THE CONCISE ROGET'S INTERNATIONAL THESAURUS®

REVISED AND UPDATED

SEVENTH EDITION

THE CONCISE ROGET'S INTERNATIONAL THESAURUS®

REVISED AND UPDATED

SEVENTH EDITION

EDITED BY

BARBARA ANN KIPFER, PH.D.

HARPER

An Imprint of HarperCollins*Publishers*

HARPER

An Imprint of HarperCollins*Publishers*
10 East 53rd Street
New York, New York 10022-5299

ISBN 978-0-06-196107-6

First Harper mass market printing: June 2011

Printed in the United States of America

Visit Harper paperbacks on the World Wide Web at
www.harpercollins.com

10 9 8 7 6 5 4 3 2 1

Contents

How to Use this Book

Like other great reference books, *Roget's International Thesaurus*® is the product of continuous improvement and long-term investment by its editors. The process began almost two centuries ago, in 1805, when Dr. Peter Mark Roget began compiling a list of useful words for his own convenience.

The revolutionary achievement of Dr. Roget was his development of a brand-new principle: *the grouping of words according to ideas*. If the user cannot find something in a reference book, it is often because of the restriction of searching alphabetically by "known" headwords. Dr. Roget's thesaurus reversed the access to allow the user to find a word from another word, or from a concept or idea. When in 1852 Roget published the first book ever to realize this concept with thoroughness and precision, he called it a *thesaurus* (from the Greek and Latin, meaning "treasury" or "storehouse"). And *thesaurus* it has remained to this day.

So successful was Roget's *Thesaurus of English Words and Phrases, Classified and Arranged so as to Facilitate the Expression of Ideas and Assist in Literary Composition* that a second edition followed one year later in 1853. By Dr. Roget's death in 1869 there had been no fewer than twenty-eight editions and printings.

Each subsequent edition introduced more efficient and useful features, all of which have contributed to the quality of the present edition. Over the years, tens of thousands of new words and phrases were added, and the numbering of the paragraphs was recently incorporated for the user's convenience. *The Concise Roget's International Thesaurus*® sixth edition is a greatly expanded and improved book, yet one which still retains Roget's brilliant organization. Prepared by Barbara Ann Kipfer, Ph.D., it has a text of over one hundred thousand words and phrases, arranged within main categories by their meanings, and a comprehensive index. The search for a word that you need is a simple, two-step process that begins in the index.

Step 1. In the index, look up the word closest to the meaning you want and note its paragraph number.

Step 2. Follow the paragraph number into the text of the thesaurus and you will find it is a **boldfaced** word among other words and phrases of similar meaning. The concise edition necessarily has a reduced index (not *all* boldfaced words are included).

Tracking down words in this way is the most obvious and direct use of the thesaurus. However, there are other ways in which the unique features of this thesaurus will help you solve word problems.

The thesaurus is a device for finding specific words or phrases for general ideas. A dictionary will tell you many things about a word—spelling, pronunciation, meaning, and origins. You use a thesaurus when you have an idea but do not know, or cannot remember, the word or phrase that expresses it best, or when you want a more accurate or effective way of saying what you mean. A thesaurus gives you possibilities, and you choose the one you think is best within your particular context. The range of possibilities includes not only meaning as we usually think of it, but the special sense and force given by nonformal words and phrases.

The Concise Roget's International Thesaurus® is an efficient word-finder because it has a structure especially designed to stimulate thought and help you organize your ideas. The backbone of this structure is the ingenious overall arrangement of the main categories, outlined in the "Synopsis of Categories," which begins on page xv. To make good use of the thesaurus's structure all you need to remember is that it contains many sequences of closely related categories. Beginning at category 48, for example, you will see **HEARING, DEAFNESS, SOUND, SILENCE, FAINTNESS OF SOUND, LOUDNESS**, etc., a procession of similar, contrasting, and opposing concepts, all dealing with the perception and quality of sounds. So when you are not quite satisfied with what you find in one place, glance at nearby categories too; it may be that your original intention was not the best. If you are having trouble framing a thought in a positive way, you may find that it can be more effectively expressed negatively. Seeing related terms and antonyms (opposites) often opens up lines of thought and chains of association that had not occurred to you.

You will have already noticed that the main categories of ideas are numbered in sequence; there are 1,075 of them in this edition. Within each main category the terms are presented by basic meaning in short numbered paragraphs. References from the index to the text are made with one-part and two-part numbers, such as 247 and 247.4, the first part being the number of the main category, the second the number of the paragraph within that main category. This system, unique to this book, makes for quick and easy pinpointing of the place where you will find the words you need.

The terms within a main category are organized by part of speech, in this order: nouns, verbs, and adjectives. When you are casting about for a way of saying something, rather than looking for a specific word, do not limit your search to the narrow area of the category suggested by the index reference, but examine the offerings in all parts of speech.

Additionally, there is a further refinement of word arrangement. The sequence of terms within a paragraph, far from being random, is determined by close, semantic relationships. The words closest in meaning are offered in clusters that are set off with semicolons; the semicolon signals a slight change in sense or application. A close examination of the clusters will make you aware of the fine distinctions between synonyms, and you will soon recognize that few words are exactly interchangeable. As an aid in focusing on the *right* word, special terms are identified by labels in angle brackets—for example, <nf> for nonformal usage, <Fr> for French terms, or <old> for older usage. A full list of bracketed abbreviations can be found on page xxix.

Cross-references are also an important feature of the text. They suggest additional meanings of the words you are examining. Notice also that the paragraphs of text are highlighted with terms in **boldface** type. The boldfaced words are those most commonly used for the idea at hand.

Thus, *The Concise Roget's International Thesaurus*® can help you in countless ways to improve your writing and speech and to enrich your active vocabulary. But you should remember the caution that very few words are true synonyms: Use the thesaurus in conjunction with a good dictionary whenever a selected word or phrase is unfamiliar to you.

Peter Roget's Preface to the First Edition *(1852)*

It is now nearly fifty years since I first projected a system of verbal classification similar to that on which the present work is founded. Conceiving that such a compilation might help to supply my own deficiencies, I had, in the year 1805, completed a classed catalog of words on a small scale, but on the same principle, and nearly in the same form, as the Thesaurus now published. I had often during that long interval found this little collection, scanty and imperfect as it was, of much use to me in literary composition, and often contemplated its extension and improvement; but a sense of the magnitude of the task, amidst a multitude of other avocations, deterred me from the attempt. Since my retirement from the duties of Secretary of the Royal Society, however, finding myself possessed of more leisure, and believing that a repertory of which I had myself experienced the advantage might, when amplified, prove useful to others, I resolved to embark in an undertaking which, for the last three or four years, has given me incessant occupation, and has, indeed, imposed upon me an amount of labor very much greater than I had anticipated. Notwithstanding all the pains I have bestowed on its execution, I am fully aware of its numerous deficiencies and imperfections, and of its falling far short of the degree of excellence that might be attained. But, in a work of this nature, where perfection is placed at so great a distance, I have thought it best to limit my ambition to that moderate share of merit which may claim in its present form; trust to the indulgence of those for whose benefit it is intended, and to the candor of critics who, while they find it easy to detect faults, can at the same time duly appreciate difficulties.

P.M. ROGET
April 29, 1852

Foreword
by Barbara Ann Kipfer, Ph.D.

In developing the concise version of the sixth edition, I chose to focus on the modernity and scope of the language coverage in *Roget's International Thesaurus*. We live in the Internet Age, making *International Thesaurus* ever more valuable. It can now be used in the wording of queries for search engines accessing the World Wide Web. To this end, I have included as many new words and phrases as possible from general vocabulary to scientific and technological terms.

I wish to acknowledge the help, support, and guidance of the late Dr. Robert L. Chapman. My editor, Greg Chaput, has worked hard to bring the project to fruition and a successful publication.

No one is luckier than I to have the time and the environment I need to complete such a massive undertaking. To that I owe gratitude to my husband and frequent collaborator, Paul Magoulas. To him and to my sons, Kyle and Keir, I would like to repay their love and encouragement.

Barbara Ann Kipfer, Ph.D.

Synopsis of Categories

Class One: THE BODY AND THE SENSES

1 Birth
2 The Body
3 Hair
4 Clothing Materials
5 Clothing
6 Unclothing

7 Nutrition
8 Eating
9 Refreshment
10 Food
11 Cooking

12 Excretion
13 Secretion

14 Bodily Development
15 Strength
16 Weakness
17 Energy
18 Power, Potency
19 Impotence

20 Rest, Repose
21 Fatigue
22 Sleep
23 Wakefulness

24 Sensation
25 Insensibility
26 Pain

27 Vision
28 Defective Vision
29 Optical Instruments
30 Blindness
31 Visibility
32 Invisibility
33 Appearance
34 Disappearance
35 Color
36 Colorlessness
37 Whiteness
38 Blackness
39 Grayness
40 Brownness
41 Redness
42 Orangeness
43 Yellowness
44 Greenness
45 Blueness
46 Purpleness
47 Variegation

48 Hearing
49 Deafness
50 Sound
51 Silence
52 Faintness of Sound
53 Loudness
54 Resonance
55 Repeated Sounds
56 Explosive Noise
57 Sibilation
58 Stridency
59 Cry, Call

60 Animal Sounds
61 Discord

62 Taste
63 Savoriness
64 Unsavoriness
65 Insipidness
66 Sweetness
67 Sourness
68 Pungency
69 Odor
70 Fragrance
71 Stench
72 Odorlessness

73 Touch
74 Sensations of Touch

75 Sex
76 Masculinity
77 Femininity
78 Reproduction, Procreation

79 Cleanness
80 Uncleanness
81 Healthfulness
82 Unhealthfulness

83 Health
84 Fitness, Exercise
85 Disease
86 Remedy
87 Substance Abuse
88 Intoxication, Alcoholic Drink
89 Tobacco
90 Health Care
91 Therapy, Medical Treatment
92 Psychology, Psychotherapy

Class Two: FEELINGS

93 Feeling
94 Lack of Feeling
95 Pleasure
96 Unpleasure
97 Pleasantness
98 Unpleasantness
99 Dislike
100 Desire
101 Eagerness
102 Indifference
103 Hate
104 Love
105 Excitement
106 Inexcitability
107 Contentment
108 Discontent
109 Cheerfulness
110 Ill Humor
111 Solemnity
112 Sadness
113 Regret
114 Unregretfulness
115 Lamentation
116 Rejoicing
117 Dullness
118 Tedium
119 Aggravation
120 Relief
121 Comfort
122 Wonder
123 Unastonishment
124 Hope
125 Hopelessness
126 Anxiety
127 Fear, Fearfulness
128 Nervousness
129 Unnervousness
130 Expectation
131 Inexpectation
132 Disappointment
133 Premonition
134 Patience
135 Impatience
136 Pride
137 Humility
138 Servility
139 Modesty
140 Vanity
141 Arrogance

Class Three: PLACE AND CHANGE OF PLACE

232 Country
233 The Country
234 Land
235 Body of Land
236 Plain
237 Highlands
238 Stream
239 Channel
240 Sea, Ocean
241 Lake, Pool
242 Inlet, Gulf
243 Marsh

Class Four:
MEASURE AND SHAPE

244 Quantity
245 Degree
246 Mean
247 Greatness
248 Insignificance
249 Superiority
250 Inferiority
251 Increase
252 Decrease
253 Addition
254 Adjunct
255 Subtraction
256 Remainder
257 Size, Largeness
258 Littleness
259 Expansion, Growth
260 Contraction
261 Distance, Remoteness

262 Form
263 Formlessness
264 Symmetry
265 Distortion
266 Structure
267 Length
268 Shortness
269 Breadth, Thickness
270 Narrowness, Thinness
271 Filament
272 Height
273 Shaft
274 Lowness
275 Depth
276 Shallowness
277 Straightness
278 Angularity
279 Curvature
280 Circularity
281 Convolution
282 Sphericity, Rotundity
283 Convexity, Protuberance
284 Concavity
285 Sharpness
286 Bluntness

287 Smoothness
288 Roughness
289 Notch
290 Furrow
291 Fold
292 Opening
293 Closure
294 Texture
295 Covering
296 Layer

297 Weight
298 Lightness

299 Rarity
300 Measurement

Class Five:
Living Things

301 Youth
302 Youngster
303 Age
304 Adult or Old Person

305 Organic Matter
306 Life
307 Death
308 Killing
309 Interment

310 Plants
311 Animals, Insects

312 Humankind

Class Six: NATURAL PHENOMENA

313 Season
314 Morning, Noon
315 Evening, Night
316 Rain
317 Air, Weather
318 Wind
319 Cloud
320 Bubble

Class Seven: BEHAVIOR AND THE WILL

321 Behavior
322 Misbehavior
323 Will
324 Willingness
325 Unwillingness
326 Obedience
327 Disobedience

328 Action
329 Inaction
330 Activity
331 Inactivity

332 Assent
333 Dissent
334 Affirmation
335 Negation, Denial

336 Imitation
337 Nonimitation

338 Compensation
339 Carefulness
340 Neglect

341 Interpretation
342 Misinterpretation
343 Communication
344 Uncommunicativeness
345 Secrecy
346 Concealment
347 Communications
348 Manifestation
349 Representation, Description
350 Misrepresentation
351 Disclosure
352 Publication
353 Messenger

354 Falseness
355 Exaggeration
356 Deception
357 Deceiver
358 Dupe
359 Resolution
360 Perseverance
361 Obstinacy
362 Irresolution
363 Changing of Mind
364 Caprice
365 Impulse
366 Leap
367 Plunge
368 Avoidance
369 Escape
370 Abandonment
371 Choice
372 Rejection

373 Custom, Habit
374 Unaccustomedness
375 Motivation, Inducement
376 Pretext
377 Allurement
378 Bribery
379 Dissuasion
380 Intention
381 Plan
382 Pursuit
383 Route, Path
384 Manner, Means
385 Provision, Equipment
386 Store, Supply
387 Use

388 Consumption
389 Misuse
390 Disuse
391 Uselessness

392 Improvement
393 Impairment
394 Relapse
395 Destruction
396 Restoration
397 Preservation
398 Rescue
399 Warning
400 Alarm
401 Haste
402 Leisure
403 Endeavor
404 Undertaking
405 Preparation
406 Unpreparedness
407 Accomplishment
408 Nonaccomplishment
409 Success
410 Failure
411 Victory
412 Defeat
413 Skill
414 Unskillfulness
415 Cunning
416 Artlessness
417 Authority
418 Lawlessness
419 Precept
420 Command
421 Demand
422 Advice
423 Council
424 Compulsion
425 Strictness
426 Laxness
427 Leniency
428 Restraint
429 Confinement
430 Freedom
431 Liberation
432 Subjection
433 Submission
434 Observance
435 Nonobservance
436 Promise
437 Compact
438 Security
439 Offer

440 Request
441 Consent
442 Refusal
443 Permission
444 Prohibition
445 Repeal
446 Promotion
447 Demotion, Deposal
448 Resignation, Retirement

449 Aid
450 Cooperation
451 Opposition
452 Opponent
453 Resistance
454 Defiance
455 Accord
456 Disaccord
457 Contention
458 Warfare
459 Attack
460 Defense
461 Combatant
462 Arms
463 Arena
464 Peace
465 Pacification
466 Mediation
467 Neutrality
468 Compromise

469 Possession
470 Possessor
471 Property
472 Acquisition
473 Loss
474 Retention
475 Relinquishment
476 Participation
477 Apportionment
478 Giving
479 Receiving
480 Taking
481 Restitution
482 Theft
483 Thief
484 Parsimony

485 Liberality
486 Prodigality

487 Celebration
488 Humorousness
489 Wit, Humor
490 Banter

491 Cowardice
492 Courage
493 Rashness
494 Caution

495 Fastidiousness
496 Taste, Tastefulness
497 Vulgarity

498 Ornamentation
499 Plainness
500 Affectation
501 Ostentation
502 Boasting
503 Bluster
504 Courtesy
505 Discourtesy
506 Retaliation
507 Revenge

508 Ridicule
509 Approval
510 Disapproval
511 Flattery
512 Disparagement
513 Curse
514 Threat
515 Fasting
516 Sobriety

Class Eight: LANGUAGE

517 Signs, Indicators
518 Meaning
519 Latent Meaningfulness
520 Meaninglessness
521 Intelligibility
522 Unintelligibility
523 Language
524 Speech
525 Imperfect Speech
526 Word
527 Nomenclature
528 Anonymity
529 Phrase
530 Grammar
531 Ungrammaticalness

532 Diction
533 Elegance
534 Inelegance
535 Plain Speech
536 Figure of Speech
537 Conciseness
538 Diffuseness
539 Ambiguity

540 Talkativeness
541 Conversation
542 Soliloquy
543 Public Speaking
544 Eloquence
545 Grandiloquence

546 Letter
547 Writing
548 Printing
549 Record
550 Recorder
551 Information
552 News
553 Correspondence
554 Book
555 Periodical
556 Treatise
557 Abridgment
558 Library

Class Nine: Human Society and Institutions

559 Relationship by Blood
560 Ancestry
561 Posterity
562 Lovemaking, Endearment

Class Ten:
VALUES AND IDEALS

636 Ethics
637 Right
638 Wrong
639 Dueness
640 Undueness
641 Duty
642 Prerogative
643 Imposition
644 Probity
645 Improbity
646 Honor

647 Insignia
648 Title

649 Justice
650 Injustice
651 Selfishness
652 Unselfishness
653 Virtue
654 Vice
655 Wrongdoing
656 Guilt
657 Innocence
658 Atonement
659 Good Person
660 Bad Person
661 Disrepute
662 Repute
663 Sensuality
664 Chastity
665 Unchastity
666 Indecency
667 Asceticism
668 Temperance
669 Intemperance
670 Moderation
671 Violence
672 Gluttony
673 Legality
674 Illegality
675 Religions, Cults, Sects
676 Theology
677 Deity
678 Mythical and Polytheistic Gods and Spirits
679 Angel, Saint
680 Evil Spirits
681 Heaven
682 Hell
683 Scripture
684 Prophets, Religious Founders
685 Sanctity
686 Unsanctity
687 Orthodoxy
688 Unorthodoxy
689 Occultism
690 Sorcery
691 Spell, Charm

692 Piety
693 Sanctimony
694 Impiety
695 Nonreligiousness

696 Worship
697 Idolatry
698 The Ministry
699 The Clergy
700 The Laity
701 Religious Rites
702 Ecclesiastical Attire
703 Religious Buildings

Class Eleven:
ARTS

704 Show Business, Theater
705 Dance
706 Motion Pictures
707 Entertainer
708 Music
709 Harmonics, Musical Elements
710 Musician
711 Musical Instruments

712 Visual Arts
713 Graphic Arts
714 Photography
715 Sculpture

Class Twelve: OCCUPATIONS AND CRAFTS

Class Thirteen: SPORTS AND AMUSEMENTS

Class Fourteen: THE MIND AND IDEAS

795 Incompleteness

796 Composition
797 Mixture
798 Simplicity
799 Complexity
800 Joining
801 Analysis
802 Separation
803 Cohesion
804 Noncohesion
805 Combination
806 Disintegration

807 Order
808 Arrangement
809 Classification
810 Disorder
811 Disarrangement
812 Continuity
813 Discontinuity
814 Precedence
815 Sequence
816 Precursor
817 Sequel
818 Beginning
819 Middle
820 End
821 Time
822 Timelessness
823 Infinity
824 Period
825 Spell
826 Interim
827 Duration
828 Transience
829 Perpetuity
830 Instantaneousness
831 Event
832 Measurement of Time
833 Anachronism
834 Previousness
835 Subsequence
836 Simultaneity
837 The Past
838 The Present
839 The Future
840 Imminence
841 Newness
842 Oldness
843 Timeliness
844 Untimeliness
845 Earliness
846 Lateness
847 Frequency
848 Infrequency
849 Repetition
850 Regularity of Recurrence
851 Irregularity of Recurrence

852 Change
853 Permanence
854 Changeableness
855 Stability
856 Continuance
857 Cessation
858 Conversion
859 Reversion
860 Revolution
861 Evolution
862 Substitution
863 Interchange

864 Generality
865 Particularity
866 Specialty
867 Conformity
868 Nonconformity
869 Normality
870 Abnormality
871 List
872 Oneness
873 Doubleness
874 Duplication
875 Bisection
876 Three
877 Triplication
878 Trisection
879 Four
880 Quadruplication
881 Quadrisection
882 Five and Over
883 Plurality
884 Numerousness
885 Fewness

886 Cause
887 Effect
888 Attribution

889 Operation
890 Productiveness
891 Unproductiveness
892 Production
893 Product
894 Influence
895 Absence of Influence
896 Tendency
897 Liability
898 Involvement
899 Concurrence
900 Counteraction
901 Support

902 Impulse, Impact
903 Reaction
904 Pushing, Throwing
905 Pulling
906 Leverage
907 Attraction
908 Repulsion
909 Ejection
910 Overrunning
911 Shortcoming
912 Elevation
913 Depression
914 Circuitousness
915 Rotation
916 Oscillation
917 Agitation
918 Spectator
919 Intellect
920 Intelligence, Wisdom
921 Wise Person
922 Unintelligence
923 Foolishness
924 Fool
925 Sanity
926 Insanity, Mania
927 Eccentricity
928 Knowledge
929 Intellectual
930 Ignorance
931 Thought
932 Idea
933 Absence of Thought
934 Intuition, Instinct
935 Reasoning
936 Sophistry
937 Topic
938 Inquiry
939 Answer
940 Solution
941 Discovery
942 Experiment

943 Comparison
944 Discrimination
945 Indiscrimination
946 Judgment
947 Prejudgment
948 Misjudgment
949 Overestimation
950 Underestimation
951 Theory, Supposition
952 Philosophy

953 Belief
954 Credulity
955 Unbelief
956 Incredulity
957 Evidence, Proof
958 Disproof
959 Qualification
960 No Qualifications

961 Foresight
962 Prediction
963 Necessity
964 Predetermination
965 Prearrangement
966 Possibility
967 Impossibility
968 Probability
969 Improbability
970 Certainty
971 Uncertainty
972 Chance

973 Truth

Class Fifteen:
SCIENCE AND TECHNOLOGY

Abbreviations Used in This Book

ADJS	adjectives	N	North, Northern
Brit	Britain, British	nf	nonformal usage
Chin	China, Chinese	old	older usage
E	East, Eastern	Pg	Portugal, Portuguese
etc	et cetera	pl	plural
fem	feminine	Russ	Russia, Russian
Fr	France, French	S	South, Southern
Ger	Germany, German	Scot	Scotland, Scottish
Gk	Greece, Greek	sing	singular
gram	grammar	Skt	Sanskrit
Heb	Hebrew	Sp	Spanish
her	heraldry	Swah	Swahili
Hindu	Hinduism	Swed	Sweden, Swedish
Ir	Ireland, Irish	tm	trademark
Ital	Italy, Italian	US	United States
L	Latin	W	West, Western
masc	masculine	Wel	Wales, Welsh

1 BIRTH

NOUNS **1** **birth,** genesis, **nativity,** nascency, **childbirth, childbearing, having a baby, giving birth, birthing,** parturition, biogenesis, the stork <nf>, patter of tiny feet; **confinement,** lying-in, being brought to bed, **childbed,** *accouchement* <Fr>; **labor,** travail, birth throes *or* pangs; **delivery,** blessed event <nf>; the Nativity; multiparity; **hatching;** littering, whelping, farrowing; active birth, alternative birth; obstetrics

VERBS **2** **be born,** have birth, come forth, issue forth, see the light of day, come into the world; **hatch;** be illegitimate *or* born out of wedlock, have the bar sinister, be born on the wrong side of the blanket, come in through a side door <nf>

3 **give birth, bear,** bear *or* have young, **have; have a baby,** bear a child, have children; drop, cast, throw, pup, whelp, kitten, foal, calve, fawn, lamb, cub, yean, farrow, litter, spawn, lay eggs; lie in, be confined, labor, travail

ADJS **4** **born,** given birth, post-natal; **hatched;** bred, begotten, cast, dropped, whelped, foaled, calved, etc; stillborn; **bearing,** giving birth, natal

2 THE BODY

NOUNS **1** **body,** the person, carcass, anatomy, frame, bodily *or* corporal *or* corporeal entity, physical self, physical *or* bodily structure, physique, soma, somatotype, bod <nf>; torso, trunk; organism, organic complex, flesh and blood <nf>; the material *or* physical part

2 **the skeleton, the bones,** one's bones, framework, frame, form, structure, shell, bony framework, endoskeleton, bag of bones; axial skeleton, appendicular skeleton, visceral skeleton; rib cage; skeletology; **bone** ; cartilage

3 **the muscles,** myon, voluntary muscle, involuntary muscle; **musculature,** physique; **connective tissue,** connectivum; thew, sinew, tendon, ligament, cartilage

4 **the skin, skin,** dermis, integument, **epidermis,** scarfskin, ecderon; hypodermis, hypoderma; dermis, derma, derm, corium, true skin, cutis, cuticle; epithelium, pavement epithelium; endothelium; mesoderm; endoderm, entoderm; blastoderm; ectoderm, epiblast, ectoblast; enderon; connective tissue; age spot, liver spot

5 <castoff skin> slough, cast, desquamation, exuviae, molt

6 **membrane,** membrana, pellicle, chorion; basement membrane, membrana propria; allantoic membrane; amnion, amniotic sac, arachnoid membrane; serous membrane, serosa, membrana serosa; **eardrum,** tympanic membrane, tympanum, membrana tympana; **mucous membrane; velum; peritoneum;** periosteum; pleura; pericardium; meninx, **meninges;** perineurium, neurilemma; conjunctiva; **hymen** *or* maidenhead

7 **member, appendage, external organ; head,** noggin *and* noodle <nf>; **arm;** forearm; wrist; elbow; upper arm, biceps; **leg,** limb, shank, gam *and* pin <nf>, legs, wheels <nf>; shin, cnemis; ankle, tarsus; calf; knee; thigh, ham; popliteal space; **hand,** paw <nf>, finger; **foot,** dog *and* puppy <nf>, toe

8 **teeth,** dentition, ivories *and* choppers <nf>, pearly whites; periodontal tissue, alveolar ridge, alveolus; **tooth,** fang, tusk; snag, snaggletooth, peg; bucktooth, gagtooth *or* gang tooth <nf>; pivot tooth; cuspid, bicuspid; canine tooth, canine, dogtooth, eyetooth, carnassial, tush <nf>; molar, grinder, gnasher; premolar; incisor, cutter, fore-tooth; wisdom tooth; milk tooth, baby tooth, deciduous tooth; permanent tooth; crown, cusp, dentine, enamel

9 **eye,** visual organ, organ of vision, oculus, optic, **orb,** peeper <nf>; clear eyes, bright eyes, starry orbs; saucer eyes, banjo eyes <nf>, popeyes, goggle eyes; naked eye, unassisted *or* unaided eye; corner of the eye; epicanthus, epicanthic fold; eyeball; retina; lens; cornea; sclera;

optic nerve; iris; pupil; eyelid, lid, nictitating membrane; choroid coat, aqueous humor, vitreous humor

10 **ear,** auditory apparatus, hearing organ, lug; external ear, **outer ear;** auricle, pinna; tragus; cauliflower ear; concha, conch, shell; ear lobe, lobe, lobule; auditory canal, acoustic *or* auditory meatus; helix; **middle ear,** tympanic cavity, tympanum; eardrum, drumhead, tympanic membrane; auditory ossicles; malleus, hammer, incus, anvil; stapes, stirrup; mastoid process; eustachian *or* auditory tube; **inner ear;** round window, secondary eardrum; oval window; bony labyrinth, membraneous labyrinth, utricle; perilymph, endolymph; vestibule; semicircular canals; cochlea; basilar membrane, organ of Corti; auditory *or* acoustic nerve

11 **nose,** nasal organ, snout, smeller, proboscis, beak, schnoz <nf>, snout, muzzle; nostril, naris, nasal cavity; olfactory nerve

12 **mouth,** oral cavity; lips, tongue, taste buds; mandible, jaw; maw; gums, periodontal tissue; uvula; teeth

13 **genitals,** genitalia, sex organs, reproductive organs, pudenda, private parts, privy parts, private parts; privates *or* meat *or* naughty bits <nf>; **crotch,** groin, pubic region, perineum, pelvis; **male organs; penis, phallus,** glans penis; gonads; **testes, testicles,** balls *and* nuts *and* rocks *and* ballocks *and* nads *and* family jewels <nf>; spermary; scrotum, bag *and* basket <nf>; vas deferens; **female organs; vulva,** cunt <nf>; **vagina;** clitoris, glans clitoridis; pudenda; labia, labia majora, labia minora, lips, nymphae; cervix; ovary; uterus, womb, fallopian tubes; secondary sex characteristic, mons pubis, mons veneris, pubic hair, beard, breasts

14 **nervous system, nerves,** central nervous system, peripheral nervous system; autonomic nervous system; sympathetic *or* thoracolumbar nervous system, parasympathetic *or* craniosacral nervous system; **nerve; neuron;** nerve cell, sensory *or* afferent neuron, sensory cell; motor *or* afferent neuron; association *or* internuncial neuron; nerve fiber, axon, dendrite, myelin *or* medullary sheath; **synapse;** effector organ; nerve trunk; **ganglion;** plexus, solar plexus; **spinal cord**

15 **brain,** encephalon; cerebrum, cerebellum, cerebral matter

16 **viscera, vitals, internal organs, insides, innards** <nf>, entrails, inwards, internals, thoracic viscera, abdominal viscera; inner mechanism, works <nf>; peritoneum, peritoneal cavity; **guts** *and* kishkes *and* giblets <nf>; **heart,** ticker *and* pump <nf>, endocardium, atria, ventricles, aorta; **lung, lungs; liver;** gallbladder; spleen; pancreas; **kidney, kidneys;** urethra

17 **digestion,** ingestion, assimilation, absorption; primary digestion, secondary digestion, peristalsis; predigestion; salivary digestion, gastric *or* peptic digestion, pancreatic digestion, intestinal digestion; digestive system, alimentary canal, gastrointestinal tract; salivary glands, gastric glands, liver, pancreas; digestive secretions, saliva, gastric juice, pancreatic juice, intestinal juice, bile

18 <digestive system> mouth, maw, salivary glands; gullet, crop, craw, **throat,** pharynx; esophagus, gorge; fauces, isthmus of the fauces; **abdomen; stomach, belly** <nf>, **midriff,** diaphragm; swollen *or* distended *or* protruding *or* prominent belly, beer belly, *embonpoint* <Fr>, **paunch,** ventripotence; underbelly; pylorus; **intestine, intestines,** entrails, **bowels;** small intestine, villus, odenum, jejunum, ileum; blind gut, cecum; foregut, hindgut; midgut, mesogaster; **appendix,** vermiform appendix *or* process; large intestine, colon, sigmoid flexure, rectum; anus

19 <nf terms> goozle, guzzle; tum, tummy, tum-tum, breadbasket, **gut,** bulge, fallen chest, corporation, spare tire, bay window, **pot,** potbelly, potgut, beerbelly, German *or* Milwaukee goiter, pusgut, swagbelly; **guts,** tripes, stuffings

20 **metabolism,** metabolic process; basal metabolism, acid-base metabolism, energy metabolism; **anabolism,** substance metabolism, constructive metabolism, assimilation; **catabolism,** destructive metabolism, disassimilation; endogenous metabolism, exogenous metabolism; pharmacokinetic metabolism; uricotelic metabolism; metabolic rate

21 **breathing, respiration,** aspiration, **inspiration, inhalation; expiration, exhalation;** insufflation, exsufflation; **breath,** wind, breath of air; three-part breath; pant, puff; wheeze, asthmatic wheeze; broken wind; gasp, gulp; snoring, snore, stertor; sniff, sniffle, snuff, snuffle; sigh, suspiration; sneeze, sternutation; cough, hack; hiccup; **artificial respiration,** kiss of life, mouth-to-mouth resuscitation; anaerobic respiration

22 <respiratory system> **lungs,** bellows <nf>; diaphragm; **windpipe, trachea**; bronchus, bronchi <pl>, bronchial tube; epiglottis

23 **duct, vessel,** canal, passage; gland; vasculature, vascularity, vascularization; vas, meatus; thoracic duct, lymphatic; pore; urethra, urete; vagina; oviduct, fallopian tube; salpinx; eustachian tube; ostium; fistula; **blood vessel; artery,** aorta, pulmonary artery, carotid; **vein,** jugular vein, vena cava, pulmonary vein; portal vein, varicose vein; venation; **capillary;** arteriole, veinlet, veinule, venule

24 <body fluids> humor, **lymph,** chyle, choler, yellow bile, black bile; rheum; serous fluid, serum; plasma; **pus, matter,** purulence; suppuration; ichor, sanies; discharge; gleet, leukorrhea, the whites; mucus; **phlegm,** snot <nf>; **saliva, spit <nf>; urine, piss <nf>; perspiration, sweat <nf>; tear,** teardrop, lachryma; **milk,** mother's milk, colostrum, lactation; **semen**; cerumen, earwax

25 **blood,** whole blood, lifeblood, vital fluid, venous blood, arterial blood, **gore;** ichor, humor; grume; **serum,** blood serum; blood substitute; **plasma,** synthetic plasma, plasma substitute, dextran, clinical dextran; **blood cell** *or* **corpuscle,** hemocyte; **red corpuscle** *or* **blood cell,** erythrocyte; **white corpuscle** *or* **blood cell,** leukocyte, blood platelet; **hemoglobin;** blood pressure; circulation; **blood group** *or* **type,** type O *or* A *or* B *or* AB; Rh-type, Rh-positive, Rh-negative; **Rh factor** *or* Rhesus factor; antigen, antibody, isoantibody, globulin; opsonin; blood grouping; blood count; hematoscope, hematoscopy, hemometer; bloodstream

ADJS 26 **skeleton, skeletal; bone,** osteal; **bony,** osseous, ossiferous; ossicular; ossified; **spinal,** myelic; **muscle, muscular,** myoid; cartilage, cartilaginous

27 **cutaneous,** cuticular; skinlike, skinny; skin-deep; **epidermal,** epidermic, ecderonic; hypodermic, hypodermal, subcutaneous; dermal, dermic; ectodermal, ectodermic; endermic, endermatic; cortical; epicarpal; testaceous; membranous

28 **eye, optic,** ophthalmic, optical; visual; **ear,** otic; aural

29 **genital;** phallic, penile, penial; testicular; scrotal; spermatic, seminal; vulvar, vulval; vaginal; clitoral; cervical; ovarian; uterine; reproductive, generative, hormonal, sexual

30 **nerve, neural,** neurological**; brain, cerebral,** cerebellar, nervous, synaptic

31 **digestive;** stomachal, stomachic, abdominal; ventral, celiac, **gastric,** ventricular; big-bellied 257.18; **metabolic,** basal metabolic, anabolic, catabolic; assimilative, dissimilative

32 **respiratory,** breathing; inspiratory, expiratory; nasal, rhinal; bronchial, tracheal; **lung,** pulmonary, pulmonic, pneumonic; puffing, huffing, snorting, wheezing, wheezy, asthmatic, stertorous, snoring, panting, heaving; sniffy, sniffly, sniffling, snuffy, snuffly, snuffling; sneezy, sternutative, sternutatory, errhine

33 **circulatory, vascular,** vascularized, circulating; vasiform; venous, veinal, venose; capillary; arterial,

aortic; **blood,** hematal, hematic; bloody, gory, sanguinary; lymphatic, rheumy, humoral, phlegmy, ichorous, serous, sanious; chylific, chylifactive, chylifactory; **puslike,** purulent, suppurated *or* suppurating, suppurative; teary, tearing, tearlike, **lachrymal,** lacrimal, lacrimatory; mucous; sweaty, perspiring; urinary

3 HAIR

NOUNS **1** **hairiness, shagginess,** hirsuteness, pilosity, fuzziness, frizziness, **furriness,** downiness, fluffiness, woolliness, fleeciness, bristliness, stubbliness, burrheadedness, mopheadedness, shockheadedness; crinosity, hispidity, villosity; hypertrichosis, pilosis, pilosism, pilosity

2 **hair,** pile, **fur** 4.2, coat, pelt, **fleece,** fuzz, wool, camel's hair, horsehair, hide; **mane;** shag, tousled *or* matted hair, **mat of hair;** pubescence, pubes, pubic hair; hairlet, villus, capillament, cilium, ciliolum 271.1; seta, setula; bristle 288.3

3 gray hair, grizzle, silver *or* silvery hair, white hair, salt-and-pepper hair *or* beard, graying temples

4 **head of hair,** head, crine; **crop,** crop of hair, mat, elflock, **thatch,** mop, **shock,** shag, fleece, **mane; locks, tresses,** crowning glory, helmet of hair

5 **lock, tress;** flowing locks, flowing tresses; **curl, ringlet,** wisp; earlock, *payess* <Yiddish>; lovelock; frizz, frizzle; crimp; ponytail

6 **tuft, flock,** fleck; forelock, widow's peak, crest, quiff <Brit>, fetlock, cowlick; **bang, bangs,** fringe

7 **braid,** plait, twist; **pigtail,** rat's-tail *or* rat-tail, tail; **queue,** cue; coil, knot; topknot, scalplock, pigtail, bunches; bun, chignon; widow's peak; dreadlock, cornrow

8 **beard, whiskers,** facial hair; beaver <nf>; full beard, chin whiskers, side whiskers; **sideburns,** burnsides, **muttonchops; goatee,** tuft; imperial, **Vandyke,** spade beard; adolescent beard, pappus, down, peach fuzz, **stubble,** bristles, five o'clock shadow, designer stubble

9 <plant beard> awn, brush, arista, pile, pappus, nettle

10 <animal and insect whiskers> tactile process, tactile hair, **feeler, antenna,** vibrissa; barb, barbel, barbule, tentacle, palpus; cat whisker

11 **mustache,** mustachio, soup-strainer <nf>, mustachios, toothbrush, handle bars *or* handlebar mustache, Fu Manchu mustache, Zapata mustache, walrus mustache, tash <nf>

12 **eyelashes, lashes,** cilia; **eyebrows,** brows

13 false hair, hair extensions, switch, fall, chignon, rat <nf>; false eyelashes

14 **wig, peruke, toupee,** hairpiece, rug *and* divot *and* doormat <nf>, hair weave; hair extensions

15 **hairdo, hairstyle, haircut,** do <nf>, **coiffure,** coif, headdress; wave; marcel, marcel wave; **permanent,** permanent wave; home permanent; cold wave; blow-drying, finger-drying

16 **feather, plume,** pinion; **quill;** pinfeather; contour feather, penna, down feather, plume feather, plumule, tail feather; filoplume; hackle; scapular; **crest,** tuft, topknot; panache

17 <parts of feathers> quill, calamus, barrel; barb, shaft, barbule, barbicel, cilium, filament, filamentule, plumule

18 **plumage, feathers,** feather, feathering; contour feathers; breast feathers, mail <of a hawk>; hackle; flight feathers; remiges, primaries, secondaries, tertiaries; covert, tectrices; speculum, wing bay

19 **down, fluff,** flue, floss, **fuzz, fur,** pile, fleece, fine hair; eiderdown, eider; swansdown; thistledown; lint

VERBS **20** grow *or* sprout hair; whisker, **bewhisker**

21 **feather, fledge,** feather out; sprout wings

22 cut *or* dress the hair, trim, **barber, coiffure,** coif, style *or* shape the hair; pompadour, wave, marcel; process, conk; **bob, shingle**

ADJS 23 **hairlike,** trichoid, capillary; filamentous, filamentary, filiform; bristlelike 288.10

24 **hairy, hirsute,** barbigerous, crinose, crinite, pubescent; pilose, pilous, pileous; **furry,** furred; bushy; villous; villose; ciliate, cirrose; hispid, hispidulous, setal; **woolly, fleecy,** lanate, lanated, flocky, flocculent, floccose; woolly-headed, woolly-haired, ulotrichous; bushy, tufty, **shaggy,** shagged; matted, tomentose; mopheaded, burrheaded, shockheaded, unshorn; **bristly** 288.9; fuzzy

25 **bearded,** whiskered, whiskery, **bewhiskered,** barbate, barbigerous; mustached *or* mustachioed; awned, awny, pappose; goateed; unshaved, **unshaven;** stubbled, stubbly, bristly

26 **wigged,** periwigged, peruked, toupeed

27 **feathery, plumy;** hirsute; featherlike, plumelike, pinnate, pennate; **downy,** fluffy, nappy, velvety, peachy, fuzzy, flossy, furry

28 **feathered, plumaged,** flighted, **pinioned, plumed,** pennate, plumate, plumose

29 **tufted, crested,** topknotted

4 CLOTHING MATERIALS

NOUNS 1 **material, fabric, cloth, textile,** textile fabric, texture, tissue, stuff, weave, weft, woof, web, **goods,** drapery, *étoffe* or *tissu* <Fr>; thread, yarn, rope; napery, table linen, felt; silk; lace; cotton; wool; polyester; nylon; rag, rags

2 **fur, pelt, hide,** coat, fell, fleece, vair <heraldry>; imitation fur, fake fur, synthetic fur; furring; peltry, skin(s); **leather**, rawhide; imitation leather, leather paper, leatherette

5 CLOTHING

NOUNS 1 **clothing, clothes, apparel, wear, wearing apparel, daywear, dress,** dressing, **raiment,** garmenture, **garb, attire, array,** habit, habiliment, fashion, style 578.1, guise, **costume,** costumery, gear, toilette, trim, bedizenment; **vestment,** vesture, investment, investiture, canonicals, liturgical garment; **garments,** robes, robing, rags <nf>, drapery, finery, feathers; toggery *or* togs *or* **duds** *or* threads <nf>, sportswear; work clothes, fatigues; linen; menswear, men's clothing, womenswear, women's clothing; unisex clothing; latest fashion

2 **wardrobe,** furnishings, things, accouterments, trappings, gear; **outfit,** livery, harness, caparison; turnout *and* getup *and* rig *and* rig-out <nf>; wedding clothes, bridal outfit, trousseau; maternity clothes

3 **garment,** vestment, vesture, robe, frock, gown, rag <nf>

4 **ready-mades,** ready-to-wear, off-the-rack clothes, off-the-peg clothes, store *or* store-bought clothes, wash-and-wear, dry goods

5 **rags, tatters,** secondhand clothes, seconds, old clothes, castoff clothes, preowned clothing, consignment clothes, Goodwill clothes; worn clothes, **hand-me-downs** *and* reach-me-downs <nf>, castoffs; slops

6 **suit**, suit of clothes, set of clothes, ensemble; **frock,** dress, rig <nf>, **costume, habit,** bib and tucker <nf>

7 **uniform, livery,** monkey suit <nf>; nurse's uniform, police officer's uniform, etc; athletic team uniform, baseball uniform, etc

8 **mufti,** civilian dress *or* clothes, **civvies** *and* cits <nf>, plain clothes

9 **costume,** costumery, character dress; outfit *and* getup *and* rig <nf>; masquerade, disguise, mask; tights, leotards; ballet skirt, tutu, bodysuit; motley, cap and bells; silks; buskin

10 **finery, frippery, fancy dress,** fine *or* full feather <nf>, investiture, regalia, caparison, fig *or* full fig <Brit nf>; **best clothes,** best bib and tucker <nf>; **Sunday best** *and* Sunday clothes *and* Sunday-go-to-meeting clothes *and* Sunday-go-to-meetings <nf>, **glad rags** <nf>, ostrich feathers <nf>, party dress, dress-up clothes, dressy clothes; power dressing

11 **formal dress,** formals, **evening dress,** evening wear, **full dress,** dress clothes, evening wear, white

tie and tails, **soup-and-fish** <nf>; dinner clothes; dress suit, full-dress suit, tail coat, tails <nf>; tuxedo, tux <nf>, dinner jacket; **regalia,** court dress; dress uniform, full-dress uniform, special full-dress uniform, social full-dress uniform; whites <nf>, dress whites, white tie; evening gown *or* dress, dinner dress *or* gown; prom dress, ball dress; morning dress, morning coat; semiformal dress; black tie, bow tie, cummerbund

12 **cloak,** overgarment

13 **outerwear; coat, jacket** ; **overcoat,** great-coat, **topcoat,** surcoat; **rainwear;** rain gear, raincoat, slicker, rainsuit, foul weather gear

14 **waistcoat,** weskit <nf>, **vest;** down vest

15 **shirt**, waist, **shirtwaist,** linen, sark *and* shift <nf>; **blouse,** bodice; pullover, shell, T-shirt; dickey; sweater

16 **dress, gown, frock; skirt**

17 **apron,** *tablier* <Fr>; pinafore, bib, tucker; smock

18 **pants, trousers,** pair of trousers *or* pants, **breeches,** britches <nf>, **pantaloons;** jeans, designer jeans, blue jeans, dungarees; **slacks;** khakis, chinos; corduroys *or* cords, flannels, ducks, pinstripes, bell-bottoms, hiphuggers, Capri pants *or* Capris, pegged pants, pedal pushers, leggings, overalls, knickers, breeches, jodhpurs, sweatpants, cargo pants, carpenter pants; shorts, short pants, Bermuda shorts, hot pants, Jamaica shorts, surfer shorts, board shorts, short shorts, cycling shorts, gym shorts

19 **waistband, belt** 280.3; **sash,** cummerbund; **loincloth,** breechcloth *or* breechclout, waistcloth, **G-string,** loinguard, dhoti, moocha; **diaper,** dydee <nf>, napkins <Brit>, nappies <Brit nf>

20 **dishabille,** *déshabillé* <Fr>, **undress,** something more comfortable; **negligee,** *négligé* <Fr>; **wrap,** wrapper; sport clothes, playwear, activewear, sportswear, casual wear, leisurewear, **casual clothes** *or* **dress,** fling-on clothes, loungewear, plain clothes, dress-down clothes, knock-around clothes, grubbies <nf>; business casual; dress-down day, casual day

21 **nightwear,** night clothes, sleepwear; **nightdress, nightgown, nightie** *and* shortie nightie <nf>, negligee, nightshirt; **pajamas,** pyjamas <Brit>, pj's <nf>, baby doll pajamas; sleepers; robe, bathrobe, dressing gown, housecoat, caftan, bed jacket

22 **underclothes,** underclothing, undergarments, underthings, bodywear, **underwear, undies** <nf>, skivvies, BVD, body clothes, smallclothes, unmentionables <nf>, tighty whities <nf>, intimate apparel, **lingerie, linen,** underlinen; flannels, woolens, long johns

23 **corset,** stays, foundation garment, corselet; **girdle,** undergirdle, panty girdle; garter belt

24 **brassiere, bra** <nf>, sports bra, bandeau, crop top, underbodice, push-up bra; padded bras, falsies <nf>

25 **headdress,** headgear, headwear, headclothes; **millinery;** headpiece, **chapeau, cap, hat,** helmet; bonnet, stocking cap, cowboy hat, visor, baseball cap; lid <nf>; headcloth, **kerchief,** bandanna, coverchief; **handkerchief**

26 **veil,** veiling, veiler, net; mantilla

27 **footwear,** footgear, *chaussure* <Fr>; **shoes, boots,** overshoes; clodhoppers *and* gunboats *and* wafflestompers *and* shitkickers <nf>, work shoes; oxfords, saddle shoes, pumps, slides, flats, slingbacks, espadrilles, high heels, platform shoes, penny loafers *or* loafers; sandals, flip-flops, zoris, jellies; athletic shoes, tennis shoes, sneakers; wooden shoes, clogs; slippers, moccasins

28 **hosiery**, legwear, pantyhose, **hose, stockings,** nylons**; socks**

29 **swimwear; bathing suit,** swimsuit, swimming suit, tank suit, tank top, *maillot* or *maillot de bain* <Fr>, one-piece suit, two-piece suit; **trunks;** bikini, string bikini *or*

string, thong; swimming trunks, surfer shorts; wet suit; coverup

30 children's wear; rompers, jumpers; creepers; layette, baby clothes, infantwear, infants' wear, baby linen; swaddling clothes, swaddle

31 <clothing accessory> scarf, belt, glove, mitten, handkerchief, sunglasses, jewelry; neckwear, tie, necktie; collar, dickey

32 garment making, **tailoring; dressmaking, the rag trade** <nf>, fashion design, haute couture, **Seventh Avenue, the garment industry,** Garment District; **millinery,** hatmaking, hatting; hosiery; **shoemaking,** bootmaking, **cobbling;** habilimentation

33 clothier, haberdasher, draper <Brit>, outfitter; costumier, costumer; glover; hosier; furrier; dry goods dealer, mercer <Brit>

34 garmentmaker, garmentworker, needleworker; cutter, stitcher, finisher

35 tailor, tailoress, *tailleur* <Fr>, sartor; fitter; busheler, bushelman; furrier, cloakmaker, outfitter

36 dressmaker, modiste, *couturière* or *couturier* <Fr>; fashion designer; seamstress 741.2

37 hatter, hatmaker, **milliner**

38 shoemaker, bootmaker, booter, **cobbler**

VERBS **39 clothe,** enclothe, **dress, garb, attire,** tire, array, **apparel,** raiment, garment, habilitate, **tog** *and* tog out <nf>, dud <nf>, robe, enrobe, invest, endue, **deck,** bedeck, dight, rag out *or* up <nf>, drape, bedrape; wrap, enwrap, lap, envelop, sheathe, shroud, enshroud, invest; wrap *or* bundle *or* muffle up; swathe, swaddle

40 cloak, mantle; coat, jacket; gown, frock; breech; shirt; **hat,** coif, bonnet, cap, hood; boot, shoe; stocking, sock

41 outfit; equip, **accouter,** uniform, caparison, rig, rig out *or* up, fit, **fit out,** turn out, **costume,** habit, suit; design; **tailor,** tailor-make, custom-make, make to order

42 dress up, get up, doll *or* **spruce up** <nf>, **primp** *and* prink *and* prank <nf>, gussy up <nf>, spiff *or* fancy *or* slick up <nf>, pretty up <nf>, deck out *or* up, trick out *or* up, tog out *or* up <nf>, rag out *or* up <nf>, fig out *or* up <nf>; dress to kill, titivate, bedeck, dizen, bedizen; overdress; put on the dog *or* style <nf>; **dress down,** underdress

43 don, put on, slip on *or* into, get on *or* into, try on, assume, dress in, adorn; change; suit up

44 wear, have on, dress in, be dressed in, put on, slip on, affect, sport <nf>; change into; try on

ADJS **45 clothing; dress,** vestiary, sartorial; **clothed, clad, dressed, attired, togged** <nf>, tired, arrayed, **garbed,** garmented, habited, habilimented, decked, bedecked, decked-out, turned-out, tricked-out, rigged-out, vested, vestmented, robed, gowned, raimented, **appareled,** invested, endued, liveried, uniformed; **costumed,** in costume, cloaked, mantled, disguised; breeched, trousered, pantalooned; coifed, capped, bonneted, hatted, hooded; **shod,** shoed, booted, *chaussé* <Fr>

46 dressed up, dolled *or* **spruced up** <nf>; spiffed *or* fancied *or* slicked up <nf>, gussied up <nf>; spruce, dressed to advantage, dressed to the nines, dressed *or* fit to kill <nf>; in Sunday best, *endimanché* <Fr>, in one's best bib and tucker <nf>, in fine *or* high feather; *en grande tenue* <Fr>, *en grande toilette* <Fr>, in full dress, in full feather, in white tie and tails, in tails; **well-dressed, chic,** *soigné* <Fr>, stylish, modish, well-turned, well turned-out, très chic; retro-chic; **dressy; overdressed**

47 in dishabille, *en déshabillé* <Fr>, **in negligee; casual,** nonformal, dress-down, sporty, in one's shirtsleeves; baggy, sloppy; skintight, décolleté, low-necked, low-cut; underdressed, half-dressed

48 tailored, custom-made, tailor-made, made-to-order, bespoke <Brit>; ready-made, store-bought *and*

off-the-rack <nf>, ready-to-wear; vestmental; sartorial

6 UNCLOTHING

NOUNS 1 **unclothing,** divestment, divestiture, divesture; **removal; stripping,** denudement, denudation; baring, stripping *or* laying bare, uncovering, **exposure,** exposing; indecent exposure, exhibitionism, flashing <nf>; decortication, excoriation; desquamation, exfoliation; exuviation, ecdysis

2 **disrobing, undressing,** undress, disrobement, unclothing; uncasing, discasing; shedding, molting, peeling; striptease, stripping; skinny-dipping <nf>, mooning <nf>, flashing <nf>

3 **nudity, nakedness,** bareness; **the nude, the altogether** *and* **the buff** <nf>, **the raw** <nf>; state of nature, state of undress, full frontal, **birthday suit** <nf>; not a stitch, not a stitch to one's name, not a stitch on one's back; full-frontal nudity; décolleté, décolletage, toplessness; nudism, naturism, gymnosophy; nudist, naturist, gymnosophist, exhibitionist; stripper, stripteaser, ecdysiast, topless dancer, lap dancer

4 **hairlessness, baldness,** acomia, alopecia; calvities; hair loss; beardlessness, bald-headedness *or* -patedness; baldhead, baldpate, baldy <nf>, skinhead; pattern baldness; shaving, tonsure, depilation; hair remover, depilatory

VERBS 5 **divest, strip, strip away, remove; uncover,** uncloak, unveil, **expose,** lay open, bare, lay *or* strip bare, strip naked, **denude,** denudate; fleece, shear; pluck; strip-search

6 **take off, remove, doff,** off with, put off, slip *or* step out of, slip off, slough off, cast off, throw off, drop; unwrap, undo

7 **undress, unclothe,** undrape, ungarment, unapparel, unarray, disarray; **disrobe;** unsheathe, discase, uncase; **strip,** strip to the buff <nf>, do a strip-tease; skinny-dip, flash <nf>, moon <nf>

8 **peel, pare, skin, strip,** flay, excoriate, decorticate, bark; scalp; depilate, shave

9 **husk, hull,** pod, **shell,** shuck

10 **shed, cast,** throw off, **slough, molt,** slough off, exuviate

11 **scale, flake,** scale *or* flake off, desquamate, exfoliate

ADJS 12 **divested, stripped, bared,** denuded, denudated, **exposed, uncovered,** stripped *or* laid bare, unveiled, showing; unsheathed, discased, uncased

13 **unclad, undressed, unclothed, unattired, disrobed,** ungarmented, undraped, ungarbed, unrobed, unappareled, uncased; **clothesless,** garbless, garmentless, raimentless; half-clothed, underclothed, *en déshabillé* <Fr>, in dishabille, nudish; low-necked, low-cut, décolleté, strapless, topless; **seminude,** scantily clad

14 **naked, nude; bare,** peeled, raw <nf>, **in the raw** <nf>, *in puris naturalibus* <L>, in a state of nature, in nature's garb; in one's birthday suit, **in the buff** *and* in native buff *and* stripped to the buff *and* **in the altogether** <nf>, with nothing on, without a stitch, without a stitch to one's name *or* on one's back; **stark-naked,** bare-ass <nf>, buck naked, bare as the back of one's hand, naked as the day one was born, naked as a jaybird <nf>, starkers <Brit nf>; topless, bare-breasted, bottomless, bare-bottomed, nudist, naturistic, gymnosophical

15 **barefoot,** barefooted, unshod; discalced, discalceate

16 bare-ankled, bare-armed, bare-backed, bare-breasted, topless, bare-chested, bare-faced, bare-handed, bare-headed, bare-kneed, bare-legged, bare-necked, bare-throated

17 **hairless,** depilous; **bald,** acomous; bald as a coot, bald as an egg; **bald-headed,** bald-pated, tonsured; **beardless,** whiskerless, shaven, clean-shaven, smooth-shaven, smooth-faced; smooth, glabrous

18 exuvial, sloughy; desquamative, exfoliatory; denudant *or* denudatory; peeling, shedding

ADVS 19 nakedly, barely, baldly

7 NUTRITION

NOUNS **1 nutrition, nourishment,** nourishing, feeding, nurture; alimentation, sustenance; **food** *or* **nutritive value, food intake;** food chain *or* cycle; food pyramid, recommended daily vitamins and minerals

2 nutritiousness, nutritiveness, **digestibility,** assimilability; healthfulness

3 nutrient, nutritive, **nutriment** 10.3, food; nutrilite, growth factor, growth regulator; **natural food,** health food ; roughage, fiber, dietary fiber

4 vitamin, vitamin complex; provitamin, provitamin A *or* carotene; food additive, vitamin supplement

5 carbohydrate, carbo *or* carbs <nf>, simple carbohydrate, complex carbohydrate; hydroxy aldehyde, hydroxy ketone, glycogen, cellulose, ketone, saccharide, monosaccharide, disaccharide, trisaccharide, polysaccharide *or* polysaccharose; **sugar;** artificial sweetener; **starch**

6 protein *or* proteid, simple protein, conjugated protein, protein structure; **amino acid**, essential amino acid; peptide, dipeptide, polypeptide, etc; globulin, collagen, gluten, immunoglobulin, hemoglobin

7 fat, glyceride, **lipid,** lipoid; lecithin; fatty acid; steroid, sterol; **cholesterol,** glycerol-cholesterol, cephalin-cholesterol; triglyceride; **lipoprotein,** high-density lipoprotein *or* HDL, low-density lipoprotein *or* LDL; polyunsaturated fat; saturated fat; unsaturated fat

8 digestion, ingestion, assimilation, absorption; primary digestion, secondary digestion; predigestion; salivary digestion, gastric *or* peptic digestion, pancreatic digestion, intestinal digestion; digestive system, alimentary canal, gastrointestinal tract; salivary glands, gastric glands, liver, pancreas; digestive secretions, saliva, gastric juice, pancreatic juice, intestinal juice, bile

9 digestant, digester, digestive; pepsin; **enzyme,** proteolytic enzyme

10 enzyme, apoenzyme, coenzyme, isoenzyme; transferase, hydrolase, lyase, isomerase, polymerase, amylase, diastase; pepsin, rennin; proenzyme, trypsin, zymogen

11 essential element, macronutrient; carbon, hydrogen, oxygen, nitrogen, calcium, phosphorus, potassium, sodium, chlorine, sulfur, magnesium; trace element, micronutrient; iron, manganese, zinc, copper, iodine, cobalt, selenium, molybdenum, chromium, silicon

12 metabolism, basal metabolism, metabolic process, acid-base metabolism, energy metabolism; **anabolism,** assimilation; **catabolism,** disassimilation

13 diet, dieting, dietary; dietetics; **regimen,** regime; bland diet; soft diet, pap, spoon food *or* meat, spoon victuals <nf>; balanced diet; diabetic diet, allergy diet, reducing diet, weight-loss diet, obesity diet; high-calorie diet, low-calorie diet, watching one's weight *or* calories, calorie-counting; liquid diet; high-protein diet, low-carbohydrate diet; low-salt diet, low-sodium diet, salt-free diet; low-fat diet, fat-free diet; low-cholesterol diet; sugar-free diet; vegetarianism, lactovegetarianism, vegan diet; macrobiotic diet; crash diet, fad diet; portion control; eating disorder, anorexia, anorexia nervosa, bulimia; diet book, calorie counter

14 vitaminization, **fortification, enrichment,** restoration

15 nutritionist, dietitian, vitaminologist, enzymologist

16 <science of nutrition> **dietetics,** dietotherapeutics, dietotherapy; vitaminology; threpsology; enzymology

VERBS **17 nourish,** feed, sustain, aliment, nutrify, nurture, provide for, fatten up; **sustain,** strengthen; cook for, wine and dine, regale, chef; force-feed

18 digest, assimilate, absorb; metabolize; predigest

19 diet, go on a diet; watch one's weight *or* calories, count calories

20 vitaminize, **fortify, enrich,** restore

ADJS **21 nutritious,** nutritive, nutrient, **nourishing;** good for, healthful;

alimentary, alimental; organic; digestible, assimilable

22 **digestive,** assimilative; peptic, eupeptic

23 **dietary,** dietetic, dietic; regiminal

8 EATING

NOUNS 1 **eating, feeding, dining,** messing; the nosebag <nf>; ingestion, consumption, consuming, deglutition; **tasting,** relishing, savoring; **gourmet eating** *or* **dining,** fine dining, gourmandise, gastronomy; nibbling, pecking, licking, **munching;** snacking; **devouring,** gobbling, wolfing, downing, gulping; **gorging, overeating,** gluttony, overconsumption; **chewing,** mastication, manducation, rumination; **feasting, regaling,** regalement; **appetite, hunger** 100.7; nutrition 7; **dieting** 7.13; gluttony 672.1; carnivorism, carnivorousness, carnivority; herbivorism, herbivority, herbivorousness, grazing, browsing, cropping, pasturing, pasture; vegetarianism, phytophagy; omnivorism, omnivorousness, pantophagy; cannibalism, anthropophagy; omophagia *or* omophagy

2 **bite, morsel, taste,** swallow; mouthful, gob <nf>, piece, slice, scrap, tidbit; nibble, munchies; cud, quid; bolus, gobbet; **chew,** chaw <nf>; nip, niblet; munch; gnash; champ, chomp <nf>; appetizer, hors d'oeuvre, amuse-bouche

3 **drinking,** imbibing, imbibition, potation; lapping, sipping, tasting, nipping, tippling; quaffing, gulping, swigging <nf>, swilling *and* guzzling <nf>, pulling <nf>; winebibbing; compotation, symposium; barhopping; drunkenness 88.1,3

4 **drink,** potation, beverage, potion, libation, oblation, thirst-quencher; draft, dram, drench, **swig** <nf>, swill *and* guzzle <nf>, quaff, tipple, **sip,** sup, suck, tot, bumper, snort *and* slug <nf>, pull <nf>, lap, gulp, slurp <nf>; nip, peg; toast, health; mixed drink, cocktail; nightcap <nf>

5 **meal, repast,** feed *and* sit-down <nf>, mess, spread <nf>, menu, table, board, meat, *repas* <Fr>; **refreshment,** refection, regalement, collation, entertainment, treat; frozen meal

6 <meals> **breakfast,** *petit déjeuner* <Fr>, continental breakfast, English breakfast, American breakfast, meat breakfast, *déjeuner à la fourchette* <Fr>, banquet, smorgasbord; power breakfast *or* lunch *or* dinner; **brunch** <nf>, Sunday brunch, elevenses <Brit nf>; **lunch, luncheon,** tiffin, hot lunch, light lunch, box lunch, brown-bag lunch, packed lunch <Brit>; blue-plate special; tapas; **tea,** teatime, high tea, afternoon tea, cream tea; **dinner,** *diner* <Fr>, evening meal, dinner party; **supper,** *souper* <Fr>; buffet supper *or* lunch; fast food, takeout, drive-through meal; precooked frozen meal, TV dinner; **picnic, cookout,** alfresco meal, fête champêtre, tailgate picnic, **barbecue,** fish fry, clambake, wiener roast *or* wienie roast; pot luck; midnight supper *or* snack; progressive dinner; dashboard *or* cupholder meal

7 **light meal, refreshments,** light repast, light lunch, spot of lunch <nf>, collation, **snack** *and* nosh <nf>, **bite** <nf>, bite to eat <nf>, *casse-croûte* <Fr>; informal meal; coffee break, tea break

8 **hearty meal, full meal,** healthy meal, large *or* substantial meal, heavy meal, nosh-up, **square meal,** man-sized meal, large order; three squares; formal meal, sit-down meal

9 **feast, banquet,** regale, buffet, smorgasbord, festal board, groaning board, spread; finger buffet; Lucullan banquet, bacchanalia; Passover; blow *or* blowout <nf>, feeding frenzy <nf>; dinner party; bean feast

10 **serving,** service; **portion, helping,** serving suggestion; second helping, seconds; **course;** dish, plate; *plat du jour* <Fr>; antepast; first course, starter, soup, entree, *entrée* <Fr>, main course, entremets, side dish, tapas; dessert

11 <manner of service> service, table service, counter service, self-

service, curb service, take-out service, drive-through; table d'hôte, ordinary; à la carte; cover, *couvert* <Fr>; cover charge; American plan, European plan

12 **tableware,** dining utensils; **silverware,** silver, silver plate, stainless-steel ware; **flatware,** flat silver; hollow ware; **cutlery,** knives, fish knife, carving knife, fruit knife, steak knife, butter knife; forks, fish fork, salad fork, fondue fork; spoons, tablespoon, teaspoon, soup spoon, dessert spoon, coffee spoon, serving spoon; chopsticks; **dishware, china, dishes,** plates, cups, saucers, bowls, fingerbowls; glasses, **glassware,** tumbler, goblet, wineglass, crystal, flute; **dish,** salad dish, fruit dish, dessert dish; **bowl,** cereal bowl, fruit bowl, punchbowl; **tea service, tea set,** tea things, tea strainer, tea-caddy, tea-cozy

13 **table linen, napery,** tablecloth, table cover, table-mat, table pad, place mat, setting; **napkin, table napkin,** serviette <Brit>

14 **menu, bill of fare,** carte, a la carte, menuboard

15 **gastronomy,** gastronomics, gastrology, **epicurism,** epicureanism

16 **eater,** feeder, consumer, devourer, partaker; **diner,** luncher; picnicker; mouth, hungry mouth, big eater; diner-out, eater-out; boarder, board-and-roomer; **gourmet,** gastronome, epicure, gourmand, connoisseur of food *or* wine, bon vivant, Lucullus, foodie, chowhound; overeater, pig *and* wolf <nf>, trencherman, big eater, **glutton** 672.3; light eater, nibbler, picky eater, fussy eater; omnivore, pantophagist; **flesh-eater, meat-eater, carnivore,** omophagist, predacean; **man-eater, cannibal; vegetarian,** lactovegetarian, vegan, fruitarian, plant-eater, **herbivore,** phytophagan, phytophage; grass-eater, graminivore; grain-eater, granivore

17 **restaurant,** eating place, eating house, dining room; eatery *and* beanery *and* hashery *and* hash house *and* greasy spoon <nf>, chain restaurant, theme restaurant; **fast-food restaurant,** takeout, hamburger joint <nf>; *trattoria* <Ital>; **lunchroom,** luncheonette; **café,** *caffè* <Ital>, roadside cafe; **tearoom,** *bistro* <Fr>; **coffeehouse,** coffeeroom, **coffee shop,** coffee bar; **tea shop,** tea-garden, teahouse; pub, tavern, brew pub, gastropub <Brit>; chop-house; **grill,** grillroom, steakhouse, carvery; brasserie; pancake house, waffle house; cookshop; buffet, smorgasbord, self-service restaurant; **lunch counter,** quick-lunch counter; salad bar; hot-dog stand, hamburger stand, drive-in restaurant, drive-in; **snack bar,** sandwich bar, *buvette* <Fr>, *cantina* <Sp>; milk bar; sushi bar; juice bar; raw bar; pizzeria; **cafeteria,** automat; mess hall, dining hall, refectory; canteen; cookhouse, cookshack, lunch wagon, chuck wagon; **diner,** dog wagon <nf>; delicatessen, deli; ice-cream parlor, soda fountain; dining car; vending machine; **kitchen** 11.4, breakfast nook, dining room, dinette

VERBS 18 **feed, dine,** wine and dine, mess; nibble, snack, graze <nf>; satisfy, gratify; regale; bread, meat; board, sustain; pasture, put out to pasture, graze, browse; forage, fodder; provision 385.9

19 **nourish, nurture,** nutrify, aliment, foster; **nurse, suckle,** lactate, breast-feed, wet-nurse, dry-nurse; fatten, fatten up, stuff, force-feed

20 **eat, feed,** fare, take, partake, partake of, *mange* <Fr>, take nourishment, subsist, break bread, break one's fast, feast on; refresh *or* entertain the inner man, feed one's face *and* put on the feed bag <nf>, fall to, pitch in <nf>; **taste,** relish, savor; hunger 100.19; get *or* have the munchies, **diet,** go on a diet, watch one's weight, count calories

21 **dine,** dinner; **sup,** breakfast; lunch; have dinner, have lunch, have breakfast; picnic, cook out; **eat out, dine out;** board; mess with, break bread with; brown-bag

22 **devour, swallow,** ingest, **consume,** take in, tuck in *or* away *and* tuck into *and* chow down <nf>, down, get down, scarf down, put away

<nf>, snarf <nf>; **eat up;** dispatch *or* dispose of <nf>

23 **gobble, gulp, bolt,** wolf, gobble *or* gulp *or* bolt *or* wolf down

24 **feast, banquet,** regale; eat heartily, have a good appetite, eat up, lick the platter *or* plate, do oneself proud <nf>, do one's duty, do justice to, clean one's plate, polish the platter, put it away <nf>

25 **stuff, gorge** 672.4, pig out <nf>, oink out <nf>, engorge, glut, guttle, binge, cram, eat one's fill, stuff *or* gorge oneself, gluttonize, eat everything in sight

26 **pick, peck** <nf>, **nibble; snack** <nf>, nosh <nf>; pick at, peck at <nf>, eat like a bird, show no appetite

27 **chew,** chew up, chaw <nf>, bite into; **masticate,** manducate; ruminate, chew the cud; **bite,** grind, champ, chomp <nf>; **munch,** crunch**;** gnash; **gnaw;** mouth, mumble; gum

28 **feed on** *or* **upon, feast on** *or* **upon,** batten upon, fatten on *or* upon; prey on *or* upon, live on *or* upon, pasture on, browse, graze, crop

29 **drink,** drink in, **imbibe,** wet one's whistle <nf>; **quaff, sip, sup,** bib, swig *and* swill *and* guzzle *and* pull *and* gulp <nf>; **suck,** suckle, suck in *or* up; drink off *or* up, toss off *or* down, knock back, drain the cup; wash down; **toast,** drink to, pledge; tipple, **booze** 88.23

30 **lap up,** sponge *or* soak up, lick, lap, slurp <nf>

ADJS **31** **eating, feeding, gastronomical, dining,** mensal, commensal, prandial, postprandial, preprandial; **nourishing, nutritious** 7.21; empty-calorie; **dietetic; omnivorous,** pantophagous, **gluttonous** 672.6; **flesh-eating, meat-eating, carnivorous,** omophagic, omophagous, predacious; **man-eating, cannibal,** cannibalistic; insect-eating, insectivorous; vegetable-eating, **vegetarian,** lactovegetarian, vegan, fruitarian; plant-eating, **herbivorous,** phytivorous, phytophagous; grass-eating, graminivorous; grain-eating, granivorous; organic

32 chewing, masticatory, masticating, manducatory; ruminant, ruminating, cud-chewing; tasting, nibbling

33 **edible, eatable,** comestible, consumable, safe to eat, esculent, digestible, gustable, esculent; kosher; **palatable,** succulent, mouth-watering, **delicious,** dainty, savory, good to eat, finger-licking; **fine, fancy, gourmet;** calorific, fattening, rich

34 **drinkable,** potable, quaffable

9 REFRESHMENT

NOUNS **1** **refreshment,** refection, refreshing, freshening up, **bracing, exhilaration, stimulation,** enlivenment, vivification, **invigoration,** reinvigoration, reanimation, rejuvenation, revival, revivification, revivescence *or* revivescency, renewal, recreation, rest and recreation, R and R; regalement, regale; **tonic,** bracer, breath of fresh air, pick-me-up *and* a shot in the arm *and* an upper <nf>; cordial

VERBS **2** **refresh, freshen,** freshen up, fresh up <nf>; **revive,** revivify, **reinvigorate,** reanimate; **exhilarate, stimulate, invigorate,** fortify, enliven, liven up, restore, animate, vivify, quicken, brisk, brisken; brace, **brace up,** buck up *and* pick up <nf>, perk up *and* chirk up <nf>, set up, set on one's legs *or* feet <nf>; renew one's strength, put *or* breathe new life into, give a breath of fresh air, blow out the cobwebs, give a shot in the arm <nf>; renew, recreate, charge *or* recharge one's batteries <nf>, give a break, give a breather; **regale, cheer,** refresh the inner man

ADJS **3** **refreshing,** refreshful, **fresh,** brisk, crisp, crispy, fortifying, zesty, zestful, **bracing, tonic,** cordial; analeptic; **exhilarating, stimulating, stimulative, stimulatory, invigorating,** rousing, energizing; regaling, cheering; rejuvenating; recreative, recreational

4 **refreshed, restored, invigorated, exhilarated,** freshened up, enlivened, stimulated, energized, recharged, animated, reanimated, **revived,** renewed, recreated, ready for more, ready for another round

5 **unwearied, untired, unfatigued, unexhausted**

10 FOOD

NOUNS **1** **food,** foodstuff, food and drink, sustenance, kitchen stuff, victualage, **comestibles, edibles,** eatables, viands, **cuisine,** ingesta <pl>; soul food; fast food, junk food; **fare,** cheer, creature comfort; provision, provender; meat, bread, daily bread, bread and butter, staff of life; health food; board, table, feast 8.9, spread <nf>; nouvelle cuisine, designer food; processed food

2 <nf terms> **grub,** grubbery, **eats, chow,** chuck, grits, groceries, nosh, the nosebag, scarf *or* scoff, nibbles, tuck <Brit>, victuals *or* vittles; fast food; Frankenfood

3 **nutriment, nourishment,** nurture; pabulum, pap; aliment, alimentation, fare; **refreshment,** refection; **sustenance,** support, keep

4 **feed, fodder, provender,** animal food; forage, pasture, eatage, pasturage; grain; corn, oats, barley, wheat, cereal grain; meal, bran, chop; **hay,** timothy, clover, straw; ensilage, silage; chicken feed, scratch, scratch feed, mash; slops, swill; pet food, dog food, cat food; bird seed

5 **provisions, groceries,** provender, supplies, stores, larder, food supply, food and drink, victuals; fresh foods, canned foods, frozen foods, dehydrated foods, precooked foods, convenience foods; commissariat, commissary, grocery

6 **rations,** board, meals, commons <chiefly Brit>, mess, allowance, allotment, food allotment; short commons <chiefly Brit>; emergency rations; K ration, C ration, garrison *or* field rations

7 **dish**, culinary preparation *or* concoction; cover, **course** 8.10; casserole; grill, broil, boil, roast, fry; **main dish, entree,** main course, *pièce de résistance* <Fr>, culinary masterpiece, dish fit for a king; hors d'oeuvre, starter, appetizer; side dish, side, salad, vegetables; dessert; dish of the day, soup of the day, specialty

8 **delicacy, dainty, goody** <nf>, treat, kickshaw, **tidbit,** titbit; gourmet food; **morsel,** choice morsel, *bonne bouche* or *amuse-gueule* <Fr>, savory; dessert; ambrosia, nectar, cate, manna

9 **appetizer,** whet, *apéritif* <Fr>; foretaste, antepast, *antipasto* <Ital>; **hors d'oeuvre;** *crostato* <Ital>, starter, nibbles, tidbits; smorgasbord; crackers and cheese, crudites, **dip,** guacamole, salsa, pâté, cheese dip, nachos, potato skins, hummus; falafel; rumaki; **pickle,** dill pickle

10 **soup,** *potage* <Fr>, *zuppa* or *minestra* <Ital>, cream soup, clear soup, consomme, stock, bouillon, broth, potage, bisque, borscht, gumbo, chowder, bouillabaisse, alphabet soup, avgolemono

11 **stew,** olla, olio, *olla podrida* <Sp>; hot pot; meat stew, *étuvée* <Fr>; Irish stew, mulligan stew *or* mulligan <nf>, burgoo; goulash, Hungarian goulash; ragout; salmi; *bouillabaisse* <Fr>, *paella* <Catalan>, oyster stew; fricassee; curry

12 sauce; tomato sauce, ketchup *or* catsup; brown sauce, Worcestershire sauce, soy sauce, Bordelaise; Tabasco sauce <TM>, barbecue sauce; tartar sauce, horseradish; condiment, dip, dressing, salsa, guacamole, pesto; applesauce; mayonnaise, salad dressing, vinaigrette; white sauce, veloute, Alfredo, Bearnaise, hollandaise, bechamel

13 **meat,** flesh, red meat, *viande* <Fr>, white meat; butcher's meat, *viande de boucherie* <Fr>; **cut of meat;** game, *menue viande* <Fr>; venison; **roast,** joint, *rôti* <Fr>; pot roast; chop, cutlet, grill; barbecue, boiled meat, *bouilli* <Fr>; forcemeat; mincemeat, mince; hash, *hachis* <Fr>; *civet* <Fr>; pemmican, jerky; sausage meat, scrapple; aspic; meat substitute, tofu, bean curd

14 **beef,** *bœuf* <Fr>; roast beef, *rosbif* <Fr>; chuck, rib roast, tenderloin, sirloin, steak, round, filet *or* fillet, beefsteak, boneless rump, shank, brisket; hamburger, ground beef; corned beef; dried beef; chipped beef; jerky, charqui; pastrami; beef extract, bouillon; suet

15 **veal,** *vitello* <Ital>, *veau* <Fr>; veal cutlet, *côtelette de veau* <Fr>; shoulder, rib roast, chops, loin, rump, shank, leg, cutlet, escallop, breast, neck; *poitrine de veau* <Fr>; fricandeau; calf's head, *tête de veau* <Fr>; calf's liver, *foie de veau* <Fr>; sweetbread, *ris de veau* <Fr>; calf's brains

16 **mutton,** *mouton* <Fr>; muttonchop; **lamb,** *agneau* <Fr>; breast of lamb, rack of lamb, crown roast, *poitrine d'agneau* <Fr>; leg of lamb, leg of mutton, *gigot* <Fr>, *jambe de mouton* <Fr>; saddle of mutton

17 **pork,** *porc* <Fr>, pig, pigmeat <nf>, spareribs, ribs

18 **steak,** *tranche* <Fr>, **beefsteak,** *bifteck* <Fr>, *tranche de bœuf* <Fr>, *bistecca* <Ital>, minute steak, filet, tournedo

19 **chop, cutlet,** *côtelette* <Fr>; pork chop, *côtelette de porc frais* <Fr>; mutton chop, *côtelette de mouton* <Fr>, scallop, papillote, Saratoga chop; veal cutlet, veal chop, *côtelette de veau* <Fr>, *Wiener Schnitzel* <Ger>

20 <variety meats> kidneys; heart; brains; liver; gizzard; tongue; sweetbread <thymus>; beef bread <pancreas>; tripe <stomach>; marrow; cockscomb; chitterlings *or* chitlins <intestines>; prairie *or* mountain oyster <testis>; haslet, giblets, *abattis* <Fr>, offal

21 **sausage,** *saucisse* <Fr>, *saucisson* <Fr>, *salsiccia* <Ital>, *Wurst* <Ger>, banger, hot dog; **pâté**

22 **poultry, fowl,** bird, edible bird, chicken, turkey, *volaille* <Fr>

23 <parts of poultry> leg, drumstick, thigh, wing, wishbone, breast; white meat, dark meat, giblets, pope's *or* parson's nose <nf>

24 **fish,** *poisson* <Fr>; seafood; fruits de mer; fried fish, broiled fish, boiled fish, poached fish, smoked fish, fish cake *or* fish ball, fish stick, fish pie; fish and chips; food fish; finnan haddie; kipper, kippered salmon *or* herring, gravlax; smoked salmon, lox; smoked herring, red herring; eel, *anguille* <Fr>; fish eggs, roe, caviar; ceviche, sushi; squid, calamari; flatfish, sole, lemon sole, Dover sole, flounder, fluke, dab, sanddab

25 **shellfish,** *coquillage* <Fr>; **mollusc,** mollusk, snail, *escargot* <Fr>

26 **eggs,** *œufs* <Fr>; fried eggs, *œufs sur le plat* <Fr>; hard- and soft-boiled eggs, *œufs à la coque* <Fr>, coddled eggs; poached eggs, over-easy, sunny-side up, *œufs pochés* <Fr>; scrambled eggs, buttered eggs, *œufs brouillés* <Fr>; dropped eggs, shirred eggs, stuffed eggs, deviled eggs; omelet *or* omelette; soufflé; Scotch egg, eggs Benedict; egg salad

27 **stuffing, dressing,** forcemeat *or* farce

28 **bread,** *pain* <Fr>, *pane* <Ital>, the staff of life; French bread, Italian bread, sourdough bread, ciabatta; loaf of bread; crust, breadcrust, crust of bread; breadstuff; **leaven,** leavening, ferment

29 **corn bread;** pone, ash pone, corn pone, corn tash, ash cake, hoecake, johnnycake; dodger, corn dodger, corn dab, hush puppy; cracklin' bread <nf>; *tortilla* <Sp>

30 **biscuit,** sinker <nf>; hardtack, sea biscuit, ship biscuit, pilot biscuit *or* bread; shortcake; **cracker,** soda cracker *or* saltine, graham cracker, *biscotto* or *biscotti* <Ital>, cream cracker, potato chip, potato crisp <Brit>, sultana, water biscuit, butter cracker, oyster cracker, pilot biscuit; wafer; rusk, zwieback, melba toast, Brussels biscuit; pretzel

31 **roll, bun, muffin;** bagel, bialy *or* bialystoker; brioche, croissant; English muffin; popover; scone; hard roll, kaiser roll, dinner roll, Parker House roll, Portuguese roll

32 **sandwich,** *canapé* <Fr>, *smörgasbord* <Swed>; club sandwich, Dagwood; hamburger, burger; subma-

rine *or* sub *or* hero *or* grinder *or* hoagy *or* poorboy; wedge; gyro; veggieburger *or* vegeburger *or* gardenburger

33 **noodles,** pasta, Italian paste, paste; **spaghetti,** spaghettini, ziti, penne, fettuccine, linguine, fusilli, radiattore, vermicelli, rigatoni, tortellini, ravioli, gnocchi, **macaroni,** lasagne; *kreplach* <Yiddish pl>, won ton; **dumpling;** spaetzle, dim sum; matzo balls, *knaydlach* <Yiddish>

34 **cereal,** breakfast food, dry cereal, hot cereal; **flour,** meal

35 **vegetables,** produce, *légumes* <Fr>, veg *and* veggies <nf>; **greens;** potherbs; **beans,** *frijoles* <Sp>, *haricots* <Fr>; leafy vegetable, stem vegetable, root vegetable, tuber, flower vegetable, seed vegetable, pulse; **potato,** spud <nf>, tater <nf>, *pomme de terre* <Fr>, Irish potato, pratie <nf>, white potato; **tomato,** love apple; mushroom; eggplant, *aubergine* <Fr>, mad apple; rhubarb, pieplant; cabbage, *Kraut* <Ger>; ratatouille, mixed vegetables

36 **rice**, white rice, long-grain rice, brown rice, wild rice, pilaf, orzo, couscous, risotto, Arborio rice

37 **salad,** *salade* <Fr>; **greens,** *crudités* <Fr>, tossed salad, chef's salad, Caesar salad; fruit salad, pasta salad, potato salad, coleslaw, Cobb salad, composed salad

38 **fruit;** produce; stone fruit, drupe, berry, pome, pepo, sorosis, syconium, hesperidium; simple fruit, true fruit, composite fruit, aggregate fruit, multiple fruit, false fruit, succulent fruit; citrus fruit; tropical fruit; dry fruit, dehiscent fruit, indehiscent fruit, fruiting body; fruit compote, fruit soup, fruit cup, fruit cocktail, fruit salad, stewed fruit

39 **nut,** *noix* <Fr>, *noisette* <Fr>; kernel, meat

40 **sweets,** sweet stuff, **confectionery; sweet, sweetmeat; confection; candy;** bonbon, comfit, confiture; **jelly, jam;** preserve, conserve; marmalade; toffee, butterscotch, caramel, dulce de leche, chocolate, fudge; gelatin, Jell-O <TM>; compote; pudding, custard, mousse; tutti-frutti; maraschino cherries; honey; icing, frosting, glaze; meringue; whipped cream

41 **pastry,** *patisserie* <Fr>; French pastry, Danish pastry; **tart,** tarlet; turnover; timbale; **pie,** *tarte* <Fr>, fruit pie, tart, single-crust pie, double-crust pie, deep-dish pie, fruit pie, custard pie, meringue pie; *quiche* or *quiche Lorraine* <Fr>; cobbler, crisp, bread pudding; patty, patty cake; patty shell, *vol-au-vent* <Fr>; rosette; dowdy, pandowdy; phyllo *or* filo, strudel, baklava; puff pastry, flake pastry; puff, cream puff, croquembouche, profiterole; cannoli, cream horn; éclair; tiramisu; croissant, scone, shortbread, brioche

42 **cake,** gâteau, torte; petit-four; layer cake, Bundt cake, pound cake, sponge cake, upside-down cake, fruitcake, gingerbread, cheesecake, shortcake, cupcake, tiramisu, brownie; petit four, madeleine; doughnut, doughnut hole

43 **cookie,** biscuit <Brit>, fortune cookie, biscotti, bar cookie, drop cookie, refrigerator *or* icebox cookie, sandwich cookie; cereal bar, energy bar

44 **doughnut,** donut, friedcake, sinker <nf>, olykoek <nf>; French doughnut, raised doughnut; glazed doughnut; doughnut hole; fastnacht; **cruller,** twister; jelly doughnut, bismarck; fritter, *beignet* <Fr>; apple fritter

45 **pancake,** griddlecake, **hot cake,** battercake, flapcake, **flapjack,** flannel cake; buckwheat cake; chapatty <India>; **waffle;** blintz, cheese blintz, *crêpe* and *crêpe suzette* <Fr>, Swedish pancake, latke

46 **pudding,** custard, mousse, flan, tapioca

47 **ice,** *glace* <Fr>, frozen dessert; **ice cream,** ice milk; **sherbet,** water ice <Brit>, Italian ice, sorbet, bombe; gelato; tortoni; parfait; sundae, ice-cream sundae, banana split; ice-cream soda; ice-cream float, frappé; ice-cream cone; frozen pudding; frozen custard, soft ice cream; frozen yogurt; ice cream sandwich

48 **dairy products,** milk products, butter, cream, yogurt; **cheese,** *fromage* <Fr>**; tofu,** bean curd

49 **beverage,** drink, thirst quencher, potation, potable, drinkable <nf>, **liquor,** liquid, hard liquor, alcoholic drink, libation, liqueur, mixed drink, cocktail, **beer,** brew, brewski <nf>, alcopop; **wine** ; **soft drink,** nonalcoholic beverage; cooler, spritzer; cold drink; carbonated water, soda water, sparkling water, tap water, spring water, mineral water, seltzer water; **soda,** pop, soda pop, tonic; milk shake *or* milkshake, shake *and* frosted <nf>; malted milk, malt <nf>, hot chocolate, cocoa; smoothie; **milk**, pasteurized milk, homogenized milk, skim milk, condensed milk, evaporated milk, lowfat milk, chocolate milk; **coffee**, cappuccino, espresso, decaffeinated coffee *or* decaf, café latté *or* latté, café au lait, java *and* joe <nf>; **tea**, iced tea; **fruit juice**, lemonade, vegetable juice, tomato juice; juice box

50 <food packaging terms> use-by date, best-before date, sell-by date

11 COOKING

NOUNS **1** **cooking, cookery, cuisine, culinary art;** food preparation, food processing; home economics, domestic science, home management, culinary science; haute cuisine, *nouvelle cuisine* <Fr>; gastronomy; catering; nutrition 7

2 <cooking technique> manner of preparation, style of recipe; baking, toasting, roasting, oven-roasting, frying, deep-frying, pan-frying, stir-frying, searing, flash-frying, blackening, smoking, curing, sautéing, boiling, parboiling, simmering, steaming, stewing, basting, braising, poaching, shirring, blanching, steaming, barbecuing, steeping, brewing, grilling, broiling, panbroiling, charbroiling, microwaving, pressure-cooking; canning, pickling, preserving

3 **cook, chef,** *cuisinier* or *cuisinière* <Fr>, kitchener, culinarian, culinary artist; **chief cook, head chef,** *chef de cuisine* <Fr>, cordon bleu cook; sous chef, apprentice chef, fry cook *or* grease-burner <nf>, short-order cook, food preparer, prep cook; **baker,** *boulanger* <Fr>, pastry cook, pastry chef, *patissier* <Fr>, saucier; caterer

4 **kitchen, cookroom,** cookery, **scullery,** cuisine; back of the house; kitchenette, cooking area; **galley;** cookhouse; **bakery,** bakehouse; barbecue; **cookware, kitchen ware,** cooker ; pots and pans; refrigerator, fridge <nf>, freezer; cookbook, recipe, receipt

VERBS **5** **cook,** prepare food, prepare, prepare a meal, do, cook up, fry up, boil up, rustle up <nf>; precook; boil, heat, heat up, stew, simmer, parboil, blanch; brew; poach, coddle; bake, fire, ovenbake; **microwave,** micro-cook, nuke <nf>; scallop; shirr; roast; toast; fry, deep-fry *or* deep-fat fry, griddle, pan, panfry; sauté, stir-fry; frizz, frizzle; sear, blacken, braise, brown; broil, grill, pan-broil; barbecue; fricassee; steam, blanch; devil; curry; baste; **do to a turn,** do to perfection, whip something up *and* throw something together <nf>

ADJS **6** **cooking, culinary,** kitchen, gastronomic, epicurean; mealtime, mensal; preprandial, postprandial, after-dinner; au naturel, a la mode, a la carte, table d'hôte

7 **cooked,** heated, stewed, fried, barbecued, curried, fricasseed, deviled, sautéed, shirred, toasted; roasted, roast; fired, pan-fried, deep-fried *or* deep-fat fried, stir-fried; broiled, grilled, pan-broiled; seared, blackened, braised, browned; boiled, simmered, parboiled; steamed; blanched; poached, coddled; baked, fired, oven-baked; scalloped

8 **done, well-done,** well-cooked; *bien cuit* <Fr>, done to a turn *or* to perfection; overcooked, **overdone,** burned; medium, medium-rare; doneness

9 **underdone,** undercooked, not done, **rare,** red, raw, *saignant* <Fr>; al dente; sodden, fallen

12 EXCRETION

<bodily discharge>

NOUNS **1** **excretion,** egestion, extrusion, **elimination, discharge,** expulsion, call of nature <nf>**; emission;** eccrisis; **exudation,** transudation; extravasation, effusion, flux, flow; ejaculation, ejection 909; **secretion** 13

2 **defecation,** dejection, **evacuation,** voidance; movement, **bowel movement** *or* BM, number two <nf>, **stool,** shit *and* crap <nf>; **diarrhea,** loose bowels, flux; trots *and* runs *and* shits *and* GI's *and* GI shits <nf>; turistas *or* tourista *and* Montezuma's revenge *and* Aztec two-step <nf>; lientery; **dysentery,** bloody flux; catharsis, purgation, purge

3 **excrement,** dejection, dejecta, dejecture, **discharge,** ejection; matter; **waste,** waste matter; **excreta,** egesta, ejecta, ejectamenta; exudation, exudate; transudation; extravasation; effluent; sewage, sewerage

4 **feces,** feculence; defecation, movement, bowel movement *or* **BM; stool, shit** <nf>, **ordure,** night soil, jakes <Brit nf>, crap *and* ca-ca *and* doo-doo *and* number two *and* poo-poo *and* poop <nf>; turd <nf>; dingleberry <nf>; **manure, dung, droppings;** cow pats, cow flops <nf>; cow chips, buffalo chips; guano; coprolite, coprolith; sewage, sewerage

5 **urine,** water, **piss** <nf>, number one, *pish* <Yiddish>, pee *and* pee-pee *and* wee-wee *and* whizz <nf>, piddle, leak, stale; **urination,** micturition, emiction, a piss *and* a pee *and* a whizz <nf>; golden shower <nf>; urea, uric acid

6 **pus; matter,** purulence, discharge, ichor, sanies; pussiness; **suppuration, festering,** rankling, mattering, running, weeping; gleet, leukorrhea

7 **sweat, perspiration,** perspiring, sweating, water, moisture, dampness, wetness; exudation, exudate; diaphoresis, sudor, sudation, sudoresis; honest sweat, the sweat of one's brow; beads of sweat, beaded brow; cold sweat; **lather,** swelter, streams of sweat; sudoresis; body odor *or* **BO,** perspiration odor

8 **hemorrhage,** hemorrhea, **bleeding;** nosebleed; ecchymosis, petechia

9 **menstruation,** menstrual discharge *or* flow *or* flux, catamenia, catamenial discharge, **the curse** <nf>, the curse of Eve; flow <nf>; **menses, monthlies,** courses, period, one's friend, time of the month, that time

10 **latrine,** convenience, **toilet,** toilet room, water closet *or* WC <nf>; **john** *and* johnny *and* **can** *and* crapper *and* head <nf>; loo <Brit nf>; **lavatory,** washroom; **bathroom,** basement; **rest room,** comfort station *or* room, commode; ladies' *or* women's *or* girls' *or* little girls' *or* powder room <nf>; men's *or* boys' *or* little boys' room <nf>, the ladies', the gents'; head; privy, outhouse, backhouse, shithouse <nf>, johnny house <nf>, earth closet <Brit>, jakes, closet *and* necessary <nf>; bog <Brit>; urinal

11 **toilet,** stool, **water closet; john** *and* johnny *and* **can** *and* crapper *and* thunderbox <nf>; latrine; commode, closetstool, potty-chair <nf>; **chamber pot,** chamber, pisspot <nf>, potty <nf>, jerry <Brit nf>, jordan <Brit nf>, thunder mug <nf>; throne <nf>; chemical toilet, chemical closet; urinal; bedpan

VERBS **12** **excrete,** egest, **eliminate, discharge,** emit, give off, pass, expel; ease *or* relieve oneself, go to the bathroom *or* toilet <nf>; **exude,** exudate, transude; weep; effuse, extravasate; answer the call of nature, pay a call, make a pit stop, make a comfort stop; **secrete** 13.5

13 **defecate, shit** *and* crap <nf>, **evacuate,** void, **stool,** dung, have a bowel movement *or* BM, move one's bowels, soil, take a shit *or* crap <nf>, ca-ca *or* number two <nf>; have the runs *or* trots *or* shits <nf>

14 **urinate, pass** *or* **make water, wet,** stale, **piss** <nf>, piddle, pee, tinkle; pee-pee *and* wee-wee *and* whizz *and* take a whizz *and* take a leak <nf>, spend a penny, pump bilge, do number one

15 **fester,** suppurate, matter, rankle, run, weep; ripen, come *or* draw to a head

16 **sweat, perspire,** exude; break out in a sweat, **get all in a lather** <nf>; sweat like a trooper *or* horse *or* pig, swelter, wilt, steam

17 **bleed, hemorrhage,** lose blood, **shed blood,** spill blood; bloody; ecchymose, extravasate

18 **menstruate,** come sick, bleed, come around, have one's period, have the curse, have one's friend, be on the rag <nf>, flow

ADJS **19** **excretory,** excretive, excretionary; eliminative, eliminant, egestive; exudative, transudative; **secretory** 13.7

20 **excremental,** excrementary; **fecal,** feculent, shitty *and* crappy <nf>, scatologic *or* scatological, stercoral, stercorous, stercoraceous, dungy; **urinary,** urinative

21 **festering,** suppurative, rankling, mattering; pussy, purulent

22 **sweaty,** perspiry <nf>; sweating, perspiring; wet with sweat, beaded with sweat, **sticky** <nf>, **clammy;** bathed in sweat, drenched with sweat, wilted; in a sweat; sudatory, sudoric, sudorific, diaphoretic

23 **bleeding, bloody,** hemorrhaging; ecchymosed; blood-borne

24 **menstrual,** catamenial, menstruating; on the rag <nf>

13 SECRETION

NOUNS **1** **secretion,** secreta, secernment; **excretion** 12; external secretion, internal secretion; exudation, transudation; lactation; weeping, lacrimation; ooze

2 digestive secretion *or* juice, salivary secretion, gastric juice, digestive juice, pancreatic juice, intestinal juice; bile, gall; endocrine; prostatic fluid, seminal fluid, semen, sperm; thyroxin; autacoid, **hormone,** chalone; mucus; tears; rheum; sebum, musk, pheromone; milk, colostrum; gland

3 **saliva, spittle, sputum, spit, expectoration**, spitting**;** phlegm, sputum; salivation, ptyalism, sialorrhea, sialagogue, **slobber,** slabber, slaver, **drivel,** dribble, **drool;** froth, foam; mouth-watering

4 endocrinology, eccrinology, hormonology

VERBS **5** **secrete,** produce, give out *or* off, exude, transude, release, emit, discharge, eject; **excrete** 12.12; water; lactate; weep, tear, cry, lacrimate; sweat, perspire; ooze

6 **salivate,** ptyalize; **slobber,** slabber, slaver, **drool, drivel,** dribble; **expectorate, spit,** spit up; spew; hawk, clear the throat

ADJS **7** **secretory,** secretive, secretional, secretionary, secreting; **excretory** 12.19; exudative, transudatory, emanative, emanatory, emanational; lymphatic, serous; seminal, spermatic; watery, watering; lactational; lacteal, lacteous, lactating; lachrymal, lacrimatory, lachrymose; rheumy; salivary, salivant, salivous, salivating, sialoid, sialagogic; sebaceous, sebiferous; sweating, sweaty, sudatory; oozing

8 **glandular,** glandulous; **endocrine,** humoral, exocrine, eccrine, apocrine, holocrine, merocrine; **hormonal** *or* hormonic; adrenal, pancreatic, gonadal; ovarian; luteal; prostatic; splenetic; thymic; thyroidal

14 BODILY DEVELOPMENT

NOUNS **1** **bodily** *or* **physical development,** growth, development 861.1, maturation, maturing, maturescence, coming of age, growing up, reaching one's full growth, upgrowth; growing like a weed <nf>; plant growth, vegetation 310.32, germination, pullulation; sexual maturity, pubescence, puberty; nubility, marriageability, marriageableness; adulthood, manhood, womanhood; reproduction, procreation 78, burgeoning, sprouting; budding, gemmation; outgrowth, excrescence; overgrowth 257.5

VERBS **2** **grow, develop,** wax, **increase** 251; gather, brew; **grow up,** mature, maturate, spring up, ripen, come of age, **shoot up,** sprout up, upshoot, upspring, upsprout, upspear, overtop, tower, get bigger, get taller; grow like a weed <nf>; burgeon, **sprout** 310.34, blossom 310.35, reproduce 78.7, procreate 78.8, grow out of, germinate, pullulate; vegetate 310.34; **flourish, thrive;** mushroom, balloon; outgrow; overgrow, hypertrophy, overdevelop, grow uncontrollably

ADJS **3 grown, full-grown, grown-up,** developed, well-developed, fully developed, **mature, adult, full-fledged,** fully fledged; **growing,** adolescent, maturescent, pubescent; nubile, marriageable; **sprouting,** crescent, budding, in full bloom, flowering 310.38, florescent, **flourishing,** blossoming, blooming, burgeoning, fast-growing, thriving; overgrown, hypertrophied, overdeveloped

15 STRENGTH

<inherent power>

NOUNS **1 strength, might,** mightiness, powerfulness, stamina; **force, potency, power** 18; **energy** 17; **vigor, vitality,** vigorousness, heartiness, lustiness, lustihood; **stoutness, sturdiness,** stalwartness, robustness, hardiness, ruggedness; **guts** *and* gutsiness <nf>, fortitude, intestinal fortitude <nf>, **toughness** 1049, **endurance, stamina,** staying *or* sticking power, stick-to-itiveness <nf>; **strength of will,** decisiveness, obstinacy 361

2 muscularity, brawniness; beefiness *and* huskiness *and* heftiness *and* burliness <nf>, thewiness, sinewiness; **brawn,** beef <nf>; **muscle,** brawn, sinew, sinews, thew, thews; musculature, build, physique; tone, elasticity 1048; brute strength

3 firmness, soundness, staunchness, stoutness, **sturdiness, stability,** solidity, **hardness** 1046, temper

4 impregnability, impenetrability, **invulnerability,** inexpugnability, inviolability; **unassailability,** unattackableness; resistlessness, **irresistibility; invincibility,** indomitability, insuperability, unconquerableness, unbeatableness; invincibility

5 strengthening, invigoration, fortification; **hardening,** toughening, firming; case hardening, tempering; **restrengthening,** reinforcement; **reinvigoration,** refreshment, revivification; fortifying

6 strong man, stalwart, tower of strength, muscle man, piledriver, bulldozer, hunk <nf>, hardbody; **giant,** Samson, Goliath; Charles Atlas, Mr Universe; superhero, Hercules, Atlas, Antaeus, Cyclops, Briareus, colossus, Polyphemus, Titan, Brobdingnagian, Tarzan, Superman; the strong, the mighty; bouncer; he-man

7 <nf terms> **hulk, powerhouse, muscle man,** man mountain, big bruiser, bruiser, strapper, strong-arm man, bully, bullyboy, ape, tough, toughie, tough guy, bozo, **goon** 671.10, gorilla, meat-eater

8 <comparisons> horse, ox, lion; pigshit <nf>; oak, heart of oak; rock, Gibraltar; iron, steel, nails; lumberjack

VERBS **9 be strong,** overpower, overwhelm; have what it takes, pack a punch

10 not weaken, not flag; **bear up, hold up,** keep up, stand up; **hold out,** stay *or* see it out, not give up, **never say die,** not let it get one down, gird up one's loins

11 <nf terms> **tough it out, hang tough, hang in,** stick *or* take it, take it on the chin, sweat it out, go *or* stay the distance

12 exert strength, put beef *or* one's back into it <nf>; use force, get tough <nf>, muscle *and* manhandle *and* strong-arm <nf>; push around

13 strengthen, invigorate, fortify, beef up <nf>, brace, batten, buttress, prop, shore up, support, undergird, brace up; gird, gird up one's loins; steel, harden, case harden, anneal, stiffen, **toughen,** temper, nerve; confirm, sustain; **restrengthen, reinforce; reinvigorate,** refresh, revive, recruit one's strength; tone; soup up, beef up

14 **proof,** insulate, weatherproof, soundproof, muffle, quietize, fireproof, waterproof, goofproof <nf>, etc

ADJS **15** **strong, forceful,** forcible, **mighty, powerful,** puissant <nf>, **potent** 18.12; **stout, sturdy, stalwart, rugged,** hale; hunky *and* husky *and* hefty *and* beefy <nf>, strapping, durable, doughty <nf>, **hardy,** hard, hard as nails, cast-iron, iron-hard, steely; **robust,** robustious, gutty *and* gutsy <nf>; strong-willed, obstinate 361.8; **vigorous, hearty,** nervy, **lusty,** bouncing, full- *or* red-blooded; bionic, sturdy as an ox, strong as a lion *or* an ox *or* a horse, strong as brandy, strong as pig-shit <nf>, strong as strong; full-strength, double-strength, industrial-strength <nf>

16 **able-bodied, well-built,** well-set, well-set-up <nf>, well-knit, of good *or* powerful physique, broad-shouldered, barrel-chested, **athletic; muscular,** well-muscled, heavily muscled, thickset, burly, **brawny;** buff; thewy, sinewy, **wiry;** muscle-bound, all muscle; strapping

17 **herculean,** Briarean, Antaean, Cyclopean, Atlantean, gigantic, gigantesque, Brobdingnagian, huge 257.20; Amazonian

18 **firm, sound, stout,** sturdy, tough, hard-boiled <nf>, **staunch, stable,** solid; sound as a dollar, solid as a rock, firm as Gibraltar, made of iron; buffed; rigid, unbreakable, infrangible; braced, buttressed

19 **impregnable,** impenetrable, **invulnerable,** inviolable, inexpugnable; **unassailable,** unattackable, insuperable, unsurmountable; resistless, **irresistible; invincible,** indomitable, **unconquerable,** unsubduable, unyielding 361.9, incontestable, unbeatable, more than a match for; overpowering, overwhelming, avalanchine

20 **resistant, proof, tight;** impervious; foolproof; shatterproof; weatherproof, dampproof, watertight, hermetically sealed, vacuum-packed, leakproof; hermetic, airtight; soundproof, noiseproof; puncture proof, holeproof; bulletproof, ballproof, shellproof, bombproof; rustproof, corrosionproof; fireproof, flameproof, fire-resisting; burglarproof

21 **unweakened, undiminished,** unallayed, unbated, unabated, unfaded, unwithered, unshaken, unworn, unexhausted; **unweakening, unflagging, unbowed;** in full force *or* swing, **going strong** <nf>; in the plenitude of power

22 <of sounds and odors> **intense, penetrating,** piercing; **loud,** deafening, thundering 56.12; **pungent,** five-alarm, three-alarm, **reeking** 69.10

ADVS **23** **strongly, stoutly, sturdily,** stalwartly, robustly, ruggedly; **mightily, powerfully, forcefully,** forcibly; **vigorously, heartily,** lustily; **soundly, firmly,** staunchly; impregnably, invulnerably, **invincibly, irresistibly,** unyieldingly; resistantly, imperviously; **intensely; loudly,** at the top of one's lungs, clamorously, deafeningly; **pungently**

16 WEAKNESS

NOUNS **1** **weakness,** weakliness, **feebleness,** enfeeblement, strengthlessness; **flabbiness, flaccidity,** softness; **impotence** *or* impotency 19; **debility,** debilitation, prostration, invalidism, collapse; **faintness,** faintishness, dizziness, lightheadedness, shakiness, gone *or* blah feeling <nf>; **fatigue** 21, exhaustion, weariness, dullness, sluggishness, languor, lassitude, **listlessness,** tiredness, languishment, atony, burn-out *or* burnout; anemia, bloodlessness, etiolation, asthenia, adynamia, cachexia *or* cachexy

2 **frailty,** slightness, **delicacy, daintiness,** lightness; **flimsiness, unsubstantiality,** wispiness, sleaziness, shoddiness; **fragility,** frangibility *or* frangibleness, brittleness, breakableness, destructibility; disintegration 806; **human frailty,** fatal flaw; gutlessness <nf>, cowardice 491; moral weakness, irresolution, **indecisiveness,** infirmity of will, velleity, changeableness 854; inherent vice

3 **infirmity, unsoundness,** incapacity, unfirmness, unsturdiness, **instability, unsubstantiality;** decrepitude; **unsteadiness, shakiness,** ricketiness, wobbliness, wonkiness <Brit nf>, weediness <nf>; caducity, senility, invalidism; wishy-washiness, insipidity, vapidity, wateriness

4 **weak point, weakness,** weak place, **weak side,** weak link, vulnerable point, chink in one's armor, Achilles' heel *or* heel of Achilles, soft underbelly; fatal flaw; feet of clay

5 **weakening, enfeeblement, debilitation,** exhaustion, inanition, attrition; languishment; **devitalization,** enervation, evisceration; fatigue; attenuation, extenuation; softening, mitigation, damping, abatement, slackening, relaxing, relaxation, blunting, deadening, dulling; **dilution,** watering, watering-down, attenuation, thinning, reduction

6 **weakling,** weak *or* meek soul, weak sister <nf>, hothouse plant, softy <nf>, softling, **jellyfish,** invertebrate, gutless wonder <nf>, **baby,** big baby, crybaby, chicken <nf>, scaredy-cat, coward, wimp, wussy, Milquetoast, sop, **milksop, namby-pamby, mollycoddle,** mama's boy, mother's boy, mother's darling, teacher's pet; sissy *and* pansy *and* pantywaist <nf>, pushover <nf>, softie, lightweight; **wimp,** poor *or* weak *or* dull tool <nf>; **nonentity,** hollow man, doormat *and* empty suit *and* nebbish *and* sad sack <nf>

7 <comparisons> kitten, reed, thread, matchwood, rope of sand; house of cards, eggshell, glass, house built on sand, sand castle, cobweb; water, milk and water, gruel, dishwater, cambric tea

VERBS 8 <be weak> **shake,** tremble, quiver, quaver, cringe, cower 491.9, totter, teeter, dodder; halt, limp; be on one's last leg, have one foot in the grave

9 <become weak> **weaken,** grow weak *or* weaker, go soft <nf>; **languish, wilt,** faint, **droop,** drop, dwindle, **sink, decline, flag, pine, fade, tail away** *or* off, fail, fall *or* drop by the wayside, ebb, wane; crumble, go to pieces, disintegrate 806.3; go downhill, hit the skids <nf>, give way, break, collapse, cave in <nf>, surrender, cry uncle <nf>; give out, have no staying power, run out of gas <nf>, conk *or* peter *or* poop *or* peg *or* fizzle out <nf>; come apart, come apart at the seams, come unstuck *or* unglued <nf>; yield; die on the vine <nf>; wear thin *or* away

10 <make weak> **weaken, enfeeble, debilitate,** unstrengthen, unsinew, undermine, soften up <nf>, unbrace, unman, unnerve, rattle, shake up <nf>, impair, **devitalize, enervate,** eviscerate; **sap,** sap the strength of, exhaust, gruel, take it out of <nf>; shake, unstring; reduce, lay low; attenuate, extenuate, mitigate, abate; blunt, deaden, dull, damp *or* dampen, take the edge off; draw the teeth, defang; cramp, cripple

11 **dilute, cut** <nf>, **reduce, thin,** thin out, attenuate, rarefy; **water,** water down, adulterate, irrigate *and* baptize <nf>; soften, muffle, mute; negate

ADJS 12 **weak,** weakly, **feeble,** debilitated, imbecile; **strengthless,** sapless, marrowless, pithless, sinewless, listless, out of gas <nf>, nerveless, lustless; **impotent, powerless** 19.13; spineless, lily-livered, whitelivered, wimpy *and* wimpish *and* chicken *and* gutless *and* wussy <nf>, cowardly 491.10; unnerved, shookup <nf>, unstrung, faint, faintish, lightheaded, dizzy, gone; dull, slack; **soft, flabby,** flaccid, unhardened; **limp,** limber, limp *or* limber as a dishrag, floppy, rubbery; **languorous,** languid, **drooping,** droopy, pooped <nf>; asthenic, anemic, bloodless, effete, etiolated; not what one used to be

13 weak as water, eak as milk and water, weak as a drink of water, weak as a child *or* baby, weak as a chicken, weak as a kitten, weak as a mouse

14 **frail, slight, delicate, dainty**; puny; light, lightweight; effeminate; namby-pamby, sissified, pansyish;

fragile, frangible, **breakable,** destructible, shattery, crumbly, brittle, fragmentable, fracturable; **unsubstantial, flimsy,** sleazy, tacky <nf>, wispy, cobwebby, gossamery, papery; gimcrack *and* gimcracky *and* cheap-jack *and* ticky-tacky <nf>; jerry-built, jerry; gimpy

15 **unsound, infirm,** unfirm, **unstable, unsubstantial,** unsturdy, unsolid, decrepit, crumbling, fragmented, fragmentary, disintegrating 806.5; poor, poorish; rotten, rotten to the core

16 **unsteady, shaky, rickety,** ricketish, wonky <Brit nf>, spindly, spidery, teetering, teetery, tottery, tottering, doddering, tumbledown, ramshackle, dilapidated, rocky <nf>; groggy, wobbly, staggery

17 **wishy-washy,** tasteless, bland, **insipid,** vapid, neutral, watery, milky, milk-and-water, mushy; halfhearted, infirm of will *or* purpose, **indecisive,** irresolute, changeable 854.7; limp-wristed, gutless

18 **weakened, enfeebled, disabled,** incapacitated, challenged <nf>, debilitated, infirm; **devitalized,** drained, exhausted, sapped, burned-out, maxed-out, used up, played out, spent, effete, etiolated; **fatigued, enervated,** eviscerated; **wasted, rundown,** worn, worn-out, worn to a frazzle <nf>; stressed out; on one's last legs

19 **diluted, cut** <nf>, **reduced, thinned,** rarefied, attenuated; adulterated; watered, watered-down

20 **weakening, debilitating, enfeebling; devitalizing,** enervating, sapping, exhausting, fatiguing, grueling, trying, draining, unnerving

21 **languishing, drooping,** sinking, declining, flagging, pining, fading, failing; on the wane

ADVS 22 **weakly, feebly,** strengthlessly, languorously, listlessly; faintly; delicately, effeminately, daintily; infirmly, unsoundly, unstably, unsubstantially, unsturdily, flimsily; shakily, unsteadily, teeteringly, totteringly

17 ENERGY

NOUNS 1 **energy, vigor, force, power, vitality,** strenuousness, **intensity, dynamism,** demonic energy; **potency** 18; **strength** 15; actual *or* kinetic energy; dynamic energy; potential energy; **energy source** 1021.1, electrical energy, hydroelectric energy *or* power, water power, nuclear energy, solar energy, wind energy, alternative energy

2 **vim, verve,** fire, adrenalin, **dash, drive; aggressiveness, enterprise,** initiative, proactiveness, thrust, spunk; **eagerness** 101, zeal, heartiness, keenness, gusto, passion

3 <nf terms> **pep,** bang, biff, get-up-and-go, ginger, gism, jazz, sizzle, kick, moxie, oomph, pepper, piss and vinegar, **pizzazz,** poop, punch, push, snap, spizzerinctum, spark, starch, steam, zing, zip, zizz, sparkle, wallop, balls, oomph, adrenaline rush

4 **animation, vivacity,** liveliness, energy, **ardor,** vitality, glow, warmth, enthusiasm, vibrancy, lustiness, robustness, mettle, **zest,** zestfulness, **gusto, élan,** éclat, impetus, impetuosity, *joie de vivre* <Fr>, *brio* <Ital>, spiritedness, **briskness,** perkiness, sprightliness, pertness, sensibility, **life, spirit,** life force, vital force *or* principle, *élan vital* <Fr>; activity 330

5 <energetic disapproval or criticism> **acrimony,** acridity, acerbity, acidity, **bitterness,** tartness, **causticity,** mordancy *or* mordacity, **virulence; harshness,** fierceness, **rigor,** roughness, **severity, vehemence,** violence 671, stringency, astringency, stridency 58.1, **sharpness, keenness, poignancy,** trenchancy; edge, point; bite, teeth, grip, sting; animosity; backstabbing

6 **energizer, stimulus,** stimulator, vitalizer, arouser, needle <nf>, restorative; **stimulant, tonic** 86.8; **activator,** motivator, motivating force, motive power; **animator,** spark plug *and* human dynamo *and* ball of fire <nf>; life, life of the party; spinach

7 <units of energy> atomerg, dinamode, dyne, erg, energid, foot-

pound, horsepower-hour, horsepower-year, joule, calorie 1019.19, kilogram-meter, kilowatt-hour, photon, quantum

8 **energizing, invigoration, animation, enlivenment,** quickening, **vitalization,** revival, revitalization; **exhilaration, stimulation**

9 **activation,** reactivation; viability

VERBS 10 **energize,** dynamize; **invigorate, animate, enliven, liven, liven up,** vitalize, quicken, goose *or* jazz up <nf>; **exhilarate, stimulate,** hearten, galvanize, enthuse, electrify, fire, build a fire under, inflame, warm, kindle, charge, charge up, psych *or* pump up <nf>, rouse, arouse, act like a tonic, be a shot in the arm <nf>, **pep** *or* snap *or* jazz *or* zip *or* perk up <nf>, put pep *or* zip into it <nf>

11 **have energy,** be energetic, be vigorous, **thrive,** burst *or* overflow with energy, flourish, tingle, feel one's oats, be up and doing, be full of beans *or* pep *or* ginger *or* zip <nf>, be full of piss and vinegar <nf>, champ at the bit <nf>; come on like gangbusters <nf>

12 **activate,** reactivate, recharge, reanimate; step on the gas <nf>

ADJS 13 **energetic, vigorous, strenuous, forceful, forcible, strong, dynamic,** kinetic, intense, acute, keen, incisive, trenchant, vivid, vibrant, passionate; **enterprising, aggressive,** proactive, activist, can-do *and* gung ho *and* take-over *and* take-charge <nf>, go-getting; **active, lively,** living, **animated, spirited,** go-go <nf>, **vivacious,** brisk, bright-eyed and bushy-tailed <nf>, feisty, lusty, **robust,** hearty, enthusiastic, mettlesome, zesty, zestful, impetuous, spanking, smacking; pumped *and* pumped up *and* jazzed-up *and* charged up *and* switched on <nf>, full-on, snappy *and* zingy *and* zippy *and* peppy <nf>, full of pep *or* pizzazz *or* piss and vinegar <nf>, full of beans <nf>

14 **acrimonious, acrid,** acidulous, acid, acerbic, **bitter,** tart, **caustic,** escharotic <med>, mordant *or* mordacious, **virulent, violent, vehement,** vitriolic; **harsh,** fierce, **rigorous,** severe, rough, stringent, astringent, strident 58.12, **sharp, keen,** sharpish, incisive, trenchant, **cutting,** biting, stinging, **scathing,** stabbing, **piercing, poignant,** penetrating, edged, double-edged

15 **energizing, vitalizing, enlivening,** quickening; tonic, bracing, rousing; **invigorating,** invigorative; **animating,** animative; **exhilarating,** exhilarative; **stimulating,** stimulative, stimulatory, vivifying; activating; viable

ADVS 16 **energetically, vigorously, strenuously, forcefully,** forcibly, intensely, like a house afire *and* like gangbusters <nf>, zestfully, lustily, heartily, keenly, passionately; **actively,** briskly; **animatedly, spiritedly,** vivaciously, with pep <nf>, *con brio* <Ital>

18 POWER, POTENCY

<effective force>

NOUNS 1 **power, potency** *or* potence, prepotency, **force, might,** mightiness, **vigor,** vitality, vim, push, drive, charge, puissance; dint, virtue; moxie *and* oomph *and* pizzazz *and* poop *and* punch *and* bang *and* clout *and* steam <nf>; powerfulness, forcefulness; virulence, vehemence; **strength** 15; **energy** 17; **virility** 76.2; cogence *or* cogency, validity, effect, impact, **effectiveness,** effectivity, effectuality, competence *or* competency; productivity, productiveness; power structure, corridors of power; **influence** 894, pull; **authority** 417, weight; **superiority** 249; power pack, amperage, wattage; main force, *force majeure* <Fr>, main strength, brute force *or* strength, compulsion, duress; muscle power, sinew, might and main, beef <nf>, strong arm; full force, full blast; power struggle; mana; charisma

2 **ability, capability, capacity,** potentiality, faculty, facility, fitness, qualification, talent, flair, genius, caliber, **competence,** competency, adequacy,

sufficiency, **efficiency,** efficacy; **proficiency** 413.1; the stuff *and* the goods *and* what it takes <nf>; susceptibility

3 **omnipotence, almightiness, all-powerfulness,** invincibility; omnicompetence

4 manpower; horsepower, brake horsepower *or* bhp, electric power, electropower, hydroelectric power; hydraulic power, water power; steam power; geothermal power; solar power; atomic power, nuclear power, thermonuclear power; rocket power, jet power; **propulsion, thrust,** impulse

5 force of inertia, *vis inertiae* <L>, torpor; dead force, *vis mortua* <L>; living force, *vis viva* <L>; force of life, *vis vitae* <L>

6 centrifugal force *or* action, centripetal force *or* action, force of gravity

7 <science of forces> dynamics, statics, mechanics

8 **empowerment, enablement;** investment, endowment, enfranchisement

9 **work force,** hands, men, manpower; **fighting force,** troops, units, the big battalions, firepower; **personnel** 577.11, human resources; **forces**

VERBS **10** **empower, enable;** invest, clothe, invest *or* clothe with power, commission, deputize, warrant; enfranchise; endue, endow, **authorize;** arm; strengthen

11 **be able,** be up to, up to, **lie in one's power; can,** may, can do; make it *or* make the grade <nf>; hack it *and* cut it *and* cut the mustard <nf>; charismatize; **wield power,** possess authority 417.13; **take charge** 417.14, get something under one's control *or* under one's thumb, hold all the aces *and* have the say-so <nf>

ADJS **12** **powerful, potent,** prepotent, powerpacked, **mighty,** irresistible, avalanchine, **forceful,** forcible, dynamic; **vigorous,** vital, **energetic,** puissant, ruling, in power; **cogent,** striking, telling, effective, impactful, valid, operative, in force; **strong;** high-powered, high-tension, high-pressure, high-performance, high-potency, bionic; **authoritative;** armipotent, mighty in battle; kick-ass <nf>

13 **omnipotent, almighty, all-powerful;** plenipotentiary, pre-eminent, absolute, unlimited, **sovereign** 417.17; **supreme** 249.13; omnicompetent

14 **able, capable, equal to,** up to, **competent,** adequate, effective, effectual, efficient, efficacious, can-do; productive; **proficient** 413.22

ADVS **15** **powerfully, potently, forcefully,** forcibly, mightily, with might and main, **vigorously, energetically,** dynamically; **cogently,** strikingly, tellingly, impactfully; **effectively,** effectually; productively; with telling effect, to good account, to good purpose, with a vengeance

16 **ably, capably, competently,** adequately, effectively, effectually, **efficiently, well; to the best of one's ability,** as lies in one's power, so far as one can, as best one can; with all one's might, with everything that is in one

17 **by force,** by main *or* brute force, by *force majeure,* with the strong arm, with a high hand, high-handedly; **forcibly,** amain, with might and main; by force of arms, at the point of the sword, by storm

19 IMPOTENCE

NOUNS **1** **impotence** *or* impotency, **powerlessness,** impuissance, forcelessness, feebleness, softness, flabbiness, wimpiness *or* wimpishness <nf>, **weakness** 16; power vacuum

2 **inability, incapability, incapacity,** incapacitation, **incompetence** *or* incompetency, inadequacy, insufficiency, ineptitude, **inferiority** 250, inefficiency, unfitness, imbecility; disability, disablement, disqualification; legal incapacity, wardship, minority, infancy

3 **ineffectiveness, ineffectualness,** ineffectuality, inefficaciousness, **inefficacy,** counterproductiveness *or* counterproductivity, invalidity, **futility, uselessness,** inutility, bootlessness, failure 410; fatuity, inanity

4 **helplessness, defenselessness,** unprotectedness, vulnerability; **debilitation,** invalidism, effeteness, etiolation, enervation; wimpiness <nf>

5 **emasculation,** demasculinization, defeminization, effeminization, neutering, maiming, castration 255.4

6 **impotent,** weakling 16.6, invalid, incompetent, unable; flash in the pan, blank cartridge, wimp *and* dud <nf>; eunuch, *castrato* <Ital>, gelding, pushover, easy mark <nf>

VERBS 7 be impotent, lack force; be ineffective, avail nothing, not work *or* do not take <nf>; **waste one's effort,** bang one's head against a brick wall, have one's hands tied, spin one's wheels, tilt at windmills, run in circles, get nowhere

8 **cannot, not be able,** be unable, not have it *and* not hack it *and* not cut it *and* not cut the mustard <nf>, not make it *and* not make the grade *and* not make the cut <nf>

9 **disable,** disenable, unfit, **incapacitate,** drain, de-energize; enfeeble, debilitate, **weaken** 16.9,10; cripple, maim, lame, hamstring, knee-cap, defang, pull the teeth of <nf>; wing, clip the wings of; **inactivate,** disarm, unarm, put out of action, put *hors de combat;* **put out of order,** put out of commission <nf>, throw out of gear; bugger *and* bugger up *and* queer *and* queer the works *and* gum up *or* screw up <nf>, throw a wrench *or* monkey wrench in the machinery <nf>, sabotage, wreck; kibosh *and* put the kibosh on <nf>; spike, spike one's guns, put a spoke in one's wheels

10 <put out of action> **paralyze,** prostrate, shoot down in flames <nf>, put *hors de combat,* knock out <nf>, break the neck *or* back of; hamstring; handcuff, tie the hands of, hobble, enchain, manacle, hog-tie <nf>, **tie hand and foot,** truss up; throttle, strangle, get a stranglehold on; muzzle, gag, silence; **take the wind out of one's sails,** deflate, knock the props out from under, undermine, cut the ground from under, not leave a leg to stand on

11 **disqualify; invalidate,** knock the bottom out of <nf>

12 **unman, unnerve, enervate,** exhaust, etiolate, **devitalize; emasculate,** cut the balls off <nf>, demasculinize, effeminize; desex, desexualize; sterilize; castrate 255.11, neuter

ADJS 13 **impotent, powerless, forceless, out of gas** <nf>; feeble, soft, flabby, **weak** 16.12, weak as a kitten, wimpy *or* wimpish <nf>, wussy

14 **unable, incapable, incompetent,** inefficient, ineffective; **unqualified,** inept, unendowed, ungifted, untalented, **unfit,** unfitted; **outmatched,** out of one's depth, in over one's head, outgunned; **inferior** 250.6

15 **ineffective, ineffectual, inefficacious,** counterproductive, feckless, not up to scratch *or* up to snuff <nf>, **inadequate** 250.7; **invalid, inoperative,** of no force; nugatory, nugacious; fatuous, fatuitous; **vain, futile, inutile, useless,** unavailing, bootless, fruitless; all talk and no action, all wind; **empty,** inane; **debilitated,** effete, enervated, etiolated, barren, sterile, washed-out <nf>

16 **disabled, incapacitated; crippled,** hamstrung; disqualified, invalidated; disarmed; paralyzed; hog-tied <nf>; prostrate, **on one's back,** on one's beam-ends; challenged

17 **out of action, out of commission** *and* out of it <nf>, out of gear; *hors de combat* <Fr>, out of the battle, off the field, out of the running; laid on the shelf, obsolete, life-expired

18 **helpless, defenseless, unprotected;** vulnerable, like a sitting duck <nf>, dead in the water <nf>, aidless, friendless, unfriended; fatherless, motherless; leaderless, guideless; **untenable,** pregnable, vulnerable; disenfranchised

19 **unmanned, unnerved, enervated,** debilitated, **devitalized;** nerveless, sinewless, marrowless, pithless, lustless; **castrated,** emasculate, emasculated, gelded, eunuchized, unsexed, deballed <nf>, demasculinized, effeminized

ADVS 20 **beyond one,** beyond one's power *or* capacity *or* ability, beyond one's depth, out of one's league <nf>, above one's head, too much for

20 REST, REPOSE

NOUNS 1 **rest, repose, ease, relaxation,** leisure, slippered *or* unbuttoned ease, decompression <nf>; **comfort** 121; comfort zone; restfulness, quiet, tranquility; inactivity 331; sleep 22

2 **respite, recess, rest, pause,** halt, stay, lull, **break,** surcease, suspension, interlude, **intermission,** spell, letup <nf>, **time out** <nf>, time to catch one's breath; **breathing spell,** breathing time, breathing place, breathing space, breath; **breather;** coffee break, tea break, cigarette break; cocktail hour, happy hour <nf>; enforced respite, downtime; R and R *or* rest and recreation

3 **vacation,** holiday <Brit>, getaway; **time off;** day off, week off, month off, etc; paid vacation, paid holiday <Brit>; personal day, personal time, personal time off; weekend; **leave, leave of absence, furlough; liberty,** shore leave; day trip, scenic route; **sabbatical,** sabbatical leave *or* year; **weekend; busman's holiday;** package tour *or* holiday; honeymoon; spring break, winter break; Cook's tour

4 **holiday, day off; red-letter day,** gala day, fete day, festival day, day of festivities, field day; national holiday, legal holiday, bank holiday <Brit>; High Holiday, High Holy Day; holy day; feast, feast day, high day, church feast, fixed feast, movable feast; half-holiday; mini-break

5 **day of rest,** *dies non* <L>; **Sabbath,** Sunday, Lord's day, First day

VERBS 6 **rest, repose,** take rest, take one's ease, **take it easy** <nf>, lay down one's tools, rest from one's labors, rest on one's oars, take life easy; go to rest, settle to rest; lie down, have a lie-down, go to bed, snuggle down, curl up, tuck up, bed, bed down, couch, recline, lounge, drape oneself, sprawl, loll; take off one's shoes, unbuckle one's belt, get *or* take a load off one's feet, put one's feet up

7 **relax,** unlax <nf>, unbend, unwind, slack, slacken, **ease; ease up, let up,** slack up, slack off, **ease off,** let down, **slow down,** take it slow, take time to catch one's breath; mellow out, chill, lay back *and* kick back *and* decompress <nf>

8 **take a rest, take a break, break, take time out** *and* grab some R and R <nf>, pause, lay off, **knock off** <nf>, recess, **take a recess,** take ten *and* take five <nf>; stop for breath, catch one's breath, breathe; stop work, suspend operations, call it a day; go to bed with the chickens, sleep in; take a nap, catch some Zs <nf>; take a moment

9 **vacation, get away from it all,** holiday, take a holiday, make holiday; **take a leave of absence,** take leave, go on leave, go on furlough, take one's sabbatical; weekend; Sunday, Christmas, etc

ADJS 10 **vacational, holiday,** ferial, festal; sabbatical; **comfortable** 121.11; **restful,** quiet 173.12

ADVS 11 **at rest, at ease,** at one's ease; abed, in bed

12 **on vacation,** on leave, on furlough; off duty, on one's own time, having a field day

21 FATIGUE

NOUNS 1 **fatigue, tiredness, weariness,** wearifulness; **burnout,** end of one's tether, overtiredness, overstrain; faintness, goneness, weakness, enfeeblement, lack of staying power, enervation, debility, debilitation 16.1; jadedness; lassitude, languor; tension fatigue, stance fatigue, stimulation fatigue; fatigue disease, fatigue syndrome *or* post-viral fatigue syndrome, chronic fatigue syndrome; combat fatigue; mental fatigue, brain fag <nf>; strain, mental strain, heart strain, eyestrain; jet lag sleepiness 22.1

2 **exhaustion,** exhaustedness, draining, inanition; **collapse, prostra-**

tion, breakdown, crack-up <nf>, nervous exhaustion *or* prostration, burn-out *or* burnout; blackout

3 **breathlessness, shortness of breath,** windedness, short-windedness; panting, gasping; dyspnea, labored breathing

VERBS 4 **fatigue, tire, weary, exhaust,** wilt, flag, jade, harass; **wear,** wear on *or* upon, **wear down; tire out, wear out, burn out; use up; do in; wind,** put out of breath; overtire, overweary, overfatigue, overstrain; weaken, enervate, debilitate 16.10; weary *or* tire to death, take it out of; prostrate; deprive of sleep

5 **burn out, get tired, grow weary, tire, weary,** fatigue, jade; **flag, droop,** faint, sink, feel dragged out, wilt; **play out,** run out, run down, burn out; gasp, wheeze, pant, puff, blow, puff and blow, puff like a grampus; collapse, break down, crack up <nf>, give out, drop, fall *or* drop by the wayside, drop in one's tracks, succumb; need a break

6 <nf terms> **beat, poop,** frazzle, fag, tucker; fag out, tucker out, knock out, do in, do up; **poop out,** peter out

ADJS 7 **tired, weary, fatigued,** wearied, weariful, jaded, run-down, good and tired; unrefreshed, unrestored, in need of rest, ready to drop; **faint,** fainting, feeling faint, **weak,** rocky <nf>, enfeebled, enervated, debilitated, seedy <nf>, weakened 16.18; drooping, droopy, wilting, flagging, sagging; languid; worn, worn-down, **worn to a frazzle** *or* shadow, toilworn, weary-worn; wayworn, way-weary; foot-weary, weary-footed, footsore; tired-armed; tired-winged, weary-winged; weary-laden

8 <nf terms> **beat, pooped, bushed,** poohed, paled, frazzled, bagged, fagged, tuckered, plumb tuckered, done, done in, all in, dead, dead beat, dead on one's feet, gone; **pooped out,** knocked out, wiped out, tuckered out, played out, fagged out; run ragged; used up, done up, beat up, washed-up, whacked out

9 tired-looking, weary-looking, tired-eyed, tired-faced, haggard, hollow-eyed, ravaged, drawn, cadaverous, worn, wan, zombiish

10 **burnt-out,** burned-out, **exhausted,** drained, **spent,** unable to go on, gone; **tired out, worn-out,** beaten; maxed-out; bone-tired, bone-weary; **dog-tired,** dog-weary; **dead-tired, tired to death,** weary unto death, dead-alive *or* dead-and-alive, more dead than alive, ready to drop, on one's last legs; prostrate

11 **overtired, overweary,** overwrought, overwearied, overstrained, overdriven, overfatigued, overspent; hackneyed

12 **breathless, winded;** wheezing, puffing, panting, **out of breath,** short of breath *or* wind, gasping for breath, agasp; short-winded, short-breathed, dyspneic

13 **fatiguing, wearying,** wearing, **tiring,** straining, stressful, trying, **exhausting,** draining, **grueling,** punishing, killing, demanding; **tiresome,** fatiguesome, **wearisome,** weariful; toilsome 725.18

ADVS 14 **out,** to the point of exhaustion

22 SLEEP

NOUNS 1 **sleepiness, drowsiness,** keif, doziness, heaviness, lethargy, oscitation, somnolence *or* somnolency, yawning, stretching, oscitancy, pandiculation; languor 331.6; sand in the eyes, heavy eyelids; REM sleep *or* rapid-eye-movement sleep *or* dreaming sleep; dormition

2 **sleep, slumber; repose,** silken repose, *somnus* <L>, the arms of Morpheus; bye-bye *or* beddy-bye <nf>; doss <Brit nf>, blanket drill *and* shut eye <nf>; light sleep, fitful sleep, **doze, drowse,** snoozle <nf>; beauty sleep <nf>; sleepwalking, somnambulism; somniloquy; **land of Nod,** slumberland, sleepland, dreamland; hibernation, winter sleep, aestivation; bedtime, sack time <nf>; unconsciousness 25.2

3 **nap, snooze** <nf>, **catnap,** wink, **forty winks** *and* some Zs <nf>, zizz <Brit nf>, wink of sleep, spot of

sleep; **siesta,** blanket drill *and* sack *or* rack time <nf>; power nap

4 sweet sleep, balmy sleep, downy sleep, soft sleep, gentle sleep, smiling sleep, golden slumbers; peaceful sleep, sleep of the just; restful sleep, good night's sleep

5 **deep sleep,** profound sleep, heavy sleep, **sound sleep,** cataphor, unbroken sleep, wakeless sleep, drugged sleep, dreamless sleep, the sleep of the dead; paradoxical *or* orthodox *or* dreaming *or* REM sleep, synchronized *or* S *or* NREM sleep; lucid dreaming

6 **stupor,** sopor, **coma, swoon,** lethargy, persistent vegetative state; **trance;** narcosis, narcohypnosis, narcoma, narcotization, narcotic stupor *or* trance; sedation; high <nf>; nod <nf>; narcolepsy; catalepsy; thanatosis, shock; sleeping sickness, encephalitis lethargica

7 **hypnosis,** mesmeric *or* **hypnotic sleep, trance,** somnipathy, hypnotic somnolence; lethargic hypnosis, somnambulistic hypnosis, cataleptic hypnosis, animal hypnosis; narcohypnosis; autohypnosis, self-hypnosis; hypnotherapy

8 **hypnotism, mesmerism;** hypnology; hypnotization, mesmerization; **animal magnetism,** od, odyl, odylic force; hypnotic suggestion, posthypnotic suggestion, autosuggestion

9 **hypnotist, mesmerist,** hypnotizer, mesmerizer; Svengali, Mesmer

10 **sleep-inducer,** sleep-producer, sleep-provoker, sleep-bringer, hypnotic, soporific, somnifacient; poppy, mandrake, mandragora, opium, opiate, morphine, morphia; nightcap; sedative 86.12; anesthetic; lullaby

11 **Morpheus,** Somnus, Hypnos; sandman, dustman <Brit>

12 **sleeper, slumberer;** sleeping beauty; **sleepyhead,** lie-abed, slugabed, sleepwalker, somnambulist; somniloquist, dreamer

VERBS 13 **sleep, slumber,** rest in the arms of Morpheus; **doze, drowse; nap, catnap,** take a nap, catch a wink, sleep soundly, **sleep like a top** *or* **log,** sleep like the dead; *dormir sur les deux oreilles* <Fr>; snore, saw wood *and* saw logs <nf>; have an early night, go to bed betimes; sleep in; oversleep

14 <nf terms> **snooze,** get some shuteye, get some sack time, flake *or* sack out, crash, catch forty winks *or* some zs, zizz <Brit>; pound the ear, kip *or* doss <Brit>, log zs

15 **hibernate,** aestivate, lie dormant

16 **go to sleep,** settle to sleep, go off to sleep, **fall asleep,** drop asleep, **drop off,** drift off, drift off to sleep; **doze off, drowse off,** nod off, dope off <nf>; close one's eyes

17 **go to bed, retire;** lay me down to sleep; bed, bed down; go night-night *and* go bye-bye *and* go beddy-bye <nf>

18 <nf terms> **hit the hay, hit the sack,** crash, turn in, crawl in, flop, sack out, sack up, kip down *or* doss down <Brit>, lights out

19 **put to bed,** bed; nestle, cradle; **tuck in**

20 **put to sleep; lull to sleep,** rock to sleep; **hypnotize, mesmerize,** magnetize; **entrance,** trance, put in a trance; narcotize, drug, dope <nf>; anesthetize, put under; sedate

ADJS 21 **sleepy, drowsy,** dozy, snoozy <nf>, **slumberous,** slumbery, dreamy, sleepful; **half asleep,** asleep on one's feet; sleepful, sleep-filled; yawny, stretchy <nf>, oscitant, yawning, napping, **nodding,** ready for bed; heavy, **heavy-eyed, heavy with sleep,** sleep-swollen, sleep-drowned, sleep-drunk, drugged with sleep; **somnolent,** soporific; **lethargic,** comatose, narcose *or* narcous, stuporose *or* **stuporous, in a stupor,** out of it <nf>; narcoleptic; cataleptic; narcotized, drugged, doped <nf>; sedated; anesthetized; **languid**

22 **asleep, sleeping, slumbering,** in the arms *or* lap of Morpheus, in the land of Nod; **sound asleep, fast asleep,** dead asleep, deep asleep, in a sound sleep, flaked-out <nf>; **unconscious, oblivious, out,** out like a light, out cold; comatose; dormant; dead, **dead to the world;** unwakened, unawakened

23 **sleep-inducing,** sleep-producing, sleep-bringing, sleep-causing, sleep-compelling, sleep-inviting, sleep-provoking, sleep-tempting; **narcotic,** hypnotic, **soporific, somniferous,** somnifacient; sedative 86.45

24 **hypnotic,** hypnoid, hypnoidal, **mesmeric;** odylic; narcohypnotic; somnambulant, somnambulic

23 WAKEFULNESS

NOUNS **1** **wakefulness,** wake; **sleeplessness,** restlessness, tossing and turning; **insomnia,** insomnolence *or* insomnolency, white night; vigilance, vigil, all-night vigil, lidless vigil, *per vigilium* <L>; insomniac; consciousness, sentience; alertness 339.5

2 **awakening, wakening,** rousing, **arousal;** rude awakening, rousting out <nf>; reveille

VERBS **3** **keep awake,** keep one's eyes open; keep alert, be vigilant 339.8; stay awake, **toss and turn, not sleep a wink,** not shut one's eyes, count sheep; have a white night

4 **awake, awaken, wake, wake up, get up,** rouse, come alive <nf>; open one's eyes, stir <nf>

5 <wake someone up> **awaken, waken, rouse, arouse,** awake, wake, **wake up,** shake up, knock up <Brit>, roust out <nf>

6 **get up, get out of bed, arise,** rise, **rise and shine** <nf>, greet the day, **turn out** <nf>; roll out *and* pile out *and* **show a leg** *and* hit the deck <nf>

ADJS **7** **wakeful, sleepless,** slumberless, **unsleeping,** insomniac, insomnious; restless; watchful, vigilant, lidless

8 **awake,** conscious, **up; wide-awake,** broad awake; sentient; alert 339.14

ADVS **9** **sleeplessly, unsleepingly; wakefully,** with one's eyes open; alertly 339.17

24 SENSATION

<physical sensibility>

NOUNS **1** **sensation, sense, feeling;** sense impression, sense-datum *or* -data, percept, perception, sense perception; experience, sensory experience, sense impression; **sensuousness,** sensuosity, sensuality; **consciousness,** awareness, apperception; response, response to stimuli

2 **sensibility,** sensibleness, physical sensibility, sentience *or* sentiency; openness to sensation, readiness of feeling, receptiveness, receptivity; sensation level, threshold of sensation, limen; impressionability, impressibility, affectibility; **susceptibility,** susceptivity, perceptibility, esthesia, aesthesia, esthesis

3 **sensitivity, sensitiveness;** perceptivity, perceptiveness, feelings; responsiveness; **tact, tactfulness, considerateness,** courtesy, politeness; **compassion, sympathy;** empathy, identification; **concern,** solicitousness, solicitude; capability of feeling, passibility; **delicacy, exquisiteness,** tenderness, fineness; **oversensitiveness,** oversensibility, hypersensitivity, **thin skin,** hyperesthesia, hyperpathia, supersensitivity, overtenderness; **irritability,** prickliness, soreness, **touchiness,** tetchiness; ticklishness, nervousness 128; allergy, anaphylaxis; sensitization; photophobia

4 **sore spot,** sore point, soft spot, raw, exposed nerve, raw nerve, nerve ending, tender spot, the quick, where the shoe pinches, where one lives *and* in the gut <nf>; agitation, agita <nf>, hot spot

5 **senses, five senses,** sensorium; touch 74, taste 62, smell 69, sight 27, hearing 48; sixth sense, second sight, extrasensory perception *or* ESP; sense *or* sensory organ, sensillum, receptor; synesthesia, chromesthesia, color hearing; phonism, photism; kinesthesia, muscle sense, sense of motion; sense organ; horse sense

VERBS **6** **sense, feel,** experience, **perceive,** apprehend, be sensible of, be conscious *or* aware of, apperceive; taste 62.7, smell 69.8, see 27.12, hear 48.11,12, touch 73.6; respond, respond to stimuli; be sensitive to, have a thing about <nf>; overreact

7 **sensitize,** make sensitive; sensibilize, sensify; **sharpen, whet, quicken,** stimulate, excite, stir, cultivate, refine

8 **touch a sore spot,** touch a soft spot, touch on the raw, touch a raw spot, touch to the quick, hit *or* touch a nerve *or* nerve ending, touch where it hurts, hit one where he lives <nf>, strike *or* hit home

ADJS 9 **sensory,** sensorial; **sensitive,** receptive, responsive; **sensuous;** sensorimotor, sensimotor; kinesthetic, somatosensory; feeling, percipient; centripetal

10 **neural, nervous,** nerval; neurologic, neurological

11 sensible, sentient, sensile; **susceptible,** susceptive; **receptive,** impressionable, impressive, impressible; **perceptive; conscious,** cognizant, **aware,** sensitive to, alive to, clued in, sussed <nf>

12 **sensitive,** responsive, sympathetic, compassionate; empathic, empathetic; passible; delicate, tactful, considerate, courteous, solicitous, tender, refined; **oversensitive, thin-skinned;** oversensible, hyperesthetic, hyperpathic, hypersensitive, supersensitive, overtender, overrefined, overwhelmed; **irritable, touchy,** irascible, tetchy <nf>, quick on the draw *or* trigger *or* uptake, itchy, ticklish, prickly; goosey <nf>, skittish; nervous; allergic, anaphylactic

13 <keenly sensitive> **exquisite,** poignant, **acute,** sharp, **keen,** biting, vivid, intense, extreme, excruciating

14 sensate, perceptible, audible, visible, tactile, palpable, tangible, noticeable

25 INSENSIBILITY

<physical unfeeling>

NOUNS 1 **insensibility,** insensibleness, **insensitivity,** insensitiveness, insentience, impassibility, lack of feeling; **unperceptiveness,** imperceptiveness, imperception, imperceptivity, impercipience, blindness, lack of concern, obtuseness; inconsiderateness; unsolicitousness; tactlessness; discourtesy, boorishness; philistinism; **unfeeling,** unfeelingness, **apathy,** affectlessness, lack of affect; thick skin *or* hide, callousness 94.3; **numbness,** dullness, hypothymia, **deadness;** pins and needles; hypesthesia; anesthesia, analgesia; narcosis, electronarcosis; narcotization; lack of awareness

2 **unconsciousness, senselessness;** nothingness, oblivion, obliviousness, indifference, heedlessness, unawareness; nirvana; **faint, swoon, blackout,** syncope, athymia, lipothymy *or* lipothymia; **coma;** torpor, **stupor;** trance; catalepsy, catatony *or* catatonia, sleep 22; knockout *or* KO *or* kayo <nf>; semiconsciousness, grayout; suspended animation

3 **anesthetic,** general anesthetic, local anesthetic, analgesic, anodyne, balm, ointment, **pain killer,** pain-reliever, antiodontalgic; tranquilizer, **sedative,** sleeping pill *or* tablet, somnifacient, knockout drops *and* Mickey Finn *and* Mickey <nf>; drug, dope <nf>, narcotic, opiate; acupuncture; desensitization; ether

VERBS 4 **deaden, numb,** benumb, blunt, dull, obtund, **desensitize;** paralyze, palsy; **anesthetize, put to sleep,** slip one a Mickey *or* Mickey Finn <nf>, chloroform, etherize; narcotize, drug, dope <nf>; freeze, **stupefy, stun,** bedaze, besot; knock unconscious, knock senseless, **knock out,** KO *and* kayo *and* lay out *and* coldcock *and* knock stiff *and* brain <nf>; concuss

5 **faint, swoon,** drop, succumb, keel over <nf>, fall in a faint, fall senseless, **pass** *or* zonk out <nf>, **black out,** dim, go out like a light; gray out

ADJS 6 **insensible, unfeeling, insensitive,** insentient, insensate, impassible; nerveless, senseless, unemotional; unsympathetic, uncompassionate; unconcerned, unsolicitous, non-caring, uncaring, impassive, cold-blooded, apathetic, hardhearted; tactless, boorish, heavy-handed; **unperceptive,** imperceptive, impercipient, blind, unmindful; thick-skinned, hardened, **dull,** obtuse, obdurate; **numb,** numbed, benumbed, dead, **deadened,** asleep, unfelt; **unfeeling, apathetic,** affectless; stoic; deaf; callous 94.12; anesthetized, narcotized, hypnotized

7 **stupefied, stunned,** dazed, bedazed, astonied

8 **unconscious, senseless, oblivious,** unaware, comatose, asleep, dead, lifeless, **dead to the world,** cold, out, **out cold;** heedless, unmindful; nirvanic; half-conscious, semiconscious; drugged, narcotized; doped *and* stoned *and* spaced out *and* strung out *and* zonked *and* zonked out *and* out of it <nf>; catatonic, cataleptic; stunned, concussed, knocked out; desensitized; out for the count <nf>

9 **deadening,** numbing, dulling; **anesthetic,** analgesic, narcotic; stupefying, stunning, numbing, mind-boggling *or* -numbing; anesthetizing, narcotizing

26 PAIN

<physical suffering>

NOUNS 1 **pain; suffering, hurt, hurting,** painfulness, misery <nf>, **distress,** dolor; **discomfort,** malaise; aches and pains; pain threshold

2 **pang,** pangs, throe, throes; seizure, spasm, paroxysm; ouch <nf>; **twinge,** twitch, wrench, jumping pain; crick, kink, hitch, cramp *or* cramps; **nip,** thrill, pinch, tweak, bite, prick, pinprick, **stab,** stitch, sharp *or* piercing *or* stabbing pain, acute pain, **shooting pain,** darting pain, fulgurant pain, lancinating pain, shooting; boring *or* terebrant *or* terebrating pain; gnawing, gnawing *or* grinding pain; stitch in the side; charley horse <nf>; phantom limb pain; hunger pang *or* pain; wandering pain; psychalgia, psychosomatic pain, soul pain, mind pain

3 **smart,** smarting, **sting,** stinging, urtication, **tingle,** tingling; **burn,** burning, burning pain, fire; pins and needles

4 **soreness, irritation,** inflammation, tenderness, sensitiveness; algesia; rankling, festering; sore; sore spot 24.4

5 **ache,** aching, throbbing, throbbing ache *or* pain, throb; **headache,** cephalalgia, misery in the head <nf>; splitting headache, **sick headache, migraine,** megrim, hemicrania; **backache; earache,** otalgia; **toothache,** odontalgia; **stomachache,** tummyache <nf>, bellyache *or* gut-ache <nf>; **colic,** collywobbles, gripes, gripe, gnawing, gnawing of the bowels, fret <nf>; **heartburn,** acid reflux, agita, pyrosis; **angina**

6 **agony, anguish, torment, torture,** ordeal, exquisite torment *or* torture, the rack, excruciation, crucifixion, martyrdom, martyrization, excruciating *or* agonizing *or* atrocious pain, hell on earth, punishment; pain in the neck

VERBS 7 **pain,** give *or* inflict pain, **hurt, wound, afflict, distress,** injure; **burn;** sting; nip, bite, tweak, pinch; pierce, prick, stab, cut, lacerate, thrash; **irritate, inflame,** sear, harshen, exacerbate, intensify; chafe, gall, fret, rasp, rub, grate; gnaw, grind; gripe; fester, rankle; **torture, torment,** rack, put to torture, put *or* lay on the rack, **agonize, harrow,** crucify, martyr, martyrize, traumatize, excruciate, wring, twist, contorse, convulse; wrench, tear, rend; prolong the agony, kill by inches

8 **suffer, feel pain,** feel the pangs, anguish 96.19; **hurt, ache,** have a misery <nf>, ail, be afflicted; **smart,** tingle; throb, pound; shoot; twinge, thrill, twitch; **wince,** blanch, shrink, make a wry face, grimace; **agonize,** writhe

ADJS 9 **pained,** in pain, **hurt,** hurting, **suffering,** afflicted, wounded, distressed, in distress; **tortured, tormented, racked, agonized, harrowed,** lacerated, crucified, martyred, martyrized, wrung, twisted, convulsed, anguished; on the rack, under the harrow; traumatized; stressed out, bothered

10 **painful;** hurtful, **hurting,** distressing, afflictive, miserable; **acute, sharp,** piercing, stabbing, shooting, stinging, biting, gnawing; **poignant,** pungent, burning, searing, **severe,** cruel, harsh, grave, hard; griping, cramping, spasmic, spasmatic, spasmodic, paroxysmal; **agonizing, excruciating,** exquisite, atrocious, torturous, tormenting, martyrizing, racking, **harrowing**, unbearable, intolerable

11 **sore, raw;** pained; smarting, tingling, **burning; irritated, inflamed, tender,** sensitive, fiery, angry, red; algetic; chafed, galled; **festering,** rankling; black-and-blue

12 **aching,** achy, **throbbing;** headachy, migrainous, backachy, toothachy, stomachachy, colicky, griping

13 **irritating,** irritative, irritant; **chafing, galling,** fretting, bothersome, rasping, boring, grating, grinding, stinging, scratchy

27 VISION

NOUNS **1** **vision, sight, eyesight,** seeing; **sightedness;** visioning; eye, power of sight, sense of sight, visual sense; **perception,** discernment; perspicacity, perspicuity, sharp *or* acute *or* keen sight, visual acuity, quick sight, 20/20 vision; farsight, farsightedness; nearsightedness; astigmatism; clear sight, unobstructed vision; rod vision, scotopia; cone vision, photopia; color vision, twilight vision, daylight vision, day vision, night vision; eye-mindedness; **field of vision,** visual field, scope, ken, purview, horizon, sweep, range; line of vision, line of sight, sight-line; peripheral vision, peripheral field; field of view 31.3; sensitivity to light, phototonus

2 **observation,** observance; **looking, watching, viewing, seeing,** witnessing, espial; **notice,** note, respect, **regard;** watch, lookout; spying, espionage

3 **look, sight,** the eye *and* a look-see *and* a gander <nf>, glad eye <nf>, dekko <Brit nf>, eye, view, regard; sidelong look; leer, leering look, lustful leer; sly look; look-in; preview; scene, prospect 33.6

4 **glance,** glance *or* flick of the eye, slant <nf>, rapid glance, cast, sideglance; **glimpse,** flash, quick sight; **peek, peep;** wink, blink, flicker *or* twinkle of an eye; casual glance, **half an eye;** *coup d'œil* <Fr>

5 **gaze, stare,** gape, goggle; sharp *or* piercing *or* penetrating look; **ogle,** glad eye, come-hither look <nf>, bedroom eyes <nf>; **glare, glower,** glaring *or* glowering look, black look, dirty look; evil eye, whammy <nf>; withering look, hostile look, chilly look, the fisheye *or* stinkeye *or* hairy eyeball <nf>; rubbernecking

6 **scrutiny,** overview, **survey,** contemplation, surveillance; **examination, inspection** 938.3, scrutiny, the once-over <nf>, visual examination, a vetting <Brit nf>, ocular inspection, eyeball inspection <nf>

7 **viewpoint, standpoint, point of view,** vantage, vantage point, perspective, point *or* coign of vantage, where one stands; bird's-eye view, worm's-eye view, fly on the wall; **outlook,** angle, slant, angle *or* field of vision, *optique* <Fr>, eyeshot; mental outlook 978.2

8 observation post *or* point *or* deck; **observatory; lookout,** outlook, overlook, scenic overlook; planetarium; **watchtower,** tower; Texas tower; beacon, lighthouse, pharos; gazebo, belvedere; bridge, conning tower, crow's nest; peephole, sighthole, spyhole, loophole; **ringside,** ringside seat; **grandstand,** bleachers, stands; **gallery,** top gallery; paradise *and* peanut gallery <nf>; window

9 **eye,** visual organ, organ of vision, oculus, optic, **orb, peeper** <nf>, baby blues <nf>; clear eyes, bright eyes, starry orbs; saucer eyes, popeyes *and* goggle eyes *and* banjo eyes *and* googly eyes *and* sparklers <nf>; naked eye, unassisted *or* unaided eye; corner of the eye; eyeball; iris; pupil; eyelid, lid, nictitating membrane; eyeglasses

10 **sharp eye,** keen eye, piercing *or* penetrating eye, gimlet eye, X-ray eye; **eagle eye,** hawkeye, peeled eye <nf>, watchful eye; **weather eye**

11 <comparisons> eagle, hawk, cat, lynx, ferret, weasel; Argus

VERBS 12 **see, behold, observe, view, witness, perceive, discern, spy,** espy, **sight,** have in sight, make out, pick out, descry, spot <nf>, twig <Brit nf>, discover, notice, take notice of, have one's eye on, distinguish, recognize, ken <nf>, **catch sight of,** get a load of <nf>, take in, get an eyeful of <nf>, look on *or* upon, cast the eyes on *or* upon, **set** *or* **lay eyes on, clap eyes on** <nf>; **glimpse,** get *or* catch a glimpse of; see at a glance, see with half an eye; see with one's own eyes

13 **look, peer,** have a look, take a gander *and* take a look <nf>, direct the eyes, turn *or* bend the eyes, cast one's eye, lift up the eyes; **look at,** take a look at, eye, **eyeball** <nf>, have a look-see <nf>, have a dekko <Brit nf>, look on *or* upon, gaze at *or* upon; **watch, observe, view, regard;** keep one's eyes peeled *or* skinned, be watchful *or* observant *or* vigilant, keep one's eyes open; keep in sight *or* view, hold in view; look after; **check** *and* **check out** <nf>, scope <nf>, scope on *or* out <nf>; keep under observation, spy on, have an eye out, keep an eye out, keep an eye on, keep a weather eye on, follow, tail *and* shadow <nf>, stake out; **reconnoiter,** scout, get the lay of the land; **peek, peep,** pry, take a peep *or* peek; play peekaboo

14 **scrutinize, survey, eye,** contemplate, look over, give the eye *or* the once-over <nf>; **ogle,** ogle at, **leer,** leer at, give one the glad eye; examine, vet <Brit nf>, **inspect** 938.24; **pore,** pore over, peruse; take a close *or* careful look; take a long, hard look; size up <nf>; take stock of; have eyes in the back of one's head

15 **gaze,** gloat, fix one's gaze, fix *or* fasten *or* rivet one's eyes upon, keep one's eyes upon, feast one's eyes on; **eye, ogle; stare,** stare at, stare hard, stare out, zone out, look, goggle, **gape, gawk** *or* gawp <nf>, gaze open-mouthed; crane, crane the neck, stand on tiptoe, rubberneck <nf>; strain one's eyes; look straight in the eye, look full in the face, hold one's eye *or* gaze, stare down

16 **glare, glower,** look daggers, look black; give one the evil eye, give one a whammy <nf>; give one the fish eye <nf>, give one a dirty look

17 **glance, glimpse,** glint, cast a glance, glance at *or* upon, give a *coup d'œil* <Fr>, take a glance at, take a squint at <nf>

18 **look askance** *or* askant, give a sidelong look; squint, look asquint; cock the eye; **look down one's nose** <nf>

19 **look away,** look aside, **avert the eyes,** look another way, break one's eyes away, stop looking, turn away from, turn the back upon; drop one's eyes *or* gaze, cast one's eyes down; avoid one's gaze

ADJS 20 **visual, ocular,** eye, eyeball <nf>; **sighted,** seeing, having sight *or* vision; **optic, optical;** ophthalmic; retinal; visible 31.6

21 **clear-sighted,** clear-eyed; twenty-twenty; **farsighted,** farseeing, telescopic; **sharp-sighted,** keen-sighted, sharp-eyed, **eagle-eyed,** hawk-eyed, ferret-eyed, lynx-eyed, cat-eyed, Argus-eyed; eye-minded, perceptive, aware

ADVS 22 **at sight,** as seen, visibly, at a glance; by sight, by eyeball <nf>, visually; at first sight, **at the first blush,** *prima facie* <L>; out of the corner of one's eye; from where one stands, from one's viewpoint *or* standpoint

28 DEFECTIVE VISION

NOUNS 1 faulty eyesight, bad eyesight, visual handicap, defect of vision *or* sight, poor sight, impaired vision, imperfect vision, blurred vision, reduced sight, partial sightedness, partial blindness; legal blindness; **astigmatism,** astigmia; nystagmus; albinism; double vision, double sight, diplopia; tunnel vision; photophobia; **blindness** 30

2 **dim-sightedness,** dull-sightedness, near-blindness, amblyopia, gravel-blindness, sand-blindness, **purblindness,** dim eyes; blurredness,

blearedness, bleariness; eyestrain, bloodshot eyes, redness, red eyes

3 **nearsightedness, myopia,** shortsightedness, short sight

4 **farsightedness,** hyperopia, l ongsightedness, long sight; presbyopia

5 strabismus, heterotropia; cast, cast in the eye; **squint,** squinch <nf>; **cross-eye, cross-eyedness;** convergent strabismus, esotropia; upward strabismus, anoöpsia; walleye, exotropia; detached retina; tic

6 <defective eyes> cross-eyes, cockeyes, squint eyes, lazy eye, swivel eyes <nf>, goggle eyes, walleyes, bug-eyes *and* popeyes <nf>, saucer eyes <nf>

7 **winking, blinking,** fluttering the eyelids, nictitation; winker; tic

VERBS 8 see badly *or* poorly, barely see, be half-blind; have a mote in the eye; see double

9 **squint,** squinch <nf>, squint the eye, look asquint, screw up the eyes, skew, goggle

10 **wink, blink,** nictitate, bat the eyes <nf>

ADJS **11** poor-sighted; visually impaired, visually handicapped, sight-impaired; legally blind; **blind** 30.9; **astigmatic, astigmatical;** nystagmic; **nearsighted, shortsighted, myopic**; **farsighted,** longsighted, presbyopic; dayblind, hereralopic; nightblind, nyctalopic; colorblind; sand-blind; **squinting,** squinty, asquint, squint-eyed, squinch-eyed <nf>, strabismal, strabismic; winking, **blinking,** blinky, blink-eyed, nictating; blinkered; photophobic

12 **cross-eyed, cockeyed,** swivel-eyed <nf>, goggle-eyed, bug-eyed *and* popeyed <nf>, **walleyed,** saucer-eyed, glare-eyed; one-eyed, monocular, cyclopean; moon-eyed

13 **dim-sighted,** dim, dull-sighted, dim-eyed, weak-eyed, feeble-eyed, mole-eyed; **purblind,** half-blind, gravel-blind, sand-blind; bleary-eyed, blear-eyed; filmy-eyed, film-eyed; snow-blind; sand-blind; bloodshot, red-eyed; dry-eyed

29 OPTICAL INSTRUMENTS

NOUNS **1 optical instrument**, optical device, viewer; **microscope** ; **spectroscope, spectrometer**

2 **lens,** glass; prism, objective prism; eyepiece, objective, condenser; mirror system, catadioptric system, telecentric system; **camera** 714.11

3 **spectacles, specs** <nf>, **glasses, eyeglasses,** pair of glasses *or* spectacles, barnacles <Brit nf>, cheaters *and* peepers <nf>; reading glasses, readers; bifocals, divided spectacles, trifocals, pince-nez, nippers <nf>; progressive lenses; lorgnette, *lorgnon* <Fr>; horn-rimmed glasses; harlequin glasses; granny glasses; mini-specs <nf>; colored glasses, sunglasses, sun-specs <nf>, dark glasses, Polaroid <TM> glasses, shades <nf>; goggles, blinkers; eyeglass, monocle, quizzing glass; thick glasses, thick-lensed glasses, thick lenses, Coke-bottle glasses <nf>; **contacts,** contact lenses, hard lenses, soft lenses, extended-wear lenses; progressive lenses

4 **telescope**, scope, **spy glass,** terrestrial telescope, glass, **field glass; binoculars,** zoom binoculars, opera glasses, binocs <nf>

5 **sight;** sighthole; finder, viewfinder; panoramic sight; bombsight; peep sight, open sight, leaf sight

6 **mirror,** glass, **looking glass,** seeing glass <Brit nf>, reflector, speculum; hand mirror, window mirror, rear-view mirror, cheval glass, pier glass, shaving mirror; steel mirror; convex mirror, concave mirror, distorting mirror

7 **optics,** optical physics; **optometry;** microscopy, microscopics; telescopy; stereoscopy; spectroscopy, spectrometry; infrared spectroscopy; spectrophotometry; electron optics; fiber optics; **photography** 714

8 **oculist,** ophthalmologist, **optometrist;** microscopist, telescopist; optician

ADJS **9 optic, optical,** ophthalmic, ophthalmologic, ophthalmological, optometrical; acousto-optic, acousto-optical; ocular, binocular, monocular

10 microscopic, telescopic, etc; stereoscopic, three-dimensional, 3-D

11 **spectacled, bespectacled,** four-eyed <nf>; goggled; monocled

30 BLINDNESS

NOUNS **1** **blindness, sightlessness,** cecity, ablepsia, unseeingness, sightless eyes, lack of vision, eyelessness; stone-blindness, total blindness; darkness, legal blindness; partial blindness, reduced sight, **blind side; blind spot;** dimsightedness; snow blindness, niphablepsia; amaurosis, *gutta serena* <L>, drop serene; cataract; glaucoma; trachoma; mental *or* psychic blindness, mind-blindness, soul-blindness, benightedness, unenlightenment, spiritual blindness; **blinding,** making blind, depriving of sight, putting out the eyes; blurring the eyes, blindfolding, hoodwinking, blinkering; tunnel vision

2 **day blindness,** hemeralopia; **night blindness,** nyctalopia; moon blindness, moon-blind

3 **color blindness;** dichromatism; monochromatism, achromatopsia; red blindness, protanopia, green blindness, deuteranopia, red-green blindness, Daltonism; yellow blindness, xanthocyanopia; blue-yellow blindness, tritanopia; violet-blindness

4 **the blind,** the sightless, the unseeing; blind man; bat, mole

5 blindfold; eye patch; blinkers, blinds, blinders, rogue's badge

6 <aids for the blind> sensory aid, **Braille,** New York point, Gall's serrated type, Boston type, Howe's American type, Moon *or* Moon's type, Alston's Glasgow type, Lucas's type, sight-saver type, Frere's type; line letter, string alphabet, writing stamps; noctograph, writing frame, embosser, high-speed embosser; visagraph; talking book; optophone, Visotoner, Optacon; personal sonar, Pathsounder; ultrasonic spectacles; cane; Seeing Eye dog, guide dog; white stick *or* cane

VERBS **7** **blind,** blind the eyes, deprive of sight, **strike blind,** render *or* make blind; darken, dim, obscure, eclipse; **put one's eyes out,** gouge; **blindfold,** blinker, hoodwink, bandage; throw dust in one's eyes, benight; **dazzle,** bedazzle, daze; glare; snow-blind

8 **be blind,** not see, walk in darkness, grope in the dark, feel one's way; go blind, lose one's sight *or* vision, black out; be blind to, close *or* shut one's eyes to, wink *or* blink at, look the other way, blind oneself to, wear blinkers *or* have blinders on, avert one's eyes; have a blind spot *or* side

ADJS **9** **blind, sightless, unsighted,** ableptical, eyeless, visionless, **unseeing,** undiscerning, unobserving, unperceiving; in darkness, rayless, bereft of light, dark <nf>; **stone-blind,** stark blind, **blind as a bat,** blind as a mole *or* an owl; amaurotic; dim-sighted 28.13; hemeralopic; nyctalopic; color-blind; glaucomatous; legally blind; mind-blind, soul-blind, mentally *or* psychically *or* spiritually blind, benighted, unenlightened

10 **blinded**, darkened, obscured; **blindfolded,** blindfold, hoodwinked, blinkered; **dazzled,** bedazzled, dazed; snow-blind, snow-blinded; sand-blind

11 **blinding,** obscuring; **dazzling,** bedazzling, stunning

31 VISIBILITY

NOUNS **1** **visibility,** visibleness, perceptibility, discernibleness, observability, detectability, visuality, seeableness; exposure; manifestation; outcrop, outcropping; the visible, the seen, what is revealed, what can be seen; revelation, epiphany

2 **distinctness, plainness,** evidence, evidentness, obviousness, patentness, manifestness, recognizability; **clearness, clarity,** crystal-clearness, lucidity, limpidity; **definiteness,** definition, sharpness, microscopical distinctness; resolution, high resolution, low resolution; **prominence, conspicuousness,** conspicuity; **exposure,** public exposure, high profile, low profile; high *or* low visibility; atmospheric visibility, seeing, ceiling, ceiling unlimited, visibility unlimited, CAVU *or* ceiling and visibility unlimited, severe clear <nf>, visibility zero

3 **field of view,** field of vision, range *or* scope of vision, visual range, **sight,** limit of vision, eyereach, **eyesight,** eyeshot, ken; **vista, view, horizon, prospect, perspective, outlook,** survey, visible horizon; range, scan, scope; line of sight, sightline, line of vision; naked eye; command, domination, outlook over; **viewpoint, observation point** 27.8

VERBS 4 **show,** show up, show through, shine out *or* through, **surface, appear** 33.8, **be visible,** be seen, be revealed, be evident, be noticeable, be obvious, meet the gaze, impinge on the eye, present to the eye, meet *or* catch *or* hit *or* strike the eye; **stand out,** stand forth, loom large, glare, **stare one in the face,** hit one in the eye, **stick out like a sore thumb;** dominate; emerge, come into view, materialize

5 **be exposed,** be conspicuous, have high visibility, stick out, hang out <nf>, crop out; live in a glass house; have *or* keep a high profile

ADJS 6 **visible,** visual, **perceptible,** perceivable, **discernible, seeable,** viewable, witnessable, beholdable, observable, detectable, noticeable, recognizable, to be seen; **in sight,** in view, in plain sight, in full view, present to the eyes, before one's eyes, under one's eyes, open, naked, outcropping, hanging out <nf>, exposed, showing, open *or* exposed to view; **evident,** in evidence, **manifest, apparent;** revealed, disclosed, unhidden, unconcealed, unclouded, undisguised

7 **distinct, plain, clear, obvious, evident, patent,** unmistakable, unmissable, not to be mistaken, much in evidence, plain to be seen, for all to see, showing for all to see, apparent, plain as a pikestaff, plain as the nose on one's face, plain as day, clear as day, plain as plain can be, big as life and twice as ugly; **definite, defined, well-defined,** well-marked, well-resolved, in focus; **clear-cut,** clean-cut; crystal-clear, clear as crystal; **conspicuous,** glaring, staring, **prominent,** pronounced, well-pronounced, in bold *or* strong *or* high relief, high-profile; identifiable, recognizable

ADVS 8 **visibly, perceptibly,** perceivably, discernibly, seeably, recognizably, observably, markedly, noticeably; **manifestly, apparently,** evidently; **distinctly, clearly,** with clarity *or* crystal clarity, **plainly,** obviously, patently, definitely, unmistakably; conspicuously, undisguisedly, unconcealedly, prominently, pronouncedly, glaringly, starkly, staringly

32 INVISIBILITY

NOUNS 1 **invisibility,** imperceptibility, unperceivability, undetectability, indiscernibility, unseeableness, viewlessness; nonappearance; disappearance 34; the invisible, the unseen; more than meets the eye; unsubstantiality 764, immateriality 1053, **secrecy** 345, **concealment** 346; hidden depths, tip of the iceberg; zero visibility

2 **inconspicuousness,** half-visibility, semivisibility, low profile, latency; **indistinctness, unclearness,** unplainness, **faintness,** paleness, feebleness, weakness, **dimness,** bedimming, bleariness, darkness, shadowiness, **vagueness,** vague appearance, indefiniteness, obscurity, uncertainty, indistinguishability; **blurriness,** blur, soft focus, defocus, **fuzziness, haziness,** mistiness, filminess, fogginess; blackout, brownout

VERBS 3 be invisible *or* unseen, escape notice; lie hid 346.8, **blush unseen;** disappear 34.2; white out, black out

4 **blur, dim, pale,** soften, film, mist, fog; defocus, lose resolution *or* sharpness *or* distinctness, go soft at the edges

ADJS **5 invisible; imperceptible,** unperceivable, **indiscernible,** undiscernible, undetectable, **unseeable,** viewless, unbeholdable, unapparent, insensible; **out of sight,** *à perte de vue* <Fr>, out of range; **secret** 345.11,15; **unseen,** sightless, unbeheld, unviewed, unwitnessed, unobserved, unnoticed, unperceived; unsubstantial, transparent; behind the curtain *or* scenes; disguised, camouflaged, hidden, **concealed** 346.11,14; undisclosed, unrevealed, *in petto* <L>; latent, unrealized, submerged

6 inconspicuous, half-visible, semivisible, low-profile; **indistinct, unclear,** unplain, **indefinite,** undefined, ill-defined, ill-marked, **faint,** pale, feeble, weak, **dim,** dark, **shadowy, vague, obscure,** indistinguishable, unrecognizable; half-seen, merely glimpsed; low-profile, half-seen, low-definition; uncertain, confused, out of focus, **blurred, blurry,** bleared, bleary, blear, **fuzzy, hazy,** misty, filmy, foggy

33 APPEARANCE

NOUNS **1 appearance, appearing,** apparition, coming, forthcoming, showing-up, coming forth, coming on the scene, making the scene <nf>, putting in an appearance, arrival; **emergence,** issuing, issuance; **arising,** rise, rising, occurrence; **materialization, materializing,** coming into being; **manifestation,** realization, incarnation, revelation, showing-forth; epiphany, theophany, avatar, ostent; **presentation, disclosure, exposure,** opening, unfolding, unfoldment, showing; rising of the curtain

2 appearance, exterior, externals, **mere externals, facade,** outside, **show, outward show, image,** display, front <nf>, outward *or* external appearance, surface appearance, surface show, vain show, apparent character, public image, window dressing, cosmetics; whitewash; whited sepulcher; **glitz** *and* tinsel <nf>, gaudiness, speciousness, meretriciousness, superficies, **superficiality;** PR *and* flack <nf>; pretense

3 aspect, look, view; feature, lineaments; **seeming, semblance, image,** imago, icon, eidolon, likeness, simulacrum; guise, mien; effect, impression, total effect *or* impression; **form, shape,** figure, configuration, gestalt; **manner,** fashion, wise, guise, style; **respect, regard,** reference, light; **phase; facet, side,** angle, viewpoint 27.7, slant *and* twist *and* spin <nf>

4 looks, features, lineaments, traits, lines; **countenance,** face, visage, feature, favor, brow, physiognomy; cast of countenance, **cut of one's jib** <nf>, facial appearance *or* expression, cast, turn; **look, air, mien,** demeanor, carriage, bearing, port, deportment, posture, stance, poise, presence; guise, garb, dress, complexion, color

5 <thing appearing> **apparition, appearance,** phenomenon, semblance; **vision, image, shape, form,** figure, presence; false image, mirage, phasm, specter, **phantom** 988.1

6 view, scene, sight; prospect, outlook, lookout, vista, perspective; scenery, scenic view; panorama, sweep; scape, **landscape,** seascape, riverscape, waterscape, airscape, skyscape, cloudscape, cityscape, townscape; bird's-eye view, worm's-eye view; best seat in the house

7 spectacle, sight; exhibit, **exhibition,** exposition, **show, stage show** 704.4, **display, presentation,** representation; dog and pony show; tableau, tableau vivant; panorama, diorama, cosmorama, myriorama, cyclorama, georama; *son et lumière* <Fr>, sound-and-light show; phantasmagoria, shifting scene, light show; psychedelic show; **pageant,** pageantry; parade, pomp

VERBS **8 appear,** become visible; **arrive, make one's appearance,** make *or* put in an appearance, appear on the scene, make the scene *and* weigh in <nf>, appear to one's eyes, meet *or* catch *or* strike the eye, **come in sight** *or* **view, show,** show oneself, show one's face, nip in <nf>, **show up** <nf>, **turn up,** come, **materialize,** pop up, present oneself, present oneself to view, **manifest oneself,** become manifest, **reveal oneself,** discover oneself, uncover oneself, declare oneself, expose *or* betray oneself, flash; **come to light,** see the light, see the light of day; **emerge,** issue, issue forth, stream forth, come forth, come to the fore, present itself, come out, come forward, come to the surface, come one's way, come to hand, come into the picture; enter 189.7, come upon the stage; **rise, arise,** rear its head; look forth, peer *or* peep out; crop out, outcrop; loom, heave in sight, appear on the horizon; crawl out of the woodwork; fade in, wax

9 **burst forth,** break forth, debouch, erupt, irrupt, explode; **pop up, bob up** <nf>, start up, spring up, burst upon the view; flare up, flash, gleam

10 appear to be, seem to be, **appear, seem, look,** feel, sound, look to be, appear to one's eyes, have *or* present the appearance of, give the feeling of, strike one as, come on as <nf>; **appear like, seem like, look like,** have *or* wear the look of, **sound like; have every appearance of,** have all the earmarks of, have all the features of, show signs of, have every sign *or* indication of; assume the guise of, take the shape of, exhibit the form of

ADJS 11 **apparent,** appearing, **seeming, ostensible;** outward, surface, superficial; material, incarnate; **visible** 31.6

ADVS 12 **apparently, seemingly, ostensibly, to** *or* by all appearances, to *or* by all accounts, to all seeming, evidently, as it seems, to the eye; on the face of it, *prima facie* <L>; on the surface, outwardly, superficially; at first sight *or* view, at the first blush

34 DISAPPEARANCE

NOUNS 1 **disappearance,** disappearing, **vanishing,** vanishment; **going, passing, departure, loss;** dissipation, dispersion; dissolution, dissolving, melting, evaporation, evanescence, dematerialization 1053.5; fade, fadeout, fading, fadeaway, blackout; wane, ebb; wipe, wipeout, wipeoff, erasure; eclipse, occultation, blocking; sunset; delitescence; vanishing point; elimination 773.2; extinction 395.6; disappearing act

VERBS 2 **disappear, vanish,** vanish from sight, do a vanishing act <nf>, depart, fly, **flee** 368.10, go, be gone, **go away,** pass, pass out *or* away, pass out of sight, exit, pull up stakes <nf>, leave the scene *or* stage, clear out, pass out of the picture, pass *or* retire from sight, become lost to sight, be seen no more, take a powder; **perish, die,** die off; die out *or* away, dwindle, wane, fade, **fade out** *or* **away,** do a fade-out <nf>; sink, sink away, dissolve, melt, melt away, dematerialize 1053.6, evaporate, evanesce, **vanish** *or* **disappear into thin air,** go up in smoke; disperse, dispel, dissipate; cease, cease to exist, **cease to be;** cease publication, go out of print, go off the air, become obsolete, close down; leave no trace; waste, waste away, erode, be consumed, wear away; undergo *or* suffer an eclipse; **hide** 346.8; blend into the background

ADJS 3 **vanishing, disappearing,** passing, fleeting, fugitive, transient, flying, fading, dissolving, melting, evaporating, evanescent, waning, here today gone tomorrow

4 **gone,** away, gone away, past and gone, extinct, missing, no more, poof <nf>, lost, lost to sight *or* view, long-lost, **out of sight; unaccounted for;** nonexistent; out of the picture

35 COLOR

NOUNS 1 **color, hue; tint,** tinct, tincture, **tinge, shade, tone,** cast; key; **coloring, coloration;** color harmony, color balance, color scheme; decorator color; **complexion,** skin color *or* coloring *or* tone, pigmentation; chromatism, chromaticism, chromism; achromatism 36.1; natural color; undercolor; pallor 36.2; color perception, color vision, color blindness

2 **warmth,** warmth of color, warm color; **blush, flush, glow,** healthy glow *or* hue

3 **softness,** soft color, subtle color, pale color, pastel, pastel color, pastel shade

4 **colorfulness,** color, bright color, pure color, **brightness, brilliance, vividness,** intensity, saturation; **richness,** gorgeousness, gaiety; riot *or* splash of color; Technicolor <TM>; Day-Glo <TM>; variegation, multicolor, polychrome; color scheme, color coordination

5 **garishness,** loudness, luridness, glitz <nf>, gaudiness 501.3; loud *or* screaming color <nf>; shocking pink, jaundiced yellow, chartreuse; clashing colors, color clash

6 **color quality;** chroma, Munsell chroma, brightness, purity, saturation; **hue,** value, lightness; colorimetric quality, chromaticity, chromaticness; tint, **tone;** chromatic color, achromatic *or* neutral color; warm color; cool color; tinge, shade

7 **color system,** chromaticity diagram, color triangle, Maxwell triangle; hue cycle, color disk, color wheel, color circle, chromatic circle, color cycle *or* gamut, color chart; Munsell scale; color solid; fundamental colors; **primary color,** primary pigment, primary; secondary color, secondary; tertiary color, tertiary; complementary color; chromaticity coordinate; color mixture curve *or* function; spectral color, spectrum color, pure *or* full color; metamer; **spectrum,** solar spectrum, color spectrum, chromatic spectrum, color index; rainbow; monochrome; demitint, half tint, halftone, mezzotint, half-light, patina; chromatic aberration

8 <coloring matter> **color, coloring, colorant,** tinction, tincture, **pigment, stain;** chromogen; **dye,** dyestuff, artificial coloring, food coloring, color filter, color gelatin; paint, distemper, tempera, enamel, glaze; coat, coating, **coat of paint; undercoat,** undercoating, **primer,** priming, prime coat, **ground, flat coat,** dead-color; interior paint, exterior paint, floor enamel; wash, wash coat, flat wash, colorwash, whitewash; opaque color, transparent color; medium, vehicle; drier; thinner; turpentine, turps <nf>; additive color, subtractive color; artist's colors, colored pencils, crayons, chalk

9 <persons according to hair color> **brunet; blond,** Goldilocks; bleached blond, peroxide blond; ash blond, platinum blond, strawberry blond, honey blond, dirty blond; **towhead; redhead,** carrottop <nf>; gray

10 <science of colors> chromatology; chromatics, chromatography, chromatoscopy, colorimetry, spectrum analysis, spectroscopy, spectrometry, spectrography; color theory

11 <applying color> **coloring,** coloration; **staining, dyeing; tie-dyeing; tinting,** tinging, tinction; pigmentation; illumination, emblazonry; color printing; lithography

12 **painting,** paint-work, coating, covering; **enameling,** glossing, glazing; **varnishing,** japanning, lacquering, shellacking; staining; **calcimining, whitewashing;** gilding; stippling; frescoing, fresco; undercoating, priming; watercoloring, gouache, oil-painting, crayoning

13 **spectrum,** rainbow; red, orange, yellow, green, blue, indigo, violet

VERBS 14 **color,** hue, lay on color; **tinge, tint,** tinct, **tincture,** tone, complexion; pigment; bedizen; variegate, colorize; **stain, dye,** dip, tie-dye; imbue; deep-dye, fast-dye, double-dye, dye in the wool, yarn-dye; ingrain, grain; shade, shadow; illuminate, emblazon; **paint,** apply paint, paint up, **coat,** cover, face, watercolor, crayon; dab, **daub,** bedaub, smear, besmear, brush on paint, slap *or* slop on paint; **enamel,** gloss, glaze; **varnish,** japan, **lacquer, shellac; white out; calcimine, whitewash,** parget; wash; **gild,** begild, engild; stipple; fresco; distemper; undercoat, prime; emblazon; color-code

15 <be inharmonious> **clash,** conflict, collide, fight

ADJS **16 chromatic,** colorational; **coloring,** colorific, colorative, tinctorial, tingent; pigmental, pigmentary; monochrome, monochromic, monochromatic; dichromatic; many-colored, parti-colored, medley *or* motley, rainbow, **variegated** 47.9, polychromatic, multicolored, kaleidoscopic, Technicolored; prismatic, spectral; matching, toning, harmonious; warm, glowing; cool, cold

17 colored, hued, in color, colorized, in Technicolor <TM>; **tinged, tinted,** tinctured, tinct, toned; **painted, enameled; stained, dyed;** tie-dyed; imbued; complexioned, complected <nf>; full-colored, full; deep, deep-colored; wash-colored; washed

18 deep-dyed, fast-dyed, double-dyed, **dyed-in-the-wool;** ingrained, ingrain; permanent, colorfast, fast, fadeless, unfading, indelible, constant

19 colorful, colory; **bright, vivid,** intense, **rich,** exotic, **brilliant,** burning, **gorgeous, gay,** bright-hued, bright-colored, rich-colored, gay-colored, high-colored, deep-colored

20 garish, lurid, loud, screaming, shrieking, glaring, flaring, flashy, glitzy <nf>, flaunting, crude, blinding, overbright, raw, gaudy 501.20; Day-Glo <TM>

21 off-color, off-tone; **inharmonious, discordant,** incongruous, **harsh,** clashing, conflicting, colliding

22 soft-colored, soft-hued, **soft,** softened, **subdued,** understated, muted, delicate, light, creamy, peaches-and-cream, **pastel, pale,** palish, subtle, mellow, delicate, quiet, tender, sweet; pearly, nacreous, mother-of-pearl, iridescent, opalescent; patinaed; somber, simple, sober, sad; flat, eggshell, semigloss, gloss; weathered, heathered

36 COLORLESSNESS

NOUNS **1 colorlessness,** lack *or* absence of color, huelessness, tonelessness, achromatism, achromaticity; dullness, lackluster 1027.5; neutral hue *or* tint

2 paleness, dimness, weakness, **faintness,** fadedness; lightness, fairness; **pallor,** pallidity, pallidness, prison pallor, **wanness, sallowness,** pastiness, ashiness; wheyface; muddiness, dullness; grayness, griseousness; **anemia,** hypochromic anemia, hypochromia, chloranemia; bloodlessness, exsanguination; **ghastliness, haggardness,** lividness, sickly hue, sickliness, deadly *or* deathly pallor, deathly hue, cadaverousness

3 decoloration, decolorizing, decolorization, discoloration, achromatization, lightening; **fading, paling; dimming, bedimming; whitening,** blanching, etiolation, whiteness, albinism, pigment deficiency; bleeding, bleeding white; weathering

4 bleach, bleaching, bleaching agent *or* substance; whitener; color remover, decolorant, decolorizer, achromatizer

VERBS **5** decolor, decolorize, discolor, achromatize, etiolate; **fade, wash out; dim, dull, tarnish,** tone down; **pale, whiten,** blanch, drain, drain of color; **bleach,** peroxide; etiolate

6 lose color, fade, fade out; **bleach,** bleach out; **pale, turn pale,** grow pale, **change color,** change countenance, turn white, **whiten, blanch,** wan; come out in the wash; discolor

ADJS **7 colorless, hueless,** toneless, uncolored, achromic, achromatic, achromatous, unpigmented; neutral; dull, flat, mat, dead, dingy, muddy, leaden, lusterless, lackluster 1027.17; **faded, washed-out,** dimmed, discolored, decolored, etiolated, weathered; **pale, dim,** weak, **faint; pallid, wan, sallow,** fallow; pale *or* blue *or* green around the gills, drained of color; **white,** white as a sheet; crystal; **pasty,** mealy, waxen; **ashen,** ashy, ashen-hued, cinereous, cineritious, gray, griseous, mousy, dingy; **anemic,** hypochromic, chloranemic; bloodless, exsanguine, exsanguinated, exsanguineous, bled white; **ghastly,** livid, lurid, **haggard,** cadaverous, unhealthy, sickly, deadly *or* deathly pale; pale as death *or* a ghost *or* a corpse; pale-faced, tallow-faced, whey-faced, white-skinned

8 **bleached,** decolored, decolorized, achromatized, whitened, blanched, lightened, bleached out, bleached white; drained, drained of color; etiolated

9 **light, fair,** light-colored, light-hued; pastel; whitish 37.8

37 WHITENESS

NOUNS 1 **whiteness, white, whitishness;** albescence; **lightness, fairness;** paleness 36.2; silveriness; snowiness, frostiness; chalkiness; pearliness; **creaminess**, off-whiteness, chalkiness; blondness; hoariness, grizzliness, canescence; milkiness, lactescence; glaucousness; glaucescence; silver; albinism, achroma, achromasia, achromatosis; albino; leukoderma, vitiligo; wheyface; white race 312.2,3

2 <comparisons> alabaster, bone, chalk, cream, ivory, lily, lime, milk, pearl, sheet, swan, sheep, fleece, flour, foam, paper, phantom, silver, snow, driven snow, tallow, teeth, wax, wool

3 **whitening,** albification, blanching; etiolation; **whitewashing; bleaching** 36.4; silvering, frosting, grizzling

4 whitening agent, whitener, whiting, whitening, **whitewash,** calcimine; pipe clay; correction fluid, Wite-Out <TM>; bleach

VERBS 5 **whiten,** white, etiolate, **blanch; bleach** 36.5; pale, blench; decolorize; fade; silver, grizzle, frost, besnow; chalk

6 **whitewash,** white, calcimine; pipeclay; clean

ADJS 7 **white,** pure white, white as alabaster or bone or chalk or snow, etc 37.2, **snow-white,** snowy, niveous, frosty, frosted; **hoary,** hoar, **grizzled,** grizzly, griseous, canescent; silver, **silvery,** silvered, argent <heraldry>, argentine; platinum; chalky, cretaceous; fleece- *or* fleecy-white; swan-white; foam-white; **milk-white,** milky, lactescent; marble, marmoreal; lily-white, white as a lily; white as a sheet, wheyfaced, ghastly; albescent; whitened, bleached, blanched, achromatic; crystal

8 **whitish,** whity, albescent; **light, fair;** pale 36.7; off-white; eggshell; glaucous, glaucescent; pearl, pearly, pearly-white, pearl-white; alabaster, alabastrine; cream, **creamy;** ivory, ivory-white; gray-white; dun-white

9 **blond** *or* blonde**;** flaxen-haired, fair-haired; artificial blond, bleached-blond, peroxide-blond; ash-blond, platinum-blond, strawberry-blond, honey-blond, blond-headed, blond-haired; **towheaded,** tow-haired; golden-haired 43.5; white-haired

10 **albino,** albinic, albinistic, albinal

38 BLACKNESS

NOUNS 1 **blackness,** nigritude, nigrescence; inkiness; **black, sable, ebony;** melanism; black race 312.2,3; darkness 1027

2 **darkness, darkishness,** darksomeness, blackishness; total darkness, lightlessness; **swarthiness,** swartness, swarth; **duskiness,** duskness; pitchiness; soberness, sobriety, **somberness,** graveness, sadness, funereality; hostility, sullenness, anger, black mood, black looks, black words

3 **dinginess, griminess, smokiness,** sootiness, fuliginousness, fuliginosity, smudginess, smuttiness, blotchiness, dirtiness, **muddiness,** murkiness

4 <comparisons> ebony *or* ebon <old>, jet, ink, sloe, pitch, tar, coal, charcoal, smoke, soot, smut, raven, obsidian, sable, crow, night, hell, sin, one's hat <Brit>, pitch

5 **blackening, darkening,** nigrification, melanization, melanism, melanosis, denigration; shading; **smudging,** smutching, **smirching;** smudge, smutch, smirch, smut

6 **blacking,** blackening, blackening agent, blackwash; charcoal, burnt cork, black ink; lampblack, carbon black, stove black, gas black, soot; japan; melanin

VERBS **7** **blacken,** black, nigrify, melanize, denigrate; **darken,** bedarken; shade, shadow; blackwash, ink, charcoal, cork; **smudge,** smutch, **smirch,** besmirch, murk, blotch, blot, dinge, dirty; smut, soot; smoke, oversmoke, singe, scorch, char; ebonize; **smear** 661.9/512.10, **blacken one's name** *or* **reputation,** give one a black eye; japan, niello

ADJS **8** **black,** black as ink or pitch or tar or coal, etc 38.4; **sable** <heraldry>, nigrous, nigrescent; **ebony,** ebon; deep black, of the deepest dye; **pitch-black, pitch-dark,** pitchy, black *or* dark as pitch, tar-black, tarry; night-black, night-dark, black *or* dark as night; midnight, black as midnight; **inky,** inky-black, atramentous, achromatic, ink-black, black as ink; **jet-black,** jet, jetty; **coal-black,** coaly, black as coal, coal-black; sloe, sloe-black, sloe-colored; raven, **raven-black,** black as a crow; blue-black, brown-black; **dark** 1027.13–16

9 **dark,** dark-colored, **darkish,** darksome, blackish; nigrescent; **swarthy,** swart; **dusky,** dusk; **somber,** sombrous, **sober, grave,** sad, funereal; hostile, sullen, angry; achromatic

10 **dark-skinned,** black-skinned, **dark-complexioned; black, colored;** swarthy, swart; melanian, melanic, melanotic, melanistic, melanous

11 **dingy, grimy, smoky,** sooty, fuliginous, **smudgy,** smutty, blotchy, dirty, **muddy,** murky, smirched, besmirched, dusky; blackened, singed, charred

12 **livid, black-and-blue**

13 **black-haired, raven-haired,** raven-tressed, black-locked, dark-haired; brunet *or* brunette

39 GRAYNESS

NOUNS **1** **grayness, gray,** grayishness, canescence; glaucousness, glaucescence; silveriness; ashiness; neutral tint; smokiness; mousiness; slatiness; leadenness; lividness, lividity; dullness, drabness, soberness, somberness; grisaille; oyster, taupe, greige; gunmetal, iron, lead, pewter, silver, slate, steel

2 **gray-haired** *or* **gray-headed person,** gray-hair, graybeard, grisard, salt-and-pepper, hoariness

VERBS **3** **gray, grizzle,** silver, frost

ADJS **4** **gray, grayish,** gray-colored, gray-hued, gray-toned, grayed, griseous; canescent; iron-gray, steely, steel-gray; Quaker-gray, Quaker-colored, acier, gray-drab; Oxford gray; dove-gray, dove-colored; pearl-gray, pearl, pearly; silver-gray, silver, silvery, silvered; **grizzly,** grizzled, grizzle; ash-gray, ashen, ashy, cinerous, cinereous, cineritious, cinereal; dusty, dust-gray; smoky, smoke-gray; charcoal-gray; slaty, slate-colored; leaden, livid, lead-gray, iron-gray; glaucous, glaucescent; wolf-gray; mousy, mouse-gray, mouse-colored; taupe; dapple-gray, dappled-gray; gray-spotted, gray-speckled, salt-and-pepper; gray-black, gray-brown, etc; taupe, ecru, greige; neutral; **dull, dingy,** dismal, **somber, sober, sad, dreary;** winter-gray, hoar, hoary, frost-gray, rime-gray

5 **gray-haired,** gray-headed, silver-headed; hoar, hoary, hoary-haired, grizzled; gray-bearded, silver-bearded, salt-and-pepper *or* pepper-and-salt; frosty

6 **gray color varieties**

ash *or* ash gray	gun metal
bat	iron
battleship gray	lead
blue-gray	light gray
cadet gray	lilac gray
charcoal gray	merle
cinder	mole gray
cloud	moleskin
crystal gray	mouse
dark gray	mushroom
dove	neutral
field gray	nutria
flint	obsidian
French gray	olive gray
glaucous gray	opal gray
granite	Oxford gray
gray *or* grey	oyster gray
gray-white	pale gray
greige *or* grege	pearl *or* pearl gray

pelican	silver
plumbago	silver-gray
powder gray	slate gray
Quaker gray	smoke gray
salt-and-pepper *or* pepper-and-salt	steel gray
	taupe
shell gray	zinc gray

40 BROWNNESS

NOUNS 1 **brownness, brownishness, brown,** browning, infuscation; brown race 312.2; ochre, sepia, raw sienna, burnt sienna, raw umber, burnt umber; caramel, pumpernickel, coffee, chocolate, paper bag

VERBS 2 **brown,** embrown, infuscate; rust; **tan, bronze,** suntan; sunburn, burn; fry, sauté, scorch, braise; toast; caramelize

ADJS 3 **brown, brownish;** cinnamon, hazel; fuscous; **brunet,** brune; tawny, fulvous; dark brown; tan, tan-colored; tan-faced, tan-skinned, tanned, sun-tanned; khaki, khaki-colored; drab, olive-drab; **dun,** dun-brown, dun-drab, dun-olive; beige, grege, buff, biscuit, mushroom; **chocolate,** chocolate-colored, chocolate-brown; cocoa, cocoa-colored, cocoa-brown; coffee, coffee-colored, coffee-brown; toast, toast-brown; nut-brown; oatmeal; walnut, walnut-brown; seal, seal-brown; fawn, fawn-colored; grayish-brown; brownish-gray, fuscous, taupe, mouse-dun, mouse-brown, tweed; snuff-colored, snuff-brown, mummy-brown; umber, umber-colored, umber-brown; olive-brown; **sepia;** sorrel; sable; yellowish-brown, brownish-yellow; lurid; brown as a berry, berry-brown

4 **reddish-brown,** rufous-brown, brownish-red; roan; henna; terra-cotta; rufous, foxy; livid-brown; **mahogany,** mahogany-brown; auburn, Titian; **russet,** russety; rust, rust-colored, rusty, ferruginous, rubiginous; liver-colored, liver-brown; **bronze,** bronze-brown, bronze-colored, bronzed, brazen; copper, coppery, copperish, cupreous, copper-colored; **chestnut,** chestnut-brown, castaneous; bay, bay-colored; bayard; sunburned, adust

5 **brunet** *or* brunette**;** brown-haired; auburn-haired; xanthous

41 REDNESS

NOUNS 1 **redness, reddishness,** rufosity, rubricity; **red,** *rouge* <Fr>, gules <heraldry>; rubicundity, **ruddiness,** color, high color, floridness, floridity; rubor, erythema, erythroderma; erythrism; reddish brown; red race 312.3; carmine, crimson, henna, rouge, vermilion, cerise; cherry, ruby, fire engine

2 **pinkness, pinkishness; rosiness; pink,** rose

3 **reddening,** rubefaction, rubification, rubescence, erubescence, rufescence; **coloring,** mantling, crimsoning, **blushing, flushing; blush,** flush, glow, bloom, rosiness; hectic, hectic flush; flush syndrome, alcohol flush syndrome; rubefacient

VERBS 4 <make red> **redden, rouge,** ruddle, rubefy, raddle, rubric; warm, inflame; crimson, encrimson; vermilion, madder, miniate, henna, rust, carmine; incarnadine, pinkify; **blush;** red-ink, red-pencil, lipstick

5 **redden,** turn *or* grow red, **color,** color up, **mantle, blush, flush, crimson;** flame, glow

ADJS 6 **red, reddish,** gules <heraldry>, red-colored, red-hued, red-dyed, red-looking; **ruddy,** ruddied, rubicund; rubric *or* rubrical, rubricate, rubricose; rufescent, rufous, rufulous; warm, hot, glowing; bright-red; fiery, flaming, flame-colored, flame-red, fire-red, red as fire, lurid, red as a hot *or* live coal; reddened, inflamed; **scarlet, vermilion, vermeil; crimson;** rubiate; maroon; damask; puce; stammel; cerise; iron-red; cardinal, cardinal-red; cherry, cherry-colored, cherry-red; carmine, incarmined; **ruby,** ruby-colored, ruby-red; wine, port-wine, wine-colored, wine-red, vinaceous; carnation, carnation-red; brick-red, bricky, tile-red, lateritious; rust, rust-red, rusty, ferruginous, rubiginous; beet-red, red as a beet;

lobster-red, red as a lobster; red as a turkey-cock; copper-red, carnelian; russet; Titian, Titian-red; infrared; reddish-amber, reddish-gray, etc; reddish-brown 40.4

7 **sanguine,** sanguineous, **blood-red,** blood-colored, bloody-red, bloody, gory, red as blood

8 **pink, pinkish,** pinky; **rose, rosy,** rose-colored, rose-hued, rose-red, roseate; primrose; flesh-colored, flesh-pink, incarnadine; coral, coral-colored, coral-red, coralline; salmon, salmon-colored, salmon-pink; damask, carnation; fuchsia

9 **red-complexioned,** ruddy-complexioned, warm-complexioned, red-fleshed, red-faced, ruddy-faced, apple-cheeked, **ruddy,** rubicund, **florid,** sanguine, full-blooded; blowzy, blowzed; rosy, **rosy-cheeked;** glowing, blooming; hectic, blushing, rouged, flushed, flush; burnt, sunburned; erythematous

10 **redheaded,** red-haired, red-polled, red-bearded; erythristic; red-crested, red-crowned, red-tufted; ginger-haired, carroty, carrot-topped, chestnut, auburn, Titian, xanthous

11 reddening, blushing, flushing, coloring; rubescent, erubescent; rubificative, rubrific; rubefacient

42 ORANGENESS

NOUNS **1** **orangeness,** oranginess; **orange**; cadmium orange, carotene

ADJS **2** **orange, orangeish,** orangey, orange-hued, reddish-yellow; ocherous *or* ochery, ochreous, ochroid, ocherish; old gold; saffron; pumpkin, pumpkin-colored; tangerine, tangerine-colored; apricot, peach, cantaloupe, salmon, mango; carroty, carrot-colored; orange-red, orange-yellow, red-orange, reddish-orange, yellow-orange

43 YELLOWNESS

NOUNS **1** **yellowness, yellowishness;** goldenness, aureateness; **yellow,** gold, or <heraldry>; gildedness; fallowness; cadmium yellow, cadmium lemon

2 yellow skin, yellow complexion, sallowness; biliousness; xanthochroism; **jaundice,** yellow jaundice, icterus, xanthoderma, xanthism; yellow race 312.2

VERBS **3** **yellow,** turn yellow; **gild,** begild, engild; aurify; sallow; **jaundice**

ADJS **4** **yellow, yellowish,** yellowy; lutescent, luteous, luteolous; xanthic, xanthous; flavescent; **gold, golden**, gold-colored, golden-yellow, gilt, gilded, auric, aureate; sunshine-yellow; **canary,** canary-yellow; citron, citron-yellow, citreous; **lemon,** lemon-colored, lemon-yellow; sulfur-colored, sulfur-yellow; mustard, mustard-yellow; pale-yellow, **sallow,** fallow; cream, creamy, cream-colored; straw, straw-colored, tow-colored; flaxen, flaxen-colored, flax-colored; sandy, sand-colored; ocherous *or* ochery, ochreous, ochroid, ocherish; buff, buff-colored, buff-yellow; honey-colored; saffron, saffron-colored, saffron-yellow; primrose, primrose-colored, primrose-yellow; topaz-yellow; greenish-yellow, chartreuse; banana; maize

5 **yellow-haired, golden-haired,** tow-headed, tow-haired, auricomous, xanthous; blond 37.9

6 yellow-faced, yellow-complexioned, sallow, yellow-cheeked; **jaundiced,** xanthodermatous, icteric, icterical, bilious

44 GREENNESS

NOUNS **1** **greenness,** viridity; greenishness, virescence, viridescence; verdantness, verdancy, **verdure,** glaucousness, glaucescence; **green,** greensickness, chlorosis, chloremia, chloranemia; chlorophyll; grass, emerald

2 **verdigris, patina,** aerugo; patination

VERBS **3** **green;** verdigris, patinate, patinize

ADJS **4** **green,** virid; **verdant,** verdurous, vert <heraldry>; grassy, leafy, leaved, foliaged; springlike, summerlike, summery, vernal, vernant, aestival; **greenish,** viridescent, virescent; **grass-green,** green as grass, grassy; citrine, citrinous; **olive,** olive-green, olivaceous; pea-green; avocado; jade; loden green; bottle-green; forest-green; sea-green; beryl-green, berylline; leek-green; holly, holly-green; ivy, ivy-green; emerald, emerald-green, smaragdine, chartreuse, yellow-green, yellowish-green, greenish-yellow; glaucous, glaucescent, glaucous-green; blue-green, bluish-green, green-blue, greenish-blue; greensick, chlorotic, chloremic, chloranemic

5 verdigrisy, verdigrised, patinous, patinaed, patinated *or* patinized, aeruginous

45 BLUENESS

NOUNS 1 **blueness, bluishness;** azureness; **blue, azure**, cyan, indigo, ultramarine; lividness, lividity; cyanosis

VERBS 2 **blue,** azure

ADJS 3 **blue, bluish,** cerulescent, cerulean, ceruleous; cyanic, cyaneous, cyanean, cyanotic; **azure** <heraldry>, azurine, azurean, azureous, azured, azure-blue, azure-colored, azure-tinted; sky-blue, sky-colored, sky-dyed; ice-blue; light-blue, lightish-blue, pale-blue; dark-blue, deep-blue, midnight-blue, navy-blue; peacock-blue, pavonine, pavonian; beryl-blue, berylline; turquoise, turquoise-blue; aquamarine; cornflower; electric-blue; ultramarine; royal-blue; indigo; sapphire, sapphire-blue, sapphirine; Wedgwood-blue, robin's-egg blue; livid

46 PURPLENESS

NOUNS 1 **purpleness, purplishness,** purpliness; **purple; violet**, lavender, lilac, magenta, mauve, amethyst; lividness, lividity, bruise

VERBS 2 **purple,** empurple, purpurate

ADJS 3 **purple,** purpure <heraldry>, purpureal, purpureous, purpurean, purpurate; royal purple; **purplish,** purply, purplescent, empurpled; **violet,** violaceous; plum, plum-colored, plum-purple; amethystine; **lavender,** lavender-blue; lilac; magenta; mauve; mulberry; orchid; pansy-purple, pansy-violet; raisin-colored; fuchsia, puce, aubergine, orchid; purple-blue; livid

47 VARIEGATION

<diversity of colors>

NOUNS 1 **variegation, multicolor;** parti-color; medley *or* mixture of colors, spectrum, rainbow of colors, rainbow, riot of color; polychrome, polychromatism; dichromatism, trichromatism, etc; dichroism, trichroism, etc

2 **iridescence,** iridization, irisation, **opalescence,** nacreousness, pearliness, chatoyancy, **play of colors** *or* **light;** light show; moiré pattern, tabby; burelé *or* burelage

3 **spottiness,** maculation, freckliness, speckliness, mottledness, mottlement, dappleness, dappledness, stippledness, spottedness, dottedness; **fleck, speck, speckle;** freckle; **spot,** dot, polka dot, macula, macule, blotch, splotch, patch, splash, bullet point; **mottle, dapple;** brindle; **stipple,** stippling, pointillism, pointillage; pinpointing; spattering

4 **check, checker,** checks, checking, checkerboard, chessboard; **plaid,** tartan; checker-work, variegated pattern, harlequin, colors in patches, crazy-work, patchwork; parquet, parquetry, marquetry, mosaic, tesserae, tessellation; crazy-paving <Brit>; hound's tooth; inlay, damascene; graph

5 **stripe, striping,** candy-stripe, pinstripe; barber pole; **streak, streaking;** striation, striature, stria; striola, striga; crack, craze, crackle, reticulation; bar, band, belt, list

6 <comparisons> spectrum, rainbow, iris, chameleon, leopard, jaguar, cheetah, ocelot, zebra, barber pole, candy cane, Dalmatian, firedog, peacock, butterfly, mother-of-pearl, nacre, tortoise shell, opal, kaleidoscope,

stained glass, serpentine, calico cat, marble, mackerel sky, confetti, crazy quilt, patchwork quilt, shot silk, moiré, watered silk, marbled paper, Joseph's coat, harlequin, tapestry; bar code, checkerboard, graph paper

VERBS 7 **variegate,** motley; parti-color; polychrome, polychromize; pattern; harlequin; **mottle, dapple,** stipple, **fleck,** flake, **speck, speckle,** bespeckle, freckle, **spot,** bespot, dot, sprinkle, blot, spangle, bespangle, pepper, stud, maculate; blotch, splotch; tattoo, stigmatize; **check, checker;** tessellate; **stripe, streak,** striate, band, bar, vein, craze; marble, marbleize; engrail; tabby

8 **opalesce,** opalize; iridesce

ADJS 9 **variegated, many-colored,** many-hued, diverse-colored, **multicolored,** multicolor, multicolorous, **varicolored,** varicolorous, polychrome, polychromic, polychromatic; parti-colored, parti-color; of all manner of colors, of all the colors of the rainbow; versicolor, versicolored, versicolorate, versicolorous; engrailed; motley, medley, harlequin; colorful, colory; daedal; crazy; thunder and lightning; kaleidoscopic, kaleidoscopical; prismatic, prismatical, prismal, spectral; shot, shot through; bicolored, bicolor, dichromic, dichromatic; tricolored, tricolor, trichromic, trichromatic; two-color *or* -colored, three-color *or* -colored, two-tone *or* -toned, etc

10 **iridescent,** iridal, iridial, iridine, iridian, iridiated; irised, irisated, **rainbowy,** rainbowlike, rainbowed; **opalescent,** opaline, opaloid; nacreous, nacry, *nacré* <Fr>, nacred, **pearly,** pearlish, mother-of-pearl; tortoise-shell; peacock-like, pavonine, pavonian; chatoyant; moiré, burelé; watered

11 **chameleonlike,** chameleonic, changeable

12 **mottled, motley; pied, piebald,** skewbald, pinto; **dappled,** dapple; calico; marbled; clouded; salt-and-pepper

13 **spotted, dotted,** polka-dot, sprinkled, peppered, studded, pocked, pockmarked; **spotty,** dotty, patchy, pocky; **speckled, specked,** speckledy, speckly, specky; **stippled,** pointillé, pointillistic; **flecked,** fleckered; spangled, bespangled; maculate, maculated, macular; punctate, punctated; freckled, frecked, freckly; blotched, blotchy, splotched, splotchy; flea-bitten; tortoiseshell; foxed

14 **checked, checkered,** checkedy, check, **plaid,** plaided; tessellated, tessellate, mosaic

15 **striped,** stripy, candy-stripe, pinstripe; **streaked,** streaky; **striated,** striate, striatal, striolate, strigate *or* strigose; barred, banded, listed; veined; **brindle,** brindled, brinded; marbled, marbleized; reticulate; tabby

48 HEARING

NOUNS 1 **hearing,** audition; sense of hearing, auditory *or* aural sense, auditory sensation; ear; listening, heeding, attention, hushed attention, rapt attention, eager attention, mind; auscultation, aural examination, examination by ear; audibility

2 **audition,** hearing, tryout, call <nf>, **audience, interview,** conference; attention, favorable attention, ear; **listening,** listening in; **eavesdropping,** overhearing, wiretapping, electronic surveillance, bugging <nf>

3 good hearing, refined *or* acute sense of hearing, sensitive ear, nice *or* quick *or* sharp *or* correct ear; **an ear for;** musical ear, ear for music, musicality; ear-mindedness; bad *or* poor ear, no ear, tin ear <nf>

4 **earshot,** earreach, **hearing,** range, auditory range, reach, carrying distance, **sound of one's voice**

5 **listener,** hearer, auditor, audient, hearkener, auditioner, earwitness; **eavesdropper,** overhearer, monitor; little pitcher with big ears, snoop <nf>, listener-in; fly on the wall <nf>

6 **audience,** auditory, **house, congregation;** studio audience, live audience, captive audience, theatregoers,

gallery, crowd, grandstand; orchestra, pit; groundling, boo-bird <nf>, spectator 918

7 **ear** 2.10, auditory apparatus, hearing organ; external ear, **outer ear;** cauliflower ear, jug ear, bat ear

8 listening device; **hearing aid,** hard-of-hearing aid; electronic hearing aid, transistor hearing aid; vacuum-tube hearing aid; ear trumpet; amplifier, speaking trumpet, megaphone; stethoscope

9 <science of hearing> otology; otoscopy, auriscopy; audiometry; otoneurology, otopathy, otography, otoplasty, otolaryngology, otorhinolaryngology, ear, nose, and throat *or* ENT; audiology; acoustic phonetics, phonetics 524.13; auriscope, otoscope, auscultator, stethoscope; audiometer

VERBS 10 **listen,** hark, **hearken, heed, hear, attend,** give attention, **give ear,** give *or* lend an ear, bend an ear; **listen to,** listen at <nf>, attend to, pay attention, give a hearing to, give audience to, sit in on; **listen in; eavesdrop,** wiretap, tap, intercept, bug <nf>; **keep one's ears open,** be all ears <nf>, listen with both ears, strain one's ears; prick up the ears, cock the ears, keep one's ear to the ground, have long ears; hang on the lips of, hang on every word; hear out; auscultate, examine by ear

11 **hear,** catch, get <nf>, take in, hear from; **overhear; hear of,** hear tell of <nf>, pick up; get an earful <nf>, get wind of, get word; have an ear for, have perfect pitch

12 be heard, **fall on the ear,** sound in the ear, catch *or* reach the ear, carry, sound, resound, echo, reverberate, come within earshot, come to one's ear, register, make an impression, get across <nf>; **have one's ear,** reach, contact, get to; make oneself heard, get through to, gain a hearing, reach the ear of; ring in the ear; caress the ear; assault *or* split *or* assail the ear

ADJS 13 **auditory,** audio, audile, **hearing, aural,** auricular, otic, audial, auditive, auditorial; audiovisual; audible; otological, otoscopic, otopathic, etc; acoustic, acoustical, phonic

14 **listening, attentive,** open-eared, **all ears** <nf>, hearing; wired

15 **eared,** auriculate; big-eared, cauliflower-eared, crop-eared, dog-eared, droop-eared, flap-eared, flop-eared, jug-earned, lop-eared, long-eared, mouse-eared, prick-eared, quick-eared; **sharp-eared;** tin-eared; ear-minded; ear-shaped, earlike, auriform

49 DEAFNESS

NOUNS 1 **deafness, hardness of hearing,** dull hearing, deaf ears; **stone-deafness;** nerve-deafness; mind deafness, word deafness; **tone deafness**, asonia, unmusicalness**;** cophosis; impaired hearing, hearing *or* auditory impairment; loss of hearing, **hearing loss; deaf-muteness,** deaf-mutism

2 **the deaf,** the hard-of-hearing; **deaf-mute**, deaf-and-dumb person; lip reader; silent person

3 deaf-and-dumb alphabet, manual alphabet, finger alphabet, fingerspelling; dactylology, sign language, American Sign Language; lip reading, oral method; hearing aid

VERBS 4 **be deaf;** have no ears, be earless; lose one's hearing, suffer hearing loss *or* impairment, go deaf; shut *or* stop *or* close one's ears, **turn a deaf ear;** fall on deaf ears; lipread, use sign language, sign

5 **deafen, stun,** split the ears *or* eardrums

ADJS 6 **deaf, hard-of-hearing,** hearing-impaired, dull *or* thick of hearing, deaf-eared, dull-eared; deafened, stunned; **stone-deaf,** deaf as a stone, deaf as a door *or* a doorknob *or* doornail, **deaf as a post,** deaf as an adder; **unhearing;** earless; word-deaf; tone-deaf, unmusical; dealfish, half-deaf, quasi-deaf; **deaf and dumb,** deaf-mute

50 SOUND

NOUNS 1 **sound,** sonance, acoustic, acoustical *or* acoustic phenomenon;

auditory phenomenon *or* stimulus, auditory effect; noise; ultrasound; sound wave, sound propagation; sound intensity, sound intensity level, amplitude, loudness 53; phone, speech sound 524.12; resonance

2 **tone, pitch, frequency,** audio frequency *or* AF; monotone, monotony, tonelessness; overtone, harmonic, partial, partial tone; undertone; fundamental tone, fundamental; intonation 524.6

3 **timbre,** tonality, **tone quality,** tone color, color, coloring, clang color *or* tint, register

4 **sounding,** sonation, sonification

5 **acoustics,** phonics, radioacoustics, acoustic theory, harmonics; acoustical engineer, acoustician; radiophonics

6 **sonics;** subsonics; **supersonics,** ultrasonics; speed of sound 174.2; sound barrier, transonic barrier, sonic barrier *or* wall; sonic boom; ultrasonic frequency, infrasonic frequency

7 <sound unit> **decibel,** db; bel, phon, sone

8 **loudspeaker, speaker,** dynamic speaker; speaker unit, speaker system; crossover network; voice coil; cone, diaphragm; acoustical network; horn <nf>; **headphone, earphone,** stereo headset, headset, ear buds

9 **microphone, mike** <nf>; radiomicrophone; concealed microphone, **bug** <nf>

10 **audio amplifier, amplifier, amp <nf>; preamplifier,** preamp <nf>

11 sound reproduction system, audio sound system; **high-fidelity** system *or* **hi-fi** <nf>; **record player, phonograph,** gramophone, Victrola; **jukebox,** nickelodeon; radio-phonograph combination; monophonic *or* monaural system, **mono** <nf>, stereophonic *or* binaural system, stereo <nf>; four-channel stereo system, discrete four-channel system, derived four-channel system, quadraphonic sound system; multitrack player *or* recorder *or* sound system; **pickup** *or* cartridge, magnetic pickup *or* cartridge, ceramic pickup *or* cartridge, crystal pickup, photoelectric pickup; stylus, needle; tone arm; turntable, transcription turntable, record changer, changer; **public-address system** *or* PA *or* PA system; sound truck; loudhailer, bullhorn; intercommunication system, **intercom** <nf>, squawk box <nf>; **tape recorder,** tape deck, cassette *or* audio-cassette player, cassette *or* audio-cassette recorder, recording system; boom box, ghetto blaster; compact disk *or* CD player; media player; iPod <TM>; hi-fi fan *or* freak <nf>, audiophile

12 **record, phonograph record,** disc, wax, long-playing record *or* LP; transcription, electrical transcription, digital transcription, digital recording; **recording,** wire recording, tape recording; digital stereo; digital disc; tape, tape cassette, cassette; tape cartridge, cartridge; digital audio tape *or* DAT, DVD; compact disk *or* CD; video-cassette recorder *or* VCR

13 **audio distortion, distortion;** interference, static 1034.21; scratching, shredding, hum, 60-cycle hum, rumble, hissing, howling, blurping, blooping, woomping, fluttering, flutter, squeals, whistles, birdies, motorboating; feedback

VERBS 14 **sound,** make a sound *or* noise, give forth *or* emit a sound; noise; speak 524.19; resound, reverberate, echo; **record,** tape, tape-record; prerecord; play back; broadcast, amplify

ADJS 15 **sounding,** sonorous, soniferous; **sounded;** tonal; monotone, monotonic, toneless, droning; voiced

16 **audible,** hearable, heard; **distinct, clear,** plain, definite, articulate; distinctive, contrastive; high-fidelity, hi-fi <nf>, stereophonic; microphonic

17 **acoustic, acoustical,** phonic, **sonic;** subsonic, supersonic, ultrasonic, hypersonic; transonic *or* transsonic, faster than sound

ADVS 18 **audibly, aloud,** out, **out loud;** distinctly, clearly, plainly

51 SILENCE

NOUNS **1** **silence,** silentness, **soundlessness,** noiselessness, **stillness, quietness,** quietude, quiescence 173, **quiet, still,** peace, **hush,** mum; lull, rest, calm; golden silence; total silence, deathlike *or* tomblike silence, dead silence, perfect silence, solemn *or* awful silence, radio silence, the quiet *or* silence of the grave *or* the tomb; dull roar; hush *or* dead of night, dead; tacitness, taciturnity, reticence, reserve; inaudibility; tranquillity; not a sound *or* peep

2 **muteness,** mutism, **dumbness,** voicelessness, tonguelessness; speechlessness, wordlessness; inarticulateness; anaudia, aphasia, aphonia; hysterical mutism; deaf-muteness 49.1; standing mute, refusal to speak, stonewalling <nf>, the code of silence *or omertà* <Ital>, keeping one's lip buttoned <nf>; laryngitis

3 **mute,** dummy; deaf-mute 49.2

4 **silencer, muffler,** muffle, **mute,** baffle *or* baffler, quietener, cushion; **damper,** damp; dampener; **soft pedal,** sordine, sourdine; hushcloth, silence cloth; **gag, muzzle;** antiknock; **soundproofing,** acoustic tile, sound-absorbing material, sound-proofing insulation

VERBS **5** **be silent,** keep silent *or* silence, **keep still** *or* **quiet; keep one's mouth shut, hold one's tongue,** keep one's tongue between one's teeth, bite one's tongue, put a bridle on one's tongue, seal one's lips, shut *or* close one's mouth, hold one's breath, muzzle oneself, **not breathe a word,** not speak, forswear speech *or* speaking, **keep mum, hold one's peace,** not let a word escape one, not utter a word, not open one's mouth, not make a sound, not make a peep; make no sign, keep to oneself; not have a word to say, be mute, stand mute; choke up, have one's words stick in one's throat; be taciturn, spare one's words, have little to say, keep one's counsel, hush up

6 <nf terms> **shut up,** keep one's trap *or* yap shut, button up, button one's lip, save one's breath, shut one's bazoo, can it, dummy up, clam up, close up like a clam, knock it off, not let out a peep, say nothing, not say 'boo', play dumb, stonewall

7 **fall silent, hush,** quiet, quieten, quiesce, **quiet down,** pipe down <nf>, check one's speech, stop talking; lose one's voice, get laryngitis

8 **silence, put to silence, hush,** hush one up, hush-hush, **shush, quiet,** quieten, **still; soft-pedal,** put on the soft pedal, play down; squash, squelch <nf>, stifle, choke, choke off, throttle, put the kibosh on <nf>, put the lid on *and* shut down on <nf>, put the damper on <nf>, **gag, muzzle,** muffle, stifle, stop one's mouth, cut one short; strike dumb *or* mute, dumbfound; tongue-tie

9 **muffle, mute, dull, soften, deaden,** quietize, cushion, baffle, damp, **dampen,** deafen; subdue, stop, tone down, **soft-pedal,** put on the soft pedal

ADJS **10** **silent, still,** stilly, **quiet,** quiescent 173.12, **hushed, soundless,** noiseless; taciturn, uncommunicative, tight-lipped, clammed up <nf>; echoless; **inaudible,** subaudible, below the limen *or* threshold of hearing, unhearable; quiet as a mouse *or* lamb, mousy; silent as a post *or* stone, so quiet that one might hear a feather *or* pin drop; silent as the grave *or* tomb, still as death; **unsounded, unvoiced,** unpronounced

11 **tacit, wordless, unspoken,** unuttered, unexpressed, unsaid, unarticulated, unvocalized; **implicit** 519.8

12 **mute, mum, dumb,** voiceless, tongueless, **speechless,** wordless, breathless, at a loss for words, choked up; inarticulate; **tongue-tied,** dumbstruck, dumbstricken, stricken dumb, **dumbfounded;** anaudic, aphasic, aphonic

ADVS **13** **silently,** in silence, **quietly, soundlessly,** noiselessly; inaudibly

52 FAINTNESS OF SOUND

NOUNS **1 faintness, lowness, softness,** gentleness, subduedness, dimness, feebleness, weakness; indistinctness, unclearness, flatness; subaudibility, inaudibility; decrescendo; distant sound

2 muffled tone, veiled voice, *voce velata* <Ital>, covered tone; **mutedness; dullness, deadness,** flatness; noise abatement, sound reduction, soundproofing

3 thud, dull thud; **thump,** flump, crump, clop, clump, clunk, plunk, tunk, plump, bump; pad, pat; **patter,** pitter-patter, pit-a-pat; **tap,** rap, **click,** tick, flick, pop, peep; tinkle, ting, clink, chink, tingaling

4 murmur, murmuring, murmuration; **mutter,** muttering; **mumble,** mumbling; soft voice, low voice, small *or* little voice; **undertone,** underbreath, bated breath; susurration, susurrus, undercurrent; **whisper,** whispering, stage whisper, breathy voice; breath, sigh, sough, exhalation, aspiration; purl, hum, moan, white noise *or* sound; nonresonance

5 ripple, splash, ripple of laughter, ripple of applause; titter, chuckle

6 rustle, rustling, froufrou, swoosh

7 hum, humming, thrumming, low rumbling, booming, bombilation, bombination, **droning, buzzing,** whizzing, whirring, purring

8 sigh, sighing, moaning, sobbing, whining, soughing

VERBS **9 steal** *or* **waft on the ear,** melt in the air, float in the air

10 murmur, mutter, mumble, maffle <Brit nf>; coo; susurrate; **lower one's voice, speak under one's breath; whisper,** whisper in the ear; breathe, sigh, aspirate

11 ripple, babble, burble, bubble, **gurgle,** guggle, **purl, trill;** lap, plash, **splash,** swish, swash, slosh, wash

12 rustle, crinkle; **swish,** whish

13 hum, thrum, bum <Brit nf>, boom, bombilate, bombinate, **drone, buzz,** whiz, whir, burr, birr, purr

14 sigh, moan, sob, whine, sough; **whimper**

15 thud, thump, patter, clop, clump, clunk, plunk, flump, crump; pad, pat; **tap,** rap, **click,** tick, tick away; pop; tinkle, clink, chink

ADJS **16 faint, low, soft, gentle, subdued, dim, feeble, weak,** faint-sounding, low-sounding, soft-sounding; soft-voiced, low-voiced, faint-voiced, weak-voiced; murmured, whispered, hushed; half-heard, barely heard, scarcely heard; distant, dying away; indistinct, unclear; barely audible, subaudible, near the limit *or* threshold of hearing; soft-pedaled, piano, pianissimo; decrescendo; unstressed, unaccented

17 muffled, muted, softened, dampened, damped, **smothered,** stifled, bated, dulled, deadened, subdued; **dull, dead, flat,** *sordo* <Ital>; nonresonant

18 murmuring, murmurous, murmurish, **muttering, mumbling;** susurrous, susurrant; **whispering,** whisper, whispery; whimpering; **rustling**

19 rippling, babbling, burbling, bubbling, **gurgling,** guggling, **purling, trilling;** lapping, splashing, plashing, sloshing, swishing

20 humming, thrumming, **droning,** booming, bombinating, **buzzing,** whizzing, whirring, purring, burring

ADVS **21 faintly, softly,** gently, subduedly, hushedly, dimly, feebly, weakly, low; piano, pianissimo; *sordo* and *sordamente* <Ital>, *à la sourdine* <Fr>

22 in an undertone, *sotto voce* <Ital>, **under one's breath,** with bated breath, in a whisper, in a stage whisper, between the teeth; aside, in an aside; out of earshot

53 LOUDNESS

NOUNS **1 loudness,** intensity, volume, amplitude, fullness; sonorousness, sonority; surge of sound, surge, swell, swelling; loudishness, high volume

2 noisiness, noisefulness, **uproariousness,** racketiness, tumultuousness, thunderousness, clamorousness, clangorousness, boisterousness, obstreperousness; vociferousness 59.5; stridency, stridor; intensity

3 **noise,** loud noise, **blast** 56.3, tintamarre, **racket, din, clamor;** outcry, **uproar,** hue and cry, noise and shouting; howl; clangor, clang, clatter, clap, jangle, rattle; roar, rumble, thunder, thunderclap 56.5; **crash, boom,** sonic boom; **bang,** percussion; brouhaha, **tumult, hubbub,** bobbery <India>, vociferation, ululation; fracas, **brawl,** commotion, drunken brawl; **pandemonium,** bedlam, hell *or* bedlam let loose; charivari, shivaree <nf>; discord 61; shattered silence; cachinnation, stertor, explosion, bombardment; crescendo, forte, fortissimo, tutti

4 <nf terms> row, flap, hullabaloo, brannigan, shindy, donnybrook, free-for-all, shemozzle, rumble, rhubarb, dustup, rumpus, ruckus, ruction, rowdydow, hell broke loose, foofooraw, hoo-ha, Katy-bar-the-door, tzimmes

5 **blare, blast,** shriek 58.4, peal; **toot,** tootle, **honk,** beep, blat, trumpet, report; bay, bray; **whistle,** tweedle, squeal; trumpet call, trumpet blast *or* blare, sound *or* flourish of trumpets, Gabriel's trumpet *or* horn, **fanfare,** tarantara, tantara, tantarara, clarion call; tattoo; taps; full blast

6 **noisemaker;** ticktack, bull-roarer, catcall, whizzer, whizgig, snapper, cricket, clapper, clack, clacker, cracker; firecracker, cherry bomb; rattle, rattlebox; horn, Klaxon <TM>; whistle, thunderer, steam whistle, siren; boiler room, boiler factory; loud-hailer, bullhorn <nf>

VERBS **7** **din; boom,** thunder 56.9; **resound,** ring, peal, ring *or* resound in the ears, din in the ear, **blast the ear,** pierce *or* split *or* rend the ears, rend *or* split the eardrums, split one's head; **deafen,** stun; blast 56.8, **bang, crash** 56.6; **rend the air** *or* skies *or* firmament, rock the sky, fill the air, make the welkin ring; shake *or* rattle the windows; awake *or* startle the echoes, set the echoes ringing, awake the dead, shatter the peace; surge, swell, rise, crescendo; **shout** 59.6

8 **drown out,** outshout, outroar, shout down, overpower, overwhelm; jam

9 **be noisy, make a noise** *or* **racket,** raise a clamor *or* din *or* hue and cry, noise, racket, **clamor,** roar, clangor; brawl, row, rumpus; **make an uproar,** kick up a dust *or* racket, kick up *or* raise a hullabaloo, raise the roof, raise Cain *or* Ned, howl like all the devils of hell, raise the devil, raise hell, whoop it up, maffick <Brit>; not be able to hear oneself think

10 **blare,** blast; shriek 58.8; **toot,** tootle, sound, peal, wind, blow, blat; pipe, trumpet, bugle, clarion; bay, bell, bray; **whistle,** tweedle, squeal; **honk,** honk *or* sound *or* blow the horn, beep; sound taps, sound a tattoo; go off

ADJS **11** **loud,** loud-sounding, forte, fortissimo, crescendo; loudish; **resounding,** ringing, plangent, pealing; full, sonorous; **deafening,** ear-deafening, **ear-splitting,** head-splitting, ear-rending, ear-piercing, piercing; **thunderous,** thundering, tonitruous, tonitruant; **crashing, booming** 56.12; window-rattling, earthshaking, enough to wake the dead *or* the seven sleepers

12 **loud-voiced, loudmouthed,** full-mouthed, full-throated, big-voiced, clarion-voiced, trumpet-voiced, trumpet-tongued, brazen-mouthed, **stentorian,** stentorious, stentorophonic, like Stentor, booming

13 **noisy,** noiseful, rackety, clattery, clangorous, clanging, **clamorous,** clamoursome <Brit nf>, clamant, blatant, blaring, brassy, brazen, blatting; uproarious, **tumultuous,** turbulent, blustering, brawling, **boisterous,** rip-roaring, rowdy, mafficking <Brit>, strepitous, strepitant, obstreperous; vociferous 59.10

ADVS **14** **loudly, aloud,** loud, lustily; **boomingly, thunderously, thunderingly; noisily,** uproariously; ringingly, resoundingly; with a loud voice, at the top of one's voice, at the pitch of one's breath, in full cry, with one wild yell, with a whoop and a hurrah; forte, *fortemente* <Ital>, fortissimo

54 RESONANCE

NOUNS **1 resonance, resoundingness,** resonancy, **sonorousness,** sonority, plangency, **vibrancy;** mellowness, richness, fullness; deepness, lowness, bassness; hollowness; **snore,** snoring

2 reverberation, resounding; rumble, rumbling, thunder, thundering, boom, booming, growl, growling, grumble, grumbling, reboation; rebound, resound, **echo,** reecho

3 ringing, tintinnabulation, **pealing, chiming, tinkling,** tingling, **jingling,** dinging, donging; **tolling,** knelling; clangor, clanking, clanging; **ring, peal, chime; toll,** knell; **tinkle,** tingle, **jingle,** dingle, ding, dingdong, ding-a-ling, ting-a-ling; clink, tink, ting, ping, chink; clank, clang; jangle, jingle-jangle; campanology, bell ringing, change ringing, peal ringing; tinnitis, ringing of *or* in the ear

4 bell, tintinnabulum; **gong,** triangle, **chimes,** door chimes, clock chimes, Westminster chimes; clapper, tongue; carillon, set of bells; ringtone

5 resonator, resounder, reverberator; **sounding board,** soundboard, sound box; resonant chamber *or* cavity; echo chamber; loud pedal, damper pedal, sustaining pedal

VERBS **6 resonate, vibrate,** pulse, throb; snore

7 reverberate, resound, sound, **rumble,** roll, boom, echo, reecho, rebound, bounce back, be reflected, be sent back, echo back, send back, return

8 ring, tintinnabulate, **peal,** sound; **toll,** knell, sound a knell; **chime;** gong; **tinkle,** tingle, **jingle,** ding, dingdong, dong; clink, tink, ting, chink; clank, clang, clangor; jangle, jinglejangle; ring changes *or* peals; ring in the ear

9 <deep voices> bass, basso, basso profundo, baritone, bass-baritone, contralto

ADJS **10 resonant, reverberant, vibrant, sonorous,** plangent, rolling; mellow, rich, full; resonating, reverberating, echoing, reechoing, vibrating, pulsing, throbbing

11 deep, deep-toned, deep-pitched, deep-sounding, deepmouthed, deep-echoing; **hollow, sepulchral; low,** low-pitched, low-toned, grave, heavy; **bass;** baritone; contralto; throaty, gravelly

12 reverberating, reverberant, reverberatory, reboant, **resounding,** rebounding, repercussive, sounding; **rumbling,** thundering, booming, growling; echoing, reechoing, echoic; undamped; persistent, lingering

13 ringing, pealing, tolling, belling, sounding, chiming; **tinkling,** tinkly, tingling, **jingling,** dinging; tintinnabular *or* tintinnabulary *or* tintinnabulous; campanological

55 REPEATED SOUNDS

NOUNS **1 staccato; drum, thrum, beat, pound, roll;** drumming, tom-tom, beating, pounding, thumping; **throb,** throbbing, pulsation 916.3; **palpitation,** flutter; sputter, spatter, splutter; **patter, pitter-patter,** pit-a-pat; rub-a-dub, rattattoo, rataplan, rat-a-tat, rat-tat, rat-tat-tat, tat-tat, tat-tat-tat; clop-clop; **tattoo,** devil's tattoo, ruff, ruffle, paradiddle; **drumbeat,** drum music; drumfire, barrage; echo, re-echo; ringtone

2 clicking, ticking, tick, ticktock, ticktack, ticktick

3 rattle, rattling, brattle, ruckle <Brit nf>, rattletybang; **clatter,** clitter, clunter <Brit nf>, **clitterclatter, chatter,** clack, clacket <nf>; racket 53.3

VERBS **4 drum, thrum, beat, pound, thump, thump out, roll; palpitate,** flutter; sputter, splatter, splutter; patter, pitter-patter, go pit-a-pat *or* pitter-patter; **throb,** pulsate 916.12; beat *or* sound a tattoo, beat a devil's tattoo, ruffle, beat a ruffle

5 tick, ticktock, ticktack, tick away

6 rattle, ruckle <Brit nf>, brattle; **clatter,** clitter, **chatter,** clack; rattle around, clatter about

ADJS **7 staccato; drumming, thrumming, beating, pounding, thump-**

ing; **throbbing;** palpitant, fluttering; sputtering, spattering, spluttering; clicking, ticking

8 **rattly,** rattling, chattering, **clattery,** clattering

56 EXPLOSIVE NOISE

NOUNS 1 **report, crash, crack, clap, bang,** wham, slam, clash, burst; **knock, rap, tap,** smack, whack, thwack, whop, whap, swap <nf>, whomp, splat, crump <Brit nf>, bump, slap, slat <Brit nf>, flap, flop

2 **snap, crack;** click, clack; **crackle,** snapping, cracking, crackling, crepitation, decrepitation, sizzling, spitting; rale

3 **detonation, blast, explosion,** fulmination, **discharge, burst, bang, pop, crack,** bark; **shot,** gunshot; backfire; volley, salvo, fusillade; displosion

4 **boom,** booming, cannonade, **peal, rumble,** grumble, growl, **roll, roar**

5 **thunder,** thundering, clap *or* crash *or* peal of thunder, **thunderclap,** thunderpeal, thundercrack, thunderstroke; peal; thunderstorm 316.3; Thor *or* Donar, Jupiter Tonans, Indra

VERBS 6 **crack, clap, crash,** wham, slam, **bang,** clash; **knock, rap, tap,** smack, whack, thwack, whop, whap, swap <nf>, whomp, splat, crump <Brit nf>, bump, slat <Brit nf>, slap, flap

7 **snap, crack;** click, clack; **crackle,** crepitate, decrepitate; spit

8 **blast, detonate, explode, discharge, burst,** go off, **bang, pop, crack,** bark, fulminate; burst on the ear

9 **boom, thunder, peal, rumble,** grumble, growl, **roll, roar;** peal

ADJS 10 **snapping, cracking, crackling,** crackly, crepitant

11 **banging,** crashing, bursting, exploding, explosive, blasting, cracking, popping; knocking, rapping, tapping; slapping, flapping, slatting <Brit nf>

12 **thundering, thunderous,** thundery, fulminating, tonitruous, tonitruant, thunderlike; **booming,** pealing, rumbling, rolling, roaring; cannonading, volleying; tonant

57 SIBILATION

<hissing sounds>

NOUNS 1 sibilation, sibilance *or* sibilancy; **hiss, hissing,** siss, sissing, white noise; hush, hushing, shush, shushing; sizz, sizzle, sizzling; fizz, fizzle, fizzling, effervescing, effervescence; swish, whish, whoosh; whiz, buzz, zip; siffle; wheeze, *râle* <Fr>, rhonchus; whistle, whistling; sneeze, sneezing, sternutation; snort; snore, stertor; **sniff,** sniffle, snuff, snuffle; spit, sputter, splutter; squash, squish, squelch; sigmatism, lisp; assibilation; frication, frictional rustling; interference, static

VERBS 2 sibilate; **hiss,** siss; hush, shush; sizzle, sizz; fizzle, fizz, effervesce; whiz, buzz, zip; swish, whish, whoosh; whistle; wheeze; sneeze; snort; snore; sniff, sniffle, snuff, snuffle; spit, sputter, splutter; squash, squish, squelch; lisp; assibilate

ADJS 3 **sibilant; hissing,** hushing, sissing; sizzling, fizzling, effervescent; **sniffing,** sniffling, snuffling; snoring; wheezing, wheezy

58 STRIDENCY

<harsh and shrill sounds>

NOUNS 1 **stridency,** stridence, stridor, stridulousness, stridulation; **shrillness,** highness, sharpness, acuteness, arguteness; **screechiness, squeakiness,** creakiness, reediness, pipingness, brassiness

2 **raucousness, harshness,** raucity; discord, cacophony 61.1; coarseness, rudeness, ugliness, roughness, gruffness; **raspiness,** scratchiness, scrapiness, **hoarseness,** huskiness, dryness; stertorousness; roupiness; gutturalness, gutturalism, gutturality, thickness, throatiness; cracked voice

3 **rasp, scratch, scrape,** grind; crunch, craunch, scrunch, crump;

burr, chirr, buzz; snore, snort, stertor; **jangle, clash, jar;** clank, clang, clangor, twang, twanging; blare, blat, bray; croak, caw, cackle; belch; growl, snarl; grumble, groan

4 **screech, shriek, scream, squeal,** shrill, keen, squeak, squawk, skirl, screak, skreak <nf>, skriech *or* skreigh, creak; bleep; **whistle,** wolf-whistle; pipe; **whine, wail, howl,** ululation, yammer; vibrato; waul, caterwaul

5 <insect sounds> **stridulation,** cricking, creaking, chirking; crick, creak, chirk, chirp, chirping, chirrup, scritch

6 <high voices> soprano, mezzo-soprano, treble; tenor, alto; male alto, countertenor; head register, head voice, head tone, falsetto

VERBS 7 **stridulate,** crick, creak, chirk, chirp, chirrup, scritch

8 **screech, shriek,** screak, skreak <nf>, creak, squeak, squawk, **scream, squeal,** shrill, keen; **whistle,** wolf-whistle; pipe, skirl; **whine,** wail, howl, wrawl <Brit nf>, yammer, ululate; waul, caterwaul; raise the roof <nf>

9 <sound harshly> **jangle, clash, jar;** blare, blat, bray; croak, caw, cackle; belch; burr, chirr, buzz; snore; growl, snarl; grumble, groan; clank, clang, clangor; twang

10 **grate, rasp, scratch, scrape,** grind; crunch, craunch, scrunch, crump

11 **grate on,** jar on, grate upon the ear, jar upon the ear, offend the ear, pierce *or* split *or* rend the ears, harrow *or* lacerate the ear, **set the teeth on edge, get on one's nerves,** jangle *or* wrack the nerves, make one's skin crawl

ADJS 12 **strident,** stridulant, stridulous; strident-voiced

13 **high,** high-pitched, high-toned, high-sounding; treble, soprano, mezzo-soprano, tenor, alto, falsetto, countertenor

14 **shrill, thin, sharp,** acute, argute, keen, keening, peeping, **piercing,** penetrating, ear-piercing, ear-splitting; **screechy,** screeching, shrieky, shrieking, **squeaky,** squeaking, screaky, creaky, creaking; whistling, piping, skirling, reedy; whining, wailing, howling, ululating, ululant; vibrato

15 **raucous,** raucid, **harsh,** harsh-sounding; coarse, rude, rough, gruff, ragged; **hoarse, husky,** roupy, cracked, dry; **guttural,** thick, throaty, croaky, croaking; choked, strangled; squawky, **squawking;** brassy, brazen, tinny, metallic; stertorous

16 **grating, jarring,** grinding; **jangling,** jangly; **rasping,** raspy; scratching, scratchy; scraping, scrappy; abrasive

59 CRY, CALL

NOUNS 1 **cry, call, shout, yell,** hoot; halloo, hollo, yo-ho, hello, hi, yo, hail; **whoop, holler** <nf>; **cheer, hurrah**, huzzah, hooray**; howl,** yowl, yawl <Brit nf>; shout-out; bawl, bellow, roar; **scream, shriek,** screech, squeal, squall, caterwaul; yelp, yap, yammer, yawp, bark; war cry, battle cry, war whoop, rallying cry; jeer, boo, hiss, razz; guffah, cachinnation; raspberry, razzing, heckling; Bronx cheer

2 **exclamation,** ejaculation, outburst, blurt, ecphonesis; expletive

3 hunting cry; tallyho, yoicks, view halloo

4 **outcry, vociferation, clamor;** hullabaloo, hubbub, brouhaha, **uproar** 53.3; **hue and cry**

5 vociferousness, vociferance, clamorousness, clamoursomeness <Brit nf>, blatancy; noisiness 53.2

VERBS 6 **cry, call, shout, yell, holler** <nf>, hoot; hail, halloo, hollo; **whoop; cheer** 116.6; **howl,** yowl, yammer, yawl <Brit nf>; squawk, yawp; **bawl, bellow,** roar, roar *or* bellow like a bull; cry *or* yell *or* scream bloody murder *or* blue murder; **scream, shriek,** screech, squeal, squall, waul, caterwaul; yelp, yap, bark; heckle

7 **exclaim,** give an exclamation, ejaculate, burst out, blurt, blurt out, jerk out, spout out; stammer out; shout out

8 vociferate, outcry, **cry out,** call out, bellow out, yell out, holler out <nf>, shout out, sing out; sound off <nf>, pipe up, **clamor,** make *or* raise a clamor; make an outcry, **raise a hue and cry,** make an uproar

9 cry aloud, raise *or* lift up the voice, give voice *or* tongue, shout *or* cry *or* thunder at the top of one's voice, split the throat *or* lungs, strain the voice *or* throat *or* vocal cords, rend the air

ADJS **10 vociferous,** vociferant, vociferating; **clamorous,** clamoursome <Brit nf>; **blatant;** obstreperous, brawling; **noisy;** crying, shouting, **yelling, hollering** <nf>, **bawling,** screaming; yelping, yapping, yappy, yammering; loud-voiced, loud-mouthed, openmouthed, stentorian, Boanergean; booming

11 exclamatory, ejaculatory, blurting

60 ANIMAL SOUNDS

NOUNS **1** animal noise; **call, cry;** mating call *or* cry; grunt, howl, bark, howling, waul, caterwaul, ululation, barking; bird song, birdcall, note, woodnote, clang; stridulation 58.5; dawn chorus; warning cry

VERBS **2** cry, call; **howl,** yowl, yawp, yawl <nf>, ululate; wail, whine, pule; **squeal,** squall, scream, screech, screak, squeak; troat; **roar; bellow,** blare, **bawl; moo,** low; **bleat,** blate, blat; **bray; whinny, neigh,** whicker, nicker, bray; **bay,** bay at the moon, bell; **bark,** woof, latrate, give voice *or* tongue; **yelp, yap,** yip; **mew,** mewl, **meow,** miaow, waul, caterwaul; weal

3 grunt, gruntle <Brit nf>, oink; **snort**

4 growl, snarl, grumble, gnarl, snap; hiss, spit

5 <birds> **warble, sing,** carol, call; pipe, whistle; **trill,** chirr, roll; **twitter,** tweet, twit, chatter, chitter; **chirp,** chirrup, chirk, **cheep,** peep, pip; **quack,** honk, cronk; **croak, caw; squawk,** scold, screech; **crow,** cock-a-doodle-doo; **cackle,** gaggle, gabble, guggle, **cluck,** clack, chuck; **gobble; hoot,** hoo; **coo; cuckoo;** drum; tu-whit tu-whoo; whoop

ADJS **6 howling,** yowling, crying, wailing, whining, puling, bawling, ululant, blatant; barking; lowing, mugient, snarling, growling; singing, humming

61 DISCORD

<dissonant sounds>

NOUNS **1 discord,** discordance *or* discordancy, **dissonance** *or* dissonancy, diaphony, **cacophony;** stridor, stridency; **inharmoniousness,** unharmoniousness, disharmony, inharmony; **unmelodiousness,** unmusicalness, unmusicality, untunefulness, tunelessness; atonality, atonalism; flatness, sharpness, sourness <nf>; dissonant chord, wolf; false note, sour note *and* clinker *and* clam <nf>, off note; cipher; dodecaphonism *or* dodecaphony

2 clash, jangle, jar; noise, mere noise, confusion *or* conflict *or* jarring *or* jostling of sounds; Babel, witches' *or* devils' chorus; harshness 58.2; clamor 53.3

VERBS **3** sound *or* strike *or* hit a sour note <nf>, hit a clinker *or* a clam <nf>; not carry a tune; **clash, jar, jangle,** conflict, jostle; grate 58.10,11; untune, unstring; hurt the ears

ADJS **4 dissonant, discordant, cacophonous**, disconsonant, diaphonic; strident, shrill, harsh, raucous, grating 58.16; **inharmonious,** unharmonious, disharmonious, disharmonic, inharmonic; **unmelodious,** immelodious, nonmelodious; **unmusical,** musicless, nonmusical, untuneful, tuneless; untunable, untuned, atonal, toneless; droning, singsong; cracked, **out of tune,** out of tone, out of pitch; **off-key, off-tone, off-pitch,** off; flat, sharp, **sour** <nf>

5 clashing, jarring, jangling, jangly, confused, conflicting, jostling, warring, ajar; **harsh,** hoarse, **grating** 58.16

62 TASTE

<sense of taste>

NOUNS 1 **taste,** *goût* <Fr>; sense of taste; **flavor,** sapor; **smack, tang; savor, relish,** sapidity, deliciousness; palate, tongue, tooth, stomach; taste in the mouth, taste perception; sweetness, sourness, bitterness, bittersweetness, saltiness; sharp taste, acid taste, tart taste, salty taste, spicy taste, sweet taste, sour taste, bitter taste, pungent taste; aftertaste; tang; savoriness 63

2 **sip, sup, lick, bite,** try, nip

3 tinge, soupçon, smack hint 248.4

4 **sample, specimen, taste,** taste test, taster, little bite, little smack, taste treat; tidbit, sampler; example 786.2; appetizer, hors d'oeuvre, canape, aperitif, starter <Brit>, tapas, little plate

5 taste bud *or* bulb *or* goblet, taste *or* gustatory cell, taste hair; **tongue,** lingua; **palate**

6 **tasting, savoring,** gustation, nibble, nip, sampling

VERBS 7 **taste,** taste of, sample, degust, partake; **savor,** savor of, relish; try; sip, sup <nf>, roll on the tongue, test; lick; smack

ADJS 8 **gustatory,** gustative; tastable, gustable

9 **flavored,** flavorous, flavory, sapid, saporous, saporific; tasty, savory, flavorful 63.9; sweet, sour, bitter, bittersweet, salt

10 **lingual,** glossal; **tonguelike,** linguiform, lingulate

63 SAVORINESS

NOUNS 1 **savoriness, palatableness,** palatability, **tastiness,** toothsomeness, goodness, good taste, right taste, **deliciousness,** gustatory delightfulness, scrumptiousness *and* yumminess <nf>, lusciousness, delectability, **flavorfulness,** flavorsomeness, flavorousness, flavoriness, good flavor, fine flavor, sapidity; full flavor, full-bodied flavor; gourmet quality; succulence, juiciness; sapidity, sapidness

2 **savor, relish, zest, gusto,** *goût* <Fr>; richness

3 **flavoring, flavor,** flavorer; **seasoning,** seasoner, **relish, condiment, spice,** condiment; flavor enhancer; artificial flavoring

VERBS 4 **taste good,** tickle *or* flatter *or* delight the palate, tempt *or* whet the appetite, make one's mouth water, melt in one's mouth

5 **savor, relish,** like, love, be fond of, be partial to, enjoy, delight in, have a soft spot for, appreciate; smack the lips; do justice to; taste 62.7

6 **savor of, taste of, smack of,** have a relish of, have the flavor of, taste like

7 **flavor,** savor; **season,** salt, pepper, **spice,** sauce

ADJS 8 **tasty,** fit to eat *and* finger-lickin' good <nf>, good-tasting, **savory,** savorous, **palatable, toothsome,** gustable, sapid, **good,** good to eat, nice, agreeable, likable, pleasing, mouth-watering, to one's taste, **delicious,** delightful, delectable, exquisite; delicate, dainty; juicy, succulent, **luscious,** lush; for the gods, ambrosial, nectarous, nectareous; fit for a king, gourmet, fit for a gourmet, of gourmet quality, epicurean; scrumptious *and* yummy <nf>

9 **flavorful, flavorsome,** flavorous, flavory, well-flavored; full-flavored, full-bodied; nutty, fruity; **rich,** rich-flavored; sapid

10 **appetizing, mouth-watering, tempting,** tantalizing, provocative, piquant

64 UNSAVORINESS

NOUNS 1 **unsavoriness, unpalatableness,** unpalatability, **distastefulness,** untastefulness; bad taste, bad taste in the mouth

2 acridness, acridity, tartness, sharpness, causticity, astringence *or* astringency, acerbity, **sourness** 67; pungency 68; **bitterness,** bitter taste; gall, gall and wormwood, wormwood, bitter pill

3 **nastiness, foulness, vileness, loathsomeness, repulsiveness, obnoxiousness,** odiousness, offensiveness,

disgustingness, nauseousness; **rankness,** rancidity, rancidness, overripeness, rottenness, malodorousness, fetor, fetidness; yuckiness <nf>; repugnance 99.2; nauseant, emetic, sickener

VERBS 4 **disgust, repel,** turn one's stomach, nauseate; make one's gorge rise; gross one out <nf>

ADJS 5 **unsavory, unpalatable, unappetizing,** untasteful, untasty, ill-flavored, foul-tasting, **distasteful,** dislikable, unlikable, uninviting, unpleasant, unpleasing, displeasing, disagreeable

6 **bitter,** bitter as gall *or* wormwood, amaroidal; **acrid,** sharp, caustic, tart, astringent; hard, harsh, rough, coarse; acerb, acerbic, sour; pungent

7 **nasty, offensive** 98.18, fulsome, noisome, noxious, rebarbative, mawkish, cloying, brackish, **foul, vile,** bad; gross *and* icky *and* yucky <nf>, **sickening, nauseating,** nauseous, nauseant, vomity *and* barfy <nf>; poisonous, toxic, rank, rancid, maggoty, weevily, spoiled, overripe, high, rotten, stinking, putrid, malodorous, fetid

8 **inedible, uneatable,** not fit to eat *or* drink, undrinkable, impotable; unfit for human consumption

65 INSIPIDNESS

NOUNS 1 **insipidness,** insipidity, **tastelessness, flavorlessness,** blandness, savorlessness, saplessness, unsavoriness, dullness; **weakness, thinness,** mildness, **wishy-washiness,** namby-pambyness; **flatness, staleness,** lifelessness, deadness; vapidity, inanity, jejunity, jejuneness; adulteration, dilution; pablum

ADJS 2 **insipid, tasteless, flavorless,** bland, nondescript, unexciting, plain, spiceless, **savorless,** sapless, unsavory, unflavored, unseasoned; pulpy, pappy, gruelly, pasty; **weak, thin,** mild, **wishy-washy,** milktoast, washy, watery, watered, watered-down, diluted, dilute, milk-and-water, dishwater; **flat, stale,** dead, *fade* <Fr>; vapid, inane, jejune; unappetizing; indifferent, characterless, neither one thing nor the other

66 SWEETNESS

NOUNS 1 **sweetness,** sweet, sweetishness, saccharinity, dulcitude; **sugariness,** syrupiness; oversweetness, mawkishness, cloyingness, sickly-sweetness; sweet tooth; confectionery, sweet-shop <Brit>, candy store, bakery

2 **sweetening,** edulcoration; sweetener; sugar, cane sugar, beet sugar, sugar lump, sugar loaf, caster sugar, granulated sugar, powdered sugar, brown sugar, turbinado sugar; sweetening agent, sugar-substitute, artificial sweetener, saccharin, aspartame, NutraSweet <TM>, cyclamates, sodium cyclamate, calcium cyclamate; molasses, blackstrap, treacle <Brit>; syrup, maple syrup, cane syrup, corn syrup, sorghum, golden syrup *or* treacle <Brit>; **honey,** honeycomb, honeypot, comb honey, clover honey; honeydew; **nectar, ambrosia;** sugarcoating; sweets, candy, dessert; sugar-making; sugaring off; saccharification

VERBS 3 **sweeten,** dulcify, edulcorate *or* dulcorate; **sugar;** honey, nectarize; sugarcoat, glaze, candy; ice, frost, glaze; mull; saccharify; sugar off

ADJS 4 **sweet,** sweetish, sweetened; sacchariferous, saccharine; **sugary,** sugared, candied, **honeyed,** syrupy; mellifluous, mellifluent; melliferous, nectarous, nectareous, ambrosial; sugarsweet, honeysweet, sweet as sugar *or* honey, sweet as a nut; sugar-coated; bittersweet; sour-sweet, sweet-sour, sweet and sour, sweet and pungent

5 **oversweet,** saccharine, rich, **cloying,** mawkish, luscious, sickly-sweet

67 SOURNESS

NOUNS 1 **sourness,** sour, sourishness, **tartness,** tartishness, acerbity, astringency, verjuice; acescency; acidity, acidulousness; hyperacidity, subacidity; vinegariness; unsweetness, **dryness; pungency** 68; greenness, unripeness; bitterness, sharpness

2 **sour; vinegar,** acidulant; **pickle,** sour pickle, dill pickle, bread-and-butter pickle; verjuice; lemon, lime, crab apple, green apple, sour cherry; aloe; sourgrass; sour balls; sourdough; sour cream, sour milk; bitters; wormwood; **acid**

3 **souring,** acidification, acidulation, acetification, acescence; fermentation; turning

VERBS 4 **sour,** turn sour *or* acid, turn, go sour, sharpen, **acidify,** acidulate, acetify; ferment; set one's teeth on edge; curdle, spoil, turn, ferment, go off, go bad, molder

ADJS 5 **sour,** soured, sourish; **tart,** tartish; tangy, pungent; crab, **crabbed;** acerb, acerbic, acerbate, acrid; acescent; **vinegarish,** vinegary, sour as vinegar; pickled; lemony; **pungent** 68.6; unsweet, unsweetened, **dry,** sec; green, unripe

6 **acid,** acidulous, acidulent, acidulated; acetic, acetous, acetose; hyperacid; subacid, subacidulous

68 PUNGENCY

NOUNS 1 **pungency, piquancy, poignancy**, spiciness; strong flavor; **sharpness, keenness,** edge, **causticity,** astringency, mordancy, severity, asperity, trenchancy, cuttingness, bitingness, penetratingness, harshness, roughness, **acridity; bitterness** 64.2; acerbity, acidulousness, acidity, **sourness** 67; aroma

2 **zest,** zestfulness, zestiness, **briskness,** liveliness, raciness; **nippiness, tanginess,** snappiness; **spiciness,** pepperiness, hotness, fieriness; **tang, spice,** relish; **nip, bite**, kick; sting, punch, snap, zip, ginger, sharpness; **kick,** guts <nf>; heat

3 **strength,** strongness; high flavor, highness, rankness, gaminess

4 **saltiness, salinity,** brininess; brackishness; **salt; brine;** pepperiness

VERBS 5 **bite, nip,** cut, penetrate, bite the tongue, sting, kick, make the eyes water, go up the nose

ADJS 6 **pungent, piquant, poignant; sharp, keen,** piercing, penetrating, nose-tickling, aromatic, stinging, **biting, acrid,** astringent, irritating, harsh, rough, **spicy**, severe, asperous, cutting, trenchant; **caustic,** vitriolic, mordant, escharotic; **bitter** 64.6; acerbic, acid, **sour**, tart, sharp

7 **zestful,** zesty, **brisk,** lively, racy, zippy, **nippy,** snappy, **tangy,** with a kick, strong; spiced, seasoned, high-seasoned, savory; **spicy,** curried, **peppery,** hot, burning, hot as pepper; mustardy; like horseradish, like Chinese mustard

8 **strong,** strong-flavored, strong-tasting; **high,** highly flavored, highy seasoned, high-tasted; **rank, gamy**, racy

9 **salty,** salt, salted, saltish, **saline, briny; brackish;** pickled

69 ODOR

NOUNS 1 **odor, smell, scent,** aroma, flavor, savor; **essence,** definite odor, redolence, effluvium, emanation, exhalation, fume, breath, subtle odor, whiff, wafture, trace, detectable odor; trail, spoor; **fragrance** 70; **stink, stench** 71, funk

2 **odorousness, smelliness,** headiness, pungency 68; aromatherapy

3 smelling, olfaction, nosing, scenting; sniffing, snuffing, snuffling, whiffing, odorizing, odorization

4 **sense of smell,** smell, smelling, scent, olfaction, olfactory sense

5 olfactory organ; olfactory pit, olfactory cell, olfactory area, **nose; nostrils,** noseholes <nf>, nares, naris, nasal cavity; olfactory nerves; **olfactories;** scent gland, pheromone

VERBS 6 <have an odor> **smell,** be aromatic, smell of, be redolent of; emit *or* emanate *or* give out a smell, reach one's nostrils, yield an odor *or* aroma, breathe, exhale; reek, **stink** 71.4; pong <Brit nf>

7 odorize; scent, aromatize, perfume 70.8

8 **smell, scent,** nose; **sniff,** snuff, snuffle, inhale, breathe, breathe in; get a noseful of, smell of, catch a smell of, get *or* take a whiff of,

whiff, get wind of, follow one's nose

ADJS 9 **odorous,** odoriferous, odiferous, odored, odorant, olent, **smelling, smelly,** smellsome, olent, **redolent, aromatic;** effluvious; **fragrant** 70.9; **stinking, malodorous** 71.5; emanative, pheromonal

10 **strong,** strong-smelling, strong-scented; **pungent,** penetrating, nose-piercing, sharp, heady; reeking, reeky; funky, foul; suffocating, stifling; noisome, noxious

11 **smellable,** sniffable, whiffable

12 **olfactory,** olfactive

13 keen-scented, quick-scented, sharp- *or* keen-nosed, **with a nose for**

70 FRAGRANCE

NOUNS 1 **fragrance,** fragrancy, **perfume, aroma,** scent, redolence, balminess, **incense, bouquet,** nosegay, sweet smell, sweet savor; **odor** 69; spice, spiciness; muskiness; fruitiness; perfume dynamics, aromatherapy

2 perfumery, *parfumerie* <Fr>; **perfume,** *parfum* <Fr>, eau de parfum, **scent, essence,** extract; aromatic, ambrosia; attar, essential *or* volatile oil; aromatic water; balsam, **balm,** aromatic gum; myrrh; bay oil, myrcia oil; champaca oil; rose oil, attar of roses, lavender oil, heliotrope, jasmine oil, bergamot oil; fixative, musk, civet, ambergris, patchouli, musk

3 **toilet water,** Florida water; rose water, *eau de rose* <Fr>; lavender water; cologne, cologne water, eau de Cologne; bay rum; **lotion,** aftershave lotion

4 **incense;** joss stick; pastille; frankincense *or* olibanum; agalloch *or* aloeswood, calambac, lignaloes *or* linaloa, sandalwood, frangipani, resin, myrrh, eucalyptus, attar, ambergris, patchouli

5 **perfumer,** *parfumeur* <Fr>; thurifer, censer bearer, censer, thurible; **perfuming,** censing, thurification, odorizing

6 <articles> perfumer, *parfumoir* <Fr>, fumigator, scenter, odorator, odorizer; atomizer, purse atomizer, spray; censer, thurible, incensory, incense burner; vinaigrette, scent bottle, smelling bottle, scent box, scent ball; scent strip; scent bag, sachet; pomander; potpourri; scratch-and-sniff; dryer sheet

VERBS 7 **be fragrant,** smell sweet, **smell good,** please the nostrils, smell like a rose

8 **perfume, scent,** cense, incense, thurify, aromatize, odorize, fumigate, embalm

ADJS 9 **fragrant, aromatic,** odoriferous, redolent, perfumy, **perfumed, scented, sweet, sweet-smelling,** sweet-scented, savory, balmy, ambrosial, incense-breathing; thuriferous; **odorous** 69.9; sweet as a rose, fragrant as new-mown hay; pungent, heady; flowery; fruity; musky; spicy; aromatherapeutic

71 STENCH

NOUNS 1 **stench, stink,** funk, malodor, fetidness, fetidity, fetor, foul *or* bad odor, offensive odor, unpleasant smell, offense to the nostrils, bad smell, niff *and* pong <Brit nf>, rotten smell, noxious stench, smell *or* stench of decay, **reek,** reeking, nidor; fug *and* frowst <Brit nf>; mephitis, miasma, graveolence, effluvium, osmidrosis; body odor *or* BO; halitosis, **bad breath,** foul breath

2 **fetidness,** fetidity, malodourousness, **smelliness,** stinkingness, **odorousness,** noisomeness, **rankness, foulness,** putridness, offensiveness; repulsiveness; **mustiness,** funkiness, must, frowst *or* frowstiness <Brit nf>, moldiness, mildew, fustiness, frowziness, stuffiness; staleness; **rancidness,** rancidity, reastiness <Brit nf>; rottenness 393.7; putrefaction, putrescence, decay, gaminess

3 **stinker,** stinkard; skunk *or* polecat *or* rotten egg; stink ball, stinkpot, stink bomb; mothball; flatus, fart, cesspool, hydrogen sulfide, sulfur dioxide

VERBS 4 **stink,** smell, **smell bad,** niffy *and* pong <Brit nf>, assail *or* offend the nostrils, stink in the nostrils, stink to heaven *or* high heaven, smell of rotten eggs; **reek;** smell up, stink up; stink out

ADJS **5 malodorous, fetid,** olid, **odorous, stinking, reeking,** reeky, nidorous, smelling, bad-smelling, **evil-smelling,** foul-smelling, ill-smelling, heavy-smelling, **smelly**, niffy *and* pongy <Brit nf>, stenchy; **foul,** vile, putrid, bad, fulsome, noisome, fecal, feculent, excremental, offensive, repulsive, noxious, sulfurous, graveolent; rotten; **rank,** strong, high, gamy; **rancid,** reasty *or* reasy <Brit nf>; **musty,** funky, fusty, frowy <nf>, frowzy, frowsty <Brit>, stuffy, moldy, mildewed, mildewy; mephitic, miasmic, miasmal; crappy; asphyxiating

72 ODORLESSNESS

NOUNS **1 odorlessness, inodorousness,** lack of smell, scentlessness, scentlessness, smell-lessness; inoffensiveness; anosmia

2 deodorizing, deodorization, fumigation, ventilation; freshness, fresh air; smoke-free area, no-smoking area

3 deodorant, deodorizer; antiperspirant; fumigant, fumigator; mouthwash, breath freshener; ventilator, air filter, air purifier

VERBS **4 deodorize,** fumigate; ventilate, freshen the air; cleanse

ADJS **5 odorless,** inodorous, nonodorous, smell-less, **scentless,** unscented; fragrance-free; smoke-free, smokeless; fumigated; neutral-smelling; inoffensive; in the fresh air

6 deodorant, deodorizing, freshening

73 TOUCH

NOUNS **1 touch;** sense of touch, tactile sense, tactual sensation, cutaneous sense; taction, **contact** 223.5; **feel,** feeling; hand-mindedness; light touch, lambency, whisper, breath, **kiss,** lip-clap <nf>, **caress,** fondling; loving touch; lick, lap; **brush,** graze, grazing, glance, glancing; stroke, rub; tap, flick; fingertip caress; tentative poke

2 touching, feeling, fingering, palpation, palpating; **handling,** manipulation, manipulating; petting, caressing, stroking, massaging, rubbing, frottage, frication, friction 1044; laying on of hands, fondling; pressure 902.2; feeling up <nf>; osteopathy, chiropractic

3 touchableness, **tangibility, palpability,** tactility, sensitivity, feel

4 feeler, tactile organ, tactor; tactile cell; tactile process, tactile corpuscle, **antenna;** tactile hair, vibrissa; cat whisker; barbel, barbule; palp, palpus; tentaculum

5 finger, digit; forefinger, index finger, index; ring finger, annulary; middle finger, medius, dactylion; little finger, pinkie *or* pinky <nf>, minimus; thumb, pollex

VERBS **6 touch, feel,** feel of, palpate; **finger,** pass *or* run the fingers over, feel with the fingertips, thumb; **handle,** palm, paw; **manipulate,** wield, ply; twiddle; poke at, prod, paw; tap, flick; come in contact 223.10

7 touch lightly, touch upon; kiss, **brush,** sweep, graze, brush by, glance, scrape, skim

8 stroke, pet, caress, fondle; **nuzzle,** nose, rub noses; feel up <nf>; rub, rub against, snuggle, massage, knead 1047.6

9 lick, lap, tongue, mouth

ADJS **10 tactile,** tactual; hand-minded

11 touchable, **palpable, tangible,** tactile, tactual; touchy-feely

12 lightly touching, lambent, playing lightly over, barely touching, grazing, skimming, tickling

74 SENSATIONS OF TOUCH

NOUNS **1 tingle,** tingling, thrill, buzz; **prickle,** prickles, prickling, pins and needles; **sting,** stinging, urtication; paresthesia

2 tickle, tickling, **titillation,** pleasant stimulation, **ticklishness,** tickliness

3 itch, itching, itchiness; pruritus; prurigo

4 creeps *and* **cold creeps** *and* shivers *and* **cold shivers** <nf>, creeping of the flesh; gooseflesh, goose bumps, goose pimples; formication

VERBS **5** **tingle,** thrill; **itch;** scratch; **prickle,** prick, sting

6 **tickle, titillate,** thrill

7 **feel creepy,** feel funny, creep, crawl, **have the creeps** *or* **cold creeps** *or* the heebie-jeebies *or* abdabs <nf>; have gooseflesh *or* goose bumps; give one the creeps *or* the willies <nf>

ADJS **8** **tingly,** tingling, atingle; **prickly,** prickling

9 **ticklish,** tickling, tickly, **titillative**

10 **itchy,** itching; pruriginous

11 **creepy, crawly,** creepy-crawly, formicative

75 SEX

NOUNS **1** **sex,** gender; male, maleness, masculinity 76, female, femaleness, femininity 77; **genitals, genitalia**

2 **sexuality,** sexual nature, sexualism, sex life, love life; sex education, birds and the bees; **love** 104, sexual activity, lovemaking 562, marriage 563; heterosexuality; homosexuality; bisexuality, ambisexuality; **carnality, sensuality** 663; sexiness, voluptuousness, flesh, fleshiness; **libido,** sex drive, sexual instinct *or* urge; **potency** 76.2; impotence; frigidity, coldness

3 **sex appeal,** sexual attraction *or* attractiveness *or* magnetism, sexiness, animal magnetism

4 **sex object;** piece *and* meat *and* piece of meat *and* ass *and* piece of ass *and* hot number <nf>; nooky *or* nookie; sex queen, sex goddess, sex kitten; hottie; skirt <nf>; hunk, sex god; beefcake *or* stud *or* stud muffin <nf>, pretty boy

5 **sexual desire,** sensuous *or* carnal desire, bodily appetite, **biological urge,** venereal appetite *or* desire, sexual longing, **lust,** desire, lusts *or* desires of the flesh, itch, horniness, lech <nf>, chemistry; **erection,** penile erection, hard-on <nf>; **passion,** carnal *or* sexual passion, fleshly lust, prurience *or* pruriency, concupiscence, hot blood, aphrodisia, the hots *and* hot pants *and* hot rocks *and* hot nuts <nf>, G-spot; lustfulness, goatishness, libidinousness; lasciviousness 665.5; **eroticism,** erotism; indecency 666; erotomania, eromania, *hysteria libidinosa* <L>; nymphomania, andromania, *furor uterinus* <L>; satyrism, satyriasis, gynecomania; infantile sexuality, polymorphous perversity; **heat,** rut, mating instinct; frenzy *or* fury of lust; estrus, estrum, estrous cycle, estral cycle

6 **aphrodisiac, love potion, philter,** love philter; cantharis, blister beetle, Spanish fly

7 **copulation, sex act,** having sex, having intercourse, *le sport* <Fr>, coupling, mating, pairing, intimacy, coition, **coitus,** pareunia, venery, copula <law>, **sex, intercourse, sexual intercourse,** cohabitation, commerce, sexual commerce, congress, sexual congress, sexual union, sexual relations, relations, marital relations, marriage act, consummation, act of love, making love, sleeping together *or* with, going to bed with, going all the way <nf>; screwing *and* balling *and* nookie *and* diddling *and* making it with <nf>; consenting adult; meat *and* ass <nf>, intimacy, connection, carnal knowledge, aphrodisia; foreplay; **oral sex,** oral-genital stimulation, fellatio, fellation, blow job <nf>, cunnilingus, sixty-nine <nf>; **anal sex,** anal intercourse, sodomy, buggery <nf>; **orgasm,** climax, sexual climax; unlawful sexual intercourse, adultery, hanky-panky, fornication 665.7; coitus interruptus, onanism; tantric sex; group sex, group grope <nf>; serial sex, gang bang <nf>; spouse swapping, wife swapping, husband swapping; casual sex, one-night stand *or* quickie; phone sex; safe sex; sex shop; **lovemaking** 562; **procreation** 78; germ cell, sperm, ovum 305.12

8 **masturbation,** autoeroticism, self-abuse, onanism, manipulation, playing with oneself, jacking off *and* jerking off *and* pulling off *and* hand job <nf>, wank <nf>; sexual fantasy; wet dream; manustupration

9 **sexlessness,** asexuality, neuterness, nonsexualness; **impotence** 19; frigidity; eunuch, spado, neuter, gelding; steer

10 **sexual preference; sexual orientation;** sexual normality, sexual nature; **heterosexuality; homosexuality,** homosexualism, homoeroticism, homophilia, *l'amour bleu* <Fr>, the love that dare not speak its name, sexual inversion, lesbianism, sapphism, tribadism; alternative lifestyle; autoeroticism; transsexuality; **bisexuality,** bisexualism, ambisexuality, ambisextrousness, amphierotism, swinging *or* going both ways <nf>; **lesbianism,** sapphism, tribadism *or* tribady; **sexual prejudice,** sexism, genderism, phallicism, heterosexism, homosexism; coming out of the closet <nf>

11 **perversion,** sexual deviation, sexual deviance, sexual perversion, sexual abnormality; sexual pathology; psychosexual disorder; sexual psychopathy, *psychopathia sexualis* <L>; paraphilia; zoophilia, zooerastia, bestiality; pedophilia; algolagnia, algolagny, **sadomasochism** *or* s and m; active algolagnia, **sadism;** passive algolagnia, **masochism;** satyrism; fetishism; narcissism; pederasty, pedophilia; exhibitionism; nymphomania; necrophilia; coprophilia; scotophilia, voyeurism; transvestitism, cross-dressing; **incest,** incestuousness, **sex crime**, sexual offense; **sexual abuse,** carnal abuse, molestation; sexual harassment; unlawful sexual intercourse, rape, date rape; cybersex

12 **intersexuality,** intersexualism, epicenism, epicenity; hermaphroditism, pseudohermaphroditism; androgynism, androgyny, gynandry, gynandrism; transsexuality, transsexualism

13 **heterosexual, straight** <nf>, breeder <nf>

14 **homosexual,** gay person, homosexualist, homophile, invert; catamite, *mignon* <Fr>, Ganymede, chicken *and* punk *and* gunsel <nf>; **bisexual,** bi-guy <nf>; **lesbian,** sapphist, tribade; gay pride, gay rights

15 <nf terms for male homosexuals> homo, queer, faggot, fag, fruit, flit, fairy, pansy, nance, auntie, queen, drag queen, closet queen, fruitcake, poof *and* poofter *and* poove <Brit>; <nf terms for female homosexuals> dyke, bull dyke, butchfemme, boondagger, diesel-dyke, lesbo, lez

16 sexual pervert; **pervert,** perve <nf>, **deviant,** deviate, sex pervert, sex fiend, sex criminal, sexual psychopath; sodomist, sodomite, sob <Brit nf>, bugger; pederast; paraphiliac; zoophiliac; pedophiliac; sadist; masochist; sadomasochist, algolagniac; fetishist; transvestite *or* TV, cross-dresser; narcissist; exhibitionist; necrophiliac; coprophiliac; scotophiliac, voyeur; erotomaniac, nymphomaniac, satyr, horndog <nf>; rapist 665.12

17 **intersex,** sex-intergrade, epicence; hermaphrodite, pseudohermaphrodite; androgyne, gynandroid; transsexual

18 **sexology,** sex study, sexologist; sexual counselor; sexual surrogate; sexual customs *or* mores *or* practices; sexual morality; new morality, sexual revolution; sexual freedom *or* liberation, free love; trial marriage

VERBS **19** sex, sexualize; genderize

20 lust, **lust after,** itch for, have a lech *and* have hot pants for <nf>, **desire; be in heat** *or* **rut,** rut, come in; get physical <nf>; get an erection, get a hard-on <nf>, tumesce

21 **copulate,** couple, **mate,** have intercourse, unite in sexual intercourse, **have sexual relations, have sex,** pair, make out <nf>, perform the act of love *or* marriage act, come together, cohabit, cohabitate, shack up <nf>, be intimate; sleep with *or* together, lie with, go to bed with, bonk; fuck *and* screw *and* lay *and* ball *and* frig *and* diddle and do it *and* **make it with** <nf>, go all the way, go to bed with, lie together, get laid <nf>; cover, mount, serve *or* service <of animals>; commit adultery, fornicate 665.19; **make love**

22 **masturbate,** play with *or* abuse oneself, jack off *and* whack off

<nf>; fellate, suck *and* suck off <nf>; sodomize, bugger *and* ream <nf>

23 **stimulate,** have foreplay; go down on, give head, suck *or* suck off

24 **climax, come,** achieve satisfaction, achieve *or* reach orgasm; **ejaculate,** get off <nf>

ADJS **25** **sexual,** sex, sexlike, gamic, coital, libidinal, **erotic,** appealing, amorous, magnetic; nuptial; venereal; **carnal, sensual** 663.5, voluptuous, fleshly; desirable, baddable; **sexy;** erogenous, erogenic, erotogenic, ginchy <nf>; sexed, oversexed, hypersexual; procreative 78.15; potent 76.13

26 **aphrodisiac,** aphroditous, **arousing,** stimulating, eroticizing, venereal

27 **lustful, prurient, hot,** steamy, sexy, concupiscent, lickerish, libidinous, **salacious** 666.9, **passionate,** hot-blooded, itching, **horny** *and* hot to trot *and* sexed-up *and* hot and bothered <nf>, excited, aroused, randy, goatish, sexed-up, randy; sex-starved, unsatisfied; lascivious 665.29; **orgasmic,** orgastic, **ejaculatory**

28 **in heat, burning, hot; in rut,** rutting, rutty, ruttish; in must, must, musty; estrous, estral, estrual

29 **unsexual,** unsexed; **sexless,** asexual, esexual, **neuter,** neutral, neutered; castrated, emasculated, eunuchized; **cold, frigid; impotent;** frustrated; undersexed

30 **homosexual,** homoerotic, gay, queer *and* limp-wristed *and* faggoty <nf>; **bisexual,** bisexed, ambisexual, ambisextrous, amphierotic, AC-DC <nf>, autoerotic; lesbian, sapphic, tribadistic; butch *and* dykey <nf>; effeminate 77.14; transvestite; outed; gay-friendly

31 hermaphrodite, hermaphroditic, pseudohermaphrodite, pseudohermaphroditic, epicene, monoclinous; androgynous, androgynal, gynandrous, gynandrian

76 MASCULINITY

NOUNS **1** **masculinity,** masculineness, maleness; **manliness,** manlihood, **manhood,** manfulness, manlikeness; mannishness; gentlemanliness, gentlemanlikeness; boyishness; tomboyishness; a guy thing <nf>

2 **male sex, male sexuality, virility,** virileness, virilism, potence *or* **potency,** sexual power, manly vigor, **machismo;** ultramasculinity; phallicism; male superiority

3 **mankind, man, men, manhood,** menfolk *or* menfolks <nf>, the sword side, patriarchy

4 **male,** male being, masculine; he, him, his, himself; **man,** male person, *homme* <Fr>, *hombre* <Sp>; **gentleman,** gent <nf>

5 <nf terms> **guy,** fellow, feller, lad, blade, chap, chappie, cat, duck, stud, joker, jasper, bugger, bastard, bloke *and* cove *and* johnny *and* bod <Brit nf>, body, dude, gent, Joe, Adam, bud

6 **real man, he-man,** *and* two-fisted man <nf>, hunk *and* jockstrap *and* jock <nf>, man with hair on his chest; caveman *and* bucko <nf>, beefcake

7 <forms of address> **Mister, Mr,** Messrs <pl>, Master; **sir,** my good man, gentleman, my dear sir *or* man; esquire; *monsieur* or *M* <Fr>, *messieurs* or *MM* <Fr pl>; *signor* and *signore* and *signorino* <Ital>; *señor* and *Sr* and *don* <Sp>, *Dom, senhor* <Pg>; *Herr* and *mein Herr* <Ger>; *mijnheer* <Dutch>, *sahib* <India>, *sri* or *babu* <Hindu>; *bwana* <Swah>

8 <male animals> cock, rooster, chanticleer; cockerel; drake; gander; peacock; tom turkey, tom, turkey-cock, gobbler, turkey gobbler; dog; boar; stag, hart, buck; stallion, studhorse, stud, top horse <nf>, entire horse, entire, colt; tomcat, tom; he-goat, billy goat, billy; boar, hog; ram, tup <Brit>; wether; bull, bullock, top cow <nf>; steer, stot <Brit nf>; drone

9 <mannish female> **amazon,** virago, androgyne; lesbian, butch *and* dyke <nf>; **tomboy,** hoyden, romp

10 **man of the family,** family man, married man, husband, widower, househusband, patriarch, paterfamilias, father, papa <nf>; son, brother, uncle, nephew, godfather, godson, grandfather, grandson, grandpa

VERBS **11** masculinize, virilize

ADJS **12** **masculine, male,** bull, he-; **manly, manlike, mannish,** manful, andric; uneffeminate; **gentlemanly,** gentlemanlike; yang

13 **virile, potent,** viripotent; ultramasculine, **macho, he-mannish** *and* hunky <nf>, two-fisted <nf>, broad-shouldered, hairy-chested

14 **mannish, mannified; unwomanly, unfeminine,** uneffeminate, viraginous; **tomboyish,** hoyden, rompish

77 FEMININITY

NOUNS **1** **femininity,** feminality, feminacy, feminineness, femaleness, femineity, feminism; **womanliness,** womanlikeness, womanishness, **womanhood,** womanity, muliebrity; girlishness, little-girlishness; maidenhood, maidenliness; **ladylikeness,** gentlewomanliness; **matronliness,** matriarchy, matronage, matronhood, matronship; the eternal feminine; a girl thing <nf>

2 **effeminacy, unmanliness,** effeminateness, epicenity, epicenism, **womanishness,** muliebrity, **sissiness** <nf>, prissiness <nf>; androgyny, girly man <nf>; feminism

3 **womankind, woman, women,** femininity, **womanhood,** womenfolk *or* womenfolks <nf>, the distaff side; **the female sex;** the second sex, **the fair sex,** the gentle sex, the softer sex, **the weaker sex,** the weaker vessel <nf>

4 **female,** female being; she, her, herself

5 **woman,** Eve, daughter of Eve, Adam's rib, *femme* <Fr>, distaff, weaker vessel; frow, *Frau* <Ger>, *vrouw* <Dutch>, *donna* <Ital>, wahine <Hawaii>; **lady,** milady, gentlewoman, *domina* <L>; feme sole *and* feme covert <law>; married woman, wife; **matron,** dame, **dowager;** squaw; unmarried woman, bachelor girl <nf>, single woman, spinster, maiden; old maid; lass, lassie, girl 302.6; career woman, businesswoman, working woman, working wife *or* mother; superwoman; liberated woman, feminist, suffragette, women's libber <nf>

6 <nf terms> **gal, dame,** hen, biddy, skirt, missy, toots, jane, broad, doll, damsel, babe, chick, wench, bird <Brit>, tomato, bitch, minx, momma, mouse, sister, squaw, toots, ball-breaker, dudette

7 **woman of the family,** married woman, wife, widow, housewife, mother, matriarch, materfamilias; daughter, sister, aunt, niece, godmother, goddaughter, grandmother, granddaughter; soccer mom

8 <forms of address> **Ms;** Miss *or* miss; Mistress, **Mrs; madam** *or* ma'am; missus; my good lady, my dear woman *or* lady, lady; *madame* or *Mme* <Fr>; *mesdames* or *Mmes* <Fr pl>; *Frau* and *Fraulein* <Ger>, *vrouw* <Dutch>, *signora* <Ital>, *señora* <Sp>, *senhora* <Pg>, *memsahib* <Hindu>; *donna* <Ital>, *doña* <Sp>, *dona* <Pg>, *mademoiselle* or *Mlle* <Fr>; *Fraülein* <Ger>; *signorina* <Ital>, *señorita* <Sp>, *senhorita* <Pg>, Dame *and* Lady <Brit>

9 <female animals> hen, biddy; guinea hen; peahen; bitch, slut, gyp; sow, gilt; ewe, ewe lamb; she-goat, nanny goat *or* nanny; doe, hind, roe; jenny; mare, brood mare; filly; cow, bossy; heifer; vixen; tigress; lioness; she-bear, she-lion, queen bee, etc

10 <effeminate male> **mollycoddle,** effeminate; **mother's darling, mother's boy, mama's boy,** Lord Fauntleroy, sissy, Percy, goody-goody, goody two-shoes; **pantywaist,** pansy, nancy *or* nance, chicken, lily; cream puff, weak sister, milksop, wussy; fag *or* queen *or* swish <nf>

11 feminization, womanization, effemination, effeminization, sissification <nf>

VERBS **12** feminize; womanize, demasculinize, effeminize, effeminatize, effeminate, soften, sissify <nf>; emasculate, castrate, geld

ADJS **13 feminine, female;** gynic, gynecic, gynecoid; muliebral, distaff, **womanly, womanish, womanlike,** petticoat; **ladylike,** gentlewomanlike, gentlewomanly; **matronly,** matronal, matronlike; **girlish,** little-girlish, kittenish; maidenly 301.11; yin

14 effeminate, womanish, fem <nf>, old-womanish, **unmanly,** muliebrous, soft, chicken, prissy, **sissified,** sissy, **sissyish**

78 REPRODUCTION, PROCREATION

NOUNS **1 reproduction, making, recreation,** remaking, refashioning, reshaping, redoing, re-formation, reworking, rejiggering <nf>; **reconstruction,** rebuilding, redesign, restructuring, *perestroika* <Russ>; **revision;** reedition, reissue, reprinting; reestablishment, **reorganization,** reinstitution, reconstitution; redevelopment; **rebirth,** renascence, resurrection, revival; regeneration, regenesis, palingenesis; **duplication** 874, **imitation** 336, **copy** 785, **repetition** 849; **restoration** 396, renovation; producing *or* making *or* creating anew *or* over *or* again *or* once more; **birth rate,** fertility rate; baby boom *or* boomlet <nf>

2 procreation, reproduction, generation, begetting, breeding, engenderment, engendering, fathering, siring, spawning; **propagation, multiplication,** proliferation; linebreeding; inbreeding, endogamy; outbreeding, xenogamy; dissogeny; crossbreeding 797.4

3 fertilization, fecundation; **impregnation,** insemination, begetting, getting with child, knocking up <nf>, mating, servicing; **pollination,** pollinization; germination; cross-fertilization, cross-pollination; self-fertilization, heterogamy, orthogamy; isogamy, artificial insemination; conjugation, zygosis; in vitro fertilization, test-tube baby technique

4 conception, conceiving, inception of pregnancy; superfetation, superimpregnation

5 pregnancy, gestation, incubation, parturiency, gravidness *or* gravidity, heaviness, greatness, bigness, the family way <nf>; brooding, sitting, covering

6 birth, generation, genesis; development; procreation; abiogenesis, archigenesis, biogenesis, blastogenesis, digenesis, dysmerogenesis, epigenesis, eumerogenesis, heterogenesis, histogenesis, homogenesis, isogenesis, merogenesis, metagenesis, monogenesis, oögenesis, orthogenesis, pangenesis, parthenogenesis, phytogenesis, sporogenesis, xenogenesis; spontaneous generation

VERBS **7 reproduce, remake,** make *or* do over, **re-create,** regenerate, resurrect, revive, re-form, refashion, **reshape,** remold, recast, rework, rejigger <nf>, redo, **reconstruct,** rebuild, redesign, restructure, **revise;** reprint, reissue; reestablish, reinstitute, reconstitute, refound, **reorganize; redevelop; duplicate** 874.3, **copy** 336.5, **repeat** 849.7, **restore** 396.11, **renovate**

8 procreate, generate, breed, beget, get, **engender; propagate, multiply;** proliferate; mother; father, sire; reproduce in kind, reproduce after one's kind; breed true; inbreed, breed in and in; outbreed; cross-pollinate, crossbreed; linebreed

9 lay <eggs>, deposit, drop, spawn

10 fertilize, fructify, fecundate, fecundify; **impregnate, inseminate,** spermatize, knock up <nf>, **get with child** *or* **young; pollinate** *or* pollinize, pollen; cross-fertilize, cross-pollinate *or* cross-pollinize

11 conceive, get in the family way <nf>; superfetate

12 be pregnant, be gravid, be great with child, **be with child** *or* **young;** be in the family way *and* have a bun in the oven *and* be expecting *and* anticipate a blessed event <nf>, be infanticipating *and* be knocked up <nf>, be blessed-eventing <nf>; gestate, breed, carry, carry young; **incubate, hatch; brood,** sit, set, cover

13 give birth 1.3

ADJS 14 **reproductive, re-creative, reconstructive,** re-formative; renascent, regenerative, resurgent, reappearing; reorganizational; revisional; **restorative** 396.22; Hydraheaded, phoenixlike

15 **reproductive, procreative,** procreant, **propagative,** life-giving; spermatic, spermatozoic, seminal, germinal, fertilizing, fecundative; multiparous

16 **genetic, generative,** genial, gametic; genital, genitive; abiogenetic, biogenetic, blastogenetic, digenetic, dysmerogenetic, epigenetic, eumerogenetic, heterogenetic, histogenetic, homogenetic, isogenetic, merogenetic, metagenetic, monogenetic, oögenetic, orthogenetic, pangenetic, parthenogenetic, phytogenetic, sporogenous, xenogenetic

17 **bred, impregnated,** inseminated; inbred, endogamic, endogamous; outbred, exogamic, exogamous; crossbred; linebred

18 **pregnant,** *enceinte* <Fr>, preggers *and* knocked-up <nf>, **with child** *or* **young, in the family way** <nf>, gestating, breeding, teeming, parturient; heavy with child *or* young, great *or* big with child *or* young, wearing her apron high, in a delicate condition, gravid, heavy, great, bigladen; carrying, carrying a fetus *or* an embryo; **expecting** <nf>, anticipating *and* anticipating a blessed event <nf>, infanticipating <nf>; superfetate, superimpregnated

79 CLEANNESS

NOUNS 1 **cleanness, cleanliness; purity,** squeaky-cleanness <nf>, pureness; **immaculateness,** immaculacy; **spotlessness,** unspottedness, stainlessness, whiteness; freshness; fastidiousness, daintiness, cleanly habits, spit and polish; asepsis, sterility, hospital cleanliness; tidiness 807.3

2 **cleansing, cleaning,** cleaning up, detersion; **purge,** purging, purgation, cleanout, cleaning out, purging, purgation, catharsis, abstersion; **purification,** purifying, lustration; expurgation, bowdlerization; housecleaning, spring-cleaning, cleanup

3 **sanitation, hygiene,** hygenics; **disinfection, decontamination, sterilization,** sanitization, antisepsis, asepsis; pasteurization; deodorization, fumigation, disinfestation, delousing; chlorination

4 **refinement, clarification, purification,** depuration; **straining,** colature; elution, elutriation; extraction 192.8; **filtering,** filtration; **percolation,** leaching, lixiviation; **sifting,** separation, **screening,** sieving, bolting, riddling, winnowing; essentialization; sublimation; **distillation,** destructive distillation

5 **washing, ablution;** lavation, laving, lavage; lavabo; **wash, washup;** soaking, soaping, lathering; dip, dipping; rinse, rinsing; sponge, sponging; shampoo, shampooing; washout, elution, elutriation; irrigation, flush, flushing, flushing out; douche, douching; enema; **scrub,** scrubbing, swabbing, mopping, scouring; **cleaning up** *or* **out,** washing up, scrubbing up *or* out, mopping up *or* down, wiping up *or* down

6 **laundering, laundry,** tubbing; **wash, washing;** washday

7 **bathing,** balneation

8 **bath,** bathe <Brit>, tub <nf>; **shower,** shower bath, needle bath, hot *or* cold shower; douche; sponge bath, sponge; hip bath, sitz bath; footbath; sweat bath, Turkish bath, hummum, Russian bath, Swedish bath, Finnish bath, sauna *or* sauna bath, steam bath, Japanese bath, hot tub, whirlpool bath, Jacuzzi <TM>, plunge bath

9 **dip, bath;** acid bath, mercury bath, fixing bath; sheepdip

10 **bathing place, bath, baths,** public baths, **bathhouse,** bagnio, sauna, Turkish baths; *balneum* and *balneae* and *thermae* <L>; mikvah <Judaism>; watering place, spa; lavatory, washroom, bathroom; steam room, sweat room, sudatorium, sudarium, sudatory, caldarium, tepidarium; rest room

11 **washery, laundry;** washhouse, washshed; **coin laundry, Laundromat** <TM>, **launderette,** coin-operated laundry, laundrette <Brit>, washateria; automatic laundry; hand laundry; car wash

12 **washbasin, washbowl,** washdish, basin; **lavatory, washstand; bathtub,** tub, bath; bidet; basin and pitcher, basin and ewer; **shower,** showers, shower room, shower bath, shower stall, shower head, shower curtain; **sink,** kitchen sink; dishwasher; washing machine, washer; piscina, lavabo, ewer, aquamanile; washtub, washboard, washpot, washing pot, wash boiler, dishpan; finger bowl; wash barrel

13 **refinery; refiner,** purifier, clarifier; **filter; strainer,** colander; **percolator,** lixiviator; **sifter, sieve, screen,** riddle, cribble; winnow, winnower, winnowing machine, winnowing basket *or* fan; cradle, rocker

14 **cleaner,** cleaner-up, cleaner-off, cleaner-out; **janitor,** janitress, custodian; cleaning woman *or* lady *or* man, housecleaner, housemaid, maid, daily *or* daily woman *and* charwoman *or* char <Brit>; window cleaner, squeegee <nf>; scrubber, swabber; shoeshiner, bootblack

15 **washer,** launderer; **laundress,** laundrywoman, **washerwoman,** washwoman; **laundryman,** washerman, washman; dry cleaner; **dishwasher,** pot-walloper *and* pearl-diver <nf>, scullion, scullery maid; dishwiper

16 **sweeper; street sweeper,** crossing sweeper, whitewing, cleanser *or* scavenger <Brit>; **chimney sweep** *or* sweeper, sweep, flue cleaner; scavenger, beachcomber; garbage collector, trash collector, sanitary engineer

17 **cleanser, cleaner;** cleaning agent; antiseptic, disinfectant; cold cream, cleansing cream, **soap, detergent,** washing powder, soap flakes, abstergent; dishwashing liquid *or* powder; shampoo; rinse; bubble bath, shower gel; **solvent;** cleaning solvent; water softener; purifier, depurant; mouthwash, gargle; dentifrice, **toothpaste, tooth powder,** whitener; abrasive, pumice, pumice stone, holystone, hearthstone, scouring powder, scouring pad; polish, varnish, wax, whitewah; purge, purgative, cathartic, enema, diuretic, emetic, nauseant, laxative; **cleaning device,** cleaning tool, cleaning cloth

VERBS **18** **clean, cleanse, purge,** deterge, depurate; **purify,** lustrate, disinfect; sweeten, **freshen;** whiten, bleach; clean up *or* out, clear out, sweep out, clean up after; houseclean, clean house, spring-clean; spruce, **tidy** 808.12; scavenge; **wipe,** wipe up *or* out, wipe off, mop *or* mop up, swab, scrub, scour; dust, dust off; steam-clean, **dry-clean;** expurgate, bowdlerize

19 **wash, bathe,** bath <Brit>, shower, lave, have *or* take a bath; **launder,** tub; wash up *or* out *or* away; **rinse,** rinse out, dip, dunk, flush, flush out, irrigate, sluice, sluice out; ritually immerse, baptize, *toivel* <Yiddish>; sponge, sponge down *or* off; **scrub,** scrub up *or* out, **swab, mop,** mop up; **scour**; hose out *or* down; rinse off *or* out; soak out *or* away; soap, lather; shampoo; syringe, douche; gargle

20 **groom,** dress, fettle <Brit nf>, **brush up; preen,** plume, titivate; manicure

21 **comb,** curry, card, hackle *or* hatchel, heckle <nf>, rake

22 **refine, clarify,** clear, purify, rectify, depurate, decrassify; try; **strain;** elute, elutriate; **extract** 192.10; **filter,** filtrate; **percolate,** leach, lixiviate; **sift,** separate, sieve, **screen,** decant, bolt, winnow; sublimate, sublime; **distill,** essentialize

23 **sweep,** sweep up *or* out, **brush,** brush off, whisk, broom; vacuum <nf>, vacuum-clean

24 **sanitize,** sanitate, hygienize; **disinfect, decontaminate, sterilize,** antisepticize, radiosterilize; autoclave, boil; pasteurize, flash-pasteurize; disinfest, fumigate, deodorize, delouse; chlorinate

ADJS **25** **clean, pure; immaculate, spotless,** stainless, pristine, white, fair, dirt-free, soil-free, fresh; **unsoiled, unsullied,** unmuddied, unsmirched, unbesmirched, unblotted, unsmudged, unstained, untarnished, **unspotted,** unblemished, unmarked, undirtied; smutless, smut-free; bleached, whitened; bright, shiny 1025.34; **unpolluted,** nonpolluted, untainted, unadulterated, **undefiled;** kosher, ritually pure *or* clean; **squeaky-clean** *and* clean as a whistle *or* a new penny *or* a hound's tooth <nf>; **sweet, fresh,** fresh as a daisy; **cleanly,** fastidious, dainty, of cleanly habits; well-washed, well-scrubbed, tubbed <nf>

26 **cleaned, cleansed,** cleaned up, cleaned out, washed, scrubbed; purged, purified; expurgated, bowdlerized; refined, filtered; spruce, spick and span, **tidy** 807.8

27 **sanitary, hygienic, prophylactic; sterile,** aseptic, antiseptic, **uninfected;** disinfected, decontaminated, sterilized; autoclaved, boiled; pasteurized

28 **cleansing, cleaning;** detergent, detersive; disinfectant, antibacterial; abstergent, abstersive, depurative; **purifying,** purificatory, lustral; expurgatory; purgative, purging, cathartic, diuretic, emetic; balneal, ablutionary

ADVS **29** **cleanly,** clean; **purely, immaculately, spotlessly**

80 UNCLEANNESS

NOUNS **1** **uncleanness,** immundity; **impurity,** unpureness; **dirtiness,** grubbiness, dinginess, griminess, messiness *and* grunginess *and* scuzziness <nf>, scruffiness, slovenliness, sluttishness, untidiness 810.6; miriness, muddiness 1062.4; uncleanliness

2 **filthiness, foulness,** vileness, scumminess <nf>, feculence, shittiness <nf>, muckiness, ordurousness, nastiness, grossness *and* yuckiness *and* ickiness <nf>; scurfiness, scabbiness; rottenness, putridness 393.7; rankness, fetidness 71.2; odiousness, repulsiveness 98.2; nauseousness, disgustingness 64.3; hoggishness, piggishness, swinishness, beastliness

3 **squalor,** squalidness, squalidity, **sordidness,** slum, hellhole; slumminess <nf>; insanitation, lack of sanitation; unhealthy conditions

4 **defilement, befoulment,** dirtying, soiling, besmirchment; **pollution, contamination, infection;** abomination; ritual uncleanness *or* impurity *or* contamination

5 **soil,** soilure, soilage, smut; **smirch, smudge,** smutch, smear, **spot,** blot, blotch, **stain** 1004.3

6 **dirt, grime;** dust; soot, smut; **mud** 1062.8

7 **filth, muck,** slime, mess, sordes, foul matter; ordure, **excrement** 12.3; mucus, snot <nf>; scurf, furfur, dandruff; scuzz *and* mung <nf>; putrid matter, pus, corruption, gangrene, decay, carrion, **rot** 393.7; **obscenity,** smut <nf> 666.4

8 **slime, slop,** scum, sludge, slush; glop *and* gunk <nf>, **muck, mire,** ooze

9 **offal,** slough, **offscourings,** scurf, scum, riffraff, scum of the earth; residue; **carrion; garbage, swill,** slop, slops, sullage; dishwater, ditchwater, bilgewater, bilge; **sewage,** sewerage; rubbish, trash, **waste, refuse** 391.4

10 **dunghill, manure pile,** midden, mixen <Brit nf>, colluvies; compost heap; kitchen midden, refuse heap

11 **sty, pigsty,** pigpen, hogpen; **stable,** Augean stables; dump *and* hole *and* shithole <nf>, rathole; tenement; warren, **slum,** rookery; the inner city, the ghetto, the slums, asphalt *or* concrete jungle; plague spot, pesthole; hovel

12 <receptacle of filth> sink; sump, **cesspool,** cesspit, septic tank; catchbasin; bilge *or* bilges; **sewer,** drain, *cloaca* and *cloaca maxima* <L>; sewage farm, purification plant; **dump,** garbage dump, dumpsite, sanitary landfill, landfill; **swamp,** bog, mire, quagmire, marsh

13 **pig, swine, hog,** slut, sloven, slattern 810.7

VERBS **14** wallow in the mire, live like a pig, roll in the dirt *or* mud

15 **dirty,** dirty up, grime, **begrime;** muck, muck up <nf>; **muddy**; mire, bemire; slime; dust; soot, smoke, besmoke

16 **soil,** besoil; black, **blacken; smirch,** besmirch, sully, slubber <Brit nf>, smutch *or* smouch, besmutch, smut, **smudge, smear,** besmear, daub, bedaub; **spot, stain** 1004.6; get one's hands dirty, dirty *or* soil one's hands

17 **defile, foul, befoul; sully;** foul one's own nest, shit where one eats <nf>, nasty *or* benasty <nf>, mess *and* mess up <nf>, make a mess of; **pollute, corrupt, contaminate, infect; taint,** tarnish, poison; profane, desecrate, unhallow

18 **spatter, splatter,** splash, **bespatter,** dabble, bedabble, spot, splotch

19 **draggle,** bedraggle, **drabble,** bedrabble, drabble in the mud

ADJS 20 **unclean, unwashed,** unbathed, unscrubbed, unscoured, unswept, unwiped; **impure,** unpure; **polluted, contaminated, infected, corrupted;** ritually unclean *or* impure *or* contaminated, *tref* <Yiddish>, nonkosher; not to be handled without gloves; **uncleanly**; septic, unhygienic, contaminated, polluted, toxic

21 **soiled, sullied, dirtied, smirched,** besmirched, smudged, spotted, **tarnished,** tainted, **stained; defiled,** fouled, **befouled;** draggled, drabbled, bedraggled

22 **dirty,** dirt-encrusted, **grimy, grubby,** grungy <nf>, scummy <nf>, smirchy, dingy, messy <nf>; scruffy, slovenly, untidy 810.15; miry, **muddy** 1062.14; **dusty;** smutty, smutchy, smudgy; sooty, smoky; snuffy

23 **filthy, foul, vile,** mucky, **nasty,** icky *and* yecchy *and* yucky *and* gross *and* grungy *and* scuzzy *and* grotty <nf>; malodorous, mephitic, rank, **fetid** 71.5; **putrid, rotten;** pollutive; nauseating, disgusting; **odious, repulsive** 98.18; **slimy**; barfy *and* vomity *and* puky <nf>; sloppy, sludgy; gloppy *and* gunky <nf>, scurfy, scabby; wormy, maggoty, flyblown; feculent, ordurous, crappy *and* shitty <nf>, excremental, excrementitious, fecal 12.20

24 **hoggish, piggish, swinish,** beastly

25 **squalid, sordid,** wretched, shabby; slumlike, slummy

ADVS 26 **uncleanly, impurely,** unpurely; **dirtily,** grimily; **filthily, foully,** nastily, vilely

81 HEALTHFULNESS

NOUNS 1 **healthfulness, healthiness, salubrity,** salubriousness, salutariness, **wholesomeness,** beneficialness, goodness

2 **hygiene,** hygienics; sanitation 79.3; public health, epidemiology; health physics; **preventive medicine,** prophylaxis, preventive dentistry, prophylactodontia; prophylactic psychology, mental hygiene; **fitness** and **exercise** 84; cleanliness

3 **hygienist,** hygeist, sanitarian; public health doctor *or* physician, epidemiologist; health physicist; preventive dentist, prophylactodontist; dental hygienist

VERBS 4 **make for health,** conduce to health, **be good for,** agree with

ADJS 5 **healthful, healthy, salubrious, salutary, wholesome,** health-preserving, health-enhancing, health-giving, life-promoting, **beneficial,** benign, good, **good for;** nutritious, nourishing, roborant; **hygienic, hygienical,** hygeian, sanitary; constitutional, for one's health; conditioning; bracing, refreshing, invigorating, tonic; what the doctor ordered

82 UNHEALTHFULNESS

NOUNS 1 **unhealthfulness, unhealthiness, insalubrity,** insalubriousness, unsalutariness, ill health, poor health, **unwholesomeness,** badness; noxiousness, noisomeness, injuriousness, harmfulness 1000.5; pathenogenicity; chronic ill health, valetudinarianism; health hazard, threat *or* danger *or* menace to health; contamination, pollution, environmental pollution, air *or* water *or* noise pollution

2 **innutritiousness, indigestibility**

3 **poisonousness, toxicity, venomousness; virulence** *or* virulency,

malignancy, noxiousness, destructiveness, deadliness, morbidity; **infectiousness,** infectivity, contagiousness, communicability; poison, venom 1001.3

VERBS **4 disagree with,** not be good for, sicken

ADJS **5 unhealthful, unhealthy, insalubrious, unsalutary, unwholesome,** peccant, bad, **bad for;** noxious, noisome, injurious, baneful, harmful 1000.12; **polluted,** contaminated, tainted, foul, septic, stagnant; unhygienic, unsanitary, insanitary; morbific, pathogenic, pestiferous

6 unnutritious, indigestible, unassimilable

7 poisonous, toxic, toxicant; **venomous,** envenomed, venenate, venenous; veneniferous, toxiferous; pollutive; **virulent, noxious, malignant,** malign, destructive, deadly; pestiferous, pestilential, pestilent; mephitic, miasmal, miasmic, miasmatic; **infectious,** infective, contagious, communicable, catching, germ-laden; mephitic; lethal, deadly

83 HEALTH

NOUNS **1 health, well-being; fitness,** health and fitness, physical fitness 84; bloom, flush, pink, glow, rosiness; mental health, emotional health; physical condition; Hygeia

2 healthiness, healthfulness, **soundness,** wholesomeness; healthy body, good *or* healthy constitution; **good health,** good state of health; **robust health,** rugged health, rude health, glowing health, picture of health; **fine fettle,** fine whack <nf>, fine *or* high feather <nf>, **good shape,** good trim, fine shape, top shape <nf>, good condition, mint condition; eupepsia, good digestion; clean bill of health

3 haleness, heartiness, robustness, vigorousness, ruggedness, **vitality,** lustiness, hardiness, strength, vigor; longevity

4 immunity, resistance, nonproneness *or* nonsusceptibility to disease; **immunization;** antibody, antigen 86.27

5 health care, health protection, health *or* medical management, **health maintenance, medical care** 91.1; **wellness,** wellness program, disease prevention, preventive medicine; health awareness program; health policy, health-care policy; allied health care; ambulatory care; palliative care; **health plan, health** *or* **medical insurance,** health service, health-care delivery service *or* plan, health maintenance organization *or* HMO, Medicare, Medicaid; National Health Service *or* NHS *or* National Health <Brit>; socialized medicine; health department, health commissioner; health club, health spa

VERBS **6 enjoy good health,** have a clean bill of health, be in the pink; be in the best of health; **feel good,** feel fine, feel fit, feel like a million dollars *or* like a million <nf>, never feel better; feel one's oats, be full of pep; burst with health, bloom, glow, flourish; keep fit, stay in shape; wear well, stay young, be well-preserved

7 get well, recover 396.20, mend, get healthy, be oneself again, feel like a new person, get back on one's feet, bounce back, get over it, perk up, get the color back in one's cheeks; recuperate 396.19

ADJS **8 healthy, healthful,** enjoying health, **fine,** in health, in shape, in condition, **fit,** fit and fine; **in good health,** in the pink of condition, in mint condition, in good case, **in good** *or* **fine shape, in fine fettle,** in A-1 condition, bursting with health, full of life and vigor, feeling one's oats; eupeptic

9 <nf terms> **in the pink,** in fine whack, in fine *or* high feather, chipper, **fit as a fiddle;** alive and kicking, bright-eyed and bushy-tailed; full of beans *or* of piss and vinegar

10 well, unailing, unsick, unsickly, unfrail; all right, doing nicely, up and about, sitting up and taking nourishment, alive and well

11 sound, whole, wholesome; unimpaired 1002.8; sound of mind and body, sound in wind and limb, sound as a dollar <nf>

12 **hale, hearty,** hale and hearty, **robust,** robustious, robustuous, vital, **vigorous, strong,** strong as a horse *or* an ox, bionic <nf>, stalwart, stout, sturdy, **rugged,** rude, hardy, lusty, bouncing, well-knit, flush; **fit,** in condition *or* shape; of good constitution

13 **fresh,** green, youthful, **blooming;** flush, flushed, **rosy,** rosy-cheeked, apple cheeked, ruddy, pink, pink-cheeked; fresh-faced, fresh as a daisy *or* rose, fresh as April

14 **immune, resistant,** nonprone *or* nonsusceptible to disease; health-conscious, health-protecting; immune response

84 FITNESS, EXERCISE

NOUNS **1 fitness, physical fitness, physical conditioning, condition, shape,** trim, tone, fettle, aerobic fitness, anaerobic fitness, cardiovascular fitness, cardiorespiratory fitness, cardio; **gymnasium, gym** <nf>, **fitness center, health club,** health spa, work-out room, weight room, exercise track *or* trail, trim trail <Brit>, *parcourse* or *parcours* <Fr>; **weight, barbell,** dumbbell, exercise machine, Nautilus <TM>, bench, exercise bike, rowing machine, stair-climbing machine, elliptical trainer, treadmill; whirlpool bath, Jacuzzi <TM>, hot tub, spa

2 **exercise,** motion, movement, maneuver; **program,** routine, drill, work-out; **exercise systems; warm-up, stretching,** warm-down; **calisthenics**, free exercise, setting-up exercise *or* set-ups, physical jerks <Brit>, daily dozen <nf>, constitutional; **parcourse exercise**; **gymnastic exercise, gymnastics;** slimnastics; **isometrics,** isometric *or* no-movement exercise; breather, wind sprint; **aerobic exercise, aerobics,** aerobic dancing *or* dance, step aerobics, dancercize *or* dancercizing, fitaerobics, jazz ballet *or* Jazzercise; Callanetics; **bodybuilding,** weightlifting, weight training, pumping iron <nf>, bench press, arm raise, curl, wrist curl; **running, jogging,** roadwork, distance running; obligate running; cross-training, interval training, *fartlek* <Swedish>; **walking,** fitness walking, healthwalking, aerobic walking, powerwalking, powerstriding; **swimming,** swimnastics, water exercise, aquaerobics; yoga, Pilates

3 **physical fitness test;** stress test, treadmill test; cardiovascular text

VERBS **4 exercise, work out,** warm up, aerobicize, stretch, lift weights, weight-train, pump iron <nf>, jog, run, bicycle, walk, fitness-walk, power-walk; practice

85 DISEASE

NOUNS **1 disease, illness, sickness, malady, ailment, indisposition, disorder,** complaint, morbidity, *morbus* <L>, **affliction,** affection, **infirmity; disability,** defect, handicap; deformity 265.3; **birth defect,** congenital defect; abnormality, condition, pathological condition; **signs, symptoms, pathology,** symptomatology, symptomology, syndrome; **sickishness,** malaise, seediness *and* rockiness *and* the pip *and* the crud *and* the creeping crud <nf>; complication, secondary disease *or* condition; plant disease, blight 1001.2

2 **fatal disease,** deadly disease, terminal disease *or* illness, hopeless condition; **death** 307, clinical death, loss of vital signs; apparent death; **brain death,** local death, somatic death; sudden death, unexplained death; liver death; serum death; thymic death *or* mors thymica; cell death, molecular death; cot death *or* crib death *or* sudden infant death syndrome *or* SIDS

3 **unhealthiness,** healthlessness; **ill health,** poor health, delicate *or* shaky *or* frail *or* fragile health; **sickliness,** peakedness <nf>, **feebleness,** delicacy, weakliness, fragility, **frailty** 16.2; **infirmity, unsoundness,** debility, debilitation, enervation, exhaustion, decrepitude;

wasting, languishing, cachexia *or* cachexy; chronic ill health, invalidity, **invalidism;** unwholesomeness, morbidity, morbidness; hypochondria, hypochondriasis, valetudinarianism, history of illness

4 **infection, contagion,** contamination, taint, virus, affliction; **contagiousness, infectiousness, communicability;** pestiferousness, epidemicity, inoculability; carrier, vector; **epidemiology**

5 **epidemic, plague, pestilence,** pest, pandemic, pandemia, scourge, bane; white plague, tuberculosis; pesthole, plague spot

6 **seizure, attack,** access, visitation; arrest; blockage, stoppage, occlusion, thrombosis, thromboembolism; **stroke,** ictus, apoplexy; **spasm, throes, fit, paroxysm, convulsion,** eclampsia, frenzy; **epilepsy,** falling sickness; tonic spasm, tetany, lockjaw, trismus, tetanus; laryngospasm, laryngismus; clonic spasm, clonus; cramp; vaginismus

7 **fever, feverishness,** febrility, febricity, pyrexia; hyperpyrexia, hyperthermia; **heat, fire, fever heat;** flush, hectic flush; calenture; delirium 926.8, ague; chill, hypothermia, shivers, shakes

8 **collapse, breakdown, crackup** <nf>, **prostration,** exhaustion, burn-out *or* burnout; nervous prostration *or* breakdown *or* exhaustion, neurasthenia; circulatory collapse

9 <disease symptoms> indication, **syndrome**; anemia; ankylosis; asphyxiation, anoxia, cyanosis; ataxia; bleeding, hemorrhage; colic; dizziness, vertigo; ague, chill, chills; hot flash, hot flush; dropsy, hydrops, edema; morning sickness; fainting; fatigue 21; headache, migraine; fever; constipation; diarrhea, flux, dysentery; indigestion, upset stomach, dyspepsia; inflammation 85.10; necrosis; insomnia; malaise; itching, pruritus; jaundice, icterus; backache, lumbago; vomiting, nausea; paralysis; skin eruption, rash; sore, abscess, discharge; hypertension, high blood pressure; hypotension, low blood pressure; tumor, growth; shock; convulsion, seizure, spasm; pain 26; fibrillation, tachycardia; shortness of breath, labored breathing, apnea, dyspnea, asthma; blennorhea; congestion, nasal discharge, rheum, sore throat, coughing, sneezing; wasting, cachexia *or* cachexy, tabes, marasmus, emaciation, atrophy; sclerosis

10 **inflammation,** inflammatory disease, -itis; muscle *or* muscular disease *or* disorder, myopathy; collagen disease, connective-tissue disease

11 **deficiency diseases**, nutritional disease, vitamin-deficiency disease, acquired immune deficiency syndrome *or* AIDS

12 **genetic disease**, gene disease, genetransmitted disease, hereditary *or* congenital disease

13 **infectious disease**, infection

14 **eye disease**, ophthalmic disease, disease of the eye *or* of vision; cataract; conjunctivitis *or* pink eye; glaucoma; sty; eye *or* visual defect, defective vision 28

15 **ear disease,** otic disease *or* disorder; **deafness; earache,** otalgia; tympanitis; otosclerosis; **vertigo,** dizziness, loss of balance; Ménière's syndrome *or* disease *or* apoplectical deafness

16 **respiratory disease, upper respiratory disease;** lung disease; cold, sinusitis; influenza, flu; bronchitis, pneumonia

17 **tuberculosis** *or* **TB,** white plague, phthisis, consumption

18 **venereal disease** *or* VD, sexually-transmitted disease *or* STD, social disease, Cupid's itch *or* Venus's curse, dose <nf>; chancre, chancroid; gonorrhea *or* clap *or* the clap *or* claps <nf>; syphilis *or* syph *or* the syph *or* the pox <nf>; herpes, crabs; acquired immune deficiency syndrome *or* AIDS

19 **cardiovascular disease;** heart disease, heart condition, heart trouble; vascular disease; hypertension *or* high blood pressure; angina *or* angina pectoris; cardiac *or* myocardial infarction; cardiac arrest; congenital heart disease; congestive heart fail-

ure; coronary *or* ischemic heart disease; coronary thrombosis; heart attack, coronary, heart failure; tachycardia; heart surgery, bypass surgery, angioplasty

20 **blood disease,** hemic *or* hematic disease, hematopathology, anemia, leukemia, lymphoma, Hodgkin's disease; blood poisoning, toxemia, septicemia; hemophilia

21 **endocrine disease,** gland *or* glandular disease, endocrinism, endocrinopathy; diabetes; goiter; hyper- *or* hypoglycemia; hyper- *or* hypothyroidism

22 **metabolic disease;** acidosis, alkalosis, ketosis, gout, podagra; galactosemia, lactose intolerance, fructose intolerance; phenylketonuria *or* PKU, maple syrup urine disease, congenital hypophosphatasia

23 **liver disease,** hepatic disease; gallbladder disease; jaundice *or* icterus

24 **kidney disease,** renal disease; nephritis

25 **neural** *or* **nerve disease,** neurological disease, neuropathy; brain disease; amyotrophic lateral sclerosis *or* Lou Gherig's disease; palsy, cerebral palsy, Bell's palsy; chorea *or* St Vitus's dance *or* the jerks <nf>; Huntington's chorea; headache, migraine; multiple sclerosis *or* MS; muscular dystrophy; Parkinson's disease *or* Parkinsonism; Alzheimer's disease; neuralgia; sciatica *or* sciatic neuritis; shingles *or* herpes zoster; spina bifida; meningitis; emotional trauma 92.17

26 **shock, trauma;** traumatism

27 **paralysis,** paralyzation, palsy, impairment of motor function; **stroke,** apoplexy; paresis; motor paralysis, sensory paralysis; hemiplegia, paraplegia, diplegia, quadriplegia; cataplexy, catalepsy; infantile paralysis, poliomyelitis, polio <nf>; atrophy, numbness

28 **heatstroke;** heat prostration *or* exhaustion; sunstroke, *coup de soleil* <Fr>, siriasis, insolation; calenture, thermic fever

29 **gastrointestinal disease,** disease of the digestive tract; stomach condition; colic; colitis; constipation *or* irregularity; diarrhea *or* dysentery *or* looseness of the bowels *or* flux, the trots *or* the shits *or* the runs <nf>, Montezuma's revenge; gastritis; gastroenteritis; indigestion *or* dyspepsia; stomachache, bellyache; cramps; heartburn, acid reflux, agita; stomach flu; ulcer, peptic ulcer, stomach cancer; food poisoning

30 **nausea,** nauseation, queasiness, squeamishness, qualmishness; qualm, pukes <nf>; motion sickness, travel sickness, **seasickness,** *mal de mer* <Fr>, airsickness, car sickness, motion discomfort; vomiting 909.8

31 **poisoning,** intoxication, venenation; septic poisoning, blood poisoning, sepsis, septicemia, toxemia, pyemia, septicopyemia; autointoxication; food poisoning, ptomaine poisoning, botulism, salmonellosis, listeriosis; milk sickness; ergotism, St Anthony's fire

32 **environmental disease, occupational disease**, disease of the workplace, environmental *or* occupational hazard, biohazard; tropical disease

33 **vitamin deficiency disease,** avitaminosis; night blindness, xerophthalmia, beriberi, pellagra, pernicious anemia, scurvy, rickets, osteomalacia

34 **allergy,** allergic disorder; allergic rhinitis, **hay fever,** rose cold, pollinosis, spring allergy; **asthma,** bronchial asthma; **hives,** urticaria; eczema; conjunctivitis; cold sore; allergic gastritis; cosmetic dermatitis; Chinese restaurant syndrome *or* Kwok's disease; allergen

35 **skin diseases;** acne, sebaceous gland disorder; dermatitis; eczema; herpes; hives; itch; psoriasis; scabies; athlete's foot; melanoma, skin cancer

36 **skin eruption,** eruption, **rash,** efflorescence, breaking out, acne, pimple; diaper rash; drug rash, vaccine rash; prickly heat, heat rash; hives, urticaria, nettle rash; papular rash; rupia

37 **sore, lesion;** pustule, papule, papula, fester, **pimple,** hickey *and* zit

<nf>; pock; ulcer, ulceration; bedsore; tubercle; blister, bleb, bulla, blain; whelk, wheal, welt, wale; **boil,** furuncle, furunculus; carbuncle; canker; canker sore; cold sore, fever blister; sty; abscess, gathering; gumboil, parulis; whitlow, felon, paronychia; bubo; chancre; soft chancre, chancroid; hemorrhoids, piles; bunion; chilblain, kibe; polyp; stigma, petechia; scab, eschar; fistula; suppuration, festering; swelling, rising 283.4

38 **trauma, wound, injury,** hurt, lesion; **cut,** incision, scratch, gash; puncture, stab, stab wound; flesh wound; **laceration,** mutilation; abrasion, scuff, scrape, chafe, gall; frazzle, fray; run, **rip,** rent, slash, **tear; burn,** scald, scorch, first- *or* second- *or* third-degree burn; flash burn; **break, fracture,** bone-fracture, comminuted fracture, compound *or* open fracture, greenstick fracture, spiral *or* torsion fracture; rupture; crack, chip, craze, check, crackle; wrench; whiplash injury *or* whiplash; concussion; **bruise, contusion,** ecchymosis, **black-and-blue mark; black eye,** shiner *and* mouse <nf>; **battering;** battered child syndrome; sprain, strain, repetitive strain injury; paper cut

39 **growth,** neoplasm; **tumor,** intumescence; benign tumor, nonmalignant tumor, innocent tumor; malignant tumor, malignant growth, metastatic tumor, **cancer,** sarcoma, carcinoma; morbid growth; excrescence, outgrowth; proud flesh; exostosis; cyst, wen; fungus, fungosity; callus, callosity, **corn,** clavus; **wart,** verruca; **mole,** nevus

40 **gangrene,** mortification, necrosis, sphacelus, sphacelation; noma; moist gangrene, dry gangrene, gas gangrene, hospital gangrene; caries, cariosity, tooth decay; slough; necrotic tissue

41 <animal diseases> anthrax, splenic fever, charbon, milzbrand, malignant pustule; malignant catarrh *or* malignant catarrhal fever; bighead; blackleg, black quarter, quarter evil *or* ill; cattle plague, rinderpest; glanders; foot-and-mouth disease, hoof-and-mouth disease, aphthous fever; distemper; gapes; heaves, broken wind; hog cholera; mad cow disease; loco, loco disease, locoism; mange, scabies; pip; rot, liver rot, sheep rot; staggers, megrims, blind staggers, mad staggers; swine dysentery, bloody flux; stringhalt; Texas fever, blackwater; John's disease, paratuberculosis, pseudotuberculosis; rabies, hydrophobia; myxomatosis

42 **germ,** pathogen, contagium, bug <nf>, disease-causing agent, disease-producing microorganism; **microbe,** microorganism; **virus,** filterable virus, nonfilterable virus, adenovirus, echovirus, reovirus, rhinovirus, enterovirus, picornavirus, retrovirus, virion, bacteriophage, phage; HIV *or* human immunodeficiency virus; rickettsia; bacterium, **bacteria,** germ, coccus, streptococcus, staphylococcus, bacillus, spirillum, vibrio, spirochete, gram-positive bacteria, gram-negative bacteria, aerobe, aerobic bacteria, anaerobe, anaerobic bacteria; protozoon, amoeba, trypanosome; fungus, mold, spore; **carcinogen,** cancer-causing agent

43 **sick person,** ill person, sufferer, victim; valetudinarian, **invalid, shut-in;** incurable, terminal case; **patient, case;** inpatient, outpatient; apoplectic, bleeder, consumptive, dyspeptic, epileptic, rheumatic, arthritic, spastic; addict; **the sick, the infirm;** hypochondriac

44 **carrier,** vector, biological vector, mechanical vector; Typhoid Mary

45 **cripple,** defective, **handicapped person,** disabled person, physically challenged, incapable; amputee; paraplegic, quadriplegic, paralytic; deformity 265.3; the crippled, the handicapped

VERBS **46** **ail, suffer,** labor under, be affected with, complain of; **feel ill,** feel under the weather, feel awful *or* feel like hell <nf>, feel something terrible, not feel like anything <nf>, feel like the walking dead; look green about the gills <nf>

47 take sick *or* **ill, sicken; catch, contract, get,** take, sicken for <Brit>, **come down with** <nf>, be stricken *or* seized by, fall a victim to; catch cold; take one's death <nf>; **break out,** break out with, break out in a rash, erupt; run a temperature, fever; be laid by the heels, be struck down, be brought down, be felled; drop in one's tracks, **collapse;** overdose *or* **OD** <nf>; go into shock, be traumatized

48 fail, weaken, sink, decline, run down, lose strength, lose one's grip, dwindle, droop, flag, wilt, wither, wither away, fade, **languish,** waste, waste away, pine, peak

49 go lame, founder

50 afflict, disorder, derange; sicken, indispose; weaken, enfeeble, enervate, reduce, debilitate, devitalize; **invalid,** incapacitate, **disable;** lay up, hospitalize

51 infect, disease, contaminate, taint, pollute; reinfect, superinfect

52 poison, empoison, envenom

ADJS **53 disease-causing, disease-producing, pathogenic;** threatening, life-threatening; unhealthful 82.5

54 unhealthy, healthless, in poor health; **infirm, unsound,** unfit, invalid, valetudinary, valetudinarian, debilitated, cachectic, enervated, exhausted, drained; shut-in, housebound, homebound, wheelchair-bound; **sickly,** peaky *or* peaked <nf>; **weakly, feeble, frail** 16.14; weakened, decrepit, with low resistance, **run-down,** reduced, reduced in health; **dying** 307.32, **terminal,** moribund, languishing, failing 16.21; pale 36.7

55 unwholesome, unhealthy, unsound, morbid, diseased, pathological

56 ill, ailing, sick, unwell, indisposed, taken ill, down, bad, on the sick list; **sickish, seedy** *and* rocky <nf>, **under the weather, out of sorts** <nf>, all-overish <nf>, below par <nf>, white as a sheet, off-color, off one's feed <nf>; not quite right, not oneself; faint, faintish, feeling faint; feeling awful *and* feeling something terrible <nf>, feel crummy *and* feel shitty <nf>; sick as a dog <nf>, laid low; in a bad way, critically ill, in danger, on the critical list, on the guarded list, in intensive care; terminal, inoperable, mortally ill, sick unto death, near death; far gone

57 nauseated, nauseous, **queasy, squeamish, qualmish,** qualmy; **sick to one's stomach;** pukish *and* puky *and* barfy <nf>; seasick, carsick, airsick, green around the gills

58 feverish, fevered, feverous, in a fever, febrile, pyretic; **flushed,** inflamed, **hot, burning,** fiery, hectic; hyperpyretic, hyperthermic; delirious 926.31

59 laid up, invalided, hospitalized, in hospital <Brit>; **bedridden, bedfast, sick abed; down,** prostrate, flat on one's back; in childbed, confined

60 diseased, morbid, pathological, bad, **infected, contaminated,** tainted, peccant, **poisoned,** septic; cankerous, cankered, ulcerous, ulcerated, ulcerative, gangrenous, gangrened, mortified, sphacelated; **inflamed;** congested; **swollen,** edematous

61 anemic, chlorotic; bilious; dyspeptic, liverish, colicky; dropsical, edematous, hydropic; gouty, podagric; neuritic, neuralgic; palsied, paralytic; pneumonic, pleuritic, tubercular, tuberculous, phthisic, consumptive; rheumatic, arthritic; rickety, rachitic; syphilitic, pocky, luetic; tabetic, tabid; allergic; allergenic; apoplectic; hypertensive; diabetic; encephalitic; epileptic; laryngitic; leprous; malarial; measly; nephritic; scabietic, scorbutic, scrofulous; variolous, variolar; tumorous; cancerous, malignant; **carcinogenic,** tumorigenic; HIV-positive

62 contagious, infectious, infective, **catching,** taking, spreading, **communicable,** zymotic, inoculable; pathogenic, germ-carrying; pestiferous, pestilent, pestilential, **epidemic,** epidemial, pandemic; epizootic, epiphytotic; endemic; sporadic; septic

86 REMEDY

NOUNS **1 remedy, cure, corrective,** alterative, remedial measure, sovereign remedy; **relief, help, aid, assistance,** succor; balm, balsam; healing agent; restorative, analeptic; healing quality *or* virtue; oil on troubled waters; specific, specific remedy; **prescription,** recipe, receipt; magic bullet

2 nostrum, patent medicine, quack remedy; snake oil

3 panacea, cure-all, universal remedy, theriac, catholicon, philosophers' stone; polychrest, broad-spectrum drug *or* antibiotic; elixir, elixir of life, *elixir vitae* <L>

4 medicine, medicament, medication, medicinal, theraputant, pharmaceutical, **drug, physic,** preparation, mixture; herbs, medicinal herbs, simples, vegetable remedies; wonder drug, miracle drug; balsam, balm; tisane, ptisan; drops; powder; inhalant; electuary, elixir, syrup, lincture, linctus; officinal; specialized drug, orphan drug; **prescription drug,** ethical drug; over-the-counter *or* OTC drug, counter drug, **nonprescription drug;** proprietary medicine *or* drug, proprietary, patent medicine; proprietary name, generic name; materia medica; pharmacognosy; **placebo,** placebo effect

5 drug, narcotic drug, controlled substance, designer drug, illegal drug, dope <nf>

6 dose, dosage, draft, potion, portion, **shot,** injection; broken dose; booster, booster dose, recall dose, booster shot; drops; inhalant

7 pill, bolus, **tablet, capsule,** time-release capsule, lozenge, dragée, troche, pastille

8 tonic, bracer, cordial, restorative, analeptic, roborant, **pick-me-up** <nf>; **shot in the arm** <nf>; stimulant; vitamin shot, herb tea, ginseng, iron

9 stimulant; Adrenalin <TM> *or* adrenaline <Brit> *or* epinephrine, aloes; amphetamine sulphate, aromatic spirits of ammonia, caffeine, dextroamphetamine sulfate *or* Dexedrine <TM>, digitalin *or* digitalis, methamphetamine hydrochloride *or* Methedrine <TM>, smelling salts *or* salts; pep pill

10 palliative, alleviative, alleviatory, lenitive, assuasive, assuager; soothing, abirritant

11 balm, lotion, salve, ointment, unguent, *unguentum* <L>, cream, balm, cerate, unction, balsam, oil, emollient, demulcent; **liniment,** embrocation; vulnerary; collyrium, eyesalve, eyebath, eyewash; ear-drops

12 sedative, sedative hypnotic, depressant, amobarbital and secobarbital, amobarbital sodium *or* Amytal <TM>, atropine, barbital *or* barbitone <Brit>, barbituric acid, belladonna, chloral hydrate *or* chloral, laudanum, meperidine *or* Demerol <TM>, morphine, pentobarbital *or* Nembutal <TM>, phenobarbital *or* Luminal <TM>, Quaalude <TM>, reserpine, scopolamine, secobarbital *or* Seconal <TM>; **sleeping pill** *or* **tablet** *or* potion; **calmative, tranquilizer,** chlorpromazine, Equanil <TM>, Librium <TM>, meprobamate, rauwolfia, reserpine, Thorazine <TM>, Triavil <TM>, Valium <TM>; abirritant, soother, soothing syrup, quietener, pacifier; **analgesic,** acetaminophen *or* Tylenol <TM>, acetanilide, acetophenetidin, aspirin *or* acetylsalicylic acid *or* Bayer <TM>, buffered aspirin *or* Bufferin <TM>, headache *or* aspirin powder, ibuprofen *or* Advil <TM> *or* Motrin <TM> *or* Nuprin <TM>, phenacetin, propoxyphene *or* Darvon <TM>, sodium salicylate; **anodyne,** paregoric; **pain killer** *and* pain pill <nf>; anti-inflammatory drug *or* agent, nonsteroidal anti-inflammatory drug *or* NSAID, muscle relaxant; alcohol, liquor 88.13

13 psychoactive drug, hallucinogen, psychedelic, psychedelic drug

14 antipyretic, febrifuge, fever-reducer, fever pill <nf>

15 anesthetic; local *or* topical *or* general anesthetic; differential anesthetic; chloroform, ether, ethyl chloride, gas, laughing gas, nitrous oxide, novocaine *or* Novocain <TM>, thiopental sodium *or* Pentothal <TM> *or* truth serum

16 **cough medicine,** cough syrup, cough drops; horehound

17 **laxative, cathartic, physic, purge, purgative,** aperient, carminative, diuretic; stool softener; milk of magnesia, castor oil, Epsom salts; nauseant, emetic; douche, enema

18 **emetic,** nauseant

19 **enema,** clyster, clysma, lavage

20 **prophylactic,** prophylaxis, **preventive,** preventative, protective

21 **antiseptic, disinfectant,** fumigant, fumigator, **germicide,** bactericide, microbicide; alcohol, carbolic acid, hydrogen peroxide, merbromin *or* Mercurochrome <TM>, tincture of iodine

22 **dentifrice, toothpaste,** tooth powder; mouthwash, gargle, fluoride, dental floss

23 **contraceptive,** birth control device, prophylactic, contraception; condom; **rubber** *and* skin *and* bag <nf>; oral contraceptive, **birth control pill, the pill** <nf>, Brompton *or* Brompton's mixture *or* cocktail, morning-after pill, abortion pill, RU-486; diaphragm, pessary; spermicide, spermicidal jelly, contraceptive foam; intrauterine device *or* IUD, Dalkon shield <TM>, Lippes loop; abortion issue, anti-choice, pro-choice, pro-life, right-to-life

24 **vermifuge,** vermicide, worm medicine, anthelminthic

25 **antacid,** gastric antacid, alkalizer

26 **antidote,** countermeasure, counterpoison, counteraction, alexipharmic, antitoxin, counterirritant, theriaca *or* theriac

27 **antitoxin,** antitoxic serum; **antivenin; serum,** antiserum; interferon; **antibody,** antigen-antibody product, anaphylactic antibody, incomplete antibody, inhibiting antibody, sensitizing antibody; gamma globulin, serum gamma globulin, immune globulin, antitoxic globulin; lysin, precipitin, agglutinin, anaphylactin, bactericidin; antiantibody; antigen, Rh antigen, Rh factor; allergen; **immunosuppressive drug**

28 **vaccination, inoculation; vaccine**

29 **antibiotic,** ampicillin, bacitracin, erythromycin, gramicidin, neomycin, nystatin, penicillin, polymyxin, streptomycin, tetracycline *or* Terramycin <TM>; **miracle drug, wonder drug,** magic bullet; bacteriostat; **sulfa drug**, sulfa, sulfanilamide, sulfonamide, sulfathiazole

30 diaphoretic, sudorific

31 vesicant, vesicatory, epispastic

32 miscellaneous drugs, anabolic steroid *or* muscle pill, antihistamine, antispasmodic, beta blocker, counterirritant, decongestant, expectorant, fertility drug *or* pill, hormone, vasoconstrictor, vasodilator, AZT, hormone replacement therapy

33 **dressing, application**; plaster, court plaster, mustard plaster, sinapism; **poultice,** cataplasm; formentation; **compress,** pledget; stupe; tent; tampon; **bandage, bandaging**, binder, cravat, triangular bandage, roller *or* roller bandage, four-tailed bandage; bandage compress, adhesive compress, adhesive bandage, Band-Aid <TM>; butterfly dressing; elastic bandage, Ace elastic bandage *and* Ace bandage <TM>, compression bandage; rubber bandage; plastic bandage *or* strip; **tourniquet;** sling; splint, brace; cast, plaster cast; tape, **adhesive tape;** lint, cotton, gauze, sponge; patch, nicotine patch

34 **pharmacology, pharmacy, pharmaceutics;** posology; materia medica

35 **pharmacist,** pharmaceutist, pharmacopolist, **druggist, chemist** <Brit>, **apothecary,** dispenser, gallipot; pharmacologist, pharmaceutical chemist, posologist; pill pusher *or* roller<nf>

36 **drugstore, pharmacy,** chemist *and* chemist's shop <Brit>, apothecary's shop, dispensary, dispensatory

37 **pharmacopoeia,** pharmacopedia, dispensatory

VERBS **38** remedy, help, relieve, cure 396.15; medicate; prescribe; treat.

ADJS **39 remedial, curative, therapeutic, healing, corrective,** disease-fighting, alterative, restorative, curing, analeptic, sanative, sanatory; salubrious, salutiferous; all-healing, panacean; adjuvant; **medicinal,** medicative, theriac, theriacal, iatric; anticancer; first-aid

40 **palliative, lenitive, alleviative, assuasive,** soothing, balmy, balsamic, demulcent, emollient, pain-relieving, analgesic, anodyne

41 **antidotal,** alexipharmic, counteractant; **antitoxic; antibiotic,** synthetic antibiotic, semisynthetic antibiotic, bacteriostatic, antimicrobial; antiluetic, antisyphilitic; antiscorbutic; antiperiodic; antipyretic, febrifugal; vermifugal, anthelmintic; **antacid**

42 **prophylactic, preventive,** protective

43 **antiseptic, disinfectant, germicidal,** bactericidal

44 **tonic, stimulating, bracing, invigorating,** stimulative, reviving, refreshing, restorative, analeptic, strengthening, roborant, corroborant

45 **sedative, calmative,** calmant, depressant, **soothing, tranquilizing, quietening; narcotic,** opiatic; **analgesic,** anodyne, paregoric; anti-inflammatory; muscle-relaxant; hypnotic, soporific, somniferous, somnifacient, sleep-inducing

46 **psychochemical,** psychoactive; ataractic; antidepressant, mood drug; hallucinogenic, **psychedelic,** mind-expanding, psychotomimetic

47 **anesthetic,** deadening, numbing

48 **cathartic,** laxative, purgative, aperient; carminative; diuretic

49 **emetic,** vomitive

87 SUBSTANCE ABUSE

NOUNS **1 substance abuse, drug abuse,** narcotics abuse, drug use, glue-sniffing, solvent abuse; **addiction, addictedness, drug addiction,** narcotic addiction, opium addiction *or* habit, opiumism, morphine addiction *or* habit, morphinism, heroin addiction *or* habit, cocaine addiction, cocainism, coke habit <nf>, crack habit, barbiturate addiction, amphetamine addiction; **habit,** drug habit, jones <nf>, drug habituation, drug dependence, physical addiction *or* dependence, psychological addiction *or* dependence, jones *and* monkey on one's back *and* Mighty Joe Young <nf>; **drug experience, drug intoxication,** high *and* buzz *and* rush <nf>; frightening drug experience, bad trip *and* bum trip *and* bummer *and* drag <nf>; **alcoholism** 88.3, alcohol abuse, drinking habit, acute alcoholism, chronic alcoholism, dipsomania, hitting the bottle <nf>, Dutch courage, hard drinking, liquid lunch, barhopping; drunk driving; **smoking,** smoking habit, one- *or* two- *or* three-pack-a-day habit, nicotine addiction 89.10, chain smoking; **tolerance,** acquired tolerance; **withdrawal, withdrawal sickness,** withdrawal syndrome, withdrawal symptoms, bogue *and* coming down *and* crash <nf>, abrupt withdrawal *and* cold turkey <nf>; **detoxification** *or* detox <nf>, drying out, taking the cure; Alcoholics Anonymous, AA; Narcotics Anonymous, NA; drug test; drug czar

2 <drug use> smoking, sniffing, injecting, snorting, freebasing, hitting up, shooting up, skin-popping, mainlining, pill-popping, banging, blowing, cocktailing; buzz, trip, acid trip, bad trip; drug pushing, drug trafficking, holding <nf>

3 **drug, narcotic,** dope <nf>, dangerous drug, controlled substance, abused substance, illegal drug, addictive drug, **hard drug;** soft drug, gateway drug; lifestyle drug; **opiate; sedative, depressant,** sedative hypnotic, **antipsychotic tranquilizer,** trank <nf>**; hallucinogen,** hallucinogenic drug, psychedelic, psychedelic drug, psychoactive drug, psychoactive chemical *or* psychochemical, psychotropic drug, psychotomimetic drug, mind-altering drug, mind-expanding drug, mind-blowing drug; designer drug; street drug; recreational drug; **stimulant; antidepressant,** Prozac <TM>; **inhalant,** volatile inhalant; drug of choice

4 <nf terms for amphetamines> bennies, benz, black mollies, brain ticklers, crank, crystal, dexies, diet pills, dolls, ecstasy, footballs, greenie,

hearts, ice, jelly beans, lid poppers, meth, pep pills, purple hearts, speed, uppers, ups, white crosses

5 <nf terms for amyl nitrate> amies, blue angels, blue devils, blue dolls, blue heavens, poppers, snappers; **barbiturates,** barbs, black beauties, candy, dolls, downers, downs, goofballs, gorilla pills, nebbies, nimbies, phennies, phenos, pink ladies, purple hearts, yellow jackets

6 <nf terms for chloral hydrate> joy juice, knockout drops, mickey, Mickey Finn, peter

7 <nf terms for cocaine> basuco, bernice, C, big C, blow, C, charlie, coke, crack, crack cocaine, jumps, dust, flake, girl, gold dust, her, jay, joy powder, lady, lady snow, nose candy, Peruvian marching powder, rock, snow, star dust, toot, white, white girl, white lady, white stuff

8 <nf terms for hashish> black hash, black Russian, hash

9 <nf terms for heroin> big H, boy, brown, caballo, crap, doojee, flea powder, garbage, H, hard stuff, henry, him, his, horse, hombre, jones, junk, mojo, P-funk, scag, schmeck, smack, white stuff

10 <nf terms for LSD> acid, big D, blotter, blue acid, blue cheer, blue heaven, California sunshine, cap, cubes, D, deeda, dots, electric Kool-Aid, haze, L, mellow yellows, orange cubes, pearly gates, pink owsley, strawberry fields, sugar, sunshine, tabs, yellow, yellow sunshine, orange sunshine

11 <nf terms for marijuana> Acapulco gold, aunt mary, bomb, boo, bush, doobie, gage, ganja, grass, grefa, hay, hemp, herb, Indian hay, J, jane, kif, mary, maryjane, mary warner, meserole, mighty mezz, moota, muggles, pod, pot, smoke, snop, tea, Texas tea, weed, yerba

12 <nf terms for marijuana cigarette> joint, joy stick, kick stick, reefer, roach, stick, twist

13 <nf terms for mescaline> beans, big chief, buttons, cactus, mesc

14 <nf terms for morphine> big M, emm, hocus, M, miss emma, miss morph, morph, moocah, white stuff

15 <nf terms for pentobarbital> nebbies, nemmies, nimby, yellow dolls, yellows

16 <nf terms for opium> black pills, brown stuff, hop, O, tar

17 <nf terms for peyote> bad seed, big chief, buttons, cactus, P, topi

18 <nf terms for phencyclidine> angel dust, animal trank, DOA, dust, elephant, hog, PCP, peace, rocket fuel, supergrass, superweed

19 <nf terms for psilocybin> magic mushroom, mushroom, shroom, STP

20 **dose,** hit *and* fix *and* toke *and* rock <nf>; **shot, injection,** bang *or* bhang <nf>; **portion, packet,** spliff *and* snort *and* blockbuster *and* toke and blast <nf>, shoot-up *and* hype <nf>, bag *and* deck <nf>, dime bag; drug house, shooting gallery *and* needle park <nf>, crack house, opium den, balloon room *and* pot party *and* dope den <nf>

21 **addict, drug addict, narcotics addict, user, drug user,** drug abuser, junkie *and* head *and* druggy *and* doper *and* toker *and* fiend *and* freak *and* space cadet <nf>; cocaine user, cokie *and* coke head *and* crackhead *and* sniffer *and* snow drifter *and* flaky <nf>; opium user, opium addict, hophead *and* hopdog *and* tar distiller <nf>; heroin user *or* addict, smackhead *and* smack-sack *and* schmecker <nf>; methedrine user *or* methhead <nf>; amphetamine user, pillhead *and* pill popper *and* speed freak <nf>; LSD user, acidhead *and* acid freak *and* tripper *and* cubehead <nf>; marijuana smoker *and* pothead <nf>; **drug seller** ***or*** dealer, pusher, contact, connection; **alcoholic, alcoholic** 88.11; **smoker,** heavy smoker, chain smoker, nicotine addict

VERBS **22** **use, be on,** get on; use occasionally *or* irregularly, have a cotton habit *and* chip *and* chippy *and* joy pop <nf>; **get a rush** ***or*** flush, go over the hump <nf>; **sniff,** snort, blow, toot, one and one <nf>; **smoke marijuana,** take on a number *and* blow a stick *and* toke *and* blast *and* weed out <nf>; **smoke opium,** blow a fill; freebase; **inject,** mainline, shoot *and* shoot up *and* jab *and* get down *and* get off <nf>, pop *and* skin pop <nf>, **take pills,** pop pills <nf>; **withdraw,** crash *and* come down <nf>, kick *or* go cold turkey *and* go a la canona *and* hang tough *and* water out <nf>, detoxify, disintoxicate, detoxicate, dry out, kick *and* kick the habit <nf>; **trip,** blow one's mind *and* wig out <nf>; **sell drugs,** deal *and* push <nf>; **buy drugs,** score *and* make *and* connect <nf>; **have drugs,** be heeled *and* carry *and* hold *and* sizzle <nf>; **drink** *or* **booze** 88.25; **smoke, smoke tobacco,** puff, puff away, drag, chainsmoke, smoke like a chimney

ADJS 23 **intoxicated,** under the influence, nodding, narcotized, poppied, far gone

24 <nf terms> **high,** bent, blasted, blind, bombed out, bonged out, buzzed, coked, coked out, flying, fried, geared, geared up, geezed, gonged, gorked, hopped-up, in a zone, junked, luded out, maxed, noddy, ripped, smashed, snowed, spaced, space out, spacey, stoned, strung out, switched on, tanked, totaled, tranqued, tripping, trippy, wankered, wired, wrecked, zoned, zoned out, zonked, zonked out

25 **addicted,** hooked *and* zunked *and* on the needle <nf>; dependency-prone; **supplied with drugs,** holding *and* heeled *and* carrying *and* anywhere <nf>; using, on, behind acid <nf>

88 INTOXICATION, ALCOHOLIC DRINK

NOUNS 1 **intoxication, inebriation, inebriety,** insobriety, besottedness, sottedness, **drunkenness, tipsiness,** befuddlement, fuddle, fuddlement, fuddledness, tipsification *and* tiddliness <nf>; a high, soaking <nf>; Dutch courage, pot-valiance *or* pot-valiancy, pot-valor; hangover, katzenjammer, morning after <nf>

2 **bibulousness,** bibacity, bibaciousness, bibulosity, sottishness; serious drinking; crapulence, crapulousness; **intemperance** 669; bacchanalianism; Bacchus, Dionysus, fondness for the bottle

3 **alcoholism, dipsomania,** oenomania, alcoholic psychosis *or* addiction, pathological drunkenness, problem drinking, heavy drinking, habitual drunkenness, ebriosity; delirium tremens 926.10; grog blossom *and* bottle nose <nf>; gin drinker's liver, cirrhosis of the liver

4 **drinking, imbibing; social drinking; tippling,** guzzling, gargling, bibing; winebibbing, winebibbery; toping; hard drinking, serious drinking <nf>; **boozing** *and* swilling <nf>, **hitting the booze** *or* **bottle** *or* **sauce** <nf>; alcoholism, Alcoholics Anonymous

5 **spree, drinking bout,** bout, **celebration,** potation, compotation, symposium, wassail, **carouse, carousal,** drunken carousal *or* revelry, revel; bacchanal, bacchanalia, bacchanalian; **debauch, orgy**

6 <nf terms> **binge, drunk,** bust, tear, **bender, toot, bat,** pub-crawl <Brit>, jag, booze-up <chiefly Brit>, brannigan, guzzle, randan, rip

7 **drink,** dram, potation, potion, libation, **nip,** draft, drop, spot, finger or two, sip, sup, suck, drench, guzzle, gargle, jigger; peg, swig, swill, pull; **snort,** jolt, **shot,** snifter, wet; quickie; round, round of drinks

8 **bracer, refresher,** reviver, pickup *and* **pick-me-up** <nf>, tonic, hair of the dog *or* hair of the dog that bit one <nf>

9 **drink, cocktail, highball,** long drink, mixed drink; liquor, spirits; **punch; eye-opener** <nf>, **nightcap** <nf>, sundowner <Brit nf>; **chaser** <nf>, *pousse-café* <Fr>, *apéritif* <Fr>; parting cup, stirrup cup, one for the road; hair of the dog; Mickey Finn *or* Mickey *and* knockout drops <nf>; mixer, chaser

10 **toast, pledge,** health

11 **drinker,** imbiber, **social drinker,** tippler, bibber; winebibber, oenophilist; **drunkard, drunk, inebriate, sot,** toper, guzzler, swiller, soaker, lovepot, tosspot, barfly, thirsty soul,

serious drinker, devotee of Bacchus; swigger; hard drinker, heavy drinker, **alcoholic, dipsomaniac, problem drinker,** chronic alcoholic, chronic drunk, pathological drinker; carouser, reveler, wassailer; bacchanal, bacchanalian; pot companion

12 <nf terms> **drunk, lush,** lusher, **soak,** sponge, hooch hound, **boozer, boozehound,** booze fighter, booze freak, dipso, juicehead, loadie, ginhound, elbow bender *or* crooker, shikker, bottle sucker, swillbelly, swillpot, swillbowl; **souse, stew,** bum, rummy, rumhound, stewbum; wino

13 **spirits, liquor,** intoxicating liquor, adult beverage, **hard liquor,** hard stuff <nf>, **whiskey,** firewater, snake juice, spiritus frumenti, usquebaugh, schnapps, ardent spirits, strong waters, **intoxicant,** toxicant, inebriant, **potable,** potation, **beverage, drink, strong drink,** strong liquor, alcoholic drink *or* beverage, **alcohol,** aqua vitae, water of life, brew, **grog,** social lubricant, nectar of the gods; **booze** <nf>; **rum,** the Demon Rum, John Barleycorn; the bottle, the cup, the cup that cheers, little brown jug; punch bowl, the flowing bowl

14 <nf terms> **likker, hooch, juice, sauce,** tiger milk, pig *or* tiger sweat, sheepdip, moonshine, white lightning; **medicine,** snake medicine, corpse reviver; **rotgut, poison,** rat poison, formaldehyde, embalming fluid, shellac, **panther piss**

15 **liqueur, cordial;** brandy, flavored brandy

16 **beer,** brew *and* brewskie *and* suds <nf>, swipes <Brit nf>; small beer; nonalcoholic beer, alcohol-free beer; draft beer, home-brew, microbrew

17 **wine,** *vin* <Fr>, *vino* <Sp, Ital>; vintage wine, nonvintage wine; the grape; red wine, white wine, rosé wine, pink wine, blush wine; dry *or* sweet wine, heavy *or* light wine, full *or* thin wine, rough *or* smooth wine, still wine, sparkling wine; extra sec *or* demi-sec *or* sec *or* brut champagne, bubbly; new wine, must; imported wine, domestic wine; fortified wine; wine of the country, *vin du campagne* <Fr>; jug wine, plonk <Brit>; Beaujolais wine

18 **bootleg liquor, moonshine** <nf>; hooch *and* shine *and* mountain dew <nf>, white lightning *or* mule <nf>; bathtub gin; home brew

19 **liquor dealer,** liquor store owner; **vintner,** wine merchant; winegrower, winemaker, wine expert, oenologist; **bartender,** mixologist, barkeeper, barkeep, barman <Brit>, tapster, publican <Brit>; barmaid, tapstress; **brewer,** brewmaster; **distiller; bootlegger, moonshiner** <nf>

20 **bar,** barroom, *bistro* <Fr>, cocktail lounge; taproom; **tavern, pub,** pothouse, alehouse, rumshop, grogshop, dramshop, groggery, gin mill <nf>, **saloon,** drinking saloon, saloon bar <Brit>; lounge bar, piano bar, sports bar, singles bar, gay bar; waterhole *or* watering hole <nf>; wine bar; public house <Brit>; public *or* local <Brit nf>; beer parlor, beer garden, rathskeller; **nightclub, cabaret;** café, wine shop; barrel house *and* honky-tonk *and* dive <nf>; **speakeasy** *and* blind tiger *and* blind pig *and* after-hours joint <nf>

21 **distillery, still,** distiller; **brewery,** brewhouse; **winery,** wine press; bottling works

VERBS 22 **intoxicate, inebriate, addle, befuddle,** bemuse, besot, go to one's head, make one see double, make one tiddly

23 <nf terms> **plaster,** pickle, swack, crock, stew, souse, stone, pollute, tipsify, booze up, boozify, fuddle, overtake

24 **tipple, drink,** dram <Brit>, nip; grog, **guzzle,** gargle; **imbibe,** have a drink *or* nip *or* dram *or* guzzle *or* gargle, soak, bib, quaff, sip, sup, lap, lap up, take a drop, slake one's thirst, cheer *or* refresh the inner man, drown one's troubles *or* sorrows, commune with the spirits; **down,** toss off *or* down, toss one's drink, knock back, throw one back, drink off *or* up, drain the cup, drink bottoms-up, drink deep; **drink**

hard, drink like a fish, drink seriously, **tope;** take to drink *or* drinking, drink one's fill

25 <nf terms> **booze,** swig, swill, moisten *or* wet one's whistle; **liquor, liquor up,** lush, souse, tank up, **hit the booze** *or* **bottle** *or* **sauce,** exercise *or* bend *or* crook *or* raise the elbow, dip the beak, splice the main brace; chug-a-lug, chug

26 **get drunk,** be stricken drunk, get high, put on a high, take a drop too much; **get plastered** *or* **pickled,** etc <nf>, tie one on *and* get a bun on <nf>

27 **be drunk,** be intoxicated, have a drop too much, have more than one can hold, have a jag on <nf>, see double, be feeling no pain; **stagger, reel; pass out** <nf>

28 **go on a spree; go on a binge** *or* **drunk** *or* **toot** *or* **bat** *or* **bender** <nf>, **carouse, spree, revel,** wassail, debauch, paint the town red <nf>, pub-crawl <Brit nf>, club-hop

29 **drink to, toast, pledge,** drink a toast to, drink *or* pledge the health of, give you

30 **distill; brew;** bootleg, moonshine <nf>, moonlight <nf>

ADJS 31 **intoxicated, inebriated,** inebriate, inebrious, **drunk, drunken,** *shikker* <Yiddish>, **tipsy,** in liquor, **in one's cups, under the influence,** the worse for liquor, having had one too many; nappy, beery; **tiddly, giddy, dizzy,** muddled, addled, flustered, bemused, reeling, seeing double; **mellow, merry,** jolly, happy, gay, glorious; **full**; **besotted,** sotted, sodden, drenched, far-gone; drunk as a lord, drunk as a fiddler *or* piper, drunk as a skunk, drunk as an owl; staggering drunk, drunk and disorderly; crapulent, crapulous; **maudlin**

32 **dead-drunk,** blind drunk, overcome, out *and* out cold *and* passed out <nf>, helpless, under the table

33 <nf terms> **fuddled,** muzzy, **boozy,** overtaken; **swacked, plastered,** shnockered, stewed, **pickled,** pissed, **soused,** soaked, boiled, fried, canned, tanked, potted, corned, bombed, ripped, smashed; bent, **crocked,** crocko, shellacked, sloshed, sozzled, zonked, tight, lushy, squiffy, afflicted, jug-bitten, oiled, lubricated, feeling no pain, polluted, raddled, organized, **high,** elevated, high as a kite, lit, **lit up,** lit to the gills, illuminated, **loaded, stinko,** tanked, tanked-up, stinking drunk, pie-eyed, pissy-eyed, shit-faced, cockeyed, cockeyed drunk, roaring *or* rip-roaring drunk, skunk-drunk; half-seas over, three sheets to the wind, well-oiled, **blotto, stiff,** blind, paralyzed, **stoned**

34 **full of Dutch courage, pot-valiant,** pot-valorous

35 **bibulous,** bibacious, drunken, sottish, liquorish, given *or* addicted to drink, **liquor-loving,** liquor-drinking, drinking, hard-drinking, swilling <nf>, toping, tippling, winebibbing

36 **intoxicating,** intoxicative, **inebriating,** inebriative, inebriant, heady

37 **alcoholic, spirituous, ardent, strong, hard,** with a kick <nf>; winy, vinous

89 TOBACCO

NOUNS 1 **tobacco,** *tabac* <Fr>, nicotine; **the weed** <nf>, fragrant weed, Indian weed *or* drug, filthy weed; carcinogenic substance; smoke, tobacco smoke, cigarette smoke, cigar smoke, pipe smoke; secondary smoke, secondhand smoke

2 <tobaccos> flue-cured *or* bright, fire-cured, air-cured; Broadleaf, Burley, Cuban, Havana, Havana seed, Latakia, Turkish, Russian, Maryland, Virginia; plug tobacco, bird's-eye, canaster, leaf, lugs, seconds, shag; pipe tobacco

3 **smoking tobacco,** smokings <nf>, smoke *and* smokes <nf>

4 **cigar,** seegar <nf>; rope *and* stinker <nf>; **cheroot, stogie,** corona, belvedere, Havana, panatella, colorado, trichinopoly; cigarillo; box of cigars, cigar box, cigar case, humidor; cigar cutter

5 **cigarette;** butt *and* cig *and* **fag** *and* coffin nail *and* cancer stick <nf>; filter tip, high tar, low tar, methol;

cigarette butt, **butt,** stub; snipe <nf>; pack *or* deck of cigarettes, box *or* carton of cigarettes, cigarette case, cigarette paper

6 **pipe,** tobacco pipe; corncob, corncob pipe, Missouri meerschaum; briar pipe, briar; clay pipe, clay, churchwarden <Brit>; meerschaum; water pipe, hookah, nargileh, kalian, hubble-bubble; peace pipe, calumet; pipe rack, pipe cleaner, tobacco pouch

7 **chewing tobacco,** eating tobacco, oral tobacco; navy *or* navy plug, cavendish, twist, pigtail, plug, cut plug; **quid,** cud, fid <Brit nf>, **chew,** chaw; tobacco juice

8 **snuff,** snoose <nf>; rappee; pinch of snuff; snuff bottle, snuffbox, snuff mill

9 **nicotine**

10 **smoking,** smoking habit, habitual smoking; chain-smoking; smoke, puff, drag <nf>; **chewing;** tobacco *or* nicotine addiction, tobaccoism, tabacosis, tabacism, tabagism, nicotinism; passive smoking

11 **tobacco user, smoker,** cigarette *or* pipe *or* cigar smoker, chewer, snuffer, snuff dipper

12 **tobacconist;** snuffman; tobacco store *or* shop, cigar store

13 **smoking room,** smoking car, **smoker;** smoke-free area, non-smoking section

VERBS **14** <use tobacco> **smoke;** inhale, puff, draw, drag <nf>, pull; smoke like a furnace *or* chimney; chain-smoke; **chew,** chaw <nf>; roll; **take snuff,** dip *or* inhale snuff

ADJS **15** **tobacco,** tobaccoy *or* tobaccoey, tobaccolike; **nicotinic;** smoking, chewing; snuffy; smoke-free, non-smoking

90 HEALTH CARE

NOUNS **1** **medicine, medical practice,** medical profession, medical care, **health care,** health-care industry, health-care delivery, primary care *or* treatment; **medical specialty** *or* **branch** ; **treatment, therapy** 91; **health insurance** 83.5, Medicare, Medicaid; **care,** nursing care, home care, outpatient care, life care; family practice, general practice

2 **surgery;** operation; cosmetic surgery, plastic surgery, facelift, liposuction, nose job <nf>, tuck <nf>

3 **dentistry**, dental medicine, dental care

4 **doctor,** doc <nf>, **physician,** Doctor of Medicine *or* **MD** *or* medical doctor, **medical practitioner, medical man, medico** <nf>, croaker *and* sawbones <nf>; **general practitioner** *or* **GP;** family doctor; country doctor; **intern; resident,** house physician, resident physician; fellow; physician in ordinary; medical attendant, attending physician; **specialist,** board-certified physician *or* specialist; **medical examiner,** coroner; oculist, **optometrist**, radiologist, anesthesiologist; health maintenance organization *or* HMO

5 **surgeon,** sawbones <nf>; operator, operative surgeon

6 **dentist,** tooth doctor; **dental surgeon,** oral surgeon, operative dentist; Doctor of Dental Surgery *or* DDS; Doctor of Dental Science *or* DDSc; Doctor of Dental Medicine *or* DMD; orthodondist, perdontist, exodontist, endodontist, prosthodontist

7 **veterinary, veterinarian, vet** <nf>, veterinary surgeon, horse doctor, animal doctor, horse whisperer

8 **health-care professional, health-care provider, physician, nurse, midwife, therapist,** therapeutist, practitioner; physical therapist, physiotherapist, speech therapist, occupational therapist

9 **healer, nonmedical therapist;** theotherapist; Christian *or* spiritual *or* divine healer; **Christian Science practitioner**; **faith healer,** witch doctor <nf>, shaman, alternative practitioner, **osteopath, chiropractor,** podiatrist, acupuncturist, etc

10 **nurse,** sister *or* nursing sister <Brit>; **probationer,** probationist, probe <nf>; caregiver, hospice caregiver; practical nurse; registered nurse *or* RN, nurse practitioner

11 <hospital staff> paramedic, emergency medical technician *or* EMT;

medevac; physician's assistant *or* PA; orderly, attendant, nurse's aide; audiologist; anesthetist; dietician, nutritionist; radiographer, X-ray technician; laboratory technician; radiotherapist; dietitian; hospital administrator; ambulance driver; custodian

12 **Hippocrates,** Galen; Aesculapius, Asclepius

13 **practice of medicine,** medical practice; general practice, restricted *or* limited practice; group practice; professional association *or* PA; family practice, private practice, health maintenance organization *or* HMO; orthodox medicine, conventional medicine, general medicine, preventive medicine, internal medicine, occupational medicine, public-health medicine, community medicine; unorthodox medicine, alternative medicine, acupuncture, faith healing, homeopathy, naturopathy, guided imagery, visualization, Ayurveda, shamanism, color therapy, art therapy, etc.

VERBS 14 **practice medicine,** doctor <nf>; examine, diagnose, screen; treat; prescribe, medicate, administer, inject; make a house call, be on call; intern; practice surgery, perform surgery, operate; practice dentistry; do a procedure

ADJS 15 **medical,** iatric, health, Hippocratic; surgical; chiropodic, pediatric, orthopedic, obstetric, obstetrical, neurological; dental; orthodontic, periodontic, prosthodontic, exodontic; osteopathic, chiropractic, naturopathic, hydropathic, allopathic, homeopathic; gynecological, internal, pathological, forensic; clinical; diagnostic; therapeutic; veterinary

91 THERAPY, MEDICAL TREATMENT

NOUNS 1 **therapy, therapeutics,** therapeusis, **treatment, medical care** *or* **treatment,** medication; noninvasive *or* nonsurgical therapy *or* treatment; disease-fighting, healing; healing arts; physical therapy, psychotherapy 92; medicines 86

2 **nonmedical therapy;** theotherapy; **healing;** Christian *or* spiritual *or* divine healing; shamanism; **faith healing**

3 **hydrotherapy,** hydrotherapeutics; hydropathy, water cure; cold-water cure; contrast bath, whirlpool bath

4 **heat therapy,** thermotherapy; heliotherapy, solar therapy; fangotherapy; hot bath, sweat bath, sunbath

5 **diathermy,** medical diathermy; electrotherapy, electrotherapeutics; **radiothermy,** high-frequency treatment; shortwave diathermy, ultrashortwave diathermy, microwave diathermy; ultrasonic diathermy; surgical diathermy, radiosurgery, electrosurgery, electrosection, electrocautery, electrocoagulation

6 **radiotherapy,** radiation therapy, radiotherapeutics; adjuvant therapy

7 **radiology,** radiography, radioscopy, radiation, fluoroscopy, etc 1037.8; diagnostic radiology, scanning, magnetic resonance imaging *or* MRI

8 <radiotherapeutic substances> radium; cobalt; radioisotope, tracer, labeled *or* tagged element, radioelement; radiocarbon, carbon 14, radiocalcium, radiopotassium, radiosodium, radioiodine; atomic cocktail

9 <diagnostic pictures and graphs> **X ray,** scan, radiograph, radiogram, roentgenogram *or* roentgenograph; photofluorograph; X-ray movie; chest X-ray; pyelogram; orthodiagram; encephalograph, encephalogram; electroencephalograph, electroencephalogram *or* EEG; electrocorticogram; electrocardiogram *or* ECG *or* EKG; electromyogram; computer-assisted tomography *or* CAT, computerized axial tomography *or* computed tomography *or* computer-assisted tomography *or* computerized tomography *or* CAT; CAT scan; magnetic resonance imaging *or* MRI; MRI scan; positron emission tomography *or* PET; PET scan; ultrasound, ultrasonography; sonogram

10 case history, medical history, anamnesis; associative anamnesis; catamnesis, follow-up

11 **diagnostics,** prognostics; symptomatology, semeiology, semeiotics

12 **diagnosis**; **examination, physical examination;** study, test, workup <nf>; medical test, laboratory test, screening, diagnostic procedure; blood test, blood work <nf>, blood count, urinalysis, uroscopy; biopsy; Pap test *or* smear; stress test; electrocardiography, electroencephalography, electromyography; mammography; pregnancy test, amniocentesis *or* amnio, ultrasound

13 **prognosis,** prognostication; prognostic, **symptom, sign**

14 **treatment,** medical treatment *or* attention *or* care; **cure,** curative measures; **medication,** medicamentation; **regimen,** regime, protocol; first aid; hospitalization; physical therapy, acupressure, shiatsu

15 **immunization;** immunization therapy, immunotherapy; vaccine therapy, vaccinotherapy; toxin-antitoxin immunization; serum therapy, serotherapy, serotherapeutics; tuberculin test, scratch test, patch test; **immunology,** immunochemistry; immunity theory, side-chain theory; immunity; immunodeficiency

16 **inoculation, vaccination; injection,** hypodermic, hypodermic injection, shot *and* bing <nf>, hypospray *or* jet injection; booster, booster shot <nf>; antitoxin, vaccine 86.28

17 <methods of injection> cutaneous, percutaneous, subcutaneous, intradermal, intramuscular, intravenous, intramedullary, intracardiac, intrathecal, intraspinal

18 **transfusion,** blood transfusion; serum; blood bank, blood donor center, bloodmobile; blood donor

19 **surgery,** surgical treatment, **operation,** surgical operation, surgical intervention, surgical technique *or* measure, the knife <nf>; **instrument,** device; respirator; unnecessary surgery, *cacoëthes operandi* <L>, tomomania; major surgery, minor surgery, laser surgery, plastic surgery

20 bloodletting, bleeding, venesection, phlebotomy; leeching; cupping

21 **hospital, clinic,** *hôpital* <Fr>, treatment center; general hospital, teaching hospital, university hospital, health center, base hospital; hospice, infirmary; nursing home, rest home, convalescent home, sanitarium, assisted living; sick bay *or* berth; trauma center; birthing center; wellness center

22 **pesthouse,** lazar house

23 **health resort, spa, watering place,** baths; mineral spring, warm *or* hot spring; pump room, pump house; yoga retreat

VERBS **24** **treat, doctor,** minister to, care for, give care to, physic; **diagnose;** nurse; **cure, remedy, heal;** dress the wounds, bandage, poultice, plaster, strap, splint; bathe; massage, rub; operate on; physic, purge; **operate,** perform a procedure; transplant, replant

25 **medicate,** medicine, drug, dope <nf>, dose; salve, oil, anoint, embrocate

26 **irradiate,** radiumize, **X-ray,** roentgenize

27 bleed, let blood, leech, phlebotomize; cup; **transfuse,** give a transfusion; perfuse

28 **immunize, inoculate, vaccinate,** shoot <nf>

29 **undergo treatment,** take the cure, doctor <nf>, take medicine; go under the knife <nf>

92 PSYCHOLOGY, PSYCHOTHERAPY

NOUNS **1** **psychology**, science of the mind, science of human behavior, mental philosophy; psychologism, pop psychology *and* psychobabble <nf>; mental states, mental processes

2 psychological school, school *or* system of psychology, psychological theory; Adlerian psychology; behaviorism *or* behavior *or* behavioristic psychology *or* stimulus-response psychology; Freudian psychology *or* Freudianism; Gestalt psychology *or* configurationism; Horneyan psychology; Jungian *or* analytical psychology; Pavlovian psychology; Reichian psychology *or* orgone theory; Skinnerian psychology; Sullivanian psychology

3 **psychiatry,** psychological medicine; neuropsychiatry; social psychiatry; prophylactic psychiatry

4 **psychosomatic medicine,** psychological medicine, medicopsychology; psychosocial medicine

5 **psychotherapy,** psychotherapeutics, mind cure, cognitive therapy

6 **psychoanalysis, analysis,** the couch <nf>, counseling, behavior therapy, behavior modification; psychoanalytic therapy, psychoanalytic method; **depth psychology,** psychology of depths; group analysis *or* psychology, family therapy; play therapy; transactional analysis; psychognosis, psychognosy; dream analysis, interpretation of dreams, dream symbolism; depth interview; hypnotherapy; meditation, transcendental meditation

7 **psychodiagnostics,** psychodiagnosis, psychological *or* psychiatric evaluation

8 **psychometrics,** psychometry, psychological measurement; **intelligence testing;** mental test, psychological screening; psychography; psychogram, psychograph, psychological profile; psychometer, IQ meter <nf>; lie detector, polygraph, psychogalvanometer, psychogalvanic skin response

9 **psychological test**, mental test; standardized test; developmental test, achievement test

10 **psychologist; psychotherapist, therapist,** psychotherapeutist; clinical psychologist; licensed psychologist, psychological practitioner; child psychologist; **psychiatrist,** alienist, somatist; neuropsychiatrist; psychopathist, psychopathologist; psychotechnologist, industrial psychologist; hypnotherapist; behavior therapist; psychobiologist, psychochemist, psychophysiologist, psychophysicist; psychographer; psychiatric social worker; **psychoanalyst, analyst; shrink** *and* headshrinker *and* shrinker <nf>; **counselor,** psychological counselor; counseling service

11 **personality tendency,** complexion, humor; somatotype; **introversion,** introvertedness, ingoingness; inner-directedness; **extroversion,** extrovertedness, outgoingness; other-directedness; syntony, ambiversion; schizothymia, schizothymic *or* schizoid personality; cyclothymia, cyclothymic *or* cycloid personality; mesomorphism, mesomorphy; endomorphism, endomorphy; ectomorphism, ectomorphy

12 <personality type> **introvert, extrovert,** syntone, ambivert; schizothyme, schizoid; cyclothymic, cyclothyme, cycloid; choleric, melancholic, sanguine, phlegmatic; endomorph, mesomorph, ectomorph; Type A; Type B

13 **pathological personality,** psychopathological personality, sick personality, psycho <nf>

14 **mental disorder, emotional disorder,** neurosis; psychonosema, psychopathyfunctional nervous disorder; reaction; emotional instability; **maladjustment,** social maladjustment; nervous *or* mental breakdown, crack-up <nf>; problems in living; brainstorm; **insanity, mental illness** 926.1; **psychosis** 926.3; **schizophrenia; paranoia** 926.4; **manic-depressive psychosis,** bipolar disorder; **depression,** melancholia 926.5; seasonal affective disorder *or* SAD, post-partum depression; melancholia *or* endogenous depression; premenstrual syndrome *or* PMS; **neurosis, psychoneurosis,** neuroticism, neurotic *or* psychoneurotic disorder; brain disease, nervous disorder; cognitive disorder, eating disorder, sleep disorder, somatoform disorder, dissociative disorder, mood disorder, anxiety disorder, sexual disorder, impulse-control disorder, conversion disorder; battle fatigue

15 **personality disorder, character disorder,** moral insanity, sociopa-

thy, **psychopathy; psychopathic personality;** sexual pathology, sexual psychopathy 75.11; compulsion, fixation, complex; obsessive-compulsive disorder; identity crisis, midlife crisis

16 **neurotic reaction,** neurosis, overreaction, disproportionate reaction, depression, mania

17 **psychological stress, stress; frustration,** external frustration, internal frustration; conflict, ambivalence, ambivalence of impulse; **trauma,** psychological *or* emotional trauma, traumatism, mental *or* emotional shock, decompensation; rape trauma syndrome; post-traumatic stress disorder; shell shock

18 **psychosomatic symptom; symptom of emotional disorder,** emotional symptom, psychological symptom; **thought disturbance,** thought disorder *or* disturbances, dissociative disorder, delirium, delusion, disorientation, hallucination; **speech abnormality**

19 **trance,** daze, stupor; catatonic stupor, catalepsy; cataplexy; dream state, reverie, daydreaming 985.2; somnambulism, sleepwalking; hypnotic trance; fugue, fugue state; **amnesia** 990.2; meditation; brown study

20 **dissociation,** mental *or* emotional dissociation, disconnection, dissociative disorder; dissociation of personality, personality disorganization *or* disintegration; **schizoid personality;** double *or* dual personality; multiple personality, split personality, alternating personality; schizoidism, schizothymia, **schizophrenia** 926.4; depersonalization; **paranoid personality; paranoia** 926.4

21 **fixation,** libido fixation *or* arrest, **arrested development;** infantile fixation, pregenital fixation, father fixation, Freudian fixation, mother fixation, parent fixation; **regression,** retreat to immaturity

22 **complex,** inferiority complex, superiority complex, parent complex, Oedipus complex, mother complex, Electra complex, father complex, Diana complex, persecution complex; castration complex; compulsion complex

23 **defense mechanism,** defense reaction; ego defense, psychotaxis; biological *or* psychological *or* sociological adjustive reactions; resistance; dissociation; **negativism, alienation; escapism,** escape mechanism, avoidance mechanism; escape, flight, **withdrawal; isolation,** emotional insulation; **fantasy,** fantasizing, escape into fantasy, dreamlike thinking, autistic *or* dereistic thinking, idealization, wishful thinking, autism, dereism; wish-fulfillment, wish-fulfillment fantasy; sexual fantasy; **compensation,** overcompensation, decompensation; substitution; **sublimation;** regression, reversion; **projection,** identification, blame-shifting; displacement; intellectualization, **rationalization**

24 **suppression, repression, inhibition,** resistance, restraint, censorship, censor; block, psychological block, blockage, blocking; denial, negation, rejection; reaction formation; rigid control; **suppressed desire**

25 **catharsis,** purgation, abreaction, motor abreaction, psychocatharsis, **emotional release,** relief of tension, outlet; release therapy, acting-out, psychodrama; imaging

26 **conditioning,** classical *or* Pavlovian conditioning; instrumental conditioning; operant conditioning; psychagogy, reeducation, reorientation; conditioned reflex, conditioned stimulus, conditioned response; reinforcement, positive reinforcement, negative reinforcement; simple reflex, unconditioned reflex, **reflex** 903.1; **behavior** 321; suggestion

27 **adjustment,** adjustive reaction; **readjustment, rehabilitation;** psychosynthesis, integration of personality; fulfillment, self-fulfillment; self-actualization, peak experience; integrated personality, syntonic personality; stress management

28 **psyche,** psychic apparatus, **personality, self,** personhood; **mind** 919.1,3,4, pneuma, soul; preconscious, foreconscious, coconscious; **subconscious, unconscious,** stream of consciousness, subconscious *or* unconscious mind, submerged mind, subliminal, subliminal self; **libido,** psychic *or* libidinal energy, motive force, vital impulse, ego-libido, object libido; **id,** primitive self, pleasure principle, life instinct, death instinct; **ego,** conscious self; **superego,** ethical self, conscience; ego ideal; ego-id conflict; anima, animus, persona; collective unconscious, racial unconscious; hive mind; psychological me; **self**

29 **engram,** memory trace, traumatic trace *or* memory; unconscious memory; archetype, archetypal pattern *or* image *or* symbol; imago, image, father image, etc; race *or* racial memory; cultural memory; **memory** 989

30 **symbol,** universal symbol, father symbol, mother symbol, phallic symbol, fertility symbol, etc; symbolism, symbolization

31 **surrogate,** substitute; father surrogate, father figure, father image; mother surrogate, mother figure, mother image

32 **gestalt,** pattern, figure, configuration, form, sensory pattern; figure-ground

33 **association, association of ideas,** chain of ideas, concatenation, mental linking; controlled association, free association, association by contiguity, association by similarity; association by sound, clang association; stream of consciousness; transference, identification, positive transference, negative transference; synesthesia 24.5

34 **cathexis,** cathection, desire concentration; charge, energy charge, cathectic energy; anticathexis, countercathexis, counterinvestment; hypercathexis, overcharge

35 psychiatric treatment, psychiatric care; psychosurgery, shock treatment, shock therapy, convulsive therapy, electroconvulsive therapy

VERBS **36** **psychologize, psychoanalyze,** analyze, counsel**;** abreact; fixate, obsess on <nf>; neuroticize

ADJS **37** **psychological; psychiatric,** neuropsychiatric; psychometric; **psychopathic,** psychopathological; **psychosomatic,** somatopsychic, psychophysical, psychophysiological, psychobiological; psychogenic, psychogenetic, functional; psychodynamic, psychoneurological, psychosexual, psychosocial, psychotechnical; **psychotic**

38 **psychotherapeutic;** psychiatric, psychoanalytic, psychoanalytical; psychodiagnostic; hypnotherapeutic

39 **neurotic, psychoneurotic,** disturbed, disordered; neurasthenic, psychasthenic; hysteric *or* hysterical, hypochondriac, phobic; deluded; dissociated; depressed, poopy <nf>; stressed

40 **introverted,** introvert, introversive, **subjective, ingoing,** inner-directed; withdrawn, isolated; Type B

41 **extroverted,** extrovert, extroversive, **outgoing,** extrospective; other-directed; Type A

42 **subconscious, unconscious;** subliminal, extramarginal; preconscious, foreconscious, coconscious

93 FEELING

NOUNS **1** **feeling, emotion,** affect, **sentiment,** affection, affections, sympathies, beliefs; affective faculty, affectivity; emotional charge, cathexis; **feelings, sensitiveness, sensibility,** susceptibility, thin skin; emotional life; the logic of the heart; **sense,** deep *or* profound sense, gut sense *or* sensation <nf>; emotional intelligence; **sensation** 24; **impression,** undercurrent, perception; hunch, intuition, feeling in one's bones, vibes <nf>, presentiment 934.3; foreboding; **reaction, response,** gut reaction <nf>; **instinct** 365.1; emotional coloring *or* shade *or* nuance, **tone;** drama queen

2 **passion,** passionateness, strong feeling, powerful emotion; **fervor, fervency,** fervidness, impassionedness, **ardor, ardency,** *empressement* <Fr>, warmth of feeling, **warmth, heat, fire,** verve, furor, **fury,** vehemence; heartiness, gusto, relish, savor; spirit, heart, soul; **liveliness** 330.2; **zeal** 101.2; **excitement** 105; **ecstasy**

3 **heart, soul, spirit,** *esprit* <Fr>, **breast, bosom,** inmost heart *or* soul, heart of hearts, secret *or* inner recesses of the heart, secret places, heart's core, heartstrings, cockles of the heart, bottom of the heart, being, innermost being, core of one's being; viscera, pit of one's stomach, **gut** *or* guts <nf>; bones

4 **sensibility, sensitivity, sensitiveness,** delicacy, fineness of feeling, tenderness, affectivity, susceptibility, impressionability 24.2

5 **sympathy, fellow feeling, sympathetic response,** good feeling, responsiveness, relating, warmth, cordiality, **caring,** concern; response, echo, chord, sympathetic chord, vibrations, vibes <nf>; **empathy,** identification; involvement, sharing; pathos

6 **tenderness,** tender feeling, softness, gentleness, delicacy; **tenderheartedness,** softheartedness, warmheartedness, tender *or* sensitive *or* warm heart, soft place *or* spot in one's heart; warmth, **fondness, weakness** 100.2

7 **bad feeling, hard feelings;** immediate dislike, disaffinity, personality conflict, bad vibes *or* chemistry *or* juju <nf>, bad blood, **hostility,** scunner, animosity 589.4; resentment, bitterness, ill will, intolerance, disappointment; **hard-heartedness** 94.3

8 **sentimentality, sentiment, sentimentalism,** oversentimentality, oversentimentalism, bathos; nostalgia, nostomania; romanticism; sweetness and light, hearts-and-flowers; bleeding heart; mawkishness, cloyingness, maudlinness, namby-pamby, namby-pambyness, namby-pambyism; mushiness *or* sloppiness <nf>; **mush** *and* slush *and* slop *and* goo *and* schmaltz <nf>; sob story *and* tearjerker <nf>, soap opera

9 **emotionalism,** emotionality, lump in one's throat; emotionalizing, emotionalization; emotiveness, emotivity; visceralness; nonrationalness, unreasoningness; demonstrativeness, making scenes, excitability; **theatrics, theatricality, histrionics, dramatics,** hamminess *and* chewing up the scenery <nf>; **sensationalism, melodrama,** melodramatics, blood and thunder; yellow journalism; emotional appeal, human interest, love interest; **overemotionalism,** hyperthymia, excess of feeling, emotional instability

VERBS **10** **feel,** entertain *or* harbor *or* cherish *or* nurture a feeling; feel deeply, feel in one's viscera *or* bones, feel in one's gut *or* guts <nf>; experience 831.8; have a sensation, get *or* receive an impression, **sense, perceive**; intuit, have a hunch

11 **respond, react,** be moved, be affected *or* touched, be inspired, echo, catch the flame *or* infection, be in tune; **respond to,** warm up to, take *or* lay to heart, open one's heart to, be turned on to <nf>, nourish in one's bosom, feel in one's breast, cherish at the heart's core, treasure up in the heart; enter into the spirit of, be imbued with the spirit of; care about, feel for, sympathize with, empathize with, identify with, relate to emotionally, dig *and* be turned on by <nf>, be involved, share; color with emotion

12 **have deep feelings, be all heart, have a tender heart,** take to heart, be a person of heart *or* sentiment; have a soft place *or* spot in one's heart; be a prey to one's feelings; love 104.18–20; hate 103.5

13 **emotionalize, emote** <nf>, give free play to the emotions, make a scene; be theatrical, theatricalize, ham it up *and* chew up the scenery <nf>; **sentimentalize,** gush *and* slobber over <nf>

14 **affect, touch, move, stir; melt, soften,** melt the heart, choke one up, give one a lump in the throat; **penetrate,** pierce, go through one, go deep; touch a chord, **touch a sympathetic chord, touch one's heart,** tug at the heart *or* heartstrings, go to one's heart, get under one's skin; come home to; **touch to the quick,**

touch on the raw, flick one on the raw, smart, sting

15 **impress, affect, strike, hit,** smite, rock; **make an impression, get to one** <nf>; make a dent in, make an impact upon, sink in <nf>, strike home, come home to, hit the mark <nf>; tell, have a strong effect, traumatize, strike hard, impress forcibly

16 **impress upon,** bring home to, make it felt; stamp, stamp on, etch, engrave, engrave on

ADJS **17** **emotional, affective,** emotive, affectional, **feeling,** sentient; soulful, of soul, of heart, of feeling, of sentiment; visceral, gut <nf>; glandular; emotiometabolic, emotiomotor, emotiomuscular, emotiovascular; demonstrative, overdemonstrative

18 **fervent, fervid, passionate, impassioned,** intense, **ardent; hearty, cordial,** enthusiastic, exuberant, unrestrained, vigorous; keen, breathless, **excited** 105.18,20,22; **lively** 330.17; zealous; **warm, burning, heated, hot, volcanic,** red-hot, fiery, flaming, glowing, ablaze, afire, on fire, boiling over, steaming, steamy; delirious, fevered, feverish, febrile, flushed; wired; intoxicated, drunk; obsessed

19 **emotionalistic,** emotive, overemotional, hysteric, hysterical, sensational, sensationalistic, melodramatic, theatric, theatrical, histrionic, dramatic, overdramatic, hammy <nf>, nonrational, unreasoning; overemotional, hyperthymic

20 **sensitive,** sensible, emotionable, passible, delicate; responsive, sympathetic, receptive; empathetic, caring; susceptible, impressionable; **tender, soft, tenderhearted, softhearted,** warmhearted

21 **sentimental,** sentimentalized, soft, **mawkish, maudlin,** cloying; sticky *and* gooey *and* schmaltzy *and* sappy *and* soppy <nf>, oversentimental, oversentimentalized, bathetic; **mushy** *or* sloppy *or* gushing *or* teary *or* beery <nf>, treacly <Brit nf>; tearjerking <nf>; namby-pamby, romantic; nostalgic, nostomanic

22 **affecting, touching, moving,** emotive, pathetic

23 **affected, moved, touched, impressed;** impressed with *or* by, penetrated with, seized with, imbued with, devoured by, obsessed, obsessed with *or* by; wrought up by; stricken, wracked, racked, torn, agonized, tortured; worked up, all worked up, wired, **excited** 105.18

24 **deep-felt,** deepgoing, from the heart, heartfelt; **deep, profound;** indelible; pervasive, pervading, absorbing; penetrating, penetrant, piercing; **poignant,** keen, sharp, acute

ADVS **25** **feelingly, emotionally,** affectively; affectingly, touchingly, movingly, **with feeling,** poignantly

26 **fervently, fervidly, passionately, impassionedly,** intensely, **ardently,** zealously; keenly, breathlessly, excitedly; warmly, heatedly, glowingly; heartily, cordially; enthusiastically, exuberantly, vigorously; kindly, heart and soul, with all one's heart, from the heart, from the bottom of one's heart

27 **sentimentally,** mawkishly, maudlinly, cloyingly; mushily *and* sloppily *and* gushingly <nf>

94 LACK OF FEELING

NOUNS **1** **unfeeling,** unfeelingness, affectlessness, lack of affect, lack of feeling *or* feeling tone, emotional deadness *or* numbness *or* paralysis, **anesthesia, emotionlessness,** unemotionalism, unexcitability; **dispassion,** dispassionateness, unpassionateness, **objectivity;** passionlessness, **spiritlessness, heartlessness,** soullessness; **coldness, coolness, frigidity,** chill, chilliness, frostiness, iciness; coldheartedness, cold-bloodedness; cold heart, cold blood; cold fish; **unresponsiveness,** unsympatheticness; lack of touch *or* contact, autism, self-absorption, withdrawal, catatonia; unimpressionableness, unimpressibility; insusceptibility, unsusceptibility; **impassiveness,** impassibility, impassivity; straight face *and* poker face <nf>, deadpan <nf>; immovability, untouchability; **dullness, obtuseness; inexcitability** 106

2 insensibility, insensibleness, **unconsciousness,** unawareness, **obliviousness,** oblivion; anesthesia, narcosis

3 callousness, insensitivity, insensitiveness, philistinism; **coarseness, brutalization, hardness,** hardenedness, **hard-heartedness, hardness of heart,** hard heart, stony-heartedness, heart of stone, stoniness, marbleheartedness, flintheartedness, flintiness; **obduracy,** obdurateness, induration, inuredness; imperviousness, **thick skin,** rhinoceros hide, thick *or* hard-shell, armor, formidable defenses

4 apathy, indifference, unconcern, lack of caring, disinterest; withdrawnness, **aloofness, detachment,** ataraxy *or* ataraxia, **dispassion; passiveness,** passivity, supineness, insouciance, nonchalance; inappetence, lack of appetite; **listlessness, spiritlessness,** burnout, blah *or* blahs <nf>, heartlessness, plucklessness, spunklessness; **lethargy, phlegm,** lethargicalness, phlegmaticalness, phlegmaticness, hebetude, **dullness,** sluggishness, languor, languidness; soporifousness, sopor, coma, comatoseness, torpidness, torpor, torpidity, **stupor,** stupefaction, narcosis; acedia, sloth; **resignation,** resignedness, stoicism; **numbness,** benumbedness; hopelessness 125

VERBS **5** not be affected by, remain unmoved, not turn a hair, not care less <nf>; have a thick skin, have a heart of stone; be cold as ice, be a cold fish, be an icicle; not affect, leave one cold *or* unmoved, unimpress, underwhelm <nf>

6 callous, harden, case harden, **harden one's heart,** ossify, steel, indurate, inure; brutalize

7 dull, blunt, desensitize, obtund, hebetate

8 numb, benumb, paralyze, **deaden,** anesthetize, freeze, **stun, stupefy,** drug, narcotize

ADJS **9 unfeeling, unemotional,** nonemotional, emotionless, affectless, emotionally dead *or* numb *or* paralyzed, anesthetized, drugged, narcotized; **unpassionate, dispassionate,** unimpassioned, **objective;** passionless, **spiritless, heartless,** soulless; lukewarm, Laodicean; **cold, cool, frigid,** frozen, chill, chilly, arctic, frosty, frosted, icy, **coldhearted, cold-blooded,** cold as charity, **unaffectionate,** unloving; **unresponsive,** unresponding, **unsympathetic;** out of touch *or* contact; in one's shell *or* armor, behind one's defenses; autistic, self-absorbed, self-centered, egocentric, catatonic; unimpressionable, unimpressible, insusceptible, unsusceptible, unperturbed, imperturbable, undisturbed; **impassive,** impassible; immovable, untouchable; dull, obtuse, blunt; **inexcitable** 106.10

10 insensible, unconscious, unaware, **oblivious,** blind to, deaf to, dead to, lost to

11 unaffected, unmoved, untouched, dry-eyed, unimpressed, unshaken, unstruck, **unstirred,** unruffled, unanimated, uninspired

12 callous, calloused, insensitive, Philistine; **thick-skinned,** pachydermatous; **hard, hard-hearted, hardened,** case-hardened, coarsened, brutalized, indurated, stony, stony-hearted, marblehearted, flinthearted, flinty, steely, impervious, inured, armored *or* steeled against, proof against, as hard as nails

13 apathetic, indifferent, unconcerned, uncaring, **disinterested, uninterested; withdrawn, aloof, detached,** Olympian, above it all; **passive,** supine; stoic, stoical; insouciant, nonchalant, blasé, **listless, spiritless,** burned-out, blah <nf>, heartless, pluckless, spunkless; **lethargic, phlegmatic,** hebetudinous, **dull,** desensitized, sluggish, torpid, languid, slack, soporific, comatose, **stupefied,** in a stupor, **numb,** numbed, benumbed; resigned; hopeless 125.12

ADVS **14 unfeelingly, unemotionally,** emotionlessly; with a straight *or* poker face <nf>, deadpan <nf>; **dispassionately,** unpassionately; **spiritlessly, heartlessly,** coldly, coldheartedly, cold-bloodedly, **in cold blood;** with dry eyes

15 **apathetically, indifferently, unconcernedly,** disinterestedly, uninterestedly, uncaringly, impassively; **listlessly, spiritlessly,** heartlessly, pluckiessly, spunklessly; **lethargically, phlegmatically,** dully, numbly

95 PLEASURE

NOUNS 1 **pleasure, enjoyment;** quiet pleasure, euphoria, well-being, good feeling, comfort zone, **contentment,** content, **ease, comfort** 121; coziness, warmth; **gratification, satisfaction,** great satisfaction, hearty enjoyment, keen pleasure *or* satisfaction, pleasance; **self-gratification,** self-indulgence; instant gratification; luxury; **relish, zest, gusto,** *joie de vivre* <Fr>; sweetness of life, *douceur de vivre* <Fr>; kicks <nf>, **fun,** entertainment, amusement 743; beer and skittles <Br>; intellectual pleasure, pleasures of the mind; **strokes** *and* stroking *and* ego massage <nf>; physical pleasure, creature comforts, bodily pleasure, sense *or* sensuous pleasure; sexual pleasure, voluptuousness, sensual pleasure, *volupté* <Fr>, animal pleasure, animal comfort, bodily comfort, fleshly *or* carnal delight; forepleasure, titillation, endpleasure, fruition; sensualism

2 **happiness, felicity, gladness, delight,** delectation; **joy, joyfulness**; **cheer,** cheerfulness, exhilaration, **exuberance, high spirits, glee,** sunshine; gaiety 109.4, overjoyfulness, overhappiness; intoxication; **rapture,** ravishment, bewitchment, **enchantment,** unalloyed happiness; elation, exaltation; **ecstasy,** ecstasies, transport; **bliss,** blissfulness; beatitude, beatification, blessedness; paradise, heaven, seventh heaven, cloud nine; smiley face; eudaimonia; happy camper

3 **treat, regalement,** regale; **feast, banquet** revelment, regale, Lucullan feast; feast *or* banquet of the soul; round of pleasures, mad round; **festivity,** fete, fiesta, festive occasion, celebration, party, merrymaking, revel, revelry, jubilation, joyance; carnival, Mardi Gras; afterparty

4 pleasure-loving, pleasure principle, hedonism, hedonics; epicureanism, Cyrenaicism, eudaemonism, eudemonism; hedonic treadmill

5 <period of pleasure> good time, fun time, happy hour, bread and circuses, *la dolce vita* <Ital>, life of Riley, easy street, bed of roses, Elysium, Elysian fields, land of milk and honey

VERBS 6 **please, pleasure, give pleasure,** afford one pleasure, be to one's liking, sit well with one, meet one's wishes, take *or* strike one's fancy, feel good *or* right, strike one right; do one's heart good, warm the cockles of one's heart, tickle pink <nf>; **suit**

7 <nf terms> **hit the spot,** be just the ticket, be just what the doctor ordered, **make a hit,** go over big, go over with a bang

8 **gratify, satisfy,** sate, satiate; slake, appease, allay, assuage, quench; regale, feed, feast; do one's heart good, warm the cockles of the heart

9 **gladden,** make happy, happify; bless, beatify; cheer 109.7

10 **delight,** delectate, **tickle, titillate, thrill, enrapture, enthrall, enchant,** entrance, fascinate, captivate, bewitch, **charm,** becharm; enravish, ravish, imparadise; ecstasiate, transport, carry away

11 <nf terms> **give one a bang** *or* kick *or* charge *or* rush, knock out, knock off one's feet *or* dead *or* for a loop, knock one's socks off, thrill to death *or* to pieces, tickle to death, tickle pink, **wow,** slay, send, freak out; **stroke,** massage one's ego

12 **be pleased, feel happy,** feel good, sing, purr, smile, laugh, be wreathed in smiles, beam; **delight,** joy, take great satisfaction; look like the cat that swallowed the canary; brim *or*

burst with joy, walk *or* tread on air, have stars in one's eyes, be in heaven *or* seventh heaven *or* paradise, be on cloud nine; fall *or* go into raptures; die with delight *or* pleasure

13 **enjoy,** pleasure in, be pleased with, receive *or* derive pleasure from, take delight *or* pleasure in, get a kick *or* boot *or* bang *or* charge *or* lift *or* rush out of <nf>; **like, love,** adore <nf>; **delight in, rejoice in,** indulge in, luxuriate in, revel in, riot in, bask in, wallow in, swim in; groove on *and* get high on <nf>; feast on, gloat over *or* on; **relish, appreciate,** roll under the tongue, do justice to, savor, smack the lips; devour, eat up

14 **enjoy oneself,** have a good time, party, live it up <nf>, have the time of one's life, have a ball *or* blast <nf>; live large

ADJS 15 **pleased, delighted; glad,** gladsome; **charmed,** intrigued <nf>; **thrilled; tickled,** tickled to death *and* tickled pink <nf>, exhilarated; **gratified, satisfied;** pleased with, taken with, favorably impressed with, sold on <nf>, turned-on; pleased as Punch, pleased as a child with a new toy; euphoric, eupeptic; **content, contented,** easy, **comfortable** 121.11, cozy, in clover, snug as a bug in a rug <nf>

16 **happy, glad, joyful, joyous,** flushed with joy, radiant, beaming, glowing, starry-eyed, sparkling, laughing, smiling, smirking, smirky, chirping, purring, singing, dancing, leaping, capering, **cheerful, gay** 109.14; **blissful,** blessed, blessed; beatified, beatific; thrice happy, happy as a lark, happy as a king, happy as the day is long, happy as a clam at high water, happy as a clam, happy as a pig in shit *or* poo <nf>, happy as a sand boy <Brit>

17 **overjoyed,** overjoyful, overhappy, brimming *or* bursting with happiness, on top of the world; **rapturous,** raptured, **enraptured, enchanted,** entranced, enravished, ravished, rapt, possessed; sent *and* high *and* freaked-out <nf>, **in raptures,** transported, in a transport of delight, **carried away,** rapt *or* ravished away, beside oneself, beside oneself with joy, all over oneself <nf>; **ecstatic,** in ecstasies, ecstasiating; rhapsodic, rhapsodical; imparadised, **in paradise,** in heaven, in seventh heaven, on cloud nine <nf>; **elated,** elate, exalted, jubilant, exultant, flushed; blessed, blessed-out

18 **pleasure-loving,** pleasure-seeking, fun-loving, hedonic, hedonistic; Lucullan; epicurean, Cyrenaic, eudaemonic; carnivalesque; living large

ADVS 19 **happily, gladly, joyfully, joyously, delightedly,** with pleasure, to one's delight; blissfully, blessedly; **ecstatically,** rhapsodically, **rapturously; elatedly,** jubilantly, exultantly

20 **for fun,** for kicks, for the hell *or* heck *or* devil of it <nf>

96 UNPLEASURE

NOUNS 1 **unpleasure, unpleasantness** 98, **lack of pleasure,** joylessness, cheerlessness; unsatisfaction, nonsatisfaction, ungratification, nongratification; grimness; discontent 108; displeasure, dissatisfaction, **discomfort,** uncomfortableness, malaise, **painfulness; disquiet,** inquietude, **uneasiness,** unease, discomposure, vexation of spirit, **anxiety;** angst, anguish, dread, nausea, existential woe, existential vacuum; the blahs <nf>; **dullness,** flatness, staleness, tastelessness, savorlessness; **boredom,** ennui, tedium, tediousness, spleen; emptiness, spiritual void, death of the heart *or* soul; unhappiness 112.2; dislike 99

2 **annoyance, vexation,** bothersomeness, exasperation, *tracasserie* <Fr>, **aggravation; nuisance, pest, bother,** botheration <nf>, public nuisance, **trouble, problem,** pain <nf>, difficulty, hot potato <nf>; **trial;** bed of nails; **bore,** crashing bore <nf>; **drag** *and* downer <nf>, royal pain; **worry,** worriment <nf>;

downside *and* the bad news <nf>; stress, fear, pressure, anxiety, angst; **headache** <nf>; **pain in the neck** *or* **in the ass** <nf>; **harassment,** molestation, persecution, dogging, hounding, harrying; devilment, bedevilment; vexatiousness 98.7; bogey *or* bogy

3 **irritation, aggravation,** exacerbation, worsening, salt in the wound, twisting the knife in the wound, embitterment, **provocation;** fret, gall, chafe; irritant; pea in the shoe

4 **chagrin, distress; embarrassment, abashment, discomfiture,** egg on one's face <nf>, disconcertion, disconcertment, discountenance, discomposure, disturbance, confusion; **humiliation, shame,** shamefacedness, mortification, red face

5 **pain, distress, grief,** stress, stress of life, suffering, passion, dolor; ache, aching; pang, wrench, throes, cramp, spasm, twinge; wound, injury, hurt; **sore,** sore spot, soreness, tender spot, tenderness, lesion; strain, sprain; cut, stroke; shock, blow, hard *or* nasty blow; malady, illness, disease, plague; bane

6 **wretchedness, despair,** bitterness, infelicity, **misery, anguish, agony, woe,** woefulness, bale, balefulness; **melancholy,** melancholia, **depression, sadness,** disappointment, **grief** 112.10; **heartache,** aching heart, heavy heart, bleeding heart, broken heart, agony of mind *or* spirit; suicidal despair, black night of the soul, **despondency,** gloom and doom, despond; **desolation,** prostration, crushing; extremity, depth of misery; sloth, acedia

7 **torment, torture**, excruciation, crucifixion, passion, laceration, clawing, lancination, flaying, excoriation; the rack, the iron maiden, thumbscrews; **persecution; martyrdom; purgatory,** living death, hell, hell upon earth; holocaust; nightmare, horror

8 **affliction,** infliction; **curse, woe,** distress, grievance, **sorrow,** *tsures* <Yiddish>; **trouble,** peck *or* pack of troubles; **care,** burden of care; **burden,** adversity, **oppression, cross, cross to bear** *or* **be borne, load**, imposition, encumbrance, weight, albatross around one's neck, millstone around one's neck; thorn, thorn in the side, crown of thorns; white elephant; bitter pill, bitter draft, bitter cup, cup *or* waters of bitterness; gall, gall and wormwood; Pandora's box

9 **trial, tribulation,** trials and tribulations; **ordeal,** fiery ordeal, the iron entering the soul, perfect storm

10 **tormentor,** torment; torturer; **nuisance, pest,** pesterer, pain *and* pain in the neck *or* ass <nf>, nag, nudzh <nf>, *nudnik* <Yiddish>, public nuisance; **tease,** teaser; annoyer, harasser, harrier, badgerer, **heckler,** plaguer, persecutor, sadist; molester, **bully**

11 **sufferer,** victim, prey; **wretch,** poor devil <nf>, object of compassion; martyr

VERBS 12 give no pleasure *or* joy *or* cheer *or* comfort, **disquiet,** discompose, leave unsatisfied; discontent; taste like ashes in the mouth; **bore,** be tedious, cheese off <Brit nf>

13 **annoy, irk, vex, nettle, provoke, pique,** miff *and* peeve <nf>, distemper, **ruffle, disturb,** discompose, **roil,** rile, **aggravate,** make a nuisance of oneself, **exasperate,** exercise, try one's patience, try the patience of a saint; **put one's back up,** make one bristle; **gripe;** give one a pain <nf>; get, get one down, **get one's goat,** get under one's skin, get in one's hair, tread on one's toes; burn up *and* brown off <nf>; **torment, molest, bother,** pother; **harass,** harry, drive up the wall <nf>, • **hound,** dog, nag, nobble <Brit nf>, nudzh <nf>, **persecute; heckle,** pick *or* prod at, rub it in *and* rub one's nose in it <nf>, badger, hector, bait, bullyrag, worry, worry at, nip at the heels of, chivy, hardly give one time to breathe, make one's life miserable, keep on at; **bug** <nf>, be on the back of *and* be at *and* ride <nf>, **pester, tease, needle,** devil, get after *or* get on <nf>, **bedevil, pick on** <nf>, tweak the nose, pluck the beard, give a bad time to <nf>;

plague, beset, beleaguer; catch in the crossfire *or* in the middle; catch one off balance, trip one up; stalk

14 **irritate, aggravate,** exacerbate, worsen, rub salt in the wound, twist the knife in the wound, step on one's corns, barb the dart; touch a soft spot *or* tender spot, touch a raw nerve, touch where it hurts; provoke, **gall, chafe, fret,** grate, grit *and* gravel <nf>, rasp; **get on one's nerves, grate on,** set on edge; **set one's teeth on edge,** go against the grain; **rub one** *or* **one's fur the wrong way**

15 **chagrin, embarrass, abash, discomfit, disconcert,** discompose, confuse, throw into confusion *or* a tizzy *or* a hissy-fit, **upset,** confound, cast down, mortify, put out, put out of face *or* countenance, put to the blush

16 **distress, afflict, trouble,** burden, give one a tough row to hoe, load with care, **bother, disturb, perturb, disquiet, discomfort, agitate, upset,** put to it; disappoint; **worry,** give one gray hair

17 **pain, grieve,** aggrieve, anguish; **hurt, wound,** bruise, **hurt one's feelings;** pierce, prick, stab, cut, sting; **cut up** <nf>, **cut to the heart,** wound *or* sting *or* cut to the quick, hit one where one lives <nf>; be a thorn in one's side

18 **torture, torment, agonize, harrow,** savage, **rack,** scarify, crucify, impale, excruciate, lacerate, claw, rip, bloody, lancinate, macerate, convulse, wring; prolong the agony, kill by inches, make life miserable *or* not worth living; martyr, martyrize; **tyrannize,** push around <nf>; punish 604.10

19 **suffer, hurt, ache, bleed;** anguish, **suffer anguish; agonize,** writhe; go hard with, have a bad time of it, go through hell; quaff the bitter cup, drain the cup of misery to the dregs, be nailed to the cross

ADJS 20 **pleasureless,** joyless, cheerless, depressed 112.22, grim; **sad, unhappy** 112.21; unsatisfied, unfulfilled, ungratified; **bored,** cheesed off <Brit nf>; anguished, anxious, suffering angst *or* dread *or* nausea, uneasy, unquiet, prey to malaise; **repelled,** revolted, **disgusted,** sickened, nauseated, nauseous

21 **annoyed, irritated,** bugged <nf>; galled, chafed; **bothered, troubled, disturbed, ruffled, roiled,** riled; **irked, vexed, piqued, nettled, provoked, peeved** *and* miffed <nf>, **griped, aggravated, exasperated;** burnt-up *and* browned-off <nf>, cheesed-off <nf>, resentful, angry 152.28

22 **distressed, afflicted, put-upon,** beset, beleaguered; caught in the middle *or* in the crossfire; **troubled, bothered, disturbed, perturbed, disquieted,** discomforted, discomposed, agitated; hung up <nf>; **uncomfortable,** uneasy, ill at ease; **chagrined, embarrassed,** abashed, discomfited, **disconcerted, upset, confused,** mortified, **put-out,** out of countenance, cast down, chapfallen

23 **pained, grieved,** aggrieved; **wounded, hurt,** injured, **bruised,** mauled; **cut,** cut to the quick; **stung;** anguished, aching, bleeding

24 **tormented, plagued, harassed, harried,** dogged, **hounded, persecuted,** beset; nipped at, worried, chivied, **heckled,** badgered, hectored, baited, bullyragged, ragged, **pestered, teased, needled,** deviled, **bedeviled, picked on** <nf>, **bugged** <nf>

25 **tortured, harrowed,** savaged, **agonized,** convulsed, wrung, racked, crucified, impaled, lacerated, excoriated, clawed, ripped, bloodied, lancinated; on the rack, under the harrow

26 **wretched, miserable; woeful,** woebegone; crushed, stricken, **cut up** <nf>, heartsick, heart-stricken, heart-struck; deep-troubled; desolate, disconsolate, suicidal

ADVS 27 to one's displeasure, to one's disgust

97 PLEASANTNESS

NOUNS 1 **pleasantness,** pleasingness, pleasance, **pleasure** 95, pleasurefulness, **pleasurableness,** pleasurability, pleasantry, felicitousness, **enjoyableness; bliss, blissfulness;** felicitousness; sweetness, mellifluousness, *douceur* <Fr>; mellowness; **agreeableness,** agreeability, complaisance, rapport, harmoniousness; compatibility; welcomeness; geniality, congeniality, cordiality, *Gemütlichkeit* <Ger>, affability, amicability, amiability; amenity, graciousness; goodness, goodliness, niceness; **fun** 743.2/95.1; heaven

2 **delightfulness,** exquisiteness, loveliness; **charm,** winsomeness, grace, **attractiveness, appeal,** appealingness, winningness; sexiness <nf>; **glamour;** captivation, enchantment, entrancement, bewitchment, witchery, enravishment; charm offensive; **fascination** 377.1; invitingness, temptingness, tantalizingness; voluptuousness, sensuousness; luxury

3 **delectability,** delectableness, deliciousness, lusciousness; tastiness, flavorsomeness, savoriness; juiciness; succulence

4 **cheerfulness;** brightness, sunniness; sunny side, bright side; fair weather

VERBS **5** make pleasant, brighten, sweeten, gild, gild the lily *or* pill; sentimentalize, saccharinize; please, gratify, satisfy; brighten one's day, make one's day <nf>

ADJS **6 pleasant, pleasing, pleasureful, pleasurable;** fair, fair and pleasant, **enjoyable,** pleasure-giving; felicitous, felicific; **likable, desirable,** to one's liking, to one's taste, to *or* after one's fancy, after one's own heart; **agreeable,** complaisant, harmonious, *en rapport* <Fr>, compatible; **blissful;** sweet, mellifluous, honeyed, dulcet; mellow; **gratifying,** satisfying, rewarding, heartwarming, grateful; **welcome,** welcome as the roses in May; genial, congenial, cordial, *gemütlich* <Ger>, affable, amiable, amicable, gracious; good, goodly, nice, fine; cheerful 109.11

7 **delightful, exquisite, lovely; thrilling,** titillative; good-natured; **charming, attractive, endearing, engaging, appealing,** prepossessing, heartwarming, sexy <nf>, **enchanting,** bewitching, witching, entrancing, enthralling, intriguing, fascinating; **captivating, irresistible, ravishing,** enravishing; **winning,** winsome, taking, fetching, heart-robbing; inviting, tempting, tantalizing; voluptuous, zaftig <nf>, sensuous; luxurious, delicious

8 <nf terms> **fun, kicky,** chewy, dishy, drooly, sexy, toast, yummy

9 **blissful,** beatific, saintly, divine; sublime; **heavenly,** idyllic, paradisal, paradisiac, paradisiacal, paradisic, paradisical, empyreal *or* empyrean, Elysian; out of sight *or* of this world <nf>

10 **delectable, delicious,** luscious; tasty, flavorsome, savory; juicy, succulent

11 **bright, sunny,** fair, mild, balmy; halcyon, Saturnian

ADVS **12 pleasantly, pleasingly, pleasurably,** fair, **enjoyably; blissfully; gratifyingly,** satisfyingly; agreeably, genially, affably, cordially, amiably, amicably, graciously, kindly; cheerfully 109.17

13 **delightfully, exquisitely; charmingly, engagingly, appealingly, enchantingly,** bewitchingly, entrancingly, intriguingly, fascinatingly; ravishingly, enravishingly; **winningly,** winsomely; invitingly, temptingly, tantalizingly, voluptuously, sensuously; luxuriously

14 **delectably,** deliciously, lusciously, tastily, succulently, savorously

98 UNPLEASANTNESS

NOUNS **1 unpleasantness,** unpleasingness, displeasingness, displeasure; **disagreeableness,** disagreeability, *désagrément* <Fr>; **abrasiveness,** woundingess, hostility, unfriendliness; **undesirability,** unappealingness, unattractiveness, unengagingness, uninvitingness, unprepossessingness; **distastefulness,** unsavoriness, unpalatability, nastiness, **undelectability; ugliness** 1015; discomfort, pain, annoyance

2 **offensiveness,** objectionability, objectionableness, unacceptability;

repugnance, contrariety, **odiousness, repulsiveness,** repellence *or* repellency, rebarbativeness, disgustingness, offensiveness, nauseousness, grossness *and* yuckiness *and* grunginess *and* scuzziness <nf>; **loathsomeness, hatefulness,** beastliness <nf>; **vileness, foulness,** putridness, putridity, rottenness, noxiousness; **nastiness,** fulsomeness, noisomeness, **obnoxiousness,** abominableness, heinousness; **contemptibleness,** contemptibility, despicability, **despicableness,** baseness, ignobleness, ignobility; unspeakableness; coarseness, grossness, crudeness, rudeness, obscenity

3 **dreadfulness, horribleness,** horridness, atrociousness, atrocity, hideousness, terribleness, awfulness <nf>; grimness, direness, banefulness

4 **harshness, agony,** agonizingness, excruciation, excruciatingness, **torture,** torturesomeness, torturousness, **torment,** tormentingness; desolation, desolateness; heartbreak, heartsickness

5 **distressfulness, distress, grievousness, grief; painfulness,** pain 26; **harshness,** bitterness, sharpness; lamentability, lamentableness, deplorability, deplorableness, pitiableness, pitifulness, pitiability, regrettableness; **woe, sadness, sorrowfulness, mournfulness,** lamentation, woefulness, woesomeness, woebegoneness, pathos, poignancy; comfortlessness, discomfort; dreariness, cheerlessness, joylessness, dismalness, **depression,** bleakness, black *or* dark cloud

6 **mortification,** humiliation, embarrassment, egg on one's face <nf>; disconcertedness, awkwardness, disappointment

7 **vexatiousness, irksomeness, annoyance,** annoyingness, aggravation, exasperation, provocation, provokingness, tiresomeness, wearisomeness; **troublesomeness, bothersomeness,** harassment; worrisomeness, plaguesomeness, peskiness *and* pestiferousness <nf>

8 **harshness, oppressiveness, burdensomeness,** onerousness, weightiness, heaviness

9 **intolerability,** intolerableness, unbearableness, insupportableness, insufferableness, **unendurability**

VERBS 10 **be unpleasant; displease,** make unpleasant; be disagreeable *or* undesirable *or* distasteful *or* abrasive

11 **offend,** give offense, **repel,** put off, turn off <nf>, **revolt, disgust,** nauseate, sicken, make one sick, make one sick to *or* in the stomach, make one vomit *or* puke *or* retch, turn the stomach, gross out <nf>; stink in the nostrils; stick in one's throat, stick in one's crop *or* craw *or* gizzard <nf>; **horrify, appall,** shock; make the flesh creep *or* crawl, make one shudder

12 **agonize,** excruciate, **torture, torment,** desolate

13 **mortify,** humiliate, embarrass, disconcert, disturb, chagrin, shame; bitch-slap <nf>

14 **distress, dismay,** grieve, mourn, lament, sorrow; pain, discomfort; get in one's hair, try one's patience, give one a hard time *or* a pain *or* a pain in the neck *or* ass *or* butt <nf>, disturb, put off

15 **vex, irk, annoy, aggravate,** exasperate, provoke, run afoul; **trouble, worry,** give one gray hair, plague, harass, bother, hassle; disappoint

16 **oppress, burden,** weigh upon, weight down, wear one down, be heavy on one, be the bane of one's existence, crush one; **tire, exhaust,** weary, wear out, wear upon one; prey on the mind, prey on *or* upon; **haunt,** haunt the memory, obsess; stalk

ADJS 17 **unpleasant, unpleasing, unenjoyable; displeasing, disagreeable; unlikable,** dislikable; **abrasive,** wounding, hostile, unfriendly; **undesirable,** unattractive, unappealing, unengaging, uninviting, unalluring; tacky *and* low rent *and* low ride <nf>; unwelcome, thankless; **distasteful,** untasteful, **unpalatable,** unsavory, unappetizing, undelicious,

undelectable; ugly 1015.6; sour, **bitter**

18 **offensive, objectionable,** objectional, **odious, repulsive,** repellent, rebarbative, **repugnant, revolting,** forbidding; **disgusting, sickening, loathsome,** gross *and* yucky *and* grungy *and* scuzzy <nf>, beastly <nf>, **vile, foul, nasty, nauseating** 64.7; grody <nf>; fulsome, mephitic, miasmal, miasmic, malodorous, stinking, fetid, noisome, noxious; coarse, gross, crude, rude, obscene; **obnoxious, abhorrent, hateful, abominable,** heinous, **contemptible, despicable,** detestable, execrable, beneath *or* below contempt, **base,** ignoble, uncouth

19 **horrid, horrible,** horrific, **horrifying,** horrendous, unspeakable, beyond words; **dreadful, atrocious, terrible, rotten,** awful *and* beastly <nf>, **hideous; tragic;** dire, grim, baneful; appalling, shocking, disgusting

20 **distressing,** distressful, dismaying; from hell <nf>; afflicting, afflictive; **painful,** sore, **harsh, bitter,** sharp; **grievous,** dolorous, dolorific, dolorogenic; **lamentable, deplorable,** regrettable, pitiable, piteous, rueful, woeful, woebegone, **sad,** sorrowful, wretched, mournful, **depressing,** depressive, disappointing; **pathetic,** affecting, touching, moving, saddening, poignant; comfortless, discomforting, uncomfortable; **desolate,** dreary, cheerless, joyless, dismal, bleak

21 **mortifying,** humiliating, **embarrassing,** crushing, disconcerting, awkward, disturbing

22 **annoying, irritating,** galling, **provoking, aggravating** <nf>, **exasperating; vexatious,** vexing, irking, **irksome,** baneful, tiresome, wearisome; **troublesome, bothersome, worrisome,** bothering, troubling, disturbing, plaguing, plaguesome, plaguey <nf>, pestilent, pestilential, **pesky** *and* pesty *and* pestiferous <nf>; tormenting, harassing, worrying; pestering, teasing; importunate, importune; distasteful

23 **agonizing, excruciating, harrowing,** racking, rending, **desolating,** consuming; **tormenting,** torturous; **heartbreaking,** heartrending, **heartsickening,** heartwounding

24 **oppressive, burdensome, crushing,** trying, onerous, heavy, weighty; **harsh,** wearing, wearying, exhausting; overburdensome, tyrannous, grinding

25 **insufferable, intolerable, insupportable, unendurable, unbearable,** past bearing, not to be borne *or* endured, for the birds <nf>, **too much** *or* a bit much <nf>, more than flesh and blood can bear, enough to drive one mad, enough to provoke a saint, enough to make a preacher swear <nf>, enough to try the patience of Job

ADVS 26 **unpleasantly, distastefully** unpleasingly; **displeasingly, offensively, objectionably,** odiously, **repulsively,** repellently, rebarbatively, repugnantly, **revoltingly, disgustingly, sickeningly, loathsomely, vilely,** foully, nastily, fulsomely, mephitically, malodorously, fetidly, noisomely, noxiously, obnoxiously, **abhorrently, hatefully, abominably,** contemptibly, **despicably, detestably,** execrably, nauseatingly

27 **horridly, horribly, dreadfully, terribly,** hideously; **tragically;** grimly, direly, banefully; appallingly, shockingly

28 **distressingly,** distressfully; **painfully,** sorely, **grievously,** lamentably, deplorably, pitiably, ruefully, woefully, sadly, pathetically; **agonizingly, excruciatingly,** harrowingly, heartbreakingly

29 **annoyingly, irritatingly, aggravatingly, provokingly, exasperatingly; vexatiously, irksomely,** tiresomely, wearisomely; **troublesomely, bothersomely,** worrisomely, regrettably

30 **insufferably, intolerably, unbearably, unendurably, insupportably**

99 DISLIKE

NOUNS 1 **dislike, distaste,** disrelish, scunner; disaffection, **disfavor,** disinclination; disaffinity; **displeasure,**

disapproval, disapprobation; instant dislike; rejection

2 **hostility,** antagonism, **enmity** 589; **hatred, hate** 103; **aversion, repugnance,** repulsion, **antipathy,** allergy <nf>, grudge, abomination, **abhorrence, horror,** mortal horror; **disgust, loathing;** nausea; shuddering, cold sweat, creeping flesh

VERBS **3 dislike,** mislike, disfavor, not like, have no liking for, be no love lost between, **have no use for** <nf>, **not care for,** have no time for, have a disaffinity for, have an aversion to, want nothing to do with, not think much of, entertain *or* conceive *or* take a dislike to, take a scunner to, not be able to bear *or* endure *or* abide, not give the time of day to <nf>, **disapprove of; disrelish,** have no taste for, not stomach, not have the stomach for, not be one's cup of tea; be hostile to, have it in for <nf>; **hate, abhor, detest, loathe** 103.5

4 **feel disgust,** be nauseated, **sicken at,** choke on, have a bellyful of <nf>; **gag, retch,** keck, heave, vomit, puke, chunder *and* hurl *and* upchuck *and* barf <nf>

5 **shudder at,** have one's flesh creep *or* crawl at the thought of; shrink from, **recoil, revolt at; grimace,** make a face, make a wry face *or* mouth, turn up one's nose, look down one's nose, look askance, raise one's eyebrows, take a dim view of, show distaste for, disapprove of

6 **repel, disgust** 98.11, gross out <nf>; leave a bad taste in one's mouth, rub the wrong way, antagonize

ADJS **7 unlikable, distasteful,** mislikable, dislikable, **uncongenial, displeasing,** unpleasant 98.17; **not to one's taste,** not one's sort, not one's cup of tea, counter to one's preferences, offering no delight, against the grain, uninviting; yucky <nf>, unlovable; **abhorrent, odious** 98.18; **intolerable** 98.25

8 **averse, allergic** <nf>, loath, reluctant, undelighted, out of sympathy, disaffected, disenchanted, **disinclined, displeased,** put off <nf>, not charmed, less than pleased; **disapproving, censorious, judgmental,** po-faced <Brit nf>; unamiable, **unfriendly, hostile** 589.10; death on, down on

9 **disliked, uncared-for, unvalued,** unprized, misprized, undervalued; **despised,** detested, lowly, spat-upon, untouchable; **unpopular, out of favor,** gone begging; **unappreciated,** misunderstood; unsung, thankless; unwept, unlamented, unmourned, undeplored, unmissed, unregretted

10 **unloved,** unbeloved, uncherished, loveless; **lovelorn,** forsaken, **rejected,** jilted, thrown over <nf>, spurned, crossed in love

11 **unwanted,** unwished, undesired; **unwelcome,** undesirous, unasked, unbidden, uninvited, uncalled-for, unasked-for

100 DESIRE

NOUNS **1 desire, wish,** wanting, grasping, **want, need,** desideration; **hope; fancy; will, mind, pleasure,** will and pleasure; heart's desire; **urge,** drive, libido, pleasure principle; concupiscence; horme; wish fulfillment, fantasy; passion, ardor, sexual desire 75.5; **curiosity,** intellectual curiosity, thirst for knowledge, lust for learning; **eagerness** 101

2 **liking, love, fondness;** infatuation, crush; **affection; relish, taste,** gusto, gust; **passion, weakness** <nf>

3 **inclination, penchant, partiality, fancy, favor, predilection, preference,** propensity, proclivity, **leaning, bent,** turn, tilt, bias, **affinity,** tendency; mutual affinity *or* attraction; **sympathy,** fascination

4 **wistfulness,** wishfulness, yearnfulness, **nostalgia;** wishful thinking; sheep's eyes, longing *or* wistful eye; daydream, daydreaming

5 **yearning, yen** <nf>; **longing,** desiderium, **hankering** <nf>, **pining,** honing <nf>, aching; languishment, languishing; **nostalgia, homesickness**; nostomania

6 **craving, coveting, lust; hunger, thirst, appetite,** appetition, appetency *or* appetence; aching void, hungry ghost; **itch, itching,** prurience *or* pruriency; lech <nf>, **sexual desire** 75.5; *cacoëthes* <L>, **mania** 926.12

7 **appetite,** stomach, relish, taste; **hunger,** hungriness; the munchies <nf>, peckishness <Brit nf>; tapeworm <nf>, eyes bigger than one's stomach, wolf in one's stomach, canine appetite; empty stomach, emptiness <nf>, hollow hunger; **thirst,** thirstiness, drought <nf>, dryness; polydipsia; torment of Tantalus; sweet tooth <nf>

8 **greed,** greediness, graspingness, **avarice, cupidity, avidity, voracity, rapacity, lust,** avariciousness, *avaritia and cupiditas* <L>; money-grubbing; avidness, esurience, wolfishness; voraciousness, ravenousness, rapaciousness, sordidness, **covetousness,** acquisitiveness; itching palm; grasping; **piggishness, hoggishness,** swinishness; **gluttony** 672, *gula* <L>; inordinate desire, furor, craze, fury *or* frenzy of desire, overgreediness; insatiable desire, insatiability; incontinence, intemperateness 669.1

9 **aspiration,** reaching high, upward looking; high goal *or* aim *or* purpose, dream, ideals, hope; **idealism** 986.7

10 **ambition,** ambitiousness, vaulting ambition; aim, target; climbing, status-seeking, social climbing, careerism; opportunism; power-hunger; noble *or* lofty ambition, magnanimity; American dream

11 <object of desire> **desire,** heart's desire, desideration, *desideratum* <L>; wish; **hope;** catch, quarry, prey, game, plum, prize, trophy, brass ring <nf>; status symbol; collectable, collectible; forbidden fruit, ideal, weakness, temptation; lodestone, magnet; golden vision, mecca, glimmering goal; land of heart's desire 986.11; something to be desired; dearest wish, ambition, the height of one's ambition; a sight for sore eyes, a welcome sight; the light at the end of the tunnel

12 **desirer,** wisher, wanter, hankerer <nf>, yearner, coveter; fancier, collector; addict, freak <nf>, glutton, greedy pig, devotee, votary; **aspirant,** aspirer, solicitant, wannabee *or* wannabe *and* hopeful *and* would-be <nf>, candidate; **lover,** love interest, swain, suitor, toyboy, squeeze <nf>

13 **desirability; agreeability,** acceptability, unobjectionableness; **attractiveness,** attraction, magnetism, **appeal,** seductiveness, provocativeness, pleasingness; likability, lovability 104.6

VERBS 14 **desire,** desiderate, be desirous of, **wish,** lust after, bay after, kill for *and* give one's right arm for <nf>, die for <nf>, **want,** have a mind to, choose <nf>; would be glad of; **like,** have *or* acquire a taste for, fancy, take to, **take a fancy** *or* a shine to, have a fancy for; have an eye to, have one's eye on; lean toward, tilt toward, have a penchant for, have a weakness *or* soft spot in one's heart for; aim at, set one's cap for, have designs on; wish very much, wish to goodness; **love** 104.18; lust; prefer, favor 371.17

15 **want to, wish to, like to,** love to, dearly love to, choose to; **itch to,** burn to; ache to, long to

16 **wish for, hope for, yearn for,** yen for *and* have a yen for <nf>, **itch for,** lust for, pant for, **long for, pine for,** hone for <nf>, ache for, be hurting for <nf>, weary for, languish for, **be dying for,** thirst for, sigh for; cry for, clamor for; spoil for <nf>

17 **want with all one's heart, want in the worst way; set one's heart on, have one's heart set on,** give one's kingdom in hell for *or* one's eyeteeth for <nf>

18 **crave, covet, hunger after,** thirst after, crave after, **lust after,** have a lech for <nf>, pant after, run mad after, **hanker for** *or* **after** <nf>; crawl after; aspire after, be consumed with desire; have an itchy *or* itching palm *and* have sticky fingers <nf>

19 **hunger,** hunger for, feel hungry, be peckish <Brit nf>; starve <nf>, be

ravenous, raven; **have a good appetite,** be a good trencherman, have a tapeworm <nf>, have a wolf in one's stomach; eye hungrily, lick one's chops <nf>; **thirst,** thirst for; lick one's lips

20 **aspire, be ambitious;** aspire to, try to reach; aim high, keep one's eyes on the stars, raise one's sights, set one's sights, reach for the sky, dream of

ADJS **21** **desirous,** desiring, lickerish, **wanting, wishing,** needing, hoping; aspirational; dying to <nf>; tempted; appetitive, desiderative, optative, libidinous, libidinal; orectic; hormic; **eager;** lascivious, **lustful**

22 **desirous of** *or* **to,** keen on, set on <nf>, bent on; fond of, with a liking for, partial to <nf>; inclined toward, leaning toward; **itching for** *or* **to,** aching for *or* to, **dying for** *or* **to;** spoiling for <nf>; mad on *or* for, wild to *or* for <nf>, crazy to *or* for <nf>

23 **wistful,** wishful; **longing, yearning,** yearnful, **hankering** <nf>, **languishing, pining,** honing <nf>; **nostalgic, homesick**

24 **craving,** coveting; **hungering,** hungry, thirsting, thirsty, athirst; **itching,** prurient; fervid; **devoured by desire,** in a frenzy *or* fury of desire, mad with lust, consumed with desire

25 **hungry,** hungering, peckish <Brit nf>; empty <nf>, unfilled; ravening, **ravenous,** voracious, sharp-set, **wolfish,** dog-hungry <nf>, hungry as a bear; **starved, famished,** starving, famishing, perishing *or* pinched with hunger; fasting, off food, unfed; keeping Lent, Lenten; underfed; half-starved, half-famished

26 **thirsty,** thirsting, athirst; **dry,** parched, droughty <nf>

27 **greedy, avaricious, avid, voracious, rapacious,** cupidinous, esurient, **ravening, grasping, grabby** <nf>, graspy, acquisitive, mercenary, sordid, overgreedy; ravenous, gobbling, devouring; miserly, money-hungry, money-grubbing, money-mad, venal; **covetous,** coveting; **piggish, hoggish,** swinish, a hog for, greedy as a hog; **gluttonous** 672.6; omnivorous, all-devouring; insatiable, insatiate, unsatisfied, unsated, unappeased, unappeasable, limitless, bottomless, unquenchable, quenchless, unslaked, unslakeable, slakeless; big-eyed <nf>

28 **aspiring, ambitious,** sky-aspiring, upward-looking, high-reaching; high-flying, social-climbing, careerist, careeristic, fast-track, fast-lane, on the make <nf>; power-hungry; would-be, wannabe

29 **desired, wanted,** coveted; **wished-for,** hoped-for, longed-for; sought after, in demand, popular

30 **desirable,** sought-after, much sought-after, to be desired, to die for <nf>, **much to be desired; enviable,** worth having; **likable, pleasing,** after one's own heart; **agreeable,** acceptable, unobjectionable, cromulent; palatable; **attractive,** taking, winning, sexy <nf>, dishy <Brit nf>, **seductive, provocative,** tantalizing, exciting; appetizing, tempting, toothsome, mouth-watering; **lovable,** adorable; buzzworthy

ADVS **31** **desirously, wistfully,** wishfully, **longingly, yearningly,** piningly, languishingly; cravingly, itchingly; hungrily, thirstily; aspiringly, ambitiously

32 **greedily, avariciously,** avidly, ravenously, raveningly, voraciously, rapaciously, **covetously,** graspingly, devouringly; wolfishly, **piggishly, hoggishly,** swinishly

101 EAGERNESS

NOUNS **1** **eagerness, enthusiasm, avidity,** avidness, keenness <chiefly Brit>, forwardness, prothymia, **readiness,** promptness, quickness, **alacrity,** cheerful readiness, *empressement* <Fr>; keen desire, **appetite** 100.7; anxiousness, anxiety; **zest,** zestfulness, gusto, verve, **liveliness,** life, **vitality,** vivacity, élan, spirit, animation; **impatience,** breathless impatience 135.1; keen interest, fascination; **craze** 926.12

2 **zeal, ardor, ardency, fervor, fervency, fervidness, spirit, warmth, fire, heat,** heatedness, **passion,** passionateness, impassionedness, heartiness, intensity, **abandon,** vehemence; intentness, resolution 359; **devotion,** devoutness, devotedness, dedication, commitment, committedness; **earnestness, seriousness,** sincerity; loyalty, faithfulness, faith, fidelity 644.7; discipleship, followership

3 **overzealousness, overeagerness,** overanxiousness, overanxiety; unchecked enthusiasm, **overenthusiasm, infatuation; overambitiousness; frenzy, fury; zealotry,** zealotism; mania, **fanaticism** 926.11

4 **enthusiast, zealot,** infatuate, energumen, rhapsodist; addict; faddist; pursuer; hobbyist, collector; **fanatic,** trainspotter <Brit nf>**;** stalker; visionary 986.13; **devotee,** votary, aficionada, aficionado, **fancier,** admirer, **follower; disciple,** worshiper, idolizer, idolater; amateur, dilettante

5 <nf terms> **fan, buff, freak,** hound, fiend, demon, nut, bug, head, junkie, groupie, rooter, booster, great one for, sucker for; fan club, fanzine; eager beaver, -aholic

VERBS 6 **jump at,** catch, grab, grab at, go for, snatch, snatch at, fall all over oneself, get excited about, go at hammer and tongs *or* tooth and nail, go hog wild <nf>; go to great lengths, lean *or* bend *or* fall over backwards; **desire** 100.14,18

7 **be enthusiastic, rave, enthuse** *and* be big for <nf>; get stars in one's eyes, **rhapsodize, carry on over** *and* rave on <nf>, make much of, **make a fuss over,** make an ado *or* much ado about, make a to-do over *and* take on over <nf>, be *or* go on over *or* about <nf>, rave about *and* whoop it up about <nf>; go nuts *or* gaga *or* ape over <nf>; gush, gush over; effervesce, bubble over

ADJS 8 **eager, anxious,** agog, all agog; **avid, keen,** forward, prompt, quick, ready, ready and willing, alacritous, bursting to, dying to, raring to, gung ho; **zestful, lively,** full of life, vital, vivacious, vivid, spirited, **animated; impatient** 135.6; breathless, panting, champing at the bit; **desirous** 100.21

9 **zealous, ardent, fervent, fervid,** perfervid, **spirited, intense,** hearty, vehement, abandoned, **passionate,** impassioned, **warm,** heated, hot, hot-blooded, red-hot, fiery, white-hot, flaming, burning, afire, aflame, on fire, like a house afire <nf>; **devout, devoted;** dedicated, committed; **earnest, sincere, serious,** in earnest; loyal, faithful 644.20; intent, intent on, resolute 359.11

10 **enthusiastic,** enthused *and* big <nf>, **gung ho** <nf>, glowing, full of enthusiasm; enthusiastic about, infatuated with

11 <nf terms> **wild about, crazy about, mad about,** ape about *or* over, gone on, all in a dither over, gaga over, starry-eyed over, all hopped up about, hepped up over, hot about *or* for *or* on, steamed up about, **turned-on, switched-on;** hipped on, **cracked on,** bugs on, freaked-out, **nuts on** *or* **over** *or* **about, keen on** *or* **about,** crazy *or* mad about

12 **overzealous,** ultrazealous, **overeager,** over-anxious; **overambitious;** overdesirous; **overenthusiastic, infatuated;** feverish, perfervid, febrile, at fever *or* fevered pitch; hectic, frenetic, furious, **frenzied,** frantic, **wild,** hysteric, hysterical, delirious; **insane** 926.26; **fanatical** 926.32

ADVS 13 **eagerly, anxiously; impatiently,** breathlessly; **avidly,** promptly, quickly, keenly, readily; zestfully, vivaciously, animatedly; **enthusiastically,** with enthusiasm; **with alacrity,** with zest, with gusto, with relish, with open arms, avidiously

14 **zealously, ardently, fervently, fervidly,** perfervidly, heatedly, heartily, vehemently, **passionately,** impassionedly; intently, intensely; **devoutly, devotedly;** earnestly, sincerely, seriously

102 INDIFFERENCE

NOUNS **1 indifference,** indifferentness; indifferentism; halfheartedness, zeallessness, perfunctoriness, fervorlessness; **coolness,** coldness, chilliness, chill, iciness, frostiness, stoicism; tepidness, **lukewarmness,** Laodiceanism; **neutrality,** neutralness; insipidity, vapidity; adiaphorism

2 unconcern, disinterest, detachment; disregard, dispassion, insouciance, **carelessness,** regardlessness; easygoingness; **heedlessness,** mindlessness, inattention 984; **unmindfulness, incuriosity** 982; **insensitivity;** disregardfulness, recklessness, negligence 340.1; *je-m'en-foutisme* or *je-m'en fichisme* <Fr>; unsolicitousness, unanxiousness; pococurantism; **nonchalance,** inexcitability 106, ataraxy *or* ataraxia, samadhi; indiscrimination, casualness 945.1; **listlessness,** lackadaisicalness, lack of feeling *or* affect, **apathy** 94.4; sloth, acedia, phlegm, lethargy

3 undesirousness, desirelessness; nirvana; lovelessness, passionlessness; uneagerness, **unambitiousness;** lack of appetite, inappetence

VERBS **4 not care, not mind, not give** *or* **care a damn,** not give a hoot *or* shit *or* crap <nf>, not care less *or* two hoots <nf>, care nothing for *or* about, not care a straw about; shrug off, dismiss; **take no interest in,** have no desire for, not think twice about, have no taste *or* relish for; hold no brief for; be halfhearted, temper one's zeal; lose interest

5 not matter to, be all one to, take it or leave it; make no difference, make no never-mind <nf>; sit on the fence, remain neutral

ADJS **6 indifferent, halfhearted,** zealless, perfunctory, fervorless; **cool, cold** 589.9; tepid, **lukewarm,** Laodicean; neither hot nor cold, neither one thing nor the other; unmoved; blah, **neuter, neutral**

7 unconcerned, uninterested, disinterested, turned-off, **dispassionate,** insouciant, **careless,** regardless; easygoing; incurious 982.3; mindless, **unmindful, heedless,** inattentive 984.6, disregardful; **devil-may-care,** reckless, negligent 340.10; unsolicitous, unanxious; pococurante, **nonchalant,** inexcitable 106.10; ataractic; **blasé,** undiscriminating, casual 945.5; **listless,** lackadaisical, sluggish; bovine; numb, **apathetic** 94.13

8 undesirous, unattracted, desireless; loveless, passionless; inappetent; nirvanic; **unenthusiastic,** uneager; **unambitious,** unaspiring

ADVS **9 indifferently, with indifference,** with utter indifference; coolly, coldly; lukewarmly, halfheartedly; perfunctorily; for all *or* aught one cares

10 unconcernedly, uninterestedly, disinterestedly, dispassionately, insouciantly, **carelessly,** regardlessly; mindlessly; **unmindfully, heedlessly,** recklessly, negligently 340.17; **nonchalantly;** listlessly, lackadaisically; numbly, **apathetically** 94.15

PHRS **11 who cares?,** I don't care, I couldn't care less <nf>; who gives a crap?; it's a matter of sublime indifference; never mind!, **what does it matter?,** what's the difference?, what's the diff? <nf>, what are the odds?, what of it?, **so what?,** what the hell <nf>, it's all one to me, it's all the same to me, it's no skin off one's nose *or* ass <nf>; like it or lump it; forget it!

12 I should worry?, I should fret?, that's your lookout, that's your problem, I feel for you but I can't reach you; that's your pigeon <nf>, that's your tough luck, tough titty *and* shit <nf>

103 HATE

NOUNS **1 hate, hatred; dislike** 99; **detestation, abhorrence, aversion, antipathy,** repugnance, **loathing,** execration, **abomination,** odium; **spite,** spitefulness, despite, despitefulness, **malice, malevolence,** malignity; vials of hate *or* wrath;

rancor, venom; misanthropy, misanthropism; misandry, misogyny; misogamy; misopedia; anti-Semitism; race hatred, racism, racialism; bigotry; phobia, Anglophobia, Russophobia, xenophobia, etc; grudge; scorn, despising, **contempt** 157; hate crime

2 **enmity** 589; bitterness, **animosity** 589.4; hatefulness

3 <hated thing> **anathema, abomination,** detestation, aversion, abhorrence, antipathy, execration, hate; peeve, pet peeve; phobia; bugbear, bête noire, bane, bitter pill; fear; dislike

4 hater, man-hater, woman-hater, misanthropist, misanthrope, misogynist, anti-Semite, racist, racialist, white supremacist, bigot, redneck <nf>; phobic, Anglophobe, xenophobe, etc; detester, loather

VERBS **5** **hate, detest, loathe, abhor,** execrate, **abominate,** hold in abomination, take an aversion to, shudder at, utterly detest, be death on, not stand, not stand the sight of, not stomach; scorn, spit on, **despise** 157.3; hate someone's guts <nf>

6 **dislike,** have it in for <nf>, feel aversion for, disrelish 99.3

ADJS **7** **hating, abhorrent,** loathing, despising, venomous, death on; averse 99.8; disgusted 96.20; scornful, **contemptuous** 157.8; antagonistic; execrative

8 **hateful, loathesome,** accursed, aversive, odious, detestable 98.18; despiteful; unlikable 99.7; **contemptible** 661.12/98.18

104 LOVE

NOUNS **1** **love, affection, attachment, devotion, fondness,** sentiment, warm feeling, soft spot in one's heart, weakness <nf>, like, **liking,** fancy, shine <nf>, amore <Ital>; **partiality, predilection;** intimacy; **passion,** tender feeling *or* passion, **ardor,** ardency, fervor, heart, flame, the real thing <nf>; physical love, Amor, Eros, bodily love, libido, sexual love, sex 75; desire, yearning 100.5; lasciviousness 665.5; charity, *caritas* <L>, brotherly love, Christian love, agape, loving concern, fellow feeling, **caring;** sentimental attachment; spiritual love, platonic love; amour-propre; **adoration,** worship, hero worship; **regard,** admiration; idolization, idolism, idolatry; popular regard, popularity; faithful love, truelove; married love, conjugal love, uxoriousness; free love, free-lovism; **lovemaking** 562; self-love, narcissism, autophilia, egotism; patriotism, love of one's country

2 **amorousness,** amativeness, lovingness, meltingness, **affection, affectionateness,** demonstrativeness; mating instinct, reproductive *or* procreative drive, libido; carnality, sexiness, goatishness, hot pants *and* horniness <nf>; romantic love, romanticism, **sentimentality,** susceptibility; lovesickness, lovelornness; ecstasy, rapture; enchantment 95.2

3 **infatuation,** infatuatedness, passing fancy; **crush** *and* mash *and* pash *and* case <nf>; **puppy love** *and* young love *and* calf love <nf>; love at first sight, *coup de foudre* <Fr>; falling in love

4 **parental love, natural affection,** mother *or* maternal love, father *or* paternal love; filial love; parental instinct; unconditional love

5 **love affair, affair,** affair of the heart, **amour, romance,** *affaire d'amour* <Fr>, romantic tie *or* bond, something between, thing <nf>, relationship, liaison, entanglement, involvement, intrigue, tryst; **dalliance,** amorous play, the love game, flirtation, hanky-panky, lollygagging <nf>; triangle, eternal triangle; illicit *or* unlawful love, forbidden *or* unsanctified love, adulterous affair, adultery, unfaithfulness, infidelity, cuckoldry; hookup <nf>; courtship, courting, wooing, pursuit, dating, dallying, betrothal, engagement, going together *and* going out with <nf>, going steady <nf>

6 **loveableness, likeableness,** lovability, likability, adoreableness, adorability, sweetness, loveliness, lovesomeness; cuddliness, cuddlesomeness; amiability, attractiveness 97.2, desirability, agreeability, amiability; **charm, appeal,** allurement 377; winsomeness, winning ways

7 Love, Cupid, Amor, Eros, Kama; Venus, Aphrodite, Astarte, Freya

8 <symbols> **cupid,** cupidon, amor, amourette, amoretto, *amorino* <Ital>; love-knot

9 **sweetheart, loved one, love, beloved, darling, dear, dear one,** dearly beloved, well-beloved, truelove, beloved object, **object of one's affections,** light of one's eye *or* life, light of love; sex object, prey, quarry, game; valentine

10 <nf terms> **sweetie, honey,** honeybunch, honey-bunny, honey bun, honeypie, hon, main squeeze, sweetie-pie, sweet patootie, tootsie, tootsie-pie, tootsy-wootsy, dearie, baby, dreamboat, heartthrob, poopsy, poopsy-woopsy, sugar, sugar-bun, sweets, cookie

11 **lover, admirer,** adorer, amorist; infatuate, paramour, **suitor, wooer,** pursuer, follower; **flirt,** coquette; vampire, vamp; conquest, catch; devotee; escort, companion, date *and* steady <nf>; significant other, soul mate, bashert <Yiddish>; squeeze <nf>; old flame <nf>, new flame <nf>; love interest; other woman

12 **beau, inamorato, swain,** suitor, escort, man, gallant, cavalier, squire, esquire, *caballero* <Sp>; *amoroso* and *cavaliere servente* <Ital>; sugar daddy <nf>; gigolo; **boyfriend** *and* **fellow** *and* young man *and* flame <nf>; old man <nf>; love-maker, lover-boy <nf>; **seducer, ladykiller,** ladies' man, sheik, philanderer, cocksman <nf>; Prince Charming, Lothario, Romeo; Casanova, Don Juan; boy toy <nf>

13 **ladylove, inamorata,** *amorosa* <Ital>, lady, mistress, ladyfriend; lass, lassie, jo, gill, jill, Dulcinea

14 <nf terms> **doll, angel,** baby, babydoll, doll-baby, buttercup, ducks, ducky, pet, snookums, snooky, **girl, girlfriend,** sweetheart, best girl, dream girl; old lady

15 **favorite,** preference; **darling,** idol, jewel, apple of one's eye, fair-haired boy, man after one's own heart; **pet,** fondling, cosset, minion; spoiled child *or* darling, *enfant gâté* <Fr>, lap dog; teacher's pet; matinee idol; tin god, little tin god

16 **fiancé, fiancée,** bride-to-be, affianced, betrothed, future, intended <nf>

17 **loving couple,** soul mates, lovebirds, turtledoves, bill-and-cooers; newlyweds, honeymooners; star crossed lovers; Romeo and Juliet, Anthony and Cleopatra, Tristan and Isolde, Abélard and Héloïse, Darby and Joan; item <nf>

VERBS **18** **love, be fond of,** be in love with, **care for, like, fancy,** have a fancy for, take an interest in, **dote on** *or* **upon,** be desperately in love, burn with love; be partial to, have a soft spot in one's heart for, have a weakness *or* fondness for; court, woo, romance

19 <nf terms> **go for,** have an eye *or* eyes for, only have eyes for, be sweet on, have a crush *or* mash *or* case on; have it bad, carry a torch *or* the torch for, have designs on

20 **cherish, hold dear,** hold in one's heart *or* affections, think much *or* the world of, prize, treasure; **admire, regard,** esteem, revere; **adore, idolize,** worship, dearly love, think worlds *or* the world of, love to distraction

21 **fall in love, lose one's heart, become enamored,** be smitten; take to, **take a liking** *or* **fancy to,** take a shine to *and* fall for <nf>, become attached to, bestow one's affections on; fall head and ears *or* head over heels in love, be swept off one's feet; cotton to <nf>

22 **enamor, endear;** win one's heart, win the love *or* affections of, take the fancy of, make a hit with <nf>; **charm,** becharm, **infatuate,** hold in thrall, command one's affection, **fascinate,** attract, allure, grow on one, strike *or* tickle one's fancy, **captivate,** bewitch, enrapture, carry away, sweep off one's feet, turn one's head, inflame with love; **seduce,** vamp <nf>, draw on, tempt, tantalize

ADJS 23 **beloved, loved, dear, darling, precious;** pet, favorite; **adored, admired,** esteemed, revered; **cherished,** prized, treasured, held dear; **well-liked,** popular; **well-beloved,** dearly beloved, dear to one's heart, after one's heart *or* own heart, dear as the apple of one's eye

24 **endearing, lovable, likable, adorable,** admirable, **lovely,** lovesome, sweet, winning, winsome; **charming;** angelic, seraphic; caressable, kissable; cuddlesome, cuddly

25 **amorous,** amatory, amative, erotic; **sexual** 75.25; loverly, loverlike; **passionate, ardent,** impassioned; desirous 100.21,22; lascivious 665.29

26 **loving,** lovesome, **fond, adoring, devoted, affectionate,** demonstrative, **romantic, sentimental, tender,** soft <nf>, melting; lovelorn, lovesick, languishing; wifely, husbandly, conjugal, uxorious, faithful; parental, paternal, maternal, filial; charitable, caritative; self-loving, narcissistic

27 **enamored, charmed,** becharmed, **fascinated, captivated,** bewitched, enraptured, enchanted; **infatuated,** infatuate; **smitten,** heartsmitten, heartstruck, lovestruck, besotted with

28 **in love,** head over heels in love, over head and ears in love

29 **fond of, enamored of,** partial to, **in love with,** attached to, wedded to, devoted to, wrapped up in; **taken with,** smitten with, struck with

30 <nf terms> **crazy about,** mad *or* nuts *or* nutty *or* wild about, swacked on, sweet on, stuck on, gone on

ADVS 31 **lovingly, fondly, affectionately, tenderly,** dearly, **adoringly,** devotedly; amorously, ardently, passionately; with love, with affection, with all one's love

105 EXCITEMENT

NOUNS 1 **excitement,** emotion, excitedness, **arousal, stimulation, exhilaration;** a high <nf>, manic state *or* condition

2 **thrill, sensation,** titillation; **tingle,** tingling; quiver, shiver, shudder, tremor, **tremor of excitement,** rush <nf>; flush, rush of emotion, surge of emotion

3 <nf terms> **kick, charge,** electricity, hullabaloo, boot, bang, belt, blast, flash, hit, jolt, large charge, rush, upper, lift; jollies

4 **agitation, perturbation,** ferment, **turbulence, turmoil,** tumult, embroilment, uproar, **commotion,** disturbance, ado, *brouhaha* <Fr>, to-do <nf>; pell-mell, **flurry,** ruffle, bustle, stir, swirl, swirling, whirl, vortex, eddy, hurry, hurry-scurry, hurly-burly; fermentation, yeastiness, effervescence, ebullience, ebullition; fume; agita <nf>

5 **trepidation,** trepidity; **disquiet,** disquietude, inquietude, **unrest, restlessness,** fidgetiness; **fidgets** *or* **shakes** *and* shivers *and* dithers *and* antsyness <nf>; **quivering, quavering, quaking,** heartquake, **shaking,** trembling; **quiver,** quaver, shiver, shudder, dread, didder <Brit nf>, twitter, **tremor,** tremble, flutter; palpitation, pitapatation <nf>, pit-a-pat, pitter-patter; **throb,** throbbing; panting, heaving

6 **dither, tizzy** <nf>, swivet, foofaraw, **pucker** <nf>, **twitter,** twitteration <nf>, **flutter, fluster,** flusteration *and* flustration <nf>, **fret, fuss,** pother, bother, lather *and* stew *and* snit <nf>, flap; emotional crisis, *crise* <Fr>

7 **fever of excitement, fever pitch,** fever, heat, fever heat, fire; sexual excitement, rut

8 **fury, furor,** furore <Brit>, fire and fury; **ecstasy,** transport, **rapture,** ravishment; intoxication, abandon; **passion, rage,** raging *or* tearing passion, towering rage *or* passion; **frenzy,** orgy, orgasm; madness, craze, **delirium,** hysteria

9 **outburst,** outbreak, **burst, flare-up,** blaze, **explosion,** eruption, irruption, upheaval, convulsion, spasm, seizure, fit, paroxysm; storm, tornado, funnel cloud, whirlwind, cyclone, hurricane, gale, tempest, gust; steroid rage, roid rage <nf>; road rage <nf>

10 **excitability,** excitableness, perturbability, agitability; emotional insta-

bility, explosiveness, eruptiveness, inflammability, combustibility, tempestuousness, violence, latent violence; **irascibility** 110.2; irritability, edginess, touchiness, prickliness, **sensitivity** 24.3; skittishness, **nervousness** 128; excessive emotion, hyperthymia, **emotionalism** 93.9

11 **excitation, excitement, arousal,** arousing, **stirring,** stirring up, working up, working into a lather <nf>, lathering up, whipping up, steaming up, **agitation, perturbation; stimulation, stimulus, exhilaration,** animation; electrification, galvanization; **provocation, irritation,** aggravation, exasperation, exacerbation, fomentation, inflammation, infuriation, **incitement** 375.4

VERBS 12 **excite, impassion, arouse, rouse, stir, stir up,** set astir, stir the feelings, stir the blood, cause a stir *or* commotion, play on the feelings; **work up,** work into, work up into a lather <nf>, lather up, whip up, **key up,** steam up; **move** 375.12; **foment, incite** 375.17; turn on <nf>; **awaken,** awake, wake, waken, wake up; call up, summon up, call forth; **kindle,** enkindle, light up, light the fuse, **fire, inflame,** heat, warm, set fire to, set on fire, fire *or* warm the blood; fan, fan the fire *or* flame, blow the coals, stir the embers, feed the fire, add fuel to the fire *or* flame, pour oil on the fire; raise to a fever heat *or* pitch, bring to the boiling point; overexcite; **annoy, incense; enrage, infuriate;** frenzy, madden

13 **stimulate, whet, sharpen,** pique, provoke, quicken, enliven, liven up, pick up, jazz up <nf>, animate, **exhilarate,** invigorate, galvanize, fillip, give a fillip to; infuse life into, give new life to, revive, renew, resuscitate

14 **agitate, perturb, disturb, trouble, disquiet, discompose,** discombobulate <nf>, unsettle, **stir, ruffle, shake, shake up, shock, upset,** make waves, jolt, jar, rock, stagger, electrify, bring *or* pull one up short, give one a turn <nf>; fuss <nf>, flutter, flurry, rattle, disconcert, **fluster**

15 **thrill, tickle,** thrill to death *or* to pieces, give a thrill, **give one a kick** *or* boot *or* charge *or* bang *or* lift <nf>; intoxicate, fascinate, titillate, take one's breath away

16 **be excitable,** excite easily; **get excited, have a fit;** catch the infection; **explode, flare up,** flash up, flame up, fire up, catch fire, take fire; **fly into a passion,** go into hysterics, have a tantrum *or* temper tantrum, come apart; ride off in all directions at once, run around like a chicken with its head cut off; **rage, rave, rant,** rant and rave, rave on, bellow, **storm,** ramp; be angry, smolder, **seethe** 152.15

17 <nf terms> **work oneself up,** work oneself into a sweat, lather, have a short fuse, get hot under the collar, run a temperature, race one's motor, get into a dither *or* tizzy *or* swivet *or* pucker *or* stew; blow up, **blow one's top** *or* stack *or* cool, **flip,** flip out, flip one's lid *or* wig, freak out, pop one's cork, wig out, blow a gasket, fly off the handle, **hit the ceiling,** go ape, go hog wild, go bananas, lose one's cool, go off the deep end

18 <be excited> **thrill,** tingle, **tingle with excitement,** glow; swell, swell with emotion, be full of emotion; thrill to; turn on to *and* get high on *and* freak out on <nf>; heave, pant; **throb,** palpitate, go pit-a-pat; **tremble, shiver, quiver, quaver, quake,** flutter, twitter, **shake,** shake like an aspen leaf, have the shakes <nf>; **fidget,** have the fidgets *and* have ants in one's pants <nf>; toss and turn, toss, tumble, twist and turn, wriggle, wiggle, writhe, squirm; twitch, jerk

19 **change color,** turn color, go all colors; **pale,** whiten, blanch, turn pale; darken, look black; turn blue in the face; **flush, blush,** crimson, glow, mantle, color, redden, turn *or* get red

ADJS 20 **excited,** impassioned; **thrilled,** agog, tingling, tingly, atingle, aquiver, atwitter; **stimulated, exhilarated, high** <nf>; manic; **moved, stirred,** stirred up, **aroused,**

roused, switched *or* turned on <nf>, on one's mettle, fired, inflamed, wrought up, **worked up,** all worked up, worked up into a lather <nf>, lathered up, whipped up, steamed up, keyed up, hopped up <nf>; turned-on <nf>; carried away; bursting, ready to burst; effervescent, yeasty, ebullient

21 **in a dither, in a tizzy** <nf>, in a swivet, in a foofaraw, **in a pucker** <nf>, in a quiver, **in a twitter,** in a flutter, all of a twitter *or* flutter, in a fluster, in a flurry, in a pother, in a bother, in a ferment, in a turmoil, in an uproar, in a stew *and* in a sweat <nf>, in a lather <nf>

22 **heated, passionate, warm, hot,** red-hot, flaming, **burning, fiery, glowing, fervent, fervid; feverish,** febrile, on fire, hectic, flushed; sexually excited, in rut 75.28; burning with excitement, het up <nf>, hot under the collar <nf>; seething, boiling, boiling over, steamy, steaming

23 **agitated, perturbed, disturbed, troubled, disquieted, upset,** antsy <nf>, unsettled, **discomposed, flustered,** ruffled, **shaken**

24 **turbulent,** tumultuous, tempestuous, boisterous, clamorous, uproarious

25 **frenzied, frantic; ecstatic,** transported, enraptured, ravished, in a transport *or* ecstasy; intoxicated, abandoned; orgiastic, orgasmic; raging, raving, roaring, bellowing, ramping, storming, howling, ranting, fulminating, frothing *or* foaming at the mouth; freaked out; **wild,** hog-wild <nf>; **violent,** fierce, ferocious, feral, **furious,** ballistic; **mad,** madding, **rabid,** maniac, maniacal, demonic, demoniacal, possessed; carried away, **distracted, delirious, beside oneself,** out of one's wits; uncontrollable, running mad, amok, berserk, hog-wild <nf>; **hysterical,** in hysterics; wild-eyed, wild-looking, haggard; blue in the face

26 **overwrought, overexcited, overstimulated, hyper** <nf>; **overcome,** overwhelmed, overpowered, overmastered; hand-wringing; **upset,** *bouleversé* <Fr>; theatrical

27 **restless,** restive, **uneasy,** unquiet, unsettled, unrestful, tense; **fidgety,** antsy <nf>, fussy, fluttery

28 **excitable, emotional,** highly emotional, overemotional, hyperthymic, perturbable, flappable <nf>, agitable; emotionally unstable; explosive, volcanic, eruptive, inflammable; irascible 110.19; irritable, edgy, touchy, wired <nf>, prickly, **sensitive** 24.13; **skittish,** startlish; **high-strung,** highly strung, on edge, high-spirited, mettlesome, high-mettled; **nervous**

29 **passionate, fiery, vehement,** hot-headed, **impetuous,** violent, volcanic, furious, fierce, **wild;** tempestuous, stormy, tornadic; simmering, volcanic, ready to burst forth *or* explode

30 **exciting, thrilling,** thrilly <nf>, **stirring, moving, breathtaking,** eye-popping <nf>; agitating, agitative, perturbing, disturbing, upsetting, troubling, gut-wrenching, disquieting, unsettling, distracting, jolting, jarring; heart-stirring, heart-thrilling, heart-swelling, heart-expanding, soul-stirring, spirit-stirring, deep-thrilling, mind-blowing <nf>; impressive, striking, telling; **provocative** 375.27, provoking, piquant, tantalizing; **inflammatory** 375.28; **stimulating,** stimulative, stimulatory; exhilarating, heady, intoxicating, maddening, ravishing; **electric,** galvanic, charged, overcharged; **overwhelming,** overpowering, overcoming, overmastering, more than flesh and blood can bear; suspensive, **suspenseful,** cliff-hanging <nf>

31 **penetrating, piercing,** stabbing, cutting, stinging, biting, keen, brisk, sharp, caustic, astringent

32 **sensational, lurid,** yellow, **melodramatic,** Barnumesque; spine-chilling, eye-popping <nf>; blood-and-thunder, cloak-and-dagger; tabloid

ADVS **33** **excitedly, agitatedly,** perturbedly; aflutter; with beating *or* leaping heart, with heart beating high, with heart going pitapat *or* pitter-patter <nf>, thrilling all over, with heart in mouth; with glistening eyes, all agog, all aquiver *or* atwitter *or* atingle; in a sweat *or* stew *or* dither *or* tizzy <nf>

34 **heatedly, passionately,** warmly, hotly, glowingly, fervently, fervidly, **feverishly**

35 **frenziedly, frantically,** wildly, furiously, violently, fiercely, madly, rabidly, distractedly, deliriously, till one is blue in the face <nf>

36 **excitingly, thrillingly,** stirringly, movingly; **provocatively,** provokingly; stimulatingly, exhilaratingly

106 INEXCITABILITY

NOUNS **1** **inexcitability,** inexcitableness, unexcitableness, **imperturbability,** imperturbableness, unflappability <nf>; steadiness, evenness; inirritability, unirritableness; **dispassion,** dispassionateness, unpassionateness, ataraxy *or* ataraxia; quietism; stoicism; **even temper,** steady *or* smooth temper, good *or* easy temper; unnervousness 129; **patience** 134; **impassiveness,** impassivity, stolidity; bovinity, dullness

2 **composure,** countenance; **calm, calmness,** calm disposition, **placidity, serenity,** tranquility, soothingness, peacefulness; mental composure, peace *or* calm of mind; calm *or* quiet mind, easy mind; resignation, resignedness, acceptance, fatalism, stoic calm; philosophicalness, philosophy, philosophic composure; **quiet,** quietness of mind *or* soul, quietude; decompression, imperturbation, indisturbance, unruffledness; **coolness,** coolheadedness, cool <nf>, sangfroid; icy calm; Oriental calm, Buddha-like composure, Buddha nature; shantih

3 **equanimity,** equilibrium, equability, balance; **levelheadedness,** level head, well-balanced *or* well-regulated mind; **poise,** aplomb, **self-possession, self-control,** self-command, self-restraint, restraint, possession, **presence of mind;** confidence, assurance, **self-confidence, self-assurance,** centered

4 **sedateness, staidness,** soberness, sobriety, sober-mindedness, **seriousness,** gravity, solemnity, sobersidedness; temperance, moderation; sobersides

5 **nonchalance,** casualness, offhandedness; easygoingness, lackadaisicalness; **indifference,** unconcern 102.2

VERBS **6** **be cool** *or* **composed,** not turn a hair, not have a hair out of place, keep one's cool <nf>, look as if butter wouldn't melt in one's mouth; **tranquilize, calm** 670.7; **set one's mind at ease** *or* **rest,** make one easy

7 **compose oneself, control oneself,** restrain oneself, collect oneself, **get hold of oneself,** get a grip on oneself <nf>, get a grip, get organized, master one's feelings, regain one's composure; **calm down, cool off,** cool down, sober down, hold *or* keep one's temper, simmer down *and* cool it <nf>; **relax,** decompress, unwind, take it easy, lay *or* kick back <nf>; **forget it,** get it out of one's mind *or* head, drop it

8 <control one's feelings> **suppress, repress,** keep under, smother, stifle, choke *or* hold back, fight down *or* back, inhibit; sublimate; get it together

9 **keep cool,** keep one's cool <nf>, **keep calm,** keep one's head, keep one's shirt on *and* hang loose <nf>, not turn a hair; take things as they come, roll with the punches <nf>; keep a stiff upper lip

ADJS **10** **inexcitable, imperturbable,** undisturbable, unflappable <nf>; **unirritable,** inirritable; **dispassionate,** unpassionate; **steady;** stoic, stoical; **even-tempered; impassive,** stolid; bovine, dull; unnervous 129.2; **patient;** long-suffering

11 **unexcited, unperturbed,** undisturbed, untroubled, unagitated, **unruffled,** unflustered, unstirred, unimpassioned

12 **calm, placid,** quiet, **tranquil, serene,** peaceful; **cool, coolheaded,**

cool as a cucumber <nf>; philosophical

13 **composed, collected,** recollected, **levelheaded; poised,** together <nf>, in equipoise, equanimous, equilibrious, **balanced,** well-balanced; **self-possessed,** self-controlled, controlled, self-restrained; confident, assured, **self-confident, self-assured;** temperate, pacific

14 **sedate, staid,** sober, sober-minded, **serious,** grave, solemn, sobersided; temperate, moderate

15 **nonchalant, blasé, indifferent,** unconcerned 102.7; **casual, offhand, relaxed, laid-back** *and* throwaway <nf>; **easygoing,** easy, free and easy, devil-may-care, lackadaisical, *dégagé* <Fr>

ADVS **16** inexcitably, **imperturbably,** inirritably, **dispassionately;** steadily; stoically; **calmly, placidly,** quietly, **tranquilly, serenely; coolly, composedly,** levelheadedly; impassively, stolidly, stodgily, stuffily

17 **sedately, staidly, soberly, seriously,** sobersidedly

18 **nonchalantly, casually, relaxedly,** offhandedly, easygoingly, lackadaisically

107 CONTENTMENT

NOUNS **1** **contentment, content,** contentedness, satisfiedness; **satisfaction,** entire satisfaction, fulfillment, gratification; ease, peace of mind, eupathy, composure 106.2; comfort 121; **quality of life;** well-being, euphoria; **happiness** 95.2; **acceptance,** resignation, reconcilement, reconciliation; clear *or* clean conscience, dreamless sleep; serenity; satiety; halcyon days

2 **complacency,** complacence; **smugness, self-complacence** *or* self-complacency, self-approval, self-approbation, **self-satisfaction, self-content,** self-contentedness self-contentness; bovinity

3 **satisfactoriness, adequacy, sufficiency** 991; **acceptability,** admissibility, **tolerability,** agreeability, unobjectionability, unexceptionability, tenability, viability; competency

VERBS **4** **content, satisfy;** gratify; put *or* set at ease, set one's mind at ease *or* rest, achieve inner harmony; indulge, satiate

5 **be content, rest satisfied, rest easy,** rest and be thankful, be of good cheer, be reconciled to, take the good the gods provide, accept one's lot, rest on one's laurels, let well enough alone, let sleeping dogs lie, take the bitter with the sweet; come to terms with oneself, learn to live in one's own skin; have no kick coming <nf>, not complain, not worry, have nothing to complain about, not sweat it *and* cool it *and* go with the flow <nf>; content oneself with, settle for; settle for less, take half a loaf, lower one's sights, cut one's losses; **be pleased** 95.12; have one's heart's desire

6 **be satisfactory, do, suffice** 991.4; **suit,** suit one down to the ground, serve, meet the needs of

ADJS **7** **content, contented, satisfied; pleased** 95.12; happy; **easy, at ease,** at one's ease, easygoing; composed 106.13; **comfortable** 121.11, of good comfort; fulfilled, gratified; euphoric, eupeptic; carefree, without care, *sans souci* <Fr>; accepting, resigned, reconciled; uncomplaining, unrepining

8 **untroubled, unbothered, undisturbed,** unperturbed 106.11, unworried, unvexed, unplagued, untormented, secure

9 **well-content, well-pleased,** well-contented, **well-satisfied,** highly satisfied, satiated, full, full-up

10 **complacent,** bovine; **smug, self-complacent, self-satisfied,** self-content, **self-contented**

11 **satisfactory, satisfying; sufficient** 991.6, sufficing, **adequate, enough,** commensurate, proportionate, proportionable, ample, equal to, competent

12 **acceptable,** admissible, **agreeable,** unobjectionable, unexceptionable, tenable, viable; **OK** *and* okay *and* all right *and* alright <nf>; **passable,** good enough, not bad, so-so; palatable

13 **tolerable, bearable, endurable,** supportable, sufferable

ADVS **14** **contentedly,** to one's heart's content; **satisfiedly,** with satisfaction; **complacently, smugly,** self-complacently, self-satisfiedly, self-contentedly

15 **satisfactorily,** satisfyingly; **acceptably, agreeably,** admissibly; sufficiently, adequately, commensurately, amply, enough; **tolerably, passably**

16 **to one's satisfaction,** to one's delight, to one's great glee; to one's taste, to the king's *or* queen's taste

108 DISCONTENT

NOUNS **1** **discontent,** discontentment, discontentedness; **dissatisfaction,** unsatisfaction, dissatisfiedness, unfulfillment; **resentment, envy** 154; **restlessness, restiveness, uneasiness,** unease; malaise; rebelliousness 327.3; disappointment 132; unpleasure 96; unhappiness 112.2; ill humor 110; **disgruntlement,** sulkiness, sourness, petulance, peevishness, querulousness; vexation of spirit; cold comfort; divine discontent; Faustianism

2 **unsatisfactoriness,** dissatisfactoriness; **inadequacy, insufficiency** 992; **unacceptability,** inadmissibility, unsuitability, undesirability, objectionability, untenability, indefensibility; **intolerability** 98.9

3 **malcontent,** *frondeur* <Fr>; **complainer,** complainant, **faultfinder, grumbler,** growler, smellfungus, griper, grouser, croaker, carper, peevish *or* petulant *or* querulous person, whiner; reactionary, reactionist; rebel 327.5; spoilsport; tough customer, dissatisfied customer, angry young man

4 <nf terms> **grouch, kvetch,** kicker, griper, moaner, moaning Minnie <Brit>, crank, crab, grump, beefer, bellyacher, bitcher, sorehead, picklepuss, sourpuss, churl

VERBS **5** **dissatisfy, discontent, disgruntle, displease,** fail to satisfy, be inadequate, not fill the bill, disappoint, leave much *or* a lot to be desired, dishearten, disillusion, put out <nf>; **be discontented, complain**

6 <nf terms> **beef, bitch, kvetch,** bellyache, boo, hiss, carp, crab, gripe, grouch, grouse, grump, have an attitude, kick, moan, piss, make a stink, squawk

ADJS **7** **discontented, dissatisfied, disgruntled,** unaccepting, unaccommodating, **displeased,** less than pleased, let down, disappointed; **unsatisfied, ungratified,** unfulfilled; resentful, dog-in-the-manger; envious 154.3; restless, restive, uneasy; rebellious 327.11; malcontent, malcontented, **complaining,** complaintful, critical of, pejorative, sour, **faultfinding,** grumbling, growling, murmuring, muttering, griping, croaking, **peevish, petulant,** sulky, brooding, **querulous,** querulant, whiny; unhappy 112.21; out of humor 110.17

8 <nf terms> **grouchy, kvetchy,** cranky, beefing, crabby, crabbing, grousing, griping, bellyaching, bitching

9 **unsatisfactory,** dissatisfactory; **unsatisfying, ungratifying,** unfulfilling; **displeasing** 98.17; disappointing, disheartening, not up to expectation, not good enough, substandard; **inadequate,** incommensurate, **insufficient** 992.9; unpopular, not up to snuff <nf>

10 **unacceptable,** inadmissible, unsuitable, undesirable, **objectionable,** exceptionable, impossible, untenable, indefensible; **intolerable** 98.25; rejected

ADVS **11** **discontentedly, dissatisfiedly**

12 **unsatisfactorily,** dissatisfactorily; **unsatisfyingly, ungratifyingly; inadequately, insufficiently; unacceptably,** nowise, inadmissibly, unsuitably, undesirably, objectionably; intolerably 98.30

109 CHEERFULNESS

NOUNS **1** **cheerfulness,** cheeriness, **good cheer, cheer,** cheery vein *or* mood; blitheness, blithesomeness; **gladness,** felicity, gladsomeness;

happiness 95.2; **pleasantness,** winsomeness, geniality, conviviality; brightness, radiance, **sunniness;** sanguineness, sanguinity, sanguine humor, euphoric *or* eupeptic mein; optimism, rosy expectation, hopefulness; **irrepressibility,** irrepressibleness

2 **good humor, good spirits**, good cheer**; high spirits, exhilaration,** rare good humor; *joie de vivre* <Fr>

3 **lightheartedness,** lightsomeness, lightness, levity; **buoyancy,** buoyance, resilience, resiliency, bounce <nf>, springiness; springy step; **jauntiness,** perkiness, debonairness, carefreeness; **breeziness,** airiness, pertness, chirpiness, light heart

4 **gaiety,** gayness, *allégresse* <Fr>; **liveliness, vivacity, vitality,** life, **animation, spiritedness, spirit,** esprit, élan, **sprightliness,** high spirits, zestfulness, zest, vim, zip <nf>, vigor, verve, gusto, **exuberance,** heartiness; **spirits,** animal spirits; piss and vinegar <nf>; **friskiness,** skittishness, coltishness, rompishness, rollicksomeness, capersomeness; **sportiveness, playfulness, frolicsomeness,** gamesomeness, kittenishness

5 **merriment,** merriness; **hilarity,** hilariousness; **joy,** joyfulness, joyousness; **glee,** gleefulness, high glee; **jollity,** jolliness, **joviality,** jocularity, jocundity; frivolity, **levity; mirth,** mirthfulness, **amusement** 743; **fun**, good time**; laughter** 116.4

VERBS **6** exude cheerfulness, radiate cheer, not have a care in the world, **beam,** burst *or* brim with cheer, glow, radiate, sparkle, sing, lilt, whistle, **chirp,** chirrup, chirp like a cricket; walk on air, dance, skip, caper, frolic, gambol, romp, caracole; **smile, laugh** 116.8; be a Pollyanna

7 **cheer, gladden, brighten,** put in good humor; **encourage, hearten,** pick up <nf>; **inspire,** inspirit, warm the spirits, **raise the spirits,** elevate one's mood, buoy up, boost, give a lift <nf>, put one on top of the world *and* on cloud nine <nf>; **exhilarate,** animate, invigorate, liven, enliven, vitalize; **rejoice,** rejoice the heart, do the heart good

8 **elate, exalt,** elevate, lift, uplift, flush

9 **cheer up, take heart,** drive dull care away; **brighten up,** light up, **perk up; buck up** *and* brace up *and* chirk up <nf>; come out of it, snap out of it <nf>, revive

10 **be of good cheer,** bear up, **keep one's spirits up,** keep one's chin up <nf>, keep one's pecker up <Brit nf>, keep a stiff upper lip <nf>, grin and bear it

ADJS **11 cheerful, cheery,** of good cheer, in good spirits; in high spirits, exalted, elated, exhilarated, high <nf>; irrepressible; **blithe,** blithesome; **glad, gladsome; happy,** happy as a clam *or* a lark, on top of the world, sitting on top of the world, sitting pretty, on cloud nine, over the moon <nf>; **pleasant, genial,** winsome; **bright, sunny,** bright and sunny, **radiant,** riant, sparkling, beaming, glowing, flushed, perky, rosy, smiling, laughing; sanguine, sanguineous, euphoric, eupeptic, ebullient, Pollyannaish, exhilarated; optimistic, hopeful; **irrepressible;** up <nf>

12 **lighthearted,** light, lightsome; **buoyant,** corky <nf>, resilient; **jaunty,** perky, **debonair, carefree,** free and easy; **breezy,** airy

13 **pert,** chirk <nf>, chirrupy, **chirpy, chipper** <nf>

14 **gay**; **spirited,** sprightly, **lively, animated, vivacious,** vital, zestful, zippy <nf>, **exuberant,** hearty; **frisky,** antic, skittish, coltish, rompish, capersome; **full of beans** *and* **feeling one's oats** <nf>, full of piss and vinegar <nf>; **sportive, playful,** playful as a kitten, kittenish, **frolicsome,** gamesome; rollicking, rollicky, rollicksome

15 **merry, mirthful, hilarious; joyful, joyous,** rejoicing; **gleeful,** gleesome; **jolly,** buxom; **jovial,** jocund, jocular; **frivolous;** laughter-loving, mirth-loving, risible; merry as a cricket *or* grig; tickled to death <nf>, tickled pink <nf>, high as a kite <nf>

16 **cheering, gladdening; encouraging, heartening,** heartwarming, uplifting; **inspiring,** inspiriting; **exhilarating,** animating, enlivening, invigorating; cheerful, cheery, glad, joyful

ADVS 17 **cheerfully,** cheerily, with good cheer, with a cheerful heart; irrepressibly; **lightheartedly,** lightly; jauntily, perkily, airily; **pleasantly,** genially, blithely; **gladly, happily, joyfully,** smilingly; optimistically, hopefully

18 **gaily, exuberantly, heartily, spiritedly, animatedly, vivaciously,** zestfully, with zest, with vim, with élan, with zip <nf>, with verve, with gusto

19 **merrily, gleefully, hilariously; jovially,** jocundly, jocularly; frivolously; **mirthfully,** laughingly

PHRS 20 cheer up!, every cloud has a silver lining; don't let it get you down, illegitimati non carborundum <L, don't let the bastards grind you down>; chin up!, buck up!, keep your pecker up! <Brit>; it's always darkest before the dawn, banzai!

110 ILL HUMOR

NOUNS 1 **ill humor,** bad humor, **bad temper,** rotten *or* ill *or* evil temper, **ill nature,** filthy *or* rotten *or* evil humor; **sourness,** biliousness, liverishness; choler, bile, gall, spleen; **abrasiveness,** causticity, corrosiveness, asperity 144.8; **anger** 152.5; discontent 108

2 **irascibility, irritability,** excitability, short *or* quick temper, short fuse <nf>; **crossness,** disagreeableness, disagreeability, gruffness, shortness, peevishness, querulousness, fretfulness, crabbedness, **crankiness, testiness,** crustiness, huffiness, huffishness, churlishness, bearishness, snappishness, waspishness; **perversity,** cross-grainedness, fractiousness

3 <nf terms> **crabbiness, grouchiness,** cantankerousness, crustiness, grumpiness *or* grumpishness, cussedness, huffiness *or* huffishness, **meanness, orneriness,** bitchiness, cussedness, feistiness, ugliness, miffiness, saltiness, scrappiness, shirtiness <Brit>, soreheadedness

4 **hot temper, temper,** quick *or* short temper, irritable temper, warm temper, fiery temper, fierce temper, short fuse <nf>, pepperiness, feistiness *and* spunkiness <nf>, **hotheadedness,** hot blood; sharp tongue

5 **touchiness, tetchiness,** ticklishness, prickliness, quickness to take offense, miffiness <nf>, **sensitiveness,** oversensitiveness, hypersensitiveness, sensitivity, oversensitivity, hypersensitivity, thin skin; temperamentalness, moodiness

6 **petulance** *or* petulancy, **peevishness,** pettishness, **querulousness, fretfulness,** resentfulness; shrewishness, vixenishness

7 **contentiousness, quarrelsomeness** 456.3; **disputatiousness, argumentativeness,** litigiousness; **belligerence,** truculence

8 **sullenness, sulkiness, surliness, moroseness, glumness,** grumness, grimness, mumpishness, dumpishness, dourness, *bouderie* <Fr>; **moodiness,** moodishness; mopishness, mopiness <nf>; dejection, melancholy 112.5

9 **scowl, frown,** lower, **glower, pout,** moue, mow, grimace, wry face; sullen looks, black looks, hangdog look, **long face**

10 **sulks,** sullens, **mopes,** mumps, dumps, grumps <nf>, frumps <Brit nf>, **blues,** blue devils, mulligrubs, **pouts**

11 <ill-humored person> **sorehead, grouch, curmudgeon, grump, crank,** crab, **crosspatch,** feist *or* fice <nf>, wasp, **bear,** grizzly bear, pit bull, junkyard dog <nf>; fury, Tartar, dragon, ugly customer <nf>; **hothead,** hotspur; fire-eater; sulker, churl, bellyacher, neurotic

12 **bitch** <nf>, **shrew, vixen,** virago, termagant, brimstone, fury, witch, beldam, cat, tigress, she-wolf, she-devil, spitfire; fishwife; **scold,** common scold, harpy, nag, Xanthippe; old bag; battle-ax <nf>

VERBS 13 have a temper, have a short fuse <nf>, have a devil in one, be possessed of the devil; be cross, get out on the wrong side of the bed

14 sulk, mope, mope around; grizzle <chiefly Brit nf>, grump *and* **grouch** *and* **bitch** <nf>, **fret;** get oneself in a sulk; have the blues, be down in the dumps

15 look sullen, look black, look black as thunder, gloom, pull *or* make *or* have a long face; **frown, scowl,** knit the brow, lower, **glower, pout,** brood, make a moue *or* mow, grimace, make a wry face, make a lip, hang one's lip, thrust out one's lower lip

16 sour, acerbate, exacerbate; **embitter,** bitter, envenom

ADJS **17 out of humor,** out of temper, out of sorts, **in a bad humor,** in a shocking humor, feeling evil <nf>; **abrasive,** caustic, corrosive, acid; angry; discontented 108.5

18 ill-humored, bad-tempered, ill-tempered, evil-humored, evil-tempered, **ill-natured,** ill-affected, ill-disposed

19 irascible, irritable, excitable, flappable <nf>; **cross, cranky, testy;** cankered, crabbed, spiteful, spleeny, splenetic, churlish, bearish, snappish, waspish; **gruff,** grumbly, grumbling, growling; **disagreeable; perverse,** fractious, cross-grained

20 <nf terms> **crabby, grouchy,** cantankerous, crusty, grumpy *or* grumpish, cussed, huffy *or* huffish, mean, mean as a junkyard dog, ornery, bitchy, feisty, ugly, miffy, salty, scrappy, shirty <Brit>, soreheaded

21 touchy, tetchy, miffy <nf>, ticklish, prickly, quick to take offense, **thin-skinned, sensitive,** oversensitive, hypersensitive, high-strung, highly strung, temperamental, prima-donnaish

22 peevish, petulant, pettish, **querulous, fretful,** resentful; catty; shrewish, vixenish, vixenly; nagging, naggy

23 sour, soured, **sour-tempered,** vinegarish; prune-faced <nf>; **choleric, dyspeptic, bilious,** liverish, jaundiced; **bitter,** embittered

24 sullen, sulky, surly, morose, dour, mumpish, dumpish, **glum,** grum, grim; **moody,** moodish; **mopish,** mopey <nf>, moping; **glowering,** lowering, **scowling, frowning;** dark, black; black-browed, beetle-browed; dejected, melancholy 112.23; somber

25 hot-tempered, hotheaded, passionate, hot, fiery, peppery, feisty, spunky <nf>, **quick-tempered, short-tempered;** hasty, quick, explosive, volcanic, combustible, vicious

26 contentious, quarrelsome 456.17; **disputatious,** controversial, litigious, polemic, polemical; **argumentative,** argumental; on the warpath, looking for trouble; scrappy <nf>; cat-and-doggish, cat-and-dog; **bellicose, belligerent**

ADVS **27 ill-humoredly, ill-naturedly; irascibly, irritably, crossly, crankily, testily,** huffily, cantankerously <nf>, crabbedly, sourly, churlishly, crustily, bearishly, snappily; perversely, fractiously, cross-grainedly

28 peevishly, petulantly, pettishly, **querulously, fretfully**

29 grouchily *and* **crabbily** *and* grumpily <nf>, grumblingly

30 sullenly, sulkily, surlily, morosely, mumpishly, glumly, grumly, grimly; moodily, mopingly; gloweringly, loweringly, scowlingly, frowningly

111 SOLEMNITY

NOUNS **1 solemnity, solemness, dignity, soberness, sobriety, gravity,** *gravitas* <L>, weightiness, **somberness, grimness; sedateness, staidness;** demureness, decorousness; **seriousness, earnestness, thoughtfulness, sober-mindedness,** sobersidedness; sobersides, humorlessness; long face, straight face; **formality** 580

VERBS **2** honor the occasion, keep a straight face, look serious, compose one's features, wear an earnest frown; repress a smile, not crack a smile <nf>, wipe the smile off one's face, keep from laughing, make a long face

ADJS **3 solemn, dignified, sober, grave,** unsmiling, weighty, **somber,** frowning, **grim; sedate, staid;** demure, decorous; **serious, earnest, thoughtful**, pensive**; sober-minded,** sober-sided; in earnest; straight-faced, long-faced, grim-faced, grim-visaged, stone-faced, stony-faced; sober as a judge, grave as an undertaker; **formal** 580.7

ADVS **4 solemnly, soberly,** gravely, somberly, grimly; **sedately, staidly,** demurely, decorously; with dignity, **seriously, earnestly,** thoughtfully, sober-mindedly, sobersidedly; with a straight face; formally 580.11

112 SADNESS

NOUNS **1 sadness,** sadheartedness, weight *or* burden of sorrow; heaviness, **heavyheartedness,** heavy heart, **heaviness of heart;** pathos, bathos

2 unhappiness, infelicity; displeasure 96.1; discontent 108; **uncheerfulness,** cheerlessness; **joylessness,** unjoyfulness; mirthlessness, unmirthfulness, humorlessness, infestivity; **grimness; wretchedness, misery**

3 dejection, depression, oppression, dejectedness, **downheartedness,** downcastness; **discouragement, disheartenment,** dispiritedness; *Schmerz* and *Weltschmerz* <Ger>; malaise 96.1; lowness, lowness *or* depression *or* oppression of spirit, downer *and* down trip <nf>; chill, chilling effect; **low spirits,** drooping spirits, sinking heart, funk; despondence *or* **despondency,** spiritlessness, heartlessness; black *or* blank despondency; demotivation, hopelessness 125, **despair** 125.2, pessimism 125.6, gloom and doom, suicidal despair, death wish, self-destructive urge; weariness of life, *taedium vitae* <L>; sloth, acedia, noonday demon

4 hypochondria, hypochondriasis, morbid anxiety; neurosis

5 melancholy, melancholia, melancholiness; **pensiveness, wistfulness,** tristfulness; **nostalgia,** homesickness, *mal du pays* <Fr>

6 blues *and* blue devils *and* mulligrubs <nf>, mumps, **dumps** <nf>, **doldrums,** dismals, dolefuls <nf>, megrims, blahs *and* mopes *and* megrims *and* sulks *and* funks<nf>

7 gloom, gloominess, darkness, murk, murkiness, **dismalness, bleakness, grimness, somberness, gravity, solemnity; dreariness,** drearisomeness; wearifulness, wearisomeness

8 glumness, grumness, **moroseness, sullenness,** sulkiness, **moodiness,** mumpishness, dumpishness; mopishness, mopiness <nf>

9 heartache, aching heart, bleeding heart, grieving heart; heartsickness, heartsoreness; **heartbreak, broken heart,** brokenheartedness, heartbrokenness

10 sorrow, sorrowing, **grief, care,** carking care, **woe;** heartgrief, heartfelt grief; languishment, pining; **anguish, misery, agony;** prostrating grief, prostration; **lamentation** 115

11 sorrowfulness, mournfulness, ruefulness, **woefulness, dolefulness**, dolorousness, **plaintiveness,** plangency, grievousness, aggrievedness, lugubriousness, funerealness; weeping and wailing and gnashing of teeth; *lacrimae rerum* <L>, **tearfulness** 115.2

12 disconsolateness, disconsolation, **inconsolability,** inconsolableness, unconsolability, comfortlessness; **desolation,** desolateness; forlornness

13 sourpuss *and* picklepuss *and* gloomy Gus <nf>, moaning Minnie <Brit nf>; mope, brooder; **melancholic,** melancholiac; depressive; Eeyore

14 killjoy, spoilsport, grinch *and* crepehanger *and* drag <nf>; damp, damper, **wet blanket,** party pooper; gloomster *and* doomster <nf>, doomsdayer, apocalypticist, apocalyptician, awfulizer <nf>, crapehanger; fussbudget, worrywart, skeleton at the feast; pessimist 125.7

VERBS **15** hang one's head, pull *or* make a long face, look blue, sing *or* get *or* have the blues <nf>; drag one down; carry the weight *or* woe of the world on one's shoulders; hang crape <nf>, apocalypticize, catastrophize, awfulize <nf>

16 **lose heart,** despond, give way, give oneself up *or* over to; despondency; **despair** 125.10, sink into despair, throw up one's hands in despair, be *or* become suicidal, lose the will to live; **droop,** sink, languish, mope; reach *or* plumb the depths, touch *or* hit bottom, hit rock bottom

17 **grieve, sorrow; weep, mourn** 115.8,10; be dumb with grief; **pine,** pine away *or* over; **brood over, mope, fret,** take on <nf>; **eat one's heart out,** break one's heart over; **agonize,** ache, bleed

18 **sadden,** darken, cast a pall *or* gloom upon, weigh *or* weigh heavy upon; **deject, depress, oppress, crush,** press down, hit one like a ton of bricks <nf>, **cast down,** lower, lower the spirits, get one down <nf>, take the wind out of one's sails, rains on one's parade, burst one's bubble, **discourage, dishearten,** take the heart out of, **dispirit;** damp, dampen, damp *or* dampen the spirits; dash, knock down, beat down; sink, sink one's soul, plunge one into despair

19 aggrieve, oppress, **grieve, sorrow,** plunge one into sorrow, embitter; draw tears, bring to tears; **anguish, tear up** *and* **cut up** <nf>, wring *or* pierce *or* lacerate *or* rend the heart, pull at the heartstrings; be cut up; afflict 96.16, torment 96.18; **break one's heart, make one's heart bleed;** desolate, leave an aching void; prostrate, break down, crush, bear down, inundate, overwhelm

ADJS **20** **sad,** saddened; sadhearted, **sad of heart; heavyhearted,** heavy; oppressed, weighed upon, weighed *or* weighted down, bearing the woe *or* weight of the world, burdened *or* laden with sorrow; sad-faced, long-faced; sad-eyed; sad-voiced

21 **unhappy, uncheerful,** uncheery, **cheerless, joyless, unjoyful,** unsmiling; mirthless, unmirthful, humorless, infestive; funny as a crutch <nf>; **grim; out of humor,** out of sorts, in bad humor *or* spirits; **sorry,** sorryish; discontented 108.5; **wretched, miserable;** pleasureless 96.20

22 **dejected, depressed, downhearted, down, downcast, cast down,** bowed down, subdued; **discouraged, disheartened, dispirited,** dashed; **low, feeling low,** low-spirited, **in low spirits; down in the mouth** <nf>, **in the doldrums, down in the dumps** *and* **in the dumps** *and* in the doleful dumps <nf>, in the depths; **despondent,** desponding; **despairing** 125.12, weary of life, suicidal, world-weary; pessimistic 125.16; spiritless, heartless, **woebegone; drooping,** droopy, languishing, pining, haggard; hypochondriac *or* hypochondriacal

23 **melancholy,** melancholic, splenetic, **blue** <nf>, funky <nf>; atrabilious, atrabiliar; **pensive, wistful,** tristful; **nostalgic,** homesick

24 **gloomy, dismal, murky, bleak, grim, somber,** sombrous, **solemn, grave;** sad, *triste* <Fr>, **funereal,** funebrial, crepehanging <nf>, saturnine; **dark,** black, gray; **dreary,** drear, drearisome; weary, weariful, wearisome

25 **glum,** grum, **morose, sullen,** sulky, mumpish, dumpish, long-faced, crestfallen, chapfallen; **moody,** moodish, **brooding,** broody; mopish, mopey <nf>, **moping**

26 **sorrowful, sorrowing,** sorrowed, **mournful, rueful, woeful, doleful, plaintive,** plangent; anguished; dolorous, **grievous, lamentable,** lugubrious; **tearful; care-worn;** grieved, **grief-stricken,** griefful, aggrieved, in grief, bereft, plunged in grief, dumb with grief, prostrated by grief, cut-up *and* torn-up <nf>, **inconsolable**

27 **sorrow-stricken,** sorrow-wounded, sorrow-struck, sorrow-torn, sorrow-worn, sorrow-wasted, sorrow-beaten, sorrow-blinded, sorrow-clouded, sorrow-shot, sorrow-burdened, sorrow-laden, sorrow-sighing, sorrow-sobbing, sorrow-sick

28 **disconsolate, inconsolable,** unconsolable, comfortless, prostrate *or* prostrated, **forlorn; desolate,** *désolé* <Fr>; sick, **sick at heart, heartsick,** soul-sick, heartsore

29 **overcome,** crushed, borne-down, overwhelmed, inundated, spazzed-out, **stricken, cut up** <nf>, **desolated,** prostrate *or* prostrated, broken-down, undone; **heart-stricken,** heart-struck; **broken-hearted,** heartbroken

30 **depressing,** depressive, depressant, **oppressive; discouraging, disheartening, dispiriting;** morale-sapping, worst-case, downbeat *or* downer <nf>

ADVS **31** **sadly, gloomily, dismally, drearily,** heavily, bleakly, grimly, somberly, sombrously, solemnly, funereally, gravely, with a long face; **depressingly**

32 **unhappily, uncheerfully,** cheerlessly, joylessly, unjoyfully

33 **dejectedly, downheartedly; discouragedly, disheartenedly, dispiritedly; despondently,** despairingly, spiritlessly, heartlessly; **disconsolately,** inconsolably, unconsolably, forlornly

34 **melancholily, pensively,** wistfully, tristfully; nostalgically

35 **glumly,** grumly, **morosely, sullenly; moodily,** moodishly, broodingly, broodily; mopishly, mopily <nf>, mopingly

36 **sorrowfully, mournfully, ruefully, woefully, dolefully, dolorously, plaintively, grievously,** grieffully, lugubriously; with a broken voice; **heartbrokenly,** brokenheartedly; **tearfully,** with tears in one's eyes

113 REGRET

NOUNS **1** **regret, regrets,** regretting, regretfulness, rue; **remorse,** remorsefulness, remorse of conscience; buyer's remorse; **shame,** shamefulness, shamefacedness, shamefastness; **sorrow, grief, sorriness,** repining; **contrition,** contriteness, attrition; bitterness; apologies; wistfulness 100.4

2 **compunction, qualm, qualms,** qualmishness, scruples, scrupulosity, scrupulousness, pang, pangs, **pangs of conscience,** throes, sting *or* pricking *or* twinge *or* twitch of conscience, touch of conscience, **voice of conscience,** pricking of heart, misgiving, better self

3 **self-reproach,** self-reproachfulness, **self-accusation, self-condemnation,** self-conviction, self-punishment, self-humiliation, self-debasement, **self-hatred,** self-flagellation; hair shirt; self-analysis, soul-searching, examination of conscience

4 **penitence, repentance, change of heart; apology,** humble *or* heartfelt apology, abject apology; better nature, good angel, guardian angel; reformation 858.2; deathbed repentance; mea culpa; **penance** 658.3; wearing a hairshirt *or* sackcloth *or* sackcloth and ashes, mortification of the flesh

5 **penitent,** confessor, **prodigal son,** prodigal returned; Magdalen

VERBS **6** **regret, deplore, repine, be sorry for; rue,** rue the day; **bemoan, bewail;** curse one's folly, **reproach oneself,** kick oneself <nf>, bite one's tongue, accuse *or* condemn *or* blame *or* convict *or* punish oneself, flagellate oneself, wear a hair shirt, make oneself miserable, humiliate *or* debase oneself, hate oneself for one's actions, hide one's face in shame; examine one's conscience, search one's soul, consult *or* heed one's better self, analyze *or* search one's motives; cry over spilled milk, waste time in regret

7 **repent, think better of,** change one's mind, have second thoughts; laugh out of the other side of one's mouth; **plead guilty,** own oneself in the wrong, humble oneself, **apologize** 658.5, beg pardon *or* forgiveness, throw oneself on the mercy of the court; **do penance** 658.6; reform

ADJS **8** **regretful, remorseful,** full of remorse, **ashamed,** shameful, shamefaced, shamefast, **sorry, rueful, repining,** unhappy about; **conscience-stricken,** conscience-smitten; **self-reproachful,** self-reproaching, self-accusing, self-condemning, self-convicting, self-punishing, self-flagellating, self-humiliating, self-debasing, self-hating; wistful 100.23

9 **penitent, repentant; penitential,** penitentiary; **contrite,** abject, humble, humbled, **sheepish, apologetic,** touched, softened, melted; atoning

10 **regrettable,** much to be regretted; **deplorable** 1000.9

ADVS 11 **regretfully, remorsefully,** sorrily, ruefully, unhappily

12 **penitently,** repentantly, penitentially; **contritely,** abjectly, **humbly, sheepishly, apologetically**

114 UNREGRETFULNESS

NOUNS 1 **unregretfulness, unremorsefulness, unsorriness,** unruefulness; **remorselessness,** regretlessness, sorrowlessness; **shamelessness,** unashamedness

2 **impenitence,** impenitentness; nonrepentance, irrepentance, unrepentance; **uncontriteness,** unabjectness; seared conscience, heart of stone, callousness 94.3; **hardness of heart,** hardness, induration, obduracy; **defiance** 454/327.2; **insolence** 142; no regrets, no remorse

VERBS 3 **harden one's heart,** steel oneself; **have no regrets,** not look backward, not cry over spilled milk; have no shame, have *or* feel no remorse; feel nothing

ADJS 4 **unregretful,** unregretting, **unremorseful, unsorry, unsorrowful,** unrueful; **remorseless,** regretless, sorrowless, griefless; unsorrowing, ungrieving, unrepining; **shameless,** unashamed

5 **impenitent, unrepentant,** unrepenting, unrecanting; **uncontrite,** unabject; untouched, unsoftened, unmelted, callous 94.12; hard, hardened, obdurate; **defiant** 454.7; **insolent** 142.9

6 **unregretted, unrepented,** unatoned

ADVS 7 **unregretfully, unremorsefully,** unruefully; **remorselessly,** sorrowlessly, impenitently, shamelessly, unashamedly; **without regret,** without looking back, **without remorse,** without compunction, without any qualms *or* scruples

115 LAMENTATION

NOUNS 1 **lamentation,** lamenting, **mourning, moaning, grieving, sorrowing, wailing, bewailing, bemoaning,** keening, howling, ululation; **sorrow** 112.10; woe, misery; threnody

2 **weeping, sobbing, crying,** bawling; blubbering, whimpering, sniveling; **tears,** flood of tears, fit of crying; cry *and* good cry <nf>; **tearfulness, weepiness** <nf>, lachrymosity, melting mood; tearful eyes, swimming *or* brimming *or* overflowing eyes; **tear,** teardrop, lachryma; lacrimatory, tear bottle

3 **lament, plaint,** *planctus* <L>; **murmur,** mutter; **moan, groan; whine, whimper; wail,** wail of woe; **sob,** *cri du coeur* <Fr>, **cry,** outcry, scream, **howl,** yowl, bawl, yawp, keen, ululation; jeremiad, tirade, dolorous tirade

4 **complaint, grievance, peeve,** pet peeve, **groan; dissent, protest** 333.2; hard luck story <nf>, sob story, sad story, tale of woe; **complaining,** scolding, groaning, **faultfinding** 510.4, sniping, destructive criticism, **grumbling, murmuring;** whining, petulance, peevishness, querulousness; backstabbing

5 <nf terms> **beef, kick, gripe,** kvetch, grouse, bellyache, howl, holler, **squawk,** bitch; **beefing, grousing, kicking, griping,** kvetching, **bellyaching,** squawking, **bitching,** yapping

6 **dirge, funeral** *or* **death song,** coronach, keen, elegy, epicedium, requiem, monody, threnody, threnode, coronach <Ir>, knell, death knell, passing bell, funeral *or* dead march, muffled drums; eulogy, funeral *or* graveside oration

7 <mourning garments> **mourning, weeds,** widow's weeds, crape, black; deep mourning; sackcloth, sackcloth and ashes; cypress, cypress lawn, yew; mourning band; mourning ring

8 **lamenter, griever, mourner** 309.7; moaner, weeper, sniveler; **complainer,** faultfinder, smellfungus, malcontent 108.3

9 <nf terms> **grouch, kvetch,** kicker, griper, moaner, moaning Minnie <Brit>, crank, crab, crybaby, blubberer, grouser, beefer, bellyacher, bitcher, sorehead, picklepuss, sourpuss, bellyacher, grumbler

VERBS **10 lament, mourn, moan, grieve, sorrow,** keen, weep over *or* for, **bewail, bemoan, deplore, repine, sigh,** rue, give sorrow words; sing the blues <nf>, elegize, dirge, knell, toll the knell; pay one's last respects; wake, hold a wake, go to a funeral, sound the last post

11 wring one's hands, tear one's hair, gnash one's teeth, beat one's breast, sing the blues

12 weep, sob, cry, bawl, boo-hoo; **blubber,** ululate, **whimper, snivel; shed tears,** drop a tear; **burst into tears,** burst out crying, give way to tears, melt *or* dissolve in tears, break down, break down and cry, turn on the waterworks <nf>; cry one's eyes out, cry oneself blind; cry before one is hurt

13 wail, ululate; **moan, groan; howl,** yowl, yawl <Brit nf>; **cry, squall, bawl,** yawp, **yell, scream,** shriek; cry out, make an outcry; bay at the moon; tirade

14 whine, whimper, yammer <nf>, pule, grizzle <chiefly Brit nf>

15 complain, groan; grumble, murmur, mutter, growl, clamor, croak, grunt, yelp; **fret,** fuss, make a fuss about, fret and fume; air a grievance, lodge *or* register a complaint; fault, find fault

16 <nf terms> **beef, bitch, kick, kvetch,** bellyache, crab, gripe, grouch, grouse, grump, have an attitude, holler, howl, moan, piss, piss and moan, make a stink, squawk, yap; raise a howl, put up a squawk *or* howl, take on, cry *or* yell *or* scream bloody murder, give one a hard time, piss *or* kick up a storm *or* row *or* fuss, make *or* raise a stink

17 go into mourning; put on mourning, wear mourning

ADJS **18 lamenting, grieving, mourning, moaning, sorrowing;** wailing, bewailing, bemoaning; **in mourning,** in sackcloth and ashes; depressed, down <nf>

19 plaintive, plangent, **mournful,** moanful, wailful, lamentive, ululant; woebegone, disconsolate; **sorrowful** 112.26; **howling,** Jeremianic; whining, whiny, whimpering, puling; **querulous, fretful,** petulant, peevish; **complaining, faultfinding** 510.23

20 <nf terms> **grouchy, kvetchy,** cranky, beefing, crabby, crabbing, grousing, griping, bellyaching, bitching

21 tearful, teary, **weepy** <nf>; lachrymal, lachrymose, lacrimatory; in the melting mood, on the edge of tears, ready to cry; **weeping,** weepy, **sobbing, crying;** blubbering, whimpering, sniveling; red-eyed; **in tears,** with tears in one's eyes, with tearful *or* watery eyes, with swimming *or* brimming *or* overflowing eyes, with eyes suffused *or* bathed *or* dissolved in tears

22 dirgelike, knell-like, elegiac, elegiacal, epicedial, threnodic, plaintive, plangent

ADVS **23 lamentingly, plaintively, mournfully,** moanfully, wailfully; **sorrowfully** 112.36; complainingly, groaningly, querulously, fretfully, petulantly, peevishly

116 REJOICING

NOUNS **1 rejoicing, jubilation,** jubilance, jubilant display, jubilee, show of joy, raucous happiness; **exultation,** elation, triumph; the time of one's life, special day; whoopee *and* hoopla <nf>, festivity 743.3,4, merriment 109.5; celebration 487

2 cheer, hurrah, huzzah, hurray, hooray, yippee, rah, cowabunga; **cry, shout, yell;** hosanna, hallelujah, alleluia, paean, paean *or* chorus of cheers, three cheers; **applause** 509.2, fanfare, shout-out; high-five <nf>

3 smile, smiling; bright smile, gleaming *or* glowing smile, beam; silly smile *or* grin; **grin,** grinning; broad grin, ear-to-ear grin, toothful grin; stupid grin, idiotic grin; sardonic grin, **smirk, simper**

4 **laughter, laughing, hilarity** 109.5, risibility; **laugh;** boff *and* boffola *and* yuck <nf>; **titter; giggle; chuckle, chortle;** cackle, crow; **snicker,** snigger, snort; ha-ha, hee-haw, hee-hee, ho-ho, tee-hee, yuk-yuk; guffaw, **horselaugh; hearty laugh, belly laugh** <nf>, Homeric laughter, cachinnation; **shout, shriek,** shout of laughter, burst *or* outburst of laughter, peal *or* roar of laughter, gales of laughter; fit of laughter, convulsion

VERBS **5** **rejoice,** jubilate, **exult, glory, joy, delight,** bless *or* thank one's stars *or* lucky stars, congratulate oneself, hug oneself, rub one's hands, clap hands; dance *or* skip *or* jump for joy, dance, skip, frisk, rollick, revel, frolic, caper, gambol, caracole, romp; sing, carol, chirp, chirrup, chirp like a cricket, whistle, lilt; make merry

6 **cheer,** give a cheer, give three cheers, **cry, shout, yell,** cry for joy, yell oneself hoarse; huzzah, hurrah, hurray, hooray; shout hosanna *or* hallelujah; **applaud** 509.10; high-five <nf>

7 **smile,** crack a smile <nf>, break into a smile; **beam,** smile brightly; **grin,** grin like a Cheshire cat *or* chessy-cat <nf>; **smirk, simper**

8 **laugh,** burst out laughing, burst into laughter, burst out, laugh outright; laugh it up <nf>; **titter; giggle; chuckle, chortle;** cackle, crow; **snicker,** snigger, snort; ha-ha, hee-haw, hee-hee, ho-ho, tee-hee, yuk-yuk; **guffaw,** belly laugh, horselaugh; **shout, shriek,** give a shout *or* shriek of laughter; **roar,** cachinnate, roar with laughter; shake with laughter, shake like jelly; be convulsed with laughter, go into convulsions, fall about <Brit nf>; burst *or* split with laughter, break up *and* crack up <nf>, split <nf>, **split one's sides,** laugh fit to burst *or* bust <nf>, bust a gut *and* pee in *or* wet one's pants laughing <nf>, **be in stitches** <nf>, hold one's sides, roll in the aisles <nf>; laugh oneself sick *or* silly *or* limp, die *or* nearly die laughing; laugh in one's sleeve, laugh up one's sleeve, laugh in one's beard

9 **make laugh, kill** *and* **slay** <nf>, break *or* crack one up <nf>, get a laugh

ADJS **10** **rejoicing,** delighting, exulting; **jubilant, exultant, elated,** elate, flushed, euphoric, ecstatic

ADVS **11** **rejoicingly,** delightingly, exultingly; **jubilantly, exultantly, elatedly**

117 DULLNESS

<being uninteresting>

NOUNS **1** **dullness, dryness,** dustiness, uninterestingness; **stuffiness, stodginess,** woodenness, stiffness; barrenness, sterility, aridity, jejunity; **insipidness,** insipidity, vapidness, vapidity, inanity, hollowness, emptiness, superficiality, **staleness, flatness,** tastelessness; characterlessness, colorlessness, pointlessness; **deadness,** lifelessness, spiritlessness, bloodlessness, paleness, pallor, etiolation, effeteness; **slowness,** pokiness, dragginess <nf>, unliveliness; **tediousness** 118.2; **dreariness,** drearisomeness, dismalness; **heaviness,** leadenness, ponderousness; inexcitability 106; solemnity 111; lowness of spirit 112.3

2 **prosaicness,** prosiness; prosaism, prosaicism, prose, plainness; **matter-of-factness,** unimaginativeness; matter of fact; **simplicity** 798, **plainness** 499

3 **triteness,** corniness *and* squareness <nf>, **banality,** banalness, unoriginality, sameness, **hackneyedness, commonplaceness,** commonness, familiarness, platitudinousness; a familiar ring; redundancy, repetition, **staleness,** mustiness, fustiness; cliché 974.3

VERBS **4** **fall flat,** fall flat as a pancake; leave one cold *or* unmoved, go over like a lead balloon <nf>, lay an egg *and* bomb <nf>, **wear thin**

5 prose, platitudinize, sing a familiar tune; pedestrianize; warm over; banalize

ADJS **6** **dull, dry,** dusty, dry as dust, mind-numbing; **stuffy, stodgy,** wooden, stiff; arid, barren, blank, sterile, jejune; **insipid,** vapid, inane, hollow, empty, superficial; ho-hum *and* blah <nf>, **flat,** tasteless; characterless, colorless, pointless; **dead,** lifeless, spiritless, bloodless, pale, pallid, etiolated, effete; cold; **slow,** poky, draggy <nf>, pedestrian, plodding, unlively; **tedious; dreary,** drearisome, dismal; **heavy,** leaden, ponderous, elephantine; dull as dish water; inexcitable 106.10; solemn 111.3; low-spirited 112.22

7 **uninteresting,** uneventful, **unexciting; uninspiring; unentertaining,** unenjoyable, **unamusing,** unfunny, unwitty

8 **prosaic,** prose, prosy, prosing, plain; **matter-of-fact,** unimaginative, unimpassioned

9 **trite;** corny *and* square *and* square-John *and* Clyde <nf>, hokey, fade, **banal,** unoriginal, platitudinous, **stereotyped,** stock, set, **commonplace, common,** truistic, twice-told, **familiar,** bromidic <nf>, old hat <nf>, back-number, bewhiskered, warmed-over, **cut-and-dried; hackneyed,** hackney; well-known 928.27; **stale,** musty, fusty; **worn,** timeworn, well-worn, moth-eaten, threadbare, **worn thin**

ADVS **10** **dully, dryly,** dustily, **uninterestingly;** stuffily, stodgily; aridly, barrenly, jejunely, **insipidly, vapidly,** inanely, hollowly, emptily, superficially, tastelessly, **colorlessly,** pointlessly; lifelessly, spiritlessly, bloodlessly, pallidly, effetely; slowly, draggily <nf>, ploddingly; **tediously;** drearily, drearisomely, dismally; heavily, ponderously

11 **tritely,** cornily <nf>, **banally,** commonplacely, commonly, familiarly, hackneyedly, unoriginally, truistically, stalely

118 TEDIUM

NOUNS **1** **tedium, monotony, humdrum,** irksomeness, irk; **sameness,** sameliness, samesomeness <nf>, wearisome sameness, more of the same, the same old thing *or* story, the same damn thing <nf>; broken record, parrot; platitude, chestnut; undeviation, unvariation, invariability; the round, the daily round *or* grind, the weary round, the treadmill, the squirrel cage, the rat race <nf>, the beaten track *or* path, drag <nf>; time on one's hands, time hanging heavily on one's hands; **protraction, prolongation** 827.2

2 **tediousness, monotonousness, unrelievedness; humdrumness,** humdrumminess; **dullness** 117; **wearisomeness,** wearifulness; **tiresomeness, irksomeness,** drearisomeness; boresomeness, boringness; prolixity, **long-windedness** 538.2; redundancy, repetition, repetitiveness, tick-tock

3 **weariness, tiredness,** wearifulness; jadedness, satiation, satiety; **boredom,** boredness; **ennui**, melancholy, life-weariness, *taedium vitae* <L>, world-weariness, *Weltschmerz* <Ger>, jadedness; languor, **listlessness** 94.4, **dispiritedness** 112.3

4 **bore,** crashing bore <nf>, frightful bore; **pest, nuisance;** dryasdust; proser, twaddler, **wet blanket;** buttonholer; bromide; egoist

5 <nf terms> **drag, drip, pill,** flat tire, deadass, deadfanny, dull tool; **headache,** pain, pain in the neck *or* ass; broken record

VERBS **6** **be tedious, drag on,** go on forever; have a certain sameness, be infinitely repetitive, do the same old thing; **weary, tire, irk,** wear, wear on *or* upon, **make one tired,** fatigue, weary *or* tire to death, jade; give one a pain in the ass *and* give one a bellyful *and* make one fed-up <nf>, **pall, satiate,** glut

7 **bore,** leave one cold, set *or* send to sleep; **bore stiff** *or* to tears *or* to death *or* to extinction <nf>, bore to distraction, bore out of one's life, bore out of all patience; buttonhole; wear out one's welcome, stay too long

8 **harp on** *or* **upon, dwell on** *or* **upon,** harp upon one *or* the same string, play *or* sing the same old song *or* tune, play the same broken record

ADJS 9 **tedious, monotonous, humdrum,** singsong, jog-trot, treadmill, unvarying, invariable, uneventful, broken-record, parrotlike, harping, everlasting, too much with us <nf>; blah <nf>, flat, **dreary,** drearisome, dry, dry-as-dust, dusty, **dull** 117.6; protracted, prolonged 827.11; prolix, **long-winded** 538.12; pedestrian, commonplace

10 **wearying,** wearing, **tiring; wearisome,** weariful, fatiguing, **tiresome, irksome; boring, boresome,** stupefyingly boring, stuporific, yawny <nf>

11 **weary,** weariful; **tired,** wearied, irked; good and tired, tired to death, weary unto death; sick, **sick of, tired of, sick and tired of;** jaded, satiated, palled, fed up <nf>, brassed off <Brit nf>; **blasé;** splenetic, melancholy, melancholic, life-weary, world-weary, tired of living, half-dead; **listless** 94.13, **dispirited** 112.22

12 **bored, uninterested;** bored stiff *or* to death *or* to extinction *or* to tears <nf>, stupefied *or* stuporous with boredom; with eyes rolling

ADVS 13 **tediously, monotonously,** harpingly, everlastingly, unvaryingly, endlessly; long-windedly; **boringly,** boresomely; **wearisomely,** fatiguingly, wearyingly, **tiresomely, irksomely,** drearisomely; dully 117.10

14 on a treadmill, in a squirrel cage, on the beaten track, on the same old round; without a change of menu *or* scenery *or* pace

PHRS 15 ho hum!, heigh ho!, what a life!, que sera sera; *plus ça change, plus c'est la même chose* <Fr, the more things change, the more they stay the same>; so what else is new?, go figure; MEGO *or* mine eyes glaze over

119 AGGRAVATION

NOUNS 1 **aggravation, worsening; exacerbation,** embittering, embitterment, souring; deterioration; **intensification, heightening,** stepping-up, sharpening, deepening, **increase,** enhancement, amplification, enlargement, magnification, augmentation, exaggeration; **exasperation, annoyance, irritation** 96.3; hassle <nf>, aggro <chiefly Brit>; deliberate aggravation, provocation; contentiousness

VERBS 2 **aggravate, worsen,** make worse; **exacerbate,** embitter, sour; deteriorate; **intensify, heighten,** step up, sharpen, make acute *or* more acute, bring to a head, deepen, **increase,** enhance, amplify, enlarge, magnify, build up, exaggerate; augment; rub salt in the wound, twist the knife, add insult to injury, inflame, pour oil on the fire, add fuel to the fire *or* flame, heat up *and* hot up <nf>; increase pressure *or* tension, tighten, tighten up, tighten the screws, put the squeeze on <nf>; bring to a head; **exasperate, annoy, irritate** 96.14; rub it in <nf>; provoke, antagonize, hassle <nf>, be an *agent provocateur*

3 **worsen,** get *or* grow worse, take a turn for the worse, deteriorate, degenerate; go from push to shove, **go from bad to worse; jump out of the frying pan and into the fire,** avoid Scylla and fall into Charybdis

ADJS 4 **aggravated, worsened, worse,** worse and worse, exacerbated, embittered, soured, deteriorated; **intensified, heightened,** stepped-up, **increased,** deepened, enhanced, amplified, magnified, enlarged, augmented, heated *or* hotted up <nf>; **exasperated, irritated, annoyed** 96.21; provoked, deliberately provoked; worse-off, out of the frying pan and into the fire

5 **aggravating,** aggravative; **exasperating,** exasperative; **annoying, irritating** 98.22; provocative; vexing, vexatious; contentious

ADVS 6 from bad to worse; aggravatingly, exasperatingly; annoyingly 98.29

120 RELIEF

NOUNS 1 **relief, easement, easing,** ease; **relaxation,** relaxing, relaxation *or* easing of tension, decompression, slackening, respite, let-up; **reduction,** diminishment, diminution, lessening, abatement, remission; **remedy** 86; **alleviation, mitigation, palliation,** softening, assuagement, allayment, defusing, appeasement, mollification, subduement; soothing, salving, anodyne; lulling; dulling, deadening, numbing, narcotizing, anesthesia, anesthetizing, analgesia; sedating, sedation; doping *or* doping up <nf>, comfort, solace, consolation; charity, benefaction

2 **release, deliverance, freeing,** removal; suspension, intermission, respite, surcease, reprieve; discharge; catharsis, purging, purgation, purge, cleansing, cleansing away, emotional release

3 **lightening, disburdening,** unburdening, unweighting, unloading, disencumbrance, disembarrassment, easing of the load, a load off one's mind, something out of one's system

4 **sense** *or* **feeling of relief,** sigh of relief

VERBS 5 **relieve,** give relief; **ease,** ease matters; **relax,** slacken; **reduce,** diminish, lessen, abate, remit, de-stress; **alleviate, mitigate, palliate,** soften, pad, cushion, assuage, allay, defuse, lay, appease, mollify, subdue, soothe; salve, pour balm into, pour oil on; poultice, foment, stupe; slake; lull; **dull, deaden,** dull *or* deaden the pain, numb, benumb, anesthetize, tranquilize; sedate, narcotize, dope *or* dope up <nf>; temper the wind to the shorn lamb, lay the flattering unction to one's soul; take the sting out of; comfort, solace, pacify

6 **release, free, deliver,** reprieve, remove, free from, liberate; suspend, intermit, give respite *or* surcease; **relax,** decompress, ease, destress; act as a cathartic, **purge, purge away, cleanse,** cleanse away; give release, cut loose

7 **lighten, disburden,** unburden, unweight, unload, unfreight, disencumber, disembarrass, ease one's load; **set one's mind at ease** *or* **rest,** set at ease, **take a load off one's mind,** smooth the ruffled brow of care; relieve oneself, let one's hair down, pour one's heart out, talk it out, let it all hang out *and* go public <nf>, get it off one's chest

8 **be relieved, feel relief,** feel better about, get something out of one's system, feel *or* be oneself again; get out from under <nf>; **breathe easy** *or* **easier,** breathe more freely, breathe again, rest easier; **heave a sigh of relief,** draw a long *or* deep breath

ADJS 9 **relieving, easing, alleviative,** alleviating, alleviatory, ameliorating, **mitigative,** mitigating, **palliative,** assuaging, lenitive, assuasive, softening, subduing, soothing, demulcent, emollient, balmy, balsamic; **remedial** 86.39; dulling, deadening, numbing; benumbing, anesthetic, analgesic, anodyne, pain killing, sedative, hypnotic; cathartic, purgative, cleansing; **relaxing**

10 **relieved,** breathing easy *or* easier *or* freely, able to breathe again, out from under *and* out of the woods <nf>; alleviated; decompressed; **relaxed**; calmed, restored

121 COMFORT

NOUNS 1 **comfort, ease, well-being;** contentment 107; clover, velvet <nf>, bed of roses; life of ease 1010.1; solid comfort

2 **comfortableness, easiness; restfulness,** reposefulness, peace, peacefulness; softness, cushiness <nf>, cushioniness; **coziness, snugness;** friendliness, warmness; **homelikeness,** homeyness <nf>, homeliness; **commodiousness,** roominess, convenience; luxuriousness 501.5; hospitality 585

3 **creature comforts, comforts, conveniences,** excellent accommodations, amenities, good things of life, cakes and ale, egg in one's beer <nf>, all the comforts of home; all the heart can desire, luxuries, the best

4 **consolation, solace,** solacement, easement, heart's ease; **encouragement,** aid and comfort, **assurance,**

reassurance, support, **comfort,** crumb *or* shred of comfort; condolence 147, sympathy; **relief** 120

5 **comforter,** consoler, solacer, encourager; the Holy Spirit *or* Ghost, the Comforter, the Paraclete

VERBS 6 **comfort, console, solace,** give *or* bring comfort, bear up; condole with, sympathize with, extend sympathy; ease, **put** *or* **set at ease;** bolster, support; relieve 120.5; **assure, reassure; encourage, hearten,** pat on the back; **cheer** 109.7; wipe away the tears

7 **be comforted, take comfort, take heart;** take hope, lift up one's heart, pull oneself together, pluck up one's spirits; *sursum corda* <L>

8 **be at ease,** be *or* feel easy, stand easy <Brit>; **make oneself comfortable,** make oneself at home, feel at home, put one's feet up, take a load off <nf>; **relax,** be relaxed; live a life of ease 1010.10

9 **snug,** snug down *or* up; tuck in

10 **snuggle, nestle, cuddle,** cuddle up, curl up; nest; bundle; snuggle up to

ADJS 11 **comfortable,** comfy <nf>; contented 107.7,9,10; **easy,** easeful; **restful,** reposeful, peaceful, **relaxing;** soft, cushioned, cushy <nf>, cushiony; comfortable as an old shoe; **cozy, snug,** snug as a bug in a rug; friendly, warm; **homelike,** homey *and* down-home <nf>, homely, lived-in; **commodious,** roomy, convenient; low-maintenance, luxurious 501.21

12 **at ease, at one's ease,** easy, relaxed, laid-back <nf>; at rest, resting easy; **at home,** in one's element; unstressed

13 **comforting, consoling,** consolatory, of good comfort; condoling, condolent, condolatory, sympathetic; **assuring, reassuring,** supportive; **encouraging, heartening; cheering** 109.16; relieving 120.9; hospitable 585.11; warm-and-fuzzy

ADVS 14 **comfortably, easily,** with ease; **restfully,** reposefully, peacefully; **cozily, snugly; commodiously,** roomily, conveniently; luxuriously, voluptuously

15 **in comfort,** in ease, **in clover, on** *or* **in velvet** <nf>, on *or* in a bed of roses

16 **comfortingly, consolingly,** assuringly, reassuringly, supportively, encouragingly, hearteningly; hospitably

122 WONDER

NOUNS 1 **wonder,** wonderment, sense of wonder, marveling, marvel, **astonishment, amazement,** amaze, **astoundment;** dumbfoundment, stupefaction; **surprise; awe,** breathless wonder *or* awe, sense of mystery, admiration; beguilement, fascination 377.1; bewilderment, puzzlement 971.3

2 **marvel, wonder, prodigy, miracle, phenomenon,** phenom <nf>; astonishment, amazement, marvelment, wonderment, wonderful thing, nine days' wonder, *annus mirabilis* <L>, amazing *or* astonishing thing, quite a thing, really something, **sensation,** rocker *and* stunner <nf>; one for the books *and* something to brag about *and* something to shout about *and* something to write home about *and* something else <nf>; **rarity,** nonesuch, nonpareil, exception, one in a thousand, one in a way, oner <Brit nf>; **curiosity, sight, spectacle,** eye-popper <nf>; wonders of the world; masterpiece, chef d-oeuvre, masterstroke

3 **wonderfulness,** wondrousness, **marvelousness,** miraculousness, phenomenalness, **prodigiousness, stupendousness, remarkableness,** extraordinariness; beguilingness, fascination, enchantingness, enticingness, seductiveness, **glamorousness; awesomeness, mysteriousness,** mystery, numinousness; **transcendence,** transcendentness, surpassingness

4 **inexpressibility, ineffability,** ineffableness, inenarrability, noncommunicability, noncommunicableness, incommunicability, incommunicableness, indescribability, indefinableness, **unutterability,**

unspeakability, unnameableness, innominability, unmentionability

VERBS **5 wonder, marvel,** be astonished *or* amazed *or* astounded, be seized with wonder; **gaze, gape,** drop one's jaw, look *or* stand aghast *or* agog, gawk, **stare,** stare open-mouthed, open one's eyes, rub one's eyes, hold one's breath; not know what to say, not know what to make of, not believe one's eyes *or* ears *or* senses

6 astonish, amaze, astound, surprise, startle, stagger, **bewilder, perplex** 971.13, flabbergast <nf>, confound, overwhelm, **boggle, boggle the mind; awe,** strike with wonder *or* awe; **dumbfound** *or* dumbfounder, strike dumb, strike dead; strike all of a heap *and* throw on one's beam ends *and* knock one's socks off *and* bowl down *or* over <nf>, dazzle, bedazzle, daze, bedaze; **stun, stupefy,** petrify, paralyze

7 take one's breath away, turn one's head, make one's head swim, make one's hair stand on end, make one's tongue cleave to the roof of one's mouth, make one stare, make one sit up and take notice, sweep *or* carry off one's feet; blow one's mind

8 beggar *or* baffle description, stagger belief

ADJS **9 wondering,** wrapped *or* rapt in wonder, marveling, **astonished, amazed, surprised, astounded,** flabbergasted <nf>, gobsmacked, **bewildered,** puzzled, confounded, **dumbfounded,** dumbstruck, staggered, overwhelmed, unable to believe one's senses *or* eyes; **aghast,** agape, agog, all agog, gazing, gaping, at gaze staring, gauping, wide-eyed, popeyed, open-eyed, open-mouthed, **breathless; thunderstruck,** wonder-struck, wonder-stricken, awestricken, awestruck, struck all of a heap <nf>; **awed, in awe,** in awe of; spellbound, fascinated, captivated, under a charm, beguiled, enthralled, enraptured, enravished, enchanted, entranced, bewitched, hypnotized, mesmerized, stupefied, lost in wonder *or* amazement; transfixed, rooted to the spot

10 wonderful, wondrous, marvelous, awesome, **miraculous,** fantastic, fabulous, ace, cool, rad *or* wicked <nf>, phenomenal, brilliant, **prodigious, stupendous,** unheard-of, wicked, unprecedented, extraordinary, exceptional, rare, unique, singular, **remarkable,** striking, **sensational,** bar none**; strange,** passing strange; **beguiling, fascinating;** incredible, inconceivable, outlandish, unimaginable, incomprehensible; **bewildering, puzzling,** enigmatic; *magnifique* <Fr>; supercalifragilisticexpialidocious *or* supercalifragilistic; must-see

11 awesome, awful, awing, awe-inspiring; **transcendent,** transcending, surpassing; **mysterious,** numinous; weird, eerie, uncanny, bizarre, bizarro <nf>; exotic; sweet <nf>

12 astonishing, amazing, surprising, startling, **astounding,** confounding, staggering, stunning <nf>, eye-opening, breathtaking, overwhelming, mind-boggling *or* –numbing, mind-blowing, jaw-dropping; **spectacular**, electrifying

13 indescribable, ineffable, inenarrable, inexpressible, unutterable, unspeakable, noncommunicable, incommunicable, indefinable, undefinable, unnameable, innominable, unwhisperable, unmentionable

ADVS **14 wonderfully,** wondrously, **marvelously, miraculously,** fantastically, fabulously, phenomenally, prodigiously, stupendously, extraordinarily, exceptionally, remarkably, strikingly, **sensationally;** strangely, outlandishly, incredibly, inconceivably, unimaginably, incomprehensibly, **bewilderingly, puzzlingly,** enigmatically; **beguilingly,** fascinatingly

15 awesomely, awfully, awingly, awe-inspiringly; **mysteriously,** numinously, weirdly, eerily, uncannily, bizarrely; **transcendently,** surpassingly, surpassing, passing *or* passing fair

16 astonishingly, amazingly, astoundingly, staggeringly, confoundingly;

surprisingly, startlingly, to one's surprise *or* great surprise, to one's astonishment *or* amazement; for a wonder, strange to say

17 **indescribably, ineffably,** inexpressibly, unutterably, **unspeakably,** inenarrably, indefinably, unnameably, unmentionably

18 in wonder, in astonishment, in amazement, in bewilderment, in awe, in admiration, with gaping mouth

19 oh!, O!, ah!, la!, lo!, lo and behold!, hello!, halloo!, hey!, whew!, phew!, wow!, yipes!, yike!

20 my!, oh, my!, dear!, dear me!, goodness!, gracious!, goodness gracious!, gee!, my goodness!, my stars!, good gracious!, good heavens!, good lack!, lackadaisy!, blimey!, my gosh!, welladay!, hoity-toity!, zounds!, 'sdeath!, gadzooks!, gad so!, bless my heart!, God bless me!, heavens and earth!, for crying out loud! <nf>, jiminy!

21 imagine!, fancy!, fancy that!, just imagine!, only think!, well!, I never!, can you feature that!, can you beat that!, it beats the Dutch!, do tell!, you don't say!, the devil *or* deuce you say!, I'll be!, what do you know!, what do you know about that!, how about that!, who would have thought it!, did you ever!, can it be!, can such things be?, will wonders never cease!, go on!

123 UNASTONISHMENT

NOUNS **1** **unastonishment, unamazement,** unamazedness, nonastonishment, nonamazement, nonamazedness, nonwonder, nonwondering, nonmarveling, unsurprise, unsurprisedness, awelessness, wonderlessness; phlegmaticness, apathy, passivity, nonchalance; **calm,** calmness, coolness, **cool** <nf>, cool *or* calm *or* nodding acceptance, composure, composedness, sangfroid, inexcitability 106, expectation 130, unimpressibleness, refusal to be impressed *or* awed *or* amazed; poker face, straight face; predictability

VERBS **2** **accept, take for granted** *or* as a matter of course *or* in stride *or* as it comes, treat as routine, show no amazement, refuse to be impressed, not blink an eye, not turn a hair, keep one's cool <nf>; see it coming

ADJS **3** **unastonished, unsurprised, unamazed,** unmarveling, unwondering, unastounded, undumbfounded, unbewildered; undazzled, undazed; unawed, aweless, wonderless, blasé; **unimpressed,** unmoved; calm, **cool,** cool as a cucumber, composed, nonchalant, inexcitable 106.10; expecting, expected 130.13,14; phlegmatic

124 HOPE

NOUNS **1** **hope, hopefulness,** hoping, **hopes,** fond *or* fervent hope, good hope, good cheer; aspiration, **desire** 100; prospect, **expectation** 130; sanguine expectation, happy *or* cheerful expectation; **trust, confidence, faith,** assured faith, **reliance,** dependence; conviction, assurance, security, well-grounded hope; assumption, presumption; auspiciousness; **promise, prospect,** good *or* bright *or* fair prospect, good *or* hopeful prognosis, best case; great expectations, good prospects, high hopes; hoping against hope, prayerful hope; doomed hope *or* hopes; greener pastures; plus side

2 **optimism,** optimisticalness, Pollyannaism, cheerful *or* bright *or* rosy outlook, rose-colored glasses; **cheerfulness** 109; bright side, silver lining; wishful thinking; philosophical optimism, Leibnizian *or* Rousseauistic optimism, Pollyanna optimism, utopianism, perfectionism, perfectibilism; millenarianism, chiliasm, millennialism

3 **ray of hope,** gleam *or* glimmer of hope; faint hope, last hope

4 airy hope, unreal hope, **dream,** false hope, golden dream, pipe dream <nf>, bubble, chimera, fool's paradise, quixotic ideal, utopia 986.11; vision, castles in the air, air castle, cloud-cuckoo-land, lotus land; American dream

5 **optimist,** hoper, Pollyanna, ray of sunshine <nf>, irrepressible optimist, Dr Pangloss, idealist; Leibnizian optimist, philosophical optimist, utopian, perfectionist, perfectibilist, perfectibilitarian; millenarian, chiliast, millennialist, millennian; aspirer, aspirant, hopeful <nf>, dreamer, visionary

VERBS 6 **hope,** be *or* live in hopes, have reason to hope, entertain *or* harbor the hope, cling to the hope, cherish *or* foster *or* nurture the hope; look for, prognosticate, **expect** 130.5; **trust,** confide, presume, feel confident, rest assured; pin one's hope upon, put one's trust in, hope in, rely on, count on, lean upon, bank on, set great store on; hope for, **aspire to, desire** 100.14; **hope against hope,** hope and pray, hope to God <nf>

7 **be hopeful, get one's hopes up,** keep one's spirits up, never say die, take heart, cheer up, buck up, be of good hope, be of good cheer, keep hoping, keep hope alive, keep the faith <nf>, keep smiling, cling to hope; **hope for the best,** knock on wood, touch wood <Brit>, cross one's fingers, keep one's fingers crossed, allow oneself to hope; clutch *or* catch at straws; wish

8 **be optimistic, look on the bright side; look through** *or* **wear rose-colored glasses,** *voir en couleur de rose* <Fr>; call the glass half full, look on the bright side, think positively *or* affirmatively, be upbeat <nf>, think the best of, **make the best of it,** say that all is for the best, put a good *or* bold face upon, put the best face upon; see the light at the end of the tunnel; count one's chickens before they are hatched, count one's bridges before they are crossed

9 **give hope, raise hope,** yield *or* afford hope, hold out hope, justify hope, inspire hope, **raise one's hopes,** raise expectations, **lead one to expect; cheer** 109.7; inspire, inspirit; **assure, reassure,** support; **promise,** hold out promise, augur well, bid fair *or* well, make fair promise, have good prospects

ADJS 10 **hopeful, hoping, in hopes,** full of hope, in good heart, of good hope, of good cheer; **aspiring** 100.28; **expectant** 130.11; **sanguine,** fond; **confident,** assured; undespairing

11 **optimistic,** upbeat *and* up <nf>, bright, sunny; bullish; **cheerful** 109.11; **rosy,** roseate, rose-colored, *couleur de rose* <Fr>; pollyannaish, Leibnizian, Rousseauistic, Panglossian; utopian 986.23, idealistic, perfectionist, perfectibilitarian, millenarian, chiliastic, millennialistic, visionary

12 **promising,** of promise, full of promise, bright with promise, pregnant of good, best-case, **favorable,** looking up; aspiring, aspirant; **auspicious, propitious** 133.17; heartening; inspiring, inspiriting, **encouraging,** cheering, reassuring, supportive; on a wing and a prayer

ADVS 13 **hopefully,** hopingly; **expectantly** 130.15; **optimistically; cheerfully** 109.17; sanguinely, fondly; confidently

125 HOPELESSNESS

NOUNS 1 **hopelessness,** unhopefulness, no hope, not a prayer *and* not a hope in hell <nf>, not the ghost of a chance; small hope, bleak outlook *or* prospect *or* prognosis, worst case, blank future, no future; losing battle; inexpectation 131; futility 391.2; impossibility 967

2 **despair, desperation,** desperateness, loss of hope; no way <nf>, no way out, no exit, despondency 112.3; disconsolateness 112.12; forlornness; letdown; cave of despair, cave of Trophonius; gloom and doom; acedia, sloth; apathy 94.4; downer <nf>

3 **irreclaimability, irretrievability,** irredeemability, irrecoverableness, unsalvageability, unsalvability; incorrigibility, irreformability; irrevocability, **irreversibility; irreparability, incurability,**

irremediableness, curelessness, remedilessness, immedicableness; unrelievability, unmitigability

4 forlorn hope, vain expectation, doomed *or* foredoomed hope, fond *or* foolish hope, futility; counsel of perfection

5 dashed hopes, blighted hope, hope deferred; disappointment 132

6 pessimism, cynicism, malism, nihilism; uncheerfulness 112.2; **gloominess,** dismalness, gloomy outlook; negativism; defeatism; retreatism, Weltschmerz

7 pessimist, cynic, malist, nihilist; killjoy 112.14, gloomy Gus *and* calamity howler *and* worrywart <nf>, seek-sorrow, Job's comforter, prophet of doom, Cassandra, Eeyore; negativist; defeatist; retreatist; loser, born loser; drag <nf>

8 lost cause, fool's errand, wild-goose chase; hopeless case, hopeless situation**; goner** *and* gone goose *or* gosling *and* dead duck <nf>; terminal case

VERBS **9 be hopeless,** have not a hope *or* prayer, have no remedy, look bleak *or* dark; **be pessimistic, look on the dark side,** be *or* think downbeat <nf>, think negatively, think *or* make the worst of, put the worst face upon, call *or* see the glass half empty; not hold one's breath

10 despair, despair of, **despond** 112.16, falter, lose hope, **lose heart, abandon hope,** give up hope, **give up,** give up all hope *or* expectation, give way *or* over, fall *or* sink into despair, give oneself up *or* yield to despair, throw up one's hands in despair, turn one's face to the wall; curse God and die, write off

11 shatter one's hopes, dash *or* crush *or* blight *or* shatter one's hope, burst one's bubble <nf>, bring crashing down around one's head, dash the cup from one's lips, disappoint 132.2, drive to despair *or* desperation

ADJS **12 hopeless,** unhopeful, without hope, affording no hope, worst-case, bleak, grim, dismal, cheerless, comfortless, down in the mouth; **desperate, despairing, in despair;** despondent 112.22; disconsolate 112.28; forlorn; apathetic 94.13

13 futile, vain 391.13; doomed, foredoomed, pointless

14 impossible, out of the question, not to be thought of, no-go *and* no-win *and* lose-lose <nf>

15 past hope, beyond recall, past praying for, beyond hope, abject; **irretrievable, irrecoverable, irreclaimable,** irredeemable, unsalvageable, unsalvable; incorrigible, irreformable; irrevocable, **irreversible; irremediable, irreparable,** inoperable, **incurable,** cureless, remediless, immedicable, beyond remedy, terminal; unrelievable, unmitigable; **ruined,** undone, kaput <nf>; lost, gone, gone to hell *and* gone to hell in a handbasket <nf>

16 pessimistic, pessimist, downbeat <nf>, **cynical,** nihilistic; uncheerful 112.21; **gloomy,** dismal, crepehanging, funereal, lugubrious; negative, negativistic; defeatist; Cassandran *or* Cassandrian, Cassandra-like

ADVS **17 hopelessly, desperately,** forlornly; impossibly

18 irreclaimably, irretrievably, irrecoverably, irredeemably, unsalvageably, unsalvably; irrevocably, **irreversibly; irremediably, incurably, irreparably**

126 ANXIETY

<troubled thought>

NOUNS **1 anxiety, anxiousness; apprehension, apprehensiveness,** antsyness <nf>, misgiving, foreboding, forebodingness, suspense, strain, tension, stress, nervous strain *or* tension; **dread, fear** 127; **concern,** concernment, anxious concern, **solicitude,** zeal 101.2; **care,** cankerworm of care; **distress,** trouble, vexation, unease; **uneasiness, perturbation, disturbance,** upset, **agitation, disquiet,** disquietude, inquietude, unquietness; **nervousness** 128; malaise, angst 96.1; pucker *and* yips *and* stew *and* all-overs <nf>, pins and needles, tenterhooks, shpilkes <nf>; overanxiety; anxious seat *or* bench; anxiety neurosis *or* hysteria; performance anxiety

2 worry, worriment <nf>, worriedness; **worries,** worries and cares, troubles, concerns; worrying, fretting; harassment, torment

3 worrier, worrywart *and* nervous Nellie <nf>, fussbudget

VERBS **4 concern,** give concern, **trouble, bother, distress, disturb, upset,** frazzle, **disquiet, agitate;** rob one of ease *or* sleep *or* rest, keep one on edge *or* on tenterhooks *or* on pins and needles *or* on shpilkes <nf>

5 <make anxious> **worry, upset, vex,** fret, agitate, get to <nf>, **harass,** harry, **torment,** dog, hound, plague, persecute, haunt, beset

6 <feel anxious> **worry,** worry oneself, worry one's head about, worry oneself sick, trouble one's head *or* oneself, be a prey to anxiety, lose sleep; have one's heart in one's mouth, have one's heart miss *or* skip a beat, have one's heart stand still, get butterflies in one's stomach; **fret, fuss, chafe,** stew *and* take on <nf>, fret and fume; tense up, bite one's nails, walk the floor, go up the wall <nf>, be on tenterhooks *or* pins and needles *or* shpilkes <nf>

ADJS **7 anxious, concerned, apprehensive,** foreboding, misgiving, suspenseful, strained, tense, tensed up <nf>, nail-biting, white-knuckle <nf>; **fearful** 127.23; **solicitous,** zealous 101.9; **troubled, bothered; uneasy, perturbed, disturbed, disquieted, agitated; nervous** 128.11; **on pins and needles,** on tenterhooks, on shpilkes <nf>, on the anxious seat *or* bench; all hot and bothered *and* in a pucker *and* in a stew <nf>; over-anxious, overapprehensive; trepidacious

8 worried, vexed, fretted; **harassed,** harried, tormented, dogged, hounded, persecuted, haunted, beset, plagued; worried sick, worried to a frazzle, worried stiff <nf>

9 careworn, heavy-laden, overburdened

10 troublesome, bothersome, **distressing,** distressful, **disturbing, upsetting, disquieting; worrisome,** worrying; fretting, chafing; **harassing,** tormenting, plaguing; **annoying** 98.22

ADVS **11 anxiously, concernedly, apprehensively,** misgivingly, **uneasily;** worriedly; solicitously, zealously 101.14

127 FEAR, FEARFULNESS

NOUNS **1 fear, fright,** affright; **scare, alarm, consternation, dismay; dread,** unholy dread, **awe; terror, horror,** horrification, mortal *or* abject fear; **phobia**, funk *or* blue funk <nf>; **panic,** panic fear *or* terror, blind panic; stampede; **cowardice** 491

2 fearfulness, frighteningness, frightfulness, awfulness, scariness, fearsomeness; alarmingness, dismayingness, disquietingness, startlingness, disconcertingness, terribleness, **dreadfulness, horror,** horribleness, **hideousness,** appallingness, direness, **ghastliness,** grimness, grisliness, **gruesomeness,** ghoulishness; **creepiness, spookiness,** eeriness, weirdness, uncanniness

3 fearfulness, afraidness; **timidity, timorousness, shyness;** shrinkingness, bashfulness, diffidence, stage fright, mike fright *and* flop sweat <nf>; skittishness, startlishness, jumpiness, goosiness <nf>; shamefacedness

4 apprehension, apprehensiveness, **misgiving, qualm,** qualmishness, funny feeling; **anxiety** 126, angst; worry; doubt 955.2, mental reservation; foreboding

5 trepidation, trepidity, perturbation, **fear and trembling; quaking, agitation** 105.4; **uneasiness, disquiet,** disquietude, inquietude; nervousness 128; palpitation, heartquake; shivers *or* cold shivers <nf>, creeps *or* cold creeps <nf>, heebie-jeebies <nf>, chills of fear *or* terror, icy fingers *or* icy clutch of dread, jimjams <nf>; horripilation, gooseflesh, goose bumps <nf>; sweat, cold sweat; thrill of fear, spasm *or* quiver of terror; sinking stomach; blood running cold, knocking knees, chattering teeth

6 **frightening, intimidation,** bullying, browbeating, cowing, bulldozing <nf>, hectoring; **demoralization,** psychological warfare, war of nerves

7 **terrorization, terrorizing,** horrification, scaremongering, panicmongering, scare tactics; **terrorism,** terror *or* terroristic tactics, rule by terror, reign of terror, sword of Damocles, war of nerves; agroterrorism, bioterrorism, cyberterrorism

8 **alarmist,** scaremonger, panicmonger; **terrorist,** bomber, assassin

9 **frightener, scarer, hair-raiser;** alarmist; scarebabe, **bogey,** bogeyman, **bugaboo,** bugbear; hobgoblin; **scarecrow; horror, terror,** holy terror; **ogre,** ogress, **monster,** vampire, werewolf, ghoul, bête noire, fee-faw-fum; incubus, succubus, nightmare; witch, goblin; **ghost,** specter, phantom, revenant; Frankenstein, Dracula, Wolf-man; mythical monsters

VERBS 10 **fear, be afraid; apprehend,** have qualms, misgive, eye askance; **dread,** stand in dread of, be in mortal dread *or* terror of, stand in awe of, stand aghast; be on pins and needles, sit upon thorns; have one's heart in one's mouth, have one's heart stand still, have one's heart skip *or* miss a beat; quake in one's boots; **sweat,** break out in a cold sweat, sweat bullets <nf>

11 **take fright,** take alarm, push *or* press *or* hit the panic button <nf>; funk *and* go into a funk <nf>, get the wind up <Brit nf>; lose courage 491.8; pale, grow *or* turn pale, change *or* turn color; look as if one had seen a ghost; freeze, be paralyzed with fear, throw up one's hands in horror, jump out of one's skin; shit in one's pants *and* shit green <nf>

12 **start,** startle, **jump,** jump out of one's skin, jump a mile, leap like a startled gazelle; **shy,** fight shy, start aside, boggle, jib; **panic,** stampede, skedaddle <nf>

13 **flinch, shrink, shy,** shy away from, draw back, recoil, funk <nf>, **quail, cringe, wince, blench, blink,** say *or* cry uncle; put one's tail between one's legs

14 **tremble, shake, quake, shiver, quiver, quaver; tremble** *or* **quake** *or* **shake** in one's boots *or* **shoes,** tremble like an aspen leaf, quiver like a rabbit, shake all over

15 **frighten,** fright, affright, funk <nf>, frighten *or* scare out of one's wits; **scare,** spook <nf>, scare one stiff *or* shitless *or* spitless <nf>, scare the life out of, scare the pants off of *and* scare hell out of *and* scare the shit out of <nf>; scare one to death, scare the daylights *or* the living daylights *or* the wits *or* the shit out of <nf>; give one a fright *or* scare *or* turn; **alarm,** disquiet, raise apprehensions; shake, stagger; **startle** 131.8; **unnerve, unman,** unstring; give one gooseflesh, horripilate, give one the creeps *or* the willies <nf>, make one's flesh creep, chill one's spine, make one's nerves tingle, curl one's hair <nf>, make one's hair stand on end, make one's blood run cold, freeze *or* curdle the blood, make one's teeth chatter, make one tremble, take one's breath away, make one shit one's pants *or* shit green <nf>

16 **put in fear,** put the fear of God into, **throw a scare into** <nf>; **panic,** stampede, send scuttling, throw blind fear into

17 **terrify, awe,** strike terror into; **horrify, appall, shock,** make one's flesh creep; **frighten out of one's wits** *or* **senses;** strike dumb, **stun, stupefy, paralyze, petrify,** freeze

18 **daunt, deter,** shake, stop, stop in one's tracks, set back; **discourage, dishearten;** faze <nf>; **awe, overawe**

19 **dismay, disconcert, appall, astound, confound, abash, discomfit, put out, take aback**

20 **intimidate, cow, browbeat, bulldoze** <nf>, bludgeon, dragoon; **bully, hector, harass,** huff; bluster, bluster out of *or* into; **terrorize,**

put in bodily fear, use terror *or* terrorist tactics, pursue a policy of *Schrecklichkeit,* systematically terrorize; threaten 514.2; **demoralize**

21 **frighten off, scare away,** bluff off, put to flight

ADJS 22 **afraid, scared,** scared to death <nf>, spooked <nf>; feared *or* afeared <nf>; fear-stricken, fear-struck; haunted with fear, phobic

23 **fearful,** fearing, fearsome, **in fear; cowardly** 491.10; **timorous, timid, shy,** rabbity *and* mousy <nf>, afraid of one's own shadow; **shrinking,** bashful, diffident; scary; **skittish,** skittery <nf>, startlish, gun-shy, jumpy, goosy <nf>; **tremulous,** trembling, trepidant, shaky, shivery; **nervous;** waiting for the bomb to drop

24 **apprehensive, misgiving,** antsy <nf>, **qualmish,** qualmy; anxious 126.7

25 **frightened,** frightened to death, affrighted, in a fright, frit <Brit nf>, in a funk *or* blue funk <nf>; **alarmed,** disquieted; consternated, **dismayed,** daunted; **startled** 131.13; more frightened than hurt

26 **terrified,** terror-stricken, terror-struck, terror-smitten, terror-shaken, terror-troubled, terror-riven, terror-ridden, terror-driven, terror-crazed, terror-haunted; awestricken, awestruck; **horrified,** horror-stricken, horror-struck; **appalled, astounded, aghast;** frightened out of one's wits *or* mind, **scared to death, scared stiff** *or* **shitless** *or* spitless <nf>; unnerved, unstrung, unmanned, undone, **cowed,** awed, **intimidated; stunned, petrified, stupefied,** paralyzed, frozen; white as a sheet, pale as death *or* a ghost, deadly pale, ashen, blanched, pallid, gray with fear

27 **panicky,** panic-prone, panicked, in a panic, panic-stricken, panic-struck, terror-stricken, out of one's mind with fear, prey to blind fear

28 **frightening, frightful; fearful,** fearsome, fear-inspiring, nightmarish, hellish; **scary,** scaring, chilling; **alarming, startling,** disquieting, dismaying, disconcerting; **unnerving, daunting,** deterring, **deterrent,** discouraging, disheartening, fazing, awing, overawing; stunning, stupefying, mind-boggling *or* –numbing, hair-raising

29 **terrifying,** terrorful, terror-striking, terror-inspiring, terror-bringing, terror-giving, terror-breeding, terror-breathing, terror-bearing, terror-fraught; **bloodcurdling, hair-raising** <nf>; petrifying, paralyzing, stunning, stupefying; **terrorizing, terror, terroristic**

30 **terrible,** terrific, tremendous; **horrid, horrible, horrifying,** horrific, horrendous; **dreadful, dread,** dreaded; **awful;** awesome, awe-inspiring; **shocking, appalling,** astounding; **dire,** direful, fell, formidable, redoubtable; **hideous, ghastly,** morbid, grim, grisly, gruesome, ghoulish, macabre

31 **creepy, spooky, eerie, weird, uncanny**

ADVS 32 **fearfully, apprehensively, diffidently,** for fear of; **timorously, timidly, shyly,** mousily <nf>, bashfully, shrinkingly; tremulously, tremblingly, quakingly, **with** *or* **in fear and trembling;** with heart in mouth, with bated breath

33 **in fear, in terror,** in awe, in alarm, in consternation; in mortal fear, in fear of one's life

34 **frightfully, fearfully; alarmingly, startlingly,** disquietingly, dismayingly, disconcertingly; **shockingly, appallingly,** astoundingly; **terribly,** terrifically, tremendously; **dreadfully, awfully; horridly, horribly,** horrifyingly, horrifically, horrendously

128 NERVOUSNESS

NOUNS 1 **nervousness, nerves,** nervosity, **disquiet, uneasiness, apprehensiveness,** disquietude, qualmishness, malaise, funny *or* creepy feeling, **qualm, qualms, misgiving;** undue *or* morbid excitability, excessive irritability, state of nerves, case of nerves, spell of nerves, attack of nerves; **agitation, trepidation; fear**

127; panic; **fidgets,** fidgetiness, jitteriness, jumpiness; nail-biting; twitching, tic, vellication; stage fright, buck fever <nf>; nervous stomach, butterflies in one's stomach <nf>

2 <nf terms> **jitters,** willies, **heebie-jeebies,** jimjams, **jumps, shakes,** quivers, trembles, dithers, collywobbles, butterflies, shivers, cold shivers, creeps, sweat, cold sweat, heebie-jeebies; antsyness, ants in one's pants, yips

3 **tension,** tenseness, tautness, **strain, stress,** stress and strain, mental strain, nervous tension *or* strain, pressure

4 frayed nerves, frazzled nerves, jangled nerves, shattered nerves, raw nerves *or* nerve endings, twanging *or* tingling nerves; neurosis; neurasthenia, nervous prostration, crackup, **nervous breakdown**

5 **nervous wreck,** wreck, a bundle of nerves

VERBS 6 **fidget,** have the fidgets; jitter, have the jitters, etc; **tense up; tremble**

7 lose self-control, go into hysterics; lose courage 491.8; **go to pieces,** have a nervous breakdown, fall apart *or* to pieces, come apart, fall *or* come apart at the seams

8 <nf terms> **crack, crack up,** go haywire, **blow one's cork** *or* mind *or* stack, **flip,** flip one's lid *or* wig, wig out, freak out, spazz out, go out of one's skull; come unglued *or* unstuck *or* unhinged, go up the wall

9 **get on one's nerves,** jangle the nerves, **grate on, jar on,** put on edge, **set one's teeth on edge, go against the grain, send one up the wall** <nf>, drive one crazy; **irritate** 96.14

10 **unnerve, unman, undo, unstring,** unbrace, reduce to jelly, **demoralize, shake, upset,** psych out <nf>, dash, knock down *or* flat, **crush,** overcome, prostrate, freak someone out

ADJS 11 **nervous,** nervy <Brit nf>; **high-strung,** overstrung, highly strung, all nerves; **uneasy, apprehensive,** qualmish, nail-biting, white-knuckle <nf>, frit <Brit nf>; nervous as a cat; **excitable; irritable,** edgy, **on edge,** nerves on edge, on the ragged edge <nf>, unhinged, wired <nf>, panicky, **fearful, frightened**

12 **jittery** <nf>, **jumpy,** twittery, skittish, skittery, trigger-happy <nf>, gun-shy; **shaky,** shivery, quivery, in a quiver; tremulous, tremulant, trembly; jumpy as a cat on a hot tin roof; **fidgety,** fidgeting; fluttery, all of a flutter *or* twitter; twitchy; **agitated;** shaking, trembling, quivering, shivering; shook up *and* all shook up <nf>

13 **tense,** tensed-up, uptight <nf>, **strained,** stretched tight, taut, unrelaxed, **under a strain**

14 **unnerved, unmanned, unstrung, undone,** reduced to jelly, unglued <nf>, panicked, **demoralized, shaken, upset,** dashed, stricken, **crushed; shot,** shot to pieces; neurasthenic, prostrate, prostrated, overcome

15 **unnerving, nerve-racking,** nerve-rending, nerve-shaking, nerve-jangling, nerve-trying, nerve-stretching; jarring, grating

ADVS 16 **nervously, shakily,** shakingly, tremulously, tremblingly, quiveringly

129 UNNERVOUSNESS

NOUNS 1 **unnervousness, nervelessness; sangfroid, calmness, inexcitability** 106; unshakiness, untremulousness; **steadiness,** steady-handedness, steady nerves; no nerves, strong nerves, iron nerves, nerves of steel, icy nerves; cool head

ADJS 2 **unnervous, nerveless,** without a nerve in one's body; strong-nerved, iron-nerved, steel-nerved; coolheaded, **calm, inexcitable** 106.10; calm, cool, and collected; cool as a cucumber <nf>; **steady,** steady as a rock, rock-steady, steady-nerved, steady-handed; unshaky, unshaken, unquivering, untremulous, without a tremor; unflinching, unfaltering, unwavering, unshrinking, unblenching, unblinking; **relaxed,** unstrained, laid-back

130 EXPECTATION

NOUNS **1** **expectation,** expectance *or* **expectancy,** state of expectancy; **predictability,** predictableness; **anticipation, prospect,** thought; contemplation; likelihood, probability 968; confidence, presumption, reliance 953.1, overreliance; certainty 970; imminence 840; unastonishment 123

2 sanguine *or* cheerful expectation, optimism, eager expectation, **hope** 124; the light at the end of the tunnel

3 **suspense,** state of suspense, cliff-hanging *and* nail-biting <nf>; **waiting,** expectant waiting, hushed expectancy; uncertainty 971, nervous expectation; **anxiety, dread, pessimism,** apprehension 126.1

4 **expectations,** prospects, outlook, hopes, apparent destiny *or* fate, future prospects; likelihoods, probabilities; prognosis; accountability, responsibility

VERBS **5** **expect,** be expectant, **anticipate, have in prospect,** face, think, **contemplate,** have in contemplation *or* mind, envision, envisage; **hope** 124.6; presume 951.10; dread; **take for granted;** not be surprised *or* a bit surprised; foresee 961.5

6 **look forward to,** reckon *or* calculate *or* count on, predict, foresee; look to, **look for, watch for,** look out for, watch out for, be on the watch *or* lookout for, keep a good *or* sharp lookout for; be ready for; forestall

7 **be expected,** be one's probable fate *or* destiny, be one's outlook *or* prospect, be in store

8 **await,** wait, wait for, wait on *or* upon, stay *or* tarry for; have *or* keep an eye out for, lie in wait for, line up for; wait around *or* about, watch, watch and wait; **bide one's time,** bide, abide, **mark time;** cool one's heels <nf>; be in suspense, be on tenterhooks, be on pins and needles, hold one's breath, bite one's nails, sweat *or* sweat out *or* sweat it *or* sweat it out <nf>; **wait up for,** stay up for, sit up for; cross one's fingers; be on the waiting list; be on standby, be on call

9 **expect to,** intend, **plan on** 380.6

10 **be as expected,** be as one thought *or* looked for, turn out that way, come as no surprise; **be just like one,** be one all over <nf>; **expect it of,** think that way about, **not put it past** <nf>; **impend,** be imminent 840.2; lead one to expect 133.12

ADJS **11** **expectant,** expecting, in expectation *or* anticipation; **anticipative,** anticipant, anticipating, anticipatory; **holding one's breath; waiting,** awaiting, waiting for; forewarned, forearmed, forestalling, ready, prepared, on standby; **looking forward to,** looking for, watching for, on the watch *or* lookout for; gaping, agape, agog, all agog, atiptoe, atingle, **eager;** sanguine, optimistic, hopeful 124.10; sure, confident 953.21/970.21; certain 970.13; unsurprised, not surprised

12 **in suspense, on tenterhooks,** on pins and needles, on tiptoe, **on edge, with bated breath,** tense, taut, with muscles tense, quivering, keyed-up, biting one's nails; anxious, **apprehensive;** dreading; **suspenseful,** cliff-hanging <nf>

13 **expected, anticipated, awaited, predicted, foreseen;** taken for granted; presumed 951.14; probable 968.6; **looked-for,** hoped-for; **due, promised;** long-expected, long-awaited, overdue; **in prospect, prospective;** in the cards; **in view,** in one's eye, on the horizon; imminent 840.3

14 **to be expected,** as expected, up to *or* according to expectation, just as one thought, just as predicted, on schedule, **as one may have suspected,** as one might think *or* suppose; **expected of,** counted on, **taken for granted;** just like one, one all over <nf>, in character

ADVS **15** **expectantly,** expectingly; anticipatively, **anticipatingly,** anticipatorily; hopefully 124.13; **with bated breath,** in hushed expectancy, with breathless expectation;

with ears pricked up, with eyes *or* ears strained

131 INEXPECTATION

NOUNS **1 inexpectation,** nonexpectation, inexpectance *or* inexpectancy, no expectation, **unanticipation; unexpectedness;** unforeseeableness, unpredictableness, unpredictability; unreadiness, unpreparedness; the unforeseen, the unlooked-for, the last thing one expects; **improbability** 969

2 surprise, surprisal, wonder; **astonishment** 122.1–2; surpriser, startler, shocker, **blow,** staggerer <nf>, **eye-opener,** revelation; **bolt out of** *or* **from the blue,** thunderbolt, thunderclap; **bombshell,** bomb; blockbuster, earthshaker; sudden turn *or* development, switch; surprise ending, kicker *or* joker *or* catch <nf>; surprise package; surprise party

3 start, shock, jar, jolt, turn, fright

VERBS **4 not expect,** hardly expect, **not anticipate, not look for,** not bargain for, **not foresee,** not think of, not see coming, have no thought of, have no expectation, think unlikely *or* improbable

5 be startled, be taken by surprise, be taken aback, be given a start, be given a turn *or* jar *or* jolt; **start,** startle, **jump,** jump a mile <nf>, jump out of one's skin; **shy,** start aside, flinch

6 be unexpected, come unawares, come as a surprise *or* shock, come out of left field <nf>, come out of nowhere, appear unexpectedly, turn up, pop up *and* bob up <nf>, drop from the clouds, appear like a bolt out of the blue, come *or* burst like a thunderclap *or* thunderbolt, burst *or* flash upon one, come *or* fall *or* pounce upon, steal *or* creep up on

7 surprise, take by surprise, do the unexpected, spring a surprise <nf>, **open one's eyes,** give one a revelation; **catch** *or* **take unawares,** catch *or* take short, take aback, pull up short, raise some eyebrows, **catch off-guard** 941.7, cross one up <nf>; throw a curve <nf>, bowl over, come from behind, come from an unexpected quarter, come out of the blue, come upon unexpectedly *or* without warning, spring *or* pounce upon; drop a bombshell, drop a brick <nf>; throw *or* knock for a loop <nf>; **blindside** <nf>, spring a mine under, ambush, bushwhack; drop in on <nf>; give a surprise party; **astonish** 122.6

8 startle, shock, electrify, jar, jolt, shake, stun, **stagger, give one a turn** <nf>, give the shock of one's life, make one jump out of his skin, take aback, take one's breath away, throw on one's beam ends, bowl down *or* over <nf>, strike all of a heap <nf>; frighten

ADJS **9 inexpectant,** nonexpectant, unexpecting; **unanticipative,** unanticipating; **unsuspecting, unaware,** unguessing; uninformed, unwarned, unforewarned, unadvised, unadmonished; unready, unprepared; off one's guard 984.8

10 unexpected, unanticipated, unlooked for, unhoped for, unprepared for, undivined, unguessed, unpredicted, **unforeseen;** unforeseeable, unpredictable, off-the-wall <nf>; **improbable** 969.3; contrary to expectation, beyond *or* past expectation, on the contrary, au contraire <Fr>, out of one's reckoning, more than expected, more than one bargained for; out of the blue, dropped from the clouds, out of left field *and* from out in left field <nf>; without warning, unheralded, unannounced; sudden 830.5; out-of-the-way, **extraordinary**

11 surprising, astonishing 122.12; eye-opening, eye-popping <nf>; **startling, shocking,** amazing, electrifying, boggling, staggering, stunning, jarring, jolting

12 surprised, struck with surprise, open-mouthed, amazed; **astonished** 122.9; **taken by surprise,** taken unawares, caught short; blindsided <nf>

13 startled, shocked, electrified, jarred, jolted, shaken, shook <nf>, staggered, **given a turn** *or* **jar** *or* **jolt,** taken aback, bowled down *or* over <nf>, struck all of a heap <nf>, able to be knocked down with a feather; speechless, flabbergasted

ADVS **14** **unexpectedly,** unanticipatedly, improbably, implausibly, unpredictably, **unforseeably,** *à l'improviste* <Fr>, **by surprise, unawares,** against *or* contrary to all expectation, on the contrary, when least expected, as no one would have predicted, without notice *or* warning, in an unguarded moment, like a thief in the night; **out of a clear sky, out of the blue, like a bolt from the blue;** all of the sudden, suddenly 830.9

15 **surprisingly, startlingly, to one's surprise,** to one's great surprise; shockingly, staggeringly, stunningly, **astonishingly** 122.16

132 DISAPPOINTMENT

NOUNS **1** **disappointment,** sad *or* sore disappointment, bitter *or* cruel disappointment, failed *or* blasted expectation, chagrin; **dashed hope, blighted hope,** betrayed hope, hope deferred, forlorn hope; dash to one's hopes; blow, buffet; **frustration,** discomfiture, bafflement, defeat, balk, foiling; **comedown,** setback, **letdown** <nf>; failure, smackdown <nf>, fizzle <nf>, fiasco; **disillusionment** 977; tantalization, mirage, tease; dissatisfaction 108.1; fallen countenance; bad news, bummer <nf>

VERBS **2** **disappoint,** defeat expectation *or* hope; **dash,** dash *or* blight *or* blast *or* crush one's hope; **balk,** bilk, **thwart, frustrate, baffle, defeat,** foil, cross; put one's nose out of joint; **let down,** cast down; **disillusion** 977.2; tantalize, tease; dissatisfy; leave in the lurch; burst someone's bubble; fail

3 **be disappointing, let one down** <nf>**, not come up to expectation,** come to nothing, not live *or* measure up to expectation, go wrong, turn sour, disappoint one's expectations, come *or* fall short; peter out *or* fizzle *or* fizzle out <nf>, not make it *and* not hack it <nf>

4 **be disappointed,** have hoped for better, not realize one's expectations, fail of one's hopes *or* ambitions, run into a stone wall, be let down; look blue, laugh on the wrong side of one's mouth <nf>; be crestfallen *or* chapfallen *or* disenchanted

ADJS **5** **disappointed,** bitterly *or* sorely disappointed; **let down,** betrayed, ill-served, ill done-by; **dashed,** blighted, blasted, crushed; **balked,** bilked, **thwarted, frustrated,** baffled, crossed, dished <Brit>, defeated, foiled; caught in one's own trap; disillusioned 977.5; disenchanted, chagrined, crestfallen, chapfallen, out of countenance; soured; dissatisfied; regretful 113.8

6 **disappointing,** not up to expectation, falling short, out of the running, not up to one's hopes, second- *or* third-best; tantalizing, teasing; **unsatisfactory,** unsatisfying; disheartening

133 PREMONITION

NOUNS **1** **premonition, presentiment,** preapprehension, forefeeling, presage, presagement; **hunch** 934.3, **feeling in one's bones;** prediction 962

2 foreboding, boding; **apprehension, misgiving,** chill *or* quiver along the spine, creeping *or* shudder of the flesh; wind of change

3 **omen, portent; augury,** auspice, soothsay, prognostic, prognostication; **premonitory sign** *or* **symptom,** premonitory shiver *or* chill, **foretoken,** foretokening, tokening, betokening, betokenment, foreshowing, prefiguration, presignifying, presignification, **preindication,** indicant, indication, **sign, token,** type, **promise,** sign of the times; **foreshadowing, adumbration,** foreshadow, shadow

4 **harbinger, forerunner, precursor,** messenger, **herald,** announcer, *buccinator novi temporis* <L>; presager, premonitor, foreshadower, apparitor

5 <omens> bird of ill omen, owl, raven, stormy petrel, Mother Carey's chicken; gathering clouds, clouds on the horizon, dark *or* black clouds, angry clouds, storm clouds, thundercloud, thunderhead; black cat; broken mirror; rainbow; ring around the moon; shooting star; halcyon bird; woolly bear, groundhog

6 **ominousness, portentousness, portent,** bodefulness, presagefulness, suggestiveness, significance, **meaning** 518, meaningfulness; fatefulness, fatality, doomfulness, sinisterness, banefulness, balefulness, direness

7 **inauspiciousness, unpropitiousness, unfavorableness, unfortunateness, unluckiness,** ill-fatedness, ill-omenedness; fatality

8 **auspiciousness, propitiousness, favorableness; luckiness, fortunateness,** prosperousness, beneficience, benignity, benignancy, benevolence; brightness, cheerfulness, cheeriness; good omen, good auspices, *auspicium melioris aevi* <L>

VERBS 9 **foreshow, presage;** omen, be the omen of; **foreshadow, adumbrate,** shadow, shadow forth, cast their shadows before; **predict** 962.9; have an intimation, have a hunch <nf>, feel *or* know in one's bones, feel the wind of change

10 **forebode, bode,** portend, croak; **threaten, menace, lower,** look black, spell trouble; **warn, forewarn,** raise a warning flag, give pause; have a premonition *or* presentiment, apprehend, preapprehend, fear for

11 **augur,** hint, divine; **foretoken, preindicate,** presignify, presign, presignal, pretypify, **prefigure,** betoken, token, typify, **signify, mean** 518.8, spell, **indicate,** point to, look like, **be a sign of,** show signs of

12 **promise, suggest, hint, imply,** give prospect of, make likely, give ground for expecting, raise expectation, **lead one to expect,** hold out hope, make fair promise, have a lot going for, have *or* show promise, **bid fair, stand fair to**

13 **herald, harbinger, forerun,** run before; speak of, announce, proclaim, preannounce; give notice, notify, talk about

ADJS 14 augured, **foreshadowed, adumbrated, foreshown; indicated, signified; preindicated,** prognosticated, **foretokened,** prefigured, pretypified, presignified; presignaled; **presaged; promised, threatened;** predicted 962.14

15 **premonitory, forewarning,** augural, monitory, warning, presageful, presaging, **foretokening, preindicative,** indicative, prognostic, prognosticative, presignificant, prefigurative; **significant, meaningful** 518.10, speaking; **foreshowing, foreshadowing;** big *or* pregnant *or* heavy with meaning; forerunning, precursory, precursive; intuitive 934.5; predictive 962.11

16 **ominous, portentous,** portending; **foreboding,** boding, **bodeful; inauspicious, ill-omened,** ill-boding, of ill *or* fatal omen, of evil portent, loaded *or* laden *or* freighted *or* fraught with doom, looming, looming over; fateful, doomful; presageful; apocalyptic; **unpropitious, unpromising, unfavorable, unfortunate, unlucky; sinister,** dark, black, gloomy, somber, dreary; **threatening, menacing, lowering;** bad, evil, ill, untoward; dire, baleful, baneful, **ill-fated,** ill-starred, evil-starred, star-crossed

17 **auspicious,** of good omen, of happy portent; **propitious, favorable,** favoring, fair, good; **promising,** of promise, full of promise; **fortunate, lucky,** prosperous; benign, benignant, bright, happy, golden, ripe

ADVS 18 **ominously, portentously, bodefully, forebodingly;** significantly, meaningly, meaningfully, speakingly, sinisterly; **threateningly, menacingly,** loweringly

19 **inauspiciously, unpropitiously, unpromisingly, unfavorably, unfortunately, unluckily**

20 **auspiciously, propitiously, promisingly, favorably; fortunately, luckily, happily;** brightly, fairly

134 PATIENCE

NOUNS 1 **patience,** patientness; **tolerance,** toleration, **acceptance; indulgence,** lenience, leniency 427; sweet reasonableness; **forbearance,** forbearing, forbearingness; **sufferance, endurance; long-suffering,** long-sufferance, longanimity; **stoicism,** fortitude, self-control; patience of Job; waiting game, waiting it out; **perseverance** 360

2 **resignation, meekness,** humility, humbleness, obedience; amenability; submission, **submissiveness** 433.3; acquiescence, compliance, uncomplainingness; **fatalism,** submission to fate *or* the inevitable *or* necessity; quietude, quietism, passivity, **passiveness** 329.1; *zitzflaysh* <Yiddish>; passive resistance, nonviolent resistance, nonresistance; Quakerism

3 **stoic,** Spartan, man of iron; Job, Griselda

VERBS 4 **be patient,** forbear, bear with composure, **wait,** wait it out, play a waiting game, wait around, wait one's turn, watch for one's moment, keep one's shirt *or* pants on <nf>, not hold one's breath <nf>; contain oneself, possess oneself, possess one's soul in patience; carry on, carry through

5 **endure, bear, stand,** support, sustain, **suffer, tolerate, abide,** bide, live with; persevere; **bear up under, bear the brunt, bear with, put up with, stand for,** tolerate, carry *or* bear one's cross, take what comes, take the bitter with the sweet, abide with, brook, brave, brave out, hang in there, keep it up

6 <nf terms> **take it,** take it on the chin, take it like a man, not let it get one down, stand the gaff; bite the bullet; hold still *or* stand still for, swallow, stick, **hang in, hang in there, hang tough,** tough *or* stick it out; lump it

7 **accept, condone, countenance;** overlook, not make an issue of, let go by, let pass; **reconcile oneself to,** resign oneself to, yield *or* submit to, obey; accustom *or* accommodate *or* adjust oneself to, sit through; accept one's fate, lay in the lap of the gods, take things as they come, roll with the punches <nf>; **make the best of it,** make the most of it, make the best of a bad bargain, make a virtue of necessity; submit with a good grace, **grin and bear it,** grin and abide, shrug, shrug it off, slough off, not let it bother one; take in good part, take in stride; rise above

8 **take, pocket, swallow,** down, stomach, eat, digest, disregard, turn a blind eye, ignore; swallow an insult, pocket the affront, turn the other cheek, take it lying down, turn aside provocation

ADJS 9 **patient,** armed with patience, with a soul possessed in patience, patient as Job, Job-like, Griselda like; **tolerant,** tolerative, tolerating, accepting; understanding, **indulgent,** lenient; **forbearing;** philosophical; **long-suffering,** longanimous; **enduring,** endurant; stoic, stoical, Spartan; disciplined, self-controlled; **persevering;** impassive

10 **resigned,** reconciled; wait-and-see; **meek,** humble; obedient, amenable, **submissive** 433.12; acquiescent, compliant; accommodating, adjusting, adapting, adaptive; unresisting, **passive** 329.6; **uncomplaining,** long-suffering

ADVS 11 **patiently,** enduringly, stoically; **tolerantly, indulgently,** longanimously, leniently, forbearantly, forbearingly, philosophically, more in sorrow than in anger; perseveringly

12 **resignedly, meekly, submissively,** passively, acquiescently, compliantly, uncomplainingly

PHRS 13 Rome wasn't built in a day; all in good time; all things come to him who waits; don't hold your breath; time will tell

135 IMPATIENCE

NOUNS 1 **impatience,** impatientness, unpatientness, breathless impatience; **anxiety, eagerness** 101; tense readiness, **restlessness,** restiveness, ants in one's pants <nf>, prothymia; **disquiet,** disquietude, unquietness, uneasiness, **nervousness** 128; sweat *and* lather *and* stew <nf>, **fretfulness,** fretting, chafing; **impetuousness** 365.2; **haste** 401; excitement 105

2 **intolerance,** intoleration, unforbearance, nonendurance

3 **the last straw,** the straw that breaks the camel's back, the limit, the limit of one's patience, all one can bear *or* stand

VERBS 4 **be impatient,** hardly wait; hasten 401.4,5; itch to, burn to; **champ at the bit, pull at the leash,** not be able to sit down *or* stand still; **chafe, fret, fuss,** squirm; **stew,** sweat, sweat and stew, get into a dither, get into a stew <nf>, work oneself into a lather *or* sweat <nf>, get excited; wait impatiently, sweat it out <nf>, pace the floor; beat the gun, jump the gun <nf>, go off half-cocked, shoot from the hip

5 **have no patience with,** be out of all patience; **lose patience,** run out of patience, be exasperated, call a halt, have had it <nf>, blow the whistle <nf>

ADJS 6 **impatient,** unpatient; breathless; champing at the bit, rarin' to go <nf>; dying, **anxious, eager;** hopped-up *and* in a lather *and* in a sweat *or* stew <nf>, excited 105.18; edgy, **on edge; restless,** restive, unquiet, uneasy, on *shpilkes* <Yiddish>; **fretful,** fretting, chafing, antsy-pantsy *and* antsy <nf>, squirming, squirmy, about to pee *or* piss one's pants <nf>; exasperated; **impetuous** 365.9; **hasty** 401.9

7 **intolerant, unforbearing, unindulgent**

ADVS 8 **impatiently,** breathlessly; **anxiously;** fretfully; restlessly, restively, uneasily; intolerantly; hastily

136 PRIDE

NOUNS 1 **pride,** proudness, pridefulness; **self-esteem, self-respect,** self-confidence, self-reliance, self-consequence, face, independence, self-sufficiency; pardonable pride; obstinate *or* stiff-necked pride, stiff-neckedness; **vanity, conceit** 140.4; haughtiness, swell, **arrogance** 141, hubris; boastfulness 502.1; purse-pride

2 **proud bearing,** pride of bearing, military *or* erect bearing, stiff *or* straight backbone, **dignity,** dignifiedness, **stateliness,** courtliness, grandeur, **loftiness;** pride of place; **nobility,** lordliness, princeliness; **majesty,** regality, kingliness, queenliness; distinction, worthiness, augustness, venerability; **sedateness, solemnity** 111, gravity, *gravitas* <L>, sobriety

3 proudling; stiff neck; egoist 140.5; boaster 502.5, peacock; the proud

VERBS 4 **be proud,** hold up one's head, hold one's head high, stand up straight, hold oneself erect, never stoop; look one in the face *or* eye; stand on one's own two feet, pay one's own way; have one's pride

5 **take pride, pride oneself, preen oneself,** plume oneself on, pique oneself, **congratulate oneself,** hug oneself; **be proud of,** glory in, exult in, **burst with pride**

6 **make proud,** do one's heart good, do one proud <nf>, **gratify, elate,** flush, turn one's head

7 save face, save one's face, preserve one's dignity, guard *or* preserve one's honor, be jealous of one's repute *or* good name, cover one's ass <nf>

ADJS 8 **proud, prideful,** proudful <nf>; **self-esteeming, self-respecting;** self-confident, self-reliant, **independent, self-sufficient;** proudhearted, proud-minded, proud-spirited, proud-blooded; proud-looking; proud as Punch, proud as Lucifer, proud as a peacock; erect, stiff-backed, **stiff-necked;** purse-proud, house-proud

9 **vain, conceited** 140.11; haughty, **arrogant** 141.9; boastful 502.10, egotistic

10 **puffed up,** swollen, bloated, swollen *or* bloated *or* puffed-up with pride; elated, flushed, flushed with pride; bigheaded, swellheaded; egotistical

11 **lofty, elevated,** triumphal, high, high-flown, highfalutin *and* highfaluting <nf>, high-toned <nf>; high-minded, lofty-minded; high-headed, high-nosed <nf>

12 **dignified, stately, imposing, grand, courtly,** magisterial, aristocratic; **noble,** ennobled, lordly, princely; **majestic,** regal, royal, kingly, queenly; worthy, **august, venerable;** statuesque; **sedate, solemn** 111.3, sober, grave

ADVS **13** **proudly,** pridefully, **with pride;** self-esteemingly, self-respectingly, self-confidently, self-reliantly, independently, self-sufficiently; erectly, with head erect, with head held high, with nose in air; stiff-neckedly; like a lord, *en grand seigneur* <Fr>

14 **dignifiedly, with dignity;** nobly, stately, imposingly, loftily, grandly, magisterially; majestically, regally, royally; worthily, augustly, venerably; sedately, solemnly, soberly, gravely

137 HUMILITY

NOUNS **1** **humility, humbleness, meekness; lowliness,** lowlihood, poorness, meanness, smallness, ingloriousness, undistinguishedness; unimportance 998; innocuousness 999.9; teachableness 570.5; submissiveness 433.3; **modesty,** unpretentiousness 139.1; plainness, simpleness, homeliness

2 **humiliation,** mortification, egg on one's face <nf>, **chagrin, embarrassment** 96.4; **abasement,** debasement, letdown, setdown, put-down *and* dump <nf>; **comedown,** descent, deflation, climb-down, wounded *or* injured pride; self-diminishment, **self-abasement, self-abnegation** 652.1; **shame, disgrace;** shamefacedness, shamefastness, hangdog look

3 **condescension,** condescendence, deigning, lowering oneself, stooping from one's high place

VERBS **4** **humiliate, humble;** mortify, **embarrass** 96.15; put out, put out of face *or* countenance; **shame, disgrace,** put to shame, put to the blush, give one a red face; **deflate,** prick one's balloon; take it out of; marginalize; make one feel small *or* this high; do down; bitch-slap <nf>

5 **abase, debase, crush,** abash, **degrade, reduce,** diminish, **demean,** lower, **bring low,** bring down, trip up, take down, set down, put in one's place, put down, diss <nf>, dump *and* dump on <nf>, knock one off his perch; take down a peg *or* notch or two <nf>, make a fool *or* an ass *or* a monkey of one; put down <nf>

6 <nf terms> beat *or* knock *or* **cut one down to size,** take the shine *or* starch out of, take the wind out of one's sails; put one's nose out of joint, put a tuck in one's tail, make one sing small, take down a rung

7 **humble oneself, demean oneself,** abase oneself, climb down *and* get down from one's high horse <nf>; put one's pride in one's pocket; **eat humble pie,** eat crow *or* dirt, eat one's words, swallow one's pride, lick the dust, take *or* eat shit <nf>; come on bended knee, come hat in hand; go down on one's knees; pull *or* draw in one's horns *and* sing small <nf>, lower one's note *or* tone, tuck one's tail; come down a peg *or* a peg or two; **deprecate** *or* **depreciate oneself,** diminish oneself, discount oneself, belittle oneself; kiss one's ass <nf> 138.7

8 **condescend, deign, vouchsafe; stoop, descend,** lower *or* demean oneself, trouble oneself, set one's dignity aside *or* to one side; **patronize;** be so good as to, so forget oneself, dirty *or* soil one's hands; talk down to, talk *de haut en bas* <Fr, from high to low>

9 **be humiliated,** be put out of countenance; **be crushed, feel small, feel cheap,** look foolish *or* silly, be ready to sink through the floor; **take shame, be ashamed, feel ashamed of oneself,** be put to the blush, have a very red face; bite one's tongue; hang one's head, hide one's face, not dare to show one's face, not have a word to say for oneself; be taken down a rung

ADJS **10** **humble, lowly,** low, **poor, mean,** small, inglorious, undistinguished; unimportant 998.16; innocuous; biddable, teachable 570.18; **modest, unpretentious** 139.9, without airs; **plain, simple,** homely; humble-looking, humble-visaged; humblest, lowliest, lowest, least

11 humble-hearted, humble-minded, humble-spirited, poor in spirit; **meek,** meek-hearted, meek-minded, meek-spirited, lamblike, Christlike; **abject,** submissive 433.12

12 **self-abasing, self-abnegating, self-deprecating,** self-depreciating 139.10, self-doubting

13 **humbled,** reduced, diminished, lowered, brought down *or* low, set down, bowed down, in the dust, cut down to size; on one's knees, on one's marrowbones <nf>

14 **humiliated,** humbled, mortified, **embarrassed, chagrined, abashed, crushed,** out of countenance; blushing, ablush, **red-faced, ashamed,** shamed, ashamed of oneself, shamefaced, shamefast; crestfallen, chapfallen, hangdog; taken down a notch

15 **humiliating,** humiliative, humbling, chastening, mortifying, **embarrassing,** crushing

ADVS **16** **humbly, meekly;** modestly 139.14; with due deference, with bated breath; submissively 433.17; **abjectly,** on bended knee, **on one's knees,** on one's marrowbones <nf>, on all fours, with one's tail between one's legs, hat-in-hand

138 SERVILITY

NOUNS **1** **servility, slavishness,** subservience *or* subserviency, menialness, abjectness, **baseness,** meanness; **submissiveness** 433.3; slavery, helotry, helotism, serfdom, peonage

2 **obsequiousness, sycophancy,** morigeration, fawningness, fawnery, **toadyism,** flunkyism; parasitism, sponging; **ingratiation,** insinuation; **truckling, fawning, toadying,** toadeating, groveling, cringing, **bootlicking** <nf>, back scratching, tufthunting <chiefly Brit old>, flattery; **apple-polishing** <nf>; ass-licking *and* ass-kissing *and* brown-nosing *and* sucking up <nf>; timeserving; obeisance, prostration; mealymouthedness

3 **sycophant, flatterer, toady,** toad, toadeater, lickspit, lickspittle, **truckler, fawner,** courtier, led captain *and* tufthunter <chiefly Brit old>, kowtower, groveler, cringer, spaniel; flunky, lackey, jackal; timeserver; creature, **puppet,** minion, lap dog, **tool,** cat's-paw, dupe, instrument, faithful servant, slave, helot, serf, peon; mealymouth

4 <nf terms> **apple-polisher, ass-kisser, brown-nose,** brown-noser, brownie, ass-licker, ass-wiper, suck-ass; **backslapper,** backscratcher, clawback, back-patter; **bootlicker,** bootlick; **handshaker; yes-man, stooge**; doormat

5 **parasite,** barnacle, leech; **sponger,** sponge <nf>, freeloader <nf>, gigolo, smell-feast; beat *and* deadbeat <nf>

6 **hanger-on, adherent,** dangler, appendage, **dependent, satellite, follower,** cohort, retainer, servant, man, shadow, tagtail, **henchman,** heeler <nf>

VERBS **7** **fawn, truckle; flatter; toady,** toadeat; **bootlick** <nf>, lickspittle, lick one's shoes, lick the feet of; **grovel,** crawl, creep, cower, cringe, crouch, stoop, kneel, bend the knee, fall on one's knees, prostrate oneself, throw oneself at the feet of, fall at one's feet, kiss *or* lick *or* suck one's ass *and* brown-nose <nf>, kiss one's feet, kiss the hem of one's garment, lick the dust, make a doormat of oneself; **kowtow,** bow, **bow and scrape**

8 **toady to, truckle to, pander to, cater to, cater for** <Brit>; **wait on** *or* **upon,** wait on hand and foot, dance attendance, do service, fetch and carry, do the dirty work of, do *or* jump at the bidding of, run after

9 **curry favor, court, pay court to,** make court to, run after <nf>, dance attendance on; **shine up to,** make up to <nf>; **suck up to** *and* **play up to** *and* act up to <nf>; be a yes-man

<nf>, agree to anything; fawn upon, fall over *or* all over <nf>; **hand-shake** *and* back-scratch *and* **polish the apple** <nf>

10 **ingratiate oneself,** insinuate oneself, worm oneself in, get into the good graces of, get in with *or* next to <nf>, **get on the good** *or* **right side of,** rub the right way <nf>

11 **attach oneself to,** pin *or* fasten oneself upon, hang about *or* around, dangle, hang on the skirts of, hang on the sleeve of, become an appendage of, **follow,** follow at heel; follow the crowd, get on the bandwagon, go with the stream, hold with the hare and run with the hounds; latch onto <nf>

12 **sponge** *and* **sponge on** *and* **sponge off of** <nf>; feed on, fatten on, batten on, live off of, use as a meal ticket; parasitize

ADJS **13** **servile, slavish,** subservient, **menial, base,** mean; **submissive** 433.12; under one's thumb

14 **obsequious, flattering,** sycophantic, sycophantical, morigerous, toadyish, fawning, truckling, ingratiating, smarmy <nf>, toadying, toadeating, **bootlicking** *and* back scratching *and* backslapping *and* ass-licking *and* brown-nosing *or* kiss-ass <nf>; **groveling,** sniveling, cringing, cowering, crouching, crawling; **parasitic,** leechlike, sponging <nf>; timeserving; **abject,** beggarly, hangdog; obeisant, prostrate, on one's knees, on one's marrowbones <nf>, on bended knee; mealymouthed; overattentive; sequacious

ADVS **15** **servilely, slavishly,** subserviently, menially, sequaciously; **submissively** 433.17

16 **obsequiously, sycophantically, ingratiatingly, fawningly, trucklingly;** hat-in-hand, cap-in-hand; **abjectly,** obeisantly, grovelingly, on one's knees; parasitically

139 MODESTY

NOUNS **1** **modesty, meekness;** humility 137; **unpretentiousness,** unassumingness, unpresumptuousness, **unostentatiousness,** unambitiousness, unobtrusiveness, unboastfulness

2 **self-effacement, self-depreciation,** self-deprecation, self-detraction, undervaluing of self, self-doubt, **diffidence;** hiding one's light under a bushel; low self-esteem, weak ego, lack of self-confidence *or* self-reliance, self-distrust; inferiority complex

3 **reserve, restraint, constraint,** backwardness, retiring disposition; low key, low visibility, low profile; reticence, reluctance, disinclination

4 **shyness, timidity,** timidness, timorousness, **bashfulness,** shamefacedness, shamefastness, pudicity, pudency, pudibundity *and* pudibundness *and* verecundity; **coyness, demureness,** demurity, skittishness, mousiness; self-consciousness, embarrassment; stammering, confusion; stagefright, mike fright *and* flop sweat <nf>

5 **blushing, flushing,** coloring, mantling, reddening, crimsoning; **blush, flush,** suffusion, red face

6 shrinking violet, modest violet, mouse

VERBS **7** **efface oneself,** depreciate *or* deprecate *or* doubt *or* distrust oneself; have low self-esteem; reserve oneself, retire, shrink, **retire into one's shell, keep in the background,** not thrust oneself forward, **keep a low profile,** keep oneself to oneself, keep one's distance, remain in the shade, take a back seat *and* play second fiddle <nf>, know one's place, hide one's face, hide one's light under a bushel, avoid the limelight, eschew self-advertisement; disincline

8 **blush, flush,** mantle, **color,** change color, color up, redden, crimson, turn red, have a red face, get red in the face, blush up to the eyes; stammer; squirm; die of embarrassment

ADJS **9** **modest, meek;** humble; **unpretentious,** unpretending, **unassuming,** unpresuming, unpresumptuous, **unostentatious,** unassuming, unobtrusive, unimposing, unboastful; unambitious, unaspiring

10 **self-effacing, self-depreciative, self-depreciating,** self-deprecating; **diffident,** deprecatory, deprecative, self-doubting, unself-confident, unsure of oneself, unself-reliant, self-distrustful, self-mistrustful; low in self-esteem

11 **reserved, restrained, constrained;** quiet; low-keyed, keeping low visibility *or* a low profile; **backward, retiring, shrinking**

12 **shy, timid,** timorous, **bashful,** shamefaced, shamefast, pudibund *and* verecund *and* verecundious; **coy, demure,** skittish, mousy; reluctant, disinclined; self-conscious, conscious, confused; stammering, inarticulate

13 **blushing,** blushful; **flushed,** aflush, red, ruddy, red-faced, red in the face; **sheepish; embarrassed**

ADVS 14 **modestly, meekly;** humbly; **unpretentiously,** unpretendingly, **unassumingly,** unpresumptuously, **unostentatiously,** unobtrusively; quietly, without ceremony, *sans façon* <Fr>

15 **shyly, timidly,** timorously, **bashfully, coyly, demurely,** diffidently; **shamefacedly,** shamefastly, **sheepishly,** blushingly, with downcast eyes

140 VANITY

NOUNS 1 **vanity, vainness;** overproudness, overweening pride; **self-importance,** consequentiality, consequentialness, **self-esteem,** high self-esteem *or* self-valuation, positive self-image, self-respect, self-assumption; **self-admiration,** self-delight, self-worship, self-endearment, **self-love,** *amour propre* <Fr>, self-infatuation, narcissism, narcism; autoeroticism, autoerotism, self-gratification; **self-satisfaction, self-content,** ego trip <nf>, self-approbation, self-congratulation, self-gratulation, self-complacency, **smugness,** complacency, self-sufficiency; vainglory, vaingloriousness; God's gift

2 **pride** 136; arrogance 141; **boastfulness** 502.1

3 **egotism, egoism,** egoisticalness, egotisticalness, **ego** <nf>, self-interest, individualism; **egocentricity,** egocentrism, self-centeredness, self-centerment, self-obsession; selfishness 651

4 **conceit, conceitedness, self-conceit, self-conceitedness, immodesty,** side, self-assertiveness; **stuck-upness** <nf>, chestiness <nf>, swelled-headedness, swelled head, swollen head, big head, large hat size; **cockiness** <nf>, pertness, perkiness; pomposity; obtrusiveness, bumptiousness; egomania, megalomania

5 **egotist, egoist, egocentric,** individualist; show-off, peacock; narcissist, narcist, Narcissus; **swellhead** <nf>, **braggart** 502.5, know-it-all *or* know-all, smart-ass *and* wise-ass <nf>, smart aleck, no modest violet, vaunter

VERBS 6 **be stuck on oneself** <nf>, be impressed *or* overly impressed with oneself; ego-trip *and* be *or* go on an ego trip <nf>; think well of oneself, think one is it *or* one's shit doesn't stink <nf>, get too big for one's breeches, have a swelled head, know it all, have no false modesty, have no self-doubt, love the sound of one's own voice, be blinded by one's own glory, lay the flattering unction to one's soul; fish for compliments; toot one's own horn, **boast** 502.6; be vain as a peacock, give oneself airs 501.14

7 **puff up, inflate,** swell; go to one's head, turn one's head

ADJS 8 **vain, vainglorious,** overproud, overweening; **self-important, self-esteeming,** having high self-esteem *or* self-valuation, self-respecting, self-assuming, consequential; **self-admiring,** self-delighting, self-worshiping, self-loving, self-endeared, self-infatuated, narcissistic, narcistic; autoerotic, masturbatory; **self-satisfied, self-content,** self-contented, self-approving, self-gratulating, self-gratulatory, self-congratulating, self-congratulatory, self-complacent, **smug,** complacent, self-sufficient

9 **proud** 136.8; arrogant 141.9; boastful 502.10

10 **egotistic, egotistical,** egoistic, egoistical, self-interested; **egocentric,** egocentristic, self-centered, self-obsessed, narcissistic, narcistic; selfish 651.5; egomaniac

11 **conceited, self-conceited, immodest,** self-opinionated; **stuck-up** <nf>, **puffed up**; swollen-headed, **swelled-headed, big-headed** *and* too big for one's shoes *or* britches *and* biggety *and* **cocky** <nf>, jumped-up <chiefly Brit nf>; pert, perk, perky; peacockish, peacocky; know-all *or* know-it-all, smart-ass *and* wise-ass <nf>, smarty, smart-alecky, smart-ass <nf>, overwise, wise in one's own conceit; aggressively self-confident, obtrusive, bumptious

12 **stuck on oneself** <nf>, impressed with oneself, pleased with oneself, full of oneself, all wrapped up in oneself

ADVS **13** **vainly,** self-importantly; **egotistically,** egoistically; **conceitedly,** self-conceitedly, immodestly; cockily <nf>, pertly, perkily

141 ARROGANCE

NOUNS **1** **arrogance,** arrogantness; overbearingness, overbearing pride, overweening pride, stiff-necked pride, assumption of superiority, domineering, domineeringness; **pride,** proudness; superbia, sin of pride, chief of the deadly sins; **haughtiness, hauteur; loftiness,** Olympian loftiness *or* detachment; **toploftiness** *and* stuckupness *and* uppishness *and* uppityness <nf>, hoity-toitiness, hoity-toity; haughty airs, airs of *de haut en bas*; cornstarchy airs <nf>; high horse <nf>; **condescension,** condescendence, patronizing, patronization, patronizing attitude; purse-pride

2 **presumptuousness,** presumption, overweening, overweeningness, assumption, total self-assurance; hubris; **insolence** 142

3 **lordliness, imperiousness,** masterfulness, magisterialness, **high-and-mightiness,** aristocratic presumption; elitism

4 **aloofness, standoffishness,** offishness <nf>, chilliness, coolness, distantness, remoteness

5 **disdainfulness, disdain,** aristocratic disdain, **contemptuousness, superciliousness,** contumeliousness, cavalierness, you-be-damnedness <nf>

6 **snobbery, snobbishness,** snobbiness, snobbism, **priggishness, priggery,** priggism; snootiness *and* snottiness *and* sniffiness *and* high-hattedness *and* high-hattiness <nf>; tufthunting

7 **snob, prig; elitist; highbrow** *and* egghead <nf>, Brahmin, mandarin; name-dropper, tufthunter <chiefly Brit old>, snoot, cold fish <nf>

VERBS **8** **give oneself airs** 501.14; **hold one's nose in the air, look down one's nose,** toss the head, bridle; mount *or* get on one's high horse *and* ride the high horse <nf>; **condescend, patronize, deign,** vouchsafe, stoop, descend, lower *or* demean oneself, trouble oneself, set one's dignity aside *or* to one side, be so good as to, so forget oneself, dirty *or* soil one's hands; deal with *or* treat *de haut en bas* <Fr, from high to low> or *en grand seigneur* <Fr, like a great lord>, talk down to, talk *de haut en bas;* feel entitled

ADJS **9** **arrogant, overbearing, superior,** domineering, **proud, haughty; lofty, top-lofty** <nf>; high-flown, high-falutin *and* high-faluting <nf>; high-headed; high-nosed *and* **stuck-up** *and* **uppish** *and* uppity *and* **upstage** <nf>; **hoity-toity,** big, big as you please, six feet above contradiction; on one's high horse; **condescending, patronizing,** *de haut en bas* <Fr>; purse-proud

10 **presumptuous,** presuming, assuming, overweening, would-be, self-elect, self-elected, self-appointed, self-proclaimed, *soi-disant* <Fr>; **insolent**

11 **lordly, imperious,** aristocratic, totally self-assured, noble; hubristic; masterful, magisterial, magistral, **high-and-mighty;** elitist; U <Brit nf>; dictatorial 417.16

12 **aloof, standoffish,** standoff, offish <nf>, chilly, cool, distant, remote, above all that; Olympian

13 **disdainful,** dismissive, **contemptuous, supercilious,** contumelious, cavalier, you-be-damned <nf>

14 **snobbish,** snobby, toffee-nosed <Brit nf>, **priggish,** snippy <nf>; **snooty** *and* **snotty** *and* sniffy <nf>; **high-hat** *and* high-hatted *and* high-hatty <nf>

ADVS 15 **arrogantly, haughtily, proudly,** aloofly; **condescendingly, patronizingly,** *de haut en bas* and *en grand seigneur* <Fr>; loftily, toploftily <nf>; imperiously, magisterially; Olympianly; **disdainfully, contemptuously,** superciliously, contumeliously; with nose in air, with nose turned up, with head held high, with arms akimbo

16 **presumptuously,** overweeningly, aristocratically; hubristically; **insolently**

17 **snobbishly,** snobbily, **priggishly;** snootily *and* snottily <nf>

142 INSOLENCE

NOUNS 1 **insolence; presumption,** presumptuousness; **audacity, effrontery,** boldness, assurance, hardihood, bumptiousness; hubris; overweening, overweeningness; **contempt** 157, **contemptuousness,** contumely; **disdain** 141.5, *sprezzatura* <Ital>; **arrogance** 141, uppishness *and* uppityness <nf>; obtrusiveness, pushiness <nf>

2 **impudence, impertinence,** flippancy, procacity *and* malapertness, pertness, **sauciness,** sassiness <nf>, **cockiness,** *and* cheekiness <nf>, freshness <nf>, chutzpa *or* hutzpa, **brazenness,** brazenfacedness, brassiness <nf>, face of brass, shamelessness, **rudeness** 505.1, **brashness,** disrespect, disrespectfulness, derision, ridicule 508

3 <nf terms> **cheek,** face, brass, **nerve, gall, chutzpah,** crust, nads <nf>, stones <nf>

4 **sauce** *and* sass *and* lip <nf>, **back talk,** backchat <nf>, mouth

5 <impudent person> malapert ; minx, hussy; whippersnapper, puppy, pup, upstart; boldface, brazenface; *chutzpadik* <Yiddish>; swaggerer 503.2

6 <nf terms> **smart aleck,** smarty, smart guy, smartmouth, smart-ass, wise-ass, smarty-pants, ho-dad, wisenheimer, wise guy, know-it-all, saucebox

VERBS 7 **have the audacity, have the cheek; have the gall** *or* a nerve *or* one's nerve <nf>; **get fresh** <nf>, get smart <nf>, forget one's place, **dare, presume,** take liberties, make bold *or* free; hold in contempt 157.3, ridicule, taunt, deride 508.8

8 **sauce** *and* sass <nf>, **talk back,** answer back, lip *and* give one the lip <nf>, mouth off <nf>, provoke

ADJS 9 **insolent,** insulting; **presumptuous,** presuming, overpresumptuous, overweening; **audacious, bold,** assured, hardy, bumptious; **contemptuous** 157.8, contumelious; **disdainful** 141.13, **arrogant** 141.9, uppish *and* uppity <nf>; hubristic; forward, pushy <nf>, obtrusive, familiar; cool, cold

10 **impudent, impertinent, pert,** malapert *and* procacious , flip <nf>, flippant, **cocky** *and* cheeky *and* **fresh** *and* facy *and* crusty *and* nervy <nf>, *chutzpadik* <Yiddish>; uncalled-for, gratuitous, biggety <nf>; **rude** 505.4, **disrespectful,** derisive 508.12, brash, bluff; **saucy,** sassy <nf>; smart *or* smart-alecky <nf>, smart-ass *or* wise-ass <nf>, snot-nosed <nf>

11 **brazen,** brazenfaced, boldfaced, barefaced, brassy <nf>, **bold,** bold as brass <nf>, unblushing, unabashed, aweless, **shameless,** dead *or* lost to shame; swaggering 503.4

ADVS 12 **insolently, audaciously,** bumptiously, contumeliously; **arrogantly** 141.15; **presumptuously,** obtrusively, pushily <nf>; **disdainfully** 141.15

13 **impudently, impertinently,** pertly, procaciously *and* malapertly , flippantly, **cockily** *and* cheekily <nf>, saucily; **rudely** 505.8, brashly, disrespectfully, contemptuously 157.9, derisively 508.15, in a

smart-alecky way <nf>, in a smart-ass fashion <nf>

14 **brazenly,** brazenfacedly, **boldly,** boldfacedly, **shamelessly,** unblushingly

143 KINDNESS, BENEVOLENCE

NOUNS 1 **kindness, kindliness,** kindly disposition; **benignity,** benignancy; **goodness, decency,** niceness; **graciousness; kindheartedness,** goodheartedness, warmheartedness, softheartedness, tenderheartedness, kindness *or* goodness *or* warmth *or* softness *or* tenderness of heart, affectionateness, warmth, **lovingkindness,** metta; soul of kindness, kind heart, heart of gold; **brotherhood,** fellow feeling, **sympathy,** fraternal feeling, feeling of kinship; **pity** 145, **mercy, compassion; humaneness,** humanity; charitableness

2 **good nature, good humor,** good disposition, grace, benevolent disposition, good temper, sweetness, sweet temper *or* nature, good-naturedness, good-humoredness, good-temperedness, bonhomie; **amiability,** affability, geniality, cordiality; **gentleness,** mildness, lenity

3 **considerateness, consideration, thoughtfulness,** courteousness, mindfulness, heedfulness, regardfulness, attentiveness, **solicitousness,** solicitude, thought, regard, concern, delicacy, **sensitivity,** tact, tactfulness; indulgence, toleration, leniency 427; complaisance, accommodatingness, **helpfulness,** obligingness, agreeableness

4 **benevolence,** benevolentness, benevolent disposition, well-disposedness, **beneficence, charity,** charitableness, **philanthropy; altruism,** philanthropism, **humanitarianism,** welfarism, do-goodism; utilitarianism, Benthamism, greatest good of the greatest number; **goodwill,** grace, brotherly *or* sisterly, love, charity, Christian charity *or* love, *caritas* <L>, love of mankind, love of man *or* humankind, good will to *or* toward man, love, flower power; BOMFOG *or* brotherhood of man and fatherhood of God; **bigheartedness,** largeheartedness, greatheartedness; hospitality; **generosity** 485.1; giving 478

5 **welfare; welfare work, social service,** social welfare, social work; child welfare, etc; commonweal, public welfare; welfare state, welfare statism, welfarism; relief, the dole, social security <Brit>

6 **benevolences,** philanthropies, charities; works, **good works,** public service

7 **act of kindness, kindness, favor,** mercy, **benefit,** benefaction, benevolence, benignity, blessing, **service,** turn, break <nf>, **good turn, good** *or* **kind deed,** *mitzvah* <Heb>, office, good *or* kind offices, obligation, grace, act of grace, courtesy, kindly act, labor of love, good work; rescue, relief, largess, donation, alms

8 **philanthropist, altruist,** benevolist, **humanitarian,** man of good will, **do-gooder,** goo-goo *and* bleeding heart <nf>, well-doer, power for good; good Samaritan; well-wisher; welfare worker, social worker, caseworker; welfare statist; almsgiver, almoner; bodhisattva; Robin Hood, Lady Bountiful; Mr Nice Guy

VERBS 9 **be kind,** be good *or* nice, show kindness; treat well, do right by; favor, oblige, accommodate

10 **be considerate,** consider, respect, regard, think of, **be thoughtful of,** have consideration *or* regard for; remember; be mindful; be at one's service, fuss over one, spoil one <nf>

11 **be benevolent, bear good will,** wish well, give one's blessing, have one's heart in the right place, have a heart of gold; practice *or* follow the golden rule, do as you would be done by, do unto others as you would have others do unto you; make love not war

12 **do a favor, do good,** do a kindness, do a good turn, do a good *or* kind deed, do good works, do a *mitzvah* <Heb>, use one's good offices, render a service, confer a benefit; benefit, help 449.11; mean well

ADJS 13 **kind, kindly,** kindly-disposed; **benign,** benignant; good as gold, **good, nice, decent; gracious; kindhearted, warm, warmhearted,** softhearted, tenderhearted, good-hearted, tender, loving, affectionate, sweet; **sympathetic,** sympathizing, **compassionate** 145.7, tolerant, merciful; brotherly, fraternal, sisterly; humane, human; charitable, caritative; Christly, Christlike; brotherly

14 **good-natured,** well-natured, **good-humored, good-tempered,** bonhomous, **sweet, sweet-tempered; amiable, affable, genial, cordial,** congenial; **gentle,** mild, mild-mannered; easy, easy-natured, easy to get along with, able to take a joke, **agreeable;** laid-back

15 **benevolent, charitable, beneficent, philanthropic, altruistic,** humanitarian; **bighearted,** largehearted, greathearted, freehearted; hospitable; **generous** 485.4; well-disposed; openhanded; almsgiving, eleemosynary; **welfare,** welfarist, welfaristic, welfare statist

16 **considerate, thoughtful,** mindful, heedful, regardful, solicitous, attentive, delicate, tactful, mindful of others; complaisant, **accommodating,** accommodative, at one's service, **helpful,** agreeable, **obliging,** indulgent, tolerant, lenient 427.7

17 **well-meaning, well-meant,** well-affected, well-disposed, **well-intentioned**

ADVS 18 **kindly,** benignly, benignantly; **good,** nicely, well, favorably; **kindheartedly, warmly,** warmheartedly, softheartedly, tenderheartedly; humanely, humanly; brotherly

19 **good-naturedly, good-humoredly,** bonhomously; **sweetly; amiably,** affably, genially, cordially; graciously, in good part

20 **benevolently, beneficently, charitably, philanthropically, altruistically,** bigheartedly, with good will

21 **considerately, thoughtfully,** mindfully, heedfully, regardfully, tactfully, **sensitively,** solicitously, attentively; well-meaningly, well-disposedly; out of consideration *or* courtesy

144 UNKINDNESS, MALEVOLENCE

NOUNS 1 **unkindness, unkindliness;** unbenignity, unbenignness; **unamiability,** uncordiality, ungraciousness, inhospitality, inhospitableness, ungeniality, unaffectionateness; unsympatheticness, uncompassionateness; disagreeableness

2 **unbenevolentness, uncharitableness,** ungenerousness

3 **inconsiderateness, inconsideration, unthoughtfulness,** unmindfulness, unheedfulness, **thoughtlessness,** heedlessness, respectlessness, disregardfulness, forgetfulness; **unhelpfulness,** unobligingness, unaccommodatingness; selfishness

4 **malevolence, ill will,** bad will, bad blood, bad temper, ill nature, ill-disposedness, ill *or* evil disposition; evil eye, stink eye <nf>, whammy <nf>, blighting glance

5 **malice, maliciousness,** maleficence; malignance *or* **malignancy,** malignity; **meanness** *and* orneriness *and* cussedness *and* bitchiness <nf>, hatefulness, nastiness, invidiousness; **wickedness,** iniquitousness 654.4; deviltry, devilry, devilment; malice prepense *or* aforethought, evil intent; **harmfulness, noxiousness** 1000.5

6 **spite,** despite; **spitefulness,** cattiness; gloating, unwholesome *or* unholy joy, *Schadenfreude* <Ger>

7 **rancor, virulence,** venomousness, **venom,** vitriol, gall, spleen, bile; sharp tongue; loathing

8 **causticity,** causticness, corrosiveness, mordancy, mordacity, bitingness; **acrimony, asperity,** acidity, acidness, acidulousness, acridity, acerbity, **bitterness,** tartness; sharpness, keenness, incisiveness, piercingness, stabbingness, trenchancy

9 **harshness, roughness,** ungentleness; **severity,** austerity, hardness, sternness, grimness, inclemency; stringency, astringency, asperity

10 heartlessness, unfeeling, unnaturalness, unresponsiveness, insensitivity, coldness, **cold-heartedness,** cold-bloodedness; **hard-heartedness,** hardness, hardness of heart, heart of stone; **callousness,** callosity; obduracy, induration; **pitilessness, unmercifulness** 146.1

11 cruelty, cruelness, sadistic *or* insensate cruelty, sadism, wanton cruelty; **ruthlessness** 146.1; inhumaneness, **inhumanity,** atrociousness; **brutality,** mindless *or* senseless brutality, brutalness, **brutishness, bestiality, animality,** beastliness; **barbarity,** barbarousness, vandalism; **savagery, viciousness, violence,** fiendishness, heinousness; **child abuse** 389.2, spousal abuse; mental abuse, mental cruelty; truculence, fierceness, ferociousness, **ferocity;** excessive force, piling on <nf>; bloodthirst, bloodthirstiness, bloodlust, bloodiness, bloody-mindedness, sanguineousness; cannibalism; crime against humanity

12 act of cruelty, atrocity, cruelty, brutality, bestiality, barbarity, inhumanity; act of terrorism

13 bad deed, disservice, ill service, **ill turn,** bad turn

14 beast, animal, brute, monster, monster of cruelty, **devil,** devil incarnate; **sadist,** torturer, tormenter; Attila, Torquemada, the Marquis de Sade; malefactor, malfeasor, malfeasant, evildoer, miscreant

VERBS **15** bear malice *or* ill will, malign; do a bad turn; **harshen, dehumanize,** brutalize, bestialize; torture, torment; **have a cruel streak,** go for the jugular, have the killer instinct; have it in for <nf>

ADJS **16 unkind, unkindly,** ill; **unbenign,** unbenignant; **unamiable,** disagreeable, **uncordial, ungracious,** inhospitable, **ungenial,** unaffectionate, unloving; **unsympathetic,** unsympathizing, **uncompassionate,** uncompassioned

17 unbenevolent, unbeneficient, **uncharitable,** unphilanthropic, unaltruistic, ungenerous

18 inconsiderate, unthoughtful, unmindful, unheedful, disregardful, **thoughtless,** heedless, respectless, mindless, unthinking, forgetful; **tactless, insensitive;** uncomplaisant; **unhelpful, unaccommodating, unobliging,** disobliging, uncooperative; selfish

19 malevolent, ill-disposed, evil-disposed, **ill-natured,** ill-affected, ill-conditioned, ill-intentioned, loathing

20 malicious, maleficent, malefic; **malignant,** malign; **mean** *and* **ornery** *and* cussed *and* bitchy <nf>, hateful, nasty, baleful, baneful, invidious; **wicked,** iniquitous 654.16; **harmful, noxious** 1000.12, toxic

21 spiteful, despiteful; **catty,** cattish, bitchy <nf>; **snide;** despiteful

22 rancorous, virulent, vitriolic; **venomous,** venenate, envenomed

23 caustic, mordant, mordacious, corrosive, corroding; **acrimonious,** acrid, acid, acidic, acidulous, acidulent, acerb, acerbate, acerbic, **bitter,** tart; **sharp,** sharpish, keen, incisive, trenchant, **cutting,** penetrating, piercing, biting, **stinging,** stabbing, **scathing, scorching,** withering, scurrilous, abusive, thersitical, foul-mouthed, harsh-tongued

24 harsh, rough, rugged, ungentle; **severe,** austere, **stringent,** astringent, hard, stern, dour, grim, inclement, unsparing

25 heartless, unfeeling, unnatural, unresponsive, insensitive, **cold,** cold of heart, coldhearted, **cold-blooded; hard, hardened,** hard of heart, **hard-hearted,** stony-hearted, marble-hearted, flint-hearted; **callous,** calloused; obdurate, indurated; **unmerciful** 146.3

26 cruel, cruel-hearted, sadistic; **ruthless** 146.3; **brutal,** brutish, brute, bestial, beastly, animal, animalistic; abusive; **mindless, soulless,** insensate, senseless, subhuman, dehumanized, brutalized; sharkish, wolfish, slavering; **barbarous,** barbaric, uncivilized, unchristian; **savage, ferocious,** feral, mean *and* mean as a junkyard dog <nf>, **vicious,** fierce, **atrocious,** truculent, fell; **inhuman,** inhumane, unhuman; fiendish, fiendlike; demoniac *or* demoniacal, diabolic, diabolical, devilish, satanic, hellish, infernal; **bloodthirsty,** bloody-minded, bloody, sanguineous, sanguinary; cannibalistic, anthropophagous; murderous; Draconian, Tartarean

ADVS **27 unkindly,** ill; **unbenignly,** unbenignantly; **unamiably,** disagreeably, uncordially, ungraciously, inhospitably, ungenially, unaffectionately, unlovingly; unsympathetically, uncompassionately

28 unbenevolently, unbeneficently, **uncharitably,** unphilanthropically, unaltruistically, ungenerously

29 inconsiderately, unthoughtfully, thoughtlessly, heedlessly, unthinkingly; unhelpfully, uncooperatively

30 malevolently, maliciously, maleficently, **malignantly; meanly** *and* ornerily *and* cussedly *and* bitchily *and* cattily <nf>, hatefully, nastily, invidiously, balefully; **wickedly,** iniquitously 654.19; **harmfully, noxiously** 1000.15, **spitefully,** in spite; with bad intent, with malice prepense *or* aforethought

31 rancorously, virulently, vitriolically; venomously, venenately

32 caustically, mordantly, mordaciously, corrosively, corrodingly; **acrimoniously,** acridly, acidly, acerbly, acerbically, **bitterly,** tartly; **sharply,** keenly, incisively, trenchantly, **cuttingly,** penetratingly, piercingly, bitingly, **stingingly,** stabbingly, **scathingly,** scorchingly, witheringly, thersitically, scurrilously, abusively

33 harshly, roughly; severely, austerely, stringently, sternly, grimly, inclemently, unsparingly

34 heartlessly, soullessly, unfeelingly, callously, cold-heartedly; coldbloodedly, **in cold blood**

35 cruelly, brutally, brutishly, bestially, animalistically, subhumanly, sharkishly, wolfishly, slaveringly; **barbarously, savagely, ferociously,** ferally, **viciously,** fiercely, **atrociously,** truculently, terroristically; **ruthlessly** 146.4; **inhumanely,** inhumanly, unhumanly; fiendishly, diabolically, devilishly

145 PITY

NOUNS **1 pity, sympathy,** feeling, fellow feeling, **commiseration,** condolence, condolences; **compassion, mercy,** empathy, ruth, rue, humanity; **sensitivity; clemency,** quarter, reprieve, mitigation, relief 120, favor, grace; **leniency,** lenity, gentleness; forbearance; **kindness, benevolence** 143; pardon, **forgiveness** 601.1; self-pity; **pathos**

2 compassionateness, mercifulness, ruthfulness, ruefulness, softheartedness, tenderness, tenderheartedness, lenity, gentleness; bowels of compassion *or* mercy; bleeding heart, soft spot

VERBS **3 pity, be** *or* **feel sorry for,** feel sorrow for; **commiserate,** compassionate; open one's heart; **sympathize, sympathize with,** feel for, weep for, lament for, bleed, bleed for, have one's heart bleed for *or* go out to, condole with 147.2

4 have pity, have mercy upon, take pity on *or* **upon;** melt, thaw; relent, forbear, relax, give quarter, spare, temper the wind to the shorn lamb, go easy on *and* let up *or* ease up on <nf>, soften, mitigate, unsteel; **reprieve, pardon,** remit, **forgive** 601.4; put out of one's misery; be cruel to be kind; give a second chance, give a break <nf>

5 <excite pity> **move, touch,** affect, reach, **soften,** unsteel, melt, melt the heart, appeal to one's better feelings; move to tears, sadden, grieve 112.17

6 beg for mercy, ask for pity, cry for quarter, beg for one's life; fall on one's knees, throw oneself at the feet of, throw oneself at someone's mercy

ADJS **7 pitying, sympathetic,** sympathizing, commiserative, condolent, understanding; **compassionate, merciful,** ruthful, rueful, **clement,** gentle, soft, melting, bleeding, tender, **tenderhearted,** softhearted, warmhearted; **humane,** human; lenient, forbearant 427.7; charitable 143.15

8 pitiful, pitiable, pathetic, piteous, touching, moving, affecting, heart-

rending, grievous, doleful 112.26, sad, heartbreaking, tearjerking <nf>
9 self-pitying, self-pitiful, sorry for oneself

ADVS **10** **pitifully,** sympathetically; **compassionately, mercifully,** ruthfully, ruefully, clemently, humanely

146 PITILESSNESS

NOUNS **1** **pitilessness, unmercifulness, uncompassionateness,** unsympatheticness, mercilessness, **ruthlessness,** unfeelingness, inclemency, relentlessness, inexorableness, unyieldingness 361.2, unforgivingness; **heartlessness,** heart of stone, hardness, steeliness, flintiness, harshness, induration, vindictiveness, **cruelty** 144.11; remorselessness, unremorsefulness; short shrift, tender mercies

VERBS **2** **show no mercy,** give no quarter, turn a deaf ear, be unmoved, claim one's pound of flesh, harden *or* steel one's heart, go by the rule book

ADJS **3** **pitiless,** unpitying, unpitiful; blind *or* deaf to pity; **unsympathetic,** unsympathizing; **uncompassionate,** uncompassioned; **merciless, unmerciful,** without mercy, unruing, **ruthless,** dog-eat-dog, vindictive; unfeeling, bowelless, inclement, relentless, inexorable, unyielding 361.9, unforgiving; **heartless,** coldhearted, hard, hard as nails, callous, steely, flinty, harsh, savage, **cruel;** remorseless, unremorseful; out for oneself

ADVS **4** **pitilessly,** unsympathetically; mercilessly, **unmercifully, ruthlessly,** uncompassionately, inclemently, relentlessly, inexorably, unyieldingly, unforgivingly; heartlessly, harshly, savagely, cruelly; remorselessly, unremorsefully

147 CONDOLENCE

NOUNS **1** **condolence, condolences,** condolement, **consolation,** comfort, balm, soothing words, **commiseration, sympathy,** sharing of grief *or* sorrow

VERBS **2** **condole with, commiserate, sympathize with,** feel with, empathize with, express sympathy for, send one's condolences; pity 145.3; **console,** wipe away one's tears, comfort, speak soothing words, bring balm to one's sorrow; sorrow with, share *or* help bear one's grief, grieve *or* weep with, grieve *or* weep for, share one's sorrow

ADJS **3** condoling, condolent, consolatory, comforting, commiserating, commiserative, **sympathetic,** empathic, empathetic; pitying 145.7

148 FORGIVENESS

NOUNS **1** **forgiveness,** forgivingness; unresentfulness, unrevengefulness, **condoning,** condonation, condonance, overlooking, disregard; **patience** 134; **indulgence, forbearance,** longanimity, long-suffering; **kindness, benevolence** 143; **magnanimity** 652.2; brooking, **tolerance** 979.4; peace talks
2 **pardon,** excuse, sparing, **amnesty,** indemnity, exemption, immunity, reprieve, grace; **absolution,** shrift, remission, remission *or* forgiveness of sin; redemption, deliverance; letting go; **exoneration, exculpation** 601.1

VERBS **3** **forgive, pardon, excuse,** give *or* grant forgiveness, spare; amnesty, grant amnesty to, grant immunity *or* exemption; hear confession, **absolve,** remit, acquit, give *or* grant absolution, shrive, grant remission; **exonerate, exculpate** 601.4; blot out one's sins, wipe the slate clean, expunge from the record
4 **condone** 134.7, **overlook, disregard, ignore,** accept, take *and* swallow *and* let go <nf>, pass over, give one another chance, let one off this time *and* let one off easy <nf>, let something go, close *or* shut one's eyes to, turn a blind eye to, **blink** *or* **wink at,** connive at; show mercy; allow for, make allowances for; bear with, endure, regard with indulgence; pocket the affront, leave unavenged, turn the other cheek, bury *or* hide one's head in the sand

5 **forget, forgive and forget,** dismiss from one's thoughts, think no more of, not give it another *or* a second thought, let it go <nf>, let it pass, **let bygones be bygones;** write off, charge off, charge to experience; bury the hatchet; make peace, make up, shake hands

ADJS **6** **forgiving,** sparing, placable, conciliatory; **kind, benevolent** 143.15; **magnanimous, generous** 652.6; **patient** 134.9; **forbearing,** longanimous, long-suffering, stoic; unresentful, unrevengeful; **tolerant** 979.11, more in sorrow than in anger; exonerative

7 **forgiven, pardoned, excused,** spared, amnestied, reprieved, remitted; overlooked, disregarded, forgotten, not held against one, wiped away, removed from the record, blotted, canceled, **condoned,** indulged; **absolved,** shriven; redeemed, delivered; exonerated, exculpated, acquitted, not guilty, innocent, cleared, absolved, vindicated, off the hook; unresented; unavenged, unrevenged; uncondemned; wiped away, swept clean

149 CONGRATULATION

NOUNS **1** **congratulation, congratulations,** congrats <nf>, gratulation, **felicitation,** blessing, **compliment,** pat on the back; good wishes, best wishes; **applause** 509.2, **praise** 509.5, flattery 511

VERBS **2** **congratulate,** gratulate, **felicitate,** bless, **compliment,** tender *or* offer one's congratulations *or* felicitations *or* compliments; shake one's hand, pat one on the back; **rejoice with one,** wish one joy; **applaud** 509.10, **praise** 509.12, flatter 511.5

ADJS **3** **congratulatory,** congratulant, congratulational; gratulatory, gratulant; **complimentary** 509.16, flattering 511.8

4 <nf terms> **congrats!, all right!, aw right!, right on!,** way to go!, attaboy!, attagirl!, good deal!, looking good!, nice going!, that's my boy!, that's my girl!, mazel tov!

150 GRATITUDE

NOUNS **1** **gratitude, gratefulness, thankfulness, appreciation, appreciativeness;** obligation, sense of obligation *or* indebtedness

2 **thanks, thanksgiving,** praise, laud, hymn, paean, benediction, eucharist; grace, prayer of thanks; **thank-you;** sincere thanks; **acknowledgment,** cognizance, **credit,** crediting, recognition; bonus, gratuity, tip; thank offering, votary offering

VERBS **3** **be grateful, be obliged,** feel *or* be *or* lie under an obligation, be obligated *or* indebted, be in the debt of, give credit *or* due credit; **be thankful,** thank God, thank one's lucky stars, thank *or* bless one's stars; **appreciate,** be appreciative of; never forget; overflow with gratitude; not look a gift horse in the mouth

4 **thank, extend gratitude** *or* **thanks,** bless; give one's thanks, **express one's appreciation; offer** *or* **give thanks,** tender *or* render thanks, return thanks; acknowledge, make acknowledgments of, credit, recognize, give *or* render credit *or* recognition, give a big hand; fall all over one with gratitude; fall on one's knees; pay tribute

ADJS **5** **grateful, thankful; appreciative,** appreciatory, sensible; **obliged, much obliged,** beholden, indebted to, crediting, under obligation, acknowledging, cognizant of; bread-and-butter

151 INGRATITUDE

NOUNS **1** **ingratitude, ungratefulness, unthankfulness,** thanklessness, unappreciation, **unappreciativeness;** nonacknowledgment, nonrecognition, denial of due *or* proper credit; grudging *or* half-hearted thanks

2 **ingrate,** ungrateful wretch, thankless wretch

VERBS **3** **be ungrateful,** feel no obligation, **not appreciate,** owe one no thanks; look a gift horse in the mouth; bite the hand that feeds one

ADJS 4 **ungrateful, unthankful,** unthanking, thankless, unappreciative, unappreciatory, unmindful, nonrecognitive, unrecognizing, ungracious, discourteous

5 unthanked, unacknowledged, unrecognized, nonrecognized, uncredited, denied due *or* proper credit, unrequited, unrewarded, forgotten, neglected, unduly *or* unfairly neglected, ignored, blanked, cold-shouldered; ill-requited, ill-rewarded

152 RESENTMENT, ANGER

NOUNS 1 **resentment,** resentfulness; **displeasure,** disapproval, disapprobation, dissatisfaction, **discontent; vexation,** irritation, **annoyance,** aggravation <nf>, exasperation; slow burn <nf>

2 **offense, umbrage, pique;** glower, scowl, angry look, dirty look <nf>, glare, frown

3 **bitterness, bitter resentment,** bitterness of spirit, heartburning; **rancor,** virulence, **acrimony,** acerbity, asperity; causticity 144.8; **choler,** gall, bile, spleen, acid, acidity, acidulousness; hard feelings, **animosity** 589.4; soreness, rankling, slow burn <nf>; gnashing of teeth

4 **indignation,** indignant displeasure, righteous indignation, grievance, grudge

5 **anger, wrath, ire,** *saeva indignatio* <L>, mad <nf>; angriness, irateness, wrathfulness, soreness <nf>; infuriation, enragement; vials of wrath, grapes of wrath; **heat,** more heat than light <nf>; pugnacity, aggro <Brit nf>, dancer <nf>

6 **temper,** dander *and* Irish <nf>, monkey <Brit nf>; bad temper 110.1

7 **dudgeon,** high dudgeon; **huff,** pique, pet, tiff, miff *and* stew <nf>, fret, **fume,** ferment

8 **fit,** fit of anger, fit of temper, rage, wax <Brit nf>, **tantrum,** temper tantrum; duck *or* cat fit *and* **conniption** *or* conniption fit *and* snit <nf>, paroxysm, convulsion; agriothymia; stamping one's foot

9 **outburst,** outburst of anger, burst, **explosion,** eruption, blowup *and* **flare-up** <nf>, access, blaze of temper; **storm, scene,** high words

10 **rage, passion; fury,** furor, frenzy; livid *or* towering rage *or* passion, blind *or* burning rage, raging *or* tearing passion, furious rage; vehemence, violence; the Furies, the Eumenides, the Erinyes; Nemesis; Alecto, Tisiphone, Megaera; steroid rage, roid rage <nf>

11 **provocation, affront, offense;** *casus belli* <L>, red rag, red rag to a bull, red flag, sore point, sore spot, tender spot, delicate subject, raw nerve, the quick, where one lives; slap in the face; last straw; incitement

VERBS 12 **resent,** be resentful, feel *or* harbor *or* nurse resentment, feel hurt, smart, feel sore *and* have one's nose out of joint <nf>; bear *or* hold *or* have a grudge, begrudge, bear malice

13 **take amiss,** take ill, **take in bad part,** take to heart, not take it as a joke, **mind; take offense, take umbrage,** get miffed *or* huffy <nf>; be cut *or* cut to the quick, get one's back up <nf>

14 <show resentment> redden, color, flush, mantle; **growl, snarl,** gnarl, **snap,** show one's teeth, spit; gnash *or* grind one's teeth; **glower,** lower, scowl, **glare, frown,** give a dirty look <nf>, look daggers; **stew,** stew in one's own juice

15 <be angry> **burn, seethe, simmer,** sizzle, smoke, smolder, steam; be pissed *or* pissed off *or* browned off <nf>, be livid, be beside oneself, **fume,** stew <nf>, boil, fret, chafe; foam at the mouth; breathe fire and fury; **rage, storm, rave,** rant, bluster; take on *and* go on *and* carry on <nf>, rant and rave, kick up a row *or* dust *or* a shindy <nf>; raise Cain *or* raise hell *or* raise the devil *or* raise the roof <nf>, tear up the earth; throw a fit, have a conniption *or* conniption fit *or* duck fit *or* cat fit <nf>, go into a tantrum; stamp one's foot

16 **vent one's anger,** vent one's rancor *or* choler *or* spleen, pour out the

vials of one's wrath; **snap at, bite** *or* **snap one's nose off, bite** *or* **take one's head off, jump down one's throat;** expend one's anger on, take it out on <nf>

17 <become angry> **anger, lose one's temper,** become irate, forget oneself, let one's angry passions rise; **get one's gorge up,** get one's blood up, **bridle,** bridle up, **bristle,** bristle up, raise one's hackles, get one's back up; reach boiling point, boil over, climb the wall, go through *or* hit the roof

18 <nf terms> **get mad** *or* **sore,** get one's Irish *or* dander *or* hackles up, get one's monkey up <Brit>; **see red, get hot under the collar,** flip out, work oneself into a lather *or* sweat *or* stew, get oneself in a tizzy, do a slow burn, blow one's cool

19 **flare up, blaze up,** fire up, flame up, spunk up, ignite, kindle, take fire

20 **fly into a rage** *or* **passion** *or* **temper,** fly out, fly off at a tangent; **fly off the handle** *and* **hit the ceiling** *and* go into a tailspin *and* have a hemorrhage <nf>; **explode, blow up** <nf>; blow one's top *or* stack <nf>, blow a fuse *or* gasket <nf>, flip one's lid *or* wig <nf>, wig out <nf>; kick *or* piss up a fuss *or* a row *or* a storm <nf>; jump down someone's throat <nf>, take it out on someone <nf>

21 **offend, give offense, give umbrage,** affront, outrage; grieve, aggrieve; wound, hurt, cut, cut to the quick, hit one where one lives <nf>, **sting,** hurt one's feelings; step *or* tread on one's toes

22 **anger, make angry, make mad,** raise one's gorge *or* choler; make one's blood boil

23 <nf terms> **piss** *or* tee off, tick off, piss, **get one's goat, get one's Irish** *or* back *or* dander *or* hackles up, **make sore,** make one hot under the collar, put one's nose out of joint, burn one up, burn one's ass *or* butt, steam

24 **provoke, incense,** arouse, inflame, embitter; **vex, irritate, annoy, aggravate** <nf>, **exasperate, nettle,** fret, chafe; **pique, peeve** *and* miff <nf>, huff; **ruffle, roil, rile** <nf>, ruffle one's feathers, **rankle;** bristle, put *or* get one's back up, set up, put one's hair *or* fur *or* bristles up; stick in one's craw <nf>; **stir up, work up,** stir one's bile, stir the blood; wave the bloody shirt

25 **enrage, infuriate, madden,** drive one mad, frenzy, lash into fury, work up into a passion, **make one's blood boil**

ADJS 26 **resentful,** resenting; **bitter,** embittered, rancorous, virulent, **acrimonious,** acerb, acerbic, acerbate; caustic; **choleric,** splenetic, acid, acidic, acidulous, acidulent; **sore** <nf>, rankled, burning *and* stewing <nf>

27 **provoked, vexed, piqued; peeved** *and* miffed *and* huffy <nf>, riled, **nettled, irritated, annoyed,** aggravated <nf>, exasperated, put-out; huffed, miffed, peeved, in a snit

28 **angry,** angered, **incensed, indignant, irate,** ireful; **livid,** livid with rage, beside oneself, **wroth, wrathful,** wrathy, **cross,** wrought-up, worked up, riled up <nf>

29 **burning, seething,** simmering, smoldering, sizzling, boiling, **steaming;** flushed with anger

30 <nf terms> **mad, sore,** mad as a hornet *or* as a wet hen *or* as hell, sore as a boil, pissed; **pissed-off** *or* PO'd *or* pissed; teed off *or* TO'd; ticked *or* ticked off, browned-off, waxy *and* stroppy <Brit>, **hot,** het up, **hot under the collar,** burned up, hot and bothered, boiling, boiling *or* hopping *or* fighting *or* roaring mad, fit to be tied, good and mad, steamed, hacked, bent out of shape, in a lather *or* lava *or* pucker, red-assed

31 **in a temper, in a huff, in a pet,** in a snit *or* a stew <nf>; in a wax <Brit nf>, **in high dudgeon**

32 **infuriated,** infuriate, in a rage *or* passion *or* fury; **furious,** fierce, wild, savage; raving mad <nf>, **rabid,** foaming *or* frothing at the mouth; **fuming,** in a fume; **enraged, raging, raving, ranting, storming;** ballistic

ADVS 33 **angrily, indignantly, irately,** wrathfully, infuriatedly, infuriately, furiously, heatedly; **in anger,** in hot blood, in the heat of passion

153 JEALOUSY

NOUNS **1 jealousy,** *jalousie* <Fr>, jealousness, heartburning, heartburn, **jaundice,** jaundiced eye, green in the eye <nf>; Othello's flaw, horn-madness; **envy** 154; crime of passion

2 suspiciousness, suspicion, doubt, misdoubt, mistrust, distrust, untrust, distrustfulness

VERBS **3** suffer pangs of jealousy, have green in the eye <nf>, be possessive *or* overpossessive, view with a jaundiced eye; **suspect,** distrust, mistrust, doubt, misdoubt, be paranoid

4 make one jealous, put someone's nose out of joint

ADJS **5 jealous, jaundiced,** jaundice-eyed, yellow-eyed, green-eyed, yellow, green, green with jealousy; horn-mad; invidious, **envious** 154.3; **suspicious,** distrustful

154 ENVY

NOUNS **1 envy,** enviousness, **covetousness;** emulousness ; invidia, deadly sin of envy, **invidiousness;** grudging, grudgingness; resentment, resentfulness; **jealousy** 153; rivalry, competitiveness; meanness, meanspiritedness, ungenerousness; penis envy, class envy

VERBS **2 envy,** be envious *or* covetous of, **covet,** cast envious eyes, desire for oneself; resent; **grudge, begrudge**; turn green with envy, be jealous, eat one's heart out

ADJS **3 envious,** envying, **invidious,** green with envy, green-eyed; **jealous** 153.4; **covetous,** desirous of; resentful; **grudging, begrudging;** mean, mean-spirited, ungenerous; stink-eyed, squint-eyed

155 RESPECT

NOUNS **1 respect, regard,** consideration, appreciation, favor; approbation, approval; **esteem,** estimation, prestige; **reverence, veneration,** awe; **deference,** deferential *or* reverential regard; **honor, homage,** duty; great respect, high regard, high opinion, **admiration;** adoration, breathless adoration, exaggerated respect, worship, hero worship, **idolization;** idolatry, deification, apotheosis; courtesy 504

2 obeisance, reverence, homage; **bow, nod, bob,** bend, inclination, inclination of the head, **curtsy, salaam, kowtow,** scrape, bowing and scraping, making a leg; **genuflection,** kneeling, bending the knee; prostration; salute, salutation, namaste; salaam, kowtow; presenting arms, dipping the colors *or* ensign, standing at attention; red carpet; **submissiveness, submission** 433; **obsequiousness, servility** 138

3 respects, regards, *égards* <Fr>; duties, *devoirs* <Fr>; attentions

VERBS **4 respect,** entertain respect for, accord respect to, **regard, esteem,** hold in esteem *or* consideration, favor, **admire,** think much of, think well of, think highly of, have *or* hold a high opinion of; **appreciate, value,** prize, treasure; **revere, reverence,** hold in reverence, **venerate, honor, look up to, defer to, bow to,** exalt, put on a pedestal, **worship,** hero-worship, deify, apotheosize, **idolize, adore,** worship the ground one walks on, stand in awe of; hold dear

5 do *or* **pay homage to,** show *or* demonstrate respect for, pay respect to, pay tribute to, **do** *or* **render honor to, do the honors for; doff one's cap to, take off one's hat to;** salute, present arms, dip the colors *or* ensign, stand at *or* to attention; give the red-carpet treatment, roll out the red carpet; fire a salute

6 bow, make obeisance, salaam, kowtow, make one's bow, bow down, **nod,** incline *or* bend *or* bow the head, bend the neck, **bob,** bob down, **curtsy,** bob a curtsy, bend, make a leg, scrape, **bow and scrape; genuflect, kneel,** bend the knee, get down on one's knees, throw oneself on one's knees, fall on one's knees, fall down before, fall at the feet of, prostrate oneself, kiss the hem of one's garment

7 **command respect,** inspire respect, stand high, impress, have prestige, rank high, be widely reputed, be up there *or* way up there <nf>; awe 122.6, overawe

ADJS **8** **respectful, regardful,** attentive; **deferential,** conscious of one's place, dutiful, honorific, ceremonious, appreciative, cap in hand; **courteous** 504.13

9 **reverent,** reverential; admiring, **adoring, worshiping,** worshipful, hero-worshiping, **idolizing,** idolatrous, deifying, apotheosizing; **venerative,** venerational, venerating; awestruck, awestricken, awed, in awe; on bended knee, god-fearing; solemn 111.3

10 **obeisant,** prostrate, on one's knees, on bended knee; **submissive** 433.12; **obsequious;** knowing one's place

11 **respected, esteemed, revered,** reverenced, adored, worshiped, **venerated, honored,** well-thought-of, admired, much-admired, appreciated, valued, prized, in high esteem *or* estimation, highly considered, well-considered, held in respect *or* regard *or* favor *or* consideration, time-honored, prestigious

12 **venerable, reverend, estimable, honorable,** worshipful, august, awe-inspiring, awesome, awful, dreadful; time-honored

ADVS **13** **respectfully,** regardfully, deferentially, reverentially; dutifully

156 DISRESPECT

NOUNS **1** **disrespect, disrespectfulness,** lack of respect, low estimate *or* esteem, **disesteem,** dishonor, **irreverence; ridicule** 508; **disparagement** 512; **discourtesy** 505; **impudence,** insolence 142; opprobrium; contempt

2 **indignity, affront, offense, injury,** humiliation; scurrility, contempt 157, contumely, despite, flout, flouting, mockery, jeering, jeer, mock, scoff, gibe, taunt, brickbat <nf>; **insult, aspersion,** uncomplimentary remark, snub, slight, slap *or* kick in the face, left-handed *or* backhanded compliment, damning with faint praise; cut; **outrage, atrocity,** enormity

3 <nf terms> **put-down,** dump, bring-down, brickbat, **dig,** dirty dig, ding, rank-out, rip, shot, slam, go-by

VERBS **4** **disrespect,** not respect, disesteem, hold a low opinion of, rate *or* rank low, hold in low esteem, not care much for, pay a lefthanded *or* backhanded compliment, damn with faint praise, hold in contempt, have no time for; **show disrespect for,** show a lack of respect for, **be disrespectful,** treat with disrespect, turn one's back on, be overfamiliar with; trifle with, make bold *or* free with, take a liberty, take liberties with, play fast and loose with; **ridicule** 508.8; **disparage** 512.8

5 **offend, affront,** give offense to, snub, slight, disoblige, outrage, step *or* tread on one's toes; dishonor, humiliate, treat with indignity; flout, mock, jeer at, scoff at, fleer at, gibe at, taunt, bitch-slap <nf>; **insult,** call names, kick *or* slap in the face, take *or* pluck by the beard; **add insult to injury;** give the cold shoulder, cut dead, spurn

6 <nf terms> **bad-mouth, put down, trash,** give the go-by, rubbish, dump on, dig at, dis *or* diss, rank out, rip *or* rip on, ride, roast, slam, hurl a brickbat

ADJS **7** **disrespectful, irreverent,** aweless; **discourteous** 505.4; **insolent, impudent;** flippant; ridiculing, **derisive** 508.12; **disparaging** 512.13

8 **insulting, insolent, abusive, offensive,** humiliating, degrading, pejorative, contemptuous 157.8, contumelious, calumnious; blasphemous; scurrilous, scurrile; backhand, backhanded, left-handed, cutting; contumacious, outrageous, atrocious, unspeakable

9 **unrespected,** disrespected, **unregarded, unrevered,** unvenerated, unhonored, unenvied; trivialized

157 CONTEMPT

NOUNS **1 contempt, disdain, scorn,** contemptuousness, disdainfulness, superciliousness, snootiness, snottiness, sniffiness, toploftiness, scornfulness, despite, contumely, sovereign contempt; snobbishness; clannishness, cliquishness, exclusiveness, exclusivity; hauteur, airs, mock, arrogance 141; **ridicule** 508; **insult** 156.2; **disparagement** 512

2 snub, rebuff, repulse; **slight,** humiliation, spurning, spurn, disregard, the go-by <nf>; cut, cut direct, **the cold shoulder** <nf>; sneer, snort, sniff; contemptuous dismissal, **dismissal** 908.2, kiss-off <nf>; **rejection** 372

VERBS **3 disdain, scorn, despise,** contemn, vilipend, disprize, misprize, rate *or* rank low, be contemptuous of, feel contempt for, **hold in contempt,** hold cheap, look down upon, think little *or* nothing of, feel superior to, be above, hold beneath one *or* beneath contempt, look with scorn upon, view with a scornful eye, mock, give one the fish-eye *or* the beady eye *or* the stink eye *or* the hairy eyeball <nf>; **put down** *or* dump on <nf>; deride, **ridicule** 508.8; **insult; disparage** 512.8; thumb one's nose at, sniff at, sneeze at, snap one's fingers at, sneer at, snort at, curl one's lip at, shrug one's shoulders at; care nothing for, couldn't care less about, think nothing of, set at naught

4 spurn, scout, **turn up one's nose at,** scorn to receive *or* accept, not want any part of; spit upon

5 snub, rebuff, cut *or* cut dead <nf>, drop, repulse; **high-hat** *and* upstage <nf>; **look down one's nose at,** look cool *or* coldly upon; cold-shoulder *or* turn a cold shoulder upon *or* **give the cold shoulder** <nf>, give *or* turn the shoulder <nf>, give the go-by *or* the kiss-off <nf>; turn one's back upon, turn away from, turn on one's heel, set one's face against, slam the door in one's face, show one his place, put one in his place, wave one aside; not be at home to, not receive

6 slight, ignore, pooh-pooh <nf>, make little of, dismiss, pretend not to see, disregard, overlook, neglect, pass by, pass up *and* give the go-by <nf>, leave out in the cold <nf>, take no note *or* notice of, look right through <nf>, pay no attention *or* regard to, refuse to acknowledge *or* recognize

7 avoid 368.6, avoid like the plague, go out of one's way to avoid, shun, dodge, steer clear of *and* have no truck with <nf>; **keep one's distance,** keep at a respectful distance, **keep** *or* **stand** *or* **hold aloof;** keep at a distance, hold *or* keep at arm's length; **be stuck-up** <nf>, act holier than thou, give oneself airs

ADJS **8 contemptuous, disdainful,** supercilious, snooty, snotty, sniffy, toplofty, toploftical, **scornful,** sneering, insulting, withering, contumelious; snobbish, snobby; clannish, cliquish, exclusive; stuck-up <nf>, **conceited** 140.11; haughty, **arrogant** 141.9

ADVS **9 contemptuously, scornfully, disdainfully;** in *or* with contempt, in disdain, in scorn; sneeringly, with a sneer, with curling lip

158 SPACE

<indefinite space>

NOUNS **1 space, extent,** extension, spatial extension, uninterrupted extension, space continuum, continuum; **expanse,** expansion; spread, breadth; depth, deeps; height, vertical space, air space; length; width; **measure,** volume; **dimension,** proportion, size; **area,** expanse tract, surface, surface *or* superficial extension; diameter, circumference; **field,** arena, sphere; capacity; acreage; **void,** empty space, emptiness, nothingness; infinite space, infinity, outer space, wastes of outer space, deep space, depths of outer space, interplanetary *or* interstellar *or* intergalactic space

2 range, scope, compass, reach, stretch, expanse; radius, sweep, carry, fetch, grasp; **gamut, scale,**

register, diapason; **spectrum,** array; tract; range of motion

3 **room, latitude,** swing, play, way; spare room, room to spare, room to swing a cat <nf>, **elbowroom,** legroom; **margin, leeway;** breathing space; sea room; headroom, clearance; windage; amplitude; headway; living space;

4 **open space,** clear space; **clearing,** clearance, glade; open country, wide-open spaces, **terrain,** prairie, steppe, plain 236; field, glade; wilderness, back country, boonies *and* boondocks <nf>, outback, desert, back o' beyond; back forty; distant prospect *or* perspective, empty view, far horizon; **territory;** living space, *Lebensraum* <Ger>; national territory, air space

5 **spaciousness, roominess, size** commodiousness, capacity, capaciousness, airiness, amplitude, extensiveness, extent, expanse; stowage, storage; seating capacity, seating

6 **fourth dimension, space-time,** time-space, space-time continuum, continuum, four-dimensional space; four-dimensional geometry, Minkowski world *or* universe; spaceworld; other continuums; **relativity,** theory of relativity, Einstein theory, principle of relativity, principle of equivalence, general theory of relativity, special *or* restricted theory of relativity, continuum theory; time warp; cosmic constant

7 **inner space,** psychological space, the realm of the mind; personal space, room to be, individual *or* private space, space <nf>; semantic space

8 intervening space; distance, interval, gap, remove; break, hiatus, lacuna, pause, interruption, intermission, lapse, blank; duration, period, span, spell, stretch, turn, while

VERBS **9** **extend, reach, stretch,** expand, sweep, spread, run, **go** *or* **go out,** cover, carry, **range,** lie; **reach** *or* stretch *or* thrust out; span, straddle, take in, hold, enclose, encompass, surround, environ, contain, hold; lengthen, widen, deepen, raise

ADJS **10** **spatial,** space, spacial; **dimensional,** proportional; two-dimensional, flat, surface *or* superficial, radial, three-dimensional *or* 3-D, spherical, cubic, volumetric; galactic, intergalactic, interstellar; stereoscopic; fourth-dimensional; space-time, spatiotemporal

11 **spacious, sizeable, roomy, commodious, capacious,** ample; **extensive,** expansive, extended, wide-ranging; far-reaching, extending, spreading, **vast,** vasty, broad, **wide,** deep, high, voluminous, cavernous; airy, lofty; oversized; amplitudinous; widespread **864.13**; **infinite** 823.3

ADVS **12** **extensively, widely,** broadly, vastly, abroad; **far and wide,** far and near; **right and left,** on all sides, on every side; infinitely

13 **everywhere,** everywheres <nf>, **here, there, and everywhere;** in every place, in every clime *or* region, in all places, in every quarter, in all quarters; **all over,** all round, all over hell *and* all over the map *and* all over the place *and* all over the ballpark *and* all over town <nf>, all over the world, the world over, on the face of the earth, under the sun, throughout the world, throughout the length and breadth of the land; from end to end, from pole to pole, from here to the back of beyond <Brit nf>, from hell to breakfast <nf>; **high and low,** upstairs and downstairs, inside and out, in every nook and cranny *or* hole and corner; **universally,** in all creation

14 **from everywhere,** everywhence, from all points of the compass, from every quarter *or* all quarters; everywhere, everywhither, to the four winds, to the uttermost parts of the earth, to hell and back <nf>

159 LOCATION

NOUNS **1** **location, situation, place, position,** spot, *lieu* <Fr>, placement, emplacement, stead; **whereabouts,** whereabout, ubicity; **area, district, region** 231; **locality, locale,** locus; venue; **abode** 228; **site,** situs; **spot, point,** pinpoint, exact spot *or* point, very spot *or* point, dot; benchmark; *locus classicus* <L>; bearings, coordinates, latitude and longitude, direction; setting, environs, environment; habitat, address

2 **station,** status, **stand, standing,** standpoint, pou sto; **viewpoint,** *optique* <Fr>, point of reference, reference-point, angle, perspective, distance; coign of vantage; **seat, post,** base, footing, ground, venue

3 **navigation,** guidance; dead reckoning, pilotage; coastal navigation; celestial guidance *or* astro-inertial guidance, celestial navigation *or* celo-navigation *or* astronavigation; consolan; loran; radar navigation; radio navigation; orienteering; **position, orientation,** lay, lie, set, **attitude,** aspect, exposure, frontage, **bearing** *or* **bearings,** radio bearing, azimuth; position line *or* line of position; **fix**

4 **place,** stead, lieu

5 **map, chart;** hachure, contour line, isoline, layer tint; **scale,** graphic scale, representative fraction; **legend;** grid line, meridian, parallel, latitude, longitude; inset; index; **projection,** map projection, azimuthal equidistant projection *or* azimuthal projection, conic projection, Mercator projection; **cartography, mapmaking;** chorography, topography, photogrammetry, phototopography; **cartographer, mapmaker, mapper;** chorographer, topographer, photogrammetrist

6 <act of placing> **placement, positioning, emplacement, situation, location, siting,** localization, **locating, placing,** putting; establishment, installation; **allocation,** collocation, **disposition,** assignment, **deployment,** posting, **stationing,** spotting; fixing, fixation, settling; deposition, reposition, **deposit,** disposal, dumping; **stowage,** storage, warehousing; loading, lading, packing

7 **establishment, foundation,** settlement, settling, colonization, population, peopling, plantation; lodgment, fixation; anchorage, mooring; **installation,** installment, inauguration, investiture, placing in office, initiation

8 **topography,** geography, topology; cartography, chorography; surveying, triangulation, navigation, geodesy; geodetic satellite, orbiting geophysical observatory *or* OGO; Global Positioning System *or* GPS; Geographic Information System

VERBS 9 **have place,** be there; have its place *or* slot, **belong, go, fit,** fit in

10 **be located** *or* **situated, lie, be found,** stand, rest, repose; lie in, have its seat in

11 **locate, situate, site, place, position;** emplace, spot <nf>, **install,** put in place; **allocate,** collocate, **dispose, deploy,** assign; **localize,** narrow *or* pin down; **map, chart,** put on the map *or* chart, put one's finger on, **fix,** assign *or* consign *or* relegate to a place; **pinpoint,** zero in on, home in on, find the spot; find *or* fix *or* calculate one's position, triangulate, survey, find a line of position, **get a fix on** *or* navigational fix, get a bearing, navigate; turn up, track down

12 **place, put, set, lay,** pose, posit, site, seat, stick <nf>, **station, post;** billet, quarter; **park,** plump down <nf>; **dump**

13 <put violently> **clap,** slap, **thrust, fling, hurl,** throw, cast, chuck, toss; **plump;** plunk *and* plank *and* plop <nf>

14 **deposit,** repose, reposit, rest, **lay,** lodge; **put down,** set down, lay down

15 **load, lade,** freight, burden; fill 794.7; **stow,** store, put in storage, warehouse; **pack,** pack away; pile, dump, heap, heap up, stack, mass; bag, sack, pocket

16 **establish, fix, plant,** ensconce, **site,** pitch, seat, **set,** spot; **found, base,** ground, lay the foundation; **build,** put up, set up; build in; **install, invest,** vest, place in office, put in

17 **settle, settle down,** sit down, locate, park <nf>, ensconce, ensconce oneself; take up one's abode *or* quarters, make one's home, **reside, inhabit** 225.7; **move,** relocate, change address, establish residence, make one's home, **take up residence,** take residence at, put up *or* live *or* stay

at, quarter *or* billet at, move in, hang up one's hat <nf>; take *or* strike root, put down roots, place oneself, plant oneself, get a footing, stand, take one's stand *or* position; **anchor,** drop anchor, come to anchor, moor; **squat;** camp, bivouac; perch, roost, nest, hive, burrow; domesticate, **set up housekeeping,** keep house; **colonize,** populate, people; **set up in business,** go in business for oneself, set up shop, hang up one's shingle <nf>

ADJS **18 located, placed, sited, situated,** situate, **positioned,** installed, emplaced, spotted <nf>, **set,** seated; **stationed, posted,** deployed, assigned, positioned, prepositioned, oriented; **established,** fixed, in place, **settled,** planted, ensconced, embosomed

19 locational, positional, situational, situal, directional; **cartographic;** topographic, geographic, chorographic, geodetic; navigational; **regional** 231.8

ADVS **20 in place,** in position, in situ, in loco

21 where, whereabouts, in what place, in which place; **whither,** to what *or* which place

22 wherever, where'er, **wheresoever,** wheresoe'er, wheresomever <nf>, whithersoever, wherever it may be; **anywhere,** anyplace <nf>

23 here, hereat, in this place, just here, on the spot; **hereabouts,** hereabout, in this vicinity, near here; somewhere about *or* near; aboard, on board, with *or* among us; **hither,** hitherward, hitherwards, hereto, hereunto, hereinto, to this place

24 there, thereat, in that place, in those parts; thereabout, **thereabouts,** in that vicinity *or* neighborhood; **thither,** thitherward, thitherwards, to that place

25 here and there, in places, in various places, in spots, *passim* <L>

26 somewhere, someplace, in some place, someplace or other

27 over, all over, here and there, on *or* in, at about, round about; through, **all through, throughout** 794.17

PHR **28** X marks the spot

160 DISPLACEMENT

NOUNS **1 dislocation, displacement;** disjointing 802.1, disarticulation, unjointing, unhinging, luxation; heterotopia; **shift, removal,** forcible shift *or* removal; knocking off course; eviction; **uprooting,** ripping out, deracination; rootlessness; **disarrangement** 811; incoherence 802.1; discontinuity 813; disruption; Doppler effect *and* red shift *and* violet shift <physics>

2 dislodgment; unplacement, **unseating,** upset, unsaddling, unhorsing, unsettling; **deposal** 447; relocation, translocation, transference, transshipment

3 misplacement, mislaying, misputting, mislocation, malposition, losing

4 displaced person *or* DP, stateless person, homeless person, bag person, Wandering Jew, man without a country, exile, drifter, vagabond, deportee, repatriate; displaced *or* deported population; *déraciné* <Fr>; refugee, evacuee; outcast; waif, stray

VERBS **5 dislocate, displace, disjoint,** disarticulate, unjoint, luxate, unhinge, put *or* force *or* push out of place, **put** *or* **throw out of joint,** throw out of gear, knock *or* throw off course, disrupt; **disarrange** 811.2

6 dislodge, unplace; evict; **uproot,** root up *or* out, deracinate; relocate; depose 447.4, **unseat,** unsaddle, unsettle; **unhorse,** dismount; throw off, buck off

7 misplace, mislay, misput, lose, lose track of

ADJS **8** dislocatory, dislocating, heterotopic

9 dislocated, displaced; disjointed, unjointed, unhinged; dislodged; out, **out of joint,** out of gear; **disarranged** 810.13

10 unplaced, unestablished, unsettled; **uprooted,** deracinated; unhoused, evicted, unharbored, houseless, made homeless, homeless, stateless, exiled, outcast, expatriated; swinging in the wind

11 **misplaced, mislaid,** misput, gone missing *or* astray; **out of place,** out of one's element, like a fish out of water, in the wrong place, in the wrong box *or* pew *and* in the right church but the wrong pew <nf>
12 **eccentric, off-center,** off-balance, unbalanced, uncentered

161 DIRECTION

<compass direction or course>

NOUNS 1 **direction,** directionality; **line,** direction line, line of direction, point, quarter, **aim, way,** track, range, **bearing,** azimuth, compass reading, **heading, course;** current, set; tendency, trend, inclination, bent, tenor, run, drift; **orientation,** lay, lie, lay of the land; steering, helmsmanship, piloting; navigation 182.1,2; line of march
2 <nautical, aviation terms> vector, tack; compass direction, azimuth, compass bearing *or* heading, magnetic bearing *or* heading, relative bearing *or* heading, true bearing *or* heading *or* course; lee side, weather side 218.3
3 **points of the compass,** cardinal points, cardinal directions, half points, quarter points, degrees, compass rose; compass card, lubber line; rhumb, loxodrome; magnetic north, true north, magnetic *or* compass directions, true directions; **north,** northward, nor'; **south,** southward; **east,** eastward, orient, sunrise; **west,** westward, occident, sunset; southeast, southwest, northeast, northwest; northing, southing, easting, westing
4 **orientation, bearings;** adaptation, adjustment, accommodation, alignment, collimation; disorientation; deviation

VERBS 5 **direct, point, aim, turn, bend, train,** fix, set, determine; point to *or* at, hold on, fix on, sight on; take aim, aim at, turn *or* train upon; directionize, give a push in the right direction; locate; guide, signpost, indicate
6 **direct to,** give directions to, lead *or* conduct to, point out to, show, **show** *or* **point the way,** steer, put on the track, put on the right track, set straight, set *or* put right
7 <have or take a direction> **bear, head, turn, point, aim,** take *or* hold a heading, lead, go, steer, direct oneself, align oneself; **incline, tend, trend,** set, dispose, verge, tend to go, pilot, navigate
8 go west, wester, go east, easter, go north, go south
9 **head for,** bear for, **go for, make for,** hit *or* hit out for <nf>, **steer for,** hold for, put for, **set out** *or* **off for,** strike out for, take off for <nf>, bend one's steps for, lay for, bear up for, bear up to, make up to, set in towards; set *or* direct *or* shape one's course for, set one's compass for, sail for 182.35; align one's march; **break for,** make a break for <nf>, run *or* dash for, make a run *or* dash for
10 **go directly, go straight,** follow one's nose, go straight on, **head straight for,** vector for, go straight to the point, steer a straight course, follow a course, keep *or* hold one's course, hold steady for, arrow for, cleave to the line, keep pointed; **make a beeline,** go as the crow flies; take the air line, stay on the beam
11 **orient,** orientate, orient *or* orientate oneself, orient the map *or* chart, **take** *or* **get one's bearings,** get the lay *or* lie of the land, see which way the land lies, see which way the wind blows; adapt, adjust, accommodate

ADJS 12 **directional,** azimuthal; **direct, straight,** arrow-straight, ruler-straight, straight-ahead, straightforward, straightaway, straightway; **undeviating,** unswerving, unveering; uninterrupted, unbroken; one-way, unidirectional, irreversible
13 **directable,** aimable, pointable, trainable; **steerable,** dirigible, guidable, leadable; **directed,** guided, aimed; well-aimed *or* -directed *or* -placed, on the mark, on the nose *or* money <nf>; **directional,** directive
14 **northern,** north, northernmost, northerly, northbound, **arctic,** boreal, hyperborean; **southern,** south, southernmost, southerly,

southbound, meridional, **antarctic,** austral; **eastern,** east, easternmost *or* eastermost, easterly, eastbound, **oriental; western,** west, westernmost, westerly, westbound, **occidental; northeastern,** northeast, northeasterly; **southeastern,** southeast, southeasterly; **southwestern,** southwest, southwesterly; **northwestern,** northwest, northwesterly; cross-country, downwind, upwind; oblique, axial, parallel

ADVS **15 north,** N, nor', northerly, northward, north'ard, norward, northwards, northwardly; north about

16 south, S, southerly, southward, south'ard, southwards, southwardly; south about

17 east, E, easterly, eastward, eastwards, eastwardly, where the sun rises; eastabout

18 west, W, westerly, westernly, westward, westwards, westwardly, where the sun sets; westabout

19 northeast *or* NE, nor'east, northeasterly, northeastward, northeastwards, northeastwardly; north-northeast *or* NNE; northeast by east *or* NE by E; northeast by north *or* NE by N

20 northwest *or* NW, nor'west, northwesterly, northwestward, northwestwards, northwestwardly; north-northwest *or* NNW; northwest by west *or* NW by W; northwest by north *or* NW by N

21 southeast *or* SE, southeasterly, southeastward, southeastwards, southeastwardly; south-southeast *or* SSE; southeast by east *or* SE by E; southeast by south *or* SE by S

22 southwest *or* SW, southwesterly, southwestward, southwestwards, southwestwardly; south-southwest *or* SSW; southwest by south *or* SW by S

23 directly, direct, straight, straightly, **straightforward,** straightforwards, **undeviatingly,** unswervingly, unveeringly; **straight ahead,** dead ahead; due, dead, due north, etc; right, forthright; in a direct *or* straight line, in line with, in a line for, **in a beeline, as the crow flies,** straight across; straight as an arrow

24 clockwise, rightward 219.7; **counterclockwise,** anticlockwise, widdershins, leftward 220.6; homeward; landward; seaward; earthward; heavenward; leeward, windward 218.9

25 in every direction, in all directions, in all manner of ways, every which way <nf>, everywhither, **everyway, everywhere,** at every turn, in all directions at once, in every quarter, on every side, all over the place *or* the ballpark *or* the map <nf>; around, all round, round about; forty ways *or* six ways from Sunday <nf>; from every quarter, everywhence; from *or* to the four corners of the earth, from *or* to the four winds

26 through, by, passing by *or* through, **by way of,** by the way of, **via;** over, around, round about, here and there in, all through

162 PROGRESSION
<motion forwards>

NOUNS **1 progression, progress,** going, going forward; **ongoing,** on-go, go-ahead <nf>, onward course, rolling, rolling on; **advance,** advancing, **advancement, promotion, furtherance,** furthering, preferment; forward motion, forwarding, forwardal; **headway,** way; **leap, jump,** forward leap *or* jump, quantum jump *or* leap, leaps and bounds, spring, forward spring; progressiveness, progressivity; **passage,** course, march, career, full career; midpassage, midcourse, midcareer; travel 177; improvement 392

VERBS **2 progress, advance, proceed, go,** go *or* move forward, step forward, go on, **go ahead,** go along, push ahead, press on, pass on *or* along, roll on; move, travel; go fast 174.8; **make progress,** come on, **get along,** come along <nf>, **get ahead;** further oneself; **make headway, roll,** gather head, gather way; make strides *or* rapid strides, cover ground, get over the ground, make good time, make the best of one's way, leap *or* jump *or* spring forward, catapult oneself forward; make up for lost time, gain ground, make up leeway, make progress against, stem

3 **march on,** run on, rub on, **jog on, roll on,** flow on; drift along, go with the stream

4 **make** *or* **wend one's way, work** *or* weave one's way, worm *or* thread one's way, inch forward, feel one's way, muddle along *or* through, slog toward; go slow 175.6; carve one's way; push *or* force one's way, fight one's way, go *or* swim against the current, swim upstream; come a long way, move up in the world; **forge ahead,** drive on *or* ahead, **push** *or* **press on** *or* **onward,** push *or* press forward, push, crowd; get somewhere, reach toward, raise one's sights

5 **advance, further, promote,** forward, hasten, contribute to, boost, foster, aid, facilitate, expedite, abet

ADJS 6 **progressive,** progressing, advancing, proceeding, **ongoing,** proceeding, oncoming, onward, forward, **forward-looking,** go-ahead <nf>; moving; go-getting <nf>

ADVS 7 **in progress,** in mid-progress, in midcourse, in midcareer, in full career; **going on;** by leaps and bounds

8 **forward, forwards, onward, onwards, forth, on,** along, **ahead;** on the way to, on the road *or* high road to, en route to *or* for

163 REGRESSION

<motion backwards>

NOUNS 1 **regression,** regress; recession 168; **retrogression,** retrocession, retroflexion, retroflection, reflux, refluence, retrogradation, retroaction, retrusion, reaction; return, reentry; **setback,** backset <nf>, throwback, **rollback;** backpedalling, backward motion, backward step; sternway; **backsliding,** lapse, relapse, recidivism, recidivation; arrested development

2 **retreat,** *reculade* <Fr>, motion from, **withdrawal,** withdrawment, strategic withdrawal, exfiltration; **retirement, fallback,** pullout, pullback; advance to the rear; rout; disengagement; **backing down** *or* **off** *or* **out** <nf>; reneging, copping *or* weaseling out <nf>, resigning, resignation

3 **reverse, reversal,** reversing, reversion, inversion; **backing,** backing up, backup, backflow; **about-face,** *volte-face* <Fr>, about-turn, right-about, right-about-face, turn to the right-about, U-turn, turnaround, turnabout, swingaround; back track, back trail; turn of the tide, reflux, refluence; role reversal

4 **countermotion,** countermovement, counteraction; recoil, rebound; countermarching

VERBS 5 **regress,** go backwards, **recede,** return, revert; **retrogress,** retrograde, retroflex, retrocede; pull back, jerk back, reach back, cock <the arm, fist, etc>; *reculer pour mieux sauter* <Fr>; fall *or* get *or* go behind, fall astern, lose ground, slip back; **backslide,** lapse, relapse, recidivate; go down the tubes *or* drain <nf>

6 **retreat,** sound *or* beat a retreat, beat a hasty retreat, **withdraw, retire,** pull out *or* back, backtrack, exfiltrate, advance to the rear, disengage; **fall back,** move back, go back, stand back; run back; **draw back,** draw off; **back out** *or* **out of** *and* back off *and* back down *or* back away<nf>; defer, give ground, give place, take a back seat, play second fiddle; resign; crawfish *or* crawfish out <nf>, turn tail <nf>

7 **reverse,** go into reverse; **back, back up,** backpedal, back off *or* away, go into reverse; **backwater,** make sternway; **backtrack,** backtrail, take the back track; countermarch; reverse one's field; take the reciprocal course; have second thoughts, think better of it, cut one's losses, go back to the drawing board

8 **turn back,** put back; double, double back, retrace one's steps; turn one's back upon; **return,** go *or* come back, go *or* come home

9 **turn round** *or* **around** *or* **about,** turn, make a U-turn, turn on a dime, turn tail, **come** *or* **go about,** put about, fetch about; veer, veer around; **swivel,** pivot, pivot about, swing, round, swing round; wheel, wheel about, double wheel, whirl, spin; heel, turn upon one's heel; recoil, rebound, quail

10 **about-face,** *volte-face* <Fr>, right-about-face, **do an about-face** *or* a right-about-face *or* an about-turn, perform a *volte-face,* **face about,** turn *or* face to the right-about, do a turn to the right-about

ADJS 11 **regressive,** recessive; **retrogressive,** retrocessive, retrograde, retral; retroactive; reactionary

12 **backward, reversed,** reflex, **turned around,** back; wrong-way, wrong-way around, counter, ass-backwards *and* bassackwards <nf>

ADVS 13 **backwards,** backward, retrally, **hindwards,** hindward, **rearwards,** rearward, arear, astern; **back,** away, fro, *à reculons* <Fr>; **in reverse,** ass-backwards <nf>; against the grain, *à rebours* <Fr>; counterclockwise, anticlockwise, widdershins; vice versa

164 DEVIATION

<indirect course>

NOUNS 1 **deviation,** deviance *or* deviancy, deviousness, **departure, digression,** diversion, **divergence,** divarication, branching off, divagation, declination, aberration, aberrancy, **variation,** indirection, exorbitation; tangent, parenthesis; detour, excursion, excursus, discursion; obliquity, bias, skew, slant; **circuitousness** 914; **wandering,** rambling, **straying,** errantry, pererration; drift, drifting, driftage; turning, shifting, swerving, swinging; **turn, corner, bend, curve,** dogleg, crook, hairpin, zigzag, twist, warp, swerve, **veer,** sheer, sweep; shift, double; tack, yaw; wandering *or* twisting *or* zigzag *or* shifting course *or* path, slalom course; long way around; margin of error

2 **deflection, bending,** deflexure, flection, flexure; torsion, distortion, contortion, torture *or* torturing, twisting, warping; skewness; **refraction, diffraction, scatter,** diffusion, dispersion; sidestep, crabwalk

VERBS 3 **deviate, depart from, vary, diverge,** divaricate, branch off, angle, angle off; **digress,** divagate, turn aside, go out of the way, detour, take a side road; **swerve, veer,** sheer, curve, **shift, turn,** trend, bend, heel, bear off; turn right, turn left, hang a right *or* left <nf>; alter one's course, make a course correction, change the bearing; tack 182.30

4 **stray,** go astray, lose one's way, err; go off on a tangent; take a wrong turn *or* turning; drift, go adrift; **wander,** wander off, ramble, rove, straggle, divagate, excurse, pererrate; meander, wind, twist, snake, twist and turn; lose one's bearings

5 **deflect,** deviate, **divert,** diverge, **bend,** curve, pull, crook, dogleg, hairpin, zigzag; **warp,** bias, twist, distort, contort, torture, skew; refract, diffract, **scatter, diffuse, disperse;** put rudder on

6 **avoid, evade, dodge,** duck <nf>, turn aside *or* to the side, draw aside, **turn away,** jib, shy, shy off; gee, haw; **sidetrack,** shove aside, shunt, switch; **avert; head off,** turn back 908.3; **step aside,** sidestep, move aside *or* to the side, sidle; **steer clear of,** make way for, get out of the way of; go off, bear off, sheer off, veer off, ease off, edge off; fly off, go *or* fly off at a tangent; glance, glance off

ADJS 7 **deviative,** deviatory, deviating, **deviant,** departing, aberrant, aberrational, aberrative, shifting, turning, swerving, veering; **digressive,** discursive, excursive, **circuitous; devious,** indirect, out-of-the-way; errant, erratic, zigzag, doglegged, **wandering,** rambling, roving, winding, twisting, meandering, snaky, serpentine, mazy, labyrinthine, vagrant, stray, desultory, planetary, undirected; out of sync <nf>; off-message

8 **deflective,** inflective, flectional, diffractive, refractive; refractile, refrangible; deflected, flexed, refracted, diffracted, scattered, diffuse, diffused, dispersed; distorted, skewed, skew; off-course, off-target, wide of the mark

9 **avertive, evasive,** dodging, dodgy, artful

165 LEADING

<going ahead>

NOUNS **1** **leading, heading,** foregoing; anteposition, the lead, *le pas* <Fr>; **preceding,** precedence 814; priority 834.1; front, point, leading edge, cutting edge, forefront, vanguard, bleeding edge, van 216.2; vaunt-courier , herald, precursor 816

VERBS **2** **lead, head,** spearhead, stand at the head, stand first, be way ahead <nf>, head the line; take the lead, go in the lead, **lead the way,** break the trail, be the bellwether, lead the pack; be the point *or* point man; lead the dance; **light the way,** show the way, beacon, guide; get before, get ahead *or* in front of, come to the front, come to the fore, lap, outstrip, pace, set the pace; not look back; get *or* have the start, get a head start, steal a march upon; **precede** 814.2, **go before** 816.3

ADJS **3** **leading, heading,** precessional, precedent, precursory, foregoing; **first, foremost,** headmost; **preceding,** antecedent 814.4; **prior** 834.4; **chief** 249.14

ADVS **4** **before** 814.6, in front, out in front, in the lead, outfront, foremost, headmost, in the the van, in the forefront, in advance 216.12

166 FOLLOWING

<going behind>

NOUNS **1** **following,** heeling, **trailing,** tailing <nf>, shadowing; **hounding, dogging,** chasing, **pursuit,** pursual, pursuance; sequence 815; sequel 817; series 812.2

2 **follower,** successor; shadow *and* tail <nf>; **pursuer,** pursuivant; **attendant** 769.4, **satellite, hanger-on,** dangler, adherent, appendage, dependent, parasite, stooge <nf>, flunky; **henchman,** ward heeler, partisan, supporter, votary, sectary; camp follower, groupy <nf>; fan *and* buff <nf>; courtier, *homme de cour* <Fr>, *cavaliere servente* <Ital>; trainbearer; **public; entourage, following** 769.6; disciple 572.2, discipleship

VERBS **3** **follow,** go after *or* behind, come after *or* behind, move behind; **pursue, shadow** *and* **tail** <nf>, **trail,** trail after, follow in the trail of, camp on the trail of, **heel,** follow *or* tread *or* step on the heels of, follow in the steps *or* footsteps *or* footprints of, tread close upon, breathe down the neck of, follow in the wake of, hang on the skirts of, stick like the shadow of, sit on the tail of, tailgate <nf>, go in the rear of, bring up the rear, eat the dust of, take *or* swallow one's dust; tag *and* **tag after** *and* tag along <nf>; string along <nf>; **dog,** bedog, **hound,** chase, chase after, get after, take out *or* take off after, **pursue;** haunt

4 **lag, lag behind, straggle,** lag back, drag, trail, **trail behind,** hang back *or* behind, loiter, linger, **loiter** *or* **linger behind,** dawdle, get behind, fall behind *or* behindhand, let grass grow under one's feet

ADJS **5** **following,** trailing, on the track *or* trail; succeeding 815.4; back-to-back <nf>, consequent, consecutive 812.9

ADVS **6** **behind, after,** in the rear, in the train *or* wake of; in back of 217.13

167 APPROACH

<motion towards>

NOUNS **1** **approach,** approaching, coming *or* going toward, coming *or* going near, proximation, appropinquation , **access,** accession, nearing; advance, oncoming; **advent, coming,** forthcoming; flowing toward, afflux, affluxion; appulse; nearness 223; imminence 840; approximation 223.1; approach shot

2 **approachability, accessibility, access,** getatableness *and* come-at-ableness <nf>, attainability, openness

VERBS 3 **approach, near, draw near** *or* nigh, go *or* come near, go *or* come toward, come closer *or* nearer, come to close quarters; **close,** close in, close in on, close with; zoom in on; **accost,** encounter, confront; proximate, appropinquate ; **advance,** come, **come forward,** come on, come up, bear up, bear down, step up; ease *or* edge *or* sidle up to; bear down on *or* upon, be on a collision course with; gain upon, narrow the gap; approximate 784.7/223.8

ADJS 4 **approaching, nearing,** advancing; attracted to, drawn to; **coming, oncoming, forthcoming,** upcoming, to come, provenient; approximate, proximate, approximative; prospective; near 223.14; imminent 840.3

5 **approachable, accessible,** getatable *and* come-at-able <nf>, attainable, open, easy to find, meet, etc

168 RECESSION

<motion from>

NOUNS 1 **recession,** recedence, receding, retrocedence, ceding; **retreat, retirement, withdrawing, withdrawal;** retraction, retractation, retractility; fleetingness, fugitiveness, fugitivity, evanescence; ebb

VERBS 2 **recede,** retrocede, cede; **retreat, retire, withdraw;** move off *or* away, stand off *or* away, stand out from the shore; go, **go away; die away,** fade away, drift away; erode, wash away; **diminish,** decline, sink, shrink, dwindle, **fade, ebb,** wane; shy away, tail away, tail off; go out with the tide, fade into the distance; pull away, widen the distance

3 **retract,** withdraw, **draw** *or* **pull back,** pull out, draw *or* pull in; draw in one's claws *or* horns; defer, take a back seat, play second fiddle, back-pedal; **shrink,** wince, cringe, flinch, shy, fight shy, duck

ADJS 4 **recessive,** recessional, recessionary; recedent, retrocedent

5 **receding, retreating,** retiring, withdrawing; shy; **diminishing, declining,** sinking, shrinking, eroding, dwindling, **ebbing,** waning; **fading,** dying; fleeting, fugitive, evanescent

6 **retractile,** retractable, retrahent

169 CONVERGENCE

<coming together>

NOUNS 1 **convergence,** converging, confluence, concourse, conflux; mutual approach, approach 167; **meeting,** congress, concurrence, coming together; **concentration,** concentralization, focalization 208.8, focus 208.4; meeting point, focal point, point of convergence, vanishing point; union, merger; crossing point, crossroads, crossing 170; collision course, narrowing gap; funnel, bottleneck; hub, spokes; asymptote; radius; tangent

VERBS 2 **converge, come together,** approach 167.3, run together, **meet,** unite, connect, merge; **cross, intersect** 170.6; fall in with, link up with; be on a collision course; go toward, narrow the gap, close with, close, close up, close in; funnel; taper, pinch, nip; centralize, center, **come to a center;** center on *or* around, concentralize, concenter, **concentrate,** come *or* tend to a point; **come to a focus** 208.10

ADJS 3 **converging,** convergent; **meeting,** uniting, merging; concurrent, confluent, mutually approaching, approaching; **crossing, intersecting** 170.8; connivent; **focal,** confocal, focusing, focused; centrolineal, centripetal; asymptotic, asymptotical; tangent, tangential, radial, radiating

170 CROSSING

NOUNS 1 **crossing, intercrossing,** intersecting, **intersection;** decussation, chiasma; traversal, transversion; cross section, transection; cruciation; **transit,** transiting; crisscross

2 **crossing,** crossway, **crosswalk, crossroad,** pedestrian crosswalk, zebra *or* zebra crossing <Brit>; *carrefour* <Fr>; **intersection,** intercrossing; level crossing, grade crossing; crossover, overpass, flyover <Brit>, viaduct, undercrossing; traffic circle, rotary, roundabout <Brit>; highway interchange, **interchange,** cloverleaf, spaghetti junction <Brit>

3 **network, webwork, weaving** 740, **meshwork,** tissue, crossing over and under, interlacement, intertwinement, intertexture, texture, reticulum, reticulation, plexus; crossing-out, cancellation, scrubbing <nf>; **net,** netting; **mesh,** meshes; **web,** webbing; weave, weft; lace, lacery, lacing, lacework; screen, screening; sieve, riddle, raddle; wicker, wickerwork; basketwork, basketry; lattice, latticework; hachure *or* hatchure, hatching, cross-hatching; trellis, trelliswork, treillage; grate, grating; grille, grillwork; **grid,** gridiron; tracery, fretwork, fret, arabesque, filigree; plexus, plexure; reticle, reticule; wattle, wattle and daub

4 **cross,** crux, cruciform; **crucifix,** rood, tree *or* rood tree ; X *or* ex, exing, T, Y; **swastika,** gammadion, fylfot; crossbones; dagger

5 **crosspiece,** traverse, transverse, transversal, transept, transom, cross bitt; diagonal; **crossbar,** crossarm; swingletree, singletree, whiffletree, whippletree; doubletree

VERBS **6** **cross, crisscross,** cruciate; **intersect,** intercross, decussate; **cut across,** crosscut; **traverse,** transverse, lie across; bar, crossbar

7 net, web, mesh; lattice, trellis; grate, grid

ADJS **8** **cross, crossing, crossed; crisscross, crisscrossed; intersecting, intersected,** intersectional; crosscut, cut across; decussate, decussated; chiasmal *or* chiasmic *or* chiastic; secant

9 **transverse,** transversal, traverse; **across,** cross, crossway, **crosswise** *or* crossways, thwart, athwart, overthwart; oblique 204.13

10 **cruciform, crosslike,** cross-shaped, cruciate, X-shaped, cross, crossed; cruciferous

11 **netlike,** retiform, plexiform; **reticulated,** reticular, reticulate; cancellate, cancellated; **netted,** netty; **meshed,** meshy; laced, lacy, lacelike; filigreed; latticed, latticelike; grated, gridded; barred, crossbarred, mullioned; streaked, striped

12 **webbed,** webby, weblike, woven, interwoven, interlaced, intertwined; web-footed, palmiped

ADVS **13** **crosswise** *or* crossways *or* crossway, decussatively; **cross, crisscross, across,** thwart, thwartly, thwartways, **athwart,** athwartwise, overthwart; **traverse,** traversely; **transverse,** transversely, transversally; obliquely 204.21; **sideways** *or* sidewise; contrariwise, contrawise; crossgrained, across the grain, against the grain; athwartship, athwartships

171 DIVERGENCE

<recession from one another>

NOUNS **1** **divergence** *or* divergency, divarication; aberration, deviation 164; **separation,** division, decentralization; centrifugence; **radial, radiating,** radiating out, raying out, beaming out; **spread,** spreading, spreading out, splaying, fanning, fanning out, deployment; ripple effect

2 **radiation,** ray, sunray, radius, spoke; radiance, diffusion, scattering, dispersion, emanation; halo, aureole, glory, corona; ripple effect

3 **forking,** furcation, bifurcation, biforking, trifurcation, divarication, triforking; **branching,** branching off *or* out, **ramification;** arborescence, arborization

4 **fork, prong,** trident; Y, V; **branch, ramification,** stem, offshoot; **crotch,** crutch; **fan, delta; groin,** inguen; furcula, furculum, **wishbone**

VERBS **5** **diverge,** divaricate; aberrate; **separate,** divide, separate off, split off; spread, **spread out,** outspread, splay, fan out, deploy; go off *or* away, **fly** *or* **go off at a tangent**; part company

6 **radiate,** radiate out, ray, ray out, beam out, diffuse, emanate, spread, disperse, scatter

7 **fork,** furcate, bifurcate, trifurcate, divaricate; **branch,** stem, ramify, branch off *or* out, spread-eagle

ADJS **8** **diverging,** divergent; divaricate, divaricating; palmate, palmated; fanlike, fan-shaped; deltoid, deltoidal, deltalike, delta-shaped; splayed; centrifugal

9 **radiating,** radial, radiate, radiated; rayed, spoked; radiative

10 **forked, forking,** furcate, biforked, bifurcate, bifurcated, forklike, trifurcate, trifurcated, tridentlike, pronged; **crotched,** Y-shaped, V-shaped; **branched, branching;** arborescent, arboreal, arboriform, treelike, tree-shaped, dendriform, dendritic; branchlike, ramous

172 MOTION

<motion in general>

NOUNS **1** **motion; movement,** moving, **momentum; stir,** unrest, restlessness; **going,** running, stirring; **operation,** operating, **working,** ticking; **activity** 330; kinesis, kinetics, kinematics; dynamics; kinesiatrics, kinesipathy, kinesitherapy, kinesiology; **actuation,** motivation; mobilization

2 **course, career,** set, midcareer, **passage, progress,** trend, **advance,** forward motion, going *or* moving on, momentum; **travel** 177; **flow,** flux, flight, **trajectory; stream, current,** run, rush, onrush, ongoing; drift, driftage; backward motion, **regression,** retrogression, sternway, backing, going *or* moving backwards; backflowing, reflowing, refluence, reflux, ebbing, subsiding, withdrawing; downward motion, **descent,** descending, sinking, plunging; upward motion, mounting, climbing, rising, **ascent,** ascending, **soaring,** mounting; oblique *or* crosswise motion; sideward *or* sidewise *or* sideways motion; radial motion, angular motion, axial motion; random motion, Brownian movement; perpetual motion

3 **mobility, motivity,** motility, movableness, movability; **locomotion;** motive power

4 **velocity** 174.1,2, rate, gait, pace, tread, step, stride, clip *and* lick <nf>

VERBS **5** **move, budge, stir;** go, run, flow, stream; **progress,** advance; wend, wend one's way; **back,** back up, regress, retrogress; ebb, subside, wane; **descend,** sink, plunge; **ascend,** mount, rise, climb, soar; go sideways, go crabwise; go round *or* around, circle, rotate, gyrate, spin, whirl; travel; move over, get over; shift, change, shift *or* change place; **speed** 174.8; **hurry** 401.5, do on the fly *or* run

6 **set in motion, move, actuate,** motivate, push, shove, nudge, **drive,** impel, propel; mobilize; dispatch; muster

ADJS **7** **moving, stirring, in motion;** transitional; **mobile,** motive, motile, motor, motorial, motoric; motivational, impelling, propelling, propellant, driving, self-propelled; traveling; **active** 330.17

8 **flowing,** fluent, passing, streaming, flying, **running, going, progressive,** rushing, onrushing; drifting; **regressive,** retrogressive, back, **backward;** back-flowing, refluent, reflowing; descending, sinking, plunging, **downward,** down-trending; ascending, mounting, rising, soaring, **upward,** up-trending; sideward, sidewise, sideways; **rotary,** rotatory, rotational, round-and-round; axial, gyrational, gyratory

ADVS **9** **under way,** under sail, on one's way, on the go *or* move *or* fly *or* run *or* march, **in motion, astir;** from pillar to post

173 QUIESCENCE

<being at rest; absence of motion>

NOUNS **1** **quiescence,** *or* quiescency, **stillness,** silence 51, quietness,

quiet, quietude; **calmness,** restfulness, **peacefulness,** imperturbability, passiveness, passivity, placidness, **placidity, tranquillity, serenity, peace, composure;** quietism, contemplation, satori, nirvana, samadhi, ataraxy *or* ataraxia; **rest, repose,** silken repose, statuelike *or* marmoreal repose; sleep, slumber 22.2

2 **motionlessness, immobility; inactivity, inaction;** fixity, fixation 855.2

3 **standstill, stand,** stillstand; **stop, halt, cessation** 857; dead stop, dead stand, full stop; deadlock, lock, dead set; gridlock, stalemate, stoppage; freeze, strike; running *or* dying down, subsidence, waning, ebbing, wane, ebb

4 **inertness, dormancy; inertia,** *vis inertiae* <L>; passiveness, passivity; suspense, abeyance, latency; torpor, apathy, indifference, indolence, lotus-eating, languor; **stagnation,** stagnancy, **vegetation;** estivation, hibernation; stasis; sloth; deathliness, deadliness; catalepsy, catatonia; entropy

5 **calm, lull,** lull *or* calm before the storm; dead calm, flat calm, oily calm, windlessness, deathlike calm; doldrums, horse latitudes; anticyclone, eye of the hurricane

6 **stuffiness, airlessness, closeness, oppressiveness,** stirlessness, oppression

VERBS 7 **be still, keep quiet,** lie still; **stop moving,** cease motion, freeze *or* seize up, come to a standstill; **rest, repose; remain, stay,** tarry; remain motionless, freeze <nf>; stand, **stand still,** be at a standstill; stand *or* stick fast, stick, stand firm, stay put <nf>; stand like a post; **not stir,** not stir a step, not move a muscle; not breathe, hold one's breath; bide, bide one's time, mark time, tread water, coast; rest on one's oars, put one's feet up, rest and be thankful

8 **quiet,** quieten, **lull, soothe,** quiesce, **calm,** calm down, tranquilize 670.7, pacify, passivize, assuage, pour oil on troubled waters; **stop** 857.7, halt, bring to a standstill; **cease** 857.6, wane, subside, ebb, run *or* die down, die off, dwindle, molder

9 **stagnate, vegetate,** fust ; estivate, hibernate; sleep, slumber; smolder, hang fire; **idle**

10 **sit,** set <nf>, **sit down, be seated,** remain seated, remain in situ; perch, roost

11 **becalm,** take the wind out of one's sails

ADJS 12 **quiescent, quiet, still,** stilly , stillish, hushed; quiet as a mouse; waning, subsiding, ebbing, dwindling, moldering; **at rest,** resting, reposing; restful, reposeful, relaxed, sedentary; cloistered, sequestered, sequestrated, isolated, secluded, sheltered; **calm, tranquil, peaceful,** peaceable, pacific, halcyon; **placid, smooth; unruffled, untroubled,** cool, undisturbed, unperturbed, unagitated, unmoved, unstirring, laidback <nf>; stolid, stoic, stoical, impassive; even-tenored; calm as a mill pond; still as death

13 **motionless, unmoving,** unmoved, moveless, **immobile,** immotive; **still, fixed, stationary, static,** at a standstill; **stock-still,** dead-still; still as a statue, statuelike; still as a mouse; at anchor, riding at anchor; **idle,** unemployed; out of commission, down

14 **inert, inactive, static, dormant,** passive, sedentary; **latent,** unaroused, suspended, abeyant, in suspense *or* abeyance; sleeping, slumbering; estivating, hibernating; smoldering; **stagnant,** standing, foul; **torpid, languorous, languid,** apathetic, phlegmatic, **sluggish,** logy, dopey <nf>, groggy, heavy, leaden, **dull,** flat, slack, tame, **dead,** lifeless; catatonic, cataleptic

15 **untraveled, stay-at-home,** stick-in-the-mud <nf>, home-keeping

16 **stuffy, airless,** breathless, breezeless, windless; **close, oppressive, stifling, suffocating;** stirless, unstirring, not a breath of air, not a leaf stirring; ill-ventilated, unventilated, unvented

17 **becalmed,** in a dead calm

ADVS **18** quiescently, **quietly,** stilly, still; **calmly, tranquilly, peacefully,** serenely; **placidly,** smoothly, unperturbedly, **coolly**

19 **motionlessly,** movelessly, stationarily, fixedly

20 **inertly, inactively,** statically, dormantly, passively, latently; stagnantly; **torpidly, languorously, languidly; like a bump on a log; sluggishly,** heavily, dully, coldly, lifelessly, apathetically, phlegmatically; stoically, stolidly, impassively

174 SWIFTNESS

NOUNS **1** **velocity, speed; rapidity,** celerity, **swiftness,** fastness, **quickness,** snappiness <nf>, **speediness;** haste 401.1, hurry, flurry, rush, precipitation; **dispatch, expedition, promptness,** promptitude, instantaneousness; flight, flit; lightning speed; fast *or* swift rate, smart *or* rattling *or* spanking *or* lively *or* snappy pace, round pace; relative velocity, angular velocity; air speed, ground speed, speed over the bottom; miles per hour, knots; rpm 915.3; momentum

2 **speed of sound, sonic speed,** Mach, Mach number, Mach one, Mach two, etc; subsonic speed; supersonic *or* ultrasonic *or* hypersonic *or* transsonic speed; transsonic barrier, sound barrier; escape velocity; speed of light, terminal velocity; warp speed, lightning speed; turbulent flow

3 **run, sprint; dash, rush,** plunge, headlong rush *or* plunge, **race, scurry, scamper,** scud, scuttle, **spurt,** burst, **burst of speed;** canter, **gallop,** lope; high lope, hand gallop, full gallop; dead run; **trot,** extended trot, dogtrot, jog trot; **full speed,** open throttle, flat-out speed <Brit>, wide-open speed, heavy right foot, maximum speed; **fast-forward;** fast track *or* lane; forced draft *and* flank speed <nautical>

4 **acceleration, quickening; pickup,** getaway; burst of speed; step-up, speedup; thrust, drive, impetus, kick-start; free fall; flying start; headlong plunge; overtaking; zip *or* zing <nf>

5 **speeder,** speedster, scorcher *and* hell-driver <nf>, **sprinter**, harrier**;** flier, goer, stepper; hummer *and* hustler *and* sizzler <nf>; **speed demon** *or* maniac <nf>**; racer, runner;** horse racer, turfman, jockey; Jehu; express messenger, courier

6 <comparisons> lightning, greased lightning <nf>, thunderbolt, flash, streak of lightning, streak, blue streak <nf>, bat out of hell <nf>, light, electricity, thought, wind, shot, bullet, cannonball, rocket, arrow, dart, quicksilver, mercury, express train, jet plane, torrent, eagle, swallow, antelope, courser, gazelle, greyhound, hare, blue darter, striped snake, scared rabbit

7 **speedometer,** accelerometer; cyclometer; tachometer; Mach meter; knotmeter, log, log line, patent log, taffrail log, harpoon log, ground log; windsock; wind gauge, anemometer

VERBS **8** **speed, go fast,** skim, **fly,** flit, fleet, wing one's way, outstrip the wind; **zoom;** make knots, foot; break the sound barrier, go at warp speed; go like the wind, go like a shot *or* flash, go like lightning *or* a streak of lightning, go like greased lightning; **rush, tear,** dash, dart, shoot, hurtle, bolt, fling, **scamper, scurry,** scour, scud, scuttle, scramble, **race,** careen; **hasten,** haste, make haste, **hurry** 401.4, hie, post, kick-start; march in quick *or* double-quick time; **run, sprint, trip,** spring, **bound,** leap; gallop, lope, canter; trot; **make time,** make good time, **cover ground,** get over the ground, **make strides** *or* **rapid strides,** make the best of one's way

9 <nf terms> **barrel,** clip, spank *or* cut along, tear *or* tear along *or* off, bowl along, thunder along, storm along, breeze *or* breeze along, tear up the track *or* road, eat up the track *or* road, scorch, sizzle, rip, zip, whiz, whisk, sweep, brush, nip, zing, fly low, highball, ball the jack, pour it on, boom, shake *or* get the lead out, lollop <Brit>, give it the gun, skedaddle, scoot, step on it, step on the gas, hump *or* hump it, stir one's stumps, hotfoot, hightail, make tracks, step lively, step, step along, carry the mail, hop, hop along, hop it, get, git, go like a bat out of hell, run like a scared rabbit, run like mad, go at full blast, go all out, go flat out, run wide open, go at full tilt *or* steam, let her out, open her up, go hell-bent for election *or* leather, get a move on, give it the gas, go like blazes *or* blue blazes, floor it, let her rip, put the pedal to the metal, tool

10 **accelerate, speed up, step up** <nf>, **hurry up, quicken; hasten** 401.4; crack on, put on, put on steam, pour on the coal, put on more speed, open the throttle; quicken one's pace; pick up speed, gain ground; race <a motor>, rev <nf>

11 <nautical terms> put on sail, crack *or* pack on sail, crowd sail, press her

12 **spurt,** make a spurt *or* dash, **dash** *or* dart *or* shoot ahead, rush ahead, put on *or* make a burst of speed; make one's move, plunge

13 **overtake, outstrip, overhaul,** catch up, **catch up with,** come up with *or* to, gain on *or* upon, pass, lap; outpace, outrun, outsail; leave behind, leave standing *or* looking *or* flat-footed; overwhelm

14 **keep up with,** keep pace with, run neck and neck

ADJS 15 **fast, swift, speedy, rapid; quick,** double-quick, express, **fleet, hasty, expeditious,** hustling, snappy <nf>, rushing, onrushing, dashing, flying, galloping, running, **agile, nimble,** lively, nimble-footed, fleet-footed, light-footed, light-legged, light of heel; winged, eagle-winged; mercurial; quick as lightning, quick as thought, swift as an arrow; **breakneck,** reckless, headlong, precipitate; quick as a wink, quick on the trigger <nf>, hair-trigger <nf>; **prompt** 845.9; rapid-response

16 **supersonic,** transonic, ultrasonic, hypersonic, faster than sound; warp; **high-speed,** high-velocity, high-geared

ADVS 17 **swiftly, rapidly, quickly,** snappily <nf>, **speedily,** with speed, **fast, quick,** apace, amain, on eagle's wings, *ventre à terre* <Fr>; at a great rate, at a good clip <nf>, with rapid strides, with giant strides, *à pas de géant* <Fr>, in seven-league boots, **by leaps and bounds,** trippingly; **lickety-split** *and* lickety-cut <nf>; hell-bent *and* hell-bent for election *and* hell-bent for leather <nf>; **posthaste,** post, **hastily,** expeditiously, promptly, with great *or* all haste, whip and spur, **hand over hand** *or* **fist;** double-quick, in double time, in double-quick time, on the double *or* the double-quick <nf>; in high gear, in high; under press of sail, all sails set, under crowded sails, under press of sail and steam, under forced draft, at flank speed <all nautical>

18 <nf terms> **like a shot, as if shot out of a cannon, like a flash,** like a streak, like a blue streak, like a streak of lightning, like lightning, like greased lightning, **like a bat out of hell, like a scared rabbit,** like a house afire, like sixty, like mad *and* **crazy** *and* fury, like sin, to beat the band *or* the Dutch *or* the deuce *or* the devil

19 **in short order, in no time,** instantaneously, immediately if not sooner, in less than no time, in nothing flat <nf>; in a jiff *or* jiffy <nf>, before you can say Jack Robinson, **in a flash,** in a twink, **in a twinkling,** *tout de suite* <Fr>, pronto <nf>, PDQ *or* pretty damn quick <nf>

20 **at full speed,** with all speed, at full throttle, **at the top of one's bent, for all one is worth** <nf>, hit the ground running <nf>, as fast as one's legs will carry one, as fast as one can lay feet to the ground; **at full blast,** at full drive *or* pelt; under full steam, in full sail; **all out** <nf>, flat out <Brit>, **wide open;** full speed ahead

175 SLOWNESS

NOUNS 1 **slowness, leisureliness,** pokiness, slackness, creeping, no hurry; **sluggishness,** sloth, torpor, laziness, idleness, indolence, sluggardy, languor, inertia, inertness, lentitude *or* lentor ; deliberateness, deliberation, circumspection, tentativeness, cautiousness, reluctance, foot-dragging <nf>; drawl; gradualism; hesitation, slow start

2 **slow motion, leisurely gait,** snail's *or* tortoise's pace; **creep, crawl; walk,** footpace, dragging *or* lumbering pace, trudge, waddle, saunter, stroll; slouch, shuffle, plod, shamble; limp, claudication, hobble; dogtrot, jog trot; jog, rack; mincing steps; slow march, dead *or* funeral march, largo, andante

3 **dawdling, lingering, loitering, tarrying,** dalliance, **dallying,** dillydallying, shillyshallying, lollygagging, dilatoriness, delaying tactic, delayed action, procrastination 846.5, lag, **lagging,** goofing off <nf>; tardiness, unhurriedness

4 **slowing, retardation,** retardment, **slackening,** flagging, slowing down *or* up; **slowdown,** slowup, **letup, letdown, slack-up, slack-off,** ease-off, ease-up; **deceleration,** negative *or* minus acceleration; **delay** 846.2, **detention, setback, holdup** <nf>, check, arrest, brake, obstruction; lag, drag

5 **slowpoke** *and* slowcoach <nf>, plodder, slow goer, slow-foot, **lingerer, loiterer, dawdler,** dawdle, **laggard,** procrastinator, foot-dragger, lollygagger, stick-in-the-mud <nf>, drone, slug, sluggard, lie-abed, sleepy-head, slow starter, goof-off <nf>, goldbrick <nf>; tortoise, snail; lardass <nf>; Sunday driver

VERBS 6 **go slow** *or* **slowly,** go at a snail's pace, take it slow, get no place fast <nf>; **drag,** drag out; **creep, crawl;** laze, idle; go dead slow, get nowhere fast; inch, inch along; worm, worm along; poke, **poke along;** shuffle *or* stagger *or* totter *or* toddle along *or* toddle off; drag along, drag one's feet, walk, traipse *and* **mosey** <nf>; **saunter, stroll, amble,** waddle, toddle <nf>; jogtrot, dogtrot; limp, hobble, claudicate; *festina lente* <L>

7 **plod,** plug <nf>, peg, shamble, **trudge,** tramp, stump, lumber; plod along, plug along <nf>, schlep <nf>; rub on, jog on, chug on

8 **dawdle, linger, loiter, tarry, delay, dally, dillydally,** shilly-shally, lollygag, waste time, **take one's time,** take one's own sweet time; goof off *or* around <nf>; lag, drag, trail; flag, falter, halt, not get started

9 **slow, slow down** *or* **up, let down** *or* **up, ease off** *or* **up, slack off** *or* **up, slacken,** relax, moderate, taper off, lose speed *or* momentum; **decelerate, retard, delay** 846.8, **detain,** impede, obstruct, arrest, stay, **check,** curb, **hold up, hold back,** keep back, set back, hold in check; draw rein, rein in; throttle down, take one's foot off the gas; idle, barely tick over; brake, **put on the brakes,** put on the drag; reef, take in sail; backwater, backpedal; lose ground; clip the wings; regress

ADJS 10 **slow, leisurely,** slack, moderate, gentle, **easy,** deliberate, go-slow, unhurried, relaxed, gradual, circumspect, tentative, cautious, reluctant, foot-dragging <nf>; **creeping, crawling; poking,** poky, slow-poky <nf>; tottering, staggering, toddling, trudging, **lumbering,** ambling, waddling, shuffling, **sauntering,** strolling; **sluggish,** languid, languorous, lazy, slothful, indolent, idle, slouchy; **slow-going, slow-moving,** slow-creeping, slow-crawling, slow-running, slow-sailing; **slow-footed,** slow-foot, slow-legged, slow-gaited, slow-paced, slow-stepped, easy-paced, slow-winged; snail-paced, snail-like, tortoiselike, turtlelike; limping, hobbling, hobbled; halting, claudicant; faltering, flagging; slow as slow, slow as molasses *or* molasses in January, slow as death, slower than the seven-year itch <nf>

11 **dawdling, lingering, loitering, tarrying, dallying, dillydallying,** shilly-shallying, lollygagging, procrastinatory *or* procrastinative, dilatory, delaying 846.17, **lagging,** dragging

12 **retarded,** slowed-down, eased, slackened; **delayed, detained,** checked, **arrested,** impeded, set back, backward, behind; late, **tardy** 846.16

ADVS **13** **slowly,** slow, **leisurely,** unhurriedly, relaxedly, easily, moderately, gently; creepingly, crawlingly; pokingly, pokily; **sluggishly,** languidly, languorously, lazily, indolently, idly, deliberately, with deliberation, circumspectly, tentatively, cautiously, reluctantly; **lingeringly,** loiteringly, tarryingly, dilatorily; limpingly, haltingly, falteringly; **in slow motion,** at a funeral pace, with faltering *or* halting steps; at a snail's *or* turtle's pace; in slow tempo, in march time; with agonizing slowness; in low gear, under easy sail

14 **gradually,** little by little 245.6

PHRS **15** **easy does it,** take it easy, go easy, slack off, slow down

176 TRANSFERAL, TRANSPORTATION

1 **transferal, transfer; transmission,** transference, transmittal, transmittance; transposition, transposal, transplacement; mutual transfer, interchange, metathesis; translocation, **transplantation,** translation; migration, transmigration; **import, importation; export, exportation;** deportation, extradition, expulsion, **transit,** transition, **passage; communication,** spread, spreading, dissemination, diffusion, contagion, ripple effect; metastasis; transmigration of souls, metempsychosis; passing over; osmosis, diapedesis; transduction, conduction, convection; transfusion, perfusion; transfer of property or right 629

2 transferability, conveyability; transmissibility, transmittability; movability, removability; **portability,** transportability; communicability, impartability; deliverability; carrying forward

3 **transportation, conveyance, transport, carrying,** bearing, packing, toting *and* lugging <nf>; **carriage,** carry, **hauling,** haulage, portage, porterage, waft, waftage; **cartage, truckage,** drayage, wagonage; ferriage, lighterage; telpherage; **freightage,** freight, expressage, railway express; **airfreight, air express,** airlift; **package freight,** package service; **shipment, shipping,** transshipment; containerization, cargo-handling; delivery 478.1; travel 177; expressage; public transportation

4 **moving, removal, movement,** relocation, shift, removement, remotion; **displacement,** delocalization

5 people mover, moving sidewalk, automated monorail; conveyor belt; **elevator**, lift <Brit>, escalator 912.4

6 **freight,** freightage; **shipment, consignment,** goods <Brit>; **cargo,** payload; lading, load, pack; **baggage, luggage,** impedimenta

7 **carrier, conveyer;** transporter, hauler, carter, wagoner, drayman, shipper, trucker, common carrier, truck driver, driver; freighter; containerizer; stevedore, cargo handler; expressman, express, messenger, courier; importer, exporter; **bearer, porter,** redcap, skycap, bell boy; bus boy; coolie; litter-bearer, stretcher-bearer; caddie; shield-bearer, gun bearer; water carrier *or* bearer, water boy, bheesty <India>; the Water Bearer, Aquarius; letter carrier 353.5; cupbearer, Ganymede, Hebe; carrier pigeon, homing pigeon

8 **beast of burden; pack** *or* **draft animal,** pack horse *or* mule, sumpter, sumpter horse *or* mule; **horse** 311.13, ass, mule; ox; camel, ship of the desert, dromedary, llama; reindeer; elephant; sledge dog, husky, malamute, Siberian husky

9 <geological terms> **deposit,** sediment; drift, silt, loess, moraine, scree, sinter; alluvium, alluvion, diluvium; detritus, debris

VERBS **10** **transfer, transmit, transpose,** translocate, transplace, metathesize, switch; **transplant,** translate; **pass,** pass over, **hand over,** turn over, carry over, carry forward, make over, consign, assign; **deliver** 478.13; pass on, pass the buck <nf>, hand forward, hand on, relay; **import, export;** deport, extradite, expel; communicate, diffuse, disseminate, spread, impart; expedite; transfuse, perfuse, transfer property or right 629

11 **remove, move, relocate, shift,** send, shunt; displace, delocalize, dislodge; **take away,** cart off *or* away, carry off *or* away; manhandle; set *or* lay *or* put aside, put *or* set to one side, side

12 **transport, convey,** freight, conduct, **take; carry, bear,** pack, tote *and* lug <nf>, manhandle; lift, waft, whisk, wing, fly; schlep <nf>

13 **haul, cart,** truck, bus; **ship,** barge, lighter, ferry; raft, float

14 **channel,** put through channels; **pipe,** tube, pipeline, flume, **siphon, funnel,** tap

15 **send,** send off *or* away, send forth; **dispatch,** transmit, remit, consign, forward; expedite; **ship,** ship off, freight, airfreight, embark, containerize, **transship,** pass along, send on; **express,** air-express; express-mail; package-express; **post, mail,** airmail, drop a letter; messenger; export; e-mail; drop-ship

16 **fetch, bring, go get,** go and get, go to get, **go after,** go fetch, **go for,** call for, pick up; **get,** obtain, procure, secure; **bring back, retrieve;** chase after, run after, shag, fetch and carry

17 **ladle, dip, scoop; bail,** bucket; **dish,** dish out *or* up; cup; **shovel,** spade, fork; spoon; **pour,** decant

ADJS **18** **transferable, conveyable; transmittable,** transmissible, transmissive, consignable, deliverable; **movable,** removable; **portable,** portative; transportable, transportative, transportive, carriageable; roadworthy, seaworthy, airworthy; importable, exportable; conductive, conductional; transposable, interchangeable; **communicable,** contagious, impartable; transfusable; metastatic *or* metastatical, metathetic *or* metathetical; mailable, expressable; assignable 629.5

ADVS **19** by transfer, from hand to hand, from door to door; by freight, by express, by rail, by trolley, by bus, by steamer, by airplane, by mail, by special delivery, by package express, by messenger, by hand; by e-mail

20 **on the way,** along the way, on the road *or* high road, **en route, in transit,** *in transitu* <L>, on the wing, as one goes; in passing, *en passant* <Fr>; in mid-progress

177 TRAVEL

NOUNS **1** **travel,** traveling, going, journeying, touring, moving, **movement, motion, locomotion, transit, progress, passage,** course, crossing; commutation, straphanging; world travel, globe-trotting <nf>; junketing, jaunting; **tourism,** touristry

2 **travels,** journeys, **journeyings, wanderings,** voyagings, transits, peregrinations, peripatetics, migrations, transmigrations; odyssey

3 **wandering, roving, roaming, rambling, gadding,** traipsing <nf>, wayfaring, flitting, straying, drifting, gallivanting, peregrination, peregrinity, pilgrimage, errantry, divagation; roam, rove, ramble; **itinerancy,** itineracy; **nomadism,** nomadization, gypsydom; vagabonding, vagabondism, vagabondage; **vagrancy,** hoboism, waltzing Matilda; bumming <nf>; the open road; wanderyear, *Wanderjahr* <Ger>; **wanderlust**

4 **migration, transmigration,** passage, trek; run <of fish>, flight <of birds and insects>; swarm, swarming <of bees>; **immigration,** in-migration; **emigration,** out-migration, expatriation; remigration; intermigration

5 **journey, trip,** *jornada* <Sp>, peregrination, sally, **trek;** road trip; progress, course, run; **tour,** grand tour; tourist season, low season, high season; tourist class; travel agency *or* bureau, holiday company <chiefly Brit>; **conducted tour,** package tour *or* holiday; **excursion, jaunt, junket, outing,** pleasure trip; sightseeing trip *or* tour, rubberneck tour <nf>; day-trip; round trip, circuit, turn; **cruise,** package cruise, cruise to nowhere; **expedition,** campaign; safari, hunting expedition, hunting trip, stalk, shoot, photography safari; **pilgrimage,** hajj; **voyage** 182.6

6 **riding, driving; motoring,** automobiling; busing; motorcycling, bicycling, cycling, pedaling, biking <nf>; **horseback riding,** horse-riding, equitation; horsemanship, manège; pony-trekking

7 **ride, drive;** spin *and* whirl <nf>; joyride <nf>; Sunday drive; airing; lift <nf>, pickup <nf>

8 **walking,** ambulation, perambulation, pedestrianism, shank's mare *or* pony <nf>, going on foot *or* afoot, footing *or* hoofing, footing it *or* hoofing it; strolling, sauntering, ambling, *flânerie* <Fr>; **tramping, marching, hiking,** backpacking, trail-hiking, footslogging, trudging, treading; lumbering, waddling; toddling, staggering, tottering; **hitchhiking** *and* hitching <nf>, thumbing *and* thumbing a ride <nf>; jaywalking

9 **nightwalking,** noctambulation, noctambulism; night-wandering, noctivagation; **sleepwalking,** somnambulation, somnambulism; sleepwalk

10 **walk,** ramble, amble, **hike, tramp,** traipse <nf>; slog, trudge, schlep <nf>; **stroll,** saunter; **promenade**; jaunt, airing; **constitutional** <nf>, stretch; turn; peripatetic journey *or* exercise, peripateticism; walking tour *or* excursion; **march,** forced march, route march; parade

11 **step, pace, stride; footstep,** footfall, tread; hoofbeat, clop; hop, jump; skip, hippety-hop <nf>

12 **gait, pace, walk, step, stride, tread;** saunter, stroll, strolling gait; shuffle, shamble, hobble, limp, hitch, waddle; totter, stagger, lurch; toddle, paddle; slouch, droop, drag; mince, mincing steps, scuttle, prance, flounce, stalk, strut, swagger; slink, slither, sidle; jog; swing, roll; amble, single-foot, rack, piaffer; trot, gallop 174.3; lock step; velocity 174.1,2; slowness 175

13 **march;** quick *or* quickstep march, quickstep, quick time; lockstep; double march, double-quick, double time; slow march, slow time; half step; goose step

14 **leg, limb, shank;** hind leg, foreleg; gamb, jamb <heraldry>; shin, cnemis; ankle, tarsus; hock, gambrel; calf; knee; thigh; popliteal space, ham, drumstick; gigot

15 <nf terms> gams, stems, trotters, hind legs, underpinnings, wheels, shanks, sticks, pins, stumps

16 **gliding, sliding,** slipping, slithering, coasting, sweeping, flowing, sailing; **skating, skiing, tobogganing, sledding,** boarding; glide, slide, slither, sweep, skim, flow

17 **creeping, crawling,** going on all fours; sneaking, stealing, slinking, sidling, gumshoeing *and* pussyfooting <nf>, walking on eggs, padding, prowling, nightwalking; worming, snaking; tiptoeing, tiptoe, tippytoe; creep, crawl, scramble, scrabble; all fours

VERBS 18 **travel, go, move, pass,** fare, wayfare, fare forth, fetch, flit, hie, sashay <nf>, cover ground; **progress** 162.2; move on *or* along, go along; wend, **wend one's way;** betake oneself, direct one's course, bend one's steps *or* course; course, run, flow, stream; roll, roll on; commute, straphang

19 <go at a given speed> **go, go at,** reach, **make, do,** hit <nf>, clip off <nf>

20 **traverse, cross, travel over** *or* through, pass through, **go** *or* **pass over, cover,** measure, transit, track, range, range over *or* through, course, do, perambulate, peregrinate, overpass, go over the ground; patrol, reconnoiter, scout; sweep, go *or* make one's rounds, scour, scour the country; ply, voyage 182.13

21 **journey, travel,** make *or* take *or* go *or* go on a journey, **take** *or* **make a trip,** fare, **wayfare, gad around** *or* about, get around *or* about, navigate, trek, jaunt, peregrinate; junket, go on a junket; **tour;** hit the trail <nf>, take the road, go on the road; **cruise, go on a cruise, voyage** 182.13; go abroad, go to foreign places *or* shores, range the world,

globe-trot <nf>; travel light, live out of a suitcase; pilgrimage, pilgrim, go on *or* make a pilgrimage; campaign, go overseas, go on an expedition, go on safari; go on a sightseeing trip, sight-see, rubberneck <nf>

22 **migrate, transmigrate,** trek; flit, take wing; run <of fish>, swarm <of bees>; **emigrate,** out-migrate, expatriate; **immigrate,** in-migrate; remigrate; intermigrate

23 **wander, roam, rove,** range, nomadize, **gad,** gad around *or* about, follow the seasons, wayfare, flit, traipse <nf>, gallivant, knock around *or* about *and* bat around *or* about <nf>, prowl, **drift, stray,** float around, straggle, **meander, ramble,** stroll, saunter, jaunt, peregrinate, pererrate, divagate, go *or* run about, go the rounds; **tramp,** hobo, bum *or* go on the bum <nf>, vagabond, vagabondize, take to the road, beat one's way; **hit the road** *or* **trail** <nf>, walk the tracks *and* count ties <nf>, pound the pavement

24 **go for an outing** *or* **airing,** take the air, get some air; go for a walk; go for a ride

25 **go to, repair to,** resort to, hie to, hie oneself to, arise and go to, direct one's course to, turn one's tracks to, make one's way to, set foot in, bend one's steps to, betake oneself to, **visit,** drop in *or* around *or* by, make the scene <nf>

26 **creep, crawl,** scramble, scrabble, grovel, **go on hands and knees,** go on all fours; worm, worm along, worm one's way, snake; inch, inch along; **sneak, steal,** steal along; pussyfoot *and* gumshoe <nf>, slink, sidle, pad, prowl, nightwalk; **tiptoe,** tippytoe, go on tiptoe

27 **walk,** ambulate, peripateticate, pedestrianize, traipse <nf>; **step, tread, pace, stride,** pad; foot, foot it; leg, leg it; hoof it, ankle, go on the heel and toe, ride shank's mare *or* pony <nf>, ride the shoeleather *or* hobnail express, stump it <nf>; peg *or* jog *or* shuffle on *or* along; perambulate; circumambulate; jaywalk; power walk, exercise walk, speed walk, race walk

28 <ways of walking> **stroll,** saunter, *flâner* <Fr>; shuffle, scuff, scuffle, straggle, shamble, slouch; stride, straddle; **trudge, plod,** peg, traipse <nf>, clump, stump, slog, footslog, drag, **lumber, barge;** stamp, stomp <nf>, tromp; swing, roll, lunge; hobble, halt, limp, hitch, lurch; totter, stagger; toddle, paddle; waddle, wobble, wamble, wiggle; link, slither, sidle; stalk; **strut, swagger;** mince, sashay <nf>, scuttle, prance, tittup, flounce, trip, skip, foot; hop, jump, hippety-hop <nf>; jog, jolt; bundle, bowl along; **amble,** pace; singlefoot, rack; piaffe, piaffer

29 **go for a walk, perambulate, take a walk, take one's constitutional** <nf>, take a stretch, stretch the legs; **promenade**, parade

30 **march,** mush, footslog, **tramp, hike,** backpack, trail-hike; route-march; file, defile, file off; **parade,** go on parade; goose-step, do the goose step; do the lock step

31 **hitchhike** *or* **hitch** <nf>, beat one's way, **thumb** *or* **thumb one's way** <nf>, **catch a ride;** hitch *or* hook *or* bum *or* cadge *or* thumb a ride <nf>

32 **nightwalk,** noctambulate; **sleepwalk,** somnambulate, walk in one's sleep

33 **ride, go for a ride** *or* **drive;** go for a spin <nf>, take *or* go for a Sunday drive; **drive, chauffeur; motor,** taxi; bus; bike *and* cycle *and* wheel *and* pedal <nf>; **motorcycle, bicycle,** mountain bike; BMX, bicycle moto-cross; go by rail, entrain; joyride *or* take a joyride <nf>; catch *or* make a train <nf>

34 **go on horseback, ride, horse-ride** pony-trek; ride bareback; mount, take horse; hack; ride hard, clap spurs to one's horse; trot, amble, pace, canter, gallop, tittup, lope; prance, frisk, curvet, piaffe, caracole

35 **glide, coast, skim,** sweep, flow; **sail, fly,** flit; **slide,** slip, skid, skitter, sideslip, slither, glissade, surf; skate, ice-skate, roller-skate, rollerblade, skateboard; ski; snowboard, board;

toboggan, sled, sleigh; bellywhop <nf>

ADJS 36 **traveling, going, moving,** trekking, passing; **progressing; itinerant,** itinerary, circuit-riding; **journeying, wayfaring,** strolling; **peripatetic;** ambulant, ambulatory; ambulative; perambulating, perambulatory; peregrine, peregrinative, pilgrimlike; locomotive; **walking, pedestrian, touring,** on tour, globe-trotting <nf>, globe-girdling, mundivagant ; touristic, touristical, touristy <nf>; expeditionary

37 **wandering, roving, roaming,** ranging, **rambling, meandering,** strolling, **straying,** straggling, shifting, flitting, landloping, errant, divagatory, discursive, circumforaneous; **gadding,** traipsing <nf>, gallivanting; **nomad,** nomadic, floating, drifting, gypsyish *or* gypsylike; **transient,** transitory, fugitive, peripatetic; **vagrant,** vagabond, vagabondish; **footloose,** footloose and fancy-free; **migratory,** migrational, transmigrant, transmigratory; viaggiatory

38 **nightwalking,** noctambulant, noctambulous; night-wandering, noctivagant; **sleepwalking,** somnambulant, somnambular

39 **creeping, crawling, on hands and knees, on all fours;** reptant, repent, reptile, reptatorial; **on tiptoe,** on tippytoe, atiptoe, tiptoeing, tiptoe, tippytoe

40 **traveled,** well-traveled, cosmopolitan

41 **wayworn,** way-weary, road-weary, leg-weary, **travel-worn,** travel-weary, travel-tired; travel-sated, travel-jaded; travel-soiled, travel-stained, dusty

ADVS 42 **on the move** *or* **go,** en route, in transit, on the wing *or* fly; on the run, on the jump <nf>, on the road, on the tramp *or* march; on the gad <nf>, on the bum <nf>

43 **on foot, afoot,** by foot, footback *or* on footback <nf>; on the heel and toe, on *or* by shank's mare *or* pony <nf>

44 **on horseback,** horseback, by horse, mounted, horse-drawn

178 TRAVELER

NOUNS 1 **traveler, goer,** viator, comer and goer, road warrior; **wayfarer, journeyer,** trekker; **tourist,** tourer; **tripper** <Brit>, day-tripper; cicerone, travel *or* tourist guide; **visitor,** visiting fireman <nf>; **excursionist, sightseer,** rubberneck *or* rubbernecker <nf>, looky-loo; **voyager,** cruise-goer, cruiser, sailor, mariner 183; **globe-trotter** <nf>, globe-girdler, world-traveler, cosmopolite; jet set, jet-setter; **pilgrim,** palmer, hajji; **passenger,** fare; **commuter,** straphanger <nf>; transient; passerby; adventurer, alpinist, climber, mountaineer, ecotourist, adventure traveler, adventure athlete; explorer, forty-niner, pioneer, pathfinder, voortrekker, trailblazer, trailbreaker; camper; fellow traveler; astronaut 1075.8

2 **wanderer, rover, roamer,** rambler, stroller, straggler, mover; **gad, gadabout** <nf>, runabout, go-about <nf>; **itinerant,** peripatetic, rolling stone, peregrine, peregrinator, bird of passage, migratory, visitant; **drifter** *and* **floater** <nf>; Wandering Jew, Ahasuerus, Ancient Mariner, Argonaut, Flying Dutchman, Oisin, Ossian, Gulliver, Ulysses, Odysseus; wandering scholar, Goliard, *vaganti* <L>; strolling player, wandering minstrel, troubadour

3 **vagabond, vagrant,** vag <nf>; **bum** *or* bummer <nf>, loafer, wastrel, losel; **tramp,** turnpiker, piker, knight of the road, easy rider, **hobo** *or* bo <nf>, rounder <nf>, stiff *or* bindlestiff <nf>; landloper, sundowner; beggar 440.8; **waif,** homeless waif, bag person, dogie, stray, waifs and strays; ragamuffin, tatterdemalion; **gamin,** gamine, urchin, street urchin, dead-end kid <nf>, mudlark, guttersnipe <nf>; beachcomber, loafer, idler; ski bum, beach bum, surf bum, tennis bum; ragman, ragpicker

4 **nomad,** Bedouin, Arab; gypsy, Bohemian, Romany

5 **migrant,** migrator, trekker; **immigrant,** in-migrant; migrant *or* migratory worker; **emigrant,** out-migrant, *émigré* <Fr>; expatriate; **evacuee,** *évacué* <Fr>; displaced person *or* DP, stateless person, exile; wetback <nf>

6 **pedestrian, walker,** walkist; foot traveler, foot passenger, hoofer <nf>, footbacker <nf>, ambulator, peripatetic; **hiker,** backpacker, trailsman, tramper; marcher, footslogger, foot soldier, infantryman, paddlefoot <nf>; **hitchhiker** <nf>; jaywalker; power walker, exercise walker, speed walker, race walker

7 **nightwalker,** noctambulist, noctambule, **sleepwalker,** somnambulist, somnambulator, somnambule

8 **rider, equestrian, horseman,** horserider, horseback rider, horsebacker, *caballero* <Sp>, cavalier, knight, chevalier; horse soldier, cavalryman, mounted policeman; horsewoman, equestrienne; cowboy, cowgirl, puncher *or* cowpuncher *or* cowpoke <nf>, *vaquero* and *gaucho* <Sp>; broncobuster <nf>, buckaroo; postilion, postboy; roughrider; **jockey;** steeplechaser; circus rider, trick rider

9 **driver,** reinsman, whip, Jehu, skinner <nf>; **coachman,** coachy <nf>, *cocher* <Fr>, *cochero* <Sp>, *voiturier* <Fr>, *vetturino* <Ital>, gharry-wallah <India>; stage coachman; charioteer; harness racer; **cabdriver,** cabman, cabby <nf>, hackman, hack *or* hacky <nf>, jarvey <Brit nf>; wagoner, wagonman, drayman, truckman; **carter,** cartman, carman; **teamster;** muleteer, mule skinner <nf>; bullwhacker; elephant driver, mahout; cameleer

10 **driver, motorist,** automobilist; **chauffeur; taxidriver,** cabdriver, cabby <nf>, hackman, **hack** *or* hacky <nf>, hackdriver, pilot <nf>; jitney driver; **truck driver, teamster,** truckman, **trucker; bus driver,** busman, bus jockey <nf>; speeder 174.5, road hog <nf>, Sunday driver, joyrider <nf>; hit-and-run driver; designated driver; backseat driver; new driver, learner

11 cyclist, cycler; **bicyclist,** bicycler, mountain biker, biker; **motorcyclist,** motorcycler, biker <nf>

12 **engineer,** engineman, engine driver <Brit>; hogger *or* hoghead <nf>; Casey Jones; **motorman;** gripman

13 **trainman,** railroad man, **railroader;** conductor, guard <Brit>; brakeman, brakie <nf>; fireman, footplate man <Brit>, stoker; smoke agent *and* bakehead <nf>; switchman; yardman; yardmaster; trainmaster, dispatcher; stationmaster; lineman; baggage man, baggagesmasher <nf>; porter, redcap; trainboy, butcher <nf>; trainspotter

179 VEHICLE

<*means of conveyance*>

NOUNS 1 **vehicle, conveyance,** carrier, means of carrying *or* transporting, means of transport, medium of transportation, carriage; public transportation; watercraft 180.1, aircraft 181

2 **wagon,** waggon <Brit>, wain; haywagon, milkwagon; dray, van, caravan; covered wagon, prairie schooner, Conestoga wagon, stagecoach

3 **cart,** two-wheeler; oxcart, horsecart, ponycart, dogcart; dumpcart; **handcart,** barrow, wheelbarrow, handbarrow; jinrikisha, ricksha; pushcart

4 **carriage,** four-wheeler, *voiture* <Fr>, gharry <India>; **chaise,** shay <nf>

5 **rig, equipage,** turnout <nf>, coach-and-four; team, pair, span; tandem, randem; spike, spike team, unicorn; three-in-hand, four-in-hand, etc; three-up, four-up, etc

6 **baby carriage,** baby buggy <nf>, perambulator, pram <Brit>; go-cart; **stroller,** walker

7 **wheelchair,** Bath chair, push chair

8 **cycle,** wheel <nf>; **bicycle,** bike <nf>, mountain bike, all-terrain bike, touring bike, racing bike, hybrid bike, mountain bike, velocipede; tandem bicycle; **tricycle,** three-wheeler, trike <nf>; BMX; **motorcycle,** motocycle, motorbike, bike *and* iron <nf>; pig <nf>, chop-

per <nf>, motorscooter, minibike, moped, dirt *or* trail bike; pedicab

9 **automobile**, **car, auto,** motorcar, motocar, autocar, **machine,** motor, motor vehicle, motorized vehicle, *voiture* <Fr>

10 <nf terms> **jalopy,** banger, bomber, beater, bus, buggy, wheels, tub, tuna wagon, heap, boat, short, crate, wreck, bomb, clunker, junker, junkheap, junkpile

11 **police car, patrol car; prowl car,** squad car, cruiser; **police van,** patrol wagon; wagon *and* paddy wagon *and* Black Maria <nf>, panda car <Brit>

12 **truck**, lorry <Brit>, *camion* <Fr>; trailer truck, truck trailer, tractor trailer, semitrailer, rig *and* semi <nf>; eighteen-wheeler <nf>; panel truck, van

13 <public vehicles> **commercial vehicle; bus,** omnibus, chartered bus, autobus, motorbus, motor coach, articulated bus, jitney <nf>; express bus, local bus; schoolbus; **cab, taxicab, taxi,** hack <nf>, gypsy cab <nf>; rental car; hired car, limousine, limo *and* stretch limo <nf>; public transportation

14 **train,** railroad train; choo-choo *and* choo-choo train <nf>; passenger train, Amtrak; aerotrain, bullet train, *train de haute vitesse* <Fr>; local, way train, milk train, accommodation train; shuttle train, shuttle; express train, express; lightning express, flier, cannonball express <nf>; local express; special, limited; parliamentary train *or* parliamentary <Brit>; freight train, goods train <Brit>, freight, freighter, rattler <nf>; baggage train, luggage train; electric train; cable railroad; funicular; cog railroad *or* railway, rack-and-pinion railroad; subway, *métro* <Fr>, tube, underground <Brit>; elevated, el <nf>; monorail; streamliner; rolling stock

15 **railway car,** car, waggon <Brit>; baggage car, boxcar, caboose, coach, gondola; diner, dining car *or* compartment; drawing room; freight car; hopper car; flatcar; parlor car; Pullman *or* Pullman car; refrigerator car *or* reefer <nf>; roomette, sleeper *or* sleeping car or *wagon-lit* <Fr>; smoker *or* smoking car *or* compartment

16 **handcar,** go-devil; push car, trolley, truck car, rubble car

17 **streetcar, trolley** *or* trolley car, **tram** *or* tramcar; electric car, electric <nf>; trolley bus, trackless trolley; horsecar, horse box <Brit>; cable car, grip car

18 **tractor,** traction engine; Caterpillar <TM>, Cat <nf>, tracked vehicle; bulldozer, dozer <nf>

19 **trailer,** trail car; house trailer, mobile home; recreation vehicle *or* RV; truck trailer, **semitrailer,** highway trailer; camp *or* camping trailer, caravan <Brit>; **camper,** camping bus

20 **sled, sleigh,** *traîneau* <Fr>, sledge, dogsled, troika; snowmobile, weasel, skimobile, bombardier <Can>; runner, blade; toboggan, skiboggan

21 **skates,** ice skates, hockey skates, figure skates; roller skates, skateboard, bob skates; **skis, snowshoes**

22 **Hovercraft** <TM>, hovercar, air-cushion vehicle *or* ACV, cushioncraft, ground-effect machine *or* GEM, captured-air vehicle *or* CAV, captured-air bubble *or* CAB, surface-effect ship

ADJS 23 **vehicular,** transportational; automotive, locomotive

180 SHIP, BOAT

NOUNS 1 **ship,** argosy, cargo ship, container ship, cruise ship, dredge, freighter, liner, merchant ship *or* merchantman, motorship, oceanographic research ship, paddle boat *or* steamer, refrigeration ship, roll-on roll-off ship *or* ro-ro, side-wheeler, supertanker, tanker, trawler, ULCC *or* ultra-large crude carrier, VLCC *or* very large crude carrier, whaler, supercargo; **boat,** ark, canoe, gondola, kayak, lifeboat, motorboat, shell, skiff, whaleboat, workboat; vessel, craft, bottom, bark, argosy, hull, hulk, keel, watercraft; tub *and* bucket *and* rustbucket *and* hooker <nf>, packet; leviathan

2 **steamer, steamboat, steamship;** motor ship

3 **sailboat, sailing vessel,** sailing boat, wind boat, ragboat <nf>, sailing yacht, sailing cruiser, sailing ship, tall *or* taunt ship, sail, sailer, **windjammer** <nf>, windship, windboat; **galley; yacht,** pleasure boat

4 **motorboat, powerboat,** speedboat, stinkpot <nf>; **launch,** motor launch, steam launch, naphtha launch; **cruiser,** power cruiser, **cabin cruiser,** sedan cruiser, outboard cruiser

5 **liner, ocean liner,** ocean greyhound <nf>, passenger steamer, floating hotel *or* palace, luxury liner; **cruise ship**

6 **warship,** war vessel, naval vessel; warship; **man-of-war,** man-o'-war, ship of war, armored vessel; USS *or* United States Ship; HMS *or* His *or* Her Majesty's Ship; line-of-battle ship, ship of the line; aircraft carrier *or* flattop <nf>, assault transport, battle cruiser, battleship, coast guard cutter, communications ship, cruiser, destroyer, destroyer escort, guided missile cruiser, heavy cruiser, patrol boat *or* PT boat, gunboat, hospital ship, minelayer, mine ship, minesweeper; icebreaker

7 **battleship,** battlewagon <nf>, capital ship; **cruiser,** battle-cruiser; **destroyer,** can *or* tin can <nf>

8 **carrier, aircraft carrier,** seaplane carrier, **flattop** <nf>

9 **submarine, sub,** submersible, underwater craft; **U-boat**, pigboat <nf>; nuclear *or* nuclear-powered submarine; Polaris submarine; Trident submarine; hunter-killer submarine

10 **ships, shipping,** merchant *or* mercantile marine, merchant navy *or* fleet, bottoms, tonnage; **fleet,** flotilla, argosy; line; fishing fleet, whaling fleet, etc; **navy** 461.26

11 **float, raft;** balsa, balsa raft, Kon Tiki; life raft, Carling float; boom; pontoon; buoy, life buoy; **life preserver** 397.6; surfboard; cork; bob

12 **rigging,** rig, **tackle,** tackling, **gear; ropework,** roping; service, serving, whipping; standing rigging, running rigging; boatswain's stores; ship chandlery

13 **spar,** timber; **mast,** pole, stick *and* tree <nf>; bare pole

14 **sail, canvas,** muslin, cloth, rag <nf>; **full** *or* **plain sail,** press *or* crowd of sail; reduced sail, reefed sail; square sail; fore-and-aft sail; luff, leech, foot, earing, reef point, boltrope, clew, cringle, head

15 **oar,** remi-; **paddle,** scull, sweep, pole; steering oar

16 **anchor,** mooring, hook *and* mudhook <nf>; **anchorage,** moorings; **berth,** slip; mooring buoy

ADJS 17 **rigged,** decked, trimmed; square-rigged, fore-and-aft rigged, Marconi-rigged, gaff-rigged, lateen-rigged

18 **seaworthy,** sea-kindly, fit for sea, **snug, bold; watertight,** waterproof; **A1,** A1 at Lloyd's; stiff, tender; weatherly; yare

19 **trim,** in trim; apoise, on an even keel

20 **shipshape,** Bristol fashion, shipshape and Bristol fashion, trim, trig, neat, tight, taut, ataunt, all ataunto, bungup and bilge-free

181 AIRCRAFT

NOUNS 1 **aircraft, airplane,** aeroplane <Brit>, **plane, ship,** fixed-wing aircraft, flying machine , *avion* <Fr>; aerodyne, heavier-than-air craft; kite <Brit nf>; **shuttle, space shuttle,** lifting body; **airplane part; flight instrument,** aircraft instrument; **aircraft engine; piston engine,** radial engine, rotary engine, pancake engine; **jet engine,** fan-jet engine, rocket motor, turbofan, turbojet, turboprop, pulse jet, ramjet, reaction engine *or* motor

2 **propeller plane,** single-prop, double-prop *or* twin-prop, multiprop; piston plane; turbo-propeller plane, turbo-prop, prop-jet; puddle jumper

3 **jet plane, jet; turbojet,** ramjet, pulse-jet, blowtorch <nf>; single-jet, twin-jet, multi-jet; jet liner, business jet; deltaplanform jet, tailless

jet, twin-tailboom jet; jumbo jet; subsonic jet; supersonic jet, supersonic transport *or* SST, Concorde

4 rocket plane, repulsor; rocket ship, spaceship 1075.2; rocket 1074.2

5 rotor plane, rotary-wing aircraft, rotocraft, rotodyne; gyroplane, gyro, **autogiro,** windmill <nf>; **helicopter,** copter *and* whirlybird *and* chop per *and* eggbeater <nf>

6 ornithopter, orthopter, wind flapper, mechanical bird

7 flying platform, flying ring, Hiller-CNR machine, flying bedstead *or* bedspring; **Hovercraft** <TM>, air car, ground-effect machine, air-cushion vehicle, hovercar, cushion-craft; flying crow's nest, flying motorcycle, flying bathtub

8 seaplane, waterplane, **hydroplane,** aerohydroplane, aeroboat, **floatplane,** float seaplane; **flying boat,** clipper, boat seaplane; **amphibian,** amphibious aircraft, triphibian

9 military aircraft, warplane, battle plane, combat plane; carrier fighter, carrier-based plane, bomber, dive bomber, fighter, helicopter gunship, jet bomber, strategic bomber, jet fighter, jet tanker, night fighter, photo-reconnaissance plane, reconnaissance fighter, spy plane, airborne warning and control systems *or* AWACS plane, Stealth Bomber, Stealth Fighter, tactical support bomber, torpedo bomber, troop carrier *or* transport; amphibian, flying boat; helicopter; suicide plane, kamikaze; bogey, bandit, enemy aircraft; air fleet, air armada; air force 461.29

10 trainer; Link trainer; **flight simulator;** dual-control trainer; basic *or* primary trainer, intermediate trainer, advanced trainer; crew trainer, flying classroom; navigator-bombardier trainer, radio-navigational trainer, etc

11 aerostat, lighter-than-air craft; **airship,** ship, dirigible balloon, **blimp** <nf>; rigid airship, semirigid airship; **dirigible,** zeppelin, Graf Zeppelin; gasbag, ballonet; hot-air balloon, **balloon,** *ballon* <Fr>

12 glider, gliding machine; **sailplane,** soaring plane; rocket glider; student glider; air train, glider train

13 parachute, chute <nf>, umbrella <nf>, brolly <Brit nf>; pilot chute, drogue chute; rip cord, safety loop, shroud lines, harness, pack, vent; parachute jump, brolly-hop <Brit nf>, base jump; sky dive; brake *or* braking *or* deceleration parachute; parawing *or* paraglider *or* parafoil

14 kite, box kite, Eddy kite, Hargrave *or* cellular kite, tetrahedral kite

182 WATER TRAVEL

NOUNS **1** water travel, travel by water, marine *or* ocean *or* sea travel, **navigation,** navigating, **seafaring, sailing,** steaming, passage making, voyaging, **cruising,** coasting, gunkholing <nf>; inland navigation; **boating, yachting,** motorboating, canoeing, rowing, sculling; circumnavigation, periplus; navigability

2 <methods> celestial navigation, astronavigation; radio navigation, radio beacon; loran; consolan, shoran; coastal *or* coastwise navigation; dead reckoning; point-to-point navigation; pilotage; sonar, radar, sofar; plane *or* traverse *or* spherical *or* parallel *or* middle *or* latitude *or* Mercator *or* great-circle *or* rhumbline *or* composite sailing; fix, line of position; sextant, chronometer, tables

3 seamanship, shipmanship; seamanliness, seamanlikeness; weather eye; sea legs

4 pilotship, pilotry, pilotage, **helmsmanship;** steerage; proper piloting

5 embarkation 188.3; disembarkation 186.2

6 voyage, ocean *or* sea trip, **cruise,** sail; course, **run, passage; crossing;** shakedown cruise; leg

7 wake, track; wash, backwash

8 <submarines> **surfacing,** breaking water; **submergence, dive;** stationary dive, running dive, crash dive

9 way, progress; headway, steerageway, sternway, leeway, driftway

10 seaway, waterway, fairway, road, channel, ocean *or* sea lane, ship route, steamer track *or* lane; crossing; approaches; navigable water

11 aquatics, **swimming, bathing,** natation, balneation, aquacize; **swim, bathe;** crawl, freestyle, trudgen, Australian crawl, breaststroke, butterfly, sidestroke, dog *or* doggie paddle, backstroke; treading water; floating; diving 367.3; wading; fin; flipper, flapper; fishtail; waterskiing, aquaplaning, surfboarding; surfing; windsurfing, boardsailing; free swimming

12 **swimmer, bather,** natator, merman, fish <nf>; bathing girl, mermaid; bathing beauty; frogman; diver 367.4

VERBS 13 **navigate, sail, cruise,** steam, run, **seafare, voyage,** ply, go on shipboard, go by ship, go on *or* take a voyage; go to sea, sail the sea, sail the ocean blue; **boat, yacht,** motorboat, canoe, row, scull; surf, windsurf, boardsail; steamboat; bear *or* carry sail; cross, traverse, make a passage *or* run; sail round, circumnavigate; coast

14 **pilot,** helm, coxswain, **steer,** guide, be at the helm *or* tiller, direct, manage, handle, run, operate, **conn** *or* cond, be at *or* have the conn; **navigate,** shape *or* chart a course

15 **anchor,** come to anchor, lay anchor, **cast anchor,** let go the anchor, drop the hook; carry out the anchor; kedge, kedge off; **dock, tie up; moor,** pick up the mooring; run out a warp *or* rope; lash, lash and tie; foul the anchor; disembark 186.8

16 **ride at anchor,** ride, lie, rest; ride easy; ride hawse full; lie athwart; set an anchor watch

17 **lay** *or* **lie to,** lay *or* lie by; lie near *or* close to the wind, head to wind *or* windward, be under the sea; lie ahull; lie off, lie off the land; lay *or* lie up

18 **weigh anchor,** up-anchor, bring the anchor home, break out the anchor, cat the anchor, break ground, loose for sea; **unmoor,** drop the mooring, cast off *or* loose *or* away

19 **get under way,** put *or* have way upon, **put** *or* **push** *or* **shove off;** hoist the blue Peter; **put to sea,** put out to sea, go to sea, head for blue water, go off soundings; **sail,** sail away; embark

20 **set sail,** hoist sail, unfurl *or* spread sail, heave out a sail, **make sail,** trim sail; square away, square the yards; **crowd** *or* **clap** *or* **crack** *or* **pack on sail,** put on <more> sail; clap on, crack on, pack on; give her beans <nf>

21 **make way,** gather way, **make headway,** make sternway; make knots, foot; **go full speed ahead,** go full speed astern; go *or* run *or* steam at flank speed

22 run, **run** *or* **sail before the wind,** run *or* sail with the wind, run *or* sail down the wind, make a spinnaker run, sail off the wind, sail free, sail with the wind aft, sail with the wind abaft the beam; tack down wind; run *or* sail with the wind quartering

23 **bring off the wind, pay off,** bear off *or* away, put the helm to leeward, bear *or* head to leeward, pay off the head

24 **sail against the wind,** sail on *or* by the wind, sail to windward, bear *or* head to windward; **bring in** *or* **into the wind,** bring by *or* on the wind, haul the wind *or* one's wind; uphelm, put the helm up; haul, haul off, haul up; **haul to, bring to, heave to;** sail in *or* into the wind's eye *or* the teeth of the wind; sail to the windward of, weather

25 **sail near the wind,** sail close to the wind, lie near *or* close to the wind, sail full and by, hold a close wind, **sail close-hauled,** close-haul; work *or* go *or* beat *or* eat to windward, **beat, ply; luff,** luff up, sail closer to the wind; sail too close to the wind, sail fine, touch the wind, pinch

26 **gain to windward of,** eat *or* claw to windward of, eat the wind out of, have the wind of, be to windward of

27 **chart** *or* **plot** *or* **lay out a course;** shape a course, lay *or* lie a course

28 take *or* follow a course, **keep** *or* **hold the course** *or* **a course,** hold on the course *or* a course, stand on *or* upon a course, stand on a straight course, maintain *or* keep the heading, keep her steady, keep pointed

29 **drift off course, yaw,** yaw off, pay off, bear off, drift, sag; sag *or* bear *or* ride *or* drive to leeward, make leeway, drive, fetch away; be set by the current, drift with the current, fall down

30 **change course,** change the heading, bear off *or* away, bear to starboard *or* port; sheer, swerve; **tack,** cast, break, yaw, slew, shift, turn; **cant,** cant round *or* across; **beat, ply; veer, wear, wear ship; jibe** *or* gybe <Brit>, jibe all standing, make a North River jibe; **put about,** come *or* go *or* bring *or* fetch about, beat about, cast *or* throw about; bring *or* swing *or* heave *or* haul round; **about ship,** turn *or* put back, turn on her heel, wind; swing the stern; box off; back and fill; stand off and on; double *or* round a point; miss stays; reroute

31 put the rudder hard left *or* right, put the rudder *or* helm hard over, put the rudder amidships, ease the rudder *or* helm, give her more *or* less rudder

32 **veer** *or* **wear short,** bring by the lee, **broach to,** lie beam on to the seas

33 <come to a stop> **fetch up, heave to,** haul up, fetch up all standing

34 **backwater,** back, reverse, go astern; **go full speed astern;** make sternway

35 **sail for, put away for, make for** *or* toward, make at, **run for,** stand for, head *or* steer toward, lay for, **lay a** *or* **one's course for,** bear up for; bear up to, **bear down on** *or* **upon,** run *or* bear in with, **close with;** make, reach, fetch, heave *or* go alongside; lay *or* go aboard; lay *or* lie in; **put in** *or* into, put into port, approach anchorage

36 **sail away from,** head *or* steer away from, run from, **stand from,** lay away *or* off from; **stand off,** bear off, put off, shove off, haul off; stand off and on

37 **clear the land,** bear off the land, lay *or* settle the land, make *or* get sea room

38 **make land,** reach land; close with the land, stand in for the land; sight land; smell land; make a landfall

39 **coast,** sail coast-wise, stay in soundings, range the coast, skirt the shore, lie along the shore, **hug the shore** *or* **land** *or* **coast**

40 **weather the storm,** weather, ride, **ride out,** outride, ride *or* ride out a storm; make heavy *or* bad weather

41 **sail into,** run down, run in *or* into, **ram; come** *or* **run foul** *or* **afoul of, collide,** fall aboard; nose *or* head into, run prow *or* end *or* head on, run head and head; run broadside on

42 **shipwreck,** wreck, pile up <nf>, cast away; **go** *or* **run aground,** ground, take the ground, beach, strand, run on the rocks; ground hard and fast

43 **careen, list, heel,** tip, cant, heave *or* lay down, lie along; be on beam ends

44 **capsize, upset,** overset, **overturn,** turn over, turn turtle, upset the boat, keel, keel over *or* up; pitchpole, somersault; **sink, founder,** be lost, go down, go to the bottom, go to Davy Jones's locker; scuttle

45 **go overboard,** go by the board, go over the board *or* side

46 **maneuver,** execute a maneuver; heave in together, keep in formation, maintain position, **keep station,** keep pointed, steam in line, steam in line of bearing; convoy

47 <submarines> **surface,** break water; **submerge, dive,** crash-dive, go below; rig for diving; flood the tanks, flood negative

48 <activities aboard ship> lay, lay aloft, lay forward, etc; traverse a yard, brace a yard fore and aft; heave, haul; kedge; warp; boom; heave round, heave short, heave apeak; log, heave *or* stream the log; haul down, board; spar down; ratline down, clap on ratlines; batten down the hatches; unlash, cut *or* cast loose; clear hawse

49 **trim ship,** trim, trim up; trim by the head *or* stern, put in proper fore-and-aft trim, give greater draft fore and aft, **put on an even keel; ballast,** shift ballast, wing out ballast; break out ballast, break bulk, shoot ballast; **clear the decks,** clear for action, take action stations

50 **reduce sail,** shorten *or* take in sail, hand a sail, **reef,** reef one's sails; double-reef; lower sail, dowse sail; run under bare poles; snug down; **furl,** put on a harbor furl

51 **take bearings,** cast a traverse; correct distance and maintain the bearings; run down the latitude, **take a sight,** shoot the sun, bring down the sun; **box the compass; take soundings** 275.9

52 **signal,** make a signal, speak, hail and speak; dress ship; unfurl *or* hoist a banner, unfurl an ensign, **break out a flag;** hoist the blue Peter; show one's colors, **exchange colors;** salute, dip the ensign

53 **row, paddle,** ply the oar, **pull, scull, punt;** give way, row away; catch *or* cut a crab *or* lobster <nf>; feather, feather an oar; sky an oar <nf>; row dry <Brit nf>; pace, shoot; ship oars

54 **float,** ride, drift; **sail, scud, run,** shoot; skim, foot; ghost, glide, slip; ride the sea, plow the deep, walk the waters

55 **pitch, toss, tumble,** toss and tumble, pitch and toss, **plunge,** hobbyhorse, pound, **rear, rock, roll, reel, swing, sway, lurch, yaw, heave,** scend, **flounder, welter, wallow;** make heavy weather

56 **swim, bathe,** go in swimming *or* bathing; tread water; **float,** float on one's back, do the deadman's float, dog-paddle; **wade,** go in wading; skinny-dip; aquacize; dive 367.6

ADJS **57** **nautical, marine, maritime, naval, navigational; seafaring, seagoing, oceangoing,** seaborne, water-borne; seamanly, seamanlike, **salty** <nf>; pelagic, oceanic 240.8

58 **aquatic, water-dwelling,** water-living, water-growing, water-loving; **swimming,** balneal, natant, natatory, natatorial; shore, seashore; tidal, estuarine, littoral, grallatorial; riverine; deep-sea 275.14

59 **navigable,** boatable

60 **floating, afloat,** awash; water-borne

61 **adrift, afloat,** unmoored, untied, loose, unanchored, aweigh; cast-off, started

ADVS **62** **on board,** on shipboard, on board ship, **aboard,** all aboard, afloat; **on deck,** topside; aloft; in sail; before the mast; athwart the hawse, athwarthawse

63 **under way,** making way, with steerageway, with way on; **at sea,** on the high seas, off soundings, in blue water; **under sail** *or* **canvas,** with sails spread; under press of sail *or* canvas *or* steam; under steam *or* power; under bare poles; on *or* off the heading *or* course; in soundings, homeward bound

64 **before the wind,** with the wind, down the wind, running free; off the wind, with the wind aft, with the wind abaft the beam, wing and wing, under the wind, under the lee; on a reach, on a beam *or* broad reach, with wind abeam

65 **against the wind,** on the wind, in *or* into the wind, up the wind, by the wind, head to wind; in *or* into the wind's eye, in the teeth of the wind

66 **near the wind,** close to the wind, **close-hauled,** on a beat, full and by

67 **coastward, landward,** to landward; **coastwise,** coastways

68 **leeward,** to leeward, alee, downwind; **windward,** to windward, weatherward, aweather, upwind

69 **aft,** abaft, baft, **astern;** fore and aft

70 **alongside,** board and board, yardarm to yardarm

71 **at anchor,** riding at anchor; lying to, hove to; lying ahull

72 **afoul,** foul, in collision; head and head, head *or* end *or* prow on; broadside on

73 **aground,** on the rocks; hard and fast

74 **overboard,** over the board *or* side, by the board; aft the fantail

183 MARINER

NOUNS **1** **mariner, seaman, sailor,** sailorman, **navigator, seafarer,** seafaring man, bluejacket, sea *or* water dog <nf>, Seabee <nf>, crewman, shipman, jack, jacky, jack afloat, jack-tar, **tar, salt** <nf>, gob, swabby, hearty, lobscouser <nf>, *matelot* <Fr>, windsailor, windjammer; limey *or* limejuicer <nf>, lascar <India>; common *or* ordinary seaman, OD; able *or* able-bodied seaman, AB; deep-sea man, saltwater *or* bluewater *or* deepwater sailor; fresh-water sailor; fair-weather sailor; whaler, fisherman, lobsterman; viking, sea rover, buccaneer, privateer, pirate; Jason, Argonaut, Ancient Mariner, Flying Dutchman; Neptune, Poseidon, Varuna, Dylan; **yachtsman, yachtswoman,** cruising sailor, racing sailor; submariner

2 <novice> **lubber, landlubber;** polliwog

3 <veteran> **old salt** *and* old sea dog *and* shellback *and* barnacle-back <nf>; **master mariner**

4 **navy man,** man-of-war's man, **bluejacket; gob** *and* swabbie *and* swabber <nf>; **marine, leatherneck** *and* gyrene *and* devil dog *or* jarhead <nf>, Royal Marine, jolly <Brit nf>; horse marine; boot <nf>; **midshipman,** midshipmate, middy <nf>; cadet, naval cadet; coastguardsman, Naval Reservist, Seabee, frogman

5 **boatman,** boatsman, boat-handler, **boater,** waterman; **oarsman,** oar, rower, sculler, punter; galley slave; **ferryman,** ferrier; **bargeman,** barger, bargee <Brit>, bargemaster; lighterman, wherryman; **gondolier,** *gondoliere* <Ital>

6 hand, **deckhand,** deckie <Brit>, roustabout <nf>; stoker, fireman, bakehead <nf>; black gang; wiper, oiler, boilerman; cabin boy; yeoman, ship's writer; purser; ship's carpenter, chips <nf>; ship's cooper, bungs *or* Jimmy Bungs <nf>; ship's tailor, snip *or* snips <nf>; steward, stewardess, commissary steward, mess steward, hospital steward; commissary clerk; mail orderly; navigator; radio operator, sparks <nf>; landing signalman; gunner, gun loader, torpedoman; afterguard; complement; watch

7 <ship's officers> **captain,** shipmaster, **master, skipper** <nf>, **commander,** the Old Man <nf>, *patron* <Fr>; navigator, navigating officer, sailing master; deck officer, officer of the deck *or* OD; watch officer, officer of the watch; **mate,** first *or* chief mate, second mate, third mate, boatswain's mate; **boatswain,** bos'n, pipes <nf>; quartermaster; sergeant-at-arms; chief engineer, engine-room officer; naval officer 575.20

8 **steersman, helmsman,** wheelman, wheelsman, boatsteerer; quartermaster; **coxswain,** cox <nf>; **pilot,** conner, sailing master; harbor pilot, docking pilot

9 **longshoreman,** wharf hand, dockhand, docker, dockworker, dockwalloper <nf>; **stevedore,** loader; **roustabout** <nf>, lumper

184 AVIATION

NOUNS 1 **aviation, aeronautics;** airplaning, skyriding, **flying, flight,** winging, volation, volitation; aeronautism, aerodromics; powered flight, jet flight, subsonic *or* supersonic flight; cruising, cross-country flying; bush flying; **gliding,** sail-planing, soaring, sailing; volplaning; ballooning, balloonery, lighter-than-air aviation; barnstorming <nf>; high-altitude flying; blind *or* instrument flight *or* flying, instrument flight rules *or* IFR; contact flying, visual flight *or* flying, visual flight rules *or* VFR, pilotage; skywriting; cloud-seeding; in-flight training, ground school; **air traffic,** airline traffic, air-traffic control, air-traffic controller; commercial aviation, general aviation, private aviation, private flying; astronautics 1075.1; air show, flying circus

2 air sciences, aeronautical sciences

3 **airmanship,** pilotship; **flight plan;** briefing, brief, rundown <nf>, debriefing; flight *or* pilot training, flying lessons; washout <nf>

4 air-mindedness, aerophilia; air legs

5 airsickness; aerophobia, aeropathy

6 **navigation,** avigation, aerial *or* air navigation; celestial navigation, astronavigation; electronic navigation, automatic electronic navigation, radio navigation, navar, radar, consolan, tacan, teleran, loran, shoran; omnidirectional range, omni-range, visual-aural range *or* VAR

7 <aeronautical organizations> Civil Aeronautics Administration *or*

CAA; Federal Aviation Agency *or* FAA; Bureau of Aeronautics; National Advisory Committee for Aeronautics; Office of Naval Research; Civil Air Patrol; Caterpillar Club; Airline Pilots Association; Air Force 461.29

8 **takeoff,** liftoff, hopoff <nf>; rollout, climb; taxiing, takeoff run, takeoff power, rotation; daisy-clipping *and* grass-cutting <nf>; ground loop; level-off; jet-assisted takeoff *or* JATO, booster rocket, takeoff rocket; catapult, electropult

9 **flight, trip, run; hop** *and* **jump** <nf>; powered flight; solo flight, **solo;** inverted flight; supersonic flight; test flight, **test hop** <nf>; **airlift;** airdrop; scheduled flight; mercy flight; charter flight; connecting flight; non-stop flight; crop-dusting; skywriting; red-eye

10 **air travel,** air transport, air transportation; **airfreight, air cargo; airline travel, airline,** airline service, air service, feeder airline, commuter airline, scheduled airline, charter airline, nonscheduled airline *or* nonsked <nf>, short-hop airline; flying circus; **shuttle,** air shuttle, shuttle service, shuttle trip; air taxi; frequent flier

11 <Air Force> **mission,** flight operation; training mission; gunnery mission; combat rehearsal, **dry run** <nf>; transition mission; reconnaissance mission, reconnaissance, observation flight, search mission; **milk run** <nf>; box-top mission <nf>; combat flight; **sortie,** scramble <nf>; **air raid;** shuttle raid; bombing mission; bombing, strafing 459.7; **air support** <for ground troops>, **air cover,** cover, umbrella, air umbrella

12 flight formation, formation flying, formation; close formation, loose formation, wing formation; V formation, echelon

13 <maneuvers> acrobatic *or* tactical evolutions *or* maneuvers, acrobatics, **aerobatics;** stunting *and* **stunt flying** <nf>, rolling, crabbing, banking, porpoising, fishtailing, diving; **dive, nose dive, power dive; zoom,** chandelle; stall, whip stall; **glide,** volplane; spiral, split 'S', lazy eight, sideslip, pushdown, pull-up, pullout; turn, vector in flight *or* VIF

14 **roll, barrel roll,** aileron roll, outside roll, **snap roll**

15 **spin,** autorotation, **tailspin,** flat spin, inverted spin, normal spin, power spin, uncontrolled spin, falling leaf; whipstall

16 **loop,** spiral loop, ground loop, normal loop, outside loop, inverted normal *or* outside loop, dead-stick loop, wingover, looping the loop; Immelmann turn, reverse turn, reversement; flipper turns

17 **buzzing,** flathatting *and* **hedgehopping** <nf>

18 **landing,** coming in <nf>, touching down, touchdown; arrival; landing run, landing pattern; approach, downwind leg, approach leg; holding pattern, stack up <nf>; ballooning in, parachute approach; blind *or* instrument landing, dead-stick landing, glide landing, stall landing, fishtail landing, sideslip landing, level *or* two-point landing, normal *or* three-point landing, Chinese landing <nf>, tail-high landing, tail-low landing, thumped-in landing <nf>, pancake landing, belly landing, crash landing, noseover, nose-up; overflight, overshoot, undershoot; practice landing, bounce drill

19 flying and landing guides marker, pylon; beacon; radio beacon, radio range station, radio marker; fan marker; radar beacon, racon; beam, radio beam; beacon lights; runway lights, high-intensity runway approach lights, sequence flashers, flare path; wind indicator, wind cone *or* sock, air sleeve; instrument landing system *or* ILS; touchdown rate of descent indicator *or* TRODI; ground-controlled approach *or* GCA; talking-down system, talking down

20 **crash, crack-up,** prang <Brit nf>; crash landing; collision, mid-air collision; near-miss, near collision

21 **blackout;** grayout; anoxia; useful consciousness; pressure suit, antiblackout suit

22 **airport, airfield, airdrome,** aerodrome <Brit>, drome, port, air har-

bor <Can>, aviation field, **landing field,** landing, field, airship station; **air terminal, jetport; air base,** air station, naval air station; airpark; **heliport,** helidrome; control tower, island; Air Route Traffic Control Center; baggage pickup, baggage carousel; airside, landside

23 **runway, taxiway,** strip, landing strip, **airstrip, flight strip,** take-off strip; fairway, launching way; stopway; clearway; transition strip; apron; **flight deck,** landing deck; helipad; ramp, apron

24 **hangar,** housing, dock, airdock, shed, airship shed; mooring mast

25 <propulsion> rocket propulsion, rocket power; **jet propulsion,** jet power; turbojet propulsion, pulse-jet propulsion, ram-jet propulsion, resojet propulsion; constant *or* ram pressure, air ram; reaction propulsion, reaction, action and reaction; aeromotor, aircraft engine, power plant

26 **lift,** lift ratio, lift force *or* component, lift direction; aerostatic lift, dynamic lift, gross lift, useful lift, margin of lift

27 **drag,** resistance; drag ratio, drag force *or* component, induced drag, wing drag, parasite *or* parasitic *or* structural drag, profile drag, head resistance, drag direction, cross-wind force

28 **drift,** drift angle; lateral drift, leeway

29 flow, air flow, laminar flow; **turbulence,** turbulent flow, burble, burble point, eddies

30 wash, wake, stream; downwash; backwash, **slipstream,** propeller race, propwash; **exhaust,** jet exhaust, blow wash; **vapor trail,** condensation trail, contrail, vortex

31 <speed> **air speed,** true air speed, operating *or* flying speed, cruising speed, knots, minimum flying speed, hump speed, peripheral speed, pitch speed, terminal speed, sinking speed, get-away *or* take-off speed, landing speed, ground speed, speed over the ground; **speed of sound** 174.2; zone of no signal, Mach cone; **sound barrier,** sonic barrier *or* wall; sonic boom, shock wave, Mach wave

32 <air, atmosphere> **airspace,** navigable airspace; aerosphere; **aerospace;** space, empty space; **weather, weather conditions; ceiling,** ballonet ceiling, service ceiling, static ceiling, absolute ceiling; ceiling and visibility unlimited *or* CAVU; severe clear <nf>; cloud layer *or* cover, ceiling zero; visibility, visibility zero; **overcast,** undercast; fog, soup <nf>; high-pressure area, low-pressure area; trough, trough line; front; **air pocket** *or* **hole,** air bump, pocket, hole, bump; **turbulence;** clear-air turbulence *or* CAT; roughness; head wind, unfavorable wind; tail wind, favorable *or* favoring wind; cross wind; atmospheric tides; jetstream

33 **airway, air lane, air line,** air route, skyway, corridor, flight path, lane, path

34 **course, heading,** vector; compass heading *or* course, compass direction, magnetic heading, true heading *or* course

35 <altitude> altitude of flight, absolute altitude, critical altitude, density altitude, pressure altitude, sextant altitude; clearance; ground elevation

VERBS **36** **fly,** be airborne, wing, take wing, wing one's way, take *or* make a flight, take to the air, take the air, volitate, be wafted; **jet;** aviate, airplane, aeroplane; travel by air, go *or* travel by airline, go by plane *or* air, take to the airways, ride the skies; hop <nf>; **soar,** drift, hover; **cruise; glide,** sailplane, sail, volplane; hydroplane, seaplane; balloon; ferry; airlift; break the sound barrier; navigate, avigate

37 **pilot,** control, be at the controls, **fly,** manipulate, drive <nf>, fly left seat; **copilot,** fly right seat; solo; **barnstorm** <nf>; fly blind, fly by the seat of one's pants <nf>; follow the beam, ride the beam, fly on instruments; fly in formation, take position; peel off

38 **take off,** hop *or* jump off <nf>, become airborne, get off *or* leave the ground, take to the air, go *or* fly aloft, clear; rotate, power off; **taxi**

39 **ascend,** climb, gain altitude, mount; **zoom,** hoick <nf>, chandelle

40 <maneuver> **stunt** <nf>, perform aerobatics; crab, fishtail; **spin,** go into a tailspin; **loop,** loop the loop; **roll,** wingover, spiral, undulate, porpoise, feather, yaw, sideslip, skid, bank, dip, crab, nose down, nose up, pull up, push down, pull out, plow, mush through

41 **dive,** nose-dive, power-dive, go for the deck; lose altitude, settle, dump altitude <nf>

42 **buzz,** flathat *and* **hedgehop** <nf>

43 **land,** set her down <nf>, **alight, light,** touch down; **descend,** come down, dump altitude <nf>, fly down; come in, come in for a landing; **level off,** flatten out; upwind, downwind; overshoot, undershoot; make a dead-stick landing; pancake, thump in <nf>; bellyland, settle down, balloon in; fishtail down; **crash-land;** ditch <nf>; nose up, nose over; talk down

44 **crash, crack up,** prang <Brit nf>, spin in, fail to pull out

45 **stall,** lose power, conk out <nf>; flame out

46 **black out,** gray out

47 **parachute, bail out, jump,** make a parachute jump, hit the silk, make a brollyhop <Brit nf>, sky-dive, base-jump

48 **brief,** give a briefing; debrief

ADJS **49** **aviation, aeronautic, aeronautical,** aerial; **aviatorial,** aviational, aviatic; aerodontic, **aerospace,** aerotechnical, aerostatic, aerostatical, aeromechanic, aeromechanical, aerodynamic, aerodynamical, avionic, aeronomic, aerophysical; aeromarine; aerobatic; airworthy, air-minded, air-conscious, aeromedical; air-wise; airsick; air-traffic; subsonic, supersonic, hypersonic; propeller, prop, jet, turbojet

50 **flying, airborne,** winging, soaring; volant, volitant, volitational, hovering, fluttering; gliding; jet-propelled, rocket-propelled

ADVS **51** **in flight, on the wing** *or* fly, while airborne

185 AVIATOR

NOUNS **1** **aviator, airman, flier, pilot,** air pilot, licensed pilot, private pilot, airline pilot, commercial pilot, aeronaut, flyboy *and* airplane driver *and* birdman <nf>; aircrew member; captain, chief pilot; copilot, second officer; flight engineer, third officer; jet pilot, jet jockey <nf>; instructor; test pilot; bush pilot; astronaut 1075.8; cloud seeder, rainmaker; cropduster; barnstormer <nf>; stunt man, stunt flier

2 **aviatrix,** aviatress, **airwoman,** birdwoman <nf>; stuntwoman

3 **military pilot,** naval pilot, combat pilot; fighter pilot; bomber pilot; observer, reconnaissance pilot; radarman; **aviation cadet,** air *or* flying cadet, pilot trainee; flyboy <nf>; ace; air force 461.29

4 **crew, aircrew,** flight crew; crewman, crewmate, crewmember, aircrewman; **navigator,** avigator; **bombardier;** gunner, machine gunner, belly gunner, tail gunner; crew chief; aerial photographer; meteorologist; **flight attendant, steward, stewardess,** hostess, air hostess, purser, stew <nf>

5 **ground crew,** landing crew, plane handlers; crew chief

6 aircraftsman, aeromechanic, aircraft mechanic, mechanic, grease monkey <nf>, ground engineer; rigger; aeronautical engineer, jet engineer, astronaut 1075.8; ground tester, flight tester; air-traffic controller

7 **balloonist,** ballooner, hot-air balloonist, aeronaut

8 **parachutist,** chutist *or* chuter <nf>, parachute jumper, sports parachutist; sky diver; **paratrooper;** paradoctor, paramedic; jumpmaster

9 <mythological fliers> Daedalus, Icarus

186 ARRIVAL

NOUNS **1** **arrival, coming, advent,** approach, appearance, **reaching; attainment, accomplishment, achievement**

2 **landing,** landfall; docking, mooring, tying up, dropping anchor; **getting off, disembarkation,** disembarkment, debarkation, coming *or* going ashore; **deplaning**, dropping *or* weighing anchor

3 **return, homecoming,** recursion; reentrance, **reentry;** remigration; prodigal's return

4 **welcome,** hero's welcome, **greetings** 585.3

5 **destination, goal,** bourn ; port, haven, harbor, anchorage, **journey's end;** end of the line, terminus, **terminal,** terminal point, home plate; stop, stopping place, last stop; **airport, air terminal** 184.22

VERBS **6** **arrive,** arrive at, arrive in, come, **come** *or* **get to,** approach, access, **reach, hit** <nf>; find, **gain,** attain, attain to, accomplish, achieve, make, **make it** <nf>, fetch, fetch up at, get there, reach one's destination, come to one's journey's end, end up; **come to rest,** settle, settle in; **make** *or* **put in an appearance, show up** <nf>, turn up, **surface,** pop *or* bob up *and* make the scene <nf>; **get in, come in,** blow in <nf>, pull in, roll in; **check in;** clock *or* punch *or* ring *or* time in <nf>, sign in; hit town <nf>; come to hand, be received

7 **arrive at,** come at, get at, **reach,** arrive upon, **come upon, hit upon,** strike upon, fall upon, light upon, pitch upon, stumble on *or* upon

8 **land,** come to land, make a landfall, set foot on dry land; reach *or* make land, make port; put in *or* into, put into port; dock, moor, tie up, anchor, drop anchor; go ashore, **disembark,** debark, unboat; **detrain,** debus, **deplane, disemplane;** alight

ADJS **9** **arriving,** approaching, entering, **coming,** incoming; inbound, inwardbound; homeward, homewardbound; immigrant

ADVS **10** **arriving,** on arrival *or* arriving

187 RECEPTION

NOUNS **1** **reception, taking in,** receipt, receiving; **welcome,** welcoming, cordial welcome, open *or* welcoming arms; hospitality; refuge 1009

2 **admission,** admittance, acceptance; immission , intromission 191.1; **installation,** installment, instatement, inauguration, initiation; baptism, investiture, ordination; enlistment, enrollment, induction

3 **entree, entrée,** in <nf>, entry, **entrance** 189, **access,** opening, **open door,** open arms; a foot in the door, opening wedge

4 **ingestion; eating** 8; **drinking** 8.3, imbibing, imbibition; engorgement, ingurgitation, engulfment; **swallowing,** gulping; swallow, gulp, slurp

5 <drawing in> **suction,** suck, sucking; **inhalation,** inhalement, inspiration, aspiration; snuff, snuffle, sniff, sniffle

6 sorption, **absorption,** adsorption, chemisorption *or* chemosorption, engrossment, digestion, **assimilation,** infiltration; **sponging, blotting; seepage,** percolation; **osmosis,** endosmosis, exosmosis, electroosmosis; absorbency; **absorbent,** adsorbent, **sponge, blotter,** blotting paper

7 <bringing in> **introduction; importing,** import, **importation**, investiture, naturalization

8 readmission; reabsorption, resorbence

9 **receptivity, receptiveness,** welcoming, welcome, invitingness, openness, hospitality, cordiality, recipience *or* recipiency; receptibility, admissibility

VERBS **10** **receive, take in; admit, let in,** immit , intromit, give entrance *or* admittance to; **welcome,** bid welcome, give a royal welcome, roll out the red carpet; give an entree, open the door to, give refuge *or* shelter *or* sanctuary to, throw open to; include

11 **ingest, eat** 8.20, tuck away, put away; imbibe, **drink; swallow, devour,** ingurgitate; **engulf,** engorge; **gulp,** gulp down, swill, swill down, wolf down, gobble

12 **draw in, suck,** suckle, suck in *or* up, aspirate, pick up; **inhale,** inspire,

breathe in; snuff, snuffle, sniff, sniffle, snuff in *or* up, slurp
13 **absorb,** adsorb, chemisorb *or* chemosorb, **assimilate,** engross, digest, **drink,** imbibe, take up *or* in, drink up *or* in, slurp up, swill up; blot, **blot up, soak up,** sponge; osmose; infiltrate, filter in; **soak in, seep in,** percolate in; internalize
14 **bring in, introduce, import**
15 readmit; reabsorb, resorb
ADJS 16 **receptive,** recipient; welcoming, open, hospitable, cordial, inviting, invitatory; introceptive; **admissive,** admissory; receivable, receptible, admissible; intromissive, intromittent; ingestive, imbibitory
17 sorbent, **absorbent,** adsorbent, chemisorptive *or* chemosorptive, **assimilative,** digestive; bibulous, imbibitory, thirsty, soaking, blotting; spongy, spongeous; osmotic, endosmotic, exosmotic; resorbent
18 **introductory,** introductive; **initiatory,** initiative, baptismal

188 DEPARTURE

NOUNS 1 **departure, leaving, going,** passing, **parting; exit,** walkout <nf>; egress 190.2; **withdrawal,** removal, retreat 163.2, retirement; evacuation, abandonment, desertion; decampment; escape, flight, getaway <nf>, elopement; exodus, hegira; migration, mass migration; defection, voting with one's feet; checkout
2 **start,** starting, start-off, setoff, setout, takeoff *and* getaway <nf>, liftoff; the starting gun *or* pistol; break; the green light
3 **embarkation,** embarkment, boarding; entrainment; enplanement *or* emplanement
4 **leave-taking, leave, parting, departure,** conge; **send-off,** Godspeed; **adieu,** one's adieus, **farewell,** aloha, **good-bye;** valedictory address, valedictory, valediction, parting words; parting *or* Parthian shot; swan song; viaticum; stirrup cup, one for the road, nightcap <nf>
5 **point of departure, starting place** *or* **point,** takeoff, **start,** base, baseline, basis; line of departure; starting line *or* post *or* gate, starting blocks, springboard, jumping-off point; stakeboat; port of embarkation
VERBS 6 **depart,** make off, begone, be off, take oneself off *or* away, take one's departure, take leave *or* take one's leave, **leave, go, go away, go off, get off** *or* **away,** get under way, come away, go one's way, go *or* get along, be getting along, go on, get on; move off *or* away, move out, march off *or* away; **pull out;** decamp; exit; take *or* break *or* tear oneself away, take oneself off, take wing *or* flight
7 <nf terms> **beat it, split,** scram, amscray, up and go, trot, toddle, stagger along, mosey *or* sashay along, buzz off, buzz along, bug out, bugger off <Brit>, beetle off, fuck off *or* f off, get rolling, hightail it, pull up stakes, check out, clear out, cut out, haul ass, hit the road *or* trail, piss off <chiefly Brit>, get lost, flake off, get going, shove off, push along, push off, get out, get *or* git, get the hell out, make oneself scarce, vamoose, take off, skip, skip out, lam, take it on the lam, powder, take a powder, take a runout powder, skedaddle, absquatulate , clock off
8 **set out, set forth,** put forth, go forth, **sally forth,** sally, issue, issue forth, launch forth, set forward, **set off,** be off, be on one's way, outset, **start, start out** *or* **off, strike out,** get off, get away, get off the dime <nf>; get the green light, break; set sail
9 **quit, vacate,** evacuate, abandon, desert, turn one's back on, walk away from, leave to one's fate, leave flat *or* high and dry; leave *or* desert a sinking ship; **withdraw,** retreat, **beat a retreat,** retire, remove; walk away, abscond, disappear, vanish; **bow out** <nf>, make one's exit; jump ship
10 **hasten off, hurry away; scamper off, dash off,** whiz off, whip off *or* away, nip *and* nip off <nf>, tear off *or* out, **light out** <nf>, dig *or* skin out *and* burn rubber <nf>, vamoose
11 **fling out** *or* **off,** flounce out *or* off
12 **run off** *or* **away,** run along, flee, take to flight, fly, take to one's heels,

cut and run *and* hightail *and* make tracks *and* absquatulate <nf>, scarper <Brit nf>; run for one's life; beat a retreat *or* a hasty retreat; run away from 368.10

13 **check out;** clock *and* ring *and* punch out <nf>, sign out

14 **decamp, break camp,** strike camp *or* tent, **pull up stakes**

15 **embark, go aboard,** board, go on board; go on shipboard, take ship; hoist the blue Peter; **entrain,** enplane *or* emplane, embus; weigh anchor, up-anchor, put to sea 182.19

16 say *or* bid good-bye *or* farewell, take leave, make one's adieus; bid Godspeed, give one a send-off *or* a big send-off, see off *or* out; drink a stirrup cup, have one for the road

17 **leave home,** go from home, leave the country, emigrate, out-migrate, expatriate, defect; vote with one's feet; burn one's bridges; leave the nest

ADJS **18** **departing, leaving; parting,** last, final, farewell; valedictory; outward-bound

19 **departed, left, gone,** gone off *or* away

ADVS **20** **hence,** thence, whence; off, **away,** forth, out; therefrom, thereof

21 **good night!,** nighty-night! <nf>, *bonne nuit!* <Fr>, *gute Nacht!* <Ger>, \e*buenas noches!* <Sp>, *buona notte!* <Ital>, lights out!

189 ENTRANCE

NOUNS **1** **entrance, entry,** access, entree, entrée; **ingress,** ingression; **admission, reception** 187; **ingoing, incoming,** income; **importation,** import, importing; **input, intake; penetration,** interpenetration, injection; infiltration, percolation, seepage, leakage; insinuation; intrusion 214; introduction, **insertion** 191

2 **influx, inflow,** inflooding, incursion, indraft, indrawing, inpour, inrun, inrush; afflux

3 **immigration,** in-migration, incoming population, foreign influx; border-crossing

4 **incomer, entrant,** comer, arrival; **visitor,** visitant; **immigrant,** inmigrant; newcomer 774.4, new girl, new boy, new kid; settler 227.9; **trespasser, intruder** 214.3

5 **entrance,** entry, gate, door, portal, **entranceway,** entryway; **inlet,** ingress, intake, adit, approach, **access,** means of access, in <nf>, way in; a foot in the door, an opening wedge, the camel's nose under the wall of the tent; **opening** 292; **passageway,** corridor, companionway, hall, hallway, passage, way; jetway, jet bridge; gangway, gangplank; **vestibule** 197.19; air lock

6 **porch,** propylaeum, portico, portecochere; **portal, threshold,** doorjamb, gatepost, doorpost, lintel; **door, doorway,** French door; **gate, gateway; hatch,** hatchway, scuttle; turnstile

VERBS **7** **enter, go in** *or* **into,** access, cross the threshold, **come in,** find one's way into, put in *or* into; be admitted, gain admission *or* admittance, have an entree, have an in <nf>; **set foot in,** step in, walk in; **get in,** jump in, leap in, hop in; **drop in,** look in, visit, drop by, pop in <nf>; **breeze in,** come breezing in; break *or* burst in, bust *or* come busting in <nf>; **barge in** *or* come barging in *and* wade in <nf>; thrust in, push *or* press in, crowd in, jam in, wedge in, pack in, squeeze in; slip *or* creep in, wriggle *or* worm oneself into, get one's foot in the door, edge in, work in, insinuate oneself, weigh in <nf>; irrupt, intrude 214.5; take in, admit 187.10; insert 191.3

8 **penetrate,** interpenetrate, **pierce,** pass *or* go through, get through, get into, make way into, make an entrance, gain entree; crash <nf>, gatecrash <nf>

9 **flow in,** inpour, **pour in,** inrush, inflow

10 **filter in, infiltrate, seep in,** percolate into, leak in, soak in, perfuse, worm one's way into, insinuate

11 **immigrate,** in-migrate; cross the border

ADJS **12** **entering,** ingressive, **incoming, ingoing;** in, inward; **inbound,** inward-bound; inflowing, influent, inflooding, inpouring, inrushing;

invasive, intrusive, irruptive; ingrowing

ADVS **13 in,** inward, inwards, inwardly; thereinto

190 EMERGENCE

NOUNS **1 emergence,** coming out, coming forth, coming into view, rising to the surface, surfacing, emerging; **issuing,** issuance, issue; extrusion; **emission,** emitting, giving forth, giving out; emanation; **vent,** venting, discharge; outbreak, breakout

2 egress, egression; **exit,** exodus; outgoing, outgo, going out; emersion <astronomy>; **departure** 188; evacuation; extraction 192; exfiltration

3 outburst 671.6, ejection 909

4 outflow, outflowing; discharge; **outpouring,** outpour; effluence, effusion, exhalation; **efflux,** effluxion, defluxion; **exhaust; runoff, flowoff;** outfall; drainage, drain; gush 238.4

5 leakage, leaking, weeping <nf>; **leak; dripping,** drippings, **drip,** dribble, drop, trickle; distillation

6 exuding, exudation, transudation; **filtration,** exfiltration, filtering; straining; **percolation,** percolating; leaching, lixiviation; effusion, extravasation; **seepage,** seep; perfusion; **oozing,** ooze; weeping, weep; **excretion** 12

7 emigration, out-migration, remigration; exile, expatriation, defection, deportation

8 export, exporting, exportation; outgoings

9 outlet, egress, **exit,** outgo, outcome, out <nf>, way out; loophole, escape; **opening** 292; outfall, estuary; chute, flume, sluice, weir, floodgate; **vent,** ventage, venthole, port; safety valve; avenue, channel; spout, tap; opening, orifice; debouch; **exhaust;** door 189.6; outgate, sally port; vomitory; emunctory; pore; blowhole, spiracle; fire escape

10 goer, outgoer, leaver, departer; **emigrant, émigré,** out-migrant, migrant; colonist; expatriate, defector, refugee, remittance man *or* woman; walk-off <nf>

VERBS **11 emerge, come out, issue,** issue forth, come into view, extrude, **come forth; surface,** rise to the surface; sally, sally forth, come to the fore; emanate, effuse, arise, come; debouch, disembogue; jump out, leap out, hop out; bail out; **burst forth, break forth, erupt;** break cover, **come out in the open;** protrude

12 exit, make an exit, **make one's exit;** egress, **go out,** get out, walk out, march out, run out, pass out, bow out *and* include oneself out <nf>; walk out on, leave cold <nf>; escape; **depart** 188.6

13 run out, empty, find vent; **exhaust, drain,** drain out; **flow out,** outflow, outpour, **pour out,** sluice out, well out, gush *or* spout out, spew, flow, pour, well, surge, gush, jet, spout, spurt, vomit forth, blow out, spew out

14 leak, leak out, drip, dribble, drop, trickle, trill, distill

15 exude, exudate, transude, transpire, reek; **emit, discharge,** give off; **filter,** filtrate, exfiltrate; strain; **percolate;** leach, lixiviate; effuse, extravasate; **seep, ooze;** bleed; weep; excrete 12.12

16 emigrate, out-migrate, remigrate; exile, expatriate, defect; deport

17 export, send abroad

ADJS **18 emerging,** emergent; **issuing,** arising, surfacing, coming, forthcoming; emanating, emanent, emanative, transeunt, transient

19 outgoing, outbound, outward-bound; **outflowing,** outpouring, effusive, effluent; effused, extravasated

20 exudative, exuding, transudative; percolative; porous, permeable, pervious, oozy, runny, weepy, leaky; excretory 12.19

ADVS **21 forth; out,** outward, outwards, outwardly

191 INSERTION

<putting in>

NOUNS **1 insertion, introduction,** insinuation, injection, infusion, perfusion, inoculation, intromission; **entrance** 189; **penetration** 292.3; interjection, interpolation 213.2; graft, grafting, engrafting, transplant, transplantation; infixing, implantation, embedment, tessellation, impactment, impaction; intercalation

2 **insert,** insertion; **inset, inlay;** gore, godet, gusset; **graft,** scion *or* cion; tessera; parentheses; filling, stuffing; inclusion, supplement; blow-in; tampon

VERBS 3 **insert, introduce,** insinuate, inject, infuse, perfuse, inoculate, intromit; **enter** 189.7; **penetrate; put in, stick in,** set in, throw in, pop in, tuck in, whip in; slip in, ease in; interject; pot, hole; import; inoculate, vaccinate; intercalate

4 **install,** instate, inaugurate, initiate, invest, ordain; enlist, enroll, induct, sign up, sign on

5 **inset, inlay; embed** *or* bed, bed in; dovetail, mount

6 **graft,** engraft, ingraft, **implant,** imp ; bud; inarch

7 **thrust in, drive in, run in, plunge in,** force in, push in, **ram in,** press in, stuff in, crowd in, squeeze in, cram in, jam in, tamp in, pound in, pack in, poke in, knock in, wedge in, blow in, impact; shoot

8 **implant,** transplant, bed out; infix 855.9; fit in, **inlay;** tessellate

192 EXTRACTION

<taking or drawing out>

NOUNS 1 **extraction, withdrawal,** removal; **drawing, pulling,** drawing out; ripping *or* tearing *or* wresting out, extracting; eradication, **uprooting,** unrooting, deracination; squeezing out, pressing out, expressing, expression; avulsion, evulsion, cutting out, exsection, extirpation, excision, enucleation; extrication, evolvement, disentanglement, unravelment; excavation, mining, quarrying, drilling; dredging; rooting out, uprooting; exit strategy

2 **disinterment, exhumation,** disentombment, **unearthing,** uncovering, digging out; graverobbing

3 **drawing,** drafting, sucking, **suction,** aspiration, pipetting; pumping, siphoning, tapping, broaching; milking; drainage, draining, emptying; cupping; bloodletting, bleeding, phlebotomy, venesection

4 **evisceration,** gutting, **disembowelment,** shelling

5 **elicitation,** eduction, drawing out *or* forth, bringing out *or* forth; **evocation,** calling forth; arousal, derivation

6 **extortion, exaction,** claim, demand; **wresting, wrenching, wringing, rending,** tearing, ripping; wrest, wrench, wring; shakedown

7 <obtaining an extract> **squeezing, pressing,** expression; **distillation;** decoction; **rendering,** rendition; **steeping,** soaking, infusion, marinating; concentration

8 **extract,** extraction; **essence, quintessence, spirit, elixir;** decoction; **distillate,** distillation, sublimate; **concentrate,** concentration; infusion; refinement, purification

9 **extractor,** separator, excavator, digger, miner; siphon; aspirator, pipette; pump, vacuum pump; press, wringer; corkscrew; forceps, pliers, pincers, tweezers; crowbar; smelter; scoop

VERBS 10 **extract, take out,** get out, **withdraw, remove;** pull, draw; **pull out, draw out,** tear out, rip out, wrest out, pluck out, pick out, weed out, rake out; **pry out,** prize out, winkle out <Brit>; **pull up,** pluck up; **root up** *or* **out, uproot,** unroot, eradicate, deracinate, pull *or* pluck out by the roots, pull *or* pluck up by the roots; cut out, excise, exsect; enucleate; gouge out, avulse, evulse; extricate, evolve, disentangle, unravel; free, liberate; **dig up** *or* **out,** grub up *or* out, excavate, **unearth,** mine, quarry; dredge, dredge up *or* out; smelt

11 **disinter, exhume,** disentomb, unbury, unsepulcher, dig up, excavate, uncover

12 **draw off, draft off,** draft, draw, draw from; **suck,** suck out *or* up, **siphon off;** pipette; vacuum; pump, pump out; tap, broach; let, let out;

bleed; let blood, venesect, phlebotomize, bleed; milk; **drain,** decant; exhaust, empty

13 **eviscerate, disembowel, gut,** shell

14 **elicit,** educe, deduce, induce, derive, obtain, procure, secure; **get from,** get out of; **evoke, call up, summon up,** call *or* summon forth, call out; rouse, arouse, stimulate; **draw out** *or* **forth,** bring out *or* forth, pry *or* prize out, winkle out <Brit>, drag out, worm out, bring to light; wangle, wangle out of, worm out of

15 **extort, exact,** squeeze, claim, demand; **wrest, wring from, wrench from, rend from,** wrest *or* tear from, force out, shake down

16 <obtain an extract> **squeeze** *or* **press out,** express, wring, wring out, bleed; **distill,** distill out, elixirate ; **filter,** filter out; decoct; **render,** melt down; refine; **steep,** soak, infuse; **concentrate,** essentialize

ADJS 17 extractive, eductive; educible; eradicative, uprooting; elicitory, **evocative,** arousing; **exacting,** exactive; **extortionate,** extortionary, extortive

18 **essential,** quintessential, pure 798.6

193 ASCENT

<motion upwards>

NOUNS 1 **ascent,** ascension, levitation, **rise, rising,** uprising, **uprise,** uprisal; **upgoing,** upgo, uphill, upslope, upping; upcoming; **taking off,** leaving the ground, takeoff; **soaring,** zooming, gaining altitude, leaving the earth behind; spiraling *or* gyring up; shooting *or* rocketing up; defying gravity; **jump,** vault, spring, saltation, **leap** 366; mount, **mounting; climb, climbing,** upclimb, anabasis, clamber, escalade; surge, upsurge, upsurgence, upleap, upshoot, uprush; **gush, jet,** spurt, spout, fountain; updraft; upswing, upsweep, bounce; upgrowth; upgrade 204.6; **uplift,** elevation 912; **uptick** <nf>, **increase** 251; surfacing, breaking the surface

2 **upturn, uptrend,** upcast, upsweep, upbend, upcurve, upsurge

3 **stairs, stairway, staircase,** *escalier* <Fr>, escalator, flight of stairs, pair of stairs; **steps,** treads and risers; stepping-stones; spiral staircase, winding staircase, cockle stairs <nf>; companionway, companion; stile; back stairs; perron; fire escape; landing, landing stage; ramp, incline

4 **ladder,** scale; stepladder, folding ladder, rope ladder, fire ladder; hook ladder, extension ladder; Jacob's ladder, companion ladder, accommodation ladder, boarding ladder, loft ladder, side ladder, gangway ladder, quarter ladder, stern ladder, folding ladder, aerial ladder

5 **step, stair, footstep,** rest, footrest, stepping-stone; **rung, round,** rundle, spoke, stave, scale; doorstep; tread; riser; bridgeboard, string; step stool

6 **climber,** ascender, upclimber, soarer; mountain climber, **mountaineer,** alpinist, rock climber, rockjock <nf>, cragsman; steeplejack; stegophilist

7 <comparisons> rocket, skyrocket; lark, skylark, eagle

VERBS 8 **ascend, rise, mount,** arise, up, uprise, levitate, upgo, **go up,** rise up, come up; go onwards and upwards; upsurge, **surge,** upstream, upheave; swarm up, upswarm, sweep up; upwind, upspin, spiral, spire, curl upwards; stand up, **rear,** rear up, **tower,** loom; upgrow, grow up

9 **shoot up, spring up,** jump up, **leap up,** vault up, start up, fly up, pop up, bob up; float up, surface, break water; **gush, jet,** spurt, fountain; upshoot, upstart, upspring, upleap, upspear, rocket, **skyrocket**

10 **take off,** leave the ground, leave the earth behind, gain altitude, claw skyward; become airborne; **soar,** zoom, fly, plane, kite, fly aloft; aspire; spire, spiral *or* gyre upward; **hover,** hang, poise, float, float in the air; rocket, skyrocket

11 **climb,** climb up, upclimb, **mount,** clamber, **clamber up,** scramble *or* scrabble up, claw one's way up, struggle up, inch up, shin, shinny *or* shin up <nf>, ramp <nf>, work *or*

inch one's way up, climb the ladder; **scale,** escalade, scale the heights; climb over, surmount, go over the top

12 **mount, get on,** climb on, back; **bestride,** bestraddle; **board,** go aboard, go on board; **get in,** jump in, hop in, pile in <nf>; surmount, remount

13 **upturn, turn up,** cock up; trend upwards, slope up; upcast, upsweep, upbend, upcurve

ADJS 14 **ascending,** in the ascendant, **mounting, rising,** uprising, upgoing, upcoming; ascendant, ascensional, ascensive, anabatic; **leaping,** springing, saltatory; spiraling, skyrocketing; **upward**; uphill, uphillward, upgrade, upsloping, gradient; uparching, rearing, rampant; climbing, scandent, scansorial; gravity-defying

15 **upturned, upcast,** uplifted, **turned-up,** retroussé

ADVS 16 **up, upward, upwards,** upwith; skyward, heavenward; uplong, upalong; upstream, upstreamward; uphill; uphillward; upstairs; up attic *and* up steps <nf>; uptown; up north

194 DESCENT

<motion downward>

NOUNS 1 **descent, descending,** descension *or* downcome , **comedown,** down; **dropping, falling,** plummeting, **drop, fall, free-fall,** *chute* <Fr>, **downfall,** debacle, **collapse,** crash; **swoop,** stoop, pounce, downrush, downflow, cascade, waterfall, cataract, **downpour,** defluxion; downturn, downcurve, downbend, downward trend, downtrend; declension, declination, inclination; gravitation; abseil, rappel; downgrade 204.5; **down tick; decrease** 252

2 **sinkage,** lowering, **decline, slump,** subsidence, submergence, lapse, decurrence, downgrade; cadence; **droop, sag,** swag; catenary; downer <nf>

3 **tumble, fall,** *culbute* <Fr>, cropper *and* **spill** <nf>, **flop** <nf>; **header** <nf>; **sprawl; pratfall** <nf>; **stumble,** trip; **dive, plunge** 367, belly flop, nosedive; forced landing

4 **slide; slip,** slippage; **glide,** coast, glissade; glissando; slither; **skid,** sideslip; **landslide,** mudslide, landslip, subsidence; **snowslide,** snowslip <Brit>; **avalanche**

VERBS 5 **descend, go** *or* **come down,** down, dip down, lose altitude, dump altitude <nf>; gravitate; **fall, drop,** precipitate, rain, rain *or* pour down, fall *or* drop down; **collapse,** crash; **swoop,** stoop, pounce; **pitch, plunge** 367.6, **plummet;** cascade, cataract; parachute; come down a peg <nf>; **fall off,** drop off; trend downward, down-tick, go downhill

6 **sink, go down,** sink down, submerge; **set, settle,** settle down; **decline,** lower, **subside,** give way, lapse, cave, cave in; **droop,** slouch, **sag,** swag; **slump,** slump down; flump, flump down; flop *and* flop down <nf>; plump, plop *or* plop down, plunk *or* plunk down <nf>; founder 367.8

7 **get down, alight,** touch down, **light; land,** settle, perch, come to rest; **dismount, get off,** uphorse; climb down; abseil, rappel

8 **tumble, fall, fall down,** come *or* fall *or* get a cropper <nf>, take a fall *or* tumble, take a flop *or* spill <nf>, precipitate oneself; fall over, tumble over, trip over; **sprawl,** sprawl out, take a pratfall <nf>, spread-eagle <nf>, measure one's length; fall headlong, **take a header** <nf>, nosedive; fall prostrate, fall flat, fall on one's face, fall flat on one's ass <nf>; **fall over,** topple down *or* over; capsize, turn turtle; **topple,** lurch, pitch, **stumble,** stagger, totter, careen, list, tilt, trip, flounder

9 **slide, slip,** slidder <nf>, slip *or* slide down; **glide,** skim, coast, glissade; **slither; skid,** sideslip; avalanche

10 **light upon,** alight upon, settle on; **descend upon, come down on, fall on,** drop on, hit *or* strike upon

ADJS 11 **descending,** descendant, on the descendant; **down,** downward, declivitous; decurrent, deciduous; **downgoing,** downcoming; down-reaching; **dropping, falling,**

plunging, plummeting, downfalling; **sinking,** downsinking, foundering, submerging, setting; declining, **subsiding;** collapsing, tumbledown, tottering; drooping, sagging; on the downgrade, downhill 204.16

12 **downcast, downturned;** hanging, down-hanging, collapsed

ADVS 13 **down, downward, downwards,** from the top down, *de haut en bas* <Fr>; adown, below; downright; downhill, downgrade; downstreet; downline; downstream; downstairs; downtown; south, down south

195 CONTAINER

NOUNS 1 **container, receptacle;** receiver 479.3, holder, vessel, utensil; repository, depository, reservoir, store; basin, pot, pan, drinking vessel, cup, glass, bottle, crockery, ladle; cask; box, case, crate, carton; bucket; bottle, can, box, pack, jar; kit; basket; luggage, suitcase, baggage, trunk; cabinet, cupboard; shelf, drawer, locker; frame; compartment; packet; cart, truck

2 **bag, sack,** sac, poke <nf>, bundle; **pocket,** fob; **balloon, bladder;** carryall, pouch; purse, handbag, tote, satchel

196 CONTENTS

NOUNS 1 **contents, content,** what is contained *or* included *or* comprised; **insides** 207.4, innards <nf>, guts, inner workings; **components, constituents, ingredients,** elements, **items, parts, divisions,** subdivisions; **inventory,** index, census, list 871; part 793; whole 792; composition 796; constitution, makeup, embodiment

2 **load, lading, cargo, freight, charge, burden; payload;** boatload, busload, carload, cartload, containerload, shipload, trailerload, trainload, truckload, vanload, wagonload; shipment, stowage, tonnage

3 **lining,** liner; **interlining,** interlineation; inlayer, inside layer, **inlay,** inlaying; **filling,** filler; **packing,** padding, wadding, **stuffing;** facing; doubling, doublure; bushing, bush; wainscot; insole; facing; innards

4 <contents of a container> cup, cupful, etc

5 <essential content> **substance, sum and substance, stuff, material, matter,** medium, building blocks, fabric; **gist, heart, soul, meat, nub;** the nitty-gritty *and* the bottom line *and* the name of the game <nf>, **core,** kernel, marrow, pith, sap, spirit, **essence,** quintessence, elixir, distillate, distillation, distilled essence, nucleus; sine qua non, irreducible *or* indispensable content

6 **enclosure,** the enclosed, yard, corral, pen

VERBS 7 **fill, pack** 794.7, **load; line,** interline, interlineate; inlay; face; wainscot, ceil; **pad,** wad, **stuff;** feather, fur; fill up, top up

197 ROOM

<compartment>

NOUNS 1 **room, chamber,** *chambre* <Fr>, *salle* <Fr>, four walls

2 **compartment,** chamber, space, enclosed space; **cavity,** hollow, hole, concavity; **cell,** cellule; booth, stall, crib, manger; box, pew; **crypt, vault**

3 **nook, corner, cranny, niche, recess,** cove, bay, oriel, alcove; cubicle, roomlet, carrel, hole-in-the-wall <nf>, cubby, **cubbyhole,** snuggery, hidey-hole <nf>

4 **hall;** assembly hall, exhibition hall, convention hall; gallery; meetinghouse, meeting room; **auditorium; concert hall; theater,** music hall; stadium, dome, sports dome, **arena** 463; lecture hall, lyceum, amphitheater; operating theater; dance hall; ballroom, grand ballroom; **chapel** 703.3

5 **parlor, living room, sitting room, morning room, drawing** *or* **withdrawing room, front room,** best room <nf>, foreroom <nf>, **salon,** saloon ; sun parlor *or* sunroom,

lounge, sun lounge, sunporch, solarium, conservatory

6 **library,** stacks; **study,** studio, *atelier* <Fr>, workroom, den; **office,** workplace, cubicle, cube farm <nf>, home office; **loft,** sail loft

7 **bedroom, boudoir,** chamber, sleeping chamber, **bedchamber,** master bedroom, guest room, sleeping room, cubicle, cubiculum; nursery; dormitory *or* dorm room

8 <private chamber> **sanctum,** sanctum sanctorum, holy of holies, adytum; **den,** retreat, closet, cabinet; cave <nf>

9 <ships> cabin, stateroom; saloon; house, deckhouse, trunk cabin, cuddy, shelter cabin

10 <trains> drawing room, stateroom, parlor car, Pullman car, roomette, bar car

11 **dining room,** *salle à manger* <Fr>, dinette; breakfast room, breakfast nook, dining hall, refectory, mess *or* messroom *or* mess hall, commons, canteen; dining car *or* diner; **restaurant, cafeteria**

12 **playroom,** recreation room, rec room <nf>, family room, game room, **rumpus room** <nf>; **gymnasium**

13 **utility room,** laundry room, sewing room, mud room

14 **kitchen** 11.4, kitchenette, galley, pantry, larder, scullery; **storeroom** 386.6, smoking room 89.13

15 **closet,** clothes closet, wardrobe, cloakroom, walk-in closet; checkroom; linen closet; dressing room, fitting room, pantry

16 **attic,** attic room, **garret, loft,** sky parlor; cockloft, hayloft; storeroom, junk room, lumber room <Brit>

17 **basement; cellar,** cellarage; subbasement; wine cellar, potato cellar, storm cellar, cyclone cellar; coal bin *or* hole, hold, hole, bunker; glory hole; panic room, safe room; man cave

18 **corridor, hall,** hallway; passage, **passageway; gallery,** loggia; arcade, colonnade, pergola, cloister, peristyle; areaway; breezeway

19 **vestibule,** portal, **portico,** entry, entryway, entrance, **entrance hall,** entranceway, **threshold; lobby, foyer;** propylaeum, stoa; narthex, galilee

20 **anteroom,** antechamber; side room, byroom; **waiting room,** transit lounge, *salle d'attente* <Fr>; **reception room,** presence chamber *or* room, audience chamber; throne room; lounge, greenroom, wardroom

21 **porch,** stoop, **veranda,** deck, piazza <nf>, patio, lanai, gallery; sleeping porch

22 **balcony,** gallery, terrace, deck

23 **floor, story,** level, flat; first floor *or* story, ground *or* street floor, *rez-de-chaussée* <Fr>; mezzanine, mezzanine floor, *entresol* <Fr>; clerestory

24 **showroom,** display room, exhibition room, gallery

25 **hospital room; ward,** maternity ward, fever ward, charity ward, prison ward, etc; private room, semi-private room; examining *or* examination room, consulting *or* consultation room, treatment room; **operating room** *or* OR, operating theater, surgery; labor room, delivery room; recovery room; emergency, emergency room; intensive care unit *or* ICU, critical care; pharmacy, dispensary; clinic, nursery; laboratory *or* blood bank; nurses' station

26 **bathroom, lavatory, washroom** 79.10, **water closet** *or* **WC,** closet, **rest room,** privy, john <nf>, comfort station, **toilet** 12.10

27 <for vehicles> **garage,** carport; coach *or* carriage house; carbarn; roundhouse; hangar; boathouse; shed

198 TOP

NOUNS **1** **top,** top side, upper side, upside; surface 206.2; superstratum; topside *or* topsides; upper story, top floor; clerestory; **roof,** ridgepole *or* roofpole; rooftop; ceiling

2 **summit,** top; **tip-top, peak,** pinnacle; **crest, brow;** ridge, edge; **crown,** cap, **tip,** point, spire, pitch; highest pitch, no place higher, **apex,** vertex, **acme,** *ne plus ultra* <Fr>, **zenith, climax,** apogee, pole;

culmination; extremity, maximum, limit, upper extremity, highest point, very top, top of the world, extreme limit, utmost *or* upmost *or* uppermost height; exosphere, **sky,** heaven *or* heavens, seventh heaven, cloud nine <nf>; meridian, noon, high noon; mountaintop; ninth degree

3 **topping,** icing, frosting; dressing, streusel

4 <top part> **head,** heading, **headpiece,** cap, *caput* <L>, capsheaf, **crown, crest;** topknot; pinhead, nailhead

5 **architectural topping, capital,** head, crown, cap; bracket capital; cornice; cymatium, clerestory

6 **head,** headpiece, **pate,** poll <nf>, crown, **sconce** *and* **noodle** *and* **noddle** *and* **noggin** *and* **bean** *and* dome <nf>; brow, ridge

7 **skull,** cranium, pericranium, epicranium; brainpan, brain box *or* case

8 **phrenology,** craniology, metoposcopy, physiognomy; phrenologist, craniologist, metoposcopist, physiognomist

VERBS 9 **top,** top off, **crown, cap,** crest, **head,** tip, peak, surmount; overtop *or* outtop, have the top place *or* spot, overarch; **culminate,** consummate, climax; ice, frost, dress; fill, top up

ADJS 10 **top,** topmost, **uppermost,** upmost, overmost, **highest;** tip-top, tip-crowning, **maximum,** maximal, ultimate; summital, apical, vertical, zenithal, climactic, climactical, **consummate;** acmic, acmatic; meridian, meridional; **head,** headmost, capital, chief, paramount, supreme, preeminent, uber; **top-level,** highest level, top-echelon, top-flight, top-ranking, top-drawer <nf>; peak, pitch, ultimate, maximum, crowning

11 **topping, crowning, capping,** heading, surmounting, overtopping *or* outtopping, overarching; **culminating,** consummating, perfecting, climaxing

12 **topped,** headed, **crowned, capped,** crested, plumed, tipped, peaked, roofed

13 **topless,** headless, crownless

14 cranial; cephalic, encephalic

ADVS 15 **atop, on top,** at *or* on the top, topside <nf>; at the top of the tree *or* ladder, on top of the roost *or* heap; on the crest *or* crest of the wave; at the head, at the peak *or* pinnacle *or* summit

199 BOTTOM

NOUNS 1 **bottom,** bottom side, **underside,** nether side, lower side, downside, **underneath,** fundament; belly, underbelly; buttocks 217.4, breech; **rock bottom, bedrock,** bed, hardpan; **grass roots;** substratum, underlayer, lowest level *or* layer *or* stratum, nethermost level *or* layer *or* stratum, basecoat; **nadir,** the pits <nf>; depths, benthos

2 **base,** basement, **foot,** footing, sole, toe; **foundation** 901.6, core, underpinning, infrastructure; baseboard, mopboard, skirt; wainscot, dado; skeleton, bare bones, chassis, frame, undercarriage, underside; keel, keelson

3 ground covering, **ground,** earth, *terra firma* <L>; **floor,** flooring; parquet; **deck; pavement,** *pavé* <Fr>, paving, surfacing, asphalt, blacktop, macadam, concrete; **cover,** carpet, floor covering; artificial turf, Astroturf <TM>

4 **bed, bottom, floor,** ground, **basin, channel,** coulee; riverbed, seabed, ocean bottom 275.4

5 **foot,** extremity, pes, pedes, *pied* <Fr>, trotter, pedal extremity, dog, tootsy <nf>; **hoof,** ungula; **paw,** pad, pug, *patte* <Fr>; forefoot, forepaw; harefoot, splay-foot, clubfoot; **toe,** digit; **heel; sole,** pedi *or* pedio; instep, arch; pastern; fetlock

VERBS 6 **base on, found on, ground on, build on,** bottom on, bed on, set on; root in; **underlie,** undergird; bottom, bottom out, hit bottom

ADJS 7 **bottom,** bottommost, **undermost,** nethermost, lowermost, deepest, **lowest; rock-bottom,** bedrock; ground, ground-level

8 **basic;** basal, basilar, base; **underlying, fundamental,** foundational, essential, elementary, elemental, primary, primal, primitive, rudimentary, original, grass-roots; supporting; radical; nadiral

9 **pedal;** plantar; footed, hoofed, ungulate, clawed, taloned; toed

200 VERTICALNESS

NOUNS **1** **verticalness,** verticality, verticalism; **erectness, uprightness;** stiffness *or* erectness of posture, position of attention, brace; straight up-and-downness, up-and-downness; steepness, sheerness, precipitousness, plungingness, **perpendicularity,** plumbness, aplomb; right angledness *or* angularity, squareness, orthogonality; Y-axis

2 **vertical, upright, perpendicular,** plumb, normal; right angle, orthodiagonal; vertical circle, azimuth circle

3 **precipice, cliff, sheer** *or* yawning cliff *or* precipice *or* drop, steep, bluff, wall, face, scar; crag; scarp, **escarpment; palisade,** palisades; brink

4 **erection,** erecting, **elevation; rearing,** raising; **uprearing,** upraising, lofting, uplifting, heaving up *or* aloft; standing on end *or* upright *or* on its feet *or* on its base *or* on its legs *or* on its bottom *or* at attention

5 **rising, uprising, ascension,** ascending, ascent; vertical height *or* dimension; **gradient,** rise, uprise

6 <instruments> square, T square, try square, set square, carpenter's square; plumb, plumb line, plumb rule, plummet, bob, plumb bob, lead

VERBS **7** **stand, stand erect, stand up, stand upright, stand up straight,** be erect, be on one's feet; hold oneself straight *or* stiff, stand ramrod-straight, have an upright carriage; stand at attention *and* brace *and* stand at parade rest <military>

8 **rise, arise,** ascend, mount, uprise, **rise up, get up,** get to one's feet; **stand up, stand on end; stick up,** cock up; bristle; **rear,** ramp, uprear, rear up, rise on the hind legs; upheave; sit up, sit bolt upright, straighten up; jump up, spring to one's feet

9 **erect, elevate, rear, raise,** pitch, **set up,** raise *or* lift *or* cast up; raise *or* heave *or* rear aloft; uprear, upraise, uplift, upheave; upright; **upend,** stand on end, stand upright *or* on end; set on its feet *or* legs *or* base *or* bottom

10 **plumb,** plumb-line, set *à plomb;* **square,** square up

ADJS **11** **vertical, upright,** bolt upright, ramrod straight, **erect,** upstanding, standing up, stand-up; rearing, rampant; **upended,** upraised, upreared; downright; up-and-down

12 **perpendicular, plumb,** straight-up-and-down, straight-up, **up-and-down;** sheer, steep, precipitous, plunging; **right-angled,** right-angle, right-angular, orthogonal, orthodiagonal

ADVS **13** **vertically, erectly,** upstandingly, uprightly, **upright,** up, stark *or* bolt upright; **on end,** up on end, right on end, endwise, endways; on one's feet *or* legs, on one's hind legs <nf>; at attention *and* braced *and* at parade rest <military>

14 **perpendicularly,** sheer, sheerly; up and down, **straight up and down; plumb,** *à plomb* <Fr>; **at right angles,** square

201 HORIZONTALNESS

NOUNS **1** **horizontalness,** horizontality; **levelness, flatness,** planeness, planarity, evenness, smoothness, flushness, alignment; unbrokenness, unrelievedness; transom

2 **recumbency,** recumbence, decumbency *or* decumbence, accumbency; accubation; **prostration,** proneness, procumbency; supineness, reclining, reclination; lying, lounging, **repose** 20; sprawl, loll; shavasana, corpse pose

3 **horizontal, plane, level, flat,** dead level *or* flat, homaloid; **horizontal**

or level plane; horizontal *or* level line; horizontal projection; horizontal surface, fascia; horizontal parallax; horizontal axis; horizontal fault; water level, sea level, mean sea level; ground, earth, steppe, **plain, flatland,** prairie, savanna, flats, sea of grass, bowling green, table, billiard table; floor, platform, ledge, terrace

4 **horizon, skyline,** rim of the horizon; sea line; apparent *or* local *or* visible horizon, sensible horizon, celestial *or* rational *or* geometrical *or* true horizon, artificial *or* false horizon; azimuth

VERBS 5 **lie, lie down,** lay <nf>, **recline, repose,** lounge, sprawl, loll, drape *or* spread oneself, spread-eagle, splay, lie limply; **lie flat** *or* prostrate *or* prone *or* supine, lie on one's face *or* back, lie on a level, hug the ground *or* deck; **grovel, crawl,** kowtow

6 **level, flatten, even, equalize,** align, smooth *or* smoothen, level out, smooth out, flush; grade, roll, roll flat, steamroller *or* steamroll; **lay,** lay down *or* out; **raze,** rase, lay level, lay level with the ground; lay low *or* flat; **fell** 913.5; deck <nf>

ADJS 7 **horizontal, level, flat,** flattened; **even,** smooth, smoothened, smoothed out; table-like, tabular; **flush;** homaloidal; **plane,** planar, plain; rolled, trodden, squashed, rolled *or* trodden *or* squashed flat, razed; flat as a pancake, flat as a table *or* billiard table *or* bowling green *or* tennis court, flat as a board, level as a plain

8 **recumbent,** accumbent, procumbent, decumbent; **prostrate, prone,** flat; **supine,** resupine; couchant, *couché* <Fr>; **lying, reclining, reposing,** flat on one's back; sprawling, lolling, lounging; corpselike; sprawled, spread, splay, splayed, draped; groveling, crawling, flat on one's belly *or* nose

ADVS 9 **horizontally, flat,** flatly, flatways, flatwise; **evenly,** flush; **level, on a level;** lengthwise, lengthways, at full length, on one's back *or* belly *or* nose

202 PENDENCY

NOUNS 1 **pendency,** pendulousness *or* pendulosity, pensileness *or* pensility; **hanging, suspension,** dangling *or* danglement, suspense, dependence *or* dependency, swinging

2 **hang, droop,** dangle, swing, fall; **sag,** swag, bag

3 **overhang, overhanging,** impendence *or* impendency, **projection,** extension, protrusion, beetling, jutting; cantilever

4 **pendant,** hanger; **hanging,** drape; **lobe,** ear lobe, lobule, lobus, lobation, lappet, wattle; lavalier *or* lavaliere; teardrop; **uvula**

5 **suspender, hanger,** supporter; **suspenders,** pair of suspenders, braces <Brit>, galluses <nf>

VERBS 6 **hang,** hang down, fall; **depend,** pend; **dangle,** swing, flap, flop <nf>; flow, drape, cascade; **droop,** lop; nod, weep; **sag,** swag, bag; **trail, drag, draggle,** drabble, daggle

7 **overhang,** hang over, hang out, **impend,** impend over, **project,** project over, beetle, **jut,** beetle *or* jut *or* thrust over, stick out over

8 **suspend, hang, hang up,** put up, fasten up; sling; oscillate, swing, sway, hover

ADJS 9 **pendent,** pendulous, pendulant, pendular, penduline, pensile; **suspended,** hung; **hanging,** pending, depending, dependent; **falling; dangling,** swinging, oscillating, falling loosely; weeping; flowing, cascading

10 **drooping, droopy,** limp, loose, nodding, floppy <nf>, loppy, lop; **sagging,** saggy, swag, sagging in folds; **bagging,** baggy, ballooning; lop-eared

11 **overhanging,** overhung, lowering, **impending,** impendent, **pending;** incumbent, superincumbent; **projecting, jutting; beetling,** beetle; beetle-browed; cantilevered

12 lobular, lobar, lobed, lobate, lobated

203 PARALLELISM
<physically parallel direction or state>

NOUNS **1 parallelism,** coextension, nonconvergence, nondivergence, collaterality, concurrence, equidistance; collineation, collimation; alignment; parallelization; parallelotropism; **analogy** 943.1

2 parallel, paralleler; parallel line, parallel dash, parallel bar, parallel file, parallel series, parallel column, parallel trench, parallel vector; parallelogram, parallelepiped *or* parallelepipedon

3 <instruments> parallel rule *or* rules *or* ruler, parallelograph, parallelometer

VERBS **4 parallel,** be parallel, coextend, run parallel, go alongside, go beside, run abreast, run side by side; match, equal

5 parallelize, place parallel to, equidistance; line up, align, realign; collineate, collimate; match; correspond, follow, equate

ADJS **6 parallel,** paralleling, parallelistic; coextending, coextensive, nonconvergent, nondivergent, **equidistant,** equispaced, collateral, concurrent; lined up, aligned; equal, even; parallelogrammical, parallelogrammatical; parallelepipedal; parallelotropic; parallelodrome, parallelinervate; analogous 943.8

ADVS **7 in parallel,** parallelwise, parallelly; side-by-side, alongside, abreast; equidistantly, nonconvergently, nondivergently; collaterally, coextensively

204 OBLIQUITY

NOUNS **1 obliquity,** obliqueness; **deviation** 164, deviance, divergence, digression, divagation, vagary, excursion, skewness, aberration, squint, declination; deflection, deflexure; nonconformity 868; diagonality, crosswiseness, transverseness; indirection, indirectness, deviousness, circumlocution, circuitousness 914; indirect question

2 inclination, leaning, lean, angularity; **slant,** slaunch <nf>, rake, **slope; tilt, tip,** pitch, **list, cant,** swag, sway; leaning tower, tower of Pisa

3 bias, bend, bent, **crook, warp, twist, turn, skew,** slue, **veer,** sheer, **swerve,** lurch; deflection

4 incline, inclination, **slope, grade,** gradient, pitch, **ramp,** launching ramp, bank, talus, gentle *or* easy slope, glacis; rapid *or* steep slope, stiff climb, scarp, chute; helicline, inclined plane <phys>; **bevel,** bezel, fleam; hillside, side; hanging gardens; shelving beach

5 declivity, descent, dip, drop, fall, falling-off *or* -away, **decline;** hang, hanging; **downgrade, downhill**

6 acclivity, ascent, climb, **rise,** rising, uprise, uprising, rising ground; **upgrade, uphill,** upgo, upclimb, uplift, steepness, precipitousness, abruptness, verticalness 200

7 diagonal, oblique, transverse, bias, bend <heraldry>, oblique line, slash, **slant,** virgule, scratch comma, serial comma, separatrix, solidus, cant; oblique angle *or* figure, rhomboid, rhombus

8 zigzag, zig, zag; zigzaggery, flexuosity, **crookedness,** crankiness; switchback, hairpin, dogleg; chevron; traverse

VERBS **9 oblique, deviate, diverge,** deflect, divagate, **bear off**, digress; angle, **angle off, swerve,** shoot off at an angle, **veer,** sheer, sway, slue, **skew, twist, turn,** bend, bias, dogleg; crook; circumlocute

10 incline, lean; slope, slant, camber, slaunch <nf>, rake, pitch, grade, bank, shelve; **tilt, tip, list, cant,** bevel, careen, keel, sidle, swag, sway; **ascend, rise,** uprise, climb, **go uphill; descend, decline,** dip, drop, fall, fall off *or* away, **go downhill;** retreat

11 cut, cut *or* slant across, cut crosswise *or* transversely *or* diagonally, catercorner, diagonalize, slash, slash across

12 zigzag, zig, zag, **stagger,** crank *or* crankle , wind in and out; traverse

ADJS **13 oblique**, obliquitous**; devious,** deviant, deviative, divergent, digressive, divagational, deflectional, excursive, off course; **indirect,** side, sidelong, roundabout; left-handed, sinister, sinistral; backhand, backhanded; circuitous 914.7

14 **askew, skew,** skewed; skew-jawed *and* skewgee *and* skew-whiff *and* askewgee *and* agee *and* agee-jawed <nf>; **awry,** wry; askance, askant, asquint, squinting, **cockeyed** <nf>; **crooked** 265.10; slaunchwise *or* slaunchways <nf>; wamperjawed *and* catawampous *and* yaw-ways <nf>, wonky <Brit nf>; wonky

15 **inclining,** inclined, inclinatory, inclinational; **leaning,** recumbent; **sloping,** sloped, aslope; raking, pitched; **slanting,** slanted, slant, aslant, slantways, slantwise; bias, biased; shelving, shelvy; **tilting,** tilted, atilt, tipped, **tipping,** tipsy, listing, **canting,** careening; sideling, sidelong; out of the perpendicular *or* square *or* plumb, bevel, beveled

16 <sloping downward> **downhill, downgrade; descending,** falling, dropping, dipping; **declining,** declined; declivous, declivitous, declivate

17 <sloping upward> **uphill, upgrade; rising,** uprising, **ascending,** climbing; acclivous, acclivitous, acclinate

18 **steep, precipitous, bluff,** plunging, abrupt, bold, **sheer,** sharp, rapid; headlong, breakneck; vertical 200.11

19 **transverse,** crosswise *or* crossways, thwart, athwart, across 170.9; **diagonal,** bendwise; catercorner *or* **catercornered** *or* cattycorner *or* cattycornered *or* kittycorner *or* kittycornered; slant, bias, biased, biaswise *or* biasways

20 **crooked, zigzag,** zigzagged, zigzaggy, zigzagwise *or* zigzagways, zigged, zagged, dogleg *or* doglegged; flexuous, twisty, hairpin, bendy, curvy, meandering; staggered, crankled ; chevrony, chevronwise *or* chevronways <architecture>

ADVS 21 **obliquely, deviously,** deviately, **indirectly,** circuitously 914.9; divergently, digressively, excursively, divagationally; **sideways** *or* sidewise, sidelong, sideling, on *or* to one side; at an angle

22 **askew, awry; askance,** askant, asquint, wonkily

23 **slantingly, slopingly,** aslant, aslope, atilt, rakingly, tipsily, slopewise, slopeways, slantwise, slantways, aslantwise, on *or* at a slant; slaunchwise *and* slaunchways <nf>; off plumb *or* the vertical; **downhill, downgrade; uphill, upgrade**

24 transversely, crosswise *or* crossways, athwart, across 170.13

25 **diagonally,** diagonalwise; **on the bias,** bias, biaswise; **cornerwise,** cornerways; catercornerways *or* **catercorner** *or* cattycorner *or* kittycorner

205 INVERSION

NOUNS 1 **inversion,** turning over *or* around *or* upside down, the other way round, inverted order; eversion, turning inside out, invagination, intussusception; introversion, turning inward; **reversing, reversal** 858.1, turning front to back *or* side to side; **reversion,** turning back *or* backwards, retroversion, retroflexion, retroflection, revulsion; devolution, atavism; recidivism; **transposition,** transposal; topsy-turvydom *or* topsy-turviness; the world turned upside-down, upside-downness, the tail wagging the dog; pronation, supination, resupination

2 **overturn, upset,** overset, **overthrow,** upturn, **turnover,** spill <nf>; subversion; **revolution** 860; **capsizing,** capsize, capsizal, turning turtle; **somersault,** somerset, *culbute* <Fr>, cartwheel, handspring; headstand, handstand; turning head over heels

3 <grammatical and rhetorical terms> metastasis, metathesis; anastrophe, chiasmus, hypallage, hyperbaton, hysteron proteron, palindrome, parenthesis, synchysis, tmesis

4 **inverse, reverse, converse, opposite** 215.5, other side of the coin *or* picture, the flip side *and* B side <nf>; counter, contrary

VERBS 5 **invert,** inverse, turn over *or* around *or* upside down; introvert, turn in *or* inward; **turn down; turn inside out,** turn out, evert, invaginate, intussuscept; **revert,** recidivate, relapse, lapse, back-slide; **reverse** 859.4, **transpose,** convert; put the cart before the horse, put in inverted order; turn into the opposite, turn about, flip-flop, turn the tables, turn the scale *or* balance; rotate, revolve, pronate, supinate, resupinate

6 **overturn, turn over, turn upside down,** turn bottom side up, upturn, **upset,** overset, **overthrow,** subvert, *culbuter* <Fr>; go *or* turn ass over elbows *or* ass over tincups <nf>, turn a somersault, go *or* turn head over heels; **turn turtle, turn topsy-turvy,** topsy-turvy, topsy-turvify, flip-flop; **tip over,** keel over, topple over; **capsize;** careen, set on its beam ends, set on its ears

ADJS 7 **inverted,** inversed, back-to-front, **backwards,** retroverted, **reversed, transposed, back side forward, tail first; inside out,** outside in, everted, invaginated, wrong side out, back-to-front; reverted, lapsed, recidivist *or* recidivistic; atavistic; devolutional; **upside-down, topsy-turvy,** ass over elbows *and* ass over tincups *and* arsy-varsy <nf>, bottom-up; **capsized,** head-over-heels; hyperbatic, chiastic, palindromic; resupinate; introverted; flipped, flip-flopped

ADVS 8 **inversely, conversely,** contrarily, contrariwise, **vice versa,** the other way around, **backwards,** turned around; **upside down,** over, **topsy-turvy; bottom up,** bottom side up; head over heels, heels over head

206 EXTERIORITY

NOUNS 1 **exteriority,** externalness, externality, **outwardness,** outerness; appearance, outward appearance, seeming, mien, **front,** manner; window-dressing, cosmetics; openness; extrinsicality 768; **superficiality, shallowness** 276; extraterritoriality, foreignness

2 **exterior,** external, **outside; surface,** superficies, covering 295, skin 2.4, outer skin *or* layer, epidermis, integument, envelope, crust, cortex, rind, shell 295.16; exoskeleton; cladding, plating; top, superstratum; **periphery, fringe,** circumference, outline, lineaments, border; **face,** outer face *or* side, facade, **front;** facet; extrados, back; store-front, shop-front, shop-window, street-front

3 **outdoors,** outside, **the out-of-doors,** the great out-of-doors, the open, **the open air;** outland, hinterland

4 **externalization,** exteriorization, bringing into the open, show, showing, display, displaying; projection; **objectification,** actualization, realization

VERBS 5 **externalize,** exteriorize, bring into the open, bring out, show, display, exhibit; **objectify,** actualize, project, realize; direct outward

6 **scratch the surface;** give a lick and a promise, do a cosmetic job, give a once-over-lightly, whitewash, give a nod

ADJS 7 **exterior, external;** extrinsic 768.3; **outer, outside, out, outward,** outward-facing, outlying, outstanding; **outermost,** outmost; front, facing; surface, superficial 276.5, epidermic, cortical, cuticular; exoskeletal; cosmetic, merely cosmetic; peripheral, **fringe,** roundabout; apparent, seeming; open 348.10, public 352.17; exomorphic

8 **outdoor, out-of-door,** out-of-doors, **outside, without-doors; open-air,** alfresco; out and about

9 extraterritorial, exterritorial; extraterrestrial, exterrestrial, extramundane; extragalactic, extralateral, extraliminal, extramural, extrapolar, extrasolar, extraprovincial, extratribal; foreign, outlandish, **alien**

ADVS 10 **externally, outwardly,** on the outside, exteriorly; **without, outside, outwards, out;** apparently, to all appearances; openly, publically, to judge by appearances; superficially, on the surface

11 **outdoors, out of doors, outside,** abroad, withoutdoors; in the open, **in the open air,** alfresco, *en plein air* <Fr>

207 INTERIORITY

NOUNS 1 interiority, internalness, internality, **inwardness, innerness,** inness; introversion, internalization; **intrinsicality** 767; depth 275

2 **interior, inside,** inner, inward, internal, intern; inner recess, recesses, **innermost** *or* **deepest recesses,** penetralia, intimate places, secret place *or* places; bosom, secret heart, heart, heart of hearts, soul, vitals, vital center; inner self, inner life, inner landscape, inner *or* interior man, inner nature; intrados; core, center 208.2

3 **inland,** inlands, **interior,** upcountry; **midland,** midlands; heartland; hinterland 233.2; Middle America

4 **insides, innards** <nf>, inwards, internals; inner mechanism, what makes it tick *and* works <nf>; **guts** <nf>, **vitals, viscera,** *kishkes* <Yiddish>, giblets; entrails, bowels, guts, enteron; tripes *and* stuffings <nf>

VERBS 5 internalize, put in, keep within; introvert, bottle up; enclose, embed, surround, contain, comprise, include, enfold, take to heart, assimilate; introspect; retreat into

ADJS 6 **interior, internal, inner, inside, inward;** intestine; **innermost,** inmost, **intimate,** private; visceral, gut <nf>; **intrinsic** 767.7; deep 275.10; central 208.11; indoor; live-in

7 **inland, interior,** up-country, upriver, landlocked; hinterland; **midland,** mediterranean; Middle American

8 intramarginal, intramural, intramundane, intramontane, intraterritorial, intracoastal, intragroupal; bicoastal

ADVS 9 **internally, inwardly,** interiorly, inly, **intimately,** deeply, profoundly, under the surface; **intrinsically** 767.10; centrally

10 **in, inside, within;** herein, therein, wherein

11 **inward, inwards, inwardly,** withinward, withinwards; inland, inshore

12 **indoors,** indoor, withindoors

208 CENTRALITY

NOUNS 1 **centrality,** centralness, middleness, central *or* middle *or* mid position; equidistance; centricity, centricality; concentricity; centripetalism

2 **center,** centrum; **middle** 819, midpoint, **heart, core, nucleus; core of one's being, where one lives; kernel; pith,** marrow, medulla; **nub, hub,** nave, axis, pivot, fulcrum; **navel,** umbilicus, omphalos, belly button <nf>; bull's-eye; dead center; omphalos; storm center, eye of the storm

3 <biological terms> central body, centriole, centrosome, centrosphere, nucleus; pressure point

4 **focus,** focal point, prime focus, point of convergence; **center of interest** *or* attention, focus of attention; center of consciousness; **center of attraction, centerpiece,** clou, mecca, cynosure; star, key figure; polestar, lodestar; magnet; center of gravity

5 **nerve center,** ganglion, center of activity, hub, epicenter, hotbed, vital center; control center, guidance center

6 **headquarters** *or* **HQ,** central station, central office, main office, central administration, seat, base, **base of operations,** center of authority; general headquarters *or* **GHQ,** command post *or* **CP,** company headquarters; where the action is <nf>; home office, central office; homeroom

7 **metropolis, capital;** art center, cultural center, medical center, shopping center, transportation center, trade center, manufacturing center, tourist center, community center, civic center, etc; capital city; holy place, place of pilgrimage

8 **centralization,** centering; nucleation; **focalization,** focus, focusing; convergence 169; **concentration,** concentralization, pooling; centralism

VERBS 9 **centralize, center,** middle; center round, center on *or* in, pivot on, revolve around

10 **focus,** focalize, come to a point *or* focus, bring to *or* into focus; bring *or* come to a head, get to the heart of the matter home in on; zero in on, pinpoint; draw a bead on *and* get a handle on <nf>; **concentrate,** concenter, get it together <nf>; **channel,** direct, canalize, channelize; converge 169.2

ADJS **11** **central,** centric, **middle** 819; centermost, middlemost, **midmost; equidistant;** centralized, concentrated; umbilical, omphalic; axial, **pivotal,** key; centroidal; centrosymmetric; geocentric, epicentral; halfway

12 **nuclear,** nucleate, core

13 **focal,** confocal; converging; centrolineal, centripetal; cynosural; pivotal

14 **concentric;** homocentric, centric; **coaxial,** coaxal

ADVS **15** **centrally,** in the center *or* middle of, at the heart of

209 ENVIRONMENT

NOUNS **1** **environment, surroundings, environs,** surround, ambience, entourage, circle, circumjacencies, circumambiencies, **circumstances,** environing circumstances, *alentours* <Fr>; **precincts,** ambit, purlieus, **milieu; neighborhood, vicinity,** vicinage, area; **suburbs,** burbs <nf>, bedroom community; outskirts, outposts, borderlands; borders, boundaries, limits, periphery, perimeter, compass, circuit; **context, situation;** habitat 228; total environment, configuration, gestalt

2 **setting, background,** backdrop, ground, surround, field, scene, arena, theater, locale, confines; back, rear, hinterland, distance; stage, stage setting, stage set, *mise-en-scène* <Fr>

3 <surrounding influence or condition> **milieu, ambience, atmosphere, climate, air,** aura, spirit, feeling, feel, quality, color, local color, sense, sense of place, note, tone, overtone, undertone, vibrations *or* vibes <nf>

4 <natural or suitable environment> **element,** medium; **the environment**

5 **surrounding, encompassment,** environment, circumambience *or* circumambiency, circumjacence *or* circumjacency; containment, **enclosure** 212; **encirclement,** cincture, encincture, circumcincture, circling, girdling, girding; **envelopment,** enfoldment, encompassment, encompassing, compassing, embracement; circumposition; circumflexion; inclusion 772, involvement 898

VERBS **6** **surround, environ,** compass, **encompass,** enclose, close; go round *or* around, compass about, outlie; **envelop,** enfold, lap, wrap, enwrap, embrace, enclasp, embosom, embay, involve, invest

7 **encircle, circle,** ensphere, belt, belt in, zone, cincture, encincture; **girdle,** gird, begird, engird, ring, band; loop; wreathe, wreathe *or* twine around

ADJS **8** **environing, surrounding,** encompassing, enclosing; **enveloping,** wrapping, enwrapping, enfolding, embracing; **encircling,** circling; bordering, peripheral, perimetric; circumjacent, circumferential, circumambient, ambient; circumfluent, circumfluous; circumflex; **roundabout,** suburban, neighboring, neighbhorhood

9 **environmental,** environal; **ecological;** green

10 **surrounded,** environed, compassed, **encompassed,** enclosed, on all sides, hemmed-in; **enveloped,** wrapped, enfolded, lapped, wreathed

11 **encircled, circled,** ringed, cinctured, encinctured, belted, girdled, girt, begirt, zoned

ADVS **12** **around,** round, **about,** round about, in the neighborhood *or* vicinity *or* vicinage; close, close about

13 **all round, all about,** on every side, on all sides, on all hands, right and left

210 CIRCUMSCRIPTION

NOUNS **1** **circumscription, limiting,** circumscribing, **bounding, demarcation,** delimitation, definition, determination, specification; limit-setting, inclusion-exclusion, circling-in *or* -out, encincture, boundary-marking; containment

2 **limitation, limiting, restriction,** restricting, confinement 212.1, prescription, proscription, restraint, discipline, moderation, continence; qualification, **hedging;** bounds 211, boundary, cap, limit 211.3; time-limit, time constraint; quota; small space 258.3; proviso, condition

3 **patent, copyright,** certificate of invention, *brevet d'invention* <Fr>; **trademark, logo** *or* logotype, registered trademark, trade name, service mark; proprietary information

VERBS 4 **circumscribe, bound; mark off** *or* mark out, stake out, lay off, rope off; **demarcate,** delimit, delimitate, draw *or* mark *or* set *or* lay out boundaries, circle in *or* out, hedge in, set the limit, mark the periphery; **define,** determine, fix, specify; surround 209.6; enclose 212.5

5 **limit, restrict, restrain, bound, confine,** cap, ground <nf>; straiten, narrow, tighten; specialize; stint, scant; **condition,** qualify, hedge, hedge about; constrain; draw the line, set an end point *or* a stopping place; set a quota; discipline, moderate, contain; restrain oneself, pull one's punches <nf>; **patent, copyright,** register

ADJS 6 **circumscribed,** circumscript; ringed *or* circled *or* hedged about; **demarcated, delimited, defined,** definite, determined, determinate, specific, stated, set, fixed; surrounded 209.10, encircled 209.11

7 **limited, restricted,** bound, **bounded, finite; confined** 212.10, prescribed, proscribed, cramped, strait, straitened, narrow; conditioned, qualified, hedged, capped; disciplined, moderated; **deprived,** in straitened circumstances, pinched, inhibiting, on short commons, on short rations, strapped; patented, registered, protected, copyrighted, proprietary

8 **restricted,** out of bounds, off-limits

9 **limiting, restricting,** defining, determining, determinative, confining; limitative, limitary, restrictive, definitive, exclusive, non-compete; frozen, rationed

10 **terminal,** limital; limitable, terminable

211 BOUNDS

NOUNS 1 **bounds, limits,** boundaries, limitations, **confines, pale,** marches, bourns, verges, edges, outlines, outer markings, skirts, outskirts, **fringes,** metes, metes and bounds; periphery, **perimeter;** coordinates, parameters; **compass, circumference,** circumscription 210

2 **outline, contour,** delineation, lines, lineaments, shapes, figure, figuration, **configuration,** gestalt; **features,** main features; **profile, silhouette;** relief; skeleton, framework, frame, armature

3 **boundary, bound, limit,** limitation, extremity 794.5; **barrier,** block, claustrum; delimitation, hedge, break *or* breakoff point, cutoff, cutoff point, terminus; time limit, time frame, term, deadline, target date, terminal date, time allotment; finish, **end** 820, tail end; **start,** starting line *or* point, mark; **limiting factor,** determinant, limit *or* boundary condition; bracket, brackets, **bookends** <nf>; threshold, limen; upper limit, ceiling, apogee, high-water mark; price cap; lower limit, floor, low-water mark, nadir; **confine,** march, mark, bourn, mete, compass, circumscription; **boundary line, line, border line,** frontier, division line, interface, break, boundary, line of demarcation *or* circumvallation; county line

4 **border,** limbus, bordure <heraldry>, **edge,** limb, **verge, brink,** brow, **brim, rim, margin,** marge, **skirt, fringe, hem,** list, selvage *or* selvedge, side; **forefront, cutting edge,** front line, new guard, vanguard 216.2; sideline; shore, bank, coast; **lip,** labium, labrum, labellum; flange; ledge; frame, enframement, mat; featheredge; ragged edge

5 **frontier, border, borderland,** border ground, marchland, march,

marches; outskirts, outpost, backwoods; frontier post, cow town; iron curtain, bamboo curtain, Berlin wall; Pillars of Hercules; three-mile *or* twelve-mile limit

6 **curb,** kerb <Brit>, curbing; border stone, curbstone, kerbstone <Brit>, edgestone

7 **edging, bordering,** bordure <heraldry>, **trimming,** binding, skirting; fringe, fimbriation, fimbria; **hem,** selvage, list, welt; frill, frilling; beading, flounce, furbelow, galloon, motif, ruffle, valance

VERBS 8 **bound,** circumscribe 210.4, surround 209.6, limit 210.5, enclose 212.5, divide, separate

9 **outline,** contour; **delineate;** silhouette, profile, limn

10 **border, edge, bound, rim, skirt, hem, hem in, ringe,** befringe, lap, list, margin, marge, marginate, march, verge, line, side; **adjoin** 223.9; **frame,** enframe, set off; trim, bind; purl; purfle

ADJS 11 **bordering, fringing,** rimming, skirting; **bounding,** boundary, **limiting,** limit, determining *or* determinant *or* determinative; threshold, liminal, limbic; extreme, terminal; **marginal, borderline,** frontier; coastal, littoral, sea-bordering

12 **bordered,** edged; margined, marged, marginate, marginated; **fringed,** befringed, trimmed, skirted, fimbriate, fimbriated

13 lipped, labial, labiate

14 outlining, delineatory; peripheral, perimetric, perimetrical, circumferential; outlined, **in outline**

ADVS 15 **on the verge, on the brink,** on the borderline, on the point, on the edge, on the ragged edge, at the threshold, at the limit *or* bound; **peripherally,** marginally, at the periphery

16 **thus far,** so far, thus far and no farther

212 ENCLOSURE

NOUNS 1 **enclosure; confinement,** containing, containment, circumscription 210, immurement, walling- *or* hedging- *or* hemming- *or* boxing- *or* fencing-in, circumvallation; **imprisonment,** incarceration, jailing, locking-up, lockdown; **siege,** besieging, beleaguerment, blockade, blockading, cordoning, quarantine, besetment; inclusion 772; **envelopment** 209.5

2 **packaging, packing,** package; boxing, crating, encasement; canning, tinning <Brit>; bottling; **wrapping,** enwrapment, bundling; shrink-wrapping

3 <enclosed place> **enclosure,** close, **confine,** precinct, enclave, pale, paling, list, cincture; jail, detention center; **cloister; pen, coop,** corral, fold; **yard,** park, court, courtyard, curtilage, toft; square, quadrangle, quad <nf>; **field,** delimited field, **arena,** theater, ground, reserve, sanctuary; **container** 195

4 **fence,** fencing, **wall,** boundary 211.3, **barrier;** stone wall; paling, palisade; rail, railing; balustrade, balustrading; moat; arcade

VERBS 5 **enclose,** close in, bound, include, **contain;** compass, encompass; **surround,** encircle 209.7; **shut** *or* **pen in,** coop in; **fence in,** wall in, wall up, rail in, rail off, screen off, curtain off; **hem** *or* **hedge in,** box in, pocket; shut *or* coop *or* mew up; pen, coop, corral, cage, impound, mew; **imprison,** incarcerate, jail, lock up, lock down; **besiege,** beset, beleaguer, leaguer, cordon, cordon off, quarantine, blockade; yard, yard up; house in; chamber; stable, kennel, shrine, enshrine; **wrap** 295.20

6 **confine, immure;** quarantine; cramp, straiten, encase; cloister, closet, cabin, crib; bury, entomb, coffin, casket; bottle up *or* in, box up *or* in

7 **fence, wall,** fence in, fence up; pale, rail, bar; pen up; hem, hem in, hedge, hedge in, hedge out; picket, palisade; bulkhead in

8 parenthesize, bracket, quote, air-quote, precede and follow, bookend

9 **package, pack, parcel;** box, box up, case, encase, crate, carton; can, tin <Brit>; bottle, jar, pot; barrel, cask, tank; sack, bag; basket, hamper;

capsule, encyst; contain; **wrap,** enwrap, bundle; shrink-wrap; bandage

ADJS **10** **enclosed,** closed-in; **confined,** bound, immured, cloistered; **imprisoned,** incarcerated, jailed; caged, cramped, restrained, corralled; besieged, beleaguered, leaguered, beset, cordoned, cordoned off, quarantined, blockaded; **shut-in,** pent-up, penned, cooped, mewed, walled- *or* hedged- *or* hemmed- *or* boxed- *or* fenced-in, fenced, walled, paled, railed, barred; hemmed, hedged

11 enclosing, confining, **cloistered,** cloisterlike, claustral, parietal, surrounding 209.8; limiting 210.9

12 **packed, packaged,** boxed, crated, canned, tinned <Brit>, parceled, cased, encased; bottled; capsuled, encapsuled; **wrapped,** enwrapped, bundled; shrink-wrapped; prepacked; vacuum-packed; bandaged, sheathed

213 INTERPOSITION

<a putting or lying between>

NOUNS **1** **interposition, interposing,** interposal, interlocation, intermediacy, interjacence; **intervention,** intervenience, intercurrence, slipping-in, sandwiching; leafing-in, interleaving, interfoliation, tipping-in; **intrusion** 214

2 **interjection, interpolation,** introduction, throwing- *or* tossing-in, **injection,** insinuation; intercalation, interlineation; **insertion** 191; interlocution, remark, parenthetical *or* side *or* incidental *or* casual remark, *obiter dictum* <L>, aside, parenthesis; episode; infix, insert

3 **interspersion, interfusion,** interlardment, interpenetration

4 **intermediary,** intermedium, mediary, medium; link, **connecting link,** tie, connection, **go-between,** liaison; middleman, middleperson, broker, agent, wholesaler, jobber, distributor; moderator, **mediator** 466.3

5 **partition, dividing wall,** division, separation, *cloison* <Fr>; **wall, barrier;** panel; paries, parietes; brattice <mining>; bulkhead; diaphragm, midriff, midsection; septum, interseptum, septulum, dissepiment; **border** 211.4, **dividing line,** property line, party wall; **buffer, bumper,** mat, fender, cushion, pad, shock pad, collision mat; buffer state

VERBS **6** **interpose, interject, interpolate,** intercalate, interjaculate; **mediate, go between,** liaise <Brit nf>; **intervene;** put between, sandwich; **insert in,** stick in, introduce in, insinuate in, sandwich in, slip in, inject in, implant in; leaf in, interleaf, tip in, interfoliate; **foist in,** fudge in, work in, drag in, lug in, drag *or* lug in by the heels, worm in, squeeze in, smuggle in, throw in, run in, thrust in, edge in, wedge in; **intrude** 214.5

7 **intersperse, interfuse,** interlard, interpenetrate; intersow, intersprinkle

8 **partition,** set apart, separate, divide; **wall off,** fence off, screen off, curtain off

ADJS **9** interjectional, interpolative, intercalary; parenthetical, episodic

10 **intervening,** intervenient, **interjacent,** intercurrent; **intermediate,** intermediary, medial, mean, medium, mesne, median, **middle**

11 partitioned, walled; mural; septal, parietal

214 INTRUSION

NOUNS **1** **intrusion,** obtrusion, **interloping;** interposition 213, interposal, imposition, insinuation, **interference,** intervention, interventionism, interruption, injection, interjection 213.2; **encroachment,** entrenchment, trespass, trespassing, unlawful entry; impingement, **infringement,** invasion, incursion, inroad, influx, irruption, infiltration; entrance 189

2 **meddling,** intermeddling; **butting-in** *and* kibitzing *and* sticking one's nose in<nf>; **meddlesomeness, intrusiveness, forwardness,** obtrusiveness; **officiousness,** impertinence, presumption, presumptuousness; inquisitiveness 981.1

3 **intruder, interloper, trespasser;** crasher *and* gate-crasher <nf>, unwelcome *or* uninvited guest; invader, encroacher, infiltrator

4 **meddler,** intermeddler; **busybody, pry,** Paul Pry, prier, Nosey Parker *or* nosey Parker *or* Nosy Parker <nf>, snoop *or* snooper, *yenta* <Yiddish>, **kibitzer** *and* backseat driver <nf>

VERBS **5** **intrude,** obtrude, **interlope;** come between, **interpose** 213.6, insert oneself, **intervene, interfere,** insinuate, impose; **encroach, infringe,** impinge, **trespass,** trespass on *or* upon, trench, entrench, invade, infiltrate; **break in upon,** break in, burst in, charge in, crash in, smash in, storm in; **barge in** <nf>, irrupt, **cut in,** thrust in 191.7, push in, press in, rush in, throng in, crowd in, squeeze in, elbow in, muscle in <nf>; **butt in** *and* **horn in** *and* chisel in *and* muscle in <nf>; appoint oneself; crash *and* crash the gates <nf>; **get in,** get in on, creep in, steal in, sneak in, slink in, slip in; foist in, worm *or* work in, edge in, put in *or* shove in one's oar; **foist oneself upon,** thrust oneself upon; put on *or* upon, impose on *or* upon, put one's two cents in <nf>

6 **interrupt, put in, cut in, break in;** jump in, chime in *and* chip in *and* put in one's two-cents worth <nf>, butt in

7 **meddle, intermeddle,** busybody, not mind one's business; **meddle with, tamper with,** mix oneself up with, inject oneself into, monkey with, fool with *or* around with <nf>, mess with *or* around with <nf>; **pry,** Paul-Pry, snoop, nose, **stick** *or* **poke one's nose in,** stick one's long nose into; have a finger in, have a finger in the pie; kibitz <nf>

ADJS **8** **intrusive,** obtrusive, **interfering,** intervenient, invasive, interruptive

9 **meddlesome,** meddling; **officious,** overofficious, self-appointed, impertinent, presumptuous; **busybody,** busy; pushing, pushy, forward; **prying,** nosy *or* nosey *and* snoopy <nf>; inquisitive 981.5

PHRS **10** <nf terms> **none of your business;** what's it to you?, **mind your own business,** keep your nose out of this, **butt out,** go soak your head, go sit on a tack, go roll your hoop, go peddle your fish, go fly a kite, go chase yourself, go jump in the lake; too many cooks spoil the broth

215 CONTRAPOSITION

<a placing over against>

NOUNS **1** contraposition, anteposition, posing against *or* over against; **opposition,** opposing, opposure; **antithesis,** contrast, ironic *or* contrastive juxtaposition; confrontment, **confrontation;** polarity, polar opposition, **polarization; contrariety** 779; contention 457; hostility 451.2

2 **opposites,** antipodes, polar opposites, contraries; **poles,** opposite poles, antipoles, counterpoles, North Pole, South Pole; antipodal points, antipoints; contrapositives <logic>; night and day, black and white; antonyms

3 opposite side, other side, the other side of the picture *or* coin, other face; **reverse, inverse, obverse, converse;** heads, tails <of a coin>; flip side *and* B-side <nf>

VERBS **4** contrapose, **oppose,** contrast, match, **set over against,** pose against *or* over against, put in opposition, set *or* pit against one another; **confront,** face, front, stand *or* lie opposite, stand opposed *or* vis-à-vis; be at loggerheads, be eyeball to eyeball, bump heads, meet head-on; counteract 451.3; contend; subtend; **polarize;** contraposit <logic>

ADJS **5** contrapositive, **opposite,** opposing, **facing,** confronting, confrontational, confrontive, eyeball-to-eyeball, one-on-one, face-to-face; **opposed,** on opposite sides, adversarial, at loggerheads, at daggers drawn, antithetic, antithetical; **reverse, inverse, obverse, converse; antipodal; polar,** polarized one-on-one, up against; love-hate

ADVS **6 opposite, poles apart,** at opposite extremes; contrary, contrariwise, counter; just opposite, **face-to-face,** vis-à-vis, *front à front* <Fr>, nose to nose, one on one, eyeball-to-eyeball, back to back

216 FRONT

NOUNS **1 front, fore,** forepart, forequarter, foreside, forefront, forehand; **priority,** anteriority; front office; **frontier** 211.5; foreland; **foreground;** proscenium; frontage; front page; frontispiece; **preface,** front matter, foreword; prefix; front view, full frontal, front elevation, front seat, front yard; **head,** heading; **face,** façade, frontal; fascia; **false front,** window dressing, display, persona; front man; bold *or* brave front, brave face; facet; obverse <of a coin or medal>, head <of a coin>; lap; front burner

2 vanguard, van, point, point man; **spearhead,** advance guard, **forefront, cutting edge,** avant-garde, outguard; scout; **pioneer,** trailblazer; **precursor** 816; **front-runner,** leader, first in line; **front,** battlefront, line, front line, forward line, battle line, line of departure, new guard; front rank, first line, first line of battle; **outpost,** farthest outpost; **bridgehead,** beachhead, airhead, railhead; advanced base

3 prow, bow, stem, rostrum, figurehead, nose, beak; bowsprit, jib boom; forecastle, forepeak; foredeck; foremast

4 face, facies, **visage;** physiognomy, phiz *and* dial <nf>; **countenance,** features, lineaments, favor; mug *and* mush *and* pan *and* kisser *and* map *and* puss <nf>

5 forehead, brow, lofty brow

6 chin, point of the chin, button <nf>

VERBS **7** be *or* stand in front, **lead, head,** head up; **get ahead of,** steal a march on, take the lead, come to the front *or* fore; forge ahead; be the front-runner, lead, lead the pack *or* field, be first; **pioneer;** front, front for, represent, speak for; spearhead; push the envelope <nf>; trailblaze

8 confront, front, affront , **face, meet, encounter,** breast, stem, brave, meet squarely, square up to, come to grips with, head *or* wade into, meet face to face *or* eyeball to eyeball *or* one-on-one, come face to face with, look in the face *or* eye, stare in the face, stand up to, stand fast, hold one's ground, hang tough *and* tough it out *and* gut it out <nf>; call someone's bluff, call *or* bring someone to account; **confront with, face with,** bring face to face with, tell one to one's face, cast *or* throw in one's teeth, present to, **put** *or* **bring before,** set *or* place before, lay before, put *or* lay it on the line; bring up, bring forward; put it to, put it up to; **challenge,** dare, defy, fly in the teeth of, throw down the gauntlet, ask for trouble, start something, do something about it

9 front on, face upon, give upon, face *or* look toward, look out upon, look over, **overlook**

ADJS **10 front, frontal, anterior; full-face, full-frontal**, physiognomic**; fore, forward,** forehand; foremost, headmost; first, earliest, **pioneering, trail-blazing, advanced**, front-running**; leading,** up-front <nf>, first, chief, head, prime, primary; **confronting,** confrontational, head-on, one-on-one *and* eyeball-to-eyeball <nf>; **ahead, in front,** one-up, one jump *or* move ahead

11 fronting, facing, looking on *or* out on, opposite

ADVS **12 before, ahead,** out *or* up ahead, **in front,** in the front, in the lead, in the van, in advance, **in the forefront,** in the foreground; **to the fore,** to the front; foremost, headmost, first; before one's face *or* eyes, under one's nose

13 frontward, frontwards, **forward,** forwards, vanward, **headward,** headwards, **onward,** onwards; **facing** 215.5

217 REAR

NOUNS **1 rear, rear end, hind end,** hind part, hinder part, afterpart, rearward, **posterior, behind,** breech, stern, tail, tail end; **afterpiece,** tailpiece, heelpiece, heel; **back,** back side, reverse <of a coin or medal>, tail <of a coin>; back door, postern, postern door; back seat, rumble seat; hindhead, occiput; wake, train; back burner; tail <of a coin>

2 rear guard, rear, rear area, backyard

3 **back,** dorsum, ridge; dorsal region, lumbar region, backbone; hindquarter; loin

4 **buttocks, rump,** bottom, posterior, derrière; croup, crupper; podex; haunches; gluteal region; nates

5 <nf terms> **ass,** arse *and* bum <chiefly Brit>, behind, backside, buns, **butt, can,** cheeks, hind end, nether cheeks, stern, tail, rusty-dusty, **fanny,** prat, keister, popo, rear, rear end, tuchis *or* tushy *or* tush

6 **tail,** cauda, caudation, caudal appendage; tailpiece, scut <of a hare, rabbit, or deer>, brush <of a fox>, fantail <of fowls>; rattail, rat's-tail; dock, stub; caudal fin; **queue,** cue, **pigtail**

7 **stern,** heel; poop, transom, counter, fantail; sternpost, rudderpost; after mast

VERBS **8** <be behind> **bring up the rear,** come last, **follow,** come after; trail, trail behind, lag behind, draggle, **straggle;** fall behind, fall back, fall astern; **back up, back,** go back, go backwards, regress 163.5, retrogress, get behind; revert 859.4

ADJS **9** **rear,** rearward, **back,** backward, retrograde, **posterior,** postern, tail; after *or* aft; **hind, hinder; hindmost,** hindermost, hindhand, posteriormost, **aftermost,** aftmost, rearmost; latter

10 <anatomy> posterial, dorsal, retral, tergal, lumbar, gluteal, sciatic, occipital

11 **tail,** caudal, caudate, caudated, tailed; taillike, caudiform

12 backswept, swept-back

ADVS **13** **behind, in the rear, in back of;** in the background; behind the scenes; behind one's back; back to back; tandem

14 **after;** aft, abaft, baft, astern; aback

15 **rearward,** rearwards, to the rear, **hindward,** hindwards, **backward,** backwards, posteriorly, retrad, tailward, tailwards

218 SIDE

NOUNS **1** **side, flank, hand;** laterality, sidedness, handedness; unilaterality, unilateralism, bilaterality, bilateralism, etc, multilaterality, many-sidedness; border 211.4; parallelism 203; bank, shore, coast; siding, planking; beam; broadside; quarter; hip, haunch; cheek, jowl, chop; temple; **profile,** side-view, half-face view; side entrance, side door; sideburns, burnsides

2 **lee side, lee,** leeward; lee shore; lee tide; lee wheel, lee helm, lee anchor, lee sheet, lee tack

3 **windward side, windward,** windwards, weather side, weather, weatherboard; weather wheel, weather helm, weather anchor, weather sheet, weather tack, weather rail, weather bow, weather deck; weather roll; windward tide, weather-going tide, windward ebb, windward flood

VERBS **4** **side, flank;** edge, skirt, border 211.10; stand side by side

5 **go sideways, sidle,** lateral, lateralize, **edge, veer, angle, slant, skew,** sidestep; go crabwise; **sideslip, skid;** make leeway

ADJS **6** **side, lateral;** flanking, skirting, facing, oblique; **beside,** to the side, off to one side; **alongside, parallel** 203.6; next-beside; **sidelong,** sideling, **sidewise,** sideway, **sideways,** sideward, **sidewards,** glancing; leeward, lee; windward, weather; side-by-side; peripheral

7 **sided, flanked,** handed; lateral; **one-sided,** unilateral, unilateralist, **two-sided, bilateral,** bilateralist, etc; dihedral, bifacial; **three-sided, trilateral,** trihedral, triquetrous; **four-sided, quadrilateral,** tetrahedral, etc; **many-sided, multilateral,** multifaceted, polyhedral; left-hand, sinistral, right-hand, dextral

ADVS 8 **laterally,** laterad; **sideways,** sideway, **sidewise, sidewards,** sideward, sideling, sidling, sidelong, aside, crabwise; side-to-side; **edgeways,** edgeway, **edgewise; widthwise, widthways, thwartwise; askance,** askant, asquint, glancingly; broadside, **broadside on,** on the beam; on its side, on its beam ends; on the other hand; right and left

9 **leeward,** to leeward, alee, downwind; **windward,** to windward, weatherward, aweather, upwind

10 **aside,** on one side, **to one side,** to the side, sidelong, on the side, on the one hand, on one hand, on the other hand; **alongside,** in parallel 203.7, side-by-side; nearby, in juxtaposition 223.21; away

PHRS 11 **side by side,** cheek to cheek, cheek by cheek, cheek by jowl, shoulder to shoulder, yardarm to yardarm

219 RIGHT SIDE

NOUNS 1 **right side, right,** off side <of a horse or vehicle>, starboard; Epistle side, decanal side; recto <books>; right field; starboard tack; right wing; right-winger, conservative, reactionary

2 **rightness,** dextrality; dexterity, **right-handedness;** dextroversion, dextrocularity, dextroduction; dextrorotation, dextrogyration

3 right-hander; righty <nf>

ADJS 4 **right, right-hand,** dextral, dexter; off, **starboard;** rightmost; dextrorse; dextropedal; dextrocardial; dextrocerebral; dextrocular; **clockwise,** dextrorotary, dextrogyrate, dextrogyratory; right-wing, right-wingish, right-of-center, conservative, reactionary, dry <Brit nf>

5 **right-handed,** dextromanual, dexterous

6 **ambidextrous,** ambidextral, ambidexter; dextrosinistral, sinistrodextral

ADVS 7 **rightward,** rightwards, rightwardly, **right, to the right,** dextrally, dextrad; on the right, dexter; starboard, astarboard

220 LEFT SIDE

NOUNS 1 **left side, left, left hand,** left-hand side, wrong side <nf>, near *or* nigh side <of a horse or vehicle>, portside, port, larboard; Gospel side, cantorial side, verso <books>; left field; port tack; left wing, left-winger, radical, liberal, progressive

2 **leftness,** sinistrality, **left-handedness;** sinistration; levoversion, levoduction; levorotation, sinistrogyration

3 **left-hander, southpaw** *and* lefty *and* portsider <nf>

ADJS 4 **left, left-hand,** sinister, sinistral; near, nigh; **larboard, port;** sinistrorse; sinistrocerebral; sinistrocular; counterclockwise, levorotatory, sinistrogyrate; left-wing, left-wingish, left-of-center, radical, liberal, progressive, wet <Brit nf>

5 **left-handed,** sinistromanual, sinistral, lefty *and* southpaw <nf>

ADVS 6 **leftward,** leftwards, leftwardly, **left, to the left,** sinistrally, sinister, sinistrad; on the left; larboard, port, aport

221 PRESENCE

NOUNS 1 **presence,** being here *or* there, hereness, thereness, physical *or* actual presence, spiritual presence; **immanence,** indwellingness, **inherence;** whereness, **immediacy;** ubiety; availability, accessibility; nearness 223; **occurrence** 831.2, existence 761; manifestness, materialness; presenteeism

2 **omnipresence,** all-presence, **ubiquity;** continuum, plenum; infinity; pluripresence

3 **permeation, pervasion,** penetration; **suffusion,** transfusion, perfusion, diffusion, imbuement; absorption; **overrunning,** overspreading, ripple effect, overswarming, whelming, overwhelming; saturation

4 **attendance,** frequenting, frequence; participation; number present; turnout *and* box office *and* draw <nf>

5 **attender, visitor,** churchgoer, moviegoer, etc; **patron; fan** *and* buff

<nf>, aficionado, supporter; **frequenter,** habitué, haunter; spectator 918; theatergoer; audience 48.6; regular customer, regular

VERBS **6 be present,** be located or situated 159.10, be there, be found, be met with; **occur** 831.5, exist 761.8; liĕ, stand, remain; fall in the way of; dwell in, indwell, inhere

7 pervade, permeate, penetrate; **suffuse,** inform, transfuse, perfuse, diffuse, leaven, imbue; **fill,** extend throughout, leave no void, occupy; **overrun,** overswarm, overspread, bespread, run through, meet one at every turn, whelm, overwhelm; creep *or* crawl *or* swarm with, be lousy with <nf>, teem with; honeycomb

8 attend, be at, be present at, find oneself at, **go** *or* **come to; appear** 33.8, turn up, set foot in, show up <nf>, show one's face, make *or* put in an appearance, give the pleasure of one's company, make a personal appearance; materialize; **visit, take in** *and* do *and* catch <nf>; sit in *or* at; be on hand, be on deck <nf>; watch, see; witness, look on, *assister* <Fr>; participate, take part

9 revisit, return to, go back to, come again

10 frequent, haunt, resort to, hang *and* hang around *and* hang about *and* hang out <nf>

11 present oneself, report; report for duty

ADJS **12 present,** attendant; **on hand,** on deck <nf>, on board, in attendance; **immediate,** immanent, indwelling, inherent, **available, accessible, at hand,** in view, within reach *or* sight *or* call, in place; intrinsic

13 omnipresent, all-present, ubiquitous, everywhere; continuous, uninterrupted, infinite

14 pervasive, pervading, suffusive, perfusive, diffusive, suffusing

15 permeated, saturated, shot through, filled with, perfused, suffused, imbued; honeycombed; crawling, creeping, swarming, teeming, lousy with <nf>

ADVS **16 here, there**

17 in person, personally, bodily, **in the flesh** <nf>, in one's own person, *in propria persona* <L>

PHRS **18** all present and accounted for; standing room only *or* SRO

222 ABSENCE

NOUNS **1 absence,** nonpresence, awayness; nowhereness, **nonexistence** 762; want, **lack,** total lack, blank, deprivation; nonoccurrence, neverness; **subtraction** 255

2 vacancy, vacuity, voidness, **emptiness,** blankness, hollowness, inanition; **bareness,** barrenness, desolateness, bleakness, desertedness; **nonoccupancy,** nonoccupation, vacancy, noninhabitance, nonresidence; job vacancy, opening, open place *or* post, vacant post

3 void, vacuum, blank, emptiness, empty space, inanity, vacuity; **nothingness;** *tabula rasa* <L>, clean *or* blank slate; **nothing** 762.2

4 absence, nonattendance, **absenting, leaving,** taking leave, **departure** 188; running away, fleeing, decamping, bolting, skedaddling, absquatulating *or* absquatulation, abscondence, scarpering <Brit nf>, desertion, defection; **disappearance** 34, escape 369; **absentation,** nonappearance, default, unauthorized *or* unexcused absence; **truancy, hooky** <nf>, French leave, **cut** <nf>; **absence without leave** *or* AWOL; **absenteeism,** truantism, absentation; **leave, leave of absence,** furlough; **vacation,** holiday, paid vacation, paid holiday, paid time off, time off, day off, comp *or* compensation time; authorized *or* excused absence, sick leave; sabbatical

5 absentee, truant, no-show, missing person

6 nobody, no one, no man, no woman, not one, not a single one *or* person, **not a soul** *or* **blessed soul** *or* **living soul,** never a one, ne'er a one, nary one <nf>, nobody on earth *or* under the sun, nobody present; nonperson, unperson; nonentity

VERBS **7 be absent, stay away,** keep away, keep out of the way, not come, not show up <nf>, not turn up, turn up missing <nf>, stay away in droves <nf>, fail to appear, default, sit out, include oneself out <nf>

8 **absent oneself, take leave** *or* **leave of absence,** go on leave *or* furlough; **vacation,** go on vacation *or* holiday, take time off, take off from work; slip off *or* away, duck *or* sneak out <nf>, slip out, make oneself scarce <nf>, leave the scene, bow out, exit, vacate, **depart** 188.6, **disappear** 34.2, escape 369.6; defect, desert

9 **play truant, go AWOL,** take French leave; play hooky, cut *or* skip <nf>, cut classes; jump ship

10 <nf terms> **split,** bugger off, fuck off, f off, make tracks, pull up stakes, push along, scarper <Brit>, push off, skedaddle *or* absquatulate , **haul ass,** bag ass, **beat it, blow,** boogie, bug out, cut, **cut out,** cut and run, peel out, bunk off *or* piss off <Brit>, scram, shove off, vamoose

ADJS 11 **absent,** not present, nonattendant, **away, gone,** departed, disappeared, vanished, absconded, out of sight; **missing,** among the missing, wanting, **lacking,** not found, nowhere to be found, omitted, taken away, subtracted, deleted; no longer present *or* with us *or* among us; long-lost; **nonexistent;** conspicuous by its absence

12 **nonresident,** not in residence, from home, **away from home,** on leave *or* vacation *or* holiday, on sabbatical leave; on tour; on the road; abroad, overseas

13 **truant,** absent without leave *or* **AWOL**

14 **vacant, empty,** hollow, inane, **bare, vacuous, void,** without content, with nothing inside, devoid, null, null and void; **blank,** clear, white, bleached; featureless, unrelieved, characterless, bland, insipid; **barren** 891.4

15 **available, open,** free, **unoccupied,** unfilled, **uninhabited,** unpopulated, unpeopled, untaken, untenanted, tenantless, untended, unmanned, unstaffed; **deserted,** abandoned, forsaken, godforsaken <nf>; untouristed

ADVS 16 **absently; vacantly, emptily,** hollowly, vacuously, blankly

17 **nowhere,** in no place, neither here nor there; nowhither

18 **away** 188.20, **elsewhere,** somewhere else, not here; elsewhither

223 NEARNESS

NOUNS 1 **nearness, closeness,** nighness, **proximity,** propinquity, intimacy, immediacy; approximation, approach, convergence; a rough idea <nf>; **vicinity,** vicinage, **neighborhood,** environs, surroundings, surround, setting, grounds, purlieus, confines, precinct; **foreground,** immediate foreground; convenience, handiness, accessibility

2 **short distance, short way,** little ways, **step,** short step, span, brief span, short piece <nf>, a little, intimate distance; shortcut; short range; close quarters *or* range *or* grips; middle distance; **stone's throw,** spitting distance <nf>, bowshot, gunshot, pistol shot; earshot, earreach, a whoop *and* a whoop and a holler *and* two whoops and a holler <nf>, ace, bit <nf>, **hair, hairbreadth** *or* **hairsbreadth,** finger's breadth *or* width, an inch; inch, millimeter, centimeter; near miss

3 **juxtaposition, apposition,** adjacency; **contiguity,** contiguousness, conterminousness *or* coterminousness; butting, abuttal, abutment; adjunction, junction 800.1, connection, union; **conjunction,** conjugation, collocation; appulse, syzygy; perigee, perihelion

4 **meeting,** meeting up, joining, joining up, **encounter;** juncture; confrontation; rencontre; near-miss, collision course, near thing, narrow squeak *or* brush

5 **contact, touch,** touching, *attouchement* <Fr>, taction, tangency, contingence; gentle *or* tentative contact, caress, brush, glance, nudge, kiss, rub, graze; impingement, impingence; osculation

6 **neighbor,** neighborer, next-door *or* immediate neighbor; borderer; abutter, adjoiner; bystander, onlooker, looker-on; tangent; buffer state; ringside seat

VERBS **7** **near, come near,** nigh, draw near *or* nigh, **approach** 167.3, come within shouting distance; **converge,** shake hands <nf>; come within an ace *or* an inch

8 **be near** *or* **around,** be in the vicinity *or* neighborhood, **approximate, approach,** get warm <nf>, come near, have something at hand *or* at one's fingertips; give *or* get a rough idea <nf>

9 **adjoin,** join, conjoin, **connect,** butt, **abut,** abut on *or* upon, be contiguous, be in contact; **neighbor,** border, **border on** *or* **upon,** verge on *or* upon; lie by, stand by

10 **contact, come in contact, touch, feel, impinge,** bump up against, hit; osculate; **graze,** caress, kiss, nudge, rub, brush, glance, scrape, sideswipe, skim, skirt, shave; grope *and* feel up *and* cop a feel <nf>; have a near miss, brush *or* graze *or* squeak by

11 **meet, encounter; come across, run across,** meet up, fall across, cross the path of; **come upon,** run upon, fall upon, light *or* alight upon; come among, fall among; **meet with,** meet up with <nf>, come face to face with, **confront,** meet head-on *or* eyeball to eyeball; **run into, bump into** *and* run smack into <nf>, join up with, come *or* run up against <nf>, run *and* fall foul of; burst *or* pitch *or* pop *or* bounce *or* plump upon <nf>; be on a collision course; reconnect

12 **stay near, keep close to;** stand by, lie by; go with, march with, follow close upon, breathe down one's neck, tread *or* stay on one's heels, stay on one's tail, tailgate <nf>; hang about *or* around, hang upon the skirts of, hover over; **cling to,** clasp, hug, huddle; hug the shore *or* land, keep hold of the land, stay inshore

13 **juxtapose,** appose, join 800.5, **adjoin, abut,** butt against, neighbor; bring near, put with, place *or* set side by side

ADJS **14** **near, close, nigh,** close-in, nearish, nighish, intimate, cheek-by-jowl, side-by-side, hand-in-hand, arm-in-arm, *bras-dessus-bras-dessous* <Fr>, shoulder-to-shoulder, neck and neck; **approaching,** nearing, approximate *or* approximating, proximate, proximal, propinque ; **short-range;** near the mark; warm *or* hot *or* burning <nf>

15 **nearby, handy, convenient,** neighboring, vicinal, propinquant *or* propinquous, ready at hand, easily reached *or* attained; accessible; one-stop; 24-hour

16 **adjacent, next,** immediate, contiguous, **adjoining, abutting; neighboring,** neighbor; in the neighborhood, in the vicinity; **juxtaposed,** juxtapositional, tangential; **bordering,** conterminous *or* coterminous, connecting; **face-to-face** 215.6; end-to-end, endways, endwise; **joined**

17 **in contact,** contacting, **touching, meeting,** contingent; impinging, impingent; tangent, tangential; osculatory; grazing, kissing, glancing, brushing, rubbing, nudging; interfacing, linking

18 **nearer,** nigher, **closer**

19 **nearest,** nighest, **closest,** nearmost, next, immediate

ADVS **20** **near, nigh, close;** hard, at close quarters; **nearby, close by,** hard by, fast by, not far *or* far off, in the vicinity *or* **neighborhood of,** at hand, at close range, **near** *or* **close at hand;** thereabout *or* thereabouts, hereabout *or* hereabouts; nearabout *or* nearabouts *or* nigh about <dial>; **about, around** <nf>, close about, along toward <nf>; at no great distance, only a step; as near as no matter *or* makes no difference <nf>; **within reach** *or* **range,** within call *or* hearing, within earshot *or* earreach, within a whoop *or* two whoops and a holler <nf>, within a stone's throw, a stone's throw away, in spitting distance <nf>, at one's elbow, at one's feet, at one's fingertips, under one's nose, at one's side, within one's grasp; just around the corner, just across the street, next-door, right next door, just next door

21 **in juxtaposition, in conjunction,** in apposition; beside

22 **nearly, near,** pretty near <nf>, close, **closely; almost,** all but, not quite, as good as, as near as makes no difference; **well-nigh, just about;** nigh, nigh hand

23 **approximately,** approximatively, practically <nf>, for practical purposes *or* all practical purposes, at a first approximation, give or take a little, **more or less;** plus-minus; **roughly,** roundly, in round numbers; **generally,** generally speaking, roughly speaking, say; in the ball-park <nf>

24 **against,** up against, on, upon, over against, opposite, nose to nose with, vis-à-vis, in contact with

25 **about, around,** just about, circa, c, somewhere about *or* near, near *or* close upon, give or take, near enough to, upwards of <nf>, -ish, -something; **in the neighborhood** *or* **vicinity of**

224 INTERVAL

<space between>

NOUNS 1 **interval, gap, space** 158, intervening *or* intermediate space, **interspace,** distance *or* space between, interstice; **clearance,** margin, leeway, headroom, **room** 158.3; discontinuity 813, jump, leap, interruption; daylight; hiatus, caesura, lacuna, intermission; half space, single space, double space, em space, en space, hair space; time interval, intermission, interim 826

2 **crack, cleft,** cranny, chink, check, craze, chap, **crevice,** fissure, scissure, incision, notch, score, cut, gash, slit, split, **rift,** rent; crack, hairline crack; **opening,** excavation, cavity, concavity, hole; **gap,** gape, **abyss,** abysm, **gulf, chasm,** void 222.3, canyon; **breach, break,** fracture, rupture; fault, flaw; slot, groove, furrow, moat, ditch, trench, dike, ha-ha; joint, seam; **valley**

VERBS 3 **interspace, space,** make a space, make room, set at intervals, dot, scatter 771.4, **space out, separate,** split off, part, dispart, set *or* keep apart

4 **cleave, crack,** check, incise, craze, **cut, cut apart,** gash, slit, **split,** rive, rent, rip open; **open; gap,** breach, break, fracture, rupture; slot, groove, furrow, ditch, trench

ADJS 5 intervallic, intervallary, interspatial, interstitial, discontinuous

6 **interspaced, spaced,** intervaled, **spaced out,** set at intervals, with intervals *or* an interval, interspacial, interstitial; dotted, scattered 771.9, **separated, parted,** disparted, split-off

7 **cleft, cut,** cloven, **cracked,** sundered, rift, riven, rent, chinky, chapped, crazed; **slit, split;** gaping, gappy; hiatal, caesural, lacunar; fissured, fissural, fissile

225 HABITATION

<an inhabiting>

NOUNS 1 **habitation,** inhabiting, inhabitation, habitancy, inhabitancy, **tenancy, occupancy,** occupation, **residence** *or* **residency,** residing, abiding, **living,** nesting, **dwelling,** commorancy <law>, lodging, staying, stopping, sojourning, staying over; squatting; cohabitation, living together, sharing quarters; living in sin; **abode, habitat** 228

2 **peopling,** peoplement, empeoplement, **population,** inhabiting; **colonization, settlement,** plantation

3 **housing,** domiciliation; lodgment, **lodging,** transient lodging, doss <Brit>, **quartering,** billeting, hospitality; living quarters; **housing development,** subdivision, tract, public housing; housing problem, housing bill

4 **camping,** tenting, **encampment,** bivouacking; camp 228.29

5 **sojourn,** sojourning, sojournment, temporary stay; **stay,** stop; **stopover,** stopoff, stayover, layover

6 **habitability,** inhabitability, **livability**

VERBS 7 **inhabit, occupy,** tenant, move in *or* into, take up one's abode, make one's home; rent, lease; **reside, live, live in, dwell, lodge, stay,** remain, abide, hang *or* hang out <nf>, domicile, domiciliate; **room,** bunk, crash <nf>, berth, doss down <Brit>; perch *and* roost *and* squat <nf>; nest; room together; cohabit, cohabitate, live together; live in sin

8 **sojourn,** stop, stay, **stop over,** stay over, lay over

9 **people,** empeople, **populate, inhabit,** denizen; colonize, **settle,** settle in, plant

10 **house,** domicile, domiciliate; provide with a roof, have as a guest *or* lodger, shelter, harbor; **lodge, quarter, put up,** billet, room, bed, berth, bunk; stable

11 **camp,** encamp, tent; pitch, **pitch camp,** pitch one's tent, drive stakes <nf>; bivouac; go camping, camp out, sleep out, rough it

ADJS 12 **inhabited, occupied,** tenanted; **peopled,** empeopled, populated, colonized, settled; populous

13 **resident,** residentiary, **in residence; residing, living, dwelling,** commorant, lodging, **staying,** remaining, abiding, living in; cohabiting, live-in

14 **housed,** domiciled, domiciliated, **lodged,** quartered, billeted; stabled

15 **habitable,** inhabitable, occupiable, lodgeable, tenantable, **livable, fit to live in, fit for occupation**; homelike 228.33

ADVS 16 **at home,** in the bosom of one's family, *chez soi* <Fr>; in one's element; back home *and* down home <nf>

226 NATIVENESS

NOUNS 1 **nativeness,** nativity, native-bornness, indigenousness *or* indigenity, aboriginality, autochthonousness, **nationality;** nativism

2 **citizenship,** native-born citizenship, citizenship by birth, citizenhood, subjecthood; civism; dual citizenship

3 **naturalization,** naturalized citizenship, citizenship by naturalization *or* adoption, nationalization, adoption, admission, affiliation, **assimilation,** denization; indigenization; Americanization, Anglicization, etc; acculturation, enculturation; papers, citizenship papers; culture shock

VERBS 4 naturalize, grant *or* confer citizenship, adopt, admit, affiliate, **assimilate**; Americanize, Anglicize, etc; acculturate, acculturize; indigenize, go native <nf>

ADJS 5 **native,** natal, **indigenous,** endemic, autochthonous; mother, maternal, original, aboriginal, primitive; native-born, natural-born, home-grown, homebred, native to the soil *or* place *or* heath

6 **naturalized,** adopted, **assimilated**; indoctrinated, Americanized, Anglicized, etc; acculturated, accultur ized; indigenized

227 INHABITANT, NATIVE

NOUNS 1 **population, inhabitants,** habitancy, dwellers, **populace, people,** whole people, people at large, citizenry, folk, souls, living souls, body, whole body, warm bodies <nf>; **public,** general public; community, society, **nation,** commonwealth, constituency, body politic, electorate; speech *or* linguistic community, ethnic *or* cultural community; colony, commune, neighborhood; nationality; **census,** head count; population statistics, demography, demographics

2 **inhabitant,** inhabiter, habitant; **occupant,** occupier, **dweller, tenant, denizen,** inmate; **resident,** residencer, residentiary, resider; townie; inpatient; resident *or* live-in maid; writer- *or* poet- *or* artist- *or* composer-in-residence; house detective; incumbent, *locum tenens* <L>; sojourner; addressee; indweller, inmate

3 **native,** indigene, autochthon, earliest inhabitant, first comer, primitive settler; primitive; **aborigine,** aboriginal; local *and* local yokel <nf>

4 **citizen, national,** subject; **naturalized citizen,** nonnative citizen, citizen by adoption, immigrant, metic;

hyphenated American, hyphenate; **cosmopolitan,** cosmopolite, citizen of the world; active citizen; dual citizen

5 **fellow citizen,** fellow countryman *or* countrywoman, **compatriot,** congener, **countryman,** countrywoman, *landsman* <Yiddish>, *paesano* <Ital>, *paisano* <Sp>; fellow townsman, home boy *and* home girl *and* hometowner <nf>

6 **townsman, townswoman,** townsperson, towny *and* towner *and* townie <nf>, **villager,** oppidan, city dweller, city person; big-city person, **city slicker** <nf>; metropolitan, urbanite; suburbanite; exurbanite; burgher, burgess, *bourgeois* <Fr>; townspeople, townfolks, townfolk

7 **householder,** homeowner, house-owner, proprietor, freeholder, occupier, addressee; cottager, cotter, cottier, crofter; head of household

8 **lodger, roomer,** paying guest; **boarder,** board-and-roomer, **transient,** transient guest *or* boarder; **renter, tenant,** leaser *or* lessee, leaseholder, time-sharer, subleaser *or* sublessee; roommate, flatmate <Brit>; visitor, guest

9 **settler,** *habitant*; **colonist,** colonizer, colonial, immigrant, incomer, planter; **homesteader; squatter,** nester; **pioneer;** sooner; precursor 816

10 wilderness settler *or* hinterlander; **frontiersman,** mountain man; **backwoodsman,** woodlander, woodsman, woodman, woodhick <nf>; **mountaineer, hillbilly** *and* ridge runner <nf>, mountain man, brush ape *and* briar-hopper <nf>; cracker *and* redneck <nf>, desert rat <nf>, clam digger <nf>, piny <nf>; country gentleman, ruralist, provincial, rustic, peasant, hayseed, hick, cottager

11 <regional inhabitants> **Easterner,** eastlander; **Midwesterner; Westerner,** westlander; **Southerner,** southlander; **Northener,** northlander, Yankee; Northman; New Englander, Down-Easter Yankee; Maritimer <Can>

228 ABODE, HABITAT

<place of habitation or resort>

NOUNS **1 abode, habitation, place, dwelling,** dwelling place, abiding place, place to live, where one lives *or* resides, where one is at home, roof, roof over one's head, **residence,** place of residence, **domicile,** *domus* <L>; **lodging,** lodgment, lodging place; seat, nest, living space, houseroom, sleeping place, place to rest one's head, crash pad <nf>; native heath, turf, home turf; **address,** permanent residence; **housing; affordable housing,** low-cost housing, low-and-middle-income housing, public housing, public-sector housing, scattersite housing; council house <Brit>; private housing, private-sector housing, market-rate housing

2 **home,** home sweet home; **fireside, hearth,** hearth and home, hearthstone, fireplace, *foyer* <Fr>, chimney corner, ingle, ingleside *or* inglenook; base, nest; **household,** ménage; **homestead,** home place, home roof, roof, rooftree, toft <Brit old>; place where one hangs one's hat; paternal roof *or* domicile, family homestead, ancestral halls; hometown, birthplace, cradle; homeland, native land, motherland, fatherland; **hominess** *or* homeyness

3 **domesticity;** housewifery, **housekeeping, homemaking;** householding, householdry

4 **quarters, living quarters; lodgings,** lodging, lodgment; diggings *and* digs <Brit nf>, pad *and* crib <nf>, room; **rooms,** berth, roost, accommodations; **housing** 225.3, shelter, *gîte* <Fr>

5 **house,** dwelling, dwelling house, *casa* <Sp, Ital>; house and grounds, house and lot, homesite; **building, structure, edifice,** fabric, erection, **hall** 197.4; roof; lodge; manor house, hall; town house, *rus in urbe* <L>, semidetached house, duplex, row house; country house, country seat; ranch house, farmhouse, farm, country house; prefabricated house, modular house; sod house, adobe house;

lake dwelling 241.3; houseboat; cave *or* cliff dwelling; penthouse; split-level; parsonage 703.7, **rectory,** vicarage, deanery, manse; official residence, the White House, Number 10 Downing Street, the Kremlin; governor's mansion; presidential palace; embassy, consulate

6 **farmstead; ranch,** *rancho* and *hacienda* <Sp>, toft *or* steading <Brit old>, grange, plantation

7 **estate; mansion,** palatial residence, stately home <Brit>, manor house; **villa, château,** *hôtel* <Fr>, resort, **castle,** tower; **palace,** *palais* <Fr>, *palazzo* <Ital>, court, great house; ancestral hall *or* seat

8 **cottage,** cot *or* cote, **bungalow,** box; **cabin,** log cabin; **second home, vacation home;** chalet, lodge, snuggery; home away from home, *pied-à-terre* <Fr>, *casita* <Sp>

9 **hut,** hutch, **shack, shanty,** crib, hole-in-the-wall <nf>, **shed; lean-to; booth,** stall; tollbooth *or* tollhouse, sentry box, gatehouse, porter's lodge; **outhouse,** outbuilding; privy; **pavilion,** kiosk; Quonset hut *or* Nissen hut; hutment

10 <Native American houses> wigwam, tepee *or* tipi, hogan, wickiup, jacal, longhouse; tupik *and* igloo <Eskimo>; ajouba

11 **hovel, dump** <nf>, rathole, hole, sty, pigsty, pigpen, tumbledown shack; squat

12 **summerhouse**, arbor, bower, **gazebo,** pergola, kiosk, alcove, retreat; **conservatory, greenhouse,** glasshouse <Brit>, lathhouse

13 **apartment, flat,** tenement, chambers <Brit>, room *or* rooms; studio apartment *or* flat; bed-sitter <Brit>, granny flat, flatlet; **suite,** suite *or* set of rooms; walkup, cold-water flat; **penthouse;** garden apartment; duplex apartment; railroad *or* shotgun flat

14 **apartment house, flats, tenement;** duplex, duplex house; tower block; apartment complex; cooperative apartment house *or* co-op <nf>, condominium *or* condo <nf>; high-rise apartment building *or* high rise

15 **inn, hotel,** hostel, hostelry, **tavern,** *posada* <Sp>; tourist hotel, *parador* <Sp>, boutique hotel; resort; **roadhouse,** caravansary *or* caravanserai, guesthouse, bed and breakfast *or* B and B; youth hostel, hospice, elder hostel; **lodging house,** rooming house; **boardinghouse,** *pension* <Fr>, *pensione* <Ital>; **dormitory,** dorm <nf>, fraternity *or* sorority house; bunkhouse; **flophouse** *and* fleabag <nf>, dosshouse <Brit nf>

16 **motel,** motor court, motor inn *or* lodge, motor hotel, auto court; boatel

17 **trailer,** house *or* camp trailer, **mobile home,** motor home, recreational vehicle *or* RV, camper, camper trailer, caravan <Brit>; trailer court *or* camp *or* park, campground

18 **habitat,** home, **range,** environment, surroundings, stamping *or* stomping grounds, locality, native environment; microhabitat, ecosystem, terrain, purlieu

19 **zoo, menagerie**, zoological garden *or* park, marine park, sea zoo, safari park; animal shelter

20 **barn, stable,** stall; **cowbarn,** cowhouse, cowshed, cowbyre, byre; mews; outbuilding

21 **kennel, doghouse;** pound, dog pound; cattery

22 **coop, chicken house** *or* **coop,** henhouse, hencote, hencoop, hennery; brooder

23 **birdhouse, aviary,** bird cage; dovecote, pigeon house *or* loft, columbary; roost, perch, roosting place; rookery, heronry; eyrie

24 vivarium, terrarium, aquarium; fishpond

25 **nest,** nidus; **beehive, apiary,** hive, bee tree, hornet's nest, wasp's nest, vespiary

26 **lair, den,** cave, **hole,** covert, mew, form; **burrow,** tunnel, earth, run, couch, lodge

27 **haunt,** purlieu, **hangout** <nf>, stamping ground *or* stomping ground <nf>; gathering place, rallying point, meeting place, clubhouse, club; casino, gambling house;

resort, health resort; **spa,** health spa, yoga retreat, baths, springs, watering place; meditation retreat

28 <disapproved place> **dive** <nf>, **den, lair,** den of thieves; hole *and* dump *and* **joint** <nf>; gyp *or* clip joint <nf>; **whorehouse,** cathouse <nf>, sporting house, brothel, bordello; stews, fleshpots

29 **camp, encampment**; bivouac; barrack *or* **barracks,** casern, *caserne* <Fr>, cantonment, lines <Brit>; hobo jungle *or* camp; detention camp, concentration camp; campground *or* campsite

30 <deities of the household> lares and penates, Vesta, Hestia

VERBS **31** **keep house,** housekeep <nf>, practice domesticity, maintain *or* run a household

ADJS **32** **residential,** residentiary, residing, in residence; domestic, domiciliary, domal; **home, household**, at home**;** mansional, manorial, palatial

33 **homelike,** homish, **homey** <nf>, homely; comfortable, friendly, cheerful, peaceful, cozy, snug, intimate; simple, plain, unpretending

34 **domesticated, tame,** tamed, broken; housebroken

229 FURNITURE

NOUNS **1** **furniture,** furnishings, movables, home furnishings, house furnishings, household effects, household goods,
office furniture, school furniture, church furniture, library furniture, furnishments ; **cabinetmaking,** cabinetwork, cabinetry; **furniture design, furniture style** ; period furniture; **piece of furniture, furniture piece,** chair, couch, sofa, bed, table, desk, cabinet, mirror, clock, screen; **suite, set of furniture,** ensemble, decor

230 TOWN, CITY

NOUNS **1** **town,** township; **city, metropolis,** metro, metropolitan area, greater city, megalopolis, supercity, conurbation, urban complex, spread city, urban sprawl *or* spread, Standard Metropolitan Statistical Area *or* SMSA, urban corridor, strip city, **municipality,** *urbs* <L>, city *or* municipal government; **borough, burg** <nf>, bourg, burgh; **suburb,** suburbia, burbs <nf>, bedroom community, slurb, commuter belt, outskirts; exurb, exurbia, bedroom town, streetcar suburb; market town <Brit>; small town; twin town; boom town, ghost town; industrial city; sister city; urbanization, citifying

2 **village, hamlet;** ham *and* thorp *and* wick ; country town, crossroads

3 <nf terms> **one-horse town,** jerkwater town, one-gas-station town, **tank town** *or* station, **whistle-stop,** jumping-off place; **hick town,** rube town, Podunk; hoosier town; wide place in the road

4 **capital,** capital city, **seat,** seat of government; **county seat** *or* county site, county town *or* shiretown <Brit>

5 **town hall, city hall, municipal building;** courthouse; police headquarters *or* station, station house, precinct house; firehouse, fire station, station house; county building, county courthouse; community center; school

6 <city districts> East Side *or* End, West Side *or* End; **downtown,** uptown, midtown; city center, main street, city centre <Brit>, urban center, central *or* center city, core, core city, inner city, suburbs, suburbia, burbs <nf>, outskirts, greenbelt, residential district, business district *or* section, shopping center, financial district, residential area; Chinatown, Little Italy, etc; **asphalt** *or* **concrete jungle,** mean streets; **slum** *or* **slums,** the other side *or* the wrong side of the tracks, blighted area *or* neighborhood *or* section, run-down neighborhood, tenement district, shanty-town, hell's kitchen *or* half-acre; favela, tenderloin, red-light district, Bowery, **skid row** *or* skid road <nf>, tin pan alley; combat zone; enterprise zone; **ghetto, inner city,** urban ghetto, barrio

7 **block,** city block, square
8 **square, plaza,** *place* <Fr>, *piazza* <Ital>, *campo* <Ital>, **marketplace,** market, mart, rialto, forum, agora
9 **circle,** circus <Brit>; crescent
10 **city planning,** urban planning; urban studies, urbanology

ADJS **11** **urban, metropolitan, municipal,** metro, burghal, **civic,** oppidan; main-street; citywide; city, town, village; citified; urbane; suburban; interurban; downtown, uptown, midtown; **inner-city,** core, core-city, ghetto; small-town; boom-town

231 REGION

NOUNS **1** **region, area, zone,** belt, **territory,** terrain; **place** 159.1; **space** 158; **country** 232, **land** 234, ground, soil; territoriality; territorial waters, twelve- *or* three-mile limit, continental shelf, offshore rights; air space; heartland; hinterland; **district, quarter, section,** sector, department, division; salient, corridor; part, parts; **neighborhood,** vicinity, vicinage, neck of the woods <nf>, stamping ground, turf <nf>, backyard <nf>, purlieu *or* purlieus; premises, confines, precincts, environs, milieu
2 **sphere,** hemisphere, orb, **orbit,** ambit, circle; **circuit,** judicial circuit, **beat, round,** walk; **realm,** demesne, **domain,** dominion, jurisdiction, bailiwick, niche, forté; border, borderland, march; **province,** precinct, department; **field,** pale, arena
3 **zone;** climate *or* clime ; **longitude,** longitude in arc, longitude in time; meridian, prime meridian; **latitude,** parallel; equator, the line; tropic, Tropic of Cancer, Tropic of Capricorn; tropics, subtropics, Torrid Zone; Temperate *or* Variable Zones; Frigid Zones, Arctic Zone *or* Circle, Antarctic Zone *or* Circle; horse latitudes, roaring forties; doldrums
4 **plot,** plot of ground *or* land, parcel of land, plat, **patch, tract, field,** enclosure; lot; air space; block, square; section, forty <sixteenth of a section>, back forty; close, quadrangle, quad, enclave, pale, *clos* <Fr>, croft <Brit>; real estate; allotment, holding, claim
5 <territorial divisions> **state, territory, province,** region, duchy, electorate, government, principality; **county,** shire, canton, *oblast* and *okrug* <Russ>, *département* <Fr>; **borough, ward,** precinct, riding, *arrondissement* <Fr>; **township,** hundred, commune, wapentake; metropolis, metropolitan area, **city, town** 230; **village,** hamlet; **district,** congressional district, electoral district, precinct; magistracy, soke, bailiwick; shrievalty, sheriffalty, sheriffwick, constablewick <Brit>; archdiocese, archbishopric, stake; **diocese,** bishopric, parish; colony
6 <regions of the world> continent, landmass; **Old World,** the old country; **New World,** America; **Northern Hemisphere,** North America; Central America; **Southern Hemisphere,** South America; Latin America; **Western Hemisphere, Occident,** West; **Eastern Hemisphere, Orient,** Levant, East, eastland; Far East, Mideast *or* Middle East, Near East; Asia, Europe, Eurasia, Asia Major, Asia Minor, Africa; Antipodes, Australia, down under <nf>, Australasia, Oceania; Arctic, Antarctica; Third World
7 <regions of the US> West, westland, wild West, West Coast, Coast, left Coast <nf>; Northwest, Pacific Northwest; Silicon Valley; Sierras; Rockies; Sunbelt; Southwest; Middle West *or* Midwest, Middle America; Great Plains, heartlands, Plains states; North Central region; Rust Belt; East, eastland, East Coast, Eastern Seaboard; Middle Atlantic; Northeast, Southeast; North, northland, Snow Belt, Frost Belt; Appalachia; South, southland, Dixie, Dixieland; Deep South, Old South; Delta, bayous; Bible Belt; borscht belt; Gulf Coast; New England, Down East, Yankeeland <nf>

ADJS **8** **regional, territorial, geographical,** areal, sectional, zonal, topographic *or* topographical
9 **local, localized,** of a place, geographically limited, topical,

vernacular, parochial, provincial, insular, limited, confined

232 COUNTRY

NOUNS 1 **country,** land; **nation,** nationality, **state,** nation-state, sovereign nation *or* state, self-governing state, polity, **body politic; power,** superpower, world power; microstate; **republic,** people's republic, **commonwealth,** commonweal; **kingdom,** sultanate; **empire,** empery; superpower, power; **realm,** dominion, domain; **principality,** principate; duchy, dukedom; grand duchy, archduchy, archdukedom, earldom, county, palatinate, seneschalty; chieftaincy, chieftainry; toparchy, *toparchia* <L>; city-state, *polis* <Gk>, free city; **province,** territory, possession; colony, settlement; protectorate, mandate, mandated territory, mandant, mandatee, mandatory; buffer state; **ally,** military ally, cobelligerent, treaty partner; satellite, puppet regime *or* government; coalition government; free nation *or* country, captive nation, iron-curtain country; nonaligned *or* unaligned *or* neutralist nation; developed nation, industrial *or* industrialized nation; underdeveloped nation, third-world nation; federation, confederation, commonwealth, commonweal, bloc, comity; United Nations

2 **fatherland,** *patria* <L>, *la patrie* <Fr>, land of our fathers, **motherland,** mother country, **native land,** native soil, one's native heath *or* ground *or* soil *or* place, the old country, country of origin, **birthplace,** cradle; **home, homeland,** home ground, God's country; the home front

3 **United States,** United States of America, US, USA, US of A <nf>, **America,** Columbia, the States, Yankeeland <nf>, Land of Liberty, the melting pot; stateside

4 **Britain, Great Britain, United Kingdom, the UK,** Britannia, Albion, Blighty <Brit nf>, Limeyland <US nf>, Tight Little Island, Land of the Rose, Sovereign of the Seas; British Empire, Commonwealth of Nations, British Commonwealth of Nations, the Commonwealth; perfidious Albion

5 <national personifications> Uncle Sam *or* Brother Jonathan <US>; John Bull <Brit>

6 nationhood, peoplehood, **nationality; statehood, nation-statehood, sovereignty,** sovereign nationhood *or* statehood, independence, self-government, self-determination; internationality, internationalism; **nationalism**

7 native, countryman, countrywoman, citizen, national; nationalist, ultranationalist; patriot

233 THE COUNTRY

NOUNS 1 **the country,** agricultural region, farm country, farmland, arable land, grazing region *or* country, rural district, rustic region, province *or* **provinces,** countryside, woodland 310.13, grassland 310.8, woods and fields, meadows and pastures, the soil, grass roots; **the sticks** *and* the tall corn *and* yokeldom *and* hickdom <nf>; cotton belt, tobacco belt, black belt, farm belt, corn belt, fruit belt, wheat belt, citrus belt; dust bowl; highlands, moors, uplands, foothills; lowlands, veld *or* veldt, savanna *or* savannah, plains, prairies, steppes, wide-open spaces

2 **hinterland, back country,** outback, upcountry, boonies *and* boondocks <nf>; **the bush,** bush country, bushveld, **woods,** woodlands, **backwoods,** forests, timbers, the big sticks <nf>, brush; wilderness, wilds, uninhabited region, virgin land *or* territory; **wasteland** 891.2; **frontier,** borderland, outpost; wild West, cow country, cow town

3 **rusticity, ruralism,** inurbanity, agrarianism, bucolicism, **provincialism,** provinciality, simplicity, pastoral simplicity, unspoiledness; yokelism, hickishness, backwoodsiness; **boorishness,** churlishness, unrefinement, uncultivation; peasantry, gaucherie; agrarian society

4 ruralization, countrification, rustication, pastoralization

VERBS **5 ruralize, countrify, rusticate,** pastoralize; farm 1069.16; return to the soil

ADJS **6 rustic, rural, country, provincial, farm, pastoral, bucolic,** Arcadian, **agrarian,** agrestic, agrestal, proto-industrial; **agricultural** 1069.20; lowland, low-lying, upland, highland, prairie, plains

7 countrified, inurbane; country-born, country-bred, upcountry; farmerish, hobnailed, clodhopping, clodhopperish; **boorish,** clownish, loutish, lumpish, lumpen, cloddish, churlish; **uncouth,** unpolished, uncultivated, uncultured, unrefined; country-style, country-fashion

8 <nf terms> **hick,** hicky, hickified, hicklike, from the sticks, rube, hayseed, yokel, yokelish, down-home, shit-kicking, hillbilly, redneck

9 hinterland, back, **back-country,** up-country, backroad, outback, wild, wilderness, virgin; wild-West, cow-country; **waste** 891.4; backwood *or* **backwoods,** back of beyond, backwoodsy; woodland, sylvan

234 LAND

NOUNS **1 land, ground,** landmass, earth, glebe , **sod,** clod, **soil, dirt,** dust, clay, marl, mold <Brit nf>; *terra* <L>, **terra firma,** terra incognita; terrain; **dry land;** arable land; marginal land; grassland 310.8, woodland 310.13; crust, earth's crust, lithosphere; regolith; topsoil, subsoil; alluvium, alluvion; eolian *or* subaerial deposit; **real estate,** real property, landholdings, acres, territory, freehold; region 231; the country 233; earth science 1071

2 shore, coast, *côte* <Fr>; **strand,** *playa* <Sp>, **beach,** beachfront, beachside shingle, plage, lido, riviera, sands, berm; waterside, **waterfront;** shoreline, coastline; foreshore; bank, embankment; riverside; lakefront, lakeshore; **seashore, coast, seacoast, seaside, seaboard,** seabeach, seacliff, seabank, sea margin, oceanfront, oceanside, seafront, shorefront, tidewater, tideland, coastland, littoral, littoral zone; sand dune, sand bar, sandbank, tombolo; wetland, wetlands; **bay,** bayfront, bayside; drowned *or* submerged coast; rockbound coast, ironbound coast; loom of the land

3 landsman, landman, **landlubber**

ADJS **4 terrestrial,** terrene , **earth, earthly,** telluric, tellurian; earthbound; sublunar, subastral; geophilous; terraqueous; fluvioterrestrial

5 earthy, earthen, soily, loamy, marly, gumbo, clayey, clayish; adobe; agrestal

6 alluvial, alluvious, estuarine, fluviomarine

7 coastal, littoral, seaside, shore, shoreside; shoreward; riparian *or* riparial *or* riparious; riverain, riverine; riverside; lakefront, lakeshore; oceanfront, oceanside; seaside, seafront, shorefront, shoreline; beachfront, beachside; bayfront, bayside; tideland, tidal, wetland

ADVS **8 on land,** on dry land, on terra firma; onshore, ashore; alongshore; shoreward; by land, overland

9 on earth, on the face of the earth *or* globe, in the world, in the wide world, in the whole wide world; **under the sun,** under the stars, beneath the sky, under heaven, below, **here below**

235 BODY OF LAND

NOUNS **1 continent, mainland,** main , landform, continental landform, landmass; North America, South America, Africa, Europe, Asia, Eurasia, Eurasian landmass, Australia, Antarctica; subcontinent, India, Greenland; peninsula; **plate,** tectonic plate, crustal plate, crustal segment, Pacific plate, American plate, African plate, Eurasian plate, Antarctic plate, Indian plate; continental divide, continental drift; plate tectonics; Gondwana, Laurasia, Pangaea

2 island, isle; islet, holm, ait <Brit nf>; continental island; oceanic island; volcanic island; **key,** cay;

sandbank, sandbar, bar; floating island; **reef,** coral reef, coral head; coral island, atoll; archipelago, island group *or* chain; insularity; islandology

3 **continental,** mainlander; continentalist

4 **islander,** islandman, island-dweller, islesman, insular; islandologist

VERBS 5 insulate, isolate, island, enisle; island-hop

ADJS 6 **continental,** mainland

7 **insular,** insulated, isolated; island, islandy *or* islandish, islandlike; islanded, isleted, island-dotted; seagirt; archipelagic *or* archipelagian

236 PLAIN

<open country>

NOUNS 1 **plain, plains,** flat country, flatland, **flats,** flat, level; champaign, champaign country, open country, **wide-open spaces; prairie,** grassland 310.8, sea of grass, **steppe, pampas,** *pampa* <Sp>, savanna, tundra, vega, campo, llano, sebkha; **veld,** grass veld, bushveld, tree veld; wold, weald; **moor,** moorland, down, **downs,** lande, **heath,** fell <Brit>; lowland, lowlands, bottomland; basin, playa; sand plain, sand flat, strand flat; tidal flat, salt marsh; salt pan; salt flat, alkali flat; **desert** 891.2; **plateau,** upland, tableland, table, **mesa,** mesilla; peneplain; coastal plain, abyssal plain, tidal plain, alluvial plain, delta, delta plain, flood plain; mare, lunar mare

ADJS 2 champaign, **plain, flat,** open; campestral *or* campestrian

237 HIGHLANDS

NOUNS 1 **highlands, uplands,** highland, upland, high country, elevated land, dome, **plateau, tableland,** mesa, upland area, downs, downland, piedmont, moor, moorland, **hills, heights,** hill *or* hilly country, downs, wold, foothills, rolling country, **mountains,** mountain *or* mountainous country, high terrain, peaks, range, *massif* <Fr>

2 **slope, declivity,** steep, versant, incline, rise, talus, brae, mountainside, hillside, bank, gentle *or* easy slope, glacis, angle of repose, steep *or* rapid slope, fall line, bluff, cliff, headland, ness, ben <Scot, Ir>; precipice, wall, palisade, scar <Brit>, escarpment, scarp, fault scarp, rim, face; upper slopes, upper reaches, timberline *or* tree line

3 **plateau, tableland,** high plateau, table, mesa, table mountain, butte, moor, fell <Brit>, hammada

4 **hill,** down <chiefly Brit>; brae *and* fell; **hillock, knob,** butte, kopje, kame, monticle, monticule, monadnock, **knoll,** hummock, hammock, eminence, rise, mound, swell, barrow, tumulus, kop, tell *or* tel, jebel; **dune,** sand dune; moraine, drumlin; anthill, molehill; **dune,** sand dune, sandhill

5 **ridge,** ridgeline, *arête* <Fr>, chine, spine, horst, kame, comb <Brit>, esker, os, cuesta, serpent kame, Indian ridge, moraine, terminal moraine; **saddle, hogback,** hog's-back, saddleback, horseback, col, watershed; **pass,** gap, notch, wind gap, water gap

6 **mountain**, mount, alp, hump, tor, height, dizzying height, nunatak, dome; **peak, pinnacle, summit** 198.2, mountaintop, point, topmost point *or* pinnacle, **crest,** spine, tor, pike <Brit>, *pic* <Fr>, *pico* <Sp>; crag, spur, cloud-capped *or* cloud-topped *or* snow-clad *or* snow-capped peak, the roof of the world; needle, aiguille, pyramidal peak, horn; fold mountain, fold-belt mountain, alpine chain, fault-block mountain, basin and range; oceanic ridge, oceanic rise; **volcano,** volcanic mountain, volcanic spine, volcanic neck; seamount, submarine mountain, guyot; **mountain range,** range, massif; **mountain system, chain,** mountain chain, cordillera, sierra, cordilleran belt, fold belt; hill heaped upon hill; divide, Continental Divide; mountain-building, orogeny, orogenesis, epeirogeny, folding, faulting,

block-faulting, volcanism; isostasy; orography, orology; acrophile

7 **valley,** vale, glen, dale, dell, hollow, holler <nf>, dip, flume, cleuch *or* corrie, cwm <Welsh>; **ravine, gorge, canyon,** box canyon, *arroyo* <Sp>, barranca, bolson, coulee, gully, gulch, combe *or* coomb *or* comb <Brit>, cirque, dingle, rift, rift valley, kloof, donga, graben, draw, wadi, basin, cirque, corrie, hanging valley; **crevasse;** chimney, ditch, chine, clough <Brit>, couloir; **defile,** pass, passage, col; **crater,** volcanic crater, caldera, meteorite *or* meteoritic crater

ADJS **8** **hilly, rolling,** undulating, upland; **mountainous,** montane, alpine, alpestrine, altitudinous; orogenic, orographic, orological, orometric

238 STREAM

<running water>

NOUNS **1** **stream, waterway, watercourse** 239.2, **channel** 239; meandering stream, flowing stream, lazy stream, racing stream, braided stream; spill stream; adolescent stream; mountain stream; **river;** navigable river, underground *or* subterranean river; dry stream, stream bed, stream channel, stream course, winterbourne, wadi, *arroyo* <Sp>; **brook,** branch; kill, bourn *or* bourne, run <Brit nf>, **creek,** crick <nf>; **rivulet,** rill, rillet, **streamlet,** brooklet, runlet, runnel, rundle <nf>, rindle <Brit nf>, beck <Brit>, gill <Brit>, burn, sike <Brit nf>; **freshet,** fresh; millstream, race; midstream, midchannel; drainage pattern, watershed; stream action, fluviation

2 **headwaters, headstream,** headwater, head, riverhead; **source,** fountainhead 886.6

3 **tributary,** feeder, **branch, fork,** prong <nf>, confluent, confluent stream, affluent, distributary; effluent, anabranch, branch feeder; bayou; billabong

4 **flow,** flowing, **flux,** fluency, profluence, fluid motion *or* movement; hydrodynamics; **stream, current,** set, trend, tide, water flow; drift, driftage; **course,** onward course, **surge, gush, rush,** onrush, spate, run, race; millrace, mill run; undercurrent, undertow; crosscurrent, crossflow; affluence, afflux, affluxion, confluence, convergence, concourse, conflux; **downflow,** downpour; defluxion; inflow 189.2; outflow 190.4

5 **torrent, river, flood,** flash flood, wall of water, waterflood, **deluge;** spate, **pour,** freshet, fresh

6 **overflow,** spillage, spill, spillover, overflowing, overrunning, alluvion, alluvium, **inundation, flood, deluge,** whelming, overwhelming, flush, washout, engulfment, submersion 367.2, cataclysm; the Flood, the Deluge; washout

7 **trickle,** tricklet, **dribble, drip,** dripping, stillicide , drop, spurtle; percolation, leaching, lixiviation; distillation, condensation, sweating; seeping, seepage

8 **lap, swash, wash, slosh, plash, splash;** lapping, washing, etc

9 **jet, spout, spurt,** spurtle, squirt, spit, spew, spray, spritz <nf>; rush, **gush,** flush; **fountain,** fount, font, *jet d'eau* <Fr>; geyser, spouter <nf>

10 **rapids, rapid,** white water, wild water; ripple, **riffle,** riff <nf>; chute, shoot, sault

11 **waterfall, cataract,** fall, **falls, Niagara, cascade,** force <Brit>, linn, sault; nappe; watershoot

12 **eddy,** back stream, gurge, **swirl,** twirl, whirl; **whirlpool,** vortex, gulf, **maelstrom;** Maelstrom, Charybdis; countercurrent, counterflow, counterflux, backflow, reflux, refluence, regurgitation, ebb, backwash, backwater, snye <Can>

13 **tide,** tidal current *or* stream, tidal flow *or* flood, **tide race; tidewater;** tideway, tide gate; **riptide,** rip, tiderip, overfalls; direct tide, opposite tide; **spring tide; high tide,** high water, full tide; **low tide,** low water; **neap tide,** neap; lunar tide, solar tide; **flood tide, ebb tide;** rise of the tide, rising tide, flux, flow, flood;

ebb, reflux, refluence; ebb and flow, flux and reflux; tidal amplitude, tidal range, intertidal zone, tidal flat, tidal pool; tideland; tide chart *or* table, tidal current chart; tide gauge, thalassometer

14 **wave, billow,** surge, **swell,** heave, undulation, lift, rise, send, scend; trough, peak; **sea,** heavy swell, ocean swell, ground swell; **roller,** roll; **comber,** comb; **surf, breakers,** spume; wavelet, **ripple,** riffle; **tidal wave,** tsunami, seismic sea wave, seiche, rogue wave; gravity wave, water wave; tide wave; bore, tidal bore, eagre, traveling wave; **whitecap,** white horse, white foam; rough *or* heavy sea, rough water, broken water, dirty water *or* sea, choppy *or* chopping sea, popple, lop, chop, choppiness, overfall, angry sea; standing wave

15 water gauge, fluviograph, fluviometer; marigraph; Nilometer

VERBS 16 **flow, stream, issue, pour, surge, run, course, rush, gush, flush, flood;** empty into, flow into, join, join with, mingle waters; set, make, trend; flow in 189.9; flow out 190.13; flow back, surge back, ebb, regurgitate; meander

17 **overflow,** flow over, wash over, **run over, well over, brim over,** lap, lap at, lap over, overbrim, overrun, pour out *or* over, **spill, slop, slosh,** spill out *or* over; **cataract, cascade; inundate,** engulf, swamp, sweep, whelm, overwhelm, **flood,** deluge, submerge 367.7

18 **trickle, dribble,** dripple, **drip,** drop, spurtle; **filter,** percolate, leach, lixiviate; distill, condense, sweat; seep, weep; **gurgle** 52.11, murmur

19 **lap, plash, splash, wash, swash, slosh**

20 **jet, spout, spurt,** spurtle, **squirt,** spit, spew, spray, spritz <nf>, play, **gush,** well, surge; vomit, vomit out *or* forth

21 **eddy,** gurge, **swirl,** whirl, purl, reel, spin

22 **billow, surge, swell,** heave, lift, rise, send, scend, toss, popple, **roll,** wave, **undulate; peak,** draw to a peak, be poised; comb, **break,** dash, crash, smash; rise and fall, ebb and flow

ADJS 23 **streamy,** rivery, brooky, creeky; streamlike, riverine, riverlike; fluvial, fluviatile *or* fluviatic, fluviomarine

24 **flowing, streaming, running, pouring,** fluxive, fluxional, coursing, racing, gushing, rushing, onrushing, surging, surgy, torrential, rough, whitewater; **fluent,** profluent, affluent, defluent, decurrent, confluent, diffluent, refluent; tidal; gulfy, vortical; meandering, mazy, sluggish, serpentine

25 **flooded,** deluged, inundated, engulfed, swamped, swept, whelmed, drowned, overwhelmed, afloat, awash; washed, water-washed; in flood, at flood, in spate

239 CHANNEL

NOUNS 1 **channel, conduit, duct,** canal, course; **way, passage, passageway;** trough, troughway, troughing; tunnel; ditch, trench 290.2; adit; ingress, entrance 189; egress, exit; **stream** 238; English Channel

2 **watercourse, waterway, aqueduct,** water channel, water gate, water carrier, culvert, **canal;** side-channel, intrariverine channel, snye <Can>; streamway, riverway; **bed,** stream bed, river bed, creek bed, runnel; water gap; dry bed, *arroyo* <Sp>, wadi, winterbourne, **gully,** gullyhole, gulch; swash, swash channel; race, headrace, tailrace; flume; sluice; spillway; spillbox; irrigation ditch, water furrow; waterworks

3 **gutter, trough,** eave *or* eaves trough; **flume,** chute, shoot; pentrough, penstock; guide

4 <metal founding> gate, ingate, runner, sprue, tedge

5 **drain,** sough <Brit nf>, sluice, scupper; **sink,** sump; piscina; **gutter,** kennel; **sewer,** cloaca, headchute; cloaca maxima

6 **tube; pipe; tubing, piping,** tubulation; tubulure; nipple, pipette, tubulet, tubule; reed, stem, straw; **hose,** hosepipe <Brit>, garden hose, fire hose; sprinkler; pipeline; catheter;

siphon; tap; efflux tube, adjutage; funnel; snorkel; siamese, siamese connection *or* joint

7 **main,** water main, gas main, fire main

8 **spout,** beak, waterspout, downspout; gargoyle

9 **nozzle,** bib nozzle, pressure nozzle, spray nozzle, nose, snout; rose, rosehead; shower head, sprinkler head

10 **valve,** gate; **faucet, spigot, tap;** cock, **petcock,** draw cock, stopcock, sea cock, drain cock, ball cock; bunghole; needle valve; valvule, valvula

11 **floodgate,** flood-hatch, gate, **head gate,** penstock, water gate, **sluice,** sluice gate; tide gate, aboiteau <Can>; weir; **lock,** lock gate, dock gate; air lock

12 **hydrant,** fire hydrant, **plug,** water plug, fireplug

13 air passage, air duct, airway, air shaft, shaft, **air hole,** air tube; speaking tube *or* pipe; **blowhole,** breathing hole, spiracle; nostril; touchhole; spilehole, **vent, venthole,** ventage, ventiduct; **ventilator,** ventilating shaft; transom, louver, louverwork; wind tunnel

14 **chimney, flue,** flue pipe, funnel, **stovepipe, stack, smokestack,** smoke pipe, smokeshaft; Charley Noble; fumarole

VERBS 15 **channel,** channelize, canalize, **conduct, convey,** put through; pipe, funnel, siphon; trench 290.3; direct 573.8

ADJS 16 **tubular,** tubate, tubiform, tubelike, pipelike; cylindrical; tubed, piped; cannular; tubal

17 **valvular,** valval, valvelike; valved

240 SEA, OCEAN

NOUNS 1 **ocean, sea,** ocean sea, great *or* main sea, **main** *or* ocean main, the bounding main, tide, salt sea, salt water, blue water, ocean blue, deep water, open sea, **the brine,** the briny *and* the big pond <nf>, the briny deep, **the deep,** the deep sea, the deep blue sea, drink *and* big drink <nf>, the herring pond <Brit nf>; **high sea, high seas;** the seven seas; hydrosphere; **ocean depths,** ocean deeps and trenches 275.1–7

2 **ocean** ; **sea,** tributary sea, gulf, bay; big pond <nf>

3 spirit of the sea, sea devil, Davy, **Davy Jones;** sea god, **Neptune,** Poseidon, Oceanus, Triton, Nereus, Oceanid, Nereid, Thetis, Amphitrite, Calypso; Varuna, Dylan; **mermaid,** siren; merman, seaman, undine, sea nymph, water sprite, sea serpent

4 <ocean zones> pelagic zone, benthic zone, estuarine area, sublittoral, littoral, intertidal zone, splash zone, supralittoral

5 ocean floor, seabed, sea bottom, benthos, Davy Jones's locker; continental shelf, continental slope, submarine canyon, land bridge, abyssal plain, abyssal hill, midoceanic ridge, oceanic ridge, oceanic trench, volcanic island, seamount, guyot, atoll

6 oceanography, thalassography, hydrography, bathymetry; marine biology; aquaculture

7 oceanographer, thalassographer, hydrographer, marine biologist, deep-sea diver, underwater explorer

ADJS 8 **oceanic, marine, maritime,** pelagic, thalassic; ocean-going, seagoing, seafaring; undersea, underwater; nautical 182.57; oceanographic, oceanographical, hydrographic, hydrographical, bathymetric, bathymetrical, bathyorographical, thalassographic, thalassographical; terriginous; deep-sea 275.14

ADVS 9 **at sea,** on the high seas; afloat 182.62; by water, by sea

10 **oversea, overseas,** beyond seas, over the water, transmarine, across the sea

11 **oceanward,** oceanwards, **seaward,** seawards, off; offshore, off soundings, out of soundings, in blue water

241 LAKE, POOL

NOUNS 1 **lake,** landlocked water, loch, lough <Ir>, mere, freshwater lake, natural lake; oxbow lake, bayou lake, glacial lake; volcanic lake; mountain lake; salt lake; tarn; inland sea; **pool,** lakelet, **pond,** pondlet, dew pond, linn, dike <Brit nf>, *étang* <Fr>; standing water, still water, stagnant water, dead water, bayou; **water** *or* watering hole, water pocket, swimming hole, aquascape; **oasis;** farm pond; fishpond; millpond, millpool; salt pond, salina, tidal pond *or* pool; backwater; **puddle,** plash, sump <nf>; **lagoon,** *laguna* <Sp>; **reservoir,** artificial *or* manmade lake; dam; **well, cistern,** tank, artesian well, flowing well, **spring**

2 **lake dweller,** lakeside dweller, lacustrian, lacustrine dweller *or* inhabitant, **pile dweller** *or* builder; laker

3 **lake dwelling,** lacustrine dwelling, **pile house** *or* **dwelling,** stilt house, palafitte; crannog <Scot, Ir>; lake house, lakeside home; lakeside village

4 limnology, limnologist; limnimeter, limnograph

ADJS 5 **lakish,** laky, lakelike; lacustrine, lacustral, lacustrian; pondy, pondlike, lacuscular; limnetic, limnologic, limnological, limnophilous; landlocked; lakeside, lake-dwelling

242 INLET, GULF

NOUNS 1 **inlet, cove,** creek <Brit>, arm of the sea, arm, armlet, canal, reach, loch, **bay, fjord** *or* fiord, bight; cove; **gulf; estuary,** firth *or* frith, bayou, mouth, outlet, *boca* <Sp>; **harbor,** natural harbor; bay; road *or* roads, roadstead; **strait** *or* straits, kyle, **narrow** *or* **narrows,** euripus, belt, gut, narrow seas; **sound**

ADJS 2 gulfy, gulflike; gulfed, bayed, embayed; estuarine, fluviomarine, tidewater

243 MARSH

NOUNS 1 **marsh,** marshland, **swamp,** swampland, wetland, fen, fenland, **morass,** mere *or* marish, **bog, mire, quagmire,** sump <nf>, wash, baygall; glade, everglade; slough, swale, wallow, hog wallow, buffalo wallow, sough <Brit>; bottom, **bottoms,** bottomland, slob land, holm <Brit>, water meadow, meadow; **moor,** moorland, moss, peat bog; salt marsh; quicksand; taiga; mud flat, **mud** 1062.8,9

VERBS 2 **mire,** bemire, sink in, **bog,** mire *or* bog down, stick in the mud; stodge

ADJS 3 **marshy, swampy,** swampish, **moory,** moorish, fenny, wetland, marish , paludal *or* paludous; **boggy,** boggish, **miry,** mirish, quaggy, quagmiry, spouty, poachy; **muddy** 1062.14; swamp-growing, uliginous

244 QUANTITY

NOUNS 1 **quantity,** quantum, amount, **whole** 792; mass, **bulk,** substance, matter, magnitude, amplitude, **extent, sum; measure,** measurement; strength, force, numbers

2 **amount,** quantity, large amount, small amount, **sum, number,** count, group, total, reckoning, **measure,** parcel, passel <nf>, **part** 793, **portion,** clutch, ration, share, issue, allotment, lot, deal; **batch,** bunch, heap <nf>, pack, mess <nf>, gob *and* chunk *and* hunk <nf>, budget , dose

3 **some,** somewhat, something; **aught; any,** anything

VERBS 4 **quantify,** quantize, **count, number off, enumerate, number** 1017.17, rate, fix; parcel, apportion, mete out, issue, allot, divide 802.18; **increase** 251.4,6, **decrease** 252.6, reduce 252.7; quantitate, **measure** 300.10; set a quota; massify

ADJS 5 **quantitative,** quantitive, quantified, quantized, measured; **some,** certain, one; a, an; **any**

ADVS 6 **approximately,** nearly, some, about, circa; more or less, *plus ou moins* <Fr>, by and large, upwards of

245 DEGREE

NOUNS 1 **degree, grade, step,** *pas* <Fr>, leap; round, rung, tread, stair; **point,** mark, peg, tick; **notch,** cut;

plane, level, plateau; **period,** space, interval; **extent, measure,** amount, ratio, proportion, stint, standard, height, pitch, reach, remove, compass, range, scale, scope, caliber; **shade,** shadow, nuance

2 **rank, standing, level,** footing, **status,** station; **position,** place, sphere, orbit, echelon; **order,** estate, precedence, condition; rate, rating; **class,** caste; **hierarchy,** power structure

3 **gradation, graduation,** grading, staging, phasing, tapering, shading, gradualism

VERBS 4 **graduate, grade,** calibrate; phase in, phase out, taper off, shade off, scale; **increase** 251, **decrease** 252.6,7; change by degrees

ADJS 5 **gradual,** gradational, calibrated, graduated, phased, staged, tapered, scalar; regular, progressive; hierarchic, hierarchical; in scale, calibrated; proportional

ADVS 6 **by degrees,** degreewise; **gradually,** gradatim; **step by step,** grade by grade, **bit by bit, little by little,** inch by inch, inchmeal, drop by drop; a little, fractionally; a little at a time, by slow degrees, by inches; slowly 175.13

7 to a degree, to some extent, in a way, in a measure, in some measure; somewhat, kind of <nf>, sort of <nf>, rather, pretty, quite, fairly; a little, a bit; slightly, scarcely, in a small degree 248.9, in a limited degree 248.10; very, extremely, to a great extent 247.15, in an extreme degree 247.22

246 MEAN

NOUNS 1 **mean, median, middle** 819; **golden mean,** *juste milieu* <Fr>; **medium,** happy medium; middle of the road, middle course, *via media* <L>; middle state *or* ground *or* position *or* echelon *or* level *or* point, midpoint; macrolevel; **average,** balance, par, normal, norm, rule, run, generality; **mediocrity,** averageness, passableness, adequacy; averaging, mediocritization; checks and balances; **center** 208.2

VERBS 2 **average,** average out, **split the difference,** take the average, strike a balance, pair off, split down the middle; strike *or* hit a happy medium; keep to the middle, avoid extremes; **do,** just do, pass, barely pass; mediocritize

ADJS 3 **medium,** mean, **intermediate,** intermediary, median, medial, mesial, mid-level, middle-echelon; **average,** normal, standard, par for the course; middle-of-the-road, moderate, fence sitting, middle-ground; **middling, ordinary,** usual, routine, common, mediocre, merely adequate, passing, banal, so-so, vanilla *or* plain vanilla <nf>; **central** 208.11

ADVS 4 **mediumly,** medianly; medially, midway 819.5, intermediately, in the mean; **centrally** 208.15

5 **on the average, in the long run, over the long haul; taking one thing with another,** taking all things together, **all in all, on the whole,** all things considered, on balance; **generally** 864.17

247 GREATNESS

NOUNS 1 **greatness, magnitude,** muchness; **amplitude,** ampleness, fullness, plenitude, great scope *or* compass *or* reach; **grandeur,** grandness; **immensity,** enormousness *or* enormity, **vastness,** vastitude, tremendousness, expanse, boundlessness, infinity 823; stupendousness, formidableness, prodigiousness, humongousness <nf>; **might,** mightiness, strength, power, intensity; **largeness** 257.6, **hugeness,** gigantism, bulk; **superiority** 249

2 **glory, eminence, preeminence, majesty, loftiness, prominence,** distinction, outstandingness, consequence, notability, high standing, illustriousness; **magnanimity,** nobility, sublimity; **fame,** renown, celebrity; heroism; fifteen minutes of fame

3 **quantity** 244, **numerousness** 884; **quantities, much, abundance,** copiousness, superabundance, superfluity, profusion, plenty, plenitude;

volume, mass, mountain, load; peck, bushel; bag, barrel, ton; world, acre, ocean, sea; flood, spate; **multitude** 884.3, countlessness 823.1

4 **lot, lots,** deal, no end of, **good** *or* **great deal, considerable,** sight, **heap, pile, stack,** loads, **raft, slew,** whole slew, spate, wad, **batch,** mess, mint, peck, pack, pot, **tidy sum,** quite a little; **oodles, gobs, scads,** bags *and* masses *and* lashings <Brit>

VERBS 5 **loom, bulk,** loom large, bulk large, stand out; **tower,** rear, soar, outsoar; **tower above,** rise above, overtop; **exceed, transcend,** outstrip; supersize

ADJS 6 **great, grand, considerable,** consequential; **mighty,** powerful, strong, irresistible, intense; main, maximum, **total, full,** plenary, comprehensive, exhaustive; grave, **serious,** heavy, deep

7 **large** 257.16, **immense, enormous, huge** 257.20; **gigantic,** mountainous, titanic, colossal, mammoth, Gargantuan, gigantesque, monster, monstrous, outsize, sizable, larger-than-life, overgrown, king-size, monumental; **massive,** massy, weighty, bulky, voluminous; **vast,** vasty, boundless, **infinite** 823.3, immeasurable, cosmic, astronomical, galactic; **spacious,** amplitudinous, extensive; **tremendous,** stupendous, awesome, prodigious, ginormous <nf>, humongous <nf>; supersized *or* supersize

8 **much, many,** beaucoup <nf>, ample, **abundant,** copious, generous, overflowing, superabundant, multitudinous, plentiful, **numerous** 884.6, countless 823.3

9 **eminent, prominent,** outstanding, standout, high, elevated, towering, soaring, overtopping, exalted, **lofty,** sublime, illustrious, august, majestic, noble, distinguished; **magnificent,** magnanimous, heroic, godlike, superb; famous, renowned, lauded, glorious

10 **remarkable, outstanding,** extraordinary, **superior** 249.12, **marked,** of mark, signal, conspicuous, **striking; notable,** much in evidence, noticeable, noteworthy; **marvelous,** wonderful, formidable, exceptional, uncommon, astonishing, appalling, humongous <nf>, fabulous, fantastic, incredible, brilliant, egregious

11 <nf terms> **terrific,** terrible, horrible, **dreadful, awful,** fearful, frightful, deadly; **whacking, thumping, rousing,** howling; awesome

12 **downright, outright, out-and-out; absolute, utter, perfect, consummate,** superlative, surpassing, the veriest, positive, definitive, classical, pronounced, decided, regular <nf>, proper <Brit nf>, precious, profound, stark; **thorough,** thoroughgoing, **complete,** total; **unmitigated,** unqualified, unrelieved, unspoiled, undeniable, unquestionable, unequivocal; **flagrant,** arrant, shocking, shattering, egregious, intolerable, unbearable, unconscionable, glaring, stark-staring, **rank,** crass, gross

13 **extreme, radical,** out of this world, way *or* far out <nf>, too much <nf>; **greatest,** furthest, **most, utmost,** uttermost, the max <nf>; **ultra,** ultra-ultra; at the height *or* peak *or* limit *or* summit *or* zenith

14 **undiminished,** unabated, unreduced, unrestricted, unretarded, unmitigated

ADVS 15 **greatly, largely,** to a large *or* great extent, in great measure, on a large scale; **much,** muchly <nf>, pretty much, very much, mucho <nf>, jolly well, so, so very much, ever so much, ever so, never so; **considerably,** considerable <nf>; abundantly, plenty <nf>, no end of, no end, not a little, galore <nf>, **a lot,** a deal <nf>, **a great deal,** *beaucoup* <Fr>; **highly,** to the skies; like *or* as all creation <nf>, like *or* as all get-out <nf>, in spades *and* with bells on *and* with bells on one's toes <nf>; **undiminishedly,** unabatedly, unreducedly, unrestrictedly, unretardedly, unmitigatedly

16 **vastly, immensely, enormously, hugely, tremendously,** gigantically, colossally, titanically, prodigiously, stupendously, humongously <nf>

17 **by far, far and away,** far, far and wide, by a long way, by a great deal, by a long shot *or* long chalk <nf>, out and away, by all odds

18 **very, exceedingly,** awfully *and* terribly *and* terrifically <nf>, **quite,** just, so, **really,** real *and* right <nf>, **pretty,** only too, mightily, **mighty** *and* almighty *and* powerfully *and* powerful <nf>

19 <in a positive degree> **positively, decidedly, clearly,** manifestly, unambiguously, patently, **obviously,** visibly, unmistakably, unquestionably, observably, **noticeably,** demonstrably, sensibly, quite; **certainly,** actually, **really, truly,** basically, verily, **undeniably,** indubitably, without doubt, assuredly, **indeed,** for a certainty, for real <nf>, seriously, in all conscience

20 <in a marked degree> **intensely, acutely,** exquisitely, **exceptionally,** surpassingly, superlatively, eminently, preeminently; **remarkably, markedly, notably, strikingly,** signally, emphatically, pointedly, prominently, conspicuously, pronouncedly, impressively, famously, glaringly; **particularly, singularly,** peculiarly; uncommonly, extraordinarily, **unusually; wonderfully,** wondrous, amazingly, magically, surprisingly, astonishingly, marvelously, exuberantly, incredibly, awesomely; **abundantly,** richly, profusely, amply, **generously,** copiously; **magnificently,** splendidly, nobly, worthily, magnanimously

21 <in a distressing degree> **distressingly, sadly, sorely, bitterly,** piteously, grievously, miserably, **cruelly,** woefully, lamentably, balefully, dolorously, shockingly; **terribly, awfully, dreadfully, frightfully, horribly,** abominably, **painfully,** excruciatingly, torturously, **agonizingly,** deathly, deadly, something awful *or* fierce *or* terrible *and* in the worst way <nf>, within an inch of one's life; shatteringly, staggeringly; **excessively,** exorbitantly, extravagantly, **inordinately,** preposterously; **unduly, improperly,** intolerably, unbearably; **inexcusably,** unpardonably, unconscionably; **flagrantly,** blatantly, egregiously; **unashamedly,** unabashedly, baldly, nakedly, brashly, openly; **cursedly,** confoundedly, **damnably,** deucedly <nf>, infernally, hellishly

22 <in an extreme degree> **extremely, utterly, totally,** in the extreme, **most,** *à outrance* <Fr, to the utmost>; mondo <nf>; **immeasurably,** incalculably, indefinitely, **infinitely;** beyond compare *or* comparison, **beyond measure,** beyond all bounds, all out <nf>, flat out <Brit nf>, full-on; **perfectly, absolutely,** essentially, fundamentally, radically; **purely, totally,** completely, to the max; unconditionally, with no strings attached, unequivocally, downright, dead; with a vengeance

23 <in a violent degree> **violently,** furiously, hotly, fiercely, severely, **desperately,** madly, **like mad** <nf>; **wildly,** demonically, like one possessed, **frantically,** frenetically, fanatically, uncontrollably

248 INSIGNIFICANCE

NOUNS 1 **insignificance,** inconsiderableness, unimportance 998, inconsequentialness, inconsequentiality, lowness, pettiness, meanness, triviality, nugacity, nugaciousness; **smallness,** tininess, diminutiveness, minuteness, exiguity *or* exiguousness; **slightness,** moderateness, scantiness, puniness, picayunishness, meanness, meagerness; daintiness, delicacy; **littleness** 258; **fewness** 885; insufficiency 992

2 **modicum,** minim; **minimum; little, bit,** little *or* wee *or* tiny bit <nf>, bite, **particle,** fragment, spot, **speck,** flyspeck, fleck, point, dot, jot, tittle, **iota,** ounce, **dab** <nf>, mote, **mite** <nf> 258.7; whit, ace, **hair,** scruple, groat, farthing, pittance, dole, trifling amount, **smidgen** *and* skosh *and* smitch *and* scooch <nf>, pinch, gobbet, dribble, driblet, dram, drop, drop in a bucket *or* in the ocean, tip of the iceberg;

grain, granule, pebble; molecule, **atom;** thimbleful, spoonful, handful, nutshell; trivia, minutiae; dwarf

3 **scrap,** tatter, smithereen <nf>, patch, **stitch, shred,** tag; snip, **snippet,** snick, chip, nip; splinter, sliver, shiver; **morsel,** *morceau* <Fr>, **crumb**

4 **hint,** *soupçon* <Fr>, **suspicion, suggestion,** intimation; tip of the iceberg; **trace, touch, dash,** cast, **smattering,** sprinkling; tinge, tincture; **taste, lick, smack,** sip, sup, **smell;** look, **thought,** idea; **shade,** shadow; gleam, spark, scintilla

5 **hardly anything, mere nothing,** next to nothing, less than nothing, **trifle,** bagatelle, **a drop in the bucket** *or* **in the ocean;** the shadow of a shade, the suspicion of a suspicion

ADJS 6 **insignificant, small, inconsiderable, inconsequential, negligible,** no great shakes, footling, one-horse *and* pint-size *and* vest-pocket <nf>; unimportant, no skin off one's nose *or* ass, **trivial,** trifling, nugacious, nugatory, petty, mean, niggling, piddling, picayune *or* picayunish, of no account, nickel-and-dime *and* penny-ante *and* Mickey-Mouse <nf>; shallow, depthless, cursory, superficial, skin-deep; **little** 258.10, **tiny** 258.11, **weeny, miniature** 258.12, **meager** 992.10, **few** 885.4; **short** 268.8; **low** 274.7

7 **dainty, delicate, gossamer, diaphanous; subtle,** subtile, tenuous, thin 270.16, rarefied 299.4

8 **mere, sheer,** stark, bare, barebones, plain, simple, unadorned, unenhanced

ADVS 9 <in a small degree> **scarcely, hardly,** not hardly <nf>, **barely,** only just, by a hair, by an ace *or* a jot *or* a whit *or* an iota, **slightly,** lightly, exiguously, fractionally, scantily, inconsequentially, **insignificantly, negligibly,** imperfectly, minimally, inappreciably, **little; minutely,** meagerly, triflingly, faintly, weakly, feebly; **a little, a bit,** just a bit, to a small extent, on a small scale; ever so little, *tant soit peu* <Fr>, as little as may be

10 <in a certain or limited degree> **to a degree, to a certain extent, to some degree,** in some measure, to such an extent, *pro tanto* <L>; **moderately,** mildly, **somewhat,** detectably, just visibly, modestly, appreciably, visibly, **fairly,** tolerably, **partially,** partly, part, in part, incompletely, not exhaustively, not comprehensively; **comparatively, relatively; merely,** simply, purely, only; **at least,** at the least, leastwise, at worst, at any rate; **at most,** at the most, at best, at the outside <nf>; in a manner, in a manner of speaking, **in a way,** after a fashion; so far, thus far

11 <in no degree> **noway,** in your dreams, noways, **nowise,** in no wise, in no case, in no respect, **by no means,** by no manner of means, **on no account, not on any account, not for anything in the world, under no circumstances,** at no hand, nohow <nf>, **not in the least,** not much, **not at all,** never, not by a damn sight <nf>, not by a long shot <nf>; not nearly, **nowhere near; not a bit,** not a bit of it, not a whit, not a speck, not a jot, not an iota, jack squat <nf>

249 SUPERIORITY

NOUNS 1 **superiority, preeminence, greatness** 247, **lead,** pride of place, transcendence *or* transcendency, ascendancy *or* ascendance, prestige, favor, prepotence *or* prepotency, preponderance; predominance *or* predominancy, hegemony; precedence 814, **priority,** prerogative, privilege, right-of-way; **excellence** 999.1, virtuosity, high caliber, inimitability, incomparability; **seniority,** precedence, deanship; clout, pull <nf>; **success** 409, accomplishment 407, **skill** 413

2 **advantage,** vantage, odds, leg up *and* inside track *and* pole position <nf>; **upper hand,** whip hand, trump hand; start, head *or* flying *or* running start; **edge,** bulge *and* jump *and* drop <nf>; **card up one's sleeve** <nf>, ace in the hole <nf>,

something extra *or* in reserve; vantage ground *or* point, coign of vantage, high ground; one-upmanship

3 **supremacy, primacy,** paramountcy, **first place,** height, acme, zenith, be-all and end-all, summit, top spot <nf>; **sovereignty, rule, hegemony, control** 417.5; kingship, **dominion** 417.6, lordship, imperium, world power; **command,** sway; **mastery,** mastership 417.7; **leadership,** headship, presidency; **authority** 417, directorship, management, jurisdiction, power, say *and* last word <nf>; influence 894; effectiveness; **maximum,** highest, most, *ne plus ultra* <Fr, no more beyond>, the max <nf>; **championship,** crown, laurels, palms, first prize, blue ribbon, new high, record

4 **superior, chief, head, boss** 575.1, employer, honcho <nf>, commander, **ruler, leader,** dean, *primus inter pares* <L, first among equals>, **master** 575; higher-up <nf>, senior, principal, big shot <nf>; superman, **genius** 413.12; prodigy, nonpareil, paragon, virtuoso, ace, **star, superstar,** champion, winner, top dog *and* top banana <nf>, one in a thousand, one in a million, etc, laureate, fugleman, Cadillac *and* Rolls-Royce *and* Mercedes-Benz <TM>, A per se, A1, A number 1, standout, moneymaker, record-breaker, the greatest *and* whizbang *and* world-beater *and* a tough act to follow <nf>; big fish in a small pond <nf>; alpha male, alpha female; supremist

5 **the best** 999.8, the top of the line <nf>; the best people, nobility 608; **aristocracy,** barons, top people <nf>, **elite,** cream, crème de la crème, top of the milk, upper crust, upper class, one's betters; **the brass** <nf>, the VIP's <nf>, higher-ups, movers and shakers, lords of creation, ruling circles, **establishment,** power elite, power structure, **ruling class,** bigwigs <nf>, big boys <nf>, authorities, powers that be, officialdom; fast track; happy few, chosen few

VERBS 6 **excel, surpass, exceed, transcend,** get *or* have the ascendancy, get *or* have the edge, have it all over <nf>, overcome, overpass, best, **better,** improve on, perfect, go one better <nf>; **cap,** trump; top, tower above *or* over, overtop; **predominate,** prevail, preponderate, carry the day; **outweigh,** overbalance, overbear

7 **best, beat, beat out, defeat** 412.6; beat all hollow <nf>, trounce, clobber *and* take to the cleaners *and* smoke *and* skin *and* skin alive <nf>, worst, whip *and* lick *and* have it all over *and* cut down to size <nf>; bear the palm, take the cake <nf>, bring home the bacon <nf>; **triumph; win** 411.3

8 **overshadow, eclipse, throw into the shade, top,** extinguish, take the shine out of <nf>; put to shame, show up <nf>, put one's nose out of joint, put down <nf>, fake out <nf>

9 **outdo, outrival,** outvie, outachieve, edge out, **outclass, outshine,** overmatch, outgun <nf>; **outstrip,** outgo, outrange, outreach, outpoint, **outperform;** outplay, overplay, outmaneuver, outwit; outrun, outstep, outpace, outmarch, run rings *or* circles around <nf>; outride, override; outjump, overjump; outleap, overleap

10 **outdistance, distance; pass, surpass,** overpass; **get ahead,** pull ahead, shoot ahead, walk away *or* off <nf>; **leave behind,** leave at the post, leave in the dust, leave in the lurch; **come to the front,** have a healthy lead <nf>, hold the field; steal a march

11 **rule, command, lead,** possess authority 417.13, have the authority, have the say *or* the last word, have the whip hand *and* hold all the aces <nf>; **take precedence, precede** 814.2; **come** *or* **rank first, outrank,** rank, rank out <nf>; **come to the fore,** come to the front, **lead** 165.2; play first fiddle, **star**

ADJS 12 **superior, greater,** better, finer; **higher,** upper, over, super, above; ascendant, in the ascendant, in ascendancy, coming <nf>; **eminent,** outstanding, rare, distinguished, marked, of choice, chosen;

surpassing, exceeding, excellent 999.12, **excelling, rivaling, eclipsing,** capping, topping, **transcending,** transcendent *or* transcendental, bad <nf>; **ahead,** a cut *or* stroke above, one up on <nf>; more than a match for

13 **superlative, supreme, greatest, best, highest,** veriest, maximal, maximum, most, utmost, outstanding, stickout <nf>; top, topmost, **uppermost,** tip-top, top-level, top-echelon, top-notch *and* top-of-the-line <nf>, **first-rate,** first-class, top of the line, highest-quality, best-quality, far and away the best, the best by a long shot *or* long chalk, head and shoulders above, of the highest type, A1, A number 1, uber

14 **chief, main, principal,** paramount, **foremost,** headmost, **leading, dominant,** crowning, capital, **cardinal;** great, arch, banner, master, magisterial; central, focal, prime, **primary,** primal, first; **preeminent,** supereminent; **predominant,** preponderant, prevailing, hegemonic *or* hegemonical; ruling, overruling; **sovereign** 417.17; topflight, highest-ranking, ranking; **star,** superstar, stellar, world-class

15 **peerless, matchless, champion; unmatched,** unmatchable, makeless , unrivaled, unparagoned, unparalleled, immortal, **unequaled,** never-to-be-equaled, unpeered, unexampled, unapproached, unapproachable, **unsurpassed, unexcelled;** unsurpassable; inimitable, **incomparable,** beyond compare *or* comparison, apples to oranges, **unique;** without equal *or* parallel, *sans pareil* <Fr>; in a class by itself, *sui generis* <L>, easily first, *facile princeps* <L>; second to none, *nulli secundus* <L>; **unbeatable,** invincible

ADVS 16 **superlatively, exceedingly, surpassingly;** eminently, egregiously, prominently; supremely, paramountly, preeminently, **the most,** transcendently, to crown all, *par excellence* <Fr>; inimitably, incomparably; to *or* in the highest degree, far and away

17 **chiefly, mainly, in the main,** in chief; dominantly, **predominantly; mostly, for the most part; principally, especially, particularly,** peculiarly; **primarily, in the first place,** first of all, **above all; indeed,** even, yea, still more, more than ever, all the more, *a fortiori* <L>; ever so, never so, no end

18 **peerlessly, matchlessly,** unmatchably; unsurpassedly, unsurpassably; inimitably, **incomparably; uniquely,** second to none, *nulli secundus* <L>; **unbeatably,** invincibly

19 **advantageously,** to *or* with advantage, favorably; melioratively, ameliorativeiy, improvingly

250 INFERIORITY

NOUNS 1 **inferiority, subordinacy,** subordination, secondariness; **juniority,** minority; **subservience, subjection,** servility, lowliness, humbleness, humility; back seat *and* second fiddle <nf>, second *or* third string <nf>, second banana; insignificance

2 **inferior, underling,** understrapper <Brit>, **subordinate,** subaltern, **junior;** secondary, second fiddle *and* second stringer *and* third stringer *and* benchwarmer *and* low man on the totem pole <nf>, loser *and* nonstarter <nf>; lightweight, follower, pawn, cog, flunky, yes-man, creature; lower class *or* orders *or* ranks, lowlife, commonalty; infrastructure *or* commonality, hoi polloi, masses; satellite; B-list, C-list, D-list; trailer trash, white trash; Eurotrash

3 **inadequacy, mediocrity** 1005, deficiency, imperfection, insufficiency 992; **incompetence** *or* incompetency, maladroitness, unskillfulness 414; **failure** 410; smallness 248.1; littleness 258; meanness, lowness, baseness, pettiness, triviality, shabbiness, vulgarity 497; **fewness** 885; subnormality

VERBS 4 **be inferior, not come up to, not measure up, fall** *or* **come short, fail** 410.9, not make *or* hack it *and* not cut the mustard *and* not make the cut <nf>, not make the grade; want, leave much to be desired, be found wanting; **not compare,** have nothing on <nf>, **not hold a candle to** <nf>, not approach, not come near; serve, subserve, rank under *or* beneath, follow, play second fiddle *and* take a back seat *and* sit on the bench <nf>

5 **bow to, hand it to** <nf>, tip the hat to <nf>, yield the palm; retire into the shade; give in <nf>, lose face; submit

ADJS 6 **inferior, subordinate,** subaltern, sub, small-scale, **secondary; junior, minor;** second *or* third string *and* one-horse *and* penny-ante *and* dinky <nf>, second *or* third rank, third-rate, low in the pecking order, low-rent *and* downscale <nf>, below the salt; **subservient,** subject, servile, low, **lowly,** humble, modest, scrub; **lesser,** less, lower, low-grade, B-list, C-list, D-list; in the shade, thrown into the shade; **common,** vulgar, **ordinary;** underprivileged, disadvantaged, nothing to write home about, crummy; **beneath one's dignity** *or* station, infra dig, demeaning; half-assed <nf>

7 **inadequate, mediocre,** deficient, imperfect, **insufficient; incompetent,** unskillful, maladroit; small, small-time, little, mean, base, petty, trivial, shabby; **not to be compared, not comparable, not a patch on** <nf>; **outclassed,** outshone, not in it *and* not in the same street *or* league with <nf>, out of it *and* out of the picture *and* **out of the running** *and* left a mile behind <nf>

8 **least, smallest,** littlest, slightest, **lowest,** shortest; minimum, minimal, minim; few 885.4; minimalistic

ADVS 9 **poorly, incompetently, inadequately,** badly, maladroitly; least of all, at the bottom of the scale, at the nadir, at the bottom of the heap *and* in the gutter <nf>; beggarly; at a disadvantage

251 INCREASE

NOUNS 1 **increase, gain,** augmentation, greatening, **enlargement, amplification, growth,** development, widening, spread, broadening, elevation, **extension,** aggrandizement, access, accession, **increment,** accretion; exponential growth; **addition** 253; **expansion** 259; **inflation,** swelling, ballooning, edema, fattening, tumescence, bloating, dilation; **multiduplication, proliferation,** productiveness 890; accruement, accrual, accumulation; **advance,** appreciation, ascent, mounting, crescendo, waxing, snowballing, **rise** *or* raise, fattening *and* boost *and* hike <nf>, **up** *and* upping <nf>, buildup; **upturn,** uptick <nf>, uptrend, upsurge, upswing; **leap,** jump; **flood,** surge, gush

2 **intensification, heightening, deepening;** tightening, turn of the screw, **strengthening,** beefing-up <nf>, enhancement, **magnification,** blowup, blowing up, exaggeration; aggravation, exacerbation, heating-up; **concentration,** condensation, consolidation; **reinforcement,** redoubling; pickup *and* step-up <nf>, **acceleration,** speedup, accelerando, escalation, upsurge; **boom, explosion,** baby boom, population explosion, information explosion

3 **gains,** winnings, cut *and* take <nf>, increase , **profits** 472.3

VERBS 4 **increase, enlarge,** aggrandize, **amplify,** amp, **augment, extend,** maximize, **add to; expand** 259.4, **inflate;** lengthen, broaden, fatten, fill out, thicken; **raise,** exalt, boost <nf>, hike *and* hike up *and* jack up *and* jump up *and* bump up *and* crank up <nf>, mark up, put up, **up** <nf>; **build, build up;** pyramid, parlay; progress

5 **intensify, heighten, deepen,** amplify, enhance, **strengthen,** beef up <nf>, aggravate, exacerbate; **exaggerate,** blow up *and* puff up <nf>, **magnify;** whet, sharpen; **reinforce,** double, redouble, triple; **concentrate,** condense, consolidate; **complicate,** ramify, make complex; give a boost to, **step up** <nf>, accelerate; key up, hop up *and* soup up *and* jazz up <nf>; add fuel to the flame *or* the fire, heat *or* hot up <nf>

6 **grow, increase, advance,** appreciate; **spread, widen,** broaden; **gain,** get ahead; wax, swell, balloon, bloat, mount, **rise,** go up, crescendo, snowball, skyrocket, mushroom; **intensify, develop,** gain strength, strengthen; accrue, accumulate; **multiply, proliferate,** breed, teem; run *or* shoot up, **boom, explode**

ADJS **7** **increased, heightened,** raised, elevated, stepped-up <nf>; **intensified,** deepened, reinforced, strengthened, fortified, beefed-up <nf>, tightened, stiffened; **enlarged, extended,** augmented, aggrandized, amplified, **enhanced,** boosted, hiked <nf>; broadened, widened, spread; **magnified, inflated, expanded,** swollen, bloated; **multiplied,** proliferated; **accelerated,** hopped-up *and* jazzed-up <nf>, cranked up

8 **increasing, rising,** fast-rising, skyrocketing, meteoric; on the upswing, on the increase, on the rise; crescent, waxing, **growing,** fast-growing, flourishing, burgeoning, blossoming, waxing, swelling, lengthening, **multiplying,** proliferating; spreading, spreading like a cancer *or* like wildfire, expanding; tightening, intensifying; incremental; **on the increase,** crescendoing, snowballing, mushrooming, growing like a mushroom

ADVS **9** **increasingly,** growingly, more, **more and more,** on and on, greater and greater, ever more; in a crescendo

252 DECREASE

NOUNS **1** **decrease,** decrescence, decrement, **diminishment,** diminution, **reduction, lessening, lowering,** waning, shrinking *or* shrinkage, withering, withering away, scaling down, scaledown, downsizing, build-down; miniaturization; downplaying, underplaying; depression, damping, dampening; **letup** <nf>, abatement, easing, easing off, slackening; de-escalation; **alleviation,** relaxation, mitigation; attenuation, extenuation, weakening, sagging, dying, dying off *or* away, trailing off, tailing off, tapering off, fadeout, languishment; depreciation, **deflation; deduction** 255.1; subtraction, **abridgment** 268.3; **contraction** 260; simplicity 798

2 **decline,** declension, **subsidence,** slump <nf>, lapse, **drop,** downtick <nf>; **collapse,** crash; dwindling, wane, ebb; downturn, downtrend, downward trend *or* curve, retreat, remission; **fall, plunge,** dive, decline and fall; decrescendo, diminuendo; catabasis, deceleration, slowdown; leveling off, bottoming out

3 **decrement, waste, loss,** dissipation, wear and tear, erosion, ablation, wearing away, depletion, corrosion, attrition, consumption, shrinkage, exhaustion; deliquescence, dissolution; extinction, consumption

4 **curtailment, retrenchment,** cut, cutback, drawdown, rollback, scaleback, pullback; moderation, restraint; abridgment; slash, slashing

5 **minimization,** minification, making light of, devaluing, undervaluing, **belittling,** belittlement, detraction; abridgment, miniaturization; qualification 959

VERBS **6** **decrease, diminish, lessen; let up,** bate, abate; **decline, subside,** shrink, wane, wither, ebb, ebb away, dwindle, languish, sink, sag, die down *or* away, wind down, taper off *and* trail off *or* away *and* tail off *or* away <nf>; **drop,** drop off, dive, take a nose dive, plummet, plunge, fall, fall off, fall away, fall to a low ebb, run low; **waste,** wear, waste *or* wear away, crumble, erode, ablate, corrode, consume, consume away, be eaten away; melt away, deliquesce; become extinct

7 **reduce, decrease, diminish, lessen,** take from; **lower, depress,** de-escalate, damp, dampen, **step down** *and* tune down *and* phase down *or* out *and* scale back *or* down *and* roll back *or* down <nf>; **downgrade;** depreciate, **deflate; curtail,** retrench; **cut,** cut down *or* back, cut down to size <nf>, trim away, chip away at, whittle away *or* down, pare, pare down, roll back <nf>; deduct 255.9; **shorten** 268.6, abridge;

compress 260.7, shrink, retrench, downsize; **simplify** 798.4

8 **abate,** bate, ease; **weaken,** dilute, water, water down, attenuate, extenuate; alleviate, mitigate, slacken, remit; enfeeble, debilitate; tail off, die off

9 **minimize,** minify, **belittle,** detract from; dwarf, bedwarf; play down, underplay, downplay, de-emphasize, play down, tone down, moderate; hush

ADJS 10 **reduced, decreased, diminished, lowered,** dropped, fallen; bated, **abated; deflated,** contracted, shrunk, shrunken; **simplified** 798.9; back-to-basics, no-frills; dissipated, **eroded,** consumed, ablated, **worn;** curtailed, shorn, retrenched, cutback; weakened, attenuated, watered-down, diluted; scaled-down, miniaturized, abridged, pared down; minimized, belittled, on a downer <nf>; **lower,** less, lesser, smaller, shorter; off-peak; downplayed, underplayed, toned down, de-emphasized

11 **decreasing, diminishing, lessening, subsiding, declining,** languishing, dwindling, waning, on the wane, on the slide, wasting; decrescent, reductive, deliquescent, **contractive;** diminuendo, decrescendo

ADVS 12 **decreasingly, diminishingly,** less, **less and less,** ever less; decrescendo, diminuendo; on a declining scale, at a declining rate

253 ADDITION

NOUNS 1 **addition,** accession, annexation, affixation, suffixation, prefixation, agglutination, attachment, junction, **joining** 800, adjunction, uniting; **increase** 251; **augmentation, supplementation, complementation,** reinforcement; superaddition, admixture, superposition, superjunction, superfetation, suppletion; juxtaposition 223.3; adjunct 254, add-on, rider, extra, accessory

2 <math terms> plus sign, plus; addend; sum, summation, total, aggregate; subtotal

3 **adding,** totalizing *or* totalization, toting up, reckoning, computation, calculation, ringing up; **adding machine,** calculator

VERBS 4 **add,** add on, plus <nf>, put with, **join** *or* **unite with, bring together, affix, attach,** annex, adjoin, append, conjoin, subjoin, prefix, suffix, infix, postfix, tag, tag on, **tack on** <nf>, slap on <nf>, hitch on <nf>, carry over; glue on, paste on, agglutinate; superpose, superadd; burden, encumber, saddle with; **complicate,** ornament, decorate

5 **add to, augment, supplement,** append; volumize; **increase** 251.4; **reinforce,** strengthen, fortify, beef up <nf>; recruit, swell the ranks of; superadd

6 **compute,** add up; sum, total, totalize, total up, tot *and* tot up *and* tote *and* tote up <nf>, tally, calculate

7 **be added,** advene, supervene

ADJS 8 **additive,** additional, additory; **cumulative,** accumulative; summative *or* summational; loaded

9 **added,** affixed, add-on, **attached,** annexed, appended, appendant; adjoined, adjunct, adjunctive, conjoined, subjoined; superadded, superposed, superjoined

10 **additional, supplementary, supplemental; extra,** plus, further, farther, fresh, **more,** new, **other,** another, ulterior; **auxiliary,** ancillary, supernumerary, contributory, **accessory,** collateral, supererogatory; **surplus,** spare, superfluous

ADVS 11 **additionally, in addition, also,** and then some, even more, more so, and also, and all <nf>, and so, **as well, too,** else, beside, **besides, to boot, not to mention, let alone, into the bargain;** on top of, over, above; **beyond, plus; extra,** on the side <nf>, for lagniappe; **more, moreover,** *au reste* <Fr>, *en plus* <Fr>, thereto, farther, further, **furthermore,** at the same time, then, again, yet; similarly, likewise, by the same token, by the same sign; item; therewith, withal ; all included, altogether; among other things, *inter alia* <L>

CONJS 12 **and, also,** and also

PHRS **13 et cetera, etc, and so forth, and so on**; et al, *et alii* <L>, and all <nf>, and others, and other things, *cum multis aliis* <L, with many others>; and everything else, **and more of the same, and the rest, and the like;** blah blah blah blah *and* dah-dah dah-dah dah-dah *and* and suchlike *or* and all that sort of thing *and* and all that *and* and all like that *and* and stuff like that *and* and all that jazz <nf>; yada yada *or* yadda yadda; **and what not** *and* and what have you *and* and I don't know what *and* and God knows what *and* and then some *and* you name it <nf>; and the following, *et sequens* <L>, et seq

254 ADJUNCT

<thing added>

NOUNS **1 adjunct, addition,** increase, **increment,** augmentation, supplementation, complementation, *additum* <L>, additament, additory, addendum, addenda <pl>, accession, fixture; **annex,** annexation; **appendage,** appendant, pendant, appanage, tailpiece, coda; undergirding, reinforcement; appurtenance, appurtenant; **accessory,** attachment; **supplement,** complement, continuation, extrapolation, extension; offshoot, side issue, corollary, sidebar <nf>, side effect, spin-off <nf>, aftereffect; **concomitant, accompaniment** 769, **additive,** adjuvant; leftover, carry-over

2 <written text> **postscript** *or* P.S., **appendix;** rider, allonge, codicil; **epilogue,** envoi, coda, tail, afterword; back matter, front matter; note, marginalia, scholia, commentary, annotation, footnote; **interpolation,** interlineation; affix, prefix, suffix, infix; subscript, superscript; enclitic, proclitic

3 <building> wing, **addition, annex,** extension, ell *or* L, outhouse, outbuilding

4 extra, bonus, signing bonus, retention bonus, **premium,** something extra, extra dash, little extra, extra added attraction, lagniappe, something into the bargain, something for good measure, baker's dozen; peripheral; added value; **padding,** stuffing, filling; trimming, **frill,** flourish, filigree, decoration, ornament; bells and whistles <nf>; superaddition; fillip, wrinkle, twist; the works <nf>; benefit, perquisite, perk; freebie <nf>

255 SUBTRACTION

NOUNS **1 subtraction, deduction,** subduction, **removal,** taking away; abstraction, ablation, sublation; erosion, abrasion, wearing, wearing away; refinement, purification; detraction

2 reduction, diminution, decrease 252, build-down, phasedown, drawdown, decrement, impairment, **cut** *or* **cutting,** curtailment, shortening, truncation; **shrinkage,** depletion, **attrition,** remission; **depreciation,** detraction, disparagement, derogation; retraction, retrenchment; **extraction**

3 excision, abscission, rescission, extirpation; **elimination,** exclusion, extinction, eradication, destruction 395, annihilation; cancellation, write-off, erasure; circumcision; **amputation,** mutilation

4 castration, gelding, emasculation, deballing <nf>, altering *and* fixing <nf>, spaying

5 <written text> **deletion,** erasure, cancellation, omission; editing, blue-penciling, striking *or* striking out; expurgation, bowdlerization, censoring *or* censorship; abridgment, abbreviation

6 <math terms> difference; subtrahend, minuend; negative; minus sign, minus

7 <thing subtracted> **deduction,** decrement, minus; refund, rebate

8 <result> **difference, remainder** 256, epact <astronomy>, discrepancy, net, balance, surplus 993.5, deficit, credit; contradistinction

VERBS **9 subtract, deduct,** subduct, take away, take from, **remove,** withdraw, abstract, debit, dock; **reduce,** shorten, curtail, retrench, lessen, **diminish, decrease,** phase down, impair, bate, abate; **depreciate,** disparage, detract, derogate; **erode,** abrade, eat *or* wear *or* rub *or* shave *or* file away; **extract,** leach, drain, wash away; thin, thin out, weed; **refine,** purify

10 **excise,** cut out, cut, extirpate, enucleate; **cancel,** write off; **eradicate,** root out, wipe *or* stamp out, **eliminate,** kill, kill off, liquidate, annihilate, knock off, destroy 395.10, extinguish; **exclude,** except, take out, cancel, cancel out, censor out, bleep out <nf>, rule out, bar, ban; set aside *or* apart, isolate, pick out, cull; **cut off** *or* **away,** shear *or* take *or* strike *or* knock *or* lop off, truncate; minus; **amputate,** mutilate, abscind; **prune,** pare, peel, clip, crop, bob, dock, lop, nip, shear, shave, strip, strip off *or* away

11 **castrate,** geld, emasculate, eunuchize, neuter, spay, fix *or* alter <nf>, unsex, desex, deball <nf>; geld, caponize; unman; sterilize

12 <written text> **delete,** erase, expunge, **cancel,** omit; **edit,** edit out, blue-pencil; strike, strike out *or* off, rub *or* blot out, cross out *or* off, kill, cut; void, rescind; **censor,** bowdlerize, expurgate; abridge, abbreviate

ADJS **13** **subtractive, reductive,** deductive, extirpative; ablative, erosive; censorial; removable, eradicable

256 REMAINDER

NOUNS **1** **remainder, remains, remnant,** relict, **residue,** residuum, residual, **rest, balance;** holdover; **leavings, leftovers, oddments; refuse,** odds and ends, scraps, rags, **rubbish, waste,** litter, orts, candle ends; scourings, offscourings; parings, sweepings, filings, shavings, sawdust; chaff, straw, stubble, husks; **debris,** detritus, ruins; end, fag end; stump, butt *or* butt end, stub, rump; survival, vestige, trace, hint, shadow, afterimage, afterglow; glut; **fossil,** relics

2 **dregs, grounds, lees,** dross, slag, draff, scoria, feces; **sediment, settlings, deposits,** deposition; precipitate, precipitation, sublimate <chem>; alluvium, alluvion, diluvium; overflow; silt, loess, moraine; scum, off-scum, froth; ash, ember, cinder, sinter, clinker; soot, smut

3 **survivor,** heir, successor, inheritor; **widow,** widower, relict, war widow, **orphan;** others, those left

4 **excess** 993, **surplus,** surplusage, overplus, overage; superfluity, redundancy, pleonasm; something for a rainy day

VERBS **5** **remain, be left** *or* **left over, survive,** subsist, rest, stay

6 **leave,** leave over, leave behind, bequeath

ADJS **7** **remaining, surviving, extant,** vestigial, over, left, **leftover, still around, remnant,** remanent, odd, on the shelf; **spare,** to spare; unused, unconsumed; **surplus,** superfluous; **outstanding,** unmet, unresolved; net; redundant

8 **residual,** residuary; sedimental, sedimentary

257 SIZE, LARGENESS

NOUNS **1** **size, largeness, bigness, greatness** 247, vastness, vastitude, **magnitude,** order of magnitude, amplitude; mass, bulk, **volume,** body; **dimensions, proportions,** dimension, caliber, scantling, proportion; **measure,** measurement 300, gauge, **scale; extent,** extension, expansion, expanse, square footage *or* yardage etc, **scope,** reach, range, ballpark <nf>, spread, coverage, area, circumference, ambit, girth, diameter, radius, boundary, border, periphery; linear measure *or* dimension, length, height, procerity <depth>; depth, breadth, width; wheelbase, wingspan

2 **capacity, volume, content,** holding capacity, cubic footage *or* yardage etc, accommodation, room, space, measure, limit, burden; gallonage, tankage; poundage, tonnage, cordage; stowage; **quantity** 244

3 **full size,** full growth; life size

4 large size, extra large size, economy size, family size, **king size,** California king size, queen size, giant size, plus size

5 **oversize,** outsize; overlargeness, overbigness; **overgrowth,** wild *or* uncontrolled growth, overdevelopment, sprawl; **overweight,** overheaviness; overstoutness, overfatness, overplumpness, bloat, bloatedness, obesity, chubbiness; gigantism, giantism, titanism; hyperplasia, hypertrophy, acromegalic gigantism, acromegaly, pituitary gigantism, normal gigantism

6 <large size> **sizableness, largeness, bigness,** greatness, grandness, grandeur, grandiosity; largishness, biggishness; voluminousness, capaciousness, generousness, copiousness, ampleness; tallness, toweringness; broadness, wideness; profundity; extensiveness, expansiveness, comprehensiveness; spaciousness 158.5; bagginess

7 <very large size> **hugeness, vastness,** vastitude; humongousness <nf>; **enormousness, immenseness, enormity, immensity,** tremendousness, **prodigiousness,** stupendousness, mountainousness; **gigantism,** giganticness, giantism, giantlikeness; monumentalism; **monstrousness, monstrosity**

8 **corpulence, obesity, stoutness,** largeness, bigness, *embonpoint* <Fr>; **fatness,** fattishness, adiposis *or* adiposity, endomorphy, fleshiness, beefiness, meatiness, heftiness, grossness; **plumpness,** buxomness, rotundity, fubsiness <Brit>, tubbiness <nf>, roly-poliness; pudginess, podginess; chubbiness, chunkiness <nf>, stockiness, squattiness, squatness, dumpiness, portliness; paunchiness, bloatedness, puffiness, pursiness, blowziness; middle-age spread; weight problem; hippiness <nf>; steatopygia *or* steatopygy; bosominess, bustiness <nf>

9 **bulkiness, bulk,** hulkingness *or* hulkiness, **massiveness,** lumpishness, clumpishness; **ponderousness,** cumbrousness, cumbersomeness; clumsiness, awkwardness, unwieldiness, clunkiness <nf>

10 **lump,** clump, **hunk** *and* **chunk** <nf>, wodge <Brit nf>; **mass,** piece, **gob** *and* glob <nf>, gobbet, dollop, cluster, gobs <nf>; batch, **wad,** heap, block, loaf; pat <of butter>; clod; nugget; **quantity** 244

11 <something large> **whopper** *and* thumper *and* lunker *and* whale *and* jumbo <nf>; monster, hulk; large part, bulk, mass, lion's share, majority, better part

12 <corpulent person> **heavyweight, pig,** porker, heavy <nf>, human *or* man mountain <nf>; big *or* large person; **fat person, fatty** *and* **fatso** <nf>, roly-poly, **tub, tub of lard,** tun, tun of flesh, whale, blimp <nf>, hippo <nf>, **potbelly,** gorbelly , swagbelly, dumpling, lardass <nf>

13 **giant**, giantess, **amazon, colossus, titan,** titaness, *nephilim* <Heb pl>, brute, hulk; long drink of water

14 **behemoth, leviathan, monster;** mammoth, mastodon; elephant, jumbo <nf>; whale; hippopotamus, hippo <nf>; **dinosaur**

VERBS 15 **size, adjust, grade,** group, range, rank, graduate, sort, match; gauge, **measure** 300.10, proportion; **bulk** 247.5; **enlarge** 259.4,5; fatten

ADJS 16 **large, sizable, big, great** 247.6, **grand,** tall <nf>, **considerable, goodly,** healthy, tidy <nf>, **substantial,** bumper; as big as all outdoors; numerous 884.6; largish, biggish; large-scale, larger than life; man-sized <nf>; large-size *or* -sized, man-sized, king-size, queen-size, plus-size; economy-size, family-size; good-sized, life-size *or* -sized

17 **voluminous, capacious, generous, ample,** copious, broad, wide, extensive, expansive, capacious, comprehensive; **spacious**

18 **corpulent, stout, fat, overweight,** fattish, **obese,** adipose, gross, fleshy, beefy, meaty, hefty, porky, porcine; paunchy, paunched, bloated, puffy, blowzy, distended, swollen, pursy; abdominous, big-bellied, full-bellied, potbellied, gorbellied <old *or* dial>, swag-bellied, pot-gutted *and* pussle-gutted <nf>, **plump, buxom,** *zaftig* <Yiddish>, pleasantly

plump, full, huggy <nf>, rotund, fubsy <Brit>, **tubby** <nf>, roly-poly; **pudgy,** podgy; thickbodied, thick-girthed, **heavyset, thickset, chubby,** chunky <nf>, fubsy <Brit nf>, **stocky,** squat, squatty, dumpy, square; pyknic, endomorphic; **stalwart, brawny, burly;** lusty, strapping <nf>; **portly,** imposing; full-figured; well-fed, corn-fed, grain-fed; chubby-faced, round-faced, moonfaced; hippy <nf>, full-buttocked, steatopygic *or* steatopygous, fat-assed *and* lard-assed <nf>, broad in the beam <nf>, well-upholstered <nf>; bosomy, full-bosomed, chesty, busty <nf>, top heavy; plump as a dumpling *or* partridge, fat as a quail, fat as a pig *or* hog, fat as brawn *or* bacon

19 **bulky, hulky,** hulking, lumpish, lumpy, lumping <nf>, clumpish, lumbering, lubberly; **massive,** massy; elephantine, hippopotamic; **ponderous,** cumbrous, cumbersome; **clumsy,** awkward, **unwieldy;** clunky <nf>

20 **huge, immense, vast, enormous,** astronomic, astronomical, humongous <nf>, jumbo <nf>, king-size, queen-size, tremendous, prodigious, stupendous, macro, mega, giga; great big, larger than life, Homeric, mighty, **titanic, colossal, monumental,** heroic, heroical, epic, epical, towering, mountainous; profound, abysmal, deep as the ocean *or* as China; **monster,** monstrous; **mammoth,** mastodonic; **gigantic, giant,** giantlike, gigantesque, gigantean; Cyclopean, Brobdingnagian, Gargantuan, Herculean, Atlantean; elephantine, jumbo <nf>; dinosaurian, dinotherian; **infinite** 823.3

21 <nf terms> **whopping, walloping, whaling, whacking,** spanking, slapping, lolloping, thumping, thundering, bumping, banging

22 **full-sized,** full-size, full-scale; **full-grown, full-fledged,** full-blown; full-formed, **life-sized,** large as life, larger than life

23 **oversize,** oversized; **outsize,** outsized, giant-size, **king-size, queen-size,** record-size, extra-large *or* XL, XXL, **overlarge,** overbig, too big; **overgrown,** overdeveloped; **overweight,** overheavy; overfleshed, overstout, overfat, overplump, overfed, obese

24 this big, so big, yay big <nf>, this size, about this size, of that order

ADVS **25** largely, on a large scale, in a big way; in the large; as can be

258 LITTLENESS

NOUNS **1** **littleness, smallness,** smallishness, **diminutiveness,** miniatureness, slightness, exiguity; puniness, pokiness, dinkiness <nf>; tininess, **minuteness;** undersize; petiteness; dwarfishness, stuntedness, runtiness, shrimpiness; **shortness** 268; **scantiness** 885.1; small scale; compactness, portability; miniaturization, microminiaturization, microscopy, micrography

2 **infinitesimalness;** undetectability, inappreciability, evanescence; intangibility, impalpability, tenuousness, imponderability; imperceptibility, invisibility

3 <small space> **tight spot** *and* corner *and* squeeze <nf>, pinch, not enough room to swing a cat <nf>; hole, pigeonhole; hole-in-the-wall; cubby, cubbyhole; dollhouse, playhouse, doghouse; no room to swing a cat

4 <small person or creature> **runt, shrimp** <nf>, wart <nf>, diminutive, wisp, chit, slip, snip, snippet, minikin , **peanut** *and* **peewee** <nf>, wee thing, pipsqueak, squirt, half pint, shorty, fingerling, small fry <nf>, dandiprat *and* tiddler <Brit old>; lightweight, featherweight; bantam, banty <nf>; pony; minnow, mini *and* minny <nf>; mouse, titmouse; nubbin, button

5 <creature small by species or birth> **dwarf,** dwarfling, **midget,** midge, **pygmy,** manikin, homunculus, atomy, micromorph, hop-o'-my-thumb; elf, gnome, brownie, hobbit, leprechaun; Lilliputian, Pigwiggen, Tom Thumb, Thumbelina, Alberich, Alviss, Andvari, Nibelung, Regin

6 **miniature,** mini; scaled-down *or* miniaturized version; microcosm, microcosmos; baby; doll, puppet, toy; microvolume; Elzevir, Elzevir edition; duodecimo, twelvemo, pocket edition

7 <minute thing> minutia, **minutiae** <pl>, minim, **drop,** droplet, **mite** <nf>, **point,** vanishing point, mathematical point, point of a pin, pinpoint, pinhead, **dot;** mote, fleck, **speck,** flyspeck, jot, tittle, jot nor tittle, iota, **trace,** trace amount, suspicion, *soupçon* <Fr>; **particle,** crumb, scrap, bite, snip, snippet; grain, grain of sand; barleycorn, millet seed, mustard seed; midge, gnat; microbe, **microorganism,** amoeba, bacillus, bacteria, diatom, germ, paramecium, protozoon, zoospore, animalcule, plankton, virus; cell; microchip; pixel

8 **atom,** atomy, monad; **molecule,** ion; nucleus; **electron,** proton, meson, neutrino, muon, quark, parton, subatomic *or* nuclear particle

VERBS 9 **make small, contract** 260.7; **shorten** 268.6; **miniaturize,** minify, minimize, scale down; **reduce** 252.7, scale back

ADJS 10 **little, small** 248.6, smallish; **slight,** exiguous; **puny, trifling,** poky, piffling *and* pindling *and* piddling *and* piddly <nf>, paltry, picayune, **dinky** <nf>, negligible; cramped, limited; one-horse, two-by-four <nf>; pintsized <nf>, half-pint; knee-high, knee-high to a grasshopper; petite; short 268.8

11 **tiny;** teeny *and* teeny-weeny *and* eentsy-weentsy <nf>, wee *and* pee-wee <nf>, bitty *and* bitsy *and* little-bitty *and* little-bitsy *and* itsy-bitsy *and* itsy-witsy <nf>, dinky <nf>; **minute,** fine

12 **miniature, diminutive, minuscule,** minuscular, mini, micro, miniaturized, subminiature, minikin , **small-scale,** minimal; pony, bantam, banty <nf>; **baby,** baby-sized; bite-sized; pocket, pocketsized, pocket-size, **vest-pocket; toy;** handy, compact, portable; duodecimo, twelvemo

13 **dwarf,** dwarfed, dwarfish, **pygmy, midget,** nanoid, elfin; Lilliputian, Tom Thumb; **undersized,** undersize, squat, dumpy; **stunted,** undergrown, runty, pint-size *or* -sized *and* sawed-off <nf>; shrunk, shrunken, wizened, shriveled; meager, scrubby, scraggy; rudimentary, rudimental

14 **infinitesimal, microscopic,** ultramicroscopic; evanescent, thin, tenuous; inappreciable; impalpable, imponderable, intangible; imperceptible, indiscernible, invisible, unseeable; atomic, subatomic; molecular; granular, corpuscular, microcosmic<al>; embryonic, germinal

15 **microbic,** microbial, **microorganic;** animalcular, bacterial; microzoic; protozoan, microzoan, amoebic *or* amoeboid

ADVS **16 small,** little, **slightly** 248.9, fractionally; **on a small scale,** in a small compass, in a small way, on a minuscule *or* infinitesimal scale; **in miniature,** in the small; in a nutshell

259 EXPANSION, GROWTH

<increase in size>

NOUNS **1 expansion, extension, enlargement, increase** 251, uptick, crescendo, upping, raising, hiking, magnification, aggrandizement, amplification, ampliation , broadening, widening; **spread,** spreading, sprawl, creeping, fanning out, dispersion, ripple effect, sprawl; buildout; **flare,** splay, ramification; deployment; augmentation, **addition** 253; adjunct 254

2 **distension,** stretching; **inflation,** sufflation, blowing up; **dilation,** dilatation, dilating; diastole; **swelling,** swelling 283.4; puffing, puff, puffiness, **bloating,** bloat, **flatulence** *or* flatulency, flatus, gassiness, windiness; **turgidity,** turgidness, turgescence; tumidness *or* tumidity, tumefaction; tumescence, intumescence; **swollenness,** bloatedness; dropsy, edema; tympanites, tympany, tympanism

3 **growth, development** 861.1; **bodily development** 14, **maturation,** maturing, coming of age, growing up, upgrowth; vegetation 310.32; repro-

duction, procreation 78, germination, pullulation; burgeoning, sprouting; budding, gemmation; outgrowth, excrescence; overgrowth 257.5

VERBS 4 <make larger> **enlarge, expand, extend, widen, broaden,** build, build up, aggrandize, **amplify,** crescendo, **magnify, increase** 251.4, augment, add to 253.5, raise, up, scale up, hike *or* hike up; develop, bulk *or* bulk up; **stretch, distend, dilate, swell, inflate,** sufflate, **blow up,** puff up, huff, puff, bloat; pump, pump up; rarefy

5 <become larger> **enlarge, expand, extend, increase,** greaten, crescendo, **develop, widen, broaden,** bulk; **stretch, distend, dilate, swell, swell up, swell out, puff up, puff out, pump up, bloat,** tumefy, balloon, fill out; snowball

6 **spread,** spread out, outspread, outstretch; **expand, extend,** widen; open, **open up,** unfold; **flare,** flare out, broaden out, splay; spraddle, sprangle, sprawl; branch, branch out, ramify; fan, fan out, disperse, deploy; spread like wildfire; overrun, overgrow

7 **grow, develop,** wax, **increase** 251; gather, brew; **grow up,** mature, spring up, ripen, come of age, **shoot up,** sprout up, upshoot, upspring, upsprout, upspear, overtop, tower; burgeon, **sprout** 310.34, blossom 310.35, reproduce 78.7, procreate 78.8, grow out of, germinate, pullulate; vegetate 310.34; **flourish, thrive,** grow like a weed; mushroom; outgrow; overgrow, hypertrophy, overdevelop, grow uncontrollably

8 **fatten,** fat, plump, pinguefy *and* engross , fill out; **gain weight,** gather flesh, take *or* put on weight, become overweight; chub out <nf>

ADJS 9 **expansive, extensive;** expansional, extensional; expansile, extensile, elastic, stretchy; expansible, inflatable, augmentative; distensive, dilatant; inflationary; developable

10 **expanded, extended, enlarged, increased** 251.7, upped, raised, hiked, **amplified,** ampliate , crescendoed, widened, broadened, built-up, beefed-up <nf>

11 **spread, spreading;** sprawling, sprawly; **outspread, outstretched,** spreadout, stretched-out, drawn-out; open, unfolded, gaping, patulous; widespread, wide-open; flared, spraddled, sprangled, splayed; flaring, flared, flared-out, spraddling, sprangling, splaying; splay; fanned, fanning; fanlike, fan-shaped, fanshape, flabelliform, deltoid

12 **grown, full-grown, grown-up, mature,** developed, well-developed, fully developed, full-fledged, of age; growing, sprouting, crescent, bud ding, flowering 310.38, florescent, **flourishing,** blossoming, blooming, burgeoning, fast-growing, thriving; overgrown, hypertrophied, overdeveloped

13 **distended, dilated, inflated,** sufflated, **blown up, puffed up, swollen,** swelled, **bloated,** turgid, tumid, plethoric, incrassate; **puffy,** pursy; flatulent, gassy, windy, ventose; tumefacient; dropsical, edematous; enchymatous; fat; puffed out, bouffant, bouffed up *and* bouffy <nf>, stuffed

260 CONTRACTION

<decrease in size>

NOUNS 1 **contraction,** contracture; systole, syneresis, synizesis, dwindling; **compression,** compressure, pressurizing, pressurization; **compacting,** compaction, compactedness; **condensation, concentration,** consolidation, solidification; **circumscription, narrowing;** reduction, diminuendo, lessening, waning; miniaturization; **decrease** 252; abbreviation, curtailment, shortening 268.3; **constriction,** stricture *or* striction, astriction, strangulation, stenosis, **choking,** choking off, coarctation; bottleneck, chokepoint, hourglass, hourglass figure, nipped *or* wasp waist; neck, cervix, isthmus, narrow place; astringency, constringency;

puckering, pursing; knitting, wrinkling

2 **squeezing,** compression, clamping *or* clamping down, tightening; **pressure,** press, crush; **pinch, squeeze, tweak, nip**; scrunch

3 **shrinking,** shrinkage, atrophy; **shriveling, withering;** searing, parching, drying *or* drying up; attenuation, thinning; wasting, consumption, emaciation, emaceration ; skin and bones; preshrinking, preshrinkage, Sanforizing <TM>

4 **collapse,** prostration, cave-in; implosion; **deflation**

5 contractibility, contractility, compactability, **compressibility,** condensability, reducibility; collapsibility; shrinkability

6 contractor, constrictor, clamp, compressor, compacter, condenser, vise, pincer, squeezer; thumbscrew; **astringent,** styptic; alum, astringent bitters, styptic pencil; tourniquet

VERBS 7 **contract, compress,** cramp, compact, condense, concentrate, consolidate, solidify; **reduce, decrease** 252; abbreviate, curtail, **shorten** 268.6; miniaturize; **constrict,** constringe, circumscribe, coarct, **narrow,** draw, draw in *or* together; strangle, strangulate, choke, choke off; **pucker,** pucker up, **purse; knit, wrinkle**

8 **squeeze,** compress, clamp, cramp, cramp up, tighten; roll *or* wad up, roll up into a ball, scrunch, ensphere; **press,** pressurize, crush, appress; tense; **pinch, tweak, nip**

9 **shrink, shrivel, wither,** sear, parch, dry up; **wizen,** weazen; consume, waste, waste away, attenuate, thin, emaciate, macerate *or* emacerate ; preshrink, Sanforize <TM>

10 **collapse, cave, cave in,** fall in; telescope; fold, fold up; implode; **deflate,** let the air out of, take the wind out of, flatten; puncture

ADJS 11 **contractive,** contractional, contractible, contractile, compactable; **astringent,** constringent, styptic; **compressible,** condensable, reducible; shrinkable; **collapsible,** foldable; deflationary; consumptive; circumscribable

12 **contracted, compressed,** cramped, compact *or* compacted, concentrated, condensed, consolidated, solidified, boiled-down; **constricted,** strangled, strangulated, choked, choked off, coarcted, **squeezed,** clamped, nipped, pinched *or* pinched-in, wasp-waisted; puckered, pursed; knitted, wrinkled; miniaturized; scaled-down; shortened, abbreviated

13 **shrunk,** shrunken; **shriveled,** shriveled up; **withered,** sear, parched, corky, dried-up; **wasted,** wasted away, consumed, emaciated, emacerated, thin, attenuated; **wizened,** wizen, weazened; preshrunk, Sanforized <TM>

14 **deflated, punctured, flat,** holed

261 DISTANCE, REMOTENESS

NOUNS 1 **distance, remoteness,** farness, far-offness, longinquity; **separation,** separatedness, divergence, clearance, margin, leeway; **extent, length,** space 158, **reach,** stretch, range, compass, span, stride, haul, a way, ways *and* piece <nf>; perspective, aesthetic distance, distancing; astronomical *or* interstellar *or* galactic *or* intergalactic distance, deep space, depths of space, **infinity** 823; **mileage,** light-years, parsecs; aloofness, standoffishness

2 **long way,** good ways <nf>, **great distance, far cry,** far piece <nf>; long step, tidy step, giant step *or* stride; long run *or* haul, long road *or* trail, day's march, miles away; marathon; far cry, long shot; long range; apogee, aphelion

3 the distance, **remote distance, offing; horizon,** the far horizon, where the earth meets the sky, vanishing point, background

4 <remote region> jumping-off place *and* godforsaken place *and* God knows where *and* the middle of nowhere <nf>, the back of beyond, the end of the rainbow, Thule *or* Ultima Thule, Timbuktu, Siberia, Darkest Africa, the South Seas, Pago Pago, the Great Divide, China, Outer Mongolia, pole, an-

tipodes, end of the earth, North Pole, South Pole, Tierra del Fuego, Greenland, Yukon, Pillars of Hercules, remotest corner of the world, four corners of the earth; outpost, outskirts; hinterland; the sticks *and* the boondocks *and* the boonies <nf>; **nowhere;** frontier, outback; the moon; outer space

VERBS 5 **reach out, stretch out,** extend, extend out, go *or* go out, range out, carry out; outstretch, outlie, outdistance, outrange

6 **extend to,** stretch to, stretch away to, **reach to,** lead to, go to, get to, come to, run to, carry to

7 **keep one's distance, distance oneself,** remain at a distance, maintain distance *or* clearance, keep at a respectful distance, separate oneself, **keep away,** stand off *or* away; keep away from, keep *or* stand clear of, **steer clear of** <nf>, hold away from, give a wide berth to, keep a good leeway *or* margin *or* offing, keep out of the way of, keep at arm's length, keep a safe distance from, not touch with a ten-foot pole <nf>, keep *or* stay *or* stand aloof; maintain one's perspective, keep one's esthetic distance

ADJS 8 **distant,** distal, **remote, removed, far, far-off,** away, **faraway,** way-off, far-flung, at a distance, exotic, separated, apart, asunder; long-distance, long-range

9 **out-of-the-way,** godforsaken, back of beyond, outlying, upcountry; **out of reach, inaccessible,** ungetatable, unapproachable, untouchable, hyperborean, antipodean

10 **thither,** ulterior; **yonder,** yon; **farther, further,** remoter, more distant; outlying

11 transoceanic, transmarine, ultramarine, oversea, overseas; transatlantic, transpacific; tramontane, transmontane, ultramontane, transalpine; transarctic, transcontinental, transequatorial, transpolar, transpontine, transmundane, ultramundane; offshore, overseas

12 **farthest, furthest,** farthermost, farthest off, furthermost, ultimate, extreme, remotest, most distant, terminal

ADVS 13 **yonder,** yon; **in the distance,** in the remote distance; **in the offing,** on the horizon, in the background

14 **at a distance, away, off,** aloof, at arm's length; distantly, remotely

15 **far, far off,** far away, **afar,** afar off, a long way off, a good ways off <nf>, a long cry to, as far as the eye can see, out of sight; clear to hell and gone <nf>

16 **far and wide,** far and near, distantly and broadly, wide, widely, broadly, abroad

17 **apart, away, aside,** wide apart, wide away

18 **out of reach,** beyond reach, **out of range,** beyond the bounds, out-of-the-way, out of the sphere of; out of sight, *à perte de vue* <Fr>; out of hearing, out of earshot *or* earreach

19 **wide, clear;** wide of the mark, abroad, all abroad, astray, afield, far afield

20 **beyond, past, over, across,** the other *or* far side of

262 FORM

NOUNS 1 **form, shape, figure;** figuration, **configuration;** formation, **conformation; structure** 266; **build,** make, frame; **arrangement** 808; makeup, format, layout; **composition** 796; cut, set, stamp, type, turn, cast, mold, impression, pattern, matrix, model, mode, modality; archetype, prototype 786.1, Platonic form *or* idea; style, fashion; aesthetic form, inner form, significant form; art form, genre

2 **contour,** *tournure* <Fr>, *galbe* <Fr>; broad lines, silhouette, profile, **outline** 211.2; organization 807.1

3 **appearance** 33, lineaments, features, physiognomy, cut of one's jib

4 <human form> **figure, form,** shape, frame, anatomy, **physique,** build, body-build, person; body 1052.3

5 **forming, shaping,** molding, modeling, fashioning, making, making up, formulation; **formation,** conformation, figuration, configuration; sculpture; morphogeny, morphogenesis; creation

6 <grammatical terms> form, morph, allomorph, morpheme; morphology, morphemics

VERBS **7** **form,** formalize, **shape, fashion,** tailor, frame, figure, **lick into shape** <nf>; work, knead; set, fix; **forge,** drop-forge; **mold,** model, sculpt *or* sculpture; cast, found; thermoform; stamp, mint; carve, whittle, cut, chisel, hew, hew out; roughhew, roughcast, rough out, block out, lay out, sketch out; hammer *or* knock out; whomp out *or* up <nf>, cobble up; create; organize 807.4, systematize

8 <be formed> **form,** take form, shape, **shape up, take shape;** materialize

ADJS **9** **formative,** formal, formational, plastic, morphotic; **formed, shaped,** patterned, fashioned, tailored, framed, structured; **forged,** molded, modeled, sculpted; cast, founded; stamped, minted; carved, cut, whittled, chiseled, hewn; roughhewn, roughcast, roughed-out, blocked-out, laid-out, sketched-out; hammered-out, knocked-out, cobbled-up; **made, produced**

10 <biological terms> plasmatic, plasmic, protoplasmic, plastic, metabolic

11 <grammatical terms> morphologic, morphological, morphemic

263 FORMLESSNESS

NOUNS **1** **formlessness, shapelessness;** unformedness, amorphousness, amorphism; misshapenness; lack of definition; **chaos** 810.2, confusion, messiness, mess, muddle 810.2, orderlessness, untidiness; **disorder** 810; entropy; anarchy 418.2; **indeterminateness, indefiniteness,** indecisiveness, vagueness, mistiness, haziness, fuzziness, blurriness, unclearness, obscurity; lumpiness, lumpishness

2 unlicked cub, diamond in the rough, raw material

VERBS **3** **deform, distort** 265.5; misshape; unform, unshape; disorder, jumble, mess up, muddle, confuse; obfuscate, obscure, fog up, blur

ADJS **4** **formless, shapeless,** structureless, unstructured, featureless, characterless, nondescript, inchoate, lumpy, lumpish, blobby *and* baggy <nf>, inform; amorphous *or* amorphic, **chaotic, orderless,** disorderly 810.13, unordered, unorganized, confused, anarchic 418.6; kaleidoscopic; **indeterminate, indefinite,** undefined, indecisive, vague, misty, hazy, fuzzy, blurred *or* blurry, unclear, obscure; obfuscatory; unfinished, undeveloped

5 **unformed, unshaped,** unshapen, unfashioned, unlicked; unstructured; uncut, unhewn

264 SYMMETRY

NOUNS **1** **symmetry,** symmetricalness, **proportion,** proportionality, **balance** 790.1, equilibrium; **regularity,** uniformity 781, evenness; equality 790; finish; harmony, congruity, consistency, conformity 867, **correspondence,** keeping; concord ; eurythmy, eurythmics; dynamic symmetry; bilateral symmetry, trilateral symmetry, etc, multilateral symmetry; parallelism 203, polarity; shapeliness

2 symmetrization, regularization, balancing, harmonization; evening, equalization; coordination, integration; **compensation,** playing off, playing off against, posing against *or* over against; counterbalance

VERBS **3** symmetrize, regularize, **balance,** balance off, compensate; harmonize; **proportion,** proportionate; even, even up, equalize; coordinate, integrate; play off, play off against

ADJS **4** **symmetric, symmetrical, balanced,** balanced off, proportioned, eurythmic, harmonious, mirror-image; **regular,** uniform 781.5, even, even-steven <nf>, equal 790.7, equal on both sides, fifty-fifty <nf>, square, squared-off; coequal, coordinate, equilateral, aligned; **well-balanced,** well-set, well-set-up <nf>; finished; enantiomorphic

5 **shapely, well-shaped, well-proportioned,** well-made, **well-**

formed, well-favored; comely; trim, trig , neat, spruce, clean, clean-cut, clean-limbed

265 DISTORTION

NOUNS **1 distortion,** torsion, twist, twistedness, **contortion, crookedness,** tortuosity; asymmetry, unsymmetry, disproportion, lopsidedness, imbalance, irregularity, skewness, **deviation; twist,** quirk, turn, screw, wring, wrench, wrest; **warp,** buckle; knot, gnarl; anamorphosis; anamorphism

2 perversion, corruption, misdirection, misrepresentation 350, misinterpretation, misconstruction; **falsification** 354.9; **twisting,** false coloring, bending the truth, **spin,** spin control, slanting, straining, torturing; misuse 389; falsehood, travesty; debasement

3 deformity, deformation, **malformation,** malconformation, monstrosity 870.6, teratology, freakishness, misproportion, **misshapenness,** misshape; **disfigurement, defacement;** mutilation, truncation; humpback, hunchback, crookback, camelback, kyphosis; swayback, lordosis; wryneck, torticollis; clubfoot, talipes, flatfoot, splayfoot; knock-knee; bowlegs; valgus; harelip; cleft palate; mutation

4 grimace, wry face, wry mouth, rictus, snarl; moue, mow, pout; scowl, frown; squint; tic

VERBS **5 distort, contort,** turn awry; **twist,** turn, screw, wring, wrench, wrest; writhe; **warp,** buckle, crumple; knot, gnarl; **crook,** bend, spring; put out of kilter

6 pervert, falsify, twist, garble, put a false construction upon, give a spin, give a false coloring, color, varnish, slant, strain, torture; put words in someone's mouth; **bias;** misrepresent 350.3, misconstrue, misinterpret, misrender, misdirect; debase; misuse 389.4; send *or* deliver the wrong signal *or* message, lead up *or* down the garden path; exaggerate

7 deform, malform, misshape, twist, torture, disproportion; **disfigure, deface;** mutilate, truncate; blemish, mar

8 grimace, make a face, make a wry face *or* mouth, pull a face, **screw up one's face,** mug <nf>, mouth, make a mouth, mop, mow, mop and mow; pout

ADJS **9** distortive, contortive, contortional, torsional

10 distorted, contorted, warped, twisted, crooked; tortuous, labyrinthine, buckled, sprung, bent, bowed; cockeyed <nf>, crazy; crunched, crumpled; unsymmetric, unsymmetrical, asymmetric, asymmetrical, nonsymmetric, nonsymmetrical; irregular, deviative, anamorphous; one-sided, lopsided; awry, askew 204.14, off-center, left *or* right of center, off-target; cockeyed

11 falsified, perverted, twisted, garbled, slanted, doctored, biased, crooked; strained, tortured; misrepresented, misquoted; half-true, partially true, falsely colored; creative <nf>

12 deformed, malformed, misshapen, misbegotten, misproportioned, ill-proportioned, ill-made, ill-shaped, **out of shape;** dwarfed, stumpy; bloated; **disfigured,** defaced, blemished, marred; mutilated, truncated; grotesque, **monstrous** 870.13; sway-backed, round-shouldered; bowlegged, bandy-legged, bandy; knock-kneed; rickety, rachitic; clubfooted, talipedic; flatfooted, splayfooted, pigeon-toed; pug-nosed, snub-nosed, simous

13 humpbacked, hunchbacked, bunchbacked, crookbacked, crookedbacked, camelback, humped, gibbous, kyphotic

266 STRUCTURE

NOUNS **1 structure, construction,** architecture, tectonics, architectonics, **frame,** make, **build,** fabric, tissue, warp and woof *or* weft, web, weave, texture, contexture, mold, **shape, pattern, plan,** fashion, arrangement, **organization** 807.1;

organism, organic structure, **constitution, composition; makeup,** getup <nf>, setup; **formation,** conformation, **format; arrangement** 808, configuration; **composition** 796; making, building, creation, production, forging, fashioning, molding, fabrication, manufacture, shaping, structuring, patterning; anatomy, physique, organic structure; form 262; **morphology,** science of structure; anatomy, histology, zootomy

2 **structure, building, edifice, construction,** construct, erection, establishment, fabric; house; tower, pile, pyramid, skyscraper, ziggurat; prefabrication, prefab, packaged house; air structure, bubble <nf>, air hall <Brit>; superstructure, structural framework; flat-slab construction, post-and-beam construction, steel-cage construction, steel construction; complex

3 **understructure,** understruction, underbuilding, undercroft, crypt; **substructure,** substruction; infrastructure, underpinning; spread foundation, footing; fill, backfill

4 **frame,** framing; braced framing; **framework, skeleton,** fabric, cadre, chassis, shell, armature; lattice, latticework, scaffold; sash, casement, case, casing; window case *or* frame, doorframe; picture frame

VERBS 5 **construct, build; structure; organize** 807.4; **form** 262.7; erect, raise, put up

ADJS 6 **structural,** formal, morphological, edificial, tectonic, textural; **anatomic,** anatomical, **organic,** organismal, organismic; **structured, patterned,** shaped, formed; **architectural,** architectonic; constructional; superstructural, substructural, infrastructural; organizational

267 LENGTH

NOUNS 1 **length,** longness, lengthiness, overall length; wheelbase; **extent,** extension, **measure, span, reach, stretch; distance** 261; footage, yardage, mileage; infinity 823; perpetuity 829; long time 827.4; linear measures; oblongness; longitude

2 a length, **piece, portion,** part; coil, **strip,** bolt, roll; run

3 **line, strip,** bar, streak; stripe 517.6; string

4 **lengthening, prolongation, elongation,** production, protraction; prolixity, prolixness; **extension,** stretching, stretching *or* spinning *or* stringing out, dragging out

VERBS 5 **be long, be lengthy, extend,** be prolonged, **stretch**, span**; stretch out,** extend out, reach out; stretch oneself, crane, crane one's neck, rubberneck; stand on tiptoes; outstretch, outreach; sprawl, straggle; last, endure

6 **lengthen, prolong,** prolongate, **elongate, extend,** expand, produce, **protract,** continue; make prolix; lengthen out, let out, **draw** *or* drag *or* stretch *or* string *or* spin out; **stretch,** draw, pull

ADJS 7 **long, lengthy;** longish, longsome; tall; **extensive, far-reaching,** fargoing, far-flung; sesquipedalian, sesquipedal; unabridged, full-length; as long as one's arm, a mile long; **time-consuming,** interminable, without end, no end of *or* to, infinite; long-lasting, enduring, long-range

8 **lengthened, prolonged,** prolongated, **elongated, extended, protracted; prolix; long-winded; drawn-out,** dragged out, long-drawn-out, stretched *or* spun *or* strung out, straggling; **stretched,** drawn, pulled

9 **oblong,** oblongated, oblongitudinal, **elongated;** rectangular; elliptical; lengthwise, lengthways, longitudinal

ADVS 10 lengthily, extensively, at length, *in extenso* <L>, *ad infinitum* <L>, ad nauseam

11 **lengthwise** *or* lengthways, longwise *or* longways, longitudinally, along, in length, at length; **endwise** *or* endways, endlong; *in extenso* <L>

268 SHORTNESS

NOUNS 1 **shortness, briefness, brevity; succinctness,** curtness, terseness, summariness, compendiousness, compactness; **conciseness** 537; **littleness** 258; transience 828, short time 828.3, instantaneousness 830; banker's hours, French hours

2 **stubbiness,** stumpiness <nf>, **stockiness, fatness** 257.8, chubbiness, chunkiness <nf>, blockiness, squatness, squattiness, dumpiness; pudginess, podginess; snubbiness; **lowness** 274

3 **shortening, abbreviation; reduction; abridgment, condensation,** compression, conspectus, epitome, epitomization, summary, summation, summarization, précis, abstract, recapitulation, recap <nf>, wrapup, synopsis, encapsulation; **curtailment,** truncation, retrenchment; telescoping; elision, ellipsis, syncope, apocope; foreshortening; cutback; docking; contraction

4 shortener, cutter, abridger; abstracter, epitomizer *or* epitomist

5 **shortcut,** cut, cutoff; shortest way; **beeline,** air line

VERBS 6 **shorten, abbreviate, cut; reduce** 260.7; **abridge, condense,** compress, contract, **boil down,** abstract, sum up, summarize, recapitulate, recap <nf>, synopsize, epitomize, encapsulate, capsulize; **curtail,** truncate, retrench; bowdlerize; elide, **cut short,** cut down, cut off short, cut back, take in; **dock,** bob, shear, shave, trim, clip, snub, nip; hem; mow, reap, **crop; prune,** poll, pollard; stunt, check the growth of; telescope; foreshorten

7 **take a short cut,** short-cut; **cut across,** cut through; **cut a corner,** cut corners; **make a beeline,** take the air line, go as the crow flies

ADJS 8 **short, brief, abbreviated,** abbreviatory; **concise** 537.6; **curt,** curtal , curtate, decurtate; **succinct, summary,** synoptic, synoptical, compendious, compact; **little** 258.10; **low** 274.7; transient 828.7, instantaneous 830.4

9 **shortened, abbreviated; abridged,** compressed, condensed, epitomized, digested, abstracted, capsule, capsulized, encapsulated; bowdlerized; nutshell, vest-pocket; **curtailed,** cut short, short-cut, **docked,** bobbed, sheared, shaved, trimmed, clipped, snub, snubbed, nipped; mowed, mown, reaped, **cropped; pruned,** polled, pollarded; elided, elliptic, elliptical; foreshortened

10 **stubby,** stubbed, stumpy <nf>, undergrown, **thickset, stocky,** blocky, **chunky** <nf>, **fat** 257.18, **chubby,** tubby <nf>, dumpy; **squat,** squatty, squattish; **pudgy,** podgy; pug, **pugged;** snub-nosed; turned-up, *retroussé* <Fr>

11 short-legged, breviped; short-winged, brevipennate

ADVS 12 **shortly, briefly,** summarily, *tout court* <Fr>, in brief compass, economically, sparely, curtly, succinctly, in a nutshell, in two *or* a few words; abbreviatedly, for short; **concisely** 537.7, compendiously, synoptically

13 **short, abruptly,** suddenly 830.9, all of a sudden

269 BREADTH, THICKNESS

NOUNS 1 **breadth, width,** broadness, wideness, fullness, amplitude, latitude, distance across *or* crosswise *or* crossways, extent, **span, expanse, spread;** beam

2 **thickness,** the third dimension, distance through, depth; **mass, bulk, body;** corpulence, fatness 257.8, bodily size; **coarseness,** grossness 294.2

3 **diameter, bore, caliber; radius,** semidiameter; handbreadth, beam

VERBS 4 **broaden, widen,** deepen; **expand,** extend, extend to the side *or* sides; **spread** 259.6, spread out *or* sidewise *or* sideways, outspread, outstretch; span

5 **thicken,** grow thick, thick; incrassate, inspissate; congeal, gel; fatten 259.8

ADJS 6 **broad, wide,** deep; broad-scale, wide-scale, wide-ranging, broad-based, exhaustive, comprehensive, in-depth, extensive; spread-out, **expansive;** spacious, **roomy;** ample, full; widespread 864.13

7 broad of beam, broad-beamed, broad-sterned, beamy, wide-set;

wide-body, wide-bodied; wide-angle, wide-screen; broad-ribbed, wide-ribbed, laticostate; broad-toothed, wide-toothed, latidentate; broad-gauge; broadloom

8 **thick,** three-dimensional; **thickset, heavyset,** thick-bodied, broad-bodied, thick-girthed; **massive, bulky** 257.19, corpulent 257.18; coarse, heavy, gross, crass, fat; full-bodied, full, viscous; **dense** 1045.12; thicknecked, bullnecked

ADVS **9** breadthwise *or* breadthways, in breadth; widthwise *or* widthways; broadwise *or* broadways; broadside, broad side foremost; side-wise *or* -ways; through, depth-wise *or* -ways, in depth

270 NARROWNESS, THINNESS

NOUNS **1 narrowness, slenderness; closeness,** nearness; **straitness,** restriction, restrictedness, limitation, strictness, confinement, circumscription; crowdedness, incapaciousness, incommodiousness, crampedness; **tightness,** tight squeeze; hair, hairbreadth *or* hairsbreadth; finger's breadth *or* width; narrow gauge

2 **narrowing, tapering,** taper; **contraction** 260, compression; stricture, constriction, strangulation, coarctation

3 <narrow place> narrow, **narrows, strait; bottleneck,** chokepoint; isthmus; channel 239, canal; pass, defile; neck, throat, craw; narrow gauge, single track

4 **thinness, slenderness, slimness, frailty,** slightness, gracility, lightness, airiness, delicacy, flimsiness, wispiness, laciness, paperiness, gauziness, gossameriness, diaphanousness, insubstantiality, ethereality, mistiness, vagueness; light *or* airy texture; **fineness** 294.3; **tenuity, rarity,** subtility, exility, exiguity; **attenuation;** dilution, dilutedness, wateriness 1061.1, weakness

5 **leanness, skinniness,** fleshlessness, slightness, frailness, twigginess, spareness, meagerness, **scrawniness, gauntness,** gangliness, lankness, **lankiness,** gawkiness, **boniness,** skin and bones; haggardness, poorness, paperiness, peakedness <nf>, puniness; undernourishment, undernutrition, underweight; hatchet face, lantern jaw

6 **emaciation,** malnutrition, emaceration , attenuation, atrophy, tabes, marasmus, anorexia nervosa

7 <comparisons> paper, wafer, lath, slat, **rail,** rake, splinter, slip, shaving, streak, vein; gruel, soup; shadow, mere shadow; **skeleton**

8 <thin person> **slim, lanky;** twiggy, **shadow, skeleton,** stick, walking skeleton, corpse, barebones, bag *or* stack of bones; rattlebones *or* **spindleshanks** *or* spindlelegs <nf>, gangleshanks *and* gammerstang <nf>, lathlegs *and* sticklegs <nf>, **beanpole,** beanstalk, broomstick, clothes pole, stilt; slip, sylph, ectomorph, long drink of water

9 **reducing, slenderizing, slimming down;** weight-watching, calorie-counting; fasting, dieting

10 **thinner,** solvent 1064.4

VERBS **11 narrow,** constrict, diminish, draw in, go in; restrict, limit, straiten, confine; **taper; contract** 260.7, compress, zip <nf>

12 **thin,** thin down, thin away *or* off *or* out, down; **rarefy,** subtilize, **attenuate;** dilute, water, water down, weaken; undernourish; **emaciate,** emacerate

13 **slenderize, reduce,** reduce *or* lose *or* take off weight, watch one's weight, lose flesh, weight-watch, count calories, diet, crash-diet; slim, **slim down,** thin down

ADJS **14 narrow, slender;** narrowish, narrowy; close, near; **tight, strait,** isthmic, isthmian; close-fitting; **restricted,** limited, circumscribed, **confined,** constricted; **cramped,** cramp; incapacious, incommodious, crowded; **meager,** scant, scanty; narrow-gauge *or* narrow-gauged, single-track; angustifoliate, angustirostrate, angustiseptal, angustisellate; stenopeic, isthmian

15 **tapered,** taper, tapering, cone- *or* wedge-shaped, attenuated, fusiform, stenosed

16 **thin, slender, slim,** gracile; thin-bodied, thin-set, ectomorphic, narrow- *or* wasp-waisted; **svelte,** slinky, sylphlike, willowy; girlish, boyish; thinnish, slenderish, slimmish; **slight,** slight-made; **frail,** delicate, light, airy, wispy, lacy, gauzy, papery, gossamer, diaphanous, insubstantial, ethereal, misty, vague, flimsy, wafer-thin, **fine; finespun,** thin-spun, fine-drawn, wiredrawn; threadlike, slender as a thread; **tenuous,** subtle, rare, **rarefied;** attenuated, attenuate, **watery, weak,** diluted, watered *or* watered-down, small

17 **lean,** lean-looking, **skinny** <nf>, fleshless, lean-fleshed, thin-fleshed, **spare,** meager, **scrawny,** scraggy, thin-bellied, **gaunt, lank, lanky,** wiry**; gangling** *and* gangly <nf>, gawky, **spindling,** spindly; flat-chested, flat <nf>; **bony, rawboned,** bare-boned, rattleboned <nf>, skeletal, **mere skin and bones, all skin and bones, nothing but skin and bones;** twiggy; **underweight,** undersized, undernourished, spidery, thin *or* skinny as a lath *or* rail; waifish

18 lean-limbed, thin-legged, lath- *or* stick-legged <nf>, spindle-legged *or* -shanked <nf>, gangle-shanked <nf>, stilt-legged

19 lean- *or* horse- *or* thin-faced, thin-featured, **hatchet-faced;** wizen- *or* weazen-faced; lean- *or* thin-cheeked; lean- *or* lantern-jawed

20 **haggard, poor,** puny, **peaked** *and* peaky <nf>, **pinched;** gaunt, drawn; shriveled, withered; **wizened,** weazeny; emaciated, emaciate, emacerated, **wasted,** attenuated, corpselike, skeletal, hollow-eyed, wraithlike, cadaverous; tabetic, tabid, marantic, marasmic; **starved,** anorexic, anorectic, starveling, starved-looking; undernourished, underfed, jejune; worn to a shadow

21 **slenderizing,** reducing, slimming

ADVS **22** **narrowly,** closely, nearly, **barely,** hardly, only just, **by the skin of one's teeth**

23 thinly, thin; meagerly, sparsely, sparingly, scantily

271 FILAMENT

NOUNS **1** **filament; fiber; thread; strand,** suture; filature; **hair** 3; artificial fiber, natural fiber, animal fiber; fibril, fibrilla; cilium, ciliolum; **tendril,** cirrus; flagellum; **web,** cobweb, gossamer, spider *or* spider's web; denier

2 **cord, line, rope, wire,** braided rope, twisted rope, flattened-strand rope, wire rope, locked-wire rope, **cable,** wire cable; **yarn,** spun yarn, skein, hank; **string, twine;** braid; **ligament,** ligature, ligation; **tendon**

3 **cordage,** cording, **ropework,** roping; tackle, tack, gear, rigging; ship's ropes

4 **strip, strap,** strop; **lace,** thong; **band,** bandage, fillet, fascia, taenia; **belt,** girdle; **ribbon,** ribband; **tape,** tapeline, tape measure; slat, lath, batten, spline, strake, plank; ligule, ligula

5 **spinner,** spinster; silkworm, spider; spinning wheel, spinning jenny, jenny, mule, mule-jenny; spinning frame, bobbin and fly frame; spinneret; rope walk

VERBS **6** <make threads> **spin; braid,** twist

ADJS **7** **threadlike,** thready; **stringy,** ropy, wiry; **hairlike** 3.23, hairy 3.24; filamentary, filamentous, filiform; fibrous, fibered, fibroid, fibrilliform; ligamental; capillary, capilliform; cirrose, cirrous; funicular, funiculate; flagelliform; taeniate, taeniform; ligulate, ligular; gossamer, gossamery, flossy, silky

272 HEIGHT

NOUNS **1** **height,** heighth <nf>, vertical *or* perpendicular distance; **highness, tallness,** procerity; **altitude, elevation,** ceiling; **loftiness,** sublimity, exaltation; hauteur, toploftiness 141.1; eminence, prominence; **stature**

2 **height, elevation,** eminence, **rise,** raise, **uprise,** lift, rising ground, vantage point *or* ground; **heights,** soaring *or* towering *or* Olympian heights, aerial heights, dizzy *or*

dizzying heights; upmost *or* uppermost *or* utmost *or* extreme height; sky, stratosphere, ether, heaven *or* heavens; **zenith, apex, acme**

3 **highlands** 237.1, highland, upland, uplands, moorland, moors, downs, wold, rolling country

4 **plateau,** tableland, table, mesa, table mountain, bench; **hill; ridge; mountain; peak; mountain range**

5 **watershed,** water parting, **divide;** Great Divide, Continental Divide

6 **tower; turret,** *tour* <Fr>; campanile, bell tower, belfry; **spire,** church spire; **lighthouse,** light tower; cupola, lantern; dome; martello, martello tower; barbican; **derrick,** pole; windmill tower, observation tower, fire tower, watch tower, control tower; **mast,** radio *or* television mast, antenna tower; water tower, standpipe; **spire,** pinnacle; **steeple,** *flèche* <Fr>; minaret; stupa, tope, pagoda; pyramid; pylon; **shaft,** pillar, column; pilaster; obelisk; monument; colossus; skyscraper

7 <tall person> **longlegs** *and* longshanks *and* highpockets *and* long drink of water <nf>; beanpole 270.8; **giant** 257.13; six-footer, seven-footer, grenadier <Brit>

8 **high tide,** high water, mean high water, flood tide, spring tide, flood; storm surge

9 <measurement of height> altimetry, hypsometry, hypsography; altimeter, hypsometer

VERBS **10 tower, soar,** spire; **rise, uprise, ascend, mount, rear;** stand on tiptoe

11 **rise above, tower above** *or* **over,** clear, overtop, o'er top, outtop, **top, surmount; overlook,** look down upon *or* over; overhang, beetle; **command,** dominate, overarch, overshadow, command a view of; bestride, bestraddle

12 <become higher> **grow,** grow up, upgrow; uprise, **rise** *or* **shoot up,** mount, sprout

13 **heighten, elevate** 912.5

ADJS **14 high,** high-reaching, high-up, **lofty, elevated,** altitudinous, altitudinal, uplifted *or* upreared, uprearing, **eminent, exalted, prominent,** supernal, **superlative,** sublime; **towering,** towery, **soaring,** spiring, aspiring, mounting, ascending; towered, turreted, steepled; **topping,** outtopping *or* overtopping; overarching, **overlooking, dominating;** airy, aerial, ethereal; Olympian; monumental, colossal; high as a steeple; topless; high-set, high-pitched; high-rise, multistory; **haughty** 141.9/157.8, toplofty

15 skyscraping, **sky-high,** heaven-reaching *or* -aspiring, heaven-high, heaven-kissing; cloud-touching *or* -topped *or* –capped, supernal; **mid-air**

16 **giant** 257.20, gigantic, colossal, statuesque, amazonian; **tall, lengthy,** long 267.7; **rangy, lanky,** lank, tall as a maypole; **gangling** *and* gangly <nf>; **long-legged,** long-limbed, leggy

17 **highland,** upland; hill-dwelling, mountain-dwelling

18 **hilly,** knobby, rolling; **mountainous,** mountained, **alpine,** alpen, alpestrine, alpigene; subalpine; monticuline, monticulous

19 **higher,** superior, greater; **over, above;** upper, upmost *or* uppermost, outtopping, overtopping, topmost; highest 198.10

20 altimetric, altimetrical, hypsometrical, hypsographic

ADVS **21 on high,** high up, high; **aloft,** aloof; **up,** upward, upwards, straight up, to the zenith; **above, over,** o'er, **overhead;** above one's head, over head and ears; skyward, airward, in the air, in the clouds; on the peak *or* summit *or* crest *or* pinnacle; upstairs, abovestairs; tiptoe, on tiptoe; on stilts; on the shoulders of; supra, *ubi supra* <L>, hereinabove, hereinbefore

273 SHAFT

NOUNS **1 shaft, pole, bar, rod, stick,** scape, scapi-; **stalk, stem;** thill; tongue, wagon tongue; flagstaff; totem pole; Maypole; utility *or* telephone *or* telegraph pole; tent pole

2 **staff,** stave; **cane, stick, walking stick,** handstaff, shillelagh; Malacca

cane; baton, marshal's baton, drum-major's baton, conductor's baton; swagger stick, swanking stick; pilgrim's staff, pastoral staff, shepherd's staff, crook; crosier, cross-staff, cross, paterissa; pikestaff, alpenstock; quarterstaff; lituus, thyrsus; **crutch,** crutch-stick

3 **beam, timber,** pole, spar

4 **post, standard, upright;** king post, queen post, crown post; newel; banister, baluster; balustrade, balustrading; gatepost, swinging *or* hinging post, shutting post; doorpost, jamb, doorjamb; signpost, milepost; stile, mullion; stanchion; hitching post, snubbing post, Samson post

5 **pillar, column,** post, pier, pilaster; colonnette, columella; caryatid; atlas, atlantes <pl>; telamon, telamones; **colonnade, arcade,** pilastrade, portico, peristyle

6 **leg,** shank; **stake,** peg; pile, spile, stud; picket, pale, palisade

274 LOWNESS

NOUNS 1 **lowness, shortness,** squatness, squattiness, stumpiness, shallowness, stuntedness; **prostration,** supineness, proneness, recumbency, proneness, reclination, **lying, lying down, reclining;** depression, debasement; subjacency

2 **low tide,** low water, mean low water, dead low water *or* tide, ebb tide, neap tide, neap, low ebb

3 lowland, **lowlands,** bottomland, swale; water meadow, piedmont, foothills, flats, depression

4 **base, bottom** 199, lowest point, nadir, depths; the lowest of the low; lowest *or* underlying level, lower strata, substratum, bedrock

VERBS 5 **lie low, squat, crouch,** lay low <nf>, couch; crawl, grovel, lie prone *or* supine *or* prostrate, hug the earth, lie down; lie under, underlie

6 lower, debase, depress 913.4; flatten

ADJS 7 **low, unelevated, flat, low-lying; short, squat,** squatty, stumpy, runty 258.13; **lowered,** debased, depressed 913.12; demoted; **reduced** 252.10; prone, supine, prostrate *or* prostrated, couchant, crouched, stooped, recumbent, bowed; laid low, knocked flat, decked <nf>; low-set, low-hung; **low-built,** low-rise, low-sized, low-statured, low-bodied; low-level, low-leveled; neap, shallow, shoal; knee-high, knee-high to a grasshopper <nf>; low-necked, low-cut, décolleté

8 **lower,** inferior, **under, nether,** subjacent; down; less advanced; earlier; substrative, rock-bottom; lowest 199.7

ADVS 9 **low,** near the ground; at a low ebb

10 **below,** down below, **under;** infra, hereunder, hereinafter, hereinbelow; thereunder; belowstairs, downstairs, below deck; underfoot; below par, below the mark

275 DEPTH

NOUNS 1 **depth, deepness,** profoundness, profundity; deep-downness, extreme innerness, deep-seatedness, deep-rootedness; bottomlessness, plumblessness, fathomlessness; subterraneity, undergroundness; interiority 207; extensiveness, unfathomableness

2 **pit, deep, depth, hole,** hollow, **cavity,** shaft, well, **gulf, chasm, abyss,** abysm, yawning abyss; crater; crevasse; valley; underground, subterrane

3 **depths,** deeps, bowels, bowels of the earth, core; bottomless pit; infernal pit, hell, nether world, underworld; dark *or* unknown *or* yawning *or* gaping depths, unfathomed deeps; outer *or* deep space

4 **ocean depths, the deep sea, the deep,** trench, deep-sea trench, hadal zone, **the deeps, the depths,** bottomless depths, inner space, abyss; bottom waters; abyssal zone, Bassalia *or* Bassalian realm, bathyal zone, pelagic zone; **seabed,** seafloor, **bottom of the sea,** ocean bottom *or* floor *or* bed, ground, benthos, benthonic division, benthonic zone; Davy Jones's locker <nf>; Mariana Trench

5 **sounding** *or* **soundings,** fathoming, depth sounding, probing; **echo**

sounding, echolocation; sonar; **depth indicator;** oceanography, bathometry, bathymetry; fathomage, water <depth of water>

6 **draft,** submergence, submersion, sinkage, **displacement**

7 **deepening, lowering, depression;** sinking, sinkage, descent; excavation, digging, mining, tunneling; drilling, probing

VERBS 8 **deepen, lower, depress, sink;** founder; countersink; **dig,** excavate, tunnel, mine, **drill;** pierce to the depths; **dive** 367.6

9 **sound, take soundings,** make a sounding, heave *or* cast *or* sling the lead, **fathom, plumb,** plumb-line, plumb the depths, probe

ADJS 10 **deep, profound,** deep-down, penetrating; deepish, deepsome; **deep-going,** deep-lying, deep-reaching; **deep-set,** deep-laid; deep-sunk, deep-sunken, deep-sinking; **deep-seated, deep-rooted,** deep-fixed, deep-settled; deep-cut, deep-engraven; knee-deep, ankle-deep, waist-deep

11 **abysmal,** abyssal, yawning, cavernous, gaping, plunging; **bottomless,** without bottom, soundless, unsounded, plumbless, **fathomless,** unfathomed, unfathomable, rock-bottom; deep as a well, deep as the sea *or* ocean, deep as hell

12 **underground, subterranean,** subterraneous, hypogeal, buried, deep-buried

13 **underwater,** subaqueous; **submarine, undersea;** submerged, submersed, immersed, buried, engulfed, inundated, flooded, drowned, sunken

14 **deep-sea,** deep-water, blue-water; oceanographic, bathyal; benthic, benthal, benthonic; abyssal, Bassalian; bathyorographic, bathyorographical, bathymetric, bathymetrical; benthopelagic, bathypelagic

15 deepest, deepmost, profoundest; bedrock, rock-bottom

ADVS 16 **deep; beyond one's depth,** out of one's depth; over one's head, over head and ears; at bottom, at the core, at rock bottom

276 SHALLOWNESS

NOUNS 1 **shallowness, depthlessness;** shoalness, shoaliness, no water, no depth; **superficiality,** exteriority, triviality, **cursoriness,** slightness; insufficiency 992; a lick and a promise *and* once-over-lightly <nf>; **surface,** superficies, skin, rind, epidermis; veneer, gloss; pinprick, scratch, mere scratch

2 **shoal, shallow,** shallows, shallow *or* shoal water, flat, shelf; **bank, bar,** sandbank, sandbar, tombolo; **reef,** coral reef; ford; wetlands, tidal flats, flats, mud flat

VERBS 3 **shoal,** shallow; fill in *or* up, silt up

4 **scratch the surface, touch upon,** hardly touch, skim, skim over, skim *or* graze the surface, hit the high spots *and* give a lick and a promise *and* give it once over lightly <nf>; trivialize, trifle

ADJS 5 **shallow,** shoal, **depthless,** not deep, unprofound; **surface,** on *or* near the surface, merely surface; **superficial, cursory,** slight, light, cosmetic, merely cosmetic, thin, jejune, trivial; **skin-deep,** epidermal; one-dimensional, trifling, trivial; ankle-deep, knee-deep; shallow-rooted, shallow-rooting; shallow-draft *or* -bottomed *or* -hulled

6 shoaly, shelfy; reefy; unnavigable; shallow-sea; neritic

277 STRAIGHTNESS

NOUNS 1 **straightness,** directness, unswervingness, lineality, **linearity,** rectilinearity; verticalness 200; flatness, horizontalness 201; perpendicularity

2 **straight line,** straight, right line, direct line; straight course *or* stretch, straightaway; **beeline,** air line; **shortcut** 268.5; great-circle course; streamline; edge, side, diagonal, secant, transversal, chord, tangent, perpendicular, normal, segment, directrix, diameter, axis, radius, vector, radius vector <all mathematics>; ray, beeline, plumb line, column

3 straightedge, rule, ruler; square, T square, triangle

VERBS **4** be straight, have no turning *or* turns; arrow; go straight, make a beeline

5 straighten, set *or* **put straight,** rectify, make right *or* good, square away; **unbend,** unkink, uncurl, unsnarl, disentangle 798.5; straighten up, square up, straighten out, extend; flatten, smooth 201.6; iron, flatten

ADJS **6 straight;** straight-lined, dead straight, straight as an edge *or* a ruler, ruler-straight, even, right, true, straight as an arrow, arrowlike; straightaway; **rectilinear,** rectilineal; **linear,** lineal, in a line; quasilinear; **direct, undeviating, unswerving,** unbending, undeflected; **unbent, unbowed,** unturned, uncurved, undistorted, uncurled; **uninterrupted, unbroken;** straight-side, straight-front, straight-cut; upright, vertical 200.11; flat, level, smooth, horizontal 201.7; plumb, true, right

ADVS **7 straight,** straightly, on the straight, unswervingly, undeviatingly, **directly;** straight to the mark; down the alley *and* down the pipe *and* in the groove *and* on the beam *and* on the money <nf>

278 ANGULARITY

NOUNS **1 angularity,** angularness, crookedness, hookedness; squareness, orthogonality, right-angledness, rectangularity; flection, flexure

2 angle, point, bight; vertex, apex 198.2; **corner,** quoin, coin, nook; **crook, hook,** crotchet; **bend,** curve, swerve, veer, inflection, deflection; ell, L; cant; furcation, bifurcation, fork 171.4; zigzag, zig, zag; chevron; elbow, knee, dogleg <nf>; crank; obtuse angle, oblique angle, acute angle, right angle, perpendicular

3 <angular measurement> goniometry; trigonometry; geometry

4 <instruments> goniometer, radiogoniometer; pantometer, clinometer, graphometer, astrolabe; azimuth compass, azimuth circle; theodolite, transit theodolite, transit, transit instrument, transit circle; sextant, quadrant; bevel, bevel square, set square, T-square; protractor, bevel protractor; graduated cylinder

VERBS **5 angle, crook, hook, bend,** elbow; crank; angle off *or* away, curve, swerve, veer, veer off, slant off, go off on a tangent; furcate, bifurcate, branch, fork 171.7; zigzag, zig, zag

ADJS **6 angular;** cornered, **crooked, hooked, bent,** flexed, flexural; akimbo; knee-shaped, geniculate, geniculated, doglegged <nf>; crotched, Y-shaped, V-shaped; furcate, furcal, forked 171.10; sharp-cornered, **sharp, pointed;** zigzag, jagged, serrate, sawtooth *or* saw-toothed; mitered

7 right-angled, rectangular, right-angular, right-angle; **orthogonal,** orthodiagonal, orthometric; **perpendicular,** normal

8 triangular, trilateral, trigonal, oxygonal, deltoid; wedgeshaped, cuneiform, cuneate, cuneated

9 quadrangular, quadrilateral, quadrate, quadriform; **rectangular, square;** foursquare, orthogonal; tetragonal, tetrahedral; **oblong;** trapezoid *or* trapezoidal, rhombic *or* rhombal, rhomboid *or* rhomboidal; **cubic** *or* **cubical,** cubiform, cuboid, cube-shaped, cubed, diced; rhombohedral, trapezohedral

10 pentagonal, hexagonal, heptagonal, octagonal, decagonal, dodecagonal, etc; pentahedral, hexahedral, octahedral, dodecahedral, icosahedral, etc

11 multilateral, multiangular, polygonal; polyhedral, pyramidal, pyramidic; prismatic, prismoid; diamond

279 CURVATURE

NOUNS **1 curvature,** curving, curvation, arcing; incurvature, incurvation; excurvature, excurvation; decurvature, decurvation; recurvature, recurvity, recurvation; rondure;

arching, vaulting, arcuation, concameration; aduncity, aquilinity, crookedness, hookedness; sinuosity, sinuousness, tortuosity, tortuousness; circularity 280; convolution 281; rotundity 282, roundness; convexity 283; concavity 284; curvaceousness

2 **curve,** sinus; **bow, arc; crook, hook;** parabola, hyperbola, witch of Agnesi; ellipse; caustic, catacaustic, diacaustic; catenary, festoon, swag; conchoid; lituus; tracery; circle 280.2; curl 281.2; coil, loop, spiral

3 **bend,** bending; **bow,** bowing, oxbow; Cupid's bow; **turn,** turning, sweep, meander, hairpin turn *or* bend, S-curve, U-turn; **flexure,** flex, **flection,** conflexure, inflection, deflection; reflection; geanticline, geosyncline; detour

4 **arch, span, vault,** vaulting, concameration, camber; ogive; apse; **dome,** cupola, geodesic dome, igloo, concha; cove; arched roof, ceilinged roof; **arcade, archway,** arcature; voussoir, keystone, skewback

5 **crescent, semicircle,** scythe, sickle, meniscus; crescent moon, halfmoon; lunula, lunule; horseshoe; rainbow

VERBS 6 **curve, turn,** arc, sweep; **crook, hook,** loop; incurve, incurvate; recurve, decurve, bend back, retroflex, detour; sag, swag <nf>; **bend,** flex; deflect, inflect; reflect, reflex; **bow,** embow; **arch,** vault; dome; **hump,** hunch; wind, curl 281.5; round 282.6

ADJS 7 **curved,** curve, curvate, curvated, **curving,** curvy, curvaceous <nf>, curvesome, curviform; curvilinear, curvilineal; wavy, undulant, billowy, billowing; sinuous, tortuous, serpentine, mazy, labyrinthine, meandering; **bent,** flexed, flexural, flexuous; incurved, incurving, incurvate, incurvated; recurved, recurving, recurvate, recurvated; geosynclinal, geanticlinal

8 **hooked, crooked, aquiline,** aduncous; **hook-shaped,** hooklike, uncinate, unciform; hamulate, hamate, hamiform; claw-like, unguiform, down-curving; **hook-nosed,** beaknosed, parrot-nosed, aquiline-nosed, Roman-nosed, crooknosed, crookbilled; **beaked,** billed; **beak-shaped,** beak-like; bill-shaped, billlike; rostrate, rostriform, rhamphoid

9 turned-up, upcurving, upsweeping, *retroussé* <Fr>

10 **bowed,** embowed, bandy; bowlike, bow-shaped, oxbow, Cupid's-bow; **convex, concave** 284.16, convexo-concave; arcuate, arcuated, arcual, arciform, arclike; **arched,** vaulted; **humped,** hunched, humpy, hunchy; gibbous, gibbose; humpbacked 265.13

11 **crescent-shaped,** crescentlike, crescent, crescentic, crescentiform; meniscoid<al>, menisciform; S-shaped, ess, S, sigmoid; **semicircular,** semilunar; horn-shaped, hornlike, horned, corniform; bicorn, two-horned; sickle-shaped, sicklelike, falcate, falciform; moonshaped, moonlike, lunar, lunate, lunular, luniform

12 lens-shaped, lenticular, lentiform, lentoid

13 parabolic, parabolical, paraboloid, saucer-shaped; elliptic, elliptical, ellipsoid; bell-shaped, bell-like, campanular, campanulate, campaniform; hyperbolic, domical

14 pear-shaped, pearlike, pyriform, ovipyriform

15 heart-shaped, heartlike; cordate, cardioid, cordiform, obcordate

16 kidney-shaped, kidneylike, reniform, nephroid

17 turnip-shaped, turniplike, napiform

18 shell-shaped, shell-like; conchate, conchiform, conchoidal, cochleated

19 shield-shaped, shieldlike, peltate; scutate, scutiform; clypeate, clypeiform, aspidate

20 helmet-shaped, helmetlike, galeiform, cassideous, galeated

280 CIRCULARITY

NOUNS 1 **circularity, roundness,** ring-shape, ringliness, annularity; annulation

2 **circle,** circus, rondure, **ring,** annulus, O, full circle; **circumference,** radius; **round,** roundel, rondelle; **cycle, circuit;** orbit 1072.16; closed

circle *or* arc; vicious circle, eternal return; magic circle, charmed circle, fairy ring; logical circle, circular reasoning, petitio principii; **wheel** 914.5; **disk,** discus, saucer; **loop,** looplet; noose, lasso; crown, diadem, coronet, corona; garland, chaplet, wreath; halo, glory, areola, aureole; annular muscle, sphincter

3 <thing encircling> **band, belt, cincture,** cingulum, **girdle, girth,** girt, zone, fascia, fillet; collar, collarband, neckband; necktie; necklace, bracelet, armlet, torque, wristlet, wristband, anklet; **ring**, earring, nose ring, finger ring; hoop; quoit; zodiac, ecliptic, equator, great circle; round trip

4 **rim,** felly, **tire**

5 circlet, **ringlet,** roundlet, annulet, eye, **eyelet,** grommet

6 **oval,** ovule, ovoid; ellipse

7 cycloid; epicycloid, epicycle; hypocycloid; lemniscate; cardioid; Lissajous figure

8 **semicircle,** half circle, hemicycle; crescent 279.5; quadrant, sextant, sector

9 <music and poetry> **round,** canon; rondo, rondino, rondeau, rondelet

VERBS **10** **circle, round;** orbit; **encircle** 209.7, surround, encompass, girdle; make a round trip, circumnavigate

ADJS **11** **circular, round,** rounded, circinate, annular, annulate, ringshaped, ringlike; annulose; disklike, discoid; cyclic, cyclical, cycloid, cycloidal; epicyclic; planetary; coronal, crownlike; orbital; circulatory, circumferential

12 **oval,** ovate, ovoid, oviform, eggshaped, obovate, ellipsoid, elliptic, prolate

281 CONVOLUTION

<complex curvature>

NOUNS **1** **convolution,** involution, circumvolution, **winding, twisting, turning; meander, meandering;** crinkle, crinkling; circuitousness, circumlocution, circumbendibus, circumambages, ambagiousness, ambages, convolutedness; Byzantinism; tortuousness, tortuosity; torsion, intorsion; sinuousness, **sinuosity,** sinuation, slinkiness; anfractuosity; snakiness; flexuousness, flexuosity; undulation, wave, waving; rivulation; **complexity** 799

2 **coil, whorl,** roll, **curl,** curlicue, ringlet, pigtail, **spiral,** helix, double helix, volute, volution, involute, evolute, gyre, scroll, turbination; **kink, twist, twirl;** screw, corkscrew, screw thread; tendril, cirrus; whirl, swirl, vortex; intricacy; squiggle; spheroid

3 curler, curling iron; curlpaper, papillote; crimper, crimping iron

VERBS **4** convolve, convolute, **wind, twine,** twirl, **twist, turn, twist and turn, meander,** crinkle; serpentine, snake, slink, worm; screw, corkscrew; whirl, swirl; whorl; scallop; wring; intort; contort; undulate, squiggle, twist and turn

5 **curl, coil;** crisp, kink, crimp, wave

ADJS **6** **convolutional,** convoluted, **winding, twisting,** twisty, **turning; meandering,** meandrous, mazy, labyrinthine; **serpentine,** snaky, anfractuous; roundabout, circuitous, ambagious, circumlocutory; labyrinthine; Byzantine; **sinuous,** sinuose, sinuate; **tortuous,** torsional; tortile; flexular, flexuous, flexuose; involutional, involute, involuted; rivose, rivulose; sigmoidal; wreathy, wreathlike; ruffled, whorled, turbinate

7 **coiled,** tortile, **snakelike, snaky,** snake-shaped, **serpentine,** serpentlike, serpentiform; anguine , anguiform; eellike, eelshaped, anguilliform; wormlike, vermiform, lumbricoid, lumbricine, lumbriciform

8 **spiral,** spiroid, volute, voluted; **helical,** helicoid, helicoidal; anfractuous; screw-shaped, corkscrew, corkscrewy; verticillate, whorled, scrolled; cochlear, cochleate; turbinal, turbinate

9 **curly, curled; kinky,** kinked; **frizzly,** frizzy, frizzled, frizzed; crisp, crispy, crisped

10 **wavy, undulant,** undulatory, undulative, undulating, undulate, undulated; **billowy,** billowing, surgy, rolling

ADVS 11 **windingly, twistingly,** sinuously, tortuously, serpentinely, meanderingly, meandrously; in waves; wavily; **in and out,** round and round

282 SPHERICITY, ROTUNDITY

NOUNS 1 **sphericity, rotundity, roundness,** ball-likeness, rotundness, orbicularness, orbicularity, orbiculation, orblikeness, **sphericalness,** sphericality, globularity, globularness, globosity, globoseness; spheroidity, spheroidicity; belly; cylindricality; convexity 283

2 **sphere; ball,** orb, orbit, **globe,** rondure; geoid; spheroid, globoid, ellipsoid, oblate spheroid, prolate spheroid; spherule, globule, globelet, orblet; glomerulus; **pellet;** boll; **bulb,** bulbil *or* bulbel, bulblet; knob, knot; **gob,** glob <nf>, blob, gobbet; pill, bolus; **balloon,** bladder, bubble; marble

3 **drop,** droplet; dewdrop, raindrop, teardrop; bead, pearl

4 **cylinder,** cylindroid, pillar, column; barrel, drum, cask; pipe, tube; roll, rouleau, roller, rolling pin; bole, trunk; rung

5 **cone,** conoid, conelet; complex cone, cone of a complex; funnel; ice-cream cone, cornet <Brit>; pine cone; cop; trumpet; top; traffic cone

VERBS 6 **round; round out, fill out;** cone

7 **ball, snowball;** sphere, spherify, globe, conglobulate; roll; bead; balloon, mushroom

ADJS 8 **rotund, round,** rounded, rounded out, round as a ball; bellied, bellylike; convex, bulging

9 **spherical,** sphereic, spheriform, spherelike, sphere-shaped; **globular, global,** globed, globose, globate, globelike, globe-shaped; orbicular, orbiculate, orbiculated, orbed, orb, orby , orblike; spheroid, spheroidal, globoid, ellipsoid, ellipsoidal; hemispheric, hemispherical; **bulbous,** bulblike, bulging; ovoid, obovoid

10 **beady,** beaded, bead-shaped, bead-like

11 **cylindric, cylindrical,** cylindroid, cylindroidal; **columnar,** columnal, columned, columelliform; **tubular,** tube-shaped; barrel-shaped, drum-shaped

12 **conical,** conic, coned, cone-shaped, conelike; conoid, conoidal; spheroconic; funnel-shaped, funnellike, funnelled, funnelform, infundibuliform, infundibular; bell-shaped

283 CONVEXITY, PROTUBERANCE

NOUNS 1 **convexity,** convexness, convexedness; excurvature, excurvation; camber; gibbousness, gibbosity; tuberousness, tuberosity; **bulging,** bulbousness, bellying, puffing, puffing out

2 **protuberance** *or* protuberancy, **projection, protrusion, extrusion;** prominence, eminence, salience, boldness, **bulging,** bellying; gibbousness, gibbosity; excrescence *or* excrescency; tuberousness, tuberosity, puffiness; salient; relief, high relief, *alto-rilievo* <Ital>, low relief, bas-relief, *basso-rilievo* <Ital>, embossment

3 **bulge,** bilge, bow, convex; **bump;** thank-you-ma'am *and* whoopdedoo <nf>, cahot <Can>; speed bump, sleeping policeman <Brit>; hill, mountain; **hump,** hunch; **lump,** clump, bunch, blob; nubbin, nubble, nub; **mole,** nevus; **wart,** papilloma, verruca; **knob,** boss, bulla, button, bulb; stud, jog, joggle, peg, dowel; flange, lip; tab, ear, flap, loop, ring, handle; knot, knur, knurl, gnarl, burl, gall; **ridge,** rib, cost- *or* costo- *or* costi-, chine, spine, shoulder; welt, wale; blister, bleb, vesicle <anat>, blain; bubble; condyle; bubo; tubercle *or* tubercule; beer belly; bandha <Skt>

4 **swelling,** swollenness, edema; **rising, lump, bump,** pimple; pock, furuncle, boil, carbuncle; corn; pustule; dilation, dilatation; turgidity, turgescence *or* turgescency, tumes-

cence, intumescence; tumor, tumidity, tumefaction; wen, cyst, sebaceous cyst; bunion; distension 259.2

5 **node,** nodule, nodulus, nodulation, nodosity

6 **breast, bosom, bust, chest,** crop, brisket; thorax; pigeon breast; **breasts,** dugs, teats; **nipple,** papilla, pap, mammilla, *mamelon* and *téton* <Fr>; mammillation, mamelonation; mammary gland, udder, bag

7 <nf terms> **tits,** titties, **boobs,** boobies, bubbies, jugs, headlights, **knockers,** knobs, *nénés* <Fr>, bazooms, bags, bazongas, coconuts, hooters; balls

8 **nose,** olfactory organ; **snout, snoot** <nf>, nozzle <nf>, **muzzle; proboscis,** antlia, **trunk; beak,** rostrum; **bill** *and* pecker <nf>; nib, neb; smeller *and* beezer *and* bugle *and* schnozzle *and* schnoz *and* schnozzola *and* conk <nf>; muffle, rhinarium; nostrils, noseholes <Brit nf>, nares

9 <point of land> **point,** hook, spur, **cape,** tongue, bill; **promontory,** foreland, **headland,** head; naze, ness; **peninsula,** chersonese; **delta; spit,** sandspit; **reef,** coral reef; breakwater 901.4

VERBS 10 **protrude, protuberate, project, extrude; stick out,** jut out, poke out, stand out, shoot out; **stick up,** bristle up, start up, cock up, shoot up

11 **bulge,** bilge, bouge <nf>, **belly,** bag, balloon, **pouch,** pooch <nf>; pout; **goggle,** bug <nf>, pop; **swell, swell up, dilate, distend,** billow; swell out, **belly out,** round out

12 **emboss, boss,** chase, raise; ridge

ADJS 13 **convex,** convexed; excurved, excurvate, excurvated; **bowed,** bowed-out, out-bowed, arched 279.10; gibbous, gibbose; humped 279.10; rotund 282.8

14 **protruding, protrusive,** protrudent; protrusile, protrusible; **protuberant,** protuberating; **projecting, extruding,** jutting, outstanding; prominent, eminent, salient, bold; prognathous; excrescent, excrescential; protrusile, emissile; sticking out

15 **bulging, swelling,** distended, bloated, potbellied, bellying, pouching; bagging, baggy; rounded, hillocky, hummocky, moutonnée; billowing, billowy, bosomy, ballooning, pneumatic; **bumpy,** bumped; bunchy, bunched; **bulbous,** bulbose; warty, verrucose, verrucated; meniscoid

16 **bulged, bulgy,** bugged-out <nf>; swollen 259.13, turgid, tumid, turgescent, tumescent, tumorous, bellied, ventricose; pouched, pooched <nf>; goggled, goggle; exophthalmic, bug-eyed <nf>, popeyed <nf>

17 **studded, knobbed, knobby,** knoblike, nubbled, nubby, nubbly, torose; **knotty, knotted; gnarled,** knurled, knurly, burled, gnarly; noded, nodal, nodiform; noduled, nodular; nodulated; bubonic; tuberculous, tubercular; tuberous, tuberose

18 **in relief,** in bold *or* high relief, bold, raised, *repoussé* <Fr>; chased, bossed, embossed, bossy

19 **pectoral,** chest, thoracic; pigeon-breasted; mammary, mammillary, mammiform; mammalian, mammate; papillary, papillose, papulous; breasted, bosomed, chested; teated, titted <nf>, nippled; busty, bosomy, chesty

20 **peninsular;** deltaic, deltal

284 CONCAVITY

NOUNS 1 **concavity, hollowness;** incurvature, incurvation; depression, impression; emptiness 222.2

2 **cavity,** concavity, concave; **hollow,** hollow shell, shell; **hole, pit, depression, dip,** sink, fold <Brit>; scoop, pocket, socket; **basin,** trough, **bowl,** punch bowl, cup, container 195; **crater;** antrum; lacuna; alveola, alveolus, alveolation; vug *or* vugg *or* vugh; crypt; armpit; socket; funnel chest *or* breast

3 **pothole, sinkhole,** pitchhole, chuckhole, **mudhole, rut** 290.1

4 **pit, well, shaft,** sump; **chasm, gulf, abyss,** abysm; **excavation,** dig, diggings, workings; mine, quarry

5 **cave, cavern,** cove, **hole, grotto,** grot, antre, subterrane; lair 228.26; **tunnel, burrow,** warren; subway;

bunker, foxhole, dugout, *abri* <Fr>; sewer

6 **indentation,** indent, indention, indenture, **dent,** dint; gouge, **furrow** 290; sunken part *or* place, **dimple; pit,** pock, pockmark; impression, impress; imprint, print; alveolus, alveolation; honeycomb, Swiss cheese; **notch** 289

7 **recess,** recession, **niche, nook,** inglenook, corner; cove, alcove; bay; pitchhole

8 <hollow in the side of a mountain> combe, cwm <Welsh>, cirque, corrie

9 **valley,** vale, dale, dell, dingle; **glen,** bottom, bottoms, bottom glade, intervale, strath, gill <Brit>, cwm <Welsh>, wadi, grove; trench, trough, lunar rill; gap, pass, ravine

10 **excavator, digger;** archaeologist; sapper; **miner;** tunneler, sandhog *and* groundhog <nf>, burrower; gravedigger; dredger; quarryman; driller; steam shovel, navvy <Brit>; dredge, dredger

11 **excavation,** digging; mining; indentation, **engraving**

VERBS 12 <be concave> **sink, dish,** cup, bowl, hollow; retreat, retire; incurve, curve inward

13 **hollow,** hollow out, concave, **dish,** cup, bowl; cave, cave in

14 **indent, dent,** dint, **depress,** press in, stamp, tamp, punch, punch in, impress, imprint; **pit;** pock, pockmark; dimple; honeycomb; **recess,** set back; set in; **notch** 289.4; engrave

15 **excavate, dig,** dig out, **scoop,** scoop out, **gouge,** gouge out, grub, shovel, spade, trowel, dike, delve, scrape, scratch, scrabble; dredge; **trench,** trough, furrow, groove; **tunnel, burrow;** drive, sink, lower; **mine,** sap; quarry; drill, bore

ADJS 16 **concave,** concaved, **incurved,** incurving, incurvate; **sunk,** sunken; retreating, recessed, retiring; **hollow,** hollowed, empty; palm-shaped; dish-shaped, dished, dishing, dishlike, bowl-shaped; bowllike, crater-shaped, craterlike, saucer-shaped; spoon-like; **cupped,** cup-shaped, scyphate; funnel-shaped, infundibular, infundibuliform; funnel-chested, funnel-breasted; boat-shaped, boatlike, navicular, naviform, cymbiform, scaphoid; **cavernous,** cavelike

17 **indented, dented,** depressed; **dimpled; pitted;** cratered; pocked, pockmarked; honeycombed, alveolar, alveolate, faveolate; **notched** 289.5; **engraved**

285 SHARPNESS

NOUNS 1 **sharpness, keenness, edge;** acuteness, acuity; **pointedness,** acumination; thorniness, prickliness, spinosity, spininess, bristliness; mucronation; denticulation, dentition; serration; cornification; acridity 68.1

2 <sharp edge> **edge, cutting edge, honed edge, knife-edge, razor-edge,** saw-edge; jagged edge; featheredge, fine edge; edge tool; sword 462.5

3 **point, tip,** cusp, vertex; acumination, mucro; **nib,** neb; needle; hypodermic needle, hypodermic syringe; **drill,** borer, auger, bit; prong, tine; **prick, prickle;** sting, acus *or* aculeus; **tooth** 2.8

4 <pointed projection> **projection,** spur, jag, **snag,** snaggle; **horn,** antler; cornicle; crag, peak, arête; spire, steeple, flèche; **cog, sprocket,** ratchet; sawtooth; harrow, rake; comb, pecten; nail, tack, pin; arrowhead; skewer, spit; tooth, snaggletooth, fang, denticle

5 **thorn, bramble, brier, nettle,** burr, awn, prickle, sticker <nf>; **spike,** spikelet, spicule, spiculum; **spine;** bristle; quill; **needle,** pine needle; **thistle,** catchweed, cleavers, goose grass, cactus; yucca, Adam's-needle, Spanish bayonet

VERBS 6 come *or* taper to a point, end in a point, acuminate; prick, prickle, sting, stick, bite; be keen, have an edge, cut, needle; bristle with

7 **sharpen, edge,** acuminate, aculeate, spiculate, taper; **whet, hone,** oilstone, file, grind; strop, strap; set, reset; **point;** barb, spur, point, file to a point

ADJS 8 **sharp, keen, edged, acute,** fine, **cutting,** knifelike, cultrate;

sharp-edged, keen-edged, razor-edged, knife-edged, sharp as broken glass; featheredged, fine-edged; acrid 68.6; two-edged, double-edged; sharp-set, sharp as a razor *or* needle *or* tack; sharpened, set

9 **pointed,** pointy, acuminate, acuate, aculeate, aculeated, acute, unbated; tapered, tapering; cusped, cuspate, cuspated, cuspidal, cuspidate, cuspidated; **sharp-pointed; needlelike,** needle-sharp, needle-pointed, needly, acicular, aciculate, aculeiform; mucronate, mucronated; acuminate; toothed; **spiked,** spiky, spiculate; **barbed, tined, pronged; horned,** horny, cornuted, corniculate, cornified, ceratoid; **spined, spiny,** spinous, hispid, acanthoid, acanthous

10 **prickly,** pricky <nf>, muricate, echinate, acanaceous, acanthous, aculeolate; pricking, stinging; **thorny,** brambly, briery, thistly, nettly, burry; bristly

11 **arrowlike,** arrowy, arrowheaded; sagittal, sagittate, sagittiform

12 **spearlike,** hastate; lancelike, lanciform, lanceolate, lanceolar; **spindle-shaped,** fusiform

13 **swordlike,** gladiate, ensate, ensiform

14 **toothlike,** dentiform, dentoid, odontoid; **toothed,** toothy, **fanged, tusked,** corniculate, denticulate, cuspidate, muricate; snaggle-toothed, snaggled, jagged; emarginate

15 **star-shaped, starlike,** star-pointed, stellate, stellular

286 BLUNTNESS

NOUNS 1 **bluntness, dullness,** unsharpness, obtuseness, obtundity; bluffness; abruptness; flatness, smoothness; toothlessness, lack of bite *or* incisiveness

VERBS 2 **blunt, dull,** disedge, retund, obtund, **take the edge off,** take the sting *or* bite out; turn, turn the edge *or* point of; weaken, repress; draw the teeth *or* fangs; bate; flatten, smooth

ADJS 3 **blunt, dull,** obtuse, obtundent; bluntish, dullish; **unsharp,** unsharpened, unwhetted; **unedged,** edgeless; rounded, faired, smoothed, streamlined; **unpointed,** pointless; blunted, dulled; blunt-edged, dull-edged; blunt-pointed, dull-pointed, blunt-ended; bluff, abrupt; flat

4 **toothless,** teethless, edentate, edental, edentulous, biteless

287 SMOOTHNESS

NOUNS 1 **smoothness, flatness, levelness,** evenness, uniformity, regularity; **sleekness,** glossiness; **slickness,** slipperiness, lubricity, oiliness, greasiness, frictionlessness; silkiness, satininess, velvetiness; glabrousness, glabriety; downiness; suavity 504.5; peacefulness, dead calm

2 **polish, gloss, glaze,** burnish, varnish, wax, enamel, **shine, luster,** finish; **patina**

3 <smooth surface> smooth, **plane, level, flat;** tennis court, bowling alley *or* green, billiard table *or* ball; slide; glass, ice; marble, alabaster, ivory; silk, satin, velvet, a baby's ass <nf>; mahogany

4 **smoother;** roller, lawn-roller; sleeker, slicker; **polish,** burnish; **abrasive,** abrader, abradant; lubricant; flattener, iron; buffer, sander, burnisher

VERBS 5 **smooth, flatten, plane,** planish, **level,** even, equalize; **dress,** dub, dab; smooth down *or* out, lay; plaster, plaster down; roll, roll smooth; harrow, drag; grade; mow, shave; lubricate, oil, grease

6 **press,** hot-press, **iron, mangle,** calender; roll

7 **polish, shine, burnish, furbish,** sleek, slick, slick down, gloss, glaze, glance, luster; **rub,** scour, **buff;** wax, varnish; finish

8 **grind, file, sand, scrape,** sandpaper, emery, pumice; levigate; abrade; sandblast

9 move smoothly; glide, skate, roll, ski, float, slip, slide, skid, coast

ADJS 10 **smooth;** smooth-textured *or* -surfaced, **even, level, plane, flat,** regular, uniform, **unbroken;** peaceful, still; unrough, unroughened, unruffled, unwrinkled, unrumpled; glabrous, glabrate, glabrescent; downy, peachlike; silky, satiny, velvety, smooth as silk *or* satin *or* velvet, smooth as a billiard ball *or* baby's ass <nf>; leiotrichous, lissotrichous; smooth-shaven 6.17; suave 504.17

11 **sleek, slick, glossy,** shiny, gleaming; silky, silken, satiny, velvety; **polished,** burnished, furbished; buffed, rubbed, finished; varnished, lacquered, shellacked, glazed, *glacé* <Fr>; **glassy,** smooth as glass

12 **slippery,** slippy, **slick,** slithery *and* sliddery <nf>, slippery as an eel; lubricous, lubric, oily, oleaginous, greasy, buttery, soaped, soapy; lubricated, oiled, greased

ADVS 13 **smoothly, evenly,** regularly, uniformly; **like clockwork,** on wheels

288 ROUGHNESS

NOUNS 1 **roughness, unsmoothness, unevenness,** irregularity, ununiformity, nonuniformity 782, inequality; **bumpiness,** pockedness, pockiness, holeyness, lumpiness, knobbliness; **abrasiveness, abrasion,** harshness, asperity; **ruggedness,** rugosity; **jaggedness,** raggedness, cragginess, scraggliness; joltiness, bumpiness; rough air, turbulence; choppiness; tooth; granulation; hispidity, bristliness, spininess, thorniness; nubbiness, nubbliness; scaliness, scabrousness

2 <rough surface> **rough,** broken ground; broken water, chop; **corrugation,** ripple, washboard; serration; gooseflesh, goose bumps, goose pimples, horripilation; tweed, corduroy, sackcloth; steel wool; sandpaper; potholed road, dirt road

3 **bristle,** barb, barbel, striga, setule, setula, seta; **stubble,** designer stubble; whiskers, five o'clock shadow

VERBS 4 **roughen,** rough, rough up, harshen; coarsen; granulate; gnarl, knob, stud, boss; pimple, horripilate; roughcast, rough-hew

5 **ruffle,** wrinkle, corrugate, crinkle, crumple, corrugate, **rumple; bristle; rub the wrong way, go against the grain,** set on edge

ADJS 6 **rough, unsmooth; uneven,** ununiform, unlevel, inequal, **broken,** irregular, textured; jolty, **bumpy,** rutty, rutted, pitted, pocky, potholed; horripilant, pimply; **corrugated,** ripply, wimpled; **choppy;** ruffled, unkempt; **shaggy,** shagged; **coarse,** rank, unrefined; unpolished; rough-grained, coarse-grained, cross-grained; grainy, granulated; rough-hewn, rough-cast; homespun, linsey-woolsey; bouclé, tweed, tweedy, corduroy

7 **rugged,** ragged, harsh; rugose, rugous, wrinkled, crinkled, crumpled, corrugated; **scratchy, abrasive,** rough as a cob <nf>; **jagged,** jaggy; **snaggy,** snagged, snaggled; scraggy, scragged, scraggly; sawtooth, sawtoothed, serrate, serrated; **craggy,** cragged; **rocky,** gravelly, stony; rockbound, ironbound

8 **gnarled,** gnarly; **knurled,** knurly; **knotted,** knotty, knobbly, nodose, nodular, studded, lumpy

9 **bristly, bristling,** bristled, hispid, hirsute, whiskery; barbellate, whiskered, glochidiate, setaceous, setous, setose; strigal, strigose, strigate, studded; **stubbled,** stubbly; hairy 3.24

10 bristlelike, setiform, aristate, setarious

ADVS 11 **roughly,** rough, in the rough; **unsmoothly,** brokenly, **unevenly,** irregularly, raggedly, choppily, jaggedly; **abrasively**

12 cross-grained, **against the grain,** the wrong way

289 NOTCH

NOUNS 1 **notch, nick,** nock, **cut,** cleft, **incision, gash,** hack, blaze, scotch, **score,** kerf, crena, depression, jag; gouge; jog, joggle; **indentation** 284.6

2 **notching, serration,** serrulation, saw, saw tooth *or* teeth; denticulation, dentil, dentil band, dogtooth; crenation, crenelation, crenature, crenulation; **scallop;** rickrack; picot edge, Vandyke edge; deckle

edge; cockscomb, crest; pinking shears

3 battlement, crenel, merlon, embrasure, castellation, machicolation; cog, zigzag

VERBS 4 **notch, nick, cut, incise, gash,** nock, slash, chop, crimp, scotch, **score,** blaze, jag, scarify, gouge; **indent** 284.14; **scallop,** crenelate, crenulate, machicolate; serrate, pink, mill, knurl, tooth, picot, Vandyke

ADJS 5 **notched, nicked,** incised, incisural, gashed, scotched, scored, chopped, blazed; **indented** 284.17; serrate, serrated, serrulated, **saw-toothed,** saw-edged, sawlike; crenate, crenated, crenulate, crenellated, battlemented, embrasured; scalloped; dentate, dentated, **toothed,** toothlike, tooth-shaped; lacerate, lacerated; **jagged,** jaggy; erose; serrated, serriform

290 FURROW

NOUNS 1 **furrow, groove,** scratch, crack, fissure, cranny, chase, chink, score, **cut,** gash, striation, streak, stria, **gouge,** slit, incision; sulcus, sulcation; wrinkle, crinkle; **rut,** ruck <nf>, wheeltrack, well-worn groove; wrinkle 291.3; **corrugation;** flute, fluting; rifling; chamfer, bezel, rabbet, dado; microgroove; **engraving** 713.2

2 **trench, trough, channel, ditch,** dike , fosse, **canal,** cut, gutter, conduit, kennel <Brit>; moat; sunk fence, ha-ha; aqueduct 239.2; entrenchment 460.5; canalization; pleat, crimp, goffer

VERBS 3 **furrow, groove,** score, scratch, incise, cut, carve, chisel, gash, striate, streak, gouge, slit, crack; plow; rifle; **channel, trough, flute,** chamfer, rabbet, dado; **trench,** canal, canalize, **ditch,** dike , gully, **rut; corrugate,** wrinkle, crinkle; wrinkle 291.6; pleat, crimp, goffer; **engrave** 713.9

ADJS 4 **furrowed, grooved,** scratched, scored, incised, cut, gashed, gouged, slit, striated, slotted; **channeled, troughed,** trenched, ditched, plowed; fluted, chamfered, rabbeted, dadoed; rifled; sulcate, sulcated; canaliculate, canaliculated; **corrugated,** corrugate; corduroy, corduroyed, **rutted,** rutty, rimose, wrinkly; wrinkled 291.8, pleated, crimped, goffered, crinkly; **engraved;** ribbed, costate

291 FOLD

NOUNS 1 **fold, double,** fold on itself, doubling, doubling over, duplicature; ply; plication, plica, plicature; flection, flexure; **crease,** creasing; crimp; **tuck, gather;** ruffle, frill, ruche, ruching; flounce; lappet; lapel; buckling, geological fold, anticline, syncline; dog-ear

2 **pleat,** pleating, plait *or* plat; accordion pleat, box pleat, knife pleat, kick pleat

3 **wrinkle, corrugation,** ridge, **furrow** 290, **crease, crimp,** ruck, **pucker,** cockle; **crinkle,** crankle, rimple, ripple, wimple; crumple, rumple; crow's-feet

4 **folding, creasing,** infolding, infoldment *or* enfoldment, envelopment; plication, plicature; paper-folding, origami

VERBS 5 **fold,** fold on itself, fold up; **double,** ply, plicate; fold over, double over *or* under, lap, turn over *or* under; **crease, crimp;** crisp; **pleat,** plait, plat <nf>; **tuck, gather,** tuck up, ruck, ruck up; ruffle, ruff, frill; flounce; twill, quill, flute; turn up *or* down, dog-ear; **fold in,** enfold *or* infold, wrap, lap; interfold

6 **wrinkle, corrugate,** shirr, ridge, **furrow, crease,** crimp, crimple, cockle, cocker, **pucker, purse; knit;** ruck, ruckle; **crumple,** rumple; **crinkle,** rimple, ripple, wimple

ADJS 7 **folded, doubled;** plicate, plicated, plical; **pleated,** plaited; **creased,** crimped; tucked, gathered; flounced, ruffled; twilled, quilled, fluted; dog-eared; foldable, folding, flexural, flexible, flectional, pliable, pliant, willowy

8 **wrinkled, wrinkly; corrugated,** corrugate; **creased,** rucked, ruched, **furrowed** 290.4, ridged; cockled,

cockly; puckered, puckery; pursed, pursy; knitted, knotted; rugged, rugose, rugous; **crinkled,** crinkly, cranklety <nf>, rimpled, rippled; crimped, crimpy; **crumpled,** rumpled

292 OPENING

NOUNS **1** **opening, aperture, hole,** hollow, **cavity** 284.2, **orifice; slot,** split, crack, check, leak, hairline crack; opening up, unstopping, uncorking, clearing, throwing open, laying open, broaching, cutting through; passageway; inlet 189.5; outlet 190.9; **gap,** gape, yawn, hiatus, lacuna, gat, space, interval; **chasm, gulf;** cleft 224.2; fontanel; foramen, fenestra; stoma; pore, porosity; fistula; **disclosure** 351; open space, clearing; window, window of opportunity

2 **gaping, yawning,** oscitation, oscitancy, dehiscence, pandiculation; **gape, yawn;** the gapes

3 **hole, perforation, penetration, piercing,** empiercement, **puncture,** goring, boring, puncturing, punching, pricking, lancing, broach, transforation, terebration; acupuncture, acupunctuation; trephining, trepanning; **impalement,** skewering, fixing, transfixion, transfixation; bore, borehole, drill hole; ear piercing, body piercing

4 **mouth;** maw, oral cavity, gob <nf>, gab; **muzzle,** jaw, lips, embouchure; bazoo *or* kisser *or* mug *or* mush *or* trap *or* yap <nf>; **jaws,** mandibles, chops, chaps, jowls; premaxilla

5 <other body orifices> pore, sweat gland; aural cavity, nasal cavity, nostril; stoma; **anus; asshole** *and* bumhole *and* bunghole <nf>; urethra; vagina

6 **door,** doorway 189.6; **entrance, entry** 189.5

7 **window,** casement; **windowpane,** window glass, pane, skylight; window frame, window ledge, windowsill, window bay

8 **porousness,** porosity; sievelikeness, cribriformity, cribrosity; screen, lattice, grate; sieve, strainer, colander; honeycomb; sponge; tea bag; filter, net

9 **permeability, perviousness**

10 **opener;** can opener, tin opener <Brit>; corkscrew, bottle screw, bottle opener, church key <nf>; **key,** clavis; latchkey; passkey, *passe-partout* <Fr>; master key, skeleton key; password, open sesame; key card, smart card; master switch

VERBS **11** **open,** ope , **open up;** lay open, throw open; fly open, spring open, swing open; **tap, broach;** cut open, cut, cleave, split, slit, crack, chink, fissure, crevasse, incise; rift, rive; tear open, rent, tear, rip, rip open, part, dispart, separate, divide, divaricate; spread, spread out, open out, splay, splay out

12 **unclose,** unshut; **unfold,** unwrap, unroll; **unstop, unclog, unblock,** clear, unfoul, free, deobstruct; **unplug,** uncork, uncap; crack; **unlock,** unlatch, undo, unbolt; unseal, unclench, unclutch; **uncover,** uncase, unsheathe, unveil, undrape, uncurtain; **disclose** 351.4, expose, reveal, bare, take the lid off, manifest; gain access

13 **make an opening,** find an opening, make place *or* space, **make way, make room**

14 **breach,** rupture; **break open,** force *or* pry *or* prize open, crack *or* split open, rip *or* tear open; break into, break through; break in, burst in, bust in <nf>, stave *or* stove in, cave in; excavate, dig

15 **perforate, pierce,** empierce, **penetrate, puncture, punch, hole,** prick; **tap, broach; stab, stick,** pink, run through; **transfix,** transpierce, fix, **impale,** spit, skewer; gore, spear, lance, spike, needle; **bore, drill,** auger; **ream,** ream out, countersink, gouge, gouge out; trepan, trephine; punch full of holes, make look like Swiss cheese *or* a sieve, **riddle, honeycomb**

16 **gape,** gap <nf>, **yawn,** oscitate, dehisce, hang open

ADJS **17** **open, unclosed,** uncovered; **unobstructed, unstopped, unclogged;** clear, cleared, free; wide-open, unrestricted; **disclosed**

348.10; bare, exposed, unhidden 348.11, naked, bald; accessible

18 **gaping, yawning,** agape, oscitant, slack-jawed, openmouthed; dehiscent, ringent; ajar, half-open, cracked

19 **apertured,** slotted, **holey;** pierced, **perforated,** perforate, holed; honeycombed, like Swiss cheese, riddled, *criblé* <Fr>, shot through, peppered; windowed, fenestrated; leaky

20 **porous,** porose; poriferous; like a sieve, sievelike, cribose, cribriform; spongy, spongelike; percolating, leachy

21 **permeable, pervious, penetrable,** openable, accessible

22 **mouthlike, oral,** orificial; mandibular, maxillary

293 CLOSURE

NOUNS 1 **closure, closing, shutting,** shutting up, occlusion; **shutdown,** shutting down, cloture; **exclusion** 773, shutting out, **ruling out;** blockade, embargo

2 **imperviousness, impermeability, impenetrability,** impassability; imperforation

3 **obstruction, clog, block,** blockade, sealing off, **blockage,** strangulation, choking, choking off, **stoppage,** stop, **bar, barrier, obstacle,** impediment; occlusion; **bottleneck,** chokepoint; **congestion,** jam, traffic jam, gridlock, rush hour; gorge; constipation, obstipation, costiveness; infarct, infarction; embolism, embolus; **blind alley,** blank wall, **dead end,** cul-de-sac, dead-end street, impasse; cecum, blind gut; standstill, deadlock, stalemate

4 **stopper,** stop, **stopple,** stopgap; **plug, cork,** bung, spike, spill, spile, tap, faucet, spigot, valve, check valve, cock, sea cock, peg, pin; lid 295.5; tamper-resistant packaging

5 stopping, **wadding, stuffing,** padding, **packing,** pack, tampon; gland; gasket; bandage, tourniquet; wedge

VERBS 6 **close, shut,** occlude; close up, shut up, contract, constrict, strangle, strangulate, choke, choke off, squeeze, squeeze shut; **exclude** 773.4, shut out, squeeze out; **rule out** 444.3; **fasten,** secure; **lock,** lock up, lock out, key, padlock, latch, bolt, bar, barricade; **seal,** seal up, seal in, seal off; button, button up; snap; zipper, zip up; batten, batten down the hatches; put *or* slap the lid on, **cover;** contain; **shut the door,** slam, clap, bang

7 **stop, stop up; obstruct, bar,** stay; **block,** block up; **clog,** clog up, foul, silt up, choke off; **choke,** choke up *or* off; **fill,** fill up; **stuff,** pack, jam; **congest,** stuff up; **plug,** plug up; stopper, stopple, **cork,** bung, spile; cover; **dam,** dam up; stanch; chink; caulk; blockade, barricade, embargo; constipate, obstipate, bind; occlude

8 close shop, **close up** *or* **down,** shut up, **shut down,** go out of business, fold *or* fold up *and* pull an el foldo <nf>, shutter, put up the shutters, discontinue; cease 857.6

ADJS 9 **closed, shut, unopen,** unopened; unvented, unventilated; fastened, secured; **excluded** 773.7, shut-out; **ruled out, barred** 444.7; contracted, constricted, choked, choked off, choked up, squeezed shut, strangulated, occluded; blank; blind, cecal, dead; dead-end, blind-alley, closed-end, closed-ended; **exclusive,** exclusionary, closed-door, in-camera, private, closed to the public; tamper-resistant

10 **unpierced,** pierceless, **unperforated,** imperforate, intact; **untrodden,** pathless, wayless, trackless

11 **stopped, stopped up; obstructed,** infarcted, **blocked; plugged,** plugged up, bunged; **clogged,** clogged up; foul, fouled; **choked,** choked up, strangulated, strangled; **full, stuffed,** packed, jammed, bumper-to-bumper <nf>, jam-packed, like sardines; **congested,** stuffed up; constipated, obstipated, costive, bound; silted up

12 **close, tight, compact,** fast, shut fast, **snug,** staunch, firm; **sealed;** hermetic, hermetical, hermetically sealed; airtight, dusttight *or* dustproof, gastight *or* gasproof, lighttight *or* lightproof, oil-tight *or*

oil-proof, raintight *or* rainproof, smoketight *or* smokeproof, stormtight *or* stormproof, watertight *or* waterproof, windtight *or* windproof; water-repellant *or* -resistant

13 **impervious, impenetrable, impermeable; impassable,** unpassable; unpierceable, unperforable; **punctureproof,** nonpuncturable, holeproof

294 TEXTURE

<surface quality>

NOUNS 1 **texture,** surface texture; **surface; finish,** feel, touch; intertexture, contexture, constitution, consistency; **grain,** granular texture, fineness *or* coarseness of grain; **weave,** woof 740.3, weftage, wale; **nap,** pile, shag, nub, knub, protuberance 283; **pit,** pock, indentation 284.6; structure 266

2 **roughness** 288; irregularity; bumpiness, lumpiness; **coarseness, grossness, unrefinement,** coarsegrainedness; cross-grainedness; **graininess,** granularity, granulation, grittiness, grit; pockiness; hardness 1046

3 **smoothness** 287, **fineness, refinement,** fine-grainedness; **delicacy, daintiness;** filminess, gossameriness 1029.1; down, **downiness,** fluff, fluffiness, velvet, velvetiness, fuzz, fuzziness, peach fuzz, peachiness; pubescence; satin, satininess; silk, silkiness; softness 1047

VERBS 4 **coarsen; grain,** granulate; tooth, **roughen** 288.4; gnarl, knob; rumple, wrinkle; smooth 287.5, flatten

ADJS 5 **textural, textured,** -surfaced

6 **rough** 288.6, **coarse, gross, unrefined, coarse-grained;** crossgrained; grained, **grainy,** granular, granulated, gritty, gravelly, gravelish

7 **nappy,** pily, **shaggy,** hairy, hirsute; nubby *or* nubbly; bumpy, lumpy; studded, knobbed; pocked, pitted 284.17; woven, matted, ribbed, twilled, tweedy, woolly; fibrous; frizzly, frizzy

8 **smooth** 287.10; **fine, refined,** attenuate, attenuated, **fine-grained; delicate, dainty; finespun,** thin-spun, fine-drawn, wiredrawn; gauzy, filmy, gossamer, gossamery 1029.4, **downy,** fluffy, velvety, velutinous, fuzzy, pubescent; satin, satiny, silky

295 COVERING

NOUNS 1 <act of covering> **covering,** coverage, obduction; **coating,** cloaking; **screening,** shielding, hiding, curtaining, **veiling,** clouding, obscuring, befogging, fogging, fuzzing, masking, mantling, shrouding, shadowing, blanketing; blocking, blotting out, eclipse, eclipsing, occultation; **wrapping,** enwrapping, enwrapment, sheathing, envelopment; **overlaying,** overspreading, laying on *or* over, superimposition, superposition; superincumbence; upholstering, upholstery; plasterwork, stuccowork, brickwork, cementwork, pargeting; incrustation; geocache, geocaching

2 **cover, covering,** coverage, covert, coverture, housing, hood, cowl, cowling, **shelter; screen,** shroud, shield, veil, pall, mantle, curtain, hanging, drape, drapery, window treatment; **coat,** cloak, mask, guise; vestment 5.1; camouflage, shroud

3 **skin,** dermis; **cuticle; rind; flesh;** bare skin *or* flesh, the buff; integument, tegument 206.4, tegmen, tegmentum, testa; scab; **pelt, hide, coat, jacket, fell, fleece, fur, hair,** vair <heraldry>; feathers, plumage; **peel, peeling, rind; skin,** epicarp; **bark;** cork, phellum; cortex, cortical tissue, epidermis; periderm, phelloderm; peridium; dermatogen; protective coloring

4 **overlayer,** overlay; appliqué, **lap, overlap,** overlapping, imbrication; **flap,** fly, tentfly; shutter

5 **cover, lid, top, cap, screw-top;** operculum; stopper 293.4

6 **roof,** roofing, roofage, top, **housetop,** rooftop; roof-deck, roof garden, penthouse; roofpole, ridgepole, rooftree; shingles, slates, tiles; eaves; **ceiling,** *plafond* <Fr>, over-

head; skylight, lantern, cupola, dome; widow's walk *or* captain's walk; canopy, awning, marquee

7 **umbrella,** gamp *or* brolly <Brit nf>, bumbershoot <nf>; **sunshade, parasol,** beach umbrella

8 **tent,** canvas; top, whitetop, round top, big top; tentage; tepee, wigwam, yurt

9 **rug, carpet,** floor cover *or* covering; carpeting, wall-to-wall carpet *or* carpeting; mat; drop cloth, ground cloth, groundsheet; **flooring,** floorboards, duckboards; **tiling; pavement,** pavé; tarpaulin

10 **blanket, coverlet,** coverlid <nf>, blankie <nf>, security blanket, space blanket, cover, covers, **spread,** robe, buffalo robe, **afghan,** rug <Brit>; lap robe; **bedspread; bedcover;** counterpane, counterpin <nf>; comfort, **comforter, down comforter,** duvet, continental quilt <Brit>, **quilt,** feather bed, eiderdown; patchwork quilt; **bedding,** bedclothes, clothes; **linen,** bed linen; **sheet,** sheeting, bedsheet, fitted sheet, contour sheet, dust ruffle; **pillowcase,** pillow slip, case, slip, sham; electric blanket

11 horsecloth, **horse blanket;** caparison, housing; **saddle blanket,** saddlecloth

12 **blanket, coating,** coat; **veneer, facing,** veneering, revetment; pellicle, **film, scum,** skin, scale; slick, oil slick; varnish, enamel, lacquer, paint 35.14

13 **plating,** plate, cladding; nickel plate, silver plate, gold plate, copperplate, chromium plate, anodized aluminum; electroplate, electroplating, electrocoating

14 **crust, incrustation** *or* encrustation, shell; piecrust, pastry shell; lithosphere, stalactite, stalagmite; scale, scab, eschar

15 **shell,** seashell, lorication, lorica, conch; test, testa, episperm, pericarp, elytron, scute, scutum; operculum; exoskeleton; **armor,** mail, **shield; carapace,** plate, chitin, scale, scute; **protective covering,** cortex, thick skin *or* hide, elephant skin

16 **hull,** shell, pod, capsule, case, **husk, shuck;** cornhusk, corn shuck; bark, jacket; chaff, bran, palea; seed coat; germ

17 **case,** casing, encasement; **sheath,** sheathing

18 **wrapper,** wrapping, gift wrapping, gift wrap, wrap; wrapping paper, tissue paper, waxed paper, aluminum foil, tin foil, plastic wrap, clingfilm <Brit>, cellophane; **binder,** binding; **bandage,** bandaging; **envelope,** envelopment; **jacket,** jacketing; dust jacket *or* cover

VERBS **19 cover,** cover up; apply to, **put on,** lay on; **superimpose,** superpose; **lay over,** overlay; **spread over,** overspread; **clothe, cloak,** mantle, muffle, blanket, canopy, cope, cowl, hood, **veil,** curtain, **screen, shield,** screen off, mask, cloud, obscure, fog, befog, fuzz; block, eclipse, occult; film, film over, scum

20 **wrap,** enwrap, wrap up, wrap about *or* around; **envelop, sheathe;** surround, encompass, lap, smother, enfold, embrace, invest; shroud, enshroud; swathe, swaddle; **box, case,** encase, **crate,** pack, embox; containerize; **package,** encapsulate

21 **top, cap,** tip, crown; put the lid on, cork, stopper, plug; hood, hat, coif, bonnet; roof, roof in *or* over; ceil; dome, endome

22 **floor; carpet; pave,** causeway, cobblestone, flag, pebble; cement, concrete; **pave, surface,** pave over, repave, resurface; blacktop, tar, asphalt, metal , macadamize

23 **face, veneer,** revet; **sheathe;** board, plank, weatherboard, clapboard, lath; shingle, shake; tile, stone, brick, slate; thatch; glass, glaze, fiberglass; paper, wallpaper; wall in *or* up

24 **coat,** spread on, **spread with;** smear, **smear on,** besmear, slap on, dab, daub, bedaub, plaster, beplaster; flow on, pour on; lay on, lay it on thick, slather; undercoat, prime; paint, enamel, gild, gloss, lacquer; butter; tar; wallpaper

25 **plaster,** parget, stucco, cement, concrete, mastic, grout, mortar; face,

line; roughcast, pebble-dash, spatter-dash
26 **plate,** chromium-plate, copperplate, gold-plate, nickel-plate, silver-plate; **electroplate, galvanize,** anodize
27 **crust, incrust,** encrust; loricate; effloresce; scab, scab over
28 **upholster,** overstuff
29 **re-cover,** reupholster, recap
30 **overlie,** lie over; **overlap,** lap, **lap over,** override, imbricate, jut, shingle; **extend over,** span, bridge, bestride, bestraddle, arch over, overarch, hang over, overhang
ADJS 31 **covered,** covert, under cover; **cloaked,** mantled, blanketed, muffled, canopied, coped, cowled, hooded, **shrouded, veiled,** clouded, obscured, fogged, fogged in; eclipsed, occulted, curtained, **screened,** screened-in, screened-off; shielded, masked; **housed;** tented, under canvas; roofed, roofed-in *or* -over, domed; walled, walled-in; **wrapped,** enwrapped, jacketed, **enveloped,** sheathed, swathed; **boxed, cased,** encased, encapsuled *or* encapsulated, **packaged; coated,** filmed, filmed-over, scummed; shelled, loricate, loricated; armored; ceiled; **floored; paved, surfaced;** plastered, stuccoed
32 **cutaneous,** cuticular; skinlike, skinny; skin-deep; **epidermal,** epidermic, dermal, dermic; ectodermal, ectodermic; endermic, endermatic; cortical; epicarpal; testaceous; hairy, furry 3.24; integumental, integumentary, tegumentary, tegumental, tegmental; vaginal; thecal
33 **plated,** chromium-plated, copper-plated, gold-plated, nickel-plated, silver-plated; electroplated, galvanized, anodized
34 upholstered, overstuffed
35 **covering, coating;** cloaking, blanketing, shrouding, obscuring, **veiling, screening,** shielding, sheltering; wrapping, **enveloping,** sheathing
36 **overlying,** incumbent, superincumbent, superimposed; **overlapping,** lapping, shingled, equitant; imbricate, imbricated; spanning, bridging; overarched, overarching

296 LAYER

NOUNS 1 **layer,** thickness; **level, tier,** stage, story, floor, gallery, step, ledge, deck, row, landing; **stratum,** strata, seam, *couche* <Fr>, vein, lode, belt, band, **bed, course,** measures; zone; shelf; **overlayer, superstratum,** overstory, topsoil, topcoat; **underlayer, substratum,** understratum, understory, underlay, undercoat; bedding; cultural layer, occupation layer, living floor
2 lamina, lamella; **sheet,** leaf, *feuille* <Fr>, foil; wafer, disk; **plate,** plating, cladding; covering 295, **coat,** coating, veneer, film, patina, scum, membrane, pellicle, sheathe, peel, skin, rind, hide; slick, oil slick; **slice,** cut, rasher, collop, sliver; **slab,** plank, deal <Brit>, slat, tablet, table; panel, pane; **fold,** lap, flap, **ply,** plait; laminate; laminated glass, safety glass; laminated wood, plywood, layered fiberglass; liner
3 **flake,** flock, floccule, flocculus; **scale, scurf,** dandruff, squama; chip; shaving, paring, swarf
4 **stratification,** layering, **lamination,** lamellation, sequence; foliation; delamination, exfoliation; desquamation, furfuration; flakiness, scaliness
VERBS 5 **layer,** lay down, lay up, **stratify,** arrange in layers *or* levels *or* strata *or* tiers, **laminate;** shingle, sandwich; flake, scale; delaminate, desquamate, exfoliate; interface
ADJS 6 **layered,** in layers; **laminated,** laminate, laminous; lamellated, lamellate, lamellar, lamelliform; plated, coated; veneered, faced; two-ply, three-ply, etc; two-level, bilevel, three-level, trilevel, etc; one-story, single story, two-story, double-story, etc; **stratified,** stratiform, straticulate; foliated, foliaceous, leaflike; terraced, multistage
7 **flaky,** flocculent, floccose; **scaly,** scurfy, squamous, lentiginous, furfuraceous, lepidote; scabby, scabious, scabrous

297 WEIGHT

NOUNS **1 weight, heaviness, weightiness, ponderousness,** ponderosity, ponderability, leadenness, heftiness *and* heft <nf>; body weight, avoirdupois <nf>, fatness 257.8, beef *and* beefiness <nf>, heft, chunk; poundage, tonnage; deadweight, live weight; gross weight, gr wt; **net weight,** neat weight, nt wt, net, nett <Brit>; short-weight; underweight; overweight; overbalance, overweightage; **solemnity, gravity** 111.1, 580.1

2 onerousness, **burdensomeness, oppressiveness, deadweight, overburden, cumbersomeness,** cumbrousness; massiveness, massiness , bulkiness 257.9, lumpishness, unwieldiness

3 <sports> bantamweight, featherweight, flyweight, heavyweight, light heavyweight, lightweight, middleweight, cruiser weight, welterweight; catchweight; fighting weight; jockey weight

4 counterbalance 900.4; makeweight; **ballast,** ballasting

5 <physics terms> **gravity, gravitation, G,** supergravity; specific gravity; gravitational field, gravisphere; gravitational pull; graviton; geotropism, positive geotropism, apogeotropism, negative geotropism; G suit, anti-G suit; **mass;** atomic weight, molecular weight, molar weight; quagma

6 weight, paperweight, letterweight; sinker, lead, plumb, plummet, bob; sash weight; sandbag

7 burden, burthen , pressure, **oppression, deadweight;** burdening, saddling, charging, taxing; overburden, overburdening, overtaxing, overweighting, weighing *or* weighting down; charge, **load,** loading, lading, freight, cargo, bale, ballast; cumber, cumbrance, **encumbrance;** incubus; incumbency *or* superincumbency ; handicap, drag, millstone; surcharge, overload

8 <systems of weight> avoirdupois weight, troy weight, apothecaries' weight; atomic weight, molecular weight; **pound, ounce, gram** etc, **unit of weight**

9 weighing, hefting <nf>, balancing; weighing-in, weigh-in, weighing-out, weigh-out; **scale,** weighing instrument

VERBS **10 weigh,** weight; **heft** <nf>, **balance,** weigh in the balance, strike a balance, hold the scales, put on the scales, lay in the scales; **counterbalance; weigh in,** weigh out; be heavy, weigh heavy, lie heavy, have weight, carry weight; **tip the scales,** turn *or* depress *or* tilt the scales, tip the balance

11 weigh on *or* **upon,** rest on *or* upon, bear on *or* upon, lie on, press, press down, press to the ground

12 weight, weigh *or* **weight down;** hang like a millstone; **ballast;** lead, sandbag

13 burden, burthen , **load,** load down *or* up, lade, cumber, **encumber, charge, freight,** tax, handicap, hamper, saddle; **oppress, weigh one down, weigh on** *or* **upon, weigh heavy on,** bear *or* rest hard upon, lie hard *or* heavy upon, press hard upon, be an incubus to; **overburden,** overweight, overtax, **overload** 993.15

14 outweigh, overweigh, overweight, overbalance, **outbalance,** outpoise, overpoise

15 gravitate, descend 194.5, drop, plunge 367.6, precipitate, sink, settle, subside; tend, tend to go, **incline,** point, head, lead, lean

ADJS **16 heavy, ponderous, massive,** massy, weighty, hefty <nf>, bulky, fat 257.18; **leaden,** heavy as lead; deadweight; heavyweight; overweight; **solemn, grave** 111.3/580.8

17 onerous, oppressive, burdensome, incumbent *or* superincumbent, **cumbersome,** cumbrous; massive; lumpish, **unwieldy;** ponderous

18 weighted, weighed *or* **weighted down; burdened, oppressed, laden,** cumbered, **encumbered,** charged, loaded, fraught, freighted, taxed, saddled, hampered; **overburdened,** overloaded, overladen, overcharged, overfreighted, overfraught, overweighted, overtaxed; borne-down, sinking, foundering

19 **weighable,** ponderable; **apprecia-ble,** palpable, sensible
20 **gravitational,** mass
ADVS 21 **heavily,** heavy, weightily, leadenly; burdensomely, onerously, oppressively; **ponderously,** cumbersomely, cumbrously

298 LIGHTNESS

NOUNS 1 **lightness, levity,** unheaviness, lack of weight; **weightlessness; buoyancy,** buoyance, floatability; levitation, ascent 193; **volatility; airiness,** ethereality; foaminess, frothiness, bubbliness, yeastiness; downiness, fluffiness, gossameriness 1029.1; softness, gentleness, delicacy, daintiness, tenderness; light touch, gentle touch; frivolousness 923.1
2 <comparisons> air, ether, feather, down, thistledown, flue, fluff, fuzz, sponge, gossamer, cobweb, fairy, straw, chaff, dust, mote, cork, chip, bubble, froth, foam, spume
3 **lightening,** easing, **easement, alleviation, relief;** disburdening, **disencumberment,** unburdening, **unloading,** unlading, unsaddling, untaxing, unfreighting; unballasting
4 **leavening, fermentation; leaven, ferment**
5 <indeterminacy of weight> **imponderableness** *or* imponderability, unweighableness *or* unweighability; imponderables, imponderabilia
VERBS 6 **lighten,** make light *or* lighter, reduce weight; unballast; **ease, alleviate, relieve; disburden, disencumber,** unburden, unload, unlade, off-load; **be light,** weigh lightly, have little weight, kick the beam; lose weight
7 **leaven,** raise, **ferment**
8 **buoy,** buoy up; float, float high, ride high, waft; **sustain, hold up,** bear up, uphold, upbear, uplift, upraise; refloat
9 **levitate, rise,** ascend 193.8; hover, **float**
ADJS 10 **light,** unheavy, imponderous, lightweight; **weightless; airy, ethereal,** aeriform; **volatile;** frothy, foamy, spumy, spumous, spumescent, bubbly, yeasty; downy, feathery, fluffy, gossamery 1029.4; *soufflé* or *moussé* or *léger* <Fr>; light as air or a feather or gossamer, etc 298.10; **frivolous** 922.20, 109.15; insubstantial
11 **lightened, eased, unburdened,** disburdened, disencumbered, unencumbered, relieved, alleviated, out from under, breathing easier; mitigated
12 **light, gentle, soft, delicate,** dainty, tender, **easy**
13 **lightweight,** bantamweight, featherweight; underweight
14 **buoyant,** floaty, floatable; floating, supernatant
15 levitative, levitational
16 **lightening, easing,** alleviating, alleviative, alleviatory, relieving, disburdening, unburdening, disencumbering
17 **leavening,** raising, **fermenting,** fermentative, working; yeasty, barmy; enzymic, diastatic
18 **imponderable,** unweighable

299 RARITY
<lack of density>

NOUNS 1 **rarity,** rareness; **thinness, tenuousness,** tenuity; **subtlety,** subtility; **fineness,** slightness, flimsiness, **unsubstantiality** *or* **insubstantiality** 764; **ethereality,** airiness, immateriality, incorporeality, bodilessness, insolidity, low density; **diffuseness,** dispersedness, scatter, scatteredness
2 **rarefaction,** attenuation, subtilization, etherealization; **diffusion,** dispersion, scattering; **thinning,** thinning-out, dilution, adulteration, watering, watering-down; decompression
VERBS 3 **rarefy, attenuate,** thin, thin out; dilute, adulterate, water, water down, cut; subtilize, **etherealize; diffuse,** disperse, scatter; expand 259.4; decompress
ADJS 4 **rare,** rarefied; **subtle; thin,** thinned, dilute, attenuated, attenuate; thinned-out, diluted, adulterated, watered, watered-down, cut;

tenuous, fine, flimsy, slight, **unsubstantial** *or* **insubstantial** 764; **airy, ethereal,** vaporous, gaseous, windy; **diffused,** diffuse, dispersed, scattered; uncompact, uncompressed, decompressed

5 rarefactive, rarefactional

300 MEASUREMENT

NOUNS **1 measurement, measure;** mensuration, measuring, **gauging;** admeasurement; metage; **estimation,** estimate, rough measure, approximation, ballpark figure <nf>; **quantification,** quantitation, quantization; **appraisal,** appraisement, **stocktaking, assay,** assaying; **assessment,** determination, rating, valuation, evaluation; assizement, assize, sizing up <nf>; **survey,** surveying; triangulation; **instrumentation;** telemetry, telemetering; metric system; metrication; English system of measurement; calibration, correction, computation, calculation

2 measure, measuring instrument, **meter, instrument, gauge,** barometer, **rule, yardstick,** measuring rod *or* stick, **standard,** norm, canon, **criterion,** test, touchstone, check, benchmark; rule of thumb; **pattern,** model, type, prototype; **scale,** graduated *or* calibrated scale; meter-reading, reading, readout, value, degree, quantity; parameter

3 extent, quantity 244, degree 245, size 257, distance 261, length 267, breadth 269; **weight** 297

4 <measures> US liquid measure, British imperial liquid measure, US dry measure, British imperial dry measure, apothecaries' measure, linear measure, square measure, circular measure, cubic measure, volume measure, area measure, surface measure, surveyor's measure, land measure, board measure

5 coordinates, Cartesian coordinates, rectangular coordinates, polar coordinates, cylindrical coordinates, spherical coordinates, equator coordinates; latitude, longitude; altitude, azimuth; declination, right ascension; ordinate, abscissa

6 waterline; watermark, tidemark, floodmark, **high-water mark;** load waterline, load line mark, Plimsoll mark *or* line

7 measurability, mensurability, computability, determinability, quantifiability

8 science of measurement, **mensuration,** metrology

9 measurer, meter, gauger; **geodesist,** geodetic engineer; **surveyor,** land surveyor, quantity surveyor; topographer, cartographer, mapmaker, oceanographer, chorographer; **appraiser, assessor;** assayer; valuer, valuator, evaluator; estimator; quantifier, actuary; timekeeper

VERBS **10 measure, gauge, quantify,** quantitate, quantize, meter, take the measure of, mensurate, triangulate, apply the yardstick to; **estimate,** make an approximation; **assess, rate, appraise, valuate, value,** evaluate, appreciate, prize; **assay;** size *or* size up <nf>, take the dimensions of; **weigh,** weigh 297.10; survey; plumb, probe, sound, fathom; span, pace, step; calibrate, graduate, grade; divide; caliper; meter; read the meter, take a reading, check a parameter; compute, calculate, reckon

11 measure off, mark off, lay off, set off, rule off; **step off,** pace off *or* out; **measure out,** mark out, lay out; put at

ADJS **12 measuring, metric, metrical,** mensural, mensurative, mensurational; valuative, valuational; **quantitative,** numerative; approximative, estimative; geodetic, geodetical, geodesic, geodesical, hypsographic, hypsographical, hypsometric, hypsometrical; topographic, topographical, chorographic, chorographical, cartographic, cartographical, oceanographic, oceanographical

13 measured, gauged, metered, **quantified;** quantitated, quantized; **appraised, assessed, valuated,** valued, rated, ranked; **assayed; surveyed,** plotted, mapped, admeasured, triangulated; known by measurement

14 **measurable,** mensurable, **quantifiable,** numerable, meterable, gaugeable, fathomable, **determinable,** computable, calculable; quantifiable, quantitatable, quantizable; estimable; assessable, appraisable, ratable; appreciable, perceptible, noticeable

ADVS 15 **measurably, appreciably, perceptibly, noticeably**

301 YOUTH

NOUNS 1 **youth, youthfulness,** youngness, **juvenility,** juvenescence, tenderness, tender age, early years, school age, *jeunesse* <Fr>, jejuneness, prime of life, flower of life, salad days, springtime *or* springtide of life, seedtime of life, flowering time, bloom, florescence, budtime, younger days, school days, golden season of life, heyday of youth *or* of the blood, young blood, early days

2 **childhood**; **boyhood; girlhood,** maidenhood *or* maidenhead, puerility; puppyhood, calfhood; subteens, pre-teens

3 **immaturity, undevelopment,** inexperience, **callowness, unripeness,** greenness, rawness, naiveté, sappiness, freshness, juiciness, dewiness; **minority,** juniority, infancy, nonage

4 **childishness,** childlikeness, **puerility; boyishness,** boylikeness; **girlishness,** girl-likeness, maidenliness

5 **infancy, babyhood,** the cradle, the crib, the nursery, incunabula

6 **adolescence,** maturation, maturement, pubescence, **puberty;** nobility; pre-teen, tweenager

7 **teens,** teen years *or* age, teenagehood, **awkward age,** age of growing pains <nf>

VERBS 8 make young, youthen, **rejuvenate,** reinvigorate; turn back the clock

ADJS 9 **young,** youngling, youngish, **juvenile,** juvenal, juvenescent, **youthful,** youthlike, in the flower *or* bloom of youth, blooming, florescent, flowering, dewy, fresh-faced; young-looking, well-preserved

10 **immature,** unadult; **inexperienced,** unseasoned, unfledged, newfledged, fledgling, **callow, unripe,** ripening, unmellowed, **raw, green,** vernal, primaveral, dewy, juicy, sappy, budding, tender, virginal, intact, innocent, naive, ingenuous, **undeveloped,** growing, unformed, unlicked, wet *or* not dry behind the ears, unprepared; **minor,** underage, underaged; unformed

11 **childish,** childlike, kiddish <nf>, **puerile; boyish,** boylike, beardless; **girlish,** girl-like, maiden, maidenly; puppyish, puppylike, puplike, calflike, coltish, coltlike; knee-high

12 **infant, infantile,** infantine, **babyish,** baby; dollish, doll-like; kittenish, kittenlike; **newborn,** neonatal; in the cradle *or* crib *or* nursery, in swaddling clothes, in diapers, in nappies <Brit>, in arms, at the breast, tied to mother's apron strings

13 **adolescent,** pubescent, nubile, pre-teen

14 **teenage,** teenaged, teenish, **in one's teens;** sweet sixteen <nf>

15 **junior,** Jr; **younger,** puisne

302 YOUNGSTER

NOUNS 1 **youngster,** young person, **youth, juvenile,** youngling, young'un <nf>, juvenal ; **stripling,** slip, sprig, sapling; fledgling; hopeful, young hopeful; **minor,** infant; **adolescent,** pubescent; **teenager,** teener, teenybopper <nf>, pre-teen, tweenager <nf>, twenty-something, thirty-something, young adult; junior, younger, youngest, baby

2 **young people, youth,** young, **younger generation,** rising *or* new generation, baby boomers *or* boomers, Generation X, Generation Y, young blood, young fry <nf>; **children,** tots, childkind; small fry *and* **kids** *and* **little kids** *and* little guys <nf>; boyhood, girlhood; babyhood

3 **child**; nipper, **kid** *and* kiddy *and* kiddo *and* kiddie <nf>, **little one,** little fellow *or* guy, little bugger <nf>, shaver *and* little shaver <nf>, little squirt <nf>, **tot, little tot,** wee tot, pee-wee, tad *or* little tad, tyke,

mite, chit <nf>, innocent, little innocent, moppet, poppet; darling, cherub, lamb, lambkin, kitten, **offspring** 561.3

4 **brat, urchin; minx, imp,** puck, elf, gamin, little monkey, **whippersnapper,** young whippersnapper, *enfant terrible* <Fr>, little terror, holy terror; spoiled brat; snotnose kid <nf>; juvenile delinquent, JD <nf>, punk *and* punk kid <nf>

5 **boy, lad,** laddie, **youth,** manchild, manling, young man, *garçon* <Fr>, *muchacho* <Sp>, schoolboy, schoolkid <nf>, fledgling, hobbledehoy; fellow 76.5; pup, puppy, whelp, cub, colt; master; sonny, sonny boy; bud *and* buddy <nf>; bub *and* bubba <nf>; buck, young buck; schoolboy

6 **girl,** girlie <nf>, **maid, maiden, lass,** girlchild, **lassie,** young thing, young creature, young lady, damsel in distress, **damsel,** damoiselle, demoiselle, *jeune fille* <Fr>, *mademoiselle* <Fr>, *muchacha* <Sp>, miss, missy, little missy, slip, wench <dial *or* nf>, colleen <Irish>

7 <nf terms> **gal,** dame, **chick,** tomato, **babe** *or* baby, **broad,** frail, **doll,** skirt, jill, chit, cutie, filly, heifer; teenybopper *and* weenybopper <nf>

8 **schoolgirl,** schoolmaid, schoolmiss, junior miss, preteen; subdebutante; bobbysoxer <nf>, **tomboy,** hoyden, romp; piece <nf>, nymphet; virgin, *virgo intacta* <L>

9 **infant, baby, babe,** babe in arms, little darling *or* angel *or* doll *or* cherub, bouncing baby, puling infant, mewling infant, babykins <nf>, baby bunting; papoose, *bambino* <Ital>; **toddler; suckling,** nursling, fosterling, weanling; neonate; yearling, yearold; premature baby, preemie <nf>, incubator baby; preschooler; crumbcrusher *and* -cruncher *and* -grinder *and* -snatcher; rug rat *and* carpet rat *and* rug ape *and* carpet ape *and* curtain-climber <nf>

10 <animals> yearling, **fledgling,** birdling, nestling; **chick,** chicky, chickling; **pullet,** fry, fryer; **duckling;** gosling, cygnet; **kitten,** kit, catling; **pup,** puppy, whelp; **cub; calf,** dogie, weaner; **colt,** foal, filly; piglet, pigling, shoat; **lamb,** lambkin; kid, yeanling; fawn; **tadpole,** polliwog; litter, nest, brood, clutch, spawn, farrow

11 <plants> **sprout, seedling,** set; sucker, shoot, slip, offshoot; **twig,** sprig, scion, sapling

12 <insects> **larva, chrysalis,** aurelia, **cocoon,** pupa, grub; nymph, nympha; wriggler, wiggler; caterpillar, maggot, grub

303 AGE

<time of life>

NOUNS 1 **age,** years; time *or* stage of life; lifetime, lifespan, life expectancy, timespan, longevity; seven ages of man: infancy, childhood, youth, adolescence, adulthood, middle age, maturity, old age, declining years, senility

2 **maturity, adulthood, majority,** adultness, grown-upness, maturation, matureness, full growth, mature age, legal age, voting age, driving age, drinking age, *legalis homo* <L>; age of consent; ripeness, ripe age, riper years, full age *or* growth *or* bloom, flower of age, **prime, prime of life,** age of responsibility, age *or* years of discretion, age of matured powers; **manhood,** man's estate, virility, *toga virilis* <L>, masculinity, maleness, manliness; **womanhood,** womanness, femininity, femaleness, womanliness

3 **seniority, eldership,** deanship, primogeniture

4 **middle age,** middle life, meridian of life, the middle years, the wrong side of forty, the dangerous age, prime of life; change of life, perimenopause, menopause, climacteric, midlife crisis

5 **old age, oldness,** eld , **elderliness,** senectitude, senescence, agedness, advanced age *or* years; superannuation, pensionable age, retirement age, age of retirement; **ripe old age,** the golden years, advanced years,

senior citizenship, hoary age, hoariness, gray *or* white hairs, grayness; **decline of life,** declining years, youth deficiency, the vale of years, threescore years and ten, the shady side <nf>; sunset *or* twilight *or* evening *or* autumn *or* winter of one's days; **decrepitude,** ricketiness, infirm old age, infirmity of age, infirmity, debility, caducity, feebleness; dotage, anecdotage, second childhood; senility 922.10, anility; **longevity,** long life, length of years, green *or* hale old age

6 maturation, development, growth, ripening, blooming, blossoming, flourishing; **mellowing,** seasoning, tempering; **aging,** senescence

7 change of life, perimenopause, **menopause,** climacteric, grand climacteric, **midlife crisis**

8 geriatrics, gerontology, geriatric medicine

VERBS **9 mature, grow up,** grow, **develop, ripen,** flower, flourish, bloom, blossom; fledge, leave the nest, put up one's hair, not be in pigtails, put on long pants; **come of age,** come to maturity, attain majority, **reach one's majority,** reach twenty-one, reach voting age, reach the age of consent, reach manhood *or* womanhood, write oneself a man, come to *or* into man's estate, put on long trousers *or* pants, assume the toga virilis, come into years of discretion, be in the prime of life, cut one's wisdom teeth *or* eyeteeth <nf>, have sown one's wild oats, settle down; **mellow,** season, temper

10 age, grow old, senesce, get on *or* along, **get on** *or* **along in years,** grow *or* have whiskers, be over the hill <nf>, turn gray *or* white; **decline,** wane, fade, fail, sink, waste away; **dodder,** totter, shake; wither, wrinkle, shrivel, wizen; **live to a ripe old age,** cheat the undertaker <nf>; be in one's dotage *or* second childhood

11 have had one's day, have seen one's day *or* best days, **have seen better days; show one's age,** show marks of age, have one foot in the grave

ADJS **12 adult, mature, of age,** out of one's teens, big, grown, **grown-up;** old enough to know better; **marriageable,** of marriageable age, marriable, nubile

13 mature, ripe, ripened, of full *or* ripe age, **developed,** fully developed, well-developed, **full-grown,** full-fledged, fully fledged, full-blown, in full bloom, in one's prime; **mellow** *or* mellowed, seasoned, tempered, aged

14 middle-aged, mid-life, *entre deux âges* <Fr>, fortyish, matronly; perimenopausal, menopausal

15 past one's prime, senescent, on the shady side <nf>, overblown, overripe, of a certain age, over the hill <nf>

16 aged, elderly, old, grown old in years, along *or* up *or* advanced *or* on in years, years old, advanced, advanced in life, **at an advanced age, ancient,** geriatric, gerontic; **venerable,** old as Methuselah *or* as God *or* as the hills; patriarchal; hoary, hoar, **gray,** white, gray- *or* white-headed, gray- *or* white-haired, gray- *or* white-crowned, gray- *or* white-bearded, gray *or* white with age; wrinkled, prune-faced <nf>; wrinkly, with crow's feet, marked with the crow's foot

17 aging, growing old, senescent, **getting on** *or* **along,** getting on *or* along *or* up in years, not as young as one used to be, long in the tooth; **declining,** sinking, waning, fading, wasting, doting

18 stricken in years, decrepit, infirm, weak, debilitated, feeble, geriatric, timeworn, the worse for wear, rusty, moth-eaten *or* mossbacked <nf>, fossilized, wracked *or* ravaged with age, run to seed; **doddering,** doddery, doddered, tottering, tottery, rickety, shaky, palsied; on one's last legs, with one foot in the grave; **wizened,** crabbed, **withered,** shriveled, like a prune, mummylike, papery-skinned; **senile** 922.23, anile

304 ADULT OR OLD PERSON

NOUNS **1** **adult, grownup,** mature man *or* woman, grown man *or* woman, big boy *and* big girl <nf>; **man, woman;** major, *legalis homo* <L>; no chicken *and* no spring chicken <nf>

2 **old man, elder, oldster** <nf>; golden-ager, senior citizen, geriatric, patron; old chap, old party, **old gentleman,** old gent <nf>, codger *and* old codger <nf>, geezer *and* old geezer <nf>, gramps <nf>, gaffer, old duffer <nf>, old dog *and* old-timer <nf>, dotard, veteran, pantaloon, man of the world, **patriarch,** graybeard *or* greybeard, reverend *or* venerable sir; grandfather, grandsire; Father Time, Methuselah, Nestor, Old Paar; sexagenarian, septuagenarian, octogenarian, nonagenarian, centenarian; curmudgeon; eld <nf>

3 **old woman, old lady,** dowager, granny, old granny, dame, **grandam,** matron, matriarch, trot *and* old trot <nf>; old dame *and* hen *and* girl <nf>; old bag *and* bat *and* battleax *and* witch <nf>; old maid; **crone,** hag, witch, beldam, frump <nf>, old wife; grandmother; woman of the world

4 <old people> the old, older generation, seniors, retirees, over-the-hill gang <nf>; Darby and Joan, Baucis and Philemon

5 **senior,** Sr, *senex* <L>, **elder,** older; dean, *doyen* <Fr>, *doyenne* <Fr>; father, sire; firstling, first-born, **eldest,** oldest

VERBS **6** **mature** 303.9; grow old 303.10

ADJS **7** **mature** 303.12; middle-aged 303.14; aged 303.16, older 842.19

305 ORGANIC MATTER

NOUNS **1** **organic matter,** animate *or* living matter, all that lives, living nature, organic nature, organized matter; **biology** 1068; **flesh, tissue,** fiber, brawn, plasm; **flora and fauna,** plant and animal life, animal and vegetable kingdom, biosphere, biota, ecosphere, noosphere; force of nature

2 **organism,** organization, organic being, life-form, form of life, **living being** *or* **thing,** being, animate being, creature, created being, **individual,** genetic individual, physiological individual, morphological individual; zoon, zooid; virus; aerobic organism, anaerobic organism; heterotrophic organism, autotrophic organism; microbe, microorganism

3 **biological classification,** taxonomy, biotaxy, kingdom, phylum, etc

4 **cell,** bioplast, cellule; procaryotic cell, eucaryotic cell; plant cell, animal cell; germ cell, somatic cell; corpuscle; unicellularity, multicellularity; germ layer, ectoderm, endoderm, mesoderm; **protoplasm,** energid; trophoplasm; chromatoplasm; germ plasm; cytoplasm; ectoplasm, endoplasm; cellular tissue, reticulum; plasmodium, coenocyte, syncytium

5 **organelle;** plastid; chromoplast, plastosome, chloroplast; mitochondrion; Golgi apparatus; ribosome; spherosome, microbody; vacuole; central apparatus, cytocentrum; centroplasm; centra body, microcentrum; centrosome; centrosphere; centriole, basal body; pili, cilia, flagella, spindle fibers; aster; kinoplasm; plasmodesmata; cell membrane

6 **metaplasm;** cell wall, cell plate; structural polysaccharide; bast, phloem, xylem, xyl- *or* xylo-, cellulose, chitin

7 **nucleus,** cell nucleus; macronucleus, meganucleus; micronucleus; nucleolus; plasmosome; karyosome, chromatin strands; nuclear envelope; chromatin, karyotin; basichromatin, heterochromatin, oxychromatin

8 **chromosome;** allosome; heterochromosome, sex chromosome, idiochromosome; W chromosome; X chromosome, accessory chromosome, monosome; Y chromosome; Z chromosome; euchromosome, autosome; homologous chromosomes;

univalent chromosome, chromatid; centromere; gene-string, chromonema; genome; chromosome complement; chromosome number, diploid number, haploid number; polyploidy

9 **genetic material, gene;** allele; operon; cistron, structural gene, regulator gene, operator gene; altered gene; deoxyribonucleic acid *or* **DNA;** DNA double helix, superhelix *or* supercoil; nucleotide, codon; ribonucleic acid *or* **RNA;** messenger RNA, mRNA; transfer RNA, tRNA; ribosomal RNA; anticodon; gene pool, gene complex, gene flow, genetic drift; genotype, biotype; **hereditary character,** heredity 560.6; genetic counseling; genetic screening; **recombinant DNA technology,** gene mapping, gene splicing; gene transplantation, gene transfer, germline insertion; intronizing, intron *or* intervening sequence; exonizing, exon; **genetic engineering,** genetic fingerprinting; designer gene

10 **gamete, germ cell,** reproductive cell; macrogamete, megagamete; microgamete; planogamete; genetoid; gamone; gametangium, gametophore; gametophyte; germ plasm, idioplasm

11 **sperm, spermatozoa, seed, semen,** jism *or* gism *and* come *or* cum *and* scum *and* spunk <nf>; seminal *or* spermatic fluid, milt; **sperm cell,** male gamete; spermatozoon, spermatozoid, antherozoid; antheridium; spermatium, spermatiophore *or* spermatophore, spermagonium; pollen; spermatogonium; androcyte, spermatid, spermatocyte

12 **ovum, egg, egg cell,** female gamete, oösphere; oöcyte; oögonium; ovicell, oöecium; ovule; stirp; ovulation; donor egg

13 **spore;** microspore; macrospore, megaspore; swarm spore, zoospore, planospore; spore mother cell, sporocyte; zygospore; sporocarp, cystocarp; basidium; sporangium, megasporangium, microsporangium; sporocyst; gonidangium; sporogonium, sporophyte; sporophore; sorus

14 **embryo,** zygote, oösperm, oöspore, blastula; **fetus,** germ, germen , rudiment; **larva,** nymph

15 **egg;** ovule; bird's egg; roe, fish eggs, caviar, spawn; **yolk,** yellow, vitellus; white, **egg white,** albumen, glair; eggshell

16 **cell division; mitosis;** amitosis; metamitosis, eumitosis; endomitosis, promitosis; haplomitosis, mesomitosis; karyomitosis; karyokinesis; interphase, prophase, metaphase, anaphase, telophase, diaster, cytokinesis; **meiosis**

ADJS 17 **organic,** organismic; organized; **animate, living,** vital, zoetic; **biological,** biotic; physiological

18 **protoplasmic,** plasmic, plasmatic; **genetic,** genic, hereditary

19 **cellular,** cellulous; unicellular, multicellular; corpuscular

20 gametic, gamic, sexual; **spermatic,** spermic, **seminal,** spermatozoal, spermatozoan, spermatozoic; sporal, sporous, sporoid; sporogenous

21 **nuclear,** nucleal, nucleary, nucleate; multinucleate; nucleolar, nucleolate, nucleolated; **chromosomal;** chromatinic; haploid, diploid, polyploid

22 **embryonic, germinal,** germinant, germinative, germinational; larval; fetal; in the bud; germiparous

23 **egglike,** ovicular, eggy; ovular; albuminous, albuminoid; yolked, yolky; oviparous

306 LIFE

NOUNS 1 **life, living, vitality,** being alive, having life, animation, animate existence; breath; liveliness, animal spirits, vivacity, spriteliness; long life, longevity; life expectancy, life-span; viability; lifetime 827.5; immortality 829.3; birth 1; existence 761

2 **life force, soul,** spirit, indwelling spirit, force of life, living force, *vis vitae* or *vis vitalis* <L>, **vital force** *or* energy, animating force *or* power *or* principle, inspiriting force *or* power *or* principle, archeus, élan vital, impulse of life, vital principle, **vital spark** *or* **flame,** spark of life, divine spark, life principle, vital

spirit, vital fluid, anima, consciousness; **breath,** life breath, **breath of life,** breath of one's nostrils, divine breath, life essence, essence of life, pneuma; prana, atman, jivatma, jiva; blood, **lifeblood,** heartblood, heart's blood; **heart,** heartbeat, beating heart; seat of life; growth force, bathmism; **life process;** biorhythm, biological clock, internal clock; life cycle

3 **the living,** the living and breathing, all animate nature, the quick; the quick and the dead

4 **living being,** human being, living person, entity, living soul, living thing, life on earth, survivor, the quick

5 life cycle, **lifetime,** longevity, life expectancy

6 vivification, vitalization, animation, quickening

7 **biosphere**, ecosphere, noosphere; biochore, biotype, biocycle

VERBS 8 **live,** be alive *or* animate *or* vital, have life, exist 761.8, be, breathe, respire, live and breathe, fetch *or* draw breath, draw the breath of life, walk the earth, subsist

9 **come to life,** come into existence *or* being, come into the world, see the light, be incarnated, **be born** *or* begotten *or* conceived; quicken; **revive, come to,** come alive, come around, regain consciousness, show signs of life; **awake, awaken;** rise again, live again, rise from the grave, resurge, resurrect, resuscitate, reanimate, return to life

10 **vivify, vitalize, energize, animate, quicken,** inspirit, invigorate, enliven, imbue *or* endow with life, give birth to, give life to, put life *or* new life into, breathe life into, give a new lease on life, bring to life, bring *or* call into existence *or* being; conceive; give birth, reproduce

11 **keep alive,** feed, nourish, provide for, keep body and soul together, endure, survive, persist, last, last out, hang on, hang in <nf>, be spared, come through, continue, carry on, have nine lives; support life; cheat death

ADJS 12 **living, alive,** having life, live, very much alive, alive and well, alive and kicking <nf>, conscious, breathing, quick , **animate,** animated, **vital,** viable, zoetic, instinct with life, imbued *or* endowed with life, vivified, enlivened, inspirited; in the flesh, among the living, in the land of the living, on this side of the grave, still with us, still breathing, above-ground, incarnate; existent 761.13; extant; long-lived, tenacious of life; capable of life *or* survival, viable

13 **life-giving,** animating, animative, quickening, vivifying, energizing

307 DEATH

NOUNS 1 **death, dying,** somatic death, clinical death, biological death, abiosis, **decease, demise;** brain death; perishing, release, **passing away,** passing, passing over, leaving life, making an end, departure, parting, going, going off *or* away, exit, ending, **end** 820, end of life, cessation of life, end of the road *or* line <nf>; **loss of life,** no life, ebb of life, expiration, expiry, **dissolution, extinction,** bane, annihilation, extinguishment, quietus; doom, crack of doom, summons of death, final summons, sentence of death, death knell, knell; **sleep, rest,** eternal rest *or* sleep, last sleep, last rest; **grave** 309.16; reward, debt of nature, last debt; last muster, last roundup, curtains <nf>, big sleep <nf>; jaws of death, hand *or* finger of death, shadow *or* shades of death; clinical death; rigor mortis; near-death experience *or* NDE; the beyond, the other side, the Great Divide

2 <personifications and symbols> **Death, Grim Reaper,** Reaper; pale horse, pale rider; angel of death, death's bright angel, Azrael; scythe *or* sickle of Death; **skull,** death's-head, grinning skull, crossbones, skull and crossbones; *memento mori* <L>; white cross; great leveler, thief in the night, Last Summoner; shadow of death, dance of death

3 river of death, Styx, Stygian shore, Acheron; Jordan, Jordan's bank; Heaven 681; Hell 682

4 early death, early grave, **untimely end,** premature death; sudden death; stroke of death, death stroke; deathblow

5 **violent death;** killing 308; suffocation, smothering, smotheration <nf>; asphyxiation; choking, choke, strangulation, strangling; drowning, watery grave; fatal accident, accidental death; starvation; liver death, serum death; megadeath; suicide, assisted suicide; murder, assassination; capital punishment, execution

6 **natural death;** easy *or* quiet *or* peaceful death *or* end, euthanasia, blessed *or* welcome release; stillbirth

7 dying day, deathday; final *or* fatal *or* last hour, dying hour, running-out of the sands, deathtime

8 moribundity, extremity, last *or* final extremity; **deathbed;** deathwatch; death struggle, agony, last agony, death agony, death throes, throes of death; last breath *or* gasp, dying breath; **death rattle,** death groan; making an end, passing, passing away, crossing the Styx; extreme unction, last rites

9 **swan song,** *chant du cygne* <Fr>, death song, final words, last words

10 **bereavement** 473.1

11 **deathliness,** deathlikeness, deadliness; **weirdness, eeriness, uncanniness,** unearthliness; ghostliness, ghostlikeness; **ghastliness, grisliness, gruesomeness,** macabreness; paleness, haggardness, wanness, luridness, pallor; cadaverousness, corpselikeness; *facies Hippocratica* <L>, Hippocratic face *or* countenance, mask of death

12 **death rate,** death toll; **mortality,** mortalness, mortality rate; extinction, dissolution, abiosis transience 828; mutability 854.1

13 **obituary,** obit <nf>, death notice, necrology, necrologue; register of deaths, roll of the dead, death roll, mortuary roll, bill of mortality; fatality list, casualty list; martyrology; death toll, body count

14 terminal case; **dying**

15 **corpse,** dead body, dead man *or* woman, dead person, **cadaver, carcass, body;** *corpus delicti* <L>; **stiff** <nf>; **the dead,** the defunct, **the deceased,** the departed, the loved one; **decedent,** the late lamented; **remains,** mortal *or* organic remains, remains, carrion, bones, skeleton, dry bones, relics, reliquiae; dust, ashes, earth, clay, tenement of clay; **carrion,** crowbait, food for worms; **mummy,** mummification; embalmed corpse

16 **dead,** the majority, the great majority; one's fathers, one's ancestors; the choir invisible

17 **autopsy, postmortem, inquest,** postmortem examination, ex post facto examination, necropsy, necroscopy; medical examiner, coroner, pathologist, mortality committee

VERBS 18 **die, decease, succumb, expire, perish,** be taken by death, up and die <nf>, cease to be *or* live, part, depart, quit this world, make one's exit, go, go the way of all flesh, go out, pass, pass on *or* over, **pass away, meet one's death** *or* **end** *or* **fate,** end one's life *or* days, depart this life, put off mortality, **lose one's life,** fall, be lost, relinquish *or* surrender one's life, resign one's life *or* being, **give up the ghost,** yield the ghost *or* spirit, yield one's breath, take one's last breath, breathe one's last, stop breathing, fall asleep, close one's eyes, take one's last sleep, pay the debt of *or* to nature, go out with the ebb, return to dust *or* the earth

19 <nf terms> **croak,** go west, kick the bucket, kick in, pop off, conk off, conk out, cop it, drop off, step off, go to the wall, go home feet first, knock off, pipe off, kick off, shove off, bow out, pass out, peg out, push up daisies, go for a burton <Brit>, belly up, go belly up, bite the dust, take the last count; flatline; check out, check in, cash in, hand *or* pass *or* cash in one's checks *or* chips; turn up one's toes; slip one's cable; buy the farm *or* the ranch, farm,

have one's time *and* have it *and* buy it <Brit>

20 **meet one's Maker,** go to glory, go to kingdom come <nf>, go to the happy hunting grounds, go to *or* reach a better place *or* land *or* life *or* world, go to one's rest *or* reward, go home, go home feet first <nf>, go to one's last home, go to one's long account, go over to *or* join the majority *or* great majority, **be gathered to one's fathers,** join one's ancestors, join the angels, join the choir invisible, die in the Lord, go to Abraham's bosom, pass over Jordan, cross the Stygian ferry, give an obolus to Charon; awake to life immortal

21 **drop dead, fall dead,** fall down dead; come to an untimely end; predecease

22 die in harness, die with one's boots on, make a good end, die fighting, die in the last ditch, die like a man

23 die a natural death; die a violent death, be killed; **starve,** famish; smother, **suffocate;** asphyxiate; choke, strangle; **drown,** go to a watery grave, go to Davy Jones's locker <nf>; catch one's death, catch one's death of cold

24 **lay down** *or* **give one's life for one's country, die for one's country,** make the supreme sacrifice, do one's bit

25 be dying, be moribund, be terminal; die out, become extinct

26 be dead, be no more, sleep *or* be asleep with the Lord, sleep with one's fathers *or* ancestors; lie in the grave, lie in Abraham's bosom <nf>

27 **bereave;** leave, leave behind; orphan, widow

ADJS **28** **deathly, deathlike,** deadly; **weird, eerie, uncanny,** unearthly; ghostly, ghostlike; **ghastly, grisly, gruesome, macabre;** pale, deathly pale, wan, lurid, blue, livid, haggard; **cadaverous,** corpselike; mortuary

29 **dead, lifeless,** breathless, without life, inanimate 1055.5, exanimate, without vital functions; **deceased, demised, defunct,** croaked <nf>, departed, departed this life, destitute of life, **gone, passed on,** passed away, gone the way of all flesh, gone west <nf>, extinct, gone before, long gone, dead and gone, done for <nf>, dead and done for <nf>, no more, finished <nf>, taken off *or* away, released, fallen, bereft of life, gone for a burton <Brit nf>; **at rest,** resting easy <nf>, still, out of one's misery; **asleep,** sleeping, reposing; asleep in Jesus, with the Lord, asleep *or* dead in the Lord; **called home,** out of the world, gone to a better world *or* place *or* land, gone but not forgotten, launched into eternity, gone to glory, taken *or* called by God, at the Pearly Gates, in Abraham's bosom, joined the choir invisible, gone to kingdom come <nf>, with the saints, sainted, numbered with the dead; in the grave, deep-sixed <nf>, six feet under *and* pushing up daisies <nf>; carrion, food for worms; martyred; death-struck, death-stricken, smitten with death; stillborn, dead on arrival, DOA; late, late lamented

30 **stone-dead;** dead as a doornail *and* dead as a dodo *and* dead as a herring *and* dead as mutton <nf>; cold, stone-cold, stiff <nf>

31 **drowned,** in a watery grave *or* bier, in Davy Jones's locker

32 **dying, terminal,** expiring, going, slipping, slipping away, sinking, sinking fast, fading, low, despaired of, given up, given up for dead, not long for this world, hopeless, bad, **moribund,** near death, deathlike, perishing, doomed, near one's end, at the end of one's rope <nf>, hanging by a thread, done for <nf>, at the point of death, **at death's door,** at the portals of death, *in articulo mortis* <L>, *in extremis* <L>, in the jaws of death, facing *or* in the face of death; **on one's last legs** <nf>, half-dead, with one foot in the grave, tottering on the brink of the grave; on one's deathbed; at the last gasp; in critical condition, mortally ill, terminal; nonviable, unviable, incapable of life

33 **mortal, perishable,** subject to death, ephemeral, transient 828.7, mutable 854.6

34 **bereaved,** bereft, deprived; widowed; orphan, **orphaned,** parentless, fatherless, motherless

35 **postmortem,** postmortal, postmortuary, postmundane, post-obit, postobituary, **posthumous**

ADVS 36 **deathly, deadly;** to the death, *à la mort* <Fr>

PHRS 37 one's hour is come, one's days are numbered, one's race is run, one's doom is sealed, life hangs by a thread, one's number is up, Death knocks at the door, Death stares one in the face, the sands of life are running out

308 KILLING

NOUNS 1 **killing, slaying, slaughter, dispatch, extermination, destruction, murder,** destruction of life, taking of life, death-dealing, dealing of death, bane; kill; **bloodshed,** bloodletting, blood, gore, flow of blood; mercy killing, euthanasia, negative *or* passive euthanasia; ritual murder *or* killing, immolation, sacrifice, religious sacrifice, crucifixion, martyrdom; *auto-da-fé* <Sp, literally, act of faith>, martyrdom, martyrization; lynching; stoning, lapidation; defenestration; braining; shooting, drive-by shooting; poisoning; execution 604.7; mass killing, biocide, ecocide, genocide; Holocaust; mass murder

2 **homicide, manslaughter; negligent homicide,** unlawful killing; **murder,** bloody murder <nf>, first-degree murder, second-degree murder, capital murder; serial killing; hit *and* bump-off *and* bumping-off *and* rubbing out *and* blowing away *and* wasting <nf>, gangland-style execution, contract murder; kiss of death; foul play; **assassination;** terrorist killing; crime of passion; removal, elimination; liquidation, purge, purging; thuggery, thuggism, thuggee; justifiable homicide

3 **butchery,** butchering, **slaughter,** shambles, occision, slaughtering, hecatomb, holocaust

4 **carnage, massacre, bloodbath, decimation,** saturnalia of blood; **mass murder, mass destruction,** mass extermination, wholesale murder, pogrom, race-murder, genocide, race extermination, ethnic cleansing, **the Holocaust,** the final solution, Roman holiday

5 **suicide,** autocide, self-murder, self-homicide, self-destruction, self-slaughter, death by one's own hand, *felo-de-se* <L>, self-immolation, self-sacrifice; slashing one's wrists, **disembowelment,** ritual suicide, self-immolation, *hara-kiri* and *seppuku* <Japanese>, suttee, sutteeism, kamikaze; car of Jagannath *or* Juggernaut; mass suicide, race suicide, suicide pact; suicide bombing

6 **suffocation,** smothering, smotheration <nf>, **asphyxiation,** asphyxia; **strangulation,** strangling, burking, throttling, stifling, garrote, garroting; **choking,** choke; **drowning**

7 **execution,** capital punishment, death penalty, legalized killing, judicial murder, judicial execution

8 **fatality,** fatal accident, violent death, **casualty,** disaster, calamity; DOA *or* dead-on-arrival

9 **deadliness, lethality,** mortality, fatality; **malignance** *or* malignancy, malignity, **virulence, perniciousness,** banefulness

10 **deathblow,** death stroke, final stroke, fatal *or* mortal *or* lethal blow, *coup de grâce* <Fr>

11 **killer, slayer, slaughterer, butcher,** bloodshedder; massacrer; **manslayer, homicide, murderer,** mankiller, bloodletter, man of blood, Cain; **assassin,** assassinator; **cutthroat,** thug, desperado, bravo, gorilla <nf>, apache, gunman; professional killer, contract killer, hired killer, hit man *or* button man *or* gun *or* trigger man *or* torpedo *or* gunsel <nf>; **hatchet man;** poisoner; strangler, hangman, garroter, burker; cannibal, maneater, anthropophagus; headhunter; mercy killer, euthanasiast; thrill killer, psychopath, homicidal maniac; serial killer; executioner 604.8; matador; exterminator, eradicator; death squad; terrorist, bomber; poison, pesticide 1001.3

12 <place of slaughter> aceldama, field of blood *or* bloodshed; **slaughterhouse,** butchery <Brit>, shambles, abattoir; bullring, arena, battleground, battlefield; stockyard; gas chamber, concentration camp, death camp, killing fields; Auschwitz, Belsen, etc

VERBS **13** **kill, slay, put to death,** deprive of life, bereave of life, **take life,** take the life of, take one's life away, **do away with,** make away with, **put out of the way,** put to sleep, end, **put an end to,** end the life of, hasten someone's end, **dispatch, do to death,** do for, finish, finish off, kill off, take off, **dispose of, exterminate, destroy,** annihilate; **liquidate,** purge; carry off *or* away, remove from life; put down, put away, put to sleep, put one out of one's misery; launch into eternity, send to glory, send to kingdom come <nf>, send to one's last account, send to one's Maker; **martyr,** martyrize; immolate, sacrifice; lynch; cut off, cut down, nip in the bud; poison; chloroform; starve; euthanatize; **execute**

14 <nf terms> **waste, zap,** nuke, rub out, croak, snuff, bump off, knock off, bushwhack, lay out, polish off, blow away, blot out, erase, wipe out, blast, do in, off, hit, ice, gun down, pick off, put to bed with a shovel, scrag, take care of, take out, take for a ride, give the business *or* works, deep-six, get, fix, settle

15 **shed blood,** spill blood, let blood, bloody one's hands with, dye one's hands in blood, have blood on one's hands, pour out blood like water, wade knee-deep in blood

16 **murder,** commit murder; **assassinate;** remove, **purge, liquidate,** eliminate, get rid of

17 **slaughter, butcher, massacre, decimate,** mow down, spare none, take no prisoners, wipe out, wipe off the face of the earth, annihilate, exterminate, liquidate, commit carnage, depopulate, murder *or* kill *or* slay en masse; purge, commit mass murder *or* destruction, murder wholesale, commit genocide, suicide-bomb

18 **strike dead,** fell, bring down, lay low; drop, drop *or* stop in one's tracks; **shoot,** shoot down, pistol, shotgun, machinegun, gun down, riddle, shoot to death; cut down, cut to pieces *or* ribbons, **put to the sword,** stab to death, jugulate, cut *or* slash the throat; **deal a death blow,** give the quietus *or coup de grâce* <Fr>, silence; knock in *or* on the head; **brain,** blow *or* knock *or* dash one's brains out, poleax; **stone,** lapidate, stone to death; defenestrate; blow up, blow to bits *or* pieces *or* kingdom come, frag; disintegrate, vaporize; burn to death, incinerate, burn at the stake

19 **strangle,** garrote, **throttle, choke,** burke; **suffocate, stifle, smother, asphyxiate,** stop the breath; **drown**

20 **condemn to death,** sign one's death warrant, strike the death knell of, finger <nf>, give the kiss of death to

21 **be killed,** get killed, die a violent death, **come to a violent end,** meet with foul play; welter in one's own blood

22 **commit suicide, take one's own life, kill oneself,** die by one's own hand, do away with oneself, put an end to oneself; blow one's brains out, take an overdose <of a drug>, overdose *or* OD <nf>; commit hara-kiri *or* seppuku; sign one's own death warrant, doom oneself; jump overboard, do oneself in *or* off oneself <nf>

ADJS **23** **deadly, deathly,** deathful, **killing, destructive,** death-dealing, death-bringing, feral , fell; savage, brutal; internecine; **fatal, mortal, lethal, malignant,** malign, **virulent, pernicious,** baneful; **life-threatening, terminal**; capital; incurable, terminal, inoperable

24 **murderous,** slaughterous; cutthroat; redhanded; **homicidal,** man-killing, death-dealing; biocidal, genocidal; suicidal, self-destructive; soul-destroying; cruel; **bloodthirsty,** bloody-minded; **bloody, gory,** sanguinary; psychopathic, pathological

309 INTERMENT

NOUNS 1 **interment, burial,** burying, inhumation, sepulture, **entombment;** encoffinment, inurning, inurnment, urn burial; primary burial; secondary burial, reburial; disposal of the dead; burial *or* funeral *or* funerary customs; mass burial, burial at sea, military burial, full military rites

2 **cremation, incineration, burning,** reduction to ashes, pyre, scattering of the ashes

3 **embalmment,** embalming; mummification

4 **last offices,** last honors, **last rites,** funeral rites, last duty *or* service, funeral service, funeral ceremony, burial service, graveside service, memorial service, exequies, **obsequies;** Office of the Dead, Memento of the Dead, requiem, requiem mass, dirge ; **extreme unction;** viaticum; funeral oration *or* sermon, eulogy; **wake,** deathwatch, Irish wake; lowering the body

5 **funeral, burial,** burying; funeral procession, cortege; dead march, muffled drum, last post <Brit>, taps; dirge; burial at sea, deep six <nf>

6 **knell,** passing bell, death bell, funeral ring, tolling, tolling of the knell, funeral hymn, dirge

7 **mourner, griever, lamenter,** keener; mute, professional mourner; **pallbearer,** bearer; eulogist, eulogizer, elegist, epitaphist, obituarist

8 **undertaker, mortician,** funeral director; embalmer; gravedigger; sexton

9 **mortuary, morgue,** deadhouse , charnel house, lichhouse <Brit nf>; ossuary *or* ossuarium; **funeral home** *or* **parlor,** undertaker's establishment; **crematorium,** crematory, cinerarium; pyre, funeral pile; burning ghat

10 **hearse,** funeral car *or* coach; catafalque

11 **coffin, casket,** burial case, box, kist; wooden kimono *or* overcoat <nf>; **sarcophagus;** mummy case

12 **urn,** cinerary urn, funerary *or* funeral urn *or* vessel, bone pot, ossuary *or* ossuarium, canopic urn *or* jar *or* vase

13 **bier,** litter

14 **graveclothes, shroud,** winding sheet, cerecloth, cerements; pall

15 **graveyard, cemetery, burial ground** *or* **place,** plot, family plot, burying place *or* ground, boneyard *and* bone orchard <nf>, burial yard, necropolis, god's acre, polyandrium, **memorial park,** city *or* village of the dead; **churchyard,** God's acre, final resting place; garden of remembrance *or* rest; **potter's field;** Golgotha, Calvary; urnfield; lychgate; columbarium, cinerarium

16 **tomb, sepulcher; grave,** gravesite, burial, pit, deep six <nf>; resting place; last home, long home, narrow house, house of death, low house, low green tent; **crypt, vault,** burial chamber; ossuary *or* ossuarium; charnel house, bone house; **mausoleum; catacombs;** mastaba; cist grave, box grave, passage grave, shaft grave, beehive tomb; catafalque; **shrine,** reliquary, monstrance, tope, stupa; cenotaph; dokhma, tower of silence; pyramid, mummy chamber; burial mound, tumulus, barrow, cist, cromlech, dolmen, menhir, cairn, tower of silence; grave pit, common grave, mass grave, open grave

17 monument, gravestone 549.12

18 **epitaph,** inscription, *hic jacet* <L>, here lies, Rest in Peace, RIP; tombstone marking

VERBS 19 **inter,** inhume, **bury,** sepulture, inearth , **lay to rest, consign to the grave,** consign to earth, lower the body, lay in the grave *or* earth, lay under the sod, put six feet under <nf>; plant <nf>; tomb, **entomb,** ensepulcher, hearse; enshrine; inurn; encoffin, coffin; hold *or* conduct a funeral

20 **cremate, incinerate, burn,** reduce to ashes, burn on the pyre

21 **lay out; embalm;** mummify; lie in state

ADJS 22 **funereal,** funeral, funerary, funebrial, funebrous *or* funebrious, *funèbre* <Fr>, feral ; burial, mortuary, exequial, obsequial; graveside;

sepulchral, tomblike; cinerary; necrological, obituary, epitaphic; **dismal** 112.24; **mournful** 112.26; dirgelike; memorial, eulogistic, elegiac

ADVS **23** beneath the sod, underground, six feet under <nf>; at rest, resting in peace

PHRS **24** **RIP,** *requiescat in pace* <L singular>, *requiescant in pace* <L plural>, rest in peace; *hic jacet* <L>, *ci-gît* <Fr>, here lies

310 PLANTS

NOUNS **1** **plants, vegetation; flora, plant life,** vegetable life; **vegetable kingdom,** plant kingdom; herbage, flowerage, verdure, greenery, greens, green plants; botany 1068.3; vegetation spirit 1069.4

2 **growth,** stand, crop; plantation, planting; **clump,** tuft, tussock, hassock

3 **plant,** green plant**; vegetable; weed;** seedling; cutting; vascular plant, herbaceous plant; seed plant, spermatophyte; gymnosperm; angiosperm, flowering plant; monocotyledon *or* monocot *or* monocotyl; dicotyledon *or* dicot *or* dicotyl; polycotyledon *or* polycot *or* polycotyl; thallophyte, fungus; gametophyte, sporophyte; exotic, hothouse plant, greenhouse plant; ephemeral, annual, biennial, triennial, perennial; evergreen, deciduous plant; cosmopolite; aquatic plant, hydrophyte, amphibian; cultivated plant, garden plant, houseplant, pot plant; food plant, cereal, vegetable, herb; medicinal plant

4 <varieties> **legume,** pulse, vetch, bean, pea, lentil; **herb**, pot-herb; succulent; **vine**, grapevine, creeper, ivy, climber, liana; **fern**, bracken; **moss; wort,** liverwort; **algae; seaweed,** kelp, sea moss, rockweed, gulfweed, sargasso *or* sargassum, sea lentil, wrack, sea wrack; **fungus,** mold, rust, smut, puffball, mushroom, toad-stool; lichen; parasitic plant, parasite, saprophyte, perthophyte, heterophyte, autophyte; plant families; fruits and vegetables

5 **grass,** gramineous *or* graminaceous plant, pasture *or* forage grass, lawn grass, ornamental grass; aftergrass, fog <nf>; **cereal,** cereal plant, farinaceous plant, **grain,** corn <Brit>; sedge; rush, reed, cane, bamboo

6 **turf, sod, sward,** greensward; divot

7 **green, lawn;** artificial turf, Astroturf <TM>; grassplot, greenyard; grounds; **common, park, village green;** golf course *or* links, fairway; bowling green, putting green; grass court

8 **grassland,** grass; parkland; **meadow,** meadow land, field, mead , swale, lea *or* ley, haugh *or* haughland, vega; crop circle; bottomland, water meadow; **pasture,** pastureland, pasturage, pasture land, park <Brit nf>; **range,** grazing, grazing land; **prairie, savanna,** savannah, **steppe,** steppeland, **pampas,** pampa, campo, llano, **veld** *or* veldt, grass veld, plain, range, champaign, campagna; herbage, verdure; moor, moorland, common, heath, downs, downland, wold

9 **shrubbery; shrub, bush;** scrub, bramble, brier, brier bush; topiary

10 **tree**, timber; shade tree, fruit tree, timber tree; softwood tree, hardwood tree; sapling, seedling; conifer *or* coniferous tree, evergreen; pollard, pollarded tree, standard; deciduous tree, borad-leaved tree; ornamental tree; Christmas tree

11 <tree parts> trunk, bole, gnarl, knot, burl, burr, crown, limb, branch, bough, twig, switch, sprig, spur, leader, leaf, needle, cone, root, tree *or* annual *or* growth ring

12 <tree groupings> **forest**, tree line *or* zone, timberline, jungle, gallery forest, fringing forest, virgin forest, primeval forest, coniferous forest; taiga, woodland, chaparral, plantation, stand, timberland, tree farm, tree nursery, orchard, orangery

13 **woodland, wood, woods, timberland; timber,** stand of timber, **forest,** forest land, forest cover, forest preserve, state *or* national forest; forestry, dendrology, silviculture;

afforestation, reforestation; boondocks <nf>; wildwood, **bush,** scrub; bushveld, tree veld; shrubland, scrubland; pine barrens, palmetto barrens; hanger; **park,** parkland, chase <Brit>; park forest; arboretum; conservation land, nature preserve; primeval forest

14 **grove, woodlet;** holt <nf>, hurst, spinney <Brit>, *tope* <India>, shaw <nf>, bosk ; **orchard;** wood lot; coppice, copse; *bocage* <Fr>

15 **thicket,** thickset, **copse, coppice,** copsewood, frith <Brit nf>; bosket *or* bosquet , boscage; covert; motte; **brake,** canebrake; chaparral; chamisal; ceja

16 **brush, scrub,** bush, **brushwood,** shrubwood, scrubwood, shrub

17 **undergrowth, underwood, underbrush,** copsewood, undershrubs, boscage, frith <Brit nf>; ground cover, tree litter, leaf litter, leaf mold, covert

18 **foliage, leafage,** leafiness, umbrage, foliation; frondage, frondescence; vernation; greenery

19 **leaf, frond;** leaflet, foliole; ligule; lamina, **blade,** leaf blade, spear, spire, pile, flag; **needle,** pine needle; floral leaf, **petal,** sepal; bract, bractlet, bracteole, spathe, involucre, involucrum, glume, lemma; cotyledon, seed leaf; stipule, stipula; scale leaf, modified leaf

20 **branch,** fork, **limb, bough;** deadwood; **twig, sprig,** switch; spray; **shoot,** offshoot, spear, frond; scion; **sprout,** sprit, slip, burgeon, thallus; sucker; **runner,** stolon, flagellum, sarmentum, sarment; bine; **tendril;** ramage; branchiness, branchedness, ramification

21 **stem, stalk, stock,** axis, *caulis* <L>; **trunk,** bole; spear, spire; straw; reed; cane; culm, haulm <Brit>; caudex; footstalk, pedicel, peduncle; leafstalk, petiole, petiolus, petiolule; seedstalk; caulicle; tigella; funicule, funiculus; stipe, anthrophore, carpophore, gynophore

22 **root,** radix, radicle; rootlet; **taproot,** tap; **rhizome,** rootstock; **tuber,** tubercle, tuberous root, root tuber; **bulb,** bulbil, corm, earthnut; lateral root, prop root, aerial root

23 **bud,** burgeon, gemma; leaf bud, foliage bud; apical bud, terminal bud, axillary bud, lateral bud, resting bud; gemmule, gemmula; plumule, acrospire; leaf bud, flower bud

24 **flower, posy, blossom, bloom,** blow ; floweret, floret, floscule; **wildflower;** garden flower, pot plant, cut flowers; **gardening,** horticulture, floriculture; hortorium; community garden

25 **bouquet, nosegay, posy,** boughpot, flower arrangement; **boutonniere,** buttonhole <Brit>; **corsage; spray; wreath;** festoon; **garland,** daisy chain, chaplet, lei; dried flower, pressed flower

26 **flowering,** florescence, efflorescence, flowerage, **blossoming, blooming;** inflorescence; **blossom, bloom,** blowing, blow, full blow; unfolding, unfoldment; anthesis, full bloom

27 <types of inflorescence> flower head; raceme, corymb, umbel, panicle, cyme, thyrse *or* thyrsus, verticillaster, spadix, verticillaster; head, capitulum; spike, spikelet; ament, catkin; strobile, cone, pine cone; ray flower, disk flower, cymose inflorescnce

28 <flower parts> petal, perianth, floral envelope; calyx, epicalyx, sepal; nectary; corolla, corolla tube, corona; androecium, anther, stamen, microsporophyll; pistil, gynoecium, ovary, ovule, micrypyle; style; stigma, carpel, megasporophyll; receptacle, torus; involucre, bract, whorl, spathe; pollen, pollen grain, pollen sac, pollen tube

29 **ear,** spike; auricle; ear of corn, mealie; **cob,** corncob

30 **seed vessel, seedcase,** seedbox, pericarp; hull, husk; **capsule, pod,** cod <nf>, seed pod, seed coat; pease cod, legume, legumen, boll, burr, follicle, silique

31 **seed; stone, pit, nut;** pip; fruit; **grain, kernel, berry;** flaxseed, linseed; hayseed; bird seed

32 **vegetation, growth;** germination, pullulation; burgeoning, sprouting; budding, luxuriation

33 <garden plants> seedling, cutting, bulb, corm, rhizome, tuber; rock plant, alpine plant, bedding plant, creeper, ground cover, turf, climber *or* climbing plant, rambler; annual, biennial, perennial; herb, flower, woody plant, succulent

VERBS **34 vegetate, grow;** germinate, pullulate; root, take root, strike root; sprout up, shoot up, upsprout, up spear; **burgeon,** put forth, burst forth; **sprout,** shoot; **bud,** gemmate, put forth *or* put out buds; **leaf,** leave, leaf out, put out *or* put forth leaves; flourish, luxuriate, riot, grow rank *or* lush; overgrow, overrun; run to seed, dehisce; photosynthesize, change color

35 flower, be in flower, **blossom, bloom,** bud, be in bloom, blow, effloresce, floreate, burst into bloom, flourish, burgeon

ADJS **36 vegetable,** vegetal, vegetative, vegetational, vegetarian; **plantlike; herbaceous,** herbal, herbous, herbose, herby; leguminous, leguminose, leguminiform; cereal, farinaceous; weedy; fruity, fruitlike; tuberous, bulbous; rootlike, rhizoid, radicular, radicated, radiciform; botanic, botanical; green, grassy, leafy, verdant

37 algal, fucoid, confervoid; phytoplanktonic, diatomaceous; fungous, fungoid, fungiform

38 floral; flowery, florid ; **flowered,** floreate, floriate, floriated; **flowering, blossoming, blooming,** abloom, bloomy, florescent, inflorescent, efflorescent, in flower, in bloom, in blossom; uniflorous, multiflorous; radiciflorous, rhizanthous; **garden,** horticultural, hortulan, floricultural; flowerlike

39 arboreal, arborical, arboresque, arboreous, arborary, arboraceous; **treelike,** arboriform, arborescent, dendroid, dendroidal, dendriform, dendritic; deciduous, nondeciduous; evergreen; softwood, hardwood; piny *or* piney; coniferous; citrous; palmate, palmaceous; **bosky,** bushy, shrubby, scrubby, scrubbly; bushlike, shrublike, scrublike

40 sylvan, silvan, sylvatic, **woodland, forest,** forestal; dendrologic, dendrological, silvicultural, afforestational, reforestational, reforested; tree-covered; **wooded,** timbered, forested, afforested, timbered, arboreous; **woody,** woodsy, bosky, bushy, shrubby, scrubby; copsy, braky; ligneous, ligniform

41 leafy, leavy , bowery; foliated, foliate, foliose, foliaged, leaved; **branched,** branchy, branching, ramified, ramate, ramous *or* ramose; twiggy

42 verdant, verdurous, verdured; **mossy,** moss-covered, moss-grown; **grassy,** grasslike, gramineous, graminaceous; turfy, swardy, turflike, caespitose, tufted; meadowy

43 luxuriant, flourishing, **rank, lush,** riotous, exuberant; dense, impenetrable, thick, heavy, gross; jungly, jungled; overgrown, overrun; **weedy,** unweeded, weed-choked, weed-ridden; gone to seed

44 perennial, ephemeral; hardy, half-hardy; **deciduous,** evergreen

311 ANIMALS, INSECTS

NOUNS **1 animal life, animal kingdom,** brute creation, **fauna,** Animalia <zoology>, animality; animal behavior, biology ; birds, beasts, and fish; the beasts of the field, the fowl of the air, and the fish of the sea; domestic animals, livestock, stock <nf>, cattle; wild animals *or* beasts, beasts of field, wildlife, denizens of the forest *or* jungle *or* wild, furry creatures; predators, beasts of prey; game, big game, small game; animal rights

2 animal, creature, critter <nf>, living being *or* thing, creeping thing; **brute, beast,** varmint <nf>, dumb animal *or* creature, dumb friend, furry friend, four-legged friend, critter <nf>; pet, companion animal, animal companion

3 <varieties> **vertebrate; invertebrate; biped, quadruped; mammal, mammalian, primate**, warm-blooded animal; chordate; **marsupial,** marsupialian; canine; **feline; rodent,** gnawer; **ungulate; ruminant;** insectivore, herbivore, carnivore, omnivore; cannibal; scavenger; reptile; amphibian; fish; aquatic; bird; cosmopolite; vermin, varmint <nf>; zooid, protist, protozoan; worm, mollusk, gastropod, arthropod, insect, arachnid; parasite, scavenger, predator, grazer; **fungi**

4 **pachyderm; elephant,** Jumbo, hathi <India>; mammoth, woolly mammoth; mastodon; **rhinoceros,** rhino; **hippopotamus,** hippo, river horse; subungulate, proboscidean, Proboscidea

5 <hoofed animals> ungulate, ungulant; odd-toed ungulate, perissodactyl; even-toed ungulate, artiodactyl; **deer, buck, doe, fawn;** red deer, **stag,** hart, hind; roe deer, roe, roebuck; musk deer; fallow deer; hog-deer; white-tailed *or* Virginia deer; mule deer; **elk,** wapiti; **moose; reindeer,** caribou; deerlet; **antelope;** gazelle, kaama, wildebeest *or* gnu, hartebeest, springbok, reebok, dik-dik, eland *or* Cape elk, koodoo; **camel,** dromedary, ship of the desert; **giraffe,** camelopard, okapi; equine, equid, horse; pig, hog, swine; camel, llama; goat, sheep

6 **cattle**, kine <old pl>, neat; beef cattle, beef, beeves <pl>; dairy cattle *or* cows; bovine animal, **bovine,** critter <nf>; **cow,** moo-cow *and* bossy <nf>; milk *or* milch cow, milker, milcher, dairy cow; **bull,** bullock, top cow <nf>; **steer,** stot <Brit nf>, **ox,** oxen <pl>; **calf, heifer,** yearling, fatling, stirk <Brit>; **dogie** *and* leppy <W US>; maverick <W US>; hornless cow, butthead *and* muley head <nf>, muley cow; zebu, Brahman; yak; musk-ox; **buffalo,** water buffalo, Indian buffalo, carabao; bison, aurochs, wisent

7 **sheep**; **lamb,** lambkin, yeanling; teg <Brit>; **ewe,** yow <nf>; ewe lamb; **ram,** tup <Brit>, wether; bellwether; mutton

8 **goat;** he-goat, buck, **billy goat** *and* billy <nf>; she-goat, doe, **nanny goat** *and* nanny <nf>; **kid,** doeling; mountain goat

9 **swine**, **pig, hog,** porker; **shoat,** piggy, piglet, pigling; sucking *or* suckling pig; gilt; **boar, sow;** barrow; wild boar, tusker, razorback; warthog, babirusa

10 **horse;** horseflesh, hoss <nf>, critter <nf>; **equine,** mount, **nag** <nf>; **steed,** prancer, dobbin; charger, courser, war-horse, destrier ; Houyhnhnm <Jonathan Swift>; **colt,** foal, filly; **mare,** brood mare; **stallion, studhorse, stud,** top horse <nf>, entire horse, entire; gelding, purebred horse, thoroughbred, blood horse; wild horse, Przewalsky's horse, tarpan; **pony,** Shetland pony, Shetland, shelty, Iceland pony, Galloway, cob; **bronco,** bronc, range horse, Indian pony, cayuse, mustang; bucking bronco, buckjumper, sunfisher, broomtail; cowcutting horse, stock horse, roping horse, cow pony, circus horse

11 <colored horses> appaloosa, bay, blood bay, bayard, chestnut, liver chestnut, gray, dapple-gray, black, grizzle, roan, sorrel, dun, buckskin, pinto, paint, piebald, skewbald, palomino, seal brown, strawberry roan, calico pony, painted pony

12 <inferior horse> **nag, plug,** hack, jade, crock, garron <Scot,Ir>, crowbait <nf>, scalawag, rosinante; goat *and* stiff *and* dog <nf>; roarer, whistler; balky horse, balker, jughead; rogue; rackabones, scrag, stack of bones

13 **workhorse,** plow horse, beast of burden; **hunter;** stalking-horse; **saddle horse,** saddler, rouncy , steed, **riding horse,** rider, palfrey, **mount;** remount; polo pony; post-horse; cavalry horse; **driving horse,** road horse, roadster, carriage horse, coach horse, gigster; hack, hackney; **draft horse,** dray horse, cart horse, shaft horse, pole horse, thill horse, thiller, fill horse *or* filler <nf>; wheelhorse, wheeler, lead, leader; pack horse, jument , sumpter, sumpter horse, bidet; pit-pony; cow pony; war-horse

14 **race horse; show-horse, gaited horse,** racer, galloper, trotter, pacer, sidewheeler <nf>; stepper, high-stepper, cob, prancer, turf horse,

sprinter; ambler, padnag, pad; racker; single-footer; steeplechaser; bangtail <nf>

15 **ass, donkey, burro,** neddy *or* cuddy <Brit nf>, moke <Brit nf>, Rocky Mountain canary <W US>; **jackass,** jack, dickey <Brit nf>; jenny, jenny ass, jennet; **mule,** sumpter mule, sumpter; hinny, jennet

16 **dog, canine, pooch** *and* bow-wow <nf>; **pup, puppy,** puppy dog *and* perp <nf>, **whelp;** bitch, gyp, slut; toy dog, lap dog; working dog; ratter; watchdog, bandog; sheep dog, shepherd *or* shepherd's dog; hound; Seeing Eye dog, guide dog; guard dog, watchdog; police dog, sled dog; gazehound, sight-hound; show dog, fancy dog, toy dog; man's best friend <nf>, bow-wow, pooch; kennel, pack of dogs

17 sporting dog, **hunting dog,** hunter, field dog, bird dog, gundog, water dog, hound, courser, setter, pointer, spaniel, retriever

18 **cur, mongrel,** lurcher <Brit>, tyke, **mutt** <nf>; pariah dog

19 **fox,** reynard; **wolf,** timber wolf, lobo <W US>, **coyote,** brush wolf, prairie wolf, medicine wolf <W US>; dingo, jackal, **hyena;** Cape hunting dog, African hunting dog

20 **cat, feline,** pussy *and* **puss** *and* **pussycat** <nf>, domestic cat, house cat, tabby, grimalkin; house cat; **kitten, kitty** *and* kitty-cat <nf>; kit, kitling <Brit nf>; **tomcat,** tom; gib *or* gib-cat <Brit nf>; mouser; ratter; Cheshire cat, Chessycat <nf>; silver cat, Chinchilla cat; blue cat, Maltese cat; tiger cat, tabby cat; tortoise-shell cat, calico cat; alley cat; Morris

21 <wild cats> **big cat, jungle cat; lion,** Leo <nf>, *simba* <Swah>; **tiger,** Siberian tiger; **leopard,** panther, jaguar, cheetah; cougar, puma, mountain lion, catamount *or* cat-a-mountain; lynx, ocelot; wildcat, bobcat, steppe cat, Pallas's cat

22 <wild animals> **bear,** bar <nf>; guinea pig, cavy; hedgehog, **porcupine,** quill pig <nf>; woodchuck, **groundhog, whistle-pig** <nf>; prairie dog, prairie squirrel; **raccoon,** coon; **opossum,** possum; **weasel,** mousehound <Brit>; **wolverine,** glutton; ferret, monk <nf>; **skunk,** polecat <nf>; zoril, stink cat, Cape polecat; foumart; **primate, simian; ape; monkey,** chimpanzee, chimp

23 **hare,** leveret, jackrabbit; **rabbit, bunny** *and* bunny rabbit <nf>, lapin; cottontail; Belgian hare, leporide; buck, doe

24 **reptile,** reptilian; **lizard;** saurian, dinosaur; crocodile, crocodilian, alligator, gator <nf>; tortoise, turtle, terrapin; cold-blooded animal, poikilotherm, Reptilia, Squamata, Rhynchocephalia, Crocodilia

25 **serpent, snake,** ophidian; **viper,** pit viper; sea snake

26 **amphibian,** batrachian, croaker, paddock <nf>; **frog,** rani-, tree toad *or* frog, bullfrog; **toad,** hoptoad *or* hoppytoad; newt, salamander; **tadpole, polliwog;** caecilian, apodan, urodele, caudate, salientian, anuran

27 **bird, fowl;** dicky-bird *and* birdy *and* birdie <nf>; fowls of the air, birdlife, avifauna, Aves, feathered friends; baby bird, chick, nestling, fledgling; wildfowl, game bird; waterfowl, water bird, wading bird, diving bird; sea bird; shore bird; migratory bird, migrant, bird of passage; **songbird,** oscine bird, warbler, passerine bird, perching bird; cage bird; flightless bird, ratite; seed-eating bird, insect-eating bird, fruit-eating bird, fish-eating bird; **raptor,** bird of prey; **eagle,** bird of Jove, eaglet; **hawk, falcon; owl,** bird of Minerva, bird of night; peafowl, peahen, **peacock,** bird of Juno; **swan,** cygnet; **pigeon, dove,** squab; stormy *or* storm petrel, Mother Carey's chicken; fulmar, Mother Carey's goose

28 **poultry, fowl,** domestic fowl, barnyard fowl, barn-door fowl, dunghill fowl; **chicken,** chick, chicky *and* chickabiddy <nf>; **cock, rooster,** chanticleer; **hen,** biddy <nf>, partlet; cockerel, pullet; setting hen, brooder, broody hen; capon, poulard; broiler, fryer, spring chicken, chicklet; roaster, stewing chicken; Bantam, banty <nf>; game fowl;

guinea fowl, guinea cock, guinea hen; **goose,** gander, gosling; **duck,** drake, duckling; **turkey,** gobbler, turkey gobbler; turkey-cock, tom, tom turkey; hen turkey; poult

29 marine animal, denizen of the deep; **whale,** cetacean; **porpoise, dolphin,** sea pig; **sea serpent,** sea snake, Loch Ness monster, sea monster, Leviathan <Bible>; **fish,** game fish, tropical fish, panfish; **shark,** man-eating shark, man-eater; **salmon,** kipper, grilse, smolt, parr, alevin; **minnow** *or* minny <nf>, fry, fingerling; **sponge; plankton,** zooplankton, nekton, benthon, benthos, zoobenthos; **crustacean,** lobster, spiny lobster, **crab,** blueclaw, Dungeness crab, king crab, spider crab, land crab, stone crab, soft-shell crab; crayfish *or* crawfish *or* crawdaddy; **mollusc,** wentletrap, whelk, snail, cockle, mussel, **clam, oyster,** razor clam, quahog, steamer, toheroa, tridachna *or* giant clam

30 **fish;** saltwater fish, marine fish, freshwater fish; jawless fish, cyclostome, cartilaginous fish, elasmobranch, selachian, holocephalan, bony fish, lobe-finned fish, crossopterygian, dipnoan, ray-finned fish, teleost fish, flying fish, mouthbreeder, flatfish; food fish, game fish, aquarium fish, tropical fish, fossil fish; shoal, school

31 **invertebrate;** lower animal, protochordate, echinoderm, arthropod, arachnid, insect, crustacean, myriapod, mollusk, worm, coelenterate, sponge, protozoan *or* protozoon

32 **insect, bug; beetle;** arthropod; hexapod, myriapod; centipede, chilopod; millipede, diplopod; social insect; **mite; arachnid, spider,** tarantula, black widow spider, daddy longlegs *or* harvestman; **scorpion; tick;** larva, maggot, nymph, **caterpillar;** winged insect, **fly,** gnat, midge, mosquito, dragonfly, butterfly, moth, bee, wasp; creepy-crawly <nf>, pest

33 **ant,** emmet <nf>, pismire, pissant *and* antymire <nf>; red ant, black ant, fire ant, house ant, agricultural ant, carpenter ant, army ant; slave ant, slave-making ant; **termite,** white ant; queen, worker, soldier

34 **bee,** honeybee, bumblebee, carpenter bee; queen, queen bee, worker, drone, Africanized bee; **wasp; hornet,** yellow jacket

35 **locust,** acridian; **grasshopper,** hopper, hoppergrass <nf>; **cricket;** cicada, cicala, dog-day cicada, seventeen-year locust; stick insect, mantis

36 **vermin;** parasite; **louse,** head louse, body louse, grayback, cootie <nf>; crab, crab louse; weevil; nit; **flea,** sand flea, dog flea, cat flea, chigoe, chigger, jigger, red bug, mite, harvest mite; **roach, cockroach,** *cucaracha* <Sp>; tick, mosquito

37 bloodsucker, parasite; **leech; tick,** wood tick, deer tick; **mosquito,** skeeter <nf>, culex; bedbug, housebug <Brit>

38 **worm;** earthworm, angleworm, fishworm, night crawler, nightwalker; measuring worm, inchworm; tapeworm, helminth

ADJS **39** **animal,** animalian, animalic, animalistic, animal-like, theriomorphic, zoic, zooidal; zoologic, zoological; **brutish, brutal,** brute, brutelike; **bestial, beastly,** beastlike; **wild,** feral; subhuman, soulless; dumb; instinctual *or* instinctive, mindless, nonrational; half-animal, half-human, anthropomorphic, therianthropic

40 **vertebrate,** chordate, mammalian; viviparous; marsupial, cetacean

41 **canine,** doggish, doggy, doglike; vulpine, foxy, foxlike; lupine, wolfish, wolflike

42 **feline,** felid, cattish, catty, catlike; kittenish; leonine, lionlike; tigerish, tigerlike

43 ursine, bearish, bearlike

44 **rodent,** rodential; verminous; mousy, mouselike; ratty, ratlike

45 ungulate, hoofed, hooved; **equine,** hippic, horsy, horselike; **equestrian;** asinine, mulish; bovid, ruminant; **bovine,** cowlike, cowish; bull-like, bullish, taurine; cervine, deerlike; caprine, caprid, hircine, goatish, goatlike; ovine, sheepish, sheeplike; porcine, swinish, piggish, hoggish

46 elephantlike, elephantine, pachydermous

47 **reptile,** reptilian, **reptilelike,** reptiloid, reptiliform; reptant, repent, creeping, crawling, slithering; **lizardlike,** saurian; crocodilian; **serpentine,** serpentile, serpentoid, serpentiform, **serpentlike; snakish, snaky, snakelike,** colubrine, ophidian, anguine ; viperish, viperous, vipery, viperine, viperoid, viperiform, viperlike; amphibian, batrachian, froggy, toadish, salamandrian

48 **birdlike,** birdy; avian, avicular; gallinaceous, rasorial; oscine, passerine, perching; columbine, columbaceous, dovelike; psittacine; aquiline, hawklike; anserine, anserous, goosy; nidificant, nesting, nest-building; nidicolous, altricial; nidifugous, precocial

49 **fishlike,** fishy; piscine, pisciform; piscatorial, piscatory; eellike; selachian, sharklike, sharkish

50 **invertebrate,** invertebral; protozoan, protozoal, protozoic; crustaceous, crustacean; molluscan, molluscoid

51 **insectile, insectlike,** buggy; verminous; lepidopterous, lepidopteran; weevily

52 **wormlike,** vermicular, vermiform; wormy

53 planktonic, nektonic, benthonic, zooplanktonic, zoobenthoic

312 HUMANKIND

NOUNS **1** **humankind, mankind, womankind,** personkind, **man,** human species, **human race,** race of man, human family, the family of man, **humanity,** human beings, mortals, earthlings, mortality, flesh, mortal flesh, clay; generation of man , *le genre humain* <Fr>, homo, genus Homo, **Homo sapiens,** Hominidae, hominids; archaic Homo; **race,** strain, stock, subrace, infrarace, subspecies; **culture** 373.2; ethnic group; ethnicity, ethnicism, roots <nf>; **society,** speech community, **ethnic group;** community, folk, persons, **the people, the populace**, world population**; nationality, nation**

2 <races of humankind> **Caucasoid** *or* **Caucasian** *or* **white race;** Nordic subrace, Alpine subrace, Mediterranean subrace; dolichocephalic people, brachycephalic people; xanthochroi, melanochroi; Archaic Caucasoid *or* archaic white *or* Australoid race; Polynesian race; **Negroid** *or* **black race;** Nilotic race, Melanesian race, Papuan race; Pygmoid race; Bushman race; **Mongoloid** *or* **Mongolian** *or* **yellow race;** Malayan *or* Malaysian *or* brown race; prehistoric races; majority, racial *or* ethnic majority; minority, racial *or* ethnic minority; persons of color

3 **Caucasian, white man** *or* **woman, white person,** paleface *and* ofay *and* the Man *and* Mister Charley *and* whitey *and* honky <nf>; Australian aborigine; **Negro, black man** *or* **woman, black,** colored person, person of color, darky *and* spade *and* nigger <nf>; African-American; negritude, Afroism, blackness; pygmy, Negrito, Negrillo; Bushman; **Native American,** Indian, American Indian, Amerindian, Amerind, Red Indian <Brit>, red man *or* woman; injun *and* redskin <nf>; Latino; Mongolian, yellow man *or* woman, **Oriental,** Asian**;** gook *and* slant-eye <nf>; Malayan, brown man; mixed race, mulatto, quadroon, half-breed

4 **the people** 606, the populace, the population, the public, the world, everyone, everybody

5 **person, human, human being, man, woman, child,** member of the human race *or* family, Adamite, daughter of Eve; ethnic; **mortal,** life, **soul,** living soul; **being,** creature, fellow creature, clay, ordinary clay, flesh and blood, the naked ape, the noble animal; **individual**; personage, **personality, personhood,** individuality; **body;** somebody, one, someone; earthling, groundling, terran, worldling, tellurian; **ordinary person;** head, hand, nose; fellow <nf> 76.5; gal <nf> 77.6

6 **human nature, humanity;** frail *or* fallen humanity, Adam, the generation of Adam, Adam's seed *or* offspring
7 **God's image, lord of creation,** God's creation; homo faber, symbol-using animal, rational animal, animal capable of reason
8 **humanness, humanity,** mortality; **human nature,** the way you are; **frailty,** human frailty, human fallibility, weakness, **human weakness,** weakness of the flesh, flesh, the weaknesses human flesh is heir to; human equation
9 humanization, humanizing; **anthropomorphism,** pathetic fallacy, anthropopathism, anthropomorphology
10 **anthropology,** science of man; social studies, cultural studies; cultural anthropology, physical anthropology, anthropogeny, anthropography, anthropogeography, human geography, demography, human ecology, anthropometry, craniometry, craniology, ethnology, ethnography, paleoanthropology, paleoethnology; material culture; behavioral science, sociology, social anthropology, social psychology, psychology 92; anatomy; **anthropologist,** ethnologist, ethnographer; sociologist; demographics, population study, population statistics; demographer
11 **humanism;** naturalistic humanism, scientific humanism, secular humanism; religious humanism; Christian humanism, integral humanism; new humanism; anthroposophy
VERBS 12 **humanize,** anthropomorphize, make human, civilize
ADJS 13 **human;** hominal; creaturely, creatural; Adamite *or* Adamitic; **frail, weak,** fleshly, finite, **mortal; only human;** earthborn, of the earth, earthy, tellurian, unangelic; humanistic; man-centered, homocentric, anthropocentric; anthropological, ethnographic, ethnological; demographic, epigraphic; social, societal, sociological
14 **manlike, anthropoid,** humanoid, hominid; anthropomorphic, anthropopathic, therioanthropic
15 **personal, individual,** private, peculiar, idiosyncratic; person-to-person, one-to-one, one-on-one
16 **public, general, common; communal, societal, social;** civic, civil; **national,** state; international, cosmopolitan, supernational, supranational
ADVS 17 **humanly,** mortally, after the manner of men

313 SEASON

<time of year>

NOUNS 1 **season,** time of year, season of the year, **period,** annual period; dry *or* rainy *or* cold season, monsoon; theatrical *or* opera *or* concert season; **social season,** the season; dead *or* off-season; baseball season, football season, basketball season, hunting season, preseason, etc; open season, closed season; seasonality, periodicity 850.2; **seasonableness** 843.1; seasonal affective disorder *or* SAD
2 **spring,** springtide, **springtime,** seedtime *or* budtime, Maytime, Eastertide; *primavera* <Ital>, prime, prime of the year, vernal equinox
3 **summer,** summertide, **summertime,** good old summertime; growing season; midsummer; **dog days,** canicular days; the silly season, high summer; summer solstice; estivation
4 **autumn, fall,** fall of the year, fall of the leaf, harvest, harvest time, harvest home; autumnal equinox
5 **Indian summer,** St Martin's summer, St Luke's summer, little summer of St Luke, St Austin's *or* St Augustine's summer
6 **winter,** wintertide, **wintertime**; midwinter; Christmastime *or* Christmastide, Yule *or* Yuletide; winter solstice; hibernation
7 **equinox,** vernal equinox, autumnal equinox; **solstice,** summer solstice, winter solstice
VERBS 8 summer, winter, overwinter, spend *or* pass the spring, summer, etc; hibernate, estivate
ADJS 9 **seasonal,** in *or* out of season, in season and out of season, off-season; early-season, mid-season,

late-season; **spring,** springlike, vernal; **summer,** summery, summerly, summerlike, canicular, aestival; midsummer; **autumn,** autumnal; **winter,** wintry, wintery, hibernal, hiemal, brumal, boreal, arctic 1023.14, winterlike, snowy, icy; midwinter; equinoctial, solstitial, periodic

314 MORNING, NOON

NOUNS **1 morning,** morn, morningtide, morning time, morntime, matins, morrow , waking time, reveille, get-up time <nf>, **forenoon;** *ante meridiem* <L> *or* **AM,** Ack Emma <Brit old>; this morning, this AM <nf>; early bird; breakfast time

2 Morning, Aurora, Eos

3 dawn, the dawn of day, dawning, **daybreak,** dayspring, day-peep, **sunrise, sunup** <nf>, cockcrowing *or* cocklight <Brit nf>, light 1025, first light, daylight, aurora; **break of day,** peep of day, **crack of dawn,** prime, prime of the morning, first blush *or* flush of the morning, brightening *or* first brightening; chanticleer *or* chantecler

4 foredawn, twilight, morning twilight, half-light, glow, dawnlight, first light, crepuscule, aurora; **the small hours;** alpenglow

5 noon, noonday, noontide, nooning <nf>, noontime, **high noon, midday,** midsun, meridian, *meridiem* <L>, twelve o'clock, 1200 hours, eight bells; noonlight; meridian devil *or daemonium meridianum* <L>**;** lunchtime; sext

ADJS **6 morning,** matin, matinal, matutinal, **antemeridian;** auroral, dawn, dawning; forenoon

7 noon, noonday, noonish, **midday,** meridian, twelve-o'clock, highnoon; noonlit

ADVS **8 in the morning,** before noon, mornings <nf>; at sunrise, at dawn, at dawn of day, at cockcrow, at first light, **at the crack** *or* **break of dawn;** with the sun, with the lark

9 at noon, at midday, at twelve-o'clock sharp

315 EVENING, NIGHT

NOUNS **1 afternoon,** *post meridiem* <L> *or* **PM;** this afternoon, this aft <nf>, this PM <nf>; matinee; siesta

2 evening, eve, even, evensong time *or* hour, **eventide,** vesper, crepuscle; **close of day,** decline *or* fall of day, shut of day, gray of the evening, grayness 39, evening's close, when day is done; **nightfall, sunset, sundown,** setting sun, going down of the sun, cockshut *and* cockshut time *and* cockshut light <nf>, retreat; shank of the afternoon *or* evening <nf>, the cool of the evening; cocktail hour, suppertime, dinnertime

3 dusk, dusking time *or* -tide, dusk-dark *and* dust-dark *and* dusty-dark <nf>, **twilight,** evening twilight, crepuscule, crepuscular light, gloam, **gloaming,** glooming; duskiness, duskishness, brown of dusk, brownness 40, candlelight, candlelighting, owllight *or* owl's light, cocklight <Brit nf>

4 night, nighttime, nighttide, lights-out, taps, bedtime, sleepy time <nf>, **darkness** 1027, blackness 38; dark of night

5 eleventh hour, curfew

6 midnight, dead of night, hush of night, the witching hour; midnight hours, small *or* wee small hours; late-night *or* midnight supper *or* snack

ADJS **7 afternoon,** postmeridian

8 evening, evensong, vesper, vespertine *or* vespertinal, vesperal; **twilight,** twilighty, twilit, crepuscular; **dusk,** dusky, duskish

9 nocturnal, night, **nightly,** nighttime; nightlong, all-night; nightfallen; midnight

10 benighted, night-overtaken

ADVS **11 nightly,** nights <nf>, at *or* by night; **overnight,** through the night, all through the night, nightlong, the whole night, all night

316 RAIN

NOUNS **1 rain, rainfall,** fall, **precipitation,** precip <nf>, moisture, wet, rainwater, raininess; **shower,**

sprinkle, flurry, patter, pitter-patter, splatter, intermittent rain *or* showers; streams of rain, sheet of rain, splash *or* spurt of rain, fine rain, light rain, occasional rain *or* showers, April showers, sun shower; **drizzle,** mizzle; **mist,** misty rain, Scotch mist; evening mist; fog drip; blood rain; raindrop, unfrozen hydrometeor; acid rain

2 **rainstorm,** brash *and* scud; **cloudburst,** rainburst, burst of rain, torrent of rain, torrential rain *or* downpour; waterspout, spout, rainspout, **downpour,** downflow, downfall, pour, pouring *or* pelting *or* teeming *or* drowning rain, spate, plash <nf>, **deluge, flood,** heavy rain, driving *or* gushing rain, drenching *or* soaking rain, drencher, soaker, gullywasher, pluviosity, goosedrownder <nf>, lovely weather for ducks

3 **thunderstorm,** thundersquall, thundergust, thundershower; electric storm

4 **wet weather, raininess,** rainy weather, stormy *or* dirty weather, rainy season, cat-and-dog weather <nf>, spell of rain, wet; rainy day; **rains,** rainy *or* wet season, spring rains, **monsoon;** predominance of Aquarius, reign of St Swithin; flood

5 **rainmaking,** seeding, cloud seeding, nucleation, artificial nucleation; **rainmaker,** rain doctor, cloud seeder; dry ice, silver iodide

6 Jupiter Pluvius, Zeus; Thor

7 **rain gauge,** pluviometer, pluvioscope, pluviograph; ombrometer, ombrograph; udometer, udomograph; hyetometer, hyetometrograph, hyetograph

8 **rainbow,** arc, double rainbow, primary rainbow, seconary rainbow, fogdog, fogbow *or* white rainbow, mistbow *or* seadog

9 <science of precipitation> hydrometeorology, hyetology, hyetography; pluviography, pluviometry, ombrology

VERBS **10 rain, precipitate,** rain down, fall; weep; **shower,** shower down; **sprinkle,** spit *and* spritz <nf>, spatter, patter, pitter-patter, plash; **drizzle,** mizzle; **pour,** stream, stream down, pour with rain, **pelt,** pelt down, drum, tattoo, come down in torrents *or* sheets *or* buckets *or* curtains, **rain cats and dogs** <nf>, rain tadpoles *or* bullfrogs *or* pitchforks *or* buckets <nf>; rainmake, seed clouds

ADJS **11 rainy, showery;** pluvious *or* pluviose *or* pluvial; **drizzly,** drizzling, mizzly, drippy; **misty,** misty-moisty; torrential, pouring, streaming, pelting, drumming, driving, blinding, cat-and-doggish <nf>; wet

12 pluviometric *or* pluvioscopic *or* pluviographic, ombrometric *or* ombrographic, udometric *or* udographic, hyetometric, hyetographic, hyetometrographic; hydrometeorological, hyetological

317 AIR, WEATHER

NOUNS **1 air;** ether; ozone <nf>; thin air, rarity

2 **atmosphere;** aerosphere, gaseous envelope *or* environment *or* medium *or* blanket, welkin, lift <nf>; biosphere, ecosphere, noosphere; air mass; atmospheric component, atmospheric gas; atmospheric layer *or* stratum *or* belt

3 **weather, climate,** clime; **the elements,** forces of nature; microclimate, macroclimate, aerology; weather situation, weather pattern, weather conditions; fair weather, calm weather, halcyon days, good weather; stormy weather 671.4; rainy weather 316.4; windiness 318.14; heat wave, hot weather 1019.7; cold wave, cold weather 1023.3

4 <weather terms> weather map; isobar, isobaric *or* isopiestic line; isotherm, isothermal line; isometric, isometric line; frontal system; high, high-pressure area, ridge; low, low-pressure area; front, wind-shift line, squall line; cold front, polar front, cold sector; warm front; occluded front, occlusion, stationary front; air mass; thermal, downdraft, updraft; cyclone, anticyclone; air pressure, air temperature, heat index, temperature-humidity index, dew-

point; humidity, relative humidity; precipitation; wind speed, wind strength, chill factor, wind-chill factor; ambient temperature; climate change

5 **meteorology,** weather science, aerology, aerography, air-mass analysis, weatherology, climatology, climatography, microclimatology, forecasting, long-range forecasting; barometry; pneumatics 1039.5; anemology 318.15; nephology 319.5 anemometry, anemology, hyetography, nephology, micrometeorology, macrometeorology, mesometeorology, agricultural meteorology, aviation meteorology, maritime meteorology, hydrometeorology, mountain meteorology, planetary meteorology, atmospheric physics

6 **meteorologist,** weather scientist, aerologist, aerographer, weatherologist; climatologist, microclimatologist; **weatherman, weather forecaster,** weather prophet; **weather report,** weather forecast; weather bureau; weather ship; weather station; weather-reporting network

7 weather forecast, forecast, weather report, regional forecast, local forecast, general outlook, travel report, boating report, small craft advisory, long-term forecast, 5-day forecast, storm watch *or* warning, tornado watch *or* warning, hurricane watch *or* warning

8 weather instrument, meteorological *or* aerological instrument; **barometer,** aneroid barometer, glass, weatherglass; barograph, barometrograph, recording barometer, mercury barometer; thermometer, thermograph; aneroidograph; vacuometer; hygrometer; wind gauge, anemometer, anemograph, wind sock, wind cone, wind sleeve, drogue, weathercock; rain gauge, pluviometer, udometer; weather balloon, radiosonde; weather satellite, weather radar; hurricane-hunter aircraft; weather vane 318.16

9 **ventilation,** cross-ventilation, **airing,** aerage, perflation, refreshment; fanning, **aeration; air conditioning,** central air conditioning, air cooling; oxygenation, oxygenization

10 **ventilator; aerator**, blower**; air conditioner,** air filter, air cooler, ventilating *or* cooling system; blower; heat pump; air passage; fan

VERBS **11** **air,** air out, **ventilate,** cross-ventilate, wind, refresh, freshen; **air-condition,** air-cool; **fan,** winnow; **aerate,** airify, aerify; oxygenate, oxygenize

ADJS **12** **airy,** aery, **aerial,** aeriform, airlike, aeriferous, **pneumatic,** ethereal; exposed, roomy, light; airish, breezy; open-air, alfresco; **atmospheric,** tropospheric, stratospheric

13 **climatal,** climatic, climatical, climatographical, **elemental;** meteorological, meteorologic, aerologic, aerological, aerographic, aerographical, climatologic, climatological; macroclimatic, microclimatic, microclimatologic; barometric, barometrical, baric, barographic; isobaric, isopiestic, isometric; high-pressure, low-pressure; cyclonic, anti-cyclonic; seasonal

318 WIND

<airflow>

NOUNS **1** **wind,** current, **air current,** current of air, **draft,** movement of air, stream, stream of air, flow of air; updraft, uprush; downdraft, downrush, microburst; indraft, inflow, inrush; crosscurrent, crosswind, undercurrent; fall wind, gravity wind, katabatic wind, anabatic wind, head wind, tail wind, following wind; wind aloft; jet stream, upper-atmosphere *or* upper-atmospheric wind, high-altitude wind, gradient wind, geostrophic wind, prevailing wind; surface wind, mountain wind, valley wind; wind shift, wind shear

2 <wind god; the wind personified> Aeolus, Boreas, Aquilo <north wind>; Eurus <east wind>; Zephyr *or* Zephyrus, Favonius <west wind>; Notus, Auster <south wind>; Caurus *or* Caecias

<northwest wind>; Afer *or* Africus <southwest wind>; Argestes <northeast wind>

3 **puff,** puff of air *or* wind, breath, breath of air, flatus, waft, capful of wind, whiff, whiffet, stir of air

4 **breeze,** light *or* gentle wind *or* breeze, softblowing wind, **zephyr,** gale , air, light air, moderate breeze; fresh *or* stiff breeze; cool *or* cooling breeze; land breeze; sea breeze, onshore breeze, ocean breeze, cat's-paw

5 **gust,** wind gust, **blast,** blow, flaw, **flurry,** scud, squall

6 **hot wind;** snow eater, thawer; chinook, **chinook wind;** simoom, samiel; foehn *or* föhn; khamsin; harmattan; sirocco *or* yugo; solano; Santa Ana; volcanic wind

7 **wintry wind,** winter wind, raw wind, chilling *or* freezing wind, bone-chilling wind, sharp *or* piercing wind, cold *or* icy wind, biting wind, the hawk <nf>, nipping *or* nippy wind; Arctic *or* boreal *or* hyperboreal *or* hyperborean blast; wind chill *or* wind chill factor

8 **north wind, norther,** mistral, bise, tramontane, Etesian winds, meltemi, vardarac, Papagayo wind; northeaster, **nor'easter,** Euroclydon *or* gregale *or* gregal *or* gregau, bura, Tehuantepec wind, Tehuantepecer; northwester, **nor'wester;** southeaster, **sou'easter;** southwester, **sou'wester,** kite-wind, libeccio; **east wind,** easter, easterly, levanter, sharav; **west wind,** wester, westerly; **south wind,** souther

9 **prevailing wind**; polar easterlies; prevailing westerlies, prevailing southwesterlies, prevailing northwesterlies, antitrades; trade winds *or* trades; antitrade winds; doldrums, wind-equator; horse latitudes, roaring forties; intertropical convergence zone *or* ITCZ; equatorial low *or* doldrums

10 <nautical terms> **headwind, beam wind, tailwind,** following wind, fair *or* favorable wind, apparent *or* relative wind, backing wind, veering wind, slant of wind; onshore wind, offshore wind, wind shear

11 **windstorm,** vortex, eddy, big *or* great *or* fresh *or* strong *or* stiff *or* high *or* howling *or* spanking wind, ill *or* dirty *or* ugly wind; storm, storm wind, stormy winds, **tempest,** tempestuous wind; williwaw; **blow,** violent *or* heavy blow; **squall,** thick squall, black squall, white squall; squall line, wind-shift line, line squall; line storm; equinoctial; **gale,** half a gale, whole gale; tropical cyclone, **hurricane,** typhoon, tropical storm, **blizzard** 1023.8; **thundersquall,** thundergust; wind shear

12 **dust storm, sandstorm,** shaitan, peesash, devil, khamsin, sirocco, simoom, samiel, harmattan

13 **whirlwind,** whirlblast, tourbillon, wind eddy; **cyclone, tornado, twister,** funnel cloud, rotary storm, typhoon, *baguio* <Sp>; sandspout, sand column, dust devil; waterspout, rainspout

14 **windiness,** gustiness; airiness, **breeziness;** draftiness

15 **anemology,** anemometry; **wind direction; wind force, Beaufort scale,** half-Beaufort scale, International scale; wind rose, barometric wind rose, humidity wind rose, hyetal *or* rain wind rose, temperature wind rose, dynamic wind rose; wind arrow, wind marker

16 **weather vane, weathercock,** vane, cock, wind vane, wind indicator, wind cone *or* sleeve *or* sock, anemoscope; anemometer, wind-speed indicator, anemograph, anemometrograph

17 **blower,** bellows; blowpipe, blowtube, blowgun

18 **fan,** flabellum; punkah, thermantidote, electric fan, blower, window fan, attic fan, exhaust fan; ventilator; windsail, windscoop, windcatcher

VERBS 19 **blow, waft; puff,** huff, whiff; whiffle; **breeze;** breeze up, freshen; **gather, brew,** set in, blow up, pipe up, come up, **blow up a storm;** bluster, squall; **storm,** rage, blast, blow great guns, blow a hurricane; blow over

20 **sigh,** sough, whisper, mutter, murmur, **sob, moan,** groan, growl,

snarl, **wail, howl,** scream, screech, shriek, **roar,** whistle, pipe, sing, sing in the shrouds

ADJS **21 windy, blowy; breezy, drafty,** airy, airish; brisk, fresh; **gusty,** blasty, puffy, flawy; **squally;** prevailing; blustery, blustering, blusterous; aeolian, favonian, boreal; ventose

22 stormy, tempestuous, raging, storming, angry; turbulent; gale-force, storm-force, hurricane-force; dirty, foul; cyclonic, tornadic, typhonic, typhoonish; inclement; rainy 316.11; cloudy 319.8

23 windblown, blown; **windswept,** bleak, raw, exposed

24 anemological, anemographic, anemometric, anemometrical

319 CLOUD

NOUNS **1 cloud,** high fog; fleecy cloud, cottony cloud, billowy cloud; **cloud bank,** cloud mass, cloud cover, cloud drift; cloud base; cloudling, cloudlet; cloudscape, cloud band; cloudland, Cloudcuckooland *or* Nephelococcygia <Aristophanes>; macerel sky, buttermilk sky

2 <cloud types> ice cloud, water cloud, storm cloud, thunderhead, thunder cloud; cirrus, cirrocumulus, altostratus, cirrostratus, altocumulus, nimbostratus, stratocumulus *or* cumulostratus, stratus, cumulus, cumulonimbus, nimbus

3 fog, pea soup *and* peasouper *and* pea-soup fog <nf>; ground fog, coastal fog, fog drip, dense fog; London fog, London special <Brit nf>, Scotch mist, brume; fog-bank; **smog** <smoke-fog>, smaze <smoke-haze>; frost smoke; mist, drizzling mist, drisk <nf>; haze, gauze, film; vapor 1067

4 cloudiness, cloud cover, **haziness, mistiness, fogginess,** nebulosity, nubilation, nimbosity, **overcast,** heavy sky, dirty sky, lowering *or* louring sky

5 nephology, nephelognosy; nephologist

6 nephelometer, nepheloscope

VERBS **7 cloud,** becloud, encloud, cloud over, overcloud, cloud up, clabber up <nf>, **overcast,** overshadow, shadow, shade, **darken** 1027.9, darken over, nubilate, obnubilate, obscure; **smoke,** oversmoke; **fog,** befog; fog in; smog; **mist,** mist over, mist up, bemist, enmist; **haze**

ADJS **8 cloudy,** nebulous, nubilous, nimbose, nebulosus, nephological; **clouded,** overclouded, **overcast;** dirty, heavy, lowering *or* louring; dark 1027.13; **gloomy** 1027.14; cloud-flecked; cirrous, cirrose; cumulous, cumuliform, stratous, stratiform, cirrocumuliform, cirrocumulous, altocumuliform, altocumulous, altostratous, cirrostratous, nimbostratous, cumulonimbiform; lenticularis, mammatus, castellatus; thunderheaded, stormy, squally

9 cloud-covered, cloud-laden, cloud-curtained, cloud-crammed, cloud-crossed, cloud-decked, cloud-hidden, cloud-wrapped, cloud-enveloped, cloud-surrounded, cloud-girt, cloud-flecked, cloud-eclipsed, **cloud-capped,** cloud-topped

10 foggy, soupy *or* pea-soupy <nf>, nubilous; fog-bound, fogged-in; smoggy; hazy, misty; so foggy the seagulls are walking, so thick you can cut it with a knife

11 nephological

320 BUBBLE

NOUNS **1 bubble,** bleb, **globule;** vesicle, bulla, **blister,** blood blister, fever blister; balloon, bladder 195.2; air bubble, soap bubble

2 foam, froth; spume, sea foam, scud; **spray, surf,** breakers, white water, spoondrift *or* **spindrift**; **suds, lather,** soap-suds; beer-suds, head; **scum,** off-scum; head, collar; puff, mousse, soufflé, meringue

3 bubbling, bubbliness, **effervescence** *or* effervescency, **sparkle,** spumescence, frothiness, frothing, foaming; **fizz,** fizzle, carbonation; ebullience *or* ebulliency; **ebullition,** boiling; **fermentation,** ferment

VERBS 4 **bubble,** bubble up, burble; **effervesce, fizz, fizzle;** hiss, **sparkle; ferment,** work; **foam, froth,** froth up; have a head, foam over; **boil,** seethe, simmer; plop, blubber; guggle, gurgle; bubble over, **boil over**

5 **foam, froth,** spume, cream; **lather,** suds, sud; scum, mantle; **aerate,** whip, beat, whisk

ADJS 6 **bubbly,** burbly, **bubbling,** burbling; **effervescent,** spumescent, **fizzy, sparkling,** *mousseux* <Fr>, *spumante* <Ital>; carbonated; ebullient; puffed, soufflé *or* souffléed, beaten, whipped, chiffon; **blistered,** blistery, blebby, vesicated, vesicular; blistering, vesicant, vesicatory

7 **foamy,** foam-flecked, **frothy,** spumy, spumous *or* spumose; yeasty, barmy; **sudsy,** suddy, **lathery,** soapy, soapsudsy, soapsuddy; heady, with a head *or* collar on

321 BEHAVIOR

NOUNS 1 **behavior, conduct, deportment, comportment, manner, manners, demeanor, mien,** *maintien* <Fr>, **carriage, bearing,** port, poise, posture, guise, **air,** address, presence; tone, style, lifestyle; way of life, habit of life, modus vivendi; **way, way of acting, ways; trait behavior,** behavior trait; methods, **method, methodology; practice,** praxis; procedure, proceeding; **actions,** acts, goings-on, doings, what one is up to, movements, moves, tactics; action, doing 328.1; activity 330; objective *or* observable behavior; motions, gestures, gesticulation, hand-waving; pose, affectation 500; pattern, behavior pattern; Type A behavior, Type B behavior; culture pattern, behavioral norm, folkway, **custom** 373

2 **good behavior,** sanctioned behavior; good citizenship; good manners, correct deportment, **etiquette** 580.3; **courtesy** 504; social behavior, sociability 582; bad *or* poor behavior, **misbehavior** 322; **discourtesy** 505

3 **behaviorism,** behavioral science, behavior *or* behavioristic psychology, Watsonian psychology, Skinnerian psychology; social science; behavior modification, behavior therapy ethology, animal behavior, human behavior, social behavior, ethology; behavior modification

VERBS 4 **behave, act, do,** go on; **behave oneself, conduct oneself,** manage oneself, **handle oneself,** guide oneself, **comport oneself, deport oneself,** demean oneself, **bear oneself, carry oneself;** acquit oneself, quit oneself ; proceed, move, swing into action; **misbehave** 322.4

5 **behave oneself, behave,** act well, clean up one's act <nf>, act one's age, **be good,** be nice, **do right,** do what is right, do the right *or* proper thing, keep out of mischief, play the game *and* mind one's P's and Q's <nf>, be on one's good *or* best behavior, play one's cards right, set a good example

6 **treat, use, do by,** deal by, **act** *or* **behave toward,** conduct oneself toward, act with regard to, conduct oneself vis-à-vis *or* in the face of; **deal with,** cope with, **handle;** respond to

ADJS 7 **behavioral;** behaviorist, behavioristic; ethological; **behaved,** behaviored, **mannered,** demeanored

322 MISBEHAVIOR

NOUNS 1 **misbehavior, misconduct,** misdemeanor ; unsanctioned *or* nonsanctioned behavior; frowned-upon behavior; **naughtiness,** badness; impropriety; venial sin; **disorderly conduct,** disorder, disorderliness, disruptiveness, disruption, **rowdiness,** rowdyism, riotousness, ruffianism, hooliganism, hoodlumism, aggro <Brit nf>; vandalism, trashing; roughhouse, horseplay; discourtesy 505; vice 654; misfeasance, malfeasance, misdoing, delinquency, **wrongdoing** 655

2 **mischief, mischievousness; devilment, deviltry,** devilry; **roguishness,** roguery, scampishness; **waggery,** waggishness; **impishness,** devilishness, puckishness, elfish-

ness; **prankishness,** pranksomeness; sportiveness, playfulness, *espièglerie* <Fr>; high spirits, youthful spirits; foolishness 923

3 **mischief-maker,** mischief, **rogue, devil,** knave, **rascal,** rapscallion, scapegrace, **scamp; wag** 489.12; buffoon 707.10; funmaker, joker, jokester, practical joker, prankster, life of the party, **cutup** <nf>; **rowdy,** ruffian, hoodlum, hood <nf>, hooligan; **imp, elf, puck,** pixie, **minx,** bad boy, bugger *and* booger <nf>, little devil, little rascal, little monkey, *enfant terrible* <Fr>

VERBS **4** **misbehave,** misdemean , **misbehave oneself, misconduct oneself,** misdemean oneself , behave ill; get into mischief; **act up** *and* make waves *and* **carry on** *and* carry on something scandalous <nf>, sow one's wild oats; **cut up** <nf>, horse around <nf>, roughhouse *and* cut up rough <nf>; rock on; play the fool 923.6

ADJS **5** **misbehaving, unbehaving; naughty, bad;** improper, not respectable; out-of-order *and* off-base *and* out-of-line <nf>; **disorderly,** disruptive, **rowdy,** rowdyish, **ruffianly**

6 **mischievous,** mischief-loving, full of mischief, full of the devil *or* old nick; **roguish,** scampish, scapegrace, arch, knavish; **devilish; impish, puckish, elfish,** elvish; **waggish, prankish,** pranky, pranksome, trickish, tricksy; **playful,** sportive, high-spirited, *espiègle* <Fr>; foolish 923.8

ADVS **7** **mischievously, roguishly,** knavishly, scampishly, devilishly; impishly, puckishly, elfishly; waggishly; prankishly, playfully, sportively, in fun

323 WILL

NOUNS **1** **will, volition; choice,** determination, **decision** 371.1; **wish, mind, fancy,** discretion, pleasure, **inclination, disposition,** liking, appetence, appetency, **desire** 100; half a mind *or* notion, idle wish, velleity; **appetite, passion, lust, sexual desire** 75.5; animus, **objective, intention** 380; **command** 420; **free choice,** one's own will *or* choice *or* discretion *or* initiative, **free will** 430.6, free hand; conation, conatus; will power, **resolution** 359; final will *or* wishes

VERBS **2** **will, wish,** see *or* think fit, think good, think proper, **choose to, have a mind to;** have half a mind *or* notion to; **choose,** determine, **decide** 371.14,16; **resolve** 359.7; command, decree; **desire** 100.14,18

3 have one's will, **have** *or* **get one's way, get one's wish, have one's druthers** <nf>, **write one's own ticket,** have it all one's way, do *or* go as one pleases, please oneself; assert oneself, take the bit in one's teeth, take charge of one's destiny; stand on one's rights; take the law into one's own hands; have the last word, impose one's will; know one's own mind

ADJS **4** **volitional, volitive; willing, voluntary;** conative; *ex gratia* <L>; intentional

ADVS **5** **at will,** at choice, at pleasure, **at one's pleasure,** at one's will and pleasure, at one's own sweet will, **at one's discretion,** *à discrétion* <Fr>, *ad arbitrium* <L>; *ad libitum* <L>, ad lib; as one wishes, as it pleases *or* suits oneself, **in one's own way,** in one's own sweet way *or* time <nf>, **as one thinks best,** as it seems good *or* best, as far as one desires; of one's own free will, of one's own accord, on one's own; without coercion, unforced

324 WILLINGNESS

NOUNS **1** **willingness, gameness** <nf>, readiness; **unreluctance,** unloathness, ungrudgingness; agreeableness, **agreeability,** favorableness; **acquiescence, consent** 441; **compliance,** cooperativeness; receptivity, receptiveness, responsiveness; amenability, tractableness, tractability, docility, biddability, biddableness, pliancy, pliability, malleability; **eagerness,** keenness, promptness, forwardness, alacrity, zeal, zealousness, ardor, enthusiasm, fervor; goodwill, cheerful consent; **willing heart** *or* **mind** *or* **humor, favorable disposition,** positive *or* right *or* receptive mood, willing ear

2 **voluntariness,** volunteering; **gratuitousness; spontaneity,** spontaneousness, unforcedness; **self-determination,** self-activity, self-action, autonomy, autonomousness, independence, free will 430.6; **volunteerism,** voluntaryism, voluntarism; volunteer; labor of love

VERBS 3 **be willing, be game** <nf>, be ready; be of favorable disposition, take the trouble, find it in one's heart, find one's heart , have a willing heart; **incline, lean;** look kindly upon; be open to, bring oneself, **agree,** be agreeable to; **acquiesce, consent** 441.2; not hesitate to, would as lief, would as leave <nf>, would as lief as not, not care *or* mind if one does <nf>; **play** *or* **go along** <nf>, do one's part *or* bit, have a good mind to; be eager, be keen, be dying to, fall all over oneself, be spoiling for, be champing at the bit; be Johnny on the spot, step into the breach; **enter with a will,** lean *or* bend over backward, go into heart and soul, go the extra mile, plunge into; **cooperate,** collaborate 450.3; lend *or* give *or* turn a willing ear

4 **volunteer,** do voluntarily, do ex gratia, **do of one's own accord,** do of one's own volition, **do of one's own free will** *or* **choice;** do independently; put forward, sacrifice oneself; offer

ADJS 5 **willing, willinghearted, ready, game** <nf>; **disposed, inclined, minded, willed,** fain *and* prone ; **well-disposed,** well-inclined, favorably inclined *or* disposed; predisposed; **favorable, agreeable, cooperative; compliant,** content , **acquiescent** 332.13, **consenting** 441.4; **eager;** keen, prompt, quick, alacritous, forward, ready and willing, zealous, ardent, enthusiastic; in the mood *or* vein *or* humor *or* mind, in a good mood; receptive, responsive; amenable, tractable, docile, pliant, in favor

6 **ungrudging,** ungrumbling, **unreluctant,** unloath, **nothing loath,** unaverse, unshrinking

7 **voluntary, volunteer;** ***ex gratia*** <L>, **gratuitous; spontaneous, free, freewill;** offered, proffered; **discretionary,** discretional, nonmandatory, **optional,** elective; arbitrary; **self-determined,** self-determining, autonomous, independent, self-active, self-acting; **unsought,** unbesought, **unasked,** unrequested, **unsolicited, uninvited,** unbidden, uncalled-for; **unforced,** uncoerced, unpressured, unrequired, uncompelled; unprompted, uninfluenced; spontaneous

ADVS 8 **willingly, with a will,** with good will, with right good will, *de bonne volonté* <Fr>; **eagerly,** with zest, with relish, with open arms, without question, zealously, ardently, enthusiastically; **readily,** promptly, at the drop of a hat <nf>

9 **agreeably, favorably, compliantly;** lief, lieve <nf>, fain, as lief, as lief as not; **ungrudgingly,** ungrumblingly, **unreluctantly, nothing loath,** without reluctance *or* demur *or* hesitation, unstintingly, unreservedly

10 **voluntarily, freely, gratuitously, spontaneously;** optionally, electively, by choice; **of one's own accord,** of one's own free will, of one's own volition, without reservation, of one's own choice, at one's own discretion; without coercion *or* pressure *or* compulsion *or* intimidation; independently

325 UNWILLINGNESS

NOUNS 1 **refusal** 442, **unwillingness, disinclination,** nolition, **indisposition,** indisposedness, **reluctance,** renitency, renitence, grudgingness, grudging consent; unenthusiasm, lack of enthusiasm *or* zeal *or* eagerness, slowness, backwardness, dragging of the feet *and* foot-dragging <nf>, apathy, indifference; sullenness, sulk, sulks, sulkiness; cursoriness, perfunctoriness; recalcitrance *or* recalcitrancy, disobedience, refractoriness, fractiousness, intractableness, indocility, mutinousness; averseness, aversion, repugnance, antipathy, distaste, disrelish, no stomach for; **obstinacy, stubbornness** 361.1; opposition 451; **resistance** 453; **disagreement,** dissent 456.3

2 **demur,** demurral, **scruple, qualm,** qualm of conscience, reservation, compunction; **hesitation,** hesitancy *or* hesitance, pause, boggle, **falter;** qualmishness, scrupulousness, scrupulosity; **stickling,** boggling; **faltering;** shrinking; shyness, **diffidence,** modesty, bashfulness, retiring disposition, restraint; recoil; **protest, objection** 333.2

VERBS 3 **refuse** 442.3, **be unwilling, would** *or* **had rather not, not care to,** not feel like <nf>, not find it in one's heart to, not have the heart *or* stomach to; **mind,** object to, draw the line at, be dead set against, **balk at;** grudge, begrudge

4 **demur, scruple,** have qualms *or* scruples; **stickle, stick at,** boggle, strain; falter, waver; **hesitate,** pause, be half-hearted, **hang back,** hang off, hold off; **fight shy of,** shy at, shy, crane, shrink, recoil, blench, flinch, wince, quail, pull back; make bones about *or* of

ADJS 5 **unwilling, disinclined, indisposed,** not in the mood, averse, not feeling like; **unconsenting** 442.6; dead set against, opposed 451.8; **resistant** 453.5; **disagreeing,** differing, at odds 456.16; disobedient, recalcitrant, refractory, fractious, sullen, sulky, indocile, mutinous; cursory, perfunctory; **involuntary, forced**

6 **reluctant,** renitent, **grudging, loath;** backward, laggard, dilatory, slow, slow to, foot-dragging; unenthusiastic, unzealous, indifferent, apathetic, perfunctory; balky, balking, restive

7 **demurring, qualmish,** boggling, stickling, hedging, squeamish, **scrupulous; diffident,** shy, modest, bashful; **hesitant,** hesitating, faltering; shrinking

ADVS 8 **unwillingly, involuntarily, against one's will,** *à contre coeur* <Fr>; under compulsion *or* coercion *or* pressure; in spite of oneself, *malgré soi* <Fr>

9 **reluctantly, grudgingly,** sullenly, sulkily; unenthusiastically, perfunctorily; with dragging feet, with a bad *or* an ill grace, **under protest;** with a heavy heart, with no heart *or* stomach; over one's dead body, not on one's life

326 OBEDIENCE

NOUNS 1 **obedience** *or* **obediency,** compliance; acquiescence, consent 441; **deference** 155.1, self-abnegation, submission, submissiveness 433.3; servility 138; eagerness *or* readiness *or* willingness to serve, **dutifulness,** duteousness; **service,** servitium, homage, fealty, **allegiance, loyalty,** faithfulness, faith, suit and service *or* suit service, observance , brand loyalty; doglike devotion *or* obedience; **conformity** 867, lockstep; law-abidingness; obeisance, good behavior, best behavior

VERBS 2 **obey, mind, heed, keep, observe,** listen *or* hearken to; **comply, conform** 867.3, walk in lockstep; stay in line *and* not get out of line *and* not get off base <nf>, **toe the line** *or* mark, come to heel, fall in, fall in line, obey the rules, follow the book, keep the law, behave, be on one's best behavior, **do what one is told;** do as one says, do the will of, defer to 155.4, do one's bidding, come at one's call, lie down and roll over for <nf>; take orders, attend to orders, do suit and service, follow the lead of; **submit** 433.6,9

ADJS 3 **obedient, compliant,** complying, allegiant; **acquiescent,** consenting 441.4, **submissive** 433.12, deferential 155.8, self-abnegating; willing, **dutiful,** duteous; under control; loyal, faithful, devoted; uncritical, unshakeable, doglike; conforming, in conformity; law-abiding

4 **at one's command,** at one's whim *or* pleasure, at one's disposal, at

one's nod, at one's call, **at one's beck and call**

5 **henpecked, tied to one's apron strings,** on a string, on a leash, in leading strings; wimpish <nf>; milk-toast *or* milquetoast, Caspar Milquetoast; under one's thumb; chicken-pecked

ADVS 6 **obediently, compliantly; acquiescently, submissively** 433.17; willingly, **dutifully,** duteously; loyally, faithfully, devotedly; in obedience to, in compliance *or* conformity with

7 at your service *or* command *or* orders, as you please, as you will, as thou wilt

327 DISOBEDIENCE

NOUNS 1 **disobedience,** nonobedience, **noncompliance; undutifulness,** unduteousness; willful disobedience; **insubordination,** indiscipline; **unsubmissiveness, intractability,** indocility 361.4, recusancy; **nonconformity** 868; **disrespect** 156; **lawlessness,** waywardness, frowardness, naughtiness; violation, transgression, infraction, infringement, lawbreaking; civil disobedience, passive resistance; uncooperativeness, noncooperation; **dereliction,** deliberate negligence, default, delinquency, nonfeasance

2 **defiance, refractoriness, recalcitrance** *or* recalcitrancy, recalcitration, defiance of authority, contumacy, **contumaciousness, obstreperousness, unruliness,** restiveness, fractiousness, orneriness *and* feistiness <nf>; wildness 430.3; **obstinacy, stubbornness** 361.1

3 **rebelliousness, mutinousness;** riotousness; insurrectionism, insurgentism; factiousness, **sedition,** seditiousness; treasonableness, traitorousness, subversiveness, subversion; extremism 611.4

4 **revolt, rebellion, revolution, mutiny, insurrection, insurgence** *or* insurgency, *émeute* <Fr>, **uprising,** rising, outbreak, general uprising, *levée en masse* <Fr>, **riot,** civil disorder; peasant revolt, *jacquerie* <Fr>; putsch, coup, coup d'état; **strike, general strike;** intifada; resistance movement, resistance; terrorism

5 **rebel,** revolter; **insurgent,** insurrectionary, insurrecto, **insurrectionist;** malcontent, *frondeur* <Fr>; **insubordinate; mutineer,** rioter, brawler; maverick <nf>, noncooperator, troublemaker, refusenik <nf>, agent provocateur; nonconformist 868.3; agitator 375.11; extremist 611.12; reactionary; revolutionary, revolutionist 860.3; traitor, subversive 357.11; freedom fighter; contra

VERBS 6 **disobey,** not mind, not heed, not keep *or* observe, not listen *or* hearken, pay no attention to, **ignore, disregard, defy,** set at defiance, fly in the face of, snap one's fingers at, scoff at, flout, go counter to, set at naught, set naught by, care naught for; be a law unto oneself, step out of line, get off-base <nf>, refuse to cooperate; not conform 868.4, hear a different drummer; **violate,** transgress 435.4; break the law 674.5; thumb one's nose at

7 **revolt, rebel,** kick over the traces, reluct, reluctate; **rise up,** rise, arise, rise up in arms, mount the barricades; mount *or* make a coup d'état; **mutiny,** mutineer ; insurge *and* insurrect , **riot,** run riot; revolutionize, revolution, revolute, subvert, overthrow 852.2; call a general strike, strike 727.5; secede, break away

ADJS 8 **disobedient, transgressive,** uncomplying, violative, lawless, wayward, froward, naughty; recusant, nonconforming 868.5; **undutiful,** unduteous; self-willed, willful, obstinate 361.8; **defiant** 454.7; **undisciplined,** ill-disciplined, indisciplined

9 **insubordinate, unsubmissive,** indocile, **uncompliant, uncooperative,** noncooperative, noncooperating, **intractable** 361.12

10 **defiant, refractory, recalcitrant, contumacious, obstreperous, unruly,** restive, impatient of control *or* discipline; fractious, ornery *and* feisty <nf>; wild, untamed 430.29

11 **rebellious,** rebel, breakaway; **mutinous,** mutineering; **insurgent, insurrectionary,** riotous, turbulent; factious, **seditious,** seditionary; revolutionary, revolutional; traitorous, treasonable, subversive; extreme, extremistic 611.20

ADVS **12** **disobediently,** uncompliantly, against *or* contrary to order and discipline; **insubordinately, unsubmissively,** indocilely, **uncooperatively;** unresignedly; disregardfully, floutingly, **defiantly;** intractably 361.17; obstreperously, contumaciously, restively, fractiously; **rebelliously,** mutinously; riotously

328 ACTION

<voluntary action>

NOUNS **1** **action, activity** 330, act, willed action *or* activity; **acting, doing,** activism, direct action, not words but action, happening; **practice,** actual practice, praxis; **exercise,** drill; **operation,** working, function, functioning; play; **operations,** affairs, workings; **business,** employment, work, occupation; **behavior** 321

2 **performance, execution,** carrying out, enactment; **transaction; discharge, dispatch;** conduct, **handling,** management, administration; **achievement, accomplishment, effectuation, implementation; commission, perpetration;** completion 407.2

3 **act, action, deed, doing,** thing, thing done, overt act; **turn; feat, stunt** *and* **trick** <nf>; **master stroke,** *tour de force* <Fr>, **exploit,** adventure, **enterprise, initiative,** achievement, accomplishment, **performance,** production, track record <nf>; gesture; effort, endeavor, job, undertaking; **transaction;** dealing, deal <nf>; passage; **operation, proceeding,** process, **step, measure, maneuver, move, movement;** policy, tactics; *démarche* <Fr>, coup, stroke; blow, go <nf>; accomplished fact, *fait accompli* <Fr>, done deal <nf>; overt act <law>; acta, *res gestae* <L>, **doings, dealings**, affairs; **works;** work, handiwork, hand

VERBS **4** **act, serve, function; operate, work, move,** practice, do one's stuff *or* one's thing <nf>; **move,** proceed; make, play, **behave** 321.4

5 **take action, take steps** *or* **measures; proceed,** proceed with, go ahead with, go with, go through with; do something, go *or* swing into action, **do something about, act on** *or* **upon,** take it on, run with it <nf>, get off the dime *or* one's ass *or* one's dead ass <nf>, get with it *or* the picture <nf>; fish or cut bait, shit or get off the pot *and* put up or shut up *and* put one's money where one's mouth is <nf>; **go,** have a go <chiefly Brit nf>, take a whack *or* a cut <nf>, lift a finger, **take** *or* **bear a hand;** play a role *or* part in; stretch forth one's hand, strike a blow; **maneuver,** make moves <nf>; get a life <nf>

6 **do, effect,** effectuate, **make; bring about,** bring to pass, **bring off, produce, deliver** <nf>, **do the trick,** put across *or* through; swing *or* swing it *and* hack it *and* cut it *and* cut the mustard <nf>; **do one's part,** carry one's weight, carry the ball <nf>, hold up one's end *or* one's end of the bargain; tear off <nf>, **achieve, accomplish,** realize 407.4; **render, pay; inflict, wreak,** do to; **commit, perpetrate;** pull off <nf>; go and do, up and do *or* take and do <nf>

7 **carry out,** carry through, go through, fulfill, work out; **bring off,** carry off; **put through,** get through; **implement; put into effect, put in** *or* **into practice,** carry into effect, execute, carry into execution, **translate into action;** suit the action to the word; rise to the occasion, come through <nf>

8 **practice, put into practice, exercise, employ, use; carry on, conduct, prosecute, wage; follow, pursue; engage in,** work at, devote oneself to, **do,** turn to, apply oneself to, employ oneself in; play at; **take up,** take to, **undertake, tackle,** take on, address oneself to, have a go at, turn one's hand to, **go in** *or* **out for** <nf>, make it one's business, follow as an occupation, set up shop; specialize in 866.4

9 **perform, execute, enact; transact; discharge, dispatch;** conduct, **manage, handle;** legislate, commission; dispose of, take care of, **deal with,** cope with; **make, accomplish,** complete 407.6

ADJS 10 **acting,** performing, practicing, serving, functioning, functional, operating, operative, operational, working, in harness; in action 889.11; behavioral 321.7

329 INACTION

<voluntary inaction>

NOUNS 1 **inaction,** passiveness, **passivity,** passivism; passive resistance, nonviolent resistance; nonresistance, nonviolence; pacifism; neutrality, neutralness, neutralism, **nonparticipation, noninvolvement;** standpattism <nf>; **do-nothingism,** do-nothingness, do-nothing policy; **laissez-faireism,** *laissez-faire* and *laissez-aller* <Fr>; watching and waiting, watchful waiting, waiting game, a wait-and-see attitude, indecision; **inertia,** inertness, **immobility,** dormancy, stagnation, stagnancy, vegetation, stasis, paralysis, standstill; **procrastination; idleness,** indolence, torpor, torpidness, torpidity, sloth; stalemate, logjam; **immobility** 853.1; equilibrium, dead center; **inactivity** 331; **quietude, serenity, quiescence** 173; **quietism,** contemplation, meditation, passive self-annihilation; leisure; contemplative life, *vita contemplativa* <L>; back burner

VERBS 2 **do nothing,** not stir, not budge, **not lift a finger** *or* **hand,** not move a foot, **sit back, sit on one's hands** <nf>, sit on one's ass *or* dead ass *or* butt *or* duff <nf>, sit on the sidelines, be a sideliner, sit it out, take a raincheck <nf>, fold one's arms, twiddle one's thumbs; **cool one's heels** *or* jets <nf>; **bide one's time, delay,** watch and wait, wait and see, play a waiting game, lie low, tread water <nf>; hang fire, not go off half-cocked; lie *or* sit back, lie *or* rest upon one's oars, rest, put one's feet up *and* kick back <nf>, be still 173.7; repose on one's laurels; drift, coast; **stagnate,** vegetate, veg out <nf>, lie dormant, hibernate; lay down on the job <nf>, idle 331.12; not stir, freeze; back-burner

3 **refrain, abstain,** hold, **spare, forbear, forgo,** keep from; hold *or* stay one's hand, sit by *or* idly by, sit on one's hands

4 **let alone,** leave alone, **leave** *or* **let well enough alone;** look the other way, not make waves, not look for trouble, not rock the boat; **let be,** leave be <nf>, let things take their course, let it have its way; leave things as they are; *laisser faire* or *laisser passer* or *laisser aller* <Fr>, live and let live; **take no part in,** not get involved in, **have nothing to do with,** have no hand in, stand *or* hold *or* remain aloof, keep out of; tolerate, sit on the fence

5 **let go,** let pass, **let slip, let slide** *and* let ride <nf>; procrastinate, sit tight, defer

ADJS 6 **passive; neutral,** neuter; standpat <nf>, **do-nothing;** *laissez-faire* and *laissez-aller* <Fr>; **inert,** like a bump on a log <nf>, immobile, dormant, stagnant, stagnating, vegetative, vegetable, static, stationary, motionless, unmoving, paralyzed, paralytic; procrastinating; **inactive, idle** 331.18; quiescent 173.12; quietist, quietistic, contemplative, meditative

ADVS 7 **at a stand** *or* **standstill,** at a halt; as a last resort

PHRS 8 if it ain't broke don't fix it, let sleeping dogs lie; *dolce far niente* <Ital>

330 ACTIVITY

NOUNS 1 **activity, action,** activeness; **movement,** motion, **stir; proceedings, doings, goings-on; activism,** political activism, judicial activism, etc; **militancy;** business 724.1

2 liveliness, animation, vivacity, vivaciousness, **sprightliness, spiritedness,** bubbliness, ebullience, effervescence, **briskness, breeziness, peppiness** <nf>; **life, spirit, verve,** energy, adrenalin; pep *and* moxie *and* oomph *and* pizzazz *and* piss and vinegar <nf>, **vim** 17.2

3 quickness, swiftness, speediness, alacrity, celerity, readiness, smartness, sharpness, briskness; **promptness,** promptitude; dispatch, expeditiousness, expedition, **agility, nimbleness, spryness,** springiness

4 bustle, fuss, flurry, flutter, fluster, scramble, ferment, stew, sweat, whirl, swirl, vortex, maelstrom, **stir,** hubbub, hullabaloo, hoo-ha *and* foofaraw *and* flap <nf>, schemozzle <Brit nf>, ado, to-do <nf>, bother, botheration <nf>, pother; fussiness, flutteriness; tumult, commotion, **agitation; restlessness,** unquiet, fidgetiness; **spurt, burst,** fit, spasm

5 busyness, press of business, hive of activity; plenty to do, many irons in the fire, much on one's plate; the battle of life, rat race <nf>

6 industry, industriousness, assiduousness, **assiduity, diligence, application,** concentration, laboriousness, sedulity, **sedulousness,** unsparingness, relentlessness, zealousness, ardor, fervor, vehemence; **energy,** energeticalness, strenuousness, strenuosity, tirelessness, indefatigability

7 enterprise, enterprisingness, dynamism, **initiative,** aggression, **aggressiveness,** killer instinct, force, forcefulness, pushfulness, pushingness, **pushiness, push, drive, hustle, go,** getup, get-up-and-get *or* **get-up-and-go** <nf>, go-ahead, go-getting, go-to-itiveness <nf>, **up-and-comingness; adventurousness,** venturousness, venturesomeness, adventuresomeness; spirit, gumption *and* spunk <nf>; **ambitiousness** 100.10

8 man *or* **woman of action, doer,** man of deeds; **hustler** *and* self-starter <nf>, bustler; go-getter *and* ball of fire *and* live wire *and* powerhouse *and* human dynamo *and* spitfire <nf>; **workaholic,** overachiever; beaver, busy bee, **eager beaver** <nf>, no slouch <nf>; operator *and* big-time operator *and* wheeler-dealer <nf>; winner <nf>; **activist,** political activist, **militant;** enthusiast 101.4; new broom, take-charge guy <nf>

9 overactivity, hyperactivity; hyperkinesia *or* hyperkinesis; franticness, frenziedness; overexertion, overextension; officiousness 214.2; a finger in every pie

VERBS **10 be busy, have one's hands full,** have many irons in the fire, have a lot on one's plate; not have a moment to spare, not have a moment to call one's own, not be able to call one's time one's own; do it on the run; have other things to do, have other fish to fry; **work, labor, drudge** 725.14; **busy oneself** 724.10,11

11 stir, stir about, **bestir oneself,** stir one's stumps <nf>, get down to business, sink one's teeth into it, take hold, be up and doing

12 bustle, fuss, make a fuss, stir, stir about, rush around *or* about, tear around, hurry about, buzz *or* whiz about, dart to and fro, run *or* go around like a chicken with its head cut off, run around in circles

13 hustle <nf>, **drive,** drive oneself, **push, scramble,** go all out <nf>, **make things hum,** step lively <nf>, make the sparks *or* chips fly <nf>, do one's damnedest <nf>; make up for lost time; press on, drive on; go ahead, forge ahead, shoot ahead, go full steam ahead

14 <nf terms> **hump,** get cutting, break one's neck, bear down on it, put one's back into it, get off the dime, get off one's ass *or* duff *or* dead ass, **hit the ball,** pour it on, lean on it, shake a leg, go to town, get the lead out, floor it, go wild, go gangbusters

15 keep going, keep on, keep on the go, keep on keeping on, keep on trucking <nf>, **carry on,** peg *or* plug away <nf>, **keep at it,** keep moving, keep driving, **keep the pot boiling,** keep the ball rolling; keep busy, **keep one's nose to the**

grindstone, stay on the treadmill, burn the candle at both ends

16 make the most of one's time, improve the shining hour, make hay while the sun shines, not let the grass grow under one's feet; get up early

ADJS **17** **active, lively, animated, spirited,** bubbly, ebullient, effervescent, **vivacious, sprightly,** chipper *and* perky <nf>, pert; **spry, breezy, brisk, energetic,** eager, keen, can-do <nf>; smacking, spanking; alive, live, full of life, full of pep *or* go *and* pizzazz *or* moxie <nf>, alive and kicking; **peppy** *and* snappy *and* zingy <nf>; frisky, bouncing, bouncy; mercurial, quicksilver; **activist,** activistic, **militant**

18 **quick, swift, speedy, expeditious, snappy** <nf>, celeritous, alacritous, dispatchful , **prompt,** ready, smart, sharp, quick on the draw *or* trigger *or* upswing <nf>; **agile, nimble, spry,** springy

19 **astir, stirring,** afoot, **on foot;** in full swing

20 **bustling,** fussing, fussy; **fidgety,** restless, fretful, jumpy, unquiet, unsettled 105.23; **agitated, turbulent**

21 **busy,** full of business; **occupied, engaged, employed, working;** at it; **at work,** on duty, on the job, in harness; involved, engagé; **hard at work, hard at it; on the move, on the go,** on the run, **on the hop** *or* **jump** <nf>, on the make <nf>; busy as a bee *or* beaver, busier than a one-armed paper hanger <nf>; up to one's ears *or* elbows *or* neck *or* eyeballs in <nf>; tied up

22 **industrious, assiduous, diligent, sedulous,** laborious, **hardworking,** workaholic; hard, unremitting, unsparing, relentless, zealous, ardent, fervent, vehement; **energetic,** strenuous; never idle; unsleeping; tireless, unwearied, unflagging, indefatigable; stick-to-it-ive <nf>

23 **enterprising, aggressive, dynamic,** activist, proactive, driving, forceful, **pushing,** pushful, **pushy, up-and-coming, go-ahead** *and* **hustling** <nf>, go-getting <nf>; adventurous, venturous, venturesome, adventuresome; **ambitious** 100.28

24 **overactive,** hyperactive, hyper <nf>; hectic, frenzied, frantic, frenetic; hyperkinetic; intrusive, officious 214.9; full of beans <nf>

ADVS **25** **actively, busily; lively,** sprightly, **briskly, breezily, energetically, animatedly, vivaciously, spiritedly,** with life and spirit, with gusto; allegro, allegretto; full tilt, in full swing, all out <nf>; like a house afire

26 **quickly, swiftly, expeditiously,** with dispatch, readily, **promptly; agilely, nimbly, spryly**

27 **industriously, assiduously, diligently, sedulously,** laboriously; unsparingly, relentlessly, zealously, ardently, fervently, vehemently; **energetically,** strenuously, tirelessly, indefatigably

331 INACTIVITY

NOUNS **1** **inactivity, inaction** 329, inactiveness; lull, suspension; suspended animation; dormancy, hibernation; immobility, motionlessness, quiescence 173; **inertia** 329.1; underactivity; back burner

2 **idleness,** unemployment, nothing to do, otiosity, inoccupation; **leisure,** leisureliness, unhurried ease; idle hands, idle hours, off hours, time on one's hands; **relaxation,** letting down, unwinding, putting one's feet up, slippered ease

3 **unemployment,** lack of work, joblessness, inoccupation; layoff, furlough; normal unemployment, seasonal unemployment, technological unemployment, cyclical unemployment; unemployment insurance; shutdown, recession, depression

4 **idling, loafing,** lazing, *flânerie* <Fr>, goofing off <nf>, slacking <nf>, goldbricking <nf>; *dolce far niente* <Ital>; trifling; dallying, dillydallying, mopery, dawdling; loitering, tarrying, lingering; lounging, **lolling**

5 **indolence, laziness, sloth,** slothfulness, bone-laziness; laggardness, slowness, dilatoriness, remissness, do-nothingness, faineancy, *fainéantise* <Fr>; inexertion, inertia; **shift-**

lessness, do-lessness <nf>; hoboism, vagrancy; spring fever; ergophobia

6 **languor,** languidness, languorousness, languishment , lackadaisicalness, lotus-eating; **listlessness,** lifelessness, inanimation, enervation, slowness, lenitude *or* lentor , **dullness, sluggishness,** heaviness, dopiness <nf>, hebetude, supineness, **lassitude, lethargy,** loginess; kef, nodding; phlegm, **apathy, indifference, passivity;** torpidness, torpor, torpidity; stupor, stuporousness, stupefaction; **sloth,** slothfulness, acedia; **sleepiness, somnolence, oscitancy, yawning, drowsiness** 22.1; **weariness, fatigue** 21; jadedness, satedness 994.2; world-weariness, ennui, boredom 118.3

7 **lazybones,** lazyboots, lazylegs, indolent, lie-abed, slugabed

8 **idler, loafer, lounger,** loller, layabout <Brit nf>, couch potato <nf>, lotus-eater, *flâneur* and *flâneuse* <Fr>, **do-nothing,** dolittle, *fainéant* <Fr>, goof-off *and* fuck-off *and* goldbrick *and* goldbricker <nf>, clock watcher; **sluggard,** slug, slouch, sloucher, lubber, stick-in-the-mud <nf>, gentleman of leisure; **time waster,** time killer; **dallier, dillydallier,** mope, moper, doodler, diddler <nf>, **dawdler,** dawdle, laggard, **loiterer,** lingerer; waiter on Providence; trifler, **putterer,** potterer

9 **bum,** stiff <nf>, derelict, skid-row bum, Bowery bum; beachcomber; **good-for-nothing,** good-for-naught, **ne'er-do-well,** wastrel; drifter, vagrant, hobo, tramp 178.3; beggar 440.8

10 homeless person; street person; shopping-bag lady *or* woman, bag person

11 **nonworker, drone;** cadger, bummer *and* moocher <nf>, **sponger,** freeloader, lounge lizard <nf>, social parasite, parasite, spiv <Brit>; beggar, mendicant, panhandler <nf>; **the unemployed;** the unemployable; the chronically unemployed, discouraged workers, lumpen proletariat; leisure class, rentiers, coupon-clippers, idle rich

VERBS 12 **idle,** do nothing, **laze,** lazy <nf>, take one's ease *or* leisure, take one's time, **loaf, lounge; lie around,** lounge around, loll around, lollop about <Brit nf>, moon, moon around, sit around, sit on one's ass *or* butt *or* duff <nf>, stand *or* hang around, **loiter about** *or* **around,** slouch, slouch around, **bum around** *and* mooch around <nf>; **shirk,** avoid work, **goof off** *and* **lie down on the job** <nf>; sleep at one's post; let the grass grow under one's feet; twiddle one's thumbs, fold one's arms; back-burner

13 **waste time,** consume time, **kill time,** idle *or* trifle *or* fritter *or* fool away time, loiter away *or* loiter out the time, beguile the time, **while away the time,** pass the time, lose time, waste the precious hours, burn daylight ; **trifle,** dabble, fribble, footle, putter, potter, piddle, diddle, doodle

14 **dally, dillydally,** piddle, diddle, diddle-daddle, doodle, **dawdle, loiter,** lollygag <nf>, linger, lag, poke, take one's time, hang around *or* about <nf>, kick around <nf>

15 **take it easy,** take things as they come, **drift,** drift with the current, go with the flow, swim with the stream, coast, lead an easy life, **live a life of ease,** eat the bread of idleness, lie *or* rest on one's oars; rest *or* repose on one's laurels, lie back on one's record

16 **lie idle, lie fallow;** aestivate, hibernate, lie dormant; lie *or* lay off, charge *or* recharge one's batteries <nf>; lie up, lie on the shelf; ride at anchor, lay *or* lie by, lay *or* lie to; have nothing to do, have nothing on <nf>

ADJS 17 **inactive,** unactive; stationary, static, at a standstill; sedentary; **quiescent,** motionless 173.13; inanimate

18 **idle,** fallow, otiose; **unemployed, unoccupied,** disengaged, *désœuvré* <Fr>, **jobless, out of work,** out of employ, out of a job, out of harness; free, available, at liberty, at leisure; at loose ends; unemployable, lumpen; leisure, leisured; off-duty,

off-work, off; housebound, shut-in; back-burnered

19 **indolent, lazy,** bone-lazy, **slothful,** workshy, ergophobic; **do-nothing,** *fainéant* <Fr>, **laggard,** slow, **dilatory,** procrastinative, remiss, slack, slacking, lax; easy; **shiftless,** do-less <nf>; **unenterprising,** nonaggressive; good-for-nothing, ne'er-do-well; drony, dronish, spivvish <Brit>, parasitic, cadging, sponging, scrounging

20 **languid, languorous, listless,** lifeless, inanimate, enervated, debilitated, **pepless** <nf>, lackadaisical, slow, wan, **lethargic,** logy, hebetudinous, supine, lymphatic, apathetic, **sluggish,** dopey <nf>, drugged, nodding, droopy, **dull,** heavy, leaden, lumpish, **torpid,** stultified, stuporous, **inert,** stagnant, stagnating, vegetative, vegetable, dormant; phlegmatic, numb, benumbed; moribund, dead, exanimate, dead to the world; sleepy, somnolent 22.21; **pooped** <nf>, weary; jaded, sated 994.6; **blasé,** world-weary, bored; out cold, comatose

332 ASSENT

NOUNS 1 **assent, acquiescence, concurrence, concurring, concurrency, compliance, agreement, acceptance,** accession, agreeance; eager *or* hearty *or* warm assent, welcome; assentation; agreement in principle, general agreement; support; **consent** 441; oral agreement, written agreement

2 **affirmative; yes,** yea, aye, amen, OK, yeah <nf>; nod, nod of assent; thumbs-up; **affirmativeness,** affirmative attitude, yea-saying; **metooism;** toadying, automatic agreement, knee-jerk assent, subservience, ass-licking <nf>

3 **acknowledgment, recognition, acceptance;** appreciation; **admission,** confession, concession, allowance; avowal, profession, declaration; shout-out

4 **ratification, endorsement, acceptance, approval, approbation** 509.1, subscription, subscribership, signing-off, imprimatur, **sanction, permission, the OK** *and* the okay *and* **the green light** *and* **the go-ahead** *and* the nod <nf>, **certification, confirmation, validation, authentication,** authorization, warrant; **affirmation,** affirmance; stamp, rubber stamp, seal *or* **stamp of approval;** seal, signet, sigil; **subscription, signature,** John Hancock <nf>; countersignature; visa, *visé* <Fr>; notarization

5 **unanimity,** unanimousness, universal *or* univocal *or* unambiguous assent; **like-mindedness, meeting of minds,** one *or* same mind; total agreement; **understanding,** mutual understanding; **concurrence, consent,** general consent, common assent *or* consent, consentaneity, **accord,** accordance, **concord,** concordance, **agreement,** general agreement; **consensus,** consensus of opinion <nf>; *consensus omnium* <L>, universal agreement *or* accord, *consensus gentium* <L>, agreement of all, shared sense, sense of the meeting; **acclamation,** general acclamation; unison, harmony, **chorus, concert,** one *or* single voice, one accord; general voice, vox pop, *vox populi* <L>

6 **assenter, consenter, accepter,** covenanter, covenantor; assentator, yea-sayer; **yes-man,** toady, creature, ass-licker *and* ass-kisser *and* brown-nose *and* boot-licker <nf>, fellow traveler, supporter

7 **endorser, subscriber, ratifier,** approver, upholder, certifier, confirmer; **signer,** signatory, the undersigned; seconder; cosigner, cosignatory, party; underwriter, guarantor, insurer; notary, notary public

VERBS 8 **assent,** give *or* yield assent, **acquiesce, consent** 441.2, **comply, accede, agree,** agree to *or* with, have no problem with; find it in one's heart; take kindly to *and* hold with <nf>; **accept,** receive, buy <nf>, take one up on <nf>; **subscribe to,** acquiesce in, abide by; yes, **say 'yes' to; nod,** nod assent, vote for, cast one's vote for, give one's voice for; welcome, hail, cheer, acclaim, applaud, accept in toto

9 **concur, accord,** coincide, **agree, agree with,** agree in opinion; enter into one's view, enter into the ideas *or* feelings of, **see eye to eye, be at one with,** be of one mind with, go with, **go along with,** fall *or* chime *or* strike in with, close with, meet, conform to, side with, join *or* identify oneself with; cast in one's lot, fall in *or* into line, lend oneself to, play *or* go along, take kindly to; **echo,** ditto <nf>, say 'ditto' to, say 'amen' to; join in the chorus, go along with the crowd <nf>, run with the pack, go *or* float *or* swim with the stream *or* current; get on the bandwagon <nf>; rubber-stamp

10 **come to an agreement, agree, concur on, settle on,** agree with, **agree on** *or* **upon, arrive at an agreement, come to an understanding, come to terms, reach an understanding** *or* **agreement** *or* **accord,** strike *or* hammer out a bargain, covenant, get together <nf>; **shake hands on,** shake on it <nf>, seal the deal; come around to

11 **acknowledge, admit, own, confess, allow,** avow, **grant,** warrant, **concede,** yield , defer; **accept, recognize;** agree in principle, express general agreement, go along with, not oppose *or* deny, agree provisionally *or* for the sake of argument; bring oneself to agree, assent grudgingly *or* under protest; let the ayes have it; acknowledge the corn

12 **ratify, endorse,** sign off on, second, support, **certify, confirm, validate, authenticate, accept,** give the nod *or* the green light *or* the go-ahead *or* the OK <nf>, give a nod of assent, give one's imprimatur, permit, give permission, **approve** 509.9; sanction, **authorize,** warrant, accredit; **pass,** pass on *or* upon, give thumbs up <nf>; amen, say amen to; visa, *visé* <Fr>; underwrite, subscribe to; **sign,** undersign, sign on the dotted line, put one's John Hancock on <nf>, initial, put one's mark *or* X *or* cross on; autograph; cosign, countersign; seal, sign and seal, set one's seal, **set one's hand and seal;** affirm, swear and affirm, take one's oath, swear to; rubber stamp <nf>; notarize

ADJS 13 **assenting, agreeing,** acquiescing, **acquiescent, compliant,** consenting, consentient, consensual, submissive, unmurmuring, conceding, concessive, assentatious, **agreed, content**

14 **accepted, approved,** received; acknowledged, admitted, allowed, granted, conceded, recognized, professed, confessed, avowed, warranted; self-confessed; **ratified, endorsed, certified,** confirmed, validated, authenticated; certificatory, confirmatory, validating, warranting; **signed,** sealed, signed and sealed, countersigned, underwritten; stamped; sworn to, notarized, affirmed, sworn and affirmed

15 **unanimous, solid,** consentaneous, **with one consent** *or* **voice;** uncontradicted, unchallenged, uncontroverted, uncontested, unopposed; **concurrent,** concordant, **of one accord; agreeing, in agreement, likeminded, of one mind,** of the same mind; of a piece, **at one,** at one with, agreed on all hands, carried by acclamation

ADVS 16 **affirmatively,** assentingly, in the affirmative

17 **unanimously,** concurrently, consentaneously, **by common** *or* **general consent,** with one consent, **with one accord,** with one voice, without contradiction, *nemine contradicente* <L>, nem con, without a dissenting voice, *nemine dissentiente* <L>, in chorus, in concert, in unison, in one voice, univocally, unambiguously, to a man, **together,** all together, all agreeing, **as one,** as one man, one and all, on all hands; by acclamation

18 <nf terms> **yeah,** yep, yup, uh-huh; yes sirree, same here, likewise, indeedy, yes indeedy, sure, sure thing, sure enough, surest thing you know; right on!, righto!; OK, okay, okey-dokey; Roger, Roger-dodger; fine; you bet!, bet your ass!, you can bet on it!, you can say that again!, you

said it!, you better believe it; capeesh?

PHRS **19** **so be it,** be it so, so mote it be , so shall it be, amen; so it is, so is it; agreed, done, that's about the size of it; *c'est bien* <Fr>; that takes care of that, that's that, that's right; that makes two of us

333 DISSENT

NOUNS **1** **dissent, dissidence,** dissentience; nonassent, nonconsent, nonconcurrence, nonagreement, agreement to disagree; minority opinion *or* report *or* position; **disagreement, difference, variance,** diversity, disparity; **dissatisfaction, disapproval,** disapprobation, red light, thumbs down; repudiation, **rejection; refusal, opposition** 451; dissension, disaccord 456; **alienation,** withdrawal, dropping out, secession; recusance *or* recusancy, **nonconformity** 868; apostasy 363.2; counterculture, underground, alternative; raspberry *or* Bronx cheer <nf>

2 **objection, protest; kick** *and* **beef** *and* **bitch** *and* squawk *and* howl <nf>, protestation; **remonstrance, remonstration,** expostulation; **challenge; demur,** demurrer; **reservation, scruple,** compunction, qualm, twinge *or* qualm of conscience; **complaint, grievance; exception;** peaceful *or* nonviolent protest; **demonstration, demo** <nf>, protest demonstration, counterdemonstration, **rally,** march, sit-in, teach-in, boycott, strike, picketing, indignation meeting; grievance committee; **rebellion** 327.4

3 **dissenter, dissident,** dissentient, recusant; **objector,** demurrer; minority *or* opposition voice; **protester,** protestant, detractor; **separatist,** schismatic; sectary, sectarian, opinionist; nonconformist 868.3, odd man out; apostate 363.5; conscientious objector, passive resister; dissatisfied customer, bellyacher <nf>

VERBS **4** **dissent,** dissent from, be in dissent, say nay, **disagree,** discord with, **differ,** not agree, disagree with, agree to disagree *or* differ; divide on, be at variance; **take exception,** withhold assent, **take issue, beg to differ,** raise an objection, rise to a point of order; be in opposition to, oppose, be at odds with; refuse to conform, kick against the pricks, march to *or* hear a different drummer, swim against the tide *or* against the current *or* upstream; **split off, withdraw,** drop out, secede, separate *or* disjoin oneself, schismatize

5 **object, protest, kick** *and* **beef** <nf>, put up a struggle *or* fight; **bitch** *and* **beef** *and* **squawk** *and* howl *and* holler *and* put up a squawk *and* raise a howl <nf>; exclaim *or* cry out against, make *or* create *or* raise a stink about <nf>; yell bloody murder <nf>; **remonstrate,** expostulate; raise *or* press objections, raise one's voice against, enter a protest; **complain,** exclaim at, state a grievance, air one's grievances; **dispute, challenge,** call in question; **demur, scruple,** boggle, dig in one's heels; **demonstrate, demonstrate against,** rally, march, sit-in, teach-in, boycott, strike, picket; **rebel** 327.7

ADJS **6** **dissenting, dissident,** dissentient, recusant; **disagreeing, differing; opposing** 451.8, in opposition; alienated; counterculture, antiestablishment, underground, alternative; breakaway <Brit>; at variance with, at odds with; schismatic, schismatical, sectarian, sectary; heterodox; nonconforming 868.5; rebellious 327.11; resistant 453.5

7 **protesting,** protestant; **objecting,** expostulative, expostulatory, remonstrative, remonstrant; under protest

334 AFFIRMATION

NOUNS **1** **affirmation,** affirmance, **assertion,** assertation, **asseveration,** averment, **declaration,** vouch , allegation; **avouchment, avowal; position, stand,** stance; profession, **statement, word,** say, saying, say-so <nf>, positive declaration *or* statement, affirmative; manifesto, position paper; statement of principles, **creed** 953.3; **pronouncement, proclamation,** announcement, annunciation, enunciation; proposition, conclusion; predication, predicate; protest, protestation; utterance, dictum, *ipse dixit* <L>; emphasis, stress; admission, confession, disclosure; mission statement

2 **affirmativeness; assertiveness,** positiveness, absoluteness, speaking out, table-thumping <nf>; definiteness

3 **deposition, sworn statement, affidavit,** statement under oath, notarized statement, sworn testimony *or* statement, affirmation; **vouching, swearing; attestation;** certification; **testimony;** authentication, validation, verification, vouch ; substantiation, proof

4 **oath, vow,** avow , **word, assurance, guarantee, warrant,** promise, solemn oath *or* affirmation *or* word *or* declaration, word of honor; **pledge** 436.1; Bible oath, ironclad oath; judicial oath, extrajudicial oath, Hippocratic oath; oath of office, official oath; oath of allegiance, loyalty oath, test oath; commitment

VERBS 5 **affirm, assert,** assever , asseverate, **aver,** state positively, protest, lay down, avouch, avow, **declare,** say, say loud and clear, say out loud, sound off <nf>, have one's say, speak, speak one's piece *or* one's mind, speak up *or* out, **state,** set down, express, put, put it, put in one's two-cents worth <nf>; **allege,** profess; stand on *or* for; predicate; issue a manifesto *or* position paper, manifesto; announce, **pronounce,** annunciate, enunciate, **proclaim; maintain,** have, **contend,** argue, **insist, hold,** submit, maintain with one's last breath

6 **depose,** depone; **testify,** take the stand, witness; **warrant, attest,** certify, **guarantee, assure; vouch, vouch for, swear, swear to,** swear the truth, **assert under oath;** make *or* take one's oath, **vow;** swear by bell, book, and candle; call heaven to witness, declare *or* swear to God, swear on the Bible, kiss the book, swear to goodness, hope to die, cross one's heart *or* cross one's heart and hope to die; swear till one is black *or* blue in the face <nf>; corroborate, substantiate

7 administer an oath, **place** *or* **put under oath,** put to one's oath, put upon oath; **swear, swear in,** adjure ; charge

ADJS 8 **affirmative,** affirming, affirmatory, certifying, certificatory; **assertive,** assertative, assertional; annunciative, annunciatory; enunciative, enunciatory; **declarative,** declaratory; predicative, predicational; **positive,** absolute, emphatic, decided, table-thumping <nf>, unambiguously, unmistakably, loud and clear; attested, corroboratory, substantiating

9 **affirmed, asserted,** asseverated, avouched, avowed, averred, **declared; alleged,** professed; **stated,** pronounced, announced, annunciated, enunciated; predicated; manifestoed; **deposed,** warranted, **attested, certified,** vouched, **vouched for,** vowed, pledged, **sworn, sworn to;** strongly worded, emphatic, underscored; allegeable

ADVS 10 **affirmatively,** assertively, assertorily, declaratively, predicatively; **positively,** absolutely, decidedly, loudly, loud and clear, at the top of one's voice *or* one's lungs; emphatically, with emphasis, pointedly; without fear of contradiction; under oath, on one's honor *or* one's word

335 NEGATION, DENIAL

NOUNS 1 **negation,** negating, abnegation; negativeness, negativity, **negativism,** negative attitude, naysaying; **obtusenss,** perversity, orneriness <nf>, cross-grainedness; **negative, no,** nay, nix <nf>; defiance; refusal; unacceptance; pessimism, defeatism; deal breaker

2 **denial, disavowal, disaffirmation,** disaffirmance, **disownment,** disallowance; disclamation, disclaimer; **renunciation, retraction,** retractation, **repudiation,** recantation;

revocation, nullification, annulment, abrogation; abjuration, abjurement, forswearing; **contradiction,** flat *or* absolute contradiction, contravention, contrary assertion, controversion, countering, crossing, gainsaying, impugnment; flat denial, emphatic denial, **refutation, disproof** 958; **apostasy, defection** 363.2; **about-face, reversal** 363.1

VERBS **3 negate,** abnegate, negative; **say 'no',** no, naysay; shake one's head, wag *or* waggle the beard, nix <nf>; refuse, reject

4 deny, not admit, not accept, refuse to admit *or* accept; **disclaim, disown, disaffirm, disavow, disallow,** abjure, forswear, **renounce, retract,** take back, recant; revoke, nullify, **repudiate; contradict,** fly in the face of, cross, assert the contrary, contravene, controvert, impugn, **dispute,** gainsay, **oppose, counter,** go counter to, go contra, contest, take issue with, join issue upon, run counter to; belie, give the lie to, give one the lie direct *or* in his throat; deprecate; **refute** 958.5, **disprove** 958.4; **reverse oneself** 363.6; **defect, apostatize** 363.7

ADJS **5 negative,** negatory, abnegative, negational; **denying, disclaiming,** disowning, disaffirming, disallowing, disavowing, renunciative, renunciatory, repudiative, recanting, abjuratory, revocative *or* revocatory; **contradictory,** contradicting, contradictive, **opposing, contrary,** contra, counter, opposite, nay-saying, refuting, adversative, repugnant; **obtuse,** perverse, ornery <nf>, cross-grained, contrarious <nf>

ADVS **6 negatively, in the negative;** in denial, in contradiction, in opposition; in no way

CONJS **7 neither,** not either, **nor,** nor yet, or not, and not, also not

8 by no means, by no manner of means; on no account, in no respect, **in no case, under no circumstances, on no condition,** no matter what; **not at all,** not in the least, **never;** in no wise, in no way, noways, noway, nohow <nf>, not even; out of the question, in your dreams; **not for the world,** not for anything in the world, not if one can help it, not if I know it, not at any price, not for love or money, not for the life of me, over one's dead body; a thousand times no; to the contrary, *au contraire* <Fr>, quite the contrary, far from it; God forbid

9 <nf terms> nope, nix, no dice, unhunh, no sirree; no way, no way José, not on your life, not by a long chalk, not by a long shot *or* sight, not by a darn *or* damn sight, not a bit of it, not much, not a chance, fat chance, nothing doing, forget it, that'll be the day, you've got to be kidding *or* joking

336 IMITATION

NOUNS **1 imitation, copying,** counterfeiting, repetition; **me-tooism** <nf>, emulation, the sincerest form of flattery, following, mirroring, reflection, echo; copycat crime <nf>; **simulation** 354.3, modeling; fakery, forgery, plagiarism, plagiarizing, plagiary; **imposture, impersonation, takeoff** *and* hit-off <nf>, **impression,** burlesque, pastiche; mimesis; parody, onomatopoeia

2 mimicry, mockery, apery, parrotry, mimetism; protective coloration *or* mimicry, aggressive mimicry, aposematic *or* synaposematic mimicry *and* cryptic mimicry <biology>, playing possum

3 reproduction, duplication, imitation 784.1, **copy** 785.1, dummy, mock-up, **replica,** facsimile, representation, paraphrase, approximation, model, version, knockoff <nf>, recording, transcript; computer model *or* simulation; parody, burlesque, pastiche, travesty 508.6

4 imitator, simulator, me-tooer <nf>, **impersonator, impostor** 357.6, **mimic,** mimicker, mimer, mime, **mocker;** ventriloquist; mockingbird, cuckoo; **parrot,** polly, poll-parrot *or* polly-parrot, **ape,** aper, monkey; **echo,** echoer, echoist; **copier,** copyist, **copycat** <nf>; **faker, imposter,** counterfeiter, forger, plagiarist; dissimulator, dissembler, deceiver, gay deceiver, hypocrite, phony <nf>, poseur; conformist, sheep, slave to fashion

VERBS **5** **imitate, copy, repeat,** ditto <nf>; do like <nf>, do <nf>, act *or* go *or* make like <nf>; **mirror, reflect; echo,** reecho, chorus; **borrow,** steal one's stuff <nf>, take a leaf out of one's book; assume, **affect; simulate;** counterfeit, fake <nf>, hoke *and* hoke up <nf>, forge, plagiarize, crib, lift <nf>; **parody,** pastiche, travesty; **paraphrase,** approximate

6 **mimic, impersonate,** mime, **ape, parrot,** copycat <nf>; do an impression; take off, hit off, hit off on, take off on, send up

7 **emulate, follow,** follow in the steps *or* footsteps of, walk in the shoes of, put oneself in another's shoes, follow in the wake of, follow the example of, follow suit, follow like sheep, jump on the bandwagon, play follow the leader; **copy after,** model after, model on, pattern after, pattern on, shape after, take after, take a leaf out of one's book, take as a model

ADJS **8** **imitation, mock, sham,** copied, fake *and* phony <nf>, counterfeit, faux, dummy, forged, plagiarized, unoriginal, ungenuine; **pseudo,** synthetic, synthetical, artificial, man-made, ersatz, hokey *and* hoked-up <nf>, quasi

9 **imitative,** simulative, me-too <nf>, derivative; **mimic,** mimetic, **apish,** parrotlike; **emulative;** echoic, onomatopoetic, onomatopoeic

10 imitable, copiable, duplicable, replicable

ADVS **11** imitatively, apishly, apewise, parrotwise; onomatopoetically; synthetically; quasi

337 NONIMITATION

NOUNS **1** **nonimitation, originality, novelty,** newness, innovation, freshness, uniqueness; **authenticity;** inventiveness, creativity, creativeness 986.3; idiosyncrasy

2 **original, model** 786, archetype, prototype 786.1, master, **pattern, mold,** pilot model; **innovation,** new departure; original thought; precedent, invention

3 **autograph,** holograph, first edition; genuine article

VERBS **4** **originate, invent; innovate; create;** revolutionize; pioneer

ADJS **5** **original, novel, unprecedented; unique,** *sui generis* <L>; new, fresh 841.7; underived, **firsthand; authentic, imaginative, creative** 986.18; **avant-garde,** revolutionary; **pioneer,** bellwether, trail-blazing, first in the field; *nouvelle* <Fr>

6 **unimitated,** uncopied, **unduplicated,** unreproduced, unprecedented, unexampled; **archetypal,** archetypical, archetypic, seminal, prototypal 786.9; **prime,** primary, primal, primitive, pristine

338 COMPENSATION

NOUNS **1** **compensation, recompense,** repayment, payback, recoup, indemnity, indemnification, measure for measure, rectification, restitution, **reparation; amends,** expiation, atonement, meed ; damage control; **redress,** satisfaction, remedy; commutation, substitution; **offsetting,** balancing, **counterbalancing,** counteraction; payback time; **retaliation** 506, revenge, *lex talionis* <L>

2 **offset,** setoff; **counterbalance,** counterpoise, equipoise, counterweight, makeweight; **balance,** ballast; **trade-off,** equivalent, consideration, something of value, *quid pro quo* <L, something for something>, tit for tat, give-and-take 863.1; retroaction

3 **counterclaim,** counterdemand

VERBS **4** **compensate,** make compensation, make good, set right, restitute, pay back, rectify, **make up for; make amends,** expiate, do penance, atone; **recompense,** pay back, repay, indemnify, cover; **trade off,** give and take; correct, **retaliate** 506.4

5 **offset** 779.4, set off, **counteract,** countervail, **counterbalance,** counterweigh, counterpoise, **balance,**

play off against, set against, set over against, equiponderate; recoup, **square,** square up, settle the score

ADJS 6 **compensating, compensatory;** recompensive, amendatory, indemnificatory, reparative, rectifying, retributive; **offsetting,** counteracting *or* counteractive, countervailing, balancing, **counterbalancing,** zero-sum; **expiatory,** penitential; **retaliatory** 506.8

ADVS 7 **in compensation,** in return, back; in consideration, for a consideration

ADVS, CONJS 8 **notwithstanding,** but, all the same <nf>, still, yet, even; **however, nevertheless,** nonetheless; **although,** when, though; howbeit, albeit; **at all events,** in any event, **in any case,** at any rate; **be that as it may,** for all that, even so, **on the other hand,** rather, again, at the same time, all the same, just the same, **however, that may be;** after all, after all is said and done

339 CAREFULNESS

<close or watchful attention>

NOUNS 1 **carefulness, care, heed, concern, regard; attention** 983; **heedfulness,** regardfulness, mindfulness, **thoughtfulness; consideration,** solicitude, caring, loving care, tender loving care, TLC <nf>, caregiving, compassion; circumspectness, circumspection; forethought, anticipation, preparedness; **caution** 494

2 **painstakingness,** painstaking, **pains; diligence,** assiduousness, assiduity, sedulousness, industriousness, industry; **thoroughness,** thoroughgoingness

3 **meticulousness,** exactingness, **scrupulousness,** scrupulosity, **conscientiousness,** punctiliousness, attention to detail, fine-tuning; **particularness,** particularity, circumstantiality; **fussiness, criticalness,** criticality; **finicalness,** finickingness, finickiness, finicality, persnicketiness <nf>; **exactness, exactitude, accuracy, preciseness, precision,** precisionism, precisianism, punctuality, correctness, prissiness; **strictness, rigor,** rigorousness, spit and polish; nicety, niceness, delicacy, detail, subtlety, refinement, minuteness, exquisiteness, elegance

4 **vigilance, wariness,** prudence, **watchfulness,** watching, observance, **surveillance; watch, vigil, lookout;** *qui vive* <Fr>; invigilation, proctoring, monitoring; inspection; watch and ward; custody, custodianship, guardianship, stewardship; **guard,** guardedness, guard duty; **sharp eye, weather eye,** peeled eye, watchful eye, eagle eye, lidless *or* sleepless *or* unblinking *or* unwinking eye

5 **alertness, attentiveness; attention** 983; **wakefulness,** sleeplessness; **readiness,** promptness, promptitude, punctuality; **quickness,** agility, nimbleness; **smartness,** brightness, keenness, sharpness, acuteness, acuity

VERBS 6 **care, mind, heed,** reck, think, consider, regard, pay heed to, take heed *or* thought of; **take an interest,** be concerned; **pay attention** 983.8

7 **be careful, take care** *or* good care, take heed, have a care, exercise care; **be cautious** 494.5; **take pains,** take trouble, **be painstaking,** go to great pains, go to great lengths, go out of one's way, go the extra mile <nf>, bend over backwards <nf>, use every trick in the book, not miss a trick; mind what one is doing *or* about, mind one's business, **mind one's P's and Q's** <nf>; **watch one's step** <nf>, pick one's steps, tread on eggs, tread warily, walk on eggshells, place one's feet carefully, feel one's way; treat gently, **handle with gloves** *or* **kid gloves**

8 **be vigilant,** be watchful, never nod *or* sleep, **be on the watch** *or* **lookout,** be on the *qui vive* <Fr>, keep a good *or* sharp lookout, keep in sight *or* view; **keep watch,** keep watch and ward, keep vigil; **watch, look sharp,** look about one, look with one's own eyes, **be on one's guard,** keep an eye out, sleep with one eye

open, have all one's eyes *or* wits about one, keep one's eye on the ball <nf>, keep one's eyes open, keep a weather eye open *and* **keep one's eyes peeled** <nf>, keep the ear to the ground, keep a nose to the wind; keep alert, **be on the alert; look out, watch out;** look lively *or* alive; stop, look, and listen

9 look after, nurture, foster, **tend, take care of** 1008.19, care for, keep an eye on

ADJS **10 careful, heedful, regardful, mindful, thoughtful, considerate, caring,** solicitous, loving, tender, curious ; circumspect; **attentive** 983.15; **cautious** 494.8

11 painstaking, diligent, assiduous, sedulous, **thorough, thoroughgoing,** operose, industrious, elaborate

12 meticulous, exacting, scrupulous, conscientious, religious, punctilious, punctual, **particular, fussy, critical, attentive,** scrutinizing; **thorough,** thoroughgoing, thorough-paced; **finical,** finicking, finicky, high-maintenance; **exact, precise,** precisionistic, precisianistic, persnickety, prissy, **accurate, correct;** close, narrow; **strict,** rigid, **rigorous,** spit-and-polish, exigent, demanding; nice, delicate, subtle, fine, refined, minute, detailed, exquisite

13 vigilant, wary, prudent, **watchful,** lidless, sleepless, observant, chary; **on the watch, on the lookout,** *aux aguets* <Fr>; **on guard,** on one's guard, guarded; with open eyes, with one's eyes open, with one's eyes peeled *or* with a weather eye open <nf>; open-eyed, sharp-eyed, keen-eyed, Argus-eyed, eagle-eyed, hawk-eyed; all eyes, all ears, **all eyes and ears;** custodial

14 alert, on the alert, on the *qui vive* <Fr>, **on one's toes, on top** *and* **on the job** *and* on the ball <nf>, **attentive; awake,** wakeful, **wide-awake,** sleepless, unsleeping, unblinking, unwinking, unnodding, alive, ready, prompt, quick, agile, nimble, quick on the trigger *or* draw *or* uptake <nf>; **smart, bright, keen, sharp**

ADVS **15 carefully, heedfully,** regardfully, **mindfully,** thoughtfully, **considerately,** solicitously, tenderly, lovingly; circumspectly; **cautiously** 494.12; **with care,** with great care; **painstakingly, diligently,** assiduously, industriously, sedulously, thoroughly, thoroughgoingly, nine ways to Sunday *and* to a t *or* a turn *and* to a fare-thee-well <nf>

16 meticulously, exactingly, scrupulously, conscientiously, religiously, punctiliously, punctually, fussily; strictly, rigorously; exactly, **accurately, precisely, with exactitude, with precision;** nicely, with great nicety, refinedly, minutely, in detail, exquisitely

17 vigilantly, warily, prudently, **watchfully,** observantly; **alertly,** attentively; sleeplessly, unsleepingly, unwinkingly, unblinkingly, lidlessly, unnoddingly

340 NEGLECT

NOUNS **1 neglect,** neglectfulness, **negligence,** inadvertence *or* inadvertency, malperformance, dereliction, *culpa* <L>, culpable negligence, criminal negligence; **remissness,** laxity, laxness, slackness, looseness, laches; unrigorousness, permissiveness; noninterference, *laissez-faire* <Fr>, nonrestriction; **disregard,** airy disregard, slighting; **inattention** 984; **oversight,** overlooking; **omission,** nonfeasance, nonperformance, lapse, failure, **default;** poor stewardship *or* guardianship *or* custody; procrastination 846.5

2 carelessness, heedlessness, unheedfulness, disregardfulness, regardlessness, ignorance; unperceptiveness, impercipience, blindness, deliberate blindess; uncaring, unsolicitude, unsolicitousness, **thoughtlessness,** tactlessness, inconsiderateness, **inconsideration;** unthinkingness, unmindfulness, oblivion, forgetfulness; **unpreparedness,** unreadiness, lack of foresight *or* forethought; **recklessness** 493.2; **indifference** 102, *je-m'en-fichisme* and *je-m'en-foutisme* <Fr>; **laziness** 331.5; perfunctoriness; cursoriness, hastiness, offhandedness, casualness; easiness; nonconcern, insouciance; abandon, careless abandon, *sprezzatura* <Ital>

3 **slipshodness,** slipshoddiness, **slovenliness,** slovenry, sluttishness, untidiness, **sloppiness** *and* **messiness** <nf>; haphazardness; slapdash, slapdashness, a lick and a promise <nf>, loose ends; bad job, sad work, botch, slovenly performance; bungling 414.4; procrastination, avoidance

4 **unmeticulousness,** unexactingness, **unscrupulousness,** unrigorousness, **unconscientiousness,** unpunctiliousness, unpunctuality, unparticularness, unfussiness, unfinicalness, **uncriticalness;** inexactness, **inexactitude,** inaccuracy, imprecision, unpreciseness

5 **neglecter,** negligent , ignorer, disregarder; *je-m'en-fichiste* and *je-m'en-foutiste* <Fr>; **procrastinator,** waiter on Providence, Micawber <Dickens>; slacker, shirker, malingerer, dodger, goof-off *and* goldbrick <nf>, idler; skimper <nf>; trifler; sloven, slob; bungler 414.8

VERBS 6 **neglect, overlook, disregard,** not heed, not attend to, take for granted, **ignore;** not care for, not take care of; **pass over,** gloss over; **let slip, let slide** <nf>, let the chance slip by, **let go,** let ride <nf>, let take its course; let the grass grow under one's feet; put off till tomorrow; not think *or* consider, not give a thought to, take no thought *or* account of, blind oneself to, turn a blind eye to, leave out of one's calculation; lose sight of, lose track of; **be neglectful** *or* **negligent,** fail in one's duty, **fail,** lapse, **default,** let go by default; not get involved; nod, nod *or* sleep through, sleep , be caught napping, be asleep at the switch <nf>

7 **leave undone,** leave, **let go,** leave half-done, pretermit, **skip,** jump, **miss, omit,** cut *and* blow off <nf>, let be *or* alone, pass over, pass up <nf>, abandon; leave a loose thread, leave loose ends, let dangle, give a lick and a promise; **slack, shirk,** malinger, goof off *and* goldbrick <nf>; trifle; **procrastinate** 846.11

8 **slight;** turn one's back on, turn a cold shoulder to, get *or* give the cold shoulder *and* get *or* give the go-by *and* cold-shoulder <nf>, leave out in the cold; not lift a finger, leave undone; scamp, skimp <nf>; slur, **slur over,** pass over, skate over <Brit>, slubber over, slip *or* **skip over,** dodge, waffle <Brit nf>, fudge, blink, carefully ignore; skim, **skim over,** skim the surface, **touch upon,** touch upon lightly *or* in passing, pass over lightly, go once over lightly, **hit the high spots** *and* **give a lick and a promise** <nf>; **cut corners,** cut a corner

9 **do carelessly,** do by halves, do in a half-assed way <nf>, do in a slipshod fashion, do anyhow, do in any old way <nf>; botch, **bungle** 414.11; **trifle with,** play *or* play at fast and loose with, mess around *or* about with *and* muck around *or* about with *and* piss around *or* about with <nf>; **do offhand,** dash off, knock off *and* throw off <nf>, **toss off** *or* **out** <nf>; **roughhew,** roughcast, rough out; **knock out** <nf>, hammer *or* pound out, bat out <nf>; toss *or* slap *or* **throw together,** knock together, cobble up, patch together, patch, patch up, fudge up, fake up, whomp up <nf>, lash up <Brit nf>, slap up <nf>; jury-rig

ADJS 10 **negligent, neglectful,** neglecting, derelict, culpably negligent; inadvertent, uncircumspec, ignorant; **inattentive** 984.6; unwary, unwatchful, asleep at the switch, off-guard, unguarded; **remiss,** slack, lax, relaxed, laid-back <nf>, loose, loosey-goosey <nf>, unrigorous, permissive, overly permissive; noninterfering, *laissez-faire* <Fr>, nonrestrictive; slighting; slurring, scamping, skimping <nf>; procrastinating 846.17

11 **careless, heedless, unheeding, unheedful, disregardful,** disregardant, regardless, **unsolicitous, uncaring;** tactless, respectless, **thoughtless, unthinking, inconsiderate,** untactful, undiplomatic, mindless of, **un-**

mindful, forgetful, oblivious; **unprepared,** unready; **reckless** 493.8; **indifferent** 102.6; lackadaisical; lazy, shirking; perfunctory, cursory, casual, offhand; easygoing, *dégagé* <Fr>, airy, flippant, insouciant, free and easy, free as a bird

12 **slipshod,** slipshoddy, **slovenly,** sloppy *and* **messy** *and* half-assed <nf>, lax, slapdash, shoddy, sluttish, untidy, messy; **clumsy, bungling** 414.20; **haphazard, promiscuous, hit-or-miss,** hit-and-miss, deficient, half-assed <nf>, botched

13 **unmeticulous, unexacting, unpainstaking, unscrupulous,** unrigorous, **unconscientious,** unpunctilious, unpunctual, **unparticular, unfussy, unfinical, uncritical;** inexact, inaccurate, unprecise

14 **neglected,** unattended to, untended, unwatched, unchaperoned, uncared-for; **disregarded,** unconsidered, unregarded, **overlooked, missed,** omitted, passed by, passed over, passed up <nf>, gathering dust, **ignored, slighted**, blanked; unasked, unsolicited; half-done, undone, left undone; deserted, abandoned; in the cold *and* out in the cold <nf>; on the shelf, shelved, pigeonholed, on hold *and* on the back burner <nf>, **put** *or* **laid aside,** sidetracked *and* sidelined <nf>, shunted

15 **unheeded, unobserved, unnoticed, unnoted, unperceived, unseen,** undiscerned, undescried, unmarked, unremarked, unregarded, unminded, unconsidered, unthought-of, unmissed

16 **unexamined, unstudied,** unconsidered, unsearched, unscanned, unweighed, unsifted, unexplored, uninvestigated, unindagated, unconned

ADVS **17** **negligently, neglectfully,** inadvertently; **remissly,** laxly, slackly, loosely; **unrigorously,** permissively; nonrestrictively; **slightingly,** lightly, slurringly; scampingly, skimpingly <nf>

18 **carelessly, heedlessly,** unheedingly, unheedfully, disregardfully, regardlessly, **thoughtlessly, unthinkingly, unsolicitously,** tactlessly, **inconsiderately,** unmindfully, forgetfully; **inattentively, unwarily,** unvigilantly, unguardedly, unwatchfully; **recklessly** 493.11; perfunctorily; once over lightly, cursorily; casually, offhand, offhandedly, airily; clumsily, bunglingly 414.24; **sloppily** *and* **messily** <nf>, sluttishly, shoddily, shabbily; haphazardly, promiscuously, hit or miss *and* hit and miss *and* helter-skelter *and* slapdash *and* anyhow *and* any old way *and* any which way <nf>

19 **unmeticulously, unscrupulously, unconscientiously,** unfussily, **uncritically;** inexactly, inaccurately, unprecisely, imprecisely, unrigorously, unpunctually

341 INTERPRETATION

NOUNS **1** **interpretation, construction, reading,** way of seeing *or* understanding *or* putting; constructionism, strict constructionism, loose constructionism; **diagnosis; definition,** description; **meaning** 518

2 **rendering, rendition; text,** edited text, diplomatic text, normalized text; **version;** reading, lection, variant, variant reading; **edition,** critical *or* scholarly edition; variorum edition *or* variorum; conflation, composite reading *or* text

3 **translation,** transcription, transliteration; Englishing; **paraphrase,** loose *or* free translation; decipherment, decoding, code cracking, unscrambling; amplification, restatement, rewording, simplification; metaphrase, literal *or* verbal *or* faithful *or* word-for-word translation; **pony** *and* trot *and* crib <nf>; interlinear, interlinear translation, bilingual text *or* edition; **gloss, glossary;** key, *clavis* <L>; lipreading

4 **explanation,** explication, unfolding, **elucidation,** illumination, enlightenment, light, **clarification,** *éclaircissement* <Fr>, simplification; take <nf>; **exposition,** expounding, exegesis; **illustration, demonstration,** exemplification; **reason,** rationale; euhemerism, demythologization, allegorization;

decipherment, decoding, cracking, unlocking, **solution** 940; editing, emendation; critical revision, recension, diaskeuasis

5 <explanatory remark> **comment, word of explanation**, explanatory remark**; annotation,** notation, **note,** note of explanation, footnote, gloss, definition, scholium; exegesis; *apparatus criticus* <L>; commentary, commentation ; legend, appendix

6 **interpretability,** interpretableness, construability; **definability, describability;** translatability; **explicability,** explainableness, accountableness

7 **interpreter,** exegete, exegetist, exegesist, hermeneut; constructionist, strict constructionist, loose constructionist; **commentator,** annotator, scholiast; critic, textual critic, **editor,** diaskeuast, emender, emendator; cryptographer, cryptologist, decoder, decipherer, cryptanalyst, lipreader; **explainer,** lexicographer, definer, **explicator,** exponent, expositor, expounder, clarifier; demonstrator, euhemerist, demythologizer, allegorist; go-between 576.4; **translator,** metaphrast, paraphrast; oneirocritic; guide, *cicerone* <Ital>, dragoman

8 <science of interpretation> exegetics, hermeneutics; tropology; criticism, literary criticism, textual criticism; paleography, epigraphy; cryptology, cryptography, cryptanalysis; lexicography; diagnostics, symptomatology, semiology, semiotics; pathognomy; physiognomics, physiognomy; metoposcopy; oneirology, oneirocriticism

VERBS **9** **interpret, diagnose; construe,** put a construction on, **take;** understand, **understand by, take to mean,** take it that; **read; read into,** read between the lines; see in a special light, read in view of, take an approach to

10 **explain, explicate, expound,** make of, exposit; **give the meaning,** tell the meaning of, **define, describe**; **spell out,** unfold; **account for,** give reason for; **clarify, elucidate,** clear up, clear the air, **cover** *and* cover the waterfront *or* the territory <nf>, **make clear,** make plain; **simplify,** popularize; **illuminate,** enlighten, give insight, **shed** *or* **throw light upon;** rationalize, euhemerize, demythologize, allegorize; tell *or* show how, show the way; **demonstrate, show, illustrate,** exemplify, represent; get to the bottom of *or* to the heart of, make sense of, make head or tails of; decipher, crack, unlock, find the key to, unravel, demystify, read between the lines, read into, **solve** 940.2; explain oneself; explain away; overinterpret

11 **comment upon,** commentate, remark upon; **annotate,** gloss; **edit,** make an edition

12 **translate, render,** transcribe, transliterate, put *or* turn into, transfuse the sense of; construe; disambiguate

13 **paraphrase, rephrase, reword, restate,** rehash; give a free *or* loose translation

ADJS **14** **interpretative,** interpretive, interpretational, exegetic, exegetical, hermeneutic, hermeneutical; constructive, constructional; **diagnostic;** symptomatological, semeiological; tropological; **definitional, descriptive**

15 **explanatory,** explaining, exegetic, exegetical, **explicative,** explicatory, defining; **expository,** expositive; **clarifying, elucidative, elucidatory; illuminating,** illuminative, enlightening; **demonstrative, illustrative,** exemplificative; glossarial, annotative, critical, editorial, scholiastic; rationalizing, rationalistic, euhemeristic, demythologizing, allegorizing

16 **translational,** translative; paraphrastic, metaphrastic; literal, word-for-word, verbatim

17 **interpretable, construable; definable,** describable; translatable, renderable; Englishable ; explainable, explicable, accountable; diagnosable

ADVS **18** **by interpretation,** as here interpreted, as here defined, according to this reading; **in explanation, to explain; that is,** that is to say, as it were, *id est* <L>, i.e.; **to wit, namely,** *videlicet* <L>, viz, *scilicet* <L>, sc; **in other words,** in words to that effect

342 MISINTERPRETATION

NOUNS 1 **misinterpretation, misunderstanding,** *malentente* <Fr>, misintelligence, **misapprehension, misreading, misconstruction,** mistaking, malobservation, **misconception; misrendering,** mistranslation, translator's error, eisegesis; misexplanation, misexplication, misexposition; misreading; misapplication; gloss; **perversion, distortion,** wrenching, twisting, contorting, torturing, squeezing, garbling; reversal; abuse of terms, misuse of words, catachresis; misquotation, miscitation; misjudgment 948; **error** 975; misrepresentation; sniglet

VERBS 2 **misinterpret, misunderstand,** misconceive, **mistake, misapprehend; misread, misconstrue,** put a false construction on, miss the point, **take wrong, get wrong,** get one wrong, take amiss, take the wrong way; **get backwards,** reverse, have the wrong way round, put the cart before the horse; misapply; misexplain, misexplicate, misexpound; **misrender,** mistranslate; quote out of context; misquote, miscite, give a false coloring, give a false impression *or* idea, gloss; misread; **garble, pervert, distort,** wrench, contort, torture, squeeze, twist the words *or* meaning, stretch *or* strain the sense *or* meaning, misdeem, **misjudge** 948.2; bark up the wrong tree; misrepresent

ADJS 3 **misinterpreted, misunderstood, mistaken, misapprehended, misread,** eisegetical, misconceived, **misconstrued; garbled,** misquoted, misrepresented, **perverted, distorted,** catachrestic, catechrestical; backwards, reversed, assbackwards <nf>

4 **misinterpretable, misunderstandable,** mistakable

343 COMMUNICATION

NOUNS 1 **communication,** communion, congress, **commerce, intercourse;** means of communication, **speaking, speech** 524, utterance, speech act, talking, linguistic intercourse, speech situation, speech circuit, converse, **conversation** 541; signalling; **contact, touch, connection; interpersonal communication, intercommunication,** intercommunion, grokking <nf>, **interplay,** interaction; **exchange,** interchange; answer, response, reply; one-way communication, two-way communication; **dealings,** dealing, **traffic, truck** <nf>; information 551; message 552.4; ESP, telepathy 689.9; writing; correspondence 553; social intercourse 582.4; media studies

2 **informing, telling,** imparting, impartation, impartment, **conveyance, transmission,** transmittal, transfer, transference, sharing, giving, sending, signaling, letting one in on; notification, alerting, **announcement** 352.2, publication 352, **disclosure** 351

3 **communicativeness, talkativeness** 540, **sociability** 582; **unreserve,** unreservedness, **unreticence, unrestraint, unconstraint,** unrestriction; **unrepression,** unsuppression; **unsecretiveness,** untaciturnity; candor, **frankness** 644.4; **openness,** plainness, freeness, outspokenness, plainspokenness; **accessibility,** approachability, conversableness; **extroversion,** outgoingness; **uncommunicativeness** 344, reserve, taciturnity

4 **communicability, impartability, conveyability, transmittability,** transmissibility, transferability; contagiousness

5 **communications,** electronic communications, communications industry, media, communications medium *or* media, mass communications, communications network; telecommunication 347.1,long-distance communication; radio communication, wire communication, broadcasting, satellite broadcasting, broadband, podcasting; information theory 551.7; signaling

VERBS 6 **communicate, be in touch** *or* **contact,** be in connection *or* intercourse, have intercourse, hold communication; **intercommunicate,** interchange, commune with; grok <nf>; commerce with, **deal with, traffic with, have dealings with, have truck with** <nf>; **speak, talk,** be in a speech situation, **converse** 541.8, pass the time of day

7 **communicate, impart, tell,** lay on one <nf>, **convey, transmit,** transfer, send, send word, deliver *or* send a signal *or* message, **disseminate,** broadcast, pass, **pass on** *or* **along, hand on; report, render, make known,** get across *or* over, let in on; give *or* send *or* leave word; **signal;** share, share with; **leak,** let slip out, **give** 478.12; tell 551.8

8 **communicate with, get in touch** *or* **contact with, contact** <nf>, **make contact with,** raise, reach, get to, get through to, get hold of, make *or* establish connection, get in connection with; **make advances,** make overtures, **approach,** make up to <nf>; relate to; keep in touch *or* contact with, maintain connection; **answer,** respond *or* reply to, get back to; **question,** interrogate; **correspond,** drop a line; reconnect

ADJS 9 **communicational, communicating,** communional; transmissional; speech, **verbal,** linguistic, oral; **conversational** 541.12; **intercommunicational,** intercommunicative, intercommunional, interactional, interactive, interacting, interresponsive, responsive, answering; questioning, interrogative, interrogatory; telepathic

10 **communicative, talkative** 540.9, gossipy, newsy; **sociable; unreserved, unreticent,** unshrinking, **unrestrained, unconstrained,** unhampered, unrestricted; demonstrative, expansive, effusive; **unrepressed, unsuppressed; unsecretive,** unsilent, untaciturn; candid, **frank** 644.17; self-revealing, self-revelatory; **open,** free, outspoken, free-speaking, free-spoken, free-tongued; **accessible, approachable,** conversable, easy to speak to; **extroverted,** outgoing; **uncommunicative** 344.8

11 **communicable, impartable, conveyable, transmittable,** transmissible, transferable; contagious

12 communicatively; verbally, talkatively, by word of mouth, orally, viva voce

344 UNCOMMUNICATIVENESS

NOUNS 1 **uncommunicativeness,** closeness, indisposition to speak, disinclination to communicate; unconversableness, **unsociability** 583; nondisclosure, **secretiveness** 345.1; lack of message *or* meaning, meaninglessness 520; miscommunication

2 **taciturnity, untalkativeness,** unloquaciousness; **silence** 51; **speechlessness,** wordlessness, dumbness, **muteness** 51.2; quietness, quietude; laconicalness, laconism, curtness, shortness, terseness; brusqueness, briefness, brevity, conciseness, economy *or* sparingness of words, pauciloquy

3 **reticence** *or* reticency; **reserve,** reservedness, restraint, low key, **constraint;** guardedness, discreetness, discretion; suppression, repression; subduedness; backwardness, retirement, low profile; **aloofness, standoffishness,** distance, remoteness, **detachment,** withdrawal, withdrawnness, reclusiveness, solitariness; impersonality; **coolness,** coldness, frigidity, iciness, frostiness, chilliness; **inaccessibility, unapproachability; undemonstrativeness,** unexpansiveness, unaffability, uncongeniality; **introversion;** modesty, bashfulness 139.4, pudency; expressionlessness, blankness, impassiveness, impassivity; straight *or* poker face, mask

4 **prevarication, equivocation,** tergiversation, **evasion,** shuffle, fencing, dodging, parrying, waffling *and* tap-dancing <nf>; *suppressio veri* <L>; weasel words

5 **man of few words,** clam <nf>, strong silent type, laconic ; Spartan, Laconian; evader, weasel

VERBS 6 **keep to oneself,** keep one's own counsel; not open one's mouth, not say a word, not breathe a word, stand mute, **hold one's tongue** 51.5, clam up <nf>; bite one's tongue; have little to say, refuse comment, say neither yes nor no, waste no words, save one's breath; retire; **keep one's distance,** keep at a distance, keep oneself to oneself, **stand aloof,** hold oneself aloof; keep secret 345.7

7 **prevaricate, equivocate,** waffle <nf>, tergiversate, evade, dodge, sidestep, pussyfoot, say in a roundabout way, parry, duck, weasel *and* weasel out <nf>, palter; hum and haw, **hem and haw,** back and fill; **mince words,** mince the truth, euphemize

ADJS 8 **uncommunicative,** indisposed *or* disinclined to communicate; unconversational, unconversable ; **unsociable** 583.5; **secretive** 345.15; meaningless 520.6

9 **taciturn, untalkative,** unloquacious, indisposed to talk; **silent, speechless,** wordless, **mum; mute** 51.12, dumb, quiet; close, **close-mouthed,** close-tongued, snug <nf>, **tight-lipped;** close-lipped, tongue-tied, word-bound; **laconic,** curt, brief, terse, brusque, short, concise, **sparing of words,** economical of words, of few words

10 **reticent, reserved,** restrained, nonassertive, low-key, low-keyed, constrained; **suppressed,** repressed; subdued; guarded, discreet; backward, **retiring,** shrinking; **aloof, standoffish,** offish <nf>, standoff, **distant,** remote, removed, **detached,** Olympian, withdrawn; impersonal; **cool,** cold, frigid, icy, frosty, chilled, chilly; **inaccessible, unapproachable,** forbidding; **undemonstrative,** unexpansive, unaffable, uncongenial, ungenial; **introverted;** modest, verecund, verecundious, *pudique* <Fr>, bashful 139.12; expressionless, blank, impassive

11 **prevaricating, equivocal,** tergiversating, tergiversant, waffling <nf>, **evasive,** weaselly, weasel-worded

345 SECRECY

NOUNS 1 **secrecy,** secretness, airtight secrecy, close secrecy; crypticness; the dark; hiddenness, hiding, **concealment** 346; **secretiveness,** closeness; discreetness, discretion, **uncommunicativeness** 344; **evasiveness,** evasion, subterfuge; hugger-mugger, hugger muggery; Area 51; back channel; down-low

2 **privacy,** retirement, isolation, sequestration, seclusion; incognito, anonymity; **confidentialness,** confidentiality; closed meeting *or* session, executive session, private conference, secret meeting

3 **veil of secrecy, veil,** curtain, pall, wraps; iron curtain, bamboo curtain; wall *or* barrier of secrecy, wall of silence; **suppression,** repression, stifling, smothering; **censorship,** blackout <nf>, **hush-up, cover-up; seal of secrecy,** official secrecy, classification, official classification; security, ironbound security; pledge *or* oath of secrecy

4 **stealth,** stealthiness, **furtiveness, clandestineness,** clandestinity, clandestine behavior, **surreptitiousness, covertness,** slyness, shiftiness, sneakiness, slinkiness, underhandedness, underhand dealing, undercover *or* underground activity, **covert activity** *or* **operation;** prowl, prowling; stalking; hugger-mugger; counterintelligence; conspiracy, cabal, intrigue; funny business <nf>; secret service, intelligence agency

5 **secret, confidence;** private *or* personal matter, privity ; trade secret; confidential *or* **privileged information** *or* **communication;** doctor-patient *or* lawyer-client confidentiality; seal *or* secret of the confessional; more than meets the eye; deep dark secret; solemn secret; guarded secret, hush-hush matter, classified information, eyes-only *or* top-secret information, restricted information; confession; inside information, inside skinny <nf>; **mystery, enigma** 522.8; the arcane, arcanum, *arcanum arcanorum* <L>; esoterica, cabala, the

occult, occultism, hermetism, hermeticism, hermetics; deep *or* profound secret, sealed book, mystery of mysteries; skeleton in the closet *or* cupboard, family secret; sealed orders, state secret

6 **cryptography,** cryptoanalysis, cryptoanalytics; **code, cipher;** secret language; code book, code word, code name; **secret writing,** coded message, cryptogram, cryptograph; secret *or* invisible *or* sympathetic ink; cryptographer

VERBS 7 **keep secret, keep mum, veil,** keep dark; keep it a deep, dark secret; secrete, **conceal;** keep to oneself 344.6, bosom, keep close, keep snug <nf>, keep back, keep from, **withhold,** hold out on <nf>; not let it go further, keep within these walls, keep within the bosom of the lodge, keep between us; **not tell,** hold one's tongue 51.5, never let on <nf>, make no sign, not breathe *or* whisper a word, clam up <nf>, be the soul of discretion; **not give away** <nf>, **keep it under one's hat** <nf>, keep under wraps <nf>, keep a lid on, keep buttoned up <nf>, keep one's own counsel; play one's cards close to the chest *or* to one's vest; play dumb; clam up; not let the right hand know what the left is doing; keep in ignorance, keep *or* leave in the dark; classify; file and forget; **have secret** *or* **confidential information,** be in on the secret *and* know where the bodies are buried <nf>; anonymize

8 **cover up,** muffle up; **hush up, hush,** hush-hush, shush, hugger-mugger; **suppress,** repress, **stifle,** muffle, **smother,** squash, quash, squelch, kill, sit on *or* upon, put the lid on <nf>; **censor,** black out <nf>

9 **tell confidentially,** tell for one's ears only, mention privately, **whisper, breathe, whisper in the ear;** tell one a secret; take aside, see one alone, talk to in private, speak in privacy; say under one's breath

10 code, encode, encipher, cipher

ADJS 11 **secret,** close, closed, closet; cryptic, dark; unuttered, unrevealed, undivulged, undisclosed, unspoken, untold; **hush-hush, top secret,** supersecret, eyes-only, classified, restricted, under wraps <nf>, under security *or* security restrictions; **censored,** suppressed, stifled, smothered, hushed-up, under the seal *or* ban of secrecy; **unrevealable, undivulgable, undisclosable, untellable,** unwhisperable, unbreatheable, unutterable; latent, ulterior, concealed, hidden 346.11; arcane, esoteric, occult, cabalistic, hermetic; enigmatic, mysterious 522.18

12 **covert, clandestine,** quiet, unobtrusive, hugger-mugger, **surreptitious, undercover,** underground, under-the-counter, under-the-table, **cloak-and-dagger** <nf>, backdoor, hole-and-corner <nf>, underhand, **underhanded; furtive, stealthy,** privy, backstairs, **sly, shifty, sneaky,** sneaking, skulking, slinking, slinky, feline

13 **private, privy, closed-door; intimate, inmost,** innermost, interior, inward, **personal; privileged,** protected; **secluded, sequestered,** isolated, withdrawn, retired; incognito, anonymous

14 **confidential,** auricular, **inside** <nf>, esoteric; close to one's chest *or* vest <nf>, under one's hat <nf>; **off the record,** not for the record, not to be minuted, within these four walls, in the bosom of the lodge, for no other ears, eyes-only, between us; not to be quoted, not for publication *or* release; not for attribution; unquotable, unpublishable, sealed; sensitive, privileged, under privilege

15 **secretive,** close-lipped, secret, close, dark; discreet; evasive, shifty; **uncommunicative, close-mouthed**

16 coded, encoded; ciphered, enciphered; cryptographic, cryptographical; hieroglyphic

ADVS 17 **secretly, in secret,** in *or* up one's sleeve, on the down-low; in the closet; with nobody the wiser; **covertly,** stownlins *and* in hidlings, **undercover,** *à couvert* <Fr>, under the cloak of; **behind the scenes,** in the background, in a corner, in the dark, in darkness, behind the veil *or* curtain, behind the veil of secrecy;

sub rosa <L>, under the rose; underground; *sotto voce* <Ital>, under the breath, with bated breath, in a whisper; off the record

18 **surreptitiously, clandestinely, secretively, furtively, stealthily, slyly,** shiftily, sneakily, sneakingly, skulkingly, slinkingly, slinkily; by stealth, **on the sly** *and* **on the quiet** *and* on the qt <nf>, *à la dérobée* <Fr>, *en tapinois* <Fr>, behind one's back, by a side door, **like a thief in the night,** underhand, underhandedly, under the table, in holes and corners *and* in a hole-and-corner way <nf>

19 **privately,** privily, **in private,** in privacy, in privy; apart, aside; **behind closed doors,** *januis clausis* <L>, *à huis clos* <Fr>, *in camera* <L>, in chambers, in secret *or* closed meeting, in executive session, in private conference

20 **confidentially, in confidence,** in strict confidence, under the seal of secrecy, **off the record; between ourselves,** strictly between us, *entre nous* <Fr>, *inter nos* <L>, for your ears *or* eyes only, between you and me, from me to you, between you and me and the bedpost *or* lamppost <nf>

346 CONCEALMENT

NOUNS 1 **concealment, hiding, secretion;** burial, burying, interment, putting away; **cover, covering,** covering up, masking, screening 295.1; mystification, obscuration; darkening, obscurement, clouding 1027.6; hiddenness, concealedness, **covertness,** occultation; eclipse; disappearance; **secrecy** 345; uncommunicativeness 344; invisibility 32; **subterfuge, deception** 356

2 **veil,** curtain, **cover, screen** 295.2, mask, camouflage; fig leaf; **wraps** <nf>; **cover, disguise**

3 **ambush,** ambushment, **ambuscade,** *guet-apens* <Fr>; surveillance, shadowing 938.9; lurking hole *or* place; blind, stalking-horse; booby trap, trap

4 **hiding place, hideaway, hideout,** hidey-hole <nf>, hiding, concealment, **cover,** secret place; safe house; drop, accommodation address <Brit>; **recess, corner,** dark corner, nook, cranny, niche; **hole,** bolt-hole, foxhole, trench, dugout, lair, den; bomb shelter, storm shelter; **asylum, sanctuary, retreat, refuge** 1009; covert, coverture, undercovert; **cache,** stash <nf>; safe-deposit box, bank vault, safe, lockbox; cubbyhole, cubby, pigeonhole; secret compartment; mother's skirts

5 **secret passage,** covert way, secret exit; **back way, back door, side door;** bolt-hole, escape route, escape hatch, escapeway; secret staircase, *escalier dérobé* <Fr>, **back stairs; underground,** underground route, underground railroad

VERBS 6 **conceal, hide,** ensconce; **cover, cover up,** blind, **screen, cloak, veil,** screen off, curtain, blanket, shroud, enshroud, envelop; **disguise, camouflage, mask,** dissemble; plain-wrap, wrap in plain brown paper; whitewash <nf>; **paper over,** gloss over, varnish, slur over; distract attention from; **obscure,** obfuscate, cloud, becloud, befog, throw out a smoke screen, shade, throw into the shade; **eclipse,** occult; put out of sight, sweep under the rug *or* carpet, keep under cover, keep under wraps; cover up one's tracks, lay a false scent, hide one's trail; hide one's light under a bushel

7 **secrete, hide away,** keep hidden, put away, store away, stow away, file and forget, bottle up, lock up, seal up, put out of sight; **keep secret** 345.7; **cache,** stash <nf>, deposit, plant <nf>; **bury;** bosom, embosom

8 <hide oneself> **hide, conceal oneself, take cover, hide out** <nf>, hide away, **go into hiding,** go to ground; stay in hiding, **lie hid** *or* **hidden,** lie *or* lay low <nf>, lie perdue, lie snug *or* close <nf>, lie doggo *and* sit tight <nf>, burrow , **hole up** <nf>, **go underground;** play peekaboo *or* bopeep *or* hide and seek; keep out of sight, retire from sight, drop from sight, disappear 34.2, crawl *or*

retreat into one's shell, keep *or* stay in the background, keep a low profile, stay in the shade; **disguise oneself,** masquerade, take an assumed name, assume a cover, change one's identity, go under an alias, remain anonymous, be incognito, go *or* sail under false colors, wear a mask; leave no address; reinvent oneself

9 **lurk,** couch; **lie in wait,** lay wait; **sneak, skulk, slink, prowl,** nightwalk, **steal, creep,** pussyfoot <nf>, gumshoe <nf>, tiptoe; stalk, shadow 938.35

10 **ambush,** ambuscade, **waylay; lie in ambush,** lay wait for, **lie in wait for,** lay for <nf>; stalk; set a trap for, still-hunt

ADJS **11** **concealed, hidden, hid,** occult, recondite , blind; **covered** 295.31; **covert, under cover,** under wraps <nf>; code-named; **obscured,** obfuscated, clouded, clouded over, wrapped in clouds, in a cloud *or* fog *or* mist *or* haze, beclouded, befogged; eclipsed, in eclipse, under an eclipse; in the wings; buried; underground; close, secluded, secluse, sequestered; in purdah, under house arrest, incommunicado; **obscure,** abstruse, mysterious 522.18; **secret** 345.11; unknown 930.16, latent 519.5

12 **unrevealed, undisclosed,** undivulged, **unexposed;** unapparent, **invisible, unseen,** unperceived, unspied, undetected; undiscovered, unexplored, untraced, untracked; unaccounted for, unexplained, unsolved

13 **disguised, camouflaged, in disguise;** masked, masquerading; **incognito,** incog <nf>, anonymous, unrecognizable; in plain wrapping *or* plain brown paper <nf>; cryptic, coded, codified

14 **in hiding,** hidden out, **under cover,** in a dark corner, lying hid, doggo <nf>; in ambush *or* ambuscade; waiting concealed, lying in wait; in the wings; lurking, skulking, prowling, sneaking, stealing; pussyfooted, pussyfoot, on tiptoe; stealthy, furtive, surreptitious 345.12

15 **concealing, hiding,** obscuring, obfuscatory; covering; unrevealing, nonrevealing, undisclosing

347 COMMUNICATIONS

NOUNS **1** **communications,** signaling, telecommunication, comms <Brit nf>, transmission; electronic communication, electrical communication; satellite communication; wire communication, wireless communication; communications engineering, communications technology; communications engineer; media, communications medium *or* media; communication or information theory 551.7; communication *or* information explosion

2 **telegraph, telegraph recorder,** ticker; **telegraphy,** telegraphics, data transmission; **teleprinter,** Telex <TM>, teletypewriter; teleprinter exchange *or* telex; wire service; code 345.6; electricity 1032; **key,** interrupter, transmitter, sender; receiver, **sounder**

3 **radio** 1034, **radiotelephony, radiotelegraphy,** wireless <Brit>, wireless telephony, wireless telegraphy; line radio, wire *or* wired radio, wired wireless <Brit>, wire wave communication; radiophotography; digital audio broadcasting *or* DAB; **television** 1035; electronics 1033

4 **telephone, phone** *and* horn <nf>, dog <Brit nf>, telephone set, handset; telephony, telephonics, telephone mechanics, telephone engineering; high-frequency telephony; receiver, telephone receiver, earpiece; mouthpiece, transmitter; telephone extension, extension; wall telephone, desk telephone; dial *or* rotary telephone, touch-tone telephone, push-button telephone, cordless phone; beeper; scrambler; telephone booth, telephone box, call box <Brit>, telephone kiosk <Brit>, public telephone, coin telephone, pay station, pay phone; mobile telephone *or* phone <nf>, cellular *or* cell telephone *or* phone <nf>, car phone, digital phone, flip phone; iPhone <TM>; SIM *or* SIM card;

speakerphone, videophone; speed calling, call forwarding, call waiting, redial, caller ID service; phone card; facsimilie transmission, fax

5 **radiophone, radiotelephone,** wireless telephone, wireless; headset, headphone 50.8

6 **intercom** <nf>, Interphone, intercommunication system

7 **telephone exchange,** telephone office, central office, **central;** automatic exchange, machine-switching office; step-by-step switching, panel switching, crossbar switching, electronic switching

8 **switchboard; PBX** *or* private branch *or* business exchange, private exchange; in *or* A board, out *or* B board

9 **telephone operator, operator,** switchboard operator, telephonist, central ; long distance; PBX operator

10 **telephone man;** telephone mechanic; telephonic engineer; lineman *or* linewoman

11 **telephoner,** phoner <nf>, caller, **party,** calling party, subscriber

12 telephone number, **phone number** <nf>, unlisted number, fax number, cell phone number; telephone directory *or* book, phone book <nf>; telephone exchange, exchange; telephone area, area code; calling zone

13 telephone call, **phone call** <nf>, **call, ring** *and* buzz <nf>; local call, toll call, long-distance call; long distance, direct distance nondialing, DDD; trunk call; station-to-station call, person-to-person call; collect call; toll-free call; mobile call; dial tone, busy signal; crank call, nuisance call; conference call, video teleconference, teleconference; hot line; chat *or* talk *or* gab line, messagerie; voicemail, phonemail; electronic mail *or* e-mail *or* email; telemarketing; direct marketing; multilevel marketing, multilevel sales; cold call; ringy-dingy *or* jingle *or* tinkle <nf>

14 **telegram, telegraph, wire** <nf>, telex; **cablegram, cable; radiogram,** radiotelegram; **day letter, night letter;** fast telegram

15 **Telephoto** <TM>, Wirephoto <TM>, Telecopier <TM>, **facsimile, fax** <nf>; telephotograph, radiophotograph

16 **telegrapher,** telegraphist, telegraph operator; **sparks** *and* brass pounder *and* dit-da artist <nf>; radiotelegrapher; wireman, wire chief

17 **line,** wire line, telegraph line, telephone line; private line, direct line; party line; hot line; trunk, trunk line; WATS *or* wide area telecommunications service, WATS line; cable, telegraph cable; transmission line, concentric cable, coaxial cable, co-ax <nf>, fiber cable, fiberoptic cable

18 computer networking, **Internet,** World Wide Web *or* WWW, electronic mail; modem; digital compression; broadband

VERBS 19 **telephone, phone** <nf>, call, call on the phone <nf>, put in *or* make a call, **call up, ring,** ring up, give a ring *or* buzz *or* call *or* tinkle *or* jingle <nf>, buzz <nf>; nonformal; listen in; hold the phone *or* wire; hang up, ring off <Brit>; cold call

20 **telegraph,** telegram, flash, **wire** *and* send a wire <nf>, telex; **cable;** Teletype; radio; sign on, sign off

ADJS 21 **communicational,** telecommunicational, **communications,** communication, signal; **telephonic,** magnetotelephonic, microtelephonic, monotelephonic, thermotelephonic; **telegraphic; Teletype;** Wirephoto, facsimile, fax; phototelegraphic, telephotographic; **radio,** wireless <Brit>; radiotelegraphic; networkable

348 MANIFESTATION

NOUNS 1 **manifestation, appearance; expression,** evincement; **indication, evidence,** proof 957, proof positive; embodiment, incarnation, bodying forth, materialization; epiphany, theophany, pneumatophany, avatar; **revelation, disclosure** 351, showing forth; dissemination, **publication** 352

2 **display, demonstration, show, showing; presentation,** showing forth, presentment, ostentation , **exhibition, exhibit, exposition,** expo, retrospective; production, performance, representation, enactment, projection; opening, unfolding, unfoldment; **showcase,** showcasing, unveiling, exposure, varnishing day, *vernissage* <Fr>

3 **manifestness, apparentness, obviousness, plainness, clearness,** crystal-clearness, perspicuity, distinctness, microscopical distinctness, patency, patentness, palpability, tangibility; evidentness, evidence , **self-evidence; openness,** openness to sight, overtness; visibility 31; unmistakableness, unquestionability 970.3

4 **conspicuousness, prominence, salience** *or* saliency, bold *or* high *or* strong relief, boldness, **noticeability,** pronouncedness, strikingness, demonstrativeness, outstandingness; highlighting, spotlighting, featuring; obtrusiveness; **flagrance** *or* flagrancy, arrantness, blatancy, notoriousness, notoriety; ostentation 501; dramatics, theatrics

VERBS **5** **manifest, show, exhibit, demonstrate, display,** breathe, unfold, develop; **present,** represent , **evince, evidence; indicate,** give sign *or* token, token, betoken, mean 518.8; **express,** show forth, set forth; show off, showcase; **make plain, make clear;** produce, bring out, roll out, trot out <nf>, bring forth, bring forward *or* to the front, put forward, bring to notice, expose to view, bring to *or* into view; **reveal, divulge, disclose** 351.4; **illuminate, highlight, spotlight, feature,** bring to the fore, place in the foreground, bring out in bold *or* strong *or* high relief; **flaunt,** dangle, wave, **flourish,** brandish, parade; affect, make a show *or* a great show of; perform, enact, dramatize; **embody,** incarnate, body forth, **materialize**

6 <manifest oneself> **come out, come into the open,** come out of the closet <nf>, come forth, **surface; show one's colors** *or* true colors, wear one's heart upon one's sleeve; **speak up, speak out,** raise one's voice, **assert oneself,** let one's voice be heard, speak one's piece *or* one's mind, **stand up and be counted,** take a stand; open up, show one's mind, have no secrets; **appear, materialize**

7 **be manifest,** be there for all to see, make an appearance, be no secret *or* revelation, **surface,** lie on the surface, be seen with half an eye; need no explanation, **speak for itself,** tell its own story *or* tale; **go without saying,** *aller sans dire* <Fr>; **leap to the eye,** *sauter aux yeux* <Fr>, **stare one in the face,** hit one in the eye, strike the eye, glare, shout; come across, project; stand out, stick out, stick out a mile, stick out like a sore thumb, hang out <nf>

ADJS **8** **manifest, apparent, evident, self-evident,** axiomatic, indisputable, **obvious, plain, clear,** perspicuous, distinct, palpable, patent, tangible; **visible, perceptible, perceivable, discernible,** seeable, observable, **noticeable, much in evidence; to be seen,** easy to be seen, plain to be seen; plain as day, plain as the nose on one's face, plain as a pikestaff, big as life, big as life and twice as ugly; **crystal-clear,** clear as crystal; **express, explicit, unmistakable,** not to be mistaken, open-and-shut <nf>; self-explanatory, self-explaining; **indubitable** 970.15

9 **manifesting, manifestative,** showing, displaying, showcasing, demonstrating, **demonstrative,** presentational, expository, expositional, exhibitive, exhibitional, **expressive;** evincive, evidential; **indicative,** indicatory; appearing, incarnating, incarnational, materializing; epiphanic, theophanic, angelophanic, Satanophanic, Christophanic, pneumatophanic; **revelational,** revelatory, **disclosive** 351.10; promulgatory 352.18; histrionic

10 **open,** overt, open to all, open as day, out of the closet <nf>; unclassified; **revealed, disclosed, exposed;** made public; bare, bald, naked

11 **unhidden, unconcealed,** unscreened, uncurtained, unshaded, veilless; **unobscure,** unobscured, undarkened, unclouded; **undisguised,** uncamouflaged

12 **conspicuous, noticeable, notable,** ostensible, **prominent, bold, pronounced, salient,** in relief, in bold *or* high *or* strong relief, **striking, outstanding,** in the foreground, sticking *or* hanging out <nf>; highlighted, spotlighted, featured; obtrusive; **flagrant,** arrant, blatant, notorious; **glaring,** staring, stark-staring

13 **manifested,** demonstrated, exhibited, shown, displayed, showcased; **manifestable,** demonstrable, exhibitable, displayable

ADVS 14 **manifestly, apparently, evidently, obviously, patently, plainly, clearly,** distinctly, **unmistakably,** expressly, explicitly, palpably, tangibly; **visibly, perceptibly,** perceivably, discernibly, observably, **noticeably**

15 **openly, overtly,** before one, **before one's eyes** *or* very eyes, under one's nose <nf>; to one's face, face-to-face; **publicly,** in public; **in the open,** out in the open, in open court, **in plain sight,** in broad daylight, in the face of day *or* heaven, for all to see, in public view, in plain view, in the marketplace; aboveboard, on the table

16 **conspicuously, prominently, noticeably,** ostensibly, **notably, markedly, pronouncedly, saliently, strikingly, boldly, outstandingly;** obtrusively; arrantly, flagrantly, blatantly, notoriously; glaringly, staringly

349 REPRESENTATION, DESCRIPTION

NOUNS 1 **representation, delineation,** presentment, drawing, **portrayal, portraiture, depiction,** depictment, rendering, rendition, characterization, charactering , picturization, figuration, limning, imaging; prefigurement; **illustration,** exemplification, demonstration; projection, **realization,** manifestation, presentment; imagery, iconography; **art** 712; **drama** 704.1; conventional representation, plan, diagram, schema, schematization, **blueprint, chart, map;** conceptual model; drawing, sketch; mind map; visual; **notation,** mathematical notation, musical notation, score, tablature; dance notation, Laban dance notation system *or* labanotation, choreography; symbolization; **writing,** script, written word, text; **writing system; alphabet,** syllabary; alphabetic symbol, syllabic symbol, letter, ideogram, pictogram, logogram, logograph, hieroglyphic *or* hieroglyph, rune; printing 548; **symbol**

2 **description, portrayal,** portraiture, **depiction,** rendering, rendition, **delineation,** limning, **representation** 349; imagery; stream of consciousness; **word painting** *or* **picture, picture, portrait, image,** photograph; evocation, impression; **sketch,** vignette, cameo; **characterization,** character, character sketch, profile; vivid description, exact description, realistic *or* naturalistic description, slice of life, *tranche de vie* <Fr>, graphic account; specification, particularization, particulars, details, itemization, catalog, cataloging; **narration;** version; air quotes

3 **account, recounting,** statement, report, word, statement of fact; play-by-play description, blow-by-blow account *or* description; case study *or* history

4 **impersonation,** personation; mimicry, mimicking, mime, miming, pantomime, pantomiming, aping, dumb show; air guitar; mimesis, **imitation** 336; personification, embodiment, incarnation, realization; **characterization,** portrayal; **acting,** playing, dramatization, enacting, enactment, performing, performance; **posing,** masquerade

5 **image, likeness; resemblance,** semblance, similitude, simulacrum; **effigy,** icon, idol; **copy** 785, fair copy; **picture; portrait,** likeness;

photograph 714.3; **perfect** *or* **exact likeness, duplicate, double**, clone; replica, facsimile; match, fellow, mate, companion, **twin;** living image, very image, very picture, living picture, dead ringer <nf>, spitting image *or* spit and image <nf>, eidetic image; miniature, model; **reflection,** shadow, mirroring; trace, tracing; rubbing

6 **figure, figurine; doll,** dolly <nf>; teddy bear; **puppet, marionette,** hand puppet, glove puppet; **mannequin** *or* manikin, model, dummy, working model, lay figure; wax figure, waxwork; scarecrow, corn dolly <Brit>, woman *or* man of straw, snowman, snowwoman, gingerbread woman *or* man, scarecrow, robot, automaton; **sculpture, bust, statue, statuette,** statuary, monument ; portrait bust *or* statue; death mask, life mask; carving, wood carving; figurehead

7 **representative,** representation, **type, specimen,** typification, embodiment, type specimen; **cross section;** exponent; **example** 786.2, exemplar; exemplification, typicality, typicalness, representativeness; epitome, quintessence, figuration; mother of all <nf>

VERBS 8 **represent, delineate, depict,** render, characterize, hit off, character , **portray, picture,** picturize, limn, draw, paint 712.19; **register,** convey an impression of; take *or* catch a likeness, capture; **notate, write,** print, map, chart, diagram, schematize; trace, trace out, trace over; rub, take a rubbing; record, photograph, film, shoot, scan; **symbolize** 517.18

9 **describe, portray, picture,** render, **depict, represent, delineate,** limn, **paint,** draw; evoke, bring to life, make one see, define; outline, sketch; **characterize,** character; **express,** set forth, give words to; **write** 547.19

10 **go for** *or* **as, pass for** *or* **as, count for** *or* **as,** answer for *or* as, stand in the place of, be taken as, be regarded as, be the equivalent of; **serve as,** be accepted for

11 **image, mirror,** hold the mirror up to nature, reflect, figure; **embody,** body forth, incarnate, **personify,** personate, impersonate; **illustrate,** demonstrate, exemplify; project, realize; shadow, shadow forth; **prefigure, pretypify,** foreshadow, adumbrate

12 **impersonate,** personate; **mimic,** mime, pantomime, take off, do *or* give an impression of, mock; ape, copy; **pose as, masquerade as,** affect the manner *or* guise of, pass for, pretend to be, represent oneself to be; **act,** enact, perform, do; **play, act as,** act *or* play a part, act the part of, act out, role-play, portray

ADJS 13 **representational, representative, depictive, delineatory, resemblant; illustrative,** illustrational; pictorial, graphic, vivid; ideographic, pictographic, figurative; **representing, portraying,** limning, illustrating; **typifying, symbolizing,** symbolic, personifying, incarnating, embodying; imitative, mimetic, simulative, apish, mimish; echoic, onomatopoeic

14 **descriptive, depictive,** expositive, **representative,** representational, **delineative; expressive, vivid, graphic,** well-drawn, detailed; realistic, naturalistic, true to life, lifelike, real-life, faithful; evocative

15 **typical,** typic, typal; exemplary, sample; **characteristic,** distinctive, distinguishing, quintessential; **realistic, naturalistic; natural, normal,** usual, regular, par for the course <nf>; **true to type, true to form,** the nature of the beast <nf>

ADVS 16 **descriptively,** representatively; **expressively, vividly, graphically;** faithfully, realistically, naturalistically

350 MISREPRESENTATION

NOUNS 1 **misrepresentation, perversion, distortion,** deformation, garbling, twisting, slanting; inaccuracy; **coloring,** miscoloring, **false coloring;** false pretenses; **falsification** 354.9, **spin,** spin control, disinformation; misteaching 569; injustice, unjust representation; misdrawing, mispainting; misstatement, misreport, misquotation, misinformation; misdirection, misguidance; nonrepresentationalism, nonrealism, abstractionism, expressionism, calculated distortion; overstatement, exaggeration, hyperbole, overdrawing; understatement, litotes, conservative estimate; adulteration, forgery, counterfeiting; cover-up, whitewash

2 bad *or* poor likeness, **daub,** botch; scribble, scratch, hen tracks *or* scratches <nf>; distortion, distorted image, false image, anamorphosis, astigmatism; **travesty,** parody, **caricature, burlesque,** gross exaggeration

VERBS **3** **misrepresent, belie,** give a wrong idea, pass *or* pawn *or* foist *or* fob off as, send *or* deliver the wrong signal *or* message; put in a false light, **pervert, distort, garble, twist,** warp, deform, wrench, slant, put a spin on, twist the meaning of; **color,** miscolor, pervert, **give a false coloring,** put a false construction *or* appearance upon, slant, falsify 354.16; misteach 569.3; **disguise,** camouflage; misstate, misreport, misquote, put words into one's mouth, quote out of context; overstate, exaggerate, overdraw, blow up, blow out of all proportion, overemphasize; understate; **travesty,** parody, **caricature, burlesque;** misinform, disinform

4 **misdraw, mispaint;** overdraw, daub, botch, butcher, scribble, scratch

351 DISCLOSURE

NOUNS **1** **disclosure,** disclosing; **revelation,** revealment, revealing, making public, publicizing, broadcasting, announcement, breaking news; apocalypse; discovery, discovering; manifestation 348; unfolding, unfoldment, **uncovering,** unwrapping, uncloaking, taking the wraps off, taking from under wraps, removing the veil, **unveiling, unmasking; exposure,** exposition, **exposé; baring,** stripping, stripping *or* laying bare; outing <nf>; **showing up**

2 **divulgence, divulging,** divulgement, divulgation, evulgation , letting out, full report; **betrayal,** unwitting disclosure, indiscretion; leak, communication leak; **giveaway** *and* dead giveaway <nf>; telltale, telltale sign, obvious clue; **blabbing** *and* blabbering <nf>, babbling; **tattling**; state's evidence

3 **confession,** confessing, shrift, **acknowledgment, admission,** concession, avowal, self-admission, self-concession, self-avowal, owning, owning up *and* coming clean <nf>, unbosoming, unburdening oneself, getting a load off one's mind <nf>, fessing up <nf>, making a clean breast, baring one's breast; rite of confession

VERBS **4** **disclose, reveal, let out, show,** impart, discover, develop , **leak,** let slip out, let the cat out of the bag *and* spill the beans <nf>; manifest 348.5; unfold, unroll; **open,** open up, lay open, break the seal, bring into the open, get out in the open, bring out of the closet; **expose, show up; bare,** strip *or* lay bare, blow the lid off *and* blow wide open *and* rip open *and* crack wide open <nf>; take the lid off, **bring to light,** bring into the open, hold up to view; hold up the mirror to; **unmask,** dismask, tear off the mask, **uncover,** unveil, take the lid off <nf>, ventilate, take out from under wraps, take the wraps off, lift *or* draw the veil, raise the curtain, let daylight in, shine some light on, unscreen, uncloak, undrape, unshroud, unfurl, unsheathe, unwrap, unpack, unkennel; put one wise *and* clue one in *and* bring one up to speed <nf>, put one in the picture <chiefly Brit nf>, open one's eyes

5 **divulge,** divulgate, evulgate ; **reveal, make known, tell,** breathe, utter, vent, ventilate, air, give vent to, **give out, let out** <Brit>, let get around, out with <nf>, come out with; break it to, **break the news;** let in on *or* to, **confide,** confide to, let one's hair down <nf>, unbosom oneself, let into the secret; **publish** 352.10

6 **betray,** inform, **inform on** 551.12, talk *and* peach <nf>; rat *and* stool *and* sing *and* squeal <nf>, turn state's evidence; leak <nf>, spill <nf>, **spill the beans** <nf>; **let the cat out of the bag** <nf>, speak before one thinks, be unguarded *or* indiscreet, kiss and tell, **give away** *and* give the show away *and* give the game away <nf>, betray a confidence, tell secrets, reveal a secret; have a big mouth *or* bazoo <nf>, **blab** *or* blabber <nf>; babble, **tattle,** tell *or* tattle on, tell tales, **tell tales out of school;** talk out of turn, let slip, let fall *or* drop; **blurt, blurt out**

7 **confess,** break down and confess, **admit, acknowledge,** tell all, avow, concede, grant, **own, own up** <nf>, let on, implicate *or* incriminate oneself, come clean <nf>; spill *and* spill it *and* spill one's guts <nf>; **tell the truth,** tell all, admit everything, let it all hang out <nf>, throw off all disguise; **plead guilty,** own oneself in the wrong, cop a plea <nf>; **unbosom oneself, make a clean breast, get it off one's chest** <nf>, **get it out of one's system** <nf>, disburden *or* unburden one's mind *or* conscience *or* heart, **get a load off one's mind** <nf>, fess up <nf>; out with it *and* spit it out *and* open up <nf>; throw oneself on the mercy of the court; **reveal oneself,** show one's colors *or* true colors, come out of the closet <nf>, show one's hand *or* cards, put *or* lay one's cards on the table

8 **be revealed, become known, surface, come to light,** appear, manifest itself, come to one's ears, transpire, **leak out, get out, come out,** out, come home to roost, come out in the wash, break forth, show its face; show its colors, be seen in its true colors, stand revealed; blow one's cover <nf>

ADJS 9 **revealed, disclosed** 348.10

10 **disclosive, revealing,** revelatory, revelational, clueful; **disclosing,** showing, exposing, betraying; kiss-and-tell; eye-opening; **talkative** 343.10/540.9; admitted, confessed, self-confessed

11 confessional, admissive

352 PUBLICATION

NOUNS 1 **publication, publishing, promulgation,** evulgation, **propagation, dissemination, diffusion, broadcast, broadcasting, spread, spreading,** spreading abroad, divulgence, disclosure, **circulation,** ventilation, airing, noising, bandying, bruiting, bruiting about, spreading the word; **display;** issue, issuance; telecasting, videocasting, podcasting, blogging; printing 548; book, periodical 555

2 **announcement,** annunciation, enunciation; **proclamation,** pronouncement, pronunciamento; edict, decree; **report,** communiqué, **declaration, statement;** public declaration *or* statement, program, programma, **notice, notification,** public notice; speech; circular, encyclical, encyclical letter; manifesto, position paper; broadside; rationale; white paper, white book; ukase, edict 420.4; bulletin board, notice board

3 **press release,** release, handout, bulletin, official bulletin, notice, public service announcement

4 **publicity,** publicness, **notoriety, fame,** famousness, renown, notoriousness, infamy, notice, public notice *or* recognition, **celebrity,** *réclame* and *éclat* <Fr>; **limelight** *and* **spotlight** <nf>, daylight, bright light, glare, public eye *or* consciousness, **exposure, currency,** common *or* public knowledge, widest *or* maximum dissemination, public forum; **ballyhoo** *and* hoopla <nf>; report, public report; cry, hue and cry; **public relations** *or* PR, flackery <nf>; **publicity story,** press notice; propaganda; **writeup, puff** <nf>, **plug** <nf>, **blurb** <nf>, hype <nf>; photo opportunity, photo op <nf>; name in bright lights <nf>

5 **promotion, buildup** *and* promo <nf>, flack <nf>, publicization, publicizing, promoting, advocating,

advocacy, bruiting, drumbeating, tub-thumping, press-agentry; **advertising,** salesmanship 734.2, Madison Avenue, hucksterism <nf>; advertising campaign; advertising agency; advertising medium *or* media; advocacy, advocacy group; product placement

6 **advertisement, ad** <nf>, advert <Brit nf>, notice; **commercial,** message, important message, message *or* words from the sponsor; spot commercial *or* spot, network commercial; infomercial; reader, reading notice; display ad; want ad <nf>, classified ad; personal ad; spread, two-page spread, testimonial; advertorial; trailer; teaser; website ad, banner ad, Yellow Pages; bumper sticker; ad creep

7 **poster, bill, placard, sign,** show card, banner, *affiche* <Fr>; **signboard, billboard,** highway sign, hoarding <Brit>; sandwich board; marquee; bulletin board

8 **advertising matter,** promotional material, public relations handout *or* release, **literature** <nf>; **leaflet,** leaf, **folder, handbill, bill, flier, throwaway, handout, circular,** pamphlet, brochure, broadside, broadsheet; insert *or* insertion, blow-in

9 **publicist,** publicizer, public relations person, public relations officer, PR person, flack *and* pitchman *or* pitchperson <nf>, public relations specialist, **publicity man** *or* agent, **press agent,** agent, flack <nf>, imagemaker; **advertiser; adman** *and* huckster *and* pitchman <nf>; ad writer <nf>, copywriter, blurb writer; **promoter, booster** <nf>, plugger <nf>; **ballyhooer** *or* **ballyhoo man** <nf>; **barker,** spieler <nf>, skywriter; billposter; signpainter; sandwich boy *or* man; spin doctor

VERBS **10** **publish, promulgate, propagate, circulate,** circularize, **diffuse, disseminate,** distribute, **broadcast,** televise, telecast, videocast, air, **spread,** spread around *or* about, spread far and wide, publish abroad, **pass the word around,** bruit, **bruit about, advertise,** repeat, retail, put about, **bandy about, noise about,** cry about *or* abroad, noise *or* sound abroad, bruit abroad, set news afloat, **spread a report; rumor,** launch a rumor, voice , whisper, buzz, **rumor about,** whisper *or* buzz about

11 **make public,** go public with <nf>; bring *or* lay *or* drag before the public, **display,** take one's case to the public, **give** *or* **put out,** give to the world, **make known; divulge** 351.5; **ventilate,** air, give air to, bring into the open, get out in the open, open up, broach, give vent to

12 **announce,** annunciate, enunciate; **declare, state,** declare roundly, affirm, pronounce, give notice; **say,** make a statement, send a message *or* signal; **report,** make an announcement *or* a report, issue a statement, publish *or* issue a manifesto, present a position paper, issue a white paper, hold a press conference

13 **proclaim,** cry, cry out, **promulgate,** give voice to; **herald,** herald abroad; **blazon,** blaze, blaze *or* blazon about *or* abroad, blare, blare forth *or* abroad, thunder, declaim, shout, trumpet, trumpet *or* thunder forth, announce with flourish of trumpets *or* beat of drum; shout from the housetops, proclaim at the crossroads *or* market cross, proclaim at Charing Cross <Brit>

14 **issue, bring out, put out, get out, launch,** get off, emit, put *or* give *or* send forth, offer to the public, pass out

15 **publicize,** give publicity; go public with <nf>; bring *or* drag into the limelight, throw the spotlight on <nf>; **advertise, promote,** build up, cry up, sell, puff <nf>, **boost** <nf>, **plug** <nf>, **ballyhoo** <nf>; put on the map, make a household word of, establish; bark *and* spiel <nf>; make a pitch for *and* beat the drum for *and* thump the tub for <nf>; **write up,** give a write-up, press-agent <nf>; circularize; bulletin; bill; **post bills,** post, post up, placard; skywrite

16 <be published> **come out, appear,** break, hit the streets <nf>, **issue,** go *or* come forth, find vent, **see the light,** see the light of day, become public; **circulate, spread,** spread about, have currency, **get around** *or* about, get abroad, get afloat, get exposure, go *or* fly *or* buzz *or* blow about, **go the rounds,** pass from mouth to mouth, be on everyone's lips, go through the length and breadth of the land; spread like wildfire; blog

ADJS **17 published, public,** made public, **circulated,** in circulation, promulgated, propagated, **disseminated,** issued, spread, diffused, distributed; in print; **broadcast,** telecast, televised; **announced,** proclaimed, declared, **stated,** affirmed; **reported,** brought to notice; common knowledge, common property, current; **open,** accessible, open to the public; hot off the press

18 publicational, promulgatory, propagatory; proclamatory, annunciatory, enunciative; declarative, declaratory; heraldic; promotional; on-message

ADVS **19 publicly, in public; openly** 348.15; in the public eye, in the glare of publicity, in the limelight *or* spotlight <nf>, reportedly

353 MESSENGER

NOUNS **1 messenger,** message-bearer, **dispatch-bearer,** commissionaire <Brit>, nuncio , **courier,** diplomatic courier, carrier, **runner,** express <Brit>, dispatch-rider, pony-express rider, post , postboy, postrider, **estafette** <Fr>; bicycle *or* motorcycle messenger; **go-between** 576.4; **emissary** 576.6; Mercury, Hermes, Iris, Pheidippides, Paul Revere; post office, courier service, package service, message service *or* center; answering service

2 herald, harbinger, forerunner, vaunt-courier; evangel, evangelist, bearer of glad tidings; herald angel, Gabriel, **buccinator** <L>

3 announcer, annunciator, enunciator; nunciate ; **proclaimer; crier, town crier,** bellman

4 errand boy, office boy, messenger-boy, copyboy; bellhop <nf>, bellboy, bellman, callboy, caller

5 postman, mailman, mail carrier, letter carrier; postmaster, postmistress; postal clerk

6 <mail carriers> carrier pigeon, carrier, homing pigeon, homer <nf>; pigeon post; post-horse, poster; post coach, mail coach; post boat, packet boat *or* ship, mail boat, mail packet, mailer ; mail train, mail car, post car, post-office car, railway mail car; mail truck; mailplane; electronic mail

354 FALSENESS

NOUNS **1 falseness, falsehood,** falsity, inveracity, untruth, **truthlessness, untrueness; fallaciousness,** fallacy, **erroneousness** 975.1; false negative, false positive

2 spuriousness, phoniness <nf>, bogusness, **ungenuineness, unauthenticity,** unrealness, artificiality, factitiousness, syntheticness

3 sham, fakery, faking, falsity, feigning, pretending; feint, pretext, **pretense,** hollow pretense, **pretension, false pretense** *or* **pretension;** humbug, humbuggery; **bluff,** bluffing, four-flushing <nf>; speciousness, meretriciousness; cheating, fraud; imposture; deception, delusion 356.1; acting, playacting; representation, **simulation,** simulacrum; dissembling, **dissemblance, dissimulation;** seeming, semblance, appearance, face, ostentation, **show, false show,** outward show, false air; window dressing, front, **false front, façade,** gloss, varnish; gilt; color, coloring, false color; masquerade, facade, disguise; posture, pose, posing, attitudinizing; mannerism, affectation 500

4 falseheartedness, falseness, doubleheartedness, doubleness of heart, doubleness, **duplicity, two-facedness,** double-facedness, **double-dealing,** ambidexterity;

double standard; **dishonesty,** improbity, lack of integrity, Machiavellianism, bad faith; low cunning, **cunning,** artifice, wile 415.3; **deceitfulness** 356.3; faithlessness, treachery 645.6

5 **insincerity, uncandidness,** uncandor, **unfrankness,** disingenuousness, indirectness; emptiness, hollowness; mockery, hollow mockery; crossed fingers, tongue in cheek, unseriousness; halfheartedness; sophistry, jesuitry, jesuitism, casuistry 936.1

6 **hypocrisy,** hypocriticalness; Tartuffery, Tartuffism, Pecksniffery, pharisaism, **sanctimony** 693, sanctimoniousness, religiosity, false piety, ostentatious devotion, pietism, Bible-thumping <nf>; **mealy-mouthedness, unctuousness,** oiliness, smarminess *or* smarm <nf>; cant, mummery, snuffling , **mouthing; lip service;** tokenism; token gesture, empty gesture; smooth tongue, smooth talk, sweet talk *and* soft soap <nf>; crocodile tears

7 **quackery, chicanery,** quackishness, quackism, **mountebankery, charlatanry,** charlatanism; **imposture; humbug,** humbuggery

8 **untruthfulness, dishonesty,** falsehood, **unveracity,** unveraciousness, truthlessness, **mendaciousness, mendacity;** credibility gap; **lying, fibbing,** fibbery, pseudology; pathological lying, habitual lying, mythomania, *pseudologia phantastica* <L>

9 **deliberate falsehood, disinformation, falsification,** disinforming, falsifying; confabulation; **perversion, distortion,** straining, **bending; misrepresentation,** misconstruction, misstatement, coloring, false coloring, miscoloring, slanting, imparting a spin <nf>; tampering, cooking *and* fiddling <nf>; stretching, fictionalization, **exaggeration** 355; **prevarication,** equivocation 344.4; **perjury,** false swearing, oath breaking, false oath, false plea

10 **fabrication, invention, concoction, disinformation;** canard, base canard; **forgery; fiction,** figment, **myth,** legend, fable, story, romanticized version, extravaganza; old wives' tale, unfact

11 **lie, falsehood,** falsity, **untruth,** false statement, untruism, mendacity, **prevarication, fib,** taradiddle *or* tarradiddle <nf>, flimflam *or* flam, a crock *and* a crock of shit <nf>, *blague* <Fr>; **fiction,** pious fiction, legal fiction; **story** <nf>, **trumped-up story,** farrago; **yarn** <nf>, **tale,** fairy tale <nf>, ghost story; farfetched story, tall tale *and* **tall story** <nf>, **cock-and-bull story,** fish story <nf>, flight of fancy; exaggeration 355; half-truth, stretching of the truth, slight stretching, white lie, little white lie; *suggestio falsi* <L>; partial truth; propaganda, rumor, gossip, empty talk; a pack of lies

12 monstrous lie, consummate lie, deep-dyed falsehood, out-and-out lie, **whopper** <nf>, gross *or* flagrant *or* shameless falsehood, downright lie, **barefaced lie, dirty lie** <nf>, big lie; **slander, libel** 512.3; the big lie; bullshit *or* load of crap <nf>

13 **fake,** fakement *and* put-up job <nf>, **phony** <nf>, **rip-off** <nf>, **sham, mock, imitation,** simulacrum, dummy; paste, tinsel, *clinquant* <Fr>, pinchbeck, shoddy, junk; **counterfeit, forgery;** put-up job *and* frame-up <nf>, put-on <nf>; **hoax, cheat, fraud, swindle** 356.8; whited sepulcher, whitewash job <nf>; impostor 357.6

14 **humbug,** humbuggery; **bunk** <nf>, **bunkum;** hooey *and* hoke *and* **hokum** <nf>, **bosh** <nf>, bull *and* **bullshit** *and* crap <nf>, baloney <nf>, flimflam, flam, smoke and mirrors <nf>, claptrap, moonshine, eyewash, hogwash, gammon <Brit nf>, *blague* <Fr>, jiggery-pokery <Brit>

VERBS 15 ring false, **not ring true**

16 **falsify, belie, misrepresent,** miscolor; misstate, misquote, misreport, miscite; overstate, understate; **pervert, distort,** strain, warp, **slant, twist,** warp, stretch the truth, impart spin <nf>; garble; put a false appearance upon, give a false coloring,

falsely color, give a color to, **color, gild,** gloss, gloss over, whitewash, varnish, paper over <nf>; fudge <nf>, dress up, titivate, embellish, embroider, trick *or* prink out; deodorize, make smell like roses; **disguise, camouflage, mask;** propagandize, gossip

17 **tamper with, manipulate, fake, juggle,** sophisticate, **doctor** *and* **cook** <nf>, rig, cook *or* juggle the books *or* the accounts <nf>; pack, stack; **adulterate;** retouch; **load; salt,** plant <nf>, salt a mine

18 **fabricate, invent, manufacture, trump up, make up, hatch, concoct, cook up** *and* make out of whole cloth <nf>, fictionalize, mythologize, fudge <nf>, fake, hoke up <nf>; **counterfeit, forge;** fantasize, fantasize about

19 **lie, tell a lie,** falsify, speak falsely, speak with forked tongue <nf>, be untruthful, trifle with the truth, deviate from the truth, **fib, story** <nf>; **stretch the truth,** strain *or* bend the truth; draw the longbow; **exaggerate** 355.3; lie flatly, lie in one's throat, lie through one's teeth, lie like a trooper, **prevaricate,** misstate, equivocate 344.7; **deceive, mislead,** tell a white lie; bullshit <nf>

20 swear falsely, forswear oneself , perjure, **perjure oneself, bear false witness**

21 **sham, fake** <nf>, **feign, counterfeit, simulate,** put up <nf>, gammon <Brit nf>; **pretend,** make a pretense, **make believe, make a show of,** make like <nf>, make as if *or* as though; go through the motions <nf>; let on, let on like <nf>; **affect,** profess, **assume,** put on; **dissimulate, dissemble,** cover up; **act, play,** play-act, **put on an act** *or* a charade <nf>, act *or* play a part; **put up a front** <nf>, put on a front *or* false front <nf>; four-flush <nf>, **bluff,** pull *or* put up a bluff <nf>; **play possum** <nf>, roll over and play dead

22 **pose as, masquerade as,** impersonate, pass for, assume the guise *or* identity of, set up for, act the part of, represent oneself to be, claim *or* pretend to be, **make false pretenses,** go under false pretenses, **sail under false colors**

23 **be hypocritical, act** *or* **play the hypocrite;** cant, be holier than the Pope *or* thou, reek of piety; shed crocodile tears, snuffle , snivel, mouth; give mouth honor, render *or* give lip service; sweet-talk, softsoap, blandish 511.5

24 **play a double game** *or* **role, play both ends against the middle,** work both sides of the street, have it both ways at once, have one's cake and eat it too, run with the hare and hunt with the hounds <Brit>; two-time <nf>

ADJS 25 **false, untrue, truthless, not true,** void *or* devoid of truth, contrary to fact, in error, **fallacious, erroneous** 975.16; unfounded 936.13; disinformative

26 **spurious, ungenuine, unauthentic,** supposititious, bastard, **pseudo, quasi,** apocryphal, **fake** <nf>, **phony** <nf>, **sham, mock, counterfeit,** colorable, **bogus,** queer <nf>, dummy, **make-believe,** so-called, **imitation** 336.8; not what it's cracked up to be <nf>; **falsified;** dressed up, titivated, embellished, embroidered; garbled; twisted, distorted, warped, perverted, slanted; half-true, falsely colored; **simulated, faked, feigned,** colored, fictitious, fictive, **counterfeited, pretended, affected, assumed, put-on; artificial, synthetic,** ersatz; unreal; factitious, unnatural, man-made; illegitimate; *soi-disant* <Fr>, self-styled; pinchbeck, brummagem <Brit>, tinsel, shoddy, tin, junky

27 **specious, meretricious,** gilded, tinsel, **seeming,** apparent, colored, colorable, plausible, **ostensible**

28 **quack, quackish; charlatan, charlatanish,** charlatanic

29 **fabricated,** invented, manufactured, **concocted, hatched, trumped-up, made-up,** put-up, cooked-up <nf>; **forged;** fictitious, fictional, fictionalized, figmental, **mythical,** fabulous, legendary; fantastic, fantasied, fancied, legendary

30 **tampered with, manipulated, cooked** *and* **doctored** <nf>, juggled, **rigged,** engineered; packed

31 **falsehearted, false,** false-principled, false-dealing; double, duplicitous, ambidextrous, **double-dealing,** doublehearted, double-minded, double-tongued, double-faced, **two-faced,** Janus-faced; Machiavellian, dishonest; **crooked, deceitful;** creative, artful, cunning, crafty 415.12; faithless, perfidious, treacherous 645.21

32 **insincere, uncandid, unfrank, mealymouthed, unctuous, oily,** disingenuous, ungenuine, pseudo, smarmy <nf>; dishonest; **empty, hollow;** tongue in cheek, unserious; sophistic *or* sophistical, jesuitic *or* jesuitical, casuistic 936.10

33 **hypocritic** *or* hypocritical, canting, Pecksniffian, pharisaic, pharisaical, pharisean, **sanctimonious, goody-goody** <nf>, goody two-shoes, holier-than-the-Pope, holier-than-thou, simon-pure; artificial, dissembling, phony

34 **untruthful, dishonest, unveracious,** unveridical, truthless, **lying, mendacious,** untrue; perjured, forsworn; prevaricating, equivocal 344.11

ADVS 35 **falsely, untruly,** truthlessly; **erroneously** 975.20; **untruthfully,** unveraciously; mendaciously; **spuriously,** ungenuinely; artificially, synthetically; unnaturally, factitiously; speciously, seemingly, apparently, plausibly, ostensibly; nominally, in name only

36 **insincerely,** uncandidly, unfrankly; emptily, hollowly; unseriously; ambiguously; **hypocritically,** mealymouthedly, unctuously

355 EXAGGERATION

NOUNS 1 **exaggeration,** exaggerating; **overstatement,** big *or* tall talk <nf>, bullshit <nf>, jive <nf>, **hyperbole,** hyperbolism; **superlative; extravagance,** profuseness, **prodigality** 486, overdoing it, going too far, overshooting; **magnification, enlargement,** amplification , dilation, dilatation, **inflation,** expansion, blowing up, puff, puffing up, aggrandizement, embellishment, elaboration, embroidery; **stretching, heightening,** enhancement; overemphasis, overstressing; overestimation 949; exaggerated lengths, **extreme,** extremism, stretch, exorbitance, inordinacy, **overkill, excess** 993; burlesque, travesty, caricature; crock <nf>, whopper, tall story; sensationalism, puffery *and* ballyhoo <nf>, touting, huckstering; grandiloquence 545, painting *or* gilding the lily; to-do *and* hype *and* hoopla <nf>

2 **overreaction, much ado about nothing,** fuss, uproar, commotion, storm *or* tempest in a teapot, making a mountain out of a molehill

VERBS 3 **exaggerate,** hyperbolize; **overstate,** overspeak , overreach, **overdraw,** overcharge; overstress, overemphasize; **overdo, carry too far, go to extremes;** push to the extreme, indulge in overkill, overestimate 949.2; gild the lily; overpraise, oversell, tout, puff *and* ballyhoo *and* hype <nf>; **stretch,** stretch the truth, stretch the point, draw the longbow, embellish; **magnify, inflate,** amplify ; aggrandize, build up; pile *or* lay it on *and* pour *or* spread *or* lay it on thick *and* lay it on with a trowel <nf>; talk big <nf>, talk in superlatives, deal in the marvelous, make much of; **overreact,** make a Federal case out of it <nf>, something out of nothing, make a mountain out of a molehill, create a tempest in a teapot *or* teacup, make too much of, cry over spilt milk; caricature, travesty, burlesque, ham, ham it up

ADJS 4 **exaggerated,** hyperbolical, **magnified,** amplified , **inflated,** aggrandized, stylized, embroidered, embellished, varnished; **stretched,** disproportionate, **blown up out of all proportion,** blown out of proportion, overblown; overpraised, oversold, overrated, touted, puff *and* puffed *and* ballyhooed <nf>, hyped <nf>; overemphasized, **overemphatic, overstressed; overemphatic, overstressed; overstated, overdrawn; overdone,** overwrought, a bit thick; caricatural, melodramatic, farfetched, too much <nf>, over the top; overestimated 949.3; overlarge, overgreat; **extreme,** pushed to the extreme, exorbitant, inordinate, **excessive** 993.16; **superlative, extravagant,** profuse, **prodigal** 486.8; high-flown, grandiloquent 545.8; overexposed

5 **exaggerating, exaggerative,** hyperbolical

356 DECEPTION

NOUNS 1 **deception,** calculated deception, **deceptiveness, subterfuge,** gimmickry *or* gimmickery, **trickiness; falseness** 354; fallaciousness, fallacy; self-deception, fond illusion, wishful thinking, willful misconception; vision, hallucination, phantasm, mirage, will-o'-the-wisp, **delusion,** delusiveness, illusion 976; deceiving, **victimization, dupery;** bamboozlement <nf>, hoodwinking; swindling, defrauding, conning, flimflam *or* flimflammery <nf>; **fooling,** befooling, tricking, **kidding** *and* putting on <nf>; spoofing *and* spoofery <nf>; bluffing; circumvention, overreaching, outwitting; ensnarement, entrapment, enmeshment, entanglement; smoke and mirrors

2 **misleading, misguidance, misdirection;** bum steer <nf>; misinformation 569.1

3 **deceit, deceitfulness, guile, falseness,** insidiousness, **underhandedness; shiftiness, furtiveness,** surreptitiousness, indirection; **hypocrisy** 354.6; **falseheartedness, duplicity** 354.4; **treacherousness** 645.6; **artfulness,** craft, guile, **cunning** 415; sneakiness 345.4; sneak attack; funny business

4 **chicanery,** chicane, **skulduggery** <nf>, knavery, **trickery,** dodgery, pettifogging, pettifoggery, *supercherie* <Fr>, **artifice,** sleight, machination; **sharp practice, underhand dealing, foul play;** connivery, connivance, collusion, conspiracy, covin <law>; fakery, charlatanism, mountebankery, quackery

5 **juggling,** jugglery, **trickery,** dirty pool <nf>, *escamotage* <Fr>, prestidigitation, conjuration, **legerdemain, sleight of hand,** smoke and mirrors <nf>; mumbo jumbo, **hocus-pocus,** hanky-panky *and* monkey business *and* hokey-pokey <nf>, nobbling *and* jiggery-pokery <Brit nf>, shenanigans <nf>

6 **trick, artifice, device,** ploy, gambit, stratagem, scheme, **design,** *ficelle* <Fr>, **subterfuge,** blind, **ruse, wile,** chouse <nf>, shift, **dodge,** artful dodge, sleight, pass, feint, fetch, chicanery; **bluff;** gimmick, joker, catch; curve, curve-ball, googly *or* bosey *or* wrong'un <Brit nf>; **dirty trick,** dirty deal, fast deal, scurvy trick; sleight of hand, sleight-of-hand trick, hocus-pocus ; juggle, juggler's trick; **bag of tricks,** tricks of the trade

7 **hoax, deception,** spoof <nf>, **humbug,** flam, **fake** *and* fakement, **rip-off** <nf>, **sham;** mare's nest; put-on <nf>

8 **fraud, fraudulence** *or* fraudulency, **dishonesty; imposture; imposition, cheat, cheating,** cozenage, **swindle,** dodge, fishy transaction, piece of sharp practice; customer-gouging, insider-trading, short weight, chiseling; **gyp joint** <nf>; **racket** <nf>, illicit business 732; **graft** <nf>, grift <nf>; bunco; card-sharping; ballot-box stuffing, gerrymandering

9 <nf terms> **gyp,** diddle, diddling, scam, flimflam flam, ramp <Brit>, snow job, song and dance, number, bill of goods, burn, the business, dipsy-doodle, double cross, fiddle, hosing, the old army game, reaming, suckering, sting, con, ripoff

10 **confidence game, con game** <nf>, **skin game** <nf>, **bunco game; shell game,** thimblerig, thimblerigging; bucket shop, boiler room <nf>; goldbrick; bait-and-switch, the wire, the pay-off, the rag, pastposting

11 **cover, disguise, camouflage,** protective coloration; **false colors, false front** 354.3; **incognito;** smoke screen; **masquerade,** masque, mummery; **mask,** visor, vizard, viz-

ard mask , false face, domino, domino mask; red herring, diversion

12 **trap, gin; pitfall,** trapfall, deadfall; flytrap, mousetrap, mole trap, rattrap, bear trap; deathtrap, firetrap; Venus's flytrap, Dionaea; Catch-22; spring gun, set gun; baited trap; **booby trap, mine; decoy** 357.5; hidden danger

13 **snare,** springe; noose, lasso, lariat; bola; **net,** trawl, dragnet, seine, purse seine, pound net, gill net; cobweb; **meshes, toils; fishhook, hook,** sniggle; **bait,** ground bait; lure, fly, jig, squid, plug, wobbler, spinner; lime, birdlime

VERBS **14** **deceive, beguile, trick, hoax, dupe,** gammon, **gull,** pigeon, play one for a fool *or* sucker, **bamboozle** *and* snow *and* **hornswoggle** *and* diddle *and* scam <nf>, nobble <Brit nf>, **humbug, take in,** put on *and* hocus-pocus <nf>, string along, **put something over** *or* **across,** slip one over on <nf>, pull a fast one on; **play games** <nf>; **delude,** mock; **betray,** let down, leave in the lurch, leave holding the bag, play one false, **double-cross** <nf>, cheat on; two-time <nf>; juggle, conjure; **bluff;** cajole, **circumvent,** get around, forestall; **overreach,** outreach, outwit, outmaneuver, outsmart

15 **fool,** befool, make a fool of, practice on one's credulity, **pull one's leg,** make an ass of; **trick; spoof** *and* **kid** *and* put one on <nf>; **play a trick on,** play a practical joke upon, send on a fool's errand, fake one out <nf>; sell one a bill of goods, give one a snow job

16 **mislead, misguide, misdirect,** lead astray, lead up the garden path, **give a bum steer** <nf>; fake someone out, feed one a line <nf>, throw off the scent, throw off the track *or* trail, put on a false scent, drag *or* draw a red herring across the trail; throw one a curve *or* curve ball <nf>, bowl a googly *or* bosey *or* wrong 'un <Brit nf>; misinform 569.3

17 **hoodwink,** blindfold, blind, blind one's eyes, blear the eyes of , throw dust in one's eyes, **pull the wool over one's eyes**

18 **cheat, victimize, gull,** pigeon, fudge, **swindle, defraud,** practice fraud upon, euchre, **con,** finagle, **fleece,** mulct, fob , **bilk,** cozen, cog , chouse, **cheat out of, do out of,** chouse out of, beguile of *or* out of; obtain under false pretenses; live by one's wits; bunco, play a bunco game; sell gold bricks <nf>; shortchange, shortweight, skim off the top; stack the cards *or* deck, pack the deal <nf>, deal off the bottom of the deck, play with marked cards; cog the dice, load the dice; thimblerig; crib <nf>; throw a fight *or* game <nf>, take a dive <nf>

19 <nf terms> **gyp, clip, scam,** rope in, hose, shave, beat, rook, flam, flimflam, diddle, dipsy-doodle, do a number on, hustle, fuck, screw, have, pull something, pull a trick *or* stunt, give the business, ramp <Brit>, stick, sting, burn, gouge, chisel, hocus, hocus-pocus, play *or* take for a sucker, make a patsy of, do, run a game on, slicker, take for a ride

20 **trap,** entrap, gin, catch, catch out, catch in a trap; catch unawares, ambush; **ensnare, snare,** hook, **hook in,** sniggle, noose; inveigle; net, mesh, enmesh, snarl , ensnarl, wind, tangle, entangle, entoil, enweb; trip, trip up; **set** *or* **lay a trap for,** bait the hook, spread the toils; lime, birdlime; **lure,** allure, **decoy** 377.3

ADJS **21** **deceptive, deceiving, misleading,** beguiling, **false, fallacious,** delusive, delusory; hallucinatory, illusive, **illusory;** tricky, trickish, tricksy , catchy; **fishy** <nf>, questionable, dubious; delusional

22 **deceitful, false; fraudulent, sharp, guileful, insidious,** slick, slippery, slippery as an eel, **shifty, tricky,** trickish, cute, finagling, chiseling <nf>; underhand, **underhanded, furtive, surreptitious,** indirect; collusive, covinous; **falsehearted, two-faced; treacherous** 645.21; sneaky 345.12; **cunning,** artful, gimmicky <nf>, **wily, crafty** 415.12; calculating, scheming, double-dealing

ADVS **23 deceptively,** beguilingly, **falsely,** fallaciously, delusively, **trickily, misleadingly,** with intent to deceive; under false colors, under cover of, under the garb of, in disguise

24 deceitfully, fraudulently, guilefully, insidiously, **shiftily, trickily; underhandedly,** furtively, surreptitiously, indirectly, like a thief in the night; **treacherously** 645.25

357 DECEIVER

NOUNS **1 deceiver, deluder,** duper, misleader, **beguiler, bamboozler** <nf>; actor, playactor <nf>, role-player; **dissembler,** dissimulator; confidence man; **double-dealer,** Machiavelli, Machiavel, Machiavellian; dodger, Artful Dodger <Charles Dickens>, **counterfeiter, forger, faker;** plagiarizer, plagiarist; entrancer, **enchanter,** charmer, befuddler, hypnotizer, mesmerizer; **seducer,** Don Juan, Casanova; tease, teaser; jilt, jilter; gay deceiver; **fooler, joker,** jokester, **hoaxer,** practical joker; spoofer *and* **kidder** *and* ragger *and* leg-puller <nf>

2 trickster, tricker; **juggler,** sleight-of-hand performer, magician, illusionist, conjurer, **prestidigitator,** *escamoteur* <Fr>, manipulator

3 cheat, cheater; two-timer <nf>; **swindler, defrauder,** cozener, juggler; **sharper, sharp,** spieler, pitchman, pitchperson; **confidence man, confidence trickster, horse trader,** horse coper <Brit>; **cardsharp,** cardsharper; thimblerigger; shortchanger; **shyster** *and* pettifogger <nf>; land shark, land pirate, land grabber, mortgage shark; carpetbagger; crimp

4 <nf terms> **gyp,** gypper, gyp artist, flimflammer, flimflam man, blackleg, chiseler, bilker, fleecer, diddler, crook, sharpie, shark, jackleg, slicker, con man, con artist, bunco, bunco artist, bunco steerer, scammer, clip artist, smoothie, dipsy-doodle, hustler, hoser

5 shill, decoy, **come-on man** <nf>, plant, capper, stool pigeon, stoolie <nf>; *agent provocateur* <Fr>

6 impostor, ringer; impersonator; pretender; sham, shammer, **humbug,** *blagueur* <Fr>, **fraud** <nf>, **fake** *and* **faker** *and* **phony** <nf>, **fourflusher** <nf>, bluff, bluffer; **charlatan, quack,** quacksalver, quackster, **mountebank,** saltimbanco; **wolf in sheep's clothing,** ass in lion's skin, jackdaw in peacock's feathers; poser, poseur; malingerer

7 masquerader, masker; **impersonator,** personator; mummer, guiser, guisard; incognito, incognita

8 hypocrite, phony <nf>, sanctimonious fraud, pharisee, whited sepulcher, **canter,** snuffler, mealy-mouth, dissembler, dissimulator, pretender, poseur, poser; Tartuffe <Molière>, Pecksniff *and* Uriah Heep <Charles Dickens>, Joseph Surface <Richard B Sheridan>; false friend, fair-weather friend; summer soldier; cupboard lover

9 liar, fibber, fibster, fabricator, fabulist, pseudologist; falsifier; **prevaricator,** equivocator, evader, mudger <Brit nf>, waffler <nf>, palterer; **storyteller;** yarner *and* yarn spinner *and* spinner of yarns <nf>, double-talker; Ananias; Satan, Father of Lies; Baron Münchausen; Sir John Mandeville; consummate liar; *menteur à triple étage* <Fr>, dirty liar; pathological liar, mythomane, mythomaniac, pseudologue, confirmed *or* habitual liar, consummate liar; **perjurer,** false witness; slanderer, libeler, libelant; bullshitter <nf>

10 traitor, treasonist, **betrayer, quisling, rat** <nf>, serpent, snake, cockatrice, **snake in the grass, double-crosser** <nf>, double-dealer; double agent; trimmer, timeserver; turncoat 363.5; informer 551.6; archtraitor; Judas, Judas Iscariot, Benedict Arnold, Quisling, Brutus; **schemer, plotter,** intriguer, *intrigant* <Fr>, conspirer, **conspirator,** conniver, machinator; pseud <nf>, two-timer <nf>

11 subversive; saboteur, fifth columnist, crypto; security risk; **collaborationist,** collaborator, fraternizer; fifth column, underground; Trojan horse; renegade

358 DUPE

NOUNS 1 **dupe, gull,** gudgeon, *gobemouches* <Fr>; **victim;** gullible *or* dupable *or* credulous person, trusting *or* simple soul, innocent, *naïf* <Fr>, babe, babe in the woods; greenhorn; toy, plaything; monkey; **fool** 924; stooge, **cat's-paw**

2 <nf terms> **sucker, patsy,** pigeon, chicken, fall guy, doormat, mug <Brit>, fish, jay <chiefly Brit>, easy mark, sitting duck, juggin <chiefly Brit>, pushover, cinch, mark, vic, easy pickings, greeny, greener, chump, boob, schlemiel, sap, saphead, prize sap, easy touch, soft touch, hornswoggler

359 RESOLUTION

NOUNS 1 **resolution,** resolve, resolvedness, **determination, decision,** fixed *or* firm resolve, will, purpose; **resoluteness, determinedness,** determinateness, decisiveness, decidedness, **purposefulness;** definiteness; closure; **earnestness, seriousness,** sincerity, devotion, dedication, commitment, total commitment; single-mindedness, relentlessness, persistence, tenacity, perseverance 360; self-will, obstinacy 361; control freak

2 **firmness,** firmness of mind *or* spirit, fixity of purpose, **staunchness,** settledness, steadiness, constancy, steadfastness, fixedness, unshakableness; **stability** 855; concentration; flintiness, steeliness; inflexibility, rigidity, unyieldingness 361.2; trueness, loyalty 644.7

3 **pluck, spunk** <nf>, **mettle, backbone** <nf>, **grit,** true grit, spirit, **stamina, guts** *and* moxie <nf>, pith , bottom, **toughness** <nf>; clenched teeth, gritted teeth; pluckiness, spunkiness <nf>, **gameness,** feistiness <nf>, mettlesomeness; courage 492

4 **willpower, will,** power, **strong-mindedness,** strength of mind, strength *or* fixity of purpose, strength, fortitude, **moral fiber; iron will,** will of iron *or* steel; a will *or* mind of one's own, law unto oneself; the courage of one's convictions, moral courage

5 **self-control, self-command, self-possession,** strength of character, self-mastery, self-government, self-domination, **self-restraint,** self-conquest, self-discipline, **self-denial;** control, restraint, constraint, discipline; composure, possession, aplomb; **independence** 430.5

6 **self-assertion,** self assertiveness, forwardness, **nerve** *and* pushiness <nf>, importunateness, importunacy; self-expression, self-expressiveness

VERBS 7 **resolve, determine, decide, will, purpose, make up one's mind,** make *or* take a resolution, make a point of; **settle,** settle on, fix, seal; conclude, come to a determination *or* conclusion *or* decision, determine once for all

8 **be determined,** be resolved, attain closure; **have a mind** *or* **will of one's own,** know one's own mind; **be in earnest, mean business** <nf>, mean what one says; have blood in one's eyes *and* be out for blood <nf>, **set one's mind** *or* **heart upon;** put one's heart into, devote *or* commit *or* dedicate oneself to, give oneself up to; buckle oneself, buckle down, buckle to; steel oneself, brace oneself, grit one's teeth, set one's teeth *or* jaw; put *or* lay *or* set one's shoulder to the wheel; take the bull by the horns, take the plunge, cross the Rubicon; nail one's colors to the mast, burn one's bridges *or* boats, go for broke *and* shoot the works <nf>, kick down the ladder, throw away the scabbard; never say die, die hard, die fighting, die with one's boots on

9 **remain firm, stand fast** *or* **firm, hold out,** hold fast, get tough <nf>, **take one's stand,** set one's back against the wall, **stand** *or* **hold one's ground,** keep one's footing, hold one's own, hang in *and* hang in there *and* hang tough <nf>, dig in, dig one's heels in; **stick to one's guns,** stick, stick with it, stick fast,

stick to one's colors, adhere to one's principles; not listen to the voice of the siren; take what comes, stand the gaff; **put one's foot down** <nf>, stand no nonsense

10 **not hesitate,** think nothing of, think little of, **make no bones about** <nf>, have *or* make no scruple of , **stick at nothing,** stop at nothing; not look back; go the whole hog <nf>, carry through, face out; go the whole nine yards <nf>

ADJS **11** **resolute, resolved, determined,** bound *and* bound and determined <nf>, **decided,** decisive, **purposeful;** definite; **earnest, serious,** sincere; devoted, dedicated, committed, wholehearted; single-minded, relentless, persistent, tenacious, persevering; **obstinate** 361.8

12 **firm, staunch,** standup <nf>, fixed, settled, steady, steadfast, constant, set *or* sot <nf>, flinty, steely; unshaken, not to be shaken, unflappable <nf>; undeflectable, **unswerving,** not to be deflected; immovable, unbending, inflexible, **unyielding** 361.9; true, committed, loyal 644.20

13 **unhesitating,** unhesitant, **unfaltering,** unflinching, unshrinking; stick-at-nothing <nf>

14 **plucky, spunky** *and* feisty *and* gutty *or* gutsy <nf>, gritty, **mettlesome,** dauntless, **game,** game to the last *or* end; **courageous** 492.16

15 **strong-willed, strong-minded,** firm-minded; **self-controlled,** controlled, self-disciplined, self-restrained; **self-possessed; self-assertive,** self-asserting, forward, pushy <nf>, importunate; self-expressive; **independent**

16 **determined upon,** resolved upon, decided upon, intent upon, fixed upon, settled upon, **set on,** dead set on <nf>, sot on <nf>, **bent on,** hell-bent on <nf>; obsessed

ADVS **17** **resolutely, determinedly, decidedly,** decisively, resolvedly, **purposefully, with a will;** firmly, steadfastly, steadily, fixedly, with constancy, staunchly; **seriously,** in all seriousness, **earnestly,** in earnest, in good earnest, sincerely; devotedly, with total dedication, committedly; hammer and tongs, tooth and nail, *bec et ongles* <Fr>; heart and soul, with all one's heart *or* might, wholeheartedly; **unswervingly;** singlemindedly, relentlessly, persistently, tenaciously, like a bulldog, like a leech, perseveringly; **obstinately, unyieldingly, inflexibly** 361.15

18 **pluckily, spunkily** *and* feistily *and* gutsily <nf>, mettlesomely, **gamely,** dauntlessly, manfully, like a man; on one's mettle; **courageously, heroically** 492.22

19 **unhesitatingly,** unhesitantly, **unfalteringly,** unflinchingly, unshrinkingly

PHRS **20** **come what may,** *venga lo que venga* <Sp>, *vogue la galère* <Fr>, **cost what it may,** *coûte que coûte* <Fr>, whatever the cost, at any price *or* cost *or* sacrifice, at all risks *or* hazards, **whatever may happen,** *ruat caelum* <L>, though the heavens may fall, at all events, live or die, survive or perish, sink or swim, rain or shine, come hell or high water; in some way or other

360 PERSEVERANCE

NOUNS **1** **perseverance, persistence** *or* persistency, insistence *or* insistency, singleness of purpose; **resolution** 359; **steadfastness, steadiness,** stability 855; **constancy, permanence** 853.1; loyalty, fidelity 644.7; **single-mindedness,** concentration, undivided *or* unswerving attention, engrossment, preoccupation 983.3; **endurance, stick-to-itiveness** <nf>, staying power, bitterendism, **pertinacity,** pertinaciousness, **tenacity,** tenaciousness, **doggedness,** unremittingness, relentlessness, dogged perseverance, bulldog tenacity, unfailing *or* leechlike grip; plodding, plugging, slogging; bidding war; **obstinacy, stubbornness** 361.1; **diligence,** application, sedulousness, sedulity, industry, industriousness, hard work, assiduousness, assiduity, unflagging efforts; **tirelessness, indefatigability, stamina; patience,** patience of Job 134.1

VERBS **2 persevere, persist, carry on,** go on, **keep on,** keep up, keep at, **keep at it,** keep going, keep driving, keep trying, try and try again, **keep the ball rolling,** keep the pot boiling, keep up the good work; not take 'no' for an answer; not accept compromise *or* defeat; **endure,** last, **continue** 827.6

3 keep doggedly at, **plod,** drudge, slog *or* slog away, soldier on, put one foot in front of the other, peg away *or* at *or* on; **plug,** plug at, plug away *or* along; pound *or* hammer away; **keep one's nose to the grindstone**

4 stay with it, hold on, hold fast, **hang on,** hang on like a bulldog *or* leech, **stick to one's guns;** not give up, **never say die,** not give up the ship, not strike one's colors; come up fighting, come up for more; **stay it out, stick out, hold out;** hold up, last out, **bear up,** stand up; **live with it,** live through it; stay the distance *or* the course; sit tight, be unmoved *or* unmoveable; brazen it out

5 prosecute to a conclusion, **go through with it, carry through, follow through, see it through,** see it out, follow out *or* up; go through with it, go to the bitter end, go the distance, go all the way, go to any length, go to any lengths; **leave no stone unturned,** leave no avenue unexplored, overlook nothing, exhaust every move; move heaven and earth, go through fire and water

6 die trying, die in the last ditch, die in harness, **die with one's boots on** *or* die in one's boots, die at one's post, die in the attempt, die game, die hard, **go down with flying colors**

7 <nf terms> **stick,** stick to it, stick with it, stick it, stick it out, hang on for dear life, hang in, hang in there, hang tough, tough it out, keep on trucking, keep on keeping on; **go the limit,** go the whole hog, go the whole nine yards, go all out, shoot the works, go for broke, go through hell and high water; work one's ass *or* butt *or* tail off

ADJS **8 persevering,** perseverant, **persistent,** persisting, insistent; **enduring,** permanent, **constant, lasting;** continuing 856.7; **stable, steady, steadfast** 855.12; immutable, inalterable; **resolute** 359.11; **diligent, assiduous, sedulous,** industrious; dogged, plodding, slogging, plugging; **pertinacious, tenacious, stick-to-itive** <nf>; loyal, faithful 644.20; **unswerving,** unremitting, unabating, unintermitting, uninterrupted; single-minded, utterly attentive; rapt, preoccupied 983.17; **unfaltering, unwavering,** unflinching; relentless, **unrelenting; obstinate,** high-maintenance, **stubborn** 361.8; **unrelaxing,** unfailing, **untiring,** unwearying, unflagging, never-tiring, **tireless,** weariless, **indefatigable,** unwearied, unsleeping, undrooping, unnodding, unwinking, sleepless; undiscouraged, undaunted, indomitable, unconquerable, invincible, game to the last *or* to the end, hanging in there; **patient,** patient as Job 134.9

ADVS **9 perseveringly, persistently,** persistingly, insistently; resolutely 359.17; loyally, faithfully, devotedly 644.25; **diligently,** industriously, assiduously, sedulously; **doggedly,** sloggingly, ploddingly; pertinaciously, tenaciously; unremittingly, unabatingly, unintermittingly, uninterruptedly; unswervingly, unwaveringly, unfalteringly, unflinchingly; relentlessly, unrelentingly; **indefatigably, tirelessly,** wearilessly, untiringly, unwearyingly, unflaggingly, unrestingly, unsleepingly; **patiently**

10 through thick and thin, through fire and water, come hell or high water, through evil report and good report, rain or shine, fair or foul, in sickness and in health; **come what may** 359.20, **all the way, down to the wire,** to the bitter end

361 OBSTINACY

NOUNS **1 obstinacy,** obstinateness, pertinacity, restiveness, **stubbornness, willfulness,** self-will, hardheadedness, **headstrongness,** strongheadness; mind *or* will of one's own, set *or* fixed mind, inflexible will; **perseverance** 360, **doggedness, determination,** tenaciousness, tenacity, bitterendism; **bullheadedness, pigheadedness, mulishness; obduracy,** unregenerateness; stiff neck, stiff-neckedness; sullenness, sulkiness; balkiness; uncooperativeness; dogmatism, opinionatedness 970.6; overzealousness, fanaticism 926.11; intolerance, bigotry 980; bloody-mindedness <Brit>

2 **unyieldingness,** unbendingness, stiff temper, **inflexibility,** inelasticity, impliability, ungivingness, **obduracy,** toughness, **firmness,** stiffness, adamantness, rigorism, **rigidity,** strait-lacedness *or* straight-lacedness, stuffiness; **hard line,** hard-bittenness, hard-nosedness <nf>; fixity; unalterability, unchangeability, immutability, immovability; irreconcilability, uncompromisingness, **intransigence** *or* intransigency, *intransigeance* <Fr>, intransigentism; **implacability,** inexorability, **relentlessness,** unrelentingness; sternness, grimness, dourness, flintiness, **steeliness**

3 **perversity,** perverseness, **contrariness, wrongheadedness, waywardness,** forwardness, difficultness, crossgrainedness, cantankerousness, feistiness *and* orneriness *and* cussedness <nf>; sullenness, sulkiness, dourness, stuffiness; irascibility 110.2

4 **ungovernability, unmanageability,** uncontrollability; indomitability, untamableness, **intractability,** refractoriness, shrewishness; incorrigibility; **unsubmissiveness,** unbiddability <Brit>, **indocility;** irrepressibility, insuppressibility; unmalleability, unmoldableness; recidivism; **recalcitrance** *or* recalcitrancy, contumacy, contumaciousness; **unruliness,** obstreperousness, restiveness, fractiousness, wildness; defiance 454; resistance 453

5 **unpersuadableness,** deafness, blindness; closed-mindedness; positiveness, dogmatism 970.6

6 <obstinate person> **mule** *and* donkey <nf>, ass, perverse fool; bullethead, pighead; hardnose <nf>, hardhead, hammerhead <nf>, hard-liner; standpat *and* **standpatter, stickler; intransigent,** maverick; dogmatist, positivist, bigot, fanatic, purist; **diehard, bitter-ender,** last-ditcher; conservative; stick-in-the-mud

VERBS 7 **balk, stickle;** hold one's ground, not budge, dig one's heels in, **stand pat** <nf>, **not yield an inch,** stick to one's guns; hold out; stand firm; take no denial, not take 'no' for an answer; take the bit in one's teeth; die hard; cut off one's nose to spite one's face; **persevere** 360.2; turn a deaf ear

ADJS 8 **obstinate, stubborn, pertinacious, restive; willful, self-willed,** strong-willed, hardheaded, **headstrong,** strongheaded, *entêté* <Fr>; **dogged,** bulldogged, **tenacious, perserving; bullheaded,** bulletheaded, **pigheaded, mulish** <nf>, stubborn as a mule; set, **set in one's ways,** case-hardened, stiff-necked; sullen, sulky; balky, balking; unregenerate, uncooperative; bigoted, intolerant 980.11, overzealous, fanatic, fanatical 926.32; dogmatic, opinionated 970.22

9 **unyielding, unbending, inflexible, hard, hard-line,** inelastic, impliable, ungiving, **firm, stiff,** rigid, rigorous, stuffy; rock-ribbed, rock-hard, rock-like; **adamant,** adamantine; unmoved, unaffected; **immovable,** not to be moved; **unalterable,** unchangeable, immutable; **uncompromising,** intransigent, irreconcilable, hard-shell *and* hard-core <nf>; implacable, inexorable, **relentless,** unrelenting; stern, grim, dour; iron, cast-iron, flinty, steely

10 **obdurate,** tough, **hard,** hard-set, hard-mouthed, hard-bitten, hard-nosed *and* hard-boiled <nf>

11 **perverse, contrary, wrongheaded, wayward, froward, difficult,** cross-grained, cantankerous, feisty, ornery <nf>; sullen, sulky, stuffy; irascible 110.19

12 **ungovernable, unmanageable, uncontrollable, indomitable,** untamable, **intractable, refractory;** shrewish; **incorrigible, unreconstructed; unsubmissive,** unbid-

dable <Brit>, **indocile;** irrepressible, insuppressible; unmalleable, unmoldable; recidivist, recidivistic; **recalcitrant,** contumacious; obstreperous, **unruly, restive,** wild, fractious, breachy <nf>; beyond control, out of hand; **resistant, resisting** 453.5; **defiant** 454.7; irascible; like a hog on ice <nf>

13 unpersuadable, deaf, blind; closed-minded; positive; dogmatic 970.22

ADVS **14 obstinately, stubbornly,** pertinaciously; willfully, headstrongly; **doggedly,** tenaciously; **bullheadedly,** pigheadedly, mulishly; unregenerately; uncooperatively; with set jaw, with sullen mouth, with a stiff neck

15 unyieldingly, unbendingly, inflexibly, adamantly, obdurately, **firmly,** stiffly, rigidly, rigorously; unalterably, unchangeably, immutably, immovably, unregenerately; uncompromisingly, intransigently, irreconcilably; implacably, inexorably, relentlessly, unrelentingly; sternly, grimly, dourly

16 perversely, contrarily, contrariwise, waywardly, wrongheadedly, frowardly, crossgrainedly, cantankerously, feistily, sullenly, sulkily

17 ungovernably, unmanageably, uncontrollably, indomitably, untamably, intractably; shrewishly; incorrigibly; unsubmissively; irrepressibly, insuppressibly; contumaciously; unrulily, obstreperously, restively, fractiously

362 IRRESOLUTION

NOUNS **1 irresolution, indecision,** unsettlement, unsettledness, irresoluteness, undeterminedness, **indecisiveness,** undecidedness, infirmity of purpose; mugwumpery, mugwumpism, fence-sitting, fence-straddling; double-mindedness, **ambivalence,** ambitendency; dubiety, dubiousness, **uncertainty** 971; **instability, inconstancy,** changeableness 854; capriciousness, mercuriality, fickleness 364.3; change of mind, second thoughts, tergiversation 363.1; fence-sitting

2 vacillation, fluctuation, oscillation, pendulation, mood swing, **wavering,** wobbling, waffling <nf>, shilly-shally, **shilly-shallying,** blowing hot and cold; equivocation 344.4; second thoughts; back-pedaling, reversal, about-face

3 hesitation, hesitance, **hesitancy,** hesitating, holding back, dragging one's feet; falter, faltering, shilly-shally, shilly-shallying; diffidence, tentativeness, caution, cautiousness

4 weak will, weak-mindedness; feeblemindedness , **weakness,** feebleness, faintness, faintheartedness, **frailty, infirmity; wimpiness** *or* wimpishness <nf>, spinelessness, invertebracy; abulia; fear 127; cowardice 491; **pliability** 1047.2

5 vacillator, shillyshallyer, shilly-shally, **waverer,** wobbler, butterfly; mugwump, fence-sitter, fence-straddler; equivocator, tergiversator, prevaricator; ass between two bundles of hay; yo-yo <nf>, flip-flopper <nf>; **wimp** <nf>, weakling, jellyfish, Milquetoast; quitter; don't know

VERBS **6 not know one's own mind,** not know where one stands, **be of two minds,** have two minds, have mixed feelings, be in conflict, be conflicted <nf>; stagger, stumble, boggle

7 hesitate, pause, falter, hang back, hover; procrastinate; shilly-shally, hum and haw, **hem and haw;** wait to see how the cat jumps *or* the wind blows, scruple, jib, demur , stick at, stickle, strain at; think twice about, stop to consider, ponder, wrinkle one's brow; debate, deliberate, see both sides of the question, balance, weigh one thing against another, consider both sides of the question, weigh the pros and cons; be divided, come down squarely in the middle, sit on *or* straddle the fence, fall between two stools; yield, back down 433.7; retreat, withdraw 163.6, wimp *or* chicken *or* cop out <nf>; pull back, drag one's feet; **flinch, shy away from, shy** 903.7, back off <nf>; fear; not face up to, hide one's head in the sand

8 **vacillate, waver, waffle** <nf>, **fluctuate,** pendulate, oscillate, wobble, wobble about, teeter, totter , dither, swing from one thing to another, **shilly-shally,** back and fill, keep off and on, will and will not, keep *or* leave hanging in midair; blow hot and cold 364.4; **equivocate** 344.7, fudge and mudge <Brit nf>; change one's mind, tergiversate; vary, **alternate** 854.5; shift, change horses in midstream, **change** 852.7

ADJS **9** **irresolute,** irresolved, **unresolved; undecided, indecisive, undetermined,** unsettled, infirm of purpose; dubious, **uncertain** 971.16; at loose ends, at a loose end; **of two minds,** in conflict, double-minded, ambivalent, ambitendent; changeable, mutable 828.7; capricious, mercurial, fickle 364.6; mugwumpian, mugwumpish, fence-sitting, fence-straddling

10 **vacillating,** vacillatory, waffling <nf>, oscillatory, wobbly, **wavering, fluctuating,** pendulating, oscillating, **shilly-shallying,** shilly-shally; inconsistent

11 **hesitant,** hesitating, pikerish; faltering; shilly-shallying; diffident, tentative, timid, cautious; scrupling, jibbing, demurring , sticking, straining, stickling

12 **weak-willed, weak-minded,** feeble-minded , weak-kneed, **weak,** wimpy *or* wimpish <nf>, feeble, faint-hearted, **frail, faint, infirm,** feeble; **spineless,** invertebrate; without a will of one's own, unable to say 'no'; abulic; afraid, **chicken** *and* chicken-hearted *and* chicken-livered <nf>, cowardly 491.10; like putty, **pliable** 1047.9

ADVS **13** **irresolutely,** irresolvedly, **undecidedly, indecisively, undeterminedly; uncertainly;** hesitantly, hesitatingly, falteringly; waveringly, vacillatingly, shilly-shally, shilly-shallyingly

363 CHANGING OF MIND

NOUNS **1** **reverse, reversal,** flip *and* flip-flop *and* U-turn <nf>, turnabout, turnaround, **about-face,** about turn <Brit>, *volte-face* <Fr>, right-about-face, right-about turn <Brit>, right-about, a turn to the right-about; tergiversation, tergiversating; **change of mind;** second thoughts, better thoughts, afterthoughts, mature judgment; paradigm shift

2 **apostasy,** recreancy; **treason,** misprision of treason, betrayal, turning traitor, turning one's coat, changing one's stripes, ratting <nf>, going over, joining *or* going over to the opposition, siding with the enemy; **defection;** bolt, bolting, secession, breakaway; **desertion** 370.2; **recidivism,** recidivation, relapse, backsliding 394.2; faithlessness, **disloyalty** 645.5

3 **recantation, withdrawal, disavowal, denial,** reneging, **unsaying, repudiation,** palinode, palinody, **retraction,** retractation; **disclaimer,** disclamation, **disownment,** disowning, abjurement, abjuration, **renunciation,** renouncement, forswearing; expatriation, self-exile

4 **timeserver,** timepleaser , temporizer, opportunist, trimmer, weathercock; mugwump; chameleon, Vicar of Bray

5 **apostate, turncoat,** turnabout, **recreant, renegade,** renegado, renegate *or* runagate , **defector,** tergiversator, tergiversant; **deserter,** turntail, quisling, fifth columnist, collaborationist, collaborator, **traitor** 357.10; strikebreaker; **bolter, seceder,** secessionist, **separatist,** schismatic; **backslider,** recidivist; reversionist; convert, proselyte

VERBS **6** **change one's mind** *or* **song** *or* **tune** *or* **note,** sing a different tune, dance to another tune; come round, wheel, do an about-face, reverse oneself, do a flip-flop *or* U-turn <nf>, go over, change sides; swing from one thing to another; think better of it, have second thoughts, be of another mind; bite one's tongue

7 **apostatize** *or* apostacize, go over, change sides, switch, switch over, change one's allegiance, **defect; turn one's coat,** turn cloak; desert *or* leave a sinking ship; secede, break away, bolt, fall off *or* away; desert

8 **recant, retract, repudiate, withdraw, take back,** unswear, renege, welsh <nf>, **abjure, disavow, disown; deny,** disclaim, unsay, unspeak; **renounce, forswear, eat one's words,** eat one's hat, swallow, eat crow, eat humble pie; **back down** *or* **out,** climb down, crawfish out <nf>, backwater, weasel

9 **be a timeserver,** trim, temporize, change with the times; sit on *or* straddle the fence

ADJS 10 **timeserving, trimming, temporizing;** supple, neither fish nor fowl

11 **apostate, recreant,** renegade, tergiversating, tergiversant; **treasonous, treasonable, traitorous,** forsworn; collaborating; faithless, **disloyal** 645.20

12 **repudiative,** repudiatory; abjuratory, renunciative, renunciatory; schismatic; **separatist,** secessionist, breakaway <nf>; **opportunistic,** mugwumpian, mugwumpish, fence-straddling, fence-sitting

364 CAPRICE

NOUNS 1 **caprice, whim,** *capriccio* <Ital>, *boutade* <Fr>, humor, **whimsy,** freak, whim-wham; **fancy,** fantasy, **conceit, notion,** flimflam, toy, freakish inspiration, crazy idea, fantastic notion, fool notion <nf>, harebrained idea, brainstorm, **vagary,** megrim; **fad, craze, passing fancy,** next big thing; **quirk, crotchet,** crank, kink; maggot, maggot in the brain, bee in one's bonnet <nf>, flea in one's nose <nf>

2 **capriciousness,** caprice, **whimsicalness,** whimsy, whimsicality; humorsomeness, **fancifulness,** fantasticality, **freakishness;** crankiness, crotchetiness, quirkiness; **moodiness,** temperamentalness, prima-donnaism; petulance 110.6; **arbitrariness,** motivelessness

3 **fickleness, flightiness,** skittishness, inconstancy, **lightness, levity,** *légèreté* <Fr>; flakiness <nf>; volatility, mercurialness, mercuriality, erraticism; **mood swing;** faddishness, faddism; **changeableness** 854; unpredictability 971.1; unreliability, undependability 645.4; coquettishness; frivolousness 922.7; purposelessness, motivelessness

VERBS 4 **blow hot and cold,** keep off and on, have as many phases as the moon, chop and change, **fluctuate** 854.5, vacillate 362.8, flip-flop <nf>; act on impulse

ADJS 5 **capricious, whimsical,** freakish, humorsome, vagarious; **fanciful, notional,** fantasied , fantastic *or* fantastical, maggoty, **crotchety,** kinky, harebrained, cranky, flaky <nf>, quirky; wanton, wayward, vagrant; **arbitrary, unreasonable,** motiveless; **moody, temperamental,** prima-donnaish; petulant 110.22; unrestrained

6 **fickle, flighty,** skittish, **light;** coquettish, flirtatious, toying; versatile, **inconstant,** erratic, **changeable** 854.7; vacillating 362.10; volatile, mercurial, quicksilver; faddish; **scatterbrained** 985.16, unpredictable; **impulsive;** idiosyncratic; unreliable, undependable 645.19; polytropic

ADVS 7 **capriciously, whimsically,** fancifully, at one's own sweet will <nf>; **flightily, lightly;** arbitrarily, unreasonably, without rhyme or reason

365 IMPULSE

NOUNS 1 **impulse;** natural impulse, blind impulse, irresistible impulse, **instinct,** urge, drive; vagrant *or* fleeting impulse; involuntary impulse, reflex, knee jerk, automatic response; gut response *or* reaction <nf>; **notion, fancy; sudden thought,** flash, inspiration, brainstorm, brain wave, quick hunch; impulse buy

2 **impulsiveness, impetuousness,** impulsivity, impetuousity; **hastiness,** overhastiness, haste, quickness, suddenness; **precipitateness,** precipitance, precipitancy, precipitation; hair-trigger; **recklessness, rashness** 493; impatience 135

3 **thoughtlessness,** unthoughtfulness, **heedlessness** 984.1, **carelessness,** inconsideration, inconsiderateness; **negligence** 102.2, caprice 364

4 **unpremeditation,** indeliberation, **undeliberateness,** uncalculatedness, undesignedness, **spontaneity, spontaneousness,** unstudiedness; involuntariness 963.5; snap judgment *or* decision; snap shot, offhand shot

5 **improvisation, extemporization,** improvision, improvising, extempore , **impromptu, ad-lib,** ad-libbing *and* playing by ear <nf>, **ad hoc measure** *or* solution, adhocracy <nf>, ad hockery *or* hocery *or* hocism <nf>; extemporaneousness, extemporariness; temporary measure *or* arrangement, pro tempore measure *or* arrangement, **stopgap, makeshift,** jury-rig; cannibalization; bricolage; jam session; thinking on one's feet

6 **improviser,** improvisator, **extemporizer,** ad-libber <nf>; cannibalizer; bricoleur; creature of impulse

VERBS 7 **act on the spur of the moment,** obey one's impulse, let oneself go; shoot from the hip <nf>, be too quick on the trigger *or* the uptake *or* the draw; **blurt out,** come out with, let slip out, say what comes uppermost, say the first thing that comes into one's head *or* to one's mind; be unable to help oneself; impulse-buy; reinvent oneself

8 **improvise, extemporize,** improvisate, improv *and* tapdance *and* talk off the top of one's head <nf>, speak off the cuff, think on one's feet, invent, make it up as one goes along, play it by ear <nf>, throw away *or* depart from the prepared text, throw away the speech, scrap the plan, **ad-lib** <nf>, **do offhand,** wing it <nf>, vamp, fake <nf>, play by ear <nf>; **dash off, strike off,** knock off, throw off, toss off *or* out; make up, whip up, **cook up,** run up, rustle up *or* whomp up <nf>, slap up *or* together *and* throw together <nf>, lash up <Brit>, cobble up; jury-rig; rise to the occasion; cannibalize

ADJS 9 **impulsive, impetuous, hasty,** overhasty, quick, sudden, snap; quick on the draw *or* trigger *or* uptake, hair-trigger; **precipitate,** headlong; **reckless, rash** 493.7; impatient 135.6

10 **unthinking, unreasoning, unreflecting,** uncalculating, unthoughtful, **thoughtless, inadvertent,** reasonless, **heedless, careless,** inconsiderate; unguarded; arbitrary, capricious 364.5

11 **unpremeditated,** unmeditated, **uncalculated,** undeliberated, **spontaneous, undesigned, unstudied;** unintentional, unintended, inadvertent, unwilled, **indeliberate,** undeliberate, collateral; **involuntary,** reflex, reflexive, knee-jerk <nf>, acting out, automatic, goose-step, lockstep; gut <nf>, unconscious; **unconsidered,** unadvised, snap, casual, offhand, throwaway <nf>; **ill-considered,** ill-advised, ill-devised; act-first-and-think-later

12 **extemporaneous, extemporary,** extempore, **impromptu,** unrehearsed, **improvised,** improvisatory, improvisatorial, improviso, *improvisé* <Fr>; **ad-lib,** *ad libitum* <L>; **ad-hoc,** stopgap, makeshift, jury-rigged; **offhand,** off the top of one's head *and* off-the-cuff <nf>, **spur-of-the-moment, quick and dirty** <nf>; catch-as-catch-can; potluck

ADVS 13 **impulsively, impetuously, hastily,** suddenly, quickly, **precipitately,** headlong; **recklessly, rashly** 493.10

14 **on impulse,** on a sudden impulse, **on the spur of the moment; without premeditation,** unpremeditatedly, uncalculatedly, undesignedly; unthinkingly, unreflectingly, unreasoningly, unthoughtfully, thoughtlessly, heedlessly, carelessly, inconsiderately, unadvisedly; unintentionally, inadvertently, without willing, indeliberately, involuntarily

15 **extemporaneously, extemporarily,** extempore, *à l'improviste* <Fr>, **impromptu, ad lib, offhand,** out of hand; at *or* on sight; by ear, off the

hip *and* off the top of one's head *and* off the cuff <nf>; at short notice

366 LEAP

NOUNS 1 **leap, jump, hop, spring, skip, bound,** bounce; **pounce;** upleap, upspring, jump-off; **hurdle; vault,** pole vault; demivolt, curvet, capriole; jeté, grand jeté, tour jeté, saut de basque; jig, galliard, lavolta, Highland fling, morris; standing *or* running *or* flying jump; long jump, broad jump, standing *or* running broad jump; high jump, standing *or* running high jump; leapfrog; jump shot; handspring; buck, buckjump; ski jump, jump turn, geländesprung, gelände jump, steeplechase; hippety-hop <nf>; jump-hop; hop, skip, and jump

2 **caper,** dido <nf>, **gambol, frisk,** curvet, cavort, capriole; **prance,** caracole; *gambade* <Fr>, gambado; falcade

3 **leaping, jumping,** bouncing, bounding, hopping, capering, cavorting, prancing, skipping, **springing,** saltation; **vaulting,** pole vaulting; **hurdling,** the hurdles, hurdle race, timber topping <nf>, steeplechase; leapfrogging; bungee-jumping

4 **jumper,** leaper, hopper; broad jumper, high jumper; **vaulter,** pole vaulter; **hurdler,** hurdle racer, timber topper <nf>; jumping jack; bucking bronco, buckjumper, sunfisher <nf>; jumping bean; kangaroo, gazelle, stag, jackrabbit, goat, frog, grasshopper, flea; salmon

VERBS 5 **leap, jump, vault, spring, skip, hop, bound,** bounce; upleap, upspring, updive; leap over, jump over, etc; overleap, overjump, overskip, leapfrog; **hurdle,** clear, negotiate; curvet, capriole; buck, buckjump; ski jump; steeplechase; start, start up, start aside; **pounce,** pounce on *or* upon; hippety-hop <nf>

6 **caper, cut capers,** cut a dido <nf>, curvet, cavort, capriole, **gambol,** gambado, **frisk,** flounce, **trip, skip,** bob, bounce, jump about; **romp,** ramp <nf>; **prance;** caracole

ADJS 7 **leaping, jumping,** springing, hopping, skipping, prancing, bouncing, bounding; saltant, saltatory, saltatorial

367 PLUNGE

NOUNS 1 **plunge, dive, pitch, drop, fall;** free-fall; header <nf>; **swoop, pounce,** stoop; swan dive, gainer, jackknife, cannonball; belly flop *and* belly buster *and* belly whopper <nf>; nose dive, power dive; parachute jump, sky dive, bungee jump; crash dive, stationary dive, running dive

2 **submergence, submersion, immersion,** immergence, engulfment, **inundation,** burial; **dipping, ducking,** dousing, sousing, dunking <nf>, sinking; **dip, duck, souse;** baptism

3 **diving,** plunging; skydiving; bungee jumping; fancy diving, high diving; scuba diving, snorkeling, skin diving, pearl diving, deep-sea diving

4 **diver,** plunger; high diver; bungee jumper; parachute jumper, jumper, sky diver, sport jumper, paratrooper, smoke jumper, paramedic; skin diver, snorkel diver, scuba diver, free diver, pearl diver, deep-sea diver, frogman

5 <diving equipment> diving bell, diving chamber, bathysphere, bathyscaphe, benthoscope, aquascope; submarine 180.9; diving boat; scuba *or* self-contained underwater breathing apparatus, Aqua-Lung <TM>; Scuba; diving goggles, diving mask, swim fins; wet suit; air cylinder; diving suit; diving helmet, diving hood; snorkel, periscope

VERBS 6 **plunge, dive, pitch, plummet, drop, fall;** skydive; bungee jump; free-fall; plump, plunk, plop; swoop, swoop down, stoop, **pounce,** pounce on *or* upon; nose-dive, make *or* take a nose dive; parachute, skydive; skin-dive; sound; take a header <nf>

7 **submerge,** submerse, **immerse,** immerge, merge, **sink,** bury, engulf, **inundate,** deluge, drown, overwhelm, whelm; **dip, duck, dunk**

<nf>, douse, souse, plunge in water; baptize

8 **sink, scuttle,** send to the bottom, send to Davy Jones's locker; **founder, go down,** go to the bottom, sink like lead, go down like a stone; get out of one's depth

ADJS **9** **submersible,** submergible, immersible, sinkable; immersive

368 AVOIDANCE

NOUNS **1** **avoidance, shunning; forbearance,** refraining; hands-off policy, **nonintervention,** noninvolvement, neutrality; **evasion,** elusion; side-stepping, getting around <nf>, **circumvention;** prevention, forestalling, forestallment; **escape** 369; evasive action, the runaround <nf>; zigzag, jink *and* juke <nf>, slip, dodge, duck, side step, shy; shunting off, sidetracking; bypassing; evasiveness, elusiveness; **equivocation** 344.4, waffle <nf>, fudging, fudge and mudge <Brit nf>; avoiding reaction, defense mechanism *or* reaction; safe distance, wide berth; cold shoulder, snub; abstinence; shyness

2 **shirking, slacking,** goldbricking <nf>, cop-out <nf>, soldiering, goofing *and* goofing off *and* fucking off <nf>; clock-watching; **malingering,** skulking <Brit>; passivity; **dodging,** ducking; welshing <nf>; truancy; tax evasion, tax dodging

3 **shirker,** shirk, **slacker,** eye-servant *or* eye-server , goof-off <nf>, soldier *or* old soldier, **goldbricker,** goldbrick <nf>; clock watcher; **welsher** <nf>; **malingerer,** skulker *or* skulk <Brit>; truant; tax dodger *or* evader

4 **flight,** fugitation, exit, quick exit, making oneself scarce *and* getting the hell out <nf>, bolt, scarpering <Brit nf>, disappearing act <nf>, hasty retreat; **running away, decampment**, bugging out <nf>**;** skedaddle *and* skedaddling *and* scramming *and* absquatulation <nf>; **elopement;** disappearance 34; French leave, absence without leave *or* AWOL; desertion 370.2; hegira; truancy, hooky *or* hookey

5 **fugitive,** fleer, person on the run, **runaway,** runagate, **bolter,** skedaddler <nf>; **absconder, eloper; refugee, evacuee,** boat person, *émigré* <Fr>; **displaced person** *or* DP, stateless person; **escapee** 369.5; illegal immigrant, wetback <nf>, day-crosser; draft dodger; truant, absentee; desserter

VERBS **6** **avoid, shun, fight shy of, shy away from,** keep from, **keep away from, circumvent,** keep clear of, avoid like the plague, **steer clear of** <nf>, give a miss to <nf>, skate around <Brit nf>, keep *or* get out of the way of, **give a wide berth,** keep remote from, stay detached from; make way for, give place to; **keep one's distance,** keep at a respectful distance, keep *or* stand *or* hold aloof; give the cold shoulder to <nf>, have nothing to do with, have no association with, not give the time of day, **have no truck with** <nf>; not meddle with, let alone, let well enough alone, keep hands off, not touch, not touch with a ten-foot pole, back off; turn away from, turn one's back upon, slam the door in one's face

7 **evade, elude,** beg, **get out of,** shuffle out of, skirt, **get around** <nf>, circumvent; take evasive action; give one the run-around; ditch *and* shake *and* shake off <nf>, get away from, give the runaround *or* the slip <nf>; throw off the scent; play at hide and seek; lead one a chase *or* merry chase, lead one a dance *or* pretty dance; escape 369.6

8 **dodge, duck; take evasive action,** juke *and* jink <nf>, zig-zag; throw off the track *or* trail; shy, shy off *or* away; swerve, sheer off; pull away *or* clear; pull back, shrink, recoil 903.6,7; **sidestep,** step aside; parry, fence, ward off; have an out *or* escape hatch; shift, shift *or* put off; **hedge,** pussyfoot <nf>, be *or* sit on the fence, beat around *or* about the bush, hem and haw, beg the question, tapdance <nf>, dance around, equivocate 344.7, fudge and mudge <Brit nf>

9 **shirk, slack, lie** *or* **rest upon one's oars,** not pull fair, not pull one's weight; **lie down on the job** <nf>; soldier, duck duty, **goof off** *and* dog it <nf>, **goldbrick** <nf>; **malinger,** skulk <Brit>; **get out of,** sneak *or* slip out of, slide out of, pass the buck, cop out <nf>, dodge, duck; welsh <nf>

10 **flee, fly, take flight,** take to flight, take wing, fugitate, **run, cut and run** <nf>, make a precipitate departure, **run off** *or* **away,** run away from, bug out <nf>, **decamp,** pull up stakes, **take to one's heels,** make off, **depart** 188.6, do the disappearing act, make a quick exit, **beat a retreat** *or* **a hasty retreat, turn tail,** show the heels, show a clean *or* light pair of heels; **run for it, bolt, run for one's life;** make a run for it; advance to the rear, make a strategic withdrawal; **take French leave,** go AWOL, slip the cable; **desert; abscond,** levant <Brit>, **elope,** run away with; skip *or* jump bail; play hooky *or* hookey

11 <nf terms> **beat it, blow, scram,** bug off, lam, book, air out, shemozzle *and* bugger off <Brit>, **take it on the lam,** take a powder *or* runout powder, make tracks, cut ass, cut and run, peel out, **split,** skin out, **skip,** skip out, duck out, duck and run, dog it, vamoose, absquatulate *and* skedaddle , **clear out,** make oneself scarce, get the hell out, make a break for it, warp out, scram

12 **slip away, steal away, sneak off,** shuffle off, slink off, slide off, slither off, skulk away, mooch off *and* duck out <nf>, slip out of

13 **not face up to,** hide one's head in the sand, not come to grips with, put off, procrastinate, temporize, waffle <nf>

ADJS 14 **avoidable, escapable,** eludible; evadable; preventable

15 **evasive, elusive,** elusory; **shifty,** slippery, slippery as an eel; cagey <nf>; shirking, malingering

16 **fugitive, runaway,** in flight, on the lam <nf>, hot <nf>; disappearing 34.3

369 ESCAPE

NOUNS 1 **escape; getaway** *and* break *and* breakout <nf>; **deliverance; delivery,** riddance, **release,** setting-free, freeing, freedom, **liberation, extrication, rescue;** emergence, issuance, issue, outlet, vent; **leakage,** leak; jailbreak, prisonbreak, break, breakout; evasion 368.1; **flight** 368.4; retreat; French leave; hooky; elopment; escapology; escapism

2 **narrow escape,** hairbreadth escape, **close call** *or* **shave** <nf>, **near miss,** near go *or* thing <Brit nf>, near *or* narrow squeak <Brit nf>, close *or* tight squeeze <nf>, squeaker <nf>

3 bolt-hole, escape hatch, fire escape, life net, lifeboat, life raft, life buoy, lifeline, sally port, slide, inflatable slide, ejection *or* ejector seat, emergency exit, escapeway, back door, trapdoor, escape hatch, secret passage

4 **loophole, way out,** way of escape, hole to creep out of, escape hatch, escape clause, saving clause, technicality; pretext 376; **alternative,** choice 371

5 **escapee,** escaper, evader; escape artist; escapologist; runaway, **fugitive** 368.5; escapist, Houdini

VERBS 6 **escape,** make *or* effect one's escape, make good one's escape; **get away, make a getaway** <nf>; **free oneself,** deliver oneself, gain one's liberty, **get free, get clear of,** bail out, **get out, get out of,** get well out of; **break loose,** cut loose, break away, break one's bonds *or* chains, slip the collar, shake off the yoke; **jump** *and* **skip** <nf>; **break jail** *or* **prison,** escape prison, fly the coop <nf>; leap over the wall; evade 368.7; flee 368.10; vamoose, take it on the lam

7 **get off, go free,** win freedom, go at liberty, **go scot free,** escape with a whole skin, escape without penalty, walk *and* beat the rap <nf>; **get away with** <nf>, get by, get by with, get off easy *or* lightly, get away with murder <nf>, **get off cheap;** cop a plea *and* cop out <nf>, get off on a technicality

8 scrape *or* squeak through, squeak by, escape with *or* by the skin of one's teeth, have a close call *or* close shave <nf>

9 **slip away, give one the slip,** slip through one's hands *or* fingers; slip *or* sneak through; **slip out of,** slide out of, crawl *or* creep out of, sneak out of, wiggle *or* squirm *or* shuffle *or* wriggle *or* worm out of, find a loophole, elude

10 **find vent,** issue forth, come forth, exit, **emerge, issue,** debouch, erupt, break out, break through, come out, run out, **leak out,** ooze out

ADJS **11** **escaped, loose,** on the loose, disengaged, out of, well out of; fled, flown; fugitive, runaway; free as a bird, scot-free, at large, **free**

370 ABANDONMENT

NOUNS **1** **abandonment, forsaking, leaving,** jilting; jettison, jettisoning, throwing overboard *or* away *or* aside, casting away *or* aside; **withdrawal,** evacuation, pulling out, absentation; cessation 857; disuse, desuetude

2 **desertion, defection,** ratting <nf>; dereliction, decampment; **secession,** bolt, breakaway, walkout; betrayal 645.8; schism, apostasy 363.2; deserter 363.5

3 <giving up> **relinquishment, surrender, resignation, renouncement,** renunciation, abdication, waiver, abjurement, abjuration, ceding, cession, handing over, standing *or* stepping down, **yielding, forswearing; withdrawing, dropping out** <nf>

4 **derelict,** castoff; jetsam, flotsam, lagan, **flotsam and jetsam;** waifs and strays; **rubbish, junk,** trash, refuse, waste, waste product, solid waste; liquid waste, wastewater; **dump,** dumpsite, garbage dump, landfill, sanitary landfill, junkheap, junkpile, scrap heap, midden; abandonee, waif, throwaway, orphan, dogie <nf>; **castaway;** foundling; wastrel, reject, deselect, **discard** 390.3

VERBS **5** **abandon, desert, forsake; quit, leave,** leave behind, take leave of, depart from, absent oneself from, turn one's back upon, turn one's tail upon, say goodbye to, bid a long farewell to, walk away, **walk** *or* **run out on** <nf>, **leave flat** *and* leave high and dry *or* holding the bag *or* in the lurch <nf>, leave one to one's fate, throw to the wolves <nf>; **withdraw, back out, drop out** <nf>, pull out, stand down <nf>; **go back on, go back on one's word;** cry off <Brit>, beg off, renege; **vacate,** evacuate; quit cold *and* leave flat <nf>, toss aside; jilt, throw over <nf>; maroon; **jettison; junk,** deep-six <nf>, **discard** 390.7; let fall into disuse *or* desuetude

6 **defect, secede, bolt,** break away; pull out <nf>, withdraw one's support, decamp; sell out *and* sell down the river <nf>, **betray** 645.14; turn one's back on; apostatize

7 **give up, relinquish, surrender, yield,** yield up, waive, **forgo, resign, renounce,** throw up, abdicate, **abjure, forswear, give up on, have done with,** give up as a bad job, cede, hand over, lay down, wash one's hands of, **write off,** drop, drop all idea of, drop like a hot potato; **cease** 857.6, **desist from,** leave off, give over; hold *or* stay one's hand, cry quits, acknowledge defeat, **throw in the towel** *or* **sponge** 433.8

ADJS **8** **abandoned, forsaken, deserted,** left; untouristed; disused; **derelict,** castaway, jettisoned; marooned; junk, junked, discarded 390.11

371 CHOICE

NOUNS **1** **choice, selection, election,** preference, decision, **pick, choosing,** free choice; alternativity; co-option, co-optation; **will,** volition, free will 430.6,7; preoption, first choice; the best 999.8

2 **option, discretion, pleasure,** will and pleasure; optionality; possible choice, alternative, alternate choice, possible action

3 **dilemma,** Scylla and Charybdis, quandary, fix, bind, the devil and the deep blue sea; *embarras de choix* <Fr>; choice of Hercules; Hobson's choice, **no choice,** only choice, zero option; limited choice, positive discrimination <Brit>, affirmative action; lesser of two evils

4 **adoption, embracement,** acceptance, espousal; affiliation

5 **preference, predilection,** proclivity, bent, affinity, prepossession, predisposition, partiality, inclination, leaning, tilt, penchant, bias, tendency, taste, favoritism; favor, fancy, preferment; prejudice; personal choice, particular choice , druthers <nf>; chosen kind *or* sort, style, one's cup of tea <nf>, type, bag *and* thing <nf>; way of life, lifestyle

6 **vote,** voting, **suffrage,** franchise, enfranchisement, voting right, right to vote; **voice, say;** representation; **poll,** polling, canvass, canvassing, division <Brit>, counting heads *or* noses *or* hands, exit poll; **ballot,** balloting, secret ballot, absentee ballot; ballot-box, voting machine; **plebiscite,** plebiscitum, **referendum;** yeas and nays, yea, aye, yes, nay, no; voice vote, *viva voce* vote; rising vote; hand vote, show of hands; absentee vote, proxy; casting vote, deciding vote; write-in vote, write-in; faggot vote <Brit old>; graveyard vote; single vote, plural vote; transferable vote, nontransferable vote; direct vote; Hare system, list system, cumulative voting, preferential voting, proportional representation; **straw vote** *or* **poll;** informal vote; record vote, snap vote

7 **selector,** chooser, optant, elector, balloter, **voter;** delegate, superdelegate; **electorate**; electoral college

8 **nomination, designation,** naming, proposal

9 **election, appointment;** political election; caucus; primary election, general election

10 **selectivity,** selectiveness, picking and choosing; **choosiness** 495.1; eclecticism; discretion, **discrimination** 944

11 **eligibility, qualification, fitness,** fittedness, **suitability,** acceptability, worthiness, desirability; competency

12 **elect,** elite, the chosen, the cream, crème de la crème; president-elect

VERBS 13 **choose, elect,** pick, go with <nf>, opt, opt for, co-opt, make *or* take one's choice, make choice of, have one's druthers <nf>, use *or* take up *or* exercise one's option, exercise one's discretion; **shop around** <nf>, pick and choose

14 **select**, make a selection; **pick,** handpick, **pick out, single out,** choose, like, choose out, smile on, give the nod <nf>, jump at, seize on; extract, excerpt; **decide between, choose up sides** <nf>, cull, glean, winnow, sift; side with; cherry-pick, separate the wheat from the chaff *or* tares, separate the sheep from the goats

15 **adopt;** approve, ratify, pass, carry, endorse, sign off on <nf>; **take up, go in for** <nf>; accept, take on up on <nf>, **embrace,** advance, espouse; affiliate

16 **decide upon, determine upon,** settle upon, fix upon, resolve upon; make *or* take a decision, **make up one's mind**

17 **prefer,** have preference, **favor, like better** *or* **best,** wish, prefer to, set before *or* above, regard *or* honor before; rather <nf>, **had** *or* **have rather,** would rather, choose rather, had sooner, had *or* would as soon; think proper, see *or* think fit, think best, please; tilt *or* incline *or* lean *or* tend toward, have a bias *or* partiality *or* penchant

18 **vote, cast one's vote,** ballot, cast a ballot; go to the polls; have a say *or* a voice; hold up one's hand, exercise one's suffrage *or* franchise, stand up and be counted; plump *or* plump for <Brit>; divide <Brit>; **poll,** canvass

19 **nominate, name, designate;** put up, propose, submit, name for office; run, run for office

20 **elect, vote in,** place in office; **appoint**

21 **put to choice,** offer, present, set before; put to vote, have a show of hands

ADJS **22 elective;** volitional, voluntary, volitive; **optional,** discretional; **alternative,** disjunctive

23 selective, selecting, choosing; eclectic *or* eclectical; elective, electoral; appointing, appointive, constituent; adoptive; exclusive, discriminating 944.7; **choosy** <nf>, particular 495.9

24 eligible, qualified, fit, fitted, **suitable,** acceptable, admissible, worthy, desirable; with voice, with vote, with voice and vote, enfranchised

25 preferable, of choice *or* preference, **better,** preferred, **to be preferred,** more desirable, favored; handpicked; preferential, preferring, favoring; not to be sniffed *or* sneezed at <nf>

26 chosen, selected, picked; select, elect; handpicked, singled-out; **adopted,** accepted, embraced, espoused, approved, ratified, passed, carried; **elected,** unanimously elected, elected by acclamation; appointed; **nominated,** designated, named

ADVS **27 at choice, at will,** at one's will and pleasure, at one's pleasure, electively, at one's discretion, at the option of, if one wishes; on approval; **optionally;** alternatively

28 preferably, by choice *or* **preference,** in preference; by vote, by election *or* suffrage; **rather than,** sooner than, first, sooner, rather, before

CONJS **29** or, either . . . or; and/or

PHRS **30** one man's meat is another man's poison, there's no accounting for taste

372 REJECTION

NOUNS **1 rejection, repudiation;** abjurement, abjuration, **renouncement** 370.3, renunciation; disownment, disavowal, disclamation, **recantation** 363.3; **exclusion,** exception 773.1; **disapproval, nonacceptance,** zero tolerance, nonapproval, declining, declination, veto, **refusal** 442; contradiction, **denial** 335.2; passing by *or* up <nf>, ignoring, nonconsideration, discounting, dismissal, disregard 984.1; throwing out *or* away, putting out *or* away, chucking *and* chucking out <nf>, heave-ho; discard 390.3; turning out *or* away, repulse, a flea in one's ear, rebuff 908.2; **spurning,** kiss-off *and* brush-off <nf>, cold shoulder, despising, despisal, contempt 157; scorn, disdain; bum's rush <nf>; excommunication

VERBS **2 reject, repudiate,** abjure, forswear, **renounce** 370.7, **disown, disclaim, recant;** vote out; except, **exclude** 773.4, deselect, include out <nf>, close out, close the door on, leave out in the cold, cut out, blackball, blacklist; **disapprove, decline, refuse** 442.3; contradict, **deny** 335.4; pass by *or* up <nf>, waive, ignore, not hear of, wave aside, brush away *or* aside *or* off, refuse to consider, discount, **dismiss,** dismiss out of hand; **disregard** 984.2; throw out *or* away, chuck *and* chuck out <nf>, **discard** 390.7; turn out *or* away, shove away, push aside, repulse, repel, slap *or* smack down <nf>, rebuff 908.2, send away with a flea in one's ear, show the door, send about one's business, send packing, excommunicate; turn one's back on; **spurn, disdain,** scorn, contemn, make a face at, turn up one's nose at, look down one's nose at, raise one's eyebrows at, **despise** 157.3

ADJS **3 rejected, repudiated; renounced,** forsworn, **disowned; denied,** refused; excluded, excepted; **disapproved, declined;** ignored, blanked, discounted, not considered, **dismissed,** dismissed out of hand; **discarded;** repulsed, rebuffed; **spurned,** snubbed, **disdained, scorned,** contemned, **despised;** out of the question, not to be thought of, declined with thanks; discarded; excommunicated

4 rejective; renunciative, abjuratory; declinatory; dismissive; contemptuous, despising, **scornful,** disdainful

373 CUSTOM, HABIT

NOUNS **1 custom, convention,** use, **usage,** standard usage, standard behavior, **wont,** wonting, **way,** established way, time-honored practice, **tradition,** standing custom, **folkway,** manner, **practice,** praxis, prescription, **observance,** ritual, rite, consuetude, **mores;** institution; unwritten law, consuetude; proper thing, what is done, **social convention** 579; bon ton, **fashion** 578; manners, protocol, etiquette 580.3; way of life, lifestyle; conformity 867; **generalization** 864.1, labeling, stereotyping

2 **culture, society, civilization;** trait, culture trait; key trait; complex, culture complex, trait-complex; culture area; culture center; shame culture, memory culture; **folkways, mores,** system of values, **ethos, culture pattern;** cultural change; cultural lag; culture conflict; acculturation, enculturation; culture contact <Brit>, cultural drift; ancient wisdom

3 **habit,** habitude, **custom, second nature,** matter of course; use, **usage,** trick, wont, **way,** practice, praxis; bad habit; stereotype; pattern, **habit pattern;** stereotyped behavior; force of habit; creature of habit; knee-jerk reaction <nf>, automatism 963.5; peculiarity, characteristic 865.4

4 **rule, norm,** procedure, **common practice,** the way things are done, form, prescribed *or* set form; common *or* ordinary run of things, matter of course, par for the course <nf>; standard operating procedure *or* SOP, standard procedure, drill; standing orders

5 **routine, run,** ritual, round, beat, track, beaten path *or* track; pattern, custom; jog trot, **rut, groove,** well-worn groove; **treadmill,** squirrel cage, hamster wheel, hedonic treadmill; the working day, nine-to-five, the grind *or* the daily grind <nf>; **red tape,** redtapeism, **bureaucracy,** bureaucratism, *chinoiseries* <Fr>

6 **customariness,** accustomedness, wontedness, **habitualness; inveteracy,** inveterateness, confirmedness, settledness, fixedness; commonness, prevalence 864.2

7 **habituation, accustoming; conditioning,** seasoning, training; **familiarization,** naturalization , breaking-in <nf>, orientation, adaptation; **domestication, taming,** breaking, housebreaking; acclimation, acclimatization; **inurement,** hardening, case hardening, seasoning, assuetude, assuefaction; adaption, adjustment, accommodation 867.1

8 **addiction** 87.1; **addict** 87.21

VERBS 9 **accustom, habituate,** wont; **condition,** season, **train;** familiarize, naturalize , break in <nf>, orient, orientate; **domesticate,** domesticize, **tame,** break, gentle, housebreak; put through the mill; acclimatize, acclimate; inure, harden, case harden; adapt, adjust, accommodate 788.7; confirm, fix, establish 855.9; acculturate, enculturate

10 **become a habit,** take root, become fixed, **grow on one,** take hold of one, take one over

11 **be used to, be wont,** wont, **make a practice of;** get used to, get into the way of, get the knack of, get the hang of <nf>, **take to,** accustom oneself to, make a practice of; catch oneself doing; contract *or* fall into a habit, addict oneself to

12 **get in a rut, be in a rut,** move *or* travel in a groove *or* rut, run on in a groove, follow the beaten path *or* track

ADJS 13 **customary, wonted,** consuetudinary; traditional, time-honored, immemorial; familiar, everyday, ordinary, **usual; established,** received, accepted, handed down, time-honored; set, prescribed, prescriptive; **normative, normal; standard,** regular, stock, regulation; prevalent, prevailing, widespread, obtaining, generally accepted, popular, **current** 864.12; **conventional** 579.5, orthodox; inside the box; conformist, conformable 867.5

14 **habitual, regular,** frequent, constant, persistent; repetitive, recurring, recurrent; stereotyped; knee-jerk <nf>, goose-step, lockstep, automatic 963.14; **routine,** usual, nine-to-five, workaday,

well-trodden, well-worn, beaten; trite, hackneyed 117.9; predictable

15 **accustomed, wont, wonted, used to; conditioned,** trained, seasoned; experienced, **familiarized,** naturalized , broken-in, run-in <nf>, oriented, orientated; acclimated, acclimatized; inured, hardened, case-hardened; adapted, adjusted, accommodated; housebroken, potty-trained

16 **used to, familiar with,** conversant with, **at home in** *or* **with,** no stranger to, an old hand at, *au fait* <Fr>

17 **habituated,** *habitué* <Fr>; **in the habit of,** used to; never free from; **in a rut**

18 **confirmed, inveterate, chronic, established,** long-established, **fixed, settled, rooted,** thorough; incorrigible, irreversible; **deep-rooted,** deep-set, deep-settled, **deep-seated,** deep-fixed, deep-dyed; **infixed, ingrained,** fast, dyed-in-the-wool, inveterate; implanted, inculcated, instilled; set, **set in one's ways,** settled in habit; addicted, given

ADVS 19 **customarily,** conventionally, accustomedly, wontedly; normatively, normally, **usually; as is the custom;** as is usual, *comme d'habitude* <Fr>; as things go, as the world goes

20 **habitually, regularly,** routinely, frequently, persistently, repetitively, recurringly; **inveterately, chronically;** from habit, **by** *or* **from force of habit,** as is one's wont

374 UNACCUSTOMEDNESS

NOUNS 1 **unaccustomedness, newness,** unwontedness, disaccustomedness, unusedness, unhabituatedness; shakiness <nf>; **unfamiliarity,** unacquaintance, unconversance, unpracticedness, newness to; inexperience 414.2; ignorance 930

VERBS 2 **disaccustom, cure, break off,** stop, **wean**

3 **break the habit, cure oneself of,** disaccustom oneself, kick a habit <nf>, wean oneself from, break the pattern, break one's chains *or* fetters; **give up,** leave off, **abandon,** drop, stop, discontinue, kick *and* shake <nf>, throw off, rid oneself of; get on the wagon, swear off 668.8

ADJS 4 **unaccustomed, new,** disaccustomed, **unused, unwonted,** unwont, wontless; uninured, unseasoned, untrained, unhardened; shaky <nf>, tyronic; unhabituated, **not in the habit of;** out of the habit of, rusty; unweaned; **unused to, unfamiliar with,** not used to, unacquainted with, unconversant with, unpracticed, new to, a stranger to; cub, greenhorn; inexperienced 414.17; ignorant 930.11

375 MOTIVATION, INDUCEMENT

NOUNS 1 **motive, reason, cause,** source, spring, mainspring; matter, score, consideration; **ground, basis** 886.1; sake; **aim, goal** 380.2, end, end in view, telos, final cause; **ideal,** principle, **ambition,** aspiration, inspiration, guiding light *or* star, lodestar; impetus; calling, vocation; intention 380; ulterior motive, hidden agenda; rationale, rational motive, justification, driving force

2 **motivation,** moving, **actuation, prompting, stimulation,** animation, triggering, setting-off, setting in motion, getting under way; direction, inner-direction, other-direction; **influence** 894; hot button; carrot

3 **inducement,** enlistment, engagement, solicitation, **persuasion,** suasion; exhortation, hortation, preaching, preachment; **selling,** sales talk, salesmanship, hard sell, high pressure, hawking, huckstering, flogging <Brit>; jawboning *and* arm-twisting <nf>; **lobbying; coaxing,** wheedling, working on <nf>, cajolery, cajolement, conning, snow job *and* smoke and mirrors <nf>, nobbling <Brit nf>, blandishment, sweet talk *and* soft soap <nf>, soft sell <nf>; **allurement** 377

4 **incitement,** incitation, **instigation, stimulation, arousal, excitement, agitation, inflammation,** excitation, fomentation, eggement, firing,

stirring, stirring-up, impassioning, whipping-up, rabble-rousing; waving the bloody shirt, rallying cry; **provocation,** irritation, exasperation; pep talk, pep rally

5 **urging, pressure,** pressing, pushing, entreaty, plea, advocacy; **encouragement,** abetment; **insistence,** instance; **goading, prodding,** exhortation, goosing <nf>, spurring, pricking, needling

6 **urge,** urgency; impulse, impulsion, compulsion; press, **pressure, drive,** push; sudden *or* rash impulse; constraint, exigency, stress, pinch

7 **incentive, inducement, encouragement,** persuasive, **invitation, provocation, incitement; stimulus, stimulation,** stimulative, fillip, whet; carrot; reward, payment 624; **profit** 472.3; bait, **lure** 377.3; palm oil <nf>, greased palm <nf>, bribe 378.2; sweetening *and* sweetener <nf>, flattery, interest, percentage, what's in it for one <nf>; offer one cannot refuse; payola <nf>, pork barrel <nf>; perk <nf>

8 **goad, spur, prod,** prick , sting, **gadfly;** oxgoad; rowel; whip, lash, gad <nf>, crack of the whip

9 **inspiration, infusion,** infection; fire, firing, spark, sparking; **animation, exhilaration,** enlivenment; afflatus, divine afflatus; genius, animus, moving *or* animating spirit; muse; the Muses; guiding light, angel

10 **prompter, mover, prime mover,** motivator, impeller, energizer, galvanizer, inducer, **actuator, animator,** moving spirit, mover and shaker <nf>; **encourager,** abettor, **inspirer,** firer, spark, sparker, spark plug <nf>; persuader, salesperson, brainwasher, spin doctor <nf>; **stimulator, gadfly; tempter** 377.4; coaxer, coax <nf>, wheedler, cajoler, pleader

11 **instigator, inciter,** exciter, urger, motivator; **provoker,** *provocateur* <Fr>, *agent provocateur* <Fr>, catalyst; **agitator, fomenter,** inflamer; agitprop; **rabble-rouser,** rouser, **demagogue; firebrand, incendiary; seditionist,** seditionary; lobbyist, activist; **troublemaker,** makebate , mischief-maker, ringleader; tactician, strategist; pressure group, special-interest group

VERBS 12 **motivate, move,** set in motion, **actuate,** move to action, **impel,** propel; **stimulate,** energize, galvanize, **animate, spark;** promote, foster; force, compel 424.4; ego-involve

13 **prompt, provoke, evoke, elicit, call up,** summon up, muster up, call forth, **inspire;** bring about, **cause**

14 **urge, press, push,** work on <nf>, twist one's arm <nf>; **sell,** flog <Brit>; **insist,** push for, not take no for an answer, **importune, nag, pressure, high-pressure,** browbeat, bring pressure to bear upon, throw one's weight around, throw one's weight into the scale, jawbone *and* build a fire under <nf>, talk round *or* around; grind in; **lobby**, pitch <nf>; hype <nf>**; coax,** wheedle, cajole, blandish, plead with, sweet-talk *and* soft-soap <nf>, **exhort,** call on *or* upon, advocate, recommend, put in a good word, buck for *and* hype <nf>; insist, insist upon

15 **goad, prod,** poke, nudge, prod at, goose <nf>, **spur** *or* spur on, encourage, prick, sting, needle; whip, lash; pick at *or* on, nibble at, nibble away at

16 **urge on** *or* **along, egg on** <nf>, hound on, hie on, hasten on, hurry on, speed on; **goad on, spur on,** drive on, whip on *or* along; cheer on, root on <nf>, root from the sidelines <nf>; aid and abet

17 **incite, instigate, put up to** <nf>; set on, sic on; **foment,** ferment, **agitate, arouse, excite, stir up,** work up, whip up, turn on; rally; **inflame,** incense, **fire,** heat, heat up, impassion; **provoke,** pique, whet, tickle; nettle; lash into a fury *or* frenzy; wave the bloody shirt; pour oil on the fire, feed the fire, add fuel to the flame, fan, fan the flame, blow the coals, stir the embers

18 **kindle,** enkindle, **fire, spark, spark off, trigger, trigger off, touch off,** set off, light the fuse, **enflame,** set afire *or* on fire, turn on <nf>

19 **rouse, arouse,** raise, raise up, **waken, awaken,** wake up, turn on <nf>, charge *or* psych *or* pump up <nf>, stir, **stir up,** set astir, **pique**

20 **inspire,** inspirit, spirit, spirit up; **fire, fire one's imagination; animate, exhilarate,** enliven; **infuse, infect,** inject, inoculate, imbue, inform

21 **encourage, hearten, embolden,** give encouragement, pat *or* clap on the back, stroke <nf>; **invite,** ask for; **abet,** aid and abet, countenance, keep in countenance; **foster, nurture,** nourish, feed

22 **induce, prompt, move one to, influence, sway,** incline, **dispose,** carry, bring, lead, **lead one to; lure; tempt;** determine, decide; enlist, procure, engage , interest in, get to do

23 **persuade, prevail on** *or* **upon,** prevail with, **sway,** convince, lead to believe, **bring round,** bring to reason, bring to one's senses; **win, win over,** win around, bring over, draw over, gain, gain over; **talk over, talk into,** argue into, out-talk <nf>; wangle, wangle into; hook and hook in <nf>, con *and* do a snow job on <nf>, nobble <Brit nf>, sell *and* sell one on <nf>, **charm, captivate;** wear down, overcome one's resistance, arm-twist *and* twist one's arm <nf>, put the screws to; **bribe** 378.3, grease *or* oil *or* cross one's palm <nf>; brainwash

24 **persuade oneself, make oneself easy about,** make sure of, make up one's mind; follow one's conscience; be persuaded, rest easy, come around, buy <nf>

ADJS 25 **motivating, motivational, motive, moving, animating, actuating, impelling, driving,** impulsive, inducive, directive; **urgent, pressing, driving;** compelling; causal, causative; goal-oriented

26 **inspiring, inspirational,** inspiriting; infusive; animating, exhilarating, enlivening

27 **provocative, provoking,** piquant, **exciting,** challenging, prompting, **rousing, stirring, stimulating,** stimulant, stimulative, stimulatory, energizing, electric, galvanizing, galvanic; **encouraging,** inviting, **alluring**; enticing; addictive

28 **incitive,** inciting, incentive; **instigative,** instigating; **agitative,** agitational; **inflammatory, incendiary,** fomenting, rabble-rousing

29 **persuasive,** suasive, persuading; wheedling, cajoling; hortative, hortatory; exhortative, exhortatory; hard-selling

30 **moved, motivated, prompted, impelled, actuated;** stimulated, animated; minded, inclined, of a mind to, with half a mind to; inner-directed, other-directed; soft <nf>

31 **inspired, fired,** afire, on fire

376 PRETEXT

NOUNS 1 **pretext, pretense, pretension,** lying pretension, **show,** ostensible *or* announced *or* public *or* professed motive; **front,** facade, ruse, **sham** 354.3; **excuse,** apology, protestation, poor excuse, lame excuse; **occasion,** mere occasion; put-off <nf>; handle, peg to hang on, leg to stand on, *locus standi* <L>; **subterfuge,** refuge, device, stratagem, feint, dipsy-doodle <nf>, swiftie, **trick** 356.6; dust thrown in the eye, smoke screen, **screen, cover,** stalking-horse, **blind;** guise, semblance; mask, cloak, veil; **cosmetics,** mere cosmetics, gloss, varnish, color, coat of paint, whitewash <nf>; spit and polish; **cover,** cover-up, cover story, alibi; band-aid

2 **claim,** profession, allegation

VERBS 3 pretext, make a pretext of, take as an excuse *or* reason *or* occasion, urge as a motive, **pretend,** make a pretense of; put up a front *or* false front; **allege, claim,** profess, purport, avow; protest too much

4 **hide under,** cover oneself with, shelter under, take cover under, wrap oneself in, cloak *or* mantle oneself with, take refuge in; conceal one's motive with; **cover,** cover up, gloss *or* varnish over, apply a coat of paint *or* whitewash, stick on a band-aid

ADJS **5** **pretexted, pretended, alleged, claimed, professed, purported,** avowed; **ostensible,** hypocritical, **specious;** so-called, in name only

ADVS **6** **ostensibly, allegedly,** purportedly, professedly, avowedly; for the record, for public consumption; under the pretext of, **as a pretext,** as an excuse, as a cover *or* a cover-up *or* an alibi

377 ALLUREMENT

NOUNS **1** **allurement, allure, enticement, inveiglement,** invitation, come-hither <nf>, blandishment, cajolery; inducement 375.7; **temptation,** tantalization; **seduction,** seducement; **beguilement,** beguiling; **fascination, captivation,** enthrallment, entrapment, snaring; **enchantment,** witchery, bewitchery, bewitchment; **attraction, interest, charm, glamour, appeal,** magnetism; charisma; star quality; wooing; flirtation

2 **attractiveness, allure,** charmingness, bewitchingness, impressiveness, **seductiveness,** winsomeness, winning ways, winningness; **sexiness,** sex appeal *or* SA <nf>

3 **lure,** charm, **come-on** <nf>, attention-getter *or* -grabber, **attraction, draw** *or* drawer *or* crowd-drawer, crowd-pleaser, headliner; clou, hook *and* gimmick <nf>, drawing card, drawcard; **decoy,** decoy duck; **bait,** ground bait, baited trap, baited hook; **snare,** trap; **endearment** 562; the song of the Sirens, the voice of the tempter, honeyed words; forbidden fruit

4 **tempter, seducer, enticer,** inveigler, **charmer,** enchanter, fascinator, tantalizer, teaser; coquette, flirt; Don Juan; Pied Piper of Hamelin; **temptress,** enchantress, seductress, **siren;** Siren, Circe, Lorelei, Parthenope; **vampire,** vamp <nf>, *femme fatale* <Fr>

VERBS **5** **lure,** allure, **entice, seduce, inveigle, decoy,** draw, **draw on, lead on;** come on to *and* give the come-on *and* give a come-hither look *and* bat the eyes at *and* make goo-goo eyes at <nf>, flirt with, flirt; **woo;** coax, cajole, blandish; **ensnare;** draw in, suck in *and* rope in <nf>; bait, offer bait to, bait the hook, angle with a silver hook

6 **attract, interest, appeal, engage,** impress, charismatize, fetch <nf>, catch *or* get one's eye, command one's attention, rivet one, attract one's interest, be attractive, take *or* tickle one's fancy; **invite,** summon, beckon; **tempt, tantalize, titillate,** tickle, **tease,** whet the appetite, make one's mouth water, dangle before one

7 **fascinate, captivate, charm,** becharm, spell, spellbind, cast a spell, put under a spell, **beguile, intrigue, enthrall,** infatuate, **enrapture, transport, enravish, entrance, enchant,** witch, **bewitch,** voodoo; carry away, sweep off one's feet, turn one's head, knock one's socks off <nf>; hypnotize, mesmerize; vamp <nf>; charismatize

ADJS **8** **alluring, fascinating, captivating, riveting, charming, glamorous,** glam <nf>, exotic, **enchanting,** spellful, spellbinding, **entrancing,** ravishing, **enravishing, intriguing, enthralling,** witching, **bewitching; attractive, interesting, appealing,** dishy <Brit nf>, sexy <nf>, engaging, taking, eye-catching, catching, fetching, winning, winsome, prepossessing; exciting; charismatic; **seductive,** seducing, **beguiling, enticing, inviting,** come-hither <nf>; flirtatious, coquettish; coaxing, cajoling, blandishing; **tempting, tantalizing,** teasing, titillating, titillative, tickling; **provocative,** *provoquant* <Fr>; appetizing, mouth-watering, piquant; **irresistible;** siren, sirenic; hypnotic, mesmeric

ADVS **9** **alluringly, fascinatingly,** captivatingly, charmingly, enchantingly, entrancingly, enravishingly, intriguingly, beguilingly, glamorously, bewitchingly; attractively, appealingly, engagingly, winsomely; **enticingly, seductively,** with bedroom eyes <nf>; **temptingly,** provocatively; **tantalizingly,** teasingly; piquantly, appetizingly; irresistibly; hypnotically, mesmerically

378 BRIBERY

NOUNS **1** **bribery,** bribing, subornation, **corruption, graft,** bribery and corruption

2 **bribe,** bribe money, sop, sop to Cerberus, gratuity, gratification , payoff <nf>, boodle <nf>; hush money <nf>; payola <nf>; protection

VERBS **3** **bribe,** throw a sop to; grease *and* **grease the palm** *or* **hand** *and* oil the palm *and* tickle the palm <nf>; **purchase;** buy *and* **buy off** *and* pay off <nf>; suborn, **corrupt,** tamper with; reach *and* get at *and* get to <nf>; approach, try to bribe; **fix, take care of**

ADJS **4** **bribable,** corruptible, purchasable, buyable; approachable; fixable; on the take *and* on the pad <nf>; **venal, corrupt,** bought and paid for, in one's pocket

379 DISSUASION

NOUNS **1** **dissuasion,** talking out of <nf>, remonstrance, expostulation, admonition, monition, dehortation, **warning,** caveat, **caution,** cautioning; intimidation, **determent,** deterrence, scaring *or* frightening off, turning around; contraindication

2 **deterrent,** determent; **discouragement,** disincentive, chilling effect, demotivation; deflection, roadblock, obstacle, red light, closed door; damp, damper, **wet blanket,** cold water, chill; alienation, disaffection

VERBS **3** **dissuade,** convince to the contrary, convince otherwise, **talk out of** <nf>; contraindicate; unconvince, unpersuade; remonstrate, expostulate, admonish, cry out against; **warn, warn off** *or* **away, caution;** enter a caveat; **intimidate,** scare *or* frighten off, daunt, cow; turn around

4 **disincline, indispose,** disaffect, disinterest; **deter,** repel, turn from, turn away *or* aside; divert, deflect; distract, put off *and* turn off <nf>; wean from; **discourage; pour** *or* **dash** *or* **throw cold water on,** throw *or* lay a wet blanket on, be a wet blanket, damp, dampen, demotivate, **cool, chill,** quench, blunt; nip in the bud; take the starch out of, take the wind out of one's sails

ADJS **5** **dissuasive,** dissuading, disinclining, unwilling, **discouraging; deterrent,** off-putting, repellent, disenchanting; expostulatory, admonitory, monitory, cautionary; intimidating

380 INTENTION

NOUNS **1** **intention, intent,** intendment, mindset, **aim,** effect, meaning, view, study, animus, **point, purpose,** function, set *or* settled *or* fixed purpose; sake; **design, plan, project,** idea, notion; **quest,** pursuit; **proposal,** prospectus; **resolve,** resolution, mind, will; **motive** 375.1; determination 359.1; desideratum, desideration, **ambition,** aspiration, **desire** 100; striving, nisus

2 **objective, object, aim, end, goal,** destination, mark, object in mind, **end in view,** telos, final cause, ultimate aim *or* purpose, mission; end in itself; **target,** butt, bull's-eye, quintain; quarry, prey, game; reason for being, *raison d'être* <Fr>; by-purpose, by-end; teleology

3 **intentionality, deliberation, deliberateness,** directedness; express intention, expressness, **premeditation, predeliberation,** preconsideration, **calculation, calculatedness, predetermination,** preresolution, forethought, aforethought, calculated risk

VERBS **4** **intend, purpose, plan,** purport, **mean,** think, **propose; resolve,** determine 359.7; project, **design,** destine; **aim,** aim at, take aim at, draw a bead on, set one's sights on, have designs on, go for, drive at, aspire to *or* after, be after, set before oneself, purpose to oneself, have every intention; harbor a design; **desire** 100.14

5 **contemplate, meditate; envisage,** envision, **have in mind, have in view;** have an eye to, have every intention, have a mind *or* notion, have half a mind *or* notion, have a good *or* great mind *or* notion

6 **plan, plan on, figure on,** plan for *or* out, count on, figure out, calculate, calculate on, reckon, do the math, reckon *or* bargain on, bargain for, bank on *or* upon, make book on <nf>, expect, foresee

7 **premeditate, calculate, preresolve, predetermine,** predeliberate, preconsider, direct oneself, forethink, work out beforehand; plan; plot, scheme

ADJS 8 **intentional, intended,** proposed, purposed, telic, **projected, designed,** of design, aimed, aimed at, **meant, purposeful,** purposive, **willful, voluntary, deliberate;** deliberated; on-message; considered, studied, advised, **calculated, contemplated, envisaged,** envisioned, meditated, **conscious,** knowing, witting; planned; teleological

9 **premeditated, predeliberated,** preconsidered, predetermined, preresolved, prepense, aforethought, foremeant

ADVS 10 **intentionally, purposely,** purposefully, purposively, pointedly, **on purpose,** with purpose, prepensely, with a view *or* an eye to, **deliberately, designedly, willfully, voluntarily,** of one's own accord *or* one's own free will; **wittingly, consciously, knowingly; advisedly, calculatedly,** contemplatedly, meditatedly, premeditatedly, **with premeditation, with intent,** with full intent, **by design,** with one's eyes open; with malice aforethought, in cold blood

381 PLAN

NOUNS 1 **plan, scheme, design,** method, **program,** device, contrivance, game, envisagement, conception, enterprise, **idea, notion;** organization, rationalization, systematization, schematization; charting, mapping, graphing, blueprinting; **planning,** calculation, figuring; planning function; long-range planning, long-range *or* long-term plan; **master plan,** the picture *and* the big picture <nf>; approach, attack, plan of attack; way, procedure; **arrangement,** prearrangement, system, disposition, layout, setup, lineup; **schedule,** timetable, timescheme, time frame; agenda, order of the day, dance card; deadline; plan of work; **schema,** schematism, scheme of arrangement; blueprint, **guideline, guidelines,** program of action; methodology; working plan, ground plan, tactical plan, strategic plan; tactics, **strategy,** game plan <nf>; mission statement; contingency plan; operations research; **intention** 380; forethought, foresight 961; back room; mise en place; Plan A, Plan B

2 **project, projection, scheme; proposal,** prospectus, proposition; scenario, **game plan** <nf>

3 **diagram, plot, chart, blueprint,** graph, bar graph, pie *or* circle graph *or* chart, area graph; flow diagram, flow chart; **table; design, pattern,** copy , cartoon; **sketch, draft, drawing,** working drawing, rough; *brouillon* and *ébauche* and *esquisse* <Fr>; **outline, delineation,** skeleton, figure, profile; house plan, ground plan, ichnography; elevation, projection; **map, chart** 159.5

4 **policy,** polity, principles, guiding principles; **procedure,** course, line, plan of action; creed 953.3; **platform,** party line; position paper; formula; rule

5 **intrigue,** web of intrigue, **plot, scheme,** deep-laid plot *or* scheme, underplot, game *or* little game <nf>, secret plan, trick, stratagem, finesse, method; counterplot; **conspiracy,** confederacy, covin, complot , cabal; **complicity, collusion, connivance; artifice** 415.3; **contrivance,** contriving; **scheming,** schemery, plotting; finagling <nf>, **machination,** manipulation, **maneuvering,** engineering, rigging; frame-up <nf>; wirepulling <nf>; inside job; expedient, last resort, eleventh-hour rescue; way out, loophole

6 **planner, designer,** deviser, contriver, framer, projector; enterpriser,

entrepreneur; intrapreneur; organizer, promoter, developer, engineer; expediter, facilitator, animator; **policymaker, decision-maker; architect, tactician, strategist, strategian**, mastermind, brains <nf>

7 **schemer, plotter,** counterplotter, finagler <nf>, Machiavelli; **intriguer,** *intrigant* and *intrigante* <Fr>, cabalist; **conspirer, conspirator,** coconspirator, **conniver;** maneuverer, machinator, operator <nf>, opportunist, pot-hunter, exploiter; wire-puller <nf>, wangler

VERBS 8 **plan, devise, contrive, design,** frame, shape, cast, concert, lay plans; organize, rationalize, systematize, schematize, methodize, configure, pull together, sort out; **arrange,** prearrange, make arrangements, set up, work up, work out; **schedule;** lay down a plan, shape *or* mark out a course; program; **calculate,** figure; **project,** cut out, make a projection, forecast , plan ahead; intend 380.4

9 **plot, scheme, intrigue,** be up to something; **conspire, connive,** collude, complot , cabal; **hatch, hatch up,** cook up <nf>, brew, concoct, hatch *or* lay a plot; **maneuver,** machinate, finesse, operate <nf>, engineer, rig, wangle <nf>, angle, finagle <nf>; frame *or* frame up <nf>; counterplot, countermine

10 **plot; map, chart** 159.11, **blueprint; diagram,** graph; **sketch,** sketch in *or* out, draw up a plan; map out, plot out, **lay out,** set out, mark out; lay off, mark off; design a prototype

11 **outline,** line, **delineate,** chalk out, brief; **sketch, draft,** trace; block in *or* out; rough in, rough out; chalk out

ADJS 12 **planned, devised, designed,** shaped, set, **blueprinted,** charted, mapped, **contrived; plotted;** premeditated; arranged; organized, rationalized, systematized, schematized, methodized, strategized; worked out, calculated, figured; **projected; scheduled,** on the agenda, in the works, in the pipeline <nf>, on the calendar, on the docket, on the anvil, on the carpet, on the tapis , *sur le tapis* <Fr>; tactical, **strategic**

13 **scheming, calculating, designing, contriving, plotting, intriguing;** resourceful; manipulatory, **manipulative;** opportunist, **opportunistic;** Machiavellian, Byzantine; **conniving,** connivent , wangling, conspiring, conspiratorial, collusive; stratagemical

14 schematic, diagrammatic

382 PURSUIT

NOUNS 1 **pursuit,** pursuing, pursuance, prosecution ; **quest,** seeking, hunting, searching, all-points bulletin; **following,** follow, follow-up; tracking, trailing, tracking down, dogging, hounding, shadowing, stalking, tailing <nf>; **chase,** hot pursuit; hue and cry; all points bulletin *or* APB, dragnet, manhunt; wild-goose chase; trainspotting, aircraft spotting

2 **hunting,** gunning, shooting, venery, cynegetics, sport, sporting; **hunt, chase,** chevy *or* chivy <Brit>, *shikar* <India>, coursing; blood sport; fox hunt, fox hunting; hawking, falconry; stalking, still hunt

3 **fishing,** fishery; **angling,** piscatology , halieutics; fly-fishing, saltwater fishing, ice fishing, competitive fishing

4 **pursuer,** pursuant, **chaser,** follower; hunter, quester, **seeker**, tracker, trailer, tail <nf>

5 **hunter, huntsman,** sportsman, **Nimrod;** huntress, sportswoman; stalker; courser; trapper; big game hunter, *shikari* <India>, white hunter; jacklighter, jacker; gamekeeper; beater, whipper-in; falconer; gundog; poacher

6 **fisher, fisherman, angler,** *piscator* <L>, piscatorian, piscatorialist; Waltonian; dibber, dibbler, troller, trawler, trawlerman, dragger, jacker, jigger, bobber, guddler, tickler, drifter, drift netter, whaler, clam digger, lobsterman, etc

7 **quarry, game, prey,** venery, beasts of venery, victim, the hunted; kill; big game, small game

VERBS **8** **pursue,** prosecute , **follow,** follow up, **go after,** take out *or* off after <nf>, bay after, run after, run in pursuit of, make after, go in pursuit of; raise the hunt, raise the hue and cry, hollo after; **chase, give chase,** chivy; hound, dog; **quest,** quest after, **seek,** seek out, hunt, **search** 938.31, send out a search party; trawl

9 **hunt,** go hunting, hunt down, chase, run, *shikar* <India>, sport; engage in a blood sport; shoot, gun; course; ride to hounds, follow the hounds; **track,** trail; **stalk,** prowl after, still-hunt; poach; hound, dog; hawk, falcon; fowl; flush, start; drive, beat; jack, jacklight; trap, ensnare

10 **fish,** go fishing, **angle;** cast one's hook *or* net; bait the hook; shrimp, whale, clam, grig, still-fish, fly-fish, troll, bob, dap, dib *or* dibble, gig, jig, etc; reel in

ADJS **11** **pursuing,** pursuant, following; **questing,** in quest of, **seeking, searching** 938.38; **in pursuit,** in hot pursuit, in full cry, tailing, chasing, trailing; hunting, cynegetic, fishing, piscatory, piscatorial, halieutic, halieutical

383 ROUTE, PATH

NOUNS **1** **route, path, way, itinerary, course,** track, run, line, road; trajectory, traject, *trajet* <Fr>; direction; circuit, tour, orbit; walk, beat, round; trade route, traffic lane, **sea lane,** shipping lane, **air lane,** flight path; path of least resistance, primrose path, garden path; shortcut, detour; line of advance, line of retreat; scenic route

2 **path, track, trail, pathway,** footpath, footway, *piste* <Fr>; walkway, catwalk, skybridge *or* skywalk *or* flying bridge *or* walkway; **sidewalk, walk,** fastwalk, *trottoir* <Fr>, foot pavement <Brit>; boardwalk; hiking trail; public walk, promenade, esplanade, alameda, parade, *prado* <Sp>, mall; towpath *or* towing path; bridle path *or* road *or* trail *or* way; bicycle path; berm; run, runway; beaten track *or* path, rut, groove; garden path

3 **passageway, pass, passage, defile; avenue, artery; corridor, aisle,** aisleway, **alley, lane,** back alley; **channel, conduit** 239.1; ford, ferry, traject, *trajet* <Fr>; opening, aperture; access, right of way, approach, inlet 189.5; exit, outlet 190.9; connection, communication; covered way, gallery, arcade, portico, colonnade, cloister, ambulatory; underpass, overpass, flyover <Brit>; tunnel, railroad tunnel, vehicular tunnel; junction, interchange, **intersection** 170.2

4 **byway, bypath,** byroad, by-lane, bystreet, side road, side street; **bypass, detour,** roundabout way; bypaths and crooked ways, side path; back way, back stairs, back door, side door; back road, back street

5 **road**, highway, roadway, carriageway <Brit>, right-of-way; **street**

6 **pavement,** paving; macadam, blacktop, bitumen, asphalt, tarmacadam, tarmac, tarvia, bituminous macadam; cement, concrete; tile, brick, paving brick; stone, paving stone, pavestone, flag, flagstone, flagging; cobblestone, cobble; road metal <Brit>; gravel; washboard; curbstone, kerbstone <Brit>, edgestone; curb, kerb <Brit>, curbing; gutter, kennel <Brit>

7 **railway**, **railroad,** rail, line, track, trackage, railway *or* railroad *or* rail line; subway; junction; terminus, terminal, the end of the line; roadway, roadbed, embankment; bridge, trestle

8 **cableway,** ropeway, wireway, wire ropeway, cable *or* rope railway, funicular *or* funicular railway; monorail; *téléphérique* <Fr>, telpher, telpherway, telpher ropeway, telpher line *or* railway; ski lift, chair lift, gondola, aerial tramway, tram

9 **bridge, span, viaduct;** cantilever bridge, clapper bridge, drawbridge, footbridge, pontoon bridge, rope bridge, skybridge *or* skywalk *or* flying bridge *or* walkway, suspension bridge, toll bridge, floating bridge, covered bridge, aqueduct; overpass, overcrossing, overbridge *or* flyover <Brit>; stepping-stone, stepstone, catwalk; Bifrost

384 MANNER, MEANS

NOUNS **1** **manner, way,** wise, **means, mode,** modality, form , **fashion, style,** tone, guise ; **method,** methodology, **system;** algorithm <math>; **approach,** attack, tack; **technique, procedure, process,** proceeding, measures, steps, course, practice; order; lines, line, line of action; *modus operandi* <L>, mode of operation *or* MO, manner of working, mode of procedure; **routine;** the way of, the how, the how-to, the drill <Brit>

2 **means,** ways, **ways and means,** means to an end; **wherewithal,** wherewith; funds 728.14; **resources,** disposable resources, capital 728.15; bankroll <nf>; stock in trade, inventory, stock, supply 386; power, capacity, ability 18.2; power base, constituency, backing, support; recourses, resorts, devices; tools of the trade, tricks of the trade, bag of tricks

3 **instrumentality, agency;** machinery, **mechanism,** modality; gadgetry <nf>; mediation, going between, intermediation, service; **expedient,** recourse, resort, device 995.2

4 **instrument, tool, implement, appliance,** device; contrivance, makeshift, lever, mechanism; **vehicle, organ; agent** 576; medium, mediator, intermedium, intermediary, intermediate, interagent, liaison, go-between 576.4; expediter, facilitator, animator; midwife, servant, slave, handmaid, handmaiden, *ancilla* <L>; **cat's-paw, puppet, dummy, pawn,** creature, minion, stooge <nf>; stalking horse; toy, plaything; gadget, contrivance; dupe 358

VERBS **5** **use, utilize,** adopt, effect; **approach, attack;** proceed, practice, go about; routinize

6 **find means, find a way,** provide *or* have the wherewithal, develop a method; enable, facilitate; get by hook or by crook, obtain by fair means or foul; beg, borrow, or steal; think laterally; network

7 be instrumental, **serve, subserve,** serve one's purpose, come in handy, stand in good stead, fill the bill; minister to, act for, act in the interests of, **promote, advance, forward, assist,** facilitate; mediate, go between; liaise

ADJS **8** modal; **instrumental, implemental;** agential, agentive, agentival; effective, efficacious; **useful,** utile, handy, employable, **serviceable; helpful,** conducive, forwarding, favoring, promoting, assisting, facilitating; subservient, ministering, ministerial; mediating, mediatorial, intermediary

ADVS **9** **how, in what way** *or* **manner,** by what mode *or* means; to what extent; in what condition; by what name; at what price; after this fashion, in this way, in such wise, along these lines; **thus, so,** just so, thus and so; as, like, on the lines of

10 **anyhow, anyway,** anywise, anyroad <Brit nf>, in any way, **by any means, by any manner of means;** in any event, at any rate, leastways <nf>, in any case; **nevertheless, nonetheless, however, regardless,** irregardless <nf>; at all, nohow <nf>

11 **somehow, in some way,** in some way or other, someway <nf>, by some means, **somehow or other,** somehow or another, in one way or another, in some such way, after a fashion; no matter how, **by hook or by crook,** by fair means or foul

12 herewith, therewith, wherewith, wherewithal; whereby, thereby, hereby

PHRS **13** it isn't what you do, it's how you do it; there's more than one way to skin a cat

385 PROVISION, EQUIPMENT

NOUNS **1** **provision,** providing; **equipment, accouterment,** fitting out, outfitting; **supply,** supplying, finding; **furnishing,** furnishment; chandlery, **retailing, selling** 734.2; **logistics;** procurement 472.1; investment, endowment, subvention, subsidy, subsidization; provisioning, victualing, purveyance, catering; armament; resupply, replenishment, reinforcement; supply line, line of supply; **preparation** 405

2 **provisions, supplies** 386.1; provender 10.4; **merchandise** 735; basics

3 **accommodations,** accommodation, facilities; **lodgings;** bed, board, full board; **room and board,** bed and board; **subsistence,** keep, fostering

4 **equipment,** matériel, equipage, munitions; **furniture, furnishings,** furnishments ; **fixtures, fittings, appointments, accouterments, appurtenances,** trappings, installations, plumbing; **appliances,** utensils, **conveniences; outfit, apparatus, rig,** machinery; stock-in-trade; **plant,** facility, facilities; paraphernalia, harness, things, **gear, stuff** <nf>, impedimenta <pl>, **tackle;** rigging; armament, munition; **kit,** duffel, effects, personal effects; government issue, military issue

5 **harness,** caparison, trappings, **tack,** tackle

6 **provider, supplier,** furnisher; donor 478.11; patron; **purveyor,** provisioner, distributor, middleman; **caterer,** victualler, sutler; *vivandier* or *vivandière* <Fr>; chandler, retailer, merchant 730.2; commissary, commissariat, quartermaster, shopkeeper, storekeeper, merchant, stock clerk, steward, manciple; grocer, vintner; procurer; megastore

VERBS 7 **provide, supply,** find, dish up *and* rustle up *and* offer up <nf>, **furnish;** accommodate; invest, endow, fund, subsidize; donate, give, afford, contribute, kick in <nf>, yield, present 478.12; make available; stock, store; provide for, make provision *or* due provision for, plenish; prepare 405.6; support, maintain, keep; fill, fill up; replenish, restock, recruit

8 **equip, furnish, outfit,** gear, **prepare, fit,** fit up *or* out, fix up <nf>, **rig,** rig up *or* out, set up, **turn out,** appoint, accouter, clothe, dress; arm, heel <nf>, munition; man, staff

9 **provision,** provender, cater, victual, plenish , serve, cook for; provide a grubstake <nf>; **board,** feed; forage; fuel, gas, gas up, fill up, top off, coal, oil, bunker; **purvey,** sell 734.8

10 **accommodate,** furnish accommodations; house, lodge 225.10; **put up,** take in, board

11 **make a living,** earn a living *or* livelihood, **make** *or* **earn one's keep**

12 **support oneself,** make one's way; **make ends meet, keep body and soul together, keep the wolf from the door,** keep *or* hold one's head above water, keep afloat; **survive, subsist, cope, eke out,** make out, scrape along, manage, get by

ADJS 13 **provided, supplied, furnished,** provisioned, purveyed, catered; perquisited; invested, endowed; **equipped, fitted,** fitted out, outfitted, rigged, accoutered; armed, heeled <nf>; staffed, manned; readied, in place, **prepared** 405.16

14 **well-provided, well-supplied, well-furnished,** well-stocked, well-found; **well-equipped, well-fitted,** well-appointed; well-armed

386 STORE, SUPPLY

NOUNS 1 **store, hoard, treasure,** treasury; plenty, plenitude, abundance, cornucopia; heap, mass, stack, pile, dump, rick; **collection, accumulation,** cumulation, **amassment,** budget, **stockpile; backlog;** repertory, repertoire; stock-in-trade; **inventory, stock,** supply on hand; lock, stock, and barrel; **stores, supplies, provisions,** provisionment, rations; larder, commissariat, commissary; munitions; matériel; material, materials 1054

2 **supply, fund, resource, resources; means, assets,** liquid assets, balance, pluses <nf>, black-ink items, financial resources, **capital,** capital goods, capitalization, available means *or* resources *or* funds, cash flow, stock in trade; venture capital; backing, support; grist, grist for the mill; holdings, property 471; labor resources

3 **reserve, reserves,** reservoir, resource; proved *or* proven reserve; **stockpile, cache,** backup, reserve supply, store, standby, safeguard, something in reserve *or* in hand, something to fall back on, reserve

fund, emergency funds, **nest egg, savings,** petty cash, sinking fund; trust fund; proved reserves; backlog, unexpended balance; ace in the hole <nf>, a card *or* ace up one's sleeve; spare *or* replacement part

4 **source of supply,** source, staple, resource; well, fountain, fount, font , spring, wellspring; mine, **gold mine, bonanza,** luau <nf>; quarry, lode, vein; oilfield, oil well, oil rig; cornucopia

5 **storage, stowage;** preservation, conservation, safekeeping, warehousing; cold storage, cold store, dry storage, dead storage; storage space, shelf-room; custody, guardianship 1008.2; sequestration, escrow

6 **storehouse, storeroom,** stockroom, box room <Brit>, lumber room, store, storage, **depository, repository,** conservatory , reservoir, repertory, depot, supply depot, supply base, magazine, *magasin* <Fr>, warehouse, megastore, big-box store, godown <Asia>; bonded warehouse, entrepôt; dock; hold, cargo dock; attic, loft, cellar, basement; closet, cupboard; wine cellar, larder; shed, stable, garage; **treasury,** treasure house, treasure room, exchequer, coffers; bank, vault 729.13, strongroom, strongbox; **archives, library,** stack room; armory, arsenal, dump; lumberyard; drawer, shelf; bin, bunker, bay, crib; rack, rick; vat, tank; elevator; crate, box; chest, **locker,** hutch; bookcase, stack; sail locker, chain locker, lazaret, lazaretto, glory hole

7 **garner, granary,** grain bin, elevator, grain elevator, **silo;** mow, haymow, hayloft, hayrick; crib, corncrib

8 **larder, pantry,** buttery <nf>; spence <Brit nf>, stillroom <Brit>; root cellar; dairy, dairy house *or* room

9 **museum; gallery,** art gallery, picture gallery, pinacotheca; science museum, natural history museum; salon; waxworks; museology, curatorship

VERBS 10 **store, stow,** lay in store; **lay in,** lay in a supply *or* stock *or* store, store away, stow away, **put away, lay away,** put *or* lay by, pack away, bundle away, lay down, stow down, salt down *or* away *and* sock away *and* squirrel away <nf>; **deposit,** reposit, lodge; **cache,** stash <nf>, bury away; **bank,** coffer, hutch ; warehouse, reservoir; file, file away

11 **store up, stock up, lay up,** put up, **save up,** hoard up, treasure up, garner up, **heap up,** pile up, build up a stock *or* an inventory, provision; **accumulate,** cumulate, **collect, amass, stockpile;** backlog; garner, gather into barns; **hoard,** treasure, save, keep, hold, squirrel, squirrel away; hide, secrete 346.7

12 **reserve, save, conserve, keep,** retain, husband, husband one's resources, keep *or* hold back, withhold; **keep in reserve,** keep in store, keep on hand, keep by one; sequester, put in escrow; **preserve** 397.7; **set** *or* **put aside,** set *or* put apart, put *or* lay *or* set by; save up, save to fall back upon, keep as a nest egg, **save for a rainy day,** provide for *or* against a rainy day

13 **have in store** *or* **reserve,** have to fall back upon, have something to draw on, have something laid by, have something laid by for a rainy day, have something up one's sleeve

ADJS 14 **stored, accumulated,** amassed, laid up, stocked; gathered, garnered, collected, heaped, piled; **stockpiled;** backlogged; **hoarded,** treasured

15 **reserved, preserved, saved,** conserved, put by *or* aside, kept, retained, held, filed, withheld, held back, kept *or* held in reserve; in storage, warehoused, mothballed; bottled, pickled, canned, refrigerated, frozen; spare

ADVS 16 **in store,** in stock, in supply, **on hand**

17 **in reserve,** back, aside, by

387 USE

NOUNS 1 **use, employment,** utilization, employ , **usage; exercise, exertion,** active use, wear; good use;

ill use, wrong use, misuse 389; hard use, hard *or* rough usage; hard wear, heavy duty; **application,** appliance, deployment; expenditure, expending, using up, exhausting, dissipation, dissipating, **consumption** 388

2 usage, treatment, handling, management; way *or* means of dealing; stewardship, custodianship, guardianship, care

3 utility, usefulness, usability, use, utilizability, avail, good, advantage, benefit, added value, **serviceability,** service, **helpfulness,** functionality, profitability, applicability, availability, **practicability,** practicality, practical utility, operability, **effectiveness,** efficacy, efficiency; readiness, availability; instrumentality; ultimate purpose

4 benefit, use, service, avail, profit, advantage, point, percentage *and* mileage <nf>, what's in it for one <nf>, convenience; interest, behalf, behoof; **value, worth,** fruitfulness; commonweal, public good

5 function, use, purpose, role, part, point, end use, immediate purpose, ultimate purpose, operational purpose, operation; work, duty, office

6 functionalism, utilitarianism; pragmatism, pragmaticism; functional design, functional furniture *or* housing, etc

7 <law terms> usufruct, imperfect usufruct, perfect usufruct, right of use, user, enjoyment of property; *jus primae noctis* <L>, *droit du seigneur* <Fr>; disposal; possession

8 utilization, using, making use of, making instrumental, using as a means *or* tool; **employment,** employing; **management,** manipulation, handling, working, operation, **exploitation,** recruiting, recruitment, calling upon, calling into service; mobilization, mobilizing

9 user, employer; **consumer,** enjoyer, exploiter; customer, client; end user

VERBS **10 use, utilize, make use of,** do with; **employ,** practice, ply, work, manage, handle, manipulate, operate, **wield,** play, exercise; **have** *or* **enjoy the use of;** exercise, **exert;** reuse, repurpose

11 apply, put to use *or* **good use,** carry out, put into execution, **put into practice** *or* **operation,** put in force, enforce; bring to bear upon

12 treat, handle, manage, use, **deal with, cope with,** come to grips with, take on, tackle <nf>, contend with, do with; steward, care for

13 spend, consume, expend, **pass,** employ, **put in;** devote, bestow, give to *or* give over to, devote *or* consecrate *or* dedicate to; while, while away, wile; dissipate, **exhaust, use up**

14 avail oneself of, make use of, resort to, put to use *or* **good use,** have recourse to, **turn to,** look to, recur to, refer to, take to <nf>, betake oneself to; revert to, fall back on *or* upon, rely on; convert *or* turn to use, put in *or* into requisition, press *or* enlist into service, lay under contribution, impress, **call upon,** call *or* bring into play, draw on *or* upon, recruit, muster; pick someone's brains

15 take advantage of, avail oneself of, make the most of, use to the full, make good use of, maximize, improve, **turn to use** *or* **profit** *or* **account** *or* **good account,** turn to advantage *or* good advantage, use to advantage, put to advantage, find one's account *or* advantage in; improve the occasion 843.8; **profit by, benefit from,** reap the benefit of; **exploit, capitalize on, make capital of,** make a good thing of <nf>, make hay <nf>, **trade on,** cash in on <nf>, play on, play off against; make the best of, make a virtue of necessity

16 <take unfair advantage of> **exploit, take advantage of, use,** make use of, **use for one's own ends;** make a paw *or* cat's-paw of, make a pawn of, sucker *and* play for a sucker <nf>; **manipulate,** work on, work upon, stroke, play on *or* upon; play both ends against the middle; **impose upon,** presume upon; use ill, ill-use, abuse, misuse 389.4; batten on; milk, bleed, bleed white <nf>; drain, suck the blood of *or* from, suck dry; exploit one's position, feather one's nest <nf>, **profiteer;** abuse

17 avail, be of use, be of service, serve, **suffice, do,** answer, **answer** *or* **serve one's purpose,** serve one's need, fill the bill *and* do the trick <nf>, suit one's purpose; bestead , **stand one in stead** *or* **good stead,** be handy, come in handy, stand one in hand <nf>; advantage, be of advantage *or* service to; **profit, benefit,** pay *and* pay off <nf>, give good returns, yield a profit, bear fruit

ADJS **18 useful,** employable, of use, of service, **serviceable,** commodious ; good for; **helpful,** of help 449.21; **advantageous, to one's advantage** *or* **profit, profitable,** remuneratory, bankable, beneficial 999.12; **practical,** banausic, pragmatical, **functional, utilitarian,** of general utility *or* application, commodious; fitting, proper, appropriate, expedient 995.5; well-used, well-thumbed; reusable, recyclable

19 using, exploitive, exploitative, manipulative, manipulatory

20 handy, convenient; available, accessible, **ready, at hand,** to hand, **on hand,** on tap, on deck <nf>, on call, at one's call *or* beck and call, at one's elbow, at one's fingertips, just around the corner, at one's disposal; versatile, adaptable, all-around <nf>, of all work; crude but effective, quick and dirty <nf>; to the purpose; fast-food, convenience; one-stop

21 effectual, effective, active, efficient, efficacious, operative; instrumental; subsidiary, subservient

22 valuable, of value, all for the best, all to the good, **profitable,** bankable, yielding a return, well-spent, **worthwhile,** rewarding; gainful, remunerative, moneymaking, lucrative

23 usable, utilizable; applicable, appliable, employable, serviceable; practical, operable; **reusable**, recyclable**; exploitable;** manipulable, pliable, compliant 433.12; at one's service

24 used, employed, exercised, exerted, **applied;** previously owned *or* preowned, secondhand 842.18

25 in use, in practice, in force, in effect, in service, in operation, in commission

ADVS **26 usefully,** to good use; **profitably, advantageously, to advantage,** to profit, to good effect; effectually, effectively, efficiently; serviceably, functionally, **practically;** handily, conveniently; by use of, by dint of

388 CONSUMPTION

NOUNS **1 consumption, consuming, using** *or* **eating up;** burning up; absorption, assimilation, digestion, ingestion, **expenditure,** expending, spending; squandering, wastefulness 486.1; finishing; **depletion,** drain, exhausting, **exhaustion,** impoverishment; **waste,** wastage, wasting away, erosion, ablation, wearing down, wearing away, attrition; throwing away

2 consumable, consumable item *or* **goods;** nonrenewable *or* nonreusable *or* nonrecyclable item *or* resource; **throwaway,** throwaway item, disposable goods *or* item; throwaway culture *or* psychology, instant obsolescence

VERBS **3 consume, spend, expend, use up;** absorb, assimilate, digest, ingest, eat, **eat up,** swallow, swallow up, gobble, gobble up; burn up; **finish,** finish off; **exhaust, deplete,** impoverish, drain, drain of resources; suck dry, bleed white <nf>, suck one's blood; wear away, erode, erode away, ablate; waste away; **throw away, squander** 486.3

4 be consumed, be used up, waste; **run out, give out,** peter out <nf>; run dry, dry up

ADJS **5 used up, consumed,** eaten up, burnt up; finished, gone; unreclaimable, irreplaceable; nonrenewable, nonrecyclable, nonreusable; **spent,** exhausted, maxed-out, effete, dissipated, depleted, impoverished, drained, worn-out; worn away, eroded, ablated; **wasted** 486.9

6 consumable, expendable, spendable; exhaustible; replaceable; disposable, throwaway, no-deposit, no-deposit-no-return

389 MISUSE

NOUNS **1 misuse, misusage, abuse,** wrong use; **misemployment, misapplication; mishandling,** mismanagement, poor stewardship; corrupt administration, malversation, breach of public trust, maladministration; diversion, defalcation, misappropriation, conversion, **embezzlement,** peculation, pilfering, fraud; perversion, prostitution; profanation, violation, pollution, fouling, befoulment, desecration, defilement, debasement; malpractice, abuse of office, malversation, misconduct, malfeasance, misfeasance

2 mistreatment, ill-treatment, maltreatment, ill-use, ill-usage, **abuse,** verbal abuse; **molesting, molestation,** child abuse *or* molestation; spousal abuse; self-abuse; **violation,** outrage, violence, injury, atrocity; cruel and unusual punishment; overuse

3 persecution, oppression, harrying, hounding, tormenting, bashing <nf>, harassment, nobbling <Brit nf>, victimization, torture; **witch-hunting,** witch-hunt, red-baiting <nf>, McCarthyism; Spanish inquisition; open season, piling on <nf>

VERBS **4 misuse, misemploy, abuse, misapply; mishandle,** mismanage, maladminister; divert, misappropriate, expropriate, convert, defalcate , embezzle, defraud, pilfer, peculate, feather one's nest <nf>; pervert, prostitute; profane, violate, pollute, foul, foul one's own nest, spoil, befoul, desecrate, defile, debase; verbally abuse, bad-mouth; misuse *or* abuse power

5 mistreat, maltreat, ill-treat, ill-use, abuse, injure, **molest;** do wrong to, do wrong by; outrage, do violence to, do one's worst to; mishandle, manhandle; buffet, batter, bruise, **savage,** manhandle, maul, knock about, rough, rough up; pollute; overuse, overwork, overtax

6 <nf terms> **screw,** screw over, shaft, kick around, stiff, give the short *or* the shitty end of the stick, fuck, fuck over

7 persecute, oppress, **torment,** victimize, play cat and mouse with, **harass,** get *or* keep after, get *or* keep at, harry, hound, beset, nobble <Brit nf>; pursue, hunt

ADVS **8** on one's back *and* on one's case *and* in one's face <nf>

390 DISUSE

NOUNS **1 disuse,** disusage, desuetude; **nonuse, nonemployment; abstinence, abstention;** neglect, inusitation; nonprevalence, unprevalence; **obsolescence,** obsoleteness, obsoletism, obsoletion, planned obsolescence; superannuation, retirement, pensioning off, early retirement; redundancy <Brit>

2 discontinuance, cessation, desisting, desistance; **abdication,** relinquishment, forebearance, resignation, renunciation, renouncement, abjurement, abjuration; waiver, nonexercise; abeyance, suspension, back burner *and* cold storage <nf>, limbo, bardo; **phaseout, abandonment** 370

3 discard, discarding, jettison, deep six <nf>, disposal, dumping, **waste disposal,** solid waste disposal, burning, incineration, ocean burning *or* incineration; compacting; **scrapping, junking** <nf>; removal, elimination 773.2; **rejection** 372; **reject,** throwaway, castaway, castoff, remains, rejectamenta <pl>; **refuse** 391.4

VERBS **4 cease to use; abdicate, relinquish; discontinue, disuse,** quit, stop, drop <nf>, give up, give over, lay off <nf>, **phase out,** phase down, put behind one, let go, leave off, come off <nf>, cut out, desist, desist from, have done with; waive , resign, renounce, abjure, neglect; nol-pros, not pursue *or* proceed with; decommission, put out of commission

5 not use, do without, dispense with, **let alone,** not touch, hold off;

abstain, **refrain,** forgo, forbear, spare, waive; keep *or* hold back, reserve, save, save up, sock *or* squirrel away, tuck away, put under the mattress, hoard; keep in hand, have up one's sleeve; see the last of

6 **put away,** lay away, **put aside,** lay *or* set *or* wave *or* cast *or* push aside, sideline <nf>, put *or* lay *or* set by; stow, store 386.10; **pigeonhole, shelve,** put on the shelf, put in mothballs; **table,** lay on the table; table the motion, pass to the order of the day; put on hold *or* on the back burner <nf>, postpone, delay 846.8

7 **discard, reject, throw away, throw out,** chuck *or* chuck away *and* shitcan *and* eighty-six <nf>, cast, cast off *or* away *or* aside; **get rid of,** get quit of, get shut *or* shet of <nf>, rid oneself of, shrug off, **dispose of,** slough, **dump, ditch** <nf>, **jettison, throw** *or* **heave** *or* **toss overboard,** deep-six <nf>, throw out the window, throw *or* cast to the dogs, cast to the winds; sell off *or* out; throw over, jilt; part with, give away; throw to the wolves, write off, walk away from, **abandon** 370.5; remove, **eliminate** 773.5

8 **scrap, junk** <nf>, consign to the scrap heap, throw on the junk heap <nf>; superannuate, retire, pension off, put out to pasture *or* grass

9 **obsolesce,** fall into disuse, go out, pass away; be superseded; superannuate

ADJS 10 **disused, abandoned,** deserted, **discontinued,** done with, derelict; out, **out of use;** old; relinquished, resigned, renounced, abjured; decommissioned, out of commission; **outworn,** worn-out, past use, not worth saving; **obsolete,** obsolescent, life-expired, superannuated, superannuate; superseded, outdated, out-of-date, outmoded, desuete; retired, pensioned off; on the shelf; written off <nf>; antique, antiquated, old-fashioned, old

11 **discarded,** rejected, **castoff,** castaway, scrapped, junked

12 **unused,** unutilized, **unemployed,** unapplied, unexercised; in abeyance, suspended; waived; **unspent,** unexpended, unconsumed; held back, held out, put by, put aside, saved, held in reserve, in hand, spare, to spare, extra, reserve; stored 386.14; untouched, unhandled; untapped; untrodden, unbeaten; **new,** brand-new, original, pristine, virgin, fresh, fresh off the assembly line, mint, in mint condition, factory-fresh; underused, underutilized

391 USELESSNESS

NOUNS 1 **uselessness,** inutility; **needlessness,** unnecessity; unserviceability, **unusability,** unemployability, inoperativeness, inoperability, disrepair; unhelpfulness; inapplicability, unsuitability, unfitness; functionlessness; otioseness, otiosity; redundancy, tautology; **superfluousness** 993.4; excess baggage

2 **futility,** vanity, emptiness, hollowness; **fruitlessness,** bootlessness, unprofitableness, profitlessness, unprofitability, otiosity, worthlessness, valuelessness; triviality, nugacity, nugaciousness; unproductiveness 891; **ineffectuality,** ineffectiveness, inefficacy 19.3; **impotence** 19.1; effeteness; **pointlessness,** meaninglessness, purposelessness, aimlessness, fecklessness; the absurd, absurdity; inanity, fatuity; vicious circle *or* cycle; **rat race** <nf>

3 **labor in vain,** labor lost, labor for naught; labor of Sisyphus, work of Penelope, Penelope's web; **wild-goose chase,** snipe hunt, bootless errand; waste of energy, waste of labor, waste of breath, waste of time, waste of effort *or* wasted effort, wasted breath, wasted labor; red herring; fool's errand; blind alley

4 **refuse, waste,** wastage, waste matter, waste stream, waste product, solid waste, liquid waste, wastewater, effluent, sewage, sludge; incinerator ash; industrial waste, hazardous waste, toxic waste, atomic waste, dumping; hazardous materials; medical waste; **offal; leavings,** sweepings, dust <Brit>, **scraps,**

orts; **garbage,** gash <nf>, swill, pigswill, slop, slops, hogwash <nf>; bilgewater; draff, lees, **dregs** 256.2; **offscourings,** scourings, rinsings, dishwater; parings, raspings, filings, shavings; **scum;** chaff, stubble, husks; weeds, tares; deadwood; rags, bones, wastepaper, shard, potsherd; scrap iron; slag, culm, slack

5 **rubbish, rubble, trash, junk** <nf>, shoddy, riffraff, raff <Brit nf>, **scrap,** dust <Brit>, **debris, litter,** lumber, clamjamfry, truck <nf>

6 **trash pile,** rubbish heap, junkheap *and* junkpile <nf>, scrap heap, dustheap, dustbin, midden, kitchen midden; wasteyard, **junkyard** <nf>, scrapyard, **dump,** dumpsite, garbage dump, landfill, sanitary land fill, toxic waste dump, dumping; garbology

7 wastepaper basket, wastebasket, shitcan <nf>; litter basket, litter bin; garbage bag, garbage can, wastebin, dustbin <Brit>, trash can; Dumpster <TM>, skip <Brit>; waste disposal unit, compactor, garbage grinder <nf>; compost, compost heap; circular file <nf>, file 13 <nf>

VERBS 8 **be useless, be futile, make no difference, cut no ice; die aborning; labor in vain, go on a wild-goose chase,** run in circles, go around in circles, fall by the wayside, spin one's wheels *and* bang one's head against a brick wall <nf>, beat the air, lash the waves, tilt at windmills, sow the sand, bay at the moon, waste one's effort *or* breath, preach *or* speak to the winds, beat *or* flog a dead horse, roll the stone of Sisyphus, carry coals to Newcastle, milk the ram, milk a he-goat into a sieve, pour water into a sieve, hold a farthing candle to the sun, look for a needle in a haystack, lock the barn door after the horse is stolen; attempt the impossible, spin one's wheels

ADJS 9 **useless,** of no use, no go <nf>; **aimless,** meaningless, **purposeless,** of no purpose, **pointless,** feckless; **unavailing,** of no avail, failed; ineffective, **ineffectual** 19.15; impotent 19.13; **superfluous** 993.17; frustaneous; dud

10 **needless, unnecessary, unessential,** nonessential, **unneeded, uncalled-for,** unrequired; unrecognized, neglected; tautological, tautologic, redundant

11 **worthless, valueless, good-for-nothing,** good-for-naught, no-good *or* NG <nf>, no-account <nf>, dear at any price, worthless as tits on a boar <nf>, not worth a dime *or* a red cent *or* a hill of beans *or* shit *or* bubkes <nf>, not worth the paper it's written on, not worthwhile, not worth having, not worth mentioning *or* speaking of, not worth a thought, not worth a rap *or* a continental *or* a damn, not worth the powder to blow it to hell, not worth the powder and shot, not worth the pains *or* the trouble, of no earthly use, fit for the junkyard <nf>; trivial, penny-ante <nf>, nugatory, nugacious; **junk** *and* **junky** <nf>; **cheap,** shoddy, trashy, **shabby**

12 **fruitless,** gainless, profitless, bootless, otiose, **unprofitable,** unremunerative, nonremunerative; uncommercial; **unrewarding,** rewardless; abortive; barren, sterile, unproductive 891.4

13 **vain, futile,** hollow, empty, idle, unavailing; absurd; inane, fatuous, fatuitous

14 **unserviceable, unusable,** unemployable, inoperative, inoperable, unworkable; out of order, out of whack *and* on the blink *and* on the fritz <nf>, in disrepair; **unhelpful,** unconducive; inapplicable; unsuitable, unfit; functionless, nonfunctional, otiose, nonutilitarian; kaput

ADVS 15 **uselessly; needlessly,** unnecessarily; bootlessly, fruitlessly; **futilely, vainly;** purposelessly, to little purpose, to no purpose, **aimlessly, pointlessly,** fecklessly; tautologically

392 IMPROVEMENT

NOUNS 1 **improvement, betterment,** bettering, change *or* turn for the better; melioration, **amelioration;** sea change; **mend,** mending, **amendment; progress,** progression, headway; breakthrough, quantum jump *or* leap; **advance,** advancement; upward mobility; **promotion, furtherance,** preferment; **rise,** ascent, **lift, uplift,** uptick <nf>, upswing, uptrend, upbeat, edification; **increase** 251, upgrade, upping *and* boost *and* pickup <nf>; gentrification; **enhancement, enrichment,** good influence; euthenics, eugenics; **restoration,** revival, retro, recovery, comeback

2 **development, refinement,** elaboration, **perfection;** beautification, embellishment; maturation, coming-of-age, ripening, evolution, seasoning

3 **cultivation, culture, refinement, polish,** civility; cultivation of the mind; **civilization;** acculturation; enculturation, socialization; enlightenment, Age of Enlightenment, Age of Reason; education 928.4

4 **revision,** revise, revisal; revised edition; **emendation, amendment, correction, corrigenda, rectification;** editing, redaction, recension, revampment, blue-penciling; **rewrite,** rewriting, rescript, rescription ; **polishing,** touching up, putting on the finishing touches, putting the gloss on, finishing, perfecting, tuning, fine-tuning; retrofitting

5 **reform, reformation;** regeneration 858.2; **transformation; conversion** 858; makeover; reformism, meliorism; gradualism, Fabianism, revisionism; utopianism; progressiveness, progressivism, progressism; radical reform, extremism, radicalism 611.4; revolution 860; quiet revolution; perestroika

6 **reformer,** reformist, meliorist; gradualist, Fabian, revisionist; utopian, utopist; progressive, progressivist, progressionist, progressist; resister, passive resister; radical, extremist 611.12; revolutionary 860.3; comeback kid

VERBS 7 <get better> **improve, grow better,** look better, show improvement, **mend,** amend , meliorate, ameliorate; **look up** *or* **pick up** *or* **perk up** <nf>; **develop,** shape up; **advance, progress, make progress, make headway, gain,** gain ground, go forward, get *or* go ahead, come on, come along *and* come along nicely <nf>, get along; make strides *or* rapid strides, take off *and* skyrocket <nf>, make up for lost time, turn around; straighten up and fly right <nf>; make the grade, graduate

8 **rally,** come about *or* round, come back, **take a favorable turn,** get over <nf>, take a turn for the better, gain strength; come a long way <nf>; **recuperate, recover** 396.20

9 **improve, better,** change for the better, make an improvement; transform, transfigure; vet; improve upon, refine upon, **mend, amend,** emend; meliorate, **ameliorate; advance, promote,** foster, favor, nurture, forward, bring forward; **lift,** elevate, **uplift,** raise, boost <nf>; upgrade; gentrify; **enhance, enrich,** fatten, lard ; make one's way, better oneself; be the making of; **reform,** put *or* set straight; reform oneself, turn over a new leaf, mend one's ways, straighten out, straighten oneself out, go straight <nf>; get it together *and* get one's ducks in a row <nf>; **civilize,** acculturate, socialize; enlighten, edify; **educate**

10 **develop,** elaborate; beautify, embellish; **cultivate;** come of age, come into its own, mature, ripen, evolve, season; gild the lily; formulate

11 **perfect, touch up,** finish, put on the finishing touches, polish *or* polish up, fine down, fine-tune <nf>, tone up, **brush up, furbish,** furbish up, spruce, **spruce up,** freshen, vamp, vamp up, rub up, brighten up, shine <nf>; retouch; **revive, renovate** 396.17; **repair, fix** 396.14; retrofit; streamline

12 **revise,** redact, recense, **revamp, rewrite,** redraft, **rework,** work over, retool; **emend, amend,** emendate, **rectify,** correct; **edit,** blue-pencil; straighten out; autocorrect

ADJS 13 **improved, bettered;** changed for the better, advanced, ameliorated, enhanced, enriched, touched up; developed, perfected; beautified, embellished; upgraded; gentrified; **reformed; transformed,** transfigured, converted; **cultivated,** cultured, **refined,** polished, emended, civilized; **educated** 928.18

14 **better,** better off, better for, all the better for; before-and-after

15 **improving, bettering;** meliorative, ameliorative, amelioratory, medial; progressive, progressing, advancing, ongoing; mending, **on the mend;** on the lift *or* rise *or* upswing *or* upbeat *or* upgrade <nf>, looking up <nf>

16 **emendatory, corrective;** revisory, revisional; reformatory, reformative, reformational; **reformist,** reformistic, progressive, progressivist, melioristic; gradualistic, Fabian, revisionist; utopian; radical 611.20; revolutionary 860.5

17 **improvable,** ameliorable, corrigible, revisable, perfectible; **emendable** 396.25; curable

393 IMPAIRMENT

NOUNS 1 **impairment, damage, injury, harm,** mischief, scathe, **hurt, detriment,** loss, weakening, sickening; **worsening,** disimprovement; disablement, incapacitation; collateral damage; encroachment, inroad, infringement 214.1; **disrepair, dilapidation,** ruinousness; breakage; **breakdown, collapse,** crash *and* crack-up <nf>; **malfunction,** glitch <nf>; bankruptcy; hurting, spoiling, ruination; sabotage, monkey-wrenching <nf>; mayhem, mutilation, crippling, hobbling, hamstringing, laming, maiming; destruction 395; the skids <nf>

2 **corruption, pollution, contamination,** vitiation, **defilement,** fouling, befouling; **poisoning,** envenoming; infection, festering, suppuration; **perversion,** prostitution, misuse 389; denaturing, adulteration

3 **deterioration, decadence** *or* decadency, **degradation, debasement,** derogation, deformation; **degeneration,** degeneracy, degenerateness, effeteness; etiolation, loss of tone, failure of nerve; depravation, depravedness; **retrogression,** retrogradation, retrocession, **regression;** devolution, involution; demotion 447; downward mobility; **decline,** declination, declension, worsening, comedown, **descent,** downtick <nf>, downtrend, downward trend, downturn, depreciation, **decrease** 252, **drop, fall, plunge,** free-fall, falling-off, lessening, slippage, slump, lapse, fading, dying, failing, failure, wane, ebb; loss of morale; shadow of one's former self

4 **waste, wastage, consumption;** withering, wasting, wasting away, atrophy, wilting, marcescence; emaciation 270.6

5 **wear,** use, hard wear, **wear and tear; erosion, weathering,** ablation, ravages of time, attrition

6 **decay, decomposition, disintegration, dissolution,** resolution, degradation, biodegradation, breakup, disorganization, **corruption, spoilage, dilapidation; corrosion,** oxidation, oxidization, rust; mildew, mold 1001.2; degradability, biodegradability; radioactive decay

7 **rot, rottenness, foulness, putridness,** putridity, rancidness, rancidity, rankness, **putrefaction,** putrescence, spoilage, decay, decomposition, moldering; carrion; dry rot, wet rot

8 **wreck, ruins, ruin, total loss;** hulk, carcass, skeleton; mere wreck, wreck of one's former self, perfect wreck; nervous wreck; rattletrap

VERBS 9 **impair, damage,** endamage, **injure, harm, hurt,** irritate; **worsen,** make worse, disimprove, deteriorate, put *or* set back, aggravate, exacerbate, embitter; **weaken; dilapidate;** add insult to injury, rub salt in the wound

10 **spoil, mar,** botch, **ruin,** wreck, blight, **play havoc with; destroy** 395.10; pollute

11 <nf terms> **screw up, foul up,** fuck up, bitch up, **blow,** louse up, queer, snafu, snarl up, balls up <Brit>, bugger, bugger up, gum up, ball up, bollix, bollix up, **mess up,** hash up, muck up; play hob with, play hell with, play merry hell with, play the devil with, rain on one's picnic *or*

parade; upset the apple cart, cook, sink, shoot down in flames; **total;** pulverize

12 **corrupt, debase, degrade,** degenerate, **deprave, debauch, defile,** violate, desecrate, profane, deflower, ravish, ravage, despoil; **contaminate,** confound, **pollute, vitiate, poison, infect, taint;** canker, ulcerate; **pervert,** warp, twist, distort; prostitute, misuse 389.4; denature; **cheapen,** devalue; coarsen, vulgarize, drag in the mud; adulterate, alloy, water, water down

13 <inflict an injury> **injure, hurt;** draw blood, wound, scotch ; **traumatize;** stab, stick, pierce, puncture; cut, incise, slit, slash, gash, scratch; abrade, eat away at, scuff, scrape, chafe, fret, gall, bark, skin; break, fracture, rupture; crack, chip, craze, check; lacerate, claw, tear, rip, rend; run; frazzle, fray; burn, scorch, scald; mutilate, maim, rough up <nf>, make mincemeat of, maul, batter, savage; sprain, strain, wrench; bloody; **blemish** 1004.4; **bruise, contuse,** bung *and* bung up <nf>; **buffet,** batter, bash <nf>, maul, pound, beat, beat black and blue; give a black eye; play havoc with

14 **cripple, lame,** maim; **hamstring,** hobble; wing; emasculate, castrate; incapacitate, **disable** 19.9

15 **undermine,** sap, mine, sap the foundations of, honeycomb; sabotage, monkey-wrench *and* throw *or* toss a monkey-wrench in the works <nf>, subvert

16 **deteriorate, sicken, worsen, get** *or* **grow worse,** get no better fast <nf>, disimprove, **degenerate;** slip back, **retrogress,** retrograde, regress, relapse, fall back; jump the track; go to the bad 395.24; let oneself go, let down, slacken; be the worse for, be the worse for wear *and* have seen better days <nf>

17 **decline, sink, fail, fall,** slip, fade, die, wane, ebb, subside, lapse, **run down,** go down, **go downhill, fall away, fall off,** go off <nf>, slide, slump, hit a slump, take a nose dive <nf>, go into a tailspin, take a turn for the worse; hit the skids <nf>; reach the depths, hit *or* touch bottom, hit rock bottom, have no lower to go

18 **languish, pine, droop, flag, wilt; fade,** fade away; **wither, shrivel,** shrink, diminish, wither *or* die on the vine, **dry up,** desiccate, wizen, wrinkle, sear; retrograde, retrogress

19 **waste, waste away, wither away,** atrophy, consume, consume away, erode away, emaciate, pine away; trickle *or* dribble away; run to waste, run to seed

20 **wear, wear away, wear down, wear off;** abrade, fret, whittle away, rub off; fray, frazzle, tatter, wear ragged; **wear out;** weather, erode, ablate

21 **corrode, erode,** eat, gnaw, eat into, eat away, nibble away, gnaw at the root of; canker; **oxidize, rust**

22 **decay, decompose, disintegrate;** biodegrade; go *or* fall into decay, go *or* fall to pieces, break up, crumble, crumble into dust; **spoil,** corrupt, canker, **go bad; rot, putrefy,** putresce; fester, suppurate, rankle <nf>; **mortify,** necrose, gangrene, sphacelate; mold, molder, molder away, rot away, rust away, mildew; gangrene

23 **break, break up,** fracture, **come apart,** come unstuck, **come** *or* **fall to pieces, fall apart, disintegrate;** burst, rupture; crack, split, fissure; snap; break open, give way *or* away, start, spring a leak, come apart at the seams, come unstuck <nf>

24 **break down, founder, collapse;** crash <nf>, cave *or* fall in, come crashing *or* tumbling down, topple, topple down *or* over, tremble *or* nod *or* totter to one's fall; totter, sway

25 get out of order, **malfunction,** get out of gear; get out of joint; go wrong

26 <nf terms> **get out of whack,** get out of kilter, get out of commission, go kaput, **go on the blink** *or* **fritz, go haywire,** fritz out, go blooey *or* kerflooey, give out, **break down,** pack up <Brit>, conk out

ADJS 27 **impaired, damaged, hurt, injured, harmed; deteriorated, worsened,** cut to the quick, aggravated, exacerbated, irritated, embittered; weakened; **worse,** worse off, the worse for, all the worse for; imperfect; lacerated, mangled, cut, split, rent, torn, slit, slashed, mutilated, chewed-up; **broken** 802.24, **shattered, smashed,** in bits, in pieces, in shards, burst, busted <nf>, ruptured, sprung; cracked, chipped, crazed, checked; burned, scorched, scalded; **damaging, injurious,** traumatic, degenerative

28 **spoiled** *or* spoilt, **marred,** botched, blighted, **ruined,** wrecked; **destroyed** 395.28

29 <nf terms> **queered, screwed up, fouled up,** loused up, snafued, buggered, buggered up, gummed up, snarled up, balled up, bollixed up, **messed up,** hashed up, mucked up, botched up; beat up, clapped-out <Brit>; **totaled,** kaput, finished, packed-up <Brit>, done for, done in, cooked, sunk, shot

30 **crippled,** game <nf>, bad, handicapped, maimed; **lame, halt,** halting, hobbling, limping; kneesprung; hamstrung; spavined; **disabled, incapacitated,** challenged; emasculated, castrated

31 **worn,** well-worn, deep-worn, worn-down, the worse for wear, dog-eared; timeworn; shopworn, shopsoiled <Brit>, shelfworn; worn to the stump, worn to the bone; **worn ragged,** worn to rags, worn to threads; **threadbare,** bare, sere

32 **shabby, shoddy, seedy,** scruffy, **tacky** <nf>, dowdy, tatty, ratty; holey, full of holes; raggedy, raggedy-ass <nf>, **ragged, tattered, torn;** patchy; **frayed, frazzled;** in rags, in tatters, in shreds; **out at the elbows,** out at the heels, **down-at-heel** *or* **-heels, down-at-the-heel** *or* **-heels**

33 **dilapidated, ramshackle,** decrepit, shacky, tottery, slummy <nf>, **tumbledown, broken-down, run-down,** in ruins, ruinous, ruined, derelict, gone to wrack and ruin, the worse for wear; **battered,** beaten up, **beat-up** <nf>

34 **weatherworn, weather-beaten, weathered,** weather-battered, weather-wasted, weather-eaten, weather-bitten, weather-scarred; eroded; **faded,** washed-out, bleached, blanched, etiolated

35 **wasted,** atrophied, shrunken; **withered,** sere, shriveled, wilted, wizened, dried-up, desiccated; wrinkled, wrinkled like a prune; brittle, papery, parchmenty; **emaciated** 270.20; starved, worn to a shadow, reduced to a skeleton, skin and bones

36 **worn-out, used up** <nf>, worn to a frazzle, frazzled, fit for the dust hole *or* wastepaper basket; **exhausted, tired,** fatigued, pooped <nf>, **spent,** effete, etiolated, played out, maxed-out, shotten <nf>, jaded, emptied, done *and* done up <nf>; **run-down,** dragged-out <nf>, laid low, at a low ebb, in a bad way, far-gone, on one's last legs

37 **in disrepair, out of order, malfunctioning,** out of working order, out of condition, out of repair, inoperative; out of tune, out of gear; out of joint; **broken** 802.24

38 <nf terms> **out of whack** *or* **kilter** *or* kelter *or* sync *or* commission, on the fritz, fritzed, on the blink, blooey, kerflooey, haywire, wonky <Brit>

39 **putrefactive,** putrefacient, rotting; **septic;** saprogenic, saprogenous; saprophilous, saprophytic, saprobic

40 **decayed, decomposed; spoiled, corrupt,** peccant, bad, **gone bad; rotten, rotting, putrid, putrefied, foul;** putrescent, **mortified,** necrosed, necrotic, sphacelated, gangrened, gangrenous; carious; cankered, ulcerated, festering, suppurating, suppurative; rotten at *or* to the core

41 **tainted, off,** blown, frowy <nf>; **stale; sour,** soured, turned; **rank,** reechy , **rancid,** strong <nf>, **high,** gamy

42 **blighted, blasted, ravaged,** despoiled; blown, **flyblown,** wormy, weevily, maggoty; **moth-eaten, worm-eaten; moldy,** moldering, **mildewed,** smutty, smutted; **musty, fusty,** frowzy *or* frowsy, frowsty <Brit>

43 **corroded, eroded,** eaten; **rusty,** rust-eaten, rust-worn, rust-cankered

44 **corrupting, corruptive;** corrosive, corroding; erosive, eroding, **damaging, injurious** 1000.12; pollutive

45 **deteriorating, worsening,** disintegrating, coming apart *or* unstuck, crumbling, cracking, fragmenting, going to pieces; **decadent, degenerate,** effete; **retrogressive,** retrograde, regressive, from better to worse; **declining, sinking, failing,** falling, waning, subsiding, **slipping,** sliding, slumping; **languishing, pining,** drooping, flagging, wilting; ebbing, draining, dwindling; **wasting,** fading, fading fast, **withering,** shriveling; tabetic, marcescent

46 **on the wane, on the decline,** on the downgrade, on the downward track, on the skids <nf>; tottering, nodding to its fall, on the way out

47 degradable, biodegradable, decomposable, putrefiable, putrescible

ADVS **48** out of the frying pan into the fire, from better to worse; for the worse

394 RELAPSE

NOUNS **1** **relapse, lapse,** falling back; **reversion, regression** 859.1; **reverse, reversal,** backward deviation, devolution, **setback,** backset; **return,** recurrence, renewal, recrudescence; throwback, atavism; recadency

2 **backsliding,** backslide; **fall, fall from grace;** lapsing, recidivism, recidivation; apostasy 363.2

3 **backslider,** recidivist, reversionist; apostate 363.5

VERBS **4** **relapse, lapse, backslide,** slide back, lapse back, **slip back,** sink back, **fall back,** have a relapse, devolve, **return to, revert to,** recur to, yield again to, fall again into, recidivate; revert, **regress** 859.4; **fall, fall from grace**

ADJS **5** **relapsing, lapsing, lapsarian, backsliding,** recidivous; recadent; recrudescent; **regressive** 859.7; apostate 363.11

395 DESTRUCTION

NOUNS **1** **destruction, ruin, ruination,** rack, **rack and ruin,** blue ruin <nf>; perdition, damnation, eternal damnation; universal ruin; **wreck;** devastation, ravage, havoc, holocaust, firestorm, hecatomb, carnage, shambles, slaughter, bloodbath, **desolation; waste, consumption;** decimation; **dissolution, disintegration,** breakup, disruption, disorganization, undoing, lysis; vandalism, depredation, spoliation, despoliation, despoilment; the road to ruin *or* wrack and ruin; iconoclasm

2 **end, fate, doom,** death, death knell, bane, deathblow, death warrant, *coup de grâce* <Fr>, final blow, quietus, cutoff, end of the world, eschaton, apocalypse

3 **fall, downfall,** prostration; **overthrow, overturn, upset, upheaval,** *bouleversement* <Fr>; convulsion, **subversion,** sabotage, monkey-wrenching <nf>

4 **debacle, disaster, cataclysm, catastrophe; breakup,** breaking up; **breakdown, collapse; crash,** meltdown, smash, **smashup,** crack-up <nf>; **wreck,** wrack, shipwreck; cave-in, cave; washout; total loss, big one

5 **demolition,** demolishment; wrecking, wreckage, leveling, razing, flattening, smashing, tearing down, bringing to the ground; **dismantlement,** disassembly, unmaking; hatchet job

6 **extinction, extermination, elimination, eradication,** extirpation; rooting out, deracination, uprooting, tearing up root and branch; **annihilation,** extinguishment, **snuffing out; abolition,** abolishment; annulment, **nullification,** voiding, **negation; liquidation, purge; suppression;** choking, choking off, suffocation, stifling, strangulation; silencing; nuclear winter

7 **obliteration, erasure, effacement,** deletion, expunction, blot , blotting, **blotting out, wiping out;** washing out *and* scrubbing <nf>, cancellation, cancel; deletion; annulment,

abrogation; palimpsest, clean slate, tabula rasa

8 **destroyer, ruiner, wrecker, bane,** wiper-out, demolisher; **vandal,** hun; exterminator, annihilator; **iconoclast,** idoloclast; biblioclast; nihilist; terrorist, syndicalist; **bomber,** dynamiter, dynamitard; burner, arsonist; loose cannon

9 **eradicator,** expunger; **eraser,** rubber, India rubber, sponge; extinguisher

VERBS **10 destroy,** deal *or* unleash destruction, unleash the hurricane, nuke <nf>; **ruin,** ruinate <nf>, bring to ruin, lay in ruins, play *or* raise hob with, throw into disorder, turn upside-down, upheave; **wreck,** wrack, shipwreck; damn, seal the doom of, **condemn,** confound; **devastate, desolate,** waste, **lay waste, ravage,** havoc, wreak havoc, despoil, depredate; vandalize; **decimate;** devour, consume, engorge, gobble, gobble up, swallow up; gut, gut with fire, incinerate, vaporize, ravage with fire and sword; dissolve, lyse

11 do for, fix <nf>, settle, sink, cook *and* cook one's goose *and* cut one down to size *and* cut one off at the knees *and* pull the plug on *and* pull the rug out from under <nf>, dish, scuttle, put the kibosh on *and* put the skids under <nf>, do in, **undo,** knock in *or* on the head, poleax, torpedo, knock out, clobber, KO *and* banjax <nf>, deal a knockout blow to, zap *and* shoot down *and* shoot down in flames <nf>; break the back of; make short work of; hamstring; **defeat** 412.6

12 put an end to, make an end of, **end, finish,** finish off <nf>, put paid to <Brit>, give the *coup de grâce* <Fr> to, give the quietus to, deal a deathblow to, dispose of, get rid of, do in, do away with; cut off, take off, be the death of, sound the death knell of; put out of the way, put out of existence, **slaughter,** make away with, off *and* waste *and* blow away <nf>, kill off, strike down, **kill** 308.13; nip, nip in the bud; cut short; scrub <nf>

13 abolish, nullify, void, abrogate, annihilate, annul, tear up, repeal, revoke, negate, negative, invalidate, **undo, cancel,** cancel out, bring to naught, put *or* lay to rest

14 exterminate, eliminate, eradicate, deracinate, **extirpate, annihilate; wipe out** <nf>; cut out, root up *or* out, uproot, pull *or* pluck up by the roots, cut up root and branch, strike at the root of, lay the ax to the root of; **liquidate,** vaporize, **purge;** remove, sweep away, wash away; wipe off the map <nf>, leave no trace

15 extinguish, quench, snuff out, put out, stamp *or* trample out, trample underfoot; **smother,** choke, stifle, strangle, suffocate; silence; **suppress, quash,** squash *and* squelch <nf>, **quell,** put down

16 obliterate, expunge, efface, erase, raze , blot, sponge, **wipe out,** wipe off the map, rub out, **blot out,** sponge out, wash away; cancel, strike out, cross out, scratch, scratch out, rule out; blue-pencil; **delete** *or* dele, kill; leave on the cutting-room floor <nf>

17 demolish, wreck, total *and* rack up <nf>, undo, unbuild, unmake, **dismantle, disassemble; take apart, tear apart, tear asunder, rend, take** *or* **pull** *or* **pick** *or* **tear to pieces,** pull in pieces, tear to shreds *or* rags *or* tatters; sunder, cleave, **split; disintegrate, fragment,** break to pieces, make mincemeat of, reduce to rubble, atomize, pulverize, **smash,** shatter 802.13

18 blow up, blast, spring, explode, blow to pieces *or* bits *or* smithereens *or* kingdom come, bomb, bombard, blitz; mine; self-destruct

19 raze, rase, **fell, level,** flatten, smash, prostrate, raze to the ground *or* dust; steamroller, bulldoze; **pull down, tear down, take down,** bring down, bring down about one's ears, bring tumbling *or* crashing down, break down, throw down, cast down, beat down, knock down *or* over; cut down, chop down, mow down; blow down; burn down

20 overthrow, overturn; upset, overset, upend, **subvert,** throw down *or*

over; undermine, honeycomb, **sap,** sap the foundations, **weaken**

21 **overwhelm,** whelm, swamp, engulf; inundate

22 <be destroyed> **fall,** fall to the ground, tumble, come tumbling *or* crashing down, topple, tremble *or* nod to its fall, bite the dust <nf>; **break up,** crumble, crumble to dust, disintegrate, go *or* fall to pieces; go by the board, go out the window *or* up the spout <nf>, go down the tube *or* tubes <nf>; self-destruct

23 **perish, expire, succumb, die, cease, end,** come to an end, go, pass, **pass away, vanish, disappear,** fade away, run out, peg *or* conk out <nf>, come to nothing *or* naught, be no more, be done for; be all over with, be all up with <nf>

24 **go to ruin, go to rack and ruin,** go to rack and manger , **go to the bad,** go wrong, **go to the dogs** *or* **pot** <nf>, go *or* run to seed, go to hell in a handbasket <nf>, go to the deuce *or* devil <nf>, go to hell <nf>, go to the wall, go to perdition *or* glory <nf>; go up <nf>, go under; **go to smash,** go to shivers, go to smithereens <nf>

25 **drive to ruin,** drive to the bad, **force to the wall,** drive to the dogs <nf>, hound *or* harry to destruction

ADJS 26 **destructive,** destroying; **ruinous,** ruining; demolishing, demolitionary; **disastrous, calamitous, cataclysmic,** cataclysmal, **catastrophic;** fatal, fateful, doomful, baneful; bad news <nf>; **deadly;** consumptive, consuming, withering; **devastating, desolating,** ravaging, wasting, wasteful, spoliative, depredatory; vandalic, vandalish, vandalistic; subversive, subversionary; nihilist, nihilistic; suicidal, self-destructive; fratricidal, internecine, internecive

27 **exterminative,** exterminatory, **annihilative, eradicative,** extirpative, extirpatory; all-destroying, all-devouring, all-consuming

28 **ruined, destroyed, wrecked, blasted, undone,** down-and-out, broken, bankrupt; spoiled; irremediable 125.15; fallen, overthrown; **devastated, desolated, ravaged,** blighted, wasted; ruinous, in ruins, gutted; gone to rack and ruin; obliterated, annihilated, liquidated, vaporized; doomed, not long for this world

29 <nf terms> **shot, done for,** done in, finished, kaput; gone to pot, gone to the dogs, gone to hell in a handbasket, phut, belly up, blooey, kerflooey, dead in the water, washed up, all washed up, history, **dead meat, down the tube** *or* **tubes,** zapped, nuked, tapped out, wiped out, rubbed out, bust

396 RESTORATION

NOUNS 1 **restoration,** restoral, **restitution, reestablishment, redintegration, reinstatement,** reinstation, reformation , reinvestment, reinvestiture, instauration, reversion, reinstitution, reconstitution, recomposition; replacement; **rehabilitation,** redevelopment, reconversion, reactivation, reenactment; improvement 392; return to normal

2 **reclamation, recovery, retrieval,** salvage, salving; redemption, salvation

3 **revival,** revivification, revivescence *or* revivescency, **renewal,** resurrection, resuscitation, restimulation, reanimation, resurgence, recrudescence, comeback; retro; **refreshment** 9; second wind; renaissance, renascence, **rebirth,** new birth; **rejuvenation,** rejuvenescence, second youth, new lease on life; **regeneration,** regeneracy, regenerateness; regenesis, palingenesis, reanimation, reincarnation; new hope, second chance

4 **renovation, renewal;** refreshment; **redecorating; reconditioning,** furbishment, refurbishment, refurbishing; retread *and* retreading <nf>; face-lifting *or* face-lift; slum clearance, urban renewal; remodeling; overhauling

5 **reconstruction, re-creation, remaking,** recomposition, remodeling, **rebuilding,** refabrication, refashioning; reassembling,

reassembly; reformation; restructuring, perestroika

6 **reparation, repair,** repairing, **fixing, mending,** making *or* setting right, repairwork; servicing, maintenance; **overhaul,** overhauling; troubleshooting <nf>; **rectification, correction, remedy;** damage control; **redress,** making *or* setting right, amends, satisfaction, compensation, **recompense;** emendation

7 **cure, curing, healing, remedy** 86; **therapy** 91

8 **recovery, rally, comeback** <nf>, return, upturn; **recuperation, convalescence**

9 **restorability, reparability,** curability, recoverability, reversibility, remediability, retrievability, redeemability, salvageability, corrigibility

10 **mender, fixer,** doctor <nf>, restorer, renovator, repairer, **repairman, repairwoman,** handyman, maintenance man *or* woman, **serviceman, servicewoman;** trouble man *and* troubleshooter <nf>; Mr Fixit *and* little Miss Fixit <nf>; **mechanic** *or* mechanician; tinker, tinkerer; cobbler; salvor, salvager

VERBS 11 **restore, put back, replace, return,** place in *status quo ante;* **reestablish,** redintegrate, reform , reenact, **reinstate,** restitute; **reinstall,** reinvest, revest, reinstitute, reconstitute, recompose, recruit, **rehabilitate,** redevelop; reintegrate, reconvert, reactivate; make as good as new; refill, replenish; give back 481.4

12 **redeem, reclaim, recover, retrieve;** ransom; rescue; salvage, salve; recycle; win back, **recoup**

13 **remedy, rectify, correct, right,** patch up, emend, amend, **redress,** make good *or* right, **put right,** set right, put *or* set to rights, put *or* set straight, set up, heal up, knit up, make all square; pay reparations, give satisfaction, requite, restitute, recompense, compensate, remunerate

14 **repair, mend, fix,** fix up <nf>, do up, doctor <nf>, put in repair, put in shape, set to rights, put in order *or* condition; **condition, recondition,** commission, put in commission, ready; **service, overhaul;** patch, **patch up;** tinker, tinker up, fiddle, fiddle around; cobble; sew up, darn; recap, retread

15 **cure,** work a cure, recure , **remedy, heal, restore to health,** heal up, knit up, bring round *or* around, pull round *or* around, give a new *or* fresh lease on life, make better, make well, fix up, pull through, set on one's feet *or* legs; snatch from the jaws of death

16 **revive,** revivify, **renew,** recruit; **reanimate,** reinspire, **regenerate, rejuvenate, revitalize,** put *or* breathe new life into, restimulate; **refresh** 9.2; **resuscitate,** bring to, bring round *or* around; recharge; **resurrect,** bring back, call back, recall to life, raise from the dead; rewarm, warm up *or* over; **rekindle,** relight, reheat the ashes, stir the embers; restore to health

17 **renovate, renew; recondition,** refit, revamp, furbish, refurbish; refresh, face-lift; fix up, upgrade

18 **remake,** reconstruct, remodel, recompose, reconstitute, re-create, **rebuild,** refabricate, re-form, refashion, reassemble

19 **recuperate,** recruit, **gain strength,** recruit *or* renew one's strength, catch one's breath, **get better; improve** 392.7; **rally, pick up,** perk up *and* brace up <nf>, bounce back, take a new *or* fresh lease on life; **take a favorable turn,** turn the corner, be out of the woods, take a turn for the better; **convalesce;** sleep it off

20 **recover, rally, revive, get well, get over, pull through,** pull round *or* around, come round *or* around <nf>, come back <nf>, make a comeback <nf>; get about, get back in shape <nf>, be oneself again, feel like a new person; **survive,** weather the storm, live through; **come to,** come to oneself, show signs of life; come up smiling <nf>, get one's second wind; come *or* pull *or* snap out of it <nf>

21 **heal, heal over,** close up, scab over, cicatrize, granulate; heal *or* right itself; **knit, set**

ADJS 22 **tonic, restorative, restitutive,** restitutory, restimulative; analeptic; reparative, reparatory; sanative; remedial, **curative** 86.39

23 **recuperative,** recuperatory; reviviscent; **convalescent;** buoyant, resilient, elastic

24 **renascent,** redivivus, redux, resurrected, renewed, revived, reborn, resurgent, recrudescent, reappearing, phoenix-like; like new; oneself again

25 **remediable, curable;** medicable, treatable; emendable, amendable, **correctable,** rectifiable, corrigible; **improvable,** ameliorable; **reparable,** repairable, **mendable, fixable;** restorable, recoverable, salvageable, retrievable, reversible, reclaimable, recyclable, redeemable; renewable; sustainable

397 PRESERVATION

NOUNS 1 **preservation,** preserval, **conservation, saving, salvation,** salvage, **keeping, safekeeping,** maintenance, upkeep, support, service; custody, custodianship, guardianship, curatorship; protectiveness, protection 1008; conservationism, environmental conservation, environmentalism, ecology; nature conservation *or* conservancy, soil conservation, forest conservation, forest management, wildlife conservation, stream conservation, water conservation, wetlands conservation; salvage; self-preservation

2 **food preservation;** storage, retention; **curing,** seasoning, salting, brining, pickling, marinating, corning; **drying,** dry-curing, jerking; dehydration, anhydration, evaporation, desiccation; **smoking,** fuming, smoke-curing, kippering; **refrigeration,** freezing, quick-freezing, blast-freezing, deep-freezing; freeze-drying, lyophilization; irradiation; **canning,** tinning <Brit>; bottling, processing, packaging; irradiation, sterilization

3 **embalming,** mummification; taxidermy, stuffing; tanning

4 **preservative,** preservative medium; salt, brine, vinegar, formaldehyde, formalin *or* formol, embalming fluid, food additive, MSG *or* monosodium glutamate

5 **preserver,** saver, conservator, keeper, safekeeper; taxidermist; lifesaver, rescuer, deliverer, savior; **conservationist,** preservationist; National Wildlife Service, Audubon Society, Sierra Club, Nature Conservancy; **ranger, forest ranger,** Smokey the Bear, fire warden, game warden

6 **life preserver,** life jacket, life vest, life belt, cork jacket, Mae West <nf>; life buoy, life ring, buoy, flotation device, floating cushion; man-overboard buoy; water wings; breeches buoy; lifeboat, life raft, rubber dinghy <Brit>; life net; lifeline; safety belt; **parachute;** ejection seat *or* ejector seat, ejection capsule

7 **preserve, reserve, reservation; park,** paradise; national park, state park; national seashore; forest preserve *or* reserve, arboretum; national *or* state forest; wilderness preserve; Indian reservation; **refuge, sanctuary** 1009.1, game preserve *or* reserve, bird sanctuary, wildlife sanctuary *or* preserve; museum, library 558, archives 549.2, bank, store 386; protected area

VERBS 8 **preserve, conserve, save,** spare; **keep,** keep safe, keep inviolate *or* intact; patent, copyright, register; not endanger, not destroy; not use up, not waste, not expend; **guard, protect** 1008.18; **maintain, sustain,** uphold, support, **keep up,** keep alive

9 **preserve, cure,** season, salt, brine, marinate *or* marinade, pickle, corn, **dry, dry-cure,** jerk, dry-salt; dehydrate, anhydrate, evaporate, desiccate; vacuum-pack; **smoke,** fume, **smoke-cure,** smoke-dry, kipper; **refrigerate,** freeze, quick-freeze, blast-freeze, keep on ice; freeze-dry, lyophilize; irradiate

10 **embalm,** mummify; stuff; tan

11 **put up,** put by, do up; **can,** tin <Brit>, bottle

ADJS **12 preservative,** preservatory, conservative, conservatory; custodial, curatorial; **conservational,** conservationist; preserving, conserving, saving, salubrious, keeping, eco-friendly, environment-friendly; **protective** 1008.23

13 preserved, conserved, **kept,** saved, spared; protected 1008.21; **untainted, unspoiled;** intact, all in one piece, undamaged 1002.8; **well-preserved,** well-conserved, **well-kept,** in a good state of preservation, none the worse for wear; embalmed, laid up in lavender, mummified, stuffed

398 RESCUE

NOUNS **1 rescue, deliverance,** delivery, **saving;** lifesaving; **extrication, release, freeing, liberation** 431; **bailout; salvation,** salvage, **redemption,** ransom; **recovery, retrieval;** good riddance; 911

2 rescuer, lifesaver, lifeguard; coast guard, lifesaving service, air-sea rescue; emergency medical technician *or* EMT; savior 592.2; lifeboat; salvager, salvor; savior; emancipator

VERBS **3 rescue,** come to the rescue, **deliver, save,** be the saving of, save by the bell, **redeem,** ransom, **salvage; recover, retrieve** 481.6; **free,** set free, **release, extricate,** extract, **liberate** 431.4; snatch from the jaws of death; save one's bacon *and* save one's neck *or* ass *and* bail one out <nf>

ADJS **4 rescuable, savable;** redeemable; deliverable, extricable; salvageable; fit for release

399 WARNING

NOUNS **1 warning, caution,** caveat, **admonition,** monition, admonishment; **notice,** notification; **word to the wise,** word of advice, *verbum sapienti* <L>, verb sap, enough said; **hint,** broad hint, measured words, flea in one's ear <nf>, little birdy <nf>, kick under the table; tip-off <nf>; **lesson,** object lesson, **example,** deterrent example, warning piece; moral, moral of the story; **alarm** 400; code red; final warning *or* notice, ultimatum; **threat** 514

2 forewarning, prewarning, **premonition,** precautioning; advance warning *or* notice, plenty of notice, prenotification; presentiment, hunch *and* funny feeling <nf>, **foreboding; portent**; evil portent

3 warning sign, premonitory sign, danger sign; preliminary sign *or* signal *or* token; **symptom,** early symptom, premonitory symptom, prodrome, prodroma, prodromata <pl>; **precursor** 816; **omen** 133.3,5; **handwriting on the wall**; straw in the wind; gathering clouds, clouds on the horizon; thundercloud, thunderhead; falling barometer *or* glass; storm *or* stormy petrel, **red light,** red flag, Very lights; quarantine flag, yellow flag, yellow jack; death's-head, skull *and* crossbones; **high sign** <nf>, **warning signal, alert,** red alert; siren, klaxon, tocsin, alarm bell, burglar alarm, car horn, fog horn; tattoo; early warning system

4 warner, cautioner, admonisher, monitor; prophet *or* messenger of doom, Cassandra, Jeremiah, Nostradamus, Ezekiel; **lookout, lookout man; sentinel, sentry; signalman,** signaler, flagman; lighthouse keeper

VERBS **5 warn, caution, advise, admonish; give warning,** give fair warning, utter a caveat, address a warning to, put a flea in one's ear <nf>, drop a hint, have a word with one, say a word to the wise; tip *and* tip off <nf>; notify, put on notice, give notice *or* advance notice *or* advance word; tell once *and* for all; issue an ultimatum; **threaten** 514.2; **alert,** warn against, put on one's guard, warn away *or* off; **give the high sign** <nf>; **put on alert,** cry havoc, sound the alarm 400.3

6 forewarn, prewarn, precaution, premonish; prenotify, tell in advance, give advance notice; **portend, forebode;** give a head's up

ADJS **7 warning,** cautioning, **cautionary; monitory,** monitorial, admonitory, admonishing, minatory; notifying, notificational; exemplary, deterrent

8 **forewarning, premonitory; portentous,** foreboding 133.16; **precautionary,** precautional; en garde; precursive, precursory, forerunning, prodromal, prodromic

400 ALARM

NOUNS 1 **alarm,** alarum, alarm signal *or* bell, **alert;** hue and cry; **red light,** danger signal, amber light, caution signal; **alarm button,** panic button <nf>, nurse's signal; **beeper,** buzzer; note of alarm; air-raid alarm; all clear; tocsin, alarm bell; signal of distress, SOS, Mayday, upside-down flag, flare; *sécurité* <Fr>, notice to mariners; storm warning, storm flag *or* pennant *or* cone, hurricane watch *or* warning *or* advisory, gale warning, small-craft warning *or* advisory, tornado watch *or* warning, winter storm watch *or* advisory, winter weather advisory, severe thunderstorm watch *or* warning; fog signal *or* alarm, foghorn, fog bell; burglar alarm; car alarm; fire alarm, fire bell, fire flag, still alarm; siren, whistle, horn, klaxon, hooter <Brit>; police whistle, watchman's rattle; alarm clock; five-minute gun, two-minute gun; lighthouse, beacon; blinking light, flashing light, occulting light

2 **false alarm,** cry of wolf; bugbear, bugaboo; bogy; flash in the pan *and* dud <nf>; false positive

VERBS 3 **alarm, alert, arouse,** put on the alert; **warn** 399.5; fly storm warnings; **sound the alarm,** give *or* raise *or* beat *or* turn in an alarm, ring *or* sound the tocsin, cry havoc, raise a hue *and* cry; give a false alarm, cry before one is hurt, **cry wolf;** frighten *or* scare out of one's wits *or* to death, **frighten,** startle 131.8

ADJS 4 **alarmed, aroused;** alerted; frit <Brit nf>, frightened to death *or* out of one's wits, **frightened; startled** 131.13

401 HASTE

<*rapidity of action*>

NOUNS 1 **haste, hurry, scurry, rush, race,** speed, dash, drive, scuttle, scamper, **scramble,** hustle <nf>, **bustle,** flutter, **flurry,** hurry-scurry, helter-skelter; no time to be lost; shotgun approach; express lane

2 **hastiness, hurriedness,** quickness, swiftness, expeditiousness, alacrity, promptness 330.3; **speed** 174.1; furiousness, feverishness; **precipitousness,** precipitance *or* precipitancy, precipitation; rapidity; suddenness, abruptness; **impetuousness** 365.2, impetuosity, **impulsiveness, rashness** 493, impulsivity; eagerness, zealousness, **overeagerness, overzealousness**

3 **hastening, hurrying,** festination, speeding, forwarding, quickening, hotfooting, **acceleration;** forced march, double time, double-quick time, double-quick; fast-forward; skedaddle <nf>

VERBS 4 **hasten,** haste, **hurry, accelerate, speed,** speed up, **hurry up,** hustle up <nf>, **rush,** quicken, hustle <nf>, bustle, bundle, precipitate, forward; **dispatch, expedite; whip,** whip along, spur, **urge** 375.14,16; push, press; crowd, stampede; **hurry on,** hasten on, drive on, hie on, push on, press on; **hurry along,** lollop <chiefly Brit>, rush along, speed along, **speed on its way; push through,** railroad <nf>, steamroll

5 **make haste, hasten,** festinate, **hurry, hurry up, race, run,** post, **rush, chase, tear, dash,** spurt, leap, plunge, **scurry,** hurry-scurry, **scamper, scramble, scuttle, hustle** <nf>, bundle, **bustle;** bestir oneself, move quickly 174.9; make for, hurry on, dash on, press *or* push on, crowd; double-time, go at the double; break one's neck *or* fall all over oneself <nf>; lose no time, not lose a moment; rush through, romp through, hurry through; dash off; make short *or* fast work of, make the best of one's time *or* way, think on one's

feet, make up for lost time; do on the run *or* on the fly

6 <nf terms> **step on it, snap to it,** hop to it, hotfoot, bear down on it, shake it up, **get moving** *or* **going,** get a move on, get cracking <chiefly Brit>, get *or* shake the lead out, get the lead out of one's ass, get one's ass in gear, give it the gun, hump, hump it, hump oneself, shag ass, tear ass, **get a hustle** *or* **wiggle on,** stir one's stumps, not spare the horses, barrel along, tear off, make tracks

7 **rush into, plunge into,** dive into, plunge, plunge ahead *or* headlong, cannonball; **not stop to think,** go off half-cocked *or* at half cock <nf>, leap before one looks, cross a bridge before one comes to it

8 **be in a hurry,** be under the gun <nf>, have no time to lose *or* spare, not have a moment to spare, hardly have time to breathe, work against time *or* the clock, work under pressure, have a deadline, do at the last moment

ADJS 9 **hasty, hurried,** festinate, **quick,** flying, **expeditious,** prompt 330.18; quick-and-dirty <nf>, **immediate,** instant, on the spot, precipitant; onrushing, **swift, speedy; urgent;** furious, feverish; slap-bang, slapdash, **cursory,** passing, cosmetic, snap <nf>, superficial; spur-of-the-moment, last-minute

10 **precipitate,** precipitant, precipitous; **sudden,** abrupt; **impetuous, impulsive, rash;** headlong, breakneck; breathless, panting

11 **hurried, rushed,** pushed, pressed, railroaded, crowded, **pressed for time,** hard-pushed *or* -pressed, hard-run; double-time, double-quick, on *or* at the double; fool-hasty

ADVS 12 **hastily, hurriedly, quickly; expeditiously,** promptly, with dispatch; all in one breath, in one word, in two words; apace, amain, hand over fist, **immediately,** instantly, in a second *or* split second *or* jiffy, at once, as soon as possible *or* **ASAP; swiftly, speedily,** on *or* at fast-forward; with haste, with great *or* all haste, in *or* with a rush, in a mad rush, at fever pitch; furiously, feverishly, in a sweat *or* lather of haste, hotfoot; by forced marches; **helter-skelter, hurry-scurry,** pellmell; slapdash, cursorily, superficially, on the run *or* fly, in passing, on the spur of the moment

13 **posthaste,** in posthaste; post, express, by express, by airmail, by return mail, by express mail; by cable, by telegraph, by fax

14 **in a hurry, in haste,** in hot haste, in all haste; in short order; against time, against the clock

15 **precipitately,** precipitantly, precipitously, slap-bang; **suddenly,** abruptly; **impetuously, impulsively, rashly; headlong,** headfirst, headforemost, head over heels, heels over head , *à corps perdu* <Fr>

16 <nf terms> **step on it!,** snap to it!, **make it snappy!, get a move on!,** get a wiggle on!, **chop-chop!, shake a leg!,** stir your stumps!, get the lead out!, **get moving!, get going!,** get cracking!, get with it!, hop to it!, move your tail!, move your fanny!, get on the ball!, don't spare the horses!

402 LEISURE

NOUNS 1 **leisure, ease, convenience,** freedom; retirement, semiretirement; rest, repose 20; **free time, spare time,** goof-off time <nf>, downtime, odd moments, idle hours; time to spare *or* burn *or* kill, time on one's hands, time at one's disposal *or* command, time to oneself; time, one's own sweet time <nf>; breathing room; all the time in the world; time off, holiday, vacation, furlough, sabbatical, leave; break, recess, breather, coffee break; day of rest; letup <nf>; couch potato

2 **leisureliness, unhurriedness,** unhastiness, hastelessness, relaxedness; **inactivity** 331; **slowness** 175; otiosity; deliberateness, deliberation; contentment

VERBS 3 **have time,** have time enough, have time to spare, have plenty of time, have nothing but time, be in no hurry; lounge, loll

4 **take one's leisure,** take one's ease, **take one's time, take one's own sweet time** <nf>, do at one's leisure *or* convenience *or* pleasure; go slow 175.6; ride the gravy train *and* lead the life of Riley <nf>, take time to smell the flowers *or* roses; put one's feet up, be a couch potato

ADJS 5 **leisure, leisured;** idle, unoccupied, free, open, spare; retired, semiretired, unemployed, in retirement; otiose; on vacation, on holiday; after-dinner

6 **leisurely, unhurried,** laid-back <nf>, unhasty, hasteless, easy, relaxed; sluggish, lazy; deliberate; inactive 331.17; **slow** 175.10

ADVS 7 **at leisure, at one's leisure, at one's convenience,** at one's own sweet time <nf>, when one gets around to it, when it is handy, when one has the time, when one has a minute to spare, when one has a moment to call one's own

403 ENDEAVOR

NOUNS 1 **endeavor,** effort, striving, struggle, strain; **all-out effort,** best effort, college try *or* old college try <nf>, valiant effort; **exertion** 725; determination, resolution 359; **enterprise** 330.7

2 **attempt, trial, effort, essay,** assay , first attempt, *coup d'essai* <Fr>; **endeavor, undertaking;** approach, move; coup, stroke 328.3, step; gambit, offer, **bid,** strong bid; experiment, tentative; tentation, trial and error

3 <nf terms> **try, whack, fling, shot, crack,** bash, belt, go, stab, leap, lick, rip, ripple, cut, hack, smack; last shot, swan song

4 **one's best, one's level best, one's utmost,** one's damndest *or* darndest <nf>, one's best effort *or* endeavor, the best one can, the best one knows how, all one can do, all one's got, all one's got in one, one's all <nf>, the top of one's bent, as much as in one lies

VERBS 5 **endeavor, strive, struggle,** strain, sweat, sweat blood, labor, get one's teeth into, come to grips with, take it on, make an all-out effort, move heaven *and* earth, **exert oneself,** apply oneself, use some elbow grease <nf>; spend oneself; seek, study, aim; resolve, be determined 359.8

6 **attempt, try, essay,** assay, offer; try one's hand *or* wings, try it on <chiefly Brit>, set about; **undertake** 404.3, **approach,** come to grips with, engage, take the bull by the horns; venture, venture on *or* upon, chance; **make an attempt** *or* **effort,** lift a finger *or* hand

7 <nf terms> **tackle, take on, make a try, give a try,** have a go <chiefly Brit>, take a shot *or* stab *or* crack *or* try *or* whack at; try on for size, **go for it,** go for the brass ring, **have a fling** *or* **go at,** give a fling *or* a go *or* a whirl, **make a stab at,** have a shot *or* stab *or* crack *or* try *or* whack at

8 **try to,** try *and* <nf>, **attempt to, endeavor to,** strive to, seek to, study to, aim to, venture to, dare to, pretend to

9 **try for, strive for,** strain for, struggle for, contend for, pull for <nf>, bid for, make a bid *or* strong bid for, make a play for <nf>

10 **see what one can do,** see what can be done, see if one can do, do what one can, use one's endeavor; try anything once; **try one's hand,** try one's luck, tempt fate; make a cautious *or* tentative move, experiment, feel one's way, test the waters, run it up the flagpole <nf>

11 **make a special effort, go out of the way,** go out of one's way, take special pains, **put oneself out,** put oneself out of the way, lay oneself out *and* fall *or* bend *or* lean over backward <nf>, fall all over oneself, trouble oneself, **go to the trouble,** take trouble, **take pains,** redouble one's efforts

12 **try hard, push** <nf>, make a bold push, **put one's back to** *or* **into,** put one's heart into, try until one is blue in the face, die trying, **try and try;** try, try again; exert oneself 725.9

13 **do one's best** *or* **level best, do one's utmost,** try one's best *or* utmost, **do**

all *or* **everything one can,** do the best one can, **do the best one knows how,** do all in one's power, do as much as in one lies, do what lies in one's power, do one's damnedest <nf>; put all one's strength into, put one's whole soul in, **strain every nerve; give it one's all**, go flat out <nf>; go for broke; be on one's mettle, **die trying**

14 <nf terms> **knock oneself out, break one's neck,** break *or* bust one's balls, bust a gut, bust one's ass *or* hump, rupture oneself, do it *or* know why not, do it *or* break a leg, do it *or* bust a gut, do *or* try one's damndest *or* darndest, go all out, go the limit, go for broke, shoot the works, give it all one's got, give it one's best shot, go for it

15 **make every effort, spare no effort** *or* **pains, go all lengths, go to great lengths,** go the whole length, go through fire *and* water, not rest, not relax, not slacken, move heaven *and* earth, leave no stone unturned, leave no avenue unexplored

ADJS 16 trial, tentative, experimental; venturesome, willing; determined, resolute 359.11; utmost, damndest

ADVS 17 **out for,** out to, trying for, **on the make** <nf>

18 **at the top of one's bent,** to one's utmost, as far as possible

404 UNDERTAKING

NOUNS 1 **undertaking, enterprise, operation,** work, **venture, project,** proposition *and* deal <nf>; matter at hand; **program, plan** 381; **affair, business, matter, task** 724.2, concern, interest; **initiative,** effort, attempt 403.2; **action** 328.3; **engagement, contract, obligation,** mission statement, **commitment** 436.2; *démarche* <Fr>

2 **adventure,** emprise, **mission;** quest, pilgrimage; expedition, exploration, escapade

VERBS 3 **undertake, assume,** accept, **take on, take upon oneself,** take in hand, take upon one's shoulders, take up, sign up, go with, **tackle,** attack; engage *or* contract *or* obligate *or* commit oneself; **put** *or* **set** *or* **turn one's hand to, engage in, devote oneself to, apply oneself to,** betake oneself to , address oneself to, give oneself up to; join oneself to, associate oneself with, take in hand, **come aboard** <nf>; busy oneself with 724.11; **take up,** move into, go into, **go in** *or* **out for** <nf>, **enter on** *or* **upon,** proceed to, embark in *or* upon, **venture upon,** go upon, launch, set forward, get going, get under way, initiate; set about, go about, lay about, go to do; **go** *or* **swing into action, set to, turn to, buckle to, fall to; pitch into** <nf>, plunge into, fall into, **launch into** *or* **upon;** go at, set at, have at <nf>, knuckle *or* buckle down to; put one's hand to the plow, put *or* lay one's shoulder to the wheel; take the bull by the horns; **endeavor, attempt**; dare, take a shot at

4 **have in hand, have one's hands in,** have on one's hands *or* shoulders

5 **be in progress** *or* **process,** be on the anvil, be in the fire, be in the works *or* hopper *or* pipeline <nf>, **be under way**

6 **bite off more than one can chew** <nf>, take on too much, overextend *or* overreach oneself, have too many irons in the fire, have too much on one's plate, stretch oneself too thin

ADJS 7 **undertaken, assumed,** accepted, **taken on** <nf>; **ventured,** attempted, chanced; **in hand,** on the anvil, in the fire, **in progress** *or* **process,** on one's plate, in the works *or* hopper *or* pipeline <nf>, on the agenda, **under way**; contractual

8 **enterprising,** venturesome, adventurous, plucky, keen, eager; resourceful, ambitious; pioneering, ground-breaking; avant-garde

405 PREPARATION

NOUNS 1 **preparation,** preparing, prep *and* prepping <nf>, **readying,** getting *or* making ready, makeready, taking measures; warm-up, getting in shape *or* condition; mobilization; walk-up, **run-up; prearrangement**

965, lead time, advance notice, warning, advance warning, alerting; **planning** 381.1; trial, dry run, **tryout** 942.3; **provision, arrangement;** preparatory *or* preliminary act *or* measure *or* step; **preliminary, preliminaries;** clearing the decks <nf>; **grounding,** propaedeutic, preparatory study *or* instruction, preparatory *or* prep school; basic training, familiarization, briefing; prerequisite; processing, treatment, pretreatment; equipment 385; training 568.3; manufacture; **spadework,** groundwork, foundation 901.6; pioneering, trailblazing, pushing the envelope <nf>; all-nighter

2 **fitting,** checking the fit, fit, fitting out; **conditioning; adaptation, adjustment,** tuning; **qualification,** capacitation, enablement; **equipment, furnishing** 385.1

3 <a preparation> **concoction,** decoction, *decoctum* <L>, brew, **confection;** solution; **composition, mixture** 797.5, combination 805

4 **preparedness, readiness; fitness,** fittedness, suitedness, suitableness, **suitability;** condition, trim; **qualification,** qualifiedness, credentials, record, track record <nf>; **competence** *or* competency, **ability, capability, proficiency,** mastery; ripeness, maturity, seasoning, fitness, tempering; emergency preparedness

5 **preparer,** preparator, preparationist; trainer, coach, instructor, mentor, teacher, tutor; **trailblazer, pathfinder; forerunner** 816.1; **paver of the way**, pioneer

VERBS **6** **prepare, make** *or* **get ready,** prep <nf>, do the prep work, trim , **ready, fix** <nf>; provide , **arrange; make preparations** *or* **arrangements,** take measures, sound the note of preparation, clear the decks <nf>, clear for action, settle preliminaries, tee up <nf>; mobilize, marshal, deploy, marshal *or* deploy one's forces *or* resources; **prearrange; plan; try out** 942.8; fix *or* ready up <nf>, put in *or* into shape; dress; treat, pretreat, process; cure, tan, taw; map out, sketch out, outline

7 **make up, get up, fix up** *and* rustle up <nf>; **concoct,** decoct, brew; **compound, compose, put together, mix;** make

8 **fit, condition, adapt, adjust,** suit, tune, attune, put in tune *or* trim *or* working order; customize; **qualify,** enable, capacitate; **equip,** fit out, supply, **furnish** 385.7,8

9 **prime, load,** charge, cock, set, precondition; wind, wind up; steam up, get up steam, warm up

10 **prepare to, get ready to,** get set for <nf>, fix to <nf>; be about to, be on the point of; ready oneself to, hold oneself in readiness

11 **prepare for, provide for,** arrange for, make arrangements *or* dispositions for, look to, look out for, see to, **make provision** *or* **due provision for;** provide against, make sure against, forearm, **provide for** *or* **against a rainy day,** prepare for the evil day; lay in provisions, lay up a store, keep as a nest egg, save to fall back upon, lay by, husband one's resources, salt *or* squirrel something away; set one's house in order, line up one's ducks

12 **prepare the way, pave the way,** smooth the path *or* road, **clear the way,** open the way, open the door to; build a bridge; **break the ice;** pioneer, go in advance, be the point, push the envelope, **blaze the trail; prepare the ground,** cultivate the soil, sow the seed; do the spadework, lay the groundwork *or* foundation, lay the first stone, provide the basis; lead up to

13 **prepare oneself,** brace oneself, **get ready, get set** <nf>, put one's house in order, strip for action, get into shape *or* condition, roll up one's sleeves, spit on one's hands, limber up, warm up, flex one's muscles, gird up one's loins, buckle on one's armor, get into harness, shoulder arms; sharpen one's tools, whet the knife *or* sword; psych oneself up <nf>; do one's homework; get one's house in order; **run up to,** build up to, gear up, tool up, rev up

14 **be prepared, be ready,** stand by, stand ready, hold oneself in readiness

15 <be fitted> **qualify, measure up,** meet the requirements, check out <nf>, have the credentials *or* qualifications *or* prerequisites; be up to *and* be just the ticket *and* fill the bill <nf>

ADJS **16 prepared, ready,** well-prepared, prepped <nf>, in readiness *or* ready state, all ready, good *and* ready, prepared *and* ready; psyched *or* pumped up <nf>, eager, keen, champing at the bit; alert, vigilant 339.13; **ripe, máture; set** *and* **all set** <nf>, on the mark *and* teed up <nf>; about to, fixing to <nf>; **prearranged; planned; primed,** loaded, cocked, **loaded for bear** <nf>; familiarized, briefed, informed, put into the picture <Brit nf>; groomed, coached; ready for anything; in the saddle, booted *and* spurred; armed *and* ready, in arms, up in arms, **armed** 460.14; in battle array, mobilized; **provided, equipped** 385.13; dressed; treated, pretreated, processed; cured, tanned, tawed; **readied,** available 221.12

17 fitted, adapted, adjusted, suited; qualified, fit, competent, able, capable, proficient; customized; checked out <nf>; well-qualified, well-fitted, well-suited

18 prepared for, ready for, alert for, set *or* all set for <nf>; loaded for, primed for; up for <nf>; equal to, up to

19 ready-made, ready-formed, ready-mixed, ready-furnished, ready-dressed; ready-built, prefabricated, prefab <nf>, preformed; ready-to-wear, ready-for-wear, off-the-rack; ready-cut, cut-and-dried; convenient, convenience, fast-food; ready-to-cook, precooked, oven-ready; instant

20 preparatory, preparative; propaedeutic; prerequisite; provident, provisional

ADJS, ADVS **21 in readiness, in store, in reserve;** in anticipation

22 in preparation, in course of preparation, **in progress** *or* **process,** under way, **going on,** in embryo, **in production,** on stream, under construction, **in the works** *or* hopper *or* pipeline <nf>, on the way, **in the making, in hand,** on the anvil, on the fire, in the oven; under revision; brewing, forthcoming

23 afoot, on foot, afloat, astir

406 UNPREPAREDNESS

NOUNS **1 unpreparedness, unreadiness,** unprovidedness, nonpreparedness, nonpreparation, lack of preparation; vulnerability 1006.4; extemporaneousness, improvisation, ad lib <nf>, planlessness, disorganization; **unfitness,** unfittedness, unsuitedness, unsuitableness, **unsuitability, unqualifiedness,** unqualification, lack of credentials, poor track record <nf>, **disqualification,** incompetence *or* incompetency, incapability; rustiness

2 improvidence, thriftlessness, unthriftiness, poor husbandry, lax stewardship; **shiftlessness,** fecklessness, thoughtlessness, heedlessness; happy-go-luckiness; hastiness 401.2; negligence 340.1

3 <raw *or* original condition> **naturalness,** inartificiality; **natural state,** nature, **state of nature,** nature in the raw; pristineness, intactness, virginity; defenselessness; natural man; artlessness 416

4 undevelopment, nondevelopment; **immaturity,** immatureness, callowness, unfledgedness, cubbishness, **rawness, unripeness, greenness; unfinish,** unfinishedness, unpolishedness, **unrefinement, uncultivation; crudity,** crudeness, **rudeness, coarseness,** roughness, the rough; **oversimplification,** oversimplicity, simplism, reductionism

5 raw material; crude, crude stuff <nf>; ore, rich ore, rich vein; unsorted *or* unanalyzed mass; rough diamond, **diamond in the rough;** unlicked cub; **virgin soil,** untilled ground

VERBS **6 be unprepared** *or* **unready,** not be ready, lack preparation; go off half-cocked *or* at half cock <nf>; be taken unawares *or* aback, be blindsided <nf>, be caught napping, be caught with one's pants down

<nf>, be surprised, drop one's guard; **extemporize,** improvise, ad-lib *and* play by ear <nf>; have no plan, be innocent of forethought; improvise

7 **make no provision,** take no thought of tomorrow *or* the morrow, seize the day, *carpe diem* <L, Horace>, let tomorrow take care of itself, live for the day, live like the grasshopper, live from hand to mouth; make it up as one goes along

ADJS 8 **unprepared, unready,** unprimed; surprised, caught short, caught napping, caught with one's pants down <nf>, taken by surprise, taken aback, taken unawares, blindsided <nf>, caught off balance, caught off base <nf>, tripped up; **unarranged,** unorganized, haphazard; makeshift, rough-and-ready, **extemporaneous,** extemporized, improvised, ad-lib *and* off the top of one's head <nf>; spontaneous, ad hoc; impromptu, snap <nf>; **unmade,** unmanufactured, unconcocted, unhatched, uncontrived, undevised, unplanned, unpremeditated, undeliberated, unstudied; hasty, precipitate 401.10; unbegun

9 **unfitted,** unfit, ill-fitted, unsuited, unadapted, unqualified, disqualified, incompetent, incapable; **unequipped, unfurnished,** unarmed, ill-equipped, ill-furnished, **unprovided,** ill-provided 992.12

10 **raw, crude; uncooked,** unbaked, unboiled; underdone, undercooked, rare, red; half-baked

11 **immature, unripe,** underripe, unripened, impubic, **raw, green,** callow, wet behind the ears, cub, cubbish, unfledged, fledgling, unseasoned, unmellowed, vulnerable; ungrown, half-grown, adolescent, juvenile, puerile, boyish, girlish, inchoate; undigested, ill-digested; half-baked <nf>; half-cocked *and* at half cock <nf>, wet behind the ears

12 **undeveloped, unfinished,** unlicked, unformed; unfashioned, unwrought, unlabored, unworked, unprocessed, untreated; unblown; uncut, unhewn; **underdeveloped;** backward, arrested, stunted; **crude, rude, coarse, unpolished, unrefined; uncultivated, uncultured; rough,** roughcast, roughhewn, **in the rough; rudimentary,** rudimental; embryonic, in embryo, fetal, *in ovo* <L>; **oversimple, simplistic,** reductive, reductionistic, unsophisticated; untrained; rusty, unpracticed; scratch <nf>

13 <in the raw *or* original state> **natural, native, in a state of nature,** in the raw; inartificial, artless 416.5; virgin, virginal, pristine, untouched, unsullied

14 **fallow,** untilled, uncultivated, unsown, unworked

15 **improvident, prodigal,** unproviding; **thriftless, unthrifty,** uneconomical; grasshopper; hand-to-mouth; **shiftless, feckless, thoughtless, heedless;** happy-go-lucky; negligent 340.10

407 ACCOMPLISHMENT

<act of accomplishing; entire performance>

NOUNS 1 **accomplishment, achievement, fulfillment, performance, execution, effectuation,** implementation, carrying out *or* through, **discharge, dispatch, consummation, realization, attainment,** production, fruition; **success** 409; track record *or* track <nf>; *fait accompli* <Fr>, accomplished fact, done deal <nf>; mission accomplished

2 **completion,** completing, **finish,** finishing, **conclusion, end,** ending, **termination,** terminus, **close, windup** <nf>, rounding off *or* out, topping off, wrapping up, wrap-up, finalization; **perfection,** culmination 1002.3; ripeness, maturity, maturation, full development; tipping point

3 **finishing touch,** final touch, last touch, last stroke, final *or* finishing stroke, finisher <nf>, craftsmanship, icing the cake, the icing on the cake; copestone, capstone, crown, crowning of the edifice; capper <nf>, climax 198.2

VERBS 4 **accomplish, achieve, effect, effectuate, compass, consummate, do, execute, produce, deliver, make,** enact, **perform, discharge, fulfill, realize, attain,** run with *and* hack *and* swing <nf>; **work,** work out; **dispatch, dispose of,** knock off <nf>, polish off <nf>, take care of <nf>, **deal with,** put away, make short work of; succeed, manage 409.12; come through *and* do the job <nf>, **do** *or* **turn the trick** <nf>

5 **bring about, bring to pass,** bring to effect, **bring to a happy issue; implement, carry out, carry through,** carry into execution; **bring off, carry off, pull off** <nf>; **put through,** get through, **put over** *or* **across** <nf>; come through with <nf>

6 **complete, perfect, finish, finish off, conclude, terminate, end,** bring to a close, carry to completion, prosecute to a conclusion; **get through, get done;** come off of, get through with, get it over, get it over with, **finish up;** clean up *and* wind up *and* button up *and* sew up *and* wrap up *and* mop up <nf>, close up *or* out; put the lid on *and* call it a day <nf>; **round off** *or* **out, wind up** <nf>, **top off;** top out, crown, cap 198.9; climax, culminate; give the finishing touches *or* strokes, **put the finishing touches** *or* **strokes on**, lick *or* whip into shape, finalize, put the icing on the cake; autocomplete

7 **do to perfection, do up brown** <nf>, **do to a turn,** do to a T *or* to a frazzle *or* down to the ground <nf>, not do by halves, do oneself proud <nf>, use every trick in the book, leave no loose ends, leave nothing hanging; go all lengths, go to all lengths, go the whole length *or* way, go the limit *and* go whole hog *and* go all out *and* shoot the works *and* go for broke <nf>

8 **ripen,** ripe <nf>, **mature,** maturate; bloom, blow, blossom, flourish; come to fruition, bear fruit; **mellow;** grow up, reach maturity, reach its season; come *or* draw to a head; bring to maturity, bring to a head

ADJS 9 **completing,** completive, completory, **finishing,** consummative, culminating, terminative, conclusive, **concluding,** fulfilling, finalizing, crowning; ultimate, **last, final,** terminal

10 **accomplished, achieved, effected,** effectuated, implemented, **consummated, executed, discharged, fulfilled, realized,** consummate, compassed, **attained; dispatched, disposed of,** set at rest; wrought, wrought out

11 **completed, done, finished, concluded, terminated, ended,** finished up; signed, sealed, *and* delivered, cleaned up *and* wound up *and* sewed *or* sewn up *and* wrapped up *and* mopped up <nf>; washed up <nf>, **through,** done with; all over with, all said *and* done, all over but the shouting; perfective

12 **complete, perfect, consummate,** polished; exhaustive, thorough 794.10; fully realized

13 **ripe, mature,** matured, maturated, seasoned; blooming, abloom; **mellow,** full-grown, fully developed

ADVS 14 **to completion,** to the end, down-the-line, to the full, to the limit; to a turn, to a T <nf>, to a finish, to a frazzle <nf>

408 NONACCOMPLISHMENT

NOUNS 1 **nonaccomplishment, nonachievement, nonperformance,** inexecution, nonexecution, nondischarging, **noncompletion,** nonconsummation, nonfulfillment, unfulfillment; nonfeasance, omission; **neglect** 340; loose ends, rough edges; endless task, work of Penelope, Sisyphean labor *or* toil *or* task; **disappointment** 132; **failure** 410

VERBS 2 neglect, leave undone 340.7, fail 410.9; be disappointed 132.4

ADJS 3 **unaccomplished, unachieved, unperformed,** unexecuted, undischarged, unfulfilled, unconsummated, unrealized, unattained; **unfinished, uncompleted, undone;**

open-ended; **neglected** 340.14; **disappointed** 132.5

409 SUCCESS

NOUNS **1** **success, successfulness,** fortunate outcome, prosperous issue, favorable termination; **prosperity** 1010; accomplishment 407; **victory** 411; the big time

2 sure success, foregone conclusion, sure-fire proposition <nf>; **winner** *and* **natural** <nf>; shoo-in *and* **sure thing** *and* sure bet *and* **cinch** *and* lead-pipe cinch <nf>

3 **great success, triumph,** resounding triumph, brilliant success, striking success, **meteoric** success; flying colors; **stardom; success story**; best seller; brief *or* momentary success, nine days' wonder, flash in the pan, fad, next big thing

4 <nf terms> smash, hit, smash hit, gas, gasser, blast, boffo, showstopper, barn-burner, howling *or* roaring success, one for the book, wow, wowser, sensation, overnight sensation, sensaysh, phenom, sockeroo

5 **score, hit, bull's-eye;** goal, touchdown; slam, grand slam; strike; hole, hole in one; home run, homer <nf>

6 <successful person> **winner,** star, star in the firmament, success, superstar *and* megastar <nf>; prizewinner, lottery winner; phenom *and* comer <nf>, whiz kid, VIP; **victor** 411.2

VERBS **7** **succeed, prevail,** be successful, be crowned with success, meet with success, do very well, do famously, deliver, come through *and* make a go of it <nf>; **go, come off,** go off; **prosper** 1010.7; fare well, work well, do *or* work wonders, go to town *or* go great guns <nf>; make a hit <nf>, click *and* connect <nf>, **catch on** *and* take <nf>, catch fire, have legs <nf>; **go over** *and* go over big *or* with a bang <nf>; pass, graduate, qualify, win one's spurs *or* wings, get one's credentials, be blooded; pass with flying colors

8 **achieve one's purpose, gain one's end** *or* **ends,** secure one's object, attain one's objective, do what one set out to do, reach one's goal, bring it off, pull it off *and* hack it *and* swing it <nf>; make one's point; play it *or* handle it just right <nf>, not put a foot wrong, play it like a master

9 **score a success,** score, notch one up <nf>, hit it, hit the mark, ring the bell <nf>, turn up trumps, break the bank *or* make a killing <nf>, hit the jackpot <nf>

10 **make good, come through, achieve success,** make a success, have a good thing going <nf>, **make it** <nf>, get into the zone *or* bubble <nf>, wing *and* cruise, <nf>, hit one's stride, **make one's mark, give a good account of oneself,** bear oneself with credit, do all right by oneself *and* **do oneself proud,** make out like a bandit <nf>; **advance, progress,** make one's way, make headway, **get on,** come on <nf>, **get ahead** <nf>; go places, **go far;** rise, **rise in the world,** work one's way up, step up, come *or* move up in the world, claw *or* scrabble one's way up, mount the ladder of success, pull oneself up by one's bootstraps; **arrive,** get there <nf>, make the scene <nf>; come out on top, come out on top of the heap <nf>; **be a success,** have it made *or* hacked *or* wrapped up <nf>, have the world at one's feet, eat *or* live high on the hog <nf>; **make a noise in the world** <nf>, cut a swath, set the world *or* river *or* Thames on fire; break through, score *or* make a breakthrough

11 **succeed with,** crown with success; **make a go of it; accomplish,** compass, **achieve** 407.4; **bring off, carry off, pull off** <nf>, turn *or* do the trick <nf>, **put through,** bring through; **put over** *or* **across** <nf>; get away with it *and* get by <nf>

12 **manage, contrive, succeed in; make out, get on** *or* **along** <nf>, come on *or* along <nf>, go on; **scrape along,** worry along, **muddle through** <Brit>, get by, **manage somehow; make it** <nf>,

make the grade, cut the mustard *and* hack it <nf>; **clear,** clear the hurdle; **negotiate** <nf>, **engineer; swing** <nf>, put over <nf>, put through

13 **win through, win out** <nf>, come through <nf>, rise to the occasion, beat the game *and* beat the system <nf>; **triumph** 411.3; weather out, **weather the storm,** live through, keep one's head above water; come up fighting *or* smiling, not know when one is beaten, persevere 360.2

ADJS 14 **successful,** succeeding, crowned with success; **prosperous,** fortunate 1010.14; **triumphant;** ahead of the game, out in front, on top, sitting on top of the world *and* sitting pretty <nf>, on top of the heap <nf>; assured of success, surefire, made; coming *and* on the up-and-up <nf>

ADVS 15 **successfully,** swimmingly <nf>, well, to some purpose, to good purpose; beyond all expectation, beyond one's fondest dreams, from rags to riches, with flying colors

410 FAILURE

NOUNS 1 **failure, unsuccessfulness,** unsuccess, successlessness, nonsuccess; no go <nf>; ill success; futility, uselessness 391; **defeat** 412; losing game, **no-win situation;** nonaccomplishment 408; **bankruptcy** 625.3

2 <nf terms> **flop,** flopperoo, megaflop, gigaflop, **bust,** frost, **fizzle,** lemon, clinker, dud, non-starter, **loser, washout,** turkey, bomb, flat failure, dull thud, total loss, black mark; game over; the pits

3 **collapse, crash,** smash, comedown, breakdown, derailment, **fall,** pratfall <nf>, stumble, tumble, **downfall,** cropper <chiefly Brit nf>; nose dive *and* tailspin <nf>; deflation, bursting of the bubble, letdown, **disappointment** 132

4 **miss,** near-miss; **slip, slipup** <nf>, slip 'twixt cup *and* lip; **error, mistake** 975.3

5 **abortion, miscarriage,** miscarrying, abortive attempt, vain attempt; wild-goose chase, merry chase; **misfire, flash in the pan,** wet squib, malfunction, glitch <nf>; **dud** <nf>; **flunk** <nf>, **washout** <nf>

6 **fiasco, botch,** botch-up, cock-up *and* balls-up <Brit nf>, bungle, hash, mess, muddle, foozle *and* bollix *and* bitch-up *and* screw-up *and* fuck-up <nf>

7 <unsuccessful person> **failure,** flash in the pan; bankrupt 625.4

8 <nf terms> **loser, non-starter,** born loser, **flop,** washout, false alarm, **dud,** also-ran, bum, dull tool, bust, schlemiel, turkey, hopeless case; underdog

VERBS 9 **fail,** be unsuccessful, fail of success, not work *and* not come off <nf>, come to grief, **lose,** not make the grade, go nowhere, be found wanting, not come up to the mark; not pass, **flunk** *and* **flunk out** <nf>; go to the wall, **go on the rocks;** labor in vain 391.8; come away empty-handed; tap out <nf>, go bankrupt 625.7

10 <nf terms> **lose out,** get left, **not make it,** not hack it, not get to first base, drop the ball, go for a Burton *and* come a cropper <Brit>, **flop,** flummox, fall flat on one's ass, lay an egg, go over like a lead balloon, draw a blank, bomb, drop a bomb; fold, fold up; take it on the chin, take the count; crap out; strike out, fan, whiff

11 **sink, founder,** go down, go under <nf>, go south; **slip,** go downhill, be on the skids <nf>

12 **fall, fall down** <nf>, fall *or* drop by the wayside, fall flat, fall flat on one's face; fall down on the job <nf>; **fall short, fall through,** fall to the ground; fall between two stools; **fall dead; collapse,** fall in; **crash,** go to smash <nf>

13 **come to nothing,** hang up *and* get nowhere <nf>; **poop out** *and* go phut <nf>; be all over *or* up with; fail miserably *or* ignominiously; fizz out *and* **fizzle** *and* **fizzle out** *and* peter out *and* poop out <nf>; **misfire,** flash in the pan, hang fire; **blow up, blow up in one's face, explode,**

end *or* **go up in smoke,** go up like a rocket *and* come down like a stick

14 miss, miss the mark, miss one's aim; slip, slip up <nf>; goof <nf>, blunder, foozle <nf>, **err** 975.9; **botch, bungle** 414.11; waste one's effort, run around in circles, spin one's wheels

15 miscarry, abort, be stillborn, die aborning; **go amiss,** go astray, **go wrong,** go on a wrong tack, take a wrong turn, derail, go off the rails

16 stall, stick, die, go dead, **conk out** <nf>, sputter *and* stop, run out of gas *or* steam, come to a shuddering halt, come to a dead stop

17 flunk *or* **flunk out** <nf>; **fail,** pluck *and* plough <Brit nf>, bust *and* wash out <nf>, bomb <nf>, flush it <nf>

ADJS **18 unsuccessful,** successless, failing; failed, manqué <Fr>, stickit; **unfortunate** 1011.14; **abortive,** miscarrying, miscarried, stillborn, died aborning; fruitless, bootless, no-win <nf>, futile, useless 391.9; lame, **ineffectual,** ineffective, inefficacious, of no effect; malfunctioning, glitchy <nf>

ADVS **19 unsuccessfully,** successlessly, **without success;** fruitlessly, bootlessly, ineffectually, ineffectively, inefficaciously, lamely; to little *or* no purpose, **in vain**

411 VICTORY

NOUNS **1 victory, triumph, conquest,** subduing, subdual; a feather in one's cap <nf>; total victory, grand slam; **championship,** crown, laurels, cup, trophy, belt, blue ribbon, first prize, flying colors; V-for-victory sign *or* V-sign, raised arms; victory lap; **winning,** win <nf>; knockout *or* KO <nf>; easy victory, walkover *and* walkaway <nf>, pushover *and* picnic <nf>; runaway victory, laugher *and* romp *and* shellacking <nf>; landslide victory, landslide; Pyrrhic victory, Cadmean victory; moral victory; winning streak <nf>; winning ways, triumphalism; **success** 409; ascendancy 417.6; mastery 612.2

2 victor, winner, victress, victrix, triumpher; **conqueror,** defeater, **vanquisher,** subduer, subjugator, *conquistador* <Sp>; top dog <nf>; master, master of the situation; hero, conquering hero; champion, champ *and* number one <nf>; easy winner, sure winner, shoo-in <nf>; pancratiast; runner-up

VERBS **3 triumph, prevail, be victorious,** come out ahead, come out on top <nf>, clean up, chain victory to one's car; **win, gain, capture, carry;** win out <nf>, **win through,** carry it, carry off *or* away; **win** *or* **carry** *or* **gain the day,** win the battle, come out first, finish in front, make a killing <nf>, remain in possession of the field; get *or* have the last laugh; **win the prize,** win the palm *or* bays *or* laurels, bear the palm, take the cake <nf>, win one's spurs *or* wings; fluke *and* win by a fluke <nf>; **win by a nose** *and* nose out *and* edge out <nf>; **succeed;** break the record, set a new mark <nf>

4 win hands down *and* win going away <nf>, win in a canter *and* walk *and* waltz <nf>, romp *or* breeze *or* waltz home <nf>, **walk off** *or* **away with,** waltz off with <nf>, walk off with the game, **walk over** <nf>; have the game in one's own hands, have it all one's way; **take** *or* **carry by storm,** sweep aside all obstacles, sweep, carry all before one, make short work of

5 defeat 412.6, **triumph over, prevail over,** best, **beat** <nf>, **get the better** *or* **best of; surmount, overcome,** outmatch, rise above

6 gain the ascendancy, come out on top <nf>, **get the advantage, gain the upper** *or* **whip hand,** dominate the field, get the edge on *or* jump on *or* drop on <nf>, get a leg up on <nf>, get a stranglehold on

ADJS **7 victorious, triumphant,** triumphal, **winning, prevailing;** conquering, vanquishing, defeating, overcoming; ahead of the game, ascendant, in the ascendant, in ascendancy, sitting on top of the world *and* sitting pretty <nf>, dominant

612.17; successful; flushed with success *or* victory

8 **undefeated, unbeaten, unvanquished, unconquered,** unsubdued, unquelled, unbowed

ADVS 9 **triumphantly,** victoriously, **in triumph;** by a mile

412 DEFEAT

NOUNS 1 **defeat; beating,** drubbing, thrashing; clobbering *and* hiding *and* lathering *and* whipping *and* lambasting *and* trimming *and* licking <nf>, trouncing; **vanquishment, conquest, conquering,** mastery, subjugation, subduing, subdual; **overthrow,** overturn, overcoming; **fall, downfall,** collapse, smash, crash, **undoing, ruin,** debacle, derailing, derailment; **destruction** 395; deathblow, quietus; Waterloo; failure 410

2 **discomfiture, rout, repulse,** rebuff; **frustration,** bafflement, confusion; **checkmate,** check, balk, foil ; **reverse,** reversal, **setback**

3 **utter defeat,** total defeat, overwhelming defeat, crushing defeat, smashing defeat, decisive defeat; no contest; **smearing** *and* **pasting** *and* creaming *and* **clobbering** *and* **shellacking** *and* whopping *and* whomping <nf>; whitewash *or* **whitewashing** <nf>, **shutout**

4 **ignominious defeat,** abject defeat, inglorious defeat, disastrous defeat, utter rout, bitter defeat, stinging defeat, embarrassing defeat

5 **loser,** defeatee <nf>; the vanquished; good loser, game loser, sport *or* **good sport** <nf>; poor sport, poor loser; **underdog, also-ran;** booby *and* duck <nf>; stooge *and* fall guy <nf>; victim 96.11

VERBS 6 **defeat, worst, best, get the better** *or* **best of,** be too good for, be too much for, be more than a match for; **outdo,** outgeneral, outmaneuver, outclass, outshine, outpoint, outsail, outrun, outfight, etc; **triumph over; knock on the head,** deal a deathblow to, put *hors de combat*; undo, ruin, destroy 395.10; beat by a nose *and* nose out *and* edge out <nf>

7 **overcome,** surmount; **overpower, overmaster,** overmatch; **overthrow, overturn,** overset; put the skids to <nf>; **upset,** trip, trip up, lay by the heels, send flying *or* sprawling; silence, floor, deck, make bite the dust; overcome oneself, master oneself; kick the habit <nf>

8 **overwhelm,** whelm, snow under <nf>, overbear, defeat utterly, deal a crushing *or* smashing defeat; **discomfit, rout, put to rout,** put to flight, scatter, stampede, panic; confound; put out of court

9 <nf terms> **clobber, trim, skin alive, beat,** skunk, drub, massacre, marmelize <Brit>, lick, whip, thrash, knock off, trim, hide, cut to pieces, run rings *or* circles around, throw for a loss, lather, trounce, **lambaste,** skin alive; fix, settle, settle one's hash, make one say 'uncle,' do in, lick to a frazzle, beat all hollow, beat one's brains out, cook one's goose, make hamburger *or* mincemeat out of, mop up the floor with, sandbag, banjax, bulldoze, steamroller, **smear,** paste, cream, **shellac,** whup, whop, whomp, shut out

10 **conquer, vanquish,** quell, **suppress, put down, subdue, subjugate,** put under the yoke, master; **reduce,** prostrate, fell, **flatten, break, smash, crush, humble,** bend, **bring one to his knees;** roll *or* trample in the dust, tread *or* trample underfoot, trample down, ride down, ride *or* run roughshod over, override; have one's way with

11 **thwart, frustrate,** dash, check, deal a check to, checkmate 1012.15

12 **lose,** lose out <nf>, lose the day, come off second best, **get** *or* **have the worst of it, meet one's Waterloo; fall,** succumb, tumble, bow, go down, go under, **bite** *or* **lick the dust,** take the count <nf>; snatch defeat from the jaws of victory; throw in the towel, say 'uncle'; have enough

ADJS 13 **lost,** unwon

14 **defeated, worsted, bested, outdone; beaten, discomfited,** put to

rout, **routed,** scattered, stampeded, panicked; confounded; **overcome, overthrown,** upset, overturned, overmatched, **overpowered, overwhelmed,** whelmed, **overmastered,** overborne, overridden; **fallen,** down; floored, silenced; **undone, done for** <nf>, **ruined,** kaput *and* on the skids <nf>, *hors de combat* <Fr>; all up with <nf>

15 <nf terms> **beat, clobbered, licked, whipped,** trimmed, sandbagged, banjaxed, done in, lathered, creamed, shellacked, trounced, lambasted, settled, fixed; skinned alive; thrown for a loss

16 **shut out,** skunked *and* blanked *and* whitewashed <nf>, scoreless, not on the scoreboard

17 **conquered, vanquished,** quelled, suppressed, put down, **subdued, subjugated,** mastered; **reduced,** prostrate *or* prostrated, felled, **flattened,** smashed, **crushed,** broken; **humbled,** brought to one's knees

18 **irresistible, overpowering, overcoming, overwhelming, overmastering,** overmatching, avalanchine

413 SKILL

NOUNS 1 **skill,** skillfulness, **expertness, expertise, proficiency,** callidity , craft, moxie <nf>, **cleverness; dexterity,** dexterousness *or* dextrousness; **adroitness,** address, **adeptness,** deftness, handiness, hand, practical ability; coordination, timing; quickness, readiness; **competence,** capability, capacity, ability; efficiency; **facility, prowess;** grace, style, finesse; **tact, tactfulness, diplomacy;** *savoir-faire* <Fr>; **artistry;** artfulness; **craftsmanship,** workmanship, artisanship; **know-how** *and* savvy *and* bag of tricks <nf>; technical skill, **technique, touch,** technical brilliance, technical mastery, **virtuosity,** bravura, wizardry; brilliance 920.2; cunning 415; **ingenuity,** ingeniousness, resource, resourcefulness, wit; **mastery,** mastership, **command,** control, grip; steady hand; marksmanship, seamanship, airmanship, horsemanship, etc

2 **agility, nimbleness, spryness,** lightness, featliness

3 **versatility, ambidexterity,** many-sidedness, all-roundedness <nf>, Renaissance versatility; **adaptability,** adjustability, flexibility; broad-gauge, many hats; Renaissance man *or* woman

4 **talent, flair,** strong flair, **gift, endowment,** dowry, dower, natural gift *or* endowment, **genius,** instinct, **faculty,** bump <nf>; **power, ability, capability, capacity,** potential; caliber; **forte,** speciality, métier, long suit, strong point, strong suit, strength; **equipment, qualification;** talents, powers, naturals , parts; the goods *and* the stuff *and* the right stuff *and* what it takes *and* the makings <nf>

5 **aptitude,** inborn *or* innate aptitude, innate ability, genius, aptness, felicity, flair; **bent, turn,** propensity, **leaning,** inclination, tendency; turn for, capacity for, gift for, genius for; feeling for, good head for, an eye for, an ear for, a hand for, a way with

6 **knack, art, hang, trick,** way; **touch,** feel

7 **art, science, craft; skill; technique,** technic, **technics,** technology, technical knowledge *or* skill, technical know-how <nf>; **mechanics,** mechanism; method

8 **accomplishment, acquirement, attainment;** finish; coup, feat, clincher, classic; hit, smash hit

9 **experience, practice,** practical knowledge *or* skill, hands-on experience <nf>, field-work; background, past experience, seasoning, tempering; backstory; **worldly wisdom,** knowledge of the world, episteme, **sophistication;** sagacity 920.4

10 **masterpiece, masterwork,** *chef d'œuvre* <Fr>; **master stroke,** *coup de maître* <Fr>; **feat,** *tour de force* <Fr>, *pièce de résistance* <Fr>, magnum opus, classic, treasure, work of art, epic, crème de la crème, artistry

11 **expert, adept,** proficient, genius; **artist, craftsman,** artisan, skilled

workman, journeyman; technician; seasoned *or* experienced hand; shark *or* sharp *or* sharpy *and* no slouch *and* tough act to follow <nf>; graduate; **professional, pro** <nf>; **jack-of-all-trades,** all-rounder, Renaissance man *or* woman, handy man; wordsmith <etc.>; **authority,** maven <nf>, know-it-all <nf>; professor; **consultant,** expert consultant, specialist, attaché, technical adviser; counselor, adviser, mentor; boffin <Brit nf>, pundit, savant 929.3; diplomatist, diplomat; politician, statesman, statesperson, elder statesman; connoisseur, cognoscente; *cordon bleu* <Fr>; marksman, crack shot, dead shot; walking encyclopedia <nf>, illuminati

12 **talented person, talent,** man *or* woman of parts, gifted person, prodigy, natural <nf>, **genius,** mental genius, intellectual genius, intellectual prodigy, mental giant; rocket scientist *and* brain surgeon <nf>; phenom <nf>; gifted child, **child prodigy,** wunderkind, whiz kid *and* boy wonder <nf>; polymath; one-trick pony

13 **master, past master**, grand master; master hand, world-class performer, champion, **good hand,** dab hand <Brit nf>, skilled *or* practiced hand, practitioner, specialist; first chair; **prodigy; wizard,** magician; **virtuoso;** maestro; **genius,** man *or* woman of genius, paragon; mastermind; master spirit, mahatma, sage 920.17

14 <nf terms> **ace, star, superstar, crackerjack,** dab, great, all-time great, topnotcher, first-rater, whiz, flash, hot stuff, pisser, piss-cutter, pistol, no slouch, world-beater, hot rock, the one who wrote the book, right person for the job, smart cookie; geek, nerd

15 **champion,** champ <nf>, victor, title-holder, world champion; **record holder,** world-record holder; laureate; medal winner, Olympic medal winner, medalist, award winner, prizeman, prizetaker, **prizewinner**, titleholder**;** most valuable player *or* MVP; hall of famer

16 **veteran,** vet <nf>, seasoned *or* grizzled veteran, **old pro** <nf>; **old hand, old-timer** <nf> one of the old guard, old stager <Brit>; old campaigner, war-horse *or* old war-horse <nf>; salt *and* old salt *and* old sea dog <nf>, shellback <nf>

17 **sophisticate,** man of experience, **man of the world;** slicker *and* city slicker <nf>, man-about-town; **cosmopolitan,** cosmopolite, citizen of the world

VERBS 18 **excel in** *or* **at, shine in** *or* **at** <nf>, be master of; write the book <nf>, have a good command of, feel comfortable with, be at home in; **have a gift** *or* **flair** *or* **talent** *or* **bent** *or* **faculty** *or* **turn for,** have a bump for <nf>, be a natural *and* be cut out *or* born to be <nf>, **have a good head for,** have an ear for, have an eye for, be born for, show aptitude *or* talent for, have something to spare; have the knack *or* touch, have a way with, have the right touch, have the hang of it, have a lot going for one <nf>, be able to do it blindfolded *or* standing on one's head <nf>; have something *or* plenty on the ball <nf>

19 **know backwards** *and* **forwards, know one's stuff** *or* **know one's onions** <nf>**, know the ropes** *and* **know all the ins** *and* **outs** <nf>, know from A to Z *or* alpha to omega, know like the back of one's hand *or* a book, know from the ground up, know all the tricks *or* moves, know all the tricks of the trade, know all the moves of the game; **know what's what, know a thing** *or* **two, know what it's all about, know the score** *and* know all the answers <nf>; have savvy <nf>; **know one's way about,** know the ways of the world, have been around <nf>, have been around the block <nf>, have been through the mill <nf>, have cut one's wisdom teeth *or* eyeteeth <nf>, be long in the tooth, **not be born yesterday;** get around <nf>

20 **exercise skill,** handle oneself well, demonstrate one's ability, **strut one's stuff** *and* hotdog *and*

grandstand *and* showboat <nf>, show expertise; cut one's coat according to one's cloth, play one's cards well

21 **be versatile,** double in brass *and* wear more than one hat <nf>

ADJS 22 **skillful, good,** goodish, excellent, **expert, proficient; dexterous,** callid , good at, **adroit, deft, adept, coordinated,** well-coordinated, **apt,** no mean, **handy;** quick, ready; **clever,** cute *and* slick *and* slick as a whistle <nf>, neat, clean; fancy, graceful, stylish; some *or* quite some *or* quite a *or* every bit a <nf>; **masterly, masterful;** magistral, magisterial; authoritative, consummate, professional; the compleat *or* the complete; crack *or* crackerjack <nf>, ace, first-rate, supreme; whiz-kid <nf>; **virtuoso,** bravura, technically superb; **brilliant** 920.14; cunning 415.12; tactful, diplomatic, politic, statesmanlike; **ingenious,** resourceful, daedal, Daedalian; **artistic; workmanlike, well-done**

23 **agile, nimble, spry,** sprightly, fleet, featly, peart <nf>, light, graceful, nimble-footed, light-footed, sure-footed; nimble-fingered, neat-fingered, neat-handed

24 **competent, capable, able, efficient, qualified, fit, fitted, suited, worthy;** journeyman; fit *or* fitted for; **equal to, up to;** up to snuff <nf>, up to the mark <nf>, *au fait* <Fr>; well-qualified, well-fitted, well-suited

25 **versatile, ambidextrous,** two-handed, **all around** <nf>, broad-gauge, **well-rounded, many-sided,** generally capable; **adaptable,** adjustable, flexible, resourceful, supple, ready for anything; amphibious

26 **skilled, accomplished; practiced; professional,** career; trained, coached, prepared, primed, finished; at one's best, at concert pitch; initiated, initiate; technical; conversant

27 **skilled in,** proficient in, adept in, versed in, **good at,** expert at, **handy at, a hand** *or* **good hand at,** master of, strong in, at home in; **up on,** well up on, well-versed 928.20

28 **experienced, practiced,** mature, matured, ripe, ripened, **seasoned,** tried, well-tried, tried *and* true, **veteran,** old, an old dog at <nf>; sagacious 920.16; **worldly, worldly-wise,** world-wise, wise in the ways of the world, knowing, shrewd, **sophisticated,** cosmopolitan, cosmopolite, blasé, dry behind the ears, not born yesterday, long in the tooth; been there done that <nf>

29 **talented, gifted, endowed,** with a flair; born for, made for, cut out for <nf>, with an eye for, with an ear for, with a bump for <nf>

30 **well-laid, well-devised,** well-contrived, well-designed, well-planned, well-worked-out; well-invented; **well-weighed, well-reasoned,** well-considered, well-thought-out, thought-out; **cunning, clever**

ADVS 31 **skillfully, expertly, proficiently,** excellently, well; **cleverly,** neatly, ingeniously, resourcefully; cunningly 415.13; **dexterously, adroitly, deftly, adeptly,** aptly, handily; agilely, nimbly, featly, spryly; **competently, capably, ably,** efficiently; **masterfully;** brilliantly, superbly, with genius, with a touch of genius; **artistically,** artfully; with skill, with consummate skill, with finesse

414 UNSKILLFULNESS

NOUNS 1 **unskillfulness,** skilllessness, **inexpertness, unproficiency, uncleverness;** unintelligence 922; inadeptness, **undexterousness,** indexterity, **undeftness;** inefficiency; **incompetence** *or* incompetency, **inability, incapability, incapacity,** inadequacy; ineffectiveness, **ineffectuality; mediocrity,** pedestrianism; **inaptitude,** inaptness, unaptness, ineptness, maladroitness; unfitness, unfittedness; untrainedness, unschooledness; thoughtlessness, inattentiveness; maladjustment; rustiness <nf>, nonuse

2 **inexperience,** unexperience, unexperiencedness, unpracticedness;

rawness, greenness, unripeness, callowness, unfledgedness, unreadiness, immaturity; ignorance 930; **unfamiliarity,** unacquaintance, unacquaintedness, unaccustomedness; rawness, greenness, **amateurishness,** amateurism, unprofessionalness, unprofessionalism

3 **clumsiness, awkwardness,** bumblingness, **maladroitness, unhandiness,** left-handedness, heavy-handedness, fumblitis *and* ham-handedness <nf>, ham-fistedness <Brit nf>; handful of thumbs; **ungainliness**, uncouthness, **ungracefulness,** gracelessness, inelegance; **gawkiness,** gawkishness; **lubberliness, oafishness,** loutishness, boorishness, clownishness, lumpishness; **cumbersomeness,** hulkiness, **ponderousness; unwieldiness, unmanageability**

4 **bungling, blundering,** boggling, **fumbling,** malperformance, muffing, **botching,** botchery, blunderheadedness; **sloppiness, carelessness** 340.2; too many cooks

5 **bungle, blunder, botch,** flub, boner *and* bonehead play <nf>, boggle, bobble *and* boo-boo *and* screw-up *and* ball-up *and* fuck-up *and* foul-up <nf>, foozle <nf>, bevue; **fumble, muff,** fluff, flop, miscue <nf>, misfire, mishit; **slip,** trip, stumble; *gaucherie* and *étourderie* and *balourdise* <Fr>; **hash** *and* **mess** <nf>; bad job, sad work, clumsy performance, poor show *or* performance; off day; **error, mistake** 975.3

6 **mismanagement, mishandling,** misdirection, misguidance, misconduct, **misgovernment,** misrule; misadministration, maladministration; malfeasance, malpractice, misfeasance, wrongdoing 655; nonfeasance, omission, **negligence,** neglect 340.6; bad policy, impolicy, inexpedience *or* inexpediency 996

7 **incompetent,** incapable; dull tool, mediocrity, duffer *and* hacker <nf>, no great shakes, no prize, no prize package, no brain surgeon, no rocket scientist; no conjuror; one who will not set the Thames on fire <Brit>; greenhorn 930.7

8 **bungler, blunderer,** blunderhead, boggler, slubberer, bumbler, hack, **fumbler, botcher;** bull in a china shop, ox; lubber, lobby, **lout, oaf,** gawk, boor, **clown,** slouch; clodhopper, clodknocker, bumpkin, yokel, geek; **clod,** clot <Brit>, **dolt,** sad sack, blockhead 924.4; awkward squad; blind leading the blind

9 <nf terms> **goof,** goofer, goofball, goofus, foul-up, fuck-up, screw-up, bobbler, bonehead, dub, jerk, bozo, foozler, clumsy, fumble-fist, klutz, **butterfingers,** muff, muffer, stumblebum, stumblebunny, duffer, lummox, **slob,** lump; gowk <Brit>, rube, hick

VERBS 10 not know how, not have the knack, not have it in one <nf>; not be up to <nf>; not be versed; muddle along, pedestrianize; show one's ignorance, not have a clue <nf>

11 **bungle, blunder,** bumble, boggle, bobble, **muff,** muff one's cue *or* lines, **fumble,** be all thumbs, have a handful of thumbs; **flounder,** muddle, lumber; stumble, **slip,** trip, trip over one's own feet, get in one's own way, miss one's footing, miscue; commit a faux pas, commit a gaffe; blunder on *or* upon *or* into; blunder away, be not one's day; **botch,** mar, **spoil, butcher, murder,** make sad work of; play havoc with, play mischief with

12 <nf terms> **goof, pull a boner,** bobble, lay an egg, put *or* stick one's foot in it, stub one's toe, step on one's schvantz *or* pecker, drop the ball, drop a pop-up, drop a brick, bonehead into it; **blow,** blow it, bitch, bitch up, hash up, **mess up,** flub, flub the dub, **make a mess** *or* **hash of,** make a faux pas, foul up, fuck up, goof up, bollix up, **screw up, louse up, gum up,** gum up the works, bugger, bugger up, play the deuce *or* devil *or* hell *or* merry hell with; go at it ass-backwards; put one's foot in one's mouth; self-destruct

13 **mismanage, mishandle, misconduct,** misdirect, misguide, **misgovern, misrule;** misadminister, maladminister; be negligent 340.6

14 not know what one is about, not know one's interest, lose one's touch, make an ass of oneself, **make a fool of oneself,** lose face, stultify oneself, have egg on one's face, put oneself out of court, stand in one's own light, not know on which side one's bread is buttered, not know one's ass from one's elbow *or* a hole in the ground, kill the goose that lays the golden egg, cut one's own throat, dig one's own grave, behave self-destructively, **play with fire,** burn one's fingers, jump out of the frying pan into the fire, lock the barn door after the horse is stolen, **count one's chickens before they are hatched,** buy a pig in a poke, aim at a pigeon and kill a crow, **put the cart before the horse,** put a square peg into a round hole, paint oneself into a corner, run before one can walk

ADJS **15 unskillful,** skill-less, artless, **inexpert, unproficient, unclever;** inefficient; **undexterous, undeft, inadept, unfacile; unapt, inapt, inept,** hopeless, half-assed *and* clunky <nf>, **poor;** mediocre, pedestrian; thoughtless, inattentive; unintelligent 922.13

16 unskilled, unaccomplished, untrained, untaught, unschooled, untutored, uncoached, unimproved, uninitiated, **unprepared,** unprimed, unfinished, unpolished; **untalented, ungifted, unendowed; amateurish,** unprofessional, unbusinesslike, semiskilled

17 inexperienced, unexperienced, unversed, unconversant, **unpracticed;** undeveloped, unseasoned; **raw, green,** green as grass, unripe, callow, unfledged, immature, unmatured, fresh, wet behind the ears, not dry behind the ears, in training, **untried;** unskilled in, unpracticed in, unversed in, unconversant with, unaccustomed to, unused to, unfamiliar *or* unacquainted with, new to, uninitiated in, a stranger to, a novice *or* tyro at; 930.11; semiskilled

18 out of practice, out of training *or* form, soft <nf>, out of shape *or* condition, stiff, **rusty;** gone *or* run to seed *and* over the hill *and* not what one used to be <nf>, losing one's touch, slipping, on the downgrade

19 incompetent, incapable, unable, inadequate, unequipped, unqualified, ill-qualified, out of one's depth, outmatched, **unfit, unfitted,** unadapted, not equal *or* up to, not cut out for <nf>; ineffective, **ineffectual;** unadjusted, maladjusted

20 bungling, blundering, blunderheaded, bumbling, fumbling, mistake-prone, accident-prone; **clumsy, awkward, uncoordinated,** maladroit, unhandy, left-hand, left-handed, heavy-handed, ham-handed <nf>, ham-fisted *and* cack-handed <Brit nf>, clumsy-fisted, butterfingered <nf>, **all thumbs,** fingers all thumbs, with a handful of thumbs; stiff; **ungainly,** uncouth, **ungraceful,** graceless, inelegant, *gauche* <Fr>; **gawky,** gawkish; **lubberly, loutish, oafish,** boorish, clownish, lumpish, slobbish <nf>; **sloppy, careless** 340.11; **ponderous, cumbersome,** lumbering, hulking, hulky; **unwieldy**

21 botched, bungled, fumbled, muffed, spoiled, **butchered,** murdered; **ill-managed,** ill-done, ill-conducted, ill-devised, ill-contrived, ill-executed; mismanaged, misconducted, **misdirected, misguided;** impolitic, ill-considered, ill-advised; negligent 340.10

22 <nf terms> **goofed-up, bobbled,** bitched, bitched-up, hashed-up, **messed-up, fouled-up, fucked-up, screwed-up, bollixed-up, loused-up,** gummed-up, buggered, buggered-up, snafued; clunky, half-assed; ass-backwards

ADVS **23 unskillfully, inexpertly, unproficiently, uncleverly;** inefficiently; **incompetently, incapably,** inadequately, unfitly; **undexterously, undeftly, inadeptly,** unfacilely; **unaptly, inaptly, ineptly,** poorly

24 clumsily, awkwardly; bunglingly, blunderingly; maladroitly, unhandily; ungracefully, gracelessly, inelegantly, uncouthly; **ponder-**

ously, cumbersomely, lumberingly, hulkingly, hulkily; ass-backwards <nf>

415 CUNNING

NOUNS **1 cunning,** cunningness, **craft, craftiness,** callidity , **artfulness, art, artifice, wiliness,** wiles, guile, **slyness,** insidiousness, suppleness, **foxiness,** slipperiness, shiftiness, trickiness; low cunning, animal cunning; gamesmanship *and* one-upmanship <nf>; **canniness, shrewdness,** sharpness, acuteness, astuteness, **cleverness** 413.1; **resourcefulness, ingeniousness, wit,** inventiveness, readiness; subtlety, subtleness, Italian hand, fine Italian hand, finesse, restraint; acuteness, cuteness *and* cutification <nf>; Jesuitism, Jesuitry, **sophistry** 936; satanic cunning, the cunning of the serpent; sneakiness, concealment, **stealthiness, stealth** 345.4; cageyness <nf>, wariness 494.2

2 Machiavellianism, Machiavellism; realpolitik; **politics, diplomacy,** diplomatics; jobbery, jobbing

3 stratagem, artifice, art , **craft, wile,** strategy, maneuver, **device,** wily device, **contrivance, expedient, design, scheme, trick,** cute trick, fetch, fakement <nf>, gimmick <nf>, **ruse, red herring, shift,** tactic, **maneuver, stroke,** stroke of policy, master stroke, **move,** coup, gambit, **ploy, dodge,** artful dodge; **game,** little game, racket *and* grift <nf>; **plot,** conspiracy, **intrigue;** sleight, feint, jugglery; method in one's madness; **subterfuge,** blind, dust in the eyes; chicanery, knavery, deceit, trickery 356.4

4 machination, manipulation, wirepulling <nf>; influence, political influence, behind-the-scenes influence *or* pressure; **maneuvering,** maneuvers, tactical maneuvers; **tactics,** devices, expedients, gimmickry <nf>; web of deceit

5 circumvention, getting round *or* around; **evasion,** elusion, the slip <nf>, pretext; the runaround *and* buck-passing *and* passing the buck <nf>; **frustration, foiling, thwarting** 1012.3; **outwitting,** outsmarting, outguessing, **outmaneuvering**

6 slyboots, sly dog <nf>, **fox,** reynard, dodger, Artful Dodger <Charles Dickens>, crafty rascal, smooth *or* slick citizen <nf>, smooth *or* cool customer <nf>, smooth operator, slickster, smoothy *or* smoothie, glib tongue, smooth *or* sweet talker, smoothie <nf>, charmer; **trickster,** shyster <nf>, shady character, Philadelphia lawyer <nf>; horse trader, Yankee horse trader, wheeler-dealer; **swindler** 357.3

7 strategist, tactician; maneuverer, machinator, manipulator, wirepuller <nf>; calculator, schemer, **intriguer**

8 Machiavellian, Machiavel, Machiavellianist; **diplomat,** diplomatist, **politician** 610; political realist; influence peddler; powerbroker, kingmaker; power behind the throne, gray eminence, *éminence grise* <Fr>

VERBS **9 live by one's wits,** fly by the seat of one's pants, play a deep game; use one's fine Italian hand, finesse; shift, dodge, twist and turn, zig and zag; have something up one's sleeve, hide one's hand, cover one's path, have an out *or* a way out *or* an escape hatch; **trick, deceive** 356.14

10 maneuver, manipulate, pull strings *or* wires; **machinate, contrive,** angle <nf>, **jockey, engineer;** play games <nf>; **plot, scheme, intrigue; finagle, wangle;** gerrymander; know a trick or two

11 outwit, outfox, outsmart, outguess, outfigure, **outmaneuver,** outgeneral, outflank, outplay, be one up on; get the better *or* best of, go one better, know a trick worth two of that; play one's trump card; **overreach,** outreach; **circumvent,** get round *or* around, **evade,** stonewall <nf>, **elude, frustrate, foil,** give the slip *or* runaround <nf>; pass the buck <nf>; pull a fast one <nf>, steal a march on; make a fool of, make a sucker *or* patsy of <nf>; be too much for, be too deep for; throw a curve <nf>, **deceive, victimize** 356.18

ADJS 12 **cunning, crafty, artful, wily,** callid , guileful, **sly,** insidious, **shifty,** pawky <Brit>, arch, **smooth, slick** *and* slick as a whistle <nf>, **slippery,** snaky, serpentine, **foxy,** vulpine, feline, no flies on <nf>; **canny, shrewd,** knowing, sharp, razor-sharp, cute *or* cutesy *or* cutesy-poo <nf>, acute, astute, **clever;** resourceful, ingenious, inventive, ready; subtle; Jesuitical, **sophistical** 936.10; **tricky,** trickish, tricksy , gimmicky <nf>; **Machiavellian,** Machiavellic, politic, diplomatic; strategic, tactical; deep, deep-laid; cunning as a fox *or* serpent, crazy like a fox <nf>, slippery as an eel, too clever by half; sneaky, clandestine, **stealthy** 345.12; cagey <nf>, wary 494.9; **scheming, designing; manipulative,** manipulatory; **deceitful**

ADVS 13 **cunningly, craftily, artfully,** wilily, guilefully, insidiously, shiftily, foxily, trickily, smoothly, slick <nf>; **slyly,** on the sly; **cannily, shrewdly,** knowingly, astutely, **cleverly;** subtlely; cagily <nf>, warily 494.13; diplomatically

416 ARTLESSNESS

NOUNS 1 **artlessness, ingenuousness, guilelessness; simplicity,** simpleness, plainness; simpleheartedness, simplemindedness; **unsophistication,** unsophisticatedness; *naïveté* <Fr>, naivety, naiveness, childlikeness; **innocence;** trustfulness, trustingness, unguardedness, unwariness, unsuspiciousness; **openness,** openheartedness, sincerity, **candor** 644.4; **integrity,** single-heartedness, singlemindedness, singleness of heart; directness, bluffness, bluntness, outspokenness

2 **naturalness,** naturalism, nature; state of nature; unspoiledness; **unaffectedness,** unaffectation, **unassumingness,** unpretendingness, unpretentiousness, undisguise; **inartificiality,** unartificialness, genuineness

3 **simple soul,** unsophisticate, naïf, **ingenue, innocent,** pure heart, **child,** mere child, infant, **babe,** baby, newborn babe, babe in the woods, lamb, dove; child of nature, noble savage; primitive; yokel, rube *and* hick <nf>; oaf, lout 924.5; dupe 358

VERBS 4 wear one's heart on one's sleeve, look one in the face, have no affectations

ADJS 5 **artless, simple,** plain, **guideless;** simplehearted, simpleminded; **ingenuous,** *ingénu* <Fr>; **unsophisticated, naive;** childlike, born yesterday; **innocent,** innocuous; trustful, trusting, unguarded, unwary, unreserved, confiding, unsuspicious, on the up and up; **open,** openhearted, sincere, candid, **frank** 644.17; single-hearted, singleminded; direct, bluff, blunt, outspoken

6 **natural,** naturelike, native; in the state of nature; primitive, primal, pristine, unspoiled, untainted, uncontaminated; **unaffected, unassuming, unpretending,** unpretentious, unfeigning, undisguising, undissimulating, undissembling, undesigning; **genuine, inartificial,** unartificial, unadorned, unvarnished, unembellished, uncontrived; homespun; **pastoral, rural,** arcadian, bucolic

ADVS 7 **artlessly, ingenuously, guilelessly;** simply, plainly; naturally, genuinely; naïvely; openly, openheartedly

417 AUTHORITY

NOUNS 1 **authority, prerogative, right, power,** faculty, competence *or* competency; **mandate,** popular authority *or* mandate, people's mandate, electoral mandate; regality, royal prerogative; constituted authority, vested authority; inherent authority; legal *or* lawful *or* rightful authority, legitimacy, law, eminent domain, divine right; derived *or* delegated authority, vicarious authority, indirect authority, constituted *or* invested authority, inherent authority;

the say *and* **the say-so** <nf>; the man <nf>, Big Brother; rubber stamp; divine right, *jus divinum* <L>; absolute power, absolutism 612.8

2 **authoritativeness, authority, power,** powerfulness, magisterialness, **potency** *or* potence, puissance, **strength,** might, mightiness, string pulling, wire pulling, clout <nf>

3 **authoritativeness, masterfulness, lordliness,** magistrality, magisterialness; **arbitrariness,** peremptoriness, imperativeness, **imperiousness,** autocraticalness, high-handedness, dictatorialness, overbearingness, overbearance, overbearing, domineering, domineeringness, tyrannicalness, authoritarianism, bossism <nf>

4 **prestige, authority, influence,** influentialness; pressure, **weight,** weightiness, moment, **consequence;** eminence, **stature,** rank, seniority, preeminence, priority, precedence; **greatness** 247; **importance, prominence** 997.2

5 **governance, authority, jurisdiction, control, command, power, rule, reign,** regnancy, **dominion, sovereignty,** empire, empery, raj <India>, imperium, **sway; government** 612; administration, disposition 573.3; **control, grip,** claws, **clutches,** hand, hands, iron hand, talons

6 **dominance** *or* dominancy, **dominion, domination; preeminence, supremacy, superiority** 249; **ascendance** *or* **ascendancy; upper** *or* **whip hand, sway; sovereignty,** suzerainty, suzerainship, **overlordship;** primacy, principality, **predominance** *or* predominancy, predomination, prepotence *or* prepotency, hegemony; preponderance; balance of power; eminent domain

7 **mastership,** masterhood, masterdom, **mastery; leadership, headship, lordship;** hegemony; supervisorship, directorship 573.4; hierarchy, nobility, aristocracy, **ruling class** 575.15; chair, chairmanship; chieftainship, chieftaincy, chieftainry, chiefery; presidentship, presidency; premiership, primeministership, prime-ministry; governorship; princeship, princedom, principality; rectorship, rectorate; suzerainty, suzerainship; regency, regentship; prefectship, prefecture; proconsulship, proconsulate; provostship, provostry; protectorship, protectorate, seneschalship, seneschalsy; pashadom, pashalic; sheikhdom; emirate, viziership, vizierate; magistrateship, magistrature, magistracy; mayorship, mayoralty; sheriffdom, sheriffcy, sheriffalty, shrievalty; consulship, consulate; chancellorship, chancellery, chancellorate; seigniory; tribunate, aedileship; deanship, decanal authority, deanery; patriarchate, patriarchy ; bishopric, episcopacy; archbishopric, archiepiscopacy, archiepiscopate; metropolitanship, metropolitanate; popedom, popeship, popehood, papacy, pontificate, pontificality; dictatorship, dictature; chess master, grand master, past master

8 **sovereignty, royalty,** regnancy, **majesty,** empire, empery, imperialism, **emperorship; kingship,** kinghood; queenship, queenhood; kaisership, kaiserdom; czardom; rajaship; sultanship, sultanate; caliphate; the throne, the Crown, the purple; royal insignia 647.3

9 **scepter, rod, staff,** wand, staff *or* rod *or* wand of office, baton, mace, truncheon, fasces; crosier, crook, cross-staff; caduceus; gavel; mantle; chain of office; portfolio

10 <seat of authority> **saddle** <nf>, **helm, driver's seat** <nf>; office of power, high office; seat, **chair,** bench; woolsack <Brit>; seat of state, seat of power; curule chair; dais; chairmanship, directorship, chieftainship, presidency, premiership, secretariat, governorship, mayoralty; consulate, proconsulate, prefecture, magistry; supremist

11 **throne,** royal seat; musnud *or* gaddi <India>; Peacock throne

12 <acquisition of authority> **accession; succession,** rightful *or* legitimate

succession; **usurpation,** arrogation, assumption, taking over, seizure, seizure of power, takeover, coup d'etat, coup, revolution, overthrowing; anointment, anointing, consecration, coronation; selection, **delegation,** deputation, devolution, devolvement, assignment, nomination, **appointment; election**, mandate; **authorization,** empowerment, permission, grant, sanction, warrant, license, charter; consignation; job sharing

VERBS **13 possess** *or* **wield** *or* **have authority, have power,** have the power, have in one's hands, have the right, have the say *or* say-so <nf>, have the whip hand, wear the crown, hold the prerogative, have the mandate; exercise sovereignty; be vested *or* invested, carry authority, have clout <nf>, have what one says go, have one's own way; show one's authority, crack the whip, throw one's weight around *and* ride herd <nf>, have under one's thumb, wear the pants, have over a barrel <nf>; **rule** 612.13, **control**, govern; supervise 573.10

14 take command, take charge, take over, take the helm, take the reins of government, take the reins into one's hand, take office, gain authority, get the power into one's hands, gain *or* get the upper hand, lead, take the lead; ascend *or* mount *or* succeed *or* accede to the throne, call the shots <nf>; **assume command,** assume, **usurp,** arrogate, seize; usurp *or* seize the throne *or* crown *or* mantle, usurp the prerogatives of the crown; seize power, execute a *coup d'état*

ADJS **15 authoritative,** clothed *or* vested *or* invested with authority, **commanding, imperative; governing, controlling,** definitive, **ruling** 612.17; **preeminent, supreme,** administrative, managerial, bureaucratic, ruling, leading, **superior** 249.12; **powerful, potent,** puissant, mighty; dominant, ascendant, hegemonic, hegemonistic; **influential, prestigious, weighty,** momentous, consequential, eminent, substantial, considerable; great 247.6; important, prominent; ranking, senior; authorized, empowered, duly constituted, competent; **official,** *ex officio* <L>; authoritarian; absolute, autocratic, monocratic; **totalitarian**

16 imperious, imperial, **masterful,** authoritative, feudal, aristocratic, **lordly,** magistral, **magisterial**, commanding; arrogant 141.9; **arbitrary, peremptory,** imperative; absolute, absolutist, absolutistic; **dictatorial, authoritarian; bossy** <nf>, **domineering, high-handed, overbearing,** overruling, imperious; autocratic, monocratic, **despotic, tyrannical;** tyrannous, grinding, oppressive 98.24; repressive, suppressive 428.11; strict, severe 425.6

17 sovereign; regal, royal, majestic, purple; **kinglike, kingly**; **imperial,** imperious *or* imperatorious ; imperatorial; monarchic *or* monarchical, monarchal, monarchial; tetrarchic; princely, princelike; **queenly,** queenlike; dynastic

ADVS **18 authoritatively,** with authority, by virtue of office; **commandingly, imperatively; powerfully, potently,** puissantly, mightily; **influentially, weightily,** momentously, consequentially; **officially,** *ex cathedra* <L>

19 imperiously, masterfully, magisterially; **arbitrarily, peremptorily; autocratically, dictatorially, highhandedly, domineeringly, overbearingly, despotically, tyrannically**

20 by authority of, in the name of, in *or* by virtue of, by the power vested in

21 in authority, in power, in charge, in control, in command, at the reins, at the head, **at the helm,** at the wheel, **in the saddle** *or* driver's seat <nf>, on the throne

418 LAWLESSNESS

<absence of authority>

NOUNS **1 lawlessness; licentiousness,** license, uncontrol, anything goes, unrestraint 430.3; indiscipline, insubordination, mutiny, disobedience 327; permissiveness; **irresponsibility,** unaccountability; willfulness, unchecked *or* rampant will; interregnum, power vacuum; defiance of authority, lack of authority, breakdown of authority, breakdown of law and order; overthrow, coup, coup d'etat

2 anarchy, anarchism, **disorderliness, unruliness,** misrule, **disorder,** disruption, disorganization, confusion, arrogation, unruliness, riot, **turmoil, chaos,** primal chaos, tohubohu; antinomianism; **nihilism;** syndicalism *and* anarcho-syndicalism *and* criminal syndicalism , lynch law, mob rule *or* law, mobocracy, ochlocracy; **law of the jungle;** dog eat dog; subversion, sedition, unrestraint, insubordination, disobedience, revolution 860; rebellion 327.4

3 anarchist, anarch; antinomian; **nihilist,** syndicalist *and* anarcho-syndicalist ; subversive, seditionary; revolutionist 860.3; mutineer, rebel 327.5

VERBS **4 reject** *or* **defy authority,** usurp power *or* authority, enthrone one's own will; **take the law in one's own hands,** act on one's own responsibility; do *or* go as one pleases, indulge oneself; be a law unto oneself, answer to no man, undermine, arrogate; resist control; overthrow, depose, topple

ADJS **5 lawless; licentious, ungoverned,** undisciplined, unrestrained; permissive; insubordinate, mutinous, disobedient 327.8; **uncontrolled,** uncurbed, unbridled, unchecked, rampant, untrammeled, unreined, unrestrained, reinless, anything goes; **irresponsible,** wildcat, unaccountable; selfwilled, willful, headstrong, heady, defiant; rebellious, riotous, seditious, insurgent

6 anarchic, anarchical, anarchial, anarchistic; **unruly, disorderly,** disorganized, chaotic; antinomian; **nihilistic**, syndicalistic, ochlocratic, mobocratic; every man for himself, ungovernable

ADVS **7 lawlessly,** licentiously; anarchically, chaotically

419 PRECEPT

NOUNS **1 precept,** prescript, **prescription, teaching; instruction, direction, charge,** commission, injunction, dictate; **order,** command 420

2 rule, law, canon, maxim, dictum, moral, moralism; **norm, standard;** formula, form; rule of action *or* conduct, moral precept; commandment, *mitzvah* <Heb>; sutra; **tradition;** ordinance, imperative, **regulation**, reg <nf>, *règlement* <Fr>; **principle,** principium, settled principle, general principle *or* truth, te net, convention; **guideline,** ground rule, rubric, protocol, working rule, working principle, standard procedure; guiding principle, golden rule, caveat emptor; **code;** gold standard

3 formula, form , **recipe,** receipt; **prescription;** formulary

ADJS **4 preceptive,** didactic, didactive, instructive, moralistic, **prescriptive;** prescript, prescribed, mandatory, hard-and-fast, binding, dictated; formulary, standard, regulation, official, authoritative, canonical, statutory, rubric, rubrical, protocolary, protocolic; **normative; conventional;** traditional

420 COMMAND

NOUNS **1 command, commandment, order,** direct order, command decision, **bidding,** behest, hest , imperative, **dictate,** dictation, **will, pleasure,** say-so <nf>, word, word of command, *mot d'ordre* <Fr>; special order; **authority** 417

2 injunction, charge, commission, **mandate**

3 direction, directive, instruction, rule, regulation; prescript, prescription, **precept** 419; general order

4 decree, decreement , decretum, decretal, rescript, fiat, **edict,** *edictum* <L>; **law** 673.3; **rule, ruling,** dictum, ipse dixit; ordinance, *ordonnance* <Fr>, appointment ; **proclamation,** pronouncement, pronunciamento, **declaration,** ukase; bull, brevet ; decree-law, *décret-loi* <Fr>; *senatus consultum* <L>, senatus consult; diktat

5 **summons, bidding, beck, call,** calling, nod, **beck and call,** preconization; **convocation,** convoking; evocation, calling forth, invocation; requisition, indent <chiefly Brit>

6 **court order,** injunction, legal order, warrant, subpoena, citation, injunction, interdict *or* interdiction

7 process server, summoner

VERBS 8 **command, order, dictate, direct, instruct,** mandate, **bid, enjoin, charge,** commission, call on *or* upon; issue a writ *or* an injunction; **decree, rule, ordain,** promulgate; give an order *or* a direct order, issue a command, say the word, give the word *or* word of command; call the shots *or* tune *or* signals *or* play <nf>; order about *or* around; **speak, proclaim, declare,** pronounce 352.12

9 **prescribe, require, demand, dictate,** impose, lay down, set, fix, appoint, make obligatory *or* mandatory; decide once and for all, carve in stone, set in concrete <nf>; authorize 443.11

10 **lay down the law,** put one's foot down <nf>, read the riot act, lower the boom <nf>, set the record straight

11 **summon, call,** demand, preconize; call for, send for *or* after, bid come; **cite, summons** <nf>, **subpoena,** serve; page; convoke, convene, call together; call away; muster, invoke, conjure; order up, summon up, muster up, call up, conjure up, magic *or* magic up <Brit>; evoke, call forth, summon forth, call out; recall, call back, call in; requisition, indent <chiefly Brit>

ADJS 12 **mandatory,** mandated, **imperative, compulsory,** prescript, prescriptive, **obligatory,** must <nf>; dictated, imposed, required, entailed, decretory; decisive, final, peremptory, absolute, eternal, written, hard-and-fast, carved in stone, set in concrete <nf>, ultimate, conclusive, binding, irrevocable, without appeal

13 **commanding,** imperious, imperative, jussive, peremptory, abrupt; **directive, instructive; mandating,** dictating, compelling, obligating, **prescriptive,** preceptive; decretory, decretive, decretal; **authoritative** 417.15

ADVS 14 **commandingly, imperatively,** peremptorily

15 **by order** *or* **command,** at the word of command, as ordered *or* required, to order; mandatorily, compulsorily, obligatorily

421 DEMAND

NOUNS 1 **demand, claim, call; requisition,** requirement, stated requirement, order, rush order, indent <chiefly Brit>; seller's market, land-office business; strong *or* heavy demand, draft, drain, levy, tax, taxing; imposition, impost, tribute, duty, dun, contribution; insistent demand, rush; exorbitant *or* extortionate demand, exaction, extortion, blackmail; **ultimatum,** nonnegotiable demand; notice, warning 399

2 **stipulation, provision,** proviso, condition; **terms;** exception, reservation; **qualification** 959

3 <nf terms> catch, **Catch-22** 356.12, kicker, zinger, snag, joker; strings, strings attached; ifs, ands, *and* buts; whereases, howevers, howsomevers

4 **insistence, exigence, importunity,** importunateness, importunacy, **demandingness,** pertinaciousness, pertinacity; pressure, pressingness, **urgency, exigency** 997.4; **persistence** 360.1

VERBS 5 **demand, ask, ask for,** make a demand; **call for,** call on *or* upon one for, appeal to one for; call out for, cry *or* cry out for, clamor for; **claim,** challenge, **require;** levy, **impose,** impose on one for; **exact, extort,** squeeze, screw; blackmail; requisition, make *or* put in **requisition,** dun, indent <chiefly Brit>, **confiscate; order,** put in *or* place an order, order up; deliver *or* issue an ultimatum; warn 399.5

6 **claim, pretend to, lay claim to, stake a claim** <nf>, put *or* have dibs on <nf>, assert *or* vindicate a claim *or* right *or* title to; have going for it *or* one <nf>; **challenge**

7 **stipulate,** stipulate for, specifically provide, set conditions *or* terms, make reservations; **qualify** 959.3

8 **insist, insist on** *or* **upon,** stick to <nf>, set one's heart *or* mind upon; **take one's stand upon,** stand on *or* upon, put *or* lay it on the line <nf>, make no bones about it; stand upon one's rights, **put one's foot down** <nf>; brook *or* take no denial, not take no for an answer; **maintain, contend,** assert; urge, press 375.14; **persist** 360.2

ADJS **9** **demanding, exacting,** exigent; draining, taxing, exorbitant, extortionate, grasping; **insistent,** instant, **importunate,** urgent, pertinacious, pressing, loud, clamant, crying, clamorous; persistent

10 **claimed,** spoken for; requisitioned; requisitorial, requisitory

ADVS **11** **demandingly, exactingly,** exigently; exorbitantly, extortionately; **insistently, importunately, urgently,** pressingly, clamorously, loudly, clamantly

12 **on demand,** at demand, **on call,** upon presentation

422 ADVICE

NOUNS **1** **advice, counsel, recommendation, suggestion,** rede <Brit>; proposition, proposal; advising, advocacy; **direction, instruction,** guidance, briefing; **exhortation,** hortation , enjoinder, expostulation, remonstrance; **sermons,** sermonizing, preaching, preachiness; **admonition,** monition, monitory *or* monitory letter, caution, caveat, **warning** 399; **idea,** thought, opinion 953.6, precept; consultancy, consultantship, **consultation,** parley 541.5, advisement; council 423; **counseling;** guidance counseling, educational counseling, vocational guidance; mentorship; constructive criticism

2 piece of advice, **word of advice, word to the wise,** words of wisdom, pearls of wisdom, *verbum sapienti* <L>, verb *or* verbum sap <nf>, word in the ear, maxim, **hint, broad hint, flea in the ear** <nf>, **tip** <nf>, one's two cents' worth <nf>, intimation, insinuation; ear worm <nf>

3 **adviser, advisor, counsel, counselor, consultant,** professional consultant, expert, maven <nf>, boffin <Brit nf>; instructor, guide, **mentor,** nestor, orienter; confidant *or* confidante, personal adviser; admonisher, monitor, Dutch uncle; Polonius, preceptist; **teacher** 571; meddler, buttinsky *and* yenta *and* kibitzer *and* backseat driver <nf>; advocate; brain trust

4 **advisee,** counselee; client

VERBS **5** **advise, counsel, recommend, suggest, advocate,** propose, submit, propound; instruct, coach, guide, direct, brief; prescribe; weigh in with advice <nf>, give a piece of advice, give a hint *or* broad hint, hint at, intimate, insinuate, put a flea in one's ear <nf>, have a word with one, speak words of wisdom; meddle, kibitz <nf>; confer, consult with 541.10

6 **admonish, exhort,** expostulate, remonstrate, preach; **enjoin, charge,** call upon one to; caution, issue a caveat, wag one's finger <nf>; advise against, warn away, warn off, **warn** 399.5, dissuade; move, prompt, **urge, incite, encourage, induce, persuade** 375.23; **implore** 440.11

7 **take** *or* **accept advice, follow advice,** follow, follow implicitly, go along with <nf>, buy *or* buy into <nf>; consult, confer; solicit advice, desire guidance, implore counsel; **be advised by;** refer to, have at one's elbow, take one's cue from; seek a second opinion; put heads together *or* have a powwow with <nf>, huddle

ADJS **8** **advisory,** recommendatory; **consultative,** consultatory, consultive; directive, instructive; **admonitory,** monitory, monitorial, cautionary, **warning** 399.7; **expostulative,** expostulatory, **remonstrative,** remonstratory, remonstrant; **exhortative,** exhortatory, hortative, hortatory, preachy <nf>, **didactic,** moralistic, sententious

PHRS **9** too many cooks spoil the broth, another country heard from

423 COUNCIL

NOUNS **1 council,** conclave, *concilium* <L>, deliberative *or* advisory body, **assembly;** deliberative assembly, consultative assembly; chamber, house; **board,** court, bench, panel; **full assembly,** plenum, plenary session; **congress,** diet, synod, senate, soviet; **legislature** 613; **cabinet,** divan, council of ministers, council of state, US Cabinet, British Cabinet; kitchen cabinet, camarilla; staff; junta, directory; Sanhedrin; privy council; common council, county council, parish council, borough *or* town council, city *or* municipal council, village council; brain trust <nf>, brains trust <Brit nf>, group *or* corps *or* body of advisers, inner circle; council of war; council fire; syndicate, **association** 617; **conference** 541.5; **assembly** 770.2; **tribunal** 595

2 committee, subcommittee, standing committee; select committee, special committee, ad hoc committee; committee of one

3 forum, conference, discussion group, buzz session <nf>, **round table, panel;** open forum, colloquium, symposium; town meeting; board meeting; **powwow** <nf>; working lunch, power lunch, power breakfast

4 ecclesiastical council, chapter, classis, conclave, conference, caucus, congregation, consistory, convention, convocation, presbytery, session, synod, vestry; parochial council, parochial church council; diocesan conference, diocesan court; provincial court, plenary council; ecumenical council; Council of Nicaea, Council of Trent, Lateran Council, Vatican Council, Vatican Two; conciliarism

ADJS **5 conciliar,** council, councilmanic, aldermanic; **consultative, deliberative, advisory;** synodal, synodic, synodical

ADVS **6 in council, in conference, in consultation, in a huddle** <nf>, in conclave; **in session,** sitting

424 COMPULSION

NOUNS **1 compulsion, obligation,** obligement; **command** 420; **necessity** 963; **inevitability** 963.7; **irresistibility, compulsiveness; forcing,** enforcement; command performance; **constraint,** coaction; **restraint** 428; obsession; self-determination

2 force, *ultima ratio* <L>; **brute force,** naked force, rule of might, big battalions, **main force,** physical force; the right of the strong, the law of the jungle; **tyranny** 612.9; steamroller <nf>, irresistible force

3 coercion, coercing, intimidation, scare tactics, headbanging *and* armtwisting <nf>, **duress; the strong arm** *and* strong-arm tactics <nf>, a pistol *or* gun to one's head, the sword, the mailed fist, the bludgeon, the boot in the face, the jackboot, the big stick, the club, *argumentum baculinum* <L>; terrorism; **pressure, high pressure,** high-pressure methods; **violence** 671; impressment

VERBS **4 compel, force, make;** have, cause, cause to; **constrain, bind,** tie, tie one's hands; **restrain** 428.7; enforce, **drive,** impel; dragoon, use force upon, force one's hand, hold a pistol *or* gun to one's head; browbeat

5 oblige, necessitate, require, exact, demand, dictate, impose, call for; take *or* brook no denial; leave no option *or* escape, admit of no option

6 press; bring pressure to bear upon, put pressure on, bear down on, bear against, bear hard upon, put under duress

7 coerce, use violence, terrorize, ride roughshod, intimidate, bully, bludgeon, blackjack; hijack, shanghai, dragoon, carjack

8 <nf terms> **twist one's arm, arm-twist, twist arms, knock *or* bang heads, knock** *or* bang heads together, strong-arm, steamroller, bulldoze, **pressure,** high-pressure, lean on, squeeze; put the screws on *or* to, get one over a barrel *or* under one's thumb, hold one's feet to the fire, turn on the heat; pull rank; ram *or* cram down one's throat

9 **be compelled, be coerced,** have to 963.10; be stuck with <nf>, can't help but

ADJS 10 **compulsory, compulsive,** compulsatory, **compelling; pressing, driving,** imperative, imperious; constraining, coactive; **restraining** 428.11; **irresistible**

11 **obligatory, compulsory,** imperative, mandatory, required, dictated, **binding;** involuntary; **necessary** 963.12; **inevitable** 963.15

12 **coercive, forcible;** steamroller *and* bulldozer *and* sledgehammer *and* strong-arm <nf>; terroristic, violent

ADVS 13 **compulsively,** compulsorily, **compellingly,** imperatively, imperiously

14 **forcibly, by force,** by main force, by *force majeure*, by a strong arm; by force of arms, *vi et armis* <L>, at gunpoint, with a pistol *or* gun to one's head, at the point of a gun, at the point of the sword *or* bayonet, at bayonet point

15 **obligatorily**, compulsorily, mandatorily, by stress of, under press of; under the lash *or* gun; of necessity

425 STRICTNESS

NOUNS 1 **strictness, severity, harshness, stringency,** astringency, **hard line; discipline,** strict *or* tight *or* rigid discipline, regimentation, spit and polish; **austerity, sternness,** grimness, ruggedness, **toughness** <nf>; **belt-tightening;** Spartanism; authoritarianism; demandingness, exactingness; **meticulousness** 339.3

2 **firmness, rigor, rigorousness,** rigidness, rigidity, stiffness, **hardness,** obduracy, obdurateness, **inflexibility,** inexorability, unyieldingness, unbendingness, impliability, unrelentingness, **relentlessness; uncompromisingness;** stubbornness, obstinacy 361; purism; precisianism, puritanism, fundamentalism, orthodoxy

3 **firm hand, iron hand,** heavy hand, strong hand, tight hand, tight rein; tight *or* taut ship

VERBS 4 **hold** *or* **keep a tight hand upon,** keep a firm hand on, keep a tight rein on, rule with an iron hand, rule with a rod of iron, knock *or* bang heads together <nf>; regiment, discipline; run a tight *or* taut ship, ride herd, keep one in line; maintain the highest standards, not spare oneself nor anyone else, go out of one's way, go the extra mile <nf>

5 **deal hardly** *or* **harshly with,** deal hard measure to, lay a heavy hand on, bear hard upon, **take a hard line,** not pull one's punches <nf>

ADJS 6 **strict, exacting,** exigent, demanding, not to be trifled with, **stringent,** astringent; disciplined, spit-and-polish; **severe, harsh,** dour, unsparing; **stern, grim, austere,** rugged, **tough** <nf>; Spartan, Spartanic; **hard-line,** authoritarian 417.16; **meticulous** 339.12

7 **firm, rigid, rigorous,** rigorist, rigoristic, stiff, **hard,** iron, steel, steely, hard-shell, obdurate, **inflexible,** ironhanded, inexorable, dour, **unyielding,** unbending, impliable, **relentless,** unrelenting, procrustean; **uncompromising;** stubborn, obstinate 361.8; purist, puristic; puritan, puritanic, puritanical, fundamentalist, orthodox; ironbound, rockbound, musclebound, ironclad <nf>; straitlaced, hidebound

ADVS 8 **strictly, severely, stringently, harshly; sternly,** grimly, **austerely,** ruggedly, toughly <nf>

9 **firmly, rigidly, rigorously,** stiffly, stiff, hardly, obdurately, **inflexibly,** impliably, inexorably, unyieldingly, unbendingly; **uncompromisingly, relentlessly,** unrelentingly; ironhandedly, with a firm *or* a strong *or* a heavy *or* a tight *or* an iron hand

426 LAXNESS

NOUNS **1 laxness, laxity, slackness, looseness,** relaxedness; loosening, relaxation; imprecision, sloppiness <nf>, carelessness, remissness, negligence 340.1; indifference 102; weakness 16; impotence 19; unrestraint 430.3

2 unstrictness, nonstrictness, undemandingness, unsevereness, unharshness; leniency 427; **permissiveness,** overpermissiveness, overindulgence, **softness;** unsternness, unaustereness; easygoingness, easiness; **flexibility,** pliancy; latitude, lenience

VERBS **3 hold a loose rein, give free rein to,** give the reins to, **give one his head,** give a free course to, give rope enough to; permit all *or* anything

ADJS **4 lax, slack, loose,** relaxed; imprecise, sloppy <nf>, careless, slipshod; remiss, negligent 340.10; indifferent 102.6; weak 16.12; impotent 19.13; untrammeled, unrestrained

5 unstrict, undemanding, **unexacting; unsevere, unharsh; unstern,** unaustere; lenient 427.7; **permissive,** overpermissive, overindulgent, **soft;** easy, easygoing, laid-back <nf>, low-maintenance, concessory; **flexible,** pliant, yielding

427 LENIENCY

NOUNS **1 leniency** *or* lenience, lenientness, lenity; **clemency,** clementness, **mercifulness,** mercy, **humaneness,** humanity, pity, **compassion** 145.1; **mildness, gentleness,** tenderness, softness, moderateness; **easiness,** easygoingness; laxness 426; **forebearance,** forbearing, patience 134; acceptance, concession, **tolerance** 979.4; kid gloves, kid-glove treatment, light hand *or* rein

2 compliance, complaisance, obligingness, accommodatingness, **agreeableness;** affability, graciosity, graciousness, generousness, decency, amiability; kindness, kindliness, benignity, **benevolence** 143

3 indulgence, humoring, obliging; favoring, gratification, pleasing; **pampering,** cosseting, **coddling,** mollycoddling, petting, **spoiling; permissiveness,** overpermissiveness, overindulgence, acquiescence; sparing the rod; laissez faire

4 spoiled child *or* **brat,** *enfant gâté* <Fr>, pampered darling, mama's boy, mollycoddle, sissy; *enfant terrible* <Fr>, naughty child, holy terror

VERBS **5 be** *or* **go easy on,** ease up on, handle with kid *or* velvet gloves, use a light hand *or* rein, slap one's wrist, spare the rod, let off the hook; **tolerate,** bear with 134.5

6 indulge, humor, oblige; favor, please, gratify, satisfy, **cater to; give way to,** yield to, let one have his own way; **pamper,** cosset, **coddle,** mollycoddle, pet, make a lap dog of, **spoil;** spare the rod; make few demands

ADJS **7 lenient, mild, gentle,** mild-mannered, tender, humane, compassionate, **clement,** merciful 145.7; soft, moderate, **easy,** easygoing; lax 426.4; forgiving 148.6; **forebearing, forbearant,** patient 134.9; accepting, **tolerant** 979.11

8 indulgent, compliant, complaisant; **obliging, accommodating, agreeable,** amiable, gracious, generous, magnanimous, benignant, affable, decent, kind, kindly, benign, benevolent 143.15; **hands-off** <nf>, permissive, overpermissive, overindulgent, spoiling

9 indulged, pampered, coddled, spoiled, spoiled rotten <nf>

428 RESTRAINT

NOUNS **1 restraint, constraint; inhibition;** legal restraint, injunction, enjoining, enjoinder, interdict, veto; **control, curb, check,** rein, arrest, arrestation; **retardation,** deceleration, slowing down; cooling *and* cooling off *and* cooling down <nf>; retrenchment, curtailment; self-control 359.5; **hindrance** 1012; rationing; thought control; restraint of trade, monopoly, protection, protectionism, protective tariff, tariff wall; clampdown *and* crackdown <nf>, proscription, **prohibition** 444

2 **suppression, repression**, oppression; **subdual,** quelling, putting down, shutting *or* closing down, smashing, crushing; quashing, squashing *and* squelching <nf>; smothering, stifling, suffocating, strangling, throttling; extinguishment, quenching; **censorship,** censoring, bleeping *or* bleeping out <nf>, blue laws

3 **restriction, limitation, confinement;** Hobson's choice, no choice, zero option; circumscription 210; stint, cramping, cramp; qualification 959

4 **shackle,** restraint, **restraints, fetter, hamper,** trammel, trammels, **manacle,** gyves, bond, **bonds,** irons, chains, ball and chain; stranglehold; **handcuffs,** cuffs, bracelets <nf>; stocks, bilbo, pillory; **tether,** spancel, leash, lead <chiefly Brit>, leading string; **rein;** hobble, hopple; strait-jacket, strait-waistcoat <Brit>, camisole; yoke, collar; bridle, halter; **muzzle, gag;** electronic ankle bracelet *and* offender's tag *and* monitor; iron rule, iron hand

5 **lock,** bolt, bar, padlock, catch, safety catch; barrier 1012.5

6 restrictionist, protectionist, monopolist; censor; screw <nf>

VERBS 7 **restrain, constrain, control, govern,** guard, contain, keep under control, put *or* lay under restraint; **inhibit,** straiten ; enjoin, clamp *or* crack down on <nf>, proscribe, prohibit 444.3; **curb, check, arrest, bridle,** get under control, rein, snub, snub in; **retard,** slow down, decelerate; **cool** *and* **cool off** *and* **cool down** <nf>; retrench, curtail; hold, **hold in,** keep, withhold, hold up <nf>, **keep from;** hinder 1012.10; **hold back, keep back,** pull, set back; **hold in, keep in,** pull in, rein in; **hold** *or* **keep in check, hold at bay,** hold in leash, tie one down, tie one's hands; hold fast, keep a tight hand on; restrain oneself, not go too far, not go off the deep end <nf>

8 suppress, repress, stultify; **keep down,** hold down, keep under; **close** *or* shut down; **subdue, quell, put down,** smash, **crush; quash, squash** *and* **squelch** <nf>; **extinguish,** quench, stanch, damp down, pour water on, dash *or* pour cold water on, drown, kill; **smother, stifle,** suffocate, asphyxiate, strangle, throttle, choke off, **muzzle, gag;** censor, bleep *or* bleep out <nf>, silence; sit on *and* sit down on *and* slap *or* smack down <nf>; jump on *and* crack down on *and* clamp down on <nf>, put *or* keep the lid on <nf>; bottle up, cork, cork up

9 **restrict, limit, narrow, confine,** tighten; ground, restrict to home, barracks, bedroom, quarters, etc; circumscribe 210.4; keep in *or* within bounds, keep from spreading, localize; **cage in,** hem, hem in, box, box in *or* up; **cramp,** stint, cramp one's style; qualify 959.3

10 **bind, restrain, tie,** tie up, put the clamps on, **strap,** lash, leash, pinion, fasten, secure, make fast; **hamper, trammel,** entrammel; rope; **chain,** enchain; **shackle, fetter, manacle,** gyve, **put in irons; handcuff, tie one's hands; tie hand and foot,** hog-tie <nf>; straitjacket; hobble, hopple, fetter, leash, put on a lead <chiefly Brit>, spancel; tether, picket, moor, anchor; tie down, pin down, peg down; get a stranglehold on, put a half nelson on <nf>; **bridle;** gag, muzzle

ADJS 11 **restraining, constraining; inhibiting,** inhibitive; **suppressive, repressive,** oppressive, stultifying; controlling, on top of <nf>, prohibitive

12 **restrictive,** limitative, restricting, **narrowing, limiting, confining,** cramping; censorial

13 **restrained, constrained, inhibited,** pent up; guarded; controlled, curbed, bridled; **under restraint,** under control, in check, under discipline; grounded, out of circulation; slowed down, retarded, arrested, in remission; in *or* on leash, in leading strings

14 **suppressed, repressed; subdued,** quelled, put down, smashed,

crushed; quashed, squashed *and* squelched <nf>; smothered, stifled, suffocated; censored

15 **restricted, limited, confined;** circumscribed 210.6, hemmed in, hedged in *or* about, boxed in; landlocked; **shut-in,** stormbound, weatherbound, windbound, icebound, snowbound; cramped, stinted; qualified 959.10; under arrest, up the river <nf>, doing time <nf>, in the big house <nf>

16 **bound, tied,** bound hand *and* foot, tied up, tied down, strapped, hampered, trammeled, shackled, handcuffed, fettered, manacled, tethered, leashed; **in bonds,** in irons *or* chains, ironbound

429 CONFINEMENT

NOUNS 1 **confinement,** locking-up, lockup, lockdown, caging, penning, putting behind barriers, impoundment, **restraint,** restriction; check, **restraint, constraint** 428.1

2 **quarantine, isolation,** cordoning off, segregation, separation, sequestration, seclusion; walling in *or* up *or* off; sanitary cordon, *cordon sanitaire* <Fr>, cordon; quarantine flag, yellow flag, yellow jack

3 **imprisonment, jailing,** incarceration, **internment,** immurement, immuration; **detention, captivity,** detainment, duress, durance, durance vile; close arrest, house arrest; term of imprisonment; preventive detention; minimum- *or* maximum-security imprisonment *or* detention; lockdown, solitary confinement

4 **commitment,** committal, consignment; recommitment, remand; mittimus <law>; institutionalization

5 **custody,** custodianship, keep , **keeping, care, change, ward,** guarding, hold, protective *or* preventive custody; protection, safekeeping 1008.1

6 **arrest,** arrestment, arrestation, pinch *and* bust *and* collar <nf>; **capture, apprehension, seizure,** netting <nf>; house arrest, protective *or* preventive custody

7 **place of confinement,** close quarters, not enough room to swing a cat; limbo, bardo, hell, purgatory; pound, pinfold *or* penfold; **cage; enclosure,** pen, coop 212.3

8 **prison,** prison house, correctional *or* correction facility, minimum- *or* maximum-security facility, **penitentiary,** pen <nf>, keep, penal institution, bastille, state prison, federal prison; house of detention *or* correction, detention center, detention home; **jail, gaol** <Brit>, jailhouse, lockup, bridewell <Brit>, county jail, city jail; maximum- *or* minimum-security prison; **military prison, guardhouse, stockade, brig; dungeon,** oubliette, black hole; **reformatory,** house of correction, reform school, training school, industrial school, borstal *or* borstal institution <Brit>; debtor's prison *and* sponging house ; **prison camp,** internment camp, detention camp, labor camp, forced-labor camp, gulag, **concentration camp;** prisoner-of-war camp *or* stockade, POW camp, prison farm; cell; bullpen; solitary confinement, the hole <nf>, solitary; **cell,** prison *or* jail cell; detention center, **detention cell,** holding cell, lockup; tank *and* drunk tank <nf>; cellblock, cellhouse; condemned cell, death cell, death house *or* row, jail cell; penal settlement *or* colony, Devil's Island, Alcatraz; halfway house, reformatory, reform school, detension home

9 <nf terms> **slammer, slam, jug,** can, coop, cooler, hoosegow, stir, clink, pokey *or* poky, nick *and* quod *and* chokey <Brit>, hoosegow; **joint,** big house, big school, big cage, big joint, brig, tank, icebox

10 **jailer, gaoler** <Brit>, correctional *or* correction *or* corrections officer; **keeper, warder,** prison guard, **turnkey,** bull *and* screw <nf>; **warden,** governor <Brit>, commandant, principal keeper; custodian, caretaker, guardian 1008.6; **guard** 1008.9

11 **prisoner, captive, inmate,** *détenu* <Fr>, cageling; arrestee; **convict,** con <nf>; **jailbird** <nf>, gaolbird <Brit nf>, stir bird <nf>, lifer, col-

lar, yardbird, lag *or* lagger <Brit>; **detainee; internee; prisoner of war** *or* POW; enemy prisoner of war *or* EPWS; political prisoner, prisoner of conscience, political detainee, terror suspect; lifer <nf>; trusty *or* trustee; condemned prisoner; parolee, ticket-of-leave man *or* ticket-of-leaver <Brit>; ex-convict; chain-gang member, hostage

VERBS 12 **confine, shut in,** shut away, coop in, hem in, fence in *or* up, wall in *or* up, rail in; **shut up, coop up, pen up,** box up, mew up, bottle up, cork up, seal up, **impound;** pen, coop, pound , crib, mew, cloister, immure, cage, cage in, encage; **enclose** 212.5; **hold, keep in,** hold *or* keep in custody, **detain,** keep in detention, constrain, ground, **restrain,** hold in restraint; check, inhibit 428.7; restrict 428.9; shackle 428.10

13 **quarantine, isolate,** segregate, separate, seclude; **cordon, cordon off,** seal off, rope off; wall off, set up barriers, put behind barriers

14 **imprison, incarcerate, intern,** immure; **jail,** gaol <Brit>, jug <nf>, put under security, put behind bars, put away, put *or* throw into jail, throw under the jailhouse <nf>; throw *or* cast in prison, clap up, clap in jail *or* prison, send up the river <nf>, send to the big house <nf>; **lock up,** lock in, bolt in, put *or* keep under lock *and* key; hold captive, hold prisoner, hold in captivity; hold under close *or* house arrest, throw in the tank *or* cooler

15 **arrest,** make an arrest, put under arrest, pick up; catch flat-footed; catch with one's pants down *or* hand in the till <nf>, catch one in the act *or* red-handed *or* in flagrante delicto, catch *or* have one dead to rights; run down, run to earth, **take captive, take prisoner, apprehend, capture,** seize, net <nf>, lay by the heels, **take into custody,** entrap

16 <nf terms> **bust, pinch,** make a pinch, nab, collar, nick, pull in, **run in,** collar

17 **commit,** consign, commit to prison, send to jail, send up *and* send up the river <nf>; commit to an institution, institutionalize; recommit, remit, remand

18 **be imprisoned, do** *or* **serve time** <nf>; pay one's debt to society, land in the cooler, lag <Brit>

ADJS 19 **confined,** in confinement, **shut-in,** pent, **pent-up,** penned in, kept in, under restraint, held, in detention; impounded; grounded, out of circulation; **detained;** restricted 428.15; cloistered, enclosed 212.10

20 **quarantined,** isolated, segregated, separated; cordoned, cordoned *or* sealed *or* roped off

21 **jailed,** jugged <nf>, **imprisoned, incarcerated, interned,** immured; **in prison,** in stir <nf>, in captivity, captive, **behind bars,** locked up, under lock *and* key, in durance vile, serving a sentence; doing time, on the inside, on ice, in the cooler, up the river, in the big house

22 **under arrest, in custody,** in hold, in charge <Brit>, under *or* in detention; under close arrest, under house arrest

430 FREEDOM

NOUNS 1 **freedom, liberty; license,** loose ; run *and* the run of <nf>; **civil liberty,** the Four Freedoms <F D Roosevelt>: freedom of speech *and* expression, freedom of worship, freedom from want, freedom from fear; freedom of movement; constitutional freedom; lack of censorship; academic freedom; artistic license, poetic license

2 **right, rights, civil rights,** civil liberties, constitutional rights, legal rights; Bill of Rights, Petition of Right, Declaration of Right, Declaration of the Rights of Man, Magna Charta *or* Carta; **unalienable rights, human rights,** natural rights; diplomatic immunity

3 **unrestraint, unconstraint,** noncoercion, nonintimidation; **unreserve,** irrepressibleness, irrepressibility, uninhibitedness, exuberance 109.4; **immoderacy, intemperance,** incontinence, uncontrol, unruliness, indiscipline; **abandon,** abandonment,

licentiousness, wantonness, riotousness, wildness; permissiveness, unstrictness, **laxness** 426; one's own way, one's own devices

4 **latitude, scope, room,** range, way, field, maneuvering space *or* room, room to swing a cat <nf>; **margin,** clearance, **space,** open space *or* field, elbowroom, breathing space *or* room, **leeway** <nf>, sea room, wide berth; **tolerance; free scope,** full *or* ample scope, **free hand,** free play, free course; **carte blanche,** blank check; no holds barred; swing, play, full swing; rope, long rope *or* tether, rope enough to hang oneself

5 **independence, self-determination, self government,** self-direction, autonomy, home rule; autarky, autarchy, self-containment, self-sufficiency; **individualism,** rugged individualism, individual freedom; **self-reliance,** self-dependence; inner-direction; no allegiance; singleness, bachelorhood; independent means

6 **free will,** free choice, **discretion,** option, choice, say, say-so *and* druthers <nf>, free decision; **full consent;** absolute *or* unconditioned *or* noncontingent free will

7 **own free will, own account, own accord, own hook** *and* own say-so <nf>, own discretion, own choice, **own initiative,** personal initiative, own responsibility, personal *or* individual responsibility, own volition, own authority, own power; own way, own sweet way <nf>; law unto oneself

8 **exemption,** exception, **immunity; release,** discharge; **franchise, license,** charter, patent, liberty; diplomatic immunity, congressional *or* legislative immunity; special case *or* privilege; grandfather clause, grandfathering; privilege; permission 443

9 **noninterference, nonintervention; isolationism; laissez-faireism,** let-alone principle *or* doctrine *or* policy, deregulation; *laissez-faire* and *laissez-aller* <Fr>; liberalism, free enterprise, free competition, self-regulating market; open market; capitalism 611.8; free trade; noninvolvement, nonalignment, neutrality

10 **liberalism,** libertarianism, latitudinarianism; broad-mindedness, open-mindedness, toleration, tolerance; unbigotedness 979.1; libertinism, **freethinking,** free thought; liberalization, **liberation** 431; nonconformity

11 **freeman,** freewoman; citizen, free citizen, burgess, bourgeois; franklin; emancipated *or* manumitted slave, freedman, freedwoman; dedititician

12 **free agent, independent, free lance; individualist,** rugged individualist; free spirit; **liberal,** libertarian, latitudinarian; libertine, freethinker; free trader; **nonpartisan,** neutral, undecided, mugwump; isolationist; nonaligned nation; third world, third force, developing world; indie <nf>; lone wolf <nf>, loner, nonconformist, one-man band

VERBS 13 **liberalize,** ease; **free, liberate** 431.4

14 **exempt, free, release,** discharge, **let go** *and* **let off** <nf>, set at liberty, spring <nf>; **excuse,** spare, except, grant immunity, make a special case of; grandfather; **dispense,** dispense from, give dispensation from; dispense with, save the necessity; remit, remise; absolve 601.4

15 **give a free hand,** let one have his head, **give one his head; give the run of** <nf>, give the freedom of; give one leeway <nf>, give full play; give one scope *or* space *or* room; **give rein** *or* **free rein to,** give the reins to, give bridle to, give one line, give one rope; **give one carte blanche, give one a blank check;** let go one's own way, let one go at will

16 **not interfere, leave** *or* **let alone, let be,** leave *or* let well enough alone, let sleeping dogs lie; **keep hands off,** not tamper, not meddle, not involve oneself, not get involved, let it ride <nf>, let nature take its course; live *and* let live, leave one to oneself, leave one in peace; mind one's own business; tolerate; **decontrol, deregulate**

17 <nf terms> **get off one's back** *or* **one's case** *or* **one's tail,** get out of one's face *or* hair, **butt out, back off,** leave be, call off the dogs, keep one's nose out, get lost, take a walk, not cramp someone's style

18 **be free,** feel free, feel free as a bird, feel at liberty; **go at large,** breathe free, breathe the air of freedom; **have free scope,** have one's druthers <nf>, have a free hand, have the run of <nf>; be at home, feel at home; be freed, be released, be exonerated, go *or* get off scot-free, walk

19 **let oneself go,** let go, let loose *and* cut loose *and* let one's hair down <nf>, **give way to,** open up, let it all hang out <nf>; go all out, go flat out <Brit>, pull out all the stops; go unrestrained, run wild, have one's fling, sow one's wild oats

20 **stand on one's own two feet, shift for oneself, fend for oneself,** stand on one's own, strike out for oneself, trust one's good right arm, look out for number one <nf>; **go it alone, be one's own man,** pull a lone oar, play a lone hand <nf>, **paddle one's own canoe** <nf>; suffice to oneself, do for oneself, make *or* pay one's own way; ask no favors, ask no quarter; **be one's own boss** <nf>, call no man master, answer only to oneself, ask leave of no man; **go one's own way,** take one's own course; do on one's own, don one's own thing, do on one's own initiative, do on one's own hook *or* say-so <nf>, do in one's own sweet way <nf>; **have a will of one's own,** have one's own way, do what one likes *or* wishes *or* chooses, do as one pleases, **go as one pleases,** please oneself <nf>, **suit oneself;** have a free mind; free-lance, be a free agent

ADJS 21 **free; at liberty, at large,** on the loose, **loose,** unengaged, disengaged, detached, unattached, uncommitted, uninvolved, clear, in the clear, go-as-you-please, easygoing, footloose, footloose *and* fancy-free, free *and* easy; free as air, free as a bird, free as the wind; scot-free; **freeborn; freed, liberated, emancipated,** manumitted, released, uncaged, sprung <nf>

22 **independent,** self-dependent; free-spirited, freewheeling, free-floating, free-standing; **self-determined,** self-directing, one's own man; free-lance; inner-directed, **individualistic;** self-governed, **self-governing, autonomous,** sovereign; stand alone, self-reliant, self-sufficient, self-subsistent, self-supporting, self-contained, autarkic, autarchic; nonpartisan, neutral, **nonaligned;** third-world, third-force

23 **free-acting,** free-going, free-moving, free-working; freehand, freehanded; **free-spoken,** outspoken, **plain-spoken, open, frank,** direct, candid, blunt 644.17

24 **unrestrained, unconstrained, unforced,** uncompelled, uncoerced; unmeasured, **uninhibited, unsuppressed, unrepressed, unreserved,** go-go <nf>, exuberant 109.14; **uncurbed, unchecked, unbridled,** unmuzzled; **unreined,** reinless; **uncontrolled,** unmastered, unsubdued, ungoverned, **unruly;** out of control, out of hand, out of one's power; **abandoned,** intemperate, immoderate, **incontinent, licentious,** loose, wanton, rampant, riotous, wild; irrepressible; lax 426.4

25 **nonrestrictive,** unrestrictive; **permissive,** hands-off <nf>; indulgent 427.8; lax 426.4; **liberal,** libertarian, latitudinarian; broad-minded, open-minded, tolerant; unbigoted 979.8; libertine; freethinking

26 **unhampered, untrammeled, unhandicapped, unimpeded,** unhindered, unprevented, unclogged, unobstructed; clear, unencumbered, unburdened, unladen, unembarrassed, disembarrassed; free-ranging, free-range

27 **unrestricted, unconfined, uncircumscribed,** unbound , unbounded, unmeasured; **unlimited,** limitless, illimitable; unqualified, unconditioned, **unconditional,** without strings, no strings, no strings attached; **absolute,** perfect, unequivocal, full, plenary; open-ended, open,

wide-open <nf>; permissive; decontrolled, deregulated

28 **unbound,** untied, **unfettered,** unshackled, unchained; unmuzzled, ungagged; uncensored; declassified

29 **unsubject,** ungoverned, unenslaved, **unenthralled;** unvanquished, unconquered, unsubdued, unquelled, **untamed,** unbroken, undomesticated, unreconstructed

30 **exempt, immune;** exempted, **released, excused,** excepted, let off <nf>, spared; grandfathered; **privileged, licensed,** favored, chartered; permitted; dispensed; **unliable,** unsubject, irresponsible, unaccountable, unanswerable

31 **quit, clear, free, rid; free of, clear of, quit of, rid of, shut of,** shed of <nf>

ADVS 32 **freely,** free; **without restraint,** without stint, **unreservedly,** with abandon; outright

33 **independently, alone, by oneself,** all by one's lonesome <nf>, under one's own power *or* steam, **on one's own** *and* **on one's own hook** <nf>, on one's own initiative, on one's own bottom ; **on one's own account** *or* **responsibility,** on one's own say-so <nf>; **of one's own free will, of one's own accord,** of one's own volition, at one's own discretion

431 LIBERATION

NOUNS 1 **liberation, freeing,** setting free, setting at liberty; **deliverance, delivery; rescue** 398; **emancipation,** disenthrallment, manumission; enfranchisement, affranchisement; Emancipation Proclamation; Nineteenth Amendment; Equal Rights Amendment; women's liberation; gay liberation; women's *or* gay *or* men's lib <nf>

2 **release, freeing,** unhanding, **loosing,** unloosing; unbinding, untying, unbuckling, unshackling, unfettering, unlashing, unstrapping, untrussing *and* unpinioning , unmanacling, **unleashing,** unchaining, untethering, unhobbling, unharnessing, unyoking, unbridling; unmuzzling, ungagging; unlocking, unlatching, unbolting, unbarring; unpenning, uncaging; **discharge, dismissal;** parole, bail; convict release, springing <nf>; demobilization, separation from the service

3 **extrication,** freeing, releasing, clearing; **disengagement, disentanglement,** untangling, unsnarling, unraveling, disentwining, disinvolvement, unknotting, disembarrassment, disembroilment; dislodgment, breaking out *or* loose, busting out *or* loose <nf>

VERBS 4 **liberate, free, deliver, set free,** set at liberty, set at large; **emancipate,** manumit, disenthrall; enfranchise, affranchise; **rescue** 398.3

5 **release, unhand, let go, let loose, turn loose,** cast loose, let out, let off, let go free, let off the hook; **discharge, dismiss;** let out on bail, grant bail to, go bail for <nf>; parole, put on parole; release from prison, spring <nf>; demobilize, separate from the service

6 **loose,** loosen, let loose, cut loose *or* free, unloose, unloosen; **unbind, untie,** unstrap, unbuckle, unlash, untruss *and* unpinion ; **unfetter, unshackle,** unmanacle, unchain, unhandcuff, untie one's hands; **unleash,** untether, unhobble; unharness, unyoke, unbridle; unmuzzle, ungag; unlock, unlatch, unbolt, unbar; unpen, uncage

7 **extricate, free, release, clear,** get out; **disengage,** disentangle, untangle, unsnarl, unravel, disentwine, disinvolve, unknot, detangle, disembarrass, disembroil; dislodge, break out *or* loose, cut loose, tear loose

8 **free oneself from,** deliver oneself from, **get free of,** get quit of, **get rid of,** get clear of, **get out of,** get well out of, get around, extricate oneself, get out of a jam <nf>; **throw off, shake off;** break out, bust out <nf>, go over the wall <nf>, **escape** 369.6; wriggle out of

9 **go free,** go scot free, go at liberty, **get off,** get off scot-free, get out of, beat the rap *and* walk <nf>

ADJS 10 **liberated, freed, emancipated, released;** delivered, rescued, ransomed, redeemed; extricated, unbound, untied, unshackled, etc; free 430.21; scot-free; on parole, out on bail

432 SUBJECTION

NOUNS **1 subjection, subjugation; domination** 612.2; **restraint, control** 428.1; **bondage, captivity; thrall, thralldom,** enthrallment; **slavery,** enslavement, master-slave relationship; **servitude,** compulsory *or* involuntary servitude, servility, bond service, indentureship; **serfdom,** serfhood, villenage, **vassalage;** helotry, helotism; debt slavery, **peonage;** feudalism, feudality; absolutism, tyranny 612.8,9; deprivation of freedom, disenfranchisement, disfranchisement

2 subservience *or* subserviency, subjecthood, subordinacy, **subordination,** juniority, **inferiority;** lower status, subordinate role, satellite status; back seat *and* second fiddle *and* hind tit <nf>; **service,** servitorship 577.12

3 dependence *or* dependency, codependency, contingency, tutelage, chargeship, wardship; apprenticeship; clientship, clientage

4 subdual, quelling, conquest, crushing, trampling *or* treading down, reduction, **humbling, humiliation; breaking, taming,** domestication, gentling; conquering 412.1; **suppression** 428.2

5 subordinate, junior, secondary, second-in-command, lieutenant, **inferior; underling,** understrapper, low man on the totem pole <nf>, errand boy, flunky, gofer <nf>, grunt <nf>; assistant, personal assistant, undersecretary, helper 616.6; strong right arm, **right-hand man** 616.7; **servant, employee** 577

6 dependent, charge, ward, client, protégé, encumbrance; pensioner, pensionary; public charge, ward of the state; child; foster child; dependency *or* dependent state, client state, satellite *or* satellite state, puppet government, creature; hanger-on, parasite

7 subject, vassal, liege, liege man, liege subject, homager; **captive; slave,** servant, chattel, chattel slave, **bondsman,** bondman, **bondslave,** theow, thrall; indentured servant; laborer, esne; bondwoman, bondswoman, bondmaid; odalisque, concubine; galley slave; **serf,** helot, villein; churl; debt slave, **peon;** conscript

VERBS **8 subjugate, subject, subordinate; dominate** 612.14; disfranchise, disenfranchise, divest *or* deprive of freedom; **enslave,** enthrall, hold in thrall, make a chattel of; take captive, lead captive *or* into captivity; **hold in subjection,** hold in bondage, **hold captive,** hold in captivity; **hold down,** keep down, keep under; **keep** *or* **have under one's thumb,** have tied to one's apron strings, hold in leash, hold in leading strings, hold in swaddling clothes, hold *or* keep at one's beck *and* call; vassalize, make dependent *or* tributary; peonize

9 subdue, master, overmaster, **quell, crush, reduce,** beat down, **break,** break down, overwhelm; tread underfoot, trample on *or* down, trample underfoot, roll in the dust, trample in the dust, drag at one's chariot wheel; oppress, **suppress** 428.8; make one give in *or* say 'uncle' <nf>, **conquer** 412.10; kick around <nf>, tyrannize 612.15; unman 19.12; bring low, **bring to terms, humble,** humiliate, take down a notch *or* peg, bend, **bring one to his knees, bend to one's will**

10 have subject, twist *or* turn *or* wind around one's little finger, make lie down *and* roll over, have eating out of one's hand, **lead by the nose,** make a puppet of, make putty of, make a sport *or* plaything of; use as a doormat, treat like dirt under one's feet, walk all over

11 domesticate, tame, break, bust *and* gentle <nf>, break in, break to harness; housebreak

12 depend on, be at the mercy of, be the sport *or* plaything *or* puppet of, be putty in the hands of; not dare to say one's soul is one's own; eat out of one's hands; play second fiddle, suck hind tit <nf>, take a back seat; pay tribute

ADJS **13 subject, dependent,** tributary, client; **subservient, subordinate, inferior;** servile; liege, **vassal,** feudal, feudatory

14 subjugated, subjected, **enslaved, enthralled, in thrall, captive,** bond, unfree; disenfranchised, disfranchised, **oppressed, suppressed** 428.14; **in subjection, in bondage, in captivity,** in slavery, in bonds, in chains; under the lash, under the heel; **in one's power,** in one's control, in one's hands *or* clutches, in one's pocket, **under one's thumb,** at one's mercy, under one's command *or* orders, at one's beck and call, at one's feet, at one's pleasure; **subordinated,** playing second fiddle; at the bottom of the ladder, sucking hind tit <nf>

15 subdued, quelled, crushed, broken, reduced, mastered, overmastered, humbled, humiliated, brought to one's knees, brought low, made to grovel; **tamed, domesticated,** broken to harness, gentled; housebroken *or* housebroke

16 downtrodden, downtrod , kept down *or* under, ground down, overborne, trampled, **oppressed; abused,** misused; **henpecked, browbeaten,** led by the nose, in leading strings, tied to one's apron strings, ordered *or* kicked around <nf>, regimented, tyrannized; slavish, servile, submissive 433.12; unmanned 19.19; treated like dirt under one's feet, treated like shit <nf>

433 SUBMISSION

NOUNS **1 submission,** submittal, **yielding; compliance,** com**plaisance, acquiescence, acceptance;** going along with <nf>, **assent** 332; **consent** 441; **obedience** 326; subjection 432; **resignation,** resignedness, stoicism, philosophical attitude; **deference,** homage, kneeling, obeisance; **passivity, unassertiveness,** passiveness, supineness, longanimity, long-suffering, long-sufferance , nonresistance, nonopposition, nonopposal, quietness, nondissent, quietude, quietism; **cowardice** 491

2 surrender, capitulation; renunciation, giving over, abandonment, relinquishment, **cession;** giving up *or* in, backing off *or* down <nf>, retreat, recession, recedence, caving in <nf>, giving up the fort, the white flag <nf>, throwing in the towel *or* sponge <nf>

3 submissiveness, docility, tractability, prostration, biddability, yieldingness, compliableness , pliancy, pliability, flexibility, malleability, moldability, ductility, plasticity, facility; agreeableness, agreeability; subservience, **servility** 138

4 manageability, governability, controllability, manipulability, manipulatability, corrigibility, untroublesomeness; **tameness,** housebrokenness; tamableness, domesticability; milk-toast, milquetoast, Caspar Milquetoast

5 meekness, gentleness, tameness, mildness, mild-manneredness, peaceableness, lamblikeness, dovelikeness, spinelessness; **self-abnegation, humility** 137

VERBS **6 submit, comply, take, accept,** go along with <nf>, suffer, bear, brook, **acquiesce,** be agreeable, accede, **assent** 332.8; **consent** 441.2; relent, **succumb,** resign, resign oneself, give oneself up, not resist; take one's medicine, swallow the pill, face the music, face the facts; **bite the bullet; knuckle down** *or* **under,** knock under , take it, swallow it; jump through a hoop, dance to another's tune; take it lying down; put up with it, grin and bear it, make the best of it, take the bitter with the sweet, shrug, shrug off, live with it; obey 326.2

7 yield, cede, give way, give ground, back down, give up, give in, cave in <nf>, withdraw from *or* quit the field, break off combat, cease resistance, have no fight left

8 surrender, give up, capitulate, acknowledge defeat, **cry quits,** cry pax <Brit>, **say 'uncle'** <nf>, beg a truce, pray for quarter, implore mercy, throw **in the towel** *or* **sponge** <nf>, show *or* wave the white flag, lower *or* haul down *or* strike one's flag *or* colors, throw down *or* lay down *or* deliver up one's arms, hand over one's sword, yield the palm, ask for mercy, pull in one's horns <nf>, come to terms; renounce, abandon, relinquish, **cede,** give over, hand over

9 **submit to, yield to, defer to,** bow to, give way to, knuckle under to, succumb to

10 **bow down,** bow, bend, stoop, crouch, **bow one's head,** bend the neck, bow submission, genuflect, curtsy; **bow to,** bend to, knuckle to <nf>, bend *or* bow to one's will, bend to one's yoke; kneel to, **bend the knee to, fall on one's knees before,** crouch before, **fall at one's feet,** throw oneself at the feet of, prostrate oneself before, **truckle to,** cringe to, cave in; **kowtow,** bow *and* scrape, grovel, do obeisance *or* homage; kiss ass <nf>; take the line of least resistance

11 **eat dirt, eat crow, eat humble pie,** lick the dust, kiss the rod, take it on the chin

ADJS 12 **submissive, compliant,** compliable , complaisant, complying, **acquiescent,** consenting 441.4; **assenting,** accepting, agreeable; subservient, abject, **obedient** 326.3; servile; **resigned,** uncomplaining; unassertive; **passive,** supine, **unresisting,** nonresisting, unresistant, nonresistant, nonresistive, long-suffering, longanimous, nonopposing, nondissenting

13 **docile, tractable,** biddable, unmurmuring, **yielding,** pliant, pliable, flexible, malleable, moldable, ductile, plastic, facile , like putty in one's hands

14 **manageable, governable, controllable,** manipulable, manipulatable, handleable, corrigible, restrainable, untroublesome; domitable, tamable, domesticable; milk-toast *or* milquetoast

15 **meek, gentle, mild,** mild-mannered, peaceable, pacific, quiet; **subdued, chastened, tame,** tamed, broken, housebroken, domesticated; lamblike, gentle as a lamb, dovelike; humble; spineless, soft, weak-kneed

16 **deferential, obeisant; subservient, obsequious,** servile 138.13; crouching, prostrate, prone, on one's belly, on one's knees, on one's marrowbones <nf>, on bended knee, bowed, bowing

ADVS 17 **submissively, compliantly,** complaisantly, acquiescently, agreeably; **obediently** 326.6; **resignedly,** uncomplainingly, with resignation; **passively,** supinely, unresistingly, unresistantly, nonresistively

18 **docilely, tractably,** biddably, **yieldingly,** pliantly, pliably, malleably, flexibly, plastically, facilely

19 **meekly, gently, tamely, mildly,** peaceably, pacifically, quietly, like a lamb

434 OBSERVANCE

NOUNS 1 **observance,** observation, honoring; **keeping,** adherence, heeding; compliance, conformance, conformity, accordance; **faith,** faithfulness, fidelity; **respect, deference** 155.1; **performance, practice,** execution, discharge, carrying out *or* through; dutifulness 641.2, acquittal *or* acquittance , fulfillment, satisfaction; heed, care 339.1; obeying the law

VERBS 2 **observe, keep, heed, follow,** keep the faith; regard, defer to, **respect** 155.4, attend to, **comply with,** conform to; hold by, **abide by,** adhere to; **live up to,** act up to, practice what one preaches, **be faithful to,** keep faith with, do justice to, do the right thing by; **fulfill,** fill, meet, satisfy; **make good,** keep *or* make good one's word *or* promise, be as good as one's word, redeem one's pledge, stand to one's engagement; keep to the spirit of, keep faith with; obey the law

3 **perform, practice,** do, execute, discharge, carry out *or* through, carry into execution, do one's duty

641.10, do one's office, fulfill one's role, discharge one's function; honor one's obligations

ADJS 4 **observant,** respectful 155.8, regardful, mindful; **faithful,** devout, devoted, true, loyal, constant; dutiful 641.13, duteous; as good as one's word; **practicing,** active; compliant, conforming; punctual, punctilious, scrupulous, meticulous, conscientious 339.12; obedient; sabbatarian

435 NONOBSERVANCE

NOUNS 1 **nonobservance,** inobservance, unobservance, nonadherence; nonconformity, disconformity, **nonconformance, noncompliance;** apostasy; inattention, indifference, **disregard** 984.2; laxity 426.1; **nonfulfillment, nonperformance,** nonfeasance, failure, **dereliction, delinquency,** omission, default, slight, oversight; **negligence; neglect** 340, laches; abandonment 370; lack of ceremony

2 **violation, infraction, breach,** breaking; **infringement, transgression, trespass,** contravention; offense 674.4; breach of promise, breach of contract, breach of trust *or* faith, bad faith, breach of privilege; breach of the peace

VERBS 3 **disregard,** lose sight of, pay no regard to; **neglect** 340.6; renege, abandon 370.5; defect 858.13; do one's own thing <nf>

4 **violate, break, breach; infringe, transgress, trespass,** contravene, trample on *or* upon, trample underfoot, do violence to, make a mockery of, outrage; defy, set at defiance, flout, set at naught, set naught by; take the law into one's own hands; break one's promise, break one's word

ADJS 5 **nonobservant,** inobservant, unobservant, nonadherent; nonconforming, unconforming, noncompliant, uncompliant; inattentive, **disregardful** 984.6; **negligent** 340.10; unfaithful, untrue, unloyal, inconstant, lapsed, renegade 858.20/363.11; contemptuous

436 PROMISE

NOUNS 1 **promise, pledge,** solemn promise, troth, plight, faith, parole, **word, word of honor,** debt of honor, solemn declaration *or* word; **oath, vow;** avouch, avouchment; **assurance, guarantee,** warranty, personal guarantee; entitlement

2 **obligation, commitment, agreement, engagement,** undertaking, recognizance, feasance; **understanding,** gentlemen's agreement, unwritten agreement, handshake; verbal agreement, nonformal agreement, pactum <law>; tacit *or* unspoken agreement; **contract** 437.1, covenant, bond; designation, committal, earmarking; promissory note

3 **betrothal,** betrothment, intention, espousal, **engagement,** handfasting *and* affiance , troth, marriage contract *or* vow, plighted troth *or* faith *or* love, exchange of vows; banns, banns of matrimony; prenuptial agreement *or* contract, prenup <nf>

VERBS 4 **promise,** give *or* make a promise, hold out an expectation; **pledge,** plight, troth, **vow; give one's word,** pledge *or* pass one's word, give one's parole, **give one's word of honor,** plight one's troth *or* faith, pledge *or* plight one's honor; cross one's heart *and* cross one's heart *and* hope to die <nf>, **swear;** vouch, avouch, **warrant, guarantee, assure;** underwrite, countersign

5 **commit, engage,** undertake, obligate, bind, **agree to,** say yes, answer for, be answerable for, take on oneself, be responsible for, be security for, go bail for, accept obligation *or* responsibility, bind oneself to, put oneself down for; have an understanding; enter into a gentlemen's agreement; take the vows *or* marriage vows; shake hands on, shake on it; contract, sign on the dotted line; designate, commit, earmark

6 **be engaged, affiance, betroth,** troth, plight one's troth, say 'I do'; **contract,** contract an engagement, pledge *or* promise in marriage; read *or* publish the banns

ADJS **7** **promissory,** votive; under *or* upon oath, on one's word, on one's word of honor, on the Book, under hand and seal, avowed

8 **promised, pledged, bound, committed,** compromised, **obligated; sworn,** warranted, **guaranteed,** assured, underwritten, cosigned; contracted 437.11; **engaged, plighted, affianced, betrothed,** intended

ADVS **9** on one's honor *or* word *or* word of honor *or* parole; solemnly

437 COMPACT

NOUNS **1** **compact, pact, contract,** legal contract, valid contract, **covenant,** convention, transaction, paction, accord, **agreement,** mutual agreement, agreement between *or* among parties, signed *or* written agreement, formal agreement, legal agreement, undertaking, stipulation; adjustment, accommodation; **understanding, arrangement, bargain,** dicker *and* **deal** <nf>, informal agreement; **settlement,** negotiated settlement; **labor contract, union contract** 727.3, wage contract, employment contract, collective agreement; deed; cartel, consortium; **protocol**; bond, binding agreement, ironclad agreement, covenant of salt; gentleman's *or* gentlemen's agreement; prenuptial agreement; licensing agreement; promise 436

2 **treaty,** international agreement, entente *or* entente cordiale <Fr>, concord, concordat, cartel, convention, consortium, protocol, paction, capitulation; **alliance, league;** nonaggression pact, mutual-defense treaty; trade agreement; arms control agreement; NATO *or* North Atlantic Treaty Organization; SEATO *or* Southeast Asia Treaty Organization; Warsaw Pact

3 signing, **signature**, sealing, closing, conclusion, solemnization; handshake

4 **execution, completion; transaction; carrying out, discharge, fulfillment,** prosecution, effectuation; enforcement; observance 434

VERBS **5** **contract,** compact, **covenant, bargain, agree, engage,** undertake, commit, mutually commit, make a deal <nf>, do a deal <Brit nf>, stipulate, agree to, bargain for, contract for; preset, prearrange, **promise** 436.4; subcontract, outsource; cut a deal <nf>

6 **treat with, negotiate, bargain,** make terms, sit down with, sit down at the bargaining table

7 **sign, shake hands** *or* shake <nf>, affix one's John Hancock <nf>, seal, formalize, make legal *and* binding, solemnize; agree on terms, come to terms, come to an agreement 332.10; strike a bargain 731.18; plea-bargain

8 **arrange, settle; adjust,** fine-tune, accommodate, reshuffle, rejigger <nf>, **compose,** fix, make up, straighten out, put *or* set straight, work out, sort out *and* square away <nf>; **conclude,** close, **close with,** settle with

9 **execute, complete, transact,** promulgate, make; close a deal; make out, fill out; **discharge, fulfill,** render, administer; **carry out,** carry through, put through, prosecute; effect, effectuate, set in motion, implement; enforce, put in force; **abide by, honor, live up to,** adhere to, live by, **observe** 434.2

ADJS **10** contractual, covenantal, conventional, consensual

11 **contracted,** compacted, **covenanted, agreed upon, bargained for,** agreed <Brit>, stipulated; engaged, undertaken; **promised** 436.8; arranged, settled; under hand and seal, **signed,** sealed, signed sealed and delivered; ratified

ADVS **12** **contractually, as agreed upon, as promised,** as contracted for, by the terms of the contract, according to the contract *or* bargain *or* agreement

438 SECURITY

<thing given as a pledge>

NOUNS **1** **security, surety,** indemnity, **guaranty, guarantee, warranty,**

insurance, warrant, assurance, underwriting; **obligation** 436.2, full faith *and* credit; **bond,** tie; stocks and bonds 738.1; national security

2 **pledge, gage,** *pignus* or *vadium* <L>; undertaking; **earnest,** earnest money, god's penny, handsel; escrow; token payment; pawn, hock <nf>; **bail,** bond, vadimonium; replevin, replevy, recognizance; mainprise; hostage, surety

3 **collateral,** collateral security *or* warranty; deposit, stake, forfeit; indemnity, IOU; caution money, caution; margin; cosigned promissory note; cosignage

4 **mortgage,** mortgage deed, deed of trust, lien, security agreement, real estate loan; vadium mortuum *or* mortuum vadium; dead pledge; vadium vivum, living pledge, antichresis; hypothec, hypothecation, bottomry, bottomry bond; adjustment mortgage, blanket mortgage, chattel mortgage, closed mortgage, participating mortgage, installment mortgage, leasehold mortgage, trust mortgage, reverse mortgage, jumbo mortgage; first mortgage, second mortgage, third mortgage; adjustable-rate mortgage *or* ARM, variable-rate mortgage *or* VRM, fixed-rate mortgage; equity loan; reverse equity

5 **lien,** general lien, particular lien; pignus legale, common-law lien, statutory lien, judgment lien, pignus judiciale, tax lien, mechanic's lien; mortgage bond

6 **guarantor,** warrantor, guaranty, guarantee; mortgagor; insurer, underwriter; sponsor, surety; godparent, godfather, godmother; bondsman, bailsman, mainpernor

7 **warrantee,** mortgagee; insuree, policyholder; godchild, godson, goddaughter

8 guarantorship, **sponsorship,** sponsion

VERBS 9 **secure, guarantee, guaranty, warrant, assure, insure,** ensure, bond, certify; countersecure; stand surety; **sponsor,** be sponsor for, sign for, sign one's note, **back,** stand behind *or* back of, stand up for; **endorse;** indemnify, countersign; sign, cosign, **underwrite,** undersign, subscribe to; confirm, attest

10 **pledge,** impignorate *and* handsel , **deposit, stake,** post, put in escrow, **put up,** put up as collateral, lay out *or* down; **pawn,** put in pawn, spout *or* put up the spout , **hock** *and* **put in hock** <nf>; mortgage, hypothecate, bottomry, bond; **put up** *or* **go bail,** bail out

ADJS 11 **secured,** covered, **guaranteed, warranted,** certified, **insured,** ensured, **assured;** certain, sure 970.13

12 **pledged,** staked, posted, deposited, in escrow, **put up,** put up as collateral; on deposit, at stake; as earnest; **pawned,** in pawn, **in hock** <nf>, hocked, up the spout

13 **in trust,** held in trust, held in pledge, fiduciary; in escrow; mortgaged

439 OFFER

NOUNS 1 **offer,** offering, proffer, presentation, **bid,** submission; **advance, overture,** approach, invitation, come-on <nf>; hesitant *or* tentative *or* preliminary approach, feeling-out, **feeler** <nf>; asking price; **counteroffer, counterproposal**

2 **proposal, proposition, suggestion,** instance; **motion,** resolution; sexual advance *or* approach *or* invitation *or* overture, indecent proposal, pass <nf>, improper suggestion; request 440

3 **ultimatum,** last *or* final word *or* offer, firm bid *or* price, sticking point, ultimation

VERBS 4 **offer, proffer, present,** tender, offer up, **put up, submit, extend,** prefer , **hold out,** hold forth, place in one's way, lay at one's feet, put *or* place at one's disposal, put one in the way of

5 **propose, submit,** prefer; **suggest,** recommend, **advance,** commend to attention, **propound, pose, put forward,** bring forward, put *or* set forth, put it to, put *or* set *or* lay *or* bring before, dish up *and* come out *or* up with <nf>; put a bee in one's

bonnet, put ideas into one's head; **bring up, broach, moot,** introduce, open up, launch, start, kick off <nf>; **move, make a motion,** offer a resolution; postulate 951.12

6 **bid,** bid for, make a bid

7 **make advances,** approach, overture, **make an overture,** throw *or* fling oneself at one <nf>; **solicit, importune**

8 <nf terms> **proposition, come on to,** hit on, put *or* make a move on, jump one's bones, make *or* throw a pass, george, **make a play for,** play footsie with, pitch, mash

9 **urge upon, press upon,** ply upon, push upon, force upon, thrust upon; **press, ply;** insist

10 **volunteer, come *or* step forward, offer *or* proffer *or* present oneself,** be at one's service, not wait to be asked, not wait for an invitation, need no prodding, step into the breach, be Johnny-on-the-spot <nf>

440 REQUEST

NOUNS 1 **request,** asking; the touch <nf>; desire, wish, expressed desire; **petition,** petitioning, impetration, address; **application; requisition,** indent <Brit>; demand 421; special request

2 **entreaty, appeal, plea, bid,** suit, call, cry, clamor, *cri du cœur* <Fr>, beseeching, impetration, obtestation; **supplication, prayer,** rogation, **beseechment,** imploring, imploration, obsecration, obtestation, adjuration, imprecation; **invocation,** invocatory plea *or* prayer; act of contrition

3 **importunity,** importunateness, urgency, pressure, high pressure *and* hard sell <nf>; **urging, pressing, plying;** buttonholing; dunning; teasing, pestering, plaguing, nagging, nudging <nf>; **coaxing,** wheedling, cajolery, cajolement, blandishment

4 **invitation, invite** *and* **bid** <nf>, engraved invitation, bidding, biddance, **call,** calling, **summons**

5 **solicitation, canvass, canvassing; suit,** addresses; **courting, wooing;** fund-raising; the touch <nf>

6 **beggary,** mendicancy, mendicity; **begging,** cadging, scrounging; mooching *and* bumming *and* panhandling <nf>

7 **petitioner, supplicant,** suppliant, suitor; **solicitor** 730.6; **applicant,** solicitant, claimant; aspirant, seeker, wannabee <nf>; candidate, postulant; bidder

8 **beggar, mendicant,** scrounger, **cadger; bum** *and* bummer *and* **moocher** *and* **panhandler** *and* sponger <nf>; *schnorrer* <Yiddish>; hobo, tramp 178.3; loafer 331.8; mendicant friar; mendicant order

VERBS 9 **request, ask,** make a request, **beg leave,** make bold to ask; **desire,** wish, wish for, express a wish for, crave; **ask for,** order, put in an order for, bespeak, call for, trouble one for; whistle for <nf>; **requisition,** make *or* put in a requisition, indent <Brit>; make application, apply for, file for, put in for; demand 421.5; pop the question <nf>

10 **petition,** present *or* prefer a petition, sign a petition, circulate a petition; **pray,** sue; **apply to, call on** *or* **upon;** memorialize

11 **entreat, implore, beseech, beg,** crave, **plead, appeal, pray, supplicate,** impetrate, obtest; adjure, conjure; invoke, imprecate , **call on** *or* **upon,** cry on *or* upon, **appeal to,** cry to, run to; go cap *or* hat in hand to; kneel to, go down on one's knees to, fall on one's knees to, go on bended knee to, throw oneself at the feet of, get *or* come down on one's marrow-bones <nf>; **plead for,** clamor for, cry for, cry out for; call for help

12 **importune, urge, press,** pressure <nf>, prod, prod at, apply *or* exert pressure, push, **ply;** dun; **beset, buttonhole,** besiege, take *or* grasp by the lapels; work on <nf>, tease, pester, plague, nag, nag at, make a pest *or* nuisance of oneself, try one's patience, bug <nf>, nudge; coax, wheedle, cajole, blandish, flatter, soft-soap <nf>

13 **invite, ask, call, summon, call in, bid come,** extend *or* issue an invitation, request the presence of, request

the pleasure of one's company, send an engraved invitation

14 **solicit, canvass; court, woo,** address, sue, sue for, pop the question <nf>, propose; **seek, bid for,** look for; **fish for,** angle for; pass the hat

15 beg, **scrounge, cadge; mooch** *and* **bum** *and* **panhandle** <nf>; **hit** *and* hit up *and* **touch** *and* put the touch on *and* make a touch <nf>; pass the hat <nf>

ADJS **16** **supplicatory, suppliant,** supplicant, supplicating, **prayerful,** precative; **petitionary; begging,** mendicant, cadging, scrounging, mooching <nf>; on one's knees *or* bended knees, on one's marrowbones <nf>; with joined *or* folded hands

17 **imploring, entreating, beseeching, begging, pleading, appealing,** precatory, precative, adjuratory

18 **importunate; teasing,** pesty, pesky <nf>, pestering, plaguing, nagging, dunning; **coaxing,** wheedling, cajoling, flattering, soft-soaping <nf>; **insistent, demanding, urgent**

19 **invitational,** inviting, invitatory

441 CONSENT

NOUNS **1** **consent, assent, agreement,** accord , acceptance, approval, blessing, approbation, sanction, **endorsement,** ratification, backing; affirmation, affirmative, affirmative voice *or* vote, yea, aye, **nod** *and* **okay** *and* **OK** <nf>, okey-dokey <nf>, go-ahead <nf>, green light <nf>; **leave, permission** 443; **willingness,** readiness, promptness, promptitude, eagerness, unreluctance, unloathness, ungrudgingness, tacit *or* unspoken *or* silent *or* implicit consent, **connivance; acquiescence, compliance;** submission 433

VERBS **2** **consent, assent,** give consent, yield assent, be willing, be amenable, be persuaded, accede to, accord to *and* grant , say yes *or* aye *or* yea, vote affirmatively, vote aye, **nod, nod assent; accept, play** *or* **go along** <nf>, **agree to, sign off on** <nf>, go along with <nf>; be in accord with, be in favor of, take kindly to, **approve of,** hold with; **approve,** give one's blessing to, **okay** *or* **OK** <nf>; sanction, **endorse, ratify;** consent to silently *or* by implication *or in petto* <Ital>; **wink at, connive at; be willing,** turn a willing ear; deign, condescend; have no objection, not refuse; permit 443.9

3 **acquiesce, comply, comply with,** fall in with, take one up on <nf>, be persuaded, come round *or* around, come over, come to <nf>, see one's way clear to; **submit** 433.6,9

ADJS **4** **consenting, assenting,** affirmative, amenable, persuaded, approving, agreeing, favorable, accordant, consentient, consentual, consentant; sanctioning, endorsing, ratifying; **acquiescent, compliant,** compliable ; submissive 433.12; **willing, agreeable,** content; ready, prompt, eager, unreluctant, unloath, nothing loath, unmurmuring, ungrudging, unrefusing; permissive 443.14

ADVS **5** **consentingly, assentingly,** affirmatively, approvingly, favorably, positively, agreeably, accordantly; acquiescently, compliantly; willingly 324.8; **yes** 332.18

442 REFUSAL

NOUNS **1** **refusal, rejection,** turndown, turning down; thumbs-down <nf>, *pollice verso* <L>; nonconsent, nonacceptance, zero tolerance; **declining,** declination, declension, declinature; **denial,** disclamation, disclaimer, disallowance; decertification, disaccreditation; **repudiation** 372.1; disagreement, dissent 333; recantation 363.3; contradiction 335.2; negation, abnegation, negative, negative answer, nay, no, nix <nf>; unwillingness 325; disobedience 327; noncompliance, noncooperation, nonobservance 435; withholding, holding back, retention, deprivation

2 **repulse, rebuff,** peremptory *or* flat *or* point-blank refusal, summary negative; a flea in one's ear; kiss-off *and* slap in the face *and* kick in the teeth <nf>; short shrift

VERBS **3** **refuse, decline,** not consent, refuse consent, **reject, turn down** <nf>, decline to accept, **not have,** not buy <nf>; not hold with, not think *or* hear of; **say no,** say nay, vote nay, vote negatively *or* in the negative, side against, disagree, beg to disagree, dissent 333.4; shake one's head, negative, negate; vote down, **turn thumbs down on;** be unwilling 325.3; turn one's back on, turn a deaf ear to, set oneself against, set one's face against, be unmoved, harden one's heart, resist entreaty *or* persuasion; stand aloof, not lift a finger, have nothing to do with, wash one's hands of; hold out against; put *or* set one's foot down, refuse point-blank *or* summarily, decline politely *or* with thanks, beg off; **repudiate,** disallow, disclaim 372.2; decertify, disaccredit

4 **deny, withhold,** hold back; grudge, begrudge; close the hand *or* purse; deprive one of; **renege**

5 **repulse, rebuff, repel,** kiss one off *and* slap one in the face *and* kick one in the teeth <nf>, send one away with a flea in one's ear, give one short shrift, shut *or* slam the door in one's face, turn one away; slap *or* smack one down <nf>; deny oneself to, refuse to receive, not be at home to, cut, **snub** 157.5; not want anything to do with

ADJS **6** **unconsenting,** nonconsenting, **negative; unwilling** 325.5; **uncompliant,** uncomplying, uncomplaisant, inacquiescent, uncooperative; disobedient; rejective, declinatory; deaf to, not willing to hear of; dissenting

PHRS **7** **I refuse, I won't,** I will not, I will do no such thing; over my dead body, far be it from me, not if I can help it, not likely, not on your life, count me out, include me out, I'm not taking any, I won't buy it, it's no go, like hell I will, I'll be hanged if I will, try and make me, you have another guess coming, you should live so long, I'll see you in hell first, nothing doing <nf>; out of the question, not to be thought of, impossible; **no,** by no means, **no way, no way José, there's no way;** in a pig's eye *or* ear *or* ass, my eye *or* ass; you've got to be kidding

443 PERMISSION

NOUNS **1** **permission, leave, allowance,** vouchsafement; **consent** 441; permission to enter, admission, ticket, ticket of admission; implied consent, clearance; approbation, blessing; **license,** liberty 430.1; **okay** *and* **OK** *and* **nod** *and* **go-ahead** *and* **green light** *and* **go sign** *and* **thumbs-up** <nf>; special permission, charter, patent, dispensation, release, waiver; zoning variance, variance

2 **sufferance, tolerance,** toleration, **indulgence;** leniency; winking, overlooking, connivance; permissiveness; dispensation, exemption

3 **authorization, authority, sanction, licensing,** countenance, **warrant,** warranty, fiat; empowerment, enabling, entitlement, enfranchisement, certification; clearance, security clearance; ratification 332.4; legalization, legitimation, decriminalization

4 **carte blanche,** blank check <nf>, freedom, **full authority,** full power, free hand, open mandate

5 **grant, concession;** charter, franchise, liberty, diploma, patent, letters patent, brevet; royal grant

6 **permit, license, warrant;** building permit, learner's permit, work permit; driver's license, marriage license, hunting license, fishing license, gaming license, etc; nihil obstat, imprimatur; credentials

7 **pass, passport, safe-conduct,** safeguard, protection; visa, entry visa, exit visa; green card; **clearance,** clearance papers; bill of health, clean bill of health, pratique, full pratique

8 **permissibility,** permissibleness, **allowableness; admissibility,** admissibleness; justifiableness, warrantableness, sanctionableness; **validity,** legitimacy, lawfulness, licitness, legality

VERBS **9** **permit, allow, admit, let,** leave <nf>, give permission, give leave, make possible; **allow** *or* **permit of;** give *or* leave room for, open the door to; consent 441.2; **grant,** accord, vouchsafe; **okay** *and* **OK** *and* **give the nod** *or* **go-ahead** *or* **green light** *or* **go sign** <nf>, say *or* give the word <nf>; dispense, release, waive

10 **suffer, countenance,** have, **tolerate, condone,** brook, endure, stomach, bear, bear with, put up with, stand for, hear of *and* go along with <nf>; indulge 427.6; shut one's eyes to, **wink at,** blink at, overlook, connive at; leave the door *or* way open to

11 **authorize, sanction, warrant;** give official sanction *or* warrant, legitimize, validate, legalize; empower, give power, enable, entitle; **license; privilege;** charter, patent, enfranchise, franchise; accredit, certificate, certify; ratify 332.12; **legalize,** legitimate, legitimize, decriminalize

12 **give carte blanche,** issue *or* accord *or* give a blank check <nf>, give full power *or* authority, give an open mandate *or* invitation, give free rein, give a free hand, leave alone, leave it to one; permit all *or* anything, open the floodgates, remove all restrictions, let someone get away with murder <nf>

13 **may,** can, have permission, **be permitted** *or* **allowed**

ADJS **14** **permissive,** admissive, permitting, allowing; consenting 441.4; **unprohibitive,** nonprohibitive; tolerating, obliging, tolerant; suffering, **indulgent,** soft, liberal, **lenient** 427.7; hands-off <nf>; lax 426.4; easy come easy go <nf>

15 **permissible, allowable, admissible;** justifiable, warrantable, sanctionable; licit, **lawful, legitimate, legal,** legitimized, legalized, legitimated, decriminalized, legit <nf>

16 **permitted, allowed,** allowable, admitted; tolerated, on sufferance; unprohibited, unforbidden, unregulated, unchecked; unconditional, without strings

17 **authorized,** empowered, entitled; **warranted, sanctioned; licensed, privileged;** chartered, patented; franchised, enfranchised; accredited, certificated

ADVS **18** **permissively,** admissively; **tolerantly, indulgently**

19 **permissibly, allowably,** admissibly; with permission, by one's leave; licitly, lawfully, legitimately, legally

PHRS **20** **by your leave,** with your permission, if you please, with respect, may I?

444 PROHIBITION

NOUNS **1** **prohibition, forbidding,** forbiddance; **ruling out, disallowance,** denial, rejection 372; refusal 442; **repression, suppression** 428.2; **ban, embargo, enjoinder, injunction,** prohibitory injunction, **proscription,** inhibition, **interdict,** *interdictum* <L>, interdiction; index, *Index Expurgatorius* and *Index Librorum Prohibitorum* <L>; gag order; **taboo;** thou-shalt-not *and* don't *and* no-no <nf>; law, statute 673.3; preclusion, exclusion, **prevention** 1012.2; forbidden fruit, contraband; sumptuary law *or* ordinance; zoning, zoning law, restrictive convenant; **forbidden ground** *or* **territory,** no-man's land <nf>, no-fly zone; curfew; restriction, circumscription

2 **veto,** negative ; absolute veto, qualified *or* limited *or* negative veto, countermand, suspensive *or* suspensory veto, item veto, pocket veto; **thumbs-down** <nf>, red light <nf>, *pollice verso* <L>; blacklist

VERBS **3** **prohibit, forbid; disallow, rule out** *or* **against,** forfend**;** deny, **reject** 372.2; say no to, **refuse** 442.3; **bar,** debar, preclude, exclude, exclude from, shut out, shut *or* close the door on, **prevent** 1012.14; **ban,** put under the ban, **outlaw,** criminalize, proscribe**; repress, suppress** 428.8; **enjoin,** put under an injunction, issue an injunction against, issue a prohibitory injunction; **proscribe,** inhibit, **interdict,** put *or* lay under an interdict *or* interdiction; put on the Index; embargo, **lay** *or* **put an embargo on; taboo**; outlaw, criminalize,

4 **not permit** *or* **allow, not have, not suffer** *or* **tolerate,** not endure, not stomach, not bear, not bear with, **not countenance,** not brook, brook no, not condone, not accept, not put up with, not go along with <nf>; not stand for *and* not hear of <nf>, put *or* set one's foot down on <nf>

5 **veto,** put one's veto upon, decide *or* rule against, **turn thumbs down on** <nf>, **negative,** kill, nix <nf>

ADJS **6** **prohibitive,** prohibitory, prohibiting, **forbidding;** inhibitive, inhibitory, **repressive, suppressive** 428.11; proscriptive, interdictive, interdictory; preclusive, exclusive, **preventive** 1012.19

7 **prohibited, forbidden,** forbade, forbid, *verboten* <Ger>, **barred; vetoed; unpermissible,** nonpermissible, not permitted *or* allowed, unchartered, **unallowed;** disallowed, ruled out, contraindicated; beyond the pale, off limits, out of bounds; unauthorized, **unsanctioned,** unlicensed; banned, under the ban, **outlawed,** contraband; taboo, untouchable; **illegal,** unlawful, illicit

445 REPEAL

NOUNS **1** **repeal, revocation,** revoke, revokement; reneging, renigging *and* going back on *and* welshing <nf>, **rescinding,** rescindment, rescission, **reversal, striking down, abrogation,** cassation; suspension; waiving, **waiver, setting aside; countermand,** counterorder; **annulment,** nullification, withdrawal, **invalidation,** voiding, voidance, vacation, vacatur, defeasance; **cancellation,** canceling, cancel, write-off; **abolition,** abolishment; **recall,** retraction, recantation 363.3

VERBS **2** **repeal, revoke, rescind, reverse, strike down, abrogate;** renege, renig *and* go back on *and* welsh <nf>; suspend; **waive, set aside; countermand,** counterorder; **abolish,** do away with; **cancel,** write off; **annul,** nullify, disannul, withdraw, **invalidate,** void, vacate, make void, declare null *and* void; **overrule,** override; **recall,** retract, recant; unwish

ADJS **3** **repealed, revoked, rescinded,** struck down, set aside; **invalid,** void, **null and void**

446 PROMOTION

NOUNS **1** **promotion, preferment, advancement, advance,** step-up *and* upping <nf>, rise, elevation, upgrading, jump, step up, step up the ladder, furtherance; **raise, boost** <nf>; kicking *or* bumping upstairs <nf>; exaltation, aggrandizement; ennoblement, knighting; graduation, passing; pay raise

VERBS **2** **promote, advance,** prefer, up *and* boost <nf>, elevate, upgrade, jump; kick *or* bump upstairs <nf>, furthering; **raise;** exalt, aggrandize; **ennoble,** knight; pass, graduate; raise one's pay, up *or* boost one's pay <nf>

447 DEMOTION, DEPOSAL

NOUNS **1** **demotion,** degrading, degradation, disgrading, downgrading, debasement; abasement, humbling, humiliation, casting down; **reduction,** bump *and* bust <nf>; stripping of rank, depluming, displuming

2 **deposal, deposition, removal,** displacement, outplacement, supplanting, supplantation, replacement, deprivation, **ousting,** unseating; **cashiering, firing** <nf>, **dismissal** 909.5; pink slip <nf>, walking papers <nf>; reduction in forces *or* RIF; forced resignation; kicking upstairs <nf>; **superannuation,** pensioning off, putting out to pasture, **retirement,** the golden handshake *or* parachute <nf>; **suspension;** impeachment; purge, **liquidation; overthrow,** overthrowal; **dethronement,** disenthronement, discrownment; **disbarment,** disbarring; unfrocking, defrocking, unchurching; deconsecration, expulsion, excommunication 909.4

VERBS **3** **demote, degrade,** disgrade, downgrade, debase, abase, humble, humiliate, **lower, reduce,** bump *and* bust <nf>; strip of rank, cut off one's spurs, deplume, displume; force out

4 **depose, remove from office,** send to the showers *and* give the gate <nf>, divest *or* deprive *or* strip of office, **remove,** displace, outplace, supplant, replace; **oust; suspend; cashier,** drum out, strip of rank, **break,** bust <nf>; give a pink slip, hand one's walking papers; **dismiss** 909.19; **purge, liquidate; overthrow; retire,** superannuate, pension, pension off, put out to pasture, give the golden handshake *or* parachute <nf>; kick upstairs <nf>; **unseat,** unsaddle; **dethrone,** disenthrone, unthrone, uncrown, discrown; **disbar; unfrock,** defrock, unchurch; strike off the roll, read out of; **expel,** excommunicate 909.17; deconsecrate

448 RESIGNATION, RETIREMENT

NOUNS 1 **resignation,** demission, **withdrawal, retirement,** pensioning, pensioning off, golden handshake *or* parachute <nf>, superannuation, emeritus status, retiracy; **abdication;** voluntary resignation; forced resignation, forced retirement, early retirement, deposal 447; relinquishment 370.3

VERBS 2 **resign,** demit, **quit,** leave, **vacate,** withdraw from; **retire,** superannuate, be superannuated, be pensioned *or* pensioned off, be put out to pasture, get the golden handshake *or* parachute <nf>; relinquish, give up 370.7; retire from office, stand down, stand *or* step aside, give up one's post, hang up one's spurs <nf>; **tender** *or* **hand in one's resignation,** send in one's papers, turn in one's badge *or* uniform; **abdicate,** renounce the throne, give up the crown; pension off 447.4; be invalided out

ADJS 3 **retired,** in retirement, superannuated, on pension, pensioned, pensioned off, emeritus, emerita <fem>

449 AID

NOUNS 1 **aid, help, assistance, support, succor, relief, comfort,** ease, remedy; mutual help *or* assistance; **service, benefit** 387.4; ministry, ministration, office, offices, good offices; yeoman's service; therapy 91; protection 1008; **bailout** <nf>, rescue 398; means to an end

2 **assist, helping hand, hand, lift; boost** *and* leg up <nf>; help in time of need; **support group,** self-help group, Alcoholics Anonymous *or* AA, Gamblers Anonymous, etc, 12-step group; tough love, intervention; social assistance, counsel, guidance, moral support, constructive criticism, tender loving care *or* TLC

3 **support, maintenance, sustainment,** sustentation, **sustenance, subsistence,** provision, total support, meal ticket <nf>; **keep, upkeep; livelihood, living,** meat, bread, daily bread; **nurture, fostering,** nurturance, nourishment, nutriture , mothering, parenting, rearing, fosterage, foster-care, **care, caring,** caregiving, tender loving care *or* TLC <nf>; manna, manna in the wilderness; economic support, price support, subsidy, subsidization, subvention, endowment, boost; **support services, social services**, welfare, relief, succor; technical support *or* tech support

4 **patronage, fosterage, tutelage, sponsorship, backing, auspices,** aegis, coattails <nf>, care, guidance, **championing, championship,** seconding; interest, advocacy, encouragement, **backing, abetment;** countenance, **favor, goodwill,** charity, **sympathy,** handout <nf>

5 **furtherance, helping along, advancement,** advance, **promotion, forwarding,** facilitation, speeding, easing *or* smoothing of the way, clearing of the track, greasing of the wheels, expedition, expediting, rushing; preferment, special *or* preferential treatment; tailwind

6 **self-help,** self-helpfulness, **self-support,** self-sustainment, self-improvement; independence 430.5

7 helper, assistant 616.6; benefactor 592; facilitator, animator

8 **reinforcements, support, relief,** auxiliaries, reserves, reserve forces, staff

9 **facility, accommodation, appliance, convenience,** amenity, appurtenance; advantage; labor-saving device, time-saving device

10 **helpfulness,** aidfulness , cooperation, goodwill, charity; serviceability, utility, **usefulness** 387.3; **advantageousness,** profitability, favorableness, beneficialness 999.1

VERBS **11** **aid, help, assist,** comfort, abet , succor, relieve, **ease,** doctor, remedy; be of some help, put one's oar in <nf>; do good, do a world of good, **benefit, avail** 999.10; **favor, befriend; give help,** render assistance, offer *or* proffer aid, come to the aid of, rush *or* fly to the assistance of, lend aid, **give** *or* **lend** *or* **bear a hand** *or* **helping hand,** stretch forth *or* hold out a helping hand, boost, cater for <chiefly Brit>; take by the hand, take in tow; **give an assist, give a leg up** *or* lift *or* boost <nf>, help a lame dog over a stile; **save,** redeem, bail out <nf>, **rescue** 398.3; protect 1008.18; set up, put on one's feet; give new life to, resuscitate, rally, reclaim, revive, **restore** 396.11,15; be the making of, set one up in business; see one through

12 **support, lend support,** give *or* furnish *or* afford support; **maintain, sustain, keep,** upkeep <Brit>; **uphold,** hold up, bear, upbear, **bear up,** bear out; reinforce, undergird, bolster, **bolster up,** buttress, shore, shore up, prop, prop up, crutch; **finance,** fund, subsidize, subvention, subventionize; comp *and* pick up the tab *or* check <nf>, give new life to

13 **back, back up, stand behind, stand back of** *or* in back of, get behind, get in behind, get in back of; stand by, stick by *and* **stick up for** <nf>, **champion; second, take the part of,** take up *or* adopt *or* espouse the cause of, take under one's wing, **go to bat for** <nf>, take up the cudgels for, run interference for <nf>, **side with,** take sides with, associate oneself with, join oneself to, align oneself with, ally with, come down *or* range oneself on the side of, find time for

14 **abet, aid** *and* **abet, encourage,** hearten, embolden, comfort ; advocate, hold a brief for <nf>, countenance, keep in countenance, **endorse, lend oneself to,** lend one's countenance to, lend one's favor *or* support to, lend one's offices, put one's weight in the scale, plump for *and* thump the tub for <nf>, lend one's name to, give one's support *or* countenance to, give moral support to, hold one's hand, make one's cause one's own, weigh in for <nf>; subscribe <Brit>, **favor, go for** <nf>, smile upon, shine upon

15 **patronize, sponsor,** take up, endow, finance

16 **foster, nurture,** nourish, mother, care for, lavish care on, feed, parent, rear, sustain, cultivate, **cherish;** pamper, coddle, cosset, fondle ; **nurse,** suckle, cradle; dry-nurse, wet-nurse; spoon-feed; take in hand

17 **be useful, further, forward, advance, promote,** stand in good stead, encourage, **boost** <nf>, favor, advantage, **facilitate,** set *or* put *or* push forward, give an impulse to; speed, expedite, quicken, hasten, lend wings to; conduce to, make for, contribute to

18 **serve, lend** *or* **give oneself,** render service to, do service for, **work for, labor in behalf of; minister to,** cater to, do for <Brit>; attend 577.13; pander to*

19 **oblige, accommodate, favor,** do a favor, do a service

ADJS **20** **helping,** assisting, serving, promoting; **assistant, auxiliary,** adjuvant, subservient, subsidiary, ancillary, accessory; ministerial, ministering, ministrant; fostering, nurtural; care, caring, care-giving; instrumental

21 **helpful, useful,** utile, aidful ; **profitable, salutary,** good for, **beneficial** 999.12; remedial, therapeutic; **serviceable, useful** 387.18; **contributory,** contributing, conducive,

constructive, positive, promotional, furthersome ; at one's service, at one's command, at one's beck *and* call; right-hand; adjuvant

22 **favorable, propitious;** kind, kindly, kindly-disposed, all for <nf>, **well-disposed,** well-affected, well-intentioned, well-meant, **well-meaning;** benevolent, beneficent, benign, benignant; friendly, amicable, neighborly; cooperative

23 self-helpful, self-helping, self-improving; **self-supporting, self-sustaining;** self-supported, self-sustained; independent

ADVS 24 **helpfully,** helpingly; **beneficially,** favorably, profitably, advantageously, to advantage, to the good; serviceably, **usefully**

25 **for, on** *or* **in behalf of,** in aid of <chiefly Brit>, in the name of, on account of, **for the sake of,** in the service of, in furtherance of, in favor of; remedial of

26 **behind, back of** <nf>, supporting, **in support of**

450 COOPERATION

NOUNS 1 **cooperation, collaboration, coaction,** concurrence, synergy, synergism; support, backup; **consensus, commonality; community,** harmony, concordance, concord, fellowship, fellow feeling, solidarity, concert, united front, **teamwork;** pulling *or* working together, communal *or* community activity, joining of forces, pooling, pooling of resources, joining of hands; bipartisanship, **mutualism,** mutuality, mutual assistance, coadjuvancy; **reciprocity;** back-scratching, give and take; joint effort, common effort, combined *or* joint operation, common enterprise *or* endeavor, collective *or* united action, mass action; job-sharing; coagency; coadministration, cochairmanship, codirectorship; duet, duumvirate; trio, triumvirate, troika; quartet, quintet, sextet, septet, octet; government by committee, coalition government; symbiosis, commensalism; **cooperativeness,** collaborativeness, team spirit, morale, esprit, *esprit de corps* <Fr>; communism, communalism, communitarianism, collectivism; quislingism; ecumenism, ecumenicism, ecumenicalism; **collusion,** complicity; networking

2 **affiliation, alliance, allying, alignment, association,** consociation, combination, union, unification, **coalition,** fusion, merger, coalescence, coadunation, amalgamation, **league, federation, confederation,** confederacy, consolidation, incorporation, inclusion, integration; hookup *and* tie-up *and* tie-in <nf>; **partnership,** copartnership, copartnery , cahoots <nf>; colleagueship, **collegialism, collegiality; fraternity,** confraternity, fraternization, fraternalism; sorority; **fellowship,** sodality; comradeship, camaraderie, freemasonry, communalism, ecumenicism; adfiliation; reaffiliation

VERBS 3 **cooperate, collaborate,** do business *and* **play ball** <nf>, coact, concur; concert, harmonize, concord; join, band, league, **associate, affiliate,** ally, **combine, unite,** fuse, merge, coalesce, amalgamate, federate, confederate, consolidate; synergize; hook up *and* tie up *and* tie in <nf>; partner, be in league, **go into partnership with,** go partners <nf>, go *or* be in cahoots with; **join together,** club together, league together, band together; **work together,** get together *and* team up *and* buddy up <nf>, work as a team, act together, act in concert, **pull together; hold together, hang together,** keep together, **stand together,** stand shoulder to shoulder; lay *or* put *or* get heads together; **close ranks,** make common cause, throw in together <nf>, unite efforts, join in, pitch in; network; reciprocate; conspire, collude, aid and abet, stonewall

4 **side with,** take sides with, **unite with; join, join with,** join up with *and* get together with *and* team up with <nf>, strike in with ; **throw in with** *and* string along with *and* swing in with <nf>, **go along with; line up with** <nf>, align with, align

oneself with, range with, range oneself with, stand up with, stand in with; **join hands with,** be hand in glove with, go hand in hand with; act with, take part with, **go in with;** cast in one's lot with, join one's fortunes with, stand shoulder to shoulder with, be cheek by jowl with, sink *or* swim with, stand *or* fall with; **close ranks with**, fall in with, make common cause with, pool one's interests with; enlist under the banner of, rally round, flock to

ADJS **5 cooperative, cooperating,** cooperant, **hand in glove;** in cahoots <nf>; **collaborative,** coactive, coacting, coefficient, synergetic, synergic, synergical, synergistic *or* synergistical; **fellow;** concurrent, concurring, concerted, **in concert; consensus,** consensual, agreeing, in agreement, of like mind; harmonious, harmonized, concordant, **common, communal,** collective; **mutual,** reciprocal; **joint, combined** 805.5; coadjuvant, coadjutant; symbiotic, symbiotical, commensal; complicit, complicitous; uncompetitive, noncompetitive, communalist, communalistic, communist, communistic, communitarian, collective, collectivist, collectivistic, ecumenic *or* ecumenical; **conniving, collusive**

ADVS **6 cooperatively,** cooperatingly, coactively, coefficiently, concurrently; in consensus, consensually; **jointly,** combinedly, **conjointly,** concertedly, in concert with; harmoniously, concordantly; communally, collectively, **together;** as one, with one voice, unanimously, in chorus, in unison, as one man, en masse; **side by side, hand in hand, hand in glove, shoulder to shoulder, back to back**

7 in cooperation, in collaboration, in partnership, in cahoots <nf>, **in collusion,** in league

451 OPPOSITION

NOUNS **1 opposition,** opposing, opposure, crossing, oppugnancy, bucking <nf>, standing against; contraposition 779.1; **resistance** 453; **noncooperation; contention** 457; negation 335; **rejection** 372, refusal; **counteraction,** counterworking 900.1; refusal 442; **contradiction,** challenge, contravention, contraversion, rebutment, rebuttal, denial, impugnation, impugnment; countercurrent, head wind; crosscurrent, undercurrent, undertow; unfriendliness, stiff opposition; contest, pageant, grudge match; line in the sand

2 hostility, antagonism, oppugnancy, oppugnance *and* oppugnation , **antipathy,** enmity, bad blood, inimicalness; **contrariness, contrariety,** orneriness <nf>, repugnance *or* repugnancy, perverseness, **obstinacy** 361; fractiousness, refractoriness, recalcitrance 327.2; uncooperativeness, noncooperation, negativeness, **obstructionism,** traversal, bloody-mindedness <Brit>; **friction, conflict,** clashing, **collision,** cross-purposes, dissension, disaccord 456; latent hostility; rivalry, vying, competition 457.2; polarity

VERBS **3 oppose, counter, cross,** go *or* act in opposition to, **go against,** run against, strive against, **run counter to,** fly in the face of, fly in the teeth of, conflict with, butt heads; kick out against, make waves <nf>, **protest** 333.5; set oneself against, set one's face *or* heart against; be *or* play at cross-purposes, **obstruct,** traverse, sabotage; **take issue with, take one's stand against,** lift *or* raise a hand against, declare oneself against, stand and be counted against, side against, vote against, vote nay, veto; make a stand against, make a dead set against; join the opposition; not put up with, not abide, not be content with; counteract, counterwork, countervail 900.6; **resist,** withstand 453.3

4 contend against, militate against, **contest, combat, battle, clash with, clash, fight against, strive against,** struggle against, labor against, **take on** <nf>, grapple with, join battle with, close with, come to close quarters with, go the the mat with

<nf>, antagonize , **fight, buck** <nf>, **counter;** buffet, beat against, beat up against, breast, stem, breast *or* stem the tide *or* current *or* flood, breast the wave, buffet the waves; rival, compete with *or* against, vie with *or* against; fight back, **resist, offer resistance** 453.3

5 **confront, affront,** front, go eyeball-to-eyeball *or* one-on-one with <nf>, take on, tackle, **meet, face, meet head-on; encounter**

6 **contradict,** cross, traverse, contravene, controvert, rebut, deny, **gainsay;** challenge, contest; oppugn, call into question; **belie,** be contrary to, come in conflict with, negate 335.3; **reject** 372.2

7 **be against,** be agin <nf>, reject; discountenance 510.11; not hold with, not have anything to do with; have a crow to pluck *or* pick, have a bone to pick

ADJS 8 **oppositional, opponent, opposing, opposed; anti** <nf>, contra, confrontational, confrontive; at odds, at loggerheads; **adverse, adversary,** adversarial, adversative, oppugnant, antithetic, antithetical, repugnant, con <nf>, **set** *or* **dead set against; contrary, counter; negative; opposite,** oppositive, death on; overthwart , cross; **contradictory;** unfavorable, unpropitious 133.16; **hostile, antagonistic,** unfriendly, enemy, inimical, alien, antipathetic, antipathetical, unsympathetic, averse; fractious, refractory, recalcitrant 327.10; uncooperative, noncooperative, **obstructive,** bloody-minded <Brit>; ornery <nf>, perverse, obstinate 361.8; **conflicting, clashing,** dissentient, disaccordant 456.15; rival, competitive

ADVS 9 **in opposition, in confrontation,** eyeball-to-eyeball *and* one-on-one <nf>, head-on, **at variance, at cross-purposes, at odds,** at issue, at war with, up in arms, with crossed bayonets, at daggers drawn, at daggers, in hostile array, poised against one another; contra, contrariwise, counter, cross, athwart; against the tide *or* wind *or* grain

452 OPPONENT

NOUNS 1 **opponent, adversary, antagonist, assailant, foe,** foeman, enemy, archenemy; adverse *or* opposing party, opposite camp, opposite *or* opposing side, **the opposition,** the loyal opposition, unfriendly <nf>; **combatant** 461

2 **competitor, contestant, contender,** corrival, vier, player, entrant; **rival,** arch-rival; emulator; the field; finalist, semifinalist, etc

3 **oppositionist,** opposer; obstructionist, obstructive, negativist, naysayer, wet noodle <nf>; contra; **objector, protester,** dissident, dissentient; **resister;** noncooperator; **disputant,** litigant, plaintiff, defendant; quarreler, irritable man, curmudgeon, scrapper <nf>, wrangler, brawler; die-hard, bitter-ender, last-ditcher, intransigent, irreconcilable

453 RESISTANCE

NOUNS 1 **resistance,** withstanding, countering, renitence *or* renitency, repellence *or* repellency; **defiance** 454; **opposing, opposition** 451; **stand; repulsion,** repulse, rebuff; **objection, protest,** remonstrance, **dispute,** challenge, **demur; complaint;** dissentience, **dissent** 333; reaction, hostile *or* combative reaction, rebellion, **counteraction** 900; revolt 327.4; recalcitrance *or* recalcitrancy, recalcitration, fractiousness, refractoriness 327.2; **reluctance** 325.1; **obstinacy** 361; passive resistance, noncooperation; uncooperativeness, negativism; obstinacy; resistance movement, passive resistance, civil disobedience, mutiny, insurrection, insurgence

VERBS 2 **resist, withstand; stand; endure** 134.5; **stand up, bear up, hold up, hold out; defy** 454.3, tell one where to get off <nf>, throw down the gauntlet; be obstinate; be proof against, bear up against; **repel,** repulse, rebuff

3 **offer resistance, fight back,** bite back, not turn the other cheek, show fight, lift *or* raise a hand, stand *or*

hold one's ground, **withstand,** stand, **take one's stand,** make a stand, make a stand against, take one's stand against, square off *and* put up one's dukes <nf>, **stand up to,** stand up against, stand at bay; front, **confront,** meet head-on, fly in the teeth *or* face of, **face up to,** face down, face out; **object, protest,** remonstrate, **dispute,** challenge, **complain,** complain loudly, exclaim at; **dissent** 333.4; revolt, mutiny; make waves <nf>; make a determined resistance; kick against, kick out against, recalcitrate; put up a fight *or* struggle <nf>, not take lying down, hang tough *and* tough it out <nf>; **revolt** 327.7; **oppose** 451.3; **contend with** 457.17; **strive against** 451.4

4 **stand fast, stand** *or* **hold one's ground,** stand firm, make a resolute stand, **hold one's own,** remain firm, stick *and* stuck fast <nf>, **stick to one's guns, stay it out, stick it out** <nf>, **hold out,** not back down, not give up, not submit, **never say die; fight to the last ditch,** die hard, sell one's life dearly, go down with flying colors, refuse to bow down

ADJS **5** **resistant, resistive,** resisting, renitent, up against, **withstanding,** repellent; obstructive, retardant, retardative; **unyielding,** unsubmissive 361.12; hard-shell, hard-nosed; rebellious 327.11; **proof against; objecting, protesting,** disputing, disputatious, complaining, dissentient, dissenting 333.6; recalcitrant, fractious, obstinate, refractory 327.10; **reluctant** 325.6; noncooperative, uncooperative; up in arms, on the barricades, not lying down; immune

454 DEFIANCE

NOUNS **1** **defiance,** defying, defial ; **daring,** daringness, **audacity,** boldness, bold front, brash bearing, brashness, brassiness <nf>, brazenness, bravado, insolence; bearding, beard-tweaking, nose-tweaking; **arrogance** 141; **sauciness,** sauce, **cheekiness** *or* cheek <nf>, rebelliousness, pertness, impudence, impertinence; bumptiousness, cockiness; **contempt,** contemptuousness, derision, **disdain,** disregard, despite; **risk-taking,** tightrope walking, funambulism; disobedience, insubordination

2 **challenge, dare,** double dare, threat, taunt; fighting words; **defy** *or* defi; gage, gage of battle, gauntlet, glove, chip on one's shoulder, slap of the glove, invitation *or* bid to combat, call to arms; war cry, war whoop, battle cry, rebel yell; back talk, insult

VERBS **3** **defy,** bid defiance, hurl defiance, snarl *or* shout *or* scream defiance; **dare,** double dare, outdare; **challenge,** call out, throw *or* fling down the gauntlet *or* glove *or* gage, stand up to, knock the chip off one's shoulder, cross swords; oppose, protest; beard, beard the lion in his den, face, face out, look in the eye, stare down, stare out <Brit>, **confront, affront,** front, say right to one's face, square up to, go eyeball-to-eyeball *or* one-on-one with <nf>; tweak the nose, pluck by the beard, slap one's face, double *or* shake one's fist at; give one the finger; **ask for it** <nf>, ask *or* look for trouble, make something of it <nf>, show fight, show one's teeth, bare one's fangs; dance the war dance; **brave** 492.10; be insubordinate

4 **flout,** disregard, **slight,** slight over, treat with contempt, set at defiance, fly in the teeth *or* face of, **snap one's fingers at; thumb one's nose at,** cock a snook at, bite the thumb at; **disdain, despise, scorn** 157.3; laugh at, laugh to scorn, laugh out of court, laugh in one's face; hold in derision, scout, scoff at, **deride** 508.8; give someone lip <nf>, sass <nf>

5 **show** *or* **put up a bold front,** bluster, throw out one's chest, strut, crow, look big, stand with arms akimbo, gasconade

6 **take a dare,** accept a challenge, **take one up on** *and* **call one's bluff** <nf>; **start something,** take up the gauntlet

ADJS **7** **defiant,** defying, challenging; **daring, bold,** brash, brassy <nf>, brazen, **audacious,** insolent; arrogant 141.9; saucy, cheeky <nf>, pert, impudent, impertinent; stubborn, obstinate; bumptious, cocky, sassy; **contemptuous,** disdainful, derisive, disregardful, greatly daring, regardless of consequences; obstreperous

ADVS **8 in defiance of,** in the teeth of, in the face of, under one's very nose

455 ACCORD

<harmonious relationship>

NOUNS **1 accord,** accordance, **concord,** concordance, **harmony,** symphony, sync <nf>; **rapport;** good vibrations <nf>, good vibes <nf>, good karma; amity 587.1; frictionlessness; *rapprochement* <Fr>; **sympathy,** empathy, identity, feeling of identity, fellow feeling, **fellowship,** kinship, togetherness, **affinity; agreement, understanding, like-mindedness, congruence;** congeniality, **compatibility; oneness,** unity, unison, union; **community,** communion, community of interests, meeting of the minds; solidarity, team spirit, esprit, *esprit de corps* <Fr>; mutuality, sharing, reciprocity, mutual supportiveness; bonds of harmony, ties of affection, cement of friendship; happy family; peace 464; **love**, charity, *caritas* <L>, brotherly love; correspondence 788.1

VERBS **2 get along,** harmonize, **agree with, agree, get along with,** get on with, cotton to *or* hit it off with <nf>, harmonize with, **be in harmony with,** be in tune with, fall *or* chime in with, blend in with, go hand in hand with, **be at one with;** sing in chorus, be on the same wavelength <nf>, see eye to eye; **sympathize,** empathize, identify with, respond to, understand one another, enter into one's views, enter into the ideas *or* feelings of; accord, correspond 788.6; reciprocate, interchange 863.4

ADJS **3 in accord,** accordant , **harmonious, in harmony,** congruous, congruent, in tune, attuned, agreeing, in concert, **in rapport,** *en rapport* <Fr>, amicable 587.15,18; frictionless; **sympathetic,** simpatico <nf>, empathic, empathetic, **understanding; like-minded,** akin, of the same mind, of one mind, at one, united, together; concordant, corresponding 788.9; agreeable, congenial, **compatible; peaceful** 464.9

456 DISACCORD

<unharmonious relationship>

NOUNS **1 disaccord, discord,** discordance *or* discordancy, asynchrony, **unharmoniousness,** inharmoniousness, disharmony, inharmony, incongruence, incongruency, disaffinity, incompatibility, incompatibleness; culture gap, generation gap, gender gap; noncooperation; **conflict,** open conflict *or* war, **friction,** rub; jar, **jarring,** jangle, clash, clashing; touchiness, strained relations, tension; bad blood; **unpleasantness;** mischief; **contention** 457; **enmity** 589; Eris, Discordia; the Apple of Discord

2 disagreement, difficulty, misunderstanding, difference, difference of opinion, agreement to disagree, **variance,** division, dividedness; cross-purposes; polarity of opinion, polarization; credibility gap, **disparity** 789.1

3 dissension, dissent, dissidence, flak <nf>; bickering, infighting, faction, factiousness, partisanship, partisan spirit; **divisiveness; quarrelsomeness;** litigiousness; pugnacity, bellicosity, combativeness, **aggressiveness,** contentiousness, belligerence; feistiness <nf>, **touchiness, irritability,** shrewishness, irascibility 110.2

4 falling-out, breach of friendship, parting of the ways, bust-up <nf>; **alienation, estrangement, disaffection,** disfavor; **breach, break, rupture, schism, split, rift,** cleft, **disunity, disunion, disruption,** separation, cleavage, divergence, division, dividedness; division in the camp, house divided against itself; open rupture, breaking off of negotiations, recall of ambassadors

5 **quarrel,** open quarrel, dustup, **dispute, argument,** polemic, argy-bargy *and* slanging match <Brit>, fliting , lovers' quarrel, **controversy,** altercation, **fight, squabble, contention,** strife, **tussle,** bicker, wrangle, snarl, **tiff, spat,** fuss; **breach of the peace; fracas,** donnybrook *or* donnybrook fair, brouhaha; dissent; broil, embroilment, imbroglio; words, sharp words, war of words, logomachy; **feud,** blood feud, vendetta; brawl 457.5; turf war

6 <nf terms> **row, rumpus,** row-de-dow, ruckus, ruction, brannigan, shindy, foofooraw, hoo-ha, barney *and* shemozzle <Brit>, set-to, run-in, **scrap, hassle,** rhubarb; knock-down-and-drag-out, knock-down-and-drag-out quarrel *or* fight; the dozens; handbags at dawn, handbag situation

7 **bone of contention,** apple of discord, sore point, tender spot, delicate *or* ticklish issue, rub, beef <nf>; **bone to pick,** crow to pluck *or* pick *or* pull; *casus belli* <L>, grounds for war

VERBS 8 **disagree, differ,** differ in opinion, hold opposite views, disaccord, **be at variance,** not get along, pull different ways, be at cross-purposes, have no measures with, misunderstand one another; **conflict, clash,** collide, jostle, jangle, jar; live like cat *and* dog, live a cat-and-dog life

9 **have a bone to pick with,** have a crow to pluck with *or* pick with *or* pull with, have a beef with <nf>

10 **fall out,** have a falling-out, **break with, split,** separate, **diverge,** divide, agree to disagree, **part company,** come to *or* reach a parting of the ways

11 **quarrel, dispute,** oppugn, flite , altercate, **fight, squabble,** tiff, spat, **bicker, wrangle,** spar, broil, have words, set to, join issue, make the fur fly; cross swords, **feud, battle; brawl; be quarrelsome** *or* contentious, be thin-skinned, be touchy *or* sensitive, get up on the wrong side of the bed

12 <nf terms> **row, scrap, hassle,** make *or* kick up a row; mix it up, lock horns, bump heads

13 **pick a quarrel,** fasten a quarrel on, look for trouble, pick a bone with, pluck a crow with; have a chip on one's shoulder; add insult to injury

14 **sow dissension,** stir up trouble, make *or* borrow trouble; **alienate, estrange,** separate, **divide, disunite,** disaffect, **come between; irritate, provoke,** aggravate; **set at odds,** set at variance; **set against,** pit against, **sic on** *or* **at, set on,** set by the ears, set at one's throat; add fuel to the fire *or* flame, fan the flame, pour oil on the blaze, light the fuse, stir the pot <nf>

ADJS 15 **disaccordant, unharmonious,** inharmonious, disharmonious, out of tune, asynchronous, unsynchronized, out of sync <nf>, **discordant,** out of accord, dissident, dissentient, **disagreeing, differing; conflicting,** clashing, colliding; like cats *and* dogs; **divided,** faction-ridden, fragmented

16 **at odds, at variance, at loggerheads,** at square , at cross-purposes; at war, at strife, at feud, at swords' points, at daggers *or* at daggers drawn, up in arms

17 **partisan,** polarizing, **divisive,** factional, factious; **quarrelsome,** bickering, disputatious, wrangling, eristic, eristical, polemical; litigious, pugnacious, combative, **aggressive,** bellicose, belligerent; feisty <nf>, touchy, irritable, shrewish, **irascible** 110.19

457 CONTENTION

NOUNS 1 **contention, contest,** contestation, combat, **fighting, conflict, strife, war, struggle,** blood on the floor, cut *and* thrust; fighting at close quarters, infighting; **warfare** 458; **hostility,** enmity 589; **quarrel, altercation, controversy,** dustup, polemic, debate, forensics, **argument, dispute, disputation;** litigation; words, war of words, paper war, logomachy; **fighting,** scrapping *and* hassling <nf>; **quarreling, bickering, wrangling, squabbling;** oppugnancy, contentiousness, disputatiousness, litigiousness, **quarrelsomeness** 456.3; cat-and-dog life; Kilkenny cats; **competitiveness,** vying, rivalrousness, competitorship; cold war; bone of contention

2 **competition, rivalry,** trying conclusions *or* the issue, vying, emulation, jockeying <nf>; cutthroat competition; run for one's money; **sportsmanship,** gamesmanship, lifemanship, one-upmanship, competitive advantage; rat race <nf>; feeding frenzy <nf>

3 **contest, engagement, encounter, match,** matching, meet, meeting, derby, pissing match *or* contest <nf>, **trial, test,** *concours* and *rencontre* <Fr>; **close contest, hard contest,** closely fought contest, close *or* tight one, horse race *and* crapshoot <nf>; fight, bout, go <nf>, tussle; joust, tilt; tournament, tourney; rally; **game** 743.9; **games,** Olympic games, Olympics, gymkhana; cookoff, Bake-Off <TM>; spelling bee

4 **fight, battle, fray,** affray, combat, action, conflict, embroilment; gun battle; **clash; brush, skirmish,** scrimmage; tussle, **scuffle, struggle,** scramble, shoving match; exchange of blows, *passage d'armes* <Fr>, passage at *or* of arms, clash of arms; **quarrel** 456.5; pitched battle; battle royal; unarmed combat; **fistfight**, punch-out *and* duke-out <nf>, punch-up <Brit nf>; **hand-to-hand fight,** stand-up fight <nf>, running fight *or* engagement; tug-of-war; bull-fight, tauromachy; dogfight, cockfight; street fight, rumble <nf>; air *or* aerial combat, sea *or* naval combat, ground combat, armored combat, infantry combat, fire fight, hand-to-hand combat, house-to-house combat; **internal struggle,** intestine *or* internecine struggle *or* combat; rhubarb <nf>

5 **free-for-all, knock-down-and-drag-out** <nf>, **brawl,** broil, melee, scrimmage, **fracas,** riot

6 **death struggle, life-and-death** *or* **life-or-death struggle, struggle** *or* **fight** *or* **duel to the death,** *guerre à mort* and *guerre à outrance* <Fr>, all-out war, total war, last-ditch fight, fight to the last ditch, fight with no quarter given

7 **duel,** single combat, monomachy, satisfaction, **affair of honor,** *affaire d'honneur* <Fr>

8 **fencing, swordplay;** swordsmanship, dueling

9 **boxing** 754, **fighting,** noble *or* manly art of self-defense, **fisticuffs, pugilism, prize-fighting,** the fights <nf>, the ring; **boxing match, prizefight,** spar, bout; shadowboxing; close fighting, infighting, the clinches <nf>; Chinese boxing; savate

10 **wrestling,** rassling <nf>, grappling, *sumo* <Japanese>; **martial arts;** catch-as-catch-can; wrestling match, wrestling meet; Greco-Roman wrestling, Cornish wrestling, Westmorland wrestling, Cumberland wrestling; professional wrestling

11 **racing, track,** track sports; **horse racing** 757, the turf, the sport of kings; dog racing, automobile racing 756

12 **race,** contest of speed *or* fleetness; derby; **horse race; automobile race**, off-road race**; heat, lap,** bell lap, victory lap; footrace, run, running event; torch race; match race, obstacle race, three-legged race, sack race, potato race; walk; ride *and* tie; endurance race, motorcycle race, bicycle race; boat race, yacht race, regatta; air race; dog race

VERBS 13 **contend, contest,** jostle; **fight, battle, combat, war, declare** *or* **go to war,** take *or* take up arms, put up a fight <nf>, open hostilities, call to arms; wage war; **strive, struggle,** scramble, go for the brass ring; make the fur *or* feathers fly, **tussle, scuffle; quarrel** 456.11; clash, collide; **wrestle,** rassle <nf>, grapple, grapple with, go to the mat with; **come to blows,** close, try conclusions, **mix it up** *and* go toe-to-toe <nf>, exchange blows *or* fisticuffs, **box,** spar, give *and* take, give one a knuckle sandwich <nf>; cut *and* thrust, **cross swords, fence,** thrust *and* parry; **joust, tilt, tourney,** run a tilt *or* a tilt at, break a lance with; **duel,** fight a duel, give satisfaction; feud; skirmish; fight one's way; fight the good fight; **brawl,** broil; **riot;** do a job on <nf>

14 **lift** *or* **raise one's hand against;** make war on; draw the sword against, take up the cudgels, couch one's lance; square up *or* off <nf>, come to the scratch; have at, jump; lay on, lay about one; **pitch into** *and* **sail into** *and* light into *and* lay into *and* rip into <nf>, strike the first blow, draw first blood, **attack** 459.14

15 **encounter, come** *or* **go up against,** fall *or* run foul *or* afoul of; close with, come to close quarters, bring to bay, meet *or* fight hand-to-hand

16 **engage, take on** <nf>, go against *or* up against, close with, try conclusions with, enter the ring *or* arena with, put on the gloves with, match oneself against; **join issue** *or* **battle, do** *or* **give battle,** engage in battle *or* combat

17 **contend with, engage with,** cope with, **fight with, strive with, struggle with,** wrestle with, grapple with, bandy with , try conclusions with, measure swords with, tilt with, **cross swords with;** exchange shots, shoot it out with <nf>; **lock horns** *and* **bump heads** <nf>, fall *or* go to loggerheads ; **tangle with** *and* **mix it up with** <nf>, have a brush with; have it out, fight *or* battle it out, settle it; **fight** *or* **go at it hammer and tongs** *or* tooth and nail, fight it out, duke it out <nf>, fight like devils, ask *and* give no quarter, make blood flow freely, battle *à outrance,* fight to the death, fight to the finish

18 **compete, contend, vie,** try conclusions *or* the issue, jockey <nf>; **compete with** *or* **against, vie with, challenge,** cope , enter into competition with, give a run for one's money, **meet;** try *or* test one another; **rival,** emulate, outvie; keep up with the Joneses

19 **race,** race with, run a race; horse-race, boat-race, etc

20 **contend for, strive for, struggle for, fight for,** vie for; stickle for, stipulate for, hold out for, make a point of

21 **dispute, contest,** oppugn, take issue with; **fight over, quarrel over, wrangle over, squabble over,** bicker over, strive *or* contend about

ADJS 22 **contending,** contesting; **contestant,** disputant; striving, struggling; fighting, battling, warring; **warlike; quarrelsome** 456.17

23 **competitive,** competitory, competing, **vying,** rivaling, **rival,** rivalrous, emulous, in competition, in rivalry; **cutthroat**

458 WARFARE

NOUNS 1 **war, warfare, warring, warmaking,** art of war, **combat, fighting,** *la guerre* <Fr>; armed conflict, armed combat, military operation, the sword, arbitrament of the sword, appeal to arms *or* the sword, resort to arms, force *or* might of arms, bloodshed; **state of war, hostilities,** belligerence *or* belligerency, open war *or* warfare *or* hostilities; **hot war, shooting war;** total war, **all-out war; wartime; battle** 457.4; **attack** 459; **war zone, theater of operations;** trouble spot; warpath; localized war, major war, world war, atomic war, nuclear war, civil war, chemical war, biological war, bacteriological warfare, war of independence, naval war; offensive warfare, preventive warfare, psychological warfare; static warfare, trench warfare, guerrilla warfare; nuclear winter; limited war

2 **battle array,** order of battle, **disposition, deployment, marshaling;** open order; close formation; echelon

3 **campaign,** war, **drive, expedition,** battle plan, hostile expedition; **crusade,** holy war, jihad

4 **operation,** action; **movement; mission; operations,** military operations, land operations, naval *or* sea operations, air operations; combined operations, joint operations, coordinated operations; active operations,

amphibious operations, airborne operations, fluid operations, major operations, minor operations, night operations, overseas operations; war plans, staff work; logistic; war game, dry run, kriegspiel, maneuver, maneuvers; **strategy, tactics; battle**

5 **military science, art** *or* rules *or* science of war, military affairs, military strategy, military tactics, military operations; siegecraft; warcraft, war, **arms,** profession of arms; **generalship,** soldiership; chivalry, knighthood, knightly skill

6 **declaration of war,** challenge; defiance 454

7 **call to arms, call-up,** call to the colors, **rally; mobilization; muster,** levy; conscription, recruitment; **rallying cry,** slogan, watchword, catchword, exhortation; battle cry, war cry, war whoop, rebel yell; banzai, gung ho, St George, Montjoie, Geronimo, go for broke; **bugle call,** trumpet call, clarion, clarion call; remember the Maine *or* the Alamo *or* Pearl Harbor; battle orders, military orders

8 **service, military service;** active service *or* duty; military duty, military obligation, compulsory service, conscription, draft, impressment; selective service, national service <Brit>; reserve status; recruiting, recruitment; enlisting, volunteering

9 **militarization,** activation, **mobilization;** war *or* wartime footing, national emergency; **war effort, war economy;** martial law, suspension of civil rights; garrison state, military dictatorship; remilitarization, reactivation; arms race; war clouds, war scare

10 **warlikeness,** unpeacefulness, war *or* warlike spirit, ferocity, fierceness; **hard line; combativeness, contentiousness; hostility, antagonism;** unfriendliness 589.1; aggression, **aggressiveness;** aggro <Brit nf>; belligerence *or* belligerency, **pugnacity,** pugnaciousness, **bellicosity, bellicoseness, truculence,** fight <nf>; chip on one's shoulder <nf>; militancy, **militarism,** martialism, militaryism; saber rattling; **chauvinism, jingoism,** hawkishness <nf>, **warmongering;** waving of the bloody shirt; warpath; war fever; oppugnancy, **quarrelsomeness** 456.3

11 <rallying devices *and* themes> battle flag, banner, colors, gonfalon, bloody shirt, bluidy sark, fiery cross *or* crostarie, atrocity story, enemy atrocities; martial music, war song, battle hymn, national anthem, military band; national honor, face; foreign threat, totalitarian threat, Communist threat, colonialist *or* neocolonialist *or* imperialist threat, Western imperialism, yellow peril; expansionism, manifest destiny; independence, self-determination

12 war-god, Mars, Ares, Odin *or* Woden *or* Wotan, Tyr *or* Tiu *or* Tiw; war-goddess, Athena, Minerva, Bellona, Enyo, Valkyrie

VERBS 13 **war, wage war, make war, carry on war** *or* **hostilities,** engage in hostilities, wield the sword; battle, **fight;** spill *or* shed blood

14 **make war on,** levy war on; **attack** 459.14,17; **declare war, challenge,** combat, attack, throw *or* fling down the gauntlet; defy 454.3; open hostilities, plunge the world into war; launch a holy war on, go on a crusade against

15 **go to war,** break *or* breach the peace, take up the gauntlet, **go on the warpath, rise up in arms, take** *or* **resort to arms,** take arms, take up arms, take up the cudgels *or* sword, fly *or* appeal to the sword, unsheathe one's weapon, come to cold steel; take the offensive, take the field

16 **campaign,** undertake operations, open a campaign, make an expedition, go on a crusade

17 **serve,** do duty; fulfill one's military obligation, wear the uniform; **soldier,** see *or* do active duty; **bear arms,** carry arms, shoulder arms, shoulder a gun, defend, protect; see action *or* combat, hear shots fired in anger

18 **call to arms, call up,** call to the colors, **rally; mobilize; muster,** levy; **conscript, recruit;** sound the call to

arms, give the battle cry, wave the bloody shirt, beat the drums, blow the bugle *or* clarion

19 militarize, activate, mobilize, go on a wartime footing, put on a war footing, call to the colors, gird *or* gird up one's loins, muster one's resources; reactivate, remilitarize, take out of mothballs *and* retread <nf>

ADJS **20 warlike, militant,** fighting, warring, battling; **martial, military,** soldierly, soldierlike; **combative, contentious,** gladiatorial; trigger-happy <nf>; **belligerent, pugnacious,** pugilistic, **truculent, bellicose,** scrappy <nf>, full of fight; **aggressive,** offensive; fierce, ferocious, savage, bloody, bloody-minded, bloodthirsty, sanguinary, sanguineous; **unpeaceful,** unpeaceable, unpacific; **hostile, antagonistic,** agonistic, **enemy,** inimical; unfriendly 589.9; **quarrelsome** 456.17; paramilitary, mercenary, soldierlike; don't ask don't tell

21 militaristic, warmongering, war-loving, warlike, saber-rattling, battle-hungry; **chauvinistic,** chauvinist, **jingoistic,** jingoist, jingoish, jingo, crusading; **hard-line, hawkish** <nf>, of the war party

22 embattled, battled, **engaged,** at grips, in combat, on the warpath, on the offensive; **arrayed, deployed,** ranged, in battle array, in the field; **militarized; armed** 460.14; war-ravaged, war-torn

ADVS **23 at war, up in arms;** in the midst of battle, in the thick of the fray *or* combat; in the cannon's mouth, at the point of the gun; at swords' points, at the point of the bayonet *or* sword

459 ATTACK

NOUNS **1 attack, assault,** assailing, assailment; offense, **offensive; aggression; onset, onslaught; strike;** surgical strike, first strike, preventive war; descent on *or* upon; **charge,** rush, dead set at, run at *or* against; **drive, push** <nf>; **sally, sortie;** infiltration; *coup de main* <Fr>; frontal attack *or* assault, head-on attack, flank attack; mass attack, kamikaze attack; banzai attack *or* charge, suicide attack *or* charge; hit-and-run attack; breakthrough; **counterattack, counteroffensive;** amphibious attack; gas attack; diversionary attack, diversion; assault *and* battery, simple assault, mugging <nf>, aggravated assault, aggravated battery, armed assault, unprovoked assault; **preemptive strike; blitzkrieg, blitz,** lightning attack, lightning war, panzer warfare, sudden *or* devastating *or* crippling attack, deep strike, shock tactics; atomic *or* thermonuclear attack, first-strike capacity, megadeath, overkill; nuclear winter; land attack, air attack, combined attack, terrorist attack, bioterror, biowarfare; personal attack

2 surprise attack, surprise, surprisal, unforeseen attack, **sneak attack** <nf>; Pearl Harbor; stab in the back; shock tactics

3 thrust, pass, lunge, swing, cut, stab, jab; feint; home thrust

4 raid, foray, razzia; **invasion, incursion,** inroad, irruption; **air raid, air strike,** air attack, shuttle raid, fire raid, saturation raid; escalade, scaling, boarding, **tank** *or* **armored attack,** panzer attack

5 siege, besiegement, beleaguerment; encompassment, investment, encirclement, envelopment; blockading, blockade; cutting of supply lines; vertical envelopment; pincer movement

6 storm, storming, taking by storm, overrunning

7 bombardment, bombing, air bombing, strategic bombing, tactical bombing, saturation bombing; strafing; terrorist attack; suicide bombing

8 gunfire, fire, firing, musketry, **shooting,** fireworks *or* gunplay <nf>; gunfight, shoot-out; **firepower,** offensive capacity, bang <nf>

9 volley, salvo, burst, spray, strafe, **fusillade,** rapid fire; cross fire; drumfire, **cannonade,** cannonry, **broadside,** enfilade; **barrage, artillery barrage;** sharpshooting, sniping

10 **stabbing,** piercing, sticking <nf>; **knifing,** bayonetting; the sword; **impalement, transfixion**
11 **stoning,** lapidation
12 **assailant,** assailer, **attacker;** assaulter, mugger <nf>; **aggressor;** invader, raider; warrior; terrorist
13 **zero hour,** H-hour; D-day, target day
VERBS 14 **attack, assault, assail,** harry, assume *or* take the offensive; commit an assault upon; **strike, hit, pound; go at, come at,** have at, **launch out against,** make a set *or* dead set at; **fall on** *or* **upon, set on** *or* **upon, descend on** *or* upon, come down on, swoop down on; pounce upon; **lift** *or* **raise a hand against,** draw the sword against, take up arms *or* the cudgels against; **lay hands on,** lay a hand on, bloody one's hands with; gang up on, attack in force; surprise, **ambush; blitz,** attack *or* hit like lightning
15 <nf terms> **pitch into, light into, lambaste,** pile into, sail into, wade into, lay into, plow into, tie into, rip into; **let one have it,** let one have it with both barrels, kick ass; **land on,** land on like a ton of bricks, climb all over, crack down on, lower the boom on, tee off on; **mug,** jump, bushwhack, sandbag, scrag; swipe at, lay at, **go for, go at;** blindside, blind-pop, sucker-punch; **take a swing** *or* **crack** *or* **swipe** *or* **poke** *or* punch *or* **shot at**
16 **lash out at, strike out at,** hit out at, let drive at, let fly at; **strike at,** hit at, poke at, thrust at, **swing at,** swing on, make a thrust *or* pass at, lunge at, aim *or* deal a blow at, flail at, flail away at, take a fling *or* shy at; cut and thrust; smite; feint
17 **launch an attack,** kick off an attack, mount an attack, **push, thrust,** mount *or* open an offensive, **drive; advance against** *or* **upon, march upon** *or* **against,** bear down upon; **infiltrate; strike;** flank; press the attack, follow up the attack; **counterattack,** retaliate, take on
18 **charge,** rush, **rush at, fly at,** run at, dash at, make a dash *or* rush at; tilt at, go full tilt at, make *or* run a tilt at, ride full tilt against; **jump off,** go over the top <nf>
19 **besiege, lay siege to,** encompass, surround, **encircle,** envelope, invest, hem in, set upon on all sides, get in a pincers, close the jaws of the pincers *or* trap; **blockade; beset, beleaguer, harry, harass,** drive *or* press one hard; soften up
20 **raid,** foray, make a raid; **invade,** inroad, make an inroad, make an irruption into; escalade, scale, scale the walls, board; storm, take by storm, overwhelm, inundate
21 **pull a gun on,** draw a gun on; **get the drop on** *and* **beat to the draw** <nf>
22 **pull the trigger, fire upon,** fire at, **shoot at,** pop at *and* take a pop at <nf>, take *or* fire *or* let off a shot at, blaze away at <nf>; **open fire,** commence firing, open up on <nf>; aim at, take aim at, level at , zero in on, take dead aim at, draw a bead on; **snipe,** snipe at; **bombard, blast, strafe, shell,** cannonade, mortar, barrage, blitz; pepper, fusillade, fire a volley; rake, enfilade; pour a broadside into; cannon; **torpedo; shoot**
23 **bomb,** drop a bomb, lay an egg <nf>; dive-bomb, glide-bomb, skip-bomb, pattern-bomb, suicide-bomb, etc; atom-bomb, hydrogen-bomb; nuke <nf>, plaster <nf>
24 **mine,** plant a mine, trigger a mine
25 **stab, stick** <nf>, **pierce,** plunge in; **run through, impale,** spit, **transfix,** transpierce; **spear,** lance, poniard, bayonet, saber, sword, put to the sword; **knife,** dirk, dagger, stiletto; spike; cut down
26 **gore,** horn, tusk
27 **pelt, stone,** lapidate , pellet; brickbat *or* egg <nf>, chuck
28 **hurl at, throw at, cast at,** heave at, fling at, sling at, toss at, shy at, fire at, let fly at; hurl against, hurl at the head of
ADJS 29 **attacking,** assailing, assaulting, charging, driving, thrusting, advancing; **invading,** invasive, invasionary, incursive, incursionary, irruptive, storming

30 **offensive, combative,** on the offensive *or* attack; **aggressive;** militant, hawkish, on the warpath

ADVS **31** **under attack, under fire;** under siege; counterattacking

460 DEFENSE

NOUNS **1** **defense,** defence <Brit>, **guard,** ward; **protection** 1008; resistance 453; self-defense, self-protection, self-preservation; deterrent capacity; defense in depth; the defensive; covering one's ass *or* rear-end <nf>; defenses, psychological defenses, ego defenses, defense mechanism, escape mechanism, avoidance reaction, negative taxis *or* tropism; bunker atmosphere *or* mentality; siege mentality

2 **military defense, national defense,** defense capability; Air Defense Command; **civil defense;** CONELRAD *or* control of electromagnetic radiation for civil defense, Emergency Broadcast System *or* EBS, Civil Defense Warning System; radar defenses, distant early warning *or* DEW Line; antimissile missile, antiballistic-missile system *or* ABM, strategic defense initiative *or* Star Wars

3 **armor,** armature; armor plate; body armor, suit of armor, plate armor; panoply, harness; **mail,** chain mail, chain armor; bulletproof vest; **battlegear; protective covering,** cortex, **thick skin,** carapace, shell 295.15; spines, needles; human shield

4 **fortification,** work, defense work, **bulwark, rampart, fence,** earthwork, stockade, **barrier** 1012.5; **enclosure** 212.3

5 **entrenchment, trench,** ditch, fosse; **moat; dugout,** *abri* <Fr>; **bunker; foxhole,** slit trench; approach trench, communication trench, fire trench, gallery, parallel, coupure; tunnel, fortified tunnel; undermining, sap, single *or* double sap, flying sap; mine, countermine

6 **stronghold,** hold, safehold, fasthold, strong point, **fastness,** keep, ward, **bastion,** donjon, **citadel, castle,** tower, tower of strength; mote *or* motte; **fort, fortress,** post; **bunker, pillbox,** blockhouse, garrison *or* trenches *or* barricades; garrison house; acropolis; peel, peel tower; rath; martello tower, martello; **bridgehead, beachhead;** safeguard

7 **defender, champion, advocate; upholder; guardian angel,** angel <nf>; **supporter** 616.9; vindicator, apologist; **protector** 1008.5; **guard** 1008.9; henchman; paladin, knight, white knight; guard dog, attack dog, junkyard dog

VERBS **8** **defend, guard, shield,** screen, secure, guard against, ward; defend tooth *and* nail *or* to the death *or* to the last breath; **safeguard, protect** 1008.18; stand by the side of, flank; **advocate, champion** 600.10; **defend oneself,** cover one's ass *or* rear-end <nf>, CYA *or* cover your ass <nf>

9 **fortify,** embattle *or* battle ; **arm; armor,** armor-plate; **man;** garrison, man the garrison *or* trenches *or* barricades; **barricade, blockade;** bulwark, wall, palisade, fence; castellate, crenellate; bank; entrench, **dig in;** mine; beef up

10 **fend off, ward off, stave off, hold off, fight off,** keep off, beat off, parry, fend, counter, turn aside; **hold** *or* **keep at bay,** keep at arm's length; **hold the fort, hold the line,** stop, check, block, hinder, obstruct; **repel, repulse, rebuff, drive back,** put back, push back; avert; go on the defensive, fight a holding *or* delaying action, fall back to prepared positions

ADJS **11** **defensive,** defending, **guarding,** shielding, screening; **protective** 1008.23; self-defensive, self-protective, self-preservative

12 **fortified,** battlemented, embattled *or* battled , entrenched; castellated, crenellated, casemated, machicolated; secured, protected

13 **armored,** armor-plated; in armor, panoplied, armed cap-a-pie, armed at all points, in harness; mailed, mailclad, ironclad; loricate, loricated

14 **armed,** heeled *and* carrying *and* gun-toting <nf>; accoutered, **in arms,** bearing *or* wearing *or* carrying arms, under arms, sword in hand; **well-armed,** heavy-armed, full-armed, bristling with arms, **armed to the teeth;** light-armed; **garrisoned,** manned

15 **defensible, defendable, tenable**

ADVS 16 **defensively, in defense,** in self-defense; **on the defensive,** on guard; **at bay,** *aux abois* <Fr>, with one's back to the wall

461 COMBATANT

NOUNS 1 **combatant, fighter, battler,** scrapper <nf>; **contestant, contender, competitor, rival,** adversary, opponent, agonist; disputant, wrangler, squabbler, bickerer, quarreler; struggler, tussler, scuffler; brawler, rioter; feuder; **belligerent,** militant; gladiator; jouster, tilter; knight, belted **knight;** swordsman, blade, sword, *sabreur* or *beau sabreur* <Fr>; fencer, foilsman, swordplayer ; duelist, dueler; gamecock, fighting cock; **tough,** rough, rowdy, **ruffian,** thug, **hoodlum, hood** <nf>, hooligan, streetfighter, bully, bullyboy, bravo; gorilla *and* goon *and* plug-ugly *and* skinhead <nf>; hatchet man *and* enforcer <nf>, strong-arm man, strong arm, strongarmer; fire-eater, swaggerer, swashbuckler

2 **boxer, pugilist,** pug *or* palooka <nf>; **street fighter,** scrapper, pit bull

3 **wrestler,** rassler *and* grunt-and-groaner <nf>, grappler, scuffler, matman

4 **bullfighter,** toreador, *torero* <Sp>; banderillero, picador, matador

5 **militarist, warmonger,** war dog *or* hound, war hawk, **hawk** <nf>; **chauvinist, jingo,** jingoist, hardliner; conquistador, privateer, pirate, buccaneer; terrorist

6 **military man** *or* **woman, serviceman, servicewoman,** navy man *or* woman; air serviceman *or* servicewoman; **soldier, warrior,** brave, fighting man, legionary, hoplite, **man-at-arms,** rifleman, rifle; ninja; **cannon fodder,** food for powder, trooper, militiaman; warrioress, Amazon; spearman, pikeman, halberdier; military training, boot camp

7 <common soldiers> **GI,** GI Joe, dough *and* doughfoot *and* Joe Tentpeg *and* John Dogface *and* grunt <nf>, **doughboy, Yank;** Tommy Atkins *or* Tommy *or* Johnny *or* swaddy <Brit>

8 **enlisted man,** noncommissioned officer 575.19; **common soldier, private, private soldier,** buck private <nf>; private first class *or* pfc

9 **infantryman, foot soldier;** light infantryman, chasseur; rifleman, rifle, musketeer; fusileer, carabineer; **sharpshooter,** marksman, expert rifleman; **sniper;** grenadier

10 <nf terms> **grunt, dogface,** footslogger, paddlefoot, doughfoot, blisterfoot, crunchie, line doggie, groundpounder

11 **artilleryman,** artillerist, **gunner,** guns <nf>, cannoneer, machine gunner; **bomber,** bomb thrower, bombardier

12 **cavalryman,** mounted infantryman, **trooper;** dragoon, light *or* heavy dragoon; lancer, lance, uhlan, hussar; cuirassier; spahi; cossack

13 **tanker,** tank corpsman, tank crewman

14 **engineer,** combat engineer, pioneer, Seabee; sapper, sapper *and* miner

15 **elite troops, shock troops,** storm troops; rapid deployment force *or* RDF; commandos, rangers, Special Forces, special ops, Green Berets, marines, paratroops; guardsmen, guards, household troops; Life Guards, Horse Guards, Foot Guards, Grenadier Guards, Coldstream Guards, Scot Guards, Irish Guards; Swiss Guards

16 **irregular,** casual; **guerrilla,** partisan, franctireur; **bushfighter,** bushwhacker <nf>; underground, resistance, maquis; Vietcong *or* VC, Charley <nf>; SWAPO *or* South West African People's Organization

guerrilla; Shining Path Guerrilla; Contra; *maquisard* <Fr>, underground *or* resistance fighter, freedom fighter; terrorist

17 **mercenary, hireling,** free lance, free companion, **soldier of fortune,** adventurer; gunman, gun, hired gun, hired killer, professional killer; terrorist

18 **recruit, rookie** <nf>, **conscript,** drafted man, **draftee, inductee, selectee, enlistee,** enrollee, trainee, boot <nf>; **raw recruit,** tenderfoot; awkward squad <nf>; draft, levy

19 **veteran, vet** <nf>, campaigner, old campaigner, old soldier, old trooper, war-horse <nf>, Veterans of Foreign Wars *or* VFW member, American Legion member

20 **defense forces, services, the service, armed forces,** armed services, fighting machine; **the military,** the military establishment; professional forces, standing forces, regular forces, reserve forces, volunteer forces; combat troops, support troops

21 **branch, branch of the service, corps** ; **service, arm of the service,** Air Force, Army, Navy, Marine Corps, Coast Guard, Merchant Marine

22 <military units> **unit, organization,** tactical unit, **outfit** <nf>; **army,** field army, army group, corps, army corps, **division,** infantry division, armored division, airborne division, triangular division, pentomic division, Reorganization Objective Army Division *or* ROAD; **regiment, battle group,** battalion, garrison, **company,** troop, brigade, legion, phalanx, cohort, **platoon,** section, **battery,** maniple; **combat team,** combat command; **task force;** commando unit, combat team; **squad,** squadron; detachment, detail, section, posse, unit, detachment; kitchen police *or* KP; column, flying column; rank, file; train, field train; cadre

23 **army,** this man's army <nf>, **soldiery, forces,** armed forces, **troops, host,** array, legions; ranks, rank *and* file; **standing army, regular army,** active forces, regulars, professional *or* career soldiers; the line, troops of the line; line of defense, first *or* second line of defense; ground forces, ground troops; storm troops, assault troops; **airborne troops,** paratroops; ski troops, mountain troops; occupation force; elite troops

24 **militia,** organized militia, national militia, mobile militia, territorial militia, reserve militia, citizen's army; home reserve; **National Guard,** Air National Guard, state guard; home guard <chiefly Brit>; minutemen, trainband, yeomanry

25 **reserves,** auxiliaries, **second line of defense,** reinforcements, ready reserves, landwehr, army reserves, home reserves, territorial reserves, territorial *or* home defense army <Brit>, supplementary reserves, organized reserves; US Army Reserve, US Naval Reserve, US Marine Corps Reserve, US Air Force Reserve, US Coast Guard Reserve, National Guard; ready reserves, standby reserves, retired reserves

26 **volunteers, enlistees,** volunteer forces, volunteer army, volunteer militia, volunteer navy

27 **navy,** naval forces, **first line of defense; fleet,** flotilla, argosy, armada, squadron, escadrille, division, task force, task group; amphibious force; mosquito fleet; support fleet, destroyer fleet, auxiliary fleet, reserve fleet, mothball fleet; United States Navy *or* USN; Royal Navy *or* RN; marine, mercantile *or* merchant marine, merchant navy, merchant fleet; naval militia; naval reserve; coast guard; Seabees, Naval Construction Battalion; admiralty; gunboat diplomacy

28 **marines,** sea soldiers, Marine Corps, Royal Marines; **leathernecks** *and* devil dogs *and* gyrenes <nf>, jollies <Brit nf>

29 **air force,** air corps, air service, air arm; US Air Force *or* USAF; strategic air force, tactical air force; squadron, escadrille, flight, wing

30 **war-horse, charger,** courser, trooper

462 ARMS

NOUNS **1** **arms, weapons,** deadly weapons, instruments of destruction, offensive weapons, **military hardware,** matériel, **weaponry, armament, munitions, ordnance,** munitions of war, *apparatus belli* <L>; musketry; missilery; small arms; side arms; stand of arms; conventional weapons, nonnuclear weapons; **nuclear weapons,** atomic weapons, thermonuclear weapons, A-weapons, strategic nuclear weapon, tactical nuclear weapon; bacteriological *or* biological weapon, chemical weapon; weapons of mass destruction; arms industry, arms maker, military-industrial complex; natural weapon; secret weapon

2 **armory, arsenal,** magazine, dump; ammunition depot, ammo dump <nf>, arms depot; park, gun park, artillery park, park of artillery; atomic arsenal, thermonuclear arsenal, gun room, powder barrel *or* keg

3 **ballistics, gunnery,** musketry, artillery; rocketry, missilery; archery

4 **fist, clenched fist; brass knuckles;** knucks *and* brass knucks <nf>, knuckles, knuckle-dusters; club, bludgeon, blackjack, truncheon, billy, blunt instrument, etc

5 **sword, blade,** cutlass, saber, rapier, foil, bayonet, machete; steel, **cold steel;** Excalibur; **knife,** switchblade, bowie knife, Swiss Army knife, box cutter**; dagger; axe**

6 **arrow, shaft, dart,** reed, **bolt;** quarrel; chested arrow, footed arrow, bobtailed arrow; arrowhead, barb; flight, volley

7 **bow,** longbow, carriage bow; **bow and arrow;** crossbow, arbalest

8 **spear,** throwing spear, javelin, lance, harpoon, sharp weapon

9 **sling, slingshot;** throwing-stick, throw stick, spear-thrower, atlatl, wommera; **catapult,** arbalest, ballista, trebuchet

10 **gun, firearm;** shooting iron *and* gat *and* rod *and* heater *and* piece <nf>; shoulder weapon *or* gun *or* arm; gun make; gun part; stun gun; automatic, BB gun, blunderbuss , Bren, Browning automatic rifle, burp gun <nf>, carbine, derringer, flintlock, forty-five *or* .45, forty-four *or* .44, Gatling gun, handgun, machine gun, musket, pistol, piece *or* equalizer <nf>, automatic, semiautomatic, repeater, revolver, rifle, Saturday night special, sawed-off shotgun, shotgun, six-gun *or* six-shooter <nf>, submachine gun, thirty-eight *or* .38, thirty-thirty *or* .30-30, thirty-two *or* .32, Thompson submachine gun *or* tommy gun <nf>, twenty-two *or* .22, Uzi submachine gun, zip gun

11 **artillery, cannon,** guns, cannonry, ordnance, engines of war, Big Bertha, howitzer; field artillery; heavy artillery, heavy field artillery; self-propelled artillery; siege artillery, bombardment weapons; breakthrough weapons; siege engine; mountain artillery, coast artillery, trench artillery, anti-aircraft artillery, flak <nf>; battery

12 **antiaircraft gun** *or* AA gun, ack-ack <nf>, pom-pom <nf>

13 **ammunition, ammo** <nf>, **powder and shot,** iron rations <nf>, round, live ammunition

14 **explosive,** high explosive; cellulose nitrate, cordite, dynamite, gelignite, guncotton, gunpowder, nitroglycerin *or* nitroglycerine, plastic explosive *or* plastique, powder, trinitrotoluene *or* trinitrotoluol *or* TNT

15 **fuse, detonator,** exploder; **cap,** blasting cap, percussion cap, mercury fulminate, fulminating mercury; electric detonator *or* exploder; detonating powder; **primer,** priming; primacord

16 **charge, load;** blast; warhead, payload

17 **cartridge,** cartouche, **shell;** ball cartridge; clip, blank cartridge, dry ammunition

18 **missile, projectile,** bolt; brickbat, stone, rock, alley apple *and* Irish confetti <nf>; boomerang; bola; throwing-stick, throw stick; **ballistic missile,** cruise missile, Exocet missile, surface-to-air missile *or* SAM, surface-to-surface missile, Tomahawk missile; **rocket** 1074.2-6, **torpedo**

19 **shot; ball,** cannonball, rifle ball, minié ball; **bullet,** slug, pellet; buckshot; dumdum bullet, expanding bullet, explosive bullet, manstopping bullet, manstopper, copkiller *or* Teflon bullet <TM>; tracer bullet, tracer; **shell,** high-explosive shell, **shrapnel**

20 **bomb,** bombshell, device <nf>; antipersonnel bomb, atomic bomb *or* atom bomb *or* A-bomb, atomic warhead, hydrogen bomb *or* H-bomb, nuclear bomb, blockbuster, depth charge *or* depth bomb *or* ash can <nf>, fire bomb *or* incendiary bomb *or* incendiary, grenade, hand grenade, pineapple <nf>, letter bomb, Molotov cocktail, napalm bomb, neutron bomb, nuclear warhead, pipe bomb, plastic *or* plastique bomb, plutonium bomb, smart bomb, stench *or* stink bomb, time bomb; clean bomb, dirty bomb; **mine**, landmine; booby trap

21 **launcher,** projector, bazooka; rocket launcher, grenade launcher, hedgehog, mine thrower, **mortar**

22 non-lethal weapon, riot control agent; stun gun, Taser <TM>, pepper spray, water cannon; rubber bullet, plastic bullet; minimal force, controlled force, soft kill, mission kill

463 ARENA

NOUNS **1** **arena, scene of action, site,** scene, setting, background, **field, ground,** terrain, sphere, place, locale, milieu, precinct, purlieu; course, range, walk ; campus; **theater,** stage, stage set *or* setting, scenery; **platform; forum,** agora, marketplace, open forum, public square; **amphitheater,** circus, **hippodrome, coliseum,** colosseum, **stadium, bowl; hall, auditorium;** gymnasium, gym <nf>, palaestra; **lists,** tiltyard, tilting ground; floor, **pit,** cockpit; bear garden; **ring,** prize ring, boxing ring, canvas, squared circle <nf>, wrestling ring, mat, bull ring; parade ground; athletic field, field, playing field; covered stadium, domed stadium; stamping ground, turf, bailiwick 894.4

2 **battlefield, battleground,** battle site, **field,** combat area, **field of battle;** field of slaughter, field of blood *or* bloodshed, aceldama, killing ground *or* field, shambles; **battlefront, the front,** front line, line, enemy line *or* lines, firing line, battle line, line of battle; battle zone, war zone, combat zone; **theater, theater of operations,** theater *or* seat of war; beachhead, bridgehead; communications zone, zone of communications; no-man's-land; demilitarized zone *or* DMZ; jump area *or* zone, landing beach

3 **campground,** camp, campsite, camping ground *or* area, encampment, bivouac, tented field

464 PEACE

NOUNS **1** **peace,** *pax* <L>; **peacetime,** state of peace, peaceable kingdom, the storm blown over; freedom from war, cessation of combat, exemption from hostilities, public tranquillity, peace movement; **harmony,** concord, accord 455; universal peace, lasting peace, Pax Romana

2 **peacefulness, tranquillity, serenity, calmness, quiet,** peace and quiet, quietude, quietness, quiescence, quiet life, restfulness, rest, stillness, silence; order, orderliness, law and order, imposed peace; no hassle <nf>

3 **peace of mind,** peace of heart, peace of soul *or* spirit, peace of God; ataraxia, shanti

4 **peaceableness, unpugnaciousness,** uncontentiousness, nonaggression; irenicism, dovelikeness, dovishness <nf>, **pacifism,** pacificism; peaceful coexistence; **nonviolence**, ahimsa; line of least resistance; meekness, lamblikeness 433.5

5 **noncombatant,** nonbelligerent, nonresistant, nonresister; **civilian,** citizen

6 **pacifist,** pacificist, peacenik <nf>, **peace lover, dove,** *and* dove of peace <nf>; pacificator, peacemaker, bridgebuilder; peacemonger; **conscientious objector,** passive resister, conchie <nf>

7 **peace treaty**, peace agreement, nonaggression pact, disarmament treaty, arms reduction, arms control; test ban; deescalation; amnesty, pardon, forgiveness, burying the hatchet <nf>

VERBS 8 **keep the peace,** remain at peace, wage peace; refuse to shed blood, keep one's sword in its sheath; forswear violence, beat one's swords into plowshares; pursue the arts of peace, pour oil on troubled waters; make love not war; defuse

ADJS 9 **pacific, peaceful, peaceable; tranquil, serene;** idyllic, pastoral; halcyon, soft, piping, **calm, quiet,** quiet as a lamb, quiescent, still, restful, **untroubled,** orderly, **at peace;** concordant 455.3; bloodless; peacetime; postwar, postbellum

10 **unbelligerent, unhostile,** unbellicose, **unpugnacious, uncontentious,** unmilitant, unmilitary, nonaggressive, noncombative, nonmilitant; noncombatant, civilian; **antiwar, pacific, peaceable,** peace-loving, dovelike; meek, passive, lamblike 433.15; pacifistic, pacifist, irenic; nonviolent; conciliatory 465.12

465 PACIFICATION

NOUNS 1 **pacification, peacemaking,** irenics, peacemongering, **conciliation, propitiation, placation, appeasement, mollification,** dulcification; **calming, soothing,** tranquilization; détente, relaxation of tension, easing of relations; mediation 466; placability; peacekeeping force, United Nations peacekeeping force

2 **peace offer,** offer of parley, parley, peace overture; peace feelers; **peace offering,** propitiatory gift; **olive branch; white flag,** truce flag, flag of truce; calumet, peace pipe, **pipe of peace;** downing of arms, hand of friendship, empty hands, outstretched hand; **cooling off, cooling-off period;** peace sign; compensation, reparation, atonement, restitution; amnesty, pardon, mercy, leniency, clemency; dove, lamb

3 **reconciliation,** reconcilement, rapprochement <Fr>, reunion, shaking of hands, making up *and* kissing *and* making up <nf>

4 **adjustment,** accommodation, resolution, composition *or* settlement of differences, compromise, arrangement, settlement, terms; consensus building, consensus seeking

5 **truce, armistice, peace; pacification,** treaty of peace, suspension *or* end of hostilities, **cease-fire,** cessation, stand-down, breathing spell, cooling-off period, lull in hostilities; Truce *or* Peace of God, Pax Dei, Pax Romana; temporary truce, temporary arrangement, *modus vivendi* <L>; hollow truce, *pax in bello* <L>; demilitarized zone, buffer zone, neutral territory; uneasy truce; peacekeeping mission

6 **disarmament,** reduction of armaments; unilateral disarmament; **demilitarization,** deactivation, disbanding, disbandment, **demobilization,** mustering out, reconversion, decommissioning; civilian life, mufti *and* civvy street <Brit>; defense cuts, arms reduction, arms control; test ban

VERBS 7 **pacify, conciliate, placate, propitiate, appease, mollify,** dulcify; **calm, settle, soothe,** tranquilize 670.7; smooth, smooth over *or* out, smooth down, smooth one's feathers; allay, lay, lay the dust; pour oil on troubled waters, pour balm on, take the edge off of, take the sting out of; cool <nf>, defuse; clear the air

8 **reconcile, bring to terms, bring together,** reunite, heal the breach; bring about a détente; **harmonize,** restore harmony, put in tune; **iron** *or* **sort out,** adjust, settle, compose, accommodate, arrange matters, settle differences, resolve, compromise; **patch things up,** make up <nf>, fix

up <nf>, patch up a friendship *or* quarrel, smooth it over; weave peace between, mediate 466.6

9 **make peace,** cease hostilities, cease fire, stand down, raise a siege; **cool it** *and* **chill out** <nf>, **bury the hatchet, smoke the peace pipe;** negotiate a peace, dictate peace; make a peace offering, hold out the olive branch, hoist *or* show *or* wave the white flag; make the world a safer place, make the lion lie down with the lamb; turn the other cheek

10 **make up** *and* **kiss** ***and*** **make up** *and* make it up *and* make matters up <nf>, **shake hands,** come round, come together, come to an understanding, **come to terms,** let the wound heal, let bygones be bygones, forgive and forget, put it all behind one, settle *or* compose one's differences, meet halfway, compromise

11 **disarm, lay down one's arms,** unarm, turn in one's weapons, down *or* ground one's arms, put down one's gun, sheathe the sword, turn swords into plowshares; **demilitarize,** deactivate, **demobilize, disband,** reconvert, decommission

ADJS 12 **pacificatory, pacific,** irenic, **conciliatory,** reconciliatory, **propitiatory,** propitiative, **placative,** placatory, **mollifying, appeasing; pacifying, soothing** 670.15, appeasable

13 **pacifiable, placable, appeasable, propitiable**

ADVS 14 **pacifically, peaceably; with no hard feelings**

466 MEDIATION

NOUNS 1 **mediation,** mediating, intermediation, **intercession; intervention,** interposition, putting oneself between, moderation, stepping in, declaring oneself in, involvement, interagency; interventionism; diplomacy, statesmanship; troubleshooting, good offices; peacekeeping mission

2 **arbitration,** arbitrament, compulsory arbitration, binding arbitration; nonbinding arbitration; umpirage, refereeship, mediatorship

3 **mediator,** intermediator, intermediate agent, intermediate, intermedium, **intermediary,** interagent, internuncio, mediatrix; **medium; intercessor,** interceder; ombudsman; intervener, **intervenor;** interventionist; **go-between,** liaison, **middleman** 576.4; connection <nf>; front *and* front man <nf>; deputy, agent 576; **spokesman, spokeswoman,** spokesperson, spokespeople; **mouthpiece; negotiator,** negotiant, negotiatress *or* negotiatrix; Little Miss Fixit; troubleshooter; spin doctor <nf>; harmonizer

4 **arbitrator,** arbiter, impartial arbitrator, third party, unbiased observer; **moderator,** moderating influence; **umpire, referee, judge;** armchair quarterback; magistrate 596.1

5 **peacemaker,** make-peace, reconciler, smoother-over, peace negotiator, mediator; **pacifier,** pacificator, peace lover, pacifist; peacekeeper, United Nations peacekeeping force; **conciliator,** propitiator, **appeaser;** marriage counselor, family counselor; guidance counselor; patcher-up

VERBS 6 **mediate,** intermediate, **intercede,** go between; **intervene,** interpose, step in, step into the breach, declare oneself a party, involve oneself, put oneself between disputants, use one's good offices, act between; butt in *and* put one's nose in <nf>; represent 576.14; **negotiate,** bargain, **treat with,** make terms, meet halfway; **arbitrate,** moderate; **umpire, referee,** judge, officiate

7 **settle, arrange,** compose, patch up, adjust, straighten out, bring to terms *or* an understanding; make peace 465.9; reconcile, conciliate

ADJS 8 **mediatory,** mediatorial, mediative, mediating, arbitral, going *or* coming between; intermediatory, intermediary, intermedial, intermediate, **middle,** intervening, mesne, interlocutory; interventional, arbitrational, arbitrative; **intercessory,** intercessional; diplomatic; pacificatory 465.12

467 NEUTRALITY

NOUNS **1 neutrality, neutralism,** strict neutrality; noncommitment, noninvolvement; **independence, nonpartisanism, unalignment, nonalignment;** anythingarianism *or* nothingarianism <nf>; mugwumpery, mugwumpism, fence-sitting *or* -straddling, fence <nf>, trimming; **evasion, cop-out** <nf>, abstention; **impartiality** 649.3, coexistence, avoidance; nonintervention, nonaggression

2 indifference, indifferentness, Laodiceanism; passiveness 329.1; apathy 94.4, phlegm, disinterest

3 middle course *or* **way,** *via media* <L>; middle ground, neutral ground *or* territory, center; meeting ground, interface; gray area, penumbra, compromise; **middle of the road,** sitting on *or* straddling the fence <nf>; medium, **happy medium;** mean, **golden mean;** moderation, moderateness 670.1; compromise 468; halfway measures, half measures, half-and-half measures

4 neutral, neuter; **independent, nonpartisan;** mugwump, fence-sitter *or* -straddler, trimmer; anythingarian *and* nothingarian <nf>; unaligned *or* nonaligned nation, third force, third world; game face

VERBS **5 remain neutral,** stand neuter, hold no brief, **keep in the middle of the road, straddle** *or* **sit on the fence** *and* sit out *and* sit on the sidelines <nf>, trim; **evade,** evade the issue, duck the issue *and* waffle *and* cop out <nf>, abstain

6 steer a middle course, hold *or* keep *or* preserve a middle course, walk a middle path, follow the via media, strike *or* preserve a balance, stay on an even keel, **strike** *or* **keep a happy medium,** keep the golden mean, steer between *or* avoid Scylla *and* Charybdis; be moderate 670.5

ADJS **7 neutral,** neuter; noncommitted, uncommitted, noninvolved, uninvolved; anythingarian *and* nothingarian <nf>; **indifferent,** Laodicean; tolerant; passive 329.6; apathetic 94.13; neither one thing nor the other, neither hot nor cold, inert; even, half-and-half, fifty-fifty <nf>; **on the fence** *or* **sidelines** <nf>, **middle-of-the-road,** centrist, center, moderate, midway; **independent, nonpartisan; unaligned, nonaligned,** third-force, third-world; **impartial** 649.9

468 COMPROMISE

<mutual concession>

NOUNS **1 compromise,** composition, adjustment, accommodation, settlement, mutual concession, give-and-take; abatement of differences; bargain, deal <nf>, arrangement, understanding; **concession,** giving way, yielding; surrender, desertion of principle, evasion of responsibility, cop-out <nf>; middle ground, happy medium; meeting halfway; trade-off; face-saver

VERBS **2 compromise,** make *or* reach a compromise, compound, compose, accommodate, adjust, settle, make an adjustment *or* arrangement, **make a deal** <nf>, do a deal <Brit nf>, come to an understanding, strike a bargain, do something mutually beneficial; plea-bargain; strike a balance, take the mean, **meet halfway,** split the difference, go fifty-fifty <nf>, give *and* take; play politics; steer a middle course 467.6; **make concessions,** make trade-off, give way, yield, wimp *or* chicken out <nf>; **surrender** 433.8, desert one's principles, evade responsibility, sidestep, duck responsibility *and* cop out *and* punt <nf>

PHRS **3** half a loaf is better than none; you can't win them all

469 POSSESSION

NOUNS **1 possession,** possessing, outright possession, free-and-clear possession; **owning,** having title to; seisin, nine points of the law, *de facto* possession, **de jure** possession, lawful *or* legal possession; property rights, proprietary rights; **title,** absolute title, free-and-clear title, original title; derivative title; adverse possession, squatting, squatterdom, **squatter's right; claim,** legal claim, lien; usucapion, usucaption , prescription; **occupancy,** occupation; **hold, holding, tenure; tenancy,** tenantry, **lease,** leasehold, sublease, underlease, undertenancy; gavelkind; villenage, villein socage, villeinhold; socage, free socage; burgage; frankalmoign, lay fee; tenure in chivalry, knight service; fee fief, fiefdom, feud, feodum; freehold, alodium; fee simple, fee tail, fee simple absolute, fee simple conditional, fee simple defeasible *or* fee simple determinable; fee position; dependency, colony, mandate; prepossession , preoccupation, preoccupancy; chose in possession, bird in hand, nine tenths of the law <nf>; **property** 471

2 **ownership, title,** possessorship, *dominium* <L>, **proprietorship,** proprietary, **property right** *or* rights; lordship, **overlordship,** seigniory; **dominion, sovereignty** 417.5; landownership, landowning, landholding, land tenure; nationalization, public domain, state ownership

3 **monopoly,** monopolization; **corner** *and* cornering *and* a corner on <nf>; exclusive possession; engrossment, forestallment

VERBS 4 **possess, have, hold,** have and hold, possess outright *or* free *and* clear, **occupy, fill, enjoy,** boast; be possessed of, have tenure of, have in hand, be seized of, have in one's grip *or* grasp, have in one's possession, be enfeoffed of; **command,** have at one's command *or* pleasure *or* disposition *or* disposal, have going for one <nf>; claim, usucapt; squat, squat on, claim squatter's rights

5 **own, have title to,** have for one's own *or* very own, have to one's name, call one's own, have the deed for, hold in fee simple, etc

6 **monopolize,** hog *and* grab all of *and* gobble up <nf>, call one's own, take it all, have all to oneself, have exclusive possession of *or* exclusive rights to; engross, forestall, tie up; **corner** *and* get a corner on *and* corner the market <nf>

7 **belong to,** pertain to, appertain to; vest in

ADJS 8 **possessed, owned,** held; in seisin, in fee, in fee simple, **free and clear; own,** of one's own, in one's name; **in one's possession, in hand,** in one's grip *or* grasp, at one's command *or* disposal; on hand, by one, in stock, in store

9 **possessing, having, holding,** having *and* holding, **occupying, owning; in possession of, possessed of,** seized of, master of; tenured; enfeoffed; endowed with, blessed with; worth; propertied, property-owning, landed, landowning, landholding

10 **possessive,** possessory, **proprietary**

11 **monopolistic,** monopolist, monopolizing, hogging *or* hoggish <nf>; exclusive

ADVS 12 **free and clear, outright;** bag and baggage; by fee simple, etc

470 POSSESSOR

NOUNS 1 **possessor, holder,** keeper, haver, enjoyer; a have <nf>

2 **proprietor,** proprietary, **owner;** *rentier* <Fr>; titleholder, deedholder; proprietress, proprietrix; **master, mistress, lord; landlord, landlady;** lord *or* lady of the manor <Brit>, man *or* lady of the house, mesne lord, mesne, feudatory, feoffee; squire, country gentleman; householder; beneficiary, cestui, cestui que trust, cestui que use

3 **landowner,** landholder, property owner, propertied *or* landed person, man of property, freeholder; landed interests, landed gentry, slumlord, rent gouger; absentee landlord

4 **tenant, occupant,** occupier, incumbent, **resident; lodger,** roomer, boarder, paying guest; **renter,** hirer <Brit>, rent-payer, **lessee,** leaseholder; subtenant, sublessee, underlessee, undertenant; tenant at sufferance, tenant at will; tenant from year to year, tenant for years, tenant for life; squatter; homesteader; squatter

5 **trustee,** fiduciary, holder of the legal estate; depository, depositary

471 PROPERTY

NOUNS **1** **property, properties, possessions, holdings,** havings, goods, chattels, goods *and* chattels, **effects,** estate and effects, what one can call one's own, what one has to one's name, all one owns *or* has, all one can lay claim to, one's all; household possessions *or* effects, lares *and* penates; hereditament, corporeal hereditament, incorporeal hereditament; acquest; acquisitions, receipts 627; **inheritance** 479.2; public property, common property

2 **belongings, appurtenances,** trappings, paraphernalia, appointments, accessories, perquisites, appendages, appanages, choses local; **things,** material things, mere things; consumer goods; choses, choses in possession, choses in action; **personal effects,** personal property, chattels personal, movables, choses transitory; what one can call one's own, what has to one's name

3 **impedimenta, luggage, dunnage, baggage,** bag and baggage, traps, tackle, apparatus, truck, gear, kit, outfit, duffel

4 **estate, interest, equity, stake,** part, percentage; **right, title** 469.1, **claim,** holding; use, trust, benefit; absolute interest, vested interest, contingent interest, beneficial interest, equitable interest; easement, right of common, common, right of entry; limitation; settlement, strict settlement; copyright, patent

5 freehold, estate of freehold; alodium, alod; frankalmoign, lay fee, tenure in *or* by free alms, appanage; mortmain, dead hand; leasehold

6 **real estate, realty,** real property, land *and* buildings, chattels real, tenements; immoveables; *praedium* <L>, landed property *or* estate, **land, lands,** property, grounds, acres; lot, lots, parcel, plot, plat, quadrat; demesne, domain ; messuage, manor, honor, toft <Brit>

7 **assets, means, resources,** total assets *or* resources; stock, stock-in-trade; worth, net worth, what one is **worth;** circumstances, funds 728.14; wealth 618; **material assets,** tangible assets, tangibles; intangible assets, intangibles; current assets, deferred assets, fixed assets, frozen assets, liquid assets, quick assets, assets *and* liabilities, net assets; assessed valuation

ADJS **8** **propertied,** proprietary; **landed;** copyrighted, patented

9 real, praedial; manorial, seignioral, seigneurial; feudal, feudatory, feodal; patrimonial

10 freehold, leasehold, copyhold; allodial

472 ACQUISITION

NOUNS **1** **acquisition,** gaining, getting, getting hold of <nf>, coming by, **acquirement, obtainment,** obtention, **attainment,** securement, winning, realization; trover; accession; addition 253; **procurement,** procural, procurance, procuration; **earnings,** making, pulling *or* dragging *or* knocking down <nf>, moneymaking, breadwinning, moneygetting, moneygrubbing

2 **collection, gathering,** gleaning, bringing together, assembling, putting *or* piecing together, **accumulation,** cumulation, **amassment,** accretion, heaping up, grubbing

3 **gain, profit,** percentage <nf>, get <Brit nf>, **take** *or* take-in *and* piece *and* slice *and* end *and* rakeoff *and* skimmings <nf>; **gains, profits, earnings, winnings, return, returns, proceeds, bottom line** <nf>, ettings, makings; **income** 624.4; **receipts** 627; **fruits,** pickings, gleanings; **booty, spoils** 482.11; pelf, lucre, filthy lucre; perquisite, perk *or* perks; **pile** *and* bundle *and* cleanup *and* killing *and* haul *and* mint <nf>; net *or* neat profit, clean *or* clear profit, net; gross profit, gross; paper profits; capital gains; interest, dividends; net profit, net revenue; getting ahead; hoard, store 386; wealth 618

4 **profitableness, profitability,** gainfulness, remunerativeness, rewardingness, bang for the buck <nf>
5 **yield, output,** make, production; **proceeds,** produce, product; **crop, harvest,** fruit, vintage, bearing; second crop, aftermath; bumper crop
6 **find,** finding, **discovery; trove,** *trouvaille* <Fr>; treasure trove, buried treasure; **windfall,** windfall money, windfall profit, found money, easy money, money in the bank, **bonus, gravy** <nf>, bunce <Brit nf>
7 **godsend, boon, blessing;** manna, manna from heaven, loaves and fishes, gift from on high; piece of luck

VERBS 8 **acquire, get, gain, obtain, secure, procure; win,** score; **earn,** make; **reap, harvest;** contract; take, catch, capture; **net;** come *or* enter into possession of, **come into, come by,** come in for, be seized of; draw, derive
9 <nf terms> **grab, latch** *or* glom on to, corral, bag, get *or* lay hold of, rake in *or* up *or* off, skim *or* skim off, catch, collar, cop, dig up, grub up, round up, drum up, get *or* lay one's hands, get *or* lay one's mitts on, get one's fingers *or* hands on, get one's hooks into, snag, snaffle, scratch together, hook, land, throw together, nab, pick up, nail, scare *or* scrape up; take home, pull *or* drag *or* knock down
10 **take possession, appropriate, take up,** take over, make one's own, move in *or* move in on <nf>, annex
11 **collect, gather, glean,** harvest, **pick, pluck,** cull, **take up,** pick up, get *or* gather in, gather to oneself, bring *or* get together, scrape together, scare up <nf>; heap up, amass, assemble, accumulate 386.11
12 **profit, make** *or* **draw** *or* **realize** *or* **reap profit, come out ahead, make money;** rake it in *and* coin money *and* make a bundle *or* pile *or* killing *or* mint *and* clean up <nf>, laugh all the way to the bank; gain by, **capitalize on,** commercialize, make capital out of, **cash in on** *and* make a good thing of <nf>, turn to profit *or* account, **realize on,** make money by, obtain a return, turn a penny *or* an honest penny; **gross, net; realize, clear;** kill two birds with one stone, turn to one's advantage; make a fast *or* quick buck <nf>; line one's pockets
13 **be profitable,** pay, repay, pay off <nf>, yield a profit, show a percentage, be gainful, be worthwhile *or* worth one's while, be a good investment show a profit, pay interest; roll in <nf>

ADJS 14 **obtainable, attainable, available,** accessible, to be had
15 **acquisitive,** acquiring; grasping, hoggy *and* grabby <nf>; greedy 100.27
16 **gainful,** productive, **profitable, remunerative, remuneratory, lucrative,** fat, **paying,** well-paying, high-yield, high-yielding, bankable; advantageous, worthwhile, rewarding; banausic, moneymaking, breadwinning

ADVS 17 **profitably, gainfully,** remuneratively, lucratively, **at a profit,** in the black; for money; advantageously, to advantage, to profit, to the good

473 LOSS

NOUNS 1 **loss, losing, privation,** getting away, losing hold of; **deprivation, bereavement,** taking away, stripping, dispossession, despoilment, despoliation, spoliation, robbery; setback, reversal; divestment, denudation; **sacrifice, forfeit, forfeiture,** giving up *or* over, denial; nonrestoration; **expense, cost, debit;** detriment, injury, damage; **destruction, ruin,** perdition, total loss, dead loss; collateral damage; losing streak <nf>; **loser** 412.5
2 **waste,** wastage, **exhaustion, depletion,** sapping, depreciation, dissipation, diffusion, **wearing, wearing away, erosion,** ablation, leaching away; molting, shedding, casting *or* sloughing off; **using, using up, consumption, expenditure, drain;** stripping, clear-cutting; impoverishment, shrinkage; leakage, evaporation; decrement, decrease 252

3 **losses,** losings; red ink; net loss, bottom line <nf>; diminishing returns; going to the wall *or* going belly up <nf>

VERBS 4 **lose,** incur loss, **suffer loss,** undergo privation *or* deprivation, be bereaved *or* bereft of, have no more, meet with a loss; drop *and* kiss good-bye <nf>; let slip, let slip through one's fingers; **forfeit,** default; **sacrifice; miss,** wander from, go astray from; **mislay,** misplace; lose out; **lose everything,** go broke *and* lose one's shirt *and* take a bath *or* to the cleaners *and* tap out *and* go to Tap City <nf>; have a setback *or* reversal

5 **waste, deplete, depreciate,** dissipate, wear, wear away, erode, ablate, consume, drain, **shrink,** dribble away; **molt, shed,** cast *or* slough off; decrease 252.6; squander 486.3; labor in vain

6 **go to waste,** come to nothing, come to naught, go up in smoke *and* go down the drain <nf>; run to waste, go to pot <nf>, run *or* go to seed, go down the tubes <nf>, go to the dogs <nf>; dissipate, leak, leak away, scatter to the winds

ADJS 7 **lost, gone;** forfeited, forfeit; by the board, out the window *and* down the drain *or* tube <nf>; **nonrenewable,** irreclaimable; long-lost; lost to; wasted, consumed, depleted, dissipated, diffused, **expended; worn away, eroded,** ablated, used, used up, shrunken; stripped, clear-cut; squandered 486.9; irretrievable 125.15; astray; the worse for wear

8 **bereft, bereaved,** divested, denuded, **deprived of,** shorn of, parted from, bereaved of, stripped of, dispossessed of, despoiled of, robbed of; **out of,** minus <nf>, wanting, lacking; cut off, cut off without a cent; out-of-pocket; **penniless, destitute, broke** *and* cleaned out *and* tapped out *and* wiped out *and* bust *and* belly up <nf>

ADVS 9 **at a loss, unprofitably,** to the bad <nf>; in the red <nf>; out, out-of-pocket

474 RETENTION

NOUNS 1 **retention,** retainment, **keeping, holding, maintenance, preservation;** prehension; keeping *or* holding in, **bottling** *or* corking up <nf>, locking in, suppression, repression, inhibition, retentiveness, retentivity; **tenacity** 803.3; adhesion; tenaciousness; detention

2 **hold, purchase, grasp, grip, clutch, clamp, clinch, clench;** seizure 480.2; bite, nip, toothhold; **cling,** clinging; toehold, foothold, footing; **clasp, hug, embrace,** bear hug, squeeze; grapple; handhold, firm hold, tight grip, iron grip, grip of iron *or* steel, death grip, stranglehold

3 <wrestling holds> half nelson, full nelson, quarter nelson, three-quarter nelson, stranglehold, toehold, flying mare, body slam, lock, hammerlock, headlock, scissors, bear hug, pin, fall

4 **clutches, claws, talons,** pounces, unguals; **nails,** fingernails; **pincers,** nippers, chelae; **tentacles; fingers,** digits, hooks <nf>; **hands,** paws *and* meathooks *and* mitts <nf>; palm; prehensile tail; **jaws,** mandibles, maxillae; **teeth,** fangs

VERBS 5 **retain, keep, save,** save up, pocket *and* hip-pocket <nf>; **maintain, preserve;** keep *or* hold in, **bottle** *or* cork up <nf>, lock in, suppress, repress, inhibit, keep to oneself; persist in; hold one's own, hold one's ground; get a foothold

6 **hold, grip, grasp, clutch,** clip, **clinch, clench;** bite, nip; grapple; **clasp, hug, embrace; cling, cling to,** cleave to, stick to, adhere to, freeze to; **hold on to,** hold fast *or* tight, hang on to, keep a firm *or* tight hold on; **hold on, hang on** <nf>, hold on like a bulldog, stick like a leech, cling like a winkle, hang on for dear life; keep hold of, never let go, not part with; **seize** 480.14

7 **hold, keep, harbor,** bear, have, have *and* hold, hold on to; **cherish,** fondle, entertain, treasure, treasure up;

foster, nurture, nurse; embrace, hug, clip <Brit nf>, cling to; bosom *or* embosom , take to the bosom

ADJS **8 retentive,** retaining, keeping, holding, gripping, grasping; **tenacious,** clinging; viselike; anal

9 prehensile, raptorial; fingered, digitate *or* digitated, digital; clawed, taloned, jawed, toothed, dentate, fanged

ADVS **10 for keeps** <nf>, to keep, **for good,** for good *and* all, for always; forever 829.12

475 RELINQUISHMENT

NOUNS **1 relinquishment, release,** giving up, letting go, dispensation; **disposal,** disposition, riddance, getting rid of, dumping 390.3; **renunciation,** forgoing, forswearing, swearing off, abstinence, resignation, abjuration, **abandonment** 370; recantation, retraction 363.3; **surrender,** cession, handover, turning over, **yielding;** sacrifice; abdication; derequisition

2 waiver, quitclaim, disclaimer, deed of release

VERBS **3 relinquish, give up,** render up, **surrender, yield,** cede, hand *or* turn over, cough up <nf>; take one's hands off, loose one's grip on; spare; resign, vacate; drop, **waive,** dispense with; **forgo,** do without, get along without, forswear, abjure, **renounce,** swear off; walk away from, **abandon** 370.5; recant, retract; disgorge, throw up; have done with, wash one's hands of, pack it in; **part with,** give away, dispose of, ditch <nf>, rid oneself of, get rid of, see the last of, dump 390.7; kiss goodbye *or* off <nf>; **sacrifice,** make a sacrifice, forfeit; quitclaim; sell off

4 release, let go, leave go <nf>, **let loose of,** unhand, unclutch, unclasp, relax one's grip *or* hold

ADJS **5 relinquished,** released, disposed of; waived, dispensed with; forgone, forsworn, renounced, abjured, **abandoned** 370.8; recanted, retracted; **surrendered,** ceded, yielded; sacrificed, forfeited

476 PARTICIPATION

NOUNS **1 participation, partaking, sharing,** having a part *or* share *or* voice, contribution, association; **involvement,** engagement; complicity; **voting** 609.18, **suffrage** 609.17; **power-sharing;** partnership, copartnership, copartnery, joint control, cochairmanship, joint chairmanship; joint tenancy, cotenancy; joint ownership, condominium *or* condo, cooperative *or* coop; communal ownership, commune

2 communion, community, communal effort *or* enterprise, **cooperation,** cooperative society, intercommunion; social life, socializing; **collectivity,** collectivism, collective enterprise, collective farm, kibbutz, kolkhoz; **democracy,** participatory democracy, town meeting, self-rule; collegiality; common ownership, public ownership, state ownership, communism, socialism 611.6; profit sharing; sharecropping

3 communization, communalization, **socialization, nationalization, collectivization**

4 participator, participant, partaker, player, sharer; party, **a party to,** accomplice, accessory; partner, copartner; cotenant; shareholder

VERBS **5 participate, take part, partake, contribute,** chip in, involve *or* engage oneself, get involved; **have** *or* **take a hand in,** get in on, have a finger in, have a finger in the pie, have to do with, have a part in, be an accessory to, be implicated in, be a party to, be a player in; **participate in,** partake of *or* in, **take part in,** take an active part in, **join, join in,** figure in, make oneself part of, join oneself to, associate oneself with, play *or* perform a part in, play a role in, get in the act <nf>; **join up,** sign on, enlist, volunteer, answer the call; climb on the bandwagon; **have a voice in,** help decide, be in on the decisions, **vote,** have suffrage, be enfranchised; **enter into,** go into; make the scene <nf>; sit in, sit on; bear a hand, pull an oar; come out of one's shell

6 **share, share in,** come in for a share, **go shares,** be partners in, have a stake in, have a percentage *or* piece of <nf>, partake in, **divide with, divvy up with** <nf>, halve, go halves; go halvers *and* **go fifty-fifty** *and* go even stephen <nf>, split the difference, **share and share alike;** do one's share *or* part, pull one's weight; cooperate 450.3; apportion 477.6

7 **communize,** communalize, **socialize, collectivize, nationalize**

ADJS 8 **participating, participative,** participant, participatory; hands-on, involved, engaged, **in** *or* **in on** <nf>; implicated, accessory; partaking, sharing

9 **communal, common,** general, public, collective, popular, social, societal; **mutual,** commutual , reciprocal, associated, **joint,** conjoint, **in common,** share *and* share alike; **cooperative** 450.5; power-sharing, profit-sharing; collectivistic, **communistic,** socialistic 611.22

477 APPORTIONMENT

NOUNS 1 **apportionment, apportioning, portioning, division,** divvy <nf>, partition, repartition, partitionment, partitioning, parceling, budgeting, rationing, **dividing, sharing,** share-out, sharing out, splitting, cutting, slicing, cutting the pie *and* divvying up <nf>; reapportionment

2 **distribution,** dispersion, **disposal,** disposition; dole, doling, doling *or* parceling out, giving out, passing around; **dispensation,** administration, issuance; disbursal, disbursement, paying out; redistribution; maldistribution; dealing, dispensing, divvying <nf>

3 **allotment, assignment, appointment,** setting aside, **earmarking,** tagging; underallotment, overallotment; appropriation; **allocation;** misallocation; reallocation

4 **dedication, commitment,** devoting, devotion, consecration

5 **portion, share, interest, part,** stake, stock, **piece,** bit, segment; **bite** *and* **cut** *and* **slice** *and* **chunk** *and* slice *and* piece of the pie *or* melon <nf>, piece of the action <nf>, **lot, allotment, end** <nf>, **proportion, percentage,** measure, quantum, **quota,** deal *or* dole , ratio, meed, moiety, mess, helping; contingent; dividend; **commission,** rake-off <nf>; equal share, half; **lion's share,** bigger half, big end <nf>; small share, modicum; **allowance, ration, budget; load, work load;** fate, destiny 964.2

VERBS 6 **apportion, portion, parcel, partition, part, divide,** share; share with, cut *or* deal one in <nf>, share *and* share alike, divide with, go halvers *or* fifty-fifty *or* even stephen with <nf>; divide into shares, **share out** *or* **around,** divide up, divvy *or* divvy up *or* out <nf>, **split,** split up, carve, cut, slice, carve up, slice up, cut up, cut *or* slice the pie *or* melon <nf>; divide *or* split fifty-fifty

7 **proportion,** proportionate, **prorate,** divide *pro rata,* appropriate

8 **parcel out, portion out,** measure out, serve out, spoon *or* ladle *or* dish out, **deal out, dole out, hand out, mete out,** ration out, give out, hand around, pass around; mete, dole, deal; **distribute,** disperse; **dispense,** dispose , issue, administer; disburse, pay out

9 **allot,** lot, **assign, appoint, set,** detail; **allocate,** make assignments *or* allocations, schedule; **set apart** *or* **aside, earmark,** tag, mark out for; demarcate, set off, mark off, portion off; assign to, appropriate to *or* for; reserve, restrict to, restrict 210.5; **ordain, destine, fate**

10 **budget, ration;** allowance, put on an allowance; divvy <nf>

11 **dedicate, commit, devote, consecrate,** set apart

ADJS 12 **apportioned,** portioned out, parceled, allocated, etc; **apportionable,** allocable, divisible, divvied <nf>, distributable, committable, appropriable, dispensable, donable, severable

13 **proportionate,** proportional; prorated, *pro rata* <L>; half; halvers *or* fifty-fifty *or* even stephen <nf>,

half-and-half, equal; **distributive,** distributional; **respective,** particular, per head, per capita, several

ADVS **14 proportionately, in proportion,** *pro rata* <L>; **distributively; respectively,** severally, each to each; share *and* share alike, in equal shares, half-and-half; fifty-fifty *and* even stephen <nf>

478 GIVING

NOUNS **1 giving, donation,** bestowal, bestowment; **endowment,** gifting <nf>, **presentation,** presentment; **award,** awarding; grant, granting; accordance, vouchsafement ; conferment, conferral; investiture; **delivery,** deliverance, surrender; **concession,** communication, impartation, impartment; **contribution,** subscription; tithing; accommodation, supplying, furnishment, provision 385; **offer** 439; **liberality** 485

2 commitment, consignment, assignment, **delegation,** relegation, commendation, remanding, **entrustment;** enfeoffment, infeudation *or* infeodation; labor of love

3 charity, almsgiving; philanthropy 143.4

4 gift, present, presentation, *cadeau* <Fr>, **offering,** fairing <Brit>; tribute, **award;** free gift, freebie *and* gimme <nf>, gift horse; oblation 696.7; handsel; box <Brit>; Christmas present *or* gift, birthday present *or* gift; peace offering; a little something; dowry; treat; goody bag

5 gratuity, largess, bounty, liberality, donative, sportula; perquisite, perks <Brit nf>; consideration, fee , **tip,** sweetener, inducement; grease *and* salve *and* palm oil <nf>; **premium, bonus,** something extra, **gravy** <nf>, bunce <Brit nf>, lagniappe; baker's dozen; honorarium; incentive pay, time and a half, double time; bribe 378.2**;** slush fund

6 donation, donative; **contribution, subscription; alms,** pittance, **charity, dole, handout** <nf>, alms fee, widow's mite, **pledge**; Peter's pence; **offering,** offertory, votive offering, collection; tithe

7 benefit, benefaction, benevolence, **blessing, favor, boon,** grace; manna, manna from heaven

8 subsidy, subvention, subsidization, support, price support, depletion allowance, tax benefit *or* write-off; **grant,** grant-in-aid, bounty; **allowance, stipend,** allotment; **aid,** assistance, financial assistance, financial aid; **help,** pecuniary aid; scholarship, fellowship; honorarium; **welfare,** public welfare, public assistance, relief, relief *or* welfare payments, welfare aid, dole, aid to dependent children, bailout, food stamps, meal ticket; guaranteed annual income; alimony, palimony; annuity; pension, old-age insurance, retirement benefits, social security, remittance; unemployment insurance; golden handcuffs; handout <nf>

9 endowment, investment, **settlement,** foundation; fund; charitable foundation; **dowry,** *dot* <Fr>, portion, marriage portion, marriage money; **dower,** widow's dower; jointure, legal jointure, thirds; appanage; community chest; charity event, fund-raiser, telethon

10 bequest, bequeathal, **legacy,** devise; inheritance 479.2; **will, testament,** last will and testament, living will; probate, attested copy; codicil

11 giver, donor, donator, gifter <nf>, presenter, bestower, conferrer, grantor, awarder, imparter, vouchsafer; fairy godmother, Lady Bountiful, Santa Claus, Robin Hood, sugar daddy <nf>; cheerful giver; **contributor, subscriber,** supporter, backer, financer, funder, angel <nf>; subsidizer; patron, patroness, Maecenas; tither; almsgiver, almoner; **philanthropist** 143.8, humanitarian; assignor, consignor; settler; testate, testator, testatrix; feoffor; good neighbor, good Samaritan

VERBS **12 give, present, donate,** slip <nf>, let have; **bestow, confer, award, allot, render,** bestow on; impart, let one know, communicate; **grant,** accord, **allow,** vouchsafe, yield, afford, make available; **tender,** proffer, offer, extend, come up with

<nf>; **issue, dispense,** administer; serve, help to; distribute; deal, dole, mete; **give out, deal out, dole out, mete out, hand** *or* dish *or* shell out <nf>, fork out *or* over *or* up <nf>; make a present of, gift *or* gift with <nf>, give as a gift; **give generously,** give the shirt off one's back; be generous *or* liberal with, give freely; pour, shower, rain, snow, heap, lavish 486.3; give in addition *or* as lagniappe, give into the bargain; regift

13 **deliver, hand, pass, reach,** forward, render, put into the hands of; transfer; **hand over,** give over, deliver over, fork over <nf>, **pass over, turn over,** come across with <nf>; hand out, give out, pass out, distribute, circulate; hand in, give in; **surrender,** resign

14 **contribute, subscribe, chip in** *and* kick in *and* pony up *and* pay up <nf>, give one's share *or* fair share; put oneself down for, pledge; contribute to, give to, donate to, gift *and* gift with <nf>; put something in the pot, sweeten the kitty

15 **furnish, supply, provide, afford,** provide for; **make available to,** put one in the way of; **accommodate with,** favor with, indulge with; **heap upon,** pour on, shower down upon, **lavish upon**

16 **commit, consign, assign, delegate,** relegate, confide, commend, remit, remand, give in charge; **entrust,** trust, give in trust; enfeoff, infeudate

17 **endow,** invest, vest; endow with, favor with, bless with, grace with, vest with; **settle on** *or* **upon; dower;** philanthropize, aid, benefit, relieve

18 **bequeath, will,** will and bequeath, **leave, devise, will to,** hand down, hand on, pass on, transmit, provide for; **make a will,** draw up a will, execute a will, make a bequest, write one's last will and testament, write into one's will; add a codicil; entail

19 **subsidize, finance,** bankroll *and* greenback <nf>, fund; angel <nf>; **aid, assist, support, help,** pay the bills, pick up the check *or* tab *and* spring for *and* pop for <nf>; pension, pension off

20 **thrust upon, force upon, press upon,** push upon, obtrude on, ram *or* cram down one's throat

21 **give away,** dispose of, part with, sacrifice, spare

ADJS **22** philanthropic, philanthropical, eleemosynary, **charitable** 143.15; giving, generous to a fault, liberal, **generous** 485.4; openhanded

23 **giveable,** presentable, bestowable; impartable, communicable; bequeathable, devisable; allowable; committable; fundable

24 **given,** allowed, accorded, granted, vouchsafed, bestowed, etc; gratuitous 634.5; God-given, providential

25 donative, contributory; concessive; testate, testamentary; intestate

26 **endowed,** dowered, subsidized, invested; dower, dowry, dotal; subsidiary, stipendiary, pensionary

ADVS **27** as a gift, gratis, on one, on the house, free, all-expense-paid; to his heirs, to the heirs of his body, to his heirs and assigns, to his executors *or* administrators and assigns

479 RECEIVING

NOUNS **1** **receiving, reception,** receival, **receipt, getting, taking; acquisition** 472; derivation; **assumption, acceptance;** admission, admittance; **reception** 187

2 **inheritance,** heritance , **heritage, patrimony, birthright, legacy, bequest,** bequeathal; reversion; entail; heirship; **succession,** line of succession, mode of succession, law of succession; primogeniture, ultimogeniture, postremogeniture, borough-English, coheirship, coparcenary, gavelkind; hereditament, corporeal *or* incorporeal hereditament; **heritable; heirloom**

3 **recipient, receiver,** accepter, getter, taker, acquirer, obtainer, procurer, donee; payee, endorsee; addressee, consignee; holder, trustee; **hearer,** viewer, beholder, audience, auditor, listener, looker, spectator; the receiving end; charity case; receiver of stolen property, fence <nf>

4 **beneficiary,** allottee, **donee, grantee,** patentee; **assignee, assign; devisee, legatee,** legatary ; trustee; feoffee; almsman, almswoman; stipendiary; pensioner, pensionary; annuitant

5 **heir,** heritor, inheritor, *heres* <L>; **heiress,** inheritress, inheritrix; coheir, joint heir, fellow heir, coparcener; heir expectant; **heir apparent,** apparent heir; **heir presumptive,** presumptive heir; statutory next of kin; legal heir, heir at law, heir general; heir by destination; heir of the body; heir in tail, heir of entail; fideicommissary heir, fiduciary heir; reversioner; remainderman; **successor,** next in line

VERBS 6 **receive, get, gain, secure,** have, come by, be in receipt of, be on the receiving end; **obtain, acquire** 472.8; **admit, accept, take,** take off one's hands; **take in** 187.10; assume, take on, take over; **derive, draw,** draw *or* derive from; have an income of, drag down *and* pull down *and* rake in <nf>, have coming in, take home; accept stolen property, fence <nf>

7 **inherit,** be heir to, **come into,** come in for, come by, fall *or* step into; step into the shoes of, succeed to

8 **be received, come in,** come to hand, pass *or* fall into one's hands, go into one's pocket, come *or* fall to one, fall to one's share *or* lot; **accrue,** accrue to

ADJS 9 **receiving,** on the receiving end; **receptive,** recipient 187.16

10 **received, accepted, admitted, recognized, approved**

480 TAKING

NOUNS 1 **taking,** possession, taking possession, taking away; **claiming,** staking one's claim; **acquisition** 472; **reception** 479.1; **theft** 482; bumming *or* mooching <nf>; moonlight requisition

2 **seizure, seizing, grab,** grabbing, snatching, snatch; **kidnapping, abduction,** forcible seizure; power grab <nf>, coup, coup d'état, seizure of power; hold 474.2; **catch,** catching; **capture,** collaring <nf>, nabbing <nf>; **apprehension,** prehension; **arrest,** arrestation, taking into custody; picking up *and* taking in *and* running in <nf>; dragnet

3 **sexual possession,** taking; sexual assault, ravishment, **rape,** violation, indecent assault, date rape *or* acquaintance rape, serial rape *or* gang bang <nf>; statutory rape; defloration, deflowerment, devirgination

4 **appropriation, taking over, takeover** <nf>, **adoption, assumption, usurpation,** arrogation; requisition, indent <Brit>; preoccupation, prepossession, preemption; **conquest,** occupation, subjugation, enslavement, colonization; infringement of copyright, plagiarism

5 **attachment, annexation,** annexure <Brit>; **confiscation,** sequestration; impoundment; **commandeering, impressment;** expropriation, nationalization, socialization, communalization, communization, collectivization; levy; distraint, distress; garnishment; execution; eminent domain, angary, right of eminent domain, right of angary

6 **deprivation, deprival,** privation, divestment, bereavement; relieving, disburdening, disburdenment; curtailment, abridgment ; disentitlement

7 **dispossession,** disseisin, expropriation; reclaiming, repossessing, **repossession,** foreclosure; **eviction** 909.2; disendowment; **disinheritance,** disherison, disownment

8 **extortion, shakedown** <nf>, **blackmail,** bloodsucking, vampirism; protection racket; badger game

9 **rapacity,** rapaciousness, ravenousness, sharkishness, wolfishness, **predaciousness,** predacity; pillaging, looting

10 **take, catch, bag,** capture, seizure, **haul;** booty 482.11; hot property

11 **taker;** partaker; **catcher, captor,** capturer; appropriator, expropriator

12 **extortionist,** extortioner, **blackmailer,** racketeer, shakedown artist <nf>, **bloodsucker,** leech, **vampire; predator,** raptor, bird of prey, beast of prey; harpy; vulture, shark;

profiteer; rack-renter; kidnapper, abductor

VERBS **13 take,** possess, take possession; **get,** get into one's hold *or* possession; pocket, palm; draw off, drain off; skim *and* skim off *and* take up front <nf>; **claim,** stake one's claim, enforce one's claim; partake; **acquire** 472.8; **receive** 479.6; **steal** 482.13

14 seize, take *or* get hold of, **lay hold of,** catch *or* grab hold of, glom *or* latch on to <nf>, **get** *or* **lay hands on,** clap hands on <nf>, put one's hands on, get into one's grasp *or* clutches; get one's fingers *or* hands on, get between one's finger *and* thumb; **grab, grasp, grip,** gripe , **grapple, snatch,** snatch up, nip, nail <nf>, **clutch,** claw, clinch, clench; **clasp, hug, embrace;** snap up, nip up, whip up, catch up; pillage, loot; take by assault *or* storm; **kidnap, abduct,** snatch <nf>, carry off; shanghai; take by the throat, throttle

15 possess sexually, take; **rape,** commit rape, commit date *or* acquaintance rape, ravish, violate, assault sexually, lay violent hands on, have one's will of; deflower, deflorate, devirginate

16 seize on *or* **upon,** fasten upon; spring *or* pounce upon, jump <nf>, swoop down upon; **catch at, snatch at,** snap at, jump at, make a grab for, scramble for

17 catch, take, catch flatfooted, land *and* nail <nf>, hook, **snag, snare,** sniggle, spear, harpoon; ensnare, enmesh, entangle, tangle, foul, tangle up with; **net,** mesh; **bag,** sack; **trap,** entrap; lasso, rope, noose

18 capture, apprehend, collar <nf>, run down, run to earth, **nab** <nf>, grab <nf>, lay by the heels, take prisoner; **arrest,** place *or* put under arrest, take into custody; pick up *or* take in *or* run in <nf>

19 appropriate, adopt, assume, usurp, arrogate, accroach; requisition, indent <Brit>; **take possession of,** possess oneself of, take for oneself, arrogate to oneself, take up, **take over, help oneself to,** make use of, make one's own, make free with, dip one's hands into; take it all, take all of, hog <nf>, monopolize, sit on; preoccupy, prepossess, preempt; jump a claim; **conquer,** overrun, occupy, subjugate, enslave, colonize; squat on; bum *or* mooch <nf>

20 attach, annex; confiscate, sequester, sequestrate, impound; **commandeer,** press, **impress;** expropriate, nationalize, socialize, communalize, communize, collectivize; exercise the right of eminent domain, exercise the right of angary; levy, distrain, replevy, replevin; garnishee, garnish

21 take from, take away from, **deprive of,** do out of <nf>, relieve of, disburden of, lighten of, ease of; **deprive, bereave, divest;** tap, milk, mine, drain, bleed, curtail, abridge ; cut off; disentitle

22 wrest, wring, wrench, **rend,** rip; **extort, exact,** squeeze, screw, **shake down** <nf>, **blackmail,** levy blackmail, badger *and* play the badger game <nf>; **force from, wrest from, wrench from, wring from, tear from, rip from, rend from,** snatch from, pry loose from

23 dispossess, disseise, expropriate, foreclose; evict 909.15; disendow; **disinherit,** disherison, **disown,** cut out of one's will, **cut off,** cut off with a shilling, cut off without a cent

24 strip, strip bare *or* clean, **fleece** <nf>, **shear,** denude, skin *and* pluck <nf>, flay, **despoil, divest,** pick clean, pick the bones of; deplume, displume; **milk; bleed, bleed white;** exhaust, drain, dry, suck dry; **impoverish,** beggar; clean out *and* take to the cleaners <nf>; eat out of house *and* home

ADJS **25 taking, catching;** private, deprivative; confiscatory, annexational, expropriatory; **thievish** 482.21; ripoff <nf>

26 rapacious, ravenous, ravening, vulturous, vulturine, sharkish, **wolfish,** lupine, predacious, **predatory,** raptorial; vampirish, **bloodsucking,** parasitic; **extortionate; grasping,** graspy, grabby <nf>, **insatiable** 100.27; all-devouring, all-engulfing

481 RESTITUTION

NOUNS **1 restitution, restoration,** restoring, giving back, sending back, remitting, remission, **return,** redress; reddition ; extradition, rendition; repatriation; recommitment, remandment, remand; satisfaction

2 reparation, recompense, paying back, squaring <nf>, repayment, reimbursement, refund, remuneration, **compensation, indemnification;** retribution, **atonement,** redress, satisfaction, **amends,** making good, **requital**; conscience money

3 recovery, regaining; **retrieval,** retrieve; **recuperation,** recoup, recoupment; **retake,** retaking, recapture; **repossession,** resumption, reoccupation; **reclamation,** reclaiming; **redemption,** ransom, salvage, trover; replevin, replevy; **revival, restoration** 396, retro

VERBS **4 restore, return, give back,** restitute, hand back, put back; take back, bring back; put the genie back into the bottle, put the toothpaste back into the tube; **remit,** send back; repatriate; extradite; recommit, remand; requite

5 make restitution, make reparation, **make amends,** make good, make up for, atone, give satisfaction, redress, **recompense,** pay back, square <nf>, repay, reimburse, refund, remunerate, **compensate, requite,** indemnify, make it up; pay damages, pay reparations; pay conscience money; overcompensate

6 recover, regain, retrieve, recuperate, **recoup, get back,** come by one's own; **redeem,** ransom; **reclaim; repossess,** resume, reoccupy; **retake,** recapture, take back; replevin, replevy; revive, renovate, **restore** 396.11,15

ADJS **7 restitutive,** restitutory, **restorative;** compensatory, indemnificatory, retributive, reparative, reparatory; reversionary, reversional, revertible; redeeming, redemptive, redemptional; reimbursable

ADVS **8 in restitution,** in reparation, in recompense, in compensation, to make up for, in return for, in retribution, in requital, in amends, in atonement, to atone for

482 THEFT

NOUNS **1 theft, thievery,** stealage, **stealing,** thieving, **purloining;** swiping *and* lifting *and* snatching *and* snitching *and* pinching <nf>; conveyance , **appropriation,** conversion, liberation *and* annexation <nf>; **pilfering,** pilferage, **filching,** scrounging <nf>; abstraction; sneak thievery; shoplifting, boosting <nf>; poaching; **graft; embezzlement** 389.1; **fraud, swindle** 356.8

2 larceny, petit *or* petty larceny, petty theft, grand larceny, grand theft, simple larceny, mixed *or* aggravated larceny; automobile theft

3 theft, robbery, robbing; bank robbery; banditry, highway robbery; **armed robbery, holdup,** assault *and* robbery, **mugging,** push-in job *or* crime; purse snatching; **pocket picking** *or* pick-pocketing, jostling; **hijacking,** asportation ; carjacking; cattle stealing, **cattle rustling** *and* cattle lifting <nf>; **extortion** 480.8; identity theft

4 <nf terms> **heist, stickup,** job, stickup job, bag job, boost, hustle, pinch, swipe, lift, burn, knockover, **ripoff;** sticky fingers

5 burglary, burglarizing, housebreaking, **breaking and entering,** break and entry, break-in, unlawful entry; second-story work <nf>; safebreaking, **safecracking, safeblowing**

6 plundering, pillaging, looting, sacking, freebooting, ransacking, rifling, spoiling, **despoliation,** despoilment, despoiling; rapine, spoliation, depredation, direption , **raiding,** ravage, ravaging, ravagement, rape, ravishment; **pillage, plunder,** sack; brigandage, brigandism, banditry; **marauding,** foraging; raid, foray, razzia

7 piracy, buccaneering, privateering, freebooting; letters of marque, letters of marque and reprisal; **air piracy,** airplane hijacking, skyjacking; carjacking

8 **plagiarism,** plagiarizing, plagiary, **piracy,** literary piracy, appropriation, borrowing, cribbing; infringement; infringement of copyright; autoplagiarism; cribbing <nf>; crib *or* cheat sheet

9 **abduction, kidnapping, snatching** <nf>; **shanghaiing,** impressment, crimping

10 **grave-robbing,** body-snatching <nf>, resurrectionism

11 **booty,** spoil, **spoils, loot, swag** <nf>, ill-gotten gains, **plunder,** prize, haul, take, pickings, stealings, stolen goods, hot goods *or* items <nf>; **boodle** *and* squeeze *and* **graft** <nf>; perquisite, perks <Brit nf>, pork barrel, spoils of office, public trough; till, public till; blackmail; hot property

12 **thievishness,** larcenousness, taking ways <nf>, light fingers, sticky fingers; kleptomania, bibliokleptomania, etc

VERBS **13** **steal, thieve, purloin, appropriate, take,** snatch, palm, **make off with,** walk off with, run off *or* away with, abstract, disregard the distinction between *meum* and *tuum*; have one's hand in the till; **pilfer, filch;** shoplift; poach; rustle; **embezzle** 389.4; defraud, swindle; **extort** 480.22

14 **rob,** commit robbery; pick pockets, jostle; hold up, stick someone up

15 **burglarize,** burgle <nf>, commit burglary, housebreak; crack *or* blow a safe

16 <nf terms> **swipe, pinch,** bag, **lift,** hook, crib, **cop,** nip, snitch, snare, boost, annex, borrow, burn, clip, **rip off,** nick *and* nobble <Brit>; **heist, knock off** *or* **over,** tip over; **stick up; mug;** roll, jackroll; do a job; cook the books; case the joint

17 **plunder, pillage, loot, sack,** ransack, rifle, freeboot, spoil, spoliate, despoil, depredate, prey on *or* upon, **raid,** reive, ravage, ravish, raven, sweep, gut; **fleece** 480.24; maraud, foray, forage

18 **pirate,** buccaneer, privateer, freeboot

19 **plagiarize, pirate,** borrow *and* crib <nf>, appropriate; **pick one's brains;** infringe a copyright

20 **abduct,** abduce, spirit away, **carry off** *or* **away,** magic away <Brit>, run off *or* away with; **kidnap,** snatch <nf>, hold for ransom; skyjack, hijack, carjack; **shanghai,** crimp, impress

ADJS **21** **thievish, thieving, larcenous, light-fingered, sticky-fingered;** kleptomaniacal, burglarious; brigandish, piratical, piratelike; fraudulent

22 **plunderous, plundering, looting,** pillaging, ravaging, marauding, spoliatory; predatory, predacious

23 **stolen,** pilfered, purloined, ripped off; pirated, plagiarized; hot <nf>

483 THIEF

NOUNS **1** **thief, robber,** stealer, purloiner, lifter <nf>, *ganef* <Yiddish>, **crook** <nf>; larcenist, larcener; **pilferer, filcher,** petty thief, chicken thief; sneak thief, prowler; shoplifter, booster <nf>; poacher; **grafter,** petty grafter; jewel thief; **swindler,** con man 357.3,4; land pirate, land shark, land-grabber; grave robber, body snatcher, resurrectionist, ghoul; embezzler, peculator, white-collar thief; den of thieves

2 **pickpocket,** cutpurse, fingersmith *and* dip <nf>; **purse snatcher;** light-fingered gentry

3 **burglar,** yegg *and* cracksman <nf>; housebreaker, cat burglar, cat man, second-story thief *or* worker; **safecracker,** safebreaker, safeblower; pete blower *or* pete man *or* peterman <nf>

4 **bandit, brigand,** dacoit; **gangster** *and* mobster <nf>, goodfella <nf>; racketeer; **thug, hoodlum** 593.4

5 **robber, holdup man** *and* stickup man <nf>; highwayman, highway robber, footpad, road agent; **mugger** <nf>, sandbagger; train robber; bank robber, **hijacker** <nf>

6 **plunderer, pillager, looter, marauder,** rifler, sacker, spoiler, despoiler, spoliator, depredator, **raider,** moss-trooper, free-booter rapparee, reiver, forayer, forager, ravisher, ravager; wrecker

7 **pirate, corsair, buccaneer, privateer,** sea rover, rover, picaroon; viking, sea king; Blackbeard, Captain Kidd, Jean Lafitte, Henry Morgan; Captain Hook, Long John Silver; air pirate, airplane hijacker, skyjacker; hijacker, carjacker; record pirate, video pirate, bootlegger

8 cattle thief, abactor, rustler *and* **cattle rustler** <nf>, poacher

9 **plagiarist,** plagiarizer, cribber <nf>, pirate, literary pirate, copyright infringer

10 abductor, kidnapper; shanghaier, snatcher *and* baby-snatcher <nf>; crimp, crimper

11 <famous thieves> Barabbas, Robin Hood, Jesse James, Clyde Barrow, John Dillinger, Claude Duval, Jack Sheppard, Willie Sutton, Dick Turpin, Jonathan Wild; Autolycus, Macheath, Thief of Baghdad, Jean Valjean, Jimmy Valentine, Raffles, Bill Sikes

484 PARSIMONY

NOUNS **1** **parsimony,** parsimoniousness; frugality 635.1; **stinting, pinching, scrimping,** skimping, cheeseparing; economy, economy of means, economy of assumption, law of parsimony, Ockham's razor, elegance

2 **niggardliness,** penuriousness, **meanness,** minginess, shabbiness, sordidness

3 **stinginess, ungenerosity, illiberality, cheapness, chintziness** *and* tightness *and* narrowness <nf>, tight purse strings, nearness, closeness, closefistedness, closehandedness , tightfistedness, hardfistedness, **miserliness,** penny-pinching, hoarding, austerity; **avarice** 100.8

4 **niggard, tightwad** *and* **cheapskate** <nf>, **miser,** hard man with a buck <nf>, **skinflint,** scrooge, penny pincher, moneygrubber <nf>, pinchfist, pinchgut , churl, curmudgeon , muckworm, save-all <nf>, Silas Marner

VERBS **5** **stint, scrimp, skimp, scamp,** scant, screw, **pinch,** starve, famish; **pinch pennies,** rub the print off a dollar bill, rub the picture off a nickel; live upon nothing; grudge, begrudge

6 **withhold,** hold back, hold out on <nf>

ADJS **7** **parsimonious, sparing,** cheeseparing, **stinting, scamping, scrimping,** skimping; frugal 635.6; too frugal, overfrugal, frugal to excess; penny-wise, penny-wise and pound-foolish; austere

8 **niggardly,** niggard, pinchpenny, penurious, **grudging, mean,** mingy, shabby, sordid

9 **stingy, illiberal, ungenerous, chintzy, miserly,** save-all, **cheap** *and* **tight** *and* narrow <nf>, **near, close, closefisted,** closehanded , tightfisted, pinchfisted, hardfisted; near as the bark on a tree; pinching, **penny-pinching; avaricious** 100.27

ADVS **10** **parsimoniously,** stintingly, scrimpingly, skimpingly

11 **niggardly, stingily,** illiberally, ungenerously, closefistedly, tightfistedly; meanly, shabbily, sordidly

485 LIBERALITY

NOUNS **1** **liberality,** liberalness, freeness, freedom; **generosity,** generousness, largeness, **unselfishness, munificence,** largess *or* largesse, charity; bountifulness, bounteousness, **bounty;** hospitality, welcome, graciousness; **openhandedness,** freehandedness, open *or* free hand, easy purse strings; **givingness;** open-heartedness, bigheartedness, largeheartedness, greatheartedness, freeheartedness; open heart, big *or* large *or* great heart, heart of gold; **magnanimity** 652.2

2 **cheerful giver,** free giver; contributor; Lady Bountiful; Santa Claus; philanthropist; almsgiver, altruist

VERBS **3** **give freely,** give cheerfully, give with an open hand, give with both hands, put one's hands in one's pockets, open the purse, loosen *or* untie the purse strings; **spare no expense,** spare nothing, not count the cost, let money be no object; **heap upon,** lavish upon, shower down upon; give the coat *or* shirt off one's back, give more than one's share, **give until it hurts;** give of oneself, give of one's substance, not hold back, offer oneself; tip well; keep the change!

ADJS **4 liberal, free,** free with one's money, free-spending; **generous, munificent,** large, princely, handsome; **unselfish,** ungrudging; **unsparing, unstinting,** stintless, unstinted; **bountiful,** bounteous, **lavish,** profuse; hospitable, gracious; **openhanded,** freehanded, open; **giving;** openhearted, **bighearted,** largehearted, greathearted, freehearted; **magnanimous** 652.6

ADVS **5 liberally, freely; generously, munificently,** handsomely; **unselfishly,** ungrudgingly; **unsparingly, unstintingly; bountifully,** bounteously, **lavishly,** profusely; hospitably, graciously; **openhandedly,** freehandedly; openheartedly, bigheartedly, largeheartedly, greatheartedly, freeheartedly; with open hands, with both hands, with an unsparing hand, without stint

486 PRODIGALITY

NOUNS **1 prodigality, overliberality,** overgenerousness, overgenerosity; profligacy, **extravagance,** pound-foolishness, recklessness, reckless spending *or* expenditure, overspending, frittering away; incontinence, intemperance 669; lavishness, profuseness, profusion; **wastefulness, waste; dissipation, squandering,** squandermania; *carpe diem* <L>; slack *or* loose purse strings, leaking purse; conspicuous consumption *or* waste; splurge, spree

2 prodigal, wastrel, waster, **squanderer; spendthrift,** wastethrift, spender, spendall, big spender <nf>; Diamond Jim Brady; prodigal son; last of the big spenders

VERBS **3 squander, lavish,** slather, blow <nf>, play ducks *and* drakes with; **dissipate,** scatter , sow broadcast, scatter to the winds, fritter away; **run through,** go through; **throw away,** throw one's money away, throw money around, **spend money like water,** hang the expense, let slip *or* flow through one's fingers, spend as if money grew on trees, spend money as if it were going out of style, spend like a drunken sailor; gamble away; burn the candle at both ends; seize the day, live for the day, let tomorrow take care of itself

4 waste, consume, spend, expend, use up, exhaust; deplete, drain, suck dry, milk dry; misuse, abuse; lose; spill, pour down the drain *or* rathole; pour water into a sieve, cast pearls before swine, kill the goose that lays the golden egg, *manger son blé en herbe* <Fr>, throw out the baby with the bath water; waste effort, labor in vain

5 fritter away, fool away, fribble away, dribble away, drivel away, **trifle away,** dally away, potter away, piss away <nf>, muddle away, diddle away <nf>, squander in dribs *and* drabs; idle away, while away

6 misspend, misapply, **throw good money after bad,** throw the helve after the hatchet, throw out the baby with the bathwater, cast pearls before swine

7 overspend, spend more than one has, spend what one hasn't got, lavish; overdraw, overdraw one's account, live beyond one's means, have champagne tastes on a beer budget

ADJS **8 prodigal, extravagant, lavish,** profuse, **overliberal,** overgenerous, overlavish, **spendthrift, wasteful,** profligate, dissipative; incontinent, intemperate 669.7; pound-foolish, penny-wise *and* pound-foolish; easy come, easy go

9 wasted, squandered, dissipated, consumed, spent, used, lost; **gone to waste,** run *or* gone to seed; down the drain *or* spout *or* rathole <nf>; misspent

487 CELEBRATION

NOUNS **1 celebration,** celebrating; **observance,** formal *or* solemn *or* ritual observance, **solemnization;**

marking *or* honoring the occasion; **commemoration,** memorialization, remembrance, memory; jubilee; red-letter day, **holiday** 20.4; anniversary; **festivity** 743.3,4; **revel** 743.6; rejoicing 116; **ceremony,** rite 580.4; religious rites 701; ovation, triumph; **tribute;** testimonial, testimonial banquet *or* dinner; toast; roast; **salute;** salvo, flourish of trumpets, fanfare, fanfaronade; dressing ship; high-five; binge *or* bender <nf>, blowout <nf>; ladies' night; **party,** afterparty

VERBS 2 **celebrate, observe, keep, mark,** solemnly mark, **honor; commemorate,** memorialize; **solemnize,** signalize, hallow, mark with a red letter, party, party down <nf>, hold jubilee, jubilize, jubilate, maffick <Brit nf>; **make merry,** make whoopie; binge <nf>; kill the fatted calf; sound a fanfare, blow the trumpet, beat the drum, fire a salute; dress ship; high-five

ADJS 3 **celebrative,** celebratory, celebrating, partying; **commemorative,** commemorating; memorial; solemn; festive, festal, gala

ADVS 4 **in honor of, in commemoration of,** in memory *or* remembrance of, to the memory of

488 HUMOROUSNESS

NOUNS 1 **humorousness, funniness,** amusingness, laughableness, laughability, hilarity, hilariousness; wittiness 489.2; **drollness,** drollery; **whimsicalness,** quizzicalness; **ludicrousness, ridiculousness, absurdity,** absurdness, quaintness, eccentricity, incongruity, bizarreness, bizarrerie; richness, pricelessness <nf>; the funny side; barrel of laughs

2 **comicalness,** comicality, funiosity; farcicalness, **farcicality,** slapstick quality, broadness

3 bathos; anticlimax, comedown, shaggy dog story

ADJS 4 **humorous, funny, amusing; witty** 489.15; **droll, whimsical,** quizzical; **laughable,** risible, good for a laugh; **ludicrous, ridiculous, hilarious, absurd,** quaint, eccentric, incongruous, bizarre

5 <nf terms> **funny ha-ha,** priceless, too funny *or* too killing for words, hardy-har *or* hardy-har-har *or* har-har-har, rich, hysterical

6 **comic** *or* **comical; farcical,** slapstick, broad; **burlesque** 508.14; tragicomic, serio-comic, mock-heroic

ADVS 7 **humorously, amusingly,** funnily, **laughably;** wittily 489.18; drolly, whimsically, quizzically; **comically,** farcically, broadly; **ludicrously, ridiculously, absurdly,** quaintly, eccentrically, incongruously, bizarrely

489 WIT, HUMOR

NOUNS 1 **wit, humor,** pleasantry, *esprit* <Fr>, salt, spice *or* savor of wit; Attic wit *or* salt, Atticism; ready wit, quick wit, nimble wit, agile wit, pretty wit; dry wit, dry humor, subtle wit; **comedy** 704.6; black humor, dark humor, sick humor, gallows humor; **satire,** sarcasm, irony; Varronnian satire, Menippean satire; **parody, lampoon,** lampoonery, travesty, **caricature, burlesque,** squib, takeoff, spoof; **farce,** mere farce; **slapstick,** slapstick humor, broad humor, black humor; visual humor, cartoon, comic strip, the funnies; stand-up comedy

2 **wittiness, humorousness** 488, **funniness;** facetiousness, pleasantry, **jocularity,** jocoseness, jocosity; **joking,** japery, joshing <nf>; smartness, cleverness, brilliance; pungency, saltiness; keenness, sharpness; keen-wittedness, quick-wittedness, nimble-wittedness

3 **drollery,** drollness; **whimsicality,** whimsicalness, humorsomeness, antic wit

4 **waggishness, waggery;** roguishness 322.2; **playfulness,** sportiveness, **levity, frivolity,** flippancy, merriment 109.5; **prankishness,** pranksomeness; trickery, trickiness, tricksiness, trickishness

5 **buffoonery,** buffoonism, clownery, clowning, clowning around,

harlequinade; **clownishness,** buffoonishness; **foolery,** fooling, **tomfoolery;** horseplay; shenanigans *and* monkey tricks *and* monkeyshines <nf>, funny business; **banter** 490

6 **joke, jest, gag** *and* one-liner <nf>, **wheeze,** jape; **fun, sport, play,** kidding; story, yarn, **funny story,** good story; dirty story *or* joke, blue story *or* joke, *double entendre* <Fr>; one-liner; shaggy-dog story; sick joke <nf>; ethnic joke; capital joke, good one, laugh, belly laugh, rib tickler, sidesplitter, thigh-slapper, howler, wow, hoot, scream, riot, panic; visual joke, sight gag <nf>; standing joke; **point,** punch line, gag line, tag line; cream of the jest; jest-book

7 **witticism, pleasantry,** *plaisanterie* and *boutade* <Fr>; **play of wit,** *jeu d'esprit* <Fr>; **crack** *and* smart crack *and* **wisecrack** <nf>; **quip,** conceit, bright *or* happy thought, bright *or* brilliant idea; **mot, bon mot,** smart saying, stroke of wit, one-liner *and* zinger <nf>; epigram, turn of thought, aphorism, apothegm; flash of wit, scintillation; sound bite; **sally,** flight of wit; **repartee,** backchat, retort, riposte, snappy comeback <nf>; facetiae <pl>, quips *and* cranks; **gibe, dirty** *or* **nasty crack** <nf>; persiflage 490.1

8 **wordplay, play on words,** *jeu de mots* <Fr>, missaying, corruption, paronomasia, *calembour* <Fr>, abuse of terms; **pun,** punning; equivoque, equivocality; anagram, logogram, logogriph, metagram; acrostic, double acrostic; amphiboly, amphibologism; palindrome; spoonerism; malapropism; Tom Swifty

9 **old joke,** old wheeze *or* turkey, **trite joke,** hoary-headed joke, joke with whiskers; **chestnut** *and* corn *and* **corny joke** *and* oldie <nf>; Joe Miller, Joe Millerism; twice-told tale, retold story, warmed-over cabbage <nf>

10 **prank, trick, practical joke,** waggish trick, *espièglerie* <Fr>, antic, caper, frolic; **monkeyshines** *and* **shenanigans** <nf>, leg-pull

11 **sense of humor, risibility,** funny bone

12 **humorist, wit, funnyman, comic,** *bel-esprit* <Fr>, life of the party; **joker,** jokester, gagman <nf>, **jester,** court jester, **quipster, wisecracker** *and* gagster <nf>; wag, wagwit; zany, madcap, cutup <nf>; **prankster; comedian,** stand-up comic *or* comedian, banana <nf>, straight man; **clown** 707.10; punster, punner; epigrammatist; satirist, ironist; burlesquer, caricaturist, cartoonist, parodist, lampooner; reparteeist; witling; gag writer <nf>, jokesmith

VERBS **13** **joke, jest, wisecrack** *and* crack wise <nf>, utter a mot, **quip,** jape, josh <nf>, fun <nf>, make fun, **kid** *or* **kid around** <nf>; **make a funny** <nf>; **crack a joke,** get off a joke, tell a good story; pun, play on words; scintillate, sparkle; **make fun of,** gibe at, fleer at, mock, scoff at, poke fun at, send up, take off, lampoon, make the butt of one's humor, be merry with; ridicule 508.8

14 **trick, play a practical joke,** play tricks *or* pranks, **play a joke** *or* **trick on,** make merry with; **clown around,** pull a stunt *or* trick; pull one's leg *and* put one on <nf>

ADJS **15** **witty, amusing,** *spirituel* <Fr>; **humorous** 488.4, **comic, comical, farcical** 488.6; **funny; jocular,** joky <nf>, **joking, jesting, jocose, tongue-in-cheek; facetious,** joshing <nf>, **whimsical, droll,** humorsome; smart, clever, brilliant, scintillating, sparkling, sprightly; keen, sharp, rapier-like, pungent, pointed, biting, mordant; teasing; satiric, **satirical, sarcastic, ironic,** ironical; salty, salt, Attic; **keen-witted, quick-witted, nimble-witted,** dry-witted, smart

16 **clownish,** buffoonish

17 **waggish;** roguish 322.6; **playful, sportive; prankish,** pranky, pranksome; tricky, trickish, tricksy

ADVS **18** **wittily, humorously; jocularly, jocosely; facetiously; whimsically, drolly**

19 **in fun, in sport, in play, in jest,** in joke, as a joke, jokingly, jestingly, with tongue in cheek; for fun, for sport

490 BANTER

NOUNS **1 banter, badinage, persiflage, pleasantry, fooling, fooling around, kidding** *and* **kidding around** <nf>, **raillery,** rallying, **sport,** good-natured banter, harmless teasing; ridicule 508; exchange, give-and-take; side-talk, **byplay,** asides; flyting, slanging, the dozens <nf>

2 bantering, twitting, chaffing, joking, jesting, japing, **fooling, teasing,** hazing; playing the dozens <nf>, backchat

3 <nf terms> **kidding,** joshing, jollying, jiving, fooling around; **ribbing,** ragging, razzing, **roasting**

4 banterer, *persifleur* <Fr>, **chaffer, twitter; kidder** *and* josher <nf>

VERBS **5 banter, twit, chaff,** rally, **joke, jest,** jape, **tease,** haze; have a slanging match, play the dozens <nf>, backchat

6 <nf terms> **kid,** jolly, josh, fool around, jive, rub, put on; **razz, roast,** ride, needle

ADJS **7 bantering, chaffing, twitting; jollying** *and* **kidding** *and* joshing etc <nf>, **fooling, teasing,** quizzical

491 COWARDICE

NOUNS **1 cowardice, cowardliness; fear** 127; **faintheartedness,** faintheart, weakheartedness, chickenheartedness, henheartedness, pigeonheartedness; **yellowness,** white-liveredness *and* lily-liveredness *and* chicken-liveredness <nf>, weak-kneedness; weakness, softness; unmanliness, unmanfulness; timidness, **timidity,** timorousness, milksoppiness, milksoppishness, milksopism, cowardship

2 uncourageousness, unvaliantness, unvalorousness, unheroicness, ungallantness, unintrepidness; **plucklessness, spunklessness** *and* gritlessness *and* gutlessness <nf>, spiritlessness, heartlessness; defeatism

3 dastardliness, pusillanimousness, **pusillanimity, poltroonery,** poltroonishness, poltroonism, baseness, abjectness, **cravenness;** desertion under fire, bugout *and* skedaddling <nf>, lack of moral fiber

4 cold feet <nf>, weak knees, **faintheart,** chicken heart, **yellow streak** <nf>, white feather; gutlessness

5 coward, jellyfish, invertebrate, faintheart, **weakling,** weak sister <nf>, milksop, milquetoast, mouse, **sissy, wimp** <nf>, baby, **big baby, chicken** <nf>; namby-pamby; **yellow-belly,** *and* white-liver *and* lily-liver *and* chicken-liver <nf>, jellyfish, white feather; fraid-cat *and* **fraidy-cat** *and* scaredy-cat <nf>; funk *and* funker <nf>

6 dastard, craven, poltroon, recreant, caitiff, arrant coward; sneak; deserter

VERBS **7 dare not; have a yellow streak** <nf>, have cold feet <nf>, be unable to say 'boo' to a goose

8 lose one's nerve, lose courage, **get cold feet** <nf>, **show the white feather;** falter, boggle, funk <nf>, **chicken** <nf>; put one's tail between one's legs, back out, funk out <nf>, **wimp** *or* **chicken out** <nf>, have no stomach for; desert under fire, turn tail, bug out *and* skedaddle <nf>, **run scared** <nf>, scuttle, retreat

9 cower, quail, cringe, crouch, skulk, sneak, slink

ADJS **10 cowardly,** coward; **afraid, fearful** 127.23; timid, timorous, overtimorous, overtimid, rabbity *and* mousy <nf>; **fainthearted,** weakhearted, chicken-hearted, henhearted, pigeonhearted; white-livered *and* lily-livered *and* chicken-livered *and* milk-livered <nf>; **yellow** *and* yellow-bellied *and* with a yellow streak <nf>; **weak-kneed, chicken** <nf>, afraid of one's shadow; weak, soft; **wimpy** *or* wimpish <nf>, unmanly, unmanful, sissy, sissified; milksoppy, milksoppish; panicky, panic-prone, funking *and* funky <nf>; daunted, dismayed, unmanned, cowed, intimidated

11 uncourageous, unvaliant, unvalorous, unheroic, ungallant, **unintrepid,**

undaring, unable to say 'boo' to a goose; unsoldierlike, unsoldierly; **pluckless,** spunkless *and* gritless <nf>, gutless <nf>, spiritless, heartless

12 **dastardly,** dastard; hit-and-run; **poltroonish,** poltroon; **pusillanimous,** base, craven, recreant, caitiff; dunghill, dunghilly

13 **cowering, quailing, cringing; skulking, sneaking, slinking,** sneaky, slinky

ADVS 14 **cravenly,** poltroonishly, like a coward, **cowardly, uncourageously,** unvaliantly, unvalorously, unheroically, ungallantly, unintrepidly, undaringly; plucklessly, spunklessly *and* gritlessly <nf>, spiritlessly, heartlessly; faintheartedly, weakheartedly, chickenheartedly; wimpishly

492 COURAGE

NOUNS 1 **courage,** courageousness, **nerve,** pluck, **bravery,** braveness, ballsiness *and* gutsiness *or* guttiness <nf>, **boldness,** nerves of steel, **valor,** valorousness, valiance, valiancy, **gallantry,** conspicuous gallantry, gallantry under fire *or* beyond the call of duty, gallantness, **intrepidity,** intrepidness, **prowess,** virtue; doughtiness, stalwartness, stoutness, stoutheartedness, lionheartedness, greatheartedness; **heroism,** heroicalness; chivalry, chivalrousness, knightliness; military *or* martial spirit, fighting spirit, soldierly quality *or* virtues; **manliness,** manfulness, **manhood,** virility, machismo; Dutch courage <nf>, pot-valor, bold front, bravado

2 **fearlessness,** dauntlessness, **undauntedness, unfearfulness,** unfearingness, unafraidness, **unapprehensiveness; confidence** 970.5; untimidness, untimorousness, unshrinkingness, unshyness, unbashfulness

3 <nf terms> **balls, guts,** intestinal fortitude, spunk, brass balls, cojones, moxie, spizzerinctum, **backbone,** chutzpah

4 **daring,** derring-do, deeds of derring-do; **bravado,** bravura; **audacity,** audaciousness, overboldness; **venturousness,** venturesomeness, risk-taking, tightrope walking, funambulism; **adventurousness,** adventuresomeness, enterprise; foolhardiness 493.3

5 **fortitude, hardihood,** hardiness; **pluckiness; spunkiness** *and* grittiness *and* nerviness <nf>, mettlesomeness; **gameness,** gaminess; grit, **stamina,** toughness, pith , **mettle,** bottom; heart, spirit, stout **heart,** heart of oak; **resolution** 359, resoluteness, tenaciousness, tenacity, pertinaciousness, pertinacity, bulldog courage, true grit, stiff upper lip

6 **exploit, feat, deed, enterprise, achievement, adventure,** act of courage, gest, **bold stroke,** heroic act *or* deed; prowess; heroics; aristeia

7 <brave person> **hero, heroine;** brave, stalwart, gallant, valiant, man *or* woman of courage *or* mettle, a man, valiant knight, good soldier, warrior, knight in shining armor; tragic hero, unsung hero; demigod, paladin; demigoddess; the brave; decorated hero; Hector, Achilles, Roland, David; lion, **tiger,** bulldog, fighting cock, gamecock; he-man; daredevil, stunt person

8 **encouragement, heartening, inspiration,** inspiriting, inspiritment, emboldening, assurance, reassurance, pat *or* clap on the back, bucking up

VERBS 9 **dare, venture, make bold to,** make so bold as to, take risks, walk the tightrope, **have the nerve, have the guts** *or* the balls <nf>, have the courage of one's convictions, be a man; defy 454.3

10 **brave, face, confront,** affront, front, look one in the eye, say to one's face, **face up to,** meet, **meet head-on** *or* boldly, square up to, stand up to *or* against, go eyeball-to-eyeball *or* one-on-one with <nf>; set at defiance 454.4; speak up, speak out, stand up and be counted; not flinch *or* shrink from, bite the bullet <nf>, look full in the face, put a bold face upon, show *or* present a bold front; head

into, face up, come to grips with, grapple with; face the music <nf>; **brazen,** brazen out *or* through; beard; put one's head in the lion's mouth, fly into the face of danger, take the bull by the horns, march up to the cannon's mouth, bell the cat, go through fire and water, court disaster, go in harm's way, throw caution to the wind, run the gauntlet, take one's life in one's hands, put one's ass *or* life on the line <nf>

11 **outbrave, outdare; outface,** face down, face out; **outbrazen,** brazen out; **outlook, outstare,** stare down, stare out <Brit>, stare out of countenance

12 **steel oneself, get up nerve,** nerve oneself, muster *or* summon up *or* gather courage, pluck up heart, screw up one's nerve *or* courage, stiffen one's backbone <nf>

13 **take courage, take heart,** pluck up courage, take heart of grace; **brace** *or* **buck up** <nf>

14 keep up one's courage, bear up, **keep one's chin up** <nf>, keep one's pecker up <Brit nf>, **keep a stiff upper lip** <nf>, hold up one's head, take what comes; hang in *or* hang in there *or* hang tough *or* stick it out <nf>, stick to one's guns, grin and bear it

15 **encourage, hearten, embolden, nerve,** pat *or* clap on the back, **assure, reassure,** bolster, support, cheer on, root for; **inspire,** inspirit; incite, exhort; buck *or* brace up <nf>; put upon one's mettle, make a man of; cheer 109.7

ADJS 16 **courageous, plucky, brave, bold, valiant, valorous, gallant, intrepid,** doughty, **hardy,** stalwart, stout, stouthearted, ironhearted, lionhearted, greathearted, bold-spirited, bold as a lion; **heroic,** herolike; **chivalrous,** chivalric, knightly, knightlike, soldierly, soldierlike; **manly,** manful, virile, macho

17 **resolute, tough, game; spirited,** spiritful, red-blooded, **mettlesome;** bulldoggish, tenacious, pertinacious

18 <nf terms> **ballsy,** gutsy, gutty, nervy, stand-up, dead game, gritty, spunky, nervy

19 **unafraid, unfearing, unfearful; unapprehensive,** undiffident; **confident** 970.21; **fearless, dauntless,** aweless, dreadless; **unfrightened,** unscared, unalarmed, unterrified; **untimid,** untimorous, unshy, unbashful

20 **undaunted, undismayed,** uncowed, unintimidated, unappalled, unabashed, unawed; **unflinching, unshrinking,** unquailing, unbowed, uncringing, unwincing, unblenching, unblinking

21 **daring, audacious,** overbold; **adventurous, venturous, venturesome,** adventuresome, enterprising; foolhardy 493.9

ADVS 22 **courageously, bravely, boldly, heroically, valiantly,** valorously, **gallantly, intrepidly,** doughtily, stoutly, hardily, stalwartly; **pluckily, spunkily** <nf>, gutsily <nf>, **resolutely, gamely,** tenaciously, pertinaciously, bulldoggishly, **fearlessly,** unfearingly, unfearfully; **daringly,** audaciously; chivalrously, knightly, yeomanly; like a man, like a soldier

493 RASHNESS

NOUNS 1 **rashness, brashness,** brazen boldness, **incautiousness,** overboldness, **imprudence, indiscretion,** injudiciousness, improvidence; irresponsibility; **unwariness,** unchariness; overcarelessness; overconfidence, oversureness, overweeningness; **impudence,** insolence 142; **gall** *and* brass *and* cheek *and* chutzpah <nf>; hubris; **temerity,** temerariousness; heroics

2 **recklessness,** devil-may-careness; heedlessness, **carelessness** 340.2; **impetuousness** 365.2, impetuosity, hotheadedness; **haste** 401, **hastiness,** hurriedness, overeagerness, overzealousness, overenthusiasm; **furiousness,** desperateness, wantonness, wildness, wild oats; frivolity; **precipitateness,** precipitousness, precipitance, precipitancy, precipitation

3 **foolhardiness,** harebrainedness; **audacity,** audaciousness; more guts

than brains <nf>, *courage fou* <Fr>; forwardness, boldness, **presumption,** presumptuousness; **daring,** daredeviltry, daredevilry, fire-eating; playing with fire, flirting with death, courting disaster, stretching one's luck, going for broke <nf>, brinkmanship, tightrope walking, funambulism; adventurousness

4 **daredevil,** devil, **madcap,** madbrain, wild man, hotspur, hellcat, rantipole, harumscarum *and* fire-eater <nf>; **adventurer,** adventuress, adventurist; brazen-face

VERBS 5 be rash, be reckless, carry too much sail, sail too near the wind, throw caution to the wind, go out of one's depth, go too far, go to sea in a sieve, take a leap in the dark, buy a pig in a poke, count one's chickens before they are hatched, catch at straws, lean on a broken reed, put all one's eggs in one basket, live in a glass house; go out on a limb <nf>, leave oneself wide open <nf>, drop one's guard, stick one's neck out *and* ask for it <nf>

6 **court danger,** ask for it, ask for trouble, mock *or* defy danger, go in harm's way, thumb one's nose at the consequences, **tempt fate** *or* **the gods** *or* **S,** tweak the devil's nose, bell the cat, play a desperate game, ride for a fall; play with fire, flirt with death, stretch one's luck, march up to the cannon's mouth, put one's head in a lion's mouth, beard the lion in his den, sit on a barrel of gunpowder, sleep on a volcano, play Russian roulette, playing with a loaded pistol *or* gun, working without a net; risk all, go for broke *and* shoot the works <nf>

ADJS 7 **rash, brash, incautious,** overbold, **imprudent, indiscreet,** injudicious, improvident; ill-considered; irresponsible; **unwary, unchary;** overcareless; overconfident, oversure, overweening, **impudent,** insolent, brazenfaced, brazen; hubristic; temerarious

8 **reckless,** devil-may-care; careless 340.11; **impetuous,** hotheaded; **hasty** 401.9, hurried, overeager, overzealous, overenthusiastic; **furious,** desperate, mad, wild, wanton, harum-scarum <nf>; precipitate, **precipitous, precipitant; headlong, breakneck;** slapdash, slap-bang; accident-prone; asking for it

9 **foolhardy, harebrained,** madcap, **wild,** wild-ass <nf>, madbrain, madbrained; **audacious;** forward, bold, **presumptuous; daring,** daredevil, risk-taking, fire-eating, death-defying; adventurous; frivolous, flippant

ADVS 10 **rashly, brashly, incautiously, imprudently, indiscreetly,** injudiciously, improvidently; **unwarily,** uncharily; overconfidently, overweeningly, **impudently,** insolently, **brazenly,** hubristically, temerariously

11 **recklessly,** happen what may; heedlessly, **carelessly** 340.18; **impetuously,** hotheadedly; **hastily,** hurriedly, overeagerly, overzealously, overenthusiastically; **furiously,** desperately, wildly, wantonly, **madly,** like mad *or* crazy *and* like there was no tomorrow <nf>; **precipitately,** precipitiously, precipitantly; **headlong,** headfirst, headforemost, **head over heels,** heels over head, *à corps perdu* <Fr>; slapdash, slap-bang *or* slam-bang <nf>; helter-skelter, ramble-scramble <nf>, hurry-scurry, holus-bolus

12 **foolhardily, daringly, audaciously,** presumptuously, harebrainedly

494 CAUTION

NOUNS 1 **caution, cautiousness;** slowness to act *or* commit oneself *or* make one's move; **care, heed, solicitude; carefulness, heedfulness,** mindfulness, regardfulness, thoroughness; paying mind *or* attention; **guardedness;** uncommunicativeness 344; **gingerliness, tentativeness,** hesitation, hesitancy, unprecipitateness; slow *and* careful steps, deliberate stages, wait-and-see attitude *or* policy; **prudence,** prudentialness, **circumspection, discretion,** canniness; **coolness, judiciousness** 920.7; calculation, **deliberateness,** deliberation, careful consideration, prior consultation; **safeness,** safety first, no room for error; **hedge, hedging,** hedging one's bets, cutting one's losses; designated driver

2 **wariness, chariness, cageyness** *and* **leeriness** <nf>; **suspicion,** suspiciousness; **distrust,** distrustfulness, mistrust, mistrustfulness; reticence, skepticism, second thoughts, reservation

3 **precaution,** precautiousness; **forethought, foresight,** foresightedness, forehandedness, forethoughtfulness; **providence,** provision, nest egg, forearming; precautions, steps, measures, steps and measures, preventive measure *or* step; **safeguard,** protection 1008, preventive measure, safety net, safety valve, sheet anchor; **insurance**; rainy-day policy; lemon law

4 **overcaution, overcautiousness, overcarefulness,** overwariness; unadventurousness

VERBS 5 **be cautious, be careful;** think twice, give it a second thought; make haste slowly, take it easy *or* slow <nf>; put the right foot forward, take one step at a time, pick one's steps, go step by step, feel one's ground *or* way; pussyfoot, tiptoe, go *or* walk on tiptoe, walk on eggs *or* eggshells *or* thin ice; pull *or* draw in one's horns; doubt, have second thoughts

6 **take precautions, take steps** *or* **measures,** take steps and measures; **prepare** *or* **provide for** *or* **against,** forearm; **guard against, make sure against,** make sure; **play safe** <nf>, anticipate; keep on the safe side; leave no stone unturned, forget *or* leave out nothing, overlook no possibility, leave no room *or* margin for error, leave nothing to chance, consider every angle; **look before one leaps;** see how the land lies *or* the wind blows, see how the cat jumps <nf>; clear the decks, batten down the hatches, shorten sail, reef down, tie in *or* tuck in *or* take in a reef, get out a sheet-anchor, have an anchor to windward; hedge, provide a **hedge,** hedge one's bets, cut one's losses; take out insurance; keep something for a rainy day; provide for

7 **beware, take care, have a care,** take heed, take heed at one's peril; keep at a respectful distance, keep out of harm's way; mind, mind one's business; **be on one's guard,** be on the watch *or* lookout, be on the *qui vive*; **look out, watch out** <nf>; **look sharp,** keep one's eyes open, keep a weather eye out *or* open <nf>, keep one's eye peeled <nf>, **watch one's step** <nf>, look about one, look over one's shoulder, keep tabs on <nf>; stop, look, and listen; not stick one's neck out <nf>, not go out on a limb <nf>, not expose oneself, not be too visible, **keep a low profile,** lie low, stay in the background, blend with the scenery; not blow one's cover <nf>; hold one's tongue 51.5

ADJS 8 **cautious, careful,** heedful, mindful, alert, regardful, **thorough; prudent, circumspect,** slow to act *or* commit oneself *or* make one's move, noncommittal, uncommitted; canny; sly, crafty, scheming; **discreet, politic, judicious** 920.19, Polonian, Macchiavelian; unadventurous, no-risk, unenterprising, undaring; **gingerly; guarded,** on guard, on one's guard; uncommunicative 344.8; **tentative,** hesistant, unprecipitate, cool; **deliberate;** safe, on the safe side, leaving no stone unturned, forgetting *or* leaving out nothing, overlooking no possibility, leaving no room *or* margin for error

9 **wary, chary, cagey** <nf>, **leery** <nf>, **suspicious,** suspecting, **distrustful,** mistrustful, shy; guarded, on guard; cautionary

10 **precautionary,** precautious, precautional; **preventive,** preemptive, prophylactic; **forethoughtful,** forethoughted, **foresighted,** foreseeing, forehanded; **provident,** provisional; anticipatory

11 **overcautious, overcareful,** overwary, unadventurous

ADVS 12 **cautiously, carefully,** heedfully, mindfully, regardfully;

prudently, circumspectly, cannily, pawkily <Brit>, **discreetly,** judiciously; **gingerly,** guardedly, easy <nf>, with caution, with care

13 **warily, charily,** cagily <nf>; **askance,** askant, suspiciously, leerily <nf>, distrustfully

495 FASTIDIOUSNESS

NOUNS 1 **fastidiousness, particularity,** particularness; **scrupulousness,** scrupulosity; punctiliousness, punctilio, spit and polish; preciseness, precision; **meticulousness, conscientiousness,** criticalness; taste 496; **sensitivity, discrimination** 944, discriminatingness, discriminativeness; **selectiveness,** selectivity, pickiness <nf>, choosiness; **strictness** 339.3, **perfectionism,** precisianism, **purism; puritanism, priggishness, prudishness, prissiness** <nf>, propriety, strait-lacedness, censoriousness, judgmentalness

2 **finicalness,** finickiness, finickingness, finicality; **fussiness,** pernicketiness *or* persnicketiness <nf>; squeamishness, queasiness

3 **nicety,** niceness, **delicacy,** delicateness, daintiness, exquisiteness, fineness, refinement, **subtlety**

4 overfastidiousness, **overscrupulousness, overparticularity, overconscientiousness,** overmeticulousness, overniceness, **overnicety; overcriticalness,** hypercriticism, hairsplitting; overrefinement, oversubtlety, supersubtlety; oversqueamishness, oversensitivity, hypersensitivity, morbid sensibility

5 **exclusiveness,** exclusivity, selectness, selectiveness, selectivity; **cliquishness,** clannishness; **snobbishness,** snobbery, snobbism; quiddity

6 **perfectionist,** precisian, precisianist, stickler, nitpicker <nf>, captious critic 946.7

7 **fussbudget, fusspot** <nf>, fuss, fusser, **fuddy-duddy** <nf>, granny, old woman, old maid; Mrs Grundy

VERBS 8 **be hard to please,** want everything just so, **fuss,** fuss over; pick *and* choose; **turn up one's nose,** look down one's nose, disdain, scorn, spurn; not dirty *or* soil one's hands

ADJS 9 **fastidious, particular, scrupulous, meticulous, conscientious,** exacting, precise, punctilious, spit-and-polish; **sensitive, discriminating** 944.7, discriminative; **selective,** picky <nf>, choosy, choicy <nf>; critical; **strict** 339.12, perfectionistic, precisianistic, puristic; puritanic, puritanical, priggish, prudish, prissy, proper, strait-laced, censorious, judgmental

10 **finical, finicky,** finicking, finikin; **fussy,** fuss-budgety <nf>; **squeamish,** pernickety *and* persnickety <nf>, difficult, hard to please

11 **nice, dainty, delicate,** *délicat* <Fr>, picture-perfect, fine, refined, exquisite, **subtle**

12 **overfastidious,** queasy, **overparticular, overscrupulous, overconscientious,** overmeticulous, **overnice,** overprecise; **overcritical,** hypercritical, ultracritical, hairsplitting; overrefined, oversubtle, supersubtle; oversqueamish, oversensitive, hypersensitive, morbidly sensitive; **compulsive,** anal, anal-compulsive

13 **exclusive,** selective, **select,** elect, elite; **cliquish,** clannish; **snobbish,** snobby; quiddative

ADVS 14 **fastidiously, particularly, scrupulously, meticulously, conscientiously,** critically, punctiliously; discriminatingly, discriminatively, selectively; **finically,** finickily, finickingly; **fussily; squeamishly,** queasily; refinedly, subtly

496 TASTE, TASTEFULNESS

NOUNS 1 **taste, good taste,** sound critical judgment, discernment *or* appreciation of excellence, preference for the best, *goût raffiné* <Fr>; **tastefulness,** quality, excellence, choiceness, **elegance,** grace, gracefulness, gracility, graciousness, graciosity, gracious living; propriety; **refinement,** finesse, **polish, culture,**

cultivation, civilizedness, refined *or* cultivated *or* civilized taste, finish; niceness, nicety, delicacy, daintiness, **subtlety, sophistication; discrimination** 944, fastidiousness 495; acquired taste, connoisseurship; etiquette

2 **decorousness, decorum,** decency, properness, propriety, rightness, right thinking, **seemliness,** becomingness, fittingness, fitness, appropriateness, suitability, meetness, happiness, felicity; gentility, genteelness; civility, urbanity 504.1

3 **restraint,** restrainedness, **understatement,** unobtrusiveness, quietness, subduedness, quiet taste; simplicity 499.1; subtlety

4 **aesthetic** *or* **artistic taste,** virtuosity, virtu, **expertise,** expertism, connoisseurship; dilettantism; fine art of living; epicurism, epicureanism; gastronomy, *friandise* <Fr>; aesthetics

5 **aesthete,** person of taste, lover of beauty

6 **connoisseur,** *connaisseur* <Fr>, *cognoscente* <Ital>; **judge,** good judge, **critic, expert,** authority, maven <nf>, arbiter, arbiter of taste, *arbiter elegantiarum* <L>, tastemaker, trend-setter; **epicure,** epicurean; **gourmet, gourmand,** *bon vivant* <Fr>, good *or* refined palate; oenophile, wine lover; virtuoso; dilettante, amateur; culture vulture <nf>; collector; gentleperson

ADJS 7 **tasteful, in good taste,** in the best taste; excellent, of quality, of the best, of the first water; **aesthetic,** artistic, pleasing, well-chosen, choice, of choice; pure, chaste; classic *or* classical, Attic, restrained, understated, unobtrusive, conservative, quiet, subdued, simple, low-key, unaffected 499.7

8 **elegant,** graceful, gracile, gracious; **refined, polished, cultivated,** civilized, **cultured;** nice, fine, delicate, dainty, **subtle, sophisticated, discriminating** 944.7, fastidious 495.9, sensitive, U <nf>

9 **decorous,** decent, proper, right, right-thinking, **seemly, becoming,** fitting, appropriate, suitable, meet, happy, felicitous; genteel; civil, urbane 504.14

ADVS 10 **tastefully, with taste,** in good taste, in the best taste; aesthetically, artistically; elegantly, gracefully; decorously, genteelly, decently, properly, seemly, becomingly; quietly, unobtrusively; simply 499.10

497 VULGARITY

NOUNS 1 **vulgarity,** vulgarness, vulgarism, commonness, meanness; **inelegance** *or* **inelegancy, indelicacy, impropriety, indecency, indecorum,** indecorousness, unseemliness, unbecomingness, unfittingness, inappropriateness, unsuitableness, unsuitability; ungentility; **untastefulness,** tastelessness, unaestheticness, unaestheticism, tackiness; low *or* bad *or* poor taste, *mauvais goût* <Fr>; vulgar taste, bourgeois taste, Babbittry, philistinism; popular taste, pop culture *and* pop <nf>; campiness, camp, high *or* low camp; baseness, kitsch

2 **coarseness, grossness,** *grossièreté* <Fr>, **rudeness, crudeness,** crudity, **crassness,** rawness, roughness, **earthiness;** ribaldness, ribaldry; raunchiness <nf>, **obscenity** 666.4; meretriciousness, **loudness** <nf>, **gaudiness** 501.3

3 **unrefinement, uncouthness, uncultivation,** uncultivatedness, unculturedness; uncivilizedness, wildness; impoliteness, incivility, ill breeding 505.1; **barbarism,** barbarousness, barbarity, philistinism, Gothicism; **savagery,** savagism; **brutality,** brutishness, bestiality, animality, **mindlessness;** Neanderthalism, troglodytism

4 **boorishness, churlishness,** carlishness, **loutishness,** lubberliness, lumpishness, cloddishness, clownishness, yokelism; ruffianism, rowdyism, hooliganism; parvenuism, arrivism, upstartness; roughness

5 **commonness, commonplaceness,** ordinariness, homeliness; **lowness, baseness, meanness; ignobility,** plebeianism

6 **vulgarian,** low *or* vulgar *or* ill-bred fellow, mucker <nf>, guttersnipe <nf>, *épicier* <Fr>; Babbitt, Philistine, bourgeois; *parvenu* and *arriviste* and *nouveau riche* <Fr>, upstart; bounder <nf>, cad, **boor,** churl, clown, **lout,** yahoo, redneck <nf>, looby, peasant, groundling, yokel; rough, **ruffian,** roughneck <nf>, **rowdy,** hooligan; vulgarist, ribald; guttermouth; rascal, rapscallion; vulgus, hoi polloi, rabble, riffraff, great unwashed, scum, huddled masses

7 **barbarian, savage,** Goth, animal, brute; Neanderthal, troglodyte

8 vulgarization, coarsening; popularization; *haute vulgarisation* <Fr>; dumbing down <nf>

VERBS **9** vulgarize, coarsen; popularize; dumb down <nf>; **pander;** commercialize

ADJS **10** **vulgar, inelegant, indelicate, indecorous, indecent, improper, unseemly,** unbeseeming, unbecoming, unfitting, inappropriate, unsuitable, **ungenteel,** undignified, discourteous; **untasteful,** tasteless, in bad *or* poor taste, tacky *and* chintzy *and* Mickey Mouse <nf>, gauche, garish; **offensive,** offensive to gentle ears

11 **coarse, gross, rude, crude, crass,** raw, rough, **earthy;** ribald; raunchy <nf>, **obscene** 666.9; meretricious, **loud** <nf>, **gaudy** 501.20; cacological, solecistic

12 **unrefined, unpolished, uncouth,** unkempt, uncombed, unlicked; **uncultivated, uncultured; uncivilized,** noncivilized; impolite, uncivil, ill-bred 505.6; **wild,** untamed; **barbarous,** barbaric, barbarian, infra dig; outlandish, Gothic; primitive; **savage, brutal,** brutish, bestial, animal, **mindless;** Neanderthal, troglodytic; wild-and-woolly, rough-and-ready

13 **boorish, churlish,** carlish, **loutish,** redneck <nf>, lubberly, lumpish, cloddish, clownish, loobyish, yokelish; rowdy, **rowdyish, ruffianly,** roughneck <nf>, hooliganish, raffish, raised in a barn

14 **common, commonplace, ordinary;** plebeian; homely, homespun; **general, public, popular,** pop <nf>; vernacular; Babbittish, Philistine, bourgeois; campy, high-camp, low-camp, kitschy

15 **low, base, mean, ignoble,** vile, scurvy, sorry, scrubby, beggarly; low-minded, base-minded

ADVS **16** **vulgarly, uncouthly, inelegantly,** indelicately, indecorously, indecently, improperly, unseemly, untastefully, offensively; **coarsely, grossly, rudely, crudely,** crassly, roughly; ribaldly

498 ORNAMENTATION

NOUNS **1** **ornamentation, ornament; decoration,** decor; **adornment, embellishment,** embroidery, elaboration; nonfunctional addition *or* adjunct; garnish, garnishment, garniture; trimming, trim; flourish; emblazonment, emblazonry; illumination; **color,** color scheme, color pattern, color compatibility, color design, color arrangement; **arrangement,** flower arrangement, floral decoration, furniture arrangement; table setting *or* decoration; window dressing; **interior decoration** *or* decorating, room decoration, interior design; feng shui; **redecoration, refurbishment** 396.4, redoing

2 **ornateness, elegance, fanciness,** fineness, **elaborateness; ostentation** 501; richness, luxuriousness, luxuriance; **floweriness,** floridness, floridity; dizenment , **bedizenment; gaudiness, flashiness** 501.3; flamboyance *or* flamboyancy, chi-chi; **overelegance,** overelaborateness, overornamentation, busyness; clutteredness; baroqueness, baroque, rococo, arabesque, moresque, chinoiserie

3 **finery,** frippery, gaudery, gaiety, bravery, trumpery, folderol, trickery, chiffon, trappings, festoons, superfluity; **frills,** frills and furbelows, bells and whistles *and* gimmickry *and* Mickey Mouse *and* glitz <nf>, **frillery,** frilling, frilliness; foofaraw <nf>, fuss <nf>, froufrou; gingerbread; tinsel, clinquant, pinchbeck, paste; gilt, gilding

4 **trinket,** gewgaw, **knickknack** *or* nicknack, knack , **gimcrack,** kickshaw, doodad, whim-wham, **bauble,** fribble, bibelot, toy, gaud; bric-a-brac; sequin

5 **jewelry,** bijouterie, ice <nf>; costume jewelry, glass, paste, junk jewelry <nf>; bling *or* bling-bling <nf>

6 **jewel,** bijou, **gem,** stone, precious stone; rhinestone; pin, brooch, stickpin, breastpin, scatter pin, chatelaine; cuff-link, tie clasp *or* clip, tie bar, tiepin *or* scarfpin, tie tack *or* tie tac; **ring,** band, wedding band, engagement ring, promise ring, mood ring, signet ring, school *or* class ring, circle, earring, nose ring; bracelet, wristlet, wristband, armlet, anklet; chain, necklace, torque; locket; beads, chaplet, wampum; bangle; charm; fob; crown, coronet, diadem, tiara; laurel

7 **motif,** ornamental motif, **figure, detail,** form, touch, repeated figure; **pattern, theme,** design, ornamental theme, ornamental *or* decorative composition; foreground detail, background detail; **background,** setting, foil, **style,** ornamental *or* decorative style, national style, **period style**

VERBS **8** **ornament, decorate, adorn, dress, trim, garnish,** array, **deck,** bedeck, dizen , bedizen; prettify, **beautify; redecorate,** refurbish, redo; gimmick *or* glitz *or* sex up <nf>; **embellish, furbish,** embroider, enrich, grace, set off *or* out, paint, color, blazon, emblazon, paint in glowing colors; **dress up; spruce up** *and* gussy up *and* doll up *and* fix up <nf>, **primp up,** prink up, prank up, trick up *or* out, deck out, bedight , fig out; primp, prink, prank, preen; smarten, smarten up, dandify, titivate, give a face lift

9 figure, filigree; **spangle, bespangle;** bead; tinsel; jewel, bejewel, gem, diamond; pavé; ribbon, beribbon; flounce; flower, garland, wreathe; feather, plume; flag; illuminate; paint 35.14; engrave

ADJS **10** **ornamental, decorative,** adorning, embellishing

11 **ornamented, adorned, decorated, embellished, bedecked,** decked out, tricked out, garnished, trimmed, dizened , bedizened; figured; flowered; festooned, befrilled, wreathed; spangled, bespangled, spangly; jeweled, bejeweled; beaded; studded; plumed, feathered; beribboned

12 **ornate, elegant, fancy,** fine, chichi, pretty-pretty; picturesque; **elaborate,** overornamented, overornate, overelegant, etc, labored, high-wrought; **ostentatious** 501.18; glitzy, flashy; **rich, luxurious,** luxuriant; **flowery,** florid; flamboyant, fussy, frilly, frilled, flouncy, gingerbread *or* gingerbready; **overelegant,** overelaborate, overlabored, overworked, overwrought, overornamented, busy; cluttered; **baroque,** rococo, arabesque, moresque, gilded; gimmicked- *or* glitzed- *or* sexed-up <nf>

499 PLAINNESS

<unaffectedness>

NOUNS **1** **plainness, simplicity** 798, **simpleness, ordinariness, commonness, commonplaceness,** homeliness, prosaicness, prosiness, matter-of-factness; **purity,** chasteness, classic *or* classical purity, Attic simplicity

2 **naturalness,** inartificiality; **unaffectedness,** unassumingness, **unpretentiousness;** directness, straightforwardness; innocence, naïveté, chasteness

3 **unadornment, unembellishment,** unadornedness, unornamentation; **no frills,** no nonsense, back-to-basics; **uncomplexity,** uncomplication, uncomplicatedness, **unsophistication,** unadulteration; bareness, baldness, nakedness, nudity, starkness, undress, beauty unadorned

4 **inornateness, unelaborateness,** unfanciness, unfussiness; **austerity,** severity, starkness, Spartan simplicity

VERBS **5** **simplify** 798.4; chasten, restrain, purify; put in words of one syllable, spell out

ADJS **6** **simple** 798.6, **plain, ordinary, nondescript, common, commonplace, prosaic,** prosy, **matter-of-fact, homely, homespun,** everyday, vanilla <nf>, conventional, workday, workaday, household, garden, common- *or* garden-variety; pure, **pure and simple,** chaste, classic *or* classical, Attic

7 **natural,** native; **inartificial,** unartificial; **unaffected, unpretentious,** unpretending, unassuming, unfeigning, direct, straightforward, honest, candid; innocent, naive

8 **unadorned, undecorated, unornamented, unembellished,** ungarnished, unfurbished, unvarnished, untrimmed; olde *and* olde-worlde <nf>; back-to-basics, no-frills, nononsense, vanilla *or* plain-vanilla *and* white-bread *or* white-bready <nf>; back-to-nature; **uncomplex,** uncomplicated, **unsophisticated,** unadulterated; **undressed,** undecked, unarrayed; bare, bald, blank, naked, nude

9 **inornate,** unornate, **unelaborate,** unfancy, unfussy; austere, monkish, cloistral, severe, stark, Spartan

ADVS **10** **plainly, simply,** ordinarily, commonly, commonplacely, prosaically, matter-of-factly

11 **unaffectedly, naturally,** unpretentiously, unassumingly, directly, straightforwardly

500 AFFECTATION

NOUNS **1** **affectation, affectedness; pretension, pretense, airs,** pretentiousness, putting on airs, put-on <nf>; **show, false show,** mere show; front, false front <nf>, **facade,** mere facade, **image,** public image; feigned belief, **hypocrisy** 354.6; la-di-da <nf>, phoniness <nf>, sham 354.3; artificiality, unnaturalness, insincerity; prunes *and* prisms, airs *and* graces; stylishness, mannerism

2 **mannerism,** *minauderie* <Fr>, **trick of behavior,** trick, **quirk,** habit, peculiarity, peculiar trait, idiosyncrasy, trademark

3 **posing, pose, posturing,** attitudinizing, attitudinarianism; peacockery, peacockishness; pompousness; putting on airs

4 **foppery, foppishness, dandyism,** coxcombry, puppyism, conceit

5 **overniceness,** overpreciseness, **overrefinement, elegance,** exquisiteness, preciousness, preciosity; goody-goodyism *and* goody-goodness <nf>; purism, formalism, formality, pedantry, precisionism, precisianism; euphuism; euphemism

6 **prudery, prudishness, prissiness, priggishness, primness, smugness, stuffiness** <nf>, old-maidishness, **straitlacedness,** stiff-neckedness, hidebound, narrowness, censoriousness, sanctimony, sanctimoniousness, **puritanism,** puritanicalness; **false modesty,** overmodesty, demureness, *mauvaise honte* <Fr>

7 **phony** *and* **fake** *and* **fraud** <nf> 354.13; affecter; mannerist; **pretender,** actor, playactor <nf>, performer; paper tiger, hollow man, straw man, man of straw, empty suit <nf>

8 **poser, poseur,** striker of poses, **posturer,** posturist, posture maker, attitudinarian, attitudinizer, bluffer

9 **dandy, fop,** coxcomb, macaroni, gallant, dude *and* swell *and* sport <nf>, ponce *and* toff <Brit nf>, exquisite, blood, fine gentleman, puppy, jackanapes, jack-a-dandy, fribble, clotheshorse, fashion plate; beau, Beau Brummel, spark, blade, ladies' man, lady-killer <nf>, masher, cocksman <nf>; man-about-town, boulevardier

10 **fine lady,** *grande dame* and *précieuse* <Fr>; belle, toast

11 **prude, prig,** priss, puritan, bluenose, goody-goody <nf>, goody two-shoes, wowser <Brit nf>, old maid; Victorian, mid-Victorian

VERBS **12** **affect, assume, put on,** assume *or* put on airs, wear, **pretend, simulate, counterfeit, sham, fake** <nf>, **feign,** make out like <nf>, make a show of, play, playact <nf>, act *or* play a part, play a scene, do a bit <nf>, put up a front <nf>, dramatize, histrionize, show off, play to the gallery, lay it on thick <nf>, overact, ham *and* ham it up *and* chew up the scenery *and* emote <nf>, tug at the heartstrings

13 **pose, posture, attitudinize,** peacock, strike a pose, strike an attitude, pose for effect

14 **mince,** mince it, prink <Brit nf>; **simper,** smirk, bridle

ADJS 15 **affected, pretentious,** la-di-da, posy <Brit nf>; mannered, *maniéré* <Fr>; **artificial, unnatural,** insincere; theatrical, stagy, histrionic; overdone, overacted, hammed up <nf>

16 **assumed, put-on, pretended,** simulated, **phony** *and* **fake** *and* **faked** <nf>, feigned, counterfeited; spurious, sham; deceptive, specious; hypocritical

17 **foppish, dandified,** dandy, coxcombical, conceited, chichi, pompous

18 <affectedly nice> **overnice,** overprecise, precious, *précieuse* <Fr>, exquisite, **overrefined, elegant,** mincing, simpering, namby-pamby; **goody-goody** *and* goody good-good <nf>; puristic, formalistic, pedantic, precisionistic, precisian, precisianistic, euphuistic, euphemistic

19 **prudish, priggish, prim, prissy, smug, stuffy** <nf>, old-maidish, **overmodest,** demure, **straitlaced,** stiff-necked, hide-bound, narrow, censorious, po-faced <Brit>, sanctimonious, **puritanical,** Victorian, mid-Victorian

ADVS 20 **affectedly, pretentiously;** elegantly, mincingly; for effect, for show

21 **prudishly, priggishly,** primly, smugly, stuffily <nf>, straitlacedly, stiffneckedly, puritanically

501 OSTENTATION

NOUNS 1 **ostentation,** ostentatiousness, ostent; **pretentiousness, pretension, pretense;** loftiness, lofty affectations, **triumphalism**

2 **pretensions,** vain pretensions; **airs,** lofty airs, airs *and* graces, vaporing, highfalutin *or* highfaluting ways <nf>, side, swank <nf>, delusions of grandeur

3 **showiness, flashiness,** flamboyance, panache, dash, jazziness <nf>, jauntiness, sportiness <nf>, gaiety, glitter, glare, dazzle, dazzlingness; extravaganza; **gaudiness,** gaudery, glitz *and* gimmickry *and* razzmatazz *and* razzledazzle <nf>, **tawdriness,** meretriciousness; gorgeousness, colorfulness; loudness <nf>, **blatancy,** flagrancy, shamelessness, brazenness, luridness, extravagance, sensationalism, obtrusiveness, vulgarness, crudeness, extravagation

4 **display, show, demonstration,** manifestation, **exhibition, parade,** *étalage* <Fr>; **pageantry,** pageant, **spectacle,** gala; vaunt, fanfaronade, blazon, flourish, flaunt, flaunting; daring, brilliancy, éclat, bravura, flair; dash *and* splash *and* splurge <nf>; figure; showmanship, **exhibitionism,** showing-off, fuss and feathers; theatrics, histrionics, dramatics, staginess, camp; false front, **sham** 354.3

5 **grandeur,** grandness, grandiosity, **magnificence,** gorgeousness, **splendor,** splendidness, splendiferousness, resplendence, brilliance, glory; nobility, proudness, **state, stateliness, majesty;** impressiveness, imposingness; **sumptuousness, elegance, elaborateness, lavishness, luxuriousness;** ritziness *or* poshness *or* plushness *or* swankness *or* swankiness <nf>; **luxury,** barbaric *or* Babylonian splendor

6 **pomp,** circumstance, pride, **state,** solemnity, formality; **pomp and circumstance**; heraldry

7 **pompousness, pomposity,** pontification, pontificality, **stuffiness** <nf>, **self-importance,** inflation; grandiloquence, bombast, turgidity, orotundity

8 **swagger, strut,** swank <nf>, bounce, brave show; swaggering, strutting; swash, **swashbucklery,** swashbuckling, swashbucklering; peacockishness, peacockery

9 **stuffed shirt** <nf>, blimp <nf>, Colonel Blimp; bloated aristocrat

10 strutter, swaggerer, swanker <Brit>, swash, swasher, **swashbuckler,** peacock, miles gloriosus

11 show-off <nf>, **exhibitionist,** flaunter; **grandstander** *or* grandstand player *or* hot dog *or* **hotshot** *or* showboat <nf>

VERBS **12 put** *or* **thrust oneself forward,** come forward, step to the front *or* fore, step into the limelight, take center stage, attract attention, make oneself conspicuous

13 cut a dash, make a show, put on a show, make one's mark, cut a swath, cut *or* **make a figure;** make a splash *or* a **splurge** <nf>; splurge *and* splash <nf>; shine, glitter, glare, dazzle

14 give oneself airs, put on airs, put on, put on side, put on the dog <nf>, put up a front <nf>, put on the ritz *and* ritz it <nf>, look big, **swank** <nf>, swell, swell it, act the grand seigneur; pontificate, play the pontiff

15 strut, swagger, swank <Brit>, prance, stalk, peacock, swash, swashbuckle

16 show off <nf>, **grandstand** *and* hotdog *and* showboat <nf>, play to the gallery *or* galleries <nf>, please the crowd, ham it up; exhibit *or* parade one's wares <nf>, strut one's stuff <nf>, go through one's paces, show what one has

17 flaunt, vaunt, **parade, display, demonstrate,** manifest, make a great show of, **exhibit,** air, put forward, put forth, hold up, flash *and* sport <nf>; advertise; **flourish,** brandish, wave; dangle, dangle before the eyes; emblazon, Zblazon forth; trumpet, trumpet forth

ADJS **18 ostentatious, pretentious,** posy <Brit nf>; **ambitious,** vaunting, **lofty, highfalutin** *and* highfaluting <nf>, **high-flown,** high-flying; **high-toned,** tony <nf>, **fancy,** classy *or* glitzy *or* flossy <nf>; Gatsbyesque

19 showy, flaunting, flashy, snazzy, flashing, glittering, **jazzy** *and* **glitzy** *and* gimmicky *and* splashy *and* splurgy <nf>; camp; exhibitionistic, showoffy <nf>, bravura; **gay,** jaunty, rakish, **dashing;** gallant, brave, daring; **sporty** *or* dressy <nf>; **frilly, flouncy,** frothy, chichi

20 gaudy, tawdry; gorgeous, colorful; **garish, loud** <nf>, **blatant, flagrant,** shameless, **brazen,** brazen-faced, lurid, extravagant, sensational, **spectacular,** glaring, flaring, flaunting, screaming <nf>, obtrusive, vulgar, crude; meretricious, low-rent *and* low-ride *and* tacky <nf>

21 grandiose, grand, magnificent, splendid, splendiferous, splendacious <nf>, **glorious,** superb, fine, superfine, fancy, superfancy, swell <nf>; **imposing, impressive,** larger-than-life, awful, awe-inspiring, awesome; **noble, proud, stately, majestic,** princely; **sumptuous, elegant, elaborate, luxurious,** luxuriant, extravagant, deluxe; executive *and* plush *and* posh *and* ritzy *and* swank *and* swanky <nf>, Corinthian; palatial, Babylonian

22 pompous, stuffy <nf>, **self-important,** impressed with oneself, pontific, pontifical; **inflated, swollen,** bloated, tumid, turgid, flatulent, gassy <nf>, stilted; grandiloquent, **bombastic** 545.9; solemn 111.3, formal

23 strutting, swaggering; swashing, **swashbuckling,** swashbucklering; peacockish, peacocky; too big for one's britches

24 theatrical, theatric, stagy, dramatic, histrionic; spectacular

ADVS **25 ostentatiously, pretentiously, loftily;** with flourish of trumpet, with beat of drum, with flying colors

26 showily, flauntingly, flashily, with a flair, glitteringly; gaily, jauntily, **dashingly;** gallantly, bravely, daringly

27 gaudily, tawdrily; gorgeously, colorfully; **garishly, blatantly, flagrantly,** shamelessly, **brazenly,** brazenfacedly, luridly, sensationally, **spectacularly,** glaringly, flaringly, obtrusively

28 grandiosely, grandly, magnificently, splendidly, splendiferously, splendaciously <nf>, gloriously, superbly; nobly, proudly, majestically;

imposingly, impressively; **sumptuously, elegantly,** elaborately, luxuriously, **extravagantly;** palatially

29 **pompously, pontifically,** stuffily <nf>, **self-importantly;** stiltedly; **bombastically** 545.12

502 BOASTING

NOUNS **1** **boasting, bragging,** vaunting; **boastfulness, braggadocio, braggartism; boast, brag,** vaunt; side, bombast, bravado, vauntery, fanfaronade, blowing-off *or* blowing *or* tooting one's own horn <nf>, gasconade, gasconism, rodomontade, fanfaronade; bluster, swagger 503.1; vanity, conceit 140.4; jactation, jactitation; heroics

2 <nf terms> **big talk,** fine talk, fancy talk, tall talk, highfalutin *or* highfaluting, **hot air,** gas, bunk, bunkum, **bullshit;** tall story, fish story; bragging rights

3 **self-approbation,** self-praise, self-laudation, self-gratulation, self-applause, self-boosting, self-puffery, self-vaunting, self-advertising, self-advertisement, self-adulation, self-glorification, self-dramatizing, self-dramatization, self-promoting, self-promotion; **vainglory,** vaingloriousness

4 **crowing,** exultation, elation, triumph, jubilation; **gloating**

5 **braggart, boaster,** brag, braggadocio, exaggerator, hector, fanfaron, Gascon, gasconader, miles gloriosus; **blowhard** *and* blower *and* big mouth *and* bullshitter *and* bullshit artist *and* hot-air artist *and* gasbag *and* windbag *and* big bag of wind *and* windjammer *and* windy <nf>; blusterer 503.2, panjandrum; Texan, Fourth-of-July orator; Braggadocchio, Captain Bobadil, Thraso, Parolles; swashbuckler, rushbuckler

VERBS **6** **boast, brag,** make a boast of, vaunt, flourish, gasconade, vapor, puff, draw the longbow, advertise oneself, **blow one's own trumpet, toot one's own horn,** sing one's own praises, exaggerate one's own merits; bluster, swagger 503.3; speak for Buncombe

7 <nf terms> **blow,** blow off, mouth off, **blow hard, talk big,** sound off, blow off *and* toot *or* blow one's own horn, **bullshit,** shoot the shit, spread oneself, lay it on thick, brag oneself up

8 **flatter oneself,** conceit oneself, **congratulate oneself,** hug oneself, shake hands with oneself, form a mutual admiration society with one self, **pat oneself on the back,** take merit to oneself; think one's shit doesn't stink <nf>

9 **exult,** triumph, glory, delight, joy, jubilate; **crow** *or* crow over, crow like a rooster *or* cock; gloat, gloat over

ADJS **10** **boastful, boasting, braggart, bragging,** thrasonical, thrasonic, big-mouthed <nf>, vaunting, vaporing, gasconading, Gascon, fanfaronading, fanfaron; vain, pompous, conceited 140.11; **vainglorious**

11 **self-approving,** self-approbatory, self-praising, self-gratulating, self-boosting, self-puffing, self-adulating, self-adulatory, self-glorifying, self-glorying, self-glorious, self-lauding, self-laudatory, self-congratulatory, self-applauding, self-flattering, self-vaunting, self-advertising, self-dramatizing, self-promoting

12 **inflated, swollen, windy** *and* gassy <nf>, **bombastic,** high-swelling, **high-flown, highfalutin** *and* highfaluting <nf>, **pretentious,** extravagant, big, tall <nf>, hyped <nf>

13 **crowing,** exultant, exulting, elated, elate, jubilant, **triumphant, flushed,** cock-a-hoop, in high feather; **gloating**

ADVS **14** **boastfully,** boastingly, braggingly, vauntingly, vaingloriously; **self-approvingly,** self-praisingly, etc

15 **exultantly,** exultingly, elatedly, jubilantly, triumphantly, triumphally, in triumph; **gloatingly**

503 BLUSTER

NOUNS **1** **bluster,** blustering, hectoring, bullying, **swagger,** swashbucklery, side; **bravado,** rant, rodomontade, fanfaronade; sputter, splutter;

fuss, bustle, fluster, flurry; bluff, bluster *and* bluff; intimidation 127.6; **boastfulness** 502.1

2 **blusterer, swaggerer,** swasher, swashbuckler, fanfaron, bravo, **bully,** bullyboy, bucko, roisterer, cock of the walk, vaporer, blatherskite <nf>; ranter, raver, hectorer, hector, Herod; slanger <Brit>; bluff, bluffer; **braggart** 502.5

VERBS 3 **bluster,** hector; **swagger,** swashbuckle; bully; bounce, vapor, roister, rollick, gasconade, kick up a dust <nf>; sputter, splutter; rant, rage, rave, rave on, storm; slang <Brit>; bluff, bluster and bluff, put up a bluff <nf>; intimidate; shoot off one's mouth, sound off, bogart <nf>, **brag** 502.6

ADJS 4 **blustering,** blustery, blusterous, hectoring, **bullying, swaggering,** swashing, swashbuckling, boisterous, roisterous, roistering, rollicking; ranting, raging, raving, storming; tumultuous; noisy

504 COURTESY

NOUNS 1 **courtesy,** courteousness, common courtesy, **politeness, civility,** *politesse* <Fr>, amenity, agreeableness, urbanity, comity, affability; graciousness, **gracefulness;** complaisance; **thoughtfulness, considerateness** 143.3, **tactfulness,** tact, consideration, **solicitousness, solicitude; respect,** respectfulness, deference; civilization, quality of life

2 **gallantry,** gallantness, **chivalry,** chivalrousness, knightliness; courtliness, courtly behavior *or* politeness; *noblesse oblige* <Fr>

3 **mannerliness, manners, good manners,** excellent *or* exquisite manners, good *or* polite deportment, good *or* polite behavior, *bienséance* <Fr>; *savoir-faire* and *savoir-vivre* <Fr>; decency; correctness, correctitude, **etiquette** 580.3

4 **good breeding, breeding; refinement, finish, polish, culture, cultivation; gentility,** gentleness, genteelness, elegance; gentlemanliness, gentlemanlikeness, ladylikeness

5 **suavity, suaveness, smoothness, smugness,** blandness; **unctuousness,** oiliness, oleaginousness, smarm *or* smarminess <nf>; **glibness,** slickness <nf>, fulsomeness; sweet talk, fair words, soft words *or* tongue, sweet *or* honeyed words *or* tongue, incense; soft soap *and* butter <nf>

6 **courtesy, civility,** amenity, urbanity, attention, polite act, act of courtesy *or* politeness, graceful gesture, pleasantry; old-fashioned courtesy *or* civility, courtliness

7 **amenities, courtesies, civilities,** gentilities, graces, elegancies; dignities; formalities, ceremonies, rites, rituals, observances

8 **regards, compliments, respects,** *égards* and *devoirs* <Fr>; **best wishes,** one's best, good wishes, best regards, kind *or* kindest regards, love, best love; greetings 585.3; remembrances, kind remembrances; compliments of the season

9 **gallant, cavalier,** chevalier, **knight**

VERBS 10 **mind one's manners,** mind one's P's and Q's <nf>; keep a civil tongue in one's head; mend one's manners; observe etiquette, observe *or* follow protocol; be polite, be considerate

11 **extend courtesy, do the honors, pay one's respects, make one's compliments,** present oneself, pay attentions to, do service, wait on *or* upon

12 **give one's regards** *or* **compliments** *or* love, give one's best regards, give one's best, send one's regards *or* compliments *or* love; wish one joy, wish one luck, bid Godspeed

ADJS 13 **courteous, polite, civil, urbane, gracious,** graceful, agreeable, affable, fair; complaisant; obliging, accommodating; **thoughtful, considerate,** tactful, solicitous; respectful, deferential, attentive

14 **gallant, chivalrous,** chivalric, knightly; **courtly; formal,** ceremonious; old-fashioned, old-world

15 **mannerly, well-mannered,** good-mannered, **well-behaved,** well- *or* fair-spoken; **correct,** correct in

one's manners *or* behavior; housebroken <nf>

16 **well-bred,** highbred, **well-brought-up; cultivated, cultured, polished, refined, genteel,** gentle; gentlemanly, gentlemanlike, ladylike

17 **suave, smooth, smug,** bland, **glib, unctuous,** oily, oleaginous, smarmy <nf>, soapy *and* buttery <nf>, fulsome, ingratiating, disarming; suave-spoken, fine-spoken, fair-spoken, soft-spoken, smooth-spoken, smooth-tongued, oily-tongued, honey-tongued, honey-mouthed, sweet-talking

ADVS 18 **courteously, politely, civilly,** urbanely, mannerly; **gallantly, chivalrously,** courtly, knightly; **graciously,** gracefully, with a good grace; complaisantly, complacently; out of consideration *or* courtesy; obligingly, accommodatingly; respectfully, attentively, deferentially

505 DISCOURTESY

NOUNS 1 **discourtesy,** discourteousness; **impoliteness,** unpoliteness; **rudeness, incivility,** inurbanity, gall, **ungraciousness, ungallantness,** uncourtesy, uncourtliness, ungentlemanliness, **unmannerliness,** mannerlessness, bad *or* ill manners, **ill breeding,** conduct unbecoming a gentleman, caddishness; inconsiderateness, inconsideration, unsolicitousness, unsolicitude, tactlessness, **insensitivity; grossness, crassness,** gross *or* crass behavior, **boorishness, vulgarity, coarseness, crudeness,** offensiveness, loutishness, nastiness

2 **disrespect**, disrespectfulness 156.1; **insolence** 142; criminal contempt

3 **gruffness, brusqueness,** *brusquerie* <Fr>, **curtness,** shortness, sharpness, abruptness, bluntness, brashness; **harshness,** roughness, severity; truculence, aggressiveness; **surliness,** crustiness, bearishness, beastliness, churlishness, crustiness

ADJS 4 **discourteous,** uncourteous; **impolite,** unpolite, inurbane; **rude, uncivil, ungracious, ungallant,** uncourtly, inaffable, uncomplaisant, unaccommodating; disrespectful; **insolent;** impertinent

5 **unmannerly,** unmannered, mannerless, **ill-mannered, ill-behaved,** ill-conditioned, bad-mannered

6 **ill-bred, ungenteel,** ungentle, caddish; **ungentlemanly,** ungentlemanlike; **unladylike,** unfeminine; **vulgar, boorish, unrefined** 497.12, **inconsiderate, unsolicitous, tactless, insensitive; gross,** offensive, crass, **coarse, crude,** loutish, nasty

7 **gruff, brusque, curt,** short, sharp, snippy <nf>, abrupt, **blunt,** bluff, brash, cavalier; **harsh,** rough, severe; truculent, aggressive; **surly,** crusty, bearish, beastly, churlish; vituperative

ADVS 8 **discourteously, impolitely, rudely,** uncivilly, ungraciously, ungallantly, ungenteelly, caddishly; inconsiderately, unsolicitously, tactlessly, insensitively

9 **gruffly, brusquely, curtly,** shortly, sharply, snippily <nf>, abruptly, bluntly, bluffly, brashly, cavalierly; harshly, crustily, bearishly, churlishly, **boorishly,** nastily

506 RETALIATION

NOUNS 1 **retaliation, reciprocation,** exchange, interchange, give-and-take; **retort, reply,** return, comeback <nf>; counter, counterblow, counterstroke, counterblast, counterpunch, recoil, boomerang, backlash

2 **reprisal, requital, retribution; recompense, compensation** 338, **reward,** comeuppance <nf>, desert, deserts, **just deserts,** what is merited, what is due *or* condign, what's coming to one *and* a dose of one's own medicine <nf>; quittance, return of evil for evil; **revenge** 507; **punishment** 604

3 **tit for tat, measure for measure,** like for like, quid pro quo, something in return, blow for blow, a Roland for an Oliver, a game two can play, **an eye for an eye,** a tooth for a tooth, law of retaliation *or* equivalent retaliation, *lex talionis* <L>, talion; game at which two can play

VERBS **4** **retaliate, retort,** counter, **strike back,** hit back at <nf>, give in return; **reciprocate,** give in exchange, give *and* take; **get** *or* **come back at** <nf>, turn the tables upon; fight fire with fire, return the compliment

5 **requite,** quit, make requital *or* reprisal *or* retribution, get satisfaction, recompense, compensate, make restitution, indemnify, reward, redress, make amends, **repay,** pay, **pay back,** pay off; **give one his comeuppance** <nf>, give one his desserts *or* just desserts, serve one right, give one what is coming to him <nf>

6 **give in kind,** cap, match, give as good as one gets *or* as was sent; repay in kind, **pay one in one's own coin** *or* **currency, give one a dose of one's own medicine** <nf>; return the like, return the compliment; return like for like, **return evil for evil;** return blow for blow, **give one tit for tat,** give a quid pro quo, give as good as one gets, give measure for measure, give *or* get an eye for an eye *and* a tooth for a tooth, follow *or* observe the *lex talionis*

7 **get even with** <nf>, even the score, **settle** *or* **settle up with, settle** *or* **square accounts** *and* settle the score *and* fix <nf>, pay off old scores, pay back in full measure, be *or* make quits; fix one's wagon <nf>, **take revenge** 507.4; **punish** 604.10

ADJS **8** **retaliatory,** retaliative; **retributive,** retributory; reparative, compensatory, restitutive, recompensing, recompensive, reciprocal; punitive; recriminatory, like for like; revengeful, vindictive

ADVS **9** **in retaliation, in exchange,** in reciprocation; **in return,** in reply; **in requital, in reprisal,** in retribution, in reparation, in amends; **in revenge,** *en revanche* <Fr>

PHRS **10** what goes around comes around, one's chickens come home to roost; the shoe is on the other foot

507 REVENGE

NOUNS **1** **revenge, vengeance, avengement,** sweet revenge, getting even, evening of the score; **wrath;** revanche, revanchism; **retaliation, reprisal** 506.2; vendetta, feud, blood feud; the wrath of God

2 **revengefulness, vengefulness, vindictiveness,** rancor, grudgefulness, irreconcilableness, unappeasableness, implacableness, implacability

3 **avenger, vindicator;** revanchist; Nemesis, the Furies, the Erinyes, the Eumenides

VERBS **4** **revenge, avenge, take** *or* **exact revenge,** have one's revenge, wreak one's vengeance; **retaliate, even the score, get even with** 506.7; launch a vendetta

5 **harbor revenge,** breathe vengeance; have accounts to settle, have a crow to pick *or* pluck *or* pull with; nurse one's revenge, brood over, dwell on *or* upon, keep the wound open, wave the bloody shirt

6 **reap** *or* **suffer** *or* **incur vengeance** *or* revenge; sow the wind and reap the whirlwind; live by the sword and die by the sword

ADJS **7** **revengeful, vengeful,** avenging; **vindictive,** vindicatory; revanchist; **punitive,** punitory; **wrathful,** rancorous, grudgeful, irreconcilable, unappeasable, implacable, unwilling to forgive and forget, unwilling to let bygones be bygones; **retaliatory** 506.8

508 RIDICULE

NOUNS **1** **ridicule, derision, mockery, raillery,** rallying, chaffing; panning *and* razzing *and* roasting *and* ragging <nf>, **scoffing, jeering, sneering,** snickering, sniggering, smirking, grinning, leering, fleering, snorting, levity, flippancy, smartness, smart-aleckiness *and* joshing <nf>, fooling, japery, twitting, taunting, booing, hooting, catcalling, hissing; **banter** 490

2 **gibe, scoff, jeer,** fleer, flout, mock, barracking <Brit>, **taunt, twit,** quip, jest, jape, put-on *and* leg-pull <nf>, foolery; **insult** 156.2; scurrility, caustic remark; **cut,** cutting remark, verbal thrust; gibing retort, rude reproach, short answer, back answer, comeback <nf>, parting shot, Parthian shot

3 **boo,** booing, **hoot, catcall; Bronx cheer** *and* **raspberry** *and* razz <nf>; **hiss, hissing,** the bird <nf>

4 scornful laugh *or* smile, snicker, snigger, **smirk,** sardonic grin, leer, fleer, **sneer,** snort

5 **sarcasm, irony, cynicism, satire,** satiric wit *or* humor, invective, innuendo; causticity 144.8

6 **burlesque, lampoon,** squib, **parody, satire, farce,** mockery, imitation, wicked imitation *or* pastiche, takeoff <nf>, black humor, **travesty, caricature**

7 **laughingstock,** jestingstock, gazingstock, derision, mockery, **figure of fun,** byword, byword of reproach, jest, joke, **butt,** target, stock, goat <nf>, toy, game, **fair game,** victim, dupe, fool, everybody's fool, monkey, mug <Brit nf>

VERBS 8 **ridicule, deride,** ride <nf>, make a laughingstock *or* a mockery of; roast <nf>, **insult** 156.5; **make fun** *or* **game of, poke fun at,** make merry with, put one on *and* pull one's leg <nf>; **laugh at,** laugh in one's face, grin at, smile at, snicker *or* snigger at; **laugh to scorn,** hold in derision, laugh out of court, hoot down; point at, point the finger of scorn; pillory

9 **scoff, jeer,** gibe, barrack <Brit>, **mock, revile, rail at, rally,** chaff, **twit, taunt,** jape, flout, scout, have a fling at, cast in one's teeth; cut at; jab, jab at, dig at, take a dig at; pooh, **pooh-pooh;** sneer, **sneer at,** fleer, curl one's lip

10 **boo, hiss, hoot,** catcall, give the raspberry *or* Bronx cheer <nf>, razz, give the bird <nf>, whistle at

11 **burlesque, lampoon, satirize, parody, caricature,** travesty, hit *or* take off on

ADJS 12 **ridiculing, derisive,** derisory; **mocking,** railing, rallying, chaffing; panning *and* razzing *and* roasting *and* ragging <nf>, **scoffing,** jeering, sneering, snickering, sniggering, smirky, smirking, grinning, leering, fleering, snorting, flippant, smart, smart-alecky *and* smart-ass *and* wise-ass <nf>; joshing *and* jiving <nf>, fooling, japing, twitting, taunting, booing, hooting, catcalling, hissing, bantering, kidding, teasing, quizzical

13 **satiric, satirical; sarcastic, ironic, ironical, sardonic, cynical,** Rabelaisian, dry; caustic

14 **burlesque, farcical, broad,** slapstick; parodic, caricatural, macaronic, doggerel

ADVS 15 **derisively, mockingly, scoffingly,** jeeringly, sneeringly

509 APPROVAL

NOUNS 1 **approval, approbation; sanction,** acceptance, countenance, **favor; admiration, esteem, respect** 155; endorsement, support, backing, vote, favorable vote, yea vote, yea, voice, adherence, blessing, seal of approval, nod *or* nod of approval, wink, stamp of approval, **OK** 332.4, rubber stamp, green light, go-ahead, thumbs up

2 **applause,** plaudit, éclat, **acclaim, acclamation; popularity;** clap, handclap, **clapping,** handclapping, clapping of hands; **cheer** 116.2; burst of applause, peal *or* thunder of applause; **round of applause, hand, big hand; ovation,** standing ovation; encore

3 **commendation,** good word, acknowledgment, recognition, appreciation; boost *and* buildup <nf>; **puff,** promotion; citation, accolade, kudos; good review; **blurb** *and* **plug** *and* promo *and* hype <nf>; honorable mention

4 **recommendation,** recommend <Brit nf>, letter of recommendation; **advocacy,** advocating, advocation, patronage; **reference, credential,** letter of reference, voucher, **testimonial;** character reference, character, certificate of character, good character; letter of introduction

5 **praise,** bepraisement; **laudation,** laud; **glorification,** glory, exaltation, extolment, magnification, **honor; eulogy,** *éloge and hommage* <Fr>, eulogium; **encomium,** accolade, kudos, panegyric; paean; **tribute,**

homage, meed of praise; congratulation 149.1; flattery 511; overpraise, excessive praise, idolizing, idolatry, deification, apotheosis, adulation, lionizing, hero worship

6 **compliment,** polite commendation, complimentary *or* flattering remark, flattery, pat on the back, stroke <nf>; **bouquet** *and* posy <nf>, trade-last <old nf>

7 **praiseworthiness, laudability,** laudableness, commendableness, estimableness, meritoriousness, exemplariness, admirability

8 commender, eulogist, eulogizer; **praiser,** lauder, laudator, extoller, encomiast, panegyrist, **booster** <nf>, puffer, promoter, champion; plugger *and* tout *and* touter <nf>; **applauder,** *claqueur* <Fr>; claque; rooter *and* fan *and* buff <nf>, adherent; admirer; appreciator; **flatterer** 138.3, 511.4, fan club

VERBS 9 **approve, approve of,** think well of, take kindly to; **sanction, accept; admire, esteem, respect** 155.4; endorse, bless, sign off on <nf>, OK 332.12; countenance, keep in **countenance;** hold with, uphold; **favor,** be in favor of, view with favor, take kindly to

10 **applaud, acclaim, hail; clap,** clap one's hands, give a hand *or* big hand, have *or* hear a hand *or* big hand for, hear it for <nf>; **cheer** 116.6; root for <nf>, cheer on; encore; cheer *or* applaud to the very echo; huzzah; raise the roof <nf>

11 **commend, speak well** *or* **highly of,** speak in high terms of, speak warmly of, have *or* say a good word for; boost *and* give a boost to <nf>, puff, promote, cry up; plug *and* tout *and* hype; pour *or* spread *or* lay it on thick <nf>; **recommend, advocate,** put in a word *or* good word for, support, back, lend one's name *or* support *or* backing to, make a pitch for <nf>; condone, bless

12 **praise,** bepraise, talk one up <nf>; **laud,** belaud; **eulogize,** panegyrize, pay tribute, salute, hand it to one <nf>; **extol, glorify,** magnify, exalt, bless; cry up, blow up, puff, puff up; boast of, brag about <nf>, make much of; celebrate, emblazon, sound *or* resound the praises of, ring one's praises, sing the praises of, trumpet, hype <nf>; praise to the skies, *porter aux nues* <Fr>; flatter 511.5; overpraise, praise to excess, idolize, deify, apotheosize, adulate, lionize, hero-worship; put on a pedestal

13 **espouse,** join *or* associate oneself with, take up, take for one's own; **campaign for, crusade for,** put on a drive for, take up the cudgels for, push for <nf>; carry the banner of, march under the banner of; beat the drum for, thump the tub for; lavish oneself on, fight the good fight for; devote *or* dedicate oneself to, spend *or* give *or* sacrifice oneself for

14 **compliment, pay a compliment,** make one a compliment, give a bouquet *or* posy <nf>, say something nice about; hand it to *and* have to hand it to <nf>, pat on the back, take off one's hat to, doff one's cap to, congratulate 149.2

15 **meet with approval,** find favor with, **pass muster,** recommend itself, do credit to; redound to the honor of; ring with the praises of

ADJS 16 **approbatory, approbative, commendatory, complimentary, laudatory,** acclamatory, felicitous, eulogistic, panegyric, panegyrical, encomiastic, **appreciative, appreciatory; admiring, regardful, respectful** 155.8; flattering 511.8

17 **approving, favorable,** favoring, in favor of, **pro,** well-disposed, well-inclined, supporting, backing, **advocating;** promoting, promotional; touting *and* puffing *and* hyping <nf>; recommending

18 **uncritical,** uncriticizing, **uncensorious,** unreproachful; overpraising, overappreciative, unmeasured *or* excessive in one's praise, idolatrous, adulatory, lionizing, hero-worshiping, fulsome; knee-jerk <nf>

19 **approved,** favored, backed, advocated, supported; favorite; **accepted,** received, admitted; **recommended,** bearing the seal of approval, highly touted <nf>, **admired** 155.11, **ap-**

plauded, well-thought-of, in good odor, **acclaimed,** cried up; **popular;** given a blessing

20 **praiseworthy**, worthy, **commendable,** estimable, **laudable,** admirable, meritorious, creditable; exemplary, model, unexceptionable; deserving, well-deserving; beyond all praise, *sans peur et sans reproche* <Fr>; **good** 999.12,13

21 **hail!,** all hail!, *ave!* <L>, *vive!* <Fr>, *viva!* or *evviva!* <Ital>, live live!, long life to!, glory be to!, honor be to!

510 DISAPPROVAL

NOUNS **1** **disapproval, disapprobation,** disfavor, disesteem, disrespect 156; dim view, poor *or* low opinion, low estimation, adverse judgment; **displeasure,** distaste, **dissatisfaction,** discontent, discontentment, discontentedness, disgruntlement, indignation, **unhappiness;** doghouse <nf>; disillusion, disillusionment, disenchantment, disappointment; disagreement, **opposition** 451, opposure; rejection, thumbs-down, exclusion, ostracism, blackballing, blackball, ban; **complaint, protest,** objection, **dissent** 333

2 **deprecation,** discommendation, dispraise, denigration, disvaluation; **ridicule** 508; depreciation, disparagement 512; **contempt** 157

3 **censure, reprehension,** stricture, reprobation, **blame, denunciation,** denouncement, decrying, decrial, bashing *and* trashing <nf>, impeachment, arraignment, indictment, **condemnation,** damnation, fulmination, anathema; castigation, flaying, skinning alive <nf>, fustigation, excoriation; pillorying

4 **criticism,** adverse criticism, harsh *or* hostile criticism, flak <nf>, bad notices, bad press, panning, brickbat, animadversion, imputation, reflection, **aspersion,** stricture, obloquy; **knock** *and* **swipe** *and* **slam** *and* **rap** *and* hit <nf>, roasting <nf>, home thrust; minor *or* petty criticism, niggle, cavil, quibble, exception, nit <nf>; **censoriousness,** reproachfulness, priggishness; **faultfinding,** taking exception, carping, caviling, pettifogging, quibbling, captiousness, niggling, nitpicking, pestering, nagging; hypercriticism, hypercriticalness, overcriticalness, hairsplitting, trichoschistism

5 **reproof,** reproval, reprobation, a flea in one's ear, **rebuke, reprimand, reproach,** reprehension, **scolding, chiding,** rating, **upbraiding,** objurgation; **admonishment, admonition; correction,** castigation, chastisement, spanking, rap on the knuckles; lecture, lesson, sermon; **disrecommendation**, low rating, adverse report, wolf ticket

6 <nf terms> piece *or* bit of one's mind, **talking-to,** speaking-to, roasting, raking-down, **raking-over,** raking over the coals, dressing, dressing-down, set-down; **bawling-out,** cussing-out, **calling-down,** jacking-up, going-over, chewing-out, chewing, reaming-out, reaming, ass-chewing, ass-reaming, what-for, ticking-off

7 **berating,** rating, tongue-lashing; **revilement, vilification,** blackening, **execration, abuse, vituperation,** invective, contumely, hard *or* cutting *or* bitter words; **tirade, diatribe,** jeremiad, screed, philippic; **attack, assault,** onslaught, assailing; **abusiveness; acrimony**

8 **reproving look,** dirty *or* nasty look <nf>, black look, frown, scowl, glare; hiss, boo; Bronx cheer *or* raspberry <nf>

9 **faultfinder,** disapprover, *frondeur* <Fr>, momus, basher *and* tracher *and* boo-bird <nf>; **critic** 946.7, criticizer, **nitpicker** <nf>, smellfungus, belittler, censor, censurer, castigator, carper, caviler, quibbler, pettifogger, detractor, cynic; **scold,** common scold; kvetch, **complainer** 108.3

VERBS **10** **disapprove, disapprove of,** not approve, raise an objection, go *or* side against, go contra; **disfavor, view with disfavor, raise one's eyebrows, frown at** *or* **on,** look black upon, look askance at, make a wry face at, grimace at, **turn up one's nose at,** shrug one's shoulders at; **take a dim view of** <nf>, not think much of, think ill of, think little of, have no respect for, have a low opinion of, not take kindly to, not hold with, hold no brief for *and* not sign off on <nf>; not hear of, not go for *and* not get all choked up over *and* be turned off by <nf>; not want *or* have any part of, wash one's hands of, dissociate oneself from; **object to,** take exception to; **oppose** 451.3, set oneself against, set one's face *or* heart against; **reject,** categorically reject, disallow, not hear of; **turn thumbs down on** *and* thumb down <nf>, vote down, veto, frown down, exclude, ostracize, blackball, ban; say no to, shake one's head at; **dissent from, protest, object** 333.4,5; turn over in one's grave

11 **discountenance,** not countenance, **not tolerate,** not brook, not condone, not suffer, not abide, not endure, not bear with, not put up with, **not stand for** <nf>

12 **deprecate,** discommend, dispraise, disvalue, not be able to say much for, denigrate, **fault,** faultfind, find fault with, put down <nf>, pick at *or* on, pick holes in, pick to pieces; **ridicule** 508.8; **depreciate, disparage** 512.8; **hold in contempt,** disdain, **despise** 157.3

13 **censure,** reprehend; **blame,** lay *or* cast blame upon; **bash** *and* trash *and* rubbish <nf>; **reproach,** impugn; **condemn,** damn, take out after; damn with faint praise; fulminate against, anathematize, anathemize, put on the Index; **denounce,** denunciate, **accuse** 599.7,9, **decry,** cry down, impeach, arraign, indict, call to account, exclaim *or* declaim *or* inveigh against, peg away at, cry out against, cry out on *or* upon, cry shame upon, raise one's voice against, raise a hue *and* cry against, shake up ; reprobate, hold up to reprobation; animadvert on *or* upon, reflect upon, cast reflection upon, cast a reproach *or* slur upon, complain against; throw a stone at, cast *or* throw the first stone

14 **criticize; pan** *and* **knock** *and* **slam** *and* hit *and* rap *and* take a rap *or* swipe at <nf>, snipe at, strike out at, tie into *and* tee off on *and* rip into *and* open up on *and* plow into <nf>; belittle

15 **find fault,** take exception, fault-find, pick holes, cut up, **pick** *or* **pull** *or* tear apart, pick *or* pull *or* **tear to pieces; tear down, carp, cavil,** quibble, **nitpick,** pick nits, pettifog, catch at straws

16 **nag,** niggle, **carp at, fuss at, fret at,** yap *or* **pick at** <nf>, peck at, nibble at, **pester, henpeck, pick on** <nf>, bug *and* hassle <nf>

17 **reprove, rebuke, reprimand,** reprehend, put a flea in one's ear, **scold, chide,** rate, **admonish, upbraid,** objurgate, have words with, take a hard line with; **lecture,** read a lesson *or* lecture to; **correct,** rap on the knuckles, **chastise,** spank, turn over one's knees; **take to task,** call to account, bring to book, call on the carpet, read the riot act, give one a tongue-lashing, tonguelash; take down, set down, set straight, straighten out

18 <nf terms> **call down** *or* **dress down, speak** *or* **talk to, tell off,** tell a thing *or* two, pin one's ears back, **give a piece** *or* **bit of one's mind, rake** *or* **haul over the coals,** rake up one side *and* down the other, give it to, let one have it, let one have it with both barrels, trim, come down on *or* down hard on, jump on *or* all over *or* down one's throat; give one a hard time *or* what for; **bawl out,** give a bawling out, chew, **chew out,** chew ass, ream, ream out, ream ass, cuss out, jack up, sit on *or* upon, lambaste, give a going-over, tell where to get off; give the deuce *or* devil, give hell, give hail Columbia

19 **berate,** rate, betongue, jaw <nf>, clapper-claw <nf>, **tongue-lash, rail at,** rag, thunder *or* fulminate against, rave against, yell at, bark *or* yelp at; **revile, vilify,** blacken, **execrate, abuse,** vituperate, load with reproaches

20 <criticize *or* reprove severely> **attack, assail; castigate, flay,** skin

alive <nf>, lash, slash, excoriate, fustigate, scarify, scathe, **roast** <nf>, scorch, blister, trounce; lay into <nf>

ADJS **21 disapproving, disapprobatory,** unapproving, turned-off, **displeased, dissatisfied,** less than pleased, discontented, disgruntled, indignant, **unhappy;** disillusioned, disenchanted, disappointed; **unfavorable,** low, poor, **opposed** 451.8, **opposing, con,** against, agin <nf>, dead set against, death on, down on, **dissenting** 333.6; **uncomplimentary;** unappreciative

22 condemnatory, censorious, censorial, damnatory, **denunciatory, reproachful,** blameful, reprobative, objurgatory, po-faced <Brit>, priggish, judgmental; deprecative, deprecatory; **derisive, ridiculing, scoffing** 508.12; **depreciative, disparaging** 512.13; **contemptuous** 157.8; invective, inveighing; reviling, vilifying, blackening, execrating, execrative, execratory, abusive, vituperative

23 critical, faultfinding, carping, picky *and* nitpicky <nf>, caviling, quibbling, pettifogging, captious, cynical; nagging, niggling; hypercritical, ultracritical, overcritical, hairsplitting, trichoschistic; abusive

24 unpraiseworthy, illaudable; uncommendable, discommendable, not good enough; objectionable, exceptionable, unacceptable, not to be thought of, beyond the pale

25 blameworthy, blamable, to blame, at fault, much at fault; **reprehensible,** censurable, reproachable, reprovable, open to criticism *or* reproach; **culpable,** chargeable, impeachable, accusable, indictable, arraignable, imputable

ADVS **26 disapprovingly, askance,** askant, **unfavorably;** censoriously, critically, reproachfully, rebukingly; captiously

511 FLATTERY

NOUNS **1 flattery, adulation; praise** 509.5; **blandishment,** palaver, **cajolery,** cajolement, wheedling, inveiglement; **blarney** *and* bunkum *and* **soft soap** *and* soap *or* butter salve <nf>, oil, grease, eyewash <nf>; strokes *and* stroking *and* ego massage <nf>, sweet talk, fair *or* sweet *or* honeyed words, soft *or* honeyed phrases, incense, pretty lies, sweet nothings; trade-last <old nf>, **compliment** 509.6; ass-kissing <nf>, ingratiation, **fawning, sycophancy** 138.2

2 unction; unctuousness, oiliness, sliminess, slobber, gush, smarm *and* smarminess <nf>; flattering tongue; insincerity 354.5

3 overpraise, overprizing, excessive praise, overcommendation, overlaudation, overestimation; idolatry 509.5

4 flatterer, *flatteur* <Fr>, adulator, courtier; **cajoler, wheedler; backslapper,** back-scratcher, yes-man, bootlicker; blarneyer *and* soft-soaper <nf>; ass-kisser <nf>, brown-noser, **sycophant** 138.3

VERBS **5 flatter,** adulate, conceit; **cajole,** wheedle, **blandish,** palaver; slaver *or* slobber over, beslobber, beslubber; oil the tongue, lay the flattering unction to one's soul, make fair weather; **praise, compliment** 509.14, praise to the skies; scratch one's back, kiss ass <nf>, fawn upon 138.9

6 <nf terms> **soft-soap,** butter, honey, **butter up,** soften up; stroke <nf>, massage the ego <nf>; **blarney,** jolly, pull one's leg; lay it on <nf>, pour *or* spread *or* lay it on thick *or* with a trowel <nf>, overdo it, soap, oil; string along, kid along; play up to, get around; suck up to

7 overpraise, overprize, overcommend, overlaud; overesteem, overestimate, overdo it, protest too much; idolize 509.12, put on a pedestal; puff

ADJS **8 flattering, adulatory; complimentary** 509.16; **blandishing, cajoling, wheedling,** blarneying *and* soft-soaping <nf>; fair-spoken, fine-spoken, smooth-spoken, smooth-tongued, **mealymouthed,** honey-mouthed, honey-tongued, honeyed, oily-tongued; fulsome, slimy, slobbery, gushing, protesting too much, smarmy <nf>, insinuating, oily, buttery <nf>, soapy <nf>, soft-soaping <nf>, **unctuous,** smooth, bland; insincere, hypocritical, tongue-in-cheek; courtly, courtierly; **fawning, sycophantic, obsequious**

512 DISPARAGEMENT

NOUNS **1 disparagement, faultfinding, depreciation, detraction,** deprecation, derogation, bad-mouthing *and* running down *and* knocking *and* putting down <nf>, **belittling;** sour grapes; slighting, minimizing, faint praise, lukewarm support, discrediting, decrying, decrial; **disapproval** 510; **contempt** 157; indignity, disgrace, comedown <nf>

2 defamation, malicious defamation, defamation of character, smear campaign, injury of *or* to one's reputation; **vilification,** revilement, defilement, blackening, denigration; smear, character assassination, *ad hominem* <L> *or* personal attack, name-calling, smear word; **muckraking, mudslinging**

3 slander, scandal, libel, traducement; calumny, calumniation; backbiting, cattiness *and* bitchiness <nf>

4 aspersion, slur, **remark, reflection,** imputation, **insinuation,** suggestion, sly suggestion, innuendo, whispering campaign; disparaging *or* uncomplimentary remark; poison-pen letter, hatchet job

5 lampoon, send-up <nf>, take-off, pasquinade, ridicule, pasquin, pasquil, squib, lampoonery, **satire,** malicious parody, **burlesque** 508.6; caricature

6 disparager, depreciator, decrier, detractor, basher *and* trasher *and* boo-bird <nf>, belittler, debunker, deflater, slighter, derogator, **knocker** <nf>, hatchet man; **slanderer,** libeler, defamer, backbiter; calumniator, traducer; **muckraker, mudslinger,** social critic; **cynic,** railer, Thersites

7 lampooner, lampoonist, **satirist,** pasquinader; poison-pen writer

VERBS **8 disparage, depreciate, belittle,** slight, minimize, make little of, degrade, debase, **run** *or* **knock down** <nf>, **put down** <nf>, sell short; **discredit,** bring into discredit, reflect discredit upon, disgrace; detract from, derogate from, cut down to size <nf>; **decry,** cry down; speak ill of; speak slightingly of, not speak well of; disapprove of 510.10; hold in contempt 157.3; submit to indignity *or* disgrace, bring down, bring low

9 defame, malign, bad-mouth *and* poor-mouth <nf>; **asperse, cast aspersions on,** cast reflections on, injure one's reputation, damage one's good name, give one a black eye <nf>; **slur,** cast a slur on, do a number *or* a job on <nf>, tear down

10 vilify, revile, defile, sully, soil, smear, smirch, besmirch, bespatter, tarnish, **blacken,** denigrate, blacken one's good name, give a black eye <nf>; **call names,** give a bad name, give a dog a bad name, stigmatize 661.9; **muckrake, throw mud at,** mudsling, heap dirt upon, drag through the mud *or* the gutter; engage in personalities

11 slander, libel; calumniate, traduce; stab in the back, backbite, speak ill of behind one's back

12 lampoon, satirize, pasquinade; parody, send up <nf>, take off; dip the pen in gall, **burlesque** 508.11

ADJS **13 disparaging, derogatory,** derogative, **depreciatory,** depreciative, deprecatory, slighting, belittling, minimizing, detractory, pejorative, back-biting, catty *and* bitchy <nf>, contumelious, contemptuous, derisive, derisory, ridiculing 508.12; **snide,** insinuating; censorious; **defamatory,** vilifying, **slanderous, scandalous, libelous;** calumnious, calumniatory; **abusive,** scurrilous, scurrile

513 CURSE

NOUNS **1 curse, malediction,** malison, damnation, denunciation, commination, imprecation, execration; blasphemy; anathema, fulmination, thundering, excommunication; ban, proscription; hex, evil eye, jinx, whammy *or* double whammy <nf>; ill wishes

2 **vilification, abuse,** revilement, **vituperation, invective,** opprobrium, obloquy, contumely, calumny, scurrility, blackguardism; **disparagement** 512; slanging match <nf>

3 **cursing,** cussing <nf>, **swearing, profanity,** profane swearing, foul *or* profane *or* obscene *or* blue *or* bad *or* strong *or* unparliamentary *or* indelicate language, vulgar language, vile language, colorful language, unrepeatable expressions, dysphemism, billingsgate, ribaldry, evil speaking, **dirty language** *or* **talk** <nf>, **obscenity,** scatology, coprology, **filthy language, filth;** foul mouth, dirty mouth <nf>

4 **oath,** profane oath, curse; cuss *or* cuss word *and* dirty word *and* four-letter word *and* **swearword** <nf>, profanity, bad word, naughty word, no-no <nf>, foul invective, **expletive, epithet,** dirty name <nf>, dysphemism, obscenity, vulgarity; F-word

VERBS 5 **curse,** accurse, **damn,** darn, **confound,** blast, anathematize, fulminate *or* thunder against, execrate, imprecate, proscribe; excommunicate; call down evil upon, call down curses on the head of; put a curse on; curse up hill *and* down dale; curse with bell, book, *and* candle; blaspheme; hex, give the evil eye, put a whammy on <nf>

6 **curse, swear, cuss** <nf>, curse *and* swear, execrate, rap out *or* rip out an oath, take the Lord's name in vain; swear like a trooper, cuss like a sailor, make the air blue, swear till one is blue in the face; **talk dirty** <nf>, scatologize, coprologize, dysphemize, use strong language; blaspheme, profane

7 **vilify, abuse, revile,** vituperate, blackguard, call names, epithet, epithetize; **swear at,** damn, cuss out <nf>

ADJS 8 **cursing, maledictory,** imprecatory, **damnatory,** denunciatory, epithetic, epithetical; **abusive,** vituperative, contumelious; calumnious, calumniatory; execratory, comminatory, fulminatory, excommunicative, excommunicatory; **scurrilous,** scurrile ; blasphemous, **profane, foul, foulmouthed, vile,** thersitical, **dirty** <nf>, **obscene,** dysphemistic, scatologic, scatological, coprological, toilet, sewer, cloacal; ribald, Rabelaisian, raw, risqué

9 **cursed,** accursed, bloody <Brit nf>, **damned, damn, damnable,** goddamned, goddamn, **execrable**

10 <euphemisms> **darned,** danged, **confounded,** deuced, blessed, **blasted,** dashed, blamed, goshdarn, doggone *or* doggoned, goldarned, goldanged, dadburned; blankety blank; ruddy <Brit>

11 <euphemistic oaths> darn!, dern!, dang!, dash!, drat!, blast!, doggone!, goldarn!, goldang!, golding!, goshdarn!, cripes!, crikey! <Brit>, golly!, gosh!, heck!, bugger it! <Brit>, goodness!, goodness gracious!, jeepers!, gee whillikers! gee whiz!

514 THREAT

NOUNS 1 **threat, menace,** threateningness, threatfulness, promise of harm, knife poised at one's throat, arrow aimed at one's heart, sword of Damocles; imminent threat, powder keg, timebomb, imminence 840; **foreboding; warning** 399; saber-rattling, muscle-flexing, woofing <nf>, bulldozing, scare tactics, **intimidation** 127.6, arm-twisting <nf>; denunciation, commination; veiled *or* implied threat, idle *or* hollow *or* empty threat; bomb threat

VERBS 2 **threaten, menace,** bludgeon, bulldoze, put the heat *or* screws *or* squeeze on <nf>, lean on <nf>; hold a pistol to one's head, terrorize, **intimidate,** twist one's arm *and* arm-twist <nf>; utter threats against, shake *or* double *or* clench one's fist at; hold over one's head; denounce, comminate; **lower,** spell *or* mean trouble, look threatening, loom, loom up; **be imminent**

840.2; **forebode** 133.10; **warn** 399.5

ADJS **3 threatening, menacing,** threatful, minatory, minacious; **lowering; imminent** 840.3; **ominous**, foreboding 133.16; denunciatory, comminatory, abusive; fear-inspiring, **intimidating,** bludgeoning, muscle-flexing, saber-rattling, bulldozing, browbeating, bullying, hectoring, blustering, terrorizing, terroristic

ADVS **4** under duress *or* threat, under the gun, at gunpoint *or* knifepoint

515 FASTING

NOUNS **1 fasting,** abstinence from food; abstemiousness, starvation; punishment of Tantalus; religious fasting; hunger strike; anorexia nervosa, bulimia nervosa

2 fast, lack of food; spare *or* meager diet, Lenten diet, Lenten fare; prison fare; short commons *or* rations, military rations, K rations; starvation diet, water diet, crash diet, bread and water, bare subsistence, bare cupboard; xerophagy, xerophagia; Barmecide *or* Barmecidal feast

3 fast day, *jour maigre* <Fr>; Lent, Good Friday, Quadragesima; Yom Kippur, Tishah B'Av *or* Ninth of Av; Ramadan; meatless day, fish day, day of abstinence

VERBS **4 fast,** not eat, go hungry, eat nothing, eat like a bird, dine with Duke Humphrey; eat sparingly, eat less, count calories

ADJS **5 fasting,** uneating, unfed; abstinent, abstemious; keeping Lent, **Lenten,** quadragesimal; underfed

516 SOBRIETY

NOUNS **1 sobriety, soberness;** unintoxicatedness, uninebriatedness, undrunkenness; abstinence, abstemiousness; temperance 668; clear head; prohibition, temperance society; nondrinker, teetotaler

VERBS **2 sober up,** sober off; sleep it off; bring one down, take off a high <nf>; dry out, clear one's head, detoxify; give up alcohol, go on the wagon

ADJS **3 sober,** in one's sober senses, in one's right mind, in possession of one's faculties; clearheaded; **unintoxicated, uninebriated,** uninebriate, uninebrious, not drunk, undrunk, undrunken, untipsy, unfuddled; stone-cold sober <nf>, **sober as a judge;** able to walk the chalk, able to walk the chalk mark *or* line <nf>; nondrinking, off the bottle, dry, straight, on the wagon <nf>, temperate 668.9, abstinent

4 unintoxicating, nonintoxicating, uninebriating; **nonalcoholic, soft**

517 SIGNS, INDICATORS

NOUNS **1 sign,** telltale sign, sure sign, tip-off <nf>, **index,** indicant, **indicator,** signal , measure; tip of the iceberg; **symptom;** note, keynote, **mark, earmark,** hallmark, **badge,** device, banner, stamp, signature, sigil, seal, trait, **characteristic,** character, peculiarity, idiosyncrasy, **property,** differentia; image, picture, **representation,** representative; **insignia** 647; notation; reference sign

2 symbol, emblem, icon, token, cipher , type; **allegory; symbolism, symbology,** iconology, iconography, charactery; conventional symbol; symbolic system; **symbolization;** semiotics, semiology; **ideogram,** logogram, pictogram; **logo** <nf>, logotype; **totem,** totem pole; love knot; symbol list

3 indication, signification, identification, differentiation, denotation, **designation,** denomination; characterization, highlighting; **specification,** naming, pointing, pointing out *or* to, fingering <nf>, picking out, selection; symptomaticness, indicativeness; **meaning** 518; hint, suggestion 551.4; **expression, manifestation** 348; show, showing, disclosure 351

4 pointer, index, **lead; direction, guide;** fist, index finger *or* mark, finger, arm; **arrow;** hand, hour hand, minute hand, gauge, **needle,** compass needle, lubber line; **signpost,** guidepost, finger post, direction post; milepost; blaze; guideboard, signboard 352.7

5 **mark, marking;** watermark; **scratch,** scratching, engraving, graving, **score,** scotch, cut, hack, gash, blaze; bar code; nick, notch 289; **scar,** cicatrix, scarification, cicatrization; **brand, earmark; stigma; stain, discoloration** 1004.2; blemish, macula, **spot,** blotch, splotch, flick, patch, splash; mottle, dapple; **dot,** point; polka dot; tittle, jot; **speck, speckle,** fleck; tick, **freckle,** lentigo, mole; **birthmark,** strawberry mark, port-wine stain, vascular nevus, nevus, hemangioma; beauty mark *or* spot; caste mark; **check,** checkmark; prick, puncture; tattoo, tattoo mark

6 **line,** score, **stroke,** slash, virgule, diagonal, **dash, stripe, strip, streak, striation,** striping, streaking, bar, band; squiggle; hairline; dotted line; lineation, delineation; sublineation, **underline,** underlining, underscore, underscoring; hatching, cross-hatching, hachure

7 **print, imprint, impress, impression;** dint, dent, indent, indentation, indention, concavity; sitzmark; **stamp,** seal, sigil, signet; colophon; **fingerprint,** finger mark, thumbprint, thumbmark, dactylogram, dactylograph; **footprint,** footmark, footstep, step, vestige; hoofprint, hoofmark; pad, paw print, pawmark, pug, pugmark; claw mark; fossil print *or* footprint, ichnite, ichnolite; **bump,** boss, stud, pimple, lump, excrescence, convexity, embossment; ecological footprint

8 **track, trail, path, course,** *piste* <Fr>, **line, wake;** vapor trail, contrail, condensation trail; **spoor,** signs, traces, **scent**

9 **clue, cue, key,** tip-off <nf>, telltale, smoking gun <nf>, straw in the wind; **trace, vestige, spoor,** scent, whiff; **lead** *and* hot lead <nf>; catchword, cue word, key word; **evidence** 957; **hint, intimation, suggestion** 551.4

10 **marker, mark;** bookmark; **landmark,** seamark; bench mark; **milestone,** milepost; cairn, menhir, catstone; **lighthouse,** lightship, tower, Texas tower; platform, watchtower, pharos; buoy, aid to navigation, bell, gong, lighted **buoy,** nun, can, spar buoy, wreck buoy, junction buoy, special-purpose buoy; seamark, watermark, tidemark; **monument** 549.12

11 **identification,** identification mark; **badge,** identification badge, identification tag, dog tag <military>, passport, personal identification number *or* PIN number *or* PIN, **identity card** *or* **ID card** *or* **ID**; Social Security number, driver's license number; card, business card, calling card, visiting card, *carte de visite* <Fr>, press card; letter of introduction; signature, initials, monogram, calligram; credentials; serial number; countersign, countermark; theme, theme tune *or* song; **criminal identification,** forensic tool, DNA print, genetic fingerprint, voiceprint; fingerprint 517.7; dental record

12 **password, watchword, countersign;** token; open sesame; secret grip; shibboleth

13 **label, tag;** ticket, docket <Brit>, tally; stamp, sticker; seal, sigil, signet; cachet; stub, counterfoil; **token,** check; **brand, brand name, trade name,** trademark name; **trademark,** registered trademark; government mark, government stamp, broad arrow <Brit>; **hallmark,** countermark; price tag; plate, bookplate, book stamp, colophon, *ex libris* <L>, logotype *or* logo; International Standard Book Number *or* ISBN; masthead, imprint, title page; letterhead, billhead; running head *or* title

14 **gesture, gesticulation; motion,** movement; carriage, bearing, posture, poise, pose, stance, way of holding oneself; body language, kinesics; beck, beckon; shrug; charade, dumb show, **pantomime;** sign language, signing, gesture language; dactylology, deaf-and-dumb alphabet; hand signal; chironomy

15 **signal, sign; high sign** *and* the wink *and* the nod <nf>; wink, flick of the

eyelash, glance, leer; look in one's eyes, tone of one's voice; nod; nudge, elbow in the ribs, poke, kick, touch; **alarm** 400; **beacon,** signal beacon, marker beacon, radio beacon, lighthouse beacon; signal light, signal lamp *or* lantern *or* light; blinker; signal fire, beacon fire, watch fire, balefire, smoke signal; **flare,** parachute flare; rocket, signal rocket, Roman candle; signal gun, signal shot; signal siren *or* whistle, signal bell, bell, signal gong, **police whistle,** watchman's rattle; fog signal *or* alarm, fog bell, **foghorn,** diaphone, fog whistle; **traffic signal,** traffic light, red *or* stop light, amber *or* caution light, green *or* go light; heliograph; signal flag; **semaphore,** semaphore telegraph, semaphore flag; **wigwag,** wigwag flag; international alphabet flag, international numeral pennant; red flag; white flag; yellow flag, quarantine flag; blue peter; pilot flag *or* jack; signal post, signal mast, signal tower; telecommunications

16 call, summons; whistle; moose call, bird call, duck call, hog call, goose call, crow call, hawk call, dog whistle; **bugle call,** trumpet call, fanfare, flourish; **reveille, taps,** last post <Brit>; alarm, alarum; **battle cry,** war cry, war whoop, rebel yell, rallying cry; call to arms; Angelus, Angelus bell

VERBS **17** **signify, betoken,** stand for, identify, differentiate, note , speak of, talk, **indicate,** be indicative of, be an indication of, be significant of, connote, denominate, argue, bespeak, be symptomatic *or* diagnostic of, symptomize, **characterize, mark,** highlight, be the mark *or* sign of, give token, **denote, mean** 518.8; testify, give evidence, bear witness to; **show, express, display, manifest** 348.5, **hint,** suggest 551.10, reveal, **disclose** 351.4; entail, involve 772.4

18 **designate, specify;** denominate, name, denote; stigmatize; **symbolize, stand for,** typify, be taken as, symbol, emblematize, figure ; **point to,** refer to, advert to, allude to, make an allusion to; pick out, select; **point out,** point at, put *or* lay one's finger on, finger <nf>

19 **mark,** make a mark, put a mark on; pencil, chalk; mark out, demarcate, delimit, define; **mark off, check, check off,** tick, tick off, chalk up; punctuate, point; **dot, spot,** blotch, splotch, dash, **speck, speckle,** fleck, freckle; mottle, dapple; blemish; **brand**, stigmatize; **stain, discolor** 1004.6; stamp, seal, punch, impress, imprint, **print, engrave; score, scratch,** gash, scotch, scar, scarify, cicatrize; nick, notch 289.4; **blaze,** blaze a trail; **line, seam,** trace, **stripe, streak, striate;** hatch; **underline, underscore;** prick, puncture, tattoo, riddle, pepper

20 **label, tag,** tab, ticket; stamp, seal; **brand, earmark;** hallmark; bar-code

21 **gesture, gesticulate; motion,** motion to; use body language; beckon, wiggle the finger at; wave the arms, wig-wag, saw the air; shrug, shrug the shoulders; pantomime, mime, mimic, imitate, ape, take off

22 **signal,** signalize, sign, give a signal, make a sign; speak; flash; **give the high sign** *or* **the nod** *or* a high five <nf>; nod; nudge, poke, kick, dig one in the ribs, touch; wink, glance, raise one's eyebrows, leer; hold up the hand; wave, wave the hand, wave a flag, **flag,** flag down; **unfurl a flag,** hoist a banner, break out a flag; **show one's colors,** exchange colors; **salute,** dip; dip a flag, hail, hail *and* speak; half-mast; give *or* sound an alarm, raise a cry; beat the drum, sound the trumpet

ADJS **23** **indicative,** indicatory, signifying; connotative, indicating, signifying, signalizing; **significant,** significative, meaningful; symptomatic, symptomatologic, symptomatological, diagnostic, pathognomonic, pathognomonical; evidential, **designative,** denotative, denominative, naming; **suggestive,** implicative; **expressive,** demonstrative, exhibitive, telltale; representative; identifying, identificational; individual, peculiar, idiosyncratic; **emblematic, sym-**

bolic, emblematical, symbolical; symbolistic, symbological, typical; figurative, figural, metaphorical; ideographic; semiotic, semantic; nominal, diagrammatic

24 **marked, designated,** flagged; signed, signposted; monogrammed, individualized, personal; own-brand, own-label; punctuated

25 **gestural,** gesticulative, gesticulatory; kinesic; pantomimic, **in pantomime,** in dumb show

518 MEANING

NOUNS 1 **meaning, significance, signification,** *significatum* <L>, *signifié* <Fr>, point, **sense,** idea, **purport, import,** where one is coming from <nf>; **reference, referent;** intension, extension; **denotation;** dictionary meaning, lexical meaning; emotive *or* affective meaning, undertone, overtone, coloring; relevance, bearing, **relation,** pertinence *or* pertinency; **substance, gist,** pith, core, spirit, essence, gravamen, last word, name of the game *and* meat *and* potatoes *and* bottom line <nf>; **drift,** tenor; sum, sum *and* substance; **literal meaning, true** *or* **real meaning, unadorned meaning; secondary meaning, connotation** 519.2; more than meets the eye, what is read between the lines; effect, force, impact, consequence, practical consequence, response; shifted *or* displaced meaning, implied meaning, **implication** 519.2; Aesopian *or* Aesopic meaning, Aesopian *or* Aesopic language; totality of associations *or* references *or* relations, value; syntactic *or* structural meaning, grammatical meaning; symbolic meaning; metaphorical *or* transferred meaning; semantic content, deep structure; semantic field, semantic domain, semantic cluster; range *or* span of meaning, scope; topic, subject matter

2 **intent, intention, purpose,** point, **aim, object,** end, **design,** plan; value, worth, use

3 **explanation, definition,** construction, sense-distinction, **interpretation** 341

4 **acceptation,** acception, accepted *or* received meaning; **usage,** acceptance

5 **meaningfulness,** suggestiveness, expressiveness, pregnancy; **significance,** significancy, significantness; intelligibility, interpretability, readability; pithiness, meatiness, sententiousness; importance, import

6 <units> sign, symbol, significant, type, token, icon, verbal icon, lexeme, sememe, morpheme, glosseme, **word,** term, phrase, utterance, lexical form *or* item, linguistic form, semantic *or* semiotic *or* semasiological unit; text; synonym, antonym; derivation, etymology

7 **semantics,** semiotic, semiotics, significs, semasiology, semiology, linguistics; lexicology

VERBS 8 **mean, signify, denote, connote,** import, spell, have the sense of, be construed as, have the force of; be talking *and* be talking about <nf>; **stand for, symbolize; imply,** suggest, argue, breathe, bespeak, betoken, **indicate; refer to; mean something,** mean a lot, have impact, come home, hit one where one lives *and* hit one close to home <nf>; get across, convey

9 **intend,** have in mind, seek to communicate

ADJS 10 **meaningful,** meaning, **significant,** significative; literal, explicit; **denotative, connotative,** denotational, connotational, intensional, extensional, associational; **referential; symbolic, metaphorical,** figurative, allegorical, idiomatic; transferred, extended; intelligible, interpretable, definable, readable; **suggestive,** indicative, **expressive; pregnant,** full of meaning, loaded *or* laden *or* fraught *or* freighted *or* heavy with significance, articulate; **pithy, meaty,** sententious, substantial, full of substance; pointed, full of point

11 **meant,** implied 519.7, **intended**

12 **semantic,** semantological, semiotic, semasiological, semiological; linguistic; lexological; **symbolic,**

signific, iconic, lexemic, sememic, glossematic, morphemic, **verbal,** phrasal, lexical, philological; structural

ADVS **13 meaningfully,** meaningly, **significantly;** suggestively, indicatively; **expressively**

519 LATENT MEANINGFULNESS

NOUNS **1 latent meaningfulness, latency,** latentness, delitescence, latent content; **potentiality,** virtuality, possibility; dormancy 173.4

2 implication, connotation, import, latent *or* underlying *or* implied meaning, ironic suggestion *or* implication, more than meets the eye, what is read between the lines; meaning 518; **suggestion,** allusion; coloration, tinge, undertone, overtone, undercurrent, more than meets the eye *or* ear, something between the lines, intimation, touch, nuance, innuendo; **code word,** weasel word; **hint** 551.4; **inference, supposition,** presupposition, assumption, presumption; secondary *or* transferred *or* metaphorical sense; innuendo; undermeaning, undermention, subsidiary sense, subsense, **subtext;** Aesopian *or* Aesopic meaning, cryptic *or* hidden *or* esoteric *or* arcane meaning, occult meaning; **symbolism, allegory**

VERBS **3 be latent, underlie, lie under the surface, lurk,** lie hid *or* low, lie beneath, hibernate, lie dormant, smolder; be read between the lines; make no sign, escape notice

4 imply, implicate, involve, import, connote, entail 772.4; mean 518.8; **suggest,** lead one to believe, bring to mind; **hint, insinuate, infer, intimate** 551.10; **allude to,** point to from afar, point indirectly to; write between the lines; allegorize; **suppose, presuppose,** assume, presume, take for granted; mean to say *or* imply *or* suggest

ADJS **5 latent, lurking,** lying low, delitescent, **hidden** 346.11, obscured, obfuscated, veiled, muffled, covert, occult, mystic , cryptic; esoteric; **underlying, under the surface,** submerged; **between the lines;** hibernating, sleeping, dormant 173.14; **potential,** unmanifested, virtual, possible

6 suggestive, allusive, allusory, **indicative, inferential; insinuating,** insinuative, insinuatory; ironic; **implicative,** implicatory, implicational; referential

7 implied, implicated, inferred, involved; **meant,** indicated; **suggested, intimated, insinuated, hinted; inferred, supposed,** assumed, presumed, presupposed, reputative; hidden, arcane, esoteric, **cryptic,** Aesopian *or* Aesopic

8 tacit, implicit, implied, understood, taken for granted

9 unexpressed, unpronounced, **unsaid, unspoken, unuttered,** undeclared, unbreathed, unvoiced, wordless, silent; **unmentioned,** untalked-of, **untold,** unsung, unproclaimed, unpublished; unwritten, unrecorded

10 symbolic, symbolical, allegoric, allegorical, figural, figurative, tropological, **metaphoric,** metaphorical, anagogic, anagogical

ADVS **11 latently,** underlyingly; **potentially,** virtually

12 suggestively, allusively, inferentially, insinuatingly; impliedly; by suggestion, by allusion, etc

13 tacitly, implicitly, unspokenly, wordlessly, silently

520 MEANINGLESSNESS

NOUNS **1 meaninglessness,** unmeaningness, **senselessness,** nonsensicality; **insignificance,** unsignificancy, irrelevance; **noise,** mere noise, static, empty sound, talking to hear oneself talk, phatic communion; inanity, emptiness, nullity; purposelessness, aimlessness, futility; dead letter; no bearing

2 nonsense, stuff and nonsense, pack of nonsense, **folderol, balderdash,** *niaiserie* <Fr>, flummery, trumpery, **rubbish,** trash, *narrishkeit* <Yiddish>, vaporing, fudge; **humbug,** gammon, hocus-pocus; fandangle; rant, claptrap, fustian, rodomontade, bombast, absurdity 923.3; stultiloquence, **twaddle,** twiddle-twaddle, fiddle-faddle, fiddledeedee, fiddlesticks, **blather, babble,** babblement, bibble-babble, **gabble,** gibble-gabble, **blabber, gibber, jabber,** prate, prattle, palaver, rigmarole *or* rigamarole, galimatias, skimble-skamble, drivel, drool; **gibberish,** jargon, mumbo jumbo, **double-talk,** evasion, equivoke, ambiguity, amphigory, gobbledygook <nf>; glossolalia, speaking in tongues; logorrhea

3 <nf terms> **bullshit,** shit, crap *or* crapola, horseshit, horsefeathers, bull, poppycock, bosh, tosh <Brit>, applesauce, bunkum, bunk, garbage, guff, hogwash, jive, bilge, piffle, moonshine, flapdoodle, a crock *or* a crock of shit, claptrap, tommyrot, rot, hogwash, malarkey, double Dutch, hokum, hooey, bushwa, balls <Brit>, blah-blah-blah, baloney, blarney, tripe, hot air, gas, wind, waffle <Brit>, yada yada

VERBS **4** **be meaningless, mean nothing,** signify nothing, not mean a thing, not convey anything; not make sense, not figure <nf>, not compute; **not register,** not ring any bells

5 **talk nonsense, twaddle, piffle,** waffle <Brit>, **blather,** blether, **blabber, babble, gabble,** gibble-gabble, **jabber, gibber,** prate, **prattle,** rattle, spiel <nf>; talk through one's hat; gas *and* bull *and* **bullshit** *and* throw the bull *and* shoot off one's mouth *and* shoot the bull <nf>; **drivel,** vapor, drool, run off at the mouth <nf>; speak in tongues; not mean what one says

ADJS **6** **meaningless,** unmeaning, **senseless,** purportless, importless, nondenotative, nonconnotative; **insignificant,** unsignificant; empty, inane, null; phatic, garbled, scrambled; **purposeless, aimless,** designless, **without rhyme or reason**

7 **nonsensical,** silly, poppycockish <nf>; **foolish, absurd;** twaddling, twaddly; rubbishy, trashy; skimble-skamble; Pickwickian

ADVS **8** **meaninglessly,** unmeaningly, nondenotatively, nonconnotatively, **senselessly, nonsensically;** insignificantly, unsignificantly; **purposelessly,** aimlessly

521 INTELLIGIBILITY

NOUNS **1** **intelligibility, comprehensibility, apprehensibility,** prehensibility, graspability, **understandability,** understandableness, knowability, cognizability, scrutability, penetrability, fathomableness, decipherability; recognizability, readability, interpretability; articulateness; open book

2 **clearness, clarity; plainness, distinctness,** microscopical distinctness, explicitness, clear-cutness, definition; **lucidity,** limpidity, pellucidity, crystal *or* crystaline clarity, crystallinity, perspicuity, perspicuousness, transpicuity, transparency; **simplicity,** straightforwardness, directness, literalness; unmistakableness, unequivocalness, unambiguousness, unambiguity; **coherence,** connectedness, consistency, structure; plain language, plain style, plain English, plain speech, unadorned style; clear, plaintext, unencoded text; lowest common denominator

3 **legibility,** decipherability, **readability**

VERBS **4** **be understandable, make sense;** be plain *or* clear, be obvious, be self-evident, be self-explanatory; **speak for itself,** tell its own tale, speak volumes, have no secrets, put up no barriers; read easily

5 <be understood> **get over** *or* **across** <nf>, come through, **register** <nf>, **penetrate, sink in,** soak in; dawn on, be glimpsed; become apparent

6 **make clear,** make it clear, **let it be understood,** make crystal-clear, make oneself understood, get *or* put over *or* across <nf>; **simplify,** put in plain words *or* plain English, put in words of one syllable, spell out <nf>; elucidate, **explain,** define, demonstrate, explicate, **clarify** 341.10; illuminate, enlighten; put one in the picture <Brit>; disambiguate; demystify, descramble;

decode, **decipher;** make available to all, popularize, vulgarize

7 **understand, comprehend, apprehend,** have, **know, conceive, realize,** appreciate, have no problem with, ken, savvy <nf>, sense, make sense out of, make something of, make out, make heads or tails of; **fathom, follow; grasp, seize,** get hold of, grasp *or* seize the meaning, be seized of, take, **take in,** catch, **catch on,** get the meaning of, latch onto; **master, learn** 570.6; **assimilate, absorb, digest**

8 <nf terms> **read one loud and clear,** read, read one, dig, get the idea, be with one, be with it, get the message, get the word, get the picture, get up to speed, get into *or* through one's head *or* thick head, get, get it, catch *or* get the drift, have it taped, have it down pat, see where one is coming from, hear loud and clear, hear what one is saying, grok, have hold of, get the hang of, get *or* have a fix on, know like the back *or* palm of one's hand, know inside out

9 **perceive, see, discern, make out,** descry; see the light, see daylight <nf>, wake up, wake up to, tumble to <nf>, come alive; **see through,** see to the bottom of, penetrate, see into, pierce, plumb; see at a glance, see with half an eye; get *or* have someone's number *and* read someone like a book <nf>

ADJS 10 **intelligible, comprehensible, apprehensible,** prehensible, graspable, **knowable,** cognizable, scrutable, **fathomable,** decipherable, plumbable, penetrable, interpretable; **understandable,** easily understood, easy to understand, exoteric; readable; articulate

11 **clear, crystal-clear,** clear as crystal, clear as day, clear as the nose on one's face; **plain, distinct,** microscopically distinct, plain as pikestaffs; **definite,** defined, well-defined, **clear-cut,** clean-cut, crisp, obvious, made easy; **direct, literal;** simple, **straightforward; explicit, express; unmistakable, unequivocal,** univocal, unambiguous, unconfused; **loud and clear** <nf>; **lucid,** pellucid, limpid, crystal-clear, crystalline, perspicuous, transpicuous, **transparent,** translucent, luminous; **coherent,** connected, consistent

12 **legible, decipherable, readable,** fair; uncoded, unenciphered, in the clear, clear, plaintext

ADVS 13 **intelligibly, understandably, comprehensibly,** apprehensibly; articulately; **clearly, lucidly,** limpidly, pellucidly, perspicuously, **simply, plainly, distinctly,** definitely; **coherently; explicitly, expressly; unmistakably, unequivocally,** unambiguously; in plain terms *or* words, in plain English, in no uncertain terms, in words of one syllable

14 **legibly,** decipherably, readably, fairly

522 UNINTELLIGIBILITY

NOUNS 1 **unintelligibility, incomprehensibility,** inapprehensibility, ungraspability, unseizability, **ununderstandability,** inconceivability, unknowability, incognizability, inscrutability, impenetrability, unfathomableness, unsearchableness, numinousness; **incoherence,** unconnectedness, ramblingness; inarticulateness; **ambiguity** 539, equivocation

2 **abstruseness,** reconditeness; crabbedness, crampedness, knottiness; **complexity,** intricacy, **complication** 799.1; **hardness, difficulty; profundity,** profoundness, deepness; esotericism, esotery

3 **obscurity,** obscuration, obscurantism, obfuscation, mumbo jumbo <nf>, mystification; perplexity; **unclearness,** unclarity, unplainness, opacity; **vagueness,** indistinctness, indeterminateness, fuzziness, shapelessness, amorphousness; murkiness, murk, mistiness, mist, fogginess, fog, darkness, dark

4 **illegibility,** unreadability; undecipherability, indecipherability; invisibility; scribble, scrawl, hen track <nf>

5 **unexpressiveness,** inexpressiveness, **expressionlessness,** impassivity;

uncommunicativeness; straight face, deadpan <nf>, poker face <nf>

6 **inexplicability,** unexplainableness, uninterpretability, indefinability, undefinability, unaccountableness; insolvability, inextricability; **enigmaticalness,** mysteriousness, mystery, strangeness, weirdness

7 <something unintelligible> Greek, Choctaw, double Dutch; gibberish, babble, jargon, garbage, gubbish, gobbledygook, noise, Babel; scramble, jumble, garble, muddle; purple prose; argot, cant, slang, secret language, Aesopian *or* Aesopic language, code, cipher, cryptogram; glossolalia, gift of tongues; enigma, riddle; double meaning

8 **enigma, mystery, puzzle,** puzzlement; Chinese puzzle, crossword puzzle, word game, jigsaw puzzle, Sudoku; **problem,** puzzling *or* baffling problem, why; question, question mark, vexed *or* perplexed question, enigmatic question, sixty-four dollar question <nf>; **perplexity;** obscure point; knot, knotty point, crux, point to be solved; **puzzler,** poser, brain twister *or* teaser <nf>, sticker <nf>; mind-boggler, **floorer** *or* **stumper** <nf>; nut to crack, **hard** *or* **tough nut to crack;** tough proposition <nf>

9 **riddle, conundrum,** paradox, charade, rebus; brainteaser, Chinese puzzle, tangram, acrostic, logogriph, anagram; riddle of the Sphinx, squaring of the circle; Sudoku, crossword

VERBS **10** **be incomprehensible, not make sense,** be too deep, go over one's head, defy comprehension, be beyond one, beat one <nf>, elude *or* escape one, lose one, need explanation *or* clarification *or* translation, be Greek to, pass comprehension *or* understanding, not penetrate, make one's head swim; **baffle, perplex** 971.13, riddle, be sphinxlike, speak in riddles; speak in tongues; talk double Dutch, babble, gibber, ramble, drivel, mean nothing

11 **not understand, be unable to comprehend,** not have the first idea, not get *or* not get it <nf>, be unable to get into *or* through one's head *or* thick skull; be out of one's depth, be at sea, be lost; **not know what to make of,** make nothing of, not have the slightest idea, not be able to account for, not make head *or* tail of, not register; be unable to see, not see the wood for the trees; go over one's head, escape one; give up, pass <nf>; rack one's brains

12 **make unintelligible, scramble,** jumble, garble, mix up; encode, encipher; **obscure,** obfuscate, mystify, shadow; **complicate** 799.3

ADJS **13** **unintelligible, incomprehensible,** inapprehensible, ungraspable, unseizable, **ununderstandable,** unknowable, incognizable; **unfathomable, inscrutable,** impenetrable, unsearchable, numinous; **ambiguous,** equivocal; **incoherent,** unconnected, rambling; **inarticulate; past comprehension,** beyond one's comprehension, beyond understanding; Greek to one; ultracrepidarian

14 **hard to understand, difficult, hard,** tough <nf>, beyond one, **over one's head,** beyond *or* out of one's depth; knotty, cramp, crabbed; intricate, **complex,** overtechnical, perplexed, **complicated** 799.4; **scrambled,** jumbled, **garbled;** Johnsonian

15 **obscure,** obscured, obfuscated; **vague, indistinct,** indeterminate, undiscernible, fuzzy, shapeless, amorphous *or* amorphic, obfuscatory; unclear, unplain, opaque, muddy, **clear as mud** *and* clear as ditch water <nf>; **dark, dim,** blind , shadowy; **murky,** cloudy, foggy, fogbound, hazy, misty, nebulous

16 **recondite, abstruse,** abstract, transcendental; **profound, deep; hidden** 346.11; arcane, **esoteric,** occult; **secret** 345.11

17 **enigmatic,** enigmatical, cryptic, cryptical; sphinxlike; **perplexing, puzzling;** riddling; logogriphic, anagrammatic, mysterious

18 **inexplicable, unexplainable,** uninterpretable, undefinable, indefinable, funny, funny peculiar <nf>, **unaccountable; insolvable,** unsolvable, insoluble, inextricable; mysterious, mystic, mystical, shrouded *or* wrapped *or* enwrapped in mystery

19 **illegible, unreadable, unclear; undecipherable,** indecipherable

20 **inexpressive,** unexpressive, impassive, po-faced <Brit>; uncommunicative; **expressionless; vacant, empty, blank;** glassy, glazed, glazed-over, fishy, wooden; deadpan, poker-faced <nf>

ADVS 21 **unintelligibly, incomprehensibly,** inapprehensibly, ununderstandably

22 **obscurely, vaguely, indistinctly,** indeterminately; **unclearly,** unplainly; illegibly

23 reconditely, **abstrusely;** esoterically, occultly

24 **inexplicably, unexplainably,** undefinably, bafflingly, **unaccountably, enigmatically; mysteriously,** mystically

25 **expressionlessly, vacantly, blankly, emptily,** woodenly, glassily, fishily

PHRS 26 **I don't understand, I can't see,** I don't see how *or* why, **it beats me** <nf>, you've got me <nf>, **it's beyond me,** it's too deep for me, it has me guessing, I don't have the first *or* foggiest idea, it's Greek to me, I'm clueless <Brit>; **I give up,** I pass <nf>

523 LANGUAGE

NOUNS 1 **language**, speech, tongue, *lingua* <L>, spoken language, natural language; **talk, parlance, locution,** phraseology, **idiom, lingo** <nf>; dialect; idiolect, personal usage, individual speech habits *or* performance, parole; code *or* system of oral communication, individual speech, competence, langue; **usage,** use of words; **language type; language family, subfamily, language group;** area language, regional language; world language, universal language; words, lexicon; foreign language

2 **dead language,** ancient language, lost language; archaic language, archaism, archaic speech; parent language; classical language; living language, vernacular; sacred language *or* tongue

3 **mother tongue,** native language *or* tongue, natal tongue, native speech, vernacular, first language

4 **standard language,** standard *or* prestige dialect, acrolect; national language, official language; educated speech *or* language; literary language, written language, formal written language, formal language; classical language; correct *or* good English, **Standard English, the King's** *or* **Queen's English,** Received Standard, Received Pronunciation

5 **nonformal language** *or* **speech,** nonformal standard speech, informal language, **spoken language, colloquial language** *or* **speech,** vernacular language *or* speech, vernacular; **slang;** colloquialism, colloquial usage, conversationalism, vernacularism; ordinary language *or* speech; nonformal English, conversational English, colloquial English, English as it is spoken

6 **substandard** *or* nonstandard language *or* **speech,** nonformal language *or* speech; vernacular language *or* speech, **vernacular,** demotic language *or* speech, vulgate, vulgar tongue, common speech, low language; uneducated speech, illiterate speech; substandard usage; basilect; **nonformal**

7 **dialect,** idiom; class dialect; regional *or* local dialect; idiolect; subdialect; folk speech *or* dialect, patois; **provincialism, localism, regionalism,** regional accent 524.8; Canadian French, French Canadian; Pennsylvania Dutch, Pennsylvania German; Yankee, New England dialect; Brooklynese; Southern dialect *or* twang; Black English, Afro-Americanese; Cockney; Yorkshire; Midland, Midland dialect; Anglo-Indian; Australian English; Gullah; Acadian, Cajun; dialect atlas, linguistic atlas; isogloss, bundle of isoglosses; speech community; linguistic community; linguistic ambience; speech *or* linguistic island, relic area; click language

8 <idioms> Anglicism, Briticism, Englishism; Americanism, Yankeeism; Westernism, Southernism; Gallicism, Frenchism; Irishism, Hibernicism; Canadianism, Scotticism, Germanism, Russianism, Latinism, etc

9 **jargon, lingo** <nf>, **slang, cant, argot, patois, patter, vernacular;** vocabulary, terminology, nomenclature, phraseology; gobbledygook, mumbo jumbo, gibberish; **nonformal;** taboo language, vulgar language; obscene language, scatology, doublespeak, bizspeak, mediaspeak, policyspeak, technospeak, technobabble, ecobabble, etc; shoptalk

10 <jargons> Academese, cinemese, collegese, constablese, ecobabble, economese, sociologese, legalese, pedagese, societyese, stagese, telegraphese, Varietyese, Wall Streetese, journalese, newspaperese, newspeak, officialese, federalese, Pentagonese, Washingtonese, medical Greek, medicalese, businessese *or* businessspeak, computerese, technobabble, technospeak, psychobabble; Yinglish, Franglais, Spanglish; Eurojargon; man-talk, bloke-talk <Brit nf>, woman-talk, hen-talk <nf>; shoptalk; pig Latin; glossolalia

11 **lingua franca,** international language, jargon, **pidgin,** trade language; auxiliary language, interlanguage; creolized language, creole language, creole; koine; diplomatic language, business language, language *or* linguistic universal; pidgin English, talkee-talkee, Bêche-de-Mer, Beach-la-mar; Kitchen Kaffir; Chinook *or* Oregon Jargon; Sabir; Esperanto; artificial language, sign language, sign, American Sign Language *or* ASL *or* Ameslan; Morse code, cryptography, cryptanalysis; computer language; shorthand, stenography

12 language family; Indo-European, Indo-Iranian, Anatolian, Hellenic, Tocharian, Italic, Celtic, Germanic, Baltic, Slavic; Finno-Ugric; Afroasiatic *or* Hamito-Semitic; Sino-Tibetan; Austronesian

13 **linguistics,** linguistic science, science of language; glottology, glossology ; linguistic analysis; linguistic terminology, metalanguage; **philology;** paleography; speech origins, language origins, bowwow theory, dingdong theory, pooh-pooh theory; language study, foreign-language study, linguistic theory

14 **language element,** morpheme, phoneme, grapheme; letter, alphabet, word, phrase, sentence; grammar, syntax, part of speech; context clue

15 **linguist,** linguistic scientist, linguistician, linguistic scholar; philologist, philologer, philologian; philologaster; **grammarian,** grammatist; grammaticaster; **etymologist,** etymologer; **lexicologist; lexicographer,** glossographer, glossarist; phoneticist, phonetician, phonemicist, phonologist, orthoepist; dialectician, dialectologist; semanticist, semasiologist; paleographer; logophile; morphologist, orthographer

16 **polyglot,** linguist, **bilingual** *or* diglot, trilingual, multilingual

17 **colloquializer;** jargonist, jargoneer, jargonizer; slangster

VERBS **18** **speak, talk,** use language, communicate orally *or* verbally; use nonformal speech *or* style, colloquialize, vernacularize; jargon, jargonize, cant; patter; utter, verbalize, articulate

ADJS **19** **linguistic,** lingual, glottological, glossological ; descriptive, structural, glottochronological, lexicostatistical, psycholinguistic, sociolinguistic, metalinguistic; **philological;** lexicological, lexicographic, lexicographical; syntactic, syntactical, **grammatical;** grammatic, semantic 518.12; phonetic 524.30, phonemic, phonological; morphological; morphophonemic, graphemic, paleographic, paleographical

20 **vernacular, colloquial, conversational, unliterary, nonformal,** informal, demotic, spoken, vulgar, vulgate; unstudied, familiar, common, everyday; jargonistic; **substandard,** nonformal, uneducated, low

21 **jargonish,** jargonal; **slang,** slangy; taboo, four-letter, obscene, vulgar; scatological; rhyming slang

22 **idiomatic; dialect,** dialectal, dialectological; provincial, regional, local

524 SPEECH
<utterance>

NOUNS 1 **speech, talk,** the power *or* faculty of speech, the verbal *or* oral faculty, talking, speaking, **discourse,** colloquy, oral communication, vocal *or* voice *or* viva-voce communication, communication, verbal intercourse; **palaver, prattle, gab** *and* jaw-jaw <nf>; rapping *and* yakking *and* yakkety-yak <nf>; **words, accents;** chatter 540.3; conversation 541; elocution 543.1; **language** 523

2 **utterance, speaking,** *parole* <Fr>, spoken language, vocalization, locution , phonation, phonetics; **speech act,** linguistic act *or* behavior; string, utterance string, sequence of phonemes, expression; **voice, tongue,** vocalism, parlance; word of mouth, parol, the spoken word; vocable, **word** 526

3 **remark, statement,** earful *and* crack *and* one's two cents' worth <nf>, **word,** say, **saying, utterance, observation, reflection, expression; note,** thought, **mention; assertion,** averment, allegation, affirmation, pronouncement, position, dictum; **declaration;** interjection, exclamation; question 938.10; answer 939; address, greeting, apostrophe; sentence, phrase; subjoinder, Parthian shot

4 articulateness, articulacy, oracy, readiness *or* facility of speech; eloquence 544; way with words, word power

5 **articulation,** uttering, phonation, voicing, giving voice, **vocalization; pronunciation, enunciation,** utterance; **delivery, attack**

6 **intonation, inflection, modulation;** intonation pattern *or* contour, intonation *or* inflection of voice, speech tune *or* melody; suprasegmental, suprasegmental phoneme; **tone, pitch;** pitch accent, tonic accent

7 manner of speaking, way of saying, mode of expression *or* speech; **tone of voice, voice,** *voce* <Ital>, **tone;** speaking voice, voice quality, vocal style, **timbre;** voice qualifier; paralinguistic communication

8 **accent,** regional accent, brogue, twang, burr, drawl, broad accent, trill, whine, nasality, stridor; **foreign accent;** guttural accent, clipped accent; broken English; speech impediment, speech defect; speech community, isogloss

9 pause, juncture, open juncture, close juncture; terminal, clause terminal, rising terminal, falling terminal; sandhi; word boundary, clause boundary; pause

10 **accent,** accentuation, stress accent; **emphasis, stress, word stress;** ictus, beat, rhythmical stress; rhythm, rhythmic pattern, **cadence;** prosody, prosodics, metrics; stress pattern; level of stress; primary stress, secondary stress, tertiary stress, weak stress

11 vowel quantity, **quantity,** mora; long vowel, short vowel, full vowel, reduced vowel

12 **speech sound,** phone, vocable, phonetic unit *or* entity; puff of air, aspiration; stream of air, airstream, glottalic airstream; articulation, manner of articulation; **stop,** plosive, explosive, mute, check, occlusive, **affricate,** continuant, **liquid,** lateral, **nasal;** point *or* place of articulation; voice, voicing; sonority; aspiration, palatalization, labialization, pharyngealization, glottalization; surd, voiceless sound; sonant, voiced sound; **consonant; semivowel,** glide, transition sound; velar, guttural, voiced consonant, frictionless continuant, labial, labio-dental, labio-nasal, spirant, sibilant, aspirate, glottal stop, fricative, sonant, polyphone; vocalic, syllabic nucleus, syllabic peak, peak; vocoid; **vowel;** monophthong, **diphthong,** triphthong; **syllable; phoneme,** segmental phoneme, morphophoneme, digraph; modification, assimilation, dissimilation; **allophone;** parasitic vowel, epenthetic vowel, svarab-

hakti vowel, prothetic vowel; vowel gradation, vowel mutation; doubletalk

13 **phonetics,** articulatory phonetics, acoustic phonetics; phonology; morphophonemics, morphophonology; orthoepy; sound *or* phonetic law; pronunciation; phonography; sound shift; umlaut, mutation, ablaut, gradation; rhotacism, betacism; Grimm's law, Verner's law, Grassmann's law

14 **phonetician,** phonetist, phoneticist; orthoepist

15 **ventriloquism,** ventriloquy; **ventriloquist**

16 talking machine, sonovox, voder, vocoder

17 **talker, speaker,** sayer, utterer, patterer; chatterbox 540.4; conversationalist 541.7

18 **vocal** *or* **speech organ,** articulator, voice, mouth; tongue, apex, tip, blade, dorsum, back; vocal cords *or* bands, vocal processes, vocal folds; voice box, larynx, Adam's apple; syrinx; arytenoid cartilages; glottis, vocal chink, epiglottis; lips, teeth, palate, hard palate, soft palate, velum, alveolus, teeth ridge, alveolar ridge, uvula; nasal cavity, oral cavity; pharynx, throat *or* pharyngeal cavity

VERBS **19** **speak, talk; patter** *or* **gab** *or* wag the tongue <nf>; mouth; chatter 540.5; converse 541.8; declaim 543.10

20 <nf terms> **yak,** yap, yakkety-yak, gab, spiel, chin, jaw, shoot off one's face *or* mouth, shoot *or* bat the breeze, beat *or* bat one's gums, bend one's ear, make chin music, rattle away, talk a blue streak, talk someone's ear *or* head off, flap one's jaw, natter <Brit>, spout off, sound off

21 **speak up, speak out, speak one's piece** *or* **one's mind, pipe up, open one's mouth,** open one's lips, say out, say loud *and* clear, say out loud, sound off, lift *or* raise one's voice, break silence, find one's tongue; take the floor; put in a word, get in a word edgewise *or* edgeway; **have one's say,** put in one's two cents worth <nf>, relieve oneself, get a load off one's mind <nf>, give vent *or* voice to, pour one's heart out

22 **say, utter, breathe,** sound, **voice,** vocalize, phonate, **articulate, enunciate, pronounce,** lip, give voice, give tongue, give utterance; whisper; **express,** give expression, verbalize, put in words, find words to express; **word,** formulate, put into words, couch, phrase 532.4; **present,** deliver; **emit,** give, raise, **let out,** out with, come *or* give out with, put *or* set forth, pour forth; throw off, fling off; chorus, chime; **tell, communicate** 343.6,7; **convey, impart, disclose** 351.4

23 **state, declare, assert,** aver, affirm, asseverate, allege; **say,** make a statement, send a message; **announce,** tell the world; **relate, recite;** quote; proclaim, nuncupate

24 **remark, comment, observe, note; mention,** speak , let drop *or* fall, say by the way, make mention of; refer to, allude to, touch on, make reference to, call attention to; muse, reflect; opine <nf>; interject; blurt, blurt out, exclaim

25 <utter in a certain way> murmur, mutter, mumble, whisper, breathe, buzz, sigh; gasp, pant; exclaim, yell 59.6; sing, lilt, warble, chant, coo, chirp; pipe, flute; squeak; cackle, crow; bark, yelp, yap; growl, snap, snarl; hiss, sibilate; grunt, snort; roar, bellow, blare, trumpet, bray, blat, bawl, thunder, rumble, boom; scream, shriek, screech, squeal, squawk, yawp, squall; whine, wail, keen, blubber, sob; drawl, twang

26 **address, speak to, talk to,** bespeak, beg the ear of; **appeal to,** invoke; apostrophize; **approach; buttonhole,** take by the button *or* lapel; take aside, talk to in private, closet oneself with; **accost, call to, hail,** halloo, greet, salute, speak, speak fair

27 **pass one's lips, escape one's lips,** fall from the lips *or* mouth

28 inflect, modulate, intonate

ADJS **29** **speech; language, linguistic,** lingual; **spoken, uttered, said,** vocalized, **voiced, verbalized,**

pronounced, sounded, articulated, enunciated; vocal, voiceful; **oral, verbal, unwritten,** *viva voce* <L>, nuncupative, parol

30 **phonetic,** phonic; articulatory, acoustic; intonated; pitched, pitch, **tonal,** tonic, oxytone, oxytonic, paroxytonic, barytone; **accented, stressed,** strong, heavy; unaccented, unstressed, weak, light, pretonic, atonic, posttonic; articulated; stopped, muted, checked, occlusive, nasal, nasalized, twangy, continuant, liquid, lateral, affricated; alveolabial, alveolar, alveolingual, etc; low, high, mid, open, broad, close; front, back, central; wide, lax, tense, narrow; voiced, sonant, voiceless, surd; rounded, unrounded, flat; aspirated; labialized; palatalized, soft, *mouillé* <Fr>; unpalatalized, hard; pharyngealized, glottalized; velar, guttural; burring, frictionless, labial, spirant, sibilant, fricative, polyphonic, polyphonous, digraphic; **consonant,** consonantal, semivowel, glide, **vowel;** vowellike, vocoid, vocalic, syllabic; monophthongal, diphthongal, triphthongal; **phonemic,** allophonic; assimilated, dissimilated

31 **speaking, talking;** articulate, talkative 540.9; **eloquent** 544.8, well-spoken; true-speaking, clean-speaking, plain-speaking, plain-spoken, **outspoken,** free-speaking, free-spoken, loud-speaking, loud-spoken, soft-speaking, soft-spoken; English-speaking, etc

32 ventriloquial, ventriloquistic

ADVS 33 **orally, vocally, verbally, by word of mouth,** *viva voce* <L>; from the lips of, from his own mouth

525 IMPERFECT SPEECH

NOUNS 1 **speech defect,** speech impediment, speech difficulty, impairment of speech; dysarthria, dysphasia, dysphrasia; dyslalia, dyslogia; idioglossia, idiolalia; **broken speech,** cracked *or* broken voice, broken tones *or* accents; indistinct *or* blurred *or* muzzy speech; loss of voice, aphonia; **nasalization,** nasal tone *or* accent, **twang,** nasal twang, talking through one's nose; **falsetto,** childish treble, artificial voice; **shake, quaver,** tremor; **lisp,** lisping; hiss, sibilation, lallation; **croak,** choked voice, hawking voice; crow; harshness, dysphonia, hoarseness 58.2; voicelessness, loss of voice

2 **inarticulateness,** inarticulacy, inarticulation; thickness of speech

3 **stammering, stuttering,** hesitation, faltering, traulism, dysphemia, *balbuties* <L>; palilalia; stammer, stutter

4 **mumbling, muttering,** maundering; unintelligible speech; droning, drone; mumble, mutter; jabber, jibber, gibber, gibbering, gabble; whispering, whisper, susurration; mouthing; murmuring

5 **mispronunciation,** misspeaking, cacology, cacoepy; lallation, lambdacism, paralambdacism; rhotacism, pararhotacism; gammacism; mytacism; **corruption,** language pollution

6 **aphasia, agraphia;** aphrasia, aphrasia paranoica; **aphonia,** loss of speech, aphonia clericorum, hysterical aphonia, stage fright, aphonia paralytica, aphonia paranoica, spastic aphonia, mutism, muteness 51.2; voiceless speech, sign language

VERBS 7 **speak poorly,** talk incoherently, be unable to put two words together; have an impediment in one's speech, have a bone in one's neck *or* throat; speak thickly; **croak; lisp; shake, quaver; drawl;** mince, clip one's words; lose one's voice, get stage fright, clank *or* clank up *and* freeze <nf>, be struck dumb

8 **stammer, stutter,** stammer out; hesitate, falter, halt, mammer <Brit nf>, stumble; hem, haw, hum, **hum and haw, hem and haw**

9 **mumble, mutter,** maunder; drone, drone on; swallow one's words, speak drunkenly *or* incoherently; jabber, gibber, gabble; splutter, sputter; blubber, sob; whisper, susurrate; murmur; babble; mouth

10 nasalize, whine, **speak through one's nose,** twang, snuffle

11 **mispronounce,** misspeak, missay, **murder the King's** *or* **Queen's English**

ADJS **12** <imperfectly spoken> inarticulate, indistinct, blurred, muzzy, unintelligible; **mispronounced; shaky,** shaking, **quavering,** breaking, cracked, tremulous, titubant; **drawling,** drawly; **lisping; throaty, guttural,** thick, velar; stifled, choked, choking, strangled; **nasal, twangy,** breathy, adenoidal, snuffling; croaking, hawking; harsh, dysphonic, hoarse 58.15

13 **stammering, stuttering,** halting, hesitating, faltering, stumbling, balbutient; **aphasic;** aphrasic; aphonic, dumb, **mute** 51.12

526 WORD

NOUNS **1** **word,** free form, minimum free form, semanteme, **term,** name, expression, locution, linguistic form, lexeme; written unit; content word, function word; *logos* <Gk>, *verbum* <L>; verbalism, vocable, utterance, articulation; **usage;** syllable, polysyllable; homonym, homophone, homograph; monosyllable; synonym; metonym; antonym; easy word, hard word

2 **root,** etymon, primitive; eponym; derivative, derivation; cognate; doublet

3 **morphology,** morphemics; morphophonemics; **morpheme;** morph, allomorph; bound morpheme *or* form, free morpheme *or* form; difference of form, formal contrast; accidence; **inflection,** conjugation, declension; paradigm; derivation, word-formation; formative; root, radical; theme, stem; word element, combining form; **affix, suffix, prefix,** infix; proclitic, enclitic; affixation, infixation, suffixation, prefixation; morphemic analysis, immediate constituent *or* IC analysis, cutting; morphophonemic analysis

4 **word form,** formation, construction; back formation; clipped word; spoonerism; **compound;** *tatpurusha, dvandva, karmadharaya, dvigu, avyayibhava, bahuvrihi* <all Skt>; endocentric compound, exocentric compound; acronym, acrostic; paronym, conjugate; proclitic, enclitic

5 **technical term,** technicality; jargon word; jargon 523.9,10

6 **barbarism, corruption, vulgarism, impropriety,** taboo word, dirty word *and* four-letter word <nf>, swearword, naughty word, bad word, obscenity, expletive; **colloquialism, slang, localism** 526.6

7 **loan word,** borrowing, borrowed word, paronym; loan translation, calque; foreignism

8 **neologism,** neology, neoterism, new word *or* term, newfangled expression; **coinage;** new sense *or* meaning; **nonce word;** ghost word *or* name

9 **catchword,** catch phrase, shibboleth, slogan, cry; **pet expression,** byword, cliché; **buzzword,** vogue word, fad word, in-word; euphemism, **code word;** commonplace, hackneyed expression

10 long word, hard word, jawbreaker *or* jawtwister *and* two-dollar *or* five-dollar word <nf>, polysyllable; sesquipedalian, sesquipedalia <pl>; lexiphanicism, grandiloquence 545

11 hybrid word, **hybrid;** macaronicism, macaronic; hybridism, contamination; blendword, blend, portmanteau word, portmanteau, portmantologism, telescope word, **counterword;** ghost word

12 **archaism,** archaicism, antiquated word *or* expression; obsoletism, obsolete

13 **vocabulary, lexis, words, word stock,** wordhoard, stock of words; phraseology; **thesaurus,** Roget's; lexicon

14 **lexicology; lexicography,** lexigraphy, glossography; onomastics 527.1, toponymics; **meaning** 518, semantics, semasiology; denotation, connotation

15 **etymology, derivation, origin,** word origin, word history, semantic history, etymon; historical linguistics, comparative linguistics; eponymy; folk etymology

16 echoic word, onomatopoeic word, onomatope; onomatopoeia; bow-wow theory

17 **neologist, word-coiner,** neoterist; phraser, phrasemaker, phrasemonger; word nerd

ADJS 18 **verbal,** vocabular, vocabulary

19 lexical, lexicologic, lexicological; lexigraphic, lexigraphical, **lexicographical,** lexicographic; glossographic, glossographical; etymological, etymologic, derivational; onomastic, onomatologic; onomasiological; echoic, onomatopoeic; conjugate, paronymous, paronymic

20 neological, neoterical

21 **morphological,** morphemic; morphophonemic; inflective, inflectional, paradigmatic, derivational; affixal, prefixal, infixal, suffixal

527 NOMENCLATURE

NOUNS 1 **nomenclature, terminology,** orismology, glossology , vocabulary, lexicon; onomatology, onomastics; toponymics, toponymy, place-names, place-naming; antonomasia; orismology; polyonymy; **taxonomy,** classification, systematics, cladistics, biosystematics, cytotaxonomy, binomial nomenclature, binomialism, Linnaean method, trinomialism; kingdom, phylum, class, order, family, genus, species

2 **naming, calling, denomination,** appellation, designation, designating, styling, terming, definition, identification; **christening,** baptism; dubbing; nicknaming

3 **name, appellation,** appellative, **denomination, designation, style,** heading, *nomen* <L>, cognomen, cognomination, full name; proper name *or* noun; moniker *and* handle <nf>; **title,** honorific; empty title *or* name; **label, tag; epithet,** byword; **scientific name,** trinomen, trinomial name, binomen, binomial name; *nomen nudum* <L>, hyponym; tautonym; typonym; middle name; eponym; namesake; secret name, cryptonym, euonym, password; professional title; title of respect *or* address; military title; place name, toponym; trade name, trademark

4 **first name,** forename, **Christian name, given name,** baptismal name; **middle name**

5 **surname, last name, family name, cognomen,** byname; **maiden name;** married name; patronym, matronym

6 <Latin terms> *praenomen, nomen, agnomen, cognomen*

7 **nickname, sobriquet,** byname, cognomen; epithet, agnomen; **pet name,** diminutive, hypocoristic, affectionate name

8 **alias, pseudonym,** anonym, **assumed name,** false *or* fictitious name, *nom de guerre* <Fr>; pen name, nom de plume; stage name, nom de théâtre <Fr>, professional name; John Doe, Jane Doe, Richard Roe

9 **misnomer,** wrong name

10 **signature,** sign manual, **autograph, hand, John Hancock** <nf>; mark, mark of signature, cross, christcross, X; initials; subscription; countersignature, countersign, countermark, counterstamp; endorsement; visa, *visé* <Fr>; monogram, cipher, device; seal, sigil, signet

VERBS 11 **name, denominate,** nominate, **designate, call, term, style, dub,** color <nf>; specify; define, identify; title, entitle; **label, tag; nickname; christen,** baptize

12 **misname,** misnomer, **miscall,** misterm, misdesignate

13 **be called, be known by** *or* as, go by, go as, **go by the name of,** go *or* pass under the name of, bear the name of, rejoice in the name of; go under an assumed *or* a false name, have an alias

ADJS 14 **named, called,** yclept , **styled, titled,** denominated, denominate , **known as,** known by the name of, designated, termed, dubbed, identified as; christened, baptized; what one may well *or* fairly *or* properly *or* fitly call

15 **nominal,** cognominal; **titular, in name only,** nominative, formal; so-called, quasi; would-be, *soi-disant* <Fr>; **self-called, self-styled,** self-christened; honorific; agnominal, epithetic, epithetical; hypocoristic, diminutive; by name, by whatever

name, under any other name; **alias,** a k a *or* also known as

16 denominative, nominative, appellative; eponymous, eponymic

17 **terminological,** nomenclatural, orismological; onomastic; toponymic, toponymous; taxonomic, classificatory, binomial, Linnaean, trinomial

528 ANONYMITY

NOUNS 1 **anonymity, anonymousness, namelessness; incognito;** cover, cover name; code name; anonym; unknown quantity, no-name; Unknown Soldier; Anon.

2 **what's-its-name** *and* **what's-his-name** *and* what's-his-face *and* what's-her-name *and* **what-you-may-call-it** *and* whatchamacallit *and* what-you-may-call-'em *and* what-d'ye-call-'em *and* what-d'ye-call-it *and* whatzit <nf>; *je ne sais quoi* <Fr>, I don't know what; such-and-such; **so-and-so,** certain person, X *or* Mr X; you-know-who

ADJS 3 **anonymous, anon; nameless, unnamed,** unidentified, undesignated, unspecified, innominate, without a name, **unknown;** undefined; unacknowledged; **incognito;** cryptonymous, cryptonymic; lesser-known

529 PHRASE

NOUNS 1 **phrase, expression, locution, utterance,** usage, term, verbalism; **word-group,** fixed expression, construction, endocentric construction, headed group, syntagm; syntactic structure; noun phrase, compound noun, verb phrase, verb complex, adverbial phrase, adjectival phrase, prepositional phrase; conditional phrase; phrasal verb; **collocation**; **clause,** coordinate clause, subordinate clause, independent clause**; sentence,** period, periodic sentence; **paragraph; idiom,** idiotism, phrasal idiom; turn of phrase *or* expression, peculiar expression, manner *or* way of speaking; set phrase *or* term; conventional *or* common *or* standard phrase; phraseogram, phraseograph; maxim, adage, moral, proverb, slogan, motto, quotation, quote, sound bite

2 **diction, phrasing;** phraseology, choice of words, wording

3 **phraser, phrasemaker,** phrasemonger, phraseman

ADJS 4 **phrasal,** phrase; phrasey

5 in set phrases *or* terms, in good set terms, in round terms

530 GRAMMAR

NOUNS 1 **grammar,** rules of language, linguistic structure, syntactic structure, sentence structure; grammaticalness, well-formedness, grammaticality, grammatical theory; **traditional grammar, school grammar;** descriptive grammar, **structural grammar;** case grammar; phrase-structure grammar; generative grammar, **transformational grammar, transformational generative grammar;** comparative grammar; tagmemic analysis; glossematics; stratificational grammar; **parsing,** construing, grammatical analysis; **morphology** 526.3; **phonology** 524.13, good grammar, good English, Standard English, correct grammar; style guide *or* sheet

2 **syntax, structure, syntactic structure,** word order, word arrangement; syntactics, syntactic analysis; immediate constituent analysis *or* IC analysis, cutting; phrase structure; surface structure, shallow structure, deep structure, underlying structure; levels, ranks, strata; tagmeme, form-function unit, slot, filler, slot *and* filler; **function, subject, predicate, complement, object,** direct object, indirect object, **modifier,** qualifier, sentence *or* construction modifier, appositive, attribute, attributive; inflection, diminuitive, intensive, formative; asyndeton, syndeton, apposition, hypotaxis, parataxis

3 **part of speech,** form class, major form class, function class; function *or* empty *or* form word; **adjective,** adjectival, attributive, derived

adjective; **adverb,** adverbial; **preposition;** verbal adjective, gerundive; **participle,** present participle, past participle, perfect participle; **conjunction,** subordinating conjunction, coordinating conjunction, conjunctive adverb, adversative conjunction, copula, copulative, copulative conjunction, correlative conjunction, disjunctive, disjunctive conjunction; **interjection,** exclamatory noun *or* adjective; **particle**

4 **verb,** transitive, transitive verb, intransitive, intransitive verb, impersonal verb, neuter verb, deponent verb, defective verb, reflexive verb, irregular verb; predicate; finite verb; linking verb, copula; helping verb; verbal, verbid, nonfinite verb form; **infinitive; auxiliary verb,** auxiliary, modal auxiliary; phrasal verb; verb phrase, phrasal verb; present participle, past participle, perfect participle

5 **noun, pronoun,** substantive, substantival, common noun, proper noun, concrete noun, abstract noun, collective noun, quotation noun, compound noun, possessive noun, hypostasis, adherent noun, adverbial noun, attributive noun; verbal noun, gerund; nominal; noun phrase; mass noun, count noun

6 **article,** definite article, indefinite article; determiner, noun determiner, determinative, post-determiner

7 **person;** first person; second person, proximate; third person; fourth person, obviative

8 number; singular, dual, trial, plural

9 **case;** common case, subject case, nominative; object *or* objective case, accusative, dative, possessive case, genitive; local case, locative, essive, superessive, inessive, adessive, abessive, lative, allative, illative, sublative, elative, ablative, delative, terminative, approximative, prolative, perlative, translative; comitative, instrumental, prepositional, vocative; oblique case

10 **gender,** masculine, feminine, neuter, common gender; grammatical gender, natural gender; animate, inanimate

11 **mood,** mode; indicative, subjunctive, imperative, conditional, potential, obligative, permissive, optative, jussive

12 **tense; present;** historical present; **past,** preterit *or* preterite; aorist; imperfect; future; **perfect,** present perfect, future perfect; past perfect, **pluperfect;** progressive tense, durative; point tense

13 **aspect;** perfective, imperfective, inchoative, iterative, frequentative, desiderative

14 **voice;** active voice, active, passive voice, passive; middle voice, middle; medio-passive; reflexive

15 **punctuation,** punctuation marks; diacritical mark *or* sign, accent; reference mark, reference; point, tittle; stop, end stop

VERBS 16 grammaticize; **parse,** analyze; inflect, **conjugate, decline; punctuate,** mark, point; parenthesize, hyphenate, bracket; diagram, notate

ADJS 17 **grammatical, syntactical,** formal, structural; correct, well-formed; tagmemic, glossematic; **functional;** substantive, nominal, pronominal; verbal, transitive, intransitive; linking, copulative; attributive, adjectival, adverbal, participial; prepositional, post-positional; conjunctive

531 UNGRAMMATICALNESS

NOUNS 1 **ungrammaticalness,** bad *or* faulty grammar, faulty syntax; lack of concord *or* agreement, incorrect usage, faulty reference, misplaced *or* dangling modifier, shift of tense, shift of structure, anacoluthon, faulty subordination, faulty comparison, faulty coordination, faulty punctuation, lack of parallelism, sentence fragment, comma fault, comma splice; abuse of terms, corruption of speech, broken speech

2 **solecism,** ungrammaticism, **misusage, missaying, misconstruction,** barbarism, infelicity; corruption; antiphrasis, spoonerism, malapropism 975.7

VERBS **3** solecize, commit a solecism, use faulty *or* inadmissable *or* inappropriate grammar, ignore *or* disdain *or* violate grammar, murder the King's *or* Queen's English, break Priscian's head

ADJS **4** **ungrammatic, ungrammatical,** solecistic, solecistical, **incorrect,** barbarous; faulty, erroneous 975.16; infelicitous, improper 789.7; careless, slovenly, slipshod 810.15; loose, imprecise 975.17

532 DICTION

NOUNS **1** **diction,** words, wordage, verbiage, word-usage, **usage,** *usus loquendi* <L>, use *or* choice of words, formulation, way of putting *or* couching, word garment, word dressing; **rhetoric,** speech, talk <nf>; **language,** dialect, parlance, locution, expression, **grammar** 530; **idiom;** composition

2 **style; mode, manner,** strain, vein; fashion, way; **rhetoric; manner of speaking,** mode of expression, literary style, style of writing, command of language *or* idiom, form of speech, expression of ideas; feeling for words *or* language, way with words, sense of language, *Sprachgefühl* <Ger>; gift of gab *or* of the gab <nf>, blarney *or* the blarney <nf>; the power *or* grace of expression; linguistic tact *or* finesse; personal style; mannerism, trick, pecularity; affectation; editorial style; inflation, exaggeration, grandiloquence 545; the grand style, the sublime style, the sublime; the plain style; **stylistics,** stylistic analysis

3 stylist, master of style; rhetorician, rhetor, rhetorizer ; mannerist; wordsmith; phrasemonger

VERBS **4** **phrase, express,** find a phrase for, give expression *or* words to, **word,** state, **frame,** conceive, style, couch, **put in** *or* **into words,** clothe *or* embody in words, couch in terms, express by *or* in words, find words to express, find words for; put, present, set out; **formulate,** formularize; paragraph; rhetorize

ADJS **5** **phrased,** expressed, worded, formulated, styled, put, presented, couched; stylistic, overdone

533 ELEGANCE

<of language>

NOUNS **1** **elegance,** elegancy; **grace,** gracefulness, gracility; **taste,** tastefulness, good taste; **correctness,** seemliness, comeliness, **propriety,** aptness, fittingness; **refinement,** precision, exactitude, lapidary quality, finish; **discrimination,** choice; **restraint; polish, finish,** terseness, neatness; smoothness, flow, **fluency; felicity,** felicitousness, **ease;** clarity, clearness, lucidity, limpidity, pellucidity, perspicuity; distinction, dignity; **purity,** chastity, chasteness; **plainness,** straightforwardness, directness, **simplicity,** naturalness, unaffectedness, Atticism, unadorned simplicity, gracility, Attic quality; classicism, classicalism; well-rounded *or* well-turned periods, flowing periods; the right word in the right place, right word at the right time, *mot juste* <Fr>; fittingness, appropriateness; classicism, Atticism

2 **harmony, proportion,** symmetry, **balance,** equilibrium, order, orderedness, measure, measuredness, concinnity; rhythm; **euphony,** sweetness, beauty

3 <affected elegance> **affectation,** affectedness, studiedness, **pretentiousness, mannerism,** posiness <Brit>, preciosity, manneredness, artifice, artfulness, **artificiality,** unnaturalness; **euphuism,** Gongorism, Marinism; **preciousness,** preciosity; euphemism; purism; overelegance, overelaboration, overniceness, overrefinement, hyperelegance, etc

4 purist, classicist, Atticist, plain stylist

5 euphuist, Gongorist, Marinist, *précieux* and *précieuse* <Fr>; phrasemaker, phrasemonger

ADJS **6** **elegant, tasteful, graceful, polished,** finished, round, terse;

neat, trim, **refined, exact,** lapidary *or* lapidarian; **restrained; clear,** lucid, limpid, pellucid, perspicuous; **simple, unaffected, natural,** unlabored, fluent, flowing, **easy; pure,** chaste; **plain,** straightforward, direct, unadorned, gracile, no-frills *and* vanilla *and* plain vanilla <nf>; classic, classical; Attic, Ciceronian, Augustan

7 **appropriate, fit, fitting,** just , **proper, correct, seemly,** comely; **felicitous,** happy, **apt, well-chosen; well-put,** well-expressed, inspired

8 **harmonious, balanced,** symmetrical, orderly, ordered, measured, concinnate, concinnous; **euphonious,** euphonic, euphonical , sweet; **smooth,** tripping, smooth-sounding, fluent, flowing, fluid; classical

9 <affectedly elegant> **affected,** euphuistic, euphuistical; elaborate, elaborated; **pretentious, mannered, artificial, unnatural,** posy <Brit>, studied; precious, *précieux* or *précieuse* <Fr>, deluxe, overnice, overrefined, overelegant, overelaborate, hyperelegant, etc; Gongoristic, Gongoresque, Marinistic

534 INELEGANCE
<of language>

NOUNS **1** **inelegance,** inelegancy; inconcinnity , infelicity; **clumsiness,** cumbrousness, clunkiness *and* klutziness <nf>, leadenness, heavy-handedness, ham-handedness, ham-fistedness <chiefly Brit>, heavy-footedness, heaviness, stiltedness, **ponderousness,** unwieldiness; sesquipedalianism, sesquipedality; turgidity, bombasticness, pompousness 545.1; **gracelessness,** ungracefulness; **tastelessness,** bad taste, impropriety, indecorousness, unseemliness; incorrectness, impurity; **vulgarity,** vulgarism, Gothicism , barbarism, barbarousness, **coarseness, unrefinement,** roughness, grossness, rudeness, crudeness, uncouthness; turgidity; dysphemism; solecism; cacology, poor diction; cacophony, uneuphoniousness, harshness; loose *or* slipshod construction, ill-balanced sentences; lack of finish *or* polish

ADJS **2** inelegant, clumsy, clunky *and* **klutzy** <nf>, heavy-handed, heavy-footed, ham-handed, ham-fisted <chiefly Brit>, graceless, ungraceful, inconcinnate *and* inconcinnous , infelicitous, unfelicitous; **tasteless,** in bad taste, offensive to ears polite; **incorrect, improper; indecorous, unseemly,** uncourtly, undignified; **unpolished, unrefined;** impure, unclassical; **vulgar,** barbarous, barbaric, rude, **crude, uncouth,** Doric, outlandish; low, gross, **coarse,** dysphemistic, doggerel; cacologic, cacological, cacophonous, uneuphonious, harsh, ill-sounding; solecistic

3 **stiff, stilted, formal,** Latinate, *guindé* <Fr>, **labored,** ponderous, elephantine, lumbering, cumbrous, leaden, heavy, unwieldy, sesquipedalian, inkhorn, turgid, bombastic, pompous 545.8; **forced,** awkward, cramped, halting; crabbed

535 PLAIN SPEECH

NOUNS **1** **plain speech,** plain speaking, plain-spokenness, plain style, unadorned style, gracility, **plain English,** plain words, common speech, vernacular, household words, words of one syllable; plainness, simpleness, simplicity; soberness, restrainedness; severity, austerity; spareness, leanness, baldness, bareness, starkness, unadornedness, naturalness, unaffectedness; **directness, straightforwardness,** calling a spade a spade, mincing no words, making no bones about it <nf>; unimaginativeness, prosaicness, matter-of-factness, prosiness, unpoeticalness; homespun, rustic style; **candor,** frankness, openness

VERBS **2** **speak plainly,** waste no words, **call a spade a spade,** come to the point, lay it on the line, not beat about the bush, mince no words, make no bones about it *and* talk turkey <nf>

ADJS **3** **plain-speaking,** simple-speaking; **plain,** common; plain-spoken; simple, unadorned, unvarnished, pure, neat; sober, severe, austere, ascetic, spare, lean, bald, bare, stark, Spartan; **natural, unaffected;** direct, straightforward, woman-to-woman, man-to-man, one-on-one; commonplace, homely, homespun, rustic; **candid,** up-front <nf>, plain-spoken, frank, straight-out <nf>, open; **prosaic,** prosing, prosy; unpoetical, unimaginative, dull, dry, matter-of-fact; point-blank

ADVS **4** **plainly, simply,** naturally, unaffectedly, matter-of-factly; in plain words, plain-spokenly, **in plain English,** in words of one syllable; **directly,** point-blank, to the point; candidly, frankly

PHRS **5** read my lips, I'll spell it out

536 FIGURE OF SPEECH

NOUNS **1** **figure of speech, figure, image,** trope, turn of expression, manner *or* way of speaking, ornament, device, flourish, flower; purple passage; imagery, nonliterality, nonliteralness, figurativeness, figurative language; figured *or* florid *or* flowery style, Gongorism, floridity, euphuism

VERBS **2** metaphorize, figure ; similize; personify, personalize; symbolize

ADJS **3** **figurative,** tropologic, tropological; **metaphorical,** trolatitious; allusive, referential; mannered, figured, ornamented, **flowery** 545.11

ADVS **4** **figuratively,** tropologically; **metaphorically;** symbolically; **figuratively speaking,** so to say *or* speak, in a manner of speaking, **as it were**

537 CONCISENESS

NOUNS **1** **conciseness,** concision, briefness, brachylogy, **brevity**; shortness, compactness; **curtness,** brusqueness, **crispness, terseness,** summariness; compression; taciturnity 344.2, reserve 344.3; **pithiness,** succinctness, pointedness, sententiousness; compendiousness; heart of the matter

2 laconicness, laconism, laconicism, economy of language *or* words; laconics; Atticism; commatism

3 **aphorism, epigram** 974.1; **abridgment** 557

4 **abbreviation,** shortening, clipping, cutting, pruning, truncation; ellipsis, aposiopesis, contraction, syncope, apocope, elision, crasis, syneresis <all rhetoric>

VERBS **5** **be brief, come to the point,** get to the bottom line *or* the nitty-gritty <nf>, **make a long story short,** cut the matter short, cut the shit <nf>, be telegraphic, waste no words, put it in few words, give more matter *and* less art; shorten, condense, **abbreviate** 268.6

ADJS **6** **concise, brief, short, condensed, compressed,** tight, close, compact; compendious 268.8; curt, brusque, **crisp, terse,** summary; taciturn 344.9; reserved 344.10; **pithy, succinct; laconic,** Spartan; **abridged, abbreviated,** vest-pocket, synopsized, shortened, clipped, cut, pruned, contracted, truncated, docked; elliptic, syncopic, aposiopestic; telegraphic; sententious, epigrammatic, epigrammatical, gnomic, aphoristic *or* aphoristical, **pointed,** to the point; brachylogous; encapsuled

ADVS **7** **concisely, briefly,** shortly, standing on one leg; laconically; curtly, brusquely, crisply, tersely, summarily; pithily, succinctly, pointedly; sententiously, aphoristically, epigrammatically

8 **in brief, in short, for short,** *tout court* <Fr>; in substance, in epitome, in outline; **in a nutshell,** in a capsule; **in a word,** in two words, in a few words, without wasting *or* mincing words; **to be brief,** to the point, to sum up, to come to the point, to cut the matter short, **to make a long story short**

538 DIFFUSENESS

NOUNS **1** **diffuseness,** diffusiveness, diffusion; shapelessness,

formlessness 263, amorphousness, blobbiness <nf>, unstructuredness; obscurity 522.3

2 **wordiness, verbosity,** verbiage, verbalism, verbality; **prolixity, long-windedness,** longiloquence, loquacity; flow *or* flux of words, cloud of words; profuseness, **profusiveness,** profusion; **effusiveness,** effusion, gush, gushing; outpour, tirade; logorrhea, verbal diarrhea, diarrhea of the mouth, **talkativeness** 540; **copiousness, exuberance,** rampancy, amplitude, extravagance, prodigality, fertility, fecundity, rankness, teemingness, prolificity, prolificacy, productivity, abundance, overflow, fluency ; superfluity, superflux, superabundance, overflow, inundation; **redundancy,** pleonasm, repetitiveness, reiterativeness, reiteration, iteration, tautology, macrology, double-talk; repetition for effect *or* emphasis, palilogy

3 discursiveness, desultoriness, digressiveness, aimlessness; **rambling**, maundering, meandering, wandering, roving

4 **digression, departure,** deviation, **discursion,** excursion, excursus, sidetrack, side path, side road, byway, bypath; episode; rambling; segue

5 **circumlocution, roundaboutness,** circuitousness, ambages ; deviousness, obliqueness, **indirection;** periphrase, periphrasis; ambagiousness

6 **amplification, expatiation, enlargement, expansion,** dilation, dilatation, dilating; **elaboration, laboring; development,** explication, unfolding, working-out, fleshing-out, detailing, filling in the empty places, filler, padding

VERBS 7 **amplify, expatiate, dilate, expand,** enlarge, **enlarge upon,** expand on, **elaborate;** relate *or* rehearse in extenso; detail, particularize; **develop,** open out, fill in, flesh out, evolve, unfold; work out, explicate; descant, relate at large

8 **protract, extend, spin out,** string out, draw out, stretch out, go on *or* be on about, **drag out,** run out, drive into the ground <nf>; pad, fill out; perorate; **speak at length,** spin a long yarn, never finish; verbify, chatter, talk one to death 540.6

9 **digress,** wander, **get off the subject, wander from the subject,** get sidetracked, excurse, ramble, maunder, stray, go astray; depart, **deviate,** turn aside, jump the track; **go off on a tangent,** go up blind alleys; segue

10 circumlocute <nf>, say in a roundabout way, talk in circles, **go round about,** go around *and* around, **beat around** *or* **about the bush,** go round Robin Hood's barn; periphrase

ADJS 11 **diffuse,** diffusive; **formless** 263.4, unstructured; **profuse,** profusive; **effusive,** gushing, gushy; copious, exuberant, extravagant, prodigal, fecund, teeming, prolific, productive, abundant, superabundant, overflowing; **redundant,** pleonastic, repetitive, reiterative, iterative, tautologous, parrotlike

12 **wordy, verbose; talkative** 540.9; **prolix,** windy <nf>, **long-winded,** longiloquent; **protracted,** extended, *de longue haleine* <Fr>, lengthy, long, **long-drawn-out,** long-spun, spun-out, endless, unrelenting; padded, filled out

13 **discursive, aimless,** loose; **rambling, maundering, wandering,** peripatetic, roving, deviating; excursive, discursive, **digressive,** deviative, **desultory,** episodic; by the way; sidetracked

14 **circumlocutory,** circumlocutional, **roundabout, circuitous,** ambagious , oblique, indirect; periphrastic

15 **expatiating,** dilative, dilatative, enlarging, amplifying, expanding; **developmental;** garrulous

ADVS 16 **at length,** *ad nauseam* <L>, at large, in full, *in extenso* <L>, in detail, on and on

539 AMBIGUITY

NOUNS 1 **ambiguity,** ambiguousness; **equivocalness,** equivocacy, equivocality; **double meaning,** amphibology, multivocality, polysemy, polysemousness; punning, paronomasia;

double reference, double entendre; twilight zone, gray area; six of one *and* half dozen of the other; inexplicitness, uncertainty 971; irony, contradiction, oxymoron, enantiosis; levels of meaning, richness of meaning, complexity of meaning

2 <ambiguous word *or* expression> **ambiguity,** equivoque, equivocal, equivocality; equivocation, amphibology, double entendre; counterword, portmanteau word; polysemant; weasel word; squinting construction; pun 489.8

VERBS 3 equivocate, weasel; ironize; have mixed feelings, be uncertain 971.9

ADJS 4 **ambiguous, equivocal,** equivocatory, dilogical; multivocal, polysemous, polysemantic, amphibolous, amphibological; two-edged, two-sided, either-or, betwixt and between; bittersweet, mixed; inexplicit, uncertain 971.16; ironic; obscure, mysterious, funny, funny peculiar <nf>, enigmatic 522.17

540 TALKATIVENESS

NOUNS 1 **talkativeness, loquacity,** loquaciousness; overtalkativeness, loose tongue, runaway tongue, big mouth <nf>; gabbiness *and* windiness *and* gassiness <nf>; **garrulousness,** garrulity; **long-windedness, prolixity, verbosity** 538.2; multiloquence, multiloquy; **volubility, fluency, glibness;** fluent tongue, flowing tongue, **gift of gab** <nf>; openness, candor, frankness 644.4; effusion, gush, slush; gushiness, **effusiveness,** communicativeness; flow *or* flux *or* spate of words; *flux de bouche* and *flux de mots* and *flux de paroles* <Fr>; **communicativeness** 343.3; gregariousness, sociability, conversableness 343.3

2 **logomania, logorrhea, diarrhea of the mouth, verbal diarrhea,** *cacoëthes loquendi* and *furor loquendi* <L>, blathering, gift of gab

3 **chatter, jabber,** gibber, **babble,** babblement, prate, **prating, prattle, palaver,** small talk, chat, natter <Brit>, **gabble, gab** *and* jaw-jaw <nf>, **blab, blabber,** blather, blether, blethers, clatter, clack, cackle, talkee-talkee; *caquet* and *caqueterie* and *bavardage* <Fr>, twaddle, twattle, **gibble-gabble, bibble-babble, chitter-chatter, prittle-prattle, tittle-tattle,** mere talk, idle talk *or* chatter; **guff** *and* **gas** *and* **hot air** *and* blah-blah *and* yak *and* yakkety-yak *and* blah-blah-blah <nf>; watercooler moment; **gossip;** nonsense 520.2

4 **chatterer, chatterbox, babbler, jabberer, prater, prattler, gabbler,** gibble-gabbler, **gabber** <nf>, **blabberer, blabber,** blatherer, patterer, word-slinger, *moulin à paroles* <Fr>, blab, rattle, bigmouth; magpie, jay, informer; **windbag** *and* gasbag *and* windjammer *and* hot-air artist *and* motor-mouth *and* ratchet-jaw *and* blabbermouth<nf>; idle chatterer, talkative person, **big** *or* **great talker** <nf>, nonstop talker, spendthrift of one's tongue

VERBS 5 **chatter, chat, prate, prattle, patter,** palaver, **babble, gab** <nf>, natter <Brit>, **gabble, gibble-gabble,** tittle-tattle, **jabber,** gibber, **blab, blabber, blather,** blether, clatter, twaddle, twattle, rattle, clack, haver <Brit>, dither, spout *or* **spout off** <nf>, hold forth, pour forth, spin out, **gush,** have a big mouth <nf>, love the sound of one's own voice, talk to hear one's head rattle <nf>; **jaw** *and* **gas** *and* yak *and* **yakkety-yak** *and* run off at the mouth *and* beat one's gums <nf>, **shoot off one's mouth** *or* **face** <nf>; reel off; **talk on,** talk away, **go on** <nf>, run on, rattle on, run on like a mill race; ramble on; talk oneself hoarse, talk till one is blue in the face, talk oneself out of breath; **talk too much; gossip;** talk nonsense 520.5

6 <nf terms> **talk one to death, talk one's head** *or* **ear off,** talk one deaf *and* dumb, talk one into a fever, talk the hind leg off a mule, like the sound of one's own voice, oil one's tongue, talk till one is blue in the face

7 **outtalk,** outspeak, **talk down,** outlast; filibuster

8 be loquacious *or* garrulous, be a windbag *or* gasbag <nf>; have a big mouth *or* bazoo <nf>

ADJS 9 **talkative, loquacious, talky,** big-mouthed <nf>, long-tongued, overtalkative, garrulous, running on, chatty; gossipy, newsy; gabby *and* windy *and* gassy <nf>, all jaw <nf>; multiloquent, multiloquious; **long-winded, prolix, verbose** 538.12; **voluble, fluent; glib,** flip <nf>, smooth; candid, frank 644.17; **effusive,** gushy; expansive, **communicative;** conversational; gregarious, sociable

10 **chattering, prattling, prating,** gabbling, jabbering, gibbering, babbling, blabbing, blabbering, blathering, babblative

ADVS 11 **talkatively, loquaciously,** garrulously; **volubly, fluently,** glibly; effusively, expansively, gushingly

541 CONVERSATION

NOUNS 1 **conversation, converse,** conversing, rapping <nf>; interlocution, colloquy; **exchange;** verbal intercourse, conversational interchange, interchange of speech, give-and-take, cross-talk, rapping <nf>, **repartee,** backchat; **discourse,** colloquial discourse; **communion, intercourse,** social intercourse, **communication** 343

2 **talk, palaver, speech, words;** confabulation, **confab** <nf>, banter, repartee; **chinfest** *and* **chinwag** *and* **talkfest** *and* **bull session** <nf>; **dialogue,** duologue, trialogue; **interview,** question-and-answer session, audience, audition, interlocution; interrogation, examination

3 **chat,** cozy chat, friendly chat *or* talk, **little talk,** coze, causerie, **visit** <nf>, gam, *tête-à-tête* <Fr>, **heart-to-heart talk** *or* heart-to-heart; pillow-talk, intimate discourse, backchat

4 **chitchat,** chitter-chatter, tittle-tattle, **small talk,** by-talk, cocktail-party chitchat, beauty-parlor chitchat, tea-table talk, table talk, idle chat *or* talk, gossip, backchat

5 **conference, congress, convention, parley, palaver, confab** <nf>, confabulation, **conclave, powwow, huddle** <nf>, **consultation,** colloquium, *pourparler* <Fr>, **meeting;** session, sitting, sit-down <nf>, séance; exchange *or* interchange of views; **council,** council of war; **discussion; interview, audience; news conference,** press conference; photo opportunity, photo op <nf>; high-level talk, conference at the summit, summit, summit conference; summitry; negotiations, bargaining, bargaining session; confrontation, eyeball-to-eyeball encounter <nf>; teleconference; council fire; conference table, negotiating table

6 **discussion, debate,** debating, **deliberation, nonformalogue,** exchange of views, canvassing, ventilation, airing, review, **treatment, consideration,** investigation, **examination, study, analysis,** logical analysis; logical discussion, dialectic; buzz session <nf>, rap *or* rap session <nf>; **panel,** panel discussion, open discussion, joint discussion, symposium, colloquium, conference, seminar; **forum,** open forum, town meeting; polemics

7 **conversationalist,** converser, conversationist; talker, discourser, verbalist, confabulator; colloquist, colloquialist, collocutor; conversational partner; interlocutor, interlocutress *or* interlocutrice *or* interlocutrix; parleyer, palaverer; dialogist; Dr Johnson; interviewer, examiner, interrogator, cross-examiner; chatterer

VERBS 8 **converse, talk together, talk** *or* **speak with,** converse with, strike up a conversation, visit with <nf>, discourse with, **commune with,** communicate with, take counsel with, commerce with, **have a talk with,** have a word with, **chin** <nf>, **chew the rag** *or* **fat** <nf>, **shoot the breeze** <nf>, hold *or* carry on *or* join in *or* engage in a conversation, exchange words; confabulate, confab <nf>, parley; colloque, colloquize; **bandy words; communicate** 343.6,7

9 **chat, visit** <nf>, gam, coze, pass the time of day, touch base with, have a friendly *or* cozy chat; **have a little talk,** have a heart-to-heart, let one's hair down; talk with one in private, talk tête-à-tête, be closeted with, make conversation *or* talk, engage in small talk; prattle, prittle-prattle, tittle-tattle; **gossip**

10 **confer,** hold a conference, parley, palaver, powwow, hold talks, hold a summit, sit down together, meet around the conference table, **go into a huddle** <nf>, deliberate, take counsel, counsel, **lay** *or* **put heads together;** collogue; **confer with,** sit down with, **consult with, advise with, discuss with, take up with,** reason with; **discuss,** talk over; **consult,** refer to, call in; compare notes, exchange observations *or* views; have conversations; negotiate, bargain

11 **discuss, debate, reason, deliberate,** deliberate upon, exchange views *or* opinions, talk, **talk over, hash over** <nf>, talk of *or* about, rap <nf>, exchange ideas, colloquize, comment upon, reason about, discourse about, **consider, treat,** dissertate on, handle, deal with, take up, **go into, examine,** investigate, talk out, brainstorm, **analyze,** sift, **study,** canvass, review, pass under review, controvert, ventilate, air, thrash *or* thresh out, hammer out, reason the point, consider the pros *and* cons; **kick** *or* **knock around** <nf>; talk shop, talk turkey

ADJS 12 conversational, colloquial, confabulatory, interlocutory; communicative; chatty, chitchatty, cozy

ADVS 13 conversationally, colloquially; *tête-à-tête* <Fr>

542 SOLILOQUY

NOUNS 1 **soliloquy,** monology, self-address; **monologue;** aside; solo; monodrama; monody; interior monologue, stream of consciousness, apostrophe, aside; one-man *or* –woman show

2 **soliloquist,** soliloquizer, Hamlet; monodist, **monologist**

VERBS 3 **soliloquize,** monologize; **talk to oneself,** say to oneself, tell oneself, think out loud *or* aloud; address the four walls, talk to the wall; have an audience of one; say aside, apostrophize; do all the talking, monopolize the conversation, hold forth without interruption

ADJS 4 soliloquizing, monologic, monological, self-addressing; apostrophic; soloistic; monodramatic; thinking aloud, talking to oneself

543 PUBLIC SPEAKING

NOUNS 1 **public speaking, declamation, speechmaking, speaking,** speechification <nf>, lecturing, speeching; after-dinner speaking; **oratory,** platform oratory *or* speaking; campaign oratory, stump speaking, the stump, the hustings <Brit>; the soap box; **elocution; rhetoric,** art of public speaking; **eloquence** 544; forensics, **debating;** speechcraft, wordcraft; **preaching,** pulpit oratory, Bible-thumping <nf>, the pulpit, homiletics; demagogism, demagogy <chiefly Brit>, demagoguery, rabble-rousing; **pyrotechnics**

2 **speech,** speeching, speechification <nf>, **talk, oration, address,** declamation, harangue; public speech *or* address, formal speech, set speech, prepared speech *or* text; welcoming address, farewell address; campaign speech, stump speech, stump oratory; soapbox oratory, tub-thumping <nf>; say; **tirade,** screed, **diatribe,** jeremiad, philippic, invective; after-dinner speech; funeral oration, eulogy; allocution, exhortation, hortatory address, forensic, forensic address; **recitation,** recital, reading; salutatory, salutatory address; valediction, valedictory, valedictory address; inaugural address, inaugural; chalk talk <nf>; pep talk <nf>; pitch, sales talk 734.5; talkathon, filibuster; peroration; debate

3 **lecture,** prelection, **discourse; sermon,** sermonette, homily, religious

or pulpit discourse, talk; preachment, preaching, preachification <nf>; **evangelism,** televison *or* TV evangelism; travel talk, travelogue

4 **speaker, talker, public speaker, speechmaker,** speecher, speechifier <nf>, spieler *and* jawsmith <nf>; after-dinner speaker, keynote speaker; **spokesperson,** spokesman, spokeswoman; **demagogue,** rabble-rouser; declaimer, ranter, tub-thumper <nf>, haranguer, spouter <nf>; valedictorian, salutatorian; panelist, debater

5 **lecturer,** praelector, discourser, reader, professor; **preacher;** sermonizer, sermonist, sermoner, homilist , pulpitarian, pulpiteer <nf>, Boanerges, hellfire preacher; **evangelist,** televison *or* TV evangelist, televangelist; **expositor,** expounder; chalk talker <nf>

6 **orator, public speaker,** platform orator *or* speaker; rhetorician, rhetor; silver-tongued orator, **spellbinder;** Demosthenes, Cicero, Franklin D Roosevelt, Winston Churchill, William Jennings Bryan, Martin Luther King; **soapbox orator,** soapboxer, stump orator

7 **elocutionist,** elocutioner; **recitationist,** reciter, diseur, diseuse; reader; improvisator

8 **rhetorician,** teacher of rhetoric, rhetor, elocutionist; speechwriter

VERBS 9 **make a speech, give a talk, deliver an address,** speechify <nf>, **speak, talk, discourse; address;** stump <nf>, go on *or* take the stump; platform, soapbox; take the floor

10 **declaim,** hold forth, **orate,** elocute <nf>, spout <nf>, spiel <nf>, mouth; **harangue, rant,** tub-thump, perorate, rodomontade; **recite,** read; debate; demagogue, rabble-rouse

11 **lecture,** prelect, read *or* deliver a lectue; **preach,** Bible-thump *and* preachify <nf>, **sermonize,** read a sermon

ADJS 12 **declamatory, elocutionary, oratorical, rhetorical,** forensic; eloquent 544.8; demagogic, demagogical

544 ELOQUENCE

NOUNS 1 **eloquence, rhetoric, silver tongue,** eloquent tongue, facundity; disertitude; **articulateness;** gift of gab <nf>, **glibness,** smoothness, slickness; **felicitousness,** felicity; **oratory** 543.1; expression, **expressiveness,** command of words *or* language, gift of gab *or* of the gab <nf>, gift of expression, vividness, graphicness; pleasing *or* effective style; **meaningfulness** 518.5

2 **fluency,** flow; **smoothness, facility, ease; grace,** gracefulness, poetry; **elegance** 533

3 **vigor, force,** power, strength, vitality, drive, sinew, sinewiness, nervousness, nervosity, vigorousness, forcefulness, effectiveness, impressiveness, pizzazz *and* punch *and* clout <nf>; incisiveness, trenchancy, cuttingness, poignancy, bitingness, bite, mordancy; strong language

4 **spirit,** pep <nf>, liveliness, raciness, sparkle, vivacity, dash, verve, vividness; piquancy, poignancy, pungency

5 **vehemence, passion,** impassionedness, enthusiasm, **ardor,** ardency, **fervor,** fervency, fire, fieriness, glow, warmth, heat

6 **loftiness,** elevation, sublimity; grandeur, **nobility,** stateliness, majesty, gravity, *gravitas* <L>, solemnity, **dignity**

VERBS 7 **have the gift of gab** *or* **of the gab** <nf>, have a tongue in one's head; **spellbind;** shine

ADJS 8 **eloquent, silver-tongued,** silver; well-speaking, well-spoken, **articulate,** facund; **glib, smooth,** smooth-spoken, smooth-tongued, **slick; felicitous;** facile, slick as a whistle <nf>, spellbinding; Demosthenic, Demosthenian; Ciceronian

9 **fluent, flowing,** tripping; **smooth,** pleasing, facile, **easy, graceful, elegant** 533.6

10 **expressive, graphic, vivid,** suggestive, imaginative; well-turned; meaningful 518.10

11 **vigorous,** strong, **powerful,** imperative, **forceful,** forcible, vital, driving, sinewy, sinewed, punchy *and*

full of piss and vinegar *and* zappy <nf>, **striking, telling, effective,** impressive; incisive, trenchant, cutting, biting, piercing, poignant, penetrating, slashing, mordant, acid, corrosive; sensational

12 **spirited, lively,** peppy *and* gingery <nf>, racy, sparkling, vivacious; piquant, poignant, pungent

13 **vehement,** emphatic, **passionate, impassioned,** enthusiastic, **ardent,** fiery, **fervent,** burning, glowing, warm; urgent, stirring, exciting, stimulating, provoking

14 **lofty, elevated, sublime, grand, majestic,** noble, stately, grave, solemn, dignified; serious, weighty; moving, inspiring

ADVS 15 **eloquently; fluently,** smoothly, glibly, trippingly on the tongue; **expressively,** vividly, graphically; **meaningfully** 518.13; **vigorously,** powerfully, forcefully, spiritedly; tellingly, strikingly, effectively, impressively; **vehemently, passionately,** ardently, fervently, warmly, glowingly, in glowing terms

545 GRANDILOQUENCE

NOUNS 1 **grandiloquence,** magniloquence, lexiphanicism, **pompousness,** pomposity, orotundity; **rhetoric;** mere rhetoric, rhetoricalness; high-flown diction, big *or* tall talk <nf>; grandioseness, grandiosity; loftiness, stiltedness; fulsomeness; **pretentiousness,** pretension, **affectation** 533.3; ostentation; **flamboyancy,** showiness, flashiness, gaudiness, meretriciousness, bedizenment, **glitz** <nf>, garishness; sensationalism, luridness, Barnumism; **inflation, inflatedness,** swollenness, turgidity, turgescence, flatulence *or* flatulency, tumidness, tumidity; sententiousness, pontification; swollen phrase *or* diction, swelling utterance; platitudinous ponderosity, polysyllabic profundity, pompous prolixity; Johnsonese; prose run mad; convolution, tortuosity, tortuousness, ostentatious complexity *or* profundity

2 **bombast,** bombastry, pomposity, **fustian,** highfalutin <nf>, **rant,** rodomontade; **hot air** <nf>; balderdash, gobbledygook <nf>, purple prose, claptrap

3 high-sounding words, lexiphanicism, hard words; **sesquipedalian word,** big *or* long word, twodollar *or* five-dollar word <nf>, **jawbreaker,** jawtwister, mouthful; antidisestablishmentarianism, honorificabilitudinitatibus, pneumonoultramicroscopicsilicovolcanoconiosis; polysyllabism, sesquipedalianism, sesquipedality; Latinate diction; academese, technical jargon; puff piece

4 **ornateness, floweriness,** floridness, floridity, lushness, luxuriance; flourish, flourish of rhetoric, flowers of speech *or* rhetoric, **purple patches** *or* **passages,** beauties, fine writing; **ornament,** ornamentation, **adornment, embellishment,** elegant variation, **embroidery, frill,** colors *or* colors of rhetoric , figure, **figure of speech** 536

5 **phrasemonger,** rhetorician; phraseman, phrasemaker, fine writer, wordspinner; euphuist, Gongorist, Marinist; pedant

VERBS 6 **talk big** <nf>, talk highfalutin <nf>, phrasemake, **pontificate, blow** <nf>, **vapor,** Barnumize; inflate, bombast, lay *or* pile it on <nf>, lay it on thick *and* lay it on with a trowel <nf>; smell of the lamp

7 **ornament, decorate, adorn, embellish, embroider,** enrich; overcharge, overlay, overload, load with ornament, festoon, weight down with ornament, flourish ; **gild,** gild the lily, trick out, varnish; paint in glowing colors, tell in glowing terms; elaborate, convolute, involve

ADJS 8 **grandiloquent,** magniloquent, **pompous, orotund; grandiose;** fulsome; lofty, elevated, tall <nf>, **stilted; pretentious, affected** 533.9; overblown, overdone, overwrought; **showy, flashy, ostentatious,** gaudy, glitzy <nf>, meretricious, flamboyant, flaming, bedizened, flaunting, garish; lurid, sensational, sensationalistic; **high-flown, high-falutin** <nf>, high-flying; high-flowing, **high-sounding, big-sounding,** great-sounding, grandisonant , sonorous; **rhetorical,** declamatory; **pedantic,** inkhorn, lexiphanic ; sententious, Johnsonian; convoluted, tortuous, labyrinthine, overelaborate, overinvolved; euphuistic, Gongoresque

9 **bombastic,** fustian, mouthy, **inflated, swollen,** swelling, turgid, turgescent, tumid, tumescent, flatulent, windy *and* gassy <nf>; overadorned, fulsome

10 sesquipedalian, sesquipedal, polysyllabic, jawbreaking *and* jawtwisting <nf>

11 **ornate,** purple <nf>, colored, **fancy;** adorned, **embellished, embroidered,** lavish, decorated, festooned, overcharged, overloaded, befrilled, flashy; **flowery, florid,** lush, luxuriant; figured, **figurative** 536.3

ADVS 12 **grandiloquently,** magniloquently, **pompously,** grandiosely, fulsomely, loftily, stiltedly, pretentiously; **ostentatiously,** showily; **bombastically,** turgidly, tumidly, flatulently, windily <nf>

13 **ornately,** fancily; **flowerily,** floridly

546 LETTER

NOUNS 1 **letter, written character, character, sign, symbol,** graph, digraph, grapheme, allograph, alphabetic character *or* symbol, phonetic character *or* symbol; diacritic, diacritical mark, vowel point; logographic *or* lexigraphic character *or* symbol; ideographic *or* ideogrammic *or* ideogrammatic character *or* symbol; initial; syllabic character *or* symbol, syllabic, syllabogram; pictographic character *or* symbol; cipher, device; monogram; graphy, *mater lectionis* <L>; **writing** 547

2 <phonetic *and* ideographic symbols> **phonogram;** phonetic symbol; **logogram,** logograph, grammalogue; word letter; **ideogram,** ideograph, phonetic, radical, determinative; **pictograph,** pictogram; **hieroglyphic,** hieroglyph, hieratic symbol, demotic character; **rune,** runic character *or* symbol; **cuneiform, character;** wedge, arrowhead, ogham; kana, hiragana, katakana; kanji; **shorthand** 547.8; hieroglyphics

3 **writing system, script, letters; alphabet,** letters of the alphabet, **ABC's;** christcross-row; **phonetic alphabet,** International Phonetic Alphabet *or* IPA; Initial Teaching Alphabet; phonemic alphabet; phonetic alphabet; runic alphabet, futhark *or* futharc; alphabetism; **syllabary;** alphabetics, alphabetology, graphemics; paleography; speech sound 524.12

4 **spelling,** orthography; phonetic spelling *or* respelling, phonetics, phonography; normalization; spelling reform; spelling match *or* bee, spelldown; bad spelling, cacography; spelling pronunciation

5 **lettering,** initialing; **inscription,** epigraph, graffito, printing, calligraphy; handwriting; alphabetization; transliteration, romanization, pinyin *or* pinyin, Wade-Giles system; transcription; phonetic transcription, phonography, lexigraphy

VERBS 6 **letter, initial, inscribe,** character, sign, mark; **capitalize; alphabetize,** alphabet; transliterate, transcribe

7 **spell,** orthographize; spell *or* respell phonetically; spell out, write out, trace out; spell backward; outspell, spell down; syllabify, syllabize, syllable, syllabicate

ADJS 8 **literal, lettered; alphabetic, alphabetical;** abecedarian; graphemic, allographic; large-lettered, majuscule, majuscular, uncial; **capital,** capitalized, upper-case; small-lettered, minuscule, minuscular, lower-case; logographic, logogrammatic, lexigraphic, ideographic, ideogrammic, ideogrammatic, pictographic; transliterated, transcribed; orthographic, spelled; symbolical, phonogramic, phonographic, cuneiform, cuneal, hieroglyphic, hieroglyphical

547 WRITING

NOUNS **1 writing,** scrivening *or* scrivenery , inscription, lettering; engrossment; pen, **pen-and-ink;** inkslinging *and* ink spilling <nf>, pen *or* pencil driving *or* pushing <nf>; **typing, typewriting;** macrography, micrography; stroke *or* dash of the pen, *coup de plume* <Fr>; secret writing, cryptography 345.6; **alphabet, writing system** 546.3; texting

2 authorship, writing, authorcraft, pencraft, wordsmanship, **composition,** the art of composition, inditing, inditement; one's pen; **creative writing,** literary art, verbal art, literary composition, literary production, verse-writing, short-story writing, novel-writing, playwriting, drama-writing; essay-writing; **expository writing;** technical writing; journalism, newspaper writing, investigative reporting, editorial-writing, feature-writing, rewriting; magazine writing; citizen journalism; blogging; content creation; **songwriting**, lyric-writing, libretto-writing; artistry, literary power, literary artistry, literary talent *or* flair, skill with words *or* language, facility in writing, ready pen; **writer's itch,** graphomania, scribblemania, graphorrhea, *cacoëthes scribendi* <L>; automatic writing; writer's cramp, graphospasm

3 handwriting, hand, script, fist <nf>, chirography, **calligraphy,** autography; **manuscript,** scrive; **autograph,** holograph; **penmanship,** penscript, pencraft; stylography; graphology, graphanalysis, graphometry; paleography

4 handwriting style; **printing,** hand-printing, block letter, **lettering; stationery; writing materials,** paper, foolscap, note paper, pad, papyrus, parchment, tracing paper, typing paper, vellum

5 <good writing> **calligraphy,** fine writing, elegant penmanship, **good hand,** fine hand, good fist <nf>, fair hand, copybook hand

6 <bad writing> **cacography, bad hand,** poor fist <nf>, cramped *or* crabbed hand, botched writing, childish scrawl, illegible handwriting, griffonage <Fr>

7 scribbling, scribblement; **scribble,** scrabble, **scrawl, scratch,** *barbouillage* <Fr>; *pattes de mouche* <Fr>, hen tracks *and* hen scratches <nf>, pothookery, pothooks, pothooks *and* hangers

8 stenography, shorthand, brachygraphy, tachygraphy; speedwriting, phonography, stenotype; contraction

9 letter, written character 546.1; **alphabet, writing system** 546.3

10 <written matter> **writing, the written word; piece;** piece of writing, text, screed; **copy, matter;** printed matter, literature, reading matter; the written word, *literae scriptae* <L>; nonfiction; fiction 722; composition, work, opus, production, literary production, literary artefact *or* artifact, lucubration, brainchild; essay, article 556.1; poem; play 704.4; letter 553.2; **document** 549.5,8; **paper,** parchment, scroll; **script,** scrip, scrive; **penscript, typescript; manuscript** *or* MS *or* Ms *or* ms, holograph, autograph; **draft,** first draft, second draft, etc, recension, **version;** edited version, finished version, final draft; transcription, transcript, fair copy, engrossment; flimsy; original, author's copy; camera-ready copy; printout, computer printout, hard copy; gray literature; blog, post

11 <ancient manuscript> **codex;** scroll; palimpsest, *codex rescriptus* <L>; papyrus, parchment

12 literature, letters, belles lettres, polite literature, humane letters, *litterae humaniores* <L>, republic of letters, writing; **work, literary work, text, literary text; works, complete works, oeuvre, canon, literary canon, author's canon;** serious literature; **classics,** ancient literature; medieval literature, Renaissance literature, etc; national literature, English literature, French literature, etc; contemporary literature; underground literature;

pseudonymous literature; folk literature, oral history; travel literature; wisdom literature; erotic literature, erotica; pornographic literature, pornography, porn *and* hard porn *and* soft porn <nf>, obscene literature, scatological literature; Weblog, blog, bulletin board; popular literature, pop literature <nf>; kitsch

13 **writer, scribbler** <nf>, **penman,** pen, penner; pen *or* pencil driver *or* pusher <nf>, word-slinger, **ink-slinger** *and* ink spiller <nf>, knight of the plume *or* pen *or* quill <nf>; **scribe, scrivener, amanuensis, secretary,** recording secretary, **clerk,** administrative assistant; letterer; **copyist,** copier, transcriber; chirographer, calligrapher

14 **writing expert,** graphologist, handwriting expert, graphometrist; paleographer

15 **author, writer,** scribe <nf>, composer, inditer; authoress, penwoman; **creative writer,** *littérateur* <Fr>, literary artist, literary craftsman *or* artisan *or* journeyman, belletrist, man of letters, literary man, literary lion; wordsmith, word painter; free lance, free-lance writer; ghostwriter, ghost <nf>; collaborator, coauthor; prose writer, logographer; fiction writer, fictioneer <nf>; story writer, **short story writer;** storyteller; **novelist;** novelettist; diarist; **newspaperman; annalist; poet** 720.11; **dramatist,** humorist 489.12; scriptwriter, scenario writer, scenarist, script doctor; nonfiction writer; article writer, magazine writer; **essayist;** monographer; reviewer, critic, literary critic, music critic, art critic, drama critic, dance critic; columnist; pamphleteer; technical writer; copywriter, advertising writer; compiler, list-maker, encyclopedist, bibliographer; blogger

16 **hack writer,** hack, literary hack, Grub Street writer <Brit>, **penny-a-liner, scribbler** <nf>, **potboiler** <nf>; blogger

17 **stenographer,** brachygrapher, tachygrapher; phonographer, stenotypist

18 **typist**, keyboarder; texter; printer

VERBS 19 **write, pen, pencil,** drive *or* push the pen *or* pencil <nf>; stain *or* spoil paper <nf>, shed *or* spill ink <nf>, **scribe,** scrive; inscribe, scroll; superscribe; enface; take pen in hand; **put in writing,** put in black and white; **draw up, draft, write out,** make out; write down, record 549.15; take down in shorthand; **type; transcribe,** copy out, engross, make a fair copy, copy; trace; **rewrite, revise, edit,** recense, make a recension, make a critical revision; highlight

20 **scribble,** scrabble, **scratch, scrawl,** make hen tracks *or* hen *or* chicken scratches <nf>, doodle

21 **write,** author, **compose, indite,** formulate, produce, prepare; dash off, knock off *or* out <nf>, throw on paper, pound *or* crank *or* grind *or* churn out; free-lance; collaborate, coauthor; ghostwrite, ghost <nf>; novelize; scenarize; pamphleteer; editorialize; blog

ADJS 22 **written,** penned, penciled, lettered, literal, graphical, typed; **inscribed;** engrossed; **in writing, in black and white,** on paper; scriptural, scriptorial, graphic; calligraphic, chirographic, chirographical; stylographic, stylographical; manuscript, autograph, autographic, holograph, holographic, holographical, in one's own hand, under one's hand; **longhand,** in longhand, in script, handwritten; **shorthand,** in shorthand; italic, italicized; cursive, running, flowing; graphologic, graphological, graphometric, graphometrical; graphoanalytic, graphoanalytical; typewritten; printed

23 **scribbled,** scrabbled, **scratched, scrawled; scribbly, scratchy, scrawly**

24 **literary,** belletristic, lettered; classical

25 auctorial, authorial; polygraphic; graphomaniac, graphomaniacal, scribblemaniac, scribblemaniacal, scripturient

26 **alphabetic**, ideographic, etc

27 stenographic, stenographical; **shorthand,** in shorthand

28 **clerical, secretarial**

548 PRINTING

NOUNS **1 printing,** publishing, publication, photographic reproduction, photochemical process, phototypography, phototypy; **photoengraving; letterpress,** relief printing, **typography,** letterpress photoengraving; zincography, photozincography; line engraving, halftone engraving; stereotypy; wood-block printing, xylotypography, chromoxylography; intaglio printing, **gravure;** rotogravure, rotary photogravure; planographic printing, planography, **lithography,** typolithography, photolithography, lithogravure, lithophotogravure; **offset printing,** offset lithography, offset, dry offset, photo-offset; photogelatin process, albertype, collotype; electronography, electrostatic printing, onset, xerography, xeroprinting; stencil, mimeograph, silk-screen printing; color printing, chromotypography, chromotypy, two-color printing, three-color printing; book printing, job printing, sheetwork; history of printing, palaeotypography; photography 714; **graphic arts, printmaking** 713.1

2 composition, typesetting, setting, composing; hand composition, machine composition; hot-metal typesetting, cold-type typesetting, photosetting, photocomposition; imposition; justification; composing stick, galley chase, furniture, quoin; typesetting machine, phototypesetter, phototypesetting machine; computer composition, computerized typesetting; composition tape; line of type, slug; layout, dummy

3 print, imprint, stamp, impression, impress, letterpress; reprint, reissue; offprint; offcut; offset, setoff, mackle; duplicate, facsimile, carbon copy, repro <nf>

4 copy, printer's copy, manuscript, typescript; **camera-ready copy; matter;** composed matter, live matter, dead matter, standing matter

5 proof, proof sheet, pull <Brit>, trial impression; galley, **galley proof,** slip; page proof, foundry proof, plate proof, stone proof, press proof, cold-type proof, color proof, computer proof, engraver's proof, reproduction *or* repro proof, blueprint, blue <nf>, vandyke, progressive proof; author's proof; revise

6 type, key in *or* key, **print, stamp, letter; type size;** type body *or* shank *or* stem, body, shank, stem, shoulder, belly, back, bevel, beard, feet, groove, nick, face, counter; ascender, descender, serif; lower case, minuscule; upper case, majuscule; capital, cap <nf>, small capital, small cap <nf>; ligature, logotype; bastard type, bottle-assed type, fat-faced type; **pi;** type lice; **font; face,** typeface; type class, roman, sans serif, script, italic, black letter; case, typecase; point, pica; en, em; typefounders, typefoundry

7 space, spacing, patent space, justifying space, justification space; spaceband, slug; quadrat, quad; em quad, en quad; em, en; three-em space, thick space; four-em space, five-em space, thin space; hair space

8 printing surface, plate, printing plate; typeform, locked-up page; duplicate plate, electrotype, stereotype, plastic plate, rubber plate; zincograph, zincotype; **printing equipment**

9 presswork, makeready; **press, printing press,** printing machine <Brit>; platen press, flatbed cylinder press, cylinder press, rotary press, web press, rotogravure press; bed, platen, web

10 printed matter; reading matter, text, letterpress <Brit>; advertising matter; advance sheets

11 press, printing office, print shop, printery, printers; publishers, **publishing house; pressroom,** composing room, proofroom

12 printer, printworker; **compositor, typesetter,** typographer, Linotyper; keyboarder; stoneman, makeup man; proofer; stereotyper, stereotypist, electrotyper; apprentice printer, devil, printer's devil; **pressman**

13 proofreader, reader, printer's reader <Brit>, copyholder; **copyreader,** copy editor

VERBS **14** **print; imprint, impress, stamp,** enstamp ; engrave; run, run off, strike; **publish, issue, put in print, bring out, put out, get out;** put to press, put to bed, see through the press; prove, proof, prove up, make *or* pull a proof, pull; overprint; reprint, reissue; mimeograph, hectograph; multigraph

15 autotype, electrotype, Linotype <TM>, monotype, palaeotype, stereotype; keyboard

16 **compose,** set, set in print; **make up,** impose; justify, overrun; pi, pi a form

17 **copy-edit; proofread,** read, read *or* correct copy; vet

18 <be printed> go to press, come off press, come out, appear in print

ADJS **19** **printed, in print;** typeset

20 **typographic, typographical;** phototypic, phototypographic; chromotypic, chromotypographic; stereotypic, palaeotypographical; **boldface,** bold-faced, blackface, black-faced, full-faced; **lightface,** light-faced; **upper-case, lower-case**

549 RECORD

NOUNS **1** **record, recording,** documentation, written word; **chronicle, annals,** history, story; roll, **rolls,** pipe roll <Brit>; account; register, registry, rota, roster, scroll, catalog, inventory, table, list 871, dossier, portfolio; letters, correspondence; **vestige, trace,** memorial, token, relic, remains; herstory <nf>; list-making, glazomania

2 **archives**, public records, government archives, government papers, presidential papers, historical documents, historical records, memorabilia; clipping; cartulary; biographical records, life records, biographical material, papers, ana; parish rolls *or* register *or* records

3 **registry**, registrar, registry office; archives, files; chancery; National Archives, Library of Congress; Somerset House <Brit>

4 **memorandum, memo** <nf>, memoir, *aide-mémoire* <Fr>, memorial; **reminder** 989.5; **note, notation,** annotation, jotting, docket, marginal note, marginalia, scholium, scholia, adversaria, footnote; jottings; **entry,** register, **registry,** item; **minutes;** inscription, personal note

5 **document,** official document, legal document, legal paper, legal instrument, **instrument,** writ, **paper,** parchment, scroll, roll, **writing,** script, scrip; holograph, chirograph; **papers,** ship's papers; docket, **file,** personal file, **dossier;** blank, form; deed, title deed, muniments; registration document, insurance papers; attachment

6 **certificate,** certification, **ticket; authority,** authorization; **credential, voucher, warrant,** warranty, testimonial, charter; note; **affidavit,** sworn statement, notarized statement, deposition, witness, attestation, *procès-verbal* <Fr>; **visa,** *visé* <Fr>; passport; **bill of health,** clean bill of health; navicert <Brit>; **diploma,** sheepskin <nf>; certificate of proficiency, testamur <Brit>; birth certificate, death certificate, marriage certificate

7 **report, bulletin, brief, statement, account,** accounting; account rendered, *compte rendu* <Fr>; **minutes,** the record, proceedings, transactions, acta; official report, annual report; report card, transcript; **yearbook,** annual; **returns,** census report *or* returns, election returns, tally; case history; book report

8 <official documents> state paper, white paper; blue book, green book, Red Book <Brit>, white book, yellow book, *livre jaune* <Fr>; gazette, official journal, Congressional Record, Hansard

9 <registers> genealogy, pedigree, studbook; Social Register, blue book; directory; Who's Who; Lloyd's Register

10 <recording media> bulletin board, notice board; scoresheet, scorecard, scoreboard; **tape,** magnetic tape, magnetic track, magnetic storage, cassette tape, videotape, ticker tape; **computer disk,** magnetic disk, diskette, floppy disk *or* floppy, hard disk, disk cartridge, CD-ROM, laser disk, optical disk; memory; computer file, database; compact disk *or* CD, multimedia CD, laser disk, DVD; phonograph record, disc *or* disk, platter <nf>; film, motion-picture film; slip, card, index card, filing card; library catalog, catalog card; microcard, microfiche, microdot, microfilm; **file** 871.3; recording instrument, photocopier, camera, videocamera, camcorder, recorder, tape recorder, wiretap, bug <nf>, answering machine, videocassette recorder *or* VCR, flight recorder, black box; voice recognition

11 <record books> **notebook, pocketbook,** pocket notebook, blankbook; loose-leaf notebook, spiral notebook; **memorandum book,** memo book <nf>, commonplace book, adversaria; address book, directory; workbook; **blotter,** police blotter; docket, court calendar; **calendar,** desk calendar, appointment calendar, appointment schedule, engagement book, agenda, agenda book, Filofax <TM>, datebook; Moleskine <TM>; **tablet,** table , writing tablet; diptych, triptych; pad, **scratch pad**, notepad; Post-it Note <TM>, sticky <nf>; **scrapbook,** memory book, **album; diary, journal,** daybook**; log,** ship's log, **logbook; account book, ledger,** daybook; **cashbook,** petty cashbook; checkbook; Domesday Book; catalog, classified catalog, index; yearbook, annual; guestbook, guest register, register, registry; cartulary *or* chartulary; art journal; blog, online journal

12 **monument,** monumental *or* memorial record, **memorial;** necrology, obituary, **memento,** remembrance, testimonial; cup, trophy, prize, ribbon, plaque; **marker;** inscription; **tablet,** stone, hoarstone <Brit>, boundary stone, memorial stone; **pillar,** stele *or* stela, shaft, column, memorial column, rostral column, manubial column; cross; war memorial; arch, memorial arch, triumphal arch, victory arch; memorial statue, bust; monolith, obelisk, **pyramid; tomb,** grave 309.16**;** tomb of unknown soldier; **gravestone, tombstone**; memorial tablet, brass; headstone, footstone; mausoleum; cenotaph; cairn, mound, barrow, cromlech, dolmen, megalith, menhir, cyclolith, earthwork, mound; **shrine,** reliquary, tope, stupa

13 recorder, registrar 550.1, blogger, listmaker

14 **registration, register, registry; recording,** record keeping, recordation; archiving; minuting, **enrollment,** matriculation, enlistment; impanelment; **listing, tabulation, cataloging,** inventorying, indexing; chronicling; **entry,** insertion, entering, posting; docketing, inscribing, **inscription; booking, logging**; recording instruments

VERBS **15** **record,** put *or* place upon record; **inscribe,** enscroll; **register, enroll,** matriculate, check in; impanel; poll; **file,** index, catalog, calendar, **tabulate, list,** docket; **chronicle,** document**;** minute, put in the minutes *or* on the record, spread on the record; commit to *or* preserve in an archive, archive; **write,** commit *or* reduce to writing, put in writing, put in black and white, put on paper; **write out; make out,** fill out; **write up,** chalk, chalk up; **write down, mark down, jot down, put down, set down, take down; note,** note down, make a note, make a memorandum; **post,** post up; **enter,** make an entry, insert, write in; **book, log;** cut, carve, grave, engrave, incise; put on tape, tape, tape-record; capture on film; record, cut; videotape; keyboard, key; diarize

ADJS **16** **recording,** recordative , registrational; certificatory

17 **recorded,** registered; inscribed, written down, down; **filed,** indexed, enrolled, **entered,** logged, booked, posted; documented, chronicled; minuted; **on record,** on file, on the books; official, legal, of record; in black and white; duly noted

18 **documentary,** documentational, documental, archival, archived; epigraphic, inscriptional; necrological, obituary; testimonial

550 RECORDER

NOUNS 1 **recorder,** recordist, record keeper; **registrar,** register, prothonotary; archivist, documentalist; master of the rolls <Brit>, *custos rotulorum* <L>; librarian, cybrarian; **clerk,** record clerk, penpusher <nf>, filing clerk; town *or* municipal clerk, county clerk; bookkeeper, accountant, tax preparer; **scribe,** scrivener; **secretary,** amanuensis; **stenographer** 547.17; notary, notary public; marker; scorekeeper, scorer, official scorer, timekeeper; engraver, stonecutter; reporter

2 **annalist,** genealogist, chronicler; cliometrician; historian

551 INFORMATION

NOUNS 1 **information,** info <nf>, gen <Brit nf>, **facts, data, knowledge** 928; public knowledge, open secret, common knowledge; general information; news, factual information, hard information; **evidence, proof** 957; **enlightenment,** light; incidental information, sidelight; **acquaintance,** familiarization, briefing; **instruction** 568.1; **intelligence,** intel <nf>**; the dope** *and* the goods *and* **the scoop** *and* the skinny *and* the straight skinny *and* the inside skinny <nf>, the know <nf>, the gen <Brit>; transmission, **communication** 343; **report, word,** message, presentation, account, **statement,** mention; white paper, white book, blue book, command paper <Brit>; dispatch, bulletin, communiqué, handout <nf>, fact sheet, release; publicity, promotional material, broadside; **notice,** notification; notice board, bulletin board; announcement, publication 352; directory, guidebook 574.10; trivia; current events, current affairs; information processing; information overload; bullet points

2 **inside information,** private *or* confidential information; **the lowdown** *and* **inside dope** *and* inside wire *and* **hot tip** *and* dirt *and* poop <nf>; insider; pipeline <nf>; privileged information, classified information; insider trading

3 **tip** *and* tip-off *and* **pointer** <nf>, clue, cue; steer <nf>; **advice;** whisper, passing word, **word to the wise,** word in the ear, bug in the ear <nf>, bee in the bonnet <nf>; warning, caution, monition, alerting, sound bite; aside

4 **hint,** gentle hint, **intimation, indication, suggestion, mere** *or* **faint suggestion, suspicion, inkling,** whisper, **glimmer, glimmering; cue, clue,** index, **symptom, sign,** spoor, track, scent, sniff, whiff, telltale, tip-off <nf>; **implication, insinuation, innuendo;** broad hint, gesture, signal, nod, wink, look, nudge, kick, prompt; disguised message, backward masking; rumor, leak, gossip

5 **informant, informer, source,** teller, interviewee, enlightener, deep throat <nf>; **adviser,** monitor; **reporter,** notifier, **announcer,** annunciator; spokesperson, spokespeople, spokeswoman, spokesman, press secretary, press officer, information officer, mouthpiece, messenger, correspondent; spin doctor <nf>; communicator, communicant, publisher; **authority,** witness, expert witness; **tipster** <nf>, **tout** <nf>; newsmonger, gossipmonger; **information medium** *or* **media, mass media,** print media, electronic media, the press, radio, television; channel, the grapevine; information network, network; information center; public relations officer *or* person; agent, handler; infopreneur

6 **informer, betrayer,** double-crosser <nf>, delator ; fifth columnist; **snitch** *and* snitcher <nf>; whistleblower <nf>; **tattler, tattletale, telltale, talebearer; blab** *or* blabber *or* blabberer *or* blabbermouth <nf>; **squealer** *and* preacher *and* **stool pigeon** *and* stoolie *and* **fink** *and* rat <nf>, nark <Brit nf>; spy 576.9; mole; grapevine, channel

7 information technology *or* IT, information *or* communication theory; data storage *or* retrieval, information retrieval, EDP *or* electronic

data processing, data processing, information processing; signal, noise; encoding, decoding; bit; redundancy, entropy; channel; information *or* communication explosion, information superhighway

VERBS **8 inform, tell, speak on** *or* **for,** apprise, **advise, advertise,** advertise of, **give word,** mention to, **acquaint, enlighten,** familiarize, brief, verse, give the facts, give an account of, give by way of information; **instruct**, educate; possess *or* seize one of the facts; **let know, have one to know, give** *or* **lead one to believe** *or* **understand;** tell once *and* for all; notify, give notice *or* notification, serve notice; **communicate** 343.6,7; bring *or* send *or* leave word; **report** 552.11; **disclose** 351.4; put in a new light, shed new *or* fresh light upon; announce, broadcast, convey, break the news

9 post *and* **keep posted** <nf>; wise up *and* clue *or* fill in *and* bring up to speed *or* date *and* put in the picture <nf>

10 hint, intimate, suggest, insinuate, imply, indicate, adumbrate, lead *or* leave one to gather, justify one in supposing, give *or* drop *or* throw out a hint, give an inkling of, signal, suggest, **hint at; leak,** let slip out; allude to, make an allusion to, glance at ; **prompt,** give the cue, put onto; put in *or* into one's head, put a bee in one's bonnet

11 tip *and* tip off *and* **give one a tip** <nf>, alert; **give a pointer to** <nf>; put hep *or* hip <nf>, **let in on,** let in on the know <nf>; let next to *and* put next to *and* **put on to** *and* put on to something hot <nf>; **confide,** confide to, entrust with information, give confidential information, mention privately *or* confidentially, whisper, buzz, breathe, whisper in the ear, **put a bug in one's ear** <nf>

12 inform on *or* **against, betray; tattle;** turn informer; testify against, **bear witness against;** turn state's evidence, turn king's *or* queen's evidence <Brit>

13 <nf terms> **sell one out** *or* **down the river,** tell on, blab, snitch, squeal, peach , sell out, sing, rat, stool, fink, nark, finger, put the finger on, blow the whistle, shop <Brit>, dime, drop a dime, spill one's guts, spill the beans, squawk, weasel, let the cat out of the bag, sell down the river

14 learn, come to know, be informed *or* **apprised of,** have it reported, get the facts, **get wise to** <nf>, **get hep to** *and* **next to** *and* **on to** <nf>, find out, get word; become conscious *or* aware of, become alive *or* awake to, awaken to, tumble to <nf>, open one's eyes to; realize, get wind of; overhear

15 know 928.12, be informed *or* apprised, have the facts, be in the know <nf>, **come to one's knowledge,** come to *or* reach one's ears; be told, **hear, overhear,** hear tell of *and* hear say <nf>; get scent *or* wind of; **know well** 928.13; have inside information, know where the bodies are buried <nf>

16 keep informed, keep posted <nf>, stay briefed, **keep up on,** keep up to date *or* au courant, keep abreast of the times; **keep track of,** keep count *or* account of, keep watch on, keep tab *or* tabs on <nf>, keep a check on, keep an eye on

ADJS **17 informed** 928.18–20; informed of, enlightened, briefed, in the know 928.16, clued-in *or* clued-up <nf>

18 informative, informing, informational, informatory; illuminating, **instructive, enlightening;** educative, educational; advisory, monitory; **communicative**

19 telltale, tattletale, kiss-and-tell

ADVS **20** from information received, according to reports *or* rumor, from notice given, as a matter of general information, by common report, from what one can gather, as far as anyone knows

552 NEWS

NOUNS **1 news, tidings, intelligence, information, word,** advice; happenings, current affairs, hard news; newsiness <nf>; newsworthiness; a nose for news; **journalism,** reportage, coverage, news coverage, news gathering; **the press,** the fourth estate, the press corps, print journalism, electronic journalism, investigative journalism, broadcast journalism, broadcast news, radio journalism, television journalism; **news medium** *or* **media,** newspaper, newsletter, newsmagazine, radio, television, press association, news service, news agency, press agency, wire service, telegraph agency; press box, press gallery; yellow press, tabloid press; pack journalism; alternative press; newsserver, multimedia; Internet forum

2 **good news,** good word, **glad tidings;** gospel, evangel; bad news

3 **news item,** piece *or* budget of news; **article, story,** piece, account; copy; scoop *and* beat <nf>, exclusive; interview; breaking story, newsbreak; feature story; follow-up, sidebar; column, editorial; spot news; photo opportunity; outtake; sound bite; media hype <nf>; factoid, data point

4 **message, dispatch, word, communication, communiqué,** advice, press *or* news release, release; press conference, news conference; express <Brit>; embassy, embassage ; **letter** 553.2; **telegram** 347.14; pneumatogram, *petit bleu* <Fr>; text message, instant message

5 **bulletin,** news report, **flash,** brief *or* news brief, update, newsfeed

6 **report, rumor,** flying rumor, unverified *or* unconfirmed report, **hearsay,** *on-dit* <Fr>, **scuttlebutt** *and* latrine rumor <nf>; **talk, whisper, buzz, rumble,** bruit, cry; idea afloat, news stirring; **common talk,** town talk, **talk of the town,** topic of the day, *cause célèbre* <Fr>; **grapevine; canard**, roorback

7 **gossip,** gossiping, gossipry, gossipmongering, newsmongering, mongering, back-fence gossip <nf>; **talebearing,** taletelling; **tattle,** tittle-tattle, chitchat, **talk,** idle talk, small talk, by-talk; piece of gossip, groundless rumor, tale, story

8 **scandal, dirt** <nf>, **malicious gossip**; juicy morsel, tidbit, choice bit of dirt <nf>; **scandalmongering;** gossip column; character assassination, **slander** 512.3; whispering campaign

9 **newsmonger, rumormonger, scandalmonger, gossip,** gossipmonger, gossiper, *yenta* <Yiddish>, quidnunc, **busybody,** tabby <nf>; **talebearer,** taleteller, telltale, **tattletale** <nf>, tattler, tittle-tattler; gossip columnist; reporter, newspaperman, newsperson, cub reporter

10 <secret news channel> **grapevine, grapevine telegraph,** channel; **pipeline;** a litle bird *or* birdie; informer, leak; insider information; contact

VERBS 11 **report,** give a report, give an account of, tell, relate, rehearse ; write up, make out *or* write up a report, publicize; editorialize; gather the news, newsgather; dig *or* dig up dirt <nf>; bring word, tell the news, break the news, give tidings of; bring glad tidings, give the good word; announce 352.12; put around, spread, **rumor** 352.10; clue in *or* clue up <nf>, **inform** 551.8

12 **gossip,** talk over the back fence <nf>; **tattle,** tittle-tattle; clatter, **talk;** retail gossip, **dish the dirt** <nf>, tell idle tales

ADJS 13 **newsworthy,** front-page, with news value, newsy, informative; reportorial

14 **gossipy,** gossiping, newsy; **talebearing,** taletelling; tabloidesque

15 **reported, rumored,** whispered; rumored about, talked about, whispered about, bruited about, bandied about; **in the news, in circulation, in the air, going around,** going about, going the rounds, **current, rife,** afloat, in every one's mouth, on all tongues, on the street, all over the town, hot off the press; made public 352.17

ADVS 16 reportedly, allegedly, as they say, as it is said, **as the story goes** *or* runs, as the fellow says <nf>, it is said

553 CORRESPONDENCE

NOUNS 1 **correspondence, letter writing,** written communication, exchange of letters, epistolary intercourse *or* communication; personal correspondence, business correspondence; mailing, mass mailing; electronic mail, e-mail; text messaging *or* texting, instant messaging

2 **letter, epistle, message, communication, dispatch, missive,** favor ; personal letter, business letter; **note, line,** chit, billet ; **reply, answer, acknowledgment,** rescript

3 **card, postcard, postal card,** lettercard <Brit>; picture postcard

4 **mail, post** <chiefly Brit>, **postal services,** letter bag; post day <Brit>; domestic mail, general delivery, snail mail <nf>, airmail, surface mail, express mail, priority mail, special handling, special delivery, first- *or* second- *or* third—*or* fourth-class mail, parcel post, registered mail, certified mail, insured mail, metered mail; mailing list; junk mail <nf>; direct mail, direct-mail advertising *or* selling, mail-order selling; mail solicitation; fan mail; electronic mail, e-mail; text message, instant message; Pony Express

5 **postage;** stamp, postage stamp; frank; postmark, cancellation; postage meter

6 **mailbox,** postbox *and* letter box <chiefly Brit>, pillar box <Brit>; letter drop, mail drop; mailing machine *or* mailer; mailbag, postbag <Brit>; e-mail box, voicemail box

7 **postal service, postal system; post office** *or* **PO**, general post office *or* GPO, sorting office, dead-letter office, sea post office, mailboat; postmaster, **mailman, postman,** mail carrier, letter carrier**;** mail clerk, post-office *or* postal clerk; messenger, courier; postal union; electronic mail service

8 **correspondent, letter writer,** writer, communicator; pen pal <nf>; addressee

9 **address,** name *and* address, direction , **destination,** superscription; zone, zip code *or* ZIP, zip plus four, postal code *or* postcode; letterhead, billhead; drop, accommodation address <Brit>; e-mail address

VERBS 10 **correspond,** correspond with, **communicate with, write, write to,** write a letter, send a letter to, send a note, **drop a line** <nf>; use the mails; keep up a correspondence, exchange letters

11 **reply, answer, acknowledge,** respond**;** reply by return mail

12 **mail, post,** dispatch, send, forward; airmail

13 **address, direct,** superscribe

ADJS 14 epistolary; **postal,** post; letter; mail-order, direct-mail, mail-in; mailable; send-in, sendable

PHRS 15 please reply, RSVP *or répondez s'il vous plaît* <Fr>

554 BOOK

NOUNS 1 **book, volume, tome;** publication, writing, **work, opus, production; title;** opusculum, opuscule; **trade book; textbook,** schoolbook, reader, grammar; **reference book,** playbook; songbook 708.28; notebook 549.11; storybook, **novel; best seller** *or* bestseller**;** coffee-table book; nonbook; **children's book,** juvenile book, juvenile; picture book; coloring book, sketchbook; prayer book, psalter, psalmbook; **classic,** the book, the bible, magnum opus, great work, standard work, definitive work

2 **publisher,** book publisher; publishing house, press, small press, vanity press; **editor,** trade editor, reference editor, juvenile editor, textbook editor, dictionary editor, college editor, line editor; acquisitions editor, executive editor, managing editor, editor-in-chief; picture editor; packager; copy editor *or* copyeditor, fact checker, proofreader; production editor, permissions editor; **printer,** book printer, typesetter, compositor; **bookbinder,** bibliopegist; **bookdealer, bookseller,** book agent, book salesman; book packager; book manufacturer, press

3 **book, printed book, bound book,** bound volume, cased book, casebound book, cloth-bound book, clothback, leather-bound book; manufactured book, finished book; packaged book;

hardcover, hardcover book, hardbound, hardbound book, hard book; **paperback,** paper-bound book; pocket book, soft-cover, soft-bound book, limp-cover book; self-published book; electronic book, e-book

4 **volume, tome;** folio; quarto *or* 4to; octavo *or* 8vo; twelvemo *or* 12mo; sextodecimo *or* sixteenmo *or* 16mo; octodecimo *or* eighteenmo *or* 18mo; imperial, super, royal, medium, crown; trim size

5 **edition,** issue; volume, number; **printing,** impression, press order, print order, print run; copy; series, set, boxed set, collection, library; library edition; back number; **trade edition,** subscription edition, subscription book; school edition, text edition

6 **rare book,** early edition; first edition; signed edition; Elzevir, Elzevir book *or* edition; Aldine, Aldine book *or* edition; manuscript, scroll, codex; incunabulum, cradle book

7 **compilation,** omnibus; symposium; collection, collectanea, miscellany; collected works, selected works, complete works, corpus, *œuvres* <Fr>, canon; **miscellanea,** analects; ana; chrestomathy, delectus; compendium, **anthology,** composition, garland, florilegium; flowers, beauties; garden; *Festschrift* <Ger>; quotation book; album, photograph album; scrapbook; yearbook; display, exhibition; series, serialization

8 **handbook, manual,** enchiridion, vade mecum, gradus, how-to book <nf>; **cookbook,** cookery book <Brit>; nature book, field guide; travel book, **guidebook** 574.10; sports book

9 **reference book,** work of reference; **encyclopedia,** cyclopedia; **concordance; catalog;** calendar; index; classified catalog, catalogue raisonné <Fr>, dictionary catalog; **directory,** city directory; telephone directory, telephone book, phone book <nf>; **atlas, gazetteer;** studbook; source book, casebook; record book 549.11; **language reference book** ; **dictionary,** lexicon, wordbook, Webster's; glossary, gloss, **vocabulary,** onomasticon, nomenclator; **thesaurus, Roget's,** storehouse *or* treasury of words, synonomicon; **almanac**

10 **textbook, text, schoolbook, manual,** manual of instruction; **primer,** alphabet book, abecedary, abecedarium; hornbook, battledore; gradus, exercise book, workbook; **grammar, reader;** spelling book, speller, casebook

11 **booklet, pamphlet, brochure, chapbook, leaflet, folder, tract;** circular 352.8; comic book

12 **makeup, design;** front matter, preliminaries, text, back matter; head, fore edge, back, tail; page, leaf, folio; type page; trim size; flyleaf, endpaper, endleaf, endsheet, signature; recto, verso *or* reverso; title page, half-title page; title, bastard title, binder's title, subtitle, running title; copyright page, imprint, printer's imprint, imprimatur, colophon; catchword, catch line; dedication, inscription; acknowledgments, preface, foreword, introduction; contents, contents page, table of contents; appendix, notes, glossary; errata; bibliography; index

13 **part, section,** book, volume; article; serial, installment, *livraison* <Fr>; fascicle; **passage,** phrase, clause, verse, paragraph, chapter, column

14 **bookbinding,** bibliopegy; **binding, cover, book cover,** case, bookcase, hard binding, soft binding, mechanical binding, spiral binding, comb binding, plastic binding; library binding; headband, footband, tailband; **jacket, book jacket, dust jacket,** dust cover, wrapper; slipcase, slipcover; book cloth, binder's cloth, binder's board, binder board; folding, tipping, gathering, collating, sewing; **signature;** collating mark, niggerhead; Smyth sewing, side sewing, saddle stitching, wire stitching, stapling, perfect binding; smashing, gluing-off, trimming, rounding, backing, lining, lining-up; casemaking, stamping, casing-in

15 <bookbinding styles> Aldine, Arabesque, Byzantine, Canevari, cottage, dentelle, Etruscan, fanfare, Grolier, Harleian, Jansenist, Maioli, pointillé, Roxburgh

16 **bookstore, bookshop,** *librairie* <Fr>, bookseller, book dealer; **bookstall,** bookstand; **book club**; bibliopole; online bookseller

17 **bookholder, bookrest,** book support, **book end; bookcase,** revolving bookcase *or* bookstand, bookrack, bookstand, **bookshelf;** stack, bookstack; book table, book tray, book truck; folder, folio; **portfolio**

18 **booklover,** philobiblist, bibliophile, bibliolater, book collector, bibliomane, bibliomaniac, bibliotaph; **bookworm,** bibliophage; bookstealer, biblioklept; word nerd

19 **bibliology,** bibliography; bookcraft, bookmaking, book printing, book production, book manufacturing, bibliogenesis, bibliogony; bookselling, bibliopolism

ADJS **20** **bibliological,** bibliographical; bibliothecal, bibliothecary; bibliopolic; bibliopegic

555 PERIODICAL

NOUNS **1** **periodical, serial, journal,** gazette; ephemeris; **magazine,** book *and* zine <nf>, webzine; pictorial; review;
organ, **house organ; trade journal,** trade magazine; academic journal; daily, weekly, biweekly, bimonthly, fortnightly, monthly, quarterly, seasonal; annual, yearbook; newsletter; daybook, diary 549.11

2 **newspaper,** news, **paper,** sheet *or* rag <nf>, **gazette,** daily newspaper, daily, weekly newspaper, weekly, local paper, neighborhood newspaper, national newspaper; newspaper of record; **tabloid,** scandal sheet, extra, special, extra edition, special edition, Sunday paper, early edition, late edition; magazine section, comics, color supplement; online edition

3 **the press,** journalism, the public press, **the fourth estate;** print medium, the print media, print journalism, the print press, the public print; Fleet Street <Brit>; **wire service,** newswire; **publishing, newspaper publishing, magazine publishing; the publishing industry, communications,** mass media, the communications industry, public communication; satellite publishing; reportage, coverage, legwork

4 **journalist, newspaperman, newspaperwoman, newsman, newswoman,** journo <Brit nf>, newspeople, inkstained wretch, pressman <Brit>, newswriter, gazetteer , gentleman *or* representative of the press, **reporter,** newshawk *and* newshound <nf>; leg man <nf>; interviewer; investigative reporter *or* journalist; **cub reporter; correspondent, foreign correspondent,** war correspondent, special correspondent, stringer; publicist; rewriter, **rewrite man;** reviser, diaskeuast; **editor,** subeditor, managing editor, city editor, news editor, sports editor, woman's editor, feature editor, **copy editor,** copyman, copy chief, slotman; reader, **copyreader;** editorial writer, leader writer <Brit>; **columnist,** paragrapher, paragraphist; freelance reporter; **photographer, news photographer,** photojournalist; paparazzo; press baron; press corps

ADJS **5** **journalistic,** journalese <nf>; **periodical,** serial; magazinish, magaziny; newspaperish, newspapery; **editorial; reportorial**

556 TREATISE

NOUNS **1** **treatise,** piece, treatment, handling, tractate, tract; contribution; examination, survey, inquiry, **discourse, discussion,** disquisition, descant, exposition, screed; homily; memoir; **dissertation, thesis; essay,** theme; pandect; excursus; **study,** lucubration, étude; **paper,** research paper, term paper, position paper; **sketch,** outline, aperçu; causerie; **monograph,** research monograph; *morceau* <Fr>, paragraph, **note;** preliminary study, introductory study, first approach, prolegomenon; **article,** feature, special article

2 **commentary,** commentation ; **comment, remark; criticism,** critique, *compte-rendu critique* <Fr>, analysis; **review,** critical review, **report,** notice, **write-up** <nf>; **editorial,** leading article *or* leader <Brit>; gloss, running commentary, Op-Ed column

3 **discourser,** discusser, disquisitor, dissertator, doctoral candidate, expositor, descanter; symposiast, discussant; essayist; monographer, monographist; tractation, tractator ; **writer, author** 547.15; scholar

4 **commentator,** commenter; expositor, expounder, exponent; annotator, scholiast; glossarist, glossographer; **critic; reviewer,** book reviewer; **editor;** editorial writer, editorialist, leader writer <Brit>; news analyst; publicist

VERBS **5** **write upon,** touch upon, **discuss, treat, treat of, deal with,** take up, handle, go into, inquire into, survey; discourse, dissert, dissertate, descant, develop at thesis; **comment upon,** commentate, remark upon, annotate; expound; **criticize, review, write up**

ADJS **6** dissertational, disquisitional, discoursive, discursive; expository, expositorial, expositive, exegetical; essayistic; monographic, commentative, commentatorial, annotative; critical, interpretive *or* interpretative; editorial

557 ABRIDGMENT

NOUNS **1** **abridgment,** compendium, compend, *abrégé* <Fr>, **condensation,** short *or* shortened version, condensed version, potted version <Brit>, abbreviation, abbreviature, diminution, brief, digest, **abstract,** epitome, **précis, capsule,** nutshell *or* capsule version, capsulization, encapsulation, sketch, thumbnail sketch, **synopsis,** conspectus, syllabus, *aperçu* <Fr>, **survey, review,** overview, pandect, bird's-eye view; **outline,** skeleton, draft, blueprint, prospectus; topical outline; head, rubric

2 **summary, résumé,** curriculum vitae *or* CV, **recapitulation, recap** <nf>, rundown, run-through; **summation;** review; sum, substance, sum *and* substance, **wrapup** <nf>; pith, meat, gist, drift, core, essence, main point 997.6

3 **excerpt, extract, selection,** extraction, excerption, snippet; passage, selected passage; **clip** <nf>, film clip, outtake, sound bite <nf>

4 **excerpts,** *excerpta* <L>, **extracts, gleanings,** cuttings, clippings, snippets, selections; flowers, florilegium, **anthology;** compendium, treasury; ephemera; fragments; analects; **miscellany,** miscellanea; **collection,** collectanea; ana

VERBS **5** **abridge, shorten** 268.6, **condense, cut, clip; summarize,** synopsize, wrap up <nf>; **outline, sketch,** sketch out, hit the high spots; capsule, capsulize, encapsulate; **put in a nutshell**

ADJS **6** **abridged,** condensed; shortened, clipped, abstracted, abbreviated, truncated, compressed; nutshell, compendious, **brief** 268.8

ADVS **7** in brief, in summary, in sum, to the point, laconically, in a nutshell 537.8

558 LIBRARY

NOUNS **1** **library,** book depository; learning center; media center, media resource center, information center; **public library**, town *or* city *or* municipal library, county library, state library; school library, community college library, college library, university library; **special library,** medical library, law library, art library, etc; **circulating library, lending library** <Brit>; rental library; **book wagon, bookmobile;** bookroom, bookery , *bibliothèque* <Fr>, bibliotheca <L>, athenaeum; reading room; **national library,** Bibliothèque Nationale, Bodleian Library, British Library, Deutsche B_cherei, Library of Congress; carrel; interlibrary loan

2 librarianship, professional librarianship; **library science,** information science, library services, library and information services, library and information studies; cybrarianship

3 librarian, professional librarian, library professional; **director, head librarian, chief librarian;** head of service; library services director; cybrarian

4 bibliography, annotated bibliography; **index**; Books in Print, Paperbound Books in Print; **publisher's catalog,** publisher's list, backlist; National Union Catalog, Library of Congress Catalog, General Catalogue of Printed Books <Brit>, Union List of Serials; **library catalog,** computerized catalog, on-line catalog, integrated online system; CD-ROM workstation

559 RELATIONSHIP BY BLOOD

NOUNS **1 blood relationship,** blood, ties of blood, consanguinity, common descent *or* ancestry, biological *or* genetic relationship, **kinship,** kindred, **relation, relationship,** sibship; propinquity; cognation; agnation, enation; filiation, affiliation; alliance, connection, **family connection** *or* tie; motherhood, maternity; fatherhood, paternity; patrocliny, matrocliny; patrilineage, matrilineage; patriliny, matriliny; patrisib, matrisib; brotherhood, brothership, fraternity; sisterhood, sistership; cousinhood, cousinship; parental unit <nf>; **ancestry** 560

2 kinfolk *and* **kinfolks** <nf>, **kinsmen, kinsfolk, kindred,** kinnery <nf>, **kin,** kith *and* kin, **family, relatives, relations, people,** immediate family, folks <nf>, connections; **blood relation** *or* **relative,** flesh, blood, flesh *and* blood, uterine kin, consanguinean; cognate; agnate, enate; kinsman, kinswoman, sib, sibling; german; near relation, distant relation; next of kin; collateral relative, collateral; distaff *or* spindle side, distaff *or* spindle kin; sword *or* spear side, sword *or* spear kin; **tribesman,** tribespeople, clansman *or* -woman; **ancestry** 560, **posterity** 561

3 brother, bub *and* bubba *and* bro *and* bud *and* buddy <nf>, frater; brethren 700.1; **sister,** sis *and* sissy <nf>; sistern <nf>; kid brother *or* sister; blood brother *or* sister, uterine brother *or* sister, brother- *or* sister-german; half brother *or* sister, foster brother *or* sister, stepbrother *or* stepsister; **aunt,** auntie <nf>; **uncle,** unc *and* uncs *and* nunks *and* nunky *and* nuncle <nf>, **nephew, niece; cousin,** cousin-german; first cousin, second cousin, etc; cousin once removed, cousin twice removed, etc; country cousin; great-uncle, granduncle; great-granduncle; great-aunt, grandaunt; great-grandaunt; grandnephew, grandniece; **father, mother; son, daughter** 561.3

4 race, people, folk, family, house, clan, tribe, nation; patriclan, matriclan, deme, sept, gens, phyle, phratry, totem; **lineage,** line, blood, strain, stock, stem, species, stirps, **breed,** brood, kind; plant *or* animal kingdom, class, order, etc 809.4; **ethnicity,** tribalism, clannishness, roots <nf>

5 family, fam <nf>, brood, nuclear family, binuclear family, extended family, one-parent *or* single-parent family; **house, household,** hearth, hearthside, ménage, people, **folk,** homefolk, folks *and* homefolks <nf>; kin, relatives, relations; **children,** issue, descendants, progeny, **offspring,** litter, get, kids <nf>

ADJS **6 related, kindred, akin;** consanguineous *or* consanguinean *or* consanguineal, consanguine, by *or* of the blood; **biological,** genetic; **natural, birth,** by birth; cognate, uterine, agnate, enate; sib, sibling; allied, affiliated, congeneric; german, germane; collateral; foster, novercal; patrilineal, matrilineal; patroclinous, matroclinous; patrilateral, matrilateral; avuncular; intimately *or* closely related, remotely *or* distantly related

7 racial, ethnic, tribal, national, family, clannish, totemic, **lineal;**

ethnic; phyletic, phylogenetic, genetic; gentile, gentilic

560 ANCESTRY

NOUNS **1 ancestry,** progenitorship; parentage, parenthood; grandparentage, grandfatherhood, grandmotherhood

2 paternity, fatherhood, fathership; natural *or* birth *or* biological fatherhood; fatherliness, paternalness; adoptive fatherhood

3 maternity, motherhood, mothership; natural *or* birth *or* biological motherhood; motherliness, maternalness; adoptive motherhood; surrogate motherhood

4 lineage, line, bloodline, descent, descendancy, line of descent, ancestral line, succession, **extraction,** derivation, birth, **blood,** breed, **family,** house, **strain,** sept, **stock,** race, stirps, seed; direct line, phylum; **branch,** stem; filiation, affiliation, apparentation; side, father's side, mother's side; enate, agnate, cognate; male line, spear *or* sword side; female line, distaff *or* spindle side; consanguinity, ancestry 560.1

5 genealogy, pedigree, stemma, genealogical tree, **family tree,** tree; genogram; descent, lineage, line, bloodline, ancestry

6 heredity, heritage, inheritance, birth; patrocliny, matrocliny; endowment, inborn capacity *or* tendency *or* susceptibility *or* predisposition; diathesis; inheritability, heritability, hereditability; Mendel's law, Mendelism *or* Mendelianism; Weismann theory, Weismannism; Altmann theory, De Vries theory, Galtonian theory, Verworn theory, Wiesner theory; **genetics,** genetic engineering, genetic fingerprinting, pharmacogenetics, genesiology, eugenics; **gene,** factor, inheritance factor, determiner, determinant; **character,** dominant *or* recessive character, allele *or* allelomorph; germ cell, germ plasm; **chromosome;** sex chromosome, X chromosome, Y chromosome; chromatin, chromatid; genetic code; DNA, RNA, replication

7 ancestors, antecedents, predecessors, ascendants, **fathers, forefathers, forebears,** progenitors, primogenitors; **grandparents,** grandfathers; patriarchs, elders

8 parent, progenitor, ancestor, procreator, begetter; natural *or* birth *or* biological parent; grandparent; ancestress, progenitress, progenitrix; stepparent; adoptive parent; surrogate parent; empty-nester

9 father, sire, genitor, paternal ancestor, pater <nf>, the old man <nf>, governor <nf>; patriarch, paterfamilias; stepfather; foster father, adoptive father; birth father

10 <nf terms> **papa,** pa, pap, pappy, **pop,** pops, **dad, daddy,** daddums, daddyo, big daddy, the old man, the governor, pater

11 mother, genetrix, dam, maternal ancestor, matriarch, materfamilias; stepmother; foster mother, adoptive mother; birth mother

12 <nf terms> **mama,** mater, the old woman, mammy, mam, **ma, mom, mommy,** mummy, mumsy, mimsy, motherkin, motherkins

13 grandfather, grandsire; old man 304.2; great-grandfather

14 <nf terms> **grandpa,** grampa, gramper, gramp, gramps, grandpapa, grandpap, grandpappy, **granddad,** granddaddy, granddada, granfer, gramfer, granther, pop, grandpop

15 grandmother, grandam; great-grandmother

16 <nf terms> **grandma,** granma, old woman 304.3; grandmamma, grandmammy, **granny,** grammy, gammy, grannam, gammer

ADJS **17 ancestral,** ancestorial, patriarchal; patrifocal; **parental,** parent; **paternal,** fatherly, fatherlike; **maternal,** motherly, motherlike; matrifocal; grandparental; grandmotherly, grandmaternal; grandfatherly, grandpaternal

18 lineal, family, familial, genealogical; kindred, akin; enate *or* enatic, agnate *or* agnatic, cognate *or* cog-

natic; direct, in a direct line; phyletic, phylogenetic; diphyletic
19 **hereditary,** patrimonial, **inherited, innate;** genetic, genic; patroclinous, matroclinous
20 **inheritable,** heritable, hereditable

561 POSTERITY

NOUNS 1 **posterity, progeny, issue, offspring,** fruit, seed, brood, breed, family; **descent,** succession; lineage 560.4, blood, bloodline; **descendants,** heirs, inheritors, sons, **children, kids** <nf>, little ones, little people <nf>, treasures, hostages to fortune, youngsters, younglings; grandchildren, great-grandchildren; new *or* young *or* rising generation
2 <of animals> **young, brood,** get, **spawn,** spat, fry; **litter,** farrow <of pigs>; clutch, hatch
3 **descendant; offspring, child, scion; son,** son *and* heir, a chip off the old block, sonny; **daughter,** heiress; grandchild, grandson, granddaughter; stepchild, stepson, stepdaughter; foster child; adopted child
4 <derived *or* collateral descendant> **offshoot**, offset, **branch,** sprout, shoot, filiation
5 **bastard,** illegitimate, illegitimate *or* bastard child, whoreson, by-blow, child born out of wedlock *or* without benefit of clergy *or* on the wrong side of the blanket, natural *or* love child, *nullius filius* <L>; illegitimacy, bastardy, bar *or* bend sinister; hellspawn
6 sonship, sonhood; daughtership, daughterhood

ADJS 7 **filial,** sonly, sonlike; **daughterly,** daughterlike

562 LOVEMAKING, ENDEARMENT

NOUNS 1 **lovemaking,** dalliance, amorous dalliance, billing and cooing; **fondling, caressing,** hugging, kissing; cuddling, snuggling, nestling, nuzzling; bundling; sexual intercourse 75.7
2 <nf terms> **making out, necking, petting,** spooning, smooching, lollygagging, canoodling, playing kissy-face *or* kissy-kissy *or* kissy-poo *or* kissy-huggy *or* lickey-face *or* smacky-lips, pitching *or* flinging woo, sucking face, swapping spit
3 **embrace, hug, squeeze,** fond embrace, embracement, clasp, enfoldment, bear hug <nf>
4 **kiss,** buss, smack, smooch <nf>, **osculation;** French kiss, soul kiss; fish-kiss; air-kiss
5 **endearment; caress,** pat; sweet talk, soft words, honeyed words, sweet nothings; line <nf>, blandishments, artful endearments; love call, mating call, wolf whistle
6 <terms of endearment> **darling, dear,** deary, **sweetheart, sweetie, sweet,** sweets, sweetkins, **honey,** hon, honeybun, honey-bunny, honeybunch, honey child, sugar, love, lover, precious, precious heart, pet, petkins, babe, **baby, doll,** baby-doll, cherub, angel, chick, chickabiddy, buttercup, duck, duckling, ducks, lamb, lambkin, snookums, poppet <Brit>
7 **courtship, courting, wooing;** court, suit, suing, amorous pursuit, addresses; gallantry; serenade
8 **proposal,** marriage proposal, offer of marriage, popping of the question; engagement 436.3
9 **flirtation, flirtiness, coquetry,** dalliance; flirtatiousness, coquettishness, coyness; sheep's eyes, goo-goo eyes <nf>, puppy-dog eyes <nf>, amorous looks, coquettish glances, come-hither look; ogle, side-glance; bedroom eyes <nf>
10 **philandering,** philander, lady-killing <nf>; lechery, licentiousness, unchastity 665
11 **flirt, coquette,** gold digger *and* vamp <nf>; strumpet, whore 665.14,16
12 **philanderer,** philander, woman chaser, **ladies' man,** heartbreaker, rake, cad, man of the world; masher, lady-killer, wolf, skirt chaser, man on the make *and* make-out artist <nf>; libertine, lecher, cocksman

<nf>, seducer 665.12, gigolo, Casanova, Don Juan, Lothario; male prostitute, stud; roving eye

13 **love letter,** billet-doux, mash note <nf>; valentine

VERBS **14** **make love,** bill *and* coo; dally, toy, trifle, wanton, make time; sweet-talk <nf>, whisper sweet nothings; go steady, keep company; copulate

15 <nf terms> **make out, neck,** pet, spoon, smooch, lollygag, canoodle, pitch *or* fling woo, play kissy-face *or* kissy-kissy *or* kissy-huggy *or* kissy-poo *or* lickey-face *or* smacky-lips, suck face, swap spit

16 **caress, pet,** pat; feel *or* feel up <nf>, **fondle,** dandle, coddle, cocker, cosset; pat on the head *or* cheek, chuck under the chin

17 **cuddle, snuggle, nestle,** nuzzle; lap; bundle

18 **embrace, hug, clasp, press, squeeze** <nf>, fold, **enfold,** bosom, embosom, put *or* throw one's arms around, take to *or* in one's arms, fold to the heart, press to the bosom

19 **kiss, osculate,** buss, smack, smooch <nf>; blow a kiss

20 **flirt, coquet; philander,** gallivant, play the field <nf>, run *or* play around, sow one's oats; **make eyes at, ogle,** eye, cast coquettish glances, cast sheep's eyes at, make goo-goo eyes at <nf>, *faire les yeux doux* <Fr>, look sweet upon <nf>; play hard to get

21 **court, woo,** sue, press one's suit, **pay court** *or* **suit to,** make suit to, cozy up to <nf>, eye up *and* chat up <Brit nf>, pay one's court to, address, pay one's addresses to, pay attention to, lay siege to, fling oneself at, throw oneself at the head of; **pursue,** follow; chase <nf>; set one's cap at *or* for <nf>; serenade; spark <nf>, squire, esquire, beau, sweetheart <nf>, swain

22 **propose, pop the question** <nf>, ask for one's hand; become engaged

ADJS **23** amatory, amative; sexual 75.25; caressive; **flirtatious,** flirty; **coquettish,** coy, come-hither

563 MARRIAGE

NOUNS **1** **marriage, matrimony, wedlock, married status,** holy matrimony, holy wedlock, match, matching, match-up, splicing <nf>, union, matrimonial union, alliance, marriage sacrament, sacrament of matrimony *or* marriage, bond *or* state of matrimony, wedding knot, conjugal bond *or* tie *or* knot, conjugality, nuptial bond *or* tie *or* knot, one flesh, alliance; married state *or* status, wedded state *or* status, wedded bliss, conjugal bliss, weddedness, wifehood, coverture, husbandhood, spousehood; coverture, cohabitation; bed, marriage bed, bridal bed, bridebed; living as man and wife, common-law marriage; tying the knot *and* getting hitched *and* getting spliced <nf>; intermarriage, mixed marriage, interfaith marriage, interracial marriage; remarriage; arranged marriage; lesbian marriage, homosexual marriage, gay marriage, civil union; miscegenation; misalliance, *mésalliance* <Fr>

2 **marriageability,** marriageableness, nubility, ripeness; age of consent

3 **wedding, marriage,** marriage *or* wedding ceremony, nuptial mass; church wedding, civil wedding, civil ceremony, courthouse wedding; espousement, bridal; banns; wedding bells, **nuptials,** spousals, espousals, marriage vows, hymeneal rites, wedding service; commitment ceremony; wedding canopy; white wedding; wedding song, marriage song, nuptial song, prothalamium, epithalamium, epithalamy, hymen, hymeneal; wedding veil, saffron veil *or* robe; bridechamber, bridal suite, nuptial apartment; **honeymoon;** forced marriage, shotgun wedding; Gretna Green wedding, elopement; wedding planner

4 **wedding party;** wedding attendant, usher; **best man,** bridesman, groomsman; paranymph; **bridesmaid,** bridemaiden, maid *or* matron of honor; attendant, flower girl, train bearer, ring bearer

5 **newlywed; bridegroom, groom; bride,** plighted bride, blushing bride; war bride, GI bride <nf>; honeymooner

6 **spouse,** espouser, espoused, **mate,** yokemate, partner, consort, **better half** <nf>, other half <nf>, one's promised, one's betrothed, soul mate, helpmate, helpmeet; old ball and chain <nf>

7 **husband, married man,** man, benedict, goodman , old man <nf>, hubby <nf>

8 **wife, married woman,** wedded wife, goodwife *or* goody , squaw, woman, lady, matron, old lady *and* old woman *and* little woman *and* ball and chain <nf>, feme, feme covert, **better half** <nf>, **helpmate,** helpmeet, rib, wife of one's bosom; wife in name only; wife in all but name, concubine, common-law wife; blushing bride, war bride, GI bride

9 **married couple,** wedded pair, bridal pair, happy couple, **man and wife,** husband and wife, man and woman, *vir et uxor* <L>, one flesh, Mr and Mrs; newlyweds, **bride and groom**, honeymooners

10 **harem, seraglio,** serai, gynaeceum; zenana, purdah

11 **monogamist,** monogynist; **bigamist;** digamist, deuterogamist; trigamist; **polygamist,** polygynist, polyandrist; Bluebeard

12 **matchmaker, marriage broker,** matrimonial agent, *shadchan* <Yiddish>; matrimonial agency *or* bureau; go-between; dating agency *or* service, lonely hearts club, computer dating

13 <god> Hymen; <goddesses> Hera, Teleia; Juno, Pronuba; Frigg

VERBS 14 <join in marriage> **marry,** wed, nuptial, **join, unite, hitch** *and* **splice** <nf>, couple, match, match up, make *or* arrange a match, join together, **unite in marriage,** join *or* unite in holy wedlock *or* matrimony, tie the knot, tie the nuptial *or* wedding knot, celebrate a marriage, make one, pronounce man and wife; give away, give in marriage; marry off, find a mate for, find a husband *or* wife for

15 <get married> **marry, wed,** contract matrimony, say "I do", mate, couple, espouse, wive, **take to wife,** take a wife *or* husband, **get hitched** *or* spliced <nf>, tie the knot, become one, be made one, pair off, give one's hand to, bestow one's hand upon, lead to the altar, take for better *or* for worse; make an honest man *or* woman of; remarry, rewed; intermarry, interwed, miscegenate

16 **honeymoon,** go on a honeymoon, consummate one's marriage; second-honeymoon

17 **cohabit,** cohabitate, live together, live as man and wife, share one's bed and board; shack up <nf>

ADJS 18 **matrimonial, marital, conjugal, connubial, nuptial,** wedded, married, hymeneal; epithalamic; **spousal;** husbandly, uxorious; bridal, wifely, uxorial; premarital, concubinal, concubinary

19 **monogamous,** monogynous, monandrous; **bigamous,** digamous; **polygamous,** polygynous, polyandrous; morganatic; miscegenetic

20 **marriageable,** nubile, eligible, ripe, of age, of marriageable age

21 **married, wedded,** newlywed, espoused, one, one bone and one flesh, mated, matched, coupled, partnered, paired, hitched *and* spliced *and* hooked <nf>

564 RELATIONSHIP BY MARRIAGE

NOUNS 1 **marriage relationship,** affinity, marital affinity; connection, family connection, marriage connection, matrimonial connection

2 **in-laws** <nf>, **relatives-in-law;** brother-in-law, sister-in-law, father-in-law, mother-in-law, son-in-law, daughter-in-law

3 stepfather, stepmother; stepbrother, stepsister; stepchild, stepson, stepdaughter

ADJS 4 **affinal,** affined, by marriage

565 CELIBACY

NOUNS **1 celibacy, singleness,** singlehood, single blessedness, single *or* unmarried *or* unwed state *or* condition; **bachelorhood,** bachelordom, bachelorism, bachelorship; **spinsterhood,** maidenhood, maidenhead, **virginity,** maiden *or* virgin state, chastity, chasteness; **monasticism,** monachism, spiritual marriage, holy orders, the veil; misogamy, misogyny; self-restraint, self-denial; sexual abstinence *or* abstention, continence 664.3

2 celibate, *célibataire* <Fr>; monk, monastic, lama, bhikkhu, priest, nun, cenobite, eremite; virgin, vestal; misogamist, misogynist; unmarried, single <nf>

3 bachelor, bach *and* old bach <nf>, single *or* unmarried man, confirmed bachelor, **single man**, unattached male; misogamist

4 single *or* unmarried woman, spinster, spinstress, **old maid,** maid, maiden, bachelor girl, single girl, lone woman, maiden lady, feme sole, unattached female; **virgin,** virgo intacta, cherry <nf>; vestal, vestal virgin

VERBS **5 be unmarried, be single, live alone,** enjoy single blessedness, **bach** *and* **bach it** <nf>, keep bachelor quarters, keep one's freedom, sit on the shelf <nf>

ADJS **6 celibate**, celibatic**; monastic,** monachal, **monkish,** cenobitic, nunnish; misogamic, misogynous; sexually abstinent *or* continent, abstinent, abstaining; self-restrained

7 unmarried, unwedded, unwed, single, sole, spouseless, wifeless, husbandless, unmated, mateless; **bachelorly,** bachelorlike; **spinsterly,** spinsterish, spinsterlike; **oldmaidish,** old-maidenish; maiden, maidenly; virgin, virginal; independent, unattached, fancy-free; on the shelf <nf>

566 DIVORCE, WIDOWHOOD

NOUNS **1 divorce,** divorcement, grasswidowhood, civil divorce, **separation,** legal *or* judicial separation, separate maintenance; interlocutory decree; dissolution of marriage; divorce decree, decree nisi, decree absolute; annulment, decree of nullity; nonconsummation of marriage, estrangement, living apart, desertion; broken marriage, broken home; breakup, split-up, split, marriage on the rocks <nf>

2 divorcé, divorced person, divorced man, divorced woman, *divorcée* <Fr>, free man *or* woman; divorcer; grass widow, grass widower

3 widowhood, viduity ; **widowerhood,** widowership; weeds, widow's weeds

4 widow, widow woman <nf>, relict; dowager, queen dowager *or* dowager queen, merry widow, war widow; **widower,** widowman <nf>

VERBS **5 divorce, separate,** part, split up *and* split the sheets <nf>, unmarry, put away, obtain a divorce, dissolve one's marriage, come to a parting of the ways, untie the knot, sue for divorce, file for divorce; have one's marriage annulled; grant a divorce, grant a final decree; grant an annulment, grant a decree of nullity, annul a marriage, put asunder, regain one's freedom; break up, split up, split, sunder; separate, live apart, part, be estranged; desert, abandon, leave, walk out

6 widow, bereave, make a widow

ADJS **7** widowly, widowish, widowlike; **widowed,** widowered; **divorced;** separated, legally separated, split, estranged; on the rocks <nf>

567 SCHOOL

NOUNS **1 school, educational institution,** teaching institution, academic *or* scholastic institution, teaching and research institution, **institute, academy,** seminary, *Schule* <Ger>, *école* <Fr>, *escuela* <Sp>; alternative school; magnet school

2 preschool, prekindergarten, pre-K, infant school <Brit>, nursery, **nursery school;** day nursery, **day-care center,** crèche; playschool; **kindergarten**

3 **elementary school, grade school** *or* graded school, the grades; **primary school;** junior school <Brit>; **grammar school;** folk school, home schooling

4 **secondary school,** middle school, **academy,** *Gymnasium* <Ger>; *lycée* <Fr>, lyceum; **high school,** high <nf>; **junior high school,** junior high <nf>, intermediate school; **senior high school,** senior high <nf>; **preparatory school,** prep school <nf>, public school <Brit>, seminary; **grammar school** <Brit>, Latin school; charter school

5 **college, university,** institution *or* institute of higher education or learning, degree-granting institution; tertiary school, graduate school, post graduate school, coeducational school; academe, academia, the groves of Academe, **the campus,** the halls of learning or ivy, ivied halls; alma mater; women's college; polytechnic, adult education, correspondence course; distance learning, distance education, e-learning, online degree, virtual classroom; professional development

6 **service school, service academy**, military academy, naval academy

7 **art school, performing arts school,** music school, conservatory, arts conservatory, school of the arts, dance school

8 **religious school**, parochial school, church-related school, church school; Sunday school

9 **reform school, reformatory,** correctional institution, industrial school, training school; borstal *or* borstal school *or* remand school <Brit>

10 **schoolhouse,** school building; little red schoolhouse; classroom building; portable classroom; hall; campus

11 **schoolroom, classroom;** recitation room; lecture room or hall; auditorium, assembly hall; theater, amphitheater

12 **governing board, board;** board of education, school board; college board, board of regents, board of trustees, board of visitors

ADJS 13 **scholastic, academic,** institutional, **school,** classroom; **collegiate; university;** preschool; interscholastic, intercollegiate, extramural; intramural

568 TEACHING

NOUNS 1 **teaching, instruction, education, schooling, tuition; edification, enlightenment,** illumination; tutelage, tutorage, tutorship; tutoring, coaching, direction, training, preparation, private teaching, teacher 571; spoon-feeding; direction, guidance; **pedagogy,** pedagogics, didactics, didacticism; scholarship; catechization; computer-aided instruction, programmed instruction; home schooling; self-teaching, self-instruction; distance education; information 551; reeducation 858.4; **school** 567; **formal education,** coursework, schoolwork

2 **inculcation, indoctrination,** catechization, inoculation, **implantation,** infixation, infixion, **impression, instillment,** instillation, impregnation, **infusion,** imbuement; absorption and regurgitation; dictation; conditioning, brainwashing; reindoctrination 858.5

3 **training, preparation,** readying <nf>, **conditioning, grooming,** cultivation, development, improvement; **discipline;** breaking, housebreaking; **upbringing, bringing-up,** fetching-up <nf>, **rearing, raising, breeding, nurture,** nurturing, fostering; **practice,** rehearsal, **exercise, drill,** drilling; **apprenticeship,** in-service training, on-the-job training; work-study; military training, basic training; manual training, sloyd; vocational training *or* education; **liberal arts,** arithmetic, astronomy, geometry, grammar, logic, music, rhetoric

4 preinstruction, pre-education; **priming,** cramming <nf>

5 **elementary education**, nursery school, preschool, primary education, home schooling**; initiation, introduction,** propaedeutic; **rudiments,** grounding, first steps,

elements, **ABC's, basics;** reading, writing, and arithmetic, **three R's;** primer, hornbook, abecedarium, abecedary

6 **instructions, directions, orders; briefing,** final instructions

7 **lesson, teaching, instruction, lecture,** lecture-demonstration, harangue, **discourse,** disquisition, exposition, **talk,** homily, **sermon,** preachment; chalk talk <nf>; skull session <nf>; **recitation,** recital; **assignment, exercise,** task, set task, homework; moral, morality, moral compass, moralization, moral lesson; object lesson

8 **study,** branch of learning, branch of knowledge; **discipline,** subdiscipline; **field, specialty,** academic specialty, area; **course,** course of study, **curriculum**, syllabus, module, department**; subject;** major, minor; requirement *or* required course, elective course, core curriculum; refresher course; summer *or* summer-session course, intersession course; crash course; gut course <nf>; correspondence course; distance-learning course; **seminar,** proseminar; professional development

9 physical education, physical culture, gymnastics, calisthenics, eurythmics

VERBS **10 teach, instruct,** give instruction, give lessons in, **educate, school; edify, enlighten,** civilize, illumine; **direct, guide;** get across, **inform** 551.8; **show,** show how, show the ropes, demonstrate; give an idea of; put in the right, set right; improve one's mind, enlarge *or* broaden the mind; sharpen the wits, open the eyes *or* mind; teach a lesson, give a lesson to; **ground,** teach the rudiments *or* elements *or* basics; catechize; teach an old dog new tricks; reeducate 858.14

11 **tutor, coach**, mentor, direct; **prime, cram** <nf>, cram with facts, stuff with knowledge

12 **inculcate, indoctrinate,** catechize, inoculate, **instill, infuse,** imbue, impregnate, **implant,** infix, impress; **impress upon the mind** *or* **memory,** urge on the mind, beat into, beat or knock into one's head, grind in, drill into, drum into one's head or skull; **condition, brainwash, program**

13 **train; drill, exercise; practice,** rehearse; keep in practice, keep one's hand in; **prepare,** ready, **condition, groom,** fit, put in tune, form, **lick into shape** <nf>; **rear, raise, bring up,** fetch up <nf>, bring up by hand, **breed; cultivate,** develop, improve; **nurture, foster,** nurse; **discipline,** take in hand; put through the mill *or* grind <nf>; break, break in, housebreak, house-train <Brit>; put to school, send to school, apprentice

14 preinstruct, pre-educate; **initiate,** introduce

15 **give instructions,** give directions; **brief,** give a briefing

16 **expound,** exposit; explain 341.10; **lecture, discourse,** harangue, hold forth, give or read a lesson; **preach,** sermonize; **moralize,** point a moral

17 **assign,** give *or* make an assignment, give homework, set a task, set hurdles; lay out a course, make a syllabus

ADJS **18 educational,** educative, educating, educatory, teaching, **instructive,** instructional, **tuitional,** tuitionary; **cultural, edifying, enlightening,** illuminating; informative, informational; edifying; didactic, preceptive; self instructional, self-teaching, autodidactic; lecturing, preaching, hortatory, exhortatory, homiletic, homiletical; initiatory, introductory, propaedeutic; **disciplinary;** coeducational; remedial

19 **scholastic, academic, schoolish, pedantic, donnish** <Brit>; **scholarly; pedagogical;** collegiate, graduate, professional, doctoral, graduate-professional, postgraduate; interdisciplinary, cross-disciplinary, transdisciplinary; curricular, intramural, extramural, varsity

20 extracurricular, extraclassroom; nonscholastic, noncollegiate

569 MISTEACHING

NOUNS **1 misteaching,** misinstruction; **misguidance,** misdirection, misleading; sophistry 935; perversion, corruption; mystification, obscuration, obfuscation, obscurantism; **misinformation,** misknowledge; the blind leading the blind; college of Laputa

2 **propaganda;** propagandism, indoctrination; brainwashing; **propagandist,** agitprop; **disinformation;** war of nerves

VERBS 3 **misteach,** misinstruct, miseducate; **misinform;** misadvise, **misguide,** misdirect, **mislead;** pervert, corrupt; mystify, obscure, obfuscate

4 **propagandize,** carry on a propaganda; indoctrinate; **disinform,** brainwash

ADJS 5 **mistaught,** misinstructed; **misinformed;** misadvised, **misguided,** misdirected, **misled**

6 misteaching, misinstructive, miseducative, **misinforming; misleading,** misguiding, misdirecting; obscuring, mystifying, obfuscatory; propagandistic, indoctrinational; disinformational

570 LEARNING

NOUNS 1 **learning,** intellectual acquirement *or* acquisition *or* attainment, stocking *or* storing the mind, mental cultivation, mental culture, improving *or* broadening the mind, acquisition of knowledge, scholarship; **mastery,** mastery of skills; **self-education,** self-instruction; **knowledge, erudition** 928.5; education 568.1; memorization 989.3; cultural literacy; professional student

2 **absorption,** ingestion, imbibing, assimilation, taking-in, getting, getting hold of, getting the hang of <nf>, soaking-up, digestion; aha moment

3 **study, studying,** application, conning; **reading, perusal;** restudy, restudying, brushing up, boning up <nf>, **review; contemplation** 931.2; **inspection** 938.3; **engrossment; brainwork, headwork,** lucubration, mental labor; exercise, **practice, drill;** grind *and* grinding *and* boning <nf>, boning up <nf>; **cramming** *and* cram <nf>, swotting <Brit nf>; extensive study, wide reading; subject 568.8

4 **studiousness, scholarliness,** scholarship; bookishness, diligence 330.6; learnedness, intellectuality, literacy, polymathy, erudition

5 **teachableness, teachability, educability,** trainableness; **aptness, aptitude,** quickness, **readiness; receptivity,** mind like a blotter, ready grasp, quick mind, quick study; **willingness, motivation,** hunger *or* thirst for learning, willingness to learn, curiosity, inquisitiveness; docility, **malleability,** moldability, pliability, facility, plasticity, **impressionability,** susceptibility, formability; brightness, cleverness, quickness, readiness, **intelligence** 920

VERBS 6 **learn,** get, get hold of <nf>, get into one's head, get through one's thick skull <nf>; **gain knowledge,** pick up information, gather *or* collect *or* glean knowledge *or* learning; stock *or* store the mind, improve *or* broaden the mind; stuff *or* cram the mind; burden *or* load the mind; **find out, ascertain, discover,** find, determine, figure out; **become informed,** gain knowledge *or* understanding of, acquire information *or* intelligence about, research, become aware of, **learn about, find out about,** do the math; acquaint oneself with, make oneself acquainted with, become acquainted with; be informed 551.14

7 **absorb, acquire, take in,** ingest, imbibe, get by osmosis, **assimilate, digest, soak up,** drink in; **soak in, seep in,** percolate in

8 **memorize** 989.16, get by rote; fix in the mind 989.17

9 **master,** attain mastery of, make oneself master of, **gain command of, become adept in,** become familiar *or* conversant with, become versed *or* well-versed in, **get up in** *or* **on,** gain a good *or* thorough knowledge of, **learn all about, get down pat** <nf>, get down cold <nf>, get taped <Brit nf>, get to the bottom *or* heart of; **get the hang** *or*

knack of; learn the ropes, learn the ins and outs; know well 928.13

10 **learn by experience,** learn by doing, **live and learn,** go through the school of hard knocks, learn the hard way <nf>; teach *or* school oneself; **learn a lesson,** be taught a lesson

11 **be taught, receive instruction,** be tutored, be instructed, undergo schooling, pursue one's education, attend classes, go to *or* attend school, take lessons, be mentored, matriculate, enroll, register; **train,** prepare oneself, ready oneself, go into training; serve an apprenticeship; apprentice, apprentice oneself to; **study with,** read with, sit at the feet of, learn from, have as one's master; monitor, audit

12 **study,** regard studiously, apply oneself to, con, crack a book *and* hit the books <nf>; **read, peruse,** go over, read up *or* read up on, have one's nose in a book <nf>; restudy, **review; contemplate** 931.12; **examine** 938.21; give mind to 983.5; **pore over,** vet <Brit nf>; be highly motivated, hunger *or* thirst for knowledge; bury oneself in, wade through, plunge into, throw oneself into; **dig** *and* **grind** *and* **bone** *and* bone up on <nf>, swot <Brit nf>; lucubrate, elucubrate, **burn the midnight oil;** make a study of; **practice, drill**

13 **browse, scan, skim, dip into,** thumb over *or* through, run over *or* through, glance *or* run the eye over *or* through, turn over the leaves, have a look at, hit the high spots, graze

14 **study up, get up,** study up on, read up on, get up on; **review, brush up,** polish up <nf>, rub up, **cram** *or* cram up <nf>, **bone up** <nf>; pull an all-nighter

15 **study to be, study for, read for,** read law, etc; **specialize in, go in for,** make one's field; major in, minor in

ADJS 16 educated, **learned** 928.21,22; knowledgeable, erudite; literate, numerate; self-taught, self-instructed, autodidactic

17 **studious,** devoted to studies, **scholarly,** scholastic, academic, professorial, tweedy, donnish <Brit>; owlish; rabbinic, mandarin; pedantic, dryasdust; bookish 928.22; diligent 330.22

18 **teachable, instructable, educable,** schoolable, trainable; **apt,** quick, **ready,** ripe for instruction; **receptive, willing,** motivated; hungry *or* thirsty for knowledge; docile, **malleable, moldable,** pliable, facile, plastic, **impressionable,** susceptible, formable; bright, clever, **intelligent** 920.12

571 TEACHER

NOUNS 1 **teacher, instructor, educator,** preceptor, **mentor; master,** maestro; **pedagogue,** pedagogist, educationist, educationalist, tutor; schoolman; **schoolteacher, schoolmaster,** schoolkeeper; abecedarian , certified *or* licensed teacher; **professor, academic,** member of academy; don <Brit>, fellow; guide 574.7, docent; rabbi, pandit, pundit, guru, *mullah* <Persian>; home tutor, private tutor, mentor

2 <woman teachers> instructress, educatress, preceptress, **mistress; schoolmistress; schoolma'am** *or* **schoolmarm**, dame, schooldame; **governess**, duenna

3 <academic ranks> professor, associate professor, assistant professor, instructor, tutor, associate, assistant, lecturer, reader <Brit>; visiting professor; emeritus, professor emeritus, retired professor

4 teaching fellow, teaching assistant *or* TA; paraeducator; teaching intern, fellow, intern; practice teacher, apprentice teacher, student *or* pupil teacher; teacher's aide, paraprofessional; monitor, proctor, prefect, praepostor <Brit>; student assistant, graduate assistant

5 **tutor,** tutorer; **coach,** coacher; **private instructor**

6 **trainer, handler, groomer;** driller, drillmaster; **coach,** athletic coach

7 **lecturer,** lector, **reader** <Brit>, praelector, **preacher,** homilist

8 principal, headmaster, headmistress, vice-principal; president, chancellor, vice-chancellor, rector, provost, master; **dean,** academic dean, dean of the faculty, dean of women, dean of men; administrator, educational administrator; administration; department head *or* chair

9 faculty, staff <Brit>, faculty members, professorate, professoriate, professors, professordom, teaching staff

10 instructorship, teachership, preceptorship, schoolmastery; **tutorship,** tutorhood, tutorage, tutelage; **professorship,** professorhood, professorate, professoriate; **chair,** endowed chair; lectureship, readership <Brit>; fellowship, research fellowship; assistantship

ADJS **11 pedagogic, pedagogical,** preceptorial, tutorial; **teacherish,** teachery, teacherlike, teachy, **schoolteacherish,** schoolteachery, **schoolmasterish,** schoolmasterly, schoolmastering, schoolmasterlike; schoolmistressy, schoolmarmish <nf>; **professorial,** professorlike, academic, tweedy, donnish <Brit>; pedantic 928.22

572 STUDENT

NOUNS **1 student, pupil, scholar,** learner, studier, educatee, **trainee,** *élève* <Fr>; tutee; inquirer; mature student, adult-education *or* continuing education student; self-taught person, autodidact; auditor; **reader,** reading enthusiast, great reader, printhead <nf>; bookworm, researcher; opsimath

2 disciple, follower, apostle; convert, proselyte 858.7; **discipleship,** disciplehood, pupilage, tutelage, studentship, followership

3 schoolchild, school kid <nf>; **schoolboy,** school lad; **schoolgirl;** day-pupil, day boy, day girl; preschool child, preschooler, nursery school child, infant <Brit>; kindergartner, grade schooler, primary schooler, intermediate schooler; secondary schooler, prep schooler, preppie <nf>, high schooler; schoolmate, schoolfellow, fellow student, classmate

4 special *or* exceptional student, gifted student; special education *or* special ed <nf> student; learning disabled *or* LD student; learning impaired student; slow learner, underachiever; handicapped *or* retarded student; emotionally disturbed student; culturally disadvantaged student

5 college student, collegian, collegiate, university student, **varsity student** <Brit nf>, college boy *or* girl; co-ed <nf>; seminarian, seminarist

6 undergraduate, undergrad <nf>, cadet, midshipman; underclassman, **freshman,** freshie <nf>, plebe, **sophomore,** soph <nf>; **upperclassman, junior, senior**

7 <Brit terms> commoner, pensioner, sizar, servitor , exhibitioner, fellow commoner; sophister *and* questionist ; wrangler, optime; passman; muggle

8 graduate, grad <nf>; **alumnus,** alumni, alumna, alumnae; old boy <Brit>; **graduate student,** grad student <nf>, master's degree candidate, doctoral candidate; **postgraduate,** postgrad <nf>; degrees; college graduate, college man *or* woman, educated man *or* woman, educated class; meritocracy

9 novice, novitiate *or* noviciate, **tyro,** abecedarian, alphabetarian, **beginner** 818.2, entrant, **neophyte, tenderfoot** *and* **greenhorn** <nf>, freshman, **fledgling;** newbie; Bambi; catechumen, initiate, debutant; new boy <Brit>, newcomer 774.4; ignoramus 930.7; **recruit, raw recruit,** inductee, **rookie** *and* yardbird <nf>, boot; **probationer,** probationist, postulant; **apprentice,** articled clerk

10 nerd *or* egghead *or* grind *or* greasy grind <nf>, swotter *or* mugger <Brit nf>; bookworm 929.4

11 class, form <Brit>, **grade;** track; year

ADJS **12 studentlike,** schoolboyish, schoolgirlish; undergraduate, graduate, postgraduate; **collegiate,** college-bred; sophomoric; sophomorical; autodidactic; **studious** 570.17; **learned, bookish** 928.22; exceptional, gifted, special

13 **probationary,** probational, on probation; in detention

573 DIRECTION, MANAGEMENT

NOUNS 1 **direction, management, managing,** managery , handling, **running** <nf>, **conduct;** governance, **command, control, chiefdom, government** 612, governance, controllership; **authority** 417; **regulation,** ordering, husbandry; manipulation, orchestration; **guidance, lead, leading; steering, navigation,** pilotage, conning, the conn, the helm, the wheel

2 **supervision, superintendence,** intendance *or* intendancy, heading, heading up *and* **bossing** *and* running <nf>; **surveillance,** oversight, eye; **charge, care, auspices, jurisdiction; responsibility,** accountability 641.2

3 **administration,** executive function *or* role, command function, say-so *and* last word <nf>; **decision-making; disposition,** disposal, **dispensation;** officiation; lawmaking, legislation, regulation

4 **directorship, leadership, managership,** directorate, headship, governorship, chairmanship, convenership <Brit>, presidency, premiership, generalship, captainship; mastership 417.7; dictatorship, sovereignty 417.8; superintendence *or* **superintendency,** intendancy, foremanship, overseership, supervisorship; stewardship, custody, guardianship, shepherding, proctorship; personnel management; collective leadership

5 **helm,** conn, rudder, tiller, wheel, steering wheel; **reins;** joystick; remote control *or* remote

6 **domestic management, housekeeping,** homemaking, housewifery, ménage, husbandry ; domestic economy, home economics

7 **efficiency engineering,** scientific management, bean-counting <nf>, industrial engineering, management engineering, management consulting; management theory; efficiency expert, management consultant; time and motion study, time-motion study, time study; therblig

VERBS 8 **direct, manage, regulate, conduct, carry on, handle, run** <nf>, be in charge; **control, command, head, govern** 612.11, rule, **boss** *and* head up *and* pull the strings *and* **mastermind** *and* quarterback *and* call the signals <nf>; **order, prescribe;** organize; lay down the law, make the rules, call the shots *or* tune <nf>; **head,** head up, office, captain, skipper <nf>; **lead,** take the lead, lead on; manipulate, maneuver, engineer; take command 417.14; be responsible for; hold the purse strings <nf>

9 **guide, steer, drive, run** <nf>; herd, counsel, advise, shepherd; channel; **pilot,** take the helm *or* wheel, be at the helm *or* wheel *or* tiller *or* rudder, hold the reins, **be in the driver's seat** <nf>; emcee

10 **supervise, superintend, boss, oversee,** overlook, ride herd on <nf>, crack the whip <nf>, stand over, keep an eye on *or* upon, keep in order; cut work out for; straw-boss <nf>; take care of 1008.19

11 **administer,** administrate; **officiate; preside,** preside over, preside at the board; chair, chairman, occupy the chair, take the chair

ADJS 12 **directing, directive,** directory, directorial; **managing, managerial; commanding, controlling, governing** 612.17; regulating, regulative, regulatory; **head, chief;** leading, guiding

13 **supervising, supervisory,** overseeing, **superintendent, boss; in charge** 417.21, in the driver's seat *and* holding the reins <nf>

14 **administrative, administrating;** ministerial, **executive; officiating, presiding**

ADVS 15 in the charge of, in the hands of, in the care of; **under the auspices of,** under the aegis of; in one's charge, on one's hands, under one's care, under one's jurisdiction

574 DIRECTOR

NOUNS **1 director,** *directeur* <Fr>, director general, **governor,** rector, **manager, administrator,** intendant, **conductor;** person in charge, responsible person, key person; ship's husband, supercargo; impresario, producer; deputy, agent 576

2 superintendent; supervisor, foreman, monitor, **head,** headman, overman, **boss,** chief, gaffer *and* ganger <Brit nf>, taskmaster; sirdar <India>, **overseer,** overlooker; inspector, surveyor; proctor; subforeman, **straw boss** <nf>; slave driver; boatswain; floorman, floorwalker, floor manager; noncommissioned officer 575.19, controller, comptroller, auditor; department head; chief cook and bottle washer <nf>

3 executive, officer, official, pinstriper <nf>, employer, company official; suit <nf>; **president,** prexy <nf>, chief executive officer *or* CEO, chief executive, chief operating officer *or* COO, managing director, director; provost, prefect, warden, archon; policy-maker, agenda-setter; magistrate; **chairman of the board; chancellor,** vice-chancellor; vice-president *or* VP *or* veep <nf>; secretary; treasurer; dean; executive officer, executive director, executive secretary; **management,** the administration 574.11

4 steward, bailiff <Brit>, reeve , factor, seneschal; majordomo, butler, housekeeper, *maître d'hôtel* <Fr>; master of ceremonies *or* MC *and* emcee <nf>, master of the revels; proctor, procurator, attorney; guardian, custodian 1008.6, executor; curator, librarian; croupier; factor

5 chairman, chairwoman, **chair,** chairperson, convener <Brit>, speaker, presiding officer; cochairman, etc

6 leader, conductor ; file leader, fugleman; pacemaker, pacesetter, honcho; bellwether, bell mare, bell cow, Judas goat; standard-bearer, torchbearer; **leader of men,** born leader, charismatic leader *or* figure, inspired leader; messiah, Mahdi; führer, duce; forerunner 816.1; ringleader 375.11; precentor, coryphaeus, choragus, symphonic conductor, choirmaster 710.18

7 guide, guider; **shepherd,** herd, herdsman, drover, cowherd, goatherd, etc; tour guide, tour director *or* conductor, cicerone, mercury , courier, dragoman; **pilot,** river pilot, navigator, **helmsman,** timoneer, steerman, steerer, coxswain, boatsteerer, boatheader; automatic pilot, Gyropilot; pointer, fingerpost <Brit>, guidepost 517.4; leader, motivator, pacesetter, standard-bearer

8 guiding star, guiding light, cynosure , **polestar,** polar star, lodestar, Polaris, **North Star**

9 compass, magnetic compass, gyrocompass, gyroscopic compass, gyrostatic compass, Gyrosin compass, surveyor's compass, mariner's compass; needle, magnetic needle; direction finder, radio compass, radio direction finder *or* RDF

10 directory, guidebook, handbook, Baedeker; city directory, business directory; telephone directory, telephone book, phone book <nf>, classified directory, Yellow Pages; **bibliography;** catalog, index, handlist, checklist, finding list; itinerary, road map, roadbook; gazetteer, reference book

11 directorate, directory, **management, the administration,** the brass *and* top brass <nf>, the people upstairs *and* the people in the front office <nf>, executive hierarchy; the executive, executive arm *or* branch; middle management; **cabinet; board,** governing board *or* body, board of directors, board of trustees, board of regents; steering committee, executive committee, interlocking directorate; cadre, executive council; infrastructure; council 423

575 MASTER

NOUNS **1 master, lord, lord and master,** overlord, seigneur, paramount, lord paramount, liege, liege lord, lord of the manor, *padrone* <Ital>, *patron* and *chef* <Fr>, patroon; **chief, boss,** sahib <India>, *bwana* <Swah>; employer; husband, man of the house, master of the house, goodman <old nf>, paterfamilias; patriarch, elder; teacher, rabbi, guru, starets; church dignitary, ecclesiarch

2 **mistress,** governess, dame , madam; **matron, housewife,** homemaker, goodwife, mistress *or* lady of the house, chatelaine; housemistress, housemother; rectoress, abbess, mother superior; great lady, first lady; materfamilias, matriarch, dowager

3 **chief,** principal, headman; **master,** dean, doyen, doyenne; high priest <nf>, superior, senior; **leader** 574.6; important person, personage 997.8; owner, landowner

4 <nf terms> **top dog,** boss man, big boy, Big Daddy, big cheese, kingpin, kingfish, el supremo, honcho *or* head honcho, top banana, big enchilada, bigwig, big gun, top gun, big shot, big wheel, VIP, himself, herself, man *or* woman upstairs, cock of the walk; queen bee, heavy momma, Big Momma, old man, quarterback, ringmaster, skipper, high priest

5 **figurehead,** nominal head, dummy, lay figure, front man *and* front <nf>, stooge *and* Charlie McCarthy <nf>, puppet, creature; straw man, lame duck

6 **governor, ruler; captain, master, commander,** commandant, commanding officer, intendant, castellan, chatelain, chatelaine; **director, manager, executive** 574.3

7 **head of state, chief of state**, leader; **premier, prime minister, chancellor,** grand vizier, dewan <India>; doge; **president,** chief executive, POTUS <nf>, the man in the White House

8 **potentate, sovereign, monarch,** absolute monarch, **ruler, prince,** dynast, **crowned head, emperor,** *imperator* <L>, king-emperor, **king,** anointed king, majesty, royalty, royal, royal personage, emperor, etc; petty king, tetrarch, kinglet; grand duke; paramount, lord paramount, suzerain, overlord, overking, high king; **chief, chieftain,** high chief; prince consort 608.7

9 <rulers> **caesar,** kaiser, **czar;** Holy Roman Emperor; Dalai Lama; **pharaoh;** pendragon, rig, ardri; **mikado,** tenno; shogun, tycoon; khan *or* cham; shah, padishah; negus; bey; sheikh; sachem, sagamore; Inca; cacique; kaid

10 <Muslim rulers> **sultan,** Grand Turk, grand seignior; caliph, imam; hakim; khan *or* cham; nizam, nabab; emir; Great Mogul, Mogul

11 **sovereign queen, sovereign princess, princess, queen,** queen regent, queen regnant, **empress,** czarina; grand duchess; queen consort

12 **regent,** protector, prince regent, queen regent

13 <regional governors> **governor,** governor-general, lieutenant governor; **viceroy,** vice-king, exarch, proconsul, khedive, stadtholder, vizier; nabob *and* nabab *and* subahdar <India>; gauleiter; eparch; palatine; tetrarch; burgrave; collector; hospodar, vaivode; dey, bey *or* beg, beglerbeg, wali *or* vali, satrap; provincial; warlord; military governor

14 **tyrant, despot,** warlord; **autocrat,** autarch; oligarch; absolute ruler *or* master *or* monarch, omnipotent *or* all-powerful ruler; **dictator,** duce, führer, commissar, pharaoh, caesar, czar; usurper, arrogator; **oppressor, hard master,** driver, **slave driver,** Simon Legree <Harriet B Stowe>; **martinet, disciplinarian,** stickler, tin god, petty tyrant

15 **the authorities, the powers that be,** ruling class *or* classes, the lords of creation, **the Establishment,** the interests, the power elite, **the power structure; they,** them; the inner circle; the ins *and* the in-group *and* those on the inside <nf>; **management, the administration;** higher echelons, top brass <nf>; higher-ups *and* the people upstairs *or* in the front office <nf>; **the top** <nf>, the corridors of power; prelacy, hierarchy; ministry; **bureau-**

cracy, officialdom; directorate 574.11

16 **official, officer,** officiary, functionary, *fonctionnaire* <Fr>, apparatchik; **public official,** public servant; officeholder, office-bearer *and* placeman <Brit>; government *or* public employee; **civil servant; bureaucrat,** politician, mandarin, redtapist, *rond-de-cuir* <Fr>, petty tyrant, jack-in-office; The Man <nf>,

17 <public officials> **minister,** secretary, secretary of state <Brit>, undersecretary, cabinet minister, cabinet member, minister of state <Brit>; chancellor; warden; archon; magistrate; syndic; commissioner; commissar; county commissioners; city manager, mayor, *maire* <Fr>, lord mayor, burgomaster; headman; **councilman,** councilwoman, councillor, city councilman, elder, city father, alderman, alderperson, bailie, selectman; supervisor, county supervisor; reeve, portreeve; legislator 610.3

18 **commissioned officer, officer,** military leader, military officer; top brass *and* the brass <nf>; **commander in chief,** generalissimo, captain general; hetman, sirdar, commanding officer, commandant; general of the army, general of the air force, five-star general <nf>, marshal, *maréchal* <Fr>, field marshal; general officer, **general,** four-star general <nf>; lieutenant general, three-star general <nf>; major general, two-star general <nf>; brigadier general, one-star general <nf>, brigadier <Brit>; field officer; **colonel,** chicken colonel <nf>; lieutenant colonel; **major;** company officer; **captain; lieutenant,** first lieutenant; second lieutenant, shavetail <nf>, subaltern *and* sublieutenant <Brit>; warrant officer, chief warrant officer; **commander,** commandant, the Old Man <nf>; **commanding officer** *or* CO; executive officer, exec <nf>; chief of staff; aide, aide-de-camp *or* ADC; officer of the day *or* OD, orderly officer <Brit>; staff officer; senior officer, junior officer; brass hat <nf>; air marshal

19 **Army noncommissioned officer,** noncom *or* NCO <nf>; centurion; sergeant, sarge <nf>, havildar <India>; sergeant major of the Army, command sergeant major, sergeant major, first sergeant, top sergeant *and* topkick *and* first man <nf>, master sergeant, sergeant first class, technical sergeant, staff sergeant, sergeant, specialist seven, platoon sergeant, mess sergeant, color sergeant, acting sergeant, lance sergeant <Brit>; **corporal,** acting corporal, lance corporal <Brit>, lance-jack <Brit nf>; **Air Force noncommissioned officer,** chief master sergeant of the Air Force, chief master sergeant, senior master sergeant, master sergeant, technical sergeant, staff sergeant, sergeant, airman first class

20 Navy *or* **naval officer; fleet admiral,** navarch, **admiral,** vice admiral, rear admiral, **commodore, captain, commander,** lieutenant commander, **lieutenant,** lieutenant junior grade, ensign; warrant officer; Navy *or* naval noncommissioned officer, master chief petty officer of the Navy, master chief petty officer, senior chief petty officer, chief petty officer, petty officer first class, petty officer second class, petty officer third class; **Marine Corps noncommissioned officer,** sergeant major of the Marine Corps, sergeant major, master gunnery sergeant, first sergeant, master sergeant, gunnery sergeant, staff sergeant, sergeant, corporal, lance corporal

21 <heraldic officials> herald, king of arms, king at arms, earl marshal; Garter, Garter King of Arms, Clarenceux, Clarenceux King of Arms, Norroy and Ulster, Norroy and Ulster King of Arms, Norroy, Norroy King of Arms, Lyon, Lyon King of Arms; College of Arms

576 DEPUTY, AGENT

NOUNS 1 **deputy, proxy, representative, substitute,** sub <nf>, vice, vicegerent, **alternate,** backup *and* stand-in <nf>, body double, alternative, alter ego, **surrogate,** procurator, secondary, understudy, pinch hitter <nf>, utility man *or* woman, scrub <nf>, reserve, the bench <nf>; assistant, right hand, second in command, number two, executive officer; exponent, advocate, pleader, paranymph, attorney, champion; **lieutenant;** aide; vicar, vicar general; locum tenens *or* locum <chiefly Brit>; amicus curiae; **puppet,** dummy, creature, cat's-paw, figurehead; stunt man *or* woman; ghost writer

2 **delegate,** legate, appointee; **commissioner,** commissary, *commissionaire* <Fr>, commissar; **messenger,** herald, **emissary, envoy; minister,** secretary

3 **agent, instrument,** implement, implementer, trustee, broker; expediter, facilitator; **tool; steward** 574.4; **functionary; official** 575.16; clerk, **secretary;** amanuensis; factor, consignee; puppet, cat's-paw; dupe 358

4 **go-between, middleman, intermediary, medium,** intermedium, intermediate, interagent, **internuncio,** broker; connection <nf>, **contact; negotiator,** negotiant; interpleader; arbitrator, mediator 466.3

5 **spokesman, spokeswoman, spokesperson,** spokespeople, official spokesman *or* -woman *or* -person, press officer, speaker, voice, mouthpiece <nf>; spin doctor <nf>; herald; messenger; proloctor, prolocutress *or* prolocutrix; reporter, rapporteur

6 **diplomat,** diplomatist, diplomatic agent, diplomatic ; **emissary, envoy, legate, minister,** foreign service officer; **ambassador,** ambassadress, ambassador-at-large; envoy extraordinary, plentipotentiary, **minister plenipotentiary;** nuncio, internuncio, apostolic delegate; vice-legate; resident, minister resident; chargé d'affaires, chargé, chargé d'affaires ad interim; secretary of legation, chancellor <Brit>; **attaché,** commercial attaché, military attaché, **consul,** consul general, vice-consul, consular agent; career diplomat

7 **foreign office, foreign service,** diplomatic service; diplomatic mission, diplomatic staff *or* corps, *corps diplomatique* <Fr>; **embassy, legation;** consular service

8 vice-president, vice-chairman, vice-governor, vice-director, vice-master, vice-chancellor, vice-premier, vice-warden, vice-consul, vice-legate; vice-regent, viceroy, vicegerent, vice-king, vice-queen, vice-reine, etc

9 **secret agent,** operative, cloak-and-dagger operative, **undercover man,** inside man <nf>; **spy,** espionage agent; counterspy, double agent; **spotter; scout,** reconnoiterer; **intelligence agent** *or* **officer;** military-intelligence man, naval-intelligence man; spymaster; spy-catcher <nf>, counterintelligence agent; agent provocateur; codetalker, windtalker

10 **detective, operative, investigator, sleuth,** Sherlock Holmes <A Conan Doyle>; police detective, Bow Street runner *or* officer <Brit old>, **plainclothesman;** private detective *or* dick, private investigator *or* PI, inquiry agent <Brit>; hotel detective, house detective, house dick <nf>, store detective; arson investigator; narcotics agent, narc <nf>; FBI agent *or* G-man <nf>; treasury agent *or* T-man <nf>; Federal *or* fed <nf>; Federal Bureau of Investigation *or* FBI; Secret Service

11 <nf terms> **dick,** gumshoe, gumshoe man, hawkshaw, sleuthhound, beagle, flatfoot, tec; eye, private eye; skip tracer, spotter

12 **secret service,** intelligence service, intelligence bureau *or* department; intelligence, military intelligence, naval intelligence; Central Intelligence Agency *or* CIA; **counterintelligence**

13 <group of delegates> **delegation, deputation, commission, mission,** legation; committee, subcommittee

VERBS **14** **represent, act for,** act on behalf of, substitute for, appear for, answer for, speak for, be the voice of, give voice to, be the mouthpiece of <nf>, hold the proxy of, hold a brief for, act in the place of, stand in the stead of, serve in one's stead, pinch-hit for <nf>; understudy, double for *and* stand in for *and* back up <nf>, substitute for; front for <nf>; deputize, commission; ghostwrite *or* ghost

15 deputize, depute, authorize, empower, charge, designate, nominate

ADJS 16 **deputy,** deputative; **acting,** representative

17 **diplomatic,** ambassadorial, consular, ministerial, plenipotentiary

ADVS 18 by proxy, indirectly; on behalf of 862.11

577 SERVANT, EMPLOYEE

NOUNS 1 **retainer,** dependent, follower; myrmidon, yeoman; vassal, liege, liege man, henchman, feudatory, homager; inferior, **underling, subordinate,** understrapper; **minion,** creature, hanger-on, lackey, flunky, stooge <nf>, drudge; peon, serf, bond servant, thrall, vassal, slave 432.7

2 **servant,** servitor, help, paid helper; **domestic,** domestic help, domestic servant, house *or* household servant; live-in help, day help; **menial,** drudge, slavey <nf>; scullion, turnspit; humble servant

3 **employee;** pensioner, **hireling, mercenary,** myrmidon; wage earner, staff member; hired man, hired hand, man *or* girl Friday, right-hand man, go-to guy, point man *or* person, assistant 616.6; worker 726, subordinate, subaltern; white-collar worker, nonmanual worker, skilled worker, semiskilled worker, unskilled worker, blue-collar worker, manual worker, laborer; part-time worker, freelance worker; hourly worker; officer worker, assistant, administrative assistant, secretary, clerk, messenger, runner, gofer

4 **man,** manservant, serving man, gillie, **boy,** *garçon* <Fr>, houseboy, houseman; butler; valet, *valet de chambre* <Fr>, gentleman, gentleman's gentleman; driver, chauffeur, coachman; gardener; handyman, odd-job man; lord-in-waiting, lord of the bedchamber, equerry; bodyguard, chaperon

5 **attendant,** tender, usher, server, squire, yeoman; errand boy *or* girl, gofer <nf>, office boy *or* girl, copyboy; page, footboy; concierge; bellboy, bellman, bellhop; cabin boy, purser; porter, redcap; printer's devil; chore boy; caddie; bootblack, boots <Brit>, shoeshine boy, shoeblack; trainbearer; cupbearer, Ganymede, Hebe; orderly, batman <Brit>; **cabin** *or* **flight attendant, steward, stewardess, hostess,** airline stewardess *or* hostess, stew <nf>, cabin crew, skycap; hat-check girl, cloakroom attendant; salesclerk *or* clerk, salesperson, sales associate, shop assistant <Brit>

6 **lackey, flunky,** livery *or* liveried servant; **footman,** *valet de pied* <Fr>

7 **waiter, waitress,** waitperson, waitron; carhop; counterman, soda jerk <nf>; busboy; headwaiter, *maître d'hôtel* <Fr>, maître d' <nf>; hostess; wine steward, sommelier; bartender, barkeeper *or* barkeep, barman, barmaid

8 **maid, maidservant,** servitress, **girl,** servant girl, *bonne* <Fr>, serving girl, wench, biddy <nf>, hired girl; lady-help <Brit>, au pair; live-in maid, live-out maid; **handmaid,** handmaiden; personal attendant; **lady's maid,** waiting maid *or* woman, gentlewoman, abigail, soubrette; lady-in-waiting, maid-in-waiting, lady of the bedchamber; companion; chaperon; betweenmaid *or* tweeny <Brit>; duenna; parlormaid; kitchenmaid, scullery maid; cook; housemaid, chambermaid, *femme de chambre* or *fille de chambre* <Fr>, upstairs maid; nursemaid 1008.8

9 **factotum, do-all** , general servant <Brit>, man of all work; maid of all work, domestic drudge, slavey <nf>, Mister Fix-it, handyman

10 **major-domo, steward,** house steward, **butler,** chamberlain, *maître d'hôtel* <Fr>, seneschal; **housekeeper**

11 **staff, personnel, employees,** help, hired help, occasional help, the help,

crew, gang, men, force, servantry, retinue 769.6

12 **service,** servanthood, servitude , servitorship, *servitium* <L>; **employment, employ; ministry, ministration, attendance,** tendance; serfdom, peonage, thralldom, slavery 432.1

VERBS 13 **serve, work for,** be in service, serve one's every need; minister *or* administer to, pander to, do service; **help** 449.11; **care for,** do for <nf>, **look after,** wait on hand and foot, take care of; **wait, wait on** *or* **upon, attend,** tend, attend on *or* upon, dance attendance upon; make oneself useful; lackey, valet, maid, chore; drudge 725.14

ADJS 14 **serving,** servitorial, servitial, **ministering,** waiting, waiting on, **attending,** attendant; in the train of, in one's pay *or* employ; helping 449.20; **menial, servile**

578 FASHION

NOUNS 1 **fashion, style, mode, vogue,** trend, prevailing taste; proper thing, ton, bon ton; design; custom 373; convention 579.1,2; the swim <nf>, current *or* stream of fashion; height of fashion; the new look, the season's look; high fashion, *haute couture* <Fr>, designer label; flavor of the month, flavor of the week; personal style, signature

2 **fashionableness,** chic, ton, bon ton, fashionability, **stylishness, modishness,** voguishness; with-itness <nf>; **popularity,** prevalence, currency 864.2

3 **smartness, chic,** elegance; style-consciousness, clothes-consciousness; **spruceness, nattiness,** neatness, trimness, sleekness, **dapperness,** jauntiness; sharpness *and* spiffiness *and* classiness *and* niftiness <nf>; swankness *and* **swankiness** <nf>; foppery, foppishness, coxcombry, dandyism; hipness <nf>

4 **the rage,** the thing, **the last word** <nf>, *le dernier cri* <Fr>, **the latest thing,** the in thing *and* the latest wrinkle <nf>

5 **fad, craze, rage;** wrinkle <nf>; new take <nf>, next big thing, new new thing; novelty 841.2; faddishness, faddiness <nf>, faddism; **faddist;** the bandwagon, me-tooism

6 **society,** *société* <Fr>, fashionable society, **polite society, high society,** high life, *beau monde* and *haut monde* <Fr>, good society; best people, people of fashion, right people; *monde* <Fr>, world of fashion, Vanity Fair; **smart set** <nf>; the Four Hundred, **upper crust** *and* upper cut <nf>; **cream of society,** *crème de la crème* <Fr>, cream of the crop, elite, carriage trade; café society, jet set, beautiful people, in-crowd, glitterati <nf>; *jeunesse dorée* <Fr>; drawing room, salon; social register; fast track

7 person of fashion, fashionable, man-about-town, man *or* woman of the world, nob, *mondain* or *mondaine* <Fr>; leader *or* arbiter of fashion, tastemaker, trendsetter, tonesetter, *arbiter elegantiae* <L>, arbiter of fashion; ten best-dressed, fashion plate, clotheshorse, sharpy <nf>, snappy dresser; Beau Brummel, fop, dandy 500.9; **socialite; clubwoman,** clubman; salonist, salonnard; jet setter; swinger <nf>; **debutante,** subdebutante, deb *and* subdeb <nf>, Sloane Ranger <Brit nf>; rag trade <nf>

VERBS 8 **catch on,** become popular, **become the rage,** catch *or* take fire

9 **be fashionable, be the style, be the rage,** be the thing; have a run; cut a figure in society <nf>, give a tone to society, set the fashion *or* style *or* tone; dress to kill

10 **follow the fashion, get in the swim** <nf>, get *or* climb *or* jump on the bandwagon <nf>, join the parade, follow the crowd, go with the stream *or* tide *or* current *or* flow; keep in step, do as others do; keep up, **keep up appearances,** keep up with the Joneses

ADJS 11 **fashionable, in fashion, smart, in style, in vogue; all the rage,** all the thing; **popular,** prevalent, current 864.12; **up-to-date,** up-to-datish, up-to-the-minute, happening <nf>, switched-on *and* hip *and* with-it *and* in <nf>, trendy <nf>, newfashioned, modern, mod <nf>, new 841.7,9,10,12–14; **in the swim;** sought-after, much sought-after

12 **stylish, modish,** voguish, vogue; dressy <nf>; *soigné* or *soignée* <Fr>; *à la mode* <Fr>, in the mode

13 **chic, smart,** elegant; style-conscious, clothes-conscious; **well-dressed,** well-groomed, *soigné* or *soignée* <Fr>, dressed to advantage, all dressed up, dressed to kill, dressed to the teeth, dressed to the nines, well-turned-out; **spruce, natty,** neat, trim, sleek, smug, trig, tricksy ; **dapper,** dashing, jaunty, braw; sharp *and* spiffy *and* classy *and* nifty *and* snazzy <nf>; **swank** *or* **swanky** <nf>, posh <nf>, ritzy <nf>, swell *and* nobby <nf>; genteel; exquisite, *recherché* <Fr>; cosmopolitan, sophisticated

14 **ultrafashionable,** ultrastylish, ultrasmart; chichi; foppish, dandified, dandyish, dandiacal

15 **trendy** <nf>, **faddish,** faddy <nf>, groovy

16 socially prominent, in society, high-society, elite; café-society, jet-set; lace-curtain, silk-stocking

ADVS **17** **fashionably, stylishly, modishly,** *à la mode* <Fr>, in the latest style *or* mode

18 **smartly,** dressily, chicly, elegantly, exquisitely; **sprucely, nattily,** neatly, trimly, sleekly; **dapperly,** jauntily, dashingly, swankly *or* swankily <nf>; foppishly, dandyishly

579 SOCIAL CONVENTION

NOUNS **1** **social convention, convention,** conventional usage, what is done, what one does, **social usage, form, formality; custom** 373; **conformism, conformity** 867; **propriety, decorum,** decorousness, correctness, *convenance* and *bienséance* <Fr>, decency, seemliness, civility , good form, etiquette 580.3; **conventionalism, conventionality, Grundyism; Mrs Grundy**

2 **the conventions, the proprieties, the mores,** the right things, accepted *or* sanctioned conduct, what is done, civilized behavior; **dictates of society,** dictates of Mrs Grundy

3 conventionalist, Grundy, Mrs Grundy; conformist 867.2

VERBS **4** **conform,** observe the proprieties, play the game, follow the rule 867.4, fall in or into line

ADJS **5** **conventional, decorous,** orthodox, **correct,** right, **right-thinking, proper,** decent, seemly, meet; **accepted, recognized,** acknowledged, received, admitted, approved, being done; *comme il faut* and *de rigueur* <Fr>; **traditional, customary;** formal 580.7; conformable 867.5

ADVS **6** **conventionally,** decorously, orthodoxly; **customarily, traditionally;** correctly, properly, as is proper, as it should be, *comme il faut* <Fr>; according to use *or* custom, according to the dictates of society *or* Mrs Grundy

580 FORMALITY

NOUNS **1** **formality, form, formalness; ceremony,** ceremonial, **ceremoniousness; the red carpet; ritual,** rituality; extrinsicality, impersonality 768.1; formalization, stylization, conventionalization; **stiffness, stiltedness,** primness, prissiness, rigidness, starchiness, buckram , **dignity,** gravity, weight, *gravitas* <L>, weighty dignity, staidness, reverend seriousness, **solemnity** 111; **pomp** 501.6; pomposity 501.7

2 **formalism, ceremonialism, ritualism;** legalism; pedantry, pedantism, pedanticism; precisianism, preciseness, preciousness, preciosity, purism; punctiliousness, punctilio, scrupulousness; overrefinement

3 **etiquette,** social code, rules *or* code of conduct; **formalities,** social procedures, social conduct *or* convention, what is done, what one does; **manners,** good manners, exquisite manners, quiet good manners, **politeness,** *politesse* <Fr>, natural politeness, comity, civility 504.1; **amenities,** decencies, civilities, elegancies, **social**

graces, mores, proprieties; decorum, good form; **courtliness,** elegance 533; **protocol,** diplomatic code; punctilio, point of etiquette; convention, social usage; table manners

4 <ceremonial function> **ceremony,** ceremonial; **rite, ritual, formality; solemnity, service, function,** office, **observance,** performance; **exercise,** exercises; **celebration,** solemnization; **liturgy,** religious ceremony; **rite of passage,** *rite de passage* <Fr>; convocation; commencement, commencement exercises; graduation, graduation exercises; baccalaureate service; inaugural, inauguration; initiation; formal, ball; wedding; funeral; set piece; empty formality or ceremony, mummery

VERBS **5 formalize,** ritualize, solemnize, **celebrate,** dignify; **observe;** conventionalize, stylize

6 stand on ceremony, observe the formalities, follow protocol, do things by the book

ADJS **7 formal,** formulary; formalist, formalistic; legalistic; pedantic, pedantical; official, stylized, conventionalized; extrinsic, outward, impersonal 768.3; surface, **superficial, nominal** 527.15

8 ceremonious, ceremonial; red-carpet; ritualistic, ritual; hieratic, hieratical, sacerdotal, liturgic; **grave, solemn** 111.3; **pompous** 501.22; **stately** 501.21; well-mannered 504.15; **conventional,** decorous 579.5

9 stiff, stilted, prim, prissy, rigid, starch, starchy, starched; buckram *and* in buckram

10 punctilious, scrupulous, precise, precisian, precisionist, precious, puristic; by-the-book; exact, **meticulous** 339.12; **orderly, methodical** 807.6

ADVS **11 formally,** in due form, in set form; **ceremoniously, ritually,** ritualistically; **solemnly** 111.4; for form's sake, *pro forma* <L>, **as a matter of form**; by the book

12 stiffly, stiltedly, starchly, primly, rigidly

581 INFORMALITY

NOUNS **1 informality, informalness, unceremoniousness; casualness,** offhandedness, **ease, easiness,** easygoingness; **relaxedness;** affability, graciousness, cordiality, sociability 582; Bohemianism, unconventionality 868.2; **familiarity; naturalness,** simplicity, plainness, homeliness, homeyness, folksiness <nf>, common touch, **unaffectedness,** unpretentiousness 499.2; unconstraint, unconstrainedness, looseness; irregularity; lack of convention, freedom, license

VERBS **2 not stand on ceremony,** let one's hair down <nf>, be oneself, be at ease, feel at home, come as you are; relax

ADJS **3 informal, unceremonious; casual, offhand,** offhanded, throwaway <nf>, unstudied, easy, easygoing, free and easy, loose, nonformal; *dégagé* <Fr>; **relaxed;** affable, gracious, cordial, sociable; Bohemian, unconventional 868.6, nonconformist; **familiar; natural,** simple, plain, homely, homey, down-home *and* folksy <nf>, *haymish* <Yiddish>; **unaffected, unassuming** 499.7; unconstrained, loose; irregular; unofficial

ADVS **4 informally, unceremoniously,** without ceremony, *sans cérémonie* and *sans façon* <Fr>; **casually,** offhand, offhandedly; relaxedly; familiarly; **naturally,** simply, plainly; **unaffectedly, unassumingly** 499.11; unconstrainedly, unofficially; *en famille* <Fr>

582 SOCIABILITY

NOUNS **1 sociability,** sociality, sociableness, fitness *or* fondness for society, socialmindedness, **gregariousness, affability,** companionability, compatibility, geniality, *Gemütlichkeit* <Ger>, **congeniality;** hospitality 585; clubbability <nf>, clubbishness, clubbiness, clubbism; intimacy, familiarity; amiability, **friendliness** 587.1; **communicativeness** 343.3; social grace, civility, urbanity, courtesy 504

2 **camaraderie,** comradery, comradeship, **fellowship, good-fellowship;** male bonding; consorting, hobnobbing, hanging *and* hanging out <nf>

3 **conviviality, joviality, jollity,** gaiety, heartiness, cheer, good cheer, festivity, partying, merrymaking, merriment, revelry

4 **social life, social intercourse,** social activity, **intercourse, communication, communion,** intercommunion, **fellowship,** intercommunication, **community,** collegiality, commerce, congress, converse, conversation, social relations

5 **social circle** *or* **set,** social class, one's crowd *or* set, clique, coterie, crowd <nf>; **association** 617

6 **association,** consociation, affiliation, bonding, social bonding, **fellowship, companionship, company, society;** fraternity, **fraternization;** membership, participation, partaking, sharing, cooperation 450

7 **visit, social call,** call; formal visit, duty visit, required visit; exchange visit; flying visit, look-in; visiting, visitation; round of visits; social round, social whirl, mad round; play date

8 **appointment, engagement, date** <nf>, double date *and* blind date <nf>; arrangement, interview, meeting, meet; fix-up; engagement book, agenda book, personal digital assistant

9 **rendezvous, tryst, assignation, meeting;** blind date; trysting place, meeting place, place of assignation; assignation house; love nest <nf>

10 **social gathering, social,** sociable, social affair, social hour, hospitality hour, affair, gathering, get-together <nf>; function; **reception,** at home, salon, levee, soiree; matinee; reunion, family reunion; wake

11 **party, entertainment,** celebration, fete, bash, party time, **festivity** 743.3,4

12 <nf terms> **brawl, bash,** blast, clambake, wingding, hoodang, blowout, shindig, shindy, do *and* bean-feast *and* knees-up *and* rave *and* rave-up <Brit>

13 **tea,** afternoon tea, five-o'clock tea, high tea, cream tea

14 bee, quilting bee, raising bee, husking bee, cornhusking, corn shucking, husking

15 **debut, coming out** <nf>, presentation

16 <sociable person> joiner, mixer *and* **good mixer** <nf>, good *or* pleasant company, excellent companion, life of the party, social butterfly, bon vivant; man-about-town, playboy, social lion, habitué; clubman, clubwoman; salonnard, salonist

VERBS **17** **associate with,** assort with, sort with, consort with, hobnob with, fall in with, socialize, interact, go around with, **mingle with, mix with, touch** *or* **rub elbows** *or* **shoulders with,** eat off the same trencher; **fraternize,** fellowship, join in fellowship; **keep company with,** bear one's company, walk hand in hand with; **join; flock together,** herd together, club together

18 <nf terms> **hang with,** hang out *or* around with, clique, clique with, gang up with, run *or* run around with, chum, chum together, pal, pal with, pal up *or* around with; take *or* tie up with, hook up with

19 **visit,** make *or* pay a visit, **call on** *or* **upon, drop in,** run *or* stop in, look in, look one up, see, stop off *or* over <nf>, drop *or* run *or* stop by, drop around *or* round; leave one's card; exchange visits

20 have *or* give a party, entertain

21 <nf terms> **throw a party; party,** have fun, live it up, have a ball, ball, boogie, jam, kick up one's heels, make whoopee, whoop it up

ADJS **22** **sociable, social,** social-minded, fit for society, fond of society, **gregarious, affable; companionable,** companionate, compatible, genial, *gemütlich* <Ger>, **congenial;** hospitable 585.11; neighborly; clubby, clubbable <nf>, clubbish; **communicative** 343.10; amiable, **friendly;** civil, urbane, courteous 504.13

23 **convivial,** boon, free and easy, hail-fellow-well-met; **jovial, jolly,** hearty, festive, gay

24 **intimate, familiar,** cozy, chatty, *tête-à-tête* <Fr>; man-to-man, woman-to-woman

ADVS **25** **sociably,** socially, gregariously, affably; friendlily, companionably, arm in arm, hand in hand, hand in glove

583 UNSOCIABILITY

NOUNS **1** **unsociability,** insociability, unsociableness, dissociability, dissociableness; **ungregariousness,** uncompanionability; unclubbableness *or* unclubbability <nf>, ungeniality, **uncongeniality;** incompatibility, social incompatibility; **unfriendliness** 589.1; **uncommunicativeness** 344; sullenness, mopishness, moroseness; self-sufficiency, self-containment; autism, catatonia; bashfulness 139.4

2 **aloofness, standoffishness,** offishness, withdrawnness, **remoteness,** distance, detachment; **coolness,** coldness, frigidity, chill, chilliness, iciness, frostiness; cold shoulder; inaccessibility, unapproachability; private world

3 seclusiveness, **seclusion** 584; exclusiveness, exclusivity

VERBS **4** **keep to oneself,** keep oneself to oneself, not mix *or* mingle, enjoy *or* prefer one's own company, stay at home, shun companionship, be a poor mixer, **stand aloof,** hold oneself aloof *or* apart, keep one's distance, keep at a distance, keep in the background, retire, retire into the shade, creep into a corner, seclude oneself, stay in one's shell; have nothing to do with 586.5, be unfriendly, not give one the time of day

ADJS **5** **unsociable,** insociable, dissociable, unsocial; **ungregarious,** nongregarious; **uncompanionable,** ungenial, uncongenial; incompatible, socially incompatible; unclubbable <nf>; **unfriendly** 589.9; **uncommunicative** 344.8; sullen, mopish, mopey, morose; close, snug; self-sufficient, self-contained; autistic, catatonic; bashful 139.12

6 **aloof, standoffish,** offish, standoff, **distant, remote,** withdrawn, removed, detached, Olympian; **cool,** cold, cold-fish, frigid, chilly, icy, frosty; seclusive; exclusive; inaccessible, unapproachable; tight-assed <nf>

584 SECLUSION

NOUNS **1** **seclusion,** reclusion, **retirement, withdrawal, retreat,** recess; renunciation *or* forsaking of the world; cocooning; **sequestration,** quarantine, separation, detachment, apartness; segregation, apartheid, Jim Crow; **isolation**; ivory tower, ivory-towerism, ivory-towerishness; **privacy,** privatism, **secrecy;** rustication; privatization; isolationism; opt-out

2 **hermitism,** hermitry, eremitism, anchoritism, anchoretism, cloistered monasticism

3 **solitude,** solitariness, **aloneness,** loneness, singleness; **loneliness, lonesomeness**

4 **forlornness, desolation;** friendlessness, kithlessness, fatherlessness, motherlessness, homelessness, rootlessness; helplessness, defenselessness; abandonment, desertion

5 **recluse, loner,** solitaire, solitary, solitudinarian; **shut-in,** invalid, bedridden invalid; cloistered monk *or* nun; **hermit,** eremite, anchorite, anchoret; marabout; hermitess, anchoress; **ascetic;** closet cynic; stylite, pillarist, pillar saint; Hieronymite, Hieronymian; Diogenes, Timon of Athens, St Simeon Stylites, St Anthony, desert saints, desert fathers; outcast, pariah 586.4; **stay-at-home, homebody; isolationist,** seclusionist; ivory-towerist, ivory-towerite; one-man band

6 **retreat** 1009.5, **hideaway, cell, ivory tower,** hidey-hole <nf>, lair, sanctum, sanctum sanctorum, inner sanctum

VERBS **7** **seclude oneself, go into seclusion, retire, go into retirement,** retire from the world, abandon *or* forsake the world, live in retirement, lead a retired life, lead a cloistered life, sequester *or* sequestrate oneself, be *or* remain incommunicado, shut oneself up, live alone, live apart, retreat to one's ivory tower; stay at home; rusticate; take the veil; cop out <nf>, opt out *or* drop out of society

ADJS 8 **secluded, seclusive, retired, withdrawn; isolated,** shut off, insular, **separate,** separated, **apart,** detached, removed; segregated, quarantined; **remote, out-of-the-way,** up-country, in a backwater, out-of-the-world, outback *and* back of beyond; **unfrequented,** unvisited, off the beaten track; untraveled

9 **private,** privatistic, reclusive; ivory-towered, ivory-towerish

10 **recluse, reclusive, sequestered, cloistered,** sequestrated, shut up *or* in; hermitlike, hermitic, hermitical, eremitic, eremitical, hermitish; anchoritic, anchoritical; stay-at-home, domestic; homebound

11 **solitary, alone; in solitude,** by oneself, all alone; **lonely, lonesome, lone;** lonely-hearts

12 **forlorn,** lorn; **abandoned, forsaken, deserted, desolate,** godforsaken <nf>, friendless, unfriended, kithless, fatherless, motherless, homeless; helpless, defenseless; outcast 586.10

ADVS 13 **in seclusion, in retirement,** in retreat, in solitude; in privacy, in secrecy

585 HOSPITALITY, WELCOME

NOUNS 1 **hospitality,** hospitableness, receptiveness; honors *or* freedom of the house; **cordiality,** amiability, graciousness, **friendliness,** neighborliness, geniality, heartiness, bonhomie, **generosity,** liberality, openheartedness, warmth, warmness, warmheartedness; open door

2 **welcome,** welcoming, **reception,** *accueil* <Fr>; cordial *or* warm *or* hearty welcome, pleasant *or* smiling reception, the glad hand <nf>, **open arms; embrace, hug;** welcome mat

3 **greetings, salutations,** salaams; **regards,** best wishes 504.8

4 **greeting, salutation,** salute, salaam; **hail, hello,** how-do-you-do; accost, address; nod, bow, bob; curtsy 155.2; wave; handshake, handclasp; namaste; open arms, embrace, hug, kiss; smile, smile *or* nod of recognition, nod

5 **host,** mine host; hostess, receptionist, greeter; landlord 470.2

6 **guest, visitor,** visitant; **caller,** company; invited guest, invitee; frequenter, habitué, haunter; uninvited guest, gate-crasher <nf>; moocher *and* freeloader <nf>; guest list

VERBS 7 **receive, admit,** accept, take in, let in, open the door to; **be at home to,** have the latchstring out, keep a light in the window, put out the welcome mat, keep the door open, keep an open house, keep the home fires burning

8 **entertain,** entertain guests, guest; host, preside, do the honors <nf>; give a party, throw a party <nf>; spread oneself <nf>

9 **welcome,** make welcome, bid one welcome, bid one feel at home, make one feel welcome *or* at home or like one of the family, do the honors of the house, give one the freedom of the house, hold out the hand, extend the right hand of friendship; glad hand *and* give the glad hand *and* glad eye <nf>; **embrace, hug, receive** *or* **welcome with open arms;** give a warm reception to, roll out the red carpet, give the red-carpet treatment, receive royally, make feel like a king *or* queen

10 **greet, hail, accost,** address; **salute,** make one's salutations; **bid** *or* **say hello,** bid good day *or* good morning, etc; exchange greetings, **pass the time of day; give one's regards** 504.12; shake hands, shake *and* give one some skin *and* give a high *or* a low five <nf>, press the flesh <nf>, press *or* squeeze one's hand; nod to, bow to; curtsy 155.6; tip the hat to, lift the hat, touch the hat *or* cap; take one's hat off to, uncover; pull *or* tug at the forelock; kiss, greet with a kiss, kiss hands *or* cheeks

ADJS 11 **hospitable, receptive,** welcoming; **cordial,** amiable, gracious, **friendly,** neighborly, genial, hearty, open, openhearted, warm, warmhearted; **generous,** liberal

12 **welcome,** welcome as the roses in May, wanted, desired, wished-for; **agreeable,** desirable, acceptable; **grateful,** gratifying, pleasing

ADVS 13 **hospitably, with open arms;** friendlily

14 **greetings!,** salutations!, **hello!,** hullo!, hail!, hey! *or* heigh!, **hi!,** aloha!, *hola!* <Sp>; **how do you do?, how are you?,** *comment allez-vous?* and *comment ça va?* <Fr>, *cómo está Usted?* <Sp>, *come sta?* <Ital>, *wie geht's?* <Ger>; **good morning!,** top of the morning!, *guten Morgen!* <Ger>; good day!, *bon jour!* <Fr>, *buenos días!* <Sp>, *buon giorno!* <Ital>, *guten Tag!* <Ger>; **good afternoon!,** *buenas tardes!* <Sp>; **good evening!,** *bon soir!* <Fr>, *buona sera!* <Ital>, *guten Abend!* <Ger>

15 <nf terms> **howdy!,** howdy-do!, how-de-do!, how-do-ye-do!, how-d'ye-do!, how you doin'?, hi ya!; how's things?, how's tricks?, how goes it?, how's every little thing?, how's the world treating you?, **yo!,** ahoy!, hey!; long time no see!

586 INHOSPITALITY

NOUNS 1 **inhospitality,** inhospitableness, unhospitableness, unreceptiveness; **uncordialness,** ungraciousness, **unfriendliness,** unneighborliness; nonwelcome, nonwelcoming

2 unhabitability, uninhabitability, unlivability

3 **ostracism,** ostracization, thumbs down; **banishment** 909.4; **proscription, ban; boycott,** boycottage; **blackball,** blackballing, blacklist; **rejection** 442.1

4 **outcast,** social outcast, outcast of society, **castaway, derelict,** Ishmael; **pariah, untouchable,** leper; outcaste; *déclassé* <Fr>; **outlaw; expellee, evictee; displaced person** *or* **DP; exile, expatriate,** man without a country; undesirable; *persona non grata* <L>, unacceptable person

VERBS 5 **have nothing to do with,** have no truck with <nf>, refuse to associate with, steer clear of <nf>, **spurn, turn one's back upon,** not give one the time of day <nf>; deny oneself to, refuse to receive, not be at home to; shut the door upon

6 **ostracize,** turn thumbs down, disfellowship; **reject** 442.3, **exile, banish** 909.17; **proscribe, ban, outlaw** 444.3, put under the ban, criminalize; **boycott, blackball,** blacklist

ADJS 7 **inhospitable,** unhospitable; **unreceptive,** closed; **uncordial,** ungracious, **unfriendly,** unneighborly

8 **unhabitable, uninhabitable,** nonhabitable, unoccupiable, untenantable, **unlivable, unfit to live in,** not fit for man or beast

9 **unwelcome, unwanted; unagreeable,** undesirable, unacceptable; **uninvited,** unasked, unbidden

10 **outcast, cast-off, castaway, derelict;** outlawed 444.7, outside the pale, outside the gates; **rejected, disowned; abandoned, forsaken**

587 FRIENDSHIP

NOUNS 1 **friendship, friendliness; amicability,** amicableness, amity, peaceableness, unhostility; **amiability,** amiableness, **congeniality,** well-affectedness; neighborliness, neighborlikeness; peaceableness; sociability 582; **affection, love** 104; **loving kindness, kindness** 143

2 **fellowship, companionship, comradeship,** colleagueship, chumship <nf>, palship <nf>, circle of friends, freemasonry, consortship, boon companionship; comradery, camaraderie, male bonding; **brotherhood, fraternity,** fraternalism, fraternization, sodality, confraternity; **sisterhood, sorority;** brotherliness, sisterliness; community of interest, *esprit de corps* <Fr>; chumminess <nf>

3 **good terms, good understanding,** good footing, friendly relations; **harmony,** compatibility, sympathy, fellow feeling, bonding, understanding, **rapport** 455.1, rapprochement; **favor, goodwill, good graces, regard,** respect, mutual regard *or* respect, favorable regard, the good *or* right side of <nf>, esprit de corps; an in <nf>;

entente, entente cordiale, hands across the sea

4 **acquaintance,** acquaintedness, close acquaintance, acquaintanceship; **introduction,** presentation, knockdown <nf>

5 **familiarity, intimacy,** intimate acquaintance, closeness, nearness, inseparableness, inseparability; affinity, special affinity, mutual affinity; chumminess <nf>, palliness *or* palsiness *or* palsy-walsiness <nf>, mateyness <Brit nf>; togetherness; conversance

6 **cordiality, geniality,** heartiness, bonhomie, ardency, warmth, warmness, affability, warmheartedness; hospitality 585

7 **devotion, devotedness;** dedication, commitment; fastness, steadfastness, firmness, constancy, staunchness; triedness, trueness, trueblueness, tried-and-trueness

8 cordial friendship, warm *or* ardent friendship, close friendship, passionate friendship, devoted friendship, bosom friendship, intimate *or* familiar friendship, sincere friendship, beautiful friendship, fast *or* firm friendship, staunch friendship, loyal friendship, lasting friendship, undying friendship, cross-sex friendship

VERBS 9 **be friends,** have the friendship of, have the ear of; be old friends *or* friends of long standing, be long acquainted, go way back; **know, be acquainted with;** associate with; cotton to *and* hit it off <nf>, get on well with, hobnob with, fraternize with, keep company with, go around with; be close friends with, be best friends, be buddies, be inseparable; **be on good terms,** enjoy good *or* friendly relations with; keep on good terms, have an in with <nf>

10 **befriend, make** *or* **win friends,** gain the friendship of, **strike up a friendship,** get to know one another, take up with <nf>, shake hands with, **get acquainted,** make *or* scrape acquaintance with, pick up an acquaintance with; win friends, win friends and influence people; break the ice; warm to

11 <nf terms> **be buddy-buddy** *or* **palsy-walsy with,** click, have good *or* great chemistry, team up; **get next to, get palsy** *or* **palsy-walsy with,** get cozy with, cozy *or* snuggle up to, get close to, get chummy with, buddy *or* pal up with, play footsie with

12 **cultivate,** cultivate the friendship of, **court,** pay court to, pay addresses to, seek the company of, **run after** <nf>, **shine up to,** make up to <nf>, play up to *and* suck up to <nf>, hold out *or* extend the right of friendship *or* fellowship; **make advances,** approach, break the ice

13 **get on good terms with, get into favor,** win the regard of, **get in the good graces of, get in good with,** get in with *or* on the in with *and* get next to <nf>, **get on the good** *or* **right side of** <nf>; stay friends with, keep in with <nf>

14 **introduce, present, acquaint,** make acquainted, give an introduction, give a knockdown <nf>, do the honors <nf>

ADJS 15 **friendly,** friendlike; **amicable, peaceable,** unhostile; **harmonious** 455.1; **amiable, congenial,** *simpático* <Sp>, *simpatico* <Ital>, *sympathique* <Fr>, pleasant, agreeable, favorable, well-affected, well-disposed, well-intentioned, well-meaning, well-meant, well-intended; brotherly, fraternal, confraternal; sisterly; neighborly, neighborlike; sociable; kind 143.13

16 **cordial, genial,** gracious, courteous, hearty, ardent, warm, warmhearted, affable; compatible, cooperative; welcoming, receptive, hospitable 585.11

17 **friends with,** friendly with, at home with; **acquainted**

18 **on good terms,** on a good footing, on friendly *or* amicable terms, **on speaking terms,** on a first-name basis, on visiting terms; **in good with,** in with *and* on the in with *and* in <nf>, **in favor, in one's good graces,** in one's good books, on the good *or* right side of <nf>, regarded highly by, on a first-name basis with, in with <nf>

19 **familiar, intimate, close,** near, inseparable, on familiar *or* intimate terms, favorite, affectionate; just between the two, one-on-one, man-to-man, woman-to-woman; hand-in-hand, hand and glove *or* hand in glove; **thick, thick as thieves** <nf>; demonstrative, backslapping, effusive

20 **chummy** <nf>, matey <Brit nf>; pally *and* palsy *and* palsy-walsy *and* buddy-buddy <nf>; companionable

21 **devoted,** dedicated, committed, **fast,** steadfast, supportive, constant, faithful, staunch, firm; tried, true, **tried and true,** true-blue, loyal, tested, trusty, trustful, trustworthy

ADVS **22** **amicably,** friendly, friendlily, friendliwise; **amiably, congenially,** pleasantly, agreeably, favorably; **cordially, genially,** heartily, ardently, warmly, with open arms; familiarly, intimately; arm in arm, hand in hand, hand in glove

588 FRIEND

NOUNS **1** **friend, acquaintance,** close acquaintance; confidant, confidante, repository; **intimate,** familiar, **close friend,** intimate *or* familiar friend; **bosom friend,** friend of one's bosom, inseparable friend, **best friend;** alter ego, other self, shadow; brother, fellow, fellowman, fellow creature, neighbor; mutual friend; **sympathizer,** well-wisher, partisan, advocate, favorer, backer, **supporter** 616.9; casual acquaintance; pickup <nf>; lover 104.12; girlfriend, boyfriend; live-in lover, POSSLQ *or* person of opposite sex sharing living quarters, significant other

2 **good friend, best friend,** great friend, **devoted friend,** warm *or* ardent friend, **faithful friend,** trusted *or* trusty friend, *fidus Achates* <L>, constant friend, staunch friend, fast friend; friend in need, friend indeed

3 **companion, fellow,** fellow companion, **comrade,** *camarade* <Fr>, amigo <nf>, mate <Brit>, comate, company, **associate** 616, peer, consociate, compeer, confrere, consort, **colleague, partner,** copartner, side partner, **crony,** old crony, gossip; girlfriend <nf>; **roommate,** chamberfellow; flatmate; bunkmate, bunkie <nf>; bedfellow, bedmate; **schoolmate,** schoolfellow, classmate, classfellow, school companion, school chum, fellow student *or* pupil; **playmate,** playfellow; **teammate,** yokefellow, yokemate; workmate, workfellow 616.5; shipmate; messmate; confederate, comrade in arms; homeboy <nf>

4 <nf terms> **pal, buddy,** bud, buddyboy, bosom buddy, asshole buddy, main man, home boy, goombah, landsman, paesan, paesano, pally, palsy-walsy, road dog, walkboy, pardner, pard, sidekick, tillicum, **chum,** ace, mate *and* butty <Brit>, my man

5 **boon companion,** boonfellow; **good fellow,** jolly fellow, hearty, *bon vivant* <Fr>; pot companion

6 <famous friendships> Achilles and Patroclus, Castor and Pollux, Damon and Pythias, David and Jonathan, Diomedes and Sthenelus, Epaminondas and Pelopidas, Hercules and Iolaus, Nisus and Euryalus, Pylades and Orestes, Theseus and Pirithoüs, Christ and the beloved disciple; the Three Musketeers

589 ENMITY

NOUNS **1** **enmity, unfriendliness,** inimicality; **uncordiality,** unamiability, ungeniality, disaffinity, incompatibility, incompatibleness; personal conflict, strain, **tension;** coolness, coldness, chilliness, chill, frost, frostiness, iciness, the freeze; inhospitality 586, unsociability 583

2 **disaccord** 456; ruffled feelings, strained relations, alienation, **disaffection, estrangement** 456.4

3 **hostility, antagonism, repugnance, antipathy,** spitefulness, spite, despitefulness, bellicosity, malice, malevolence, malignity, **hatred, hate** 103; dislike; **conflict, contention** 457, collision, clash, clashing, **friction;** quarrelsomeness 456.3; belligerence, intolerance; state of war

4 **animosity,** animus; **ill will,** ill feeling, bitter feeling, **hard feelings,** no love lost; **bad blood,** ill blood, feud, blood feud, vendetta; **bitterness,** sourness, soreness, **rancor,** resentment, acrimony, virulence, venom, vitriol

5 **grudge, spite,** crow to pick *or* pluck *or* pull, bone to pick; peeve *and* pet peeve <nf>; peevishness

6 **enemy, foe,** foeman, **adversary, antagonist,** unfriendly <nf>; bitter enemy; sworn enemy; open enemy; secret enemy; public enemy, public enemy number one; archenemy, devil; the other side, the opposition, opponent, rival; **bane** 395.8, bête noire; no friend

VERBS **7** **antagonize,** set against, make enemies, set at odds, set at each other's throat, sick on each other <nf>; aggravate, exacerbate, heat up, **provoke,** envenom, **embitter,** infuriate, irritate, madden; divide, disunite, **alienate,** estrange 456.14; be alienated *or* estranged, draw *or* grow apart

8 **bear ill will,** bear malice, have it in for <nf>, hold it against, be down on <nf>; **bear** *or* **harbor** *or* **nurse a grudge,** owe a grudge, have a bone to pick with; no love is lost between; have a crow to pick *or* pluck *or* pull with; pick a quarrel; take offense, take umbrage; scorn, **hate** 103.5

ADJS **9** **unfriendly, inimical, unamicable; uncordial,** unamiable, ungenial, incompatible; strained, tense; discordant, unharmonious; cool, cold, chill, chilly, frosty, icy; inhospitable 586.7; unsociable 583.5

10 **hostile, antagonistic,** repugnant, antipathetic, set against, ill-disposed, acrimonious, snide, spiteful, despiteful, malicious, malevolent, malignant, hateful, full of hate *or* hatred; virulent, **bitter,** sore, sour, rancorous, acrid, caustic, venomous, vitriolic; conflicting, clashing, colliding; resentful, grudging, peevish; quarrelsome 456.17, contentious; **provocative,** off-putting; belligerent, bellicose

11 **alienated, estranged,** pffft <nf>, disaffected, separated, divided, disunited, torn, at variance; irreconcilable; distant; not on speaking terms

12 **at outs, on the outs** <nf>, at enmity, at variance, **at odds,** at loggerheads, at cross-purposes, at sixes and sevens, at each other's throats, at swords points, at daggers drawn, at war; on bad terms, in bad with <nf>

13 **on bad terms,** not on speaking terms, on the outs; in bad with <nf>, in bad odor with, in one's bad *or* black books, on one's shitlist *or* drop-dead list <nf>

ADVS **14** **unamicably,** inimically; **uncordially,** unamiably, ungenially; coolly, coldly, chillily, frostily; **hostilely, antagonistically**

590 MISANTHROPY

NOUNS **1** **misanthropy,** misanthropism, people-hating, Timonism, cynicism, antisociality, antisocial sentiments *or* attitudes; unsociability 583; **man-hating,** misandry; **woman-hating,** misogyny; **sexism,** sex discrimination, sexual stereotyping, male *or* female chauvinism

2 **misanthrope,** misanthropist, people-hater, cynic, Timon, Timonist; **man-hater,** misandrist; **woman-hater,** misogynist; **sexist,** male *or* female chauvinist, chauvinist

ADJS **3** **misanthropic,** people-hating, Timonist, Timonistic, cynical, **antisocial;** unsociable 583.5; **man-hating,** misandrist; **woman-hating,** misogynic, misogynistic, misogynous; **sexist,** male- *or* female-chauvinistic, chauvinistic

591 PUBLIC SPIRIT

NOUNS **1** **public spirit,** social consciousness *or* responsibility; **citizenship, good citizenship,** citizenism, civism; altruism

2 **patriotism,** love of country; **nationalism,** nationality, ultranationalism superpatriotism; Americanism, Anglicism, Briticism, etc; **chauvinism, jingoism,** overpatriotism; patriotics, flag-waving; saber-rattling

3 **patriot;** nationalist; ultranationalist; **chauvinist,** chauvin, **jingo,** jingoist; patrioteer <nf>, flag waver, superpatriot, hard hat <nf>, hundred-percenter, hundred-percent American; hawk

ADJS 4 **public-spirited, civic; patriotic; nationalistic;** ultranationalist, ultranationalistic; overpatriotic, superpatriotic, flagwaving, **chauvinist, chauvinistic,** jingoist, jingoistic; hawkish

592 BENEFACTOR

NOUNS 1 **benefactor,** benefactress, **benefiter,** succorer, befriender; ministrant, ministering angel; Samaritan, **good Samaritan; helper,** aider, assister, help, aid, helping hand; Johnny-on-the-spot <nf>, jack-at-a-pinch <old Brit nf>, fairy godmother; **patron, backer** 616.9, angel *and* cash cow <nf>; **good person** 659

2 **savior, redeemer,** deliverer, **liberator,** rescuer, freer, **emancipator,** manumitter

VERBS 3 **benefit, aid,** assist, succor; befriend, take under one's wing; back, support; save the day, save one's neck *or* skin *or* bacon

ADJS 4 benefitting, aiding, befriending, assisting; backing, supporting; saving, salving, salvational, redemptive, redeeming; liberating, freeing, emancipative, emancipating, manumitting

ADVS 5 by one's aid *or* good offices, with one's support, on one's shoulders *or* coattails

593 EVILDOER

NOUNS 1 **evildoer, wrongdoer,** worker of ill *or* evil, **malefactor,** malfeasant, malfeasor, misfeasor, malevolent, public enemy, **sinner, villain,** villainess, transgressor, delinquent, culprit; bad *or* bad guy *and* baddy *and* meany *and* wrongo *and* black hat <nf>, wrong'un <Brit nf>, villain; **criminal,** outlaw, felon, **crook** <nf>, lawbreaker, perpetrator, perp <nf>, gangster *and* mobster <nf>; racketeer, thief, robber, burglar, rapist, murderer, con; terrorist; **bad person** 660; deceiver 357

2 **troublemaker, mischief-maker;** holy terror; agitator 375.11

3 **ruffian,** rough, bravo, **rowdy, thug,** desperado, cutthroat, kill-crazy animal, mad dog; gunman; bully, bullyboy, bucko; devil, hellcat, hell-raiser; killer; gang member, gangster

4 <nf terms> **roughneck, tough,** bruiser, mug, mugger, bimbo, bozo, ugly customer, **hoodlum, hood, hooligan,** gorilla, ape, plug-ugly, strong-arm man, muscle man, **goon;** gun, gunsel, trigger man, rodman, torpedo, hatchet man; hellion, terror, holy terror, shtarker, ugly customer

5 **savage, barbarian, brute, beast, animal,** tiger, shark, hyena; wild man; cannibal, man-eater, anthropophagite; **wrecker, vandal,** nihilist, destroyer

6 **monster, fiend,** fiend from hell, **demon, devil,** devil incarnate, hellhound, hellkite; **vampire,** lamia, **harpy, ghoul;** werewolf, ape-man; ogre, ogress; Frankenstein's monster

7 **witch, hag, vixen,** hellhag, hellcat, she-devil, virago, brimstone, termagant, grimalkin, Jezebel, beldam, she-wolf, tigress, wildcat, bitchkitty <nf>, siren, fury

594 JURISDICTION

<administration of justice>

NOUNS 1 **jurisdiction,** legal authority *or* power *or* right *or* sway, the confines of the law; original *or* appellate jurisdiction, exclusive *or* concurrent jurisdiction, civil *or* criminal jurisdiction, common-law *or* equitable jurisdiction, *in rem* jurisdiction, *in personam* jurisdiction, subject-matter juristiction, territorial jurisdiction; voluntary jurisdiction; mandate, cognizance

2 **judiciary,** judicial *or* legal *or* court system, judicature, judicatory, court, the courts; criminal-justice system; **justice,** the wheels of justice, judicial process; judgment 946

3 **magistracy,** magistrature, magistrateship; **judgeship,** justiceship; mayoralty, mayorship

4 **bureau, office, department;** secretariat, ministry, commissariat; municipality, bailiwick; constabulary, constablery, sheriffry, sheriffalty, shrievalty; constablewick, sheriffwick

VERBS 5 **administer justice,** administer, administrate; preside, preside at the board; **sit in judgment** 598.18; **judge** 946.8

ADJS 6 **jurisdictional,** jurisdictive; **judicatory,** judicatorial, judicative, **juridic** *or* **juridical**; jural, jurisprudential, **judicial, judiciary;** magisterial; forensic

595 TRIBUNAL

NOUNS 1 **tribunal, forum, board,** curia, Areopagus; judicature, judicatory, judiciary 594.2; council 423; inquisition, the Inquisition

2 **court, law court, court of law** *or* **justice,** court of arbitration, legal tribunal, judicature; **United States court**, federal court; **British court**, Crown court; high court, trial court, court of record, superior court, inferior court; criminal court, civil court

3 <ecclesiastical courts> Papal Court, Curia, Rota, Sacra Romana Rota, Court of Arches *and* Court of Peculiars <Brit>

4 **military court, court-martial,** general *or* special *or* summary court-martial, drumhead court-martial; naval court, captain's mast

5 **seat of justice, judgment seat,** mercy seat, siege of justice ; **bench;** woolsack <Brit>

6 **courthouse, court;** county *or* town hall, town house; **courtroom;** jury box; bench, bar; witness stand *or* box, dock

ADJS 7 **tribunal, judicial,** judiciary, court, curial; appellate

596 JUDGE, JURY

NOUNS 1 **judge, magistrate, justice,** adjudicator, bencher, man *or* woman on the bench, presiding officer, beak <Brit nf>; **justice of the peace** *or* **JP;** arbiter, arbitrator, moderator; umpire, referee; his *or* her honor, your honor, his *or* her worship, his lordship; Mr Justice; critic 946.7; **special judge**

2 <historical> tribune, praetor, ephor, archon, syndic, podesta; Areopagite; justiciar, justiciary; dempster, deemster, doomster, doomsman

3 <Muslim> mullah, ulema, hakim, mufti, cadi

4 Chief Justice, Associate Justice, Justice of the Supreme Court; Lord Chief Justice, Lord Justice, Lord Chancellor, Master of the Rolls, Baron of the Exchequer; Judge Advocate General

5 Pontius Pilate, Solomon, Minos, Rhadamanthus, Aeacus

6 jury, **panel,** jury of one's peers, country, twelve men in a box, twelve good men and true; inquest; jury panel, jury list, venire facias; hung *or* deadlocked jury; grand jury, petit jury, common jury, special jury *or* blue-ribbon jury *or* struck jury

7 **juror, juryman, jurywoman,** venire-man *or* -woman, talesman; foreman of the jury, foreman *or* foreperson; grand-juror, grand-juryman; petit-juror, petit-juryman; recognitor

597 LAWYER

NOUNS 1 **lawyer, attorney, attorney-at-law,** barrister, barrister-at-law, **counselor,** counselor-at-law, **counsel,** legal counsel *or* counselor, legal adviser, law officer, legal expert, **solicitor, advocate, pleader;** member of the bar, legal practitioner, officer of the court; smart lawyer, pettifogger, Philadelphia lawyer; Juris Doctor *or* Jur.D., proctor, procurator; friend at *or* in court, amicus curiae; deputy, agent 576; intercessor 466.3; sea lawyer, latrine *or* guardhouse lawyer <nf>, self-styled lawyer, legalist; public prosecutor, public defender, defense lawyer *or* attorney, prosecuting attorney, trial lawyer *or* attorney;

judge advocate, district attorney *or* DA, attorney general

2 legist, jurist, jurisprudent, jurisconsult; law member of a court-martial

3 <nf terms> **shyster, mouthpiece, ambulance chaser,** lip, fixer, legal eagle, ambulance chaser

4 **bar,** legal profession, members of the bar; representation, counsel, pleading, attorneyship; **practice,** legal practice, criminal practice, corporate practice, etc; legal-aid *or* pro bono practice; **law firm,** legal firm, partnership

VERBS **5** **practice law,** practice at the bar; be admitted to the bar; take silk <Brit>

ADJS **6** **lawyerly,** lawyerlike, barristerial; representing, of counsel

598 LEGAL ACTION

NOUNS **1** **lawsuit, suit,** suit in *or* at law; countersuit; **litigation, prosecution, action, legal action,** proceedings, legal proceedings, legal process, legal procedure, due process, course of law; legal remedy; **case, court case,** cause, cause in court, legal case; **judicial process;** claim, counterclaim; test case; one's day in court

2 **summons, subpoena,** writ of summons; **writ, warrant**

3 **arraignment, indictment, impeachment; complaint, charge** 599.1; presentment; information; bill of indictment, true bill; **bail** 438.2

4 **jury selection, impanelment,** venire, venire facias, venire facias de novo, jury service, sequestration

5 **trial, jury trial,** trial by jury, trial at the bar, trial by law, **hearing, inquiry, inquisition,** inquest, assize; court-martial; **examination,** cross-examination; retrial; mistrial; change of venue; civil trial, criminal trial, bench trial

6 **pleadings,** arguments at the bar; **plea,** pleading, argument; **defense,** statement of defense; demurrer, general *or* special demurrer; refutation 958.2; rebuttal 939.2

7 **declaration, statement,** allegation, allegation *or* statement of facts, procès-verbal; **deposition,** affidavit; claim; complaint; bill, bill of complaint; libel, narratio; nolle prosequi, nol pros; nonsuit

8 **testimony; evidence** 957;, cross-examination, direct examination; **argument,** presentation of the case; resting of the case; **summing up,** summation, closing arguments, jury instructions, charge to the jury, charging of the jury

9 **judgment, decision,** landmark decision; **verdict,** directed verdict, special verdict, sealed verdict, **sentence** 946.5; acquittal 601; condemnation 602, penalty 603

10 **appeal,** appeal motion, application for retrial, appeal to a higher court; writ of error; certiorari, writ of certiorari

11 **litigant, litigator,** litigationist; suitor, **party,** party to a suit, suitor; injured *or* aggrieved party, **plaintiff** 599.5; **defendant** 599.6; witness; accessory, accessory before *or* after the fact; panel, parties litigant

12 <legal terms> motion for summary judgment, search warrant, bench warrant, discovery, written interrogatories, witness list, plea bargaining, objection, perjury

VERBS **13** **sue, litigate, prosecute,** go into litigation, **bring suit,** put in suit, sue *or* prosecute at law, **go to law,** seek in law, appeal to the law, seek justice *or* legal redress, implead, **bring action against,** bring legal action, start an action, prosecute a suit against, take *or* institute legal proceedings against; law *or* have the law in <nf>; take to court, bring into court, hale *or* haul *or* drag into court, bring a case before the court *or* bar, bring before a jury, bring to justice, bring to trial, **put on trial,** bring to the bar, take before the judge; set down for hearing; implead, seek legal protection

14 **summons, issue a summons,** subpoena

15 **arraign, indict, impeach,** cite, serve notice on, find an indictment against, present a true bill, claim, prefer *or* file a claim, have *or* pull up <nf>, bring up for investigation; press charges, **prefer charges** 599.7

16 select *or* **impanel a jury,** impanel, panel

17 call to witness, bring forward, put on the stand; swear in 334.7; take oath; take the stand, testify

18 try, try a case, conduct a trial, bring to trial, put on trial, **hear,** give a hearing to, sit on; charge the jury, deliver one's charge to the jury; **judge, sit in judgment**

19 plead, enter a plea *or* **pleading,** implead, conduct pleadings, argue at the bar; **plead** *or* **argue one's case,** stand trial, present one's case, make a plea, tell it to the judge <nf>; hang the jury <nf>; rest, rest one's case; sum up one's case; throw oneself on the mercy of the court

20 bring in a verdict, judge, **pass** *or* **pronounce sentence** 946.13; acquit 601.4; convict 602.3; penalize 603.4

ADJS **21** litigious, litigant, litigatory, litigating; causidical, lawyerly; litigable, actionable, justicble, prosecutable; prosecutorial; **moot,** sub judice; unactionable, unprosecutable, unlitigable, frivolous, without merit

PHRS **22 in litigation,** in court, in chancery, in jeopardy, **at law,** litigated, coram judice, brought before the court *or* judge, at bar, at the bar, **on trial,** up for investigation *or* hearing, before the court *or* bar *or* judge

599 ACCUSATION

NOUNS **1 accusation,** accusal, finger-pointing <nf>, **charge, complaint,** plaint, count, **blame, imputation,** delation, reproach, taxing; **accusing, bringing of charges,** laying of charges, bringing to book; **denunciation,** denouncement; **impeachment, arraignment, indictment,** bill of indictment, true bill; **allegation,** allegement; **imputation,** ascription; **insinuation, implication, innuendo,** veiled accusation, unspoken accusation; information, information against, bill of particulars; charge sheet; specification; gravamen of a charge; prosecution, suit, lawsuit 598.1

2 incrimination, crimination, **inculpation,** implication, **citation,** involvement, impugnment; attack, assault; **censure** 510.3

3 recrimination, retort, countercharge

4 trumped-up charge, false witness; **put-up job** *and* **frame-up** *and* **frame** <nf>; false charge

5 accuser, accusant, accusatrix; incriminator, delator, allegator, impugner; informer 551.6; impeacher, indictor; **plaintiff, complainant,** claimant, appellant, petitioner, libelant, suitor, **party,** party to a suit, pursuer; **prosecutor,** the prosecution; hostile witness

6 accused, defendant, respondent, codefendant, corespondent, libelee, appellee, suspect, culprit, prisoner, prisoner before the court, accused person; prime suspect

VERBS **7 accuse,** bring accusation; **charge, press charges, prefer** *or* **bring charges,** lay charges; complain, **lodge a complaint,** lodge a plaint; **impeach, arraign, indict,** bring in *or* hand up an indictment, return a true bill, article, **cite,** cite on several
counts; book; **denounce,** denunciate; **finger** *and* point
the finger at *and* put *or* lay the finger on <nf>, throw the book at <nf>, **testify against** 551.12; **impute,** ascribe; allege, insinuate, imply; bring to book; tax, task, take to task *or* account; **reproach,** twit, taunt with; report, put on report

8 blame, blame on *or* upon <nf>, lay on, hold against, **put** *or* **place** *or* lay the blame on, lay *or* cast blame upon, place *or* fix the blame *or* responsibility for; fasten on *or* upon, pin *or* hang on <nf>

9 accuse of, charge with, tax *or* task with, saddle with, lay to
one's charge, place to one's account, lay at one's door, bring home to, cast *or* throw in one's teeth, throw up to one, throw *or* thrust in the face of

10 incriminate, criminate, **inculpate,** implicate, involve; cry out against, cry out on *or* upon, cry shame upon, raise one's voice against; attack, assail, impugn; **censure** 510.13; throw a stone at, cast *or* throw the first stone

11 **recriminate,** countercharge, retort an accusation

12 **trump up a charge, bear false witness; frame** *and* frame up *and* set up *and* put up a job on <nf>, plant evidence

ADJS 13 **accusing, accusatory,** accusatorial, accusative, pointing to; imputative, denunciatory; recriminatory; prosecutorial; **condemnatory**

14 **incriminating,** incriminatory, criminatory; delatorian; inculpative, inculpatory

15 **accused, charged, blamed,** tasked, taxed, reproached, **denounced, impeached, indicted, arraigned; under a cloud** *or* a cloud of suspicion, under suspicion; incriminated, recriminated, inculpated, implicated, involved, in complicity; **cited,** impugned; under attack, under fire

600 JUSTIFICATION

NOUNS 1 **justification, vindication; clearing,** clearing of one's name *or* one's good name, clearance, purging, purgation, destigmatizing, destigmatization, **exculpation** 601.1; no bill, failure to indict; explanation, rationalization; reinstatement, restitution, restoration, **rehabilitation**

2 **defense, plea,** pleading; argument, statement of defense; answer, reply, counterstatement, response, riposte; grounds; **refutation** 958.2, **rebuttal** 939.2; demurrer, general *or* special demurrer; denial, objection, exception; **special pleading;** self-defense, plea of self-defense, Nuremberg defense, the devil-made-me-do-it defense, blame-the-victim defense

3 **apology,** apologia, apologetic; amende

4 **excuse, cop-out** *and* **alibi** *and* **out** <nf>; lame excuse, poor excuse, likely story, sob story; escape hatch, way out; credibility gap

5 **extenuation, mitigation, palliation,** softening; extenuative, palliative, saving grace; **whitewash, whitewashing,** decontamination; gilding, gloss, varnish, color, putting the best color on; qualification, allowance; extenuating circumstances, mitigating circumstances, diminished responsibility; five second rule; dichaeologia

6 **warrant, reason,** good reason, **cause,** call, **right, basis,** substantive *or* material basis, **ground, grounds,** foundation, substance

7 **justifiability, vindicability, defensibility;** explainability, explicability; **excusability,** pardonableness, forgivableness, remissibility, veniality; warrantableness, allowableness, admissibility, reasonableness, reasonability, legitimacy

8 **justifier, vindicator; defender,** pleader; **advocate,** successful advocate *or* defender, proponent, **champion; apologist,** apologizer, apologetic, excuser; whitewasher

VERBS 9 **justify, vindicate,** do justice to, make justice *or* right prevail; fail to indict, no-bill; **warrant,** account for, show sufficient grounds for, give good reasons for; **rationalize,** explain; cry sour grapes; get off the hook <nf>, find an out, **exculpate** 601.4; **clear,** clear one's name *or* one's good name, purge, destigmatize, reinstate, restore, rehabilitate

10 **defend,** offer *or* say in defense, allege in support *or* vindication, **support, uphold, sustain, maintain,** assert, stick up for; **answer,** reply, respond, riposte, counter; refute 958.5, **rebut** 939.5; **plead for,** make a plea, offer as a plea, plead one's case *or* cause, put up a front *or* a brave front; **advocate,** champion, go to bat for <nf>, espouse, join *or* associate oneself with, stand *or* stick up for, speak up for, contend for, speak for, argue for, urge reasons for, put in a good word for

11 **excuse,** alibi <nf>, offer excuse for, give as an excuse, cover with excuses, **explain,** offer an explanation; plead ignorance *or* insanity *or* diminished responsibility; **apologize for,** make apology for; alibi out of

<nf>, crawl *or* worm *or* squirm out of, lie out of, have an out *or* alibi *or* story <nf>

12 **extenuate, mitigate, palliate,** soften, lessen, diminish, **ease,** mince; **soft-pedal;** slur over, ignore, pass by in silence, give the benefit of the doubt, not hold it against one, **explain away, gloss** *or* **smooth over,** put a gloss upon, put a good face upon, varnish, **white-wash,** color, lend a color to, put the best color *or* face on, show in the best colors, show to best advantage; **allow for,** make allowance for; give the Devil his due

ADJS 13 **justifying,** justificatory; **vindicative,** vindicatory, rehabilitative; refuting 958.6; defensive; **excusing,** excusatory; **apologetic, apologetical; extenuating,** extenuative, **palliative**

14 **justifiable, vindicable, defensible; excusable, pardonable, forgivable,** expiable, remissible, exemptible, venial; **condonable,** dispensable; **warrantable,** allowable, admissible, reasonable, colorable, legitimate; innocuous, unobjectionable, inoffensive

601 ACQUITTAL

NOUNS 1 **acquittal,** acquittance, acquitment; **exculpation,** disculpation, verdict of acquittal *or* not guilty; **exoneration, absolution, vindication, remission,** compurgation, purgation, purging; **clearing,** clearance, destigmatizing, destigmatization, quietus; **pardon, excuse, forgiveness, free pardon; discharge, release, dismissal,** setting free; quashing of the charge *or* indictment; assoilment; grace

2 **exemption, immunity,** impunity, nonliability, dispensation, waiver; diplomatic immunity; **amnesty,** indemnity, nonprosecution, non prosequitur, nolle prosequi; stay; dispensation; freedom

3 **reprieve,** respite, grace, remit

VERBS 4 **acquit, clear, exculpate, exonerate, absolve,** give *or* grant absolution, bring in *or* return a verdict of not guilty; **vindicate,** justify; **pardon, excuse, forgive,** show mercy; remit, grant remission, remit the penalty of; amnesty, grant or extend amnesty; **discharge, release, dismiss, free, set free,** let off <nf>, let go, let off scot-free, spare; quash the charge *or* indictment, withdraw the charge; **exempt,** grant immunity, exempt from, dispense from; clear the skirts of, shrive, purge; blot out one's sins, wipe the slate clean; **whitewash,** decontaminate; destigmatize; non-pros; assoil

5 **reprieve,** respite, give *or* grant a reprieve; stay

602 CONDEMNATION

NOUNS 1 **condemnation, damnation, doom,** guilty verdict, verdict of guilty; proscription, excommunication, anathematizing; **denunciation,** denouncement; **censure** 510.3; **conviction; sentence, judgment,** rap <nf>; capital punishment, corporal punishment, death penalty, death sentence, death warrant, burning at the stake; curse

2 attainder, attainture, attaintment; bill of attainder; civil death

VERBS 3 **condemn, damn, doom; denounce,** denunciate; **censure** 510.13; **convict,** find guilty, bring home to; proscribe, excommunicate, anathematize; blacklist, put on the Index; reprobate; pronounce judgment 946.13; **sentence,** pronounce sentence, pass sentence on; penalize 603.4; attaint; sign one's death warrant

4 **stand condemned,** be convicted, be found guilty

ADJS 5 **condemnatory, damnatory,** denunciatory, proscriptive; **censorious**

6 convicted, condemned, guilty, blameworthy, liable, sentenced

603 PENALTY

NOUNS 1 **penalty,** penalization, penance, penal retribution; **sanctions,** penal *or* punitive measures; **punishment** 604; **reprisal** 506.2, retaliation

506, compensation, price; the devil to pay

2 **handicap,** disability, **disadvantage** 1012.6

3 **fine,** monetary *or* financial penalty, mulct, amercement, sconce, **damages,** punitive damages, compensatory damages; distress, distraint; forfeit, forfeiture; escheat, escheatment

VERBS 4 **penalize,** put *or* impose *or* inflict a penalty *or* sanctions on; **punish** 604.10; **handicap,** put at a disadvantage

5 **fine,** mulct, amerce, sconce, estreat, pillory; distrain, levy a distress; award damages

ADVS 6 **on pain of,** under *or* upon pain of, **on** *or* **under penalty of**

604 PUNISHMENT

NOUNS 1 **punishment,** punition, **chastisement, chastening, correction, discipline,** disciplinary measure *or* action, **castigation,** infliction, scourge, ferule, what-for <nf>; pains, pains and punishments; pay, payment; crime fighting; **retribution,** retributive justice, nemesis; judicial punishment; punishment that fits the crime, condign punishment, well-deserved punishment; **penalty,** penal retribution; penalization; penology; cruel and unusual punishment; judgment; what's coming to one, **just desserts, desserts**

2 <forms of punishment> penal servitude, jailing, imprisonment, incarceration, confinement; hard labor, rock pile, chain gang, labor camp; galleys; torture, torment, martyrdom; the gantlet, keelhauling, tar-and-feathering, railriding, picketing, the rack, impalement, dismemberment; walking the plank; house arrest; exile

3 **slap,** smack, whack, whomp, **cuff, box,** buffet, belt; blow 902.4; **rap on the knuckles,** box on the ear, slap in the face; slap on the wrist, token punishment

4 **corporal punishment, whipping, beating, thrashing, spanking, flogging,** paddling, flagellation, scourging, flailing, trouncing, basting, bastinado, drubbing, buffeting, belaboring; **lashing, lacing,** stripes; horse-whipping, strapping, belting, rawhiding, cowhiding; **switching; clubbing,** cudgeling, caning, truncheoning, fustigation, bastinado; pistol-whipping; battery; dusting

5 <nf terms> **licking,** larruping, walloping, whaling, lathering, leathering, **hiding, tanning, dressing-down**, chewing out**; paddling,** swingeing; grounding

6 <old nf terms> strap oil, hazel oil, hickory oil, birch oil; dose of strap oil, etc

7 **capital punishment, execution;** legal *or* judicial murder, extreme penalty, death sentence *or* penalty *or* warrant; **hanging,** the gallows, the rope *or* noose; summary execution; **lynching,** necktie party *or* sociable <nf>, vigilanteism, vigilante justice; the necklace; **crucifixion,** impalement; **electrocution,** the chair <nf>, the hot seat <nf>; gassing, the gas chamber; lethal injection; **decapitation,** decollation, beheading, the guillotine, the ax, the block; **strangling,** strangulation, garrote; **shooting,** fusillade, firing squad; **burning,** burning at the stake; **poisoning,** hemlock; stoning, lapidation; drowning; defenestration

8 **punisher,** discipliner, chastiser, chastener; **executioner,** executionist, deathsman , Jack Ketch <Brit>; **hangman; lyncher;** electrocutioner; headsman, **beheader,** decapitator; strangler, garroter; sadist, torturer; hatchet man, hit man <nf>

9 **penologist;** jailer 429.10

VERBS 10 **punish, chastise, chasten, discipline, correct, castigate, penalize**, reprimand**; take to task,** bring to book, bring *or* call to account; deal with, settle with, settle *or* square accounts, **give one his desserts** *or* **just desserts,** serve one right; inflict upon, visit upon; teach *or* give one a lesson, make an example of; pillory; masthead; reduce to the ranks

11 <nf terms> **attend to,** do for, take care of, serve one out, **give it to,** take *or* have it out of; pay, pay out, **fix, settle,** fix one's wagon, settle one's hash, settle the score, give one his gruel, make it hot for one, **give one his comeuppance;** lower the boom, put one through the wringer, come down on *or* down hard on, throw the book at, throw to the wolves; **give what-for,** give a going-over, climb one's frame, let one have it, tell off, light into, lay into, land on, mop *or* wipe up the floor with, skin live, have one's hide

12 **slap,** smack, whack, thwack, whomp, **cuff, box,** buffet; strike 902.13; slap the face, box the ears, give a rap on the knuckles

13 **whip,** give a whipping *or* beating *or* thrashing, **beat, thrash, spank, flog,** scourge, flagellate, flay, flail, whale; **smite,** thump, trounce, baste, **pummel,** pommel, **drub, buffet, belabor,** lay on; **lash, lace,** cut, stripe; horsewhip; knout; **strap,** belt, rawhide, cowhide; **switch,** birch, give the stick; **club, cudgel,** cane, truncheon, fustigate, bastinado; pistol-whip

14 **thrash soundly, batter,** bruise

15 <nf terms> **beat up,** rough up, clobber, marmelize <Brit>, work over, lick, larrup, wallop, whop, swinge, beat one's brains out, whale, whale the tar out of, beat *or* kick the shit out of, beat to a jelly, **beat black and blue, knock one's lights out, nail,** welt, trim, flax, lather, leather, **hide,** tan, **tan one's hide,** dress down, **kick ass,** give a dressing-down, knock head, knock heads together; **paddle; lambaste, clobber,** dust one's jacket, give a dose of birch oil *or* strap oil *or* hickory oil *or* hazel oil, take it out of one's hide *or* skin

16 **torture,** put to the question; rack, put on *or* to the rack; dismember, tear limb from limb; draw and quarter, break on the wheel, tar and feather, ride on a rail, picket, keelhaul, impale, grill, thumbscrew, persecute, work over

17 **execute, put to death,** inflict capital punishment; **electrocute,** burn *and* fry <nf>; send to the gas chamber; **behead, decapitate,** decollate, guillotine, bring to the block; **crucify; shoot,** execute by firing squad; burn, **burn at the stake; strangle,** garrote, bowstring; stone, lapidate; defenestrate; send to the hot seat <nf>

18 **hang,** hang by the neck; **string up** *and* scrag *and* stretch <nf>; gibbet, noose, neck, bring to the gallows; **lynch;** hang, draw, and quarter

19 **be hanged,** suffer hanging, **swing,** dance upon nothing, kick the air *or* wind *or* clouds

20 **be punished, suffer,** suffer for, **suffer the consequences** *or* **penalty,** get it *and* **catch it** <nf>, get *or* catch it in the neck <nf>, catch hell *or* the devil <nf>, get *or* take a licking *or* shellacking <nf>; **get one's desserts** 639.6; get it coming and going <nf>, be doubly punished, sow the wind and reap the whirlwind; get hurt, get one's fingers burned, have *or* get one's knuckles rapped

21 **take one's punishment,** bow one's neck, take the consequences, **take one's medicine** *or* what is coming to one, swallow the bitter pill *or* one's medicine, pay the piper, face the music <nf>, stand up to it, make one's bed and lie on it, get what one is asking for; take the rap <nf>, take the fall <nf>

22 **deserve punishment, have it coming** <nf>, be for it *or* in for it, be heading for a fall, be cruising for a bruising <nf>

ADJS **23** **punishing, chastising,** chastening, corrective, disciplinary, correctional; retributive; grueling <nf>; **penal, punitive,** punitory, inflictive; castigatory; baculine; penological; capital; corporal

605 INSTRUMENTS OF PUNISHMENT

NOUNS **1** **whip, lash, scourge,** flagellum, strap, thong, rawhide, cowhide, blacksnake, kurbash, sjambok, belt, razor strap; knout; bullwhip, bullwhack; horsewhip; crop; quirt; rope's end; cat, cat-o'-nine-tails; whiplash; bastinado

2 **rod, stick, switch; paddle,** ruler, ferule, pandybat; birch, rattan; cane; club

3 <devices> **pillory, stocks,** finger pillory; cucking stool, ducking stool, trebuchet; whipping post, branks, triangle *or* triangles, wooden horse, treadmill, crank

4 <instruments of torture> **rack,** wheel, Iron Maiden of Nuremberg; screw, thumbscrew; boot, iron heel, scarpines; Procrustean bed *or* bed of Procrustes

5 <instruments of execution> **scaffold; block, guillotine,** ax, maiden; **stake; cross; gallows,** gallows-tree, gibbet, tree, drop; **hangman's rope, noose,** rope, halter, hemp, hempen collar *or* necktie *or* bridle <nf>; **electric chair,** death chair, the chair <nf>, hot seat <nf>; **gas chamber,** lethal chamber, death chamber; the necklace, the needle

606 THE PEOPLE

<the population>

NOUNS 1 **the people, the populace, the public,** the general public, people in general, everyone, everybody; **the population,** the citizenry, the whole people, the polity, the body politic; **the community, the commonwealth, society,** the society, the social order *or* fabric, the nation; the commonalty *or* commonality, commonage, commoners, commons, demos <Gk>; **common people, ordinary people** *or* **folk, persons, folk, folks,** gentry; the common sort, plain people *or* folks, the common run <nf>, the rank and file, the boy *or* girl next door, Brown Jones and Robinson, John Q. Public, Middle America; Tom, Dick, and Harry; the salt of the earth, Everyman, Everywoman, the man *or* woman in the street, the common man, you and me, John Doe, Joe Sixpack *or* Joe Schmo <nf>, *vulgus* <L>, the third estate; **the upper class; the middle class; the lower class;** demography, demographics; social anthropology

2 **the masses, the hoi polloi**, the many, **the multitude,** the crowd, **the mob,** the horde, the million, **the majority,** the mass of the people, the herd, the great unnumbered, the great unwashed, **the vulgar** *or* **common herd**, vulgar masses; *profanum vulgus* and *ignobile vulgus* and *mobile vulgus* <L>; audience, followers

3 **rabble,** rabblement, rout, ruck, common ruck, canaille, *racaille* <Fr>, ragtag <nf>, **ragtag and bobtail;** rag, tag, and bobtail; **riffraff, trash,** raff, chaff, **rubbish,** dregs, sordes, offscourings, off-scum, **scum, scum of the earth, dregs** *or* **scum** *or* **off-scum** *or* **offscourings of society,** swinish multitude, vermin, cattle; colluvies

4 **the underprivileged,** the disadvantaged, the poor, ghetto-dwellers, slum-dwellers, welfare cases, chronic poor, underclass, depressed class, poverty subculture, the wretched of the earth, outcasts, the homeless, the dispossessed, bag people, the powerless, the unemployable, lumpen, the lumpenproletariat *or* lumpenprole <nf>, lower orders, second-class citizens, the have-nots, small potatoes

5 **common man, commoner,** little man, **little fellow, average man,** ordinary man, typical man, **man in the street,** one of the people, man of the people, man in the street, regular guy, regular joe, Everyman, ham-and-egger; **plebeian,** pleb <slang>; **proletarian,** prole <Brit nf>, *roturier* <Fr>; ordinary *or* average Joe *and* Joe Doakes *and* Joe Sixpack <nf>, John Doe, Jane Doe, John Smith, Mr *or* Mrs Brown *or* Smith, Joe Blow, John Q. Public, Mr Nobody; nonentity; muggle; bourgeois

6 **peasant, countryman,** countrywoman, **provincial,** son of the soil, tiller of the soil; **peon,** hind, fellah, muzhik, serf, villein, churl; **farmer** 1069.5, **hick** *and* yokel *and* rube *and* hayseed *and* shit-kicker <nf>,

bumpkin, country bumpkin, rustic, clod, **clodhopper** <nf>, hillbilly *and* woodhick <nf>, **boor,** clown, lout, looby; townie

7 **upstart, parvenu,** adventurer, sprout <nf>; *bourgeois gentilhomme* <Fr>, would-be gentleman; *nouveau riche* and *nouveau roturier* <Fr>, *arriviste* <Fr>, **newly-rich,** pig in clover <nf>; **social climber,** climber, name-dropper, tufthunter, status seeker

ADJS 8 **populational,** population; **demographic,** demographical; national, societal; **popular,** public, mass, grass-roots, cultural, **common,** common as dirt, commonplace, communal, folk, tribal, **plain, ordinary, lowly,** low, mean, base; **humble,** homely; rank-and-file, provincial, of the people; second-class, **lowborn,** lowbred, baseborn, earthborn, earthy, of humble birth, plebeian; third-estate; ungenteel, shabby-genteel, uncultured; **vulgar, rude,** coarse, below the salt; **parvenu, upstart,** risen from the ranks, jumped-up <nf>; newly-rich, *nouveau-riche* <Fr>; non-U <Brit>

607 SOCIAL CLASS AND STATUS

NOUNS 1 **class, social class, economic class,** social group *or* grouping, status group, accorded status, social category, order, grade, caste, estate, rank; **status, social status, economic status,** socioeconomic status *or* background, standing, footing, prestige, rank, ranking, place, station, position, level, degree, stratum; **social structure, hierarchy,** pecking order, social stratification, social system, social gamut, social differentiation, social pyramid, class structure, class distinction, status system, power structure, ranking, stratification, social network, ordering, social scale, gradation, division, social inequality, inequality, haves and have-nots; **social bias, class conflict,** class identity, class difference, class prejudice, class struggle, class politics; ageism; **mobility, social mobility,** upward mobility, downward mobility, vertical mobility, horizontal mobility; social justice

2 **upper class, upper classes, aristocracy,** patriciate, second estate, ruling class, ruling circles, elite, elect, the privileged, the classes, the quality, the better sort, upper circles, upper cut *and* upper crust *and* crust *and* cream <nf>, upper-income group *or* higher-income group, gentlefolk, gentility, lords of creation; **high society,** high life, the Four Hundred, bon ton, *haut monde* <Fr>, First Families of Virginia *or* FFV; Social Register, Bluebook; nobility, gentry 608; status symbol; social ladder

3 **aristocracy, aristocratic status,** aristocraticalness, aristocraticness, high status, high rank, quality, high estate, gentility, social distinction, social prestige; **birth,** high birth, distinguished ancestry *or* descent *or* heritage *or* blood, blue blood, silk stocking

4 **aristocrat, patrician,** Brahmin, blue-blood, thoroughbred, member of the upper class, socialite, swell *and* upper-cruster <nf>, grandee, grand dame, dowager, magnifico, lord of creation; **gentleman, lady,** person of breeding; trophy wife <nf>; debutante

5 **middle class,** middle order *or* orders, lower middle class, upper middle class, bourgeoisie, educated class, professional class, middle-income group, white-collar workers, salaried workers; suburbia; Middle America, silent majority; white bread <nf>; third estate

6 **bourgeois,** member of the middle class, white-collar worker 726.2, salaried worker; pillar of society, solid citizen

7 **lower class, lower classes,** lower orders, plebeians, plebs, workers, working class, working people, proletariat, proles <Brit nf>, rank and file, grass roots, laboring class *or* classes, toilers, toiling class *or* classes, the other half, low-income group, wage-earners, hourly worker, blue-collar worker; bottom feeder

8 the underclass, the underprivileged

9 worker 726.2, **workman, working man, working woman,** working girl, proletarian, laborer, laboring man, toiler, stiff *and* working stiff <nf>, artisan, mechanic, industrial worker, factory worker; grunt worker or grunt <nf>

ADJS **10 upper-class, aristocratic, patrician, upscale;** gentle, genteel, of gentle blood; gentlemanly, gentlemanlike; ladylike, quite the lady; **wellborn, well-bred, blue-blooded,** of good breed; **thoroughbred,** purebred, pure-blooded, *pur sang* <Fr>, full-blooded; **highborn,** highbred; born to the purple, born with a silver spoon in one's mouth; **high-society,** socialite, hoity-toity <nf>, posh; **middle-class, bourgeois,** *petit-bourgeois* <Fr>, petty-bourgeois, suburban, white-bread <nf>; **working class, blue collar,** proletarian, lower-class, born on the wrong side of the tracks; **class-conscious; mobile, socially mobile,** upwardly mobile, downwardly mobile, vertically mobile, horizontally mobile, déclassé

608 ARISTOCRACY, NOBILITY, GENTRY

<*noble rank or birth*>

NOUNS **1 aristocracy, nobility,** titled aristocracy, hereditary nobility, noblesse; **royalty; elite,** upper class, elect, the classes, **upper classes** *or* circles, upper cut *and* **upper crust** <nf>, upper ten <Brit nf>, **upper ten thousand,** the Four Hundred, Social Register <TM>, high society, high life, *haut monde* <Fr>; old nobility, *ancienne noblesse* <Fr>, *noblesse de robe* and *noblesse d'épée* <Fr>, *ancien régime* <Fr>; First Families of Virginia *or* FFV; **peerage,** baronage, lords temporal and spiritual; baronetage; knightage, chivalry; gentlefolk, beau monde, jet set

2 nobility, nobleness, aristocracy, aristocraticalness; **gentility,** genteelness; quality, rank, virtue, distinction; birth, high *or* noble birth, ancestry, high *or* honorable descent; lineage, pedigree; blood, **blue blood;** royalty 417.8

3 gentry, gentlefolk, gentlefolks, gentlepeople, better sort; lesser nobility, *petite noblesse* <Fr>; *samurai* <Japanese>; landed gentry, squirearchy

4 nobleman, noble, gentleman; peer; aristocrat, patrician, Brahman, **blue blood,** titled person, thoroughbred, silk-stocking, lace-curtain, swell *and* upper-cruster <nf>, life peer; **grandee,** magnifico, magnate, optimate; **lord,** laird, lordling; seignior, seigneur, *hidalgo* <Sp>; **duke,** grand duke, archduke, marquis, **earl, count,** viscount, **baron,** daimio, **baronet;** squire; esquire, armiger; palsgrave, waldgrave, margrave, landgrave; jet-setter, patrician

5 knight, cavalier, chevalier, *caballero* <Sp>; **knight-errant,** knight-adventurer; companion; bachelor, knight bachelor; baronet, knight baronet; banneret, knight banneret; Bayard, Gawain, Lancelot, Sidney, Sir Galahad, Don Quixote

6 noblewoman, peeress, gentlewoman; lady, dame, *doña* <Sp>, khanum; **duchess,** grand duchess, archduchess, marchioness, marquise, viscountess, **countess, baroness,** margravine

7 prince, knez, atheling, sheikh, sherif, mirza, khan, emir, shahzada <India>; princeling, princelet; crown prince, heir apparent; heir presumptive; prince consort; prince regent; **king;** princes of India; Muslim rulers 575.10

8 princess, *princesse* <Fr>, *infanta* <Sp>, rani *and* maharani *and* begum *and* shahzadi *and* kumari *or* kunwari *and* raj-kumari *and* malikzadi <India>; crown princess; **queen** 575.11

9 <rank or office> lordship, ladyship; dukedom, marquisate, earldom, barony, baronetcy; viscountship, viscountcy, viscounty; knighthood, knight-errantship; seigniory, seigneury, seignioralty; pashaship, pashadom; peerage; princeship, princedom; kingship, queenship 417.8

ADJS 10 **noble,** ennobled, titled, of rank, high, exalted; **aristocratic, patrician; gentle,** genteel, of gentle blood; gentlemanly, gentlemanlike; ladylike, quite the lady; knightly, chivalrous; ducal, archducal, princely, princelike; **regal** 417.17, kingly, kinglike; queenly, queenlike; titled

11 **wellborn, well-bred, blue-blooded,** well-connected, of good breed; **thoroughbred,** purebred, pureblooded, *pur sang* <Fr>, fullblooded; **highborn,** highbred; born to the purple, high-caste, of good family; classy <nf>, U <Brit>

609 POLITICS

NOUNS 1 **politics,** polity, the art of the possible; practical politics, *Realpolitik* <Ger>; empirical politics; **party** *or* **partisan politics, partisanism; politicization;** reform politics; multiparty politics; power politics; machine politics, bossism <nf>, Tammany Hall, Tammanism <nf>; confrontation *or* confrontational *or* confro politics; **interest politics,** single-issue politics, interest-group politics, pressure-group politics, PAC *or* political action committee politics; consensus politics; fusion politics; career politics; petty politics, peanut politics <nf>, pork-barrel politics; kid-glove politics <nf>; silk-stocking politics <nf>; ward politics; electronic *or* technological politics; public affairs, civic affairs

2 **political science,** poli-sci <nf>, **politics, government, civics;** political philosophy, political theory; political behavior; political economy, comparative government, international relations, public administration; political geography, geopolitics; realpolitik

3 **statesmanship, statecraft,** political *or* governmental leadership, national leadership; transpartisan *or* suprapartisan leadership; kingcraft, queencraft; senatorship

4 **policy, polity,** public policy; line, **party line,** party principle *or* doctrine *or* philosophy, **position,** bipartisan policy; noninterference, nonintervention, *laissez-faire* <Fr>, laissez-faireism; free enterprise; go-slow policy; government control, governmentalism; planned economy, managed currency, price supports, pump-priming <nf>; autarky, economic self-sufficiency; free trade; protection, protectionism; bimetallism; strict constructionism; localism, sectionalism, states' rights, nullification; political correctness

5 **foreign policy, foreign affairs;** world politics; **diplomacy,** diplomatic *or* diplomatics ; shirt-sleeve diplomacy; shuttle diplomacy; dollar diplomacy, dollar imperialism; gunboat diplomacy; brinkmanship; **nationalism, internationalism;** expansionism, imperialism, manifest destiny, colonialism, neocolonialism; spheres of influence; balance of power; containment; deterrence; militarism, preparedness; tough policy, the big stick <nf>, twisting the lion's tail; brinksmanship; nonresistance, isolationism, neutralism, coexistence, peaceful coexistence; détente; compromise, appeasement; peace offensive; good-neighbor policy; open-door policy, open door; diplomatic doctrine; Monroe Doctrine; Truman Doctrine; Eisenhower Doctrine; Nixon Doctrine

6 **program;** Square Deal <Theodore Roosevelt>, New Deal <Franklin D Roosevelt>, Fair Deal <Harry S Truman>, New Frontier <John F Kennedy>, Great Society <Lyndon B Johnson>; austerity program; Thatcherism <Brit>

7 **platform,** party platform, **program,** declaration of policy; **plank; issue;** keynote address, keynote speech; position paper

8 **political convention, convention;** conclave, powwow <nf>; national convention, quadrennial circus

<nf>; state convention, county convention, preliminary convention, nominating convention; constitutional convention

9 **caucus,** legislative *or* congressional caucus, packed caucus; secret caucus

10 **candidacy,** candidature <chiefly Brit>, **running, running for office,** throwing *or* tossing one's hat in the ring <nf>, standing *or* standing for office <Brit>

11 **nomination,** caucus nomination, direct nomination, petition nomination; acceptance speech

12 **electioneering,** campaigning, politicking <nf>, **stumping** *and* **whistle-stopping** <nf>; **rally,** clambake <nf>; campaign dinner, fundraising dinner

13 **campaign,** all-out campaign, hard-hitting campaign, hoopla *or* hurrah campaign <nf>; **canvass, solicitation;** front-porch campaign; grassroots campaign; stump excursion *and* stumping tour *and* whistle-stop campaign <nf>; TV *or* media campaign; campaign commitments *or* promises; campaign fund, campaign contribution; campaign button

14 **smear campaign,** mudslinging campaign, negative campaign; **whispering campaign;** muckraking, **mudslinging** *and* **dirty politics** *and* **dirty tricks** *and* dirty pool <nf>, character assassination; political canard, roorback; last-minute lie

15 **election,** general election, by-election; congressional election, presidential election; partisan election, nonpartisan election; **primary,** primary election; direct primary, open primary, closed primary, nonpartisan primary, mandatory primary, optional primary, preference primary, presidential primary, presidential preference primary, runoff primary; caucus 609.9; runoff, runoff election; disputed *or* contested election; referendum; close election, horse race *and* toss-up <nf>

16 **election district, precinct, ward, borough;** congressional district; safe district; swing district <nf>; close borough *and* pocket borough *and* rotten borough <Brit>; gerrymander, gerrymandered district, shoestring district; silk-stocking district *or* ward; single-member district *or* constituency; body politic

17 **suffrage, franchise, the vote,** right to vote; universal suffrage, manhood suffrage, woman *or* female suffrage; suffragism, suffragettism; suffragist, woman-suffragist, suffragette; household franchise; one man one vote

18 **voting,** going to the polls, casting one's ballot; preferential voting, preferential system, alternative vote; proportional representation *or* PR, cumulative system *or* voting, Hare system, list system; single system *or* voting, single transferrable vote; plural system *or* voting; single-member district 609.16; absentee voting; proxy voting, card voting; voting machine; election fraud, colonization, floating, repeating, ballot-box stuffing; **vote** 371.6

19 **ballot, slate, ticket,** proxy <nf>; straight ticket, split ticket; Australian ballot; office-block ballot; Indiana ballot, party-column ballot; absentee ballot; long ballot, blanket ballot, jungle ballot <nf>; short ballot; nonpartisan ballot; sample ballot; party emblem

20 **polls,** poll, polling place, polling station <Brit>, balloting place; voting booth, polling booth; ballot box; voting machine; pollbook

21 **returns,** election returns, **poll,** count, official count; **recount;** landslide, tidal wave

22 **electorate,** electors; **constituency,** constituents; electoral college

23 **voter, elector, balloter;** registered voter; fraudulent voter, floater, repeater, ballot-box stuffer; proxy

24 **political party, party,** major party, minor party, third party, splinter party; party in power, opposition party, loyal opposition; **fraction, camp; machine,** political *or* party machine, Tammany Hall; city hall; one-party system, two-party system, multiple party system, multiparty system; right, left, center; new left;

right-wing *or* left-wing conspiracy; popular front; bloc, coalition

25 **partisanism,** partisanship, partisanry; Republicanism; Conservatism, Toryism; Liberalism; Whiggism, Whiggery

26 **nonpartisanism, independence,** neutralism; mugwumpery, mugwumpism

27 **partisan, party member,** party man *or* woman; regular, stalwart, loyalist; wheelhorse, party wheelhorse; heeler, ward heeler, **party hack;** party faithful; right-winger, left-winger; Democrat, Republican

28 **nonpartisan, independent, neutral, mugwump,** undecided *or* uncommitted voter, centrist, swing vote, superdelegate

29 **political influence, wire-pulling** <nf>; **social pressure, public opinion, special-interest pressure,** group pressure; **influence peddling; lobbying,** lobbyism; **logrolling,** back scratching; political corruption

30 **wire-puller** <nf>; **influence peddler,** four-percenter, power broker, fixer <nf>, five-percenter <nf>; logroller

31 **pressure group,** interest group, special-interest group, political action committee *or* PAC, single-issue group; **special interest;** vested interest; financial interests, farm interests, labor interests, etc; minority interests, ethnic vote, black vote, etc; **Black Power,** White Power, Polish Power, etc

32 **lobby,** legislative lobby, special-interest lobby; **lobbyist,** registered lobbyist, lobbyer, parliamentary agent <Brit>

33 **front, movement,** coalition, political front; popular front, people's front, communist front, etc; grassroots movement, ground swell, the silent majority; youth crusade *or* movement

34 <political corruption> **graft,** boodling <nf>, jobbery; pork-barrel legislation *or* pork-barreling; political intrigue

35 **spoils of office; graft,** boodle <nf>; slush fund <nf>; campaign fund, campaign contribution; public tit *and* public trough <nf>; spoils system; cronyism, nepotism

36 **political patronage, patronage, favors of office, pork** *and* **pork barrel** <nf>, plum, melon <nf>

37 **political** *or* **official jargon; officialese** *and* federalese *and* Washingtonese *and* gobbledygook <nf>; bafflegab <nf>; political doubletalk, doublespeak, bunkum <nf>; pussyfooting; pointing with pride and viewing with alarm; new world order

VERBS 38 **politick** <nf>, politicize; look after one's fences *and* mend one's fences <nf>; caucus; gerrymander, lobby

39 **run for office,** run; **throw** *or* **toss one's hat in the ring** <nf>, go into politics, announce for, enter the lists *or* arena, stand *and* stand for office <Brit>; contest a seat <Brit>; take the field

40 **electioneer, campaign; stump** *and* take the stump *and* take to the stump *and* stump the country *and* take to the hustings *and* hit the campaign trail *and* **whistle-stop** <nf>; **canvass,** go to the voters *or* electorate, solicit votes, ring doorbells; shake hands and kiss babies

41 **support, back** *and* **back up** <nf>, come out for, **endorse;** go with the party, follow the party line; **get on the bandwagon** <nf>; **nominate, elect, vote** 371.18,20

42 **hold office,** hold *or* occupy a post, fill an office, be the incumbent, be in office, be elected, be voted in

ADJS 43 **political,** politic; governmental, civic; geopolitical; statesmanlike; diplomatic; suffragist; politico-commercial, politico-diplomatic, politico-ecclesiastical, politico-economic, politico-ethical, politico-geographical, politico-judicial, politico-military, politico-moral, politico-religious, politico-scientific, politico-social, politico-theological; politically correct

44 **partisan, party;** bipartisan, biparty, two-party

45 **nonpartisan, independent,** neutral, mugwumpian *and* mugwumpish <nf>, **on the fence**

610 POLITICIAN

NOUNS 1 **politician,** politico, political leader, professional politician; party leader, party boss *and* party chieftain <nf>; machine *or* clubhouse politician, **political hack,** Tammany man ; **pol** <nf>; old campaigner, war-horse; wheelhorse; reform politician, reformer, advocate; campaigner

2 **statesman,** stateswoman, statesperson, solon, public man *or* woman, national leader; elder statesman; ruler; governor, executive, administrator, leader; president, vice president; prime minister, premier

3 **legislator, lawmaker,** legislatrix, solon, lawgiver; solon; **congressman,** congresswoman, Member of Congress; **senator; representative;** Speaker of the House; majority leader, minority leader; floor leader; whip, party whip; Member of Parliament *or* MP; state senator, assemblyman, assemblywoman, chosen; freeholder, councilman, alderman, alderperson, selectman, selectperson, city father

4 <petty politician> **two-bit** *or* **peanut politician** <nf>, politicaster, statemonger , political dabbler; **hack,** political hack, **party hack**

5 <corrupt politician> **dirty** *or* **crooked politician** *and* jackleg politician <nf>; **grafter,** boodler <nf>; spoilsman, spoilsmonger; influence peddler 609.30

6 <political intriguer> strategist, machinator, gamesman, wheeler-dealer <nf>; operator *and* finagler *and* **wire-puller** <nf>; **logroller,** pork-barrel politician; Machiavellian; behind-the-scenes operator, gray eminence, *éminence grise* <Fr>, power behind the throne, kingmaker <nf>, **powerbroker** 894.6

7 <political leader> **boss** <nf>, higher-up *or* man higher up <nf>, cacique *and* sachem ; keynoter <nf>, policy maker; standard-bearer; ringleader 375.11; **big shot** 997.9

8 **henchman,** cohort, hanger-on, buddy *and* sidekick <nf>; heeler *and* **ward heeler** <nf>; hatchet man; partner in crime

9 **candidate, aspirant,** hopeful *and* political hopeful *and* wannabee <nf>, office seeker *or* hunter, baby kisser <nf>; running mate; leading candidate, head of the ticket *or* slate; **dark horse;** stalking-horse; favorite son; presidential timber; defeated candidate, also-ran *and* dud <nf>

10 **campaigner,** electioneer, **stumper** <nf>, whistle-stopper <nf>, stump speaker *or* orator <nf>

11 **officeholder,** office-bearer <Brit>, jack-in-office, elected official, public servant, public official, **incumbent;** holdover, lame duck; new broom <nf>; president-elect; ins, the powers that be

12 **political worker, committeeman,** committeewoman, precinct captain, precinct leader, district leader; party chairperson, state chairperson, national chairperson, chairperson of the national committee; speechwriter; political philosopher

VERBS 13 go into politics; **run,** get on the ticket, run for office; **campaign,** stump

ADJS 14 **statesmanlike,** statesmanly

611 POLITICO-ECONOMIC PRINCIPLES

NOUNS 1 **conservatism, conservativeness, rightism;** standpattism <nf>, unprogressiveness, backwardness; **ultraconservatism, reaction,** arch-conservative, reactionism, reactionarism, reactionaryism, reactionariness, die-hardism <nf>

2 **moderatism, moderateness,** middle-of-the-roadism; middle of the road, moderate position, via media, **center,** centrism; third force, nonalignment

3 **liberalism, progressivism, leftism; left, left wing,** progressiveness

4 **radicalism, extremism,** ultraism; radicalization; revolutionism; ultraconservatism 611.1; extreme left, extreme left wing, left-wing extrem-

ism, loony left <Brit nf>; New Left, Old Left; Jacobinism, sans-culottism, *sans-culotterie* <Fr>; **anarchism, nihilism,** syndicalism *and* anarcho-syndicalism *and* criminal syndicalism ; extreme rightism, radical rightism, know-nothingism; extreme right, extreme right wing; social Darwinism; laissez-faireism 329.1; **royalism, monarchism;** Toryism, Bourbonism

5 **communism, Bolshevism, Marxism,** Marxism-Leninism, Leninism, Trotskyism, Stalinism, Maoism, Titoism, Castroism, revisionism; Marxian socialism; dialectical materialism; democratic centralism; dictatorship of the proletariat; **Communist Party;** Communist International, Comintern; Communist Information Bureau, Cominform; iron curtain 1012.5

6 **socialism,** collective ownership, collectivization, public ownership; **collectivism;** creeping socialism; state socialism; guild socialism; Fabian socialism, Fabianism; utopian socialism; Marxian socialism, Marxism 611.5; phalansterism; Owenism; Saint-Simonianism, Saint-Simonism; **nationalization**

7 **welfarism,** welfare statism; womb-to-tomb security, cradle-to-grave security; social welfare; social security, social insurance; old-age and survivors insurance; unemployment compensation, unemployment insurance; workmen's compensation, workmen's compensation insurance; health insurance, Medicare, Medicaid, state medicine, **socialized medicine;** sickness insurance; public assistance, **welfare, relief,** welfare payments, aid to dependent children *or* ADC, old-age assistance, aid to the blind, aid to the permanently and totally disabled; guaranteed income, guaranteed annual income; welfare state; welfare capitalism

8 **capitalism,** capitalistic system, **free enterprise,** private enterprise, free-enterprise economy, free-enterprise system, free economy; finance capitalism; *laissez-faire* <Fr>, laissez-faireism; private sector; private ownership; state capitalism; **individualism,** rugged individualism

9 **conservative,** conservatist, **rightist, rightwinger;** dry <Brit nf>; standpat *and* standpatter <nf>; hard hat; social Darwinist; ultraconservative, archconservative, extreme right-winger, **reactionary,** reactionarist, reactionist, diehard; **royalist, monarchist,** Bourbon, Tory, imperialist; **right, right wing; radical right**

10 **moderate,** moderatist, moderationist, **centrist,** middle-of-the-roader <nf>; independent; center

11 **liberal,** liberalist, wet <Brit nf>, **progressive,** progressivist, **leftist, left-winger;** welfare stater; Lib-Lab <Brit nf>; **left**

12 **radical, extremist,** ultra, ultraist; **revolutionary,** revolutionist; subversive; extreme left-winger, left-wing extremist, **red** <nf>, Bolshevik; yippie; Jacobin, sansculotte; **anarchist,** nihilist; mild radical, parlor Bolshevik <nf>, pink *and* parlor pink *and* pinko <nf>; lunatic fringe

13 **Communist,** Bolshevist; Bolshevik, **Red** *and* commie *and* bolshie <nf>; Marxist, Leninist, Marxist-Leninist, Trotskyite *or* Trotskyist, Stalinist, Maoist, Titoist, Castroite, revisionist; card-carrying Communist, avowed Communist; fellow traveler, Communist sympathizer, comsymp <nf>

14 **socialist,** collectivist; social democrat; state socialist; Fabian, Fabian socialist; Marxist 611.13; utopian socialist; Fourierist, phalansterian; Saint-Simonian; Owenite

15 **capitalist;** coupon-clipper <nf>; rich man 618.7

VERBS 16 **politicize;** democratize, republicanize, socialize, communize; nationalize 476.7; deregulate, privatize, denationalize; radicalize

ADJS 17 **conservative, right-wing,** right of center, dry <Brit nf>; old-line, die-hard, unreconstructed, standpat <nf>, unprogressive, nonprogressive; ultraconservative, **reactionary,** reactionist

18 **moderate,** centrist, middle-of-the-road <nf>, independent

19 **liberal, liberalistic,** liberalist, wet <Brit nf>, bleeding-heart <nf>; **progressive,** progressivistic; **leftist, left-wing,** on the left, left of center

20 **radical, extreme, extremist,** extremistic, ultraist, ultraistic; revolutionary, revolutionist; subversive; ultraconservative 611.17; extreme left-wing, **red** <nf>; anarchistic, nihilistic, syndicalist *and* anarcho-syndicalist ; mildly radical, pink <nf>

21 **Communist, communistic,** Bolshevik, Bolshevist, commie *and* bolshie *and* Red <nf>; **Marxist,** Leninist, Marxist-Leninist, Trotskyite *or* Trotskyist, Stalinist, Maoist, Titoist, Castroite; revisionist

22 **socialist, socialistic,** collectivistic; social-democratic; Fabian; Fourieristic, phalansterian; Saint-Simonian

23 **capitalist, capitalistic,** bourgeois, individualistic, nonsocialistic, free-enterprise, private-enterprise

612 GOVERNMENT

NOUNS **1 government,** governance, **discipline, regulation; direction, management, administration,** dispensation, disposition, oversight, **supervision** 573.2; **regime,** regimen; **rule, sway, sovereignty, reign,** regnancy, regency; empire, empery, dominion, dynasty, regime, regimen; social order, civil government, political government, political system; form *or* system of government, political organization, polity, political party; local government, state government, national government, world government, international government

2 **control, mastery, mastership, command, power, jurisdiction, dominion, domination; hold, grasp,** grip, gripe, command; hand, hands, iron hand, clutches; talons, claws; helm, reins of government

3 **the government, the authorities; the powers that be,** national government, central government, the Establishment; the corridors of power, government circles; Uncle Sam, Washington; John Bull, the Crown, His *or* Her Majesty's Government, Whitehall

4 <kinds of government> **federal government,** federation, federalism; **constitutional government**, majority rule**; republic,** commonwealth; **democracy,** representative government, representative democracy, direct *or* pure democracy, town-meeting democracy; **parliamentary government;** social democracy, welfare state; mob rule, tyranny of the majority, mobocracy <nf>, ochlocracy; minority government; pantisocracy; aristocracy, hierarchy, oligarchy, elitism, plutocracy, minority rule; feudal system; monarchy, monarchical government, absolute monarchy, constitutional monarchy, limited monarchy, kingship, queenship; dictatorship, tyranny, autocracy, autarchy; dyarchy, duarchy, duumvirate; triarchy, triumvirate; **totalitarian government** *or* regime, totalitarianism, police state, despotism; **fascism, communism;** stratocracy, demagogy, **military government,** militarism, garrison state; martial law, rule of the sword; regency; hierocracy, theocracy, thearchy; patriarchy, patriarchate; gerontocracy; technocracy, meritocracy; **autonomy, self-government,** autarchy, self-rule, self-determination, home rule; heteronomy, dominion rule, colonial government, colonialism, neocolonialism; provisional government; coalition government; tribalism, tribal system, clan system; isocracy, egalitarianism; caretaker government, interregnum, provisional government, coalition government

5 <government by women> matriarchy, matriarchate, gynarchy, gynocracy, gynecocracy; petticoat government

6 **supranational government,** supergovernment, **world government,** World Federalism; League of Nations, United Nations 614

7 <principles of government> democratism, power-sharing, republicanism; constitutionalism, rule of law, parliamentarism, parliamentarian-

ism; monarchism, royalism; feudalism, feudality; imperialism; fascism, neofascism, Nazism, national socialism; statism, governmentalism; collectivism, communism 611.5, socialism 611.6; federalism; centralism; pluralism; politico-economic principles 611; glasnost

8 **absolutism, dictatorship, despotism,** tyranny, autocracy, autarchy, monarchy, absolute monarchy; **authoritarianism;** totalitarianism; one-man rule, one-party rule; Caesarism, Stalinism, kaiserism, czarism; benevolent despotism, paternalism

9 **despotism, tyranny, fascism,** domineering, domination, oppression; heavy hand, high hand, iron hand, iron heel *or* boot; big stick, *argumentum baculinum* <L>; **terrorism,** reign of terror; thought control

10 **officialism, bureaucracy;** beadledom, bumbledom; **red-tapeism** *and* red-tapery *and* **red tape** <nf>; federalese, official jargon 609.37

VERBS 11 **govern, regulate; wield authority** 417.13; **command,** officer, captain, **head, lead,** be master, be at the head of, **preside over,** chair; **direct, manage, supervise, administer,** administrate 573.11; discipline; stand over

12 **control, hold in hand,** have in one's power, be in power, have power, gain a hold upon; hold the reins, hold the helm, call the shots *or* tune *and* be in the driver's seat *or* saddle <nf>; direct, have control of, **have under control, have in hand** *or* **well in hand;** be master of the situation, have it all one's own way, have the game in one's own hands, hold all the aces <nf>; pull the strings *or* wires

13 **rule, sway,** hold sway, **reign,** bear reign, have the sway, wield the scepter, wear the crown, sit on the throne; rule over, overrule

14 **dominate, predominate,** preponderate, prevail; **have the ascendancy, have the upper** *or* **whip hand,** get under control, have on the hip ; **master,** have the mastery of; bestride; dictate, lay down the law; **rule the roost** *and* wear the pants *and* crack the whip *and* ride herd <nf>; take the lead, play first fiddle; **lead by the nose, twist** *or* **turn around one's little finger; keep under one's thumb,** bend to one's will

15 **domineer,** domineer over, **lord it over;** browbeat, order around, henpeck <nf>, intimidate, bully, cow, bulldoze <nf>, walk over, walk all over; castrate, unman; daunt, terrorize; **tyrannize,** tyrannize over, push *or* kick around <nf>, despotize; **grind,** grind down, break, **oppress,** suppress, repress, weigh *or* press heavy on; keep under, keep down, beat down, clamp down on <nf>; overbear, overmaster, overawe; override, ride over, trample *or* stamp *or* tread upon, trample *or* tread down, **trample** *or* **tread underfoot,** keep down, crush under an iron heel, **ride roughshod over;** hold *or* keep a tight hand upon, rule with a rod of iron, rule with an iron hand *or* fist; enslave, subjugate 432.8; compel, coerce 424.7

ADJS 16 **governmental,** gubernatorial; **political, civil,** civic; **official,** bureaucratic, administrative; democratic, republican, fascist, fascistic, oligarchal, oligarchic, oligarchical, aristocratic, aristocratical, theocratic, **federal,** federalist, federalistic, **constitutional,** parliamentary, parliamentarian; monarchic *or* monarchical, monarchial, monarchal ; autocratic, monocratic, absolute; **authoritarian;** despotic, **dictatorial; totalitarian;** pluralistic; paternalistic, patriarchal, patriarchic, patriarchical; matriarchal, matriarchic, matriarchical; heteronomous; autonomous, self-governing, self-ruling, autarchic; executive, presidential; gubernatorial

17 **governing, controlling, regulating,** regulative, regulatory, **commanding; ruling, reigning, sovereign,** regnant, regnal, titular; **master, chief,** general, **boss, head; dominant, predominant,** predominate, preponderant, preponderate, prepotent, prepollent, prevalent, **leading,**

paramount, supreme, number one <nf>, hegemonic, hegemonistic; ascendant, in the ascendant, in ascendancy; at the head, in chief; in charge 417.21

18 **executive, administrative,** ministerial; official, bureaucratic; **supervisory, directing, managing** 573.12

ADVS 19 **under control, in hand,** well in hand; **in one's power,** under one's control

613 LEGISLATURE, GOVERNMENT ORGANIZATION

NOUNS 1 **legislature**, legislative body; **parliament, congress, assembly,** general assembly, house of assembly, legislative assembly, **national assembly, chamber of deputies,** federal assembly, diet, soviet, court; unicameral legislature, bicameral legislature; legislative chamber, **upper chamber** *or* **house**, **lower chamber** *or* **house** ; state legislature, state assembly; provincial legislature, provincial parliament; city council, city board, board of aldermen, common council, commission; representative town meeting, town meeting

2 United States Government, Federal Government; Cabinet ; Executive Department, executive branch; government agency; legislature; Congress, Senate, Upper House, Senate committee; House of Representatives, House, Lower House, House of Representatives committee; Supreme Court

3 **cabinet,** ministry, British cabinet, **council,** advisory council, council of state, privy council, divan; shadow cabinet; kitchen cabinet, camarilla

4 **capitol, statehouse; courthouse;** city hall

5 **legislation, lawmaking,** legislature ; **enactment,** enaction, constitution, passage, passing; **resolution,** concurrent resolution, joint resolution; act 673.3

6 <legislative procedure> introduction, first reading, committee consideration, tabling, filing, second reading, deliberation, **debate,** third reading, **vote,** division, roll call; **filibustering,** filibuster, talkathon <nf>; cloture 857.5; **logrolling;** steamroller methods; guillotine <Brit>

7 **veto,** executive veto, absolute veto, qualified *or* limited veto, suspensive *or* suspensory veto, item veto, pocket veto; veto power; veto message; senatorial courtesy

8 **referendum,** constitutional referendum, statutory referendum, optional *or* facultative referendum, compulsory *or* mandatory referendum; **mandate; plebiscite,** plebiscitum; initiative, direct initiative, indirect initiative; recall

9 **bill,** omnibus bill, hold-up bill, companion bills amendment; **clause, proviso;** enacting clause, dragnet clause, escalator clause, saving clause; **rider;** joker <nf>; **calendar, motion;** question, previous question, privileged question

VERBS 10 **legislate,** make *or* enact laws, **enact, pass,** constitute, ordain, put in force; **put through, jam** *or* **steamroller** *or* **railroad through** <nf>, lobby through; table, pigeonhole; take the floor, get the floor, have the floor; yield the floor; **filibuster; logroll,** roll logs; **veto, pocket, kill; decree** 420.8

ADJS 11 **legislative,** legislatorial, lawmaking; deliberative; **parliamentary, congressional;** senatorial; bicameral, unicameral

614 UNITED NATIONS, INTERNATIONAL ORGANIZATIONS

NOUNS 1 **United Nations** *or* **UN;** League of Nations

2 <UN organs> Secretariat; General Assembly; Security Council; Trusteeship Council; International Court of Justice; **United Nations agency**, Economic and Social Council or ECOSOC, ECOSOC commission

3 international organization, non-UN international organization

615 COMMISSION

NOUNS **1** **commission,** commissioning, **delegation,** devolution, devolvement, vesting, investing, investment, investiture; **deputation;** commitment, entrusting, entrustment, **assignment,** consignment, consignation; **errand, task, office; care,** cure, **responsibility,** purview, jurisdiction; **mission,** legation, embassy; **authority** 417; **authorization,** empowerment, power to act, full power, plenipotentiary power, vicarious *or* delegated authority; **warrant,** license, **mandate, charge, trust,** brevet, exequatur; **agency,** agentship, factorship; regency, regentship; lieutenancy; trusteeship, executorship; **proxy,** procuration, **power of attorney**

2 **appointment, assignment,** designation, **nomination,** naming, selection, tabbing <nf>; **ordainment,** ordination; posting, transferral

3 **installation,** installment, **instatement,** induction, placement, **inauguration,** investiture, taking office; **accession,** accedence; coronation, crowning, enthronement

4 **engagement, employment, hiring, appointment,** taking on <nf>, recruitment, recruiting; executive recruiting, executive search; retaining, retainment, briefing <Brit>; preengagement, bespeaking; reservation, booking; exercise, function

5 executive search agency *or* firm; executive recruiter, executive recruitment consultant, executive development specialist; **headhunter** *and* body snatcher *and* flesh peddler *and* talent scout <nf>

6 **rental, rent; lease,** let <Brit>; hire, hiring; sublease, subrent; **charter,** bareboat charter; lend-lease

7 **enlistment, enrollment; conscription, draft, drafting, induction,** impressment, press; call, draft call, call-up, summons, call to the colors, letter from Uncle Sam <nf>; **recruitment,** recruiting; **muster,** mustering, mustering in, levy, levying; mobilization; selective service, compulsory military service

8 indenture, binding over; **apprenticeship**

9 **assignee, appointee,** selectee, nominee, candidate; licensee, licentiate; deputy, agent 576

VERBS **10** **commission, authorize,** empower, accredit; **delegate,** devolute, devolve, devolve upon, vest, invest; depute, **deputize; assign,** consign, **commit, charge, entrust,** give in charge; license, charter, warrant; detail, detach, post, transfer, send out, mission, send on a mission

11 **appoint, assign,** designate, **nominate,** name, select, tab <nf>, elect; **ordain,** ordinate

12 **install,** instate, induct, **inaugurate,** invest, put in, place, **place in office;** chair; crown, throne, enthrone, anoint

13 **be instated, take office,** accede; take *or* mount the throne; attain to

14 **employ, hire,** give a job to, take into employment, take into one's service, take on <nf>, recruit, headhunt <nf>, **engage,** sign up *or* on <nf>; retain, brief <Brit>; bespeak, preengage; sign up for <nf>, **reserve,** book

15 **rent, lease, let** <Brit>, hire, job, **charter; sublease, sublet,** underlet

16 **rent out, rent; lease,** lease out; let *and* let off *and* let out <Brit>; **hire out,** hire; charter; **sublease, sublet,** underlet; lend-lease, lease-lend; lease-back; farm, farm out; job

17 **enlist,** list , **enroll, sign up** *or* **on** <nf>; **conscript, draft, induct,** press, impress, commandeer; detach, detach for service; summon, call up, call to the colors; **mobilize,** call to active duty; **recruit, muster,** levy, raise, muster in; join 617.14

18 indenture, article, bind, bind over; **apprentice**

ADJS **19** **commissioned, authorized, accredited;** delegated, deputized, appointed; devolutionary

20 **employed, hired, hireling, paid,** mercenary; rented, leased, let <Brit>; sublet, underlet, subleased; chartered

21 **indentured,** articled, bound over; **apprenticed, apprentice,** prentice *or* 'prentice

ADVS **22** **for hire,** for rent, to let, to lease

616 ASSOCIATE

NOUNS **1** **associate, confederate,** consociate, **colleague,** fellow member, **companion, fellow,** bedfellow, **crony,** consort, cohort, compeer, compatriot, confrere, brother, brother-in-arms, **ally,** adjunct, coadjutor; comrade in arms, **comrade** 588.3

2 **partner,** pardner *or* pard <nf>, copartner, side partner, buddy <nf>, **sidekick** *and* sidekicker <nf>; **mate; business partner,** nominal *or* holding-out *or* ostensible *or* quasi partner, general partner, special partner, silent partner, secret partner, dormant *or* sleeping partner

3 **accomplice,** cohort, confederate, fellow conspirator, coconspirator, partner *or* accomplice in crime; *particeps criminis* and *socius criminis* <L>; **accessory,** accessory before the fact, accessory after the fact; **abettor**

4 **collaborator,** cooperator; coauthor; **collaborationist;** quisling, partner in crime

5 **co-worker, workfellow, workmate, fellow worker, buddy** <nf>, butty <Brit nf>; **teammate, yokefellow,** yokemate; benchfellow, shopmate

6 **assistant, helper,** auxiliary, aider, **aid,** aide, paraprofessional; **help, helpmate, helpmeet;** deputy, **agent** 576; **attendant, second,** acolyte; best man, groomsman, paranymph; **servant, employee** 577; adjutant, aide-de-camp; lieutenant, executive officer; coadjutant, coadjutor; coadjutress, coadjutrix; sidesman <Brit>; supporting actor *or* player; supporting instrumentalist, sideman; suffragan; special assistant

7 **right-hand man** *or* **woman, right hand,** strong right hand *or* arm, **man** *or* **gal Friday,** fidus Achates, second self, alter ego, confidant; Boswell

8 **follower, disciple,** adherent, votary; **man, henchman,** camp follower, hanger-on, devotee, satellite, creature, lackey, flunky, stooge <nf>, jackal, minion, myrmidon; yes-man <nf>, sycophant 138.3; goon <nf>, thug 593.3; puppet, cat's-paw; dummy, figurehead

9 **supporter, upholder,** maintainer, sustainer; support, **mainstay, standby** <nf>, stalwart, reliance, dependence; **abettor, seconder,** second; endorser, sponsor; **backer, promoter,** angel <nf>, rabbi <nf>; **patron,** Maecenas; friend at *or* in court; **champion,** defender, apologist, **advocate,** exponent, **protagonist; well-wisher,** favorer, encourager, sympathizer; **partisan,** sider , sectary, votary; **fan** *and* buff <nf>, aficionado, **admirer,** lover

617 ASSOCIATION

NOUNS **1** **association, society,** body, organization; **alliance, coalition, league, union;** council; **bloc,** axis; **partnership; federation, confederation,** confederacy; grouping, assemblage 770; **combination,** combine; **unholy alliance, gang** *and* **ring** *and* mob <nf>; machine, **political machine;** economic community, common market, free trade area, customs union; credit union; cooperative, cooperative society, consumer cooperative, Rochdale cooperative; syndicate, guild; college, **group,** corps, band 770.3; labor union 727

2 **community, society, commonwealth,** social system; body; **kinship group, clan,** sept, moiety, clan, tribe, totemic *or* totemistic group, phyle, phratry *or* phratria, gens, caste, subcaste, endogamous group; **family,** extended family, nuclear family, binuclear family; order, **class, social class** 607.1, economic class; colony, settlement; **commune,** ashram

3 **fellowship,** sodality; **society,** guild, order; **brotherhood, fraternity,** confraternity, confrerie, fraternal order *or* society; **sisterhood, sorority; club,** country club, lodge; peer group; secret society, **cabal**

4 **party, interest, camp, side;** interest group, lobby, pressure group, ethnic group; minority group, vocal minority; political action committee *or* PAC; silent majority; **faction,** division, **sect,** wing, **caucus,** splinter, splinter group, breakaway group, offshoot; **political party** 609.24

5 **school, sect,** class, order; **denomination, communion,** confession, faith, church; **persuasion, ism; disciples, followers,** adherents

6 **clique, coterie, set, circle,** ring, junto, junta, cabal, camarilla, **clan,** group, grouping, cult; **crew** *and* mob *and* **crowd** *and* **bunch** *and* outfit <nf>; cell; cadre, cohort, inner circle; closed *or* charmed circle; in-group, in-crowd, popular crowd, we-group; elite, elite group; leadership group; **old-boy network;** peer group, age group

7 **team, outfit,** squad, string, corps; eleven, nine, eight, five, etc; **crew,** rowing crew; varsity, first team, first string; bench, reserves, second team, second string, third string; platoon, troupe; complement; **cast,** company

8 **organization,** establishment, **foundation, institution, institute**

9 **company, firm, business firm, concern, house**; **business, industry, enterprise,** business establishment, commercial enterprise; **trust, syndicate, cartel,** combine, pool, consortium, plunderbund <nf>; combination in restraint of trade; chamber of commerce, junior chamber of commerce; trade association

10 **branch, organ, division,** wing, arm, offshoot, **affiliate; chapter,** lodge, post; chapel; **local;** branch office; virtual office

11 **member,** affiliate, belonger, insider, initiate, one of us, cardholder, card-carrier, card-carrying member; **enrollee,** enlistee; **associate,** socius, **fellow;** brother, sister; comrade; honorary member; life member; member in good standing, dues-paying member; charter member; clubman, clubwoman, clubber <nf>; fraternity man, fraternity *or* frat brother, Greek <nf>, sorority woman; sorority sister, guildsman; committeeman; conventionist, conventioner, conventioneer; joiner <nf>; pledge

12 **membership,** members, associates, affiliates, body of affiliates, constituency

13 **partisanism,** partisanship, **partiality; factionalism, sectionalism,** faction; sectarianism, denominationalism; **cliquism,** cliquishness, cliqueyness; **clannishness,** clanship; exclusiveness, exclusivity; ethnocentricity; party spirit, *esprit de corps* <Fr>; the old college spirit

VERBS **14** **join,** join up <nf>, **enter, go into,** come into, get into, make oneself part of, swell the ranks of; **enlist, enroll, affiliate, sign up** *or* **on** <nf>, take up membership, take out membership; inscribe oneself, put oneself down; associate oneself with, affiliate with, league with, team *or* team up with; sneak in, creep in, insinuate oneself into; **combine, associate** 805.4

15 **belong,** hold membership, be a member, be on the rolls, be inscribed, subscribe, hold *or* carry a card, be in <nf>

ADJS **16** **associated, corporate,** incorporated; **combined** 805.5; non-profit-making, non-profit, not-for-profit

17 **associational, social, society, communal;** organizational; coalitional; sociable

18 **cliquish,** cliquey, **clannish;** ethnocentric; exclusive

19 **partisan,** party; **partial,** interested; **factional, sectional,** sectarian, sectary, denominational

ADVS **20** **in association, conjointly** 450.6

618 WEALTH

NOUNS **1** **wealth, riches, opulence** *or* opulency 991.2, **luxuriousness** 501.5; richness, wealthiness; **prosperity,** prosperousness, **affluence,** comfortable *or* easy circumstances, independence; **money,** lucre, pelf, gold, mammon; **substance, property, possessions,** material wealth;

assets 728.14; **fortune, treasure,** handsome fortune; full *or* heavy *or* well-lined *or* bottomless *or* fat *or* bulging purse, deep pockets <nf>; *embarras de richesses* <Fr>, money to burn <nf>; high income, six-figure income; high tax bracket, upper bracket; old money, new money

2 **large sum,** good sum, tidy sum *and* **pretty penny, king's ransom;** heaps of gold; thousands, millions, cool million, billion, etc

3 <nf terms> **bundle, big bucks,** megabucks, gigabucks, big money, serious money, gobs, heaps, heavy lettuce, heavy jack, heavy money, important money, pot, potful, power, mint, barrel, raft, load, **loads,** pile, wad, wads, nice hunk of change, packet <Brit>, long green, deep pockets

4 <rich source> **mine,** mine of wealth, **gold mine,** bonanza, luau <nf>, lode, rich lode, mother lode, pot of gold, Eldorado, Golconda, Seven Cities of Cibola; gravy train <nf>; rich uncle; golden goose; cash cow <nf>

5 **the golden touch,** Midas touch; philosophers' stone; Pactolus

6 **the rich, the wealthy,** the well-to-do, the well-off, the haves <nf>, privileged class; jet set, glitterati, country-club set, beau monde; **plutocracy,** timocracy

7 **rich man** *or* **woman,** wealthy man *or* woman, warm man *or* woman <Brit nf>, **moneyed man** *or* **woman,** man *or* woman of wealth, **man** *or* **woman of means** *or* **substance,** fat cat <nf>, richling, deep pocket *and* moneybags *and* Mr Moneybags <nf>, tycoon, magnate, baron, Daddy Warbucks <Harold Gray>, coupon-clipper, **nabob; capitalist, plutocrat,** bloated plutocrat; **millionaire,** multimillionaire, megamillionaire, millionairess, multibillionaire, multimillionairess, billionaire; parvenu; vulgarian; nouveau riche

8 Croesus, Midas, Plutus, Timon of Athens; Rockefeller, Vanderbilt, Whitney, DuPont, Ford, Getty, Rothschild, Onassis, Hughes, Hunt, Trump; Sergey Brin and Larry Page, Bill Gates, Warren Buffett

VERBS 9 **enrich, richen;** endow

10 **grow rich, get rich,** fill *or* line one's pockets, feather one's nest, **make** *or* **coin money,** have a gold mine, have the golden touch, **make a fortune,** make one's pile <nf>; **strike it rich;** come into money; make good, get on in the world, do all right by oneself *and* rake it in <nf>; hit the jackpot, clean up <nf>

11 **have money,** command money, **be loaded** *and* have deep pockets <nf>, have the wherewithal, have means, have independent means; **afford,** well afford

12 **live well,** live high, live high on the hog <nf>, **live in clover,** live the life of Riley, roll *or* wallow in wealth, roll *or* live in the lap of luxury; have all the money in the world, have a mint, have money to burn <nf>

13 worship mammon, worship the golden calf, worship the almighty dollar

ADJS 14 **wealthy, rich, affluent,** affluential, **moneyed** *or* **monied,** in funds *or* cash, **well-to-do,** well-to-do in the world, **well-off, well-situated, prosperous,** comfortable, provided for, well provided for, fat, **flush,** flush with *or* of money, abounding in riches, worth a great deal, in clover, frightfully rich, rich as Croesus; independent, independently rich, independently wealthy; **luxurious** 501.21; **opulent** 991.7; privileged, born with a silver spoon in one's mouth; higher-income, upper-income, well-paid

15 <nf terms> **loaded, well-heeled, filthy rich,** warm <Brit>, flush, in the money *or* dough *or* chips *or* gravy, well-fixed, worth a bundle, made of money, **rolling in money,** rolling *or* wallowing in it, disgustingly rich, big-rich, rich-rich, oofy, lousy rich, upscale

619 POVERTY

NOUNS 1 **poverty,** poorness, impecuniousness, impecuniosity; **straits,** dire straits, difficulties, **hardship**

1011.1; financial distress *or* embarrassment, **embarrassed** *or* **reduced** *or* **straitened circumstances,** tight squeeze, hard pinch, crunch <nf>, cash *or* credit *or* budget crunch <nf>; cash-flow shortage, cash-flow blowout <nf>; slender *or* narrow means, insolvency, light purse; unprosperousness; broken fortune; genteel poverty; vows of poverty, voluntary poverty

2 indigence, penury, pennilessness, penuriousness, moneylessness; **pauperism,** pauperization, **impoverishment,** grinding *or* crushing poverty, chronic pauperism, subsistence level, poverty line; **beggary,** beggarliness, mendicancy; **destitution, privation, deprivation; neediness, want,** need, lack, pinch, gripe, necessity, dire necessity, disadvantagedness, necessitousness, **homelessness; hand-to-mouth existence,** bare subsistence, wolf at the door, bare cupboard, empty purse *or* pocket

3 the poor, the needy, the have-nots <nf>, the down-and-out, the disadvantaged, the underprivileged, the distressed, the underclass; the urban poor, ghetto-dwellers, barrio-dwellers; welfare rolls, welfare clients, welfare families; the homeless, the ranks of the homeless, bag people; the other America; the forgotten man; depressed population, depressed area, chronic poverty area; underdeveloped nation, Third World, developing world; cardboard city

4 poor person, poorling, poor devil, down-and-out *or* down-and-outer, **pauper,** indigent, penniless man, hard case, starveling; homeless person, bag woman *or* lady, bag person, shopping-bag lady, shopping-cart woman *or* lady, street person, skell <nf>; hobo, bum; **beggar** 440.8; welfare client; almsman, almswoman, charity case, casual; bankrupt 625.4

VERBS **5 be poor,** be hard up <nf>, find it hard going, have seen better days, be on one's uppers, be pinched *or* strapped, **be in want,** want, need, lack; **starve,** not know where one's next meal is coming from, **live from hand to mouth,** eke out *or* squeeze out a living; **not have a penny** *or* **sou,** not have a penny to bless oneself with, not have one dollar to rub against another; sing for one's supper; go on welfare, use food stamps

6 impoverish, reduce, **pauperize, beggar;** eat out of house and home; cut off without a penny; **bankrupt** 625.8

ADJS **7 poor, ill off,** badly *or* poorly off, hard up <nf>, downscale, impecunious, **unmoneyed; unprosperous;** reduced, in reduced circumstances; **straitened, in straitened circumstances,** narrow, in narrow circumstances, feeling the pinch, strapped, **financially embarrassed** *or* distressed, **pinched,** squeezed, put to one's shifts *or* last shifts, at the end of one's rope, on the edge *or* ragged edge <nf>, down to bedrock, in Queer Street; short, **short of money** *or* **funds** *or* **cash,** out-of-pocket; unable to make ends meet, unable to keep the wolf from the door; poor as a church mouse; house-poor; land-poor

8 indigent, poverty-stricken; needy, necessitous, **in need, in want,** disadvantaged, deprived, underprivileged; **beggared,** beggarly, mendicant; **impoverished, pauperized,** starveling; ghettoized; bereft, bereaved; stripped, fleeced; **down at heels,** down at the heel, on *or* down on one's uppers, out at the heels, out at elbows, in rags; on welfare, on relief, on the bread line, on the dole <Brit>

9 destitute, down-and-out, in the gutter; **penniless,** moneyless, fortuneless, out of funds, **without a sou,** without a penny to bless oneself with, without one dollar to rub against another; insolvent, in the red, **bankrupt** 625.11; homeless; propertyless, landless

10 <nf terms> **broke, dead broke,** bust, busted, dirt poor, **flat, flat broke,** flat on one's ass, flat-ass, down for the count, belly up, stone *or* stony broke, stony, **strapped,**

skint <Brit>, hurting, beat, oofless; down to one's last penny *or* cent, cleaned out, tapped out, Tap City, oofless, wasted, wiped out, without a pot to piss in

620 LENDING

NOUNS 1 **lending, loaning;** money-lending, lending at interest; advance, advancing, advancement; **usury,** loan-sharking *and* shylocking <nf>; pawnbroking, hocking; **interest,** interest rate, lending rate, the price of money; points, mortgage points

2 **loan,** the lend <nf>, **advance,** accommodation; lending on security; lend-lease

3 **lender, loaner;** loan officer; commercial banker; **moneylender,** moneymonger; money broker; banker 729.11; **usurer,** shylock *and* loan shark <nf>; **pawnbroker;** uncle <nf>; mortgagee, mortgage holder; creditor; financier

4 **lending institution,** savings and loan association *or* thrift *or* thrift institution *or* savings institution; savings and loan *or* thrift industry; building society <Brit>; finance company *or* corporation, loan office, mortgage company; commercial bank, **bank** 729.13; **credit union; pawnshop, pawnbroker,** pawnbrokery, **hock shop** <nf>, *mont-de-piété* <Fr>, sign of the three balls; World Bank

VERBS 5 **lend, loan, advance,** accommodate with; loan-shark <nf>; float *or* negotiate a loan; lend-lease, lease-lend; give credit

ADJS 6 **loaned, lent**, on loan, on credit

ADVS 7 **on loan,** on security; in advance

621 BORROWING

NOUNS 1 **borrowing,** money-raising; touching *or* hitting *or* hitting up <nf>; financing, mortgaging; installment buying, installment plan, hire purchase <Brit>; debt, debtor 623.4; debt counseling

2 **adoption, appropriation, taking,** deriving, **derivation, assumption; imitation,** simulation, copying, mocking; borrowed plumes; a leaf from someone else's book; adaptation; plagiarism, plagiary, pastiche, pasticcio; infringement, pirating; cribbing, lifting

VERBS 3 **borrow,** borrow the loan of, get on credit *or* trust, get on tick *and* get on the cuff <nf>; get a loan, float *or* negotiate a loan, go into the money market, **raise money; touch** *and* hit up *and* hit one for *and* put the arm *or* bite *or* touch on <nf>; run into debt 623.6; pawn 438.10

4 **adopt, appropriate,** take, take on, take over, assume, make use of, take a leaf from someone's book, derive from; **imitate,** simulate, copy, mock, steal one's stuff <nf>; plagiarize, steal; pirate, infringe, crib, lift; adapt, parody

622 FINANCIAL CREDIT

NOUNS 1 **credit, trust,** tick <nf>; borrowing power *or* capacity; commercial credit, cash credit, bank credit, book credit, tax credit, investment credit; credit line, line of credit; installment plan, installment credit, consumer credit, store credit, hire purchase plan <Brit>, never-never <Brit nf>; **credit standing,** standing, **credit rating,** rating, Dun and Bradstreet rating, solvency 729.7; credit squeeze, insolvency; credit risk; credit bureau *or* agency; credit insurance, credit life insurance; credit union, cooperative credit union

2 **account,** credit account, charge account; bank account, savings account, checking account; share account; bank balance; expense account; current *or* open account; installment plan

3 **credit instrument;** paper credit; **letter of credit,** *lettre de créance* <Fr>, circular note; credit slip, credit memorandum, deposit slip, certificate of deposit; share certificate; negotiable instrument 728.11; **credit card,** plastic <nf>, plastic money *or* credit, bank card, affinity

card, custom credit card, gold card, platinum card, charge card, charge plate; debit card; smart card, supersmart card; phonecard; automated teller machine *or* ATM, cash machine

4 **creditor,** creditress; debtee; mortgagee, mortgage-holder; noteholder; credit man; bill collector, collection agent; loan shark; pawnbroker; dunner, dun

VERBS 5 **credit, credit with; credit to one's account,** place to one's credit *or* account

6 **give** *or* **extend credit** *or* a line of credit; sell on credit, trust, entrust; give tick <nf>; carry, carry on one's books

7 **receive credit,** take credit, **charge,** charge to one's account, keep an account with, go on tick <nf>, buy on credit, buy on the cuff <nf>, buy on the installment plan, buy on time, defer payment, put on layaway; go in hock for <nf>; have one's credit good for

ADJS 8 **credited,** of good credit, **well-rated**

ADVS 9 **to one's credit** *or* **account,** to the credit *or* account of, to the good

10 **on credit, on account, on trust,** on tick *and* **on the cuff** <nf>; on terms, on good terms, on easy terms, on budget terms, in installments, on time

623 DEBT

NOUNS 1 **debt, indebtedness,** indebtment, **obligation, liability,** financial commitment, due, **dues,** score, pledge, unfulfilled pledge, amount due, outstanding debt; **bill, bills,** chits <nf>, **charges;** floating debt; funded debt, unfunded debt; accounts receivable; accounts payable; borrowing 621; maturity; bad debts, uncollectibles, frozen assets; **national debt,** public debt; deficit, national deficit; megadebt <nf>; debt explosion

2 **arrears,** arrear, arrearage, back debts, back payments; the red; **deficit,** default, deferred payments; cash *or* credit crunch <nf>; overdraft, bounced *or* bouncing check, rubber check <nf>; dollar gap, unfavorable trade balance *or* balance of payments; deficit financing

3 **interest, premium, price, rate;** interest rate, rate of interest, prime interest rate *or* **prime rate,** bank rate, lending rate, borrowing rate, the price of money; discount rate; annual percentage rate *or* APR; **usury** 620.1, excessive *or* exorbitant interest; points, mortgage points; simple interest, compound interest; net interest, gross interest; compensatory interest; lucrative interest; penal interest

4 **debtor,** borrower; mortgagor; insolvent

VERBS 5 **owe, be indebted,** be obliged *or* obligated for, be financially committed, lie under an obligation, be bound to pay, owe money

6 **go in debt,** get into debt, run into debt, plunge into debt, incur *or* contract a debt, go in hock <nf>, be overextended, **run up a bill** *or* a score *or* an account *or* a tab; run *or* show a deficit, operate at a loss; borrow; overspend, overdraw

7 **mature, accrue, fall due**

ADJS 8 **indebted, in debt,** plunged in debt, in difficulties, embarrassed, in embarrassed circumstances, in the hole *and* in hock <nf>, in the red, in dire straits, **insolvent**, encumbered, mortgaged, mortgaged to the hilt, tied up, involved; deep in debt, involved *or* deeply involved in debt, burdened with debt, head over heels *or* up to one's ears in debt <nf>; cash poor

9 **chargeable, obligated, liable,** pledged, responsible, answerable for

10 **due, owed, owing, payable,** receivable, redeemable, mature, **outstanding, unpaid,** in arrear *or* arrears, back

624 PAYMENT

NOUNS 1 **payment, paying,** paying off, paying up <nf>, payoff; **defrayment,** defrayal; paying out, doling out, **disbursal** 626.1; **discharge, settlement, clearance, liquidation,**

amortization, amortizement, retirement, satisfaction; quittance; acquittance *or* acquitment or acquittal ; **debt service, interest payment,** sinking-fund payment; **remittance;** installment, installment plan, layaway plan; hire purchase *or* hire purchase plan *or* never-never <Brit>; regular payments, monthly payments, weekly payments, quarterly payments, etc; down payment, deposit, earnest, earnest money, binder; god's penny; the King's shilling <Brit>; **cash,** hard cash, spot cash, cash payment, cash on the nail *and* cash on the barrelhead <nf>; pay-as-you-go; prepayment; **postponed** *or* **deferred payment,** contango *or* carryover *and* continuation *and* backwardation <Brit>; payment in kind; accounts receivable, receivables

2 **reimbursement,** recoupment, recoup, return, restitution, settlement; payment in lieu; **refund,** refundment; kickback <nf>; payback, chargeback, **repayment** 481.2

3 **recompense, remuneration, compensation;** requital, requitement, quittance, **retribution, reparation, redress,** satisfaction, **atonement, amends,** return, restitution 481; blood money, wergild ; **indemnity,** indemnification; price, consideration; **reward,** meed, guerdon; honorarium; workmen's compensation *or* comp <nf>, solatium, damages, smart money; salvage

4 **pay, payment, remuneration, compensation,** total compensation, wages plus fringe benefits, financial package, pay and allowances, financial remuneration; rate of pay; **salary, wage, wages, income, earnings,** hire; real wages, purchasing power; payday, pay check, pay envelope, pay packet <Brit>; take-home pay *or* income, wages after taxes, pay *or* income *or* wages after deductions, net income *or* wages *or* pay *or* earnings, taxable income; gross income; living wage; minimum wage, base pay; portal-to-portal pay; severance pay, discontinuance *or* dismissal wage, golden parachute; wage scale; escalator plan, escalator clause, sliding scale; guaranteed income, guaranteed annual income, negative income tax; fixed income; wage freeze, wage rollback, wage reduction, wage control; guaranteed annual wage, guaranteed income plan; overtime pay; danger money, combat pay, flight pay; back pay; strike pay; **payroll;** golden handcuffs; royalty, advance

5 **fee, stipend, allowance,** emolument, tribute, honorarium; **reckoning,** account, bill; assessment, scot; initiation fee, footing ; retainer, retaining fee; hush money, blackmail; blood money; mileage

6 <extra pay or allowance> **bonus, premium, fringe benefit** *or* **benefits,** bounty, perquisite, perquisites, perks <nf>, gravy <nf>, lagniappe, solatium; **tip** 478.5; overtime pay; bonus system; health insurance, life insurance, disability insurance; profit-sharing; holidays, vacation time, flextime *or* flexitime; pension program

7 **dividend; royalty; commission,** rake-off *and* cut <nf>

8 <the bearing of another's expense> **treat,** standing treat, picking up the check *or* tab <nf>; paying the bills, maintenance; child support, support 449.3; subsidy 478.8

9 **payer,** remunerator, compensator, recompenser; paymaster, purser, bursar, cashier, treasurer 729.12; defrayer; liquidator; **taxpayer, ratepayer** <Brit>

VERBS 10 **pay,** render, tender; **recompense, remunerate, compensate, reward,** guerdon, indemnify, satisfy; salary, fee; remit; prepay; pay by *or* in installments, pay on, pay in; make payments to *or* towards *or* on

11 **repay,** pay back, restitute, **reimburse,** recoup; **requite,** quit, **atone,** redress , **make amends,** make good, make up for, make up to, make restitution, make reparation 481.5; pay in kind, pay one in his own coin,

give tit for tat; **refund,** kick back <nf>

12 **settle with,** reckon with, account with , pay out, **settle** *or* **square accounts with,** square oneself with, get square with, **get even with,** get quits with; even the score <nf>, wipe *or* clear off old scores, pay old debts, clear the board

13 **pay in full, pay off, pay up** <nf>, **discharge, settle,** square, **clear, liquidate, amortize,** retire, take up, lift, take up and pay off, honor, acquit oneself of ; satisfy; meet one's obligations *or* commitments, redeem, redeem one's pledge *or* pledges, tear up *or* burn one's mortgage, have a mortgage-burning party, settle *or* square accounts, make accounts square, strike a balance; pay the bill, pay the shot

14 **pay out, fork out** *or* **over** <nf>, **shell out** <nf>; **expend** 626.5

15 **pay over,** hand over; ante, **ante up,** put up; put down, lay down, lay one's money down, show the color of one's money

16 <nf terms> **kick in, fork over,** pony up, pay up, cough up, stump up <Brit>, come across, come through with, come across with, come down with, come down with the needful, plank down, plunk down, post, tickle *or* grease the palm, cross one's palm with, lay on one; pay to the tune of

17 **pay cash,** make a cash payment, cash, **pay spot cash, pay cash down,** pay cash on the barrelhead <nf>, plunk down the money *and* put one's money on the line <nf>, pay at sight; pay in advance; pay as you go; pay cash on delivery *or* pay COD

18 **pay for,** pay *or* stand the costs, **bear the expense** *or* **cost,** pay the piper <nf>; **finance, fund** 729.16; **defray,** defray expenses; pay the bill, **foot the bill** *and* pick up the check *or* tab *and* spring *or* pop for <nf>; honor a bill, acknowledge, redeem; pay one's way; pay one's share, chip in <nf>, go Dutch <nf>, Dutch-treat, go halvsies <nf>

19 **treat,** treat to, **stand treat,** go treat, stand to <nf>, pick up the check *or* tab <nf>, pay the bill, set up, blow to <nf>; stand drinks; maintain, support 449.12; subsidize 478.19

20 **be paid, draw wages,** be salaried, work for wages, be remunerated, collect for one's services, **earn,** get an income, pull down *and* drag down <nf>

ADJS **21** **paying, remunerative, remuneratory; compensating,** compensative, compensatory, disbursing; retributive, retributory; **rewarding,** rewardful; lucrative, moneymaking, profitable, gainful; repaying, satisfying, reparative; bankable

22 **paid, paid-up,** discharged, settled, liquidated, acquitted , paid in full, receipted, remitted; **spent, expended;** salaried, waged, hired; compensated; prepaid, postpaid

23 **unindebted,** unowing, **out of debt,** above water, out of the hole *or* the red <nf>, **clear,** all clear, free and clear, all straight; solvent 729.18

ADVS **24** **in compensation,** as compensation, in recompense, for services rendered, for professional services, **in reward,** in requital, in reparation, in retribution, in restitution, in exchange for, **in amends,** in atonement, to atone for

25 **cash,** cash on the barrelhead <nf>, strictly cash; **cash down, money down,** down; cash on delivery *or* **COD;** on demand, on call; pay-as-you-go

625 NONPAYMENT

NOUNS **1** **nonpayment, default, delinquency,** delinquence , nondischarge of debts, nonremittal, failure to pay; defection; protest, repudiation; dishonor, dishonoring; bad debt, uncollectible, dishonored *or* protested bill; tax evasion; creative accounting

2 **moratorium,** grace period; embargo, freeze; **write-off,** cancellation, obliteration 395.7

3 **insolvency, bankruptcy,** receivership, Chapter 11, **failure; crash,**

collapse, bust <nf>, ruin; run on a bank; insufficient funds, overdraft, overdrawn account, not enough to cover, bounced *or* bouncing check, bad check, kited *or* rubber check; Chapter 7, Chapter 13

4 **insolvent,** insolvent debtor; **bankrupt,** failure; **loser,** heavy loser, lame duck <nf>

5 **defaulter,** delinquent, nonpayer; **welsher** <nf>, levanter; tax evader, tax dodger *or* cheat <nf>

VERBS 6 **not pay;** dishonor, repudiate, disallow, protest, stop payment, refuse to pay; **default, welsh** <nf>, levant; button up one's pockets, draw the purse strings; **underpay;** bounce *or* kite a check <nf>

7 **go bankrupt, go broke** <nf>, go into receivership, become insolvent *or* bankrupt, **fail,** break, bust <nf>, crash, collapse, **fold, fold up,** belly up *and* go up *and* go belly up *and* **go under** <nf>, shut down, shut one's doors, go out of business, **be ruined,** go to ruin, go on the rocks, go to the wall, go to pot <nf>, go to the dogs, go bust <nf>; take a bath *and* be taken to the cleaners *and* be cleaned out *and* lose one's shirt *and* tap out <nf>

8 **bankrupt, ruin, break,** bust *and* wipe out <nf>; put out of business, drive to the wall, scuttle, sink; impoverish 619.6

9 **declare a moratorium; write off, forgive,** absolve, **cancel,** nullify, wipe the slate clean; wipe out, obliterate 395.16

ADJS 10 **defaulting,** nonpaying, **delinquent;** behindhand, in arrear *or* arrears, in hock, in the red

11 **insolvent, bankrupt,** in receivership, in the hands of receivers, belly-up <nf>, broken, **broke** *and* busted <nf>, **ruined,** failed, out of business, unable to pay one's creditors, unable to meet one's obligations, illiquid, on the rocks; destitute 619.9

12 **unpaid, unremunerated,** uncompensated, unrecompensed, **unrewarded,** unrequited; underpaid

13 **unpayable,** irredeemable, inconvertible

626 EXPENDITURE

NOUNS 1 **expenditure, spending,** expense, disbursal, **disbursement;** debit, debiting; budgeting, scheduling; costing, costing-out; **payment** 624; deficit spending; **use** 387; **consumption** 388

2 **spendings,** disbursements, payments, outgoings, outgo, outflow, **outlay,** money going out; capital outlay *or* expenditure

3 **expenses, costs,** charges, disbursals, **liabilities**, damages <nf>**; expense, cost,** burden of expenditure; budget, budget item, budget line, line item; **overhead,** operating expense *or* expenses *or* costs *or* budget, general expenses; expense account, swindle sheet <nf>; business expenses, nonremunerated business expenses, out-of-pocket expenses; direct costs, indirect costs; distributed costs, undistributed costs; material costs; labor costs; carrying charge; unit cost; replacement cost; prime cost; cost of living, cost-of-living index, cost-of-living allowance *or* COLA, inflation

4 **spender,** expender, expenditor, disburser, buyer, purchaser; spend-all, spendthrift

VERBS 5 **spend, expend, disburse, pay out,** fork out *or* over <nf>, shell out <nf>, **lay out,** outlay; go to the expense of; **pay** 624.10; put one's hands in one's pockets, open the purse, loosen *or* untie the purse strings *and* throw money around <nf>, go on a spending spree, splurge, spend money like a drunken sailor *and* spend money as if it were going out of style <nf>, go *or* run through, be out of pocket, **squander** 486.3; **invest,** sink money in <nf>, put out; throw money away; **incur costs** *or* **expenses;** budget, schedule, cost, cost out; **use** 387.10; **consume**

6 **be spent,** burn in one's pocket, burn a hole in one's pocket

7 **afford,** well afford, spare, spare the price, bear, stand, support, endure, undergo, meet the expense of, swing

627 RECEIPTS

NOUNS 1 **receipts,** receipt, **income, revenue, profits, earnings, returns, proceeds,** avails , **take,** takings, intake, take *or* take-in <nf>, get <Brit nf>; credit, credits; gains 472.3; gate receipts, gate, box office; net receipts, net; gross receipts, gross; national income; net income, gross income, gross profit margin; earned income, take-home pay, unearned income; **dividend** 738.7, dividends, payout, payback; interest; royalties, commissions; receivables; disposable income; make, produce, **yield, output** 893.2, bang for the buck <nf>, fruits, first fruits; bonus, premium; income; legacy; winnings

2 <written acknowledgment> **receipt, acknowledgment, voucher,** warrant <Brit>; canceled check, bank statement; proof of purchase; **receipt in full,** receipt in full of all demands, release, acquittance, quittance, discharge

VERBS 3 **receive** 479.6, **pocket, acquire** 472.8; earn; accrue; acknowledge receipt of, receipt, mark paid

4 **yield, bring in, afford, pay,** pay off <nf>, **return; gross, net**

628 ACCOUNTS

NOUNS 1 **accounts; outstanding accounts,** uncollected *or* unpaid accounts; **accounts receivable,** receipts, assets; **accounts payable,** expenditures, liabilities; **budget,** budgeting; costing out

2 **account, reckoning, tally, rendering-up, score;** account current; account rendered, *compte rendu* <Fr>, account stated; balance, trial balance

3 **statement, bill,** itemized bill, bill of account, **account, reckoning, check,** *l'addition* <Fr>, score *or* tab <nf>; **dun; invoice,** manifest, bill of lading

4 **account book, ledger, journal,** daybook; **register,** registry, **record book,** books; inventory, catalog; **log,** logbook; **cashbook; bankbook,** passbook; balance sheet; cost sheet, cost card

5 **entry,** item, line item, minute, note, notation; single entry, double entry; **credit, debit**

6 **accounting, accountancy, bookkeeping,** double-entry bookkeeping *or* accounting, single-entry bookkeeping *or* accounting; comptrollership *or* controllership; business *or* commercial *or* monetary arithmetic; cost accounting, costing <Brit>, cost system, cost-accounting system; **audit, auditing;** stocktaking, inspection of books

7 **accountant, bookkeeper;** tax preparer**; clerk,** actuary , registrar, recorder, journalizer; calculator, reckoner; cost accountant, cost keeper; certified public accountant *or* CPA; chartered accountant *or* CA <Brit>; **auditor,** bank examiner; bank accountant; actuary; accountant general; comptroller *or* controller; statistician; investment manager, money manager; financial advisor

VERBS 8 **keep accounts, keep books,** make up *or* cast up *or* render accounts; make an entry, enter, post, post up, journalize, book, docket, log, note, minute; **credit, debit;** charge off, write off; capitalize; carry, carry on one's books; carry over; **balance,** balance accounts, balance the books, strike a balance; close the books, close out

9 **take account of, take stock,** overhaul; **inventory; audit,** examine *or* inspect the books

10 **falsify accounts,** garble accounts, cook *or* doctor accounts <nf>, cook the books <nf>, salt, fudge; surcharge

11 **bill,** send a statement; **invoice;** call, call in, demand payment, **dun**

ADJS 12 accounting, bookkeeping; budget, budgetary

629 TRANSFER OF PROPERTY OR RIGHT

NOUNS 1 **transfer,** transference; **conveyance,** conveyancing; **giving** 478; **delivery,** deliverance; **assignment,** assignation; **consignment,** consignation; conferment, conferral, settling, settlement; vesting; bequeathal 478.10; **sale** 734; surrender, cession; transmission, transmittal; disposal, disposition, deaccession, deaccessioning; demise; alienation, abalienation; amortization, amortizement; enfeoffment; deeding; bargain and sale; lease and release; **exchange,** barter, trading; entailment

2 devolution, succession, reversion; shifting use, shifting trust

VERBS **3** **transfer, convey, deliver,** hand, pass, negotiate; **give** 478.12-14,16,21; **hand over, turn over, pass over; assign, consign,** confer, settle, settle on; cede, surrender; bequeath 478.18; entail; **sell** 734.8,11,12, sell off, deaccession; **make over, sign over,** sign away; transmit, **hand down, hand on, pass on,** devolve upon; demise; alienate, alien, abalienate, amortize; enfeoff; **deed,** deed over, give title to; **exchange,** barter, trade, trade away

4 **change hands,** change ownership; devolve, pass on, descend, succeed

ADJS **5** **transferable, conveyable,** negotiable, alienable; **assignable,** consignable; devisable, bequeathable; heritable, inheritable

630 PRICE, FEE

NOUNS **1** **price, cost, expense,** expenditure, **charge,** damage *and* score *and* tab <nf>; rate, figure, amount; **quotation,** quoted price, price tag *and* **ticket** *and* **sticker** <nf>; **price list,** price range, prices current; stock market quotations; standard price, asking price, list price, sale price, selling price, market price

2 **worth, value,** account, rate; face value, face; par value; market value; street value; fair value; net worth; conversion factor *or* value; monetary value; money's worth, pennyworth, value received; bang for the buck <nf>; going rate; trade-in price

3 **valuation, evaluation,** value-setting, value-fixing, pricing, price determination, **assessment, appraisal,** appraisement, estimation, rating, bond rating; unit pricing, dual pricing

4 **price index,** business index; wholesale price index; consumer price *or* retail price index; cost-of-living index; stock market index; price level; price ceiling, ceiling price, ceiling, top price; floor price, floor, bottom price; demand curve; rising prices, **inflation,** inflationary spiral

5 **price controls,** price-fixing, valorization; managed prices, fair-trading, fair trade, fair-trade agreement; **price supports,** rigid supports, flexible supports; price freeze; rent control; prix fixe

6 **fee, dues, toll, charge, charges, demand, exaction,** exactment, scot, shot, scot and lot; hire; **fare,** carfare; user fee; airport fee *or* charge; license fee; entrance *or* entry *or* admission fee, admission; cover charge; portage, towage; wharfage, anchorage, dockage; pilotage; storage, cellarage; brokerage; salvage; service fee *or* charge; commission, cut

7 freightage, freight, haulage, carriage, cartage, drayage, expressage, lighterage; poundage, tonnage

8 **rent, rental;** rent-roll; rent charge; rack rent, quitrent; ground rent, wayleave rent

9 **tax, taxation, duty, tribute,** taxes, rates <Brit>, contribution, **assessment, revenue enhancement,** cess <Brit>, **levy, toll, impost,** imposition; tax code, tax law; **tithe;** indirect taxation, direct taxation; **tax burden,** overtaxation, undertaxation; bracket *or* tax-bracket creep; progressive taxation, graduated taxation; regressive taxation; tax withholding; tax return, separate returns, joint return; tax evasion *or* avoidance; tax haven *or* shelter; **tax deduction, deduction; tax write-off,** write-off, tax relief; tax exemption, tax-exempt status; tax structure, tax base; taxable income *or* goods *or* land *or* property, ratables

10 **tax collector,** taxer, taxman, publican; collector of internal revenue, internal revenue agent, revenuer; tax farmer, farmer; assessor, **tax assessor;** exciseman <Brit>, revenuer; Internal Revenue Service *or* IRS; Inland Revenue *or* IR <Brit>; **customs agent; customs,** US Customs Service, Bureau of Customs and Excise <Brit>; customhouse; taxpayer

VERBS **11 price,** set *or* name a price, fix the price of; place a value on, **value, evaluate,** valuate, **appraise, assess, rate,** prize, apprize; quote a price; set an arbitrary price on, control *or* manage the price of, valorize; mark up, mark down, **discount;** fair-trade; reassess

12 charge, demand, ask, require; overcharge, undercharge; **exact, assess, levy, impose; tax,** assess a tax upon, slap a tax on <nf>, lay *or* put a duty on, make dutiable, subject to a tax *or* fee *or* duty, collect a tax *or* duty on; tithe; prorate, assess *pro rata;* charge for, stick for <nf>

13 cost, sell for, fetch, bring, bring in, stand one *and* set *or* move one back <nf>, knock one back <Brit nf>; **come to,** run to *or* into, **amount to,** mount up to, come up to, total up to

ADJS **14 priced, valued,** evaluated, assessed, appraised, rated, prized; **worth,** valued at; good for; ad valorem, pro rata

15 chargeable, taxable, ratable <Brit>, assessable, dutiable, leviable, declarable; tithable

16 tax-free, nontaxable, nondutiable, tax-exempt; deductible, tax-deductible; duty-free

ADVS **17 at a price,** for a consideration; to the amount of, to the tune of *and* in the neighborhood of <nf>

631 DISCOUNT

NOUNS **1 discount, cut, deduction,** price reduction, slash, abatement, reduction, price reduction, price-cutting, price-cut, rollback <nf>; underselling; **rebate,** rebatement; bank discount, cash discount, chain discount, time discount, trade discount; write-off, charge-off; **depreciation; allowance,** concession; set-off; drawback, **refund,** kickback <nf>; **premium,** percentage, agio; trading stamp; bank rate, bank discount

VERBS **2 discount, cut, deduct,** bate, abate; **take off,** write off, charge off; knock down <nf>; **depreciate,** reduce; sell at a loss; **allow,** make allowance; rebate, **refund,** kick back <nf>; take a premium *or* percentage

ADVS **3 at a discount,** at a reduction, at a reduced rate, below par, below *or* under cost; cost-efficient

632 EXPENSIVENESS

NOUNS **1 expensiveness, costliness, dearness,** high *or* great cost, highness, stiffness *or* **steepness** <nf>, priceyness; **richness, sumptuousness,** sumptuosity, **luxuriousness;** pretty penny <nf>

2 preciousness, dearness, value, high *or* great value, **worth,** extraordinary worth, price *or* great price , **valuableness; pricelessness, invaluableness**

3 high price, high *or* big price tag *and* big ticket *and* big sticker price <nf>, **fancy price,** good price, steep *or* stiff price <nf>, luxury price, a pretty penny *or* an arm and a leg <nf>, exorbitant *or* unconscionable *or* extortionate price; famine price, scarcity price; rack rent; bracket creep; inflationary prices, rising *or* soaring *or* spiraling prices, soaring costs; sellers' market; **inflation,** cost *or* cost-push inflation *or* cost-push, demand-pull inflation, inflationary trend *or* pressure, hot economy, inflationary spiral, inflationary gap; reflation; stagflation, slumpflation

4 exorbitance, exorbitancy , **extravagance,** excess, **excessiveness,** inordinateness, immoderateness, immoderation, undueness, unreasonableness, outrageousness, preposterousness; unconscionableness, extortionateness

5 overcharge, surcharge, overassessment; gouging *or* price-gouging; **extortion,** extortionate price; **holdup** *and* armed robbery *and* highway robbery <nf>; profiteering, rack-rent; ripoff <nf>

VERBS **6** **cost much,** cost money *and* cost you <nf>, be dear, cost a pretty penny *or* an arm and a leg *or* a packet <nf>, **run into money;** be overpriced, price out of the market

7 **overprice,** set the price tag too high; **overcharge,** surcharge, overtax; **hold up** *and* **soak** *and* **stick** *and* **sting** *and* **clip** <nf>, **make pay through the nose, gouge;** commit highway robbery; victimize, rip off, swindle 356.18; exploit, skin <nf>, **fleece,** screw *and* put the screws to <nf>, bleed, bleed white; profiteer; rack *or* rack up the rents, rack rent; double-charge; profiteer

8 **overpay,** overspend, pay too much, pay more than it's worth, **pay dearly,** pay exorbitantly, pay, **pay through the nose,** be had *or* taken <nf>

9 **inflate,** heat *or* heat up the economy; reflate

ADJS **10** **precious, dear, valuable,** worthy, rich, golden, of great price , worth a pretty penny <nf>, worth a king's ransom, worth its weight in gold, good as gold, precious as the apple of one's eye; **priceless, invaluable,** inestimable, without *or* **beyond price,** not to be had for love or money, not for all the tea in China

11 **expensive, dear, costly,** of great cost, dear-bought, **high, high-priced,** premium, at a premium, top; big ticket <nf>, **fancy** *and* stiff *and* steep <nf>, pricey; beyond one's means, not affordable, more than one can afford, sky-high; unpayable; upmarket, upscale <nf> rich, sumptuous, executive *and* posh <nf>, **luxurious** 501.21, gold-plated

12 **overpriced,** grossly overpriced, **exorbitant, excessive, extravagant, inordinate, immoderate,** undue, unwarranted, unreasonable, fancy, unconscionable, outrageous, preposterous, out of bounds, out of sight <nf>, **prohibitive; extortionate,** cutthroat, **gouging, usurious,** exacting; **inflationary,** spiraling, skyrocketing, mounting; stagflationary, slumpflationary; reflationary

ADVS **13** **dear, dearly;** at a high price, at great cost, at a premium, at a great rate, at heavy cost, at great expense

14 **preciously, valuably,** worthily; pricelessly, invaluably, inestimably

15 **expensively,** richly, sumptuously, luxuriously

16 **exorbitantly, excessively,** grossly, **extravagantly, inordinately,** immoderately, unduly, unreasonably, unconscionably, outrageously, preposterously; **extortionately,** usuriously, gougingly

633 CHEAPNESS

NOUNS **1** **cheapness, inexpensiveness,** affordableness, affordability, reasonableness, modestness, moderateness, nominalness; drug *or* glut on the market; shabbiness, shoddiness 998.2

2 **low price, nominal price,** reasonable price, modest *or* manageable price, sensible price, moderate price; low *or* nominal *or* reasonable charge; bargain prices, budget prices, economy prices, easy prices *or* terms, popular prices, rock-bottom prices; buyers' market; low *or* small price tag *and* low sticker price *and* low tariff <nf>; **reduced price,** cut price, sale price; cheap *or* reduced rates; bargain rate; cut price *or* rate

3 **bargain,** advantageous purchase, **buy** <nf>, **good buy, steal** <nf>; money's worth, pennyworth, good pennyworth; special offer; loss leader

4 **cheapening, depreciation, devaluation,** reduction, lowering; deflation, deflationary spiral, cooling *or* cooling off of the economy; **buyers' market; decline,** plummet, plummeting, plunge, dive, nose dive *and* slump *and* sag <nf>, free fall; price fall, break; **price cut** *or* **reduction,** cut, slash, **markdown;** oversupply

VERBS **5** **be cheap,** cost little, not cost anything *and* cost nothing *and* next to nothing <nf>; **go dirt cheap** *or* for a song *or* for nickels and dimes *or* for peanuts <nf>, buy at a bargain, buy for a mere nothing; get one's money's worth, get a good pennyworth; buy at wholesale prices *or* at cost

6 **cheapen, depreciate, devaluate,** lower, reduce, devalue, **mark down, cut prices, cut,** slash, shave, trim, pare, underprice, knock the bottom out of <nf>, knock down <nf>; deflate, cool *or* cool off the economy; beat down; come down *or* fall in price; **fall,** decline, plummet, dive, nose-dive <nf>, drop, crash, head for the bottom, plunge, sag, slump; break, give way; reach a new low; unload

ADJS 7 **cheap, inexpensive,** unexpensive, **low, low-priced,** bargain, frugal, reasonable, sensible, manageable, modest, moderate, affordable, to fit the pocketbook, budget, easy, economy, economic, economical; within means, within reach *or* easy reach; nominal, token; austere; worth the money, well worth the money; cheap *or* good at the price, cheap at half the price; shabby, shoddy, cheapo <nf>; deflationary

8 **dirt cheap,** cheap as dirt, dog-cheap <nf>, **a dime a dozen,** bargain-priced, bargain-basement, five-and-ten, dime-store

9 **reduced,** cut, cut-price, slashed, **marked down;** cut-rate; half-price; priced to go; giveaway, sacrificial; **lowest,** rock-bottom, bottom; deep-discount

ADVS 10 **cheaply, cheap,** on the cheap <Brit nf>; **inexpensively,** reasonably, moderately, nominally; **at a bargain,** *à bon marché* <Fr>, for a song *or* mere song <nf>, for pennies *or* nickels and dimes *or* peanuts <nf>, at small cost, at a low price, at budget prices, at piggy-bank prices, at a sacrifice; at cost *or* cost price, at prime cost, wholesale, at wholesale; at reduced rates

634 COSTLESSNESS

<absence of charge>

NOUNS 1 **costlessness,** gratuitousness, gratuity, **freeness,** expenselessness, complimentariness, no charge; free ride <nf>; freebie *and* gimme <nf>; labor of love; **gift** 478.4

2 **complimentary ticket, pass,** comp <nf>, free pass *or* ticket, paper <nf>, free admission, guest pass *or* ticket, Annie Oakley <nf>; discount ticket, twofer <nf>

3 **freeloader,** free rider, pass holder, deadhead <nf>, sponger

VERBS 4 **give, present** 478.12, comp <nf>; freeload, sponge

ADJS 5 **gratuitous, gratis, free, free of charge,** for free, for nothing, free for nothing, free for the asking, free gratis *and* free gratis for nothing <nf>, for love, free as air; freebie *and* freebee *and* freeby <nf>; costless, expenseless, untaxed, without charge, free of cost *or* expense, all-expense-paid; no charge; unbought, unpaid-for; **complimentary, on the house, comp** <nf>, given 478.24; giftlike; eleemosynary, charitable 143.15

ADVS 6 **gratuitously, gratis, free, free of charge,** for nothing, for the asking, at no charge, without charge, with the compliments of the management, as our guest, on the house

635 THRIFT

NOUNS 1 **thrift, economy, thriftiness,** economicalness, savingness, sparingness, unwastefulness, **frugality,** frugalness; tight purse strings; parsimony, **parsimoniousness** 484.1; false economy; carefulness, care, chariness, canniness; **prudence,** providence, forehandedness; **husbandry,** management, good management *or* stewardship, custodianship, prudent *or* prudential administration; **austerity,** austerity program, belt-tightening; economic planning; economy of means 484.1

2 **economizing,** economization, reduction of spending or government spending; **cost-effectiveness; saving,** scrimping, skimping <nf>, scraping, sparing, cheeseparing; **retrenchment, curtailment,** reduction of expenses, cutback, rollback, slowdown, cooling, cooling off *or* down, low growth rate; reduction in

forces *or* RIF; budget, spending plan

3 **economizer,** economist , **saver,** string-saver, skimper

VERBS 4 **economize, save,** make *or* enforce economies; **scrimp, skimp** <nf>, **scrape,** scrape and save; **manage, husband,** husband one's resources, conserve; budget; live frugally, get along on a shoestring, get by on little; keep within compass , keep *or* stay within one's means *or* budget, balance income with outgo, live within one's income, make ends meet, cut one's coat according to one's cloth, keep *or* stay ahead of the game; put something aside, **save up,** save for a rainy day, have a nest egg; supplement *or* eke out one's income

5 **retrench, cut down,** cut *or* pare down expenses, **curtail expenses; cut corners, tighten one's belt,** cut back, roll back, take a reef, slow down

ADJS 6 **economical, thrifty, frugal,** economic, unwasteful, conserving, **saving,** economizing, spare, **sparing;** Scotch; **prudent,** prudential, provident, forehanded; careful, chary, canny; scrimping, skimping <nf>, cheeseparing, austere; penny-wise; **parsimonious** 484.7; **cost-effective, cost-efficient; efficient,** labor-saving, time-saving, money-saving

ADVS 7 **economically, thriftily, frugally,** husbandly ; **cost-effectively, cost-efficiently;** prudently, providently; carefully, charily, cannily; sparingly, with a sparing hand

636 ETHICS

NOUNS 1 **ethics, principles,** standards, norms, principles of conduct *or* behavior, principles of professional practice; **morals,** moral principles; code, ethical *or* moral code, **ethic,** code of morals *or* ethics, ethical system, value system, values, axiology; **norm,** behavioral norm, normative system; moral climate, **ethos,** *Zeitgeist* <Ger>; Ten Commandments, decalogue; social ethics, professional ethics, bioethics, medical ethics, legal ethics, business ethics, etc

2 ethical *or* moral philosophy, ethonomics, aretaics, eudaemonics, casuistry, deontology, empiricism, evolutionism, hedonism, ethical formalism, intuitionism, perfectionism, Stoicism, utilitarianism, categorical imperative, golden rule; egoistic ethics, altruistic ethics; Christian ethics; situation ethics; comparative ethics

3 **morality, morals,** morale; virtue 653; ethicality, ethicalness; scruples, good conscience, moral fiber, moral compass

4 **amorality,** unmorality; amoralism; moral delinquency, moral turpitude

5 **conscience,** grace, **sense of right and wrong,** moral sense, sense of right and wrong; inward monitor, inner arbiter, moral censor, censor, ethical self, superego; **voice of conscience,** still small voice within, wee small voice, guardian *or* good angel; inner light, light within; tender conscience; clear *or* clean conscience; social conscience; conscientiousness 644.2; twinge of conscience 113.2

ADJS 6 **ethical, moral,** moralistic; ethological; axiological

637 RIGHT

NOUNS 1 **right,** rightfulness, rightness; what is right *or* proper, what should be, what ought to be, the seemly, the thing, the right *or* proper thing, the right *or* proper thing to do, what is done

2 **propriety, decorum, decency,** good behavior *or* conduct, correctness, correctitude, rightness, properness, decorousness, goodness, goodliness, niceness, seemliness, cricket <Brit nf>; fitness, fittingness, appropriateness, expediency, suitability 995.1; normativeness, normality; proprieties, decencies; rightmindedness, **righteousness** 653.1

ADJS 3 **right,** rightful; fit, suitable 995.5; **proper, correct, decorous,** good, nice, decent, seemly, **due,**

appropriate, fitting, condign, **right and proper,** as it should be, as it ought to be, expedient, up to par, *comme il faut* <Fr>; kosher *and* according to Hoyle <nf>; in the right; normative, normal; rightminded, right-thinking, **righteous**

ADVS 4 **rightly, rightfully,** right; **by rights,** by right, with good right, **as is right** *or* **only right; properly,** correctly, as is proper *or* fitting, **duly, appropriately,** fittingly, condignly, **in justice,** in equity; in reason, in all conscience

638 WRONG

NOUNS 1 **wrong,** wrongfulness, wrongness; **impropriety, indecorum;** incorrectness, improperness, indecorousness, unseemliness; unfitness, unfittingness, inappropriateness, unsuitableness, unsuitability 996.1; infraction, violation, delinquency, criminality, illegality, unlawfulness; abnormality, deviance *or* deviancy, aberrance *or* aberrancy; sinfulness, wickedness, unrighteousness; **dysfunction,** malfunction, out of order; maladaptation, maladjustment; malfeasance, malversation, malpractice; malformation

2 **abomination, horror,** terrible thing; **scandal, disgrace, shame, pity,** atrocity, profanation, desecration, violation, sacrilege, infamy, ignominy

ADJS 3 **wrong, wrongful; improper, incorrect, indecorous,** undue, unseemly; unfit, unfitting, inappropriate, unsuitable 996.5; delinquent, criminal, illegal, unlawful; fraudulent, creative <nf>; abnormal, deviant, aberrant; **dysfunctional,** out of order; **evil, sinful, wicked, unrighteous;** not the thing, hardly the thing, not done, not cricket <Brit>; **off-base** *and* **out-of-line** *and* **off-color** *and* off the beam <nf>; abominable, terrible, scandalous, disgraceful, immoral, shameful, shameless, atrocious, sacrilegious, infamous, ignominious; maladapted, maladjusted, unjust

ADVS 4 **wrongly, wrongfully,** wrong; **improperly,** incorrectly, indecorously; unjustly

639 DUENESS

NOUNS 1 **dueness, entitlement,** entitledness, deservingness, deservedness, meritedness, expectation, just *or* justifiable expectation, expectations, outlook, prospect, prospects; **justice** 649

2 **due,** one's due, what one merits *or* is entitled to, what one has earned, what is owing, what one has coming, what is coming to one, acknowledgment, cognizance, recognition, credit, crediting; **right**

3 **desserts,** just desserts, deservings, merits, dues, due reward *or* punishment, **comeuppance** <nf>, all that is coming to one, what's coming to one; the wrath of God; retaliation 506, vengeance 507.1

VERBS 4 **be due,** be one's due, **be entitled to,** have a right or title to, have a rightful claim to *or* upon, claim as one's right, **have coming,** come by honestly

5 **deserve, merit,** earn, rate *and* be in line for <nf>, **be worthy of,** be deserving, richly deserve

6 **get one's desserts,** get one's dues, **get one's comeuppance** *and* get his *or* hers <nf>, get what is coming to one; get justice; serve one right, be rightly served; get for one's pains, reap the fruits *or* benefit of, reap where one has sown, come into one's own

ADJS 7 **due, owed, owing,** payable, redeemable, coming, **coming to**

8 **rightful,** condign, appropriate, proper; fit, becoming 995.5; **fair, just** 649.7

9 **warranted, justified, entitled,** qualified, worthy; **deserved, merited,** richly deserved, earned, well-earned

10 **due, entitled to,** with a right to; **deserving, meriting, meritorious, worthy of;** attributable, ascribable

ADVS 11 **duly,** rightfully, condignly, as is one's due *or* right

PHRS **12** what's sauce for the goose is sauce for the gander; give the devil his due; give credit where credit is due; he's made his bed let him lie in it; let the punishment fit the crime

640 UNDUENESS

NOUNS **1** **undueness, undeservedness,** undeservingness, unentitledness, unentitlement, unmeritedness, unwarrantedness; disentitlement; lack of claim *or* title, false claim *or* title, invalid claim *or* title, no claim *or* title, empty claim *or* title; unearned increment; **inappropriateness** 996.1; **impropriety** 638.1; **excess** 993

2 **presumption,** assumption, **imposition; license,** licentiousness, **undue liberty,** liberties, familiarity, **presumptuousness,** freedom *or* liberty abused, hubris; lawlessness 418; injustice 650

3 **usurpation, arrogation,** seizure, unlawful seizure, **appropriation,** assumption, adoption, infringement, encroachment, invasion, trespass, trespassing; playing God

4 **usurper,** arrogator, pretender

VERBS **5** **not be entitled to,** have no right *or* title to, have no claim upon, not have a leg to stand on

6 **presume, assume, venture, hazard, dare,** pretend, attempt, **make bold** *or* so bold, make free, **take the liberty,** take upon oneself, go so far as to

7 **presume on** *or* **upon, impose on** *or* **upon,** encroach upon, obtrude upon; **take liberties,** take a liberty, overstep, overstep one's rights *or* bounds *or* prerogatives, make free with *or* of, abuse one's rights, abuse a privilege, give an inch and take an ell; take for granted, presuppose; **inconvenience,** bother, trouble, cause to go out of one's way

8 <take to oneself unduly> **usurp, arrogate,** seize, grab *and* latch on to <nf>, **appropriate,** assume, adopt, take over, arrogate *or* accroach to oneself, pretend to, infringe, encroach, invade, trespass; play God

ADJS **9** **undue, unowed, unowing,** not coming, not outstanding; **undeserved, unmerited,** unearned; **unwarranted, unjustified,** unprovoked; unentitled, undeserving, unmeriting, nonmeritorious, unworthy; preposterous, outrageous

10 **inappropriate** 996.5; **improper** 638.3; **excessive** 993.16

11 **presumptuous, presuming,** licentious; hubristic 493.7

PHRS **12** give him an inch he'll take a mile; let a camel get his nose under the tent and he'll come in

641 DUTY

<moral obligation>

NOUNS **1** **duty, obligation,** charge, **onus, burden,** mission, devoir, must, ought, imperative, bounden duty, proper *or* assigned task, what ought to be done, what one is responsible for, where the buck stops <nf>, deference, respect 155, fealty, allegiance, loyalty, homage; devotion, dedication, **commitment;** self-commitment, self-imposed duty; **business** 724.1, function, province, place 724.3; ethics 636; line of duty; call of duty; duties and responsibilities, assignment, work-load; burden of proof; civic duty

2 **responsibility,** incumbency; **liability, accountability,** accountableness, answerability, answerableness, amenability; product liability; **responsibleness, dutifulness,** duteousness, devotion *or* dedication to duty, sense of duty *or* obligation, code of honor, inner voice

VERBS **3** **should, ought to,** had best, had better, be expedient

4 **behoove, become,** befit, beseem, be bound, be obliged *or* obligated, be under an obligation; **owe it to,** owe it to oneself; must

5 **be the duty of, be incumbent on** *or* **upon,** be his *or* hers to, fall to, stand on *or* upon, be a must *or* an imperative for, duty calls one to

6 **be responsible for, answer for,** stand responsible for, **be liable for,** be answerable *or* accountable for;

be on the hook for *and* take the heat *or* rap for <nf>

7 **be one's responsibility,** be one's office, be one's charge *or* mission, be one's concern, **rest with,** lie upon, devolve upon, rest on the shoulders of, lie on one's head *or* one's door *or* one's doorstep, fall to one *or* to one's lot

8 **incur a responsibility,** become bound to, become sponsor for

9 **take** *or* **accept the responsibility, take upon oneself,** take upon one's shoulders, commit oneself; be where the buck stops <nf>; **answer for,** respect *or* defer to one's duty; sponsor, be *or* stand sponsor for; do at one's own risk *or* peril; **take the blame,** be in the hot seat *or* on the spot *and* take the heat *or* rap for <nf>

10 **do one's duty,** perform *or* fulfill *or* discharge one's duty, do what one has to do, pay one's dues <nf>, **do what is expected,** do the needful, do the right thing, do justice to, **do** *or* **act one's part,** play one's proper role; answer the call of duty, do one's bit *or* part; walk the walk

11 **meet an obligation,** satisfy one's obligations, stand to one's engagement, stand up to, **acquit oneself, make good,** redeem one's pledge

12 **obligate, oblige, require,** make incumbent *or* imperative, tie, **bind,** pledge, commit, saddle with, put under an obligation; call to account, hold responsible *or* accountable *or* answerable

ADJS 13 **dutiful, duteous;** moral, ethical; conscientious, scrupulous, observant; obedient 326.3; deferential, respectful 155.8

14 **incumbent on** *or* **upon,** chargeable to, behooving

15 **obligatory, binding, imperative,** imperious, peremptory, mandatory, compulsory, must, *de rigueur* <Fr>; **necessary,** required 963.13

16 **obliged, obligated,** obligate, **under obligation; bound, duty-bound,** in duty bound, tied, pledged, committed, saddled, beholden, bounden; **obliged to,** beholden to, bound *or* bounden to, **indebted to**

17 **responsible, answerable; liable, accountable,** incumbent, amenable, unexempt from, chargeable, on one's head, at one's doorstep, on the hook <nf>; responsible for, at the bottom of; to blame

ADVS 18 **dutifully, duteously, in the line of duty,** as in duty bound; beyond the call of duty

642 PREROGATIVE

NOUNS 1 **prerogative, right, due,** droit; power, authority, prerogative of office; faculty, appurtenance; **claim,** proper claim, demand, **interest, title,** pretension, pretense, prescription; birthright; natural right, presumptive right, inalienable right, exclusive right; divine right; vested right *or* interest; property right; conjugal right; royal charter

2 **privilege, license, liberty, freedom, immunity;** franchise, patent, copyright, grant, warrant, blank check, carte blanche; favor, indulgence, **special favor,** dispensation

3 **human rights,** rights of man; constitutional rights, rights of citizenship, **civil rights** 430.2, civil liberties; rights of minorities, minority rights; gay rights; Bill of Rights

4 **women's rights,** rights of women; **feminism, women's liberation,** women's lib <nf>, womanism, women's movement *or* liberation movement, sisterhood

5 women's rightist, **feminist,** women's liberationist, women's liberation advocate *or* adherent *or* activist, womanist, women's libber *and* libber <nf>; suffragette, suffragist

VERBS 6 have *or* claim *or* assert a right, exercise a right; defend a right

643 IMPOSITION

<*a putting or inflicting upon*>

NOUNS 1 **imposition, infliction,** laying on *or* upon, charging, taxing, tasking; burdening, weighting *or* weighting down, freighting, loading *or* loading down, heaping on *or* upon, imposing an onus; **exaction,**

demand 421; unwarranted demand, obtrusiveness, presumptuousness 142.1; inconvenience, trouble, bother, pain <nf>; inconsiderateness 144.3

2 administration, giving, bestowal; applying, application, dosing, dosage, meting out, prescribing; **forcing,** forcing on *or* upon, enforcing; regimentation

3 **charge, duty, tax,** task; **burden,** weight, freight, cargo, load, onus

VERBS **4** **impose, impose on** *or* **upon, inflict on** *or* **upon, put on** *or* **upon, lay on** *or* **upon,** enjoin; **put, place, set, lay,** put down; **levy, exact, demand** 421.1; **tax,** task, **charge,** burden with, weight *or* freight with, weight down with, yoke with, **fasten upon,** saddle with, stick with <nf>; subject to

5 **inflict, wreak, do to,** bring, bring upon, bring down upon, bring on *or* down on one's head, visit upon

6 **administer, give, bestow; apply, put on** *or* **upon,** lay on *or* upon, dose, dose with, dish out <nf>, mete out, prescribe, regiment; **force, force upon,** impose by force *or* main force, strongarm <nf>, force down one's throat, enforce upon

7 **impose on** *or* **upon, take advantage of** 387.16; **presume upon** 640.7; **deceive,** play *or* work on, out on *or* upon, put over *or* across <nf>; palm *or* pass *or* fob off on, fob *or* foist on; shift the blame *or* responsibility, **pass the buck** <nf>

ADJS **8** **imposed, inflicted,** piled *or* heaped on; burdened with, stuck with <nf>; self-inflicted; exacted, demanded

644 PROBITY

NOUNS **1** **probity,** truthfulness, assured probity, **honesty, integrity, rectitude, uprightness,** upstandingness, erectness, **virtue,** virtuousness, **righteousness, goodness;** cleanness, **decency; honor,** honorableness, worthiness, estimableness, reputability, nobility; unimpeachableness, unimpeachability, irreproachableness, irreproachability, blamelessness; immaculacy, unspottedness, stainlessness, pureness, purity; respectability; principles, high principles, high ideals, high-mindedness; **character,** good *or* sterling character, moral strength, moral excellence; **fairness,** justness, justice 649; gentrification

2 **conscientiousness, scrupulousness,** scrupulosity, **scruples,** punctiliousness, meticulousness; scruple, point of honor, punctilio; qualm 325.2; twinge of conscience 113.2; overconscientiousness, overscrupulousness; fastidiousness 495

3 **honesty, veracity,** veraciousness, verity, **truthfulness,** truth, veridicality, truth-telling, truth-speaking; truth-loving; credibility, absolute credibility; objectivity

4 **candor, candidness, frankness,** plain dealing; sincerity, genuineness, authenticity; ingenuousness; artlessness 416; **openness,** openheartedness; freedom, freeness; **unreserve,** unrestraint, unconstraint; **forthrightness, directness, straightforwardness; outspokenness,** plainness, plainspokenness, plain speaking, plain speech, roundness, broadness; **bluntness,** bluffness, brusqueness

5 **undeceptiveness, undeceitfulness, guilelessness**

6 **trustworthiness,** faithworthiness, trustiness, trustability, **reliability, dependability,** dependableness, sureness; answerableness, responsibility 641.2; unfalseness, unperfidiousness, untreacherousness; incorruptibility, inviolability

7 **fidelity, faithfulness, loyalty,** faith; **constancy, steadfastness,** staunchness, firmness; trueness, troth, true blue; good faith, *bona fides* <L>, *bonne foi* <Fr>; **allegiance, fealty, homage;** bond, tie; attachment, adherence, adhesion; devotion, devotedness

8 **person** *or* **man** *or* **woman of honor,** man of his word, woman of her word; gentleman; **honest man,** good man; **lady, real lady; honest woman, good woman;** salt of the earth; square *or* straight shooter *and*

straight arrow <nf>; true blue, truepenny; trusty, faithful

VERBS **9 keep faith,** not fail, **keep one's word** *or* **promise,** keep troth, show good faith, be as good as one's word, one's word is one's bond, redeem one's pledge, play by the rules, acquit oneself, make good; practice what one preaches

10 shoot straight <nf>, draw a straight furrow, **put one's cards on the table,** level with one <nf>, play it straight <nf>, shoot from the hip <nf>

11 speak *or* **tell the truth,** speak *or* tell true, paint in its true colors, tell the truth and shame the devil; tell the truth, the whole truth, and nothing but the truth, stick to the facts

12 be frank, speak plainly, speak out, speak one's mind, say what one thinks, **call a spade a spade,** tell it like it is, make no bones about it, not mince words

ADJS **13 honest, upright,** uprighteous, **upstanding,** erect, right, **righteous, virtuous, good,** clean, squeaky-clean <nf>, **decent; honorable,** full of integrity, **reputable,** estimable, creditable, worthy, noble, sterling, manly, yeomanly; Christian <nf>; unimpeachable, beyond reproach, irreproachable, squeaky-clean <nf>, blameless, immaculate, spotless, stainless, unstained, unspotted, unblemished, untarnished, unsullied, undefiled, pure; **respectable,** highly respectable; **ethical, moral; principled, high-principled,** high-minded, right-minded; uncorrupt, uncorrupted, inviolate; truehearted, true-blue, true-souled, true-spirited; true-dealing, true-disposing, true-devoted; **law-abiding,** law-loving, law-revering; **fair, just** 649.7

14 straight, square, foursquare, straight-arrow <nf>, honest and aboveboard, right as rain; **fair and square; square-dealing,** square-shooting, straight-shooting, up-and-up, **on the up-and-up** *and* **on the level,** *and* on the square <nf>; **aboveboard, open and aboveboard;** bona fide, good-faith; authentic, all wool and a yard wide, veritable, genuine; single-hearted; honest as the day is long

15 conscientious, tender-conscienced; **scrupulous,** careful 339.10; punctilious, punctual, meticulous, religious, strict, nice; fastidious 495.9; overconscientious, overscrupulous

16 honest, veracious, truthful, true, true to one's word, veridical; truth-telling, truth-speaking, truth-declaring, truth-passing, truth-bearing, truth loving, truth-seeking, truth-desiring, truth-guarding, truth-filled; true-speaking, true-meaning, true-tongued

17 candid, frank, sincere, genuine, ingenuous, frankhearted; **open,** openhearted, transparent, open-faced; artless 416.5; **straightforward, direct,** up-front *and* straight <nf>, **forthright,** downright, straight-out <nf>, straight-from-the-shoulder; plain, broad, round; **unreserved,** unrestrained, unconstrained, unchecked; unguarded, uncalculating; free; **outspoken, plain-spoken,** free-spoken, free-speaking, free-tongued; explicit, unequivocal; **blunt,** bluff, brusque; heart-to-heart

18 undeceptive, undeceitful, undissembling, undissimulating, undeceiving, undesigning, uncalculating; **guileless,** unbeguiling, unbeguileful; unassuming, unpretending, unfeigning, undisguising, unflattering; undissimulated, undissembled; unassumed, unaffected, unpretended, unfeigned, undisguised, unvarnished, untrimmed

19 trustworthy, trusty, trustable, faithworthy, **reliable, dependable, responsible,** straight <nf>, sure, to be trusted, **to be depended** *or* **relied upon,** to be counted *or* reckoned on, as good as one's word; tried, true, **tried and true,** tested, proven; unfalse, unperfidious, untreacherous; incorruptible, inviolable

20 faithful, loyal, devoted, allegiant; **true, true-blue,** true to one's colors; **constant, steadfast,** unswerving, steady, consistent, stable, unfailing, staunch, firm, solid

ADVS 21 **honestly, uprightly, honorably,** upstandingly, erectly, **virtuously, righteously, decently,** worthily, reputably, nobly; unimpeachably, irreproachably, blamelessly, immaculately, unspottedly, stainlessly, purely; high-mindedly, morally; **conscientiously, scrupulously,** punctiliously, meticulously, fastidiously 495.14

22 **truthfully, truly,** veraciously; to tell the truth, to speak truthfully; in truth, in sooth , of a truth, with truth, in good *or* very truth; objectively

23 **candidly, frankly, sincerely,** genuinely, in all seriousness *or* soberness, from the heart, in all conscience; in plain words *or* English, straight from the shoulder, not to mince the matter, not to mince words, without equivocation, with no nonsense, all joking aside *or* apart; **openly,** openheartedly, **unreservedly,** unrestrainedly, unconstrainedly, **forthrightly, directly, straightforwardly, outspokenly, plainly,** plain-spokenly, uninhibitedly, broadly, roundly, **bluntly,** bluffy, brusquely

24 **trustworthily,** trustily, **reliably, dependably, responsibly;** undeceptively, undeceitfully, guilelessly; incorruptibly, inviolably

25 **faithfully, loyally,** devotedly; **constantly, steadfastly,** steadily, responsibly, consistently, unfailingly, unswervingly, staunchly, firmly; in *or* with good faith, *bona fide* <L>

645 IMPROBITY

NOUNS 1 **improbity,** untruthfulness, **dishonesty,** dishonor; **unscrupulousness,** unconscientiousness; **corruption,** corruptness, corruptedness; **crookedness,** criminality, feloniousness, **fraudulence** *or* fraudulency, underhandedness, unsavoriness, fishiness *and* shadiness <nf>, indirection, shiftiness, slipperiness, deviousness, evasiveness, unstraightforwardness, trickiness

2 **knavery, roguery, rascality,** rascalry, **villainy,** reprobacy, scoundrelism; chicanery 356.4; knavishness, roguishness, scampishness, villainousness, charlatanism; **baseness, vileness,** degradation, turpitude, moral turpitude

3 **deceitfulness; falseness** 354; perjury, forswearing, untruthfulness 354.8, credibility gap; inveracity; mendacity, mendaciousness; **insincerity,** unsincereness, uncandidness, uncandor, unfrankness, disingenuousness; hypocrisy; sharp practice 356.4; fraud 356.8; artfulness, craftiness 415.1; intrigue

4 **untrustworthiness,** unfaithworthiness, untrustiness, **unreliability, undependability,** irresponsibility

5 **infidelity, unfaithfulness,** unfaith, faithlessness, cheating, trothlessness; **inconstancy, unsteadfastness,** fickleness; **disloyalty,** unloyalty; **falsity,** falseness, untrueness; disaffection, recreancy, dereliction; bad faith, *mala fides* <L>, Punic faith; breach of promise, breach of trust *or* faith, barratry; breach of confidence

6 **treachery,** treacherousness; **perfidy,** perfidiousness, falseheartedness 354.4, two-facedness, doubleness, sycophancy, false face; **duplicity, double-dealing,** foul play, dirty work *and* dirty pool *and* dirty trick *and* dirty game <nf>; broken promise, breach of promise, breach of faith

7 **treason,** petty treason, misprision of treason, high treason; lese majesty, sedition; quislingism, fifth-column activity; collaboration, fraternization; subversion, subversiveness, subversivism

8 **betrayal,** betrayment, letting down <nf>, **double cross** *and* sellout <nf>, Judas kiss, kiss of death, stab in the back

9 **corruptibility, venality,** bribability, purchasability

10 criminal 660.9, perpetrator, perp <nf>, scoundrel 660.3, traitor 357.10, deceiver 357

VERBS 11 <be dishonest> live by one's wits; shift, shift about, evade; deceive; cheat; falsify; lie; sail under false colors, put on a false face, pass oneself off as

12 **be unfaithful,** not keep faith *or* troth, **go back on** <nf>, **fail,** break one's word *or* promise, renege, go back on one's word <nf>, break faith, betray, perjure *or* forswear oneself; forsake, desert 370.5; pass the buck <nf>; shift the responsibility *or* blame; cheat *and* cheat on *and* two-time <nf>

13 **play one false,** prove false; **stab one in the back,** backstab, knife one <nf>; bite the hand that feeds one; play dirty pool <nf>; shift *or* move the goalposts *and* change the rules <nf>; bamboozle

14 **betray, double-cross** *and* two-time <nf>, sell out *and* sell down the river <nf>, turn in; **mislead,** lead one down the garden path; let down; inform on 551.12

15 **act the traitor,** turn against, go over to the enemy, turn one's coat, sell oneself, sell out <nf>; collaborate, fraternize

ADJS **16** **dishonest, dishonorable; unconscientious,** unconscienced, conscienceless, unconscionable, shameless, without shame *or* remorse, **unscrupulous, unprincipled,** unethical, immoral, amoral; **corrupt,** corrupted, rotten, bottom-dwelling; **crooked, criminal,** felonious, **fraudulent,** creative <nf>, underhand, underhanded; shady <nf>, up to no good, not kosher <nf>, unsavory, dark, sinister, insidious, indirect, slippery, devious, tricky, shifty, evasive, unstraightforward; fishy <nf>, questionable, suspicious, doubtful, dubious, hinky <nf>; ill-gotten, ill-got

17 **knavish, roguish, scampish, rascally, scoundrelly,** blackguardly, villainous, reprobate, recreant, **base, vile,** degraded; **infamous, notorious**

18 **deceitful;** falsehearted; perjured, forsworn, untruthful 354.34; **insincere,** unsincere, uncandid, unfrank, disingenuous; artful, crafty 415.12; calculating, scheming; **tricky,** cute *and* dodgy <nf>, slippery as an eel

19 **untrustworthy,** unfaithworthy, untrusty, trustless, **unreliable, undependable,** fly-by-night, irresponsible, unsure, not to be trusted, not to be depended *or* relied upon

20 **unfaithful,** faithless, of bad faith, trothless; **inconstant, unsteadfast,** fickle; **disloyal,** unloyal; false, **untrue,** not true to; disaffected, recreant, derelict, barratrous; two-timing <nf>

21 **treacherous, perfidious,** falsehearted; **shifty,** slippery, tricky; **double-dealing,** double, ambidextrous; **two-faced**

22 **traitorous,** turncoat, double-crossing *and* two-timing <nf>, betraying; Judas-like, Iscariotic; **treasonable,** treasonous; quisling, quislingistic, fifth-column, Trojan-horse; subversive, seditious

23 **corruptible, venal,** bribable, purchasable, on the pad <nf>, mercenary, hireling

ADVS **24** **dishonestly, dishonorably; unscrupulously,** unconscientiously; **crookedly,** criminally, feloniously, **fraudulently,** underhandedly, like a thief in the night, insidiously, deviously, shiftily, evasively, fishily <nf>, suspiciously, dubiously, by fair means or foul; **deceitfully;** knavishly, roguishly, villainously; basely, vilely; infamously, notoriously

25 **perfidiously,** falseheartedly; **unfaithfully,** faithlessly; **treacherously;** traitorously, treasonably

646 HONOR

<token of esteem>

NOUNS **1** **honor,** great honor, distinction, glory, credit, ornament

2 **award, reward, prize;** first prize, second prize, etc; blue ribbon; consolation prize; booby prize; Nobel Prize, Pulitzer Prize; sweepstakes; jackpot; Oscar, Academy Award, Emmy, Tony; gold medal; Olympic Gold *or* Silver *or* Bronze medal

3 **trophy,** laurel, **laurels,** bays, palm, palms, crown, chaplet, wreath, garland, **feather in one's cap** <nf>; civic crown *or* garland *or* wreath; **cup,** loving cup, pot <nf>; America's Cup, Old Mug; **belt,** championship belt, black belt, brown belt, etc; banner, flag

4 **citation,** eulogy, mention, honorable mention, kudos, **accolade, tribute, praise** 511.1

5 **decoration,** decoration of honor, order, ornament; ribbon, riband; blue ribbon, *cordon bleu* <Fr>; red ribbon, red ribbon of the Legion of Honor; cordon, grand cordon; garter; star, gold star

6 **medal, military honor**, order, medallion; military medal, service medal, war medal, soldier's medal; lifesaving medal, Carnegie hero's medal; police citation, departmental citation; spurs, stripes, pips, star, gold star

7 scholarship, fellowship; grant

VERBS **8** **honor, do honor,** pay regard to, give *or* pay *or* render honor to, **recognize; cite; decorate,** pin a medal on; crown, crown with laurel; hand it to *or* take off one's hat to one <nf>, pay tribute, praise 511.5; give credit where credit is due; give one the red carpet treatment, roll out the red carpet

ADJS **9** **honored, distinguished;** laureate, crowned with laurel

10 **honorary, honorific, honorable**

ADVS **11** **with honor,** with distinction; *cum laude, magna cum laude, summa cum laude, insigne cum laude, honoris causa* <all L>

647 INSIGNIA

NOUNS **1** **insignia, regalia,** ensign, **emblem, badge, symbol,** logo <nf>, marking, attribute; badge of office, mark of office, chain, chain of office, collar; wand, verge, *fasces* <L>, **mace, staff, baton;** livery, uniform, mantle, dress; tartan, tie, old school tie, regimental tie, club tie; ring, school ring, class ring; pin, button, lapel pin *or* button; cap and gown, mortarboard; cockade; brassard; figurehead, eagle; cross 170.4, skull and crossbones, swastika, hammer and sickle, rose, thistle, shamrock, fleur-de-lis, caduceus; medal, **decoration** 646.5; **heraldry,** armory, blazonry, sigillography, sphragistics

2 <heraldry terms> heraldic device, achievement, bearings, coat of arms, arms, armorial bearings, armory, blazonry, blazon; hatchment; shield, escutcheon, scutcheon, lozenge; charge, field; crest, torse, wreath, garland, bandeau, chaplet, mantling, helmet; crown, coronet; device, motto; pheon, broad arrow; animal charge, lion, unicorn, griffin, yale, cockatrice, falcon, alerion, eagle, spread eagle; marshaling, quartering, impaling, impalement, dimidiating, differencing, difference; ordinary, bar, bend, bar sinister, bend sinister, baton, chevron, chief, cross, fess, pale, paly, saltire; subordinary, billet, bordure, canton, flanch, fret, fusil, gyron, inescutcheon, mascle, orle, quarter, rustre, tressure; fess point, nombril point, honor point; cadency mark, file, label, crescent, mullet, martlet, annulet, fleur-de-lis, rose, cross moline, octofoil; tincture, gules, azure, vert, sable, purpure, tenne; metal, or, argent; fur, ermine, ermines, erminites, erminois, pean, vair; heraldic officials 575.21; Hershey bar *or* pip *or* hash mark <nf>

3 <royal insignia> **regalia**; scepter, rod, rod of empire; orb; armilla; purple, ermine, robe of state *or* royalty, robes of office; purple pall; crown, royal crown, coronet, tiara, diadem; cap of maintenance *or* dignity *or* estate, triple plume, Prince of Wales's feathers; uraeus; seal, signet, great seal, privy seal; throne; badge of office

4 <ecclesiastical insignia> tiara, triple crown; ring, keys; miter, crosier, crook, pastoral staff; pallium; cardinal's hat, red hat

5 <military insignia> insignia of rank, grade insignia, chevron, stripe; star, bar, eagle, spread eagle, chicken <nf>, pip <Brit>, oak leaf; branch of service insignia, insignia of branch *or* arm; unit insignia, organization insignia, shoulder patch, patch; shoulder sleeve insignia, badge, aviation badge *or* wings; parachute badge, submarine badge; service stripe, hash mark <nf>, overseas bar, Hershey bar <nf>; epaulet

6 <national insignia> American eagle, British lion and unicorn, Canadian maple leaf, English rose, French fleur-de-lis, Irish shamrock, Japanese rising sun, Nazi swastika, Roman eagle, Russian bear, Scottish thistle, Soviet hammer and sickle, Swiss cross, Welsh leek *or* daffodil

7 **flag, banner,** oriflamme, **standard,** gonfalon *or* gonfanon, guidon, *vexillum* <L>, *labarum* <L>; **pennant,** pennon, pennoncel, banneret *or* bannerette, banderole, swallowtail, burgee, ensign, **streamer; bunting;** coachwhip, long pennant; **national flag, colors;** royal standard; **ensign,** merchant flag, jack, Jolly Roger, black flag; house flag; Old Glory, Stars and Stripes, Star-Spangled Banner, red, white, and blue <US>; Stars and Bars <Confederacy>; tricolor, *le drapeau tricolore* <Fr>; Union Jack, Union Flag, white *or* red *or* blue ensign <Brit>; yellow flag, white flag; vexillology; signal, 517.15

648 TITLE

<appellation of dignity or distinction>

NOUNS **1** **title, honorific, honor,** title of honor; **handle** *and* handle to one's name <nf>; courtesy title

2 <honorifics> Excellency, Eminence, Reverence, Grace, Honor, Worship, Your *or* His *or* Her Excellency; Lord, My Lord, milord, Lordship, Your *or* His Lordship; Lady, My Lady, milady, Ladyship, Your *or* Her Ladyship; Highness, Royal Highness, Imperial Highness, Serene Highness, Your *or* His *or* Her Highness; Majesty, Royal Majesty, Imperial Majesty, Serene Majesty, Your *or* His *or* Her Majesty

3 Sir, sire, sirrah; Esquire; Master, Mister 76.7; mirza, effendi, sirdar, emir, khan, sahib

4 Mistress, Ms, madame 77.8

5 <ecclesiastical titles> Reverend, His Reverence, His Grace; Monsignor; Holiness, His Holiness; Dom, Brother, Sister, Father, Mother; Rabbi

6 **degree, academic degree** ; **bachelor,** baccalaureate, *baccalaureus* <L>, bachelor's degree; **master,** master's degree; **doctor,** doctorate, doctor's degree, doctoral degree; terminal degree

ADJS **7** **titular,** titulary; honorific; honorary

8 the Noble, the Most Noble, the Most Excellent, the Most Worthy, the Most Worshipful; the Honorable, the Most Honorable, the Right Honorable; the Reverend, the Very Reverend, the Right Reverend, the Most Reverend

649 JUSTICE

NOUNS **1** **justice, justness; equity,** equitableness, level playing field <nf>; **evenhandedness,** measure for measure, give-and-take; balance, equality 790; **right, rightness,** rightfulness, meetness, properness, propriety, what is right; dueness 639; justification, **justifiableness,** justifiability, warrantedness, warrantability, defensibility; poetic justice; retributive justice, nemesis; summary justice, drumhead justice, rude justice; scales of justice; lawfulness, legality 673

2 **fairness,** fair-mindedness, candor; the fair thing, the right *or* proper thing, the handsome thing <nf>; level playing field, **square deal** *and* **fair shake** <nf>; **fair play,** cricket <nf>; sportsmanship, good sportsmanship, sportsmanliness, sportsmanlikeness

3 **impartiality,** detachment, **dispassion,** loftiness, Olympian detachment, **dispassionateness, disinterestedness,** disinterest, unbias, unbiasedness, a fair field and no favor; **neutrality** 467; selflessness, unselfishness 652

4 <personifications> Justice, Justitia, blind *or* blindfolded Justice;

Rhadamanthus, Minos; <deities> Jupiter Fidius, Deus Fidius; Fides, Fides publica Romani, Fides populi Romani; Nemesis, Dike, Themis; Astraea

VERBS **5** **be just, be fair,** do the fair thing, do the handsome thing <nf>, do right, be righteous, do it fair and square, do the right thing by; **do justice to,** see justice done, see one righted *or* redressed, redress a wrong *or* an injustice, remedy an injustice, serve one right, shoot straight with *and* **give a square deal** *or* **fair shake** <nf>; give the Devil his due; give and take; bend *or* lean over backwards, go out of one's way, go the extra mile <nf>

6 **play fair, play the game** <nf>, be a good sport, show a proper spirit; judge on its own merits, hold no brief

ADJS **7** **just, fair,** square, **fair and square; equitable,** balanced, level <nf>, **even,** evenhanded; **right, rightful;** justifiable, justified, warranted, warrantable, defensible; **due** 639.7,10, deserved, merited; meet, meet and right, right and proper, fit, **proper, good,** as it should *or* ought to be; lawful, legal 673.11

8 fair-minded; **sporting,** sportsmanly, sportsmanlike; square-dealing *and* square-shooting <nf>

9 **impartial, impersonal, evenhanded,** equitable, **dispassionate, disinterested,** detached, objective, lofty, Olympian; **unbiased,** uninfluenced, unswayed; **neutral** 467.7; selfless, unselfish 652.5

ADVS **10** **justly, fairly,** fair, in a fair manner; rightfully, rightly, duly, deservedly, meetly, properly; **equitably, equally, evenly,** upon even terms; justifiedly, justifiably, warrantably, warrantedly; **impartially, impersonally, dispassionately, disinterestedly,** without distinction, without regard *or* respect to persons, without fear or favor

11 **in justice,** in equity, in reason, in all conscience, in all fairness, **to be fair,** as is only fair *or* right, as is right *or* just *or* fitting *or* proper

650 INJUSTICE

NOUNS **1** **injustice, unjustness; inequity,** iniquity, inequitableness, iniquitousness; inequality 791, inequality of treatment *or* dealing; **wrong, wrongness,** wrongfulness, unmeetness, improperness, **impropriety;** undueness 640; what should not be, what ought not *or* must not be; unlawfulness, illegality 674

2 **unfairness;** unsportsmanliness, **unsportsmanlikeness;** foul play, foul, a hit below the belt, dirty pool <nf>

3 **partiality, onesidedness; bias,** leaning, inclination, tendentiousness; undispassionateness, undetachment, interest, involvement, **partisanism,** partisanship, *parti pris* <Fr>; unneutrality; **slant,** angle, spin <nf>; **favoritism,** preference, nepotism; unequal *or* preferential treatment, discrimination, unjust legal disability, inequality

4 **injustice, wrong, injury,** grievance, disservice; raw *or* rotten deal *and* bad rap <nf>; imposition; mockery *or* miscarriage of justice; great wrong, grave *or* gross injustice; atrocity, outrage

5 **unjustifiability, unwarrantability,** indefensibility; **inexcusability,** unconscionableness, **unpardonability,** unforgivableness, inexpiableness, irremissibility

VERBS **6** not play fair, hit below the belt, give a raw deal *or* rotten deal *or* bad rap <nf>

7 **do one an injustice, wrong,** do wrong, do wrong by, **do one a wrong,** do a disservice; do a great wrong, do a grave *or* gross injustice, commit an atrocity *or* outrage

8 **favor,** prefer, show preference, **play favorites,** treat unequally, discriminate; **slant,** angle, put on spin <nf>

ADJS **9** **unjust, inequitable,** unequitable, iniquitous, **unbalanced, discriminatory, uneven, unequal** 791.4; **wrong, wrongful,** unrightful; **undue** 640.9, unmeet, undeserved, unmerited; unlawful, illegal 674.6

10 **unfair,** not fair; **unsporting,** unsportsmanly, **unsportsmanlike,** not done, not kosher <nf>, not cricket

<Brit nf>; **dirty** <nf>, foul, below the belt; sexist

11 **partial, interested,** involved, **partisan,** unneutral, **one-sided,** all on *or* way over to one side, undetached, unobjective, **undispassionate, biased,** tendentious, tendential, warped, influenced, swayed, slanted

12 **unjustifiable, unwarrantable,** unallowable, unreasonable, indefensible; **inexcusable,** unconscionable, **unpardonable, unforgivable,** inexpiable, irremissible

ADVS 13 **unjustly, unfairly;** wrongfully, wrongly, undeservedly; inequitably, iniquitously, unequally, unevenly; partially, interestedly, one-sidedly, undispassionately; **unjustifiably, unwarrantably,** unallowably, unreasonably, indefensibly; inexcusably, unconscionably, unpardonably, unforgivably, inexpiably, irremissibly

651 SELFISHNESS

NOUNS 1 **selfishness,** selfism, **self-seeking,** self-serving, self-pleasing, **self-indulgence,** hedonism; self-advancement, self-promotion, self-advertisement; **careerism,** personal ambition; **narcissism, self-love,** self-devotion, self-jealousy, **self-consideration,** self-solicitude, self-sufficiency, self-absorption, ego trip, self-occupation; self-containment, self-isolation; autism, catatonia, remoteness 583.2; **self-interest,** self-concern, self-interestedness, interest; self-esteem, self-admiration 140.1; **self-centeredness, self-obsession, narcissism, egotism** 140.3; **avarice, greed,** graspingness, grabbiness <nf>, acquisitiveness, possessiveness, covetousness; **individualism** 430.5, personalism, privatism, private *or* personal desires, private *or* personal aims; looking out for number one; me generation, entitlement generation

2 **ungenerousness, unmagnanimousness, illiberality,** meanness, smallness, littleness, paltriness, minginess, pettiness; **niggardliness, stinginess** 484.3

3 **self-seeker,** self-pleaser, self-advancer; member of the me generation, member of the entitlement generation; **narcissist, egotist** 140.5; timepleaser, timeserver, temporizer; fortune hunter, moneygrubber, tufthunter, name-dropper; self-server, careerist; opportunist; monopolist, hog, road hog; dog in the manger; **individualist,** loner *and* lone wolf <nf>

VERBS 4 **please oneself,** gratify oneself; ego-trip *and* be *or* go on an ego trip <nf>, be full of oneself; indulge *or* pamper *or* coddle oneself, consult one's own wishes, look after one's own interests, know which side one's bread is buttered on, take care of *or* look out for number one *or* numero uno <nf>, think only of oneself; want everything, have one's cake and eat it; covet; monopolize, hog

ADJS 5 **selfish, self-seeking, self-serving,** self-advancing, self-promoting, self-advertising, careerist, opportunistic, ambitious for self, **self-indulgent,** self-pleasing, hedonistic, self-jealous, self-sufficient, **self-interested,** self-considerative, self-besot, self-devoted, self-occupied, self-absorbed, wrapped up in oneself, self-contained, autistic, remote 583.6; self-esteeming, self-admiring 140.8; **self-centered, self-obsessed, narcissistic, egotistical** 140.10; possessive; **avaricious, greedy,** covetous, grasping, graspy *and* grabby <nf>, acquisitive; **individualistic,** personalistic, privatistic

6 **ungenerous, illiberal,** unchivalrous, mean, small, little, paltry, mingy, petty; **niggardly, stingy** 484.9

ADVS 7 **selfishly, for oneself,** in one's own interest, from selfish *or* interested motives, to gain some private ends

652 UNSELFISHNESS

NOUNS 1 **unselfishness, selflessness;** self-subjection, self-subordination, self-suppression, self-abasement, self-effacement; **humility** 137; modesty 139; self-neglect, self-neglectfulness, self-forgetfulness; **self-renunciation,** self-renouncement; **self-denial,** self-abnegation, self-effacement; **self-sacrifice,** sacrifice, self-immolation, self-devotion, devotion, dedication, commitment, consecration; disinterest, disinterestedness; unpossessiveness, unacquisitiveness; **altruism** 143.4; martyrdom

2 **magnanimity,** magnanimousness, greatness of spirit *or* soul, **generosity,** generousness, openhandedness, **liberality,** liberalness; **bigness, bigheartedness,** greatheartedness, largeheartedness, big *or* large *or* great heart, greatness of heart; noble-mindedness, **high-mindedness, idealism; benevolence** 143.4; **nobleness,** nobility, princeliness, greatness, **loftiness,** elevation, exaltation, sublimity; chivalry, chivalrousness, knightliness, errantry, knight-errantry; heroism; consideration, considerateness, compassion

VERBS **3** not have a selfish bone in one's body, think only of others; be generous to a fault; put oneself out, go out of the way, lean over backwards; sacrifice, make a sacrifice; subject oneself, subordinate oneself, abase oneself; show compassion; take a backseat

4 observe the golden rule, do as one would be done by, do unto others as you would have others do unto you

ADJS **5** **unselfish, selfless;** self-unconscious, self-forgetful, self-abasing, self-effacing; **altruistic** 143.15, **humble; unpretentious, modest** 139.9; self-neglectful, self-neglecting; **self-denying,** self-renouncing, self-abnegating, self-abnegatory, self-effacing; **self-sacrificing,** self-immolating, sacrificing, self-devotional, self-devoted, devoted, dedicated, committed, consecrated, unsparing of self, disinterested; unpossessive, unacquisitive; ready to die for, martyred

6 **magnanimous,** great-souled *or* -spirited; **generous,** generous to a fault, openhanded, **liberal; big, bighearted,** greathearted, largehearted, great of heart *or* soul; noble-minded, **high-minded, idealistic,** public-spirited**; benevolent** 143.15, **noble,** princely, handsome, great, high, elevated, **lofty,** exalted, sublime; chivalrous, knightly; heroic

ADVS **7** **unselfishly, altruistically,** forgetful of self; for others

8 **magnanimously, generously,** openhandedly, **liberally; bigheartedly,** greatheartedly, largeheartedly; **nobly,** handsomely; chivalrously, knightly

653 VIRTUE

<moral goodness>

NOUNS **1** **virtue, virtuousness, goodness, righteousness,** rectitude, right conduct *or* behavior, the straight and narrow, the right thing, integrity; probity 644; **morality,** moral fiber *or* rectitude *or* virtue *or* excellence, morale; **saintliness,** saintlikeness, angelicalness; **godliness** 692.2; aretaics

2 **purity,** immaculacy, immaculateness, spotlessness, unspottedness; upstandingness; **uncorruptness,** uncorruptedness, incorruptness; angel, saint, good egg <nf>; **unsinfulness, sinlessness,** unwickedness, uniniquitousness; undegenerateness, undepravedness, undissoluteness, undebauchedness; **chastity** 664; guiltlessness, innocence 657

3 **cardinal virtues,** natural virtues; prudence, justice, temperance, fortitude; theological virtues *or* supernatural virtues; faith, hope, charity *or* love

VERBS **4** **be good,** do no evil, do the right thing; keep in the right path, walk the straight path, follow the straight and narrow, keep on the straight and narrow way *or* path, fly right, resist temptation; fight the good fight

ADJS **5** **virtuous, good, moral; upright, honest** 644.13,14,16; **righ-**

teous, just, straight, rightminded, right-thinking; **angelic,** seraphic; **saintly,** saintlike; **godly** 692.9; irreproachable; goody-goody

6 **chaste, immaculate, spotless, pure** 664.4; **clean,** squeaky-clean <nf>; guiltless, **innocent** 657.6; pure as the driven snow

7 **uncorrupt,** uncorrupted, incorrupt, incorrupted; **unsinful,** sinless; **unwicked,** uniniquitous, unerring, unfallen; undegenerate, undepraved, undemoralized, undissolute, undebauched

654 VICE

<moral badness>

NOUNS 1 **vice,** viciousness; criminality, **wrongdoing** 655; **immorality,** unmorality, **evil; amorality** 636.4; **unvirtuousness,** ungoodness; **unrighteousness, ungodliness,** unsaintliness, unangelicalness; **uncleanness, impurity, unchastity** 665, fallenness, fallen state, lapsedness; waywardness, wantonness, prodigality; delinquency, moral delinquency; peccability; backsliding, recidivism; **evil nature, carnality** 663.2

2 **vice, weakness,** weakness of the flesh, **flaw,** moral flaw *or* blemish, **frailty, infirmity; failing,** failure; weak point, weak side, foible; bad habit, besetting sin; **fault, imperfection** 1003; laxity, lack of principle

3 **iniquity, evil,** bad, wrong, error, obliquity, villainy, knavery, reprobacy, peccancy, **abomination, atrocity, infamy,** shame, disgrace, scandal, unforgivable *or* cardinal *or* mortal sin, **sin** 655.2; seven deadly sins, pride, covetousness *or* avarice, lust, anger, gluttony, envy, sloth

4 **wickedness, badness,** naughtiness, **evilness, viciousness, sinfulness, iniquitousness,** wicked ways; **baseness,** rankness, **vileness,** foulness, arrantness, nefariousness, **heinousness,** infamousness, villainousness, flagitiousness; fiendishness, hellishness; devilishness, devilry, deviltry; bad egg <nf>

5 **turpitude, moral turpitude; corruption,** corruptedness, corruptness, rottenness, moral pollution *or* pollutedness, lack *or* absence of moral fiber; **decadence** *or* decadency, debasement, **degradation,** demoralization, abjection; **degeneracy,** degenerateness, degeneration, reprobacy, **depravity,** depravedness, depravation, corruption, perversion; **dissoluteness, profligacy;** abandonment, abandon; notoriety

6 **obduracy, hardheartedness, hardness, callousness,** heartlessness, hardness of heart, heart of stone

7 **sewer, gutter, pit, sink, sink of corruption**, sinkhole; **den of iniquity,** den, **fleshpot,** hellhole; hole *and* joint *and* the pits <nf>; Sodom, Gomorrah, Babylon; **brothel** 665.9; road to hell; hellhole

VERBS 8 **do wrong, sin** 655.4; misbehave, misdemean *and* misdo

9 **go wrong,** stray, go astray, **err,** deviate, deviate from the path of virtue, leave the straight and narrow, step out of line, get or go off base <nf>; **fall,** fall from grace, **lapse,** slip, trip; **degenerate; go to the bad** 395.24, go to the dogs; **relapse,** recidivate, backslide 394.4

10 **corrupt; sully, soil, defile;** demoralize, vitiate; mislead; seduce, tempt

ADJS 11 vice-prone, vice-laden, vicious, **steeped in vice; immoral,** unmoral; **amoral,** nonmoral; unethical

12 **unvirtuous,** virtueless, ungood; **unrighteous, ungodly,** unsaintly, unangelic; morally weak, lax; **unclean, impure,** spotted, flawed, blemished, maculate , **unchaste** 665.23; fleshly, carnal 663.6, wayward, wanton, prodigal; erring, **fallen, lapsed,** postlapsarian; frail, weak, infirm; Adamic; peccable; **relapsing, backsliding,** recidivist, recidivistic; of easy virtue 665.26

13 **diabolic, diabolical, devilish,** demonic, demoniac, demoniacal, **satanic,** Mephistophelian; **fiendish,** fiendlike; **hellish,** hellborn, **infernal**

14 **corrupt,** corrupted, vice-corrupted, polluted, morally polluted, rotten, tainted, contaminated, vitiated; warped, perverted; **decadent,** debased, degraded, reprobate, **depraved, debauched,** debaucherous, **dissolute, degenerate,** profligate, abandoned, gone to the bad *or* dogs, sunk *or* steeped in iniquity, rotten at *or* to the core, in the sewer *or* gutter

15 **evil-minded,** evilhearted, **blackhearted; base-minded,** low-minded; low-thoughted, dirty *or* dirty-minded <nf>; crooked

16 **wicked, evil, vicious, bad, naughty, wrong, sinful, iniquitous,** peccant, reprobate; dark, black; **base, low, vile,** foul, rank, flagrant, arrant, nefarious, **heinous,** villainous, criminal, up to no good, knavish, flagitious; abominable, atrocious, monstrous, unspeakable, execrable, damnable; shameful, disgraceful, scandalous, **infamous, unpardonable,** unforgivable; **improper,** reprehensible, blamable, blameworthy, unworthy

17 **hardened, hard, case-hardened, obdurate,** inured, indurated; **callous,** calloused, **seared; hardhearted,** heartless; **shameless,** lost to shame, blind to virtue, lost to all sense of honor, conscienceless, unblushing, **brazen**

18 **irreclaimable,** irredeemable, unredeemable, unregenerate, **irreformable,** incorrigible, past praying for; shriftless, graceless; **lost**

ADVS 19 **wickedly, evilly, sinfully, iniquitously,** peccantly, **viciously;** basely, vilely, foully, rankly, arrantly, flagrantly, flagitiously

655 WRONGDOING

NOUNS 1 **wrongdoing, evildoing, wickedness,** misdoing , wrong conduct, **misbehavior** 322, **misconduct,** misdemeaning, misfeasance, malfeasance, malversation, **malpractice,** evil courses, machinations of the devil; **sin; crime, criminality,** lawbreaking, feloniousness, trespass, offense, transgression, infringement, infraction, breach, encroachment; criminal tendency; habitual criminality, criminosis; viciousness, **vice** 654; misprision, negative *or* positive misprision, misprision of treason *or* felony

2 **misdeed, misdemeanor,** misfeasance, malfeasance, malefaction, criminal *or* guilty *or* sinful act, **offense,** injustice, injury, **wrong, iniquity, evil,** peccancy, *malum* <L>; tort; **error, fault,** breach; **impropriety,** slight *or* minor wrong, venial sin, **indiscretion,** peccadillo, misstep, trip, slip, lapse; **transgression,** trespass; **sin; cardinal** *or* **deadly** *or* **mortal sin,** grave *or* heavy sin, unutterable sin, unpardonable *or* unforgivable *or* inexpiable sin, original sin, capital sin, carnal sin; sin against the Holy Ghost; sin of commission; sin of omission, nonfeasance, omission, failure, dereliction, delinquency; **crime, felony;** capital crime; white-collar crime, execu-crime; computer crime; copycat crime <nf>; war crime, crime against humanity, genocide, terrorism; **outrage, atrocity,** enormity

3 **original sin,** fall from grace, fall, fall of man, fall of Adam *or* Adam's fall, sin of Adam; **cardinal sins,** lust, gluttony, greed, sloth, wrath, envy, pride

VERBS 4 **do wrong,** do amiss, misdo , misdemean oneself, **misbehave** 322.4, **err,** offend; **sin,** commit sin; **transgress,** trespass

ADJS 5 **wrongdoing, evildoing,** malefactory, malfeasant; **wrong,** iniquitous, **sinful, wicked** 654.16; **criminal,** felonious, criminous ; crime-infested, crime-ridden

656 GUILT

NOUNS 1 **guilt, guiltiness; criminality,** peccancy; guilty *or* wrongful *or* criminal involvement; **culpability,** reprehensibility, blamability, blameworthiness; chargeability, answerability, much to answer for; censurability, censurableness, reproachability, reproachableness, reprovability, reprovableness, inculpation, implication, involvement, complicity, impeachability, impeachableness, indictability, indictableness, arraignability, arraignableness; bloodguilt *or* -guiltiness, red-handedness, dirty hands, red *or* bloody hands; much to answer for; **ruth**, ruefulness, remorse, guilty conscience, guilt feelings; onus, burden

VERBS **2** be guilty, look guilty, have no alibi, look like the cat that swallowed the canary, blush, stammer; have on one's hands *or* to one's discredit, have much to answer for; have a red face; be caught in the act *or* flatfooted *or* redhanded, be caught with one's pants down *or* with one's hand in the till *or* with one's hand in the cookie jar <nf>; guilt someone <nf>

ADJS **3** **guilty,** guilty as hell, peccant, **criminal, to blame, at fault,** faulty, in the wrong, on one's head; **culpable,** reprehensible, censurable, reproachable, reprovable, inculpated, implicated, involved, impeachable, indictable, arraignable; red-handed, bloodguilty; caught in the act *or* flatfooted *or* red-handed, caught with one's pants down *or* with one's hand in the till *or* with one's hand in the cookie jar <nf>

ADVS **4** **red-handed,** red-hand, **in the act,** in the very act, *in flagrante delicto* <L>

5 **guilty,** shamefacedly, sheepishly, with a guilty conscience

657 INNOCENCE

NOUNS **1** **innocence,** innocency, innocentness; unfallen *or* unlapsed *or* prelapsarian state, state of grace; unguiltiness, **guiltlessness,** faultlessness, blamelessness, reproachlessness, **sinlessness,** offenselessness; **spotlessness,** stainlessness, taintlessness, unblemishedness; **purity,** cleanness, cleanliness, whiteness, immaculateness, immaculacy, impeccability; clean hands, clean slate, clear conscience, nothing to hide

2 childlikeness 416.1; lamblikeness, dove-likeness, angelicness; unacquaintance with evil, uncorruptedness, incorruptness, pristineness, undefiledness; naiveté

3 **inculpability,** unblamability, unblamableness, **unblameworthiness,** irreproachability, irreproachableness, impeccability, impeccableness, unexceptionability, unexceptionableness, **irreprehensibility,** irreprehensibleness, uncensurability, uncensurableness, unimpeachability, unimpeachableness, unindictableness, unarraignableness

4 **innocent,** baby, babe, babe in arms, newborn babe, infant, babe in the woods, child, mere child, lamb, dove, angel; virgin

VERBS **5** know no wrong, have clean hands, have a clear conscience, look as if butter would not melt in one's mouth; have nothing to hide

ADJS **6** **innocent;** unfallen, unlapsed, prelapsarian; **unguilty,** not guilty, **guiltless, faultless, blameless,** reproachless, **sinless,** offenseless, with clean hands; clear, in the clear; without reproach, *sans reproche* <Fr>; innocent as a lamb, lamblike, dovelike, angelic, childlike 416.5; unacquainted with *or* untouched by evil, uncorrupted, incorrupt, pristine, undefiled; innocuous

7 **spotless,** stainless, taintless, unblemished, unspotted, **untainted, unsoiled, unsullied, undefiled,** wemless; **pure, clean, immaculate,** impeccable, white, pure *or* white as driven snow, squeaky-clean <nf>

8 **inculpable,** unblamable, unblameworthy, **irreproachable,** beyond reproach, irreprovable, **irreprehensible,** uncensurable, unimpeachable, unindictable, unarraignable, unobjectionable, unexceptionable, above suspicion, squeaky-clean <nf>, with clean hands

ADVS **9** **innocently, guiltlessly, unguiltily,** with a clear conscience; **unknowingly,** unconsciously, unawares

658 ATONEMENT

NOUNS 1 **atonement, reparation, amends,** making amends, **restitution, propitiation, expiation, redress, recompense,** compensation, setting right, making right *or* good, making up, squaring, redemption, reclamation, satisfaction, quittance; making it quits; indemnity, indemnification; compromise, composition; expiatory offering *or* sacrifice, piaculum, peace offering; eye for an eye, measure for measure; conciliation, propitiation

2 **apology, excuse,** regrets; acknowledgment, penitence, contrition, breast-beating, *mea culpa* <L>, confession 351.3; abject apology

3 **penance,** penitence, repentance; penitential act *or* exercise, **mortification,** maceration, flagellation, lustration; sacrifice, offering, peace offering; **asceticism** 667, **fasting** 515; **purgation,** purgatory; **sackcloth and ashes;** hair shirt; **Lent;** Day of Atonement, Yom Kippur

VERBS 4 **atone, atone for, propitiate, expiate,** compensate, restitute, recompense, redress, redeem, repair, satisfy, give satisfaction, **make amends, make reparation** *or* **compensation** *or* **expiation** *or* **restitution,** make good *or* right, rectify, set right, **make up for,** make matters up, square, square things, make it quits, pay the forfeit *or* penalty, pay one's dues <nf>, pay back, wipe off old scores; wipe the slate clean; set one's house in order; live down, unlive; reconcile, propitiate

5 **apologize, beg pardon, ask forgiveness,** beg indulgence, express regret; take back; get *or* fall down on one's knees, get down on one's marrowbones <nf>, come hat in hand; confess, admit

6 **do penance,** flagellate oneself, mortify oneself, mortify one's flesh, make oneself miserable, shrive oneself, purge oneself, cleanse oneself of guilt, stand in a white sheet, repent in sackcloth and ashes, wear a hair shirt, wear sackcloth *or* sackcloth and ashes; receive absolution; regret, show remorse *or* compunction

ADJS 7 **atoning, propitiatory, expiatory,** piacular, reparative, reparatory, restitutive, restitutory, restitutional, redressing, recompensing, compensatory, compensational, righting, squaring, conciliatory; redemptive, redeeming, reclamatory, satisfactional; **apologetic, apologetical;** repentant, repenting; **penitential,** purgative, purgatorial; lustral, lustrative, lustrational, cleansing, purifying; ascetic

659 GOOD PERSON

NOUNS 1 good person, fine person, good *or* fine man *or* woman *or* child, worthy, prince, nature's nobleman *or* -woman, man *or* woman after one's own heart; *persona grata* <L>, acceptable person; **good fellow,** capital fellow, **good sort,** right sort, a decent sort of fellow, good lot <Brit nf>, no end of a fellow; real person, real man *or* woman, mensch <nf>, cool cat <nf>; **gentleman,** perfect gentleman, a gentleman and a scholar; **lady,** perfect lady; **gem,** jewel, pearl, diamond; rough diamond, diamond in the rough; honest man 644.8

2 <nf terms> **good guy,** crackerjack, brick, trump, good egg, stout fellow, nice guy, Mr Nice Guy, good Joe, likely lad, no slouch, doll, living doll, pussycat, **sweetheart, sweetie**

3 **good** *or* **respectable citizen,** excellent *or* exemplary citizen, good neighbor, burgher, taxpayer, **pillar of society,** pillar of the church, salt of the earth; Christian *and* true Christian <nf>

4 **paragon, ideal,** beau ideal, nonpareil, person to look up to, *chevalier sans peur et sans reproche* <Fr>, **good example, role model,** shining example, gold standard; exemplar, epitome; **model, pattern, standard,** norm, mirror; *Übermensch* <Ger>; **standout,** one in a thousand *or* ten thousand, man of men, a man among men, woman of women, a woman among women

5 **hero, god, demigod,** phoenix; **heroine, goddess,** demigoddess; **idol;** fairy godmother

6 holy man; great soul, mahatma; guru; saint, angel 679

660 BAD PERSON

NOUNS **1** bad person, bad man *or* woman *or* child, unworthy *or* disreputable person, unworthy, disreputable, **undesirable,** *persona non grata* <L>, unacceptable *or* unwanted *or* objectionable person, baddy *and* wrongo *and* bad news <nf>; bad egg, bad example

2 **wretch,** mean *or* miserable wretch, **beggarly fellow, beggar, blighter** <Brit nf>; **bum** *and* bummer *and* lowlifer *and* lowlife *and* **mucker** <nf>, caitiff, budmash <India>, pilgarlic; devil, **poor devil,** *pauvre diable* <Fr>, poor creature, *mauvais sujet* <Fr>; **sad case,** sad sack *and* sad sack of shit <nf>; **good-for-nothing, good-for-naught, no-good** <nf>, **ne'er-do-well,** wastrel, *vaurien* <Fr>, worthless fellow; **derelict,** skid-row bum, Bowery bum, tramp, hobo, beachcomber, **drifter,** drunkard, vagrant, vag <nf>, vagabond, truant, stiff *and* bindlestiff <nf>; human wreck; trailer trash, white trash

3 **rascal,** precious rascal, rogue, knave, **scoundrel,** villain, blackguard, **scamp, scalawag** <nf>, rapscallion, **devil;** shyster; sneak

4 **reprobate,** recreant, **miscreant,** bad *or* sorry lot <Brit nf>, bad egg *and* wrongo *and* wrong number <nf>, bad'un *or* wrong'un <Brit nf>; scapegrace, black sheep; lost soul, lost sheep, *âme damnée* <Fr>, backslider, recidivist, fallen angel; degenerate, pervert; profligate, **lecher** 665.11; trollop, **whore** 665.14,16; **pimp** 665.18

5 <nf terms> **asshole, prick, bastard, son of a bitch** *or* SOB, **jerk, horse's ass,** creep, motherfucker, mother, dork, **shit,** turd, birdturd, shithead, shitface, cuntface, dickhead, fart, **louse, meanie, heel, shitheel, rat,** rat bastard, **stinker,** stinkard, pill, bugger, dirtbag, dweeb, twerp, sleaze, sleazoid, sleazebag, bad lot <Brit>; **hood, hooligan** 593.4

6 beast, **animal; cur,** dog, hound, whelp, mongrel; **reptile,** viper, serpent, snake; vermin, varmint <nf>, hyena; **swine,** pig; **skunk,** polecat; insect, worm

7 cad, bounder *and* rotter <nf>

8 **wrongdoer, malefactor, sinner,** transgressor, delinquent; malfeasor, misfeasor, nonfeasor; misdemeanant, misdemeanist; **culprit, offender; evil person, evil man** *or* **woman** *or* **child, evildoer** 593

9 **criminal, felon, perpetrator, crook** *and* perp <nf>, public enemy, **lawbreaker,** scofflaw; **gangster** *and* mobster *and* wiseguy <nf>, **racketeer; swindler** 357.3; thief 483; thug 593.3; **desperado,** desperate criminal; **outlaw,** fugitive, **convict,** jailbird, gaolbird <Brit>; gallows bird <nf>; **traitor,** betrayer, quisling, Judas, double-dealer, two-timer <nf>, **deceiver** 357; stalker

10 **the underworld,** gangland, gangdom, **organized crime,** organized crime family, the rackets, the mob, the syndicate, the Mafia, Cosa Nostra, Black Hand; **gangsterism; gangster,** ganglord, gangleader, caporegime *or* capo, button man, soldier

11 **the wicked,** the bad, the evil, the unrighteous, the reprobate; sons of men, sons of Belial, sons *or* children of the devil, limbs *or* get *or* imps of Satan, children of darkness; **scum of the earth,** dregs of society

661 DISREPUTE

NOUNS **1** **disrepute, ill repute,** bad repute, bad *or* poor reputation, evil repute *or* reputation, ill fame, shady *or* unsavory reputation, **bad name,** bad odor, bad report, bad character; **disesteem, dishonor,** public dishonor, **discredit; disfavor,** ill-favor; disapprobation 510.1

2 **disreputability,** disreputableness, **notoriety;** discreditableness, dishonorableness, unsavoriness,

unrespectability; disgracefulness, **shamefulness**

3 **baseness, lowness, meanness, crumminess** <nf>, poorness, pettiness, paltriness, smallness, littleness, pokiness, cheesiness <nf>, beggarliness, **shabbiness, shoddiness, squalor,** scrubbiness, scumminess, scabbiness, scurviness, scruffiness, shittiness <nf>; **abjectness, wretchedness,** miserableness, despicableness, contemptibleness, contemptibility, abominableness, execrableness, obnoxiousness; **vulgarity,** tastelessness, crudity, crudeness, tackiness *and* chintziness <nf>; **vileness** 98.2, foulness, rankness, fulsomeness, grossness, nefariousness, heinousness, **atrociousness,** monstrousness, enormity; degradation, debasement, depravity

4 **infamy,** infamousness; **ignominy,** ignominiousness; ingloriousness, **ignobility,** odium, obloquy, opprobrium; depluming, displuming, loss of honor *or* name *or* repute *or* face; degradation, comedown <nf>, **demotion** 447

5 **disgrace, scandal, humiliation; shame,** dirty shame *and* low-down dirty shame <nf>, crying *or* burning shame; **reproach,** byword, byword of reproach, a disgrace to one's name

6 **stigma,** stigmatism, onus; **brand,** badge of infamy; **slur,** reproach, censure, reprimand, imputation, aspersion, reflection, stigmatization; pillorying; **black eye** <nf>, black mark; **disparagement** 512; **stain, taint,** attaint, **tarnish,** blur, **smirch,** smutch *or* smooch, smudge, **smear,** spot, blot, blot on *or* in one's escutcheon *or* scutcheon; bend *or* bar sinister <heraldry>; baton *and* champain *and* point champain <heraldry>; mark of Cain; broad arrow <Brit>; shady past

VERBS 7 **incur disgrace,** incur disesteem *or* dishonor *or* discredit, get a black eye <nf>, be shamed, earn a bad name *or* reproach *or* reproof, forfeit one's good opinion, fall into disrepute, seal one's infamy; lose one's good name, **lose face,** lose countenance, lose credit, **lose caste; disgrace oneself,** lower oneself, demean oneself, drag one's banner in the dust, degrade *or* debase oneself, act beneath oneself, dirty *or* soil one's hands, get one's hands dirty, sully *or* lower oneself, derogate, stoop, descend, ride to a fall, fall from one's high estate, fall from grace *or* favor, foul one's own nest; **scandalize,** make oneself notorious, put one's good name in jeopardy; compromise oneself; raise eyebrows, cause eyebrows to raise, cause tongues to wag

8 **disgrace, dishonor, discredit,** reflect discredit upon, bring into discredit, reproach, cast reproach upon, be a reproach to; **shame, put to shame,** impute shame to, hold up to shame; hold up to public shame *or* public scorn *or* public ridicule, pillory, bring shame upon, **humiliate** 137.4; **degrade, debase** 447.3, deplume, displume, defrock, unfrock, bring low

9 **stigmatize, brand; stain, besmirch,** smirch, tarnish, taint, attaint, blot, **blacken, smear,** bespatter, desecrate, **sully,** soil, defile, vilify, **slur,** cast a slur upon, blow upon; disapprove 510.10; **disparage, defame** 512.9; censure, reprimand, **give a black eye** <nf>, give a black mark, put in one's bad *or* black books; give a bad name, give a dog a bad name; expose, expose to infamy; pillory, gibbet; burn *or* hang in effigy; **skewer,** impale, crucify

ADJS 10 **disreputable, discreditable, dishonorable,** unsavory, shady, **seamy, sordid; unrespectable, ignoble, ignominious, infamous,** inglorious; notorious; unpraiseworthy; derogatory 512.13

11 **disgraceful, shameful,** pitiful, deplorable, opprobrious, sad, sorry, too bad; degrading, debasing, demeaning, beneath one, beneath one's dignity, *infra indignitatem* <L>, infra dig <nf>, unbecoming, unworthy of one; cheap, gutter; **humiliating,** humiliative; **scandalous,** shocking, outrageous

12 **base, low,** low rent *and* low ride *and* low-down *and* cotton-picking <nf>, **mean,** crummy <nf>, poor, petty, paltry, small, little, **shabby, shoddy, squalid,** lumpen, scrubby, scummy, scabby, **scurvy,** scruffy, mangy <nf>, measly *and* cheesy <nf>, poky, beggarly, **wretched, miserable,** abject, **despicable, contemptible,** abominable, execrable, obnoxious, **vulgar,** tasteless, crude, **tacky** *and* chintzy <nf>; **disgusting, odious** 98.18, vile, foul, **dirty,** rank, fulsome, gross, flagrant, grave, arrant, nefarious, heinous, reptilian, **atrocious,** monstrous, unspeakable, unmentionable; degraded, debased, depraved

13 **in disrepute,** in bad repute, in bad odor; **in disfavor,** in discredit, **in bad** <nf>, in one's bad *or* black books, out of favor, out of countenance, at a discount; **in disgrace,** in Dutch *and* **in the doghouse** <nf>, under a cloud; scandal-plagued *or* -ridden; stripped of reputation, disgraced, discredited, dishonored, shamed, loaded with shame, unable to show one's face; **in trouble**

14 **unrenowned,** renownless, nameless, inglorious, **unnotable, unnoted,** unnoticed, unremarked, **undistinguished, unfamed,** uncelebrated, unsung, unhonored, unglorified, unpopular; no credit to; **unknown,** little known, obscure, unheard-of, *ignotus* <L>

ADVS 15 **disreputably, discreditably, dishonorably, unrespectably, ignobly, ignominiously, infamously,** ingloriously

16 **disgracefully, scandalously,** shockingly, deplorably, outrageously; **shamefully,** to one's shame, to one's shame be it spoken

17 **basely, meanly,** poorly, pettily, **shabbily, shoddily,** scurvily, **wretchedly, miserably,** abjectly, **despicably, contemptibly,** abominably, execrably, obnoxiously, **odiously** 98.26, **vilely,** foully, grossly, flagrantly, arrantly, nefariously, heinously, **atrociously,** monstrously

662 REPUTE

NOUNS 1 **repute, reputation; name,** character, figure; **fame,** famousness, **renown, kudos,** report, **glory;** éclat, **celebrity, popularity,** recognition, a place in the sun; popular acceptance *or* favor, vogue; **acclaim, public acclaim,** réclame, **publicity; notoriety,** notoriousness, talk of the town; **exposure;** play *and* air-play <nf>

2 **reputability,** reputableness; good reputation, good name, **good** *or* **high repute,** good report, good track record <nf>, good odor, face, fair name, name to conjure with; good reference; good color

3 **esteem,** estimation, **honor, regard, respect,** approval, approbation, account, favor, consideration, **credit,** credibility, points *and* Brownie points <nf>

4 **prestige, honor; dignity; rank, standing,** stature, high place, eminence, position, station, face, **status**

5 **distinction, mark, note; importance, consequence,** significance; **notability, prominence, eminence, preeminence, greatness,** conspicuousness, outstandingness; **stardom;** elevation, exaltation, exaltedness, loftiness, high and mightiness <nf>; nobility, grandeur, sublimity; excellence 999.1, supereminence 999.2

6 **illustriousness, luster,** brilliance *or* brilliancy, radiance, splendor, resplendence *or* resplendency, refulgence *or* refulgency, refulgentness, **glory,** blaze of glory, nimbus, halo, aura, envelope; charisma, mystique, glamour, numinousness, magic; cult of personality, personality cult; claim to fame; fifteen minutes of fame

7 <posthumous fame> **memory, remembrance,** blessed *or* sacred memory, legend, heroic legend *or* myth; **immortality,** lasting *or* undying fame, niche in the hall of fame, secure place in history; immortal name

8 **glorification, ennoblement,** dignification, **exaltation,** elevation, enskying, enskyment, magnification, aggrandizement; enthronement;

immortalization, enshrinement; beatification, canonization, sainting, sanctification; **deification, apotheosis;** lionization

9 **celebrity,** man *or* woman of mark *or* note, person of note *or* consequence, **notable, notability, luminary, great man** *or* **woman,** eminence, master spirit, worthy, name, **big name,** figure, public figure, **somebody; important person, VIP** *and* **standout** <nf>, personage 997.8, one in a hundred *or* thousand *or* million etc; cynosure, model, very model, ideal type, **idol,** popular idol, tin god *or* little tin god <nf>; lion, social lion, pillar of the community; hero, heroine, popular hero, pop hero <nf>, folk hero, superhero; **star, superstar,** megastar, hot stuff <nf>; cult figure *or* hero; **immortal;** luminaries, galaxy, pleiad, constellation; celebutante; semicelebrity; favorite

VERBS 10 **be somebody,** be something, **impress,** charismatize; **figure,** make *or* cut a figure, cut a dash *and* make a splash <nf>, **make a noise in the world,** make *or* leave one's mark; live, **flourish; shine,** glitter, gleam, glow

11 **gain recognition,** be recognized, get a reputation, **make a name** *or* make a name for oneself, make oneself known, come into one's own, come to the front *or* fore, come into vogue; **burst onto the scene,** become an overnight celebrity, come onto the scene <nf>, come out of the woods *or* out of nowhere *or* out of left field <nf>; make points *or* Brownie points <nf>

12 **honor,** confer *or* bestow honor upon; **dignify,** adorn, grace; **distinguish,** signalize, confer distinction on, give credit where credit is due

13 **glorify,** glamorize; **exalt,** elevate, ensky, raise, uplift, set up, **ennoble,** aggrandize, magnify, exalt to the skies; crown; throne, enthrone; immortalize, enshrine, hand one's name down to posterity, make legendary; beatify, canonize, saint, sanctify; **deify,** apotheosize, apotheose; **lionize**

14 **reflect honor,** lend credit *or* distinction, shed a luster, redound to one's honor, give one a reputation

ADJS 15 **reputable,** highly reputed, of repute, **estimable, esteemed,** much *or* highly esteemed, **honorable,** honored; **meritorious,** worth one's salt, noble, worthy, creditable; respected, respectable, highly respectable; revered, reverend, venerable, venerated, worshipful; **well-thought-of,** highly regarded, held in esteem, in good odor, in favor, in high favor; in one's good books; prestigious

16 **distinguished,** distingué; **noted, notable,** marked, of note, of mark; **famous,** famed, honored, **renowned, celebrated, popular,** in favor, acclaimed, much acclaimed, sought-after, hot *and* world-class <nf>, **notorious, well-known,** best-known, in everyone's mouth, on everyone's tongue *or* lips, talked-of, talked-about; far-famed, far-heard; fabled, legendary, mythical

17 **prominent, conspicuous, outstanding,** stickout <nf>, much in evidence, to the front, in the limelight <nf>; **important,** consequential, significant

18 **eminent, high, exalted,** elevated, enskyed, lofty, sublime, held in awe, awesome; immortal; **great,** big <nf>, **grand;** excellent 999.12, 15, supereminent, mighty, high and mighty <nf>; glorified, ennobled, magnified, aggrandized; enthroned, throned; immortalized, shrined, enshrined; beatified, canonized, sainted, sanctified; **idolized, godlike, deified,** apotheosized

19 **illustrious,** lustrous, glorious, brilliant, radiant, splendid, splendorous, splendrous, splendent, resplendent, bright, shining; charismatic, glamorous, numinous, magic, magical

ADVS 20 **reputably, estimably, honorably,** nobly, respectably, worthily, creditably

21 **famously, notably, notedly, notoriously,** popularly, celebratedly; **prominently, eminently,** conspicuously, outstandingly; **illustriously,** gloriously

663 SENSUALITY

NOUNS 1 **sensuality,** sensualness, sensualism; appetitiveness, appetite; **voluptuousness,** luxuriousness, luxury; **unchastity** 665; **pleasure-seeking;** sybaritism; **self-indulgence, hedonism,** Cyrenaic hedonism, Cyrenaicism, ethical hedonism, psychological hedonism, hedonics, hedonic calculus; epicurism, epicureanism; pleasure principle; **instant gratification;** sensuousness 24.1

2 **carnality,** carnal-mindedness; **fleshliness,** flesh; animal *or* carnal nature, the flesh, the beast, Adam, the Old Adam, the offending Adam, fallen state *or* nature, lapsed state *or* nature, postlapsarian state *or* nature; **animality, animalism, bestiality,** beastliness, brutishness, **brutality;** coarseness, grossness; swinishness; **earthiness,** unspirituality, nonspirituality, materialism; erotica

3 **sensualist, voluptuary, pleasure-seeker,** sybarite, Cyrenaic, Sardanapalus, Heliogabalus, **hedonist,** *bon vivant* <Fr>, carpet knight; epicure, epicurean; gourmet, gourmand; swine

VERBS 4 sensualize, carnalize, coarsen, brutify; *carpe diem* <L, seize the day>, live for the moment

ADJS 5 **sensual,** sensualist, sensualistic; appetitive; **voluptuous,** luxurious; **unchaste** 665.23, **hedonistic, pleasure-seeking,** pleasure-bent, bent on pleasure, luxury-loving, hedonic, epicurean, sybaritic; Cyrenaic; sensory, sensuous

6 **carnal,** carnal-minded, **fleshly,** bodily, physical; Adamic, fallen, lapsed, postlapsarian; animal, animalistic; **brutish, brutal,** brute; **bestial,** beastly, beastlike; Circean; coarse, gross; swinish; orgiastic; **earthy,** unspiritual, nonspiritual, material, materialistic

664 CHASTITY

NOUNS 1 **chastity, virtue,** virtuousness, honor; **purity,** cleanness, cleanliness; whiteness, snowiness; **immaculacy,** immaculateness, spotlessness, stainlessness, taintlessness, blotlessness, unspottedness, unstainedness, unblottedness, untaintedness, unblemishedness, unsoiledness, unsulliedness, undefiledness, untarnishedness; uncorruptness; sexual innocence, innocence 657

2 **decency, seemliness, propriety, decorum,** decorousness, elegance, delicacy; **modesty,** shame, pudicity, pudency

3 **continence** *or* continency; abstemiousness, abstaining, abstinence 668.2; celibacy; **virginity,** intactness, maidenhood, maidenhead; Platonic love; marital fidelity *or* faithfulness

ADJS 4 **chaste, virtuous; pure,** purehearted, pure in heart; **clean,** cleanly; **immaculate, spotless,** blotless, stainless, taintless, white, snowy, pure *or* white as driven snow; **unsoiled, unsullied, undefiled,** untarnished, unstained, unspotted, untainted, unblemished, unblotted, uncorrupt; sexually innocent, innocent 657.6

5 **decent, modest, decorous,** delicate, elegant, proper, becoming, seemly

6 **continent;** abstemious, abstinent 668.10; celibate; virginal, **virgin,** maidenly, vestal, intact; Platonic

7 **undebauched, undissipated, undissolute,** unwanton, unlicentious

665 UNCHASTITY

NOUNS 1 **unchastity,** unchasteness; unvirtuousness; **impurity,** uncleanness, uncleanliness, taintedness, soiledness, sulliedness; **indecency** 666

2 **incontinence,** uncontinence; intemperance 669; unrestraint 430.3

3 **profligacy, dissoluteness, licentiousness,** license, unbridledness, wildness, fastness, rakishness, gallantry, **libertinism,** libertinage; **dissipation, debauchery,** debauchment; venery, wenching, whoring, womanizing

4 **wantonness, waywardness; looseness,** laxity, lightness, loose morals, easy virtue, whorishness,

chambering, **promiscuity,** sleeping around *and* swinging <nf>

5 **lasciviousness, lechery, lecherousness, lewdness,** bawdiness, **dirtiness,** salacity, salaciousness, **carnality,** animality, fleshliness, **sexuality, sexiness, lust, lustfulness**; **obscenity** 666.4; **prurience** *or* pruriency, sexual itch, concupiscence, lickerishness, libidinousness, randiness, horniness <nf>, lubricity, lubriciousness, **sensuality,** eroticism, goatishness; satyrism, satyriasis, gynecomania; nymphomania, *furor uterinus* <L>, hysteromania, uteromania, clitoromania; erotomania, eroticomania, aphrodisiomania

6 **seduction,** seducement, **betrayal; violation,** abuse; **debauchment, defilement,** ravishment, ravage, despoilment, fate worse than death; priapism; defloration, deflowering; **rape,** sexual *or* criminal assault; date *or* acquaintance rape

7 <illicit sexual intercourse> **adultery,** criminal conversation *or* congress *or* cohabitation, extramarital *or* premarital sex, extramarital *or* premarital relations, extracurricular sex *or* relations <nf>, **fornication;** free love, free-lovism; **incest;** concubinage; cuckoldry

8 **prostitution, harlotry,** whoredom, **street-walking;** soliciting, solicitation; Mrs Warren's profession; whoremonging, whoremastery, pimping, pandering

9 **brothel, house of prostitution,** house of assignation, house of joy *or* ill repute *or* ill fame, **whorehouse,** bawdyhouse, massage parlor, sporting house, disorderly house, **cathouse, bordello,** bagnio, stew, dive, den of vice, den *or* sink of iniquity, crib, joint; panel house *or* den; red-light district, tenderloin, stews, street of fallen women

10 **libertine, swinger** <nf>, **profligate, rake,** rakehell, rip <nf>, **roué,** wanton, womanizer, cocksman <nf>, walking phallus, debauchee, rounder , **wolf** <nf>, woman chaser, skirt chaser <nf>, gay dog, gay deceiver, gallant, philanderer, loverboy <nf>, lady-killer, Lothario, Don Juan, Casanova

11 **lecher, satyr, goat,** old goat, **dirty old man;** whorer *or* whoremonger , whoremaster, whorehound <nf>; Priapus; gynecomaniac; erotomaniac, eroticomaniac, aphrodisiomaniac

12 **seducer, betrayer,** deceiver; **debaucher, ravisher,** ravager, violator, despoiler, defiler; raper, **rapist**

13 **adulterer, cheater, fornicator; adulteress,** fornicatress, fornicatrix

14 **strumpet, trollop, wench, hussy, slut, jade, baggage,** *cocotte* <Fr>, grisette; **tart** *and* **chippy** *and* **floozy** *and* broad <nf>, bitch, drab, trull, quean, harridan, Jezebel, harlot, wanton, whore <nf>, bad woman, **loose woman,** easy woman <nf>, easy lay <nf>, woman of easy virtue, frail sister; pickup; nymphomaniac, nymphet, nympho <nf>, hysteromaniac, uteromaniac, clitoromaniac; nymphet

15 **demimonde,** demimondaine, demirep; **courtesan,** adventuress, **seductress,** femme fatale, vampire, vamp, temptress; hetaera, houri, harem girl, odalisque; Jezebel, Messalina, Delilah, Thais, Phryne, Aspasia, Lais

16 **prostitute, harlot, whore,** *fille de joie* <Fr>, daughter of joy, lady of the evening, call girl *and* B-girl <nf>, **scarlet woman,** unfortunate woman, painted woman, fallen woman, erring sister, **streetwalker,** hustler *and* **hooker** <nf>, woman of the town, *poule* <Fr>, stew, meretrix, Cyprian, Paphian; white slave

17 **mistress,** woman, **kept woman,** kept mistress, **paramour,** concubine, doxy, playmate, spiritual *or* unofficial wife; live-in lover <nf>; other woman <nf>

18 **procurer, pimp,** pander *or* panderer, *maquereau* <Fr>, mack *or* mackman, ponce <Brit nf>; **bawd; gigolo,** fancy man; procuress, **madam** <nf>; white slaver

VERBS **19 be promiscuous,** sleep around *and* swing <nf>; **debauch, wanton,** rake, chase women, womanize, whore, sow one's wild oats;

philander; dissipate 669.6; fornicate, **cheat, commit adultery,** get a little on the side <nf>; grovel, wallow, wallow in the mire

20 **seduce, betray, deceive,** mislead, lead astray, lead down the garden *or* the primrose path; **debauch, ravish,** ravage, despoil, ruin; deflower, pop one's cherry <nf>; **defile,** soil, sully; **violate,** abuse; **rape,** force

21 **prostitute oneself,** sell *or* peddle one's ass <nf>, streetwalk; pimp, procure, pander

22 **cuckold;** wear horns, wear the horn

ADJS 23 **unchaste, unvirtuous,** unvirginal; **impure, unclean; indecent** 666.5; soiled, sullied, smirched, besmirched, defiled, tainted, maculate

24 **incontinent,** uncontinent; **orgiastic;** intemperate 669.7; unrestrained

25 **profligate, licentious,** unbridled, untrammeled, uninhibited, free; **dissolute, dissipated, debauched,** abandoned; **wild, fast,** gallant, gay, rakish; rakehell, rakehellish, rakehelly

26 **wanton, wayward,** Paphian; **loose,** lax, slack, loose-moraled, of loose morals, of easy virtue, easy <nf>, **light,** no better than she should be, whorish, chambering, **promiscuous**

27 freeloving; **adulterous,** illicit, extramarital, premarital; incestuous

28 **prostitute, prostituted, whorish, harlot,** scarlet, fallen, meretricious, streetwalking, hustling <nf>, on the town *or* streets, on the *pavé,* in the life

29 **lascivious, lecherous, sexy, salacious, carnal,** animal, **sexual, lustful,** ithyphallic, **hot,** horny *and* sexed-up *and* hot to trot <nf>; prurient, itching, itchy <nf>; concupiscent, lickerish, libidinous, randy, horny <nf>, lubricious; **lewd, bawdy,** adult, X-rated, hard, pornographic, porno <nf>, **dirty, obscene** 666.9; erotic, **sensual,** fleshly; goatish, satyric, priapic, gynecomaniacal; nymphomaniacal, hysteromaniacal, uteromaniacal, clitoromaniacal; erotomaniacal, eroticomaniacal, aphrodisiomaniacal

666 INDECENCY

NOUNS 1 **indecency, indelicacy,** inelegance *or* inelegancy, **indecorousness,** indecorum, **impropriety** 638.1, inappropriateness, unseemliness, indiscretion, indiscreetness; **unchastity** 665

2 **immodesty,** unmodestness, impudicity; exhibitionism; **shamelessness,** unembarrassedness; **brazenness** 142.2, brassiness, pertness, forwardness, boldness, procacity, bumptiousness; **flagrancy,** notoriousness, scandal, scandalousness

3 **vulgarity** 497, **uncouthness, coarseness, crudeness, grossness,** rankness, rawness, raunchiness <nf>; **earthiness,** frankness; **spiciness, raciness,** saltiness

4 **obscenity, dirtiness,** bawdry, raunch <nf>, **ribaldry, pornography,** porno *and* porn <nf>, hard *or* hard-core pornography, soft *or* soft-core pornography, salacity, **smut, dirt, filth; lewdness, bawdiness,** salaciousness, **smuttiness, foulness, filthiness,** nastiness, vileness, offensiveness; scurrility, fescenninity; Rabelaisianism; erotic art *or* literature, pornographic art or literature; sexploitation; blue movie *and* dirty movie *and* porno film *and* skin flick <nf>, adult movie, stag film <nf>, X-rated movie; pornographomania, erotographomania, iconolagny, erotology; **dirty talk, scatology** 523.9

ADJS 5 **indecent, indelicate, inelegant, indecorous, improper,** inappropriate, **unseemly, unbecoming,** indiscreet

6 **immodest,** unmodest; exhibitionistic; **shameless,** unashamed, unembarrassed, unabashed, unblushing, **brazen,** brazenfaced, brassy; **forward,** bold, pert, procacious , bumptious; **flagrant,** notorious, scandalous

7 **risqué,** risky, **racy,** salty, spicy, **off-color,** suggestive, scabrous

8 **vulgar, uncouth, coarse, gross,** rank, raw, broad, low, foul, gutter; **earthy,** frank, pulling no punches

9 **obscene, lewd, adult, bawdy,** ithyphallic, **ribald, pornographic,**

salacious, sultry <nf>, lurid, **dirty, smutty,** raunchy <nf>, blue, smoking-room, impure, unchaste, unclean, **foul, filthy, nasty,** vile, fulsome, offensive, unprintable, unrepeatable, not fit for mixed company; scurrilous, scurrile, Fescennine; **foulmouthed,** foul-tongued, foul-spoken; Rabelaisian

667 ASCETICISM

NOUNS 1 **asceticism,** ascetism, **austerity, self-denial,** self-abnegation, **rigor; puritanism,** eremitism, anchoritism, anchorite *or* anchoritic monasticism, monasticism, monachism; austerity; Sabbatarianism; Albigensianism, Waldensianism, Catharism; Yoga; mortification, self-mortification, maceration, flagellation; **abstinence** 668.2; belt-tightening, fasting 515; voluntary poverty, mendicantism, Franciscanism; Trappism

2 **ascetic, puritan,** Sabbatarian; Albigensian, Waldensian, Catharist; **abstainer** 668.4; anchorite, **hermit** 584.5; yogi, yogin; sannyasi, bhikshu, dervish, fakir, flagellant, Penitente; Buddha, bodhi; eremite; mendicant, Franciscan, Discalced *or* barefooted Carmelite; Trappist

VERBS 3 deny oneself; abstain, tighten one's belt; flagellate oneself, wear a hair shirt, make oneself miserable

ADJS 4 **ascetic, austere,** self-denying, self-abnegating, **rigorous, rigoristic; puritanical,** eremitic, anchoritic, Sabbatarian; **penitential;** Albigensian, Waldensian, Catharist; **abstinent** 668.10; mendicant, discalced, barefoot, wedded to poverty, Franciscan; Trappist; flagellant; eremitic, eremitical

668 TEMPERANCE

NOUNS 1 **temperance,** temperateness, **moderation,** moderateness, middle way, sophrosyne; golden mean, via media, *juste milieu* <Fr>; nothing in excess, sobriety, soberness, frugality, forbearance, abnegation; renunciation, renouncement, forgoing; denial, **self-denial;** restraint, constraint, **self-restraint; self-control,** self-reining, self-mastery, **discipline,** self-discipline

2 **abstinence,** abstention, abstainment, **abstemiousness,** refraining, refrainment, avoidance, eschewal, denying *or* refusing oneself, saying no to, passing up <nf>; **total abstinence, teetotalism,** nephalism, Rechabitism; the pledge; Encratism, Shakerism; Pythagorism, Pythagoreanism; sexual abstinence, celibacy 565; chastity 664; gymnosophy; Stoicism; vegetarianism, veganism, fruitarianism; plain living, spare diet, simple diet; Spartan fare, Lenten fare; fish day, banyan day; fast 515.2,3; **continence** 664.3; **asceticism** 667; smokeout

3 **prohibition,** prohibitionism; Eighteenth Amendment, Volstead Act

4 **abstainer,** abstinent; **teetotaler,** teetotalist, sobersides <nf>; nephalist, Rechabite, hydropot, water-drinker; vegetarian, vegan, fruitarian, pescetarian; banian, banya; gymnosophist; Pythagorean, Pythagorist; Encratite, Apostolici, Shaker; **ascetic** 667.2; nonsmoker, nondrinker, etc; moderationist

5 **prohibitionist, dry** <nf>; Anti-Saloon League; Women's Christian Temperance Union *or* WCTU

VERBS 6 **restrain oneself,** constrain oneself, curb oneself, hold back, **avoid excess; limit oneself, restrict oneself; control oneself,** control one's appetites, repress *or* inhibit one's desires, contain oneself, discipline oneself, master oneself, exercise self-control *or* self-restraint, keep oneself under control, keep in *or* within bounds, keep within compass *or* limits, know when one has had enough, **deny** *or* refuse oneself, **say no** *or* just say no; live plainly *or* simply *or* frugally; mortify oneself, mortify the flesh, control the fleshy lusts; control the carnal man *or* the old Adam; eat to live, not live to eat; eat sparingly, diet; tighten one's belt

7 **abstain,** abstain from, refrain, **refrain from, forbear, forgo,** spare, withhold, hold back, **avoid, shun,** eschew, **pass up** <nf>, **keep from,** keep *or* stand *or* hold aloof from, have nothing to do with, take no part in, have no hand in, **let alone,** let well enough alone, let go by, **deny oneself,** do without, go without, make do without, not *or* never touch, keep hands off; fast

8 **swear off, renounce,** forswear, **give up,** abandon, stop, discontinue; take the pledge, get on the wagon *or* water wagon <nf>, go on the wagon <nf>; **kick** *and* kick the habit <nf>, dry out

ADJS **9** **temperate, moderate,** sober, frugal, restrained, **sparing,** stinting, measured

10 **abstinent,** abstentious, **abstemious;** teetotal, sworn off, on the wagon *or* water wagon <nf>; nephalistic, Rechabite; Encratic, Apostolic, Shaker; Pythagorean; sexually abstinent, celibate, chaste; Stoic; fasting; vegetarian, veganistic, vegan, fruitarian; Spartan, Lenten; maigre, meatless; **continent** 664.6; **ascetic**

11 prohibitionist, antisaloon, dry <nf>

ADVS **12** **temperately, moderately, sparingly,** stintingly, frugally, in moderation, within compass *or* bounds

669 INTEMPERANCE

NOUNS **1** **intemperance,** intemperateness, **indulgence, self-indulgence**, self-absorption; instant gratification; **overindulgence,** overdoing; **unrestraint,** unconstraint, indiscipline, uncontrol; **immoderation,** immoderacy, immoderateness; inordinacy, inordinateness; **excess, excessiveness,** too much, too-muchness <nf>; addiction; prodigality, extravagance; crapulence *or* crapulency, crapulousness; **incontinence** 665.2; **swinishness, gluttony** 672; **drunkenness** 88.1

2 **dissipation, licentiousness; riotous living,** free living, high living <nf>, fast *or* killing pace, fast lane <nf>, burning the candle at both ends; **debauchery,** debauchment; **carousal** 88.5, carousing, carouse; **debauch, orgy,** saturnalia; hedonism, sybaritism

3 **dissipater,** rounder , free liver, high liver <nf>; nighthawk *and* nightowl <nf>; debauchee; **playboy,** partyer, partygoer, party girl, party animal; pleasure-seeker

VERBS **4** **indulge,** indulge oneself, indulge one's appetites, deny oneself nothing *or* not at all; **give oneself up to,** give free course to, give free rein to; live well *or* high, live high on the hog <nf>, live it up <nf>, live off the fat of the land; indulge in, luxuriate in, wallow in; roll in; look out for number one

5 **overindulge, overdo, carry to excess,** carry too far, go the limit, go whole hog <nf>, know no limits, not know when to stop, bite off more than one can chew, spread oneself too thin; dine not wisely but too well; live above *or* beyond one's means; binge <nf>

6 **dissipate,** plunge into dissipation, **debauch, wanton, carouse,** run riot, live hard *or* fast, squander one's money in riotous living, burn the candle at both ends, keep up a fast *or* killing pace, not know when to stop, sow one's wild oats, have one's fling, **party** <nf>

ADJS **7** **intemperate, indulgent, self-indulgent; overindulgent,** overindulging, unthrifty, unfrugal, **immoderate,** inordinate, **excessive,** too much, prodigal, extravagant, extreme, unmeasured, unlimited; crapulous, crapulent; undisciplined, uncontrolled, unbridled, unconstrained, uninhibited, **unrestrained; incontinent** 665.24; **swinish, gluttonous** 672.6; bibulous; party-hearty

8 **licentious, dissipated, riotous, dissolute, debauched;** free-living, high-living <nf>

9 **orgiastic,** saturnalian, corybantic

ADVS **10** **intemperately,** prodigally, **immoderately,** inordinately, excessively, **in** *or* **to excess,** to extremes, beyond all bounds *or* limits, without restraint; high, high on the hog <nf>

670 MODERATION

NOUNS 1 **moderation,** moderateness; **restraint,** constraint, control; **judiciousness,** prudence; steadiness, evenness, balance, equilibrium, **stability** 855; **temperateness,** temperance, sobriety; self-abnegation, self-restraint, self-control, self-denial; abstinence, continence, abnegation; **mildness,** lenity, gentleness; calmness, serenity, tranquillity, repose, calm, cool <nf>; unexcessiveness, unextremeness, unextravagance, nothing in excess; **happy medium, golden mean,** *juste-milieu* <Fr>, middle way *or* path, *via media* <L>, balancing act <nf>; moderationism, **conservatism** 853.3; **nonviolence,** pacifism, pacification, peace movement, ahimsa; impartiality, neutrality, dispassion; irenics, ecumenism

2 modulation, **abatement,** remission, **mitigation,** diminution, defusing, de-escalation, **reduction,** lessening, falling-off; **relaxation,** relaxing, slackening, **easing,** loosening, letup *and* letdown <nf>; **alleviation,** assuagement, allayment, palliation, leniency, relenting, lightening, **tempering, softening,** moderating, moderative, subdual; **deadening, dulling,** damping, blunting; drugging, narcotizing, sedating, sedation; **pacification, tranquilization,** tranquilizing, mollification, demulsion, dulcification, **quieting,** quietening, lulling, **soothing, calming,** hushing

3 **moderator, mitigator,** modulator, stabilizer, temperer, assuager; **mediator, bridge-builder,** calming *or* restraining hand, wiser head; **alleviator,** alleviative, palliative, lenitive; **pacifier, soother,** comforter, peacemaker, pacificator, dove of peace, mollifier; **drug,** anodyne, dolorifuge, soothing syrup, **tranquilizer,** calmative; **sedative** 86.12; balm, salve; cushion, shock absorber

4 **moderate,** moderatist, moderationist, middle-of-the-roader, **centrist,** neutral, compromiser; **conservative** 853.4

VERBS 5 **be moderate, keep within bounds,** keep within compass; practice self-control *or* self-denial, live within one's means, live temperately, do nothing in excess, strike a balance, strike *or* keep a happy medium, seek the golden mean, steer *or* preserve an even course, keep to the middle path *or* way, steer *or* be between Scylla and Charybdis; keep the peace, not resist, espouse *or* practice nonviolence, be pacifistic; not rock the boat *and* not make waves *or* static <nf>; cool it *and* keep one's cool <nf>, keep one's head *or* temper; sober down, settle down; remit, relent; take in sail; go out like a lamb; be conservative 853.6

6 **moderate, restrain,** constrain, control, **keep within bounds; modulate, mitigate,** defuse, abate, weaken, **diminish, reduce,** de-escalate, slacken, lessen, slow down; **alleviate,** assuage, allay, lay, lighten, palliate, extenuate, **temper,** attemper, lenify; **soften, subdue,** tame, hold in check, keep a tight rein, chasten, underplay, play down, downplay, de-emphasize, tone *or* tune down; turn down the volume, lower the voice; **drug,** narcotize, sedate, tranquilize, deaden, dull, blunt, obtund, take the edge off, take the sting *or* bite out; smother, suppress, stifle; **damp, dampen,** bank the fire, reduce the temperature, throw cold water on, throw a wet blanket on; sober, sober down *or* up; clear the air

7 **calm,** calm down, **stabilize, tranquilize, pacify,** mollify, appease, dulcify; **quiet,** hush, still, rest, compose, **lull, soothe,** gentle, rock, cradle, rock to sleep; cool, **subdue,** quell; ease, steady, smooth, smoothen, smooth over, smooth down, even out; keep the peace, be the dove of peace, pour oil on troubled waters, pour balm into

8 **cushion,** absorb the shock, **soften the blow,** break the fall, deaden, damp *or* dampen, soften, suppress, neutralize, offset; show pity *or* mercy *or* consideration *or* sensitivity, temper the wind to the shorn lamb

9 **relax,** unbend; ease, **ease up,** ease off, **let up,** let down; abate, bate, remit, mitigate; **slacken,** slack, slake, slack off, slack up; loose, **loosen;** unbrace, unstrain, unstring

ADJS 10 **moderate, temperate,** sober; **mild,** soft, bland, **gentle,** tame; mild as milk *or* mother's milk, mild as milk and water, gentle as a lamb; nonviolent, peaceable, peaceful, pacifistic; **judicious, prudent**

11 **restrained,** constrained, limited, controlled, **stable,** in control, in hand; tempered, **softened,** hushed, **subdued,** quelled, chastened

12 **unexcessive,** unextreme, unextravagant, **conservative;** reasonable

13 **equable,** even, low-key *or* low-keyed, **cool,** even-tempered, levelheaded, dispassionate; tranquil, reposeful, serene, calm 173.12

14 **mitigating,** assuaging, abating, **diminishing, reducing,** lessening, allaying, **alleviating, relaxing, easing;** tempering, **softening,** chastening, **subduing;** deadening, dulling, blunting, damping, dampening, cushioning

15 **tranquilizing,** pacifying, mollifying, appeasing; cooling-off; **calming,** lulling, gentling, rocking, cradling, hushing, quietening, stilling; **soothing,** soothful, restful; dreamy, drowsy

16 **palliative, alleviative,** alleviatory, assuasive, lenitive, **calmative,** calmant, **narcotic, sedative,** demulcent, anodyne; antiorgastic, anaphrodisiac

ADVS 17 **moderately, in moderation,** restrainedly, subduedly, in *or* within reason, within bounds *or* compass, in balance; **temperately,** soberly, prudently, judiciously, dispassionately; composedly, calmly, coolly, evenly, steadily, equably, tranquilly, serenely; soothingly, conservatively

671 VIOLENCE

<*vehement action*>

NOUNS 1 **violence, vehemence, virulence, venom, furiousness, force, rigor,** roughness, harshness, ungentleness, ẽxtremity, impetuosity, inclemency, **severity, intensity,** acuteness, **sharpness; acrimony** 17.5; fierceness, ferociousness, ferocity, furiousness, viciousness, insensateness, savagery, destructiveness, **destruction, vandalism; terrorism, barbarity, brutality, atrocity,** inhumanity, bloodlust, killer instinct, murderousness, malignity, mercilessness, pitilessness, mindlessness, animality, brutishness; **rage,** raging, **anger** 152

2 **turbulence, turmoil,** chaos, upset, **fury, furor, rage, frenzy, passion,** fanaticism, zealousness, zeal, tempestuousness, storminess, wildness, tumultuousness, **tumult, uproar,** racket, cacophony, pandemonium, hubbub, **commotion, disturbance, agitation,** bluster, broil, brawl, embroilment, brouhaha, fuss, flap <Brit nf>, **row, rumpus,** ruckus <nf>, foofaraw <nf>, **ferment,** fume, boil, boiling, seething, ebullition, fomentation; all hell let loose

3 **unruliness, disorderliness,** obstreperousness, Katy-bar-the-door <nf>; **riot, rioting;** looting, pillaging, plundering, rapine; wilding <nf>; laying waste, sowing with salt, sacking; scorched earth; **attack** 459, **assault,** onslaught, battering; **rape, violation,** forcible seizure; **killing** 308, butchery, massacre, slaughter

4 **storm, tempest,** squall, line squall, **tornado, cyclone, hurricane,** tropical cyclone, typhoon, storm-center, tropical storm, eye of the storm *or* hurricane, war of the elements; stormy weather, rough weather, foul weather, dirty weather; rainstorm 316.2; thunderstorm 316.3; windstorm 318.11; **snowstorm** 1023.8; **firestorm**

5 **upheaval, convulsion,** cataclysm, catastrophe, disaster; meltdown; **fit,** spasm, **paroxysm,** apoplexy, stroke; climax; **earthquake,** quake, temblor, diastrophism, epicenter, shock wave; tidal wave, *tsunami* <Japanese>

6 **outburst, outbreak, eruption,** debouchment, eructation, belch, spew; **burst,** dissilience *or* dissiliency;

meltdown, atomic meltdown; **torrent,** rush, gush, spate, cascade, spurt, jet, rapids, **volcano,** volcan, burning mountain

7 explosion, discharge, blowout, blowup, detonation, fulmination, **blast, burst, report** 56.1; flash, flash *or* flashing point, flare, flare-up, fulguration; bang, boom 56.4; backfire

8 concussion, shock, impact, crunch, smash; percussion, repercussion

9 <violent person> berserk *or* berserker; **hothead,** hotspur; **devil, demon, fiend, brute,** hellhound, hellcat, hellion, hell-raiser; **beast,** wild beast, tiger, dragon, mad dog, wolf, monster, mutant, savage; **rapist, mugger, killer;** Mafioso, hit man <nf>, contract killer, hired killer, hired gun; **fury,** virago, vixen, termagant, beldam, she-wolf, tigress, witch; firebrand, revolutionary 860.3, **terrorist,** incendiary, bomber, guerrilla, suicide bomber

10 <nf terms> **goon, gorilla,** ape, knuckle dragger, muscle man, plug-ugly, shtarker, cowboy, bimbo, bozo, bruiser, hardnose, tough guy, tough, hoodlum, hood, meat-eater, gunsel, terror, holy terror, fire-eater, spitfire, tough *or* ugly customer

VERBS **11 rage, storm, rant, rave,** roar; **rampage,** ramp, **tear,** tear around; go *or* carry on <nf>; come in like a lion; **destroy, wreck,** wreak havoc, ruin; sow chaos *or* disorder; **terrorize,** sow terror, vandalize, barbarize, brutalize; **riot,** loot, burn, pillage, sack, lay waste; **slaughter, butcher; rape,** violate; **attack, assault,** batter, savage, mug, maul, hammer; go for the jugular

12 seethe, boil, fume, foam, simmer, stew, ferment, stir, churn, see red

13 erupt, burst forth *or* **out, break out, blow out** *or* **open,** eruct, belch, **vomit,** spout, spew, disgorge, **discharge,** eject, throw *or* hurl forth

14 explode, blow up, burst, go off, go up, blow out, blast, bust <nf>; **detonate,** fulminate; **touch off,** trigger, trip, set off, let off; **discharge,** fire, shoot; backfire; melt down

15 run amok, go berserk, go on a rampage, cut loose, run riot, run wild

ADJS **16 violent, vehement, virulent, venomous, severe, rigorous, furious, fierce, intense,** sharp, acute, keen, cutting, splitting, piercing; **destructive;** rough, bruising, tough <nf>; **drastic,** extreme, outrageous, excessive, exorbitant, unconscionable, intemperate, immoderate, extravagant; acrimonious 17.14; on the warpath

17 unmitigated, unsoftened, untempered, unallayed, unsubdued, unquelled; unquenched, unextinguished, unabated; unmixed, unalloyed; **total**

18 turbulent, tumultuous, raging, chaotic, hellish, anarchic, **storming,** stormy, **tempestuous,** troublous, **frenzied, wild, wild-eyed, frantic, furious,** infuriate, insensate, **mad,** demented, insane, enraged, ravening, raving, slavering; **angry; blustering,** blustery, blusterous; **uproarious,** rip-roaring <nf>; pandemoniac

19 unruly, disorderly, obstreperous; **unbridled; riotous,** wild, rampant; **terroristic,** anarchic, nihilistic, revolutionary 860.5

20 boisterous, rampageous, rambunctious <nf>, on the rampage, rumbustious, roisterous, wild, rollicking, **rowdy,** rough, hoody <nf>, harum-scarum <nf>; knockabout, rough-and-tumble, knock-down-and-drag-out <nf>

21 savage, fierce, ferocious, vicious, murderous, cruel, atrocious, mindless, brutal, brutish, **bestial,** insensate, monstrous, mutant, inhuman, pitiless, ruthless, merciless, bloody, sanguinary, kill-crazy <nf>; malign, malignant; feral, ferine; **wild,** untamed, tameless, undomesticated, ungentle; **barbarous,** barbaric; **uncivilized,** noncivilized

22 fiery, heated, inflamed, flaming, scorching, hot, red-hot, white-hot; **fanatic, zealous,** totally committed, hard-core, hard-line, ardent, passionate; **hotheaded**

23 **convulsive,** cataclysmic, disastrous, upheaving; seismic; **spasmodic,** paroxysmal, spastic, jerky, herky-jerky <nf>; orgasmic

24 **explosive,** bursting, detonating, explosible, explodable, fulminating, fulminant, fulminatory; cataclysmic; dissilient; **volcanic,** eruptive

ADVS **25** **violently, vehemently, virulently, venomously, rigorously, severely, fiercely, drastically; furiously,** wildly, madly, **like mad,** like fury <nf>, like blazes; all to pieces, with a vengeance

26 **turbulently, tumultuously,** riotously, uproariously, stormily, tempestuously, troublously, **frenziedly, frantically, furiously, ragingly, enragedly, madly; angrily** 152.33

27 **savagely, fiercely, ferociously, atrociously, viciously, murderously,** brutally *or* brutishly, mindlessly, bestially, barbarously, inhumanly, insensately, ruthlessly, pitilessly, mercilessly; **tooth and nail,** tooth and claw, *bec et ongles* <Fr>

672 GLUTTONY

NOUNS **1** **gluttony,** gluttonousness, **greed,** greediness, voraciousness, voracity, ravenousness, edacity, crapulence *or* crapulency, gulosity, rapacity, insatiability; omnivorousness; big appetite, **piggishness, hoggishness,** swinishness; **overindulgence, overeating;** eating disorder, polyphagia, hyperphagia, bulimia, bulimia nervosa, binge-purge syndrome, binging <nf>; **intemperance** 669

2 **epicurism, epicureanism, gourmandise;** gastronomy

3 **glutton,** greedy eater, big *or* hearty *or* good eater <nf>, trencherman, trencherwoman, belly-god, gobbler, greedygut *or* greedyguts <nf>, gorger, **gourmand,** gourmandizer, gormand, gormandizer, guttler, cormorant, bon vivant; animal, **hog** *and* **pig** *and* chow hound *and* khazer *and* gobbler *and* wolf <nf>; omnivore; binger

VERBS **4** **gluttonize,** gormandize, **indulge one's appetite,** live to eat, love to eat; **gorge,** engorge, glut, cram, stuff, batten, guttle, guzzle, **devour,** raven, bolt, gobble, gulp, **wolf,** gobble *or* gulp *or* bolt *or* wolf down, eat like a horse, tuck into, stuff oneself *and* hog it down *and* eat one's head off *and* fork *or* shovel it in <nf>, eat one out of house and home, wipe the plate clean

5 **overeat,** overgorge, **overindulge, make a pig** *or* **hog of oneself, pig out** *or* pork out *or* scarf out <nf>; glut oneself, stuff oneself

ADJS **6** **gluttonous, greedy,** voracious, ravenous, edacious, esurient, rapacious, insatiable, polyphagic, bulimic, hyperphagic, Apician, **piggish, hoggish,** swinish; crapulous, crapulent; intemperate 669.7; omnivorous, all-devouring; **gorging,** cramming, glutting, guttling, stuffing, guzzling, wolfing, bolting, **gobbling, gulping,** gluttonizing; binging <nf>

7 overfed, overgorged, overindulged

ADVS **8** **gluttonously, greedily,** voraciously, ravenously, edaciously; **piggishly, hoggishly, swinishly**

673 LEGALITY

NOUNS **1** **legality, legitimacy, lawfulness, legitimateness, licitness,** rightfulness, validity, scope, applicability; **jurisdiction** 594; actionability, justiciability, **constitutionality,** constitutional validity; letter of the law; legal process, legal form, **due process;** legalism, constitutionalism; **justice** 649

2 **legalization, legitimation, legitimatization, decriminalization;** money-washing *or* -laundering; validation; authorization, sanction; legislation, enactment, authority, license, warrant

3 **law,** *lex* and *jus* <L>, **statute,** rubric, **canon,** institution; **ordinance; act, enactment, measure,** legislation; **rule, ruling; prescript,** prescription; **regulation,** *règlement* <Fr>, reg <nf>; **dictate,** dictation; form, formula, formulary, formality;

standing order; bylaw; **edict, decree** 420.4; **bill;** manifesto, order, standing order, rescript, precept

4 **law,** legal system, system of laws, legal branch *or* specialty

5 **code, digest,** pandect, capitulary, **body of law,** corpus juris, legal code, code of laws, digest of law; **codification; civil code, penal code;** Justinian Code; Napoleonic code, *Code Napoléon* <Fr>; lawbook, statute book, compilation; Blackstone; Uniform Code of Military Justice; written law, unwritten law, statute law, common law, private law, international law, military law, commercial law, contracts law, criminal law, civil law, labor law, constitutional law; law of the land; canon

6 **constitution,** written constitution, unwritten constitution; law and equity; charter, codification, codified law; constitutional amendment; Bill of Rights, constitutional guarantees; constitutional interpretation

7 **jurisprudence, law,** legal science; nomology, nomography; **forensic science,** science of law, forensic *or* legal medicine, medical jurisprudence, medico-legal medicine; forensic psychiatry; forensic *or* legal chemistry; criminology; constitutionalism, penology

8 <codes of law> Constitution of the U.S., Bill of Rights; Corpus Juris Civilis, Codex Juris Canonici, Digest *or* Pandects of Justinian; Law of Moses, Ten Commandments, Pentateuch, Torah, Koran *or* Qur'an, the Bible; Code of Hammurabi, Magna Carta, Napoleonic Code

VERBS 9 **legalize, legitimize,** legitimatize, legitimate, make legal, declare lawful, **decriminalize;** wash *or* launder money; validate; **authorize, sanction**, license, warrant; constitute, ordain, establish, put in force; prescribe, formulate; regulate, make a regulation, bring within the law; **decree; legislate, enact; enforce; litigate** 598.13, take legal action

10 **codify,** digest; compile, publish

ADJS 11 **legal, legitimate,** legit *and* kosher <nf>, competent, by right, de jure, **licit, lawful,** rightful, according to law, within the law; **actionable,** litigable, justiciable, within the scope of the law; **enforceable,** legally binding; **judicial,** juridical; **authorized, sanctioned,** valid, applicable, warranted; **constitutional;** statutory, statutable; legalized, legitimized, decriminalized; **legislative, lawmaking;** lawlike; **just** 649.7

12 jurisprudent, jurisprudential; **legalistic; forensic;** nomistic, nomothetic; criminological

ADVS 13 **legally, legitimately, licitly, lawfully,** by law, *de jure* <L>, in the eyes of the law, within the law

674 ILLEGALITY

NOUNS 1 **illegality, unlawfulness, illicitness, lawlessness,** wrongfulness; unauthorization, impermissibility, **unconstitutionality;** legal *or* technical flaw, legal irregularity; **outlawry; anarchy,** collapse *or* breakdown *or* paralysis of authority, anomie; illicit business 732

2 **illegitimacy, illegitimateness,** illegitimation; **bastardy,** bastardism; bend *or* bar sinister, baton

3 **lawbreaking, violation,** breach *or* violation of law, infringement, contravention, infraction, **transgression,** trespass, trespassing, offense, breach, nonfeasance, encroachment; vice, fraud; crime, **criminality,** criminalism, habitual criminality, delinquency; flouting *or* making a mockery of the law

4 **offense, wrong,** illegality; **violation** 435.2; **wrongdoing** 655; much to answer for; **crime, felony; misdemeanor;** tort; delict, delictum

VERBS 5 **break** *or* **violate the law,** breach the law, infringe, contravene, infract, violate 435.4, **transgress, trespass,** disobey the law, offend against the law, flout the law, make a mockery of the law, fly in the face of the law, set the law at defiance, snap one's fingers at the law, set the law at naught, circumvent the law, disregard the law, **take the law into**

one's own hands, twist *or* torture the law to one's own ends *or* purposes; commit a crime; have much to answer for; live outside the law

ADJS 6 **illegal, unlawful, illegitimate, illicit,** nonlicit, nonlegal, lawless, wrongful, fraudulent, creative <nf>, **against the law; unauthorized,** unallowed, impermissible, unwarranted, unwarrantable, unofficial, unlicensed; unstatutory, instatutory, injudicial, extrajudicial; **unconstitutional,** nonconstitutional; flawed, irregular, contrary to law; actionable, chargeable, justiciable, litigable; triable, punishable; **criminal, felonious; outlaw, outlawed; contraband,** bootleg, black-market; under-the-table, under-the-counter; unregulated, unchartered; anarchic, anarchistic, anomic

7 **illegitimate, spurious,** false; **bastard,** misbegot, **misbegotten,** miscreated, gotten on the wrong side of the blanket, baseborn, born out of wedlock, without benefit of clergy

ADVS 8 **illegally, unlawfully, illegitimately, illicitly;** impermissibly; criminally, feloniously; contrary to law, in violation of law, against the law

675 RELIGIONS, CULTS, SECTS

NOUNS 1 **religion,** religious belief *or* faith, **belief, faith,** teaching, doctrine, creed, credo, dogma, theology 676, orthodoxy 687; system of beliefs, belief system; persuasion, tradition

2 **cult, ism;** cultism; **mystique**

3 **sect**, sectarism, religious order, **denomination, persuasion,** faction, **church,** communion, community, group, fellowship, affiliation, order, school, party, society, body, organization; branch, variety, version, segment; offshoot; **schism,** division

4 **sectarianism,** sectarism, **denominationalism,** partisanism, the clash of creeds; schismatism; syncretism, eclecticism

5 **theism; monotheism; polytheism,** multitheism, myriotheism; **ditheism,** dyotheism, dualism; **tritheism;** tetratheism; **pantheism,** cosmotheism, theopantism, acosmism; physitheism, psychotheism, animotheism; physicomorphism; hylotheism; anthropotheism, anthropomorphism; anthropolatry; allotheism; monolatry, henotheism; autotheism; zootheism, theriotheism; **deism**

6 **animism, animistic religion** *or* cult; voodooism, voodoo, hoodoo, wanga, juju, jujuism, obeah, obeahism; shamanism; fetishism, totemism; nature worship, naturism; primitive religion

7 **Christianity**, Christianism, Christendom; Latin *or* Roman *or* Western Christianity; Eastern *or* Orthodox Christianity; Protestant Christianity; Judeo-Christian religion *or* tradition *or* belief; fundamentalism, Christian fundamentalism

8 **Catholicism,** Catholicity; **Roman Catholicism,** Romanism, Rome; papalism; popery *and* popeism *and* papism *and* papistry <nf>; ultramontanism; Catholic Church, **Roman Catholic Church,** Church of Rome; Eastern Rites, Uniate Rites, Uniatism, Alexandrian *or* Antiochian *or* Byzantine Rite

9 Orthodoxy; **Eastern Orthodox Church, Holy Orthodox Catholic Apostolic Church,** Greek Orthodox Church, Russian Orthodox Church; patriarchate of Constantinople, patriarchate of Antioch, patriarchate of Alexandria, patriarchate of Jerusalem

10 **Protestantism,** Reform, Reformationism; Evangelicalism; Zwinglianism; dissent 333; apostasy 363.2; new theology

11 **Anglicanism;** High-Churchism, Low-Churchism; Anglo-Catholicism; Church of England, Established Church; High Church, Low Church; Broad Church, Free Church

12 **Judaism;** Hebraism, Hebrewism; Israelitism; Orthodox Judaism, Conservative Judaism, Reform Judaism, Reconstructionism; Hasidism; rabbinism, Talmudism; Pharisaism; Sadduceeism; Karaism *or* Karaitism

13 **Islam, Muslimism,** Islamism, Moslemism, Muhammadanism, Mohammedanism; Sufism, Wahabiism, Sunnism, Shi'ism, Druzism; Black Muslimism; Muslim fundamentalism, militant Muslimism

14 <other religions> **Christian Science; Mormonism;** New Thought, Higher Thought, Practical Christianity, Mental Science, Divine Science Church; Buddhism, Zen Buddhism; Hinduism; Sikhism; Shintoism; Jainism; Rastafarianism; Zoroastrianism; Confucianism; Taoism

15 **religionist,** religioner; zealot, iconoclast; **believer** 692.4; worshiper; cultist

16 **theist; monotheist; polytheist,** multitheist, myriotheist; ditheist, dualist; tritheist; tetratheist; **pantheist,** cosmotheist; psychotheist; physitheist; hylotheist; anthropotheist; anthropolater; allotheist; henotheist; autotheist; zootheist, theriotheist; **deist**

17 **Christian,** Nazarene, Nazarite; practicing Christian; Christian sectarian

18 **sectarian,** sectary, **denominationalist,** factionist, schismatic

19 **Catholic,** Roman Catholic *or* RC <nf>, Romanist, papist <nf>; ultramontane; Eastern-Rite Christian, Uniate

20 **Protestant,** non-Catholic, Reformed believer, Reformationist, Evangelical; Zwinglian; dissenter 333.3; apostate 363.5; Anglican, Episcopalian, Unitarian, born-again Christian

21 **Jew, Hebrew,** Judaist, Israelite; Orthodox *or* Conservative *or* Reform Jew, Reconstructionist; Hasid; Zionist; Essene; Rabbinist, Talmudist; Pharisee; Sadducee; Karaite

22 **Mormon,** Latter-day Saint, Josephite <nf>

23 **Muslim,** Muhammadan *and* Mohammedan <nf>, Mussulman, Moslem, Islamite; Shi'ite, Shia, Sectary; Motazilite, Sunni, Sunnite, Wahhabi, Sufi, Druze; dervish; abdal; Black Muslim; Muslim fundamentalist *or* militant

24 **Christian Scientist,** Christian Science Practitioner; Buddhist, Zen Buddhist; Hindu; Sikh; Shintoist; Jainist; Rastafarian; Zoroastrian; Confucianist; Taoist

ADJS 25 **religious, theistic; monotheistic; polytheistic,** ditheistic, tritheistic; **pantheistic,** cosmotheistic; physicomorphic; anthropomorphic, anthropotheistic; **deistic;** theophoric

26 **sectarian,** sectary, **denominational,** schismatic, schismatical

27 **nonsectarian, undenominational, nondenominational;** interdenominational

28 **Protestant,** non-Catholic, Reformed, Reformationist, Evangelical; Lutheran, Calvinist, Calvinistic, Zwinglian; dissentient 333.6; apostate 363.11

29 **Catholic; Roman Catholic** *or* RC <nf>, Roman; Romish *and* popish *and* papish *and* papist *and* papistical <nf>; ultramontane

30 **Jewish, Hebrew,** Judaic, Judaical, Israelite, Israelitic, Israelitish; Orthodox, Conservative, Reform, Reconstructionist; Hasidic

31 **Muslim, Islamic,** Moslem, Islamitic, Islamistic, Muhammadan, Mohammedan; Shiite, Sunni, Sunnite

32 <Oriental> Buddhist, Buddhistic; Brahmanic, Brahmanistic; Vedic, Vedantic; Confucian, Confucianist; Taoist, Taoistic, Shintoist, Shintoistic; Zoroastrian, Zarathustrian, Parsee

676 THEOLOGY

NOUNS 1 **theology** <see list>, **religion, divinity;** theologism; doctrinism, doctrinalism; religious studies, religious education

2 **doctrine, dogma** 953.2; **creed,** credo; credenda, articles of religion *or* faith; Apostles' Creed, Nicene Creed, Athanasian Creed; Catechism

3 **theologian,** theologist, theologizer, theologer, theologician, theologue; **divine;** scholastic, schoolman; theological *or* divinity student, theological, theologue; canonist

ADJS 4 **theological, religious; divine;** doctrinal, doctrinary, ecclesiological; canonic *or* canonical; physicotheological

677 DEITY

NOUNS **1** **deity, divinity,** divineness, supernatural being, immortal; **godliness,** godlikeness; **godhood,** godhead, godship, Fatherhood; heavenliness; divine essence; **transcendence;** god, goddess

2 **God;** Lord, Maker, Creator, Supreme Being, Almighty, King of Kings, Lord of Lords; Jehovah; *Yahweh, Adonai, Elohim* <all Heb>; **Allah;** the Great Spirit, Manitou, Prime Mover

3 <Hinduism> **Brahma,** the Supreme Soul, the Essence of the Universe; **Atman,** the Universal Ego *or* Self; **Vishnu,** the Preserver; **Siva,** the Destroyer, the Regenerator

4 <Buddhism> **Buddha,** the Blessed One, the Teacher, **the Lord Buddha,** bodhisattva, bodhi

5 <Zoroastrianism> **Ahura Mazda,** Ormazd, Mazda, the Lord of Wisdom, the Wise Lord, the Wise One, the King of Light, the Guardian of Mankind

6 <Christian Science> **Mind, Divine Mind,** Spirit, Soul Principle, Life, Truth, Love

7 **world spirit** *or* **soul,** *anima mundi* <L>, universal life force, world principle, **world-self,** universal ego *or* self, infinite spirit, supreme soul *or* principle, **oversoul, nous, Logos,** World Reason

8 **Nature, Mother Nature,** Dame Nature, Natura, Great Mother

9 **Godhead, Trinity;** Trimurti, Hindu trinity *or* triad

10 **Christ**, Jesus Christ, Son of God, Emmanuel, Redeemer, Messiah; the Way, the Truth, and the Life; Light of the World

11 **the Word, Logos,** the Word Made Flesh, **the Incarnation,** God Incarnate, the Hypostatic Union

12 God the Holy Ghost, **the Holy Ghost, the Holy Spirit,** the Spirit of God, the Spirit of Truth, the Paraclete, the Comforter, the Intercessor, the Dove

13 <divine functions> creation, preservation, dispensation; **providence, divine providence,** dealings *or* dispensations *or* visitations of providence

14 <functions of Christ> salvation, redemption; atonement, propitiation; mediation, intercession; judgment

15 <functions of the Holy Ghost> inspiration, unction, regeneration, sanctification, comfort, consolation, grace, witness

ADJS **16** **divine,** heavenly, celestial, empyrean; **godly, godlike** 692.9; **transcendent,** superhuman, supernatural; self-existent; Christly, Christlike, redemptive, salvational, propitiative, propitiatory, mediative, mediatory, intercessive, intercessional; incarnate, incarnated, made flesh; messianic

17 **almighty, omnipotent,** all-powerful; creating, creative, making, shaping; **omniscient,** providential, all-wise, all-knowing, all-seeing; **infinite,** boundless, limitless, unbounded, unlimited, undefined, omnipresent, ubiquitous; perfect, sublime; eternal, everlasting, timeless, perpetual, immortal, permanent; one; immutable, unchanging, changeless, eternally the same; supreme, sovereign, highest; holy, hallowed, sacred, numinous; glorious, radiant, luminous; majestic; good, just, loving, merciful; triune, tripersonal, three-personed, three-in-one

678 MYTHICAL AND POLYTHEISTIC GODS AND SPIRITS

NOUNS **1** **the gods,** the immortals; the major deities, the greater gods, *di majores* <L>; the minor deities, the lesser gods, *di minores* <L>; pantheon; theogony; **spirits,** animistic spirit *or* powers, manitou, huaca, nagual, mana, pokunt, tamanoas, wakan, zemi

2 **god,** *deus* <L>; **deity, divinity,** immortal, heathen god, pagan deity *or* divinity; **goddess,** *dea* <L>; deva, devi, the shining ones; **idol,** false god, devil-god

3 godling, godlet, godkin; **demigod,** half-god, hero; cult figure; demigoddess, heroine

4 **god, goddesses; Greek and Roman deities** ; **Norse and Germanic deities** ; **Celtic deities** ; **Hindu deities** ; **avatars of Vishnu; Egyptian deities** ; **Semitic deities; Chinese deities; Japanese deities; specialized** *or* **tutelary deities**

5 **spirit,** intelligence, supernatural being; **genius,** daemon, demon; atua; **specter** 988; **evil spirits** 680

6 **elemental,** elemental spirit; sylph, spirit of the air; gnome, spirit of the earth, earth-spirit; salamander, fire-spirit; undine, water spirit, water-sprite

7 **fairyfolk,** elfenfolk, **the little people** *or* **men,** the good folk *or* people, denizens of the air; **fairyland,** faerie

8 **fairy, sprite, fay,** fairy man *or* woman; **elf, brownie, pixie, gremlin,** ouphe, hob, cluricaune, puca *or* pooka *or* pwca, kobold, nisse, peri; **imp, goblin** 680.8; **gnome,** dwarf; **sylph,** sylphid; **banshee; leprechaun;** fairy queen; Ariel, Mab, Oberon, Puck, Titania, Béfind, Corrigan, Finnbeara; little green men

9 **nymph;** nymphet, nymphlin; **dryad,** hamadryad, wood nymph; vila *or* willi; tree nymph; oread, mountain nymph; limoniad, meadow *or* flower nymph; Napaea, glen nymph; Hyades; Pleiades, Atlantides

10 **water god, water spirit** *or* **sprite** *or* **nymph;** undine, nix, nixie, kelpie; **naiad,** limniad, fresh-water nymph; Oceanid, Nereid, sea nymph, ocean nymph, **mermaid,** sea-maid, sea-maiden, siren; Thetis; **merman,** man fish; **Neptune**; Oceanus, Poseidon, Triton; Davy Jones, Davy

11 **forest god, sylvan deity,** vegetation spirit *or* daemon, field spirit, fertility god, corn spirit, **faun, satyr,** silenus, panisc, paniscus, panisca; **Pan,** Faunus; Cailleac; Priapus; Vitharr *or* Vidar, the goat god; Jack-in-the-green, Green Man, little green man

12 **familiar spirit,** familiar; **genius, good genius,** daemon, demon, *numen* <L>, totem; **guardian, guardian spirit, guardian angel,** angel, good angel, ministering angel, **fairy godmother;** guide, control, attendant godling *or* spirit, invisible helper, special providence; **tutelary** *or* **tutelar god** *or* **genius** *or* **spirit;** *genius tutelae, genius loci, genius domus, genius familiae* <all L>; **household gods;** *lares familiaris, lares praestites, lares compitales, lares viales, lares permarini* <all L>; penates, lares and penates; ancestral spirits; manes, pitris

13 **Santa Claus,** Santa, Saint Nicholas, Saint Nick, Kriss Kringle, Father Christmas

14 **mythology,** mythicism; **legend, lore, folklore,** mythical lore; fairy lore, fairyism; mythologist; urban legend *or* myth

ADJS 15 **mythic, mythical, mythological; fabulous, legendary;** folkloric

16 **divine, godlike**

17 **fairy,** faery, **fairylike,** fairyish, fay; sylphine, sylphish, sylphy, sylphidine, sylphlike; **elfin,** elfish, elflike; gnomish, gnomelike; pixieish

18 nymphic, nymphal, nymphean, nymphlike

679 ANGEL, SAINT

NOUNS 1 **angel,** celestial, celestial *or* heavenly being; messenger of God; **seraph,** seraphim <pl>, angel of love; **cherub, cherubim** <pl>, angel of light; principality, archangel; recording angel; **saint,** beatified soul, canonized mortal; patron saint; martyr; redeemed *or* saved soul, soul in glory; guardian angel, divine messenger

2 **heavenly host,** host of heaven, choir invisible, angelic host, heavenly hierarchy, Sons of God, ministering spirits; Amesha Spentas

3 <celestial hierarchy> seraphim, cherubim, thrones; dominations *or* dominions, virtues, powers; principalities, archangels, angels; angelology

4 Azrael, angel of death, death's bright angel; Abdiel, Chamuel,

Gabriel, Jophiel, Michael, Raphael, Uriel, Zadkiel

5 **the Madonna;** the Immaculate Conception; Mariology; Mariolatry

ADJS 6 **angelic,** angelical, **seraphic, cherubic; heavenly, celestial;** archangelic; **saintly, sainted,** full of grace, beatified, canonized; martyred; saved, redeemed, glorified, in glory

680 EVIL SPIRITS

NOUNS 1 **evil spirits, demons, demonkind,** powers of darkness, spirits of the air, host of hell, hellish host, hellspawn, denizens of hell, inhabitants of Pandemonium, souls in hell, damned spirits, lost souls, the lost, the damned

2 **devil,** *diable* <Fr>, *diablo* <Sp>, *diabolus* <L>

3 **Satan**, Satanas

4 Beelzebub, Belial, Eblis, Azazel, Ahriman *or* Angra Mainyu; Mephistopheles, Mephisto; Shaitan, Sammael, Asmodeus; Abaddon, Apollyon; Lilith; Aeshma, Pisacha, Putana, Ravana

5 <gods of evil> Set, Typhon, Loki; Nemesis; gods of the nether world; Namtar, Azazel, Asmodeus, Baba Yaga

6 **demon, fiend,** fiend from hell, **devil,** Satan, daeva, rakshasa, dybbuk, shedu, gyre, bad *or* evil *or* unclean spirit; **hellion** <nf>, hellhound, hellkite ; she-devil; cacodemon, incubus, succubus; **jinni,** genie, genius, jinniyeh, afreet *or* afrit; evil genius; barghest; **ghoul,** lamia, Lilith, yogini, Baba Yaga, **vampire,** the undead

7 **imp, pixie, sprite, elf, puck,** kobold, *diablotin* <Fr>, tokoloshe, poltergeist, **gremlin,** Dingbelle, Fifinella, **bad fairy,** bad peri; little *or* young devil, devilkin, deviling; erlking; Puck, Robin Goodfellow, Hob, Hobgoblin

8 **goblin, hobgoblin,** hob, ouphe

9 **bugbear, bugaboo, bogey,** bogle, boggart; **booger, bugger,** bug , **booger-man, bogeyman, boogeyman;** bête noire, fee-faw-fum, Mumbo Jumbo

10 **Fury,** avenging spirit; the Furies, the Erinyes, the Eumenides, the Dirae; Alecto, Megaera, Tisiphone

11 **changeling,** elf child; shape-shifter

12 **werefolk, were-animals; werewolf,** lycanthrope, *loup-garou* <Fr>; werejaguar, jaguar-man, uturuncu; wereass, werebear, werecalf, werefox, werehyena, wereleopard, weretiger, werelion, wereboar, werecrocodile, werecat, werehare

13 **devilishness,** demonishness, **fiendishness;** devilship, devildom; horns, the cloven hoof, the Devil's pitchfork

14 **Satanism,** diabolism, devil-worship, **demonism, devilry, diablerie, demonry;** demonomy, demonianism; black magic; Black Mass; sorcery 690; demonolatry, demon *or* devil *or* chthonian worship; demonomancy; demonology, diabolology *or* diabology, demonography, devil lore

15 **Satanist,** Satan-worshiper, diabolist, devil-worshiper, demonist; **demonomist,** demoniast; demonologist, demonologer; demonolater, chthonian, demon worshiper; sorcerer 690.5

VERBS 16 **demonize, devilize,** diabolize; possess, **obsess; bewitch,** bedevil

ADJS 17 **demoniac** *or* **demoniacal,** demonic *or* demonical, demonish, demonlike; **devilish,** devil-like; **satanic, diabolic, diabolical; hellish** 682.8; **fiendish,** fiendlike; ghoulish, ogreish; foul, unclean, damned; inhuman

18 **impish, puckish, elfish,** elvish; mischievous 322.6

681 HEAVEN

<abode of the deity and blessed dead>

NOUNS 1 **Heaven**

2 **the hereafter,** the afterworld, immortal life, life to come, immortality, eternal life, the afterlife 839.2, life after death

3 Holy City, **Zion,** New Jerusalem, Heavenly *or* Celestial City, Kingdom

of God, City Celestial, Heavenly City of God, City of God, *Civitas Dei* <L>

4 **heaven of heavens, seventh heaven,** the empyrean, throne of God, God's throne, celestial throne, the great white throne

5 <Christian Science> bliss, harmony, spirituality, the reign of Spirit, the atmosphere of Soul

6 <Mormon> celestial kingdom, terrestrial kingdom, telestial kingdom

7 <Muslim> Alfardaws, Assama *or* Assuma; Falak al Aflak

8 <Hindu, Buddhist, and Theosophical> nirvana; Buddha-field; devaloka, land of the gods; kamavachara, kamaloka; devachan; samadhi

9 <mythological> Olympus, Mount Olympus; Elysium, Elysian fields; fields of Aalu; Islands *or* Isles of the Blessed, Happy Isles, Fortunate Isles *or* Islands; Avalon; garden *or* abode of the Gods, garden of the Hesperides, Bower of Bliss; Tir-na-n'Og, Annwfn

10 <Norse> Valhalla, Asgard, Fensalir, Glathsheim, Vingolf, Valaskjalf, Hlithskjalf, Thruthvang *or* Thruthheim, Bilskirnir, Ydalir, Sökkvabekk, Breithablik, Folkvang, Sessrymnir, Noatun, Thrymheim, Glitnir, Himinbjorg, Vithi

11 <removal to heaven> **apotheosis, resurrection, translation,** gathering, **ascension,** the Ascension; **assumption,** the Assumption; removal to Abraham's bosom

ADJS **12** **heavenly,** heavenish; **paradisal, paradisaic, paradisaical,** paradisiac, paradisiacal, paradisic, paradisical; **celestial,** supernal, ethereal; empyrean, empyreal; **unearthly,** unworldly; **otherworldly,** extraterrestrial, extramundane, transmundane, transcendental; Elysian, Olympian; blessed, beatified, beatific *or* beatifical, glorified, in glory; from on high

ADVS **13** **celestially,** paradisally, supernally, ethereally; in heaven, in Abraham's bosom, *in sinu Abraham* <L>, on high, among the blest, in glory

682 HELL

NOUNS **1** **hell, Hades,** Sheol, Gehenna, Tophet, Abaddon, Naraka, jahannan, avichi, **perdition,** Pandemonium, **inferno,** the pit, **the bottomless pit,** the abyss, **nether world,** lower world, underworld, infernal regions, abode *or* world of the dead, abode of the damned, eternal damnation, place of torment, the grave, shades below; **purgatory; limbo,** bardo

2 **hellfire,** fire and brimstone, lake of fire and brimstone, everlasting fire *or* torment

3 <mythological> **Hades,** Orcus, Tartarus, Avernus, Acheron, pit of Acheron; Amenti, Aralu; Hel, Niflhel, Niflheim, Naströnd

4 <rivers of Hades> Styx, Stygian creek; Acheron, River of Woe; Cocytus, River of Wailing; Phlegethon, Pyriphlegethon, River of Fire; Lethe, River of Forgetfulness

5 <deities of the nether world> Pluto, Orcus, Hades *or* Aides *or* Aidoneus, Dis *or* Dis pater, Rhadamanthus, Erebus, Charon, Cerberus, Minos; Osiris; Persephone, Proserpine, Proserpina, Persephassa, Despoina, Kore *or* Cora; Hel, Loki; Satan 680.3

VERBS **6** **damn,** doom, send *or* consign to hell, cast into hell, doom to perdition, condemn to hell *or* eternal punishment

7 go to hell *or* to the devil, be damned, go the other way *or* to the other place <nf>

ADJS **8** **hellish, infernal,** sulfurous, brimstone, fire-and-brimstone; chthonic, chthonian; pandemonic, pandemoniac; devilish; Plutonic, Plutonian; Tartarean; Stygian; Lethean; Acherontic; purgatorial, hellborn

ADVS **9** **hellishly, infernally,** in hell, in hellfire, below, in torment

683 SCRIPTURE

NOUNS **1** **scripture, scriptures, sacred writings** *or* **texts, bible;** canonical writings *or* books, sacred canon

2 **Bible, Holy Bible, Scripture, the Scriptures, Holy Scripture,** Holy Writ, the Book, the Good Book, the Book of Books, the Word, the Word of God; Vulgate, Septuagint, Douay Bible, Authorized *or* King James Version, Revised Version, American Revised Version; Revised Standard Version; Jerusalem Bible; Testament; canon

3 **Old Testament,** Tenach; Hexateuch, Octateuch; Pentateuch, Chumash, Five Books of Moses, **Torah,** the Law, the Jewish *or* Mosaic Law, Law of Moses; the Prophets, Nebiim, Major *or* Minor Prophets; the Writings, Hagiographa, Ketubim; Apocrypha, noncanonical writings

4 **New Testament; Gospels,** Evangels, the Gospel, Good News, Good *or* Glad Tidings; Synoptic Gospels, Epistles, Pauline Epistles, Catholic Epistles, Johannine Epistles; Acts, Acts of the Apostles; Apocalypse, Revelation

5 <Jewish> Torah, **Talmud,** Targum, Mishnah, Gemara; Masorah, Bahir, Midrash

6 <Islamic> **Koran,** Qur'an, Hadith, Sunna

7 <other texts> sacred text, scripture, sacred writings, canonical writings, canon; Avesta, **Zend-Avesta;** Granth, Adigranth; Tao Té Ching; Analects of Confucius; the Eddas; Arcana Caelestia; **Book of Mormon;** Science and Health with Key to the Scriptures

8 <Hindu> **the Vedas, Veda,** Rig-Veda, Yajur-Veda, Sama-Veda, Atharva-Veda, sruti; Brahmana, Upanishad, Aranyaka; Samhita; shastra, Smriti, Purana, Tantra, Agama; Bhagavad-Gita

9 <Buddhist> Tripitaka; Vinaya Pitaka, Sutta Pitaka, Abhidamma Pitaka; Dhammapada, Jataka; The Diamond Sutra, The Heart Sutra, The Lotus Sutra, Prajnaparamita Sutra

10 **revelation, divine revelation; inspiration,** afflatus, divine inspiration; theopneusty, theopneustia; theophany, theophania, epiphany; **mysticism,** direct *or* immediate intuition *or* communication, mystical experience, mystical intuition, contemplation, ecstasy; **prophecy,** prophetic revelation, apocalypse

ADJS **11** **scriptural, Biblical,** Old-Testament, New-Testament, Gospel, Mosaic, Yahwist, Yahwistic, Elohist; **revealed, revelational;** prophetic, apocalyptic, apocalyptical; **inspired,** theopneustic; evangelic, evangelical, evangelistic, gospel; apostolic, apostolical; textual, textuary; canonical; Bible-thumping <nf>

12 Talmudic, Mishnaic, Gemaric, Masoretic; rabbinic

13 epiphanic, mystic, mystical

14 Koranic; Avestan; Eddic; Mormon

15 Vedic; tantrist

684 PROPHETS, RELIGIOUS FOUNDERS

NOUNS **1** **prophet** 962.4, *vates sacer* <L>; Old Testament prophets ; minor prophets

2 <Christian founders> **evangelist, apostle, disciple,** saint; Matthew, Mark, Luke, John; Paul; Peter; **the Fathers, fathers of the church**

3 Martin Luther, John Calvin, John Wycliffe, Jan Hus, John Wesley, John Knox, George Fox <Protestant reformers>; Emanuel Swedenborg <Church of the New Jerusalem>; Mary Baker Eddy <Christian Science>; Joseph Smith <Church of Jesus Christ of Latter-day Saints>

4 Buddha, Gautama Buddha <Buddhism>; Mahavira *or* Vardhamana *or* Jina <Jainism>; Mirza Ali Muhammad of Shiraz *or* the Bab <Babism>; Muhammad *or* Mohammed <Islam>; Confucius <Confucianism>; Lao-tzu <Taoism>; Zoroaster *or* Zarathustra <Zoroastrianism>; Nanak <Sikhism>

685 SANCTITY

<sacred quality>

NOUNS **1** **sanctity,** sanctitude; **sacredness, holiness,** hallowedness, numinousness; sacrosanctness, sacrosanctity; heavenliness, transcendence, divinity, divineness 677.1; venerableness, **venerability, blessedness;** awesomeness, awfulness; inviolableness, **inviolability;** ineffability, unutterability, unspeakability, inexpressibility, inenarrableness; godliness 692.2; odor of sanctity

2 **the sacred,** the holy, the holy of holies, the numinous, the ineffable, the unutterable, the unspeakable, the inexpressible, the inenarrable, the transcendent

3 **sanctification, hallowing; purification;** beatitude, blessing; **glorification,** exaltation, enskying; **consecration,** dedication, devotion, setting apart; sainting, canonization, enshrinement; **sainthood, beatification; blessedness; grace,** state of grace; justification, justification by faith, justification by works

4 **redemption,** redeemedness, **salvation,** conversion, regeneration, new life, reformation, adoption; **rebirth, new birth, second birth, reincarnation,** spiritual rebirth; circumcision, spiritual purification *or* cleansing; spiritual awakening, metanoia

VERBS **5** **sanctify, hallow; purify,** cleanse, wash one's sins away; **bless,** beatify; **glorify,** exalt, ensky; **consecrate,** dedicate, devote, set apart; **beatify, saint, canonize;** enshrine

6 **redeem,** regenerate, reform, convert, save, give salvation

ADJS **7** **sacred, holy,** numinous, **sacrosanct, religious, spiritual,** heavenly, divine; faith-based; **venerable,** awesome, awful; inviolable, **inviolate,** untouchable; **ineffable,** unutterable, unspeakable, inexpressible, inenarrable

8 **sanctified, hallowed; blessed,** consecrated, devoted, dedicated, set apart; **glorified, exalted,** enskied; **saintly,** sainted, beatified, canonized

9 **redeemed, saved,** converted, regenerated, regenerate, justified, reborn, born-again, renewed; circumcised, spiritually purified *or* cleansed

686 UNSANCTITY

NOUNS **1** **unsanctity,** unsanctitude; **unsacredness, unholiness,** unhallowedness, unblessedness; profanity, profaneness; unregenerateness, reprobation; **worldliness,** secularity, secularism; secular humanism

2 **the profane,** the unholy; the temporal, the secular, **the worldly,** the fleshly, the mundane; the world, the flesh, and the devil

ADJS **3** **unsacred,** nonsacred, **unholy,** unhallowed, unsanctified, unblessed; profane, **secular, temporal, worldly,** fleshly, mundane; unsaved, unredeemed, unregenerate, reprobate

687 ORTHODOXY

NOUNS **1** **orthodoxy,** orthodoxness, orthodoxism; **soundness,** soundness of doctrine, rightness, right belief *or* doctrine; **authoritativeness,** authenticity, canonicalness, canonicity; traditionalism; the truth, religious truth, gospel truth

2 **the faith, true faith,** apostolic faith, primitive faith; old-time religion, faith of our fathers

3 **the Church, the true church,** Holy Church, Church of Christ, the Bride of the Lamb, body of Christ, temple of the Holy Ghost, body of Christians, members in Christ, disciples *or* followers of Christ; apostolic church; universal church, the church universal; church visible, church invisible; church militant, church triumphant

4 **true believer,** orthodox Christian; Sunni Muslim; Orthodox Jew; orthodox, orthodoxian, orthodoxist; textualist, textuary; canonist; fundamentalist; the orthodox

5 **strictness,** strict interpretation, scripturalism, evangelicalism; hyperorthodoxy, puritanism, puritanicalness, purism; staunchness; straitlacedness, stiff-neckedness, hideboundness; hard line <nf>; **bigotry** 980.1; **dogmatism** 970.6; **fundamentalism,** literalism, precisianism; bibliolatry; Sabbatarianism; sabbatism

6 **bigot** 980.5; **dogmatist** 970.7

ADJS 7 **orthodox,** orthodoxical; of the faith, of the true faith; **sound,** firm, faithful, true, true-blue, right-thinking; Christian; **evangelical; scriptural,** canonical; traditional, traditionalistic; literal, textual; standard, customary, conventional; **authoritative,** authentic, accepted, received, approved; correct, right, proper

8 **strict,** scripturalistic, evangelical; hyperorthodox, puritanical, purist *or* puristic, straitlaced, staunch; hidebound, hardline <nf>, creedbound; **bigoted** 980.10; **dogmatic** 970.22; **fundamentalist,** precisianist *or* precisianistic, literalist *or* literalistic; Sabbatarian

688 UNORTHODOXY

NOUNS 1 **unorthodoxy, heterodoxy;** unorthodoxness, **unsoundness,** un-Scripturality; **unauthoritativeness,** unauthenticity, uncanonicalness, uncanonicity; **nonconformity** 868

2 **heresy,** false doctrine, **misbelief; fallacy, error** 975

3 **infidelity,** infidelism; unchristianity; gentilism; **atheism, unbelief** 695.5

4 **paganism, heathenism;** paganry, heathenry; pagandom, heathendom; pagano-Christianism; allotheism; animism, animatism; idolatry 697

5 **heretic, misbeliever;** heresiarch; nonconformist 868.3; antinomian, Albigensian, Arian, Donatist, etc

6 **gentile;** non-Christian; **non-Jew,** goy, goyim, non-Jewish man *or shegets* <Yiddish>, non-Jewish woman *or shiksa* <Yiddish>; non-Muslim, non-Moslem, non-Muhammadan, non-Mohammedan, kaffir; zendik, zendician, zendikite; non-Mormon; infidel; unbeliever 695.11

7 **pagan, heathen;** allotheist; animist; idolater 697.4

VERBS 8 **misbelieve, err,** stray, deviate, wander, go astray, stray from the path, step out of line <nf>, go wrong, fall into error; be wrong, be mistaken, be in error; serve Mammon

ADJS 9 **unorthodox,** nonorthodox, **heterodox, heretical; unsound; unscriptural,** uncanonical, apocryphal; **unauthoritative,** unauthentic, unaccepted, unreceived, unapproved; **fallacious,** erroneous 975.16; antinomian, Albigensian, Arian, Donatist, etc

10 **infidel,** infidelic, misbelieving; **atheistic,** unbelieving 695.19; **unchristian,** non-Christian; gentile, non-Jewish, goyish, uncircumcised; non-Muslim, non-Muham-madan, non-Mohammedan, non-Moslem, non-Islamic; non-Mormon

11 **pagan, paganish,** paganistic; **heathen, heathenish;** pagano-Christian; allotheistic; animist, animistic; idolatrous 697.7

689 OCCULTISM

NOUNS 1 **occultism, esoterics,** esotericism, esoterica, esoterism, esotery; cabalism, cabala *or* kabala *or* kabballa; yoga, yogism, yogeeism; **theosophy,** anthroposophy; symbolics, symbolism; anagogics; anagoge; hermetics; shamanism, spiritism, animism; mystery, mystification; hocus-pocus, mumbo jumbo; mysticism 683.10

2 **supernaturalism,** supranaturalism, preternaturalism, **transcendentalism; the supernatural,** the supersensible, the paranormal

3 **metaphysics,** hyperphysics, transphysical science, the first philosophy *or* theology

4 **psychics,** psychism, psychicism; **parapsychology, psychical** *or* **psychic research;** metapsychics, metapsychism, metapsychology; psychosophy; panpsychism; psychic monism

5 **spiritualism,** spiritism; mediumism; necromancy; séance, sitting; spirit 988.1

6 psychic *or* psychical phenomena, spirit manifestation; materialization; spirit rapping, table tipping *or* turning; poltergeistism, poltergeist;

telekinesis, psychokinesis, power of mind over matter, telesthesia, teleportation; levitation; trance speaking, glossolalia; psychorrhagy; hallucination, déjà vu; séance; automatism, psychography, automatic *or* trance *or* spirit writing; Ouija board, Ouija; planchette; out-of-body experience; cosmic vibration, synchronicity; UFO sighting, alien encounter

7 **ectoplasm,** exteriorized protoplasm; aura, emanation, effluvium; ectoplasy; bioplasma

8 **extrasensory perception** *or* ESP; **clairvoyance,** lucidity, second sight, insight, sixth sense, inner sense, third eye, the force <nf>; intuition 934; foresight 961; premonition 133.1; clairsentience, clairaudience, crystal vision, psychometry, metapsychosis, feyness

9 **telepathy, mental telepathy, mind reading,** thought transference, telepathic transmission; telergy, telesthesia; telepathic dream, telepathic hallucination, cosmic consciousness

10 **divination** 962.2; **sorcery** 690

11 **occultist,** esoteric, mystic, mystagogue, cabalist, supernaturalist, transcendentalist; adept, mahatma; yogi, yogin, yogist; theosophist, anthroposophist; fork bender, unspeller

12 **parapsychologist;** psychist, psychicist; **metapsychist;** panpsychist; **metaphysician,** metaphysicist

13 **psychic; spiritualist,** spiritist, **medium,** ecstatic, spirit rapper, automatist, psychographist; necromancer

14 **clairvoyant;** clairaudient, clairsentient; seer, prophet; psychometer, psychometrist

15 **telepathist, mental telepathist, mind reader,** thought reader

16 **diviner** 962.4; **sorcerer** 690.5

17 **astral body,** astral, linga sharira, design body, subtle body, vital body, etheric body, bliss body, Buddhic body, spiritual body, soul body; kamarupa, desire *or* kamic body; causal body; mental *or* mind body

18 <seven principles of man, theosophy> spirit, atman; mind, manas; soul, buddhi; life principle, vital force, prana; astral body, linga sharira; physical *or* dense *or* gross body, sthula sharira; principle of desire, kama

19 **spiritualization,** etherealization, idealization; **dematerialization,** immaterialization, unsubstantialization; **disembodiment,** disincarnation

VERBS 20 **spiritualize,** spiritize; etherealize; idealize; **dematerialize,** immaterialize, unsubstantialize; **disembody,** disincarnate; teleport

21 practice spiritualism, hold a séance *or* sitting; call up spirits 690.11

22 **telepathize, read one's mind**

ADJS 23 **occult, esoteric, esoterical, mysterious,** mystic, mystical, recondite, obscure, arcane; anagogic, anagogical; metaphysic, metaphysical; cabalic, cabalistic; **paranormal, supernatural** 870.15; theosophical, theosophist, anthroposophical

24 **psychic, psychical, spiritual; spiritualistic,** spiritistic; mediumistic; **clairvoyant,** second-sighted, clairaudient, clairsentient, **telepathic; extrasensory,** psychosensory; supersensible, supersensual, pretersensual; telekinetic, psychokinetic; automatist; unconscious, subconscious; transphysical

690 SORCERY

NOUNS 1 **sorcery, necromancy, magic,** sortilege, **wizardry,** theurgy, gramarye , rune, glamour; **witchcraft,** spellcraft, spellbinding, spellcasting; **witchery,** witchwork, bewitchery, enchantment; possession; **voodooism, voodoo,** hoodoo, wanga, juju, jujuism, obeah, obeahism; shamanism; magism, magianism; fetishism; totemism; vampirism; thaumaturgy, thaumaturgia, thaumaturgics, thaumaturgism; theurgy; alchemy; white *or* natural magic; sympathetic magic, chaos magic; **divination** 962.2; spell, charm 691

2 **black magic,** the black art; **diabolism, demonism,** diablerie, demonology, Satanism

3 <practices> magic circle; ghost dance; Sabbath, coven, witches' Sabbath *or* Sabbat; ordeal, ordeal by battle *or* fire *or* water *or* lots; Halloween, Walpurgis Night, witching hour, black mass

4 **conjuration,** conjurement, evocation, invocation; **exorcism,** exorcisation; exsufflation; **incantation** 691.4

5 **sorcerer, necromancer, wizard, wonder-worker,** warlock, theurgist; warlock, male witch; thaumaturge, thaumaturgist, miracle- *or* wonder-worker; alchemist; **conjurer; diviner** 962.4; dowser, water witch *or* diviner; diabolist; Faust, Comus

6 **magician,** mage, magus; Merlin; prestidigitator, illusionist 357.2

7 **shaman,** shamanist; **voodoo,** voodooist, wangateur, **witch doctor,** obeah doctor, **medicine man,** mundunugu, isangoma; witch-hunter, witch-finder; exorcist, exorciser; unspeller

8 **sorceress,** shamaness; **witch,** witchwoman <nf>, witchwife, **hex, hag,** lamia; witch of Endor; coven, witches' coven, Weird Sisters

9 **bewitcher, enchanter, charmer, spellbinder; enchantress, siren,** vampire; Circe; Medusa, Medea, Gorgon, Stheno, Euryale

VERBS **10** sorcerize, shamanize; make *or* work magic, wave a wand, rub the ring *or* lamp; ride a broomstick; alchemize

11 **conjure, conjure up,** evoke, invoke, raise, summon, call up; **call up spirits,** conjure *or* conjure up spirits, summon spirits, raise ghosts, evoke from the dead

12 **exorcise,** lay; lay ghosts, **cast out devils;** unspell

13 cast a spell, wave a wand, bewitch 691.9

ADJS **14** sorcerous, necromantic, **magic, magical,** magian, numinous, thaumaturgic, thaumaturgical, miraculous, wizardlike, wizardly; alchemical, alchemistic, alchemistical; shaman, shamanic, shamanist *or* shamanistic; witchlike, witchy, witch; necromantic; voodoo, hoodoo <nf>, voodooistic; incantatory, incantational, spellbinding, hypnotic, autohypnotic; talismanic, fetishistic

691 SPELL, CHARM

NOUNS **1** **spell,** magic spell, **charm,** glamour, weird *or* cantrip, wanga; hand of glory; evil eye, whammy <nf>; **hex, jinx, curse; exorcism**

2 **bewitchment, witchery, bewitchery; enchantment, entrancement,** fascination, captivation; illusion, maya; bedevilment; **possession, obsession**

3 **trance, ecstasy,** ecstasis, transport, mystic transport, seance; meditation, contemplation; **rapture;** yoga trance, dharana, dhyana, samadhi; hypnosis 22.7

4 **incantation, conjuration,** magic words *or* formula, invocation, evocation, chant; hocus-pocus, abracadabra, mumbo jumbo; open sesame, abraxas, paternoster

5 **charm, amulet, talisman, fetish,** periapt, phylactery; **voodoo, hoodoo,** juju, obeah, mumbo jumbo; **good-luck charm,** good-luck piece, **lucky piece** *or* **charm,** rabbit's-foot, lucky bean, four-leaf clover, whammy <nf>; mascot; madstone; love charm, philter; scarab, scarabaeus, scarabee; veronica, sudarium; swastika, fylfot, gammadion; potion; bell, book, and candle

6 **wish-bringer,** wish-giver; **wand, magic wand,** Aaron's rod; Aladdin's lamp, magic ring, magic belt, magic spectacles, magic carpet, seven-league boots; wishing well, wishing stone, wishing cap, Fortunatus's cap; cap of darkness, Tarnkappe, Tarnhelm; fern seed; **wishbone,** wishing bone, merrythought <Brit>

VERBS **7** **cast a spell,** spell, **spellbind; entrance,** trance, put in a trance; **hypnotize, mesmerize**

8 **charm,** becharm, **enchant, fascinate,** captivate, glamour

9 **bewitch,** witch, **hex, jinx;** voodoo, hoodoo; **possess, obsess;** bedevil, diabolize, demonize; hagride;

overlook, look on with the evil eye, cast the evil eye

10 **put a curse on,** put a hex on, put a juju on, put obeah on, give the evil eye, give the *malocchio,* give a whammy <nf>

ADJS 11 **bewitching, witching;** illusory, illusive, illusionary; **charming, enchanting, entrancing, spellbinding, fascinating,** glamorous, Circean

12 **enchanted, charmed,** becharmed, charmstruck, charm-bound; **spellbound,** spell-struck, spell-caught; **fascinated,** captivated; **hypnotized, mesmerized;** under a spell, in a trance

13 **bewitched,** witched, witch-charmed, witch-held, witch-struck; hag-ridden; **possessed,** taken over, obsessed

692 PIETY

NOUNS 1 **piety, piousness,** pietism; **religion, faith; religiousness, religiosity,** religionism, religious-mindedness; theism; love of God, adoration; **devoutness,** devotion, devotedness, worship 696, worshipfulness, prayerfulness, cultism; faithfulness, dutifulness, observance, churchgoing, conformity 867; sanctimony; **reverence,** veneration; discipleship, followership; daily communion; deism, mysticism, spirituality

2 **godliness,** godlikeness; fear of God; **sanctity,** sanctitude; odor of sanctity, beauty of holiness; **righteousness, holiness,** goodness; **spirituality,** spiritual-mindedness, holy-mindedness, heavenly-mindedness, godly-mindedness; **purity,** pureness, pure-heartedness, pureness of heart; **saintliness,** saintlikeness; saintship, sainthood; angelicalness, seraphicalness; heavenliness; **unworldliness,** unearthliness, other-worldliness

3 **zeal,** zealousness, zealotry, zealotism; unction; **evangelism, revival,** evangelicalism, revivalism; pentecostalism, charismatic movement; charismatic renewal, baptism in the spirit; charismatic gift, gift of tongues, glossolalia; **overreligiousness, religiosity,** overpiousness, overrighteousness, **overzealousness,** overdevoutness; bibliolatry; fundamentalism, militance, **fanaticism** 926.11; **sanctimony** 693

4 **believer,** truster, accepter, receiver; God-fearing man, pietist, religionist, saint, theist; **devotee,** devotionalist, votary; **zealot,** zealotist, fundamentalist, militant; **churchgoer,** churchman, churchite; pillar of the church; communicant, daily communicant; **convert,** proselyte, neophyte, catechumen; **disciple,** follower, servant, faithful servant; **fanatic**

5 **the believing, the faithful,** the righteous, the good; the elect, the chosen, the saved; the children of God, the children of light; Christendom, the Church 687.3

VERBS 6 **be pious, be religious; have faith,** trust in God, love God, fear God; witness, bear witness, affirm, **believe** 953.10; keep the faith, fight the good fight, let one's light shine, praise and glorify God, walk humbly with one's God; be observant, follow righteousness

7 **be converted, get religion** <nf>, receive *or* accept Christ, stand up for Jesus, be washed in the blood of the Lamb; be born again, see the light, meet God, enter the church

ADJS 8 **pious,** pietistic; **religious,** religious-minded; theistic; **devout,** devoted, devotional, dedicated, worshipful, prayerful, cultish, cultist, cultistic; **reverent,** reverential, venerative, venerational, adoring, solemn; faithful, dutiful, worshipful; orthodox; affirming, witnessing, believing 953.21; keeping the faith; **observant, practicing**

9 **godly, godlike; God-fearing; righteous, holy,** good; **spiritual,** spiritual-minded, holy-minded, godly-minded, heavenly-minded; **pure,** purehearted, pure in heart; **saintly,** saintlike; **angelic, angelical,** seraphic, seraphical; heavenly; **unworldly,** unearthly, other-

wordly, not of the earth, not of this world

10 **regenerate,** regenerated, **converted, redeemed, saved,** God-fearing, theopathic, humble, prostrate; reborn, **born-again;** sanctified 685.8

11 **zealous,** zealotical; ardent, unctuous; **overreligious,** ultrareligious, overpious, overrighteous, **overzealous,** overdevout; holier-than-thou; crusading, missionary, Bible-thumping; **fanatical** 926.32; sanctimonious 693.5

693 SANCTIMONY

NOUNS **1** **sanctimony, sanctimoniousness; pietism,** piety, **piousness,** pietisticalness, false piety; religionism, religiosity; **self-righteousness;** goodiness *and* goody-goodiness <nf>; pharisaism, pharisaicalness; Tartuffery, Tartuffism; **falseness, insincerity, hypocrisy** 354.6; affectation 500; **cant,** mummery, snivel, snuffle; unction, unctuousness, oiliness, smarm *and* smarminesss <nf>, mealymouthedness

2 **lip service, mouth honor,** mouthing, lip homage *or* worship *or* devotion *or* praise *or* reverence; formalism, solemn mockery; BOMFOG *or* brotherhood of man and fatherhood of God

3 **pietist,** religionist, **hypocrite,** religious hypocrite, canting hypocrite, pious fraud, religious *or* spiritual humbug, whited sepulcher, **pharisee,** Holy Willie <Robert Burns>; bleeding heart <nf>; **canter,** ranter, snuffler, sniveler; dissembler, dissimulator; affecter, poser 500.8; **lip server,** lip worshiper, formalist; Pharisee, scribes and Pharisees; Tartuffe, Pecksniff, Mawworm, Joseph Surface

VERBS **4** be sanctimonious, be hypocritical; cant, snuffle, snivel; give mouth honor, render *or* pay lip service

ADJS **5** **sanctimonious,** sanctified, **pious, pietistic, pietistical,** self-righteous, pharisaic, pharisaical, **holier-than-thou,** holier-than-the-pope <nf>; goody *and* goody-goody *and* goo-goo <nf>; **false, insincere, hypocritical** 354.33; affected 500.15; Tartuffish, Tartuffian; canting, sniveling, unctuous, mealy-mouthed, smarmy <nf>

694 IMPIETY

NOUNS **1** **impiety, impiousness;** ungodliness, godlessness; **irreverence,** undutifulness; desertion, renegadism, apostasy, recreancy; backsliding, recidivism, lapse, fall *or* lapse from grace; **atheism, irreligion; unsanctity** 686

2 **sacrilege, blasphemy,** blaspheming, impiety; **profanity,** profaneness; sacrilegiousness, blasphemousness; **desecration, profanation;** tainting, pollution, contamination

3 sacrilegist, **blasphemer,** Sabbath-breaker; deserter, renegade, apostate, recreant; backslider, recidivist; **atheist,** unbeliever 695.11

VERBS **4** **desecrate, profane,** dishonor, unhallow, commit sacrilege

5 **blaspheme;** vilify, abuse 513.7; curse, swear 513.6; take in vain; taint, pollute, contaminate

ADJS **6** **impious, irreverent,** undutiful; **profane,** profanatory; **sacrilegious, blasphemous;** renegade, apostate, recreant, backsliding, recidivist *or* recidivistic, lapsed, fallen, lapsed *or* fallen from grace; atheistic, **irreligious** 695.17; **unsacred** 686.3

695 NONRELIGIOUSNESS

NOUNS **1** **nonreligiousness, unreligiousness; undevoutness;** indevoutness, indevotion, undutifulness, nonobservance; adiaphorism, indifferentism, Laodiceanism, lukewarm piety; indifference 102; **laicism,** unconsecration; **deconsecration, secularization,** laicization, desacralization

2 **secularism, worldliness,** earthliness, earthiness, mundaneness;

unspirituality, carnality; worldly-mindedness, earthly-mindedness, carnal-mindedness; materialism, Philistinism

3 **ungodliness,** godlessness, **unrighteousness, irreligion, unholiness,** unsaintliness, unangelicalness; unchristianliness, un-Christliness; impiety 694; **wickedness, sinfulness** 654.4

4 **unregeneracy,** unredeemedness, **reprobacy,** gracelessness, shriftlessness

5 **unbelief, disbelief** 955.1; infidelity, infidelism, faithlessness; **atheism;** nullifidianism, minimifidianism

6 **agnosticism; skepticism, doubt, incredulity,** Pyrrhonism, Humism; scoffing 508.1

7 **freethinking,** free thought, **latitudinarianism; humanism,** secular humanism; areligious

8 antireligion; antichristianism, antichristianity; antiscripturism

9 **iconoclasm,** iconoclasticism, image breaking

10 **irreligionist; worldling,** earthling; **materialist;** iconoclast, idoloclast; anti-Christian, antichrist

11 **unbeliever, disbeliever,** nonbeliever; **atheist, infidel, pagan, heathen**, heretic; nullifidian, minimifidian; secularist; **gentile** 688.6

12 **agnostic; skeptic, doubter,** dubitante, **doubting Thomas,** scoffer, Pyrrhonist, Humist

13 **freethinker, latitudinarian,** *esprit fort* <Fr>; humanist, secular humanist

VERBS 14 **disbelieve,** doubt 955.6; scoff 508.9; **laicize,** deconsecrate, **secularize,** desacralize

ADJS 15 **nonreligious, unreligious,** having no religious preference; **undevout,** indevout, indevotional, undutiful, nonobservant, nonpracticing; adiamorphic, indifferentist *or* indifferentistic, Laodicean, lukewarm, indifferent 102.6; unconsecrated, **deconsecrated, secularized,** laicized, desacralized

16 **secularist, secularistic, worldly, earthly,** earthy, terrestrial, **mundane,** temporal; **unspiritual, profane,** carnal, **secular;** humanistic, secular-humanistic; worldly minded, earthly minded, carnal-minded; **materialistic,** material, Philistine

17 **ungodly,** godless, **irreligious, unrighteous, unholy,** unsaintly, unangelic, unangelical; impious 694.6; **wicked, sinful** 654.16

18 **unregenerate,** unredeemed, **unconverted,** godless, reprobate, graceless, shriftless, **lost, damned;** lapsed, fallen, recidivist, recidivistic

19 **unbelieving, disbelieving, faithless; infidel,** infidelic; **pagan, heathen; atheistic,** atheist; nullifidian, minimifidian

20 **agnostic; skeptic, skeptical, doubtful, dubious, incredulous,** Humean, Pyrrhonic; Cartesian

21 **freethinking, latitudinarian**

22 **antireligious;** antichristian; antiscriptural; **iconoclastic**

696 WORSHIP

NOUNS 1 **worship,** worshiping, **adoration, devotion, homage, veneration, reverence,** honor; adulation, esteem; cult, cultus, cultism; latria, dulia, hyperdulia; falling down and worshiping, prostration; co-worship; idolatry 697

2 **glorification,** glory, **praise,** extolment, laudation, laud, exaltation, magnification, dignification

3 **paean,** laud; hosanna, hallelujah, alleluia; **hymn,** hymn of praise, **doxology, psalm, anthem,** motet, canticle, chorale; **chant,** versicle; mantra, Vedic hymn *or* chant; plainsong, carol, gospel song; Introit, Miserere; Gloria, Gloria in Excelsis, Gloria Patri; Te Deum, Agnus Dei, Benedicite, Magnificat, Nunc Dimittis; response, responsory, report, answer; Trisagion; antiphon, antiphony; offertory, offertory sentence *or* hymn; hymnody, hymnology, hymnography, psalmody; hymnal

4 **prayer,** praying, **supplication, invocation,** imploration, impetration, entreaty, beseechment, appeal, petition, suit, aid prayer, bid *or* bidding prayer, request, petitionary prayer, act of contrition, penitential prayer,

orison, obsecration, obtestation, confession, rogation, **devotions;** genuflection, prostration; silent prayer, meditation, contemplation, communion; intercession *or* intercessory prayer, suffrage; **grace, thanks, thanksgiving;** litany; breviary, canonical prayers; collect, collect of the Mass, collect of the Communion; Angelus; Paternoster, the Lord's Prayer; Hail Mary, Ave, Ave Maria; Kyrie Eleison; Pax; chaplet; rosary, beads, beadroll; Kaddish, Mourner's Kaddish; prayer wheel *or* machine

5 **benediction, blessing,** benison, invocation, benedicite; sign of the cross; laying on of hands

6 **propitiation,** appeasement 465.1; atonement 658

7 **oblation, offering, sacrifice, immolation,** incense; libation, drink offering; burnt offering, holocaust; thank offering, votive *or* ex voto offering; heave offering, peace offering, sacramental offering, sin *or* piacular offering, whole offering; human sacrifice, mactation, infanticide, hecatomb; self-sacrifice, self-immolation; sutteeism; scapegoat, suttee; offertory, collection; penitence

8 divine service, **service,** public worship, **liturgy** 701.3, office, duty, exercises, **devotions;** meeting; church service, church, celebration; **revival,** revival meeting, camp meeting, tent meeting, praise meeting; watch meeting, watch-night service, watch night; **prayer meeting,** prayers, prayer, call to prayer; morning devotions *or* services *or* prayers, matins, lauds; prime, prime song; tierce, undersong; sext; none, nones; novena; evening devotions *or* services *or* prayers, vesper, vespers, vigils, evensong; compline, night song *or* prayer; bedtime prayer; Mass; pilgrimage, hajj

9 **worshiper,** adorer, venerator, votary, adulator, communicant, daily communicant, celebrant, churchgoer, chapelgoer, parishioner, follower; prayer, suppliant, supplicant, supplicator, petitioner; orans, orant; beadsman; revivalist, evangelist; congregation; **idolater** 697.4; flock, sheep, congregation, concourse, minyan

10 <sacred object> cross, crucifix, chalice, relic, incense, holy water, thurible, censer, chrism, rosary beads, votive candle, vigil light; phylactery, tefillin, mezuzah, menorah; totem, talisman, charm, amulet

VERBS 11 **worship, adore, reverence, venerate, revere, honor,** respect, adulate, do *or* pay homage to, pay divine honors to, do service, lift up the heart, bow down and worship, humble oneself before, prostrate, genuflect; **idolize** 697.5

12 **glorify, praise, laud, exalt, extol,** magnify, bless, celebrate; praise God, praise *or* glorify the Lord, bless the Lord, praise God from whom all blessings flow; praise Father, Son, and Holy Ghost; give thanks; sing praises, sing the praises of, sound *or* resound the praises of; doxologize, hymn

13 **pray, supplicate,** invoke, petition, make supplication, *daven* <Yiddish>; **implore, beseech** 440.11, obtest; offer a prayer, send up a prayer, commune with God; **say one's prayers;** tell one's beads, recite the rosary; **say grace, give** *or* **return thanks;** pray over

14 **bless, give one's blessing,** give benediction, confer a blessing upon, invoke benefits upon; cross, make the sign of the cross over *or* upon; lay hands on

15 **propitiate,** make propitiation; appease 465.7; **offer sacrifice,** sacrifice, make sacrifice to, immolate before, offer up an oblation

ADJS 16 **worshipful,** worshiping; **adoring,** adorant; **devout,** devotional; pious; **reverent,** reverential, dedicated; **venerative,** venerational; solemn; at the feet of; **prayerful,** praying, penitent, **supplicatory,** supplicant, suppliant; precatory, precative, imploring, honoring, on one's knees, on bended knee; prone *or* prostrate before, in the dust; blessing, benedictory, benedictional; propitiatory; anthemic

17 O Lord!, our Father which art in heaven!; God grant!, pray God that!; God bless!, God save!, God forbid!

697 IDOLATRY

NOUNS **1** **idolatry,** idolatrousness, idolism, idolodulia, **idol worship;** heathenism, paganism; image worship, iconolatry, iconoduly; cult, cultism; totemism; **fetishism** *or* fetichism; **demonism,** demonolatry, demon *or* devil worship, Satanism; animal worship, snake worship, fire worship, pyrolatry, Parsiism, Zoroastrianism; sun worship, star worship, Sabaism; tree worship, plant worship, Druidism, nature worship; phallic worship, phallicism; hero worship; idolomancy

2 **idolization,** fetishization; **deification,** apotheosis

3 **idol; fetish,** totem, joss; **graven image, golden calf**, effigy; devil-god; Baal, Jaganatha *or* Juggernaut; sacred cow

4 **idolater,** idolatress, idolizer, idolatrizer, iconolater, cultist, idolist, idol worshiper, image-worshiper; fetishist, totemist; demon *or* devil worshiper, demonolater, chthonian; animal worshiper, zoolater, theriolater, therolater, snake worshiper, ophiolater; fire worshiper, pyrolater, Parsi, Zoroastrian; sun worshiper, heliolater; star worshiper, Sabaist; tree worshiper, arborolater, dendrolater, plant worshiper, Druid, nature worshiper; phallic worshiper; anthropolater, archaeolater, etc; groupie, hero-worshiper

VERBS **5** **idolatrize,** idolize, idolify, idol; fetishize, fetish, totemize; **make an idol of, deify,** apotheosize; idealize, lionize, hero-worship, look up to

6 **worship idols,** worship the golden calf, *adorer le veau d'or* <Fr>

ADJS **7** **idolatrous,** idolatric *or* idolatrical, **idol worshiping;** idolistic, idolizing, iconolatrous, cultish, fetishistic, totemistic; heathen, pagan; demonolatrous, chthonian; heliolatrous; bibliolatrous; zoolatrous; hero-worshiping, lionizing

698 THE MINISTRY

NOUNS **1** **the ministry, pastorate,** pastorage, pastoral care, cure *or* care of souls, **the Church,** the cloth, the pulpit, the desk; **priesthood,** priestship; apostleship; call, vocation, sacred calling; holy orders; rabbinate

2 ecclesiasticalism, ecclesiology, priestcraft

3 **clericalism,** sacerdotalism; priesthood; priestism; episcopalianism; ultramontanism

4 **monasticism,** monachism, monkery, **monkhood,** friarhood; celibacy 565

5 ecclesiastical office, church office, dignity

6 **papacy,** papality, **pontificate,** popedom, the Vatican, Apostolic See, See of Rome, the Church

7 hierarchy, hierocracy; theocracy

8 **diocese, see,** archdiocese, bishopric, archbishopric; province; synod, conference; **parish**

9 **benefice,** living, **incumbency,** glebe, advowson; curacy, cure, charge, cure *or* care of souls; prelacy, rectory, vicarage

10 **holy orders, orders** 699.4, major orders, apostolic orders, minor orders; calling, election, nomination, appointment, preferment, induction, institution, installation, investiture; conferment, presentation; **ordination,** ordainment, consecration, canonization, reading in <Brit>

VERBS **11** **be ordained, take holy orders,** take orders, take vows, read oneself in <Brit>; **take the veil,** wear the cloth

12 **ordain,** frock, **canonize, consecrate;** saint

ADJS **13** **ecclesiastic, ecclesiastical, churchly; ministerial, clerical,** sacerdotal, **pastoral; priestly,** priestish; prelatic, prelatical, prelatial; episcopal, episcopalian; archiepiscopal; primatal, primatial, primatical; canonical; capitular, capitulary; abbatical, abbatial; ultramontane; **evangelistic;** rabbinic, rabbinical; priest-ridden; parochial

14 **monastic,** monachal, **monasterial, monkish;** conventual

15 **papal, pontific, pontifical,** apostolic, apostolical; **popish** *or* papist *or* papistic *or* papistical *or* papish <nf>

16 **hierarchical,** hierarchal, hieratic; hierocratic; theocratic, theocratist

17 **ordained;** in orders, in holy orders, of the cloth

699 THE CLERGY

NOUNS 1 **clergy, ministry,** the cloth; clerical order, clericals; **priesthood;** priestery; presbytery; prelacy; Sacred College; rabbinate; hierocracy, pastorage; clerical venue

2 **clergyman,** clergywoman, clergyperson, man *or* woman of the cloth, **divine, ecclesiastic, churchman, cleric,** clerical; clerk, clerk *or* person in holy orders, tonsured cleric; **minister, minister of the Gospel, parson, pastor,** *abbé* and *curé* <Fr>, **rector,** curate, vicar, man *or* woman of God, servant of God, shepherd, sky pilot *and* Holy Joe <nf>, reverend <nf>; supply minister *or* preacher, supply clergy; **chaplain;** military chaplain, padre <nf>; the Reverend, the Very *or* Right Reverend; Doctor of Divinity *or* DD; elder

3 **preacher,** sermoner, sermonizer, sermonist, homilist; pulpiter, pulpiteer; predicant, predikant; preaching friar; circuit rider; televison *or* TV preacher, telepreacher <nf>

4 holy orders, major orders, priest *or* presbyter, deacon *or* diaconus, subdeacon *or* subdiaconus; minor orders, acolyte *or* acolytus, exorcist *or* exorcista, reader *or* lector, doorkeeper *or* ostiarius; ordinand, candidate for holy orders

5 **priest, father,** father in Christ, **padre,** cassock, presbyter; curé, parish priest; confessor, father confessor, spiritual father *or* director *or* leader, holy father; penitentiary

6 **evangelist,** revivalist, evangel, evangelicalist; **missionary,** missioner; missionary apostolic, missionary rector, colporteur; television *or* TV evangelist, televangelist <nf>

7 benefice-holder, beneficiary, **incumbent;** resident, residentiary

8 church dignitary, ecclesiarch, ecclesiast, hierarch; minor *or* lay officer

9 <Catholic> pope, pontiff; cardinal, dean, archbishop, bishop, provost, high priest, ecclesiarch, canon, monsignor

10 <Mormon> deacon, teacher, priest, elder, Seventy, high priest, bishop, patriarch, apostle; Aaronic priesthood, Melchizedek priesthood

11 <Jewish> **rabbi,** rebbe, rabbin; chief rabbi; *baal kore* <Yiddish>; cantor; priest, high priest; maggid; Levite; scribe

12 <Muslim> imam, qadi, sheikh, mullah, murshid, mufti, hajji, muezzin, dervish, abdal, fakir, santon, ayatollah

13 <Hindu> Brahman, pujari, purohit, pundit, guru, bashara, vairagi *or* bairagi, Ramwat, Ramanandi; sannyasi; yogi, yogin; bhikshu, bhikhari

14 <Buddhist> bonze, bhikku, poonghie, talapoin, bodhisattva, guru; lama; Grand Lama, Dalai Lama, Panchen Lama

15 <pagan> Druid, Druidess; flamen; hierophant, hierodule, hieros, daduchus, mystes, epopt

16 **religious,** *religieux* <Fr>; **monk,** monastic, lama, bhikkhu; brother, lay brother; cenobite, conventual; caloyer, hieromonach; **mendicant, friar;** pilgrim, palmer; stylite, pillarist, pillar saint; beadsman; prior, claustral *or* conventual prior, grand prior, general prior; abbot; lay abbot, abbacomes; hermit 584.5; ascetic 667.2; celibate 565.2

17 **nun,** sister, *religieuse* <Fr>, clergywoman, conventual; abbess, prioress; **mother superior,** lady superior, superioress, the reverend mother, holy mother; canoness, regular *or* secular canoness; novice, postulant

700 THE LAITY

NOUNS 1 **the laity, lay persons,** laymen, laywomen, nonclerics, nonordained persons, seculars, temporalty; brothers, sisters, brethren, sistren <nf>, people; flock, fold, sheep; **congregation,** parishioners, churchgoers, assembly; minyan; **parish,** society; class

2 **layman,** layperson, laic, secular, churchman, **parishioner,** church member; brother, sister, lay brother, lay sister; laywoman, churchwoman; catchumen; communicant

ADJS 3 **lay,** laic *or* laical; **nonecclesiastical,** nonclerical, nonministerial, nonpastoral, nonordained; nonreligious; **secular,** secularist; secularistic; temporal, popular, civil; congregational

701 RELIGIOUS RITES

NOUNS 1 **ritualism,** rituality, ritualization, **ceremonialism, formalism,** liturgism; symbolism, symbolics; **cult,** cultus, cultism; sacramentalism, sacramentarianism; sabbatism, Sabbatarianism; ritualization, **solemnization,** solemn observance, **celebration;** liturgics, liturgiology

2 **ritualist, ceremonialist,** celebrant, liturgist, **formalist,** formulist, formularist; sacramentalist, sacramentarian; sabbatist, Sabbatarian; High-Churchman, High-Churchist; crucifer, thurifer, acolyte

3 **rite, ritual,** rituality, **liturgy,** holy rite; service, order of worship; **ceremony, ceremonial; observance,** ritual observance; **formality,** solemnity; **form,** formula, formulary, form of worship *or* service, mode of worship; prescribed form; service, function, duty, office, practice; **sacrament,** sacramental, mystery; ordinance; institution

4 **seven sacraments,** mysteries: baptism, confirmation, the Eucharist, penance, extreme unction, holy orders, matrimony

5 **unction,** sacred unction, sacramental anointment, chrism *or* chrisom, chrismation, chrismatory; **extreme unction, last rites,** viaticum; ointment; chrismal

6 **baptism,** baptizement; **christening; immersion,** total immersion; **sprinkling,** aspersion, aspergation; affusion, infusion; baptism for the dead; baptismal regeneration; baptismal gown *or* dress *or* robe, chrismal; baptistery, baptistry, **font; confirmation,** bar *or* bas mitzvah <Jewish>

7 **Eucharist, Lord's Supper, Last Supper, Communion,** Holy Communion, **the Sacrament,** the Holy Sacrament; intinction; consubstantiation, impanation, subpanation, transubstantiation; real presence; elements, consecrated elements, bread and wine, body and blood of Christ; Host, wafer, loaf, bread, altar bread, consecrated bread; Sacrament Sunday

8 **Mass,** *Missa* <L>, Eucharistic rites; **the Liturgy,** the Divine Liturgy; **parts of the Mass,** High Mass, Low Mass

9 <non-Christian rites> initiation, rite of passage; circumcision; bar mitzvah *and* bas mitzvah <Jewish>; Kaddish, shivah; female circumcision; ritual cleaning, ritual bathing; fertility rite; sun dance, rain dance, war dance, ghost dance, potlatch; witches' Sabbath, black mass; hara-kiri

10 **sacred object** *or* **article; ritualistic manual,** Book of Common Prayer, breviary, canon, haggadah <Jewish>, missal *or* Mass book, book of hours, lectionary, prayer book; siddur *and* mahzor <Jewish>

11 **psalter, psalmbook;** Psalm Book, Book of Common Order; the Psalms, Book of Psalms, the Psalter, the Psaltery

12 **holy day,** hallowday <nf>, holytide, holiday; feast, fast, fast day; Sabbath; Sunday, Lord's day; saint's day; church calendar, ecclesiastical calendar

13 Christian holy days ; Jewish holy days

14 <Muslim holy days> Ramadan <month>, Bairam, Muharram

VERBS 15 **celebrate, observe, keep, solemnize;** ritualize; celebrate Mass; communicate, administer Communion; attend Communion, receive the Sacrament, partake of the Lord's Supper; attend Mass

16 **minister, officiate,** do duty, **perform a rite,** perform service *or*

divine service; administer a sacrament, administer the Eucharist, etc; anoint, chrism, bless; confirm, impose, lay hands on; make the sign of the cross

17 **baptize, christen;** dip, immerse; sprinkle, asperge; circumcise

18 **confess,** make confession, receive absolution; **shrive,** hear confession; **absolve,** administer absolution; administer extreme unction

ADJS 19 **ritualistic, ritual; ceremonial, ceremonious; formal,** formular, formulaic, formulary; liturgic, liturgical, **liturgistic, liturgistical;** solemn, consecrated; High-Church; **sacramental,** sacramentarian; eucharistic, eucharistical, baptismal; paschal, Passover; matrimonial, nuptial; funereal

702 ECCLESIASTICAL ATTIRE

NOUNS 1 **canonicals,** clericals <nf>, robes, cloth; **vestments,** vesture; regalia; liturgical garments, ceremonial attire; pontificals, pontificalia, episcopal vestments; habit, veil

2 **robe,** frock, mantle, gown, cloak, surplice, scapular, cassock, cope, hood, clerical collar, etc

3 **staff,** pastoral staff, **crosier, cross,** cross-staff, crook, paterissa

ADJS 4 **vestmental,** vestmentary

703 RELIGIOUS BUILDINGS

NOUNS 1 **church,** kirk, bethel, **meetinghouse,** church house, **house of God,** place of worship, house of worship *or* prayer; conventicle; **mission;** basilica, major *or* patriarchal basilica, minor basilica; **cathedral,** cathedral church; collegiate church

2 **temple,** fane; **tabernacle; synagogue,** *shul* <Yiddish>; **mosque,** masjid; dewal, girja; pagoda; kiack; pantheon; wat, ziggurat, pantheon

3 **chapel,** chapel of ease, chapel royal, side chapel, school chapel, sacrament chapel, Lady chapel, oratory, oratorium; chantry; sacellum, sacrarium

4 **shrine,** holy place, dagoba, cella, naos; sacrarium, sanctum sanctorum, holy of holies, delubrum; tope, stupa; reliquary, *reliquaire* <Fr>

5 **sanctuary, holy of holies, sanctum, sanctum sanctorum,** adytum, sacrarium

6 **cloister, monastery, house, abbey,** friary; priory, priorate; lamasery; **convent, nunnery;** ashram, hermitage, retreat

7 **parsonage, pastorage,** pastorate, manse, **church house,** clergy house; presbytery, **rectory,** vicarage, deanery; glebe; chapter house; deanery, manse

8 bishop's palace; **Vatican;** Lambeth, Lambeth Palace

9 <church interior> vestry, sacristy, sacrarium, sanctuary, diaconicon *or* diaconicum; baptistery; aisle, ambry, apse, blindstory, chancel, choir, choir screen, cloisters, confessional, confessionary , crypt, Easter sepulcher, narthex, nave, porch, presbytery, rood loft, rood stair, rood tower *or* spire *or* steeple, transept, triforium; organ loft

10 <church furnishings> piscina; stoup, holy-water stoup *or* basin; baptismal font; patent; reredos; jube, rood screen, rood arch, chancel screen; altar cloth, cerecloth, chrismal; communion *or* sacrament cloth, corporal, fanon, oblation cloth; rood cloth; baldachin; kneeling stool, *prie-dieu* <Fr>; prayer rug *or* carpet *or* mat

11 <vessels> cruet; chalice; ciborium, pyx; chrismal, chrismatory; monstrance, ostensorium; reliquary; font, holy-water font

12 **altar,** scrobis; bomos, eschara, hestia; **Lord's table,** holy table, **Communion table,** chancel table, table of the Lord, God's board; rood altar; altar desk, missal stand; credence, prothesis, table *or* altar of prothesis, predella; superaltar, retable, retablo, ancona, gradin; altarpiece, altar side, altar rail, altar carpet, altar stair; altar facing *or* front, frontal; altar slab, altar stone, mensal

13 **pulpit, rostrum,** ambo; **lectern,** desk, reading desk

14 <seats> **pew; stall;** mourners' bench, anxious bench *or* seat, penitent form; amen corner; sedilia

ADJS 15 **churchly,** churchish, **ecclesiastical;** churchlike, templelike; cathedral-like, cathedralesque; tabernacular; synagogical, synagogal; pantheonic

16 **claustral, cloistered; monastic,** monachal, **monasterial; coventual,** conventical

704 SHOW BUSINESS, THEATER

NOUNS 1 **show business,** show biz <nf>, the entertainment industry; **the theater, the footlights, the stage, the boards,** the bright lights, Broadway, the Great White Way, the scenes , traffic of the stage; avant-garde theater, contemporary theater, experimental theater, total theater, epic theater, theater of the absurd, theater of cruelty, guerrilla theater, street theater; stagedom, theater world, stage world, stageland, playland; **drama,** legitimate stage *or* theater, legit <nf>, off Broadway, off-off-Broadway; music *or* musical theater, fringe theater; café theater, dinner theater; regional theater; repertory drama *or* theater, stock; summer theater, summer stock, straw hat *or* straw hat circuit <nf>; **vaudeville,** variety; **burlesque; circus,** carnival; magic show; theatromania, theatrophobia

2 **dramatics;** dramatization, dramaticism, dramatism; **theatrics,** theatricism, **theatricalism,** theatricality, staginess; theatricals, amateur theatricals; **histrionics,** histrionism; dramatic *or* histrionic *or* Thespian art; dramatic stroke, *coup de théâtre* <Fr>; **melodramatics,** sensationalism; **dramaturgy,** dramatic structure, play construction, dramatic form; dramatic irony, tragic irony

3 **theatercraft, stagecraft,** stagery, scenecraft; **showmanship**

4 **stage show, show; play,** stage play, piece, vehicle, work; **hit** *or* hit show <nf>, gasser <nf>, success, critical success, audience success, word-of-mouth success, box-office hit, long run; short run, failure, **flop** *and* bomb *and* turkey <nf>

5 **tragedy,** tragic drama, melodrama; tragic flaw; buskin, cothurnus; tragic muse, Melpomene

6 **comedy;** comic relief; comic muse, Thalia; black comedy *or* humor, satire, farce; sock, coxcomb, cap and bells, motley, bladder, slapstick, burlesque; historic comedy

7 **act, scene, number, turn,** bit *and* shtick <nf>, routine <nf>; curtain raiser *or* lifter; introduction; expository scene; monologue, soliloquy; **prologue,** epilogue; **entr'acte,** intermezzo, intermission, interlude, *divertissement* <Fr>, *divertimento* <Ital>, climax; **finale,** afterpiece; exodus, exode; chaser <nf>; curtain call, curtain; encore, ovation; hokum *or* hoke act <nf>; song and dance; burlesque act; stand-up comedy act; sketch, skit

8 **acting, playing,** playacting, performing, **performance,** taking a role *or* part, role-playing; **representation, portrayal, characterization,** interpretation, projection, enactment; **impersonation,** personation, miming, mimicking, mimicry, mimesis; pantomiming, mummery; Method acting; improvisation; ham *and* hammy acting *and* hamming *or* hamming up <nf>, camping it up <nf>, overacting, histrionics; stage presence; stage directions, **business,** stage business, *jeu de théâtre* <Fr>, acting device; stunt *and* gag <nf>; hokum *or* hoke <nf>; buffoonery, slapstick; patter; stand-up comedy; crossover

9 **repertoire, repertory;** stock

10 **role, part,** piece <nf>; cue, **lines,** side; cast; **character,** person, personage; lead, starring *or* lead *or* leading role, fat part, leading man, leading woman *or* lady, hero, heroine; antihero; title role, top billing, protagonist, principal character; supporting role, supporting character; ingenue, *jeune première* or *jeune premier* <Fr>, romantic lead; <Fr>; *soubrette* <Fr>; villain, heavy <nf>, bad guy <nf>, antagonist, deuteragonist; bit, bit part, minor role, speaking part; feed *or* feeder, straight part; walking part, walk-on,

extra; double, stand-in, stunt person, stunt man *or* woman, understudy; top banana, second banana; chorus, Greek chorus; stock part *or* character; **actor** 707.2

11 **engagement,** playing engagement, booking; **run; stand,** one-night stand *or* one-nighter; **circuit,** barnstorming, vaudeville circuit, borscht circuit; **tour, bus-and-truck, production tour;** date, gig <nf>

12 theatrical performance, **performance, show, presentation,** presentment, **production,** entertainment, stage presentation *or* performance; bill; **exhibit, exhibition;** benefit performance, benefit; personal appearance; showcase, tryout, preview; premiere, premier performance, debut, opening night; farewell performance, swan song <nf>; command performance; matinee; sellout, full house

13 **production,** mounting, staging, putting on; stage management; **direction,** *mise-en-scène* <Fr>; blocking; **rehearsal,** dress rehearsal, walk-through, run-through, technical *or* tech rehearsal *or* run, final dress, gypsy rehearsal *or* run-through *or* run

14 **theater, playhouse, house,** theatron, odeum; **auditorium; opera house,** opera; **hall,** music hall, concert hall; **amphitheater;** circle theater, arena, stadium, theater-in-the-round; vaudeville theater; burlesque theater; **little theater,** community theater; open-air theater, outdoor theater; Greek theater; children's theater; Elizabethan theater, Globe Theatre; showboat; dinner theater; cabaret, nightclub, club, night spot, *boîte de nuit* <Fr>

15 **auditorium**, seating; parquet, orchestra, **pit** <Brit>; **orchestra circle,** parquet circle, parterre; **dress circle;** fauteuil *or* theatre stall *or* **stall** <Brit>; **box,** box seat, **loge,** *baignoire* <Fr>; stage box; proscenium boxes, parterre boxes; balcony, gallery, mezzanine; **peanut gallery** *and* paradise <nf>; standing room; box office

16 **stage,** the boards; acting area, playing *or* performing area; thrust stage, three-quarter-round stage, theater-in-the-round; apron, passerelle, apron stage, forestage; proscenium stage, proscenium arch, proscenium; bridge; revolving stage; orchestra, pit, orchestra pit; **bandstand,** shell, band shell; stage right, R; stage left, L, upstage, downstage, backstage, center stage; **wings,** coulisse; dressing room, greenroom; flies, fly gallery, fly floor; gridiron, grid <nf>, board, lightboard, switchboard; dock; prompter's box; curtain, grand drape, safety curtain, asbestos curtain, fire curtain; stage door

17 <stage requisites> **property, prop;** practical piece *or* prop <nf>, hand-prop; costume 5.9; theatrical makeup, makeup, greasepaint, blackface, clown white; spirit gum

18 stage lighting, lights, instruments; **footlights,** foots <nf>, floats; floodlight, flood; bunch light; battens, houselights; **limelight,** follow spot, spotlight *or* spot <nf>, following spot <nf>, arc light, arc, klieg *or* kleig light; color filter, color wheel, medium, gelatin *or* gel; projector, stroboscope *or* strobe *or* strobe light; lightboard; dimmer; marquee; light plot

19 **setting, stage setting,** stage set, **set,** *mise-en-scène* <Fr>; location, locale

20 **scenery,** decor; **scene;** screen, **flat;** cyclorama *or* cyc; batten; side scene, **wing,** coulisse; border; tormentor, **teaser;** wingcut, woodcut; transformation, transformation scene; flipper; counterweight; **curtain,** rag <nf>, hanging; **drop,** drop scene, drop curtain, scrim, cloth; **backdrop,** back cloth <Brit>; act drop *or* curtain; tab, tableau curtain

21 **playbook, script,** text, **libretto;** promptbook; book, book of words; **score; scenario,** continuity, shooting script; scene plot; lines, actor's lines, cue, sides; stage direction; prompt book

22 **dramatist; playwright,** playwriter, dramaturge; doctor *and* play doctor *and* play fixer <nf>; dramatizer; **scriptwriter, scenario writer,**

scenarist, **scenarioist, screenwriter; gagman,** gag writer, joke writer, jokesmith; **librettist;** tragedian, comedian; farcist, *farceur* and *farceuse* <Fr>, farcer; melodramatist; monodramatist; mimographer; **choreographer**

23 theater man, theatrician; **showman,** exhibitor, **producer, impresario; director,** auteur; stage director, **stage manager;** set designer, scenewright; costume designer, costumer, *costumier* and *costumière* <Fr>, wardrobe master *or* mistress; dresser; hair *or* wigmaker *or* designer; makeup artist, visagiste; propsmaster *or* propsmistress; prompter; callboy; playreader; master of ceremonies, MC *or* emcee <nf>; box-office staff; ticket collector; usher, usherer, usherette, doorkeeper; ringmaster, equestrian director; barker, ballyhoo man *and* spieler <nf>

24 stage technician, stagehand, stage crew, machinist , sceneman, scene master, **sceneshifter;** flyman; carpenter; **electrician;** sound man; scene painter, scenic artist, scenewright

25 agent, actor's agent, playbroker, tenpercenter <nf>; **booking agent;** advance agent, advance man; press agent; publicity man *or* agent; business manager, publicity manager

26 patron, patroness; **backer, angel** <nf>, promoter; Dionysus

27 playgoer, theatergoer; attender 221.5, spectator 918, audience 48.6, house; moviegoer, **motion-picture fan** <nf>; first-nighter; standee, groundling ; *claqueur* <Fr>, hired applauder; pass holder, deadhead <nf>, stage-door Johnny; critic, reviewer, talent scout

VERBS **28 dramatize,** theatricalize; melodramatize; scenarize; **present, stage, produce, mount, put on,** put on the stage, adapt for the stage; **put on a show;** try out, preview; give a performance; premiere; **open,** open a show, open a show cold <nf>; set the stage; ring up the curtain, ring down the curtain; **star, feature** <nf>, bill, **headline,** give top billing to; succeed, make *or* be a hit *and* have legs <nf>, be a gas *or* gasser *and* run out of gas <nf>; fail, flop *and* bomb *and* bomb out <nf>; script

29 act, perform, play, playact, tread the boards, strut one's stuff <nf>; appear, **appear on the stage;** act like a trouper; register; emotionalize, emote <nf>; pantomime, mime; patter; sketch; troupe, barnstorm <nf>; improvise, ad-lib, wing it <nf>; steal the show, upstage, steal the spotlight; **debut,** make one's debut *or* bow, come out, take the stage, make an entrance; act as foil *or* feeder, stooge <nf>, be straight man for; **star,** play the lead, get top billing, have one's name in lights, costar, understudy

30 enact, act out; represent, depict, portray; act *or* play *or* perform a part *or* role, role-play, take a part, sustain a part, act *or* play the part of; create a role *or* character; **impersonate,** personate; play opposite, support

31 overact, overdramatize, chew up the scenery <nf>, act all over the stage; **ham** *and* ham it up <nf>, camp it up; play to the gallery; **mug** <nf>, grimace; spout, rant, roar, declaim; milk a scene, milk it; **underact,** underplay, fluff, go blank, throw away <nf>

32 rehearse, practice, go through, walk *or* run through, go over; block; go through one's part, read one's lines; learn one's lines, memorize, con *or* study one's part; be a fast *or* slow study; interpret the part, get into character

ADJS **33 dramatic,** dramatical , **dramaturgic, dramaturgical; theatric, theatrical, histrionic, thespian;** scenic; **stagy;** theaterlike, stagelike; rehearsed, staged, interpreted, improvised; **spectacular; melodramatic;** ham *or* hammy *or* campy <nf>; overacted, overplayed, milked <nf>; underacted, underplayed, thrown away; musical, choral; **operatic;** choreographic, terpsichorean; ballet, balletic; legitimate; stellar, all-star; stagestruck, starstruck; stageworthy, actor-proof

34 **tragic,** heavy; buskined, cothurned; tragicomic *or* tragicomical

35 **comic, light;** tragicomical, **farcical, slapstick;** camp *or* campy <nf>; burlesque

ADVS **36** **on the stage** *or* boards, before an audience, before the footlights; **in the limelight** *or* spotlight; onstage; downstage, upstage; backstage, off stage, behind the scenes; down left *or* DL; down right *or* DR; up left *or* UL; up right *or* UR

705 DANCE

NOUNS **1** **dancing,** terpsichore, dance; the light fantastic; **choreography;** dance drama, choreodrama; **hoofing** <nf>

2 **dance, hop** <nf>, dancing party, **shindig** *and* shindy <nf>; **ball,** *bal* <Fr>; masked ball, masque, mask, masquerade ball, masquerade, *bal masqué* <Fr>, *bal costumé* <Fr>, fancy-dress ball, cotillion *or* cotillon; promenade, **prom** <nf>, formal <nf>; country dance, square dance, barn dance, hoedown; mixer, stag dance; record hop; dinner-dance, tea dance, *thé dansant* <Fr>, dinner dance

3 **dancer,** danseur, terpsichorean, **hoofer** <nf>, step dancer, tap dancer, clog dancer, go-go dancer, foxtrotter, etc; **ballet dancer; ballerina,** danseur, danseuse, coryphée; *première danseuse* and *danseur noble* <Fr>, corps de ballet; twinkletoes <nf>; classical dancer; **modern dancer;** *corps de ballet* <Fr>; figurant, figurante; **chorus girl, chorine,** chorus boy *or* man; chorus line; geisha *or* geisha girl; nautch girl, bayadere; hula girl; taxi dancer; topless dancer; burlesque dancer, strip-teaser, stripper *and* bump-and-grinder <nf>; choreographer

4 **ballroom, dance hall,** dancery; dance palace; discotheque, disco; dance floor; nightclub, casino

VERBS **5** **dance, trip the light fantastic,** go dancing, trip, skip, hop, foot, prance <nf>, **hoof** *and* hoof it <nf>, clog, tap-dance, fold-dance, etc; shake, shimmy, shuffle; waltz, one-step, two-step, foxtrot, etc; choreograph

ADJS **6** **dancing, dance, terpsichorean;** balletic; choreographic

706 MOTION PICTURES

NOUNS **1** **motion pictures, movies, the movies, the pictures,** moving pictures, films, the films, the cinema, the screen, the big screen, the silver screen, the flicks *and* the flickers <nf>, motion-picture industry, moviedom, filmdom, Hollywood; **motion picture, movie, picture, film,** flick *and* flicker <nf>, picture show, motion-picture show, moving-picture show, photoplay, photodrama; **sound film,** silent film *or* silent; cinéma vérité *or* direct cinema; vérité; magic realism; **documentary film** *or* **movie,** docudrama, docutainment; **feature,** feature film, feature-length film, main attraction; theatrical film, big-screen film; **motion-picture genre** *or* **type;** TV film *or* movie, made-for-television movie *or* film, cable movie, miniseries; **short,** short movie, short subject; preview, sneak preview; independent film, indie; **B-movie,** B-picture, Grade B movie, low-budget picture; **educational film** *or* **movie,** training film, promotional film, trigger film; **underground film** *or* **movie,** experimental film *or* movie, avant-garde film *or* movie, representational film, art film *or* movie, surrealistic film *or* movie; **cartoon,** animated cartoon, animation, cel animation, claymation, computer graphics; animatron, audioanimatron; video <nf>, rental movie, pay-per-view movie, video-on-demand; **rated movie** *or* **film,** rating system, rating, G *or* general audience, PG *or* parental guidance suggested, PG-13 *or* parents strongly cautioned, R *or* restricted *or* children under 17 require accompanying parent or guardian, NC-17 *or* X *or* no children under 17 admitted; filmmaking, cinema

2 <movie type> drama, comedy, musical, love story, mystery, thriller, adventure, actioner, romance, Western, shoot-em-up <nf>, historical film, epic film, futuristic film, science-fiction *or* sci-fi film, foreign *or* foreign-language film, film noir, cult movie, girl *or* chick flick; date movie; art movie, buddy film

3 **script, screenplay,** motion-picture play *or* script, shooting script, storyboard, scenario, treatment, original screenplay, screen adaptation; plot, subplot, story; **dialogue,** book, lines; **role,** lead, romantic lead, stock character, ingenue, soubrette, cameo, bit, silent bit

4 **motion-picture studio, movie studio,** film studio, dream factory <nf>, animation studio, lot, back lot, sound stage, location; **set, motion-picture set, film set,** *mise-en-scène* <Fr>, properties *or* props, set dressing; **motion-picture company, film company,** production company; **producer,** filmmaker, moviemaker, **director,** auteur, screenwriter *or* scriptwriter *or* scenarist, editor *or* film editor, **actor, actress, film actor, film actress,** player, cinemactor, cinemactress, star, starlet, character actor, featured player, supporting actor *or* actress, supporting player, bit player, extra; **crew,** film crew

5 **motion-picture photography, photography,** cinematography, camera work, cinematics, camera work, camera angle, camera position, **shot, take,** footage, retake; screen test; **special effects,** rear-screen projection, mechanical effects, optical effects, process photography, FX; **color photography,** Technicolor *and* CinemaScope <TM>; black-and-white, color, colorization; **cameraman** *or* **camerawoman, motion-picture cameraman** *or* **camerawoman,** cinematographer, director of photography *or* DP, first cameraman, lighting cameraman

6 **motion-picture editing, film editing, editing,** cutting, arranging, synchronizing; **transition,** fade, fade-out/fade-in, dissolve, lap *or* overlap dissolve, out-focus-dissolve, match dissolve, cross-dissolve, mix; colorizing, colorization; freeze-frame; McGuffin

7 **motion-picture theater, movie theater,** picture theater *or* house, film theater, cinema <Brit>, movie house *or* palace, dream palace <nf>, circuit theater, drive-in theater *or* movie, grind house <nf>, fleapit <Brit>, Cineplex, multiplex; **screen,** movie screen, motion-picture screen, silver screen, aspect ratio *or* format, screen proportion, widescreen, Cinerama *and* Cinemascope *and* VistaVision *and* Ultra-Panavision <trademarks>

VERBS **8 film, shoot,** cinematize, filmmake; colorize

ADJS **9 motion-picture, movie, film,** cinema, cinematic, filmistic, filmic; colorized; black-and-white; animated; animatronic, audioanimatronic

707 ENTERTAINER

NOUNS **1 entertainer,** public entertainer, performer; artist, artiste; impersonator, female impersonator; **vaudevillian,** vaudevillist; dancer 705.3, hoofer <nf>; song and dance man; chorus girl, show girl, chorine <nf>; coryphée; chorus boy *or* man; burlesque queen <nf>, **stripteaser,** exotic dancer, ecdysiast; stripper *and* peeler *and* stripteuse *and* bump-and-grinder <nf>; dancing girl, nautch girl, belly dancer; go-go dancer; geisha, geisha girl; mountebank; **magician,** conjurer, prestidigitator, sleight-of-hand artist; circus performer, clown; mummer, guiser, guisard; singer, musician 710; performance artist

2 **actor, actress, player,** stage player *or* performer, playactor, histrion, histrio, thespian, Roscius, theatrical <nf>, trouper; child actor; mummer, pantomime, pantomimist; monologist, diseur, diseuse, reciter; dramatizer; mime, mimer, mimic; strolling player, stroller; barnstormer <nf>; character actor *or* actress, character man *or* woman, character; **villain,** antagonist, **bad guy** *or* **heavy** *or* black hat <nf>, villainess; juvenile,

ingenue; *jeune premier* and *jeune première* <Fr>; soubrette; foil, feeder *and* stooge <nf>, straight man *or* person; utility man *or* person; protean actor; featured actor, leading man *or* lady, lead actor *or* actress; Method actor; matinee idol <nf>, star of stage and screen; romantic lead

3 circus artist *or* performer; trapeze artist, aerialist, flier <nf>; high-wire artist, tightrope walker, slack-roper artist, equilibrist; **acrobat,** tumbler; bareback rider; juggler; lion tamer, sword swallower; snake charmer; clown; ringmaster, equestrian director

4 **motion-picture actor,** movie actor; **movie star,** film star; starlet; day player, under-five player, contract player

5 ham *or* ham actor <nf>; grimacer

6 **lead,** leading man *or* lady, leading actor *or* actress, principal, **star,** superstar, megastar, headliner, headline *or* feature attraction; costar; **hero, heroine,** protagonist; juvenile lead, *jeune premier* or *jeune première* <Fr>; first tragedian, heavy lead <nf>; **prima donna,** diva, singer 710.13; première danseuse, prima ballerina, *danseur noble* <Fr>

7 **supporting actor** *or* **actress; support,** supporting cast; **supernumerary,** super *or* supe <nf>, spear-carrier <nf>, **extra;** bit player; walking gentleman *or* lady <nf>, walk-on, mute; figurant, figurante; **understudy, stand-in,** standby, substitute, swing

8 **tragedian,** tragedienne

9 **comedian,** comedienne, **comic, funnyman;** farcist, farcer, *farceur* and *farceuse* <Fr>; stand-up comic *or* comedian <nf>, light comedian, genteel comedian, low comedian, slapstick comedian, hokum *or* hoke comic <nf>

10 **buffoon,** *buffo* <Ital>, **clown, fool, jester, zany, merry-andrew,** jack-pudding, pickle-herring, **motley fool,** motley, wearer of the cap and bells; harlequin; Pierrot; Pantaloon, Pantalone; Punch, Punchinello, Pulcinella, Polichinelle; Punch and Judy; Hanswurst; Columbine; Harlequin; Scaramouch

11 **cast,** cast of characters, characters, persons of the drama, *dramatis personae* <L>; supporting cast; **company,** acting company, outfit, **troupe;** repertory company, stock company, touring company; ensemble, chorus, *corps de ballet* <Fr>; circus troupe

708 MUSIC

NOUNS **1 music,** harmonious sound; music appreciation, music theory

2 **melody,** melodiousness, **tunefulness,** musicalness, musicality; **tune, tone,** musical sound, musical quality, tonality; sweetness, dulcetness, mellifluence, mellifluousness

3 **harmony, concord,** concordance, concert, consonance *or* consonancy, consort, accordance, **accord,** monochord, concentus, symphony, diapason; synchronism, synchronization; **attunement,** tune, attune; chime, chiming; unison, unisonance, homophony, monody; **euphony;** chime; light *or* heavy harmony; two-part *or* three-part harmony, etc; harmony *or* music of the spheres; harmonics 709

4 **air,** aria, **tune, melody,** line, melodic line, refrain, note, **song,** solo, solo part, soprano part, treble, lay, descant, lilt, **strain,** measure; canto, cantus

5 **piece,** opus, **composition,** production, work; **score; arrangement,** adaptation, orchestration, harmonization, setting; **form**; transcription, accompaniment

6 **classical music,** classic; concert music, serious music, longhair music <nf>, symphonic music, chamber music, operatic music; semiclassic, semiclassical music

7 **popular music,** pop music, pop, light music, popular song *or* air *or* tune, **ballad;** hit, song hit, hit tune; Tin Pan Alley; karaoke; hip hop, rap music, gangsta rap; ambient music, mood music; chartbuster

8 **dance music,** ballroom music, **dances;** syncopated music,

syncopation; ragtime *or* rag, doo-wop; modern dance music

9 **jazz;** hot jazz, Dixieland, Basin Street, New Orleans, Chicago, traditional jazz *or* trad <Brit nf>; **swing,** jive <nf>; bebop, bop <nf>; mainstream jazz; avant-garde jazz, the new music <nf>, modern jazz, progressive jazz, third-stream jazz, cool jazz, acid jazz; boogie *or* boogie-woogie; rhythm-and-blues *or* R and B, blues; walking bass, stride *or* stride piano

10 **rock-and-roll, rock music,** rock-'n'-roll, rock, hard rock, soft rock, acid rock, folk rock, country rock, rockabilly, hard core, full-tilt boogie, heavy metal, punk rock, New Wave, fusion, grunge, alternative rock

11 **folk music,** folk songs, ethnic music, ethnomusicology; folk ballads, balladry; border ballads; country music, hillbilly music; country-and-western music, western swing; old-time country music *or* old-timey music; bluegrass; field holler; ethnic music, soul, reggae, ska

12 **march,** martial *or* military music; military march, quick *or* quickstep march; processional march, recessional march; funeral *or* dead march; wedding march

13 **vocal music, song; singing,** caroling, warbling, lyricism, vocalism, **vocalization;** operatic singing, bel canto, coloratura, bravura; choral singing; folk singing; croon, crooning; yodel, yodeling; scat, scat singing; intonation; hum, humming; solmization, tonic sol-fa, solfeggio, solfège, sol-fa, sol-fa exercise

14 **song,** lay, *chanson* <Fr>, carol, **ditty,** canticle, lilt; **ballad,** ballade, *ballata* <Ital>; *canzone* <Ital>; canzonet, *canzonetta* <Ital>; aubade, serenade, lullaby, barcarole, glee, lay, chantey *or* chanty *or* shantey, chant, plainsong, canticle, chorale, carol, hymn, psalm, anthem

15 **solo;** karaoke; **aria;** operatic aria

16 <Italian terms for arias> arietta, arioso; aria buffa, aria da capo, aria d'agilità, aria da chiesa, aria d'imitazione, aria fugata, aria parlante; bravura, aria di bravura; coloratura, aria di coloratura; cantabile, aria cantabile; recitativo

17 **sacred music, church music,** liturgical music; **hymn,** hymn-tune, hymnody, hymnology; **psalm,** psalmody; **chorale,** choral fantasy, anthem; motet; **oratorio;** passion; **mass;** requiem mass, requiem, missa brevis, missa solemnis; offertory, offertory sentence *or* hymn; **cantata;** doxology, introit, canticle, paean, prosodion; recessional

18 **part music,** polyphonic music, part song, part singing, ensemble music, ensemble singing; **duet,** duo, *duettino* <Ital>; **trio,** terzet, *terzetto* <Ital>; **quartet; quintet; sextet,** sestet; **septet,** septuor; **octet;** cantata, lyric cantata; madrigal, *madrigaletto* <Ital>; **chorus** 710.16, chorale, glee club, choir; choral singing; four-part, soprano-alto-tenor-base *or* SATB; barbershop quartet

19 **round, rondo,** rondeau, **roundelay,** catch, troll; rondino, rondoletto; **fugue,** canon, fugato

20 **polyphony,** polyphonism; **counterpoint,** contrapunto; **plainsong,** Gregorian chant, Ambrosian chant; *faux-bourdon* <Fr>; musica ficta, false music

21 monody, monophony, homophony

22 **part,** melody *or* voice part, **voice** 709.5, **line;** descant, canto, cantus, cantus planus *or* firmus, plain song, plain chant; prick song, cantus figuratus; soprano, tenor, treble, alto, contralto, baritone, bass, bassus; undersong; drone; **accompaniment;** continuo, basso continuo, figured bass, thorough bass; ground bass, basso ostinato; drone, drone bass, bourdon, burden

23 **response,** responsory report, answer; echo; antiphon, antiphony, antiphonal chanting *or* singing

24 **passage, phrase,** musical phrase, strain, part, motive, motif, theme, subject, figure; leitmotiv; **movement;** introductory phrase, anacrusis; statement, exposition, development, variation; division; period, musical sentence; section; **measure;**

figure; **verse, stanza;** burden, bourdon; **chorus, refrain,** response; folderol, **ornament** 709.18, cadence 709.23, harmonic close, resolution; **coda,** tailpiece; ritornello; intermezzo, interlude; bass passage; tutti, tutti passage; bridge, bridge passage

25 <fast, slow, etc passages> presto, prestissimo; allegro, allegretto; scherzo, scherzando; adagio, adagietto; andante, andantino; largo, larghetto, larghissimo; crescendo; diminuendo, decrescendo; rallentando, ritardando; ritenuto; piano, pianissimo; forte, fortissimo; staccato, marcato, marcando; pizzicato; spiccato; legato; stretto

26 **overture, prelude, introduction,** operatic overture, dramatic overture, concert overture, voluntary, descant, vamp; curtain raiser

27 **impromptu, extempore, improvisation, interpolation;** cadenza; **ornament** 709.18, flourish, ruffles and flourishes, grace note, appoggiatura, mordent, upper mordent, inverted mordent; **run,** melisma; vamp; lick, hot lick, riff

28 **score,** musical score *or* copy, **music,** notation, musical notation, written music, copy, draft, transcript, transcription, version, edition, text, arrangement; part; full *or* orchestral score, compressed *or* short score, piano score, vocal score, instrumental score; tablature, lute tablature; opera score, opera; **libretto;** sheet music; **songbook,** songster; hymnbook, hymnal; music paper; music roll

29 **staff,** stave <Brit>; line, ledger line; bar, bar line; space, degree; brace

30 **execution, performance; rendering,** rendition, music-making, **touch, expression;** fingering; pianism; intonation; repercussion; pizzicato, staccato, spiccato, parlando, legato, cantando, rubato, demilegato, mezzo staccato, slur; glissando

31 **musicianship;** musical talent *or* flair, musicality; virtuosity; pianism; musical ear, ear for music; musical sense, sense of rhythm; absolute *or* perfect pitch; relative pitch

32 musical occasion; choral service, service of lessons and carols, service of song, sing <nf>, singing, community singing *or* sing, singfest, songfest, sing-in; karaoke; folk-sing *and* hootenanny <nf>; **festival,** music festival; opera festival; folk-music festival, jazz festival, rock festival; jam session <nf>

33 **performance,** musical performance, **program,** musical program, program of music; **concert,** symphony concert, chamber concert; philharmonic concert, philharmonic; popular concert, pops *and* pop concert <nf>, promenade concert, prom <nf>; band concert; **recital;** service of music; concert performance <of an opera>; **medley,** potpourri; swan song, farewell performance

34 **musical theater, music theater, lyric theater,** musical stage, lyric stage; **music drama,** lyric drama; song-play, **opera,** grand opera, light opera, ballad opera; comic opera, *opéra bouffe* <Fr>, *opera buffa* <Ital>; **operetta; musical comedy; musical;** Broadway musical; musical drama; **ballet,** *opéra ballet* <Fr>, comedy ballet, *ballet d'action* <Fr>, *ballet divertissement* <Fr>; dance drama; chorus show; **song-and-dance act;** minstrel, minstrel show

VERBS **35** **harmonize,** be harmonious, be in tune *or* concert, chord, **accord,** symphonize, synchronize, **chime, blend,** blend in, symphonize, segue; tune, attune, atone, sound together, sound in tune; assonate; melodize, musicalize

36 **tune, tune up,** attune, atone, chord, **put in tune;** voice, string; tone up, tone down

37 **strike up,** strike up a tune, **strike up the band,** break into music, pipe up, pipe up a song, yerk out <nf>, **burst into song**

38 **sing, vocalize,** carol, descant, lilt, troll, line out *and* belt out *and* tear off <nf>; **warble,** trill, tremolo, quaver, shake; **chirp,** chirrup, twit <Brit nf>, **twitter;** pipe, whistle, tweedle, tweedledee; **chant; intone,** intonate;

croon; hum; yodel; roulade; chorus, choir, sing in chorus; **hymn,** anthem, psalm; sing the praises of; minstrel; ballad; **serenade;** sol-fa, do-re-mi, solmizate

39 **play, perform, execute, render,** do; interpret; make music; concertize; symphonize; chord; accompany; play by ear; play at, pound out *and* saw away at <nf>

40 **strum, thrum, pluck,** plunk, **pick,** twang, sweep the strings

41 **fiddle** <nf>, play violin *or* the violin; scrape *and* saw <nf>

42 **blow a horn,** sound *or* wind the horn, sound, blow, wind, **toot,** tootle, pipe, tweedle; bugle, carillon, clarion, fife, flute, trumpet, whistle; bagpipe, doodle <Brit nf>; lip, tongue, double-tongue, triple-tongue

43 **syncopate,** play jazz, swing, jive <nf>, rag <nf>, jam <nf>, riff <nf>

44 **beat time,** keep time, tap, tap out the rhythm, keep tempo; count, count the beats; beat the drum, **drum** 55.4, play drum *or* the drums, thrum, beat, thump, pound; tomtom; ruffle; beat *or* sound a tattoo

45 **conduct, direct,** lead, wield the baton

46 **compose, write, arrange, score, set, set to music,** put to music; musicalize, melodize, **harmonize; orchestrate;** instrument, instrumentate; **adapt,** make an adaptation; transcribe, transpose

ADJS 47 **musical, musically inclined,** musicianly, with an ear for music; virtuoso, virtuose, virtuosic; **music-loving,** music-mad, musicophile, philharmonic; absolute, aleatory, aleatoric

48 **melodious,** melodic; **musical,** music-like; **tuneful,** tunable; fine-toned, tonal, **pleasant-sounding,** agreeable-sounding, pleasant, appealing, agreeable, catchy, singable; **euphonious** *or* euphonic, **lyric, lyrical,** melic; **lilting,** songful, songlike; **sweet, dulcet,** sweet-sounding, achingly sweet, sweet-flowing; honeyed, mellifluent, mellifluous, mellisonant, music-flowing; rich, mellow; sonorous, canorous; golden, golden-toned; silvery, silver-toned; sweet-voiced, golden-voiced, silver-voiced, silver-tongued, golden-tongued, music-tongued; ariose, arioso, cantabile

49 **harmonious,** harmonic, symphonious; harmonizing, **chiming,** blending, well-blended, blended; **concordant,** consonant, accordant, according, **in accord,** in concord, in concert; synchronous, synchronized, in sync <nf>, symphonic, **in tune,** tuned, attuned; in unison, in chorus; unisonous, unisonant; homophonic, monophonic, monodic; assonant, assonantal; rhythmic

50 **vocal,** singing; **choral,** choric; four-part; operatic; hymnal; psalmic, psalmodic, psalmodial; sacred, liturgical; treble, soprano, tenor, alto, falsetto; coloratura, lyric, bravura, dramatic, heroic; baritone; bass

51 **instrumental,** orchestral, symphonic, concert; dramatico-musical; jazz, syncopated, jazzy, rock, swing

52 **polyphonic, contrapuntal**

ADJS, ADVS 53 <directions, style> legato; staccato; spiccato; pizzicato; forte, fortissimo; piano, pianissimo; sordo; crescendo, accrescendo; decrescendo, diminuendo, morendo; dolce; amabile; affettuoso, con affetto; amoroso, con amore lamentabile; agitato, con agitazione; leggiero; agilmente, con agilità; capriccioso, a capriccio; scherzando, scherzoso; appassionato, appassionatamente; abbandono; brillante; parlando; a cappella; trillando, tremolando, tremoloso; sotto voce; stretto

54 <slowly> largo, larghetto, allargando; adagio, adagietto; andante, andantino, andante moderato; calando; a poco; lento; ritardando, rallentando; downtempo

55 <fast> presto, prestissimo; veloce; accelerando; vivace, vivacissimo; desto, con anima, con brio; allegro, allegretto; affrettando, moderato

709 HARMONICS, MUSICAL ELEMENTS

NOUNS **1 harmonics,** harmony; melodics; rhythmics; musicality; music, **music theory,** theory; musicology; musicography

2 harmonization; orchestration, instrumentation; arrangement, setting, adaptation, transcription; accompaniment; harmonic progression, chordal progression; phrasing, modulation, intonation, preparation, suspension, solution, resolution; tone painting

3 tone, tonality 50.3

4 pitch, tuning, tune, **tone, key, note,** register, tonality; height, depth; pitch range, tessitura; classical pitch, high pitch, diapason *or* normal *or* French pitch, international *or* concert *or* new philharmonic pitch, standard pitch, low pitch, Stuttgart *or* Scheibler's pitch, philharmonic pitch, philosophical pitch; temperament, equal temperament; absolute pitch, perfect pitch

5 voice, *voce* <Ital>; *voce di petto* <Ital>, chest voice; *voce di testa* <Ital>, head voice; **soprano,** mezzo-soprano, dramatic soprano, soprano spinto, lyric soprano, coloratura soprano; boy soprano; male soprano, castrato; alto, contralto; tenor, lyric tenor, operatic tenor, heldentenor *or* heroic tenor *or* Wagnerian tenor; countertenor *or* male alto; baritone, light *or* lyric baritone; **bass,** basso, basso profundo, basso cantante *or* lyric bass, basso buffo *or* comic bass; treble, falsetto, castrato

6 scale, gamut, register, compass, range, diapason; diatonic scale, chromatic scale, modal scale, enharmonic scale, major scale, minor scale, natural *or* harmonic *or* melodic minor, whole-tone scale; great scale; octave scale, dodecuple scale, pentatonic scale; tetrachordal scale; twelve-tone *or* dodecuple scale, tone block, tone row, tone cluster

7 sol-fa, tonic sol-fa, do-re-mi; Guidonian syllables, ut, re, mi, fa, sol, la; sol-fa syllables, do, re, mi, fa, sol, la, ti *or* si, do; solmization, solfeggio; fixed-do system, movable-do system; solmization; bobization

8 <diatonic series> tetrachord, chromatic tetrachord, enharmonic tetrachord, Dorian tetrachord; hexachord, hard hexachord, natural hexachord, soft hexachord; pentachord

9 octave, *ottava* <Ital>, eighth; *ottava alta* <Ital>, *ottava bassa* <Ital>; small octave, great octave; contraoctave, subcontraoctave, double contraoctave; one-line octave, two-line octave, four-line octave, two-foot octave, four-foot octave; tenor octave

10 mode, octave species; major mode, minor mode; Greek mode, Ionian mode, Dorian mode, Phrygian mode, Lydian mode, mixolydian mode, Aeolian mode, Locrian mode; hypoionian mode, hypodorian mode, hypophrygian mode, hypolydian mode, hypoaeolian mode, hypomixolydian mode, hypolocrian mode; Gregorian *or* ecclesiastical *or* church *or* medieval mode; plagal mode, authentic mode; Indian *or* Hindu mode, raga

11 form, arrangement, pattern, model, design; song *or* lied form, primary form; **sonata form,** sonata allegro, ternary form, symphonic form, canon form, toccata form, fugue form, rondo form

12 notation, character, mark, symbol, signature, sign, *segno* <Ital>; proportional notation; chart *or* paper <nf>, dot; custos, direct; cancel; bar, measure; measure *or* time signature, key signature; tempo mark, metronome *or* metronomic mark; fermata, hold, pause; *presa* <Ital>, lead; slur, tie, ligature, vinculum, enharmonic tie; swell; accent, accent mark, expression mark; ledger, staff, stave, line, space, brace, rest, interval

13 clef; C clef, soprano clef, alto *or* viola clef, tenor clef; F *or* bass clef, G *or* treble clef

14 note, musical note, notes of a scale; **tone** 50.2; **sharp, flat, natural;**

accidental; double whole note, breve; whole note, semibreve; half note, minim; quarter note, crotchet; eighth note, quaver; sixteenth note, semiquaver; thirty-second note, demisemiquaver; sixty-fourth note, hemidemisemiquaver; tercet, triplet; sustained note, dominant, dominant note; enharmonic, enharmonic note; separation, hammering, staccato, spiccato; connected, smooth, legato; responding note, report; shaped note, patent note

15 **key,** key signature, tonality, sharps and flats; **keynote,** tonic; tonic key; major, minor, major *or* minor key, tonic major or minor; supertonic, mediant, submediant, dominant, subdominant, subtonic; pedal point, organ point

16 **harmonic,** harmonic tone, overtone, upper partial tone; flageolet tone

17 **chord,** *concento* <Ital>, combination of tones *or* notes; major *or* minor chord, primary *or* secondary chord, tonic chord, dominant chord; tertiary chord, third, fourth, etc; interval, major *or* minor interval

18 **ornament,** grace, arabesque, embellishment, *fioritura* <Ital>; **flourish,** roulade, flight, run; passage, division 708.24; florid phrase *or* passage; coloratura; incidental, incidental note; grace note, appoggiatura, arpeggio, acciaccatura; rubato; mordent, single mordent, double *or* long mordent; inverted mordent, pralltriller; turn, back *or* inverted turn; cadence, cadenza

19 **trill,** trillo; trillet, *trilleto* <Ital>; **tremolo,** tremolant, tremolando; quaver, quiver, tremble, tremor, flutter, falter, shake; **vibrato**

20 **interval,** degree, **step,** note, tone; second, third, fourth, fifth, sixth, seventh, octave; prime *or* unison interval, major *or* minor interval, harmonic *or* melodic interval, enharmonic interval, diatonic interval; parallel *or* consecutive intervals, parallel fifths, parallel octaves; whole step, major second; half step, halftone, semitone, minor second; augmented interval; diminished interval; diatonic semitone, chromatic semitone, less semitone, quarter semitone, tempered *or* mean semitone; quarter step, enharmonic diesis; diatessaron, diapason; *tierce de Picardie* <Fr> *or* Picardy third; augmented fourth *or* tritone

21 **rest,** pause; whole rest, breve rest, semibreve rest, half rest, minim, quarter rest, eighth rest, sixteenth rest, thirty-second rest, sixty-fourth rest

22 **rhythm, beat, meter, measure,** number *or* numbers, movement, **lilt, swing;** prosody, metrics; rhythmic pattern *or* phrase

23 cadence *or* cadency, authentic cadence, plagal cadence, mixed cadence, perfect *or* imperfect cadence, half cadence, deceptive *or* false cadence, interrupted *or* suspended cadence

24 **tempo, time, beat,** time pattern, timing; time signature; simple time *or* measure, compound time *or* measure; two-part *or* duple time, three-part *or* triple time, triplet, four-part *or* quadruple time, five-part *or* quintuple time, six-part *or* sextuple time, seven-part *or* septuple time, nine-part *or* nonuple time; two-four time, six-eight time, etc; tempo rubato, rubato; mixed times; **syncopation,** syncope; **ragtime,** rag <nf>; waltz time, three-four *or* three-quarter time, andante tempo, march tempo, etc; largo, etc; presto, etc

25 **accent,** accentuation, rhythmical accent *or* accentuation, ictus, emphasis, stress arsis, thesis

26 **beat,** throb, pulse, pulsation; downbeat, upbeat, offbeat; bar beat

ADJS 27 **tonal,** tonic; chromatic, enharmonic; semitonic

28 **rhythmic, rhythmical,** cadent, cadenced, **measured, metric, metrical;** in rhythm, in numbers; beating, throbbing, pulsing, pulsating, pulsative, pulsatory

29 **syncopated; ragtime,** ragtimey <nf>; **jazz;** jazzy *and* jazzed *and* jazzed up <nf>, hot, swingy <nf>

ADVS 30 **in time,** in tempo 709.24, *a tempo* <Ital>

710 MUSICIAN

NOUNS 1 **musician,** musico, **music maker,** professional musician; performer, executant, interpreter, tunester, artiste, artist, concert artist, player, **virtuoso,** virtuosa; maestro; recitalist; **soloist,** duettist; singer; street musician, busker <chiefly Brit>

2 **popular** *or* pop musician; ragtime musician; **jazz musician, jazzman;** swing musician; big-band musician; **rock** *or* **rock'n'roll musician**

3 **player, instrumentalist,** instrumental musician; bandman, bandsman; orchestral musician; symphonist; concertist; accompanist, accompanyist

4 **wind player,** wind-instrumentalist, horn player, French-horn player *or* hornist, horner, piper, tooter; bassoonist, bugler, clarinetist, cornettist, fifer, oboist, piccoloist, saxophonist, trombonist; trumpeter, trumpet major; fluegelhornist; flutist *or* flautist

5 **string musician,** strummer, picker <nf>, thrummer, twanger; banjoist, banjo-picker <nf>, citharist, guitarist, guitar-picker <nf>, classical guitarist, folk guitarist, lute player, lutenist, lutist, lyrist, mandolinist, theorbist; violinist, fiddler <nf>; bass violinist, bassist, bass player, contrabassist; violoncellist, cellist, celloist; violist; harpist, harper; zitherist, psalterer

6 xylophonist, marimbaist, vibist *or* vibraphonist

7 **pianist,** pianiste, pianofortist, piano player, ivory tickler *or* thumper <nf>; keyboard player *or* keyboardist; harpsichordist, clavichordist, monochordist; accordionist, concertinist

8 **organist,** organ player

9 organ-grinder, hurdy-gurdist, hurdy-gurdyist, hurdy-gurdy man

10 **drummer, percussionist,** tympanist *or* timpanist, kettle-drummer; taborer

11 **cymbalist,** cymbaler; bell-ringer, **carilloneur,** campanologist, campanist; triangle player

12 **orchestra, band, ensemble,** combo <nf>, group; strings, woodwind *or* woodwinds, brass *or* brasses, string *or* woodwind *or* brass section, string *or* woodwind *or* brass choir; desks; garage band

13 **singer, vocalist,** vocalizer, voice, songster, songbird, warbler, lead singer, backup vocalist, caroler, melodist, minstrel, cantor; songstress, singstress, cantatrice, chanteuse, song stylist, canary <nf>; chanter, chantress; aria singer, lieder singer, opera singer, diva, prima donna; improvisator; rap singer; blues singer, torch singer <nf>; crooner, rock *or* rock-and-roll singer; yodeler; country singer, folk singer *or* folkie <nf>; psalm singer, hymner; Meistersinger; **singing voice, voice** 709.5

14 **minstrel, ballad singer,** balladeer, **bard,** rhapsode, rhapsodist; wandering *or* strolling minstrel, **troubadour,** trovatore, trouvère, minnesinger, scop, gleeman, fili, jongleur; street singer, wait; serenader; **folk singer,** folk-rock singer; country-and-western singer

15 **choral singer,** choir member, chorister, chorus singer, choralist; choirman, **choirboy; chorus girl,** chorine <nf>

16 **chorus, chorale, choir,** choral group, choral society, oratorio society, chamber chorus, men's *or* women's chorus, male chorus, mixed chorus, ensemble, voices; **glee club,** *Liedertafel* and *Liederkranz* <Ger>, singing club *or* society; *a cappella* choir; choral symphony

17 **conductor,** leader, maestro, symphonic conductor, **music director,** director; **orchestra leader, band leader, bandmaster,** band major, drum major

18 **choirmaster,** choral director *or* conductor, chorus master, song leader; choir chaplain, minister of music, precentor, cantor, chorister

19 **concertmaster,** concertmeister, first violinist; first chair

20 **composer, scorer, arranger,** musicographer; melodist, melodizer;

harmonist, harmonizer; **orchestrator;** adapter; symphonist; tone poet; ballad maker *or* writer, balladeer, balladist, balladmonger; madrigalist; lyrist; hymnist, hymnographer, hymnologist; contrapuntist; song writer *or* songwriter, songsmith, tunesmith; lyricist, librettist; musicologist, ethnomusicologist; music teacher

21 **music lover,** philharmonic person, **music fan** *and* music buff <nf>, musicophile; musicmonger; concertgoer, operagoer, opera lover; tonalist

22 <patrons> the Muses, the Nine, sacred Nine, tuneful Nine, Pierides; Apollo, Apollo Musagetes; Orpheus; Erato, Euterpe, Polymnia *or* Polyhymnia, Terpsichore, St Cecilia

23 **songbird,** singing bird, **songster,** feathered songster, warbler; nightingale, Philomel; bulbul, canary, cuckoo, lark, mavis, mockingbird, oriole, ringdove, song sparrow, thrush

711 MUSICAL INSTRUMENTS

1 **musical instrument,** instrument of music; electronic instrument, synthesizer, Mellotron <TM>, Moog synthesizer <TM>

2 **string** *or* **stringed instrument,** chordophone; strings, string choir

3 **harp, lyre**

4 **plucked stringed instrument**

5 **viol** *or* violin family, chest of viols; Stradivarius, Stradivari, Strad <nf>; Amati, Cremona, Guarnerius; bow, fiddlestick, fiddlebow; bridge, sound hole, soundboard, fingerboard, tuning peg, scroll; string, G string, D string, A string, E string

6 **wind instrument,** wind; aerophone; **horn,** pipe, tooter; mouthpiece, embouchure, lip, chops <nf>; valve, bell, reed, double reed, key, slide

7 **brass wind** brass *or* brass-wind instrument; brasses, brass choir

8 **woodwind**, wood *or* woodwind instrument; woods, woodwind choir; reed instrument, **reed;** double-reed instrument, **double reed; single-reed instrument,** single reed

9 **bagpipe** *or* bagpipes, pipes, union pipes, war pipes, Irish pipes, doodlesack; cornemuse, musette; sordellina; chanter, drone; pipe bag

10 **mouth organ,** mouth harp, harp, French harp <nf>, **harmonica,** harmonicon; jaws *or* Jew's harp, mouth bow; kazoo

11 **accordion,** piano accordion; **concertina;** squeeze box <nf>; mellophone; bandonion

12 keyboard instrument, **piano, harpsichord, clavichord, player piano;** music roll, piano player roll

13 **organ,** keyboard wind instrument

14 **hurdy-gurdy,** vielle, **barrel organ,** hand organ, grind organ, street organ

15 **music box,** musical box; orchestrion, orchestrina

16 **percussion instrument**, percussion, **drum;** drumstick, jazz stick, tymp stick

17 **keyboard,** fingerboard; console, **keys,** manual, claviature; piano keys, ivories <nf>, eighty-eight <nf>, organ manual, great, swell, choir, solo, echo; pedals

18 **carillon,** chimes 711.18, chime of bells; electronic carillon

19 **organ stop,** stop rank, register

20 string, chord, steel string, wound string, nylon string; fiddlestring, catgut; horsehair; music wire, piano wire

21 plectrum, plectron, pick

22 <aids> metronome, rhythmometer; tone measurer, monochord, sonometer; tuning fork, tuning bar, diapason; pitch pipe, tuning pipe; mute; music stand, music lyre; baton, conductor's baton, stick <nf>; MIDI

712 VISUAL ARTS

NOUNS 1 **visual arts; art, artwork,** the arts; **fine arts,** *beaux arts* <Fr>; arts of design, **design,** designing; art form; abstract art, representative art; **graphic arts** 713; plastic art; **arts and crafts;** decorative arts; primitive art, cave art; folk art; calligraphy; commercial art, applied art, industrial art; modern art; sculpture 715; ceramics 742; photography 714;

etching, engraving 713.2; decoration 498.1; artist 716

2 **craft, manual art,** industrial art, **handicraft,** arts and crafts, artisan work, craftwork, artisanship; industrial design; woodcraft, woodwork, carpentry, woodworking, metalcraft, stonecraft; ceramics, glassmaking

3 <act or art of painting> **painting,** coloring; the brush

4 <art of drawing> **drawing, draftsmanship, sketching, delineation; black and white,** charcoal; mechanical drawing, drafting; freehand drawing, life drawing

5 scenography, ichnography, orthographic *or* orthogonal projection

6 **artistry, art, talent,** artistic skill, flair, artistic flair, artistic invention; artiness *and* arty-craftiness *and* artsy-craftsiness <nf>; artistic temperament, artistic taste; virtu, artistic quality

7 **style;** lines; genre; **school,** movement ; the grand style

8 **treatment; technique,** draftsmanship, brushwork, painterliness; **composition, design,** arrangement; grouping, balance; **color,** values; atmosphere, tone; shadow, shading; **line;** perspective

9 **work of art, object of art,** objet d'art, art object, art work, artistic production *or* creation, piece, **work, study, design, composition;** creation, brainchild; virtu, article *or* object *or* piece of virtu; **masterpiece,** *chef d'œuvre* <Fr>, masterwork, master , old master, classic; museum piece; grotesque; statue; mobile, stabile; nude, still life; pastiche, *pasticcio* <Ital>; artware, artwork; bric-a-brac; kitsch

10 **picture; image, likeness, representation,** tableau; photograph 714.3; **illustration,** illumination; miniature; copy, reproduction; print, color print; engraving 713.2, stencil, block print; daub; abstraction, abstract; mural, fresco, wall painting; cyclorama, panorama; montage, collage, assemblage; still life, study in still life; tapestry, mosaic, stained glass, stained glass window, **icon,** altarpiece, diptych, triptych

11 **scene, view, scape; landscape;** waterscape, riverscape, seascape, seapiece; airscape, skyscape, cloudscape; snowscape; cityscape, townscape; farmscape; pastoral; treescape; diorama; exterior, interior

12 **drawing; delineation;** line drawing; **sketch, draft; black and white,** chiaroscuro; **charcoal, crayon, pen-and-ink,** pencil drawing, charcoal drawing, pastel, pastel painting, crayon drawing; silhouette; vignette; doodle; rough draft *or* copy, rough outline, study, design; caricature; cartoon, sinopia, **study,** design; *brouillon* and *ébauche* and *esquisse* <Fr>; diagram, graph; mechanical drawing; silver-print drawing, tracing; doodle, graffito, scribble

13 **painting, canvas,** easel-picture; **oil painting,** oil; **watercolor,** water, aquarelle, wash, wash drawing; acrylic; finger painting; tempera, egg tempera; *gouache* <Fr>; sand painting

14 **portrait, portraiture, portrayal;** head; profile; silhouette, shadow figure; nude; miniature

15 **cartoon, caricature; comic strip;** comic section, comics, funny paper *and* funnies <nf>; comic book; animated cartoon, animation

16 <visual arts> animation, architecture, basketry, body decoration, bookbinding, calligraphy, caricature, clothing *or* fashion design, decorative arts, crafts, drawing, enamelwork, floral decoration, furnishings design, furniture design, glass design, graphic arts, illustration, intaglio, interior design, jewelry design, lacquerwork, landscape design, lithography, metalwork, mixed media, mosaic, painting, photography, plastic art, pottery, printmaking, relief *or* engraving, screen printing, sculpture, serigraphy, tapestry, typography, woodcut

17 **studio,** *atelier* <Fr>; **gallery** 386.9

18 <art equipment> palette; easel; paintbox; art paper, drawing paper, watercolor paper, tracing paper; sketchbook, sketchpad; canvas, artists' canvas; canvas board;

scratchboard; lay figure; camera obscura, camera lucida; maulstick; palette knife, spatula; brush, paintbrush; air brush, spray gun; pencil, drawing pencil; pen, ink, marker, highlighter; crayon, charcoal, chalk, pastel; stump; painter's cream; ground; pigments, medium; siccative, drier; fixative, varnish; **paint** 35.8

VERBS **19 portray, picture,** picturize, **depict, limn,** draw *or* paint a picture; **paint** 35.14; brush, brush in; color, tint, colorize; spread *or* lay on a color; **daub** <nf>; scumble; **draw, sketch, delineate; draft;** pencil, chalk, crayon, charcoal; draw in, pencil in; dash off, scratch <nf>; doodle; design; diagram; cartoon; copy, trace; stencil; touch up; hatch, crosshatch, shade; doodle

ADJS **20 artistic,** painterly; **arty** *or* arty-crafty *or* artsy-craftsy *or* artsy-fartsy <nf>; **art-minded,** art-conscious; imaginative, creative, stylized, **aesthetic; tasteful; beautiful; decorative, ornamental** 498.10; **well-composed,** well-grouped, well-arranged, well-varied; of consummate art; in the grand style

21 pictorial, pictural, **graphic, picturesque;** picturable; photographic 714.17; scenographic; painty, pastose; scumbled; monochrome, polychrome; freehand

713 GRAPHIC ARTS

NOUNS **1 graphic arts, graphics,** graphic design; **printmaking; painting; drawing; relief-carving; photography** 714; **printing** 548; computer graphics, digital art, graphic artist 716.8

2 engraving, engravement, graving, enchasing, **tooling,** chiseling, incising, incision, lining, scratching, slashing, scoring; **inscription,** inscript; type-cutting; **marking,** line, scratch, slash, score; hatching, cross-hatching; etch, etching; stipple, stippling; tint, demitint, half tint; burr; photoengraving 548.1

3 lithography, planography, autolithography, artist lithography; chromolithography; photolithography, offset lithography 548.1

4 stencil printing, stencil; silk-screen printing, serigraphy; monotype; glass printing, decal, decalcomania; cameography

5 print, numbered print, imprint, impression, first impression, impress; negative; color print; **etching; lithograph;** autolithograph; chromolithograph; lithotype; crayon engraving, graphotype; **block, block print,** linoleum-block print, rubber-block print, wood engraving, **woodprint,** xylograph, **cut, woodcut,** woodblock; vignette

6 plate, steel plate, copperplate, chalcograph; zincograph; stone, lithographic stone; printing plate 548.8

7 proof, artist's proof, proof before letter, open-letter proof, remarque proof

8 engraving tool, graver, burin, tint tool, style, point, etching point, needle, etching needle; etching ball; etching ground *or* varnish; scorper; rocker; **die,** punch, stamp, intaglio, seal

VERBS **9 engrave, grave, tool, enchase, incise, sculpture, inscribe,** character, **mark,** line, crease, score, scratch, scrape, cut, carve, chisel; groove, furrow 290.3; stipple, cribble; hatch, crosshatch; lithograph, autolithograph; **be a printmaker** *or* graphic artist; make prints *or* graphics; print 548.14

10 etch, eat, eat out, corrode, bite, bite in

ADJS **11 engraved, graven,** graved, glypt-*or* glypto-; tooled, enchased, chased, inscribed, incised, marked, lined, creased, cut, carved, glyphic, **sculptured,** insculptured; grooved, furrowed 290.4; **printed, imprinted, impressed, stamped,** numbered

12 glyptic, glyptical, glyptographic, lapidary, lapidarian; xylographic, wood-block; lithographic, autolithographic, chromolithographic; aquatint, aquatinta, mezzotint

714 PHOTOGRAPHY

NOUNS **1** **photography**, picture-taking; **cinematography,** motion-picture photography; color photography, black-and-white photography; photochromy, heliochromy; **3-D,** three-dimensional photography; photofinishing; photogravure; radiography, X-ray photography; photogrammetry, phototopography; digital photography; point-and-click, point-and-shoot

2 photographer 716.5, shutter-bug <nf>, photojournalist, press photographer, paparazzo, lensman, shooter *and* photog <nf>; digital artist

3 **photograph, photo** <nf>, heliograph, **picture,** shot <nf>, **snapshot,** snap <nf>, image; black-and-white photograph; color photograph, color print, heliochrome; Polaroid <TM>; slide, diapositive, transparency; candid photograph; take; still, still photograph; photomural; montage, photomontage; aerial photograph, photomap; facsimile *or* fax transmission; telephotograph, Telephoto <TM>, Wirephoto <TM>; photomicrograph, microphotograph; metallograph; microradiograph; electron micrograph; photochronograph, chronophotograph; radiograph, X ray; **portrait**, closeup**;** action shot, action sequence; pinup <nf>, cheesecake *and* beefcake <nf>; police photograph, **mug** *or* mug shot <nf>; rogues' gallery; photobiography

4 **tintype** *or* ferrotype, ambrotype, **daguerreotype,** calotype *or* talbotype, collotype *or* albertype *or* artotype *or* heliotype, photocollotype, autotype, vitrotype

5 **print,** photoprint, positive; glossy, matte, semi-matte; **enlargement, blowup;** photocopy, Photostat <TM>, photostatic copy, stat <nf>, Xerox <TM>, Xerox copy; microfilm, microfiche, microphotocopy, microprint, microcopy; blueprint, cyanotype; **slide,** transparency, lantern slide; contact printing, projection printing; photogravure; hologram; double exposure

6 shadowgraph, shadowgram, skiagraph, skiagram; radiograph, radiogram, scotograph; **X ray,** X-ray photograph, roentgenograph, roentgenogram; photofluorogram; photogram

7 spectrograph, spectrogram; spectroheliogram

8 <motion pictures> **shot; take, retake;** close-up, long shot, medium shot, full shot, group shot, deuce shot, matte shot, process shot, boom shot, travel shot, trucking shot, follow-focus shot, pan shot *or* panoramic shot, rap shot, reverse *or* reverse-angle shot, wild shot, zoom shot; motion picture; kinescope

9 **exposure,** time exposure; shutter speed; f-stop, lens opening; film rating, **film speed,** film gauge, ASA number, **DIN** *or Deutsche Industrie Normen* number, DX code; exposure meter, light meter

10 **film; negative;** printing paper, photographic paper; **plate;** dry plate; vehicle; motion-picture film, panchromatic film, monochromatic film, orthochromatic film, black-and-white film, color film, color negative film, color reversal film, Polaroid film <TM>; microfilm, bibliofilm; sound-on-film, sound film; sound track, soundstripe; Super-8, videotape, 35mm; roll, cartridge; pack, bipack, tripack; frame; emulsion, dope, backing

11 **camera,** Kodak *and* Polaroid <TM>; digital camera, digicam; disposable camera; photo booth; video camera, camcorder; TV camera, motion-picture camera, cinematograph *or* kinematograph <Brit>; security camera; scanner

12 **projector;** motion-picture projector, cineprojector, cinematograph *or* kinematograph <Brit>, vitascope; **slide projector,** magic lantern, stereopticon; slide viewer

13 **processing solution;** developer, soup <nf>; fixer, fixing bath, sodium thiosulfate *or* sodium hyposulfite *or* hypo; acid stop, stop bath, short-stop, short-stop bath; emulsion

VERBS **14** **photograph, shoot** <nf>, **take a photograph,** take a picture, take one's picture; **snap,** snapshot, snapshoot; **film,** get *or* capture on film; **mug** <nf>; daguerreotype, talbotype, calotype; Photostat <TM>; xerox; microfilm; photomap; pan; **X-ray,** radiograph, roentgenograph

15 **process; develop; print;** blueprint; **blow up, enlarge**

16 **project, show, screen**

ADJS **17** **photographic,** photo; **photogenic,** picturesome; photosensitive, photoactive; panchromatic; telephotographic, telephoto; tintype; three-dimensional, 3-D

715 SCULPTURE

NOUNS **1** **sculpture, sculpturing;** plastic art, **modeling; statuary; stonecutting;** gem-cutting, masonry; **carving,** stone carving, bone-carving, cameo carving, scrimshaw, *taille directe* <Fr>, whittling, wood-carving *or* xyloglyphy; embossing, **engraving** 713.2, **chasing,** toreutics, founding, casting, molding, plaster casting, lost-wax process, *cire perdue* <Fr>; soft sculpture; ice sculpture; sculptor 716.6

2 <sculptured piece> **sculpture; glyph; statue;** marble, bronze, terra cotta, scrimshaw, woodcarving; mobile, stabile; cast 785.6; found object, *objet trouvé* <Fr>; collage, assemblage

3 **relief,** relievo; **embossment,** boss; half relief, *mezzo-rilievo* <Ital>; high relief, *alto-rilievo* <Ital>; low relief, bas-relief, *basso-rilievo* <Ital>, *rilievo stiacciato* <Ital>; sunk relief, *cavo-rilievo* <Ital>, coelanaglyphic sculpture, **intaglio,** *intaglio rilievo* or *intaglio rilevato* <Ital>; *repoussé* <Fr>; glyph, anaglyph; glyptograph; **mask;** plaquette; **medallion; medal; cameo,** cameo glass, sculptured glass; cut glass

4 <tools, materials> chisel, point, mallet, burin, modeling tool, spatula; cutting torch, welding torch, soldering iron; solder; modeling clay, Plasticine <TM>, sculptor's wax; plaster

VERBS **5** **sculpture,** sculp *or* sculpt <nf>, insculpture ; **carve,** chisel, cut, grave, engrave, chase; weld, solder; assemble; **model, mold;** cast, found

ADJS **6** **sculptural,** sculpturesque, sculptitory; statuary; **statuesque,** statuelike; **monumental,** marmoreal; plastic

7 **sculptured,** sculpted; sculptile; **molded, modeled,** ceroplastic; **carved,** chiseled; **graven,** engraven, engraved, incised; in relief, in high *or* low relief; glyphic, glyptic, anaglyphic, anaglyptic; anastatic; embossed, chased, hammered, toreutic; *repoussé* <Fr>; tactile

716 ARTIST

NOUNS **1** **artist,** *artiste* <Fr>, creator, maker; master, **old master;** dauber, daubster; copyist; **craftsman, artisan** 726.6

2 **limner,** delineator, depicter, picturer, portrayer, imager; **illustrator;** illuminator; calligrapher; commercial artist; drawer, renderer, doodler, scribbler; pastelist

3 **draftsman,** draftswoman, **sketcher, delineator; graphic artist;** drawer, architectural draftsman; crayonist, charcoalist, pastelist; **cartoonist, caricaturist**, animator

4 **painter,** *artiste-peintre* <Fr>; **colorist;** luminist, luminarist; **oil painter,** oil-colorist; **watercolorist;** aquarellist; finger painter; monochromist, polychromist; genre painter, historical painter, landscape painter, landscapist, miniaturist, portrait painter, portraitist, marine painter, still-life painter, animal painter, religious painter; pavement artist; sign painter; scene painter, scenewright, scenographer

5 **photographer,** photographist, lensman, **cameraperson**, camerawoman, cameraman**; cinematographer;** snapshotter, snap shooter, shutterbug <nf>; daguerreotypist, calotypist, talbotypist; skiagrapher, shadowgraphist, radiographer, X-ray technician; digital artist

6 **sculptor,** sculptress, sculpturer; earth artist, environmental artist; statuary; figurer, figurist, *figuriste* <Fr>, **modeler,** molder, wax modeler, clay modeler; graver, chaser, carver; molder, caster; stonecutter, mason, monumental mason, wood carver, xyloglyphic artist, whittler; ivory carver, bone carver, shell carver; gem carver, glyptic *or* glyptographic artist; engraver, etcher; lapidary

7 **ceramist, ceramicist, potter;** china decorator *or* painter, tile painter, majolica painter; glassblower, glazer, glass decorator, pyroglazer, glass cutter; enamelist, enameler

8 **printmaker,** graphic artist; **engraver,** graver, burinist; inscriber, carver; **etcher;** line engraver; **lithographer,** autolithographer, chromolithographer; serigrapher, silk-screen artist; cerographer, cerographist; chalcographer; gem engraver, glyptographer, lapidary; wood engraver, xylographer; pyrographer, xylopyrographer; zincographer

9 **designer, stylist,** styler; costume designer, dress designer, *couturier* <Fr>, *couturière* <Fr fem>; furniture designer, rug designer, textile designer

10 **architect,** civil architect; landscape architect, landscape gardener; city *or* urban planner, urbanist; functionalist

11 **decorator,** expert in decor, ornamentist, ornamentalist; **interior decorator** *or* designer, house decorator, room decorator, floral decorator, table decorator; window decorator *or* dresser; confectionery decorator

717 ARCHITECTURE, DESIGN

NOUNS 1 **architecture,** architectural design, building design, the art and technique of building; **architectural science,** architectural engineering, structural engineering, architectural technology, building science, building technology; architectonics, tectonics; **architectural style** ; **architectural specialty**; landscape architecture, landscape gardening 1069.2

2 **architectural element; ornamentation, architectural ornamentation;** column order, Doric, Ionic, Corinthian, Composite; **type of construction**, building type

3 **architect**, architectress, building designer**;** landscape architect, landscape gardener 1069.6; architectural engineer; city *or* urban planner, urbanist, urbanologist

4 **design, styling,** patterning, planning, shaping, **design specialty**

5 <design specialties> accessory design, appearance design, architectural design, automotive design, book design, clothing design, costume design, ergonomics *or* ergonomy *or* human engineering *or* human factors engineering, fashion design, furniture design, graphics design, industrial *or* product design, interior design, jewelry design, landscape architecture, lighting design, package design, pottery design, reverse engineering, stage design, textile design, typographic design

6 **designer, stylist,** styler

ADJS 7 **architectural,** architectonic, tectonic; **design, designer**

718 LITERATURE

NOUNS 1 **literature, letters, belles lettres,** polite literature, humane letters, *litterae humaniores* <L>, republic of letters; **work, literary work, text, literary text; works, complete works, oeuvre, canon, literary canon, author's canon;** serious literature; **classics,** ancient literature; medieval literature, Renaissance literature, etc; national literature, English literature, French literature, etc; ethnic literature, black *or* Afro-American literature, Latino literature, etc; contemporary literature; underground literature; pseudonymous literature; folk literature; travel literature; wisdom literature; erotic literature, erotica; pornographic literature, pornography, porn *and* hard porn *and* soft porn <nf>, obscene literature, scatological literature; popular literature, pop literature <nf>; chick lit; kitsch

2 **authorship, writing,** authorcraft, pencraft, wordsmanship, **composition,** the art of composition, inditing, inditement; one's pen; **creative writing,** literary art, verbal art, literary composition, literary production, verse-writing, short-story writing, novel-writing, playwriting, drama-writing; essay-writing; **expository writing;** technical writing; journalism, newspaper writing, editorial-writing, feature-writing, rewriting; magazine writing; songwriting, lyric-writing, libretto-writing; artistry, literary power, literary artistry, literary talent *or* flair, skill with words *or* language, facility in writing, ready pen; **writer's itch,** graphomania, scribblemania, graphorrhea, *cacoëthes scribendi* <L>

3 **writer, scribbler** <nf>, **penman,** pen, penner; pen *or* pencil driver *or* pusher <nf>, word-slinger, **ink-slinger** *and* ink spiller *and* ink-stained wretch <nf>, knight of the plume *or* pen *or* quill <nf>

4 **author, writer,** scribe <nf>, composer, inditer, penman, wordsmith, compiler; authoress, penwoman; **creative writer,** *littérateur* <Fr>, literary artist, literary craftsman *or* artisan *or* journeyman, belletrist, man of letters, literary scholar; wordsmith, word painter; freelance, freelance writer; ghostwriter, ghost <nf>; collaborator, coauthor; prose writer, logographer; fiction writer, fictioneer <nf>; story writer, **short story writer;** storyteller, narrator; **novelist;** novelettist; diarist; chronicler, historian, historiographer; biographer; **newspaperman; annalist; poet** 720.11; **dramatist,** humorist 489.12; scriptwriter, scenario writer, scenarist; nonfiction writer; article writer, magazine writer; **essayist;** monographer; reviewer, critic, literary critic, music critic, art critic, drama critic, dance critic; cultural commentator; columnist; pamphleteer; technical writer; copywriter, advertising writer; compiler, encyclopedist, bibliographer

5 **hack writer,** hack, literary hack, Grub Street writer <Brit>, **penny-a-liner, scribbler** <nf>, **potboiler** <nf>

VERBS 6 **write,** author, pen, **compose, indite,** formulate, produce, prepare; dash off, knock off *or* out <nf>, throw on paper, pound *or* crank *or* grind *or* churn out; freelance; compile; collaborate, coauthor; ghostwrite, ghost <nf>; novelize; scenarize; pamphleteer; editorialize

ADJS 7 **literary,** belletristic, lettered; classical

8 auctorial, authorial

719 HISTORY

NOUNS 1 **history,** the historical discipline, the investigation of the past, the record of the past, the story of mankind, study of the past; historical research; **annals, chronicles,** memorabilia, chronology; chronicle, record 549; historical method, historical approach, philosophy of history, **historiography;** cliometrics; documentation, recording; narrative history, **oral history,** oral record, survivors' *or* witnesses' accounts; **biography, memoir,** memorial, **life,** story, **life story,** adventures, fortunes, reminiscences, experiences; résumé, vita, curriculum vitae *or* CV; life and letters, track record <nf>; legend, saint's legend, hagiology, hagiography; **autobiography, memoirs,** memorials, archive; **journal, diary,** confessions; **profile, biographical sketch;** obituary, necrology, martyrology; photobiography; case history; historiography, theory of history; epigraphy, archaeology; Clio, Muse of history; **the past** 837; **record, recording** 549.1; herstory <nf>

2 **story, tale, yarn, account, narrative,** narration, chronicle, tradition, legend, folk tale, folk history; **anecdote,** anecdotage; **epic,** epos, **saga;** minutes, notes; file, dossier; etymology

3 **historian,** cliometrician, historiographer; **chronicler,** annalist, recorder, archivist; **biographer,** memorialist, Boswell; autobiographer, autobiographist; diarist, Pepys; epigrapher, archaeologist

VERBS 4 **chronicle,** write history, historify; historicize; biograph, biography, biographize; immortalize; compile; document, report **record** 549.15

5 **narrate, tell, relate, recount,** report, **recite,** rehearse, give an account of; commentate, voice over

ADJS 6 **historical, historic,** historied, historically accurate; fact-based; historicized; historiographical; cliometric; **chronicled;** chronologic, chronological; **traditional, legendary;** biographical, autobiographic, autobiographical; documentary, documented, archival; hagiographic, hagiographical, martyrologic, martyrological; necrologic, necrological; retro

7 **narrative,** narrational; **fictional**

ADVS 8 **historically,** historically speaking; as chronicled, as history tells us, according to *or* by all accounts; as the record shows; retrospectively

720 POETRY

NOUNS 1 **poetry,** poesy, **verse, song, rhyme**

2 **poetics,** poetcraft, versecraft, versification, versemaking, *ars poetica* <L>; **poetic language,** poetic diction, poeticism; **poetic license, poetic justice**

3 **bad poetry,** doggerel, versemongering, poetastering, poetastery; poesy; crambo, crambo clink *or* jingle, Hudibrastic verse; nonsense verse, amphigory; macaronics, macaronic verse; lame verses, limping meters, halting meters

4 **poem, verse, rhyme;** verselet, versicle; lyric poem, dramatic poem, narrative poem

5 **book of verse,** garland, **collection, anthology;** poetic works, poesy, epos

6 **metrics, prosody, versification; scansion,** scanning; metrical pattern *or* form, prosodic pattern *or* form, meter, numbers, measure; quantitative meter, syllabic meter, accentual meter, accentual-syllabic meter, duple meter, triple meter; free verse, *vers libre* <Fr>; alliterative meter

7 **meter, measure,** numbers; **rhythm, cadence,** movement, lilt, jingle, swing; sprung rhythm; **accent,** accentuation, metrical accent, stress, emphasis, ictus, **beat;** arsis, thesis; quantity, mora; metrical unit; **foot, metrical foot** ; triseme, tetraseme; metrical group, metron, colon, period; dipody, syzygy, tripody, tetrapody, pentapody, hexapody, heptapody; monometer, dimeter, trimeter, tetrameter, pentameter, hexameter, heptameter, octameter; **iambic pentameter, dactylic hexameter;** Alexandrine; Saturnian meter; elegiac, elegiac couplet *or* distich, elegiac pentameter; heroic couplet; sprung rhythm; counterpoint; caesura, diaeresis, masculine caesura, feminine caesura; catalexis; anacrusis

8 **rhyme;** clink, crambo; **consonance, assonance; alliteration;** eye rhyme; male *or* masculine *or* single rhyme, female *or* feminine *or* double rhyme; initial rhyme, end rhyme; tail rhyme, rhyme royal; broken rhyme, half rhyme, near rhyme, pararhyme, slant rhyme; internal rhyme; terza rima, ottava rima; rime riche, identical rhyme; rhyme scheme; rhyming dictionary; unrhymed poetry, blank verse

9 <poetic divisions> **measure, strain; syllable; line;** verse; stanza, stave; strophe, antistrophe, epode; **canto,** book; **refrain, chorus,** burden; envoi; monostich, distich, tristich, tetrastich, pentastich, hexastich, heptastich, octastich; **couplet;** triplet, tercet, *terza rima* <Ital>; **quatrain;** sextet, sestet; septet; octave, octet,

ottava rima <Ital>; rhyme royal; Spenserian stanza

10 **Muse;** the Muses, Pierides, *Camenae* <L>; Apollo, Apollo Musagetes; Calliope, Polyhymnia, Erato, Euterpe; Helicon, Parnassus; Castilian Spring, Pierian Spring, Hippocrene; Bragi; **poetic genius,** poesy, afflatus, fire of genius, **creative imagination** 986.2, **inspiration** 920.8

11 **poet,** poetess, poetress , maker ; ballad maker; **bard, minstrel,** scop, fili, baird, skald, **jongleur, troubadour,** *trovatore* <Ital>, trouveur, *trouvère* <Fr>, minnesinger; minor poet, major poet, arch-poet; laureate, **poet laureate;** occasional poet; **lyric poet;** epic poet; pastoral poet, pastoralist, idyllist, bucoliast ; rhapsodist, rhapsode; vers-librist, *vers libriste* <Fr>; elegist, librettist; lyricist, lyrist; odist; satirist; sonneteer; modernist, imagist, symbolist; Parnassian; beat poet

12 **bad poet;** rhymester, rhymer; metrist; versemaker, versesmith, versifier, verseman, versemonger; poetling, **poetaster,** poeticule; balladmonger

VERBS 13 **poetize, versify,** verse, write *or* compose poetry, build the stately rime, sing deathless songs, make immortal verse; tune one's lyre, climb Parnassus, mount Pegasus; **sing**; elegize; poeticize

14 **rhyme,** assonate, alliterate; **scan;** jingle; cap verses *or* rhymes

ADJS 15 **poetic, poetical,** poetlike; **lyrical, narrative,** dramatic, lyricodramatic; bardic; runic, skaldic; epic, heroic; mock-heroic, Hudibrastic; pastoral, bucolic, eclogic, idyllic, Theocritean; didactic; elegiac, elegiacal; dithyrambic, rhapsodic, rhapsodical, Alcaic, Anacreontic, Homeric, Pindaric, sapphic; Castalian, Pierian; Parnassian, Sapphic; poetico-mythological; poetico-mystical, poetico-philosophic; comic, concrete, epic, erotic, folk, metaphysical, nonsense, pattern, satirical, tragic

16 **metric, metrical, prosodic, prosodical; rhythmic, rhythmical, measured,** cadenced, scanning, scanned; accentual; iambic, dactylic, spondaic, pyrrhic, trochaic, anapestic, antispastic, etc

17 **rhyming; assonant,** assonantal; **alliterative,** onomatopoeic**;** resonant; jingling; musical, lilting

ADVS 18 **poetically, lyrically; metrically, rhythmically,** in measure; musically

721 PROSE

NOUNS 1 **prose**; prose fiction, nonfiction prose, expository prose; prose rhythm; prose style; poetic prose, polyphonic prose, prose poetry

2 **prosaism, prosaicism, prosaicness,** prosiness, pedestrianism, **unpoeticalness; matter-of-factness,** unromanticism, unidealism; **unimaginativeness** 987; **plainness,** commonness, commonplaceness, unembellishedness; insipidness, flatness, vapidity; **dullness** 117

VERBS 3 **prose,** write prose *or* in prose; pedestrianize

ADJS 4 **prose,** in prose; unversified, nonpoetic, nonmetricalf

5 **prosaic, prosy, prosing;** unpoetical, poetryless; **plain, common, commonplace, ordinary,** unembellished, mundane; **matter-of-fact, unromantic, unidealistic,** unimpassioned; pedestrian, **unimaginative** 987.5; insipid, vapid, flat; humdrum, tiresome, **dull** 117.6

722 FICTION

NOUNS 1 **fiction,** narrative, narrative literature, imaginative narrative, prose fiction; **narration,** relation, relating, recital, rehearsal, telling, retelling, recounting, recountal, review, portrayal, graphic narration, description, delineation, presentation; **storytelling,** tale-telling, yarnspinning *and* yarning <nf>; narrative poetry; operatic libretto; computer *or* interactive fiction; pulp fiction

2 **narration, narrative, relation, recital,** rehearsal, telling, retelling, recounting, recountal, review; **story-**

telling, tale-telling, yarn spinning *or* yarning <nf>

3 **story, short story,** tale, narrative, yarn, account, narration, chronicle, relation, version; **novel,** *roman* <Fr>

4 <story elements> **plot,** fable, argument, story, line, story line, subplot, secondary plot, mythos; **structure,** plan, architecture, architectonics, scheme, design; **subject, topic, theme,** motif; thematic development, development, continuity; **action,** movement; incident, episode; **complication;** rising action, turning point, climax, defining moment, falling action, switch <nf>; recognition; denouement, catastrophe; *deus ex machina* <L>; catharsis; device, contrivance, **gimmick** <nf>; angle *and* slant *and* twist <nf>; **character,** characterization; **speech,** dialogue; **tone, atmosphere,** mood; **setting,** locale, world, milieu, background, backstory, region, local color

5 **narrator,** relator, reciter, recounter, *raconteur* <Fr>; **anecdotist; storyteller,** storier, taleteller, teller of tales, spinner of yarns *and* yarn spinner <nf>; word painter; **persona,** central consciousness, the I of the story; point-of-view ; **author, writer,** short-story writer, **novelist,** novelettist, fictionist; fabulist, fableist, fabler, mythmaker, mythopoet; romancer, romancist; sagaman

VERBS **6** **narrate, tell, relate, recount,** report, **recite,** rehearse, give an account of; tell a story, unfold a tale, a tale unfold, fable, fabulize; storify, fictionalize; romance; novelize; mythicize, mythify, mythologize, allegorize; retell

ADJS **7** **fictional,** fictionalized; **novelistic,** novelized, novelettish; mythical, mythological, **legendary, fabulous;** mythopoeic, mythopoetic *or* mythopoetical; **allegorical** *or* allegoric, parabolic *or* parabolical; **romantic,** romanticized; historical, historicized, fact-based

8 **narrative, narrational;** storied, storified; **anecdotal,** anecdotic; epic *or* epical

723 CRITICISM OF THE ARTS

NOUNS **1** **criticism,** criticism of the arts, esthetic *or* artistic criticism, aesthetic *or* artistic evaluation, aesthetic *or* artistic analysis, aesthetic *or* artistic interpretation, critical commentary, critique, critical analysis, critical interpretation, critical evaluation, metacriticism, exegetics, hermeneutics; **art criticism,** formalist criticism, expressionist criticism, neoformalist criticism; music criticism; dramatic criticism; dance criticism; aesthetios

2 **review,** critical notice, commentary, *compte rendu critique* <Fr>, critical treatment *or* treatise

3 **literary criticism,** Lit-Crit <nf>, literary analysis *or* evaluation *or* interpretation *or* exegetics *or* hermeneutics, poetics; **critical approach** *or* **school**; **literary theory,** theory of literature, critical theory, theory of criticism

4 **critic,** interpreter, exegete, analyst, explicator, theoretician, aesthetician; reviewer

VERBS **5** **criticize,** critique, evaluate, interpret, explicate, analyze, judge; theorize

ADJS **6** **critical,** evaluative, interpretive, exegetical, analytical, explicative

724 OCCUPATION

NOUNS **1** **occupation, work, job, employment,** business, employ, **activity, function,** enterprise, undertaking, **affairs,** labor; thing *and* bag <nf>; **affair, matter, concern,** concernment, **interest,** lookout <nf>; what one is doing *or* about; **commerce** 731

2 **task, work, stint, job,** labor, toil, industry, piece of work, **chore,** chare, odd job; **assignment, charge,** project, errand, **mission,** commission, **duty,** service, exercise; things to do, matters in hand, irons in the fire, fish to fry; homework, take-home work; busywork, makework

3 **function, office, duty, job,** province, place, **role,** *rôle* <Fr>, part; **capacity,** character, **position**

4 <sphere of work or activity> **field, sphere,** profession, trade, province, bailiwick, turf <nf>, department, area, discipline, subdiscipline, orb, orbit, realm, arena, domain, walk; **specialty, niche,** speciality <Brit>, line of country <Brit nf>; beat, round; shop; corporate culture; bricks and mortar, bricks and clicks

5 **position, job,** employment, gainful employment, situation; **office, post, place,** station, berth, billet, **appointment,** engagement, gig <nf>; incumbency, tenure; opening, vacancy; second job, moonlighting <nf>

6 **vocation, occupation, business, work, line, line of work,** line of business *or* endeavor, number <nf>, walk, **walk of life, calling,** mission, **profession, practice, pursuit, specialty,** specialization, *métier* <Fr>, mystery , **trade,** racket *and* game <nf>; **career,** lifework, life's work; career track, Mommy track <nf>; **craft,** art, handicraft; careerism, career building

7 **avocation, hobby,** hobbyhorse , sideline, by-line, side interest, pastime, spare-time activity, outside interest; amateur pursuit, amateurism; unpaid work, volunteer work

8 **professionalism,** professional standing *or* status

9 **nonprofessionalism, amateurism,** amateur standing *or* status

VERBS 10 **occupy, engage, busy,** devote, spend, **employ,** occupy oneself, busy oneself, go about one's business, devote oneself; pass *or* employ *or* spend the time; occupy one's time, take up one's time; attend to business, attend to one's work; mind one's business, mind the store <nf>, stick to one's last *or* knitting <nf>; telecommute

11 **busy oneself with, do,** occupy *or* engage oneself with, employ oneself in *or* upon, pass *or* employ *or* spend one's time in; **engage in, take up,** devote oneself to, apply oneself to, address oneself to, have one's hands in, turn one's hand to; concern oneself with, make it one's business; **be about, be doing,** be occupied with, be engaged *or* employed in, be at work on; practice, follow as an occupation

12 **work,** work at, work for, have a job, be employed, **ply one's trade,** labor in one's vocation, do one's number <nf>, follow a trade, practice a profession, carry on a business *or* trade, keep up; **do** *or* **transact business,** carry on *or* conduct business; set up shop, set up in business, hang out one's shingle <nf>; stay employed, hold down a job <nf>; moonlight <nf>, consult; labor, toil 725.13,14

13 **officiate, function, serve; perform as, act as,** act *or* play one's part, **do duty,** discharge *or* perform *or* exercise the office *or* duties *or* functions of, serve in the office *or* capacity of

14 **hold office,** fill an office, occupy a post

ADJS 15 **occupied, busy,** working; practical, realistic 987.6; banausic, moneymaking, breadwinning, utilitarian 387.18; materialistic 695.16; workaday, workday, prosaic 117.8; **commercial** 731.22

16 **occupational, vocational,** functional; **professional,** pro <nf>; official; technical, industrial; all in the day's work

17 **avocational,** hobby, amateur, nonprofessional

ADVS 18 **professionally,** vocationally; as a profession *or* vocation; in the course of business

725 EXERTION

NOUNS 1 **exertion, effort, energy,** elbow grease; **endeavor** 403; **trouble, pains;** great *or* mighty effort, might and main, muscle, one's back, nerve, and sinew, hard *or* strong *or* long pull

2 **strain,** straining, **stress,** stressfulness, **stress and strain,** taxing, **tension,** stretch, rack; tug, pull, haul, heave; overexertion, overstrain, overtaxing, overextension, overstress

3 **struggle, fight, battle, tussle, scuffle, wrestle,** hassle <nf>

4 **work, labor, employment, industry, toil,** moil, travail, toil and trouble,

sweat of one's brow; **drudgery, sweat,** slavery, spadework, shitwork <nf>, rat race <nf>; treadmill; unskilled labor, hewing of wood *and* drawing of water; dirty work, grunt work *and* donkey work *and* shitwork *and* scut work <nf>, thankless task; **makework,** tedious *or* stupid *or* idiot *or* tiresome work, humdrum toil, grind <nf>, fag <chiefly Brit>; rubber room work *or* job *or* assignment, no-work job; **manual labor,** handwork, handiwork; forced labor; hand's turn, stroke of work, stroke; lick *and* lick of work *and* stitch of work <nf>; man-hour; **workload,** work schedule; task 724.2; fatigue 21

5 **hard work** *or* **labor, backbreaking work,** moil, warm work, uphill work, long haul, hard *or* tough grind <nf>, the hard way; **hard job** 1013.2; labor of Hercules; **laboriousness, toilsomeness,** effortfulness, **strenuousness, arduousness,** operosity, operoseness; onerousness, oppressiveness, burdensomeness; troublesomeness

6 **exercise** 84, exercising; **practice, drill, workout**, preparation; yoga; constitutional <nf>, stretch; violent exercise; physical education

7 exerciser; horizontal bar, parallel bars, horse, side horse, long horse, rings; trapeze; trampoline; Indian club; medicine ball; punching bag; rowing machine; weight, dumbbell, barbell

VERBS 8 **exert, exercise, ply, employ, use, put forth,** put out *and* make with <nf>; practice

9 **exert oneself,** use some elbow grease <nf>, spread oneself, put forth one's strength, bend every effort, bend might and main, spare no effort, put on a full-court press <nf>, tax one's energies, break a sweat <nf>; put *or* lay oneself out <nf>, go all out <nf>; endeavor 403.4; **do one's best; apply oneself,** come to grips with; hump *and* hump it *and* hump oneself <nf>, **buckle** *or* **knuckle** *or* bear <nf>, lay to; lay to the oars, ply the oar

10 **strain, tense, stress, stretch, tax,** press, rack; **pull, tug,** haul, **heave;** strain the muscles, strain every nerve *or* every nerve and sinew; put one's back into it <nf>; sweat blood; overwork, work night and day, take on too much, spread oneself too thin, overexert, overstrain, overtax, overextend; drive *or* whip *or* flog oneself

11 **struggle, strive, contend, fight, battle,** buffet, scuffle, tussle, wrestle, hassle <nf>, work *or* fight one's way, agonize, huff and puff, grunt and sweat, sweat it <nf>, make heavy weather of it

12 **work, labor;** busy oneself 724.10,11; turn a hand, do a hand's turn, do a lick of work, earn one's keep; chore, do the chores, char *or* do chars, chare <Brit>

13 **work hard; scratch** *and* **hustle** *and* **sweat** <nf>, **slave, sweat and slave** <nf>, slave away, toil away, hammer at; **hit the ball** *and* bear down *and* pour it on <nf>; burn the candle at both ends; work one's head off <nf>, work one's fingers to the bone, break one's back, bust one's hump *or* ass <nf>; put one's heart and soul into it; beaver *or* beaver away <Brit nf>, work like a beaver, work like a horse *or* cart horse *or* dog, work like a slave *or* galley slave, work like a coal heaver, work like a Trojan; work overtime, be a workaholic <nf>, overwork, do double duty, work double hours *or* tides, **work day and night,** work late, **burn the midnight oil;** persevere; lucubrate, elucubrate; overwork 993.10

14 **drudge, grind** *and* **dig** <nf>, fag <Brit>, **grub, toil,** moil, toil and moil, travail, **plod, slog, peg, plug** <nf>, hammer, peg away *or* along, plug away *or* along <nf>, hammer away, pound away, struggle along, struggle on, work away; **get** *or* **keep one's nose to the grindstone;** wade through

15 **set to work, get rolling, get busy, get down to business** *or* **work,** roll up one's sleeves, spit on one's hands, gird up one's loins; **fall to work, fall to, buckle** *or* **knuckle down to** <nf>, **turn to, set to** *or*

about, put *or* set one's hand to, start in, set up shop, enter on *or* upon, launch into *or* upon; **get on the job** *and* get going <nf>; **go to it** *and* **get with it** *and* get cracking *and* have at it *and* get one's teeth into it <nf>; hop *or* jump to it <nf>; **attack,** set at, **tackle** <nf>; **plunge into,** dive into; **pitch in** *or* **into** <nf>; light into *and* wade into *and* tear into *and* sail into <nf>, put *or* lay one's shoulder to the wheel, put one's hand to the plow; take on, undertake 404.3

16 **task, work, busy,** keep busy, fag <Brit>, sweat <nf>, **drive, tax;** overtask, overtax, **overwork,** overdrive; burden, oppress 297.13

ADJS 17 **laboring, working; struggling, striving,** straining; **drudging, toiling,** slaving, sweating *and* grinding <nf>, grubbing, **plodding,** slogging, pegging, plugging <nf>, persevering; hardworking; busy, industrious, hard at it

18 **laborious, toilsome, arduous, strenuous,** painful, effortful, operose, troublesome, onerous, oppressive, burdensome; wearisome, tiring, exhausting; **heavy,** hefty <nf>, tough <nf>, uphill, **backbreaking,** grueling, punishing, crushing, killing, Herculean; uphill; **labored,** forced, strained; straining, tensive, painstaking, **intensive;** hard-fought, hard-won, hard-earned

ADVS 19 **laboriously, arduously, toilsomely, strenuously,** operosely; effortfully, with effort, **hard,** by the sweat of one's brow; the hard way; with all one's might, for all one is worth, with a will, **with might and main,** with a strong hand, manfully; **hammer and tongs, tooth and nail,** *bec et ongles* <Fr>, heart and soul; **industriously** 330.27

726 WORKER, DOER

NOUNS 1 **doer, agent,** actor, **performer, worker, practitioner,** perpetrator; **producer, maker,** creator, fabricator, **author,** mover, prime mover; go-getter; architect; **agent,** medium; **executor,** executant, executrix; **operator,** operative, operant, hand; subject *and* agent <gram>; coworker, colleague

2 **worker, laborer, toiler,** moiler; member of the working class, proletarian, prole <Brit nf>, blue-collar *or* lunch-bucket worker, laboring man; stiff *and* working stiff <nf>; **workman, working man; workwoman, working woman,** workfolk, workpeople; working girl, workgirl; **factory worker,** industrial worker; autoworker, steelworker; construction worker; **commuter;** home worker, telecommuter; **office worker, white-collar worker;** career woman, career girl; **jobholder,** wageworker, **wage earner,** salaried worker; **breadwinner;** wage slave; employee, servant 577; **hand, workhand**, hourly worker**; laborer,** common laborer, **unskilled laborer,** navvy <Brit>, day laborer, roustabout; casual, casual laborer; **agricultural worker** 1069.5; migrant worker, migrant; menial, flunky; piece-worker, jobber; factotum, jack-of-all-trades; full-time worker, part-time worker; temporary employee, temporary, office temporary, temp <nf>; freelance worker, freelance, freelancer, self-employed person, independent contractor, consultant; volunteer; domestic worker, clerical worker, sales worker, service worker, repair worker, artistic worker, technical worker; **labor force, work force,** crew, shop floor <Brit>, factory floor; personnel; labor market

3 **drudge, grub, hack, fag, plodder, slave,** galley slave, **workhorse,** beast of burden, slogger; grind *and* greasy grind <nf>, swot <Brit nf>; slave labor, sweatshop labor; busy bee *and* beaver *and* ant <nf>

4 **professional,** member of a learned profession, professional practitioner; businessman, businesswoman, career woman; executive; pro *and* old pro <nf>, seasoned professional; gownsman; doctor, lawyer, member of the clergy, teacher, accountant; social worker; health-care profes-

sional, military professional; law-enforcement professional, etc

5 **amateur, nonprofessional, layman,** member of the laity, laic

6 **skilled worker,** skilled laborer, **journeyman,** mechanic; **craftsman, handicraftsman;** craftswoman; craftsperson; craftspeople; **artisan,** artificer, artist; **maker**; **wright; technician;** apprentice, prentice <nf>; **master,** master craftsman, master workman, master carpenter, etc

7 **engineer,** professional engineer; **technician,** technical worker, techie <nf>; engineering, technology

8 **smith;** farrier <Brit>, forger, forgeman, metalworker; Vulcan, Hephaestus, Wayland *or* Völund

727 UNIONISM, LABOR UNION

NOUNS 1 **unionism,** trade unionism, trades unionism <Brit>, labor unionism; **unionization; collective bargaining; arbitration,** nonbinding arbitration; industrial relations, labor relations, work relations; employee rights, employer rights; salary negotiations, labor negotiations, negotiated *or* negotiation points, employee demands, management demands

2 **labor union,** trade union, trades union <Brit>; organized labor; collective bargaining; **craft union,** guild, horizontal union; **industrial union,** vertical union; **local,** union local, local union; company union

3 **union shop,** preferential shop, **closed shop;** open shop; nonunion shop; **labor contract, union contract,** sweetheart contract, yellow-dog contract; maintenance of membership

4 **unionist, labor unionist, trade unionist, union member,** trades unionist <Brit>, organized *or* unionized worker, cardholder; shop steward, bargainer, negotiator; business agent; union officer; union *or* labor organizer, organizer, labor union official; union contractor

5 **strike, walkout** *or* tie-up <nf>, industrial action <Brit>, **job action;** slowdown, rulebook slowdown, sick-in *and* sickout *and* blue flu <nf>; work stoppage, sit-down strike, sit-down, wildcat strike, outlaw strike, called strike, organized strike; sympathy strike; **slowdown,** work-to-rule, rule-book slowdown; general strike; **boycott,** boy-cottage, picketing, picket; buyer's *or* consumer's strike; **lock-out;** revolt 327.4

6 **striker,** picket; sitdown striker; holdout <nf>

7 <strike enforcer> **picket; goon** <nf>, strong-arm man; flying squadron *or* squad, goon squad <nf>

8 **strikebreaker, scab** *and* **rat** *and* **fink** *and* scissorbill <nf>, goon, **blackleg** <Brit>

VERBS 9 **organize, unionize;** bargain, bargain collectively; arbitrate; submit to arbitration

10 **strike, go on strike, go out, walk, walk out;** hit the bricks <nf>, shut it down; slow down; sit down; **boycott;** picket; hold out <nf>; **lock out;** revolt 327.7

11 **break a strike; scab** *and* **rat** *and* **fink** <nf>, **blackleg** <Brit>

728 MONEY

NOUNS 1 **money, currency, legal tender, medium of exchange,** circulating medium, sterling <Brit>, **cash,** hard cash, cold cash; specie, coinage, mintage, coin of the realm, gold; **silver;** dollars; pounds, shillings, and pence; **the wherewithal,** the wherewith; lucre, **filthy lucre** <nf>, the almighty dollar, pelf, root of all evil, mammon; **hard currency,** soft currency; fractional currency; managed currency; necessity money, scrip, emergency money; monetary unit, monetary denomination

2 <nf terms> **dough, bread, jack, kale,** bucks, scratch, change, mazuma, mopus, gelt, gilt, coin, spondulicks, oof, ooftish, wampum, possibles, moolah, boodle, blunt, dinero, do-re-mi, **sugar,** brass, tin, rocks, simoleons, shekels, berries, chips, **bucks,** green, green stuff, the

needful, grease, ointment, palm oil, gravy, cabbage, lettuce, whip-out, the necessary, loot

3 **wampum,** wampumpeag, peag, sewan, roanoke, shell money; cowrie

4 **specie,** hard money; coinage; coin, piece, piece of money, piece of silver *or* gold; roll of coins, rouleau; **gold piece;** ten-dollar gold piece, eagle; five-dollar gold piece, half eagle; twenty-dollar gold piece, double eagle; guinea, sovereign, pound sovereign, crown, half crown; doubloon; ducat; napoleon, louis d'or; moidore

5 **paper money;** cash; **bill,** dollar bill, etc; **note,** negotiable note *or* instrument, legal-tender note; **bank note,** bill of exchange, Federal Reserve note; national bank note; government note, treasury note; silver certificate; gold certificate; scrip; fractional note, shinplaster <nf>; fiat money, assignat

6 <nf terms> **folding money, green stuff,** the long green, folding green, lean green, mint leaves, lettuce, greenbacks, frogskins, skins

7 <US denominations> mill; cent, penny, copper, red cent <nf>; five cents, nickel; ten cents, dime; twenty-five cents, quarter, two bits <nf>; fifty cents, half-dollar, four bits <nf>; dollar, dollar bill; buck *and* smacker *and* frogskin *and* fish *and* skin <nf>; silver dollar, beau dollar , cartwheel *and* iron man <nf>; two-dollar bill, two-spot <nf>; five-dollar bill; fiver *and* five-spot *and* fin <nf>; ten-dollar bill; tenner *and* ten-spot *and* sawbuck <nf>; twenty-dollar bill, double sawbuck <nf>; fifty-dollar bill, half a C <nf>; hundred-dollar bill; C *and* C-note *and* century *and* bill <nf>; five hundred dollars, half grand <nf>, five-hundred-dollar bill, half G <nf>; thousand dollars, G *and* grand <nf>, thousand-dollar bill, G-note *and* yard *and* big one <nf>

8 <British denominations> mite; farthing; halfpenny *or* ha'penny, bawbee <nf>, mag *or* meg <nf>; penny; pence, p; new pence, np; two-pence *or* tuppence; threepence *or* thrippence, threepenny bit *or* piece; fourpence, fourpenny, groat; sixpence, tanner <nf>, teston; shilling, bob <nf>; florin; half crown, half-dollar <nf>; crown, dollar <nf>; pound, quid <nf>; guinea; fiver <£5>, tenner <£10>, pony <£25>, monkey <£500>, plum <£100,000>, marigold <£1,000,000> <nf>

9 **foreign money,** foreign denominations; **convertibility, foreign exchange;** rate of exchange *or* exchange rate; parity of exchange; agio

10 **counterfeit,** counterfeit money, funny *or* phony *or* bogus money <nf>, false *or* bad money, queer <nf>, base coin, green goods <nf>; **forgery,** bad check, rubber check *and* bounced check *and* kite <nf>

11 **negotiable instrument** *or* **paper,** commercial paper, paper, bill; **bill of exchange,** bill of draft; certificate, certificate of deposit *or* CD; **check,** cheque <Brit>; blank check; bank check, teller's check; treasury check; cashier's check, certified check; traveler's check *or* banker's check; letter of credit, commercial letter of credit; **money order** *or* MO; postal order *or* postoffice order <Brit>; draft, warrant, voucher, debenture; **promissory note, note, IOU;** note of hand; credit note; acceptance, acceptance bill, bank acceptance, trade acceptance; due bill; demand bill, sight bill, demand draft, sight draft; time bill, time draft; exchequer bill *or* treasury bill <Brit>; checkbook

12 **token, counter,** slug; **scrip, coupon; check, ticket,** tag; hat check, baggage check

13 **sum,** amount of money; round sum, lump sum

14 **funds, finances, moneys,** exchequer, purse, budget, pocket; treasury, treasure, substance, **assets,** resources, total assets, worth, net worth, **pecuniary resources, means,** available means *or* resources *or* funds, cash flow, wherewithal, command of money; balance; pool, **fund, kitty** <nf>, petty cash; war chest; checking account, bank account; Swiss bank account,

unnumbered *or* unregistered bank account; reserves, cash reserves; savings, savings account, nest egg <nf>; life savings; bottom dollar <nf>; automated teller machine *or* ATM

15 **capital, fund;** moneyed capital; principal, corpus; circulating capital, floating capital; fixed capital, working capital, equity capital, **risk** *or* **venture capital;** capital structure; capital gains distribution; capitalization

16 **money market,** supply of short-term funds; tight money, cheap money; **borrowing** 621; **lending** 620; discounting, note discounting, note shaving, dealing in commercial paper

17 **bankroll;** roll *or* wad <nf>

18 **cash, ready money** *or* **cash,** the ready <nf>, available funds, money in hand, cash in hand, balance in hand, immediate resources, **liquid assets,** cash supply, **cash flow;** treasury

19 **petty cash, pocket money, pin money,** spending money, mad money, cheddar <nf>, **change,** small change, pocket change; nickels and dimes *and* chicken feed *and* peanuts <nf>, pittance

20 precious metals; **gold,** yellow stuff <nf>; nugget, gold nugget; **silver, copper, nickel,** coin gold *or* silver; bullion, ingot, bar

21 standard of value, gold standard, silver standard; monometallism, bimetallism; money of account

22 <science of coins> **numismatics,** numismatology; numismatist, numismatologist

23 monetization; issuance, circulation; remonetization; demonetization; revaluation, devaluation

24 **coining,** coinage, mintage, striking, stamping; **counterfeiting, forgery;** coin-clipping

25 **coiner,** minter, mintmaster, moneyer; **counterfeiter, forger;** coin-clipper

VERBS **26** monetize; **issue,** utter, **circulate;** remonetize, reissue; demonetize; revalue, devalue, devaluate

27 discount, discount notes, deal in commercial paper, shave; borrow, lend 620.5

28 **coin, mint;** print, stamp; **counterfeit, forge;** utter, pass *or* shove the queer <nf>; pass a bad check, kite a check

29 **cash,** cash in <nf>, liquidate, convert into cash, realize

ADJS **30** **monetary, pecuniary,** nummary, nummular, **financial,** fiduciary; capital; fiscal; sumptuary; numismatic; sterling

31 convertible, liquid, negotiable

729 FINANCE, INVESTMENT

NOUNS **1** **finance, finances, money matters;** world of finance, financial world, financial industry, **high finance,** investment banking, international banking, Wall Street banking, Lombard Street; the gnomes of Zurich; economics 731; purse strings

2 **financing, funding, backing,** financial backing, **sponsorship, patronization,** support, financial support; **stake** *and* **grubstake** <nf>; subsidy 478.8; **capitalizing,** capitalization, provision of capital; deficit financing

3 personal finance; bank account, savings account, checking account; telebanking; budget; pension, 401K, Individual Retirement Account *or* IRA, Keogh plan

4 **investment, venture, risk,** plunge <nf>, speculation; prime investment; ethical *or* conscience investment; money market, mutual fund, stock market, bond market; **divestment,** disinvestment

5 **banking,** money dealing, money changing; investment banking; banking industry

6 **financial condition,** state of the exchequer; **credit rating,** Dun & Bradstreet rating

7 **solvency,** soundness, solidity; credit standing, creditworthiness; unindebtedness

8 **crisis,** financial crisis; dollar crisis, dollar gap

9 **financier,** moneyman, **capitalist,** finance capitalist; Wall Streeter; investor; financial expert, economist, authority on money and banking; international banker

10 **financer, backer,** funder, **sponsor, patron, supporter,** angel <nf>, Maecenas; cash cow *and* staker *and* grubstaker <nf>, money-maker, money-spinner, meal ticket <nf>; **fundraiser**

11 **banker, money dealer,** moneymonger; money broker; discounter, note broker, bill broker <Brit>; moneylender 620.3; money changer, cambist; investment banker; bank president, bank manager, bank officer, loan officer, trust officer, banking executive; bank clerk, cashier, teller

12 **treasurer,** financial officer, bursar, purser, purse bearer, **cashier,** cashkeeper; accountant, auditor, controller *or* comptroller, bookkeeper; chamberlain, curator, steward, trustee; depositary, depository; receiver, liquidator; **paymaster;** Secretary of the Treasury, Chancellor of the Exchequer

13 **treasury, treasure-house;** subtreasury; **depository,** repository; storehouse 386.6; gold depository, Fort Knox; **strongbox, safe,** money chest, **coffer, locker, chest;** piggy bank, penny bank, bank; **vault,** strong room; safe-deposit *or* safety-deposit box *or* vault; cashbox, coin box, cash register, **till;** bursary; exchequer, fisc; **public treasury,** public funds, taxpayer funds *or* money, pork barrel, public crib *or* trough *or* till <nf>

14 **bank,** banking house, lending institution, savings institution; automated teller machine *or* ATM, cash machine; **central bank,** Bank of England *or* the Old Lady of Threadneedle Street, Bank of France; Federal Reserve Bank *or* System; World Bank, International Monetary Fund; clearing house

15 **purse, wallet, pocketbook, bag, handbag,** clutch, shoulder bag, porte-monnaie, **billfold,** money belt, money clip, poke <nf>, **pocket;** fanny pack; moneybag; purse strings

VERBS **16** **finance, back, fund, sponsor, patronize, support,** provide for, capitalize, provide capital *or* money for, pay for, bankroll <nf>, angel <nf>, put up the money, hold the purse strings; **stake** *or* **grubstake** <nf>; subsidize 478.19; set up, set up in business; refinance

17 **invest,** place, put, sink; **risk, venture;** make an investment, lay out money, place out *or* put out at interest; reinvest, roll over, plow back into <nf>; **invest in, put money in,** sink money in, pour money into, tie up one's money in; buy in *or* into, buy a piece *or* share of; financier; plunge <nf>, speculate 737.23; play the big board, play the stock exchange

ADJS **18** **solvent, sound,** substantial, solid, good, sound as a dollar, creditworthy; **able to pay,** good for, unindebted 624.23, out of the hole *or* the red

19 **insolvent,** unsound, indebted 623.8

20 financial, monetary, fiscal, pecuniary, economic; bull, bear

730 BUSINESSMAN, MERCHANT

NOUNS **1** **businessman,** businesswoman, businessperson, businesspeople; enterpriser, entrepreneur, man of commerce; small *or* little businessman; big businessman, magnate, tycoon <nf>, baron, king, top executive, business leader; director, manager 574.1; big boss; **industrialist,** captain of industry; banker, financier; robber baron; intrapreneur

2 **merchant,** merchandiser, marketer, **trader,** trafficker, **dealer,** monger, chandler; **tradesman,** tradeswoman; **storekeeper, shopkeeper;** regrater; **wholesaler,** jobber, middleman; importer, exporter; **distributor; retailer,** retail merchant, retail dealer *or* seller; **dealership, distributorship;** franchise; concession

3 **salesman,** seller, salesperson, salesclerk; **saleswoman,** saleslady, salesgirl; **clerk,** shop clerk, store clerk, shop assistant; floorwalker; **agent, sales agent,** selling agent; sales engineer; sales manager; salespeople, sales force, sales personnel; scalper *and* ticket scalper <nf>

4 traveling salesman, traveler, commercial traveler, traveling agent, traveling man *or* woman, road warrior, knight of the road, bagman <Brit>, drummer ; detail man; door-to-door salesman, canvasser

5 vendor, peddler, huckster, hawker, butcher , higgler, cadger, colporteur, chapman <Brit>; cheap-jack *and* cheap-john <nf>; coster *or* costermonger <Brit>; sidewalk salesman

6 solicitor, canvasser

7 <nf terms> tout, touter, **pitch-man** *or* **-woman** *or* person, barker, spieler, ballyhooer, **ballyhoo man**

8 auctioneer, auction agent

9 broker, note broker, bill broker <Brit>, discount broker, cotton broker, hotel broker, insurance broker, mortgage broker, diamond broker, furniture broker, ship broker, grain broker; stockbroker 737.10; pawnbroker 620.3; money broker, money changer, cambist; land broker, real estate broker, realtor, real estate agent, estate agent <Brit>

10 ragman, old-clothesman, rag-and-bone man <Brit>; **junkman,** junk dealer

11 tradesmen, tradespeople, tradesfolk, **merchantry**

ADJS **12 business, commercial,** mercantile; entrepreneurial; auctionary

731 COMMERCE, ECONOMICS

NOUNS **1 commerce, trade, traffic,** truck, intercourse, **dealing, dealings; business,** business dealings *or* affairs *or* relations, commercial affairs *or* relations; the business world, the world of trade *or* commerce, the marketplace, marketspace; merchantry, mercantile business; **market,** marketing, state of the market, buyers' market, sellers' market; **industry** 725.4; big business, small business; fair trade, free trade, reciprocal trade, unilateral trade, multilateral trade; most favored nation; balance of trade; restraint of trade; market leader; market indicator

2 trade, trading, doing business, trafficking; barter, bartering, **exchange,** interchange, swapping <nf>; give-and-take, horse trading <nf>, **dealing, deal-making,** wheeling and dealing <nf>; **buying and selling; wholesaling,** jobbing; brokerage, agency; **retailing,** merchandising 734.2; commercial trade, export and import

3 negotiation, bargaining, haggling, higgling, **dickering, chaffering,** chaffer, haggle; hacking out *or* working out *or* hammering out a deal, coming to terms; horse trading; collective bargaining, package bargaining, pattern bargaining

4 transaction, business *or* commercial transaction, **deal,** business deal, negotiation , operation, turn; package deal

5 bargain, deal <nf>, dicker; agreement, contract; **trade, swap** <nf>; horse trade <nf>; trade-in; blind bargain, pig in a poke; hard bargain

6 custom, customers, clientele, patronage, patrons, trade; **goodwill,** repute, good name

7 economy, economic system, market, capitalist *or* capitalistic economy, free-enterprise *or* free-trade *or* private-enterprise economy, market economy, free-market economy, socialist *or* socialistic economy, collectivized economy; hot *or* overheated economy; healthy *or* sound economy, weak economy; **gross national product** *or* **GNP;** economic sector, public sector, private sector; economic self-sufficiency, autarky; economic policy, fiscal policy, monetary policy; microeconomics, macroeconomics; privatization, nationalization, denationalization, supply-side economics; economic theory; open market

8 standard of living, standard of life, standard of comfort; real wages, take-home pay *or* take-home; **cost of living;** cost-of-living index, consumer price index

9 economic indicator, econometrics; gross national product *or* GNP, price index, consumer price index, retail price index, cost-of-living index; unemployment rate, national debt, budget deficit

10 **business cycle, economic cycle,** business fluctuations; peak, peaking; low, bottoming out <nf>; prosperity, boom <nf>; boomlet *or* miniboom; crisis, **recession, depression,** slowdown, cooling off, slump *and* bust <nf>, downturn, downtick <nf>; upturn, uptick <nf>, expanding economy, recovery; **growth,** economic growth, business growth, high growth rate, expansion, market expansion, **economic expansion; trade cycle;** trade deficit, trade gap, balance of payments; **monetary cycle; inflation,** deflation, stagflation

11 **economics,** eco *or* econ <nf>, economic science, the dismal science; political economy; dynamic economics; theoretical economics, plutology; classical economics; Keynesian economics, Keynesianism; supply side economics; econometrics; economism, economic determinism

12 **economist,** economic expert *or* authority; political economist

13 **commercialism,** mercantilism; industrialism; mass marketing, guerrilla marketing

14 **commercialization;** industrialization

VERBS 15 **trade, deal, traffic, truck, buy and sell, do business; barter; exchange,** change, interchange, give in exchange, take in exchange, **swap** <nf>, switch; swap horses *and* horse-trade <nf>; trade off; trade in; trade sight unseen, make a blind bargain, sell a pig in a poke; marketize; **ply one's trade** 724.12

16 **deal in, trade in, traffic in, handle,** carry, be in; market, merchandise, **sell,** retail, wholesale, job

17 **trade with, deal with, traffic with, traffic in, do business with,** have dealings with, have truck with, transact business with; frequent as a customer, shop at, trade at, **patronize,** take one's business *or* trade to; open an account with, have an account with; export, import; market, merchandise

18 **bargain, drive a bargain, negotiate, haggle,** higgle, chaffer, huckster, **deal, dicker,** barter, make a deal, do a deal <Brit>, hack out *or* work out *or* hammer out a deal, do a deal; **bid,** bid for, cheapen, beat down; underbid, outbid; drive a hard bargain; hold out for

19 **strike a bargain,** make a bargain, make a dicker, **make a deal,** get oneself a deal, put through a deal, shake hands, shake on it <nf>; bargain for, agree to; **come to terms** 332.10; be a bargain, be a go *and* be a deal <nf>, be on <nf>; network

20 put on a business basis *or* footing, make businesslike; commercialize; industrialize

21 <adjust the economy> cool *or* cool off the economy; heat *or* heat up the economy

ADJS 22 **commercial, business, trade,** trading, **mercantile,** merchant; commercialistic, mercantilistic; industrial; wholesale, retail

23 **economic**, fiscal, monetary, pecuniary, financial, budgetary; inflationary, deflationary; socio-economic, politico-economic *or* -economical

732 ILLICIT BUSINESS

NOUNS 1 illicit business, illegitimate business, illegal operations, illegal commerce *or* traffic, shady dealings, **racket** <nf>; **the rackets** <nf>, the syndicate, **organized crime, Mafia,** Cosa Nostra; **black market,** gray market; **drug** *or* **narcotics traffic;** narcoterrorism; **prostitution,** streetwalking; **pimping,** traffic in women, white slavery; usury 623.3, loansharking *and* shylocking <nf>; protection racket; bootlegging, moonshining <nf>; gambling 759.1; spam, computer virus *or* worm

2 **smuggling,** contrabandage, contraband; narcotics smuggling, dope smuggling <nf>, jewel smuggling, cigarette smuggling; gunrunning, rumrunning

3 **contraband,** smuggled goods; narcotics, drugs, dope <nf>, jewels, cigarettes; bootleg liquor; stolen goods *or* property, hot goods *or* items <nf>

4 **racketeer;** Mafioso; **black marketeer,** gray marketeer; bootlegger,

moonshiner <nf>; pusher *and* dealer <nf>, narcotics *or* dope *or* drug pusher <nf>; **drug lord;** Medellin cartel

5 **smuggler,** contrabandist, runner; drug smuggler, mule <nf>; gunrunner, rumrunner

6 **fence,** receiver, **receiver of stolen goods,** swagman *and* swagsman <nf>, bagman, bagwoman

VERBS 7 <deal in illicit goods> push *and* shove <nf>; **sell under the counter; black-market,** black-marketeer; bootleg, moonshine <nf>; fence <nf>; spam

8 **smuggle,** run, sneak

733 PURCHASE

NOUNS 1 **purchase, buying, purchasing**, acquisition**; shopping, marketing;** shopping around, comparison shopping; window-shopping; impulse buying; shopping spree, retail therapy; repurchase, rebuying; mail-order buying, catalog shopping; teleshopping, home shopping, online shopping; installment buying, hire purchase <Brit>; layaway purchase; **buying up,** cornering, coemption ; **buying** *or* **purchasing power; consumerism;** consumer society, consumer sovereignty, consumer power, acquisitive society; retail *or* consumer price index; wholesale price index; shopping list

2 **option,** first option, **first refusal,** refusal, preemption, right of preemption, prior right of purchase

3 **market,** public, purchasing public, target audience; urban market, rural market, youth market, suburban market, etc; **clientele, customers,** clientage, **patronage, custom,** trade; carriage trade; demand, consumer demand

4 **customer, client; patron,** patronizer <nf>, regular customer *or* buyer, regular; clientele; **prospect;** mark *or* sucker <nf>

5 **buyer,** purchaser, emptor, **consumer,** vendee; **shopper,** marketer; shopaholic; bargain-hunter; bidder; window-shopper, browser; purchasing agent, customer agent, personal shopper

6 by-bidder, decoy, come-on man *and* shill <nf>

VERBS 7 **purchase, buy,** procure, make *or* complete a purchase, make a buy, make a deal for, blow oneself to <nf>; **buy up,** regrate, **corner,** monopolize, engross, hoard; buy out; buy in, buy into, buy a piece of; repurchase, rebuy, buy back; buy on credit, buy on the installment plan, charge; buy sight unseen *or* blind; trade up

8 **shop, market, go shopping,** go marketing; **shop around;** window-shop, comparison-shop, **browse, graze;** impulse-buy; shop till one drops *and* hit the shops <nf>

9 **bid,** make a bid, offer, offer to buy, make an offer; give the asking price; by-bid, shill <nf>; bid up; bid in

ADJS 10 **purchasing, buying,** in the market; cliental

11 **bought,** store-bought, boughten *or* store-boughten <nf>, purchased

734 SALE

NOUNS 1 **sale; wholesale, retail; market, demand,** outlet; buyers' market, sellers' market; mass market; conditional sale; tie-in sale, tie-in; turnover; bill of sale; cash sale, cash-andcarry

2 **selling, merchandising, marketing; wholesaling,** jobbing; **retailing;** direct selling; sell-through; telemarketing; mail-order selling, direct-mail selling, catalog selling, direct marketing; viral marketing; television *or* video selling; online selling, e-commerce; **vending, peddling, hawking, huckstering;** hucksterism; market *or* marketing research, consumer research, consumer preference study, consumer survey, data warehousing; sales campaign, promotion, sales promotion; **salesmanship,** high-pressure salesmanship, hard sell <nf>, low-pressure salesmanship, soft sell <nf>; cold call; sellout; branding

3 **sale,** sellout, closing-out sale, going-out-of-business sale,

inventory-clearance sale, distress sale, fire sale; bazaar; rummage sale, white elephant sale, garage sale, tag sale, yard sale, flea market; tax sale

4 **auction,** auction sale, vendue, outcry, sale at *or* by auction, sale to the highest bidder; Dutch auction; **auction block, block**

5 **sales talk, sales pitch,** patter; **pitch** *or* spiel *or* ballyhoo <nf>

6 **sales resistance,** consumer *or* buyer resistance

7 **salability,** salableness, commerciality, merchandisability, **marketability,** vendibility

VERBS 8 **sell, merchandise, market,** move, turn over, sell off, make *or* effect a sale; convert into cash, turn into money; **sell out,** close out; sell up <Brit>; **retail,** sell retail, sell over the counter; **wholesale,** sell wholesale, job, be jobber *or* wholesaler for; dump, unload, flood the market with, get rid of; sacrifice, sell at a sacrifice *or* loss; sell off, remainder; resell, sell over; undersell, undercut, cut under; sell short; sell on consignment; telemarket

9 **vend,** dispense, **peddle, hawk, huckster;** tout

10 **put up for sale,** put up, ask bids *or* offers for, offer for sale, offer at a bargain

11 **auction, auction off, auctioneer,** sell at auction, sell by auction, put up for auction, **put on the block,** bring under the hammer; knock down, sell to the highest bidder

12 **be sold, sell,** bring, realize, sell for; change hands; sell like hotcakes, be in demand

ADJS 13 **sales,** selling, market, **marketing, merchandising, retail,** retailing, wholesale, wholesaling; vending

14 **salable, marketable,** retailable, merchandisable, merchantable, commercial, vendible; in demand

15 **unsalable,** nonsalable, **unmarketable;** on one's hands, on the shelves, not moving, not turning over, unbought, unsold

ADVS 16 **for sale,** to sell, up for sale, in *or* on the market, in the marts of trade; at a bargain, marked down

17 **at auction,** at outcry, at public auction *or* outcry, by auction, **on the block,** under the hammer

735 MERCHANDISE

NOUNS 1 **merchandise, commodities, wares, goods,** effects, vendibles; **items,** oddments; **consumer goods,** consumer items, retail goods, goods for sale; **stock, stock-in-trade;** staples; **inventory; line,** line of goods; sideline; job lot; mail-order goods, catalog goods; **luxury goods,** high-ticket *or* big-ticket *or* upscale items

2 **commodity, ware,** vendible, **product, article, item,** article of commerce *or* merchandise; staple, staple item, standard article; special, feature, leader, lead item, loss leader; seconds; drug, drug on the market

3 **dry goods, soft goods;** textiles; yard goods, white goods, linens, napery; men's wear, ladies' wear, children's wear, infants' wear; sportswear, sporting goods; leatherware, leather goods

4 **hard goods, durables, durable goods;** fixtures, white goods, **appliances** 385.4; tools and machinery 1040; **hardware,** ironmongery <Brit>; sporting goods, **housewares,** home furnishings, kitchenware; tableware, dinnerware; flatware, hollow ware; metalware, brassware, copperware, silverware, ironware, tinware; woodenware; glassware; chinaware, earthenware, clayware, stoneware, graniteware; enamelware; ovenware

5 **furniture** 229, furnishings, home furnishings

6 **notions, sundries,** novelties, knickknacks, odds and ends; toilet goods, toiletries; cosmetics; giftware

7 **groceries,** grocery <Brit>, food items, edibles, victuals, baked goods, packaged goods, canned goods, tinned goods <Brit>; green goods, **produce,** truck

736 MARKET
<place of trade>

NOUNS **1 market, mart, store, shop,** salon, boutique, wareroom, emporium, house, establishment, *magasin* <Fr>; **retail store; wholesale house, discount store, discount house, outlet store;** warehouse, megastore; mail-order house; **general store,** country store; **department store;** warehouse store, superstore, megastore**; co-op** <nf>, cooperative; **variety store,** variety shop, **dime store; ten-cent store** *or* five-and-ten *or* five-and-dime <nf>, thrift store *or* shop; convenience store, corner store, mom-and-pop store; chain store; concession; **trading post,** post; **supermarket,** grocery store; factory outlet, outlet store

2 marketplace, mart, market, open market, market overt, agora; **shopping center, shopping plaza** *or* **mall,** plaza, mall, arcade, shopping *or* shop *or* commercial complex; factory outlet center; warehouse; emporium, rialto; staple; **bazaar, fair,** trade fair, show, auto show, boat show, etc, exposition; flea market, flea fair, street market, farmers' market, fish market, meat market, *marché aux puces* <Fr>; trading post; home shopping, e-commerce *or* electronic commerce

3 booth, stall, stand; newsstand, kiosk, news kiosk; pushcart; roadside stand

4 vending machine, vendor, coin machine, coin-operated machine, slot machine, **automat;** redeemer *or* reverse vending machine

5 salesroom, wareroom; showroom; auction room

6 counter, shopboard ; notions counter; showcase; peddler's cart, pushcart

737 STOCK MARKET

NOUNS **1 stock market, the market, Wall Street;** securities market, commodity market; ticker market; open market, competitive market; steady market, strong market, hard *or* stiff market; unsteady market, spotty market; weak market; long market; top-heavy market; market index, stock price index, Dow-Jones Industrial Average

2 active market, brisk market, lively market

3 inactive market, slow market, stagnant market, flat market, tired market, sick market; investors on the sidelines

4 rising market, booming market, buoyant market; **bull market,** bullish market, bullishness

5 declining market, sagging market, retreating market, off market, soft market; **bear market,** bearish market, bearishness; **slump,** sag; break, break in the market; profit-taking, selloff; **crash,** smash

6 rigged market, manipulated market, pegged market, put-up market; **insider trading**

7 stock exchange, exchange, Wall Street, change <Brit>, **stock market,** bourse, **board;** the Exchange, New York Stock Exchange, the Big Board; American Stock Exchange, Amex, curb, curb market, curb exchange; over-the-counter market, telephone market, outside market; third market; exchange floor; commodity exchange, pit, corn pit, wheat pit, etc; quotation board; **ticker,** stock ticker; ticker tape

8 financial district, Wall Street, the Street; Lombard Street

9 stockbrokerage, brokerage, brokerage house, brokerage office; wire house; bucket shop *and* boiler room <nf>

10 stockbroker, sharebroker <Brit>, **broker,** jobber, stockjobber, dealer, stock dealer; Wall Streeter; stock-exchange broker, *agent de bourse* <Fr>; floor broker, floor trader, floorman, specialist, market maker; pit man; curb broker; odd-lot dealer; two-dollar broker; day trader, night trader; broker's agent, customer's broker *or* customer's man, registered representative; bond crowd

11 **speculator,** adventurer, operator; big operator, smart operator; **plunger,** gunslinger; scalper; stag <Brit>; lame duck; margin purchaser; **arbitrager** *or* arbitrageur *or* arb <nf>; inside trader

12 **bear,** short, short seller; shorts, short interest, short side; short account, bear account

13 **bull,** long, longs, long interest, long side; long account, bull account

14 **stockholder,** stockowner, **shareholder, shareowner;** bondholder, coupon-clipper <nf>; stockholder of record

15 **stock company,** joint-stock company; issuing company; stock insurance company

16 **trust,** investment company; investment trust, holding company; closed-end investment company, closed-end fund; open-end fund, mutual fund, money-market fund; unit trust <Brit>; load fund, no-load fund, low-load fund, back-end fund; growth fund, income fund, dual purpose fund; trust fund; blind trust

17 **pool,** bear pool, bull pool, blind pool

18 **stockbroking,** brokerage, stockbrokerage, jobbing, stockjobbing, stockjobbery, stock dealing; bucketing, legal bucketing

19 **trading,** stock-market trading, market-trading; computer *or* programmed selling; playing the market <nf>; **speculation,** stockjobbing, stockjobbery; **venture,** flutter; flier, plunge; scalping; liquidation, profit taking; **arbitrage,** arbitraging; buying in, covering shorts; short sale; spot sale; round trade *or* transaction, turn; risk *or* venture capital, equity capital; money-market trading, foreign-exchange trading, agiotage; **buyout, takeover,** hostile takeover, takeover bid; leveraged buyout; greenmail; **leverage**

20 **manipulation, rigging; raid,** bear raid, bull raid; **corner,** corner in, corner on the market, monopoly; washing, washed *or* wash sale

21 **option,** stock option, right, **put, call,** put and call, right of put and call; straddle, spread; strip; strap

22 **panic,** bear panic, rich man's panic

VERBS **23** **trade, speculate,** venture, operate, **play the market,** buy *or* sell *or* deal in futures; **arbitrage; plunge,** take a flier <nf>; scalp; bucket, bucketshop; stag *or* stag the market <Brit>; trade on margin; pyramid; be long, go long, be long of the market, be on the long side of the market; be short, be short of the market, be on the short side of the market; margin up, apply *or* deposit margin; wait out the market, hold on; be caught short, miss the market, overstay the market; scoop the market, make a scoop *or* killing *or* bundle *or* pile <nf>

24 **sell,** convert, liquidate; throw on the market, dump, unload; **sell short,** go short, make a short sale; cover one's short, fulfill a short sale; make delivery, clear the trade; close out, sell out, terminate the account

25 manipulate the market, **rig the market; bear, bear the market;** bull, **bull the market;** raid the market; hold *or* peg the market; whipsaw; wash sales

26 corner, get a corner on, **corner the market;** monopolize, engross; buy up, absorb

738 SECURITIES

NOUNS **1** **securities**, stocks and bonds, investment securities; arbitrage, program trading

2 **stock**, shares <Brit>, equity, equity security, corporate stock; stock split, split; reverse split; stock list; stock ledger, share ledger <Brit>; **holdings, portfolio,** investment portfolio

3 **share, lot;** preference share; dummy share; holding, holdings, stockholding, stockholdings; block; round lot, full lot, even lot, board lot; odd lot, fractional lot

4 **stock certificate,** certificate of stock; street certificate; interim certificate; **coupon**

5 **bond** ; nominal rate, coupon rate, current yield, yield to maturity

6 **issue,** issuance; **flotation;** stock issue, secondary issue; bond issue; poison pill <nf>

7 **dividend;** regular dividend; extra dividend, special dividend, plum *and* melon <nf>; payout ratio; cumulative dividend, accumulated dividends, accrued dividends; interim dividend; cash dividend; stock dividend; optional dividend; scrip dividend; liquidating dividend; phony dividend; **interest** 623.3; **return, yield,** return on investment, payout, payback

8 **assessment**, Irish dividend

9 **price, quotation;** bid-and-asked prices, bid price, asked *or* asking *or* offering price; actual *or* delivery *or* settling price, put price, call price; opening price, closing price; high, low; market price, quoted price, flash price; issue price; fixed price; parity; **par,** issue par; par value, nominal value, face value; stated value; book value; market value; bearish prices, bullish prices; swings, fluctuations; flurry, flutter; rally, decline

10 **margin;** thin margin, shoestring margin; exhaust price

11 <commodities> spots, spot grain, etc; futures, future grain, etc

VERBS **12** **issue, float,** put on the market; issue stock, go public <nf>; float a bond issue

13 **declare a dividend,** cut a melon <nf>

ADVS **14** dividend off, ex dividend; dividend on, cum dividend; coupon off, ex coupon; coupon on, cum coupon; warrants off, ex warrants; warrants on, cum warrants; when issued

739 WORKPLACE

NOUNS **1** **workplace,** worksite, **workshop, shop;** shop floor, workspace, working space, work area, loft; **bench,** workbench, worktable; counter, worktop; **work station; desk,** desktop; **workroom; studio,** *atelier* <Fr>, library; parlor, beauty parlor, funeral parlor, etc; **establishment, facility,** installation; **company,** institution, house, firm, concern, agency, organization, **corporation; financial institution, stock exchange** 737.7, **bank** 729.14; **market, store** 736.1, mall, shopping mall, megamall, retail park; **restaurant, eating place** 8.17; hotel, motel; gas station; construction site, building site; dockyard, shipyard; farm, ranch, nursery; power station; government office; office park, science park; virtual company

2 hive, hive of industry, beehive; factory *or* mill *or* manufacturing town; hub of industry, center of manufacture, industrial town

3 **plant, factory, works,** manufactory , manufacturing plant, installation, shop floor, job site, *usine* <Fr>; main plant, assembly plant, subassembly plant, feeder plant; foreign-owned plant, transplant; push-button plant, automated *or* cybernated *or* automatic *or* robot factory; assembly *or* production line; defense plant, munitions plant, armory, arsenal; **power plant** 1032.19; atomic energy plant; **machine shop; mill,** sawmill, flour mill, etc; **yard,** yards, railroad yard, brickyard, shipyard, dockyard, boatyard; rope-walk; mint; refinery, oil refinery, sugar refinery, etc; distillery, brewery, winery; boilery; bindery, bookbindery; packinghouse; cannery; dairy, creamery; pottery; tannery; sweatshop; **factory district,** industrial zone *or* area, industrial park, industrial estate <Brit>; factory belt, manufacturing quarter; enterprise zone

4 **foundry,** works, metalworks; steelworks, steelyard, steel mill; refinery, forge, furnace, bloomery; smelter; smithy, smithery, stithy, blacksmith shop *or* blacksmith's shop; brickworks; quarry, mine, colliery, coal mine; mint

5 **repair shop,** fix-it shop <nf>; **garage;** roundhouse; hangar

6 **laboratory, lab** <nf>; research laboratory, research installation *or* facility *or* center *or* park

7 **office,** shop <nf>; home *or* head *or* main office, headquarters, executive office, corporate *or* company headquarters; office suite, executive suite; chambers <chiefly Brit>; cubicle, closet, cabinet , **study,** den, carrell; **embassy,** consulate, legation, chancery, chancellery; box office, booking office, ticket office; branch, branch office, local office, subsidiary office, bureau, business house; office *or* executive park; virtual office

8 <home workplace> **home office,** office, den, study; kitchen, laundry room, sewing room, workbench

740 WEAVING

NOUNS 1 **weaving,** weave, warpage, weftage, warp and woof *or* weft, texture, tissue; **fabric, web,** webbing; **interweaving,** interweavement, intertexture; **interlacing,** interlacement, interlacery; crisscross; **intertwining,** intertwinement; intertieing, interknitting, interthreading, intertwisting; **lacing,** enlacement; **twining,** entwining, entwinement; wreathing, knitting, twisting; **braiding,** plaiting, plashing

2 **braid,** plait, pigtail, **wreath,** wreathwork

3 **warp; woof, weft,** filling; shoot, pick

4 **weaver,** interlacer, webster , knitter, spinner; weaverbird, weaver finch, whirligig beetle

5 **loom,** weaver; hand loom; Navajo loom; knitting machine; spinning wheel; shuttle, distaff

VERBS 6 **weave,** loom, tissue; **interweave, interlace, intertwine,** interknit, interthread, intertissue, intertie, intertwist; inweave, intort; web, net; **lace,** enlace; **twine,** entwine; **braid,** plait, pleach, **wreathe,** raddle, **knit,** twist, mat, wattle; crisscross; twill, loop, noose; splice; felt, mat, brush, nap; interconnect

ADJS 7 **woven,** loomed, textile; **interwoven, interlaced,** interthreaded, **intertwined,** interknit, intertissued, intertied, intertwisted; handwoven; **laced,** enlaced; **wreathed,** fretted, raddled, knit, knitted; **twined,** entwined; **braided,** plaited, platted, pleached; hooked; webbed; loomed

8 **weaving, twining,** entwining; **intertwining, interlacing,** interweaving, crosswise, crossways

741 SEWING

NOUNS 1 **sewing, needlework,** stitchery, stitching; mending, basting, darning, hemming, quilting, embroidery, cross-stitching, needlepoint; **fancywork;** tailoring, garment making 5.32; suture

2 **sewer, needleworker, seamstress,** sempstress, needlewoman; seamster, sempster, **tailor,** needleman , needler <Brit>; embroiderer, embroideress; knitter; garmentmaker 5.34

3 **sewing machine,** sewer, embroidery hoop

VERBS 4 **sew, stitch,** needle; mend, baste; stitch up, sew up; **tailor**

742 CERAMICS

NOUNS 1 **ceramics, pottery;** potting

2 **ceramic ware, ceramics; pottery, crockery; china, porcelain;** enamelware; refractory, cement; bisque, biscuit; pot, crock, vase, urn, jug, bowl; tile, tiling; brick, firebrick, refractory brick, adobe; glass 1029.2; industrial ceramics; ceramist, ceramicist, potter

3 <materials> **clay**; potter's clay *or* earth, fireclay, refractory clay; argil, adobe, terra cotta; porcelain clay, kaolin, china clay, china stone, marl, feldspar, petuntze *or* petuntse; flux; slip; glaze, overglaze, underglaze; crackle

4 **potter's wheel,** wheel; kick wheel, pedal wheel, hand-turned wheel, power wheel

5 **kiln, oven, stove, furnace;** acid kiln, brick kiln, cement kiln, enamel kiln, muffle kiln, limekiln, bottle kiln, beehive kiln, reverberatory, reverberatory kiln; pyrometer, pyrometric cone, Seger cone

VERBS 6 pot, shape, **throw,** throw *or* turn a pot; cast, mold; **fire,** bake; glaze

ADJS 7 **ceramic,** earthen, clay, enamel, china, porcelain; fired, baked, glazed; refractory; hand-, turned, hand-painted, thrown; industrial

743 AMUSEMENT

NOUNS 1 **amusement, entertainment, diversion,** solace, divertisement, *divertissement* <Fr>, **recreation, relaxation,** regalement; **pastime,** *passe-temps* <Fr>; **mirth** 109.5; **pleasure, enjoyment** 95.1; clubbing

2 **fun,** action <nf>; funmaking, fun and games, **play, sport,** game; **good time,** lovely time, pleasant time; big time *and* **high time** *and* high old time <nf>, picnic *and* laughs *and* lots of laughs *and* ball <nf>, great fun, time of one's life; a short life and a merry one; wild oats

3 **festivity, merrymaking, merriment, gaiety, jollity,** jollification <nf>, **joviality, conviviality,** whoopee *and* hoopla <nf>; larking <nf>, cavorting, skylarking, racketing, mafficking <Brit nf>, holidaymaking; **revelry,** revelment, reveling, revels; nightlife

4 **festival, festivity,** festive occasion, *fiesta* <Sp>, **fete,** gala, **gala affair, blowout** <nf>, **jamboree** <nf>; **high jinks,** do, great doings <nf>; *fête champêtre* <Fr>; **feast, banquet** 8.9; picnic 8.6; party 582.11; waygoose <Brit nf>, wayzgoose; fair, carnival; kermis; Oktoberfest <Ger>; Mardi Gras; Saturnalia; harvest festival, harvest home <Brit>; **field day;** gala day, feria

5 **frolic, play,** romp, rollick, frisk, gambol, caper, dido <nf>

6 **revel, lark, escapade,** ploy; **celebration** 487; **party** 582.11; **spree, bout, fling,** wingding *and* randan <nf>, randy; **carouse, drinking bout** 88.5

7 **round of pleasure,** mad round, **whirl,** merry-go-round, the rounds, the dizzy rounds

8 **sports** 744; **athletics,** agonistics; athleticism

9 **game;** card game; board game; parlor game, role-playing game; children's game; computer game, video game; gambling game; table game; word game, Scrabble <tm>; indoor game, outdoor game; **play; contest** 457.3; race 457.12; **event, meet; bout, match,** go <nf>; gambling 759

10 **tournament,** tourney, gymkhana, **field day;** rally; **regatta**

11 **playground,** playscape; field, athletic field, playing field; football field, gridiron; baseball field, diamond; infield, outfield; soccer field; archery ground, cricket ground, polo ground, croquet ground *or* lawn, bowling green; bowling alley; links, golf links, golf course; fairway, putting green; **gymnasium,** gym <nf>; **court,** badminton court, basketball court, tennis court, racket court, squash court; billiard parlor, poolroom, pool hall; racecourse, track, course turf, oval; stretch; rink, glaciarium, ice rink, skating rink; skateboard park; **playroom** 197.12

12 **swimming pool, pool,** swimming bath <Brit>, plunge, plunge bath, natatorium; swimming hole; wading pool, kiddy pool; lap pool; wave pool; infinity pool

13 **entertainment; entertainment industry, show business,** show biz <nf>; **theater;** dinner theatre; **cabaret, tavern, roadhouse;** café dansant, chantant; big dance <nf>; nightclub, night spot *or* nitery *and* hot spot <nf>, *boîte* and *boîte de nuit* <Fr>; juke joint <nf>, discothèque or disco <nf>; dance hall, dancing pavilion, ballroom, dance floor; casino; **resort** 228.27

14 **park,** public park, pleasure garden *or* ground, pleasance, paradise, common, commons, playground; **amusement park,** Tivoli, fun fair, carnival; fairground; **theme park,** safari park

15 ride, merry-go-round, carousel, roundabout, ride, whirligig, whip, flying horses; Ferris wheel; seesaw, teeter-totter; slide; swing; roller coaster; chutes, chute-the-chute; funhouse, arcade, video arcade; -drome

16 **toy, plaything,** sport; bauble, knickknack, gimcrack, gewgaw, kickshaw,

whim-wham, trinket; **doll,** action figure, paper doll, golliwog, rag doll, stuffed animal, teddy bear, puppet, glove puppet, marionette, toy soldier, tin soldier; dollhouse, doll carriage; hobbyhorse, cockhorse, rocking horse; hoop, hula hoop; top, spinning top, teetotum; pinwheel; jack-in-the-box; jacks, jackstones; jackstraws, pick-up sticks; blocks; checkerboard, chessboard; marble, mig, agate, steelie, taw; pop-gun, BB gun, air gun; slingshot, catapult <Brit>; ball; blocks, building blocks

17 **chessman,** man, piece; **bishop, knight, king, queen, pawn, rook** *or* castle

18 **player, frolicker,** frisker, **funmaker,** funster, gamboler; **pleasure-seeker,** pleasurer, pleasurist, **playboy** <nf>; **reveler, celebrant, merrymaker,** rollicker, skylarker, **carouser,** cutup <nf>; contestant 452.2

19 **athlete,** jock <nf>, **player,** sportsman, sportswoman, contender, amateur athlete, professional athlete, competitor, sportsman; letter man

20 **master of ceremonies, MC** *or* **emcee** <nf>, compère <Brit>, marshal; **toastmaster;** host, master of the revels, revel master; Lord of Misrule, Abbot of Unreason; social director

VERBS 21 **amuse, entertain, divert,** regale, beguile, solace, recreate, refresh, enliven, exhilarate, put in good humor; **relax,** loosen up; **delight, tickle, titillate,** tickle pink *or* to death <nf>, tickle the fancy; **make one laugh, strike one as funny,** raise a smile *or* laugh, convulse, set the table on a roar, be the death of; wow *and* slay *and* knock dead *and* kill *and* break one up *and* crack one up *and* fracture one <nf>; have them rolling in the aisles; keep them in stitches

22 **amuse oneself,** pleasure oneself, take one's pleasure, give oneself over to pleasure; get one's kicks *or* jollies <nf>; **relax,** let oneself go, loosen up; **have fun, have a good time,** have a ball *and* have lots of laughs <nf>, live it up *and* laugh it up <nf>; drown care, drive dull care away; beguile the time, kill time, while away the time; get away from it all

23 **play, sport, disport; frolic, rollick, gambol, frisk, romp, caper,** cut capers <nf>, lark about <Brit nf>, antic, curvet, cavort, caracole, flounce, trip, skip, dance; **cut up** <nf>, cut a dido <nf>, horse around <nf>, fool around, futz around <nf>, carry on <nf>

24 **make merry, revel, roister,** jolly, lark <nf>, skylark, **make whoopee** <nf>, let oneself go, **blow** *or* **let off steam;** cut loose, let loose, let go, let one's hair down <nf>, whoop it up, **kick up one's heels;** hell around *and* raise hell *and* blow off the lid <nf>; step out <nf>, go places and do things, go on the town, see life, **paint the town red** <nf>; go the dizzy rounds, go on the merry-go-round <nf>; **celebrate** 487.2; spree, **go on a spree,** go on a bust *or* toot *or* bender *or* binge *or* rip *or* tear <nf>; carouse, jollify <nf>, wanton, debauch, pub-crawl <chiefly Brit>, club-hop; **sow one's wild oats, have one's fling**

25 feast, banquet

ADJS 26 **amused,** entertained; diverted, **delighted,** tickled, tickled pink *or* to death <nf>, titillated

27 **amusing, entertaining, diverting,** beguiling; **fun,** funsome *and* more fun than a barrel of monkeys <nf>; recreative, recreational; **delightful,** titillative, titillating; humorous 488.4

28 **festive, festal; merry, gay, jolly, jovial, joyous, joyful,** gladsome, convivial, gala, hilarious; merrymaking, on the loose <nf>; on the town, out on the town

29 **playful, sportive,** sportful; **frolicsome,** gamesome, rompish, larkish, capersome; waggish 322.6

30 **sporting,** sports; **athletic,** agonistic; **gymnastic,** palaestral; **acrobatic**

ADVS 31 **in fun,** for amusement, for fun, for the fun of it; for kicks *and* for laughs <nf>, for the devil *or* heck *or* hell of it <nf>; just to be doing

744 SPORTS

NOUNS 1 **sport, sports, athletics,** athletic competition, game, sports activity, play, contest, match; round, set, tournament; aeronautical *or* air sport ; animal sport ; water *or* aquatic sport ; **ball game; track and field** 755; **gymnastics** ; indoor sport; **outdoor sport** ; **winter sport** ; contact sport; **combat sport,** martial art ; **decathlon; triathlon,** biathlon; **bicycling,** bicycle touring, cross-country cycling, cyclo-cross, bicycle moto-cross, road racing, off-road racing, track racing; **motor sport,** automobile racing 756, go-carting, jet-skiing, water skiing, motorcycling, moto-cross, dirt-biking, snowmobiling, soapbox racing; **in-line skating** *or* blading *or* Rollerblading <TM>, roller skating, roller hockey, skateboarding; **target sport,** archery, field archery, darts, marksmanship, target shooting, skeet shooting, trap shooting; **throwing sport** ; **weightlifting, bodybuilding,** iron-pumping <nf>, Olympic lifting, powerlifting, weight training; blood sport; extreme sport

VERBS 2 **play, compete;** practice, train, work out; try out, go out for; follow

745 BASEBALL

NOUNS 1 **baseball, ball,** the national pastime, hardball; **organized baseball, league,** loop, circuit, **major league,** big league, the majors *and* the big time *and* the bigs <nf>, professional baseball, the National League *or* Senior Circuit, the American League *or* Junior Circuit; **minor league,** triple-A, the minors *and* bush leagues *and* the bushes <nf>, college baseball; Little League baseball; division championship, playoff, League Championship Series, league championship *or* pennant, World Series, All-Star Game; fantasy baseball; **farm team,** farm club, farm, farm system; rotisserie league; **ball park, ball field,** field, park; **stands, grandstand,** boxes, lower deck, upper deck, outfield stands, bleachers; **diamond;** dugout; **home plate, the plate,** platter *and* dish <nf>; **base line, line,** base path; **base, bag,** sack, **first,** first base, **second,** second base, keystone *and* keystone sack <nf>, **third,** third base, hot corner <nf>; **infield,** infield grass *or* turf; **outfield,** warning track, fences; foul line, foul pole; **mound,** pitcher's mound, hill; **equipment,** gear

2 **baseball team, team, nine,** roster, squad, the boys of summer, **club,** ball club, personnel, crew; **starting lineup, lineup batting order; starter, regular;** substitute, sub, utility player, benchwarmer *and* bench jockey <nf>, the bench; **pitcher,** hurler <nf>, motion, pitching motion, herky-jerky motion <nf>, **right-hander,** right-hand pitcher, righty <nf>, **left-hander, left-hand pitcher, lefty** *and* **southpaw** *and* portsider <nf>; **starting pitcher, starter,** fifth starter, spot starter; starting rotation, rotation, pitching rotation; **relief pitcher, reliever,** fireman *and* closer *and* stopper <nf>, long reliever, middle *or* inner reliever, short reliever, the bull pen; **battery; catcher,** backstop *and* receiver <nf>; **fielder,** glove man, outfielder, infielder, cover man, cut-off man, relay man; **first baseman,** first bagger *and* first sacker <nf>; **second baseman,** second bagger *and* second sacker *and* keystone bagger *and* keystone sacker <nf>; **third baseman,** third bagger *and* third sacker *and* hot-corner man <nf>; shortstop; **outfielder,** left fielder, center fielder, right fielder; pinch hitter; designated hitter *or* DH *or* desi; **batter, hitter,** man at the plate, man in the box *or* batter's box, **stance,** batting stance, pull hitter, power hitter, long-ball hitter, slugger <nf>, spray hitter, contact hitter, banjo hitter <nf>, switch hitter, leadoff hitter, cleanup hitter, closer; base runner, runner, designated runner; **manager, pilot, coach,** batting coach,

pitching coach, bench coach, bullpen coach, first-base coach, third-base coach; official scorer; scout, talent scout

3 **game, ball game,** play, strategy; **umpire,** home-plate umpire, plate umpire, umpire in chief, umpire crew, first-base umpire, second-base umpire, third-base umpire; **pitch,** set, windup, kick, delivery, stuff, offering; **strike zone,** wheelhouse *and* kitchen <nf>; **throwing arm,** arm, cannon *and* soupbone <nf>; **balk; count,** balls and strikes, full count; **hit, base hit,** tater *and* bingle *and* dinger <nf>, opposite-field hit; hard-hit ball, shot *and* bullet *and* scorcher <nf>; **single,** seeing-eye hit *and* excuse-me hit *and* banjo hit <nf>; **double,** two-base hit, two-base shot, two-bagger; **triple,** three-base hit *or* three-base shot, three-bagger; **home run, homer,** four-bagger, long ball, tater *and* round trip *and* round tripper *and* circuit clout *and* big salami *and* dinger <nf>, one you can hang the wash on <nf>, grand-slam home run, grand-slammer, cheap homer *and* Chinese homer <nf>; **fly,** pop fly, pop-up, can of corn *and* looper *and* blooper *and* bloop *and* Texas Leaguer *and* banjo hit <nf>, sacrifice fly *or* sac fly <nf>; **line drive, liner,** line shot, rope *and* clothesline <nf>; **ground ball,** grounder, wormburner <nf>, slow roller, roller, bunt, drag bunt, bleeder *and* squibbler *and* nubber *and* dying quail <nf>, come-backer, chopper; **foul ball, foul; base on balls, walk,** intentional pass, free ticket *and* free ride <nf>; error, passed ball, unearned run, earned run; **out,** strikeout *or* K *or* punchout, put-out, foul-out, force-out, double play, DP, double killing *and* twin killing <nf>, triple play, triple killing <nf>, assist; **catch,** shoestring catch, basket catch, circus catch; squeeze play, hit-and-run play, pickoff play, pickoff, pitch-out; **base runner,** baseburner <nf>, pinch-runner; **run;** complete game; **inning,** frame, top of the inning, bottom of the inning, extra innings

4 **statistics,** averages, stats and numbers <nf>, percentages; batting average, earned-run average *or* ERA, slugging average *or* slugging percentage, fielding average, run batted in *or* RBI, ribby <nf>; **the record book,** the book

VERBS 5 **play,** play ball, take the field; **umpire,** call balls and strikes, officiate; **pitch, throw,** deliver, fire, offer, offer up, bring it *and* burn it *and* throw smoke *and* blow it by *and* throw seeds <nf>; throw a bean ball, dust the batter off, back the batter off; **relieve,** put out the fire <nf>; **bat, be up,** step up to the plate, be in the batter's box; **hit,** belt *and* clout *and* connect <nf>, golf, chop, tomahawk; **fly,** hit a fly, sky it *and* pop *and* pop up <nf>; **ground,** bounce, lay it down, lay down a bunt; sacrifice, hit a sacrifice fly; **hit,** get a base hit, put on one's hitting shoes <nf>; **connect,** blast it *and* cream it *and* tear the cover off *and* hit it right on the screws *and* hit it right on the button *and* hit with the good wood *and* get good wood on it <nf>; **hit a home run, homer,** hit it out; **single, double, triple;** get aboard, be a base runner; **walk, get a free ride** *or* free pass <nf>; **strike out,** go down *or* out on strikes, go down swinging, fan *and* whiff <nf>, be called out on strikes, be caught looking <nf>; ground out, fly out, pop out; catch, haul in, grab *and* glove *and* flag down <nf>; misplay, make an error, bobble *and* boot <nf>; take a trip to the showers <nf>

746 FOOTBALL

NOUNS 1 **football, ball,** American football; **organized football, college football,** NCAA football, conference, league; conference championship, post-season game, bowl invitation, Cotton Bowl, Gator Bowl, Orange Bowl, Rose Bowl, Sugar Bowl, Fiesta Bowl, national championship *or* mythical national championship; **professional football,** pro football <nf>, National Football League *or* NFL; division championship, playoff, Super Bowl,

Super Bowl championship, Pro Bowl; high school football; Pop Warner football, Pee Wee football; **stadium,** bowl, domed stadium, dome; **field, gridiron; line,** sideline, end line, end zone, goal line, goalpost, crossbar, yard line, midfield stripe, inbounds marker *or* hash mark; **equipment**, gear, armament; official, sideline crew, chain gang <nf>, zebra <nf>; fantasy football; arena football

2 **football team, eleven,** team, squad, roster, personnel; first team, regulars, starting lineup, offensive team *or* platoon, defensive team *or* platoon, special team, kicking team; substitute *or* sub, benchwarmer; **ball,** football, pigskin *and* oblate spheroid <nf>; **line, linemen, forward wall,** offensive linemen, front four, **end, tackle, nose tackle, guard, noseguard, center,** flanker, **tight end; backfield,** back, **quarterback,** signal-caller *or* field general <nf>, passer; **halfback, fullback,** kicker, punter, tailback, plunging back, slotback, flanker back, running back, wingback, blocking back, linebacker, defensive back, cornerback, safety, free safety, strong safety, weak safety; **pass receiver, receiver,** wide receiver *or* wide out, primary receiver

3 **game,** strategy, game plan, ball control; **official**, zebra <nf>; **kickoff,** kick, coin-toss *or* -flip, place kick, squib kick, free kick, onside kick, runback, kickoff return; **play**, down, first down, second down, third down, fourth down; **line,** line of scrimmage *or* scrimmage line, flat; **lineup, formation** ; **pass from center, snap,** hand-to-hand snap; live ball, ball in play, ball out of play, dead ball, play stopped, ball whistled dead; **running play, passing play, kick; ball-carrier,** ballhandling, tuck, feint, hand-off, pocket, straightarm; **block,** blocking, body block, brush block, chop block, cross block, lead block, screen block, shoulder block; **tackle,** neck tackle, shirt tackle, face-mask tackle, sack; **yardage,** gain, loss, long yardage, short yardage; **forward pass, pass,** pass pattern, pitchout, screen pass, quick release, bomb <nf>, incomplete pass, completed pass, pass completion; **pass rush,** blitz; **possession,** loss of possession, turnover, fumble, pass interception, interception, turnover; in bounds, out of bounds; **penalty**, infraction, foul, flag on the play; **punt, kick,** quick kick, squib kick *or* knuckler; punt return, fair catch; **touchdown,** conversion, field goal, safety; **period, quarter, half,** halftime, intermission, two-minute warning, thirty-second clock, sudden-death overtime; **gun,** final gun

4 **statistics, averages,** stats *and* numbers <nf>, average running yardage, average passing yardage, average punting yardage, average punt-return yardage

VERBS 5 **play,** kick, kick off, run, scramble, pass, punt; complete a pass, catch a pass; **block, tackle,** double-team, blindside, sack, blitz, red-dog; **lose possession,** fumble, bobble <nf>, give up the ball; **score,** get on the scoreboard; **officiate,** blow the whistle, whistle the ball dead, drop a flag, call a penalty

747 BASKETBALL

NOUNS 1 **basketball,** hoop, hoop sport, ball, b-ball, hoops; **organized basketball, college basketball,** NCAA *or* National Collegiate Athletic Association; **professional basketball,** pro basketball <nf>, National Basketball Association *or* NBA; **tournament,** competition, championship, Olympic Games, NCAA *or* National Collegiate Athletic Association Tournament, March Madness, Sweet 16, Final Four; NIT *or* National Invitational Tournament, NAIA *or* National Association of Intercollegiate Athletics Tournament; **basketball court, court,** hardwood *and* pine <nf>, forecourt, midcourt, backcourt, end line *or* base line, sideline, basket *or* hoop, iron <nf>, backboard, glass

<nf>, defensive board, offensive board, free throw line, charity line <nf>, free throw lane *or* foul lane, key *and* keyhole <nf>, foul line *or* the line

2 **basketball team, five,** team, roster, squad, personnel; **basketball player,** hoopster, cager, hoopster *or* hooper, center, right forward, left forward, corner man, right guard, left guard, point guard, shooting guard, point player *or* playmaker, swingman, trailer, backcourt man, disher-upper, gunner, sixth man

3 **basketball game,** game, play, strategy, defense, offense ; **official, referee,** umpire, official scorekeeper, timer; **foul,** violation, infraction; **play, strategy,** running game, fast break, passing game, draw and kick game; **jump,** center jump, jump ball, live ball; **pass,** passing, pass ball, assist, bounce pass, dish *and* feed <nf>; rebound; **tactics, action,** dribble, fake, hand-off, ball control, ball-handling, boxing out, sky shot *or* air ball, clear-out *or* outlet pass, basket hanging, freelancing, pivot *or* post, high post, low post, one-on-one, screening, pick, pick and roll, trap, turnover, steal *or* burn, out-of-bounds, dead ball, throw-in, corner throw, buzzer play; **restrictions,** three-second rule, five-second rule, ten-second rule, twenty-four-second rule, thirty-second rule; **shot, score, basket** *or* **field goal,** bucket <nf>, three-point play *or* three-pointer, free throw *or* foul shot; **quarter,** half, overtime period *or* overtime

VERBS 4 **play,** play basketball, play ball, ride the pine <nf>, **dribble,** fake, pass, dish <nf>, work the ball around, take it coast to coast, give and go, sky it, clear the ball, hand off, **guard,** play tight, play loose, double-team, hand-check, block, screen, pick, press, set a pick, steal, burn, freelance, shoot, score, sink one *and* can *and* swish <nf>, finger-roll, tip it in, use the backboard, dunk, slam dunk, make a free throw, shoot a brick <nf>, rebound, clear the board, freeze the ball, kill the clock; **foul,** commit a foul *or* violation, foul out

748 TENNIS

NOUNS 1 **tennis,** lawn tennis, indoor tennis, outdoor tennis, singles, doubles, mixed doubles, Canadian doubles, team tennis; court *or* real *or* royal tennis; table tennis, Ping-Pong <TM>; **organized tennis,** International Tennis Federation *or* ITF, United States Tennis Association *or* USTA; **tournament,** tennis competition, championship, crown, match, trophy; **tennis ball, ball, tennis racket, racket**, aluminum racket, Fiberglas racket, graphite racket, wooden racket, bat <nf>, sweet spot; **tennis court, court,** sideline, alley, doubles sideline, baseline, center mark, service line, half court line, backcourt, forecourt, midcourt, net, band; **surface,** slow surface, fast surface, grass surface *or* grass *or* grass court, hard court, clay court, competition court, all-weather court; squash, squash racquets, squash tennis, badminton

2 **game,** strategy, serve-and-volley, power game; **official, umpire,** baseline umpires *or* linesmen, line umpires *or* linesmen, service-line umpire *or* linesman, net-court judge; **play,** coin-toss, racket-flip, grip, Eastern grip, Continental grip, Western grip, two-handed grip, **stroke, shot,** service *or* serve, return, spin, top-spin, let ball *or* let, net-cord ball, rally, fault, double fault, foot fault; error, unforced error; **score, point,** service ace *or* ace, love, deuce, advantage *or* ad, game point, service break, break point, set point, match point, tiebreaker, lingering death <nf>, game, set, match; Van Alen Streamlined Scoring System *or* VASSS

VERBS 3 **play tennis, play,** serve, return, drive, volley, smash, lob, place the ball, serve and volley, play serve-and-volley tennis, fault, foot-fault, double-fault, make an unforced error; **score** *or* **make a point,** score, ace one's opponent, break service, break back

749 HOCKEY

NOUNS 1 **hockey,** ice hockey, Canadian national sport; **professional hockey,** National Hockey League *or* NHL, Clarence Campbell Conference, Smythe Division, Norris Division, Prince of Wales Conference, Patrick Division, Adams Division; **amateur hockey,** bantam hockey, midget hockey, pee-wee hockey, junior hockey, Canadian Amateur Hockey Association, Amateur Hockey Association of the United States, International Ice Hockey Federation; **competition,** series, championship, cup, Olympic Games, Stanley Cup, All-Star Game; **rink,** ice rink, hockey rink, boards, end zone, defending *or* defensive zone, attacking *or* offensive zone, neutral zone *or* center ice, blue line, red line, goal line, crease, goal *and* net *and* cage, face-off spot, face-off circle, penalty box, penalty bench, players' bench; **equipment,** gear ; floor hockey

2 **hockey team, team, skaters, squad, bench; line,** forward line, center, forward, winger, right wingman, left wingman, linesman; **defense,** defender, right defenseman, left defenseman, goaltender *or* goalie, goalkeeper, goalminder; specialized player, playmaker, penalty killer, point *or* point man, enforcer <nf>

3 **game,** match; **referee,** linesman, goal judge, timekeepers, scorer; **foul,** penalty, infraction, offside, icing *or* icing the puck; **play,** skating, stick *or* puck handling, ragging, deking, checking, backchecking, forechecking, passing, shooting; **pass,** blind pass, drop pass, through-pass; **check** ; **offense,** breakout, Montreal offense, headmanning, Toronto offense, playoff hockey, give-and-go, breakaway, peel-off, screening; **shot,** slap shot, wrist shot, backhand shot, flip, sweep shot; power play; **score,** point, finish off a play, feed, assist, hat trick; **period,** overtime *or* overtime period, sudden death overtime, shoot-out

4 **field hockey,** banty *or* bandy, hurley *or* hurling, shinty *or* shinny; International Hockey Board, *Fédération Internationale de Hockey* <Can>, International Federation of Women's Hockey Associations, United States Field Hockey Association, Field Hockey Association of America; **hockey field,** field, pitch, goal line, center line, center mark, bully circle, sideline, 7-yard line, alley, 25-yard line, striking *or* shooting circle, goalpost, goal, goal mouth; **equipment,** gear, stick, ball, shin pads

5 **team,** attack, outside left, inside left, center forward, inside right, outside right, defense, left halfback, center halfback, right halfback, left fullback, wing half, right fullback, goalkeeper

6 **game,** match; **umpire,** timekeeper; **foul,** infraction, advancing, obstructing, sticks, undercutting, **penalty,** free hit, corner hit, defense hit, penalty bully, penalty shot; **play, bully, bully-off,** pass-back, stroke, marking, pass, tackle, circular tackle, out-of-bounds, roll-in *or* push-in, hit-in; **goal,** point, score; **period,** half

VERBS 7 **play, skate,** pass, check, block, stick-handle *or* puck-handle, face off, rag, deke, give-and-go, headman, break out, shoot, score, clear, dig, freeze the puck, center, ice *or* ice the puck; tackle, mark; make a hat trick

750 BOWLING

NOUNS 1 **bowling,** kegling *or* kegeling <nf>, tenpin bowling *or* tenpins, candlepin bowling *or* candlepins, duckpin bowling *or* duckpins, fivepin bowling, rubberband duckpin bowling, ninepins, skittles <Brit>; **bowling organization,** league, American Bowling Congress *or* ABC, Women's International Bowling Congress *or* WIBC, American Junior Bowling Congress; amateur bowling, league bowling; **professional bowling,** pro bowling <nf>, tour, Professional Bowlers Association *or* PBA, Professional Women's Bowling Association; **tournament,** competition, match-play tournament, round-robin tournament; **alley, lane,** gutter, foul line, rear cushion, bed, spot, pin spot, 1-3-strike pocket; **equipment, pin,** candlepin, duckpin, fivepin, rubber-band duckpin, tenpin; automatic pinsetter; **ball,** two-hole ball, three-hole ball, bowling shoes; bowling bag

2 **game** *or* string, frame; **delivery,** grip, two-finger grip, three-finger grip, conventional grip, semi-fingertip grip, full-fingertip grip, **approach,** three-step approach *or* delivery, four-step approach, five-step approach, push-away, downswing, backswing, timing step, release, follow-through, straight ball, curve ball, backup, hook ball, gutter ball; **pocket,** Brooklyn side, Brooklyn hit *or* Jersey hit *or* crossover, **strike** *or* ten-strike, mark, double, turkey, foundation; **spare,** mark, leave, spare leave, split, railroad, open frame; **score,** pinfall, miss, perfect game *or* 300 game, Dutch

3 **lawn bowling,** green bowling, lawn bowls, bowling on the green, bowls; American Lawn Bowling Association; **bowling green,** green, crown green, level green, rink, ditch; **ball,** bowl, jack *or* kitty, mat *or* footer; **team,** side, rink, lead *or* leader, second player, third player, skip

751 GOLF

NOUNS **1** golf, the royal and ancient; **professional golf,** pro golf <nf>, tour, Professional Golfers Association of America *or* PGA, Ladies' Professional Golfers' Association *or* LPGA; **amateur golf,** club, United States Golf Association *or* USGA; **tournament**, championship, title, cup; **golf course,** course, links, 9-hole course, 18-hole course, penal course, strategic course, green, tee, teeing ground, back *or* championship marker, middle *or* men's marker, front *or* womens' marker, hole, par-3 hole, par-4 hole, par-5 hole, front nine *or* side, back nine *or* side, water hole, fairway, dogleg, obstruction, rub of the green, casual water, rough, hazard, water hazard, bunker, sand hazard, sand trap, beach <nf>, collar, apron, fringe, putting green, grass green, sand green, out of bounds, pin, flagstick, flag, lip, cup; **equipment** ; nineteenth hole; miniature golf, putt-putt

2 **golfer,** player, scratch golfer *or* player, handicapped golfer, dub *and* duffer *and* hacker <nf>, linksman, putter; **team,** twosome, threesome, foursome; caddie

3 **round,** 9 holes, 18 holes, 72 holes, match, stroke play, match play, medal play, four-ball match, three-ball match, best ball, mixed foursome, Scotch foursome; **official,** referee, official observer, marker; **play,** golfing grip, overlapping *or* Vardon grip, reverse overlap, interlocking grip, full-finger grip, address, stance, closed stance, square stance, open stance, waggle, swing, backswing, downswing, follow-through, pivot, body pivot, tee-off; **stroke, shot,** backspin, bite, distance, carry, run, lie, plugged lie, blind, stymie; **score,** scoring, strokes, eagle, double eagle, birdie, par, bogey, double bogey, penalty, hole-in-one *and* ace, halved hole, gross, handicap, net

VERBS **4** **play, shoot,** tee up, tee off, drive, hit, sclaff, draw, fade, pull, push, hook, slice, top, sky, loft, dunk, putt, can <nf>, borrow, hole out, sink, shoot par, eagle, double eagle, birdie, par, bogey, double bogey, make a hole in one, ace; play through; concede, default

752 SOCCER

NOUNS **1** **soccer,** football, association football <Brit>, soccer football; **league,** college soccer, Intercollegiate Soccer Football Association of America, NCAA *or* National Collegiate Athletic Association, Federation of International Football Associations *or* FIFA; **tournament,** competition, championship, cup; **professional soccer,** pro soccer, North American Soccer League *or* NASL; **soccer field,** field, soccer pitch, pitch, goal line, touch line, halfway line, penalty area, penalty spot *or* penalty-kick mark, goal area, goal, goalpost, crossbar, 6-yard box, 18-yard box, corner area, corner flag, center mark, center circle; **equipment,** gear, ball, suit, uniform, shirt, shorts, knee socks, shin guards, soccer shoes

2 **team,** squad, side, footballer <Brit>, forward, striker, outside right, inside right, center forward, lineman, mid fielder, inside left, outside left, right half, center half, left half, defender, back, center back, right back, left back, winger, back four, sweeper, stopper, goalkeeper *or* goaltender *or* goalie

3 **game, match; official,** referee, linesman; **play,** coin-toss *or* -flip, 3-3-4 offense, 5-2 offense, man-to-man offense, kickoff, kick, throw-in, goal kick, corner kick *or* corner, offside, ball-control, pass, back-heel pass, outside-of-the-foot pass, push pass, back pass, tackle, sliding tackle, sliding block tackle, trap, chest trap, thigh trap, breakaway, header *or* head, shot, save; **rule,** law; **foul** ; **penalty,** caution, red card, free kick, direct free kick, indirect free kick, caution, penalty kick, yellow card; **goal,** score, point, tie-breaker, series of penalty kicks, shootout, bonus point; **period,** quarter, overtime period

VERBS **4** **play,** kick, kick off, trap, pass, dribble, screen, head, center, clear, mark, tackle, save

753 SKIING

NOUNS **1** skiing, snow-skiing, Alpine skiing, downhill skiing, **Nordic skiing,** cross-country skiing *or* langlauf, snowboarding, ski-jumping, jumping, freestyle skiing *or* hotdog skiing *or* hotdogging, ballet skiing, mogul skiing, skijoring, helicopter skiing *or* heli-skiing, off-trail skiing, mountain skiing, grass-skiing, ski mountaineering; **organized skiing,** competitive skiing, *Fédération Internationale de Ski* <Fr> *or* FIS, International Freestyle Skiers Association, World Hot Dog Ski Association; **competition, championship,** cup, race; **slope,** ski slope, ski run, nursery *or* beginner's slope, expert's slope, intermediate slope, expert's trail, marked trail, moguled trail, course, trail, mogul; **ski lift, lift,** ski tow, rope tow, J-bar, chairlift, T-bar, poma; **race course,** downhill course, slalom course, giant slalom course, super giant slalom course, parallel *or* dual slalom course; starting gate, fall line, drop *or* vertical drop, control gate, obligatory gate, flagstick, open gate, closed *or* blind gate, hairpin, flush, H, men's course, women's course, **ski-jump,** ramp, inrun, outrun, hill rating, 60 point hill, normal hill, big hill, cross-country course; equipment, gear

2 **skier,** snow-skier, cross-country skier, ski-jumper, racer, downhill racer, slalom racer, giant slalom racer, mogul racer, snowboarder, freestyle skier, touring skier, forerunner, forejumper, skimeister

3 **race,** downhill race, slalom, giant slalom, super giant slalom *or* super G, slalom pole, rapid slalom pole, parallel *or* dual slalom, Alpine race, cross-country race, biathlon; **technique,** style, Arlberg technique, Lilienfeld technique, wedeln, **position,** tuck *and* egg, Vorlage, sitting position, inrun position, fish position, flight position; **maneuver, turn**

VERBS **4** **ski,** run, schuss, traverse, turn, check; hot dog, ski freestyle; snowboard

754 BOXING

NOUNS **1** **boxing, prizefighting,** fighting, pugilism, noble *or* manly art of self-defense, the noble *or* sweet science, fisticuffs, the fistic sport, the fights *and* the fight game <nf>, the ring; **amateur boxing,** Olympic Games, International Amateur Boxing Association *or* IABA,

Amateur Athletic Union *or* AAU, Gold *or* Golden Gloves; **professional boxing,** International Boxing Federation, World Boxing Council *or* WBC, World Boxing Association *or* WBA, European Boxing Union, club boxing *or* fighting; Queensbury rules, Marquess of Queensbury rules; shadowboxing; **boxing ring, ring,** prize ring, square circle *or* ring, canvas, corner, ropes, bell; **equipment, gloves,** mitts *and* mittens <nf>, boxing shorts, tape, bandages, sparring helmet, mouthpiece; boxing purse

2 **boxer, fighter,** pugilist, prizefighter, pug *and* palooka <nf>, slugger, mauler; **weight** ; division; **manager; trainer; handler,** second, sparring partner

3 **fight, match, bout,** prizefight, battle, duel, slugfest *or* haymaker <nf>; **official, referee,** ref <nf>, judge, timekeeper; **strategy, fight-plan, style,** stance, footwork, **offense, punch**, blow, belt and biff and sock <nf>, sparring, jabbing, socking, pummeling; **defense,** blocking, ducking, parrying, slipping, feint, clinching; **foul** ; **win, knockout** *or* **KO**, technical knockout *or* TKO, decision, unanimous decision, split decision, win on points; **round,** canto *and* stanza <nf>

VERBS 4 **fight, box,** punch, spar, mix it up <nf>, prizefight, jab, sock, clinch, break, block, catch, slip a punch, duck, feint, parry, heel, thumb, knock down, knock out, slug, maul, land a rabbit punch, hit below the belt; go down, go down for the count, hit the canvas <nf>, shadow-box

755 TRACK AND FIELD

NOUNS 1 **track, track and field,** athletics <Brit>; governing organization, International Athletic Federation *or* IAAF, Amateur Athletic Union of the US *or* AAU, Amateur Athletic Federation of Canada, Amateur Athletic Union of Canada, National Federation of State High School Athletic Associations; **games,** competition, cup; **stadium, arena,** oval, armory, field house; **track,** oval, lane, start line, starting block, finish line, **infield**; lap, lap of honor, victory lap

2 **track meet, meet,** games, program; **running event**, race, run *or* running, heat, sprint racing, middle-distance running, long-distance running, relay racing, hurdles, cross-country racing; **field event** ; **all-around event,** decathlon, heptathlon, pentathlon ; triathlon, biathlon ; **walking, race walking,** the walk, heel-and-toe racing

756 AUTOMOBILE RACING

NOUNS 1 **automobile racing, auto racing, car racing,** motor sport; Indy car racing, stock-car racing, drag racing, Formula car racing, midget-car racing, hot-rod racing, autocross, go-karting; **racing association; race,** competition, championship; **track,** speedway, Indianapolis Motor Speedway *or* the Brickyard <nf>, closed course, road course *or* circuit, dirt track, grasstrack, super speedway; **car, racing car,** racer; **racing engine**; **supercharger,** turbocharger, blower *and* windmill <nf>; **tires, racing tires,** shoes <nf>, slicks; **body,** body work, spoiler, sidepod, roll bar, roll cage; **wheel,** wire wheel *or* wire, magnesium wheel *or* mag; **fuel, racing fuel,** methanol, nitromethane *or* nitro, blend, pop *and* juice <nf>

2 **race driving, racing driver, driver,** fast driver *or* leadfoot <nf>, slow driver *or* balloon foot, novice driver *or* yellowtail; off-roading

3 **race, driving, start,** Le Mans start, flying start, paced start, grid start; **position,** qualifying, qualifying heat, starting grid, inside position, pole *or* pole position, bubble; **track,** turn, curve, hairpin, switchback, banked turn, corner, chicane, groove, shut-off, drift, straightaway *or* chute, pit, pit area; **signal,** black flag, white flag, checkered flag; **lap,** pace lap, victory lap *or* lane

VERBS **4 drive, race,** start, jump, rev, accelerate, put the hammer down <nf>, slow down, back off, stroke it, draft, fishtail, nerf, shut the gate

ADVS **5 at top speed,** flat-out, full-bore, ten-tenths ride the rail, spin, spin out, crash, t-bone

757 HORSE RACING

NOUNS **1 horse racing, the turf,** the sport of kings, the turf sport, the racing world *or* establishment; **flat racing; harness racing,** trotting, pacing; steeplechase, hurdle race, point-to-point race; **Jockey Club,** Trotting Horse Club, Thoroughbred Racing Association *or* TRA, Thoroughbred Racing Protective Bureau *or* TRPB, state racing commission; **General Stud Book, American Stud Book,** Wallace's Trotting Register; **Triple Crown,** Kentucky Derby, Preakness Stakes, Belmont Stakes; Grand National, Derby, 2000 Guineas, Sty Leger, Gold Cup Race, Oaks; **racetrack, track,** racecourse, turf, oval, course, strip; rail, inside rail, infield, paddock, post; turf track, steeplejack course; gate *and* barrier; **track locations** *and* **calls; track conditions**, footing; racing equipment, tack

2 jockey, jock, rider, race rider, pilot, bug boy <nf>, money rider; apprentice jockey, bug <nf>; breeder, owner; trainer; steward, racing secretary; **railbird** and race bird <nf>, turf-man; **racehorse, pony,** thoroughbred, standardbred, mount, flyer, running horse, trotter, pacer, quarter horse, bangtail *and* daisy-cutter and filly *and* gee-gee <nf>; **sire, dam,** stallion, stud, stud horse, racing stud, mare, brood mare, gelding, ridgeling *or* rigling; **horse,** aged horse, three-year-old, sophomore, two-year-old, juvenile, colt, racing colt, filly, baby, foal, tenderfoot, bug, maiden *or* maiden horse, yearling, weanling; **favorite,** chalk, choice, odds-on favorite, public choice, top horse; runner, front-runner, pacesetter; strong horse, router, stayer; winner *or* win horse, place horse, show horse, also-ran; **nag** *and* race-nag *and* beagle *and* beetle *and* hayburner *and* nine of hearts *and* palooka *and* pelter *and* pig *and* plater *and* selling plater <nf>; **rogue,** bad actor, cooler

3 horse race, race; race meeting, race card, scratch sheet; **starters,** field, weigh-in *or* weighing-in, post parade, post time, post position *or* PP; **start, break,** off; easy race, romp, shoo-in, armchair ride, hand ride; **finish,** dead heat, blanket finish, photo finish, Garison finish; **dishonest race,** boat race *and* fixed race <nf>

4 statistics, records, condition book, chart, **form, racing form,** daily racing form, past performance, **track record,** dope *or* tip *or* tout sheet <nf>, par time, parallel-time chart; **betting;** pari-mutuel 759.4; horse-racing bets

VERBS **5 race, run; start, break, be off;** air *and* breeze; make a move, drive, extend, straighten out; fade, come back; screw in *or* through; ride out, run wide; **win,** romp *or* breeze in; **place, show,** be in the money; be out of the money

ADJS **6 winning, in the money;** losing, out of the money; on the chinstrap; out in front, on the Bill Daley

758 CARDPLAYING

NOUNS **1 cardplaying** *or* card playing, shuffling, cutting, cut, dealing, deal; **card game,** game; gambling 759, gambling games

2 card, playing card, board, pasteboard; **deck, pack; suit,** hearts, diamonds, spades, clubs, puppy-feet <nf>; hand; **face card,** blaze, coat card, coat, count card, court card, paint, paint-skin, picture card, redskin; **king,** figure, cowboy *and* sergeant from K Company <nf>, one-eyed king, king of hearts *or* suicide king; queen, bitch *and* hen *and* lady *and* mop-squeezer *and* whore <nf>, queen of spades, Black Maria *and* Maria *and* slippery Anne <nf>; **jack,** knave, boy *and* fishhook *and* j-bird *and* j-boy *and* john <nf>, one-eyed jack, jack of trumps *or* right bower, left bower; **joker,** bower, best bower; spot card, rank card, plain card; **ace,** bull *and* bullet *and* seed *and* spike <nf>, ace of diamonds *or* pig's eye <nf>, ace of clubs *or* puppyfoot <nf>; **two, deuce,** two-spot, duck <nf>, two of spades *or* curse of Mexico <nf>; **three, trey,** three-spot; **four,** four-spot, four of clubs *or* devil's bedposts <nf>; **five,** five-spot, fever <nf>; **six,** six-spot; **seven,** seven-spot, fishhook <nf>; **eight,** eight-spot; **nine,** nine-spot, nine of diamonds *or* curse of Scotland <nf>; **ten,** ten-spot; wild card

3 **bridge,** auction bridge, contract bridge, rubber bridge, duplicate *or* tournament bridge; **bridge player,** partner, dummy, North and South, East and West, left hand opponent *or* LHO, bidder, responder, declarer, senior, dummy; **suit,** major suit, minor suit, trump suit *or* trumps, lay suit *or* plain suit *or* side suit; **call, bid** ; pass; **hand** ; **play,** lead, opening lead, **trick,** quick trick *or* honor trick, high-card trick, overtrick, odd trick, finesse, ruff, crossruff; **score,** adjusted score, grand slam, little slam *or* small slam, game, rubber, premium, honors *or* honors cards, yarborough, set *or* setback

4 **poker,** draw poker, stud poker, five-card stud, six-card stud, seven-card stud, eight-card stud, strip poker; poker hand, five of a kind, straight flush, royal flush, four of a kind, full house, full boat, flush, straight, three of a kind, two pairs, one pair; pot, jackpot, pool, ante, chip, stake, call, checking, raise

VERBS 5 **shuffle,** make up, make up the pack, fan *and* wash <nf>; cut; **deal,** serve, pitch <nf>

759 GAMBLING

NOUNS 1 **gambling, playing, betting, action,** wagering, punting, hazarding, risking, staking, gaming, laying, taking *or* giving *or* laying odds, sporting ; **speculation, play;** drawing *or* casting lots, tossing *or* flipping a coin, sortition

2 **gamble, chance, risk, risky thing, hazard; gambling** *or* **gambler's chance,** betting proposition, bet, matter of chance, sporting chance, **luck of the draw,** hazard of the die, roll *or* cast *or* throw of the dice, turn *or* roll of the wheel, turn of the table, turn of the cards, fall of the cards, flip *or* toss of a coin, toss-up, toss; heads or tails, touch and go; blind bargain, pig in a poke; leap in the dark, shot in the dark; potshot, random shot, potluck; **speculation, venture,** flier *and* plunge <nf>; calculated risk; uncertainty 971; fortune, luck 972.1

3 **bet, wager, stake,** hazard, lay, play *and* chunk *and* shot <nf>; cinch bet *or* sure thing, mortal cinch *and* mortal lock *and* nuts <nf>; long shot; **ante;** parlay, double or nothing; **dice bet, craps bet,** golf bet, **horse-racing bet, poker bet,** roulette bet, telebet

4 **betting system; pari-mutuel,** off-track betting *or* OTB; perfecta, exacta, win, place, show, all-way bet, daily double

5 **pot, jackpot, pool, stakes, kitty; bank;** office pool

6 **gambling odds, odds,** price; **even** *or* **square odds**, even break; **short odds, long odds,** long shot; even chance, good chance, small chance, no chance 972.10; **handicapper,** odds maker, pricemaker

7 **gambling game**, game of chance, game, friendly game; card games

8 **dice, bones** *and* rolling bones *and* ivories *and* babies *and* cubes *and* devil's bones *or* teeth *and* galloping dominoes *and* golf balls *and* marbles and Memphis dominoes and Mississippi marbles and Missouri marbles <nf>, **craps,** crap shooting, crap game, bank craps *or* casino craps, muscle craps, African dominoes *and* African golf *and* alley craps *and* army craps *and* blanket craps *and* army marbles *and* Harlem tennis *and* poor man's roulette <nf> floating crap game, floating game, sawdust game; poker dice; **false** *or* crooked *or* loaded dice

9 <throw of dice> **throw, cast, rattle, roll, shot,** hazard of the die; dice points and rolls

10 **poker,** draw poker *or* draw *or* five-card draw *or* open poker, stud poker *or* stud *or* closed poker, five-card stud *or* seven-card stud, up card *or* open card, down card *or* closed card; common *or* community *or* communal card; highball, high-low, lowball; **straight** *or* **natural poker**, wild-card poker; **poker hand,** duke *and* mitt <nf>, good hand *or* cards, lock *or* cinch *or* cinch hand *or* iron-clad hand *or* iron duke *or* mortal cinch *or* nut hand *or* nuts *or* immortals; bad hand *or* cards, trash *and* rags <nf>; **openers,** progressive openers, bet, raise *or* kick *or* bump *or* pump *or* push, showdown

11 **blackjack** *or* **twenty-one** *or* vingt-et-un; deal, card count, stiff, hard seventeen, hard eighteen, soft count, soft hand, soft eighteen, hit, blackjack *or* natural *or* snap *or* snapper, California blackjack; cut card *or* indicator card *or* sweat card; card-counting *or* ace-count *or* number count

12 **roulette,** American roulette, European roulette; **wheel,** American wheel, European wheel, wheel well, canoe, fret; **layout,** column, damnation alley, outside; zero, double zero, knotholes *or* house numbers

13 **cheating,** cheating scheme, cheating method, angle, con *and* grift *and* move *and* racket *and* scam *and* sting <nf>; deception 356

14 **lottery,** drawing, sweepstakes *or* sweepstake *or* sweep; draft lottery; **raffle; state lottery,** Lotto, Pick Six, Pick Four; tombola <Brit>; number lottery, numbers pool, **numbers game** *or* **policy,** Chinese lottery <nf>; interest lottery, Dutch *or* class lottery; tontine; grab bag *or* barrel *or* box

15 **bingo,** slow death <nf>, beano, keno, lotto; bingo card, banker, counter

16 <gambling device> gambling wheel, wheel of fortune, big six wheel, Fortune's wheel, raffle wheel *or* paddle wheel; roulette wheel, American wheel, European wheel; raffle wheel; cage, birdcage; goose *or* shaker, gooseneck; pinball machine; slot machine, slot, the slots, one-armed bandit <nf>; **layout** *or* green cloth, gambling table, craps table, Philadelphia layout, roulette table; **cheating device,** gaff *and* gimmick *and* tool <nf>

17 pari-mutuel, pari-mutuel machine, totalizator, totalizer, tote *and* tote board <nf>, odds board

18 **chip, check, counter** bean *and* fish <nf>

19 **casino, gambling house, house,** store *and* shop <nf>, gaming house, betting house, betting parlor, gambling den, gambling hall, sporting house , gambling hell <nf>; luxurious casino, carpet joint *and* rug joint <nf>; honest gambling house, right joint <nf>; disreputable gambling house, crib *and* dive *and* joint *and* sawdust joint *and* store *and* toilet <nf>; illegal gambling house, cheating gambling house, brace house *and* bust-out joint *and* clip joint *and* deadfall *and* flat joint *and* flat store *and* hell *and* juice joint *and* low den *and* nick joint *and* peek store *and* skinning house *and* snap house *and* sneak joint *and* steer joint *and* wire joint *and* wolf trap <nf>; **handbook, book,** sports book, bookie joint <nf>, racebook, horse parlor, horse room, off-track betting parlor, OTB

20 **bookmaker, bookie** <nf>, turf accountant; **tout,** turf consultant; numbers runner; bagman

21 **gambler, player,** gamester, sportsman *or* sporting man , sport, hazarder ; **speculator,** venturer, adventurer; **bettor,** wagerer, punter; high-stakes gambler, money player, high roller, plunger; petty gambler, low roller, piker *and* tinhorn *and* tinhorn gambler <nf>; professional gambler, pro *and* nutman <nf>; skillful gambler, sharp, shark, sharper, dean *and* professor *and* river gambler *and* dice gospeller *and* sharpie <nf>; cardsharp *or* cardshark, cardsharper; card counter, counter, caser, matrix player; crap shooter *and* boneshaker <nf>;

compulsive gambler; spectator, kibitzer, lumber *and* sweater *and* wood <nf>

22 **cheater,** cheat, air bandit *and* bilk *and* bunco artist *and* dildock *and* grec *and* greek *and* grifter *and* hustler *and* mechanic *and* mover *and* rook *and* worker <nf>; deceiver 357; **dupe, victim,** coll *and* flat *and* john *and* lamb *and* lobster *and* mark *and* monkey *and* patsy *and* **sucker** <nf>

VERBS 23 **gamble,** game, sport , play, **try one's luck** *or* **fortune; speculate; run** *or* **bank a game;** draw lots, draw straws, lot, cut lots, **cast lots;** cut the cards *or* deck; match coins, toss, flip a coin, call, call heads or tails; shoot craps, play at dice, roll the bones <nf>; play the ponies <nf>; raffle off

24 **chance, risk, hazard,** set at hazard, **venture,** wager, take a flier <nf>; **gamble on,** take a gamble on; **take a chance,** take one's chance, take the chances of, try the chance, **chance it**; **take** *or* **run the risk,** run a chance; **take chances,** tempt fortune; **leave** *or* **trust to chance** *or* **luck,** rely on fortune, take a leap in the dark; buy a pig in a poke; take potluck; raise the stakes, up the ante

25 **bet, wager, gamble, hazard, stake,** punt, lay, lay down, put up, **make a bet, lay a wager,** give *or* take *or* lay odds, make book, get a piece of the action <nf>; plunge <nf>; **bet on** *or* **upon, back;** bet *or* play against; play *or* follow the ponies <nf>; parlay; **ante, ante up; cover, call,** match *or* meet a bet, see, fade; **check, sandbag** <nf>, **pass,** stand pat *or* stand stiff; betcha

26 **cheat, pluck** *and* skin *and* rook <nf>; load the dice, mark the cards

ADJS 27 speculative, **uncertain** 971.16; **hazardous, risky** 1006.10, dicey <nf>; **lucky,** winning, hot *and* red hot *and* on a roll <nf>; **unlucky**, losing, cold <nf>

760 OTHER SPORTS

NOUNS 1 **billiards**, pool, pocket billiards, snooker; billiard table, pool table, pocket, cue ball, cue stick, chalk; pool hall, billiards club

2 **boating**, sailing, canoeing, rowing, sculling, windsurfing, sailboarding, surfing, rafting, whitewater rafting; yachting, competitive sailing, day sailing; sailboat, canoe, catamaran, rowboat,kayak; regatta, America's Cup; sailor, yachtsman, yachtswoman, canoeist, rower, oarsman *or* oar, sculler, windsurfer, surfer, sailboarder; mariner, boater

3 **martial arts**; judo, the way of gentleness; karate, the way of the empty hand, sport karate, recreational karate; tae kwon do, the way of the foot and fist; aikido, the way of harmony of the spirit, competition aikido; belt, grade, dan grade; dojo

4 **fencing**; foil fencing, épée fencing, saber fencing, *escrime* <Fr>; en garde, parry, riposte, thrust, feint, lunge

5 **gymnastics**; floor exercise, tumbling, vaulting, trampolining, balance beam, horizontal bar, uneven parallel bars, pommel *or* side horse, stationary rings

6 **mountain climbing**, mountaineering, rock climbing, bouldering, free climbing, clean climbing, aid climbing, big wall climbing, snow climbing, ice climbing, Alpine-style climbining, alpinism; climbing expedition, base camp, advance camp; rock face

7 **ice skating**, figure skating, free skating, pairs skating, ice dancing, speed skating; Olympic skating, professional skating; compulsory figure, loop, salchow, jump, axel jump, double axel, triple axel, toe jump, spin, camel spin, lay-back spin, sit spin

8 **swimming**, natation; synchronized swimming, diving, scuba, snorkeling, skinny-dipping <nf>, dogpaddling, Olympic swimming; crawl *or* American crawl *or* Australian crawl, back crawl, backstroke, breaststroke, butterfly stroke; flutter kick, scissors kick, back kick, wedge kick, frog kick, whip kick; lifeguarding, lifesaving; swimming pool, natatorium

761 EXISTENCE

NOUNS **1 existence, being;** subsistence, entity, essence, esse, isness, absolute *or* transcendental essence, *l'être* <Fr>, pure being, noumenon; **occurrence,** presence, monadism; **materiality** 1052, **substantiality** 763; **life** 306

2 reality, actuality, factuality, empirical *or* demonstrable *or* objective existence, the here and now; historicity; necessity; the real thing, the genuine article; facticity; **truth** 973; **authenticity;** sober *or* grim reality, hardball and the nitty-gritty <nf>, not a dream, more truth than poetry; thing, something, ens, entity, being, object, substance, phenomenon

3 fact, the case, fact *or* truth of the matter, not opinion, not guesswork, what's what *and* where it's at <nf>; **matter of fact**; **bare fact,** naked fact, bald fact, **simple fact,** sober fact, simple *or* sober truth; **cold fact,** hard fact, **stubborn fact, brutal fact,** painful fact, the nitty-gritty *and* the bottom line <nf>; **actual fact,** positive fact, absolute fact; **self-evident fact,** axiom, postulate, premise, accomplished fact, *fait accompli* <Fr>; **accepted fact,** conceded fact, admitted fact, fact of experience, well-known fact, established fact, inescapable fact, irreducible fact, indisputable fact, undeniable fact; **demonstrable fact,** provable fact; empirical fact; protocol, protocol statement *or* sentence *or* proposition; given fact, given, donné datum, **circumstance** 766; **salient fact,** significant fact; factlet, factoid, fact bite

4 the facts, information 551, the particulars, the details, the specifics, **the data;** the dope *and* the scoop *and* the score *and* the skinny *and* the inside skinny <nf>; the picture <nf>, the gen <Brit nf>, what's what <nf>; the fact *or* facts *or* truth of the matter, the facts of the case, the whole story <nf>; essentials, basic *or* essential facts, brass tacks *or* nitty-gritty <nf>; fact sheet

5 self-existence, uncreated being, noncontingent existence, aseity, innascibility

6 mere existence, simple existence, **vegetable existence, vegetation,** mere tropism; couch potato

7 (philosophy of being) ontology, metaphysics, existentialism

VERBS **8 exist, be,** be in existence, be extant, have being; breathe, **live** 306.8; subsist, stand, obtain, hold, prevail, be the case; **occur,** be present, be there, be found, be true, be met with, happen to be

9 live on, continue to exist, persist, last, stand the test of time, abide, endure 827.6

10 vegetate, merely exist, just be, pass the time

11 exist in, consist in, subsist in, lie in, rest in, repose in, reside in, abide in, inhabit, dwell in, **inhere in,** be present in, be a quality of, be comprised in, be contained in, be constituted by, be coextensive with

12 become, come to be, go, get, get to be, turn out to be, materialize; be converted into, turn into 858.17; grow 861.5; be changed

ADJS **13 existent, existing,** in existence, de facto; **subsistent,** subsisting; **being,** in being; **living** 306.12; **present, extant, prevalent, current,** in force *or* effect, afoot, on foot, under the sun, on the face of the earth

14 self-existent, self-existing, innascible; uncreated, increate

15 real, actual, factual, veritable, for real <nf>, de facto, simple, sober, **hard; absolute, positive; self-evident,** axiomatic; accepted, conceded, stipulated, given; admitted, well-known, **established, inescapable, indisputable, undeniable; demonstrable,** provable; empirical, **objective,** historical; **true** 973.13; honest-to-God <nf>, genuine, card-carrying <nf>, **authentic; substantial** 763.6

ADVS **16 really, actually; factually; genuinely,** veritably, basically, **truly; in reality,** in actuality, in effect, in fact, de facto, in point of fact, as a matter of fact; positively, absolutely; no buts about it <nf>; no ifs, ands, or buts <nf>; obviously, manifestly 348.14

762 NONEXISTENCE

NOUNS **1** **nonexistence,** nonsubsistence; **nonbeing,** unbeing, notbeing, nonentity; **nothingness,** nothing, nullity, nihility, invalidity; vacancy, deprivation, emptiness, inanity, vacuity 222.2; vacuum, void 222.3; nix <nf>; negativeness, negation, negativity; nonoccurrence, nonhappening; **unreality,** nonreality, unactuality; nonpresence, absence 222

2 **nothing, nil,** *nihil* <L>, *nada* <Sp>, **naught, aught;** zero, 0, cipher; nothing whatever, nothing at all, nothing on earth *or* under the sun, no such thing; thing of naught 764.2

3 <nf terms> **zilch, zip,** zippo, nix, goose egg, Billy be damn, diddly, shit, diddly shit, squat, diddly squat, Sweet Fanny Adams <Brit>, bubkes, beans, a hill of beans, a hoot, **a fart,** a fuck, fuck all *and* bugger all <Brit>, jack-shit, a rat's ass, chopped liver

4 **none,** not any, none at all, not a one, not a blessed one <nf>, never a one, ne'er a one, nary one <nf>; **not a bit,** not a whit, not a hint, not a smitch *or* smidgen <nf>, not a speck, not a mite, not a particle, not an iota, not a jot, not a one, not a sausage <Brit>, not a scrap, not a trace, not a lick *or* a whiff <nf>, not a shadow, not a suspicion, not a shadow of a suspicion, neither hide nor hair

VERBS **5** **not exist,** not be in existence, not be met with, not occur, not be found, found nowhere, be absent *or* lacking *or* wanting, be null and void

6 **cease to exist** *or* **be, be annihilated,** be destroyed, **be wiped out,** be extirpated, be eradicated; **go, vanish,** be no more, leave no trace; **vanish, disappear** 34.2, evaporate, fade, fade away *or* out, fly, flee, dissolve, melt away, die out *or* away, pass, pass away, pass out of the picture <nf>, turn to nothing *or* naught, peter out <nf>, come to an end, wind down, tail off *and* trail off <nf>, reach an all-time low; **perish, expire,** pass away, **die** 307.18

7 **annihilate** 395.13, **exterminate** 395.14, eradicate, extirpate, **eliminate,** liquidate, **wipe out, stamp out,** waste *and* take out *and* nuke *and* zap <nf>, put an end to 395.12

ADJS **8** **nonexistent,** unexistent, inexistent, nonsubsistent, unexisting, without being, nowhere to be found; **minus, missing,** lacking, wanting; **null, void,** devoid, empty, inane, vacuous; **negative,** less than nothing; absent

9 **unreal,** unrealistic, unactual, not real; merely nominal; **immaterial** 1053.7; **unsubstantial** 764.5; **imaginary, imagined,** make believe, **fantastic, fanciful, fancied** 986.19–22; illusory

10 **uncreated, unmade,** unborn, unbegotten, unconceived, unproduced

11 **no more, extinct, defunct, dead** 307.29, expired, passed away; vanished, gone glimmering; perished, obsolete, annihilated; gone, all gone; all over with, had it <nf>, finished *and* phut *and* pffft *and* kaput <nf>, down the tube *and* down the drain *and* up the spout <nf>, done for *and* dead and done for <nf>

ADVS **12** **none, no,** not at all, in no way, to no extent

763 SUBSTANTIALITY

NOUNS **1** **substantiality,** substantialness; materiality 1052; **substance, body,** mass; **solidity,** density, concreteness, **tangibility,** palpability, ponderability; **sturdiness, stability,** soundness, firmness, steadiness, stoutness, toughness, **strength,** durability

2 **substance, stuff, fabric, material, matter** 1052.2, medium, the tangible; **elements,** constituent elements, constituents, ingredients, components, atoms, building blocks, parts

3 **something, thing,** an existence; **being, entity,** unit, individual, entelechy, monad; **person,** persona, personality, body, soul; **creature,** created being, contingent being; **organism,** life form, living thing, life; **object** 1052.4

4 **embodiment, incarnation,** materialization, substantiation, concretization, hypostasis, reification

VERBS **5** **embody,** incarnate, **materialize,** concretize, body forth, lend substance to, reify, entify, hypostatize

ADJS **6** **substantial,** substantive; **solid, concrete; tangible,** sensible, appreciable, palpable, ponderable; **material** 1052.10; **real** 761.15; **created,** creatural, organismic *or* organismal, contingent

7 **sturdy,** stable, **solid,** sound, firm, steady, tough, stout, **strong,** rugged; **durable,** lasting, enduring; **hard, dense,** unyielding, steely, adamantine; **well-made,** well-constructed, well-built, well-knit; **well-founded,** well-established, well-grounded; **massive,** bulky, heavy, chunky

ADVS **8** **substantially,** essentially, materially

764 UNSUBSTANTIALITY

NOUNS **1** **unsubstantiality,** insubstantiality, unsubstantialness; **immateriality** 1053; bodilessness, incorporeality, unsolidity, unconcreteness; **intangibility,** impalpability, imponderability; **thinness, tenuousness,** attenuation, tenuity, evanescence, subtlety, subtility, fineness, airiness, mistiness, vagueness, ethereality; **fragility, frailness; flimsiness** 16.2; **transience** 828, **ephemerality,** ephemeralness, fleetingness, fugitiveness

2 thing of naught, nullity, zero; **nonentity, nobody** *and* nonstarter *and* nebbish <nf>, nonperson, unperson, cipher, man of straw, jackstraw , lay figure, puppet, dummy, hollow man; flash in the pan, dud <nf>; **trifle** 998.5; *nugae* <L>; nothing 762.2

3 **spirit,** air, **thin air,** breath, mere breath, smoke, vapor, mist, ether, **bubble, shadow,** mere shadow; illusion 976; phantom 988.1

VERBS **4** **spiritualize, disembody,** dematerialize; etherealize, **attenuate,** subtilize, rarefy, fine, refine; **weaken,** enervate, sap

ADJS **5** **unsubstantial,** insubstantial, nonsubstantial, unsubstanced; intangible, impalpable, imponderable; **immaterial** 1053.7; **bodiless,** incorporeal, unsolid, unconcrete; weightless 298.10; **transient** 828.7, ephemeral, fleeting, fugitive

6 **thin, tenuous,** subtile, subtle, evanescent, fine, overfine, refined, rarefied; **ethereal,** airy, windy, spirituous, vaporous, gaseous; air-built, cloud-built; **chimerical,** gossamer, gossamery, gauzy, shadowy, phantomlike 988.7; dreamlike, **illusory, unreal;** fatuous, fatuitous, inane; **imaginary,** fanciful 986.20

7 **fragile, frail** 1050.4; **flimsy,** shaky, weak, papery, paper-thin, **unsound,** infirm 16.15

8 **baseless, groundless,** ungrounded, **without foundation,** unfounded, not well-founded, built on sand

765 STATE

NOUNS **1** **state,** mode, modality; **status, situation,** status quo *or* status in quo, position, standing, footing, location, bearings, spot, walk of life; **rank,** estate, station, place, place on the ladder, **standing; condition,** circumstance 766; **case, lot; predicament, plight,** pass, pickle *and* picklement *and* fix *and* jam *and* spot *and* bind <nf>

2 **the state of affairs,** the nature *or* shape of things, the way it shapes up <nf>, the way of the world, how things stack up <nf>, **how things stand,** how things are, the way of things, the way it is, like it is, where it's at <nf>, **the way things are,** the way of it, the way things go, how it goes, the way the cookie crumbles, **how it is,** the status quo *or* status in quo, the size of it <nf>; how the land lies, the lay of the land; shape, phase, state of the art; state of mind

3 **good condition, bad condition;** adjustment, fettle, form, order, repair, **shape** <nf>, trim

4 **mode, manner, way,** tenor, vein, fashion, style, lifestyle, way of life, preference, thing and bag <nf>; **form,** shape, guise, complexion, make-up; **role,** capacity, character, part; modus vivendi, modus operandi

VERBS **5** **be in** *or* **have** a certain state, be such *or* so *or* thus, **fare,** go on *or* along; **enjoy** *or* **occupy** a certain position; **get on** *or* **along,** come on *or* along <nf>; **manage** <nf>, **contrive, make out** <nf>, come through, get by; **turn out,** come out, stack up <nf>, shape up <nf>

ADJS **6** conditional, modal, formal, situational, statal

7 **in condition** *or* **order** *or* repair *or* shape; **out of order,** out of commission *and* **out of kilter** *or* kelter *and* out of whack <nf>

766 CIRCUMSTANCE

NOUNS **1** **circumstance, occurrence, occasion, event** 831, **incident;** juncture, conjuncture, contingency, eventuality; **condition** 765.1

2 **circumstances,** total situation, existing conditions *or* situation, set of conditions, terms of reference, **environment** 209, environing circumstances, context, frame, setting, surround, surrounding conditions, parameters, status quo *or* status in quo, setup; state of affairs; **the picture,** the whole picture, full particulars, ins and outs, ball game <nf>, the score <nf>, how things stand, the way the cookie crumbles, the whole nine yards, lay of the land, layout, play-by-play description, blow-by-blow account

3 **particular, instance, item, detail,** point, count, case, fact, matter, article, datum, element, part, ingredient, factor, facet, aspect, thing; **respect, regard,** angle; minutia, minutiae <pl>, trifle, petty *or* trivial matter; incidental, minor detail

4 **circumstantiality,** particularity, specificity, thoroughness, minuteness of detail; accuracy

5 **circumstantiation,** itemization, particularization, specification, spelling-out, detailing, anatomization, atomization, analysis 801

VERBS **6** **itemize, specify,** circumstantiate, particularize, **spell out, detail,** go *or* enter into detail, descend to particulars, give full particulars, put in context, atomize, anatomize; **analyze** 801.6; **cite,** instance, adduce, document, give *or* quote chapter and verse; **substantiate**

ADJS **7** **circumstantial,** conditional, provisional; **incidental,** occasional, contingent, adventitious, **accidental, chance,** fortuitous, casual, aleatory, aleatoric, unessential *or* inessential *or* nonessential; background

8 environmental, environing, surrounding, conjunctive, conjoined, contextual, attending, attendant, limiting, determining, parametric; grounded, based

9 **detailed, minute, full, particular,** meticulous, fussy, finicky *or* finicking *or* finical, persnickety, picayune, picky <nf>, nice , precise, exact, specific, special

ADVS **10** **thus, thusly,** <nf>, in such wise, thuswise, this way, this-a-way <nf>, thus and thus, thus and so, **so,** just so, like so *and* yea <nf>, like this, like that, just like that; similarly 784.18, precisely

11 **accordingly, in that case, in that event, at that rate,** that being the case, such being the case, that being so, **under the circumstances,** the condition being such, as it is, as matters stand, as the matter stands, **therefore** 888.7, **consequently; as the case may be,** as it may be, according to circumstances; as it may happen *or* turn out, as things may fall; **by the same token,** equally

12 **circumstantially,** conditionally, provisionally; provided 959.12

13 **fully, in full, in detail,** minutely, specifically, particularly, in particular, wholly 792.13, *in toto* <L>, completely 794.14, **at length,** *in extenso* <L>, *ad nauseam* <L>

767 INTRINSICALITY

NOUNS **1** **intrinsicality,** internality, innerness, **inwardness; inbeing,** indwelling, immanence; **innateness, inherence,** indigenousness; essentiality, fundamentality; **subjectivity,** internal reality, nonobjectivity

2 **essence, substance,** stuff, very stuff, inner essence, essential nature, quiddity, esse; **quintessence, epitome,** embodiment, incarnation, model, pattern, purest type, typification, perfect example *or* exemplar, elixir, flower; **essential,** principle, essential principle, fundamental, hypostasis, postulate, axiom; **gist,** gravamen, **nub** <nf>, nucleus, center, focus, kernel, **core, pith,** meat; **heart,** soul, heart and soul, spirit, sap, lifeblood, marrow, entelechy

3 <nf terms> meat and potatoes, **nuts and bolts**, the nitty-gritty, the guts, the name of the game, the bottom line, where it's at, what it's all about, the ball game, the payoff, the score, where the rubber meets the road; back to basics; mother of all

4 **nature, character, quality,** suchness; **constitution,** crasis , composition, **characteristics,** makeup, constituents, building blocks; physique 262.4, physio; **build,** body-build, somatotype, frame, constitution, genetic make-up, system; complexion , humor *and* humors ; **temperament,** temper, fiber, **disposition,** spirit, ethos, genius, dharma; **way, habit,** tenor, cast, hue, tone, grain, vein, streak, stripe, mold, brand, stamp; **kind** 809.3, **sort, type,** ilk; **property, characteristic** 865.4; **tendency** 896; the way of it, the nature of the beast <nf>

5 **inner nature,** inside, insides <nf>, internal *or* inner *or* esoteric *or* intrinsic reality, iniety, true being, essential nature, what makes one tick <nf>, center of life, vital principle, nerve center; **spirit, indwelling spirit, soul, heart, heart and soul, breast, bosom, inner person,** heart of hearts, insight, secret heart, inmost heart *or* soul, secret *or* innermost recesses of the heart, heart's core, bottom *or* cockles of the heart; vitals, the quick, depths of one's being, guts *and* kishkes <nf>, where one lives <nf>; **vital principle,** archeus, life force, *élan vital* <Fr>

VERBS 6 **inhere,** indwell, belong to *or* permeate by nature, makes one tick <nf>; run in the blood, run in the family, inherit, be born so, have it in the genes, be made that way, be built that way <nf>, be part and parcel of

ADJS 7 **intrinsic,** internal, **inner,** inward; **inherent,** resident, implicit, immanent, indwelling; inalienable, unalienable, uninfringeable, unquestionable, unchallengeable, irreducible, qualitative; **ingrained,** in the very grain; infixed, implanted, inwrought, deep-seated; **subjective,** esoteric, private, secret

8 **innate, inborn,** born, congenital; **native, natural,** natural to, connatural, native to, indigenous; **constitutional,** bodily, physical, temperamental, organic; **inbred, genetic, hereditary,** inherited, bred in the bone, in the blood, running in the blood *or* race *or* strain, radical, rooted; connate, connatal, coeval; **instinctive,** instinctual, atavistic, primal

9 **essential,** of the essence, **fundamental; primary,** primitive, primal, elementary, elemental, simple, barebones *and* no-frills *and* bread-and-butter <nf>, original, *ab ovo* <L>, **basic, gut** <nf>, basal, underlying; **substantive,** substantial, material; constitutive, constituent; mandatory, compulsory; must-have

ADVS 10 **intrinsically, inherently,** innately; internally, inwardly, immanently; originally, primally, primitively; **naturally, congenitally,** genetically, **by birth, by nature**

11 **essentially, fundamentally, primarily, basically; at bottom,** *au fond* <Fr>, at heart; in essence, at the core, in substance, in the main; substantially, materially, most of all; per se, of *or* in itself, as such, qua

768 EXTRINSICALITY

NOUNS 1 **extrinsicality,** externality, outwardness, extraneousness, otherness, discreteness; foreignness;

objectivity, nonsubjectivity, impersonality

2 **nonessential,** inessential *or* unessential, nonvitalness, carrying coals to Newcastle, gilding the lily; **accessory, extra,** collateral; the other, not-self; **appendage,** appurtenance, auxiliary, supernumerary, **supplement,** addition, addendum, superaddition, adjunct 254; **subsidiary,** subordinate, secondary; **contingency,** contingent, incidental, accidental, accident, happenstance, mere chance; **superfluity,** superfluousness; fifth wheel *and* tits on a boar <nf>; triviality

ADJS 3 **extrinsic, external,** outward, outside, outlying; **extraneous,** foreign; **objective,** nonsubjective, impersonal, extraorganismic *or* extraorganismal; not of this world

4 **unessential,** inessential *or* nonessential, unnecessary, nonvital, superfluous; **accessory, extra,** collateral, auxiliary, supernumerary; adventitious, appurtenant, adscititious; **additional, supplementary,** supplemental, superadded, supervenient, make-weight; **secondary,** subsidiary, subordinate; **incidental,** circumstantial, contingent; trivial, throwaway; **accidental, chance,** fortuitous, casual, aleatory, aleatoric; **indeterminate, unpredictable,** capricious

769 ACCOMPANIMENT

NOUNS 1 **accompaniment,** concomitance *or* concomitancy, withness and togetherness <nf>; synchronism, **simultaneity** 836, simultaneousness; coincidence, co-occurrence, concurrence, concurrency, coexistence, symbiosis; parallelism; coagency

2 **company, association,** consociation, **society,** community; **companionship, fellowship,** consortship, partnership; cohabitation

3 **attendant,** concomitant, corollary, **accessory,** appendage; **adjunct** 254

4 **accompanier, accompanist; attendant, companion, fellow, mate,** comate, consort, **partner;** companion piece

5 **escort, conductor, usher,** shepherd; **guide,** tourist guide, cicerone; **squire,** esquire, swain, cavalier; **chaperon,** duenna; **bodyguard,** guard, **convoy**, muscle <nf>**;** companion, sidekick <nf>, fellow traveler, travel companion, satellite, outrider; third wheel

6 **attendance, following, cortege, retinue, entourage,** suite, followers, followership, rout, train, body of retainers; **court,** cohort; parasite 138.5

VERBS 7 **accompany,** bear *or* keep one company, **keep company with,** companion, go *or* travel *or* run with, go together, go along for the ride <nf>, **go along with, attend,** wait on *or* upon; **associate with,** assort with, sort with, **consort with,** couple with, hang around with *and* hang out with *and* hang with <nf>, go hand in hand with; **combine** 805.3, **associate**, consociate, confederate, flock *or* band *or* herd together

8 **escort, conduct,** have in tow <nf>, marshal, **usher,** shepherd, **guide, lead; convoy,** guard; **squire,** esquire, **attend,** wait on *or* upon, **take out** <nf>; **chaperon;** attend, dance attendance on

ADJS 9 **accompanying, attending, attendant, concomitant,** accessory, collateral; **combined** 805.5, **associated**, coupled, paired; **fellow, twin, joint, joined** 800.13, conjoint, hand-in-hand, hand-in-glove, mutual; **simultaneous, concurrent,** coincident, synchronic, synchronized; correlative; parallel; complementary, accessory

ADVS 10 **hand in hand** *or* glove, arm in arm, side by side, cheek by jowl, shoulder to shoulder; therewith, therewithal, herewith

11 **together, collectively, mutually,** jointly, unitedly, in conjunction, conjointly, *en masse* <Fr>, communally, corporately, **in a body,** all at once, *ensemble* <Fr>, in association, in company; simultaneously, coincidentally, concurrently, at once

770 ASSEMBLAGE

NOUNS 1 **assemblage, assembly, collection, gathering,** ingathering, forgathering, **congregation**, assembling; concourse, concurrence, conflux, confluence, convergence; collocation, juxtaposition, junction 800.1; combination 805; mobilization, call-up, muster, *attroupement* <Fr>; roundup, rodeo, corralling, shepherding, marshaling; **comparison** 943; canvass, census, data-gathering, survey, inventory

2 **assembly** <of persons>, *assemblée* <Fr>, **gathering, forgathering, congregation,** congress, conference, convocation, concourse, **meeting,** meet, **get-together** *and* turnout <nf>; convention, conventicle, synod, council, diet, **conclave,** levee; caucus; mass meeting, **rally,** sit-in, demonstration, demo <nf>; **session,** séance, sitting, sit-down <nf>; **panel,** forum, symposium, colloquium; committee, commission; plenum, quorum; **party, festivity** 743.4, fete, at home, housewarming, soiree, reception, **dance,** ball, prom, do <chiefly Brit>, shindig *and* brawl <nf>; rendezvous, date, assignation

3 **company, group,** grouping, groupment, network, **party, band, knot, gang, crew,** complement, cast, outfit, pack, cohort, troop, troupe, tribe, **body,** corps, stable, bunch and mob and crowd <nf>; squad, platoon, battalion, regiment, brigade, division, fleet; **team,** squad, string; covey, bevy; posse, detachment, contingent, detail, *posse comitatus* <L>; phalanx; **party, faction,** movement, wing, persuasion; in-group, old-boy network, out-group, peer group, age group; coterie, salon, clique, **set;** junta, cabal

4 **throng, multitude, horde,** host, heap <nf>, army, panoply, legion; flock, cluster, galaxy; **crowd,** press, crush, flood, spate, deluge, mass, surge, storm, squeeze; **mob,** mass, rabble, rout, ruck, jam, *cohue* <Fr>, everybody and his uncle *or* his brother <nf>, all and them some

5 <animals> **flock, bunch, pack,** colony, host, troop, army, **herd, drove,** drive, drift, trip; pride <of lions>, sloth <of bears>, skulk <of foxes>, gang <of elk>, kennel <of dogs>, clowder <of cats>, pod <of seals>, gam <of whales>, **school** *or* shoal <of fish>, etc; <animal young> **litter**

6 <birds, insects> **flock,** flight, **swarm,** cloud; covey <of partridges>, bevy <of quail>, skein <of geese in flight>, gaggle <of geese on water>, watch <of nightingales>, charm <of finches>, murmuration <of starlings>, spring <of teal>; hive <of bees>, plague <of locusts>

7 **bunch, group,** grouping, groupment, crop, **cluster, clump,** knot, wad; grove, copse, thicket; **batch, lot,** slew <nf>, **mess** <nf>; tuft, wisp; tussock, hassock; shock, stook; arrangement, nosegay, posy, spray

8 **bundle,** bindle <nf>, **pack, package,** packet, deck, budget, **parcel,** fardel <nf>, sack, bag, poke <nf>, rag-bag <nf>, bale, truss, **roll,** rouleau, bolt; fagot, fascine, fasces; quiver, sheaf; bouquet, nosegay, posy

9 **accumulation,** cumulation, gathering, **amassment,** congeries, acervation, collection, collecting, grouping; agglomeration, conglomeration, glomeration, conglomerate, agglomerate; **aggregation,** aggregate; conglobation; **mass, lump,** gob <nf>, chunk *and* hunk <nf>, wad; snowball; stockpile, stockpiling

10 **pile, heap, stack**, mass; **mound, hill;** molehill, anthill; bank, embankment, dune; haystack, hayrick, haymow, haycock, cock, mow, rick; drift, snowdrift; pyramid

11 **collection,** collector's items, collectibles *or* collectables; **holdings,** fund, treasure, hoard; corpus, corpora, **body,** data, raw data; compilation, collectanea; ana; anthology, florilegium, treasury, store, stockpile; *Festschrift* <Ger>; chrestomathy; **museum, library,** zoo, menagerie, aquarium

12 **set, suit, suite, series,** outfit *and* kit <nf>
13 **miscellany,** miscellanea, collectanea; **assortment, medley, variety, mixture** 797; mixed bag, hodgepodge, conglomerate, **conglomeration,** omnium-gatherum <nf>, potpourri, smorgasboard; **sundries,** oddments, **odds and ends**, bits and pieces
14 <a putting together> **assembly,** assemblage; assembly line, production line; assembly-line production
15 **collector,** gatherer, accumulator, connoisseur, fancier, enthusiast, pack rat *and* magpie <nf>, hoarder; beachcomber; collection agent, bill collector, dunner; tax collector, tax man, exciseman <Brit>, customs agent, *douanier* <Fr>; **miser** 484.4

VERBS 16 **come together, assemble, congregate, collect,** come from far and wide, come *or* arrive in a body; league 805.4, ally; **unite** 800.5; muster, **meet, gather, forgather,** gang up <nf>, mass, amass; **merge,** converge, flow together, fuse; group, flock, flock together; herd together; **throng, crowd,** swarm, teem, hive, surge, seethe, mill, stream, horde; **be crowded,** be mobbed, burst at the seams, be full to overflowing; **cluster,** bunch, bunch up, clot; gather around, gang around <nf>; rally, rally around; **huddle,** go into a huddle, close ranks; rendezvous, date; **couple,** copulate, link, link up
17 **convene, meet,** hold a meeting *or* session, sit; **convoke,** summon, call together
18 <bring *or* gather together> **assemble, gather;** drum up, muster, rally, **mobilize; collect,** collect up, fundraise, take up a collection, raise, take up; **accumulate,** cumulate, **amass,** mass, bulk, batch; agglomerate, conglomerate, aggregate; **combine** 805.3, **network, join** 800.5, **bring together,** get together, **gather together,** draw *or* lump *or* batch *or* bunch together, pack, pack in, cram, cram in; **bunch,** bunch up; **cluster,** clump; **group,** aggroup; **gather in,** get *or* whip in; scrape *or* scratch together, scrape up, together, rake *or* dredge *or* dig up; round up, corral, drive together; **put together,** make up, compile, colligate; collocate, **juxtapose,** pair, match, partner; hold up together, **compare** 943.4
19 **pile, pile on, heap, stack,** heap *or* pile *or* stack up; mound, hill, bank, bank up; rick; pyramid; drift; stockpile, build up
20 **bundle,** bundle up, **package,** parcel, parcel up, **pack,** bag, sack, truss, truss up; bale; wrap, **wrap up,** do *or* tie *or* bind up; roll up

ADJS 21 **assembled, collected, gathered;** congregate, congregated; meeting, in session; **combined** 805.5; **joined** 800.13; joint, leagued 805.6; **accumulated,** cumulate, massed, **amassed;** heaped, stacked, piled; glomerate, agglomerate, conglomerate, aggregate; **clustered,** bunched, lumped, clumped, knotted; bundled, packaged, wrapped up; fascicled, fasciculated; herded, shepherded, rounded up
22 **crowded, packed, crammed;** bumper-to-bumper <nf>, jam-packed, packed *or* crammed like sardines <nf>, chockablock; **compact,** firm, solid, dense, close, serried; **teeming, swarming, crawling,** seething, bristling, populous, milling, **full** 794.11
23 **cumulative,** accumulative, total, overall

771 DISPERSION

NOUNS 1 **dispersion** *or* **dispersal, scattering,** scatter, scatteration, diffraction; ripple effect; **distribution, spreading,** strewing, sowing, broadcasting, **broadcast, spread,** narrowcast, publication 352, **dissemination,** propagation, dispensation; **radiation,** divergence 171; expansion, splay; **diffusion,** circumfusion; **dilution,** attenuation, thinning, thinning-out, watering, watering-down, weakening; **evaporation,** volatilization, dissipation; fragmentation, shattering, pulverization; sprinkling, spattering; peppering, buckshot *or* shotgun pattern; deployment; diaspora

2 **decentralization,** deconcentration

3 **disbandment,** dispersion *or* dispersal, diaspora, separation, parting; breakup, split-up <nf>; **demobilization,** deactivation, **release,** detachment; dismissal 909.5; dissolution, disorganization, disintegration 806; population drift, urban sprawl, sprawl

VERBS 4 **disperse, scatter,** diffract; **distribute, broadcast, sow,** narrowcast, disseminate, propagate, pass around *or* out, publish 352.10; **diffuse, spread,** dispread, circumfuse, strew, bestrew, dot; **radiate,** diverge 171.5; expand, splay, branch *or* fan *or* spread out; **issue, deal out,** dole out, retail, utter, dispense; sow broadcast, scatter to the winds; overscatter, overspread, oversow; sunder, hive off <nf>

5 **dissipate, dispel,** dissolve, attenuate, dilute, thin, thin out, water, water down, weaken; **evaporate,** volatilize; drive away, clear away, cast forth, blow off

6 **sprinkle,** besprinkle, asperge, **spatter,** splatter, splash; **dot,** spot, speck, speckle, freckle, stud; **pepper,** powder, dust; flour, crumb, bread, dredge

7 **decentralize,** deconcentrate

8 **disband, disperse, scatter, separate, part,** break up, split up; part company, go separate ways, bug out <nf>; **demobilize,** demob <nf>, deactivate, muster out, debrief, **release,** detach, discharge, let go; dismiss 909.18; **dissolve,** disorganize, disintegrate 806.3

ADJS 9 **dispersed, scattered, distributed,** dissipated, disseminated, strown, strewn, broadcast, **spread,** dispread; **widespread,** diffuse, discrete, sparse; **diluted,** thinned, thinned-out, watered, watered-down, weakened; **sporadic;** straggling, straggly; all over the lot *or* place <nf>, few and far between, from hell to breakfast <nf>

10 **sprinkled,** spattered, splattered, asperged, splashed, **peppered,** spotted, dotted, powdered, dusted, specked, speckled, **studded,** freckled

11 dispersive, **scattering, spreading,** diffractive *or* diffractional, **distributive,** disseminative, diffusive, dissipative, attenuative

ADVS 12 **scatteringly, dispersedly,** diffusely, sparsely, **sporadically,** *passim* <L>, **here and there;** in places, **in spots** <nf>; at large, everywhere, throughout, wherever you look *or* turn <nf>, in all quarters

772 INCLUSION

NOUNS 1 **inclusion, comprisal, comprehension,** coverage, envisagement, embracement, encompassment, incorporation, embodiment, assimilation, reception; **membership,** participation, admission, admissibility, eligibility, legitimation, legitimization; **power-sharing,** enablement, enfranchisement; **completeness** 794, **inclusiveness, comprehensiveness,** exhaustiveness; **whole** 792; openness, toleration *or* tolerance; universality, generality; inclusivism

2 **entailment, involvement, implication;** assumption, presumption, presupposition, subsumption

VERBS 3 **include, comprise, contain, comprehend,** hold, **take in; cover,** cover a lot of ground <nf>, occupy, take up, fill; fill in *or* out, build into, **complete** 794.6; **embrace,** encompass, enclose, encircle, incorporate, assimilate, embody, constitute, admit, receive, envisage; **legitimize,** legitimatize; **share power,** enable, enfranchise, cut in *and* deal in *and* give a piece of the action <nf>; among, count in, work in; **number among,** take into account *or* consideration

4 <include as a necessary circumstance *or* consequence> **entail, involve, implicate,** imply, assume, presume, presuppose, subsume, affect, take in, contain, comprise, **call for, require,** take, bring, lead to

ADJS 5 **included, comprised,** comprehended, envisaged, embraced, encompassed, added-in, covered, subsumed; bound up with, forming *or* making a part of, built-in, tucked-in, integrated; **involved** 898.4

6 **inclusive, including, containing, comprising, covering, embracing,** encompassing, enclosing, encircling, assimilating, incorporating, envisaging; counting, numbering; broad-brush *and* ballpark <nf>, all-in

7 **comprehensive, sweeping, complete** 794.9; whole 792.9; **all-comprehensive,** all-inclusive 864.14, non-exclusive; without omission *or* exception, **overall,** universal, global, wall-to-wall <nf>, around-the-world, **total,** blanket, omnibus, umbrella, across-the-board; encyclopedic, compendious; synoptic; bird's-eye, panoramic

773 EXCLUSION

NOUNS 1 **exclusion, barring,** debarring, debarment, preclusion, exception, omission, nonadmission, cutting-out, leaving-out, omission; **restriction, circumscription,** narrowing, demarcation; **rejection,** repudiation; **ban,** bar, taboo, injunction; relegation; prohibition, embargo, blockade; boycott, lockout; inadmissibility, excludability, exclusivity

2 **elimination, riddance,** culling, culling out, winnowing-out, shakeout, eviction, chasing, bum's rush <nf>; **severance** 802.2; withdrawal, **removal,** detachment, disjunction 802.1; discard, eradication, clearance, **ejection,** expulsion, suspension; **deportation, exile,** expatriation, ostracism, outlawing *or* outlawry; disposal, disposition; **liquidation, purge;** obliteration

3 **exclusiveness, narrowness,** tightness; **insularity,** snobbishness, parochialism, ethnocentrism, ethnicity, xenophobia, know-nothingism; special case, exemption; **segregation, separation, separationism,** division; **isolation,** insulation, seclusion; quarantine; racial segregation, apartheid, color bar, Jim Crow, race hatred; **out-group; outsider,** nonmember, stranger, the other, they; **foreigner, alien** 774.3, outcast 586.4, outlaw; *persona non grata* <L>; blacklist, blackball; monopoly; sexual discrimination

VERBS 4 **exclude, bar,** debar, bar out, lock out, **shut out, keep out,** count out <nf>, close the door on, close out, cut out, cut off, preclude; **reject, repudiate,** blackball *and* turn thumbs down on <nf>, read *or* drum out, ease *or* freeze out and leave *or* keep out in the cold <nf>, cold-shoulder, send to Coventry <Brit>, ostracize, wave off *or* aside; **ignore,** turn a blind eye, turn a deaf ear, filter out, tune out; **ban,** prohibit, proscribe, taboo, **leave out,** omit, pass over, ignore; relegate; **blockade,** embargo; **tariff,** trade barrier

5 **eliminate, get rid of,** rid oneself of, **get quit of,** get shut of <nf>, **dispose of, remove,** abstract, eject, expel, give the bum's rush <nf>, kick downstairs, cast off *or* out, chuck <nf>, throw over *or* overboard <nf>; **deport, exile,** outlaw, expatriate; clear, clear out, clear away, clear the decks; **weed out,** pick out; **cut out,** strike off *or* out, elide, censor; eradicate, root up *or* out; **purge, liquidate**

6 **segregate, separate,** separate out *or* off, divide, cordon, cordon off; **isolate,** insulate, seclude; **set apart,** keep apart; **quarantine,** put in isolation; put beyond the pale, ghettoize; **set aside,** lay aside, put aside, keep aside, box off, wall off, fence off; **sort** *or* **pick out,** cull out, sift, screen, sieve, bolt, riddle, winnow, winnow out; thresh, thrash, gin

ADJS 7 **excluded, barred,** debarred, precluded, kept-out, **shut-out, left-out,** left out in the cold <nf>, passed-over; not included, not in it, not in the picture <nf>; excepted, excused; **ignored;** cold-shouldered; relegated; **banned,** prohibited, proscribed, tabooed; **expelled,** ejected, **purged,** liquidated; deported; exiled; **blockaded,** embargoed

8 segregated, separated, cordoned-off, divided; isolated, insulated, secluded; **set apart,** sequestered; **quarantined; ghettoized,** beyond the pale; peripheral

9 exclusive, excluding, exclusory; seclusive, preclusive, exceptional, inadmissible, prohibitive, preventive, prescriptive, restrictive; separative, segregative, closed-door; select, selective; narrow, insular, parochial, ethnocentric, xenophobic, snobbish; racist, sexist

774 EXTRANEOUSNESS

NOUNS **1 extraneousness, foreignness;** otherness, alienism, alienage, alienation, **extrinsicality** 768, **exteriority** 206; nonassimilation, nonconformity; intrusion

2 intruder, foreign body *or* element, foreign intruder *or* intrusion, interloper, encroacher; **impurity,** blemish 1004; speck 258.7, spot, macula, blot; mote, splinter *or* sliver, **weed,** misfit 789.4; oddball 870.4; black sheep

3 alien, stranger, foreigner, outsider, non-member, not one of us, not our sort, not the right sort, the other, outlander, *Uitlander* <Afrikaans>, tramontane, ultramontane, barbarian, *gringo* <Sp>; **exile,** outcast, outlaw, wanderer, refugee, émigré, displaced person *or* DP, *déraciné* <Fr>; the Wandering Jew

4 newcomer, new arrival, *novus homo* <L>; *arriviste* <Fr>, Johnny-come-lately <nf>, new boy *or* man, new kid; **tenderfoot,** greenhorn; settler, emigrant, immigrant; recruit, rookie <nf>; **intruder, squatter,** gate-crasher, stowaway

ADJS **5 extraneous, foreign, alien,** strange, exotic, foreign-looking; unearthly, extraterrestrial 1072.26; exterior, **external;** extrinsic 768.3; ulterior, outside, outland, outlandish; barbarian, barbarous, barbaric; foreign-born; intrusive

ADVS **6** abroad, in foreign parts; oversea, **overseas,** beyond seas; on one's travels

775 RELATION

NOUNS **1 relation, relationship, connection;** relatedness, connectedness, **association** 617, **affiliation,** filiation, bond, union, alliance, **tie,** tie-in <nf>, link, linkage, linking, linkup, liaison, **addition** 253, adjunct 254, junction 800.1, **combination** 805, assemblage 770; deduction 255.1, disjunction 802.1, **contrariety** 779, **disagreement** 789, negative *or* bad relation; **positive** *or* **good relation, affinity, rapport,** mutual attraction, sympathy, accord 455; **closeness,** propinquity, **proximity,** approximation, contiguity, nearness 223, intimacy; **relations, dealings,** affairs, business, transactions, doings *and* truck <nf>, intercourse; **similarity** 784, homology

2 relativity, dependence, contingency; **relativism,** indeterminacy, uncertainty, variability, variance; **interrelation, correlation** 777

3 kinship, common source *or* stock *or* descent *or* ancestry, consanguinity, agnation, cognation, enation, relationship by blood 559; family relationship, affinity 564.1

4 relevance, pertinence, pertinency, cogency, relatedness, materiality, **appositeness,** germaneness; application, applicability, effect, appropriateness; **connection,** reference, **bearing,** concern, concernment, interest, respect, regard

VERBS **5 relate to,** refer to, **apply to, bear on** *or* **upon,** respect, regard, **concern, involve,** touch, affect, interest; **pertain, pertain to,** appertain, appertain to, belong to, fit; **agree, agree with,** answer to, correspond to, chime with; **have to do with,** have connection with, link with *or* link up with, connect, reconnect, put in context, tie in with <nf>, liaise with <nf>, deal with, treat of, touch upon

6 relate, associate, connect, interconnect, ally, link, link up, wed, marry, marry up, weld, bind, tie, couple, bracket, equate, identify; bring into relation with, bring to bear upon, apply; **parallel,** parallelize, draw a parallel; symmetrize; **interrelate,** relativize, **correlate** 777.4

ADJS 7 **relative, comparative** relational; **relativistic,** indeterminate, uncertain, variable; **connective, linking,** associative; **relating,** pertaining, appertaining, pertinent, referring, referable

8 **approximate,** approximating, approximative, proximate; **near, close** 223.14; **comparable,** relatable, commensurable; **proportional,** proportionate, proportionable; correlative; **like,** homologous, **similar** 784.10

9 **related, connected; linked,** tied, coupled, knotted, twinned, wedded, wed, married *or* married up, welded, conjugate, bracketed, bound, yoked, spliced, conjoined, conjoint, conjunct, joined 800.13; **associated, affiliated,** filiated, **allied,** associate, affiliate; interlocked, **interrelated,** interlinked, involved, implicated, overlapping, interpenetrating, relevant, **correlated;** in the same category, of that kind *or* sort *or* ilk, corresponding; parallel, collateral; **congenial,** *en rapport* <Fr>, sympathetic, compatible, affinitive

10 **kindred, akin, related,** of common source *or* stock *or* descent *or* ancestry, agnate, cognate, enate, connate, connatural, congeneric *or* congenerous, consanguine *or* consanguineous, genetically related, by blood 559.6, affinal 564.4

11 **relevant, pertinent,** appertaining, **germane, apposite,** cogent, material, admissible, applicable, applying, pertaining, belonging, involving, appropriate, **apropos,** *à propos* <Fr>, to the purpose, **to the point,** in point, *ad rem* <L>

ADVS 12 **relatively,** comparatively, proportionately, not absolutely, to a degree, to an extent, to some extent; **relevantly,** pertinently, appositely, germanely

776 UNRELATEDNESS

NOUNS 1 **unrelatedness,** irrelativeness, irrelation; **irrelevance,** irrelevancy, impertinence, inappositeness, uncogency, ungermaneness, immateriality, inapplicability; inconnection *or* disconnection, disconnect <nf>, inconsequence, independence; **unconnectedness,** separateness, delinkage, discreteness, dissociation, disassociation, disjuncture, disjunction 802.1

2 **misconnection,** misrelation, wrong *or* invalid linking, **mismatch,** mismatching, misalliance, *mésalliance* <Fr>; misapplication, misapplicability, misreference

3 **an irrelevance** *or* irrelevancy, quite another thing, something else again *and* a whole nother thing *and* a whole different story *and* a whole different ball game <nf>

VERBS 4 **not concern,** not involve, not imply, not implicate, not entail, not relate to, not connect with, have nothing to do with, have no business with, cut no ice *and* make no never mind <nf>, have no bearing

5 foist, drag in 213.6; impose on 643.7

ADJS 6 **unrelated,** irrelative, unrelatable, unrelational, **unconnected,** unallied, unlinked, **unassociated,** unaffiliated *or* disaffiliated; disrelated, disconnected, dissociated, detached, discrete, disjunct, removed, **separated,** segregated, apart, other, independent, marked off, bracketed; **isolated,** insular; **foreign, alien,** strange, exotic, outlandish; incommensurable, incomparable; inconsistent, inconsonant; extraneous 768.3

7 **irrelevant,** irrelative; **impertinent, inapposite,** ungermane, uncogent, inconsequent, inapplicable, immaterial, inappropriate, inadmissible; wide of *or* away from the point, *nihil ad rem* <L>, **beside the point,** beside the mark, wide of the mark, **beside the question,** off the subject, off-topic, not to the purpose, **nothing to do with the case,** not at issue, out-of-the-way; **unessential,** nonessential, extraneous, extrinsic 768.3; incidental, parenthetical

8 **farfetched, remote,** distant, out-of-the-way, strained, forced, dragged

in, neither here nor there, brought in from nowhere; **imaginary** 986.19; improbable 969.3

ADVS **9 irrelevantly,** irrelatively, impertinently, inappositely, ungermanely, uncogently, amiss; without connection, without reference *or* regard

777 CORRELATION

<reciprocal or mutual relation>

NOUNS **1 correlation,** corelation; correlativity, correlativism; **reciprocation,** reciprocity, reciprocality, two-edged sword, relativity 775.2; **mutuality,** communion, community, commutuality, common ground; **common denominator,** common factor; proportionality, direct *or* inverse relationship, direct *or* inverse ratio, direct *or* inverse proportion, covariation; **equilibrium, balance,** symmetry 264; **correspondence, equivalence,** equipollence, coequality

2 interrelation, interrelationship; **interconnection,** interlocking, interdigitation, intercoupling, interlinking, interlinkage, interalliance, interassociation, interaffiliation, interdependence, interdependency, codependency; dovetail

3 interaction, interworking, intercourse, intercommunication, **interplay;** alternation, seesaw; **meshing,** intermeshing, mesh, engagement; **complementation,** complementary relation, complementary distribution; **interweaving,** interlacing, intertwining 740.1; **interchange** 863, tit for tat, trade-off, *quid pro quo* <L>; **concurrence** 899, coaction, **cooperation** 450, compromise; codependency

4 correlate, correlative; **correspondent,** analogue, counterpart; reciprocator, reciprocatist; each other, one another

VERBS **5 correlate,** corelate; **interrelate, interconnect,** interassociate, interlink, intercouple, interlock, interdigitate, interally, intertie, interjoin, interdepend; interface; find common ground; dovetail

6 interact, interwork, **interplay;** mesh, intermesh, engage, fit, fit like a glove, dovetail, mortise; **interweave,** interlace, intertwine; **interchange;** coact, **cooperate;** codepend

7 reciprocate, correspond, correspond to, respond to, answer, answer to, go tit-for-tat; **complement,** coequal; **cut both ways,** cut two ways; counteract

ADJS **8 correlative,** corelative, correlational, corelational; **correlated,** corelated; **interrelated, interconnected,** internetworked, interassociated, interallied, interaffiliated, interlinked, interlocked, intercoupled, intertied, interdependent; interchanged, converse

9 interacting, interactive, interworking, interplaying; in gear, in mesh; dovetailed, mortised; cooperative, **cooperating** 450.5

10 reciprocal, reciprocative, tit-for-tat, seesaw, seesawing; **corresponding,** correspondent, answering, analogous, homologous, equipollent, tantamount, equivalent, coequal; **complementary,** complemental

11 mutual, commutual, **common, joint, communal,** shared, sharing, conjoint; respective, two-way, cooperative

ADVS **12 reciprocally,** back and forth, backward and forward, backwards and forwards, alternately, seesaw, to and fro; vice versa,

13 mutually, commonly, communally, **jointly;** respectively, each to each; *entre nous* <Fr>, *inter se* <L>

778 SAMENESS

NOUNS **1 sameness, identity,** identicalness, selfsameness, indistinguishability, undifferentiation, nondifferentiation, two peas in a pod; **coincidence,** correspondence, agreement, congruence; **equivalence, equality** 790, coequality; **synonymousness,** synonymity, synonymy; **oneness, unity,** homogeneity, consubstantiality; isogeny; homogeny

2 identification, likening, unification, coalescence, combination, union, fusion, merger, blending, melding, synthesis

3 **the same, selfsame,** very same, one and the same, identical same, no other, none other, very *or* actual thing, a distinction without a difference, the same difference <nf>; **equivalent** 784.3; **synonym;** homonym, homograph, homophone; ditto <nf>, *idem* <L>, *ipsissima verba* <L, the very words>; **duplicate,** double, clone *and* cookie-cutter copy <nf>, *Doppelgänger* <Ger>, twin, very image, look-alike, dead ringer <nf>, the image of, the picture of, spitting image *and* spit and image <nf>, **exact counterpart, copy** 785.1,3–5, replica, facsimile, carbon copy

VERBS **4** **coincide, correspond,** agree, chime with, match, tally, go hand in glove with, twin; complement

5 **identify,** make one, **unify,** unite, join, combine, coalesce, synthesize, merge, blend, meld, fuse 805.3

6 **reproduce,** copy, reduplicate, **duplicate,** ditto <nf>, clone

ADJS **7** **identical,** identic; **same, selfsame,** one, **one and the same,** all the same, all one, of the same kidney; **indistinguishable,** without distinction, without difference, undifferent, undifferentiated; **alike, all alike, like** 784.10, just alike, exactly alike, like two peas in a pod; **duplicate,** reduplicated, copied, twin; **homogeneous,** consubstantial; redundant, tautological

8 **coinciding,** coincident, coincidental; **corresponding,** correspondent, congruent; complementary; **synonymous, equivalent,** six of one and half a dozen of the other <nf>; **equal** 790.7, coequal, coextensive, coterminous; in *or* at parity

ADVS **9** **identically,** synonymously, **alike;** coincidentally, correspondently, correspondingly, congruently; **equally** 790.11, coequally, coextensively, coterminously; on the same footing, on all fours with; **likewise,** the same way, just the same, as is, ditto, same here <nf>; *ibid* and *ibidem* <L>

779 CONTRARIETY

NOUNS **1** **contrariety, oppositeness, opposition** 451; **antithesis, contrast,** contraposition 215, counterposition, contradiction, contraindication, contradistinction; **antagonism,** repugnance, oppugnance, oppugnancy, **hostility,** perversity, nay-saying, negativeness, orneriness <nf>, inimicalness, **antipathy,** scunner <nf>; **confrontation,** showdown, standoff, Mexican standoff <nf>, clashing, collision, cross-purposes 456.2, conflict; polarity; discrepancy, inconsistency, **disagreement** 789; antonymy

2 **the opposite, the contrary, the antithesis, the reverse,** the other way round *or* around, the inverse, the converse, the obverse, the counter; **the other side,** the mirror *or* reverse image, the other side of the coin, the flip *or* B side <nf>; the direct *or* polar opposite, the other *or* opposite extreme, other end of the spectrum; antipode, antipodes; countercheck *or* counterbalance *or* counterpoise, offset, setoff; **opposite pole,** antipole, counterpole, counterpoint; opposite number <nf>, vis-à-vis; **antonym,** opposite, opposite term, counterterm

3 (contrarieties when joined *or* coexisting) self-contradiction, **paradox** 789.2, antinomy, oxymoron, ambivalence, **irony,** enantiosis, equivocation, **ambiguity**

VERBS **4** **go contrary to, run counter to,** counter, contradict, contravene, controvert, fly in the face of, be *or* play at cross-purposes, go against; **oppose,** be opposed to, go *or* run in opposition to, run counter to, side against; **conflict with,** come in conflict with, oppugn, conflict, clash; contrast with, **offset,** set off, countercheck *or* counterbalance, countervail; **counteract,** counterwork; counterpose *or* contrapose, counterpoise, juxtapose in opposition

5 reverse, invert, obvert, transpose 205.5, flip <nf>

ADJS **6** **contrary;** contrarious, perverse, **opposite,** antithetic, antithetical, **contradictory,** counter, contrapositive, contrasted; **converse, reverse,** obverse, inverse; **adverse,** adversative *or* adversive, adversarial, **opposing, opposed,** oppositive, oppositional; anti <nf>, dead against; **antagonistic,** repugnant, oppugnant, perverse, contrarious, ornery <nf>, nay-saying, negative, hostile, combative, bellicose, belligerent, inimical, antipathetic, antipathetical, discordant; inconsistent, discrepant, conflicting, clashing, at cross-purposes, confronting, **confrontational,** confrontive, squared off <nf>, face to face, vis-à-vis, eyeball to eyeball *and* toe-to-toe <nf>, at loggerheads; contradistinct; antonymous; countervailing, counterpoised, balancing, counterbalancing, compensating

7 **diametric, diametrical, diametrically opposite,** diametrically opposed, at opposite poles, in polar opposition, antipodal *or* antipodean; retrograde; opposite as black and white *or* light and darkness *or* day and night *or* fire and water *or* the poles, etc

8 self-contradictory, **paradoxical,** antinomic, oxymoronic, ambivalent, **ironic;** equivocal, **ambiguous**

ADVS **9** contrarily, contrariwise, counter, conversely, inversely, **vice versa,** topsy-turvy, upside down, arsy-varsy <nf>, **on the other hand,** *per contra* <L>, **on** *or* **to the contrary,** *tout au contraire* <Fr>, at loggerheads, in flat opposition; rather, nay rather, quite the contrary, otherwise 780.11, just the other way, just the other way around, **oppositely,** just the opposite *or* reverse; by contraries, by way of opposition; against the grain, *à rebours* <Fr>; contrariously, perversely, ornerily <nf>

780 DIFFERENCE

NOUNS **1** **difference,** otherness, separateness, discreteness, distinctness, **distinction;** unlikeness, **dissimilarity** 787; **variation,** variance, variegation, variety, **mixture** 797, **heterogeneity, diversity; deviation,** divergence *or* divergency, departure; **disparity,** gap, inequality 791, odds; **discrepancy,** inconsistency, inconsonance, incongruity, discongruity, unconformity *or* nonconformity, disconformity, **strangeness** 870.1, unorthodoxy 688, incompatibility, irreconcilability; culture gap; **disagreement, dissent** 333, disaccord *or* disaccordance, inaccordance, discordance, dissonance, inharmoniousness, inharmony; **contrast,** opposition, **contrariety** 779; a far cry, a whale of a difference <nf>; difference of opinion, biodiversity

2 **margin,** wide *or* narrow margin, **differential;** differentia, distinction, point of difference; **nicety, subtlety,** refinement, delicacy, nice *or* fine *or* delicate *or* **subtle distinction,** fine point; shade *or* particle of difference, **nuance,** hairline; **seeming difference,** distinction without a difference

3 **a different thing,** a different story <nf>, **something else,** something else again <nf>, *tertium quid* <L, a third something>, *autre chose* <Fr>, another kettle of fish <nf>, another tune, different breed of cat <nf>, another can of worms, horse of a different color, bird of another feather; **nothing of the kind,** no such thing, **quite another thing; other, another,** tother *and* whole nother thing *and* different ball game *and* whole different ball game <nf>, special case, exception to the rule

4 **differentiation,** differencing, **discrimination,** distinguishing, **distinction;** demarcation, limiting, drawing the line; **separation, separateness,** discreteness 802.1, division, atomization, anatomization, analysis, disjunction, segregation, severance, severalization; **modification, alteration, change** 852, tweak, variation, diversification, disequalization; **particularization,** specification, individualization, individuation, personalization, specialization

VERBS 5 **differ, vary,** diverge, stand apart, be distinguished *or* distinct; **deviate from,** diverge from, divaricate from, depart from; **disagree with,** disaccord with, conflict with, contrast with, stand over against, clash with, jar with; not be like, bear no resemblance to 787.2, not square with, not accord with, not go on all fours with; ring the changes

6 **differentiate,** difference; **distinguish, make a distinction, discriminate, secern; separate,** sever, severalize, segregate, divide; **demarcate,** mark, mark out *or* off, set off, set apart, draw a line, set limits; **modify,** vary, diversify, disequalize, **change** 852.6,7; **particularize,** individualize, individuate, personalize, specify, specialize; atomize, analyze, anatomize, disjoin; split hairs, sharpen *or* refine a distinction, chop logic

ADJS 7 **different,** differing; unlike, not like, **dissimilar** 787.4; **distinct,** distinguished, differentiated, discriminated, discrete, separated, separate, disjoined 802.21, widely apart; **various,** variant, varying, varied, heterogeneous, multifarious, motley, assorted, variegated, diverse, divers, **diversified** 783.4; **several,** many; **divergent,** deviative, diverging, deviating, departing; **disparate,** unequal 791.4; **discrepant,** inconsistent, inconsonant, incongruous, incongruent, unconformable, incompatible, irreconcilable; **disagreeing,** in disagreement; **at odds,** at variance, clashing, inaccordant, disaccordant, discordant, dissonant, inharmonious, out of tune; **contrasting,** contrasted, poles apart, poles asunder, worlds apart; **contrary** 779.6; **discriminable,** separable, severable

8 **other, another,** whole nother <nf>, else, otherwise, other than *or* from; not the same, not the type <nf>, not that sort, of another sort, of a sort *and* of sorts <nf>; **unique,** one of a kind, rare, **special,** peculiar, *sui generis* <L, of its own kind>, in a class by itself

9 **differentiative,** differentiating, diacritic, diacritical, differential; **distinguishing,** discriminating, discriminative, discriminatory, characterizing, individualizing, individuating, personalizing, differencing, separative; diagnostic; **distinctive,** contrastive, characteristic, peculiar, idiosyncratic

ADVS 10 **differently,** diversely, variously; in a different manner, in another way, with a difference; differentiatingly, distinguishingly

11 **otherwise,** in other ways, **in other respects;** elsewise, else, or else; than; other than; **on the other hand;** contrarily 779.9; alias

781 UNIFORMITY

NOUNS 1 **uniformity, evenness,** equability; **steadiness,** stability 855, steadfastness, firmness, unbrokenness, seamlessness, constancy, unwaveringness, undeviatingness, persistence, perseverance, continuity, **consistency;** consonance, correspondence, accordance; unity, **homogeneity,** consubstantiality, monolithism; **equanimity,** equilibrium, unruffledness, serenity, tranquility, calm, calmness, cool <nf>

2 **regularity, constancy,** invariability, unvariation, undeviation, even tenor *or* pace, smoothness, clockwork regularity; **sameness** 778, **monotony,** monotonousness, undifferentiation, the same old thing <nf>, the daily round *or* routine, the treadmill; monotone, drone, dingdong, singsong, monologue

VERBS 3 **persist, prevail,** persevere, run true to form *or* type, continue the same; drag on *or* along; hum, drone

4 **make uniform,** uniformize; **regulate,** regularize, normalize, stabilize, damp; **even, equalize,** symmetrize, harmonize, balance, balance up, equilibrize; **level,** level out *or* off, smooth, smooth out, even, even out, flatten; **homogenize, assimilate,** standardize, stereotype; clone <nf>

ADJS 5 **uniform, equable,** equal, **even; level,** flat, smooth; **regular, constant,** steadfast, persistent, continuous; **unvaried,** unruffled, unbroken, seamless, undiversified, undifferentiated, unchanged; invariable, unchangeable, immutable; **unvarying,** undeviating, unchanging, steady, stable; cloned *or* clonish *and* cookie-cutter <nf>; **ordered,** balanced, measured; **orderly,** methodical, systematic, mechanical, faceless, robotlike, automatic; **consistent,** consonant, correspondent, accordant, homogeneous, **alike,** all alike, all of a piece, of a piece, consubstantial, monolithic; nonsexist, inclusive, nondiscriminatory

6 **same,** wall-to-wall, back-to-back; **monotonous, humdrum,** unrelieved, repetitive, drab, gray, ho-hum <nf>, samey <Brit nf>, usual, as usual; tedious, boring

ADVS **7** **uniformly,** equably, **evenly;** monotonously, in a rut *or* groove, dully, tediously, routinely, unrelievedly

8 **regularly; constantly, steadily,** continually; **invariably,** without exception, at every turn, every time one turns around, all the time, all year round, week in week out, year in year out, day in day out, never otherwise; methodically, orderly, systematically; **always** 829.11; like clockwork

782 NONUNIFORMITY

NOUNS **1** **nonuniformity, unevenness, irregularity,** raggedness, crazy-quilt, choppiness, jerkiness, **disorder** 810; **difference** 780; inequality; **inconstancy, inconsistency,** variability, changeability, changeableness, mutability, capriciousness, mercuriality, wavering, **instability, unsteadiness; variation, deviation,** deviance, divergence, differentiation, divarication, ramification; versatility, **diversity,** diversification, nonformalization; **nonconformity,** nonconformism, unconformity, unconformism, **unorthodoxy; pluralism,** variegation, variety, variousness, motleyness, dappleness; multiculturalism, multiculturism

VERBS **2** **diversify, vary,** variegate 47.7, chop and change, waver, mutate; **differentiate,** divaricate, diverge, ramify; **differ** 780.5; dissent 333.4; **disunify,** break up, break down, fragment, partition, **analyze** 801.6

ADJS **3** **nonuniform,** ununiform, **uneven, irregular,** ragged, erose, choppy, jerky, jagged, rough, disorderly, unsystematic; **different** 780.7, unequal, unequable; **inconstant, inconsistent, variable,** varying, **changeable,** changing, mutable, capricious, impulsive, mercurial, erratic, spasmodic, sporadic, wavery, wavering, **unstable, unsteady;** deviating, deviative, deviatory, divergent, divaricate, ramified; **diversified,** variform, diversiform, nonformal; **nonconformist,** unorthodox; **pluralistic,** variegated, various, motley 47.9,12; multicultural, multiracial

ADVS **4** **nonuniformly,** ununiformly, unequally, **unevenly, irregularly,** inconstantly, **inconsistently,** unsteadily, erratically, spasmodically, by fits and starts, capriciously, impulsively, sporadically; unsystematically, chaotically, helter-skelter, higgledy-piggledy; in all manner of ways, every which way <nf>, all over the shop *and* all over the ball park <nf>; here there and everywhere

783 MULTIFORMITY

NOUNS **1** **multiformity,** multifariousness, **variety,** nonuniformity 782, **diversity,** diversification, variation, variegation 47, variability, versatility, proteanism, manifoldness, multiplicity, heterogeneity; omniformity, omnifariousness; pluralism, multiculturalism; everything but the kitchen sink <nf>, all colors of the rainbow, polymorphism, heteromorphism; allotropy *or* allotropism <chemistry>; Proteus, shapeshifting, shapeshifter

VERBS **2** **diversify, vary,** change form, change shape, shift shape, ring changes, cover the spectrum,

variegate 47.7; branch out, spread one's wings; have many irons in the fire

ADJS 3 **multiform,** diversiform, variable, versatile; **protean,** proteiform; **manifold,** multifold, multiplex, multiple, multifarious, multiphase; polymorphous, polymorphic, heteromorphous, heteromorphic, metamorphic; omniform, omniformal, omnifarious, omnigenous; allotropic *or* allotropical <chemistry>

4 **diversified, varied, assorted,** heterogeneous, nonuniform; **various,** many and various, divers , diverse, sundry, **several, many;** of all sorts *or* conditions *or* kinds *or* shapes *or* descriptions *or* types; multiethnic, multicultural; multifunctional

ADVS 5 **variously, severally,** sundrily, multifariously, diversely, manifoldly

784 SIMILARITY

NOUNS 1 **similarity, likeness,** alikeness, **sameness,** similitude; **resemblance,** semblance; **analogy, correspondence,** conformity, accordance, agreement, comparability, commensurability, comparison, **parallelism, parity,** community, alliance, consimilarity; **approximation,** approach, closeness, nearness; assimilation, likening, **simile, metaphor**, parable, allegory**; simulation, imitation,** copying, aping, mimicking, taking-off, takeoff, burlesque, pastiche; identity 778.1; equivalence; synonymy

2 kinship, affinity, connection, family resemblance *or* likeness, family favor, generic *or* genetic resemblance; connaturality *or* connaturalness, connature, connateness, congeneracy; compatibility

3 likeness, like, the like of *or* **the likes of** <nf>, point of likeness, point in common; suchlike, such; **analogue, parallel;** cognate, congener; **counterpart, complement, correspondent,** pendant, similitude, tally; **approximation,** rough idea, sketch; coordinate, reciprocal, obverse, equivalent; correlate, correlative; **close imitation** *or* reproduction *or* copy *or* facsimile *or* replica, near duplicate, simulacrum; **close match, match-up, fellow, mate;** soul mate, kindred spirit *or* soul, **companion, twin,** brother, sister, brother *or* sister under the skin; *mon semblable* <Fr>, second self, alter ego; a chip off the old block; **look-alike,** the image of, the picture of, shadow, another edition; related form

4 **close** *or* **striking resemblance,** startling *or* marked *or* decided resemblance; close *or* near likeness; **faint** *or* **remote resemblance,** mere hint *or* shadow

5 **set,** group, matching pair *or* set, his and hers <nf>, couple, pair, twins, look-alikes, two of a kind, birds of a feather, peas in a pod

6 (of words or sounds) assonance, alliteration, rhyme, slant rhyme, near rhyme, jingle, clink; pun, paronamasia

VERBS 7 **resemble,** be like, bear resemblance; put one in mind of <nf>, remind one of, bring to mind, be reminiscent of, suggest, evoke, call up, call to mind; **look like,** favor <nf>, mirror; **take after,** favor, partake of, follow, appear *or* seem like, sound like; savor *or* smack of, be redolent of; **have all the earmarks of,** have every appearance of, have all the features of, have all the signs of, have every sign *or* indication of; **approximate,** approach, near, come near, come close; **compare with,** stack up with <nf>; **correspond, match, parallel**, connect, relate**;** not tell apart, not tell one from the other; **imitate** 336.5, **simulate,** copy, ape, mimic, take off, counterfeit; nearly reproduce *or* duplicate *or* reduplicate

8 **similarize,** approximate, assimilate, bring near; connaturalize

9 **assonate,** alliterate, rhyme, chime; pun

ADJS 10 **similar, like, alike,** something like, not unlike; **resembling,** resemblant, following, favoring <nf>, savoring *or* smacking of, suggestive of, **on the order of;** consimilar; **simulated, imitated,** imitation, copied, aped, mimicked, taken off, fake *or* phony <nf>, counterfeit, **mock,** synthetic, ersatz; nearly reproduced *or* duplicated *or* reduplicated; uniform with, homogeneous, identical 778.7

11 **analogous,** comparable; **corresponding,** correspondent, equivalent; **parallel,** paralleling; **matching,** cast in the same mold, of a kind, of a size, of a piece; duplicate, twin, of the same hue *or* stripe; mix-and-match

12 **such as,** suchlike, so

13 **akin,** affinitive, related; connatural, connate, cognate, agnate, enate, conspecific, correlative; congenerous, congeneric, congenerical; brothers *or* sisters under the skin

14 **approximating,** approximative, approximate, approximable; **near, close;** much of a muchness <Brit nf>, much the same, much at one, nearly the same, same but different; quasi, pseudo

15 **very like, mighty like,** powerful like <nf>, uncommonly like, remarkably like, extraordinarily like, strikingly like, **ridiculously like, for all the world like,** as like as can be; a lot alike, pretty much the same, the same difference *and* damned little difference <nf>; near-equal; as like as two peas in a pod, *comme deux gouttes d'eau* <Fr, like two drops of water>; faintly *or* remotely like

16 **lifelike,** speaking, faithful, living, breathing, to the life, **true to life** *or* nature; **realistic, natural**

17 (of words or sounds) assonant, assonantal, alliterative, alliteral; **rhyming,** jingling, chiming, punning

ADVS **18** **similarly,** correspondingly, **like, likewise,** either; in the same manner, **in like manner,** in kind; in that way, like that, like this; **thus** 766.10; so; by the same token, by the same sign; identically 778.9

19 so to speak, in a manner of speaking, **as it were,** in a manner, in a way; kind of *and* sort of <nf>

785 COPY

NOUNS **1** **copy, representation, facsimile, image, likeness** 784.3, resemblance, semblance, similitude, picture, portrait, life mask, death mask, icon, simulacrum, twin; ectype; pastiche; fair copy, faithful copy; certified copy; **imitation** 336.3, **counterfeit** 354.13, forgery, fake *and* phony <nf>

2 reproduction, duplication, reduplication; reprography; transcription; tracing, rubbing; mimeography, xerography, hectography

3 **duplicate, duplication,** dupe and ditto <nf>; **double,** cookie-cutter copy, clone; representation, **reproduction, replica,** repro <nf>, carbon copy, reduplication, facsimile, model, **counterpart;** a chip off the old block; triplicate, quadruplicate, etc; repetition 849

4 **transcript, transcription,** apograph, tenor <law>; **transfer,** tracing, rubbing, **carbon copy,** carbon; manifold ; microcopy, microform; microfiche, fiche; recording

5 **print,** offprint; **impression,** impress; **reprint,** proof, reproduction proof, repro proof *and* repro <nf>, second edition; photostatic copy, Photostat <TM>, stat <nf>; mimeograph copy, Ditto copy <TM>, hectograph copy, xerographic copy, Xerox copy <TM> *or* Xerox <TM>, carbon copy; **facsimile,** fax <nf>; **photograph,** positive, negative, print, enlargement, contact print, photocopy

6 **cast,** casting; mold, **molding,** die, stamp, seal

7 **reflection,** reflex; **shadow,** silhouette, outline 211.2; **echo**

VERBS **8** **copy, reproduce,** replicate, **duplicate,** dupe <nf>; clone; reduplicate; **transcribe;** trace; double; triplicate, quadruplicate, etc; manifold , multigraph, mimeograph, mimeo, Photostat <TM>, stat <nf>, facsimile, fax <nf>, hectograph, ditto, Xerox <TM>, carbon-copy; microcopy, microfilm

ADVS **9** in duplicate, in triplicate, etc

786 MODEL

<thing copied>

NOUNS **1** **model, pattern, standard, criterion,** classic example, rule, mirror, paradigm; showpiece, showplace; **original,** urtext, *locus classicus* <L>; **type, prototype,** antetype, **archetype,** genotype, biotype, type specimen, type species; **precedent**

2 **example,** exemplar; **representative,** type, symbol, emblem, exponent; **exemplification,** illustration, demonstration, explanation; **instance,** relevant instance, **case,** typical example *or* case, case in point, object lesson

3 **sample, specimen;** piece, taste, swatch; instance, for-instance <nf>

4 **ideal,** *beau ideal*, ego ideal, ideal type, acme, highest *or* perfect *or* best type; cynosure, apotheosis, idol; **shining example,** role-model, **hero, superhero; model,** the very model, mirror, paragon, epitome; cult figure

5 artist's model, dressmaker's model, photographer's model, mannequin; dummy, lay figure; clay model, wood model, pilot model, mock-up

6 **mold, form** 262, cast, template, matrix, negative; **die,** punch, stamp, intaglio, seal, mint; last, shoe last

VERBS 7 **set an example,** set the pace, lead the way; **exemplify,** epitomize, fit the pattern; **emulate,** follow, hold up as a model, model oneself on

ADJS 8 **model, exemplary,** precedential, typical, paradigmatic, representative, standard, normative, classic; ideal

9 **prototypal,** prototypic, prototypical, archetypal, archetypic, archetypical, antitypic, antitypical

787 DISSIMILARITY

NOUNS 1 **dissimilarity,** unsimilarity; **dissimilitude,** dissemblance, **unresemblance; unlikeness,** unsameness; **disparity,** diversity, divergence, gap, **contrast, difference** 780; nonuniformity 782; uncomparability, uncomparableness, incomparability, incomparableness, uncommensurableness, uncommensurability, incommensurableness, incommensurability, no resemblance, no common ground; culture gap; **disguise,** dissimilation, camouflage, masking; cosmetics; poor imitation, bad likeness *or* copy, botched copy, mere caricature *or* counterfeit

VERBS 2 **not resemble, bear no resemblance,** not look like, **not compare with; differ** 780.5; have little *or* nothing in common; diverge, deviate

3 disguise, dissimilate, camouflage; do a cosmetic job on; vary 852.6

ADJS 4 **dissimilar,** unsimilar, unresembling, unresemblant; **unlike, unalike,** unidentical; **disparate,** diverse, divergent, **contrasting, different** 780.7; nonuniform 782.3; scarcely like, hardly like, a bit *or* mite different; **off,** a bit on the off side, offbeat <nf>; unmatched, odd, counter, out

5 **nothing like,** not a bit alike, not a bit of it, **nothing of the sort,** nothing of the kind, something else, something else again <nf>, different as night from day, quite another thing, cast in a different mold, not the same thing at all; not so you could tell it *and* not that you would know it and **far from it** *and* far other <nf>; way off, away off, a mile off, way out, no such thing, no such a thing <nf>

6 **uncomparable,** not comparable, not to be compared, incomparable; incommensurable, uncommensurable, uncommensurate, incommensurate; unrelated, extraneous

ADVS 7 **dissimilarly, differently** 780.10, with a difference, disparately, contrastingly

788 AGREEMENT

NOUNS 1 **agreement, accord** 455, accordance; **concord,** concordance; **harmony, cooperation** 450, peace 464, *rapport* <Fr>, concert, consort, **consonance,** unisonance, **unison,** union, chorus, oneness; **correspondence,** coincidence, intersection, overlap, parallelism, symmetry, tally, equivalence 778.1; congeniality, compatibility, affinity; **conformity,** conformance, conformation, uniformity 781; congruity, congruence, congruency; **consistency,** self-consistency, coherence; synchronism, sync <nf>, timing; **assent** 332

2 understanding, entente; mutual *or* cordial understanding, consortium, *entente cordiale* <Fr>; **compact** 437

3 <general agreement> consensus, consentaneity, consentaneousness, *consensus omnium* <L, consent of all> *and consensus gentium* <L, consent of the people>, sense, **unanimity** 332.5; **likemindedness,** meeting *or* intersection *or* confluence of minds, sense of the meeting; family feeling; good vibrations <nf>

4 adjustment, adaptation, mutual adjustment, **compromise,** coaptation, arbitration, arbitrament; **regulation,** attunement, harmonization, **coordination,** accommodation, squaring, integration, assimilation; reconciliation, reconcilement, synchronization; consensus-building *or* -seeking

5 fitness *or* fittedness, **suitability, appropriateness,** propriety, admissibility; **aptness,** aptitude, qualification; **relevance** 775.4, felicity, appositeness, applicability

VERBS **6 agree, accord** 455.2, **harmonize, concur** 332.9, have no problem with, go along with <nf>, **cooperate** 450.3, **correspond, conform,** coincide, parallel, intersect, overlap, **match,** tally, hit, register, lock, interlock, check <nf>, square, dovetail, jibe <nf>; **be consistent,** cohere, stand *or* hold *or* hang together, fall in together, fit together, chime, chime with, chime in with; **assent** 332.8, come to an agreement 332.10, be of one *or* the same *or* like mind, subscribe to, see eye to eye, sing in chorus, have a meeting of the minds, climb on the bandwagon; **go together,** go with, conform with, be uniform with, square with, sort *or* assort with, go on all fours with, consist with, register with, answer *or* respond to

7 <make agree> **harmonize,** coordinate, bring into line, accord, make uniform 781.4, equalize 790.6, similarize, assimilate, homologize; pull together; **adjust, set,** regulate, **accommodate, reconcile,** synchronize, sync <nf>; adapt, fit, tailor, measure, proportion, adjust to, trim to, cut to, gear to, key to; fix, **rectify**, true, true up, right, set right, make plumb; **tune,** attune, put in tune

8 suit, fit, suit *or* fit to a tee, fit like a glove, **qualify, do,** serve, answer, be OK <nf>, do the job *and* do the trick *and* fill the bill *and* cut the mustard <nf>

ADJS **9 agreeing, in agreement; in accord, concurring,** positive, affirmative, in rapport, *en rapport* <Fr>, **in harmony,** in accordance, in sync <nf>, **at one,** on all fours, of one *or* the same *or* like mind, **likeminded,** consentient, consentaneous, **unanimous** 332.15, unisonous *or* unisonant; **harmonious,** accordant, **concordant,** consonant; **consistent,** self-consistent; uniform, coherent, conformable, of a piece, equivalent, **coinciding** 778.8, coincident, corresponding *or* correspondent; answerable, reconcilable; commensurate, proportionate; **congruous,** congruent; **agreeable,** congenial, compatible, cooperating *or* cooperative 450.5, coexisting *or* coexistent, symbiotic; **synchronized,** synchronous, synchronic; empathetic

10 apt, apposite, appropriate, suitable; applicable, relevant, pertinent, likely, sortable, seasonable, opportune; **fitting,** befitting, **suiting,** becoming; **fit,** fitted, qualified, **suited,** adapted, geared, tailored, dovetailing, meshing; **right,** just right, well-chosen, **pat,** happy, felicitous, just what the doctor ordered <nf>; to the point, to the purpose, *ad rem* <L>, *à propos* <Fr>, **apropos**, on the button *and* on the money <nf>, spot-on <Brit nf>

ADVS **11 in step,** in concert, **in unison,** in chorus, **in line, in conformity, in keeping,** hand in glove, just right; with it <nf>; **unanimously, as one, with one voice, harmoniously,** concordantly, consonantly, in synchronization, in sync <nf>, **by consensus;** agreeably, congenially, compatibly; fittingly

PHRS **12** that's it, that's the thing, that's just the thing, that's the very thing, that's the idea *and* that's the ticket <nf>; right on <nf>; touché

789 DISAGREEMENT

NOUNS **1 disagreement, discord,** discordance *or* discordancy; **disaccord** 456, disaccordance, inaccordance; disunity, disunion; **disharmony,** unharmoniousness; dissonance, dissidence; **jarring,** clashing; **difference** 780, **variance,** divergence, diversity; **disparity,** discrepancy, inequality; antagonism, **opposition** 451, **conflict,** controversy, faction, oppugnancy, repugnance, dissension 456.3, argumentation 935.4; **dissent** 333, negation 335, contradiction; parting of the ways

2 inconsistency, incongruity, asymmetry, inconsonance, incoherence; **incompatibility,** irreconcilability, incommensurability; disproportion, disproportionateness, nonconformity *or* unconformity, nonconformability *or* unconformability, heterogeneity, heterodoxy, unorthodoxy, heresy; self-contradiction, paradox, antinomy, oxymoron, **ambiguity** 539.2, ambivalence, equivocality, equivocalness, mixed message *or* signal

3 unfitness, inappropriateness, unsuitability, impropriety; **inaptness,** inaptitude, **inappositeness, irrelevance** *or* irrelevancy, infelicity, uncongeniality, inapplicability, inadmissibility; abnormality, anomaly; **maladjustment,** misjoining, misjoinder; mismatch, mismatchment; misalliance, *mésalliance* <Fr>

4 misfit, nonconformist, individualist, inner-directed person, oddball <nf>; **freak,** sport, anomaly; naysayer, crosspatch, dissenter; a fish out of water, a square peg in a round hole <nf>

VERBS **5 disagree, differ** 780.5, vary, not see eye-to-eye, be at cross-purposes, tangle assholes <nf>, **disaccord** 456.8, **conflict,** clash, **jar,** jangle, jostle, collide, square off, cross swords, break, break off; **mismatch,** mismate, mismarry, misally; part company, split up; **dissent** 333.4, agree to disagree, object, **negate** 335.3, **contradict,** counter; be *or* march out of step

ADJS **6 disagreeing, differing** 780.7, **discordant** 456.15, disaccordant; dissonant, dissident; **inharmonious,** unharmonious, disharmonious; discrepant, disproportionate; divergent, variant; at variance, **at odds,** at war, at daggers drawn, at opposite poles, at loggerheads, at cross-purposes; **hostile,** antipathetic, antagonistic, repugnant; inaccordant, out of accord, out of whack <nf>; **jarring,** clashing, grating, jangling; **contradictory, contrary; disagreeable,** cross, cranky, disputatious, ornery <nf>, negative, uncongenial, incompatible; immiscible <chem>

7 inappropriate, inapt, unapt, inapposite, misplaced, **irrelevant,** malapropos, *mal à propos* <Fr>; **unsuited,** ill-suited; **unfitted,** ill-fitted; **maladjusted,** unadapted, ill-adapted; ill-sorted, ill-assorted, ill-chosen; ill-matched, ill-mated, mismatched, mismated, mismarried, misallied; **unfit,** inept, unqualified; unfitting, unbefitting; **unsuitable,** improper, **unbecoming,** unseemly; infelicitous, inapplicable, inadmissible; **unseasonable, untimely,** ill-timed; **out of place,** out of line, out of keeping, out of character, out of proportion, out of joint, out of tune, out of time, out of season, out of its element

8 inconsistent, incongruous, inconsonant, inconsequent, incoherent, **incompatible,** irreconcilable; incommensurable, incommensurate; disproportionate, out of proportion, self-contradictory, paradoxical, oxymoronic, **absurd; abnormal,** anomalous; misfiting; ambivalent, ambiguous

9 nonconformist, individualistic, inner-directed, perverse; **unorthodox,** heterodox, heretical

790 EQUALITY

NOUNS **1 equality, parity,** par, equation, **identity** 778.1; equivalence *or* equivalency, convertibility, **correspondence,** parallelism, equipollence, coequality; **likeness,** levelness, evenness, coextension; **balance,** poise, equipoise, **equilibrium,** equiponderance; symmetry, proportion; level playing field; **justice** 649, equity, equal rights

2 equating, equation; equalizing, equilibration, evening, evening up; coordination, integration, accommodation, adjustment; **even break** *and* fair shake <nf>, affirmative action, equal opportunity

3 the same 778.3; **tie, draw, standoff** *and* Mexican standoff *and* wash *and* dead heat <nf>, stalemate, deadlock, impasse, neck-and-neck race, photo finish, even money; tied *or* knotted score, deuce; a distinction without a difference, six of one and half a dozen of the other, Tweedledum and Tweedledee

4 equal, match, mate, twin, fellow, **like, equivalent,** opposite number, counterpart, answer <nf>, vis à vis, equipollent, coequal, parallel, ditto <nf>; synonym; **peer,** compeer, colleague, peer group

VERBS **5 equal, match, rival, correspond, be even-steven,** be tantmount to, be equal to; **keep pace with, keep step with, run abreast; amount to,** come to, come down to, run to, reach, touch; **measure up to,** come up to, stack up with <nf>, match up with; lie on a level with, **balance, parallel,** ditto <nf>; break even <nf>; **tie, draw,** knot; go shares, go halves, go Dutch

6 equalize; equate; even, equal out, equal, even up, even off, square, level, level out, level off, make both ends meet, synchronize; **balance,** strike a balance, poise, balance out, balance the accounts, balance the books; **compensate,** make up for, counterpoise; countervail, counterbalance, cancel; coordinate, integrate, proportion; fit, accommodate, adjust

ADJS **7 equal, equalized,** like, **alike, even,** level, par, **on a par,** at par, at parity, au pair, commensurate, proportionate, flush; on the same level, on the same plane, on the same *or* equal footing; on terms of equality, **on even** *or* **equal terms,** on even ground; on a level, on a level playing field, on a footing, in the same boat; **square,** quits, zero-sum, even-steven <nf>; half-and-half, **fifty-fifty;** nip and tuck, **drawn, tied,** neck-and-neck <nf>, abreast, too close to call, deadlocked, stalemated, knotted

8 equivalent, tantamount, equiparant, equipollent, coequal, coordinate; **identical** 778.7; corresponding *or* correspondent; convertible, much the same, as broad as long, neither more nor less, **all one,** all the same, neither here nor there

9 balanced, poised, apoise, **on an even keel**; equibalanced, equiponderant *or* equiponderous

10 equisized, equidimensional, equiproportional, equispaced; equiangular, isogonic, isometric; equilateral, equisided; coextensive

ADVS **11 equally, correspondingly, proportionately,** equivalently, **evenly; identically** 778.9; without distinction, indifferently; to the same degree, *ad eundem* <L>; as, **so;** as well; to all intents and purposes, other things being equal, *ceteris paribus* <L>; as much as to say

12 to a standoff <nf>, to a tie *or* draw

791 INEQUALITY

NOUNS **1 inequality, disparity, unevenness, contrariety** 779, **difference** 780; **irregularity,** nonuniformity 782, heterogeneity; **disproportion,** asymmetry; **unbalance,** imbalance, disequilibrium, overbalance, inclination of the balance, overcompensation, tippiness; **inadequacy,** insufficiency, shortcoming; **odds,** handicap; **injustice,** inequity, tilting of the scales, unfair discrimination, second-class citizenship, untouchability; unfair advantage, loaded dice

VERBS 2 **unequalize,** disproportion
3 **unbalance,** disbalance, disequilibrate, overbalance, overcompensate, **throw off balance,** upset, skew, destabilize

ADJS 4 **unequal,** disparate, **uneven; irregular** 782.3; disproportionate, **out of proportion,** skew, skewed, asymmetric *or* asymmetrical; mismatched *or* ill-matched, ill-sorted; **inadequate,** insufficient; at a disadvantage
5 **unbalanced, ill-balanced,** overbalanced, off-balance, tippy, listing, heeling, leaning, canting, top-heavy, off-center; **lopsided,** slaunchways *and* cockeyed *and* skewgee *and* skygodlin <nf>, skew-whiff <Brit nf>; **unstable,** unsteady, tender <nautical>

ADVS 6 **unequally,** disparately, disproportionately, variously, **unevenly;** nonuniformly 782.4

792 WHOLE

NOUNS 1 **whole, totality, entirety,** collectivity; complex; integration, embodiment; **unity, integrity, wholeness;** organic unity, oneness; integer
2 **total, sum,** sum total, sum and substance, **the amount,** whole *or* gross amount, grand total; entity
3 **all, the whole, the entirety, everything,** all the above *or* all of the above <nf>, the aggregate, the assemblage, one and all, all and sundry, each and every <nf>, complete works; **package,** set, complement, package deal; **the lot,** the corpus, all she wrote <nf>, **the ensemble; be-all,** be-all and end-all, beginning and end, A to Z, A to izzard, the whole range *or* spectrum, length and breadth, sum and substance; everything from soup to nuts *and* everything but the kitchen sink <nf>; grand design, world view, big picture
4 <nf terms> **whole bunch, whole mess, whole caboodle, the kit and caboodle, whole kit and caboodle,** whole kit and boodle, whole bit *or* shtick, whole megillah, **whole shooting match,** whole hog, whole animal , **whole deal,** whole schmear, **whole shebang,** whole works, the works, the full monty <Brit nf>, whole ball of wax, whole show, whole nine yards
5 **wholeness,** totality, **completeness** 794, **unity, fullness,** inclusiveness, exhaustiveness, comprehensiveness; holism, holistic *or* total approach; universality
6 **major part, best part,** better part, **most; majority,** generality, plurality; **bulk, mass,** body, main body; **lion's share; substance,** gist, meat, essence, thrust, gravamen

VERBS 7 **form** *or* **make a whole,** constitute a whole; **integrate,** unite, form a unity
8 **total, amount to, come to, run to** *or* **into,** mount up to, add up to, tot *or* tot up to <nf>, tote *or* tote up to <nf>, reckon up to <nf>, aggregate to; aggregate, unitize; **number, comprise,** contain, encompass

ADJS 9 <not partial> **whole, total, entire,** aggregate, gross, all; integral, integrated; **one,** one and indivisible; **inclusive,** all-inclusive, **exhaustive,** comprehensive, omnibus, all-embracing, across-the-board, global; holistic; universal
10 intact, untouched, undamaged 1002.8, all in one piece <nf>, unimpaired, virgin, pristine, unspoiled, pure
11 undivided, uncut, unsevered, unclipped, uncropped, unshorn; **undiminished,** unreduced, complete
12 **unabridged,** uncondensed, unexpurgated

ADVS 13 <not partially> **wholly, entirely,** all; **totally,** *in toto* <L>, from start to finish, from soup to nuts <nf>, from A to Z, from A to izzard, across the board; **altogether, all put together,** in its entirety, *tout ensemble* <Fr>; **in all,** on all counts, in all respects, at large; **as a whole, in the aggregate,** in the lump, in the gross, in bulk, in the mass, *en masse* <Fr>, *en bloc* <Fr>; **collectively, corporately,** bodily, in a body, as a body; lock, stock, and barrel; hook, line, and sinker

14 **on the whole, in the long run, over the long haul, all in all,** to all intents and purposes, on balance, **by and large, in the main, mainly, mostly, chiefly,** substantially, essentially, effectually, **for the most part,** almost entirely, for all practical purposes, **virtually;** approximately, nearly, all but

793 PART

NOUNS **1 part, portion, fraction;** percentage; **division** 802.1; **share,** parcel, dole, quota, piece *or* piece of the action <nf>; cut *and* slice *and* vigorish <nf>; **section,** sector, **segment;** quarter, quadrant; **item,** detail, particular, installment; **subdivision,** subset, subgroup, subspecies; detachment, contingent; focus group; **cross section,** sample, random sample, sampling; **component** 796.2, module, constituent, ingredient; **adjunct** 254; **remainder** 256; minority

2 <part of writing> section, front *or* back matter, prologue, epilogue, foreword, preface, introduction, afterword, text, chapter, verse, article; sentence, clause, phrase, segment, string, constituent, paragraph, passage; number, book, fascicle; sheet, folio, page, signature, gathering

3 piece, particle, bit, scrap 248.3, bite, **fragment, morsel, crumb,** shard, potsherd, snatch, snack, appetizer; **cut,** cutting, clip, clipping, paring, shaving, rasher, snip, snippet, chip, slice, collop, dollop, scoop; **tatter, shred,** stitch; **splinter,** sliver; **shiver, smithereen** <nf>; **lump,** gob <nf>, gobbet, **hunk, chunk; stump,** butt, end, butt-end, fag-end, tail-end; modicum 248.2, moiety; bits and pieces, odds and ends; sound bite, outtake

4 member, organ; appendage; **limb; branch,** imp, bough, twig, sprig, spray, switch; runner, tendril; **offshoot,** ramification, scion, spur; **arm** 906.5, **leg,** tail; hand 474.4; **wing,** pinion; lobe, lobule, hemisphere; facet, feature, integrant, integral part

5 dose, portion; slug *and* shot *and* nip *and* snort *and* dram <nf>; helping

VERBS **6 separate,** apportion, share, share out, distribute, cut, cut up, slice, slice up, divide 802.18; **analyze** 801.6

ADJS **7 partial,** part; **fractional,** sectional, componential, partitive; segmentary, segmental, modular; **fragmentary;** incomplete 795.4, open-ended

ADVS **8 partly, partially,** part, **in part**

9 piece by piece, bit by bit, part by part, **little by little,** inch by inch, foot by foot, drop by drop; **piecemeal,** piecewise, bitwise, inchmeal, by inchmeal; **by degrees,** by inches; **by** *or* **in snatches,** by *or* in installments, in lots, in small doses, in driblets, in dribs and drabs; in detail

794 COMPLETENESS

NOUNS **1 completeness, totality; wholeness** 792.5, **entireness, entirety; unity,** integrity, integrality, undividedness, intactness, untouchedness, unbrokenness; solidity, solidarity; **thoroughness,** exhaustiveness, unstintedness, inclusiveness, comprehensiveness, universality; pervasiveness, ubiquity, omnipresence; **universe,** cosmos, plenum

2 fullness, full; **amplitude, plenitude;** impletion, **repletion,** plethora; saturation, saturation point, satiety, congestion

3 full measure, fill, full house; max <nf>; **load, capacity, complement,** lading, **charge;** the whole bit <nf>; bumper, brimmer; bellyful *and* snootful <nf>, skinful *or* mouthful <nf>; **crush,** cram <nf>, jam-up <nf>

4 completion, fulfillment, consummation, culmination, perfection, realization, actualization, fruition, **accomplishment** 407, topping-off, closure

5 limit, end 820, **extremity,** extreme, **acme,** apogee, climax, **maximum,** max <nf>, ceiling, **peak,** summit,

pinnacle, crown, top; **utmost,** uttermost, utmost extent, highest degree, nth degree *or* power, *ne plus ultra* <L>; **all, the whole** 792.3, the whole hog <nf>

VERBS **6** <make whole> **complete,** bring to completion *or* fruition, mature; **fill in, fill out,** piece out, top off, eke *or* eke out, round out; **make up,** make good, replenish, refill; **accomplish** 407.4, fulfill

7 **fill, charge, load,** lade, freight, weight; **stuff, wad,** pad, **pack,** crowd, **cram,** jam, jam-pack, ram in, chock; **fill up,** fill to the brim, brim, top up *or* top off, fill to overflowing, fill the measure of; supercharge, saturate, satiate, congest; overfill 993.15, make burst at the seams, surfeit

8 <be thorough> **go to all lengths, go all out, go the limit** <nf>, go the whole way, **go the whole hog** <nf>, cover a lot of ground, make a federal case of *and* make a big deal of *and* do up brown *and* do with a vengeance <nf>, **see it through** <nf>, follow out *or* up, follow *or* prosecute to a conclusion; leave nothing undone, not overlook a bet *and* use every trick in the book <nf>; **move heaven and earth, leave no stone unturned;** put the finishing touches to

ADJS **9** **complete, whole, total,** global, **entire,** intact, solid; **full, full-fledged,** full-dress, **full-scale;** full-grown, mature, matured, ripe, developed; **uncut,** unabbreviated, undiminished, unexpurgated

10 **thorough, thoroughgoing,** thorough-paced, exhaustive, intensive, broad-based, wall-to-wall <nf>, house-to-house *and* door-to-door <nf>, A-to-Z, comprehensive, all-embracing, all-encompassing, omnibus, radical, sweeping; **pervasive,** all-pervading, ubiquitous, omnipresent, **universal; unmitigated, unqualified, unconditional,** unrestricted, unreserved, **all-out,** balls-out <Br>, wholesale, whole-hog <nf>; **out-and-out, through-and-through,** outright, downright, straight; congenital, born, **consummate,** unmitigated, unalloyed, perfect, veritable, egregious, deep-dyed, dyed-in-the-wool; **utter, absolute, total; sheer,** clear, clean, **pure,** plumb <nf>, **plain,** regular <nf>

11 **full,** filled, **replete,** plenary, capacity, flush, round; **brimful,** brimming; **chock-full,** chock-a-block, chuck-full, **cram-full,** topful, no room to spar; **jam-full, jam-packed, overcrowded;** stuffed, overstuffed, **packed, crammed,** *farci* <Fr>; **swollen** 259.13, bulging, bursting, bursting at the seams, ready to burst, full to bursting, fit to bust <nf>; as full as a tick, packed like sardines *or* herrings; standing room only *or* SRO; **saturated,** satiated, soaked; fully laden, coming out of one's ears; congested; overfull 993.20, surfeited

12 **fraught,** freighted, **laden, loaded, charged,** burdened; heavy-laden; full-laden, full-fraught, full-charged, super-charged

13 **completing, fulfilling,** filling; completive *or* completory, consummative *or* consummatory, culminative, perfective; **complementary,** complemental

ADVS **14** **completely, totally,** globally, **entirely, wholly, fully,** integrally, roundly, **altogether,** hundred percent, **exhaustively,** inclusively, comprehensively, bag and baggage *and* lock, stock, and barrel <nf>; **unconditionally,** unrestrictedly, unreservedly, with no strings attached, no ifs, ands, or buts; **one and all;** outright, *tout à fait* <Fr>; **thoroughly,** inside out <nf>; in full, in full measure; to the hilt

15 **absolutely, perfectly, quite,** right, stark, clean, sheer, plumb <nf>, plain; irretrievably, unrelievedly, irrevocably

16 **utterly, to the utmost,** all the way, **all out,** flat out <Brit>, *à outrance* <Fr>, *à toute outrance* <Fr>, hammer and tongs and tooth and nail <nf>, **to the full, to the limit,** to the max <nf>, mondo <nf>, to the backbone, to the marrow, to the nth degree *or* power, to the sky *or* skies, to the top of one's bent, **to a fare-thee-well,** to a fare-you-well *or* fare-ye-well, to beat the band *or* the Dutch *and* nine ways to Sunday <nf>, with a vengeance, all hollow <nf>

17 **throughout, all over,** overall, **inside and out, through and through;** through thick and thin, down to the ground <nf>, **from the ground up,** from the word 'go' *and* from the git-go <nf>; **to the end** *or* **bitter end,** to the death; **at full length,** *in extenso* <L>, *ad infinitum* <L>; every inch, every whit, every bit; root and branch, head and shoulders, heart and soul; to the brim, to the hilt, neck deep, up to the ears, up to the eyes; **in every respect,** in all respects, you name it <nf>; **on all counts,** at all points, for good and all

18 **from beginning to end, from start to finish,** from end to end, **from first to last, from A to Z,** from A to izzard, from soup to nuts *and* from hell to breakfast <nf>, from cover to cover; **from top to bottom,** *de fond en comble* <Fr>; from top to toe, **from head to foot,** *a capite ad calcem* <L>, cap-a-pie; **from stem to stern,** from clew to earing, fore and aft; from soup to nuts <nf>

795 INCOMPLETENESS

NOUNS 1 **incompleteness,** incompletion; **deficiency,** defectiveness, imperfection, **inadequacy;** underdevelopment, hypoplasia, **immaturity,** callowness, arrestment; **sketchiness,** scrappiness, patchiness; short measure *or* weight; lick and a promise

2 <part lacking> **deficiency,** want, **lack, need, deficit,** defect, **shortage,** shortfall, underage; wantage, outage, ullage, slippage; defalcation, arrearage, default; **omission,** gap, hiatus, hole, vacuum, break, lacuna, discontinuity 813, interval

VERBS 3 **lack** 992.7, want, want for; fall short 911.2; be arrested, underdevelop, undergrow

ADJS 4 **incomplete, uncompleted, deficient,** defective, unfinished, imperfect, unperfected, **inadequate; undeveloped,** underdeveloped, undergrown, stunted, hypoplastic, **immature,** callow, infant, arrested, embryonic, **wanting, lacking,** needing, missing, **partial,** part, failing; in default, in arrear *or* arrears; **in short supply,** scanty; **short,** scant, shy <nf>; **sketchy,** patchy, scrappy; left hanging

5 **mutilated,** garbled, hashed, **mangled, butchered,** docked, hacked, lopped, truncated, castrated, cut short; abridged

ADVS 6 **incompletely, partially,** by halves, by *or* in half measures, in installments, in *or* by bits and pieces; **deficiently,** imperfectly, inadequately

796 COMPOSITION

<manner of being composed>

NOUNS 1 **composition, constitution, construction,** formation, fabrication, fashioning, shaping, organization; **embodiment,** incorporation, incarnation; **make, makeup,** getup *or* setup <nf>; **building,** buildup, structure, structuring, shaping-up, compiling; **assembly,** assemblage, putting *or* piecing together; synthesis, syneresis; **combination** 805; **compound** 797.5; **junction** 800.1; **mixture** 797

2 **component, constituent, ingredient,** integrant, makings and fixings <nf>, **element, factor, part** 793, player, module, part and parcel; appurtenance, adjunct 254; **feature,** aspect, specialty, circumstance, detail, item

VERBS 3 **compose, constitute,** construct, fabricate; **incorporate,** embody, incarnate; **form, organize,** structure, shape, shape up; **enter into,** go into, go to make up; **make, make up, build,** build up, assemble, put *or* piece together, compile; **consist of,** be a feature of, form a part of, combine *or* unite in, merge in;

consist, be made up of, be constituted of, contain; **synthesize; combine** 805.3; join 800.5; **mix**

ADJS **4 composed of,** formed of, **made of,** made up of, made out of, compact of, consisting of; composing, comprising, constituting, including, inclusive of, containing, incarnating, embodying, subsuming; contained in, embodied in

5 component, constituent, modular, integrant, integral; **formative,** elementary

797 MIXTURE

NOUNS **1** mixture, mixing, blending; **admixture,** composition, commixture, immixture, intermixture, **mingling,** minglement, commingling *or* comminglement, intermingling *or* interminglement, interlarding *or* interlardment; **eclecticism,** syncretism; **pluralism,** melting pot, multiculturism *or* multiculturalism, ethnic *or* racial *or* cultural diversity; **fusion,** interfusion, conflation; amalgamation, **integration,** alloyage, coalescence; **merger, combination** 805

2 imbuement, impregnation, infusion, suffusion, decoction, infiltration, instillment, instillation, permeation, pervasion, interpenetration, penetration; saturation, steeping, soaking, marination

3 adulteration, corruption, contamination, denaturalization, **pollution, doctoring** <nf>; fortifying, lacing, spiking <nf>; **dilution,** cutting <nf>, watering, watering down; debasement, bastardizing

4 crossbreeding, crossing, **interbreeding,** miscegenation; **hybridism,** hybridization, mongrelism, mongrelization; intermarriage

5 compound, mixture, admixture, intermixture, immixture, commixture, **composite, blend,** meld, composition, confection, concoction, **combination,** combo <nf>, ensemble, marriage; amalgam, alloy; paste, magma; cocktail

6 hodgepodge, hotchpotch, hotchpot; **medley, miscellany,** mélange, pastiche, **conglomeration, assortment,** assemblage, mixed bag, ragbag, grab bag, olio, *olla podrida* <Sp>, **scramble, jumble,** mingle-mangle, **mix,** mishmash, **mess,** can of worms <nf>, dog's breakfast <Can nf>, mare's nest, rat's nest, hurrah's nest <nautical nf>, hash, patchwork, salad, gallimaufry, salmagundi, sundries, **potpourri,** stew, gumbo, sauce, slurry, omnium-gatherum, Noah's ark, **odds and ends,** oddments, all sorts, everything but the kitchen sink <nf>, all colors of the rainbow, broad spectrum, what you will

7 <slight admixture> **tinge, tincture, touch, dash, smack,** taint, tinct, tint, **trace,** vestige, hint, inkling, intimation, soupçon, suspicion, suggestion, whiff, modicum, thought, shade, tempering; sprinkling, seasoning, sauce, spice, infusion

8 hybrid, crossbreed, cross, mixed-blood, mixblood, **half-breed,** half-bred, half blood, half-caste; **mongrel,** cur; *ladino* <Sp>; mustee *or* mestee, *mestizo* <Sp>, *mestiza* <Sp fem>, *métis* <Fr>, *métisse* <Fr fem>; Eurasian; **mulatto,** high yellow <nf>, quadroon, quintroon, octoroon; sambo, zambo; griffe; zebrule, zebrass, cattalo, mule, hinny, liger, tigon; tangelo, citrange, plumcot; alley cat

9 mixer, blender, beater, agitator, food processor, shaker; cement mixer, eggbeater, churn; homogenizer, colloid mill, emulsifier; crucible, melting pot

VERBS **10 mix,** admix, commix, immix, **intermix, mingle,** bemingle, commingle, immingle, **intermingle,** interlace, interweave, intertwine, interlard, intersperse, interleave; syncretize; **blend,** interblend, stir in; **amalgamate, integrate,** alloy, coalesce, **fuse, merge,** meld, compound, compose, conflate, concoct; **combine** 805.3; mix up, hash, stir up, **scramble,** conglomerate, shuffle, **jumble,** jumble up, mingle-mangle, throw *or* toss together, entangle; knead, work; homogenize, emulsify

11 **imbue,** imbrue, **infuse,** suffuse, transfuse, breathe, **instill,** infiltrate, **impregnate, permeate,** pervade, penetrate, leaven; **tinge, tincture,** entincture, temper, color, dye, flavor, season, dredge, besprinkle; **saturate,** steep, decoct, brew

12 **adulterate, corrupt,** contaminate, **debase,** infect, denaturalize, pollute, denature, bastardize, **tamper with, doctor** *and* doctor up <nf>; **fortify,** spike <nf>, pep up <nf>, lace; **dilute,** cut <nf>, water, water down <nf>

13 **hybridize, crossbreed, cross, interbreed,** miscegenate, mongrelize

ADJS **14** **mixed, mingled,** blended, compounded, amalgamated; **combined** 805.5; **composite,** compound, **complex,** many-sided, multifaceted, intricate; **conglomerate,** pluralistic, multiracial, multicultural, multiethnic, multinational, heterogeneous, varied, **miscellaneous,** medley, motley, dappled, patchy, sundry, divers; promiscuous, indiscriminate, **scrambled, jumbled,** thrown together; half-and-half, fifty-fifty <nf>; amphibious; equivocal, **ambiguous,** ambivalent, ironic; syncretic, eclectic

15 **hybrid, mongrel,** interbred, **crossbred,** crossed, cross; **half-breed,** half-bred, half-blooded, half-caste

16 miscible, mixable, assimilable, integrable

798 SIMPLICITY

<freedom from mixture or complexity>

NOUNS **1** **simplicity, purity,** simpleness, **plainness,** no frills, starkness, severity; unmixedness, monism; **unadulteration,** unsophistication, unspoiledness, intactness, fundamentality, elementarity, primitiveness *or* primitivity, primariness, naturalness; **singleness,** oneness, unity, integrity, homogeneity, uniformity 781; homeyness, unpretentiousness; unadornment; rusticity

2 **simplification,** streamlining, refinement, purification, distillation; **disentanglement,** disinvolvement; uncluttering, unscrambling, unsnarling, unknotting; stripping, stripping away *or* down, paring down, narrowing, confining, bracketing; **analysis** 801; deconstruction

3 **oversimplification, oversimplicity,** oversimplifying; **simplism,** reductivism; intellectual childishness *or* immaturity, conceptual crudity

VERBS **4** **simplify,** streamline, **reduce,** reduce to elements *or* essentials, factorize; purify, refine, distill; strip, strip down; narrow, confine, bracket, zero in <nf>; streamline; oversimplify; **analyze** 801.6

5 **disinvolve,** disintricate, unmix, disembroil, **disentangle,** untangle, **unscramble, unsnarl,** unknot, untwist, unbraid, unweave, untwine, unwind, uncoil, unthread, **unravel,** ravel; **unclutter,** clarify, clear up, disambiguate, sort out, get to the core *or* nub *or* essence

ADJS **6** **simple, plain,** bare, bare-bones and no-frills <nf>, mere; **single,** uniform, homogeneous, of a piece; **pure,** simon-pure, pure and simple; **essential,** elementary, indivisible, **primary,** primal, primitive, prime, pristine, **irreducible, fundamental,** basic, rustic; undifferentiable *or* undifferentiated, undifferenced, monolithic; **austere**, chaste, unadorned, uncluttered, spare, stark, severe; homely, homespun, grass-roots, back-to-nature, bread-and-butter, down-home *and* vanilla *or* plain-vanilla *and* white-bread <nf>; beginning, entry-level; common *or* garden, everyday; unpretentious; unadorned, natural

7 **unmixed, unmingled,** unblended, **uncombined,** uncompounded; unleavened; **unadulterated,** unspoiled, untouched, intact, virgin, uncorrupted, unsophisticated, unalloyed, untinged, undiluted, unfortified; **clear,** clarified, purified, refined, **distilled,** rectified; **neat, straight,** absolute, sheer, naked, bare

8 **uncomplicated, uninvolved,** incomplex, straightforward

9 **simplified,** streamlined, stripped down

10 **oversimplified,** oversimple; **simplistic,** reductive; intellectually childish *or* immature, conceptually crude

ADVS 11 **simply, plainly, purely;** merely, barely; **singly, solely,** only, **alone,** exclusively, just, simply and solely

799 COMPLEXITY

NOUNS 1 **complexity, complication, involvement,** complexness, involution, convolution, tortuousness, Byzantinism, *chinoiserie* <Fr>, tanglement, **entanglement,** perplexity, **intricacy,** intricateness, ramification, crabbedness, technicality, subtlety

2 **complex,** perplex <nf>, tangle, tangled skein, **mess** *and* snafu *and* fuck-up <nf>, ravel, snarl, snarl-up; knot, Gordian knot; **maze,** meander, Chinese puzzle, **labyrinth;** webwork, mesh; **wilderness, jungle,** morass, quagmire; Rube Goldberg contraption, Heath Robinson device <Brit>, wheels within wheels; mare's nest, rat's nest, hurrah's nest <nautical nf>, can of worms <nf>, snake pit; hard nut to crack, riddle of the Sphinx, squaring the circle

VERBS 3 **complicate, involve, perplex,** ramify; **confound, confuse,** muddle, **mix up,** mess up *and* ball up *and* bollix up *and* screw up *and* foul up *and* fuck up *and* snafu *and* muck up *and* louse up <nf>, implicate; **tangle,** entangle, embrangle, **snarl, snarl up,** ravel, knot, tie in knots

ADJS 4 **complex, complicated,** many-faceted, multifarious, ramified, perplexed, **confused,** confounded, **involved,** implicated, crabbed, **intricate,** elaborate, involuted, convoluted, multilayered, multilevel; **mixed up,** balled up *and* bollixed up *and* screwed up *and* loused up *and* fouled up *and* fucked up *and* snafued *and* mucked up *and* messed up *and* FUBAR <nf>; **tangled,** entangled, tangly, embrangled, **snarled,** knotted, matted, twisted, raveled; mazy, daedal, **labyrinthine,** labyrinthian, meandering; **devious,** roundabout, deep-laid, Byzantine, subtle

5 **inextricable,** irreducible, unknottable, unsolvable

800 JOINING

NOUNS 1 **joining, junction,** joinder, jointure, **connection, union,** unification, bond, bonding, connectedness *or* connectivity, conjunction, conjoining, conjugation, liaison, marriage, hookup <nf>, splice, tie, tie-up *and* tie-in <nf>, knotting, entanglement, commerce; merger, merging; symbiosis; **combination** 805; conglomeration, **aggregation,** agglomeration, congeries; **coupling,** copulation, accouplement, coupledness, **bracketing,** yoking, pairing, splicing, wedding; **linking,** linkup, linkage, bridging, **concatenation,** chaining, articulation, agglutination; **meeting,** meeting place *or* point, confluence, convergence, concurrence, concourse, gathering, massing, clustering; communication, intercommunication, intercourse

2 **interconnection,** interface, interjoinder, **interlinking,** interlocking, interdigitation; **interassociation,** interaffiliation

3 **fastening, attachment, affixation,** annexation; ligature, ligation, ligating; **binding,** bonding, gluing, sticking, tying, lashing, splicing, knotting, linking, trussing, girding, hooking, clasping, zipping, buckling, buttoning; knot ; adhesive 803.4; splice, bond, fastener, Velcro

4 **joint,** join, joining, **juncture, union, connection,** link, connecting link, **coupling, accouplement;** clinch, embrace; articulation <anatomy and botany>, symphysis <anatomy>; **pivot, hinge; knee; elbow; wrist; ankle; knuckle; hip; shoulder; neck,** cervix; ball-and-socket joint, pivot joint, hinged joint, gliding joint; toggle joint; connecting rod, tie rod; seam, suture, stitch, closure, mortise and tenon, miter, butt, scârf, dovetail, rabbet, weld; boundary, interface

VERBS 5 **put together, join,** conjoin, **unite,** unify, bond, **connect,** associate, league, band, merge, **assemble,** accumulate; **join up,** become a part of, associate oneself, enter into, come aboard <nf>; **gather,** mobilize, marshal, mass, amass, **collect,** conglobulate; **combine** 805.3; **couple,** pair, accouple, copulate, conjugate, marry, wed, tie the knot <nf>, **link,** link up, build bridges, yoke, knot, splice, tie, chain, bracket, ligate; **concatenate,** articulate, agglutinate; glue, tape, cement, solder, weld; **put together,** fix together, lay together, piece together, clap together, tack together, stick together, lump together, roll into one; bridge over *or* between, span; **include,** encompass, take in, cover, embrace, comprise

6 **interconnect, interjoin,** interface, mesh, intertie, interassociate, interaffiliate, **interlink,** interlock, interdigitate

7 **fasten, fix, attach, affix,** annex, put to, set to; graft, engraft; **secure,** anchor, moor; cement, knit, set, grapple, belay, **make fast;** clinch, clamp, cramp; tighten, trim, trice up, screw up; cinch *or* cinch up

8 **hook,** hitch; **clasp,** hasp, clip, snap; **button,** buckle, zipper; lock, latch; **pin,** skewer, peg, nail, nail up, tack, staple, toggle, screw, bolt, rivet; **sew,** stitch; **wedge,** jam, stick; rabbet, butt, scarf, mortise, miter, dovetail; batten, batten down; cleat; **hinge,** joint, articulate

9 **bind, tie,** brace, truss, **lash,** leash, rope, strap, lace, wire, chain; handcuff; **splice,** bend; **gird,** girt, belt, girth, girdle, band, cinch; **tie up,** bind up, do up, batten; **wrap,** wrap up, bundle; shrink-wrap; **bandage,** bandage up, swathe, swaddle

10 **yoke, hitch up,** hook up; harness, harness up; halter, bridle; saddle; tether, fetter

11 <be joined> **join, connect, unite, meet,** meet up, link up, merge, converge, **come together;** communicate, intercommunicate, network, interface; knit, grow together; cohere, adhere, hang *or* hold together, clinch, embrace

ADJS 12 **joint, combined,** joined, **conjoint,** conjunct, conjugate, corporate, compact, cooperative, cooperating; concurrent, coincident; inclusive, comprehensive; coherent

13 **joined, united, connected,** copulate, **coupled,** linked, knit, bridged, tightknit, knitted, bracketed, associated, conjoined, incorporated, integrated, **merged,** gathered, assembled, accumulated, **collected; associated,** joined up, on board; **allied,** leagued, banded together; hand-in-hand, hand-in-glove, intimate, liaising; unseparated, undivided; **wedded,** matched, married, paired, yoked, mated; **tied, bound,** knotted, spliced, lashed; yogic

14 **fast, fastened, fixed,** secure, firm, close, tight, set, zipped up; **bonded,** glued, cemented, taped; **jammed,** wedged, stuck, frozen, seized, seized up

15 **inseparable,** impartible, **indivisible,** undividable, indissoluble, inalienable, inseverable, bound up in *or* with

16 **joining, connecting,** meeting; **communicating,** intercommunicating; **connective,** connectional; conjunctive, combinative, combinatorial, copulative, linking, bridging, binding; yogic

17 jointed, articulate

ADVS 18 **jointly,** conjointly, corporately, **together; in common,** in partnership, mutually, in concord; **all together,** as one, in unison, in agreement, in harmony; concurrently, at once, at *or* in one fell swoop

19 **securely, firmly, fast,** tight; **inseparably,** indissolubly

801 ANALYSIS

NOUNS 1 **analysis,** analyzation, **breakdown,** breaking down, breakup, breaking up; anatomy, anatomizing, dissection; separation, **division, subdivision,** segmentation, reduction to elements *or* parts; chemical analysis, **assay *or*** assaying, resolution, titration, docimasy, qualitative analysis, quantitative analysis, volumetric analysis, gravimetric analysis; ultimate analysis, proximate analysis; microanalysis, semimicroanalysis; profiling; racial profiling

2 **itemization,** enumeration, detailing, breakout, isolation; outlining, schematization, blocking, blocking out; resolution; scansion, parsing

3 **classification, categorization, sorting,** taxonomy, sorting out, sifting, sifting out, grouping, factoring, winnowing, shakeout, pigeonholing, categorizing; **weighing, evaluation,** gauging, assessment, appraisal, position statement *or* paper, **judgment** 946; impact statement

4 **outline**, structural outline, **plan,** scheme, schema, chart, flow chart, graph; table, table of contents, index; **diagram,** block diagram, exploded view, **blueprint; catalog,** *catalogue raisonné* <Fr>

5 **analyst, analyzer, examiner** 938.16; taxonomist

VERBS 6 **analyze, break down,** break up, anatomize, dissect, atomize, unitize; **divide, subdivide,** segment; assay, titrate; separate, make discrete, isolate, reduce, reduce to elements, resolve

7 **itemize,** enumerate, factorize, number, detail, break out; **outline,** schematize, block out, diagram, graph, chart; resolve; scan, parse

8 **classify,** class, **categorize,** catalog, sort, sort out, sift, group, factor, winnow, thrash out; weigh, weigh up, **evaluate, judge,** gauge 946.9, assess, appraise 946.9

ADJS 9 **analytical,** analytic; segmental; classificatory, enumerative; schematic

ADVS 10 **analytically,** by parts *or* divisions *or* sections; by categories *or* types

802 SEPARATION

NOUNS 1 **separation, disjunction,** severalty, disjointure, disjointing, split-up, splitting-up, demerger, delinkage, disarticulation, **disconnection,** disconnectedness, discontinuity, incoherence, disengagement, disunion, nonunion, disassociation, segregation; **parting,** alienation, estrangement, **removal,** withdrawal, isolation, detachment, sequestration, abstraction; **subtraction** 255; divorce, divorcement; **division,** subdivision, partition, compartmentalization, segmentation, marking off; districting, zoning; **dislocation,** luxation; separability, partibility, dividableness, divisibility; separatism; **separateness,** discreteness, singleness, monism, unitariness

2 **severance,** disseverment *or* disseverance, **sunderance,** scission, fission, cleavage, dichotomy, parting; **cutting, slitting,** slashing, **splitting,** slicing; **rending, tearing,** ripping, laceration, hacking, chopping, butchering, mutilation; section, resection; **surgery**

3 **disruption, dissolution,** abruption, cataclasm; revolution 860; **disintegration** 806, breakup, crack-up, shattering, splintering, fragmentizing, fragmentation; **bursting,** dissilience *or* dissiliency; **scattering,** dispersal, diffusion; **stripping,** scaling, exfoliation

4 **break,** breakage, **breach,** burst, **rupture, fracture; crack,** cleft, **fissure, cut, split,** slit; slash, slice; **gap, rift,** rent, rip, tear; chip, splinter, scale; dividing line, caesura, solidus

5 **dissection, analysis** 801, vivisection, resolution, breakdown, diaeresis; anatomy

6 **disassembly, dismantlement,** taking down *or* apart, dismemberment, dismounting; undoing, unbuilding; **stripping,** stripping away *or* down, divestiture, divestment, defoliation, deprivation; disrobing, unclothing, doffing

7 **separator,** sieve, centrifuge, ultracentrifuge; creamer, cream separator; breaker, stripper, mincer; slicer, cutter, microtome; analyzer

VERBS 8 **separate, divide, disjoin, disunite,** draw apart, dissociate, disassociate, grow apart, **disjoint,** disengage, disarticulate, **disconnect;** uncouple, unyoke; **part,** cut the knot, **divorce,** estrange; **alien-**

ate, segregate, separate off, factor out, sequester, isolate, curtain off, shut off, set apart *or* aside, split off, cut off *or* out *or* loose *or* adrift; **withdraw, leave, depart,** take one's leave, cut out *and* split <nf>; pull out *or* away *or* back, stand apart *or* aside *or* aloof, step aside; subtract 255.9; delete 255.12; **expel,** eject, throw off *or* out, cast off *or* out

9 **come apart,** spring apart, fly apart, come unstuck, come unglued, come undone, come apart at the seams, **come** *or* **drop** *or* fall to pieces, **disintegrate, come to pieces,** go to pieces, fall apart, fall apart at the seams, fall to pieces, atomize, unitize, fragmentize, pulverize, break up, bust up <nf>, unravel; come *or* fall off, peel off, carry away; get loose, give way, start

10 **detach, remove,** disengage, take *or* lift off, doff; **unfasten, undo,** unattach, unfix; **free, release,** liberate, loose, unloose, unleash, unfetter; **unloosen,** loosen; cast off, weigh anchor; **unhook,** unhitch, unclasp, unclinch, unbuckle, unbutton, unsnap, unscrew, unpin, unbolt; **untie,** unbind, unknit, unbandage, unlace, unzip, unstrap, unchain; unstick, unglue

11 **sever, dissever,** cut off *or* away *or* loose, shear off, hack through, hack off, ax, amputate; **cleave, split,** fissure; sunder, cut in two, dichotomize, halve, bisect; **cut,** incise, carve, **slice,** pare, prune, trim, trim away, resect, excise 255.10; slit, snip, lance, scissor; **chop, hew,** hack, **slash;** gash, whittle, butcher; saw, jigsaw; **tear, rend,** rive, rend asunder

12 **break, burst,** bust <nf>, breach; **fracture, rupture; crack,** split, check, craze, fissure; snap; chip, scale, exfoliate

13 **shatter, splinter,** shiver, break to *or* into pieces, fragmentize, break to *or* into smithereens <nf>; **smash,** crush, crunch, squash, squish <nf>; **disrupt,** demolish, break up, smash up; **scatter,** disperse, diffuse; **fragment,** fission, atomize; **pulverize** 1051.9, grind, cut to pieces, mince, make mincemeat of, make hamburger of <nf>

14 **tear** *or* **rip apart,** take *or* pull apart, **pick** *or* **rip** *or* **tear to pieces,** tear to rags *or* tatters, **shred,** rip to shreds; **dismember,** tear limb from limb, draw and quarter; **mangle,** lacerate, mutilate, maim; skin, flay, strip, peel, denude, defoliate

15 **disassemble,** take apart *or* down, tear down; **dismantle, demolish,** dismount, unrig <nautical>

16 **disjoint,** unjoint, **unhinge,** disarticulate, **dislocate,** luxate, throw out of joint, unseat

17 **dissect, analyze** 801.6, vivisect, anatomize, break down

18 **apportion, portion,** section, partition, compartmentalize, segment; **divide,** divide up, divvy *and* divvy up <nf>, **parcel,** parcel up *or* out, **split,** split up, cut up, subdivide; district, zone

19 **part company, part, separate,** split up, dispel, disband, scatter, **disperse,** break up, break it up <nf>, **go separate ways,** diverge

ADJS 20 **separate, distinct, discrete; unjoined, unconnected, unattached,** unaccompanied, unattended, unassociated; **apart,** asunder, **in two;** discontinuous, noncontiguous, divergent; **isolated,** insular, detached, detachable, freestanding, free-floating, autonomous; **independent,** self-contained, standalone <nf>; noncohesive, noncohering, incoherent 804.4; bipartite, dichotomous, multipartite, multisegmental; **subdivided,** partitioned, curtained-off, marked-off, compartmentalized

21 **separated,** disjoined, disjoint, disjointed, disjunct, **disconnected,** disengaged, detached, **disunited, divided,** removed, divorced, **alienated,** estranged, distanced, **segregated,** sequestered, isolated, cloistered, shut off; **scattered,** dispersed, helter-skelter; disarticulated, dislocated, luxated, out of joint

22 **unfastened, unbound,** uncaught, unfixed, **undone, loose, free,** loosened, unloosened, clear; **untied, unbound,**

unknit, unleashed, unfettered, unchained, unlaced, unbandaged, unhitched; unstuck, unglued; unclasped, unclinched, unbuckled, unbuttoned, unzipped, unsnapped; unscrewed, unpinned, unbolted; **unanchored,** adrift, afloat, floating, free, free-floating

23 **severed, cut,** cleaved, cleft, cloven, riven, hewn, sheared; **splintered,** shivered, cracked, **split,** slit, reft; **rent, torn;** tattered, shredded, in shreds; quartered, **dismembered,** in pieces

24 **broken,** busted <nf>, **burst, ruptured,** dissilient; sprung; **shattered,** broken up, broken to pieces *or* bits, fragmentized, fragmentary, fragmented, in shards, in smithereens <nf>

25 **separating, dividing,** parting, distancing; separative, disjunctive

26 **separable,** severable, **divisible,** alienable, cleavable, partible; **fissionable,** fissile, scissile; dissoluble, dissolvable

ADVS 27 **separately,** severally, piecemeal, one by one; **apart,** adrift, asunder, **in two,** in twain; apart from, away from, aside from; abstractly, in the abstract, objectively, impersonally

28 **disjointedly,** unconnectedly, sporadically, spasmodically, discontinuously, by bits and pieces, by fits and starts

29 **to pieces,** all to pieces, **to bits, to smithereens** <nf>, to splinters, to shards, to tatters, to shreds

803 COHESION

NOUNS 1 **cohesion,** cohesiveness, **coherence, adherence, adhesion, sticking,** sticking together, cling, clinging, binding, colligation, inseparability; cementation, conglutination, agglutination; concretion, condensation, accretion, solidification, set, congelation, congealment, clotting, coagulation, curdling; **conglomeration,** conglobation, compaction, agglomeration, consolidation; inspissation, incrassation; **clustering,** massing, bunching, nodality; colloidality, emulsification

2 **consistency 788.1, connection, connectedness; junction 800.1; continuity, seriality, sequence 815, sequentialness, consecutiveness 812.1, orderliness**

3 **tenacity,** tenaciousness, **adhesiveness,** cohesiveness, retention, adherence; **tightness,** snugness; stickiness, **tackiness,** gluiness, gumminess, **viscidity,** consistency, viscosity, glutinosity, mucilaginousness; gelatinousness, jellylikeness, gelatinity; pulpiness; persistence *or* persistency, **stick-to-itiveness** <nf>, toughness, **stubbornness, obstinacy 361**, bulldoggedness *or* bulldoggishness, bullheadedness

4 <something adhesive or tenacious> **adhesive,** adherent, adherer; **bulldog,** barnacle, leech, limpet, remora; burr, cocklebur, clotbur, bramble, brier, prickle, thorn; sticker, bumper sticker, decalcomania, decal <nf>; **glue, cement,** gluten, mucilage, epoxy resin, paste, stickum *and* gunk <nf>; gum; resin, tar; **plaster,** adhesive plaster, court plaster; putty, size; syrup, molasses, honey; mucus; thickener; pulper; fixative; tape, Scotch tape <TM>, masking tape; Velcro <TM>; Band-Aid <TM>

5 **conglomeration,** consolidation, **conglomerate,** breccia <geology>, agglomerate, agglomeration, aggregate, congeries, cluster, bunch, mass, clot; concrete, concretion; compaction

VERBS 6 **cohere, adhere, stick, cling,** cleave, hold; **persist,** stay, stay put <nf>; cling to, freeze to <nf>; hang on, hold on; take hold of, clasp, grasp, hug, embrace, clinch; **stick together, hang** *or* **hold together;** grow to, grow together; **solidify, set,** conglomerate, agglomerate, conglobate; **congeal,** coagulate, clabber <nf>, **clot; cluster,** mass, bunch

7 **be consistent** 788.6, **connect,** connect with, follow; **join** 800.11, link up

8 **hold fast, stick close,** stick like glue, stick like a wet shirt *or* wet T-shirt *or* second skin, hug *or* mold

to the figure; stick closer than a brother, stick like a barnacle *or* limpet *or* leech, cling like ivy *or* a burr, hold on like a bulldog

9 **stick together, cement, bind, colligate, paste, glue,** agglutinate, conglutinate, gum; **weld,** fuse, **solder,** braze; gum up <nf>

ADJS 10 **cohesive,** cohering, coherent; adhering, **sticking, clinging,** inseparable, cleaving, holding together; **cemented,** stuck, agglutinative, agglutinated, agglutinate, conglutinate, conglutinated; **concrete, condensed, solidified, set, congealed,** clotted, coagulated; conglomerated, conglobate, **compacted, consolidated,** agglomerated; **clustered,** massed, bunched, nodal

11 **consistent** 788.9, **connected;** continuous 812.8, **serial,** uninterrupted, contiguous, sequential, sequent, **consecutive** 812.9; orderly, tight; **joined** 800.13

12 **adhesive, adherent,** stickable, self-adhesive, retentive; **tenacious,** clingy; **sticky, tacky,** gluey, gummy, gummous, glutenous, **viscid,** viscous, viscose, glutinous; inspissate, incrassate; colloidal; gooey *and* gunky <nf>; **persistent,** tough, **stubborn, obstinate** 361.8, bulldoggish *or* bulldogged *or* bulldoggy, bullheaded; stick–to-it-ive <nf>

804 NONCOHESION

NOUNS 1 **noncohesion,** uncohesiveness, incoherence, inconsistency, discontinuity 813, nonadhesion, unadhesiveness, unadherence, untenacity, immiscibility; **separateness,** discreteness, aloofness, standoffishness <nf>; **disjunction** 802.1, unknitting, unraveling, dismemberment; **dislocation; dissolution, chaos** 810.2, anarchy, **disorder** 810, confusion, entropy; **scattering,** dispersion *or* dispersal; diffusion

2 **looseness, slackness,** bagginess, **laxness,** laxity, relaxation, floppiness; sloppiness, shakiness, ricketiness

VERBS 3 **loosen, slacken, relax;** slack, slack off; ease, ease off, let up; **loose, free,** let go, unleash; **disjoin,** unknit, unravel, dismember, undo, unfasten, unpin; **sow confusion,** open Pandora's box; unstick, unglue; **scatter,** disperse, diffuse

ADJS 4 **incoherent,** uncoherent, noncoherent, **inconsistent, uncohesive, unadhesive,** nonadhesive, noncohesive, nonadherent, like grains of sand, **untenacious, unconsolidated,** tenuous; unjoined 802.20, disconnected, unconnected, unraveled, dismembered, gapped, open; **disordered** 810.12, chaotic, anarchic, anomic, confused; **discontinuous** 813.4, broken, detached, discrete, aloof, standoffish <nf>

5 **loose, slack, lax, relaxed,** easy, sloppy; shaky, rickety; flapping, streaming; loose-fitting, hanging, drooping, dangling; bagging, baggy

805 COMBINATION

NOUNS 1 **combination,** combine, combo <nf>, composition, compounding; **union, unification,** marriage, wedding, coupling, accouplement, linking, linkage, yoking; **incorporation,** aggregation, agglomeration, conglomeration, congeries; **amalgamation, consolidation,** assimilation, **integration,** solidification, **encompassment,** inclusion, ecumenism; **junction** 800.1; conjunction, conjugation; **alliance,** affiliation, reaffiliation, **association** 617, **merger,** league, hookup <nf>, tie-up <nf>; **taking** 480, buyout, takeover, leveraged buyout; **federation, confederation,** confederacy; collaboration; federalization, centralization, cartel; **fusion,** blend, blending, meld, melding; coalescence, coalition; **synthesis,** syncretism, syneresis, syncrasy; syndication; **conspiracy,** cabal, junta; package, package deal; collection; **agreement** 788; **addition** 253

2 **mixture** 797, **compound** 797.5

VERBS 3 **combine, unite, unify,** marry, wed, couple, link, yoke, yoke together; **incorporate, amalgamate,**

consolidate, assimilate, **integrate,** solidify, coalesce, compound, put *or* lump together, roll into one, come together, make one, unitize; **connect, join** 800.5; **mix; add** 253.4; **merge,** meld, **blend,** stir in, merge *or* blend *or* meld *or* shade into, **fuse,** flux, melt into one, conflate; interfuse, interblend; **encompass,** include, comprise; **take,** take over, buy out; **synthesize,** syncretize; syndicate; reembody

4 **league, ally, affiliate, associate,** consociate; unionize, organize, cement a union; **federate, confederate,** federalize, centralize; **join forces,** join *or* unite with, join *or* come together, join up with <nf>, hook up with <nf>, tie up *or* in with <nf>, **throw in with** <nf>, stand up with, go *or* be in cahoots <nf>, **pool one's interests, join fortunes with,** stand together, close ranks, make common cause with; **marry, wed, couple, yoke,** yoke together, link; **band together,** club together, bunch, bunch up <nf>, gang up <nf>, gang, club; team with, **team up with** <nf>, couple, pair, double up, buddy up <nf>, pair off, partner; go in partnership, go in partners <nf>; **conspire,** cabal, put heads together

ADJS 5 **combined, united, amalgamated, incorporated, consolidated, integrated,** assimilated, one, unitary, unitive, unitized, **joined** 800.13, joint 800.12, conjoint; conjunctive, combinative *or* combinatory, connective, conjugate; **merged,** blended, fused; **mixed; synthesized,** syncretized, syncretistic, eclectic

6 **leagued,** enleagued, **allied, affiliated,** affiliate, **associated,** associate, corporate; federated, confederated, federate, confederate; **in league,** in cahoots <nf>, in with; **conspiratorial,** cabalistic; partners with, in partnership; teamed, coupled, paired, married, wed, wedded, yoked, yoked together, linked, linked up

7 **combining, uniting,** unitive, unitizing, incorporating; merging, blending, fusing; combinative, combinatory; associative; federative, federal; corporative, incorporative, corporational; coalescent, symphystic

806 DISINTEGRATION

NOUNS 1 **disintegration, decomposition, dissolution, decay,** coming-apart, resolution, disorganization, degradation, breakup, breakdown, fragmentation, atomization; corruption; ruin**, ruination, destruction** 395; **erosion,** corrosion, crumbling, dilapidation, wear, wear and tear, waste, wasting, wasting away, ablation, ravagement, ravages of time; **disjunction** 802.1; **incoherence** 804.1; **impairment** 393

2 dissociation; electrolysis, catalysis, dialysis, hydrolysis, proteolysis, thermolysis, photolysis <all chemistry>, catabolism; catalyst, hydrolyst <chemistry>; hydrolyte <chemistry>; **decay,** fission <physics>, splitting, atom smashing

VERBS 3 **disintegrate, decompose, decay,** biodegrade, dissolve, come apart, disorganize, **break up** 395.22, go to rack and ruin 395.24, crack up, disjoin, unknit, split, fission, atomize, **come** *or* **fall to pieces; erode,** corrode, ablate, consume, wear *or* waste away, molder, molder away, crumble, crumble into dust

4 <chemical terms> dissociate; catalyze, dialyze, hydrolyze, electrolyze, photolyze; split, fission, atomize

ADJS 5 **disintegrative,** decomposing, disintegrating, disruptive, disjunctive; **destructive, ruinous** 395.26; chaotic; **erosive,** corrosive, ablative; resolvent, solvent, separative; **dilapidated,** disintegrated, ruinous, shacky, worn-out, worn, clapped-out <Brit nf>, moldering, ravaged, wrecked, totaled <nf>; disintegrable, decomposable, degradable, biodegradable

6 <chemical terms> dissociative; catalytic, dialytic, hydrolytic, proteolytic, thermolytic, electrolytic, photolytic; catabolic

807 ORDER

NOUNS **1 order, arrangement** 808; **organization** 808.2; **disposition,** disposal, deployment, marshaling; prioritization, putting in order; **formation, structure, configuration,** array, makeup, lineup, setup, layout; system, scheme, schedule; routine, even tenor, standard operating procedure; **peace,** quiet, quietude, **tranquillity; regularity,** uniformity 781; symmetry, proportion, concord, **harmony,** order, the music of the spheres, Tao *or* Dào; chronological order

2 continuity, logical order, serial order, reverse order, ascending *or* descending order, alphabetical order, numerical order; **degree** 245; **hierarchy,** pecking order, **gradation,** subordination, superordination, rank, place, position, status; progression; **sequence** 815; category, class

3 orderliness, trimness, tidiness, neatness; good shape <nf>, good condition, fine fettle, good trim, apple-pie order <nf>, a place for everything and everything in its place; **discipline,** method, methodology, methodicalness, system, systematicness; anality, compulsiveness, compulsive neatness

VERBS **4 order, arrange** 808.8, get it together <nf>, **organize, regulate;** dispose, deploy, marshal; form, form up, configure, structure, array, pull it together, get *or* put one's ducks in a row <nf>, straighten it out, get *or* put one's house in order, run a tight ship, line up, set up, lay out; **pacify,** quiet, cool off *or* down <nf>, **tranquilize; regularize,** harmonize; **systematize,** methodize, normalize, standardize, routinize; hierarchize, categorize, classify, grade, rank, prioritize

5 form, take form, take order, **take shape,** crystallize, **shape up;** arrange *or* range itself, place itself, take its place, fall in, **fall** *or* **drop into place,** fall into line *or* order *or* series, fall into rank, take rank; come together, draw up, gather around, rally round; put to rights, whip into shape

ADJS **6 orderly,** ordered, **regular, well-regulated, well-ordered, methodical, formal,** regular as clockwork, punctilious, uniform 781.5, **systematic,** symmetrical, **harmonious;** businesslike, routine, steady, normal, habitual, usual, en règle, in hand; **arranged** 808.14; scientific, businesslike

7 in order, in trim, to rights *and* in apple-pie order <nf>; **in condition,** in good condition, in kilter *or* kelter <nf>, in shape, in good shape <nf>, in perfect order, in good form, in fine fettle, in good trim, in the pink <nf>, in the pink of condition; **in repair,** in commission, in adjustment, in working order, fixed; up to scratch *or* snuff <nf>

8 tidy, trim, natty, neat, spruce, sleek, slick *and* slick as a whistle <nf>, smart, trig, dinky <Brit nf>, snug, tight, **shipshape,** shipshape and Bristol fashion; **well-kept,** well-kempt, well-cared-for, well-groomed; neat as a button *or* pin <nf>, not a hair out of place

ADVS **9 methodically, systematically, regularly,** through channels, uniformly, harmoniously, like clockwork

10 in order, in turn, in sequence, in succession, hierarchically, in series, seriatim <L>; step by step, by stages

808 ARRANGEMENT

<putting in order>

NOUNS **1 arrangement, ordering,** structuring, shaping, forming, configurating, configuration, constitution; **disposition, disposal, deployment,** placement, marshaling, **arraying; distribution,** collation, collocation, allocation, allotment, apportionment; **formation,** formulation, **configuration,** form, array; regimentation; syntax; **order** 807

2 organization, methodization, ordering, planning, charting, codification, regulation, regularization, routinization, normalization, rationalization; **adjustment,** harmonization, tuning, fine-tuning, tune-up, tinkering; **systematization,** ordination, coordination

3 **grouping, classification** 809, categorization, taxonomy; **gradation,** subordination, superordination, **ranking,** placement; **sorting,** sorting out, assortment, sifting, screening, triage, culling, selection, shakeout

4 **table,** code, digest, **index, inventory,** census; table of organization

5 **arranger, organizer,** coordinator, personal organizer; spreadsheet; **sorter,** sifter, **sieve,** riddle, **screen,** bolter, colander, grate, grating

6 <act of making neat> **cleanup,** red-up <nf>; tidy-up, trim-up, police-up <nf>

7 **rearrangement, reorganization,** reconstitution, **reordering, restructuring,** *perestroika* <Russ>, shake-up <nf>; **redeployment,** redisposition, realignment

VERBS 8 **arrange,** order 807.4, reduce to order, **put** *or* **get** *or* **set in order,** right, prioritize, put first things first, get one's ducks in a row <nf>; **put** *or* **set to rights, get it together** <nf>, **pull it together,** put in *or* into shape, whip into shape <nf>, sort out <chiefly Brit>, unsnarl, make sense out of <nf>

9 **dispose, distribute, fix, place,** set out, collocate, allocate, **compose,** space, **marshal,** rally, array; align, line, **line up,** form up, range; regiment; **allot, apportion,** parcel out, deal, **deal out**

10 **organize,** methodize, **systematize,** rationalize, regularize, get *or* put one's house in order; **harmonize,** synchronize, **tune,** tune up; **regularize,** routinize, normalize, standardize; **regulate,** adjust, coordinate, fix, settle; **plan,** chart, codify

11 **classify** 809.6, **group,** categorize; grade, gradate, rank, subordinate; **sort,** sort out <chiefly Brit>, assort; **separate,** divide; collate; **sift,** size, sieve, **screen,** bolt, riddle

12 tidy, **tidy up,** neaten, trim, **put in trim,** trim up, trig up <chiefly Brit>, **straighten up,** fix up <nf>, **clean up,** police *and* police up <nf>, groom, spruce *and* spruce up <nf>, **clear up,** clear the decks

13 **rearrange, reorganize,** reconstitute, **reorder, restructure,** reshuffle, rejigger <nf>, tinker *or* tinker with, tune, tune up, fine-tune; **shake up,** shake out; redispose, redistribute, reallocate, realign

ADJS 14 **arranged, ordered, disposed,** configured, composed, constituted, fixed, placed, aligned, ranged, arrayed, marshaled, grouped, ranked, **graded;** organized, methodized, **regularized,** routinized, normalized, standardized, **systematized;** regulated, harmonized, synchronized; **classified** 809.8, categorized, **sorted,** assorted; **orderly** 807.6

15 **organizational,** formational, structural

809 CLASSIFICATION

NOUNS 1 **classification, categorization,** classing, placement, ranging, **pigeonholing,** compartmentalizing, **sorting, grouping; grading,** stratification, ranking, rating, classing; division, subdivision; **cataloging,** codification, tabulation, rationalization, indexing, filing; **taxonomy,** typology; hierarchy; analysis 801, **arrangement** 808

2 **class, category, head, order, division,** branch, set, **group,** grouping, bracket, pigeonhole; **section,** heading, rubric, **label,** title; **grade,** rank, rating, status, estate, stratum, level, station, position; **caste,** clan, race, strain, blood, kin, sept; **subdivision,** subgroup, suborder, subclass, subcategory, subset; hyponym, hypernym, superordinate, subordinate

3 **kind, sort, ilk, type,** breed of cat <nf>, lot <nf>, **variety, species, genus,** *genre* <Fr>, phylum, denomination, designation, description, style, strain, manner, **nature, character,** persuasion, the like *or* likes of <nf>; **stamp, brand,** feather, color, stripe, line, grain, kidney; **make,** mark, label, shape, cast, form, mold, model;

tribe, clan, race, strain, blood, kin, breed; league, realm, domain, sphere

4 **hierarchy,** class structure, power structure, pyramid, establishment, pecking order; natural hierarchy, order *or* chain of being, domain, realm, **kingdom,** animal kingdom, vegetable kingdom, mineral kingdom; the order of things

5 <botanical and zoological classifications, in descending order> **kingdom;** subkingdom, **phylum** <zoology>, branch <botany>; superclass, **class,** subclass, superorder, **order,** suborder, superfamily, **family,** subfamily, tribe, subtribe, **genus,** subgenus, series, section, superspecies, **species;** subspecies, **variety**, subvariety, scion; biotype, genotype

VERBS 6 **classify,** class, assign, designate; **categorize,** type, put down as, **pigeonhole,** place, **group, arrange** 808.8, range; **order** 807.4, put in order, rank, rate, **grade; sort,** assort; distribute; **divide, analyze** 801.6, subdivide, break down; **catalog,** list, file, tabulate, rationalize, **index,** alphabetize, digest, codify

ADJS 7 **classificational,** classificatory; **categorical, taxonomic** *or* **taxonomical,** typologic *or* typological; ordinal; divisional, divisionary, subdivisional; **typical,** typal; **special,** specific, characteristic, particular, peculiar, denominative, differential, distinctive, defining, varietal

8 **classified,** classed, **cataloged, pigeonholed,** indexed, ordered, sorted, assorted, **graded, grouped,** ranked, rated, stratified, hierarchic, hierarchical, pyramidal; placed; filed, on file; tabular, indexical

ADVS 9 **any kind** *or* sort, **of any description, at all,** whatever, soever, whatsoever

810 DISORDER

NOUNS 1 **disorder, disorderliness, disarrangement,** derangement, disarticulation, disjunction 802.1, **disorganization;** discomposure, **dishevelment, disarray,** upset, disturbance, discomfiture, disconcertedness; **irregularity,** randomness, turbulence, perturbation, ununiformity *or* nonuniformity, unsymmetry *or* nonsymmetry, no rhyme or reason, **disproportion, disharmony;** indiscriminateness, promiscuity, promiscuousness, haphazardness; butterfly effect; **randomness,** randomicity, vagueness, trendlessness; entropy; **disruption** 802.3, destabilization, **incoherence** 804.1, unintelligibility; untogetherness <nf>; disintegration 806

2 **confusion, chaos,** anarchy, misrule, license, madhouse; **Babel,** cognitive dissonance; **muddle,** morass, **mix-up** *and* foul-up *and* fuck-up *and* snafu *and* screw-up <nf>, ball-up <nf>, balls-up <Brit nf>, hoo-ha *and* fine how-de-do <nf>, pretty kettle of fish, pretty piece of business, nice piece of work; kafuffle, kerfuffle

3 **jumble, scramble, tumble, snarl-up, mess,** bloody *or* holy *or* unholy *or* god-awful mess <nf>, pickle <nf>, shemozzle <Brit>, **turmoil,** welter, mishmash, hash, helter-skelter, farrago, crazy-quilt, higgledy-piggledy; shambles, tohubohu; **clutter, litter, hodgepodge** 797.6, rat's nest, mare's nest, hurrah's nest <nautical>; topsy-turviness *or* topsy-turvydom, arsy-varsiness, hysteron proteron

4 **commotion, hubbub, Babel, tumult,** turmoil, **uproar, racket,** riot, **disturbance, rumpus** <nf>, ruckus *and* ruction <nf>, disruption, **fracas, hassle,** shemozzle <Brit nf>, shindy <nf>, hullabaloo, rampage; **ado,** to-do <nf>, trouble, bother, pother, dustup <Brit nf>, stir <nf>, **fuss,** brouhaha, foofaraw <nf>; **row** *and* hassle <nf>, **brawl,** free-for-all <nf>, donnybrook *or* donnybrook fair, broil, embroilment, melee, scramble; helter-skelter, pell-mell, **roughhouse, rough-and-tumble**

5 **pandemonium, hell, bedlam,** witches' Sabbath, Babel, confusion of tongues; **cacophony,** din, noise, static, racket

6 slovenliness, **slipshodness,** carelessness, negligence; **untidiness,** uneatness, looseness, **messiness** <nf>,

sloppiness, dowdiness, seediness, **shabbiness,** tawdriness, chintziness <nf>, shoddiness, tackiness <nf>, grubbiness <nf>, frowziness, blowziness; **slatternliness,** frumpishness <nf>, sluttishness; **squalor,** squalidness, sordidness; derangement

7 **slob** <nf>, **slattern, sloven,** frump <nf>, sloppy Joe, schlep, schlump; drab, **slut, trollop; pig,** swine; **litterbug**

VERBS **8** lapse into disorder, fall into confusion, come apart, come apart at the seams, dissolve into chaos, slacken 804.3, come unstuck *or* unglued <nf>, disintegrate 806.3, degenerate, detune, untune

9 **disorder, disarrange** 811.2, **disorganize,** dishevel; **confuse** 811.3, sow confusion, open Pandora's box, **muddle,** jumble, jumble up, mix up; **discompose** 811.4, **upset,** destabilize, unsettle, **disturb,** perturb

10 **riot, roister,** roil, carouse; **create a disturbance, make a commotion,** make trouble, cause a stir *or* commotion, **make an ado** *or* **to-do,** create a riot, **cut loose, run wild, run riot,** run amok, go on a rampage, go berserk

11 <nf terms> **kick up a row,** kick up a shindy *or* a fuss *or* a storm, piss up a storm, **raise the devil,** raise the deuce *or* dickens, raise a rumpus *or* a storm, raise a ruckus, raise Cain, **raise hell,** raise sand, raise the roof, whoop it up, hell around, horse around *or* about; **carry on,** go on, maffick <Brit>; **cut up,** cut up rough, roughhouse

ADJS **12** **unordered, orderless, disordered, unorganized, random, entropic, unarranged,** ungraded, unsorted, unclassified; untogether <nf>; **unmethodical,** immethodical; **unsystematic,** systemless, nonsystematic; disjunct, unjoined 802.20; disarticulated, **incoherent** 804.4; discontinuous; **formless,** amorphous, inchoate, shapeless; ununiform *or* nonuniform, unsymmetrical *or* nonsymmetrical, disproportionate, misshapen; **irregular, haphazard,** desultory, **erratic,** sporadic, spasmodic, fitful, promiscuous, indiscriminate, casual, frivolous, capricious, random, hit-or-miss, vague, dispersed, wandering, planless, undirected, **aimless,** straggling, straggly; senseless, meaningless, gratuitous

13 **disorderly, in disorder,** disordered, **disorganized, disarranged, discomposed,** dislocated, deranged, convulsed; **upset, disturbed,** perturbed, unsettled, discomfited, disconcerted; **turbulent,** turbid, roily; out of order, **out of place,** misplaced, shuffled; **out of kilter** *or* **kelter** <nf>, **out of whack** <nf>, out of gear, out of joint, out of tune, on the fritz <nf>, haywire; **cockeyed** *and* skewgee *and* slaunchways *and* skygodlin <nf>, skew-whiff <Brit <nf>, awry, amiss, askew, on the blink and haywire <nf>

14 **disheveled, mussed up** <nf>, messed up <nf>, slobby <nf>, **rumpled,** tumbled, ruffled, snarled, snaggy; **tousled,** tously; uncombed, shaggy, matted; windblown

15 **slovenly, slipshod, careless, loose, slack,** nonformal, negligent; **untidy, unsightly,** unneat, slobby *and* scuzzy <nf>, **unkempt; messy** <nf>, mussy <nf>, **sloppy** <nf>, scraggly, poky, seedy <nf>, **shabby,** shoddy, schlocky <nf>, lumpen, chintzy, grubby <nf>, **frowzy, blowzy,** tacky <nf>; **slatternly, sluttish, frumpish,** frumpy, draggletailed, drabbletailed, draggled, bedraggled; down at the heel, out at the heels, out at the elbows, in rags, ragged, raggedy-ass *or* ragged-ass <nf>, raggedy, tattered; **squalid,** sordid; dilapidated, ruinous, **beat-up** *and* shacky <nf>

16 **confused, chaotic,** anarchic, **muddled, jumbled,** scattered, scatterbrained, helter-skelter <nf>, higgledy-piggledy, hugger-mugger, skimble-skamble, in a mess; **topsy-turvy,** arsy-varsy, upside-down, ass-backwards <nf>; **mixed up, balled** *or* **bollixed up** <nf>, **screwed up** <nf>, mucked up <nf>, **fouled up** *and* fucked up *and* snafu <nf>; discomposed, discombobulated

ADVS 17 **in disorder, in disarray, in confusion,** Katy bar the door <nf>, in a jumble, in a tumble, in a muddle, in a mess; higgledy-piggledy, helter-skelter <nf>, hugger-mugger, skimble-skamble, harum-scarum <nf>, willy-nilly <nf>, all over, all over hell <nf>, **all over the place, all over the shop** <nf>

18 **haphazardly, unsystematically,** unmethodically, irregularly, desultorily, **erratically,** capriciously, promiscuously, indiscriminately, **sloppily** <nf>, **carelessly,** randomly, **fitfully;** by *or* at intervals, sporadically, spasmodically, by fits, **by fits and starts,** by *or* in snatches, in spots <nf>; every now and then *and* every once in a while <nf>; **at random,** at haphazard, **by chance, hit *or* miss**

19 **chaotically, anarchically,** turbulently, **riotously; confusedly,** dispersedly, vaguely, wanderingly, **aimlessly,** planlessly, senselessly

811 DISARRANGEMENT

<bringing into disorder>

NOUNS 1 **disarrangement, derangement,** misarrangement, convulsion, dislocation; **disorganization,** shuffling; **discomposure,** disturbance, perturbation, disconcertedness; **disorder** 810; insanity 926

VERBS 2 **disarrange, derange,** misarrange; **disorder,** disorganize, disorient, throw out of order, put out of gear, dislocate, upset the apple-cart, **disarray; dishevel,** rumple, ruffle; tousle <nf>, muss *and* **muss up** <nf>, mess *and* **mess up** <nf>; **litter, clutter,** scatter

3 **confuse, muddle, jumble,** confound, garble, tumble, scramble, snarl, tie in knots, fumble, pi; **shuffle,** riffle; **mix up,** snarl up, **ball** *or* **bollix up** <nf>, **foul up** *and* fuck up *and* **screw up** *and* muck up *and* snafu <nf>; make a hash *or* mess of <nf>, play hob with <nf>; disrupt

4 **discompose,** throw into confusion, **upset, unsettle, disturb,** trip up, perturb, trouble, distract, throw <nf>, throw into a tizzy *or* snit *or* stew <nf>, agitate, convulse, embroil; **psych** *and* spook *and* bug <nf>; put out, inconvenience

ADJS 5 **disarranged** 810.13, **confused** 810.16, **disordered** 810.12

812 CONTINUITY

<uninterrupted sequence>

NOUNS 1 **continuity, uninterruption,** uninterruptedness, uninterrupted course, featurelessness, unrelievedness, monotony, unintermittedness, unbrokenness, **uniformity** 781, undifferentiation; fullness, plenitude; seamlessness, jointlessness, gaplessness, smoothness; **consecutiveness,** successiveness; continuousness, **endlessness, ceaselessness, incessancy; constancy** 847.2, continualness, constant flow; steadiness, steady state, equilibrium, stability 855

2 **series, succession,** run, **sequence,** consecution, progression, course, gradation; one thing after another; **continuum,** plenum; lineage, descent, filiation; **connection, concatenation,** catenation, catena, **chain,** chaining, linkup, articulation, reticulation, nexus; chain reaction, powder train; **train,** range, rank, **file, line, string,** thread, queue, **row,** bank, tier; windrow, swath; single file, Indian file; array; **round, cycle,** rotation, routine, the daily grind <nf>, recurrence, periodicity, flywheel effect, pendulum; endless belt *or* chain, M–bius band *or* strip, *la ronde* <Fr>, endless round; gamut, spectrum, scale; drone, monotone, hum, buzz

3 **procession, train, column, line, string, cortège;** stream, steady stream; cavalcade, caravan, motorcade; **parade,** pomp; dress parade; promenade, review, march-past, flyover, flypast <Brit>, funeral; skimmington <Brit>; chain gang, coffel; mule train, pack train; queue, crocodile <Brit>

VERBS 4 **continue,** be **continuous,** not stop, **connect, connect up, concatenate,** continuate, catenate, join

800.5, link *or* link up, **string together,** string, thread, chain *or* chain up, follow in *or* form a series, run on, maintain continuity

5 **align, line, line up,** string out, rank, array, range, arrange, get *or* put in a row

6 **line up, get in** *or* **get on line,** queue *or* queue up <Brit>, enqueue, make *or* form a line, get in formation, get in line, **fall in,** fall in *or* into line, fall into rank, take rank, take one's place

7 **file,** defile, file off; **parade,** go on parade, promenade, march past, fly over, fly past <Brit>

ADJS 8 **continuous,** continued, **continual,** continuing; **uninterrupted, unintermittent,** unintermitted, featureless, unrelieved, monotonous; **connected, joined** 800.13, linked, chained, concatenated, catenated, articulated; **unbroken,** serried, **uniform** 781.5, homogeneous, homogenized, cloned *or* clonish *and* cookie-cutter <nf>, undifferentiated, wall-to-wall *and* back-to-back <nf>, seamless, jointless, gapless, smooth, unstopped; unintermitting, unremitting; **incessant, constant,** steady, stable, **ceaseless,** unceasing, **endless,** unending, never-ending, **interminable,** perpetual, perennial; **cyclical,** repetitive, **recurrent,** periodic; straight, running, **nonstop; round-the-clock,** twenty-four-hour, all-hours; immediate, direct

9 **consecutive, successive,** successional, back-to-back <nf>, in order, running; progressive; **serial,** ordinal, seriate, catenary; sequent, **sequential;** linear, lineal, in-line; chronological

ADVS 10 **continuously, continually; uninterruptedly, unintermittently; without cease,** without stopping, with every other breath, without a break, back-to-back *and* wall-to-wall <nf>, unbrokenly, gaplessly, seamlessly, jointlessly, **connectedly,** together, cumulatively, on end; unceasingly, **endlessly,** *ad infinitum* <L>, perennially, **interminably,** again and again, repeatedly, time after time, time and again, time and time again, repetitively, cyclically, monotonously, unrelievedly, week in week out, year in year out, year-round, on and on, at *or* on a stretch; round the clock, all day long, all the livelong day, 24-7 *or* 24/7

11 **consecutively, progressively,** sequentially, successively, **in succession,** one after the other, back-to-back <nf>, **in turn,** turn about, turn and turn about; step by step; running, hand running <nf>; **serially,** in a series, *seriatim* <L>; **in a line,** in a row, in column, in file, in a chain, in single file, in Indian file

813 DISCONTINUITY

<interrupted sequence>

NOUNS 1 **discontinuity,** discontinuousness, discontinuation, discontinuance, noncontinuance; **incoherence** 804.1, **disconnectedness,** disconnection, delinkage, decoupling, discreteness, **disjunction** 802.1; **nonuniformity** 782; irregularity, **intermittence,** fitfulness 851.1; brokenness; nonseriality, nonlinearity, non sequitur; incompleteness 795; episode, parenthesis; time lag, time warp; broken thread, missing link; digression, non sequitur, parenthesis

2 **interruption, suspension, break,** fissure, breach, gap, hiatus, lacuna, caesura, crevasse; **interval, pause,** interim 826, lull, cessation, letup <nf>, **intermission**

VERBS 3 **discontinue, interrupt** 857.10, **break,** break off, **disjoin,** disconnect; **disarrange** 811.2; intermit 851.2; pause; digress

ADJS 4 **discontinuous,** noncontinuous, unsuccessive, **incoherent** 804.4, nonserial, nonlinear, nonsequential, discontinued, **disconnected,** unconnected, unjoined 802.20, delinked, decoupled, *décousu* <Fr>, **broken;** nonuniform 782.3, irregular; broken, broken off, fragmentary, **interrupted,** suspended; disjunctive, discrete, discretive; **intermittent, fitful** 851.3, stop-and-go, on-again off-again; scrappy, snatchy, spotty, patchy, jagged; choppy, chopped-off, herky-jerky <nf>, jerky, spasmodic; episodic, parenthetic

ADVS **5** **discontinuously, disconnectedly,** brokenly, fragmentarily; at intervals; **haphazardly** 810.18, randomly, occasionally, infrequently, now and then, now and again, intermittently, fitfully, **by fits and starts,** by fits, by snatches, by catches, by jerks, spasmodically, episodically, by skips, skippingly, *per saltum* <L>; willy-nilly, **here and there,** in spots, sporadically, patchily

814 PRECEDENCE

<in order>

NOUNS **1** **precedence** *or* precedency, antecedence *or* antecedency, anteposition, anteriority, precession; the lead, front position, front seat, pole position, first chair; **priority,** preference, urgency; top priority, taking precedence, preemption; prefixation, prothesis; **superiority** 249; **dominion** 417.6; **precursor** 816; prelude 816.2; preliminaries, run-up *and* walk-up <nf>; preceding 165.1

VERBS **2** **precede,** antecede, **come first,** come *or* go before, **go ahead of, go in advance,** stand first, stand at the head, **head,** head up <nf>, front, **lead** 165.2, take precedence, have priority, preempt; lead off, kick off, usher in; pilot, lead the way, blaze a trail, spearhead; head the table *or* board, sit on the dais; rank, outrank, rate; anticipate, foreshadow

3 <place before> **prefix, preface,** premise, prelude, prologize, preamble, introduce

ADJS **4** **preceding,** precedent, **prior,** antecedent, anterior, precessional, **leading** 165.3; preemptive; **preliminary,** precursory, prevenient, prefatory, exordial, prelusive, preludial, proemial, preparatory, initiatory, propaedeutic, inaugural; **first, foremost,** headmost, **chief** 249.14

5 **former,** foregoing, erstwhile, onetime, late, previous; aforesaid, aforementioned, beforementioned, above-mentioned, aforenamed, forenamed, forementioned, said, named, same

ADVS **6** **before** 216.12; above, hereinbefore, hereinabove, *supra* <L>, *ante* <L>

815 SEQUENCE

NOUNS **1** **sequence,** logical sequence, **succession,** successiveness, consecution, **consecutiveness,** following, coming after, accession; descent, lineage, line, family tree; **series** 812.2, serialization; **order,** order of succession; **priority**; **progression,** procession, rotation; **continuity** 812; **continuation,** prolongation, extension, posteriority; suffixation, subjunction, postposition; subsequence, sequel; cycle, process

VERBS **2** **succeed, follow, ensue,** come *or* go after, **come next; inherit,** take the mantle of, step into the shoes *or* place of, take over; segue; tailgate, follow on the heels of, tail <nf>

3 <place after> suffix, append, subjoin

ADJS **4** **succeeding, successive, following, ensuing,** sequent, sequential, sequacious, posterior, **subsequent,** consequent; proximate, **next;** appendant, suffixed, postpositive, postpositional; serial; progressive; tailgating

816 PRECURSOR

NOUNS **1** **precursor, forerunner,** foregoer, *voorlooper* <Dutch>, vaunt-courier, avant-courier, front- *or* lead-runner; pioneer, voortrekker <Dutch>, frontiersman, bushwhacker; scout, pathfinder, explorer, point, point man, trailblazer *or* trailbreaker, guide; **leader** 574.6, leadoff man *or* woman, bellwether, fugleman; **herald,** announcer, *buccinator* <L>, messenger, harbinger, stormy petrel; **predecessor,** forebear, precedent, antecedent, **ancestor; vanguard, avant-garde,** avant-gardist, innovator, groundbreaker; prequel

2 **curtain raiser,** countdown, run-up *and* walk-up <nf>, lead-in, warm-up, kickoff, opening gun *or* shot; **opening episode,** first episode, prequel; **prelude, preamble, preface,** prologue, foreword, introduction, *avant-propos* <Fr>, protasis, proem, proemium, prolegomenon *or* prolegomena, exordium; **prefix,** prefixture; frontispiece; **preliminary,** front matter; overture, voluntary, verse; premise, presupposition, postulate, prolepsis; **innovation, breakthrough** <nf>, leap

VERBS **3 go before, pioneer,** blaze *or* break the trail, break new ground, be in the van *or* vanguard; guide; **lead** 165.2, lead *or* show the way; **precede** 814.2; herald, count down, run up, lead in, forerun, usher in, introduce

ADJS **4 preceding** 814.4; preliminary, exploratory, pioneering, trailblazing, door-opening, kickoff, inaugural; **advanced,** avant-garde, original 337.5

817 SEQUEL

NOUNS **1 sequel,** sequela *or* sequelae, sequelant, sequent, sequitur, **consequence** 887.1; **continuation,** continuance, **follow-up** *or* **follow-through** <nf>, perseverance; caboose; **supplement,** addendum, appendix, back matter; postfix, suffix; postscript *or* PS, subscript, postface; postlude, **epilogue,** conclusion, peroration, codicil; refrain, chorus, coda; envoi, colophon, tag; afterthought, second thought, double take <nf>, *arrière-pensée* <Fr>, *esprit d'escalier* <Fr>; parting *or* Parthian shot; last words, swan song, dying words, famous last words

2 afterpart, afterpiece; **wake,** trail, train, queue; **tail,** tailpiece, rear, rear end; tab, tag, trailer

3 aftermath, afterclap, afterglow, afterimage, aftereffect, side effect, byproduct, spin-off, aftertaste; **aftergrowth,** aftercrop; **afterbirth,** placenta, secundines; afterpain

4 successor, replacement, backup, backup man *or* woman, substitute, stand-in; **descendant,** posterity, **heir,** inheritor

VERBS **5 succeed,** follow, come next, come after, come on the heels of; **follow through,** carry through, take the next step, drop the other shoe

818 BEGINNING

NOUNS **1 beginning, commencement, start,** running *or* flying start, starting point, square one <nf>, **outset,** outbreak, **onset,** oncoming, get-go; dawn; **creation, foundation, establishment, establishing, institution, origin,** origination, setting-up, setting in motion; **launching,** launch, launch *or* launching pad; alpha, A; **opening,** rising of the curtain; day one; first crack out of the box <nf>, leadoff, kickoff *and* jump-off *and* send-off *and* start-off *and* take-off *and* blast-off *and* git-go <nf>, the word 'go' <nf>; fresh start, new departure; **opening wedge,** leading edge, cutting edge, thin end of the wedge; entry level, bottom rung, bottom of the ladder, low place on the totem pole; daybreak

2 beginner, neophyte, tyro; newcomer 774.4, new arrival, Johnny-come-lately <nf>; entry-level employee, low man on the totem pole; entrant, **novice,** novitiate, probationer, catechumen; **recruit,** raw recruit, rookie <nf>; **apprentice,** trainee, learner, student; baby, infant, newborn; nestling, fledging; freshman 572.6; tenderfoot, greenhorn, greeny <nf>, initiate; debutant, deb <nf>; starter

3 first, first ever, prime, primal, primary, **initial,** alpha; **initiation,** initialization, first move, opening move, gambit, **first step,** baby step, *le premier pas* <Fr>, openers, starters, first lap, first round, first inning, first stage, first leg; breaking-in, warming-up; first blush, first glance, first sight, first impression; early days

4 origin, origination, **genesis, inception,** incipience *or* incipiency, inchoation; **divine creation,** creationism, creation science; **birth,** birthing, bearing, parturition, pregnancy, nascency *or* nascence, nativity; **infancy,** babyhood, childhood, youth; freshman year; incunabula, beginnings, cradle; fountainhead, wellspring, source

5 **inauguration,** installation *or* installment, induction, **introduction,** initiation; inception; setting in motion; embarkation *or* embarkment, **launching,** floating, flotation, unveiling; debut, first appearance, coming out <nf>; opener <nf>, preliminary, curtain raiser *or* lifter; maiden speech, inaugural address

6 **basics, essentials, rudiments, elements, nuts and bolts** <nf>; **principles,** principia, first principles, first steps, **outlines, primer,** hornbook, first reader, grammar, alphabet, **ABC's,** abecedarium; introduction, induction; groundwork, spacework

VERBS 7 **begin, commence, start; start up, kick** *or* **click in** <nf>; **start in, start off, start out, set out,** set sail, set in, set to *or* about, go *or* swing into action, get to *or* down to, **turn to,** fall to, pitch in <nf>, dive in <nf>, plunge into, head into <nf>, **go ahead,** let her rip <nf>, fire *or* blast away <nf>, take *or* jump *or* kick *or* tee *or* blast *or* send off <nf>, get the show on the road <nf>, get *or* set *or* start the ball rolling <nf>, roll it *and* let it roll <nf>

8 **make a beginning,** make a move <nf>, **start up,** get going <nf>, get off, set forth, set out, launch forth, get off the ground <nf>, **get under way,** set up shop, get in there <nf>; set a course, **get squared away** <nf>; make an auspicious beginning, **get off to a good start,** make a dent; get in on the ground floor <nf>; **break in, warm up,** get one's feet wet <nf>, cut one's teeth

9 enter, **enter on** *or* **upon** *or* **into, embark in** *or* **on** *or* **upon,** take up, go into, have a go at <chiefly Brit>, take a crack *or* whack *or* shot at <nf>; **debut,** make one's debut

10 **initiate, originate, create,** invent; **precede** 814.2, **take the initiative, take the first step,** take the lead, pioneer 816.3; **lead,** lead off, lead the way; **ahead,** head up <nf>, stand at the head, stand first; **break the ice,** take the plunge, break ground, cut the first turf, lay the first stone, get one's feet wet

11 **inaugurate,** institute, **found, establish,** set up <nf>; **install,** initiate, induct; **introduce,** broach, bring up, lift up, raise; **launch,** float; christen <nf>; **usher in,** ring in <nf>; **set on foot,** set abroach, set agoing, turn on, kick-start *and* jump-start <nf>, start up, start going, start the ball rolling <nf>, get cracking <nf>

12 **open,** open up, breach, open the door to, cut the ribbon; open fire

13 **originate, take** *or* **have origin,** be born, take birth, get started, come into the world, **become,** come to be, get to be <nf>, see the light of day, rise, **arise,** take rise, take its rise, **come forth, issue,** issue forth, come out, spring *or* crop up; burst forth, break out, erupt, irrupt; debut

14 **engender, beget, procreate** 78.8; **give birth to, bear,** birth, bring to birth, bring into the world; father, mother, sire

ADJS 15 **beginning, initial,** initiatory *or* initiative; incipient, inceptive, **introductory,** inchoative, inchoate; inaugural *or* inauguratory; **prime,** primal, **primary,** primitive, primeval; **original, first,** first ever, first of all; aboriginal, autochthonous; **elementary,** elemental, **fundamental,** foundational; **rudimentary,** rudimental, abecedarian; **ancestral,** primogenital *or* primogenitary; **formative, creative,** procreative, inventive; embryonic, in embryo, in the bud, budding, fetal, gestatory, parturient, pregnant, in its infancy, formative; infant, infantile, incunabular; **natal,** nascent, prenatal, antenatal, neonatal; early; pregame

16 **preliminary, prefatory,** preludial, proemial, precursory, preparatory; entry-level, door-opening; prepositive, prefixed

17 **first, foremost,** front, frontal, upfront <nf>, **head, chief, principal,**

premier, **leading, main,** flagship, foremost; maiden

ADVS **18 first,** firstly, **at first,** first off, first thing, for openers *or* starters <nf>, as a gambit, up front <nf>, **in the first place,** first and foremost, before everything, *primo* <L>; **principally,** mainly, chiefly, most of all; **primarily,** initially; **originally, in the beginning,** *in limine* <L>, **at the start,** at first glance *or* first blush, at the outset, at the first go-off <nf>; from the ground up, from the foundations, from the beginning, **from scratch** <nf>, from the first, **from the word 'go'** *and* from the get-go <nf>, *ab origine* <L>, *ab initio* <L>; *ab ovo* <L>

819 MIDDLE

NOUNS **1 middle,** median, midmost, **midst;** thick, thick of things; **center** 208.2, inside; **heart, core,** nucleus, kernel, heart of the matter; **mean** 246, midpoint; interior 207.2; midriff, diaphragm; **waist,** waistline, zone, girth, tummy *and* belly girt <nf>; equator; diameter; midday, midnight

2 mid-distance, middle distance; **equidistance; half,** moiety; **middle ground,** middle of the road, centrism; halfway point *or* place, midway, midcourse, midstream, halfway house; bisection; neutral ground, gray area, hâppy medium; middle way

VERBS **3** seek the middle, bisect, split down the middle; center, focus; average 246.2; double, fold, middle <nautical>; straddle, compromise

ADJS **4 middle, medial,** median, mesial, middling, mediocre, average, **medium** 246.3, mezzo <music>, **mean,** mid; **midmost,** middlemost; **central** 208.11, core, nuclear; focal, pivotal; interior, inside, internal; **intermediate,** intermediary; equidistant, halfway, midway, equatorial, diametral, midfield, midcourse, midstream; midland, mediterranean; midships, amidships; centrist, moderate, middle-of-the-road; center-seeking, centripetal

ADVS **5 midway, halfway, in the middle,** betwixt and between <nf>, halfway in the middle <nf>; plump *or* smack *or* slap- *or* smack-dab in the middle <nf>; half-and-half, neither here nor there, *mezzo-mezzo* <Ital>; medially, mediumly; in the mean; *in medias res* <L>; **in the midst of,** in the thick of; midships, amidships

820 END

NOUNS **1 end,** end point, ending, perfection, be-all and end-all, **termination, terminus, terminal,** terminating, term, period, **expiration,** expiry, phaseout, phasedown, discontinuation, closeout, **cessation** 857, ceasing, consummation, culmination, close, **conclusion, finish, finis, finale,** the end, finishing, finalizing *or* finalization, a wrap <nf>, quietus, stoppage, windup *and* payoff <nf>, curtain, curtains <nf>, all she wrote <nf>, fall of the curtain, end of the road *or* line <nf>; decease, taps, **death** 307; **last,** demise, last gasp *or* breath, final twitch, last throe, last legs, last hurrah <nf>; omega, &Omega$, izzard, Z; **goal,** destination, stopping place, resting place, finish line, tape *and* wire <nf>, journey's end, last stop; denouement, catastrophe, apocalypse, final solution, resolution; last *or* final words, peroration, swan song, dying words, envoi, coda, epilogue; **fate, destiny,** last things, eschatology, last trumpet, Gabriel's trumpet, crack of doom, doom; **effect** 887; **happy ending,** Hollywood ending, walking into the sunset

2 extremity, extreme; limit 794.5, ultimacy, definitiveness, **boundary,** farthest bound, jumping-off place, Thule, *Ultima Thule* <L>, **pole; tip,** point, nib; tail, **tail end,** butt end, tag, tag end, fag end; bitter end; stub, stump, butt; bottom dollar <nf>, bottom of the barrel <nf>

3 close, closing, cessation; decline, lapse; **homestretch, last lap** *or* **round** *or* **inning** <nf>, ninth inning, last stage; beginning of the end; deadline, closing time

4 **finishing stroke,** ender, **end-all,** quietus, stopper, **deathblow,** death stroke, *coup de grâce* <Fr>, kiss of death, mortal blow; **finisher,** clincher, equalizer, crusher, **settler;** knockout *and* knockout blow <nf>; sockdolager, KO *or* kayo *and* kayo punch <nf>; final stroke, finishing *or* perfecting *or* crowning touch, last dab *or* lick <nf>, last straw <nf>

VERBS 5 **end, terminate,** determine, close, close out, close the books on, phase out *or* down, **finish, conclude,** finish with, resolve, finish *or* wind up <nf>; **put an end to,** put a period to, put paid to <Brit>, put *or* lay to rest, **make an end of,** bring to an end, bring to a close *or* halt, end up; **get it over,** get over with *or* through with <nf>, be done with; bring down *or* drop the curtain; put the lid on <nf>, fold up <nf>, wrap *and* wrap up <nf>, sew up <nf>; call off <nf>, call all bets off <nf>; **dispose of,** polish off <nf>; kibosh *and* put the kibosh on <nf>, put the skids under <nf>; **stop, cease** 857.6; perorate; abort; scrap *and* scratch <nf>; **kill** 308.13, extinguish, scrag *and* waste *and* take out *and* zap <nf>, **give the quietus,** put the finisher *or* settler on <nf>, knock on *or* in the head, knock out <nf>, kayo *or* KO <nf>, shoot down *and* shoot down in flames <nf>, stop dead in one's tracks, wipe out <nf>; **cancel, delete,** expunge, censor, censor out, blank out, erase

6 **come to an end, draw to a close, expire, die** 307.18, come to rest, end up, land up; lapse, become void *or* extinct *or* defunct, run out, run its course, have its time *and* have it <nf>, pass, **pass away,** die away, wear off *or* away, go out, blow over, be all over, be no more; peter out, fizzle out

7 **complete** 794.6, perfect, finish, finish off, finish up, polish of, put the last *or* final *or* finishing touches on, finalize <nf>

ADJS 8 **ended, at an end, terminated, concluded, finished, complete** 794.9, perfected, settled, decided, set at rest; **over, all over,** all up <nf>; all off <nf>, all bets off <nf>; **done,** done with, over with, over and done with, through *and* through with <nf>; wound up <nf>, washed up <nf>; all over but the shouting <nf>; **dead 307.29, defunct,** extinct; **finished,** defeated, out of action, disabled, *hors de combat* <Fr>; **canceled, deleted,** expunged, censored *or* censored out, blanked *or* blanked out, bleeped *or* bleeped out; scrapped

9 <nf terms> **belly-up, dead meat,** kaput, shot, done for, SOL *or* shit out of luck, scragged, shot down, shot down in flames, down in flames, wasted, zapped, pffft *or* phut, wiped out, washed up, down and out, down the tubes, totaled

10 **ending, closing, concluding, finishing,** culminating *or* culminative, consummative *or* consummatory, **ultimate,** definitive, perfecting *or* perfective, terminating, crowning, capping, conclusive

11 **final, terminal,** terminating *or* terminative, determinative, definitive, **conclusive; last,** last-ditch <nf>, last but not least, eventual, farthest, extreme, boundary, border, limbic, limiting, polar, endmost, ultimate; caudal, tail, tail-end

ADVS 12 **finally,** in fine; **ultimately, eventually, as a matter of course; lastly,** last, **at last,** at the last *or* end *or* conclusion, at length, at long last; **in conclusion, in sum;** conclusively, once and for all

13 **to the end, to the bitter end, all the way,** to the last gasp, the last extremity, **to a finish,** *à outrance* <Fr>, till hell freezes over <nf>

PHRS 14 **that's all for, that's final, that's that,** that's all she wrote *and* that buttons it up <nf>, that's the end of the matter, so much for that, nuf said *and* enough said <nf>; the subject is closed, the matter is ended, the deal is off <nf>

821 TIME

NOUNS **1** **time, duration,** *durée* <Fr>, lastingness, continuity 812, term, while, tide, space; real time; psychological time; biological time; tense 530.12; **period** 824, time frame, timespan; time warp; cosmic time; kairotic time; quality time; space-time 158.6; the past 837, the present 838, the future 839; time-binding; **chronology** 832.1, chronometry, chronography, horology; tempo; time travel

2 Time, **Father Time,** Cronus, Kronos

3 tract of time, corridors of time, whirligig of time, glass *or* hourglass of time, sands of time, ravages of time, noiseless foot of Time, scythe of Time, time's winged chariot

4 **passage of time, course of time, lapse of time,** progress of time, process of time, succession of time, time-flow, flow *or* flowing *or* flux of time, sweep of time, stream *or* current *or* tide of time, time and tide, march *or* step of time, flight of time, time's caravan; timeframe

VERBS **5** **elapse,** lapse, **pass, expire,** run its course, run out, go *or* pass by; **flow,** tick away *or* by *or* on, run, proceed, advance, roll *or* press on, roll by, flit, fly, slip, slide, glide; drag by *or* on; **continue** 812.4, last, **endure,** go *or* run *or* flow on

6 **spend time, pass time, put in time,** employ *or* use time, fill *or* occupy time, kill time <nf>, consume time, take time, take up time, while away the time; find *or* look for time; race with *or* against time, buy time, work against time, run out of time, make time stand still; weekend, winter, summer; keep time, mark time, measure time

ADJS **7** **temporal, chronological,** timewise; chronometric, chronographic; durational, durative; lasting, continuous 812.8; temporary, pending

ADVS **8** **when, at which time,** what time *and* whenas , at which moment *or* instant, on which occasion, **upon which, whereupon,** at which, in which time, at what time, in what period, on what occasion, whenever

9 **at that time,** on that occasion, at the same time as, at the same time *or* moment that, then, concurrently, simultaneously, contemporaneously

10 in the meantime, meanwhile 826.5; during the time; for the duration; at a stretch

11 **then,** thereat, thereupon, **at that time,** at that moment *or* instant, in that case *or* instance, on that occasion; **again,** at another time, at some other time, anon

12 **whenever,** whene'er, whensoever, whensoe'er, **at whatever time,** at any time, anytime, no matter when; if ever, once

13 in the year of our Lord, *anno Domini* <L>, AD, in the Common *or* Christian Era, CE; *ante Christum* <L>, AC, before Christ, BC, before the Common *or* Christian era, BCE; *anno urbis conditae* <L>, AUC; *anno regni* <L>, AR

14 **until, till,** to, unto, **up to,** up to the time of

15 CONJS **when, while,** whilst <chiefly Brit>, the while; **during the time that,** at the time that, at the same time that, at *or* during which time; **whereas, as long as,** as far as

16 PHRS **time flies,** *tempus fugit* <L>, time runs out, time marches on

822 TIMELESSNESS

NOUNS **1** **timelessness,** neverness, datelessness, eternity 829.1,2; no time, no time at all, running out of time; time out of time, stopping time; everlasting moment; immortality

2 <a time that will never come> Greek calends *or* kalends, when hell freezes over, the thirtieth of February

ADJS **3** **timeless, dateless**

ADVS **4** **never,** ne'er, **not ever,** at no time, on no occasion, not at all; **nevermore;** never in the world, never on earth; not in donkey's years <Brit>, never in all one's born days <nf>, never in my life, *jamais de la vie* <Fr>

5 without date, *sine die* <L>, open, openended

823 INFINITY

NOUNS **1** **infinity,** infiniteness, infinitude, the all, the be-all and end-all; **boundlessness, limitlessness, endlessness;** illimitability, interminability, termlessness; **immeasurability,** unmeasurability, immensity, incalculability, innumerability, incomprehensibility; measurelessness, countlessness, unreckonability, numberlessness; exhaustlessness, inexhaustibility; universality; **all-inclusiveness,** all-comprehensiveness; **eternity** 829.1,2, **perpetuity** 829, forever; eons; vastness; bottomless pit

VERBS **2** **have no limit** *or* **bounds** *or* end, know no limit *or* bounds *or* end, be without end, **go on and on,** go on forever, never cease *or* end; last forever, perpetuate

ADJS **3** **infinite, boundless, endless, limitless,** termless, shoreless; unbounded, uncircumscribed, **unlimited,** illimited, infinitely continuous *or* extended, stretching *or* extending everywhere, without bound, without limit *or* end, no end of *or* to, bottomless; illimitable, **interminable,** interminate; **immeasurable,** incalculable, unreckonable, innumerable, incomprehensible, beyond comprehension, unfathomable; measureless, countless, sumless; **unmeasured,** unmeasurable, immense, unplumbed, untold, unnumbered, without measure *or* number *or* term; exhaustless, inexhaustible; **all-inclusive,** all-comprehensive 864.14, **universal** 864.14; **perpetual, eternal** 829.7; mind-boggling <nf>

ADVS **4** **infinitely, illimitably,** boundlessly, limitlessly, **interminably; immeasurably,** measurelessly, immensely, incalculably, innumerably, incomprehensibly; **endlessly,** without end *or* limit; *ad infinitum* <L>, to infinity; **forever, eternally** 829.10, in perpetuity

824 PERIOD

<portion or point of time>

NOUNS **1** **period, point, juncture,** stage; **interval,** lapse of time, time frame, space, span, timespan, stretch, time-lag, time-gap; **time,** while, **moment,** minute, instant, hour, day, **season;** psychological moment; pregnant *or* fateful moment, fated moment, kairos, moment of truth; **spell** 825

2 <periods> **moment, second,** millisecond, microsecond, nanosecond; **minute,** New York minute <nf>; hour, man-hour; **day,** sun; weekday; **week;** fortnight; **month,** moon, lunation; calendar month, lunar month; **quarter; semester,** trimester, term, session, academic year; **year,** annum, sun, twelvemonth; common year, regular year, intercalary year, leap year, bissextile year, defective year, perfect *or* abundant year; solar year, lunar year, sidereal year; fiscal year; calendar year; quinquennium, lustrum, luster; **decade,** decennium, decennary; **century; millennium**

3 **term,** time, duration, **tenure;** spell 825

4 **age, generation,** time, day, date, cycle; eon *or* aeon; Platonic year, great year, *annus magnus* or *annus mirabilis* <L>

5 **era, epoch, age;** Golden Age, Silver Age; Ice Age, glacial epoch; Stone Age, Bronze Age, Iron Age, steel Age; Middle Ages, Dark Ages; Era of Good Feeling; Jacksonian Age; Reconstruction Era *and* Gilded Age <1870s and 1880s>; Gay Nineties *and* Naughty Nineties *and* Mauve Decade *and* Golden Age *and* Gilded Age <1890s>; Roaring Twenties *and* Golden Twenties *and* Mad Decade *and* Age of the Red-Hot Mamas *and* Jazz Age *and* Flapper Era <1920s>; Depression Era; New Deal Era; Prohibition Era

6 <modern age> Technological Age, Automobile Age, Air Age, Jet Age, Supersonic Age, Atomic Age, Electronic Age, Computer Age, Space Age, Age of Anxiety, Age of Aquarius

825 SPELL

<period of duty, etc>

NOUNS 1 **spell,** fit, stretch, go <nf>

2 **turn, bout, round, inning,** innings <Brit>, time, time at bat, place, say, whack *and* go <nf>; opportunity, chance; **relief, spell;** one's turn, one's move <nf>, one's say

3 **shift,** work shift, **tour,** tour of duty, stint, bit, **watch, trick,** time, **turn,** relay, spell *or* turn of work; day shift, night shift, swing shift, graveyard shift <nf>, dogwatch, anchor watch; lobster trick *or* tour, sunrise watch; split shift, split schedule; flextime *or* flexitime; halftime, part-time, full-time; **overtime**

4 **term,** time; **tenure,** continuous tenure, tenure in *or* of office; **enlistment, hitch** <nf>, tour; prison term, stretch <nf>; fiscal year; biorhythm, circadian rhythm, biological clock

VERBS 5 **take one's turn,** have a go <nf>; **take turns,** alternate, turn and turn about; **time off, spell** *and* **spell off** <nf>, **relieve,** cover, **fill in for,** take over for; put in one's time, work one's shift; **stand one's watch** *or* **trick,** keep a watch; have one's innings <Brit>; do a stint; hold office, have tenure *or* tenure of appointment; **enlist**, sign up; re-enlist, re-up <nf>; do a hitch <nf>, do a tour *or* tour of duty; serve *or* do time

826 INTERIM

<intermediate period>

NOUNS 1 **interim, interval, interlude, intermission,** pause, break, **time-out,** recess, coffee break, halftime *or* halftime intermission, interruption; **lull,** quiet spell, resting point, point of repose, plateau, letup, relief, vacation, holiday, time off, off-time; downtime; **respite** 20.2; **intermission,** interval <Brit>, entr'acte; *intermezzo* <Ital>; interregnum

2 **meantime, meanwhile,** while, the while

VERBS 3 **intervene,** interlude, interval; **pause,** break, **recess,** declare a recess; call a halt *or* break *or* intermission; **call time** *or* time-out; take five *and* ten, etc *and* take a break <nf>

ADJS 4 **interim, temporary,** tentative, provisional, provisory

ADVS 5 **meanwhile, meantime, in the meanwhile** *or* **meantime,** in the interim, *ad interim* <L>; between acts *or* halves *or* periods, betweenwhiles, betweentimes, between now and then; till *or* until then; *en attendant* <Fr>, in the intervening time, during the interval, at the same time, for the nonce, for a time *or* season; *pendente lite* <L>

827 DURATION

NOUNS 1 **durability, endurance,** duration, durableness, **lastingness,** *longueur* <Fr>, perenniality, abidingness, long-lastingness, perdurability; **continuance,** perseverance, maintenance, **steadfastness,** constancy, **stability** 855, **persistence, permanence** 853, standing, long standing; **longevity,** long-livedness; **antiquity, age; survival,** survivability, viability, defiance *or* defeat of time; **service life,** serviceable life, useful life, shelf life, mean life; **perpetuity** 829

2 **protraction, prolongation**, continuation, extension, lengthening, drawing- *or* stretching- *or* dragging- *or* spinning-out, lingering; perpetuation; procrastination 846.5

3 **length of time,** distance of time, vista *or* stretch *or* desert of time; corridor *or* tunnel of time

4 **long time,** long while, long; **age** and **ages** <nf>, **aeon, century, eternity,** years, **years on end,** time immemorial, coon's age <nf>, donkey's years <Brit nf>, month of Sundays <nf>, right smart spell <nf>

5 **lifetime, life,** life's duration, life expectancy, lifespan, expectation of life, period of existence, all the days of one's life; **generation, age;** all one's born days *or* natural life <nf>

VERBS **6 endure, last** *or* **last out,** bide, **abide,** dwell, perdure, **continue,** run, extend, **go on,** carry on, hold on, keep on, stay on, run on, stay the course, go the distance, go through with, grind *or* slog on, grind *or* plug away; live, **live on,** continue to be, subsist, exist, tarry; get *or* keep one's head above water; **persist,** persevere; hang in *and* hang in there *and* hang tough <nf>; maintain, sustain, **remain, stay,** keep, hold, stand, prevail, last long, hold out; **survive,** defy *or* defeat time; live to fight another day; perennate; live on, live through; wear, wear well; stand the test of time

7 linger on, linger, tarry, go on, **go on and on, wear on,** crawl, creep, drag, **drag on,** drag along, drag its slow length along, drag a lengthening chain

8 outlast, outstay, last out, outwear, **outlive, survive**

9 protract, prolong, continue, **extend, lengthen,** lengthen out, **draw out, spin out,** drag *or* stretch out; linger on, dwell on; dawdle, procrastinate, temporize, drag one's feet

ADJS **10 durable,** perdurable, **lasting, enduring,** perduring, **abiding, continuing,** remaining, staying, **stable** 855.12, persisting, **persistent,** perennial; inveterate, agelong; **steadfast, constant,** intransient, immutable, unfading, evergreen, sempervirent, **permanent** 853.7, perennial, **long-lasting,** long-standing, of long duration *or* standing, diuturnal; long-term; **long-lived,** tough, hardy, vital, longevous *or* longeval; **ancient,** aged, antique; macrobiotic; chronic; **perpetual** 829.7

11 protracted, prolonged, extended, lengthened; **long,** overlong, time-consuming, interminable, marathon, lasting, **lingering,** languishing; long-continued, long-continuing, long-pending; drawn- *or* stretched- *or* dragged- *or* spun-out, long-drawn, **long-drawn-out;** long-winded, prolix, verbose 538.12

12 daylong, nightlong, weeklong, monthlong, yearlong

13 lifelong, livelong, lifetime, for life

ADVS **14 for a long time, long, for long, interminably,** unendingly, undyingly, persistently, protractedly, enduringly; for ever so long <nf>, for many a long day, for life *or* a lifetime, for an age *or* ages, for a coon's *or* dog's age <nf>, for a month of Sundays <nf>, for donkey's years <Brit nf>, **forever and a day, forever and ever, for years on end, for days on end,** etc; all the year round, all the day long, the livelong day, as the day is long; morning, noon, and night; hour after hour, day after day, month after month, year after year; day in day out, month in month out, year in year out; till hell freezes over <nf>, till you're blue in the face <nf>, till the cows come home <nf>, till shrimps learn to whistle <nf>, till doomsday, from now till doomsday, from here to eternity, till the end of time; since time began, from way back, long ago, long since, time out of mind, time immemorial

828 TRANSIENCE
<short duration>

NOUNS **1 transience** *or* transiency, transientness, **impermanence** *or* impermanency, transitoriness, changeableness 854, rootlessness, **mutability, instability, temporariness,** fleetingness, **momentariness;** finitude; **ephemerality,** ephemeralness, short duration; evanescence, volatility, fugacity, **short-livedness; mortality,** death, perishability, corruptibility, caducity; **expedience** 995, ad hoc, ad hockery *or* ad hocism, adhocracy; fugacity, fugaciousness; one-hit wonder

2 brevity, briefness, shortness; swiftness 174, fleetness

3 short time, little while, little, **instant, moment** 830.3, mo <nf>, small space, span, spurt, **short spell;** no time, less than no time; bit *or* **little bit,** a breath, the wink of an eye, pair of winks <nf>; **two shakes** *and* two shakes of a lamb's tail <nf>, half a mo <nf>; just a second

4 **transient,** transient guest *or* boarder, temporary lodger; **sojourner;** passer, passerby; **wanderer; vagabond,** drifter, derelict, homeless person, bag person, tramp, hobo, bum <nf>; caller, guest, visitor

5 **ephemeron,** ephemera, ephemeral; ephemerid, ephemeris, ephemerides <pl>; mayfly; bubble, smoke; nine days' wonder, flash in the pan, passing fancy; snows of yesteryear, *neiges d'antan* <Fr>; shooting star, meteor; ship that passes in the night

VERBS 6 <be transient> **flit, fly,** fleet; **pass, pass away, vanish, evaporate,** dissolve, evanesce, disappear, fade, melt, sink; fade like a shadow *or* dream, vanish like a dream, vanish into thin air, burst like a bubble, **go up in smoke,** melt like snow

ADJS 7 **transient, transitory,** transitive; **temporary,** temporal; **impermanent,** unenduring, undurable, nondurable, nonpermanent; frail, brittle, fragile, insubstantial; changeable 854.6, **mutable, unstable,** inconstant 854.7; capricious, fickle, impulsive, impetuous; **short-lived, ephemeral,** fly-by-night, evanescent, volatile, **momentary;** deciduous; **passing,** fleeting, flitting, flying, fading, dying; fugitive, fugacious; perishable, mortal, corruptible; here today and gone tomorrow; **expedient** 995.5, ad-hoc

8 **brief, short,** short-time, quick, brisk, swift, fleet, speedy; meteoric, cometary, flashing, flickering; short-term, short-termed

ADVS 9 **temporarily,** for the moment, for the time, *pro tempore* <L>, pro tem, for the nonce, **for the time being,** for a time, awhile

10 **transiently,** impermanently, evanescently, transitorily, changeably, mutably, ephemerally, fleetingly, flittingly, flickeringly, **briefly, shortly,** swiftly, quickly, **for a little while,** for a short time; **momentarily,** for a moment; **in an instant** 830.7

829 PERPETUITY

<*endless duration*>

NOUNS 1 **perpetuity,** perpetualness; **eternity,** eternalness, sempiternity, infinite duration; everness, foreverness, **everlastingness, permanence** 853, ever-duringness, duration 827, perdurability, indestructibility; **constancy,** stability, immutability, continuance, perseverance, continualness, perennialness *or* perenniality, **ceaselessness,** unceasingness, incessancy; timelessness 822; **endlessness,** never-endingness, **interminability; infinity** 823; coeternity

2 **forever, an eternity,** endless time, **time without end**

3 **immortality,** eternal life, **deathlessness,** imperishability, undyingness, incorruptibility *or* incorruption, athanasy *or* athanasia, life everlasting; eternal youth, fountain of youth

4 **perpetuation,** preservation, eternalization, immortalization; eternal recreation, eternal return *or* recurrence; steady-state universe

VERBS 5 **perpetuate, preserve,** preserve from oblivion, keep fresh *or* alive, perennialize, **eternalize,** eternize, **immortalize;** monumentalize; freeze, embalm

6 last *or* endure forever, **go on forever,** go on and on, live forever, **have no end,** have no limits *or* bounds *or* term, never cease *or* end *or* die *or* pass

ADJS 7 **perpetual, everlasting,** ever-living, ever-being, ever-abiding, ever-during, ever-durable, permanent 853.7, perdurable, indestructible; **eternal,** sempiternal, eterne , **infinite** 823.3, aeonian *or* eonian; dateless, ageless, timeless, immemorial; **endless,** unending, never-ending, without end, **interminable,** nonterminous, nonterminating; **continual,** continuous, steady, **constant, ceaseless,** nonstop, unceasing, neverceasing, **incessant,** unremitting, unintermitting, uninterrupted; coeternal

8 **perennial,** indeciduous, **evergreen,** sempervirent, ever-new, ever-young; ever-blooming, ever-bearing

9 **immortal,** everlasting, **deathless,** undying, never-dying, **imperishable,** incorruptible, amaranthine; fadeless, **unfading,** never-fading, ever-fresh; frozen, embalmed

ADVS **10** **perpetually,** in perpetuity, **everlastingly, eternally, permanently** 853.9, perennially, perdurably, indestructibly, **constantly,** continually, steadily, **ceaselessly,** unceasingly, never-ceasingly, **incessantly,** never-endingly, **endlessly,** unendingly, **interminably,** without end, world without end, time without end; **infinitely,** ad infinitum <L> 823.4

11 **always, all along,** all the time, all the while, at all times, *semper et ubique* <L, always and everywhere>; ever and always, **invariably,** without exception, never otherwise, *semper eadem* <L, ever the same; Elizabeth I>

12 **forever, forevermore, for ever and ever,** forever and aye; forever and a day <nf>, now and forever; **ever, evermore,** ever and anon, ever and again; aye, for aye; **for good,** for keeps <nf>, for good and all, for all time; throughout the ages, from age to age, in all ages; **to the end of time,** till time stops *or* runs out, to the crack of doom, to the last trumpet, till doomsday; till you're blue in the face <nf>, till hell freezes over <nf>, till the cows come home <nf>

13 **for life,** for all one's natural life, for the term of one's days, while life endures, while one draws breath, in all one's born days <nf>; from the cradle to the grave, from the womb to the tomb; **till death,** till death do us part

830 INSTANTANEOUSNESS

<*imperceptible duration*>

NOUNS **1** **instantaneousness** *or* **instantaneity,** momentariness, **momentaneousness** , **immediateness** *or* immediacy, near-simultaneity *or* -simultaneousness; instant gratification; simultaneity 836

2 **suddenness, abruptness, precipitateness,** precipitance *or* precipitancy; **unexpectedness,** unanticipation, inexpectation 131

3 **instant, moment, second,** sec <nf>, split second, millisecond, microsecond, nanosecond, half a second, half a mo <Brit nf>, minute, **trice,** twinkle, **twinkling, twinkling** *or* **twinkle of an eye,** twink, **wink,** bat of an eye <nf>, **flash,** crack, tick, stroke, coup, breath, twitch; two shakes of a lamb's tail *and* two shakes *and* shake *and* half a shake *and* **jiffy** *and* jiff *and* half a jiffy <nf>

ADJS **4** **instantaneous,** instant, momentary, momentaneous , **immediate,** presto, quick as thought *or* lightning; lightning-like, lightning-swift; nearly simultaneous; simultaneous; split-second; urgent, on-the-spot; fast-food, convenience-food; ready-to-wear, off-the-rack

5 **sudden, abrupt,** precipitant, **precipitate, precipitous; hasty,** headlong, impulsive, impetuous; speedy, swift, quick; **unexpected** 131.10, unanticipated, unpredicted, unforeseen, unlooked-for; **surprising** 131.11, startling, electrifying, shocking, nerve-shattering

ADVS **6** **instantly,** instanter, momentaneously , momentarily, momently, **instantaneously, immediately, right off the bat** <nf>; on the instant, on the dot <nf>, on the nail

7 **quickly, in an instant, in a trice, in a second,** in a moment, in a mo *or* half a mo <Brit nf>, in a bit *or* little bit, in a jiff *or* jiffy *or* half a jiffy <nf>, in a flash, in a wink <nf>, in a twink, **in a twinkling, in the twinkling of an eye, as quick as a wink,** as quick as greased lightning <nf>, in two shakes *or* a shake *or* half a shake <nf>, in two shakes of a lamb's tail <nf>, before you can say 'Jack Robinson' <nf>; **in no time,** in less than no time, in nothing flat <nf>, in short order; at the drop of a hat *or* handkerchief, like a shot, like a shot out of hell <nf>; with the speed of light

8 **at once,** at once and on the spot, **then and there, now, right now, right away, right off,** straightway, straightaway, forthwith, this minute, this very minute, **without delay,** without the least delay, in a hurry <nf>, *pronto* <Sp>, *subito* <Ital>; **simultaneously,** at the same instant, in the same breath; **all at once,** all together, at one time, at a stroke, at one stroke, at a blow, at one blow, at one swoop; at one jump, *per saltum* <L>, *uno saltu* <L>

9 **suddenly,** sudden, of a sudden, on a sudden, **all of a sudden, all at once: abruptly,** sharp; **precipitously** *or* precipitately, precipitantly, impulsively, impetuously, hastily; dash; smack, bang, slap, plop, plunk, plump, pop; **unexpectedly** 131.14, out of a clear blue sky, when least expected, before you know it; on short notice, without notice *or* warning, without further ado, unawares, **surprisingly** 131.15, startlingly, like a thunderbolt *or* thunderclap, like a flash, like a bolt from the blue

10 PHRS no sooner said than done

831 EVENT

NOUNS **1** **event, eventuality,** eventuation, effect 887, issue, outcome, result, aftermath, consequence; **realization,** materialization, coming to be *or* pass, incidence; contingency, contingent; accident 972.6

2 event, **occurrence, incident, episode, experience, adventure,** hap, **happening,** happenstance, **phenomenon,** fact, matter of fact, reality, particular, circumstance, **occasion,** turn of events; **nonevent,** pseudo-event, media event *or* happening, photo opportunity; what's happening

3 **affair, concern, matter,** thing, concernment, interest, **business,** job <nf>, **transaction,** proceeding, doing; current affairs *or* events; cause célèbre, matter of moment

4 **affairs, concerns, matters,** circumstances, relations, **dealings, proceedings,** doings, goings-on <nf>; course *or* run of events, run of things, the way of things, the way things go, what happens, current of events, march of events; the world, life, the times; order of the day; **conditions, state of affairs,** environing *or* ambient phenomena, state *or* condition of things

VERBS **5** **occur, happen** 972.11, hap, eventuate, **take place,** come *or* go down <nf>, go on, **transpire,** be realized, come, **come off** <nf>, **come about,** come true, **come to pass,** pass, pass off, go off, fall, **befall,** betide; **be found,** be met with

6 **turn up, show up** <nf>, **come along,** come one's way, cross one's path, come into being *or* existence, chance, **crop up,** spring up, pop up <nf>, arise, come forth, come *or* draw on, appear, approach, materialize, present itself, be destined for one

7 **turn out, result** 887.4

8 **experience, have, know, feel,** taste; **encounter, meet,** meet with, meet up with <nf>, run up against <nf>; **undergo, go through,** pass through, be subjected to, be exposed to, stand under, labor under, **endure, suffer,** sustain, pay, spend

ADJS **9** **happening, occurring, current, actual,** passing, taking place, on, **going on,** ongoing <nf>, **prevalent, prevailing,** that is, that applies, in the wind, afloat, afoot, under way, in hand, **on foot,** ado, doing; incidental, circumstantial, accompanying; accidental; occasional; resultant; eventuating

10 **eventful, momentous, stirring,** bustling, full of incident; phenomenal

11 **eventual, coming, final,** last, **ultimate; contingent,** collateral, secondary, indirect

ADVS **12** **eventually, ultimately, finally, in the end, after all is said and done, in the long run, over the long haul;** in the course of things, in the natural way of things, as things go, as times go, as the world goes, as the tree falls, the way the cookie crumbles <nf>, as things turn out, as it may be *or* happen *or* turn out, as luck *or* fate *or* destiny wills

CONJS **13 in the event that, if, in case,** if it should happen that, just in case, in any case, in either case, in the contingency that, in case that; provided 959.12

832 MEASUREMENT OF TIME

NOUNS **1 chronology,** timekeeping, timing, clocking, horology, **chronometry,** horometry, chronoscopy, chronography; watch- *or* clockmaking; scheduling, calendarmaking; **dating,** carbon-14 dating, radiocarbon dating, dendrochronology

2 time of day, time 821, **the time,** the exact time; time of night; **hour,** minute; stroke of the hour, time signal, bell

3 standard time, civil time, zone time, slow time <nf>; mean time, solar time, mean solar time, sidereal time, apparent time, local time; military time, 24-hour clock, 12-hour clock; universal time *or* Greenwich time *or* Greenwich mean time *or* GMT, Eastern time, Central time, Mountain time, Pacific time; Atlantic time; Alaska time, Yukon time; daylight-saving time; fast time <nf>, summer time <Brit>; **time zone**

4 date, point of time, time, day; postdate, antedate; datemark; date line, International Date Line; calends, nones, ides; name day, saint's day; red-letter day, anniversary

5 epact, annual epact, monthly *or* menstrual epact

6 timepiece, timekeeper, **timer, chronometer,** ship's watch; horologe, horologium; **clock,** Big Ben, ticker <nf>, **watch,** turnip <nf>; hourglass, sundial; watch *or* clock movement, clockworks, watchworks

7 almanac, The Old Farmer's Almanac, Nautical Almanac, Poor Richard's Almanac, World Almanac

8 calendar, calends; calendar stone, chronogram; almanac *or* astronomical calendar, ephemeris; perpetual calendar; Chinese calendar, church *or* ecclesiastical calendar, Cotsworth calendar, Gregorian calendar, Hebrew *or* Jewish calendar, Hindu calendar, international fixed calendar, Julian calendar, Muslim calendar, Republican *or* Revolutionary calendar, Roman calendar, ordo calendar

9 chronicle, chronology, register, registry, record; **annals,** journal, diary; time sheet, time book, **log,** daybook; timecard, time ticket, clock card, check sheet; datebook; date slip; **timetable,** schedule, timeline, time schedule, time chart, schedule; time scale; time study, motion study, time and motion study

10 chronologist, chronologer, chronographer, horologist, horologer; watchmaker *or* clockmaker; timekeeper, timer; chronicler, annalist, diarist, historian, historiographer; calendar maker, calendarist

VERBS **11 time, fix** *or* **set the time,** mark the time; **keep time,** mark time, measure time, beat time; **clock** <nf>; watch the clock; set the alarm; synchronize

12 punch the clock and punch in and punch out and **time in** and **time out** <nf>; ring in, ring out; clock in, clock out; check in, check out; check off

13 date, be dated, date at *or* from, date back, bear a date of, bear the date of, carry a date; fix *or* set the date, make a date; **predate,** backdate, antedate; **postdate; update,** bring up to date; datemark; date-stamp; dateline

14 chronologize, chronicle, calendar, intercalate

ADJS **15 chronologic<al>,** temporal, timekeeping; **chronometric<al>,** chronoscopic, chronographic *or* chronographical, chronogrammatic *or* chronogrammatical, horologic *or* horological, horometric *or* horometrical, metronomic *or* metronomical, calendric *or* calendrical, intercalary *or* intercalated; dated; annalistic, diaristic; calendarial

ADVS **16 o'clock,** of the clock, by the clock; half past, half *or* half after <Brit>; a quarter of *or* to, a quarter past *or* after

833 ANACHRONISM

<false estimation or knowledge of time>

NOUNS **1 anachronism,** chronological *or* historical error, **mistiming, misdating,** misdate, postdating, antedating; parachronism, metachronism, prochronism; prolepsis, anticipation; earliness, lateness, tardiness, unpunctuality

VERBS **2 mistime, misdate;** antedate, foredate, postdate; lag

ADJS **3 anachronous** *or* anachronistical *or* **anachronistic,** parachronistic, metachronistic, prochronistic, unhistorical, unchronological; **mistimed, misdated;** antedated, foredated, postdated; ahead of time, **beforehand, early;** behind time, **behindhand, late,** unpunctual, tardy; **overdue,** past due; unseasonable, out of season; **dated,** out-of-date

834 PREVIOUSNESS

NOUNS **1 previousness,** earliness 845, antecedence *or* antecedency, priority, **anteriority, precedence** *or* precedency 814, precession; *status quo ante* <L>, previous *or* prior state, earlier state; preexistence; **anticipation,** predating, antedating; antedate; **past times** 837.1

2 antecedent, precedent, premise; forerunner, **precursor** 816, ancestor

VERBS **3 be prior,** be before *or* early *or* earlier, come on the scene *or* appear earlier, **precede, antecede, forerun,** come *or* go before, set a precedent; **herald,** usher in, proclaim, announce; **anticipate,** antedate, predate; **preexist**

ADJS **4 previous, prior, early** 845.7, **earlier,** *ci-devant* or *ci-dessus* <Fr>, **former,** fore, prime, first, **preceding** 165.3, foregoing, above, anterior, **anticipatory,** antecedent; **preexistent;** older, elder, senior

5 prewar, ante-bellum, before the war; prerevolutionary; premundane *or* antemundane; prelapsarian, before the Fall; antediluvian, before the Flood; protohistoric, prehistoric 837.10; precultural; pre-Aryan; pre-Christian; premillenarian, premillennial; anteclassical, preclassical, pre-Roman, pre-Renaissance, pre-Romantic, pre-Victorian, etc

ADVS **6 previously,** priorly, **hitherto, heretofore,** thitherto, theretofore; **before, early** 845.11, **earlier,** ere, erenow, ere then, *or* ever; already, yet; before all; **formerly** 837.13

835 SUBSEQUENCE

<later time>

NOUNS **1 subsequence,** posteriority, **succession, ensuing, following** 166, sequence, coming after, supervenience, supervention; lateness 846; afterlife, next life; remainder 256, hangover <nf>; postdating; postdate; future time 839.1

2 sequel 817, **follow-up,** sequelae, **aftermath; consequence, effect** 887; **posterity,** offspring, descendant, heir, inheritor; **successor;** replacement, line, **lineage,** dynasty, family

VERBS **3 come** *or* **follow** *or* **go after, follow, follow on** *or* **upon, succeed,** replace, take the place of, displace, overtake, supervene; **ensue,** issue, emanate, attend, **result;** follow up, trail, track, come close on *or* tread on the heels of, dog the footsteps of; **step into** *or* **fill the shoes of,** don the mantle of, assume the robe of

ADJS **4 subsequent, after, later,** after-the-fact, *post factum* and *ex post facto* <L>, posterior, **following, succeeding,** successive, sequent, lineal, consecutive, ensuing, attendant; **junior,** cadet, puisne <law>, younger

5 posthumous, afterdeath; **postprandial,** postcibal, postcenal, afterdinner; **post-war,** *postbellum* <L>, after the war; **postdiluvian,** postdiluvial, after the flood, postlapsarian, after the Fall, post-industrial, postmodern, post-millenial, etc

ADVS **6 subsequently, after, afterwards,** after that, after all, **later, next,** since; **thereafter,** thereon, thereupon, therewith, **then;** in the process *or* course of time, as things worked out, in the sequel; at a subsequent *or* later time, in the aftermath; *ex post facto* <L>; hard on the heels *or* on the heels

7 **after which, on** *or* **upon which, whereupon,** whereon, whereat, whereto, whereunto, wherewith, wherefore, on, upon; hereinafter

836 SIMULTANEITY

NOUNS 1 **simultaneity** *or* **simultaneousness,** coincidence, co-occurrence, concurrence *or* concurrency, concomitance *or* concomitancy; **coexistence; contemporaneousness** *or* contemporaneity, coetaneousness *or* coetaneity, coevalness *or* coevalneity; unison; **synchronism,** synchronization, sync <nf>; isochronism; accompaniment 769, agreement 788

2 **contemporary,** coeval, concomitant, compeer; age group, peer group

3 **tie,** dead heat, draw, wash <nf>

VERBS 4 **coincide,** co-occur, concur; **coexist;** coextend; **synchronize,** isochronize, put *or* be in phase, be in time, keep time, time; contemporize; **accompany** 769.7, **agree** 788.6, match, go along with, go hand in hand, keep pace with, keep in step; sync <nf>

ADJS 5 **simultaneous, concurrent,** co-occurring, coinstantaneous, concomitant; **tied,** neck-and-neck; coexistent, coexisting; **contemporaneous,** contemporary, coetaneous, coeval; coterminous, conterminous; unison, unisonous; photo-finish; isochronous, isochronal; coeternal; accompanying 769.9, collateral; agreeing 788.9

6 **synchronous,** synchronized, synchronic *or* synchronal, in sync <nf>, isochronal, isochronous; **in time,** in step, in tempo, in phase, with *or* on the beat, in sync <nf>

ADVS 7 **simultaneously, concurrently,** coinstantaneously; **together,** all together, **at the same time,** at one and the same time, as one, as one man, in concert with, in chorus, with one voice, in unison, in a chorus, in the same breath; at one time, at a clip <nf>; synchronously, **synchronically,** isochronously, in phase, **in sync** <nf>, with *or* on the beat, on the downbeat

837 THE PAST

NOUNS 1 **the past,** past, foretime, former times, past times, times past, water under the bridge, **days** *or* **times gone by, bygone times** *or* **days,** bygones, **yesterday, yesteryear;** recent past, just *or* only yesterday; history, past **history;** dead past, dead hand of the past; the years that are past

2 **old** *or* **olden times,** early times, **old** *or* **olden days,** the olden time, times of old, **days of old, days** *or* **times of yore,** yore, yoretime, foretime, eld , good old times *or* days, the way it was, glory days, lang syne *or* auld lang syne, **the long ago,** time out of mind, days beyond recall; the old story, the same old story

3 **antiquity, ancient times,** time immemorial, ancient history, prehistory, protohistory, remote age *or* time, remote *or* far *or* dim *or* **distant past,** distance of time, past age, way back when; geological past, ice age; ancientness 842.1

4 **memory** 989, **remembrance, recollection, reminiscence, fond remembrance, retrospection,** retrospective, musing on the past, looking back, reprise; **reliving,** reexperiencing; revival 396.3; youth 301

5 <grammatical terms> past tense, preterit, perfect tense, past perfect tense, pluperfect, historical present tense, past progressive tense, past participle; aorist; perfective aspect; preterition

VERBS 6 **pass,** be past, **be a thing of the past,** be history, elapse, lapse, slip by *or* away, be gone, fade, fade away, be dead and gone, be all over, have run its course, have run out, have had its day; pass into history; **disappear** 34.2; **die** 307.18

ADJS 7 **past, gone,** by, **gone-by, bygone,** gone glimmering, bypast, ago, **over,** departed, passed, passed away, elapsed, lapsed, vanished, faded, no more, lost forever, long gone, irrecoverable, never to return, not coming back; **dead** 307.29, dead as a dodo, expired, extinct, dead and buried, defunct, deceased; run out, blown over, finished, forgotten, wound up; **passé, obsolete,** has-been, dated, antique, **antiquated**

8 **reminiscent** 989.21, **retrospective, remembered** 989.22, **recollected; relived, reexperienced; restored, revived**; retro; diachronic

9 <grammatical terms> past, preterit *or* preteritive, pluperfect, past perfect; aorist, aoristic; perfective

10 **former,** past, fore, **previous,** late, recent, **once, onetime,** sometime, **erstwhile,** then, quondam; obsolescent; retired, emeritus, superannuated; **prior** 834.4; **ancient, immemorial,** early, primitive, primeval, prehistoric; **old,** olden

11 **foregoing,** aforegoing, **preceding** 814.4; last, latter

12 **back,** backward, into the past; early; retrospective, retro, retroactive, *ex post facto* <L>, *a priori* <L>

ADVS 13 **formerly, previously, priorly** 834.6; **earlier, before,** before now, erenow, erst, whilom, erewhile, **hitherto, heretofore,** thitherto, aforetime, beforetime, **in the past,** in times past; then; **yesterday,** only yesterday, recently; **historically,** prehistorically, in historic *or* prehistoric times

14 **once,** once upon a time, one day, one fine morning, time was

15 **ago, since,** gone by; back, back when; backward, to *or* into the past; **retrospectively,** reminiscently, retroactively

16 **long ago,** long since, **a long while** *or* **time ago,** some time ago *or* since, some time back, a way *or* away back <nf>, ages ago, **years ago,** donkey's years ago <Brit nf>; **in times past,** in times gone by, in the old days, in the good old days; **anciently, of old, of yore,** in ancient times, in olden times, in the olden times, **in days of yore,** early, in the memory of man, time out of mind

17 **since,** ever since, until now; **since long ago, long since,** from away back <nf>, since days of yore, ages ago, **from time immemorial,** from time out of mind, aeons ago, since the world was made, since the world was young, since time began, since the year one, since Hector was a pup and since God knows when <nf>

838 THE PRESENT

NOUNS 1 **the present,** presentness, present time, the here and now; **now,** the present juncture *or* occasion, the present moment, the present hour *or* minute, this instant *or* second *or* moment, **the present day** *or* **time** etc; **the present age**; **today,** this day, **this day and age; this point,** this stage, this hour, **now,** nowadays, the now, the way things are, the nonce, **the time being; the times,** our times, these days, modern times; **contemporaneousness** *or* contemporaneity, nowness, actuality, topicality; **newness** 841, modernity; the Now Generation, the me generation; historical present *and* present tense <gram>, present participle

ADJS 2 **present, immediate,** latest, current, running, extant, **existent,** existing, actual, topical, being, that is, as is, that be; **present-day,** present-time, present-age, **modern** 841.13, modern-day; **contemporary,** contemporaneous; up-to-date, up-to-the-minute, fresh, with it <nf>, **new** 841.7

ADVS 3 **now, at present, at this point,** at this juncture, at this stage *or* at this stage of the game, on the present occasion, **at this time,** at this moment *or* instant, at the present time; **today,** this day, in these days, **in this day and age,** in our time, **nowadays;** this night, **tonight;** here, hereat, **here and now,** *hic et nunc* <L>, even now, but now, **just now,** as of now, as things are;

on the spot; for the nonce, for the time being; for this occasion; in the moment

4 **until now, hitherto,** till now, thitherto, **hereunto,** heretofore, until this time, by this time, **up to now,** up to the present, up to this time, to this day, to the present moment, to this very instant, **so far,** thus far, **as yet, to date,** yet, already, still, now *or* then as previously

839 THE FUTURE

NOUNS 1 **the future,** future, futurify, what is to come, imminence 840, subsequence 835, eventuality 831.1, **hereafter,** aftertime, afteryears, **time to come,** years to come, etc; **futurism,** futuristics; **tomorrow,** the morrow, the morning after, *mañana* <Sp>; **immediate** *or* **near future,** time just ahead, immediate prospect, offing, next period; **distant future,** remote *or* deep *or* far future, long run, long term; **by-and-by,** the sweet by-and-by <nf>; time ahead, course ahead, **prospect,** outlook, anticipation, expectation, project, probability, prediction, extrapolation, forward look, foresight, prevision, prevenience, envisionment, envisagement, prophecy, divination, clairvoyance, crystal ball; what is to be *or* come; determinism; future tense, future perfect; futurism; the womb of time

2 **destiny** 964.2, **fate,** doom, karma, kismet, what bodes *or* looms, what is fated *or* destined *or* doomed, what is written, what is in the books; the Fates, the Parcae *or* Parcae Fates, Lachesis, Clotho, Atropos, Moira, Moirai, **the hereafter,** the great hereafter, a better place, Paradise, Heaven, Elysian Fields, Happy Isles, the Land of Youth *or* Tir na n'Og, Valhalla; Hades, the Underworld, Hell, Gehenna; **the afterworld,** the otherworld, **the next world,** the world to come, life *or* world beyond the grave, **the beyond,** the great beyond, the unknown, the great unknown, **the grave,** home *or* abode *or* world of the dead, eternal home; **afterlife, postexistence,** future state, **life to come,** life after death

3 **doomsday,** doom, day of doom, day of reckoning, crack of doom, trumpet *or* trump of doom; **Judgment Day,** Day of Judgment, the Judgment; eschatology, last things, **last days**

4 **futurity;** ultimateness, eventuality, finality

5 **advent, coming, approach of time,** time drawing on

VERBS 6 **come,** come on, **approach,** near, **draw on** *or* **near;** be to be *or* come; be fated *or* destined *or* doomed, be in the books, be in the cards; **loom,** threaten, await, stare one in the face, be imminent 840.2; lie ahead *or* in one's course, lie just around the corner; **predict,** foresee, envision, envisage, see ahead, previse, foretell, prophesy; **anticipate, expect,** hope, hope for, look for, look forward to, **project,** plot, plan, scheme, think ahead, extrapolate, take the long view

7 **live on,** postexist, survive, get by *or* through, make it <nf>

ADJS 8 **future, later,** hereafter; **coming, forthcoming, imminent** 840.3, approaching, nearing, close at hand, waiting in the wings, nigh, **prospective; eventual** 831.11, ultimate, to-be, **to come; projected,** plotted, planned, looked- *or* hoped-for, desired, emergent, **predicted,** prophesied, foreseen, anticipated, anticipatory, previsional, prevenient, envisioned, envisaged, probable, extrapolated; determined, fatal, fatidic, fated, destinal, destined, doomed; eschatological; futuristic

ADVS 9 **in the future,** in aftertime, **afterward** *or* afterwards, **later,** at a later time, after a time *or* while, anon; **by and by,** in the sweet by-and-by <nf>; **tomorrow,** *mañana* <Sp>, the day after tomorrow; *proximo* <L>, prox, **in the near** *or* **immediate future,** just around the corner, **imminently** 840.4, **soon, before long;** probably, predictably, hopefully; fatally, by destiny *or* necessity

10 in future, **hereafter,** hereinafter, thereafter, **henceforth, henceforward** *or* henceforwards, thence, **thenceforth,** thenceforward *or* thenceforwards, over the long haul *or* short haul <nf>, from this time forward, from this day on *or* forward, from this point, from this *or* that time, from then on, **from here** *or* **now on, from now on in** <nf>, from here in *or* out <nf>, from this moment on

11 **in time, in due time,** in due season *or* course, all in good time, **in the fullness of time,** in God's good time, in the course *or* process of time, **eventually** 831.12, **ultimately,** in the long run

12 **sometime, someday, some of these days,** one of these days, some fine day *or* morning, one fine day *or* morning, some sweet day, sometime *or* other, somewhen, **sooner** *or* **later,** when all is said and done

840 IMMINENCE

<future event>

NOUNS **1** **imminence** *or* **imminency,** impendence *or* impendency, forthcomingness; **forthcoming,** coming, **approach, loom;** immediate *or* near future; futurity 839.1

VERBS **2** **be imminent, impend, overhang,** hang *or* lie over, **loom,** hang over one's head, hover, **threaten, menace,** lower; brew, gather; **come** *or* **draw on,** draw near *or* nigh, rush up on one, forthcome, **approach, loom up, near,** be on the horizon, be in the offing, be just around the corner, await, face, **confront, loom,** stare one in the face, be in store, breathe down one's neck, be about to be borning

ADJS **3** **imminent, impending,** impendent, **overhanging,** hanging over one's head, waiting, lurking, **threatening, looming,** lowering, **menacing,** lying in ambush; **brewing,** gathering, preparing; **coming, forthcoming, upcoming, to come,** about to be, about *or* going to happen, **approaching, nearing,** looming, looming up, looming in the distance *or* future; **near, close,** immediate, instant, soon to be, **at hand,** near at hand, close at hand; **in the offing,** on the horizon, **in prospect,** already in sight, just around the corner, in view, in one's eye, in store, in reserve, **in the wind,** in the womb of time; on the knees *or* lap of the gods, in the cards <nf>; that will be, that is to be; future 839.8

ADVS **4** **imminently,** impendingly; **any time,** any time now, any moment, any second, any minute, any hour, any day; **to be expected,** as may be expected, as may be

CONJS **5** **on the point of, on the verge of,** on the eve of

841 NEWNESS

NOUNS **1** **newness,** freshness, maidenhood, dewiness, pristineness, mint condition, new-mintedness, newbornness, virginity, intactness, greenness, immaturity, rawness, callowness, brand-newness; presentness, nowness; **recentness,** recency, lateness; **novelty,** gloss of novelty, newfangledness *or* newfangleness; originality 337.1; **uncommonness,** unusualness, strangeness, unfamiliarity

2 **novelty, innovation,** neology, neologism, newfangled device *or* contraption <nf>, neoism, neonism, **new** *or* **latest wrinkle** <nf>, **the last word** *or* **the latest thing** <nf>, *dernier cri* <Fr>; what's happening *and* what's in *and* the in thing *and* where it's at <nf>; new ball game; new look, latest fashion *or* fad; advance guard, vanguard, **avant-garde**; neophilia, neophiliac; start-up

3 **modernity,** modernness; modernism; modernization, updating, *aggiornamento* <Ital>; state of the art; postmodernism, space age

4 **modern,** modern man; modernist; modernizer; neologist, neoterist, neology, neologism, neoterism, neoteric; modern *or* rising *or* new generation; neonate, fledgling, stripling, neophyte, *novus homo* <L>, new man, upstart, *arriviste* <Fr>, *nouveau riche* <Fr>, parvenu; Young Turk, bright young man, comer <nf>; trendsetter; new kid on the block <nf>

VERBS **5 innovate, invent,** make from scratch *or* from the ground up, coin, new-mint, mint, inaugurate, neologize, neoterize; **renew,** renovate 396.17; give a new lease on life

6 modernize, streamline; update, **bring up to date,** keep *or* stay current, move with the times

ADJS **7 new,** young, **fresh,** fresh as a daisy, fresh as the morning dew; **unused, firsthand, original;** untried, untouched, unhandled, unhandseled, untrodden, unbeaten; virgin, virginal, intact, maiden, maidenly; green, vernal; dewy, pristine, ever-new, sempervirent, evergreen; **immature,** undeveloped, raw, callow, fledgling, unfledged, nestling; neological, neologistic, neophytic

8 fresh, additional, further, other, another; **renewed**

9 new-made, new-built, new-wrought, new-shaped, new-mown, new-minted, new-coined, uncirculated, in mint condition, mint, new-begotten, new-grown, new-laid; **newfound;** newborn, neonatal, new-fledged; **new-model,** late-model, like new, factory-new, factory-fresh, oven-fresh, in its original carton

10 <nf terms> **brand-new,** fire-new, **brand-spanking new,** spanking, **spanking new; just out; hot,** hottest, hot off the fire *or* griddle *or* spit, hot off the press; newfangled *or* newfangle

11 novel, original, unique, different; strange, unusual, uncommon; unfamiliar, unheard-of; **first, first ever** 818.15

12 recent, late, newly come, of yesterday; latter, later

13 modern, contemporary, present-day, present-time, twentieth-century, latter-day, space-age, neoteric, now <nf>, topical, **newfashioned,** fashionable, modish, mod, *à la mode* <Fr>, **up-to-date,** up-to-datish, **up-to-the-minute, in,** abreast of the times; **advanced,** progressive, forward-looking, modernizing, **avant-garde;** ultramodern, ultra-ultra, ahead of its time, far out, way out, modernistic, modernized, streamlined; postmodern, trendy, faddish

14 state-of-the-art, newest, latest, the very latest, up-to-the-minute, last, most recent, newest of the new, farthest out

ADVS **15 newly,** freshly, new, **anew,** once more, from the ground up, from scratch <nf>, *ab ovo* <L>, *de novo* <L>, **afresh, again;** as new

16 now, recently, lately, latterly, **of late,** not long ago, a short time ago, the other day, only yesterday; just now, right now <nf>; neoterically

842 OLDNESS

NOUNS **1 oldness, age,** eld , hoary eld; elderliness, seniority, senior citizenship, senility, **old age** 303.5; **ancientness, antiquity,** dust of ages, rust *or* cobwebs of antiquity; venerableness, eldership, primogeniture, great *or* hoary age; old order, old style, *ancien régime* <Fr>; **primitiveness,** primordialism *or* primordiality, aboriginality; atavism

2 tradition, custom, immemorial usage, immemorial wisdom**;** Sunna <Muslim>; Talmud *and* Mishnah <Jewish>, ancient wisdom, ways of the fathers; traditionalism *or* traditionality; oral tradition; myth, mythology, legend, lore, folklore, folktale, folk motif, folk history; racial memory, archetypal myth *or* image *or* pattern, archetype; collective unconscious; hive mind

3 antiquation, superannuation, staleness, disuse; **old-fashionedness,** unfashionableness, out-of-dateness; **old-fogyishness,** fogyishness, stuffiness, stodginess, fuddy-duddiness

4 antiquarianism; classicism, medievalism, Pre-Raphaelitism, longing *or* yearning *or* nostalgia for the past; **archaeology;** Greek archaeology,

Roman archaeology, etc, Assyriology, Egyptology, Sumerology; crisis archeology, industrial archeology, underwater *or* marine archeology, paleology, epigraphy, paleontology, human paleontology, paleethnology, paleonanthropology, paleoethnography; paleozoology, paleornithology, prehistoric anthropology

5 **antiquarian,** antiquary, *laudator temporis* acti <L>; dryasdust, the Rev Dr Dryasdust, Jonathan Oldbuck, Herr Teufelsdr–ckh; **archaeologist;** classicist, medievalist, Miniver Cheevy, Pre-Raphaelite; antique dealer, antique collector, antique-car collector; archaist

6 **antiquity, antique,** archaism; **relic,** relic of the past; **remains,** survival, vestige, ruin *or* ruins; old thing, oldie and golden oldie <nf>; monument; **fossil,** index fossil, zone fossil, trace fossil, fossil record; petrification, petrified wood, petrified forest; **artifact,** artefact, eolith, mezzolith, microlith, neolith, paleolith, plateaulith; cave painting, petroglyph; ancient manuscript 547.11; museum piece

7 **ancient,** man *or* woman *or* person of old, old Homo, **prehistoric mankind** ; preadamite, antediluvian; anthropoid, humanoid, primate, fossil man, protohuman, prehuman, missing link, apeman, hominid; **primitive, aboriginal,** aborigine, bushman, autochthon; **caveman,** cave dweller, troglodyte; bog man, bog body, Lindow man; Stone Age man, Bronze Age man, Iron Age man

8 <antiquated person> back number <nf>; pop *and* pops *and* dad <nf>, dodo *and* old dodo <nf>; fossil *and* antique *and* relic <nf>; **mossback** <nf>, longhair *and* square <nf>, **mid-Victorian,** antediluvian; old liner, old believer, conservative, hard-shell, traditionalist, reactionary; has-been; **fogy, old fogy,** regular old fogy, old poop *or* crock <nf>, **fud** and **fuddy-duddy** <nf>, eld <nf>; granny <nf>, **old woman,** matriarch; **old man,** patriarch, elder, old-timer <nf>, Methuselah

VERBS **9** **age,** grow old 303.10, grow *or* have whiskers; **antiquate,** fossilize, date, **superannuate,** outdate; obsolesce, go out of use *or* style, molder, fust, rust, fade, perish; lose currency *or* novelty; become obsolete *or* extinct; belong to the past, be a thing of the past; deteriorate, crumble

ADJS **10** **old, age-old,** auld, olden , old-time, old-timey <nf>; **ancient,** antique, archaic, venerable, hoary; of old, of yore; dateless, timeless, ageless; **immemorial,** old as Methuselah *or* Adam, old as God, old as history, old as time, old as the hills, out of the Ark; **elderly** 303.16

11 **primitive,** prime, primeval, primogenial, primordial, pristine; atavistic; **aboriginal,** autochthonous; ancestral, patriarchal; **prehistoric,** protohistoric, preglacial, preadamite, antepatriarchal; prehuman, protohuman, humanoid; archetypal

12 **traditional;** mythological, heroic; **legendary,** unwritten, oral, handed down; true-blue, tried and true; **prescriptive, customary,** conventional, understood, admitted, recognized, acknowledged, received; **hallowed, time-honored,** immemorial; **venerable,** hoary, worshipful; **longstanding, of long standing,** long-established, established, fixed, inveterate, rooted; folk, of the folk, folkloric, legendary

13 **antiquated,** grown old, **superannuated, antique, old,** age-encrusted, of other times, old-world; Victorian, mid-Victorian; historic, classical, medieval, Gothic; antediluvian; **fossil,** fossilized, petrified

14 **stale, fusty, musty,** rusty, dusty, moldy, mildewed; **worn, timeworn,** time-scarred; **moth-eaten,** moss-grown, crumbling, moldering, gone to seed, dilapidated, ruined, ruinous

15 **obsolete, passé, extinct,** gone out, gone-by, dead, past, run out, **outworn**

16 **old-fashioned,** old-fangled, old-timey <nf>, **dated, out, out-of-date, outdated, outmoded,** out of style *or* fashion, out of use, disused, out of season, **unfashionable,** styleless, **behind the times,** of the old school, old hat *and* back-number *and* has-been <nf>

17 **old-fogyish,** fogyish, old-fogy; fuddy-duddy, square *and* corny *and* cornball <nf>; **stuffy, stodgy; aged** 303.16, senile, bent *or* wracked *or* ravaged with age

18 **secondhand, used,** worn, previously owned, **unnew,** not new, pawed-over; hand-me-down and reach-me-down <nf>

19 **older,** senior, Sr, major, elder, dean; **oldest,** eldest; first-born, firstling, primogenitary; former 837.10

20 **archaeological,** paleological; antiquarian; archaic; paleolithic, eolithic, neolithic, mezzolithic

ADVS **21** anciently 837.16

843 TIMELINESS

NOUNS **1** **timeliness, seasonableness, opportuneness,** convenience; **expedience** *or* **expediency,** meetness, fittingness, fitness, appropriateness, rightness, propriety, suitability; **favorableness, propitiousness,** auspiciousness, felicitousness; **ripeness,** pregnancy, cruciality, criticality, criticalness, expectancy, loadedness, chargedness

2 **opportunity, chance, time, occasion; opening,** room, scope, space, place, liberty; clear stage, fair field, level playing field, fair game, fair shake *and* even break <nf>; **opportunism;** equal opportunity, nondiscrimination, affirmative action, positive discrimination <Brit>; trump card; a leg up, stepping-stone, rung of the ladder; time's forelock; window of opportunity

3 **good opportunity, good chance,** favorable opportunity, golden opportunity, well-timed opportunity, the chance of a lifetime, a once-in-a-lifetime chance, happy coincidence, lucky break; suitable occasion, proper occasion, suitable *or* proper time, **good time,** high time, due season; propitious *or* well-chosen moment; window of opportunity

4 **crisis, critical point,** crunch, crucial period, climax, climacteric; **turning point,** hinge, turn, turn of the tide, cusp, nexus; **emergency, exigency,** juncture *or* conjuncture *or* convergence of events, critical juncture, crossroads; **pinch,** clutch <nf>, rub, push, pass, strait, extremity, spot <nf>; **emergency,** state of emergency, red alert, race against time

5 **crucial moment,** critical moment, loaded *or* charged moment, decisive moment, kairotic moment, kairos, pregnant moment, defining moment, turning point, climax, **moment of truth,** crunch *and* when push comes to shove <nf>, when the balloon goes up <Brit nf>, point of no return; **psychological moment,** right moment; nick of time, eleventh hour; **zero hour,** H-hour, D-day, A-day, target date, deadline; crisis management

VERBS **6** **be timely,** suit *or* befit the time *or* season *or* occasion, come *or* fall just right

7 **take** *or* **seize the opportunity,** use the occasion, take the chance; take the bit in the teeth, leap into the breach, take the bull by the horns, bite the bullet, **make one's move,** cross the Rubicon, *prendre la balle au bond* <Fr, take the ball on the rebound>; **commit oneself,** make an opening, drive an entering wedge

8 **improve the occasion,** turn to account *or* good account, avail oneself of, **take advantage of,** put to advantage, profit by, **cash in** *or* **capitalize on;** take time by the forelock, seize the opportunity, seize the present hour, *carpe diem* <L, seize the day>, make hay while the sun shines; strike while the iron is hot; not be caught flatfooted, not be behindhand, not be caught looking <nf>, don't let the chance slip by, get going *and* get off the dime <nf>

ADJS **9** **timely, well-timed, seasonable, opportune,** *in loco* <L>, convenient; **expedient,** meet, fit, fitting, befitting, suitable, sortable, appropriate; **favorable, propitious,** ripe, auspicious, lucky, providential, heaven-sent, fortunate, happy, felicitous; heaven-sent

10 **critical, crucial,** pivotal, climactic, climacteric *or* climacterical, decisive; pregnant, kairotic, loaded, charged; exigent, emergent; eleventh-hour

11 **incidental, occasional, casual,** accidental; parenthetical, by-the-way

ADVS **12** **opportunely, seasonably, propitiously,** auspiciously, in proper time *or* season, in due time *or* course *or* season, in the fullness of time, **in good time,** all in good time; in the nick of time, just in time, at the eleventh hour; now *or* never

13 **incidentally, by the way, by the by; while on the subject,** speaking of, *à propos* <Fr>, apropos *or* apropos of; **in passing,** *en passant* <Fr>; parenthetically, by way of parenthesis, *par parenthése* <Fr>; for example, *par exemple* <Fr>

14 a bird in the hand is worth two in the bush, better late than never, every minute *or* moment counts; live for the moment, you can't take it with you

844 UNTIMELINESS

NOUNS **1** **untimeliness, unseasonableness,** inopportuneness, inopportunity, unripeness, inconvenience; **inexpedience,** irrelevance *or* irrelevancy; **awkwardness,** inappropriateness, impropriety, unfitness, unfittingness, wrongness, unsuitability; **unfavorableness,** unfortunateness, inauspiciousness, unpropitiousness, infelicity; **intrusion,** interruption; **prematurity** 845.2; **lateness** 846, afterthought, thinking too late, *l'esprit de l'escalier* <Fr>; anachronism; staircase wit

2 **wrong time, bad time,** wrong *or* bad *or* poor timing, unsuitable time, unfortunate time; evil hour, unlucky day *or* hour, off-year, *contretemps* <Fr>; inopportune moment

VERBS **3** **ill-time, mistime,** miss the time; **lack the time,** not have time, have other *or* better things to do, be otherwise occupied, be engaged, be preoccupied, have other fish to fry <nf>

4 **talk out of turn,** speak inopportunely, interrupt, **put one's foot in one's mouth** <nf>, intrude, butt in *and* stick one's nose in <nf>, **go off half-cocked** <nf>, open one's big mouth *or* big fat mouth <nf>; blow it <nf>, speak too late *or* too soon

5 **miss an opportunity, miss the chance, miss out, miss the boat,** miss one's turn, lose the opportunity, ignore opportunity's knock, lose the chance, blow the chance <nf>, throw away *or* waste *or* neglect the opportunity, allow the occasion to go by, let slip through one's fingers, be left at the starting gate *or* post, be caught looking <nf>, oversleep, lock the barn door after the horse is stolen

ADJS **6** **untimely, unseasonable, inopportune, ill-timed,** ill-seasoned, mistimed, unripe, unready, ill-considered, too late *or* soon, out of phase *or* time *or* sync; ill-starred; **inconvenient,** unhandy, discommodious; **inappropriate,** irrelevant, improper, unfit, wrong, out of line, off-base, unsuitable, **inexpedient,** unfitting, unbefitting, untoward, malapropos, *mal à propos* <Fr>, intrusive; **unfavorable,** unfortunate, infelicitous, inauspicious, **unpropitious,** unhappy, unlucky, misfortuned; **premature** 845.8; not in time, **late** 846.16

ADVS **7** **inopportunely, unseasonably,** inconveniently, inexpediently; **unpropitiously,** inauspiciously, unfortunately, in an evil hour, at just the wrong time

845 EARLINESS

NOUNS **1** **earliness,** early hour, time to spare; **head start,** running start, ground floor, first crack, early start, beginnings, first *or* early stage, very beginning, preliminaries; **anticipation, foresight,** prevision, prevenience; advance notice, lead time, a stitch in time, readiness, preparedness, preparation; first light

2 **prematurity,** prematureness; **untimeliness** 844; precocity, **precociousness,** forwardness; precipitation, precipitancy, haste, hastiness, **overhastiness,** rush, impulse, impulsivity, impulsiveness

3 **promptness, promptitude, punctuality,** punctualness, readiness; instantaneousness 830, immediateness *or* immediacy, summariness, decisiveness, **alacrity, quickness** 174.1, speediness, swiftness, rapidity, expeditiousness, expedition, dispatch

4 **early bird** <nf>, early riser, early *or* first comer, first arrival, first on the scene; Johnny-on-the-spot <nf>; **precursor** 816

VERBS 5 **be early,** be ahead of time, take time by the forelock, be up and stirring, be beforehand *or* betimes, be ready and waiting, be off and running; gain time, draw on futurity *or* on the future; get there first; get a wiggle on *or* hop to it <nf>

6 **anticipate, foresee,** foreglimpse, previse, see the handwriting on the wall, foretaste, pave the way for, prevent ; **forestall,** forerun, go before, **get ahead of,** win the start, break out ahead, get a head start, steal a march on, beat someone to the punch *or* the draw <nf>; **jump the gun,** beat the gun, go off half-cocked <nf>; preempt; take the words out of one's mouth

ADJS 7 **early,** bright and early and with the birds <nf>, **beforetime,** in good time *or* season; **forehand,** forehanded; foresighted, **anticipative** *or* **anticipatory,** prevenient, previsional

8 **premature, too early, too soon,** oversoon; previous and a bit previous <nf>, prevenient; **untimely; precipitate,** hasty 830.5, **overhasty,** too soon off the mark, too quick on the draw *or* trigger *or* uptake <nf>; **unprepared,** unripe, impulsive, rushed, unmatured; unpremeditated, unmeditated, ill-considered, **half-cocked** and **half-baked** <nf>, unjelled, uncrystallized, not firm; **precocious, forward, advanced,** far ahead, born before one's time

9 **prompt, punctual, immediate, instant,** instantaneous 830.4, **quick** 174.15, speedy, swift, expeditious, summary, decisive, apt, alert, **ready,** alacritous, Johnny-on-the-spot <nf>; as soon as possible *or* ASAP

10 **earlier,** previous 834.4

ADVS 11 **early, bright and early, beforehand, beforetime,** early on, betimes, precociously, **ahead of time,** foresightedly, in advance, in anticipation, ahead, before, **with time to spare**

12 **in time, in good time, soon enough,** time enough, early enough; just in time, **in the nick of time,** with no time to spare, just under the wire, without a minute to spare

13 **prematurely, too soon, oversoon,** untimely, too early, before its *or* one's time; **precipitately,** impulsively, in a rush, hastily, **overhastily;** at half cock <nf>

14 **punctually, precisely,** exactly, sharp; **on time,** on the minute *or* instant, to the minute *or* second, **on the dot** <nf>, spot on *and* bang on <Brit nf>, at the gun

15 **promptly, without delay,** without further delay *or* ado, directly, **immediately,** immediately if not sooner <nf>, **instantly** 830.6, instanter, on the instant, on the spot, **at once,** right off, **right away, straightway,** straightaway, **forthwith,** *pronto* <Sp>, *subito* <Ital>, PDQ *or* pretty damned quick <nf>, **quickly,** swiftly, speedily, with all speed, **summarily,** decisively, smartly, expeditiously, apace, in no time, in less than no time; no sooner said than done

16 **soon, presently, directly, shortly,** in a short time *or* while, **before long,** ere long, in no long time, in a while, **in a little while, after a while, by and by,** anon, betimes, *bientôt* <Fr>, in due time, in due course, at the first

opportunity; in a moment *or* minute, *tout à l'heure* <Fr>

PHRS **17** the early bird gets the worm

846 LATENESS

NOUNS **1 lateness, tardiness, belatedness, unpunctuality;** late hour, small hours; eleven hour, last minute, high time; unreadiness, unpreparedness; untimeliness 844

2 delay, stoppage, jam *and* logjam <nf>, obstruction, tie-up *and* bind <nf>, **block,** blockage, **hang-up** <nf>; delayed reaction, double take, afterthought; **retardation** *or* retardance, slow development, slowdown *and* slow-up <nf>, slowness, lag, time lag, lagging, dragging, dragging one's feet and foot-dragging <nf>, pigeonholing; **detention,** suspension, holdup <nf>, **obstruction, hindrance;** delaying action, delaying tactics; **wait, halt, stay, stop,** downtime, break, pause, interim 826, respite; reprieve, stay of execution; moratorium; **red tape,** red-tapery, red-tapeism, bureaucratic delay, *paperasserie* <Fr>; delay of game

3 waiting, cooling one's heels <nf>, **tarrying,** tarriance ; **lingering, dawdling,** dalliance, dallying, dillydallying; back burner

4 postponement, deferment *or* **deferral,** prorogation, putting-off, tabling, holding up, holding in suspension, carrying over; **prolongation,** protraction, continuation, extension of time; **adjournment** *or* adjournal, adjournment sine die

5 procrastination, cunctation, hesitation 362.3; **temporization, a play for time, stall** *and* tap-dancing <nf>; Micawberism, Fabian policy; **dilatoriness,** slowness, backwardness, remissness, slackness, laxness

6 latecomer, late arrival, Johnny-come-lately; slow starter, dawdler, dallier, dillydallier; late bloomer *or* developer; retardee; late riser, slugabed; ten o'clock scholar

VERBS **7 be late, not be on time,** be overdue, be behindhand, show up late, miss the boat; keep everyone waiting; **stay late,** stay up late *or* into the small hours, burn the midnight oil, keep late hours; get up late, keep banker's hours; oversleep

8 delay, retard, detain, make late, slacken, lag, drag, drag one's feet and stonewall <nf>, dilly-dally, slow down, **hold up** <nf>, hold *or* keep back, check, **stay, stop,** arrest, impede, **block,** hinder, obstruct, throw a monkey wrench in the works <nf>, confine; tie up with red tape

9 postpone, delay, defer, put off, give one a rain check <nf>, shift off, hold off *or* up <nf>, prorogue, put on hold *or* ice *or* the back burner <nf>, reserve, waive, **suspend,** hang up, stay, hang fire; protract, drag *or* stretch out <nf>, **prolong, extend,** spin *or* string out, continue, adjourn, recess, take a recess, prorogue; **hold over,** lay over, stand over, let the matter stand, **put aside,** lay *or* set *or* push aside, lay *or* set by, **table,** lay on the table, pigeonhole, **shelve,** put on the shelf, put on ice <nf>; consult one's pillow about, sleep on

10 be left behind, be outrun *or* outdistanced, make a slow start, be slow *or* late *or* last off the mark, be left at the post *or* starting gate; bloom *or* develop late

11 procrastinate, be dilatory, hesitate, let something slide, hang, hang back, hang fire; **temporize,** gain *or* make time, **play for time,** drag one's feet <nf>, hold off <nf>; **stall,** stall off, **stall for time,** stall *or* stooge around *and* tap-dance <nf>; talk against time, filibuster

12 wait, delay, stay, bide, abide, **bide** *or* **abide one's time; take one's time,** take time, mark time; **tarry, linger, loiter,** dawdle, dally, dillydally; hang around *or* about *or* out <nf>, stick around <nf>; **hold on** <nf>, sit tight <nf>, hold one's breath; wait a minute *or* second, wait up; hold everything *and* hold your horses *and* hold your water *and* keep your shirt on <nf>; wait *or* stay up, sit up; **wait and see,** bide the issue, see which way the cat jumps, see how the cookie crumbles *or* the ball bounces <nf>, let sleeping dogs lie; wait for something to turn up; **await** 130.8

13 wait impatiently, tear one's hair *and* sweat it out *and* champ *or* chomp at the bit <nf>

14 be kept waiting, be stood up <nf>, be left; **cool one's heels** <nf>

15 **overstay,** overtarry

ADJS **16** **late, belated, tardy,** slow, slow on the draw *or* uptake *or* trigger <nf>, **behindhand,** never on time, backward, back, **overdue, long-awaited, untimely; unpunctual,** unready; latish; **delayed,** detained, **held up** <nf>, **retarded, arrested,** blocked, **hung up** *and* in a bind <nf>, obstructed, stopped, jammed, congested; weather-bound; **postponed, in abeyance,** held up, put off, **on hold** *or* put on hold <nf>, on the back burner *or* put on the back burner <nf>; delayed-action; moratory

17 **dilatory, delaying,** Micawberish; slow *or* late *or* last off the mark; **procrastinating,** procrastinative *or* procrastinatory, go-slow; **obstructive,** obstructionist *or* obstructionistic, bloody-minded <Brit nf>; **lingering,** loitering, lagging, dallying, dillydallying, **slow,** sluggish, laggard, foot-dragging, shuffling, backward; easygoing, **lazy, lackadaisical; remiss,** slack, work-shy, lax

18 later 835.4; last-minute, eleventh-hour, deathbed

ADVS **19** **late, behind, behindhand, belatedly,** backward, slow, **behind time,** after time; far on, deep into; late in the day, at the last minute, at the eleventh hour, none too soon, in the nick of time, under the wire

20 **tardily, slow, slowly,** deliberately, dilatorily, sluggishly, lackadaisically, leisurely, at one's leisure, lingeringly; until all hours, into the night

847 FREQUENCY

NOUNS **1** **frequency,** frequence, **oftenness; commonness,** usualness, prevalence, **common occurrence,** routineness, habitualness; **incidence,** relative incidence; radio frequency

2 **constancy, continualness,** steadiness, sustainment, **regularity,** noninterruption *or* uninterruption, nonintermission *or* unintermission, incessancy, ceaselessness, constant flow, continuity 812; perpetuity 829; repetition 849; **rapidity** 174.1; rapid recurrence *or* succession, rapid *or* quick fire, tattoo, **staccato,** chattering, stuttering; **vibration,** shuddering, juddering <Brit>, pulsation, **oscillation** 916

VERBS **3** be frequent, occur often, have a high incidence, continue 812.4, recur 850.5; shudder, judder <Brit>, vibrate, oscillate 916.10; frequent, hang out at <nf>

ADJS **4** **frequent,** oftentime, many, many times, **recurrent,** recurring, **oft-repeated,** thick-coming; **common,** of common occurrence, not rare, thick on the ground <Brit>, **prevalent,** usual, routine, habitual, ordinary, everyday; frequentative <gram>

5 **constant, continual** 812.8, **perennial; steady,** sustained, **regular;** periodic; **incessant, ceaseless, unceasing,** unintermitting, unintermittent *or* unintermitted, unremitting, relentless, unrelenting, unchanging, unvarying, uninterrupted, unstopped, unbroken; **perpetual** 829.7; repeated 849.12; **rapid, staccato,** stuttering, chattering, machine gun; pulsating, juddering <Brit>, vibrating, **oscillating** 916.15

ADVS **6** **frequently, commonly,** usually, ordinarily, routinely, habitually; **often,** oft, **oftentimes,** oft times; **repeatedly** 849.16, **again and again, time after time; most often** *or* frequently, in many instances, **many times,** many a time, full many a time, many a time and oft, as often as can be, as often as not, more often than not; **in quick** *or* **rapid succession;** often enough, not infrequently, not seldom, unseldom; as often as you wish *or* like, whenever you wish *or* like

7 **constantly, continually** 812.10, **steadily,** sustainedly, **regularly,** as regular as clockwork, with every other breath, every time one turns around, right along <nf>, unvaryingly, uninterruptedly, unintermittently, **incessantly,** unceasingly, **ceaselessly,** without cease *or* ceasing, perennially, all the time, at all times, ever, ever and anon, on and on, without letup *or* break *or* intermission, without stopping; **perpetually, always** 829.11; **rapidly;** all year round, every day, every hour, every moment; daily, hourly, daily and hourly; **night and day,** day and night; **morning, noon, and night;** hour after hour, day after day, month after month, year after year; **day in day out,** month in month out, year in year out

848 INFREQUENCY

NOUNS 1 **infrequency,** infrequence, unfrequentness, seldomness; occasionalness; **rarity, scarcity, scarceness,** rareness, **uncommonness,** uniqueness, unusualness; **sparsity** 885.1; **slowness** 175; one-time offer

ADJS 2 **infrequent,** unfrequent, **rare,** scarce, scarce as hens' teeth, scarcer than hens' teeth, **uncommon,** unique, unusual, almost unheard-of, seldom met with, seldom seen, few and far between, **sparse** 885.5; one-time, one-shot, once in a lifetime; **slow** 175.10; like snow in August; unprecedented

3 **occasional, casual, incidental; odd,** sometime, extra, side, off, off-and-on, out-of-the-way, spare, sparetime, **part-time**

ADVS 4 **infrequently,** unfrequently, **seldom, rarely, uncommonly,** scarcely, hardly, **scarcely** *or* **hardly ever,** very seldom, not often, only now and then, at infrequent intervals, unoften, off-and-on; **sparsely** 885.8

5 **occasionally,** on occasion, **sometimes, at times,** at odd times, every so often <nf>, at various times, on divers occasions, **now and then,** every now and then <nf>, now and again, **once in a while,** every once in a while <nf>, every now and then, every now and again, once and again, once *or* twice, betweentimes, betweenwhiles, at intervals, **from time to time;** only occasionally, only when the spirit moves, only when necessary, only now and then, at infrequent intervals, once in a blue moon *and* once in a coon's age <nf>; irregularly, sporadically

6 **once, one-time,** on one occasion, just *or* only once, just this once, once and no more, once for all, once and for all *or* always

849 REPETITION

NOUNS 1 **repetition, reproduction,** duplication 874, reduplication, doubling, redoubling; **recurrence,** reoccurrence, cyclicality, return, reincarnation, rebirth, reappearance, renewal, resumption; resurfacing, reentry; echo, reecho, parroting; ditto; do-over; regurgitation, rehearsal, rote recitation; **quotation; imitation** 336; plagiarism 621.2; reexamination, second *or* another look

2 **iteration, reiteration, recapitulation,** recap and wrapup <nf>, retelling, recounting, recountal, **recital, rehearsal, restatement,** rehash <nf>; reissue, reprint; review, summary, précis, résumé, summing up, peroration; going over *or* through, practicing; reassertion, reaffirmation; elaboration, dwelling upon; **copy** 785

3 **redundancy, tautology,** tautologism, pleonasm, macrology, battology; stammering, stuttering; padding, filling, filler, expletive

4 **repetitiousness,** repetitiveness, stale *or* unnecessary repetition; harping; **monotony,** monotone, drone; **tedium** 118, daily round *or* grind, same old story; **humdrum,** dingdong, singsong, chime, jingle, jingle-jangle, trot, pitter-patter; **rhyme, alliteration,** assonance, slant *or* near rhyme; hamster wheel, treadmill; echolalia, **repeated sounds** 55

5 **repeat,** repetend, bis, ditto <nf>, echo; **refrain,** burden, chant, undersong, chorus, bob; bob wheel, bob and wheel; ritornel; rerun; rehash; reprint, reissue; remake; second helping

6 **encore,** repeat performance, repeat, **reprise;** replay, replaying, return match; repeat order

VERBS **7** **repeat, redo,** do again, do over, do a repeat, **reproduce, duplicate** 874.3, reduplicate, double, redouble, ditto <nf>, **echo, parrot,** reecho; **rattle off,** reel off, regurgitate; renew, reincarnate, revive; come again *and* run it by again <nf>, say again, repeat oneself, **quote,** repeat word for word *or* verbatim, repeat like a broken record; **copy, imitate** 336.5; plagiarize 621.4, 336.5; **reexamine,** take *or* have a second look, take *or* have another look

8 **iterate, reiterate, rehearse, recapitulate, recount,** rehash <nf>, **recite, retell,** retail, **restate,** reword, review, run over, sum up, summarize, précis, resume, encapsulate; reissue, reprint; do *or* say over again, **go over** *or* **through,** practice, say over, go over the same ground, give an encore, quote oneself, go the same round, fight one's battles over again; **tautologize,** battologize, pad, fill; **reaffirm,** reassert

9 **dwell on** *or* **upon,** insist upon, **harp on,** beat a dead horse, have on the brain, constantly recur *or* revert to, labor, belabor, hammer away at, always trot out, sing the same old song *or* tune, play the same old record, plug the same theme, never hear the last of; **thrash** *or* **thresh over,** cover the same ground, go over again and again, go over and over

10 **din, ding;** drum 55.4, beat, hammer, pound; **din in the ear,** din into, drum into, say over and over

11 <be repeated> **repeat, recur,** reoccur, **come again,** come round again, go round again, come up again, resurface, reenter, **return, reappear, resume;** resound, reverberate, echo; revert, turn *or* go back; keep coming, come again and again, happen over and over, run through like King Charles's head

ADJS **12** **repeated,** reproduced, doubled, redoubled; **duplicated,** reduplicated; regurgitated, recited by rote; **echoed,** reechoed, parroted; **quoted,** plagiarized; **iterated, reiterated,** reiterate; retold, **twice-told;** warmed up *or* over, *réchauffé* <Fr>

13 **recurrent,** recurring, **returning,** reappearing, revenant, ubiquitous, ever-recurring, cyclical, periodic, yearly, monthly, weekly, daily, circadian, thick-coming, frequent, incessant, continuous 812.8, year-to-year, month-to-month, week-to-week, etc; haunting, thematic

14 **repetitious,** repetitive, repetitional *or* repetitionary, repeating, recursive; **duplicative,** reduplicative; **imitative** 336.9, parrotlike; echoing, reechoing, echoic; **iterative, reiterative,** reiterant; recapitulative, recapitulatory; battological, **tautological** *or* **tautologous, redundant;** hamster-wheel

15 **monotonous,** monotone; **tedious;** harping, labored, belabored, cliché-ridden; **humdrum,** singsong, chiming, chanting, dingdong <nf>, jog-trot, jingle-jangle; **rhymed, rhyming, alliterative,** alliterating, assonant

ADVS **16** **repeatedly, often, frequently, recurrently, every time one turns around,** with every other breath, like a tolling bell, **again and again, over and over,** over and over again, many times over, time and again, **time after time,** times without number, **ad nauseam;** year in year out, week in week out, etc, year after year, day after day, day by day; **many times,** several times, a number of times, many a time, many a time and oft, full many a time and oft; every now and then, every once in a while; recursively

17 **again,** over, over again, **once more,** *encore* and *bis* <Fr>, two times, twice over, ditto; **anew,** *de novo* <L>, afresh; from the beginning, *da capo* <Ital>

850 REGULARITY OF RECURRENCE

NOUNS 1 **regularity,** regularness, clockwork regularity, predictability, punctuality, smoothness, **steadiness, evenness, unvariableness, methodicalness,** systematicalness; **repetition** 849; **uniformity** 781; **constancy** 847.2; usual suspects

2 **periodicity,** periodicalness; cyclical motion, piston motion, pendulum motion, regular wave motion, undulation, **pulsation; intermittence** *or* intermittency, alternation; rhythm 709.22, meter, beat; **oscillation** 916; **recurrence,** go-round, reoccurrence, reappearance, return, the eternal return, **cyclicalness,** cyclicality, seasonality; resurfacing, reentry

3 **round, revolution, rotation, cycle,** circle, wheel, **circuit; beat,** upbeat, downbeat, thesis, arsis, **pulse;** systole, diastole; course, series, **bout, turn,** rota <Brit>, spell 825

4 **anniversary, commemoration;** immovable feast, annual holiday; biennial, triennial, quadrennial, quinquennial, sextennial, septennial, octennial, nonennial, decennial, tricennial, jubilee, silver jubilee, golden jubilee, diamond jubilee; centennial, centenary; quasquicentennial; sesquicentennial; bicentennial, bicentenary; tercentennial, tercentenary, tricentenary; quincentennial, quincentenary; **wedding anniversary,** silver wedding anniversary, golden wedding anniversary; **birthday,** birthdate, natal day, b-day <nf>; saint's day, name day; leap year, bissextile day; annual holiday, government holiday, bank holiday; **religious holiday,** holy day

VERBS 5 <occur periodically> **recur, reoccur, return, repeat** 849.7, reappear, **come again,** come up again, be here again, resurface, reenter, **come round** *or* **around,** come round again, come in its turn; **rotate, revolve,** turn, circle, wheel, cycle, **roll around,** roll about, wheel around, go around, go round; **intermit,** alternate, **come and go,** ebb and flow; undulate 916.11; **oscillate** 916.10, **pulse, pulsate** 916.12; commute, shuttle

ADJS 6 **regular, systematic** *or* systematical, methodical, ordered, orderly, regular as clockwork; everyday; **uniform** 781.5; **constant** 847.5

7 **periodic** *or* periodical, seasonal, epochal, **cyclic** *or* cyclical, serial, isochronal, metronomic; measured, steady, even, **rhythmic** *or* rhythmical 709.28; **recurrent,** recurring, reoccurring; **intermittent,** reciprocal, alternate, every other; circling, wheeling, rotary, rotational, wavelike, undulant, undulatory, oscillatory 916.15, pulsing, beating 916.18

8 **momentary,** momently, **hourly; daily,** diurnal, quotidian, circadian, nightly, tertian; biorhythmic; **weekly,** tertian, hebdomadal, hebdomadary; biweekly, semiweekly; fortnightly; **monthly,** menstrual, catamenial, estrous; bimonthly, semimonthly; quarterly; biannual, semiannual, semiyearly, half-yearly, semestral; **yearly, annual;** perennial; biennial, triennial, decennial, etc; centennial, centenary; bissextile; secular

ADVS 9 **regularly, systematically, methodically,** like clockwork, at regular intervals, punctually, steadily; at stated times, at fixed *or* established periods; intermittently, every so often, every now and then; **uniformly** 781.7; **constantly** 847.7

10 **periodically, recurrently, seasonally,** cyclically, epochally; rhythmically, on the beat, in time, synchronously, **hourly, daily,** etc; every hour, every day, etc; hour by hour, day by day, etc; from hour to hour, from day to day, *de die in diem* <L>

11 **alternately, by turns, in turns, in rotation,** turn about, **turn and turn about,** reciprocally, every other, one after the other; to and fro, up and down, from side to side; off and on, make and break, round and round

PHRS 12 **what goes around comes around,** *plus ça change plus c'est la même chose* <Fr>

851 IRREGULARITY OF RECURRENCE

NOUNS **1 irregularity,** unmethodicalness, unsystematicness; **inconstancy, unevenness, unsteadiness,** uncertainty, desultoriness; **variability,** capriciousness, unpredictability, whimsicality, eccentricity, stagger, wobble, weaving, erraticness; roughness; **fitfulness, sporadicity** *or* sporadicalness, spasticity, jerkiness, fits and starts, patchiness, spottiness, choppiness, brokenness, disconnectedness, discontinuity 813; **intermittence, fluctuation; nonuniformity** 782; arrhythmia *and* fibrillation <medical>; assymetry; unusualness

VERBS **2 intermit, fluctuate,** vary, lack regularity, go by fits and starts; break, disconnect

ADJS **3 irregular,** unregular, unsystematic, unmethodical *or* immethodical; **inconstant, unsteady, uneven, unrhythmical,** unmetrical, rough, unequal, uncertain, unsettled; **variable,** deviative, heteroclite; **capricious, erratic,** off-again-on-again, eccentric; wobbly, wobbling, weaving, staggering, lurching, careening; **fitful, spasmodic** *or* spasmodical, spastic, spasmic, **jerky,** herky-jerky <nf>, halting; **sporadic,** patchy, spotty, scrappy, snatchy, catchy, choppy, halting, **broken, disconnected, discontinuous** 813.4; **nonuniform** 782.3; **intermittent,** intermitting, **desultory, fluctuating, wavering,** wandering, rambling, veering; flickering, guttering; haphazard, disorderly

ADVS **4 irregularly,** unsystematically, unmethodically; **inconstantly, unsteadily, unevenly,** unrhythmically, roughly, uncertainly; **variably,** capriciously, unpredictably, whimsically, eccentrically, wobblingly, lurchingly, erratically; **intermittently, disconnectedly, discontinuously** 813.5; **nonuniformly** 782.4; **brokenly, desultorily,** patchily, spottily, in spots, in snatches; **by fits and starts,** by fits, by jerks, by snatches, by catches; **fitfully, sporadically, jerkily, spasmodically,** haltingly; **off and on,** at irregular intervals, sometimes and sometimes not; when the mood strikes, when the spirit moves, at random

852 CHANGE

NOUNS **1 change, alteration, modification; variation,** variety, difference, diversity, diversification; **deviation,** diversion, aberrance *or* aberrancy, **divergence; switch, switchover, changeover, turn,** change of course, turnabout, about-face, U-turn, **reversal,** flip-flop <nf>; apostasy, defection, change of heart, change of mind; **shift,** transition, **modulation,** qualification; **conversion, renewal,** revival, revivification, retro; remaking, reshaping, re-creation, redesign, restructuring, *perestroika* <Russ>; role reversal; realignment, **adaptation, adjustment,** accommodation, fitting, tweaking, tweak; **reform,** reformation, **improvement,** amelioration, melioration, mitigation, constructive change, **betterment,** change for the better; **take** *and* **new take** <nf>; **social mobility,** vertical mobility, horizontal mobility, upward *or* downward mobility; gradual change, progressive change, **continuity** 812; **degeneration, deterioration,** worsening, degenerative change, change for the worse, disorder 810, entropy; changeableness 854; rolling stone

2 revolution, revolt, **break,** break with the past, sudden change, radical *or* revolutionary *or* violent *or* total change, catastrophic change, **upheaval,** overthrow, **quantum jump** *or* **leap,** sea change; **discontinuity** 813

3 transformation, transmogrification; **translation;** metamorphosis, metamorphism; makeover; **mutation,** transmutation, permutation, vicissitude; **mutant,** mutated form, sport; **transfiguration** *or* transfigurement; metathesis, transposition, translocation, **displacement,** metastasis, heterotopia; **transubstantiation,**

consubstantiation; transanimation, transmigration, reincarnation, metempsychosis avatar; metasomatism, metasomatosis; catalysis; metabolism, anabolism, catabolism; metagenesis; transformism; redecoration

4 **innovation, introduction,** discovery, invention, launching; neologism, neoterism, coinage; **breakthrough,** leap, quantum jump *or* leap, new phase; **novelty** 841.2

5 transformer, transmogrifier, **innovator,** innovationist, introducer; precursor 816; **alterant,** alterer, alterative, **agent,** catalytic agent, catalyst; the wind *or* winds of change; **leaven,** yeast, ferment; **modifier,** modificator; magician

VERBS 6 **be changed, change, undergo a change,** go through a change, sing *or* dance to a different tune <nf>, be converted into, turn into 858.17; **alter,** mutate, modulate; transmutate; **vary,** checker, diversify; **deviate, diverge,** turn, take a turn, take a new turn, turn aside, turn the corner, **shift,** veer, jibe, tack, come about, come round *or* around, haul around, chop, chop and change, swerve, warp; change sides, change horses in midstream; **revive,** be renewed, feel like a new person; **improve,** ameliorate, meliorate, mitigate, turn the corner; **degenerate, deteriorate, worsen;** hit bottom, bottom out <nf>, reach the nadir, flop <nf>

7 **change, work** *or* **make a change, alter,** change someone's tune; **mutate; modify;** adapt; modulate, accommodate, adjust, fine-tune, fit, **qualify; vary, diversify; convert, renew, recast, revamp** <nf>, change over, exchange, **revive;** remake, reshape, re-create, redesign, **rebuild,** reconstruct, restructure; realign; refit; **reform, improve,** better, ameliorate, meliorate, mitigate; **revolutionize,** turn upside down, subvert, overthrow, break up; worsen, deform, denature; ring the changes; give a turn to, give a twist to, turn the tide, turn the tables, turn the scale *or* balance; shift the scene; shuffle the cards; turn over a new leaf; **about-face,** do an about-face, do a 180 <nf>, change direction, reverse oneself, turn one's coat, sing *or* dance to a different tune, flip-flop <nf>, make a U-turn, change one's mind

8 **transform, transfigure, transmute,** transmogrify; **translate;** transubstantiate, metamorphose; metabolize; perform magic, conjure

9 **innovate,** make innovations, invent, discover, make a breakthrough, make a quantum jump *or* leap, **pioneer** 816.3, **revolutionize, introduce,** introduce new blood; neologize, neoterize, coin

ADJS 10 **changed, altered, modified,** qualified, **transformed,** transmuted, **metamorphosed;** translated, metastasized; deviant, aberrant, mutant; divergent; **converted, renewed,** revived, **rebuilt**, remodeled**; reformed,** improved, **better,** ameliorative, ameliatory; before-and-after; **degenerate, worse,** unmitigated; subversive, **revolutionary**; changeable 854.6,7

11 **innovational**, innovative, ameliorative

12 **metamorphic, metabolic,** anabolic, catabolic; metastatic, **catalytic**

13 presto, presto chango, hey presto <Brit>

PHRS 14 the shoe is on the other foot

853 PERMANENCE

NOUNS 1 **permanence** *or* permanency, **immutability, changelessness,** unchangingness, invariableness *or* invariability; **unchangeableness,** unchangeability, unchangingness, inalterability *or* inalterableness, inconvertibility *or* inconvertibleness; **fixedness, constancy,** steadfastness, firmness, solidity, immovableness *or* immovability, persistence *or* persistency, establishment, faithfulness, **lastingness, abidingness, endurance,** duration, continuance, perseverance, continuity, standing, long standing, inveteracy; durableness, durability 827.1; **perpetualness** 829.1; **stability** 855; **unchangeability** 855.4;

immobility, stasis, frozenness, hardening, **rigidity; quiescence,** torpor, coma

2 **maintenance, preservation** 397, **conservation**

3 **conservatism, conservativeness,** opposition *or* resistance to change, unprogressiveness, fogyism, fuddy-duddyism, backwardness, old-fashionedness, standpattism <nf>; ultraconservatism, arch-conservatism; misocainea, misoneism; political conservatism, rightism 611.1; laissez-faireism 329.1; old school tie <Brit>

4 **conservative,** conservatist; conservationist; ultraconservative, arch-conservative, knee-jerk conservative <nf>, **diehard,** standpat *and* standpatter <nf>, **old fogy,** fogy, stick-in-the-mud <nf>, mossback <nf>, *laudator temporis acti* <L>, rightist, right-winger 611.9; old school

VERBS 5 **remain, endure** 827.6, last, stay, persist, bide, abide, stand, hold, subsist; be ever the same; take root, be here to stay; cast in stone

6 **be conservative,** save, preserve, oppose change, stand on ancient ways; stand pat *and* stand still <nf>; **let things take their course,** leave things as they are, let be, let *or* leave alone, stick with it *and* let it ride <nf>, follow a hands-off policy, let well enough alone, do nothing; stop *or* turn back the clock

ADJS 7 **permanent, changeless, unchanging, immutable,** unvarying, unshifting; unchanged, unchangeable, unvaried, **unaltered,** inalterable, inviolate, undestroyed, intact; **constant, persistent,** sustained, fixed, firm, solid, steadfast, like the Rock of Gibraltar, faithful; unchecked, unfailing, unfading; **lasting, enduring,** abiding, remaining, staying, continuing; **durable** 827.10, entrenched; **perpetual** 829.7; stable 855.12; **unchangeable** 855.17; **immobile, static,** stationary, frozen, **rigid,** rocklike; **quiescent,** torpid, comatose, vegetable

8 **conservative, preservative,** old-line, **diehard,** standpat <nf>, opposed to change; backward, backward-looking, old-fashioned, **unprogressive,** nonprogressive, unreconstructed, status-quo, stuck-in-the-mud; ultraconservative, misoneistic, fogyish, **old-fogyish; right-wing** 611.17; *laissez-faire* <Fr>, hands-off; noninvasive, noninterventionist

ADVS 9 **permanently,** abidingly, lastingly, steadfastly, unwaveringly, changelessly, unchangingly; enduringly, **perpetually,** invariably, **forever, always** 829.11; statically, rigidly, inflexibly

10 *in status quo* <L>, as things are, **as is, as usual,** as per usual <nf>; at a stand *or* standstill, without a shadow of turning

PHRS 11 *plus ça change, plus c'est la même chose* <Fr, the more it changes, the more it's the same thing>; if it isn't broken don't fix it, let sleeping dogs lie

854 CHANGEABLENESS

NOUNS 1 **changeableness,** changefulness, **changeability, alterability,** convertibility, modifiability; **mutability,** permutability, impermanence, **transience,** transitoriness; mobility, motility, movability; plasticity, malleability, workability, rubberiness, fluidity; **resilience, adaptability,** adjustability, **flexibility,** suppleness; **nonuniformity** 782

2 **inconstancy, instability,** changefulness, unstableness, **unsteadiness,** unsteadfastness, unfixedness, unsettledness, rootlessness; **uncertainty,** undependability, inconsistency, shiftiness, unreliability; **variability,** variation, variety, restlessness, deviability; unpredictability, irregularity 851.1; **desultoriness,** waywardness, wantonness; **erraticism, eccentricity;** freakishness, freakery; flightiness, impulsiveness *or* impulsivity, mercuriality, moodiness, whimsicality, **capriciousness,** caprice, **fickleness** 364.3

3 **changing, fluctuation,** vicissitude, **variation, shiftingness;** alternation, oscillation, **vacillation,** pendulation; **mood swings; wavering,** shifting,

shuffling, teetering, tottering, seesawing, teeter-tottering; **exchange,** trading, musical chairs; bobbing and weaving

4 <comparisons> rollercoaster, Proteus, kaleidoscope, chameleon, shifting sands, rolling stone, April showers, cloud shapes, feather in the wind; water; wheel of fortune; whirligig; mercury, quicksilver; the weather, weathercock, weather vane; moon, phases of the moon; iridescence

VERBS 5 **change, fluctuate, vary; shift; alternate, vacillate,** tergiversate, oscillate, pendulate, waffle <Brit nf>, blow hot and cold <nf>; ebb and flow, wax and wane; go through phases, waver, shuffle, swing, sway, wobble, wobble about, flounder, stagger, teeter, totter, **seesaw, teeter-totter;** back and fill, turn, blow hot and cold, ring the changes, have as many phases as the moon; **exchange,** trade, play musical chairs; metamorphose

ADJS 6 **changeable, alterable,** alterative, modifiable; mutable, permutable, impermanent, transient, **transitory,** rollercoaster; **variable,** checkered, ever-changing, many-sided, kaleidoscopic, variegated; **movable,** mobile, motile; plastic, malleable, rubbery, fluid; **resilient, adaptable,** adjustable, **flexible,** supple, able to adapt, able to roll with the punches *or* bend without breaking; protean, proteiform; metamorphic; **nonuniform** 782.3

7 **inconstant, changeable, changeful, changing, shifting,** uncertain, inconsistent, in a state of flux; **shifty,** unreliable, undependable; **unstable, unfixed,** infirm, restless, **unsettled,** unstaid, **unsteady,** wishy-washy, spineless, shapeless, amorphous, indecisive, irresolute, waffling <Brit nf>, blowing hot and cold <nf>, like a feather in the wind, unsteadfast, unstable as water; **variable,** deviable, dodgy <nf>; unaccountable, unpredictable; vicissitudinous *or* vicissitudinary; whimsical, **capricious, fickle** 364.6, off-again-on-again; **erratic, eccentric,** freakish; volatile, giddy, dizzy, ditzy <nf>, scatterbrained, mercurial, moody, flighty, impulsive, impetuous; **fluctuating,** alternating, **vacillating, wavering,** wavery, wavy, mazy, flitting, flickering, guttering, fitful, shifting, shuffling; irregular, spasmodic 851.3; **desultory,** rambling, roving, vagrant, homeless, wanton, wayward, wandering, afloat, adrift; **unrestrained, undisciplined,** irresponsible, uncontrolled, fast and loose

ADVS 8 **changeably, variably, inconstantly,** shiftingly, shiftily, uncertainly, **unsteadily,** unsteadfastly, whimsically, capriciously, desultorily, erratically, waveringly; **impulsively, impetuously,** precipitately; back and forth, to and fro, in and out, off and on, on and off, round and round

855 STABILITY

NOUNS 1 **stability, firmness, soundness, substantiality, solidity; security,** secureness, securement; **rootedness,** fastness; reliability 970.4; **steadiness,** steadfastness; constancy 847.2, invariability, undeflectability; **imperturbability,** unflappability <nf>, nerve, steady *or* unshakable nerves, nerves of steel, unshakableness, unsusceptibility, unimpressionability, stolidness *or* stolidity, stoicism, **cool** <nf>, *sang-froid* <Fr>; iron will; **equilibrium, balance,** stable state, stable equilibrium, homeostasis; steady state; emotional stability, balanced personality; aplomb; **uniformity** 781

2 **fixity,** fixedness, fixture, fixation; infixion, implantation, embedment; **establishment, stabilization,** confirmation, entrenchment; inveteracy, deep-rootedness, **deep-seatedness**

3 **immobility,** immovability, unmovability, immovableness, irremovability, immotility; inextricability; **firmness,** solidity, unyieldingness, rigidity, **inflexibility** 1046.3; inertia, *vis inertiae* <L>, inertness; immobilization

4 unchangeableness, unchangeability, unalterability, inalterability, unmodifiability, **immutability,** incommutability, inconvertibility; nontransferability; lastingness, **permanence** 853; irrevocability, indefeasibility, **irreversibility;** irretrievability, unreturnableness, unrestorableness; intransmutability

5 indestructibility, imperishability, incorruptibility, inextinguishability, immortality, **deathlessness;** invulnerability, invincibility, inexpugnability, impregnability; ineradicability, indelibility, ineffaceability, inerasableness

6 <comparisons> rock, Rock of Gibraltar, bedrock, pillar *or* tower of strength, foundation; leopard's spots

VERBS **7 stabilize,** stabilitate *or* stabilify ; **firm, firm up** <nf>; **steady, balance,** counterbalance; ballast; **immobilize,** freeze, keep, retain; **transfix,** stick, hold, pin *or* nail down <nf>; set *or* cast *or* write in stone

8 secure, make sure *or* secure, firm up, tie, tie off *or* up, chain, tether; cleat, belay; **wedge, jam, seize; make fast, fasten,** fasten down; **anchor,** moor; batten *and* batten down; **confirm,** ratify

9 fix, define, set, **settle; establish,** found, ground, lodge, seat, **entrench; root;** infix, ingrain, set in, plant, implant, engraft, bed, embed; **print,** imprint, **stamp,** inscribe, **etch,** engrave, impress; deep-dye, **dye in the wool;** stereotype

10 <become firmly fixed> **root, take root,** strike root, settle down; **stick,** stick fast; seize, seize up, freeze; **catch, jam,** lodge, foul

11 stand fast, stand *or* remain firm, **stand pat** <nf>, stay put <nf>, hold fast, not budge, not budge an inch, **stand** *or* **hold one's ground,** persist, persevere, hold one's own, dig in one's heels, take one's stand, **stick to one's guns,** put one's foot down <nf>; **hold out,** stick *or* gut *or* tough it out and hang tough <nf>, stay the course; **hold up; weather,** weather the storm, ride it out, get home free <nf>; be imperturbable, be unflappable *and* not bat an eye *or* eyelash *and* keep one's cool <nf>

ADJS **12 stable, substantial, firm, solid, sound,** stabile; firm as Gibraltar, solid as a rock, rock-like, built on bedrock; **fast, secure; steady,** unwavering, steadfast; **balanced,** in equilibrium, in a stable state; **well-balanced; imperturbable,** unflappable <nf>, unshakable, **cool** <nf>, unimpressionable, unsusceptible, impassive, stolid, stoic; without nerves, without a nerve in one's body, unflinching, iron-willed; **reliable** 970.17, predictable; fiducial

13 established, stabilized, **entrenched,** vested, firmly established; **well-established,** well-founded, **well-grounded,** on a rock, in *or* on bedrock, aground; old-line, long-established; **confirmed, inveterate; settled, set;** well-settled, well-set, in place, entrenched; **rooted,** well-rooted; **deep-rooted, deep-seated,** deep-set, deep-settled, deep-fixed, deep-dyed, deep-engraven, deep-grounded, deep-laid; **infixed, ingrained,** implanted, engrafted, embedded, ingrown, inwrought; impressed, indelibly impressed, imprinted; engraved, etched, graven, embossed; **dyed-in-the-wool**

14 fixed, fastened, anchored, riveted; **set, settled, stated;** staple

15 immovable, unmovable, **immobile,** immotile, unmoving, **irremovable, stationary,** frozen, not to be moved, at a standstill, on dead center; **firm, unyielding,** adamant, adamantine, rigid, **inflexible** 1046.12; pat, standpat <nf>; at anchor

16 stuck, fast, stuck fast, **fixed, transfixed, caught,** fastened, tied, chained, tethered, anchored, moored, held, inextricable; **jammed,** impacted, congested, packed, wedged; seized, seized up, frozen; aground, grounded, stranded, high and dry

17 unchangeable, not to be changed, changeless, unchanged, unchanging, unvarying, unvariable, **unalterable,** unaltered, unalterative, **immutable,** incommutable, inconvertible, unmodifiable; insusceptible of change; **constant, invariable,** undeviating, undeflectable; lasting, unremitting, **permanent** 853.7; irrevocable, indefeasible, **irreversible,** nonreversible, reverseless; irretrievable, unrestorable, unreturnable, nonreturnable; intransmutable, inert, noble <chemistry>

18 **indestructible,** undestroyable, **imperishable,** nonperishable, incorruptible; **deathless,** immortal, undying; **invulnerable, invincible,** inexpugnable, impregnable, indivisible; **ineradicable,** indelible, ineffaceable, inerasable; **inextinguishable,** unquenchable, quenchless, undampable

PHRS 19 **stet, let it stand; what's done is done**

856 CONTINUANCE

<continuance in action>

NOUNS 1 **continuance, continuation, ceaselessness,** unceasingness, uninterruptedness, unremittingness, **continualness** 812.1; **prolongation, extension, protraction, perpetuation,** lengthening, spinning *or* stringing out; **survival** 827.1, holding out, hanging on *or* in; **maintenance,** sustenance, sustained action *or* activity; pursuance; run, way, straight *or* uninterrupted course; **progress,** progression; **persistence, perseverance** 360; **endurance** 827.1, **stamina,** staying power; **continuity** 812; **repetition** 849

2 **resumption, recommencement,** rebeginning, reestablishment, revival, recrudescence, resuscitation, **renewal,** reopening, reentrance, reappearance; **fresh start,** new beginning; another try, another shot *or* crack *or* go <nf>

VERBS 3 **continue** 812.4, keep *or* stay with it, keep *or* stay at it, carry on; **remain,** bide, **abide, stay,** tarry, linger; **go on,** go along, **keep on,** keep on keeping on, keep going, carry on, see it through, stay on, hold on, hold one's way *or* course *or* path, hold steady, run on, jog on, drag on, bash ahead *or* on <nf>, slog on, soldier on, plug away <nf>, grind away *or* on, stagger on, put one foot in front of the other; never cease, cease not; **endure** 827.6

4 **sustain, protract, prolong, extend,** perpetuate, lengthen, spin *or* string out; **maintain,** keep, hold, retain, preserve; **keep up,** keep going, keep alive, **survive** 827.6

5 **persist, persevere,** keep at it 360.2, stick it out, stick to it, stick with it, never say die, see it through, hang in *and* hang tough *and* not know when one is licked <nf>; survive, make out, manage, get along, get on, eke out an existence, keep the even tenor of one's way; go on, go on with, go on with the show <nf>, press on; perseverate, iterate, reiterate, **harp,** go on about, chew one's ear off *and* run off at the mouth <nf>, beat a dead horse

6 **resume, recommence,** rebegin, **renew,** reestablish; **revive,** resuscitate, recrudesce; reenter, reopen, **return to,** go back to, begin again, take up again, make a new beginning, make a fresh start, start all over, have another try, have another shot *or* crack *or* go <nf>

ADJS 7 **continuing, abiding** 827.10; staying, remaining, sticking; **continuous** 812.8, **ceaseless, unceasing,** unending, endless, incessant, unremitting, steady, sustained, protracted, undying, indefatigable, **persistent; repetitious, repetitive** 849.14; **resumed,** recommenced, rebegun, renewed, reopened

857 CESSATION

NOUNS 1 **cessation, discontinuance,** discontinuation, phaseout, phasedown, scratching and scrubbing and breakoff <nf>; **desistance,** desinence, cease, surcease, **ceasing,** ending, halting, stopping, termination; **close,** closing, shutdown; sign-off; log-off; **relinquishment,** renunciation, abandonment, breakup

2 **stop,** stoppage, **halt, stay, arrest,** check, cutoff <nf>; stand, **standstill;** full stop, dead stop, screaming

or grinding *or* shuddering *or* squealing halt; **strike** 727.5, walkout, work stoppage, sit-down strike, lockout; sick-out and blue flu <nf>; **end,** ending, endgame, final whistle, gun, bell, checkmate; **tie,** stalemate, deadlock, wash *and* toss-up <nf>, standoff *and* Mexican standoff <nf>; **terminal,** end of the line, rest stop, stopping place, terminus, closure

3 **pause, rest, break,** caesura, fermata, **recess, intermission,** interim 826, intermittence, interval, interlude, *intermezzo* <Ital>; **respite,** letup <nf>; **interruption, suspension,** time-out, break in the action, breathing spell *or* space, cooling-off period; **postponement** 846.4, rain-out; **remission;** abeyance, stay, drop, lull, lapse; truce, cease-fire, stand-down; **vacation, holiday,** time off, day off, recess, playtime, leisure

4 <grammatical terms> pause, juncture, boundary, caesura; <punctuation> stop *or* point *or* period, comma, serial comma, Oxford comma, colon, semicolon

5 <legislatures> **cloture,** clôture <Fr>; cloture by compartment, kangaroo cloture; guillotine <Brit>; closure of debate

VERBS 6 **cease, discontinue, end, stop, halt,** end-stop, terminate, close the books on, close the books, put paid to <Brit>, abort, cancel, scratch *and* scrub <nf>, hold, **quit,** stay, belay <nf>; **desist, refrain,** leave off, lay off <nf>, give over, **have done with;** cut it out *and* drop it *and* knock it off <nf>, relinquish, renounce, abandon; **come to an end** 820.6, draw to a close; hang up, ring off <nf>

7 **stop, come to a stop** *or* **halt,** halt, stop in one's tracks, skid to a stop, stop dead, **stall; bring up, pull up,** pull in, head in, draw up, **fetch up; stop short,** come up short, bring up short, come to a screaming *or* squealing *or* grinding *or* shuddering halt, stop on a dime <nf>, come to a full stop, put on the brake, come to a standstill, grind to a halt, fetch up all standing; **stick,** jam, hang fire, seize, seize up, freeze; **cease fire,** stand down; run into a brick wall

8 <stop work> **lay off, knock off** <nf>, call it a day <nf>, call it quits <nf>; lay down one's tools, **shut up shop,** close shop, shut down, lock up, close down, secure <nautical nf>; **strike,** walk out, call a strike, go *or* go out on strike, stand down; work to rule

9 **pause, rest,** let up *and* take it easy <nf>, **relax,** rest on one's oars; **recess,** take *or* call a recess; call time-out; **take a break,** break, take five *or* ten; hang fire; catch one's breath, take a breather

10 **interrupt, suspend,** intermit, **break, break off,** take a break <nf>, cut off, break *or* snap the thread

11 **put a stop to, call a halt to,** get it over with, blow the whistle on <nf>, **put an end to** 820.5, put paid to <Brit nf>, call off the dogs <nf>; **stop, stay, halt, arrest, check,** flag down, wave down; block, brake, dam, stem, stem the tide *or* current; pull up, draw rein, put on the brakes, hit the brake pedal; **bring to a stand** *or* **standstill,** bring to a close *or* halt, freeze, bring to, bring up short, **stop dead** *or* dead in one's tracks, set one back on his heels, stop cold, stop short, cut short, check in full career; checkmate, stalemate, deadlock; thwart; do in <nf>

12 **turn off, shut off,** shut, shut down, close; **phase out,** phase down, taper off, wind up *or* down; **kill, cut,** cut off short, switch off

13 <nf terms> **cut it out!,** cool it!, bag it!, chill out!, call it quits!, can it!, turn it off!, chuck it!, stow it!, drop it!, lay off!, all right already!, come off it!, **knock it off!,** break it off!, break it up!

858 CONVERSION

<change to something different>

NOUNS 1 **conversion,** reconversion, **change-over,** turning into, becoming; convertibility; **change** 852, sea change, **transformation,** transubstantiation, transmutation, metamorphosis; **transition,** transit, **switch** *and* **switchover** <nf>, passage, **shift; reversal,** about-face *and* flip-flop <nf>, role reversal, *volte-face* <Fr>; makeover, do-over, complete change, 360-degree change, 360 <nf>; **relapse,** lapse, descent; **breakthrough; growth,** progress, development; transcendence; **resolution** 940.1; reduction, simplification; **assimilation,** naturalization, adoption, assumption; processing; alchemy

2 **new start, new beginning,** fresh start, clean slate, square one <nf>; **reformation, reform, regeneration, revival, reclamation,** redemption, amendment, improvement 392, renewal, recrudescence, **rebirth,** renascence, new birth, **change of heart;** change of mind *or* commitment *or* allegiance *or* loyalty *or* conviction

3 apostasy, renunciation, **defection, desertion,** treason, crossing-over, abandonment; degeneration 393.3

4 **rehabilitation,** reconditioning, recovery, readjustment, reclamation, restoration; **reeducation,** reinstruction; **repatriation**

5 **indoctrination,** reindoctrination, counterindoctrination; **brainwashing,** menticide; subversion, alienation, corruption

6 **conversion,** proselytization, proselytism, evangelization, persuasion 375.3; indoctrination; spiritual rebirth

7 **convert, proselyte,** neophyte, catechumen, disciple, new man *or* woman, born-again person

8 **apostate, defector,** turncoat, traitor, deserter, **renegade**

9 **converter, proselyter,** proselytizer, **missionary, apostle, evangelist,** televangelist; reformer, rehabilitator

10 <instruments> philosopher's stone, melting pot, crucible, alembic, test tube, caldron, retort, mortar; potter's wheel, anvil, lathe; converter, transformer, transducer, engine, motor, machine 1040.3

VERBS 11 **convert,** reconvert; **change over,** switch *and* switch over <nf>, **shift,** slide into**; do over,** re-do, make over, rejigger <nf>; **change, transform** 852.6,8, transmute, metamorphose; **change into, turn into, become,** resolve into, assimilate to, bring to, reduce to, naturalize; **make,** render; **reverse,** do an about-face; change one's tune, sing a different tune, dance to another tune; turn back 859.5

12 **re-form,** remodel, reshape, refashion, recast; regroup, redeploy, rearrange 808.13; **renew,** new-model; be reborn, be born again, be a new person, feel like a new person; get it together *and* get one's act *or* shit together *and* get one's ducks in a row <nf>; **regenerate, reclaim,** redeem, amend, set straight; **reform, rehabilitate,** set on the straight and narrow, make a new man of, restore self-respect; mend *or* change one's ways, **turn over a new leaf,** put on the new man, undergo a personality change

13 **defect,** renege, wimp *or* chicken *or* cop out <nf>, turn one's coat, desert, apostatize, change one's colors, turn against, turn traitor; leave *or* desert a sinking ship; lapse, relapse; degenerate

14 **rehabilitate,** recondition, reclaim, recover, restore, readjust; **reeducate,** reinstruct; **repatriate**

15 **indoctrinate, brainwash,** reindoctrinate, counterindoctrinate; subvert, alienate, win away, corrupt

16 **convince, persuade,** wean, bring over, sweep off one's feet <nf>, **win over;** proselyte, **proselytize,** evangelize

17 be converted into, **turn into** *or* **to, become** 761.12, **change into,** alter into, run *or* fall *or* pass into, slide *or* glide into, **grow into,** ripen into, **develop** *or* **evolve into,** merge *or* blend *or* melt into, shift into, lapse into, open into, resolve itself *or* settle into, come round to

ADJS 18 **convertible,** changeable, resolvable, transmutable, **transformable, transitional, modifiable;** reformable, reclaimable, renewable

19 **converted, changed, transformed;** naturalized, assimilated; **reformed,**

regenerated, renewed, redeemed, reborn, born-again; liquidated; brainwashed

20 **apostate, treasonable, traitorous,** degenerate, **renegade**

859 REVERSION

<change to a former state>

NOUNS 1 **reversion,** reverting, retroversion, retrogradation, **retrogression,** retrocession, regress, **relapse** 394, **regression, backsliding,** lapse, slipping back, backing, recidivism, recidivation; reconversion; **reverse, reversal,** turnabout, about-face, right about-face, 180-degree shift *or* change, flip-flop <nf>, **turn; return,** returning, retreat; disenchantment; **reclamation, rehabilitation,** redemption, return to the fold; **reinstatement,** restitution, restoration; retroaction; turn of the tide

2 **throwback,** atavism

3 **returnee, repeater;** prodigal son, lost lamb; reversioner, reversionist; recidivist, habitual criminal *or* offender, two-time loser <nf>; backslider

VERBS 4 **revert,** retrovert, **regress, retrogress,** retrograde, retrocede, **reverse, return,** return to the fold; backslide, slip back, recidivate, lapse, lapse back, relapse 394.4

5 **turn back, change back, go back, hark back,** cry back, break back, **turn,** turn around *or* about; make a round trip; do an about-face *and* flip-flop *and* do a flip-flop *and* hang a 180<nf>, ricochet; undo, turn back the clock, put the genie back into the bottle, put the toothpaste back into the tube; go back to go *or* to square one *or* to the drawing board <nf>

6 **revert to, return to,** recur to, go back to; hark *or* cry back to

ADJS 7 **reversionary,** reversional, **regressive,** recessive, **retrogressive, retrograde;** reactionary; recidivist *or* recidivistic, recidivous, lapsarian; retroverse, retrorse; retroactive; atavistic; revertible, returnable, reversible, recoverable

860 REVOLUTION

<sudden or radical change>

NOUNS 1 **revolution, radical** *or* **total change, violent change,** striking alteration, sweeping change, clean sweep, clean slate, square one <nf>, tabula rasa; transilience, quantum leap *or* jump; **overthrow,** overturn, upset, *bouleversement* <Fr>, convulsion, spasm, subversion, coup d'état; breakup, breakdown; **cataclysm, catastrophe,** debacle, *débâcle* <Fr>; **revolution,** revolutionary war, war of national liberation; bloodless revolution, palace revolution; technological revolution, electronic *or* communications *or* computer *or* information revolution; green revolution; counterrevolution; **revolt** 327.4, reign of terror

2 **revolutionism,** revolutionariness, anarchism, syndicalism, terrorism

3 **revolutionist, revolutionary,** revolutionizer; **rebel** 327.5; anarchist, anarch, syndicalist, criminal syndicalist, terrorist 671.9; subversive; red; revolutionary junta

VERBS 4 **revolutionize, make a radical change,** make a clean sweep, break with the past; **overthrow, overturn,** throw the rascals out *and* let heads roll <nf> *boulverse* <Fr>, upset; revolt 327.7

ADJS 5 **revolutionary;** revulsive, revulsionary; transilient; subversive, insurgent; cataclysmic, catastrophic; **radical,** sweeping 794.10; **insurrectionary** 327.11

6 **revolutionist, revolutionary,** anarchic *or* anarchical, syndicalist, terrorist *or* terroristic, agin the government <nf>; Bolshevistic, Bolshevik; sans-culottic, sans-culottish; Jacobinic *or* Jacobinical, Carbonarist, Fenian, Marxist, Leninist, Communist, Trotskyist *or* Trotskyite, Guevarist, Castroist *or* Castroite, Maoist, Vietcong, Mau-Mau

861 EVOLUTION

NOUNS 1 **evolution, evolving,** evolvement; evolutionary change, gradual change, step-by-step change, peaceful *or* nonviolent change; **development, growth,** rise, incremental change, developmental change, natural growth *or* development; flowering, blossoming; ripening, coming of age, maturation 303.6; accomplishment 407; **advance,** advancement, furtherance; **progress,** progression; **elaboration,** enlargement, amplification, **expansion;** devolution, degeneration 393.3

2 **unfolding,** unfoldment, unrolling, unfurling, unwinding; revelation, gradual revelation

3 <biological terms> **genesis;** phylogeny, phylogenesis; ontogeny, ontogenesis; physiogeny, physiogenesis; **biological evolution,** speciation, convergent evolution, parallel evolution; natural selection, adaptation; horotely, bradytely, tachytely; gradualism; microevolution, macroevolution; polygenesis, polygeny

4 **evolutionism,** theory of evolution; **Darwinism,** Darwinianism, punctuated equilibrium, Neo-Darwinism, organic evolution, survival of the fittest; Haeckelism, Lamarckism *or* Lamarckianism, Neo-Lamarckism, Lysenkoism, Weismannism, Spencerianism; social Darwinism, social evolution

VERBS **5** **evolve; develop, grow,** wax, change gradually *or* step-by-step; **progress, advance,** come a long way; accomplish 407.4; ripen, mellow, mature 303.9, maturate; flower, bloom, blossom, bear fruit; degenerate

6 **elaborate, develop, work out,** enlarge, enlarge on *or* upon, amplify, **expand,** expand on *or* upon, detail, go *or* enter into detail, go into, flesh out, **pursue,** spell out <nf>; complete 407.6

7 unfold, unroll, unfurl, unwind, unreel, uncoil, reveal, reveal *or* expose gradually

ADJS **8** **evolutionary,** evolutional, evolutionist *or* evolutionistic; **evolving, developing, unfolding; maturing,** maturational, maturative; **progressing, advancing;** devolutionary, degenerative; genetic, phylogenetic, ontogenetic, physiogenetic; horotelic, bradytelic, tachytelic

862 SUBSTITUTION

<change of one thing for another>

NOUNS **1** **substitution, exchange, change,** switch, switcheroo <nf>, swap, commutation, subrogation; **surrogacy;** vicariousness, **representation,** deputation, **delegation;** deputyship, **agency, power of attorney; supplanting,** supplantation, succession; **replacement,** displacement, shuffle; provision, provisionalness *or* provisionality, adhocracy, ad hockery *or* ad hocery, ad hocism; superseding, supersession *or* supersedure; tit for tat, *quid pro quo* <L>; job sharing; novation

2 **substitute,** sub <nf>, **substitution, replacement,** backup, second *or* third string <nf>, secondary, utility player, succedaneum; **change, exchange; ersatz,** phony *and* fake <nf>, counterfeit, imitation 336, copy 785; surrogate; reserves, bench <nf>, backup, backup personnel, spares; **alternate,** alternative, next best thing, lesser of two evils; **successor,** supplanter, superseder, capper <nf>; **proxy,** dummy, ghost; vicar, agent, representative; **deputy** 576; locum tenens, vice, vice-president, vice-regent, etc; **relief,** fill-in, **stand-in, understudy, pinch hitter** *or* runner <nf>; double; **equivalent,** equal; ringer <nf>; ghostwriter; **analogy,** comparison; **metaphor,** metonymy, euphemism, synecdoche <all grammar>; **symbol, sign,** token, icon; makeshift 995.2

3 **scapegoat, goat** <nf>, fall guy *and* can-carrier *and* patsy *and* catch dog <nf>, whipping boy, lamb to the slaughter

VERBS **4** **substitute, exchange, change,** take *or* ask *or* offer in exchange, switch, swap, ring in <nf>, **put in the place of,** change for, make way for, give place to; commute, redeem, compound for; **pass off,** pawn *or* foist *or* palm *or* fob off; rob Peter to pay Paul; dub in; make do with, shift with, put up with; shuffle

5 **substitute for,** sub for <nf>, subrogate; **act for,** double for *or* as, stand *or* sit in for, understudy for, fill in for, serve as proxy, don the mantle of, change places with, swap places with <nf>, stand in the stead of, step into *or* fill the shoes of, pinch-hit *and* pinch-run <nf>; deputize; relieve, spell *and* spell off <nf>, cover for; ghost, ghostwrite; **represent** 576.14; **supplant, supersede,** succeed, **replace,** displace, **take the place of,** crowd out, cut out <nf>

6 <nf terms> **cover up for,** front for; **take the rap for** *and* take the fall for <nf>, carry the can *and* be the goat *or* patsy *or* fall guy <nf>

7 **delegate, deputize,** depute, **commission,** give the nod to <nf>, designate an agent *or* a proxy

ADJS 8 **substitute, alternate, alternative,** other, tother <nf>, equivalent, token, dummy, pinch, utility, backup, secondary; ad hoc, provisional; **vicarious,** ersatz, mock, phony *and* fake *and* bogus <nf>, counterfeit, imitation 336.8; **proxy,** deputy; makeshift, reserve, **spare,** stopgap, temporary, provisional, tentative

9 **substitutional,** substitutionary, substitutive, provisional, supersessive; **substituted,** substituent

10 **replaceable,** substitutable, supersedable, expendable

ADVS 11 **instead, rather,** *faute de mieux* <Fr>; in its stead *or* place; in one's stead, in one's behalf, in one's place, in one's shoes; by proxy; as an alternative; *in loco parentis* <L>

863 INTERCHANGE

<double or mutual change>

NOUNS 1 **interchange, exchange,** counterchange; **transposition,** transposal; mutual transfer *or* replacement; mutual admiration, mutual support; **cooperation** 450; commutation, permutation, intermutation; alternation; **interplay, tradeoff, compromise, reciprocation** 777.1, reciprocality, reciprocity, mutuality, two-way traffic, alternation; *give-and-take,* something for something, *quid pro quo* <L>, measure for measure, tit for tat, an eye for an eye; retaliation, *lex talionis* <L>; cross fire; battledore and shuttlecock; repartee

2 **trading, swapping** <nf>; trade, swap <nf>, even trade, even-steven trade, **switch;** barter 731.2; logrolling, back scratching, pork barrel; pawning, castling <chess>

3 **interchangeability,** exchangeability, changeability, standardization; convertibility, commutability, permutability

VERBS 4 **interchange, exchange,** change, counterchange; alternate; **transpose;** convert, commute, permute; **trade, swap** <nf>, **switch;** bandy, bandy about, play at battledore and shuttlecock; **reciprocate, trade off,** compromise, settle, settle for, respond, keep a balance; **give and take,** give tit for tat, give as much as one takes, give as good as one gets, return the compliment *or* favor, pay back, compensate, **requite,** return; **retaliate,** get back at, get even with, be quits with; logroll, scratch each other's back, **cooperate** 450.3

ADJS 5 **interchangeable, exchangeable,** changeable, standard; equivalent; **even,** equal; returnable, **convertible,** commutable, permutable; commutative; retaliatory, equalizing; **reciprocative** *or* **reciprocating, reciprocatory, reciprocal, traded-off**, two-way; **mutual,** give-and-take; **exchanged, transposed,** switched, **swapped** <nf>, traded, **interchanged;** requited, reciprocated

ADVS 6 **interchangeably, exchangeably; in exchange, in return; even, evenly,** *au pair* <Fr>; **reciprocally,** mutually; **in turn,** each in its turn, every one in his turn, by turns, turn about, turn and turn about

PHRS 7 one good turn deserves another; you scratch my back I scratch yours

864 GENERALITY

NOUNS 1 **generality, universality,** cosmicality, inclusiveness 772.1; worldwideness, globality *or* globalism, ecumenicity *or* ecumenicalism; catholicity; **internationalism,** cosmopolitanism; **generalization,** universalization, globalization, ecumenization, internationalization; **labeling,** stereotyping

2 **prevalence, commonness,** commonality, usualness, **currency,** occurrence; **extensiveness,** widespreadness, pervasiveness, sweepingness, rifeness, rampantness; **normality,** normalness, averageness, ordinariness, routineness, habitualness, standardness

3 **average,** ruck, **run,** general *or* common *or* average *or* ordinary run, **run of the mill;** any Tom, Dick, or Harry; Everyman; common *or* average man, the man in the street, John Q Public, John *or* Jane Doe, ordinary Joe, Joe Six-pack, Joe Blow, lowest common denominator; girl next door; everyman, everywoman; *homme moyen sensuel* <Fr>

4 **all, everyone, everybody, each and every one, one and all,** all comers *and* all hands *and* every man Jack *and* every mother's son <nf>, every living soul, **all the world,** everyone and his brother, *tout le monde* <Fr>, the devil and all <nf>, **whole, totality** 792.1; **everything,** all kinds *or* all manner of things; you name it *and* what have you *and* all the above <nf>; Anytown

5 **any, anything,** any one, aught, either; **anybody, anyone**

6 **whatever,** whate'er, **whatsoever,** whatsoe'er, **what, whichever,** anything soever which, no matter what *or* which, what have you, what you will

7 **whoever,** whoso, **whosoever, whomever,** whomso, **whomsoever,** anyone, no matter who, anybody

8 <idea *or* expression> **generalization,** general idea, **abstraction,** generalized proposition; glittering generality, sweeping statement, vague generalization; **truism, platitude, conventional wisdom,** commonplace, *lieu commun* <Fr>, *locus communis* <L>; **cliché,** tired cliché, bromide, trite *or* hackneyed expression; labeling, stereotyping

VERBS 9 **generalize, universalize,** catholicize, ecumenicize, globalize, internationalize; **broaden, widen, expand,** extend, spread; make a generalization, deal in generalities *or* abstractions; **label,** stereotype

10 **prevail, predominate, obtain,** dominate, reign, rule; be in force *or* effect; be the rule *or* fashion, be the rage *or* thing <nf>, have currency, be in <nf>

ADJS 11 **general, generalized, nonspecific,** generic, **indefinite,** indeterminate, vague, abstract, nebulous, unspecified, undifferentiated, featureless, uncharacterized, bland, neutral

12 **prevalent, prevailing, common,** popular, **current,** running; regnant, reigning, **ruling, predominant,** predominating, **dominant; rife, rampant,** pandemic, epidemic, besetting; **ordinary, normal, average, usual,** routine, standard, par for the course <nf>, stereotyped, stereotypical; public, communal

13 **extensive, broad, wide,** liberal, diffuse, large-scale, broad-scale, broad-scope, broadly-based, wide-scale, **sweeping; cross-disciplinary,** interdisciplinary; widespread, far-spread, far-stretched, **far-reaching,** far-going, far-embracing, far-extending, far-spreading, far-flying, far-ranging, **far-flung,** wide-flung, wide-reaching, wide-extending, wide-extended, wide-ranging, wide-stretching; **wholesale, indiscriminate;** rife; panoramic, bird's-eye

14 **universal,** cosmic *or* cosmical, heaven-wide, galactic, planetary, world-wide, transnational, planet-wide, **global; total,** allover, holistic; catholic, **all-inclusive,** all-including, **all-embracing,** all-encompassing, all-comprehensive, all-comprehending, all-filling, all-pervading, all-covering, encyclope-

dic; nonsectarian, nondenominational, ecumenic *or* ecumenical; omnipresent, ubiquitous; **cosmopolitan,** international; **national,** nation-wide, country-wide, state-wide

15 **every, all,** any, whichever, whichsoever; **each,** each one; every one, each and every, each and all, **one and all, all and sundry,** all and some

16 **trite, commonplace,** hackneyed, platitudinous, truistic, overworked, quotidian; common *or* garden

ADVS 17 **generally, in general; generally speaking,** speaking generally, **broadly,** broadly speaking, **roughly,** roughly speaking, as an approximation; **usually, as a rule, ordinarily, commonly, normally,** routinely, as a matter of course, in the usual course; **by and large,** at large, altogether, overall, over the long haul <nf>, **all things considered,** taking one thing with another, taking all things together, on balance, **all in all,** taking all in all, taking it for all in all, **on the whole,** as a whole, **in the long run,** for the most part, for better *or* for worse; **prevailingly, predominantly, mostly,** chiefly, mainly

18 **universally,** galactically, cosmically; **everywhere, all over,** the world over, all over the world, internationally; in every instance, without exception, **invariably, always,** never otherwise

865 PARTICULARITY

NOUNS 1 **particularity, individuality, singularity, differentiation,** differentness, distinctiveness, uniqueness; identity, individual *or* separate *or* concrete identity; **personality,** personship, personal identity; soul; **selfness,** selfhood, ipseity, **egohood,** self-identity; oneness 872.1, wholeness, integrity; personal equation, human factor; **nonconformity** 868; **individualism,** particularism; nominalism

2 **speciality, specialness,** specialty, specificality, **specificness,** definiteness; special case; specialty of the house, soup du jour, flavor of the month, today's specials

3 **the specific,** the special, **the particular,** the concrete, the individual, the unique

4 **characteristic, peculiarity, singularity,** particularity, specialty, individualism, **character,** property, nature, **trait,** quirk, point of character, bad point, good point, saving grace, redeeming feature, mannerism, keynote, trick, **feature,** distinctive feature, lineament; claim to fame, expertise, métier, forte; **mark,** marking, **earmark,** hallmark, index, signature; badge, token; **brand,** cast, stamp, cachet, seal, mold, cut, figure, shape, configuration; impress, impression; differential, differentia; **idiosyncrasy,** idiocrasy, eccentricity, peculiarity; **quality, property, attribute;** savor, flavor, taste, gust, aroma, odor, smack, tang, taint

5 **self, ego; oneself, I,** myself, me, my humble self, number one <nf>, yours truly <nf>; yourself, himself, herself, itself; ourselves, yourselves; themselves; you; he, she; him, her; they, them; it; inner self, inner man; subliminal *or* subconscious self; superego, better self, ethical self; other self, alter ego, alter, *alterum* <L>; inner child, child within

6 **specification, designation, stipulation,** specifying, designating, stipulating, singling-out, featuring, highlighting, focusing on, denomination; **allocation,** attribution, fixing, selection, assignment, pinning down; specifications, particulars, minutiae, fine print

7 **particularization, specialization;** individualization, peculiarization, personalization; localization; itemization 766.5; special interest, pursuit, vocation, field

8 **characterization,** distinction, **differentiation;** definition, description

VERBS 9 **particularize, specialize; individualize,** peculiarize, personalize; **descend to particulars,** go into detail, get precise, get down to brass tacks *or* to cases <nf>, get down to the nitty-gritty <nf>, come to the point, lay it on the line <nf>, spell out; **itemize** 766.6, detail, spell out

10 **characterize, distinguish, differentiate, define, describe; mark, earmark,** mark off, mark out, demarcate, **set apart,** make special *or* unique; keynote <nf>, sound the keynote, set the tone *or* mood, set the pace; be characteristic, **be a feature** *or* **trait of**

11 **specify,** specialize, **designate, stipulate,** determine, single out, feature, highlight, focus on, mention, select, pick out, **fix,** set, assign, pin down; **name,** denominate, name names, state, mark, check, check off, **indicate, signify,** point out, put *or* lay one's finger on; mention, cite, quote, attribute

ADJS 12 **particular, special, especial, specific, express,** precise, **concrete; singular, individual,** individualist *or* individualistic, unique; **personal,** private, intimate, inner, solipsistic, esoteric; respective, several; **fixed, definite, defined,** distinct, different, different as night and day, determinate, certain, absolute; **distinguished,** noteworthy, **exceptional, extraordinary;** minute, detailed

13 **characteristic, peculiar, singular,** single, quintessential, intrinsic, unique, qualitative, **distinctive,** marked, distinguished, notable, nameable; appropriate, proper; idiosyncratic, idiocratic, **in character, true to form**, typical

14 **this,** this and no other, this one, this single; **these; that,** that one; those

ADVS 15 **particularly, specially, especially, specifically, expressly,** concretely, exactly, precisely, **in particular,** to be specific; **definitely, distinctly; minutely,** in detail, item by item, singly, separately

16 **personally,** privately, idiosyncratically, **individually; in person,** in the flesh, *in propria persona* <L>; as for me, for all of me, **for my part, as far as I am concerned**

17 **characteristically, peculiarly,** singularly, intrinsically, **uniquely,** markedly, **distinctively,** in its own way, like no other

18 **namely,** nominally, **that is to say,** *videlicet* <L>, viz, *scilicet* <L>, scil, sc, **to wit**

19 **each, apiece;** severally, respectively, one by one, each to each; *per annum* or *per diem* or *per capita* <L>

866 SPECIALTY

<object of special attention or preference>

NOUNS 1 **specialty,** speciality, **line, pursuit, pet subject, business, line of business, line of country** <Brit>, **field,** area, main interest; **vocation** 724.6; **forte, métier, strong point,** long suit; specialism, specialization; technicality; **way,** manner, **style,** type; **lifestyle,** way of life, preferences; cup of tea *and* bag *and* thing *and* thang *and* weakness <nf>

2 **special, feature,** main feature; **leader,** lead item, leading card

3 **specialist,** specializer, **expert, authority,** savant, scholar, connoisseur, maven <nf>; technical expert, technician, techie <nf>, nerd <nf>; pundit, critic; amateur, dilettante; fan, buff, freak *and* nut <nf>, aficionado

VERBS 4 **specialize, feature; narrow, restrict,** limit, confine; specialize in, **go in for,** be into <nf>, have a weakness *or* taste for, be strong in, follow, pursue, **make one's business;** major in, minor in; do one's thing <nf>

ADJS 5 **specialized,** specialist, specialistic; down one's alley <nf>, cut out for one, fits one like a glove; technical; **restricted, limited,** confined; **featured,** feature; **expert, authoritative,** knowledgeable

867 CONFORMITY

NOUNS 1 **conformity; conformance,** conformation, other-directedness; **compliance,** acquiescence, goose step, lockstep, obedience, observance, subordination, traditionalism, **orthodoxy;** strictness; **accordance,** accord, **correspondence,** harmony, agreement, **uniformity** 781; **consistency,** congruity; **accommodation,** adaptation, adaption, pliancy, malleability, flexibility, adjustment; reconciliation, reconcilement; **conventionality** 579.1

2 **conformist,** conformer, sheep, trimmer, parrot, yes-man, organization man, company man, lackey; **conventionalist,** Mrs Grundy, Babbitt, Philistine, middle-class type, button-down *or* white-bread type <nf>, **bourgeois,** burgher, Middle American, plastic person *and* clone *and* square <nf>, three-piecer *and* yuppie <nf>, Barbie Doll <trademark nf>; model child; teenybopper <nf>; **formalist,** methodologist, perfectionist, precisianist *or* precisian, stick-in-the-mud; anal character, compulsive character; pedant

VERBS 3 **conform, comply, correspond,** accord, harmonize; **adapt,** adjust, **accommodate,** bend, meet, suit, fit, shape; **comply with,** agree with, tally with, chime *or* fall in with, go by, be guided *or* regulated by, observe, follow, bend, yield, take the shape of; **adapt to,** adjust to, gear to, assimilate to, **accommodate to** *or* **with; reconcile,** settle, compose; rub off corners; **make conform,** shape, lick into shape, mold, force into a mold; straighten, rectify, correct, **discipline**

4 **follow the rule, toe the mark,** do it according to Hoyle *or* by the book <nf>, play the game <nf>; go through channels; **fit in, follow the crowd,** go with the crowd, follow the fashion, swim *or* go with the stream *or* tide *or* current, get on the bandwagon, trim one's sails to the breeze, follow the beaten path, **do as others do, get** *or* **stay in line,** fall in *or* into line, fall in with; run true to form; **keep in step,** goose-step, walk in lockstep; keep up to standard, pass muster, come up to scratch <nf>

ADJS 5 **conformable, adaptable,** adaptive, adjustable; **compliant,** pliant, complaisant, malleable, flexible, plastic, acquiescent, unmurmuring, other-directed, submissive, tractable, obedient

6 **conformist, conventional** 579.5, bourgeois, plastic *and* square *and* straight *and* white-bread *and* white-bready *and* button-down *and* buttoned-down <nf>, cloned *and* clonish *and* cookie-cutter <nf>; **orthodox,** traditionalist *or* traditionalistic; kosher; **formalistic,** legalistic, precisianistic, anal, compulsive; pedantic, stuffy *and* hidebound <nf>, strait-laced, uptight <nf>; in accord, in keeping, in line, in step, in lockstep; **corresponding,** accordant, concordant, harmonious

ADVS 7 conformably, conformingly, in conformity, **obediently, pliantly,** flexibly, malleably, complaisantly, yieldingly, **compliantly,** submissively; **conventionally,** traditionally; anally, **compulsively;** pedantically

8 **according to rule,** *en règle* <Fr>, according to regulations; **according to Hoyle** *and* **by the book** *and* by the numbers <nf>

PHRS 9 **don't rock the boat, don't make waves,** get in line, shape up, shape up *or* ship out <nf>; when in Rome do as the Romans do

868 NONCONFORMITY

NOUNS 1 **nonconformity,** unconformity, nonconformism, **inconsistency,** incongruity; **inaccordance,** disaccord, disaccordance; originality 337.1; **nonconformance,** disconformity; **nonobservance, noncompliance,** nonconcurrence, **dissent** 333, **protest** 333.2, rebellion, disagreement, contrariety, recalcitrance, refractoriness, recusance *or* recusancy; **deviation** 870.1, deviationism

2 **unconventionality, unorthodoxy** 688, revisionism, heterodoxy, heresy, originality, Bohemianism, beatnikism, hippiedom, counterculture, iconoclasm; eccentricity; alternative lifestyle *or* society *or* medicine

3 **nonconformist,** unconformist, **original,** eccentric, gonzo <nf>, deviant, deviationist, maverick <nf>, rebel, dropout, Bohemian, beatnik, free

spirit, freethinker, independent, hippie, hipster, freak <nf>, flower child, New-Age Traveler; **misfit,** square peg in a round hole, fish out of water; *enfant terrible* <Fr>; **dissenter** 333.3; **heretic** 688.5; sectary, sectarian; nonjuror

VERBS **4 not conform,** nonconform, not comply; **get out of line** *and* **rock the boat** *and* make waves <nf>, **leave the beaten path, go out of bounds,** upset the apple cart, break step, break bounds; drop out, opt out; **dissent** 333.4, swim against the current *or* against the tide *or* upstream, **protest** 333.5

ADJS **5 nonconforming,** unconforming, nonconformable, unadaptable, unadjustable; **uncompliant,** unsubmissive; **nonobservant;** contrary, recalcitrant, refractory, recusant; **deviant,** deviationist, atypic *or* atypical, unusual; **dissenting** 333.6, **dissident;** antisocial

6 unconventional, unorthodox, eccentric, gonzo <nf>, heterodox, heretical; unfashionable, not done, not kosher, not cricket <Brit nf>; offbeat <nf>, way out *and* far out *and* kinky *and* out in left field <nf>, fringy, breakaway, **out-of-the-way; original,** maverick, Bohemian, beat, hippie, counterculture; **nonformal,** free and easy <nf>; outside the box

7 out of line, out of keeping, out of order *or* place, misplaced, **out of step,** out of turn <nf>, out of tune

869 NORMALITY

NOUNS **1** normality, normalness, typicality, normalcy, naturalness; health, wholesomeness, propriety, regularity; naturalism, naturism, realism; order 807

2 usualness, ordinariness, commonness, commonplaceness, averageness, mediocrity; generality 864, prevalence, currency

3 the normal, the usual, the ordinary, the common, the commonplace, the day-to-day, the way things are, the normal order of things; common *or* garden variety, the run of the mine *or* the mill

4 rule, law, principle, standard, criterion, canon, code, code of practice, maxim, prescription, guideline, rulebook, the book <nf>, regulation, reg *or* regs <nf>; norm, model, rule of behavior, ideal, ideal type, specimen type, exemplar; rule *or* law *or* order of nature, natural *or* universal law; form, formula, formulary, formality, prescribed *or* set form; standing order, standard operating procedure; hard-and-fast rule, Procrustean law

5 normalization, standardization, regularization; codification, formalization

VERBS **6** normalize, standardize, regularize; codify, formalize

7 do the usual thing, make a practice of, carry on, carry on as usual, do business as usual

ADJS **8** normal, natural; general 864.11; typical, unexceptional; normative, prescribed, model, ideal, desired, white-bread *or* white-bready <nf>; naturalistic, naturistic, realistic; orderly 807.6

9 usual, regular; customary, habitual, accustomed, wonted, normative, prescriptive, standard, regulation, conventional; common, commonplace, ordinary, average, everyday, mediocre, familiar, household, vernacular, stock; prevailing, predominating, current, popular; universal 864.14

ADVS **10** normally, naturally; normatively, prescriptively, regularly; typically, usually, commonly, ordinarily, customarily, habitually, generally; mostly, chiefly, mainly, for the most part, most often *or* frequently; as a rule, as a matter of course; as usual, as per usual <nf>; as may be expected, to be expected, as things go

870 ABNORMALITY

NOUNS **1 abnormality,** abnormity; **unnaturalness,** unnaturalism, strangeness; **anomaly,** anomalousness, anomalism; **aberration,** aberrance *or* aberrancy; **atypicality,** atypicalness; **irregularity, deviation,** divergence, **difference** 780;

eccentricity, erraticism, unpredictability, unpredictableness, randomness, chaos; **monstrosity,** teratism, amorphism, heteromorphism; **subnormality; inferiority** 250; **superiority** 249; **derangement** 811.1

2 **unusualness, uncommonness,** unordinariness, unwontedness, exceptionalness, exceptionality, extraordinariness; **rarity,** rareness, **uniqueness; prodigiousness,** marvelousness, wondrousness, fabulousness, mythicalness, remarkableness, stupendousness; **incredibility** 955.3, increditability, inconceivability, **impossibility** 967

3 **oddity, queerness,** curiousness, quaintness, **peculiarity, absurdity** 967.1, singularity; **strangeness,** outlandishness; bizarreness, *bizarrerie* <Fr>; fantasticality, anticness; **freakishness, grotesqueness,** grotesquerie, strangeness, weirdness, gonzo <nf>, monstrousness, monstrosity, malformation, deformity, teratism

4 <odd person> oddity, **character** <nf>, type, **case** <nf>, natural, original, odd fellow, queer specimen; **oddball** *and* **weirdo** <nf>, odd *or* queer fish, queer duck, rum one <Brit nf>; **rare bird,** *rara avis* <L>; flake, eccentric 927.3; *meshuggenah* <Yiddish>; **freak** *and* **screwball** *and* **crackpot** and **kook** *and* **nut** *and* bird *and* gonzo <nf>; **fanatic, crank,** zealot; **outsider, alien,** foreigner; **alien,** extraterrestrial, Martian, little green man, visitor from another planet; pariah, loner, lone wolf, solitary, hermit; hobo, tramp; maverick; **outcast,** outlaw, scapegoat; **nonconformist** 868.3

5 <odd thing> **oddity, curiosity, wonder,** funny *or* peculiar *or* strange thing; **abnormality, anomaly; rarity,** improbability, exception, one in a thousand *or* million; **prodigy,** prodigiosity; curio, conversation piece; museum piece

6 **monstrosity, monster,** miscreation, abortion, teratism, abnormal *or* defective birth, abnormal *or* defective fetus; **freak,** freak of nature, *lusus naturae* <L>

7 **supernaturalism,** supernaturalness, supernaturality, supranaturalism, supernormalness, **preternaturalism,** supersensibleness, superphysicalness, superhumanity; **the paranormal;** numinousness; **unearthliness,** unworldliness, **otherworldliness,** eeriness; transcendentalism; New Age; the supernatural, **the occult,** the supersensible; **paranormality;** supernature, supranature; **mystery,** mysteriousness, miraculousness, strangeness; faerie, witchery, elfdom

8 **miracle, sign, signs and portents, prodigy, wonder,** wonderwork, ferlie; thaumatology, thaumaturgy; fantasy, enchantment

ADJS 9 **abnormal, unnatural; anomalous,** anomalistic; **irregular,** eccentric, erratic, deviative, divergent, **different** 780.7; **aberrant,** stray, straying, wandering; heteroclite, heteromorphic; formless, shapeless, amorphous; **subnormal**

10 **unusual,** unordinary, **uncustomary,** unwonted, **uncommon, unfamiliar,** atypic *or* atypical, unheard-of, *recherché* <Fr>; **rare, unique,** *sui generis* <L, of its own kind>; **out of the ordinary,** out of this world, out-of-the-way, out of the common, out of the pale, **off the beaten track,** offbeat, breakaway; unexpected, not to be expected, unthought-of, undreamed-of

11 **odd, queer, peculiar, absurd** 967.7, **singular, curious, oddball** <nf>, weird *and* kooky *and* freaky *and* freaked-out <nf>, quaint, **eccentric,** gonzo <nf>, funny, rum <Brit nf>; **strange, outlandish, off-the-wall** <nf>, surreal, not for real <nf>, passing strange; **weird,** unearthly; off, out

12 **fantastic,** fantastical, fanciful, antic, **unbelievable** 955.10, **impossible, incredible,** logic-defying, incomprehensible, unimaginable, unexpected, unaccountable, inconceivable

13 **freakish,** freak *or* freaky <nf>; **monstrous, deformed,** malformed, misshapen, **misbegotten,** teratogenic, teratoid; **grotesque, bizarre,** bizarre <nf>, baroque, rococo

14 **extraordinary, exceptional, remarkable,** noteworthy, **wonderful, marvelous,** fabulous, mythical, legendary; **stupendous,** stupefying, prodigious, portentous, phenomenal; unprecedented, unexampled, unparalleled, not within the memory of man; indescribable, unspeakable, ineffable

15 **supernatural,** supranatural, **preternatural; supernormal,** hypernormal, preternormal, **paranormal; superphysical,** hyperphysical; numinous; supersensible, **supersensual,** pretersensual; **superhuman,** preterhuman, unhuman, nonhuman; **supramundane,** extramundane, transmundane, extraterrestrial; **unearthly, unworldly, otherworldly, eerie;** fey; psychical, **spiritual, occult; transcendental; mysterious,** arcane, esoteric

16 **miraculous, wondrous,** wonderworking, thaumaturgic *or* thaumaturgical, necromantic, **prodigious; magical,** enchanted, bewitched

ADVS **17** **unusually, uncommonly, incredibly, unnaturally,** abnormally, unordinarily, **uncustomarily,** unexpectedly; **rarely, seldom,** seldom if ever, once in a thousand years, hardly, hardly ever

18 **extraordinarily, exceptionally, remarkably, wonderfully, marvelously,** prodigiously, fabulously, unspeakably, ineffably, phenomenally, stupendously

19 **oddly, queerly, peculiarly, singularly, curiously,** quaintly, **strangely,** outlandishly, **fantastically,** fancifully; **grotesquely, monstrously; eerily, mysteriously,** supernaturally

871 LIST

NOUNS **1** **list, enumeration, itemization,** listing, shopping *or* grocery list; laundry list; want list *and* wish list; hit list *and* shit list *and* drop-dead list *and* enemies list <nf>; blacklist; to-do list; items, **schedule, agenda; register,** registry; **inventory,** repertory, tally; database *and* data base; **spreadsheet,** electronic spreadsheet; **checklist;** tally sheet; active list, civil list <Brit>, retired list, sick list; waiting list; blacklist; short list; reading list; syllabus; A-list, B-list, etc

2 **table,** contents, table of contents; computer listing, menu; chart

3 **catalog;** classified catalog, *catalogue raisonné* <Fr>; **card catalog, bibliography,** finding list, handlist, reference list; filmography, discography; publisher's catalog *or* list; **file,** filing system, letter file, pigeonholes

4 **dictionary,** word list, **lexicon, glossary, thesaurus, Roget's, vocabulary,** terminology, nomenclator; promptorium, gradus; **gazetteer; almanac**; telephone directory, address book; book of lists

5 **bill,** statement, account, itemized account, invoice; ledger, books; **bill of fare, menu,** carte, wine list, dessert menu; **bill of lading,** manifest, waybill, docket

6 **roll, roster,** scroll, rota; **roll call,** muster, **census,** nose *or* head count <nf>, **poll,** questionnaire, returns, census report *or* returns; property roll, tax roll, cadastre; muster roll; checkroll, checklist; jury list *or* panel; calendar, docket, **agenda,** order of business; daybook, journal, agenda book, diary; **program,** dramatis personae, credits, lineup; honor roll, dean's list; timetable, schedule, itinerary, prospectus

7 **index, listing,** tabulation; **cataloging, itemization,** filing, card file, card index, Rolodex <TM>, thumb index, indexing; **registration,** registry, enrollment

VERBS **8** **list, enumerate, itemize, tabulate, catalog,** tally; **register,** post, enter, **enroll, book;** impanel; **file,** pigeonhole, classify; **index;** inventory; calendar; score, keep score; **schedule,** program, put on the agenda; diarize; short-list

ADJS **9** **listed, enumerated, entered, itemized, cataloged,** tallied, inventoried; filed, **indexed, tabulated; scheduled,** programmed; put on the agenda; inventorial, glossarial, cadastral, classificatory, taxonomic; registered, recorded, noted

872 ONENESS

<state of being one>

NOUNS 1 **oneness, unity, singleness,** singularity, **individuality,** identity, selfsameness; **particularity** 865; **uniqueness;** intactness, inviolability, purity, simplicity 798, irreducibility, **integrity,** integrality; **unification,** uniting, integration, fusion, combination 805; **solidification,** solidity, solidarity, **indivisibility,** undividedness, **wholeness** 792.5; univocity, organic unity; uniformity 781

2 **aloneness,** loneness, **loneliness, lonesomeness,** soleness, singleness; **privacy,** solitariness, **solitude;** separateness, aloofness, detachment, seclusion, sequestration, **withdrawal, alienation,** standing *or* moving *or* keeping apart, **isolation**; celibacy, single blessedness

3 **one, I, 1, unit,** ace, atom; monad; one and only, none else, no other, nothing else, nought beside

4 **individual,** single, unit, **integer, entity,** singleton, **item,** article, point, module; person, wight , persona, soul, body, warm body <nf>; **individuality,** personhood; isolated case, single instance

VERBS 5 **unify,** reduce to unity, unitize, make one; **integrate, unite** 805.3

6 **stand alone,** stand *or* move *or* keep apart, keep oneself to oneself, withdraw, alienate *or* seclude *or* sequester *or* isolate oneself, feel out of place; individuate, become an individual; go solo, paddle one's own canoe, do one's own thing <nf>

ADJS 7 **one, single, singular, individual, sole, unique,** a certain, **solitary, lone;** exclusive; **integral,** indivisible, irreducible, monadic, monistic, unanalyzable, noncompound, atomic, unitary, unitive, unary, undivided, solid, whole-cloth, seamless, uniform 781.5, simple 798.6, whole 792.9; an, any, any one, either

8 alone, solitary, solo, *solus* <L>; isolated, insular, apart, separate, separated, alienated, withdrawn, aloof, standoffish, detached, removed; **lone, lonely, lonesome,** lonely-hearts; **private,** reserved, reticent, reclusive, shy, nonpublic, ungregarious; **friendless,** kithless, homeless, rootless, companionless, **unaccompanied,** unescorted, unattended; **unaided,** unassisted, unabetted, unsupported, unseconded; **single-handed,** solo, one-man, one-woman, one-person

9 **sole, unique,** singular, absolute, unrepeated, **alone,** lone, **only,** only-begotten, **one and only,** first and last; odd, impair, unpaired, azygous; celibate

10 **unitary, integrated,** integral, integrant; **unified,** united, rolled into one, composite

11 **unipartite,** unipart, **one-piece;** monadic *or* monadal; **unilateral, one-sided;** unilateralist, uniangulate, unibivalent, unibranchiate, unicameral, unicellular, unicuspid, unidentate, unidigitate; **unidimensional, unidirectional;** uniflorous, unifoliate, unifoliolate, unigenital, uniglobular, unilinear, uniliteral, unilobed, unilobular, unilocular, unimodular, unimolecular, uninuclear, uniocular, unisexual, unisex; unipolar, **univalent, univocal;** one-size; monolingual, monochromatic

12 **unifying, uniting,** unific; **combining,** combinative 805.5,7, combinatory; connective, connecting, connectional; conjunctive 800.16, conjunctival; coalescing, coalescent

ADVS 13 **singly, individually,** particularly, severally, one by one, one at a time; **singularly,** in the singular; **alone,** by itself, *per se* <L>; **by oneself,** by one's lonesome <nf>, on one's own, under one's own steam, **single-handedly, solo,** unaided; separately, apart; **once** 848.6

14 **solely, exclusively, only,** merely, **purely,** simply; **entirely,** wholly, totally; **integrally, indivisibly,** irreducibly, unanalyzably, undividedly

873 DOUBLENESS

NOUNS **1 doubleness, duality,** dualism, duplexity, **twoness;** twofoldness, biformity; polarity; conjugation, pairing, coupling, yoking; **doubling,** duplication 874, twinning, bifurcation; **dichotomy,** bisection 875, halving, splitting down the middle *or* fifty-fifty; **duplicity,** two-facedness, double-think, hypocrisy, Dr. Jekyll and Mr. Hyde; **irony,** enantiosis, ambiguity, equivocation, equivocality, **ambivalence;** Janus

2 two, 2, II, twain ; **couple, pair, matching pair, twosome,** set of two, duo, duet, brace, team, span, yoke, double harness; match, matchup, mates; **couplet,** distich, double, doublet; duad, dyad; the two, **both;** Darby and Joan; tandem

3 deuce; pair, doubleton; **craps** *and* **snake eyes** <gambling>

4 twins, pair of twins <nf>, identical twins, fraternal twins, exact mates, look-alikes, dead ringers <nf>, mirror image, carbon copy, Doppelganger, spit and image *or* spitting image; Tweedledum and Tweedledee, Siamese twins; Twin stars, Castor and Pollux, Gemini

VERBS **5 double,** duplicate, replicate, dualize, twin; **halve,** split down the middle *or* fifty fifty <nf>, bifurcate, dichotomize, bisect, transect; team, **yoke,** yoke together, span, double-team, double-harness; **mate, match,** couple, conjugate; **pair,** pair off, pair up, couple up, team up, match up, buddy up <nf>; talk out of both sides of one's mouth at once; square; copy, mirror, echo

ADJS **6 two,** twain ; **dual, double,** duple, duplex, doubled, twinned, duplicated, replicated, dualized; **dualistic;** dyadic; duadic; biform; bipartite, bipartisan, bilateral, either-or, two-sided, double-sided, binary; dichotomous; bifurcated, bisected, dichotomized, split down the middle *or* fifty fifty <nf>; twin, identical, matched, twinned, duplicated; **two-faced,** duplicitous, hypocritical, double-faced, Janus-like; second, secondary; two-way, two-ply, dual-purpose, two-dimensional

7 both, the two, the pair; for two, tête-à-tête, *à deux* <Fr>

8 coupled, paired, yoked, yoked together, matched, matched up, mated, paired off, paired up, teamed up, buddied up <nf>; **bracketed;** conjugate, conjugated; biconjugate, bigeminate; bijugate

PHRS **9** it takes two to tango *and* it's not a one-way street <nf>

874 DUPLICATION

NOUNS **1 duplication, reduplication,** replication, conduplication; **reproduction, repro** <nf>, **doubling;** twinning, gemination, ingemination; **repetition** 849, iteration, reiteration, echoing; **imitation** 336, parroting; **copying** 336.1; **duplicate** 785.3

2 repeat, encore, repeat performance; echo; do-over, retry

VERBS **3 duplicate,** dupe <nf>, ditto <nf>; **double,** double up; multiply by two; twin, geminate, ingeminate; **reduplicate, reproduce,** replicate, redouble; **repeat** 849.7; **copy,** carbon-copy

ADJS **4 double, doubled, duplicate,** duplicated, reproduced, replicated, cloned, twinned, geminate, geminated, dualized

ADVS **5 doubly; twofold,** as much again, twice as much; twice, two times

6 secondly, second, secondarily, **in the second place** *or* instance

7 again, another time, **once more,** once again, over again, yet again, *encore* and *bis* <Fr>; **anew,** afresh, new, freshly, newly

875 BISECTION

NOUNS **1 bisection,** halving, bipartition, bifidity; **dichotomy, halving, division, in half** *or* **by two,** splitting *or* dividing *or* cutting in two, splitting *or* dividing fifty-fifty <nf>; subdivision; bifurcation, forking, ramification, branching

2 **half,** moiety; hemisphere, semisphere, semicircle, **fifty percent;** half-and-half *and* fifty-fifty <nf>

3 bisector, diameter, equator, halfway mark, divider, partition 213.5, line of demarcation, boundary 211.3

VERBS **4** **bisect, halve, divide, in half** *or* **by two,** transect, subdivide; cleave, fission, **divide** *or* split *or* **cut in two,** share and share alike, go halfers *or* go Dutch <nf>, **dichotomize;** bifurcate, fork, ramify, branch

ADJS **5** **half, part, partly, partial,** halfway

6 **halved, bisected, divided;** dichotomous; bifurcated, forked *or* forking, ramified, branched, branching; riven, **split,** cloven, cleft

7 **bipartite,** bifid, biform, bicuspid, biaxial, bicameral, binocular, binomial, binominal, biped, bipetalous, bipinnate, bisexual, bivalent, unibivalent

ADVS **8** **in half,** in halves, **in two,** in twain, by two, down the middle; half-and-half *and* fifty-fifty <nf>; apart, asunder

876 THREE

NOUNS **1** **three,** 3, III, **trio,** trey, **threesome,** trialogue, set of three, tierce <cards>, leash, troika; **triad,** trilogy, trine, **trinity,** triunity, ternary, ternion; **triplet,** tercet, terzetto; trefoil, shamrock, clover; tripod, trivet; **triangle,** tricorn, trihedron, trident, trisul, triennium, trimester, trinomial, trionym, triphthong, triptych, triplopy, trireme, triseme, triskelion, triumvirate; triple crown, triple threat; trey *and* threespot <cards>, deuce-ace <dice>; triple-decker; menage a trois; hat trick

2 **threeness,** triplicity, triality, tripleness, trebleness, threefoldness; triunity, trinity

ADJS **3** **three, triple,** triplex, trinal, trine, trial; triadic *or* triadical; triune, three-in-one, *tria juncta in uno* <L>; triform; treble; triangular, deltoid, fan-shaped; triannual; trifold

877 TRIPLICATION

NOUNS **1** **triplication,** triplicity, trebleness, **threefoldness;** triplicate

VERBS **2** **triplicate, triple, treble, multiply by three,** threefold; cube

ADJS **3** **triple,** triplicate, **treble, threefold,** trifold, triplex, trinal, trine, tern, ternary, ternal, ternate; threeply; trilogic *or* trilocial

4 **third, tertiary**

ADVS **5** **triply, trebly,** trinely; **threefold; thrice,** three times, again and yet again

6 **thirdly,** in the third place

878 TRISECTION

NOUNS **1** **trisection,** tripartition, trichotomy, trifurcation

2 **third,** tierce, third part, one-third; *tertium quid* <L, a third something>

VERBS **3** **trisect, divide in thirds** *or* **three,** third, trichotomize; trifurcate

ADJS **4** **tripartite,** trisected, triparted, **three-parted,** trichotomous; three-sided, trihedral, trilateral; **three-dimensional;** three-forked, three-pronged, trifurcate; trident, tridental, tridentate, trifid; tricuspid; three-footed, tripodic, tripedal; trifoliate, trifloral, triflorate, triflorous, tripetalous, triadelphous, triarch; trimerous, 3-merous; three-cornered, tricornered, tricorn; trigonal, trigonoid; triquetrous, triquetral; trigrammatic, triliteral; *triangular,* triangulate, deltoid

879 FOUR

NOUNS **1** **four,** 4, IV, tetrad, quatern, quaternion, quaternary, quaternity, **quartet, quadruplet, foursome;** quatre; Little Joe *and* Little Joe from Kokomo *and* Little Dick Fisher <gambling>; quadrennium; tetralogy; tetrapody; tetraphony, four-part diaphony; quadrille, square dance; quatrefoil *or* quadrifoil, four-leaf clover; tetragram, tetragrammaton; quadrangle, quad <nf>, rectangle; tetrahedron; tetragon, square; biquadrate;

quadrinomial; quadrature, squaring; quadrilateral
2 **fourness,** quaternity, quadruplicity, fourfoldness
VERBS 3 **square, quadrate,** form *or* make four; form fours *or* squares; **cube, dice**
ADJS 4 **four;** foursquare; quaternary, quartile, quartic, quadric, quadratic; tetrad, tetradic; quadrinomial, biquadratic; tetractinal, four-rayed, **quadruped,** four-legged; quadrivalent, tetravalent; quadrilateral 278.9

880 QUADRUPLICATION

NOUNS 1 **quadruplication,** quadruplicature, quadruplicity, fourfoldness
VERBS 2 **quadruple, quadruplicate,** fourfold, form *or* make four, multiply by four; quadrate, biquadrate, quadruplex
ADJS 3 **quadruplicate, quadruple,** quadraple, **quadruplex, fourfold,** four-ply, four-part, tetraploid, quadrigeminal, biquadratic

881 QUADRISECTION

NOUNS 1 **quadrisection,** quadripartition, **quartering**
2 **fourth,** one-fourth, **quarter,** one-quarter, fourth part, twenty-five percent, twenty-five cents, two bits <old nf>; quartern; quart; farthing; quarto *or* 4to *or* 4
VERBS 3 **divide by four** *or* **into four; quadrisect, quarter**
ADJS 4 **quadrisected, quartered,** quarter-cut; quadripartite, quadrifid, quadriform; quadrifoliate, quadrigeminal, quadripinnate, quadriplanar, quadriserial, quadrivial, quadrifurcate, quadrumanal *or* quadrumanous
5 **fourth, quarter**
ADVS 6 **fourthly,** in the fourth place; quarterly, by quarters

882 FIVE AND OVER

NOUNS 1 **five,** V, cinque <cards and dice>, Phoebe *and* Little Phoebe *and* fever <gambling>; quintet, fivesome, quintuplets, quints <nf>, cinquain, quincunx, pentad; fifth; **five dollars,** fiver *and* fin *and* finniff *and* five bucks <nf>; pentagon, pentahedron, pentagram; pentapody, pentameter, pentastich; pentarchy; Pentateuch; pentachord; pentathlon; five-pointed star, pentacle, pentalpha, mullet <heraldry>; five-spot <nf>; quinquennium
2 **six,** VI, sixie from Dixie *and* sister Hicks *and* Jimmy Hicks *and* Captain Hicks <gambling>, **half a dozen, sextet,** sestet, sextuplets, hexad; hexagon, hexahedron, hexagram, six-pointed star, estoile <heraldry>, Jewish star, star of David, *Magen David* <Heb>; hexameter, hexapody, hexastich; hexapod; hexarchy; Hexateuch; hexastyle; hexachord; six-shooter; sixth sense; six-pack
3 seven, VII, heptad, little natural <crapshooting>; septet, heptad; heptagon, heptahedron; heptameter, heptastich; septemvir, heptarchy; Septuagint, Heptateuch; heptachord; **week;** seven deadly sins; seven seas; Seven Wonders of the World
4 **eight,** VIII, ogdoad, eighter *or* Ada from Decatur <crapshooting>, Ada Ross *and* Ada Ross the stable hoss <gambling>; octad, octonary; octagon, octahedron; octastylos *or* oktostylos; octave, octavo *or* 8vo; octachord; octet *or* octal, octameter; Octateuch; piece of eight; Eightfold Path
5 **nine,** IX, niner <radio communication>, Nina from Carolina *and* Nina Ross the stable hoss *and* Nina Nina ocean liner <gambling>; ennead; nonagon *or* enneagon, enneahedron; novena; enneastylos; nine days' wonder
6 **ten,** X, Big Dick *and* Big Dick from Battle Creek <gambling>; decade; decagon, decahedron; decagram, decigram, decaliter, deciliter, decare, decameter, decimeter, decastere; decapod; decastylos; decasyllable; decemvir, decemvirate, decurion; decennium, decennary; Ten Commandments *or* Decalogue; tithe; decathlon

7 <eleven to ninety> **eleven; twelve, dozen,** boxcar *and* boxcars <gambling>, duodecimo *or* twelvemo *or* 12mo; **teens; thirteen,** long dozen, baker's dozen; **fourteen,** two weeks, fortnight; **fifteen,** quindecima, quindene, quindecim, quindecennial; **sixteen,** sixteenmo *or* 16mo; **twenty, score; twenty-four,** four and twenty, two dozen, twenty-fourmo *or* 24mo; **twenty-five,** five and twenty, quarter of a hundred *or* century; thirty-two, thirty-twomo *or* 32mo; **forty,** twoscore, quadragenarian; **fifty,** L, half a hundred; **sixty,** sexagenary; Sexagesima; sexagenarian, threescore; **sixty-four,** sixty-fourmo *or* 64mo *or* sexagesimo-quarto; **seventy,** septuagenarian, threescore and ten; **eighty,** octogenarian, fourscore; **ninety,** nonagenarian, four-score and ten

8 **hundred, century,** C, one C <nf>; centennium, centennial, centenary; centenarian; cental, centigram, centiliter, centimeter, centare, centistere; hundredweight *or* cwt; hecatomb; centipede; centumvir, centumvirate, centurion; <120> great *or* long hundred; <144> gross; <150> sesquicentennial, sesquicentenary; <200> bicentenary, bicentennial; <300> tercentenary, tercentennial, etc

9 **five hundred,** D, five centuries; five C's <nf>

10 **thousand,** M, chiliad; **millennium;** G *and* grand *and* thou *and* yard <nf>; chiliagon, chiliahedron *or* chiliaüdron; chiliarchia *or* chiliarch; millepede; milligram, milliliter, millimeter, kilogram *or* kilo, kiloliter, kilometer; kilocycle, kilohertz; kilobyte; gigabyte; **ten thousand,** myriad; **one hundred thousand,** lakh <India>

11 **million;** ten million, crore <India>

12 **billion,** thousand million, milliard

13 trillion, quadrillion, quintillion, sextillion, septillion, octillion, nonillion, decillion, undecillion, duodecillion, tredecillion, quattuordecillion, quindecillion, sexdecillion, septendecillion, octodecillion, novemdecillion, vigintillion; googol, googolplex; zillion *and* jillion <nf>

14 <division into five *or* more parts> quinquesection, quinquepartition, sextipartition, etc; decimation, decimalization; fifth, sixth, etc; **tenth, tithe,** decima

VERBS **15** <divide by five, etc> quinquesect; decimalize

16 <multiply by five, etc> fivefold, sixfold, etc; quintuple, quintuplicate; sextuple, sextuplicate; centuple, centuplicate

ADJS **17** **fifth,** quinary; **fivefold, quintuple,** quintuplicate; quinquennial; quinquepartite, pentadic, quinquefid; quincuncial, pentastyle; pentad, pentavalent, quinquevalent; pentagonal

18 **sixth,** senary; **sixfold, sextuple;** sexpartite, hexadic, sextipartite, hexapartite; hexagonal, hexahedral, hexangular; hexad, hexavalent; sextuplex, hexastyle; sexennial; hexatonic

19 **seventh,** septimal; **sevenfold, septuple,** septenary; septempartite, heptadic, septemfid; heptagonal, heptahedral, heptangular; heptamerous; hebdomal

20 **eighth,** octonary; **eightfold, octuple;** octadic; octal, octofid, octaploid; octagonal, octahedral, octan, octangular; octosyllabic; octastyle

21 **ninth,** novenary, nonary; **ninefold, nonuple,** enneadic; enneahedral, enneastyle, nonagonal

22 **tenth,** denary, **decimal,** tithe; **tenfold, decuple;** decagonal, decahedral; decasyllabic; decennial

23 **eleventh,** undecennial, undecennary

24 **twelfth,** duodenary, duodenal; duodecimal

25 thirteenth, fourteenth, etc; eleventeenth, umpteenth <nf>; in one's teens

26 **twentieth,** vicenary, vicennial, vigesimal, vicesimal

27 **sixtieth,** sexagesimal, sexagenary

28 **seventieth,** septuagesimal, septuagenary

29 **hundredth,** centesimal, **centennial,** centenary, centurial; **hundredfold,**

centuple, centuplicate; secular; centigrado
30 **thousandth,** millenary, **millennial; thousandfold**
31 millionth; billionth, quadrillionth, quintillionth, etc

883 PLURALITY
<more than one>

NOUNS 1 **plurality,** pluralness; a greater number, a certain number; **several,** some, a few 885.2, more; plural number, the plural; compositeness, nonsingleness, nonuniqueness; **pluralism** 782.1, variety; numerousness 884
2 **majority,** plurality, more than half, the greater number, the greatest number, **most,** preponderance *or* preponderancy, greater *or* better part, **bulk, mass;** lion's share
3 pluralization, plurification
4 **multiplication,** multiplying, proliferation, **increase** 251; duplication 874; multiple, multiplier, multiplicand, product, factor; factorization, exponentiation; multiplication table; lowest *or* least common multiple, greatest common divisor, highest *or* greatest common factor; prime factor, submultiple, power, square, cube, fourth power, exponent, index, square root, cube root, surd, root mean square, factorial

VERBS 5 **pluralize,** plurify ; raise to *or* make more than one
6 **multiply,** proliferate, **increase** 251.4,6, duplicate 874.3

ADJS 7 **plural,** pluralized, more than one, more, several, severalfold; **some,** certain; not singular, composite, nonsingle, nonunique; plurative <logic>; **pluralistic** 782.3, various; many, beaucoup <nf>, numerous 884.6
8 **multiple,** multiplied, multifold, **manifold** 884.6; **increased** 251.7; multinomial *and* polynomial <mathematics>
9 **majority, most,** the greatest number

ADVS 10 **in the majority;** and others, et al, et cetera; plurally

884 NUMEROUSNESS

NOUNS 1 **numerousness, multiplicity, manyness,** manifoldness, multifoldness, multitudinousness, multifariousness, teemingness, swarmingness, rifeness, profuseness, profusion; **plenty, abundance** 991,2; **countlessness,** innumerability, infinitude, infinity
2 <indefinite number> **a number,** a certain number, one or two, two or three, **a few, several,** parcel, passel <nf>; eleventeen *and* umpteen <nf>; lots
3 <large number> **multitude, throng** 770.4; a many, numbers, quantities, lots 247.4, flocks, **scores,** scads, oodles**;** an abundance of, all kinds *or* sorts of, no end of, quite a few, tidy sum; muchness, any number of, **large amount; host, army,** more than one can shake a stick at, fistful *and* slew *and* shitload *and* shithouse full <nf>, legion, rout, ruck, mob, jam, clutter; **swarm, flock** 770.5, flight, cloud, hail, bevy, covey, shoal, hive, nest, pack, litter, bunch 770.7; a world of, a mass of, worlds of, masses of; small fortune
4 <immense number> **a myriad,** a thousand, **a thousand and one,** *a lakh* <India>, *a crore* <India>, a million, a billion, a quadrillion, a nonillion, etc 882.11–13; umpteen, a zillion *or* jillion *or* gazillion *or* bazillion <nf>; googol, googolplex

VERBS 5 **teem with,** overflow with, **abound with,** burst with, bristle with, pullulate with, **swarm with,** throng with, creep with, **crawl with, be alive with, have coming out of one's ears** *and* **have up the gazoo** *and* **kazoo** <nf>; clutter, crowd, jam, pack, overwhelm, overflow; multiply 883.6; outnumber; overcrowd

ADJS 6 **numerous, many, manifold,** not a few, no few; **very many,** full many, **ever so many,** considerable *and* quite some <nf>, quite a few; **multitudinous,** multitudinal, multifarious, multifold, multiple, **myriad,** thousand, million, billion; zillion *and* jillion <nf>; heaped-up; numerous as the stars, numerous as the sands, numerous as the hairs on the head

7 **several,** divers, **sundry,** various; fivish, sixish, etc; some five *or* six, etc; upwards of

8 **abundant,** copious, ample, plenteous, **plentiful** 991.7, thick on the ground <Brit>

9 **teeming, swarming, crowding,** thronging, overflowing, overcrowded, overwhelming, bursting, **crawling, alive with,** lousy with <nf>, populous, prolific, proliferating, crowded, packed, jammed, bumper-to-bumper <nf>, jam-packed, like sardines in a can <nf>, thronged, studded, bristling, rife, lavish, prodigal, superabundant, **profuse,** in profusion, thick, **thick with,** thick-coming, thick as hail *or* flies

10 **innumerable, numberless,** unnumbered, countless, uncounted, **uncountable,** unquantifiable, unreckonable, untold, incalculable, immeasurable, unmeasured, measureless, inexhaustible, endless, infinite, without end *or* limit, more than one can tell, more than you can shake a stick at <nf>, no end of *or* to; countless as the stars *or* sands; **astronomical,** galactic; millionfold, trillionfold, etc

11 **and many more,** *cum multis aliis* <L>, and what not, and heaven knows what

ADVS 12 **numerously,** multitudinously, **profusely,** swarmingly, teemingly, thickly, copiously, **abundantly, prodigally; innumerably,** countlessly, infinitely, incalculably, inexhaustibly, immeasurably; in throngs, in crowds, in swarms, in heaps, *acervatim* <L>; **no end** <nf>

885 FEWNESS

NOUNS 1 **fewness,** infrequency, **sparsity,** sparseness, **scarcity, paucity, scantiness, meagerness,** miserliness, niggardliness, tightness, thinness, stringency, restrictedness; chintziness *and* chinchiness *and* stinginess <nf>, scrimpiness *and* skimpiness <nf>; **rarity,** exiguity; smallness 258.1; unsubstantiality *or* insubstantiality; skeleton staff

2 **a few,** too few, mere *or* piddling *or* piddly few, only a few, **small number,** limited *or* piddling *or* piddly number, not enough to count *or* matter, not enough to shake a stick at, **handful, scattering,** corporal's guard, sprinkling, trickle; low *or* poor turnout, too few to mention

3 **minority,** least; the minority, the few; minority group; minimum; less, least

ADJS 4 **few, not many;** hardly *or* scarcely any, precious little *or* few, of small number, to be counted on one's fingers, too few

5 **sparse,** scant, **scanty,** exiguous, **infrequent,** sporadic, scarce, scarce as hen's teeth <nf>, poor, piddling, piddly, thin, slim, **meager**, not much; miserly, niggardly, cheeseparing, tight; chintzy *and* chinchy *and* stingy <nf>, scrimpy *and* skimpy <nf>, skimping *and* scrimping <nf>; **scattered,** sprinkled, spotty, **few and far between; rare,** seldom met with, seldom seen, not thick on the ground <Brit>

6 **fewer, less,** smaller, not so much *or* many, reduced, minimal

7 **minority,** least

ADVS 8 **sparsely,** *sparsim* <L>, **scantily, meagerly,** exiguously, piddlingly; stingily *and* scrimpily *and* skimpily <nf>, thinly; **scarcely,** rarely, infrequently; **scatteringly,** scatterdly, spottily, in dribs and drabs *and* in bits and pieces <nf>, here and there, in places, in spots

886 CAUSE

NOUNS 1 **cause, occasion,** antecedents, **grounds,** ground, background, backstory, stimulus, base, **basis,** element, principle, factor; **determinant,** determinative; causation, causality, cause and effect, karma; etiology

2 **reason,** reason why, rationale, reason for *or* behind, underlying

reason, rational ground, **explanation,** answer, **the why,** the wherefore, the whatfor *or* whyfor <nf>, **the why and wherefore,** the idea <nf>, the big idea <nf>; stated cause, pretext, pretense, excuse

3 **immediate cause,** proximate cause, trigger, spark; **domino effect,** causal sequence, chain *or* nexus of cause and effect, ripple effect, slippery slope, contagion effect, knock-on *or* knock-on effect <chiefly Brit>; transient cause, occasional cause; formal cause; efficient cause; ultimate cause, immanent cause, remote cause, causing cause, *causa causans* <L>, first cause; **final cause,** *causa finalis* <L>, **end,** end in view, teleology; provocation, **last straw,** straw that broke the camel's back, match in the powder barrel; butterfly effect *or* strange attraction *or* sensitive dependence on initial conditions; planetary influence, astrological influence

4 **author,** agent, **originator,** generator, begetter, engenderer, producer, maker, beginner, **creator,** mover, inventor; **parent, mother, father,** sire; **prime mover,** *primum mobile* <L>; causer, effector; inspirer, instigator, catalyst, mobilizer; motivator, inspiration

5 **source, origin,** genesis, original, origination, **derivation, rise, beginning,** conception, inception, commencement, **head;** provenance, provenience, background; **root,** radix, radical, taproot, grass roots; stem, stock; etymology

6 **fountainhead,** headwater, headstream, riverhead, springhead, headspring, **mainspring,** wellspring, wellhead, well, **spring, fountain,** fount, font, *fons et origo* <L>; mine, quarry

7 **vital force** *or* **principle,** *élan vital* <Fr>, reproductive urge, a gleam in one's father's eye <nf>; **egg,** ovum 305.12, **germ,** germen , spermatozoon 305.11, nucleus 305.7, **seed; embryo** 305.14; bud 310.23; loins; **womb,** matrix, uterus

8 **birthplace, breeding place,** breeding ground, birthsite, rookery, hatchery; **hotbed,** forcing bed; incubator, brooder; **nest,** nidus; **cradle,** nursery

9 <a principle *or* movement> **cause, principle,** interest, issue, burning issue, commitment, faith, great cause, lifework; reason for being, *raison d'être* <Fr>; **movement,** mass movement, activity; **drive, campaign, crusade;** zeal, passion, fanaticism

VERBS **10** **cause,** be the cause of, lie at the root of; **bring about, bring to pass,** effectuate, **effect,** bring to effect, realize; **impact,** impact on, influence; **occasion, make, create, engender,** generate, **produce,** breed, work, do; **originate,** give origin to, give occasion to, **give rise to,** spark, spark off, set off, trigger, trigger off; **give birth to, beget,** bear, bring forth, labor *or* travail and bring forth, author, **father,** sire, sow the seeds of; gestate, **conceive,** have the idea, have a bright idea <nf>; set up, set afloat, **set on foot;** found, establish, inaugurate, institute; engineer

11 **induce,** lead, procure, get, obtain, contrive, **effect,** bring, **bring on,** draw on, **call forth, elicit, evoke, provoke,** inspire, influence, instigate, egg on, **motivate;** draw down, open the door to; suborn; superinduce; incite, kindle

12 **determine,** decide, turn the scale, have the last word, tip the scale; **necessitate,** entail, require; contribute to, have a hand in, lead to, conduce to; **advance, forward,** influence, subserve; **spin off,** hive off <Brit>

ADJS **13** **causal,** causative; chicken-and-egg <nf>; occasional; originative, institutive, constitutive; **at the bottom of,** behind the scenes; **formative,** determinative, effectual, decisive, pivotal; etiological

14 **original, primary,** primal, primitive, pristine, primo <nf>, primeval, aboriginal, **elementary,** elemental, **basic,** basal, **rudimentary,** crucial, central, radical, **fundamental;** embryonic, in embryo, *in ovo* <L>, germinal, seminal, pregnant; **generative,** genetic, protogenic; effectual

887 EFFECT

NOUNS **1 effect, result,** resultant, **consequence,** consequent, sequent, sequence, sequel, sequela, sequelae; event, eventuality, eventuation, **upshot, outcome,** logical outcome, possible outcome, scenario; **outgrowth,** spin-off, offshoot, offspring, issue, aftermath, legacy; side effect; **product** 893, precipitate, distillate, **fruit,** first fruits, crop, harvest, payoff; development, corollary; derivative, derivation, by-product; net result, end result; karma

2 impact, force, **repercussion,** reaction; backwash, backlash, reflex, recoil, response; mark, print, imprint, impress, impression; significance, import, meaning

3 aftereffect, aftermath, aftergrowth, aftercrop, **afterclap,** aftershock, afterimage, afterglow, aftertaste; wake, trail, track; domino effect

VERBS **4 result, ensue, issue, follow,** attend, accompany; **turn out, come out,** fall out, redound, **work out,** pan out <nf>, fare; have a happy result, turn out well, come up roses <nf>; turn out to be, prove, prove to be; **become of,** come of, come about; **develop,** unfold; **eventuate,** terminate, end; **end up,** land up <Brit>, come out, wind up

5 result from, be the effect of, be due to, originate in *or* from, **come from,** come out of, grow from, **grow out of,** follow from *or* on, proceed from, descend from, emerge from, issue from, ensue from, emanate from, flow from, **derive from,** accrue from, rise *or* arise from, take its rise from, **spring from, stem from,** sprout from, bud from, germinate from; **spin off; depend on,** hinge *or* pivot *or* turn on, hang on, be contingent on; pay off, bear fruit

ADJS **6 resultant, resulting, following, ensuing; consequent,** consequential, following, sequent, sequential, sequacious; necessitated, entailed, required; **final;** derivative, derivational

ADVS **7 consequently, as a result,** as a consequence, in consequence, in the event, naturally, *naturellement* <Fr>, necessarily, of necessity, inevitably, of course, as a matter of course, and so, it follows that; **therefore; accordingly** 766.11; **finally**

CONJS **8 resulting from,** coming from, arising from, deriving *or* derivable from, consequent to, in consequence of; **owing to, due to;** attributed *or* attributable to, dependent *or* contingent on; **caused by,** occasioned by, **at the bottom of;** required by, entailed by, following from, following strictly from

PHRS **9** one thing leads to another, *post hoc, ergo propter hoc* <L>, what goes up must come down <nf>, what goes around comes around <nf>

888 ATTRIBUTION

<assignment of cause>

NOUNS **1 attribution, assignment,** assignation, **ascription, imputation,** arrogation, placement, application, attachment, saddling, **charge, blame; indictment; responsibility,** answerability; **credit,** honor; accounting for, reference to, derivation from, connection with; guilt by association; etiology

2 acknowledgment, citation, tribute; confession; **reference;** trademark, signature; **by-line,** credit line

VERBS **3 attribute, assign, ascribe, impute,** give, place, put, apply, attach, refer

4 attribute to, ascribe to, impute to, assign to, **lay to,** put *or* set down to, apply to, refer to, point to; **pin on,** pinpoint <nf>, fix on *or* upon, attach to, acrete to, connect with, fasten upon, hang on <nf>, **saddle on** *or* **upon,** place upon, **father upon,** settle upon, saddle with; blame, **blame for,** blame on *or* upon, charge on *or* upon, place *or* put the blame on, place the blame *or* responsibility for, indict, **fix the responsibility for,** point to one, put the finger on *and* finger <nf>, fix the burden of, **charge to,** lay to one's charge, place to one's account, set to the account of, account for, lay at the door of, bring home to; acknowledge, confess; **credit** *or* **accredit with;** put words in one's mouth

5 **trace to,** follow the trail to; **derive from,** trace the origin *or* derivation of; affiliate to, filiate to, father, fix the paternity of

ADJS 6 **attributable, assignable, ascribable, imputable,** traceable, referable, accountable, explicable; owing, **due,** assigned *or* referred to, derivable from, derivative, derivational; **charged,** alleged, imputed, putative; **credited, attributed**

ADVS 7 **hence, therefore,** therefor, **wherefore,** wherefrom, whence, then, thence, *ergo* <L>, for which reason; **consequently** 887.7; **accordingly** 766.11; **because of that,** for that, by reason of that, for that reason, for the reason that, in consideration of something, from *or* for that cause, **on that account,** on that ground, thereat; **because of this, on this account,** for this cause, on account of this, *propter hoc* <L>, for this reason, hereat; thus, thusly <nf>, thuswise; on someone's head, on *or* at someone's doorstep

8 **why,** whyever, whyfor *and* for why <nf>, how come <nf>, how is it that, **wherefore, what for,** for which, **on what account,** on account of what *or* which, for what *or* whatever reason, from what cause, *pourquoi* <Fr>

CONJS 9 **because,** *parce que* <Fr>, **since,** as, for, **whereas, inasmuch as, forasmuch as, insofar as, insomuch as,** as things go; in that, for the cause that, for the reason that, in view of the fact that, taking into account that, **seeing that,** seeing as how <nf>, being as how <nf>; **resulting from** 887.8

889 OPERATION

NOUNS 1 **operation, functioning, action, performance,** performing, **working, work,** workings, exercise, practice; agency; implementation; operations; **management** 573, **direction, conduct, running, carrying-on** *or* **-out,** execution, seeing to, overseeing, oversight; **handling,** manipulation; responsibility 641.2; **occupation** 724; joint operation

2 **process, procedure,** proceeding, course; what makes it tick; **act,** step, measure, initiative, *démarche* <Fr>, move, maneuver, motion

3 **workability, operability,** operativeness, performability, negotiability <nf>, manageability, compassability, manipulatability, maneuverability; **practicability, feasibility,** viability

4 **operator,** operative, operant; **handler,** manipulator; **manager** 574.1, **executive** 574.3; functionary, agent; driver

VERBS 5 **operate, function, run, work; manage, direct** 573.8, **conduct; carry on** *or* **out** *or* **through,** make go *or* work, carry the ball <nf>, perform; **handle,** manipulate, maneuver; deal with, see to, take care of; occupy oneself 724.10; be responsible for 641.6

6 operate on, **act on** *or* **upon, work on, affect, influence,** bear on, impact, impact on; have to do with, treat, focus *or* concentrate on; bring to bear on

7 <be operative> **operate, function, work, act, perform, go, run,** be in action *or* operation *or* commission; percolate *and* perk *and* tick <nf>; be effective, go into effect, have effect, take effect, militate; be in force; have play, have free play

8 **function as,** work as, **act as,** act *or* play the part of, have the function *or* role *or* job *or* mission of; do one's thing <nf>

ADJS 9 **operative, operational,** go <nf>, **functional, practical,** in working order; **effective,** effectual, efficient, efficacious; relevant, significant

10 **workable, operable,** operatable, **performable,** actable, **doable,** manageable, compassable, negotiable, manipulatable, maneuverable; **prac-**

ticable, feasible, practical, viable, useful

11 **operating, operational, working, functioning,** operant, functional, acting, active, running, **going,** going on, ongoing; **in operation,** in action, **in practice, in force,** in play, in exercise, at work, on foot; **in process,** in the works, on the fire, in the pipe *or* pipeline <nf>, in hand, up and going

12 operational, functional; **managerial** 573.12; agential, agentive *or* agentival; manipulational

890 PRODUCTIVENESS

NOUNS 1 **productiveness, productivity,** productive capacity; **fruitfulness,** fructification, procreativeness, progenitiveness, **fertility,** fecundity, fecundation, prolificness, prolificity, prolificacy; **pregnancy; luxuriance, exuberance,** generousness, bountifulness, plentifulness, plenteousness, richness, lushness, **abundance** 991.2, superabundance, copiousness, teemingness, swarmingness, uberty; teeming womb *or* loins

2 proliferation, multiplication, fructification, pullulation, teeming; **reproduction** 78, **production** 892

3 **fertilization, enrichment,** fecundation; propagation, pollination; insemination; impregnation 78.3

4 **fertilizer,** dressing, top dressing, enricher, richener, procreator, propagator; organic fertilizer, manure, muck, mulch, night soil, dung, guano, compost, leaf litter, leaf mold, humus, peat moss, castor-bean meal, bone meal, fish meal; commercial fertilizer, inorganic fertilizer, chemical fertilizer, phosphate, superphosphate, ammonia, nitrogen, nitrate, potash, ammonium salts, sulfate, lime, marl

5 <goddesses of fertility> Demeter, Ceres, Isis, Astarte *or* Ashtoreth, Venus of Willenburg; <gods> Frey, Priapus, Dionysus, Pan, Baal; fertility cult

6 <comparisons> rabbit, Hydra, warren, seed plot, hotbed, rich soil, land flowing with milk and honey

VERBS 7 **produce, be productive, proliferate,** pullulate, fructify, be fruitful, **multiply,** procreate, propagate, generate, multiply, mushroom, spin off, hive off <Brit>, engender, beget, teem; **reproduce** 78.7,8

8 **fertilize, enrich,** make fertile, richen, fatten, feed; fructify, fecundate, fecundify, prolificate; inseminate, impregnate 78.10; pollinate, germinate, seed; cross-fertilize, cross-pollinate; dress, top-dress; manure, compost, feed, mulch, marl

ADJS 9 **productive, fruitful,** fructiferous, fecund; **fertile, pregnant,** seminal, **rich,** flourishing, thriving, blooming; **prolific,** proliferous, uberous, **teeming,** swarming, bursting, bursting out, plenteous, **plentiful,** copious, generous, bountiful, **abundant** 991.7, **luxuriant, exuberant, lush,** superabundant; creative

10 **bearing, yielding, producing;** fruitbearing, fructiferous

11 **fertilizing, enriching,** richening, fattening, fecundatory, fructificative, **seminal,** germinal

891 UNPRODUCTIVENESS

NOUNS 1 **unproductiveness,** unproductivity, ineffectualness 19.3; **unfruitfulness,** fruitlessness, **barrenness,** nonfruition, dryness, aridity, dearth, famine; sterileness, **sterility,** unfertileness, **infertility,** infecundity; wasted *or* withered loins, dry womb; **birth control, contraception,** family planning, planned parenthood; abortion; impotence 19, incapacity

2 **wasteland, waste,** desolation, barren *or* **barrens,** barren land; heath; **desert,** Sahara, sands, desert sands, badlands, dust bowl, salt flat, Death Valley, Arabia Deserta, lunar waste *or* landscape; desert island; wilderness, howling wilderness, wild, wilds; treeless plain; bush, brush, outback; fallowness, aridness; desertification, desertization

VERBS 3 be unproductive, **come to nothing,** come to naught, prove infertile, hang fire <nf>, flash in the pan, fizzle *or* peter out <nf>; **lie fallow;** stagnate, run to seed

ADJS 4 **unproductive,** nonproductive *or* nonproducing; **infertile, sterile,** unfertile *or* nonfertile, **unfruitful,** unfructuous, acarpous <botany>, infecund, unprolific *or* nonprolific; **impotent,** gelded 19.19; **ineffectual** 19.15; **barren, desert, arid,** dry, dried-up, sere, exhausted, drained, leached, sucked dry, wasted, gaunt, **waste, desolate,** jejune; **childless,** issueless, without issue, *sine prole* <L>; fallow, unplowed, unsown, untilled, uncultivated, unfecundated; celibate; virgin; menopausal

5 **uncreative,** noncreative, nonseminal, nongerminal, unfructified, unpregnant; uninventive, unoriginal, derivative

892 PRODUCTION

NOUNS 1 **production, creation, making, origination, invention, conception,** innovation, originating, engenderment, engendering, genesis, beginning; **devising,** hatching, fabrication, **concoction,** coinage, mintage, **contriving,** contrivance; **authorship;** creative effort, **generation** 78.6; improvisation, making do; **gross national product** *or* **GNP,** net national product *or* NNP, national production of goods and services

2 **production, manufacture** *or* **manufacturing, making, producing,** devising, design, fashioning, framing, forming, formation, formulation; engineering, tooling-up; processing, conversion; casting, **shaping,** molding; machining, milling, finishing; **assembly,** composition, elaboration; **workmanship, craftsmanship, skill** 413; **construction, building,** erection, architecture; **fabrication,** prefabrication; handiwork, handwork, handicraft, crafting; **mining,** extraction, smelting, **refining; growing,** cultivation, **raising,** harvesting

3 **industrial production, industry, mass production,** volume production, **assembly-line production;** production line, assembly line; modular production *or* assembly, standardization; division of labor, industrialization; heavy industry; light industry; **cottage industry;** piecework, farmed-out work

4 **establishment, foundation,** constitution, institution, installation, formation, **organization,** inauguration, **inception, setting-up,** realization, materialization, effectuation; spinning-off, hiving-off <Brit>

5 **performance, execution, doing, accomplishment, achievement,** productive effort *or* effect, realization, bringing to fruition, fructification, effectuation, operation 889; overproduction, glut; underproduction, scarcity; **productiveness** 890, fructuousness

6 **bearing, yielding, birthing; fruition,** fruiting, fructification

7 **producer, maker,** craftsman, wright, smith; **manufacturer,** industrialist; **creator,** begetter, engenderer, **author,** mother, **father,** sire; **ancestors** 560.7; **precursor** 816; **originator,** initiator, establisher, inaugurator, introducer, institutor, beginner, mover, prime mover, motive force, instigator; **founder,** organizer, founding father, founding *or* founder member, founding partner, cofounder; **inventor,** discoverer, deviser; developer; engineer; **builder,** constructor, artificer, **architect,** planner, **conceiver,** designer, **shaper,** master *or* leading spirit; executor, executrix; facilitator, animator; **grower,** raiser, cultivator; effector, realizer; **apprentice, journeyman, master,** master craftsman *or* workman, artist, past master

VERBS 8 **produce, create, make, manufacture, form,** formulate, evolve, mature, elaborate, fashion, **fabricate,** prefabricate, cast, shape, configure, carve out, mold, extrude, frame; **construct, build,** erect, put up, set up, run up, raise, rear; make up, get up, prepare, compose, write, indite, devise, design, concoct, compound, churn out *and* crank out *and* pound out *and* hammer out *and* grind out *and* rustle up *and* gin up

<nf>; **put together, assemble,** piece together, patch together, whomp up *and* fudge together *and* slap up *or* together <nf>, improvise 365.8; **make to order,** custom-make, custom-build, purpose-build <Brit>

9 **process,** convert 858.11; mill, machine; carve, chisel; **mine,** extract, pump, smelt, **refine; raise,** rear, **grow,** cultivate, harvest

10 **establish, found,** constitute, institute, install, form, **set up, organize,** equip, endow, inaugurate, realize, materialize, effect, effectuate

11 **perform, do,** work, act, execute, **accomplish, achieve** 407.4, **deliver,** come through with, realize, engineer, effectuate, **bring about,** bring to fruition *or* into being, cause; mass-produce, volume-produce, industrialize; overproduce; underproduce; **be productive** 890.7

12 **originate, invent, conceive,** discover, **make up, devise, contrive,** concoct, fabricate, coin, mint, frame, hatch, hatch *or* cook up, strike out; improvise, make do with; think up, think out, dream up, **design,** plan, formulate, set one's wits to work; **generate, develop,** mature, **evolve;** breed, engender, beget, spawn, hatch; bring forth, give rise to, give being to, bring *or* call into being; procreate 78.8

13 **bear, yield, produce,** furnish; **bring forth,** usher into the world; fruit, **bear fruit,** fructify; spawn

ADJS **14** **productional, creational,** formational; executional; **manufacturing,** manufactural, fabricational, **industrial,** smokestack

15 **constructional, structural,** building, housing, edificial; **architectural,** architectonic

16 **creative, originative,** causative, **productive** 890.9, **constructive,** formative, fabricative, demiurgic; inventive; generative 78.16

17 **produced, made, caused, brought about;** effectuated, executed, performed, done; grown, raised

18 **made,** man-made; **manufactured,** created, crafted, formed, shaped, molded, cast, forged, machined, milled, fashioned, **built, constructed,** fabricated; **mass-produced,** volume-produced, assembly-line; **well-made,** well-built, well-constructed; **homemade,** homestyle, homespun, **handmade,** handcrafted, handicrafted, self-made, DIY *or* do it yourself; machine-made; **processed; assembled,** put together; **custom-made,** custom-built, purpose-built <Brit>, custom, made to order, bespoke; **ready-made,** ready-formed, ready-prepared, ready-to-wear, ready-for-wear, off-the-shelf, off-the-rack; prefabricated, prefab <nf>; **mined,** extracted, smelted, **refined; grown, raised,** harvested, gathered

19 **invented,** originated, **conceived,** discovered, newfound; fabricated, coined, minted, new-minted; **made-up,** made out of whole cloth

20 **manufacturable, producible,** productible

ADVS **21** **in production;** in the works, in hand, on foot; under construction; in the pipeline; on-line

893 PRODUCT

NOUNS **1** **product,** end product, production, manufacture, wares; **work,** *œuvre* <Fr>, **handiwork, artifact; creation;** creature; **offspring,** child, fruit, fruit of one's loins; **result, effect** 887, issue, outgrowth, outcome; **invention,** origination, coinage, mintage *or* new mintage, brainchild; **concoction,** composition; opus, opuscule; apprentice work; journeyman work; **masterwork, masterpiece,** *chef d'œuvre* <Fr>, work of an artist *or* a master *or* a past master, crowning achievement; piece of work; gross national product 892.1

2 **production,** produce, proceeds, net, **yield, output,** throughput; **crop,** harvest, take <nf>, return, bang <nf>

3 **extract, distillation,** essence; **by-product,** secondary *or* incidental product, spin-off, outgrowth, offshoot; **residue,** leavings, waste, waste product, industrial waste, solid waste, lees, dregs, ash, slag

4 <amount made> make, making; batch, lot, run, boiling

894 INFLUENCE

NOUNS **1** **influence,** influentiality; **power** 18, force, clout <nf>, potency, pressure, effect, indirect *or* incidental power, **say,** the final say, the last word, say-so *and* a lot to do with *or* to say about <nf>, veto power; **prestige,** favor, good feeling, credit, esteem, repute, personality, leadership, charisma, magnetism, charm, enchantment; **weight,** moment, consequence, importance, eminence; **authority** 417, control, domination, hold; **sway** 612.1, reign, rule; **mastery,** ascendancy, supremacy, dominance, predominance, preponderance; upper hand, whip hand, trump card; leverage, purchase; **persuasion** 375.3, suasion, suggestion, subtle influence, insinuation

2 **favor,** special favor, **interest; pull** *and* drag *and* suction <nf>; **connections,** the right people, inside track <nf>; amicus curiae

3 **backstairs influence,** intrigues, deals, schemes, **games,** Machiavellian *or* Byzantine intrigues, ploys, sway; **wires** *and* **strings** *and* ropes <nf>; **wire-pulling** <nf>; **influence peddling;** lobby, lobbying, lobbyism; Big Brother

4 **sphere of influence,** orbit, ambit; bailiwick, vantage, stamping ground, footing, **territory,** turf, home turf, constituency, **power base**, niche

5 **influenceability,** swayableness, movability; **persuadability,** persuadableness, persuasibility, suasibility, openness, open-mindedness, get-at-ableness <Brit nf>, perviousness, accessibility, receptiveness, responsiveness, amenableness; **suggestibility, susceptibility,** impressionability, malleability; weakness 16; putty in one's hands

6 <influential person *or* thing> **influence,** good influence; bad influence, sinister influence; **person** *or* **woman** *or* **man of influence,** an influential, an affluential, a presence, a palpable presence, a mover and shaker <nf>, a person to be reckoned with, a player *or* player on the scene, major player; heavyweight, big wheel *and* biggie *and* heavy *or* big *or* long-ball hitter *and* piledriver *and* big fish in a small pond <nf>, very important person *or* VIP <nf>, big shot *or* bigwig *or* big cheese *or* big kahuna <nf>; wheeler-dealer <nf>, influencer, **wire-puller** <nf>; **powerbroker; power behind the throne,** gray eminence, éminence grise <Fr>, hidden hand, manipulator, friend at *or* in court, kingmaker; **influence peddler,** five-percenter, lobbyist; Svengali, Rasputin; **pressure group,** special-interest group, special interests, single-issue group, PAC *or* political action committee; lobby; the Establishment, big government; ingroup, court, powers that be 575.15, superpower, lords of creation; **key,** key to the city, access, open sesame

VERBS **7** **influence,** make oneself felt, **affect,** weigh with, **sway,** bias, bend, incline, dispose, predispose, **move,** prompt, lead; color, tinge, tone, slant, impart spin; **induce, persuade** 375.23, jawbone *and* twist one's arm *and* hold one's feet to the fire <nf>, work, work *or* bend to one's will; lead by the nose <nf>, wear down, soften up; win friends and influence people, ingratiate oneself

8 <exercise influence over> **govern** 612.11, **rule, control** 612.12, order, **regulate,** direct, guide; **determine,** decide, dispose; have the say *or* say-so, have veto power over, have the last word, call the shots *and* be in the driver's seat *and* wear the pants <nf>; charismatize

9 **exercise** *or* **exert influence, use one's influence, bring pressure to bear upon,** lean on <nf>, act on, **work on,** bear upon, throw one's weight around *or* into the scale, say a few words to the right person *or* in the right quarter; charismatize; draw, draw on, lead on, magnetize; **approach,** go up to with hat in hand, make advances *or* overtures, make up to *or* get cozy with <nf>; get at *or* get the ear of <nf>; **pull strings** *or* **wires** *or* **ropes,** wire-pull

<nf>; lobby, lobby through; wheel and deal <nf>

10 **have influence, be influential, carry weight, weigh, tell, count,** cut ice, throw a lot of weight <nf>, have a lot to do with *or* say about <nf>; be the decisive factor *or* the one that counts, have pull *or* suction *or* drag *or* leverage <nf>; have a way with one, have personality *or* magnetism *or* charisma, charm the birds out of the trees, charm the pants off one <nf>, be persuasive; have an in <nf>, have the inside track <nf>; have full play; have friends in high places

11 have influence *or* power *or* a hold over, have pull *or* clout with <nf>; **lead by the nose, twist** *or* **turn** *or* **wind around one's little finger,** have in one's pocket, keep under one's thumb, make sit up and beg *or* lie down and roll over; hypnotize, mesmerize, **dominate** 612.14

12 gain influence, **get in with** <nf>, ingratiate oneself with, get cozy with <nf>; make peace, **mend fences;** gain a footing, take hold, move in, take root, strike root in, make a dent in; gain a hearing, make one's voice heard, make one sit up and take notice, be listened to, be recognized; get the mastery *or* control of, get the inside track <nf>, gain a hold upon; change the preponderance, turn the scale *or* balance, turn the tables

ADJS 13 **influential, powerful** 18.12, affluential, potent, strong, to be reckoned with; **effective,** effectual, efficacious, telling; **weighty,** momentous, important, consequential, substantial, earth-shattering, **prestigious,** estimable, authoritative, reputable; **persuasive,** suasive, personable, **winning,** magnetic, charming, enchanting, charismatic

14 <in a position of influence> **well-connected,** favorably situated, near the seat of power; **dominant** 612.17, **predominant,** preponderant, prepotent, prepollent, regnant, ruling, swaying, prevailing, prevalent, on the throne, in the driver's seat <nf>; **ascendant,** in the ascendant, in ascendancy

15 **influenceable, swayable, movable; persuadable,** persuasible, suasible, open, open-minded, pervious, accessible, receptive, responsive, amenable; **under one's thumb,** in one's pocket, on one's payroll; coercible, bribable, compellable, vulnerable; **plastic, pliant,** pliable, malleable; **suggestible, susceptible, impressionable,** weak 16.12

895 ABSENCE OF INFLUENCE

NOUNS 1 **lack of influence** *or* **power** *or* **force,** uninfluentiality, **unauthoritativeness,** powerlessness, forcelessness, impotence 19, impotency; **ineffectiveness,** inefficaciousness, inefficacy, ineffectuality; **no say,** no say-so, nothing to do with *or* say about <nf>; unpersuasiveness, lack of personality *or* charm, lack of magnetism *or* charisma; **weakness** 16, wimpiness *or* wimpishness <nf>

2 **uninfluenceability,** unswayableness, unmovability; **unpersuadability,** impersuadability, impersuasibility, unreceptiveness, imperviousness, unresponsiveness; unsuggestibility, **unsusceptibility,** unimpressionability; invulnerability; **obstinacy** 361

ADJS 3 **uninfluential, powerless,** forceless, impotent 19.13; **weak** 16.12, wimpy *or* wimpish <nf>; unauthoritative; **ineffective,** ineffectual, inefficacious; **of no account,** no-account, without any weight, featherweight, lightweight

4 **uninfluenceable, unswayable, unmovable; unpliable,** unyielding, inflexible; **unpersuadable** 361.13, impersuadable, impersuasible, unreceptive, unresponsive, unamenable; impervious, closed to; **unsuggestible, unsusceptible,** unimpressionable; invulnerable; **obstinate** 361.8

5 **uninfluenced, unmoved, unaffected, unswayed**

896 TENDENCY

NOUNS 1 **tendency, inclination, leaning,** penchant, proneness, conatus, weakness, susceptibility; liability

897, readiness, willingness, eagerness, aptness, aptitude, **disposition, proclivity, propensity,** predisposition, **predilection,** a thing for <nf>, affinity, prejudice, **liking,** delight, soft spot, penchant; **yen,** lech <nf>, hunger, thirst; instinct *or* feeling for, sensitivity to; **bent, turn, bias,** slant, tilt, spin <nf>, cast, warp, twist, leaning; probability 968; diathesis <medicine>, tropism <biology>

2 trend, drift, course, current, flow, stream, mainstream, main current, movement, glacial movement, motion, run, **tenor,** tone, **set,** set of the current, swing, bearing, line, direction, the general tendency *or* drift, the main course, the course of events, the way the wind blows, **the way things go,** sign of the times, spirit of the age *or* time, time spirit, *Zeitgeist* <Ger>; climate; the way it looks

VERBS **3 tend,** have a tendency, **incline,** be disposed, **lean, trend,** have a penchant, set, **go,** head, lead, point, verge, turn, warp, tilt, bias, bend to, work *or* gravitate *or* set toward; show a tendency *or* trend *or* set *or* direction, swing toward, point to, look to; **conduce,** contribute, serve, redound to; bode well

ADJS **4 tending;** tendentious *or* tendential; **leaning, inclining,** inclinatory, inclinational; **mainstream,** main-current, mainline

5 inclined to, leaning to, prone to, disposed to, drawn to, predisposed to, given to; **apt to, likely to, liable to** 897.6, calculated to, minded to, ready to, in a fair way to

897 LIABILITY

NOUNS **1 liability, likelihood** *or* **likeliness; probability** 968, contingency, chance 972, eventuality 831.1; weakness, **proneness** 896.1; **possibility** 966; **responsibility** 641.2, legal responsibility; **indebtedness** 623.1, financial commitment *or* obligation, pecuniary obligation

2 susceptibility, liability, susceptivity, liableness, **openness, exposure; vulnerability** 1006.4

VERBS **3 be liable; be subjected** *or* **subjected to,** be a pawn *or* plaything of, be the prey of, lie under; **expose oneself to, lay** *or* **leave oneself open to,** open the door to; **gamble,** stand to lose *or* gain, stand a chance, **run the chance** *or* **risk,** let down one's guard *or* defenses; **admit of,** open the possibility of, be in the way of, bid *or* stand fair to; **owe,** be in debt *or* indebted for

4 incur, contract, invite, welcome, run, **bring on, bring down,** bring upon *or* down upon, bring upon *or* down upon oneself; **be responsible for** 641.6; fall into, fall in with; get, gain, acquire

ADJS **5 liable, likely, prone; probable; responsible,** legally responsible, answerable; **in debt, indebted,** financially burdened, heavily committed, overextended; **exposed, susceptible, at risk,** overexposed, open, like a sitting duck, **vulnerable**

6 liable to, subject to, standing to, in a position to, incident to, dependent on; **susceptible** *or* **prone to,** susceptive to, **open** *or* vulnerable *or* **exposed to,** naked to, in danger of, within range of, at the mercy of; **capable of,** ready for; **likely to, apt to** 896.5; obliged to, responsible *or* answerable for

CONJS **7 lest,** that, **for fear that**

898 INVOLVEMENT

NOUNS **1 involvement,** involution, **implication, entanglement,** enmeshment, engagement, involuntary presence *or* cooperation, embarrassment; relation 775; **inclusion** 772; **absorption** 983.3

VERBS **2 involve, implicate,** tangle, **entangle,** embarrass, enmesh, engage, **draw in,** drag *or* hook *or* suck into, catch up in, **make a party to;** interest, concern; **absorb** 983.13

3 be involved, be into <nf>, partake, participate, take an interest, interest oneself, have a role *or* part

ADJS **4 involved, implicated;** interested, concerned, a party to; **included** 772.5

5 **involved in, implicated in,** tangled *or* entangled in, enmeshed in, **caught up in,** tied up in, wrapped up in, all wound up in, dragged *or* hooked *or* sucked into; in deep, deeply involved, **up to one's neck** *or* **ears in,** up to one's elbows *or* ass in, head over heels in, **absorbed in** 983.17, immersed *or* submerged in, far-gone

899 CONCURRENCE

NOUNS **1** **concurrence, collaboration,** coaction, **co-working,** collectivity, combined effort *or* operation, united *or* concerted action, concert, synergy; **cooperation** 450; **agreement** 788; me-tooism; **coincidence,** simultaneity 836, synchronism; concomitance, accompaniment 769; **union,** junction 800.1, **conjunction,** combination 805, association, alliance, consociation; conspiracy, collusion, cahoots <nf>; concourse, confluence; **accordance** 455.1, concordance, correspondence, consilience; symbiosis, parasitism; saprophytism; meeting of the minds

VERBS **2** **concur, collaborate,** coact, **co-work,** synergize; **cooperate** 450.3; conspire, collude, connive, be in cahoots <nf>, go in together; **combine** 805.3, **unite, associate** 805.4, coadunate, join, conjoin; harmonize; **coincide,** synchronize, happen together; **accord** 455.2, correspond, **agree** 788.6

3 go with, **go along with, go hand in hand with,** be hand in glove with, team *or* join up with, buddy up with <nf>; keep pace with, run parallel to

ADJS **4** **concurrent,** concurring; **coacting,** coactive, **collaborative,** collective, **co-working,** cooperant, synergetic *or* synergic *or* synergistic; **cooperative** 450.5; conspiratorial, collusive; **united, joint,** conjoint, **combined, concerted,** associated, associate, coadunate; **coincident,** synchronous, synchronic, in sync, coordinate; concomitant, accompanying 769.9; meeting, uniting, combining; **accordant, agreeing** 788.9, concordant, harmonious, consilient, at one with; symbiotic, parasitic, saprophytic

ADVS **5** **concurrently,** coactively, **jointly, conjointly, concertedly,** in concert, in harmony *or* unison with, synchronously, **together; with one accord,** with one voice, as one, as one man; hand in hand, hand in glove, shoulder to shoulder, cheek by jowl

900 COUNTERACTION

NOUNS **1** **counteraction, counterworking; opposition** 451, opposure, counterposition *or* contraposition, confutation, **contradiction; antagonism,** repugnance, oppugnance *or* oppugnancy, **antipathy, conflict, friction,** interference, clashing, collision; reaction, repercussion, **backlash, recoil,** kick, backfire, boomerang effect; resistance, recalcitrance, dissent 333, revolt 327.4, perverseness, nonconformity 868, crankiness, crotchetiness, orneriness <nf>, renitency; going against the current *or* against the tide, swimming upstream; **contrariety** 779

2 **neutralization, nullification, annulment,** cancellation, voiding, invalidation, vitiation, frustration, thwarting, undoing; **offsetting,** counterbalancing, countervailing, balancing; negation; equilibrium

3 **counteractant,** counteractive, **counteragent;** counterirritant; **antidote,** remedy, preventive *or* preventative, prophylactic, contraceptive; **neutralizer,** nullifier, offset; antacid, buffer

4 **counterforce,** countervailing force, counterinfluence, counterpressure; countercheck; counterpoise, counterbalance, counterweight; countercurrent, crosscurrent, undercurrent; counterblast; headwind, foul wind, crosswind; friction, drag

5 **countermeasure, counterattack,** counterstep; **counterblow** *or* counterstroke *or* countercoup *or* counterblast, counterfire; counterrevolution, counterinsurgency; counterterrorism; counterculture; **retort,** comeback <nf>; defense 460

VERBS **6** **counteract,** counter, counterwork, counterattack, countervail; counterpose *or* contrapose, **oppose,** antagonize, **go in opposition to, go** *or* **run counter to, go** *or* **work against,** go clean counter to, go *or* fly in the face of, run against, beat against, militate against; **resist,** fight back, bite back, lift a hand against, defend oneself; **dissent,** dissent from; **cross,** confute, **contradict,** contravene, oppugn, **conflict,** be antipathetic *or* hostile *or* inimical, interfere *or* conflict with, come in conflict with, **clash,** collide, meet head-on, lock horns; rub *or* go against the grain; swim upstream *or* against the tide *or* against the current; boomerang; countercheck

7 **neutralize, nullify, annul, cancel,** cancel out, negate, negative, negativate, invalidate, vitiate, void, frustrate, stultify, thwart, come *or* bring to nothing, undo; **offset, counterbalance** 338.5; buffer

ADJS **8** counteractive *or* counteractant, **counteracting, counterworking, counterproductive,** countervailing; **opposing,** oppositional; contradicting, contradictory; **antagonistic,** hostile, antipathetic, inimical, oppugnant, repugnant, **conflicting, clashing;** reactionary; resistant, recalcitrant, dissentient, dissident, revolutionary, breakaway, nonconformist, perverse, cranky, crotchety, ornery <nf>, renitent

9 **neutralizing, nullifying,** stultifying, annulling, canceling, negating, invalidating, vitiating, voiding; equalizing; **balanced,** counterbalanced, poised, in poise, offset, **zero-sum;** **offsetting,** counterbalancing, countervailing; antacid, buffering; antidotal

ADVS **10** counteractively, antagonistically, opposingly, **in opposition to, counter to**

901 SUPPORT

NOUNS **1** **support, backing, aid** 449; upholding, upkeep, carrying, carriage, maintenance, **sustaining,** sustainment, sustenance, sustentation; **reinforcement,** backup; subsidy, subvention; **support services, infrastructure; moral support;** emotional *or* psychological support, security blanket <nf>; reassurance; **power base, constituency, party;** supportive relationship, supportive therapy; strokes <nf>; **approval** 509; **assent, concurrence** 332.1; **reliance** 953.1; life-support, life-sustainment

2 **supporter, support; upholder,** bearer, carrier, sustainer, maintainer; staff 273.2, stave, cane, stick, walking stick, alpenstock, crook, crutch; **advocate** 616.9; **stay, prop,** fulcrum, **bracket, brace,** bracer, guy, guywire *or* guyline, shroud, rigging, standing rigging; ballast; bulwark, anchor; buttress, shoulder, arm, good right arm; mast, sprit, yard, yardarm; **mainstay,** backbone, spine, neck, cervix; athletic supporter, jock and jockstrap <nf>, G-string <nf>; brassiere, bra <nf>, bandeau, corset, girdle, foundation garment; **reinforcement,** reinforce, reinforcing, reinforcer, strengthener, stiffener; back, backing; rest, resting place

3 <mythology> Atlas, Hercules, Telamon, Chukwa *or* The Tortoise which Supports the Earth

4 **buttress,** buttressing; abutment, shoulder; **bulwark,** rampart; **embankment,** bank, retaining wall, bulkhead, bulkheading, plank buttress, piling; **breakwater**, seawall, mole, **jetty**, jutty, groin; **pier,** pier buttress, buttress pier; flying buttress, *arc-boutant* <Fr>, arch buttress; hanging buttress; **beam**

5 **footing, foothold, toehold,** hold, perch, **purchase** 906.2; **standing,** stand, stance, standing place, pou sto, *point d'appui* <Fr>, *locus standi* <L>; footrest, footplate, footrail

6 **foundation,** *fond* <Fr>, firm foundation, **base, basis, footing,** basement, pavement, **ground,** grounds, **groundwork, seat,** sill, floor *or* flooring, fundament; bed, bedding; **substructure,** substruction, substratum; infrastructure; **understruc-**

ture, understruction, underbuilding, undergirding, undercarriage, underpinning, bearing wall; stereobate, stylobate; firm *or* solid ground, *terra firma* <L>; solid rock *or* bottom, rock bottom, bedrock; hardpan; riprap; **fundamental** 997.6, **principle, premise** 957.1; grounds, precedent; root, radical; rudiment

7 **foundation stone,** footstone; **cornerstone, keystone,** headstone, first stone, quoin; roadbed

8 **base, pedestal; stand,** standard; **shaft** 273, **upright, column, pillar, post,** jack, pole, staff, stanchion, pier, pile *or* piling, king-post, queen-post, pilaster, newel-post, banister, baluster, balustrade, colonnade, caryatid; dado, die; plinth, subbase; surbase; socle; **trunk,** stem, **stalk,** pedicel, peduncle, footstalk

9 **sill,** groundsel; mudsill; window sill; doorsill, threshold; doorstone

10 **frame,** underframe, infrastructure, chassis, **skeleton;** armature; **mounting,** mount, **backing, setting;** surround

11 **handle, hold,** grip, grasp, haft, helve

12 **scaffold,** scaffolding, *échafaudage* <Fr>; stage, staging

13 **platform; stage,** estrade, dais, floor; **rostrum, podium, pulpit,** speaker's platform *or* stand, **soapbox** <nf>; hustings, **stump;** tribune, tribunal; emplacement; catafalque; landing stage, landing; heliport, landing pad; launching pad; **terrace,** step terrace, deck; **balcony, gallery**

14 **shelf, ledge,** shoulder, corbel, beam-end; mantel, mantelshelf, mantelpiece; retable, superaltar, gradin, predella; hob

15 **table,** board, **stand; bench,** workbench; **counter,** bar, buffet; **desk,** writing table, **secretary,** *secrétaire* <Fr>, escritoire; **lectern,** reading stand, ambo, reading desk

16 **trestle, horse; sawhorse,** buck *or* sawbuck; clotheshorse; trestle board *or* table, trestle and table; trestlework, trestling; A-frame

17 **seat, chair;** saddle, howdah

18 <saddle parts> **pommel,** horn; jockey; girth, girt, surcingle, bellyband; cinch, stirrup

19 sofa, **bed; couch;** the sack *and* the hay *and* kip *and* doss <nf>; futon; bedstead; **litter, stretcher,** gurney

20 **bedding,** underbed, underbedding; **mattress,** paillasse, pallet; air mattress, foam rubber mattress, innerspring mattress; sleeping bag; pad, mat, rug; litter, bedstraw; **pillow,** cushion, bolster; **springs,** bedsprings, box springs; futon

VERBS **21** **support, bear,** carry, **hold, sustain, maintain, bolster, reinforce,** back, back up, shoulder, give *or* furnish *or* afford *or* supply *or* lend support; go to bat for <nf>; **hold up, bear up,** bolster up, keep up, buoy up, keep afloat, back up; **uphold,** upbear, upkeep; **brace, prop,** crutch, buttress; shore, **shore up;** stay, mainstay; underbrace, undergird, underprop, underpin, underset; **underlie,** be at the bottom of, form the foundation of; cradle; cushion, pillow; **subsidize;** subvene; assent 332.8; concur 332.9; **approve** 509.9

22 **rest on, stand on, lie on,** recline on, repose on, bear on, **lean on,** abut on; **sit on,** perch, ride, piggyback on; **straddle,** bestraddle, stride, bestride; be based on, rely on

ADJS **23** **supporting, supportive, bearing,** carrying, burdened; **holding,** upholding, maintaining, sustaining, sustentative, suspensory; bracing, propping, shoring, bolstering, buttressing; life-sustaining; collaborative, corroborative, cooperative

24 **supported, borne,** upborne, held, buoyed-up, **upheld, sustained,** maintained; **braced,** guyed, stayed, propped, shored *or* shored up, bolstered, buttressed; based *or* founded *or* grounded on

ADVS **25** **on, across, astride, astraddle,** straddle, straddle-legged, straddleback, on the back of; horseback, on horseback; pickaback *or* piggyback

902 IMPULSE, IMPACT
<driving and striking force>

NOUNS **1 impulse,** impulsion, impelling force, impellent; **drive,** driving force *or* power; **motive power, power** 18; **force,** irresistible force; clout <nf>; **impetus; momentum;** moment, moment of force; propulsion 904.1; incitement 375.4, incentive 375.7, compulsion 424

2 thrust, push, shove, boost <nf>; **pressure; stress;** press; **prod, poke, punch, jab,** dig, nudge; **bump,** jog, joggle, jolt; **jostle,** hustle; **butt,** bunt; head <of water, steam, etc>

3 impact, collision, clash, appulse, **encounter,** meeting, impingement, **bump, crash,** crump, whomp; **carom,** carambole, cannon; sideswipe <nf>; smash *and* crunch <nf>; **shock, brunt; concussion,** percussion; **thrusting, ramming,** bulling, **bulldozing,** shouldering, muscling, steamrollering, railroading; hammering, smashing, mauling, sledgehammering; onslaught 459.1

4 hit, blow, stroke, knock, rap, pound, slam, bang, crack, **whack, smack, thwack,** smash, dash, swipe, swing, **punch, poke, jab,** dig, drub, thump, pelt, cut, chop, dint, slog; drubbing, drumming, tattoo, fusillade; beating 604.4

5 <nf terms> **sock,** bang, bash, bat, belt, bonk, bust, clip, clout, duke, swat, yerk, plunk, larrup, paste, lick, biff, clump, clunk, clonk, wallop, whop, slam, slug, whomp, swack

6 punch, boxing punch, blow, belt, sock

7 tap, rap, pat, dab, chuck, touch, tip; love-tap; **snap, flick, flip,** fillip, flirt, whisk, brush; **peck,** pick

8 slap, smack, flap; **box, cuff,** buffet; **spank;** whip, **lash,** cut, stripe

9 kick, boot; punt, drop kick, place kick, kicking, calcitration

10 stamp, stomp <nf>, drub, clump, clop

VERBS **11** impel, give an impetus, **set going** *or* agoing, put *or* set in motion, give momentum; **drive, move,** animate, actuate, forward; **thrust,** power; drive *or* whip on; goad; **propel;** motivate, incite 375.17; compel 424.4

12 thrust, push, shove, boost <nf>; press, stress, **bear,** bear upon, bring pressure to bear upon; **ram,** ram down, tamp, pile drive, jam, crowd, cram; bull, bulldoze, muscle, steamroller, railroad; **drive, force,** run; **prod, goad, poke, punch, jab,** dig, nudge; **bump,** jog, joggle, jolt, shake, rattle; **jostle,** hustle, hurtle; elbow, shoulder; **butt,** bunt, buck <nf>, run *or* bump *or* butt against, bump up against, knock *or* run one's head against; assault

13 collide, come into collision, be on a collision course, **clash,** meet, encounter, confront each other, impinge; percuss, concuss; **bump, hit, strike, knock, bang; run into, bump into,** bang into, slam into, smack into, **crash into, impact,** smash into, dash into, carom into, cannon into <Brit>; rear-end; **hit against,** strike against, knock against; foul, fall *or* run foul *or* afoul of; hurtle, hurt; **carom,** cannon <chiefly Brit>; **sideswipe** <nf>; **crash,** smash, crump, whomp; smash up *or* crack up *or* crunch <nf>

14 hit, strike, knock, knock down *or* out, smite; land a blow, draw blood; **poke, punch, jab,** thwack, **smack,** clap, crack, swipe, **whack;** deal, fetch, swipe at, take a punch at, throw one at <nf>, deal *or* fetch a blow, hit a clip <nf>, let have it; **thump,** snap; strike at 459.16

15 <nf terms> **belt,** bat, clout, bang, slam, bash, biff, paste, wham, whop, clump, bonk, wallop, clip, cut, plunk, swat, soak, sock, slog, slug, yerk , clunk, clonk

16 pound, beat, hammer, maul, sledgehammer, **knock, rap, bang,** thump, **drub,** buffet, **batter,** pulverize, paste <nf>, patter, pommel, pummel, pelt, baste, lambaste; thresh, thrash; flail; spank, flap; whip

17 <nf terms> **clobber,** knock for a loop, marmelize <Brit>, knock cold, dust off, bash up, punch out, rough up, slap down, smack down, sandbag, work over, deck, coldcock, wallop, larrup

18 **tap, rap, pat,** dab, chuck, touch, tip; **snap, flick, flip,** fillip, tickle, flirt, whisk, **graze,** brush; bunt; **peck,** pick, beak

19 **slap, smack,** flap; **box, cuff,** buffet; **spank;** whip

20 **club,** cudgel, blackjack, sandbag, cosh <Brit>

21 **kick,** boot, kick about *or* around, calcitrate ; kick downstairs ; kick out; knee

22 **stamp,** stomp <nf>, trample, tread, drub, clump, clop

ADJS 23 **impelling,** impellent; impulsive, pulsive, **moving,** motive, animating, actuating, **driving;** thrusting

24 concussive, percussive, crashing, smashing

903 REACTION

NOUNS 1 **reaction, response,** respondence, feedback; reply, answer 939.1, **rise** <nf>; **reflex,** reflection, **reflex action;** echo, bounce back, reverberation, resonance, sympathetic vibration; return; reflux, refluence; action and reaction; opposite response, negative response, retroaction, revulsion; predictable response, automatic *or* autonomic reaction, knee-jerk *and* knee-jerk response <nf>, spontaneous *or* unthinking response, spur-of-the-moment response; conditioned reflex

2 **recoil, rebound,** resilience, repercussion, *contrecoup* <Fr>; **bounce, bound, spring,** bounce-back; **repulse, rebuff; backlash,** backlashing, kickback, **kick,** a kick like a mule <nf>, recalcitration ; **backfire, boomerang;** ricochet, carom, cannon <Brit>

3 <a drawing back *or* aside> **retreat,** recoil, fallback, pullout, pullback, contingency plan, backup plan; evasion, avoidance, sidestepping; **flinch,** wince, cringe; **side step,** shy; **dodge, duck** <nf>

4 **reactionary,** reactionist, recalcitrant

VERBS 5 **react, respond,** reply, answer, riposte, snap back, come back at <nf>; rise to the fly, take the bait; go off half-cocked *or* at half cock

6 **recoil, rebound,** resile; **bounce, bound, spring; spring** *or* **fly back,** bounce *or* bound back, snap back; repercuss, have repercussions; **kick,** kick back, kick like a mule <nf>, recalcitrate ; **backfire, boomerang;** backlash, lash back; ricochet, carom, cannon *and* cannon off <Brit>

7 **pull** *or* **draw back,** retreat, recoil, fade, **fall back,** reel back, hang back, start back, shrink back, give ground; **shrink, flinch, wince, cringe,** blink, blench, quail; **shy,** shy away, start *or* turn aside, evade, avoid, sidestep, weasel, weasel out, cop out <nf>; **dodge, duck** <nf>; jib, swerve, sheer off, give a wide berth

8 get a reaction, get a response, evoke a response, ring a bell, strike a responsive chord, strike fire, strike *or* hit home, hit a nerve, get a rise out of <nf>

ADJS 9 **reactive,** reacting, merely reactive; **responsive,** respondent, responding, antiphonal; **quick on the draw** *or* trigger *or* uptake; **reactionary;** retroactionary, retroactive; revulsive; **reflex,** reflexive, knee-jerk <nf>; refluent

10 recoiling, rebounding, **resilient; bouncing,** bouncy, bounding, springing, springy; repercussive; recalcitrant

ADVS 11 **on the rebound,** on the return, on the bounce; on the spur of the moment, off the top of the head

904 PUSHING, THROWING

NOUNS 1 **pushing, propulsion, propelling; shoving,** butting; **drive, thrust,** motive power, driving force, means of propulsion; **push, shove;** butt, bunt; shunt, impulsion 902.1

2 **throwing, projection,** jaculation, ejaculation, trajection, flinging, slinging, **pitching, tossing,** casting, hurling, lobbing, chucking, chunking <nf>, heaving, firing *and* burning *and* pegging <nf>; bowling,

rolling; **shooting,** firing, gunnery, gunning, musketry; trap-shooting, skeet *or* skeet shooting; archery

3 **throw, toss, fling, sling, cast, hurl,** chuck, chunk <nf>, lob, **heave,** shy, **pitch,** peg <nf>; **flip;** put, shot-put; <football> pass, forward pass, lateral pass, lateral; <tennis> serve, service; bowl; <baseball> pitch

4 **shot,** discharge; ejection 909; detonation 56.3; gunfire; gun, cannon; bullet; **salvo, volley,** fusillade, tattoo, spray; bowshot, gunshot, stoneshot, potshot

5 **projectile;** ejecta, ejectamenta; **missile;** ball; discus, quoit

6 **propeller,** prop <nf>, airscrew, prop-fan; propellant, propulsor, driver; screw, wheel, screw propeller, twin screws; bow thruster; paddle wheel; turbine; fan, impeller, rotor; piston

7 **thrower, pitcher,** hurler, bowler <cricket>, chucker, chunker <nf>, **heaver, tosser,** flinger, slinger, caster, jaculator, ejaculator; bowler; shot-putter; javelin thrower; discus thrower, discobolus

8 **shooter,** shot; **gunner,** gun, **gunman; rifleman,** musketeer, carabineer, pistoleer; cannoneer, artilleryman; Nimrod, hunter 382.5; trapshooter; archer, bowman, toxophilite; **marksman, markswoman,** targetshooter, **sharpshooter,** sniper; good shot, dead shot, deadeye, **crack shot**

VERBS **9 push, propel,** impel, **shove,** thrust 902.11; **drive, move,** forward, advance, traject; sweep, sweep along; butt, bunt; shunt; pole, row; pedal, treadle; **roll,** troll, bowl, trundle

10 **throw, fling, sling, pitch, toss, cast, hurl, heave, chuck,** chunk *and* peg <nf>, lob, shy, fire, burn, pepper <nf>, launch, dash, let fly, let go, let rip, let loose; catapult; **flip,** snap, jerk; bowl; pass; serve; put, put the shot; bung <Brit nf>; dart, lance, tilt; fork, pitchfork; pelt 459.27

11 **project,** jaculate, ejaculate

12 **shoot, fire,** fire off, let off, let fly, **discharge,** eject 909.13; detonate 56.8; gun <nf>, pistol; sharpshoot; shoot at 459.22, gun for <nf>; strike, hit, plug <nf>; shoot down, fell, drop, stop in one's tracks; **riddle, pepper,** pelt, pump full of lead <nf>; snipe, pick off; torpedo; pot; potshoot, potshot, take a potshot; load, prime, charge; cock

13 **start,** start off, start up, give a start, crank up, give a push *or* shove <nf>, jump-start, kick-start, **put** *or* **set in motion, set on foot,** set going *or* agoing, start going; **kick off** *and* **start the ball rolling** <nf>; get off the ground *or* off the mark, **launch,** launch forth *or* out, float, set afloat; send, send off *or* forth; bundle off

ADJS **14 propulsive,** propulsory, **propellant,** propelling; **motive; driving, pushing, shoving**

15 **projectile,** trajectile, jaculatory, ejaculatory; **ballistic,** missile; ejective

16 jet-propelled, rocket-propelled, steam-propelled, gasoline-propelled, gas-propelled, diesel-propelled, wind-propelled, self-propelled, etc

17 <means of propulsion> battery, diesel, diesel-electric, electric, gas *or* gasoline, gravity, jet, plasma-jet, prop-fan, pulse-jet, ram-jet, reaction, resojet, rocket, spring, steam, turbofan, turbojet, turbopropeller *or* turboprop, wind

905 PULLING

NOUNS **1 pulling, traction, drawing,** draft, dragging, heaving, tugging, towing; pulling *or* tractive power, **pull;** tug-of-war; towing, towage; towrope, towbar, towing cable *or* hawser; tow car, wrecker; **hauling,** haulage, drayage; man-hauling, man-haulage; attraction 907; extraction 192

2 **pull, draw, heave, haul, tug,** tow, lug, a long pull *and* a strong pull, strain, drag

3 **jerk, yank** <nf>, quick *or* sudden pull; **twitch,** tweak, pluck, hitch, wrench, snatch, start, bob; **flip,** flick, flirt, flounce; jig, **jiggle;** jog, joggle

VERBS **4 pull, draw, heave, haul,** hale, lug, **tug, tow,** take in tow; trail, train; **drag,** man-haul, draggle, snake <nf>; troll, trawl

5 **jerk,** yerk <nf>, **yank** <nf>; **twitch,** tweak, pluck, snatch, hitch, wrench, snake <nf>; **flip,** flick, flirt, flounce; **jiggle,** jig, jigget, jigger; jog, joggle

ADJS **6** **pulling, drawing,** tractional, tractive, hauling, tugging, towing, towage; man-hauled

906 LEVERAGE

<mechanical advantage applied to moving or raising>

NOUNS **1** **leverage,** fulcrumage; **pry,** prize <nf>

2 **purchase, hold,** advantage; **foothold,** toehold, footing; differential purchase; collier's purchase; traction

3 **fulcrum, axis, pivot,** bearing, rest, resting point, *point d'appui* <Fr>; thole, tholepin, rowlock, oarlock

4 **lever; pry,** prize <nf>; **bar,** pinch bar, crowbar, crow, pinchbar, iron crow, wrecking bar, ripping bar, claw bar; cant hook, peavey; **jimmy;** handspike, marlinespike; boom, spar, beam, outrigger; pedal, treadle, crank; limb

5 **arm;** forearm; wrist; elbow; upper arm, biceps

6 **tackle,** purchase

7 *windlass; capstan* <nautical>; **winch,** crab; reel; Chinese windlass, Spanish windlass

VERBS **8** get a purchase, get leverage, get a foothold; **pry,** prize, **lever,** wedge; pry *or* prize out; **jimmy,** crowbar, pinchbar

9 reel in, wind in, bring in, draw in, pull in, crank in, trim, tighten, tauten, draw taut, take the strain; windlass, winch, crank, reel; tackle

907 ATTRACTION

<a drawing toward>

NOUNS **1** **attraction,** traction 905.1, attractiveness, attractivity; mutual attraction *or* magnetism; pulling power, **pull,** drag, draw, tug; magnetism 1032.7; gravity, gravitation; centripetal force; capillarity, capillary attraction; adduction; **affinity, sympathy; allurement** 377; come-on

2 attractor, attractant, attrahent; adductor; cynosure, focus, center, center of attraction *or* attention; crowd-pleaser *or* drawer, charismatic figure; drawing card; side show; freak show; **lure** 377.3

3 **magnet,** artificial magnet, field magnet, bar magnet, horseshoe magnet, electromagnet, solenoid, paramagnet, permanent magnet, keeper, superconducting magnet, electromagnetic lifting magnet, magnetic needle; lodestone, magnetite; magnetic pole, magnetic north; lodestar, polestar; siderite

VERBS **4** **attract, pull, draw,** drag, tug, pull *or* draw towards, have an attraction; **magnetize,** magnet, be magnetic; **lure;** adduct

ADJS **5** attracting, drawing, pulling, dragging, tugging; eye-catching; **attractive, magnetic;** charismatic; magnetized, attrahent; sympathetic; **alluring;** adductive, adducent; associative

ADVS **6** attractionally, attractively; magnetically; charismatically

908 REPULSION

<a thrusting away>

NOUNS **1** **repulsion,** repellence *or* repellency, **repelling;** mutual repulsion, polarization; disaffinity; centrifugal force; magnetic repulsion, diamagnetism; antigravity; repulsive force; ejection 909

2 **repulse, rebuff; dismissal,** cold shoulder, snub, spurning, brush-off, cut; kiss-off <nf>; turn-off <nf>; rejection; refusal; discharge 909.5

VERBS **3** **repulse, repel, rebuff, turn back,** put back, beat back, force *or* drive *or* push **or** thrust back; drive away, chase, chase off *or* away; send off *or* away, send about one's business, **send packing,** pack off, dismiss; snub, cut, brush off, drop; kiss off <nf>, show someone the door; spurn, refuse; **ward off,** hold off, keep off, fend off, fight off, drive off, push off, keep at arm's length; slap *or* smack down <nf>; eject 909.13, discharge 909.19

ADJS **4** **repulsive,** repellent, **repelling;** diamagnetic, of opposite polarity, centrifugal, abducent, abductive; off-putting

ADVS **5** repulsively, repellently

909 EJECTION

NOUNS **1** **ejection,** ejectment, throwing out, **expulsion, discharge,** extrusion, obtrusion, detrusion, **ousting, ouster,** removal, kicking *or* booting *or* chucking out <nf>; throwing *or* kicking downstairs; the boot *and* the bounce *and* the bum's rush *and* the old heave-ho <nf>, the chuck *or* the push <Brit nf>; defenestration; **rejection** 372; jettison

2 **eviction,** ousting, dislodgment, dispossession, expropriation; **ouster,** throwing overboard

3 **depopulation,** dispeoplement, unpeopling; devastation, desolation

4 **banishment,** relegation, exclusion 773; **excommunication,** disfellowship; **disbarment,** unfrocking, defrocking; proscription; **expatriation, exile,** exilement; outlawing *or* outlawry, fugitation; **ostracism,** ostracization, thumbs-down, thumbing-down, *pollice verso* <L>, blackballing, silent treatment, sending to Coventry, cold shoulder; **deportation,** transportation, **extradition;** rustication; degradation, **demotion** 447, stripping, depluming, displuming; deprivation

5 **dismissal, discharge,** forced separation, *congé* <Fr>; outplacement; **firing** *and* canning <nf>, **cashiering,** drumming out, dishonorable discharge, rogue's march; disemployment, **layoff,** removal, surplusing, displacing, furloughing; suspension; **retirement;** marching orders, the elbow, the bounce, **the sack** *and* the chuck <Brit nf>, heave-ho <nf>; the boot *and* the gate *and* the ax *and* the sack <nf>; walking papers *or* ticket <nf>, pink slip <nf>; deposal 447

6 **evacuation, voidance,** voiding; **elimination,** removal; **clearance, clearing,** clearage; unfouling, freeing; scouring *or* cleaning out, unclogging; exhaustion, exhausting, venting, emptying, depletion; **unloading,** off-loading, discharging cargo *or* freight; draining, drainage; egress 190.2; **excretion,** defecation 12.2,4

7 **disgorgement,** disemboguement, expulsion, ejaculation, **discharge,** emission; **eruption,** eructation, extravasation, **blowout, outburst;** outpour, jet, spout, squirt, spurt

8 **vomiting,** vomition, **disgorgement, regurgitation,** egestion, emesis, the pukes *and* the heaves <nf>; **retching,** heaving, gagging; nausea; vomit, vomitus, puke *and* puking *and* barf *and* barfing <nf>, spew, egesta; the dry heaves <nf>; vomiturition

9 **belch, burp** <nf>, belching, wind, gas, eructation; **hiccup**

10 **fart** <nf>, **flatulence** *or* flatulency, flatuosity, flatus, breaking wind, passing gas, gas, wind

11 **ejector,** expeller, -fuge; **ouster,** evictor; **bouncer** *and* chucker <nf>, chucker-out <Brit nf>

12 **dischargee,** expellee; ejectee; evictee

VERBS **13** **eject, expel, discharge,** extrude, obtrude, detrude, exclude, **reject,** cast, remove; **oust, bounce** *and* give the hook <nf>, **put out, turn out,** thrust out; **throw out,** run out <nf>, cast out, chuck out, give the chuck to <Brit nf>, toss out, heave out, throw *or* kick downstairs; kick *or* boot out <nf>; give the bum's rush *or* give the old heave-ho *or* throw out on one's ear <nf>; defenestrate; jettison, throw overboard, discard, junk, throw away; **be rid of,** be shut of, see the last of

14 **drive out, run out,** chase out, chase away, run off, **rout out;** drum out, read out; freeze out <nf>, push out, force out, send packing, send about one's business; **hunt out,** harry out; **smoke out,** drive into the open; run out of town, ride on a rail

15 **evict, oust,** dislodge, dispossess, put out, turn out, **turn out of doors,** turn out of house and home, turn *or* put out bag and baggage, throw into the street; unhouse, unkennel

16 **depopulate,** dispeople, unpeople; devastate, desolate

17 **banish, expel, cast out,** thrust out, relegate, **ostracize,** disfellowship, exclude, send down, **blackball,** spurn, thumb down, turn thumbs down on, snub, cut, give the cold shoulder, send to Coventry, give the silent treatment; **excommunicate; exile, expatriate, deport,** transport, send away, **extradite; deport; outlaw,** fugitate, ban, proscribe; rusticate

18 **dismiss, send off** *or* **away, turn off** *or* **away,** bundle, bundle off *or* out, hustle out, pack off, **send packing,** send about one's business, send to the showers <nf>; bow out, **show the door,** show the gate; **give the gate** *or* the air <nf>

19 **dismiss, discharge, expel, cashier,** drum out, disemploy, outplace, separate forcibly *or* involuntarily, **lay off,** suspend, surplus, furlough, turn off, make redundant, riff <nf>, turn out, release, let go, let out, remove, displace, replace, strike off the rolls, give the pink slip ; unfrock, defrock; degrade, demote, strip, deplume, displume, deprive; depose, disbar 447.4; break, bust <nf>; **retire,** put on the retired list; pension off, superannuate, put out to pasture; read out of; kick upstairs

20 <nf terms> **fire, can, sack, bump,** bounce, kick, boot, give the ax, give the gate, give one the sack *or* the ax *or* the boot *or* the gate *or* the air *or* one's walking papers, send one to the showers, show one the door *or* gate

21 **do away with, exterminate, annihilate;** purge, liquidate; **shake off,** shoo, dispel; **throw off,** fling off, cast off; **eliminate, get rid of** 773.5; throw away 390.7

22 **evacuate, void; eliminate,** remove; **empty,** empty out, deplete, **exhaust,** vent, drain; **clear, purge,** clean *or* scour out, clear off *or* away, clear, unfoul, unclog, flush out, blow, blow out, sweep out, make a clean sweep, clear the decks; defecate 12.13

23 **unload,** off-load, unlade, unpack, disburden, unburden, **discharge, dump;** unship, break bulk; pump out

24 **let out, give vent to,** give out *or* off, throw off, blow off, **emit, exhaust,** evacuate, let go; **exhale,** expire, breathe out, let one's breath out, blow, puff; fume, steam, vapor, smoke, reek; open the sluices *or* floodgates, turn on the tap

25 **disgorge,** debouch, disembogue, **discharge, exhaust, expel,** ejaculate, throw out, **cast forth,** send out *or* forth; **erupt,** eruct, **blow out,** extravasate; **pour out** *or* **forth,** pour, outpour, decant; spew, jet, spout, squirt, **spurt;** cough up

26 **vomit,** spew, **disgorge, regurgitate,** egest, **throw up,** bring up, be sick <Brit>, sick up <Brit nf>, cast *or* heave the gorge; **retch,** keck, **heave, gag;** reject; be seasick, feed the fish

27 <nf terms> **puke,** upchuck, chuck up, urp, oops, oops up, shoot *or* blow *or* toss one's cookies *or* lunch, barf, ralph, ralph up, blow grits, cough up

28 **belch, burp** <nf>, eruct, eructate; **hiccup**

29 <nf terms> **fart,** let *or* lay *or* cut a fart <nf>, let *or* break wind, cut the cheese

ADJS **30** **ejective, expulsive,** ejaculative, emissive, extrusive; eliminant; vomitive, vomitory; eructative; flatulent, flatuous; **rejected** 372.3, rejective

31 <nf terms> **beat it!, scram!,** buzz off!, bug off!, shoo!, skiddoo!, skedaddle!, vamoose!, cheese it!, make yourself scarce!, **get lost!,** take a walk!, take a hike!, go chase yourself!, go play in the traffic!, get the hell out!, push off!, shove off!, take a powder!, blow!

910 OVERRUNNING

NOUNS **1** **overrunning, overgoing, overpassing;** overrun, overpass;

overspreading, overgrowth; inundation, whelming, overwhelming; burying, burial; seizure, taking 480; overflowing 238.6; exaggeration 355; surplus, excess 993; superiority 249

2 **infestation,** infestment; **invasion,** swarming, swarm, teeming, ravage, plague; **overrunning, overswarming,** overspreading; lousiness, pediculosis

3 **overstepping, transgression, trespass,** inroad, usurpation, incursion, intrusion, **encroachment,** infraction, **infringement**

VERBS 4 **overrun, overgo, overpass,** overreach, go beyond; overstep, overstride, overstep the mark *or* bounds; overleap, overjump; **overshoot,** overshoot the mark, overshoot the field; exaggerate 355.3; superabound, exceed, **overdo** 993.10

5 **overspread,** bespread, spread over, spill over; **overgrow,** grow over, run riot, cover, swarm over, teem over

6 **infest, beset,** invade, swarm, ravage, plague; **overrun, overswarm,** overspread; **creep with, crawl with,** swarm with; seize 480.14

7 **run over,** overrun; **ride over,** override, **run down,** ride down; **trample, trample on** *or* **upon,** trample down, tread upon, step on, walk on *or* over, trample underfoot, **ride roughshod over;** hit-and-run; **inundate, whelm, overwhelm;** overflow 238.17; shout down

8 **pass, go** *or* **pass by,** get *or* shoot ahead of; bypass; **pass over, cross,** go across, ford; step over, overstride, bestride, straddle

9 **overstep, transgress, trespass,** intrude, break bounds, overstep the bounds, go too far, know no bounds, **encroach, infringe,** invade, breach, irrupt, make an inroad *or* incursion *or* intrusion, advance upon; usurp

ADJS 10 **overrun, overspread,** overpassed, bespread; overgrown; inundated, whelmed, overwhelmed; buried

11 **infested,** beset, ravaged, teeming, lagued; lousy, pediculous, pedicular; wormy, grubby; ratty

911 SHORTCOMING

<motion or action short of>

NOUNS 1 **shortcoming,** falling short, not measuring up, coming up short, **shortfall; shortage,** short measure, underage, deficit, limitation; **inadequacy** 795.1; insufficiency 992; delinquency; **default,** defalcation; arrear, **arrears,** arrearage; decline, slump; defectiveness, imperfection 1003; **inferiority** 250; **undercommitment; failure** 410

VERBS 2 **fall short, come short, run short,** stop short, not make the course, not reach; not measure up, not hack it *and* not make the grade *and* not make the cut <nf>, not make it, not make out; want, want for, lack, not have it <nf>, **be found wanting,** not answer, not fill the bill, not suffice; not reach to, not stretch; decline, lag, lose ground, slump, collapse, fall away, run out of gas *or* steam; **lose out, fail** 410.9

3 **fall through,** fall down, **fall to the ground,** fall flat, **collapse,** break down; get bogged down, get mired, get mired down, get hung up, come to nothing, come to naught, end up *or* go up in smoke; **fizzle** *or* peter *or* poop out <nf>; not make it; fall *or* drop by the wayside, end

4 **miss, miscarry, go amiss,** go astray, **miss the mark,** miss by a mile <nf>; misfire; **miss out,** miss the boat *or* bus; miss stays, miss one's mooring

ADJS 5 **short of,** short, fresh *or* clean out of <nf>, not all *or* what it is cracked up to be; **deficient, inadequate** 795.4; **insufficient** 992.9; undercommitted; **inferior** 250.6; **lacking,** wanting, minus; unreached

ADVS 6 **behind, behindhand, in arrears** *or* arrear

7 **amiss, astray, beside the mark,** below the mark, beside the point, far

from it, to no purpose, in vain, vainly, fruitlessly, bootlessly

912 ELEVATION

<act of raising>

NOUNS **1** **elevation, raising, lifting,** upping, boosting *and* hiking <nf>; **rearing,** escalation, **erection;** uprearing, uplifting; upbuoying; **uplift,** upheaval, upthrow, upcast, upthrust; **exaltation;** apotheosis, deification; beatification, canonization; enshrinement, assumption; *sursum corda* <L>; height 272; ascent 193; increase 251; antigravity; orogeny

2 **lift, boost** *and* **hike** <nf>, hoist, heave; a leg up; promotion

3 **lifter, erector;** crane, derrick, gantry crane, crab; **jack,** jackscrew; **hoist,** lift, hydraulic lift; forklift; hydraulic tailgate; lever 906.4; windlass 906.7; tackle; yeast, leaven

4 **elevator,** *ascenseur* <Fr>, **lift** <Brit>; escalator, moving staircase *or* stairway, ski lift, chair lift; dumbwaiter

VERBS **5** **elevate, raise, rear,** escalate, up, boost *and* hike <nf>; **erect, heighten, lift,** levitate, boost <nf>, **hoist,** heist <nf>, heft, heave; raise up, rear up, lift up, hold up, set up; stick up, cock up, perk up; buoy up, upbuoy; **upraise, uplift,** uphold, uprear, uphoist; upheave, upthrow, upcast; throw up, cast up; jerk up, hike <nf>; knock up, lob, loft; sky <nf>

6 **exalt,** elevate, ensky; deify, apotheosize; beatify, canonize; enshrine; put on a pedestal

7 **give a lift,** give a boost, give a leg up <nf>, **help up,** put on; mount, horse; enhance, upgrade

8 **pick up,** take up, pluck up, **gather up;** draw up, fish up, haul up, drag up; dredge, dredge up

ADJS **9** **raised, lifted, elevated;** upraised, **uplifted,** upcast; **reared,** upreared; rearing, rampant; upthrown, upflung; **exalted, lofty;** deified, apotheosized; canonized, sainted, beatified; enshrined, sublime; antigravitational; stilted, on stilts; erect, upright 200.11; high 272.14

10 elevating, elevatory, escalatory; lifting; **uplifting;** erective, erectile; levitative

913 DEPRESSION

<act of lowering>

NOUNS **1** **depression, lowering; sinking;** ducking, submergence, pushing *or* thrusting under, downthrust, down-thrusting, detrusion, pushing *or* pulling *or* hauling down; reduction, de-escalation, diminution; demotion 447, debasement, degradation; concavity, hollowness 284.1; descent 194; decrease 252; deflation; sinkhole, crater

2 **downthrow,** downcast; **overthrow,** overturn 205.2; **precipitation,** fall, downfall; downpour, downpouring

3 **crouch, stoop,** bend, squat; **bow,** genuflection, kneeling, kowtow, kowtowing, salaam, reverence, obeisance, **curtsy;** bob, duck, nod; prostration, supination; crawling, groveling; abasement, self-abasement

VERBS **4** **depress, lower,** let *or* take down, debase, de-escalate, **sink,** bring low, deflate, reduce, couch; pull *or* haul down, take down a peg <nf>; bear down, downbear, squash; thrust *or* press *or* push down, detrude; indent 284.14

5 **fell, drop, bring down,** fetch down, down <nf>, take down, take down a peg, lay low, reduce to the ranks, cashier; **raze,** rase, raze to the ground; **level,** lay level; pull down, pull about one's ears; **cut down,** chop down, hew down, whack down <nf>, mow down; **knock down,** dash down, send headlong, **floor,** deck *and* lay out <nf>, lay by the heels, ground, **bowl down** *or* **over** <nf>; trip, trip up, topple, tumble; **prostrate,** supinate; throw, **throw** *or* fling *or* cast down, **precipitate;** bulldog; spread-eagle <nf>, pin, pin down; blow over *or* down

6 **overthrow,** overturn 205.6; depose 447.4; demote 447.3

7 **drop, let go of,** let drop *or* fall

8 **crouch, duck,** cringe, **cower; stoop, bend, stoop down, squat,** squat down, get down, hunker *and* hunker down *and* get down on one's hunkers <nf>; hunch, hunch down, hunch over, scrooch *or* scrouch down <nf>

9 **bow, bend, kneel,** genuflect, bend the knee, **curtsy,** make a low bow, make a leg, make a reverence *or* an obeisance, salaam, bob, duck; **kowtow,** prostrate oneself; crawl, grovel; wallow, welter

10 **sit down,** seat oneself, park oneself <nf>, **be seated** 173.10

11 **lie down,** couch, drape oneself, **recline** 201.5; prostrate, supinate, prone <nf>; flatten oneself, prostrate oneself; hit the ground *or* the dirt <nf>

ADJS 12 **depressed, lowered,** debased, reduced, **fallen,** deflated; sunk, **sunken,** submerged; downcast, downthrown; prostrated, prostrate 201.8; low, at a low ebb; falling, precititous

914 CIRCUITOUSNESS

NOUNS 1 **circuitousness,** circuity, circuition ; **roundaboutness,** indirection, ambagiousness , meandering, deviance *or* deviancy, **deviation** 164; deviousness, **digression,** circumlocution 538.5; **excursion,** excursus; **circling, wheeling,** circulation, rounding, orbit, **orbiting; spiraling,** spiral, gyring, gyre; circumambulation, circumambience *or* circumambiency, circumflexion, circumnavigation, circummigration; turning, **turn** 164.1; circularity 280; convolution 281

2 **circuit, round,** revolution, **circle,** full circle, go-round, **cycle,** orbit, ambit; pass; round trip, *aller-retour* <Fr>; **beat,** rounds, **walk,** tour, turn, lap, loop; round robin; traffic circle, roundabout, rotary

3 **detour, bypass, roundabout way,** roundabout, ambages , circuit, circumbendibus <nf>, the long way around, digression, deviation, excursion

VERBS 4 **go roundabout,** meander, deviate, go around Robin Hood's barn, take *or* go the long way around, twist and turn; **detour,** make a detour, **go around,** go round about, go out of one's way, **bypass;** deviate 164.3; digress 538.9; **talk in circles,** say in a roundabout way; equivocate 936.9, shilly-shally; dodge 368.8

5 **circle, circuit,** describe a circle, make a circuit, move in a circle, **circulate; go round** *or* **around,** go about; **wheel,** orbit, go into orbit, round; make a pass; come full circle, close the circle, make a round trip, return to the starting point; cycle; spiral, gyre; go around in circles, chase one's tail, go round and round; revolve 915.9; **compass,** encompass, encircle, surround; skirt, flank; go the round, make the round of, make one's rounds, circuiteer ; lap; circumambulate, circummigrate; circumnavigate, girdle, girdle the globe

6 **turn, go around, round,** turn *or* round a corner, corner, round a bend, double *or* round a point

ADJS 7 **circuitous, roundabout, out-of-the-way, devious, oblique, indirect,** ambagious , meandering, backhanded; **deviative** 164.7, **deviating,** digressive, discursive, excursive; equivocatory 936.14; evasive 368.15; vacillating 362.10; **circular** 280.11, **round,** wheel-shaped, O-shaped; spiral, helical; orbital; rotary 915.15

8 circumambient, circumambulatory, circumforaneous, circumfluent, circumvolant, circumnavigatory, circumnavigable

ADVS 9 **circuitously, deviously, obliquely,** ambagiously **indirectly, round about,** about it *and* about, round Robin Hood's barn, in a roundabout way, by a side door, by a side wind; circlewise, wheelwise

915 ROTATION

NOUNS 1 **rotation, revolution,** roll, **gyration, spin,** circulation; axial motion, rotational motion, angular motion, angular momentum, angular velocity; circumrotation, circumgyration, circumvolution, full circle; **turning, whirling,** swirling, **spinning,** wheeling, reeling, whir; **spiraling,** twisting upward *or* downward, gyring, volution, turbination; centrifugation; swiveling, pivoting, swinging; **rolling,** trolling, trundling, bowling, volutation

2 **whirl,** wheel, reel, **spin, turn,** round; spiral, helix, helicoid, gyre; pirouette; **swirl,** twirl, **eddy,** gurge, surge; vortex, **whirlpool,** maelstrom, Charybdis; dizzy round, rat race; tourbillion, **whirlwind** 318.13, twister; rotary, roundabout, traffic circle

3 revolutions, **revs** <nf>; revolutions per minute *or* rpm

4 **rotator, rotor; roller,** rundle; **whirler,** whirligig, **top,** whirlabout; **merry-go-round,** carousel, roundabout; **wheel,** disk; Ixion's wheel; rolling stone; revolving door; spit, rotisserie; whirling dervish

5 **axle, axis; pivot,** gudgeon, trunnion, **swivel, spindle,** arbor, pole, radiant; fulcrum 901.2; pin, pintle; **hub,** nave; axle shaft, axle spindle, axle bar, axle-tree; distaff; mandrel; gimbal; **hinge,** hingle <nf>; rowlock, oarlock

6 **axle box,** journal, journal box; hotbox; universal joint

7 **bearing,** ball bearing, journal bearing, saw bearing, tumbler bearing, main bearing, needle bearing, roller bearing, thrust bearing, bevel bearing, bushing; jewel; headstock

8 <science of rotation> trochilics, gyrostatics

VERBS 9 **rotate, revolve, spin, turn,** round, **go round** *or* **around,** turn round *or* around; **spiral, gyrate,** gyre, whirl like a dervish; circumrotate, circumvolute; circle, circulate; **swivel, pivot, wheel,** swing; pirouette, turn a pirouette; wind, twist, screw, crank; wamble

10 **roll,** trundle, troll, **bowl;** roll up, **furl**

11 **whirl,** whirligig, twirl, **wheel, reel, spin,** spin like a top *or* teetotum, whirl like a dervish; centrifuge, centrifugate; **swirl,** gurge, surge, **eddy,** whirlpool

12 <move around in confusion> **seethe, mill,** mill around *or* about, stir, roil, moil, be turbulent

13 <roll about in> **wallow, welter,** grovel, roll, flounder, tumble

ADJS 14 **rotating, revolving, turning,** gyrating; **whirling, swirling,** twirling, **spinning,** wheeling, **reeling; rolling,** trolling, bowling

15 **rotary, rotational,** rotatory, rotative; trochilic, vertiginous; circumrotatory, circumvolutory, circumgyratory; spiral, spiralling, helical, gyral, gyratory, gyrational, gyroscopic, gyrostatic; whirly, swirly, gulfy; whirlabout, whirligig; vortical, cyclonic, tornadic, whirlwindy, whirlwindish

ADVS 16 **round, around,** round about, **in a circle; round and round,** in circles, like a horse in a mill; in a whirl, in a spin; head over heels, heels over head; clockwise, counterclockwise, anticlockwise, widdershins

916 OSCILLATION

<motion to and fro>

NOUNS 1 **oscillation, vibration,** vibrancy; to-and-fro motion; harmonic motion, simple harmonic motion; libration, nutation; pendulation; **fluctuation,** vacillation, wavering 362.2; electrical oscillation, mechanical oscillation, oscillating current; libration of the moon, libration in latitude *or* longitude; vibratility; **frequency,** frequency band *or* spectrum; resonance, resonant *or* resonance frequency; **periodicity** 850.2

2 **waving,** wave motion, **undulation,** undulancy; **brandishing, flourishing,** flaunting, shaking, swaying; brandish, flaunt, flourish; wave 238.14

3 **pulsation, pulse, beat, throb;** beating, throbbing; systole, diastole; rat-a-tat, staccato, rataplan, drumming 55.1; **rhythm, tempo** 709.24; **palpitation,** flutter, arrhythmia,

pitter-patter, pit-a-pat; fibrillation, ventricular fibrillation, tachycardia, ventricular tachycardia <all medicine>; **heartbeat,** heartthrob

4 **wave,** wave motion, ray; transverse wave, longitudinal wave; electromagnetic wave, electromagnetic radiation; **light** 1025; **radio wave** 1034.11; mechanical wave; acoustic wave, **sound wave** 50.1; transverse wave; seismic wave, **shock wave;** de Broglie wave; diffracted wave, guided wave; one- *or* two- *or* three-dimensional wave; periodic wave; standing wave, node, antinode; sea wave, surface wave, **tidal wave,** tsunami, seismic sea wave; traveling wave; surge, storm surge; amplitude, crest, trough; scend; **surf,** roller, curler, comber, whitecap, white horse; tube; wavelength; frequency, frequency band *or* spectrum; resonance, resonant *or* resonance frequency; period; wave number; diffraction; reinforcement, interference; in phase, out of phase; wave equation, Schrödinger equation; Huygens' principle

5 **alternation, reciprocation;** regular *or* rhythmic play, **coming and going,** to-and-fro, back-and-forth, ebb and flow, *va-et-vien* <Fr>, flux and reflux, systole and diastole, ups and downs, wax and wane, systole and diastole; sine wave, Lissajous figure *or* curve; **seesawing,** teetering, tottering, **teeter-tottering;** seesaw, teeter, teeter-totter, wigwag; zig-zag, zig-zagging, zig, zag

6 **swing,** swinging, **sway,** swag; **rock, lurch, roll, reel,** careen; wag, waggle; wave, waver; swing of the pendulum

7 seismicity, seismism; seismology, seismography, seismometry

8 <instruments> oscilloscope, oscillograph, oscillometer; wavemeter; harmonograph; vibroscope, vibrograph; kymograph; seismoscope, seismograph, seismometer; wave gauge

9 **oscillator, vibrator;** pendulum, pendulum wheel; metronome; swing; seesaw, teeter, teeter-totter, teeterboard, teetery-bender; rocker, rocking chair, cradle; rocking stone, logan stone, shuttle; shuttlecock

VERBS 10 **oscillate, vibrate,** librate, nutate; pendulate; **fluctuate,** vacillate, waver, wave; resonate; **swing, sway,** swag, dangle, **reel, rock, lurch, roll,** careen, toss, pitch; **wag,** waggle; **wobble,** coggle, wamble; **bob,** bobble; squeg; shake, flutter 916.11

11 **wave, undulate; brandish, flourish,** flaunt, shake, swing, wield; float, fly; **flap, flutter;** wag, wigwag

12 **pulsate, pulse, beat, throb,** not miss a beat; **palpitate,** go pit-a-pat; miss a beat; beat time, beat out, tick, ticktock; drum 55.4

13 **alternate,** reciprocate, swing, **go to and fro,** to-and-fro, **come and go,** pass and re-pass, ebb and flow, wax and wane, ride and tie, hitch and hike, back and fill; **seesaw,** teeter, **teeter-totter;** shuttle, shuttlecock, battledore and shuttlecock; **wigwag,** wibble-wabble; zigzag

14 <move up and down> **pump, shake,** bounce

ADJS 15 **oscillating,** oscillatory; **vibrating,** vibratory, harmonic; vibratile; librational, libratory; nutational; **periodic,** pendular, pendulous; **fluctuating,** fluctuational, fluctuant; wavering; vacillating, vacillatory; resonant

16 **waving, undulating,** undulatory, undulant; seismic

17 **swinging, swaying,** dangling, **reeling, rocking, lurching,** careening, **rolling,** tossing, pitching

18 pulsative, pulsatory, pulsatile; **pulsating, pulsing, beating, throbbing, palpitating,** palpitant, pit-a-pat, staccato; rhythmic 709.28

19 **alternate, reciprocal,** reciprocative; sine-wave; **back-and-forth, to-and-fro,** up-and-down, seesaw

20 seismatical, seismological, seismographic, seismometric; succussive, succussatory, sussultatory

ADVS 21 **to and fro, back and forth,** backward and forward, backwards and forwards, **in and out, up and down,** seesaw, shuttlewise, from side to side, from pillar to post, off and on, ride and tie, hitch and hike, round and round, like buckets in a well

917 AGITATION
<irregular motion>

NOUNS **1 agitation, perturbation,** hecticness, conturbation ; **frenzy, excitement** 105; **trepidation** 127.5, trepidity, fidgets *and* jitters *and* ants in the pants <nf>, antsiness *and* jitteriness <nf>, heebie-jeebies <nf>, jumpiness, nervousness, yips <nf>, nerviness <Brit>, nervosity, twitter, upset; **unrest, malaise, unease,** restlessness; fever, feverishness, febrility; **disquiet,** disquietude, inquietude, discomposure, handwringing; **stir, churn, ferment,** fermentation, foment; seethe, seething, ebullition, boil, boiling; embroilment, roil, turbidity, fume, **disturbance, commotion,** moil, **turmoil, turbulence** 671.2, **swirl, tumult,** tumultuation, hubbub, shemozzle <Brit nf>, rout, fuss, row, to-do, bluster, fluster, flurry, flutteration, hoo-ha *and* flap <nf>, bustle, brouhaha, bobbery, hurly-burly; maelstrom; **disorder** 810

2 shaking, quaking, palsy, **quivering, quavering, shivering, trembling,** tremulousness, **shuddering, vibration;** juddering <Brit>, succussion; jerkiness, fits and starts, spasms; jactation, jactitation; joltiness, bumpiness, the shakes *and* the shivers *and* the cold shivers <nf>, ague, chattering; chorea, rigor, St Vitus's dance; delirium tremens *or* the DT's

3 shake, quake, quiver, quaver, falter, **tremor, tremble, shiver, shudder,** twitter, didder, dither; **wobble; bob,** bobble; **jog,** joggle; **shock, jolt,** jar, jostle; **bounce,** bump; **jerk, twitch,** tic, grimace, rictus, vellication; jig, jiggle; the shakes <nf>

4 flutter, flitter, flit, **flicker, waver,** dance; shake, quiver 917.3; **sputter, splutter; flap,** flop <nf>; **beat,** beating; **palpitation,** throb, pit-a-pat, pitter-patter

5 twitching, jerking, vellication; **fidgets,** fidgetiness; itchiness, formication, pruritus

6 spasm, convulsion, cramp, **paroxysm,** throes; **orgasm,** sexual climax; epitasis, eclampsia; **seizure,** grip, attack, **fit,** access, ictus; epilepsy, falling sickness; stroke, apoplexy

7 wiggle, wriggle; wag, waggle; writhe, **squirm**

8 flounder, flounce, stagger, totter, stumble, falter; wallow, welter; **roll, rock, reel, lurch,** careen, **swing, sway; toss, tumble,** pitch, plunge

9 <instruments> **agitator,** shaker, jiggler, vibrator; beater, stirrer, paddle, whisk, eggbeater; churn; blender

VERBS **10 agitate, shake, disturb, perturb,** shake up, perturbate, **disquiet, discompose, upset, trouble, unsettle, stir,** swirl, flurry, flutter, flutter the dovecot, fret, roughen, ruffle, rumple, ripple, ferment, convulse; **churn,** whip, whisk, beat, paddle; **excite** 105.12; **stir up,** cause a stir *or* commotion, muddy the waters, shake up a hornet's nest <nf>; work up, shake up, churn up, whip up, beat up; roil, rile <nf>; disarrange 811.2

11 shake, quake, vibrate, jactitate; **tremble, quiver, quaver,** falter, **shudder, shiver,** twitter, didder, chatter; shake in one's boots *or* shoes, quake *or* shake *or* tremble like an aspen leaf, have the jitters *or* the shakes <nf>, have ants in one's pants <nf>; have an ague; **wobble; bob,** bobble; jiggle, **jog,** joggle; **shock, jolt,** jar, jostle, hustle, jounce, **bounce,** jump, bump

12 flutter, flitter, flit, flick, **flicker,** gutter, bicker, wave, **waver,** dance; **sputter, splutter; flap,** flop <nf>, flip, beat, slat; **palpitate,** pulse, throb, pitter-patter, go pit-a-pat

13 twitch, jerk, vellicate; itch; **jig, jiggle,** jigger *or* jigget <nf>; **fidget,** have the fidgets

14 wiggle, wriggle; wag, waggle; **writhe, squirm,** twist and turn; have ants in one's pants <nf>

15 flounder, flounce, **stagger,** totter, stumble, falter, blunder, wallop; **struggle,** labor; **wallow, welter;**

roll, rock, reel, lurch, careen, career, **swing, sway; toss, tumble,** thrash about, **pitch, plunge,** pitch and plunge, toss and tumble, toss and turn, be the sport of winds and waves; **seethe**

ADJS **16 agitated, disturbed, perturbed, disquieted, discomposed, troubled, upset, ruffled,** flurried, flustered, unsettled; stirred up, shaken, shaken up, all worked up, all shook up <nf>; troublous, feverish, fidgety *and* jittery *and* antsy <nf>, jumpy, nervous, nervy <Brit>, restless, uneasy, unquiet, unpeaceful; all of a twitter <nf>, all of a flutter, giddy, in a spin; turbulent; excited 105.18,20,22

17 shaking, vibrating, chattering; **quivering, quavering, quaking, shivering, shuddering, trembling, tremulous,** palsied, aspen; succussive, succussatory; **shaky,** quivery, quavery, shivery, trembly; wobbly; juddering

18 fluttering, flickering, wavering, guttering, dancing; sputtering, spluttering, sputtery; fluttery, flickery, bickering, flicky, wavery, unsteady, desultory

19 jerky, herky-jerky <nf>, twitchy *or* twitchety, jerking, **twitching, fidgety, jumpy,** jiggety <nf>, vellicative; **spastic, spasmodic,** eclamptic, orgasmic, convulsive; fitful, saltatory

20 jolting, jolty, **joggling,** joggly, jogglety, jouncy, **bouncy, bumpy,** choppy, rough; **jarring,** bone-bruising

21 wriggly, wriggling, crawly, creepy-crawly <nf>; **wiggly,** wiggling; squirmy, squirming; writhy, writhing, antsy <nf>

ADVS **22 agitatedly, troublously, restlessly,** uneasily, unquietly, unpeacefully, nervously, feverishly; **excitedly**

23 shakily, quiveringly, quaveringly, quakingly, **tremblingly,** shudderingly, tremulously; flutteringly, waveringly, unsteadily, desultorily; **jerkily,** spasmodically, fitfully, by jerks, by snatches, saltatorily, by fits and starts

918 SPECTATOR

NOUNS **1 spectator, observer; looker, onlooker,** looker-on, **watcher,** gazer, gazer-on, gaper, goggler, eyer, **viewer,** seer, beholder, perceiver, percipient; spectatress, spectatrix; **witness, eyewitness; bystander,** passerby; innocent bystander; sidewalk superintendent; kibitzer; girl-watcher, ogler, drugstore cowboy <nf>; bird-watcher; **viewer,** television-viewer, televiewer, video-gazer, TV-viewer, couch potato <nf>, armchair quarterback; peeping tom

2 attender 221.5, attendee; theatergoer; **audience** 48.6, house, crowd, gate, fans

3 sightseer, excursionist, **tourist,** rubberneck *or* **rubbernecker** <nf>; slummer; tour group

4 sightseeing, rubbernecking <nf>, lionism <Brit nf>; **tour,** walking tour, bus tour, sightseeing tour *or* excursion, **rubberneck tour** <nf>; grand tour, globetrotting; spectator sport

VERBS **5** spectate <nf>, witness, **see** 27.12, look on, eye, **ogle, gape;** take in, **look at, watch;** attend 221.8

6 sightsee, see the sights, take in the sights, lionize *or* see the lions <Brit nf>; **rubberneck** <nf>; go slumming; go on a tour, join a tour; take the grand tour, globe-trot

ADJS **7** spectating, spectatorial; onlooking; sight-seeing, rubberneck <nf>; passing by, caught in the cross-fire *or* in the middle

919 INTELLECT

<mental faculty>

NOUNS **1 intellect, mind,** *mens* <L>; mental *or* intellectual faculty, nous, **reason, rationality,** rational *or* reasoning faculty, power of reason, *esprit* <Fr>, *raison* <Fr>, ratio, discursive reason, **intelligence,** mentality, mental capacity, **understanding,** reasoning, intellection, conception; cognition, perception; **brain, brains,** brainpower, smarts *and* gray matter <nf>; **thought** 931; head, headpiece

2 **wits, senses, faculties,** parts, capacities, intellectual gifts *or* talents, mother wit; intellectuals ; consciousness 928.2

3 **inmost mind,** inner recesses of the mind, mind's core, deepest mind, center of the mind; inner man; subconscious, subconscious mind, inmost heart

4 **psyche, spirit,** spiritus, **soul,** geist, *âme* <Fr>, **heart, mind,** inner mind, inner being, anima, *anima humana* <L>, animus; tabula rasa; shade, shadow, manes; breath, pneuma, breath of life, divine breath; *atman* and *purusha* and *buddhi* and *jiva* and *jivatma* <all Skt>; *ba* and *khu* <Egyptian myth>; *ruach* and *nephesh* <Hebrew>; spiritual being, inner man; **ego,** the self, the I

5 **life principle,** vital principle, vital spirit *or* soul, *élan vital* <Fr>, **vital force,** *prana* <Hindu>; essence *or* substance of life, individual essence; divine spark, vital spark *or* flame; chi *or* qi, tao, ahimsa

6 **brain** 2.15, seat *or* organ of thought; sensory, sensorium; encephalon; gray matter, head, cerebrum, pate *and* sconce *and* noddle <nf>; noodle *or* noggin *or* bean *or* upper story <nf>; sensation 24

ADJS **7** **mental, intellectual, rational, reasoning, thinking,** noetic, conceptive, conceptual, phrenic; intelligent 920.12; noological; endopsychic, psychic, psychical, psychologic, psychological, spiritual; cerebral; subjective, internal

920 INTELLIGENCE, WISDOM
<mental capacity>

NOUNS **1** **intelligence, understanding, comprehension,** apprehension, mental *or* intellectual grasp, prehensility of mind, intellectual power, brainpower, thinking power, power of mind *or* thought; ideation, conception; integrative power, esemplastic power; rationality, reasoning *or* deductive power, ratiocination; **sense, wit,** mother wit, natural *or* native wit; **intellect** 919; **intellectuality,** intellectualism; capacity, mental capacity, **mentality,** caliber, reach *or* compass *or* scope of mind; **IQ** *or* intelligence quotient, mental ratio, mental age; sanity 925; knowledge 928

2 **smartness, braininess,** smarts *and* savvy <nf>, **brightness, brilliance, cleverness,** aptness, aptitude, native cleverness, mental alertness, nous, **sharpness, keenness,** acuity, acuteness; high IQ, **mental ability** *or* **capability,** gift, gifts, giftedness, **talent, flair, genius;** quickness, nimbleness, quickness *or* nimbleness of wit, adroitness, dexterity; sharp-wittedness, keen-wittedness, quick-wittedness, nimble-wittedness; nimble mind, mercurial mind, quick parts, clear *or* quick thinking; ready wit, quick wit, sprightly wit, *esprit* <Fr>

3 **shrewdness, artfulness, cunning,** cunningness, canniness, **craft, craftiness,** wiliness, guilefulness, slickness <nf>, **slyness,** pawkiness <Brit>, foxiness <nf>, peasant *or* animal cunning, low cunning; subtility, subtilty, **subtlety;** insinuation, insidiousness, deviousness

4 **sagacity,** sagaciousness, **astuteness, acumen,** longheadedness; **foresight,** foresightedness, providence; **farsightedness,** farseeingness, longsightedness; **discernment, insight,** intuition, penetration, acuteness, acuity; perspicacity, perspicaciousness, perspicuity, perspicuousness; incisiveness, trenchancy, cogency; **percipience** *or* percipiency, **perception,** apperception; **sensibility** 24.2

5 **wisdom,** ripe wisdom, seasoned understanding, mellow wisdom, wiseness, sageness, sagacity, sapience, good *or* sound understanding; Sophia <female personification of wisdom>; erudition 928.5; **profundity,** profoundness, depth; broadmindedness 979; **conventional wisdom,** received wisdom, prudential judgment

6 **sensibleness, reasonableness,** reason, rationality, sanity, saneness,

soundness; practicality, practical wisdom, practical mind; **sense,** good *or* common *or* plain sense, **horse sense** <nf>; due sense of; level head, cool head, **levelheadedness,** balance, coolheadedness, coolness; soberness, sobriety, **sobermindedness;** savvy, smarts

7 **judiciousness, judgment,** good *or* sound judgment, cool judgment, soundness of judgment, discernment; **prudence,** prudentialism, providence, policy, polity; weighing, consideration, circumspection, circumspectness, reflection, reflectiveness, **thoughtfulness; discretion,** discreetness; **discrimination**

8 **genius**, spirit, soul; daimonion, demon, daemon; **inspiration,** afflatus, divine afflatus; Muse; fire of genius; **creativity;** talent 413.4; creative thought 986.2

9 <intelligent being> **intelligence, intellect,** head, brain, mentality, consciousness; wise man 921; intellectual, thinker, academic, savant, scholar, walking encyclopedia; adept, maven

VERBS 10 **have all one's wits about one,** have all one's marbles *and* have smarts *or* savvy <nf>, have a head on one's shoulders **and** have one's head screwed on right <nf>; have method in one's madness; use one's head *or* wits, get *or* keep one's wits about one; know what's what, know the score <nf>, be wise as a serpent *or* an owl; be reasonable, listen to reason; be realistic, get real

11 be brilliant, **scintillate,** sparkle, coruscate

ADJS 12 **intelligent,** intellectual ; ideational, conceptual, conceptive, discursive; sophic, noetic, phrenic; **knowing, understanding, reasonable, rational, sensible, bright;** sane 925.4; not so dumb <nf>, strong-minded

13 **clear-witted,** clearheaded, cleareyed, clear-sighted; no-nonsense; awake, **wide-awake,** alive, **alert,** on the ball <nf>

14 **smart, brainy** <nf>, **bright, brilliant,** scintillating; **clever,** apt, **gifted,** talented; **sharp,** keen; **quick,** nimble, adroit, astute, dexterous; **sharp-witted,** keen-witted, needle-witted, **quick-witted,** quickthinking, steel-trap, nimble-witted, quick on the trigger *or* uptake <nf>; smart as a whip, sharp as a tack <nf>; nobody's fool *and* no dumbbell *and* not born yesterday <nf>, all there <nf>; nerdy, nerdish, nerdlike

15 **shrewd, artful, cunning, knowing, crafty, wily,** guileful, canny, slick, sly, pawky <Brit>, smart as a fox, foxy *and* crazy like a fox <nf>; **subtle,** subtile; insinuating, insidious, devious, Byzantine, calculating

16 **sagacious, astute,** longheaded, argute; **understanding, discerning,** penetrating, incisive, acute, trenchant, cogent, piercing; **foresighted,** foreseeing; forethoughted, forethoughtful, provident; **farsighted,** farseeing, longsighted; **perspicacious,** perspicuous; **perceptive, percipient,** apperceptive, appercipient

17 **wise, sage,** sapient, seasoned, **knowing,** knowledgeable; **learned** 928.21; **profound,** deep; wise as an owl *or* a serpent, wise as Solomon; wise beyond one's years, in advance of one's age, wise in one's generation; broad-minded 979.8

18 **sensible, reasonable,** reasoning, **rational, logical; practical,** pragmatic; philosophical; commonsense, commonsensical <nf>; **levelheaded,** balanced, coolheaded, cool, clearheaded, **sound, sane,** sober, **soberminded,** well-balanced, lucid; realistic, ratiocinative; well thought-out; profound

19 **judicious,** judicial, judgmatic, judgmatical, **prudent,** prudential, politic, careful, provident, **considerate,** circumspect, sapient, **thoughtful,** reflective, reflecting; **discreet;** discriminative, discriminating; **well-advised,** well-judged, enlightened

ADVS 20 **intelligently, understandingly,** knowingly, discerningly; **reasonably,** rationally, sensibly; **smartly, cleverly; shrewdly,** artfully, cunningly; **wisely,** sagaciously, astutely; **judiciously, prudently,** discreetly, providently, considerately, circumspectly, thoughtfully

921 WISE PERSON

NOUNS **1** **wise man, wise woman, sage,** sapient, man *or* woman of wisdom; **master, mistress,** authority, mastermind, master spirit of the age, oracle; **philosopher,** thinker, lover of wisdom; rabbi; doctor; great soul, mahatma, guru, rishi; elder, wise old man, elder statesman; philosopher king; illuminate; seer; mentor; intellect, man of intellect; mandarin, **intellectual** 929; savant, **scholar** 929.3; logician, dialectician, sophist, syllogist, metaphysician; adept

2 Solomon, Socrates, Plato, Mentor, Nestor, Confucius, Buddha, Gandhi, Albert Schweitzer, Martin Luther King Jr

3 **the wise,** the intelligent, the sensible, the prudent, the knowing, the understanding

4 Seven Wise Men of Greece, Seven Sages, Seven Wise Masters; Solon, Chilon, Pittacus, Bias, Periander, Epimenides, Cleobulus, Thales

5 Magi, Three Wise Men, Wise Men of the East, Three Kings; Three Kings of Cologne; Gaspar *or* Caspar, Melchior, Balthasar

6 **wiseacre,** wisehead, wiseling, **witling,** wisenheimer <nf>, wise guy, smart ass <nf>; wise fool; Gothamite, wise man of Gotham, wise man of Chelm

922 UNINTELLIGENCE

NOUNS **1** **unintelligence,** unintellectuality , unwisdom, unwiseness, intellectual *or* mental weakness; **senselessness, witlessness, mindlessness,** brainlessness, primal stupidity, reasonlessness, lackwittedness, lackbrainedness, slackwittedness, slackmindedness; **irrationality; ignorance** 930; **foolishness** 923; incapacity, ineptitude; low IQ, low mental age

2 **unperceptiveness,** imperceptiveness, insensibility, impercipience *or* impercipiency, undiscerningness, unapprehendingness, **incomprehension,** nonunderstanding; **blindness,** mindblindness, purblindness; **unawareness,** lack of awareness, unconsciousness, lack of consciousness; **shortsightedness,** nearsightedness, dim-sightedness

3 **stupidity,** stupidness, *bêtise* <Fr>, **dumbness** <nf>, **doltishness,** boobishness, duncery , dullardism, blockishness, cloddishness, lumpishness, sottishness, **asininity,** ninnyism, simplemindedness, simpletonianism; oafishness, oafdom, yokelism, loutishness; **density,** denseness, opacity; grossness, crassness, crudeness, boorishness; **dullness,** dopiness <nf>, **obtuseness,** sluggishness, bovinity, cowishness, slowness, lethargy, stolidity, hebetude; **dim-wittedness,** dimness, **dull-wittedness,** slow-wittedness, beef-wittedness, dull-headedness, **thick-wittedness,** thick-headedness, unteachability, ineducability; wrongheadedness

4 <nf terms> **blockheadedness,** woodenheadedness, klutziness, dunderheadedness, goofiness, jolterheadedness *or* joltheadedness <Brit>, chowderheadedness, chuckleheadedness, beetleheadedness, chumpiness, numskulledness *or* numskullery, cabbageheadedness, sapheadedness, muttonheadedness, meatheadedness, fatheadedness, boneheadedness, knuckleheadedness, blunderheadedness

5 **muddleheadedness,** addleheadedness, addlepatedness, puzzleheadedness

6 **empty-headedness,** empty-mindedness, absence of mind, airheadedness *and* bubbleheadedness <nf>; **vacuity,** vacuousness, vacancy, vacuum, emptiness, mental void, blankness, hollowness, inanity, vapidity, jejunity

7 **superficiality, shallowness, unprofundity,** lack of depth, unprofoundness, thinness; shallow-wittedness, shallow-mindedness; **frivolousness,** flightiness, lightness, fluffiness, frothiness, volatility, dizziness *and* ditziness <nf>

8 **feeblemindedness,** weak-mindedness; infirmity, weakness, feebleness, softness, mushiness <nf>

9 **mental deficiency,** mental retardation, amentia, mental handicap, subnormality, mental defectiveness; brain damage; **arrested development,** infantilism, retardation, retardment, backwardness; **simple-mindedness,** simple-wittedness, simpleness, simplicity; **idiocy,** idiotism , profound idiocy, **imbecility, half-wittedness,** blithering idiocy; moronity, moronism, **cretinism;** mongolism, mongolianism, mongoloid idiocy, Down's syndrome; insanity 926

10 **senility,** senilism, senile weakness, senile debility, caducity, decrepitude, senectitude, decline; **childishness, second childhood, dotage, dotardism;** anility; senile dementia, senile psychosis, Alzheimer's disease

11 **puerility,** puerilism, immaturity, **childishness; infantilism,** babyishness

VERBS 12 **be stupid,** show ignorance, not have all one's marbles; drool, slobber, drivel, dither, blither, blather, maunder, dote, burble; not see an inch beyond one's nose, not have enough sense to come in out of the rain, not find one's way to first base; lose one's mind *or* marbles; not be all there; have a low IQ

ADJS 13 **unintelligent,** unintellectual , **unthinking, unreasoning, irrational,** unwise, inept, **not bright;** ungifted, untalented; **senseless,** insensate; **mindless, witless, reasonless, brainless,** pin-brained, pea-brained, of little brain, headless, empty-headed; **lackwitted,** lackbrained, slackwitted, slackminded, lean-minded, lean-witted, short-witted; **foolish** 923.8; **ignorant** 930.11

14 **undiscerning, unperceptive,** imperceptive, impercipient, insensible, unapprehending, uncomprehending, nonunderstanding; **shortsighted,** myopic, nearsighted, dim-sighted; **blind,** purblind, mind-blind, blind as a bat; blinded, blindfold, blindfolded

15 **stupid, dumb,** dullard, **doltish,** blockish, klutzy *and* klutzish <nf>, duncish, duncical, cloddish, clottish <Brit>, chumpish <nf>, lumpish, **oafish,** boobish, sottish, **asinine,** lamebrained, Boeotian; **dense,** thick <nf>, opaque, gross, crass, fat; bovine, cowish, beef-witted, beef-brained, beefheaded; unteachable, ineducable; wrongheaded

16 **dull,** dull of mind, **dopey** <nf>, **obtuse,** blunt, dim, wooden, heavy, sluggish, slow, **slow-witted,** hebetudinous, **dim-witted, dull-witted,** blunt-witted, dull-brained, dull-headed, dull-pated, **thick-witted,** thick-headed, thick-pated, thick-skulled, thick-brained, fat-witted, gross-witted, gross-headed

17 <nf terms> **blockheaded,** wooden-headed, stupidheaded, dumbheaded, dunderheaded, blunderheaded, clueless *or* jolterheaded *or* joltheaded *or* jingle-brained <Brit>, chowder-headed, chuckleheaded, beetle-headed, nitwitted, numskulled, cabbageheaded, pumpkin-headed, sapheaded, lunkheaded, mutton-headed, meatheaded, fatheaded, boneheaded, knuckleheaded, clod-pated; dead from the neck up, dead above *or* between the ears, muscle-bound between the ears; feather-headed, airheaded, bubbleheaded, out to lunch, lunchy, dufus, dufus-assed, spastic, spazzy, three bricks shy of a load, without brain one, not playing with a full deck, not sixteen ounces to the pound, not all there, soft in the head

18 **muddleheaded, fuddlebrained** *and* scramblebrained <nf>, mixed-up, muddled, addled, addleheaded, **addlepated,** addlebrained, muddy-brained, puzzleheaded, blear-witted; dizzy <nf>, muzzy, foggy

19 **empty-headed,** empty-minded, empty-noddled, empty-pated, empty-skulled; **vacuous,** vacant, empty, hollow, inane, vapid, jejune, blank, airheaded *and* bubbleheaded

<nf>; **rattlebrained,** rattleheaded; scatterbrained 985.16

20 **superficial, shallow, unprofound;** shallow-witted, shallow-minded, shallow-brained, shallow-headed, shallow-pated; **frivolous,** dizzy *and* ditzy <nf>, flighty, light, volatile, frothy, fluffy, **feather-brained, birdwitted, birdbrained**

21 **feebleminded, weak-minded,** weak, feeble, infirm, soft, soft in the head, weak in the upper story <nf>

22 **mentally deficient,** mentally defective, mentally handicapped, retarded, **mentally retarded**, backward, arrested, subnormal, not right in the head, **not all there** <nf>; **simpleminded,** simplewitted, simple, simpletonian; **half-witted,** half-baked <nf>; **idiotic, moronic, imbecile,** imbecilic, cretinous, cretinistic, mongoloid, spastic <nf>; crackbrained, cracked, crazy; babbling, driveling, slobbering, drooling, blithering, dithering, maundering, burbling; brain-damaged

23 **senile,** decrepit, doddering, doddery; **childish,** childlike, in one's second childhood, **doting**

24 **puerile,** immature, **childish;** childlike; **infantile,** infantine; **babyish,** babish

ADVS 25 **unintelligently, stupidly;** insensately, foolishly

923 FOOLISHNESS

NOUNS 1 **foolishness, folly,** foolery, foolheadedness, **stupidity, asininity,** *niaiserie* <Fr>; *bêtise* <Fr>; **inanity, fatuity,** fatuousness; ineptitude; **silliness; frivolousness,** frivolity, giddiness; triviality, triflingness, nugacity, desipience; **nonsense,** tomfoolery, poppycock; **senselessness, insensateness, witlessness, thoughtlessness,** brainlessness, mindlessness; **idiocy, imbecility; craziness, madness,** lunacy, **insanity,** daftness; **eccentricity, queerness,** crankiness, crackpottedness; weirdness; screwiness *and* nuttiness *and* wackiness *and* goofiness *and* daffiness *and* battiness *and* sappiness <nf>; zaniness, zanyism, **clownishness, buffoonery,** clowning, fooling *or* horsing *or* dicking around <nf>

2 **unwiseness,** unwisdom, **injudiciousness, imprudence;** indiscreetness, **indiscretion,** inconsideration, thoughtlessness, witlessness, inattention, unthoughtfulness, lack of sensitivity; **unreasonableness, unsoundness, unsensibleness,** senselessness, reasonlessness, **irrationality, unreason,** inadvisability; recklessness; childishness, immaturity, puerility, callowness; gullibility, bamboozlability <nf>; inexpedience 996; unintelligence 922; pompousness, stuffiness

3 **absurdity,** absurdness, **ridiculousness;** ludicrousness 488.1; **nonsense,** nonsensicality, stuff and nonsense, codswallop <Brit nf>, horseshit *and* bullshit <nf>; **preposterousness,** fantasticalness, monstrousness, wildness, **outrageousness**

4 <foolish act> **folly, stupidity,** act of folly, absurdity, *sottise* <Fr>, foolish *or* stupid thing, dumb thing to do <nf>; fool *or* fool's trick, dumb trick <nf>; **imprudence, indiscretion,** imprudent *or* unwise step; blunder 975.5, blooper <nf>, gaffe

5 stultification; infatuation; trivialization

VERBS 6 **be foolish;** be stupid 922.12; **act** *or* **play the fool;** get funny, do the crazy act *or* bit *or* shtick <nf>; **fool,** tomfool <nf>, **trifle,** frivol; **fool** *or* **horse around** <nf>, dick around <nf>, clown, clown around; **make a fool of oneself,** make a monkey of oneself <nf>, stultify oneself, invite ridicule, put oneself out of court, play the buffoon; **lose one's head, take leave of one's senses,** go haywire; pass from the sublime to the ridiculous; strain at a gnat and swallow a camel; tilt at windmills; tempt fate, never learn

7 stultify, infatuate, turn one's head, befool; gull, dupe; **make a fool of,** make a monkey of *and* play for a sucker *and* put on <nf>

ADJS 8 **foolish,** fool <nf>, foolheaded <nf>, **stupid, dumb** <nf>, clueless

<Brit nf>, **asinine,** wet <Brit>; buffoonish; **silly,** apish, dizzy <nf>; **fatuous,** fatuitous, inept, **inane;** futile; **senseless, witless, thoughtless,** insensate, brainless; **idiotic,** moronic, imbecile, imbecilic, spastic <nf>; **crazy, mad,** daft, **insane;** infatuated, besotted, credulous, gulled, befooled, beguiled, fond, doting, gaga; sentimental, maudlin; dazed, fuddled

9 <nf terms> **screwy, nutty,** cockeyed, wacky, goofy, daffy, loony, batty, sappy, kooky, flaky, damnfool, out of it, out to lunch, lunchy, dorky, dippy, bird-brained, spaced-out, doodle-brained, lame, ditzy, dizzy, loony-tune, dopey, fluffheaded, loopy, scatty, zerking

10 **unwise,** injudicious, **imprudent,** unpolitic, impolitic, contraindicated, **counterproductive;** indiscreet; inconsiderate, thoughtless, mindless, witless, unthoughtful, unthinking, unreflecting, unreflective; **unreasonable, unsound, unsensible,** senseless, insensate, reasonless, **irrational,** reckless, inadvisable; inexpedient 996.5; **ill-advised, ill-considered,** ill-gauged, ill-judged, ill-imagined, ill-contrived, ill-devised, on the wrong track, unconsidered; unadvised, misadvised, misguided; undiscerning; unforseeing, unseeing, shortsighted, myopic; suicidal, self-defeating

11 **absurd, nonsensical,** insensate, ridiculous, laughable, ludicrous 488.4; **foolish, crazy;** preposterous, cockamamie <nf>, fantastic, fantastical, grotesque, monstrous, wild, weird, **outrageous,** incredible, beyond belief, outré <Fr>, extravagant, **bizarre;** high-flown

12 foolable, befoolable, gullible, bamboozlable <nf>; naive, artless, guileless, inexperienced, impressionable; malleable, like putty; persuasible, biddable

ADVS **13** **foolishly, stupidly,** sillily, idiotically; **unwisely,** injudiciously, imprudently, indiscreetly, inconsiderately; myopically, blindly, senselessly, unreasonably, thoughtlessly, witlessly, imsensately, unthinkingly; absurdly, ridiculously

924 FOOL

NOUNS **1** **fool, damn fool,** tomfool, perfect fool, born fool; *schmuck* <Yiddish>; **ass,** jackass, stupid ass, egregious ass; zany, **clown, buffoon,** doodle; sop, milksop; mome , mooncalf, softhead; figure of fun; **lunatic** 926.15; **ignoramus** 930.7

2 **stupid person, dolt, dunce,** clod, Boeotian, **dullard,** *niais* <Fr>, donkey, yahoo, thickwit, **dope, nitwit,** dimwit, lackwit, half-wit, lamebrain, putz, lightweight, witling

3 <nf terms> **chump, boob,** booby, sap, prize sap, klutz, basket case, dingbat, dingdong, ding-a-ling, **ninny,** ninnyhammer, **nincompoop,** looby, noddy, saphead, mutt, jerk, jerk-off, asshole, goof, schlemiel, sawney <Brit>, galoot, gonzo, dumbo, dweeb, dropshop, dipshit, nerd, twerp, yo-yo

4 <nf terms> **blockhead, airhead,** bubblehead, fluffhead, featherhead, woodenhead, dolthead, dumbhead, dummy, dum-dum, dumbo, dumb cluck, dodo head, doodoohead, dumbbell, dumb bunny, stupidhead, dullhead, bufflehead, bonehead, jughead, thickhead, thickskull, numskull, putz, lunkhead, chucklehead, knucklehead, chowderhead, headbanger *and* jolterhead <Brit>, muttonhead, beefhead, meathead, noodle, noodlehead, thimblewit, pinhead, pinbrain, peabrain, cabbagehead, pumpkin head, fathead, blubberhead, muddlehead, puzzlehead, addlebrain, addlehead, addlepate, tottyhead , puddinghead, stupe, mushhead, blunderhead, dunderhead, dunderpate, clodpate, clodhead, clodpoll, jobbernowl *and* gaby *and* gowk <Brit>, vegetable, dimbulb, twit, sucker

5 **oaf, lout,** boor, lubber, oik <Brit>, **gawk,** gawky, **lummox,** yokel, rube, hick, hayseed, bumpkin, clod, clodhopper

6 **silly,** silly Billy <nf>, **silly ass, goose**

7 **scatterbrain,** scatterbrains *and* shatterbrain *or* shatterplate , ditz <nf>, **rattlebrain,** rattlehead, rattlepate, **harebrain,** featherbrain, shallowbrain, shallowpate , featherhead, giddybrain, giddyhead, giddypate, **flibbertigibbet**

8 **idiot,** driveling *or* blithering *or* adenoidal *or* congenital idiot; **imbecile, moron, half-wit,** natural, natural idiot, born fool, natural-born fool, mental defective, defective; cretin, mongolian *or* mongoloid idiot, basket case *and* spastic *and* spaz <nf>; simpleton, simp <nf>, juggins *and* jiggins <nf>, clot *and* berk <Brit nf>, golem

9 **dotard,** senile; fogy, **old fogy,** fuddy-duddy, old fart *or* fud

925 SANITY

NOUNS 1 **sanity, saneness,** sanemindedness, soundness, **soundness of mind,** soundmindedness, sound mind, healthy mind, right mind <nf>, senses, reason, **rationality,** reasonableness, intelligibility, lucidity, coherence, stability, balance, wholesomeness; normalness, normality, normalcy; **mental health;** mental hygiene; mental balance *or* poise *or* equilibrium; sobriety, sober senses; a sound mind in a sound body, a healthy mind in a healthy body; contact with reality; lucid interval; knowing right from wrong; good sense, common sense, wits

VERBS 2 **come to one's senses,** sober down *or* up, recover one's sanity *or* balance *or* equilibrium, get things into proportion; see in perspective; have all one's marbles <nf>; have a good head on one's shoulder; have one's wits about one

3 **bring to one's senses,** bring to reason

ADJS 4 **sane,** sane-minded, not mad, **rational,** reasonable, sensible, **lucid,** normal, wholesome, clearheaded, clearminded, sober, balanced, **sound,** mentally sound, of sound mind, *compos mentis* <L>, sound-minded, healthy-minded, right, right in the head, **in one's right mind,** in possession of one's faculties *or* senses, together *and* all there <nf>; in touch with reality; with both oars in the water *and* playing with a full deck <nf>

926 INSANITY, MANIA

NOUNS 1 **insanity,** insaneness, unsaneness, **lunacy, madness,** *folie* <Fr>, **craziness, daftness,** oddness, strangeness, queerness, abnormality; loss of touch *or* contact with reality, loss of mind *or* reason; dementedness, dementia, athymia, brainsickness, mindsickness, mental sickness, sickness; **criminal insanity,** homicidal mania, hemothymia; **mental illness, mental disease;** brain damage; rabidness, **mania,** furor; alienation, aberration, mental disturbance, **derangement,** distraction, disorientation, mental derangement *or* disorder, unbalance, mental instability, unsoundness, **unsoundness of mind;** unbalanced mind, diseased *or* unsound mind, **sick mind,** disturbed *or* troubled *or* clouded mind, shattered mind, mind overthrown *or* unhinged, darkened mind, disordered mind *or* reason; senselessness, witlessness, reasonlessness, irrationality; possession, pixilation; mental deficiency 922.9

2 <nf terms> **nuttiness,** craziness, daffiness, battiness, screwiness, goofiness, kookiness, wackiness, dottiness, pottiness, *mishegas* <Yiddish>, looniness, lunchiness, balminess; bats in the belfry, a screw loose, one wheel in the sand, one sandwich short of a picnic; lame brains

3 **psychosis,** psychopathy, psychopathology, psychopathic condition; certifiability; **neurosis;** psychopathia sexualis, sexology 75.18; pathological drunkenness *or* intoxication, dipsomania; pharmacopsychosis, drug addiction 87.1; moral insanity, psychopathic personality, *folie du doute* and *folie à deux* <Fr>, abulia 362.4

4 **schizophrenia, dementia praecox,** mental dissociation, dissociation of

personality; catatonic schizophrenia, catatonia, residual schizophrenia, hebephrenia, hebephrenic schizophrenia; schizothymia; schizophasia; thought disorder; schizoid personality, split personality, schizotypal personality; **paranoia,** paraphrenia, paranoiac *or* paranoid psychosis; paranoid schizophrenia; schizoaffective disorder

5 **depression, melancholia,** depressive psychosis, dysthymia, barythymia, lypothymia; melancholia hypochrondriaca; involutional melancholia *or* psychosis; stuporous melancholia, melancholia attonita; flatuous melancholia; melancholia religiosa; postpartum depression; **manic-depressive disorder, manic-depression, bipolar disorder;** cyclothymia, poikilothymia, mood swings

6 **rabies, hydrophobia,** lyssa, canine madness; dumb *or* sullen rabies, paralytic rabies; furious rabies

7 **frenzy, furor,** fury, maniacal excitement, fever, **rage; seizure,** attack, acute episode, episode, **fit,** paroxysm, spasm, **convulsion; snit,** *crise* <Fr>; amok, murderous insanity *or* frenzy, homicidal mania, hemothymia; psychokinesia; furor epilepticus

8 **delirium,** deliriousness, brainstorm; calenture of the brain, afebrile delirium, lingual delirium, delirium mussitans; incoherence, wandering, raving, ranting; exhaustion delirium *or* infection, exhaustion psychosis

9 **delirium tremens,** mania *or* dementia a potu, delirium alcoholicum *or* ebriositatis

10 <nf terms> **the DT's,** the horrors, the shakes, the heebie-jeebies, the jimjams, the screaming meemies; blue Johnnies, blue devils, pink elephants, pink spiders, snakes, snakes in the boots, wigout

11 **fanaticism,** fanaticalness, **rabidness, overzealousness,** overenthusiasm, ultrazealousness, zealotry, zealotism, bigotry, perfervidness; extremism, extremeness, extravagance, excessiveness, overreaction; overreligiousness 692.3

12 **mania, craze, infatuation, enthusiasm,** passion, fascination, crazy fancy, bug <nf>, rage, furor; manic psychosis; megalomania

13 **obsession,** prepossession, preoccupation, **hang-up** <nf>, **fixation,** tic, complex, fascination; hypercathexis; **compulsion,** morbid drive, obsessive compulsion, irresistible impulse; **monomania,** ruling passion, fixed idea, *idée fixe* <Fr>, one-track mind; **possession**

14 **insane asylum,** asylum, lunatic asylum, **madhouse,** mental institution, mental home, bedlam; **bughouse** *and* nuthouse *and* laughing academy *and* **loony bin** *and* **booby hatch** *and* funny farm <nf>; mental hospital, psychopathic hospital *or* ward, psychiatric hospital *or* ward; padded cell, rubber room

15 **lunatic, madman, madwoman,** dement, phrenetic *and* fanatic , *fou* and *aliéné* <Fr>, non compos, *bacayaro* <Japanese>; bedlamite, Tom o' Bedlam; demoniac, energumen; mental case, **maniac,** raving lunatic; homicidal maniac, psychopathic killer, berserk *or* berserker; borderline case; mental defective, idiot 923.8; hypochondriac; melancholic, depressive; neurotic; headcase

16 <nf terms> **nut,** nutso, nutter, nutball, nutbar, nutcase, loon, loony, loony tune, headcase <Brit>, crazy, psycho, crackpot, screwball, weirdie, weirdo, kook, flake, crackbrain, *meshugana* <Yiddish>, fruitcake, schizo, wack, wacko, wigger, sickie, sicko, space cadet

17 **psychotic,** psycho <nf>, mental, mental case, certifiable case, **psychopath,** psychopathic case; psychopathic personality; paranoiac, paranoid; schizophrenic, schizophrene, schizoid; schiz *and* schizy *and* schizo <nf>; catatoniac; hebephreniac; manic-depressive; megalomaniac

18 **fanatic,** infatuate, **bug** <nf>, **nut** <nf>, **buff** *and* **fan** <nf>, freak <nf>, *fanatico* and *aficionado* <Sp>, devotee, **zealot, enthusiast,** energumen; monomaniac, crank <nf>; lunatic fringe

19 psychiatry, alienism, psychiatric care, psychotherapy; psychiatrist, alienist, psychotherapist

VERBS **20** **be insane, be out of one's mind,** not be in one's right mind, not be right in the head, **not be all there** <nf>, have a demon *or* devil; have bats in the belfry *and* have a screw loose, not have all one's buttons *or* marbles <nf>, not play with a full deck *and* not have both oars in the water <nf>; **wander, ramble; rave,** rage, **rant,** have a fit; dote, babble; drivel, drool, slobber, slaver; froth *or* foam at the mouth, run mad, run amok, go berserk

21 **go mad, take leave of one's senses,** lose one's mind *or* senses *or* reason *or* wits, **crack up,** go off one's head <nf>

22 <nf terms> **go crazy, go bats,** go cuckoo, go bughouse, go nuts, go nutso, go out of one's gourd *or* skull *or* tree, go off one's nut *or* rocker, go off the track *or* trolley, go off the deep end, blow one's top *or* stack, pop one's cork, flip one's lid *or* wig, wig out, go ape *or* apeshit, schiz out, go bananas, go crackers *and* go bonkers <Brit>, go bonzo, blow one's mind, freak out, flip out, go hog wild, go round the bend <Brit>, have a screw loose, have bats in one's belfry, have rocks in one's head, lose one's marbles

23 addle the wits, **affect one's mind, go to one's head**

24 **madden,** dement, **craze,** mad , make mad, send mad, **unbalance,** unhinge, undermine one's reason, **derange,** distract, frenzy, shatter, **drive insane** *or* mad *or* **crazy,** put *or* send out of one's mind, overthrow one's mind *or* reason, drive up the wall <nf>

25 **obsess, possess,** beset, infatuate, **preoccupy,** be uppermost in one's thoughts, have a thing about <nf>; grip, hold, get a hold on, not let go; **fixate; drive,** compel, impel

ADJS **26** **insane,** unsane, **mad,** stark-mad, mad as a hatter, mad as a march hare, **stark-staring mad,** maddened, **sick,** crazed, **lunatic,** moonstruck, **daft, non compos mentis,** non compos, *baca* <Japanese>, **unsound,** of unsound mind, **demented, deranged,** deluded, disoriented, unhinged, **unbalanced,** unsettled, distraught, wandering, mazed, crackbrained, brainsick, sick *or* soft in the head, not right, not in one's right mind, **touched,** touched in the head, **out of one's mind,** out of one's senses *or* wits, bereft of reason, reasonless, irrational, deprived of reason, senseless, witless; hallucinated; manic; queer, queer in the head, odd, strange, off, flighty ; abnormal 870.9, mentally deficient 922.22

27 <nf terms> **crazy, nutty,** daffy, dotty, dippy, crazy as a bedbug *or* coot *or* loon, loony, loony-tune, goofy, wacky, balmy *or* barmy, flaky, kooky, potty, batty, ape, apeshit, wiggy, lunchy, out to lunch, bonzo, bats, nuts, nutso, nutty as a fruitcake, fruity, fruitcakey, screwy, screwball, screwballs, crackers <Brit>, bananas, bonkers <Brit>, loopy, beany, buggy, bughouse, bugs, cuckoo, slaphappy, flipped, freaked-out, off-the-wall, gaga, haywire, off in the upper story, off one's nut *or* rocker, off the track *or* trolley, off the hinges, round the bend <Brit>, minus some buttons, nobody home, with bats in the belfry, just plain nuts, loco, mental <Brit>, psycho, cracked, not right in the head, tetched, off one's head, out of one's head, out of one's gourd *or* skull, out of one's tree, not all there, *meshuga* or *meshugga* <Yiddish>, not tightly wrapped, three bricks shy of a load, rowing with one oar in the water, up the wall, off the wall, schizzy, schizoid, schizo

28 **psychotic, psychopathic, psychoneurotic, mentally ill,** mentally sick, certifiable; sociopathic; traumatized, deluded, disturbed, neurotic; schizophrenic, schizoid, schiz *or* schizy <nf>; hypochondriacal; dissociated, disconnected; depressed, depressive; manic; manic-depressive; maniacal; paranoiac, **paranoid;** catatonic; brain-damaged, brain-injured

29 **possessed,** possessed with a demon *or* devil, **pixilated, bedeviled,** demonized, devil-ridden, demonic, demonical, demoniacal

30 **rabid, maniac** *or* **maniacal,** manic, raving mad, stark-raving mad, **frenzied, frantic,** frenetic; **mad,** madding, **wild, furious, violent;** desperate; hysterical, **beside oneself,** like one possessed, uncontrollable; **raving, raging,** ranting; frothing *or* foaming at the mouth; **amok, berserk,** running wild; maenadic, corybantic, bacchic, Dionysiac

31 **delirious,** out of one's head <nf>, off one's head <nf>, off, deluded; **giddy,** dizzy, lightheaded; hallucinating, **wandering, rambling, raving, ranting,** babbling, incoherent

32 **fanatic, fanatical, rabid; overzealous,** ultrazealous, **overenthusiastic,** zealotic, bigoted, perfervid; **extreme,** extremist, extravagant, inordinate; **unreasonable, irrational; wild-eyed,** wild-looking, haggard; overreligious

33 **obsessed, possessed,** prepossessed, infatuated, preoccupied, fixated, **hung up** <nf>, besotted, gripped, held, fussy; monomaniac *or* monomaniacal; anal-retentive

34 **obsessive,** obsessional; **obsessing, possessing, preoccupying,** gripping, holding; driving, impelling, **compulsive, compelling;** anal-retentive

ADVS **35** madly, insanely, crazily; deliriously; fanatically, rabidly, etc

36 **manias by subject**

927 ECCENTRICITY

NOUNS **1** eccentricity, idiosyncrasy, idiocrasy, erraticism, erraticness, queerness, oddity, peculiarity, strangeness, singularity, freakishness, freakiness, quirkiness, crotchetiness, dottiness, crankiness, crankism, crackpotism; whimsy, whimsicality; abnormality, anomaly, unnaturalness, irregularity, deviation, deviancy, differentness, divergence, aberration; nonconformity, unconventionality 868.2

2 quirk, idiosyncrasy, twist, kink, crank, quip, trick, mannerism, crotchet, conceit, whim, maggot, maggot in the brain, bee in one's bonnet *or* head <nf>

3 eccentric, erratic, character; odd person 870.4; nonconformist 868.3, recluse 584.5

4 freak, character, crackpot, nut, screwball, weirdie, weirdo, kook, queer potato, oddball, flake, strange duck, odd fellow, crank, bird, goofus, wack, wacko

ADJS **5** eccentric, erratic, idiocratic, idiocratical, idiosyncratic, idiosyncratical, queer, queer in the head, odd, peculiar, strange, fey, singular, anomalous, freakish, funny; unnatural, abnormal, irregular, divergent, deviative, deviant, different, exceptional; unconventional 868.6; crotchety, quirky, dotty, maggoty <Brit>, cranky, crank, crankish, whimsical, twisted; solitary, reclusive, antisocial

6 <nf terms> kooky, goofy, birdy, funny, kinky, loopy, goofus, haywire, squirrely, screwy, screwball, nutty, wacky, flaky, oddball, wacko, lunch, out to lunch, nobody home, weird

928 KNOWLEDGE

NOUNS **1** **knowledge,** knowing, knowingness, ken; **command,** reach; **acquaintance, familiarity,** intimacy; private knowledge, privity; **information,** data, database, datum, items, facts, factual base, corpus; **certainty, sure** *or* **certain knowledge** 970.1; protocol, protocol statement *or* sentence *or* proposition; intelligence; practical knowledge, **experience, know-how, expertise,** métier; technic, technics, technique; self-knowledge; *ratio cognoscendi* <L>

2 **cognizance;** cognition, noesis; **recognition, realization; perception,** insight, apperception, sudden insight, illumination, dawning, aha reaction, flashing <nf>; **consciousness, awareness,** mindfulness, note, notice; altered state of consciousness *or* ASC; **sense,** sensibility; appreciation, appreciativeness

3 **understanding, comprehension, apprehension,** intellection, prehension; conception, conceptualization, ideation; hipness *and* savvy <nf>; **grasp,** mental grasp, grip, **command,** mastery; precognition, familiarity, foreknowledge 961.3, clairvoyance 689.8; intelligence, wisdom 920; savoir-faire; 101 <nf>

4 **learning, enlightenment, education, schooling, instruction,** edification, illumination; acquirements, acquisitions, attainments, accomplishments, skills; sophistication; store of knowledge; liberal education; acquisition of knowledge 570.1

5 **scholarship, erudition,** eruditeness, **learnedness,** reading, letters; **intellectuality,** intellectualism; **literacy;** computer literacy, computeracy, numeracy; **culture, literary culture, high culture,** book learning, booklore; **bookishness,** bookiness, **pedantry,** pedantism, donnishness <Brit>; bluestockingism; bibliomania, book madness, bibliolatry, bibliophilism; classicism, classical scholarship, humanism, humanistic scholarship

6 **profound knowledge,** deep knowledge, total command *or* mastery; specialism, specialized *or* special knowledge; expertise, proficiency 413.1; wide *or* vast *or* extensive knowledge, generalism, general knowledge, interdisciplinary *or* cross-disciplinary knowledge; **encyclopedic knowledge,** polymathy, polyhistory, pansophy; **omniscience,** all-knowingness

7 slight knowledge 930.5

8 tree of knowledge, tree of knowledge of good and evil; forbidden fruit; bo *or* bodhi tree

9 **lore, body of knowledge,** corpus, body of learning, store of knowledge, system of knowledge, treasury of information; common knowledge; **canon;** literature, literature of the field, publications, materials; bibliography; encyclopedia, cyclopedia

10 **science,** ology, **art, study, discipline; field,** field of inquiry, concern, province, domain, area, arena, sphere, branch *or* field of study, branch *or* department of knowledge, specialty, academic specialty, academic discipline; **technology, technics,** technicology, high technology, high-tech *or* hi-tech <nf>; social science, natural science; applied science, pure science, experimental science; Big Science

11 **scientist,** man of science; **technologist;** practical scientist, experimental scientist; boffin <Brit>; savant, **scholar** 929.3; authority, expert, maven <nf>; technocrat; intellectual; egghead <nf>

VERBS **12** **know, perceive, apprehend,** prehend, cognize, recognize, discern, see, make out; conceive, conceptualize; **realize, appreciate, understand, comprehend,** fathom; dig *and* savvy <nf>; wot *or* wot of <Brit nf>, ken; have, possess, **grasp,** seize, have hold of; have knowledge of, be informed, be apprised of, command, master, have a good command of, have information about, be acquainted with, be conversant with, be cognizant of, be conscious *or* aware of; know something by heart *or* by rote *or* from memory

13 **know well, know full well,** know damn well *or* darn well <nf>, have a good *or* thorough knowledge of, be well-informed, be learned in, be proficient in, **be up on** <nf>, be master of, command, be thoroughly grounded in, retain, **have down pat** *or* **cold** <nf>, have it taped <Brit nf>, have at one's fingers' ends *or* fingertips, have in one's head, **know by heart** *or* rote, **know like a book,** know like the back of one's hand, **know backwards,** know backwards and forwards, **know inside out,** know down to the ground <nf>, **know one's stuff** *and* know one's onions <nf>, know a thing *or* two, know one's way around; be expert in; **know the ropes,** know all the ins and outs, know the score <nf>, know all the answers <nf>; know what's what

14 learn 570.6; come to one's knowledge 551.15

ADJS **15** **knowing,** knowledgeable, informed; **cognizant, conscious, aware, mindful, sensible;** intelligent 920.12; **understanding, comprehending,** apprehensive, apprehending; **perceptive,** insightful, apperceptive, percipient, perspicacious, appercipient, prehensile; shrewd, sagacious, wise 920.17; omniscient, all-knowing

16 **cognizant of, aware of, conscious of, mindful of, sensible to** *or* **of, appreciative of,** appreciatory of, no stranger to, seized of <Brit>; privy to, in the secret, let into, in the know <nf>, behind the scenes *or* curtain; alive to, awake to; **wise to** <nf>, hep to *and* on to <nf>; streetwise, street-smart; apprised of, informed of; undeceived, undeluded

17 <nf terms> **hep, hip,** on the beam, go-go, **with it,** into, really into, groovy; chic, clued-up, clued in, in the know, trendy

18 **informed, enlightened, instructed,** versed, well-versed, educated, schooled, **taught;** posted, briefed, primed, trained; **up on,** up-to-date, abreast of, *au courant* <Fr>, *au fait* <Fr>, in the picture, wise to <nf>

19 **versed in, informed in,** read *or* well-read in, up on, strong in, at home in, master of, expert *or* authoritative in, proficient in, **familiar with,** at home with, **conversant with, acquainted with,** intimate with

20 **well-informed,** well-posted, well-educated, **well-grounded, well-versed, well-read,** widely read

21 **learned, erudite, educated, cultured,** cultivated, lettered, literate, civilized, **scholarly,** scholastic, studious; wise 920.17; **profound,** deep, abstruse; **encyclopedic,** pansophic, polymath *or* polymathic, polyhistoric

22 **book-learned,** book-read, **literary,** book-taught, book-fed, book-wise, book-smart, **bookish,** booky, book-minded; book-loving, bibliophilic, bibliophagic; **pedantic,** donnish <Brit>, scholastic, inkhorn; **bluestocking**

23 **intellectual,** intellectualistic; **highbrow** *and* highbrowed *and* highbrowish <nf>; elitist

24 **self-educated,** self-taught, autodidactic

25 **knowable,** cognizable, recognizable, **understandable, comprehensible,** apprehendable, apprehensible, prehensible, graspable, seizable, discernible, conceivable, appreciable, perceptible, distinguishable, ascertainable, discoverable

26 **known, recognized,** ascertained, conceived, grasped, apprehended, prehended, seized, perceived, discerned, appreciated, **understood, comprehended,** realized; pat *and* **down pat** <nf>

27 **well-known,** well-understood, well-recognized, **widely known,** commonly known, universally recognized, generally *or* universally admitted; **familiar,** familiar as household words, household, **common, current; proverbial;** public, notorious; known by every schoolboy; talked-of, talked-about, in everyone's mouth, **on everyone's tongue** *or* **lips;** commonplace, trite 117.9, hackneyed, platitudinous, truistic

28 **scientific; technical, technological,** technicological; high-tech *or* hi-tech <nf>; **scholarly;** disciplinary

ADVS **29** **knowingly, consciously, wittingly,** with forethought, understandingly, intelligently, studiously, learnedly, eruditely, as every schoolboy knows

30 to one's knowledge, **to the best of one's knowledge,** as far as one can see *or* tell, as far as one knows, as well as can be said

929 INTELLECTUAL

NOUNS **1** **intellectual, intellect,** intellectualist, literate, member of the intelligentsia, white-collar intellectual; brainworker, thinker; brain *and* rocket scientist *and* brain surgeon <nf>; **pundit, Brahmin, mandarin,** egghead *and* pointyhead <nf>; **highbrow** <nf>; wise man 921.1

2 **intelligentsia,** literati, illuminati; intellectual elite; clerisy; literati

3 **scholar,** scholastic , clerk *or* learned clerk ; a gentleman and a scholar; student 572; **learned man,** man of learning, giant of learning, colossus of knowledge, mastermind, **savant,** pundit; genius 413.12; polymath, polyhistor *or* polyhistorian, **mine of information,** walking encyclopedia; literary man, *littérateur* <Fr> *or* litterateur, **man of letters;** philologist, philologue; philomath, lover of learning; philosopher, philosophe; bookman; **academician,** academic, schoolman; classicist, classicalist, Latinist, humanist; Renaissance man *or* woman

4 **bookworm,** bibliophage; **grind** *and* greasy grind <nf>; **booklover, bibliophile,** bibliophilist, philobiblist, bibliolater, bibliolatrist; bibliomaniac, bibliomane

5 **pedant; formalist, precisionist,** precisian, purist, *précieux* <Fr>, **bluestocking,** *bas bleu* <Fr>, *précieuse* <Fr fem>; Dr Pangloss <Voltaire>, Dryasdust <Rev Dr Carlyle>

6 **dilettante, half scholar,** sciolist, **dabbler,** dabster, amateur, trifler, smatterer; grammaticaster, philologaster, criticaster, philosophaster, Latinitaster

930 IGNORANCE

NOUNS **1** **ignorance,** ignorantness, **unknowingness,** unknowing, nescience; lack of information, knowledge-gap, hiatus of learning; empty-headedness, blankmindedness, vacuousness, vacuity, inanity; tabula rasa; **unintelligence** 922; **unacquaintance, unfamiliarity; greenness,** greenhornism, rawness, callowness, unripeness, green in the eye, **inexperience** 414.2; innocence, ingenuousness, simpleness, simplicity; crass *or* gross *or* primal *or* pristine ignorance; ignorantism, knownothingism, obscurantism; agnosticism

2 **incognizance, unawareness, unconsciousness, insensibility,** unwittingness, nonrecognition; deniability; nonrealization, incomprehension; **unmindfulness;** mindlessness; blindness 30, deafness 49

3 **unenlightenment, benightedness,** benightment, dark, darkness; savagery, barbarism, paganism, heathenism, Gothicism; age of ignorance, dark age; rural idiocy

4 **unlearnedness, inerudition,** ineducation, unschooledness, unletteredness; **unscholarliness,** unstudiousness; **illiteracy,** illiterateness, functional illiteracy, semiliteracy; **unintellectuality,** unintellectualism, Philistinism, bold ignorance

5 **slight knowledge,** vague notion, imperfect knowledge, a little learning, glimmering, glimpse , smattering, **smattering of knowledge,** smattering of ignorance, **half-learning,** semi-learning, semi-ignorance, sciolism; **superficiality,** shallowness, surface-scratching; **dilettantism,** dilettantship, amateurism

6 **the unknown,** the unknowable, the strange, the unfamiliar, the incalculable; **matter of ignorance,** sealed book, riddle, enigma, mystery, puzzle 971.3; *terra incognita* <L>, unexplored ground *or* territory; frontier, frontiers of knowledge, **unknown quantity,** x, y, z, n; dark horse; guesswork, anybody's guess; complete blank; closed *or* sealed book; all Greek <nf>

7 **ignoramus, know-nothing;** no scholar, puddinghead, dunce, fool 924; simpleton; **illiterate;** aliterate; **lowbrow** <nf>; unintelligentsia, illiterati; **greenhorn,** greeny <nf>, beginner, tenderfoot, neophyte, novice, duffer <nf>; **dilettante,** dabbler 929.6; layperson; **middlebrow** <nf>

VERBS **8** **be ignorant,** be green, have everything to learn, **know nothing,** know from nothing <nf>; wallow in ignorance; not know any better; **not know what's what,** not know what it is all about, not know the score <nf>, not be with it <nf>, not know any of the answers; not know the time of day *or* what o'clock it is, not know beans, not know the first thing about, not know one's ass from one's elbow <nf>, not know the way home, not know enough to come in out of the rain, not know chalk from cheese, **not know up from down,** not know which way is up

9 **be in the dark,** be blind, labor in darkness, walk in darkness, be benighted, grope in the dark, have nothing to go on, have a lot to learn

10 **not know,** not rightly know <nf>, know not, know not what, know nothing of, wot not of <Brit nf>, be innocent of, have no idea *or* notion *or* conception, **not have the first idea, not have the least** *or* **remotest idea,** be clueless *and* not have a clue <nf> not have idea one, not have the foggiest <nf>, **not pretend to say,** not take upon oneself to say; be stumped; not know the half of it; not know from Adam, not know from the man in the moon; wonder, wonder whether; half-know, have a little learning, scratch the surface, know a little, smatter, dabble, toy with, coquet with; pass, give up

ADJS **11** **ignorant,** nescient, **unknowing, know-nothing;** simple, **dumb** <nf>, empty, empty-headed, blank, blank-minded, vacuous, inane, **unintelligent** 922.13; **ill-informed, uninformed, unenlightened,** unilluminated, unapprized, unposted <nf>, clueless <nf>, pig-ignorant <Brit nf>; **unacquainted, unconversant,** unversed, uninitiated, **unfamiliar,** strange to; **inexperienced** 414.17; **green,** callow, innocent, ingenuous, gauche, awkward, naive, unripe, raw; groping, tentative, unsure

12 **unaware, unconscious, insensible, unknowing, incognizant;** mindless, witless; unprehensive, unrealizing, nonconceiving, **unmindful,** unwitting, unsuspecting; unperceiving, impercipient, unhearing, unseeing, uninsightful; unaware of, in ignorance of, unconscious of, unmindful of, insensible to, out of it <nf>, not with it <nf>; **blind to, deaf to,** dead to, a stranger to; asleep, napping, **off one's guard,** caught napping, caught tripping; tamasic, indifferent

13 **unlearned, inerudite,** unerudite, **uneducated,** unschooled, uninstructed, untutored, unbriefed, untaught, unedified, unguided; ill-educated, misinstructed, misinformed, mistaught, led astray; hoodwinked, deceived; **illiterate,** functionally illiterate, unlettered, grammarless; **unscholarly,** unscholastic, unstudious; **unliterary, unread,** unbookish, unbook-learned, bookless , unbooked; **uncultured,** uncultivated, unrefined, rude, Philistine; barbarous, pagan, heathen; Gothic; nonintellectual, **unintellectual; lowbrow** *and* lowbrowed *and* lowbrowish <nf>; lesser-known

14 **half-learned,** half-baked <nf>, half-cocked *and* half-assed <nf>, sciolistic; semiskilled; **shallow, superficial;** immature, sophomoric, sophomorical; **dilettante,** dilettantish, smattering, dabbling, amateur, amateurish, inexperienced; **wise in one's own conceit**

15 **benighted, dark,** in darkness, in the dark

16 **unknown,** unbeknown <nf>, unheard , **unheard-of,** unapprehended, unapparent, unperceived, unsuspected; unexplained, unascertained; uninvestigated, unexplored; unidentified, unclassified, uncharted, unfathomed, unplumbed, virgin, untouched; undisclosed, unrevealed, undivulged, undiscovered, unexposed, sealed; **unfamiliar,** strange; incalculable, **unknowable,** incognizable, undiscoverable; enigmatic 522.17, mysterious, puzzling

ADVS **17** **ignorantly, unknowingly,** unmindfully, unwittingly, witlessly, unsuspectingly, **unawares;** unconsciously, insensibly; for anything *or* aught one knows, not that one knows

931 THOUGHT

<exercise of the intellect>

NOUNS **1** **thought, thinking, cogitation,** cerebration, ideation, noesis, mentation, intellection, intellectualization, ratiocination; using one's head *or* noodle <nf>; workings of the mind; **reasoning** 935; **brainwork, headwork,** mental labor *or* effort, mental act *or* process, act of thought, mental *or* intellectual exercise; deep-think <nf>; **way of thinking,** logic, habit of thought *or* mind, thought-pattern; heavy thinking, straight thinking; conception, conceit , conceptualization; abstract thought, imageless thought; excogitation, thinking out *or* through; thinking aloud; **idea** 932; creative thought 986.2

2 consideration, contemplation, reflection, speculation, meditation, musing, rumination, deliberation, lucubration, brooding, study, **pondering,** weighing, revolving, turning over in the mind, looking at from all angles, noodling *or* noodling around <nf>; lateral thought *or* thinking; advisement, counsel

3 thoughtfulness, contemplativeness, speculativeness, reflectiveness; **pensiveness,** wistfulness, reverie, musing, melancholy; **preoccupation, absorption, engrossment,** abstraction, brown study, intense *or* deep *or* profound thought; **concentration,** study, close study; deep thinking

4 thoughts, burden of one's mind, mind's content; inmost *or* innermost thoughts *or* mind, secret thoughts, mind's core, one's heart of hearts; **train of thought,** current *or* flow of thought *or* ideas, succession *or* sequence *or* chain of thought *or* ideas; **stream of consciousness; association,** association of ideas

5 mature thought, developed thought, ripe idea; **afterthought,** *arrière-pensée* <Fr>, *esprit d'escalier* <Fr>, second thought *or* thoughts; **reconsideration,** reappraisal, revaluation, rethinking, re-examination, review, thinking over

6 introspection, self-communion, self-counsel, self-consultation, subjective inspection *or* speculation, head trip <nf>; meditation

7 subject for thought, food for thought, something to chew on, something to get one's teeth into

VERBS **8 think, cogitate,** cerebrate, put on one's thinking *or* considering cap <nf>, intellectualize, ideate, conceive, conceptualize, form ideas, entertain ideas; **reason** 935.15; **use one's head** *or* brain, use one's noodle *or* noggin <nf>, use *or* exercise the mind, set the brain *or* wits to work, bethink oneself, have something on one's mind, have a lot on one's mind

9 think hard, think one's head off, **rack** *or* **ransack one's brains,** crack one's brains <nf>, **beat** *or* **cudgel one's brains,** work one's head to the bone, do some heavy thinking, bend *or* apply the mind, knit one's brow; sweat *or* stew over <nf>, hammer *or* hammer away at; puzzle, **puzzle over**

10 concentrate, concentrate the mind *or* thoughts, concentrate on *or* upon, attend closely to, brood on, **focus on** *or* **upon,** give *or* devote the mind to, glue the mind to, cleave to the thought of, fix the mind *or* thoughts upon, bend the mind upon, bring the mind to bear upon; get to the point; gather *or* collect one's thoughts, pull one's wits together, focus *or* fix one's thoughts, marshal *or* arrange one's thoughts *or* ideas

11 think about, cogitate, **give** *or* **apply the mind to,** put one's mind to, apply oneself to, bend *or* turn the mind *or* thoughts to, direct the mind upon, **give thought to, trouble one's head about,** occupy the mind *or* thoughts with; think through *or* out, puzzle out, sort out, reason out, excogitate, ratiocinate, work out, take stock of

12 consider, contemplate, speculate, reflect, wonder, study, ponder, perpend, **weigh, deliberate, debate, meditate, muse, brood, ruminate,** chew the cud <nf>, digest; introspect, be abstracted; wrinkle one's brow; fall into a brown study, retreat into one's mind *or* thoughts; **toy with, play with,** play around with, flirt *or* coquet with the idea

13 think over, ponder over, brood over, muse over, mull over, reflect over, con over, **deliberate over,** run over, **meditate over,** ruminate over, chew over, digest, turn over, **revolve,** revolve *or* turn over in the mind, deliberate upon, meditate upon, muse on *or* upon, bestow thought *or* consideration upon, noodle *or* noodle around <nf>

14 take under consideration, entertain, take under advisement, take under active consideration, inquire into, **think it over,** have a look at *and* see about <nf>; **sleep upon,** consult with *or* advise with *or* take counsel of one's pillow

15 reconsider, re-examine, review; revise one's thoughts, reappraise, revaluate, rethink; view in a new light, have second thoughts, think better of

16 think of, bethink oneself of, seize on, flash on <nf>; tumble to <nf>; **entertain the idea of,** entertain thoughts of; conceive of; have an idea of, have thoughts about; **have in mind, contemplate, consider, have under consideration;** take it into one's head; **bear in mind, keep in mind,** hold the thought; harbor an idea, keep *or* hold an idea, cherish *or* foster *or* nurse *or* nurture an idea; ideate, premise, theorize, invent

17 <look upon mentally> **contemplate, look upon, view, regard,** see, view with the mind's eye, **envisage,** envision, **visualize** 986.15, imagine, image; meditate

18 occur to, occur to one's mind, occur, **come to mind,** rise to mind, rise in the mind, come into one's head, impinge on one's consciousness, claim one's mind *or* thoughts, pass through one's head *or* mind, dawn upon one, **enter one's mind,** pass in the mind *or* thoughts, cross one's mind, race *or* tumble through the mind, flash on *or* across the mind; **strike,** strike one, strike the mind, grab one <nf>, **suggest itself,** present itself, offer itself, present itself to the mind *or* thoughts, give one pause

19 impress, make an impression, strike, grab <nf>, hit; catch the thoughts, arrest the thoughts, seize one's mind, sink *or* penetrate into the mind, embed itself in the mind, lodge in the mind, **sink in** <nf>

20 occupy the mind *or* thoughts, engage the thoughts, monopolize the thoughts, fasten itself on the mind, seize the mind, fill the mind, take up one's thoughts; **preoccupy,** occupy, **absorb, engross,** absorb *or* enwrap *or* engross the thoughts, obsess the mind, run in the head; foster in the mind; come uppermost, be uppermost in the mind; have in *or* on one's mind, **have on the brain** <nf>, have constantly in one's thoughts

ADJS **21 cognitive,** prehensive, **thought,** conceptive, conceptual, conceptualized, ideative, ideational, noetic, **mental,** cerebral; **rational** 935.18, logical, ratiocinative; **thoughtful,** cogitative, **contemplative, reflective, speculative, deliberative, meditative, ruminative,** ruminant, in a brown study, museful ; **pensive,** wistful, musing; introspective; thinking, reflecting, contemplating, pondering, deliberating, excogitating, excogitative, meditating, ruminating, musing; reasoned, cogitative; studious, studying; sober, serious, deepthinking; concentrating, focused, on task, concentrative, concentrated, attentive

22 absorbed *or* engrossed in thought, **absorbed, engrossed,** introspective, rapt, **wrapped in thought, lost in thought,** pensive, abstracted, immersed in thought, buried in thought, engaged in thought, occupied, **preoccupied**

ADVS **23 thoughtfully,** contemplatively, reflectively, meditatively, ruminatively, musefully , cogitatively, introspectively; **pensively,** wistfully; on reconsideration, on second thought

24 on one's mind, on the brain *and* on one's chest <nf>, in the thoughts; in the heart, *in petto* <Ital>, in one's inmost *or* innermost thoughts

932 IDEA

NOUNS **1 idea; thought,** mental *or* intellectual object, **notion, concept,** conception, conceit, fancy; **perception, sense, impression,** mental impression, image, **mental image,** picture in the mind, mental picture, representation, recept, visualization; imago, ideatum, noumenon, essence; memory trace; **sentiment,** apprehension; reflection, observation; **opinion** 953.6; viewpoint, point of view; supposition, **theory** 951; plan, scheme

2 <philosophy> ideatum, ideate; noumenon; universal, universal concept *or* conception; idée-force; Platonic idea *or* form, archetype, prototype, subsistent form, eternal object, transcendent universal, eternal universal, pattern, model, exemplar, ideal, transcendent idea *or* essence, universal essence, innate idea; Aristotelian form, form-giving cause, formal cause; complex idea, simple idea; percept; construct of memory and association; Kantian idea, supreme principle of pure reason, regulative first principle, highest unitary principle of thought, transcendent nonempirical concept; Hegelian idea, highest category, the Absolute, the Absolute Idea, the Self-determined, the realized ideal; logical form *or* category; noosphere; history of ideas; **idealism** 1053.3

3 abstract idea, abstraction, general idea, generality, abstract

4 main idea, intellectual *or* philosophical basis, leading *or* principal idea, fundamental *or* basic idea, *idée-maitresse* <Fr>, guiding principle, crowning principle, **big idea** <nf>, precept, premise

5 novel idea, intellectual *or* conceptual breakthrough, new *or* **latest wrinkle** <nf>, new slant *or* twist *or* take <nf>

6 good idea, great idea, not a bad idea; **bright thought,** bright *or* brilliant idea, **insight; brainchild** *and* **brainstorm** <nf>, brain wave <nf>, **inspiration;** quantum leap

7 absurd idea, crazy idea, fool notion *and* brainstorm <nf>

8 ideology, system of ideas, body of ideas, system of theories; world view; philosophy; **ethos**

ADJS **9** ideational, ideal, **conceptual, conceptive,** notional, fanciful, imaginative; **intellectual; theoretical** 951.13; **ideological**

10 ideaed, notioned, thoughted

933 ABSENCE OF THOUGHT

NOUNS **1 thoughtlessness,** thoughtfreeness; **vacuity,** vacancy, **emptiness of mind, empty-headedness,** blankness, mental blankness, blankmindedness; fatuity, inanity, foolishness 923; tranquillity, calm of mind, meditation; **nirvana,** ataraxia, calm *or* tranquillity of mind; **oblivion,** forgetfulness, lack *or* loss of memory, amnesia; mental block; quietism, passivity, apathy; blank mind, fallow mind, tabula rasa; unintelligence 922; ignorance; head in the clouds

VERBS **2 not think, make the mind a blank,** let the mind lie fallow; **not think of,** not consider, be unmindful of; **not enter one's mind** *or* **head,** be far from one's mind *or* head *or* thoughts; pay no attention *or* mind

3 get it off one's mind, get it off one's chest <nf>, clear the mind, relieve one's mind; **put it out of one's thoughts,** dismiss from the mind *or* thoughts, push from one's thoughts, put away thought

ADJS **4 thoughtless, thoughtfree,** incogitant, **unthinking,** unreasoning; unideaed; unintellectual; **vacuous,** vacant, blank, blankminded, relaxed, empty, **empty-headed,** fallow, fatuous, inane 922.19; unoccupied; calm, tranquil; nirvanic; oblivious, ignorant; quietistic, passive

5 unthought-of, undreamed-of, unconsidered, unconceived, unconceptualized; unimagined, unimaged; imageless

934 INTUITION, INSTINCT

NOUNS **1 intuition, intuitiveness, sixth sense;** intuitive reason *or* knowledge, direct perception *or* apprehension, immediate apprehension *or* perception, unmediated perception *or* apprehension, subconscious perception, unconscious *or* subconscious knowledge, immediate cognition, knowledge without thought *or* reason, flash of insight; intuitive understanding, tact, spontaneous sense; **revelation,** epiphany, moment of illumination; **insight,** inspiration, aperçu; precognition, anticipation, a priori knowledge; woman's intuition; second sight, second-sightedness, precognition 961.3, clairvoyance 689.8, extrasensory perception, presentiment; intuitionism, intuitivism; noology

2 instinct, natural instinct, unlearned capacity, innate *or* inborn proclivity, native *or* natural tendency, **impulse,** blind *or* unreasoning impulse, vital impulse; **libido, id,** primitive self; archetype, archetypal pattern *or* idea; unconscious *or* subconscious urge *or* drive; collective unconscious, race memory; **reflex,** spontaneous reaction, unthinking response, knee-jerk, Pavlovian response, gut reaction <nf>

3 hunch <nf>, sense, **presentiment, premonition,** preapprehension, intimation, foreboding; suspicion, **impression,** intuition, intuitive impression, **feeling,** forefeeling, vague feeling *or* idea, funny feeling <nf>, feeling in one's bones, gut feeling <nf>, flash

VERBS **4 intuit, sense, feel,** feel intuitively, **feel** *or* **know in one's bones** <nf>, **have a feeling,** have a funny feeling <nf>, **get** *or* **have the impression, have a hunch** <nf>, just know, know instinctively; grok <nf>; perceive, divine

ADJS **5 intuitive,** intuitional, sensing, sensitive, perceptive, feeling; second-sighted, precognitive 961.7, telepathic, clairvoyant

6 instinctive, natural, **inherent, innate,** unlearned; unconscious, subliminal; **involuntary, automatic,** spontaneous, impulsive, reflex, knee-jerk <nf>; **instinctual,** libidinal

ADVS **7 intuitively,** by intuition; **instinctively,** automatically, spontaneously, on *or* by instinct, **instinctually**

935 REASONING

NOUNS **1 reasoning, reason,** logical thought, discursive reason, rationalizing, rationalization, ratiocination; the divine faculty; **rationalism, rationality,** discourse *or* discourse of reason ; sweet reason, reasonableness; demonstration, proof 957; specious reasoning, sophistry 936; philosophy 952

2 logic, logics; **dialectics,** dialectic, dialecticism; art of reason, science of discursive thought; formal logic, material logic; doctrine of terms, doctrine of the judgment, doctrine of inference, traditional *or* Aristotelian logic, Ramist *or* Ramistic logic, modern *or* epistemological logic, pragmatic *or* instrumental *or* experimental logic; psychological logic, psychologism; symbolic *or* mathematical logic, logistic; propositional calculus, calculus of individuals, functional calculus, combinatory logic, algebra of relations, algebra of classes, set theory, Boolean algebra; mereology

3 <methods> a priori reasoning, a fortiori reasoning, a posteriori reasoning; discursive reasoning; **deduction, deductive reasoning,** syllogism, syllogistic reasoning; hypothetico-deductive method; **induction, inductive reasoning,** epagoge; philosophical induction, inductive *or* Baconian method; **inference; generalization,** particularization; synthesis, analysis; hypothesis and verification

4 argumentation, argument, controversy, dispute, disagreement, disputation, polemic, debate, disceptation , eristic, art of dispute; **contention, wrangling, bickering,** hubbub 53.3, quibble, bicker, setto

<nf>, rhubarb *and* hassle <nf>, passage of arms; war of words, verbal engagement *or* contest, logomachy, flyting; paper war, *guerre de plume* <Fr>; adversarial procedure, confrontational occasion; academic disputation, defense of a thesis; defense, apology, apologia, apologetics; dialectics, dialecticism; pilpul, casuistry; polemics, litigation; examination, cross-examination

5 **argument,** *argumentum* <L>; **case, plea,** pleading, *plaidoyer* <Fr>, brief; special pleading; **reason, consideration; refutation,** elenchus, ignoratio elenchi; stance, position; grounds, evidence; pros, cons, **pros and cons;** talking point; **dialogue,** reasoning together, dialectic; formal argument; rationale, pretext, premise

6 **syllogism;** prosyllogism; mode; figure; mood; pseudosyllogism, paralogism; sorites, progressive *or* Aristotelian sorites, regressive *or* Goclenian sorites; categorical syllogism; enthymeme; dilemma; **rule,** rule of deduction, transformation rule; modus ponens, modus tollens

7 **premise, proposition, position,** assumed position, sumption, **assumption,** supposal, presupposition, **hypothesis, thesis, theorem,** lemma, **statement,** affirmation, categorical proposition, premise, assertion, basis, ground, foundation; **postulate, axiom, postulation,** postulatum; data; major premise, minor premise; first principles; a priori principle, apriorism; philosophical proposition, philosopheme; hypothesis ad hoc; sentential *or* propositional function, truth-function, truth table, truth-value

8 **conclusion** 946.4

9 **reasonableness,** reasonability, **logicalness,** logicality, **rationality, sensibleness, soundness,** justness, justifiability, admissibility, cogency; sense, common **sense,** sound sense, sweet reason, **logic, reason;** plausibility 968.3

10 **good reasoning, right thinking,** sound reasoning, ironclad reasoning, irrefutable logic; cogent argument, **cogency;** strong argument, knockdown argument; good case, good reason, sound evidence, strong point

11 **reasoner,** ratiocinator, **thinker; rationalist;** rationalizer; synthesizer; **logician,** logistician; logicaster; dialectician; syllogist, syllogizer; sophist 936.6; philosopher 952.8

12 **arguer, controversialist, disputant, plaintiff, defendant, debater,** eristic, argufier <nf>, advocate, wrangler, proponent, litigator, mooter, lawyer, jurist, Philadelphia lawyer <nf>, guardhouse *or* latrine *or* forecastle lawyer <nf>, disceptator , pilpulist, casuist; polemic, polemist, polemicist; logomacher, logomachist; apologist

13 **contentiousness,** litigiousness, **quarrelsomeness,** argumentativeness, disputatiousness, testiness, feistiness <nf>, combativeness; ill humor 110

14 **side,** interest; **the affirmative,** pro, yes, aye, yea; **the negative,** con, no, nay

VERBS **15 reason;** logicalize, logicize; rationalize, provide a rationale; intellectualize; bring reason to bear, apply *or* use reason, put two and two together; construe, **deduce, infer, generalize; synthesize, analyze, work out; theorize,** hypothesize; premise; philosophize; syllogize; ratiocinate

16 **argue,** argufy <nf>, **dispute,** discept , dissent, disagree, logomachize, polemize, polemicize, moot, **bandy words, chop logic, plead,** pettifog <nf>, join issue, give and take, cut and thrust, try conclusions, cross swords, lock horns, **contend, contest,** spar, **bicker, wrangle,** hassle <nf>, have it out, have words; thrash out; take one's stand upon, **put up an argument** <nf>; take sides, take up a side; argue to no purpose; **quibble, squabble, cavil** 936.9; litigate

17 **be reasonable, be logical, make sense,** figure <nf>, **stand to reason,** be demonstrable, be irrefutable; hold

good, hold water <nf>; have a leg to stand on; show wisdom

ADJS **18 reasoning, rational,** ratiocinative *or* ratiocinatory; analytic, analytical; conceptive, conceptual; cerebral, noetic, phrenic

19 argumentative, argumental, dialectic, dialectical, controversial, disputatious, contentious, quarrelsome, dissenting, disputing, litigious, combative, factious, testy, feisty <nf>, petulant, ill-humored 110.18, eristic, eristical, polemic, polemical, logomachic, logomachical, pilpulistic, pro and con; diectic, apodeictic, aporetic; at cross-purposes, at odds

20 logical, reasonable, rational, cogent, sensible, sane, wise, sound, well-thought-out, legitimate, just, justifiable, admissible; credible 953.24; plausible 968.7; as it should be, as it ought to be; well-argued, **well-founded, well-grounded**

21 reasoned, advised, considered, calculated, meditated, contemplated, deliberated, studied, weighed, thought-out, well-reasoned

22 dialectic, dialectical, maieutic; syllogistic, syllogistical, enthymematic, enthymematical, soritical, epagogic, inductive, deductive, inferential, synthetic, synthetical, analytic, analytical, discursive, heuristic; a priori, a fortiori, a posteriori; categorical, hypothetical, propositional, postulated, conditional

23 deducible, derivable, inferable; sequential, following

ADVS **24 reasonably, logically, rationally,** by the rules of logic, **sensibly,** sanely, soundly; syllogistically, analytically; realistically, pragmatically, plausibly; **in reason,** in all reason, within reason, within the bounds *or* limits of reason, within reasonable limitations, **within bounds,** within the bounds of possibility, as far as possible, in all conscience

936 SOPHISTRY

<specious reasoning>

NOUNS **1 sophistry,** sophistication, sophism, philosophism, **casuistry,** Jesuitry, Jesuitism, subtlety, oversubtlety; **false** *or* **specious reasoning, rationalization,** evasive reasoning, vicious reasoning, sophistical reasoning, special pleading; **fallacy,** fallaciousness; **speciousness,** speciosity, superficial *or* apparent soundness, plausibleness, plausibility; **insincerity, disingenuousness; equivocation,** equivocalness; fudging *and* waffling <nf>, fudge and mudge <Brit nf>; perversion, distortion, misapplication; vicious circle, circularity; mystification, obfuscation, obscurantism; reduction, trivialization

2 illogicalness, illogic, illogicality, **unreasonableness, irrationality, reasonlessness, senselessness, unsoundness,** unscientificness, invalidity, untenableness, inconclusiveness; **inconsistency,** incongruity, antilogy; invalidity

3 <specious argument> **sophism,** sophistry, insincere argument, mere rhetoric, philosophism, solecism; paralogism, pseudosyllogism; claptrap, moonshine, empty words, doubletalk, doublespeak; bad case, weak point, flawed argument, circular argument; **fallacy,** logical fallacy, formal fallacy, material fallacy, verbal fallacy; *argumentum ad hominem, argumentum ad baculum, argumentum ad captandum, argumentum ad captandum vulgus* <all L>, crowd-pleasing argument, argument by analogy, *tu quoque* <L>, argument, *petitio principii* <L>, begging the question, **circular argument,** undistributed middle, *non sequitur* <L>, *hysteron proteron* <Gk>, *post hoc* and *ergo propter hoc* <L>, paradox; contradition in terms

4 quibble, quiddity, quodlibet, quillet , Jesuitism, **cavil;** quip, quirk, shuffle, dodge

5 quibbling, caviling, boggling, captiousness, nit-picking, **bickering; logic-chopping,** choplogic, **hairsplitting,** trichoschistism; subterfuge, chicane, chicanery, pettifoggery; **equivocation,** tergiversation, prevarication, **evasion, hedging, pussyfooting** <nf>, **sidestepping,**

dodging, shifting, shuffling, fencing, parrying, boggling, paltering, beating around the bush

6 **sophist,** sophister, philosophist , **casuist,** Jesuit; choplogic , logic-chopper; paralogist

7 **quibbler, caviler,** pettifogger, hairsplitter, captious *or* picayune critic, nitpicker; **equivocator,** Jesuit, mystifier, mystificator, obscurantist, prevaricator, palterer, tergiversator, shuffler, mudger <Brit nf>; **hedger;** pussyfoot *or* **pussyfooter** <nf>, waffler <nf>

VERBS 8 reason speciously, reason ill, paralogize, reason in a circle, argue insincerely, pervert, distort, misapply; explain away, rationalize; prove that black is white and white black; not have a leg to stand on

9 **quibble, cavil, bicker,** boggle, chop logic, **split hairs,** nitpick, pick nits; Jesuitize; **equivocate,** mystify, obscure, prevaricate, tergiversate, doubletalk, doublespeak, tap-dance <nf>, misrepresent, misinform, fudge, palter, fence, parry, shift, shuffle, **dodge,** shy, **evade,** sidestep, hedge, skate around <Brit nf>, pussyfoot <nf>, evade the issue; twist, slant; **beat about** *or* **around the bush,** avoid the issue, not come to the point, **beg the question;** pick holes in, pick to pieces; blow hot and cold; strain at a gnat and swallow a camel

ADJS 10 **sophistical,** sophistic, philosophistic, philosophistical , casuistic, casuistical, Jesuitic, Jesuitical, **fallacious, specious,** colorable, plausible, hollow, superficially *or* apparently sound; deceptive, illusive, empty; overrefined, oversubtle, **insincere, disingenuous**

11 **illogical, unreasonable, irrational, reasonless,** contrary to reason, **senseless,** without reason, **without rhyme** *or* **reason; unscientific,** nonscientific, unphilosophical; **invalid,** inauthentic, unauthentic, faulty, flawed, paralogical, fallacious; inconclusive, inconsequent, inconsequential, not following; **inconsistent,** incongruous, absonant , loose, unconnected; contradictory, **self-contradictory,** self-annulling, self-refuting, oxymoronic

12 **unsound, unsubstantial,** insubstantial, weak, feeble, poor, flimsy, unrigorous, inconclusive, unproved, unsustained, poorly argued

13 **baseless, groundless,** ungrounded, **unfounded,** ill-founded, unbased, **unsupported,** unsustained, invalid, **without foundation,** without basis *or* sound basis; **untenable, unsupportable,** unsustainable; **unwarranted,** idle, empty, vain

14 **quibbling, caviling, equivocatory,** equivocal, captious, nitpicky *and* nit-picking <nf>, bickering; picayune, petty, trivial, trifling; paltering, shuffling, hedging, pussyfooting <nf>, **evasive; hairsplitting,** trichoschistic, logic-chopping, choplogic *or* choplogical

ADVS 15 **illogically, unreasonably, irrationally, reasonlessly, senselessly;** baselessly, groundlessly; untenably, unsupportably, unsustainably; out of all reason, out of all bounds

937 TOPIC

NOUNS 1 **topic, subject,** subject of thought, **matter, subject matter,** what it is about, **concern,** focus of interest *or* attention, discrete matter, category; field, branch, discipline; **theme,** burden, **text,** motif, motive, angle, business at hand, **case,** matter in hand, **question, problem, issue,** bone of contention; **point,** point at issue, point in question, topic for discussion, main point, gist 997.6; plot; item on the agenda; head, heading, chapter, rubric, category; contents, substance, meat, essence, material part, basis; living issue, topic of the day; thesis

2 **caption, title, heading, head,** superscription, rubric; **headline;** overline; banner, banner head *or* line, streamer; **scarehead,** screamer; spread, spreadhead; drop head, dropline, hanger; running head *or* title, jump head; **subhead, subheading,** subtitle; legend, motto, epigraph; title page

VERBS 3 focus on, have regard to, distinguish, lift up, set forth, specify, zero in on <nf>, center on, be concerned with; include; caption, title, head, head up <nf>; **headline;** subtitle, subhead

ADJS 4 **topical, thematic**

938 INQUIRY

NOUNS 1 **inquiry,** inquiring, probing, **inquest** 307.17, inquirendo; inquisition; interpellation; inquiring mind; analysis 801

2 **examination,** school examination, examen, **exam** <nf>, **test, quiz;** oral examination, oral, doctor's oral, master's oral, viva voce examination, viva <nf>; catechesis, catchization; **audition, hearing;** multiple-choice test, multiple-guess test <nf>; written examination, written <nf>, blue book <nf>, test paper; course examination, midterm, midyear, midsemester; qualifying examination, preliminary examination, prelim <nf>; take-home examination; unannounced examination, pop *or* shotgun *or* surprise quiz <nf>; final examination, **final** <nf>, comprehensive examination, comps <nf>, great go *or* greats <Oxford>; honors <Brit>, tripos <Cambridge>

3 **examination, inspection, scrutiny; survey, review, perusal,** look-over, once over *and* look-see <nf>, perlustration, **study,** look-through, scan, run-through; visitation; overhaul, overhauling; quality control; confirmation, cross-check

4 **investigation,** indagation , **research,** legwork <nf>, inquiry into; data-gathering, gathering *or* amassing evidence; perscrutation, **probe,** searching investigation, close inquiry, exhaustive study; police inquiry *or* investigation, criminal investigation, detective work, detection, sleuthing; investigative bureau *or* agency, bureau *or* department of investigation; legislative investigation, Congressional investigation, hearing; witch-hunt, fishing expedition, Inquisition

5 preliminary *or* tentative examination; quick *or* cursory inspection, glance, quick look, first look, once-over-lightly <nf>

6 **checkup, check;** spot check; physical examination, **physical,** physical checkup, health examination; self-examination; exploratory examination; testing, drug testing, alcohol testing, random testing; bench test

7 **re-examination,** reinquiry, recheck, **review,** reappraisal, revaluation, rethinking, revision, rebeholding, second *or* further look

8 **reconnaissance;** recce *and* recco *and* recon <nf>; **reconnoitering,** reconnoiter, exploration, **scouting;** exploratory survey

9 **surveillance,** shadowing, following, trailing, tailing <nf>, 24-hour surveillance, observation, stakeout <nf>; **spying, espionage,** espial, **intelligence,** military intelligence, intelligence work, cloak-and-dagger work <nf>; intelligence agency, secret service, secret police; counterespionage, counterintelligence; wiretap, wiretapping, bugging <nf>, electronic surveillance; tagging

10 **question, query, inquiry, demand** , **interrogation,** interrogatory; interrogative; frequently asked question *or* FAQ; **problem, issue, topic** 937, case *or* point in question, bone of contention, controversial point, question before the house, debating point, controversy, question *or* point at issue, **moot point** *or* case, question mark, *quodlibet* <L>; difficult question, vexed *or* knotty question, burning question; sixty-four-thousand-dollar question; leader, leading question; feeler, trial balloon, fishing question; trick question, poser, stumper, tough nut to crack, conundrum, enigma, mind-boggler <nf>; trivia question; cross-question, rhetorical question; cross-interrogatory; catechism, catechizing; easy question

11 **interview,** press conference, press opportunity, photo opportunity, photo op <nf>

12 **questioning, interrogation, querying,** asking, seeking, pumping,

probing, inquiring; **quiz,** quizzing, **examination;** challenge, dispute; interpellation, bringing into question; catechizing, catechization; catechetical method, Socratic method *or* induction

13 **grilling,** the grill <nf>, inquisition, pumping; police interrogation; **the third-degree** <nf>; direct examination, redirect examination, **cross-examination,** cross-interrogation, **cross-questioning**

14 **canvass, survey, inquiry, questionnaire,** questionary; exit poll; **poll, public-opinion poll,** opinion poll *or* survey, statistical survey, opinion sampling, voter-preference survey; consumer-preference survey, market-research survey; consumer research, market research

15 **search,** searching, **quest, hunt,** hunting, stalk, stalking, still hunt, dragnet, posse, search party; search warrant; search-and-destroy operation *or* mission; **rummage, ransacking,** turning over *or* upside down; **forage;** house-search, perquisition, domiciliary visit; exploration, probe; **body search,** frisk *and* toss *and* shake *and* shakedown *and* skin-search *and* bodyshake *and* pat-down search <nf>; all-points bulletin

16 **inquirer, asker, prober,** querier, querist, **questioner,** questionist, interrogator; interviewer; interrogatrix; interpellator; **quizzer,** examiner, catechist; inquisitor, inquisitionist; cross-questioner, cross-interrogator, **cross-examiner;** interlocutor; **pollster,** poller, sampler, canvasser, opinion sampler; **interviewer; detective** 576.10; **secret agent** 576.9; quiz-master

17 **examiner,** examinant, **tester; inspector,** scrutinizer, scrutator, scrutineer, quality-control inspector; **monitor,** reviewer; fact-checker; check-out pilot; observer; visitor, visitator; **investigator,** indagator ; editor, copy editor, proofreader

18 seeker, hunter, searcher, perquisitor; rummager, ransacker; digger, delver; zetetic; **researcher, fact finder,** researchist, research worker, market researcher, consumer researcher; surveyor

19 **examinee,** examinant, examinate, questionee, quizzee; interviewee; informant, subject, interviewee; witness; candidate; defendant, plaintiff, suspect

VERBS **20** **inquire, ask, question, query; make inquiry,** take up *or* institute *or* pursue *or* follow up *or* conduct *or* carry on an inquiry, ask after, inquire after, ask about, ask questions, put queries; inquire of, require an answer, ask a question, put a question to, pose *or* set *or* propose *or* propound a question; bring into question, interpellate; **demand, want to know;** introspect

21 **interrogate, question, query, quiz, test, examine;** catechize; **pump,** pump for information, shoot questions at, pick the brains of, worm out of; interview; draw one out

22 **grill,** put on the grill <nf>, inquisition, pump, make inquisition; roast <nf>, put the pressure on *and* put the screws to *and* go over <nf>; **cross-examine, cross-question,** cross-interrogate, cross <nf>; third-degree <nf>, give *or* put through the third degree <nf>; put to the question; extract information, pry *or* prize out; run *or* put through the mill <nf>

23 **investigate,** indagate , sift, **explore, look into,** peer into, **search into, go into, delve into,** dig into, poke into, pry into; fact-find; **probe, sound, plumb, fathom; check into, check on, check out,** nose into, see into; poke about, root around *or* about, scratch around *or* about, cast about *or* around

24 **examine, inspect, scrutinize, survey,** canvass, **look at,** peer at, eyeball <nf>, **observe, scan, peruse, study; look over,** give the once-over <nf>, run the eye over, cast *or* pass the eyes over, scope out <nf>; go over, run over, pass over, pore over; overlook, overhaul; **monitor, review,** pass under review; set an examination, give an examination; **take stock of,** size *or* **size up,** take the measure <nf>; **check, check**

out, check over *or* **through; check up on;** autopsy, postmortem 307.17; soul-search

25 **make a close study of, research, scrutinize,** examine thoroughly, vet <Brit>, **go deep into,** look closely at, probe; examine point by point, go over with a fine-tooth comb, go over step by step, subject to close scrutiny, view *or* try in all its phases, get down to nuts and bolts <nf>; perscrutate, perlustrate

26 **examine cursorily,** take a cursory view of, give a quick *or* cursory look, give a once-over-lightly <nf>, give a dekko <Brit nf>, **scan, skim, skim over** *or* **through,** slur, slur over, slip *or* skip over *or* through, **glance at,** give the once-over <nf>, pass over lightly, zip through, **dip into, touch upon,** touch upon lightly *or* in passing, **hit the high spots; thumb through,** flip through the pages, turn over the leaves, leaf *or* page *or* flick through

27 **re-examine,** recheck, reinquire, **reconsider,** reappraise, revaluate, rethink, **review,** revise, rebehold, take another *or* a second *or* a further look; retrace, retrace one's steps, go back over; rejig *or* rejigger <nf>; take back to the old drawing board

28 **reconnoiter,** make a reconnaissance, case <nf>, scout, **scout out,** spy, **spy out,** play the spy, peep; **watch,** put under surveillance, stake out <nf>; bug <nf>; check up on, check up

29 **canvass, survey,** make a survey; **poll,** conduct a poll, sample, **questionnaire** <nf>

30 **seek, hunt,** look , **quest, pursue,** go in pursuit of, follow, go in search of, prowl after, see to, try to find; **look up, hunt up; look for,** look around *or* about for, look for high and low, look high and low, search out, **search for,** seek for, **hunt for,** cast *or* beat about for; shop around for; **fish for, angle for,** bob for, dig for, delve for, go on a fishing expedition; **ask for,** inquire for; **gun for,** go gunning for; still-hunt <nf>

31 **search, hunt, explore;** research; read up on; **hunt through, search through, look through, go through;** dig, delve, burrow, root, pick over, poke, pry; look round *or* around, poke around, nose around, smell around; beat the bushes; forage; frisk <nf>

32 **grope,** grope for, **feel for,** fumble, grabble, scrabble, feel around, poke around, pry around, beat about, grope in the dark; **feel** *or* **pick one's way**

33 **ransack, rummage, rake, scour, comb;** rifle; **look everywhere,** look into every hole and corner, **look high and low,** look upstairs and downstairs, **look all over,** look all over hell <nf>, search high heaven, turn upside down, turn inside out, **leave no stone unturned;** shake down *and* shake *and* toss <nf>

34 **search out, hunt out, spy out,** scout out, **ferret out,** fish out, pry out, winkle out <Brit nf>, dig out, root out, grub up

35 **trace, stalk, track, trail; follow,** follow up, shadow, tail <nf>, dog the footsteps of, have *or* keep an eye on; nose, nose out, **smell** *or* **sniff out,** follow the trail *or* scent *or* spoor of; follow a clue; **trace down, hunt down, track down, run down, run to earth**

ADJS 36 **inquiring, questioning, querying,** quizzing; **quizzical, curious; interrogatory,** interrogative, interrogational; inquisitorial, inquisitional; visitatorial, visitorial; catechistic, catechistical, catechetic, catechetical

37 **examining,** examinational; scrutatorial, examinatorial; **testing,** trying, **tentative;** groping, feeling; inspectional; **inspectorial;** interpellant; **investigative,** indagative ; zetetic; heuristic, investigatory, investigational; **exploratory,** explorative, explorational; fact-finding; analytic, analytical; curious

38 **searching, probing, prying, nosy** <nf>; poking, digging, fishing, delving; in search *or* quest of, looking for, **out for,** on the lookout for, **in the market for,** loaded *or* out for bear <nf>; all-searching; fact-finding, knowledge-seeking

ADVS **39 in question, at issue,** in debate *or* dispute, **under consideration,** under active consideration, **under advisement,** *subjudice* <L>, under examination, under investigation, under surveillance; up *or* open for discussion; **before the house, on the docket, on the agenda, on the table, on the floor**

939 ANSWER

NOUNS **1 answer, reply, response,** responsion, replication; answering, respondence; riposte, **uptake** <nf>, **retort, rejoinder,** reaction 903, return, **comeback** *and* **take** <nf>, back answer, short answer, back talk, backchat <nf>; **repartee,** backchat, clever *or* ready *or* witty reply *or* retort, snappy comeback <nf>, witty repartee; yes-and-no answer, evasive reply; **acknowledgment,** receipt, confirmation; rescript, rescription; antiphon; **echo,** reverberation 54.2

2 rebuttal, counterstatement, counterreply, counterclaim, counterblast, counteraccusation, countercharge, *tu quoque* <L, you too>, defense, contraremonstrance; **rejoinder,** replication, defense, rebutter, surrebutter *or* surrebuttal, surrejoinder; confutation, refutation; last word, parting shot

3 answerer, replier, responder, **respondent,** responser; defendant

VERBS **4 answer,** make *or* give answer, return answer, return for answer, offer, proffer, **reply, respond,** say, say in reply; **retort,** riposte, **rejoin,** return, throw back, flash back; come back *and* come back at *and* come right back at <nf>, answer back *and* talk back *and* shoot back <nf>, **react; acknowledge,** make *or* give acknowledgement; echo, reecho, reverberate 54.7

5 rebut, make a rebuttal; **rejoin,** surrebut, surrejoin; counterclaim, countercharge; confute, refute; have the last word, have the final say; fire the parting shot; lip off <nf>

ADJS **6 answering, replying, responsive,** respondent, responding; rejoining, returning; antiphonal; echoing, echoic, reechoing 54.10; confutative, refutative; acknowledging, confirming

ADVS **7** in answer, in reply, in response, in return, in rebuttal

940 SOLUTION

<answer to a problem>

NOUNS **1 solution,** resolution, **answer, reason, explanation** 341.4; **finding,** conclusion, determination, ascertainment, verdict, judgment; **outcome, upshot,** denouement, **result,** issue, end 820, end result; accomplishment 407; **solving,** working, **working-out,** finding-out, resolving, **clearing up,** cracking; **unriddling,** riddling, unscrambling, unraveling, sorting out, untwisting, unspinning, unweaving, untangling, disentanglement; **decipherment, deciphering, decoding,** decryption; interpretation 341; **happy ending** *or* outcome, the answer to one's prayers, the light at the end of the tunnel; possible solution, **scenario**

VERBS **2 solve, resolve,** find the solution *or* answer, problem-solve, **clear up,** get, get right, do, work, **work out, find out, figure out,** dope *and* dope out <nf>; **straighten out, iron out,** sort out, puzzle out; debug; psych *and* psych out <nf>; **unriddle,** riddle, unscramble, undo, untangle, disentangle, untwist, unspin, unweave, **unravel,** ravel, ravel out; **decipher, decode,** decrypt, crack, do the math; **make out,** interpret 341.9; **answer, explain** 341.10; unlock, pick *or* open the lock; find the key of, find a clue to; **get to the bottom *or* heart of, fathom,** plumb, bottom; have it, hit it, hit upon a solution, hit the nail on the head, hit it on the nose <nf>; guess, divine, guess right; end happily, work out right *and* come up roses <nf>

ADJS **3 solvable,** soluble, **resolvable,** open to solution, capable of solution, workable, doable, answerable; explainable, explicable, determinable, ascertainable; **decipherable,** decodable

941 DISCOVERY

NOUNS **1** **discovery, finding, detection,** spotting, catching, catching sight of, sighting, espial; recognition, determination, distinguishment; locating, **location; disclosure, exposure, revelation, uncovering, unearthing,** digging up, exhumation, excavation, bringing to light *or* view; **find,** trove, treasure trove, *trouvaille* <Fr>, strike, lucky strike; accidental *or* chance discovery, happening *or* stumbling upon, tripping over, casual discovery; serendipity; **learning, finding out,** determining, becoming conscious *or* cognizant of, becoming aware of; self-discovery; realization, enlightenment; rediscovery; invention; archaeology

VERBS **2** **discover, find,** get; strike, hit; put *or* lay one's hands on, lay one's fingers on, **locate** 159.11; **hunt down,** search out, trace down, track down, **run down, run** *or* **bring to earth;** trace; **learn, find out,** determine, become cognizant *or* conscious of, become aware of, get it <nf>; discover *or* find out the hard way, discover to one's cost; discover *or* find oneself; rediscover; invent

3 **come across, run across, meet with,** meet up with <nf>, fall in with, **encounter, run into,** bump into <nf>, come *or* run up against <nf>, **come on** *or* **upon, hit on** *or* **upon,** strike on, light on *or* upon, alight on *or* upon, fall on, tumble on *or* upon; **chance on** *or* **upon,** happen on *or* upon *or* across, **stumble on** *or* **upon,** *or* **across** *or* **into,** stub one's toe on *or* upon, trip over, bump up against, blunder upon, discover serendipitously

4 **uncover, unearth, dig up,** disinter, exhume, excavate; **disclose, expose, reveal,** blow the lid off, crack wide open, **bring to light,** lay bare; **turn up,** root up, rootle up <Brit>, fish up; worm out, ferret out, winkle out <Brit>, pry out

5 **detect, spot,** <nf>, **see, lay eyes on,** catch sight of, catch a glimpse of, perceive, **spy,** espy, descry, sense, pick up, notice, discern, **perceive, make out, recognize,** distinguish, identify

6 **scent,** catch the scent of, sniff, smell, get a whiff of <nf>, **get wind of;** sniff *or* scent *or* smell out, nose out; be on the right scent, be near the truth, be warm <nf>, burn <nf>, have a fix on, place

7 **catch,** catch out; catch off side, catch off base; catch tripping, **catch napping, catch off-guard,** catch asleep at the switch; **catch at,** catch in the act, **catch red-handed,** catch in *flagrante delicto,* **catch with one's pants down** <nf>, catch flat-footed, have the goods on <nf>, ensnare

8 <detect the hidden nature of> **see through, penetrate,** see as it really is, see in its true colors, see the inside of, read between the lines, see the cloven hoof; open the eyes to, tumble to, catch on to, wise up to <nf>; **be on to, be wise to, be hep to** <nf>, have one's measure, **have one's number,** have dead to rights <nf>, read someone like a book

9 **turn up, show up,** be found; discover itself, expose *or* betray itself; hang out <nf>; materialize, **come to light,** come out; come along, come to hand; show one's true colors

ADJS **10** on the right scent, **on the right track,** on the trail of; **hot** *and* **warm** <nf>; **discoverable,** determinable, findable, **detectable,** spottable, disclosable, exposable, locatable, **discernible;** exploratory

942 EXPERIMENT

NOUNS **1** **experiment, experimentation;** experimental method; testing, trying, trying-out, **trial;** research and development *or* R and D; running it up the flagpole <nf>, trying it on *or* out <nf>, exploration, bench test; **trial and error,** hit and miss, cut and try <nf>; empiricism, experimentalism, pragmatism, instrumentalism; **rule of thumb;** tentativeness, tentative method; control experiment, controlled experiment, **control;** experimental design; experimental proof *or* verification; noble experiment; single-blind experiment, double-blind experiment; guesswork

2 **test, trial, try;** essay; check; docimasy , assay; determination, blank determination; **proof,** verification; touchstone, standard, criterion 300.2; crucial test; acid test, litmus *or* litmus paper test; ordeal, crucible; probation; **feeling out, sounding out;** test case; first *or* rough draft, rough sketch, mock-up; stab *and* crack *and* whack <nf>; *brouillon* <Fr>; trial balloon

3 **tryout,** workout, **rehearsal,** practice; pilot plan *or* program; **dry run,** dummy run, practice run; road test; **trial run,** practical test; shakedown, shakedown cruise, bench test; flight test, test flight *or* run; audition, hearing

4 **feeler, probe,** sound, sounder; **trial balloon,** *ballon d'essai* <Fr>, pilot balloon, barometer; weather vane, weathercock; straw to show the wind, straw vote; sample, random sample, experimental sample

5 **laboratory, lab** <nf>, research laboratory, research center *or* establishment *or* facility *or* institute, experiment station, field station, research and development *or* R and D establishment; **proving ground;** think tank <nf>, workshop

6 **experimenter,** experimentist, experimentalist, empiricist, bench scientist, **researcher,** research worker, R and D worker; experimental engineer; **tester,** tryer-out, test driver, test pilot; essayer; assayer; analyst, analyzer, investigator

7 **subject, experimental subject,** experimentee, testee, patient, sample; laboratory animal, experimental *or* test animal, **guinea pig,** lab rat

VERBS 8 **experiment,** experimentalize, **research,** make an experiment, **run an experiment,** run a sample *or* specimen; **test, try,** essay, cut and try <nf>, **test** *or* **try out,** have a dry run *or* dummy run *or* rehearsal *or* test run, rehearse; run it up the flagpole and see who salutes <nf>; put to the test, **put to the proof, prove, verify,** validate, substantiate, confirm, put to trial, bring to test, make a trial of, give a trial to; **give a try,** have a go, give it a go <nf>, have *or* take a stab *or* crack *or* whack at <nf>; sample, taste; assay; play around *or* fool around with <nf>; try out under controlled conditions; give a tryout *or* workout <nf>, **road-test,** shake down; try one out, put one through his paces; experiment *or* practice upon; try it on; try on, try it for size <nf>; try one's strength, see what one can do; send up a trial balloon

9 **sound out, check out, feel out, sound,** get a sounding *or* reading *or* sense, probe, **feel the pulse,** read; **put** *or* **throw out a feeler,** put out feelers, send up a trial balloon, fly a kite; **see which way the wind blows,** see how the land lies, test out, test the waters; take a straw vote, take a random sample, use an experimental sample

10 **stand the test, stand up, hold up, hold up in the wash,** pass, **pass muster,** get by <nf>, make it *and* hack it *and* cut the mustard <nf>, meet *or* satisfy requirements

ADJS 11 **experimental, test, trial;** pilot; testing, proving, trying; probative, probatory, verificatory; probationary; **tentative,** provisional; empirical; trial-and-error, hit-or-miss, cut-and-try; heuristic

12 **tried, well-tried, tested, proved,** verified, confirmed, tried and true

ADVS 13 **experimentally,** by rule of thumb, by trial and error, by hit and miss, hit *or* miss, by guess and by God

14 **on trial,** under examination, **on** *or* **under probation,** under suspicion, **on approval**

943 COMPARISON

NOUNS 1 **comparison,** compare, examining side by side, matching, matchup, holding up together, proportion , comparative judgment *or* estimate; **likening,** comparing, **analogy;** parallelism; comparative relation; weighing, balancing; opposing, opposition, **contrast;** contrastiveness, distinctiveness, distinction 944.3; confrontment, confrontation; **relation** 775, relating, relativism; correlation 777; simile, similitude, metaphor, allegory, figure *or* trope of comparison; comparative degree; comparative method; comparative linguistics, comparative grammar, comparative literature, comparative anatomy, etc

2 **collation,** comparative scrutiny, point-by-point comparison; **verification, confirmation, checking;** check, cross-check

3 **comparability,** comparableness, comparativeness; analogousness, equivalence, **commensurability;** proportionateness *or* proportionability ; ratio, proportion, balance; **similarity** 784

VERBS **4** **compare, liken,** assimilate, similize, liken to, compare with; **make** *or* **draw a comparison,** run a comparison, do a comparative study, bring into comparison; **analogize,** bring into analogy; relate 775.6; metaphorize; **draw a parallel,** parallel; **match,** match up; examine side by side, view together, hold up together; weigh *or* measure against; confront, bring into confrontation, **contrast, oppose,** set in opposition, set off against, set in contrast, **put** *or* **set over against,** set *or* place against, counterpose; compare and contrast, note similarities and differences; **weigh,** balance

5 **collate,** scrutinize comparatively, compare point by point, painstakingly match; **verify, confirm, check, cross-check**

6 **compare notes,** exchange views *or* observations, match data *or* findings, put heads together <nf>

7 be comparable, compare, compare to *or* **with,** not compare with 787.2, admit of comparison, be commensurable, be of the same order *or* class, be worthy of comparison, be fit to be compared; **measure up to, come up to,** match up with, stack up with <nf>, hold a candle to <nf>; **match, parallel;** vie, vie with, rival; **resemble** 784.7

ADJS **8** **comparative, relative** 775.7, **comparable,** commensurate, commensurable, parallel, matchable, **analogous;** analogical; collatable; **correlative;** much at one, much of a muchness <nf>; **similar** 784.10; something of the sort *or* to that effect

9 **incomparable,** incommensurable, not to be compared, of different orders; apples and oranges; **unlike, dissimilar** 787.4

ADVS **10** **comparatively, relatively;** comparably; dollar for dollar, pound for pound, ounce for ounce, etc; on the one hand, on the other hand

944 DISCRIMINATION

NOUNS **1** **discrimination,** discriminateness, discriminatingness, discriminativeness; seeing *or* making distinctions, appreciation of differences; analytic power *or* faculty; **criticalness; finesse,** refinement, delicacy; niceness of distinction, nicety, subtlety, refined discrimination, critical niceness; **tact, tactfulness,** feel, feeling, sense, **sensitivity** 24.3, **sensibility** 24.2; intuition, instinct 934; appreciation, appreciativeness; judiciousness 920.7; taste, discriminating taste, aesthetic *or* artistic judgment; palate, fine *or* refined palate; ear, good ear, educated ear; eye, good eye; connoisseurship, savvy <nf>, selectiveness, fastidiousness 495

2 **discernment,** critical discernment, penetration, **perception,** perceptiveness, **insight,** perspicacity; **flair; judgment,** acumen 920.4; analysis 801

3 **distinction,** contradistinction, distinctiveness ; **distinguishment, differentiation** 780.4, winnowing, shakeout, separation, separationism, division, segregation, segregationism, demarcation; nice *or* subtle *or* fine distinction, **nuance,** shade of difference, microscopic distinction; hairsplitting, trichoschistism

VERBS **4 discriminate, distinguish,** draw *or* make distinctions, contradistinguish, compare and contrast, pick and choose, secern, distinguish in thought, **separate,** separate out, divide, analyze 801.6, subdivide, **segregate,** sever, severalize, **differentiate,** demark, demarcate, mark the interface, set off, **set apart,** grade, graduate, sift, sift out, sieve, sieve out, winnow, screen, screen out, sort, classify, sort out; **pick out, select** 371.14; separate the sheep from the goats, separate the men from the boys, separate the wheat from the tares *or* chaff, winnow the chaff from the wheat; **draw the line,** fix *or* set a limit; **split hairs,** draw *or* make a fine *or* overfine *or* nice *or* subtle distinction, subtilize

5 be discriminating, discriminate, exercise discrimination, tell which is which; **be tactful,** show *or* exercise tact; be tasteful, use one's palate; shop around, pick and choose; use advisedly

6 distinguish between, make *or* **draw a distinction,** appreciate differences, see nuances *or* shades of difference, see the difference, tell apart, tell one thing from another, know which is which, know what's what <nf>, not confound *or* mix up; know one's ass from one's elbow <nf>

ADJS **7 discriminating, discriminate,** discriminative, selective; discriminatory; **tactful, sensitive;** appreciative, appreciatory; **critical;** distinctive , **distinguishing;** differential; precise, accurate, exact; nice, fine, delicate, subtle, subtile, refined; fastidious 495.9; distinctive, contrastive

8 discerning, perceptive, perspicacious, insightful; **astute, judicious** 920.19; perfectionist, choosy

9 discriminable, distinguishable, separable, differentiable, contrastable, opposable

ADVS **10 discriminatingly,** discriminatively, discriminately; with finesse; **tactfully; tastefully**

945 INDISCRIMINATION

NOUNS **1 indiscrimination,** indiscriminateness, undiscriminatingness, undiscriminativeness, unselectiveness, **uncriticalness, unparticularness;** syncretism; unfastidiousness; lack of refinement, coarseness *or* crudeness *or* crudity of intellect; **casualness,** promiscuousness, **promiscuity; indiscretion,** indiscreetness, **imprudence** 923.2; **untactfulness,** tactlessness, lack of feeling, insensitivity, **insensibility** 25, unmeticulousness, unpreciseness 340.4, inexactitude; **generality** 864, catholicity, catholic tastes; indifference; color blindness, tonedeafness; impartiality

2 indistinction, indistinctness, vagueness 32.2; **indefiniteness** 971.4; uniformity 781; facelessness, impersonality; indistinguishableness, **undistinguishableness,** indiscernibility; a distinction without a difference; randomness, generality, universality

VERBS **3 confound, confuse,** mix, mix up, muddle, tumble, jumble, jumble together, **blur,** blur distinctions, overlook distinctions; lump together, take as one, roll into one

4 use loosely, use unadvisedly

ADJS **5 undiscriminating, indiscriminate,** indiscriminative, undiscriminative, undifferentiating, unselective; wholesale, **general** 864.11, **blanket; uncritical,** uncriticizing, undemanding, nonjudgmental; **unparticular,** unfastidious; unsubtle; **casual, promiscuous;** undiscerning; unexacting, unmeticulous 340.13; **indiscreet,** undiscreet, **imprudent; untactful,** tactless, insensitive; catholic; indifferent; color-blind

6 indistinguishable, undistinguishable, undistinguished, indiscernible, **indistinct,** indistinctive, **without distinction,** not to be distinguished, undiscriminated, nondiscriminatory, inclusive, unindividual, unindividualized, undifferentiated, **alike,** six of one and half a dozen of the other <nf>; desultory; undefined, indefinite; faceless, impersonal; standard, interchangeable, stereotyped, uniform 781.5; random; miscellaneous, motley

946 JUDGMENT

NOUNS 1 **judgment,** judging, adjudgment, adjudication, judicature, deeming ; judgment call <nf>; arbitrament, arbitration 466.2; **resolution** 359; good judgment 920.7; **choice** 371; **discrimination** 944

2 **criticism; censure** 510.3; **approval** 509; **critique,** review, notice, critical notice, report, comment; book review, critical review, thumbnail review; literary criticism, art criticism, music criticism, etc, critical journal, critical bibliography

3 **estimate, estimation; view, opinion** 953.6; **assessment,** assessing, **appraisal,** appraisement, appraising, appreciation, reckoning, **stocktaking,** valuation, valuing, **evaluation,** evaluating, value judgment, evaluative criticism, analyzing, weighing, weighing up, gauging, ranking, rank-ordering, **rating;** measurement 300; comparison 943; second opinion; public opinion

4 **conclusion, deduction, inference,** consequence, consequent, corollary; derivation, illation; induction; judgment day

5 **verdict, decision,** resolution , **determination, finding,** holding; diagnosis, prognosis; **decree, ruling,** consideration, order, **pronouncement,** deliverance; **award,** action, **sentence; condemnation,** doom; dictum; precedent; edict, decree; execution of judgment

6 **judge,** judger, adjudicator, justice; arbiter 596.1; referee, umpire

7 **critic,** criticizer; connoisseur, cognoscente <Ital>; literary critic, man of letters; textual critic; editor; social critic, muckraker; captious critic, smellfungus, caviler, carper, faultfinder; criticaster, criticule, critickin; **censor,** censurer; **reviewer, commentator,** commenter; scholiast, annotator

VERBS 8 **judge,** exercise judgment *or* the judgment; make a judgment call <nf>; adjudge, adjudicate; be judicious *or* judgmental; **consider, regard,** hold, **deem, esteem, count, account,** think of; allow <nf>, **suppose, presume** 951.10, opine, form an opinion, give *or* pass *or* express an opinion, weigh in *and* put in one's two cents' worth <nf>

9 **estimate,** form an estimate, make an estimation; **reckon,** call, guess, figure <nf>; **assess, appraise,** give an appreciation, **gauge, rate, rank,** rank-order, put in rank order, class, mark, **value,** deem, **evaluate,** valuate, place *or* set a value on, weigh, weigh up, prize, appreciate; size up *or* take one's measure <nf>, **measure** 300.10

10 **conclude,** draw a conclusion, be forced to conclude, **come to** *or* **arrive at a conclusion, come up with a conclusion** *and* **end up** <nf>; find, hold; deduce, derive, take as proved *or* demonstrated, extract, **gather,** collect, glean, fetch; **infer,** draw an inference; induce; **reason,** reason that; put two and two together

11 **decide, determine; find,** hold, ascertain; **resolve** 359.7, **settle,** fix; make a decision, come to a decision, **make up one's mind,** settle one's mind, come down <nf>, settle the matter

12 **sit in judgment,** hold the scales, hold court; **hear,** give a hearing to; **try** 598.18; **referee, umpire,** officiate; arbitrate 466.6

13 **pass judgment, pronounce judgment,** utter a judgment, deliver judgment; agree on a verdict, return a verdict, hand down a verdict, **bring in a verdict, find,** find for *or* against; pronounce on, act on, **pronounce,** report, **rule,** decree, order; **sentence,** pass sentence, hand down a sentence, doom, condemn; charge the jury

14 **criticize,** critique; **censure** 510.13, pick holes in, pick to pieces; **approve** 509.9; **review;** comment upon, annotate; moralize upon; pontificate; vet <nf>

15 **rank, rate,** count, be regarded, be thought of, be in one's estimation

ADJS **16** **judicial, judiciary,** judicative, judgmental; juridic, juridical, juristic, juristical; **judicious** 920.19; **evaluative; critical; approbatory** 509.16

ADVS **17** **all things considered, on the whole, taking one thing with another,** on balance, taking everything into consideration *or* account; everything being equal, other things being equal, *ceteris paribus* <L>, taking into account, considering, after all, this being so; therefore, wherefore; on the one hand, on the other hand, having said that; *sub judice* <L>, in court, before the bench *or* bar *or* court

947 PREJUDGMENT

NOUNS **1** **prejudgment,** prejudication, forejudgment; **preconception, presumption, supposition, presupposition,** presupposal, presurmise, preapprehension, prenotion, **prepossession; predilection,** predisposition; preconsideration, **predetermination,** predecision, preconclusion, premature judgment; ulterior motive, hidden agenda, *parti pris* <Fr>, an ax to grind, **prejudice** 980.3

VERBS **2** **prejudge,** forejudge; **preconceive, presuppose, presume,** presurmise; **be predisposed;** predecide, predetermine, preconclude, judge beforehand *or* prematurely, judge before the evidence is in, have one's mind made up; **jump to a conclusion,** go off half-cocked *or* at half cock *and* beat the gun *and* jump the gun *and* shoot from the hip <nf>

ADJS **3** **prejudged,** forejudged, **preconceived,** preconceptual, **presumed, presupposed,** presurmised; predetermined, predecided, preconcluded, judged beforehand *or* prematurely; **predisposed,** predispositional; prejudicial, prejudging, prejudicative

948 MISJUDGMENT

NOUNS **1** **misjudgment,** poor judgment, error in judgment, warped *or* flawed *or* skewed judgment; **miscalculation,** miscomputation, **misreckoning, misestimation,** misappreciation, misperception, misevaluation, misvaluation, misconjecture, wrong impression; **misreading,** wrong construction, misconstruction, **misinterpretation** 342; **inaccuracy, error** 975; unmeticulousness 340.4; injudiciousness 923.2; wrong end of the stick

VERBS **2** **misjudge,** judge amiss, **miscalculate, misestimate, misreckon,** misappreciate, misperceive, get a wrong impression, misevaluate, misvalue, miscompute, misdeem, misesteem, misthink, misconjecture; **misread,** misconstrue, put the wrong construction on things, get wrong, misread the situation *or* case; **misinterpret** 342.2; err 975.9; fly in the face of facts; get hold of the wrong end of the stick <nf>

949 OVERESTIMATION

NOUNS **1** **overestimation,** overestimate, **overreckoning,** overcalculation, **overrating,** overassessment, overvaluation, overappraisal; overreaction; **overstatement, exaggeration** 355, hype <nf>

VERBS **2** **overestimate, overreckon,** overcalculate, overcount, overmeasure, see more than is there; **overrate,** overassess, overappraise, overesteem, **overvalue,** overprize, overprice, think *or* make too much of, put on a pedestal, idealize, see only the good points of; overreact to; **overstate, exaggerate** 355.3; pump up *and* jump up *and* make a big deal *or* Federal case <nf>; hype <nf>

ADJS **3** **overestimated, overrated,** puffed up, pumped up <nf>, overvalued, on the high side; **exaggerated** 355.4

950 UNDERESTIMATION

NOUNS **1** **underestimation,** misestimation, underestimate, **underrating,** underreckoning, undervaluation, misprizing, misprizal, misprision; **belittlement, depreciation,** deprecation, **minimization,** disparagement 512; conservative estimate; negative outlook, pessimism

VERBS 2 **underestimate,** misestimate, **underrate,** underreckon, **undervalue,** underprize, **misprize,** underprice; **make little of,** set at little, set at naught, set little by, attach little importance to, not do justice to, sell short, think little of, make *or* think nothing of, see less than is there, miss on the low side, set no store by, make light of, shrug off, soft-pedal <nf>; **depreciate, deprecate,** minimize, belittle, bad-mouth *and* poor-mouth *and* put down *and* run down <nf>, take someone for an idiot *or* a fool; disparage 512.8; play down, understate

ADJS 3 **underestimated, underrated,** undervalued, on the low side; unvalued, unprized, misprized; underpriced, cheap

951 THEORY, SUPPOSITION

NOUNS 1 **theory,** theorization; theoretics, theoretic, theoric ; **hypothesis,** hypothecation, hypothesizing; **speculation,** mere theory; doctrinairism, doctrinality, doctrinarity; analysis, **explanation,** abstraction; theoretical basis *or* justification; body of theory, theoretical structure *or* construct; unified theory

2 **theory, explanation,** proposed *or* tentative explanation, rationalization, proposal, proposition, statement covering the facts *or* evidence; **hypothesis,** working hypothesis

3 **supposition, supposal,** supposing; **presupposition,** presupposal; **assumption, presumption, conjecture, inference, surmise, guesswork; postulate,** postulation, *postulatum* <L>, set of postulates; **proposition, thesis, concept, premise** 935.7; **axiom** 974.2

4 **guess, conjecture,** unverified supposition, perhaps, speculation, guesswork, surmise, educated guess; guesstimate *and* hunch *and* shot *and* stab <nf>; rough guess, wild guess, blind guess, bold conjecture, shot in the dark <nf>, crude estimate

5 <vague supposition> **suggestion,** bare suggestion, **suspicion, inkling, hint, clue, sense, feeling, feeling in one's bones, intuition** 934, **intimation, impression, notion,** mere notion, hunch *and* sneaking suspicion <nf>, instinct, trace of an idea, half an idea, vague idea, hazy idea, **idea** 932

6 supposititiousness, presumptiveness, presumableness, theoreticalness, hypotheticalness, conjecturableness, speculativeness

7 **theorist, theorizer,** theoretic, **theoretician,** notionalist ; **speculator;** hypothesist, hypothesizer; doctrinaire, doctrinarian; inquirer; synthesizer; armchair authority *or* philosopher; thinker; researcher, experimenter

8 **supposer,** assumer, surmiser, **conjecturer, guesser,** guessworker, speculator, gambler

VERBS 9 **theorize, hypothesize, hypothecate,** form a hypothesis, **speculate,** postulate, have *or* entertain a theory, espouse a theory, generalize

10 **suppose, assume, presume, surmise,** expect, **suspect, infer, understand, gather, conclude, deduce, consider,** reckon, reason, derive, divine, imagine, **fancy,** dream, conceive, **believe, deem,** repute, feel, **think,** be inclined to think, opine, say, daresay, be afraid <nf>; take, take it, take it into one's head, take for, take to be, take for granted, take as a precondition, **presuppose, presurmise,** prefigure; provisionally accept *or* admit *or* agree to, take one up on <nf>, grant, stipulate, take it as given, let, let be, say *or* assume for argument's sake, say for the hell of it <nf>; draw a mental picture

11 **conjecture, guess,** guesstimate <nf>, give a guess, talk off the top of one's head <nf>, hazard a conjecture, venture a guess, risk assuming *or* stating, tentatively suggest, go out on a limb <nf>

12 **postulate, predicate, posit,** set forth, lay down, put forth, assert; pose, advance, **propose, propound** 439.5

ADJS **13** **theoretical, hypothetical,** hypothetic; postulatory, notional; **speculative, conjectural,** blue-sky; impressionistic, intuitive 934.5; general, generalized, abstract, ideal; unverified, merely theoretical, academic, moot; impractical, armchair, thought-provoking

14 **supposed,** suppositive, **assumed, presumed, conjectured, inferred,** understood, deemed, **reputed,** reputative, putative, alleged, accounted as; suppositional, supposititious; assumptive, **presumptive;** guessed; given, granted, taken as *or* for granted, agreed, stipulated; **postulated,** postulational, premised; granted for the sake of argument

15 **supposable, presumable,** assumable, conjecturable, surmisable, imaginable, premissable

ADVS **16** **theoretically, hypothetically,** *ex hypothesi* <L>, notionally, conceptually, ideally; **in theory,** in idea, in the ideal, in the abstract, on paper, in Never-Neverland <nf>

17 **supposedly,** supposably, **presumably,** presumedly, assumably, assumedly, presumptively, assumptively, reputedly, presumingly; suppositionally, supposititiously; **seemingly,** in seeming, quasi; as it were; on the assumption that

18 conjecturably, **conjecturally;** to guess, to make a guess, **as a guess,** as a rough guess *or* an approximation, speculatively

CONJS **19** **supposing,** supposing that, **assuming that,** allowing that, if we assume that, let's say that, granting *or* granted that, given that, on the assumption *or* supposition that; if, as if, as though, by way of hypothesis

952 PHILOSOPHY

NOUNS **1** **philosophy**; philosophical inquiry *or* investigation, philosophical speculation; inquiry *or* investigation into first causes; branch of philosophy, department *or* division of philosophy; school of philosophy, philosophic system, school of thought; philosophic doctrine, philosophic theory; theory of knowledge; philosophastry, philosophastering; sophistry 936

2 **viewpoint**, point of view, outlook, attitude, opinion; feeling, sentiment, idea, thought, notion; tenet, dogma, doctrine, canon, principle; assertion, proposition, premise, assumption, precept, thesis, postulate, hypothesis, concept; supposition, presupposition, conjecture, speculation; maxim, axiom; rationalization, justification; conclusion, judgment; philosophical system, belief system, value system, set of beliefs *or* values, ethics, morals, school of thought, moral code, code of conduct, value judgment, standards, principles, ideology

3 Platonic philosophy, Platonism, philosophy of the Academy; Aristotelian philosophy, Aristotelianism, philosophy of the Lyceum, Peripateticism, Peripatetic school; Stoic philosophy, Stoicism, philosophy of the Porch *or* Stoa; Epicureanism, philosophy of the Garden

4 **materialism; idealism** 1053.3

5 monism, philosophical unitarianism, mind-stuff theory; pantheism, cosmotheism; hylozoism

6 pluralism; dualism, mind-matter theory

7 <political and economic philosophy> anarchism, capitalism, collectivism, communism, internationalism, isolationism, Marxism, monetarism, nationalism, socialism, utilitarianism, utopianism

8 **philosopher,** philosophizer, philosophe; philosophaster; **thinker,** speculator; casuist; metaphysician, cosmologist, logician, dialectician, syllogist; sophist 936.6; idealist, idealogue, visionary, dreamer

VERBS **9** **philosophize,** reason 935.15, probe

ADJS **10** **philosophical,** philosophic, sophistical 936.10; philosophicohistorical, philosophicolegal, philosophicojuristic, philosophicopsychological, philosophicoreligious, philosophicotheological; notional, abstract, esoteric, ideological, ideational, hypothetical, theoretical

11 absurdist, acosmistic, aesthetic, African, agnostic, Alexandrian, analytic, animalistic, animist *or* animistic, atomistic, etc

12 Aristotelian, Peripatetic; Augustinian, Averroist *or* Averroistic, Bergsonian, Berkeleian, Cartesian, Comtian, Hegelian, Neo-Hegelian, Heideggerian, Heraclitean, Humean, Husserlian, Kantian, Leibnizian, Parmenidean, Platonic, Neoplatonic, pre-Socratic, Pyrrhonic, Pyrrhonian, Pythagorean, Neo-Pythagorean, Sartrian, Schellingian, Schopenhauerian, Scotist, Socratic, Spencerian, Thomist *or* Thomistic, Viconian, Wittgensteinian

953 BELIEF

NOUNS **1** **belief,** credence, credit, believing, faith, trust; hope; **confidence,** assuredness, convincedness, persuadedness, **assurance;** sureness, surety, **certainty** 970; **reliance, dependence,** reliance on *or* in, dependence on, stock *and* store <nf>; acceptation, acception, acceptance; reception, acquiescence; blind faith, full faith and credit; suspension of disbelief; fideism; **credulity** 954

2 **a belief, tenet, dogma,** precept, **principle, principle** *or* **article of faith,** premise, canon, maxim, axiom; **doctrine,** teaching

3 **system of belief; religion, faith** 675.1, belief-system; **school, cult, ism,** philosophy, **ideology**, world view; political faith *or* belief *or* philosophy; **creed, credo,** credenda, dogma, canon; articles of religion, articles of faith, creedal *or* doctrinal statement, formulated *or* stated belief; gospel; catechism

4 **statement of belief** *or* **principles, manifesto,** position paper; solemn declaration; deposition, affidavit, sworn statement

5 **conviction, persuasion, certainty; firm belief,** moral certainty, implicit *or* staunch belief, settled judgment, mature judgment *or* belief, fixed opinion, unshaken confidence, steadfast faith, rooted *or* deep-rooted belief

6 **opinion, sentiment, feeling, sense, impression,** reaction, **notion, idea, thought,** mind, thinking, **way of thinking, attitude,** stance, posture, position, mindset, **view,** viewpoint, eye, sight, lights, observation, **conception,** concept, conceit, **estimation,** estimate, consideration, angle, **theory** 951, conjecture, supposition, assumption, presumption, **conclusion, judgment** 946, personal judgment; **point of view** 978.2; public opinion, public belief, general belief, prevailing belief *or* sentiment, *consensus gentium* <L>, common belief, community sentiment, popular belief, conventional wisdom, vox pop, *vox populi* <L>, climate of opinion; ethos; mystique; anecdotal evidence

7 **profession, confession,** declaration, **profession** *or* **confession** *or* **declaration of faith**

8 **believability, persuasiveness,** believableness, convincingness, **credibility, credit, trustworthiness, plausibility,** tenability, acceptability, conceivability; **reliability** 970.4

9 **believer, truster;** religious believer; true believer; the assured, the faithful, the believing; fideist; ideologist, ideologue; conformist; innocent, naÔf

VERBS **10** **believe, credit, trust, accept,** receive, buy <nf>; give credit *or* credence to, give faith to, put faith in, take stock in *or* set store by <nf>, take to heart, attach weight to; be led to believe; accept implicitly, believe without reservation, rest assured, take for granted, take *or* accept for gospel, take as gospel truth <nf>, take *or* accept on faith, take on trust *or* credit, pin one's faith on; take at face value; **take one's word for,** trust one's word, take at one's word; fall for; **buy** *and* **buy into** <nf>, **swallow** 954.6; **be certain** 970.9

11 **think, opine, be of the opinion, be persuaded, be convinced;** be afraid <nf>, **have the idea,** have an idea, **suppose, assume, presume, judge** 946.8, **guess, surmise, suspect,** have a hunch <nf>, have an inkling, expect <nf>, have an impression, be under the impression, have a sense *or* the sense, conceive, ween *and* trow , **imagine, fancy,** daresay; **deem, esteem, hold, regard, consider, maintain,** reckon, estimate; hold as, account as, set down as *or* for, view as, look upon as, take for, take, take it, get it into one's head

12 **state, assert,** swear, swear to God <nf>, declare, **affirm,** vow, avow, avouch, warrant, asseverate, confess, be under the impression, profess, express the belief, swear to a belief; depose, make an affidavit *or* a sworn statement

13 **hold the belief, have the opinion,** entertain a belief *or* an opinion, adopt *or* embrace a belief, take as an article of faith; foster *or* nurture *or* cherish a belief, be wedded to *or* espouse a belief; get hold of an idea, get it into one's head, form a conviction

14 **be confident,** have confidence, **be satisfied, be convinced, be certain,** be easy in one's mind about, be secure in the belief, **feel sure, rest assured,** rest in confidence; doubt not, **have no doubt,** have no misgivings *or* diffidence *or* qualms, have no reservations, have no second thoughts

15 **believe in, have faith in,** pin one's faith to, confide in, **have confidence in,** place *or* repose confidence in, place reliance in, put onself in the hands of, **trust in,** put trust in, have simple *or* childlike faith in, rest in, repose in *or* hope in ; give *or* get the benefit of the doubt

16 **rely on** *or* **upon, depend on** *or* **upon,** place reliance on, rest on *or* upon, repose on, lean on, **count on,** calculate on, reckon on, **bank on** *or* **upon** <nf>; **trust to** *or* **unto, swear by,** take one's oath upon; **bet on** *and* gamble on *and* lay money on *and* bet one's bottom dollar on *and* make book on <nf>; take one's word for

17 **trust, confide in, rely on, depend on,** repose, place trust *or* confidence in, have confidence in, **trust in** 953.15, trust utterly *or* implicitly, deem trustworthy, think reliable *or* dependable, take one's word, take at one's word

18 **convince; convert, win over,** lead one to believe, bring over, bring round, take in, talk over, talk around, bring to reason, bring to one's senses, **persuade, lead to believe, give to understand; satisfy, assure;** put one's mind at rest on; sell *and* sell one on <nf>; make *or* carry one's point, bring *or* drive home to; cram down one's throat *and* beat into one's head <nf>; be convincing, carry conviction; inspire belief *or* confidence; evangelize, proselytize, propagandize

19 **convince oneself, persuade oneself,** sell oneself <nf>, make oneself easy about, make oneself easy on that score, satisfy oneself on that point, make sure of, make up one's mind

20 **find credence, be believed,** be accepted, be received; be swallowed *and* **go down** *and* pass current <nf>; produce *or* carry conviction; have the ear of, gain the confidence of

ADJS 21 **believing,** of belief, preceptive, principled; attitudinal; **believing, undoubting, undoubtful,** doubtless ; faithful , God-fearing, pious, pietistic, observant, **devout;** under the impression, impressed with; **convinced, confident,** positive, dogmatic, secure, **persuaded,** sold on, **satisfied, assured;** born-again; **sure, certain** 970.13; fideistic

22 **trusting, trustful,** trusty , **confiding, unsuspecting, unsuspicious,** without suspicion; childlike, innocent, guileless, naive 416.5; **knee-jerk, credulous** 954.8; relying, depending, reliant, dependent; gullible, naive

23 **believed, credited, held, trusted, accepted;** received, of belief, authoritative, maintained; **undoubted,** unsuspected, **unquestioned,** undisputed, uncontested

24 **believable, credible,** creditable; **tenable,** conceivable, **plausible,** colorable, realistic; worthy of faith, trustworthy, trusty; fiduciary;

reliable 970.17; unimpeachable, unexceptionable, **unquestionable** 970.15

25 fiducial, fiduciary; convictional

26 **convincing,** convictional, well-founded, **persuasive,** assuring, impressive, satisfying, satisfactory, confidence-building; decisive, absolute, conclusive, determinative; authoritative

27 **doctrinal, creedal,** preceptive, canonical, dogmatic, confessional, mandatory, of faith

ADVS 28 **believingly, undoubtingly,** undoubtfully, without doubt *or* question *or* quibble, unquestioningly; **trustingly,** trustfully, unsuspectingly, unsuspiciously; piously, devoutly; with faith; **with confidence,** on *or* upon trust, on faith, on one's say-so

29 **in one's opinion, to one's mind,** in one's thinking, **to one's way of thinking,** the way one thinks, **in one's estimation,** according to one's lights, **as one sees it, to the best of one's belief;** in the opinion of, in the eyes of

954 CREDULITY

NOUNS 1 **credulity, credulousness,** inclination *or* disposition to believe, ease of belief, will *or* willingness to believe, wishful belief *or* thinking; **blind faith,** unquestioning belief, knee-jerk response *or* agreement <nf>; uncritical acceptance, premature *or* unripe acceptation, hasty *or* rash conviction; **trustfulness, trustingness, unsuspiciousness,** unsuspectingness; uncriticalness, unskepticalness; overcredulity, overcredulousness, overtrustfulness, overopenness to conviction *or* persuasion, gross credulity; infatuation, fondness, dotage; one's blind side

2 **gullibility, dupability,** bamboozlability <nf>, cullibility , **deceivability,** seduceability, persuadability, hoaxability; biddability; easiness <nf>, softness, weakness; **simpleness,** simplicity, **ingenuousness, unsophistication; greenness,** naïveness, **naïveté,** naivety

3 **superstition,** superstitiousness; popular belief, **old wives' tale;** tradition, lore, folklore; charm, spell 691

4 trusting soul; **dupe** 358; sucker *and* patsy *and* easy mark *and* pushover<nf>

VERBS 5 **be credulous,** accept unquestioningly; not boggle at anything, **believe anything,** be easy of belief *or* persuasion, be uncritical, believe at the drop of a hat, be a dupe, think the moon is made of green cheese, buy a pig in a poke

6 <nf or nf terms> kid oneself, fall for, swallow, swallow anything, swallow whole, not choke *or* gag on; swallow hook, line, and sinker; eat up, lap up, devour, gulp down, gobble up *or* down, buy, buy into, bite, nibble, rise to the fly, take the bait, swing at, go for, tumble for, be taken in, be suckered, be a sucker *or* a patsy *or* an easy mark

7 **be superstitious;** knock on wood, keep one's fingers crossed

ADJS 8 **credulous, knee-jerk** <nf>, easy of belief, ready *or* inclined to believe, easily taken in; **undoubting** 953.21; **trustful, trusting; unsuspicious, unsuspecting;** unthinking, uncritical, unskeptical; overcredulous, overtrustful, overtrusting, overconfiding; fond, infatuated, doting; **superstitious**

9 **gullible, dupable,** bamboozlable <nf>, cullible , **deceivable, foolable, deludable, exploitable,** victimizable, seduceable, persuadable, hoaxable, humbugable, hoodwinkable; biddable; soft, easy <nf>, **simple; ingenuous, unsophisticated, green, naive** 416.5

955 UNBELIEF

NOUNS 1 **unbelief, disbelief,** nonbelief, unbelievingness, discredit; refusal *or* inability to believe; **incredulity** 956; **unpersuadedness,** unconvincedness, lack of conviction; **denial** 335.2, **rejection** 372; misbelief, heresy 688.2; infidelity, atheism, **agnosticism** 695.6; minimifidianism, nullifidianism

2 **doubt, doubtfulness, dubiousness,** dubiety; half-belief; **reservation, question,** question in one's mind; **skepticism,** skepticalness; total skepticism, Pyrrhonism; **suspicion,** suspiciousness, wariness, leeriness, **distrust, mistrust, misdoubt,** distrustfulness, mistrustfulness; **misgiving,** self-doubt, diffidence; qualm; scruple *and* scrupulousness ; hesitation; apprehension 127.4; **uncertainty** 971; shadow of doubt, credibility gap

3 **unbelievability,** unbelievableness, **incredibility, implausibility,** impossibility, improbability, inconceivability, untenableness, untenability; unpersuasiveness, unconvincingness; **doubtfulness, questionableness;** credibility gap; unreliability 971.6

4 doubter, doubting Thomas; scoffer, skeptic, cynic, pooh-poohser, naysayer, disbeliever, nonbeliever, unbeliever 695.11

VERBS **5** **disbelieve,** unbelieve, misbelieve, **not believe,** find hard to believe, not admit, refuse to admit, not buy <nf>, take no stock in *and* set no store by <nf>; **discredit,** refuse to credit, refuse to give credence to, give no credit *or* credence to; gag on, **not swallow** 956.3; negate, **deny** 335.4, naysay, say nay; scoff at, pooh-pooh; **reject** 372.2

6 **doubt, be doubtful, be dubious, be skeptical,** doubt the truth of, beg leave to doubt, **have one's doubts,** have *or* harbor *or* entertain doubts *or* suspicions, half believe, have reservations, **take with a grain of salt,** be from Missouri <nf>, scruple , **distrust, mistrust,** misgive, cross one's fingers; **be uncertain** 971.9; **suspect,** smell a rat *and* see something funny <nf>; **question,** query, **challenge, contest, dispute,** cast doubt on, greet with skepticism, keep one's eye on, treat with reserve, bring *or* call into question, raise a question, throw doubt upon, awake a doubt *or* suspicion; **doubt one's word,** give one the lie; doubt oneself, be diffident

7 **be unbelievable,** be incredible, be hard to swallow, defy belief, pass belief, be hard to believe, strain one's credulity, **stagger belief;** shake one's faith, undermine one's faith; perplex, boggle the mind, stagger, fill with doubt

ADJS **8** **unbelieving, disbelieving,** nonbelieving; faithless, without faith; unconfident, unconvinced, unconverted; nullifidian, minimifidian, creedless; **incredulous** 956.4; repudiative; **heretical** 688.9; **irreligious** 695.17

9 **doubting, doubtful, in doubt, dubious; questioning; skeptical,** Pyrrhonic, from Missouri <nf>; **distrustful, mistrustful, untrustful,** mistrusting, untrusting; **suspicious,** suspecting, scrupulous , shy, wary, leery; **agnostic; uncertain**

10 **unbelievable, incredible,** unthinkable, **implausible,** unimaginable, inconceivable, not to be believed, **hard to believe,** hard of belief, beyond belief, unworthy of belief, not meriting *or* not deserving belief, tall <nf>; **defying belief,** staggering belief, passing belief; **mind-boggling,** preposterous, absurd, ridiculous, unearthly, ungodly; **doubtful, dubious,** doubtable, dubitable, **questionable,** problematic, problematical, **unconvincing,** open to doubt *or* suspicion; **suspicious,** suspect, funny; so-called, self-styled; thin *and* a bit thin <nf>; thick *and* a bit thick *and* a little too thick <nf>

11 under a cloud, unreliable

12 **doubted, questioned,** disputed, contested, moot; **distrusted,** mistrusted; **suspect,** suspected, **under suspicion,** under a cloud; **discredited,** exploded, rejected, **disbelieved**

ADVS **13** **unbelievingly,** doubtingly, **doubtfully, dubiously,** questioningly, **skeptically,** suspiciously; **with a grain of salt,** with reservations, with some allowance, with caution

14 **unbelievably, incredibly,** unthinkably, implausibly, inconceivably, unimaginably, staggeringly

956 INCREDULITY

NOUNS 1 **incredulity, incredulousness,** uncredulousness, refusal *or* disinclination to believe, resistance *or* resistiveness to belief, toughmindedness, hardheadedness, **inconvincibility,** unconvincibility, unpersuadability, unpersuasibility; **suspiciousness,** suspicion, wariness, leeriness, guardedness, cautiousness, caution; **skepticism** 955.2

2 **ungullibility,** uncullibility , **undupability, undeceivability,** unhoaxability, unseduceability; **sophistication**

VERBS 3 **refuse to believe,** resist believing, **not allow oneself to believe,** be slow to believe *or* accept; not kid oneself <nf>; **disbelieve** 955.5; **be skeptical** 955.6; **not swallow,** not be able to swallow *or* down <nf>, not go for *and* **not fall for** <nf>, not be taken in by; **not accept, not buy** *or* **buy into** <nf>, **reject** 372.2

ADJS 4 **incredulous,** uncredulous, **hard of belief,** shy of belief, disposed to doubt, indisposed *or* disinclined to believe, unwilling to accept; impervious to persuasion, **inconvincible,** unconvincible, unpersuadable, unpersuasible; **suspicious, suspecting,** wary, leery, cautious, guarded; **skeptical** 955.9

5 **ungullible,** uncullible , **undupable, undeceivable, unfoolable, undeludable,** unhoaxable, unseduceable, hoaxproof; **sophisticated, wise, hardheaded,** practical, realistic, tough-minded; nobody's fool, not born yesterday, nobody's sucker *or* patsy <nf>

957 EVIDENCE, PROOF

NOUNS 1 **evidence, proof; reason to believe,** reason, grounds for belief; **ground, grounds,** material grounds, **facts, data,** information, record, premises, basis for belief; piece *or* item of evidence, **fact,** datum, relevant fact; **indication, manifestation, sign, symptom,** mark, token, mute witness; body of evidence, documentation; muniments, title deeds and papers; chain of evidence; **clue;** exhibit; intelligence; lowdown <nf>

2 **testimony, attestation,** attest , **witness;** testimonial, testimonium ; **statement, declaration, assertion,** asseveration, affirmation 334, avouchment, avowal, averment, allegation, admission, **disclosure** 351, profession, word; confession; **deposition,** legal evidence, sworn evidence *or* testimony; *procès-verbal* <Fr>; compurgation; affidavit, sworn statement; instrument in proof, *pièce justificative* <Fr>

3 **proof, demonstration,** ironclad proof, incontrovertible proof, proof positive, conclusive proof; **determination, establishment, settlement; conclusive evidence,** indisputable evidence, incontrovertible evidence, damning evidence, unmistakable sign, sure sign, absolute indication, smoking gun <nf>; open-and-shut case; burden of proof, onus, *onus probandi* <L>; the proof of the pudding

4 **confirmation, substantiation,** proof, proving, proving out, bearing out, affirmation, attestation, **authentication, validation, certification,** ratification, **verification; corroboration, support,** supporting evidence, corroboratory evidence, fortification, buttressing, bolstering, backing, backing up, reinforcement, undergirding, strengthening, circumstantiation, fact sheet; **documentation;** proof of purchase

5 **citation,** cite <nf>, **reference,** quotation; **exemplification,** instance, example, case, case in point, particular, item, illustration, demonstration; cross reference

6 **witness, eyewitness,** spectator, earwitness; **bystander,** passerby; **deponent, testifier,** attestant, attester, attestator, voucher, swearer; **informant,** informer; character witness; cojuror, compurgator

7 **provability, demonstrability,** determinability; confirmability, supportability, verifiability

VERBS 8 **evidence, evince,** furnish evidence, **show, go to show, mean,** tend to show, witness to, testify to; **demonstrate, illustrate,** exhibit, manifest, display, express, set forth; approve; **attest; indicate, signify,** signalize, symptomatize, mark, **denote, betoken, point to,** give indication of, show signs of, bear on, touch on; **connote, imply, suggest,** involve; argue, breathe, tell, bespeak; **speak for itself,** speak volumes

9 **testify, attest, give evidence,** witness, witness to, **give** *or* **bear witness; disclose** 351.4; vouch, state one's case, **depose,** depone, **warrant, swear,** take one's oath, acknowledge, avow, **affirm,** avouch, aver, allege, asseverate, **certify, give one's word;** turn state's evidence, rat *and* squeal *and* sing <nf>; grass <Brit nf>

10 **prove, demonstrate, show,** afford proof of, prove to be, prove true; **establish,** fix, **determine, ascertain,** make out, remove all doubt; **settle,** settle the matter; **set at rest;** clinch *and* cinch *and* nail down <nf>; **prove one's point,** make one's case, bring home to, make good, have *or* make out a case; hold good, hold water; follow, follow from, follow as a matter of course

11 **confirm,** affirm, **attest,** warrant, uphold <Brit nf>, **substantiate, authenticate, validate, certify,** ratify, **verify;** circumstantiate, **corroborate, bear out,** support, buttress, **sustain,** fortify, bolster, back, back up, reinforce, undergird, strengthen; **document;** probate, prove; double-check

12 **adduce,** produce, **advance, present,** bring to bear, **offer,** proffer, invoke, obtest, allege , plead, **bring forward,** bring on; rally, marshal, deploy, array; call to witness, call to *or* put in the witness box

13 **cite, name,** call to mind; **instance,** cite a particular *or* particulars, cite cases *or* a case in point, itemize, particularize, produce an instance, give a for-instance <nf>; **exemplify,** example , **illustrate,** demonstrate; **document; quote,** quote chapter and verse

14 **refer to,** direct attention to, **appeal to,** invoke; make reference to; cross-refer, make a cross-reference; reference, cross-reference

15 **have evidence** *or* **proof,** have a case, possess incriminating evidence, **have something on** <nf>; **have the goods on** *and* have dead to rights *or* bang to rights <nf>

ADJS **16** **evidential,** evidentiary, **factual,** symptomatic, **significant, relevant, indicative,** attestative, attestive, probative; founded on, grounded on, based on; implicit, suggestive; material, telling, convincing, weighty; overwhelming, damning; **conclusive,** determinative, **decisive,** final, incontrovertible, irresistible, indisputable, irrefutable, sure, certain, absolute; documented, documentary; **valid, admissible;** adducible; firsthand, authentic, reliable 970.17, empirical, eyewitness; hearsay, circumstantial, presumptive, nuncupative, cumulative, ex parte

17 **demonstrative,** demonstrating, demonstrational, telltale; evincive, apodictic

18 **confirming,** confirmatory, confirmative, certificatory; substantiating, **verifying,** verificative; **corroborating,** corroboratory, **corroborative,** supportive, **supporting**

19 **provable, demonstrable,** demonstratable, apodictic, evincible, attestable, **confirmable,** checkable, **substantiatable, establishable,** supportable, sustainable, **verifiable,** validatable, authenticatable

20 **proved, proven, demonstrated,** shown; **established,** fixed, **settled, determined,** nailed down <nf>, ascertained; evident, self-evident; **confirmed, substantiated,** attested, **authenticated, certified, validated, verified;** circumstantiated, **corroborated,** borne out; cross-checked, double-checked; collated; ostensible

21 **unrefuted,** unconfuted, unanswered, uncontroverted, uncontradicted, **undenied; unrefutable** 970.15

ADVS **22** **evidentially,** according to the evidence, on the evidence, as attested by, judging by; **in confirmation, in corroboration of, in support of;** at first hand, at second hand; dead to rights *or* bang to rights *and* with a smoking gun *and* with one's pants down <nf>

23 **to illustrate,** to prove the point, as an example, as a case in point, to name an instance, by way of example, **for example, for instance,** to cite an instance, as an instance, e.g., *exempli gratia* <L>; as, **thus**

24 **which see, q.v.,** *quod vide* <L>; *loco citato* <L>, loc cit; *opere citato* <L>, op cit

PHRS **25 it is proven,** *probatum est* <L>, there is nothing more to be said, it must follow; QED, *quod erat demonstrandum* <L>

958 DISPROOF

NOUNS **1 disproof,** disproving, disproval, **invalidation,** disconfirmation, explosion, negation, redargution ; exposure, exposé; *reductio ad absurdum* <L>; circumstantial evidence, hearsay evidence, inadmissible evidence, incriminating evidence

2 **refutation, confutation,** confounding, refutal, **rebuttal, answer,** complete answer, crushing *or* effective rejoinder, squelch, comeback; discrediting; **overthrow,** overthrowal, upset, upsetting, subversion, undermining, demolition; renunciation; contention; **contradiction,** controversion, **denial** 335.2

3 **conclusive argument, elenchus, knockdown argument, floorer,** sockdolager <nf>; **clincher** *or* crusher *or* **settler** *and* finisher *and* squelcher <nf>

VERBS **4 disprove, invalidate,** disconfirm, discredit, prove the contrary, belie, give the lie to, redargue ; **negate,** negative; **expose, show up;** explode, blow up, blow sky-high, **puncture,** deflate, **shoot** *or* **poke full of holes, cut to pieces, cut the ground from under; knock the bottom out of** <nf>, knock the props *or* chocks out from under, knock down, take the ground from under, undercut, cut the ground from under one's feet, not leave a leg to stand on, have the last word, leave nothing to say, put *or* lay to rest

5 **refute, confute, confound, rebut,** parry, answer, **answer conclusively,** dismiss, dispose of; **overthrow,** overturn, overwhelm, upset, subvert, defeat, demolish, undermine; argue down, argue into a corner; show what's what; floor *and* finish *and* settle *and* squash *and* squelch <nf>, crush, smash all opposition; silence, put *or* reduce to silence, shut up, stop the mouth of; nonplus, take the wind out of one's sails; **contradict,** controvert, counter, run counter, **deny** 335.4

ADJS **6 refuting, confuting,** confounding, confutative, refutative, refutatory, discomfirmatory; contradictory, contrary 335.5

7 **disproved,** disconfirmed, **invalidated,** negated, negatived, discredited, belied; **exposed,** shown up; **punctured,** deflated, **exploded; refuted,** confuted, confounded; **upset, overthrown,** overturned; **contradicted,** disputed, denied, impugned; dismissed, discarded, rejected 372.3

8 **unproved,** not proved, unproven, **undemonstrated,** unshown, not shown; **untried,** untested; **unestablished,** unfixed, **unsettled, undetermined,** unascertained; **unconfirmed, unsubstantiated,** unattested, **unauthenticated,** unvalidated, uncertified, **unverified; uncorroborated,** unsustained, **unsupported,** unsupported by evidence, **groundless,** without grounds *or* basis, **unfounded** 936.13; **inconclusive,** indecisive; **moot,** sub judice; not following

9 **unprovable,** controvertible, **undemonstrable,** undemonstratable, unattestable, unsubstantiatable, **unsupportable,** unconfirmable, unsustainable, unverifiable

10 **refutable,** confutable; **disprovable,** defeasible

959 QUALIFICATION

NOUNS **1 qualification, limitation, limiting, restriction,** circumscription, **modification,** hedge, hedging; setting conditions, conditionality, provisionality, circumstantiality; specification; **allowance, concession,** cession, grant; grain of salt; **reservation, exception,** waiver, exemption; **exclusion,** ruling out, including out <nf>; specialness, special circumstance, special case, special treatment; **mental reservation,** salvo , *arrière-pensée* <Fr>, crossing one's fingers; extenuating circumstances

2 **condition, provision, proviso, stipulation,** whereas; definition; frame of reference; **specification,** parameter, given, *donnée* <Fr>, **limitation,** limiting condition, boundary condition; **contingency, circumstance** 766; **catch** *and* joker *and* kicker *and* string *and* a string to it <nf>; **requisite, prerequisite,** obligation; *sine qua non* <L>, *conditio sine qua non* <L>; clause, escape clause, escapeway, escape hatch, saving clause; escalator clause; **terms,** provisions; grounds; small *or* fine print *and* fine print at the bottom <nf>; ultimatum

VERBS **3** **qualify, limit,** condition , hedge, hedge about, **modify, restrict,** restrain, circumscribe, delimit, set limits *or* conditions, box in <nf>, narrow, set criteria; adjust to, regulate by; alter 852.6; **temper, season,** leaven, soften, modulate, moderate, assuage, **mitigate,** palliate, abate, reduce, diminish

4 **make conditional,** make contingent, **condition;** make it a condition, attach a condition *or* proviso, **stipulate;** insist upon, make a point of; **have a catch** *and* have a joker *or* kicker *and* have a joker in the deck *and* have a string attached <nf>; cross one's fingers behind one's back

5 **allow for, make allowance for,** make room for, provide for, open the door to, take account of, **take into account** *or* **consideration, consider,** consider the circumstances; allow, **grant, concede,** admit, admit exceptions, see the special circumstances; **relax,** relax the condition, **waive, set aside,** ease, lift temporarily, pull one's punches <nf>; disregard, **discount,** leave out of account; consider the source, take with a grain of salt

6 **depend,** hang, rest, hinge; **depend on** *or* **upon, hang on** *or* **upon, rest on** *or* **upon,** rest with, repose upon, lie on, lie with, stand on *or* upon, be based on, be bounded *or* limited by, be dependent on, be predicated on, **be contingent** *or* **conditional on; hinge on** *or* **upon, turn on** *or* **upon, revolve on** *or* **upon,** have as a fulcrum

ADJS **7** **qualifying,** qualificative, qualificatory, **modifying,** modificatory, altering; **limiting, limitational, restricting,** limitative, restrictive, bounding; circumstantial, contingent; **extenuating,** extenuatory, **mitigating,** mitigative, mitigatory, modulatory, palliative, assuasive, lenitive, softening

8 **conditional, provisional,** provisory, stipulatory; parametric; specificative; **specified, stipulated,** defined, fixed, stated, given; **temporary,** expedient

9 **contingent, dependent, depending;** contingent on, **dependent on, depending on,** predicated on, based on, hanging *or* hinging on, turning on, revolving on; depending on circumstances; circumscribed by, hedged *or* hedged about by; boxed in <nf>; **subject to,** incidental to, incident to

10 **qualified, modified, conditioned, limited, restricted,** delimited, hedged, hedged about; **tempered, seasoned,** leavened, palliative, softened, moderated, **mitigated,** modulated

ADVS **11** **conditionally, provisionally, with qualifications,** with a string *or* catch *or* joker *or* kicker to it <nf>; with a reservation *or* an exception, with a grain of salt; **temporarily,** for the time being

CONJS **12** **provided,** provided that, provided always, **providing,** with this proviso, it being provided; **on condition,** on condition that, **with the stipulation,** with the understanding, according as, subject to

13 **granting, admitting, allowing,** admitting that, allowing that, seeing that; exempting, waiving

14 if, an *or* an' , if and when, only if, if only, if and only if, if it be so, if it be true that, if it so happens *or* turns out

15 **so,** just so, so that , **so as, so long as, as long as**

16 **unless,** unless that, **if not, were it not,** were it not that; **except, excepting,** except that, with the exception that, save, **but; without,** absent

960 NO QUALIFICATIONS

NOUNS **1** **unqualifiedness,** unlimitedness, **unconditionality,** unrestrictedness, **unreservedness,** uncircumscribedness; categoricalness; **absoluteness,** definiteness, **explicitness;** decisiveness

ADJS **2** **unqualified, unconditional,** unconditioned, **unrestricted,** unhampered, **unlimited,** uncircumscribed, unmitigated, **categorical,** straight, **unreserved,** without reserve; unaltered, unadulterated, intact; **implicit,** unquestioning, undoubting, unhesitating; **explicit, express, unequivocal,** clear, unmistakable; **peremptory,** indisputable, inappealable; **without exception,** admitting no exception, unwaivable; **positive, absolute, flat,** definite, definitive, determinate, decided, decisive, fixed, final, conclusive; **complete, entire, whole, total,** global; **utter,** perfect, downright, outright, out-and-out, straight-out <nf>, all-out, flat-out <nf>

ADVS **3** <nf terms> **no ifs, ands,** ***or*** **buts; no strings attached,** no holds barred, no catch *or* joker *or* kicker, no joker in the deck, no small print *or* fine print, no fine print at the bottom; downright, that's that, what you see is what you get

961 FORESIGHT

NOUNS **1** **foresight,** foreseeing, looking ahead, **prevision,** divination 962.2, forecast; **prediction** 962; **foreglimpse,** foreglance, foregleam; preview, prepublication; **prospect,** prospection; **anticipation,** contemplation, envisionment, envisagement; **foresightedness; farsightedness,** longsightedness, farseeingness; sagacity, providence, discretion, preparation, provision, forehandedness, readiness, consideration, prudence 920.7

2 **forethought, premeditation,** predeliberation, preconsideration 380.3; caution 494; lead time, advance notice; run-up; plan, long-range plan, contingency plan; prospectus

3 **foreknowledge,** foreknowing, forewisdom, **precognition,** prescience, presage, presentiment, foreboding; clairvoyance 689.8; foreseeability 962.8; insight; premonition, expectation

4 **foretaste,** antepast , prelibation

VERBS **5** **foresee,** see beforehand *or* ahead, foreglimpse, foretaste, **anticipate,** contemplate, envision, envisage, **look forward to,** look ahead, look beyond, look *or* pry *or* peep into the future; **predict** 962.9; think ahead *or* beforehand; have an eye to the future

6 **foreknow,** know beforehand, precognize, know in advance, have prior knowledge; smell in the wind, scent from afar; **have a presentiment, have a premonition** 133.10; see the handwriting on the wall, have a hunch *or* feel in one's bones <nf>, just know, intuit 934.4

ADJS **7** **foreseeing, foresighted; foreknowing, precognizant,** precognitive, prescient; divinatory 962.11; **forethoughted,** forethoughtful; anticipant, anticipatory, expectant; **farseeing, farsighted,** longsighted; sagacious, provident, providential, forehanded, prepared, ready, prudent 920.19; intuitive 934.5; clairvoyant, telepathic

8 foreseeable 962.13; foreseen 962.14; predictable; intuitable

ADVS **9** **foreseeingly, foreknowingly,** with foresight; against the time when, for a rainy day

962 PREDICTION

NOUNS **1 prediction, foretelling,** foreshowing, forecasting, **prognosis,** prognostication, presage , presaging; **prophecy,** prophesying, vaticination; **soothsaying,** soothsay; prefiguration, prefigurement, prefiguring; preshowing, presignifying, presigning ; **forecast, promise;** apocalypse; prospectus; foresight 961; presentiment, foreboding; omen 133.3,5; **guesswork,** speculation, guestimation <nf>, hunch, feeling; **probability** 968, statistical prediction, actuarial prediction; improbability 969

2 divination, divining; **augury,** haruspication, haruspicy, pythonism, mantic, mantology ; **fortunetelling,** crystal gazing, palm-reading, palmistry, tea-leaf reading, tarot reading, I Ching; crystal ball; astrology, horoscopy, astrology 1072.20; sorcery 690; clairvoyance 689.8, telepathy

3 dowsing, witching, water witching; **divining rod** *or* stick, wand, witch *or* witching stick, dowsing rod, doodlebug; water diviner, dowser, water witch *or* witcher; hydromancy

4 predictor, foreteller, prognosticator, seer, foreseer, forecaster, foreknower, presager , prefigurer; **forecaster;** prophet, prophesier, soothsayer, *vates* <L>; **diviner,** divinator; augur; psychic 689.13; clairvoyant; prophetess, seeress, divineress, pythoness; Druid; **fortuneteller;** crystal gazer; palmist; geomancer; haruspex *or* aruspex, astrologer 1072.23; weather prophet 317.6; prophet of doom, calamity howler, Cassandra; prophets 684; speculator

5 <nf terms> **dopester, tipster, tout** *or* touter

6 sibyl; Pythia, Pythian, Delphic sibyl; Babylonian *or* Persian sibyl, Cimmerian sibyl, Cumaean sibyl, Erythraean sibyl, Hellespontine *or* Trojan sibyl, Libyan sibyl, Phrygian sibyl, Samian sibyl, Tiburtine sibyl

7 oracle; Delphic *or* Delphian oracle, Python, Pythian oracle; Delphic tripod, tripod of the Pythia; Dodona, oracle *or* oak of Dodona; sage

8 predictability, divinability, foretellableness, **calculability, foreseeability,** foreknowableness

VERBS **9 predict,** make a prediction, **foretell, soothsay,** prefigure, **forecast, prophesy, prognosticate,** call <nf>, make a prophecy *or* prognosis, vaticinate, forebode, presage, see ahead, see *or* tell the future, read the future, see in the crystal ball; **foresee** 961.5; dope *and* dope out <nf>; call the turn *and* call one's shot <nf>; **divine;** witch *or* dowse for water; **tell fortunes,** fortune-tell, cast one's fortune; read one's hand, read palms, read tea leaves, cast a horoscope *or* nativity; **guess,** speculate, guesstimate <nf>, make an educated guess; **bet, bet on, gamble**

10 portend, foretoken 133.11, foreshow, foreshadow

ADJS **11 predictive,** predictory, predictional; **foretelling,** forewarning, forecasting; prefiguring, prefigurative, presignifying, presignificative; **prophetic,** prophetical, fatidic, fatidical, apocalyptic, apocalyptical; vatic, vaticinatory, vaticinal, mantic, sibyllic, sibylline, fatidic, fatidical; **divinatory, oracular,** auguring, augural; haruspical; **foreseeing** 961.7; presageful, presaging; **prognostic,** prognosticative, prognosticatory; fortunetelling; weather-wise

12 ominous, premonitory, foreboding 133.16, unfavorable, adverse

13 predictable, divinable, foretellable, calculable, anticipatable; **foreseeable, foreknowable,** precognizable; **probable** 968.6; improbable 969.3

14 predicted, prophesied, presaged, **foretold, forecast,** foreshown; foreseen, foreglimpsed, **foreknown**

963 NECESSITY

NOUNS **1 necessity,** necessariness, necessitude , necessitation, entailment; mandatoriness, mandatedness, obligatoriness, **obligation,** obligement; compulsoriness, **compulsion, duress** 424.3

2 **requirement, requisite,** requisition; **necessity, need, want,** occasion; need for, **call for, demand,** demand for; desideratum, desideration; **prerequisite,** prerequirement; **must,** must item; sine qua non; **essential,** indispensable, must-have; the necessary, the needful; necessities, necessaries, essentials, bare necessities, fundamentals

3 **needfulness,** requisiteness; **essentiality,** essentialness, vitalness; **indispensability,** indispensableness; irreplaceability; irreducibleness, irreducibility

4 **urgent need, dire necessity; exigency** *or* exigence, **urgency,** imperative, imperativeness, immediacy, pressingness, pressure; matter of necessity, case of need *or* emergency, **matter of life and death; predicament** 1013.4

5 **involuntariness,** unwilledness, **instinctiveness;** compulsiveness; reflex action, Pavlovian reaction, conditioning, automatism; echolalia, echopraxia; automatic writing; **instinct,** impulse 365; blind impulse *or* instinct, knee-jerk reaction, sheer chemistry

6 **choicelessness,** no choice, no alternative, lack of choice, **Hobson's choice,** only choice, zero option, coercion; Catch-22; that *or* nothing; not a pin to choose, six of one and half a dozen of the other, distinction without a difference; indiscrimination 945

7 **inevitability,** inevitableness, **unavoidableness,** necessity, inescapableness, inevasibleness, unpreventability, undeflectability, ineluctability; irrevocability, indefeasibility; uncontrollability; relentlessness, inexorability, unyieldingness, inflexibility; fatedness, fatefulness, **certainty,** sureness; *force majeure* <Fr>, vis major, act of God, inevitable accident, unavoidable casualty; **predetermination;** God's will, will of Allah; doom, karma, one's lot, **fate** 964.2

VERBS 8 **necessitate, oblige,** dictate, **constrain;** coerce, impel, force, mandate; insist upon, **compel** 424.4

9 **require, need, want,** lack, must have, feel the want of, have occasion for, be in need of, be hurting for <nf>, stand in need of, not be able to dispense with, not be able to do without; **call for,** cry for, cry out for, clamor for; **demand,** ask, claim, exact; prerequire ; need *or* want doing, take doing <nf>, be indicated

10 **be necessary,** lie under a necessity, be one's fate; be a must <nf>; can't be avoided, can't be helped; be under the necessity of, be in for; be obliged, **must,** need *or* needs must , **have to,** have got to <nf>, should, need, **need to,** have need to; not able to keep from, not able to help, **cannot help but,** cannot do otherwise; be forced *or* driven

11 **have no choice** *or* **alternative,** have one's options reduced *or* closed *or* eliminated, have no option but, cannot choose but, be robbed *or* relieved of choice; be pushed to the wall, be driven into a corner; take it *or* leave it *and* like it *or* lump it <nf>, have that *or* nothing

ADJS 12 **necessary, obligatory, compulsory,** entailed, mandatory, fundamental; **exigent, urgent,** necessitous, importunate, **imperative;** choiceless, without choice, out of one's hands *or* control

13 **requisite, needful, required, needed,** necessary, **wanted, called for,** indicated, imperative; **essential, vital, indispensable,** unforgoable, irreplaceable; irreducible, irreductible; prerequisite

14 **involuntary, instinctive, automatic, mechanical,** reflex, reflexive, knee-jerk <nf>, autonomic, conditioned; **unconscious,** unthinking, blind; **unwitting,** unintentional, independent of one's will, unwilling, unwilled, against one's will, collateral; compulsory, **compulsive;** forced; **impulsive** 365.9

15 **inevitable, unavoidable,** necessary, **inescapable,** inevasible, unpreventable, undeflectable, ineluctable, irrevocable, indefeasible; uncontrolla-

ble, unstoppable; relentless, inexorable, unyielding, inflexible; irresistible, resistless; **certain,** fateful, **sure,** sure as fate, sure as death, sure as death and taxes; preordained, predestined, **destined, fated** 964.9; necessitarian, deterministic

ADVS **16** **necessarily, needfully,** requisitely; **of necessity,** from necessity, need *or* needs , perforce; without choice; **willy-nilly,** *nolens volens* <L>, willing *or* unwilling, *bon gré mal gré* <Fr>, whether one will *or* not; come what may; compulsorily

17 **if necessary, if need be,** if worst comes to worst; for lack of something better, *faute de mieux* <Fr>

18 **involuntarily, instinctively, automatically, mechanically,** by reflex, reflexively; blindly, **unconsciously,** unthinkingly, without premeditation; **unwittingly,** unintentionally; **compulsively; unwillingly** 325.8

19 **inevitably, unavoidably,** necessarily, **inescapably,** come hell *or* high water <nf>, inevasibly, unpreventably, ineluctably; irrevocably, indefeasibly; uncontrollably; relentlessly, inexorably, unyieldingly, inflexibly; fatefully, **certainly, surely**

PHRS **20** **it is necessary, it must be,** if need be, it needs must be *or* it must needs be , it will be, there's no two ways about it, it must have its way; it cannot be helped, there is no helping it *or* help for it, that's the way the cookie crumbles *or* the ball bounces <nf>, what will be will be, it's God's will; the die is cast; it is fated 964.11

964 PREDETERMINATION

NOUNS **1** **predetermination, predestination,** foredestiny, **preordination,** foreordination, foreordainment; decree; foregone conclusion, par for the course <nf>, preconceived notion *or* opinion; **necessity** 963; foreknowledge, prescience 961.3

2 **fate,** fatality, **fortune, lot,** cup, portion, appointed lot, **karma**, kismet, weird, future 839; **destiny,** destination, **end,** final lot; **doom,** foredoom , God's will, will of Heaven; **inevitability** 963.7; the handwriting on the wall; book of fate; Fortune's wheel, wheel of fortune *or* chance; astral influences, stars, planets, constellation, astrology 1072.20; unlucky day, ides of March, Friday, Friday the thirteenth, *dies funestis* <L>

3 **Fates,** *Fata* <L>, Parcae, Clotho, Lachesis, Atropos; Nona, Decuma, Morta; Weird Sisters, Weirds; Norns; Urdur, Verthandi, Skuld; Fortuna, Lady *or* Dame Fortune, *Tyche* <Gk>; Providence, Heaven

4 **determinism, fatalism,** necessitarianism, necessarianism, predeterminism; predestinarianism, Calvinism, election

5 **determinist, fatalist,** necessitarian, necessarian; predestinationist, predestinarian, Calvinist

VERBS **6** **predetermine, predecide,** preestablish, preset; **predestine,** predestinate, **preordain,** foreordain; agree beforehand, preconcert

7 **destine, predestine,** necessitate 963.8, destinate , **ordain,** fate, mark, appoint, decree, intend; come with the territory <nf>; have in store for; **doom,** foredoom

ADJS **8** **determined, predetermined, predecided,** preestablished, **predestined,** predestinate, **preordained,** foreordained; foregone; open-and-shut; arranged

9 **destined, fated,** fateful, fatal , ordained, written, in the cards, marked, appointed , in store, cut-and-dried; **doomed,** foredoomed, devoted; inevitable 963.15

10 **deterministic, fatalistic,** necessitarian, necessarian

PHRS **11** **it is fated, it is written,** it's in the cards; what will be will be, *che sarà sarà* <Ital>, *que será será* <Sp>; *c'est la vie* and *c'est la guerre* <Fr>

965 PREARRANGEMENT

NOUNS **1** **prearrangement,** preordering, preconcertedness; premeditation, plotting, planning, scheming; directed verdict; **reservation,** booking; overbooking

2 <nf terms> **put-up job,** packed *or* rigged game *or* jury, packed deal, stacked deck, cold deck, boat race, tank job; **frame-up,** frame, setup

3 **schedule, program,** programma, **bill,** card, **calendar,** docket, slate; playbill; batting order, **lineup, roster,** rota <chiefly Brit>; blueprint, budget; **prospectus;** schedule *or* program of operation, **order of the day,** things to be done, **agenda,** list of agenda; protocol; laundry list *and* wish list <nf>; **bill of fare, menu,** *carte du jour* <Fr>

VERBS 4 **prearrange,** precontrive, predesign , preorder, preconcert; premeditate, plot, plan, scheme; **reserve,** book, overbook

5 <nf terms> **fix, rig,** pack, cook, cook up; **stack the cards,** colddeck, pack the deal; put in the bag, sew up; frame, frame-up, set up; **throw,** tank, go in the tank, hold a boat race

6 **schedule, line up** <nf>, **slate, book,** book in, bill, program, calendar, docket, budget, put on the agenda

ADJS 7 **prearranged,** precontrived, predesigned , preordered, preconcerted, cut out; premeditated, plotted, planned, schemed; cut-and-dried, cut-and-dry

8 <nf terms> **fixed, rigged, put-up,** packed, stacked, cooked, cooked-up; **in the bag,** on ice, iced, cinched, sewed up; **framed, framed-up,** set-up

9 **scheduled, slated,** booked, billed, booked-in, to come

966 POSSIBILITY

NOUNS 1 **possibility,** possibleness, **the realm of possibility,** the domain of the possible, conceivableness, **conceivability,** thinkability, thinkableness, imaginability; **probability, likelihood** 968.1; what may be, what might be, what is possible, what one can do, what can be done, the possible, the attainable, the feasible; **potential, potentiality,** virtuality; contingency, eventuality; **chance, prospect, odds; outside chance** <nf>, off chance, remote possibility, ghost of a chance; hope, outside hope, small hope, slim odds; **good possibility, good chance,** safe bet, even chance 972.7; bare possibility 972.9

2 **practicability, practicality, feasibility; workability,** operability, actability, performability, realizability, negotiability; **viability,** viableness; **achievability,** doability, compassability, **attainability;** surmountability, superability; realm of possibility

3 **accessibility,** access, **approachability, openness,** reachableness, come-at-ableness *and* get-at-ableness <nf>; **penetrability,** perviousness; **obtainability,** obtainableness, **availability, donability, procurability,** procurableness, securableness, getableness, acquirability

VERBS 4 **be possible,** could be, might be, **have** *or* **stand a chance** *or* **good chance, bid fair to**

5 make possible, **enable,** permit, permit of, clear the road *or* path for, smooth the way for, open the way for, open the door to, open up the possibility of, give a chance to

ADJS 6 **possible,** within the bounds *or* realm *or* range *or* domain of possibility, in one's power, in one's hands, humanly possible; **probable, likely** 968.6; **conceivable,** conceivably possible, **imaginable, thinkable,** cogitable; plausible 968.7; **potential,** virtual; contingent; able, apt

7 **practicable, practical, feasible; workable,** actable, performable, effectible , realizable, compassable, operable, negotiable, doable, swingable, bridgeable; **viable; achievable, attainable;** surmountable, superable, overcomable

8 **accessible, approachable,** come-at-able *and* get-at-able <nf>, **reachable,** within reach; **open,** open to; **penetrable,** get-in-able <nf>, pervious; **obtainable, attainable, available,** procurable, securable, findable, easy to come by, getable, to be had, donable

ADVS 9 **possibly, conceivably,** imaginably, feasibly; within the realm of possibility; **perhaps,** perchance, haply; maybe, it may be, for all *or* aught one knows

10 **by any possibility, by any chance,** by any means, **by any manner of means;** in any way, in any possible way, **at any cost, at all,** if at all, ever; on the bare possibility, on the off chance; by merest chance

11 **if possible,** if humanly possible, **God willing,** *Deo volente* <L>, wind and weather permitting, Lord willing and the creek don't rise

967 IMPOSSIBILITY

NOUNS 1 **impossibility,** impossibleness, the realm *or* domain of the impossible, **inconceivability,** unthinkability, unimaginability, what cannot be, what can never be, what cannot happen, hopelessness, Chinaman's chance *and* a snowball's chance in hell *and* no way in hell <nf>, **no chance** 972.10; **self-contradiction,** unreality, absurdity, paradox, oxymoron, logical impossibility; impossible, the impossible, impossibilism; no-no <nf>

2 **impracticability,** unpracticability, **impracticality, unfeasibility; unworkability,** inoperability, unperformability; **unachievability, unattainability;** unrealizability, uncompassability; insurmountability, **insuperability**

3 **inaccessibility,** unaccessibility; **unapproachability,** un-come-at-ableness <nf>, unreachableness; **impenetrability,** imperviousness; **unobtainability,** unobtainableness, **unattainability, unavailability,** unprocurableness, unsecurableness, ungettableness <nf>, unacquirability; undiscoverability, unascertainableness

VERBS 4 **be impossible,** be an impossibility, **not have a chance,** be a waste of time; **contradict itself,** be a logical impossibility, be a paradox; fly in the face of reason

5 **attempt the impossible,** try for a miracle, look for a needle in a haystack *or* in a bottle of hay, try to be in two places at once, try to fetch water in a sieve *or* catch the wind in a net *or* weave a rope of sand *or* get figs from thistles *or* gather grapes from thorns *or* make bricks from straw *or* make cheese of chalk *or* make a silk purse out of a sow's ear *or* change the leopard's spots *or* get blood from a turnip; ask the impossible, cry for the moon; turn back time; walk on water

6 **make impossible, rule out,** disenable, disqualify, close out, **bar,** prohibit, put out of reach, leave no chance, make things difficult

ADJS 7 **impossible, not possible,** beyond the bounds of possibility *or* reason, contrary to reason, at variance with the facts; **inconceivable, unimaginable, unthinkable, not to be thought of, out of the question;** hopeless; **absurd,** ridiculous, preposterous; **self-contradictory,** paradoxical, oxymoronic, logically impossible; **ruled-out,** excluded, closed-out, **barred,** prohibited, forbidden; self-contradictory, self-defeating

8 **impracticable, impractical, unpragmatic, unfeasible; unworkable,** unviable, unperformable, inoperable, undoable, unnegotiable, unbridgeable; **unachievable, unattainable,** uneffectible ; unrealizable, uncompassable; insurmountable, unsurmountable, **insuperable,** unovercomable; **beyond one,** beyond one's power, beyond one's control, out of one's depth, too much for

9 **inaccessible,** unaccessible; **unapproachable,** un-come-at-able <nf>; **unreachable,** beyond reach, out of reach; **impenetrable,** impervious; closed to, denied to, lost to, closed forever to; **unobtainable, unattainable, unavailable,** unprocurable, unsecurable, ungettable <nf>, unacquirable; not to be had, **not to be had for love *or* money;** undiscoverable, unascertainable; back-ordered

ADVS 10 **impossibly, inconceivably,** unimaginably, unthinkably; not at any price

PHRS **11** no can do, no way, no way José <nf>, yeah right <nf>

968 PROBABILITY

NOUNS **1** **probability, likelihood,** likeliness, liability, aptitude, verisimilitude; **chance, odds; expectation, outlook,** prospect; favorable prospect, well-grounded hope, some *or* reasonable hope, fair expectation; **good chance** 972.8; presumption, presumptive evidence; tendency; probable cause, reasonable ground *or* presumption; leaning; probabilism; possibility 966

2 **mathematical probability,** statistical probability, statistics, **predictability;** probability theory, game theory, theory of games; operations research; probable error, standard deviation; stochastic *or* statistical independence, stochastic variable; probability curve, frequency curve, frequency polygon, frequency distribution, probability function, probability density function, probability distribution, cumulative distribution function; **statistical mechanics,** quantum mechanics, uncertainty *or* indeterminancy principle, Maxwell-Boltzmann distribution law, Bose-Einstein statistics, Fermi-Dirac statistics; **mortality table,** actuarial table, life table, combined experience table, Commissioners Standard Ordinary table; blip, hiccup

3 **plausibility; reasonability** 935.9; **credibility** 953.8; verisimilitude

VERBS **4** **be probable, seem likely,** could be, offer a good prospect, offer the expectation, have *or* run a good chance, be in the running, come as no surprise; **promise,** be promising, make fair promise, **bid fair to,** stand fair to, show a tendency, be in the cards, have the makings of, have favorable odds, lead one to expect; **make probable,** probabilize, make more likely, smooth the way for; increase the chances

5 **think likely, daresay,** venture to say; anticipate; **presume,** suppose 951.10

ADJS **6** **probable, likely, liable, apt,** verisimilar, in the cards, odds-on; **promising, hopeful,** fair, in a fair way; foreseeable, **predictable; presumable,** presumptive; **statistical,** actuarial; mathematically *or* statistically probable, predictable within limits; prone, apt

7 **plausible,** colorable, apparent ; **reasonable** 935.20; credible 953.24; **conceivable** 966.6

ADVS **8** **probably, in all probability** *or* **likelihood,** likely, **most likely, very likely;** as likely as not, very like *and* like enough *and* like as not <nf>; **doubtlessly,** doubtless, **no doubt,** indubitably; **presumably,** presumptively; by all odds, ten to one, a hundred to one, dollars to doughnuts

PHRS **9there is reason to believe,** I am led to believe, it can be supposed, it would appear, it stands to reason, it might be thought, one can assume, appearances are in favor of, the chances *or* odds are, you can bank on it, you can make book on it, you can bet on it, you can bet your bottom dollar, you can just bet, you can't go wrong; I daresay, I venture to say

969 IMPROBABILITY

NOUNS **1** **improbability, unlikelihood,** unlikeliness; **doubtfulness,** dubiousness, **questionableness; implausibility,** incredibility 955.3; little expectation, low order of probability, poor possibility, bare possibility, faint likelihood, poor prospect, poor outlook, a ghost of a chance, fat chance <nf>, chance in a million; long shot; **small chance** 972.9; Hollywood ending

VERBS **2** **be improbable, not be likely,** be a stretch of the imagination, strain one's credulity, go beyond reason, go beyond belief, go far afield, go beyond the bounds of reason *or* probability, be far-fetched *or* fetched from afar, be a long shot

ADJS **3** **improbable, unlikely,** unpromising, hardly possible, logic-defying, scarcely to be expected *or* anticipated; statistically improbable; **doubtful,** dubious, **questionable,** doubtable, dubitable, more than doubtful; far-fetched, **implausible,** incredible 955.10; unlooked-for, unexpected, unpredictable; back-ordered

PHRS 4 **not likely!,** no fear!, never fear!, I ask you!, you should live so long! <nf>, don't hold your breath!, don't bet *or* make book on it <nf>

970 CERTAINTY

NOUNS 1 **certainty, certitude,** certainness, **sureness,** surety, **assurance, assuredness,** certain knowledge; **positiveness, absoluteness, definiteness,** dead *or* moral *or* absolute certainty; unequivocalness, unmistakableness, unambiguity, nonambiguity, univocity, univocality; **infallibility,** infallibilism, inerrability, inerrancy; **necessity,** determinacy, determinateness, noncontingency, Hobson's choice, ineluctability, predetermination, predestination, **inevitability** 963.7; **truth** 973; **proved fact,** probatum

2 <nf terms> **sure thing,** dead certainty, dead cert <Brit nf>, dead-sure thing, sure bet, sure card, aces wired, cinch, lead-pipe cinch, dead cinch, lock, mortal lock, shoo-in, open-and-shut case

3 **unquestionability, undeniability,** indubitability, indubitableness, **indisputability,** incontestability, incontrovertibility, **irrefutability,** unrefutability, unconfutability, irrefragability, unimpeachability; **doubtlessness, questionlessness; demonstrability,** provability, verifiability, confirmability; factuality, **reality,** actuality 761.2

4 **reliability, dependability, dependableness, validity, trustworthiness,** faithworthiness; unerringness; predictability, calculability; stability, substantiality, firmness, **soundness,** solidity, staunchness, steadiness, **steadfastness;** secureness, **security;** invincibility 15.4; **authoritativeness, authenticity**

5 **confidence,** confidentness, conviction, belief 953, fixed *or* settled belief, **sureness, assurance, assuredness,** surety, security, certitude; **faith,** subjective certainty; trust 953.1; **positiveness, cocksureness; self-confidence, self-assurance, self-reliance;** poise 106.3; courage 492; **overconfidence, oversureness,** overweening , overweeningness, hubris; pride 136, arrogance 141, pomposity 501.7, self-importance 140.1

6 **dogmatism,** dogmaticalness, pontification, **positiveness,** positivism, peremptoriness, **opinionatedness,** self-opinionatedness; bigotry; infallibilism

7 **dogmatist,** dogmatizer, opinionist, doctrinaire, bigot; positivist; infallibilist

8 **ensuring, assurance;** reassurance, reassurement; **certification;** ascertainment, **determination,** establishment; **verification, corroboration,** substantiation, validation, collation, check, cross-check, double-check, checking; independent *or* objective witness; **confirmation**

VERBS 9 **be certain, be confident,** feel sure, rest assured, have sewed up <nf>, **have no doubt,** doubt not; know, just know, know for certain; **bet on** *and* gamble on *and* bet one's bottom dollar on *and* bet the ranch on <nf>; admit of no doubt; **go without saying,** *aller sans dire* <Fr>, be axiomatic *or* apodictic, bet one's life <nf>

10 **dogmatize,** lay down the law, pontificate, oracle, oraculate, proclaim, assert oneself

11 **make sure, make certain,** make sure of, make no doubt, make no mistake; remove *or* dismiss *or* expunge *or* erase all doubt; **assure, ensure,** insure, **certify; ascertain, get a fix** *or* **lock on** <nf>; **find out,** get at, see to it, see that; **determine,** decide, **establish,** settle, fix, lock in *and* nail down *and* clinch *and* cinch <nf>, pin down, clear up, sort out, set at rest; assure *or* satisfy oneself, make oneself easy about *or* on that score; **reassure**

12 **verify, confirm,** test, prove, audit, **collate,** validate, check, check up *or* on *or* out <nf>, check over *or* through, **double-check,** triple-check, cross-check, recheck, check and doublecheck, check up and down, check over and through, check in and out, measure twice cut once

ADJS 13 **certain, sure,** sure-enough <nf>; well-founded; bound; **positive, absolute, definite,** perfectly sure, apodictic; decisive, conclusive; clear, clear as day, clear and distinct, unequivocal, unmistakable, unambiguous, nonambiguous, univocal; **necessary,** determinate, ineluctable, predetermined, predestined, **inevitable** 963.15; true 973.13

14 <nf terms> dead sure, sure as death, sure as death and taxes, sure as fate, sure as can be, sure as shooting, sure as God made little green apples, sure as hell *or* the devil, shit-sure, as sure as I live and breathe

15 **obvious, patent, unquestionable, unexceptionable, undeniable, self-evident,** axiomatic; indubitable, unarguable, indisputable, incontestable, **irrefutable,** unrefutable, unconfutable, incontrovertible, irrefragable, unanswerable, inappealable, unimpeachable, absolute; admitting no question *or* dispute *or* doubt *or* denial; **demonstrable,** demonstratable, provable, verifiable, testable, confirmable; well-founded, well-established, well-grounded; factual, **real,** historical, actual 761.15

16 **undoubted,** not to be doubted, indubious, **unquestioned, undisputed, uncontested,** uncontradicted, unchallenged, uncontroverted, uncontroversial; **doubtless, questionless,** beyond a shade *or* shadow of doubt, past dispute, beyond question

17 **reliable, dependable, sure,** surefire <nf>, **trustworthy, trusty,** faithworthy, **to be depended** *or* **relied upon,** to be counted *or* reckoned on; predictable, calculable; **secure, solid, sound, firm,** fast, **stable, substantial,** staunch, steady, **steadfast, faithful, unfailing;** true to one's word; invincible

18 **authoritative, authentic,** magisterial, **official;** cathedral, ex cathedra; standard, approved, accepted, received, pontific; from *or* straight from the horse's mouth

19 **infallible, inerrable,** inerrant, unerring

20 **assured,** made sure; **determined, decided, ascertained; settled, established,** fixed, cinched *and* iced *and* sewed up *and* taped <nf>, set, stated, determinate, secure; **certified,** attested, guaranteed, warranted, tested, tried, proved; wired *and* cinched *and* open-and-shut *and* nailed down *and* in the bag *and* on ice <nf>

21 **confident, sure,** secure, **assured,** reassured, decided, determined; **convinced,** persuaded, positive, **cocksure; unhesitating,** unfaltering, unwavering; **undoubting** 953.21; **self-confident, self-assured, self-reliant,** sure of oneself; poised 106.13; unafraid; **overconfident, oversure,** overweening, hubristic; proud 136.8, arrogant 141.9, pompous 501.22, self-important 140.8

22 **dogmatic, dogmatical,** dogmatizing, pronunciative, didactic, **positive,** positivistic, peremptory, pontifical, oracular; **opinionated,** opinioned, opinionative, conceited 140.11; **self-opinionated,** self-opinioned; doctrinarian, doctrinaire; bigoted

ADVS 23 **certainly, surely, assuredly, positively, absolutely, definitely,** decidedly; without batting an eye <nf>; decisively, distinctly, clearly, unequivocally, unmistakably; **for certain,** for sure *and* for a fact <nf>, in truth, certes *or* forsooth , and no mistake <nf>; **for a certainty,** to a certainty, *à coup sûr* <Fr>; **most certainly,** most assuredly; **indeed,** indeedy <nf>; truly; **of course,** as a matter of course; **by all means,** by all manner of means; at any rate, at all events; nothing else but <nf>, no two ways about it, no buts about it <nf>; no ifs, ands, *or* buts

24 **surely, sure, to be sure,** sure enough, for sure <nf>; sure thing *and* surest thing you know <nf>

25 **unquestionably, without question, undoubtedly, beyond the shadow of a doubt, beyond a reasonable doubt, indubitably, admittedly, undeniably,** unarguably, indisputably, incontestably, incontrovertibly, irrefutably, irrefragably; **doubtlessly,** doubtless, **no doubt, without doubt,** beyond doubt *or* question, out of question

26 **without fail,** unfailingly, whatever may happen, **come what may,** come hell *or* high water <nf>; cost what it may, *coûte que coûte* <Fr>; rain *or* shine, live *or* die, sink *or* swim

PHRS 27 **it is certain,** there is no question, there is not a shadow of doubt, that's for sure <nf>; that goes without saying, *cela va sans dire* <Fr>; that is evident, that leaps to the eye, *cela saute aux yeux* <Fr>

971 UNCERTAINTY

NOUNS 1 **uncertainty, incertitude, unsureness,** uncertainness; indemonstrability, unverifiability, unprovability, unconfirmability; **unpredictability,** unforeseeableness, incalculability, unaccountability; **indetermination,** indeterminacy, indeterminism; **relativity,** relativism, contingency, conditionality; **randomness, chance,** chanciness, hit-or-missness, **luck;** entropy; **indecision,** indecisiveness, undecidedness, undeterminedness; **hesitation, hesitancy; suspense,** suspensefulness, agony *or* state of suspense; **fickleness, capriciousness,** whimsicality, **erraticness,** erraticism, **changeableness** 854; **vacillation, irresolution** 362; trendlessness; Heisenberg *or* indeterminacy *or* uncertainty principle; question mark; back order; mixed blessing

2 **doubtfulness, dubiousness, doubt,** dubiety, dubitancy, dubitation ; **questionableness, disputability,** contestability, controvertibility, refutability, confutability, deniability; disbelief 955.1

3 **bewilderment,** disconcertion, disconcertedness, disconcert, disconcertment, **embarrassment, confoundment,** discomposure, unassuredness, **confusion,** cognitive dissonance; **perplexity, puzzlement,** baffle, **bafflement,** predicament, plight, **quandary, dilemma,** horns of a dilemma, nonplus; **puzzle,** problem, riddle, conundrum, mystery, enigma; fix *and* jam *and* pickle *and* scrape *and* stew <nf>; perturbation, **disturbance, upset, bother,** pother

4 **vagueness, indefiniteness, indecisiveness,** indeterminateness, indeterminableness, indefinableness, **unclearness, indistinctness,** haziness, fogginess, mistiness, murkiness, blurriness, fuzziness; **obscurity,** obscuration; **looseness, laxity, inexactness,** inaccuracy, imprecision; **broadness, generality,** sweepingness; ill-definedness, amorphousness, shapelessness, blobbiness; inchoateness, disorder, incoherence

5 **equivocalness,** equivocality, polysemousness, ambiguity 539

6 **unreliability, undependability, untrustworthiness,** unfaithworthiness, treacherousness, treachery; **unsureness, insecurity, unsoundness, infirmity,** insolidity, unsolidity, **instability,** insubstantiality, unsubstantiality, **unsteadfastness,** unsteadiness, desultoriness, shakiness; **precariousness,** hazard, danger, risk, riskiness, diceyness *and* dodginess <Brit nf>, knife-edge, moment of truth, tightrope walking, peril, perilousness, ticklishness, slipperiness, shiftiness, shiftingness; speculativeness; **unauthoritativeness,** unauthenticity

7 **fallibility,** errability, errancy, liability to error

8 <an uncertainty> **gamble, guess,** piece of guesswork, question mark, estimate, guesstimate *and* ball-park figure <nf>; **chance, wager; toss-up** *and* **coin-toss** <nf>, **touch**

and go; contingency, double contingency, possibility upon a possibility; **question, open question;** undecided issue, loose end; wild guess; **gray area,** twilight zone, borderline case; blind bargain, pig in a poke, sight-unseen transaction; leap in the dark; enigma

VERBS **9 be uncertain, feel unsure; doubt,** have one's doubts, **question,** puzzle over, agonize over; **wonder,** wonder whether, wrinkle one's brow; not know what to make of, not be able to make head *or* tail of; be at sea, float in a sea of doubt; be at one's wit's end, **not know which way to turn,** be of two minds, be at sixes and sevens, not know where one stands, have mixed feelings, not know whether one stands on one's head *or* one's heels, be in a dilemma *or* quandary, flounder, grope, beat about, thrash about, not know whether one is coming *or* going, go around in circles; go off in all directions at once

10 hang in doubt, hang over one's head, stop to consider, think twice; **falter,** dither, **hesitate, vacillate** 362.8

11 depend, all depend, be contingent *or* conditional on, hang on *or* upon; **hang, hang in the balance,** be touch and go, tremble in the balance, **hang in suspense; hang by a thread,** cliffhang, hang by a hair, hang by the eyelids

12 bewilder, disconcert, discompose, **upset,** perturb, **disturb, dismay,** tie one in knots; abash, **embarrass, put out,** pother, **bother,** moider <Brit nf>, flummox <nf>, keep one on tenterhooks

13 perplex, baffle, confound, daze, amaze , maze, addle, fuddle, muddle, **mystify, puzzle,** nonplus, put to one's wit's end; keep one guessing, keep in suspense

14 <nf terms> **stump,** boggle <Brit>, buffalo, bamboozle, stick, floor, throw, get, beat, beat the shit out of, lick

15 make uncertain, obscure, muddle, muddy, fuzz, fog, **confuse** 985.7

ADJS **16 uncertain, unsure; doubting, agnostic, skeptical,** unconvinced, unpersuaded; chancy, dicey <Brit>, touch-and-go; **unpredictable,** unforeseeable, incalculable, uncountable, unreckonable, unaccountable, undivinable; indemonstrable, unverifiable, unprovable, unconfirmable; **equivocal,** polysemous, inexplicit, imprecise, ambiguous; **fickle, capricious,** whimsical, **erratic,** variable, wavering, irresponsible, changeable 854.6; **hesitant,** hesitating; **indecisive, irresolute** 362.9

17 doubtful, iffy <nf>; **in doubt,** *in dubio* <L>; dubitable, doubtable, **dubious, questionable, problematic, problematical, speculative,** conjectural, suppositional; debatable, moot, arguable, **disputable,** contestable, controvertible, **controversial,** refutable, confutable, deniable; mistakable; **suspicious,** suspect; open to question *or* doubt; in question, in dispute, at issue

18 undecided, undetermined, unsettled, unfixed, unestablished; untold, uncounted; pendent, dependent, **pending,** depending, contingent, conditional, conditioned; **open,** in question, at issue, **in the balance, up in the air,** up for grabs <nf>, in limbo, **in suspense,** in a state of suspense, suspenseful

19 vague, indefinite, indecisive, indeterminate, indeterminable, **undetermined,** unpredetermined, undestined; **random,** stochastic, entropic, **chance,** chancy <nf>, dicey *and* dodgy <Brit nf>, aleatory *or* aleatoric, hit-or-miss; indefinable, undefined, ill-defined, unclear, unplain, **indistinct,** fuzzy, **obscure, confused, hazy,** shadowy, shadowed forth, misty, foggy, fog-bound, murky, blurred, blurry, veiled; **loose, lax, inexact, inaccurate,** imprecise; nonspecific, unspecified; **broad, general,** sweeping; amorphous, shapeless, blobby; inchoate, disordered, orderless, chaotic, incoherent

20 unreliable, undependable, untrustworthy, unfaithworthy, treacherous, unsure, not to be depended *or* relied on; **insecure, unsound, in-**

firm, unsolid, **unstable,** unsubstantial, insubstantial, **unsteadfast,** unsteady, desultory, shaky; **precarious,** hazardous, dangerous, perilous, risky, ticklish; shifty, shifting, slippery, slippery as an eel; provisional, tentative, temporary

21 **unauthoritative, unauthentic, unofficial,** nonofficial, apocryphal; **uncertified, unverified,** unchecked, unconfirmed, uncorroborated, unauthenticated, unvalidated, unattested, unwarranted; **undemonstrated, unproved**

22 **fallible, errable,** errant, liable *or* open to error, error-prone

23 **unconfident, unsure, unassured, insecure,** unsure of oneself; unselfconfident, unselfassured, unselfreliant

24 **bewildered, dismayed,** distracted, distraught, abashed, **disconcerted, embarrassed,** discomposed, **putout, disturbed, upset,** perturbed, **bothered,** all hot and bothered <nf>; **confused** 985.12; clueless, without a clue, guessing, mazed, in a maze; turned around, going around in circles, like a chicken with its head cut off <nf>; in a fix *or* stew *or* pickle *or* jam *or* scrape <nf>; **lost,** astray, abroad, adrift, **at sea,** off the track, out of one's reckoning, out of one's bearings, disoriented

25 **in a dilemma,** on the horns of a dilemma; **perplexed, confounded, mystified, puzzled, nonplussed, baffled,** bamboozled <nf>, buffaloed <nf>; **at a loss, at one's wit's end,** fuddled, addled, muddled, dazed; **on tenterhooks,** in suspense; with bated breath

26 <nf terms> **beat,** licked, stuck, floored, stumped, thrown, buffaloed, boggled <Brit>

27 **bewildering, confusing, distracting, disconcerting,** discomposing, **dismaying, embarrassing,** disturbing, **upsetting,** perturbing, bothering; **perplexing, baffling, mystifying, mysterious, puzzling,** funny, funny peculiar, confounding; **problematic** *or* problematical; intricate 799.4; **enigmatic** 522.17

ADVS **28** **uncertainly,** in an uncertain state, **unsurely; doubtfully, dubiously;** in suspense, at sea, on the horns of a dilemma, at sixes and sevens; perplexedly, disconcertedly, confusedly, dazedly, mazedly, in a daze, in a maze, around in circles

29 **vaguely, indefinitely,** indeterminably, indefinably, **indistinctly,** indecisively, **obscurely; broadly, generally,** in broad *or* general terms

972 CHANCE

<absence of assignable cause>

NOUNS **1** **chance,** happenstance, hap; **luck;** good luck *or* fortune, serendipity, happy chance, dumb luck <nf>, rotten *and* tough luck <nf>; **fortune,** fate, **destiny,** whatever comes, lot 964.2; **fortuity, randomness,** randomicity, fortuitousness, adventitiousness, indeterminateness *or* indeterminacy, problematicness, uncertainty 971, flukiness <nf>, casualness, flip of a coin, crazy quilt, patternlessness, trendlessness, accidentality; break <nf>, the breaks <nf>, run of luck, the luck of the draw, the rub of the green, run *or* turn of the cards, fall *or* throw of the dice, the way things fall, the way the cards fall, how they fall, the way the cookie crumbles *or* the ball bounces <nf>; uncertainty principle, principle of indeterminacy, Heisenberg's principle; **probability** 968, stochastics, theory of probability, law of averages, statistical probability, actuarial calculation; random sample, **risk, risk-taking, chancing, gamble** 759.2; **opportunity** 843.2

2 Chance, Fortune, Lady *or* Dame Fortune, wheel of fortune, Fortuna, the fickle finger of fate <nf>; Luck, Lady Luck

3 **purposelessness, causelessness,** randomness, dysteleology, **unpredictability** 971.1, designlessness, **aimlessness;** lack of motive, no attributable cause, nonintention

4 **haphazard,** chance-medley <law>, **random;** random shot; potluck; spin of the wheel

5 **vicissitudes,** vicissitudes of fortune, ins and outs, **ups and downs,** ups and downs of life, chapter of accidents, feast and famine; **chain of circumstances,** concatenation of events, chain reaction, vicious circle, causal nexus, **domino effect**

6 <chance event> **happening,** hap, happenstance; **fortuity, accident,** casualty, adventure, hazard; contingent, contingency; **fluke** <nf>, freak, freak occurrence *or* accident, coincidence; chance hit, lucky shot, long shot, one in a million, long odds

7 **even chance,** even break *and* fair shake <nf>, even *or* square odds, level playing field, touch and go, odds; **half a chance,** fifty-fifty; toss, **toss-up,** standoff <nf>

8 **good chance, sporting chance,** good opportunity, good possibility; odds-on, odds-on chance, **likelihood, possibility** 966, probability 968, favorable prospect, well-grounded hope; **sure bet,** sure thing *and* dollars to doughnuts <nf>; **best bet,** main chance, winning chance

9 **small chance,** little chance, dark horse, **poor prospect** *or* prognosis, poor lookout <nf>, little opportunity, poor possibility, **unlikelihood, improbability** 969, hardly a chance, not half a chance; **off chance, outside chance** <nf>, **remote possibility,** bare possibility, a ghost of a chance, slim chance, gambling chance, **fighting chance** <nf>; poor bet, long odds, long shot <nf>, hundred-to-one shot <nf>, one chance in a million

10 **no chance,** not a Chinaman's chance *and* not a snowball's chance in hell <nf>, not a prayer; **impossibility** 967, hopelessness

VERBS 11 **chance,** bechance , betide, come *or* happen by chance, hap, hazard, **happen** 831.5, happen *or* fall on, come, come *or* happen along, bump into <nf>, **turn up,** pop up <nf>, **befall;** fall to one's lot, be one's fate

12 **risk,** take a chance, run a risk, push *or* press one's luck, lay one's ass on the line *and* put one's money where one's mouth is <nf>, **gamble, bet** 759.25; risk one's neck *and* shoot the works *and* go for broke <nf>; **predict** 962.9, prognosticate, make book <nf>; call someone's bluff

13 have a chance *or* an opportunity, **stand a chance, run a good chance, bid** *or* **stand fair to,** admit of; be in it *or* in the running <nf>; have *or* take a chance at, have a fling *or* shot at <nf>; have a small *or* slight chance, be a dark horse, barely have a chance

14 **not have** *or* **stand a chance,** have no chance *or* opportunity, not have a prayer, not have a Chinaman's chance <nf>, not stand a snowball's chance in hell <nf>; not be in it <nf>, be out of it <nf>, **be out of the running**

ADJS 15 **chance;** chancy <nf>, dicey <Brit nf>, **risky** <nf>; **fortuitous, accidental,** aleatory *or* aleatoric; **lucky,** fortunate, blessed by fortune, serendipitous; **casual,** adventitious, incidental, contingent, iffy <nf>; **causeless,** uncaused; indeterminate, undetermined; **unexpected** 131.10, **unpredictable,** unforeseeable, unlooked-for, **unforeseen; fluky** <nf>; fatal, fatidic, destinal

16 **purposeless, causeless,** designless, **aimless,** driftless, undirected, objectless, unmotivated, mindless; **haphazard, random,** dysteleological, stochastic, stray, inexplicable, unaccountable, promiscuous, indiscriminate, casual, leaving much to chance

17 **unintentional,** unintended, **unmeant, unplanned,** undesigned, unpurposed, unthought-of; **unpremeditated,** unmeditated, unprompted, unguided, unguarded; **unwitting, unthinking,** unconscious, involuntary; collateral

18 impossible 967.7; **improbable** 969.3; certain 970.13; **probable** 968.6

ADVS 19 **by chance,** perchance, **by accident, accidentally, casually,** incidentally, by coincidence, **unpredictably, fortuitously, out of a clear blue sky;** by a piece of luck, by a fluke <nf>, by good fortune; **as**

it chanced, as luck would have it, by hazard, as it may happen, as it may be, as the case may be, as it may chance, as it may turn up *or* out; somehow, in some way, in some way *or* other, somehow *or* other, for some reason

20 **purposelessly, aimlessly; haphazardly, randomly,** dysteleologically, stochastically, inexplicably, unaccountably, promiscuously, indiscriminately, casually, **at haphazard, at random,** at hazard

21 **unintentionally, without design, unwittingly,** unthinkingly, unexpectedly, unconsciously, involuntarily

PHR 22 it's a crapshoot

973 TRUTH

<conformity to fact or reality>

NOUNS 1 **truth, trueness, verity,** veridicality, conformity to fact *or* reality *or* the evidence *or* the data, simple *or* unadorned truth, very truth, sooth *or* good sooth ; more truth than poetry; **unerroneousness, unfalseness,** unfallaciousness; historical truth, **objective truth, actuality,** historicity, impersonality; **fact, actuality, reality** 761.2, the real world, things as they are; the true, ultimate truth; eternal verities; truthfulness, veracity 644.3

2 **a truth, a self-evident truth, an axiomatic truth, an axiom;** a premise, a given, a donnée *or* donné, an accomplished fact *or fait accompli* <Fr>

3 **the truth,** the truth of the matter, the case; the home truth, the unvarnished truth, the simple truth, the basic truth, indisputable truth, the unadorned truth, the naked truth, the plain truth, the unqualified truth, the honest truth, the sober truth, the exact truth, the straight truth; the absolute truth, the intrinsic truth, the unalloyed truth, the cast-iron truth, the hard truth, the stern truth, gospel, gospel truth, Bible truth, revealed truth; the whole truth and nothing but the truth

4 <nf terms> **what's what,** how it is, how things are, like it is, where it's at, the straight of it, the straight goods *or* skinny *or* scoop, the honest-to-God truth, God's truth, the real thing, the very model, the genuine article, the very thing, it, the article, the goods, the McCoy, the real McCoy, no imitation, chapter and verse, the gospel, the gospel truth, the lowdown, the skinny

5 **accuracy, correctness,** care for truth, attention to fact, right, subservience to the facts *or* the data, **rightness, trueness, rigor, rigorousness, exactness, exactitude; preciseness, precision;** mathematical precision, pinpoint accuracy *or* precision, scientific exactness *or* exactitude; factualness, factualism; **faultlessness,** perfection, absoluteness, flawlessness, impeccability, unimpeachability; **faithfulness, fidelity;** literalness, literality, literalism, textualism, the letter, literal truth; strictness, severity, rigidity; niceness, nicety, delicacy, subtlety, fineness, refinement; **meticulousness** 339.3; attention to detail; pinpoint accuracy, mathematical precision, clockwork precision

6 **validity, soundness,** solidity, substantiality, **justness;** authority, **authoritativeness; cogency,** weight, force, persuasiveness

7 **genuineness, authenticity,** bona fides, bona fideness, **legitimacy; realness, realism,** photographic realism, absolute realism, realistic representation, **naturalism,** naturalness, truth to nature, **lifelikeness,** truth to life, slice of life, *tranche de vie* <Fr>, kitchen sink, true-to-lifeness, verisimilitude, *vraisemblance* <Fr>, faithful rendering, verism, verismo, faithfulness; absolute likeness, **literalness,** literality, literalism, truth to the letter; socialist realism; inartificiality, unsyntheticness; **unspuriousness,** unspeciousness, unfictitiousness, artlessness, unaffectedness; **honesty, sincerity;** unadulteration 798.1

VERBS 8 **be true,** be the case; conform to fact, square *or* chime with the facts *or* evidence; **prove true,** prove to be, **prove out,** be so in fact; **hold true, hold good, hold water** <nf>, hold *or* stick together <nf>, **hold up, hold up in the wash** <nf>, wash <nf>, **stand up,** stand the test, be consistent *or* self-consistent, **hold,** remain valid; **be truthful**

9 seem true, ring true, sound true, **carry conviction,** convince, persuade, win over, hold *or* have the ring of truth

10 **be right, be correct,** be just right, get it straight; be OK <nf>, add up; **hit the nail on the head,** hit it on the nose *or* on the money *and* say a mouthful <nf>, hit the bull's-eye, score a bull's-eye

11 **be accurate, dot one's i's and cross one's t's,** draw *or* cut it fine <nf>, be precise; make precise, precise, particularize; stick to the letter, go by the book

12 **come true, come about,** attain fulfillment, **turn out, come to pass** *or* **to be,** happen as expected, become a reality

ADJS 13 **true, truthful; unerroneous,** not in error, in conformity with the facts *or* the evidence *or* reality, on the up-and-up *or* strictly on the up-and-up <nf>; gospel, **hard,** cast-iron; unfalse, unfallacious, unmistaken; **real, veritable,** veracious, sure-enough <nf>, objective, true to the facts, in conformity with the facts *or* the evidence *or* the data *or* reality, **factual, actual** 761.15, effectual, **historical,** documentary; objectively true; **certain,** undoubted, unquestionable 970.15; unrefuted, unconfuted, undenied; **ascertained, proved, proven, verified,** validated, **certified,** demonstrated, confirmed, determined, established, attested, substantiated, **authenticated,** corroborated; true as gospel; substantially true, categorically true; **veracious** 644.16

14 **valid, sound, well-grounded, well-founded,** conforming to the facts *or* the data *or* the evidence *or* reality, hard, solid, substantial; consistent, self-consistent, logical; **good, just,** sufficient; **cogent, weighty, authoritative; legal, lawful,** legitimate, **binding**

15 **genuine, authentic,** veridic, veridical, **real, natural, realistic, naturalistic,** true to reality, **true to nature, lifelike,** true to life, verisimilar, veristic; **literal,** following the letter, letter-perfect, *au pied de la lettre* <Fr>, true to the letter; verbatim, verbal, word-perfect, **word-for-word;** true to the spirit; **legitimate,** rightful, lawful; **bona fide,** card-carrying <nf>, **good,** sure-enough <nf>, **sincere, honest;** candid, honest-to-God <nf>; **inartificial, unsynthetic;** unspurious, unspecious, unsimulated, unfaked, unfeigned, **undisguised, uncounterfeited, unpretended, unaffected, unassumed; unassuming, simple,** unpretending, unfeigning, undisguising; **unfictitious,** unfanciful, unfabricated, unconcocted, uninvented, unimagined; unromantic; **original,** unimitated, uncopied; unexaggerated, undistorted; unflattering, unvarnished, uncolored, unqualified; **unadulterated** 798.7, honest-to-goodness; **pure,** simon-pure; **sterling,** twenty-four carat, all wool *and* a yard wide <nf>

16 **accurate, correct, right,** proper, just; all right *or* OK *or* okay <nf>, just right as rain, right, dead right, on target *and* on the money *and* on the nose *and* on the button <nf>, bang on <Brit nf>, straight, straight-up-and-down; **faultless,** flawless, impeccable, unimpeachable, unexceptionable; **absolute, perfect,** letter-perfect; **meticulous** 339.12; factual, literal

17 **exact, precise,** express; even, square; absolutely *or* definitely *or* positively right; **faithful;** direct; **unerring, undeviating, constant; infallible, inerrant, inerrable; strict,** close, severe, **rigorous,** rigid; mathematically exact, mathematical; mechanically *or* micrometrically precise; scientifically exact, scientific; religiously exact, religious; **nice,** delicate, subtle, **fine,** refined; pinpoint, microscopic

ADVS 18 **truly, really,** really-truly <nf>, **verily,** veritably, forsooth *or* in very sooth , **in truth,** in good *or* very truth, **actually,** historically, objectively, impersonally, rigorously, strictly, strictly speaking, unquestionably, without question, **in reality, in fact,** factually, technically, in point of fact, as a matter of fact, for that matter, for the matter of that, to tell the truth, if you want to know the truth, to state the fact *or* truth, of a truth, with truth; **indeed,** indeedy <nf>; **certainly; indubitably, undoubtedly** 970.25; no buts about it <nf>, nothing else but

19 **genuinely, authentically, really,** naturally, **legitimately, honestly,** veridically; warts and all; unaffectedly, unassumedly, from the heart, in one's heart of hearts, with all one's heart and soul

20 **accurately, correctly,** rightly, properly, straight; **perfectly, faultlessly,** flawlessly, impeccably, unimpeachably, unexceptionably; **just right,** just so; **so,** sic

21 **exactly, precisely,** to a T, expressly; **just, dead,** right, straight, even, square, **plumb,** directly, squarely, point-blank; unerringly, undeviatingly; verbatim, **literally,** *literatim* <L>, verbally, word-perfectly, word for word, word by word, word for word and letter for letter, *verbatim et litteratim* <L>, in the same words, *ipsissimis verbis* <L>, to the letter, according to the letter, *au pied de la lettre* <Fr>; **faithfully, strictly, rigorously,** rigidly; **definitely, positively, absolutely; in every respect,** in all respects, for all the world, neither more nor less

22 **to be exact, to be precise, strictly, technically, strictly speaking,** not to mince the matter, by the book

23 **to a nicety,** to a T *or* tittle, to a turn, to a hair, to *or* within an inch

PHRS 24 **right!, that's right, that is so,** amen!, that's it, that's just it, just so, it is that, *c'est ça* <Fr>; **you are right,** right you are, right as rain, it is for a fact, you speak truly, as you say, **right;** believe it *or* not; touché!

25 <nf terms> **right on!,** you better believe it!, you've got something there, I'll say, I'll tell the world, I'll drink to that, righto, quite, rather!, you got it!, you said it, you said a mouthful, now you're talking, you can say that again, you're not kidding, that's for sure, ain't it the truth?, you're damn tootin', don't I know it?, you're telling me?, you're not just whistling Dixie, bet your ass *or* sweet ass *or* bippy *or* boots *or* life *or* you bet the rent, fucking ay, fucking ay right

974 WISE SAYING

NOUNS 1 **maxim, aphorism,** apothegm *or* apophthegm, **epigram, dictum, adage, proverb,** gnome, words of wisdom, **saw, saying,** witticism, sentence, expression, phrase, catchword, catchphrase, word, byword, mot, motto, moral; **precept,** prescript, teaching, text, verse, sutra, distich, sloka; golden saying, proverbial saying; common *or* current saying, stock saying, pithy saying, wise saying *or* expression, oracle, sententious expression *or* saying; **conventional wisdom, common knowledge; ana, analects, proverbs, wisdom, wisdom literature, collected sayings**

2 **axiom, truth,** a priori truth, postulate, truism, self-evident truth, general *or* universal truth, home truth, obvious truth, intrinsic truth; elephant in the room; theorem; **proposition;** brocard, **principle,** *principium* <L>, settled principle; **formula; rule, law,** dictate , **dictum;** golden rule

3 **platitude, cliché, saw, old saw, commonplace, banality,** bromide, **chestnut** <nf>, corn <nf>, triticism , tired phrase, trite saying, hackneyed *or* stereotyped saying, stock phrase, commonplace expression, *lieu commun* <Fr>, *locus communis* <L>, **familiar tune** *or* **story, old song** *or* **story,** old song and dance <nf>, twice-told tale, retold story; reiteration 849.2; prosaicism, prosaism; prose; old joke 489.9

4 **motto, slogan,** watchword, catchword, catchphrase, tag line *or* tag, byword; **device;** epithet; inscription, epigraph

VERBS **5** aphorize, apothegmatize, epigrammatize, coin a phrase; proverb

ADJS **6** **aphoristic, proverbial,** epigrammatic, epigrammatical, **axiomatical; sententious, pithy,** gnomic, pungent, succinct, enigmatic, pointed; formulistic, formulaic; **cliché** *or* clichéd, banal, tired, stock, trite, tritical , **platitudinous** 117.9

ADVS **7** **proverbially,** to coin a phrase, in a nutshell, **as the saying is** *or* **goes,** as they say, as the fellow says <nf>, as it has been said, as it was said of old

975 ERROR

NOUNS **1** **error, erroneousness; untrueness,** untruthfulness, **untruth; wrongness, wrong; falseness, falsity; fallacy, fallaciousness,** self-contradiction; fault, **faultiness,** defectiveness; **sin** 655.1, sinfulness, peccancy, flaw, flawedness, *hamartia* <Gk>; misdoing, misfeasance; errancy, aberrancy, aberration, **deviancy,** wrongdoing; **heresy,** unorthodoxy, heterodoxy; perversion, **distortion; mistaking,** misconstruction, misapplication, misprision ; **delusion, illusion** 976; misjudgment 948; **misinterpretation** 342; faulty reasoning, flawed logic; fallibility, human error

2 **inaccuracy,** inaccurateness, **incorrectness, uncorrectness, inexactness,** unfactualness, inexactitude, **unpreciseness,** imprecision, unspecificity, looseness, laxity, unrigorousness; tolerance, allowance; negligence; approximation; **deviation,** standard deviation, probable error, predictable error, range of error; uncertainty 971

3 **mistake, error,** *erratum* <L>, *corrigendum* <L>; **fault,** *faute* <Fr>; gross error, bevue; human error; **misconception, misapprehension, misunderstanding;** misstatement, misquotation; misreport; **misprint, typographical error,** typo <nf>, printer's error, typist's error; clerical error; misidentification; **misjudgment, miscalculation** 948.1; misplay; misdeal; miscount; misuse; failure, miss, miscarriage

4 **slip,** slipup *and* miscue <nf>; **lapse,** *lapsus* <L>, **oversight,** omission, balk , inadvertence *or* inadvertency, loose thread; **misstep,** trip, stumble, false *or* wrong step, wrong *or* bad *or* false move; false note; **slip of the tongue,** *sus linguae* and *lapsus linguae* <L>; **slip of the pen,** *lapsus calami* <L>; Freudian slip

5 **blunder, faux pas,** gaffe, solecism; stupidity, indiscretion 923.4; **botch, bungle** 414.5

6 <nf terms> **goof, boo-boo,** muff, flub, foozle, bloomer, bloop, blooper, boot, bobble, boner, bonehead play *or* trick, dumb trick, boob stunt, fool mistake; howler, clanger <Brit>, screamer; fuck-up, screw-up, foul-up, snafu, muck-up, balls-up <Brit>, louse-up; pratfall, whoops

7 **grammatical error, solecism,** anacoluthon, anacoluthia, misusage, faulty syntax, missaying, mispronunciation; **bull, Irish bull,** fluff, **malapropism,** malaprop, Mrs Malaprop <R B Sheridan>; Pickwickian sense; spoonerism, marrow-sky; hypercorrection, hyperform; folk etymology; catachresis; misspelling

VERBS **8** **not hold water** *and* not hold together <nf>, not stand up, not square, not figure <nf>, not add up, **not hold up, not hold up in the wash** *and* not wash <nf>

9 **err,** fall into error, **go wrong, go amiss,** go astray, go *or* get out of line, go awry, stray, get off-base <nf>, **deviate,** wander, transgress, sin; **lapse, slip, slip up,** trip, stumble; **miscalculate** 948.2

10 **be wrong, mistake oneself, be mistaken, be in error, be at fault,** be out of line, be off the track, be in the wrong, miss the truth, miss the point, miss by a mile <nf>, have another think coming <nf>; take wrong, receive a false impression, take the shadow for the substance, misconstrue, misinterpret, be misled, be misguided; deceive oneself, be deceived, delude oneself; labor under a false impression, get it wrong

11 bark up the wrong tree, back the wrong horse, count one's chickens before they are hatched

12 **misdo,** do amiss; misuse, misemploy, misapply; misconduct, mismanage; miscall, miscount, miscalculate, misdeal, misplay, misfield; misprint, miscite, misquote, misread, misreport, misspell

13 **mistake, make a mistake;** miscue *and* make a miscue <nf>; **misidentify; misunderstand,** misapprehend, misconceive, **misinterpret** 342.2; **confuse** 811.3, mix up, not distinguish

14 **blunder, make a blunder, make a faux pas,** blot one's copy book, make a colossal blunder, make a false *or* wrong step, make a misstep; **misspeak,** misspeak oneself, trip over one's tongue; embarrass oneself, have egg on one's face <nf>; blunder into; **botch, bungle** 414.11

15 <nf terms> **make** *or* **pull a boner** *or* boo-boo *or* blooper; drop a brick <Brit>, goof, fluff, duff <Brit>, foozle, boot, bobble, blow, blow it, drop the ball; fuck up, screw up, foul up, muck up, louse up; put *or* stick one's foot in it *or* in one's mouth; muff one's cue, muff *or* blow *or* fluff one's lines, fall flat on one's face *or* ass, step on one's dick, trip up

ADJS **16** **erroneous, untrue,** not true, **not right;** unfactual, **wrong,** all wrong; peccant, perverse, corrupt; **false, fallacious,** self-contradictory; **illogical** 936.11; **unproved** 958.8; **faulty,** faultful, flawed, defective, **at fault;** out, off, all off, off the track *or* rails; wide , wide of the mark, beside the mark; amiss, awry, askew, deviant, deviative, deviational; erring, errant, **aberrant;** straying, astray, adrift; **heretical,** unorthodox, heterodox; abroad, all abroad; perverted, **distorted; delusive,** deceptive, **illusory**

17 **inaccurate, incorrect, inexact,** unfactual, **unprecise,** imprecise, unspecific, loose, lax, unrigorous; negligent; **vague;** approximate, approximative; out of line, out of plumb, out of true, out of square; off-base <nf>

18 **mistaken, in error, erring,** under an error, **wrong, all wet** <nf>, full of bull *or* shit *or* hot air *or* it *or* prunes *or* crap *or* beans <nf>; off *or* out in one's reckoning; in the wrong box, in the right church but the wrong pew

19 **unauthentic** *or* **inauthentic, unauthoritative, unreliable** 971.20; **misstated,** misreported, miscited, misquoted, **garbled;** unfounded 936.13; spurious

ADVS **20** **erroneously, falsely,** by mistake, fallaciously; faultily, faultfully; **untrue** , untruly; **wrong,** wrongly; **mistakenly;** amiss, astray, on the wrong track

21 **inaccurately, incorrectly,** inexactly, unprecisely, by guess and by God *or* by golly <nf>

PHRS **22** **you are wrong, you are mistaken,** you're all wet *or* you're way off *or* you have another guess coming *or* don't kid yourself <nf>

976 ILLUSION

NOUNS **1** **illusion, delusion,** deluded belief; **deception** 356, **trick;** self-deception, self-deceit, self-delusion; dereism, autism; **misconception, misbelief,** false belief, wrong impression, warped *or* distorted conception; **bubble, chimera,** vapor; wishful thinking, *ignis fatuus* <L>, will-o'-the-wisp; **dream,** dream vision; dreamworld, dreamland, dreamscape; **daydream;** pipe dream *and* trip <nf>; fool's paradise, castle in the air, fond illusion, dreamscape; maya, confabulation

2 **illusoriness,** illusiveness, delusiveness; **falseness,** fallaciousness; **unreality,** unactuality; unsubstantiality, airiness, immateriality; **idealization** 986.7; **seeming,** semblance, simulacrum, **appearance,** false *or* specious appearance, show, false show, false light; **magic, sorcery** 690, illusionism, sleight of hand, prestidigitation, magic show, magic act; magician, **sorcerer** 690.5, illusionist, Prospero; magus, wizard, conjuror

3 **fancy, phantasy, imagination** 986

4 **phantom, phantasm,** phantasma, wraith, specter; shadow, shade; phantasmagoria; **fantasy,** wildest dream; **figment of the imagination** 986.5, phantom of the mind; **apparition, appearance; vision,** waking dream, image ; shape, form, figure, presence; eidolon, idolum

5 **optical illusion, trick of eyesight;** afterimage, spectrum, ocular spectrum

6 **mirage,** fata morgana, will-o'-the-wisp, looming

7 **hallucination;** hallucinosis; tripping <nf>, mind-expansion; consciousness-expansion; delirium tremens 926.10; dream 986.9

VERBS 8 **go on a trip** *and* **blow one's mind** <nf>, freak out <nf>; **hallucinate;** expand one's consciousness; make magic, prestidigitate

ADJS 9 **illusory,** illusive; illusional, illusionary; Barmecide *or* Barmecidal; **delusory,** delusive; delusional, delusionary, deluding; dereistic, autistic; **dreamy, dreamlike; visionary; imaginary** 986.19; **erroneous** 975.16; **deceptive;** self-deceptive, self-deluding; **chimeric, chimerical, fantastic; unreal,** unactual, unsubstantial 764.5, airy; unfounded 936.13; **false,** fallacious, misleading; **specious, seeming,** apparent, ostensible, supposititious, all in the mind; spectral, apparitional, phantom, phantasmal; phantasmagoric, surreal

10 **hallucinatory,** hallucinative, hallucinational; hallucinogenic, psychedelic, consciousness-expanding, mind-expanding, mind-blowing <nf>

977 DISILLUSIONMENT

NOUNS 1 **disillusionment,** disillusion, **disenchantment,** undeception, unspelling, return to reality, loss of one's illusions, loss of innocence, cold light of reality, enlightenment, bursting of the bubble; awakening, rude awakening, bringing back to earth; disappointment 132; debunking <nf>

VERBS 2 **disillusion,** disillude, disillusionize; **disenchant,** unspell, uncharm, break the spell *or* charm; **disabuse, undeceive;** correct, **set right** *or* **straight,** put straight, tell the truth, enlighten, let in on, put one wise <nf>; clear the mind of; open one's eyes, awaken, wake up, unblindfold; disappoint 132.2; dispel *or* dissipate one's illusions, rob *or* strip one of one's illusions; bring one back to earth, let down easy <nf>; **burst** *or* **prick the bubble,** puncture one's balloon <nf>; let the air out of, take the wind out of; knock the props out from under, take the ground from under; debunk <nf>; expose, show up 351.4

3 be disillusioned, be disenchanted, get back to earth, get one's feet on the ground, have one's eyes opened, return to *or* embrace reality; charge to experience; have another thing *or* guess coming <nf>

ADJS 4 **disillusioning,** disillusive, disillusionary, **disenchanting,** disabusing, undeceiving, enlightening

5 disillusioned, disenchanted, unspelled, uncharmed, disabused, undeceived, stripped *or* robbed of illusion, enlightened, set right, put straight; with one's eyes open, sophisticated, **blasé;** disappointed 132.5

978 MENTAL ATTITUDE

NOUNS 1 **attitude,** mental attitude; psychology; **position, posture,** stance; **way of thinking; feeling, sentiment,** the way one feels; feeling tone, affect, affectivity, emotion, emotivity; opinion 953.6

2 **outlook,** mental outlook; **point of view, viewpoint, standpoint, perspective,** *optique* <Fr>; position, stand, place, situation; side; footing, basis; where one is *or* sits *or* stands; **view,** sight, light, eye; respect, regard; angle, angle of vision, slant, way of looking at things, slant on things, where one is coming from

<nf>; **frame of reference,** intellectual *or* ideational frame of reference, framework, arena, world, universe, world *or* universe of discourse, system, reference system; phenomenology

3 disposition, character, nature, temper, temperament, mettle, constitution, complexion *and* humor , makeup, stamp, type, stripe, kidney, make, mold; **turn of mind, inclination,** mind, **tendency,** grain, vein, set, mental set, mindset, **leaning,** animus, propensity, proclivity, predilection, preference, predisposition; **bent, turn, bias,** slant, cast, warp, twist; idiosyncrasy, eccentricity, individualism; diathesis, aptitude; strain, streak

4 mood, humor, feeling, feelings, temper, frame of mind, state of mind, mental state, mindset, morale, cue *or* frame , tone, note, **vein; mind,** heart, spirit *or* **spirits**

5 <pervading attitudes> **climate,** mental *or* intellectual climate, spiritual climate, moral climate, mores, norms, climate of opinion, **ethos,** ideology, world view; *Zeitgeist* <Ger>, spirit of the time *or* the age

VERBS **6 take the attitude,** feel about it, look at it, **view,** look at in the light of; **be disposed to,** tend *or* incline toward, prefer, lean toward, be bent on

ADJS **7 attitudinal; temperamental, dispositional,** inclinational, constitutional; emotional, affective; mental, intellectual, ideational, ideological; spiritual; characteristic 865.13; innate

8 disposed, dispositioned, **predisposed, prone, inclined, given,** bent, bent on, apt, likely, **minded, in the mood** *or* **humor**

ADVS **9 attitudinally; temperamentally, dispositionally,** constitutionally; emotionally; mentally, intellectually, ideationally, ideologically; morally, spiritually; **by temperament** *or* **disposition,** by virtue of mind-set, by the logic of character *or* temperament; from one's standpoint *or* viewpoint *or* angle, from where one stands *or* sits, from where one is; within the frame of reference *or* framework *or* reference system *or* universe of discourse

979 BROAD-MINDEDNESS

NOUNS **1 broad-mindedness,** wide-mindedness, large-mindedness; **breadth,** broadness, broad gauge, latitude; **unbigotedness,** unhideboundness, unprovincialism, noninsularity, unparochialism, cosmopolitanism; ecumenicity, ecumenicism, ecumenicalism, ecumenism; broad mind, spacious mind

2 liberalness, liberality, catholicity, **liberalmindedness;** liberalism, libertarianism, latitudinarianism; freethinking, free thought

3 open-mindedness, openness, receptiveness, receptivity; persuadableness, persuadability, persuasibility; open mind

4 tolerance, toleration; **indulgence,** lenience or **leniency** 427, condonation, lenity; **forbearance, patience,** long-suffering; easiness, **permissiveness; charitableness,** charity, **generousness, magnanimity** 652.2; **compassion** 427.1, sympathy; sensitivity

5 unprejudicedness, unbiasedness; impartiality 649.3, evenhandedness, equitability, **justice** 649, **fairness** 649.2, justness, **objectivity, detachment, dispassionateness, disinterestedness,** impersonality; indifference, neutrality; unopinionatedness

6 liberal, liberalist; libertarian; freethinker, latitudinarian, ecumenist, ecumenicist; big person, broad-gauge person; bleeding heart, bleeding-heart liberal

VERBS **7 keep an open mind,** be big <nf>, judge not, not write off, suspend judgment, listen to reason, open one's mind to, see both sides, judge on the merits; **live and let live;** lean over backwards, **tolerate** 134.5; **accept,** be easy with, **view with indulgence, condone,** brook, abide with, be content with; **live with** <nf>; shut one's eyes to, look the other way, wink at, blink at, **overlook, disregard, ignore**

ADJS 8 **broad-minded,** wide-minded, large-minded, **broad, wide,** wide-ranging, broad-gauged, catholic, spacious of mind; **unbigoted,** unfanatical, **unhidebound,** unprovincial, cosmopolitan, noninsular, unparochial; ecumenistic, ecumenical

9 **liberal, liberal-minded,** liberalistic; libertarian; freethinking, latitudinarian; bleeding-heart

10 **open-minded, open, receptive,** rational, admissive; **persuadable,** persuasible; unopinionated, **unopinioned,** unwedded to an opinion; **unpositive, undogmatic;** uninfatuated, unbesotted, unfanatical

11 **tolerant** 134.9, tolerating; **indulgent, lenient** 427.7, **condoning;** forbearing, forbearant , **patient, long-suffering; charitable, generous, magnanimous** 652.6; compassionate 427.7, sympathetic, sensitive

12 **unprejudiced, unbiased, unprepossessed, unjaundiced; impartial,** evenhanded, **fair, just** 649.7, equitable, **objective, dispassionate, impersonal, detached, disinterested;** indifferent, neutral; **unswayed, uninfluenced,** undazzled; non-sexist, inclusive

13 **liberalizing, liberating, broadening,** enlightening

980 NARROW-MINDEDNESS

NOUNS 1 **narrow-mindedness,** narrowness, illiberality, uncatholicity; little-mindedness, **small-mindedness, smallness, littleness, meanness, pettiness;** close-mindedness; **bigotry,** bigotedness, fanaticism, *odium theologicum* <L>; insularity, insularism, provincialism, parochialism; **hideboundness,** strait-lacedness, stuffiness <nf>; authoritarianism; **shortsightedness,** nearsightedness, purblindness; blind side, blind spot, tunnel vision, blinders; closed mind, mean mind, petty mind, shut mind; narrow views *or* sympathies, cramped ideas; *parti pris* <Fr>, an ax to grind

2 **intolerance,** intoleration; **uncharitableness,** ungenerousness; unforbearance; noncompassion, insensitivity

3 **prejudice,** prejudgment, forejudgment, **predilection, prepossession,** preconception; **bias,** bent, leaning, inclination, twist; **jaundice,** jaundiced eye; **partiality,** partialism, partisanship, favoritism, onesidedness, undispassionateness, undetachment

4 **discrimination,** social discrimination, minority prejudice; xenophobia, know-nothingism; **chauvinism,** ultranationalism, superpatriotism; fascism; **class consciousness,** class prejudice, class distinction, class hatred, class war; anti-Semitism; red-baiting <nf>; **racism,** racialism, race hatred, **race prejudice,** race snobbery, racial discrimination; white *or* black supremacy, white *or* black power; **color line,** color bar; **social barrier,** Jim Crow, Jim Crow law; **segregation,** apartheid; sex discrimination, sexism, manism, masculism, male chauvinism, feminism, womanism; ageism, age discrimination; class prejudice, class hatred, social prejudice; glass ceiling

5 **bigot,** intolerant, illiberal, little person, Archie Bunker <nf>; **racist,** racialist, racial supremacist, white *or* black supremacist, pig <nf>; **chauvinist,** ultranationalist, jingo, superpatriot; **sexist,** male chauvinist, male chauvinist pig *or* MCP <nf>, manist, masculist, feminist, female chauvinist, womanist, **dogmatist, doctrinaire** 970.7; fanatic

VERBS 6 **close one's mind,** shut the eyes of one's mind, take narrow views, put on blinders, blind oneself, have a blind side *or* spot, have tunnel vision, constrict one's views; not see beyond one's nose *or* an inch beyond one's nose; **view with a jaundiced eye,** see but one side of the question, look only at one side of the shield

7 **prejudge,** forejudge, judge beforehand, precondemn, prejudicate , take one's opinions ready-made, accede to prejudice

8 **discriminate against, draw the line,** draw the color line; bait, **bash;** red-bait

9 **prejudice,** prejudice against, prejudice the issue, prepossess, **jaundice, influence, sway, bias,** bias one's judgment; warp, twist, bend, distort

ADJS 10 **narrow-minded,** narrow, narrow-gauged, closed, closed-minded, cramped, constricted, po-faced <Brit>, *borné* <Fr>, little-minded, small-minded, mean-minded, petty-minded, narrow-hearted, narrow-souled, narrow-spirited, mean-spirited, small-souled; **small, little, mean, petty;** uncharitable, ungenerous; bigot, **bigoted,** fanatical; **illiberal,** unliberal, uncatholic; provincial, insular, parochial; **hidebound,** creed-bound, **straitlaced,** stuffy <nf>; authoritarian; **shortsighted,** nearsighted, purblind; deaf, deaf-minded, deaf to reason

11 **intolerant,** untolerating; **unindulgent,** uncondoning, unforbearing

12 **discriminatory; prejudiced,** prepossessed, **biased, jaundiced,** colored; **partial,** one-sided, partisan; influenced, swayed, warped, twisted; interested, nonobjective, **undetached,** undispassionate; xenophobic, know-nothing; **chauvinistic,** ultranationalist, superpatriotic; **racist,** racialist, anti-Negro, antiblack, antiwhite; anti-Semitic; sexist; dogmatic, doctrinaire, **opinionated** 970.22

981 CURIOSITY

NOUNS 1 **curiosity,** curiousness, **inquisitiveness; interest,** interestedness, lively interest; thirst *or* desire *or* lust *or* itch for knowledge, mental acquisitiveness, inquiring *or* curious mind; **attention** 983; **alertness, watchfulness,** vigilance; **nosiness** *and* snoopiness <nf>, prying, snooping <nf>; eavesdropping; officiousness, meddlesomeness 214.2; **morbid curiosity, ghoulishness;** voyeurism, scopophilia, prurience, prurient interest; rubbernecking <nf>

2 inquisitive person, quidnunc; **inquirer,** questioner, querier, querist, inquisitor, inquisitress; detective; **busybody,** gossip, *yenta* <Yiddish>, **pry,** Paul Pry, **snoop,** snooper, nosy Parker <nf>; eavesdropper; sightseer; rubbernecker *or* rubberneck <nf>; watcher, Peeping Tom, voyeur, scopophiliac; Lot's wife; explorer

VERBS 3 **be curious, want to know, take an interest in,** take a lively interest, burn with curiosity; be alert, alert oneself, watch, be watchful, be vigilant; prick up one's ears, keep one's ear to the ground; eavesdrop; interrogate, quiz, question, inquire, query; keep one's eyes open, keep one's eye on, stare, gape, peer, gawk, rubber *and* rubberneck <nf>; seek, dig up, dig around for, nose out, nose around for; investigate

4 **pry, snoop,** peep, peek, spy, nose, nose into, have a long *or* big nose, poke *or* stick one's nose in; meddle 214.7

ADJS 5 **curious, inquisitive,** inquisitorial, inquiring, interested, quizzical; **alert,** keen, tuned in <nf>, **attentive** 983.15; burning with curiosity, eaten up *or* consumed with curiosity, curious as a cat; agape, agog, all agog, openmouthed, open-eyed; gossipy; overcurious, supercurious; morbidly curious, **morbid, ghoulish; prurient,** itchy, voyeuristic, scopophiliac; rubbernecking <nf>

6 **prying,** snooping, **nosy** *and* **snoopy** <nf>; meddlesome 214.9

982 INCURIOSITY

NOUNS 1 **incuriosity,** incuriousness, **uninquisitiveness;** boredom; **inattention** 984; **uninterestedness,** disinterest, disinterestedness, **unconcern,** uninvolvement, detachment, **indifference** 102, indifferentness, indifferentism, uncaring, **apathy,** passivity, passiveness, impassivity, impassiveness, listlessness, stolidity, **lack of interest;** carelessness, heedlessness, regardlessness, insouciance, unmindfulness; unperturbability; aloofness, detachment, withdrawal, reclusiveness; intellectual inertia; catatonia, autism; gullibility, credulity, blind faith; objectivity

VERBS 2 **take no interest in, not care;** mind one's own business, pursue the even tenor of one's way, glance neither to the right nor to the left, keep one's nose out, keep an open mind; be indifferent, not care less <nf>, lack emotion; disregard; take it *or* leave it; take on trust; live and let live

ADJS 3 **incurious, uninquisitive,** uninquiring; bored; **inattentive** 984.6; **uninterested,** unconcerned, disinterested, uninvolved, nonaligned, detached, **indifferent,** impersonal, **apathetic,** passive, impassive, stolid, phlegmatic, imperturbable, listless; careless, heedless, regardless, insouciant, mindless, unmindful; aloof, detached, distant, withdrawn, reclusive, sequestered, eremitic; catatonic, autistic; apathetic, not bothered; lackadaisical; unbiased, objective

983 ATTENTION

NOUNS 1 **attention, attentiveness,** mindfulness, regardfulness, heedfulness; **attention span; heed,** ear; consideration, thought, mind; **awareness, consciousness, alertness** 339.5; **observation,** observance, advertence, advertency, **note, notice,** remark, put one's finger on, **regard,** respect; **intentness,** intentiveness, concentration; diligence, assiduity, assiduousness, earnestness; **care** 339.1; **curiosity** 981

2 **interest, concern,** concernment; **curiosity** 981; **enthusiasm,** passion, ardor, zeal; cathexis; matter of interest, special interest; solicitude

3 **engrossment, absorption, intentness,** single-mindedness, **concentration, application,** study, studiousness, **preoccupation,** engagement, **involvement, immersion,** submersion; obsession, monomania; rapt attention, absorbed attention *or* interest; deep study, deep *or* profound thought, contemplation, meditation

4 **close attention,** close study, scrutiny, fixed regard, rapt *or* fascinated attention, whole *or* total *or* undivided attention; minute *or* meticulous attention, attention to detail, microscopic *or* microscopical scrutiny, finicalness, finickiness; constant *or* unrelenting attention, close observance, harping, strict attention; special consideration

VERBS 5 **attend to,** look to, **see to,** advert to, be aware of; **pay attention to,** pay regard to, give mind to, pay mind to <nf>, not forget, spare a thought for, **give heed to;** bethink, bethink oneself; have a look at; **turn to,** give thought to, trouble one's head about; give one's mind to, direct one's attention to, turn *or* bend *or* set the mind *or* attention to; **devote oneself to,** devote the mind *or* thoughts to, fix *or* rivet *or* focus the mind *or* thoughts on, set one's thoughts on, apply the mind *or* attention to, apply oneself to, **occupy oneself with, concern oneself with,** give oneself up to, be absorbed *or* engrossed in, be into <nf>; sink one's teeth, take an interest in, take hold of; **have a lot on one's mind** *or* **plate;** be preoccupied with; **lose oneself in; hang on one's words,** hang on the lips; **drink in,** drink in with rapt attention; be solicitous, suck up to <nf>, brown-nose <nf>

6 **heed, attend,** be heedful, tend, **mind, watch, observe, regard,** look, see, view, mark, remark, animadvert , **note, notice,** take note *or* notice, get a load of <nf>

7 **hearken to,** hark, **listen, hear,** give ear to, lend an ear to, incline *or* bend an ear to, prick up the ears, strain one's ears, **keep one's ears open,** unstopper one's ears, have *or* keep an ear to the ground, listen with both ears, **be all ears**

8 **pay attention** *or* **heed, take heed,** give heed, **look out, watch out** <nf>, **take care** 339.7; look lively *or* alive, **look sharp,** stay *or* be alert, sit up and take notice; be on the ball *or* keep one's eye on the

ball *or* not miss a trick *or* not overlook a bet <nf>, keep a weather eye out *or* on; miss nothing; get after, seize on, keep one's eyes open 339.8; attend to business, mind one's business; pay close *or* strict attention, strain one's attention, not relax one's concern, give one's undivided attention, give special attention to, dance attendance on; keep in the center of one's attention, keep uppermost in one's thought; **concentrate on,** focus *or* fix on; **study,** scrutinize, survey; be obsessed with; cathect

9 **take cognizance of, take note** *or* **notice of,** take heed of, **take account of, take into consideration** *or* **account, bear in mind,** keep *or* hold in mind, reckon with, keep in sight *or* view, not lose sight of, have in one's eye, have an eye to, have regard for

10 **call attention to,** direct attention to, **bring under** *or* **to one's notice,** hold up to notice, bring to attention, **mention,** mention in passing, touch on; **single out,** pick out, lift up, focus on, call *or* bring to notice, direct to the attention, **feature,** highlight, brightline; **direct to,** address to; **mention,** specify, mention in passing, touch on, cite, **refer to,** allude to; **alert one,** call to one's attention, put one wise *and* put one on <nf>; **point out, point to,** point at, put *or* lay one's finger on; **excite** *or* **stimulate attention,** drum up attention

11 **meet with attention,** fall under one's notice; **catch the attention,** strike one, impress one, draw *or* hold *or* focus the attention, take *or* catch *or* meet *or* strike the eye, get *or* catch one's ear, attract notice *or* attention, arrest *or* engage attention, fix *or* rivet one's attention, arrest the thoughts, awaken the mind *or* thoughts, **excite notice,** arouse notice, arrest one's notice, invite *or* solicit attention, claim *or* demand attention, act as a magnet

12 **interest, concern,** involve in *or* with, affect the interest, give pause; **pique, titillate,** tantalize, tickle, tickle one's fancy, **attract,** invite, **fascinate, provoke, stimulate, arouse, excite,** pique one's interest, excite interest, excite *or* whet one's interest, arouse one's passion *or* enthusiasm, turn one on <nf>

13 **engross, absorb,** immerse, **occupy, preoccupy, engage,** involve, monopolize, exercise, take up; **obsess; grip, hold, arrest, hold the interest, fascinate, enthrall,** spellbind, **hold spellbound,** grab <nf>, charm, enchant, mesmerize, hypnotize, catch; absorb the attention, claim one's thoughts, engross the mind *or* thoughts, engage the attention, involve the interest, occupy the attention, monopolize one's attention, engage the mind *or* thoughts

14 **come to attention,** stand at attention

ADJS 15 **attentive, heedful, mindful, regardful,** advertent; intent, intentive, on top of <nf>, diligent, assiduous, intense, earnest, concentrated; **careful** 339.10, on guard, vigilant; **observing,** observant; watchful, aware, conscious, alert 339.14; **curious** 981.5; agog, openmouthed; open-eared, open-eyed, **all eyes, all ears,** all eyes and ears; on the job <nf>, on the ball *and* Johnny-on-the-spot <nf>; **meticulous** 339.12, sedulous, nice, finical, finicky, finicking, niggling

16 **interested,** concerned; **alert to, sensitive to, on the watch; curious** 981.5; tantalized, piqued, titillated, tickled, **attracted,** fascinated, excited, turned-on <nf>; keen on *or* about, enthusiastic, passionate; fixating, cathectic

17 **engrossed, absorbed,** totally absorbed, single-minded, **occupied, preoccupied, engaged,** devoted, devoted to, intent, intent on, monopolized, obsessed, monomaniacal, swept up, taken up with, **involved, caught up in,** wrapped in, **wrapped up in,** engrossed in, **absorbed in** *or* with *or* by, **lost in, immersed in,** submerged in, buried in; over head and ears in, head over heels in <nf>, up to one's elbows in, up to one's ears in; contemplating, contemplative,

studying, studious, meditative, meditating; solicitous, indulgent

18 **gripped, held, fascinated, enthralled, rapt, spellbound,** charmed, enchanted, mesmerized, **hypnotized,** fixed, caught, riveted, **arrested,** switched on <nf>

19 **interesting, stimulating, provocative,** provoking, thought-provoking, thought-challenging, thought-inspiring; **titillating,** tickling, **tantalizing, inviting, exciting; piquant,** lively, racy, juicy, succulent, spicy, rich; readable

20 **engrossing, absorbing,** consuming, **gripping,** riveting, holding, **arresting,** engaging, attractive, **fascinating, enthralling, spellbinding,** enchanting, magnetic, hypnotic, mesmerizing, mesmeric; obsessive, obsessing

ADVS 21 **attentively,** with attention; **heedfully,** mindfully, regardfully, advertently; observingly, observantly; **interestedly,** with interest; **raptly,** with rapt attention; engrossedly, absorbedly, preoccupiedly; devotedly, **intently,** without distraction, **with undivided attention**

22 **hey!, hail!, ahoy!, hello!,** hollo!, hallo!, halloo!, halloa!, ho!, heigh!, hi!, hist!; hello there!, ahoy there!, yo!

984 INATTENTION

NOUNS 1 **inattention,** inattentiveness, **heedlessness, unheedfulness, unmindfulness, thoughtlessness,** inconsideration; **incuriosity** 982, **indifference** 102; inadvertence *or* inadvertency; unintentness, unintentiveness; disregard, disregardfulness, regardlessness, apathy; **flightiness** 985.5, giddiness 985.4, lightmindedness, dizziness *and* ditziness <nf>, scattiness <Brit nf>; levity, frivolousness, flippancy; shallowness, superficiality; **inobservance,** unobservance, nonobservance; **unalertness,** unwariness, unwatchfulness; **obliviousness,** unconsciousness, unawareness; **carelessness,** negligence 340.1, oversight; distraction, **absentmindedness, woolgathering, daydreaming** 985.2, head in the clouds; attention deficit disorder *or* ADD, attention deficit hyperactivity disorder *or* ADHD

VERBS 2 **be inattentive, pay no attention,** pay no mind <nf>, not attend, not notice, **take no note** *or* **notice of,** take no thought *or* account of, miss, not heed, give no heed, pay no regard to, not listen, hear nothing, not hear a word; **disregard, overlook, ignore,** pass over *or* by, have no time for, let pass *or* get by *or* get past; think little of, think nothing of, **slight,** make light of; **close** *or* **shut one's eyes to,** see nothing, be blind to, turn a blind eye, **look the other way, blink at, wink at,** connive at; stick *or* bury *or* hide one's head in the sand; **turn a deaf ear to,** stop one's ears, let come in one ear and go out the other, tune out <nf>; let well enough alone; not trouble oneself with, not trouble one's head with *or* about; **be unwary,** be off one's guard, be caught out

3 **wander, stray,** divagate, wander from the subject, ramble; have no attention span, have a short attention span, let one's attention wander, allow one's mind to wander, get off the track <nf>; **fall asleep at the switch** <nf>, woolgather, **daydream** 985.9

4 **dismiss,** dismiss *or* drive from one's thoughts; **put out of mind,** put out of one's head *or* thoughts, wean *or* force one's thoughts from, **think no more of, forget, forget it,** forget about it, **let it go** <nf>, let slip, not give it another *or* a second thought, **drop the subject,** give it no more thought, obliviate; turn one's back upon, turn away from, turn one's attention from, walk away, abandon, leave out in the cold <nf>; put *or* set *or* lay aside, push *or* thrust aside *or* to one side, wave aside; put on the back burner *or* on hold <nf>; **turn up one's nose at,** sneeze at; **shrug off, brush off** *or* **aside** *or* **away,** blow off *and* laugh off *or* away <nf>, dismiss with a laugh; slight

157.6, kiss off *and* slap *or* smack down <nf>

5 **escape notice** *or* **attention,** escape one, get by, be missed, pass one by, not enter one's head, never occur to one, fall on deaf ears, not register, go over one's head

ADJS 6 **inattentive, unmindful,** inadvertent, thoughtless, **incurious** 982.3, **indifferent** 102.6; **heedless,** unheeding, unheedful, regardless, *distrait* <Fr>, **disregardful,** disregardant; **unobserving,** inobservant, unobservant, unnoticing, unnoting, unremarking, unmarking; **distracted** 985.10; **careless, negligent** 340.10; **scatterbrained, giddy** 985.16, ditzy <nf>, scatty <Brit nf>, flighty; absent-minded, out to lunch <nf>

7 **oblivious, unconscious,** insensible, dead to the world, out of it *and* not with it <nf>; blind, deaf; **preoccupied** 985.11; in a world of one's own

8 **unalert, unwary, unwatchful, unvigilant,** uncautious, incautious; **unprepared,** unready; unguarded, **off one's guard,** off-guard; **asleep,** sleeping, nodding, napping, **asleep at the switch** *and* asleep on the job *and* **not on the job** *and* goofing off *and* looking out the window <nf>; daydreaming, woolgathering

985 DISTRACTION, CONFUSION

NOUNS 1 **distraction,** distractedness, **diversion,** separation *or* withdrawal of attention, divided attention, competing stimuli; too much on one's mind *or* on one's plate, cognitive dissonance, sensory overload; inattention 984

2 **abstractedness, abstraction, preoccupation, absorption,** engrossment, depth of thought, fit of abstraction; **absentmindedness, absence of mind; bemusement,** musing, musefulness ; **woolgathering,** mooning <nf>, moonraking , stargazing, **dreaming, daydreaming,** fantasying, pipe-dreaming <nf>, castle-building; **brown study,** study, reverie, muse, dreamy abstraction, quiet *or* muted ecstasy, trance; dream, **daydream,** fantasy, pipe dream <nf>; daydreamer, Walter Mitty

3 **confusion, fluster,** flummox <nf>, **flutter,** flurry, ruffle; disorientation, **muddle, muddlement,** fuddle *and* fuddlement <nf>, befuddlement, muddleheadedness, daze, maze <nf>; unsettlement, disorganization, **disorder,** chaos, **mess** *and* mix-up *and* snafu <nf>, balls-up *and* shemozzle <Brit nf>, shuffle, jumble, **discomfiture, discomposure, disconcertion,** discombobulation <nf>, **bewilderment, embarrassment, disturbance,** perturbation, **upset,** frenzy, pother, bother, botheration *and* stew <nf>, pucker ; tizzy *and* swivet *and* sweat <nf>; haze, fog, mist, cloud; maze; **perplexity** 971.3

4 **dizziness, vertigo,** vertiginousness, spinning head, swimming, swimming of the head, **giddiness,** wooziness <nf>, **lightheadedness;** tiddliness <Brit nf>, **drunkenness** 88.1,3

5 **flightiness, giddiness,** volatility, mercuriality; **thoughtlessness,** witlessness, brainlessness, emptyheadedness, frivolity, frivolousness, dizziness *and* ditziness <nf>, scattiness <Brit nf>, foolishness 923; **scatterbrain, flibbertigibbet** 924.7

VERBS 6 **distract, divert,** detract, distract the attention, divert *or* detract attention, divert the mind *or* thoughts, draw off the attention, call away, take the mind off of, relieve the mind of, cause the mind to stray *or* wander, put off the track, derail, throw off the scent, lead the mind astray, beguile; throw off one's guard, catch off balance, put off one's stride, trip up

7 **confuse,** throw into confusion *or* chaos, entangle, **mix up, fluster;** flummox <nf>, **flutter,** put into a flutter, **flurry, rattle, ruffle,** moider <Brit nf>; **muddle,** fuddle <nf>, **befuddle, addle,** addle the wits, **daze,** maze, **dazzle,** bedazzle; **upset, unsettle,** raise hell, disorganize; throw into a tizzy *or* swivet; **disconcert, discomfit, discompose,** discombobulate <nf>, disorient, disorientate,

bewilder, embarrass, put out, disturb, perturb, bother, pother, bug <nf>; fog, mist, cloud, becloud; **perplex** 971.13

8 **dizzy, make one's head swim,** cause vertigo, send one spinning, whirl the mind, swirl the senses, make one's head reel *or* whirl *or* spin *or* revolve, go to one's head; **intoxicate** 88.22

9 **muse, moon** <nf>, **dream, daydream,** pipe-dream <nf>, fantasy; abstract oneself, be lost in thought, let one's attention wander, let one's mind run on other things, dream of *or* muse on other things; **wander, stray, ramble,** divagate, let one's thoughts *or* mind wander, give oneself up to reverie, **woolgather, go woolgathering,** let one's wits go bird's nesting, **be in a brown study,** be absent, be somewhere else, stargaze, be out of it *and* be not with it <nf>

ADJS 10 **distracted, distraught,** *distrait* <Fr>; **wandering, rambling; wild, frantic, beside oneself**

11 **abstracted, bemused,** museful , **musing, preoccupied, absorbed, engrossed,** taken up; **absent-minded, absent,** faraway, elsewhere, somewhere else, not there; pensive, meditative; lost, **lost in thought,** wrapped in thought; rapt, transported, ecstatic; dead to the world, **unconscious, oblivious; dreaming, dreamy,** drowsing, dozing, nodding, half-awake, betwixt sleep and waking, napping; **daydreaming,** daydreamy, pipe-dreaming <nf>; **woolgathering,** mooning *and* moony <nf>, moonraking , castle-building, in the clouds, off in the clouds, stargazing, in a reverie

12 **confused, mixed-up,** crazy mixed-up <nf>; **flustered,** fluttered, **ruffled, rattled,** fussed <nf>; **upset, unsettled,** off-balance, off one's stride; **disorganized, disordered,** disoriented, disorientated, chaotic, jumbled, in a jumble, shuffled; shaken, shook <nf>, **disconcerted, discomposed,** discombobulated <nf>, **embarrassed, put-out, disturbed, perturbed,** bothered, all hot and bothered <nf>; in a stew *or* botheration <nf>, in a pucker ; in a tizzy *or* swivet *or* sweat <nf>, in a pother; **perplexed**

13 **muddled,** in a muddle; fuddled <nf>, **befuddled;** muddleheaded, fuddlebrained <nf>; puzzleheaded, puzzlepated; **addled,** addleheaded, addlepated, addlebrained; adrift, at sea, foggy, fogged, in a fog, hazy, muzzy <nf>, misted, misty, cloudy, beclouded

14 **dazed,** mazed, **dazzled,** bedazzled, in a daze; **silly,** knocked silly, cockeyed <nf>; **groggy** <nf>, **dopey** <nf>, woozy <nf>; **punch-drunk** *and* punchy *and* **slap-happy** <nf>

15 **dizzy, giddy,** vertiginous, spinning, swimming, turned around, going around in circles; lightheaded, tiddly <Brit nf>, **drunk, drunken** 88.31

16 scatterbrained, shatterbrained *or* shatterpated , rattlebrained, rattleheaded, rattlepated, scramblebrained, harebrain, harebrained, **giddy, dizzy** *and* ditzy *and* gaga <nf>, scatty <Brit nf>, giddybrained, giddy-headed, giddy-pated, giddy-witted, giddy as a goose, fluttery, frivolous, featherbrained, featherheaded; **thoughtless, witless, brainless, empty-headed** 922.19

17 **flighty,** volatile, mercurial

986 IMAGINATION

NOUNS 1 **imagination,** imagining, imaginativeness, **fancy, fantasy,** conceit ; mind's eye; flight of fancy, fumes of fancy; fantasticism

2 **creative thought,** conception; lateral thinking, association of ideas; productive *or* constructive *or* creative imagination, creative power *or* ability, esemplastic imagination *or* power, shaping imagination, poetic imagination, artistic imagination, blue-sky thinking; mythopoeia; mythification, mythicization; inspiration, stimulus, muse; Muses: Calliope <epic poetry>, Clio <history>, Erato <lyric and love poetry>, Euterpe <music>, Mel-

pomene <tragedy>, Polyhymnia <sacred song>, Terpsichore <dancing and choral song>, Thalia <comedy>, Urania <astronomy>; genius 920.8; afflatus, divine afflatus; frenzy, ecstasy

3 **invention, inventiveness, originality, creativity, fabrication,** creativeness, **ingenuity;** productivity, prolificacy, **fertility,** fecundity; rich *or* teeming imagination, fertile *or* pregnant imagination, seminal *or* germinal imagination, fertile mind; imagineering; **fiction,** fictionalization

4 **lively imagination,** active fancy, **vivid imagination,** colorful *or* highly colored *or* lurid imagination, warm *or* ardent imagination, fiery *or* heated imagination, excited imagination, bold *or* daring *or* wild *or* fervent imagination; verve, vivacity of imagination

5 **figment of the imagination,** creature of the imagination, creation *or* coinage of the brain, fiction of the mind, maggot , whim, whimsy, figment, imagination, invention; caprice, vagary; brainchild; **imagining,** fancy, idle fancy, vapor, imagery; **fantasy, make-believe;** fabrication; phantom, vision, apparition, insubstantial image, eidolon, **phantasm** 976.4; **fiction,** myth, romance; wildest dreams, stretch of the imagination; **chimera, bubble, illusion** 976; hallucination, delirium, sick fancy; trip *or* drug trip <nf>

6 **visualization, envisioning,** envisaging, picturing, objectification, imaging, calling to *or* before the mind's eye, figuring *or* portraying *or* representing in the mind; depicting *or* delineating in the imagination; conceptualization; **picture, vision, image,** mental image, mental picture, visual image, visualization, vivid *or* lifelike image, eidetic image, concept, **conception,** mental representation *or* presentation; image-building, **imagery,** word-painting; poetic image, poetic imagery; imagery study; imagism, imagistic poetry

7 **idealism, idealization; ideal,** ideality; rose-colored glasses; visionariness, **utopianism;** flight of fancy, play of fancy, imaginative exercise; **romanticism,** romanticizing, romance; **quixotism,** quixotry; dreamery; **impracticality,** unpracticalness, **unrealism,** unreality; **wishful thinking,** wish fulfillment, wish-fulfillment fantasy, dream come true; autistic thinking, dereistic thinking, autism, dereism, autistic distortion

8 **dreaminess,** dreamfulness, musefulness, pensiveness; dreamlikeness; **dreaming, musing; daydreaming,** pipe-dreaming <nf>, dreamery, fantasying, castlebuilding

9 **dream; reverie, daydream, pipe dream** <nf>, wishful thinking; **brown study** 985.2; **vision; nightmare,** incubus, bad dream

10 **air castle, castle in the air,** castle in the sky *or* skies, castle in Spain; Xanadu *and* pleasure dome of Kubla Khan, pie in the sky, end of the rainbow

11 **utopia** *or* Utopia, **paradise, heaven** 681, **heaven on earth;** millennium, kingdom come; dreamland, dream world, lotus land, land of dreams, land of enchantment, land of heart's desire, wonderland, cloudland, fairyland, land of faerie, faerie; Eden, Garden of Eden; the Promised Land, land of promise, land of plenty, land of milk and honey, Canaan, Goshen; Shangri-la, Atlantis, Arcadia, Agapemone, Camelot, Avalon, Happy Valley, land of Prester John, El Dorado, Emerald City, Treasure Island, Wonderland, Seven Cities of Cibola, Quivira; Laputa; Cockaigne, Big Rock-Candy Mountain, Fiddler's Green, never-never land, Neverland, Cloudcuckooland *or* Nephelococcygia, Erewhon, Land of Youth, Fountain of Youth; dystopia *or* kakotopia; Pandemonium; Middle Earth

12 **imaginer, fancier,** fantast; fantasist; mythmaker, mythopoet; mythifier, mythicizer; **inventor; creative artist,** composer, poet, creative writer; imagineer

13 **visionary, idealist;** prophet, **seer; dreamer, daydreamer,** dreamer of dreams, castle-builder, lotus-eater, **wishful thinker; romantic,** romanticist, romancer; Quixote, Don Quixote; utopian, utopianist, utopianizer; escapist, ostrich; enthusiast, rhapsodist

VERBS **14** **imagine, fancy, conceive,** conceit , conceptualize, ideate, figure to oneself; **invent, create, originate, make,** think up, dream up, shape, mold, coin, hatch, concoct, fabricate, produce; **suppose** 951.10; **fantasize;** fictionalize; use one's imagination; give free rein to the imagination, let one's imagination riot *or* run riot *or* run wild, allow one's imagination to run away with one; experience imaginatively *or* vicariously

15 **visualize,** vision, **envision, envisage, picture, image,** objectify; picture in one's mind, picture to oneself, **view with the mind's eye,** contemplate in the imagination, form a mental picture of, represent, **see,** just see, have a picture of; call up, summon up, conjure up, **call to mind,** realize; have an inspiration

16 **idealize,** utopianize, quixotize, rhapsodize; **romanticize,** romance; paint pretty pictures of, paint in bright colors; see through rose-colored glasses; **build castles in the air** *or* **Spain;** live in a dream world

17 **dream;** dream of, dream on; **daydream,** pipe-dream <nf>, get *or* have stars in one's eyes, have one's head in the clouds, indulge in wish fulfillment; fantasy, conjure up a vision; blow one's mind *and* go on a trip *and* trip *and* freak out <nf>

ADJS **18** **imaginative,** conceptual, conceptive, ideational, ideative, notional; perceptive; **inventive, original,** innovative, originative, esemplastic, shaping, **creative, ingenious, resourceful; productive, fertile,** fecund, prolific, seminal, germinal, teeming, pregnant; **inspired,** visioned

19 **imaginary,** imaginational, notional; **imagined, fancied; unreal,** unrealistic, airy-fairy <Brit>, unactual, nonexistent, never-never; visional, supposititious, **all in the mind; illusory;** not of this world

20 **fanciful, notional,** notiony <nf>, whimsical, maggoty <Brit>; airy-fairy <nf>; brain-born; fancy-bred, fancy-born, fancy-built, fancy-framed, fancy-woven, fancy-wrought; dream-born, dream-built, dream-created; **fantastic, fantastical,** fantasque, extravagant, preposterous, outlandish, wild, baroque, rococo, florid; Alice-in-Wonderland, bizarre, grotesque, Gothic

21 **fictitious, make-believe, figmental,** fictional, fictive, fabricated, fictionalized; nonhistorical, nonfactual, nonactual, nonrealistic; **fabulous, mythic, mythical,** mythological, legendary; mythified, mythicized

22 **chimeric, chimerical, aerial, ethereal,** phantasmal; vaporous, vapory; gossamer; air-built, cloud-built, cloud-born, cloud-woven

23 **ideal, idealized;** utopian, Arcadian, Edenic, paradisal; pie in the sky <nf>; heavenly, celestial; millennial

24 **visionary, idealistic, quixotic; romantic, romanticized,** romancing, romanticizing; poetic *or* poetical; storybook; **impractical, unpractical, unrealistic;** wish-fulfilling, autistic, dereistic; starry-eyed, dewy-eyed; in the clouds, with one's head in the clouds; airy, **otherworldly,** transmundane, transcendental

25 **dreamy, dreamful; dreamy-eyed,** dreamy-minded, dreamy-souled; dreamlike; day-dreamy, **dreaming, daydreaming,** pipe-dreaming <nf>, castle-building; **entranced,** tranced, in a trance, dream-stricken, enchanted, spellbound, spelled, charmed

26 **imaginable, fanciable, conceivable, thinkable,** cogitable; **supposable** 951.15

987 UNIMAGINATIVENESS

NOUNS **1** **unimaginativeness,** unfancifulness; **prosaicness,** prosiness, prosaism, prosaicism, unpoeticalness; **staidness, stuffiness** <nf>;

stolidity; **dullness, dryness;** aridness, aridity, barrenness, infertility, infecundity; **unoriginality,** uncreativeness, uninventiveness, dearth of ideas

2 <practical attitude> **realism,** realisticness, **practicalness, practicality, practical-mindedness,** sober-mindedness, sobersidedness, **hardheadedness, matter-of-factness;** down-to-earthness, earthiness, worldliness, secularism; real world, the here and now; nuts and bolts, no nonsense, no frills; **pragmatism,** pragmaticism, positivism, scientism; unidealism, unromanticalness, unsentimentality; sensibleness, saneness, reasonableness, rationality; freedom from illusion, lack of sentimentality; lack of feeling 94

3 **realist,** pragmatist, positivist, practical person, hardhead

VERBS **4** **keep both feet on the ground,** stick to the facts, call a spade a spade; **come down to earth,** come down out of the clouds, know when the honeymoon is over.

ADJS **5** **unimaginative, unfanciful;** unidealized, unromanticized; **prosaic,** prosy, prosing, unpoetic, unpoetical; **literal,** literal-minded; earthbound, mundane; **staid, stuffy** <nf>; stolid; **dull, dry;** arid, barren, infertile, infecund; **unoriginal,** uninspired; hedged, undaring, unaspiring, **uninventive** 891.5

6 **realistic,** realist, **practical;** pragmatic, pragmatical, scientific, scientistic, positivistic; **unidealistic,** unideal, **unromantic, unsentimental, practical-minded,** sober-minded, sobersided, **hardheaded,** straight-thinking, **matter-of-fact, down-to-earth, with both feet on the ground;** worldly, earthy, secular; sensible, sane, reasonable, rational, sound, sound-thinking; **reductive, simplistic**

988 SPECTER

NOUNS **1** **specter, ghost,** spectral ghost, **spook** <nf>, **phantom,** phantasm, phantasma, **wraith, shade,** shadow, fetch, **apparition,** appearance, presence, shape, form, eidolon, idolum, revenant, larva; **spirit;** sprite, shrouded spirit, disembodied spirit, departed spirit, restless *or* wandering spirit *or* soul, soul of the dead, dybbuk; oni; Masan; astral spirit, astral; unsubstantiality, immateriality, incorporeal, incorporeity, incorporeal being *or* entity; walking dead man, zombie; jinn *or* dijn, genie; duppy; vision, theophany; materialization; haunt *or* hant <nf>; banshee; poltergeist; control, guide; manes, lemures; grateful dead

2 White Lady, White Lady of Avenel, White Ladies of Normandy; Brocken specter; Wild Hunt; Flying Dutchman

3 **double,** etheric double *or* self, cowalker, *Doppelgänger* <Ger>, doubleganger, fetch, wraith

4 **eeriness, ghostliness, weirdness, uncanniness, spookiness** <nf>

5 **possession,** spirit control; obsession,

VERBS **6** **haunt,** hant <nf>, spook <nf>; **possess,** control; obsess

ADJS **7** **spectral,** specterlike; **ghostly,** ghostish, ghosty, ghostlike; **spiritual, psychic,** psychical; **phantomlike,** phantom, phantomic *or* phantomical, phantasmal, phantasmic, **wraithlike,** wraithy, shadowy; etheric, ectoplasmic, astral, ethereal 764.6; incorporeal 1053.7; **occult, supernatural** 870.15

8 **disembodied,** bodiless, immaterial 1053.7, discarnate, decarnate, decarnated

9 **weird, eerie,** eldritch, **uncanny,** unearthly, macabre; **spooky** *and* spookish *and* hairy <nf>

10 **haunted,** spooked *and* spooky <nf>, spirit-haunted, ghost-haunted, specter-haunted; **possessed,** ghost-ridden; obsessed

989 MEMORY

NOUNS **1** **memory, remembrance, recollection,** mind, *souvenir* <Fr>; memory trace, engram; mind's eye, eye of the mind, mirror of the mind, tablets of the memory; corner *or* recess of the memory, inmost recesses of the memory; Mnemosyne, mother of the Muses; short-term memory, long-term memory, anterograde memory; computer memory, information storage; group memory, collective memory, mneme, racial memory; atavism; cover *or* screen memory, affect memory; eye *or* visual memory, kinesthetic memory; skill, verbal response, emotional response

2 **retention, retentiveness,** retentivity, memory span; good memory, retentive memory *or* mind; total memory, eidetic memory *or* imagery, photographic memory, total recall; camera-eye

3 **remembering, remembrance, recollection,** recollecting, exercise of memory, **recall,** recalling; reflection, reconsideration; **retrospect,** retrospection, hindsight, looking back, harking back; flashback, **reminiscence,** review, contemplation of the past, review of things past, nostalgia; **memoir; memorization,** memorizing, **rote,** rote memory, rote learning, learning by heart, commitment to memory; déjà vu

4 **recognition, identification, reidentification,** distinguishment; realization 928.2

5 **reminder, remembrance,** remembrancer; **prompt,** prompter, tickler; prompting, cue, hint; jogger <nf>, flapper; *aide-mémoire* <Fr>, **memorandum** 549.4

6 **memento, remembrance, token, trophy, souvenir, keepsake, relic,** favor, token of remembrance; commemoration, memorial 549.12; *memento mori* <L>; **memories, memorabilia,** memorials; history, memoirs

7 memorability, rememberability

8 mnemonics, memory training, mnemotechny, mnemotechnics, mnemonization; mnemonic, mnemonic device, *aide-mémoire* <Fr>

VERBS 9 **remember, recall, recollect,** flash on *and* mind <nf>; have a good *or* ready memory, remember clearly, remember as if it were yesterday; have total recall, remember everything; reflect; **think of,** bethink oneself ; **call** *or* **bring to mind,** recall to mind, call up, summon up, conjure up, evoke, reevoke, revive, recapture, call back, bring back; **think back,** go back, **look back,** cast the eyes back, carry one's thoughts back, look back upon things past, use hindsight, retrospect, **see in retrospect,** go back over, hark back, retrace, reconstruct, review, hark back, turn back time; review, review in retrospect; write one's memoirs

10 **reminisce,** rake *or* dig up the past

11 **recognize, know, tell, distinguish, make out; identify, place,** have; spot *and* nail *and* peg *and* cotton on <nf>, **reidentify,** know again, recover *or* recall knowledge of, know by sight; realize 928.12

12 **keep in memory, bear in mind,** keep *or* hold in mind, hold *or* retain the memory of, **keep in view,** have in mind, hold *or* carry *or* retain in one's thoughts, store in the mind, **retain, keep;** tax *or* burden the memory, **treasure, cherish,** treasure up in the memory, enshrine *or* embalm in the memory, cherish the memory of; keep up the memory of, keep the memory alive, keep alive in one's thoughts; brood over, dwell on *or* upon, fan the embers, let fester in the mind, let rankle in the breast

13 **be remembered,** sink in, penetrate, make an impression; live *or* dwell in one's memory, be easy to recall, remain in one's memory, be green *or* fresh in one's memory, stick in the mind, remain indelibly impressed on the memory, be stamped on one's memory, **never be forgotten; haunt one's thoughts,** obsess, run in the head, be in one's thoughts, be on one's mind; be burnt into one's memory, plague one; be like King Charles's head; **rankle,** rankle in the breast, fester in the mind

14 **recur,** recur to the mind, return to mind, come back, resurface, reenter

15 **come to mind,** pop into one's head, come to me, come into one's head, flash on the mind, pass in review

16 **memorize, commit to memory,** con; study; **learn by heart,** get by

heart, learn *or* get by rote, get word-perfect *or* letter-perfect, learn word for word, learn verbatim; know by heart *or* from memory, have by heart *or* rote, have at one's fingers' ends *or* tips; repeat by heart *or* rote, give word for word, recite, repeat, parrot, repeat like a parrot, say one's lesson, rattle *or* reel off; be a quick study; retain

17 fix in the mind *or* memory, instill, infix, inculcate, impress, imprint, stamp, inscribe, etch, grave, engrave; **impress on the mind, get into one's head,** drive *or* hammer into one's head, get across, get into one's thick head *or* skull <nf>; **burden the mind with,** task the mind with, load *or* stuff *or* cram the mind with; inscribe *or* stamp *or* rivet in the memory, set in the tablets of memory, etch indelibly in the mind

18 refresh the memory, review, restudy, **brush up, rub up,** polish up *and* bone up <nf>, get up on; **cram** <nf>, swot up <Brit nf>

19 remind, put in mind, remember, put in remembrance, bring back, bring to recollection, refresh the memory of; **remind one of, recall,** suggest, **put one in mind of; take one back,** carry back, carry back in recollection; **jog the memory,** awaken *or* arouse the memory, flap the memory, give a hint *or* suggestion, refresh one's memory; **prompt,** prompt the mind, give the cue, hold the promptbook; nudge, pull by the sleeve, nag; brush up; make a note

20 try to recall, think hard, rack *or* ransack one's brains, **cudgel one's brains,** crack one's brains <nf>; have on the tip of one's tongue, have on the edge of one's memory *or* consciousness

ADJS **21 recollective, memoried;** mnemonic; retentive; **retrospective,** in retrospect; **reminiscent,** nostalgic, **mindful, remindful, suggestive,** redolent, evocative

22 remembered, recollected, recalled; retained, pent-up in the memory, kept in remembrance, enduring, lasting, **unforgotten;** present to the mind, lodged in one's mind, stamped on the memory; vivid, eidetic, fresh, green, alive

23 remembering, mindful, keeping *or* bearing in mind, holding in remembrance; unable to forget, haunted, plagued, obsessed, nagged, rankled

24 memorable, rememberable, recollectable; notable

25 unforgettable, never to be forgotten, never to be erased from the mind, **indelible,** indelibly impressed on the mind, fixed in the mind; haunting, persistent, recurrent, nagging, plaguing, rankling, festering; obsessing, obsessive

26 memorial, commemorative

ADVS **27 by heart,** *par cœur* <Fr>, **by rote, by** *or* **from memory,** without book; **memorably;** rememberingly

28 in memory of, to the memory of, in remembrance *or* commemoration, *in memoriam* <L>; *memoria in aeterna* <L>, in perpetual remembrance

990 FORGETFULNESS

NOUNS **1 forgetfulness,** unmindfulness, absentmindedness, **memorylessness;** short memory, short memory span, little retentivity *or* recall, mind *or* memory like a sieve; loose memory, vague *or* fuzzy memory, dim *or* hazy recollection; **lapse of memory,** decay of memory; **obliviousness, oblivion,** nirvana; obliteration; Lethe, Lethe water, waters of Lethe *or* oblivion, river of oblivion; insensibility; trance; nepenthe; **forgetting;** heedlessness 340.2; forgiveness 148; senior moment, memory lapse

2 loss of memory, memory loss, amnesia, failure, blackout; **memory gap,** blackout <nf>; fugue; agnosia, unrecognition, body-image agnosia, ideational agnosia, astereognosis *or* astereocognosy; paramnesia, retrospective falsification, false memory, misremembrance; amnesiac

3 block, blocking, **mental block,** memory obstruction; repression, suppression, defense mechanism, conversion, sublimation, symbolization

VERBS **4** **be forgetful,** suffer memory loss, be absentminded, have a short memory, have a mind *or* memory like a sieve, have a short memory span, be unable to retain, have little recall, forget one's own name, be oblivious; misremember

5 **forget,** clean forget <nf>; **not remember,** disremember *and* disrecollect <nf>, fail to remember, forget to remember, **have no remembrance *or* recollection of,** be unable to recollect *or* recall, draw a blank <nf>; lose, lose sight of, lose one's train of thought, lose track of what one was saying; have on the tip of the tongue; blow *or* go up in *or* fluff one's lines, forget one's lines, dry up; misremember, misrecollect

6 efface *or* erase from the memory, consign to oblivion, unlearn, obliterate, **dismiss from one's thoughts** 984.4; **forgive** 148.3,5

7 **be forgotten, escape one,** miss, **slip one's mind,** fade *or* die away from the memory, slip *or* escape the memory, drop from one's thoughts; fall *or* sink into oblivion, go in one ear and out the other

ADJS **8** **forgotten,** clean forgotten <nf>, **unremembered,** disremembered *and* disrecollected <nf>, **unrecollected, unretained, unrecalled,** past recollection *or* recall, out of the mind, lost, erased, effaced, obliterated, gone out of one's head *or* recollection, beyond recall, consigned to oblivion, buried *or* sunk in oblivion; out of sight out of mind; misremembered, misrecollected; half-remembered; on the tip of one's tongue

9 **forgetful, forgetting,** inclined to forget, **memoryless, unremembering, unmindful,** absentminded, **oblivious,** insensible to the past, with a mind *or* memory like a sieve; blank, vacant, vacuous, emptyheaded, absent-minded; suffering from *or* stricken with amnesia, amnesic, amnestic; blocked, repressed, suppressed, sublimated, converted; heedless 340.11; Lethean; in a trance, preoccupied, spaced-out <nf>, out to lunch <nf>

10 **forgettable,** unrememberable, unrecollectable; effaceable, eradicable, erasable

ADVS **11** **forgetfully,** forgettingly, unmindfully, absentmindedly, **obliviously**

991 SUFFICIENCY

NOUNS **1** **sufficiency,** sufficientness, **adequacy,** adequateness, **enough,** a competence *or* competency; satisfactoriness, satisfaction, satisfactory amount, enough to go around; good *or* adequate supply; exact measure, right amount, no more and no less; bare sufficiency, minimum, bare minimum, just enough, enough to get by on, enough to live on; self-sufficiency

2 **plenty,** plenitude, plentifulness, plenteousness, muchness ; myriad, myriads, numerousness 884; **amplitude,** ampleness; substantiality, substantialness; **abundance, copiousness;** exuberance, riotousness; **bountifulness,** bounteousness, liberalness, **liberality,** generousness, **generosity; lavishness, extravagance, prodigality;** luxuriance, fertility, teemingness, productiveness 890; **wealth, opulence** *or* opulency, richness, affluence; more than enough; maximum; **fullness,** full measure, repletion, repleteness; **overflow, outpouring,** flood, inundation, flow, shower, spate, stream, gush, avalanche; landslide; **prevalence,** profuseness, **profusion,** riot; **superabundance** 993.2; **overkill;** no end of, great abundance, great plenty, quantities, much, as much as one could wish, one's fill, more than one can shake a stick at, lots, a fistful <nf>, **scads** 247.4; bumper crop, rich harvest, foison ; rich vein, bonanza, oodles *and* luau <nf>; an ample sufficiency, enough and to spare, enough and then some; fat of the land

3 cornucopia, horn of plenty, horn of Amalthea, endless supply, bottomless well *or* pit

VERBS **4** **suffice, do,** just do, serve, **answer,** quench; work, be equal to, **avail;** answer *or* serve the purpose, do the trick <nf>, **suit;** qualify, meet, fulfill, **satisfy,** meet requirements; **pass muster,** make the grade *or* the cut *and* hack it *and* cut the mustard *and* **fill the bill** <nf>, measure up to, prove acceptable; get by *and* scrape by <nf>, do it, do'er <nf>, do in a pinch, **pass,** pass in the dark <nf>; hold, stand, stand up, take it, bear; stretch <nf>, reach, go around; rise to the occasion

5 **abound,** be plentiful, exuberate , teem, **teem with,** creep with, crawl with, swarm with, be lousy with <nf>, bristle with; proliferate 890.7; **overflow,** run over, flood; flow, stream, rain, **pour,** shower, gush; flow with milk and honey, rain cats and dogs *and* stink of *and* roll in <nf>

ADJS **6** **sufficient,** sufficing; **enough, ample,** substantial, **plenty, satisfactory, adequate,** decent, due; competent, up to the mark, up to snuff; commensurate, proportionate, corresponding 788.9; suitable, fit 788.10; good, **good enough,** plenty good enough <nf>; sufficient for *or* to *or* unto, up to, equal to; barely sufficient, minimal, minimum; hand-to-mouth

7 **plentiful,** plenty, **plenteous,** plenitudinous; **galore** *and* a gogo *and* up the gazoo *or* kazoo *and* up to the ass in <nf>, in plenty, in quantity *or* quantities, aplenty <nf>; numerous 884.6; beaucoup <nf>, much, many 247.8; **ample,** all-sufficing; wholesale; well-stocked, well-provided, well-furnished, well-found; abundant, abounding, **copious,** exuberant, riotous; flush; **bountiful,** bounteous, **lavish, generous, liberal, extravagant, prodigal; luxuriant,** fertile, productive 890.9, **rich,** fat, **wealthy, opulent, affluent;** maximal; **full,** replete, well-filled, running over, overflowing; inexhaustible, exhaustless, bottomless; **profuse,** profusive, effuse, diffuse; **prevalent,** prevailing, rife, rampant, epidemic; lousy with <nf>, teeming 884.9; **superabundant** 993.19; a dime a dozen

ADVS **8** **sufficiently, amply,** substantially, **satisfactorily, enough;** competently, **adequately;** minimally

9 **plentifully,** plenteously, **aplenty** <nf>, **in plenty,** in quantity *or* quantities, in good supply; **abundantly,** in abundance, copiously, no end <nf>; **superabundantly** 993.24; **bountifully,** bounteously, **lavishly, generously, liberally, extravagantly, prodigally;** maximally; **fully,** in full measure, to the full, overflowingly; inexhaustibly, exhaustlessly, bottomlessly; exuberantly, luxuriantly, riotously; richly, opulently, affluently; **profusely,** diffusely, effusely; beyond one's wildest dreams, beyond the dreams of avarice

992 INSUFFICIENCY

NOUNS **1** **insufficiency, inadequacy,** insufficientness, inadequateness; short supply, seller's market; none to spare; unsatisfactoriness, nonsatisfaction, nonfulfillment, coming *or* falling short *or* shy, slippage, shortfall; **undercommitment;** disappointment, too little too late; a band-aid <nf>, a drop in the bucket *or* the ocean, a lick and a promise, a cosmetic measure; **incompetence,** incompetency, unqualification, unsuitability 789.3

2 **meagerness,** exiguousness, exiguity, scrimpiness, skimpiness, scantiness, spareness; meanness, miserliness, niggardliness, narrowness <nf>, stinginess, parsimony; smallness, slightness, puniness, paltriness; thinness, leanness, slimness, slim pickings <nf>, slenderness, scrawniness; jejuneness, jejunity; austerity; skeleton crew, corporal's guard

3 **scarcity,** scarceness; **sparsity,** sparseness; **scantiness,** scant sufficiency; **dearth, paucity,** poverty; **rarity,** rareness, uncommonness

4 **want, lack, need, deficiency, deficit, shortage, shortfall,** wantage, **incompleteness,** defectiveness, shortcoming 911, imperfection; **absence** 222, omission; **destitution,** impoverishment, beggary, deprivation; starvation, famine, drought, drying-up

5 **pittance,** dole, scrimption <nf>; drop in the bucket *or* the ocean; **mite,** bit 248.2; short allowance, short commons, half rations, cheeseparings and candle ends; mere subsistence, starvation wages; widow's mite

6 **dietary deficiency,** vitamin deficiency; undernourishment, undernutrition, **malnutrition,** malnourishment, starvation diet, half rations, bread and water; Lenten fare, Spartan fare

VERBS 7 **want, lack, need, require;** miss, feel the want of, be sent away empty-handed; run short of

8 **be insufficient,** not qualify, be found wanting, leave a lot to be desired, kick the beam, not make it *and* not hack it *and* not make the cut *and* not cut it *and* not cut the mustard <nf>, be beyond one's depth *or* ken, be in over one's head, **fall short,** fall shy, come short, not come up to; run short; want, want for, lack, fail, fail of *or* in; cramp one's style <nf>

ADJS 9 **insufficient,** unsufficing, **inadequate;** found wanting, defective, incomplete, imperfect, deficient, lacking, failing, wanting; **too few,** undersupplied, low on, light on; **too little,** not enough, precious little, a trickle *or* mere trickle; **unsatisfactory,** unsatisfying; cosmetic, merely cosmetic, surface, superficial, symptomatic, merely symptomatic; **incompetent,** unequal to, unqualified, not up to it, not up to snuff, beyond one's depth *or* over one's head, outmatched; short-staffed, understaffed, short-handed

10 **meager, slight,** scrimpy, skimp, skimpy, exiguous; scant, **scanty,** spare; miserly, niggardly, stingy, narrow <nf>, parsimonious, mean; hard to find, out of stock; austere, Lenten, Spartan, abstemious, ascetic; stinted, frugal, sparing; poor, impoverished; small, puny, paltry; thin, lean, slim, slender, scrawny; dwarfish, dwarfed, stunted, undergrown; straitened, limited; jejune, watered, watery, unnourishing, unnutritious; subsistence, starvation

11 **scarce, sparse, scanty; in short supply,** at a premium; **rare,** uncommon, infrequent; scarcer than hen's teeth <nf>; not to be had, not to be had for love *or* money, not to be had at any price; out of print, out of stock *or* season, nonexistent; few and far between

12 **ill-provided,** ill-furnished, ill-equipped, ill-found, ill off; **unprovided,** unsupplied, unreplenished; bare-handed; unfed, underfed, undernourished; shorthanded, undermanned; **empty-handed, poor,** pauperized, impoverished, beggarly; hungry, starved, half-starved, on short commons, starving, starveling, famished, anorectic

13 **wanting, lacking, needing, missing, in want of;** for want of, in default of, in the absence of; short, **short of,** scant of; shy, **shy of** *or* **on; out of,** clean *or* fresh out of <nf>, destitute of, bare of, void of, empty of, devoid of, forlorn of, bereft of, deprived of, denuded of, unpossessed of, unblessed with, bankrupt in; out of pocket; at the end of one's rope *or* tether

ADVS 14 **insufficiently; inadequately,** unsubstantially, incompletely

15 **meagerly, slightly,** sparely, punily, scantily, poorly, frugally, sparingly

16 **scarcely, sparsely, scantily,** skimpily, scrimpily; **rarely,** uncommonly

993 EXCESS

NOUNS 1 **excess, excessiveness, inordinance,** inordinateness, nimiety, **immoderateness,** immoderacy, immoderation, **extravagance** *or* extravagancy, intemperateness, incontinence, overindulgence, **intemperance** 669; unrestrainedness, abandon; gluttony 672; **extreme,** extremity, **extremes; boundlessness** 823.1; overlargeness, overgreatness, monstrousness, enormousness 247.1; overgrowth, overdevelopment, hypertrophy, gigantism, giantism, elephantiasis; **overmuch,** overmuchness, too much, too-muchness; **exorbitance** *or* exorbitancy, undueness, **outrageousness,** unconscionableness, **unreasonableness;** radicalism, extremism 611.4; egregiousness; fabulousness, hyperbole, **exaggeration** 355

2 **superabundance,** overabundance, superflux, **plethora,** redundancy, overprofusion, too many, too much, too much of a good thing, **overplentifulness,** overplenteousness, overplenty, **oversupply,** overstock, overaccumulation, **oversufficiency,** overmuchness, overcopiousness, overlavishness, overluxuriance, overbounteousness, overnumerousness; lavishness, **extravagance** *or* extravagancy, **prodigality; plenty** 991.2; **more than enough, enough and to spare,** enough in all conscience; **overdose,** overmeasure, one too many; too much of a good thing, egg in one's beer <nf>; more than one knows what to do with, drug on the market; spate, avalanche, landslide, deluge, flood, inundation; *embarras de richesses* <Fr>, embarrassment of riches, money to burn <nf>; overpopulation; spare tire, fifth wheel; lagniappe

3 **overfullness,** plethora, **surfeit, glut;** satiety 994; engorgement, repletion, congestion; hyperemia; **saturation,** supersaturation; **overload,** overburden, overcharge, surcharge, overfreight, overweight; **overflow,** overbrimming, overspill; **insatiability,** insatiableness; all the market can bear

4 **superfluity,** superfluousness, fat; **redundancy,** redundance; unnecessariness, needlessness; fifth wheel *and* tits on a boar <nf>; featherbedding, payroll padding; duplication, duplication of effort, overlap; **luxury,** extravagance, frill *and* **frills** *and* bells and whistles *and* gimcrackery <nf>; frippery, froufrou, overadornment, bedizenment, gingerbread; **ornamentation, embellishment** 498.1; expletive, **padding, filling;** pleonasm, tautology; verbosity, prolixity 538.2; more than one really wants to know

5 **surplus,** surplusage, leftovers, plus, **overplus,** overstock, **overage,** overset, overrun, **overmeasure, oversupply;** margin; **remainder, balance, leftover, extra, spare,** something extra *or* to spare; bonus, dividend; lagniappe <nf>; gratuity, tip, *pourboire* <Fr>

6 **overdoing,** overcarrying, **overreaching,** supererogation; **overkill;** piling on <nf>, overimportance, overemphasis; overuse; overreaction; **overwork, overexertion,** overexercise, overexpenditure, overtaxing, overstrain, tax, strain; too much on one's plate, too many irons in the fire, too much at once; **overachievement,** overachieving

7 **overextension, overdrawing,** drawing *or* spreading too thin, **overstretching,** overstrain, overstraining, stretching, straining, stretch, strain, tension, extreme tension, snapping *or* breaking point; **overexpansion;** inflation, distension, overdistension, edema, turgidity, swelling, bloat, bloating 259.2

VERBS 8 **superabound,** overabound, **know no bounds, swarm,** pullulate, run riot, luxuriate, **teem;** overflow, flood, overbrim, overspill, spill over, overrun, overspread, overswarm, overgrow, fill, saturate; meet one at every turn; hang heavy on one's hands, remain on one's hands; burst at the seams

9 **exceed, surpass, pass, top, transcend, go beyond;** overpass, overstep, overrun, **overreach,** overshoot, overshoot the mark

10 **overdo, go too far,** do twice over, do it to death <nf>, pass all bounds, know no bounds, overact, **carry too far,** overcarry, go to an extreme, **go to extremes,** go overboard, go *or* jump off the deep end; **run** *or* **drive into the ground; make a big deal of** *and* **make a Federal case of** <nf>; overemphasize, overstress; max out; overplay, overplay one's

hand <nf>; **overreact,** protest too much; overreach oneself; **overtax,** overtask, overexert, overexercise, overstrain, overdrive, overspend, exhaust, overexpend, overuse; overtrain; **overwork,** overlabor; overelaborate, overdevelop, tell more than one wants to know; overstudy; burn the candle at both ends; **spread oneself too thin, take on too much,** have too much on one's plate, have too many irons in the fire, do too many things at once; **exaggerate** 355.3; **overindulge** 669.5

11 **pile it on,** lay it on, **lay it on thick,** lay it on with a trowel <nf>, talk too much, exaggerate

12 **carry coals to Newcastle,** teach fishes to swim, teach one's grandmother to suck eggs, kill the slain, beat *or* flog a dead horse, labor the obvious, butter one's bread on both sides, preach to the converted, paint *or* gild the lily

13 **overextend, overdraw, overstretch, overstrain,** stretch, strain; reach the breaking *or* snapping point; **overexpand,** overdistend, overdevelop, inflate, swell 259.4

14 **oversupply, overprovide,** overlavish, overfurnish, overequip; **overstock;** overprovision, overprovender; overdose; flood the market, oversell; **flood, deluge,** inundate, engulf, swamp, whelm, overwhelm; lavish with, be prodigal with

15 **overload,** overlade, **overburden,** overweight, **overcharge,** surcharge; **overfill,** stuff, crowd, cram, jam, pack, jam-pack, **congest,** choke; **overstuff,** overfeed; gluttonize 672.4; **surfeit, glut, gorge,** satiate 994.4; **saturate,** soak, drench, supersaturate, supercharge

ADJS 16 **excessive, inordinate, immoderate,** overweening, hubristic, **intemperate, extravagant,** incontinent; unrestrained, unbridled, abandoned; gluttonous 672.6; **extreme; overlarge, overgreat,** overbig, larger than life, monstrous, enormous, jumbo, elephantine, gigantic 247.7; overgrown, overdeveloped, hypertrophied; **overmuch,** too much, a bit much, de trop; **exorbitant, undue, outrageous,** unconscionable, **unreasonable;** fancy *and* high *and* stiff *and* steep <nf>; **out of bounds** *or* **all bounds,** out of sight *and* out of this world <nf>, **boundless** 823.3; egregious; fabulous, hyperbolic, hyperbolical, **exaggerated** 355.4

17 **superfluous, redundant; excess, in excess,** duplicative; unnecessary, unessential, nonessential, **needless,** otiose, expendable, dispensable, needless, unneeded, gratuitous, uncalled-for; expletive; pleonastic, tautologous, tautological; verbose, prolix 538.12; *de trop* <Fr>, supererogatory, supererogative; spare, to spare; on one's hands

18 **surplus,** overplus; **remaining,** unused, **leftover;** over, **over and above; extra, spare,** supernumerary, for lagniappe <nf>, as a bonus

19 **superabundant,** overabundant, plethoric, **overplentiful,** overplenteous, overplenty, **oversufficient, overmuch; lavish, prodigal,** overlavish, overbounteous, overgenerous, overliberal; overcopious, overluxuriant, riotous, overexuberant; overprolific, overnumerous; **swarming,** pullulating, **teeming,** overpopulated, overpopulous; plentiful 991.7

20 **overfull, overloaded, overladen, overburdened,** overfreighted, overfraught, overweighted, **overcharged,** surcharged, **saturated,** drenched, soaked, supersaturated, supercharged; **surfeited, glutted,** gorged, overfed, bloated, replete, swollen, **satiated** 994.6, **stuffed,** overstuffed, **crowded, overcrowded, crammed,** jammed, packed, jam-packed, like sardines in a can *or* tin, bumper-to-bumper <nf>; choked, **congested,** stuffed up; **overstocked, oversupplied; overflowing,** in spate, running over, filled to overflowing; plethoric, hyperemic; **bursting,** ready to burst, bursting at the seams, at the bursting point, overblown, distended, **swollen, bloated** 259.13

21 **overdone,** overwrought; overdrawn, overstretched, overstrained; overwritten, overplayed, overacted

ADVS 22 **excessively, inordinately, immoderately, intemperately,** overweeningly, hubristically, **overly,** over, **overmuch,** too much; **too,** too-too <nf>; **exorbitantly, unduly, unreasonably,** unconscionably, **outrageously**

23 **in** *or* **to excess, to extremes,** to the extreme, all out *and* to the max <nf>, flat out <Brit nf>, to a fault, too far, out of all proportion

24 **superabundantly,** overabundantly, **lavishly, prodigally, extravagantly;** more than enough, plentifully 991.9; without measure, out of measure, beyond measure

25 **superfluously, redundantly,** supererogatorily; tautologously; unnecessarily, needlessly, beyond need, beyond reason, to a fare-thee-well <nf>

994 SATIETY

NOUNS 1 **satiety, satiation, satisfaction, fullness, surfeit, glut,** repletion, engorgement; contentment; **fill, bellyful** *and* skinful <nf>; **saturation,** oversaturation, saturatedness, supersaturation; saturation point; more than enough, enough in all conscience, all one can stand *or* take; too much of a good thing, much of a muchness <nf>

2 **satedness,** surfeitedness, cloyedness, jadedness; overfullness, fedupness <nf>

3 cloyer, surfeiter, sickener; **overdose;** a diet of cake; warmed-over cabbage

VERBS 4 **satiate, sate, satisfy,** slake, allay; **surfeit, glut, gorge,** engorge; **cloy,** jade, pall; **fill,** fill up; saturate, oversaturate, supersaturate; **stuff,** overstuff, cram; **overfill,** overgorge, overdose, overfeed

5 **have enough,** have about enough of, have quite enough, **have one's fill;** have too much, have too much of a good thing, **have a bellyful** *or* skinful <nf>, have an overdose, **be fed up** <nf>, have all one can take *or* stand, have it up to here *and* up the gazoo *or* kazoo <nf>, have had it

ADJS 6 **satiated, sated, satisfied,** slaked, allayed; **surfeited, gorged,** replete, engorged, **glutted; cloyed,** jaded; **full,** full of, with one's fill of, **overfull,** saturated, oversaturated, supersaturated; **stuffed,** overstuffed, crammed, overgorged, overfed; **fed up** *and* fed to the gills *or* fed to the teeth *and* stuffed to the gills <nf>; **with a bellyful** *or* skinful <nf>, with enough of; disgusted, **sick of,** tired of, sick and tired of

7 **satiating,** sating, satisfying, filling; surfeiting, overfilling; jading, **cloying,** cloysome

995 EXPEDIENCE

NOUNS 1 **expedience** *or* **expediency, advisability,** politicness, **desirability,** recommendability; **fitness, fittingness, appropriateness,** propriety, decency , seemliness, **suitability,** rightness, feasibility, **convenience;** seasonableness, timeliness, **opportuneness; usefulness** 387.3; **advantage, advantageousness,** beneficialness, **profit,** profitability, percentage *and* mileage <nf>, worthwhileness, fruitfulness; wisdom, prudence 920.7; **temporariness, provisionality**

2 **expedient, means,** means to an end, **provision, measure, step, action,** effort, **stroke,** stroke of policy, coup, **move,** countermove, **maneuver,** demarche, course of action; tactic, **device,** contrivance, artifice, stratagem, **shift; gimmick** *and* dodge *and* trick <nf>; **resort,** resource; answer, solution; quick-and-dirty solution <nf>; working proposition, working hypothesis; **temporary expedient, improvisation,** ad hoc measure, ad hoc *or* ad hockery *or* ad hocism; **fix** *and* **quick fix** <nf>, jury-rigged expedient, **makeshift,** stopgap, shake-up, jury-rig; last expedient, **last resort** *or* resource, *pis aller* <Fr>, last shift, trump

VERBS 3 **expedite one's affair,** work to one's advantage, not come amiss, come in handy, be just the thing, be just what the doctor ordered <nf>, fit to a T *or* like a glove *or* like a second skin; forward, advance, promote, profit, advantage, benefit; **work, serve,** answer, answer *or* serve one's purpose, fill the bill *and* do the trick <nf>; suit the occasion, **be fitting,** fit, befit, be right

4 **make shift, make do,** make out <nf>, rub along <Brit>, cope, manage, manage with, get along on, get by on, do with; do as well as *or* the best one can; use a last resort, scrape the bottom of the barrel

ADJS 5 **expedient, desirable,** to be desired, much to be desired, **advisable, politic,** recommendable; **appropriate, meet, fit, fitting,** befitting, **right, proper,** good, decent , **becoming,** seemly, likely, congruous, **suitable,** sortable, feasible, doable, swingable <nf>, **convenient,** happy, heaven-sent, felicitous; timely, seasonable, opportune, well-timed, in the nick of time; **useful** 387.18; **advantageous,** favorable; **profitable,** fructuous, worthwhile, worth one's while; **wise** 920.17

6 **practical,** practicable, pragmatic *or* pragmatical, banausic; feasible, workable, operable, realizable; **efficient,** effective, **effectual**

7 **makeshift,** makeshifty, **stopgap,** band-aid <nf>, improvised, improvisational, **jury-rigged; last-ditch; ad hoc;** quick *and* dirty <nf>; temporary, provisional, tentative

ADVS 8 **expediently, fittingly,** fitly, **appropriately, suitably,** sortably, congruously, rightly, properly, decently , feasibly, conveniently; practically; seasonably, opportunely; desirably, advisably; advantageously, to advantage, all to the good; as a last resort

PHRS 9 there's more than one way to skin a cat, where there's a will there's a way

996 INEXPEDIENCE

NOUNS 1 **inexpedience** *or* inexpediency, **undesirability, inadvisability,** impoliticness *or* impoliticalness; **unwiseness** 923.2; **unfitness, unfittingness, inappropriateness, unaptness, unsuitability,** incongruity, **unmeetness,** wrongness, unseemliness; **inconvenience** *or* inconveniency, awkwardness; ineptitude, inaptitude; unseasonableness, untimeliness, inopportuneness; unfortunateness, infelicity; disadvantageousness, unprofitableness, unprofitability, worthlessness, futility, uselessness 391

2 **disadvantage, drawback, liability; detriment,** impairment, prejudice, loss, damage, hurt, harm, mischief, injury; **a step back** *or* **backward,** a loss of ground; **handicap** 1012.6, disability; drag, millstone around one's neck

3 **inconvenience,** discommodity, incommodity, disaccommodation , **trouble, bother;** inconvenientness, inconveniency, **unhandiness,** awkwardness, clumsiness, unwieldiness, troublesomeness, clunkiness <nf>; gaucheness, gaucherie

VERBS 4 **inconvenience,** put to inconvenience, **put out, discommode,** incommode, disaccommodate , disoblige, **burden, embarrass; trouble, bother,** put to trouble, put to the trouble of, **impose upon;** harm, disadvantage 1000.6

ADJS 5 **inexpedient, undesirable, inadvisable, counterproductive,** impolitic, impolitical, unpolitic, not to be recommended, contraindicated; **impractical, impracticable,** dysfunctional, unworkable; **ill-advised, ill-considered, unwise; unfit, unfitting,** unbefitting, **inappropriate, unsuitable,** unmeet, inapt, inept, unseemly, **improper, wrong,** bad, out of place, out of order, incongruous, ill-suited; malapropos, *mal à propos* <Fr>, inopportune, untimely, ill-timed, badly timed, unseasonable; infelicitous, unfortunate, unhappy; unprofitable 391.12; futile 391.13

6 **disadvantageous,** unadvantageous, **unfavorable;** unprofitable, profitless, unrewarding, worthless, useless 391.9; **detrimental,** deleterious, injurious, harmful, prejudicial, disserviceable

7 **inconvenient, incommodious,** discommodious; **unhandy, awkward,** clumsy, unwieldy, troublesome, onerous; gauche

ADVS 8 **inexpediently, inadvisably,** impoliticly *or* impolitically, **undesirably; unfittingly, inappropriately, unsuitably,** ineptly, inaptly, incongruously; inopportunely, unseasonably; infelicitously, unfortunately, unhappily

9 **disadvantageously,** unadvantageously, unprofitably, unrewardingly; uselessly 391.15; **inconveniently,** unhandily, with difficulty, ill

997 IMPORTANCE

NOUNS 1 **importance, significance, consequence,** consideration, **import,** note, mark, **moment, weight, gravity;** materiality; concern, concernment, interest; **first order,** high order, high rank; **priority,** primacy, precedence, preeminence, paramountcy, superiority, **supremacy;** value, worth, merit, excellence 999.1; self-importance 140.1; emphasis, oomph <nf>; front burner

2 **notability, noteworthiness,** remarkableness, salience, memorability; **prominence, eminence, greatness,** distinction, magnitude; prestige, esteem, repute, reputation, honor, glory, renown, dignity, **fame** 662.1; **stardom,** celebrity, celebrity-hood, superstardom; semicelebrity

3 **gravity, graveness, seriousness,** solemnity, weightiness; *gravitas* <L>, grave affair; no joke, no laughing matter, nothing to sneeze at <nf>, hardball <nf>, matter of life and death, heavy scene <nf>

4 **urgency,** imperativeness, exigence *or* exigency; **momentousness, crucialness, cruciality;** consequentiality, consequentialness; **press,** pressure, high pressure, **stress,** tension, **pinch;** clutch *and* crunch <nf>; **crisis, emergency;** moment of truth, turning point, climax, defining moment; crunch

5 **matter of importance** *or* **consequence,** thing of interest, point of interest, matter of concern, object of note, one for the book *and* something to write home about <nf>, something special, no tea party, no picnic; not chicken feed <nf>; vital concern *or* interest; notabilia, memorabilia, great doings

6 **salient point,** cardinal point, high point, great point, key point; important thing, chief thing, **the point, main point,** main thing, essential matter, **essence,** the name of the game *and* the bottom line *and* what it's all about *and* where it's at <nf>, substance, gravamen, *sine qua non* <L>, issue, real issue, front-burner issue <nf>, prime issue; **essential,** fundamental, substantive point, material point; **gist, nub** <nf>, **heart,** meat, pith, kernel, **core; crux,** crucial *or* pivotal *or* critical point, pivot; turning point, **climax, cusp, crisis;** keystone, cornerstone; landmark, milestone, bench mark; linchpin; secret weapon, trump card

7 **feature, highlight,** high spot, main attraction, centerpiece, pièce de résistance; outstanding feature; best part, cream

8 **personage, important person,** person of importance *or* consequence, **great man** *or* **woman,** man *or* woman of mark *or* note, **somebody, notable,** notability, figure; **celebrity,** famous person, person of renown, personality; name, big name, megastar, nabob, **mogul,** captain of industry, panjandrum, person to be reckoned with, very important person, heavyweight; sachem; mover and shaker, lord of creation; **worthy,** pillar of society, salt of the earth, elder, father; **dignitary,** dignity; **magnate;** tycoon <nf>, baron; power; power elite, Establishment; interests; brass, top brass; top people, the great; ruling circle, lords of creation; the top, the summit

9 <nf terms> **big shot,** wheel, **big wheel,** big boy, big cat, big fish, biggie, big cheese, big noise, big-timer, big-time operator, **bigwig,** big man, big gun, **high-muck-a-muck** *or* high-muckety-muck, kingpin, lion, something, **VIP,** brass hat, high

man on the totem pole, suit; sacred cow, little tin god, tin god; big man on campus *or* BMOC; 800-pound gorilla; queen bee, heavy momma; first fiddle; mega-

10 **chief, principal,** chief executive, chief executive officer *or* CEO, paramount, lord of the manor, overlord, **king,** queen, monarch, electronics king, etc; leading light, luminary, master spirit, **star,** superstar, superman, superwoman, prima donna, lead 707.6

11 <nf terms> **boss, honcho,** big enchilada, biggest frog in the pond, big man, top *or* high man on the totem pole, top dog, Mr Big, head cheese, his nibs, himself, man upstairs

VERBS **12 matter,** import , signify, **count, tell, weigh, carry weight,** cut ice *and* cut some ice <nf>, be prominent, stand out, mean much; be something, be somebody, amount to something; have a key to the executive washroom; be featured, star, get top billing, take the limelight

13 **value, esteem, treasure, prize,** appreciate, respect, **rate highly,** think highly of, think well of, **think much of,** set store by; give *or* attach *or* ascribe importance to; make much of, make a fuss *or* stir about, make an ado *or* much ado about; hold up as an example

14 **emphasize, stress,** lay emphasis *or* stress upon, feature, highlight, brightline, place emphasis on, give emphasis to, **accent, accentuate, punctuate, point up,** bring to the fore, put in the foreground, put in bright lights; prioritize; **highlight,** spotlight; **star, underline, underscore,** italicize; overemphasize, overstress, overaccentuate, hammer home, rub in; harp on; dwell on, belabor; attach too much importance to, make a big deal *or* Federal case of <nf>, make a mountain out of a molehill; pull no punches <nf>

15 **feature,** headline <nf>; **star,** give top billing to

16 **dramatize, play up** <nf>, splash, make a production of; put on the map

ADJS **17 important, major, consequential, momentous, significant, considerable,** substantial, material, **great,** grand, big; superior, world-shaking, earthshaking; big-time *and* big-league *and* major-league *and* heavyweight <nf>; high-powered <nf>, double-barreled <nf>; bigwig *and* bigwigged <nf>; name *and* big-name <nf>, self-important 140.8; mega; A-1 <nf>

18 **of importance, of significance, of consequence,** of note, of moment, of weight; of concern, of concernment, of interest, not to be overlooked *or* despised, not hay *and* not chopped liver *and* not to be sneezed at <nf>; viable

19 **notable, noteworthy, celebrated, remarkable, marked, standout** <nf>, of mark, signal; **memorable,** rememberable, unforgettable, classic, historic, never to be forgotten; striking, telling, salient; **eminent, prominent,** conspicuous, noble, **outstanding, distinguished;** prestigious, esteemed, estimable, elevated, sublime, reputable 662.15; **extraordinary,** *extraordinaire* <Fr>, out of the ordinary, **exceptional, special,** rare; top-ten

20 **weighty,** heavy, **grave,** sober, sobering, **solemn, serious,** earnest; portentous, fateful, fatal; formidable, awe-inspiring, imposing, larger than life; world-shaking, earth-shattering

21 **emphatic, decided, positive, forceful,** forcible; **emphasized, stressed,** accented, accentuated, punctuated, pointed; underlined, underscored, starred, italicized, highlighted; red-letter, in red letters, in letters of fire

22 **urgent, imperative,** imperious, **compelling, pressing,** high-priority, high-pressure, crying, clamorous, insistent, instant, exigent; crucial, critical, pivotal, acute; fateful

23 **vital, all-important,** crucial, of vital importance, life-and-death *or* life-or-death; earth-shattering, epoch-making; **essential,** fundamental, indispensable, basic, substantive, bedrock, material; **central,** focal; bottom-line *and* meat-and-potatoes *and* gut <nf>; grass-roots

24 **paramount, principal, leading, foremost, main, chief,** number one <nf>, premier, **prime, primary,** preeminent, **supreme,** capital , cardinal; highest, uppermost, topmost, toprank, ranking, of the first rank, world-class, **dominant,** predominant, master, controlling, **overruling,** overriding, all-absorbing

ADVS **25** **importantly, significantly,** consequentially, materially, momentously, greatly, grandly; eminently, prominently, conspicuously, outstandingly, saliently, signally, notably, markedly, remarkably

26 **at the decisive moment,** in the clutch *and* when the chips are down *and* when push comes to shove <nf>

998 UNIMPORTANCE

NOUNS **1** **unimportance, insignificance,** inconsequence, inconsequentiality, indifference, **immateriality;** inessentiality; ineffectuality; unnoteworthiness, unimpressiveness; inferiority, secondariness, low order of importance, low priority, dispensability, expendability, marginality; lack of substance; **smallness,** littleness, slightness, inconsiderableness, negligibility; irrelevancy, meaninglessness; **pettiness,** puniness, pokiness, picayune, picayunishness; marginalization; irrelevance 776.1

2 **paltriness,** poorness, **meanness,** sorriness, sadness, pitifulness, contemptibleness, pitiableness, despicableness, miserableness, wretchedness, vileness, crumminess <nf>, shabbiness, shoddiness, cheapness, cheesiness, beggarliness, worthlessness, uselessness, unworthiness, meritlessness; tawdriness, meretriciousness, gaudiness 501.3

3 **triviality,** trivialness, triflingness, nugacity, nugaciousness; **superficiality,** shallowness; slightness, slenderness, slimness, flimsiness; **frivolity,** frivolousness, lightness, levity; **foolishness,** silliness; inanity, emptiness, vacuity; triteness, vapidity; vanity, idleness, futility; **much ado about nothing,** tempest *or* storm in a teacup *or* teapot, much cry and little wool, piss *and* wind *and* big deal <nf>; pettiness; snap of the fingers

4 **trivia,** triviata, **trifles; trumpery,** *nugae* <L>, gimcrackery, knickknackery, bric-a-brac; **rubbish,** trash, chaff; peanuts *and* chicken feed *and* chickenshit *and* Mickey Mouse <nf>, small change; small beer; froth; minutiae, details, minor details; inessential, nonessential

5 **trifle, triviality, oddment, bagatelle,** fribble, **gimcrack, gewgaw,** frippery, froth, **trinket,** bibelot, curio, **bauble,** gaud, toy, **knickknack,** knickknackery, kickshaw, minikin , whim-wham, folderol; pin, button, hair, straw, rush, feather, fig, bean, hill of beans <nf>, molehill, row of pins *or* buttons <nf>, sneeshing <Brit nf>, pinch of snuff; bit, snap; a curse, a continental, a hoot *and* a damn *and* a darn *and* a shit <nf>, a tinker's damn; picayune, rap, sou, halfpenny, farthing, brass farthing, cent, red cent, two cents, twopence *or* tuppence <Brit>, penny, dime, plugged nickel; peppercorn; drop in the ocean *or* the bucket; fleabite, pinprick; joke, jest, farce, mockery, child's play; small potatoes

6 **an insignificancy,** an inessential, a marginal matter *or* affair, a trivial *or* paltry affair, a small *or* trifling *or* minor matter, **no great matter;** a little thing, *peu de chose* <Fr>, hardly *or* scarcely anything, matter of no importance *or* consequence, matter of indifference; **a nothing, a big nothing, a naught,** a mere nothing, nothing in particular, nothing to signify, nothing to speak *or* worth speaking of, nothing to think twice about, nothing to boast of, nothing to write home about, thing of naught, *rien du tout* <Fr>, nullity, nihility; **technicality,** mere technicality; red herring

7 **a nobody, insignificancy,** hollow man, jackstraw , **nonentity,** nonperson, empty suit *and* nebbish <nf>, an obscurity, a nothing, cipher, little man, nobody one knows; lightweight, mediocrity; whippersnapper *and* whiffet *and* pip-squeak *and* squirt *and* shrimp *and* scrub *and* runt <nf>; squit <Brit nf>, punk <nf>; small potato, small potatoes; **the little fellow,** the little guy <nf>, **the man in the street;** common man 864.3; man of straw, dummy, figurehead; **small fry,** Mr and Mrs Nobody, John Doe and Richard Roe *or* Mary Roe; Tom, Dick, and Harry; Brown, Jones, and Robinson

8 **trifling,** dallying, **dalliance,** flirtation, flirtiness, coquetry; toying, fiddling, playing, fooling, **puttering,** tinkering, pottering, piddling; dabbling, smattering; loitering, idling 331.4

9 <nf terms> **monkeying, monkeying around,** buggering around, diddling around, fiddling around, frigging *or* fricking around, horsing around, fooling around, kidding around, messing around, pissing around, playing around, screwing around, mucking around, farting around; jerking off

10 **trifler, dallier,** fribble; **putterer,** potterer, piddler, tinkerer, smatterer, dabbler; amateur, dilettante, Sunday painter; **flirt, coquet**

VERBS 11 **be unimportant,** be of no importance, not signify, **not matter,** not count, signify nothing, matter little, **not make any difference; cut no ice, not amount to anything,** make no never mind *and* not amount to a hill of beans *or* a damn <nf>; have no clout *or* pull

12 **attach little importance to,** give little weight to; make little of, underplay, de-emphasize, downplay, play down, **minimize,** marginalize, disregard, **make light of,** think little of, throw away, **make** *or* **think nothing of,** take no account of, set little by, set no store by, set at naught; snap one's fingers at; not care a straw about; not give a shit *or* a hoot *or* two hoots for <nf>, not give a damn about, not give a dime a dozen for; bad-mouth <nf>, deprecate, depreciate 512.8; **trivialize**

13 **make much ado about nothing,** make mountains out of molehills, have a storm *or* tempest in a teacup *or* teapot

14 **trifle, dally; flirt, coquet; toy,** fribble, **play, fool,** play at, **putter, potter,** tinker, **piddle; dabble,** smatter; toy with, fiddle with, fool with, play with; idle, loiter 331.12,13; nibble, niggle, nickel-and-dime <nf>

15 <nf terms> **monkey, monkey around,** fiddle, fiddle around, fiddle-faddle, frivol, horse around, fool around, play around, mess around, kid around, **screw around,** muck around, muck about <Brit>, fart around, piss around, bugger around, diddle around, frig around; jerk off

ADJS 16 **unimportant, of no importance,** of little *or* small importance, of no great importance, **of no account,** of no significance, of no concern, of no matter, of little *or* no consequence, no great shakes <nf>; no skin off one's nose *or* elbow *or* ass <nf>; inferior, secondary, of a low order of importance, low-priority, expendable; marginal; one-dimensional, two-dimensional; not apropos, not related, irrelevant

17 **insignificant** 248.6, **inconsequential, immaterial,** of no consequence, insubstantial; nonessential, unessential, inessential, **not vital,** back-burner <nf>, dispensable; unnoteworthy, unimpressive; **inconsiderable,** inappreciable, negligible; **small, little,** minute, footling, petit, minor, inferior; technical

18 <nf terms> **measly, small-time, two-bit,** Mickey Mouse, chickenshit, nickel-and-dime, low-rent, piddly, pissy-ass, dinky, poky <Brit>, tinhorn, punk; not worth a dime *or* a red cent *or* beans *or* a hill of beans *or* bubkes *or* shit, not worth a second thought; **one-horse, two-by-four,** jerkwater

19 **trivial, trifling;** fribble, fribbling, nugacious, nugatory; catchpenny; **slight,** slender, flimsy; **superficial, shallow; frivolous, light,** windy, airy, frothy; idle, futile, vain, otiose; **foolish,** fatuous, asinine, **silly; inane,** empty, vacuous; trite, vapid; unworthy of serious consideration

20 **petty, puny, piddling,** piffling, niggling, pettifogging, technical, picayune, picayunish; small-beer

21 **paltry, poor,** common, **mean, sorry, sad,** pitiful, pitiable, pathetic, **despicable, contemptible,** beneath contempt, **miserable, wretched,** beggarly, vile, **shabby,** scrubby, scruffy, shoddy, scurvy, scuzzy <nf>, scummy, **crummy** *and* cheesy <nf>, **trashy,** rubbishy, garbagey <nf>, trumpery, gimcracky <nf>; tinpot <nf>; **cheap,** worthless, valueless, twopenny *or* twopenny-halfpenny <Brit>, two-for-a-cent *or* -penny, dime-a-dozen; tawdry, meretricious, gaudy 501.20; mickey mouse *or* rinky-dink <nf>

22 **unworthy, worthless,** meritless, unworthy of regard *or* consideration, beneath notice; no great shakes <nf>

ADVS **23** **unimportantly, insignificantly, inconsequentially,** immaterially, unessentially; **pettily,** paltrily; **trivially,** triflingly; superficially, shallowly; frivolously, lightly, idly

PHRS **24** **it does not matter,** it matters not, it does not signify, mox nix <nf>, **it is of no consequence** *or* **importance, it makes no difference,** it makes no never mind <nf>, it cannot be helped, it is all the same; *n'importe* and *de rien* and *ça ne fait rien* <Fr>; it will all come out in the wash <nf>, it will be all the same a hundred years from now

25 **no matter, never mind,** think no more of it, do not give it another *or* a second thought, don't lose any sleep over it, let it pass, let it go <nf>, ignore it, forget it <nf>, skip it *and* drop it <nf>; fiddle-dee-dee

26 **what does it matter?, what matter?, what's the difference?,** what's the diff? <nf>, what do I care?, what of it?, what boots it?, what's the odds?, so what?, what else is new?; for aught one cares, big deal <nf>

999 GOODNESS

<good quality or effect>

NOUNS **1** **goodness, excellence, quality,** class <nf>; **virtue,** grace; **merit,** desert; **value, worth; fineness,** goodliness, fairness, niceness; **superiority,** first-rateness, **skillfulness** 413.1, proficiency; wholeness, **soundness,** healthiness 81.1; **virtuousness** 653.1; **kindness, benevolence,** benignity 143.1; beneficialness, helpfulness 449.10; favorableness, auspiciousness 133.8; expedience, advantageousness 995.1; **usefulness** 387.3; pleasantness, agreeableness 97.1; cogency, validity; profitableness, rewardingness 472.4

2 **superexcellence,** supereminence, preeminence, supremacy, primacy, paramountcy, peerlessness, unsurpassedness, matchlessness, superfineness; **superbness,** exquisiteness, **magnificence,** splendidness, splendiferousness, marvelousness, distinction

3 **tolerableness,** tolerability, goodishness, passableness, fairishness, **adequateness, satisfactoriness,** acceptability, admissibility; sufficiency 991

4 **good, welfare,** well-being, **benefit;** public weal, common good; **interest, advantage; behalf,** behoof, edification; blessing, benison, boon; **profit,** avail , gain, betterment; world of good; favor, advantage; use, usefulness

5 **good thing,** a thing to be desired; **treasure,** gem, jewel, diamond, pearl; boast, pride, **pride and joy;** prize, trophy, plum; winner *and* no slouch *and* nothing to sneeze at <nf>; catch, find <nf>, *trouvaille* <Fr>; godsend, windfall; tour de force, chef-d'oeuvre, masterpiece; bestseller; collector's item; hit

6 **first-rater, topnotcher, world-beater; wonder, prodigy,** genius, virtuoso, **star, superstar;** luminary, leading light, one in a thousand *or* a million; hard *or* tough act to follow <nf>; good egg

7 <nf terms> **dandy, jim dandy, dilly, humdinger, pip,** pippin, **peach,** ace, beaut, **lulu, daisy,** darb, doozy, honey, sweetheart, dream, lollapalooza, bitch, hot shit *or* poo, pisser, pistol, corker, whiz, blinger, **crackerjack,** knockout, something else, something else again, barnburner, killer, killer-diller, smash, smash hit, the nuts, the cat's pajamas *or* balls *or* meow, bitch-kitty, whiz, whizbang, wow, wowser

8 **the best,** the very best, the best ever, the top of the heap *or* the line <nf>, head of the class, tops; **quintessence,** essence, prime, optimum, superlative; **choice, pick, select, elect, elite,** *corps d'élite* <Fr>, chosen; **cream, flower,** fat; cream *or* pick of the crop, *crème de la crème* <Fr>, grade A, salt of the earth; *pièce de résistance* <Fr>; prize, champion, queen; nonesuch, paragon, nonpareil; gem of the first water

9 **harmlessness,** hurtlessness, uninjuriousness, **innocuousness,** benignity, benignancy; unobnoxiousness, inoffensiveness; innocence; heart of gold, kindness of heart, milk of human kindness

VERBS **10** **do good, profit,** avail; do a world of good; **benefit, help, serve,** be of service, advance, advantage, favor 449.11,14,17,19; be the making of, make a man *or* woman of; do no harm, break no bones

11 **excel, surpass,** outdo, pass, do *or* go one better, transcend; do up brown *or* in spades <nf>, do with a vengeance; be as good as, equal, emulate, rival, vie, vie with, challenge comparison, go one-on-one with <nf>; **make the most of, optimize,** exploit; cream off <Brit>, skim off the cream

ADJS **12** **good, excellent,** *bueno* <Sp>, *bon* <Fr>, bonny <Brit>, **fine, nice,** goodly, fair; **splendid, capital, grand,** elegant <nf>, braw, famous <nf>, noble; royal, regal, fit for a king; very good, *très bon* <Fr>; boo-yah <nf>; commendable, laudable, estimable 509.20; skillful 413.22; **sound,** healthy 81.5; virtuous; kind, benevolent 143.15; beneficial, helpful 449.21; profitable; favorable, auspicious 133.17; expedient, advantageous 995.5; useful 387.18; pleasant 97.6; cogent, valid 973.14

13 <nf terms> **great,** swell, dandy, bitchin', jim dandy, neat, neato, cool, super, super-duper, bully , tough, mean, gnarly, heavy, bad, groovy, out of sight, fab, fantabulous, marvy, gear, something else, ducky, dynamite, keen, killer, hot, nifty, sexy, spiffy, spiffing, ripping, nobby, peachy, peachy-keen, delicious, scrumptious, not too shabby, tits, out of this world, hunky-dory, crackerjack, boss, stunning, corking, smashing, solid, all wool and a yard wide; rum *or* wizard <Brit>; bang-up, jam-up, slap-up, ace-high, fine and dandy, just dandy, but good, OK, okay, A-OK; copacetic, peachy keen; phat

14 **superior,** above par, head and shoulders above, **crack** <nf>; **high-grade, high-class,** high-quality, high-caliber, high-test, **world-class,** grade A; impressive

15 **superb,** super <nf>, **superexcellent, supereminent,** superfine, **exquisite; magnificent,** splendid, splendiferous, tremendous, immense, **marvelous, wonderful,** glorious, divine, heavenly, terrific, sensational; sterling, golden; gilt-edged *and* gilt-edge, blue-chip; of the highest type, of the best sort, of the first water, as good as good can be, as good as they come, as good as they make 'em *and* out of this world <nf>

16 **best,** very best, greatest *and* top-of-the-line <nf>, **prime,** optimum, optimal; **choice, select, elect,** elite, **picked,** handpicked; **prize, champion; supreme,** paramount, **unsurpassed,** surpassing, unparalleled, unmatched, unmatchable, matchless, makeless , **peerless;** quintessential; for the best, all for the best

17 **first-rate, first-class,** in a class by itself; of the first *or* highest degree; unmatched, matchless; champion, record-breaking

18 <nf terms> **A-1, A number one,** primo, first-chop, tip-top, top-notch, topflight, top-drawer, tops; topping *or* top-hole <Brit>

19 **up to par,** up to standard, **up to snuff** <nf>; **up to the mark,** up to the notch *and* **up to scratch** <nf>

20 **tolerable, goodish, fair, fairish,** moderate, tidy <nf>, **decent,** respectable, presentable, good enough, **pretty good, not bad,** not amiss, not half bad, not so bad, **adequate, satisfactory, all right,** OK *or* okay <nf>; better than nothing; **acceptable,** admissible, **passable,** unobjectionable, unexceptionable; workmanlike; sufficient 991.6

21 **harmless,** hurtless, unhurtful; well-meaning, well-meant; **uninjurious,** undamaging, **innocuous,** innoxious, innocent; unobnoxious, inoffensive; nonmalignant, **benign;** nonpoisonous, nontoxic, nonvirulent, nonvenomous

ADVS 22 **excellently, nicely,** finely, **capitally, splendidly, famously,** royally; **well,** very well, **fine** <nf>, right, aright; one's best, at one's best, at the top of one's bent

23 **superbly,** exquisitely, **magnificently,** tremendously, immensely, terrifically, **marvelously, wonderfully,** gloriously, divinely

24 **tolerably, fairly,** fairishly, moderately, respectably, **adequately, satisfactorily,** passably, **acceptably,** unexceptionably, presentably, decently; fairly well, well enough, pretty well; **rather, pretty**

1000 BADNESS

<bad quality or effect>

NOUNS 1 **badness, evil,** evilness, viciousness, damnability, reprehensibility; moral badness, dereliction, peccancy, iniquity, sinfulness, wickedness 654.4; unwholesomeness, unhealthiness 82.1; inferiority 1005.3; unskillfulness 414.1; unkindness, malevolence 144; inauspiciousness, unfavorableness 133.7; inexpedience 996; unpleasantness 98; invalidity 19.3; inaccuracy 975.2; improperness 638.1; deviltry

2 **terribleness, dreadfulness,** direness, **awfulness** <nf>, horribleness; **atrociousness, outrageousness,** heinousness, nefariousness; **notoriousness, egregiousness,** scandalousness, shamefulness, **infamousness; abominableness,** odiousness, **loathsomeness, detestableness,** despicableness, contemptibleness, hatefulness; **offensiveness,** grossness, obnoxiousness; squalor, squalidness, sordidness, **wretchedness,** filth, **vileness,** fulsomeness, **nastiness,** rankness, **foulness,** noisomeness; disgustingness, repulsiveness; uncleanness 80; beastliness, bestiality, brutality; **rottenness** *and* lousiness <nf>; the pits <nf>; shoddiness, shabbiness; scurviness, **baseness** 661.3; **worthlessness** 998.2

3 **evil, bad, wrong, ill; harm, hurt, injury, damage, detriment; destruction** 395; despoliation; mischief, havoc; outrage, atrocity; crime, foul play; abomination, grievance, vexation, woe, crying evil; poison 1001.3; blight, venom, toxin, **bane** 1001; **corruption,** pollution, infection, befoulment, defilement; environmental pollution, fly in the ointment, worm in the apple *or* rose; skeleton in the closet; snake in the grass, Pandora's Box; ills the flesh is heir to; the worst; *annus horribilis* <L>

4 **bad influence,** malevolent influence, evil star, **ill wind;** evil genius, **hoodoo** *and* **jinx** <nf>, **Jonah; curse,** enchantment, whammy *and* double *or* triple whammy <nf>, spell, hex, voodoo; **evil eye**; malediction; collateral damage

5 **harmfulness, hurtfulness,** injuriousness, banefulness, balefulness, detrimentalness, deleteriousness, perniciousness, mischievousness, noxiousness, venomousness, poisonousness, toxicity, virulence, noisomeness, **malignance** *or* **malignancy, malignity, viciousness;** unhealthiness 82.1; disease 85; deadliness, lethality 308.9; ominousness 133.6

VERBS 6 work evil, do ill; **harm, hurt; injure,** scathe, wound, **damage; destroy** 395.10; despoil, prejudice, disadvantage, impair, disserve, distress; **wrong,** do wrong, do wrong by, aggrieve, do evil, do a mischief, do an ill office to; **molest,** afflict; lay a hand on; get into trouble; **abuse,** bash <nf>, batter, outrage, violate, maltreat, mistreat 389.5; torment, **harass,** hassle <nf>, persecute, savage, crucify, torture 96.18; play mischief *or* havoc with, wreak havoc on, play hob with <nf>; **corrupt,** deprave, taint, pollute, infect, befoul, defile; poison, envenom, blight; **curse,** put a whammy on <nf>, give the evil eye, hex, jinx, bewitch; spell *or* mean trouble, threaten, menace 514.2; doom; condemn 602.3

ADJS **7** **bad, evil, ill,** untoward, black, sinister; **wicked, wrong,** peccant, iniquitous, **vicious; sinful** 654.16; criminal; unhealthy 82.5; **inferior** 1005.9; unskillful 414.15; unkind, malevolent 144.19; inauspicious, unfavorable 133.16; inexpedient 996.5; unpleasant 98.17; invalid 19.15; inaccurate 975.17; improper 638.3

8 <nf terms> **lousy,** punk, bum, badass, shitty, crappy, cruddy, cheesy, dog-ass, gnarly, gross, raunchy, piss-poor, rat-ass, **crummy,** grim, low-rent, low-ride, putrid, icky, skanky, yecchy, vomity, barfy, stinking, stinky, creepy, hairy, god-awful, gosh-awful

9 **terrible, dreadful,** awful <nf>, dire, horrible, horrid; atrocious, outrageous, heinous, villainous, nefarious; enormous, monstrous; **deplorable,** lamentable, regrettable, pitiful, pitiable, woeful, woesome , grievous, sad 98.20; flagrant, **scandalous,** shameful, **shocking,** infamous, **notorious,** arrant, **egregious;** unclean 80.20; shoddy, schlocky <nf>, shabby, scurvy, **base** 661.12; **odious, obnoxious,** offensive, gross, **disgusting,** repulsive, loathsome, **abominable, detestable, despicable, contemptible,** beneath contempt, hateful; blameworthy, **reprehensible;** rank, fetid, foul, filthy, vile, fulsome, noisome, **nasty,** squalid, sordid, **wretched;** beastly, brutal; as bad as they come, as bad as they make 'em <nf>, as bad as bad can be; worst; too bad; below par, subpar, not up to scratch *or* snuff *or* the mark, poor-quality, **worthless**

10 **execrable, damnable;** damned, accursed, cursed 513.9; infernal, hellish, devilish, fiendish, satanic, ghoulish, demoniac, demonic, demonical, diabolic, diabolical, unholy, ungodly

11 evil-fashioned, ill-fashioned, evil-shaped, ill-shaped, evil-qualitied, evil-looking, ill-looking, evil-favored, ill-favored, evil-hued, evil-faced, evil-minded, evil-eyed, ill-affected , evil-gotten, ill-gotten, ill-conceived

12 **harmful, hurtful,** scatheful, **baneful,** baleful, distressing, **injurious, damaging, detrimental,** deleterious, counterproductive, **pernicious,** mischievous; noxious, mephitic, venomous, venenate, poisonous, venenous, veneniferous, toxic, virulent, noisome; malignant, malign, malevolent, malefic, vicious; prejudicial, disadvantageous, disserviceable; corruptive, corrupting, corrosive, corroding; deadly, lethal; ominous 133.16

ADVS **13** **badly,** bad <nf>, ill, evil, evilly, wrong, wrongly, amiss; to one's cost

14 **terribly, dreadfully,** dreadful <nf>, **horribly,** horridly, **awfully** <nf>, **atrociously, outrageously;** flagrantly, scandalously, shamefully, shockingly, infamously, notoriously, egregiously, grossly, offensively, nauseatingly, fulsomely, odiously, **vilely,** obnoxiously, **disgustingly,** loathsomely; wretchedly, sordidly, shabbily, basely, abominably, detestably, despicably, contemptibly, foully, nastily; brutally, bestially, savagely, viciously; something fierce *or* terrible <nf>

15 **harmfully, hurtfully, banefully,** balefully, **injuriously, damagingly, detrimentally,** deleteriously, counterproductively, **perniciously,** mischievously; noxiously, venomously, poisonously, toxically, virulently, noisomely; **malignantly,** malignly, malevolently, malefically, **viciously;** prejudicially, disadvantageously, disserviceably; corrosively, corrodingly

1001 BANE

NOUNS **1** **bane, curse, affliction,** infliction, visitation, **plague, pestilence,** pest, calamity, **scourge**, torment, open wound, running sore, grievance, woe, burden, crushing burden; disease 85; death 307; evil, harm 1000.3; destruction 395; vexation 96.2; thorn, thorn in the flesh *or* side, pea in the shoe; bugbear, **bête noire,** bogy, bogeymen, nemesis, arch-nemesis

2 **blight,** blast; canker, cancer; mold, fungus, mildew, smut, must, rust; rot, dry rot; **pest;** worm, worm in the apple *or* rose; moth

3 **poison, venom,** venin, virus , toxic, toxin, toxicant; eradicant, **pesticide; insecticide,** insect powder, bug bomb <nf>; roach powder, roach paste; stomach poison, contact poison, systemic insecticide *or* systemic, fumigant, chemosterilant; chlorinated hydrocarbon insecticide, organic chlorine; organic phosphate insecticide; carbamate insecticide, sheepdip; termiticide, miticide, acaricide, vermicide, anthelminthic; rodenticide, ratsbane, rat poison; **herbicide,** defoliant, Agent Orange, paraquat, **weed killer;** fungicide; microbicide, germicide, antiseptic, disinfectant, antibiotic; **toxicology;** toxic waste, **environmental pollutant;** hemlock, arsenic, cyanide; carcinogen

4 **miasma, mephitis,** malaria ; effluvium, exhaust, exhaust gas; coal gas, chokedamp, blackdamp, firedamp; air *or* atmospheric pollution, smoke, smog, exhaust fumes, carbon monoxide; secondhand smoke; acid rain

5 sting, stinger, dart; **fang,** tang <nf>; beesting, snakebite

1002 PERFECTION

NOUNS **1** **perfection, faultlessness, flawlessness,** defectlessness, indefectibility, impeccability, absoluteness; infallibility; spotlessness, stainlessness, taintlessness, purity, immaculateness; sinlessness; chastity 664

2 **soundness, integrity, intactness, wholeness,** entireness, completeness; **fullness,** plenitude; finish; mint condition

3 **acme of perfection, pink, pink of perfection, culmination,** perfection, height, top, acme, ultimate, summit, pinnacle, peak, highest pitch, climax, consummation, *ne plus ultra* <L>, **the last word,** a dream come true

4 pattern *or* standard *or* mold *or* norm of perfection, very model, quintessence; archetype, prototype, exemplar, mirror, **epitome;** *ne plus ultra* <L>, perfect specimen, highest type, **classic,** masterwork, masterpiece, *chef d'œuvre* <Fr>, crowning achievement, showpiece; **ideal** 786.4; role model; **paragon** 659.4; a 10 <nf>

VERBS **5** **perfect,** develop, flesh out, ripen, mature; improve 392.7; crown, culminate, put on the finishing touch; lick *or* whip into shape, fine-tune; complete 407.6; do to perfection 407.7

ADJS **6** **perfect, ideal, faultless, flawless,** unflawed, defectless, not to be improved, picture-perfect, **impeccable,** absolute; **just right,** just so; spotless, stainless, taintless, unblemished, untainted, unspotted, immaculate, **pure,** uncontaminated, unadulterated, unmixed; sinless; chaste 664.4; indefective , indefectible, trouble-free; infallible; beyond all praise, irreproachable, unfaultable, *sans peur et sans reproche* <Fr>, **matchless, peerless** 249.15; A-1, world-class, number-one

7 **sound, intact, whole, entire, complete,** integral; **full;** total, utter, unqualified 960.2

8 **undamaged, unharmed, unhurt, uninjured,** unscathed, **unspoiled,** virgin, inviolate, **unimpaired;** harmless, scatheless; **unmarred,** unmarked, unscarred, unscratched, undefaced, unbruised; **unbroken,** unshattered, untorn; undemolished, undestroyed; undeformed, unmutilated, unmangled, unmaimed; unfaded, unworn, unwithered, bright, fresh, untouched, pristine, mint; none the worse for wear, right as rain

9 **perfected, finished,** polished, refined; done to a T *or* to a turn; **classic, classical,** masterly, masterful, expert, proficient; ripened, ripe, matured, mature, developed, fully developed; thorough-going, thorough-paced; **consummate,** quintessential, archetypical, exemplary, model

ADVS 10 **perfectly,** ideally; **faultlessly, flawlessly, impeccably; just right;** spotlessly; immaculately, purely; infallibly; **wholly, entirely, completely, fully,** thoroughly, totally, absolutely 794.15

11 **to perfection, to a turn, to a T,** to a finish, to a nicety; to a fare-thee-well *or* fare-you-well *or* fare-ye-well <nf>; to beat the band <nf>

1003 IMPERFECTION

NOUNS 1 **imperfection,** imperfectness, room for improvement; **unperfectedness; faultiness, defectiveness,** defectibility; **shortcoming, deficiency,** lack, want, shortage, **inadequacy,** inadequateness; erroneousness, **fallibility;** inaccuracy, inexactness, inexactitude 975.2; **unsoundness,** incompleteness, patchiness, sketchiness, unevenness; **impairment** 393; **mediocrity** 1005; immaturity, undevelopment 406.4; impurity, adulteration 797.3

2 **fault,** *faute* <Fr>, **defect, deficiency, inadequacy,** imperfection, kink, defection , hangup; **flaw,** hole, bug <nf>; something missing; catch <nf>, fly in the ointment, problem, little problem, curate's egg <Brit>, snag, drawback; **crack,** rift; **weakness,** frailty, infirmity, failure, **failing, foible, shortcoming;** weak point, Achilles' heel, vulnerable place, chink in one's armor, weak link, soft spot, underbelly; **blemish,** taint 1004.3; **malfunction,** glitch <nf>

VERBS 3 **fall short,** come short, miss, miss out, miss the mark, miss by a mile <nf>, not qualify, fall down <nf>, **not measure up,** not come up to par, not come up to the mark, not come up to scratch *or* to snuff <nf>, not pass muster, not bear inspection, not hack it *and* not make it *and* not cut it *and* not make the cut <nf>; not make the grade; fail

ADJS 4 **imperfect,** not perfect, less than perfect; good in parts; unperfected; **defective, faulty, inadequate, deficient,** short, not all it's cracked up to be <nf>, lacking, wanting, found wanting; off; erroneous, **fallible;** inaccurate, inexact, imprecise 975.17; **unsound, incomplete,** unfinished, partial, patchy, sketchy, uneven, unthorough; makeshift 995.7; **damaged, impaired** 393.27; mediocre 1005.7; **blemished** 1004.8; half-baked <nf>, immature, undeveloped 406.12; impure, adulterated, mixed

ADVS 5 **imperfectly, inadequately,** deficiently; **incompletely,** partially; **faultily, defectively**

1004 BLEMISH

NOUNS 1 **blemish, disfigurement,** disfiguration, **defacement;** scar, keloid, cicatrix; needle scar, track *or* crater <nf>; scratch; scab; blister, vesicle, bulla, bleb; weal, wale, welt, wen, sebaceous cyst; port-wine stain *or* mark, hemangioma, strawberry mark, macula; pock, pustule; pockmark, pit; nevus, birthmark, mole; freckle, lentigo; milium, whitehead, blackhead, comedo, pimple, zit <nf>, hickey <nf>, sty; crud; wart, verruca; **crack,** craze, check, rift, split; **deformity,** deformation, warp, twist, kink, **distortion; flaw, defect, fault** 1003.2

2 **discoloration,** discolorment, discolor ; bruise; foxing

3 **stain, taint, tarnish;** mark, brand, **stigma;** maculation, macule, macula; **spot, blot,** blur, **blotch,** patch, speck, speckle, fleck, flick, flyspeck; daub, dab; **smirch, smudge,** smutch *or* smouch, smut, **smear;** splotch, splash, splatter, spatter; bloodstain; eyesore; caste mark, tattoo, brand

VERBS 4 **blemish, disfigure,** deface, **flaw, mar;** scab; scar, cicatrize, scarify; **crack,** craze, check, split; **deform,** warp, twist, kink, **distort**

5 **spot,** bespot, **blot, blotch, speck, speckle,** bespeckle, maculate ; freckle; flyspeck; **spatter, splatter,** splash, splotch

6 **stain,** bestain, **discolor,** smirch, besmirch, **taint,** attaint, **tarnish; mark, stigmatize,** brand; smear, besmear, daub, bedaub, slubber <Brit nf>; blur, slur <nf>; **darken, blacken;** smoke, besmoke; scorch, singe, sear; dirty, **soil** 80.16

7 **bloodstain, bloody,** ensanguine

ADJS 8 **blemished, disfigured,** defaced, **marred,** scarred, keloidal, cicatrized, scarified, stigmatized, scabbed, scabby; pimpled, pimply; cracked, crazed, checked, split; deformed, warped, twisted, kinked, distorted; **faulty, flawed, defective** 1003.4

9 **spotted, spotty,** maculate, maculated, macular, blotched, **blotchy,** splotched, splotchy; **speckled,** speckly, bespeckled; freckled, freckly, freckle-faced; spattered, splattered, splashed

10 **stained, discolored,** foxed, foxy, **tainted, tarnished,** smirched, besmirched; stigmatized, stigmatic, stigmatiferous; darkened, blackened, murky, smoky, inky; polluted, **soiled** 80.21

11 **bloodstained,** blood-spattered, **bloody,** sanguinary, **gory,** ensanguined

1005 MEDIOCRITY

NOUNS 1 **mediocrity,** mediocreness, fairishness, modestness, modesty, moderateness, middlingness, **indifference;** respectability, passableness, **tolerableness** 999.3; **dullness,** lackluster, tediousness 117.1

2 **ordinariness,** averageness, normalness, normality, **commonness, commonplaceness;** unexceptionality, unremarkableness, unnoteworthiness; conventionality

3 **inferiority,** inferiorness, **poorness,** lowliness, humbleness, **baseness, meanness, commonness,** coarseness, tackiness, tack; **second-rateness,** third-rateness, fourth-rateness

4 **low grade,** low class, low quality, poor quality; second best, next best

5 **mediocrity, second-rater,** third-rater, fourth-rater, nothing *or* nobody special, no great shakes <nf>, no prize, no prize package, no brain surgeon, no rocket scientist, not much of a bargain, small potatoes *and* small beer <nf>; tinhorn <nf>; **nobody, nonentity** 998.7; middle class, bourgeoisie, burgherdom; suburbia, the burbs <nf>; Middle America, silent majority

6 **irregular,** second, third; schlock <nf>

ADJS 7 **mediocre, middling, indifferent, fair, fairish, fair to middling** <nf>, moderate, modest, medium, betwixt and between; respectable, passable, tolerable; so-so, *comme ci comme ça* <Fr>; of a kind, of a sort, of sorts <nf>; nothing to brag about, not much to boast of, nothing to write home about; bush-league; dull, lackluster, tedious 117.6; insipid, vapid, wishy-washy, namby-pamby

8 **ordinary, average,** normal, **common, commonplace,** garden *and* garden-variety <nf>, run-of-mine *or* -mill, run-of-the-mine *or* -mill, vanilla <nf>; **unexceptional, unremarkable, unnoteworthy,** unspectacular, nothing *or* nobody special *and* no great shakes <nf>, no prize, no prize package, no brain surgeon, no rocket scientist; conventional; middle-class, bourgeois, plastic <nf>; suburban; usual, regular

9 **inferior, poor,** punk <nf>, **base, mean, common,** coarse, cheesy *and* tacky <nf>, tinny; shabby, seedy; cheap, Mickey Mouse <nf>, paltry; irregular; second-best; **second-rate,** third-rate, fourth-rate; **second-class,** third-class, fourth-class, etc; **low-grade, low-class,** low-quality, low-test, low-rent *and* low-ride <nf>

10 **below par,** below standard, **below the mark** <nf>, substandard, **not up to scratch** *or* snuff *or* the mark

<nf>, not up to sample *or* standard *or* specification, off

ADVS 11 **mediocrely, middlingly,** fairly, fairishly, middling well, fair to middling <nf>, moderately, modestly, **indifferently, so-so;** passably, **tolerably**

12 **inferiorly, poorly,** basely, meanly, commonly

1006 DANGER

NOUNS 1 **danger, peril, endangerment, imperilment, jeopardy, hazard, risk,** cause for alarm, **menace, threat** 514; **crisis, emergency,** hot spot, nasty *or* tricky spot, pass, pinch, strait, plight, predicament 1013.4; powder keg, time bomb; dangerous *or* unpredictable *or* uncontrollable person, loose cannon <nf>; rocks *or* breakers *or* white water ahead, gathering clouds, storm clouds; dangerous ground, yawning *or* gaping chasm, quicksand, thin ice; hornet's nest; house of cards, cardhouse; hardball <nf>, no tea party, no picnic; desperate situation; hazardous materials

2 **dangerousness, hazardousness, riskiness, treachery, precariousness** 971.6, chanciness, dodginess <chiefly Brit nf>, diceyness <nf>, **perilousness; unsafeness,** unhealthiness <nf>; criticalness; **ticklishness,** slipperiness, touchiness, delicacy, ticklish business *and* shaky ground <nf>; **insecurity,** unsoundness, instability, unsteadiness, shakiness, totteriness, wonkiness <Brit nf>; sword of Damocles; **unreliability,** undependability, untrustworthiness 971.6; **unsureness,** unpredictability, **uncertainty,** doubtfulness, dubiousness 971.2

3 **exposure, openness,** liability, nonimmunity, susceptibility; **unprotectedness, defenselessness,** nakedness, helplessness; lamb, sitting duck; roadkill <nf>; naiveté

4 **vulnerability,** pregnability, penetrability, assailability, vincibility; weakness 16; vulnerable point, **weak link, weak point, soft spot,** heel of Achilles, chink, chink in one's armor; tragic flaw, fatal flaw

5 <hidden danger> snags, rocks, reefs, ledges; coral heads; shallows, shoals; sandbank, sandbar, sands; quicksands; crevasses; rockbound *or* ironbound coast, lee shore; undertow, undercurrent; **pitfall;** snake in the grass; trap, booby trap, springe, snare, tripwire, pitfall; snarling dog, ticking package; cloud on the horizon

VERBS 6 **endanger, imperil,** peril; **risk, hazard, gamble, gamble with; jeopardize,** jeopard, jeopardy, compromise, put in danger, **put in jeopardy,** put on the spot *and* lay on the line <nf>; **expose,** lay open; incur danger, run into *or* encounter danger

7 **take chances, take a chance, chance, risk, stake, gamble,** hazard, press *or* push one's luck, **run the chance** *or* **risk** *or* **hazard;** risk one's neck, run a risk, go out on a limb, stick one's neck out<nf>, **expose oneself,** bare one's breast, lower one's guard, **lay oneself open to,** leave oneself wide open, open the door to, let oneself in for; drive recklessly; **tempt Providence** *or* **fate,** forget the odds, **defy danger,** skate on thin ice, court destruction, dance on the razor's edge, go in harm's way, hang by a hair *or* a thread, stand *or* sleep on a volcano, sit on a barrel of gunpowder, build a house of cards, put one's head in the lion's mouth, march up to the cannon's mouth, play with fire, go through fire and water, go out of one's depth, go to sea in a sieve, carry too much sail, sail too near the wind; risk one's life, throw caution to the wind, **take one's life in one's hand, dare, face up to, brave** 492.10

8 **be in danger,** be in peril, be *in extremis,* be in a desperate case, have one's name on the danger list, have the chances *or* odds against one, have one's back to the wall, have something hanging over one's head; be despaired of; hang by a thread; tremble on the verge, totter on the

brink, teeter on the edge; feel the ground sliding from under one; have to run for it; race against time *or* the clock; be threatened, be on the spot *or* in a bind <nf>

ADJS **9** **dangerous,** dangersome <nf>, **perilous,** periculous, parlous, jeopardous, bad, ugly, serious, critical, explosive, attended *or* beset *or* fraught with danger; alarming, too close for comfort *or* words, **menacing, threatening** 514.3

10 **hazardous, risky, chancy,** dodgy <chiefly Brit nf>, dicey <nf>, hairy <nf>, aleatory, aleatoric, riskful, full of risk; **adventurous,** venturous, venturesome; **speculative,** wildcat

11 **unsafe,** unhealthy <nf>; **unreliable, undependable, untrustworthy,** treacherous, **insecure, unsound,** unstable, unsteady, shaky, tottery, wonky <Brit nf>, rocky; **unsure, uncertain,** unpredictable, doubtful, dubious; on the brink *or* verge

12 **precarious, ticklish, touchy,** touch-and-go, **critical, delicate;** slippery, slippy; on thin ice, on slippery ground; hanging by a thread, trembling in the balance; nerve-racking

13 **in danger, in jeopardy, in peril, at risk,** in a bad way; **endangered, imperiled, jeopardized,** *in periculo* <L>, at the last extremity, *in extremis* <L>, in deadly peril, *in periculo mortis* <L>, in desperate case; threatened, up against it, in a bad way, on the spot *and* on *or* in the hot seat <nf>; sitting on a powder keg; between the hammer and the anvil, between Scylla and Charybdis, between two fires, between the devil and the deep blue sea, between a rock and a hard place <nf>; in a predicament 1013.21; cornered

14 **unprotected, unshielded, unsheltered,** uncovered, unscreened, **unguarded, undefended,** unattended, unwatched, unfortified; armorless, unarmored, **unarmed,** bare-handed, weaponless; guardless, ungarrisoned, insecure, **defenseless, helpless;** unwarned, unsuspecting

15 **exposed, open,** out in the open, naked, bare; out on a limb <nf>; liable, susceptible, nonimmune

16 **vulnerable,** naïve, **pregnable,** penetrable, expugnable; assailable, attackable, surmountable; conquerable, beatable <nf>, vincible; weak 16.12–13

ADVS **17** **dangerously, perilously, hazardously, riskily,** critically, unsafely; **precariously,** ticklishly; at gun point

1007 SAFETY

NOUNS **1** **safety,** safeness, **security,** surety , assurance; risklessness, immunity, clear sailing; **protection,** safeguard 1008.3; harmlessness 999.9; airworthiness, crashworthiness, roadworthiness, seaworthiness; invulnerability 15.4; safety in numbers; wide berth, safe distance; safekeeping

VERBS **2** **be safe, be on the safe side; keep safe, come through;** weather, ride out, weather the storm; keep one's head above water, tide over; keep a safe distance; land on one's feet; save one's bacon <nf>, save one's neck; lead a charmed life, have nine lives

3 **play safe** <nf>, **keep on the safe side,** give danger a wide berth, watch oneself, watch out, take precautions 494.6, demand assurances; assure oneself, make sure, keep an eye *or* a weather eye out, look before one leaps; **save, protect** 1008.18

ADJS **4** **safe, secure, safe and sound,** not at risk; immune, immunized; insured; **protected** 1008.21; on the safe side; unthreatened, unmolested; unhurt, unharmed, unscathed, intact, untouched, with a whole skin, undamaged, whole

5 **unhazardous, undangerous, unperilous, unrisky,** riskless, **unprecarious;** fail-safe, trouble-free; recession-proof; guaranteed, warranteed; dependable, reliable, trustworthy, sound, stable, steady, firm 970.17; as safe as houses; harmless; invulnerable; -proof

6 **in safety, out of danger,** past danger, out of the meshes *or* toils, in, home, out of the woods *and* over the hump *or* home free <nf>, free and dry <Brit nf>, **in the clear, out of harm's reach** *or* **way;** under cover, under lock and key; in shelter, in harbor *or* port, at anchor *or* haven, in the shadow of a rock; on sure *or* solid ground, on *terra firma,* high and dry, above water; in safe keeping

7 **snug, cozy,** home free; crashworthy, roadworthy, airworthy, seaworthy, seakindly

ADVS **8** **safely, securely,** reliably, dependably; with safety, **with impunity**

PHRS **9** the danger is past, the storm has blown over, the coast is clear

1008 PROTECTION

NOUNS **1** **protection, guard, shielding, safekeeping; policing, law enforcement; patrol, patroling,** community policing, professional *or* bureaucratic policing; eye, protectiveness, watchfulness, vigilance, watchful eye, shepherding; house-sitting <nf>; protective custody; **safeguarding, security,** security industry, public safety, safety 1007; **shelter, cover,** shade, shadow , windbreak, lee; **refuge** 1009; preservation 397; **defense** 460; protective coating, Teflon coating <TM>

2 **protectorship, guardianship,** stewardship, custodianship; **care, charge, keeping, nurture, nurturing, nurturance, custody, fostering, fosterage,** cocooning, fatherly *or* motherly eye; **hands,** safe hands, wing; **auspices, patronage, tutelage, guidance; ward,** wardship, wardenship, watch and ward; cure, pastorship, pastorage, pastorate; **oversight,** jurisdiction, management, ministry, administration, government, governance; **child care,** infant care, daycare, family service, aftercare; baby-sitting, baby-minding <Brit>

3 **safeguard,** palladium, **guard,** preventive measure, precautionary steps, **precaution**; **shield, screen,** aegis; umbrella, protective umbrella; patent, copyright; **bulwark** 460.4; backstop; fender, mudguard, **bumper, buffer, cushion,** pad, padding; seat *or* safety belt; protective clothing; shin guard, knuckle guard, knee guard, nose guard, hand guard, arm guard, ear guard, finger guard, foot guard; goggles, mask, face mask, welder's mask, fencer's mask; safety shoes; helmet, hard hat <nf>, crash helmet, sun helmet; cowcatcher, pilot; dashboard; windshield, windscreen <Brit>; dodger *and* cockpit dodger <Brit>; life preserver 397.6; lifeline, safety rail, guardrail, handrail; governor; safety, safety switch, interlock; safety valve, safety plug; fuse, circuit breaker; insulation; safety glass, laminated glass; lightning rod, lightning conductor; **anchor,** bower, sea anchor, sheet anchor, drogue; **parachute; safety net;** prophylactic, preventive 86.20; contraceptive 86.23

4 **insurance,** assurance <Brit>; **annuity,** variable annuity; **social security** 611.7; nest egg, savings account, provision; **insurance company,** stock company, mutual company; **insurance policy,** policy, certificate of insurance; deductible; insurance man, underwriter, insurance broker, insurance agent, insurance adjuster, actuary; lemon law

5 **protector, keeper,** protectress, safekeeper, minder; patron, patroness; tower, pillar, strong arm, tower of strength, rock; champion, **defender** 460.7

6 **guardian, warden,** governor; **custodian,** steward, **keeper, caretaker,** warder <Brit>, attendant; caregiver; next friend, prochein ami, guardian *ad litem;* **curator,** conservator; janitor; castellan; **shepherd,** herd, cowherd; **game warden,** gamekeeper; **ranger,** forest ranger, forester; lifeguard, lifesaver <Brit>; air warden; guardian angel

7 **chaperon,** duenna; **governess;** escort

8 **nurse, nursemaid,** nurserymaid, nanny <chiefly Brit>, amah, ayah, mammy <nf>; dry nurse, wet nurse; **baby-sitter,** baby-minder <Brit>, sitter <nf>

9 **guard,** guarder, guardsman , warder; **outguard, outpost; picket,** outlying picket, inlying picket, outrider; advance guard, **vanguard,** van; **rear guard;** coast guard; armed guard, security guard; jailer 429.10; bank guard; railway *or* train guard; goalkeeper, goaltender, goalie <nf>; garrison; cordon, *cordon sanitaire* <Fr>

10 **watchman, watch,** watcher; watchkeeper; **lookout,** lookout man; **sentinel,** picket, **sentry; scout,** vedette; **point,** forward observer, spotter; **patrol, patrolman,** patroller, roundsman; night watchman, Charley <nf>; fireguard, fire patrolman, fire warden; airplane spotter; Argus

11 **watchdog,** bandog, guard dog, attack dog; sheep dog; Cerberus

12 **doorkeeper, doorman, gatekeeper,** Cerberus, warden, **porter, janitor,** commissionaire <Brit>, *concierge* <Fr>, ostiary, usher; receptionist

13 **picket, picketer,** demonstrator, picket line; counterdemonstrator

14 **bodyguard,** safeguard; **convoy, escort;** guards, praetorian guard; guardsman; yeoman *or* yeoman of the guard *or* beefeater, gentleman-at-arms, Life Guardsman <all England>

15 **policeman, policewoman, constable, officer,** police officer, *flic* <Fr nf>, *gendarme* <Fr>; peace officer, law enforcer, law enforcement agent, arm of the law; military policeman *or* MP; detective 576.10; police matron; patrolman, police constable <Brit>; trooper, mounted policeman, state police, state trooper; reeve, portreeve; **sheriff, marshal;** deputy sheriff, deputy, bound bailiff, catchpole, beagle <nf>, bombailiff <Brit nf>; sergeant, police sergeant; roundsman; lieutenant, police lieutenant; captain, police captain; inspector, police inspector; superintendent, chief of police; commissioner, police commissioner; government man, federal, fed *and* G-man <nf>; narc <nf>; **bailiff,** tipstaff, tipstaves <pl>; mace-bearer, lictor, sergeant at arms; beadle; traffic officer, meter maid; dective

16 <nf terms> cop, copper, John Law, bluecoat, bull, flatfoot, gumshoe, gendarme, shamus, dick, pig, flattie, bizzy *and* bobby *and* peeler <Brit>, Dogberry; the cops, the law, the fuzz, feds, heat; New York's finest; tec, op

17 **police, police force,** law enforcement agency; the force, forces of law and order, long arm of the law; **constabulary;** state police, troopers *or* state troopers, highway patrol, county police, provincial police; security force; special police; tactical police, riot police; SWAT *or* special weapons and tactics, SWAT team, **posse,** *posse comitatus* <L>; **vigilantes,** vigilance committee; secret police, political police; Federal Bureau of Investigation *or* FBI; military police *or* MP; shore patrol *or* SP; Scotland Yard <Brit>; Gestapo <Ger>; Royal Canadian Mounted Police *or* RCMP *and* Mounties <Can>; Interpol, International Criminal Police Commission; neighborhood watch

VERBS **18** **protect, guard, safeguard, secure, keep,** bless, make safe, **police, enforce the law;** keep from harm; **insure,** underwrite; ensure, guarantee 438.9; patent, copyright, register; **cushion;** champion, go to bat for <nf>; ride shotgun <nf>, fend, defend 460.8; **shelter, shield, screen, cover,** cloak, shroud , temper the wind to the shorn lamb; **harbor, haven;** nestle; compass about, fence; arm, armor; put in a safe place, keep under cover

19 **care for, take care of;** preserve, conserve; provide for, support; take charge of, **take under one's wing,** make one a protégé; **look after,** see after, **attend to, minister to,** look *or* see to, look *or* watch out for <nf>, have *or* keep an eye on *or* upon, keep a sharp eye on *or* upon, **watch over,** keep watch over, **watch, mind, tend;** keep tab *or* tabs on <nf>; **shepherd,** ride herd on <nf>; **chaperon,** matronize; baby-sit <nf>; **foster, nurture, cherish,**

nurse; mother, be a mother *or* father to

20 **watch, keep watch, keep guard,** keep watch over, keep vigil, keep watch and ward; stand guard, stand sentinel; be on the lookout 339.8; mount guard; **police,** patrol, pound a beat <nf>, go on one's beat

ADJS 21 **protected, guarded,** safeguarded, defended; safe 1007.4–6; patented, copyrighted; **sheltered, shielded,** screened, covered, cloaked; policed; armed 460.14; invulnerable

22 **under the protection of,** under the shield of, under the auspices of, under the aegis of, **under one's wing,** under the wing of, under the shadow of one's wing

23 **protective, custodial,** guardian, tutelary; curatorial; vigilant, watchful, on the watch, on top of; prophylactic, preventive; immunizing; protecting, guarding, safeguarding, sheltering, **shielding,** screening, covering; fostering, parental; defensive 460.11; Teflon-coated <TM>

1009 REFUGE

NOUNS 1 **refuge, sanctuary,** safehold, **asylum, haven, port,** harborage, **harbor;** harbor of refuge, port in a storm, snug harbor, safe haven; game sanctuary, bird sanctuary, preserve, forest preserve, game preserve; stronghold 460.6; **political asylum;** Rock of Gibraltar

2 **recourse, resource, resort;** last resort *or* resource, *dernier ressort* and *pis aller* <Fr>; **hope; expedient** 995.2

3 **shelter, cover, covert,** coverture; concealment 346; *abri* <Fr>, dugout, cave, earth, funk hole <Brit nf>, foxhole; **bunker;** trench; storm cellar, storm cave, cyclone cellar; air-raid shelter, bomb shelter, bombproof, fallout shelter, safety zone *or* isle *or* island; stockade, fort

4 **asylum, home,** retreat; **poorhouse,** almshouse, workhouse <Brit>, poor farm; **orphanage; hospice,** hospitium; old folks' home, rest home, nursing home, old soldiers' home, sailors' snug harbor; foster home; safe house; halfway house; retirement home *or* village *or* community, life-care home, continuing-care retirement community *or* CCRC

5 **retreat,** recess, hiding place, **hideaway,** hideout, hidey-hole <nf>, priest hole; **sanctum, inner sanctum, sanctum sanctorum,** holy ground, holy of holies, adytum; private place, privacy , secret place; **den,** lair, mew; safe house; **cloister,** hermitage, ashram, cell; **ivory tower;** study, library

6 **harbor, haven, port, seaport,** port of call, free port, treaty port, home port; hoverport; harborage, **anchorage,** anchorage ground, protected anchorage, moorage, moorings; **roadstead,** road, roads; berth, slip; **dock,** dockage, marina, basin; dry dock; shipyard, dockyard; **wharf, pier,** quay; harborside, dockside, pierside, quayside, landing, landing place *or* stage, jetty, jutty ; breakwater, mole, groin; seawall, embankment, bulkhead

VERBS 7 **take refuge, take shelter,** seek refuge, **claim sanctuary,** claim refugee status, ask for political asylum, seek asylum; run into port; fly to, throw oneself into the arms of; bar the gate, lock *or* bolt the door, raise the drawbridge, let the portcullis down; take cover 346.8

8 **find refuge** *or* sanctuary, make port, reach safety; seclude *or* sequester oneself, dwell *or* live in an ivory tower; make port

1010 PROSPERITY

NOUNS 1 **prosperity,** prosperousness, thriving *or* flourishing condition; **success** 409; **welfare, well-being,** weal, happiness, felicity; quality of life; comfortable *or* easy circumstances, **comfort, ease,** security; **life of ease,** life of Riley <nf>, **the good life; clover** *and* **velvet** <nf>, **bed of roses, luxury,** lap of luxury, Easy Street *and* Fat City *and* hog heaven <nf>; the affluent life, gracious life, gracious living; fat of the land;

fleshpots, fleshpots of Egypt; milk and honey, loaves and fishes; a chicken in every pot, a car in every garage; purple and fine linen; high standard of living; upward mobility; **affluence, wealth** 618

2 **good fortune** *or* **luck,** happy fortune, **fortune, luck,** the breaks <nf>; **fortunateness, luckiness,** felicity ; blessing, smiles of fortune, fortune's favor

3 **stroke of luck,** piece of good luck; blessing; **fluke** *and* lucky strike *and* scratch hit *and* **break** <nf>, **good** *or* **lucky break** <nf>; **run** *or* **streak of luck** <nf>; bonanza; Midas touch

4 **good times,** piping times, bright *or* palmy *or* halcyon days, days of wine and roses, rosy era; heyday; prosperity, era of prosperity; fair weather, sunshine; golden era, **golden age,** golden time, golden days, Saturnian age, reign of Saturn, *Saturnia regna* <L>; honeymoon; holiday; prime, youth; age of Aquarius, millennium; **utopia** 986.11; **heaven** 681

5 **roaring trade, land-office business** <nf>, bullishness, bull *or* bullish market, seller's market; **boom,** booming economy, expanding economy

6 **lucky dog** <nf>, lucky devil, fortune's favorite, favorite of the gods, fortune's child, destiny's darling

VERBS **7** **prosper,** enjoy prosperity, **fare well,** get on well, do well, have it made *or* hacked <nf>, have a good thing going, have everything going one's way, get on swimmingly, go great guns <nf>; **turn out well, go well,** take a favorable turn; **succeed;** come on *or* along <nf>, come a long way, get on <nf>; **advance,** progress, make progress, make headway, get ahead <nf>, move up in the world, pull oneself up by one's own boot-straps

8 **thrive, flourish,** boom; blossom, bloom, flower; batten, fatten, grow fat; be fat, dumb, and happy <nf>

9 **be prosperous, make good, make one's mark,** rise *or* get on in the world, make a noise in the world <nf>, do all right by oneself <nf>, **make one's fortune;** grow rich; drive a roaring trade, do a land-office business <nf>, rejoice in a seller's market

10 **live well, live in clover** *or* on velvet <nf>, **live a life of ease,** live *or* lead the life of Riley, **live high, live high on the hog** <nf>, live on *or* off the fat of the land, ride the gravy train *and* piss on ice <nf>, roll in the lap of luxury; bask in the sunshine, have one's place in the sun; have a good *or* fine time of it

11 **be fortunate, be lucky,** be in luck, luck out <nf>, have all the luck, have one's moments <nf>, **lead** *or* **have a charmed life;** fall into the shithouse *and* come up with a five-dollar gold piece <nf>; **get a break** *and* get the breaks <nf>; hold aces *and* turn up trumps *or* roses <nf>; have a run of luck *and* hit a streak of luck <nf>; have it break good for one <nf>, have a stroke of luck; strike it lucky *and* make a lucky strike *and* strike oil <nf>, **strike it rich** <nf>, hit it big <nf>, strike a rich vein, come into money, drop into a good thing

ADJS **12** **prosperous,** in good case; **successful,** rags-to-riches; **well-paid, high-income,** higher-income, well-heeled *and* upscale <nf>; **affluent, wealthy; comfortable,** comfortably situated, **easy;** on Easy Street *and* in Fat City *and* in hog heaven <nf>, **in clover** *and* **on velvet** <nf>, on a bed of roses, in luxury, high on the hog <nf>; up in the world, on top of the heap <nf>

13 **thriving, flourishing, prospering, booming** <nf>; vigorous, exuberant; in full swing, going strong <nf>; halcyon, palmy, balmy, rosy, piping, clear, fair; blooming, blossoming, flowering, fruiting; fat, sleek, in good case; fat, dumb, and happy <nf>

14 **fortunate, lucky, providential; in luck; blessed,** blessed with luck, favored; born under a lucky star, born with a silver spoon in one's mouth, born on the sunny side of the hedge; out of the woods, over the hump; **auspicious**

ADVS 15 **prosperously, thrivingly, flourishingly,** boomingly, swimmingly <nf>

16 **fortunately, luckily, providentially**

1011 ADVERSITY

NOUNS 1 **adversity,** adverse circumstances, difficulties, hard knocks *and* rough going <nf>, **hardship, trouble,** troubles, **rigor,** vicissitude, care, stress, pressure, stress of life; hard case *or* plight, **hard life,** dog's life, vale of tears; wretched *or* miserable *or* hard *or* unhappy lot, tough *or* hard row to hoe <nf>, ups and downs of life, things going against one; bitter cup, bitter pill; bummer *and* downer <nf>; the bad part, the downside <nf>; annoyance, irritation, aggravation; **difficulty** 1013; **trial,** tribulation, cross, bane, curse, blight, **affliction** 96.8; plight, predicament 1013.4; the pits <nf>, raw deal <nf>; turkey shoot <nf>

2 **misfortune, mishap,** ill hap, **misadventure, mischance,** *contretemps* <Fr>, grief; **disaster, calamity, catastrophe,** meltdown, cataclysm, **tragedy;** missed chance; **shock, blow,** hard *or* nasty *or* staggering blow; **accident,** casualty, collision, crash, plane *or* car crash; **wreck,** shipwreck; smash *and* smashup *and* crack-up *and* pileup <nf>; bad news <nf>

3 **reverse, reversal,** reversal of fortune, **setback,** check, severe check, backset *and* throwback <nf>; **comedown,** descent, down

4 **unfortunateness, unluckiness,** lucklessness, ill success; unprosperousness; starcrossed *or* ill-fated life; inauspiciousness 133.7

5 **bad luck,** ill luck, **hard luck,** hard lines <Brit>, **tough** *or* **rotten luck** <nf>, raw deal <nf>, bad *or* tough *or* rotten break <nf>, bad patch, devil's own luck; **ill fortune,** bad fortune, evil fortune, evil star, ill wind, evil dispensation; frowns of fortune

6 **hard times,** bad times, sad times; evil day, ill day; rainy day; hard *or* stormy *or* heavy weather, storm clouds; **depression,** recession, **slump,** economic stagnation, **bust** <nf>; rough patch, bad spell; winter of discontent

7 **unfortunate,** poor unfortunate, the plaything *or* toy *or* sport of fortune, fortune's fool; **loser** *and* sure loser *and* non-starter <nf>, born loser; hard case *and* sad sack *and* hard-luck guy <nf>; *schlemiel* or *schlimazel* <Yiddish>; odd man out; the underclass, the dispossessed, the homeless, the wretched of the earth; victim 96.11, victim of fate; martyr

VERBS 8 **go hard with,** go ill with; run one hard; **oppress, weigh on** *or* **upon,** weigh heavy on, weigh down, **burden,** overburden, load, overload, bear hard upon, lie on, lie hard *or* heavy upon; try one, put one out

9 **have trouble;** be born to trouble, be born under an evil star; **have a hard time of it,** be up against it <nf>, make heavy weather of it, meet adversity, have a bad time, lead *or* live a dog's life, have a tough *or* hard row to hoe; bear the brunt, bear more than one's share; be put to one's wit's end, not know which way to turn; **be unlucky, have bad** *or* **rotten luck,** be misfortuned, get the short *or* shitty end of the stick <nf>, hit the skids <nf>

10 **come to grief,** have a mishap, suffer a misfortune, fall, be stricken, be staggered, be shattered, be poleaxed, be felled, come a cropper <Brit nf>, be clobbered <nf>; run aground, go on the rocks *or* shoals, split upon a rock; sink, drown; **founder**

11 **fall on evil days, go** *or* **come down in the world,** go downhill, slip, be on the skids <nf>, come down, have a comedown, fall from one's high estate; deteriorate, **degenerate,** run *or* go to seed, sink, decline; **go to pot** <nf>, go to the dogs, go belly up <nf>; reach the depths, touch bottom, hit rock bottom; have seen better days

12 bring bad luck; hoodoo *and* hex *and* jinx *and* Jonah *and* put the jinx on <nf>; put the evil eye on, whammy

<nf>, put the *or* a double whammy on <nf>

ADJS 13 **adverse, untoward, detrimental, unfavorable;** sinister; hostile, antagonistic, inimical; contrary, counter, counteractive, conflicting, opposing, opposed, opposite, in opposition; **difficult, troublesome, troublous, hard,** trying, rigorous, stressful; wretched, miserable 96.26; **not easy;** harmful 1000.12

14 **unfortunate, unlucky, unprovidential,** unblessed, **unprosperous,** sad, unhappy, hapless, fortuneless, misfortuned, luckless, donsie <Brit nf>; **out of luck,** short of luck; **down on one's luck** <nf>, badly *or* ill off, down in the world, in adverse circumstances; underprivileged, depressed; ill-starred, evil-starred, born under a bad sign, born under an evil star, planet-stricken, planet-struck, star-crossed; fatal, dire, doomful, funest , **ominous, inauspicious** 133.16; **in a jam** *and* in a pickle *or* pretty pickle *and* in a tight spot *and* between a rock *and* a hard place <nf>, between the devil and the deep blue sea, caught in the crossfire *or* middle; up a tree *and* up the creek *or* up shit creek without a paddle *and* up to one's ass in alligators <nf>

15 **disastrous, calamitous, catastrophic, cataclysmic,** cataclysmal, **tragic,** ruinous, wreckful , fatal, dire, black, woeful, sore, baneful, grievous; destructive 395.26; **life-threatening, terminal**

ADVS 16 **adversely, untowardly,** detrimentally, **unfavorably;** contrarily, conflictingly, opposingly, oppositely

17 **unfortunately, unluckily,** unprovidentially, sadly, unhappily, **as ill luck would have it;** by ill luck, by ill hap; in adverse circumstances, if worse comes to worse

18 **disastrously,** calamitously, catastrophically, cataclysmically, grievously, woefully, sorely, banefully, tragically, crushingly, shatteringly

1012 HINDRANCE

NOUNS 1 **hindrance,** hindering, **hampering,** let, let *or* hindrance; **check, arrest,** arrestment, arrestation; fixation; **impediment,** holdback; **resistance, opposition** 451; suppression, **repression, restriction, restraint** 428; **obstruction,** blocking, blockage, clogging, occlusion; **bottleneck,** traffic jam, gridlock; speed bump, sleeping policeman <Brit>; **interruption,** interference; **retardation,** retardment, **detention,** detainment, **delay,** holdup, setback; **inhibition;** constriction, squeeze, stricture, cramp, stranglehold; **closure,** closing up *or* off; obstructionism, bloody-mindedness <Brit>, negativism, foot-dragging <nf>, nuisance value

2 **prevention, stop, stoppage, stopping,** arrestation, estoppel; stay, staying, halt, halting; **prohibition,** forbiddance; debarment; **determent,** deterrence, **discouragement; forestalling, preclusion, obviation,** foreclosure

3 **frustration, thwarting, balking, foiling; discomfiture, disconcertion,** bafflement, confounding; **defeat,** upset; check, checkmate, balk, foil ; derailing, derailment; vicious circle

4 **obstacle, obstruction,** obstructer; **hang-up** <nf>; **block,** blockade, cordon, curtain; **difficulty,** hurdle, hazard, bed of nails; **deterrent,** determent; **drawback,** objection; **stumbling block,** stumbling stone, stone in one's path; fly in the ointment, one small difficulty, **hitch,** hang-up <nf>, **catch,** joker <nf>, a "but," a "however"; bureaucracy, red tape, regulations

5 **barrier, bar;** gate, portcullis; **fence, wall,** stone wall, brick wall, impenetrable wall; seawall, jetty, groin, mole, breakwater; **bulwark, rampart,** defense, buffer, bulkhead, parapet, breastwork, work, earthwork, mound; bank, embankment, levee, dike; ditch, moat; dam, weir, leaping weir, barrage, milldam, beaver dam, cofferdam, wicket dam, shutter dam, bear-trap dam, hydraulic-fill dam, rock-fill dam, arch dam, arch-gravity dam, gravity dam; boom, jam, logjam; roadblock; speed

bump; backstop; iron curtain, bamboo curtain; glass ceiling

6 **impediment,** embarrassment, hamper; encumbrance, cumbrance; **trouble,** difficulty 1013; **handicap,** disadvantage, inconvenience, penalty; white elephant; **burden,** burthen , imposition, onus, cross, weight, deadweight, ball and chain, millstone around one's neck; **load,** pack, cargo, freight, charge; impedimenta, lumber; technical difficulty, flat tire, gremlin, glitch, bug <nf>, hiccup <nf>

7 **curb, check,** countercheck, arrest, **stay, stop,** damper, holdback; **brake,** clog, drag, drogue, remora; chock, scotch, spoke, spoke in one's wheel; doorstop; check-rein, bearing rein, martingale; bit, snaffle, pelham, curb bit; shackle, chain, fetter, trammel 428.4; sea anchor, drift anchor, drift sail, drag sail *or* sheet; boot *or* Denver boot

8 **hinderer,** impeder, **marplot,** obstructer; frustrater, thwarter; obstructionist, negativist; filibuster, filibusterer

9 **spoilsport,** wet blanket, **killjoy,** grouch, grinch *and* sourpuss <nf>, malcontent, **dog in the manger** <nf>, party pooper <nf>

VERBS 10 **hinder, impede, inhibit, arrest, check,** countercheck, scotch, **curb,** snub; **resist, oppose** 451.3; stonewall <nf>, stall, stall off; **suppress, repress** 428.8; **interrupt,** intercept ; intervene, interfere, intermeddle, meddle 214.7; damp, dampen, pour *or* dash *or* throw cold water; **retard,** slacken, **delay,** detain, **hold back, keep back,** set back, hold up <nf>; **restrain** 428.7; keep *or* hold in check, bottle up, dam up

11 **hamper, impede, cramp,** embarrass; trammel, entrammel, enmesh, entangle, ensnarl, entrap, entwine, involve, entoil, toil, net, lime, tangle, snarl; fetter, shackle; **handcuff,** tie one's hands; **encumber,** cumber, **burden,** lumber, **saddle with,** weigh *or* weight down, press down; hang like a millstone round one's neck; **handicap,** put at a disadvantage; lame, cripple, hobble, hamstring; cramp one's style, crab one's deal; gum up *or* gum up the works <nf>

12 **obstruct, get** *or* **stand in the way; dog, block,** block the way, put up a roadblock, blockade, block up, occlude; **jam,** crowd, pack; **bar,** barricade, bolt, lock; **debar,** shut out; shut off, **close,** close off *or* up, close tight, shut tight; constrict, squeeze, squeeze shut, **strangle,** strangulate, **stifle,** suffocate, **choke,** choke off, chock; stop up 293.7

13 **stop, stay, halt,** bring to a stop, put a stop *or* end to, bring to a shuddering *or* screeching halt <nf>; **brake,** slow down, put on the brakes, hit the brakes <nf>; **block, stall, stymie,** deadlock; nip in the bud

14 **prevent, prohibit, forbid; bar,** estop; save, help, **keep from; deter, discourage,** dishearten; **avert, parry, keep off, ward off, stave off, fend off,** fend, repel, deflect, turn aside; **forestall,** foreclose, **preclude,** exclude, debar, **obviate,** anticipate; rule out

15 **thwart, frustrate, foil, cross, balk;** spike, scotch, checkmate; **counter,** contravene, counteract, countermand, counterwork; stand in the way of, confront, brave, defy, challenge; **defeat** 412.6; **discomfit,** upset, **disrupt, confound,** flummox <nf>, discountenance, put out of countenance, **disconcert, baffle,** nonplus, perplex, stump <nf>; throw on one's beam ends, trip one up, throw one for a loss <nf>; **circumvent,** elude; sabotage, **spoil, ruin,** dish <nf>, dash, blast; **destroy** 395.10; throw a wrench in the machinery, **throw a monkey wrench** *or* **spanner** <Brit> **into the works** <nf>; put a spoke in one's wheel, scotch one's wheel, spike one's guns, put one's nose out of joint <nf>, upset one's applecart; **derail;** take the wind out of one's sails, steal one's thunder, cut the ground from under one, knock the chocks *or* props from under one, knock the bottom out of <nf>; tie one's hands, clip one's wings

16 <nf terms> **queer, crab, foul up, louse up,** snafu, bollix *or* bollix up, gum, **gum up,** gum up the works; crimp, cramp, **put a crimp in,** cramp one's style; cook one's goose, cut one down to size; give one a hard time

ADJS **17 hindering,** troublesome; **inhibitive,** inhibiting, suppressive, repressive; constrictive, strangling, stifling, choking; restrictive 428.12; **obstructive,** obstructing, occlusive, obstruent ; cantankerous <nf>, bloody-minded <Brit>, contrary, crosswise; interruptive, interrupting; in the way

18 hampering, impeding, counterproductive, impedimental, impeditive; onerous, oppressive, burdensome, cumbersome, cumbrous, encumbering

19 preventive, preventative, avertive, prophylactic; **prohibitive, forbidding; deterrent,** deterring, **discouraging;** preclusive, forestalling; foot-dragging

20 frustrating, confounding, disconcerting, baffling, defeating

ADVS **21** under handicap, at a disadvantage, on the hip , with everything against one

1013 DIFFICULTY

NOUNS **1 difficulty,** difficultness; **hardness, toughness** <nf>, strain, the hard way <nf>, **rigor,** rigorousness, ruggedness; **arduousness,** laboriousness, strenuousness, toilsomeness, severity; **troublesomeness,** bothersomeness; onerousness, oppressiveness, burdensomeness; formidability, hairiness <nf>; complication, intricacy, **complexity** 799; abstruseness 522.2

2 tough proposition *and* tough one *and* toughie <nf>, large *or* tall order <nf>; **hard job, tough job** *and* heavy lift <nf>, big undertaking, backbreaker, ballbuster <nf>, **chore,** man-sized job; brutal task, Herculean task, Augean task; uphill work *or* going, rough go <nf>, **heavy sledding,** hard pull <nf>, dead lift ; tough lineup to buck <nf>, hard road to travel; hard *or* tough nut to crack *and* hard *or* tough row to hoe *and* hard row of stumps <nf>; bitch <nf>; **handful** <nf>, all one can manage, no easy task

3 trouble, the matter; headache <nf>, problem, besetment, **inconvenience,** disadvantage; the bad part, the downside <nf>; **ado,** great ado; peck of troubles; hornet's nest, Pandora's box, can of worms <nf>; **evil** 1000.3; **bother, annoyance** 98.7; **anxiety, worry** 126.2

4 predicament, plight, spot of trouble, **strait,** straits, parlous straits, tightrope, knife-edge, thin edge; **pinch, bind,** pass, clutch, situation, emergency; pretty pass, nice *or* pretty predicament, pretty *or* fine state of affairs, **sorry plight;** slough, quagmire, morass, swamp, quicksand; **embarrassment,** embarrassing position *or* situation; **complication,** imbroglio; the devil to pay

5 <nf terms> **pickle,** crunch, hobble, pretty pickle, fine kettle of fish, how-do-you-do, fine how-do-you-do; **spot, tight spot; squeeze, tight squeeze,** ticklish *or* tricky spot, hot spot, hot seat, sticky wicket <Brit>; **scrape, jam, hot water,** tail in a gate, tit in the wringer; **mess,** holy *or* unholy mess, mix, stew; hell to pay; no-win situation

6 impasse, corner *and* **box** *and* **hole** <nf>, cleft stick; **cul-de-sac, blind alley, dead end,** dead-end street, blank wall; **extremity, end of one's rope** *or* **tether,** wit's end, nowhere to turn; **stalemate,** deadlock; stand, standoff, standstill, logjam, halt, stop

7 dilemma, horns of a dilemma, double bind, damned-if-you-do-and-damned-if-you-don't, no-win situation, **quandary,** nonplus, conundrum; **vexed question,** thorny problem, knotty point, knot, crux, node, nodus, Gordian knot, hard nut to crack, can of worms, headache, poser, teaser, perplexity, puzzle, enigma 522.8; paradox, oxymoron; asses' bridge, *pons asinorum* <L>; bad hair day; trilemma, tetralemma

8 **crux, hitch, pinch, rub,** snag, hurdle, catch, joker <nf>, where the shoe pinches, complication

9 **unwieldiness, unmanageability; unhandiness,** inconvenience, impracticality; **awkwardness, clumsiness; cumbersomeness,** ponderousness, bulkiness, hulkiness; ham-handedness

VERBS 10 **be difficult, present difficulties, pose problems, take some doing** <nf>

11 **have difficulty, have trouble,** have a rough time <nf>, hit a snag, have a hard time of it, have one's hands full, have one's work cut out, get off to a bad start *or* on the wrong foot; be hard put, have much ado with; labor under difficulties, labor under a disadvantage, have the cards stacked against one *and* have two strikes against one <nf>; struggle, **flounder,** beat about, make heavy weather of it; have one's back to the wall, not know where to turn, come to a dead end *or* standstill, not know whether one is coming *or* going, go around in circles, swim against the current; walk a tightrope, walk on eggshells *or* hot coals, dance on a hot griddle

12 **get into trouble,** plunge into difficulties; **let oneself in for, put one's foot in it** <nf>; **get in a jam** *or* **hot water** *or* **the soup** <nf>, **get into a scrape** <nf>, **get in a mess** *or* **hole** *or* **box** *or* **bind** <nf>; paint oneself into a corner <nf>, get one's ass in a bind *and* put oneself in a spot <nf>, put one's foot in one's mouth, strike a bad patch, be up a tree; have a tiger by the tail; burn one's fingers; get all tangled *or* snarled *or* wound up, get all balled *or* bollixed up <nf>

13 **trouble,** beset; **bother,** pother, get one down, <nf>, **disturb, perturb,** irk, plague, **torment,** drive one up the wall <nf>, give one gray hair, make one lose sleep; **harass, vex, distress** 96.16; inconvenience, **put out,** put out of the way, discommode 996.4; **concern, worry** 126.5; **puzzle, perplex** 971.13; put to it, give one trouble, complicate matters; give one a hard time *and* give one a bad time *and* make it tough for <nf>; be too much for; ail, be the matter; tree <nf>

14 **cause trouble,** bring trouble; ask for trouble, ask for it <nf>, bring down upon one, bring down upon one's head, bring down around one's ears; **stir up a hornet's nest,** kick up *or* piss up a fuss *or* storm *or* row <nf>; stir up a hornet's nest, open Pandora's box, open a can of worms <nf>, put fire to tow; **raise hob** *or* **hell** <nf>; raise merry hell *and* play hob *and* play hell <nf>, play the deuce *or* devil <nf>

15 **put in a hole** <nf>, put in a spot <nf>; **embarrass; involve,** enmesh, entangle

16 **corner,** run *and* drive into a corner <nf>, **tree** <nf>, chase up a tree *or* stump <nf>, drive *or* force to the wall, push one to the wall, put one's back to the wall, have one on the ropes <nf>

ADJS 17 **difficult,** difficile; **not easy,** no picnic, hairy; **hard, tough** *and* **rough** *and* **rugged** <nf>, rigorous, brutal, severe; wicked *and* mean *and* hairy <nf>, **formidable; arduous, strenuous, toilsome, laborious,** operose, Herculean; steep, uphill; hard-fought; hard-earned; jawbreaking; knotty, knotted; thorny, spiny, set with thorns; delicate, ticklish, tricky, sticky <nf>, critical, easier said than done, like pulling teeth; exacting, demanding; intricate, complex 799.4; abstruse 522.16; hard-ass <nf>

18 **troublesome,** besetting; **bothersome,** irksome, vexatious, painful, plaguey <nf>, problematic, annoying 98.22; **burdensome,** oppressive, onerous, heavy *and* hefty <nf>, crushing, backbreaking; **trying,** grueling

19 **unwieldy, unmanageable, unhandy;** inconvenient, impractical; **awkward, clumsy, cumbersome,** unmaneuverable; contrary, perverse, crosswise; ponderous, bulky, hulky, hulking, ungainly

20 **troubled,** trouble-plagued, beset, sore beset; **bothered, vexed,** irked,

annoyed 96.21; plagued, **harassed** 96.24; distressed, perturbed 96.22; inconvenienced, embarrassed; put to it *and* hard put to it <nf>; **worried, anxious** 126.6,7; puzzled

21 **in trouble, in deep trouble, in a predicament, in a sorry plight,** in a pretty pass; in deep water, out of one's depth

22 <nf terms> **in deep shit** *or* doo-doo, in a jam, in a pickle, in a pretty pickle, in a spot, in a tight spot, in a fix, in a hole, in a bind, in a box; in a mess, in a scrape, in hot water, in the soup; up a tree, up to one's ass in alligators, up the creek, up shit creek without a paddle, in Dutch, on the spot, behind the eight ball, on Queer Street, out on a limb, on the hot seat

23 **in a dilemma,** dilemmatic, on the horns of a dilemma, **in a quandary;** between two stools; between Scylla and Charybdis, between the devil and the deep blue sea, between a rock and a hard place <nf>

24 **at an impasse, at one's wit's end, at a loss,** at a stand *or* standstill, deadlocked; **nonplussed,** at a nonplus; **baffled, perplexed, bewildered,** mystified, stuck *and* stumped <nf>, stymied

25 **cornered,** in a corner, with one's back to the wall; **treed** *and* **up a tree** *and* up a stump <nf>; **at bay,** *aux abois* <Fr>

26 **straitened,** reduced to dire straits, in desperate straits, **pinched,** sore *or* sorely pressed, **hard-pressed, hard up** <nf>, **up against it** <nf>; driven from pillar to post; **desperate, in extremities,** *in extremis* <L>, **at the end of one's rope** *or* **tether**

27 **stranded, grounded,** aground, **on the rocks,** high and dry; **stuck,** stuck *or* set fast; foundered, swamped; castaway, marooned, wrecked, shipwrecked

ADVS 28 **with difficulty,** difficultly, with much ado; hardly, painfully; the hard way, **arduously, strenuously, laboriously,** toilsomely

29 **unwieldily, unmanageably, unhandily,** inconveniently; **awkwardly, clumsily, cumbersomely;** ponderously

1014 FACILITY

NOUNS 1 **facility, ease, easiness,** facileness, effortlessness; lack of hindrance, **smoothness,** freedom; clear coast, clear road *or* course; smooth road, royal road, highroad; easy going, plain sailing, smooth *or* straight sailing; clarity, intelligibility 521; uncomplexity, uncomplicatedness, **simplicity** 798

2 **handiness, wieldiness,** wieldableness, handleability, manageability, **manageableness,** maneuverability; **convenience,** practicality, practicableness, untroublesomeness; **flexibility,** pliancy, **pliability,** ductility, malleability; adaptability, feasibility

3 **easy thing,** mere child's play, simple matter, mere twist of the wrist; easy target, sitting duck <nf>; sinecure; open road

4 <nf terms> **cinch, snap,** pushover, breeze, waltz, duck soup, velvet, picnic, pie, cherry pie, apple pie, cakewalk, piece of cake <Brit>, kid stuff, turkey shoot, no-brainer, setup, high road, walkover, no sweat

5 **facilitation, facilitating, easing,** smoothing, smoothing out, smoothing the way; **speeding,** expediting, expedition, quickening, hastening; streamlining; lubricating, greasing, oiling

6 **disembarrassment, disentanglement, disencumbrance,** disinvolvement, uncluttering, uncomplicating, unscrambling, unsnarling, disburdening, unburdening, unhampering; **extrication,** disengagement, **freeing,** clearing; deregulation; **simplification** 798.2

VERBS 7 **facilitate, ease; grease the wheels** <nf>; **smooth, smooth** *or* **pave the way,** ease the way, grease *or* soap the ways <nf>, prepare the way, **clear the way,** make all clear for, make way for; run interference for <nf>, open the way, open the door to; not stand in the way of; **open up, unclog,** unblock, unjam, unbar, loose 431.6; **lubricate,** make frictionless *or* dissipationless, remove friction, grease, oil; **speed, expedite,** quicken, hasten; **help**

along, help on its way; **aid** 449.11; **explain,** make clear 521.6; **simplify** 798.4

8 **do easily,** make short work of, do with one's hands tied behind one's back, do with both eyes shut, do standing on one's head, do hands down, sail *or* dance *or* waltz through, wing it <nf>, take to like a duck to water

9 **disembarrass, disencumber, unload,** relieve, disburden, unhamper, get out from under; **disentangle,** disembroil, disinvolve, unclutter, unscramble, unsnarl; **extricate,** disengage, **free,** free up, clear; liberate 431.4

10 **go easily, run smoothly,** work well, work like a machine, go like clockwork *or* a sewing machine; present no difficulties, give no trouble, be painless, be effortless; flow, roll, glide, slide, coast, sweep, sail

11 **have it easy, have it soft** <nf>, have it all one's own way, have the game in one's hands, have it in the bag; win easily; breeze in <nf>, walk over the course <nf>, win in a walk *or* in a canter *or* hands down <nf>

12 **take it easy** *and* **go easy** <nf>, swim with the stream, drift with the current, go with the tide; cool it *and* not sweat it <nf>; take the line of least resistance; take it in one's stride, make little *or* light of, think nothing of

ADJS 13 **easy, facile, effortless,** smooth, painless; soft <nf>, cushy <nf>; plain, uncomplicated, straightforward, **simple** 798.6, Mickey Mouse <nf>, simple as ABC <nf>, easy as pie *and* easy as falling off a log <nf>, downhill all the way, like shooting fish in a barrel, like taking candy from a baby, no sooner said than done; **clear;** glib; **light,** unburdensome; nothing to it; casual, throwaway <nf>

14 **smooth-running,** frictionless, dissipationless, easy-running, easy-flowing; well-lubricated, well-oiled, well-greased

15 **handy, wieldy,** wieldable, handleable; tractable; flexible, pliant, yielding, malleable, ductile, pliable, **manageable,** maneuverable; **convenient,** foolproof, goofproof <nf>, practical, untroublesome, user-friendly; adaptable, feasible

ADVS 16 **easily,** facilely, **effortlessly, readily, simply,** lightly, swimmingly <nf>, without difficulty; no sweat *and* like nothing *and* slick as a whistle <nf>; hands down <nf>, with one hand tied behind one's back, with both eyes closed, standing on one's head; like a duck takes to water; **smoothly,** frictionlessly, like clockwork; on easy terms

1015 UGLINESS

NOUNS 1 **ugliness, unsightliness, unattractiveness,** uncomeliness, unhandsomeness, unbeautifulness, unprettiness, unloveliness, unaestheticness, unpleasingness 98.1; unprepossessingness, ill-favoredness, inelegance; **homeliness,** plainness; unshapeliness, shapelessness; ungracefulness, gracelessness, clumsiness, ungainliness 414.3; **uglification, uglifying, disfigurement,** defacement; dysphemism; cacophony

2 **hideousness,** horridness, horribleness, frightfulness, dreadfulness, terribleness, awfulness <nf>; **repulsiveness** 98.2, repugnance, repugnancy, repellence, repellency, offensiveness, forbiddingness, loathsomeness; ghastliness, gruesomeness, grisliness; **deformity,** misshapenness

3 forbidding countenance, vinegar aspect, wry face, face that would stop a clock

4 **eyesore,** blot, blot on the landscape, blemish, **sight** <nf>, **fright, horror, mess,** no beauty, no beauty queen, ugly duckling; baboon; **scarecrow,** gargoyle, monster, **monstrosity,** teratism; witch, bag *and* dog <nf>, **hag,** harridan; something the cat dragged in, back end of a bus

VERBS 5 **offend,** offend the eye, offend one's aesthetic sensibilities, **look bad;** look something terrible *and* look like hell *and* look like the devil *and* look a sight *or* a fright *or* a mess *or* like something the cat dragged in <nf>; **uglify, disfigure,** deface, blot, blemish, mar, scar, spoil; dysphemize

ADJS 6 **ugly, unsightly, unattractive, unhandsome, unpretty, unlovely,** uncomely, **inelegant; unbeautiful,** unbeauteous, beautiless, unaesthetic, unpleasing 98.17; **homely, plain;** not much to look at, not much for looks, short on looks <nf>, hard on the eyes <nf>; ugly as sin, ugly as the wrath of God, ugly as hell, homely as a mud fence, homely enough to sour milk, homely enough to stop a clock, not fit to be seen, grotty <nf>; **uglified, disfigured,** defaced, blotted, blemished, marred, spoiled; dysphemized, dysphemistic; cacophonous, cacophonic

7 **unprepossessing, ill-favored,** hard-favored, evil-favored, ill-featured; ill-looking, evil-looking; hard-featured, hard-visaged; grim, grim-faced, grim-visaged; hatchet-faced, horse-faced

8 **unshapely,** shapeless, **ill-shaped,** ill-made, ill-proportioned; **deformed,** misshapen, misproportioned, malformed, misbegotten; grotesque, scarecrowish, gargoylish; monstrous, teratic, cacogenic

9 **ungraceful,** ungraced, graceless; clumsy, clunky <nf>, **ungainly** 414.20

10 **inartistic,** unartistic, **unaesthetic; unornamental, undecorative**

11 **hideous, horrid, horrible, frightful, dreadful, terrible, awful** <nf>; **repulsive** 98.18, repellent, repelling, rebarbative, **repugnant,** offensive, foul, forbidding, loathsome, loathly , revolting; **ghastly,** gruesome, grisly

ADVS 12 **uglily,** homelily, uncomelily, **unattractively, unhandsomely, unbeautifully, unprettily**

13 **hideously, horridly, horribly, frightfully, dreadfully, terribly, awfully** <nf>; **repulsively, repugnantly,** offensively, forbiddingly, loathsomely, revoltingly; gruesomely, ghastly

1016 BEAUTY

NOUNS 1 **beauty, beautifulness,** beauteousness, **prettiness, handsomeness, attractiveness** 97.2, **loveliness, pulchritude, charm,** grace, elegance, exquisiteness; bloom, glow; the beautiful; source of aesthetic pleasure *or* delight; beauty unadorned

2 **comeliness, fairness,** sightliness, personableness, becomingness, pleasingness 97.1, goodliness, bonniness, agreeability, agreeableness; charisma

3 **good looks,** good appearance, good effect; good proportions, aesthetic proportions; **shapeliness,** good figure, good shape, *belle tournure* <Fr>, nice body, lovely build, physical *or* bodily charm, curvaceousness, curves <nf>, pneumaticness, sexy body, sexiness; good bone structure; 10 <nf>; bodily grace, **gracefulness,** gracility; good points, **beauties, charms, delights,** perfections, good features, delicate features

4 **daintiness, delicacy,** delicateness; **cuteness** *or* cunningness <nf>

5 **gorgeousness,** ravishingness; **gloriousness,** heavenliness, sublimity; **splendor,** splendidness, splendiferousness, splendorousness *or* splendrousness, sublimeness, resplendence; **brilliance,** brightness, radiance, luster; **glamour** 377.1

6 **thing of beauty,** vision, picture <nf>, poem, eyeful <nf>, **sight for sore eyes** <nf>, cynosure; masterpiece

7 **beauty, charmer,** *charmeuse* <Fr>; beauty queen, beauty contest winner, beauty pageant winner, Miss America, Miss USA, Miss World, Miss Universe, bathing beauty; **glamour girl,** cover girl, model, arm candy <nf>; sex goddess; **belle,** reigning beauty, great beauty, lady fair; beau ideal, paragon; enchantress

8 <nf terms> **doll, dish, cutie,** angel, angelface, babyface, beaut, honey, dream, looker, good-looker, stunner, dazzler; dreamboat, hunk; fetcher,

bird *and* crumpet <Brit>, peach, knockout, raving beauty, centerfold, pinup girl, pinup, bunny, cutie *or* cutesy pie, cute *or* slick chick, pussycat, sex kitten, ten; treasure; hottie, it girl, babe

9 <famous beauties> Venus, Venus de Milo; Aphrodite; Adonis, Hyperion, Narcissus; Astarte; Freya; Helen of Troy, Cleopatra; the Graces, houri, peri

10 **beautification,** prettification, cutification <nf>, **adornment;** decoration 498.1; **beauty care,** beauty treatment, cosmetology; facial <nf>; manicure; hairdressing; cosmetic surgery, plastic surgery

11 **makeup, cosmetics, beauty products, beauty-care products;** war paint *and* drugstore complexion <nf>; pancake makeup; powder, talcum, talcum powder; foundation, base; rouge, blush *or* blusher, paint; lip rouge, **lipstick,** lip color; **nail polish;** greasepaint, clown white; eye makeup, eyeliner, mascara, eye shadow, kohl; cold cream, hand cream *or* lotion, vanishing cream, foundation cream; mudpack; eyebrow pencil; puff, powder puff; makeup brush; compact, vanity case; toiletries, shampoo, soap, deodorant, perfume

12 **beautician,** beautifier, cosmetologist, makeup artist, cosmetician; hairdresser, *coiffeur* and *coiffeuse* <Fr>, hairstylist; barber; manicurist, pedicurist

13 **beauty parlor** *or* salon *or* shop, *salon de beauté* <Fr>, hairdressing salon, hair salon; barbershop, barber

14 **hairdressing,** hair styling, hair coloring, barbering; shave, depilation, tweezing, electrolysis, waxing; hair replacement; hairstyle, hairdo; haircut, trim, permanent, perm; crop, bob, cut, ponytail, plait, cornrows, braids, pigtails, bangs, chignon, bun, beehive, pompadour, pageboy, dreadlocks, sideburns, crewcut, number one buzz, number three buzz, flattop, ducktail, DA, Mohawk, Afro

VERBS **15** **beautify, prettify,** cutify <nf>, pretty up *or* gussy up *or* doll up <nf>, grace, **adorn; decorate** 498.8; set off, set off to advantage *or* good advantage, become one; **glamorize; make up,** paint *and* put on one's face <nf>, titivate, cosmetize, cosmeticize; primp

16 **look good;** look like a million *and* look fit to kill *and* knock dead *and* knock one's eyes out <nf>; take the breath away, beggar description; shine, beam, **bloom, glow**

ADJS **17** **beautiful, beauteous,** endowed with beauty; **pretty, handsome, attractive** 97.7, pulchritudinous, **lovely, graceful,** gracile; elegant; esthetic, aesthetically appealing; **cute;** pretty as a picture; tall dark and handsome; picturesque, scenic

18 **comely, fair, good-looking, nice-looking,** well-favored, **personable,** presentable, agreeable, becoming, pleasing 97.6, goodly, bonny, likely <nf>, **sightly;** pleasing to the eye, lovely to behold; **shapely,** well-built, built, well-shaped, well-proportioned, well-made, well-formed, stacked *or* well-stacked <nf>, shapely, curvaceous, curvy <nf>, pneumatic, amply endowed, built for comfort *or* built like a brick shithouse <nf>, buxom, callipygian, callipygous; Junoesque, statuesque, goddess-like; slender 270.16; Adonis-like, hunky <nf>

19 **fine, exquisite,** flowerlike, **dainty, delicate;** *mignon* <Fr>

20 **gorgeous, ravishing; glorious,** heavenly, divine, sublime; **resplendent,** splendorous *or* splendrous, splendiferous, **splendid; brilliant,** bright, radiant, shining, beaming, glowing, blooming, abloom, sparkling, **dazzling; glamorous;** babelicious <nf>

21 <nf terms> **eye-filling, easy on the eyes,** not hard to look at, drop-dead gorgeous, long on looks, looking fit to kill, dishy <chiefly Brit>; cutesy, cutesy-poo; raving, devastating, **stunning,** killing

22 **beautifying,** cosmetic; decorative 498.10; cosmetized, cosmeticized, beautified, made-up, mascaraed, titivated

ADVS **23** **beautifully,** beauteously, **prettily, handsomely, attractively, becomingly,** comelily; elegantly, exquisitely; charmingly, enchantingly

24 **daintily, delicately; cutely**

25 **gorgeously, ravishingly;** ravingly *and* devastatingly *and* stunningly <nf>; **gloriously,** divinely, sublimely; **resplendently,** splendidly, splendorously, splendrously; **brilliantly,** brightly, radiantly, glowingly, **dazzlingly**

1017 MATHEMATICS

NOUNS **1** **mathematics**, math, maths <Brit nf>, mathematic, **numbers, figures;** pure mathematics, abstract mathematics, applied mathematics, higher mathematics, elementary mathematics, classical mathematics, metamathematics, new mathematics; algorithm, logarithm; mathematical element

2 <mathematical operations> notation, **addition** 253, **subtraction** 255, **multiplication, division,** numeracy, calculation, computation, reckoning, proportion, practice, equation, extraction of roots, inversion, reduction, involution, evolution, approximation, interpolation, extrapolation, transformation, differentiation, integration; arithmetic operation, algebraic operation, logical operation, associative operation, distributive operation

3 **number**, **numeral,** *numero* <Sp, Ital>, no *or* n, digit, binary digit *or* bit, **cipher,** character, symbol, sign, notation, figure, base; decimal

4 <number systems> **Arabic numerals,** algorism *or* algorithm, Roman numerals; **decimal system,** binary system, octal system, duodecimal system, hexadecimal system; place-value notation, positional notation, fixed-point notation, floating-point notation

5 large number, astronomical number, boxcar number <nf>, zillion *and* jillion <nf>; googol, googolplex; infinity, infinite number, transfinite number, infinitude 823.1; billion, trillion, etc 882.12-13

6 **sum,** summation, difference, product, **number, count,** x number, n number; account, cast, **score, reckoning, tally,** tale, the story *and* whole story *and* all she wrote <nf>, the bottom line <nf>, **aggregate, amount,** quantity 244; **whole** 792, **total** 792.2, running total; box score <nf>

7 **ratio, rate, proportion; quota,** quotum; **percentage,** percent; **fraction,** proper fraction, improper fraction, compound fraction, continued fraction, decimal fraction; common *or* vulgar fraction; geometric ratio *or* proportion, arithmetical proportion, harmonic proportion; rule of three; numerator, denominator; body mass index

8 **series, progression;** arithmetical progression, geometrical progression, harmonic progression; Fibonacci numbers

9 **numeration, enumeration, numbering, counting,** count, accounting, census, inventorying, telling, tally, tallying, scoring; page numbering, pagination, foliation; counting on the fingers, dactylonomy; **measurement** 300; quantification, quantifying, quantization

10 **calculation, computation, estimation, reckoning,** figuring, number work, mental arithmetic, calculus; adding, footing, casting, ciphering, totaling, toting *or* totting <nf>; rounding up, rounding down, rounding off

11 **summation, summary, summing, summing up, recount,** recounting, rehearsal, capitulation, **recapitulation,** recap *and* rehash <nf>, statement, **reckoning, count,** bean-counting <nf>, repertory, census, inventory, head count, nose count, body count; account, accounts; **table,** reckoner, ready reckoner

12 **division**; long division, short division, divisibility; quotient, ratio, proportion, percentage, fraction; reciprocal, inverse, dividend, divisor, aliquot part, remainder, residue;

numerator, denominator, common denominator

13 **account of, count of,** a reckoning of, **tab** *or* **tabs of** <nf>, tally of, check of, track of

14 **figures, statistics,** indexes *or* indices; vital statistics

15 **calculator**, **computer** 1042.2; estimator, figurer, reckoner, abacist, pollster; statistician, actuary; number-cruncher <nf>; accountant, bookkeeper 628.7

16 **mathematician, arithmetician;** geometer, geometrician; algebraist, trigonometrician, statistician, geodesist, mathematical physicist, topologist; analyst

VERBS 17 **number,** numerate, number off, **enumerate, count, tell, tally,** give a figure to, put a figure on, call off, name, call over, run over; **count noses** *or* **heads** <nf>, call the roll; census, poll; page, paginate, foliate; **measure** 300.10; **round,** round out *or* off *or* down; quantify, quantitate, quantize

18 **calculate, compute, estimate, reckon, figure,** solve, reckon at, put at, cipher, cast, tally, score; **figure out,** do the math, work out, dope out <nf>, determine; take account of, figure in *and* figure on <nf>; arithmetize; **add,** add up, sum, **subtract,** take away, **multiply, divide,** multiply out, cross-multiply, times, algebraize, extract roots, raise to the power of, cube, square, decimalize; factor, factor out, factorize; **measure** 300.10

19 **sum up,** sum, summate, say it all <nf>; aggregate, **figure up,** cipher up, reckon up, **count up, add up,** foot up, cast up, score up, **tally up; total,** total up, tote *or* tot up <nf>; **summarize, recapitulate,** recap *and* rehash <nf>, **recount,** rehearse, recite, relate; detail, itemize, inventory; round up, round down, round off

20 **keep account of,** keep count of, **keep track of, keep tab** *or* **tabs** <nf>, keep tally, keep a check on *or* of

21 **check, verify** 970.12, double-check, check on *or* out; **prove,** demonstrate; balance, balance the books; **audit,** overhaul; take stock, inventory

ADJS 22 **mathematical,** numeric *or* numerical, numerary, arithmetic *or* arithmetical, algebraic *or* algebraical, geometric *or* geometrical, trigonometric *or* trigonometrical, analytic *or* analytical, combinatorial, topological, statistical

23 **numeric** *or* **numerical,** numeral, numerary, numerative; **odd,** impair, **even,** pair; arithmetical, algorismic *or* algorithmic; **cardinal, ordinal;** figural, **figurate,** figurative, **digital;** aliquot, submultiple, **reciprocal,** prime, fractional, decimal, exponential, **logarithmic,** logometric, differential, integral; positive, negative; rational, irrational, transcendental; surd, radical; real, imaginary; possible, impossible, finite, infinite, transfinite; integral, whole; decenary, binary, ternary; signed, unsigned, nonnegative

24 **numerative, enumerative; calculative,** computative, estimative; **calculating,** computing, computational, estimating; statistical; quantifying, quantizing

25 **calculable,** computable, **reckonable,** estimable, countable, numberable, enumerable, numerable; **measurable,** mensurable, quantifiable; addable, subtractive, multipliable, dividable

1018 PHYSICS

NOUNS 1 **physics;** natural *or* physical science; philosophy *or* second philosophy *or* natural philosophy *or* physic ; **branch of physics** ; physical theory, quantum theory, relativity theory, special relativity theory, general relativity theory, unified field theory, grand unified theory *or* GUT, superunified theory *or* theory of everything *or* TOE, eightfold way, string theory, superstring theory, kinetic theory, wave theory, electromagnetic theory

2 **physicist,** aerophysicist, astrophysicist, biophysicist, etc

ADJS 3 **physical;** aerophysical, astrophysical, biophysical, etc

1019 HEAT

NOUNS **1 heat, hotness,** heatedness; superheat, superheatedness; calidity *or* caloric ; **warmth,** warmness; incalescence; radiant heat, thermal radiation, induction heat, convector *or* convected heat, coal heat, gas heat, oil heat, hot-air heat, steam heat, electric heat, solar heat, dielectric heat, ultraviolet heat, atomic heat, molecular heat; latent heat, specific heat; animal heat, body heat, blood heat, hypothermia; fever heat, fever, pyrexia, feverishness, flush, calescence; heating, burning 1020.5; smoke detector

2 <metaphors> **ardor,** ardency, **fervor,** fervency, fervidness, fervidity; eagerness 101; excitement 105; **anger** 152.5,8,9; **sexual desire** 75.5; love 104

3 temperature, temp <nf>; room temperature, comfortable temperature; comfort index, temperature-humidity index *or* THI; flash point; boiling point; melting point, freezing point; dew point; recalescence point; zero, absolute zero; thermometry, pyrometry

4 lukewarmness, tepidness, tepidity; tepidarium

5 torridness, torridity; extreme heat, intense heat, torrid heat, red heat, white heat, tropical heat, sweltering heat, African heat, Indian heat, Bengal heat, summer heat, oppressive heat; **hot wind** 318.6; incandescence, flash point

6 sultriness, stuffiness, closeness, oppressiveness; humidity, humidness, mugginess, stickiness <nf>, swelter, fug; tropical heat; overheating

7 hot weather, sunny *or* sunshiny weather; sultry weather, stuffy weather, humid weather, muggy weather, sticky weather <nf>, HHH <nf>; summer, midsummer, high summer; Indian Summer, **dog days,** canicular days, canicule; **heat wave,** hot wave, hot spell, warm front, heat haze; broiling sun, midday sun; vertical rays; warm weather, fair weather; global warming, greenhouse effect

8 hot day, summer day; **scorcher** *and* **roaster** *and* broiler *and* sizzler *and* swelterer <nf>

9 hot air, superheated air; thermal; firestorm

10 hot water, boiling water; **steam,** vapor; volcanic water; hot *or* warm *or* thermal spring, thermae; geyser, Old Faithful; steaminess; boiling point

11 <hot place> **oven, furnace,** fiery furnace, inferno, hell; heater, warmer, burner; steam bath, sauna, solarium; **tropics,** subtropics, Torrid Zone, Sahara, Dearth Valley; equator; melting point

12 glow, incandescence, fieriness; **flush, blush, bloom,** redness 41, rubicundity, rosiness; whiteness 37; thermochromism; hectic, hectic flush; sunburn

13 fire; blaze, flame, ingle, devouring element; **combustion, ignition,** ignition temperature *or* point, flash *or* flashing point; **conflagration;** flicker 1025.8, wavering *or* flickering flame; smoldering fire, sleeping fire; marshfire, fen fire, ignis fatuus, will-o'-the-wisp; fox fire; witch fire, St Elmo's fire, corposant; **cheerful fire,** cozy fire, crackling fire; **roaring fire,** blazing fire; **raging fire,** sheet of fire, sea of flames; bonfire, balefire; beacon fire, beacon, signal beacon, watch fire; towering inferno; alarm fire, two-alarm fire, three-alarm fire, etc; wildfire, prairie fire, forest fire; backfire; brushfire; open fire; campfire; smudge fire; death fire, pyre, funeral pyre, crematory; burning ghat; fireball; first-degree burn, second-degree burn, third-degree burn

14 flare, flare-up, **flash,** flash fire, **blaze,** burst, outburst; deflagration

15 spark, sparkle; **scintillation,** scintilla; ignescence

16 coal, live coal, brand, firebrand, **ember,** burning ember; **cinder**

17 fireworks, pyrotechnics *or* pyrotechny

18 <perviousness to heat> transcalency; adiathermancy, athermancy

19 **thermal unit;** British thermal unit *or* BTU; Board of Trade unit *or* BOT; centigrade thermal unit; centigrade *or* Celsius scale, Fahrenheit scale; **calorie,** mean calorie, centuple *or* rational calorie, small calorie, large *or* great calorie, kilocalorie, kilogram-calorie; therm; joule

20 **thermometer,** thermal detector; mercury, glass; thermostat; calorimeter; thermograph, thermostat

21 <science of heat> thermochemistry, thermology, thermotics, thermodynamics; volcanology; pyrology, pyrognostics; pyrotechnics *or* pyrotechny, ebulliometry; calorimetry

VERBS **22** <be hot> **burn** 1020.24, **scorch,** parch, scald, **swelter, roast,** toast, cook, bake, fry, broil, sizzle, boil, seethe, simmer, stew; **be in heat;** shimmer with heat, give off waves of heat, radiate heat; **blaze,** combust, spark, **catch fire, flame** 1020.23, flame up, **flare,** flare up; **flicker** 1025.26; **glow,** incandesce, flush, blush, bloom; smolder; steam; sweat 12.16; gasp, pant; **suffocate, stifle,** smother, choke; keep warm; run a temperature; sunbathe

23 **smoke, fume,** reek, smolder; smudge; carbonize

ADJS **24** **warm,** calid , **thermal,** thermic; **toasty** <nf>, warm as toast; **sunny,** sunshiny, sunbaked; fair, mild, genial; summery, aestival; **temperate,** warmish; balmy, **tropical,** equatorial, subtropical; semitropical; **tepid, lukewarm,** luke; room-temperature; blood-warm, blood-hot; unfrozen

25 **hot, heated, torrid,** thermal, thermic; **sweltering,** sweltry, canicular; **burning,** parching, scorching, searing, scalding, blistering, baking, roasting, toasting, broiling, grilling, simmering, sizzling; **boiling,** seething, ebullient; **piping hot,** scalding hot, burning hot, roasting hot, scorching hot, sizzling hot, smoking hot; **red-hot,** white-hot; ardent; flushed, sweating, sweaty, sudorific; overwarm, overhot, overheated; hot as fire, hot as a three-dollar pistol <nf>, hot as hell *or* blazes, hot as the hinges of hell, hot enough to roast an ox, hot enough to fry an egg on, so hot you can fry eggs on the sidewalk <nf>, like a furnace *or* an oven; feverish; hot and humid, HHH <nf>

26 **fiery,** igneous, firelike, pyric; combustive, conflagrative

27 **burning, ignited,** kindled, enkindled, **blazing,** ablaze, ardent, flaring, flaming, aflame, inflamed, alight, **afire, on fire,** in flames, in a blaze, flagrant ; conflagrant, comburent; live, living; molten; **glowing,** aglow, in a glow, incandescent, candescent, candent; sparking, scintillating, scintillant, ignescent; **flickering,** aflicker, guttering; unquenched, unextinguished; slow-burning; **smoldering; smoking,** fuming, reeking

28 **sultry, stifling, suffocating, stuffy, close,** oppressive, steamy; **humid, sticky** <nf>, **muggy**

29 warm-blooded, hot-blooded

30 isothermal, isothermic; centigrade, Fahrenheit

31 diathermic, diathermal, transcalent; adiathermic, adiathermal, athermanous

32 pyrological, pyrognostic, pyrotechnic *or* pyrotechnical; pyrogenic *or* pyrogenous *or* pyrogenetic; thermochemical; thermodynamic, thermodynamical

1020 HEATING

NOUNS **1** **heating, warming,** calefaction, torrefaction, increase *or* raising of temperature; superheating; pyrogenesis; decalescence, recalescence; preheating; **heating system**, heating method; solar radiation, insolation; dielectric heating; induction heating; heat exchange; cooking 11

2 **boiling,** seething, **stewing,** ebullition, ebullience *or* ebulliency, coction; decoction; **simmering;** boil; simmer

3 **melting, fusion,** liquefaction, liquefying, liquescence, running; **thawing,** thaw; liquation; fusibility; thermoplasticity

4 **ignition, lighting,** lighting up *or* off, **kindling,** firing; reaching flash point *or* flashing point

5 **burning, combustion,** blazing, flaming; **scorching,** parching, singeing; **searing,** branding; **blistering,** vesication; **cauterization,** cautery; **incineration; cremation;** suttee, self-cremation, self-immolation; the stake, burning at the stake, *auto da fe* <Pg>; scorification; carbonization; oxidation, oxidization; calcination; cupellation; deflagration; distilling, distillation; refining, smelting; pyrolysis; cracking, thermal cracking, destructive distillation; **spontaneous combustion,** thermogenesis

6 **burn,** scald, scorch, singe; sear; brand; sunburn, sunscald; windburn; mat burn; first- *or* second- *or* third-degree burn

7 **incendiarism, arson,** torch job <nf>, fire-raising <Brit>; **pyromania;** pyrophilia; pyrolatry, fire worship

8 **incendiary, arsonist,** torcher <nf>; pyromaniac, firebug <nf>; pyrophile, fire buff <nf>; pyrolater, fire worshiper

9 **flammability, inflammability,** combustibility; spontaneous combustion

10 **heater, warmer; stove, oven, furnace; cooker,** cookery; firebox; tuyere, tewel ; burner, jet, gas jet, pilot light *or* burner, element, heating element, Bunsen burner; heat lamp; heating pipe, steam pipe, hot-water pipe; heating duct, caliduct

11 **fireplace, hearth,** ingle; **fireside,** hearthside, ingleside, inglenook, ingle cheek, chimney corner; hearthstone; hob, hub; fireguard, fireboard, fire screen, fender; chimney, chimney piece, chimney-breast, chimney-pot, chimney-stack, flue, grate; smokehole; brazier, kiln, smelter, forge; pyre

12 **fire iron; andiron,** firedog; tongs, pair of tongs, fire tongs, coal tongs; poker, stove poker, salamander, fire hook; lifter, stove lifter; pothook, crook, crane, chain; trivet, tripod; spit, turnspit; grate, grating; gridiron, grid, griddle, grill, griller; damper

13 **incinerator,** cinerator, burner; solid-waste incinerator, garbage incinerator; **crematory,** cremator, crematorium, burning ghat; calcinatory

14 **blowtorch,** blowlamp <Brit>, blast lamp, torch, alcohol torch, butane torch; soldering torch; blowpipe; **burner; welder;** acetylene torch *or* welder, cutting torch *or* blowpipe, oxyacetylene blowpipe *or* torch, welding blowpipe *or* torch

15 cauterant, cauterizer, cauter, cautery, thermocautery, actual cautery; hot iron, **branding iron,** brand iron, brand; moxa; electrocautery; **caustic, corrosive,** mordant, escharotic, potential cautery; acid; lunar caustic; radium

16 <products of combustion> scoria, sullage, slag, dross; **ashes,** ash; **cinder,** clinker, coal; coke, charcoal, brand, lava, carbon, calx; **soot,** smut, coom <Brit nf>; **smoke,** smudge, fume, reek

VERBS 17 **heat,** raise *or* increase the temperature, heat up, hot *or* hot up <Brit>, **warm,** fire, fire up, stoke up; chafe; take the chill off; tepefy; gas-heat, oil-heat, hot-air-heat, hot-water-heat, steam-heat, electric-heat, solar-heat; superheat; overheat; preheat; **reheat,** recook, warm over *or* up; mull; steam; foment; cook 11.5; glow; cook, roast, toast, bake, braise, broil, fry

18 <metaphors> **excite, inflame;** incite, **kindle, arouse** 375.17,19; anger, **enrage**

19 insolate, sun-dry; **sun,** bask, bask in the sun, sun oneself, sunbathe, suntan, get a tan, tan

20 **boil, stew, simmer, seethe;** distill; scald, parboil, steam

21 **melt,** melt down, liquefy; **run,** colliquate, **fuse,** flux; refine, smelt; render; **thaw,** thaw out, unfreeze; defrost, de-ice

22 **ignite, set fire to, fire, set on fire, set alight, kindle,** enkindle, inflame, **light,** light up, strike a light, put a match *or* torch to, torch <nf>, touch off, **burn,** conflagrate; **build a fire;** rekindle, relight, relume; feed, feed

the fire, **stoke,** stoke the fire, add fuel to the flame; bank; poke *or* stir the fire, blow up the fire, fan the flame; open the draft; reduce to ashes

23 **catch fire,** catch on fire, catch, take fire, **burn, flame,** combust, blaze, **blaze up, burst into flames,** go up in flames

24 **burn,** torrefy, **scorch, parch, sear; singe,** swinge; **blister,** vesicate; **cauterize,** brand, burn in; char, coal, carbonize; scorify; calcine; pyrolyze, crack; solder, weld, fuse, lag; vulcanize; cast, found; oxidize, oxidate; deflagrate; cupel; burn off; blaze, flame 1019.22

25 **burn up,** incendiarize, **incinerate, cremate,** consume, burn *or* reduce to ashes, **burn to a crisp,** burn to a cinder; **burn down,** burn to the ground, **go up in smoke;** burn at the stake

ADJS **26** **heating, warming,** chafing, calorific; calefactory, calefactive, calefacient, calorifacient, calorigenic; fiery, burning 1019.25,27; cauterant, cauterizing; calcinatory

27 **inflammatory,** inflammative, **inflaming, kindling,** enkindling, lighting; **incendiary,** incendive; arsonous

28 **flammable, inflammable, combustible,** burnable

29 **heated,** het *or* het up <nf>, hotted up <Brit>, **warmed,** warmed up, centrally heated, gas-heated, oil-heated, kerosene-heated, hot-water-heated, hot-air-heated, steam-heated, solar-heated, electric-heated, baseboard-heated; superheated; overheated; preheated; **reheated,** recooked, **warmed-over,** *réchauffé* <Fr>; hot 1019.25

30 **burned, burnt,** burned to the ground, incendiarized, torched <nf>, burned-out *or* -down, gutted; **scorched, blistered, parched, singed, seared, charred,** pyrographic, adust; sunburned; **burnt-up,** incinerated, cremated, consumed, consumed by fire; ashen, ashy, carbonized, pyrolyzed, pyrolytic

31 **molten, melted,** fused, liquefied; liquated; meltable, fusible; thermoplastic

1021 FUEL

NOUNS **1** **fuel,** energy source; heat source, firing, combustible *or* inflammable *or* flammable material, burnable, combustible, inflammable, flammable; fossil fuel, nonrenewable energy *or* fuel source; alternate *or* alternative energy source *or* alternate energy, renewable energy *or* fuel source; solar energy, solar radiation, insolation; wind energy; geothermal energy, geothermal heat, geothermal gradient; synthetic fuels *or* synfuels; solid fuel; fuel starter; fuel additive, dope, fuel dope; propellant; **oil** 1056; gas 1067

2 slack, coal dust, coom *or* comb <Brit nf>, culm

3 **firewood,** stovewood, wood; woodpile; kindling, **kindlings,** kindling wood; brush, brushwood; fagot, bavin <Brit>; log, backlog, yule log *or* yule clog

4 **lighter,** light, igniter, sparker; pocket lighter, cigar *or* cigarette lighter, butane lighter; **torch,** flambeau, taper, spill; brand, **firebrand;** portfire; **flint,** flint *and* steel; **detonator,** fuse, spark plug, ignition system

5 **match,** matchstick, lucifer; friction match, locofoco *and* vesuvian *and* vesta *and* fusee *and* Congreve *or* Congreve match ; safety match; matchbook

6 **tinder,** touchwood; **punk,** spunk, German tinder, amadou; tinder fungus; pyrotechnic sponge; tinderbox

7 renewable energy, soft energy; solar power, solar energy, alternate energy; photovoltaic cell, solar cell; wind power; geothermal energy; water power, hydroelectric power; wave power, tidal power; biomass

VERBS **8** **fuel,** fuel up; fill up, top off; refuel; coal, oil; **stoke, feed,** add fuel to the flame; detonate, explode

ADJS **9** **fuel,** energy, heat; fossil-fuel; alternate- *or* alternative-energy; oil-fired, coal-fired, etc; gas-powered, oil-powered, wind-powered, etc; water-driven, hydroelectric, etc; wood-burning; coaly, carbonaceous, carboniferous; anthracite; clean-burning; bituminous; high-sulfur; lignitic; peaty; gas-guzzling

1022 INCOMBUSTIBILITY

NOUNS **1 incombustibility, uninflammability,** noninflammability, **nonflammability;** unburnableness; fire resistance

2 extinguishing, extinguishment, extinction, **quenching,** dousing <nf>, **snuffing,** putting out; **choking, damping, stifling, smothering,** smotheration; controlling; fire fighting; going out, dying, burning out, flame-out, burnout

3 extinguisher, fire extinguisher; fire apparatus, fire engine, hook-and-ladder, ladder truck; ladder pipe, snorkel, deluge set, deck gun; pumper, super-pumper; **foam,** carbon-dioxide foam, Foamite <TM>, foam extinguisher; dry-powder extinguisher; carbon tetrachloride, carbon tet; water, soda, acid, wet blanket; sprinkler, automatic sprinkler, sprinkler system, sprinkler head; hydrant, fire hydrant, fireplug; fire hose

4 fire fighter, fireman, fire-eater <nf>; pumpman; forest fire fighter, fire warden, fire-chaser, smokechaser, smokejumper; volunteer fireman, vamp <nf>; fire department, fire brigade <chiefly Brit>

5 fireproofing; fire resistance; fireproof *or* fire-resistant *or* fire-resisting *or* fire-resistive *or* fire-retardant material, fire retardant; asbestos; amianthus, earth flax, mountain flax; asbestos curtain, fire wall; fire break, fire line

VERBS **6 fireproof,** flameproof

7 fight fire; extinguish, put out, quench, out, douse <nf>, **snuff,** snuff out, blow out, stamp out; stub out, dinch <nf>; **choke, damp, smother, stifle,** slack; bring under control, contain

8 burn out, go out, die, die out *or* down *or* away; fizzle *and* **fizzle out** <nf>; flame out

ADJS **9 incombustible, noncombustible, uninflammable,** noninflammable, noncombustive, **nonflammable,** unburnable; asbestine, asbestous, asbestoid, asbestoidal; amianthine

10 fireproof, flameproof, fireproofed, fire-retarded, fire-resisting *or* -resistant *or* -resistive, fire-retardant

11 extinguished, quenched, snuffed, **out;** contained, under control

1023 COLD

NOUNS **1 cold, coldness; coolness,** coolth, freshness; low temperature, arctic temperature, drop *or* decrease in temperature, lack of heat; **chilliness,** nippiness, freshness, crispness, briskness, sharpness, bite; **chill, nip,** sharp air; **frigidity, iciness,** frostiness, extreme *or* intense cold, gelidity, algidity, algidness; **rawness,** bleakness, keenness, sharpness, bitterness, severity, inclemency, rigor; freezing point; cryology; cryonics; cryogenics; absolute zero

2 <sensation of cold> **chill,** chilliness, chilling; shivering, chills, **shivers,** cold shivers, shakes, didders <Brit nf>, dithers, chattering of the teeth; creeps, **cold creeps** <nf>; **gooseflesh, goose pimples,** goose *or* duck bumps <nf>, horripilation; **frostbite, chilblains,** kibe, cryopathy; ache, aching; ice-cream headache

3 cold weather, bleak weather, raw weather, bitter weather, wintry weather, arctic weather, **freezing weather,** zero weather, subzero weather; **cold wave,** snap, **cold snap,** cold spell, cold front; **freeze,** frost, hard frost, deep freeze, arctic frost, big freeze, hard freeze; winter, wintriness, depths of winter, hard winter, arctic conditions; wintry wind 318.7; coolness, chill, nip in the air, chilliness, nippiness; chill factor, wind-chill factor; ice age

4 <cold place> Siberia, Hell, Novaya Zemlya, Alaska, Iceland, the Hebrides, Greenland, the Yukon, Tierra del Fuego, Lower Slobbovia <Al Capp>; North Pole, South Pole; Frigid Zones; the Arctic, Arctic Circle *or* Zone; Antarctica, the Antarctic; Antarctic Circle *or* Zone;

tundra; the freezer, the deep-freeze, igloo

5 **ice,** frozen water; ice needle *or* crystal; **icicle,** iceshockle <Brit nf>; cryosphere; ice sheet, ice field, ice barrier, ice front; **floe, ice floe,** sea ice, ice island, ice raft, ice pack; ice foot, ice belt; shelf ice, sheet ice, pack ice, bay ice, berg ice, field ice; **iceberg,** berg, growler; calf; snowberg; **icecap,** *jokul* <Iceland>; ice pinnacle, serac, nieve penitente; **glacier,** glacieret, glaciation, ice dike; piedmont glacier; icefall; ice banner; ice cave; **sleet,** glaze, glazed frost, verglas; snow ice; névé, black ice, granular snow, firn; ground ice, anchor ice, frazil; lolly; sludge, slob *or* slob ice <chiefly Can>; ice cubes; crushed ice; Dry Ice <TM>, solid carbon dioxide; icequake; ice storm, freezing rain

6 **hail,** hailstone; soft hail, graupel, snow pellets, tapioca snow; **hailstorm**

7 **frost,** Jack Frost; **hoarfrost,** hoar, rime, rime frost, white frost; black frost; hard frost, sharp frost; killing frost; frost smoke; frost line; permafrost; silver frost; glaze frost; ground frost

8 **snow;** granular snow, corn snow, spring corn, spring snow, powder snow, wet snow, tapioca snow; **snowfall; snowstorm,** snow blast, snow squall, snow flurry, flurry, snow shower, blizzard, whiteout; **snowflake,** snow-crystal, flake, crystal; snow dust; **snowdrift,** snowbank, snow cover, snowscape, snow blanket, snow mantle, snow wreath <Brit nf>, driven snow, drifting snow; snowcap; snow banner; snow blanket; snow bed, snowpack, snowfield, mantle of snow; snowscape; snowland; snowshed; snow line; snowball, snowman; snowslide, snowslip, avalanche; snow slush, **slush,** slosh, snowmelt, melt, meltwater; snowbridge; snow fence; snowhouse, igloo; mogul

VERBS 9 freeze, be cold, grow cold, lose heat; **shiver, quiver,** shiver to death, quake, shake, tremble, shudder, didder <Brit nf>, dither; **chatter; chill,** have a chill, have the cold shivers; **freeze,** freeze to death, freeze one's balls off <nf>, die *or* perish with the cold, horripilate, have goose pimples, have goose *or* duck bumps <nf>; have chilblains; get frostbite

10 <make cold> **freeze, chill,** chill to the bone *or* marrow, make one shiver, make one's teeth chatter; **nip,** bite, cut, **pierce,** penetrate, penetrate to the bone, go through *or* right through; freshen; air-condition; glaciate; freeze-dry; **freeze** 1024.11; frost, frostbite; numb, benumb; **refrigerate** 1024.10

11 **hail, sleet, snow;** snow in; snow under; **frost,** ice, ice up, ice over, glaze, glaze over, freeze over

ADJS 12 **cool,** coolish, temperate; chill, **chilly,** parky <Brit nf>; **fresh,** brisk, crisp, bracing, sharpish, **invigorating,** stimulating

13 **unheated,** unwarmed; unmelted, unthawed

14 **cold, freezing,** freezing cold, **crisp, brisk,** nipping, **nippy, snappy** <nf>, **raw, bleak, keen, sharp,** bitter, biting, pinching, cutting, **piercing,** penetrating, perishing; inclement, severe, rigorous; snowcold; sleety; slushy; **icy,** icelike, **ice-cold,** glacial, ice-encrusted; cryospheric; supercooled; **frigid,** bitter *or* bitterly cold, gelid, algid; below zero, subzero; numbing; **wintry,** wintery, winterlike, winterbound, hiemal, brumal, hibernal; **arctic,** Siberian, boreal, hyperborean; stone-cold, cold as death, cold as ice, cold as marble, cold as charity

15 <nf terms> **cold as hell,** cold as a welldigger's ass, cold as a witch's tit *or* kiss, cold enough to freeze the tail *or* balls off a brass monkey, cold as a bastard *or* a bitch, colder than hell *or* the deuce *or* the devil

16 <feeling cold> **cold, freezing; cool, chilly,** nippy; **shivering,** shivery, shaky, dithery; algid, aguish, aguey; chattering, with chattering teeth; **frozen** 1024.14, half-frozen, frozen to death, chilled to the bone, blue with cold, *figé de froid* <Fr>, so cold one could spit ice cubes

17 **frosty,** frostlike; **frosted,** frosted-over, frost-beaded, frost-covered, frost-chequered, rimed, **hoary,** hoar-frosted, rime-frosted; frost-riven, frost-rent; frosty-faced, frosty-whiskered; frostbound, frost-fettered

18 **snowy,** snowlike, niveous, nival; snow-blown, snow-drifted, snow-driven; **snow-covered**, snow-clad, snow-mantled, snow-robed, snow-blanketed, snow-sprinkled, snow-lined, snow-encircled, snow-laden, snow-loaded, snow-hung; **snow-capped,** snow-peaked, snow-crested, snow-crowned, snow-tipped, snow-topped; snow-bearded; snow-feathered; snow-still

19 frozen out *or* in, **snowbound,** snowed-in, **icebound**

20 **cold-blooded,** hypothermic, heterothermic, poikilothermic; cryogenic; cryological

1024 REFRIGERATION

<reduction of temperature>

NOUNS **1** **refrigeration,** infrigidation, reduction of temperature; **cooling, chilling; freezing,** glacification, glaciation, congelation, congealment; refreezing, regelation; mechanical refrigeration, electric refrigeration, electronic refrigeration, gas refrigeration; food freezing, quick freezing, deep freezing, sharp freezing, blast freezing, dehydrofreezing; adiabatic expansion, adiabatic absorption, adiabatic demagnetization; cryogenics; super-cooling; air conditioning, **air cooling,** *climatisation* <Fr>; climate control

2 refrigeration anesthesia, crymoanesthesia, hypothermia *or* hypothermy; crymotherapy, cryo-aerotherapy; cold cautery, cryocautery; cryopathy

3 **cooler,** chiller; water cooler, air cooler, air conditioner; ventilator; fan; surface cooler; ice cube, ice pail *or* bucket, wine cooler; ice bag, ice pack, cold pack

4 **refrigerator,** refrigeratory, **icebox,** ice chest; Frigidaire <TM>, fridge <nf>, electric refrigerator, electronic refrigerator, gas refrigerator, refrigerator-freezer; refrigerator car, refrigerator truck, reefer <nf>; freezer ship; ice house

5 **freezer, deep freeze,** deep-freezer, quick-freezer, sharp-freezer; ice-cream freezer; ice machine, ice-cube machine, freezing machine, refrigerating machine *or* engine; **ice plant,** icehouse, refrigerating plant

6 **cold storage; frozen-food locker,** locker, freezer locker, locker plant; coolhouse; coolerman; frigidarium; cooling tower

7 <cooling agent> **coolant; refrigerant;** cryogen; ice, Dry Ice <TM>, ice cubes; freezing mixture, liquid air, ammonia, carbon dioxide, Freon <TM>, ether; ethyl chloride; liquid air, liquid oxygen *or* lox, liquid nitrogen, liquid helium, etc

8 **antifreeze,** coolant, radiator coolant, alcohol, ethylene glycol

9 refrigerating engineering, refrigerating engineer

VERBS **10** **refrigerate; cool, chill;** refresh, freshen; ice, ice-cool; water-cool, air-cool; **air-condition;** ventilate

11 **freeze** 1023.9,10, ice, glaciate, congeal; **deep-freeze,** quick-freeze, sharp-freeze, blast-freeze; freeze solid; freeze-dry; **nip,** blight, blast; refreeze, regelate

ADJS **12** **refrigerative,** refrigeratory, refrigerant, frigorific, algific; **cooling, chilling; freezing,** congealing; quick-freezing, deep-freezing, sharp-freezing, blast-freezing; freezable, glaciable

13 **cooled, chilled; air-conditioned;** iced, ice-cooled; air-cooled, water-cooled; super-cooled

14 **frozen,** frozen solid, glacial, gelid, congealed; icy, ice-cold, icy-cold, ice, icelike; deep-frozen, quick-frozen, sharp-frozen, blast-frozen; frostbitten, frostnipped

15 antifreeze, antifreezing

1025 LIGHT

NOUNS **1** **light,** radiant *or* luminous energy, visible radiation, radiation in the visible spectrum, **illumination,** illuminance, **radiation, radiance** *or* radiancy, irradiance *or* irradiancy, irradiation, emanation; light wave; highlight; sidelight; photosensitivity; light source 1026; **invisible light,** black light, infrared light, ultraviolet light

2 **shine,** shininess, **luster, sheen, gloss,** glint, glister; **glow, gleam,** flush, sunset glow; light emission; lambency; **incandescence,** candescence; shining light; afterglow; skylight, air glow, night glow, day glow, twilight glow

3 **lightness, luminousness,** lightedness, luminosity, luminance; **lucidity,** lucence *or* lucency, translucence *or* translucency; backlight

4 **brightness, brilliance** *or* brilliancy, **splendor,** radiant splendor, **glory, radiance** *or* radiancy, resplendence *or* resplendency, **vividness,** luminance, contrast, flamboyance *or* flamboyancy; effulgence, refulgence *or* refulgency, fulgentness, fulgidity, fulgor; **glare,** blare, blaze; bright light, brilliant light, blazing light, glaring light, dazzling light, blinding light; TV lights, Klieg light, footlights, house lights; streaming light, flood of light, burst of light

5 **ray,** radiation 1037, **beam, gleam,** leam, **stream, streak, pencil, patch,** ray of light, beam of light; ribbon, ribbon of light, streamer, stream of light; electromagnetic radiation; violet ray, ultraviolet ray, infrared ray, X ray, gamma ray, invisible radiation; actinic ray *or* light, actinism; atomic beam, atomic ray; laser beam; solar rays; photon; visible spectrum

6 **flash, blaze, flare, flame, gleam, glint, glance;** blaze *or* flash *or* gleam of light; green flash; solar flare, solar prominence, facula; Bailey's beads

7 **glitter, glimmer, shimmer, twinkle, blink; sparkle,** spark; **scintillation,** scintilla; coruscation; **glisten,** glister, spangle, tinsel, glittering, glimmering, shimmering, twinkling; stroboscopic *or* strobe light <nf>, blinking; firefly, glowworm

8 **flicker, flutter, dance, quiver;** flickering, fluttering, bickering, guttering, dancing, quivering, lambency; wavering *or* flickering light, play, play of light, dancing *or* glancing light; light show

9 **reflection;** reflected *or* incident light; reflectance, albedo; blink, iceblink, ice sky, snowblink, waterblink, water sky

10 **daylight,** dayshine, day glow, light of day; day, daytime, daytide; **natural light; sunlight, sunshine,** shine; noonlight, white light, midday sun, noonday *or* noontide light; broad day *or* daylight, full sun; bright time; dusk, twilight 315.3; the break *or* crack of dawn, cockcrow, dawn 314.3; sunburst, sunbreak; **sunbeam,** sun spark, ray of sunshine; green flash; solar energy; ambient light

11 **moonlight, moonshine,** moonglow; **moonbeam,** moonrise

12 **starlight,** starshine; earthshine

13 **luminescence;** luciferin, luciferase; phosphor, luminophor; **ignis fatuus, will-o'-the-wisp,** will-with-the-wisp, wisp, jack-o'-lantern, marshfire; friar's lantern; fata morgana; fox fire; St Elmo's light *or* fire, corona discharge, wild fire, witch fire, corposant; double corposant; bioluminescence, thermoluminescence, fluorescence, phosphorescence, radioluminescence

14 **halo, nimbus,** aura, **aureole,** circle, ring, glory; **rainbow,** solar halo, lunar halo, ring around the sun *or* moon; white rainbow *or* fogbow; **corona,** solar corona, lunar corona; parhelion, parhelic circle *or* ring, mock sun, sun dog; anthelion, antisun, countersun; paraselene, mock moon, moon dog

15 <nebulous light> nebula 1072.7; zodiacal light, gegenschein, counterglow, streamers

16 polar lights, **aurora; northern lights, aurora borealis,** merry dancers; southern lights, **aurora australis;** aurora polaris; aurora

glory; streamer *or* curtain *or* arch aurora; polar ray

17 **lightning, flash** *or* **stroke of lightning,** fulguration, fulmination, bolt, lightning strike, **bolt of lightning,** streak, bolt from the blue, **thunderbolt,** thunderstroke, thunderball, fireball, firebolt, levin bolt *or* brand; fork *or* forked lightning, chain lightning, globular *or* ball lightning, summer *or* heat lightning, sheet lightning, dark lightning; Jupiter Fulgur *or* Fulminator; Thor

18 **iridescence,** opalescence, nacreousness, pearliness; **rainbow;** nacre, mother-of-pearl; nacreous *or* mother-of-pearl cloud

19 **lighting, illumination,** artificial light *or* lighting; lamp light, arc light, calcium light, candlelight, electric light, fluorescent light, gaslight, incandescent light, mercury-vapor light, neon light, sodium light, strobe light, torchlight, streetlight, floodlight, spotlight; Christmas tree lights, safety light; tonality; light and shade, black and white, chiaroscuro, clairobscure, contrast, highlights; photoemission, light-emitting diode *or* LED, liquid-crystal display *or* LCD, light pen

20 **illuminant,** luminant; electricity; gas, illuminating gas; oil, petroleum, benzine; gasoline, petrol <Brit>; kerosene, paraffin <Brit>, coal oil; light source 1026; fire, lantern

21 <measurement of light> **candle power,** luminous intensity, luminous power, luminous flux, flux, intensity, light; quantum, **light quantum, photon;** unit of light, unit of flux; lux, candle-meter, lumen meter, lumeter, lumen, candle lumen; **exposure meter,** light meter, ASA scale, Scheiner scale

22 <science of light> photics, photology, photometry; **optics,** geometrical optics, physical optics; dioptrics, catoptrics, fiber optics; actinology, actinometry; heliology, heliometry, heliography

23 <light units> *bougie décimale* <Fr>, British candle, candle, candle-foot, candle-hour, decimal candle, foot-candle, Hefner candle, international candle, lamp-hour, lumen-hour

VERBS 24 **shine,** shine forth, **burn, give light,** incandesce; glow, beam, gleam, glint, luster, glance; **flash, flare, blaze, flame,** fulgurate; **radiate,** shoot, shoot out rays, send out rays; spread *or* diffuse light; be bright, shine brightly, beacon; **glare;** daze, blind, dazzle, bedazzle

25 **glitter, glimmer, shimmer, twinkle, blink,** spangle, tinsel, coruscate; **sparkle,** spark, **scintillate; glisten,** glister, glisk

26 **flicker,** bicker, gutter, **flutter, waver, dance,** play, quiver

27 **luminesce,** phosphoresce, fluoresce; iridesce, opalesce

28 **grow light,** grow bright, light, **lighten,** brighten; dawn, break

29 **illuminate,** illumine, illume, luminate, **light, light up, lighten,** enlighten, brighten, brighten up, irradiate; bathe *or* flood with light; relumine, relume; **shed light upon,** cast *or* throw light upon, shed luster on, shine upon, overshine; spotlight, highlight; floodlight; beacon

30 **strike a light,** light, **turn** *or* **switch on the light,** open the light <nf>, make a light, shine a light

ADJS 31 **luminous,** luminant, luminative, luminificent, luminiferous, luciferous *or* lucific , luciform, illuminant; **incandescent,** candescent; **lustrous,** orient; **radiant,** irradiative; **shining,** shiny, burning, lamping, streaming; **beaming,** beamy; **gleaming,** gleamy, glinting; **glowing,** aglow, suffused, blushing, flushing; rutilant, rutilous; **sunny, sunshiny,** bright and sunny, light as day; starry, starlike, starbright

32 **light,** lightish, lightsome; **lucid,** lucent, luculent, relucent; translucent, translucid, pellucid, diaphanous, transparent; **clear,** serene; **cloudless,** unclouded, unobscured

33 **bright, brilliant, vivid, splendid,** splendorous, splendent, **resplendent,** bright and shining; fulgid , fulgent, effulgent, refulgent; **flamboyant,** flaming; **glaring,** glary,

garish; **dazzling,** bedazzling, blinding, pitiless; shadowless, shadeless

34 **shiny,** shining, **lustrous, glossy,** glassy, *glacé* <Fr>, bright as a new penny, **sheeny, polished,** burnished, shined

35 **flashing,** flashy, **blazing, flaming, flaring, burning,** fulgurant, fulgurating; aflame, ablaze; meteoric

36 **glittering, glimmering, shimmering, twinkling, blinking, glistening,** glistering; glittery, glimmery, glimmerous, shimmery, twinkly, blinky, spangly, tinselly; **sparkling, scintillating,** scintillant, scintillescent, coruscating, coruscant

37 **flickering,** bickering, **fluttering, wavering, dancing,** playing, quivering, lambent; flickery, flicky <nf>, aflicker, fluttery, wavery, quivery; blinking, flashing, stroboscopic

38 **iridescent,** opalescent, nacreous, pearly, pearl-like; rainbowlike

39 **luminescent,** photogenic; autoluminescent, bioluminescent

40 **illuminated,** luminous, **lightened,** enlightened, brightened, **lighted,** lit, **lit up,** well-lit, flooded *or* bathed with light, floodlit; irradiated, irradiate; **alight, glowing,** aglow, lambent, suffused with light; ablaze, blazing, in a blaze, fiery; lamplit, lanternlit, candlelit, torchlit, gaslit, firelit; sunlit, moonlit, starlit; spangled, bespangled, tinseled, studded; starry, starbright, star-spangled, star-studded

41 **illuminating,** illumining, **lighting, lightening,** brightening

42 **luminary,** photic; photologic *or* photological; photometric *or* photometrical; heliological, heliographic; actinic, photoactinic; catoptric *or* catoptrical; luminal

43 photosensitive; photophobic; phototropic

1026 LIGHT SOURCE

NOUNS 1 **light source,** source of light, **luminary,** illuminator, luminant, illuminant, incandescent body *or* point, **light,** glim; **lamp,** light bulb, electric light bulb, lantern, candle, taper, torch, flame; match; **fluorescent light, fluorescent tube,** fluorescent lamp; starter, ballast; fire 1019.13; sun, moon, stars 1072.4

2 **candle,** taper; dip, farthing dip, tallow dip; tallow candle; wax candle, bougie; soy candle; rush candle, rushlight; corpse candle; votary candle

3 **torch,** flaming torch, flambeau, cresset, link ; **flare,** signal flare, fusee; beacon

4 **traffic light** *or* light, stop-and-go light; stop *or* red light, go *or* green light, caution *or* amber light, pedestrian light

5 **firefly,** lightning bug, lampyrid, **glowworm,** fireworm; fire beetle; lantern fly, candle fly; luciferin, luciferase; phosphor, luminophor

6 **chandelier,** gasolier, electrolier, hanging *or* ceiling fixture, luster; corona, corona lucis, crown, circlet; light holder, light fixture, candlestick; torchiere

7 **wick,** taper; candlewick, lampwick

1027 DARKNESS, DIMNESS

NOUNS 1 **darkness, dark, lightlessness; obscurity,** obscure, tenebrosity, tenebrousness, leadenness; **night** 315.4, dead of night, deep night; sunlessness, moonlessness, starlessness; **pitch-darkness,** pitch-blackness, utter *or* thick *or* total darkness, intense darkness, velvet darkness, Cimmerian *or* Stygian *or* Egyptian darkness, Stygian gloom, Erebus; **blackness,** swarthiness 38.2; darkest hour

2 **darkishness,** darksomeness, **duskiness,** duskness; **murkiness, murk; dimness,** dim, dimming; **semidarkness,** semidark, partial darkness, bad light, dim light, half-light, *demi-jour* <Fr>; gloaming, crepuscular light, **dusk,** twilight 314.4/315.3; romantic lighting, dimmed lights

3 **shadow, shade, shadiness;** umbra, umbrage, umbrageousness; thick *or* dark shade, gloom; mere shadow; penumbra; silhouette; skiagram, skiagraph

4 **gloom, gloominess, somberness,** sombrousness, somber; lowering, lower

5 **dullness, flatness,** lifelessness, **drabness, deadness,** somberness, **lackluster, lusterlessness,** lack of sparkle *or* sheen; matte, matte finish

6 **darkening, dimming, bedimming; obscuration,** obscurement, obumbration, obfuscation; eclipsing, occulting, blocking the light; **shadowing, shading,** overshadowing, overshading, overshadowment, **clouding,** overclouding, obnubilation, gathering of the clouds, overcast; blackening 38.5; extinguishment 1022.2; hatching, cross-hatching

7 **blackout,** dimout, brownout; fadeout

8 **eclipse,** occultation; total eclipse, partial eclipse, central eclipse, annular eclipse; solar eclipse, lunar eclipse

VERBS **9** **darken,** bedarken; **obscure,** obfuscate, obumbrate; **eclipse,** occult, occultate, block the light; **black out,** brown out; black, brown; blot out; **overcast,** darken over; **shadow, shade,** cast a shadow, spread a shadow *or* shade over, encompass with shadow, overshadow; **cloud,** becloud, encloud, cloud over, overcloud, obnubilate; gloom, begloom, somber, cast a gloom over, murk; **dim, bedim,** dim out; mattify; blacken 38.7

10 **dull,** mat, deaden; **tone down**

11 turn *or* switch off the light, close the light <nf>; extinguish 1022.7

12 **grow dark, darken,** darkle, lower *or* lour; gloom , gloam; dusk; **dim, grow dim;** go out

ADJS **13** **dark, black,** darksome, darkling; **lightless,** beamless, rayless, unlighted, **unilluminated,** unlit; obscure, caliginous, **obscured,** obfuscated, eclipsed, occulted, clothed *or* shrouded *or* veiled *or* cloaked *or* mantled in darkness; tenebrous, tenebrific, tenebrious, tenebrose; Cimmerian, Stygian; **pitch-dark,** pitch-black, pitchy, dark as pitch, dark as the inside of a black cat; ebon, ebony; night-dark, night-black, dark *or* black as night; night-clad, night-cloaked, night-enshrouded, night-mantled, night-veiled, night-hid, night-filled; sunless, moonless, starless

14 **gloomy,** gloomful , glooming, dark and gloomy, Acheronian, Acherontic, **somber,** sombrous; lowering; **funereal;** stormy, cloudy, clouded, overcast; ill-lighted, ill-lit

15 **darkish,** darksome, **semidark; dusky,** dusk; fuscous, subfuscous, subfusc; **murky,** murksome, murk ; **dim,** dimmed, bedimmed, dimmish, dimpsy <Brit nf>, half-lit, semidark; dark-colored 38.9

16 **shadowy, shady, shadowed, shaded,** casting a shadow, tenebrous, darkling, umbral, umbrageous; overshadowed, overshaded, obumbrate, obumbrated; penumbral

17 **lackluster, lusterless; dull, dead,** deadened, **lifeless,** somber, **drab,** wan, **flat,** mat, murky

18 obscuring, obscurant

ADVS **19** **in the dark,** darkling, in darkness; in the night, in the dark of night, in the dead of night, at *or* by night; dimly, wanly

1028 SHADE

<a thing that shades>

NOUNS **1** **shade,** shader, **screen, light shield, curtain,** drape, drapery, blind *or* blinds, veil; **awning,** sunblind <Brit>; **sunshade,** parasol, **umbrella,** beach umbrella; cover 295.2; shadow 1027.3; partial eclipse

2 **eyeshade,** eyeshield, visor, bill; goggles, colored spectacles, smoked glasses, dark glasses, **sunglasses,** shades <nf>

3 **lamp shade;** moonshade; globe, light globe

4 **light filter,** filter, diffusing screen; smoked glass, frosted glass, ground glass; stained glass; butterfly; gelatin filter, celluloid filter; frosted lens; lens hood; sunscreen; sun roof

VERBS **5** **shade, screen,** veil, curtain, shutter, draw the curtains, put up *or* close the shutters; cover 295.19; **shadow** 1027.9; cast a shadow

ADJS **6 shading, screening,** veiling, curtaining; shadowing; covering

7 shaded, screened, veiled, curtained; sunproof; visored; shadowed, shady 1027.16

1029 TRANSPARENCY

NOUNS **1 transparency,** transparence, transpicuousness, show-through, transmission *or* admission of light; **lucidity,** pellucidity, **clearness, clarity,** limpidity; nonopacity, uncloudedness; **crystallinity,** crystal-clearness; **glassiness,** glasslikeness, vitreousness, vitrescence; vitreosity, hyalescence; **diaphanousness,** diaphaneity, sheerness, thinness, **gossameriness,** filminess, gauziness; colorlessness

2 transparent substance, diaphane; **glass**, glassware, glasswork; vitrics; stemware; window, pane, windowpane, light, windowlight, shopwindow; vitrine; showcase, display case; watch crystal *or* glass; water, air

VERBS **3** be transparent, show through; pass *or* transmit light; vitrify; reveal; crystallize

ADJS **4 transparent,** transpicuous, light-pervious; show-through, see-through, peekaboo, revealing; **lucid,** lucent, pellucid, **clear,** limpid; nonopaque, colorless, unclouded, **crystalline,** crystal, **crystal-clear,** clear as crystal; **diaphanous,** diaphane , sheer, thin; **gossamer,** gossamery, filmy, flimsy, gauzy, open-textured; insubstantial

5 glass, glassy, glasslike, clear as glass, vitric, vitreous, vitriform, hyaline, hyalescent; hyalinocrystalline

1030 SEMITRANSPARENCY

NOUNS **1 semitransparency,** semipellucidity, semidiaphaneity; semiopacity

2 translucence, translucency, lucence, lucency, translucidity, pellucidity, lucidity; transmission *or* admission of light; milkiness, pearliness, opalescence

VERBS **3 frost,** frost over

ADJS **4 semitransparent,** semipellucid, semidiaphanous, semiopaque; frosty, frosted; milky, pearly, opalescent, opaline

5 translucent, lucent, translucid, lucid, pellucid; semitranslucent, semipellucid

1031 OPAQUENESS

NOUNS **1 opaqueness,** opacity, intransparency, nontranslucency, imperviousness to light, adiaphanousness; roil, roiledness, turbidity, turbidness; cloudiness; blackness; **darkness, obscurity,** inscrutability, **dimness** 1027

VERBS **2** opaque, **darken, obscure** 1027.9; **cloud,** becloud; devitrify

ADJS **3 opaque,** intransparent, nontransparent, nontranslucent, adiaphanous, impervious to light, impenetrable; **dark,** black, **obscure** 1027.13, lightproof; **cloudy,** roiled, roily, grumly, turbid; covered; semiopaque

1032 ELECTRICITY, MAGNETISM

NOUNS **1 electricity; electrical science ; electrical** *or* **electric unit,** unit of measurement

2 current, electric current, current flow, amperage, electric stream *or* flow, juice <nf>; power source, power supply

3 electric *or* **electrical field,** static field, electrostatic field, field of electrical force; tube of electric force, electrostatic tube of force; **magnetic field,** magnetic field of currents; **electromagnetic field;** variable field; static electricity

4 circuit, electrical circuit, path

5 charge, electric *or* **electrical charge,** positive charge, negative charge; live wire

6 discharge, arc, electric discharge; **shock,** electroshock, galvanic shock

7 magnetism, magnetic attraction; **electromagnetism;** magnetization; diamagnetism, paramagnetism, ferromagnetism; residual magnetism, magnetic remanence; magnetic memory, magnetic retentiveness; magnetic elements; magnetic dip *or* inclination, magnetic variation *or* declination; hysteresis, magnetic hysteresis, hysteresis curve, magnetic friction, magnetic lag *or* retardation, magnetic creeping; permeability, magnetic permeability, magnetic conductivity; magnetic circuit, magnetic curves, magnetic figures; magnetic flux, gilbert, weber, maxwell; magnetic moment; magnetic potential; magnetic viscosity; magnetics

8 **polarity,** polarization; **pole, positive pole, anode, negative pole, cathode,** magnetic pole, magnetic axis; north pole, N pole; south pole, S pole

9 **magnetic force** *or* **intensity,** magnetic flux density, gauss, oersted; magnetomotive force; magnetomotivity; magnetic tube of force; line of force; **magnetic field, electromagnetic field**

10 electromagnetic radiation, light, radio wave, microwave, infrared radiation, visible radiation, ultraviolent radiation *or* UV, UVA, UVB, X-rays, gamma rays; radar; electromagnetic spectrum, visible spectrum, radio spectrum

11 **electroaffinity,** electric attraction; electric repulsion

12 **voltage,** volt, **electromotive force** *or* EMF, electromotivity, potential difference; **potential, electric potential;** tension, high tension, low tension

13 **resistance,** ohm, ohms, ohmage, ohmic resistance, electric resistance; surface resistance, skin effect, volume resistance; insulation resistance; reluctance, magnetic **reluctance** *or* resistance; specific reluctance, reluctivity; **reactance,** inductive reactance, capacitive reactance; **impedance**

14 **conduction,** electric conduction; **conductance,** conductivity, mho; superconductivity; gas conduction, ionic conduction, metallic conduction, liquid conduction, photoconduction; **conductor,** semiconductor, superconductor; **nonconductor,** dielectric, insulator

15 **induction;** electrostatic induction, magnetic induction, electromagnetic induction, electromagnetic induction of currents; self-induction, mutual induction; **inductance,** inductivity, henry

16 **capacitance,** capacity, farad; collector junction capacitance, emitter junction capacitance, resistance capacitance

17 **gain,** available gain, current gain, operational gain

18 **electric power, wattage,** watts; electric horsepower; hydroelectric power, hydroelectricity; power load

19 **powerhouse, power station, power plant,** central station; oil-fired power plant, coal-fired power plant; hydroelectric plant; nuclear *or* atomic power plant; power grid, distribution system

20 **blackout, power failure,** power cut, power loss; **brownout,** voltage drop, voltage loss

21 **electrical device,** electrical appliance; **battery**, accumulator, storage battery, storage device; **electric meter,** meter; **wire, cable,** electric wire, electric cord, cord, power cord, power cable

22 **electrician, electrotechnician;** radio technician 1034.24; wireman; **lineman,** linesman; rigger; groundman; power worker

23 **electrotechnologist,** electrobiologist, electrochemist, electrometallurgist, electrophysicist, electrophysiologist, **electrical engineer**

24 **electrification,** electrifying, supplying electricity

25 **electrolysis;** ionization; galvanization, electrogalvanization; electrocoating, electroplating, electrogilding, electrograving, electroetching; ion, cation, anion; electrolyte, ionogen; nonelectrolyte

VERBS **26** **electrify, galvanize,** energize, **charge;** wire, wire up; shock; **generate,** step up, amplify, stiffen; step down; plug in, loop in; switch on *or* off, turn on *or* off, turn on *or* off the juice <nf>, power down, power up; short-circuit, short

27 magnetize; electromagnetize; demagnetize, degauss

28 electrolyze; ionize; galvanize, electrogalvanize; electroplate, electrogild

29 insulate, isolate; **ground**

ADJS **30 electric, electrical, electrifying;** galvanic, voltaic; dynamoelectric, hydroelectric, photoelectric, piezoelectric, etc; electrothermal, electrochemical, electromechanical, electropneumatic, electrodynamic, static, electrostatic; electromotive; electrokinetic; electroscopic, galvanoscopic; electrometric, galvanometric, voltametric; **electrified,** electric-powered, battery-powered, cordless; solar-powered

31 magnetic, electromagnetic; diamagnetic, paramagnetic, ferromagnetic; **polar**

32 electrolytic; hydrolytic; ionic, anionic, cationic; ionogenic

33 electrotechnical; electroballistic, electrobiological, electrochemical, electrometallurgical, electrophysiological

34 charged, electrified, live, hot; high-tension, low-tension

35 positive, plus, electropositive; **negative,** minus, electronegative

36 nonconducting, nonconductive, insulating, dielectric

1033 ELECTRONICS

NOUNS **1 electronics,** radionics, radioelectronics; electron physics, electrophysics, electron dynamics; electron optics; semiconductor physics, transistor physics; photoelectronics, photoelectricity; microelectronics; electronic engineering; avionics; electron microscopy; nuclear physics 1038; radio 1034; television 1035; radar 1036; automation 1041

2 <electron theory> electron theory of atoms, electron theory of electricity, electron theory of solids, free electron theory of metals, band theory of solids

3 electron, negatron, cathode particle, beta particle; thermion; electron capture, electron transfer; electron spin; electron state, energy level; ground state, excited state; electron pair, lone pair, shared pair, electron-positron pair, duplet, octet; electron cloud; shells, electron layers, electron shells, valence shell, valence electrons, subvalent electrons; electron affinity, relative electron affinity

4 electronic effect; Edison effect, thermionic effect, photoelectric effect

5 electron emission; thermionic emission; photoelectric emission, photoemission; collision emission, bombardment emission, secondary emission; field emission; grid emission, thermionic grid emission; electron ray, electron beam, cathode ray, anode ray, positive ray, canal ray; glow discharge, cathode glow, cathodoluminescence, cathodofluorescence; electron diffraction

6 electron flow, electron stream, electron *or* **electronic current;** electric current 1032.2; electron gas, electron cloud, space charge

7 electron volt; ionization potential; input voltage, output voltage; base signal voltage, collector signal voltage, emitter signal voltage; battery supply voltage; screen-grid voltage; inverse peak voltage; voltage saturation

8 electronic circuit, transistor circuit, semiconductor circuit; vacuum-tube circuit, thermionic tube circuit; **printed circuit, microcircuit; chip, silicon chip,** microchip; **circuitry**

9 conductance, electronic conductance; **resistance,** electronic resistance

10 electron tube, vacuum tube, tube, valve <Brit>, thermionic tube; radio tube, television tube; **special-purpose tube; vacuum tube component**

11 photoelectric tube *or* **cell, phototube,** photocell; electron-ray tube, **electric eye;** photosensitivity, **photosensitive devices**

12 transistor, semiconductor *or* solid-state device

13 electronic device, electronic meter, electronic measuring device; **elec-**

tronic tester, electronic testing device

14 **electronics engineer,** electronics physicist

ADJS 15 **electronic;** photoelectronic, **photoelectric;** autoelectronic; microelectronic; thermoelectronic; thermionic; anodic, cathodic; transistorized

1034 RADIO

NOUNS 1 **radio, wireless** <Brit>; radiotelephony, radiotelegraphy; radio communications, telecommunication 347.1

2 radiotechnology, radio engineering, communication engineering; radio electronics, radioacoustics; radiogoniometry

3 **radio, radio receiver** ; radio telescope; **radio set, receiver,** receiving set, **wireless** *and* wireless set <Brit>, set; cabinet, console, housing; chassis; receiver part

4 **radio transmitter, transmitter;** transmitter part; microphone 50.9, radiomicrophone; **antenna,** aerial

5 radiomobile, mobile transmitter, remote-pickup unit

6 **radio station,** transmitting station, **studio,** studio plant; AM station, FM station, shortwave station, ultrahigh-frequency station, clear-channel station; direction-finder station, RDF station; relay station, radio relay station, microwave relay station; amateur station, ham station <nf>, ham shack <nf>; pirate radio station, offshore station; Internet radio; satellite radio

7 **control room,** mixing room, monitor room, monitoring booth; **control desk,** console, master control desk, instrument panel, control panel *or* board, jack field, mixer <nf>

8 **network,** net, radio links, **hookup,** communications net, circuit, network stations, network affiliations, affiliated stations; coaxial network, circuit network, coast-to-coast hookup, satellite network

9 **radio circuit,** radio-frequency circuit, audio-frequency circuit, superheterodyne circuit, amplifying circuit; electronic circuit 1033.8

10 **radio signal,** radio-frequency *or* RF signal, direct signal, shortwave signal, AM signal, FM signal; reflected signal, bounce; unidirectional signal, beam; signal-noise ratio; **radio-frequency** *or* **RF amplifier,** radio-frequency *or* RF stage; radio silence

11 **radio wave,** electric wave, electro magnetic wave, hertzian wave; shortwave, long wave, microwave, high-frequency wave, low-frequency wave, medium wave; ground wave, sky wave; carrier, carrier wave; **wavelength**

12 **frequency;** radio frequency *or* RF, intermediate frequency *or* IF, audio frequency *or* AF; high frequency *or* HF; very high frequency *or* VHF; ultrahigh frequency *or* UHF; superhigh frequency *or* SHF; extremely high frequency *or* EHF; medium frequency *or* MF; low frequency *or* LF; very low frequency *or* VLF; upper frequencies, lower frequencies; **carrier frequency;** spark frequency; spectrum, frequency spectrum; cycles, CPS, hertz, Hz, **kilohertz, kilocycles; megahertz, megacycles**

13 **band,** frequency band, standard band, broadcast band, amateur band, citizens band, police band, shortwave band, FM band; **channel,** radio channel, broadcast channel

14 **modulation;** amplitude modulation *or* AM; frequency modulation *or* FM; phase modulation *or* PM; sideband, side frequency, single sideband, double sideband

15 **amplification,** radio-frequency *or* RF amplification, audio-frequency *or* AF amplification, intermediate-frequency *or* IF amplification, high-frequency amplification

16 **radio broadcasting, broadcasting,** the air waves, radiocasting; **airplay, airtime;** commercial radio, public radio, college radio, satellite radio, Citizens Band *or* CB, amateur radio, ham radio; AM broadcasting, FM broadcasting, shortwave broadcasting, public broadcasting; **transmission, radio**

transmission; direction *or* beam transmission, asymmetric *or* vestigial transmission; multipath transmission, multiplex transmission; mixing, volume control, sound *or* tone control, fade-in, fade-out; broadcasting regulation, Federal Communications Commission *or* FCC

17 **pickup,** outside pickup, **remote pickup,** spot pickup

18 **radiobroadcast, broadcast,** radiocast, **radio program;** rebroadcast, rerun; simulcast; electronic *or* broadcast journalism, broadcast news, newscast, newsbreak, newsflash; all-news radio *or* format; sportscast; **talk radio;** talk show, audience-participation show, call-in *or* phone-in show, interview show; network show; commercial program, commercial; sustaining program, sustainer; serial, soap opera <nf>; taped program, canned show <nf>, electrical transcription; sound effects

19 **signature, station identification,** call letters, call sign; theme song; **station break,** pause for station identification

20 **commercial,** commercial announcement, commercial message, message, **spot announcement,** spot *and* plug <nf>

21 **reception; fading,** fade-out; **drift,** creeping, crawling; **interference,** noise interference, station interference; **static,** atmospherics, noise; blasting, blaring; blind spot; **jamming,** deliberate interference

22 **radio listener,** listener-in *and* tuner-inner <nf>; radio audience, listeners, **listenership**

23 **broadcaster,** radiobroadcaster, radiocaster; newscaster, sportscaster; commentator, news commentator; anchor, news anchor, anchorman *or* anchorwoman; host, talk-show host, talk jockey <nf>; veejay *or* VJ; announcer, voiceover; disk jockey *or* DJ *or* deejay <nf>; shock jock <nf>; master of ceremonies, MC *or* emcee <nf>; program director, programmer; sound-effects man, sound man

24 **radioman,** radio technician, radio engineer; radiotrician, radio electrician, radio repairman; **radio operator;** control engineer, volume engineer; mixer; **amateur radio operator, ham** *and* ham operator <nf>, radio amateur; Amateur Radio Relay League *or* ARRL; monitor; radiotelegrapher 347.16

VERBS 25 **broadcast,** radiobroadcast, radiocast, simulcast, **radio, wireless** <Brit>, radiate, **transmit,** send; narrowcast; shortwave; beam; newscast, sportscast, put *or* go on the air, sign on; go off the air, sign off

26 **monitor,** check

27 **listen in, tune in;** tune up, tune down, tune out, tune off

ADJS 28 **radio, wireless** <Brit>; radiosonic; neutrodyne; heterodyne; superheterodyne; shortwave; radiofrequency, audio-frequency; high-frequency, low-frequency, etc; radiogenic

1035 TELEVISION

NOUNS 1 **television, TV, video,** telly <Brit nf>; the small screen *or* the tube <nf>, the boob tube <nf>; **network television,** free television, local television; the dream factory; subscription television, pay TV; cable television, cable TV, cable-television system *or* cable system, cable; closed-circuit television *or* closed circuit TV; public-access television *or* public-access TV; public broadcasting; satellite broadcasting, satellite television; digital television; high-definition television, HDTV

2 **television broadcast, telecast, TV show;** direct broadcast, live show <nf>; taped show, canned show <nf>; prime time, prime-time show *or* attraction; syndicated program; television drama *or* play, teleplay, made-for-television *or* –TV movie; telefilm; series, dramatic series, miniseries; situation comedy *or* sitcom <nf>; variety show; game show; **serial,** daytime serial, soap opera *or* soap <nf>; reality televi-

sion; quiz show; giveaway show; panel show; talk show; electronic *or* broadcast journalism, broadcast news, newscast, news show; documentary, docudrama; telethon; public service announcement; edutainment, infotainment; film pickup; colorcast; simulcast; childrens' television, kidvid <nf>; television *or* TV performer, television *or* TV personality; news anchor, anchor, anchor man, anchor woman, anchor person; ratings, Nielsen rating, sweeps; people meter

3 **televising, telecasting;** facsimile broadcasting; monitoring, mixing, shading, blanking, switching; scanning, parallel-line scanning, interlaced scanning

4 <transmission> photoemission, audioemission; television channel, TV band; video *or* picture channel, audio *or* sound channel, video frequency; picture carrier, sound carrier; beam, scanning beam, return beam; triggering pulse, voltage pulse, output pulse, timing pulse, equalizing pulse; synchronizing pulse, vertical synchronizing pulse, horizontal synchronizing pulse; video signal, audio signal; IF video signal, IF audio signal; synchronizing signal, blanking signal

5 <reception> **picture, image; color television,** dot-sequential *or* field-sequential *or* line-sequential color television; **black-and-white television;** HDTV *or* high-definition television; definition, blacker than black synchronizing; shading, black spot, hard shadow; test pattern, scanning pattern, grid; vertical interference, rain; granulation, scintillation, snow, snowstorm; flare, bloom, woomp; picture shifts, blooping, rolling; double image, multiple image, ghost; video static, noise, picture noise; signal-to-noise ratio; fringe area

6 **television studio, TV station**

7 **mobile unit, TV mobile;** video truck, audio truck, transmitter truck

8 **transmitter,** televisor; audio transmitter, video transmitter; transmitter part, adder, encoder; television mast, television tower; satellite transmitter

9 **relay links, boosters,** booster amplifiers, relay transmitters, **booster** *or* **relay stations;** microwave link; aeronautical relay, stratovision; communication satellite, satellite relay; Telstar, Intelsat, Syncom; Comsat

10 **television camera,** telecamera, pickup camera, pickup; **camera tube**, iconoscope, orthicon, vidicon; video camera, camcorder; mobile camera

11 **television receiver, television** *or* **TV set,** TV, telly <Brit nf>, televisor, boob tube *and* idiot box <nf>; **picture tube**, cathode-ray tube, kinescope, monoscope, projection tube; receiver part, amplifier, detector, convertor, electron tube, deflector, synchronizer, limiter, mixer; portable television *or* TV set; digital television; **screen,** telescreen, videoscreen; raster; **video-cassette recorder** *or* **VCR,** videorecorder, video-tape recorder; video tape, video-cassette; videophone, Picturephone <TM>; satellite dish, dish <nf>; television recording, videocassette, videocassette recorder *or* VCR, videotape

12 televiewer, viewer; television *or* viewing audience; viewership

13 **television technician,** TV man *or* woman, television *or* TV repairman *or* repairwoman, television engineer; monitor, sound *or* audio monitor, picture *or* video monitor; pickup unit man, cameraman, camerawoman, sound man, sound woman; media personality, host, newscaster, newsreader, commentator, announcer

VERBS **14** **televise, telecast;** colorcast; simulcast

15 **teleview,** watch television *or* TV; telerecord, record, tape; channel-surf, graze <nf>; zap <nf>

ADJS **16** **televisional,** televisual, televisionary, **video;** telegenic, videogenic; in synchronization, in sync <nf>, locked in

1036 RADAR, RADIOLOCATORS

NOUNS 1 **radar,** radio detection *and* ranging; **radar set,** radiolocator <Brit>; radar part; oscilloscope, radarscope; radar antenna; radar reflector

2 airborne radar, aviation radar; **navar,** navigation *and* ranging; **teleran,** television radar air navigation; radar bombsight, K-1 bombsight; radar dome, radome

3 **loran,** long range aid to navigation; **shoran,** short range aid to navigation; GEE navigation, consolan

4 **radiolocator;** direction finder, radio direction finder *or* RDF; radiogoniometer, high-frequency direction finder *or* HFDF, huff-duff <nf>; radio compass, wireless compass <Brit>

5 **radar speed meter,** electronic cop <nf>; radar highway patrol; radar detector, Fuzzbuster <TM>

6 **radar station,** control station; Combat Information Center *or* CIC; Air Route Traffic Control Center *or* ARTCC; beacon station, display station; fixed station, home station; portable field unit, mobile trailer unit; tracking station; direction-finder station, radio compass station; triangulation stations

7 **radar beacon, racon;** transponder; radar beacon buoy, marker buoy, radar marked beacon, ramark

8 <radar operations> data transmission, scanning, scan conversion, flector tuning, signal modulation, triggering signals; phase adjustment, locking signals; triangulation, three-pointing; mapping; range finding; tracking, automatic tracking, locking on; precision focusing, pinpointing; radar-telephone relay; radar navigation

9 <applications> detection, interception, ranging, ground control of aircraft, air-traffic control, blind flying, blind landing, storm tracking, hurricane tracking; radar fence *or* screen; radar astronomy

10 **pulse,** radio-frequency *or* RF pulse, high-frequency *or* HF pulse, intermediate-frequency *or* IF pulse, trigger pulse, echo pulse

11 **signal,** radar signal; transmitter signal, output signal; return signal, echo signal, video signal, reflection, picture, target image, display, signal display, trace, reading, return, **echo, bounces, blips, pips;** spot, CRT spot; three-dimensional *or* 3-D display, double-dot display; deflection-modulated *or* DM display, intensity-modulated *or* IM display; radio-frequency *or* RF echoes, intermediate-frequency *or* IF signal; beat signal, Doppler signal, local oscillator signal; beam, beavertail beam

12 **radar interference,** deflection, refraction, superrefraction; atmospheric attenuation, signal fades, blind spots, false echoes; clutter, ground clutter, sea clutter

13 <radar countermeasure> **jamming, radar jamming;** tinfoil, aluminum foil, chaff, window <Brit>

14 **radar technician,** radar engineer, radarman; air-traffic controller; jammer

VERBS 15 **transmit, send,** radiate, beam; **jam**

16 **reflect,** return, echo, bounce back

17 **receive, tune in,** pick up, spot, home on; pinpoint; identify, trigger; lock on; sweep, scan; map

1037 RADIATION, RADIOACTIVITY

NOUNS 1 **radiation,** radiant energy; ionizing radiation; **radioactivity,** activity, radioactive radiation *or* emanation, atomic *or* nuclear radiation; natural radioactivity, artificial radioactivity; curiage; specific activity, high-specific activity; actinic radiation, ultra-violet *or* violet radiation; radiotransparency, radiolucence *or* radiolucency; radiopacity; radiosensitivity, radiosensibility; half-life; radiocarbon dating; contamination, decontamination; saturation point; radiac *or* radioactivity detection identification *and* computation; fallout 1038.16; China syndrome, nuclear winter

2 **radioluminescence, autoluminescence;** cathode luminescence; Cerenkov radiation, synchrotron radiation

3 **ray, radiation**, cosmic ray bombardment, electron shower; electron emission 1033.5

4 **radioactive particle;** alpha particle, beta particle; heavy particle; high-energy particle; meson, mesotron; cosmic particle, solar particle, aurora particle, V-particle

5 <radioactive substance> **radiator;** alpha radiator, beta radiator, gamma radiator; fluorescent paint, radium paint; radium; fission products; radiocarbon, radiocopper, radioiodine, radiothorium, etc; mesothorium; **radioactive element**, radioelement; radioisotope; tracer, tracer element, tracer atom; radioactive waste

6 <units of radioactivity> curie, dose equivalent, gray, half-life, megacurie, microcurie, millicurie, multicurie, rad, roentgen

7 **counter, radioscope,** radiodetector, **atom-tagger;** ionization chamber; ionizing event; X-ray spectrograph, X-ray spectrometer

8 **radiation physics,** radiological physics; radiobiology, radiochemistry, radiometallography, radiography, roentgenography, roentgenology, radiometry, spectroradiometry, radiotechnology, radiopathology; radiology; radiotherapy; radioscopy, curiescopy, roentgenoscopy, radiostereoscopy, fluoroscopy, photofluorography, orthodiagraphy; X-ray photometry, X-ray spectrometry; tracer investigation, atom-tagging; **unit of radioactivity** ; exposure, dose, absorbed dose

9 **radiation physicist;** radiobiologist, radiometallographer, radiochemist, etc; radiologist

VERBS **10** **radioactivate,** activate, **irradiate,** charge; radiumize; **contaminate,** poison, infect

ADJS **11** **radioactive,** activated, radioactivated, irradiated, charged, **hot; contaminated,** infected, poisoned; exposed; radiferous; radioluminescent, autoluminescent

12 **radiable;** radiotransparent, radioparent, radiolucent; radiopaque, radium-proof; radiosensitive

1038 NUCLEAR PHYSICS

NOUNS **1** **nuclear physics,** particle physics, nucleonics, atomics, atomistics, atomology, atomic science; quantum mechanics, wave mechanics; molecular physics; thermionics; mass spectrometry, mass spectrography; radiology 1037.8

2 <atomic theory> quantum theory, Bohr theory, Dirac theory, Rutherford theory, Schrödinger theory, Lewis-Langmuir *or* octet theory, Thomson's hypothesis; law of conservation of mass, law of definite proportions, law of multiple proportions, law of Dulong and Petit, law of parity, correspondence principle; Standard Model; supersymmetry theory, unified field theory; atomism; quark model

3 **atomic scientist, nuclear physicist,** particle physicist; radiologist 1037.9

4 **atom**; tracer, tracer atom, tagger atom; atomic model, nuclear atom; nuclide; **ion; shell,** subshell, planetary shell, valence shell; **atomic unit;** atomic constant; atomic mass, atomic weight, atomic number, proton number, mass number, nucleon number, neutron number

5 **isotope;** protium, deuterium *or* heavy hydrogen *and* tritium <of hydrogen>; radioactive isotope, **radioisotope;** carbon 14, strontium 90, uranium 235; artificial isotope; isotone; isobar, isomer, nuclear isomer

6 **elementary particle,** fundamental particle, atomic particle, **subatomic particle**, subnuclear particle, ultraelementary particle; **atomic nucleus, nucleus**; **nuclear particle,** nucleon; proton, neutron ; deuteron *or* deuterium nucleus, triton *or* tritium nucleus, alpha particle *or* helium nucleus; **nuclear force,** weak force *or* weak nuclear force, strong force *or* strong nuclear force; weak interaction, strong interaction; fifth force; nucleosynthesis; nuclear resonance, Mössbauer effect, nuclear magnetic resonance *or* NMR; strangeness; charm

7 atomic cluster, molecule; radical, simple radical, compound radical, chain, straight chain, branched chain, side chain; ring, closed chain, cycle; homocycle, heterocycle; benzene ring *or* nucleus, Kekulé formula; lattice, space-lattice

8 **fission, nuclear fission,** fission reaction; **atom-smashing,** atom-chipping, **splitting the atom;** atomic reaction; atomic disintegration *or* decay, alpha decay, beta decay, gamma decay; stimulation, dissociation, photodisintegration, ionization, nucleization, cleavage; neutron reaction, proton reaction, etc; reversible reaction, nonreversible reaction; thermonuclear reaction; **chain reaction;** exchange reaction; breeding; disintegration series; bombardment, atomization; bullet, target; proton gun

9 **fusion, nuclear fusion,** fusion reaction, thermonuclear reaction, thermonuclear fusion, laser-induced fusion, cold fusion

10 **fissionable material,** nuclear fuel; fertile material; **critical mass,** noncritical mass; parent element, daughter element; end product

11 **accelerator**, **particle accelerator,** atomic accelerator, atom smasher, atomic cannon

12 mass spectrometer, mass spectrograph

13 **reactor**, **nuclear reactor, pile,** atomic pile, reactor pile, chain-reacting pile, chain reactor, **furnace,** atomic *or* nuclear furnace, neutron factory; fast pile, intermediate pile, slow pile; lattice; bricks; rods; radioactive waste

14 atomic engine, **atomic** *or* **nuclear power plant,** reactor engine

15 **atomic energy, nuclear energy** *or* **power,** thermonuclear power; activation energy, binding energy, mass energy; energy level; atomic research, atomic project; Atomic Energy Commission *or* AEC

16 **atomic explosion, atom blast, A-blast; thermonuclear explosion,** hydrogen blast, **H-blast;** ground zero; blast wave, Mach stem; Mach front; mushroom cloud; **fallout,** airborne radioactivity, fission particles, dust cloud, radioactive dust; flash burn; **atom bomb** *or* **atomic bomb** *or* **A-bomb, hydrogen bomb,** thermonuclear bomb, nuke <nf>; A-bomb shelter, fallout shelter

VERBS 17 **atomize,** nucleize; activate, accelerate; bombard, cross-bombard; cleave, fission, **split** *or* **smash the atom**

ADJS 18 **atomic;** atomistic; atomiferous; monatomic, diatomic, triatomic, tetratomic, pentatomic, hexatomic, heptatomic; heteratomic, heteroatomic; subatomic, subnuclear, ultraelementary; dibasic, tribasic; cyclic, isocyclic, homocyclic, heterocyclic; isotopic, isobaric, isoteric

19 **nuclear, thermonuclear,** isonuclear, homonuclear, heteronuclear, extranuclear

20 **fissionable,** fissile, scissile

1039 MECHANICS

NOUNS 1 **mechanics** ; leverage 906; tools and machinery 1040

2 **statics**

3 **dynamics**, **kinetics,** energetics

4 **hydraulics, fluid dynamics,** hydromechanics, hydrokinetics, fluidics, hydrodynamics, hydrostatics; hydrology, hydrography, hydrometry, fluviology

5 **pneumatics,** pneumatostatics; aeromechanics, aerophysics, aerology, aerometry, aerography, aerotechnics, aerodynamics, aerostatics

6 **engineering,** mechanical engineering, jet engineering, etc; engineers

ADJS 7 **mechanical,** mechanistic, mechanized; locomotive, locomotor; motorized, power-driven; hydraulic, electronic; labor-saving; zoomechanical, biomechanical, aeromechanical, hydromechanical, etc; souped-up

8 **static;** biostatic, electrostatic, geostatic, etc

9 **dynamic, dynamical, kinetic, kinetical, kinematic, kinematical;**

geodynamic, radiodynamic, electrodynamic, etc

10 **pneumatic,** pneumatological; aeromechanical, aerophysical, aerologic, aerological, aerotechnical, aerodynamic, aerostatic, aerographic, aerographical

11 hydrologic, hydrometric, hydrometrical, hydromechanic, hydromechanical, hydrodynamic, hydrostatic, hydraulic

1040 TOOLS, MACHINERY

NOUNS **1 tool, instrument, implement, utensil; apparatus, device,** mechanical device, contrivance, contraption <nf>, gadget, gizmo, gimcrack, gimmick <nf>, means, mechanical means; gadgetry; **hand tool; power tool;** machine tool; speed tool; precision tool *or* instrument; garden tool, agricultural tool; **mechanization,** mechanizing; motorizing

2 cutlery, edge tool; **knife, ax,** dagger, sword, blade, cutter, whittle; steel, cold steel, naked steel; shiv *and* pigsticker *and* toad stabber *and* toad sticker <nf>; perforator, piercer, puncturer, point; sharpener; **saw;** trowel; shovel; plane; drill; valve 239.10

3 machinery, enginery; **machine, mechanism,** mechanical device; heavy machinery, earthmoving machinery, earthmover; farm machinery; mill; welder; pump; **engine,** motor; engine part; power plant, **power source,** drive, motive power, prime mover; **appliance,** convenience, facility, utility, home appliance, mechanical aid; fixture; labor-saving device

4 mechanism, machinery, **movement,** movements, **action, motion, works,** workings, inner workings, what makes it work, innards, nuts and bolts, what makes it tick; drive train, power train; wheelwork, **wheelworks,** wheels, gear, wheels within wheels, epicyclic train; clockworks, watchworks, servomechanism 1041.13; robot, automaton

5 simple machine; lever, wheel and axle, pulley, inclined plane; machine part, gear, gearwheel, shaft, crank, rod, hub, cam, coupling, bearing, ball bearing, roller bearing, journal, bush, differential

6 machine tool; drill, press drill, borer, lathe, mill, broaching machine, facing machine, threading machine, tapping machine, grinder, planer, shaper, saw

7 hand tool; hammer, screwdriver, drill, punch, awl, wrench, pliers, clamp, vise, chisel, wedge, ax, knife, saw, lever, crowbar, jack, pulley, wheel

8 garden tool; spade, shovel, trowel, fork, rake, hoe, tiller, plow, hedge trimmer, shears, lawn mower

9 gear, gearing, gear train; gearwheel, cogwheel, rack; **gearshift;** low, intermediate, high, neutral, reverse; differential, differential gear *or* gearing; **transmission,** gearbox; automatic transmission; selective transmission; standard transmission, stick shift, manual transmission, five-speed, five on the floor; synchronized shifting, synchromesh; spur gear, rack and pinion, helical gear, bevel gear, skew gear, worm gear, internal gear, external gear; gear tooth

10 clutch, cone clutch, plate clutch, dog clutch, disk clutch, multiple-disk clutch, rim clutch, friction clutch, cone friction clutch, slip friction clutch, spline clutch, rolling-key clutch

11 tooling, tooling up; **retooling;** instrumentation, industrial instrumentation; servo instrumentation

12 mechanic, mechanician; grease monkey <nf>; artisan, artificer; machinist, machiner; auto mechanic, aeromechanic, etc

VERBS **13 tool,** tool up, instrument; retool; **machine,** mill; **mechanize,** motorize; sharpen

ADJS **14 mechanical;** machinelike; power, powered, power-driven, motor-driven, motorized; **mechanized,** mechanistic; electronic; labor-saving

1041 AUTOMATION

NOUNS 1 **automation,** automatic control; robotization, cybernation; **self-action,** self-activity; self-movement, self-motion, **self-propulsion;** self-direction, self-determination, self-government, automatism, self-regulation; automaticity, automatization; servo instrumentation; computerization

2 autonetics, automatic *or* automation technology, automatic electronics, automatic engineering, automatic control engineering, servo engineering, **servomechanics,** system engineering, systems analysis, feedback system engineering; **cybernetics;** telemechanics; radiodynamics, radio control; systems planning, systems design; circuit analysis; bionics; communication *or* communications theory, information theory

3 **automatic control,** cybernation, servo control, robot control, robotization; cybernetic control; electronic control, electronic-mechanical control; feedback control, digital feedback control, analog feedback control; cascade control, piggyback control <nf>; supervisory control; action, control action; derivative *or* rate action, reset action; control agent; control means

4 semiautomatic control; **remote control,** push-button control, remote handling, tele-action; radio control; telemechanics; telemechanism; telemetry, telemeter, telemetering; transponder; bioinstrument, bioinstrumentation

5 control system, **automatic control system,** servo system, robot system; closed-loop system; open-sequence system; linear system, nonlinear system; carrier-current system; integrated system, complex control system; data system, data-handling system, data-reduction system, data-input system, data-interpreting system, digital data reducing system; process-control system, annunciator system, flow-control system, motor-speed control system; automanual system; automatic telephone system; electrostatic spraying system; automated factory, automatic *or* robot factory, push-button plant; servo laboratory, servolab; electronic banking; electronic cottage

6 **feedback,** closed sequence, feedback loop, closed loop; multiple-feed closed loop; process loop, quality loop; feedback circuit, current-control circuit, direct-current circuit, alternating-current circuit, calibrating circuit, switching circuit, flip-flop circuit, peaking circuit; multiplier channels; open sequence, linear operation; positive feedback, negative feedback; reversed feedback, degeneration

7 <functions> accounting, analysis, automatic electronic navigation, automatic guidance, braking, comparison of variables, computation, coordination, corrective action, fact distribution, forecasts, impedance matching, inspection, linear *or* nonlinear calibrations, manipulation, measurement of variables, missile guidance, output measurement, processing, rate determination, record keeping, statistical communication, steering, system stabilization, ultrasonic *or* supersonic flow detection

8 **process control,** bit-weight control, color control, density control, dimension control, diverse control, end-point control, flavor control, flow control, fragrance control, hold control, humidity control, light-intensity control, limit control, liquid-level control, load control, pressure control, precision-production control, proportional control, quality control, quantity control, revolution control, temperature control, time control, weight control

9 variable, process variable; simple variable, complex variable; manipulated variable; steady state, transient state

10 values, target values; set point; differential gap; proportional band; dead band, dead zone; neutral zone

11 time constants; time lead, gain; time delay, dead time; lag, process lag,

hysteresis, holdup, output lag; throughput

12 automatic device, automatic; semiautomatic; self-actor, self-mover; **robot, automation,** mechanical man; cyborg; bionic man, bionic woman

13 **servomechanism,** servo; cybernion, automatic machine; **servomotor;** synchro, selsyn, autosyn; synchronous motor, synchronous machine

14 **system component; control mechanism; regulator, control,** controller, **governor;** servo control, servo regulator; control element

15 **automatic detector;** automatic analyzer; automatic indicator

16 **control panel,** console; coordinated panel, graphic panel; panelboard, set-up board

17 **computer, computer science** 1042, electronic computer, electronic brain; electronic organizer; information machine, thinking machine; computer unit, hardware, computer hardware

18 <automatic devices> automatic pilot *or* autopilot, automaton, guided missile, robot, self-starter, speedometer

19 **control engineer,** servo engineer, system engineer, systems analyst, automatic control system engineer, feedback system engineer, automatic technician, robot specialist; computer engineer, computer technologist, computer technician, **computer programmer;** cybernetic technologist, cyberneticist

VERBS **20** **automate,** automatize, robotize; robot-control, servo-control; program; computerize

21 **self-govern,** self-control, **self-regulate,** selfdirect

ADJS **22** **automated,** cybernated, robotized; **automatic,** automatous, **spontaneous; self-acting,** self-active; **self-operating,** self-operative, self-working; **self-regulating,** self-regulative, self-governing, self-directing; **self-regulated, self-controlled,** self-governed, self-directed, self-steered; self-adjusting, self-closing, self-cocking, self-cooking, self-dumping, self-emptying, self-lighting, self-loading, self-opening, self-priming, self-rising, self-sealing, self-starting, self-winding, automanual; semiautomatic; computerized, computer-controlled

23 **self-propelled,** self-moved, horseless; **self-propelling,** self-moving, self-propellent; self-driven, self drive; **automotive,** automobile, automechanical; **locomotive,** locomobile

24 **servomechanical,** servo-controlled; **cybernetic;** isotronic

25 **remote-control,** remote-controlled, telemechanic; telemetered, telemetric; by remote control

1042 COMPUTER SCIENCE

NOUNS **1** **computer science,** computer systems *and* applications, computer hardware *and* software, computers, digital computers, computing, machine computation, number-crunching <nf>; **computerization,** digitization; **data processing,** electronic data processing *or* EDP, data storage and retrieval; data bank; **information science,** information processing, informatics; computer security; computer crime *or* fraud, computer virus *or* worm; hacking

2 **computer,** electronic data processor, information processor, electronic brain, digital computer, general purpose computer, analog computer, hybrid computer, machine, **hardware,** computer hardware, microelectronics device; **processor,** central processing unit *or* CPU, multiprocessor, microprocessor, coprocessor, mainframe computer *or* mainframe, dataflow computer, hybrid computer, work station, minicomputer, microcomputer, personal computer *or* PC, home computer, desktop computer, laptop computer, notebook computer, briefcase computer, graphics tablet, pocket computer, handheld computer, personal organizer, personal digital assistant *or* PDA, minisupercomputer, superminicomputer, supermicrocomputer, supercomputer, graphoscope, array processor, neurocomputer, neural computer; multimedia computer; neural net *or* network, semantic net *or* network; management information system *or* MIS; clone; abacus, calculator

3 **circuitry,** circuit, integrated circuit, logic circuit, **chip,** silicon chip, gallium arsenide chip, semiconductor chip, hybrid chip, wafer chip, superchip, microchip, neural network chip, transputer, **board,** printed circuit board *or* PCB, card, motherboard; **peripheral,** peripheral device *or* unit, input device, output device; expansion slot; **port,** channel interface, serial interface, serial port, parallel port; **read-write head;** vacuum tube, transistor, bus, LED, network adapter, small computer systems interface *or* SCSI, register

4 **input device,** keyboard, keypad; reader, tape reader, card punch, scanner, optical scanner, optical character reader, optical character recognition *or* OCR device, data tablet *or* tablet, touchscreen, light pen, mouse, joystick, trackball, wand

5 **drive, disk drive,** floppy disk drive, hard disk drive *or* Winchester drive *or* hard drive, tape drive, removable drive, flash drive, external hard drive

6 **disk, magnetic disk, floppy disk** *or* floppy <nf> *or* diskette, minifloppy, microfloppy, hard *or* fixed *or* Winchester disk, removable disk, optical disk, disk pack; magnetic tape *or* mag tape <nf>, magnetic tape unit, magnetic drum; CD-ROM, compact-disk read-only memory, magneto-optical disk

7 **memory, storage,** memory bank, memory chip, firmware; **main memory,** main storage *or* store, cache memory *or* cache, random-access memory *or* RAM, read-only memory *or* ROM, programmable read-only memory *or* PROM, semiconductor memory, magnetic core memory, core, core storage *or* store, solid-state memory, auxiliary *or* secondary memory, disk pack, magnetic disk, primary storage, backing store, read/write memory, optical disk memory, bubble memory; read-only memory *or* ROM, programmable read-only memory *or* PROM

8 **retrieval, access,** random access, sequential access, direct access, data capture, capture

9 **output device,** peripheral, terminal, workstation, video terminal, video display terminal *or* VDT, video display unit *or* VDU, visual display unit *or* VDU, graphics terminal, **monitor,** screen, display, cathode ray tube *or* CRT, monochrome monitor, color monitor, RGB monitor, active matrix display, window; **printer,** color printer, **serial printer,** character printer, impact printer, dot-matrix printer, daisywheel *or* printwheel printer, drum printer, **line printer,** line dot-matrix printer, chain printer, **page printer,** nonimpact printer, laser printer, electronic printer, graphics printer, color graphics printer, ink-jet printer, thermal printer, bubble-jet printer, electrostatic printer; plotter; **modem** *or* modulator-demodulator

10 **forms, computer forms, computer paper,** continuous stationery

11 **software, program,** computer program, source program, object program, binary file, binary program; program suite, suite of applications; bundle; software package, courseware, groupware, routine, subroutine, intelligent agent *or* agent, autonomous agent; application software; applet; authoring software; shareware, freeware

12 **systems program, operating system** *or* **OS,** disk operating system *or* DOS, system software; Microsoft <TM> disk operating system *or* MS-DOS <TM>; UNIX; control program monitor *or* CPM; **word processor,** text editor, editor, print formatter, WYSIWYG *or* what-you-see-is-what-you-get word processor, post-formatted word processor; spreadsheet, electronic spreadsheet, desktop publishing program, database management system *or* DBMS, authoring tool, utility program, screen saver, computer game; **computer application**, applications pro-

gram, application software, bootloader *or* bootstrap loader

13 **language**, assembler *or* assemblage language, programming language, machine language, machine-readable language, conventional programming language, computer language, high-level language, fourth generation language, macro language, preprocessor language, compiler, interpreter, low-level language, application development language, assembly language, assembly code, object code, job-control language *or* JCL, procedural language, problem-oriented language, query language; **computer** *or* **electronic virus,** computer worm, phantom bug, Trojan horse, logic bomb; source code, machine code; loader, parser, debugger; Java, HTML, SGML

14 **bit, binary digit,** infobit, kilobit, megabit, gigabit, terbit; **byte,** kilobyte, megabyte

15 **data, information,** database, data capture, database management, data warehousing, file, record, data bank, input, input-output *or* I/O; **file,** data set, record, data record, data file, text file

16 **network, computer network,** communications network, local area network *or* LAN, workgroup computing, mesh; neural network, neural net; **on-line system,** interactive system, on-line service; intranet; Internet

17 **programmer, liveware,** wetware; software engineer, computer engineer, computer scientist; systems programmer, system software specialist, application programmer, systems analyst, systems engineer, system operator *or* sysop; computer designer, computer architect, operator, technician, key puncher, keyboarder; techie; hacker <nf>; spammer

18 <computer terms> access, archive, authoring, backup, bandwidth, batch processing, baud rate, benchmark, beta test, binary tree, bit, bitmap, block, bookmark, boot, bootstrap, bug, byte, cgi, click, clickthrough, clock rate, command, compatibility, computerate, computer-friendly, computer-literate, controller, crash, cursor, desktop, diagnostic, diff, digital, direct access, directory, display, domain name, dot-com, download, downtime, drag and drop, emulator, escape key, field, file, file folder, file format, file sharing, footprint, FTP, function key, gigabyte, gopher, graphics, grep, hacking, helpdesk, home page, hot key, icon, input, interactive, interface, job, key, kilobyte, login, logon, logoff, megabyte, menu, message board, millennium bug, morphing, mouse potato, multimedia, multitasking, mouse potato <nf>, output, parity, password, plug-and-play, portal site, power user, pulldown, queue, random access, real time, record, save, scrollable, search engine, search engine optimization, sector, sequential access, signature, sleep mode, smiley, spell-checker, task bar, toolbar, toolkit, turnkey operation, upload, URL, username, virus, WYSIWYG *or* what you see is what you get

19 <computer communications> Internet, the Net <nf>, World Wide Web *or* Web *or* WWW, cyberspace, information superhighway; Internet service provider *or* ISP, electronic mail *or* e-mail *or* email, mailbox, website, communications protocol; compression, encryption; intranet; Usenet; local area network *or* LAN, wide area network *or* WAN, file server, client-server; browser; gateway; search engine; bulletin board service *or* BBS, chat room, newsgroup, workgroup; netizen, surfer; spam; wiki; Weblog *or* blog; DSL, cable modem

20 artificial intelligence, knowledge engineering, knowledge representation, intelligent retrieval, natural language processing, expert systems, speech synthesis, robotics, hypertext, hypermedia, intelligent agent

VERBS **21** **computerize,** digitize; **program,** boot, boot up, initialize, log in, log out, run, load, download, upload, **compute,** crunch numbers

<nf>; capture; **keyboard,** key in, input; browse, surf; search, google; cut and paste; export, import; bookmark

ADJS **22 computerized;** wired; machine-usable, computer-usable; computer-aided, computer-assisted; computer-driven, computer-guided, computer-controlled, computer-governed; computer-literate, computerate

1043 ENGINEERING

NOUNS **1 engineering**, mechanical engineering, civil engineering, chemical engineering, electrical engineering, mining and metallurgy, industrial engineering; automotive engineering, aerospace engineering, aeronautical engineering, astronautical engineering, marine engineering, agricultural engineering; structural engineering, transportation engineering, hydraulic engineering, geotechnical engineering, construction engineering; material engineering, biochemical engineering, environmental engineering

2 engineer, registered engineer; mechanical engineer, civil engineer, chemical engineer, electrical engineer, mining engineer, metallurgical engineer, industrial engineer; automotive engineer, aerospace engineer, aeronautical engineer, astronautical engineer, marine engineer, agricultural engineer; structural engineer, transportation engineer, hydraulic engineer, construction engineer; material engineer, biochemical engineer, biomedical engineer, environmental engineer; electronics engineer; mechanic, technician

3 <engine types> internal-combustion, external-combustion; Wankel, reciprocating, steam, gasoline, diesel, jet, turboprop, turbojet, rocket, Stirling, locomotive; automotive, aircraft, marine, railroad

VERBS **4** engineer, construct, build, erect, survey, map, excavate, dig, grade, dredge, drill, tunnel, blast, pave; process, manufacture, measure; reverse-engineer

1044 FRICTION

NOUNS **1 friction, rubbing,** rub, frottage; frication *and* confrication *and* perfrication ; **drag,** skin friction; **resistance,** frictional resistance; static friction, rolling friction, internal friction, sliding friction, slip friction

2 abrasion, attrition, erosion, wearing away, wear, detrition, ablation; rubbing against *or* together; ruboff; corrosion; erasure, erasing, rubbing away *or* off *or* out, obliteration; **grinding, filing,** rasping, limation; fretting; galling; **chafing, chafe;** levigation; **scraping,** grazing, scratching, scuffing; scrape, scratch, **scuff;** scrubbing, scrub; scouring, scour; **polishing,** burnishing, sanding, smoothing, dressing, buffing, shining; sandblasting; abrasive; brass-rubbing, heelball rubbing, graphite rubbing

3 massage, massaging, stroking, kneading; **rubdown;** backrub; massotherapy, massage therapy; whirlpool bath, Jacuzzi <TM>; vibrator; facial massage, facial

4 massager, **masseur, masseuse,** massage therapist**;** massotherapist

5 <mechanics> force of friction; force of viscosity; coefficient of friction; friction head; friction clutch, friction drive, friction gearing, friction pile, friction saw, friction welding

VERBS **6 rub,** frictionize; **massage,** knead, rub down; caress, pet, stroke 73.8; pulverize; smooth, iron

7 abrade, abrase, gnaw, gnaw away; **erode,** erode away, ablate, wear, wear away, corrode; erase, rub away *or* off *or* out, rub against; **grind, rasp, file, grate; chafe,** fret, gall; **scrape,** scratch, **graze,** raze , **scuff,** bark, skin; **fray,** frazzle; **scrub, scour**

8 buff, burnish, polish, rub up, sandpaper, **sand,** smooth, dress, shine, furbish, sandblast; brush, curry

ADJS **9 frictional,** friction; fricative; **rubbing**

10 abrasive, abradant, attritive, gnawing, erosive, ablative; scraping; **grinding, rasping;** chafing, fretting, galling

1045 DENSITY

NOUNS 1 **density,** denseness, **solidity, solidness,** firmness, **compactness, closeness,** spissitude ; **congestion,** congestedness, crowdedness, jammedness; **impenetrability,** impermeability, imporosity; hardness 1046; incompressibility; specific gravity, relative density; **consistency,** consistence, thick consistency, thickness; viscidity, viscosity, **viscousness, thickness,** gluiness, ropiness

2 **indivisibility, inseparability,** impartibility, infrangibility, indiscerptibility; indissolubility; cohesion, coherence 803; unity 792.1; insolubility, infusibility

3 **densification, condensation, compression, concentration,** inspissation, concretion, consolidation, conglobulation; hardening, **solidification** 1046.5; agglutination, clumping, clustering

4 **thickening,** inspissation; congelation, **congealment, coagulation,** clotting, **setting,** concretion; gelatinization, gelatination, jellification, jellying, **jelling,** gelling; **curdling,** clabbering; **distillation**

5 **precipitation,** deposit, sedimentation; precipitate

6 **solid,** solid body, body, mass, bulk; lump, clump, cluster; block, cake; node, knot; concrete, concretion; conglomerate, conglomeration

7 **clot,** coagulum, coagulate; blood clot, grume, embolus, crassamentum; **coagulant,** coagulator, clotting factor, coagulase, coagulose, thromboplastin *or* coagulin; casein, caseinogen, paracasein, legumin; **curd,** clabber, loppered milk *and* bonnyclabber <nf>, clotted cream, Devonshire cream

8 <instruments> densimeter, densitometer; aerometer, hydrometer, lactometer, urinometer, pycnometer

VERBS 9 **densify,** inspissate, densen; **condense, compress,** compact, **consolidate, concentrate,** come to a head; **congest; squeeze, press, crowd,** cram, jam, pack, ram down; steeve; pack *or* jam in; **solidify** 1046.8

10 **thicken,** thick ; inspissate, incrassate; **congeal, coagulate, clot,** set, concrete; gelatinize, gelatinate, jelly, jellify, **jell,** gel; **curdle,** curd, clabber, lopper <nf>; cake, lump, clump, cluster, knot

11 **precipitate,** deposit, sediment, sedimentate

ADJS 12 **dense, compact, close;** close-textured, close-knit, close-woven, tight-knit; serried, **thick, heavy,** massy, thickset, thick-packed, thick-growing, thick-spread, thick-spreading; **condensed, compressed,** compacted, concrete, consolidated, concentrated; **crowded, jammed,** packed, jam-packed, packed *or* jammed in, packed *or* jammed in like sardines; **congested,** crammed, crammed full; **solid,** firm, substantial, massive; impenetrable, impermeable, imporous, nonporous; hard 1046.10; incompressible; viscid, viscous, ropy, gluey; thick enough to be cut with a knife <nf>

13 **indivisible,** nondivisible, undividable, **inseparable,** impartible, infrangible, indiscerptible, indissoluble; cohesive, coherent 803.10; unified; insoluble, indissolvable, infusible

14 **thickened,** inspissate *or* inspissated, incrassate; **congealed, coagulated, clotted,** grumous; **curdled,** curded, clabbered; **jellied,** jelled *or* gelled, gelatinized; lumpy, lumpish; caked, cakey; coagulant, coagulating

ADVS 15 **densely,** compactly, **close,** closely, **thick,** thickly, heavily; solidly, firmly

1046 HARDNESS, RIGIDITY

NOUNS 1 **hardness,** durity , induration; **callousness,** callosity; stoniness, rock-hardness, flintiness, steeliness; **strength, toughness** 1049; solidity, impenetrability, density 1045; restiveness, resistance 453; obduracy 361.1; hardness of heart 94.3

2 **rigidity, rigidness,** rigor ; **firmness,** renitence *or* renitency, incompressibility; nonresilience *or* nonresiliency,

inelasticity; **tension,** tensity, **tenseness,** tautness, tightness

3 **stiffness, inflexibility,** unpliability, unmalleability, intractability, unbendingness, unlimberness, starchiness; **stubbornness,** unyieldingness 361.2; **unalterability,** immutability; immovability 855.3; inelasticity, irresilience *or* irresiliency; inextensibility *or* unextensibility, unextendibility, inductility

4 **temper,** tempering; chisel temper, die temper, razor temper, saw file temper, set temper, spindle temper, tool temper; precipitation hardening, heat treating; hardness test, Brinell test; hardness scale, Brinell number *or* Brinell hardness number *or* Bhn; indenter; hardener, hardening, hardening agent

5 **hardening, toughening,** induration, firming; **strengthening; tempering,** case hardening, steeling; seasoning; **stiffening,** rigidification, starching; **solidification, setting,** curing, caking, concretion; crystallization, granulation; callusing; sclerosis, arteriosclerosis, atherosclerosis, hardening of the arteries; lithification; lapidification ; **petrification,** fossilization, ossification; glaciation; cornification, hornification; calcification; vitrification, vitrifaction

6 <comparisons> stone, rock 1059, adamant, granite, flint, marble, diamond; steel, iron, nails; concrete, cement; brick; oak, heart of oak; bone; Mohs' scale

VERBS **7** **harden,** indurate, firm, **toughen** 1046.7; **callous; temper,** anneal, oil-temper, heat-temper, **case-harden,** steel; season; **petrify,** lapidify , fossilize; lithify; vitrify; calcify; ossify; cornify, hornify

8 **solidify,** concrete, **set,** take a set, cure, cake; condense, thicken 1045.10; **crystallize,** granulate, candy; hard-boil; anneal; freeze

9 **stiffen,** rigidify, starch; **strengthen, toughen** 1046.7; back, brace, reinforce, shore up; **tense, tighten,** tense up, tension; trice up, screw up

ADJS **10** **hard, solid,** dure , lacking give, **tough** 1049.4; resistive, resistant, steely, steellike, iron-hard, ironlike; **stony,** rocky, stonelike, rock-hard, rocklike, lapideous, lapidific, lapidifical, lithoid *or* lithoidal; diamondlike, adamant, adamantine; flinty, flintlike; marble, marblelike; granitic, granitelike; gritty; concrete, cement, cemental; horny; bony, osseous, ossific; petrifactive; vitreous; hard-boiled; hard as nails or a rock, etc 1046.6; dense 1045.12; obdurate 361.10; hard-hearted 94.12

11 **rigid, stiff, firm,** renitent, incompressible; **tense, taut, tight,** unrelaxed; nonresilient, inelastic; **rodlike,** virgate; ramrod-stiff, ramrodlike, pokerlike; stiff as a poker *or* rod *or* board, stiff as buckram; starched, starchy

12 **inflexible,** unflexible, **unpliable, unpliant, unmalleable, intractable,** untractable, intractile, **unbending,** unlimber, **unyielding** 361.9, ungiving, **stubborn, unalterable,** immutable; **immovable** 855.15; **adamant,** adamantine; **inelastic,** nonelastic, irresilient; inextensile, inextensible, unextensible, inextensional, unextendible, nonstretchable, inductile; intransigent

13 **hardened, toughened,** steeled, indurate, indurated, fortified; **callous,** calloused; **solidified,** set; crystallized, granulated; petrified, lapidified , fossilized; vitrified; sclerotic; ossified; cornified, hornified; calcified; crusted, crusty, incrusted; **stiffened, strengthened,** rigidified, backed, reinforced; frozen solid

14 **hardening, toughening,** indurative; petrifying, petrifactive

15 **tempered, case-hardened,** heat-treated, **annealed,** oil-tempered, heat-tempered, tempered in fire; seasoned; indurate, indurated

1047 SOFTNESS, PLIANCY

NOUNS **1** **softness,** give, nonresistiveness, insolidity, unsolidity, nonrigidity; **gentleness,** easiness, delicacy, tenderness; lenity, leniency 427; mellowness; fluffiness, flossiness, downiness, featheriness; velvetiness, plushiness, satininess, silkiness; sponginess, pulpiness

2 **pliancy, pliability, plasticity, flexibility, flexility,** flexuousness, bendability, ductility, ductibility , tensileness, tensility, tractility, **tractability,** amenability, adaptability, facility, give, **suppleness,** willowiness, **litheness, limberness; elasticity** 1048, **resilience,** springiness, resiliency, rubberiness; sponginess, pulpiness, doughiness, compressibility; malleability, moldability, fictility, sequacity ; **impressionability,** susceptibility, responsiveness, receptiveness, sensibility, sensitiveness; formability, formativeness; extensibility, extendibility; agreeability 324.1; submissiveness 433.3

3 **flaccidity,** flaccidness, **flabbiness, limpness,** rubberiness, floppiness; **looseness,** laxness, laxity, laxation, relaxedness, relaxation

4 <comparisons> putty, clay, dough, blubber, rubber, wax, butter, soap, pudding; velvet, plush, satin, silk; wool, fleece; pillow, cushion; kapok; baby's bottom; puff; fluff, floss, flue; down, feathers, feather bed, eiderdown, swansdown, thistledown; breeze, zephyr; foam; snow

5 **softening,** softening-up; **easing,** padding, cushioning; mollifying, mollification; **relaxation,** laxation; mellowing; tenderizing

VERBS **6** **soften,** soften up; unsteel; **ease,** cushion; gentle, mollify, milden; **subdue,** tone *or* tune down; mellow; tenderize; **relax,** laxate, loosen; limber, limber up, supple; massage, knead, plump, plump up, fluff, fluff up, shake up; **mash,** whip, **smash,** squash, pulp, pulverize; masticate, macerate; thaw, liquefy

7 **yield, give,** relent, relax, bend, unbend, give way; comply; mellow, loosen up, chill out <nf>; submit 433.6,9

ADJS **8** **soft,** nonresistive, nonrigid; mild, **gentle, easy, delicate, tender;** complaisant 427.8; mellow, mellowy ; **softened,** mollified; whisper-soft, soft as putty or clay or dough, etc 1047.4, soft as a kiss *or* a sigh *or* a whisper *or* a baby's bottom

9 **pliant, pliable, flexible,** flexile, flexuous, **plastic, elastic** 1048.7, **ductile,** sequacious *or* facile , tractile, **tractable, yielding,** giving, bending; adaptable, **malleable,** moldable, shapable, fabricable, fictile; compliant 324.5, submissive 433.12; **impressionable,** impressible, susceptible, responsive, receptive, sensitive; **formable,** formative; **bendable; supple,** willowy, **limber; lithe,** lithesome, lissome, double-jointed, loose-limbed, whippy; **elastic,** resilient, springy; extensile, extensible, extendible; putty, waxy, doughy, pasty, puttylike

10 **flaccid, flabby, limp,** rubbery, flimsy, floppy; **loose,** lax, relaxed, slack, unstrung

11 **spongy,** pulpy, pithy, medullary; edematous; foamy; juicy

12 **pasty, doughy;** loamy, clayey, argillaceous

13 **squashy,** squishy, squushy, squelchy, mooshy

14 **fluffy,** flossy, **downy,** pubescent, feathery; fleecy, flocculent, woolly, lanate; furry

15 **velvety,** velvetlike, velutinous; plushy, plush; **satiny,** satinlike; cottony; **silky,** silken, silklike, sericeous, soft as silk

16 **softening, easing;** subduing, mollifying, emollient; demulcent; **relaxing,** loosening

ADVS **17** **softly, gently,** easily, delicately, tenderly; compliantly 324.9, submissively 433.17

1048 ELASTICITY

NOUNS **1** **elasticity, resilience** *or* resiliency, **give;** snap, **bounce,** bounciness; **stretch, stretchiness,** stretchability; extensibility; tone, tonus, tonicity; **spring, springiness;** rebound 903.2; **flexibility** 1047.2; **adaptability,** responsiveness; **buoyancy** *or* buoyance; **liveliness** 330.2

2 **stretching;** extension; distension 259.2; **stretch, tension, strain**

3 **elastic;** elastomer; **rubber,** gum elastic; stretch fabric, latex, spandex; gum, chewing gum 1062.6; whalebone, baleen; rubber band, rubber ball, handball, tennis ball; sponge rubber, crepe rubber; spring; springboard; trampoline; racket, battledore; gutta-percha; neoprene; spring, shock absorber

VERBS 4 **stretch;** extend; distend 259.4; flex

5 **give,** yield 1047.7; bounce, spring, snap back, recoil, rebound, spring back 903.6

6 **elasticize;** rubberize, rubber; vulcanize, plasticize

ADJS 7 **elastic, resilient, springy,** bouncy; **stretchable, stretchy,** stretch; extensile; **flexible** 1047.9; flexile; **adaptable,** adaptive, responsive; buoyant; lively 330.17; tensile

8 rubber, **rubbery,** rubberlike; rubberized

1049 TOUGHNESS

NOUNS 1 **toughness, resistance, ruggedness; strength, hardiness, vitality, stamina** 15.1, sturdiness; stubbornness, stiffness; **unbreakableness** *or* **unbreakability,** infrangibility; cohesiveness, tenacity, viscidity 803.3; durability, lastingness 827.1; **hardness** 1046; **leatheriness,** leatherlikeness; stringiness; staying power

2 <comparisons> leather; gristle, cartilage

VERBS 3 **toughen,** harden, stiffen, work-harden, **temper,** strengthen; season; be tough; **endure, hang tough** <nf>

ADJS 4 **tough, resistant;** shockproof, shock-resistant, impactproof, impact-resistant; stubborn, stiff; **heavy-duty;** hard *or* tough as nails; **strong, hardy,** vigorous; cohesive, **tenacious,** viscid; **durable,** lasting 827.10; untiring; **hard** 1046.10; chewy <nf>; leathery, leatherlike, coriaceous, tough as leather; sinewy, wiry; gristly, cartilaginous; stringy, fibrous; long-lasting

5 **unbreakable,** nonbreakable, infrangible, unshatterable, shatterproof, chip-proof, fractureproof; bulletproof, bombproof, fireproof; indestructible

6 **toughened,** hardened, tempered, annealed; seasoned; casehardened; vulcanized

1050 BRITTLENESS, FRAGILITY

NOUNS 1 **brittleness, crispness,** crispiness; **fragility, frailty,** damageability, delicacy 16.2, flimsiness, **breakability,** breakableness, frangibility, fracturableness, crackability, crackableness, crunchability, crushability, crushableness; lacerability; fissility; friability, friableness, crumbliness 1051, flakiness; vulnerableness, **vulnerability** 1006.4; inelasticity

2 <comparisons> eggshell, old bone, piecrust, peanut brittle; matchwood, balsa, old paper, parchment, rice paper, dead leaf; glass, glass jaw, china, ice, icicle, glass house; house of cards; lamina, shale, slate, pottery

VERBS 3 **break, shatter,** fragment, fragmentize, fragmentate, fall to pieces, shard, fracture, chip off, flake, shiver, **disintegrate** 806.3

ADJS 4 **brittle, crisp,** crispy; **fragile, frail,** delicate 16.14, flimsy, **breakable,** frangible, crushable, crackable, crunchable, fracturable; lacerable; **shatterable,** shattery, shivery, splintery; friable, crumbly 1051.13, flaky; fissile, scissile; brittle as glass; **vulnerable** 1006.16; waferthin, papery; inelastic

1051 POWDERINESS, CRUMBLINESS

NOUNS 1 **powderiness,** pulverulence, dustiness; chalkiness; **mealiness,** flouriness, branniness; efflorescence, bloom

2 **granularity, graininess,** granulation; **sandiness, grittiness,** gravelliness, sabulosity, sandiness

3 **friability,** pulverableness, crispness, crumbliness, flakiness; brittleness 1050

4 **pulverization,** comminution, trituration, attrition, detrition; levigation;

reduction to powder *or* dust, pestling; fragmentation, sharding; brecciation; atomization, micronization; **powdering, crumbling,** flaking; abrasion 1044.2; **grinding,** milling, grating, shredding; granulation, granulization; **beating, pounding, shattering,** flailing, mashing, smashing, crushing; disintegration 806, decomposition

5 **powder, dust,** chalk; dust ball *or* kitten *or* bunny, slut's wool <Brit nf>, lint; efflorescence; **crumb,** crumble; **meal,** bran, flour, farina, grist; grits, groats; filings, raspings, sawdust; soot, smut; **particle, particulate,** particulates, airborne particles, air pollution; fallout; cosmic dust; dust cloud, dust devil; spore, pollen

6 **grain,** granule, granulet; **grit, sand; gravel,** shingle; detritus, debris; breccia, collapse breccia; speck, mote, particle

7 **pulverizer,** comminutor, triturator, levigator; **crusher; mill; grinder;** granulator, pepper grinder, pepper mill; **grater,** cheese grater, nutmeg grater; **shredder;** pestle, **mortar and pestle; masher;** pounder; grindstone, millstone, quern, quernstone, muller; roller, steamroller; hammer; abrasive

8 koniology; konimeter

VERBS 9 **pulverize, powder,** comminute, triturate, contriturate, levigate, bray, pestle, disintegrate, reduce to powder *or* dust, grind to powder *or* dust, grind up; **fragment,** shard, shatter; brecciate; atomize, micronize; **crumble,** crumb, chip, flake; **granulate,** granulize, grain; **grind, grate, shred,** abrade 1044.7; **mill,** flour; **beat, pound, mash, smash, crush,** crunch, flail, squash, scrunch <nf>; grate, shred, mince, kibble

10 <be reduced to powder> **powder,** come *or* fall to dust, **crumble,** crumble to *or* into dust, **disintegrate** 806.3, fall to pieces, break up; effloresce; granulate, grain

ADJS 11 **powdery, dusty,** powder, pulverulent, pulverous, lutose; **pulverized,** pulverant, powdered, disintegrated, comminute, gone to dust, reduced to powder, dust-covered; **particulate; ground, grated,** pestled, milled, stone-ground, comminuted, triturated, levigated; sharded, **crushed; fragmented; shredded;** sifted; **fine,** impalpable; **chalky,** chalklike; **mealy,** floury, farinaceous; branny; furfuraceous, scaly, scurfy; flaky 296.7; detrited, detrital; scobiform, scobicular; efflorescent

12 **granular, grainy,** granulate, **granulated; sandy, gritty,** sabulous, arenarious, arenaceous, arenose; shingly, shingled, pebbled, pebbly; **gravelly;** breccial, brecciated

13 **pulverable, pulverizable,** pulverulent, triturable, **friable,** crimp, crisp, **crumbly**

1052 MATERIALITY

NOUNS 1 **materiality,** materialness; **corporeity,** corporality, corporeality, corporealness, bodiliness, embodiment, existence; **substantiality** 763, concreteness 763.1; **physicalness,** physicality; tangibility; palpability

2 **matter, material,** materiality, **substance** 763.2, **stuff,** hyle; raw material, organic matter; **primal matter,** initial substance, xylem; brute matter; **element;** chemical element 1060.2; the four elements; earth, air, fire, water; elementary particle, fundamental particle; elementary unit, building block, unit of being, monad; constituent, component; **atom** 1038.4; atomic particle 1038.6; **molecule;** material world, physical world, real world, nature, natural world; hypostasis, substratum; plenum; antimatter

3 **body,** physical body, material body, corpus <nf>, anatomy <nf>, person, **figure, form,** frame, **physique,** carcass <nf>, bones, flesh, clay, clod, hulk; soma; **torso, trunk;** warm body <nf>

4 **object, article, thing,** material thing, affair, something, entity; whatsit <nf>, what's-its-name 528.2; something *or* other, *eppes* <Yiddish>, *quelque chose* <Fr>;

artifact; inanimate object; animate being

5 <nf terms> **gadget** 1040.1; thingum, **thingamabob,** thingumadad, thingy, thingumadoodle, **thingamajig** *or* thingumajig, thingumajigger, thingumaree, thingummy, **doodad,** dofunny, **dojigger,** dojiggy, domajig, domajigger, **dohickey** *or* doohickey, dowhacky, flumadiddle, gigamaree, **gimmick, gizmo,** dingus, hickey, jigger, hootmalalie, hootenanny, whatchy, widget, whatsis *or* whatsit, gismo *or* gizmo, deely-bobber

6 **materialism,** physicism, epiphenomenalism, identity theory of mind, atomism, mechanism; physicalism, behaviorism, instrumentalism, pragmatism, pragmaticism; historical materialism, dialectical materialism, Marxism; **positivism,** logical positivism, positive philosophy, empiricism, **naturalism;** realism, natural realism, commonsense realism, commonsense philosophy, naïve realism, new realism, critical realism, representative realism, epistemological realism; substantialism; hylomorphism; hylotheism; hylozoism; worldliness, earthliness, animalism, secularism, temporality

7 **materialist,** physicist, atomist; historical *or* dialectical materialist, Marxist; **naturalist;** realist, natural realist, commonsense realist, commonsense philosopher, epistemological realist; humanist, positivist; physical scientist

8 **materialization,** corporealization; substantialization, substantiation; **embodiment, incorporation,** personification, **incarnation,** manifestation; **reincarnation,** reembodiment, transmigration, metempsychosis

VERBS 9 **materialize** 763.5, corporalize; substantialize, substantify, substantiate; **embody** 763.5, body, **incorporate,** corporify, personify, **incarnate; reincarnate,** reembody, transmigrate; externalize

ADJS 10 **material,** materiate, hylic, **substantial** 763.6, tangible; **corporeal,** corporeous, corporal, **bodily; physical,** somatic, somatical, somatous; **fleshly;** worldly, earthly, here-and-now, **secular,** temporal, **unspiritual,** nonspiritual; empirical, spatiotemporal; objective, clinical

11 **embodied,** bodied, **incorporated, incarnate**

12 **materialist** *or* **materialistic,** atomistic, mechanist, mechanistic; Marxian, Marxist; **naturalist, naturalistic, positivist, positivistic;** commonsense, **realist,** realistic; hylotheistic; hylomorphous; hylozoic, hylozoistic

1053 IMMATERIALITY

NOUNS 1 **immateriality,** immaterialness; incorporeity, incorporeality, incorporealness, **bodilessness; unsubstantiality** 764, unsubstantialness; **intangibility,** impalpability, imponderability; inextension, nonextension; nonexteriority, nonexternality; **unearthliness, unworldliness,** ethereality, unreality; **supernaturalism** 689.2; **spirituality,** spiritualness, spirituousness , otherworldliness, ghostliness, shadowiness; occultism 689, the occult, occult phenomena; ghost-raising, ghost-hunting, ghostbusting <nf>; psychism, psychics, psychic *or* psychical research, psychicism; spirit world, astral plane

2 incorporeal, incorporeity, immateriality, unsubstantiality 764

3 **immaterialism, idealism,** philosophical idealism, metaphysical idealism; objective idealism; absolute idealism; epistemological idealism; monistic idealism, pluralistic idealism; critical idealism; transcendental idealism; subjectivism; solipsism; subjective idealism; **spiritualism;** personalism; panpsychism, psychism, animism, hylozoism, animatism; Platonism, Platonic realism, Berkeleianism, Cambridge Platonism, Kantianism, Hegelianism, New England Transcendentalism; Neoplatonism; Platonic idea *or* ideal *or* form, pure form, form, universal; transcendental object; transcendental

4 immaterialist, **idealist;** Berkeleian, Platonist, Hegelian, Kantian; Neoplatonist; **spiritualist;** psychist, panpsychist, animist; **occultist** 689.11; medium; ghost-raiser, ghost-hunter, ghostbuster <nf>

5 dematerialization; **disembodiment,** disincarnation; **spiritualization**

VERBS 6 dematerialize, immaterialize, unsubstantialize, insubstantialize, desubstantialize, **disembody,** disincarnate; **spiritualize,** spiritize; meditate

ADJS 7 **immaterial,** nonmaterial; **unsubstantial** 764.5, insubstantial, **intangible,** impalpable, imponderable; unextended, extensionless; **incorporeal,** incorporate, incorporeous; **bodiless,** unembodied, without body, asomatous; **disembodied,** disbodied, discarnate, decarnate, decarnated; metaphysical; **unphysical,** nonphysical; **unfleshly;** airy, ghostly, spectral, phantom, shadowy, ethereal; **spiritual,** astral, psychic *or* psychical; **unearthly, unworldly, otherworldly,** extramundane, transmundane; supernatural; **occult;** parapsychological

8 **idealist, idealistic,** immaterialist, immaterialistic; solipsistic; spiritualist, spiritualistic; panpsychist, panpsychistic; animist, animistic; Platonic, Platonistic, Berkeleian, Hegelian, Kantian; Neoplatonic, Neoplatonistic

1054 MATERIALS

NOUNS 1 **materials,** substances, stuff, matter; **raw material, staple, stock,** grist, basic material; material resources *or* means; store, supply 386; strategic materials; matériel; natural resource

2 <building materials> sticks and stones, lath and plaster, bricks and mortar, wattle and daub; **roofing,** roofage, tiles, shingles; walling, siding; **flooring,** pavement, paving material, paving, paving stone; masonry, stonework, flag, flagstone, ashlar, stone 1059.1; covering materials; mortar, plasters; **cement, concrete,** cyclopean concrete, ferroconcrete, prestressed concrete, reinforced concrete, slag concrete, cinder concrete; brick, firebrick; cinder block, concrete block; clinker, adobe, clay; **tile,** tiling; glass, steel, slate, cobble, tar, asphalt, gravel

3 **wood, lumber, timber,** forest-product; hardwood, softwood; stick, stick of wood, stave; billet; log, pole, post, beam 273.3, **board,** plank; deal; two-by-four, three-by-four, etc; slab, puncheon; slat, splat, lath; boarding, timbering, timberwork, planking; lathing, lathwork; sheeting; paneling, panelboard, panelwork; plywood, plyboard; sheathing, sheathing board; siding, sideboard; weatherboard, clapboard; shingle, shake; log; driftwood; firewood, kindling, stovewood; cordwood; cord, cordage; brushwood; dead wood; pulpwood, sapwood, alburnum, heartwood, duramen; early wood, late wood, springwood, summerwood

4 cane, bamboo, rattan

5 **paper,** paper stock, stock; sheet, leaf, page; quire, ream, stationery; cardboard

6 **plastic** ; thermoplastic; thermosetting plastic; resin plastic; cellulose plastic; protein plastic; cast plastic, molded plastic, extruded plastic; molding compounds; laminate; adhesive; plasticizer; polymer; **synthetic;** synthetic fabric *or* textile *or* cloth; synthetic rubber

VERBS 7 gather *or* procure materials; **store, stock,** stock up 386.11, lay in, restock; **process,** utilize

1055 INORGANIC MATTER

NOUNS 1 **inorganic matter,** nonorganic matter; inanimate *or* lifeless *or* nonliving matter, inorganized *or* unorganized matter, inert matter, dead matter, **brute matter;** mineral kingdom *or* world; matter, mere matter

2 **inanimateness,** inanimation, **lifelessness,** inertness; **insensibility,** insentience, insensateness,

senselessness, unconsciousness, unfeelingness

3 inorganic chemistry; chemicals 1060

ADJS **4** **inorganic,** unorganic, nonorganic; **mineral,** nonbiological; nonbiodegradable; unorganized, inorganized; material 1052.10

5 **inanimate,** inanimated, unanimated, exanimate, azoic, nonliving, dead, **lifeless,** soulless; inert; insentient, unconscious, nonconscious, **insensible,** insensate, senseless, unfeeling; dumb, mute

1056 OILS, LUBRICANTS

NOUNS **1** **oil,** *oleum* <L>; **fat,** lipid, **grease;** sebum, tallow, vegetable oil, animal oil; **ester,** glyceryl ester; fixed oil, fatty oil, nonvolatile oil, volatile oil, essential oil; saturated fat, hydrogenated fat, unsaturated fat, polyunsaturated fat; drying oil, semidrying oil, nondrying oil; glycerol, wax

2 **lubricant,** lubricator, lubricating oil, lubricating agent, antifriction; graphite, plumbago, black lead; silicone; glycerin *or* glycerine; silicone; wax, cerate; mucilage, mucus, synovia; spit, spittle, saliva; Vaseline <TM>, petroleum jelly, K-Y <TM>; soap, lather

3 **ointment, balm, salve, lotion, cream, unguent,** unguentum, inunction, inunctum, unction, chrism *or* chrisom; soothing syrup, lenitive, embrocation, demulcent, emollient, liniment; spikenard, nard; balsam; **pomade,** pomatum, brilliantine; styling mousse, styling gel; cold cream, hand lotion, face cream, lanolin; eyewash, collyrium; sun-block, sun-tan lotion, tanning cream

4 **petroleum,** rock oil, fossil oil, shale oil, coal oil; **fuel;** fuel oil; mineral oil; crude oil, crude; motor oil; gasoline *or* gas; kerosene, paraffin

5 **oiliness, greasiness, unctuousness,** unctiousness, unctuosity; **fattiness,** fatness, pinguidity; richness; sebaceousness; adiposis, adiposity; **soapiness,** saponacity *or* saponaceousness; smoothness, slickness, sleekness, **slipperiness,** lubricity; waxiness; creaminess; soapiness, saponaceousness

6 **lubrication,** lubricating, **oiling, greasing,** lubrification ; nonfriction; lubricity, lube <nf>, grease *or* lube job <nf>; **anointment,** unction, inunction; chrismatory, chrismation

7 lubritorium, lubritory; grease rack, grease pit; lubricator, oilcan, grease gun

VERBS **8** **oil,** grease; **lubricate,** lubrify ; **anoint,** salve, unguent, embrocate, dress, pour oil *or* balm upon; smear, daub; slick, slick on <nf>; pomade; lard; glycerolate, glycerinate, glycerinize; wax, beeswax; smooth the way *and* soap the way *and* grease the wheels <nf>; soap, lather

ADJS **9** **oily, greasy; unctuous,** unctional; unguinous; **oleaginous,** oleic; unguentary, **unguent,** unguentous; chrismal, chrismatory; **fat, fatty,** adipose; pinguid, pinguedinous, pinguescent; rich; sebaceous; blubbery, tallowy, suety; lardy, lardaceous; buttery, butyraceous; soapy, saponaceous; paraffinic; mucoid; smooth, slick, sleek, **slippery;** sebaceous; creamy; waxy, waxen, cereous, cerated

10 **lubricant,** lubricating, **lubricative,** lubricatory, lubricational; lenitive, unguentary, emollient, soothing, moisturizing

1057 RESINS, GUMS

NOUNS **1** **resin; gum,** gum resin; oleoresin; hard *or* varnish resin, vegetable resin; synthetic resin, plastic, resinoid; resene; **rosin,** colophony, colophonium, colophonone, resinate

VERBS **2** resin, resinize, resinate; rosin

ADJS **3** **resinous,** resinic, resiny; resinoid; rosiny; **gummy,** gummous, gumlike; pitchy

1058 MINERALS, METALS

NOUNS **1** **mineral** ; inorganic substance, lifeless matter found in nature; extracted matter *or* material; **mineral world** *or* **kingdom;** mineral resources; mineraloid, gel mineral, mineral aggregate; mineralization; crystalline element *or* compound; inorganic mineral, natural mineral, silicate, carbonate, oxide, sulfide, sulfate etc

2 **ore**, mineral; mineral-bearing material; unrefined *or* untreated mineral; natural *or* native mineral

3 **metal,** elementary metal ; metallics; native metals, alkali metals, earth metals, alkaline-earth metals, noble metals, precious metals, base metals, rare metals, rare-earth metals *or* elements; metalloid, semimetal, nonmetal; gold *or* silver bullion; gold dust; leaf metal, metal leaf, metal foil; metalwork, metalware; metallicity, metalleity

4 **alloy,** alloyage, fusion, compound; **amalgam**

5 **cast, casting; ingot, bullion;** pig, sow; sheet metal; button, gate, regulus

6 **mine,** pit; **quarry; diggings, workings;** open cut, opencast; bank; shaft; coal mine, colliery; strip mine; gold mine, silver mine, etc

7 **deposit,** mineral deposit, pay dirt; **vein, lode,** seam, dike, ore bed; shoot *or* chute, ore shoot *or* chute; chimney; stock; placer, placer deposit, placer gravel; country rock; lodestuff, gangue, matrix, veinstone

8 **mining;** coal mining, gold mining, etc; long-wall mining; room-and-pillar mining; strip mining; placer mining; hydraulic mining; prospecting; mining claim, lode claim, placer claim; gold fever; gold rush

9 **miner,** mineworker, pitman; coal miner, collier <Brit>; gold miner, gold digger; gold panner; placer miner; quarry miner; **prospector,** desert rat <nf>, sourdough; wildcatter; **forty-niner;** hand miner, rockman, powderman, driller, draw man; butty

10 **mineralogy;** mineralogical chemistry; crystallography; **petrology,** petrography, micropetrography; **geology;** mining geology, mining engineering

11 **metallurgy;** metallography, metallurgical chemistry, metallurgical engineering, physical metallurgy, powder metallurgy, electrometallurgy, hydrometallurgy, pyrometallurgy, production metallurgy, extractive metallurgy

12 **mineralogist; metallurgist,** electrometallurgist, metallurgical engineer; **petrologist,** petrographer; **geologist;** mining engineer

VERBS **13** mineralize; petrify 1046.7

14 **mine;** quarry; pan, pan for gold; prospect; hit pay dirt; mine out

ADJS **15** **mineral;** inorganic 1055.4; mineralized, petrified; asbestine, carbonous, graphitic, micaceous, alabastrine, quartzose, silicic; sulfurous, sulfuric; ore-bearing, ore-forming

16 **metal, metallic,** metallike, metalline, metalloid *or* metalloidal, metalliform; semimetallic; nonmetallic; metallo-organic *or* metallorganic, organometallic; bimetallic, trimetallic; metalliferous, metalbearing

17 brass, brassy, brazen; bronze, bronzy; copper, coppery, cuprous, cupreous; gold, golden, gilt, aureate; nickel, nickelic, nickelous, nickeline; silver, silvery; iron, ironlike, ferric, ferrous, ferruginous; steel, steely; tin, tinny; lead, leaden; pewter, pewtery; mercurial, mercurous, quicksilver; gold-filled, gold-plated, silver-plated, etc

18 **mineralogical, metallurgical,** petrological, crystallographic

1059 ROCK

NOUNS **1** **rock, stone** ; living rock, rock formation; **igneous rock,** plutonic *or* abyssal rock, hypabyssal rock, magmatic rock, acid rock, mafic rock, felsic rock, ultrabasic rock, ultramafic rock; volcanic rock, extrusive *or* effusive rock, scoria; magma, intrusive rock; granite, basalt, porphyry, **lava,** aa *and* pahoehoe <Hawaiian>; **sedimentary rock,** lithified sediment, stratified rock, clastic rock, nonclastic rock; limestone, sandstone; **metamorphic rock,** schist, gneiss; conglomerate, pudding stone, breccia, rubble, rubblestone, scree, talus, tuff, tufa, brash; sarsen, sarsen stone, druid stone; monolith; crag, craig; bedrock; mantlerock, regolith; saprolite, geest, laterite; building stone

2 **sand;** grain of sand; sands of the sea; sand pile, sand dune, sand hill; sand reef, sandbar

3 **gravel,** shingle, chesil <Brit>

4 **pebble,** pebblestone, gravelstone; jackstone *and* checkstone <nf>; fingerstone; slingstone; drakestone; spall

5 **boulder,** river boulder, shore boulder, glacial boulder

6 geological sediment, organic sediment, inorganic sediment, oceanic sediment, alluvial deposit, lake sediment, glacial deposit, eolian deposit; mud, sand, silt, clay, loess; rock, boulder, stone, gravel, granule, pebble

7 **precious stone, gem, gemstone** ; stone: crystal, crystal lattice, crystal system; semiprecious stone; gem of the first water; birthstone

8 petrification, petrifaction, lithification, crystallization; rock cycle, sedimentation, deposition, consolidation, cementation, compaction, magmatism, metamorphosis, recrystallization, foliation

9 geology, geoscience, petrology, crystallography; petrochemistry; petrogenesis

VERBS **10** petrify, lithify, crystallize, turn to stone; harden 1046.7

ADJS **11** **stone, rock,** lithic; petrified; petrogenic, petrescent; adamant, adamantine; flinty, flintlike; marbly, marblelike; granitic, granitelike; slaty, slatelike

12 **stony, rocky,** lapideous; stonelike, rocklike, lithoid *or* lithoidal; sandy, gritty 1051.12; gravelly, shingly, shingled; pebbly, pebbled; porphyritic, trachytic; crystal, crystalline; bouldery, rock- *or* boulder-strewn, rock-studded, rock-ribbed; craggy; monolithic

1060 CHEMISTRY, CHEMICALS

NOUNS **1** **chemistry,** chemical science, science of substances, science of matter; branch of chemistry

2 **element**, chemical element; table of elements, periodic table, periodic table of elements; **radical group;** free radical, diradical; **ion,** anion, cation; atom 1038.4; **molecule,** macromolecule; trace element, microelement, micronutrient, minor element; **chemical, chemical compound;** organic chemical, biochemical, inorganic chemical; fine chemicals, heavy chemicals; agent, **reagent;** metal, nonmetal, semimetal, metalloid, heavy metal, alkali metal, noble metal; alkaline-earth element, transition element, noble gas, rare-earth element, lanthanide, actinide, transuranic element, supertransuranic element, superheavy element; inert gas, rare gas; period, short period, long period; family, group; s-block, p-block, d-block, f-block; chemical equation

3 **acid;** hydracid, oxyacid, sulfacid; acidity; **base, alkali,** nonacid; pH; neutralizer, antacid; alkalinity

4 **valence,** valency <Brit>, positive valence, negative valence; monovalence, univalence, bivalence, trivalence, tervalence, quadrivalence, tetravalence, etc, multivalence, polyvalence; covalence, electrovalence

5 **atomic weight,** atomic mass, atomic volume, mass number; **molecular weight,** molecular mass, molecular volume; atomic number, valence number

6 **chemicalization,** chemical process, chemical action, chemism; **chemical apparatus,** beaker, Bunsen burner, burette, centrifuge, condenser, crucible, graduated cylinder *or* graduate, pipette, test tube

7 chemist, chemical scientist; agricultural chemist, analytical chemist, astrochemist, biochemist, inorganic chemist, organic chemist, physical chemist, physiochemist, theoretical chemist, etc

VERBS **8** **chemicalize,** chemical; alkalize, alkalinize, alkalify; acidify, acidulate, acetify; borate, carbonate, chlorinate, hydrate, hydrogenate, hydroxylate, nitrate, oxidize, reduce, pepsinate, peroxidize, phosphatize, sulfate, sulfatize, sulfonate; calcify, carburize, deuterate, esterify, fluorinate, fluoridate, halogenate, tritrate; isomerize, metamerize, polymerize, copolymerize, homopolymerize; ferment, work; catalyze 806.4; electrolyze; bond, intercalate, invert, neutralize, ionize

ADJS 9 **chemical;** astrochemical, biochemical, chemicobiologic; physicochemical, physiochemical, chemicophysical, chemicobiological, chemicophysiologic *or* chemicophysiological, chemicodynamic, chemicoengineering, chemicomechanical, chemicomineralogical, chemicopharmaceutical, chemurgic, electrochemical, iatrochemical, chemotherapeutic *or* chemotherapeutical, chemophysiologic *or* chemophysiological, macrochemical, microchemical, physicochemical, phytochemical, photochemical, radiochemical, thermochemical, zoochemical; organic, inorganic; elemental, elementary; acid; alkaline, alkali, nonacid, basic; isomeric, isomerous, metameric, metamerous, heteromerous, polymeric, polymerous, copolymeric, copolymerous, monomeric, monomerous, dimeric, dimerous, etc

10 valent; univalent, monovalent, monatomic, bivalent, trivalent, tervalent, quadrivalent, tetravalent, etc, multivalent, polyvalent; covalent, electrovalent

1061 LIQUIDITY

NOUNS 1 **liquidity, fluidity,** fluidness, liquidness, liquefaction 1064; wateriness; rheuminess, runniness; **juiciness,** sappiness, succulence; milkiness, lactescence; lactation; chylifaction, chylification; serosity; suppuration; **moisture, wetness** 1065.1; **fluency,** flow, flowage, flux, fluxion, fluxility ; **circulation;** turbulence, turbidity, turbulent flow; streamline flow; hemorrhage; suppuration, secretion; liquid state; solubleness; fluid mechanics, hydrology

2 **fluid, liquid;** liquor 10.49, drink, beverage; liquid extract, fluid extract, condensation; **juice, sap,** latex, extract; milk, whey, buttermilk, ghee; water 1065.3; **body fluid, blood;** stock, meat juice, gravy, sauce, soup; semiliquid 1062.5; fluid mechanics, hydraulics, etc 1039.4; solvent, liquefier, liquefacient; solution, infusion, decoction

3 flowmeter, fluidmeter, hydrometer, sphygmomanometer

ADJS 4 **fluid,** fluidal, fluidic, **fluent, flowing,** fluxible *or* fluxile , fluxional, fluxionary, runny; circulatory, **circulation,** turbid; **liquid,** liquidy; watery 1065.16; **juicy,** sappy, succulent, moist; **wet** 1065.15; uncongealed, unclotted; rheumy; bloody; liquefied, liquefying, liquefiable

5 **milky,** lacteal, lacteous, **lactic;** lactescent, lactiferous; milk, milch

1062 SEMILIQUIDITY

NOUNS 1 **semiliquidity,** semifluidity; butteriness, creaminess; pulpiness 1063

2 **viscosity,** viscidity, viscousness, slabbiness, lentor ; thickness, spissitude , heaviness, stodginess; **stickiness, tackiness,** glutinousness, glutinosity, toughness, tenaciousness, tenacity, **adhesiveness,** clinginess, clingingness, **gumminess,** gauminess <nf>, gumlikeness; **ropiness, stringiness;** clamminess, sliminess, mucilaginousness; gooeyness *and* gunkiness <nf>; **gluiness,** gluelikeness; syrupiness, treacliness <Brit>; gelatinousness, jellylikeness, gelatinity, gelation; colloidality; doughiness, pastiness; **thickening,** curdling, clotting, coagulation, incrassation, inspissation, clabbering *and* loppering *or* lobbering <nf>, jellification

3 **mucosity,** mucidness, mucousness, pituitousness , snottiness <nf>; **sliminess**

4 **muddiness,** muckiness, miriness, **slushiness,** sloshiness, sludginess,

sloppiness, slobbiness, slabbiness , squashiness, squelchiness, **ooziness**; **turbidity,** turbidness, dirtiness

5 **semiliquid,** semifluid; **goo** *and* goop *and* gook *and* gunk *and* glop <nf>, sticky mess, gaum <nf>; **paste,** pap, pudding, putty, **butter,** cream; **pulp** 1063.2; **jelly,** gelatin *or* gelatine, jell, gel, jam, agar, isinglass; **glue;** size; **gluten;** mucilage; mucus; **dough,** batter; mousse, pudding; **syrup,** molasses, treacle <Brit>, honey; egg white, albumen, glair; starch, cornstarch; **curd,** clabber, bonnyclabber; gruel, porridge, loblolly <nf>; soup, gumbo, gravy, purée, pulp; yogurt

6 **gum** 1057.1, chewing gum, bubble gum; chicle, chicle gum

7 **emulsion,** emulsoid; emulsification; emulsifier; **colloid,** colloider

8 **mud, muck, mire, slush, slosh,** sludge, squash, swill, **slime; slop, ooze, mire;** clay, slip; gumbo; gook *or* gunk *or* gook *or* glop *or* guck <nf>

9 **mud puddle, puddle,** loblolly <nf>, slop; **mudhole,** slough, muckhole, chuckhole, chughole <nf>; hog wallow

VERBS 10 **emulsify,** emulsionize; colloid, colloidize; cream; churn, whip, beat up; **thicken,** inspissate, incrassate, curdle, clot, coagulate, congeal, clabber *and* lopper <nf>; jell, jelly, jellify, gel

ADJS 11 **semiliquid,** semifluid, semifluidic; buttery; creamy; emulsive, colloidal; **pulpy** 1063.6; half-frozen, half-melted

12 **viscous, viscid,** viscose, slabby; **thick,** heavy, stodgy, soupy, thickened, inspissated, incrassated; curdled, clotted, grumous, coagulated, clabbered *and* loppered <nf>; **sticky, tacky,** tenacious, adhesive, clingy, clinging, tough; gluey, gluelike, glutinous, glutenous, glutinose; gumbo, gumbolike; **gummy,** gaumy <nf>, gummous, gumlike, **syrupy;** treacly <Brit>; ropy, stringy; mucilaginous, clammy, slimy, slithery; gooey *and* gunky *and* gloppy *and* goopy *and* gooky <nf>; **gelatinous,** jellylike, jellied, jelled; tremelloid *or* tremellose; glairy; **doughy, pasty;** starchy, amylaceous; pulpy, soft, mushy

13 **mucous,** muculent, mucoid, mucinous, pituitous , phlegmy, snotty <nf>; mucific, muciferous

14 **slimy; muddy,** miry, mucky, **slushy, sloshy,** sludgy, sloppy, slobby, slabby , splashy, **squashy,** squishy, **squelchy, oozy,** sloughy, plashy, sposhy <nf>; **turbid, dirty**

1063 PULPINESS

NOUNS 1 **pulpiness,** pulpousness; softness 1047; flabbiness; **mushiness,** mashiness, squashiness, creaminess; **pastiness,** doughiness; **sponginess,** pithiness; fleshiness, overripeness, succulence

2 **pulp, paste, mash, mush,** smash, squash, crush; tomato paste *or* pulp; pudding, porridge, sponge; sauce, butter; poultice, cataplasm, plaster; pith; paper pulp, wood pulp, sulfate pulp, sulfite pulp, rag pulp; pulpwood; pulp lead, white lead; dental *or* tooth pulp

3 **pulping,** pulpification, pulpefaction; blending, steeping; digestion; **maceration,** mastication

4 **pulper,** pulpifier, macerator, pulp machine *or* engine, digester; **masher,** smasher, potato masher, ricer, beetle; blender, food processor, food mill

VERBS 5 **pulp,** pulpify; **macerate,** masticate, chew; regurgitate; **mash,** smash, squash, crush

ADJS 6 **pulpy,** pulpous, pulpal, pulpar, pulplike, pulped; **pasty,** doughy; pultaceous; **mushy;** macerated, masticated, chewed; regurgitated; **squashy,** squelchy, squishy; soft, flabby; fleshy, succulent; **spongy,** pithy

1064 LIQUEFACTION

NOUNS 1 **liquefaction,** liquefying, liquidizing, liquidization, fluidification, fluidization; liquescence *or* liquescency, deliquescence, deliquiation *and* deliquium ; **solution,** dissolution, dissolving; **infusion,** soaking, steeping, brewing; **melting,** thawing, running, fusing, fusion; decoagulation, unclotting; solubilization; colliquation; lixiviation, percolation, leaching

2 **solubility,** solubleness, dissolvability, dissolvableness, dissolubility, dissolubleness; meltability, fusibility

3 **solution;** decoction, infusion, mixture; chemical solution; lixivium, leach, leachate; **suspension,** colloidal suspension; **emulsion,** gel, aerosol

4 **solvent**, dissolvent, dissolver, dissolving agent, resolvent, resolutive, **thinner,** diluent; anticoagulant; liquefier, liquefacient; menstruum; universal solvent, alkahest; flux

VERBS 5 **liquefy,** liquidize, liquesce, fluidify, fluidize; **melt, run,** thaw, colliquate; melt down; fuse, flux; deliquesce; **dissolve,** solve; thin, cut; solubilize; hold in solution; unclot, decoagulate; leach, lixiviate, percolate; **infuse,** decoct, steep, soak, brew

ADJS 6 **liquefied, melted, molten,** thawed; unclotted, decoagulated; in solution, in suspension, liquescent, deliquescent; colloidal

7 **liquefying,** liquefactive; colliquative, melting, fusing, thawing; **dissolving,** dissolutive, dissolutional

8 **solvent,** dissolvent, resolvent, resolutive, thinning, cutting, diluent; alkahestic

9 liquefiable; **meltable,** fusible, thawable; **soluble, dissolvable,** dissoluble; water-soluble

1065 MOISTURE

NOUNS 1 **moisture,** damp, wet; **dampness, moistness,** moistiness, **wetness,** wettedness, wettishness, **wateriness,** humor *or* humectation ; soddenness, soppiness, soppingness, sogginess; swampiness, bogginess, marshiness; dewiness; mistiness, fogginess 319.4; raininess, pluviosity, showeriness; rainfall; exudation 190.6; secretion 13

2 **humidity,** humidness, **dankness,** dankishness, **mugginess,** closeness, stickiness, sweatiness; absolute humidity, relative humidity; dew point, saturation, saturation point; humidification

3 **water,** *aqua* <L>, *agua* <Sp>, *eau* <Fr>; Adam's ale *or* wine, H_2O; hydrol; hard water, soft water; heavy water; water supply, water system, waterworks; drinking water, tap water; rain water, rain 316; snowmelt, melt water; **groundwater,** underground water, subsurface water, subterranean water; water table, aquifer, artesian basin, artesian spring, sinkhole; spring water, well water; seawater, salt water; limewater; fresh water; standing water; mineral water *or* waters; soda water, carbonated water; steam, water vapor; hydrosphere; hydrometeor; head, hydrostatic head; hydrothermal water; distilled water; wetting agent, wetting-out agent, liquidizer, moisturizer; humidifier; bottled water, commercially bottled water, designer water <nf>; water cycle, hydrological cycle, evaporation, transpiration, precipitation, runoff, percolation

4 **dew, dewdrops,** dawn *or* morning dew, night dew, evening damp; fog drip, false dew; guttation; haze, mist, fog, cloud

5 **sprinkle, spray,** sparge, shower; spindrift, spume, froth, foam; **splash,** plash, swash, slosh; **splatter,** spatter

6 **wetting, moistening, dampening,** damping; humidification; dewing, bedewing; **watering, irrigation;** hosing, wetting *or* hosing down; **sprinkling, spraying,** spritzing <nf>, sparging, aspersion, aspergation; **splashing,** swashing, splattering, spattering; affusion, baptism; bath, bathing, rinsing, laving; **flooding,** drowning, inundation, deluge; **immersion, submersion** 367.2

7 **soaking,** soakage, soaking through, sopping, **drenching,** imbruement, sousing; ducking, dunking <nf>; soak, drench, souse; **saturation,** permeation; waterlogging; **steeping,** maceration, seething, infusion, brewing, imbuement; injection,

impregnation; infiltration, percolation, leaching, lixiviation; pulping 1063.3

8 **sprinkler,** sparger, sparge, sprayer, speed sprayer, concentrate sprayer, mist concentrate sprayer, spray, spray can, atomizer, aerosol; nozzle; aspergil, aspergillum; **shower,** shower bath, shower head, needle bath; syringe, fountain syringe, douche, enema, clyster; sprinkling *or* watering can; water pistol *or* gun, squirt gun; lawn sprinkler; sprinkling system, sprinkler head; hydrant, irrigator

9 <sciences> hygrology, hygrometry, psychrometry, hydrography, hydrology; hydraulics; hydrotherapy, hydrotherapeutics, taking the waters

10 <instruments> hygrometer, hair hygrometer, hygrograph, hygrodeik, hygroscope, hygrothermograph; psychrometer, sling psychrometer; hydrostat; rain gauge *or* pluviometer; hydrograph; humidor; hygrostat

VERBS 11 be damp, not have a dry thread; **drip,** weep; **seep, ooze,** percolate; exude 190.15; sweat; secrete 13.5

12 **moisten, dampen,** moisturize, damp, **wet,** wet down; humidify, humect *or* humectate ; **water, irrigate;** dew, bedew; **sprinkle,** besprinkle, **spray,** spritz <nf>, sparge, asperge; bepiss; **splash,** dash, **swash, slosh, splatter, spatter,** bespatter; dabble, paddle; slop, slobber; hose, hose down; syringe, douche; sponge; dilute, adulterate

13 **soak, drench,** imbrue, **souse, sop,** sodden; **saturate,** permeate; **bathe,** lave, wash, rinse, douche, flush; water-soak, waterlog; **steep,** seethe, macerate, infuse, imbue, brew, impregnate, inject, injest; infiltrate, percolate, leach, lixiviate

14 **flood,** float, **inundate, deluge,** turn to a lake *or* sea, swamp, whelm, overwhelm, drown; duck, dip, dunk <nf>; **submerge** 367.7; sluice, pour on, flow on; rain 316.10

ADJS 15 **moist,** moisty; **damp,** dampish; **wet,** wettish; undried, tacky; **humid, dank, muggy, sticky;** dewy, bedewed, roric *and* roriferous ; rainy 316.11; marshy, swampy, fenny, boggy

16 **watery,** waterish, **aqueous, aquatic;** liquid; **splashy,** plashy, sloppy, swashy <Brit>; hydrous, hydrated; hydraulic; moist; hydrodynamic, hydraulic

17 **soaked, drenched,** soused, bathed, steeped, macerated; **saturated,** permeated; **watersoaked, waterlogged; soaking, sopping; wringing wet,** soaking wet, sopping wet, wet to the skin, like a drowned rat; **sodden,** soppy, **soggy,** soaky; dripping, **dripping wet;** dribbling, seeping, weeping, oozing; flooded, overflowed, whelmed, swamped, engulfed, inundated, deluged, drowned, submerged, submersed, immersed, dipped, dunked <nf>; awash, weltering

18 wetting, dampening, moistening, watering, humectant; **drenching, soaking,** sopping; **irrigational,** irriguous

19 hygric, hygrometric, hygroscopic, hygrophilous, hygrothermal

1066 DRYNESS

NOUNS 1 **dryness, aridness,** aridity, waterlessness, siccity; **drought;** juicelessness, saplessness; **thirst,** thirstiness, dehydration, xerostomia; corkiness; watertightness, watertight integrity; parchedness

2 <comparisons> desert, dust, bone, parchment, stick, mummy, biscuit, cracker

3 **drying, desiccation,** drying up, exsiccation; **dehydration,** anhydration; evaporation; air-drying; blow-drying; freeze-drying; insolation, sunning; drainage; withering, mummification; dehumidification; blotting

4 **drier,** desiccator, desiccative, siccative, exsiccative, exsiccator, **dehydrator,** dehydrant; dehumidifier; evaporator; hair-drier, blow-dryer; clothes dryer; tumbler-dryer; absorbent; clothesline

VERBS 5 thirst; drink up, soak up, sponge up; parch

6 **dry, desiccate,** exsiccate, dry up, **dehydrate,** anhydrate; evaporate;

dehumidify; air-dry; drip-dry; dry off; insolate, sun, sun-dry; hang out to dry, air; spin-dry, tumbler-dry; blow-dry; freeze-dry; smoke, smoke-dry; cure; torrefy, burn, fire, kiln, **bake, parch,** scorch, sear; **wither, shrivel;** wizen, weazen; mummify; sponge, blot, soak up; **wipe,** rub, swab, brush; towel; drain 192.12; evaporate

ADJS 7 **dry, arid; waterless,** unwatered, undamped, anhydrous; **bone-dry,** dry as dust, dry as a bone; like parchment, parched; droughty; juiceless, sapless; moistureless; **thirsty,** thirsting, athirst; high and dry; sandy, dusty; desert, Saharan

8 rainless, fine, fair, bright and fair, pleasant

9 **dried, dehydrated, desiccated,** dried-up, exsiccated; evaporated; squeezed dry; **parched, baked,** sunbaked, burnt, scorched, **seared,** sere, sun-dried, adust; wind-dried, air-dried; drip-dried; blow-dried; freeze-dried; **withered, shriveled,** wizened, weazened; corky; mummified

10 **drying, dehydrating, desiccative,** desiccant, exsiccative, exsiccant, siccative, siccant; evaporative

11 **watertight, waterproof,** moistureproof, dampproof, leakproof, seepproof, dripproof, stormproof, stormtight, rainproof, raintight, showerproof, floodproof; dry-shod

1067 VAPOR, GAS

NOUNS 1 **vapor,** volatile; **fume, reek,** exhalation, breath, effluvium, expiration; fluid; **miasma,** mephitis, malaria , fetid air, fumes; **smoke,** smudge; smog; wisp *or* plume *or* puff of smoke; **damp,** chokedamp, blackdamp, firedamp, afterdamp; **steam,** water vapor; **cloud** 319

2 **gas** ; rare *or* noble *or* inert gas, halogen gas; fluid, compressible fluid; **atmosphere, air** 317; pneumatics, aerodynamics 1039.5

3 **vaporousness,** vaporiness; vapor pressure *or* tension; **aeriness; ethereality,** etherialism; **gaseousness,** gaseous state, gassiness, gaseity; **gas,** stomach gas, gassiness, flatulence, flatus, wind, windiness, farting <nf>, flatuosity ; burping; fluidity

4 **volatility,** vaporability, vaporizability, evaporability

5 **vaporization, evaporation,** volatilization, gasification; sublimation; distillation, fractionation; etherification; aeration, aerification; fluidization; atomization; exhalation; fumigation; smoking; steaming; etherealization; exhalation

6 vaporizer, evaporator; atomizer, aerosol, spray; propellant; condenser; still, retort

7 vaporimeter, manometer, pressure gauge; gas meter, gasometer; pneumatometer, spirometer; aerometer, airometer; eudiometer

VERBS 8 **vaporize, evaporate,** volatilize, **gasify;** sublimate, sublime; distill, fractionate; etherify; **aerate,** aerify; carbonate, oxygenate, hydrogenate, chlorinate, halogenate, etc; atomize, spray; fluidize; **reek, fume;** exhale, give off, emit, send out, exhale; **smoke; steam;** fumigate, perfume; **etherize**

ADJS 9 **vaporous,** vaporish, vapory, vaporlike; **airy, aerial, ethereal,** atmospheric; **gaseous,** in the gaseous state, gasified, gassy, gaslike, gasiform, fizzy, carbonated; vaporing; **reeking,** reeky; miasmic *or* miasmal *or* miasmatic, mephitic, fetid, effluvial; **fuming,** fumy; smoky, smoking, smoggy; steamy, steaming; ozonic; oxygenous; oxyacetylene; pneumatic, aerostatic, aerodynamic

10 **volatile,** volatilizable; **vaporable,** vaporizable, vaporescent, vaporific; **evaporative,** evaporable

1068 BIOLOGY

NOUNS 1 **biology**, biological science, life science, the science of life, the study of living things; **botany**, plant biology, phytobiology, phytology, plant science; **plant kingdom,** vegetable kingdom; **plants** 310, flora, plantlife; **zoology**, animal biology, animal science; **animal kingdom,** kingdom Animalia, phylum, class,

order, family, genus, species; **animals** 311, fauna, animal life
2 **biologist, naturalist,** life scientist; **botanist,** plant scientist, plant biologist, phytobiologist, phytologist; **zoologist,** animal biologist, animal scientist <for other agent NOUNS add -ist *or* -er to names of branches listed>
3 life science; natural history, biological science; anatomy, biochemistry, biology, biophysics, botany, cell biology, embryology, ethnobiology, microbiology, paleontology, pathology, physiology, zoology; taxonomy, systematics; nanoscience

ADJS 4 **biological,** biologic, microbiological; **botanical,** botanic, plant, phytological, phytologic, phytobiological; **zoological,** zoologic, faunal <for other ADJS add -ic *or* -ical to the names of branches listed>

1069 AGRICULTURE

NOUNS 1 **agriculture, farming**, husbandry; cultivation, culture, geoponics, tillage, tilth; green revolution; agrology, agronomy, agronomics, agrotechnology, agricultural science, agroscience, agriscience; thremmatology; agroecosystem; agrogeology, agricultural geology; agrochemistry; agricultural engineering; agricultural economics; rural economy *or* economics, farm economy *or* economics, agrarian economy *or* economics, agrarianism, agrarian society; agribusiness *or* agrobusiness, agribiz <nf>, agroindustry; sharecropping; intensive farming, factory farming, mixed farming, crop farming, organic farming, subsistence farming
2 **horticulture, gardening;** landscape gardening, landscape architecture, groundskeeping; truck gardening, market gardening, olericulture; flower gardening, flower-growing, floriculture; viniculture, viticulture; orcharding, fruit-growing, pomiculture, citriculture; arboriculture, silviculture; indoor gardening
3 **forestry,** arboriculture, tree farming, silviculture, forest management; Christmas tree farming; forestation, afforestation, reforestation; lumbering, logging; deforestation; woodcraft
4 <agricultural deities> vegetation spirit *or* daemon, fertility god *or* spirit, year-daemon, forest god *or* spirit, green man, corn god, Ceres, Demeter, Gaea, Triptolemus, Dionysus, Persephone, Kore, Flora, Aristaeus, Pomona, Frey
5 **agriculturist,** agriculturalist; agrologist, agronomist; **farmer,** granger, husbandman, **yeoman,** cultivator, tiller, sodbuster, **tiller of the soil;** rural economist, agrotechnician; boutique farmer, contour farmer, crop-farmer, dirt farmer <nf>, truck farmer, etc; gentleman-farmer; **peasant**, countryman, rustic; **grower,** raiser; **planter,** tea-planter, coffee-planter, etc; peasant holder *or* proprietor; tenant farmer, crofter <Brit>, peasant farmer; sharecropper, cropper, collective farm worker, *kibbutznik* <Yiddish>; **agricultural worker, farm worker,** farmhand, farm laborer, migrant *or* migratory worker *or* laborer, bracero, picker; plowman, plowboy; farmboy, farmgirl; planter, sower; reaper, harvester, harvestman; haymaker
6 **horticulturist, nurseryman, gardener,** grower, green thumb, propagator; landscape gardener, landscapist, landscape architect; truck gardener, market gardener, olericulturist; **florist,** floriculturist; vinegrower, viniculturist, viticulturist, vintager; *vigneron* <Fr>; vinedresser; orchardist, orchardman, fruitgrower
7 **forester;** arboriculturist, arborist, silviculturist, dendrologist, verderer, tree farmer, topiarist; conservationist; **ranger,** forest ranger, forest manager; woodsman, woodman <Brit>, woodcraftsman, woodlander; **logger, lumberman,** timberman, lumberjack, lumberer; woodcutter, wood chopper; tapper; tree surgeon
8 **farm,** farmplace, farmstead, farmhold , farmery <Brit>, farmlet; **grange**, pen <Jamaica>; boutique farm, crop farm, dirt farm, tree

farm, etc; **plantation,** cotton plantation, etc, *hacienda* <Sp>; croft, homecroft <Brit>; **homestead,** steading; toft <Brit>; mains <Brit nf>; demesne, homefarm, demesne farm, manor farm; **barnyard,** farmyard, barton <Brit nf>; collective farm, *kibbutz* <Heb>; farmland, cropland, arable land, plowland, fallow; grassland, pasture 310.8

9 **field, tract,** plat, **plot, patch,** piece *or* parcel of land; cultivated land; clearing; hayfield, corn field, wheat field, etc; paddy, paddy field, rice paddy

10 **garden,** *jardin* <Fr>; bed, **flower bed,** border, ornamental border; paradise; garden spot; **vineyard,** vinery, grapery, grape ranch; herbarium; botanical garden; compost pile *or* heap, seed tray

11 **nursery; conservatory, greenhouse,** glasshouse <Brit>, forcing house, summerhouse, lathhouse, **hothouse,** coolhouse; potting shed; force *or* forcing bed, forcing pit, **hotbed,** cold frame; seedbed; cloche; pinery, orangery

12 **growing, raising,** rearing, cultivation; **green thumb**

13 **cultivation,** cultivating, culture, **tilling,** dressing, working; harrowing, plowing, contour plowing, furrowing, listing, fallowing, weeding, hoeing, pruning, thinning; overcropping, overcultivation; irrigation, overirrigation

14 **planting,** setting; **sowing, seeding,** semination, insemination; breeding, hydridizing; **dissemination,** broadcast, broadcasting; transplantation, resetting; retimbering, reforestation

15 **harvest,** harvesting, **reaping, gleaning,** gathering, cutting; nutting; cash crop, root crop, **crop** 472.5

VERBS 16 **farm, ranch,** work the land; **grow, raise,** rear; crop; dry-farm; sharecrop; **garden; have a green thumb**

17 **cultivate,** culture, **dress, work, till,** till the soil, dig, delve, spade; mulch; **plow,** plow in, plow under, plow up, list, fallow, backset <W US>, double-dig, rototill, fork; take cuttings, graft; irrigate; **harrow,** rake; **weed,** weed out, hoe, cut, prune, thin, thin out; force; overcrop, overcultivate; slash and burn; top-dress, compost, fertilize 890.8

18 **plant,** implant , **set,** put in; **sow, seed,** seed down, seminate, inseminate; **disseminate,** broadcast, sow broadcast, scatter seed; drill; bed; dibble; transplant, reset, pot, **transplant;** vernalize; **forest,** afforest; deforest; retimber, reforest

19 **harvest, reap,** crop, **glean, gather,** gather in, bring in, get in the harvest, reap and carry; **pick,** pluck; dig, grabble; mow, cut; hay; nut; crop herbs

ADJS 20 **agricultural, agrarian,** agro-, geoponic, geoponical, agronomic, agronomical; farm, **farming;** arable; rustic, bucolic **rural** 233.6

21 **horticultural;** olericultural; vinicultural, viticultural; arboricultural, silvicultural

1070 ANIMAL HUSBANDRY

NOUNS 1 **animal husbandry,** animal rearing *or* raising *or* culture, stock raising, **ranching;** zooculture, zootechnics, zootechny; thremmatology; gnotobiotics; herding, grazing, keeping flocks and herds, running livestock, livestock farming; transhumance; breeding, stockbreeding, stirpiculture; horse training, dressage, manÈge; horsemanship; pisciculture, fish culture; apiculture, bee culture, beekeeping; cattle raising; sheepherding; stock farming, fur farming; factory farming; pig-keeping; dairy-farming, chicken-farming, pig-farming, etc; cattle-ranching, mink-ranching, etc

2 **stockman,** stock raiser, stockkeeper; breeder, stockbreeder; sheepman; cattleman, cow keeper, cowman, grazier <Brit>; **rancher,** ranchman, ranchero; ranchhand; dairyman, dairy farmer; milkmaid; **stableman,** stableboy, **groom,** hostler, equerry; trainer, breaker, tamer; broncobuster *and* buckaroo <nf>; **blacksmith,** horseshoer, farrier

3 **herder, drover, herdsman,** herdboy; **shepherd,** shepherdess, **sheepherder,** sheepman; goatherd; swineherd, pigman, pigherd, hogherd; gooseherd, gooseboy, goosegirl; swanherd; **cowherd,** neatherd <Brit>; cowboy, cowgirl, cowhand, puncher *and* **cowpuncher** *and* cowpoke <nf>, waddy <W US>, cowman, cattleman, vaquero <Sp>, gaucho; horseherd, **wrangler,** horse wrangler

4 **apiarist,** apiculturist, **beekeeper,** beeherd

5 **farm,** stock farm, animal farm; **ranch,** rancho, rancheria; horse farm, stable, stud farm; **cattle ranch;** dude ranch; pig farm, piggery; chicken farm *or* ranch, turkey farm, duck farm, poultry farm; sheep farm *or* ranch; fur farm *or* ranch, mink farm *or* ranch; **dairy farm;** factory farm; animal enclosure

VERBS 6 **raise, breed,** rear, grow, hatch, feed, nurture, fatten; keep, run; ranch, farm; culture; back-breed

7 **tend; groom,** rub down, brush, curry, currycomb; water, drench, feed, fodder; bed, bed down, litter; milk; harness, saddle, hitch, bridle, yoke; gentle, handle, manage; tame, train, break

8 **drive, herd,** drove <Brit>, herd up, punch cattle, **shepherd,** ride herd on; spur, goad, prick, lash, whip; wrangle, round up; corral, cage

1071 EARTH SCIENCE

NOUNS 1 **earth science, earth sciences** ; geoscience; geography, geology, rock hunting *and* rock hounding <nf>, geological science, oceanography, oceanographic science, meteorology, atmospheric science, planetary science, space science

2 **earth scientist,** geoscientist; **geologist,** rock hound *and* rock hunter <nf>, **geographer, oceanographer, astronomer,** star-gazer <nf>, **meteorologist,** weather man <for other agent NOUNS, add -ist *or* -er to names of branches listed below>

1072 THE UNIVERSE, ASTRONOMY

NOUNS 1 **universe, world, cosmos,** cosmological model; creation, created universe, created nature, all, **all creation,** all tarnation <nf>, all *or* everything that is, all being, totality, totality of being, sum of things; omneity, allness; nature, system; wide world, whole wide world; plenum; **macrocosm,** macrocosmos, megacosm; metagalaxy; open universe, closed universe, inflationary universe, flat universe, oscillating universe, steady-state universe, expanding universe, pulsating universe; Einsteinian universe, Newtonian universe, Friedmann universe; Ptolemaic universe, Copernican universe; sidereal universe

2 **the heavens,** heaven, **sky, firmament;** empyrean, welkin, *caelum* <L>, lift *or* lifts <nf>; **the blue,** blue sky, azure, cerulean, the blue serene; **ether, air,** hyaline; vault, cope, canopy, vault *or* canopy of heaven, starry sphere, celestial sphere, starry heaven *or* heavens; Caelus

3 **space, outer space,** cosmic space, deep space, empty space, ether space, pressureless space, celestial spaces, interplanetary *or* interstellar *or* intergalactic *or* intercosmic space, metagalactic space, **the void,** the void above, ocean of emptiness; chaos; outermost reaches of space; astronomical unit, light-year, parsec; interstellar medium; close encounter

4 **stars,** fixed stars, starry host; music *or* harmony of the spheres; orb, sphere; **heavenly body,** celestial body *or* sphere; **comet; comet cloud; morning star,** daystar, Lucifer, Phosphor, Phosphorus; **evening star,** Vesper, Hesper, Hesperus, Venus; **North Star,** polestar, polar star, lodestar, Polaris; Dog Star, Sirius, Canicula; Bull's Eye, Aldebaran

5 **constellation, configuration,** asterism, stellar group, stellar population; zodiacal constellation; cluster, **star cluster,** galactic cluster, open

cluster, globular cluster, stellar association, supercluster; Magellanic clouds

6 **galaxy, island universe,** galactic nebula; spiral galaxy *or* nebula, spiral; barred spiral galaxy *or* nebula, barred spiral; elliptical *or* spheroidal galaxy; disk galaxy; irregular galaxy; radio galaxy; lenticular galaxy, active galaxy; Seyfert galaxy, starburst galaxy; **the Local Group; the Galaxy, the Milky Way,** the galactic circle, *Via Lactea* <L>; galactic cluster, supergalaxy; great attractor; chaotic attractor; continent of galaxies, great wall *or* sheet of galaxies; galactic coordinates, galactic pole, galactic latitude, galactic longitude; galactic noise, cosmic noise; galactic nucleus, active galactic nucleus; cosmic string; Hubble classification

7 **nebula,** nebulosity; gaseous nebula; hydrogen cloud; dark nebula; dust cloud; dark matter; interstellar cloud; planetary nebula; whirlpool nebula; cirro-nebula; ring nebula; diffuse nebula; emission nebula; reflection nebula; absorption nebula; galactic nebula; anagalactic nebula; bright diffuse nebula; dark nebula, dark cloud, coalsack; Nebula of Lyra *or* Orion, Crab Nebula, the Coalsack, Black Magellanic Cloud; nebulous stars; nebular hypothesis

8 **star** ; **quasar,** quasi-stellar radio source; **pulsar,** pulsating star, eclipsing binary X-ray pulsar; luminary; Nemesis, the Death Star; Hawking radiation; magnitude, stellar magnitude, visual magnitude; relative magnitude, absolute magnitude, apparent nebula; star *or* stellar populations; mass-luminosity law; spectrum-luminosity diagram, Hertzsprung-Russell diagram; star catalog, star atlas, star chart, sky atlas, sky survey, Messier catalog, Dreyer's New General Catalog *or* NGC; star cloud, star cluster, globular cluster, open cluster; Pleiades *or* Seven Sisters, Hyades, Beehive; stellar evolution, stellar birth, protostar, molecular cloud, main sequence, gravitational collapse, dying star, red giant, whife dwarf; nova, supernova, supernova remnant, neutron star, pulsar, **black hole,** giant black hole, mini-black hole, starving black hole, supermassive black hole, frozen black hole, event horizon, singularity, white hole, active galactic nucleus

9 **planet,** wanderer, wandering star, terrestrial planet, inferior planet, superior planet, secondary planet, major planet; minor planet, planetoid, asteroid; asteroid belt; Earth; Jupiter; Mars, the Red Planet; Mercury; Neptune; Pluto; Saturn; Uranus; Venus; solar system; syzygy

10 **Earth, planet Earth,** third planet, the world, *terra* <L>; **globe,** terrestrial globe, Spaceship Earth, the blue planet; geosphere, biosphere, magnetosphere; vale, vale of tears; Mother Earth, Ge *or* Gaea *or* Gaia, Tellus *or* Terra; whole wide world, four corners of the earth, the length and breadth of the land

11 **moon, satellite,** natural satellite; orb of night, queen of heaven, queen of night; silvery moon; **new moon,** wet moon; **crescent moon,** crescent, increscent moon, increscent, waxing moon, waxing crescent moon, first quarter, last quarter; decrescent moon, decrescent, waning moon, waning crescent moon; gibbous moon; **half-moon,** demilune; **full moon, harvest moon,** hunter's moon; horned moon; **eclipse,** lunar eclipse, eclipse of the moon; artificial satellite 1075.6

12 <moon goddess, the moon personified> Diana, Phoebe, Cynthia, Artemis, Hecate, Selene, Luna, Astarte, Ashtoreth; man in the moon

13 **sun;** orb of day, daystar; sunshine, solar radiation, sunlight; solar disk; photosphere, chromosphere, corona; sunspot; sunspot cycle; solar flare, solar prominence; solar wind; **eclipse,** eclipse of the sun, solar eclipse, total eclipse, partial eclipse, central eclipse, annular eclipse; corona, solar corona, Baily's beads

14 <sun god *or* goddess, the sun personified> Sol, Helios, Hyperion, Titan, Phaëthon, Phoebus, Phoebus

Apollo, Apollo, Ra *or* Amen-Ra, Shamash, Surya, Savitar, Amaterasu

15 **meteor;** falling *or* shooting star, meteoroid, fireball, bolide; **meteorite,** meteorolite; micrometeoroid, micrometeorite; aerolite; chondrite; siderite; siderolite; tektite; meteor dust, cosmic dust; meteor trail, meteor train; meteor swarm; meteor *or* meteoric shower; radiant, radiant point; meteor crater

16 **orbit, circle, trajectory;** circle of the sphere, great circle, small circle; **ecliptic; zodiac;** zone; meridian, celestial meridian; colures, equinoctial colure, solstitial colure; equator, celestial equator, equinoctial, equinoctial circle *or* line; equinox, vernal equinox, autumnal equinox; longitude, celestial longitude, geocentric longitude, heliocentric longitude, galactic longitude, astronomical longitude, geographic *or* geodetic longitude; apogee, perigee; aphelion, perihelion; period; revolution, eccentric inclination, rotation, rotational axis, rotational period; parabolic orbit, hyperbolic orbit

17 **observatory,** astronomical observatory; radio observatory, orbiting astronomical observatory *or* OAO, orbiting solar observatory *or* OSO; ground-based observatory, optical observatory, infrared observatory; **planetarium;** orrery; **telescope,** astronomical telescope; planisphere, astrolabe, flux collector; reflector, refractor, Newtonian telescope, Cassegrainian telescope; **radio telescope,** radar telescope; **spectroscope,** spectrograph; spectrohelioscope, spectroheliograph; coronagraph; heliostat, coelostat; **observation;** seeing, bright time, dark time

18 **cosmology,** cosmography, **cosmogony;** stellar cosmogeny, astrogony; cosmism, cosmic philosophy, cosmic evolution; nebular hypothesis; **big bang** *or* expanding universe theory, oscillating *or* pulsating universe theory, steady state *or* continuous creation theory, plasma theory; creationism, creation science

19 **astronomy, stargazing,** uranology, starwatching, astrognosy, astrography, uranography, uranometry; astrophotography, stellar photometry; spectrography, spectroscopy, radio astronomy, radar astronomy, X-ray astronomy; **astrophysics,** solar physics; celestial mechanics, gravitational astronomy; astrolithology; meteoritics; astrogeology; stellar statistics; astrochemistry, cosmochemistry; optical astronomy, observational astronomy; infrared astronomy, ultraviolet astronomy; exobiology, astrobotany

20 **astrology,** astromancy, **horoscopy;** astrodiagnosis; natural astrology; judicial *or* mundane astrology; genethliacism, genethlialogy, genethliacs, genethliac astrology; **horoscope,** nativity; zodiac, **signs of the zodiac; house,** mansion; house of life, mundane house, planetary house *or* mansion; aspect

21 **cosmologist;** cosmogenist, cosmogener; cosmographer, cosmographist; cosmic philosopher, cosmist

22 **astronomer,** stargazer, observer, uranologist, uranometrist, uranographer, uranographist, astrographer, astrophotographer; radio astronomer, radar astronomer; **astrophysicist,** solar physicist; astrogeologist; cosmochemist

23 **astrologer,** astrologian, astromancer, stargazer, Chaldean, astroalchemist, horoscoper, horoscopist, genethliac

ADJS 24 **cosmic,** cosmical, **universal;** cosmologic *or* cosmological, cosmogonal, cosmogonic *or* cosmogonical; cosmographic, cosmographical

25 **celestial, heavenly, empyrean,** empyreal; uranic; **astral, starry, stellar,** stellary, sphery; star-spangled, star-studded; cometary; galactic, intergalactic, extragalactic; side-real; zodiacal; equinoctial; **astronomic** *or* **astronomical,** astrophysical, astrologic *or* astrological, astrologistic, astrologous; **planetary,** planetarian, planetal, circumplanetary; planetoidal, planetesimal, asteroidal; **solar,** heliacal; terrestrial; **lunar,** lu-

nular, lunate, lunulate, lunary, cislunar, translunar, Cynthian; semilunar; meteoric, meteoritic; extragalactic, anagalactic; galactic; nebular, nebulous, nebulose; interstellar, intersidereal; interplanetary; intercosmic

26 **extraterrestrial,** exterrestrial, extraterrene, extramundane, alien, space; **transmundane, otherworldly,** transcendental; extrasolar

ADVS 27 **universally,** everywhere

1073 THE ENVIRONMENT

NOUNS 1 **the environment,** the natural world, the ecology, global ecology, ecosystem, global ecosystem, the biosphere, the ecosphere, the balance of nature, macroecology, microecology; **ecology,** bioregion; **environmental protection,** environmental policy; **environmental control,** environmental management; environmental assessment, environmental auditing, environmental monitoring, environmental impact analysis; emission control; **environmental science**, environmentology

2 **environmental destruction,** ecocide, ecocatastrophe; environmental pollution, pollution, contamination; **air pollution,** atmospheric pollution, air quality; **water pollution,** stream pollution, lake pollution, ocean pollution, groundwater pollution, pollution of the aquifer; **environmental pollutant** ; eutrophication; **biodegradation,** biodeterioration, microbial degradation

3 **environmentalist,** conservationist, preservationist, nature-lover, environmental activist, doomwatcher <Brit>, duck-squeezer *and* ecofreak *and* tree-hugger *and* eagle freak <nf>; Green Panther

1074 ROCKETRY, MISSILERY

NOUNS 1 **rocketry,** rocket science *or* engineering *or* research *or* technology; **missilery,** missile science *or* engineering *or* research *or* technology; rocket *or* missile testing; ground test, firing test, static firing; rocket *or* missile project *or* program; instrumentation; telemetry

2 **rocket, rocket engine** *or* **motor,** reaction engine *or* motor; rocket thruster, thruster; retrorocket; rocket exhaust; plasma jet, plasma engine; ion engine; jetavator

3 **rocket, missile**, **ballistic missile, guided missile; torpedo;** projectile rocket, ordnance rocket, combat *or* military *or* war rocket; bird <nf>; **payload; warhead,** nuclear *or* thermonuclear warhead, atomic warhead; multiple *or* multiple-missile warhead

4 **rocket bomb,** flying bomb *or* torpedo, cruising missile; **robot bomb,** robomb, V-weapon, P-plane; **buzz-bomb,** bumblebomb, doodle-bug

5 **multistage rocket, step rocket;** two- *or* three-stage rocket, two- *or* three-step rocket; single-stage rocket, single-step rocket, one-step rocket; **booster,** booster unit, booster rocket, takeoff booster *or* rocket; piggyback rocket

6 **test rocket,** research rocket, high-altitude research rocket, registering rocket, instrument rocket, instrument carrier, test instrument vehicle, rocket laboratory; probe

7 **proving ground,** testing ground; firing area; impact area; control center, mission control, bunker; radar tracking station, tracking station, visual tracking station; meteorological tower

8 **rocket propulsion,** reaction propulsion, jet propulsion, blast propulsion; **fuel, propellant,** solid fuel, liquid fuel, hydrazine, liquid oxygen *or* lox; charge, propelling *or* propulsion charge, powder charge *or* grain, high-explosive charge; **thrust,** constant thrust; **exhaust,** jet blast, backflash

9 **rocket launching** *or* **firing,** ignition, launch, shot, shoot; countdown; **lift-off,** blast-off; guided *or* automatic control, programming; flight, trajectory; **burn; burnout,** end of burning; velocity peak; altitude peak, ceiling; descent; airburst; impact

10 **rocket launcher,** projector; **launching** *or* **launch pad,** launching

platform *or* rack, firing table; **silo;** takeoff ramp; tower projector, launching tower; launching mortar, launching tube, projector tube, firing tube; rocket gun, bazooka, antitank rocket; superbazooka; multiple projector, calliope, Stalin organ, Katusha; antisubmarine projector, Mark 10, hedgehog <nf>; Minnie Mouse launcher, mousetrap <nf>; Meilewagon

11 rocket scientist *or* technician, rocketeer *or* rocketer, rocket *or* missile man, rocket *or* missile engineer

VERBS **12 rocket, skyrocket**

13 launch, project, **shoot, fire,** blast off; abort

1075 SPACE TRAVEL

NOUNS **1 space travel, astronautics,** cosmonautics, **space flight,** navigation of empty space; interplanetary travel, space exploration; manned flight; space walk; space navigation, astrogation; **space science,** space technology *or* engineering; **aerospace science,** aerospace technology *or* engineering; space *or* aerospace research; space *or* aerospace medicine, bioastronautics; astrionics; escape velocity; rocketry 1074; multistage flight, step flight, shuttle flights; trip to the moon, trip to Mars, grand tour; space terminal, target planet; space age; space tourism, astrotourism

2 spacecraft, spaceship, space rocket, rocket ship, manned rocket, interplanetary rocket; rocket 1074.2; orbiter; **shuttle,** space shuttle; **capsule, space capsule,** ballistic capsule; **nose cone, heat shield,** heat barrier, thermal barrier; module, command module, lunar excursion module *or* LEM, lunar module *or* LM; moon ship, Mars ship, etc; deep-space ship; exploratory ship, reconnaissance rocket; ferry rocket, tender rocket, tanker ship, fuel ship; **multistage rocket** 1074.5, shuttle rocket, retrorocket, rocket thruster *or* thruster, attitude-control rocket, main rocket; **burn;** space docking, docking, docking maneuver; **orbit,** parking orbit, geostationary orbit; earth orbit, apogee, perigee; lunar *or* moon orbit, apolune, perilune, apocynthion, pericynthion; **guidance system,** terrestrial guidance; soft landing, hard landing; injection, insertion, lunar insertion, Earth insertion; **reentry, splashdown**

3 flying saucer, unidentified flying object *or* UFO; foo fighter

4 rocket engine 1074.2; atomic power plant; solar battery; power cell

5 space station, astro station, **space island,** island base, cosmic stepping-stone, halfway station, advance base; manned station; inner station, outer station, transit station, space airport, **spaceport,** spaceport station, space platform, space dock, launching base, research station, space laboratory, space observatory; tracking station, radar tracking station; radar station, radio station; radio relay station, radio mirror; space mirror, solar mirror; moon station, moon base, lunar base, lunar city, observatory on the moon

6 artificial satellite, satellite, space satellite, robot satellite, unmanned satellite, sputnik; communications satellite, active communications satellite, communications relay satellite, weather satellite, earth satellite, astronomical satellite, meteorological satellite, geostationary satellite, geosynchronous satellite, spy satellite, orbiting observatory, space observatory, geophysical satellite, navigational satellite, geodetic satellite, research satellite, interplanetary monitoring satellite, automated satellite; **probe, space probe,** geo probe, interplanetary explorer, planetary probe; orbiter, lander

7 <satellite telemetered recorders> micro-instrumentation; aurora particle counter, cosmic ray counter, gamma ray counter, heavy particle counter, impulse recorder, magnetometer, solar ultraviolet detector, solar X-ray detector, telecamera

8 astronaut, astronavigator, cosmonaut, **spaceman, spacewoman,** space crew member, shuttle crew member, space traveler, rocketeer, rocket pilot; space doctor; space crew; planetary colony, lunar colony; extraterrestrial visitor, alien, saucerman, man from Mars, Martian, little green man; close encounter

9 rocketry, rocket propulsion; burn, thrust, escape velocity, orbit, parking orbit, transfer orbit, insertion, injection, trajectory, flyby, rendezvous, docking, reentry, splashdown, soft landing, hard landing; launch vehicle, multistage rocket, payload, retrorocket, solid rocket booster, engine, booster, propellant, liquid fuel, solid fuel; **rocket society,** American Rocket Society, American Interplanetary Society, British Interplanetary Society

10 <space hazards> cosmic particles, intergalactic matter, aurora particles, radiation, cosmic ray bombardment; rocket *or* satellite debris, space junk <nf>; meteors, meteorites; asteroids; meteor dust impacts, meteoric particles, space bullets; extreme temperatures; the bends, blackout, weightlessness

11 **space suit,** pressure suit, G suit, anti-G suit; space helmet

VERBS **12** travel in space, go into outer space; launch, lift off, blast off, enter orbit, orbit the earth, go into orbit, orbit the moon, etc; navigate in space, astrogate; escape earth, break free, leave the atmosphere, shoot into space; rocket to the moon, park in space, hang *or* float in space, space-walk

ADJS **13** **astronautical,** cosmonautical, spacetraveling, spacefaring; astrogational; rocketborne, spaceborne; extravehicular

Index

How to Use This Index

Numbers after index entries refer to main categories and paragraphs within the thesaurus, not to page numbers. The number before the decimal point refers to the main category in which synonyms and related words are found. The number after the decimal point refers to the paragraph or paragraphs within the main category. For example, look at the index entry for **ability**:

ability 18.2

This entry listing tells you that you can find words related to **ability** in paragraph 2 of category 18.

Words, of course, frequently have more than one meaning. Each of those meanings may have synonyms or associated related words. For example, look at the entry for **absorb**:

absorb 187.13, 570.7

This tells you that you will find synonyms for **absorb** in category 187, paragraph 13. It also tells you that you will find additional synonyms in category 570, paragraph 7.

Words that appear in bold capital letters are main categories. Due to space constraints, not all words in the thesaurus are included in this index, just the most common ones.

To make it easier to find phrases, we have indexed them according to their first word, unless that first word is an article such as **a, the,** or **an**. You do not have to guess what the key word of the phrase is to find it in the index. Simply look up the first word of the phrase. For example, **give birth** will be found in the Gs, **INORGANIC MATTER** in the Is, and **let out** in the Ls.